Second Edition — 1988

Baseball Card Price Guide

By
Bob Lemke
and
Dan Albaugh

Special consultants:
☆ **Bill Bossert**
☆ **Keith Mitchell**
☆ **John Spalding**

Copyright MCMLXXXVIII by Krause Publications, Inc.
Library of Congress Catalog Number: 87-080033
International Standard Book Number: 0-87341-105-6

Acknowledgements

Dozens of individuals have made countless valuable contributions which have been incorporated into the first two editions of the *Sports Collectors Digest Baseball Card Price Guide*. While all cannot be individually acknowledged, special appreciation is extended to the following principal contributors who have exhibited a special dedication by creating, revising or verifying listings and technical data, reviewing market valuations or loaning cards for photography.

Ken Agona
(Sports Cards Plus)
Gary Agostino
Lisa Albano
Mark Anker
Steve Applebaum
John Beisiegel
Karen Bell
Cathy Black
Mike Bodner
Brian Boston
Mike Boyd
Lou Brown
Dan Bruner
(The Card King)
Greg Bussineau
(Superior Sports Cards)
Tony Carrafiell
(Delco Sports Cards)
Lee Champion
Dwight Chapin
Chriss Christiansen
Shane Cohen
(Grand Slam Sports Collectibles)
Charles Conlon
Bryan Couling
Clyde Cripe
Jim Cumpton
Tom Daniels
(T&J Sports Cards)
Tom Day
(Major League Marketing)
Dick DeCourcy
(Georgia Music & Sports)
Larry Dluhy
(Texas Trading Cards)
John Dorsey
Curtis Earl
Joe Esposito
(B&E Collectibles)
Doak Ewing
David Festberg
(Baseball and Hobby Shop)
Jay Finglass
Jeff Fritsch
Larry Fritsch
Tom Galic
Tony Galovich
(American Card Exchange)
Richard Gilkeson
Jack Goodman
Bill Goodwin
(St. Louis Baseball Cards)

Mike Gordon
Howard Gordon
Paul Green
Wayne Grove
(First Base)
Gerry Guenther
Don Guilbert
Tom Guilfoile
David Hall
Joel Hall
Walter Hall
(Hall's Nostalgia)
Gary Hamilton
Rick Hawksley
Herbert Hecht
Ron Hosmer
Marvin Huck
Barb Johnson
Jim Johnston
Stewart Jones
Larry Jordon
Judy Kay
(Kay's Baseball Cards)
Allan Kaye
Michael Keedy
Rick Keplinger
John King
John Kittleson
(Sports Collectibles)
Bob Koehler
David Kohler
(Sportscards Plus)
Lee Lasseigne
Morley Leeking
Don Lepore
(Card Collectors Co.)
Rod Lethbridge
Howie Levy
(Blue Chip Sportcard)
Neil Lewis
(Leaf, Inc.)
Rob Lifson
Lew Lipset
Norman Liss
(Topps, Inc.)
Jeff Litteral
Mark MacRae
Bill Mastro
Don McPherson
John Mehlin
Susie Melum
Blake Meyer
(Lone Star Sportcard Co.)
Dick Millerd
J.A. Monaco
Joe Morano
Brian Morris
Mike Mowery

Vincent Murray
(Fleer Corp.)
David Musser
(D.M.B.'s Baseball Cards)
Steve Myland
Chuck Nobriga
Joe Pasternack
(Card Collectors Co.)
Donald Peck
(Fleer Corp.)
Marty Perry
Tom Pfirrman
(Baseball Card Corner)
Fred Rapoport
(Yesterday's Heroes)
Tom Reid
Bob Richardson
Gavin Riley
Ron Ritzler
Mike Rodell
Mike Rogers
Chris Ronan
Alan Rosen
John Rumierz
Jon Sands
(Howard's Coin Shop)
Kevin Savage
(The Sports Gallery)
Stephen Schauer
Dave Schwartz
(Dave's Sportscards)
Robert Scott
Corey Shanus
Dan Shedrick
(Major League Marketing)
Max Silberman
Barry Sloate
Kevin Spears
Gene Speranza
David Spivack
Don Steinbach
(Sports Collectors Store)
Larry Stone
Doug Stultz
Joe Szeremet
K.J. Terplak
Jack Urban
Pete Waldman
Gary Walter
Ken Weimer
Dale Weselowski
(Ab D. Cards of Winnipeg)
E.C. Wharton-Tigar
Charles Williamson
Kit Young
Ted Zanidakis

BASEBALL CARD HISTORY

In 1887 — exactly 100 years ago — the first nationally distributed baseball cards were issued by Goodwin & Co., of New York City. The 1½x2½'' cards featured posed studio photographs glued to stiff cardboard. They were inserted into cigarette packages with such exotic brand names as Old Judge, Gypsy Queen and Dog's Head. Poses were formal, with artificial backgrounds and bare-handed players fielding balls suspended on strings to simulate action.

Then, as now, baseball cards were intended to stimulate product sales. What could be more American than using the diamond heroes of the national pastime to gain an edge on the competition? It is a tradition that has continued virtually unbroken for a century.

Following Goodwin's lead a year later, competitors began issuing baseball cards with their cigarettes, using full-color lithography to bring to life painted portraits of the era's top players.

After a few short years of intense competition, the cigarette industry's leading firms formed a monopoly and cornered the market. By the mid-1890s, there was little competition, and no reason to issue baseball cards. The first great period of baseball card issue came to an end.

The importing of Turkish tobaccos in the years just prior to 1910 created a revolution in American smoking habits. With dozens of new firms entering the market, the idea of using baseball cards to boost sales was revived.

In the years from 1909-1912, dozens of different sets of cards were produced to be given away in cigarette packages. There was greater than ever variety in sizes, shapes and designs, from the extremely popular 1½x2⅝'' color-litho-graphed set of 500+ players which collectors call T-206, to the large (5¾x8'') Turkey Red brand cards. There were double-folders, featuring two players on the same card, and triple-folders, which had two player portraits and an action scene. Gold ink and embossed designs were also tried to make each competing company's cards attractive and popular.

It was this era that saw the issue of the "King of Baseball Cards," the T-206 Honus Wagner card, worth $25,000.

The zeal with which America's young-sters pursued their fathers, uncles and neighbors for cigarette cards in the years just prior to World War I convinced the nation's confectioners that baseball cards could also be used to boost candy sales.

While baseball cards had been produced by candy companies on a limited basis as far back as the 1880s, by the early 1920s, the concept was being widely used in the industry. The highly competitive caramel business was a major force in this new marketing strategy, offering a baseball card in each package of candy. Not to be outdone, Cracker Jack began including baseball cards in each box. The 1914-1915 Cracker Jack cards are important because they were the most popular of the candy cards to include players from a short-lived third major league, the Federal League.

Generally, candy cards of the era were not as colorful or well-printed as the earlier tobacco cards, due to shortages of paper and ink-making ingredients caused by World War I.

The association of bubblegum and baseball cards is a phenomenon of only the past half-century. In the early 1930s, techniques were developed using rubber tree products to give gum the elasticity necessary for blowing bubbles.

During this era the standard method of selling a slab of bubblegum and a baseball card in a colorfully wax-wrapped 1¢ package was developed. Bubblegum — and baseball card — production in this era was centered in Massachusetts, where National Chicle Company (Cambridge) and Goudey Gum Company (Boston) were headquartered.

Most bubblegum cards produced in the early 1930s featured a roughly square (about 2½'') format, with players depicted in colorful paintings. For the first time, considerable attention was paid to the backs of the cards, where biographical details, career highlights and past season statistics were presented.

In 1939, a new company entered the baseball card market — Gum, Inc., of Philadelphia. Its "Play Ball" gum was the major supplier of baseball cards until 1941, when World War II caused a shortage of the materials necessary both for the production of bubblegum and the printing of baseball cards.

Three years after the end of World War II baseball cards returned on a national scale, with two companies competing for the bubblegum market. In Philadelphia, the former Gum, Inc., reappeared on the market as Bowman Gum Inc.

Bowman's first baseball card set appeared in 1948, very similar in format

to the cards which had existed prior to the war, black-and-white player photos on nearly square (2x2½'') cardboard. The '48 Bowman effort was modest, with only 48 cards. The following year, color was added to the photos. For 1950, Bowman replaced the re-touched photos with original color paintings of players, many of which were repeated a year later in the 1951 issue. Also new for 1951 was a larger card size, 2x3⅛.''

Bowman had little national competition in this era. In 1948-1949, Leaf Gum in Chicago produced a 98-card set that is the only bubblegum issue of the era to include a Joe DiMaggio card.

While Bowman dominated the postwar era through 1951, in that year Topps began production of its first baseball cards, issuing three different small sets of cards and serving warning that it was going to become a major force in the baseball card field.

In 1952, Brooklyn-based Topps entered the baseball card market in a big way. Not only was its 407-card set the largest single-year issue ever produced, but its 2⅝x3¾'' format was the largest-size baseball card ever offered for over-the-counter sale. Other innovations in Topps' premiere issue for 1952 included the first-ever use of team logos in card design, and on the back of the card, the first use of line statistics to document the player's previous year and career performance. By contrast, Bowman's set for 1952 remained in the smaller format, had 72 fewer cards and showed little change in design from 1951.

Just as clearly as Topps won the 1952 baseball card battle, Bowman came back in 1953 with what is often considered the finest baseball card set ever produced. For the first time ever, actual color photographs were reproduced on baseball cards in Bowman's 160-card set. To allow the full impact of the new technology, there were no other design elements on the front of the card, and Bowman adopted a larger format, 2½x3¾.''

And so the competition went for five years, each company trying to gain an edge by signing players to exclusive contracts and creating new and exciting card designs each year. Gradually, Topps became the dominant force in the baseball card market. In late 1955, Bowman admitted defeat and the company was sold to Topps.

Baseball cards entered a new era in 1957. After years of intense competition, Topps enjoyed a virtual monopoly that was rarely seriously challenged in the next 25 years. One such challenge in the opening years of the 1960s came from Post cereal, which from 1961-1963 issued 200-card sets on the backs of its cereal boxes.

In 1957, Topps' baseball cards were issued in a new size — 2½x3½'' — that would become the industry-wide standard that prevails to this day. It was also that year that Topps first used full-color photographs for its cards, rather than paintings or re-touched black-and-white photos. Another innovation in the 1957 set was the introduction of complete major and/or minor league statistics on the card backs. This feature quickly became a favorite with youngsters and provided fuel for endless schoolyard debates about whether one player was better than another.

In the ensuing five years, major league baseball underwent monumental changes. In 1958, the Giants and Dodgers left New York for California. In 1961-1962 expansion came to the major leagues, with new teams springing up from coast to coast and border to border.

The Topps baseball cards of the era preserve those days when modern baseball was in its formative stages.

In 1963, for the first time in seven years, it looked as if there might once again be two baseball card issues to choose from. After two years of issuing ''old-timers'' card sets, Fleer issued a 66-card set of current players. Topps took Fleer to court, where the validity of Topps' exclusive contracts with baseball players to appear on bubblegum cards was upheld. It was the last major challenge to Topps for nearly 20 years.

The 1960s offered baseball card collecting at its traditional finest. Youngsters would wait and worry through the long winter, watching candy store shelves for the first appearance of the brightly colored 5¢ card packs in the spring. A cry of, ''They're in!'' could empty a playground in seconds as youngsters rushed to the corner store to see what design innovations Topps had come up with for the new year. Then, periodically through the summer, new series would be released, offering a new challenge to complete. As the season wore down, fewer and fewer stores carried the final few series, and it became a real struggle to complete the ''high numbers'' from a given year's set. But it was all part of the fun of buying baseball cards in the 1960s.

The early 1970s brought some impor-

tant changes to the baseball card scene. The decade's first two Topps' issues were stunning in that the traditional white border was dropped in favor of gray in 1970, and black in 1971. In 1972, Topps' card design was absolutely psychedelic, with brightly colored frames around the player photos, and comic book typography popping out all over. The design for the 1973 cards was more traditional, but the photos were not. Instead of close-up portraits or posed "action" shots, many cards in the 1973 Topps set featured actual game action photos. Unfortunately, too many of those photos made it hard to tell which player was which, and the set was roundly panned by collectors.

But most significantly, 1973 marked the last year in which baseball cards were issued by series through the course of the summer. On the positive side, this eliminated the traditionally scarce "high numbers" produced toward the end of the season. On the negative side, it meant players who had been traded in the pre-season could no longer be shown in their "correct" uniforms, and outstanding new players had to wait a full year before their rookie cards would debut.

This marketing change made a significant impact on the hobby and helped spur a tremendous growth period in the late 1970s. By offering all of its cards at once, Topps made it easy for baseball card dealers to offer complete sets early in the year. Previously, collectors had to either assemble their sets by buying packs of cards, or wait until all series had been issued to buy a set from a dealer. It was in this era that many of today's top baseball card dealers got their start or made the switch to baseball cards as a full-time business.

During this era, the first significant national competition to Topps' baseball card monopoly in many years was introduced. Hostess bakery products company began distributing baseball cards printed on the bottoms of packages of its snack cakes, while the Kellogg's company distributed simulated 3-D cards in boxes of its cereals. The eagerness with which collectors gobbled up these issues showed that the hobby was ready for a period of unprecedented growth.

The baseball card hobby literally boomed in 1981. A Federal court broke Topps' monopoly on the issue of baseball cards with bubblegum and Fleer of Philadelphia and Donruss of Memphis, entered the field as the first meaningful competition in nearly 20 years.

That same year also marked a beginning of the resurgence in the number of regional baseball card issues. Over the next few years, dozens of such sets came onto the market, helping to boost sales of everything from snack cakes to soda pop and police public relations. By 1984, more than half of the teams in the major leagues were issuing some type of baseball cards on a regional basis. The hobby had not enjoyed such diversity of issue since the mid-1950s.

While yet another court decision cost Fleer and Donruss the right to sell their baseball cards with bubblegum, both companies remained in the market and gained strength.

Topps' major contribution in this era was the introduction of annual "Traded" sets which offered cards of the year's new rookies as well as cards of traded players in their "correct" uniforms.

The mid-1980s have seen continued strong growth in the number of active baseball card collectors, as well as the number of new baseball card issues.

Topps, still the industry's leader, expanded the number and variety of its baseball issues with many different test issues and on-going specialty sets, including oversize cards, 3-D plastic cards, metal "cards" and much more.

After three years of over-production of its baseball card sets, Donruss in 1984 significantly limited the number of cards printed, creating a situation in which demand exceeded supply, causing the value of Donruss cards to rise above Topps for the first time. The company has maintained that policy since, making Donruss issues a perennial challenge for collectors to complete.

In 1984, Fleer followed Topps' lead and produced a season's-end "Update" set. Because the quantity of sets printed was extremely limited, and because it contains many of today's hottest young players, the 1984 Fleer Update set has become the most valuable baseball card issue produced in recent times.

In 1986, a fourth company joined the baseball "card wars." Called "Sportflics," the cards were produced by a subsidiary of the Wrigley Gum company, and featured three different photos on each card in a simulated 3-D effect.

Baseball card collecting entered its second century in 1987 and the hobby has never been stronger. It is the fastest growing hobby in the country. With more collectors and more new cards than ever before, 1988 looks like another growth year for baseball cards.

 # *WELCOME*

To the 1988 Sports Collectors Digest Price Guide. One of the most comprehensive publications on the market today. I'm sure this guide will reflect a major upward trend in the hobby. Here are my plans for 1988, a year in which I feel will see our hobby soar to even greater heights.

AUCTION

My auction, which showcases the finest collectables in the hobby, will continue to be held quarterly. Auction previews will appear in the SCD two weeks prior to actual date. In addition, check my show calendar for some lots can be viewed at conventions around the country.

SALES

My sales for 1987 were in excess of 2.5 million dollars. In 1988 I will continue to bring you, the collecting hobby, the finest in quality collectables. Look for my tables at shows throughout the United States, nobody does it better, **Bar None.**

PURCHASES

An unbelievable 1987 has seen my purchases soar to over 2 million dollars for the first time. No other dealer can or will make that claim, and I **prove** it in writing. If it's quality memorabilia, cards, publications, uniforms, you have for sale, look to the leading buyer in the hobby, the buying machine, Mr. Mint!!!

ALAN ROSEN
THE MILLION DOLLAR DEALER
28 Hilton Place, Montvale, NJ 07645
201-307-0700

HOW TO USE THIS CATALOG

This catalog has been uniquely designed to serve the needs of both beginning and advanced collectors. It provides a comprehensive guide to more than 100 years of baseball card issues, arranged so that even the most novice collector can consult it with confidence and ease.

The following explanations summarize the general practices used in preparing this catalog's listings. However, because of specialized requirements which may vary from card set to card set, these must not be considered ironclad. Where these standards have been set aside, appropriate notations are incorporated.

ARRANGEMENT

Because the most important feature in identifying, and pricing, a baseball card is its set of origin, this catalog has been alphabetically arranged according to the name by which the set is most popularly known to collectors.

Those sets that were issued for more than one year are then listed chronologically, from earliest to most recent.

Within each set, the cards are listed by their designated card number, or in the absence of card numbers, alphabetically according to the last name of the player pictured.

IDENTIFICATION

While most modern baseball cards are well identified on front, back or both, as to date and issuer, such has not always been the case. In general, the back of the card is more useful in identifying the set of origin than the front. The issuer or sponsor's name will usually appear on the back since, after all, baseball cards were first issued as a promotional item to stimulate sales of other products. As often as not, that issuer's name is the name by which

the set is known to collectors and under which it will be found listed in this catalog.

Virtually every set listed in this catalog is accompanied by a photograph of a representative card. If all else fails, a comparison of an unknown card with the photos in this book will usually produce a match.

As a special feature, each set listed in this catalog has been cross-indexed by its date of issue. This will allow identification in some difficult cases since a baseball card's general age, if not specific year of issue, can usually be fixed by studying the biographical or statistical information on the back of the card. The last year mentioned in either bio or stats is usually the year which preceded the year of issue.

PHOTOGRAPHS

A photograph of the front and back of at least one representative card from virtually every set listed in this catalog has been incorporated into the listings to aid in identification.

Photographs have been printed in reduced size. The actual size of cards in each set is given in the introductory text preceding its listing.

DATING

The dating of baseball cards by year of issue on the front or back of the card itself is a relatively new phenomenon. In most cases, to accurately determine a date of issue for an unidentified card, it must be studied for clues. As mentioned, the biography, career summary or statistics on the back of the card are the best way to pinpoint a year of issue. In most cases, the year of issue will be the year after the last season mentioned on the card.

Luckily for today's collector, earlier generations have done much of the research in determining year of issue for those cards which bear no clues. The painstaking task of matching players' listed and/or pictured team against their career records often allowed an issue date to be determined.

In some cases, particular card sets were issued over a period of more than one calendar year, but since they are collected together as a single set, their specific year of issue is not important. Such sets will be listed with their complete known range of issue years, as 1909-1911 T-206, or 1948-1949 Leaf, etc.

NUMBERING

While many baseball card issues as far back as the 1880s have contained card numbers assigned by the issuer, to facilitate the collecting of a complete set, the practice has by no means been universal. Even today, not every set bears card numbers.

Logically, those baseball cards which were numbered by their manufacturer are presented in that numerical order within the listings of this catalog. The many unnumbered issues, however, have been assigned *SCD Price Guide* numbers to facilitate their universal identification within the hobby, especially when buying and selling by mail. In all cases, numbers which have been assigned, or which otherwise do not appear on the card through error or by design, are shown in this catalog within parentheses. In virtually all cases, unless a more natural system suggested itself by the unique nature of a particular set, the assignment of *SCD Price Guide* numbers by the cataloging staff has been done by alphabetical arrangement of the player's last names or the card's principal title.

Significant collectible variations of any particular card are noted within the listings by the application of a suffix letter within parentheses.

The identification of player by full name on the front of his baseall card has been a common practice only since the 1920s. Prior to that, the player's last name and team were the more usual information found on the card front.

As a standard practice, the listings in the *SCD Price Guide* present the player's name exactly as it appears on the front of

NAMES

the card, if his full name is given there. If the player's full name only appears on the back, rather than the front, of the card, the listing corresponds to that designation.

In cases where only the player's last name is given on the card, the cataloging staff has included the first name by which he was most often known for ease of identification.

Cards which contain misspelled first or last name, or even wrong initials, will have included in their listings the incorrect information, with a correction accompanying in parentheses. This extends, also, to cases where the name on the card does not correspond to the player actually pictured.

GRADING

It is necessary that some sort of card grading standard be used so that buyer and seller (especially when dealing by mail) may reach an informed agreement on the value of a card. Each card set's listings are priced in the three grades of preservation in which those cards are most commonly encountered in the day to day buying and selling of the hobby marketplace.

Older cards are listed in grades of Near Mint (NR MT), Excellent (EX) and Very Good (VG), reflecting the basic fact that few cards were able to survive for 25, 50 or even 100 years in a close semblance to the condition of their original issue. The pricing of cards in these three conditions will allow readers to accurately price cards which fall in intermediate grades, such as EX-MT, or VG-EX.

More recent issues, which have been preserved in top condition in considerable number, are listed in the grades of Mint (MT), Near Mint and Excellent, reflective of the fact that there exists in the current market little or no demand for cards of the recent past in grades below Excellent.

In general, although grades below Very Good are not priced in this catalog, close approximations of low-grade card values may figured on the following formula: Good condition cards are valued at about 50% of VG price, with Fair cards priced about 50% of Good. Cards in Poor condition have no market value except in the cases of the rarest and most expensive cards. In such cases, value has to be

negotiated individually.

For the benefit of the reader, we present herewith the grading guide which was originally formulated by *Baseball Cards* magazine and *Sports Collectors Digest* in 1981, and has been continually refined since that time. These grading definitions have been used in the pricing of cards in this catalog, but they are by no means a universally accepted grading standard. The potential buyer of a baseball card should keep that in mind when encountering cards of nominally the same grade, but at a price which differs widely from that quoted in this book. Ultimately, the collector, himself, must formulate his own personal grading standards in deciding whether cards available for purchase meet the needs of his own collection.

No collector or dealer is required to adhere to the grading standards presented herewith — or to any other published grading standards — but all are invited to do so. The staff of the *SCD Price Guide* is eager to work toward the development of a standardized system of card grading that will be consistent with the realities of the hobby marketplace. Contact the authors.

Mint (MT): A perfect card. Well-centered, with parallel borders which appear equal to the naked eye. Four sharp, square corners. No creases, edge dents, surface scratches, paper flaws, loss of luster, yellowing or fading, regardless of age. No imperfectly printed card — out of register, badly cut or ink-flawed — or card stained by contact with gum, wax or other substances can be considered truly Mint, even if new out of the pack.

Near Mint (NR MT): A nearly perfect card. At first glance, a Near Mint card appears perfect; upon closer examination, however, a minor flaw will be discovered. On well-centered cards, three of the four corners must be perfectly sharp; only one corner showing a minor imperfection upon close inspection. A slightly off-center card with one or more borders being noticeably unequal — but still present — would also fit this grade.

Excellent (EX): Corners are still fairly sharp with only moderate wear. Card borders may be off center. No creases. No gum, wax or product stains, front or back.

Surfaces may show slight loss of luster from rubbing across other cards.

Very Good (VG): Shows obvious handling. Corners rounded and/or perhaps showing minor creases. Other minor creases may be visible. Surfaces may exhibit loss of luster, but all printing is intact. May show gum, wax or other packaging stains. No major creases, tape marks or extraneous markings or writing. Exhibits honest wear.

Good (G): A well-worn card, but exhibits no intentional damage or abuse. May have major or multiple creases. Corners rounded well beyond the border.

Fair: Shows excessive wear, along with damage or abuse. Will show all of the wear characteristics of a Good card, along with such damage as thumb tack holes in or near margins, evidence of having been taped or pasted, perhaps small tears around the edges, or creases so heavy as to break the cardboard. Backs may show minor added pen or pencil writing, or be missing small bits of paper. Still, a basically complete card.

Poor: A card that has been tortured to death. Corners or other areas may be torn off. Card may have been trimmed, show holes from paper punch or have been used for BB gun practice. Front may have extraneous pen or pencil writing, or other defacement. Major portions of front or back design may be missing. Not a pretty sight.

In addition to these seven widely-used grading terms, collectors will often encounter intermediate grades, such as VG-EX (Very Good to Excellent), EX-MT (Excellent to Mint), or NR MT-MT (Near Mint to Mint). Persons who describe a card with such grades are usually trying to convey that the card has all the characteristics of the lower grade, with enough of the higher grade to merit mention. Such cards are usually priced at a point midway between the two grades.

VALUATIONS

Values quoted in this book represent the current retail market and are compiled from recommendations provided and verified through the authors' day to day involvement in the publication of the

BILL HENDERSON'S CARDS
"King of the Commons"
2320 Ruger Ave. - KG2, Janesville, WI 53545
1-608-755-0922

"ALWAYS BUYING" Call or Write for Quote | **"ALWAYS BUYING" Call or Write for Quote**

	HI # OR SCARCE SERIES	COMMONS EACH	EX/MT TO MINT CONDITION GROUP LOTS FOR SALE				VG Condition		
				50 Diff.	100 Diff.	300 Asst.	500 Asst.	50	100 Different	200
1948 Bowman (37-48) $15.00		10.00	—	—	—	—	—	—	—	—
1949 Bowman (145-240) 35.00-40.00		10.00	(109-144) 8.00	450.00	—	—	—	270.00	—	—
1950-51 Bowman (50 1-22, 51 253-324) 22.00		10.00	51 (2-36) 12.00	450.00	—	—	—	270.00	—	—
1952 Topps (311-407) 135.00		15.00	(2-80) 35.00	675.00	—	—	—	485.00	—	—
1952 Bowman (217-252) 15.00		10.00	—	450.00	—	—	—	270.00	—	—
1953 Topps (220-280) 32.00		10.00	—	450.00	—	—	—	270.00	—	—
1953 Bowman (129-160) 25.00		15.00	(113-128) 30.00	675.00	—	—	—	405.00	—	—
1954 Topps ....—		5.00	(51-75) 7.00	225.00	440.00	—	—	135.00	—	—
1954 Bowman ....—		4.00	(129-224) 5.00	180.00	350.00	—	—	108.00	—	—
1955 Topps (161-210) 10.00		5.00	(151-160) 7.50	225.00	440.00	—	—	135.00	—	—
1955 Bowman (225-320) ....8.00-10.00 Umps		3.00	(2-96) 4.00	135.00	265.00	775.00	—	80.00	158.00	—
1956 Topps ....—		3.00	(181-260) 5.00	135.00	265.00	775.00	—	80.00	158.00	—
1957 Topps (265-351) 10.00		2.50	(353-407) 3.00	115.00	220.00	645.00	—	70.00	132.00	—
1958 Topps ....—		1.50	(1-110) 2.00	68.00	132.00	385.00	—	40.00	80.00	—
1959 Topps (507-572) 5.50		1.25	(1-110) 1.50	58.00	110.00	325.00	530.00	35.00	68.00	130.00
1960 Topps (523-572) 5.00		1.00	(441-506) 1.50	45.00	88.00	258.00	425.00	27.00	59.00	100.00
1961 Topps (523-589) 15.00		1.00	(371-522) 1.25	45.00	88.00	258.00	425.00	27.00	53.00	100.00
1962 Topps (523-590) 5.00		1.00	(371-522) 1.25	45.00	88.00	258.00	425.00	27.00	53.00	100.00
1963 Topps (447-576) 5.00		.60	(197-446) 75	27.00	53.00	155.00	—	16.00	30.00	—
1964 Topps (523-587) 2.50		.50	(371-522) 80	23.00	44.00	130.00	215.00	14.00	26.00	50.00
1965 Topps (523-598) (447-522 100) 2.50		.50	(199-446) 75	23.00	44.00	130.00	215.00	14.00	26.00	50.00
1966 Topps (523-598) 10.00		.50	(447-522) 1.50	23.00	44.00	130.00	215.00	14.00	26.00	50.00
1967 Topps (534-609) 5.00		.50	(458-533) 1.50	23.00	44.00	130.00	215.00	14.00	26.00	50.00
1968 Topps ....—		.40	(458-533) 60	18.00	35.00	100.00	170.00	11.00	20.00	38.00
1969 Topps ....—		.40	(219-327) 60	18.00	35.00	100.00	170.00	11.00	20.00	38.00
1970 Topps (634-720) 1.50		.30	(553-636) 75	14.00	26.00	78.00	125.00	—	16.00	30.00
1971 Topps (644-752) 1.50		.30	(524-643) 75	14.00	26.00	78.00	125.00	—	16.00	30.00
1972 Topps (657-787) 1.50		.30	(526-656) 75	14.00	26.00	78.00	125.00	—	16.00	30.00
1973 Topps (528-660) 1.25		.25	(397-528) 40	11.00	20.00	65.00	105.00	—	12.00	22.00
1974 Topps ....—		.25	—	11.00	20.00	65.00	105.00	—	12.00	22.00
1975 Topps (8-132 30) ....—		.25	—	11.00	20.00	65.00	105.00	—	12.00	22.00
1976-77 ....—		.20	—	—	18.00	50.00	85.00	—	10.00	18.00
1978-1980 ....—		.15	—	—	13.00	38.00	65.00	—	8.00	15.00
1981 thru 1988 Topps, Fleer or Donruss Specify Year & Company except below		.10	—	—	8.00 Per Yr.	22.00 Per Yr.	35.00 Per Yr.	—	5.00	10.00
1984-86 Donruss ....—		.15	—	7.00	13.00	38.00	60.00	—	—	—

SPECIAL IN VG CONDITION-POSTPAID

250	58-62	......150.00
500	58-62	......290.00
250	60-69	......85.00
500	60-69	......160.00
1000	60-69	......310.00
250	70-79	......28.00
500	70-79	......55.00
1000	70-79	......100.00
250	80-84	......12.00
500	80-84	......22.00
1000	80-84	......40.00

These lots are all different.
Special 1 Different from each year 1967-86 from above $100.00 postpaid.
Special 100 Different from each year 1956-86 from above $1400.00 postpaid.
Special 10 Different from each year 1956-86 from above $150.00 postpaid.
All lot groups are my choice only.
All assorted lots will contain as many different as possible
Please list alternates whenever possible.
Send your want list and I will fill them at the above price for commons. High numbers, specials, scarce series, and stars extra.
Minimum order $7.50 - Postage and handling .50 per 100 cards (minimum $1.75)
Have thousands of star and super star cards. Call or send for star list.
Also interested in purchasing your collection.
*Groups include various years of my choice.
ANY CARD NOT LISTED ON PRICE SHEET IS PRICED AT CURRENT SCD GUIDE

SETS AVAILABLE
POSTAGE $2.50 PER SET
1979 Topps $125.00
1980 Topps 125.00
1981 Topps 90.00
1982 Topps 90.00
1983 Topps 100.00
1984 Topps 90.00
1985 Topps 100.00
1986 Topps 28.00
1987 Topps 25.00
1988 Topps 20.00
(Prices subject to change without notice.)

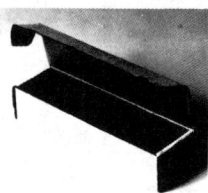

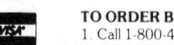

hobby's leading advertising periodicals, as well as the input of specialized consultants.

It should be stressed, however, that this book is intended to serve only as an aid in evaluating cards; actual market conditions are constantly changing. This is especially true of the cards of current players, whose on-field performance during the course of a season can greatly affect the value of their cards — upwards or downwards.

Publication of this catalog is not intended as a solicitation to buy or sell the listed cards by the authors, publishers or contributors.

Again, the values listed here are **retail** prices; what a collector can expect to pay when buying a card from a dealer. The **wholesale** price; that which a collector can expect to receive from a dealer when selling cards will be significantly lower. Most dealers operate on a 100% mark-up, generally paying about 50% of a card's retail value. On some high-demand cards, dealers will pay up yo 75% or even 100% or more of retail value, anticipating continued price increases. Conversely, for many low-demand cards, such as common players' cards of recent years, dealers may pay 25% or even less of retail.

It should also be noted that with several hundred thousand valuations quoted in this book, there are bound to be a few compilation or typographical errors which will creep into the final product; a fact readers should remember if they encounter a listing at a fraction of, or several times, the card's actual current retail price. The authors welcome the correction of any such errors discovered; use the post-paid response card bound into the book, or write: SCD Price Guide, 700 E. State St., Iola, WI 54990.

SETS

Collectors may note that the complete set prices quoted in these listings are usually significantly lower than the total of the value of the individual cards which comprise the set.

This reflects two factors in the baseball card market. First, a seller is often willing to take a lower composite price for a complete set as a "volume discount," and to avoid inventorying a large number of common player or other lower-demand cards.

Second, to a degree, the value of common cards can be said to be inflated as a result of having a built-in overhead charge to justify the dealer's time in sorting cards, carrying them in stock and filling orders. This accounts for the fact that even brand new baseball cards, which cost the dealer around ½¢ apiece when bought in bulk, carry individual price tags of 3¢ or higher.

ERRORS/ VARIATIONS

It is often hard for the beginning collector to understand that an error on a baseball card, in and of itself, does not usually add premium value to that card. It is usually only when the correcting of an error in a subsequent printing creates a variation that premium value attaches to an error.

Minor errors such as wrong stats or personal data, misspellings, inconsistencies, etc. — usually affecting the back of the card — are very common, especially in recent years. Unless a corrected variation was also printed, these errors are not noted in the listings of this book because they are not generally perceived by collectors to have premium value.

On the other hand, major effort has been expended to include the most complete listings ever for collectible variation cards. Many scarce and valuable variations — dozens of them never before cataloged — are included in these listings because they are widely collected and often have significant premium value.

COUNTERFEITS/ REPRINTS

As the value of baseball cards has risen in the past 10-20 years, certain cards and sets have become too expensive for the average collector to obtain. This, along with changes in the technology of color printing, have given rise to increasing

numbers of counterfeit and reprint cards.

While both terms describe essentially the same thing — a modern copy which attempts to duplicate as closely as possible an original baseball card — there are differences which are important to the collector.

Generally, a counterfeit is made with the intention of deceiving somebody into believing it is genuine, and thus paying large amounts of money for it. The counterfeiter takes every pain to try to make his fakes look as authentic as possible. In recent years, the 1963 Pete Rose, 1984 Donruss Don Mattingly and more than 30 superstar cards of the late 1960s-early 1980s have been counterfeited — all were quickly detected because of the differences in quality of cardboard on which they were printed.

A reprint, on the other hand, while it may have been made to look as close as possible to an original card, is made with the intention of allowing collectors to buy them as substitutes for cards they may never be otherwise able to afford. The big difference is that a reprint is generally marked as such, usually on the back of the card. In other cases, like the Topps 1952 reprint set, the replicas are printed in a size markedly different from the originals.

Collectors should be aware, however, that unscrupulous persons will sometimes cut off or otherwise obliterate the distinguishing word — ''Reprint,'' ''Copy,'' — or modern copyright date on the back of a reprint card in an attempt to pass it as genuine.

A collector's best defense against reprints and counterfeits is to acquire a knowledge of the ''look'' and ''feel'' of genuine baseball cards of various eras and issues.

UNLISTED CARDS

It is not the intention of this book to present a listing of every baseball card made in the past century. Indeed, such a listing would be impossible. Rather, the scope of this book is intended to present the cards which today's collectors most

often encounter; those which are most often bought, sold and traded in the hobby marketplace.

The publishers are at work compiling listings for the hundreds of sets and tens of thousands of cards which fall outside the scope of the present volume. It is intended that at a future date, a much more comprehensive catalog, covering virtually every printed cardboard item with a baseball player's picture on it, will result.

Readers who have cards or sets which are not covered in this edition are invited to correspond with the authors for purposes of adding to the compilation work now in progress. Address: SCD Price Guide, 700 E. State St., Iola, WI 54990.

Contributions will be acknowledged in future editions.

COLLECTOR ISSUES

There exists within the hobby a great body of cards which do not fall under the scope of this catalog by virtue of their nature of having been issued solely for the collector market. Known as ''collector issues,'' these cards and sets are distinguished from ''legitimate'' issues in not having been created as a sales promotional item for another product or service — bubblegum, soda, snack cakes, dog food, cigarettes, gasoline, etc.

By their nature, and principally because the person issuing them is always free to print and distribute more of the same if they should ever attain any real value, collector issues are generally regarded by collectors as having little or no premium value.

NEW ISSUES

Because new baseball cards are being issued all the time, the cataloging of them remains an on-going challenge. The publishers will attempt to keep abreast of new issues so that they may be added to future editions of this book.

Readers are invited to submit news of new issues, especially limited-edition or regionally issued cards to the authors. Address: SCD Price Guide, 700 E. State St., Iola, WI 54990.

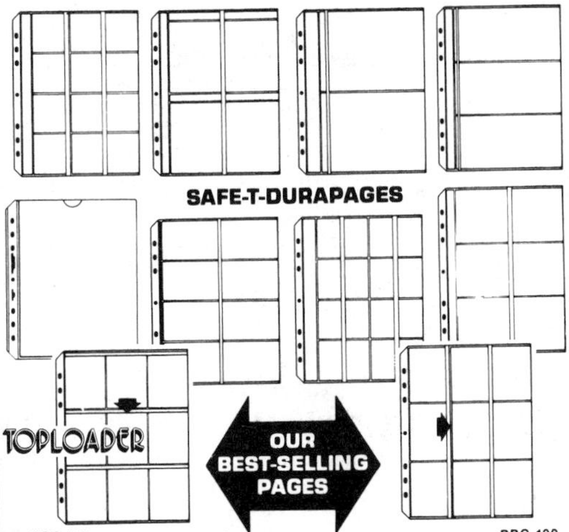

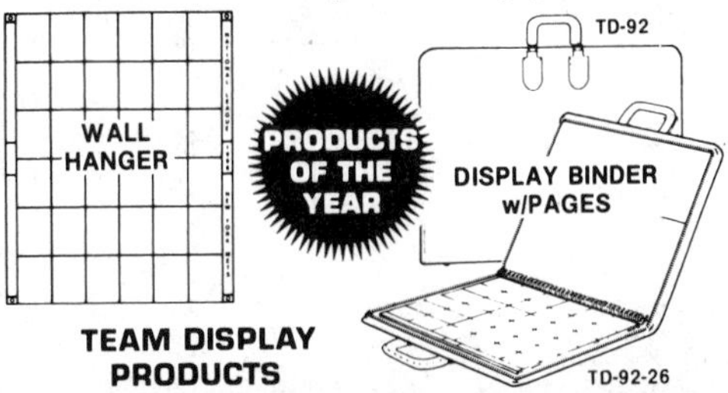

1983 Affiliated Food Stores Rangers

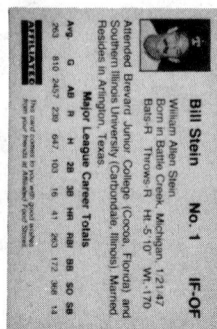

This 28-card set, featuring the Texas Rangers, was issued as a promotion by the Affiliated Food Stores chain of Arlington, Tex. late during the 1983 baseball season. Complete sets were given out free to youngsters thirteen and under at the 9/3/83 Rangers game. The cards measure 2⅜" by 3½" and feature a full-color photo on the front. Also on the front, located inside a blue box, is the player's name, uniform number, and the words "1983 Rangers". The card backs contain a small player photo plus biographical and statistical information, along with the Affiliated logo and a brief promotional message. A total of 10,000 sets were reportedly printed. Cards are numbered by the players' uniform numbers in the checklist that follows.

		MT	NR MT	EX
Complete Set:		8.50	6.50	3.50
Common Player:		.10	.08	.04
1	Bill Stein	.10	.08	.04
2	Mike Richardt	.10	.08	.04
3	Wayne Tolleson	.10	.08	.04
5	Billy Sample	.10	.08	.04
6	Bobby Jones	.10	.08	.04
7	Bucky Dent	.20	.15	.08
8	Bobby Johnson	.10	.08	.04
9	Pete O'Brien	1.00	.70	.40
10	Jim Sundberg	.15	.11	.06
11	Doug Rader	.15	.11	.06
12	Dave Hostetler	.10	.08	.04
14	Larry Biittner	.10	.08	.04
15	Larry Parrish	.35	.25	.14
17	Mickey Rivers	.20	.15	.08
21	Odell Jones	.10	.08	.04
24	Dave Schmidt	.15	.11	.06
25	Buddy Bell	.35	.25	.14
26	George Wright	.10	.08	.04
28	Frank Tanana	.20	.15	.08
29	John Butcher	.10	.08	.04
32	Jon Matlack	.15	.11	.06
40	Rick Honeycutt	.20	.15	.08
41	Dave Tobik	.10	.08	.04
44	Danny Darwin	.20	.15	.08
46	Jim Anderson	.10	.08	.04
48	Mike Smithson	.10	.08	.04
49	Charlie Hough	.25	.20	.10
---	Coaching Staff (Rich Donnelly, Glenn Ezell, Merv Rettenmund, Dick Such, Wayne Terwilliger)	.10	.08	.04

1955 Armour Coins

In 1955, Armour inserted a plastic "coin" in their packages of hot dogs. A raised profile of a ballplayer is on the front of each coin along with the player's name and team. The coin backs list the player's name, position, birthplace and date, batting and throwing preference, and 1954 hitting or pitching record. The coins, which measure 1½" in diameter and are unnumbered, came in a variety of colors. Common colors are aqua, dark blue, light green, orange, red, and yellow. Scarce colors are black, pale blue, lime green, very dark green, gold, pale orange, pink, silver, and tan. Scarce colors are double the value of the coins listed in the checklist that follows. Twenty-four different players are included in the set. Variations can be found for the Kuenn and Mantle coins. The Kuenn coin comes with the letters in his name bunched closely together (condensed) or spread apart (spaced). The Mantle coin can be found with his last name spelled correctly or misspelled "Mantel."

		NR MT	EX	VG
Complete Set:		500.00	250.00	150.00
Common Player:		10.00	5.00	3.00
(1)	John "Johnny" Antonelli	12.00	6.00	3.50
(2)	Larry "Yogi" Berra	28.00	14.00	8.50
(3)	Delmar "Del" Crandall	12.00	6.00	3.50
(4)	Lawrence "Larry" Doby	15.00	7.50	4.50
(5)	James "Jim" Finigan	10.00	5.00	3.00
(6)	Edward "Whitey" Ford	28.00	14.00	8.50
(7)	James "Junior" Gilliam	18.00	9.00	5.50
(8)	Harvey "Kitten" Haddix	10.00	5.00	3.00
(9)	Ranson "Randy" Jackson (name actually Ransom)	18.00	9.00	5.50
(10)	Jack "Jackie" Jensen	15.00	7.50	4.50
(11)	Theodore "Ted" Kluszewski	15.00	7.50	4.50
(12a)	Harvey E. Kuenn (spaced letters in name)	20.00	10.00	6.00
(12b)	Harvey E. Kuenn (condensed letters in name)	30.00	15.00	9.00
(13a)	Charles "Mickey" Mantel (incorrect spelling)	60.00	30.00	18.00
(13b)	Charles "Mickey" Mantle (correct spelling)	200.00	100.00	60.00
(14)	Donald "Don" Mueller	18.00	9.00	5.50
(15)	Harold "Pee Wee" Reese	22.00	11.00	6.50
(16)	Allie P. Reynolds	15.00	7.50	4.50
(17)	Albert "Flip" Rosen	15.00	7.50	4.50
(18)	Curtis "Curt" Simmons	10.00	5.00	3.00
(19)	Edwin "Duke" Snider	35.00	17.50	10.50
(20)	Warren Spahn	25.00	12.50	7.50
(21)	Frank J. Thomas	25.00	12.50	7.50
(22)	Virgil "Fire" Trucks	10.00	5.00	3.00
(23)	Robert "Bob" Turley	15.00	7.50	4.50
(24)	James "Mickey" Vernon	10.00	5.00	3.00

1959 Armour Coins

After a three-year layoff, Armour once again inserted plastic baseball "coins" into their hot dog packages. The coins retained their 1½" size but did not include as much detailed information as in 1955. Missing from the coins' backs is information such as birthplace and date, team, and batting and throwing preference. The fronts contain the player's name and, unlike 1955, only the team nickname is given. The set consists of twenty coins which come in a myriad of

		NR MT	EX	VG
Complete Set:		925.00	463.00	278.00
Common Player:		5.00	2.50	1.50
(1a)	Hank Aaron (Braves)	20.00	10.00	6.00
(1b)	Hank Aaron (Milwaukee Braves)	50.00	25.00	15.00
(2)	Bob Allison	10.00	5.00	3.00
(3)	Ernie Banks	10.00	5.00	3.00
(4)	Ken Boyer	8.00	4.00	2.50
(5)	Rocky Colavito	10.00	5.00	3.00
(6)	Gene Conley	8.00	4.00	2.50
(7)	Del Crandall	6.00	3.00	1.75
(8)	Bud Daley	650.00	325.00	195.00
(9a)	Don Drysdale (L.A condensed)	12.00	6.00	3.50
(9b)	Don Drysdale (space between L. and A.)			
		18.00	9.00	5.50
(10)	Whitey Ford	12.00	6.00	3.50
(11)	Nellie Fox	8.00	4.00	2.50
(12)	Al Kaline	18.00	9.00	5.50
(13a)	Frank Malzone (Red Sox)	5.00	2.50	1.50
(13b)	Frank Malzone (Boston Red Sox)			
		18.00	9.00	5.50
(14)	Mickey Mantle	45.00	22.00	13.50
(15)	Ed Mathews	15.00	7.50	4.50
(16)	Willie Mays	35.00	17.50	10.50
(17)	Vada Pinson	8.00	4.00	2.50
(18)	Dick Stuart	8.00	4.00	2.50
(19)	Gus Triandos	5.00	2.50	1.50
(20)	Early Wynn	12.00	6.00	3.50

colors. Common colors are navy blue, royal blue, dark green, orange, red, and pale yellow. Scarce colors are pale blue, cream, grey-green, pale green, dark or light pink, pale red, tan, and translucent coins of any color with or without multi-colored flecks in the plastic mix. Scarce colors are double the value listed for coins in the checklist that follows. In 1959, Armour had a write-in offer of ten coins for one dollar. The same ten players were part of the write-in offer, accounting for why half of the coins in the set are much more plentiful than the other.

		NR MT	EX	VG
Complete Set:		275.00	137.00	82.00
Common Player:		5.00	2.50	1.50
(1)	Hank Aaron	25.00	12.50	7.50
(2)	John Antonelli	12.00	6.00	3.50
(3)	Richie Ashburn	12.00	6.00	3.50
(4)	Ernie Banks	30.00	15.00	9.00
(5)	Don Blasingame	5.00	2.50	1.50
(6)	Bob Cerv	5.00	2.50	1.50
(7)	Del Crandall	12.00	6.00	3.50
(8)	Whitey Ford	25.00	12.50	7.50
(9)	Nellie Fox	10.00	5.00	3.00
(10)	Jackie Jensen	20.00	10.00	6.00
(11)	Harvey Kuenn	12.00	6.00	3.50
(12)	Frank Malzone	5.00	2.50	1.50
(13)	Johnny Podres	12.00	6.00	3.50
(14)	Frank Robinson	15.00	7.50	4.50
(15)	Roy Seivers	5.00	2.50	1.50
(16)	Bob Skinner	5.00	2.50	1.50
(17)	Frank Thomas	12.00	6.00	3.50
(18)	Gus Triandos	5.00	2.50	1.50
(19)	Bob Turley	15.00	7.50	4.50
(20)	Mickey Vernon	12.00	6.00	3.50

1986 Ault Foods Blue Jays

The Ault Foods Blue Jays set is comprised of 24 full-color stickers. Designed to be placed in a special album, the stickers measure 2'' by 3'' in size. The attractive album measures 9'' by 12'' and is printed on glossy stock. While the stickers carry no information except for the player's last name and uniform number, the 20-page album contains extensive personal and statistical information about each of the 24 players.

1960 Armour Coins

The 1960 Armour coin issue was identical in number and style to the 1959 set. The unnumbered coins, which measure 1½'' in diameter, once again came in a variety of colors. Common colors for 1960 are dark blue, light blue, dark green, light green, red-orange, dark red, and light yellow. Scarce colors are aqua, grey-blue, cream, tan, and dark yellow. Scarce colors are double the value of the coins in the checklist that follows. The Daley coin is very scarce, although it is not exactly known why. Theories for the scarcity center on broken printing molds, contract disputes, and that the coin was only inserted in a test product that quickly proved to be unsuccessful. As in 1959, a mail-in offer for ten free coins was made available by Armour. The set price for the 1960 Armour set does not include the three more difficult variations.

		MT	NR MT	EX
Complete Set:		30.00	22.00	12.00
Common Player:		.60	.45	.25
Album:		5.00	3.75	2.00
1	Tony Fernandez	2.25	1.75	.90
5	Rance Mulliniks	.60	.45	.25
7	Damaso Garcia	.90	.70	.35
11	George Bell	5.00	3.75	2.00
12	Ernie Whitt	.90	.70	.35
13	Buck Martinez	.60	.45	.25
15	Lloyd Moseby	1.25	.90	.50
16	Garth Iorg	.60	.45	.25
17	Kelly Gruber	.90	.70	.35
18	Jim Clancy	1.25	.90	.50
22	Jimmy Key	1.50	1.25	.60
23	Cecil Fielder	.90	.70	.35
25	Steve Davis	.60	.45	.25
26	Willie Upshaw	.90	.70	.35
29	Jesse Barfield	3.00	2.25	1.25
31	Jim Acker	.60	.45	.25
33	Doyle Alexander	1.25	.90	.50
36	Bill Caudill	.60	.45	.25
37	Dave Stieb	1.50	1.25	.60

		MT	NR MT	EX
39	Don Gordon	.60	.45	.25
44	Cliff Johnson	.60	.45	.25
46	Gary Lavelle	.60	.45	.25
50	Tom Henke	1.25	.90	.50
53	Dennis Lamp	.60	.45	.25

1914 B18 Blankets

These 5¼'' flannels were issued in 1914 with several popular brands of tobacco. The flannels, whose ACC designation is B18, picked up the nickname blankets because many of the square pieces of cloth were sewn together to form pillow covers or bed spreads. Different color combinations on the flannels exist for all ten teams included in the set. The complete set price in the checklist that follows does not include higher priced variations.

		NR MT	EX	VG
	Complete Set:	2500.00	1250.00	375.00
	Common Player:	10.00	5.00	3.00
(1a)	Babe Adams (purple pennants)	25.00	12.50	7.50
(1b)	Babe Adams (red pennants)	30.00	15.00	9.00
(2a)	Sam Agnew (purple basepaths)	25.00	12.50	7.50
(2b)	Sam Agnew (red basepaths)	30.00	15.00	9.00
(3a)	Eddie Ainsmith (green pennants)	10.00	5.00	3.00
(3b)	Eddie Ainsmith (brown pennants)	10.00	5.00	3.00
(4a)	Jimmy Austin (purple basepaths)	25.00	12.50	7.50
(4b)	Jimmy Austin (red basepaths)	30.00	15.00	9.00
(5a)	Del Baker (white infield)	10.00	5.00	3.00
(5b)	Del Baker (brown infield)	50.00	25.00	15.00
(5c)	Del Baker (red infield)	125.00	62.00	37.00
(6a)	Johnny Bassler (purple pennants)	25.00	12.50	7.50
(6b)	Johnny Bassler (yellow pennants)	50.00	25.00	15.00
(7a)	Paddy Bauman (Baumann) (white infield)	10.00	5.00	3.00
(7b)	Paddy Bauman (Baumann) (brown infield)	50.00	25.00	15.00
(7c)	Paddy Bauman (Baumann) (red infield)	125.00	62.00	37.00
(8a)	Luke Boone (blue infield)	12.00	6.00	3.50
(8b)	Luke Boone (green infield)	12.00	6.00	3.50
(9a)	George Burns (brown basepaths)	12.00	6.00	3.50
(9b)	George Burns (green basepaths)	12.00	6.00	3.50
(10a)	Tioga George Burns (white infield)	10.00	5.00	3.00
(10b)	Tioga George Burns (brown infield)	50.00	25.00	15.00
(11a)	Max Carey (purple pennants)	45.00	22.00	13.50

		NR MT	EX	VG
(11b)	Max Carey (red pennants)	60.00	30.00	18.00
(12a)	Marty Cavanaugh (Kavanagh) (white infield)	10.00	5.00	3.00
(12b)	Marty Cavanaugh (Kavanagh) (brown infield)	60.00	30.00	18.00
(12c)	Marty Cavanaugh (Kavanagh) (red infield)	125.00	62.00	37.00
(12d)	Marty Kavanaugh (Kavanagh)	10.00	5.00	3.00
(13a)	Frank Chance (green infield)	30.00	15.00	9.00
(13b)	Frank Chance (brown pennants, blue infield)	30.00	15.00	9.00
(13c)	Frank Chance (yellow pennants, blue infield)	125.00	62.00	37.00
(14a)	Ray Chapman (purple pennants)	25.00	12.50	7.50
(14b)	Ray Chapman (yellow pennants)	50.00	25.00	15.00
(15a)	Ty Cobb (white infield)	125.00	62.00	37.00
(15b)	Ty Cobb (brown infield)	250.00	125.00	75.00
(15c)	Ty Cobb (red infield)	625.00	312.00	187.00
(16a)	King Cole (blue infield)	12.00	6.00	3.50
(16b)	King Cole (green infield)	12.00	6.00	3.50
(17a)	Joe Connolly (white infield)	10.00	5.00	3.00
(17b)	Joe Connolly (brown infield)	50.00	25.00	15.00
(18a)	Harry Coveleski (white infield)	12.00	6.00	3.50
(18b)	Harry Coveleski (brown infield)	58.00	29.00	17.50
(19a)	George Cutshaw (blue infield)	12.00	6.00	3.50
(19b)	George Cutshaw (green infield)	12.00	6.00	3.50
(20a)	Jake Daubert (blue infield)	18.00	9.00	5.50
(20b)	Jake Daubert (green infield)	18.00	9.00	5.50
(21a)	Ray Demmitt (white infield)	10.00	5.00	3.00
(21b)	Ray Demmitt (brown infield)	50.00	25.00	15.00
(22a)	Bill Doak (purple pennants)	25.00	12.50	7.50
(22b)	Bill Doak (yellow pennants)	50.00	25.00	15.00
(23a)	Cozy Dolan (purple pennants)	25.00	12.50	7.50
(23b)	Cozy Dolan (yellow pennants)	50.00	25.00	15.00
(24a)	Larry Doyle (brown basepaths)	12.00	6.00	3.50
(24b)	Larry Doyle (green basepaths)	12.00	6.00	3.50
(25a)	Art Fletcher (brown basepaths)	12.00	6.00	3.50
(25b)	Art Fletcher (green basepaths)	12.00	6.00	3.50
(26a)	Eddie Foster (brown pennants)	10.00	5.00	3.00
(26b)	Eddie Foster (green pennants)	10.00	5.00	3.00
(27a)	Del Gainor (white infield)	10.00	5.00	3.00
(27b)	Del Gainor (brown infield)	50.00	25.00	15.00
(28a)	Chick Gandil (brown pennants)	12.00	6.00	3.50
(28b)	Chick Gandil (green pennants)	12.00	6.00	3.50
(29a)	George Gibson (purple pennants)	25.00	12.50	7.50
(29b)	George Gibson (red pennants)	30.00	15.00	9.00
(30a)	Hank Gowdy (white infield)	12.00	6.00	3.50
(30b)	Hank Gowdy (brown infield)	50.00	25.00	15.00
(30c)	Hank Gowdy (red infield)	125.00	62.00	37.00
(31a)	Jack Graney (purple pennants)	25.00	12.50	7.50
(31b)	Jack Graney (yellow pennants)	50.00	25.00	15.00
(32a)	Eddie Grant (brown basepaths)	12.00	6.00	3.50
(32b)	Eddie Grant (green basepaths)	12.00	6.00	3.50
(33a)	Tommy Griffith (white infield, green pennants)	10.00	5.00	3.00
(33b)	Tommy Griffith (white infield, red pennants)	125.00	62.00	37.00
(33c)	Tommy Griffith (brown infield)	50.00	25.00	15.00
(34a)	Earl Hamilton (purple basepaths)	25.00	12.50	7.50
(34b)	Earl Hamilton (red basepaths)	30.00	15.00	9.00
(35a)	Roy Hartzell (blue infield)	12.00	6.00	3.50
(35b)	Roy Hartzell (green infield)	12.00	6.00	3.50
(36a)	Miller Huggins (purple pennants)	45.00	22.00	13.50
(36b)	Miller Huggins (yellow pennants)	90.00	45.00	27.00
(37a)	John Hummel (brown infield)	12.00	6.00	3.50
(37b)	John Hummel (green infield)	12.00	6.00	3.50
(38a)	Ham Hyatt (purple pennants)	25.00	12.50	7.50
(38b)	Ham Hyatt (red pennants)	30.00	15.00	9.00
(39a)	Shoeless Joe Jackson (purple pennants)	190.00	95.00	57.00
(39b)	Shoeless Joe Jackson (yellow pennants)	250.00	125.00	75.00
(40a)	Bill James (white infield)	10.00	5.00	3.00
(40b)	Bill James (brown infield)	50.00	25.00	15.00
(41a)	Walter Johnson (brown pennants)	190.00	95.00	57.00
(41b)	Walter Johnson (green pennants)	190.00	95.00	57.00
(42a)	Ray Keating (blue infield)	12.00	6.00	3.50
(42b)	Ray Keating (green infield)	12.00	6.00	3.50

Complete set prices do not include the higher priced variations, unless noted otherwise.

	NR MT	EX	VG
(43a) Joe Kelley (Kelly) (purple pennants)			
	25.00	12.50	7.50
(43b) Joe Kelley (Kelly) (red pennants)			
	30.00	15.00	9.00
(44a) Ed Konetchy (purple pennants)	25.00	12.50	7.50
(44b) Ed Konetchy (red pennants)	30.00	15.00	9.00
(45a) Nemo Leibold (purple pennants)	25.00	12.50	7.50
(45b) Nemo Leibold (yellow pennants)	50.00	25.00	15.00
(46a) Fritz Maisel (blue infield)	12.00	6.00	3.50
(46b) Fritz Maisel (green infield)	12.00	6.00	3.50
(47a) Les Mann (white infield)	10.00	5.00	3.00
(47b) Les Mann (brown infield)	50.00	25.00	15.00
(48a) Rabbit Maranville (white infield)	30.00	15.00	9.00
(48b) Rabbit Maranville (brown infield)	90.00	45.00	27.00
(48c) Rabbit Maranville (red infield)	140.00	70.00	42.00
(49a) Bill McAllister (McAllester) (purple pennants)			
	25.00	12.50	7.50
(49b) Bill McAllister (McAllester) (red pennants)			
	30.00	15.00	9.00
(50a) George McBride (brown pennants)			
	10.00	5.00	3.00
(50b) George McBride (green pennants)			
	10.00	5.00	3.00
(51a) Chief Meyers (brown basepaths)	12.00	6.00	3.50
(51b) Chief Meyers (green basepaths)	12.00	6.00	3.50
(52a) Clyde Milan (brown pennants)	10.00	5.00	3.00
(52b) Clyde Milan (green pennants)	10.00	5.00	3.00
(53a) Dots Miller (purple pennants)	25.00	12.50	7.50
(53b) Dots Miller (yellow pennants)	50.00	25.00	15.00
(54a) Otto Miller (blue infield)	12.00	6.00	3.50
(54b) Otto Miller (green infield)	12.00	6.00	3.50
(55a) Willie Mitchell (purple pennants)	25.00	12.50	7.50
(55b) Willie Mitchell (yellow pennants)	50.00	25.00	15.00
(56a) Danny Moeller (brown pennants)			
	10.00	5.00	3.00
(56b) Danny Moeller (green pennants)	10.00	5.00	3.00
(57a) Ray Morgan (brown pennants)	10.00	5.00	3.00
(57b) Ray Morgan (green pennants)	10.00	5.00	3.00
(58a) George Moriarty (white infield)	10.00	5.00	3.00
(58b) George Moriarty (brown infield)	50.00	25.00	15.00
(58c) Geroge Moriarty (red infield)	125.00	62.00	37.00
(59a) Mike Mowrey (purple pennants)	25.00	12.50	7.50
(59b) Mike Mowrey (red pennants)	30.00	15.00	9.00
(60a) Red Murray (brown basepaths)	12.00	6.00	3.50
(60b) Red Murray (green basepaths)	12.00	6.00	3.50
(61a) Ivy Olson (purple pennants)	25.00	12.50	7.50
(61b) Ivy Olson (yellow pennants)	50.00	25.00	15.00
(62a) Steve O'Neill (purple pennants)	25.00	12.50	7.50
(62b) Steve O'Neill (red pennants)	50.00	25.00	15.00
(63a) Marty O'Toole (purple pennants)			
	25.00	12.50	7.50
(63b) Marty O'Toole (red pennants)	30.00	15.00	9.00
(64a) Roger Peckinpaugh (blue infield)	12.00	6.00	3.50
(64b) Roger Peckinpaugh (green infield)			
	12.00	6.00	3.50
(65a) Hub Perdue (white infield)	10.00	5.00	3.00
(65b) Hub Perdue (brown infield)	50.00	25.00	15.00
(66a) Del Pratt (purple pennants)	25.00	12.50	7.50
(66b) Del Pratt (yellow pennants)	30.00	15.00	9.00
(67a) Hank Robinson (purple pennants)			
	25.00	12.50	7.50
(67b) Hank Robinson (yellow pennants)			
	50.00	25.00	15.00
(68a) Nap Rucker (blue infield)	12.00	6.00	3.50
(68b) Nap Rucker (green infield)	12.00	6.00	3.50
(69a) Slim Sallee (purple pennants)	25.00	12.50	7.50
(69b) Slim Sallee (yellow pennants)	50.00	25.00	15.00
(70a) Howard Shanks (brown pennants)			
	10.00	5.00	3.00
(70b) Howard Shanks (green pennants)			
	10.00	5.00	3.00
(71a) Burt Shotton (purple basepaths)	25.00	12.50	7.50
(71b) Burt Shotton (red basepaths)	30.00	15.00	9.00
(72a) Red Smith (blue infield)	12.00	6.00	3.50
(72b) Red Smith (green infield)	12.00	6.00	3.50
(73a) Fred Snodgrass (brown basepaths)			
		6.00	3.50
(73b) Fred Snodgrass (green basepaths)			
	12.00	6.00	3.50
(74a) Bill Steele (purple pennants)	25.00	12.50	7.50
74b Bill Steele (yellow pennants)	50.00	25.00	15.00
(75a) Casey Stengel (white infield)	39.00	19.50	11.50
(75b) Casey Stengel (brown infield)	125.00	62.00	37.00
(76a) Jeff Sweeney (blue infield)	12.00	6.00	3.50
(76b) Jeff Sweeney (green infield)	12.00	6.00	3.50
(77a) Jeff Tesreau (brown basepaths)	12.00	6.00	3.50
(77b) Jeff Tesreau (green basepaths)	12.00	6.00	3.50
(78a) Terry Turner (purple pennants)	25.00	12.50	7.50
(78b) Terry Turner (yellow pennants)	50.00	25.00	15.00
(79a) Lefty Tyler (white infield)	10.00	5.00	3.00
(79b) Lefty Tyler (brown infield)	50.00	25.00	15.00

	NR MT	EX	VG
(79c) Lefty Tyler (red infield)	125.00	62.00	37.00
(80a) Jim Viox (purple pennants)	25.00	12.50	7.50
(80b) Jim Viox (red pennants)	30.00	15.00	9.00
(81a) Bull Wagner (blue infield)	12.00	6.00	3.50
(81b) Bull Wagner (green infield)	12.00	6.00	3.50
(82a) Bobby Wallace (purple basepaths)			
	45.00	22.00	13.50
(82b) Bobby Wallace (red basepaths)	50.00	25.00	15.00
(83a) Dee Walsh (purple basepaths)	25.00	12.50	7.50
(83b) Dee Walsh (red basepaths)	30.00	15.00	9.00
(84a) Jimmy Walsh (blue infield)	12.00	6.00	3.50
(84b) Jimmy Walsh (green infield)	12.00	6.00	3.50
(85a) Bert Whaling (white infield)	10.00	5.00	3.00
(85b) Bert Whaling (brown infield)	50.00	25.00	15.00
(85c) Bert Whaling (red infield)	125.00	62.00	37.00
(86a) Zach Wheat (blue infield)	30.00	15.00	9.00
(86b) Zach Wheat (green infield)	30.00	15.00	9.00
(87a) Possum Whitted (purple pennants)			
	25.00	12.50	7.50
(87b) Possum Whitted (yellow pennants)			
	50.00	25.00	15.00
(88a) Gus Williams (purple basepaths)	25.00	12.50	7.50
(88b) Gus Williams (red basepaths)	30.00	15.00	9.00
(89a) Owen Wilson (purple pennants)	25.00	12.50	7.50
(89b) Owen Wilson (yellow pennants)	50.00	25.00	15.00
(90a) Hooks Wiltse (brown basepaths)	12.00	6.00	3.50
(90b) Hooks Wiltse (green basepaths)	12.00	6.00	3.50

1948 Babe Ruth Story

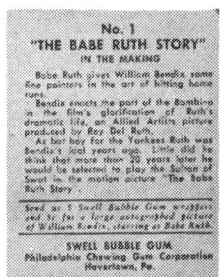

The Philadelphia Gum Co., in 1948, created a card set about the movie "The Babe Ruth Story", which starred William Bendix and Claire Trevor. The set, whose ACC designation is R421, contains 28 black and white, numbered cards which measure 2" by 2½". The Babe Ruth Story set was originally intended to consist of sixteen cards. Twelve additional cards (#'s 17-28) were added when Ruth died before the release of the film. The card backs included an offer for an autographed photo of William Bendix, starring as the Babe, for five Swell Bubble gum wrappers and five cents.

	NR MT	EX	VG
Complete Set:	625.00	313.00	188.00
Common Player: 1-16	8.00	4.00	2.50
Common Player: 17-28	25.00	12.50	7.50
1 "The Babe Ruth Story" In The Making			
	20.00	6.00	2.50
2 Bat Boy Becomes the Babe... William Bendix	10.00	4.00	2.50
3 Claire Hodgson...Claire Trevor	8.00	4.00	2.50
4 Babe Ruth and Claire Hodgson	8.00	4.00	2.50
5 Brother Matthias...Charles Bickford			
	8.00	4.00	2.50
6 Phil Conrad...Sam Levene	8.00	4.00	2.50
7 Night Club Singer...Gertrude Niesen			
	8.00	4.00	2.50
8 Baseball's Famous Deal...Jack Dunn (William Frawley)	8.00	4.00	2.50
9 Mr. & Mrs. Babe Ruth	8.00	4.00	2.50
10 Babe Ruth, Claire Ruth, and Brother Matthias	8.00	4.00	2.50
11 Babe Ruth and Miller Huggins (Fred Lightner)	8.00	4.00	2.50
12 Babe Ruth At Bed Of Ill Boy Johnny Sylvester (Gregory Marshall)	8.00	4.00	2.50

		NR MT	EX	VG
13	Sylvester Family Listening To Game			
		8.00	4.00	2.50
14	"When A Feller Needs a Friend" (With Dog At Police Station)	8.00	4.00	2.50
15	Dramatic Home Run	8.00	4.00	2.50
16	The Homer That Set the Record (#60)			
		8.00	4.00	2.50
17	"The Slap That Started Baseball's Famous Career"	25.00	12.50	7.50
18	The Babe Plays Santa Claus	25.00	12.50	7.50
19	Meeting Of Owner And Manager	25.00	12.50	7.50
20	"Broken Window Paid Off"	25.00	12.50	7.50
21	Babe In A Crowd Of Autograph Collectors			
		25.00	12.50	7.50
22	Charley Grimm And William Bendix			
		25.00	12.50	7.50
23	Ted Lyons And William Bendix	30.00	15.00	9.00
24	Lefty Gomez, William Bendix, And Bucky Harris	35.00	17.50	10.50
25	Babe Ruth and William Bendix	55.00	27.00	16.50
26	Babe Ruth And William Bendix	55.00	27.00	16.50
27	Babe Ruth And Claire Trevor	60.00	27.00	16.50
28	William Bendix, Babe Ruth, And Claire Trevor	70.00	30.00	16.50

1987 Baseball Super Stars Discs

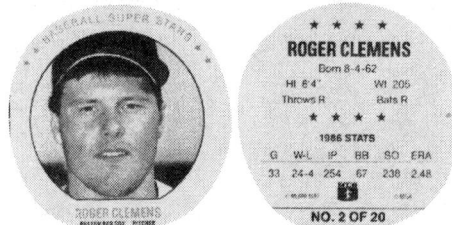

Produced by Mike Schecter and Associates, the "Baseball Super Stars" disc set was released as part of a promotion for various brands of iced tea mixes in many parts of the country. Among the brands participating in the promotion were Acme, Alpha Beta, Bustelo, Key, King Kullen, Lady Lee, Our Own and Weis. The discs were issued in three-part folding panels, with each disc measuring 2½" in diameter. The disc fronts feature a full-color photo inside a bright yellow border. Two player discs were included in each panel along with a coupon disc offering either an uncut press sheet of the set or a facsimile autographed ball.

		MT	NR MT	EX
Complete Panel Set:		6.00	4.50	2.50
Complete Singles Set:		2.00	1.50	.80
Common Panel:		.25	.20	.10
Common Single Player:		.05	.04	.02
Panel		.90	.70	.35
1	Darryl Strawberry	.15	.11	.06
2	Roger Clemens	.20	.15	.08
Panel		.35	.25	.14
3	Ron Darling	.08	.06	.03
4	Keith Hernandez	.10	.08	.04
Panel		.90	.70	.35
5	Tony Pena	.05	.04	.02
6	Don Mattingly	.30	.25	.12
Panel		.90	.70	.35
7	Eric Davis	.20	.15	.08
8	Gary Carter	.12	.09	.05
Panel		.80	.60	.30
9	Dave Winfield	.12	.09	.05
10	Wally Joyner	.20	.15	.08
Panel		.50	.40	.20
11	Mike Schmidt	.15	.11	.06
12	Robby Thompson	.05	.04	.02
Panel		.80	.60	.30
13	Wade Boggs	.20	.15	.08
14	Cal Ripken Jr.	.12	.09	.05
Panel		.90	.70	.35
15	Dale Murphy	.20	.15	.08

		MT	NR MT	EX
16	Tony Gwynn	.15	.11	.06
Panel		.80	.60	.30
17	Jose Canseco	.20	.15	.08
18	Rickey Henderson	.12	.09	.05
Panel		.25	.20	.10
19	Lance Parrish	.08	.06	.03
20	Dave Righetti	.08	.06	.03

1934-36 Batter-Up

National Chicle's 192-card "Batter-Up" set was issued from 1934 through 1936. The blank-backed cards are die-cut, enabling collectors of the era to fold the top of the card over so that it could stand upright on its own support. The cards can be found in black and white or a variety of color tints. Card numbers 1-80 measure 2⅜" by 3¼" in size, while the high numbered cards (81-192) measure ¼" smaller in width. The high numbered cards are significantly more difficult to find than the lower numbers. The set's ACC designation is R318.

		NR MT	EX	VG
Complete Set:		11000.00	5500.00	3300.
Common Player: 1-80		25.00	12.50	7.50
Common Player: 81-192		50.00	25.00	15.00
1	Wally Berger	60.00	18.00	7.50
2	Ed Brandt	35.00	12.50	7.50
3	Al Lopez	40.00	20.00	12.00
4	Dick Bartell	25.00	12.50	7.50
5	Carl Hubbell	60.00	30.00	18.00
6	Bill Terry	60.00	30.00	18.00
7	Pepper Martin	30.00	15.00	9.00
8	Jim Bottomley	40.00	20.00	12.00
9	Tommy Bridges	30.00	15.00	9.00
10	Rick Ferrell	40.00	20.00	12.00
11	Ray Benge	25.00	12.50	7.50
12	Wes Ferrell	30.00	15.00	9.00
13	Bill Cissell	25.00	12.50	7.50
14	Pie Traynor	50.00	25.00	15.00
15	Roy Mahaffey	25.00	12.50	7.50
16	Chick Hafey	40.00	20.00	12.00
17	Lloyd Waner	40.00	20.00	12.00
18	Jack Burns	25.00	12.50	7.50
19	Buddy Myer	25.00	12.50	7.50
20	Bob Johnson	30.00	15.00	9.00
21	Arky Vaughn (Vaughan)	40.00	20.00	12.00
22	Red Rolfe	35.00	17.50	10.50
23	Lefty Gomez	60.00	30.00	18.00
24	Earl Averill	40.00	20.00	12.00
25	Mickey Cochrane	60.00	30.00	18.00
26	Van Mungo	30.00	15.00	9.00
27	Mel Ott	70.00	35.00	21.00
28	Jimmie Foxx	90.00	45.00	27.00
29	Jimmy Dykes	30.00	15.00	9.00
30	Bill Dickey	80.00	40.00	24.00
31	Lefty Grove	60.00	30.00	18.00
32	Joe Cronin	50.00	25.00	15.00
33	Frankie Frisch	60.00	30.00	18.00
34	Al Simmons	40.00	20.00	12.00
35	Rogers Hornsby	80.00	40.00	24.00
36	Ted Lyons	40.00	20.00	12.00
37	Rabbit Maranville	40.00	20.00	12.00
38	Jimmie Wilson	25.00	12.50	7.50
39	Willie Kamm	25.00	12.50	7.50
40	Bill Hallahan	30.00	15.00	9.00

#	Player	NR MT	EX	VG
41	Gus Suhr	25.00	12.50	7.50
42	Charlie Gehringer	60.00	30.00	18.00
43	Joe Heving	25.00	12.50	7.50
44	Adam Comorosky	25.00	12.50	7.50
45	Tony Lazzeri	40.00	20.00	12.00
46	Sam Leslie	25.00	12.50	7.50
47	Bob Smith	25.00	12.50	7.50
48	Willis Hudlin	25.00	12.50	7.50
49	Carl Reynolds	25.00	12.50	7.50
50	Fred Schulte	25.00	12.50	7.50
51	Cookie Lavagetto	30.00	15.00	9.00
52	Hal Schumacher	30.00	15.00	9.00
53	Doc Cramer	25.00	12.50	7.50
54	Si Johnson	25.00	12.50	7.50
55	Ollie Bejma	25.00	12.50	7.50
56	Sammy Byrd	35.00	17.50	10.50
57	Hank Greenberg	60.00	30.00	18.00
58	Bill Knickerbocker	25.00	12.50	7.50
59	Billy Urbanski	25.00	12.50	7.50
60	Ed Morgan	25.00	12.50	7.50
61	Eric McNair	25.00	12.50	7.50
62	Ben Chapman	35.00	17.50	10.50
63	Roy Johnson	25.00	12.50	7.50
64	"Dizzy" Dean	225.00	112.00	67.00
65	Zeke Bonura	25.00	12.50	7.50
66	Firpo Marberry	25.00	12.50	7.50
67	Gus Mancuso	25.00	12.50	7.50
68	Joe Vosmik	25.00	12.50	7.50
69	Earl Grace	25.00	12.50	7.50
70	Tony Piet	25.00	12.50	7.50
71	Rollie Hemsley	25.00	12.50	7.50
72	Fred Fitzsimmons	30.00	15.00	9.00
73	Hack Wilson	50.00	25.00	15.00
74	Chick Fullis	25.00	12.50	7.50
75	Fred Frankhouse	25.00	12.50	7.50
76	Ethan Allen	25.00	12.50	7.50
77	Heinie Manush	40.00	20.00	12.00
78	Rip Collins	30.00	15.00	9.00
79	Tony Cuccinello	30.00	15.00	9.00
80	Joe Kuhel	25.00	12.50	7.50
81	Thomas Bridges	60.00	30.00	18.00
82	Clinton Brown	50.00	25.00	15.00
83	Albert Blanche	50.00	25.00	15.00
84	"Boze" Berger	50.00	25.00	15.00
85	Goose Goslin	90.00	45.00	27.00
86	Vernon Gomez	110.00	55.00	33.00
87	Joe Glen (Glenn)	70.00	35.00	21.00
88	"Cy" Blanton	50.00	25.00	15.00
89	Tom Carey	50.00	25.00	15.00
90	Ralph Birkhofer	50.00	25.00	15.00
91	Frank Gabler	50.00	25.00	15.00
92	Dick Coffman	50.00	25.00	15.00
93	Ollie Bejma	50.00	25.00	15.00
94	Leroy Earl Parmalee	50.00	25.00	15.00
95	Carl Reynolds	50.00	25.00	15.00
96	Ben Cantwell	50.00	25.00	15.00
97	Curtis Davis	50.00	25.00	15.00
98	Wallace Moses, Billy Webb	60.00	30.00	18.00
99	Ray Benge	50.00	25.00	15.00
100	"Pie" Traynor	110.00	55.00	33.00
101	Phil. Cavarretta	60.00	30.00	18.00
102	"Pep" Young	50.00	25.00	15.00
103	Willis Hudlin	50.00	25.00	15.00
104	Mickey Haslin	50.00	25.00	15.00
105	Oswald Bluege	50.00	25.00	15.00
106	Paul Andrews	50.00	25.00	15.00
107	Edward A. Brandt	50.00	25.00	15.00
108	Dan Taylor	50.00	25.00	15.00
109	Thornton T. Lee	50.00	25.00	15.00
110	Hal Schumacher	60.00	30.00	18.00
111	Minter Hayes, Ted Lyons	90.00	45.00	27.00
112	Odell Hale	50.00	25.00	15.00
113	Earl Averill	90.00	45.00	27.00
114	Italo Chelini	50.00	25.00	15.00
115	Ivy Andrews, Jim Bottomley	90.00	45.00	27.00
116	Bill Walker	50.00	25.00	15.00
117	Bill Dickey	175.00	87.00	52.00
118	Gerald Walker	60.00	30.00	18.00
119	Ted Lyons	90.00	45.00	27.00
120	Elden Auker (Eldon)	50.00	25.00	15.00
121	Wild Bill Hallahan	60.00	30.00	18.00
122	Freddy Lindstrom	90.00	45.00	27.00
123	Oral C. Hildebrand	50.00	25.00	15.00
124	Luke Appling	90.00	45.00	27.00
125	"Pepper" Martin	70.00	35.00	21.00
126	Rick Ferrell	90.00	45.00	27.00
127	Ival Goodman	50.00	25.00	15.00
128	Joe Kuhel	50.00	25.00	15.00
129	Ernest Lombardi	90.00	45.00	27.00
130	Charles Gehringer	140.00	70.00	42.00
131	Van L. Mungo	70.00	35.00	21.00

#	Player	NR MT	EX	VG
132	Larry French	50.00	25.00	15.00
133	"Buddy" Myer	50.00	25.00	15.00
134	Mel Harder	60.00	30.00	18.00
135	Augie Galan	50.00	25.00	15.00
136	"Gabby" Hartnett	110.00	55.00	33.00
137	Stan Hack	60.00	30.00	18.00
138	Billy Herman	90.00	45.00	27.00
139	Bill Jurges	60.00	30.00	18.00
140	Bill Lee	50.00	25.00	15.00
141	"Zeke" Bonura	50.00	25.00	15.00
142	Tony Piet	50.00	25.00	15.00
143	Paul Dean	90.00	45.00	27.00
144	Jimmy Foxx	200.00	100.00	60.00
145	Joe Medwick	90.00	45.00	27.00
146	Rip Collins	60.00	30.00	18.00
147	Melo Almada	50.00	25.00	15.00
148	Allan Cooke	50.00	25.00	15.00
149	Moe Berg	60.00	30.00	18.00
150	Adolph Camilli	60.00	30.00	18.00
151	Oscar Melillo	50.00	25.00	15.00
152	Bruce Campbell	50.00	25.00	15.00
153	Lefty Grove	140.00	70.00	42.00
154	John Murphy	70.00	35.00	21.00
155	Luke Sewell	60.00	30.00	18.00
156	Leo Durocher	140.00	70.00	42.00
157	Lloyd Waner	90.00	45.00	27.00
158	Guy Bush	50.00	25.00	15.00
159	Jimmy Dykes	60.00	30.00	18.00
160	Steve O'Neill	50.00	25.00	15.00
161	Gen. Crowder	50.00	25.00	15.00
162	Joe Cascarella	50.00	25.00	15.00
163	"Bud" Hafey	50.00	25.00	15.00
164	"Gilly" Campbell	50.00	25.00	15.00
165	Ray Hayworth	50.00	25.00	15.00
166	Frank Demaree	50.00	25.00	15.00
167	John Babich	50.00	25.00	15.00
168	Marvin Owen	50.00	25.00	15.00
169	Ralph Kress	50.00	25.00	15.00
170	"Mule" Haas	50.00	25.00	15.00
171	Frank Higgins	50.00	25.00	15.00
172	Walter Berger	50.00	25.00	15.00
173	Frank Frisch	140.00	70.00	42.00
174	Wess Ferrell (Wes)	60.00	30.00	18.00
175	Pete Fox	50.00	25.00	15.00
176	John Vergez	50.00	25.00	15.00
177	William Rogell	50.00	25.00	15.00
178	"Don" Brennan	50.00	25.00	15.00
179	James Bottomley	90.00	45.00	27.00
180	Travis Jackson	90.00	45.00	27.00
181	Robert Rolfe	70.00	35.00	21.00
182	Frank Crosetti	90.00	45.00	27.00
183	Joe Cronin	110.00	55.00	33.00
184	"Schoolboy" Rowe	70.00	35.00	21.00
185	"Chuck" Klein	90.00	45.00	27.00
186	Lon Warneke	50.00	25.00	15.00
187	Gus Suhr	50.00	25.00	15.00
188	Ben Chapman	70.00	35.00	21.00
189	Clint. Brown	50.00	25.00	15.00
190	Paul Derringer	60.00	30.00	18.00
191	John Burns	60.00	25.00	15.00
192	John Broaca	110.00	35.00	21.00

1959 Bazooka

MICKEY MANTLE
OUTFIELD · N.Y. YANKEES

The 1959 Bazooka set, consisting of 23 full color, unnumbered cards, was issued on boxes of Bazooka one-cent bubblegum. The individually wrapped pieces of Bazooka gum were produced by Topps Chewing Gum. The blank-backed cards measure 2 13/16'' x 4 15/16''. Nine cards were first issued, with 14 being added to the set later. The nine more plentiful cards are #'s 1, 5, 8, 9, 14, 15, 16, 17 and 22. Complete boxes would command a 75% premium over the prices in the checklist that follows.

		NR MT	EX	VG
Complete Set:		3400.00	1700.00	1020.
Common Player:		45.00	22.00	13.50
(1a)	Hank Aaron (name in white)	225.00	112.00	67.00
(1b)	Hank Aaron (name in yellow)	225.00	112.00	67.00
(2)	Richie Ashburn	150.00	75.00	45.00
(3)	Ernie Banks	275.00	137.00	82.00
(4)	Ken Boyer	125.00	62.00	37.00
(5)	Orlando Cepeda	55.00	27.00	16.50
(6)	Bob Cerv	90.00	45.00	27.00
(7)	Rocco Colavito	125.00	62.00	37.00
(8)	Del Crandall	45.00	22.00	13.50
(9)	Jim Davenport	45.00	22.00	13.50
(10)	Don Drysdale	175.00	87.00	52.00
(11)	Nellie Fox	150.00	75.00	45.00
(12)	Jackie Jensen	125.00	62.00	37.00
(13)	Harvey Kuenn	125.00	62.00	37.00
(14)	Mickey Mantle	400.00	200.00	120.00
(15)	Willie Mays	225.00	112.00	67.00
(16)	Bill Mazeroski	45.00	22.00	13.50
(17)	Roy McMillan	45.00	22.00	13.50
(18)	Billy Pierce	125.00	62.00	37.00
(19)	Roy Sievers	125.00	62.00	37.00
(20)	Duke Snider	250.00	125.00	75.00
(21)	Gus Triandos	125.00	62.00	37.00
(22)	Bob Turley	55.00	27.00	16.50
(23)	Vic Wertz	90.00	45.00	27.00

		NR MT	EX	VG
6	Dick Stuart	8.00	4.00	2.50
Panel		80.00	40.00	24.00
7	Bob Clemente	30.00	15.00	9.00
8	Yogi Berra	30.00	15.00	9.00
9	Ken Boyer	8.00	4.00	2.50
Panel		40.00	20.00	12.00
10	Orlando Cepeda	12.00	6.00	3.50
11	Gus Triandos	8.00	4.00	2.50
12	Frank Malzone	8.00	4.00	2.50
Panel		60.00	30.00	18.00
13	Willie Mays	30.00	15.00	9.00
14	Camilo Pascual	6.00	3.00	1.75
15	Bob Cerv	6.00	3.00	1.75
Panel		60.00	30.00	18.00
16	Vic Power	6.00	3.00	1.75
17	Larry Sherry	6.00	3.00	1.75
18	Al Kaline	30.00	15.00	9.00
Panel		65.00	32.00	19.50
19	Warren Spahn	20.00	10.00	6.00
20	Harmon Killebrew	25.00	12.50	7.50
21	Jackie Jensen	12.00	6.00	3.50
Panel		90.00	45.00	27.00
22	Luis Aparicio	20.00	10.00	6.00
23	Gil Hodges	25.00	12.50	7.50
24	Richie Ashburn	25.00	12.50	7.50
Panel		60.00	30.00	18.00
25	Nellie Fox	25.00	12.50	7.50
26	Robin Roberts	25.00	12.50	7.50
27	Joe Cunningham	6.00	3.00	1.75
Panel		60.00	30.00	18.00
28	Early Wynn	20.00	10.00	6.00
29	Frank Robinson	20.00	10.00	6.00
30	Rocky Colavito	12.00	6.00	3.50
Panel		175.00	87.00	52.00
31	Mickey Mantle	100.00	50.00	30.00
32	Glen Hobbie	6.00	3.00	1.75
33	Roy McMillan	6.00	3.00	1.75
Panel		40.00	20.00	12.00
34	Harvey Kuenn	12.00	6.00	3.50
35	Johnny Antonelli	6.00	3.00	1.75
36	Del Crandall	6.00	3.00	1.75

1960 Bazooka

Three-card panels were found on the bottoms of Bazooka bubblegum boxes in 1960. The blank-backed set is comprised of 36 cards with the card number being located at the bottom of each full-color card. The individual cards measure 1 13/16'' by 2 3/4''; the panels measure 2¾'' by 5½'' in size. Prices, in the checklist that follows, are given for complete panels and individual cards.

		NR MT	EX	VG
Complete Panel Set:		1000.00	500.00	300.00
Complete Singles Set:		650.00	325.00	195.00
Common Panel:		40.00	20.00	12.00
Common Single Player:		6.00	3.00	1.75
Panel		60.00	30.00	18.00
1	Ernie Banks	30.00	15.00	9.00
2	Bud Daley	6.00	3.00	1.75
3	Wally Moon	6.00	3.00	1.75
Panel		70.00	35.00	21.00
4	Hank Aaron	30.00	15.00	9.00
5	Milt Pappas	8.00	4.00	2.50

1961 Bazooka

Similar in design to the 1960 Bazooka set, the 1961 edition consists of 36 cards issued in panels of three on the bottom of Bazooka bubblegum boxes. The full-color cards, which measure 1 13/16'' by 2 3/4'' individually and 2¾'' by 5½'' as panels, are numbered 1 through 36. The backs are blank.

		NR MT	EX	VG
Complete Panel Set:		900.00	450.00	270.00
Complete Singles Set:		550.00	275.00	165.00
Common Panel:		40.00	20.00	12.00
Common Single Player:		6.00	3.00	1.75
Panel		175.00	87.00	52.00
1	Art Mahaffey	8.00	4.00	2.50
2	Mickey Mantle	100.00	50.00	30.00
3	Ron Santo	8.00	4.00	2.50
Panel		55.00	27.00	16.50
4	Bud Daley	6.00	3.00	1.75
5	Roger Maris	30.00	15.00	9.00
6	Eddie Yost	6.00	3.00	1.75
Panel		40.00	20.00	12.00

		NR MT	EX	VG
7	Minnie Minoso	12.00	6.00	3.50
8	Dick Groat	8.00	4.00	2.50
9	Frank Malzone	8.00	4.00	2.50
Panel		50.00	25.00	15.00
10	Dick Donovan	6.00	3.00	1.75
11	Ed Mathews	20.00	10.00	6.00
12	Jim Lemon	6.00	3.00	1.75
Panel		40.00	20.00	12.00
13	Chuck Estrada	6.00	3.00	1.75
14	Ken Boyer	8.00	4.00	2.50
15	Harvey Kuenn	12.00	6.00	3.50
Panel		55.00	27.00	16.50
16	Ernie Broglio	6.00	3.00	1.75
17	Rocky Colavito	12.00	6.00	3.50
18	Ted Kluszewski	20.00	10.00	6.00
Panel		80.00	40.00	24.00
19	Ernie Banks	30.00	15.00	9.00
20	Al Kaline	30.00	15.00	9.00
21	Ed Bailey	6.00	3.00	1.75
Panel		60.00	30.00	18.00
22	Jim Perry	6.00	3.00	1.75
23	Willie Mays	30.00	15.00	9.00
24	Bill Mazeroski	12.00	6.00	3.50
Panel		55.00	27.00	16.50
25	Gus Triandos	6.00	3.00	1.75
26	Don Drysdale	20.00	10.00	6.00
27	Frank Herrera	8.00	4.00	2.50
Panel		55.00	27.00	16.50
28	Earl Battey	6.00	3.00	1.75
29	Warren Spahn	20.00	10.00	6.00
30	Gene Woodling	8.00	4.00	2.50
Panel		50.00	25.00	15.00
31	Frank Robinson	20.00	10.00	6.00
32	Pete Runnels	6.00	3.00	1.75
33	Woodie Held	6.00	3.00	1.75
Panel		55.00	27.00	16.50
34	Norm Larker	6.00	3.00	1.75
35	Luis Aparicio	20.00	10.00	6.00
36	Bill Tuttle	6.00	3.00	1.75

		NR MT	EX	VG
(4)	Earl Battey	6.00	3.00	1.75
(5)	Warren Spahn	20.00	10.00	6.00
(6)	Lee Thomas	6.00	3.00	1.75
Panel		40.00	20.00	12.00
(7)	Orlando Cepeda	12.00	6.00	3.50
(8)	Woodie Held	6.00	3.00	1.75
(9)	Bob Aspromonte	10.00	5.00	3.00
Panel		90.00	45.00	27.00
(10)	Dick Howser	8.00	4.00	2.50
(11)	Bob Clemente	30.00	15.00	9.00
(12)	Al Kaline	30.00	15.00	9.00
Panel		60.00	30.00	18.00
(13)	Joey Jay	6.00	3.00	1.75
(14)	Roger Maris	30.00	15.00	9.00
(15)	Frank Howard	12.00	6.00	3.50
Panel		60.00	30.00	18.00
(16)	Sandy Koufax	35.00	17.50	10.50
(17)	Jim Gentile	6.00	3.00	1.75
(18)	Johnny Callison	10.00	5.00	3.00
Panel		40.00	20.00	12.00
(19)	Jim Landis	6.00	3.00	1.75
(20)	Ken Boyer	12.00	6.00	3.50
(21)	Chuck Schilling	10.00	5.00	3.00
Panel		175.00	87.00	52.00
(22)	Art Mahaffey	8.00	4.00	2.50
(23)	Mickey Mantle	100.00	50.00	30.00
(24)	Dick Stuart	8.00	4.00	2.50
Panel		60.00	30.00	18.00
(25)	Ken McBride	6.00	3.00	1.75
(26)	Frank Robinson	20.00	10.00	6.00
(27)	Gil Hodges	25.00	12.50	7.50
Panel		60.00	30.00	18.00
(28)	Milt Pappas	8.00	4.00	2.50
(29)	Hank Aaron	30.00	15.00	9.00
(30)	Luis Aparicio	20.00	10.00	6.00
Panel		250.00	125.00	75.00
(31)	Johnny Romano	20.00	10.00	6.00
(32)	Ernie Banks	90.00	45.00	27.00
(33)	Norm Siebern	20.00	10.00	6.00
Panel		50.00	25.00	15.00
(34)	Ron Santo	12.00	6.00	3.50
(35)	Norm Cash	12.00	6.00	3.50
(36)	Jim Piersall	12.00	6.00	3.50
Panel		60.00	30.00	18.00
(37)	Don Schwall	10.00	5.00	3.00
(38)	Willie Mays	30.00	15.00	9.00
(39)	Norm Larker	6.00	3.00	1.75
Panel		60.00	30.00	18.00
(40)	Bill White	12.00	6.00	3.50
(41)	Whitey Ford	25.00	12.50	7.50
(42)	Rocky Colavito	12.00	6.00	3.50
Panel		250.00	125.00	75.00
(43)	Don Zimmer	25.00	12.50	7.50
(44)	Harmon Killebrew	90.00	45.00	27.00
(45)	Gene Woodling	20.00	10.00	6.00

1962 Bazooka

KEN BOYER
ST. LOUIS CARDINALS   3rd base

In 1962, Bazooka increased the size of its set to 45 full-color cards. The set is unnumbered and was issued in panels of three on the bottoms of bubble-gum boxes. The individual cards measure 1 13/16'' by 2 3/4'' in size, whereas the panels are 2¾'' by 5½''. In the checklist that follows the cards have been numbered by panel using the name of the player who appears on the left side of the panel. Panel #'s 1-3, 31-33 and 43-45 were supposedly issued in shorter supply and command a higher price.

		NR MT	EX	VG
Complete Panel Set:		1650.00	825.00	495.00
Complete Singles Set:		1000.00	500.00	300.00
Common Panel:		40.00	20.00	12.00
Common Single Player:		6.00	3.00	1.75
Panel		250.00	125.00	75.00
(1)	Bob Allison	25.00	12.50	7.50
(2)	Ed Mathews	90.00	45.00	27.00
(3)	Vada Pinson	35.00	17.50	10.50
Panel		40.00	20.00	12.00

1963 Bazooka

FRANK ROBINSON
CINN. REDS   OF

NO. 31 OF 36 CARDS

The 1963 Bazooka issue reverted back to a 12-panel, 36-card set, but saw a change in the size of the cards. Individual cards measure 1 9/16'' by 2 1/2'', while panels are 2 1/2'' by 4 11/16'' in size. The card design was altered also, with the player's name, team and position situated in a white oval space at the bottom of the card. The full-color, blank-backed set was numbered 1-36. Five Bazooka All-Time Greats cards were inserted in each box of bubblegum.

		NR MT	EX	VG
Complete Panel Set:		900.00	450.00	270.00
Complete Singles Set:		550.00	275.00	165.00
Common Panel:		30.00	15.00	9.00
Common Single Player:		5.00	2.50	1.50
Panel		200.00	100.00	60.00
1	Mickey Mantle (batting righty)	100.00	50.00	30.00
2	Bob Rodgers	5.00	2.50	1.50
3	Ernie Banks	25.00	12.50	7.50
Panel		50.00	25.00	15.00
4	Norm Siebern	5.00	2.50	1.50
5	Warren Spahn (portrait)	20.00	10.00	6.00
6	Bill Mazeroski	12.00	6.00	3.50
Panel		55.00	27.00	16.50
7	Harmon Killebrew (batting)	20.00	10.00	6.00
8	Dick Farrell (portrait)	5.00	2.50	1.50
9	Hank Aaron (glove in front)	25.00	12.50	7.50
Panel		50.00	25.00	15.00
10	Dick Donovan	5.00	2.50	1.50
11	Jim Gentile (batting)	5.00	2.50	1.50
12	Willie Mays (bat in front)	25.00	12.50	7.50
Panel		60.00	30.00	18.00
13	Camilo Pascual (hands at waist)	5.00	2.50	1.50
14	Bob Clemente (portrait)	25.00	12.50	7.50
15	Johnny Callison (wearing pinstripe uniform)	8.00	4.00	2.50
Panel		90.00	45.00	27.00
16	Carl Yastrzemski (kneeling)	40.00	20.00	12.00
17	Don Drysdale	15.00	7.50	4.50
18	Johnny Romano (portrait)	5.00	2.50	1.50
Panel		30.00	15.00	9.00
19	Al Jackson	8.00	4.00	2.50
20	Ralph Terry	8.00	4.00	2.50
21	Bill Monbouquette	5.00	2.50	1.50
Panel		55.00	27.00	16.50
22	Orlando Cepeda	12.00	6.00	3.50
23	Stan Musial	30.00	15.00	9.00
24	Floyd Robinson (no pinstripes on uniform)	5.00	2.50	1.50
Panel		40.00	20.00	12.00
25	Chuck Hinton (batting)	5.00	2.50	1.50
26	Bob Purkey	5.00	2.50	1.50
27	Ken Hubbs	12.00	6.00	3.50
Panel		55.00	27.00	16.50
28	Bill White	8.00	4.00	2.50
29	Ray Herbert	5.00	2.50	1.50
30	Brooks Robinson (glove in front)	30.00	15.00	9.00
Panel		50.00	25.00	15.00
31	Frank Robinson (batting, uniform number doesn't show)	20.00	10.00	6.00
32	Lee Thomas	5.00	2.50	1.50
33	Rocky Colavito (Detroit)	8.00	4.00	2.50
Panel		60.00	30.00	18.00
34	Al Kaline (kneeling)	30.00	15.00	9.00
35	Art Mahaffey	8.00	4.00	2.50
36	Tommy Davis (batting follow-thru)	8.00	4.00	2.50

Consisting of 41 cards, the Bazooka All-Time Greats set was issued as inserts (5 per box) in boxes of Bazooka bubble gum. A black and white head-shot of the player is placed inside a gold plaque within a white border. The card backs have black print on white and yellow and contain a brief biography of the player. The numbered cards measure 1 9/16" by 2 1/2" in size. The cards are found with silver fronts instead of gold. The silver are worth double the values listed in the following checklist.

		NR MT	EX	VG
Complete Set:		175.00	88.00	53.00
Common Player:		2.50	1.25	.70
1	Joe Tinker	3.50	1.75	1.00
2	Harry Heilmann	2.50	1.25	.70
3	Jack Chesbro	3.00	1.50	.90
4	Christy Mathewson	5.00	2.50	1.50
5	Herb Pennock	3.00	1.50	.90
6	Cy Young	5.00	2.50	1.50
7	Big Ed Walsh	2.50	1.25	.70
8	Nap Lajoie	3.50	1.75	1.00
9	Eddie Plank	2.50	1.25	.70
10	Honus Wagner	5.00	2.50	1.50
11	Chief Bender	2.50	1.25	.70
12	Walter Johnson	5.00	2.50	1.50
13	Three-Fingered Brown	2.50	1.25	.70
14	Rabbit Maranville	2.50	1.25	.70
15	Lou Gehrig	15.00	7.50	4.50
16	Ban Johnson	2.50	1.25	.70
17	Babe Ruth	25.00	12.50	7.50
18	Connie Mack	5.00	2.50	1.50
19	Hank Greenberg	3.50	1.75	1.00
20	John McGraw	3.50	1.75	1.00
21	Johnny Evers	2.50	1.25	.70
22	Al Simmons	2.50	1.25	.70
23	Jimmy Collins	2.50	1.25	.70
24	Tris Speaker	3.50	1.75	1.00
25	Frank Chance	2.50	1.25	.70
26	Fred Clarke	2.50	1.25	.70
27	Wilbert Robinson	2.50	1.25	.70
28	Dazzy Vance	2.50	1.25	.70
29	Pete Alexander	3.50	1.75	1.00
30	Judge Landis	2.50	1.25	.70
31	Wee Willie Keeler	2.50	1.25	.70
32	Rogers Hornsby	3.50	1.75	1.00
33	Hugh Duffy	2.50	1.25	.70
34	Mickey Cochrane	3.50	1.75	1.00
35	Ty Cobb	15.00	7.50	4.50
36	Mel Ott	3.50	1.75	1.00
37	Clark Griffith	2.50	1.25	.70
38	Ted Lyons	2.50	1.25	.70
39	Cap Anson	3.50	1.75	1.00
40	Bill Dickey	3.50	1.75	1.00
41	Eddie Collins	3.50	1.75	1.00

1964 Bazooka

The 1964 Bazooka set is identical in design and size to the previous year's effort. However, different photographs were used from year to year by Topps, issuer of Bazooka bubblegum. The 1964 set consists

1963 Bazooka All-Time Greats

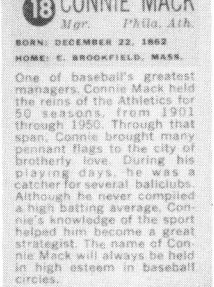

of 36 full-color, blank-backed cards numbered 1 through 36. Individual cards measure 1 9/16'' by 2 1/2''; three-card panels measure 2 1/2'' by 4 11/16''. Sheets of ten full-color baseball stamps were inserted in each box of bubblegum.

		NR MT	EX	VG
Complete Panel Set:		950.00	475.00	285.00
Complete Singles Set:		575.00	287.00	172.00
Common Panel:		30.00	15.00	9.00
Common Single Player:		5.00	2.50	1.50
Panel		200.00	100.00	60.00
1	Mickey Mantle (portrait)	100.00	50.00	30.00
2	Dick Groat	10.00	5.00	3.00
3	Steve Barber	8.00	4.00	2.50
Panel		40.00	20.00	12.00
4	Ken McBride	5.00	2.50	1.50
5	Warren Spahn (head to waist shot)			
		20.00	10.00	6.00
6	Bob Friend	6.00	3.00	1.75
Panel		60.00	30.00	18.00
7	Harmon Killebrew (portrait)	25.00	12.50	7.50
8	Dick Farrell (hands above head)	5.00	2.50	1.50
9	Hank Aaron (glove to left)	25.00	12.50	7.50
Panel		55.00	27.00	16.50
10	Rich Rollins	5.00	2.50	1.50
11	Jim Gentile (portrait)	5.00	2.50	1.50
12	Willie Mays (looking to left)	30.00	15.00	9.00
Panel		55.00	27.00	16.50
13	Camilo Pascual (pitching follow-thru)			
		5.00	2.50	1.50
14	Bob Clemente (throwing)	25.00	12.50	7.50
15	Johnny Callison (batting, screen showing)			
		10.00	5.00	3.00
Panel		75.00	37.00	22.00
16	Carl Yastrzemski (batting)	40.00	20.00	12.00
17	Billy Williams (kneeling)	15.00	7.50	4.50
18	Johnny Romano (batting)	5.00	2.50	1.50
Panel		55.00	27.00	16.50
19	Jim Maloney	5.00	2.50	1.50
20	Norm Cash	12.00	6.00	3.50
21	Willie McCovey	25.00	12.50	7.50
Panel		30.00	15.00	9.00
22	Jim Fregosi (batting)	6.00	3.00	1.75
23	George Altman	5.00	2.50	1.50
24	Floyd Robinson (wearing pinstripe uniform)			
		5.00	2.50	1.50
Panel		30.00	15.00	9.00
25	Chuck Hinton (portrait)	5.00	2.50	1.50
26	Ron Hunt (batting)	8.00	4.00	2.50
27	Gary Peters (pitching)	5.00	2.50	1.50
Panel		55.00	27.00	16.50
28	Dick Ellsworth	5.00	2.50	1.50
29	Elston Howard (holding bat)	12.00	6.00	3.50
30	Brooks Robinson (kneeling with glove)			
		30.00	15.00	9.00
Panel		70.00	35.00	21.00
31	Frank Robinson (uniform number shows)			
		20.00	10.00	6.00
32	Sandy Koufax (glove in front)	35.00	17.50	10.50
33	Rocky Colavito (Kansas City)	12.00	6.00	3.50
Panel		60.00	30.00	18.00
34	Al Kaline (holding two bats)	30.00	15.00	9.00
35	Ken Boyer (head to waist shot)	12.00	6.00	3.50
36	Tommy Davis (batting)	8.00	4.00	2.50

1964 Bazooka Stamps

Occasionally mislabeled "Topps Stamps", the 1964 Bazooka Stamps set was produced by Topps, but was found only in boxes of 1¢ Bazooka bubble gum. Issued in sheets of ten, 100 color stamps make up the set. Each stamp measures 1'' by 1½'' in size. While the stamps are not individually numbered, the sheets are numbered one through ten. The stamps are commonly found as complete sheets of ten and are priced in that fashion in the checklist that follows.

		NR MT	EX	VG
Complete Sheet Set:		350.00	175.00	105.00
Common Sheet:		12.00	6.00	3.50
1	Max Alvis, Ed Charles, Dick Ellsworth, Jimmie Hall, Frank Malzone, Milt Pappas, Vada Pinson, Tony Taylor, Pete Ward, Bill White	12.00	6.00	3.50
2	Bob Aspromonte, Larry Jackson, Willie Mays, Al McBean, Bill Monbouquette, Bobby Richardson, Floyd Robinson, Frank Robinson, Norm Siebern, Don Zimmer	35.00	17.50	10.50
3	Ernie Banks, Bob Clemente, Curt Flood, Jesse Gonder, Woody Held, Don Lock, Dave Nicholson, Joe Pepitone, Brooks Robinson, Carl Yastrzemski	50.00	25.00	15.00
4	Hank Aguirre, Jim Grant, Harmon Killebrew, Jim Maloney, Juan Marichal, Bill Mazeroski, Juan Pizarro, Boog Powell, Ed Roebuck, Ron Santo	30.00	15.00	9.00
5	Jim Bouton, Norm Cash, Orlando Cepeda, Tommy Harper, Chuck Hinton, Albie Pearson, Ron Perranoski, Dick Radatz, Johnny Romano, Carl Willey	18.00	9.00	5.50
6	Steve Barber, Jim Fregosi, Tony Gonzalez, Mickey Mantle, Jim O'Toole, Gary Peters, Rich Rollins, Warren Spahn, Dick Stuart, Joe Torre	75.00	37.00	22.00
7	Felipe Alou, George Altman, Ken Boyer, Rocky Colavito, Jim Davenport, Tommy Davis, Bill Freehan, Bob Friend, Ken Johnson, Billy Moran	18.00	9.00	5.50
8	Earl Battey, Ernie Broglio, Johnny Callison, Donn Clendenon, Don Drysdale, Jim Gentile, Elston Howard, Claude Osteen, Billy Williams, Hal Woodeshick	25.00	12.50	7.50
9	Hank Aaron, Jack Baldschun, Wayne Causey, Moe Drabowsky, Dick Groat, Frank Howard, Al Jackson, Jerry Lumpe, Ken McBride, Rusty Staub	35.00	17.50	10.50
10	Ray Culp, Vic Davalillo, Dick Farrell, Ron Hunt, Al Kaline, Sandy Koufax, Ed Mathews, Willie McCovey, Camilo Pascual, Lee Thomas	35.00	17.50	10.50

1965 Bazooka

The 1965 Bazooka set is identical to the 1963 and 1964 sets. Different players were added each year and different photographs were used for those players being included again. Individual cards cut from the boxes measure 1 9/16'' by 2 1/2''. Complete three-card panels measure 2 1/2'' by 4 11/16''. Thirty-six full-color, blank-backed, numbered cards comprise the set. Prices are given for individual cards and complete panels in the checklist that follows.

		NR MT	EX	VG
Complete Panel Set:		900.00	450.00	270.00
Complete Singles Set:		550.00	275.00	165.00
Common Panel:		30.00	15.00	9.00
Common Single Player:		5.00	2.50	1.50
Panel		175.00	87.00	52.00
1	Mickey Mantle (batting lefty)	100.00	50.00	30.00
2	Larry Jackson	5.00	2.50	1.50
3	Chuck Hinton	5.00	2.50	1.50
Panel		30.00	15.00	9.00
4	Tony Oliva	8.00	4.00	2.50
5	Dean Chance	5.00	2.50	1.50
6	Jim O'Toole	5.00	2.50	1.50
Panel		60.00	30.00	18.00
7	Harmon Killebrew (bat on shoulder)	20.00	10.00	6.00
8	Pete Ward	5.00	2.50	1.50
9	Hank Aaron (batting)	30.00	15.00	9.00
Panel		55.00	27.00	16.50
10	Dick Radatz	5.00	2.50	1.50
11	Boog Powell	8.00	4.00	2.50
12	Willie Mays (looking down)	30.00	15.00	9.00
Panel		55.00	27.00	16.50
13	Bob Veale	5.00	2.50	1.50
14	Bob Clemente (batting)	25.00	12.50	7.50
15	Johnny Callison (batting, no screen in background)	10.00	5.00	3.00
Panel		30.00	15.00	9.00
16	Joe Torre	8.00	4.00	2.50
17	Billy Williams (batting)	15.00	7.50	4.50
18	Bob Chance	5.00	2.50	1.50
Panel		40.00	20.00	12.00
19	Bob Aspromonte	8.00	4.00	2.50
20	Joe Christopher	8.00	4.00	2.50
21	Jim Bunning	12.00	6.00	3.50
Panel		50.00	25.00	15.00
22	Jim Fregosi (portrait)	8.00	4.00	2.50
23	Bob Gibson	20.00	10.00	6.00
24	Juan Marichal	20.00	10.00	6.00
Panel		30.00	15.00	9.00
25	Dave Wickersham	5.00	2.50	1.50
26	Ron Hunt (throwing)	8.00	4.00	2.50
27	Gary Peters (portrait)	5.00	2.50	1.50
Panel		60.00	30.00	18.00
28	Ron Santo	12.00	6.00	3.50
29	Elston Howard (with glove)	12.00	6.00	3.50
30	Brooks Robinson (portrait)	30.00	15.00	9.00
Panel		70.00	35.00	21.00
31	Frank Robinson (portrait)	20.00	10.00	6.00
32	Sandy Koufax (hands over head)	35.00	17.50	10.50
33	Rocky Colavito (Cleveland)	12.00	6.00	3.50
Panel		60.00	30.00	18.00
34	Al Kaline (portrait)	30.00	15.00	9.00
35	Ken Boyer (portrait)	12.00	6.00	3.50
36	Tommy Davis (fielding)	8.00	4.00	2.50

1966 Bazooka

HARMON KILLEBREW
MINN. TWINS OF
NO. 11 OF 48 CARDS

The 1966 Bazooka set was increased to 48 cards. Issued in panels of three on the bottoms of boxes of bubblegum, the full-color cards are blank-backed and numbered. Individual cards measure 1 9/16'' by 2 1/2'', whereas panels measure 2 1/2'' by 4 11/16''.

		NR MT	EX	VG
Complete Panel Set:		1200.00	600.00	360.00
Complete Singles Set:		750.00	375.00	225.00
Common Panel:		30.00	15.00	9.00
Common Single Player:		5.00	2.50	1.50
Panel		55.00	27.00	16.50
1	Sandy Koufax	35.00	17.50	10.50
2	Willie Horton	8.00	4.00	2.50
3	Frank Howard	8.00	4.00	2.50
Panel		40.00	20.00	12.00
4	Richie Allen	8.00	4.00	2.50
5	Mel Stottlemyre	10.00	5.00	3.00
6	Tony Conigliaro	12.00	6.00	3.50
Panel		175.00	87.00	52.00
7	Mickey Mantle	100.00	50.00	30.00
8	Leon Wagner	5.00	2.50	1.50
9	Ed Kranepool	10.00	5.00	3.00
Panel		60.00	30.00	18.00
10	Juan Marichal	20.00	10.00	6.00
11	Harmon Killebrew	25.00	12.50	7.50
12	Johnny Callison	10.00	5.00	3.00
Panel		50.00	25.00	15.00
13	Roy McMillan	8.00	4.00	2.50
14	Willie McCovey	20.00	10.00	6.00
15	Rocky Colavito	12.00	6.00	3.50
Panel		50.00	25.00	15.00
16	Willie Mays	30.00	15.00	9.00
17	Sam McDowell	8.00	4.00	2.50
18	Vern Law	6.00	3.00	1.75
Panel		35.00	17.50	10.50
19	Jim Fregosi	8.00	4.00	2.50
20	Ron Fairly	8.00	4.00	2.50
21	Bob Gibson	20.00	10.00	6.00
Panel		60.00	30.00	18.00
22	Carl Yastrzemski	40.00	20.00	12.00
23	Bill White	8.00	4.00	2.50
24	Bob Aspromonte	8.00	4.00	2.50
Panel		50.00	25.00	15.00
25	Dean Chance (California)	5.00	2.50	1.50
26	Bob Clemente	25.00	12.50	7.50
27	Tony Cloninger	5.00	2.50	1.50
Panel		50.00	25.00	15.00
28	Curt Blefary	5.00	2.50	1.50
29	Milt Pappas	8.00	4.00	2.50
30	Hank Aaron	30.00	15.00	9.00
Panel		40.00	20.00	12.00
31	Jim Bunning	8.00	4.00	2.50
32	Frank Robinson (portrait)	20.00	10.00	6.00
33	Bill Skowron	8.00	4.00	2.50
Panel		55.00	27.00	16.50
34	Brooks Robinson	25.00	12.50	7.50
35	Jim Wynn	8.00	4.00	2.50
36	Joe Torre	8.00	4.00	2.50
Panel		145.00	72.00	43.00
37	Jim Grant	5.00	2.50	1.50
38	Pete Rose	75.00	37.00	22.00
39	Ron Santo	8.00	4.00	2.50
Panel		40.00	20.00	12.00
40	Tom Tresh	8.00	4.00	2.50
41	Tony Oliva	8.00	4.00	2.50
42	Don Drysdale	20.00	10.00	6.00
Panel		30.00	15.00	9.00
43	Pete Richert	5.00	2.50	1.50
44	Bert Campaneris	8.00	4.00	2.50
45	Jim Maloney	5.00	2.50	1.50
Panel		60.00	30.00	18.00
46	Al Kaline	30.00	15.00	9.00
47	Eddie Fisher	5.00	2.50	1.50
48	Billy Williams	15.00	7.50	4.50

Definitions for grading conditions are located in the Introduction of this price guide.

1967 Bazooka

The 1967 Bazooka set is identical in design to the Bazooka sets of 1964-66. Issued in panels of three on the bottoms of bubblegum boxes, the set is made up of 48 full-color, blank-backed, numbered cards. Individual cards measure 1 9/16'' by 2 1/2''; complete panels measure 2 1/2'' by 4 11/16'' in size.

		NR MT	EX	VG
Complete Panel Set:		1200.00	600.00	360.00
Complete Singles Set:		725.00	362.00	217.00
Common Panel:		30.00	15.00	9.00
Common Single Player:		5.00	2.50	1.50
Panel		30.00	15.00	9.00
1	Rick Reichardt	5.00	2.50	1.50
2	Tommy Agee	5.00	2.50	1.50
3	Frank Howard	12.00	6.00	3.50
Panel		35.00	17.50	10.50
4	Richie Allen	8.00	4.00	2.50
5	Mel Stottlemyre	10.00	5.00	3.00
6	Tony Conigliaro	12.00	6.00	3.50
Panel		175.00	87.00	52.00
7	Mickey Mantle	100.00	50.00	30.00
8	Leon Wagner	5.00	2.50	1.50
9	Gary Peters	5.00	2.50	1.50
Panel		60.00	30.00	18.00
10	Juan Marichal	20.00	10.00	6.00
11	Harmon Killebrew	20.00	10.00	6.00
12	Johnny Callison	10.00	5.00	3.00
Panel		50.00	25.00	15.00
13	Denny McLain	12.00	6.00	3.50
14	Willie McCovey	20.00	10.00	6.00
15	Rocky Colavito	12.00	6.00	3.50
Panel		60.00	30.00	18.00
16	Willie Mays	30.00	15.00	9.00
17	Sam McDowell	8.00	4.00	2.50
18	Jim Kaat	15.00	7.50	4.50
Panel		35.00	17.50	10.50
19	Jim Fregosi	8.00	4.00	2.50
20	Ron Fairly	8.00	4.00	2.50
21	Bob Gibson	20.00	10.00	6.00
Panel		60.00	30.00	18.00
22	Carl Yastrzemski	40.00	20.00	12.00
23	Bill White	8.00	4.00	2.50
24	Bob Aspromonte	8.00	4.00	2.50
Panel		50.00	25.00	15.00
25	Dean Chance (Minnesota)	5.00	2.50	1.50
26	Bob Clemente	25.00	12.50	7.50
27	Tony Cloninger	5.00	2.50	1.50
Panel		50.00	25.00	15.00
28	Curt Blefary	5.00	2.50	1.50
29	Phil Regan	5.00	2.50	1.50
30	Hank Aaron	30.00	15.00	9.00
Panel		40.00	20.00	12.00
31	Jim Bunning	8.00	4.00	2.50
32	Frank Robinson (batting)	20.00	10.00	6.00
33	Ken Boyer	8.00	4.00	2.50
Panel		55.00	27.00	16.50
34	Brooks Robinson	25.00	12.50	7.50
35	Jim Wynn	8.00	4.00	2.50
36	Joe Torre	8.00	4.00	2.50
Panel		140.00	70.00	42.00
37	Tommy Davis	6.00	3.00	1.75
38	Pete Rose	75.00	37.00	22.00
39	Ron Santo	6.00	3.00	1.75
Panel		40.00	20.00	12.00
40	Tom Tresh	8.00	4.00	2.50

		NR MT	EX	VG
41	Tony Oliva	8.00	4.00	2.50
42	Don Drysdale	20.00	10.00	6.00
Panel		30.00	15.00	9.00
43	Pete Richert	5.00	2.50	1.50
44	Bert Campaneris	6.00	3.00	1.75
45	Jim Maloney	5.00	2.50	1.50
Panel		60.00	30.00	18.00
46	Al Kaline	30.00	15.00	9.00
47	Matty Alou	8.00	4.00	2.50
48	Billy Williams	15.00	7.50	4.50

1968 Bazooka

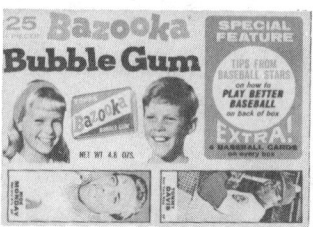

The design of the 1968 Bazooka set is radically different from previous years. The player cards are situated on the sides of the boxes with the box back containing "Tipps From The Topps." Four unnumbered player cards, measuring 1¼'' by 3⅛'', are featured on each box. The box back includes a small player photo plus illustrated tips on various aspects of the game of baseball. The boxes are numbered 1-15 on the tips panels. There are 56 different player cards in the set, with four of the cards (Agee, Drysdale, Rose, Santo) being used twice to round out the set of fifteen boxes.

		NR MT	EX	VG
Complete Box Set:		2100.00	1050.00	630.00
Complete Singles Set:		1300.00	650.00	390.00
Common Box:		110.00	55.00	33.00
Common Single Player:		5.00	2.50	1.50
Box		175.00	87.00	52.00
1	Maury Wills (Bunting)	20.00	10.00	6.00
(1)	Clete Boyer	9.00	4.50	2.75
(2)	Paul Casanova	7.00	3.50	2.00
(3)	Al Kaline	25.00	12.50	7.50
(4)	Tom Seaver	50.00	25.00	15.00
Box		150.00	75.00	45.00
2	Carl Yastrzemski (Batting)	50.00	25.00	15.00
(5)	Matty Alou	9.00	4.50	2.75
(6)	Bill Freehan	9.00	4.50	2.75
(7)	Jim Hunter	20.00	10.00	6.00
(8)	Jim Lefebvre	7.00	3.50	2.00
Box		110.00	55.00	33.00
3	Bert Campaneris (Stealing bases)			
		20.00	10.00	6.00
(9)	Bobby Knoop	7.00	3.50	2.00
(10)	Tim McCarver	12.00	6.00	3.50
(11)	Frank Robinson	20.00	10.00	6.00
(12)	Bob Veale	7.00	3.50	2.00
Box		90.00	45.00	27.00
4	Maury Wills (Sliding)	20.00	10.00	6.00
(13)	Joe Azcue	7.00	3.50	2.00
(14)	Tony Conigliaro	12.00	6.00	3.50
(15)	Ken Holtzman	9.00	4.50	2.75
(16)	Bill White	9.00	4.50	2.75

		NR MT	EX	VG
Box		150.00	75.00	45.00
5	Julian Javier (The Double Play)	20.00	10.00	6.00
(17)	Hank Aaron	35.00	17.50	10.50
(18)	Juan Marichal	20.00	10.00	6.00
(19)	Joe Pepitone	12.00	6.00	3.50
(20)	Rico Petrocelli	9.00	4.50	2.75
Box		175.00	87.00	52.00
6	Orlando Cepeda (Playing 1st Base)	25.00	12.50	7.50
(21)	Tommie Agee	5.00	2.50	1.50
(22)	Don Drysdale	10.00	5.00	3.00
(23)	Pete Rose	60.00	30.00	18.00
(24)	Ron Santo	5.00	2.50	1.50
Box		110.00	55.00	33.00
7	Bill Mazeroski (Playing 2nd Base)	20.00	10.00	6.00
(25)	Jim Bunning	12.00	6.00	3.50
(26)	Frank Howard	12.00	6.00	3.50
(27)	John Roseboro	9.00	4.50	2.75
(28)	George Scott	9.00	4.50	2.75
Box		150.00	75.00	45.00
8	Brooks Robinson (Playing 3rd Base)	50.00	25.00	15.00
(29)	Tony Gonzalez	7.00	3.50	2.00
(30)	Willie Horton	9.00	4.50	2.75
(31)	Harmon Killebrew	25.00	12.50	7.50
(32)	Jim McGlothlin	7.00	3.50	2.00
Box		110.00	55.00	33.00
9	Jim Fregosi (Playing Shortstop)	20.00	10.00	6.00
(33)	Max Alvis	7.00	3.50	2.00
(34)	Bob Gibson	20.00	10.00	6.00
(35)	Tony Oliva	12.00	6.00	3.50
(36)	Vada Pinson	12.00	6.00	3.50
Box		110.00	55.00	33.00
10	Joe Torre (Catching)	25.00	12.50	7.50
(37)	Dean Chance	7.00	3.50	2.00
(38)	Tommy Davis	9.00	4.50	2.75
(39)	Ferguson Jenkins	15.00	7.50	4.50
(40)	Rick Monday	9.00	4.50	2.75
Box		275.00	137.00	82.00
11	Jim Lonborg (Pitching)	25.00	12.50	7.50
(41)	Curt Flood	9.00	4.50	2.75
(42)	Joel Horlen	7.00	3.50	2.00
(43)	Mickey Mantle	125.00	62.00	37.00
(44)	Jim Wynn	7.00	3.50	2.00
Box		150.00	75.00	45.00
12	Mike McCormick (Fielding the Pitcher's Position)	20.00	10.00	6.00
(45)	Bob Clemente	30.00	15.00	9.00
(46)	Al Downing	9.00	4.50	2.75
(47)	Don Mincher	7.00	3.50	2.00
(48)	Tony Perez	15.00	7.50	4.50
Box		175.00	87.00	52.00
13	Frank Crosetti (Coaching)	35.00	17.50	10.50
(49)	Rod Carew	35.00	17.50	10.50
(50)	Willie McCovey	25.00	12.50	7.50
(51)	Ron Swoboda	7.00	3.50	2.00
(52)	Earl Wilson	7.00	3.50	2.00
Box		150.00	75.00	45.00
14	Willie Mays (Playing the Outfield)	50.00	25.00	15.00
(53)	Richie Allen	12.00	6.00	3.50
(54)	Gary Peters	7.00	3.50	2.00
(55)	Rusty Staub	10.00	5.00	3.00
(56)	Billy Williams	20.00	10.00	6.00
Box		175.00	87.00	52.00
15	Lou Brock (Base Running)	40.00	20.00	12.00
(57)	Tommie Agee	5.00	2.50	1.50
(58)	Don Drysdale	10.00	5.00	3.00
(59)	Pete Rose	60.00	30.00	18.00
(60)	Ron Santo	5.00	2.50	1.50

	NR MT	EX	VG
Complete Box Set:	150.00	75.00	45.00
Common Box:	8.00	4.00	2.50

		NR MT	EX	VG
1	No-Hit Duel By Toney And Vaughn (Mordecai Brown, Ty Cobb, Willie Keeler, Eddie Plank)	12.00	6.00	3.50
2	Alexander Conquers Yanks (Rogers Hornsby, Ban Johnson, Walter Johnson, Al Simmons)	8.00	4.00	2.50
3	Yanks Lazzeri Sets A.L. Hit Record (Hugh Duffy, Lou Gehrig, Tris Speaker, Joe Tinker)	12.00	6.00	3.50
4	Home Run Almost Hit Out Of Stadium (Grover Alexander, Chief Bender, Christy Mathewson, Cy Young)	8.00	4.00	2.50
5	Four Consecutive Homers By Gehrig (Frank Chance, Mickey Cochrane, John McGraw, Babe Ruth)	18.00	9.00	5.50
6	No-Hit Game By Walter Johnson (Johnny Evers, Walter Johnson, John McGraw, Cy Young)	8.00	4.00	2.50
7	Twelve RBI's By Bottomley (Ty Cobb, Eddie Collins, Johnny Evers, Lou Gehrig)	12.00	6.00	3.50
8	Ty Ties Record (Mickey Cochrane, Eddie Collins, Met Ott, Honus Wagner)	8.00	4.00	2.50
9	Babe Ruth Hits Three Homers In Game (Cap Anson, Jack Chesbro, Al Simmons, Tris Speaker)	18.00	9.00	5.50
10	Calls Shot In Series Game (Nap Lajoie, Connie Mack, Rabbit Maranville, Ed Walsh)	18.00	9.00	5.50
11	Ruth's 60th Homer Sets New Record (Frank Chance, Nap Lajoie, Mel Ott, Joe Tinker)	18.00	9.00	5.50
12	Double Shutout By Ed Reulbach (Rogers Hornsby, Rabbit Maranville, Christy Mathewson, Honus Wagner)	8.00	4.00	2.50

1971 Bazooka Unnumbered Set

1969-70 Bazooka

Issued over a two-year span, the 1969-70 Bazooka set utilized the box bottom and sides. The box bottom, entitled "Baseball Extra", features an historic event in baseball. The bottom panels are numbered 1 through 12. Two "All-Time Greats" cards were located on each side of the box. These cards are not numbered and have no distinct borders. Individual cards measure 1¼" by 3⅛"; the "Baseball Extra" panels measure 3" by 6¼". The prices in the checklist that follows are for complete boxes only. Cards/panels cut from the boxes have a greatly reduced value - 25% of the complete box prices for all cut pieces.

The final Bazooka set was issued in 1971, consisting of 36 full-color, blank-backed, unnumbered cards. Issued in panels of three on the bottoms of Bazooka bubblegum boxes, individual cards measure 2'' by 2⅝'' whereas complete panels measure 2 5/8'' by 5 5/16''. In the checklist that follows, the cards have been numbered by panel using the name of the player who appears on the left portion of the panel.

was released. The set is comprised of 48 cards as opposed to the 36 cards which make up the unnumbered set. Issued in panels of three, the nine cards not found in the unnumbered set are 1-3, 13-15 and 43-45. All other cards are identical to those found in the unnumbered set. The cards, which measure 2'' by 2⅝'', contain full-color photos and are blank-backed.

		NR MT	EX	VG
Complete Panel Set:		300.00	150.00	90.00
Complete Singles Set:		175.00	87.00	52.00
Common Panel:		10.00	5.00	3.00
Common Single Player:		1.25	.60	.40
Panel		25.00	12.50	7.50
(1)	Tommie Agee	1.25	.60	.40
(2)	Harmon Killebrew	6.50	3.25	2.00
(3)	Reggie Jackson	8.00	4.00	2.50
Panel		40.00	20.00	12.00
(4)	Bert Campaneris	1.25	.60	.40
(5)	Pete Rose	20.00	10.00	6.00
(6)	Orlando Cepeda	3.00	1.50	.90
Panel		20.00	10.00	6.00
(7)	Rico Carty	2.00	1.00	.60
(8)	Johnny Bench	10.00	5.00	3.00
(9)	Tommy Harper	1.25	.60	.40
Panel		20.00	10.00	6.00
(10)	Bill Freehan	2.00	1.00	.60
(11)	Roberto Clemente	10.00	5.00	3.00
(12)	Claude Osteen	1.25	.60	.40
Panel		15.00	7.50	4.50
(13)	Jim Fregosi	2.00	1.00	.60
(14)	Billy Williams	5.00	2.50	1.50
(15)	Dave McNally	1.25	.60	.40
Panel		30.00	15.00	9.00
(16)	Randy Hundley	1.25	.60	.40
(17)	Willie Mays	12.00	6.00	3.50
(18)	Jim Hunter	5.00	2.50	1.50
Panel		15.00	7.50	4.50
(19)	Juan Marichal	5.00	2.50	1.50
(20)	Frank Howard	3.00	1.50	.90
(21)	Bill Melton	1.25	.60	.40
Panel		30.00	15.00	9.00
(22)	Willie McCovey	6.50	3.25	2.00
(23)	Carl Yastrzemski	12.00	6.00	3.50
(24)	Clyde Wright	1.25	.60	.40
Panel		15.00	7.50	4.50
(25)	Jim Merritt	1.25	.60	.40
(26)	Luis Aparicio	5.00	2.50	1.50
(27)	Bobby Murcer	3.00	1.50	.90
Panel		10.00	5.00	3.00
(28)	Rico Petrocelli	2.00	1.00	.60
(29)	Sam McDowell	2.00	1.00	.60
(30)	Clarence Gaston	1.25	.60	.40
Panel		30.00	15.00	9.00
(31)	Brooks Robinson	6.50	3.25	2.00
(32)	Hank Aaron	12.00	6.00	3.50
(33)	Larry Dierker	1.25	.60	.40
Panel		15.00	7.50	4.50
(34)	Rusty Staub	2.00	1.00	.60
(35)	Bob Gibson	6.50	3.25	2.00
(36)	Amos Otis	1.25	.60	.40

1971 Bazooka Numbered Set

TOM SEAVER

The 1971 Bazooka Numbered Set is a proof set produced by the company after the unnumbered set

		NR MT	EX	VG
Complete Panel Set:		525.00	262.00	157.00
Complete Singles Set:		325.00	162.00	97.00
Common Panel:		15.00	7.50	4.50
Common Single Player:		1.75	.90	.50
Panel		40.00	20.00	12.00
1	Tim McCarver	6.00	3.00	1.75
2	Frank Robinson	13.00	6.50	4.00
3	Bill Mazeroski	6.00	3.00	1.75
Panel		40.00	20.00	12.00
4	Willie McCovey	9.00	4.50	2.75
5	Carl Yastrzemski	18.00	9.00	5.50
6	Clyde Wright	1.75	.90	.50
Panel		20.00	10.00	6.00
7	Jim Merritt	1.75	.90	.50
8	Luis Aparicio	7.00	3.50	2.00
9	Bobby Murcer	4.25	2.25	1.25
Panel		15.00	7.50	4.50
10	Rico Petrocelli	2.75	1.50	.80
11	Sam McDowell	2.75	1.50	.80
12	Clarence Gaston	1.75	.90	.50
Panel		40.00	20.00	12.00
13	Ferguson Jenkins	6.00	3.00	1.75
14	Al Kaline	13.00	6.50	4.00
15	Ken Harrelson	4.00	2.00	1.25
Panel		35.00	17.50	10.50
16	Tommie Agee	1.75	.90	.50
17	Harmon Killebrew	9.00	4.50	2.75
18	Reggie Jackson	12.00	6.00	3.50
Panel		20.00	10.00	6.00
19	Juan Marichal	7.00	3.50	2.00
20	Frank Howard	4.25	2.25	1.25
21	Bill Melton	1.75	.90	.50
Panel		40.00	20.00	12.00
22	Brooks Robinson	9.00	4.50	2.75
23	Hank Aaron	18.00	9.00	5.50
24	Larry Dierker	1.75	.90	.50
Panel		20.00	10.00	6.00
25	Jim Fregosi	2.75	1.50	.80
26	Billy Williams	7.00	3.50	2.00
27	Dave McNally	1.75	.90	.50
Panel		30.00	15.00	9.00
28	Rico Carty	2.75	1.50	.80
29	Johnny Bench	15.00	7.50	4.50
30	Tommy Harper	1.75	.90	.50
Panel		55.00	27.00	16.50
31	Bert Campaneris	1.75	.90	.50
32	Pete Rose	30.00	15.00	9.00
33	Orlando Cepeda	4.25	2.25	1.25
Panel		50.00	25.00	15.00
34	Maury Wills	6.00	3.00	1.75
35	Tom Seaver	20.00	10.00	6.00
36	Tony Oliva	6.00	3.00	1.75
Panel		30.00	15.00	9.00
37	Bill Freehan	2.75	1.50	.80
38	Roberto Clemente	15.00	7.50	4.50
39	Claude Osteen	1.75	.90	.50
Panel		20.00	10.00	6.00
40	Rusty Staub	2.75	1.50	.80
41	Bob Gibson	9.00	4.50	2.75
42	Amos Otis	1.75	.90	.50
Panel		20.00	10.00	6.00
43	Jim Wynn	2.50	1.25	.70
44	Rich Allen	6.00	3.00	1.75
45	Tony Conigliaro	4.00	2.00	1.25
Panel:		40.00	20.00	12.00
46	Randy Hundley	1.75	.90	.50
47	Willie Mays	18.00	9.00	5.50
48	Jim Hunter	7.00	3.50	2.00

NOTE: A card number in parentheses ( ) indicates the set is unnumbered.

1958 Bell Brand Dodgers

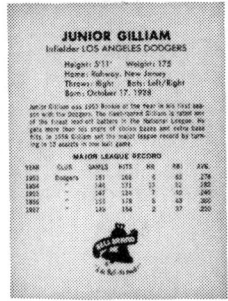

Celebrating the Dodgers first year of play in Los Angeles, Bell Brand inserted ten different unnumbered cards in their bags of potato chips and corn chips. The cards, which measure 3'' by 4'', have a sepia colored photo inside a ¼'' inch green woodgrain border. The card backs feature statistical and biographical information and include the Bell Brand logo. Roy Campanella is included in the set despite a career-ending car wreck that prevented him from ever playing in Los Angeles.

		NR MT	EX	VG
Complete Set:		700.00	350.00	210.00
Common Player:		25.00	12.50	7.50
1	Roy Campanella	70.00	35.00	21.00
2	Gino Cimoli	90.00	45.00	27.00
3	Don Drysdale	60.00	30.00	18.00
4	Junior Gilliam	30.00	15.00	9.00
5	Gil Hodges	60.00	30.00	18.00
6	Sandy Koufax	75.00	37.00	22.00
7	Johnny Podres	90.00	45.00	27.00
8	Pee Wee Reese	60.00	30.00	18.00
9	Duke Snider	125.00	62.00	37.00
10	Don Zimmer	25.00	12.50	7.50

1960 Bell Brand Dodgers

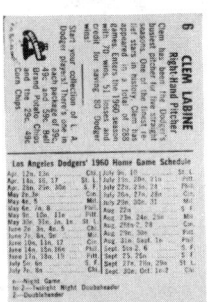

Bell Brand returned with a baseball card set in 1960 that was entirely different in style to their previous effort. The cards, which measure 2½'' by 3½'', feature beautiful, full-color photos. The backs carry a short player biography, the 1960 Dodgers home schedule, and the Bell Brand logo. Twenty different numbered cards were inserted in various size bags of potato chips and corn chips. Although sealed in cellophane, the cards were still subject to grease stains. Card #'s 6, 12 and 18 are the scarcest in the set.

	NR MT	EX	VG
Complete Set:	450.00	225.00	135.00
Common Player:	10.00	5.00	3.00

		NR MT	EX	VG
1	Norm Larker	10.00	5.00	3.00
2	Duke Snider	30.00	15.00	9.00
3	Danny McDevitt	10.00	5.00	3.00
4	Jim Gilliam	16.00	8.00	4.75
5	Rip Repulski	10.00	5.00	3.00
6	Clem Labine	55.00	27.00	16.50
7	John Roseboro	10.00	5.00	3.00
8	Carl Furillo	16.00	8.00	4.75
9	Sandy Koufax	30.00	15.00	9.00
10	Joe Pignatano	10.00	5.00	3.00
11	Chuck Essegian	10.00	5.00	3.00
12	John Klippstein	55.00	27.00	16.50
13	Ed Roebuck	10.00	5.00	3.00
14	Don Demeter	10.00	5.00	3.00
15	Roger Craig	12.00	6.00	3.50
16	Stan Williams	10.00	5.00	3.00
17	Don Zimmer	12.00	6.00	3.50
18	Walter Alston	70.00	35.00	21.00
19	Johnny Podres	16.00	8.00	4.75
20	Maury Wills	20.00	10.00	6.00

1961 Bell Brand Dodgers

The 1961 Bell Brand set is identical in format to the previous year, although printed on thinner stock. Cards can be distinguished from the 1960 set by the 1961 schedule on the backs. The cards, which measure 2 7/16'' by 3 1/2'', are numbered by the player's uniform number. Twenty different cards were inserted into various size potato chip and corn chip packages, each card being sealed in a cellophane wrapper.

		NR MT	EX	VG
Complete Set:		250.00	160.00	80.00
Common Player:		8.00	5.25	2.65
3	Willie Davis	10.00	6.25	3.75
4	Duke Snider	25.00	13.00	7.75
5	Norm Larker	8.00	5.25	3.25
8	John Roseboro	8.00	5.75	3.50
9	Wally Moon	8.00	5.75	3.50
11	Bob Lillis	8.00	5.75	3.25
12	Tom Davis	10.00	6.25	3.75
14	Gil Hodges	16.00	9.75	5.75
16	Don Demeter	8.00	5.25	3.25
19	Jim Gilliam	12.00	6.50	4.00
22	John Podres	12.00	6.75	4.00
24	Walter Alston	16.00	8.75	5.25
30	Maury Wills	16.00	9.75	5.75
32	Sandy Koufax	25.00	14.50	8.75
34	Norm Sherry	8.00	5.25	3.25
37	Ed Roebuck	8.00	5.25	3.25
38	Roger Craig	10.00	5.75	3.50
40	Stan Williams	8.00	5.25	3.25
43	Charlie Neal	8.00	5.25	3.25
51	Larry Sherry	8.00	5.25	3.25

1962 Bell Brand Dodgers

The 1962 Bell Brand set is identical in style to the previous two years and cards can be distinguished by the 1962 Dodgers schedule on the back. The set con-

WALLY MOON
OUTFIELDER   L.A. DODGERS

sists of twenty cards, each measuring 2 7/16'' by 3 1/2'' and numbered by the player's uniform number. Printed on glossy stock, the 1962 set was less susceptible to grease stains.

		NR MT	EX	VG
Complete Set:		250.00	125.00	75.00
Common Player:		8.00	4.00	2.50
3	Willie Davis	10.00	5.00	3.00
4	Duke Snider	20.00	10.00	6.00
6	Ron Fairly	8.00	4.00	2.50
8	John Roseboro	8.00	4.00	2.50
9	Wally Moon	8.00	4.00	2.50
12	Tom Davis	10.00	5.00	3.00
16	Ron Perranoski	10.00	5.00	3.00
19	Jim Gilliam	12.00	6.00	3.50
20	Daryl Spencer	8.00	4.00	2.50
22	John Podres	12.00	6.00	3.50
24	Walter Alston	15.00	7.50	4.50
25	Frank Howard	10.00	5.00	3.00
30	Maury Wills	15.00	7.50	4.50
32	Sandy Koufax	25.00	12.50	7.50
34	Norm Sherry	8.00	4.00	2.50
37	Ed Roebuck	8.00	4.00	2.50
40	Stan Williams	8.00	4.00	2.50
51	Larry Sherry	8.00	4.00	2.50
53	Don Drysdale	18.00	9.00	5.50
56	Lee Walls	8.00	4.00	2.50

1951 Berk Ross

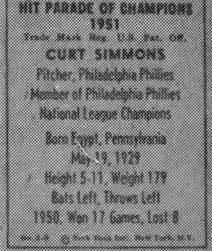

Entitled "Hit Parade of Champions", the 1951 Berk Ross set features 72 stars of various sports. The cards, which measure 2 1/16'' by 2 1/2'' and have tinted color photographs, were issued in boxes containing two-card panels. The issue is divided into four subsets with the first ten players of each series being baseball players. Only the baseball players are listed in the checklist that follows. Complete panels are valued 50% higher than the sum of the individual cards.

		NR MT	EX	VG
Complete Set:		425.00	212.00	127.00
Common Player:		6.00	3.00	1.75
1-1	Al Rosen	10.00	5.00	3.00
1-2	Bob Lemon	10.00	5.00	3.00
1-3	Phil Rizzuto	15.00	7.50	4.50

		NR MT	EX	VG
1-4	Hank Bauer	10.00	5.00	3.00
1-5	Billy Johnson	8.00	4.00	2.50
1-6	Jerry Coleman	8.00	4.00	2.50
1-7	Johnny Mize	15.00	7.50	4.50
1-8	Dom DiMaggio	8.50	4.25	2.50
1-9	Richie Ashburn	8.50	4.25	2.50
1-10	Del Ennis	7.00	3.50	2.00
2-1	Stan Musial	40.00	20.00	12.00
2-2	Warren Spahn	15.00	7.50	4.50
2-3	Tommy Henrich	10.00	5.00	3.00
2-4	Larry "Yogi" Berra	25.00	12.50	7.50
2-5	Joe DiMaggio	65.00	32.00	19.50
2-6	Bobby Brown	10.00	5.00	3.00
2-7	Granville Hamner	6.00	3.00	1.75
2-8	Willie Jones	6.00	3.00	1.75
2-9	Stanley Lopata	6.00	3.00	1.75
2-10	Mike Goliat	6.00	3.00	1.75
3-1	Ralph Kiner	15.00	7.50	4.50
3-2	Billy Goodman	6.00	3.00	1.75
3-3	Allie Reynolds	10.00	5.00	3.00
3-4	Vic Raschi	10.00	5.00	3.00
3-5	Joe Page	8.00	4.00	2.50
3-6	Eddie Lopat	10.00	5.00	3.00
3-7	Andy Seminick	6.00	3.00	1.75
3-8	Dick Sisler	6.00	3.00	1.75
3-9	Eddie Waitkus	6.00	3.00	1.75
3-10	Ken Heintzelman	6.00	3.00	1.75
4-1	Gene Woodling	10.00	5.00	3.00
4-2	Cliff Mapes	8.00	4.00	2.50
4-3	Fred Sanford	8.00	4.00	2.50
4-4	Tommy Bryne	8.00	4.00	2.50
4-5	Eddie (Whitey) Ford	20.00	10.00	6.00
4-6	Jim Konstanty	7.00	3.50	2.00
4-7	Russ Meyer	6.00	3.00	1.75
4-8	Robin Roberts	15.00	7.50	4.50
4-9	Curt Simmons	7.00	3.50	2.00
4-10	Sam Jethroe	8.50	4.25	2.50

1952 Berk Ross

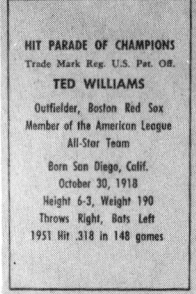

HIT PARADE OF CHAMPIONS
Trade Mark Reg. U.S. Pat. Off.

TED WILLIAMS
Outfielder, Boston Red Sox
Member of the American League
All-Star Team

Born San Diego, Calif.
October 30, 1918
Height 6-3, Weight 190
Throws Right, Bats Left
1951 Hit .318 in 148 games

Although the card size is different (2'' by 3''), the style of the fronts and backs of the 1952 Berk Ross set is similar to the previous year's effort. Seventy-two unnumbered cards make up the set. Rizzuto is included twice in the set and the Blackwell and Fox cards have transposed backs. The cards were issued individually rather than as two-card panels like in 1951.

		NR MT	EX	VG
Complete Set:		2500.00	1250.00	750.00
Common Player:		9.00	4.50	2.75
(1)	Richie Ashburn	23.00	11.50	7.00
(2)	Hank Bauer	15.00	7.50	4.50
(3)	Larry "Yogi" Berra	50.00	25.00	15.00
(4)	Ewell Blackwell (photo actually Nelson Fox)	12.00	6.00	3.50
(5)	Bobby Brown	15.00	7.50	4.50
(6)	Jim Busby	9.00	4.50	2.75
(7)	Roy Campanella	60.00	30.00	18.00
(8)	Chico Carrasquel	9.00	4.50	2.75
(9)	Jerry Coleman	12.00	6.00	3.50
(10)	Joe Collins	12.00	6.00	3.50
(11)	Alvin Dark	12.00	6.00	3.50
(12)	Dom DiMaggio	15.00	7.50	4.50
(13)	Joe DiMaggio	350.00	175.00	105.00

		NR MT	EX	VG
(14)	Larry Doby	12.00	6.00	3.50
(15)	Bobby Doerr	20.00	10.00	6.00
(16)	Bob Elliot (Elliott)	9.00	4.50	2.75
(17)	Del Ennis	10.00	5.00	3.00
(18)	Ferris Fain	9.00	4.50	2.75
(19)	Bob Feller	50.00	25.00	15.00
(20)	Nelson Fox (photo actually Ewell			
	Blackwell)	15.00	7.50	4.50
(21)	Ned Garver	9.00	4.50	2.75
(22)	Clint Hartung	9.00	4.50	2.75
(23)	Jim Hearn	9.00	4.50	2.75
(24)	Gil Hodges	25.00	12.50	7.50
(25)	Monte Irvin	20.00	10.00	6.00
(26)	Larry Jansen	9.00	4.50	2.75
(27)	George Kell	20.00	10.00	6.00
(28)	Sheldon Jones	9.00	4.50	2.75
(29)	Monte Kennedy	9.00	4.50	2.75
(30)	Ralph Kiner	20.00	10.00	6.00
(31)	Dave Koslo	9.00	4.50	2.75
(32)	Bob Kuzava	12.00	6.00	3.50
(33)	Bob Lemon	20.00	10.00	6.00
(34)	Whitey Lockman	9.00	4.50	2.75
(35)	Eddie Lopat	15.00	7.50	4.50
(36)	Sal Maglie	12.00	6.00	3.50
(37)	Mickey Mantle	350.00	175.00	105.00
(38)	Billy Martin	35.00	17.50	10.50
(39)	Willie Mays	225.00	112.00	67.00
(40)	Gil McDougal (McDougald)	15.00	7.50	4.50
(41)	Orestes Minoso	12.00	6.00	3.50
(42)	Johnny Mize	25.00	12.50	7.50
(43)	Tom Morgan	12.00	6.00	3.50
(44)	Don Mueller	9.00	4.50	2.75
(45)	Stan Musial	150.00	75.00	45.00
(46)	Don Newcombe	15.00	7.50	4.50
(47)	Ray Noble	9.00	4.50	2.75
(48)	Joe Ostrowski	12.00	6.00	3.50
(49)	Mel Parnell	9.00	4.50	2.75
(50)	Vic Raschi	15.00	7.50	4.50
(51)	Pee Wee Reese	30.00	15.00	9.00
(52)	Allie Reynolds	15.00	7.50	4.50
(53)	Bill Rigney	10.00	5.00	3.00
(54)	Phil Rizzuto (bunting)	35.00	17.50	10.50
(55)	Phil Rizzuto (swinging)	35.00	17.50	10.50
(56)	Robin Roberts	20.00	10.00	6.00
(57)	Eddie Robinson	9.00	4.50	2.75
(58)	Jackie Robinson	150.00	75.00	45.00
(59)	Elwin "Preacher" Roe	12.00	6.00	3.50
(60)	Johnny Sain	12.00	6.00	3.50
(61)	Albert "Red" Schoendienst	12.00	6.00	3.50
(62)	Duke Snider	60.00	30.00	18.00
(63)	George Spencer	9.00	4.50	2.75
(64)	Eddie Stanky	12.00	6.00	3.50
(65)	Henry Thompson	9.00	4.50	2.75
(66)	Bobby Thomson	15.00	7.50	4.50
(67)	Vic Wertz	10.00	5.00	3.00
(68)	Waldon Westlake	9.00	4.50	2.75
(69)	Wes Westrum	10.00	5.00	3.00
(70)	Ted Williams	225.00	112.00	67.00
(71)	Gene Woodling	15.00	7.50	4.50
(72)	Gus Zernial	9.00	4.50	2.75

1986 Big League Chew

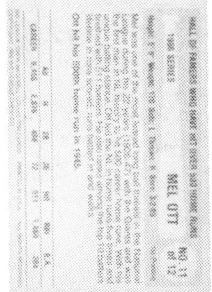

The 1986 Big League Chew set consists of twelve cards featuring the players who have hit 500 or more career home runs. The cards, which measure 2½'' by 3½'', were inserted in specially marked packages of Big League Chew, the shredded bubble gum devel-

oped by former major leaguer Jim Bouton. The set is entitled "Home Run Legends" and was available through a write-in offer on the package. Recent-day players in the set are shown in color photos, while the older sluggers are pictured in black and white.

		MT	NR MT	EX
	Complete Set:	5.00	3.75	2.00
	Common Player:	.35	.25	.14
1	Hank Aaron	.60	.45	.25
2	Babe Ruth	.70	.50	.30
3	Willie Mays	.60	.45	.25
4	Frank Robinson	.35	.25	.14
5	Harmon Killebrew	.35	.25	.14
6	Mickey Mantle	.70	.50	.30
7	Jimmie Foxx	.35	.25	.14
8	Ted Williams	.70	.50	.30
9	Ernie Banks	.35	.25	.14
10	Eddie Mathews	.35	.25	.14
11	Mel Ott	.35	.25	.14
12	500-HR Group Card	.50	.40	.20

1987 Boardwalk and Baseball

The 33-card "Top Run Makers" set was produced by Topps for distribution by the recreation amusement park "Boardwalk and Baseball", located near Orlando, Fla. The cards, which measure 2½'' by 3½'', feature fronts which contain full color player photos and the park's logo (B/B). The card backs are printed in black and pink on white stock and offer personal data and career statistics. The set was issued in a specially designed box.

		MT	NR MT	EX
	Complete Set:	5.00	3.75	2.00
	Common Player:	.09	.07	.04
1	Mike Schmidt	.40	.30	.15
2	Eddie Murray	.40	.30	.15
3	Dale Murphy	.50	.40	.20
4	Dave Winfield	.30	.25	.12
5	Jim Rice	.35	.25	.14
6	Cecil Cooper	.12	.09	.05
7	Dwight Evans	.15	.11	.06
8	Rickey Henderson	.40	.30	.15
9	Robin Yount	.30	.25	.12
10	Andre Dawson	.25	.20	.10
11	Gary Carter	.35	.25	.14
12	Keith Hernandez	.30	.25	.12
13	George Brett	.50	.40	.20
14	Bill Buckner	.09	.07	.04
15	Tony Armas	.09	.07	.04
16	Harold Baines	.15	.11	.06
17	Don Baylor	.12	.09	.05
18	Steve Garvey	.35	.25	.14
19	Lance Parrish	.20	.15	.08
20	Dave Parker	.20	.15	.08
21	Buddy Bell	.09	.07	.04
22	Cal Ripken	.40	.30	.15
23	Bob Horner	.15	.11	.06
24	Tim Raines	.35	.25	.14
25	Jack Clark	.20	.15	.08
26	Leon Durham	.12	.09	.05
27	Pedro Guerrero	.15	.11	.06
28	Kent Hrbek	.15	.11	.06

		MT	NR MT	EX
29	Kirk Gibson	.25	.20	.10
30	Ryne Sandberg	.30	.25	.12
31	Wade Boggs	.70	.50	.30
32	Don Mattingly	1.25	.90	.50
33	Darryl Strawberry	.50	.40	.20

1987 Bohemian Hearth Bread Padres

 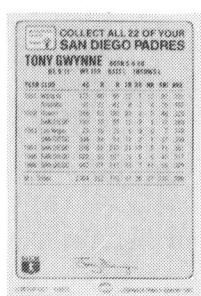

Bohemian Hearth Bread Company of San Diego issued a 22-card set highlighting the San Diego Padres. Produced in conjunction with Mike Schecter Associates, the cards are the standard 2½" by 3½" size. The card fronts contain a full-color photo encompassed by a yellow border. The Bohemian Hearth Bread logo is located in the upper left corner of the card. The card backs are printed in light brown ink on a cream color card stock and carry player personal and statistical information.

		MT	NR MT	EX
Complete Set:		25.00	18.50	10.00
Common Player:		.50	.40	.20
1	Garry Templeton	1.25	.90	.50
4	Jose Cora	1.00	.70	.40
5	Randy Ready	.50	.40	.20
6	Steve Garvey	3.00	2.25	1.25
7	Kevin Mitchell	2.00	1.50	.80
8	John Kruk	3.00	2.25	1.25
9	Benito Santiago	5.00	3.75	2.00
10	Larry Bowa	1.25	.90	.50
11	Tim Flannery	.50	.40	.20
14	Carmelo Martinez	1.00	.70	.40
16	Marvell Wynne	.50	.40	.20
19	Tony Gwynn	5.00	3.75	2.00
21	James Steels	1.00	.70	.40
22	Stan Jefferson	1.50	1.25	.60
30	Eric Show	1.00	.70	.40
31	Ed Whitson	.50	.40	.20
34	Storm Davis	.50	.40	.20
37	Craig Lefferts	.50	.40	.20
40	Andy Hawkins	.50	.40	.20
41	Lance McCullers	1.25	.90	.50
43	Dave Dravecky	1.00	.70	.40
54	Rich Gossage	2.00	1.50	.80

1947 Bond Bread Jackie Robinson

The major league's first black player, Jackie Robinson, was featured in a thirteen card set issued by Bond Bread in 1947. The cards, which measure 2¼" by 3½", are black and white photos of Robinson in various action and portrait poses. The unnumbered cards bear three different backs which contain advertising for Bond Bread. Four of the thirteen cards make use of a horizontal format. Card #6 in the checklist below is believed to have been issued in greater quantity and perhaps was a promotional card. The back of

this card is the only one in the set containing a short biography of Jackie. The ACC designation for the set is D302.

		NR MT	EX	VG
Complete Set:		3150.00	1575.00	945.00
Common Player:		150.00	75.00	45.00
(1)	Batting (awaiting pitch)	250.00	125.00	75.00
(2)	Batting Follow-Thru (white shirtsleeves)			
		250.00	125.00	75.00
(3)	Batting Follow-Thru (no shirtsleeves)			
		250.00	125.00	75.00
(4)	Leaping (scoreboard in background)			
		250.00	125.00	75.00
(5)	Leaping (no scoreboard)	250.00	125.00	75.00
(6)	Portrait (facsimile autograph)	150.00	75.00	45.00
(7)	Portrait (holding glove in air)	250.00	125.00	75.00
(8)	Running (down the baseline)	250.00	125.00	75.00
(9)	Running (about to catch ball)	250.00	125.00	75.00
(10)	Sliding (umpire in picture)	250.00	125.00	75.00
(11)	Stretching For Throw (ball in glove)			
		250.00	125.00	75.00
(12)	Stretching For Throw (no ball visible)			
		250.00	125.00	75.00
(13)	Throwing (ball in hand)	250.00	125.00	75.00

1948 Bowman

 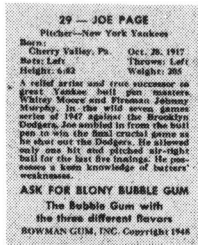

Bowman Gum Co.'s premiere set was produced in 1948, making it one the first major issues of the post-war period. Forty-eight black and white cards comprise the set, with each card measuring 2 1/16" by 2 1/2" in size. The card backs, printed in black ink on grey stock, include the card number and the player's name, team, position, and a short biography. Twelve cards (7, 8, 13, 16, 20, 22, 24, 26, 28, 29, 30 and 34) were printed in shorter supply when they were removed from the 36-card printing sheet to make room for the set's high numbers (#'s 37-48). These 24 cards command a higher price than the remaining cards in the set.

	NR MT	EX	VG
Complete Set:	1500.00	525.00	300.00
Common Player: 1-36	10.00	5.00	3.00
Common Player: 37-48	15.00	7.50	4.50

		NR MT	EX	VG
1	Bob Elliott	50.00	7.00	4.25
2	Ewell (The Whip) Blackwell	14.00	6.00	3.50
3	Ralph Kiner	40.00	20.00	12.00
4	Johnny Mize	35.00	17.50	10.50
5	Bob Feller	60.00	30.00	18.00
6	Larry (Yogi) Berra	175.00	70.00	44.00
7	Pete (Pistol Pete) Reiser	32.00	16.00	9.50
8	Phil (Scooter) Rizzuto	110.00	44.00	28.00
9	Walker Cooper	10.00	5.00	3.00
10	Buddy Rosar	10.00	5.00	3.00
11	Johnny Lindell	15.00	7.50	4.50
12	Johnny Sain	16.00	8.00	4.75
13	Willard Marshall	22.00	11.00	6.50
14	Allie Reynolds	20.00	10.00	6.00
15	Eddie Joost	10.00	5.00	3.00
16	Jack Lohrke	22.00	11.00	6.50
17	Enos (Country) Slaughter	35.00	17.50	10.50
18	Warren Spahn	60.00	30.00	18.00
19	Tommy (The Clutch) Henrich	20.00	10.00	6.00
20	Buddy Kerr	22.00	11.00	6.50
21	Ferris Fain	12.00	6.00	3.50
22	Floyd (Bill) Bevins (Bevens)	30.00	15.00	9.00
23	Larry Jansen	10.00	5.00	3.00
24	Emil (Dutch) Leonard	22.00	11.00	6.50
25	Barney McCoskey (McCosky)	10.00	5.00	3.00
26	Frank Shea	30.00	15.00	9.00
27	Sid Gordon	10.00	5.00	3.00
28	Emil (The Antelope) Verban	22.00	11.00	6.50
29	Joe Page	30.00	15.00	9.00
30	"Whitey" Lockman	22.00	11.00	6.50
31	Bill McCahan	10.00	5.00	3.00
32	Bill Rigney	12.00	6.00	3.50
33	Bill (The Bull) Johnson	15.00	7.50	4.50
34	Sheldon (Available) Jones	22.00	11.00	6.50
35	George (Snuffy) Stirnweiss	15.00	7.50	4.50
36	Stan Musial	225.00	90.00	56.00
37	Clint Hartung	15.00	7.50	4.50
38	Al "Red" Schoendienst	25.00	12.50	7.50
39	Augie Galan	15.00	7.50	4.50
40	Marty Marion	20.00	10.00	6.00
41	Rex Barney	18.00	9.00	5.50
42	Ray Poat	15.00	7.50	4.50
43	Bruce Edwards	15.00	7.50	4.50
44	Johnny Wyrostek	15.00	7.50	4.50
45	Hank Sauer	15.00	7.50	4.50
46	Herman Wehmeier	15.00	7.50	4.50
47	Bobby Thomson	25.00	12.50	7.50
48	George "Dave" Koslo	40.00	9.00	4.50

1949 Bowman

No. 29 of a Series of 240
RALPH KINER
Outfielder—Pittsburgh Pirates
Born Santa Rita, N. M., Octoer 27, 1922
Bats, Right; Throws, Right. Ht. 6 1½; Wt. 195
He is already being called another Babe Ruth.
His amazing clouting drove out 51 home runs in
1947 to tie Johnny Mize. He also led the
National League in home runs. Second player
since 1900 to do this as a rookie. He joined the
club in 1943 but due to Uncle Sam's prior
claim on him it was not until 1946 that he appeared in a game for the Pirates. Last season he
batted .265 and hit 40 homers, again tying
Johnny Mize for the lead.

BASEBALL GAME AND BANK

(Not valid where contrary to State laws)
Offer expires 12.31.49 ©Bowman Gum, Inc., 1949

In 1949, Bowman increased the size of its issue to 240 numbered cards. The cards, which measure 2 1/16'' by 2 1/2'', are black and white photos overprinted with various pastel colors. Beginning with card #109 in the set, Bowman inserted the players' names on the card fronts. Twelve cards (#'s 4, 78, 83, 85, 88, 98, 109, 124, 126, 127, 132 and 143), which were produced in the first four series of printings, were reprinted in the seventh series with either a card front or back modification. These variations are noted in the checklist that follows. Card #'s 1-3 and 5-73 can be found with either white or grey backs. The complete set value in the following checklist does not include the higher priced variation cards.

	NR MT	EX	VG
Complete Set:	8500.00	2975.00	1700.
Common Player: 1-36	10.00	5.00	3.00

		NR MT	EX	VG
Common Player: 37-73		12.00	6.00	3.50
Common Player: 74-144		10.00	5.00	3.00
Common Player: 145-240		40.00	20.00	12.00
1	Vernon Bickford	50.00	7.50	3.00
2	Carroll "Whitey" Lockman	15.00	5.00	3.00
3	Bob Porterfield	15.00	7.50	4.50
4a	Jerry Priddy (no name on front)	12.00	6.00	3.50
4b	Jerry Priddy (name on front)	30.00	15.00	9.00
5	Hank Sauer	10.00	5.00	3.00
6	Phil Cavarretta	12.00	6.00	3.50
7	Joe Dobson	10.00	5.00	3.00
8	Murry Dickson	10.00	5.00	3.00
9	Ferris Fain	12.00	6.00	3.50
10	Ted Gray	10.00	5.00	3.00
11	Lou Boudreau	24.00	12.00	7.25
12	Cass Michaels	10.00	5.00	3.00
13	Bob Chesnes	10.00	5.00	3.00
14	Curt Simmons	15.00	7.50	4.50
15	Ned Garver	10.00	5.00	3.00
16	Al Kozar	10.00	5.00	3.00
17	Earl Torgeson	10.00	5.00	3.00
18	Bobby Thomson	18.00	9.00	5.50
19	Bobby Brown	20.00	10.00	6.00
20	Gene Hermanski	12.00	6.00	3.50
21	Frank Baumholtz	10.00	5.00	3.00
22	Harry "P-Nuts" Lowrey	10.00	5.00	3.00
23	Bobby Doerr	24.00	12.00	7.25
24	Stan Musial	200.00	80.00	50.00
25	Carl Scheib	10.00	5.00	3.00
26	George Kell	24.00	12.00	7.25
27	Bob Feller	65.00	32.00	19.50
28	Don Kolloway	10.00	5.00	3.00
29	Ralph Kiner	30.00	15.00	9.00
30	Andy Seminick	10.00	5.00	3.00
31	Dick Kokos	10.00	5.00	3.00
32	Eddie Yost	10.00	5.00	3.00
33	Warren Spahn	70.00	35.00	21.00
34	Dave Koslo	10.00	5.00	3.00
35	Vic Raschi	20.00	10.00	6.00
36	Harold "Peewee" Reese	60.00	30.00	18.00
37	John Wyrostek	12.00	6.00	3.50
38	Emil "The Antelope" Verban	12.00	6.00	3.50
39	Bill Goodman	12.00	6.00	3.50
40	George "Red" Munger	12.00	6.00	3.50
41	Lou Brissie	12.00	6.00	3.50
42	Walter "Hoot" Evers	12.00	6.00	3.50
43	Dale Mitchell	12.00	6.00	3.50
44	Dave Philley	12.00	6.00	3.50
45	Wally Westlake	12.00	6.00	3.50
46	Robin Roberts	75.00	37.00	22.00
47	Johnny Sain	18.00	9.00	5.50
48	Willard Marshall	12.00	6.00	3.50
49	Frank Shea	18.00	9.00	5.50
50	Jackie Robinson	275.00	110.00	69.00
51	Herman Wehmeier	12.00	6.00	3.50
52	Johnny Schmitz	12.00	6.00	3.50
53	Jack Kramer	12.00	6.00	3.50
54	Marty "Slats" Marion	16.00	8.00	4.75
55	Eddie Joost	12.00	6.00	3.50
56	Pat Mullin	12.00	6.00	3.50
57	Gene Bearden	12.00	6.00	3.50
58	Bob Elliott	12.00	6.00	3.50
59	Jack "Lucky" Lohrke	12.00	6.00	3.50
60	Larry "Yogi" Berra	125.00	50.00	32.00
61	Rex Barney	14.00	7.00	4.25
62	Grady Hatton	12.00	6.00	3.50
63	Andy Pafko	14.00	7.00	4.25
64	Dom "The Little Professor" DiMaggio	18.00	9.00	5.50
65	Enos "Country" Slaughter	30.00	15.00	9.00
66	Elmer Valo	12.00	6.00	3.50
67	Alvin Dark	16.00	8.00	4.75
68	Sheldon "Available" Jones	12.00	6.00	3.50
69	Tommy "The Clutch" Henrich	20.00	10.00	6.00
70	Carl Furillo	24.00	12.00	7.25
71	Vern "Junior" Stephens	12.00	6.00	3.50
72	Tommy Holmes	14.00	7.00	4.25
73	Billy Cox	14.00	7.00	4.25
74	Tom McBride	10.00	5.00	3.00
75	Eddie Mayo	10.00	5.00	3.00
76	Bill Nicholson	10.00	5.00	3.00
77	Ernie (Jumbo and Tiny) Bonham	10.00	5.00	3.00
78a	Sam Zoldak (no name on front)	12.00	6.00	3.50
78b	Sam Zoldak (name on front)	30.00	15.00	9.00
79	Ron Northey	10.00	5.00	3.00
80	Bill McCahan	10.00	5.00	3.00
81	Virgil "Red" Stallcup	10.00	5.00	3.00
82	Joe Page	16.00	8.00	4.75
83a	Bob Scheffing (no name on front)	12.00	6.00	3.50

		NR MT	EX	VG
83b	Bob Scheffing (name on front)	30.00	15.00	9.00
84	Roy Campanella	175.00	70.00	44.00
85a	Johnny "Big John" Mize (no name on front)	30.00	15.00	9.00
85b	Johnny "Big John" Mize (name on front)	80.00	40.00	24.00
86	Johnny Pesky	12.00	6.00	3.50
87	Randy Gumpert	10.00	5.00	3.00
88a	Bill Salkeld (no name on front)	12.00	6.00	3.50
88b	Bill Salkeld (name on front)	30.00	15.00	9.00
89	Mizell "Whitey" Platt	10.00	5.00	3.00
90	Gil Coan	10.00	5.00	3.00
91	Dick Wakefield	10.00	5.00	3.00
92	Willie "Puddin-Head" Jones	10.00	5.00	3.00
93	Ed Stevens	10.00	5.00	3.00
94	James "Mickey" Vernon	12.00	6.00	3.50
95	Howie Pollett	10.00	5.00	3.00
96	Taft Wright	10.00	5.00	3.00
97	Danny Litwhiler	10.00	5.00	3.00
98a	Phil Rizzuto (no name on front)	40.00	20.00	12.00
98b	Phil Rizzuto (name on front)	100.00	40.00	25.00
99	Frank Gustine	10.00	5.00	3.00
100	Gil Hodges	60.00	30.00	18.00
101	Sid Gordon	10.00	5.00	3.00
102	Stan Spence	10.00	5.00	3.00
103	Joe Tipton	10.00	5.00	3.00
104	Ed Stanky	12.00	6.00	3.50
105	Bill Kennedy	10.00	5.00	3.00
106	Jake Early	10.00	5.00	3.00
107	Eddie Lake	10.00	5.00	3.00
108	Ken Heintzelman	10.00	5.00	3.00
109a	Ed Fitzgerald (Fitz Gerald) (script name on back)	12.00	6.00	3.50
109b	Ed Fitzgerald (Fitz Gerald) (printed name on back)	30.00	15.00	9.00
110	Early Wynn	30.00	15.00	9.00
111	Al "Red" Schoendienst	16.00	8.00	4.75
112	Sam Chapman	10.00	5.00	3.00
113	Ray Lamanno	10.00	5.00	3.00
114	Allie Reynolds	20.00	10.00	6.00
115	Emil "Dutch" Leonard	10.00	5.00	3.00
116	Joe Hatten	12.00	6.00	3.50
117	Walker Cooper	10.00	5.00	3.00
118	Sam Mele	10.00	5.00	3.00
119	Floyd Baker	10.00	5.00	3.00
120	Cliff Fannin	10.00	5.00	3.00
121	Mark Christman	10.00	5.00	3.00
122	George Vico	10.00	5.00	3.00
123	Johnny Blatnick	10.00	5.00	3.00
124a	Danny Murtaugh (script name on back)	12.00	6.00	3.50
124b	Danny Murtaugh (printed name on back)	30.00	15.00	9.00
125	Ken Keltner	12.00	6.00	3.50
126a	Al Brazle (script name on back)	12.00	6.00	3.50
126b	Al Brazle (printed name on back)	30.00	15.00	9.00
127a	Henry "Heeney" Majeski (script name on back)	12.00	6.00	3.50
127b	Henry "Heeney" Majeski (printed name on back)	30.00	15.00	9.00
128	Johnny Vander Meer	16.00	8.00	4.75
129	Bill "The Bull" Johnson	16.00	8.00	4.75
130	Harry "The Hat" Walker	12.00	6.00	3.50
131	Paul Lehner	10.00	5.00	3.00
132a	Al Evans (script name on back)	12.00	6.00	3.50
132b	Al Evans (printed name on back)	30.00	15.00	9.00
133	Aaron Robinson	10.00	5.00	3.00
134	Hank Borowy	10.00	5.00	3.00
135	Stan Rojek	10.00	5.00	3.00
136	Henry "Hank" Edwards	10.00	5.00	3.00
137	Ted Wilks	10.00	5.00	3.00
138	Warren "Buddy" Rosar	10.00	5.00	3.00
139	Hank "Bow-Wow" Arft	10.00	5.00	3.00
140	Rae Scarborough (Ray)	10.00	5.00	3.00
141	Ulysses "Tony" Lupien	10.00	5.00	3.00
142	Eddie Waitkus	10.00	5.00	3.00
143a	Bob Dillinger (script name on back)	12.00	6.00	3.50
143b	Bob Dillinger (printed name on back)	30.00	15.00	9.00
144	Milton "Mickey" Haefner	10.00	5.00	3.00
145	Sylvester "Blix" Donnelly	40.00	20.00	12.00
146	Myron "Mike" McCormick	45.00	22.00	13.50
147	Elmer "Bert" Singleton	40.00	20.00	12.00
148	Bob Swift	40.00	20.00	12.00
149	Roy Partee	50.00	25.00	15.00
150	Alfred "Allie" Clark	40.00	20.00	12.00
151	Maurice "Mickey" Harris	40.00	20.00	12.00
152	Clarence Maddern	40.00	20.00	12.00

		NR MT	EX	VG
153	Phil Masi	40.00	20.00	12.00
154	Clint Hartung	40.00	20.00	12.00
155	Fermin "Mickey" Guerra	40.00	20.00	12.00
156	Al "Zeke" Zarilla	40.00	20.00	12.00
157	Walt Masterson	40.00	20.00	12.00
158	Harry "The Cat" Brecheen	40.00	20.00	12.00
159	Glen Moulder	40.00	20.00	12.00
160	Jim Blackburn	40.00	20.00	12.00
161	John "Jocko" Thompson	40.00	20.00	12.00
162	Elwin "Preacher" Roe	55.00	27.00	16.50
163	Clyde McCullough	40.00	20.00	12.00
164	Vic Wertz	45.00	22.00	13.50
165	George "Snuffy" Stirnweiss	50.00	25.00	15.00
166	Mike Tresh	40.00	20.00	12.00
167	Boris "Babe" Martin	40.00	20.00	12.00
168	Doyle Lade	40.00	20.00	12.00
169	Jeff Heath	40.00	20.00	12.00
170	Bill Rigney	45.00	22.00	13.50
171	Dick Fowler	40.00	20.00	12.00
172	Eddie Pellagrini	40.00	20.00	12.00
173	Eddie Stewart	40.00	20.00	12.00
174	Terry Moore	45.00	22.00	13.50
175	Luke Appling	60.00	30.00	18.00
176	Ken Raffensberger	40.00	20.00	12.00
177	Stan Lopata	40.00	20.00	12.00
178	Tommy Brown	45.00	22.00	13.50
179	Hugh Casey	45.00	22.00	13.50
180	Connie Berry	40.00	20.00	12.00
181	Gus Niarhos	50.00	25.00	15.00
182	Hal Peck	40.00	20.00	12.00
183	Lou Stringer	40.00	20.00	12.00
184	Bob Chipman	40.00	20.00	12.00
185	Pete Reiser	45.00	22.00	13.50
186	John "Buddy" Kerr	40.00	20.00	12.00
187	Phil Marchildon	40.00	20.00	12.00
188	Karl Drews	40.00	20.00	12.00
189	Earl Wooten	40.00	20.00	12.00
190	Jim Hearn	40.00	20.00	12.00
191	Joe Haynes	40.00	20.00	12.00
192	Harry Gumbert	40.00	20.00	12.00
193	Ken Trinkle	40.00	20.00	12.00
194	Ralph Branca	55.00	27.00	16.50
195	Eddie Bockman	40.00	20.00	12.00
196	Fred Hutchinson	45.00	22.00	13.50
197	Johnny Lindell	50.00	25.00	15.00
198	Steve Gromek	40.00	20.00	12.00
199	Cecil "Tex" Hughson	40.00	20.00	12.00
200	Jess Dobernic	40.00	20.00	12.00
201	Sibby Sisti	40.00	20.00	12.00
202	Larry Jansen	40.00	20.00	12.00
203	Barney McCosky	40.00	20.00	12.00
204	Bob Savage	40.00	20.00	12.00
205	Dick Sisler	40.00	20.00	12.00
206	Bruce Edwards	45.00	22.00	13.50
207	Johnny "Hippity" Hopp	40.00	20.00	12.00
208	Paul "Dizzy" Trout	45.00	22.00	13.50
209	Charlie "King Kong" Keller	55.00	27.00	16.50
210	Joe "Flash" Gordon	45.00	22.00	13.50
211	Dave "Boo" Ferris	40.00	20.00	12.00
212	Ralph Hamner	40.00	20.00	12.00
213	Charles "Red" Barrett	40.00	20.00	12.00
214	Richie Ashburn	175.00	87.00	52.00
215	Kirby Higbe	40.00	20.00	12.00
216	Lynwood "Schoolboy" Rowe	40.00	20.00	12.00
217	Marino Pieretti	40.00	20.00	12.00
218	Dick Kryhoski	50.00	25.00	15.00
219	Virgil "Fire" Trucks	45.00	22.00	13.50
220	Johnny McCarthy	40.00	20.00	12.00
221	Bob Muncrief	40.00	20.00	12.00
222	Alex Kellner	40.00	20.00	12.00
223	Bob Hoffman (Hofman)	40.00	20.00	12.00
224	Leroy "Satchel" Paige	750.00	300.00	188.00
225	Gerry Coleman	55.00	27.00	16.50
226	Edwin "Duke" Snider	525.00	210.00	131.00
227	Fritz Ostermueller	40.00	20.00	12.00
228	Jackie Mayo	40.00	20.00	12.00
229	Ed Lopat	60.00	30.00	18.00
230	Augie Galan	40.00	20.00	12.00
231	Earl Johnson	40.00	20.00	12.00
232	George McQuinn	50.00	25.00	15.00
233	Larry Doby	70.00	35.00	21.00
234	Truett "Rip" Sewell	45.00	22.00	13.50
235	Jim Russell	40.00	20.00	12.00
236	Fred Sanford	50.00	25.00	15.00
237	Monte Kennedy	40.00	20.00	12.00
238	Bob Lemon	150.00	75.00	45.00
239	Frank McCormick	50.00	20.00	12.00
240	Norman "Babe" Young (photo actually Bobby Young)	80.00	25.00	15.00

1949 Bowman Pacific Coast League

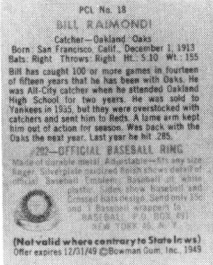

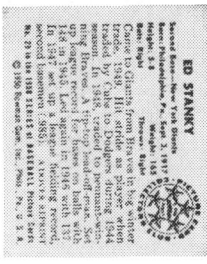

One of the scarcest issues of the post-war period, the 1949 Bowman PCL set was issued only on the West Coast. Like the 1949 Bowman regular issue, the cards contain black and white photos overprinted with various pastel colors. Thirty-six cards, which measure 2 1/16'' by 2 1/2'', make up the set. It is believed that the cards may have been issued only in sheets and not sold in gum packs.

		NR MT	EX	VG
Complete Set:		5500.00	3575.00	1800.
Common Player:		150.00	97.50	49.50
1	Lee Anthony	150.00	75.00	45.00
2	George Metkovich	150.00	75.00	45.00
3	Ralph Hodgin	150.00	75.00	45.00
4	George Woods	150.00	75.00	45.00
5	Xavier Rescigno	150.00	75.00	45.00
6	Mickey Grasso	150.00	75.00	45.00
7	Johnny Rucker	150.00	75.00	45.00
8	Jack Brewer	150.00	75.00	45.00
9	Dom D'Allessandro	150.00	75.00	45.00
10	Charlie Gassaway	150.00	75.00	45.00
11	Tony Freitas	150.00	75.00	45.00
12	Gordon Maltzberger	150.00	75.00	45.00
13	John Jensen	150.00	75.00	45.00
14	Joyner White	150.00	75.00	45.00
15	Harvey Storey	150.00	75.00	45.00
16	Dick Lajeski	150.00	75.00	45.00
17	Albie Glossop	150.00	75.00	45.00
18	Bill Raimondi	150.00	75.00	45.00
19	Ken Holcombe	150.00	75.00	45.00
20	Don Ross	150.00	75.00	45.00
21	Pete Coscarart	150.00	75.00	45.00
22	Tony York	150.00	75.00	45.00
23	Jake Mooty	150.00	75.00	45.00
24	Charles Adams	150.00	75.00	45.00
25	Les Scarsella	150.00	75.00	45.00
26	Joe Marty	150.00	75.00	45.00
27	Frank Kelleher	150.00	75.00	45.00
28	Lee Handley	150.00	75.00	45.00
29	Herman Besse	150.00	75.00	45.00
30	John Lazor	150.00	75.00	45.00
31	Eddie Malone	150.00	75.00	45.00
32	Maurice Van Robays	150.00	75.00	45.00
33	Jim Tabor	150.00	75.00	45.00
34	Gene Handley	150.00	75.00	45.00
35	Tom Seats	150.00	75.00	45.00
36	Ora Burnett	150.00	75.00	45.00

1950 Bowman

The quality of the 1950 Bowman issue showed a marked improvement over the company's previous efforts. The cards are beautiful color art reproductions of actual photographs and measure 2 1/16'' by 2 1/2'' in size. The card backs include the same type of information as found in the previous year's issue but are designed in a horizontal format. Cards found in the first two series of the set (#'s 1-72) are the scarcest in the issue. The backs of the final 72 cards in the set (#'s 181-252) can be found with or without the copyright line at the bottom of the card, the ''without'' version being the less common.

		NR MT	EX	VG
Complete Set:		5200.00	1825.00	1050.
Common Player: 1-72		20.00	10.00	6.00
Common Player: 73-252		10.00	5.00	3.00
1	Mel Parnell	150.00	13.50	6.00
2	Vern Stephens	30.00	10.00	6.00
3	Dom DiMaggio	27.00	13.50	8.00
4	Gus Zernial	20.00	10.00	6.00
5	Bob Kuzava	20.00	10.00	6.00
6	Bob Feller	75.00	37.00	22.00
7	Jim Hegan	20.00	10.00	6.00
8	George Kell	32.00	16.00	9.50
9	Vic Wertz	20.00	10.00	6.00
10	Tommy Henrich	32.00	16.00	9.50
11	Phil Rizzuto	60.00	30.00	18.00
12	Joe Page	27.00	13.50	8.00
13	Ferris Fain	22.00	11.00	6.50
14	Alex Kellner	20.00	10.00	6.00
15	Al Kozar	20.00	10.00	6.00
16	Roy Sievers	27.00	13.50	8.00
17	Sid Hudson	20.00	10.00	6.00
18	Eddie Robinson	20.00	10.00	6.00
19	Warren Spahn	70.00	35.00	21.00
20	Bob Elliott	20.00	10.00	6.00
21	Harold Reese	80.00	40.00	24.00
22	Jackie Robinson	250.00	100.00	63.00
23	Don Newcombe	35.00	17.50	10.50
24	Johnny Schmitz	20.00	10.00	6.00
25	Hank Sauer	20.00	10.00	6.00
26	Grady Hatton	20.00	10.00	6.00
27	Herman Wehmeier	20.00	10.00	6.00
28	Bobby Thomson	27.00	13.50	8.00
29	Ed Stanky	22.00	11.00	6.50
30	Eddie Waitkus	20.00	10.00	6.00
31	Del Ennis	20.00	10.00	6.00
32	Robin Roberts	50.00	25.00	15.00
33	Ralph Kiner	45.00	22.00	13.50
34	Murry Dickson	20.00	10.00	6.00
35	Enos Slaughter	35.00	17.50	10.50
36	Eddie Kazak	20.00	10.00	6.00
37	Luke Appling	32.00	16.00	9.50
38	Bill Wight	20.00	10.00	6.00
39	Larry Doby	27.00	13.50	8.00
40	Bob Lemon	45.00	22.00	13.50
41	Walter "Hoot" Evers	20.00	10.00	6.00
42	Art Houtteman	20.00	10.00	6.00
43	Bobby Doerr	32.00	16.00	9.50
44	Joe Dobson	20.00	10.00	6.00
45	Al "Zeke" Zarilla	20.00	10.00	6.00
46	Larry "Yogi" Berra	200.00	80.00	50.00
47	Jerry Coleman	32.00	16.00	9.50
48	Leland "Lou" Brissie	20.00	10.00	6.00
49	Elmer Valo	20.00	10.00	6.00
50	Dick Kokos	20.00	10.00	6.00
51	Ned Garver	20.00	10.00	6.00
52	Sam Mele	20.00	10.00	6.00
53	Clyde Vollmer	20.00	10.00	6.00
54	Gil Coan	20.00	10.00	6.00
55	John "Buddy" Kerr	20.00	10.00	6.00
56	Del Crandell (Crandall)	27.00	13.50	8.00
57	Vernon Bickford	20.00	10.00	6.00
58	Carl Furillo	32.00	16.00	9.50
59	Ralph Branca	32.00	16.00	9.50
60	Andy Pafko	22.00	11.00	6.50
61	Bob Rush	20.00	10.00	6.00
62	Ted Kluszewski	27.00	13.50	8.00
63	Ewell Blackwell	22.00	11.00	6.50
64	Alvin Dark	27.00	13.50	8.00
65	Dave Koslo	20.00	10.00	6.00
66	Larry Jansen	20.00	10.00	6.00
67	Willie Jones	20.00	10.00	6.00
68	Curt Simmons	22.00	11.00	6.50
69	Wally Westlake	20.00	10.00	6.00
70	Bob Chesnes	20.00	10.00	6.00

		NR MT	EX	VG			NR MT	EX	VG
71	Al Schoendienst	27.00	13.50	8.00	162	Eddie Yost	10.00	5.00	3.00
72	Howie Pollet	20.00	10.00	6.00	163	Earl Torgeson	10.00	5.00	3.00
73	Willard Marshall	10.00	5.00	3.00	164	Sibby Sisti	10.00	5.00	3.00
74	Johnny Antonelli	15.00	7.50	4.50	165	Bruce Edwards	12.00	6.00	3.50
75	Roy Campanella	150.00	60.00	38.00	166	Joe Hatten	12.00	6.00	3.50
76	Rex Barney	12.00	6.00	3.50	167	Elwin Roe	20.00	10.00	6.00
77	Edwin "Duke" Snider	125.00	50.00	32.00	168	Bob Scheffing	10.00	5.00	3.00
78	Mickey Owen	10.00	5.00	3.00	169	Hank Edwards	10.00	5.00	3.00
79	Johnny Vander Meer	12.00	6.00	3.50	170	Emil Leonard	10.00	5.00	3.00
80	Howard Fox	10.00	5.00	3.00	171	Harry Gumbert	10.00	5.00	3.00
81	Ron Northey	10.00	5.00	3.00	172	Harry Lowrey	10.00	5.00	3.00
82	Carroll Lockman	10.00	5.00	3.00	173	Lloyd Merriman	10.00	5.00	3.00
83	Sheldon Jones	10.00	5.00	3.00	174	Henry Thompson	10.00	5.00	3.00
84	Richie Ashburn	25.00	12.50	7.50	175	Monte Kennedy	10.00	5.00	3.00
85	Ken Heintzelman	10.00	5.00	3.00	176	Sylvester Donnelly	10.00	5.00	3.00
86	Stan Rojek	10.00	5.00	3.00	177	Hank Borowy	10.00	5.00	3.00
87	Bill Werle	10.00	5.00	3.00	178	Eddy Fitzgerald (Fitz Gerald)	10.00	5.00	3.00
88	Marty Marion	12.00	6.00	3.50	179	Charles Diering	10.00	5.00	3.00
89	George Munger	10.00	5.00	3.00	180	Harry Walker	12.00	6.00	3.50
90	Harry Brecheen	12.00	6.00	3.50	181	Marino Pieretti	10.00	5.00	3.00
91	Cass Michaels	10.00	5.00	3.00	182	Sam Zoldak	10.00	5.00	3.00
92	Hank Majeski	10.00	5.00	3.00	183	Mickey Haefner	10.00	5.00	3.00
93	Gene Bearden	10.00	5.00	3.00	184	Randy Gumpert	10.00	5.00	3.00
94	Lou Boudreau	25.00	12.50	7.50	185	Howie Judson	10.00	5.00	3.00
95	Aaron Robinson	10.00	5.00	3.00	186	Ken Keltner	12.00	6.00	3.50
96	Virgil "Fire" Trucks	12.00	6.00	3.50	187	Lou Stringer	10.00	5.00	3.00
97	Maurice McDermott	10.00	5.00	3.00	188	Earl Johnson	10.00	5.00	3.00
98	Ted Williams	300.00	120.00	75.00	189	Owen Friend	10.00	5.00	3.00
99	Billy Goodman	10.00	5.00	3.00	190	Ken Wood	10.00	5.00	3.00
100	Vic Raschi	20.00	10.00	6.00	191	Dick Starr	10.00	5.00	3.00
101	Bobby Brown	20.00	10.00	6.00	192	Bob Chipman	10.00	5.00	3.00
102	Billy Johnson	15.00	7.50	4.50	193	Harold "Pete" Reiser	12.00	6.00	3.50
103	Eddie Joost	10.00	5.00	3.00	194	Billy Cox	15.00	7.50	4.50
104	Sam Chapman	10.00	5.00	3.00	195	Phil Cavaretta (Cavarretta)	12.00	6.00	3.50
105	Bob Dillinger	10.00	5.00	3.00	196	Doyle Lade	10.00	5.00	3.00
106	Cliff Fannin	10.00	5.00	3.00	197	Johnny Wyrostek	10.00	5.00	3.00
107	Sam Dente	10.00	5.00	3.00	198	Danny Litwhiler	10.00	5.00	3.00
108	Rae Scarborough (Ray)	10.00	5.00	3.00	199	Jack Kramer	10.00	5.00	3.00
109	Sid Gordon	10.00	5.00	3.00	200	Kirby Higbe	10.00	5.00	3.00
110	Tommy Holmes	12.00	6.00	3.50	201	Pete Castiglione	10.00	5.00	3.00
111	Walker Cooper	10.00	5.00	3.00	202	Cliff Chambers	10.00	5.00	3.00
112	Gil Hodges	50.00	25.00	15.00	203	Danny Murtaugh	12.00	6.00	3.50
113	Gene Hermanski	12.00	6.00	3.50	204	Granville Hamner	10.00	5.00	3.00
114	Wayne Terwilliger	10.00	5.00	3.00	205	Mike Goliat	10.00	5.00	3.00
115	Roy Smalley	10.00	5.00	3.00	206	Stan Lopata	10.00	5.00	3.00
116	Virgil "Red" Stallcup	10.00	5.00	3.00	207	Max Lanier	10.00	5.00	3.00
117	Bill Rigney	12.00	6.00	3.50	208	Jim Hearn	10.00	5.00	3.00
118	Clint Hartung	10.00	5.00	3.00	209	Johnny Lindell	10.00	5.00	3.00
119	Dick Sisler	10.00	5.00	3.00	210	Ted Gray	10.00	5.00	3.00
120	John Thompson	10.00	5.00	3.00	211	Charlie Keller	10.00	5.00	3.00
121	Andy Seminick	10.00	5.00	3.00	212	Gerry Priddy	10.00	5.00	3.00
122	Johnny Hopp	10.00	5.00	3.00	213	Carl Scheib	10.00	5.00	3.00
123	Dino Restelli	10.00	5.00	3.00	214	Dick Fowler	10.00	5.00	3.00
124	Clyde McCullough	10.00	5.00	3.00	215	Ed Lopat	20.00	10.00	6.00
125	Del Rice	10.00	5.00	3.00	216	Bob Porterfield	15.00	7.50	4.50
126	Al Brazle	10.00	5.00	3.00	217	Casey Stengel	65.00	32.00	19.50
127	Dave Philley	10.00	5.00	3.00	218	Cliff Mapes	15.00	7.50	4.50
128	Phil Masi	10.00	5.00	3.00	219	Hank Bauer	30.00	15.00	9.00
129	Joe "Flash" Gordon	12.00	6.00	3.50	220	Leo Durocher	25.00	12.50	7.50
130	Dale Mitchell	10.00	5.00	3.00	221	Don Mueller	10.00	5.00	3.00
131	Steve Gromek	10.00	5.00	3.00	222	Bobby Morgan	12.00	6.00	3.50
132	James Vernon	12.00	6.00	3.50	223	Jimmy Russell	12.00	6.00	3.50
133	Don Kolloway	10.00	5.00	3.00	224	Jack Banta	12.00	6.00	3.50
134	Paul "Dizzy" Trout	12.00	6.00	3.50	225	Eddie Sawyer	10.00	5.00	3.00
135	Pat Mullin	10.00	5.00	3.00	226	Jim Konstanty	12.00	6.00	3.50
136	Warren Rosar	10.00	5.00	3.00	227	Bob Miller	10.00	5.00	3.00
137	Johnny Pesky	12.00	6.00	3.50	228	Bill Nicholson	10.00	5.00	3.00
138	Allie Reynolds	20.00	10.00	6.00	229	Frank Frisch	25.00	12.50	7.50
139	Johnny Mize	40.00	20.00	12.00	230	Bill Serena	10.00	5.00	3.00
140	Pete Suder	10.00	5.00	3.00	231	Preston Ward	10.00	5.00	3.00
141	Joe Coleman	10.00	5.00	3.00	232	Al "Flip" Rosen	30.00	15.00	9.00
142	Sherman Lollar	12.00	6.00	3.50	233	Allie Clark	10.00	5.00	3.00
143	Eddie Stewart	10.00	5.00	3.00	234	Bobby Shantz	15.00	7.50	4.50
144	Al Evans	10.00	5.00	3.00	235	Harold Gilbert	10.00	5.00	3.00
145	Jack Graham	10.00	5.00	3.00	236	Bob Cain	10.00	5.00	3.00
146	Floyd Baker	10.00	5.00	3.00	237	Bill Salkeld	10.00	5.00	3.00
147	Mike Garcia	12.00	6.00	3.50	238	Vernal Jones	10.00	5.00	3.00
148	Early Wynn	30.00	15.00	9.00	239	Bill Howerton	10.00	5.00	3.00
149	Bob Swift	10.00	5.00	3.00	240	Eddie Lake	10.00	5.00	3.00
150	George Vico	10.00	5.00	3.00	241	Neil Berry	10.00	5.00	3.00
151	Fred Hutchinson	12.00	6.00	3.50	242	Dick Kryhoski	10.00	5.00	3.00
152	Ellis Kinder	10.00	5.00	3.00	243	Johnny Groth	10.00	5.00	3.00
153	Walt Masterson	10.00	5.00	3.00	244	Dale Coogan	10.00	5.00	3.00
154	Gus Niarhos	10.00	5.00	3.00	245	Al Papai	10.00	5.00	3.00
155	Frank "Spec" Shea	15.00	7.50	4.50	246	Walt Dropo	12.00	6.00	3.50
156	Fred Sanford	15.00	7.50	4.50	247	Irv Noren	10.00	5.00	3.00
157	Mike Guerra	10.00	5.00	3.00	248	Sam Jethroe	12.00	6.00	3.50
158	Paul Lehner	10.00	5.00	3.00	249	George Stirnweiss	10.00	5.00	3.00
159	Joe Tipton	10.00	5.00	3.00	250	Ray Coleman	10.00	5.00	3.00
160	Mickey Harris	10.00	5.00	3.00	251	John Lester Moss	15.00	5.00	3.00
161	Sherry Robertson	10.00	5.00	3.00	252	Billy DeMars	70.00	7.50	3.00

1951 Bowman

JAMES VERNON
First Base—Washington Senators
Born: Marcus Hook, Pa., April 22, 1918
Height: 6-2   Weight: 180
Bats: Left   Throws: Left

James "Mickey" Vernon batted .281 in 118 games in 1950.
Drove in 75 runs. Tied for
top fielding percentage in the
League with a .991 mark. Began the season with Cleveland, but after 28 games was
switched back to Washington
where all of major-league
career has been spent except
1949 which was with Cleveland. First full season in the
majors: 1941. Top AL batter,
1946. In service 2 years.

No. 65 in the 1951 SERIES
BASEBALL
PICTURE CARDS
©1951 Bowman Gum, Inc. Phila., Pa., U.S.A.

In 1951, Bowman increased the numbers of cards
in its set for the third consecutive year when it issued
324 cards. The cards were, like 1950, color art reproductions of actual photographs but now measured 2
1/16'' by 3 1/8'' in size. The player's name was situated in a small, black box on the card front. Several of
the card fronts are enlargements of the 1950 version.
The higher numbered series of the set (#'s 253-324),
which includes the rookie cards of Mantle and Mays,
are the scarcest of the issue.

	NR MT	EX	VG
Complete Set:	11000.00	3850.00	2200.
Common Player: 1-36	10.00	5.00	3.00
Common Player: 37-252	10.00	5.00	3.00
Common Player: 253-324	30.00	15.00	9.00

		NR MT	EX	VG
1	Ed "Whitey" Ford	600.00	30.00	15.00
2	Larry "Yogi" Berra	175.00	50.00	30.00
3	Robin Roberts	30.00	15.00	9.00
4	Del Ennis	12.00	5.00	3.00
5	Dale Mitchell	12.00	5.00	3.00
6	Don Newcombe	20.00	10.00	6.00
7	Gil Hodges	40.00	20.00	12.00
8	Paul Lehner	12.00	5.00	3.00
9	Sam Chapman	12.00	5.00	3.00
10	Al "Red" Schoendienst	18.00	9.00	5.50
11	George "Red" Munger	12.00	5.00	3.00
12	Hank Majeski	12.00	5.00	3.00
13	Ed Stanky	15.00	7.50	4.50
14	Alvin Dark	18.00	9.00	5.50
15	Johnny Pesky	15.00	7.50	4.50
16	Maurice McDermott	12.00	5.00	3.00
17	Pete Castiglione	12.00	5.00	3.00
18	Gil Coan	12.00	5.00	3.00
19	Sid Gordon	12.00	5.00	3.00
20	Del Crandall	15.00	7.50	4.50
21	George "Snuffy" Stirnweiss	12.00	5.00	3.00
22	Hank Sauer	12.00	5.00	3.00
23	Walter "Hoot" Evers	12.00	5.00	3.00
24	Ewell Blackwell	15.00	7.50	4.50
25	Vic Raschi	20.00	10.00	6.00
26	Phil Rizzuto	40.00	20.00	12.00
27	Jim Konstanty	12.00	5.00	3.00
28	Eddie Waitkus	12.00	5.00	3.00
29	Allie Clark	12.00	5.00	3.00
30	Bob Feller	60.00	30.00	18.00
31	Roy Campanella	100.00	40.00	25.00
32	Duke Snider	90.00	36.00	23.00
33	Bob Hooper	12.00	5.00	3.00
34	Marty Marion	15.00	7.50	4.50
35	Al Zarilla	12.00	5.00	3.00
36	Joe Dobson	12.00	5.00	3.00
37	Whitey Lockman	10.00	5.00	3.00
38	Al Evans	10.00	5.00	3.00
39	Ray Scarborough	10.00	5.00	3.00
40	Dave "Gus" Bell	12.00	6.00	3.50
41	Eddie Yost	12.00	6.00	3.50
42	Vern Bickford	10.00	5.00	3.00
43	Billy DeMars	10.00	5.00	3.00
44	Roy Smalley	10.00	5.00	3.00
45	Art Houtteman	10.00	5.00	3.00
46	George Kell	25.00	12.50	7.50
47	Grady Hatton	10.00	5.00	3.00
48	Ken Raffensberger	10.00	5.00	3.00
49	Jerry Coleman	15.00	7.50	4.50

		NR MT	EX	VG
50	Johnny Mize	35.00	17.50	10.50
51	Andy Seminick	10.00	5.00	3.00
52	Dick Sisler	10.00	5.00	3.00
53	Bob Lemon	30.00	15.00	9.00
54	Ray Boone	12.00	6.00	3.50
55	Gene Hermanski	12.00	6.00	3.50
56	Ralph Branca	15.00	7.50	4.50
57	Alex Kellner	10.00	5.00	3.00
58	Enos Slaughter	30.00	15.00	9.00
59	Randy Gumpert	10.00	5.00	3.00
60	Alfonso Carrasquel	10.00	5.00	3.00
61	Jim Hearn	10.00	5.00	3.00
62	Lou Boudreau	25.00	12.50	7.50
63	Bob Dillinger	10.00	5.00	3.00
64	Bill Werle	10.00	5.00	3.00
65	Mickey Vernon	12.00	6.00	3.50
66	Bob Elliott	10.00	5.00	3.00
67	Roy Sievers	12.00	6.00	3.50
68	Dick Kokos	10.00	5.00	3.00
69	Johnny Schmitz	10.00	5.00	3.00
70	Ron Northey	10.00	5.00	3.00
71	Jerry Priddy	10.00	5.00	3.00
72	Lloyd Merriman	10.00	5.00	3.00
73	Tommy Byrne	15.00	7.50	4.50
74	Billy Johnson	15.00	7.50	4.50
75	Russ Meyer	10.00	5.00	3.00
76	Stan Lopata	10.00	5.00	3.00
77	Mike Goliat	10.00	5.00	3.00
78	Early Wynn	30.00	15.00	9.00
79	Jim Hegan	10.00	5.00	3.00
80	Harold "Peewee" Reese	45.00	22.00	13.50
81	Carl Furillo	18.00	9.00	5.50
82	Joe Tipton	10.00	5.00	3.00
83	Carl Scheib	10.00	5.00	3.00
84	Barney McCosky	10.00	5.00	3.00
85	Eddie Kazak	10.00	5.00	3.00
86	Harry Brecheen	12.00	6.00	3.50
87	Floyd Baker	10.00	5.00	3.00
88	Eddie Robinson	10.00	5.00	3.00
89	Henry Thompson	10.00	5.00	3.00
90	Dave Koslo	10.00	5.00	3.00
91	Clyde Vollmer	10.00	5.00	3.00
92	Vern "Junior" Stephens	12.00	6.00	3.50
93	Danny O'Connell	10.00	5.00	3.00
94	Clyde McCullough	10.00	5.00	3.00
95	Sherry Robertson	10.00	5.00	3.00
96	Sandalio Consuegra	10.00	5.00	3.00
97	Bob Kuzava	10.00	5.00	3.00
98	Willard Marshall	10.00	5.00	3.00
99	Earl Torgeson	10.00	5.00	3.00
100	Sherman Lollar	12.00	6.00	3.50
101	Owen Friend	10.00	5.00	3.00
102	Emil "Dutch" Leonard	10.00	5.00	3.00
103	Andy Pafko	12.00	6.00	3.50
104	Virgil "Fire" Trucks	12.00	6.00	3.50
105	Don Kolloway	10.00	5.00	3.00
106	Pat Mullin	10.00	5.00	3.00
107	Johnny Wyrostek	10.00	5.00	3.00
108	Virgil Stallcup	10.00	5.00	3.00
109	Allie Reynolds	18.00	9.00	5.50
110	Bobby Brown	18.00	9.00	5.50
111	Curt Simmons	12.00	6.00	3.50
112	Willie Jones	10.00	5.00	3.00
113	Bill "Swish" Nicholson	10.00	5.00	3.00
114	Sam Zoldak	10.00	5.00	3.00
115	Steve Gromek	10.00	5.00	3.00
116	Bruce Edwards	12.00	6.00	3.50
117	Eddie Miksis	12.00	6.00	3.50
118	Preacher Roe	18.00	9.00	5.50
119	Eddie Joost	10.00	5.00	3.00
120	Joe Coleman	10.00	5.00	3.00
121	Gerry Staley	10.00	5.00	3.00
122	Joe Garagiola	40.00	20.00	12.00
123	Howie Judson	10.00	5.00	3.00
124	Gus Niarhos	10.00	5.00	3.00
125	Bill Rigney	12.00	6.00	3.50
126	Bobby Thomson	18.00	9.00	5.50
127	Sal Maglie	15.00	7.50	4.50
128	Ellis Kinder	10.00	5.00	3.00
129	Matt Batts	10.00	5.00	3.00
130	Tom Saffell	10.00	5.00	3.00
131	Cliff Chambers	10.00	5.00	3.00
132	Cass Michaels	10.00	5.00	3.00
133	Sam Dente	10.00	5.00	3.00
134	Warren Spahn	40.00	20.00	12.00
135	Walker Cooper	10.00	5.00	3.00
136	Ray Coleman	10.00	5.00	3.00
137	Dick Starr	10.00	5.00	3.00
138	Phil Cavarretta	12.00	6.00	3.50
139	Doyle Lade	10.00	5.00	3.00
140	Eddie Lake	10.00	5.00	3.00

		NR MT	EX	VG			NR MT	EX	VG
141	Fred Hutchinson	12.00	6.00	3.50	232	Nelson Fox	35.00	17.50	10.50
142	Aaron Robinson	10.00	5.00	3.00	233	Leo Durocher	25.00	12.50	7.50
143	Ted Kluszewski	18.00	9.00	5.50	234	Clint Hartung	10.00	5.00	3.00
144	Herman Wehmeier	10.00	5.00	3.00	235	Jack "Lucky" Lohrke	10.00	5.00	3.00
145	Fred Sanford	15.00	7.50	4.50	236	Warren "Buddy" Rosar	10.00	5.00	3.00
146	Johnny Hopp	15.00	7.50	4.50	237	Billy Goodman	10.00	5.00	3.00
147	Ken Heintzelman	10.00	5.00	3.00	238	Pete Reiser	15.00	7.50	4.50
148	Granny Hamner	10.00	5.00	3.00	239	Bill MacDonald	10.00	5.00	3.00
149	Emory "Bubba" Church	10.00	5.00	3.00	240	Joe Haynes	10.00	5.00	3.00
150	Mike Garcia	12.00	6.00	3.50	241	Irv Noren	10.00	5.00	3.00
151	Larry Doby	15.00	7.50	4.50	242	Sam Jethroe	15.00	7.50	4.50
152	Cal Abrams	12.00	6.00	3.50	243	John Antonelli	15.00	7.50	4.50
153	Rex Barney	12.00	6.00	3.50	244	Cliff Fannin	10.00	5.00	3.00
154	Pete Suder	10.00	5.00	3.00	245	John Berardino	15.00	7.50	4.50
155	Lou Brissie	10.00	5.00	3.00	246	Bill Serena	10.00	5.00	3.00
156	Del Rice	10.00	5.00	3.00	247	Bob Ramazotti	10.00	5.00	3.00
157	Al Brazle	10.00	5.00	3.00	248	Johnny Klippstein	15.00	7.50	4.50
158	Chuck Diering	10.00	5.00	3.00	249	Johnny Groth	10.00	5.00	3.00
159	Eddie Stewart	10.00	5.00	3.00	250	Hank Borowy	10.00	5.00	3.00
160	Phil Masi	10.00	5.00	3.00	251	Willard Ramsdell	10.00	5.00	3.00
161	Wes Westrum	12.00	6.00	3.50	252	Homer "Dixie" Howell	10.00	5.00	3.00
162	Larry Jansen	10.00	5.00	3.00	253	Mickey Mantle	4700.00	1645.00	940.00
163	Monte Kennedy	10.00	5.00	3.00	254	Jackie Jensen	55.00	27.00	16.50
164	Bill Wight	10.00	5.00	3.00	255	Milo Candini	30.00	15.00	9.00
165	Ted Williams	275.00	110.00	69.00	256	Ken Silvestri	30.00	15.00	9.00
166	Stan Rojek	10.00	5.00	3.00	257	Birdie Tebbetts	30.00	15.00	9.00
167	Murry Dickson	10.00	5.00	3.00	258	Luke Easter	32.00	16.00	9.50
168	Sam Mele	10.00	5.00	3.00	259	Charlie Dressen	35.00	17.50	10.50
169	Sid Hudson	10.00	5.00	3.00	260	Carl Erskine	40.00	20.00	12.00
170	Sibby Sisti	10.00	5.00	3.00	261	Wally Moses	30.00	15.00	9.00
171	Buddy Kerr	10.00	5.00	3.00	262	Gus Zernial	30.00	15.00	9.00
172	Ned Garver	10.00	5.00	3.00	263	Howie Pollett (Pollet)	30.00	15.00	9.00
173	Hank Arft	10.00	5.00	3.00	264	Don Richmond	30.00	15.00	9.00
174	Mickey Owen	10.00	5.00	3.00	265	Steve Bilko	30.00	15.00	9.00
175	Wayne Terwilliger	10.00	5.00	3.00	266	Harry Dorish	30.00	15.00	9.00
176	Vic Wertz	12.00	6.00	3.50	267	Ken Holcombe	30.00	15.00	9.00
177	Charlie Keller	12.00	6.00	3.50	268	Don Mueller	30.00	15.00	9.00
178	Ted Gray	10.00	5.00	3.00	269	Ray Noble	30.00	15.00	9.00
179	Danny Litwhiler	10.00	5.00	3.00	270	Willard Nixon	30.00	15.00	9.00
180	Howie Fox	10.00	5.00	3.00	271	Tommy Wright	30.00	15.00	9.00
181	Casey Stengel	60.00	30.00	18.00	272	Billy Meyer	30.00	15.00	9.00
182	Tom Ferrick	15.00	7.50	4.50	273	Danny Murtaugh	32.00	16.00	9.50
183	Hank Bauer	20.00	10.00	6.00	274	George Metkovich	30.00	15.00	9.00
184	Eddie Sawyer	10.00	5.00	3.00	275	Bucky Harris	40.00	20.00	12.00
185	Jimmy Bloodworth	10.00	5.00	3.00	276	Frank Quinn	30.00	15.00	9.00
186	Richie Ashburn	18.00	9.00	5.50	277	Roy Hartsfield	30.00	15.00	9.00
187	Al "Flip" Rosen	18.00	9.00	5.50	278	Norman Roy	30.00	15.00	9.00
188	Roberto Avila	12.00	6.00	3.50	279	Jim Delsing	30.00	15.00	9.00
189	Erv Palica	12.00	6.00	3.50	280	Frank Overmire	30.00	15.00	9.00
190	Joe Hatten	12.00	6.00	3.50	281	Al Widmar	30.00	15.00	9.00
191	Billy Hitchcock	10.00	5.00	3.00	282	Frank Frisch	45.00	22.00	13.50
192	Hank Wyse	10.00	5.00	3.00	283	Walt Dubiel	30.00	15.00	9.00
193	Ted Wilks	10.00	5.00	3.00	284	Gene Bearden	30.00	15.00	9.00
194	Harry "Peanuts" Lowrey	10.00	5.00	3.00	285	Johnny Lipon	30.00	15.00	9.00
195	Paul Richards	15.00	7.50	4.50	286	Bob Usher	30.00	15.00	9.00
196	Bill Pierce	15.00	7.50	4.50	287	Jim Blackburn	30.00	15.00	9.00
197	Bob Cain	10.00	5.00	3.00	288	Bobby Adams	30.00	15.00	9.00
198	Monte Irvin	25.00	12.50	7.50	289	Cliff Mapes	40.00	20.00	12.00
199	Sheldon Jones	10.00	5.00	3.00	290	Bill Dickey	90.00	45.00	27.00
200	Jack Kramer	10.00	5.00	3.00	291	Tommy Henrich	45.00	22.00	13.50
201	Steve O'Neill	10.00	5.00	3.00	292	Eddie Pellagrini	30.00	15.00	9.00
202	Mike Guerra	10.00	5.00	3.00	293	Ken Johnson	30.00	15.00	9.00
203	Vernon Law	15.00	7.50	4.50	294	Jocko Thompson	30.00	15.00	9.00
204	Vic Lombardi	10.00	5.00	3.00	295	Al Lopez	40.00	20.00	12.00
205	Mickey Grasso	10.00	5.00	3.00	296	Bob Kennedy	30.00	15.00	9.00
206	Conrado Marrero	10.00	5.00	3.00	297	Dave Philley	30.00	15.00	9.00
207	Billy Southworth	10.00	5.00	3.00	298	Joe Astroth	30.00	15.00	9.00
208	Blix Donnelly	10.00	5.00	3.00	299	Clyde King	35.00	17.50	10.50
209	Ken Wood	10.00	5.00	3.00	300	Hal Rice	30.00	15.00	9.00
210	Les Moss	10.00	5.00	3.00	301	Tommy Glaviano	30.00	15.00	9.00
211	Hal Jeffcoat	10.00	5.00	3.00	302	Jim Busby	30.00	15.00	9.00
212	Bob Rush	10.00	5.00	3.00	303	Marv Rotblatt	30.00	15.00	9.00
213	Neil Berry	10.00	5.00	3.00	304	Allen Gettel	30.00	15.00	9.00
214	Bob Swift	10.00	5.00	3.00	305	Willie Mays	1100.00	440.00	275.00
215	Kent Peterson	10.00	5.00	3.00	306	Jim Piersall	50.00	25.00	15.00
216	Connie Ryan	10.00	5.00	3.00	307	Walt Masterson	30.00	15.00	9.00
217	Joe Page	15.00	7.50	4.50	308	Ted Beard	30.00	15.00	9.00
218	Ed Lopat	18.00	9.00	5.50	309	Mel Queen	30.00	15.00	9.00
219	Gene Woodling	18.00	9.00	5.50	310	Erv Dusak	30.00	15.00	9.00
220	Bob Miller	10.00	5.00	3.00	311	Mickey Harris	30.00	15.00	9.00
221	Dick Whitman	10.00	5.00	3.00	312	Gene Mauch	40.00	20.00	12.00
222	Thurman Tucker	10.00	5.00	3.00	313	Ray Mueller	30.00	15.00	9.00
223	Johnny Vander Meer	15.00	7.50	4.50	314	Johnny Sain	35.00	17.50	10.50
224	Billy Cox	15.00	7.50	4.50	315	Zack Taylor	30.00	15.00	9.00
225	Dan Bankhead	15.00	7.50	4.50	316	Duane Pillette	30.00	15.00	9.00
226	Jimmy Dykes	15.00	7.50	4.50	317	Forrest Burgess	40.00	20.00	12.00
227	Bobby Schantz (Shantz)	15.00	7.50	4.50	318	Warren Hacker	30.00	15.00	9.00
228	Cloyd Boyer	10.00	5.00	3.00	319	Red Rolfe	30.00	15.00	9.00
229	Bill Howerton	10.00	5.00	3.00	320	Hal White	30.00	15.00	9.00
230	Max Lanier	10.00	5.00	3.00	321	Earl Johnson	30.00	15.00	9.00
231	Luis Aloma	10.00	5.00	3.00	322	Luke Sewell	30.00	15.00	9.00

		NR MT	EX	VG
323	Joe Adcock	50.00	20.00	12.00
324	Johnny Pramesa	70.00	20.00	9.00

1952 Bowman

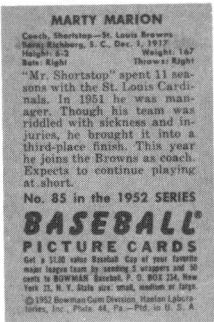

Bowman reverted back to a 252-card set in 1952, but retained the card size (2 1/16'' by 3 1/8'') employed the preceding year. The cards, which are color art reproductions of actual photographs, feature a facsimile autograph on the fronts. Artwork for fifteen cards that were never issued was uncovered several years ago and a set featuring those cards was subsequently made available to the collecting public.

		NR MT	EX	VG
Complete Set:		5900.00	2050.00	1175.
Common Player: 1-36		12.00	6.00	3.50
Common Player: 37-216		10.00	5.00	3.00
Common Player: 217-252		20.00	10.00	6.00
1	Larry "Yogi" Berra	375.00	45.00	26.00
2	Bobby Thomson	25.00	10.00	6.00
3	Fred Hutchinson	14.00	7.00	4.25
4	Robin Roberts	30.00	15.00	9.00
5	Orestes Minoso	25.00	12.50	7.50
6	Virgil "Red" Stallcup	12.00	6.00	3.50
7	Mike Garcia	14.00	7.00	4.25
8	Harold "Pee Wee" Reese	60.00	30.00	18.00
9	Vern Stephens	12.00	6.00	3.50
10	Bob Hooper	12.00	6.00	3.50
11	Ralph Kiner	30.00	15.00	9.00
12	Max Surkont	12.00	6.00	3.50
13	Cliff Mapes	12.00	6.00	3.50
14	Cliff Chambers	12.00	6.00	3.50
15	Sam Mele	12.00	6.00	3.50
16	Omar Lown	12.00	6.00	3.50
17	Ed Lopat	20.00	10.00	6.00
18	Don Mueller	12.00	6.00	3.50
19	Bob Cain	12.00	6.00	3.50
20	Willie Jones	12.00	6.00	3.50
21	Nelson Fox	20.00	10.00	6.00
22	Willard Ramsdell	12.00	6.00	3.50
23	Bob Lemon	30.00	15.00	9.00
24	Carl Furillo	20.00	10.00	6.00
25	Maurice McDermott	12.00	6.00	3.50
26	Eddie Joost	12.00	6.00	3.50
27	Joe Garagiola	35.00	17.50	10.50
28	Roy Hartsfield	12.00	6.00	3.50
29	Ned Garver	12.00	6.00	3.50
30	Al "Red" Schoendienst	20.00	10.00	6.00
31	Eddie Yost	12.00	6.00	3.50
32	Eddie Miksis	12.00	6.00	3.50
33	Gil McDougald	30.00	15.00	9.00
34	Al Dark	16.00	8.00	4.75
35	Gran Hamner	12.00	6.00	3.50
36	Cass Michaels	12.00	6.00	3.50
37	Vic Raschi	18.00	9.00	5.50
38	Whitey Lockman	10.00	5.00	3.00
39	Vic Wertz	12.00	6.00	3.50
40	Emory Church	10.00	5.00	3.00
41	Chico Carrasquel	10.00	5.00	3.00
42	Johnny Wyrostek	10.00	5.00	3.00
43	Bob Feller	55.00	27.00	16.50
44	Roy Campanella	90.00	36.00	23.00
45	Johnny Pesky	12.00	6.00	3.50
46	Carl Scheib	10.00	5.00	3.00

		NR MT	EX	VG
47	Pete Castiglione	10.00	5.00	3.00
48	Vern Bickford	10.00	5.00	3.00
49	Jim Hearn	10.00	5.00	3.00
50	Gerry Staley	10.00	5.00	3.00
51	Gil Coan	10.00	5.00	3.00
52	Phil Rizzuto	40.00	20.00	12.00
53	Richie Ashburn	18.00	9.00	5.50
54	Billy Pierce	12.00	6.00	3.50
55	Ken Raffensberger	10.00	5.00	3.00
56	Clyde King	12.00	6.00	3.50
57	Clyde Vollmer	10.00	5.00	3.00
58	Hank Majeski	10.00	5.00	3.00
59	Murray Dickson (Murry)	10.00	5.00	3.00
60	Sid Gordon	10.00	5.00	3.00
61	Tommy Byrne	10.00	5.00	3.00
62	Joe Presko	10.00	5.00	3.00
63	Irv Noren	10.00	5.00	3.00
64	Roy Smalley	10.00	5.00	3.00
65	Hank Bauer	18.00	9.00	5.50
66	Sal Maglie	15.00	7.50	4.50
67	Johnny Groth	10.00	5.00	3.00
68	Jim Busby	10.00	5.00	3.00
69	Joe Adcock	12.00	6.00	3.50
70	Carl Erskine	18.00	9.00	5.50
71	Vernon Law	12.00	6.00	3.50
72	Earl Torgeson	10.00	5.00	3.00
73	Jerry Coleman	18.00	9.00	5.50
74	Wes Westrum	12.00	6.00	3.50
75	George Kell	25.00	12.50	7.50
76	Del Ennis	12.00	6.00	3.50
77	Eddie Robinson	10.00	5.00	3.00
78	Lloyd Merriman	10.00	5.00	3.00
79	Lou Brissie	10.00	5.00	3.00
80	Gil Hodges	40.00	20.00	12.00
81	Billy Goodman	10.00	5.00	3.00
82	Gus Zernial	10.00	5.00	3.00
83	Howie Pollet	10.00	5.00	3.00
84	Sam Jethroe	10.00	5.00	3.00
85	Marty Marion	12.00	6.00	3.50
86	Cal Abrams	12.00	6.00	3.50
87	Mickey Vernon	12.00	6.00	3.50
88	Bruce Edwards	10.00	5.00	3.00
89	Billy Hitchcock	10.00	5.00	3.00
90	Larry Jansen	10.00	5.00	3.00
91	Don Kolloway	10.00	5.00	3.00
92	Eddie Waitkus	10.00	5.00	3.00
93	Paul Richards	12.00	6.00	3.50
94	Luke Sewell	10.00	5.00	3.00
95	Luke Easter	12.00	6.00	3.50
96	Ralph Branca	18.00	9.00	5.50
97	Willard Marshall	10.00	5.00	3.00
98	Jimmy Dykes	12.00	6.00	3.50
99	Clyde McCullough	10.00	5.00	3.00
100	Sibby Sisti	10.00	5.00	3.00
101	Mickey Mantle	1000.00	350.00	200.00
102	Peanuts Lowrey	10.00	5.00	3.00
103	Joe Haynes	10.00	5.00	3.00
104	Hal Jeffcoat	10.00	5.00	3.00
105	Bobby Brown	18.00	9.00	5.50
106	Randy Gumpert	10.00	5.00	3.00
107	Del Rice	10.00	5.00	3.00
108	George Metkovich	10.00	5.00	3.00
109	Tom Morgan	15.00	7.50	4.50
110	Max Lanier	10.00	5.00	3.00
111	Walter "Hoot" Evers	10.00	5.00	3.00
112	Forrest "Smokey" Burgess	12.00	6.00	3.50
113	Al Zarilla	10.00	5.00	3.00
114	Frank Hiller	10.00	5.00	3.00
115	Larry Doby	15.00	7.50	4.50
116	Duke Snider	75.00	37.00	22.00
117	Bill Wight	10.00	5.00	3.00
118	Ray Murray	10.00	5.00	3.00
119	Bill Howerton	10.00	5.00	3.00
120	Chet Nichols	10.00	5.00	3.00
121	Al Corwin	10.00	5.00	3.00
122	Billy Johnson	10.00	5.00	3.00
123	Sid Hudson	10.00	5.00	3.00
124	George Tebbetts	12.00	6.00	3.50
125	Howie Fox	10.00	5.00	3.00
126	Phil Cavarretta	12.00	6.00	3.50
127	Dick Sisler	10.00	5.00	3.00
128	Don Newcombe	18.00	9.00	5.50
129	Gus Niarhos	10.00	5.00	3.00
130	Allie Clark	10.00	5.00	3.00
131	Bob Swift	10.00	5.00	3.00
132	Dave Cole	10.00	5.00	3.00
133	Dick Kryhoski	10.00	5.00	3.00
134	Al Brazle	10.00	5.00	3.00
135	Mickey Harris	10.00	5.00	3.00
136	Gene Hermanski	10.00	5.00	3.00
137	Stan Rojek	10.00	5.00	3.00

		NR MT	EX	VG
138	Ted Wilks	10.00	5.00	3.00
139	Jerry Priddy	10.00	5.00	3.00
140	Ray Scarborough	10.00	5.00	3.00
141	Hank Edwards	10.00	5.00	3.00
142	Early Wynn	30.00	15.00	9.00
143	Sandalio Consuegra	10.00	5.00	3.00
144	Joe Hatten	10.00	5.00	3.00
145	Johnny Mize	40.00	20.00	12.00
146	Leo Durocher	25.00	12.50	7.50
147	Marlin Stuart	10.00	5.00	3.00
148	Ken Heintzelman	10.00	5.00	3.00
149	Howie Judson	10.00	5.00	3.00
150	Herman Wehmeier	10.00	5.00	3.00
151	Al "Flip" Rosen	18.00	9.00	5.50
152	Billy Cox	12.00	6.00	3.50
153	Fred Hatfield	10.00	5.00	3.00
154	Ferris Fain	12.00	6.00	3.50
155	Billy Meyer	10.00	5.00	3.00
156	Warren Spahn	45.00	22.00	13.50
157	Jim Delsing	10.00	5.00	3.00
158	Bucky Harris	18.00	9.00	5.50
159	Dutch Leonard	10.00	5.00	3.00
160	Eddie Stanky	12.00	6.00	3.50
161	Jackie Jensen	15.00	7.50	4.50
162	Monte Irvin	25.00	12.50	7.50
163	Johnny Lipon	10.00	5.00	3.00
164	Connie Ryan	10.00	5.00	3.00
165	Saul Rogovin	10.00	5.00	3.00
166	Bobby Adams	10.00	5.00	3.00
167	Bob Avila	10.00	5.00	3.00
168	Preacher Roe	18.00	9.00	5.50
169	Walt Dropo	10.00	5.00	3.00
170	Joe Astroth	10.00	5.00	3.00
171	Mel Queen	10.00	5.00	3.00
172	Ebba St. Claire	10.00	5.00	3.00
173	Gene Bearden	10.00	5.00	3.00
174	Mickey Grasso	10.00	5.00	3.00
175	Ransom Jackson	10.00	5.00	3.00
176	Harry Brecheen	12.00	6.00	3.50
177	Gene Woodling	18.00	9.00	5.50
178	Dave Williams	10.00	5.00	3.00
179	Pete Suder	10.00	5.00	3.00
180	Eddie Fitzgerald (Fitz Gerald)	10.00	5.00	3.00
181	Joe Collins	15.00	7.50	4.50
182	Dave Koslo	10.00	5.00	3.00
183	Pat Mullin	10.00	5.00	3.00
184	Curt Simmons	12.00	6.00	3.50
185	Eddie Stewart	10.00	5.00	3.00
186	Frank Smith	10.00	5.00	3.00
187	Jim Hegan	10.00	5.00	3.00
188	Charlie Dressen	15.00	7.50	4.50
189	Jim Piersall	15.00	7.50	4.50
190	Dick Fowler	10.00	5.00	3.00
191	Bob Friend	15.00	7.50	4.50
192	John Cusick	10.00	5.00	3.00
193	Bobby Young	10.00	5.00	3.00
194	Bob Porterfield	10.00	5.00	3.00
195	Frank Baumholtz	10.00	5.00	3.00
196	Stan Musial	250.00	100.00	63.00
197	Charlie Silvera	15.00	7.50	4.50
198	Chuck Diering	10.00	5.00	3.00
199	Ted Gray	10.00	5.00	3.00
200	Ken Silvestri	10.00	5.00	3.00
201	Ray Coleman	10.00	5.00	3.00
202	Harry Perkowski	10.00	5.00	3.00
203	Steve Gromek	10.00	5.00	3.00
204	Andy Pafko	12.00	6.00	3.50
205	Walt Masterson	10.00	5.00	3.00
206	Elmer Valo	10.00	5.00	3.00
207	George Strickland	10.00	5.00	3.00
208	Walker Cooper	10.00	5.00	3.00
209	Dick Littlefield	10.00	5.00	3.00
210	Archie Wilson	10.00	5.00	3.00
211	Paul Minner	10.00	5.00	3.00
212	Solly Hemus	10.00	5.00	3.00
213	Monte Kennedy	10.00	5.00	3.00
214	Ray Boone	12.00	6.00	3.50
215	Sheldon Jones	10.00	5.00	3.00
216	Matt Batts	10.00	5.00	3.00
217	Casey Stengel	80.00	40.00	24.00
218	Willie Mays	450.00	180.00	113.00
219	Neil Berry	25.00	12.50	7.50
220	Russ Meyer	25.00	12.50	7.50
221	Lou Kretlow	25.00	12.50	7.50
222	Homer "Dixie" Howell	25.00	12.50	7.50
223	Harry Simpson	25.00	12.50	7.50
224	Johnny Schmitz	27.00	13.50	8.00
225	Del Wilber	25.00	12.50	7.50
226	Alex Kellner	25.00	12.50	7.50
227	Clyde Sukeforth	25.00	12.50	7.50
228	Bob Chipman	25.00	12.50	7.50

		NR MT	EX	VG
229	Hank Arft	25.00	12.50	7.50
230	Frank Shea	25.00	12.50	7.50
231	Dee Fondy	25.00	12.50	7.50
232	Enos Slaughter	45.00	22.00	13.50
233	Bob Kuzava	32.00	16.00	9.50
234	Fred Fitzsimmons	25.00	12.50	7.50
235	Steve Souchock	25.00	12.50	7.50
236	Tommy Brown	25.00	12.50	7.50
237	Sherman Lollar	27.00	13.50	8.00
238	Roy McMillan	27.00	13.50	8.00
239	Dale Mitchell	25.00	12.50	7.50
240	Billy Loes	32.00	16.00	9.50
241	Mel Parnell	27.00	13.50	8.00
242	Everett Kell	25.00	12.50	7.50
243	George "Red" Munger	25.00	12.50	7.50
244	Lew Burdette	35.00	17.50	10.50
245	George Schmees	25.00	12.50	7.50
246	Jerry Snyder	25.00	12.50	7.50
247	John Pramesa	25.00	12.50	7.50
248	Bill Werle	25.00	12.50	7.50
249	Henry Thompson	25.00	12.50	7.50
250	Ivan Delock	25.00	12.50	7.50
251	Jack Lohrke	32.00	12.50	7.50
252	Frank Crosetti	80.00	20.00	12.00

1953 Bowman Color

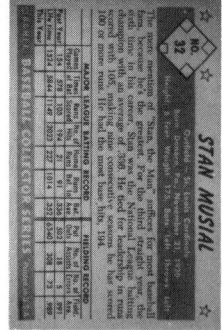

The first set of current major league players featuring actual color photographs, the 160-card 1953 Bowman Color set remains one of the most popular issues of the post-war era. The set is greatly appreciated for its uncluttered look; card fronts that contain no names, teams or facsimile autographs. Bowman increased the size of their cards to a 2½'' by 3¾'' size in order to better compete with Topps Chewing Gum. Bowman copied an idea from the 1952 Topps set and developed card backs that gave player career and previous year statistics. The high-numbered cards (#'s 113-160) are the scarcest of the set, with #'s 113-128 being exceptionally difficult to find.

		NR MT	EX	VG
Complete Set:		5900.00	2050.00	1175.
Common Player: 1-112		15.00	7.50	4.50
Common Player: 113-128		30.00	15.00	9.00
Common Player: 129-160		25.00	12.50	7.50
1	Davey Williams	50.00	10.00	4.50
2	Vic Wertz	20.00	8.50	5.00
3	Sam Jethroe	15.00	7.50	4.50
4	Art Houtteman	15.00	7.50	4.50
5	Sid Gordon	15.00	7.50	4.50
6	Joe Ginsberg	15.00	7.50	4.50
7	Harry Chiti	15.00	7.50	4.50
8	Al Rosen	20.00	10.00	6.00
9	Phil Rizzuto	55.00	27.00	16.50
10	Richie Ashburn	25.00	12.50	7.50
11	Bobby Shantz	17.00	8.50	5.00
12	Carl Erskine	25.00	12.50	7.50
13	Gus Zernial	15.00	7.50	4.50
14	Billy Loes	17.00	8.50	5.00
15	Jim Busby	15.00	7.50	4.50
16	Bob Friend	17.00	8.50	5.00

		NR MT	EX	VG
17	Gerry Staley	15.00	7.50	4.50
18	Nelson Fox	25.00	12.50	7.50
19	Al Dark	17.00	8.50	5.00
20	Don Lenhardt	15.00	7.50	4.50
21	Joe Garagiola	35.00	17.50	10.50
22	Bob Porterfield	15.00	7.50	4.50
23	Herman Wehmeier	15.00	7.50	4.50
24	Jackie Jensen	20.00	10.00	6.00
25	Walter "Hoot" Evers	15.00	7.50	4.50
26	Roy McMillan	15.00	7.50	4.50
27	Vic Raschi	25.00	12.50	7.50
28	Forrest "Smoky" Burgess	17.00	8.50	5.00
29	Roberto Avila	15.00	7.50	4.50
30	Phil Cavarretta	17.00	8.50	5.00
31	Jimmy Dykes	17.00	8.50	5.00
32	Stan Musial	225.00	90.00	56.00
33	Harold "Peewee" Reese	80.00	40.00	24.00
34	Gil Coan	15.00	7.50	4.50
35	Maury McDermott	15.00	7.50	4.50
36	Orestes Minoso	20.00	10.00	6.00
37	Jim Wilson	15.00	7.50	4.50
38	Harry Byrd	15.00	7.50	4.50
39	Paul Richards	17.00	8.50	5.00
40	Larry Doby	20.00	10.00	6.00
41	Sammy White	15.00	7.50	4.50
42	Tommy Brown	15.00	7.50	4.50
43	Mike Garcia	17.00	8.50	5.00
44	Hank Bauer, Yogi Berra, Mickey Mantle			
		225.00	90.00	56.00
45	Walt Dropo	15.00	7.50	4.50
46	Roy Campanella	130.00	52.00	33.00
47	Ned Garver	15.00	7.50	4.50
48	Hank Sauer	15.00	7.50	4.50
49	Eddie Stanky	17.00	8.50	5.00
50	Lou Kretlow	15.00	7.50	4.50
51	Monte Irvin	25.00	12.50	7.50
52	Marty Marion	17.00	8.50	5.00
53	Del Rice	15.00	7.50	4.50
54	Chico Carrasquel	15.00	7.50	4.50
55	Leo Durocher	25.00	12.50	7.50
56	Bob Cain	15.00	7.50	4.50
57	Lou Boudreau	25.00	12.50	7.50
58	Willard Marshall	15.00	7.50	4.50
59	Mickey Mantle	850.00	300.00	150.00
60	Granny Hamner	15.00	7.50	4.50
61	George Kell	25.00	12.50	7.50
62	Ted Kluszewski	20.00	10.00	6.00
63	Gil McDougald	25.00	12.50	7.50
64	Curt Simmons	17.00	8.50	5.00
65	Robin Roberts	35.00	17.50	10.50
66	Mel Parnell	17.00	8.50	5.00
67	Mel Clark	15.00	7.50	4.50
68	Allie Reynolds	25.00	12.50	7.50
69	Charlie Grimm	17.00	8.50	5.00
70	Clint Courtney	15.00	7.50	4.50
71	Paul Minner	15.00	7.50	4.50
72	Ted Gray	15.00	7.50	4.50
73	Billy Pierce	17.00	8.50	5.00
74	Don Mueller	15.00	7.50	4.50
75	Saul Rogovin	15.00	7.50	4.50
76	Jim Hearn	15.00	7.50	4.50
77	Mickey Grasso	15.00	7.50	4.50
78	Carl Furillo	25.00	12.50	7.50
79	Ray Boone	17.00	8.50	5.00
80	Ralph Kiner	35.00	17.50	10.50
81	Enos Slaughter	35.00	17.50	10.50
82	Joe Astroth	15.00	7.50	4.50
83	Jack Daniels	15.00	7.50	4.50
84	Hank Bauer	25.00	12.50	7.50
85	Solly Hemus	15.00	7.50	4.50
86	Harry Simpson	15.00	7.50	4.50
87	Harry Perkowski	15.00	7.50	4.50
88	Joe Dobson	15.00	7.50	4.50
89	Sandalio Consuegra	15.00	7.50	4.50
90	Joe Nuxhall	17.00	8.50	5.00
91	Steve Souchock	15.00	7.50	4.50
92	Gil Hodges	55.00	27.00	16.50
93	Billy Martin, Phil Rizzuto	85.00	42.00	25.00
94	Bob Addis	15.00	7.50	4.50
95	Wally Moses	15.00	7.50	4.50
96	Sal Maglie	17.00	8.50	5.00
97	Eddie Mathews	55.00	27.00	16.50
98	Hector Rodriguez	15.00	7.50	4.50
99	Warren Spahn	50.00	25.00	15.00
100	Bill Wight	15.00	7.50	4.50
101	Al "Red" Schoendienst	20.00	10.00	6.00
102	Jim Hegan	15.00	7.50	4.50
103	Del Ennis	15.00	7.50	4.50
104	Luke Easter	15.00	7.50	4.50
105	Eddie Joost	15.00	7.50	4.50
106	Ken Raffensberger	15.00	7.50	4.50

		NR MT	EX	VG
107	Alex Kellner	15.00	7.50	4.50
108	Bobby Adams	15.00	7.50	4.50
109	Ken Wood	15.00	7.50	4.50
110	Bob Rush	15.00	7.50	4.50
111	Jim Dyck	15.00	7.50	4.50
112	Toby Atwell	15.00	7.50	4.50
113	Karl Drews	30.00	15.00	9.00
114	Bob Feller	150.00	60.00	38.00
115	Cloyd Boyer	30.00	15.00	9.00
116	Eddie Yost	30.00	15.00	9.00
117	Duke Snider	350.00	140.00	88.00
118	Billy Martin	150.00	60.00	38100.
119	Dale Mitchell	30.00	15.00	9.00
120	Marlin Stuart	30.00	15.00	9.00
121	Yogi Berra	325.00	130.00	81.00
122	Bill Serena	30.00	15.00	9.00
123	Johnny Lipon	30.00	15.00	9.00
124	Charlie Dressen	35.00	17.50	10.50
125	Fred Hatfield	30.00	15.00	9.00
126	Al Corwin	30.00	15.00	9.00
127	Dick Kryhoski	30.00	15.00	9.00
128	Whitey Lockman	30.00	15.00	9.00
129	Russ Meyer	27.00	13.50	8.00
130	Cass Michaels	25.00	12.50	7.50
131	Connie Ryan	25.00	12.50	7.50
132	Fred Hutchinson	27.00	13.50	8.00
133	Willie Jones	25.00	12.50	7.50
134	Johnny Pesky	27.00	13.50	8.00
135	Bobby Morgan	27.00	13.50	8.00
136	Jim Brideweser	32.00	16.00	9.50
137	Sam Dente	25.00	12.50	7.50
138	Bubba Church	25.00	12.50	7.50
139	Pete Runnels	27.00	13.50	8.00
140	Alpha Brazle	25.00	12.50	7.50
141	Frank "Spec" Shea	25.00	12.50	7.50
142	Larry Miggins	25.00	12.50	7.50
143	Al Lopez	40.00	20.00	12.00
144	Warren Hacker	25.00	12.50	7.50
145	George Shuba	27.00	13.50	8.00
146	Early Wynn	75.00	37.00	22.00
147	Clem Koshorek	25.00	12.50	7.50
148	Billy Goodman	25.00	12.50	7.50
149	Al Corwin	25.00	12.50	7.50
150	Carl Scheib	25.00	12.50	7.50
151	Joe Adcock	32.00	16.00	9.50
152	Clyde Vollmer	25.00	12.50	7.50
153	Ed "Whitey" Ford	250.00	100.00	63.00
154	Omar "Turk" Lown	25.00	12.50	7.50
155	Allie Clark	25.00	12.50	7.50
156	Max Surkont	25.00	12.50	7.50
157	Sherman Lollar	27.00	13.50	8.00
158	Howard Fox	25.00	12.50	7.50
159	Mickey Vernon (Photo actually Floyd Baker)	32.00	13.50	8.00
160	Cal Abrams	50.00	16.00	7.50

1953 Bowman Black & White

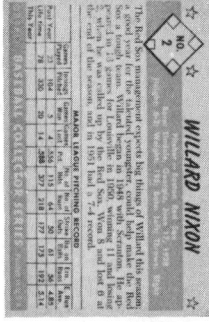

The 1953 Bowman Black & White set is similar in all respects to the 1953 Bowman Color set, except that it lacks in color. Purportedly, high costs in producing the color series forced Bowman to issue the set in black and white. Sixty-four cards, which measure 2½'' by 3¾'', comprise the set.

		NR MT	EX	VG
Complete Set:		1975.00	700.00	400.00
Common Player:		22.00	11.00	6.50
1	Gus Bell	70.00	16.00	8.00
2	Willard Nixon	32.00	11.00	6.50
3	Bill Rigney	27.00	13.50	8.00
4	Pat Mullin	22.00	11.00	6.50
5	Dee Fondy	22.00	11.00	6.50
6	Ray Murray	22.00	11.00	6.50
7	Andy Seminick	22.00	11.00	6.50
8	Pete Suder	22.00	11.00	6.50
9	Walt Masterson	22.00	11.00	6.50
10	Dick Sisler	22.00	11.00	6.50
11	Dick Gernert	22.00	11.00	6.50
12	Randy Jackson	22.00	11.00	6.50
13	Joe Tipton	22.00	11.00	6.50
14	Bill Nicholson	22.00	11.00	6.50
15	Johnny Mize	65.00	32.00	19.50
16	Stu Miller	22.00	11.00	6.50
17	Virgil Trucks	27.00	13.50	8.00
18	Billy Hoeft	22.00	11.00	6.50
19	Paul LaPalme	22.00	11.00	6.50
20	Eddie Robinson	22.00	11.00	6.50
21	Clarence "Bud" Podbielan	22.00	11.00	6.50
22	Matt Batts	22.00	11.00	6.50
23	Wilmer Mizell	22.00	11.00	6.50
24	Del Wilber	22.00	11.00	6.50
25	John Sain	40.00	20.00	12.00
26	Preacher Roe	35.00	17.50	10.50
27	Bob Lemon	60.00	30.00	18.00
28	Hoyt Wilhelm	60.00	30.00	18.00
29	Sid Hudson	22.00	11.00	6.50
30	Walker Cooper	22.00	11.00	6.50
31	Gene Woodling	35.00	17.50	10.50
32	Rocky Bridges	22.00	11.00	6.50
33	Bob Kuzava	32.00	16.00	9.50
34	Ebba St. Clair (St. Claire)	22.00	11.00	6.50
35	Johnny Wyrostek	22.00	11.00	6.50
36	Jim Piersall	32.00	16.00	9.50
37	Hal Jeffcoat	22.00	11.00	6.50
38	Dave Cole	22.00	11.00	6.50
39	Casey Stengel	225.00	90.00	56.00
40	Larry Jansen	22.00	11.00	6.50
41	Bob Ramazotti	22.00	11.00	6.50
42	Howie Judson	22.00	11.00	6.50
43	Hal Bevan	22.00	11.00	6.50
44	Jim Delsing	22.00	11.00	6.50
45	Irv Noren	32.00	16.00	9.50
46	Bucky Harris	35.00	17.50	10.50
47	Jack Lohrke	22.00	11.00	6.50
48	Steve Ridzik	22.00	11.00	6.50
49	Floyd Baker	22.00	11.00	6.50
50	Emil "Dutch" Leonard	22.00	11.00	6.50
51	Lou Burdette	32.00	16.00	9.50
52	Ralph Branca	35.00	17.50	10.50
53	Morris Martin	22.00	11.00	6.50
54	Bill Miller	32.00	16.00	9.50
55	Don Johnson	22.00	11.00	6.50
56	Roy Smalley	22.00	11.00	6.50
57	Andy Pafko	27.00	13.50	8.00
58	Jim Konstanty	27.00	13.50	8.00
59	Duane Pillette	22.00	11.00	6.50
60	Billy Cox	27.00	13.50	8.00
61	Tom Gorman	32.00	16.00	9.50
62	Keith Thomas	22.00	11.00	6.50
63	Steve Gromek	27.00	11.00	6.50
64	Andy Hansen	45.00	13.50	6.50

1954 Bowman

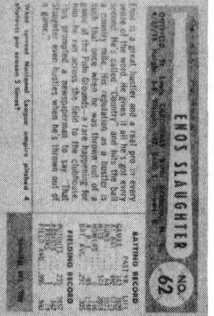

Bowman's 1954 set consists of 224 full color cards that measure 2½" by 3¾". It is believed that contractual problems caused the pulling of card #66 Ted Williams from the set, creating one of the most sought-after scarcities of the post-war era. The Williams card was replaced by #66 Jim Piersall (who is also #210) in subsequent print runs. The set contains over forty variations, most involving statistical errors on the card backs that were corrected. Neither variation carries a premium value as both varieties appear to have been printed in equal amounts. The complete set price that follows does not include all variations or #66 Williams.

		NR MT	EX	VG
Complete Set:		2600.00	900.00	525.00
Common Player: 1-224		5.00	2.50	1.50
1	Phil Rizzuto	80.00	12.50	7.50
2	Jack Jensen	10.00	3.50	2.00
3	Marion Fricano	5.00	2.50	1.50
4	Bob Hooper	5.00	2.50	1.50
5	William Hunter	5.00	2.50	1.50
6	Nelson Fox	12.00	6.00	3.50
7	Walter Dropo	5.00	2.50	1.50
8	James F. Busby	5.00	2.50	1.50
9	Dave Williams	5.00	2.50	1.50
10	Carl Daniel Erskine	8.00	4.00	2.50
11	Sid Gordon	5.00	2.50	1.50
12a	Roy McMillan (551/1290 At Bat)	6.00	3.00	1.75
12b	Roy McMillan (557/1296 At Bat)	6.00	3.00	1.75
13	Paul Minner	5.00	2.50	1.50
14	Gerald Staley	5.00	2.50	1.50
15	Richie Ashburn	12.00	6.00	3.50
16	Jim Wilson	5.00	2.50	1.50
17	Tom Gorman	8.00	4.00	2.50
18	Walter "Hoot" Evers	5.00	2.50	1.50
19	Bobby Shantz	7.00	3.50	2.00
20	Artie Houtteman	5.00	2.50	1.50
21	Victor Wertz	6.00	3.00	1.75
22a	Sam Mele (213/1661 Putouts)	6.00	3.00	1.75
22b	Sam Mele (217/1665 Putouts)	6.00	3.00	1.75
23	Harvey Kuenn	12.00	6.00	3.50
24	Bob Porterfield	5.00	2.50	1.50
25a	Wes Westrum (1.000/.987 Field Avg.)	6.00	3.00	1.75
25b	Wes Westrum (.982/.986 Field Avg.)	6.00	3.00	1.75
26a	Billy Cox (1.000/.960 Field Avg.)	7.00	3.50	2.00
26b	Billy Cox (.972/.960 Field Avg.)	7.00	3.50	2.00
27	Richard Roy Cole	5.00	2.50	1.50
28a	Jim Greengrass (Birthplace Addison, N.J.)	6.00	3.00	1.75
28b	Jim Greengrass (Birthplace Addison, N.Y.)	6.00	3.00	1.75
29	Johnny Klippstein	5.00	2.50	1.50
30	Delbert Rice Jr.	5.00	2.50	1.50
31	"Smoky" Burgess	6.00	3.00	1.75
32	Del Crandall	6.00	3.00	1.75
33a	Victor Raschi (no traded line)	10.00	5.00	3.00
33b	Victor Raschi (with traded line)	15.00	7.50	4.50
34	Sammy White	5.00	2.50	1.50
35a	Eddie Joost (quiz answer is 8)	6.00	3.00	1.75
35b	Eddie Joost (quiz answer is 33)	6.00	3.00	1.75
36	George Strickland	5.00	2.50	1.50
37	Dick Kokos	5.00	2.50	1.50
38a	Orestes Minoso (.895/.961 Field Avg.)	8.00	4.00	2.50
38b	Orestes Minoso (.963/.963 Field Avg.)	8.00	4.00	2.50
39	Ned Garver	5.00	2.50	1.50
40	Gil Coan	5.00	2.50	1.50
41a	Alvin Dark (.986/.960 Field Avg.)	8.00	4.00	2.50
41b	Alvin Dark (.968/.960 Field Avg.)	8.00	4.00	2.50
42	Billy Loes	7.00	3.50	2.00
43a	Robert B. Friend (20 shutouts in quiz question)	7.00	3.50	2.00
43b	Robert B. Friend (16 shutouts in quiz question)	7.00	3.50	2.00
44	Harry Perkowski	5.00	2.50	1.50
45	Ralph Kiner	20.00	10.00	6.00
46	Eldon Repulski	5.00	2.50	1.50
47a	Granville Hamner (.970/.953 Field Avg.)	6.00	3.00	1.75
47b	Granville Hamner (.953/.951 Field Avg.)	6.00	3.00	1.75
48	Jack Dittmer	5.00	2.50	1.50
49	Harry Byrd	8.00	4.00	2.50
50	George Kell	20.00	10.00	6.00

#	Player	NR MT	EX	VG
51	Alex Kellner	5.00	2.50	1.50
52	Myron N. Ginsberg	5.00	2.50	1.50
53a	Don Lenhardt (.969/.984 Field Avg.)	6.00	3.00	1.75
53b	Don Lenhardt (.966/.983 Field Avg.)	6.00	3.00	1.75
54	Alfonso Carrasquel	5.00	2.50	1.50
55	Jim Delsing	5.00	2.50	1.50
56	Maurice M. McDermott	5.00	2.50	1.50
57	Hoyt Wilhelm	20.00	10.00	6.00
58	"Pee Wee" Reese	30.00	15.00	9.00
59	Robert D. Schultz	5.00	2.50	1.50
60	Fred Baczewski	5.00	2.50	1.50
61a	Eddie Miksis (.954/.962 Field Avg.)	6.00	3.00	1.75
61b	Eddie Miksis (.954/.961 Field Avg.)	6.00	3.00	1.75
62	Enos Slaughter	20.00	10.00	6.00
63	Earl Torgeson	5.00	2.50	1.50
64	Ed Mathews	25.00	12.50	7.50
65	Mickey Mantle	525.00	210.00	105.00
66a	Ted Williams	1500.00	600.00	375.00
66b	Jimmy Piersall	80.00	40.00	24.00
67a	Carl Scheib (.306 Pct. with two lines under bio)	6.00	3.00	1.75
67b	Carl Scheib (.306 Pct. with one line under bio)	6.00	3.00	1.75
67c	Carl Scheib (.300 Pct.)	6.00	3.00	1.75
68	Bob Avila	6.00	3.00	1.75
69	Clinton Courtney	5.00	2.50	1.50
70	Willard Marshall	5.00	2.50	1.50
71	Ted Gray	5.00	2.50	1.50
72	Ed Yost	5.00	2.50	1.50
73	Don Mueller	5.00	2.50	1.50
74	James Gilliam	10.00	5.00	3.00
75	Max Surkont	5.00	2.50	1.50
76	Joe Nuxhall	6.00	3.00	1.75
77	Bob Rush	5.00	2.50	1.50
78	Sal A. Yvars	5.00	2.50	1.50
79	Curt Simmons	6.00	3.00	1.75
80a	John Logan (106 Runs)	6.00	3.00	1.75
80b	John Logan (100 Runs)	6.00	3.00	1.75
81a	Jerry Coleman (1.000/.975 Field Avg.)	8.00	4.00	2.50
81b	Jerry Coleman (.952/.975 Field Avg.)	8.00	4.00	2.50
82a	Bill Goodman (.965/.986 Field Avg.)	6.00	3.00	1.75
82b	Bill Goodman (.972/.985 Field Avg.)	6.00	3.00	1.75
83	Ray Murray	5.00	2.50	1.50
84	Larry Doby	8.00	4.00	2.50
85a	Jim Dyck (.926/.956 Field Avg.)	6.00	3.00	1.75
85b	Jim Dyck (.947/.960 Field Avg.)	6.00	3.00	1.75
86	Harry Dorish	5.00	2.50	1.50
87	Don Lund	5.00	2.50	1.50
88	Tommy Umphlett	5.00	2.50	1.50
89	Willie May (Mays)	175.00	70.00	44.00
90	Roy Campanella	75.00	37.00	22.00
91	Cal Abrams	5.00	2.50	1.50
92	Kenneth David Raffensberger	5.00	2.50	1.50
93a	Bill Serena (.983/.966 Field Avg.)	6.00	3.00	1.75
93b	Bill Serena (.977/.966 Field Avg.)	6.00	3.00	1.75
94a	Solly Hemus (476/1343 Assists)	6.00	3.00	1.75
94b	Solly Hemus (477/1343 Assists)	6.00	3.00	1.75
95	Robin Roberts	20.00	10.00	6.00
96	Joe Adcock	7.00	3.50	2.00
97	Gil McDougald	12.00	6.00	3.50
98	Ellis Kinder	5.00	2.50	1.50
99a	Peter Suder (.985/.974 Field Avg.)	6.00	3.00	1.75
99b	Peter Suder (.978/.974 Field Avg.)	6.00	3.00	1.75
100	Mike Garcia	6.00	3.00	1.75
101	Don James Larsen	8.00	4.00	2.50
102	Bill Pierce	6.00	3.00	1.75
103a	Stephen Souchock (144/1192 Putouts)	6.00	3.00	1.75
103b	Stephen Souchock (147/1195 Putouts)	6.00	3.00	1.75
104	Frank Spec Shea	5.00	2.50	1.50
105a	Sal Maglie (quiz answer is 8)	7.00	3.50	2.00
105b	Sal Maglie (quiz answer is 1904)	7.00	3.50	2.00
106	"Clem" Labine	7.00	3.50	2.00
107	Paul E. LaPalme	5.00	2.50	1.50
108	Bobby Adams	5.00	2.50	1.50
109	Roy Smalley	5.00	2.50	1.50
110	Al Schoendienst	10.00	5.00	3.00
111	Murry Monroe Dickson	5.00	2.50	1.50
112	Andy Pafko	6.00	3.00	1.75
113	Allie Reynolds	10.00	5.00	3.00
114	Willard Nixon	5.00	2.50	1.50
115	Don Bollweg	5.00	2.50	1.50
116	Luscious Luke Easter	5.00	2.50	1.50
117	Dick Kryhoski	5.00	2.50	1.50
118	Robert R. Boyd	5.00	2.50	1.50
119	Fred Hatfield	5.00	2.50	1.50
120	Mel Hoderlein	5.00	2.50	1.50
121	Ray Katt	5.00	2.50	1.50
122	Carl Furillo	10.00	5.00	3.00
123	Toby Atwell	5.00	2.50	1.50
124a	Gus Bell (15/27 Errors)	6.00	3.00	1.75
124b	Gus Bell (11/26 Errors)	6.00	3.00	1.75
125	Warren Hacker	5.00	2.50	1.50
126	Cliff Chambers	5.00	2.50	1.50
127	Del Ennis	6.00	3.00	1.75
128	Ebba St Claire	5.00	2.50	1.50
129	Hank Bauer	10.00	5.00	3.00
130	Milt Bolling	5.00	2.50	1.50
131	Joe Astroth	5.00	2.50	1.50
132	Bob Feller	40.00	20.00	12.00
133	Duane Pillette	5.00	2.50	1.50
134	Luis Aloma	5.00	2.50	1.50
135	Johnny Pesky	6.00	3.00	1.75
136	Clyde Vollmer	5.00	2.50	1.50
137	Elmer N. Corwin Jr.	5.00	2.50	1.50
138a	Gil Hodges (.993/.991 Field Avg.)	30.00	15.00	9.00
138b	Gil Hodges (.992/.991 Field Avg.)	30.00	15.00	9.00
139a	Preston Ward (.961/.992 Field Avg.)	6.00	3.00	1.75
139b	Preston Ward (.990/.992 Field Avg.)	6.00	3.00	1.75
140a	Saul Rogovin (7-12 Won/Lost with 2 Strikeouts)	6.00	3.00	1.75
140b	Saul Rogovin (7-12 Won/Lost with 62 Strikeouts)	6.00	3.00	1.75
140c	Saul Rogovin (8-12 Won/Lost)	6.00	3.00	1.75
141	Joe Garagiola	25.00	12.50	7.50
142	Al Brazle	5.00	2.50	1.50
143	Puddin Head Jones	5.00	2.50	1.50
144	Ernie Johnson	5.00	2.50	1.50
145a	Billy Martin (.985/.983 Field Avg.)	30.00	15.00	9.00
145b	Billy Martin (.983/.982 Field Avg.)	30.00	15.00	9.00
146	Dick Gernert	5.00	2.50	1.50
147	Joe DeMaestri	5.00	2.50	1.50
148	Dale Mitchell	5.00	2.50	1.50
149	Bob Young	5.00	2.50	1.50
150	Cass Michaels	5.00	2.50	1.50
151	Patrick J. Mullin	5.00	2.50	1.50
152	Mickey Vernon	6.00	3.00	1.75
153a	Whitey Lockman (100/331 Assists)	6.00	3.00	1.75
153b	Whitey Lockman (102/333 Assists)	6.00	3.00	1.75
154	Don Newcombe	10.00	5.00	3.00
155	Frank J. Thomas	6.00	3.00	1.75
156a	Everett Lamar Bridges (320/467 Assists)	6.00	3.00	1.75
156b	Everett Lamar Bridges (328/475 Assists)	6.00	3.00	1.75
157	Omar Lown	5.00	2.50	1.50
158	Stu Miller	5.00	2.50	1.50
159	John Lindell	5.00	2.50	1.50
160	Danny O'Connell	5.00	2.50	1.50
161	Yogi Berra	65.00	32.00	19.50
162	Ted Lepcio	5.00	2.50	1.50
163a	Dave Philley (152 Games with no traded line)	7.00	3.50	2.00
163b	Dave Philley (152 Games with traded line)	10.00	5.00	3.00
163c	Dave Philley (157 Games with traded line)	7.00	3.50	2.00
164	Early "Gus" Wynn	20.00	10.00	6.00
165	Johnny Groth	5.00	2.50	1.50
166	Sandalio Consuegra	5.00	2.50	1.50
167	Bill Hoeft	5.00	2.50	1.50
168	Edward Fitzgerald (Fitz Gerald)	5.00	2.50	1.50
169	Larry Jansen	5.00	2.50	1.50
170	Edwin D. Snider	60.00	30.00	18.00
171	Carlos Bernier	5.00	2.50	1.50
172	Andy Seminick	5.00	2.50	1.50
173	Dee V. Fondy Jr.	5.00	2.50	1.50
174a	Peter Paul Castiglione (.966/.959 Field Avg.)	6.00	3.00	1.75
174b	Peter Paul Castiglione (.970/.959 Field Avg.)	6.00	3.00	1.75
175	Melvin E. Clark	5.00	2.50	1.50
176	Vernon Bickford	5.00	2.50	1.50

		NR MT	EX	VG
177	Edward Ford	40.00	20.00	12.00
178	Del Wilber	5.00	2.50	1.50
179a	Morris Martin (44 ERA)	6.00	3.00	1.75
179b	Morris Martin (4.44 ERA)	6.00	3.00	1.75
180	Joe Tipton	5.00	2.50	1.50
181	Lester Moss	5.00	2.50	1.50
182	Sherman Lollar	6.00	3.00	1.75
183	Matt Batts	5.00	2.50	1.50
184	Mickey Grasso	5.00	2.50	1.50
185a	Daryl Spencer (.941/.944 Field Avg.)	6.00	3.00	1.75
185b	Daryl Spencer (.933/.936 Field Avg.)	6.00	3.00	1.75
186	Russell Meyer	7.00	3.50	2.00
187	Verne Law (Vern)	6.00	3.00	1.75
188	Frank Smith	5.00	2.50	1.50
189	Ransom Jackson	5.00	2.50	1.50
190	Joe Presko	5.00	2.50	1.50
191	Karl A. Drews	5.00	2.50	1.50
192	Selva L. Burdette	7.00	3.50	2.00
193	Eddie Robinson	8.00	4.00	2.50
194	Sid Hudson	5.00	2.50	1.50
195	Bob Cain	5.00	2.50	1.50
196	Bob Lemon	20.00	10.00	6.00
197	Lou Kretlow	5.00	2.50	1.50
198	Virgil Trucks	6.00	3.00	1.75
199	Steve Gromek	5.00	2.50	1.50
200	C. Marrero	5.00	2.50	1.50
201	Bob Thomson	7.00	3.50	2.00
202	George Shuba	7.00	3.50	2.00
203	Vic Janowicz	5.00	2.50	1.50
204	Jack Collum	5.00	2.50	1.50
205	Hal Jeffcoat	5.00	2.50	1.50
206	Steve Bilko	5.00	2.50	1.50
207	Stan Lopata	5.00	2.50	1.50
208	Johnny Antonelli	6.00	3.00	1.75
209	Gene Woodling (photo reversed)	10.00	5.00	3.00
210	Jimmy Piersall	10.00	5.00	3.00
211	Alfred James Robertson Jr.	5.00	2.50	1.50
212a	Owen L. Friend (.964/.957 Field Avg.)	6.00	3.00	1.75
212b	Owen L. Friend (.967/.958 Field Avg.)	6.00	3.00	1.75
213	Dick Littlefield	5.00	2.50	1.50
214	Ferris Fain	6.00	3.00	1.75
215	Johnny Bucha	5.00	2.50	1.50
216a	Jerry Snyder (.988/.988 Field Avg.)	6.00	3.00	1.75
216b	Jerry Snyder (.968/.968 Field Avg.)	6.00	3.00	1.75
217a	Henry Thompson (.956/.951 Field Avg.)	6.00	3.00	1.75
217b	Henry Thompson (.958/.952 Field Avg.)	6.00	3.00	1.75
218	Preacher Roe	10.00	5.00	3.00
219	Hal Rice	5.00	2.50	1.50
220	Hobie Landrith	5.00	2.50	1.50
221	Frank Baumholtz	5.00	2.50	1.50
222	Memo Luna	5.00	2.50	1.50
223	Steve Ridzik	7.00	2.50	1.50
224	William Bruton	20.00	3.50	1.75

1955 Bowman

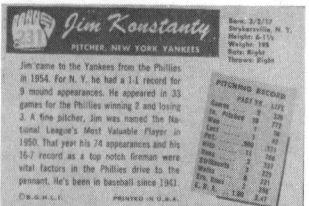

Bowman produced its final baseball card set in 1955, a popular issue which has player photographs placed inside a television set design. The set consists of 320 cards that measure 2½'' by 3¾'' in size. The high numbered cards (#'s 225-320) are scarcer in the set and include 31 umpire cards.

		NR MT	EX	VG
Complete Set:		3300.00	1150.00	650.00
Common Player: 1-224		5.00	2.50	1.50
Common Player: 225-320		8.00	4.00	2.50
1	Hoyt Wilhelm	65.00	12.00	5.50
2	Al Dark	12.00	4.00	2.50
3	Joe Coleman	5.00	2.50	1.50
4	Eddie Waitkus	5.00	2.50	1.50
5	Jim Robertson	5.00	2.50	1.50
6	Pete Suder	5.00	2.50	1.50
7	Gene Baker	5.00	2.50	1.50
8	Warren Hacker	5.00	2.50	1.50
9	Gil McDougald	10.00	5.00	3.00
10	Phil Rizzuto	25.00	12.50	7.50
11	Billy Bruton	5.00	2.50	1.50
12	Andy Pafko	6.00	3.00	1.75
13	Clyde Vollmer	5.00	2.50	1.50
14	Gus Keriazakos	5.00	2.50	1.50
15	Frank Sullivan	6.00	3.00	1.75
16	Jim Piersall	7.00	3.50	2.00
17	Del Ennis	6.00	3.00	1.75
18	Stan Lopata	5.00	2.50	1.50
19	Bobby Avila	5.00	2.50	1.50
20	Al Smith	5.00	2.50	1.50
21	Don Hoak	7.00	3.50	2.00
22	Roy Campanella	45.00	22.00	13.50
23	Al Kaline	40.00	20.00	12.00
24	Al Aber	5.00	2.50	1.50
25	Orestes "Minnie" Minoso	8.00	4.00	2.50
26	Virgil Trucks	6.00	3.00	1.75
27	Preston Ward	5.00	2.50	1.50
28	Dick Cole	5.00	2.50	1.50
29	Al "Red" Schoendienst	10.00	5.00	3.00
30	Bill Sarni	5.00	2.50	1.50
31	Johnny Temple	5.00	2.50	1.50
32	Wally Post	5.00	2.50	1.50
33	Nelson Fox	10.00	5.00	3.00
34	Clint Courtney	5.00	2.50	1.50
35	Bill Tuttle	5.00	2.50	1.50
36	Wayne Belardi	5.00	2.50	1.50
37	Harold "Pee Wee" Reese	30.00	15.00	9.00
38	Early Wynn	18.00	9.00	5.50
39	Bob Darnell	6.00	3.00	1.75
40	Vic Wertz	6.00	3.00	1.75
41	Mel Clark	5.00	2.50	1.50
42	Bob Greenwood	5.00	2.50	1.50
43	Bob Buhl	6.00	3.00	1.75
44	Danny O'Connell	5.00	2.50	1.50
45	Tom Umphlett	5.00	2.50	1.50
46	Mickey Vernon	6.00	3.00	1.75
47	Sammy White	5.00	2.50	1.50
48a	Milt Bolling (Frank Bolling back)	6.00	3.00	1.75
48b	Milt Bolling (Milt Bolling back)	15.00	7.50	4.50
49	Jim Greengrass	5.00	2.50	1.50
50	Hobie Landrith	5.00	2.50	1.50
51	Elvin Tappe	5.00	2.50	1.50
52	Hal Rice	5.00	2.50	1.50
53	Alex Kellner	5.00	2.50	1.50
54	Don Bollweg	5.00	2.50	1.50
55	Cal Abrams	5.00	2.50	1.50
56	Billy Cox	5.00	2.50	1.50
57	Bob Friend	6.00	3.00	1.75
58	Frank Thomas	5.00	2.50	1.50
59	Ed "Whitey" Ford	30.00	15.00	9.00
60	Enos Slaughter	18.00	9.00	5.50
61	Paul LaPalme	5.00	2.50	1.50
62	Royce Lint	5.00	2.50	1.50
63	Irv Noren	8.00	4.00	2.50
64	Curt Simmons	6.00	3.00	1.75
65	Don Zimmer	10.00	5.00	3.00
66	George Shuba	6.00	3.00	1.75
67	Don Larsen	10.00	5.00	3.00
68	Elston Howard	15.00	7.50	4.50
69	Bill Hunter	8.00	4.00	2.50
70	Lou Burdette	7.00	3.50	2.00
71	Dave Jolly	5.00	2.50	1.50
72	Chet Nichols	5.00	2.50	1.50
73	Eddie Yost	5.00	2.50	1.50
74	Jerry Snyder	5.00	2.50	1.50
75	Brooks Lawrence	5.00	2.50	1.50
76	Tom Poholsky	5.00	2.50	1.50
77	Jim McDonald	5.00	2.50	1.50

		NR MT	EX	VG
78	Gil Coan	5.00	2.50	1.50
79	Willie Miranda	5.00	2.50	1.50
80	Lou Limmer	5.00	2.50	1.50
81	Bob Morgan	5.00	2.50	1.50
82	Lee Walls	5.00	2.50	1.50
83	Max Surkont	5.00	2.50	1.50
84	George Freese	5.00	2.50	1.50
85	Cass Michaels	5.00	2.50	1.50
86	Ted Gray	5.00	2.50	1.50
87	Randy Jackson	5.00	2.50	1.50
88	Steve Bilko	5.00	2.50	1.50
89	Lou Boudreau	15.00	7.50	4.50
90	Art Ditmar	5.00	2.50	1.50
91	Dick Marlowe	5.00	2.50	1.50
92	George Zuverink	5.00	2.50	1.50
93	Andy Seminick	5.00	2.50	1.50
94	Hank Thompson	5.00	2.50	1.50
95	Sal Maglie	7.00	3.50	2.00
96	Ray Narleski	5.00	2.50	1.50
97	John Podres	10.00	5.00	3.00
98	James "Junior" Gilliam	10.00	5.00	3.00
99	Jerry Coleman	8.00	4.00	2.50
100	Tom Morgan	8.00	4.00	2.50
101a	Don Johnson (Ernie Johnson (Braves) on front.)	6.00	3.00	1.75
101b	Don Johnson (Don Johnson (Orioles) on front.)	15.00	7.50	4.50
102	Bobby Thomson	7.00	3.50	2.00
103	Eddie Mathews	20.00	10.00	6.00
104	Bob Porterfield	5.00	2.50	1.50
105	Johnny Schmitz	5.00	2.50	1.50
106	Del Rice	5.00	2.50	1.50
107	Solly Hemus	5.00	2.50	1.50
108	Lou Kretlow	5.00	2.50	1.50
109	Vern Stephens	5.00	2.50	1.50
110	Bob Miller	5.00	2.50	1.50
111	Steve Ridzik	5.00	2.50	1.50
112	Gran Hamner	5.00	2.50	1.50
113	Bob Hall	5.00	2.50	1.50
114	Vic Janowicz	5.00	2.50	1.50
115	Roger Bowman	5.00	2.50	1.50
116	Sandalio Consuegra	5.00	2.50	1.50
117	Johnny Groth	5.00	2.50	1.50
118	Bobby Adams	5.00	2.50	1.50
119	Joe Astroth	5.00	2.50	1.50
120	Ed Burtschy	5.00	2.50	1.50
121	Rufus Crawford	5.00	2.50	1.50
122	Al Corwin	5.00	2.50	1.50
123	Marv Grissom	5.00	2.50	1.50
124	Johnny Antonelli	6.00	3.00	1.75
125	Paul Giel	5.00	2.50	1.50
126	Billy Goodman	5.00	2.50	1.50
127	Hank Majeski	5.00	2.50	1.50
128	Mike Garcia	6.00	3.00	1.75
129	Hal Naragon	5.00	2.50	1.50
130	Richie Ashburn	10.00	5.00	3.00
131	Willard Marshall	5.00	2.50	1.50
132a	Harvey Kueen (incorrect spelling on back)	7.00	3.50	2.00
132b	Harvey Kuenn (correct spelling on back)	15.00	7.50	4.50
133	Charles King	5.00	2.50	1.50
134	Bob Feller	30.00	15.00	9.00
135	Lloyd Merriman	5.00	2.50	1.50
136	Rocky Bridges	5.00	2.50	1.50
137	Bob Talbot	5.00	2.50	1.50
138	Davey Williams	5.00	2.50	1.50
139	Billy & Bobby Shantz	7.00	3.50	2.00
140	Bobby Shantz	6.00	3.00	1.75
141	Wes Westrum	6.00	3.00	1.75
142	Rudy Regalado	5.00	2.50	1.50
143	Don Newcombe	8.00	4.00	2.50
144	Art Houtteman	5.00	2.50	1.50
145	Bob Nieman	5.00	2.50	1.50
146	Don Liddle	5.00	2.50	1.50
147	Sam Mele	5.00	2.50	1.50
148	Bob Chakales	5.00	2.50	1.50
149	Cloyd Boyer	5.00	2.50	1.50
150	Bill Klaus	5.00	2.50	1.50
151	Jim Brideweser	5.00	2.50	1.50
152	Johnny Klippstein	5.00	2.50	1.50
153	Eddie Robinson	8.00	4.00	2.50
154	Frank Lary	7.00	3.50	2.00
155	Gerry Staley	5.00	2.50	1.50
156	Jim Hughes	6.00	3.00	1.75
157a	Ernie Johnson (Don Johnson (Orioles) picture on front)	6.00	3.00	1.75
157b	Ernie Johnson (Ernie Johnson (Braves) picture on front)	15.00	7.50	4.50
158	Gil Hodges	25.00	12.50	7.50
159	Harry Byrd	5.00	2.50	1.50
160	Bill Skowron	10.00	5.00	3.00
161	Matt Batts	5.00	2.50	1.50
162	Charlie Maxwell	5.00	2.50	1.50
163	Sid Gordon	5.00	2.50	1.50
164	Toby Atwell	5.00	2.50	1.50
165	Maurice McDermott	5.00	2.50	1.50
166	Jim Busby	5.00	2.50	1.50
167	Bob Grim	8.00	4.00	2.50
168	Larry "Yogi" Berra	45.00	22.00	13.50
169	Carl Furillo	10.00	5.00	3.00
170	Carl Erskine	8.00	4.00	2.50
171	Robin Roberts	17.00	8.50	5.00
172	Willie Jones	5.00	2.50	1.50
173	Al "Chico" Carrasquel	5.00	2.50	1.50
174	Sherman Lollar	6.00	3.00	1.75
175	Wilmer Shantz	5.00	2.50	1.50
176	Joe DeMaestri	5.00	2.50	1.50
177	Willard Nixon	5.00	2.50	1.50
178	Tom Brewer	5.00	2.50	1.50
179	Hank Aaron	90.00	45.00	27.00
180	Johnny Logan	5.00	2.50	1.50
181	Eddie Miksis	5.00	2.50	1.50
182	Bob Rush	5.00	2.50	1.50
183	Ray Katt	5.00	2.50	1.50
184	Willie Mays	80.00	40.00	24.00
185	Vic Raschi	6.00	3.00	1.75
186	Alex Grammas	5.00	2.50	1.50
187	Fred Hatfield	5.00	2.50	1.50
188	Ned Garver	5.00	2.50	1.50
189	Jack Collum	5.00	2.50	1.50
190	Fred Baczewski	5.00	2.50	1.50
191	Bob Lemon	17.00	8.50	5.00
192	George Strickland	5.00	2.50	1.50
193	Howie Judson	5.00	2.50	1.50
194	Joe Nuxhall	6.00	3.00	1.75
195a	Erv Palica (no traded line on back)	7.00	3.50	2.00
195b	Erv Palica (traded line on back)	15.00	7.50	4.50
196	Russ Meyer	6.00	3.00	1.75
197	Ralph Kiner	17.00	8.50	5.00
198	Dave Pope	5.00	2.50	1.50
199	Vernon Law	6.00	3.00	1.75
200	Dick Littlefield	5.00	2.50	1.50
201	Allie Reynolds	10.00	5.00	3.00
202	Mickey Mantle	300.00	120.00	60.00
203	Steve Gromek	5.00	2.50	1.50
204a	Frank Bolling (Milt Bolling back)	6.00	3.00	1.75
204b	Frank Bolling (Frank Bolling back)	15.00	7.50	4.50
205	Eldon "Rip" Repulski	5.00	2.50	1.50
206	Ralph Beard	5.00	2.50	1.50
207	Frank Shea	5.00	2.50	1.50
208	Eddy Fitzgerald (Fitz Gerald)	5.00	2.50	1.50
209	Forrest "Smoky" Burgess	6.00	3.00	1.75
210	Earl Torgeson	5.00	2.50	1.50
211	John "Sonny" Dixon	5.00	2.50	1.50
212	Jack Dittmer	5.00	2.50	1.50
213	George Kell	17.00	8.50	5.00
214	Billy Pierce	6.00	3.00	1.75
215	Bob Kuzava	5.00	2.50	1.50
216	Preacher Roe	6.00	3.00	1.75
217	Del Crandall	6.00	3.00	1.75
218	Joe Adcock	6.00	3.00	1.75
219	Whitey Lockman	5.00	2.50	1.50
220	Jim Hearn	5.00	2.50	1.50
221	Hector "Skinny" Brown	5.00	2.50	1.50
222	Russ Kemmerer	5.00	2.50	1.50
223	Hal Jeffcoat	5.00	2.50	1.50
224	Dee Fondy	5.00	2.50	1.50
225	Paul Richards	10.00	5.00	3.00
226	W.F. McKinley (umpire)	10.00	5.00	3.00
227	Frank Baumholtz	8.00	4.00	2.50
228	John M. Phillips	8.00	4.00	2.50
229	Jim Brosnan	10.00	5.00	3.00
230	Al Brazle	8.00	4.00	2.50
231	Jim Konstanty	12.00	6.00	3.50
232	Birdie Tebbetts	8.00	4.00	2.50
233	Bill Serena	8.00	4.00	2.50
234	Dick Bartell	8.00	4.00	2.50
235	J.A. Paparella (umpire)	10.00	5.00	3.00
236	Murray Dickson (Murry)	8.00	4.00	2.50
237	Johnny Wyrostek	8.00	4.00	2.50
238	Eddie Stanky	9.00	4.50	2.75
239	Edwin A. Rommel (umpire)	10.00	5.00	3.00
240	Billy Loes	10.00	5.00	3.00
241	John Pesky	9.00	4.50	2.75
242	Ernie Banks	200.00	80.00	50.00
243	Gus Bell	9.00	4.50	2.75
244	Duane Pillette	8.00	4.00	2.50
245	Bill Miller	8.00	4.00	2.50
246	Hank Bauer	16.00	8.00	4.75

		NR MT	EX	VG
247	Dutch Leonard	8.00	4.00	2.50
248	Harry Dorish	8.00	4.00	2.50
249	Billy Gardner	8.00	4.00	2.50
250	Larry Napp (umpire)	10.00	5.00	3.00
251	Stan Jok	8.00	4.00	2.50
252	Roy Smalley	8.00	4.00	2.50
253	Jim Wilson	8.00	4.00	2.50
254	Bennett Flowers	8.00	4.00	2.50
255	Pete Runnels	9.00	4.50	2.75
256	Owen Friend	8.00	4.00	2.50
257	Tom Alston	8.00	4.00	2.50
258	John W. Stevens (umpire)	10.00	5.00	3.00
259	Don Mossi	9.00	4.50	2.75
260	Edwin H. Hurley (umpire)	10.00	5.00	3.00
261	Walt Moryn	9.00	4.50	2.75
262	Jim Lemon	9.00	4.50	2.75
263	Eddie Joost	8.00	4.00	2.50
264	Bill Henry	8.00	4.00	2.50
265	Albert J. Barlick (umpire)	10.00	5.00	3.00
266	Mike Fornieles	8.00	4.00	2.50
267	George (Jim) Honochick (umpire)	25.00	12.50	7.50
268	Roy Lee Hawes	8.00	4.00	2.50
269	Joe Amalfitano	8.00	4.00	2.50
270	Chico Fernandez	9.00	4.50	2.75
271	Bob Hooper	8.00	4.00	2.50
272	John Flaherty (umpire)	10.00	5.00	3.00
273	Emory "Bubba" Church	8.00	4.00	2.50
274	Jim Delsing	8.00	4.00	2.50
275	William T. Grieve (umpire)	10.00	5.00	3.00
276	Ivan Delock	8.00	4.00	2.50
277	Ed Runge (umpire)	10.00	5.00	3.00
278	Charles Neal	12.00	6.00	3.50
279	Hank Soar (umpire)	10.00	5.00	3.00
280	Clyde McCullough	8.00	4.00	2.50
281	Charles Berry (umpire)	10.00	5.00	3.00
282	Phil Cavarretta	9.00	4.50	2.75
283	Nestor Chylak (umpire)	10.00	5.00	3.00
284	William A. Jackowski (umpire)	10.00	5.00	3.00
285	Walt Dropo	8.00	4.00	2.50
286	Frank E. Secory (umpire)	10.00	5.00	3.00
287	Ron Mrozinski	8.00	4.00	2.50
288	Dick Smith	8.00	4.00	2.50
289	Arthur J. Gore (umpire)	10.00	5.00	3.00
290	Hershell Freeman	8.00	4.00	2.50
291	Frank Dascoli (umpire)	10.00	5.00	3.00
292	Marv Blaylock	8.00	4.00	2.50
293	Thomas D. Gorman (umpire)	10.00	5.00	3.00
294	Wally Moses	8.00	4.00	2.50
295	E. Lee Ballanfant (umpire)	10.00	5.00	3.00
296	Bill Virdon	20.00	10.00	6.00
297	L.R. "Dusty" Boggess (umpire)	10.00	5.00	3.00
298	Charlie Grimm	9.00	4.50	2.75
299	Lonnie Warneke (umpire)	10.00	5.00	3.00
300	Tommy Byrne	12.00	6.00	3.50
301	William R. Engeln (umpire)	10.00	5.00	3.00
302	Frank Malzone	12.00	6.00	3.50
303	J.B. "Jocko" Conlan (umpire)	30.00	15.00	9.00
304	Harry Chiti	8.00	4.00	2.50
305	Frank Umont (umpire)	10.00	5.00	3.00
306	Bob Cerv	12.00	6.00	3.50
307	R.A. "Babe" Pinelli (umpire)	10.00	5.00	3.00
308	Al Lopez	25.00	12.50	7.50
309	Hal H. Dixon (umpire)	10.00	5.00	3.00
310	Ken Lehman	9.00	4.50	2.75
311	Lawrence J. Goetz (umpire)	10.00	5.00	3.00
312	Bill Wight	8.00	4.00	2.50
313	A.J. Donatelli (umpire)	10.00	5.00	3.00
314	Dale Mitchell	8.00	4.00	2.50
315	Cal Hubbard (umpire)	25.00	12.50	7.50
316	Marion Fricano	8.00	4.00	2.50
317	Wm. R. Summers (umpire)	10.00	5.00	3.00
318	Sid Hudson	8.00	4.00	2.50
319	Albert B. Schroll	10.00	4.00	2.50
320	George D. Susce, Jr.	30.00	5.00	2.50

the New York players can also be found on cards in the 1954 Dan-Dee Potato Chips and 1953-55 Stahl-Meyer Franks sets.

		NR MT	EX	VG
Complete Set		6775.00	3387.00	2032.
Common Player		100.00	50.00	30.00
(1)	Hank Bauer	150.00	75.00	45.00
(2)	James Busby	100.00	50.00	30.00
(3)	Tommy Byrne	100.00	50.00	30.00
(4)	John Dixon	100.00	50.00	30.00
(5)	Carl Erskine	125.00	62.00	37.00
(6)	Edward Fitzgerald (Fitz Gerald)	100.00	50.00	30.00
(7)	Newton Grasso	100.00	50.00	30.00
(8)	Melvin Hoderlein	100.00	50.00	30.00
(9)	Gil Hodges	250.00	125.00	75.00
(10)	Monte Irvin	150.00	75.00	45.00
(11)	Whitey Lockman	100.00	50.00	30.00
(12)	Mickey Mantle	1500.00	750.00	450.00
(13)	Conrado Marrero	100.00	50.00	30.00
(14)	Walter Masterson	100.00	50.00	30.00
(15)	Carmen Mauro	100.00	50.00	30.00
(16)	Willie Mays	750.00	375.00	225.00
(17)	Mickey McDermott	100.00	50.00	30.00
(18)	Gil McDougald	150.00	75.00	45.00
(19)	Julio Moreno	100.00	50.00	30.00
(20)	Don Mueller	100.00	50.00	30.00
(21)	Don Newcombe	125.00	62.00	37.00
(22)	Robert Oldis	100.00	50.00	30.00
(23)	Erwin Porterfield	100.00	50.00	30.00
(24)	Phil Rizzuto	200.00	100.00	60.00
(25)	James Runnels	100.00	50.00	30.00
(26)	John Schmitz	100.00	50.00	30.00
(27)	Angel Scull	100.00	50.00	30.00
(28)	Frank Shea	100.00	50.00	30.00
(29)	Albert Sima	100.00	50.00	30.00
(30)	Duke Snider	375.00	187.00	112.00
(31)	Charles Stobbs	100.00	50.00	30.00
(32)	Willard Terwilliger	100.00	50.00	30.00
(33)	Joe Tipton	100.00	50.00	30.00
(34)	Thomas Umphlett	100.00	50.00	30.00
(35)	Gene Verble	100.00	50.00	30.00
(36)	James Vernon	125.00	62.00	37.00
(37)	Clyde Volmer (Vollmer)	100.00	50.00	30.00
(38)	Edward Yost	100.00	50.00	30.00

1953-54 Briggs Meats

The Briggs Meat set was issued over a two-year span (1953-54) and features 26 players from the Washington Senators and 12 from the New York City area baseball teams. The set was issued in two-card panels on hot dog packages sold in the Washington, D.C. vicinity. The color cards, which are blank-backed and measure 2¼'' by 3½'', are printed on waxed cardboard. The style of the Senators cards in the set differs from that of the New York players. Poses for

1977 Burger King Yankees

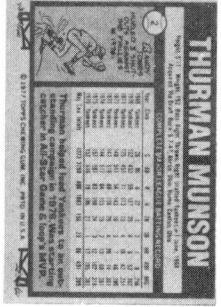

The first Topps-produced set for Burger King restaurants was issued in the New York area in 1977 and featured the A.L. champion New York Yankees. Twenty-two players plus an unnumbered checklist were issued at the beginning of the promotion with card #23 Lou Piniella being added to the set at a later date. The Piniella card was issued in limited quantities. The cards, numbered 1 through 23 and 2½'' by 3½'' in size, have fronts identical to the regular 1977 Topps set except for the following numbers: 2, 6, 7, 13, 14, 15, 17, 20 and 21. These cards feature different poses or major picture-cropping variations. It should be noted that very minor cropping variations between the regular Topps sets and the Burger King issues exist throughout the years the BK sets were produced.

		NR MT	EX	VG
Complete Set:		36.00	18.00	11.00
Common Player:		.30	.15	.09
1	Yankees Team (Billy Martin)	.90	.45	.25
2	Thurman Munson	3.50	1.75	1.00
3	Fran Healy	.30	.15	.09
4	Jim Hunter	1.00	.50	.30
5	Ed Figueroa	.30	.15	.09
6	Don Gullett	.70	.35	.20
7	Mike Torrez	.70	.35	.20
8	Ken Holtzman	.50	.25	.15
9	Dick Tidrow	.30	.15	.09
10	Sparky Lyle	.50	.25	.15
11	Ron Guidry	1.25	.60	.40
12	Chris Chambliss	.50	.25	.15
13	Willie Randolph	.80	.40	.25
14	Bucky Dent	.80	.40	.25
15	Graig Nettles	1.25	.60	.40
16	Fred Stanley	.30	.15	.09
17	Reggie Jackson	3.50	1.75	1.00
18	Mickey Rivers	.50	.25	.15
19	Roy White	.50	.25	.15
20	Jim Wynn	.70	.35	.20
21	Paul Blair	.70	.35	.20
22	Carlos May	.30	.15	.09
23	Lou Piniella	20.00	10.00	6.00
---	Checklist	.04	.02	.01

1978 Burger King Astros

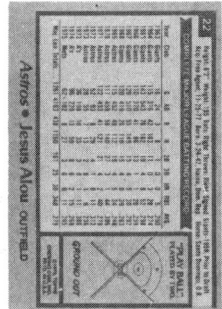

JESUS ALOU

Burger King restaurants in the Houston area distributed a Topps-produced 23-card set showcasing the Astros in 1978. The cards are standard size (2½'' by 3½'') and are numbered 1 through 22. The checklist card is unnumbered. The card fronts are identical to the regular 1978 Topps set with the exception of card numbers 21 and 22, which had different poses. Although not noted in the following checklist, it should be remembered that very minor picture-cropping variations between the regular Topps issues and the 1977-80 Burger King sets do exist.

	NR MT	EX	VG
Complete Set:	9.00	4.50	2.75
Common Player:	.30	.15	.09

		NR MT	EX	VG
1	Bill Virdon	.50	.25	.15
2	Joe Ferguson	.30	.15	.09
3	Ed Herrmann	.30	.15	.09
4	J.R. Richard	.60	.30	.20
5	Joe Niekro	.60	.30	.20
6	Floyd Bannister	.70	.35	.20
7	Joaquin Andujar	.60	.30	.20
8	Ken Forsch	.40	.20	.12
9	Mark Lemongello	.30	.15	.09
10	Joe Sambito	.40	.20	.12
11	Gene Pentz	.30	.15	.09
12	Bob Watson	.60	.30	.20
13	Julio Gonzalez	.30	.15	.09
14	Enos Cabell	.40	.20	.12
15	Roger Metzger	.30	.15	.09
16	Art Howe	.30	.15	.09
17	Jose Cruz	.90	.45	.25
18	Cesar Cedeno	.80	.40	.25
19	Terry Puhl	.50	.25	.15
20	Wilbur Howard	.30	.15	.09
21	Dave Bergman	.50	.25	.15
22	Jesus Alou	.50	.25	.15
---	Checklist	.04	.02	.01

1978 Burger King Rangers

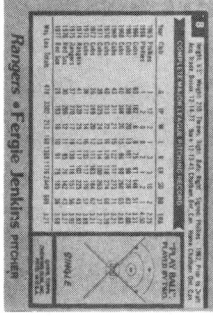

FERGIE JENKINS

Issued by Burger King restaurants in the Dallas-Fort Worth area, this 23-card Topps-produced set features the Texas Rangers. The cards are standard size (2½'' x 3½'') and are identical in style to the regular 1978 Topps set with the following exceptions: #'s 5, 8, 10, 12, 17, 21 and 22. An unnumbered checklist card was included with the set.

		NR MT	EX	VG
Complete Set:		9.00	4.50	2.75
Common Player:		.30	.15	.09
1	Billy Hunter	.40	.20	.12
2	Jim Sundberg	.50	.25	.15
3	John Ellis	.30	.15	.09
4	Doyle Alexander	.70	.35	.20
5	Jon Matlack	.50	.25	.15
6	Dock Ellis	.30	.15	.09
7	George Medich	.30	.15	.09
8	Fergie Jenkins	.90	.45	.25
9	Len Barker	.50	.25	.15
10	Reggie Cleveland	.50	.25	.15
11	Mike Hargrove	.40	.20	.12
12	Bump Wills	.60	.30	.20
13	Toby Harrah	.50	.25	.15
14	Bert Campaneris	.50	.25	.15
15	Sandy Alomar	.30	.15	.09
16	Kurt Bevacqua	.30	.15	.09
17	Al Oliver	.90	.45	.25
18	Juan Beniquez	.40	.20	.12
19	Claudell Washington	.50	.25	.15
20	Richie Zisk	.40	.20	.12
21	John Lowenstein	.50	.25	.15
22	Bobby Thompson	.50	.25	.15
---	Checklist	.04	.02	.01

1978 Burger King Tigers

 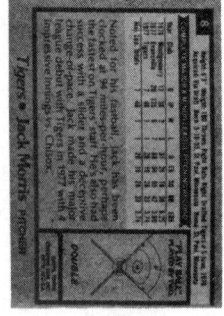

JACK MORRIS

Rookie cards of Morris, Trammell and Whitaker make the Topps-produced 1978 Burger King Detroit Tigers issue the most popular of the BK sets. Twenty-two player cards and an unnumbered checklist make up the set which was issued in the Detroit area. The cards, which measure 2½'' by 3½'', are identical to the regular 1978 Topps issue with the following exceptions - card #'s 6, 7, 8, 13, 15 and 16. Collectors are reminded that numerous minor picture-cropping variations between the regular Topps issues and the Burger King sets appear from 1977 through 1980.These very minor variations are not noted in the following checklist.

		NR MT	EX	VG
Complete Set:		40.00	20.00	12.00
Common Player:		.30	.15	.09
1	Ralph Houk	.40	.20	.12
2	Milt May	.30	.15	.09
3	Johnny Wockenfuss	.30	.15	.09
4	Mark Fidrych	.70	.35	.20
5	Dave Rozema	.30	.15	.09
6	Jack Billingham	.70	.35	.20
7	Jim Slaton	.70	.35	.20
8	Jack Morris	6.50	3.25	2.00
9	John Hiller	.50	.25	.15
10	Steve Foucault	.30	.15	.09
11	Milt Wilcox	.30	.15	.09
12	Jason Thompson	.40	.20	.12
13	Lou Whitaker	8.00	4.00	2.50
14	Aurelio Rodriguez	.70	.35	.20
15	Alan Trammell	16.00	8.00	4.75
16	Steve Dillard	.30	.15	.09
17	Phil Mankowski	.70	.35	.20
18	Steve Kemp	.40	.20	.12
19	Ron LeFlore	.40	.20	.12
20	Tim Corcoran	.70	.35	.20
21	Mickey Stanley	.40	.20	.12
22	Rusty Staub	.50	.25	.15
---	Checklist	.04	.02	.01

1978 Burger King Yankees

 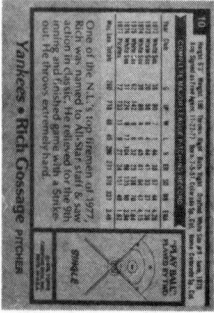

RICH GOSSAGE

Produced by Topps for Burger King outlets in the New York area for the second year in a row, the 1978 Yankees set contains twenty-two cards plus an unnumbered checklist. The cards are numbered 1 through 22 and are the standard size of 2½'' by 3½''. The cards feature the same pictures found in the regular 1978 Topps set except for numbers 10, 11 and 16. Only those variations containing different poses or major picture-cropping differences are noted. Numerous minor picture-cropping variations, that are very insignificant in nature, exist between the regular Topps sets and the Burger King issues of 1977-80.

		NR MT	EX	VG
Complete Set:		10.00	5.00	3.00
Common Player:		.30	.15	.09
1	Billy Martin	.80	.40	.25
2	Thurman Munson	2.00	1.00	.60
3	Cliff Johnson	.30	.15	.09
4	Ron Guidry	1.25	.60	.40
5	Ed Figueroa	.30	.15	.09
6	Dick Tidrow	.30	.15	.09
7	Jim Hunter	1.00	.50	.30
8	Don Gullett	.30	.15	.09
9	Sparky Lyle	.50	.25	.15
10	Rich Gossage	1.25	.60	.40
11	Rawly Eastwick	.50	.25	.15
12	Chris Chambliss	.50	.25	.15
13	Willie Randolph	.50	.25	.15
14	Graig Nettles	.80	.40	.25
15	Bucky Dent	.50	.25	.15
16	Jim Spencer	.50	.25	.15
17	Fred Stanley	.30	.15	.09
18	Lou Piniella	.80	.40	.25
19	Roy White	.50	.25	.15
20	Mickey Rivers	.50	.25	.15
21	Reggie Jackson	2.00	1.00	.60
22	Paul Blair	.30	.15	.09
---	Checklist	.04	.02	.01

1979 Burger King Phillies

 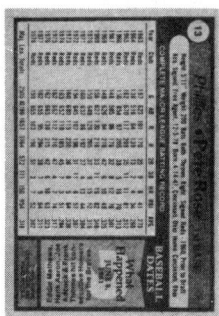

N.L. ALL-STAR
PETE ROSE 1B
PHILLIES

Twenty-two Philadelphia Phillies players were featured in the 1979 Burger King issue given out in the Philadelphia area. The Topps-produced set, whose cards measure 2½'' by 3½'', also includes an unnumbered checklist. The cards are identical to the regular 1979 Topps set except in seven instances. Card numbers 1, 11, 12, 13, 14, 17 and 22 have different poses. Very minor picture-cropping variations between the regular Topps issues and the Burger King sets can be found throughout the four years the cards were produced, but only those variations featuring major changes are noted in the following checklist.

		NR MT	EX	VG
Complete Set:		7.00	3.50	2.00
Common Player:		.20	.10	.06
1	Danny Ozark	.30	.15	.09
2	Bob Boone	.30	.15	.09
3	Tim McCarver	.30	.15	.09
4	Steve Carlton	1.50	.70	.45

		NR MT	EX	VG
5	Larry Christenson	.20	.10	.06
6	Dick Ruthven	.20	.10	.06
7	Ron Reed	.20	.10	.06
8	Randy Lerch	.20	.10	.06
9	Warren Brusstar	.20	.10	.06
10	Tug McGraw	.40	.20	.12
11	Nino Espinosa	.40	.20	.12
12	Doug Bird	.40	.20	.12
13	Pete Rose	3.50	1.75	1.00
14	Manny Trillo	.40	.20	.12
15	Larry Bowa	.50	.25	.15
16	Mike Schmidt	2.00	1.00	.60
17	Pete Mackanin	.40	.20	.12
18	Jose Cardenal	.20	.10	.06
19	Greg Luzinski	.40	.20	.12
20	Garry Maddox	.30	.15	09
21	Bake McBride	.20	.10	.06
22	Greg Gross	.50	.25	.15
---	Checklist	.04	.02	.01

1980 Burger King Phillies

Philadelphia-area Burger King outlets issued a 23-card set featuring the Phillies for the second year in a row in 1980. The Topps-produced set, whose cards measure 2½" by 3½", contains 22 player cards and an unnumbered checklist. The card fronts are identical in design to the regular 1980 Topps sets with the following exceptions - card numbers 1, 3, 8, 14 and 22 feature new poses. Collectors should note that very minor picture-cropping variations between the regular Topps issues and the Burger King sets exist in all years. Those minor differences are not noted in the checklist that follows. The 1980 Burger King sets were the first to include the Burger King logo on the card backs.

		NR MT	EX	VG
Complete Set:		6.00	3.00	1.75
Common Player:		.15	.08	.05
1	Dallas Green	.30	.15	.09
2	Bob Boone	.25	.13	.08
3	Keith Moreland	.40	.20	.12
4	Pete Rose	2.75	1.50	.80
5	Manny Trillo	.20	.10	.06
6	Mike Schmidt	2.00	1.00	.60
7	Larry Bowa	.40	.20	.12
8	John Vukovich	.30	.15	.09
9	Bake McBride	.15	.08	.05
10	Garry Maddox	.20	.10	.06
11	Greg Luzinski	.30	.15	.09
12	Greg Gross	.15	.08	.05
13	Del Unser	.15	.08	.05
14	Lonnie Smith	.40	.20	.12
15	Steve Carlton	1.25	.60	.40
16	Larry Christenson	.15	.08	.05
17	Nino Espinosa	.15	.08	.05
18	Randy Lerch	.15	.08	.05
19	Dick Ruthven	.15	.08	.05
20	Tug McGraw	.30	.15	.09
21	Ron Reed	.15	.08	.05
22	Kevin Saucier	.30	.15	.09
---	Checklist	.04	.02	.01

1979 Burger King Yankees

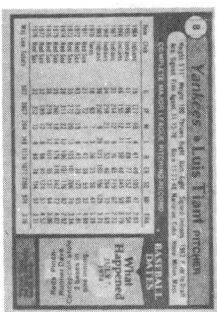

The New York Yankees were featured in a Topps-produced Burger King set for the third consecutive year in 1979. Once again, 22 numbered player cards and an unnumbered checklist made up the set. The cards, which measure 2½" by 3½", are identical to the 1979 Topps regular set except for card numbers 4, 8, 9 and 22 which included new poses. Only different poses or major picture-cropping variations between the regular Topps set and the Burger King issue are recognized in the checklist that follows. Numerous minor picture-cropping variations between the regular Topps issue and the Burger King sets of 1977-80 exist.

		NR MT	EX	VG
Complete Set:		10.00	5.00	3.00
Common Player:		.30	.15	.09
1	Yankees Team (Bob Lemon)	.50	.25	.15
2	Thurman Munson	2.00	1.00	.60
3	Cliff Johnson	.30	.15	.09
4	Ron Guidry	2.00	1.00	.60
5	Jay Johnstone	.40	.20	.12
6	Jim Hunter	.90	.45	.25
7	Jim Beattie	.30	.15	.09
8	Luis Tiant	.70	.35	.20
9	Tommy John	.90	.45	.25
10	Rich Gossage	.90	.45	.25
11	Ed Figueroa	.30	.15	.09
12	Chris Chambliss	.50	.25	.15
13	Willie Randolph	.50	.25	.15
14	Bucky Dent	.50	.25	.15
15	Graig Nettles	.70	.35	.20
16	Fred Stanley	.30	.15	.09
17	Jim Spencer	.30	.15	.09
18	Lou Piniella	.70	.35	.20
19	Roy White	.50	.25	.15
20	Mickey Rivers	.50	.25	.15
21	Reggie Jackson	2.00	1.00	.60
22	Juan Beniquez	.50	.25	.15
---	Checklist	.04	.02	.01

1980 Burger King Pitch, Hit & Run

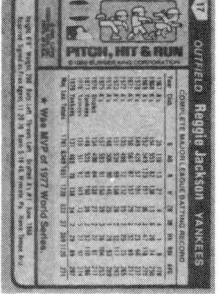

In 1980, Burger King issued, in conjunction with its "Pitch, Hit & Run" promotion, a Topps-produced 34-card set featuring pitchers (card #'s 1-11), hitters (#'s 12-22), and base stealers (#'s 23-33). The card fronts, which carry the Burger King logo, are identical in nature to the regular 1980 Topps set except for numbers 1, 4, 5, 7, 9, 10, 16, 17, 18, 22, 23, 27, 28, 29 and 30, which feature different poses. The cards, which are numbered 1 through 33, measure 2½" by 3½" in size. An unnumbered checklist was included with the set.

		NR MT	EX	VG
Complete Set:		12.00	6.00	3.50
Common Player:		.20	.10	.06
1	Vida Blue	.40	.20	.12
2	Steve Carlton	1.00	.50	.30
3	Rollie Fingers	.30	.15	.09
4	Ron Guidry	.60	.30	.20
5	Jerry Koosman	.30	.15	.09
6	Phil Niekro	.40	.20	.12
7	Jim Palmer	.80	.40	.25
8	J.R. Richard	.20	.10	.06
9	Nolan Ryan	1.00	.50	.30
10	Tom Seaver	1.00	.50	.30
11	Bruce Sutter	.25	.13	.08
12	Don Baylor	.25	.13	.08
13	George Brett	1.25	.60	.40
14	Rod Carew	.90	.45	.25
15	George Foster	.25	.13	.08
16	Keith Hernandez	.80	.40	.25
17	Reggie Jackson	2.00	1.00	.60
18	Fred Lynn	.50	.25	.15
19	Dave Parker	.40	.20	.12
20	Jim Rice	.80	.40	.25
21	Pete Rose	2.50	1.25	.70
22	Dave Winfield	1.00	.50	.30
23	Bobby Bonds	.30	.15	.09
24	Enos Cabell	.20	.10	.06
25	Cesar Cedeno	.25	.13	.08
26	Julio Cruz	.20	.10	.06
27	Ron LeFlore	.30	.15	.09
28	Dave Lopes	.30	.15	.09
29	Omar Moreno	.30	.15	.09
30	Joe Morgan	.70	.35	.20
31	Bill North	.20	.10	.06
32	Frank Taveras	.20	.10	.06
33	Willie Wilson	.25	.13	.08
---	Checklist	.04	.02	.01

1982 Burger King Braves

A set consisting of 27 "Collector Lids" featuring the Atlanta Braves was issued by Burger King restaurants in 1982. The lids, which measure 3⅜" in diameter, were placed on a special Coca-Cola cup which listed the scores of the Braves' season-opening 13-game win streak. A black and white photo plus the player's name, position, height, weight, and 1981 statistics are found on the lid front. The unnumbered, blank-backed lids also contain logos for Burger King, Coca-Cola, and the Major League Baseball Players Association.

		MT	NR MT	EX
Complete Set:		40.00	30.00	16.00
Common Player:		1.00	.70	.40
(1)	Steve Bedrosian	2.25	1.75	.90
(2)	Bruce Benedict	1.00	.70	.40
(3)	Tommy Boggs	1.00	.70	.40
(4)	Brett Butler	2.00	1.50	.80
(5)	Rick Camp	1.00	.70	.40
(6)	Chris Chambliss	1.25	.90	.50
(7)	Ken Dayley	1.00	.70	.40
(8)	Gene Garber	1.00	.70	.40
(9)	Preston Hanna	1.00	.70	.40
(10)	Terry Harper	1.00	.70	.40
(11)	Bob Horner	3.50	2.75	1.50
(12)	Al Hrabosky	1.25	.90	.50
(13)	Glenn Hubbard	1.25	.90	.50
(14)	Randy Johnson	1.00	.70	.40
(15)	Rufino Linares	1.00	.70	.40
(16)	Rick Mahler	1.50	1.25	.60
(17)	Larry McWilliams	1.00	.70	.40
(18)	Dale Murphy	12.00	9.00	4.75
(19)	Phil Niekro	5.00	3.75	2.00
(20)	Biff Pocoroba	1.00	.70	.40
(21)	Rafael Ramirez	1.25	.90	.50
(22)	Jerry Royster	1.00	.70	.40
(23)	Ken Smith	1.00	.70	.40
(24)	Bob Walk	1.00	.70	.40
(25)	Claudell Washington	1.25	.90	.50
(26)	Bob Watson	1.00	.70	.40
(27)	Larry Whisenton	1.00	.70	.40

1982 Burger King Indians

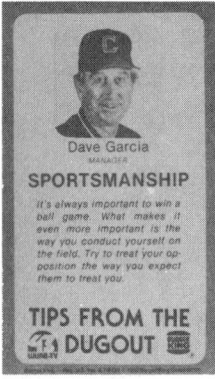

The 1982 Burger King Indians set was sponsored by WUAB-TV and Burger Kings in the Cleveland vicinity. The cards' green borders encompass a large yellow area which contains a black and white photo plus a baseball tip. Manager Dave Garcia and his four coaches provide the baseball hints. The cards, which measure 3" x 5", are unnumbered and blank-backed.

		MT	NR MT	EX
Complete Set:		4.00	2.95	2.20
Common Player:		.30	.22	.17
(1)	Dave Garcia (Be In The Game)	.30	.25	.15
(2)	Dave Garcia (Sportsmanship)	.30	.25	.15
(3)	Johnny Goryl (Rounding The Bases)	.30	.25	.15
(4)	Johnny Goryl (3rd Base Running)	.30	.25	.15
(5)	Tom McCraw (Follow Thru)	.30	.25	.15
(6)	Tom McCraw (Selecting A Bat)	.30	.25	.15
(7)	Tom McCraw (Watch The Ball)	.30	.25	.15
(8)	Mel Queen (Master One Pitch)	.30	.25	.15
(9)	Mel Queen (Warm Up)	.30	.25	.15
(10)	Dennis Sommers (Get Down On A Ground Ball)	.30	.25	.15
(11)	Dennis Sommers (Protect Your Fingers)	.30	.25	.15
(12)	Dennis Sommers (Tagging First Base)	.30	.25	.15

1986 Burger King

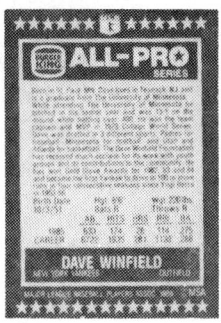

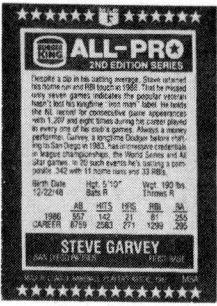

and, as with many MSA issues, all team insignias have been airbrushed away.

Burger King restaurants in the Pennsylvania and New Jersey areas issued a 20-card set entitled "All-Pro Series". The cards were issued with the purchase of a Whopper sandwich and came in folded panels of two cards each, along with a coupon card. The card fronts feature a color photo and contain the player's name, team and position plus the Burger King logo. Due to a licensing problem, the team insignias on the players' caps have been airbrushed away. The card backs feature black print on white stock and contain brief biographical and statistical information.

		MT	NR MT	EX
Complete Panel Set:		10.00	7.50	4.00
Complete Singles Set:		6.00	4.50	2.50
Common Panel		.75	.60	.30
Common Single Player		.10	.08	.04
Panel		1.00	.70	.40
1	Tony Pena	.10	.08	.04
2	Dave Winfield	.20	.15	.08
Panel		2.00	1.50	.80
3	Fernando Valenzuela	.20	.15	.08
4	Pete Rose	.50	.40	.20
Panel		1.50	1.25	.60
5	Mike Schmidt	.40	.30	.15
6	Steve Carlton	.30	.25	.12
Panel		.70	.50	.30
7	Glenn Wilson	.10	.08	.04
8	Jim Rice	.25	.20	.10
Panel		1.25	.90	.50
9	Wade Boggs	.40	.30	.15
10	Juan Samuel	.10	.08	.04
Panel		1.50	1.25	.60
11	Dale Murphy	.40	.30	.15
12	Reggie Jackson	.30	.25	.12
Panel		1.25	.90	.50
13	Kirk Gibson	.20	.15	.08
14	Eddie Murray	.30	.25	.12
Panel		1.00	.70	.40
15	Cal Ripken, Jr.	.30	.25	.12
16	Willie McGee	.10	.08	.04
Panel		1.50	1.25	.60
17	Dwight Gooden	.40	.30	.15
18	Steve Garvey	.25	.20	.10
Panel		2.50	2.00	1.00
19	Don Mattingly	1.00	.70	.40
20	George Brett	.40	.30	.15

1987 Burger King

The 1987 Burger King "All-Pro 2nd Edition Series" set was part of a giveaway promotion at participating Burger King restaurants. The set is comprised of 20 players on 10 different panels. The cards measure 2½" by 3½" each with a 3-card panel (includes a coupon card) measuring 7⅝" by 3½". The card fronts feature a full-color photo and the Burger King logo surrounded by a blue star and stripes border. The backs contain black print on white stock and carry a brief player biography and 1986 and career statistics. The set was produced by Mike Schecter Associates

		MT	NR MT	EX
Complete Panel Set:		6.00	4.50	2.50
Complete Singles Set:		2.00	1.50	.80
Common Panel:		.25	.20	.10
Common Single Player:		.05	.04	.02
Panel		.90	.70	.35
1	Wade Boggs	.20	.15	.08
2	Gary Carter	.15	.11	.06
Panel		1.00	.70	.40
3	Will Clark	.25	.20	.10
4	Roger Clemens	.20	.15	.08
Panel		.50	.40	.20
5	Steve Garvey	.15	.11	.06
6	Ron Darling	.08	.06	.03
Panel		.25	.20	.10
7	Pedro Guerrero	.08	.06	.03
8	Von Hayes	.05	.04	.02
Panel		.60	.45	.25
9	Rickey Henderson	.15	.11	.06
10	Keith Hernandez	.12	.09	.05
Panel		.60	.45	.25
11	Wally Joyner	.20	.15	.08
12	Mike Krukow	.05	.04	.02
Panel		1.00	.70	.40
13	Don Mattingly	.30	.25	.12
14	Ozzie Smith	.08	.06	.03
Panel		.50	.40	.20
15	Tony Pena	.05	.04	.02
16	Jim Rice	.15	.11	.06
Panel		.80	.60	.30
17	Ryne Sandberg	.15	.11	.06
18	Mike Schmidt	.15	.11	.06
Panel		.70	.50	.30
19	Fernando Valenzuela	.12	.09	.05
20	Darryl Strawberry	.15	.11	.06

1933 Butter Cream

The 1933 Butter Cream set consists of 29 unnumbered, black and white cards which measure 1¼" by 3½" size. The card backs feature a contest sponsored by the Butter Cream Confectionary Corp. in which the collector was to estimate the players' statistics by a specific date. Two different backs are known - 1) estimate through Sept. 1 and no company address and 2) estimate through Oct.1 with the Butter Cream address. The ACC designation for the set is R306.

		NR MT	EX	VG
Complete Set:		8000.00	4000.00	2400.
Common Player:		200.00	100.00	60.00
(1)	Earl Averill	325.00	162.00	97.00
(2)	Ed. Brandt	200.00	100.00	60.00
(3)	Guy T. Bush	200.00	100.00	60.00
(4)	Gordon Cochrane	400.00	200.00	120.00
(5)	Joe Cronin	400.00	200.00	120.00
(6)	George Earnshaw	200.00	100.00	60.00
(7)	Wesley Ferrell	200.00	100.00	60.00
(8)	"Jimmy" E. Foxx	500.00	250.00	150.00
(9)	Frank C. Frisch	400.00	200.00	120.00
(10)	Charles M. Gelbert	200.00	100.00	60.00

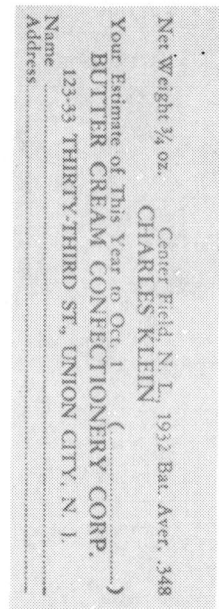

		NR MT	EX	VG
(11)	"Lefty" Robert M. Grove	400.00	200.00	120.00
(12)	Leo Charles Hartnett	325.00	162.00	97.00
(13)	"Babe" Herman	225.00	112.00	67.00
(14)	Charles Klein	325.00	162.00	97.00
(15)	Ray Kremer	200.00	100.00	60.00
(16)	Fred C. Linstrom (Lindstrom)	325.00	162.00	97.00
(17)	Ted A. Lyons	325.00	162.00	97.00
(18)	"Pepper" John L. Martin	225.00	112.00	67.00
(19)	Robert O'Farrell	200.00	100.00	60.00
(20)	Ed. A. Rommel	200.00	100.00	60.00
(21)	Charles Root	200.00	100.00	60.00
(22)	Harold "Muddy" Ruel	200.00	100.00	60.00
(23)	"Al" Simmons	325.00	162.00	97.00
(24)	"Bill" Terry	400.00	200.00	120.00
(25)	George E. Uhle	200.00	100.00	60.00
(26)	Lloyd J. Waner	325.00	162.00	97.00
(27)	Paul G. Waner	325.00	162.00	97.00
(28)	"Hack" Wilson	325.00	162.00	97.00
(29)	Glen. Wright	200.00	100.00	60.00

1986 CBS Radio Sports

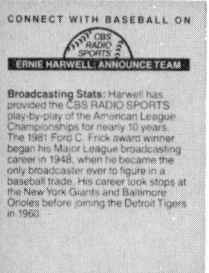

For the second consecutive year, CBS Radio Sports issued a 5-card set featuring announcers used by the network for the Game of the Week and post-season broadcasts. The cards, which were included in a custom-designed wrapper, were sent to CBS radio affiliates as part of a promotion for the Game of the Week. The color cards measure 2½'' by 3½'' in size.

		MT	NR MT	EX
Complete Set:		5.00	3.70	2.75
Common Player:		.50	.37	.28
(1)	Sparky Anderson	2.50	2.00	1.50
(2)	Jack Buck	.60	.45	.35
(3)	Howard David	.50	.40	.30
(4)	Ernie Harwell	.60	.45	.35
(5)	Ted Robinson	.50	.40	.30

1986 Cain's Potato Chips Tigers

For the second year in a row, player discs of the Detroit Tigers were found in boxes of Cain's Potato Chips sold in the Detroit area. Twenty discs make up the set which is branded as a "1986 Annual Collectors' Edition". The discs, which measure 2¾'' in diameter, have fronts which contain a color photo plus the player's name, team and position. The Cain's logo and the Major League Baseball Players Association's logo also appear on the cards' fronts. The backs, which display black print on white stock, contain player information plus the card number.

		MT	NR MT	EX
Complete Set:		40.00	30.00	16.00
Common Player:		1.00	.70	.40
1	Tom Brookens	1.00	.70	.40
2	Willie Hernandez	1.50	1.25	.60
3	Dave Bergman	1.00	.70	.40
4	Lou Whitaker	3.50	2.75	1.50
5	Dave LaPoint	1.00	.70	.40
6	Lance Parrish	3.50	2.75	1.50
7	Randy O'Neal	1.00	.70	.40
8	Nelson Simmons	1.00	.70	.40
9	Larry Herndon	1.50	1.25	.60
10	Doug Flynn	1.00	.70	.40
11	Jack Morris	3.50	2.75	1.50
12	Dan Petry	1.50	1.25	.60
13	Walt Terrell	1.50	1.25	.60
14	Chet Lemon	1.50	1.25	.60
15	Frank Tanana	1.50	1.25	.60
16	Kirk Gibson	3.50	2.75	1.50
17	Darrell Evans	2.75	2.00	1.00
18	Dave Collins	1.00	.70	.40
19	John Grubb	1.00	.70	.40
20	Alan Trammell	4.00	3.00	1.50

NOTE: A card number in parentheses ( ) indicates the set is unnumbered.

1987 Cain's Potato Chips Tigers

Player discs of the Detroit Tigers were inserted in boxes of Cain's Potato Chips for the third consecutive year. The 1987 edition is made up of 20 round cards, each measuring 2¾'' in diameter. The discs, which were packaged in a cellophane wrapper, feature a full-color photo surrounded by an orange border. The backs are printed in red on white stock. The set was produced by Mike Schecter and Associates.

		MT	NR MT	EX
Complete Set:		20.00	15.00	8.00
Common Player:		.60	.45	.25
1	Tom Brookens	.60	.45	.25
2	Darnell Coles	.75	.60	.30
3	Mike Heath	.60	.45	.25
4	Dave Bergman	.60	.45	.25
5	Dwight Lowry	.60	.45	.25
6	Darrell Evans	1.25	.90	.50
7	Alan Trammell	2.50	2.00	1.00
8	Lou Whitaker	2.00	1.50	.80
9	Kirk Gibson	2.50	2.00	1.00
10	Chet Lemon	.75	.60	.30
11	Larry Herndon	.60	.45	.25
12	John Grubb	.60	.45	.25
13	Willie Hernandez	.75	.60	.30
14	Jack Morris	2.00	1.50	.80
15	Dan Petry	.75	.60	.30
16	Walt Terrell	.75	.60	.30
17	Mark Thurmond	.60	.45	.25
18	Pat Sheridan	.60	.45	.25
19	Eric King	.75	.60	.30
20	Frank Tanana	.75	.60	.30

1984 Cereal Series

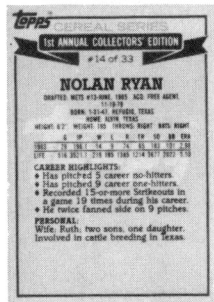

The Topps-produced 1984 Cereal Series set is identical to the Ralston Purina set from the same year in nearly all aspects. On the card fronts the words "Ralston Purina Company" have been replaced by "Cereal Series" and Topps logos have been substituted for Ralston checkerboard logos. The set is comprised of 33 cards, each measuring 2½'' by 3½.'' The cards were inserted in unmarked boxes of Chex brand cereals.

		MT	NR MT	EX
Complete Set		10.00	7.50	4.00
Common Player		.20	.15	.08
1	Eddie Murray	.70	.50	.30
2	Ozzie Smith	.30	.25	.12
3	Ted Simmons	.20	.15	.08
4	Pete Rose	1.00	.70	.40
5	Greg Luzinski	.20	.15	.08
6	Andre Dawson	.30	.25	.12
7	Dave Winfield	.50	.40	.20
8	Tom Seaver	.50	.40	.20
9	Jim Rice	.50	.40	.20
10	Fernando Valenzuela	.40	.30	.15
11	Wade Boggs	1.25	.90	.50
12	Dale Murphy	.90	.70	.35
13	George Brett	.90	.70	.35
14	Nolan Ryan	.50	.40	.20
15	Rickey Henderson	.70	.50	.30
16	Steve Carlton	.50	.40	.20
17	Rod Carew	.60	.45	.25
18	Steve Garvey	.50	.40	.20
19	Reggie Jackson	.60	.45	.25
20	Dave Concepcion	.20	.15	.08
21	Robin Yount	.40	.30	.15
22	Mike Schmidt	.90	.70	.35
23	Jim Palmer	.40	.30	.15
24	Bruce Sutter	.20	.15	.08
25	Dan Quisenberry	.20	.15	.08
26	Bill Madlock	.20	.15	.08
27	Cecil Cooper	.20	.15	.08
28	Gary Carter	.50	.40	.20
29	Fred Lynn	.30	.25	.12
30	Pedro Guerrero	.30	.25	.12
31	Ron Guidry	.30	.25	.12
32	Keith Hernandez	.40	.30	.15
33	Carlton Fisk	.30	.25	.12

1985 Circle K

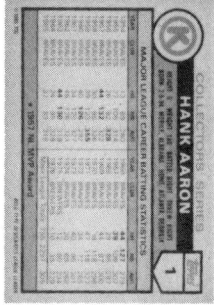

Produced by Topps for Circle K stores, this 33-card set was entitled "Baseball All Time Home Run Kings". The cards, which measure 2½'' by 3½'', are numbered on the back according to the player's position on the all-time career home run list. Joe DiMaggio, who ranked 31st, was not included in the set. The set is skip-numbered from 30 to 32. The glossy card fronts contain the player's name in the lower left corner and feature a color photo, although black and white photos were utilized for a few of the homer kings who played before 1960. The card backs have blue and red print on white stock and contain the player's career batting statistics. The set was issued with a specially designed box.

		MT	NR MT	EX
Complete Set:		7.00	5.25	2.75
Common Player:		.15	.11	.06
1	Hank Aaron	.50	.40	.20
2	Babe Ruth	.90	.70	.35
3	Willie Mays	.50	.40	.20
4	Frank Robinson	.25	.20	.10
5	Harmon Killebrew	.25	.20	.10
6	Mickey Mantle	1.50	1.25	.60
7	Jimmie Foxx	.25	.20	.10

		MT	NR MT	EX
8	Willie McCovey	.25	.20	.10
9	Ted Williams	.50	.40	.20
10	Ernie Banks	.25	.20	.10
11	Eddie Mathews	.25	.20	.10
12	Mel Ott	.20	.15	.08
13	Reggie Jackson	.30	.25	.12
14	Lou Gehrig	.50	.40	.20
15	Stan Musial	.50	.40	.20
16	Willie Stargell	.20	.15	.08
17	Carl Yastrzemski	.50	.40	.20
18	Billy Williams	.20	.15	.08
19	Mike Schmidt	.40	.30	.15
20	Duke Snider	.40	.30	.15
21	Al Kaline	.25	.20	.10
22	Johnny Bench	.30	.25	.12
23	Frank Howard	.15	.11	.06
24	Orlando Cepeda	.15	.11	.06
25	Norm Cash	.15	.11	.06
26	Dave Kingman	.15	.11	.06
27	Rocky Colavito	.15	.11	.06
28	Tony Perez	.15	.11	.06
29	Gil Hodges	.20	.15	.08
30	Ralph Kiner	.20	.15	.08
32	Johnny Mize	.20	.15	.08
33	Yogi Berra	.30	.25	.12
34	Lee May	.15	.11	.06

1987 Classic Baseball

 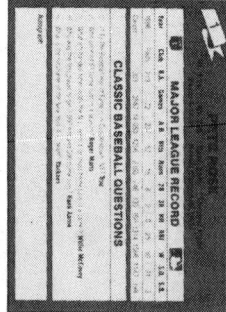

Pete Rose

The "Classic Major League Baseball Board Game" set consists of 100 full-color cards which are used to play the game. Game participants are required to answer trivia questions found on the backs of the cards. The attractive cards measure 2½" by 3½" and are printed on glossy card stock. The card backs carry the player's career statistics besides the Classic Baseball Questions. The game was produced by Game Time, Ltd. of Marietta, Ga. and sold for $19.95 in most retail outlets.

		MT	NR MT	EX
Complete Set:		16.00	12.00	6.50
Common Player:		.08	.06	.03
1	Pete Rose	.60	.45	.25
2	Len Dykstra	.15	.11	.06
3	Darryl Strawberry	.70	.50	.30
4	Keith Hernandez	.40	.30	.15
5	Gary Carter	.50	.40	.20
6	Wally Joyner	1.25	.90	.50
7	Andres Thomas	.15	.11	.06
8	Pat Dodson	.15	.11	.06
9	Kirk Gibson	.30	.25	.12
10	Don Mattingly	1.50	1.25	.60
11	Dave Winfield	.40	.30	.15
12	Rickey Henderson	.60	.45	.25
13	Dan Pasqua	.15	.11	.06
14	Don Baylor	.15	.11	.06
15	Bo Jackson	1.00	.70	.40
16	Pete Incaviglia	.70	.50	.30
17	Kevin Bass	.08	.06	.03
18	Barry Larkin	.40	.30	.15
19	Dave Magadan	.40	.30	.15
20	Steve Sax	.20	.15	.08
21	Eric Davis	1.25	.90	.50

		MT	NR MT	EX
22	Mike Pagliarulo	.15	.11	.06
23	Fred Lynn	.20	.15	.08
24	Reggie Jackson	.50	.40	.20
25	Larry Parrish	.08	.06	.03
26	Tony Gwynn	.60	.45	.25
27	Steve Garvey	.40	.30	.15
28	Glenn Davis	.20	.15	.08
29	Tim Raines	.40	.30	.15
30	Vince Coleman	.20	.15	.08
31	Willie McGee	.15	.11	.06
32	Ozzie Smith	.20	.15	.08
33	Dave Parker	.25	.20	.10
34	Tony Pena	.08	.06	.03
35	Ryne Sandberg	.30	.25	.12
36	Brett Butler	.08	.06	.03
37	Dale Murphy	.70	.50	.30
38	Bob Horner	.20	.15	.08
39	Pedro Guerrero	.25	.20	.10
40	Brook Jacoby	.15	.11	.06
41	Carlton Fisk	.20	.15	.08
42	Harold Baines	.15	.11	.06
43	Rob Deer	.15	.11	.06
44	Robin Yount	.30	.25	.12
45	Paul Molitor	.15	.11	.06
46	Jose Canseco	1.25	.90	.50
47	George Brett	.70	.50	.30
48	Jim Presley	.15	.11	.06
49	Rich Gedman	.08	.06	.03
50	Lance Parrish	.20	.15	.08
51	Eddie Murray	.50	.40	.20
52	Cal Ripken, Jr.	.50	.40	.20
53	Kent Hrbek	.25	.20	.10
54	Gary Gaetti	.20	.15	.08
55	Kirby Puckett	.50	.40	.20
56	George Bell	.50	.40	.20
57	Tony Fernandez	.20	.15	.08
58	Jesse Barfield	.20	.15	.08
59	Jim Rice	.40	.30	.15
60	Wade Boggs	1.25	.90	.50
61	Marty Barrett	.08	.06	.03
62	Mike Schmidt	.70	.50	.30
63	Von Hayes	.15	.11	.06
64	Jeff Leonard	.08	.06	.03
65	Chris Brown	.15	.11	.06
66	Dave Smith	.08	.06	.03
67	Mike Krukow	.08	.06	.03
68	Ron Guidry	.20	.15	.08
69	Rob Woodward	.15	.11	.06
70	Rob Murphy	.15	.11	.06
71	Andres Galarraga	.15	.11	.06
72	Dwight Gooden	.90	.70	.35
73	Bob Ojeda	.08	.06	.03
74	Sid Fernandez	.15	.11	.06
75	Jesse Orosco	.08	.06	.03
76	Roger McDowell	.15	.11	.06
77	John Tutor (Tudor)	.15	.11	.06
78	Tom Browning	.08	.06	.03
79	Rick Aguilera	.15	.11	.06
80	Lance McCullers	.15	.11	.06
81	Mike Scott	.20	.15	.08
82	Nolan Ryan	.30	.25	.12
83	Bruce Hurst	.08	.06	.03
84	Roger Clemens	.70	.50	.30
85	Oil Can Boyd	.08	.06	.03
86	Dave Righetti	.20	.15	.08
87	Dennis Rasmussen	.08	.06	.03
88	Bret Saberhagen (Saberhagen)	.25	.20	.10
89	Mark Langston	.15	.11	.06
90	Jack Morris	.15	.11	.06
91	Fernando Valenzuela	.25	.20	.10
92	Orel Hershiser	.15	.11	.06
93	Rick Honeycutt	.08	.06	.03
94	Jeff Reardon	.15	.11	.06
95	John Habyan	.08	.06	.03
96	Goose Gossage	.20	.15	.08
97	Todd Worrell	.20	.15	.08
98	Floyd Youmans	.15	.11	.06
99	Don Aase	.08	.06	.03
100	John Franco	.15	.11	.06

1987 Classic Baseball
Travel Edition

Game Time, Ltd. of Marietta, Ga. issued as an update to their Classic Baseball Board Game a 50-card set entitled "Travel Edition." The cards measure 2½" by 3½" and feature the same outstanding qual-

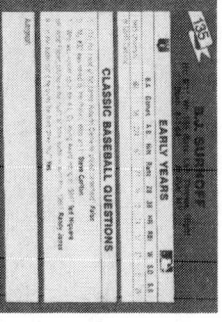

1981 Coca-Cola

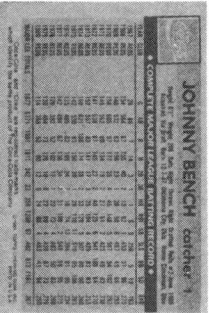

ity characteristic of the first release. Numbered from 101 to 150, the "Travel Edition" is an extension of the original set. Besides updating player trades and show-casing rookies, the set offers several highlights from the 1987 season including Andre Dawson's beaning. All new trivia questions are contained on the card backs.

		MT	NR MT	EX
Complete Set:		7.00	5.25	2.75
Common Player:		.08	.06	.03
101	Mike Schmidt	.70	.50	.30
102	Eric Davis	1.25	.90	.50
103	Pete Rose	.60	.45	.25
104	Don Mattingly	1.50	1.25	.60
105	Wade Boggs	1.25	.90	.50
106	Dale Murphy	.70	.50	.30
107	Glenn Davis	.20	.15	.08
108	Wally Joyner	1.25	.90	.50
109	Bo Jackson	1.00	.70	.40
110	Cory Snyder	.70	.50	.30
111	Jim Lindeman	.25	.20	.10
112	Kirby Puckett	.50	.40	.20
113	Barry Bonds	.40	.30	.15
114	Roger Clemens	.70	.50	.30
115	Oddibe McDowell	.20	.15	.08
116	Bret Saberhagen	.25	.20	.10
117	Joe Magrane	.40	.30	.15
118	Scott Fletcher	.08	.06	.03
119	Mark McLemore	.08	.06	.03
120	Who Me? (Joe Niekro)	.30	.25	.12
121	Mark McGwire	1.50	1.25	.60
122	Darryl Strawberry	.70	.50	.30
123	Mike Scott	.20	.15	.08
124	Andre Dawson	.50	.40	.20
125	Jose Canseco	1.25	.90	.50
126	Kevin McReynolds	.20	.15	.08
127	Joe Carter	.20	.15	.08
128	Casey Candaele	.15	.11	.06
129	Matt Nokes	1.00	.70	.40
130	Kal Daniels	.70	.50	.30
131	Pete Incaviglia	.80	.60	.30
132	Benito Santiago	.50	.40	.20
133	Barry Larkin	.40	.30	.15
134	Gary Pettis	.08	.06	.03
135	B.J. Surhoff	.70	.50	.30
136	Juan Nieves	.20	.15	.08
137	Jim Deshaies	.20	.15	.08
138	Pete O'Brien	.15	.11	.06
139	Kevin Seitzer	1.50	1.25	.60
140	Devon White	.70	.50	.30
141	Rob Deer	.15	.11	.06
142	Kurt Stillwell	.30	.25	.12
143	Edwin Correa	.25	.20	.10
144	Dion James	.15	.11	.06
145	Danny Tartabull	.30	.25	.12
146	Jerry Browne	.15	.11	.06
147	Ted Higuera	.20	.15	.08
148	Jack Clark	.20	.15	.08
149	Ruben Sierra	1.00	.70	.40
150	McGwire/Davis (Eric Davis, Mark McGwire)	1.50	1.25	.60

Definitions for grading conditions are located in the Introduction of this price guide.

In 1981, Topps produced for Coca-Cola, 12-card sets for eleven various American and National League teams. The sets include eleven player cards and one unnumbered header card. The card fronts, which measure 2½" by 3½", are identical in style to the 1981 Topps regular issue save for the Coca-Cola logo. The backs differ only from the '81 Topps regular set in that they are numbered 1-11 and and carry the Coca-Cola trademark and copyright line. The backs of the header cards contain an offer for 132-card uncut sheets of 1981 Topps baseball cards.

		MT	NR MT	EX
Complete Set:		18.00	13.50	7.25
Common Player:		.06	.05	.02
Boston Red Sox				
1	Tom Burgmeier	.06	.05	.02
2	Dennis Eckersley	.10	.08	.04
3	Dwight Evans	.60	.45	.25
4	Bob Stanley	.10	.08	.04
5	Glenn Hoffman	.06	.05	.02
6	Carney Lansford	.20	.15	.08
7	Frank Tanana	.10	.08	.04
8	Tony Perez	.20	.15	.08
9	Jim Rice	1.25	.90	.50
10	Dave Stapleton	.06	.05	.02
11	Carl Yastrzemski	1.50	1.25	.60
---	Header Card	.03	.02	.01
Chicago Cubs				
1	Tim Blackwell	.06	.05	.02
2	Bill Buckner	.15	.11	.06
3	Ivan DeJesus	.06	.05	.02
4	Leon Durham	.20	.15	.08
5	Steve Henderson	.06	.05	.02
6	Mike Krukow	.10	.08	.04
7	Ken Reitz	.06	.05	.02
8	Rick Reuschel	.15	.11	.06
9	Scot Thompson	.06	.05	.02
10	Dick Tidrow	.06	.05	.02
11	Mike Tyson	.06	.05	.02
---	Header Card	.03	.02	.01
Chicago White Sox				
1	Britt Burns	.10	.08	.04
2	Todd Cruz	.06	.05	.02
3	Rich Dotson	.20	.15	.08
4	Jim Essian	.06	.05	.02
5	Ed Farmer	.06	.05	.02
6	Lamar Johnson	.06	.05	.02
7	Ron LeFlore	.10	.08	.04
8	Chet Lemon	.10	.08	.04
9	Bob Molinaro	.06	.05	.02
10	Jim Morrison	.06	.05	.02
11	Wayne Nordhagen	.06	.05	.02
---	Header Card	.03	.02	.01
Cincinnati Reds				
1	Johnny Bench	.80	.60	.30
2	Dave Collins	.10	.08	.04
3	Dave Concepcion	.15	.11	.06
4	Dan Driessen	.10	.08	.04
5	George Foster	.25	.20	.10
6	Ken Griffey	.15	.11	.06

		MT	NR MT	EX
7	Tom Hume	.06	.05	.02
8	Ray Knight	.10	.08	.04
9	Ron Oester	.06	.05	.02
10	Tom Seaver	.70	.50	.30
11	Mario Soto	.10	.08	.04
---	Header Card	.03	.02	.01

Detroit Tigers

1	Champ Summers	.06	.05	.02
2	Al Cowens	.06	.05	.02
3	Rich Hebner	.06	.05	.02
4	Steve Kemp	.10	.08	.04
5	Aurelio Lopez	.06	.05	.02
6	Jack Morris	.35	.25	.14
7	Lance Parrish	.35	.25	.14
8	Johnny Wockenfuss	.06	.05	.02
9	Alan Trammell	.50	.40	.20
10	Lou Whitaker	.35	.25	.14
11	Kirk Gibson	.40	.30	.15
---	Header Card	.03	.02	.01

Houston Astros

1	Alan Ashby	.06	.05	.02
2	Cesar Cedeno	.15	.11	.06
3	Jose Cruz	.15	.11	.06
4	Art Howe	.06	.05	.02
5	Rafael Landestoy	.06	.05	.02
6	Joe Niekro	.15	.11	.06
7	Terry Puhl	.06	.05	.02
8	J.R. Richard	.15	.11	.06
9	Nolan Ryan	.60	.45	.25
10	Joe Sambito	.06	.05	.02
11	Don Sutton	.35	.25	.14
---	Header Card	.03	.02	.01

Kansas City Royals

1	Willie Aikens	.06	.05	.02
2	George Brett	1.50	1.25	.60
3	Larry Gura	.06	.05	.02
4	Dennis Leonard	.10	.08	.04
5	Hal McRae	.15	.11	.06
6	Amos Otis	.10	.08	.04
7	Dan Quisenberry	.20	.15	.08
8	U.L. Washington	.06	.05	.02
9	John Wathan	.10	.08	.04
10	Frank White	.10	.08	.04
11	Willie Wilson	.15	.11	.06
---	Header Card	.03	.02	.01

New York Mets

1	Neil Allen	.06	.05	.02
2	Doug Flynn	.06	.05	.02
3	Dave Kingman	.15	.11	.06
4	Randy Jones	.06	.05	.02
5	Pat Zachry	.06	.05	.02
6	Lee Mazzilli	.10	.08	.04
7	Rusty Staub	.15	.11	.06
8	Craig Swan	.06	.05	.02
9	Frank Taveras	.06	.05	.02
10	Alex Trevino	.06	.05	.02
11	Joel Youngblood	.06	.05	.02
---	Header Card	.03	.02	.01

Philadelphia Phillies

1	Bob Boone	.10	.08	.04
2	Larry Bowa	.15	.11	.06
3	Steve Carlton	.60	.45	.25
4	Greg Luzinski	.15	.11	.06
5	Garry Maddox	.10	.08	.04
6	Bake McBride	.06	.05	.02
7	Tug McGraw	.15	.11	.06
8	Pete Rose	2.00	1.50	.80
9	Mike Schmidt	1.50	1.25	.60
10	Lonnie Smith	.10	.08	.04
11	Manny Trillo	.10	.08	.04
---	Header Card	.03	.02	.01

Pittsburgh Pirates

1	Jim Bibby	.06	.05	.02
2	John Candelaria	.10	.08	.04
3	Mike Easler	.10	.08	.04
4	Tim Foli	.06	.05	.02
5	Phil Garner	.06	.05	.02
6	Bill Madlock	.15	.11	.06
7	Omar Moreno	.06	.05	.02
8	Ed Ott	.06	.05	.02
9	Dave Parker	.35	.25	.14
10	Willie Stargell	.40	.30	.15
11	Kent Tekulve	.10	.08	.04
---	Header Card	.03	.02	.01

St. Louis Cardinals

		MT	NR MT	EX
1	Bob Forsch	.10	.08	.04
2	George Hendrick	.10	.08	.04
3	Keith Hernandez	.45	.35	.20
4	Tom Herr	.15	.11	.06
5	Sixto Lezcano	.06	.05	.02
6	Ken Oberkfell	.10	.08	.04
7	Darrell Porter	.10	.08	.04
8	Tony Scott	.06	.05	.02
9	Lary Sorensen	.06	.05	.02
10	Bruce Sutter	.15	.11	.06
11	Garry Templeton	.15	.11	.06
---	Header Card	.03	.02	.01

1982 Coca-Cola Reds

 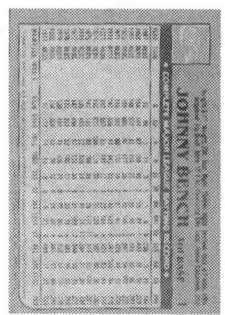

Produced by Topps for Coca-Cola, the set consists of 23 cards featuring the Cincinnati Reds and was distributed in the Cincinnati area. The cards, which are 2½'' by 3½'' in size, are identical in design to the regular 1982 Topps set but have a Coca-Cola logo on the fronts and red backs. An unnumbered header is included in the set.

		MT	NR MT	EX
	Complete Set:	5.00	3.75	2.00
	Common Player:	.08		
1	Johnny Bench	1.00	.70	.40
2	Bruce Berenyi	.08	.06	.03
3	Larry Biittner	.08	.06	.03
4	Cesar Cedeno	.15	.11	.06
5	Dave Concepcion	.25	.20	.10
6	Dan Driessen	.15	.11	.06
7	Greg Harris	.08	.06	.03
8	Paul Householder	.08	.06	.03
9	Tom Hume	.08	.06	.03
10	Clint Hurdle	.08	.06	.03
11	Jim Kern	.08	.06	.03
12	Wayne Krenchicki	.08	.06	.03
13	Rafael Landestoy	.08	.06	.03
14	Charlie Leibrandt	.15	.11	.06
15	Mike O'Berry	.08	.06	.03
16	Ron Oester	.08	.06	.03
17	Frank Pastore	.08	.06	.03
18	Joe Price	.08	.06	.03
19	Tom Seaver	1.00	.70	.40
20	Mario Soto	.20	.15	.08
21	Alex Trevino	.08	.06	.03
22	Mike Vail	.08	.06	.03
---	Header Card	.04	.03	.02

1982 Coca-Cola/Brigham's Red Sox

Coca-Cola, in conjunction with Brigham's Ice Cream stores, issued a 23-card set in the Boston area featuring Red Sox players. The Topps-produced cards, which measure 2½'' by 3½'', are identical in style to the regular 1982 Topps set but contain the Coca-Cola and Brigham's logos in the corners. The

cards were distributed in three-card cello packs including a unnumbered header card.

		MT	NR MT	EX
Complete Set:		5.00	3.75	2.00
Common Player:		.08	.06	.03
1	Gary Allenson	.08	.06	.03
2	Tom Burgmeier	.08	.06	.03
3	Mark Clear	.15	.11	.06
4	Steve Crawford	.08	.06	.03
5	Dennis Eckersley	.15	.11	.06
6	Dwight Evans	.80	.60	.30
7	Rich Gedman	.30	.25	.12
8	Garry Hancock	.08	.06	.03
9	Glen Hoffman (Glenn)	.08	.06	.03
10	Carney Lansford	.20	.15	.08
11	Rick Miller	.08	.06	.03
12	Reid Nichols	.08	.06	.03
13	Bob Ojeda	.30	.25	.12
14	Tony Perez	.30	.25	.12
15	Chuck Rainey	.08	.06	.03
16	Jerry Remy	.08	.06	.03
17	Jim Rice	1.00	.70	.40
18	Bob Stanley	.15	.11	.06
19	Dave Stapleton	.08	.06	.03
20	Mike Torrez	.08	.06	.03
21	John Tudor	.30	.25	.12
22	Carl Yastrzemski	1.25	.90	.50
---	Header Card	.05	.04	.02

1985 Coca-Cola White Sox

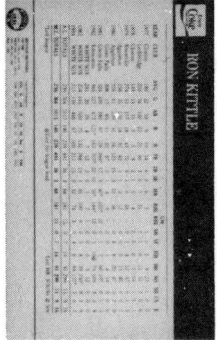

Featuring past and present White Sox players, the cards in this set were given out on Tuesday night home games. The cards, which measure 2⅝'' by 4⅛'', contain a color photo of a current Sox member. A red box at the bottom of the card carries the team logo, the player's name, uniform number and position, plus a small oval portrait of a past Sox player. The card backs contain the Coca-Cola logo and the lifetime hitting or pitching statistics for the current and past player. The set is numbered in the checklist that follows by the player's uniform number with the last three cards being unnumbered. Complete sets

were available through a fan club offer found in White Sox programs.

		MT	NR MT	EX
Complete Set:		14.00	10.50	5.50
Common Player:		.25	.20	.10
0	Oscar Gamble (Zeke Bonura)	.25	.20	.10
1	Scott Fletcher (Luke Appling)	.40	.30	.15
3	Harold Baines (Bill Melton)	.80	.60	.30
5	Luis Salazar (Chico Carrasquel)	.25	.20	.10
7	Marc Hill (Sherm Lollar)	.25	.20	.10
8	Daryl Boston (Jim Landis)	.35	.25	.14
10	Tony LaRussa (Al Lopez)	.40	.30	.15
12	Julio Cruz (Nellie Fox)	.40	.30	.15
13	Ozzie Guillen (Luis Aparicio)	.80	.60	.30
17	Jerry Hairston (Smoky Burgess)	.25	.20	.10
20	Joe DeSa (Carlos May)	.25	.20	.10
22	Joel Skinner (J.C. Martin)	.25	.20	.10
23	Rudy Law (Bill Skowron)	.25	.20	.10
24	Floyd Bannister (Red Faber)	.35	.25	.14
29	Greg Walker (Dick Allen)	.70	.50	.30
30	Gene Nelson (Early Wynn)	.35	.25	.14
32	Tim Hulett (Pete Ward)	.25	.20	.10
34	Richard Dotson (Ed Walsh)	.35	.25	.14
37	Dan Spillner (Thornton Lee)	.25	.20	.10
40	Britt Burns (Gary Peters)	.25	.20	.10
41	Tom Seaver (Ted Lyons)	.80	.60	.30
42	Ron Kittle (Minnie Minoso)	.40	.30	.15
43	Bob James (Hoyt Wilhelm)	.40	.30	.15
44	Tom Paciorek (Eddie Collins)	.35	.25	.14
46	Tim Lollar (Billy Pierce)	.25	.20	.10
50	Juan Agosto (Wilbur Wood)	.25	.20	.10
72	Carlton Fisk (Ray Schalk)	.70	.50	.30
---	Comiskey Park	.25	.20	.10
---	Ribbie and Roobarb (mascots)	.25	.20	.10
---	Nancy Faust (organist)	.25	.20	.10

1986 Coca-Cola White Sox

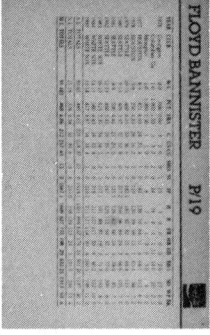

For the second year in a row, Coca-Cola, in conjunction with the Chicago White Sox, issued a 30-card set. As in 1985, cards were given out at the park on Tuesday nights games. Full sets were again available through a fan club offer found in the White Sox program. The cards, which measure 2⅝'' by 4⅛'', feature 25 players plus other White Sox personnel. The card fronts feature a color photo (an action shot in most instances) and a white bar at the bottom. A black and white bat with ''SOX'' shown on the barrel is located within the white bar, along with the player's name, position and uniform number. The white and grey backs with black print include the Coca-Cola trademark. Lifetime statistics are shown on all player cards, but there is no personal information such as height, weight or age. The non-player cards are blank-backed save for the name and logo at the top. The checklist below is numbered by the players' uniform numbers, with the last five cards of the set being unnumbered.

	MT	NR MT	EX
Complete Set:	12.00	9.00	4.75
Common Player:	.25	.20	.10

		MT	NR MT	EX
1	Wayne Tolleson	.25	.20	.10
3	Harold Baines	.60	.45	.25
7	Marc Hill	.25	.20	.10
8	Daryl Boston	.35	.25	.14
12	Julio Cruz	.25	.20	.10
13	Ozzie Guillen	.45	.35	.20
17	Jerry Hairston	.25	.20	.10
19	Floyd Bannister	.35	.25	.14
20	Reid Nichols	.25	.20	.10
22	Joel Skinner	.25	.20	.10
24	Dave Schmidt	.25	.20	.10
26	Bobby Bonilla	.40	.30	.15
29	Greg Walker	.40	.30	.15
30	Gene Nelson	.25	.20	.10
32	Tim Hulett	.25	.20	.10
33	Neil Allen	.25	.20	.10
34	Richard Dotson	.35	.25	.14
40	Joe Cowley	.25	.20	.10
41	Tom Seaver	.70	.50	.30
42	Ron Kittle	.35	.25	.14
43	Bob James	.25	.20	.10
44	John Cangelosi	.40	.30	.15
50	Juan Agosto	.25	.20	.10
52	Joel Davis	.25	.20	.10
72	Carlton Fisk	.50	.40	.20
---	Ribbie & Roobarb (mascots)	.25	.20	.10
---	Nancy Faust (organist)	.25	.20	.10
---	Ken "Hawk" Harrelson	.30	.25	.12
---	Tony LaRussa	.30	.25	.12
---	Minnie Minoso	.30	.25	.12

1987 Coca-Cola Tigers

 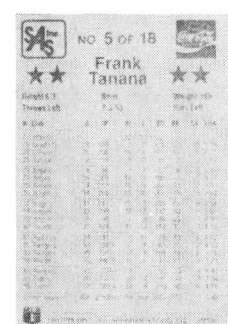

Coca-Cola and S. Abraham & Sons, Inc. issued a set of 18 baseball cards featuring members of the Detroit Tigers. The set is comprised of six 4-part folding panels. Each panel includes three player cards (each 2½'' by 3½'') and one team logo card. A bright yellow border surrounds the full-color photo. The backs are designed on a vertical format and contain personal data and career statistics. The set was produced by Mike Schecter and Associates.

		MT	NR MT	EX
Complete Set:		6.00	4.50	2.50
Complete Singles Set:		2.00	1.50	.80
Common Panel:		.60	.45	.25
Common Single Player:		.05	.04	.02
Panel		1.00	.70	.40
1	Kirk Gibson	.40	.30	.15
2	Larry Herndon	.08	.06	.03
3	Walt Terrell	.10	.08	.04
Panel		1.25	.90	.50
4	Alan Trammell	.50	.40	.20
5	Frank Tanana	.10	.08	.04
6	Pat Sheridan	.05	.04	.02
Panel		.90	.70	.35
7	Jack Morris	.30	.25	.12
8	Mike Heath	.05	.04	.02
9	Dave Bergman	.05	.04	.02
Panel		.60	.45	.25
10	Chet Lemon	.10	.08	.04
11	Dwight Lowry	.08	.06	.03
12	Dan Petry	.10	.08	.04

		MT	NR MT	EX
Panel		.80	.60	.30
13	Darrell Evans	.20	.15	.08
14	Darnell Coles	.10	.08	.04
15	Willie Hernandez	.10	.08	.04
Panel		1.00	.70	.40
16	Lou Whitaker	.30	.25	.12
17	Tom Brookens	.05	.04	.02
18	John Grubb	.05	.04	.02

1987 Coca-Cola White Sox

 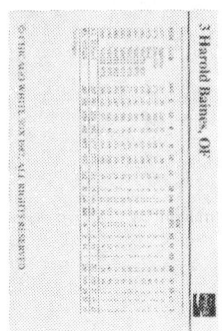

3 Harold Baines, OF

The Chicago White Sox Fan Club, in conjunction with Coca-Cola, offered members a set of 30 trading cards. For the $10 membership fee, fans received the set plus additional fan club gifts and privileges. The cards, which measure 2⅝'' by 4'', feature full-color photos inside a blue and red border. The backs include the player's name, position, uniform number and statistics. The Coca-Cola logo is also included on the card backs.

		MT	NR MT	EX
Complete Set:		12.00	9.00	4.75
Common Player:		.25	.20	.10
1	Jerry Royster	.25	.20	.10
3	Harold Baines	.60	.45	.25
5	Ron Karkovice	.30	.25	.12
8	Daryl Boston	.25	.20	.10
10	Fred Manrique	.35	.25	.14
12	Steve lyons	.25	.20	.10
13	Ozzie Guillen	.40	.30	.15
14	Russ Morman	.30	.25	.12
15	Donnie Hill	.25	.20	.10
16	Jim Fregosi	.30	.25	.12
17	Jerry Hairston	.25	.20	.10
19	Floyd Bannister	.35	.25	.14
21	Gary Redus	.30	.25	.12
22	Ivan Calderon	.40	.30	.15
25	Ron Hassey	.25	.20	.10
26	Jose DeLeon	.25	.20	.10
29	Greg Walker	.40	.30	.15
32	Tim Hulett	.25	.20	.10
33	Neil Allen	.25	.20	.10
34	Rich Dotson	.35	.25	.14
36	Ray Searage	.25	.20	.10
37	Bobby Thigpen	.35	.25	.14
40	Jim Winn	.25	.20	.10
43	Bob James	.25	.20	.10
50	Joel McKeon	.30	.25	.12
52	Joel Davis	.25	.20	.10
72	Carlton Fisk	.50	.40	.20
---	Ribbie & Roobarb (mascots)	.25	.20	.10
---	Nancy Faust (organist)	.25	.20	.10
---	Minnie Minoso	.30	.25	.12

1914 Cracker Jack

The 1914 Cracker Jack set, whose ACC designation is E145-1, is one of the most popular of the ''E'' card sets and features baseball stars from the American, National and Federal Leagues. The cards, which mea-

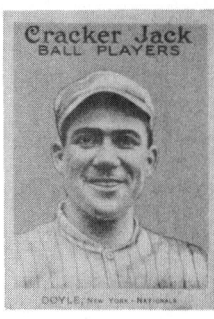
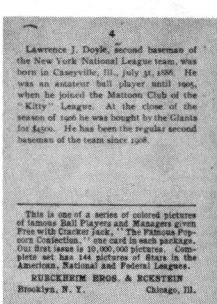

Cracker Jack
BALL PLAYERS

Lawrence J. Doyle, second baseman of the New York National League team, was born in Caseyville, Ill., July 31, 1886. He was an amateur ball player until 1905, when he joined the Mattoon Club of the "Kitty" League. At the close of the season of 1906 he was bought by the Giants for $4500. He has been the regular second baseman of the team since 1908.

This is one of a series of colored pictures of famous Ball Players and Managers given Free with Cracker Jack, "The Famous Popcorn Confection," one card in each package. Our first issue is 10,000,000 pictures. Complete set has 144 pictures of Stars in the American, National and Federal Leagues.
RUECKHEIM BROS. & ECKSTEIN
Brooklyn, N. Y.   Chicago, Ill.

DOYLE, NEW YORK—NATIONAL

sure 2¼'' by 3'' and were printed on thin stock, were found in boxes of Cracker Jack. The 1914 issue consists of 144 cards with tinted color photographs on a red background. The numbered backs feature a short biography plus an advertisement. The advertising on the low-numbered cards in the set indicate that 10 million cards were issued, while the high-numbered cards boast that 15 million were printed.

		NR MT	EX	VG
	Complete Set:	15000.00	7500.00	4500.
	Commmon Player:	60.00	30.00	18.00
1	Otto Knabe	90.00	40.00	19.50
2	Home Run Baker	90.00	45.00	27.00
3	Joe Tinker	90.00	45.00	27.00
4	Larry Doyle	65.00	32.00	19.50
5	Ward Miller	60.00	30.00	18.00
6	Eddie Plank	110.00	55.00	33.00
7	Eddie Collins	110.00	55.00	33.00
8	Rube Oldring	60.00	30.00	18.00
9	Artie Hoffman (Hofman)	60.00	30.00	18.00
10	Stuffy McInnis	60.00	30.00	18.00
11	George Stovall	60.00	30.00	18.00
12	Connie Mack	160.00	80.00	48.00
13	Art Wilson	60.00	30.00	18.00
14	Sam Crawford	90.00	45.00	27.00
15	Reb Russell	60.00	30.00	18.00
16	Howie Camnitz	60.00	30.00	18.00
17a	Roger Bresnahan (no number on back)			
		110.00	55.00	33.00
17b	Roger Bresnahan (number on back)			
		110.00	55.00	33.00
18	Johnny Evers	90.00	45.00	27.00
19	Chief Bender	110.00	55.00	33.00
20	Cy Falkenberg	60.00	30.00	18.00
21	Heinie Zimmerman	60.00	30.00	18.00
22	Smoky Joe Wood	65.00	32.00	19.50
23	Charles Comiskey	110.00	55.00	33.00
24	George Mullen (Mullin)	60.00	30.00	18.00
25	Mike Simon	60.00	30.00	18.00
26	Jim Scott	60.00	30.00	18.00
27	Bill Carrigan	60.00	30.00	18.00
28	Jack Barry	60.00	30.00	18.00
29	Vean Gregg	75.00	37.00	22.00
30	Ty Cobb	1100.00	550.00	330.00
31	Heinie Wagner	60.00	30.00	18.00
32	Mordecai Brown	90.00	45.00	27.00
33	Amos Strunk	60.00	30.00	18.00
34	Ira Thomas	60.00	30.00	18.00
35	Harry Hooper	90.00	45.00	27.00
36	Ed Walsh	90.00	45.00	27.00
37	Grover C. Alexander	160.00	80.00	48.00
38	Red Dooin	75.00	37.00	22.00
39	Chick Gandil	65.00	32.00	19.50
40	Jimmy Austin	75.00	37.00	22.00
41	Tommy Leach	60.00	30.00	18.00
42	Al Bridwell	60.00	30.00	18.00
43	Rube Marquard	110.00	55.00	33.00
44	Jeff Tesreau	60.00	30.00	18.00
45	Fred Luderus	60.00	30.00	18.00
46	Bob Groom	60.00	30.00	18.00
47	Josh Devore	75.00	37.00	22.00
48	Harry Lord	160.00	80.00	48.00
49	Dots Miller	60.00	30.00	18.00
50	John Hummell (Hummel)	60.00	30.00	18.00
51	Nap Rucker	60.00	30.00	18.00
52	Zach Wheat	90.00	45.00	27.00
53	Otto Miller	60.00	30.00	18.00
54	Marty O'Toole	60.00	30.00	18.00

		NR MT	EX	VG
55	Dick Hoblitzel (Hoblitzell)	75.00	37.00	22.00
56	Clyde Milan	60.00	30.00	18.00
57	Walter Johnson	425.00	212.00	127.00
58	Wally Schang	60.00	30.00	18.00
59	Doc Gessler	60.00	30.00	18.00
60	Rollie Zeider	160.00	80.00	48.00
61	Ray Schalk	90.00	45.00	27.00
62	Jay Cashion	160.00	80.00	48.00
63	Babe Adams	60.00	30.00	18.00
64	Jimmy Archer	60.00	30.00	18.00
65	Tris Speaker	250.00	125.00	75.00
66	Nap Lajoie	325.00	162.00	97.00
67	Doc Crandall	60.00	30.00	18.00
68	Honus Wagner	400.00	200.00	120.00
69	John McGraw	160.00	80.00	48.00
70	Fred Clarke	90.00	45.00	27.00
71	Chief Meyers	60.00	30.00	18.00
72	Joe Boehling	60.00	30.00	18.00
73	Max Carey	90.00	45.00	27.00
74	Frank Owens	60.00	30.00	18.00
75	Miller Huggins	90.00	45.00	27.00
76	Claude Hendrix	60.00	30.00	18.00
77	Hughie Jennings	90.00	45.00	27.00
78	Fred Merkle	65.00	32.00	19.50
79	Ping Bodie	60.00	30.00	18.00
80	Ed Reulbach	60.00	30.00	18.00
81	Jim Delehanty (Delahanty)	60.00	30.00	18.00
82	Gavvy Cravath	65.00	32.00	19.50
83	Russ Ford	60.00	30.00	18.00
84	Elmer Knetzer	60.00	30.00	18.00
85	Buck Herzog	60.00	30.00	18.00
86	Burt Shotten	65.00	32.00	19.50
87	Hick Cady	60.00	30.00	18.00
88	Christy Mathewson	450.00	225.00	135.00
89	Larry Cheney	60.00	30.00	18.00
90	Frank Smith	60.00	30.00	18.00
91	Roger Peckinpaugh	65.00	32.00	19.50
92	Al Demaree	75.00	37.00	22.00
93	Del Pratt	160.00	80.00	48.00
94	Eddie Cicotte	75.00	37.00	22.00
95	Ray Keating	60.00	30.00	18.00
96	Beals Becker	60.00	30.00	18.00
97	Rube Benton	60.00	30.00	18.00
98	Frank Laporte (LaPorte)	60.00	30.00	18.00
99	Frank Chance	450.00	225.00	135.00
100	Tom Seaton	60.00	30.00	18.00
101	Wildfire Schulte	60.00	30.00	18.00
102	Ray Fisher	60.00	30.00	18.00
103	Shoeless Joe Jackson	1000.00	500.00	300.00
104	Vic Saier	60.00	30.00	18.00
105	Jimmy Lavender	60.00	30.00	18.00
106	Joe Birmingham	60.00	30.00	18.00
107	Tom Downey	60.00	30.00	18.00
108	Sherry Magee	80.00	40.00	24.00
109	Fred Blanding	60.00	30.00	18.00
110	Bob Bescher	60.00	30.00	18.00
111	Nixey Callahan	160.00	80.00	48.00
112	Jeff Sweeney	60.00	30.00	18.00
113	George Suggs	60.00	30.00	18.00
114	George Moriarity (Moriarty)	60.00	30.00	18.00
115	Ad Brennan	60.00	30.00	18.00
116	Rollie Zeider	60.00	30.00	18.00
117	Ted Easterly	60.00	30.00	18.00
118	Ed Konetchy	75.00	37.00	22.00
119	George Perring	60.00	30.00	18.00
120	Mickey Doolan	60.00	30.00	18.00
121	Hub Perdue	75.00	37.00	22.00
122	Donie Bush	60.00	30.00	18.00
123	Slim Sallee	60.00	30.00	18.00
124	Earle Moore (Earl)	60.00	30.00	18.00
125	Bert Niehoff	75.00	37.00	22.00
126	Walter Blair	60.00	30.00	18.00
127	Butch Schmidt	60.00	30.00	18.00
128	Steve Evans	60.00	30.00	18.00
129	Ray Caldwell	60.00	30.00	18.00
130	Ivy Wingo	60.00	30.00	18.00
131	George Baumgardner	60.00	30.00	18.00
132	Les Nunamaker	60.00	30.00	18.00
133	Branch Rickey	160.00	80.00	48.00
134	Armando Marsans	75.00	37.00	22.00
135	Bill Killifer (Killefer)	60.00	30.00	18.00
136	Rabbit Maranville	90.00	45.00	27.00
137	Bill Rariden	60.00	30.00	18.00
138	Hank Gowdy	65.00	32.00	19.50
139	Rebel Oakes	60.00	30.00	18.00
140	Danny Murphy	60.00	30.00	18.00
141	Cy Barger	60.00	30.00	18.00
142	Gene Packard	60.00	30.00	18.00
143	Jake Daubert	75.00	32.00	19.50
144	Jimmy Walsh	90.00	30.00	18.00

1915 Cracker Jack

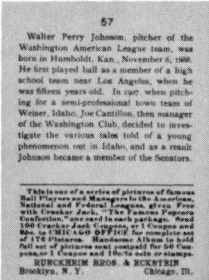

57

Walter Perry Johnson, pitcher of the Washington American League team, was born in Humboldt, Kan., November 6, 1887. He first played ball as a member of a high school team near Los Angeles, when he was fifteen years old. In 1907, when pitching for a semi-professional town team of Weiser, Idaho, Joe Cantillon, then manager of the Washington Club, decided to investigate the various talent told of a young phenomenon out in Idaho, and as a result Johnson became a member of the Senators.

This is one of a series of pictures of famous Ball Players and Managers in the American, National and Federal Leagues, given Free with Cracker Jack, "The Famous Popcorn Confection," once and in each package. Send 100 Cracker Jack Coupons, or 1 Coupon and 80c. to THE CARD OFFICE for complete set of 176 Pictures. Handsome Album to hold full set of pictures sent postpaid for 50 Coupons, or 1 Coupon and 10c. in coin or stamps. RUECKHEIM BROS. & ECKSTEIN, Brooklyn, N. Y. Chicago, Ill.

JOHNSON, WASHINGTON—BASE CARD

The 1915 Cracker Jack set (E145-2) is a re-issue of the 1914 edition with some card additions and deletions, team designation changes, and new poses. A total of 176 cards comprise the set. The deletions involve card #'s 48, 60, 62, 99 and 111. Cards can be distinguished as either 1914 or 1915 by the backs. The advertising on the backs of the 1914 cards call the set complete at 144 pictures, while the 1915 version notes 176 pictures. A complete set and an album was available from the company.

		NR MT	EX	VG
	Complete Set:	15000.00	7500.00	4500.
	Common Player: 1-144	50.00	25.00	15.00
	Common Player: 145-176	80.00	40.00	24.00
1	Otto Knabe	80.00	30.00	15.00
2	Home Run Baker	80.00	40.00	24.00
3	Joe Tinker	80.00	40.00	24.00
4	Larry Doyle	55.00	27.00	16.50
5	Ward Miller	50.00	25.00	15.00
6	Eddie Plank	100.00	50.00	30.00
7	Eddie Collins	100.00	50.00	30.00
8	Rube Oldring	50.00	25.00	15.00
9	Artie Hoffman (Hofman)	50.00	25.00	15.00
10	Stuffy McInnis	50.00	25.00	15.00
11	George Stovall	50.00	25.00	15.00
12	Connie Mack	140.00	70.00	42.00
13	Art Wilson	50.00	25.00	15.00
14	Sam Crawford	80.00	40.00	24.00
15	Reb Russell	50.00	25.00	15.00
16	Howie Camnitz	50.00	25.00	15.00
17	Roger Bresnahan	80.00	40.00	24.00
18	Johnny Evers	80.00	40.00	24.00
19	Chief Bender	100.00	50.00	30.00
20	Cy Falkenberg	50.00	25.00	15.00
21	Heinie Zimmerman	50.00	25.00	15.00
22	Smoky Joe Wood	55.00	27.00	16.50
23	Charles Comiskey	100.00	50.00	30.00
24	George Mullen (Mullin)	50.00	25.00	15.00
25	Mike Simon	50.00	25.00	15.00
26	Jim Scott	50.00	25.00	15.00
27	Bill Carrigan	50.00	25.00	15.00
28	Jack Barry	50.00	25.00	15.00
29	Vean Gregg	65.00	32.00	19.50
30	Ty Cobb	950.00	475.00	285.00
31	Heinie Wagner	50.00	25.00	15.00
32	Mordecai Brown	80.00	40.00	24.00
33	Amos Strunk	50.00	25.00	15.00
34	Ira Thomas	50.00	25.00	15.00
35	Harry Hooper	80.00	40.00	24.00
36	Ed Walsh	80.00	40.00	24.00
37	Grover C. Alexander	140.00	70.00	42.00
38	Red Dooin	65.00	32.00	19.50
39	Chick Gandil	55.00	27.00	16.50
40	Jimmy Austin	65.00	32.00	19.50
41	Tommy Leach	50.00	25.00	15.00
42	Al Bridwell	50.00	25.00	15.00
43	Rube Marquard	100.00	50.00	30.00
44	Jeff Tesreau	50.00	25.00	15.00
45	Fred Luderus	50.00	25.00	15.00
46	Bob Groom	50.00	25.00	15.00
47	Josh Devore	65.00	32.00	19.50
48	Steve O'Neill	75.00	37.00	22.00
49	Dots Miller	50.00	25.00	15.00
50	John Hummell (Hummel)	50.00	25.00	15.00
51	Nap Rucker	50.00	25.00	15.00
52	Zach Wheat	80.00	40.00	24.00

		NR MT	EX	VG
53	Otto Miller	50.00	25.00	15.00
54	Marty O'Toole	50.00	25.00	15.00
55	Dick Hoblitzel (Hoblitzell)	65.00	32.00	19.50
56	Clyde Milan	50.00	25.00	15.00
57	Walter Johnson	325.00	162.00	97.00
58	Wally Schang	50.00	25.00	15.00
59	Doc Gessler	50.00	25.00	15.00
60	Oscar Dugey	75.00	37.00	22.00
61	Ray Schalk	80.00	40.00	24.00
62	Willie Mitchell	75.00	37.00	22.00
63	Babe Adams	50.00	25.00	15.00
64	Jimmy Archer	50.00	25.00	15.00
65	Tris Speaker	200.00	100.00	60.00
66	Nap Lajoie	250.00	125.00	75.00
67	Doc Crandall	50.00	25.00	15.00
68	Honus Wagner	350.00	175.00	105.00
69	John McGraw	140.00	70.00	42.00
70	Fred Clarke	80.00	40.00	24.00
71	Chief Meyers	50.00	25.00	15.00
72	Joe Boehling	50.00	25.00	15.00
73	Max Carey	80.00	40.00	24.00
74	Frank Owens	50.00	25.00	15.00
75	Miller Huggins	80.00	40.00	24.00
76	Claude Hendrix	50.00	25.00	15.00
77	Hughie Jennings	80.00	40.00	24.00
78	Fred Merkle	60.00	30.00	18.00
79	Ping Bodie	50.00	25.00	15.00
80	Ed Reulbach	50.00	25.00	15.00
81	Jim Delehanty (Delahanty)	50.00	25.00	15.00
82	Gavvy Cravath	55.00	27.00	16.50
83	Russ Ford	50.00	25.00	15.00
84	Elmer Knetzer	50.00	25.00	15.00
85	Buck Herzog	50.00	25.00	15.00
86	Burt Shotten	55.00	27.00	16.50
87	Hick Cady	50.00	25.00	15.00
88	Christy Mathewson	400.00	200.00	120.00
89	Larry Cheney	50.00	25.00	15.00
90	Frank Smith	50.00	25.00	15.00
91	Roger Peckinpaugh	55.00	27.00	16.50
92	Al Demaree	65.00	32.00	19.50
93	Del Pratt	75.00	37.00	22.00
94	Eddie Cicotte	60.00	30.00	18.00
95	Ray Keating	50.00	25.00	15.00
96	Beals Becker	50.00	25.00	15.00
97	Rube Benton	50.00	25.00	15.00
98	Frank Laporte (LaPorte)	50.00	25.00	15.00
99	Hal Chase	125.00	62.00	37.00
100	Tom Seaton	50.00	25.00	15.00
101	Wildfire Schulte	50.00	25.00	15.00
102	Ray Fisher	50.00	25.00	15.00
103	Shoeless Joe Jackson	900.00	450.00	270.00
104	Vic Saier	50.00	25.00	15.00
105	Jimmy Lavender	50.00	25.00	15.00
106	Joe Birmingham	50.00	25.00	15.00
107	Tom Downey	50.00	25.00	15.00
108	Sherry Magee	55.00	27.00	16.50
109	Fred Blanding	50.00	25.00	15.00
110	Bob Bescher	50.00	25.00	15.00
111	Herbie Moran	75.00	37.00	22.00
112	Jeff Sweeney	50.00	25.00	15.00
113	George Suggs	50.00	25.00	15.00
114	George Moriarity (Moriarty)	50.00	25.00	15.00
115	Ad Brennan	50.00	25.00	15.00
116	Rollie Zeider	50.00	25.00	15.00
117	Ted Easterly	50.00	25.00	15.00
118	Ed Konetchy	65.00	32.00	19.50
119	George Perring	50.00	25.00	15.00
120	Mickey Doolan	50.00	25.00	15.00
121	Hub Perdue	65.00	32.00	19.50
122	Donie Bush	50.00	25.00	15.00
123	Slim Sallee	50.00	25.00	15.00
124	Earle Moore (Earl)	50.00	25.00	15.00
125	Bert Niehoff	65.00	32.00	19.50
126	Walter Blair	50.00	25.00	15.00
127	Butch Schmidt	50.00	25.00	15.00
128	Steve Evans	50.00	25.00	15.00
129	Ray Caldwell	50.00	25.00	15.00
130	Ivy Wingo	50.00	25.00	15.00
131	George Baumgardner	50.00	25.00	15.00
132	Les Nunamaker	50.00	25.00	15.00
133	Branch Rickey	140.00	70.00	42.00
134	Armando Marsans	65.00	32.00	19.50
135	Bill Killifer (Killefer)	50.00	25.00	15.00
136	Rabbit Maranville	80.00	40.00	24.00
137	Bill Rariden	50.00	25.00	15.00
138	Hank Gowdy	55.00	27.00	16.50
139	Rebel Oakes	50.00	25.00	15.00
140	Danny Murphy	50.00	25.00	15.00
141	Cy Barger	50.00	25.00	15.00
142	Gene Packard	50.00	25.00	15.00
143	Jake Daubert	55.00	27.00	16.50

		NR MT	EX	VG
144	Jimmy Walsh	50.00	25.00	15.00
145	Ted Cather	80.00	40.00	24.00
146	Lefty Tyler	80.00	40.00	24.00
147	Lee Magee	80.00	40.00	24.00
148	Owen Wilson	80.00	40.00	24.00
149	Hal Janvrin	80.00	40.00	24.00
150	Doc Johnston	80.00	40.00	24.00
151	Possum Whitted	80.00	40.00	24.00
152	George McQuillen (McQuillan)	80.00	40.00	24.00
153	Bill James	80.00	40.00	24.00
154	Dick Rudolph	80.00	40.00	24.00
155	Joe Connolly	80.00	40.00	24.00
156	Jean Dubuc	80.00	40.00	24.00
157	George Kaiserling	80.00	40.00	24.00
158	Fritz Maisel	80.00	40.00	24.00
159	Heinie Groh	80.00	40.00	24.00
160	Benny Kauff	80.00	40.00	24.00
161	Edd Rousch (Roush)	110.00	55.00	33.00
162	George Stallings	80.00	40.00	24.00
163	Bert Whaling	80.00	40.00	24.00
164	Bob Shawkey	80.00	40.00	24.00
165	Eddie Murphy	80.00	40.00	24.00
166	Bullet Joe Bush	85.00	42.00	25.00
167	Clark Griffith	110.00	55.00	33.00
168	Vin Campbell	80.00	40.00	24.00
169	Ray Collins	80.00	40.00	24.00
170	Hans Lobert	80.00	40.00	24.00
171	Earl Hamilton	80.00	40.00	24.00
172	Erskine Mayer	80.00	40.00	24.00
173	Tilly Walker	80.00	40.00	24.00
174	Bobby Veach	80.00	40.00	24.00
175	Joe Benz	90.00	40.00	24.00
176	Hippo Vaughn	110.00	50.00	24.00

		MT	NR MT	EX
Panel		3.50	2.75	2.00
9	Hank Aaron	.20	.15	.11
10	Ernie Banks	.10	.08	.06
11	Ralph Kiner	.10	.08	.06
12	Eddie Mathews	.10	.08	.06
13	Willie Mays	.20	.15	.11
14	Robin Roberts	.10	.08	.06
15	Duke Snider	.10	.08	.06
16	Warren Spahn	.10	.08	.06
---	Advertising Card	.02	.02	.01

1954 Dan-Dee Potato Chips

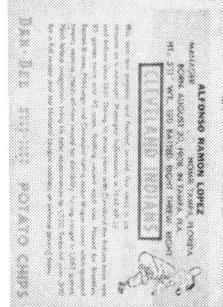

AL LOPEZ

Issued in bags of potato chips, the cards in this 29-card set are commonly found with grease stains despite their waxed surface. The unnumbered cards, which measure 2½'' by 3⅝'', feature full color photos. The card backs contain player statistical and biographical information. The set consists mostly of players from the Indians and Pirates. Photos of the Yankees players were also used for the Briggs Meats and Stahl-Meyer Franks sets. Cooper and Smith are the scarcest cards in the set.

		NR MT	EX	VG
Complete Set		4000.00	2000.00	1200.
Common Player		40.00	20.00	12.00
(1)	Bob Avila	40.00	20.00	12.00
(2)	Hank Bauer	60.00	30.00	18.00
(3)	Walker Cooper	300.00	150.00	90.00
(4)	Larry Doby	65.00	32.00	19.50
(5)	Luke Easter	50.00	25.00	15.00
(6)	Bob Feller	125.00	62.00	37.00
(7)	Bob Friend	50.00	25.00	15.00
(8)	Mike Garcia	50.00	25.00	15.00
(9)	Sid Gordon	50.00	25.00	15.00
(10)	Jim Hegan	40.00	20.00	12.00
(11)	Gil Hodges	150.00	75.00	45.00
(12)	Art Houtteman	40.00	20.00	12.00
(13)	Monte Irvin	75.00	37.00	22.00
(14)	Paul LaPalm (LaPalme)	50.00	25.00	15.00
(15)	Bob Lemon	90.00	45.00	27.00
(16)	Al Lopez	80.00	40.00	24.00
(17)	Mickey Mantle	1100.00	550.00	330.00
(18)	Dale Mitchell	40.00	20.00	12.00
(19)	Phil Rizzuto	100.00	50.00	30.00
(20)	Curtis Roberts	50.00	25.00	15.00
(21)	Al Rosen	65.00	32.00	19.50
(22)	Red Schoendienst	60.00	30.00	18.00
(23)	Paul Smith	400.00	200.00	120.00
(24)	Duke Snider	175.00	87.00	52.00
(25)	George Strickland	40.00	20.00	12.00
(26)	Max Surkont	50.00	25.00	15.00
(27)	Frank Thomas	110.00	55.00	33.00
(28)	Wally Westlake	40.00	20.00	12.00
(29)	Early Wynn	90.00	45.00	27.00

1982 Cracker Jack

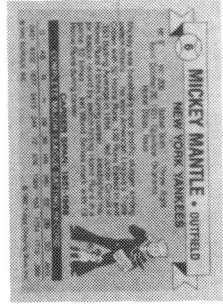

The Topps-produced 1982 Cracker Jack set was issued to promote the first "Old Timers Baseball Classic", held in Washington, D.C. Sixteen cards comprise the set which was issued in two sheets of eight cards, plus an advertising card located in the center. The individual cards are 2½'' by 3½'' in size with the complete sheets measuring 7½'' by 10½''. Cards 1-8 feature American League players with 9-16 being former National League stars. The card fronts feature a full color photo inside a Cracker Jack border. The backs contain the Cracker Jack logo plus a short player biography and his lifetime pitching or batting record. Complete sheets were available through a write-in offer.

		MT	NR MT	EX
Complete Panel Set:		7.00	5.25	3.75
Complete Singles Set:		3.00	2.25	1.65
Common Single Player:		.05	.04	.03
Panel		4.00	3.00	2.25
1	Larry Doby	.05	.04	.03
2	Bob Feller	.10	.08	.06
3	Whitey Ford	.10	.08	.06
4	Al Kaline	.10	.08	.06
5	Harmon Killebrew	.10	.08	.06
6	Mickey Mantle	.75	.40	.30
7	Tony Oliva	.05	.04	.03
8	Brooks Robinson	.10	.08	.06

1987 David Berg Hot Dogs Cubs

(8) ANDRE DAWSON, OF

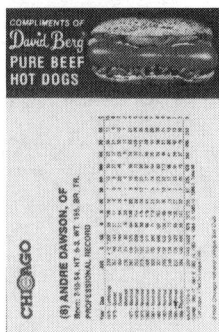

COMPLIMENTS OF David Berg PURE BEEF HOT DOGS

(8) ANDRE DAWSON, OF

HAROLD (PIE) TRAYNOR
PITTSBURGH PIRATES

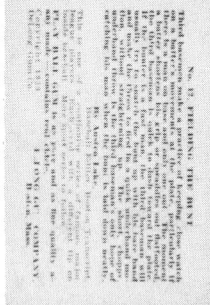

Changing sponsors from Gatorade to David Berg Pure Beef Hot Dogs, the Chicago Cubs handed out a 26-card set of baseball cards to fans attending the July 29th game at Wrigley Field. The cards are printed in full-color on white stock and measure 2⅞'' by 4¼'' in size. The set is numbered by the players' uniforms numbers. The card backs contain player personal and statistical information, plus a full-color picture of a David Berg hot dog in a bun with all the garnishings. The set marked the sixth consecutive year the Cubs held a baseball card giveaway promotion.

		MT	NR MT	EX
Complete Set:		8.00	6.00	3.25
Common Player:		.10	.08	.04
1	Dave Martinez	.70	.50	.30
4	Gene Michael	.10	.08	.04
6	Keith Moreland	.35	.25	.14
7	Jody Davis	.35	.25	.14
8	Andre Dawson	1.00	.70	.40
10	Leon Durham	.50	.40	.20
11	Jim Sundberg	.10	.08	.04
12	Shawon Dunston	.60	.45	.25
19	Manny Trillo	.15	.11	.06
20	Bob Dernier	.15	.11	.06
21	Scott Sanderson	.10	.08	.04
22	Jerry Mumphrey	.15	.11	.06
23	Ryne Sandberg	2.00	1.50	.80
24	Brian Dayett	.10	.08	.04
29	Chico Walker	.15	.11	.06
31	Greg Maddux	.30	.25	.12
33	Frank DiPino	.10	.08	.04
34	Steve Trout	.25	.20	.10
36	Gary Matthews	.25	.20	.10
37	Ed Lynch	.10	.08	.04
39	Ron Davis	.10	.08	.04
40	Rick Sutcliffe	.70	.50	.30
46	Lee Smith	.35	.25	.14
47	Dickie Noles	.10	.08	.04
49	Jamie Moyer	.20	.15	.08
---	The Coaching Staff (Johnny Oates, Jim Snyder, Herm Starrette, John Vukovich, Billy Williams)	.15	.11	.06

1933 DeLong

The DeLong Gum Company of Boston, Mass. was among the first to sell baseball cards with gum. It issued a set of 24 cards in 1933, the same year the Goudey Gum Co. issued its premiere set, making both companies pioneers in the field. The DeLong cards measure 2'' by 3'' and feature black and white player photos on a color background. The photos show the players in various action poses and position them in the middle of a miniature stadium setting so that they appear to be giant in size. Most of the cards in the set are vertically designed, but a few are horizontal. The backs of the cards, written by Austen Lake, editor of

the Boston Transcript, contain a series of sports tips to help youngsters become better ballplayers. Lake later wrote the tips that appeared on the backs of the Diamond Stars cards issued by National Chicle from 1934-36. The ACC designation for this set is R333. The checklist below gives the players' names exactly as they appear on the fronts of the cards.

		NR MT	EX	VG
Complete Set:		5500.00	2750.00	1650.
Common Player:		125.00	62.00	37.00
1	"Marty" McManus	150.00	75.00	45.00
2	Al Simmons	200.00	100.00	60.00
3	Oscar Melillo	125.00	62.00	37.00
4	William (Bill) Terry	200.00	100.00	60.00
5	Charlie Gehringer	200.00	100.00	60.00
6	Gordon (Mickey) Cochrane	200.00	100.00	60.00
7	Lou Gehrig	1000.00	500.00	300.00
8	Hazen S. (Kiki) Cuyler	175.00	87.00	52.00
9	Bill Urbanski	125.00	62.00	37.00
10	Frank J. (Lefty) O'Doul	150.00	75.00	45.00
11	Freddie Lindstrom	175.00	87.00	52.00
12	Harold (Pie) Traynor	200.00	100.00	60.00
13	"Rabbit" Maranville	175.00	87.00	52.00
14	Vernon "Lefty" Gomez	200.00	100.00	60.00
15	Riggs Stephenson	125.00	62.00	37.00
16	Lon Warneke	125.00	62.00	37.00
17	Pepper Martin	150.00	75.00	45.00
18	Jimmy Dykes	125.00	62.00	37.00
19	Chick Hafey	175.00	87.00	52.00
20	Joe Vosmik	115.00	57.00	34.00
21	Jimmy Foxx	325.00	162.00	97.00
22	Charles (Chuck) Klein	175.00	87.00	52.00
23	Robert (Lefty) Grove	200.00	100.00	60.00
24	"Goose" Goslin	175.00	87.00	52.00

1934-36 Diamond Stars

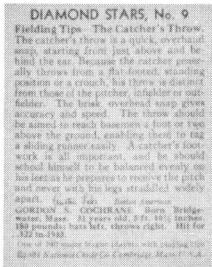

DIAMOND STARS, No. 9

Issued from 1934 through 1936, the Diamond Stars set (ACC designation R327) consists of 108 cards. Produced by National Chicle, the numbered cards measure 2⅜'' by 2⅞'' and are color art reproductions of actual photographs. The year of issue can be determined by the player's statistics found on the reverse of the card. The backs feature either a player biography or a baseball playing tip. Some cards in the set can be found with either green or blue printing on the backs. Artwork for twelve cards that were never issued was uncovered several years ago and a set featuring those cards was subsequently made available to the collecting public.

	NR MT	EX	VG
Complete Set:	6000.00	3000.00	1800.
Common Player: 1-48	15.00	7.50	4.50
Common Player: 49-72	20.00	10.00	6.00
Common Player: 73-96	32.00	16.00	9.50
Common Player: 85-96	50.00	25.00	15.00
Common Player: 97-108	120.00	60.00	36.00

		NR MT	EX	VG
1a	"Lefty" Grove (1934 green back)	250.00	30.00	15.00
1b	"Lefty" Grove (1935 green back)	250.00	30.00	15.00
2a	Al Simmons (1934 green back)	35.00	17.50	10.50
2b	Al Simmons (1935 green back)	35.00	17.50	10.50
2c	Al Simmons (1936 blue back)	35.00	17.50	10.50
3a	"Rabbit" Maranville (1934 green back)	35.00	17.50	10.50
3b	"Rabbit" Maranville (1935 green back)	35.00	17.50	10.50
4a	"Buddy" Myer (1934 green back)	15.00	7.50	4.50
4b	"Buddy" Myer (1935 green back)	15.00	7.50	4.50
4c	"Buddy" Myer (1936 blue back)	15.00	7.50	4.50
5a	Tom Bridges (1934 green back)	20.00	10.00	6.00
5b	Tom Bridges (1935 green back)	20.00	10.00	6.00
5c	Tom Bridges (1936 blue back)	20.00	10.00	6.00
6a	Max Bishop (1934 green back)	15.00	7.50	4.50
6b	Max Bishop (1935 green back)	15.00	7.50	4.50
7a	Lew Fonseca (1934 green back)	20.00	10.00	6.00
7b	Lew Fonseca (1935 green back)	20.00	10.00	6.00
8a	Joe Vosmik (1934 green back)	15.00	7.50	4.50
8b	Joe Vosmik (1935 green back)	15.00	7.50	4.50
8c	Joe Vosmik (1936 blue back)	15.00	7.50	4.50
9a	"Mickey" Cochrane (1934 green back)	50.00	25.00	15.00
9b	"Mickey" Cochrane (1935 green back)	50.00	25.00	15.00
9c	"Mickey" Cochrane (1936 blue back)	50.00	25.00	15.00
10a	Roy Mahaffey (1934 green back)	15.00	7.50	4.50
10b	Roy Mahaffey (1935 green back)	15.00	7.50	4.50
10c	Roy Mahaffey (1936 blue back)	15.00	7.50	4.50
11a	Bill Dickey (1934 green back)	60.00	30.00	18.00
11b	Bill Dickey (1935 green back)	60.00	30.00	18.00
12a	"Dixie" Walker (1934 green back)	25.00	12.50	7.50
12b	"Dixie" Walker (1935 green back)	25.00	12.50	7.50
12c	"Dixie" Walker (1936 blue back)	25.00	12.50	7.50
13a	George Blaeholder (1934 green back)	15.00	7.50	4.50
13b	George Blaeholder (1935 green back)	15.00	7.50	4.50
14a	Bill Terry (1934 green back)	50.00	25.00	15.00
14b	Bill Terry (1935 green back)	50.00	25.00	15.00
15a	Dick Bartell (1934 green back)	15.00	7.50	4.50
15b	Dick Bartell (1935 green back)	15.00	7.50	4.50
16a	Lloyd Waner (1934 green back)	35.00	17.50	10.50
16b	Lloyd Waner (1935 green back)	35.00	17.50	10.50
16c	Lloyd Waner (1936 blue back)	35.00	17.50	10.50
17a	Frankie Frisch (1934 green back)	50.00	25.00	15.00
17b	Frankie Frisch (1935 green back)	50.00	25.00	15.00
18a	"Chick" Hafey (1934 green back)	35.00	17.50	10.50
18b	"Chick" Hafey (1935 green back)	35.00	17.50	10.50
19a	Van Mungo (1934 green back)	20.00	10.00	6.00
19b	Van Mungo (1935 green back)	20.00	10.00	6.00
20a	"Shanty" Hogan (1934 green back)	15.00	7.50	4.50
20b	"Shanty" Hogan (1935 green back)	15.00	7.50	4.50
21a	Johnny Vergez (1934 green back)	15.00	7.50	4.50
21b	Johnny Vergez (1935 green back)	15.00	7.50	4.50
22a	Jimmy Wilson (1934 green back)	15.00	7.50	4.50

		NR MT	EX	VG
22b	Jimmy Wilson (1935 green back)	15.00	7.50	4.50
22c	Jimmy Wilson (1936 blue back)	15.00	7.50	4.50
23a	Bill Hallahan (1934 green back)	15.00	7.50	4.50
23b	Bill Hallahan (1935 green back)	15.00	7.50	4.50
24a	"Sparky" Adams (1934 green back)	15.00	7.50	4.50
24b	"Sparky" Adams (1935 green back)	15.00	7.50	4.50
25	Walter Berger	15.00	7.50	4.50
26a	"Pepper" Martin (1935 green back)	20.00	10.00	6.00
26b	"Pepper" Martin (1936 blue back)	20.00	10.00	6.00
27	"Pie" Traynor	50.00	25.00	15.00
28	"Al" Lopez	50.00	25.00	15.00
29	Robert Rolfe	25.00	12.50	7.50
30a	"Heinie" Manush (1935 green back)	35.00	17.50	10.50
30b	"Heinie" Manush (1936 blue back)	35.00	17.50	10.50
31a	"Kiki" Cuyler (1935 green back)	35.00	17.50	10.50
31b	"Kiki" Cuyler (1936 blue back)	35.00	17.50	10.50
32	Sam Rice	35.00	17.50	10.50
33	"Schoolboy" Rowe	20.00	10.00	6.00
34	Stanley Hack	20.00	10.00	6.00
35	Earle Averill	35.00	17.50	10.50
36a	Earnie Lombardi	35.00	17.50	10.50
36b	Ernie Lombardi	35.00	17.50	10.50
37	"Billie" Urbanski	15.00	7.50	4.50
38	Ben Chapman	25.00	12.50	7.50
39	Carl Hubbell	50.00	25.00	15.00
40	"Blondy" Ryan	15.00	7.50	4.50
41	Harvey Hendrick	15.00	7.50	4.50
42	Jimmy Dykes	20.00	10.00	6.00
43	Ted Lyons	35.00	17.50	10.50
44	Rogers Hornsby	80.00	40.00	24.00
45	"Jo Jo" White	15.00	7.50	4.50
46	"Red" Lucas	15.00	7.50	4.50
47	Cliff Bolton	15.00	7.50	4.50
48	"Rick" Ferrell	40.00	20.00	12.00
49	"Buck" Jordan	20.00	10.00	6.00
50	"Mel" Ott	65.00	32.00	19.50
51	John Whitehead	20.00	10.00	6.00
52	George Stainback	20.00	10.00	6.00
53	Oscar Melillo	20.00	10.00	6.00
54a	"Hank" Greenburg	65.00	32.00	19.50
54b	"Hank" Greenberg	65.00	32.00	19.50
55	Tony Cuccinello	20.00	10.00	6.00
56	"Gus" Suhr	20.00	10.00	6.00
57	"Cy" Blanton	20.00	10.00	6.00
58	Glenn Myatt	20.00	10.00	6.00
59	Jim Bottomley	40.00	20.00	12.00
60	Charley "Red" Ruffing	50.00	25.00	15.00
61	"Billie" Werber	20.00	10.00	6.00
62	Fred M. Frankhouse	20.00	10.00	6.00
63	"Stonewall" Jackson	40.00	20.00	12.00
64	Jimmie Foxx	110.00	55.00	33.00
65	"Zeke" Bonura	20.00	10.00	6.00
66	"Ducky" Medwick	50.00	25.00	15.00
67	Marvin Owen	20.00	10.00	6.00
68	"Sam" Leslie	20.00	10.00	6.00
69	Earl Grace	20.00	10.00	6.00
70	"Hal" Trosky	20.00	10.00	6.00
71	"Ossie" Bluege	20.00	10.00	6.00
72	"Tony" Piet	20.00	10.00	6.00
73a	"Fritz" Ostermueller (1935 green back)	32.00	16.00	9.50
73b	"Fritz" Ostermueller (1935 blue back)	32.00	16.00	9.50
73c	"Fritz" Ostermueller (1936 blue back)	32.00	16.00	9.50
74a	Tony Lazzeri (1935 green back)	50.00	25.00	15.00
74b	Tony Lazzeri (1935 blue back)	50.00	25.00	15.00
74c	Tony Lazzeri (1936 blue back)	50.00	25.00	15.00
75a	Irving Burns (1935 green back)	32.00	16.00	9.50
75b	Irving Burns (1935 blue back)	32.00	16.00	9.50
75c	Irving Burns (1936 blue back)	32.00	16.00	9.50
76a	Bill Rogell (1935 green back)	32.00	16.00	9.50
76b	Bill Rogell (1935 blue back)	32.00	16.00	9.50
76c	Bill Rogell (1936 blue back)	32.00	16.00	9.50
77a	Charlie Gehringer (1935 green back)	65.00	32.00	19.50
77b	Charlie Gehringer (1935 blue back)	65.00	32.00	19.50
77c	Charlie Gehringer (1936 blue back)	65.00	32.00	19.50
78a	Joe Kuhel (1935 green back)	32.00	16.00	9.50
78b	Joe Kuhel (1935 blue back)	32.00	16.00	9.50
78c	Joe Kuhel (1936 blue back)	32.00	16.00	9.50
79a	Willis Hudlin (1935 green back)	32.00	16.00	9.50

		NR MT	EX	VG
79b	Willis Hudlin (1935 blue back)	32.00	16.00	9.50
79c	Willis Hudlin (1936 blue back)	32.00	16.00	9.50
80a	Louis Chiozza (1935 green back)			
		32.00	16.00	9.50
80b	Louis Chiozza (1935 blue back)	32.00	16.00	9.50
80c	Louis Chiozza (1936 blue back)	32.00	16.00	9.50
81a	Bill DeLancey (1935 green back)	32.00	16.00	9.50
81b	Bill DeLancey (1935 blue back)	32.00	16.00	9.50
81c	Bill DeLancey (1936 blue back)	32.00	16.00	9.50
82a	John Babich (1935 green back)	32.00	16.00	9.50
82b	John Babich (1935 blue back)	32.00	16.00	9.50
82c	John Babich (1936 blue back)	32.00	16.00	9.50
83a	Paul Waner (1935 green back)	60.00	30.00	18.00
83b	Paul Waner (1935 blue back)	60.00	30.00	18.00
83c	Paul Waner (1936 blue back)	60.00	30.00	18.00
84a	Sam Byrd (1935 green back)	32.00	16.00	9.50
84b	Sam Byrd (1935 blue back)	32.00	16.00	9.50
84c	Sam Byrd (1936 blue back)	32.00	16.00	9.50
85	Julius Solters	50.00	25.00	15.00
86	Frank Crosetti	65.00	32.00	19.50
87	Steve O'Neil (O'Neill)	50.00	25.00	15.00
88	Geo. Selkirk	60.00	30.00	18.00
89	Joe Stripp	50.00	25.00	15.00
90	Ray Hayworth	50.00	25.00	15.00
91	Bucky Harris	65.00	32.00	19.50
92	Ethan Allen	50.00	25.00	15.00
93	Alvin Crowder	50.00	25.00	15.00
94	Wes Ferrell	50.00	25.00	15.00
95	Luke Appling	65.00	32.00	19.50
96	Lew Riggs	50.00	25.00	15.00
97	"Al" Lopez	160.00	80.00	48.00
98	"Schoolboy" Rowe	120.00	60.00	36.00
99	"Pie" Traynor	250.00	125.00	75.00
100	Earle Averill (Earl)	200.00	100.00	60.00
101	Dick Bartell	120.00	60.00	36.00
102	Van Mungo	120.00	60.00	36.00
103	Bill Dickey	325.00	162.00	97.00
104	Robert Rolfe	130.00	65.00	39.00
105	"Ernie" Lombardi	160.00	80.00	48.00
106	"Red" Lucas	120.00	60.00	36.00
107	Stanley Hack	120.00	60.00	36.00
108	Walter Berger	160.00	70.00	36.00

1981 Donruss

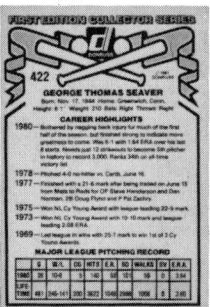

TOM SEAVER PITCHER

The Donruss Co. of Memphis, Tenn. produced its premiere baseball card issue in 1981 with a set that consisted of 600 numbered cards and five unnumbered checklists. The cards, which measure 2½" by 3½", are printed on thin stock. The card fronts contain the Donruss logo plus the year of issue. The card backs are designed on a vertical format and have black print on red and white. The set, entitled "First Edition Collector Series", contains nearly 40 variations, those being first printing errors that were corrected in a subsequent print run. The cards were issued in gum wax packs, with hobby dealer sales being coordinated by TCMA of Amawalk, N.Y. The complete set price does not include the higher priced variations.

	MT	NR MT	EX
Complete Set:	22.00	16.50	8.75
Common Player:	.06	.05	.02

		MT	NR MT	EX
1	Ozzie Smith	.40	.30	.15
2	Rollie Fingers	.25	.20	.10
3	Rick Wise	.08	.06	.03
4	Gene Richards	.06	.05	.02
5	Alan Trammell	.40	.30	.15
6	Tom Brookens	.08	.06	.03
7a	Duffy Dyer (1980 Avg. .185)	1.00	.70	.40
7b	Duffy Dyer (1980 Avg. 185)	.10	.08	.04
8	Mark Fidrych	.08	.06	.03
9	Dave Rozema	.06	.05	.02
10	Ricky Peters	.06	.05	.02
11	Mike Schmidt	1.00	.70	.40
12	Willie Stargell	.40	.30	.15
13	Tim Foli	.06	.05	.02
14	Manny Sanguillen	.06	.05	.02
15	Grant Jackson	.06	.05	.02
16	Eddie Solomon	.06	.05	.02
17	Omar Moreno	.06	.05	.02
18	Joe Morgan	.30	.25	.12
19	Rafael Landestoy	.06	.05	.02
20	Bruce Bochy	.06	.05	.02
21	Joe Sambito	.06	.05	.02
22	Manny Trillo	.08	.06	.03
23a	Dave Smith (incomplete box around stats)			
		1.00	.70	.40
23b	Dave Smith (complete box around stats)			
		.25	.20	.10
24	Terry Puhl	.06	.05	.02
25	Bump Wills	.06	.05	.02
26a	John Ellis (Danny Walton photo - with bat)			
		1.25	.90	.50
26b	John Ellis (John Ellis photo - with glove)			
		.10	.08	.04
27	Jim Kern	.06	.05	.02
28	Richie Zisk	.08	.06	.03
29	John Mayberry	.08	.06	.03
30	Bob Davis	.06	.05	.02
31	Jackson Todd	.06	.05	.02
32	Al Woods	.06	.05	.02
33	Steve Carlton	.50	.40	.20
34	Lee Mazzilli	.08	.06	.03
35	John Stearns	.06	.05	.02
36	Roy Jackson	.06	.05	.02
37	Mike Scott	.35	.25	.14
38	Lamar Johnson	.06	.05	.02
39	Kevin Bell	.06	.05	.02
40	Ed Farmer	.06	.05	.02
41	Ross Baumgarten	.06	.05	.02
42	Leo Sutherland	.06	.05	.02
43	Dan Meyer	.06	.05	.02
44	Ron Reed	.08	.06	.03
45	Mario Mendoza	.06	.05	.02
46	Rick Honeycutt	.08	.06	.03
47	Glenn Abbott	.06	.05	.02
48	Leon Roberts	.06	.05	.02
49	Rod Carew	.60	.45	.25
50	Bert Campaneris	.10	.08	.04
51a	Tom Donahue (incorrect spelling)	1.00	.70	.40
51b	Tom Donohue (Donohue on front)	.10	.08	.04
52	Dave Frost	.06	.05	.02
53	Ed Halicki	.06	.05	.02
54	Dan Ford	.06	.05	.02
55	Garry Maddox	.10	.08	.04
56a	Steve Garvey ("Surpassed 25 HR..." on back)			
		1.75	1.25	.70
56b	Steve Garvey ("Surpassed 21 HR..." on back)			
		.60	.45	.25
57	Bill Russell	.08	.06	.03
58	Don Sutton	.30	.25	.12
59	Reggie Smith	.10	.08	.04
60	Rick Monday	.10	.08	.04
61	Ray Knight	.10	.08	.04
62	Johnny Bench	.50	.40	.20
63	Mario Soto	.10	.08	.04
64	Doug Bair	.06	.05	.02
65	George Foster	.20	.15	.08
66	Jeff Burroughs	.08	.06	.03
67	Keith Hernandez	.40	.30	.15
68	Tom Herr	.10	.08	.04
69	Bob Forsch	.08	.06	.03
70	John Fulgham	.06	.05	.02
71a	Bobby Bonds (lifetime HR 986)	1.00	.70	.40
71b	Bobby Bonds (lifetime HR 326)	.15	.11	.06
72a	Rennie Stennett ("...breaking broke leg..." on back)	1.00	.70	.40
72b	Rennie Stennett ("...breaking leg..." on back)	.10	.08	.04
73	Joe Strain	.06	.05	.02
74	Ed Whitson	.08	.06	.03
75	Tom Griffin	.06	.05	.02
76	Bill North	.06	.05	.02

		MT	NR MT	EX
77	Gene Garber	.06	.05	.02
78	Mike Hargrove	.08	.06	.03
79	Dave Rosello	.06	.05	.02
80	Ron Hassey	.06	.05	.02
81	Sid Monge	.06	.05	.02
82a	Joe Charboneau ("For some reason, Phillies..." on back)	1.00	.70	.40
82b	Joe Charboneau ("Phillies..." on back)	.15	.11	.06
83	Cecil Cooper	.15	.11	.06
84	Sal Bando	.10	.08	.04
85	Moose Haas	.06	.05	.02
86	Mike Caldwell	.06	.05	.02
87a	Larry Hisle ("...Twins with 28 RBI." on back)	1.00	.70	.40
87b	Larry Hisle ("...Twins with 28 HR" on back)	.10	.08	.04
88	Luis Gomez	.06	.05	.02
89	Larry Parrish	.10	.08	.04
90	Gary Carter	.50	.40	.20
91	Bill Gullickson	.30	.25	.12
92	Fred Norman	.06	.05	.02
93	Tommy Hutton	.06	.05	.02
94	Carl Yastrzemski	.80	.60	.30
95	Glenn Hoffman	.08	.06	.03
96	Dennis Eckersley	.10	.08	.04
97a	Tom Burgmeier (Throws: Right)	1.00	.70	.40
97b	Tom Burgmeier (Throws: Left)	.10	.08	.04
98	Win Remmerswaal	.06	.05	.02
99	Bob Horner	.30	.25	.12
100	George Brett	.80	.60	.30
101	Dave Chalk	.06	.05	.02
102	Dennis Leonard	.08	.06	.03
103	Renie Martin	.06	.05	.02
104	Amos Otis	.10	.08	.04
105	Graig Nettles	.15	.11	.06
106	Eric Soderholm	.06	.05	.02
107	Tommy John	.20	.15	.08
108	Tom Underwood	.06	.05	.02
109	Lou Piniella	.15	.11	.06
110	Mickey Klutts	.06	.05	.02
111	Bobby Murcer	.10	.08	.04
112	Eddie Murray	.70	.50	.30
113	Rick Dempsey	.08	.06	.03
114	Scott McGregor	.10	.08	.04
115	Ken Singleton	.10	.08	.04
116	Gary Roenicke	.08	.06	.03
117	Dave Revering	.06	.05	.02
118	Mike Norris	.06	.05	.02
119	Rickey Henderson	.70	.50	.30
120	Mike Heath	.06	.05	.02
121	Dave Cash	.06	.05	.02
122	Randy Jones	.08	.06	.03
123	Eric Rasmussen	.06	.05	.02
124	Jerry Mumphrey	.08	.06	.03
125	Richie Hebner	.06	.05	.02
126	Mark Wagner	.06	.05	.02
127	Jack Morris	.30	.25	.12
128	Dan Petry	.10	.08	.04
129	Bruce Robbins	.06	.05	.02
130	Champ Summers	.06	.05	.02
131a	Pete Rose ("...see card 251." on back)	2.25	1.75	.90
131b	Pete Rose ("...see card 371." on back)	1.25	.90	.50
132	Willie Stargell	.40	.30	.15
133	Ed Ott	.06	.05	.02
134	Jim Bibby	.06	.05	.02
135	Bert Blyleven	.15	.11	.06
136	Dave Parker	.30	.25	.12
137	Bill Robinson	.06	.05	.02
138	Enos Cabell	.08	.06	.03
139	Dave Bergman	.06	.05	.02
140	J R Richard	.10	.08	.04
141	Ken Forsch	.08	.06	.03
142	Larry Bowa	.15	.11	.06
143	Frank LaCorte (photo actually Randy Niemann)	.06	.05	.02
144	Dennis Walling	.06	.05	.02
145	Buddy Bell	.15	.11	.06
146	Ferguson Jenkins	.20	.15	.08
147	Danny Darwin	.08	.06	.03
148	John Grubb	.06	.05	.02
149	Alfredo Griffin	.08	.06	.03
150	Jerry Garvin	.06	.05	.02
151	Paul Mirabella	.06	.05	.02
152	Rick Bosetti	.06	.05	.02
153	Dick Ruthven	.06	.05	.02
154	Frank Taveras	.06	.05	.02
155	Craig Swan	.06	.05	.02
156	Jeff Reardon	.75	.60	.30

		NR MT	EX	VG
157	Steve Henderson	.06	.05	.02
158	Jim Morrison	.06	.05	.02
159	Glenn Borgmann	.06	.05	.02
160	Lamarr Hoyt (LaMarr)	.10	.08	.04
161	Rich Wortham	.06	.05	.02
162	Thad Bosley	.06	.05	.02
163	Julio Cruz	.06	.05	.02
164a	Del Unser (no 3B in stat heads)	1.00	.70	.40
164b	Del Unser (3B in stat heads)	.10	.08	.04
165	Jim Anderson	.06	.05	.02
166	Jim Beattie	.06	.05	.02
167	Shane Rawley	.10	.08	.04
168	Joe Simpson	.06	.05	.02
169	Rod Carew	.60	.45	.25
170	Fred Patek	.06	.05	.02
171	Frank Tanana	.10	.08	.04
172	Alfredo Martinez	.06	.05	.02
173	Chris Knapp	.06	.05	.02
174	Joe Rudi	.10	.08	.04
175	Greg Luzinski	.15	.11	.06
176	Steve Garvey	.50	.40	.20
177	Joe Ferguson	.06	.05	.02
178	Bob Welch	.10	.08	.04
179	Dusty Baker	.10	.08	.04
180	Rudy Law	.06	.05	.02
181	Dave Concepcion	.15	.11	.06
182	Johnny Bench	.50	.40	.20
183	Mike LaCoss	.08	.06	.03
184	Ken Griffey	.12	.09	.05
185	Dave Collins	.08	.06	.03
186	Brian Asselstine	.06	.05	.02
187	Garry Templeton	.10	.08	.04
188	Mike Phillips	.06	.05	.02
189	Pete Vukovich	.08	.06	.03
190	John Urrea	.06	.05	.02
191	Tony Scott	.06	.05	.02
192	Darrell Evans	.15	.11	.06
193	Milt May	.06	.05	.02
194	Bob Knepper	.08	.06	.03
195	Randy Moffitt	.06	.05	.02
196	Larry Herndon	.08	.06	.03
197	Rick Camp	.06	.05	.02
198	Andre Thornton	.10	.08	.04
199	Tom Veryzer	.06	.05	.02
200	Gary Alexander	.06	.05	.02
201	Rick Waits	.06	.05	.02
202	Rick Manning	.06	.05	.02
203	Faul Molitor	.20	.15	.08
204	Jim Gantner	.08	.06	.03
205	Paul Mitchell	.06	.05	.02
206	Reggie Cleveland	.06	.05	.02
207	Sixto Lezcano	.06	.05	.02
208	Bruce Benedict	.06	.05	.02
209	Rodney Scott	.06	.05	.02
210	John Tamargo	.06	.05	.02
211	Bill Lee	.08	.06	.03
212	Andre Dawson	.35	.25	.14
213	Rowland Office	.06	.05	.02
214	Carl Yastrzemski	.80	.60	.30
215	Jerry Remy	.06	.05	.02
216	Mike Torrez	.08	.06	.03
217	Skip Lockwood	.06	.05	.02
218	Fred Lynn	.20	.15	.08
219	Chris Chambliss	.08	.06	.03
220	Willie Aikens	.06	.05	.02
221	John Wathan	.08	.06	.03
222	Dan Quisenberry	.20	.15	.08
223	Willie Wilson	.15	.11	.06
224	Clint Hurdle	.06	.05	.02
225	Bob Watson	.08	.06	.03
226	Jim Spencer	.06	.05	.02
227	Ron Guidry	.25	.20	.10
228	Reggie Jackson	.70	.50	.30
229	Oscar Gamble	.08	.06	.03
230	Jeff Cox	.06	.05	.02
231	Luis Tiant	.12	.09	.05
232	Rich Dauer	.06	.05	.02
233	Dan Graham	.06	.05	.02
234	Mike Flanagan	.10	.08	.04
235	John Lowenstein	.06	.05	.02
236	Benny Ayala	.06	.05	.02
237	Wayne Gross	.06	.05	.02
238	Rick Langford	.06	.05	.02
239	Tony Armas	.10	.08	.04
240a	Bob Lacy (incorrect spelling)	1.00	.70	.40
240b	Bob Lacey (correct spelling)	.10	.08	.04
241	Gene Tenace	.08	.06	.03
242	Bob Shirley	.06	.05	.02
243	Gary Lucas	.10	.08	.04
244	Jerry Turner	.06	.05	.02
245	John Wockenfuss	.06	.05	.02

#	Name	MT	NR MT	EX
246	Stan Papi	.06	.05	.02
247	Milt Wilcox	.08	.06	.03
248	Dan Schatzeder	.06	.05	.02
249	Steve Kemp	.08	.06	.03
250	Jim Lentine	.06	.05	.02
251	Pete Rose	1.00	.70	.40
252	Bill Madlock	.15	.11	.06
253	Dale Berra	.06	.05	.02
254	Kent Tekulve	.08	.06	.03
255	Enrique Romo	.06	.05	.02
256	Mike Easler	.10	.08	.04
257	Chuck Tanner	.08	.06	.03
258	Art Howe	.06	.05	.02
259	Alan Ashby	.06	.05	.02
260	Nolan Ryan	.50	.40	.20
261a	Vern Ruhle (Ken Forsch photo - head shot)	1.25	.90	.50
261b	Vern Ruhle (Vern Ruhle photo - waist to head shot)	.10	.08	.04
262	Bob Boone	.10	.08	.04
263	Cesar Cedeno	.12	.09	.05
264	Jeff Leonard	.12	.09	.05
265	Pat Putnam	.06	.05	.02
266	Jon Matlack	.08	.06	.03
267	Dave Rajsich	.06	.05	.02
268	Billy Sample	.06	.05	.02
269	Damaso Garcia	.20	.15	.08
270	Tom Buskey	.06	.05	.02
271	Joey McLaughlin	.06	.05	.02
272	Barry Bonnell	.06	.05	.02
273	Tug McGraw	.10	.08	.04
274	Mike Jorgensen	.06	.05	.02
275	Pat Zachry	.06	.05	.02
276	Neil Allen	.08	.06	.03
277	Joel Youngblood	.06	.05	.02
278	Greg Pryor	.06	.05	.02
279	Britt Burns	.10	.08	.04
280	Rich Dotson	.20	.15	.08
281	Chet Lemon	.08	.06	.03
282	Rusty Kuntz	.06	.05	.02
283	Ted Cox	.06	.05	.02
284	Sparky Lyle	.10	.08	.04
285	Larry Cox	.06	.05	.02
286	Floyd Bannister	.10	.08	.04
287	Byron McLaughlin	.06	.05	.02
288	Rodney Craig	.06	.05	.02
289	Bobby Grich	.10	.08	.04
290	Dickie Thon	.08	.06	.03
291	Mark Clear	.08	.06	.03
292	Dave Lemanczyk	.06	.05	.02
293	Jason Thompson	.08	.06	.03
294	Rick Miller	.06	.05	.02
295	Lonnie Smith	.08	.06	.03
296	Ron Cey	.12	.09	.05
297	Steve Yeager	.06	.05	.02
298	Bobby Castillo	.06	.05	.02
299	Manny Mota	.08	.06	.03
300	Jay Johnstone	.10	.08	.04
301	Dan Driessen	.08	.06	.03
302	Joe Nolan	.06	.05	.02
303	Paul Householder	.06	.05	.02
304	Harry Spilman	.06	.05	.02
305	Cesar Geronimo	.06	.05	.02
306a	Gary Mathews (Mathews on front)	1.25	.90	.50
306b	Gary Matthews (Matthews on front)	.10	.08	.04
307	Ken Reitz	.06	.05	.02
308	Ted Simmons	.15	.11	.06
309	John Littlefield	.06	.05	.02
310	George Frazier	.06	.05	.02
311	Dane Iorg	.06	.05	.02
312	Mike Ivie	.06	.05	.02
313	Dennis Littlejohn	.06	.05	.02
314	Gary LaVelle (Lavelle)	.06	.05	.02
315	Jack Clark	.25	.20	.10
316	Jim Wohlford	.06	.05	.02
317	Rick Matula	.06	.05	.02
318	Toby Harrah	.08	.06	.03
319a	Dwane Kuiper (Dwane on front)	1.00	.70	.40
319b	Duane Kuiper (Duane on front)	.10	.08	.04
320	Len Barker	.08	.06	.03
321	Victor Cruz	.06	.05	.02
322	Dell Alston	.06	.05	.02
323	Robin Yount	.40	.30	.15
324	Charlie Moore	.06	.05	.02
325	Lary Sorensen	.06	.05	.02
326a	Gorman Thomas ("...30-HR mark 4th..." on back)	1.25	.90	.50
326b	Gorman Thomas ("...30-HR mark 3rd..." on back)	.12	.09	.05
327	Bob Rodgers	.08	.06	.03
328	Phil Niekro	.30	.25	.12
329	Chris Speier	.08	.06	.03
330a	Steve Rodgers (Rodgers on front)	1.00	.70	.40
330b	Steve Rogers (Rogers on front)	.10	.08	.04
331	Woodie Fryman	.08	.06	.03
332	Warren Cromartie	.06	.05	.02
333	Jerry White	.06	.05	.02
334	Tony Perez	.20	.15	.08
335	Carlton Fisk	.20	.15	.08
336	Dick Drago	.06	.05	.02
337	Steve Renko	.06	.05	.02
338	Jim Rice	.50	.40	.20
339	Jerry Royster	.06	.05	.02
340	Frank White	.10	.08	.04
341	Jamie Quirk	.06	.05	.02
342a	Paul Spittorff (Spittorff on front)	1.00	.70	.40
342b	Paul Splittorff (Splittorff on front)	.10	.08	.04
343	Marty Pattin	.06	.05	.02
344	Pete LaCock	.06	.05	.02
345	Willie Randolph	.10	.08	.04
346	Rick Cerone	.08	.06	.03
347	Rich Gossage	.20	.15	.08
348	Reggie Jackson	.70	.50	.30
349	Ruppert Jones	.06	.05	.02
350	Dave McKay	.06	.05	.02
351	Yogi Berra	.15	.11	.06
352	Doug Decinces (DeCinces)	.10	.08	.04
353	Jim Palmer	.40	.30	.15
354	Tippy Martinez	.06	.05	.02
355	Al Bumbry	.08	.06	.03
356	Earl Weaver	.10	.08	.04
357a	Bob Picciolo (Bob on front)	1.00	.70	.40
357b	Rob Picciolo (Rob on front)	.10	.08	.04
358	Matt Keough	.06	.05	.02
359	Dwayne Murphy	.08	.06	.03
360	Brian Kingman	.06	.05	.02
361	Bill Fahey	.06	.05	.02
362	Steve Mura	.06	.05	.02
363	Dennis Kinney	.06	.05	.02
364	Dave Winfield	.40	.30	.15
365	Lou Whitaker	.30	.25	.12
366	Lance Parrish	.35	.25	.14
367	Tim Corcoran	.06	.05	.02
368	Pat Underwood	.06	.05	.02
369	Al Cowens	.06	.05	.02
370	Sparky Anderson	.10	.08	.04
371	Pete Rose	1.00	.70	.40
372	Phil Garner	.08	.06	.03
373	Steve Nicosia	.06	.05	.02
374	John Candelaria	.10	.08	.04
375	Don Robinson	.08	.06	.03
376	Lee Lacy	.08	.06	.03
377	John Milner	.06	.05	.02
378	Craig Reynolds	.06	.05	.02
379a	Luis Pujois (Pujois on front)	1.00	.70	.40
379b	Luis Pujols (Pujols on front)	.10	.08	.04
380	Joe Niekro	.12	.09	.05
381	Joaquin Andujar	.10	.08	.04
382	Keith Moreland	.40	.30	.15
383	Jose Cruz	.12	.09	.05
384	Bill Virdon	.08	.06	.03
385	Jim Sundberg	.08	.06	.03
386	Doc Medich	.06	.05	.02
387	Al Oliver	.15	.11	.06
388	Jim Norris	.06	.05	.02
389	Bob Bailor	.06	.05	.02
390	Ernie Whitt	.08	.06	.03
391	Otto Velez	.06	.05	.02
392	Roy Howell	.06	.05	.02
393	Bob Walk	.10	.08	.04
394	Doug Flynn	.06	.05	.02
395	Pete Falcone	.06	.05	.02
396	Tom Hausman	.06	.05	.02
397	Elliott Maddox	.06	.05	.02
398	Mike Squires	.06	.05	.02
399	Marvis Foley	.06	.05	.02
400	Steve Trout	.08	.06	.03
401	Wayne Nordhagen	.06	.05	.02
402	Tony Larussa (LaRussa)	.08	.06	.03
403	Bruce Bochte	.06	.05	.02
404	Bake McBride	.06	.05	.02
405	Jerry Narron	.06	.05	.02
406	Rob Dressler	.06	.05	.02
407	Dave Heaverlo	.06	.05	.02
408	Tom Paciorek	.08	.06	.03
409	Carney Lansford	.10	.08	.04
410	Brian Downing	.10	.08	.04
411	Don Aase	.08	.06	.03
412	Jim Barr	.06	.05	.02
413	Don Baylor	.15	.11	.06

		MT	NR MT	EX
414	Jim Fregosi	.08	.06	.03
415	Dallas Green	.08	.06	.03
416	Dave Lopes	.10	.08	.04
417	Jerry Reuss	.10	.08	.04
418	Rick Sutcliffe	.25	.20	.10
419	Derrel Thomas	.06	.05	.02
420	Tommy LaSorda (Lasorda)	.10	.08	.04
421	Charlie Leibrandt	.40	.30	.15
422	Tom Seaver	.50	.40	.20
423	Ron Oester	.06	.05	.02
424	Junior Kennedy	.06	.05	.02
425	Tom Seaver	.50	.40	.20
426	Bobby Cox	.06	.05	.02
427	Leon Durham	.70	.50	.30
428	Terry Kennedy	.08	.06	.03
429	Silvio Martinez	.06	.05	.02
430	George Hendrick	.08	.06	.03
431	Red Schoendienst	.08	.06	.03
432	John LeMaster	.06	.05	.02
433	Vida Blue	.12	.09	.05
434	John Montefusco	.08	.06	.03
435	Terry Whitfield	.06	.05	.02
436	Dave Bristol	.06	.05	.02
437	Dale Murphy	.90	.70	.35
438	Jerry Dybzinski	.06	.05	.02
439	Jorge Orta	.06	.05	.02
440	Wayne Garland	.06	.05	.02
441	Miguel Dilone	.06	.05	.02
442	Dave Garcia	.06	.05	.02
443	Don Money	.08	.06	.03
444a	Buck Martinez (photo reversed)	1.00	.70	.40
444b	Buck Martinez (photo correct)	.10	.08	.04
445	Jerry Augustine	.06	.05	.02
446	Ben Oglivie	.08	.06	.03
447	Jim Slaton	.06	.05	.02
448	Doyle Alexander	.12	.09	.05
449	Tony Bernazard	.08	.06	.03
450	Scott Sanderson	.08	.06	.03
451	Dave Palmer	.08	.06	.03
452	Stan Bahnsen	.06	.05	.02
453	Dick Williams	.08	.06	.03
454	Rick Burleson	.08	.06	.03
455	Gary Allenson	.06	.05	.02
456	Bob Stanley	.08	.06	.03
457a	John Tudor (lifetime W/L 9.7)	1.25	.90	.50
457b	John Tudor (lifetime W/L 9-7)	.75	.60	.30
458	Dwight Evans	.15	.11	.06
459	Glenn Hubbard	.08	.06	.03
460	U L Washington	.06	.05	.02
461	Larry Gura	.08	.06	.03
462	Rich Gale	.06	.05	.02
463	Hal McRae	.12	.09	.05
464	Jim Frey	.06	.05	.02
465	Bucky Dent	.10	.08	.04
466	Dennis Werth	.06	.05	.02
467	Ron Davis	.08	.06	.03
468	Reggie Jackson	.70	.50	.30
469	Bobby Brown	.06	.05	.02
470	Mike Davis	.30	.25	.12
471	Gaylord Perry	.30	.25	.12
472	Mark Belanger	.08	.06	.03
473	Jim Palmer	.40	.30	.15
474	Sammy Stewart	.06	.05	.02
475	Tim Stoddard	.06	.05	.02
476	Steve Stone	.08	.06	.03
477	Jeff Newman	.06	.05	.02
478	Steve McCatty	.06	.05	.02
479	Billy Martin	.12	.09	.05
480	Mitchell Page	.06	.05	.02
481	Cy Young 1980 (Steve Carlton)	.35	.25	.14
482	Bill Buckner	.12	.09	.05
483a	Ivan DeJesus (lifetime hits 702)	1.00	.70	.40
483b	Ivan DeJesus (lifetime hits 642)	.10	.08	.04
484	Cliff Johnson	.06	.05	.02
485	Lenny Randle	.06	.05	.02
486	Larry Milbourne	.06	.05	.02
487	Roy Smalley	.08	.06	.03
488	John Castino	.06	.05	.02
489	Ron Jackson	.06	.05	.02
490a	Dave Roberts (1980 highlights begins "Showed pop...")	1.00	.70	.40
490b	Dave Roberts (1980 highlights begins "Declared himself...")	.10	.08	.04
491	MVP (George Brett)	.60	.45	.25
492	Mike Cubbage	.06	.05	.02
493	Rob Wilfong	.06	.05	.02
494	Danny Goodwin	.06	.05	.02
495	Jose Morales	.06	.05	.02
496	Mickey Rivers	.08	.06	.03
497	Mike Edwards	.06	.05	.02
498	Mike Sadek	.06	.05	.02

		MT	NR MT	EX
499	Lenn Sakata	.06	.05	.02
500	Gene Michael	.08	.06	.03
501	Dave Roberts	.06	.05	.02
502	Steve Dillard	.06	.05	.02
503	Jim Essian	.06	.05	.02
504	Rance Mulliniks	.06	.05	.02
505	Darrell Porter	.08	.06	.03
506	Joe Torre	.08	.06	.03
507	Terry Crowley	.06	.05	.02
508	Bill Travers	.06	.05	.02
509	Nelson Norman	.06	.05	.02
510	Bob McClure	.06	.05	.02
511	Steve Howe	.15	.11	.06
512	Dave Rader	.06	.05	.02
513	Mick Kelleher	.06	.05	.02
514	Kiko Garcia	.06	.05	.02
515	Larry Biittner	.06	.05	.02
516a	Willie Norwood (1980 highlights begins "Spent most...")	1.00	.70	.40
516b	Willie Norwood (1980 highlights begins "Traded to...")	.10	.08	.04
517	Bo Diaz	.08	.06	.03
518	Juan Beniquez	.06	.05	.02
519	Scot Thompson	.06	.05	.02
520	Jim Tracy	.06	.05	.02
521	Carlos Lezcano	.06	.05	.02
522	Joe Amalfitano	.06	.05	.02
523	Preston Hanna	.06	.05	.02
524a	Ray Burris (1980 highlights begins "Went on...")	1.00	.70	.40
524b	Ray Burris (1980 highlights begins "Drafted by...")	.10	.08	.04
525	Broderick Perkins	.06	.05	.02
526	Mickey Hatcher	.08	.06	.03
527	John Goryl	.06	.05	.02
528	Dick Davis	.06	.05	.02
529	Butch Wynegar	.08	.06	.03
530	Sal Butera	.06	.05	.02
531	Jerry Koosman	.12	.09	.05
532a	Jeff Zahn (Geoff) (1980 highlights begins "Was 2nd in...")	1.00	.70	.40
532b	Jeff Zahn (Geoff) (1980 highlights begins "Signed a 3 year...")	.10	.08	.04
533	Dennis Martinez	.08	.06	.03
534	Gary Thomasson	.06	.05	.02
535	Steve Macko	.06	.05	.02
536	Jim Kaat	.15	.11	.06
537	Best Hitters (George Brett, Rod Carew)	1.00	.70	.40
538	Tim Raines	5.00	3.75	2.00
539	Keith Smith	.06	.05	.02
540	Ken Macha	.06	.05	.02
541	Burt Hooton	.08	.06	.03
542	Butch Hobson	.06	.05	.02
543	Bill Stein	.06	.05	.02
544	Dave Stapleton	.10	.08	.04
545	Bob Pate	.06	.05	.02
546	Doug Corbett	.06	.05	.02
547	Darrell Jackson	.06	.05	.02
548	Pete Redfern	.06	.05	.02
549	Roger Erickson	.06	.05	.02
550	Al Hrabosky	.08	.06	.03
551	Dick Tidrow	.06	.05	.02
552	Dave Ford	.06	.05	.02
553	Dave Kingman	.15	.11	.06
554a	Mike Vail (1980 highlights begins "After...")	1.00	.70	.40
554b	Mike Vail (1980 highlights begins "Traded...")	.10	.08	.04
555a	Jerry Martin (1980 highlights begins "Overcame...")	1.00	.70	.40
555b	Jerry Martin (1980 highlights begins "Traded...")	.10	.08	.04
556a	Jesus Figueroa (1980 highlights begins "Had...")	1.00	.70	.40
556b	Jesus Figueroa (1980 highlights begins "Traded...")	.10	.08	.04
557	Don Stanhouse	.06	.05	.02
558	Barry Foote	.06	.05	.02
559	Tim Blackwell	.06	.05	.02
560	Bruce Sutter	.15	.11	.06
561	Rick Reuschel	.10	.08	.04
562	Lynn McGlothen	.06	.05	.02
563a	Bob Owchinko (1980 highlights begins "Traded...")	1.00	.70	.40
563b	Bob Owchinko (1980 highlights begins "Involved...")	.10	.08	.04
564	John Verhoeven	.06	.05	.02
565	Ken Landreaux	.08	.06	.03
566a	Glen Adams (Glen on front)	1.00	.70	.40
566b	Glenn Adams (Glenn on front)	.10	.08	.04

		MT	NR MT	EX
567	Hosken Powell	.06	.05	.02
568	Dick Noles	.06	.05	.02
569	Danny Ainge	.30	.25	.12
570	Bobby Mattick	.06	.05	.02
571	Joe LeFebvre (Lefebvre)	.10	.08	.04
572	Bobby Clark	.06	.05	.02
573	Dennis Lamp	.06	.05	.02
574	Randy Lerch	.06	.05	.02
575	Mookie Wilson	.40	.30	.15
576	Ron LeFlore	.08	.06	.03
577	Jim Dwyer	.06	.05	.02
578	Bill Castro	.06	.05	.02
579	Greg Minton	.06	.05	.02
580	Mark Littell	.06	.05	.02
581	Andy Hassler	.06	.05	.02
582	Dave Stieb	.20	.15	.08
583	Ken Oberkfell	.08	.06	.03
584	Larry Bradford	.06	.05	.02
585	Fred Stanley	.06	.05	.02
586	Bill Caudill	.06	.05	.02
587	Doug Capilla	.06	.05	.02
588	George Riley	.06	.05	.02
589	Willie Hernandez	.10	.08	.04
590	MVP (Mike Schmidt)	.60	.45	.25
591	Cy Young 1980 (Steve Stone)	.08	.06	.03
592	Rick Sofield	.06	.05	.02
593	Bombo Rivera	.06	.05	.02
594	Gary Ward	.08	.06	.03
595a	Dave Edwards (1980 highlights begins "Sidelined...")	1.00	.70	.40
595b	Dave Edwards (1980 highlights begins "Traded...")	.10	.08	.04
596	Mike Proly	.06	.05	.02
597	Tommy Boggs	.06	.05	.02
598	Greg Gross	.06	.05	.02
599	Elias Sosa	.06	.05	.02
600	Pat Kelly	.06	.05	.02
---a	Checklist 1-120 (51 Tom Donohue)	1.25	.90	.50
---b	Checklist 1-120 (51 Tom Donahue)	.10	.08	.04
---	Checklist 121-240	.06	.05	.02
---a	Checklist 241-360 (306 Gary Mathews)	.70	.50	.30
---b	Checklist 241-360 (306 Gary Matthews)	.10	.08	.04
---a	Checklist 361-480 (379 Luis Pujois)	.70	.50	.30
---b	Checklist 361-480 (379 Luis Pujols)	.10	.08	.04
---a	Checklist 481-600 (566 Glen Adams)	.70	.50	.30
---b	Checklist 481-600 (566 Glenn Adams)	.10	.08	.04

1982 Donruss

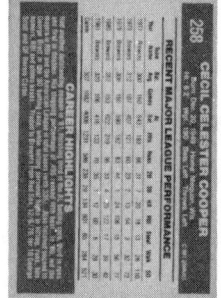

Using card stock thicker than the previous year, Donruss issued a 660-card set which included 653 numbered cards and seven unnumbered checklists. The cards, which measure 2½'' by 3½'', were sold with puzzle pieces rather than gum as a result of a law suit by Topps. The puzzle pieces (three pieces on one card per pack) featured Babe Ruth. The first 26 cards of the set, entitled Diamond Kings, showcase the artwork of Dick Perez of Perez-Steele Galleries. The card fronts display the Donruss logo and the year of issue. The card backs have black and blue ink on

white stock and include the player's career highlights. The complete set price does not include the higher priced variations.

		MT	NR MT	EX
Complete Set:		20.00	15.00	8.00
Common Player:		.06	.05	.02
1	Pete Rose (DK)	1.25	.90	.50
2	Gary Carter (DK)	.40	.30	.15
3	Steve Garvey (DK)	.50	.40	.20
4	Vida Blue (DK)	.12	.09	.05
5a	Alan Trammel (DK) (name incorrect)	1.50	1.25	.60
5b	Alan Trammell (DK) (name correct)	.40	.30	.15
6	Len Barker (DK)	.08	.06	.03
7	Dwight Evans (DK)	.15	.11	.06
8	Rod Carew (DK)	.50	.40	.20
9	George Hendrick (DK)	.08	.06	.03
10	Phil Niekro (DK)	.30	.25	.12
11	Richie Zisk (DK)	.08	.06	.03
12	Dave Parker (DK)	.30	.25	.12
13	Nolan Ryan (DK)	.50	.40	.20
14	Ivan DeJesus (DK)	.08	.06	.03
15	George Brett (DK)	.70	.50	.30
16	Tom Seaver (DK)	.50	.40	.20
17	Dave Kingman (DK)	.15	.11	.06
18	Dave Winfield (DK)	.40	.30	.15
19	Mike Norris (DK)	.08	.06	.03
20	Carlton Fisk (DK)	.25	.20	.10
21	Ozzie Smith (DK)	.20	.15	.08
22	Roy Smalley (DK)	.08	.06	.03
23	Buddy Bell (DK)	.15	.11	.06
24	Ken Singleton (DK)	.10	.08	.04
25	John Mayberry (DK)	.08	.06	.03
26	Gorman Thomas (DK)	.12	.09	.05
27	Earl Weaver	.10	.08	.04
28	Rollie Fingers	.20	.15	.08
29	Sparky Anderson	.10	.08	.04
30	Dennis Eckersley	.10	.08	.04
31	Dave Winfield	.40	.30	.15
32	Burt Hooton	.08	.06	.03
33	Rick Waits	.06	.05	.02
34	George Brett	.70	.50	.30
35	Steve McCatty	.06	.05	.02
36	Steve Rogers	.08	.06	.03
37	Bill Stein	.06	.05	.02
38	Steve Renko	.06	.05	.02
39	Mike Squires	.06	.05	.02
40	George Hendrick	.08	.06	.03
41	Bob Knepper	.08	.06	.03
42	Steve Carlton	.50	.40	.20
43	Larry Biittner	.06	.05	.02
44	Chris Welsh	.06	.05	.02
45	Steve Nicosia	.06	.05	.02
46	Jack Clark	.25	.20	.10
47	Chris Chambliss	.08	.06	.03
48	Ivan DeJesus	.06	.05	.02
49	Lee Mazzilli	.08	.06	.03
50	Julio Cruz	.06	.05	.02
51	Pete Redfern	.06	.05	.02
52	Dave Stieb	.12	.09	.05
53	Doug Corbett	.06	.05	.02
54	Jorge Bell	8.00	6.00	3.25
55	Joe Simpson	.06	.05	.02
56	Rusty Staub	.12	.09	.05
57	Hector Cruz	.06	.05	.02
58	Claudell Washington	.10	.08	.04
59	Enrique Romo	.06	.05	.02
60	Gary Lavelle	.06	.05	.02
61	Tim Flannery	.06	.05	.02
62	Joe Nolan	.06	.05	.02
63	Larry Bowa	.15	.11	.06
64	Sixto Lezcano	.06	.05	.02
65	Joe Sambito	.06	.05	.02
66	Bruce Kison	.06	.05	.02
67	Wayne Nordhagen	.06	.05	.02
68	Woodie Fryman	.08	.06	.03
69	Billy Sample	.06	.05	.02
70	Amos Otis	.08	.06	.03
71	Matt Keough	.06	.05	.02
72	Toby Harrah	.08	.06	.03
73	Dave Righetti	1.50	1.25	.60
74	Carl Yastrzemski	.80	.60	.30
75	Bob Welch	.10	.08	.04
76a	Alan Trammel (name incorrect)	1.25	.90	.50
76b	Alan Trammell (name correct)	.40	.30	.15
77	Rick Dempsey	.08	.06	.03
78	Paul Molitor	.20	.15	.08
79	Dennis Martinez	.08	.06	.03

#	Player	MT	NR MT	EX
80	Jim Slaton	.06	.05	.02
81	Champ Summers	.06	.05	.02
82	Carney Lansford	.08	.06	.03
83	Barry Foote	.06	.05	.02
84	Steve Garvey	.50	.40	.20
85	Rick Manning	.06	.05	.02
86	John Wathan	.08	.06	.03
87	Brian Kingman	.06	.05	.02
88	Andre Dawson	.35	.25	.14
89	Jim Kern	.06	.05	.02
90	Bobby Grich	.10	.08	.04
91	Bob Forsch	.08	.06	.03
92	Art Howe	.06	.05	.02
93	Marty Bystrom	.06	.05	.02
94	Ozzie Smith	.15	.11	.06
95	Dave Parker	.30	.25	.12
96	Doyle Alexander	.12	.09	.05
97	Al Hrabosky	.08	.06	.03
98	Frank Taveras	.06	.05	.02
99	Tim Blackwell	.06	.05	.02
100	Floyd Bannister	.10	.08	.04
101	Alfredo Griffin	.08	.06	.03
102	Dave Engle	.06	.05	.02
103	Mario Soto	.10	.08	.04
104	Ross Baumgarten	.06	.05	.02
105	Ken Singleton	.10	.08	.04
106	Ted Simmons	.15	.11	.06
107	Jack Morris	.30	.25	.12
108	Bob Watson	.08	.06	.03
109	Dwight Evans	.15	.11	.06
110	Tom Lasorda	.10	.08	.04
111	Bert Blyleven	.15	.11	.06
112	Dan Quisenberry	.20	.15	.08
113	Rickey Henderson	.60	.45	.25
114	Gary Carter	.40	.30	.15
115	Brian Downing	.10	.08	.04
116	Al Oliver	.15	.11	.06
117	LaMarr Hoyt	.08	.06	.03
118	Cesar Cedeno	.12	.09	.05
119	Keith Moreland	.12	.09	.05
120	Bob Shirley	.06	.05	.02
121	Terry Kennedy	.08	.06	.03
122	Frank Pastore	.06	.05	.02
123	Gene Garber	.06	.05	.02
124	Tony Pena	.25	.20	.10
125	Allen Ripley	.06	.05	.02
126	Randy Martz	.06	.05	.02
127	Richie Zisk	.08	.06	.03
128	Mike Scott	.15	.11	.06
129	Lloyd Moseby	.25	.20	.10
130	Rob Wilfong	.06	.05	.02
131	Tim Stoddard	.06	.05	.02
132	Gorman Thomas	.12	.09	.05
133	Dan Petry	.10	.08	.04
134	Bob Stanley	.08	.06	.03
135	Lou Piniella	.15	.11	.06
136	Pedro Guerrero	.40	.30	.15
137	Len Barker	.08	.06	.03
138	Richard Gale	.06	.05	.02
139	Wayne Gross	.06	.05	.02
140	Tim Wallach	1.25	.90	.50
141	Gene Mauch	.08	.06	.03
142	Doc Medich	.06	.05	.02
143	Tony Bernazard	.08	.06	.03
144	Bill Virdon	.08	.06	.03
145	John Littlefield	.06	.05	.02
146	Dave Bergman	.06	.05	.02
147	Dick Davis	.06	.05	.02
148	Tom Seaver	.50	.40	.20
149	Matt Sinatro	.06	.05	.02
150	Chuck Tanner	.08	.06	.03
151	Leon Durham	.15	.11	.06
152	Gene Tenace	.08	.06	.03
153	Al Bumbry	.08	.06	.03
154	Mark Brouhard	.06	.05	.02
155	Rick Peters	.06	.05	.02
156	Jerry Remy	.06	.05	.02
157	Rick Reuschel	.10	.08	.04
158	Steve Howe	.08	.06	.03
159	Alan Bannister	.06	.05	.02
160	U L Washington	.06	.05	.02
161	Rick Langford	.06	.05	.02
162	Bill Gullickson	.12	.09	.05
163	Mark Wagner	.06	.05	.02
164	Geoff Zahn	.06	.05	.02
165	Ron LeFlore	.08	.06	.03
166	Dane Iorg	.06	.05	.02
167	Joe Niekro	.12	.09	.05
168	Pete Rose	1.00	.70	.40
169	Dave Collins	.08	.06	.03
170	Rick Wise	.08	.06	.03
171	Jim Bibby	.06	.05	.02
172	Larry Herndon	.08	.06	.03
173	Bob Horner	.30	.25	.12
174	Steve Dillard	.06	.05	.02
175	Mookie Wilson	.12	.09	.05
176	Dan Meyer	.06	.05	.02
177	Fernando Arroyo	.06	.05	.02
178	Jackson Todd	.06	.05	.02
179	Darrell Jackson	.06	.05	.02
180	Al Woods	.06	.05	.02
181	Jim Anderson	.06	.05	.02
182	Dave Kingman	.15	.11	.06
183	Steve Henderson	.06	.05	.02
184	Brian Asselstine	.06	.05	.02
185	Rod Scurry	.06	.05	.02
186	Fred Breining	.06	.05	.02
187	Danny Boone	.06	.05	.02
188	Junior Kennedy	.06	.05	.02
189	Sparky Lyle	.10	.08	.04
190	Whitey Herzog	.10	.08	.04
191	Dave Smith	.10	.08	.04
192	Ed Ott	.06	.05	.02
193	Greg Luzinski	.15	.11	.06
194	Bill Lee	.08	.06	.03
195	Don Zimmer	.06	.05	.02
196	Hal McRae	.12	.09	.05
197	Mike Norris	.06	.05	.02
198	Duane Kuiper	.06	.05	.02
199	Rick Cerone	.08	.06	.03
200	Jim Rice	.40	.30	.15
201	Steve Yeager	.06	.05	.02
202	Tom Brookens	.06	.05	.02
203	Jose Morales	.06	.05	.02
204	Roy Howell	.06	.05	.02
205	Tippy Martinez	.06	.05	.02
206	Moose Haas	.06	.05	.02
207	Al Cowens	.06	.05	.02
208	Dave Stapleton	.06	.05	.02
209	Bucky Dent	.10	.08	.04
210	Ron Cey	.12	.09	.05
211	Jorge Orta	.06	.05	.02
212	Jamie Quirk	.06	.05	.02
213	Jeff Jones	.06	.05	.02
214	Tim Raines	.90	.70	.35
215	Jon Matlack	.08	.06	.03
216	Rod Carew	.50	.40	.20
217	Jim Kaat	.15	.11	.06
218	Joe Pittman	.06	.05	.02
219	Larry Christenson	.06	.05	.02
220	Juan Bonilla	.10	.08	.04
221	Mike Easler	.10	.08	.04
222	Vida Blue	.12	.09	.05
223	Rick Camp	.06	.05	.02
224	Mike Jorgensen	.06	.05	.02
225	Jody Davis	.50	.40	.20
226	Mike Parrott	.06	.05	.02
227	Jim Clancy	.10	.08	.04
228	Hosken Powell	.06	.05	.02
229	Tom Hume	.06	.05	.02
230	Britt Burns	.08	.06	.03
231	Jim Palmer	.40	.30	.15
232	Bob Rodgers	.08	.06	.03
233	Milt Wilcox	.08	.06	.03
234	Dave Revering	.06	.05	.02
235	Mike Torrez	.08	.06	.03
236	Robert Castillo	.06	.05	.02
237	Von Hayes	.90	.70	.35
238	Renie Martin	.06	.05	.02
239	Dwayne Murphy	.08	.06	.03
240	Rodney Scott	.06	.05	.02
241	Fred Patek	.06	.05	.02
242	Mickey Rivers	.08	.06	.03
243	Steve Trout	.08	.06	.03
244	Jose Cruz	.12	.09	.05
245	Manny Trillo	.08	.06	.03
246	Lary Sorensen	.06	.05	.02
247	Dave Edwards	.06	.05	.02
248	Dan Driessen	.08	.06	.03
249	Tommy Boggs	.06	.05	.02
250	Dale Berra	.06	.05	.02
251	Ed Whitson	.08	.06	.03
252	Lee Smith	.60	.45	.25
253	Tom Paciorek	.08	.06	.03
254	Pat Zachry	.06	.05	.02
255	Luis Leal	.06	.05	.02
256	John Castino	.06	.05	.02
257	Rich Dauer	.06	.05	.02
258	Cecil Cooper	.15	.11	.06
259	Dave Rozema	.06	.05	.02
260	John Tudor	.15	.11	.06
261	Jerry Mumphrey	.08	.06	.03

#	Player	MT	NR MT	EX
262	Jay Johnstone	.10	.08	.04
263	Bo Diaz	.08	.06	.03
264	Dennis Leonard	.08	.06	.03
265	Jim Spencer	.06	.05	.02
266	John Milner	.06	.05	.02
267	Don Aase	.08	.06	.03
268	Jim Sundberg	.08	.06	.03
269	Lamar Johnson	.06	.05	.02
270	Frank LaCorte	.06	.05	.02
271	Barry Evans	.06	.05	.02
272	Enos Cabell	.08	.06	.03
273	Del Unser	.06	.05	.02
274	George Foster	.20	.15	.08
275	Brett Butler	.50	.40	.20
276	Lee Lacy	.08	.06	.03
277	Ken Reitz	.06	.05	.02
278	Keith Hernandez	.40	.30	.15
279	Doug DeCinces	.10	.08	.04
280	Charlie Moore	.06	.05	.02
281	Lance Parrish	.35	.25	.14
282	Ralph Houk	.08	.06	.03
283	Rich Gossage	.20	.15	.08
284	Jerry Reuss	.10	.08	.04
285	Mike Stanton	.06	.05	.02
286	Frank White	.10	.08	.04
287	Bob Owchinko	.06	.05	.02
288	Scott Sanderson	.08	.06	.03
289	Bump Wills	.06	.05	.02
290	Dave Frost	.06	.05	.02
291	Chet Lemon	.08	.06	.03
292	Tito Landrum	.06	.05	.02
293	Vern Ruhle	.06	.05	.02
294	Mike Schmidt	.80	.60	.30
295	Sam Mejias	.06	.05	.02
296	Gary Lucas	.06	.05	.02
297	John Candelaria	.10	.08	.04
298	Jerry Martin	.06	.05	.02
299	Dale Murphy	.90	.70	.35
300	Mike Lum	.06	.05	.02
301	Tom Hausman	.06	.05	.02
302	Glenn Abbott	.06	.05	.02
303	Roger Erickson	.06	.05	.02
304	Otto Velez	.06	.05	.02
305	Danny Goodwin	.06	.05	.02
306	John Mayberry	.08	.06	.03
307	Lenny Randle	.06	.05	.02
308	Bob Bailor	.06	.05	.02
309	Jerry Morales	.06	.05	.02
310	Rufino Linares	.06	.05	.02
311	Kent Tekulve	.08	.06	.03
312	Joe Morgan	.30	.25	.12
313	John Urrea	.06	.05	.02
314	Paul Householder	.06	.05	.02
315	Garry Maddox	.10	.08	.04
316	Mike Ramsey	.06	.05	.02
317	Alan Ashby	.06	.05	.02
318	Bob Clark	.06	.05	.02
319	Tony LaRussa	.08	.06	.03
320	Charlie Lea	.06	.05	.02
321	Danny Darwin	.08	.06	.03
322	Cesar Geronimo	.06	.05	.02
323	Tom Underwood	.06	.05	.02
324	Andre Thornton	.10	.08	.04
325	Rudy May	.08	.06	.03
326	Frank Tanana	.10	.08	.04
327	Davey Lopes	.10	.08	.04
328	Richie Hebner	.06	.05	.02
329	Mike Flanagan	.10	.08	.04
330	Mike Caldwell	.06	.05	.02
331	Scott McGregor	.10	.08	.04
332	Jerry Augustine	.06	.05	.02
333	Stan Papi	.06	.05	.02
334	Rick Miller	.06	.05	.02
335	Graig Nettles	.15	.11	.06
336	Dusty Baker	.10	.08	.04
337	Dave Garcia	.06	.05	.02
338	Larry Gura	.08	.06	.03
339	Cliff Johnson	.06	.05	.02
340	Warren Cromartie	.06	.05	.02
341	Steve Comer	.06	.05	.02
342	Rick Burleson	.08	.06	.03
343	John Martin	.06	.05	.02
344	Craig Reynolds	.06	.05	.02
345	Mike Proly	.06	.05	.02
346	Ruppert Jones	.06	.05	.02
347	Omar Moreno	.06	.05	.02
348	Greg Minton	.06	.05	.02
349	Rick Mahler	.25	.20	.10
350	Alex Trevino	.06	.05	.02
351	Mike Krukow	.08	.06	.03
352a	Shane Rawley (Jim Anderson photo - shaking hands)	1.25	.90	.50
352b	Shane Rawley (correct photo - kneeling)	.15	.11	.06
353	Garth Iorg	.06	.05	.02
354	Pete Mackanin	.06	.05	.02
355	Paul Moskau	.06	.05	.02
356	Richard Dotson	.10	.08	.04
357	Steve Stone	.08	.06	.03
358	Larry Hisle	.08	.06	.03
359	Aurelio Lopez	.06	.05	.02
360	Oscar Gamble	.08	.06	.03
361	Tom Burgmeier	.06	.05	.02
362	Terry Forster	.08	.06	.03
363	Joe Charboneau	.08	.06	.03
364	Ken Brett	.08	.06	.03
365	Tony Armas	.10	.08	.04
366	Chris Speier	.08	.06	.03
367	Fred Lynn	.20	.15	.08
368	Buddy Bell	.15	.11	.06
369	Jim Essian	.06	.05	.02
370	Terry Puhl	.06	.05	.02
371	Greg Gross	.06	.05	.02
372	Bruce Sutter	.15	.11	.06
373	Joe Lefebvre	.06	.05	.02
374	Ray Knight	.10	.08	.04
375	Bruce Benedict	.06	.05	.02
376	Tim Foli	.06	.05	.02
377	Al Holland	.06	.05	.02
378	Ken Kravec	.06	.05	.02
379	Jeff Burroughs	.08	.06	.03
380	Pete Falcone	.06	.05	.02
381	Ernie Whitt	.08	.06	.03
382	Brad Havens	.06	.05	.02
383	Terry Crowley	.06	.05	.02
384	Don Money	.08	.06	.03
385	Dan Schatzeder	.06	.05	.02
386	Gary Allenson	.06	.05	.02
387	Yogi Berra	.15	.11	.06
388	Ken Landreaux	.08	.06	.03
389	Mike Hargrove	.08	.06	.03
390	Darryl Motley	.10	.08	.04
391	Dave McKay	.06	.05	.02
392	Stan Bahnsen	.06	.05	.02
393	Ken Forsch	.08	.06	.03
394	Mario Mendoza	.06	.05	.02
395	Jim Morrison	.06	.05	.02
396	Mike Ivie	.06	.05	.02
397	Broderick Perkins	.06	.05	.02
398	Darrell Evans	.15	.11	.06
399	Ron Reed	.08	.06	.03
400	Johnny Bench	.50	.40	.20
401	Steve Bedrosian	.80	.60	.30
402	Bill Robinson	.06	.05	.02
403	Bill Buckner	.12	.09	.05
404	Ken Oberkfell	.08	.06	.03
405	Cal Ripken, Jr.	8.00	6.00	3.25
406	Jim Gantner	.08	.06	.03
407	Kirk Gibson	.40	.30	.15
408	Tony Perez	.20	.15	.08
409	Tommy John	.20	.15	.08
410	Dave Stewart	.40	.30	.15
411	Dan Spillner	.06	.05	.02
412	Willie Aikens	.06	.05	.02
413	Mike Heath	.06	.05	.02
414	Ray Burris	.06	.05	.02
415	Leon Roberts	.06	.05	.02
416	Mike Witt	.90	.70	.35
417	Bobby Molinaro	.06	.05	.02
418	Steve Braun	.06	.05	.02
419	Nolan Ryan	.50	.40	.20
420	Tug McGraw	.12	.09	.05
421	Dave Concepcion	.15	.11	.06
422a	Juan Eichelberger (Gary Lucas photo - white player)	1.25	.90	.50
422b	Juan Eichelberger (correct photo - black player)	.08	.06	.03
423	Rick Rhoden	.10	.08	.04
424	Frank Robinson	.12	.09	.05
425	Eddie Miller	.06	.05	.02
426	Bill Caudill	.06	.05	.02
427	Doug Flynn	.06	.05	.02
428	Larry Anderson (Andersen)	.10	.08	.04
429	Al Williams	.06	.05	.02
430	Jerry Garvin	.06	.05	.02
431	Glenn Adams	.06	.05	.02
432	Barry Bonnell	.06	.05	.02
433	Jerry Narron	.06	.05	.02
434	John Stearns	.06	.05	.02
435	Mike Tyson	.06	.05	.02
436	Glenn Hubbard	.08	.06	.03

#	Player	MT	NR MT	EX
437	Eddie Solomon	.06	.05	.02
438	Jeff Leonard	.10	.08	.04
439	Randy Bass	.06	.05	.02
440	Mike LaCoss	.08	.06	.03
441	Gary Matthews	.10	.08	.04
442	Mark Littell	.06	.05	.02
443	Don Sutton	.30	.25	.12
444	John Harris	.06	.05	.02
445	Vada Pinson	.08	.06	.03
446	Elias Sosa	.06	.05	.02
447	Charlie Hough	.10	.08	.04
448	Willie Wilson	.15	.11	.06
449	Fred Stanley	.06	.05	.02
450	Tom Veryzer	.06	.05	.02
451	Ron Davis	.06	.05	.02
452	Mark Clear	.08	.06	.03
453	Bill Russell	.08	.06	.03
454	Lou Whitaker	.30	.25	.12
455	Dan Graham	.06	.05	.02
456	Reggie Cleveland	.06	.05	.02
457	Sammy Stewart	.06	.05	.02
458	Pete Vuckovich	.08	.06	.03
459	John Wockenfuss	.06	.05	.02
460	Glenn Hoffman	.06	.05	.02
461	Willie Randolph	.10	.08	.04
462	Fernando Valenzuela	.80	.60	.30
463	Ron Hassey	.06	.05	.02
464	Paul Splittorff	.08	.06	.03
465	Rob Picciolo	.06	.05	.02
466	Larry Parrish	.10	.08	.04
467	Johnny Grubb	.06	.05	.02
468	Dan Ford	.06	.05	.02
469	Silvio Martinez	.06	.05	.02
470	Kiko Garcia	.06	.05	.02
471	Bob Boone	.10	.08	.04
472	Luis Salazar	.06	.05	.02
473	Randy Niemann	.06	.05	.02
474	Tom Griffin	.06	.05	.02
475	Phil Niekro	.30	.25	.12
476	Hubie Brooks	.25	.20	.10
477	Dick Tidrow	.06	.05	.02
478	Jim Beattie	.06	.05	.02
479	Damaso Garcia	.08	.06	.03
480	Mickey Hatcher	.08	.06	.03
481	Joe Price	.06	.05	.02
482	Ed Farmer	.06	.05	.02
483	Eddie Murray	.60	.45	.25
484	Ben Oglivie	.08	.06	.03
485	Kevin Saucier	.06	.05	.02
486	Bobby Murcer	.10	.08	.04
487	Bill Campbell	.06	.05	.02
488	Reggie Smith	.10	.08	.04
489	Wayne Garland	.06	.05	.02
490	Jim Wright	.06	.05	.02
491	Billy Martin	.12	.09	.05
492	Jim Fanning	.06	.05	.02
493	Don Baylor	.15	.11	.06
494	Rick Honeycutt	.08	.06	.03
495	Carlton Fisk	.20	.15	.08
496	Denny Walling	.06	.05	.02
497	Bake McBride	.06	.05	.02
498	Darrell Porter	.08	.06	.03
499	Gene Richards	.06	.05	.02
500	Ron Oester	.06	.05	.02
501	Ken Dayley	.20	.15	.08
502	Jason Thompson	.06	.05	.02
503	Milt May	.06	.05	.02
504	Doug Bird	.06	.05	.02
505	Bruce Bochte	.06	.05	.02
506	Neil Allen	.06	.05	.02
507	Joey McLaughlin	.06	.05	.02
508	Butch Wynegar	.08	.06	.03
509	Gary Roenicke	.08	.06	.03
510	Robin Yount	.40	.30	.15
511	Dave Tobik	.06	.05	.02
512	Rich Gedman	.40	.30	.15
513	Gene Nelson	.12	.09	.05
514	Rick Monday	.10	.08	.04
515	Miguel Dilone	.06	.05	.02
516	Clint Hurdle	.06	.05	.02
517	Jeff Newman	.06	.05	.02
518	Grant Jackson	.06	.05	.02
519	Andy Hassler	.06	.05	.02
520	Pat Putnam	.06	.05	.02
521	Greg Pryor	.06	.05	.02
522	Tony Scott	.06	.05	.02
523	Steve Mura	.06	.05	.02
524	Johnnie LeMaster	.06	.05	.02
525	Dick Ruthven	.06	.05	.02
526	John McNamara	.06	.05	.02
527	Larry McWilliams	.06	.05	.02
528	Johnny Ray	.80	.60	.30
529	Pat Tabler	.60	.45	.25
530	Tom Herr	.10	.08	.04
531a	San Diego Chicken (trademark symbol on front)	1.25	.90	.50
531b	San Diego Chicken (no trademark symbol)	.50	.40	.20
532	Sal Butera	.06	.05	.02
533	Mike Griffin	.06	.05	.02
534	Kelvin Moore	.06	.05	.02
535	Reggie Jackson	.60	.45	.25
536	Ed Romero	.06	.05	.02
537	Derrel Thomas	.06	.05	.02
538	Mike O'Berry	.06	.05	.02
539	Jack O'Connor	.06	.05	.02
540	Bob Ojeda	.60	.45	.25
541	Roy Lee Jackson	.06	.05	.02
542	Lynn Jones	.06	.05	.02
543	Gaylord Perry	.30	.25	.12
544a	Phil Garner (photo reversed)	1.25	.90	.50
544b	Phil Garner (photo correct)	.10	.08	.04
545	Garry Templeton	.10	.08	.04
546	Rafael Ramirez	.10	.08	.04
547	Jeff Reardon	.20	.15	.08
548	Ron Guidry	.25	.20	.10
549	Tim Laudner	.20	.15	.08
550	John Henry Johnson	.06	.05	.02
551	Chris Bando	.06	.05	.02
552	Bobby Brown	.06	.05	.02
553	Larry Bradford	.06	.05	.02
554	Scott Fletcher	.30	.25	.12
555	Jerry Royster	.06	.05	.02
556	Shooty Babbitt	.06	.05	.02
557	Kent Hrbek	2.50	2.00	1.00
558	Yankee Winners (Ron Guidry, Tommy John)	.15	.11	.06
559	Mark Bomback	.06	.05	.02
560	Julio Valdez	.06	.05	.02
561	Buck Martinez	.06	.05	.02
562	Mike Marshall	1.00	.70	.40
563	Rennie Stennett	.06	.05	.02
564	Steve Crawford	.06	.05	.02
565	Bob Babcock	.06	.05	.02
566	Johnny Podres	.08	.06	.03
567	Paul Serna	.06	.05	.02
568	Harold Baines	.40	.30	.15
569	Dave LaRoche	.06	.05	.02
570	Lee May	.08	.06	.03
571	Gary Ward	.10	.08	.04
572	John Denny	.08	.06	.03
573	Roy Smalley	.08	.06	.03
574	Bob Brenly	.35	.25	.14
575	Bronx Bombers (Reggie Jackson, Dave Winfield)	.40	.30	.15
576	Luis Pujols	.06	.05	.02
577	Butch Hobson	.06	.05	.02
578	Harvey Kuenn	.08	.06	.03
579	Cal Ripken, Sr.	.10	.08	.04
580	Juan Berenguer	.08	.06	.03
581	Benny Ayala	.06	.05	.02
582	Vance Law	.12	.09	.05
583	Rick Leach	.12	.09	.05
584	George Frazier	.06	.05	.02
585	Phillies Finest (Pete Rose, Mike Schmidt)	.70	.50	.30
586	Joe Rudi	.10	.08	.04
587	Juan Beniquez	.06	.05	.02
588	Luis DeLeon	.08	.06	.03
589	Craig Swan	.06	.05	.02
590	Dave Chalk	.06	.05	.02
591	Billy Gardner	.06	.05	.02
592	Sal Bando	.08	.06	.03
593	Bert Campaneris	.10	.08	.04
594	Steve Kemp	.08	.06	.03
595a	Randy Lerch (Braves)	1.25	.90	.50
595b	Randy Lerch (Brewers)	.08	.06	.03
596	Bryan Clark	.10	.08	.04
597	Dave Ford	.06	.05	.02
598	Mike Scioscia	.06	.05	.02
599	John Lowenstein	.06	.05	.02
600	Rene Lachmann (Lachemann)	.06	.05	.02
601	Mick Kelleher	.06	.05	.02
602	Ron Jackson	.06	.05	.02
603	Jerry Koosman	.12	.09	.05
604	Dave Goltz	.08	.06	.03
605	Ellis Valentine	.06	.05	.02
606	Lonnie Smith	.08	.06	.03
607	Joaquin Andujar	.10	.08	.04
608	Garry Hancock	.06	.05	.02
609	Jerry Turner	.06	.05	.02
610	Bob Bonner	.06	.05	.02

		MT	NR MT	EX
611	Jim Dwyer	.06	.05	.02
612	Terry Bulling	.06	.05	.02
613	Joel Youngblood	.06	.05	.02
614	Larry Milbourne	.06	.05	.02
615	Phil Roof (Gene)	.06	.05	.02
616	Keith Drumwright	.06	.05	.02
617	Dave Rosello	.06	.05	.02
618	Rickey Keeton	.06	.05	.02
619	Dennis Lamp	.06	.05	.02
620	Sid Monge	.06	.05	.02
621	Jerry White	.06	.05	.02
622	Luis Aguayo	.10	.08	.04
623	Jamie Easterly	.06	.05	.02
624	Steve Sax	1.25	.90	.50
625	Dave Roberts	.06	.05	.02
626	Rick Bosetti	.06	.05	.02
627	Terry Francona	.12	.09	.05
628	Pride of the Reds (Johnny Bench, Tom Seaver)	.35	.25	.14
629	Paul Mirabella	.06	.05	.02
630	Rance Mulliniks	.06	.05	.02
631	Kevin Hickey	.06	.05	.02
632	Reid Nichols	.06	.05	.02
633	Dave Geisel	.06	.05	.02
634	Ken Griffey	.12	.09	.05
635	Bob Lemon	.12	.09	.05
636	Orlando Sanchez	.06	.05	.02
637	Bill Almon	.06	.05	.02
638	Danny Ainge	.20	.15	.08
639	Willie Stargell	.30	.25	.12
640	Bob Sykes	.06	.05	.02
641	Ed Lynch	.10	.08	.04
642	John Ellis	.06	.05	.02
643	Fergie Jenkins	.15	.11	.06
644	Lenn Sakata	.06	.05	.02
645	Julio Gonzales	.06	.05	.02
646	Jesse Orosco	.20	.15	.08
647	Jerry Dybzinski	.06	.05	.02
648	Tommy Davis	.08	.06	.03
649	Ron Gardenhire	.06	.05	.02
650	Felipe Alou	.08	.06	.03
651	Harvey Haddix	.08	.06	.03
652	Willie Upshaw	.15	.11	.06
653	Bill Madlock	.15	.11	.06
---a	Checklist 1-26 DK (5 Trammel)	.70	.50	.30
---b	Checklist 1-26 DK (5 Trammell)	.08	.06	.03
---	Checklist 27-130	.06	.05	.02
---	Checklist 131-234	.06	.05	.02
---	Checklist 235-338	.06	.05	.02
---	Checklist 339-442	.06	.05	.02
---	Checklist 443-544	.06	.05	.02
---	Checklist 545-653	.06	.05	.02

1983 Donruss

 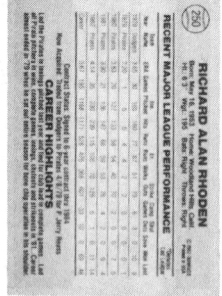

The 1983 Donruss set consists of 653 numbered cards plus seven unnumbered checklists. The cards, which measure 2½'' by 3½'', were issued with puzzle pieces (three pieces on one card per pack) that featured Ty Cobb. The first 26 cards in the set are once again the Diamond King series. The card fronts display the Donruss logo and the year of issue. The card backs have black print on yellow and white and include statistics, career highlights, and the player's contract status. (DK) in the checklist that follows indicates cards which belong to the Diamond King series.

		MT	NR MT	EX
Complete Set:		28.00	21.00	11.00
Common Player:		.06	.05	.02
1	Fernando Valenzuela (DK)	.40	.30	.15
2	Rollie Fingers (DK)	.20	.15	.08
3	Reggie Jackson (DK)	.50	.40	.20
4	Jim Palmer (DK)	.40	.30	.15
5	Jack Morris (DK)	.30	.25	.12
6	George Foster (DK)	.20	.15	.08
7	Jim Sundberg (DK)	.08	.06	.03
8	Willie Stargell (DK)	.30	.25	.12
9	Dave Stieb (DK)	.12	.09	.05
10	Joe Niekro (DK)	.12	.09	.05
11	Rickey Henderson (DK)	.60	.45	.25
12	Dale Murphy (DK)	.80	.60	.30
13	Toby Harrah (DK)	.08	.06	.03
14	Bill Buckner (DK)	.12	.09	.05
15	Willie Wilson (DK)	.15	.11	.06
16	Steve Carlton (DK)	.40	.30	.15
17	Ron Guidry (DK)	.25	.20	.10
18	Steve Rogers (DK)	.08	.06	.03
19	Kent Hrbek (DK)	.40	.30	.15
20	Keith Hernandez (DK)	.40	.30	.15
21	Floyd Bannister (DK)	.10	.08	.04
22	Johnny Bench (DK)	.40	.30	.15
23	Britt Burns (DK)	.08	.06	.03
24	Joe Morgan (DK)	.30	.25	.12
25	Carl Yastrzemski (DK)	.80	.60	.30
26	Terry Kennedy (DK)	.08	.06	.03
27	Gary Roenicke	.08	.06	.03
28	Dwight Bernard	.06	.05	.02
29	Pat Underwood	.06	.05	.02
30	Gary Allenson	.06	.05	.02
31	Ron Guidry	.25	.20	.10
32	Burt Hooton	.08	.06	.03
33	Chris Bando	.06	.05	.02
34	Vida Blue	.12	.09	.05
35	Rickey Henderson	.60	.45	.25
36	Ray Burris	.06	.05	.02
37	John Butcher	.06	.05	.02
38	Don Aase	.08	.06	.03
39	Jerry Koosman	.12	.09	.05
40	Bruce Sutter	.15	.11	.06
41	Jose Cruz	.12	.09	.05
42	Pete Rose	1.00	.70	.40
43	Cesar Cedeno	.12	.09	.05
44	Floyd Chiffer	.06	.05	.02
45	Larry McWilliams	.06	.05	.02
46	Alan Fowlkes	.06	.05	.02
47	Dale Murphy	.90	.70	.35
48	Doug Bird	.06	.05	.02
49	Hubie Brooks	.12	.09	.05
50	Floyd Bannister	.10	.08	.04
51	Jack O'Connor	.06	.05	.02
52	Steve Senteney	.06	.05	.02
53	Gary Gaetti	1.50	1.25	.60
54	Damaso Garcia	.08	.06	.03
55	Gene Nelson	.06	.05	.02
56	Mookie Wilson	.10	.08	.04
57	Allen Ripley	.06	.05	.02
58	Bob Horner	.30	.25	.12
59	Tony Pena	.10	.08	.04
60	Gary Lavelle	.06	.05	.02
61	Tim Lollar	.06	.05	.02
62	Frank Pastore	.06	.05	.02
63	Garry Maddox	.10	.08	.04
64	Bob Forsch	.08	.06	.03
65	Harry Spilman	.06	.05	.02
66	Geoff Zahn	.06	.05	.02
67	Salome Barojas	.06	.05	.02
68	David Palmer	.08	.06	.03
69	Charlie Hough	.10	.08	.04
70	Dan Quisenberry	.20	.15	.08
71	Tony Armas	.10	.08	.04
72	Rick Sutcliffe	.12	.09	.05
73	Steve Balboni	.15	.11	.06
74	Jerry Remy	.06	.05	.02
75	Mike Scioscia	.06	.05	.02
76	John Wockenfuss	.06	.05	.02
77	Jim Palmer	.40	.30	.15
78	Rollie Fingers	.20	.15	.08
79	Joe Nolan	.06	.05	.02
80	Pete Vuckovich	.08	.06	.03
81	Rick Leach	.06	.05	.02
82	Rick Miller	.06	.05	.02
83	Graig Nettles	.15	.11	.06
84	Ron Cey	.12	.09	.05
85	Miguel Dilone	.06	.05	.02
86	John Wathan	.08	.06	.03
87	Kelvin Moore	.06	.05	.02
88a	Byrn Smith (first name incorrect)	.90	.70	.35

		MT	NR MT	EX
88b	Bryn Smith (first name correct)	.08	.06	.03
89	Dave Hostetler	.06	.05	.02
90	Rod Carew	.50	.40	.20
91	Lonnie Smith	.08	.06	.03
92	Bob Knepper	.08	.06	.03
93	Marty Bystrom	.06	.05	.02
94	Chris Welsh	.06	.05	.02
95	Jason Thompson	.06	.05	.02
96	Tom O'Malley	.06	.05	.02
97	Phil Niekro	.30	.25	.12
98	Neil Allen	.06	.05	.02
99	Bill Buckner	.12	.09	.05
100	Ed VandeBerg (Vande Berg)	.10	.08	.04
101	Jim Clancy	.10	.08	.04
102	Robert Castillo	.06	.05	.02
103	Bruce Berenyi	.06	.05	.02
104	Carlton Fisk	.20	.15	.08
105	Mike Flanagan	.10	.08	.04
106	Cecil Cooper	.15	.11	.06
107	Jack Morris	.30	.25	.12
108	Mike Morgan	.10	.08	.04
109	Luis Aponte	.06	.05	.02
110	Pedro Guerrero	.25	.20	.10
111	Len Barker	.08	.06	.03
112	Willie Wilson	.15	.11	.06
113	Dave Beard	.06	.05	.02
114	Mike Gates	.06	.05	.02
115	Reggie Jackson	.50	.40	.20
116	George Wright	.06	.05	.02
117	Vance Law	.08	.06	.03
118	Nolan Ryan	.40	.30	.15
119	Mike Krukow	.08	.06	.03
120	Ozzie Smith	.15	.11	.06
121	Broderick Perkins	.06	.05	.02
122	Tom Seaver	.40	.30	.15
123	Chris Chambliss	.08	.06	.03
124	Chuck Tanner	.08	.06	.03
125	Johnnie LeMaster	.06	.05	.02
126	Mel Hall	.50	.40	.20
127	Bruce Bochte	.06	.05	.02
128	Charlie Puleo	.12	.09	.05
129	Luis Leal	.06	.05	.02
130	John Pacella	.06	.05	.02
131	Glenn Gulliver	.06	.05	.02
132	Don Money	.08	.06	.03
133	Dave Rozema	.06	.05	.02
134	Bruce Hurst	.10	.08	.04
135	Rudy May	.08	.06	.03
136	Tom LaSorda (Lasorda)	.10	.08	.04
137	Dan Spillner (photo actually Ed Whitson)	.06	.05	.02
138	Jerry Martin	.06	.05	.02
139	Mike Norris	.06	.05	.02
140	Al Oliver	.15	.11	.06
141	Daryl Sconiers	.06	.05	.02
142	Lamar Johnson	.06	.05	.02
143	Harold Baines	.15	.11	.06
144	Alan Ashby	.06	.05	.02
145	Garry Templeton	.10	.08	.04
146	Al Holland	.06	.05	.02
147	Bo Diaz	.08	.06	.03
148	Dave Concepcion	.15	.11	.06
149	Rick Camp	.06	.05	.02
150	Jim Morrison	.06	.05	.02
151	Randy Martz	.06	.05	.02
152	Keith Hernandez	.40	.30	.15
153	John Lowenstein	.06	.05	.02
154	Mike Caldwell	.06	.05	.02
155	Milt Wilcox	.08	.06	.03
156	Rich Gedman	.10	.08	.04
157	Rich Gossage	.20	.15	.08
158	Jerry Reuss	.10	.08	.04
159	Ron Hassey	.06	.05	.02
160	Larry Gura	.08	.06	.03
161	Dwayne Murphy	.08	.06	.03
162	Woodie Fryman	.08	.06	.03
163	Steve Comer	.06	.05	.02
164	Ken Forsch	.08	.06	.03
165	Dennis Lamp	.06	.05	.02
166	David Green	.10	.08	.04
167	Terry Puhl	.06	.05	.02
168	Mike Schmidt	.60	.45	.25
169	Eddie Milner	.15	.11	.06
170	John Curtis	.06	.05	.02
171	Don Robinson	.08	.06	.03
172	Richard Gale	.06	.05	.02
173	Steve Bedrosian	.12	.09	.05
174	Willie Hernandez	.08	.06	.03
175	Ron Gardenhire	.06	.05	.02
176	Jim Beattie	.06	.05	.02
177	Tim Laudner	.08	.06	.03

		MT	NR MT	EX
178	Buck Martinez	.06	.05	.02
179	Kent Hrbek	.30	.25	.12
180	Alfredo Griffin	.08	.06	.03
181	Larry Andersen	.06	.05	.02
182	Pete Falcone	.06	.05	.02
183	Jody Davis	.12	.09	.05
184	Glenn Hubbard	.08	.06	.03
185	Dale Berra	.06	.05	.02
186	Greg Minton	.06	.05	.02
187	Gary Lucas	.06	.05	.02
188	Dave Van Gorder	.06	.05	.02
189	Bob Dernier	.15	.11	.06
190	Willie McGee	1.50	1.25	.60
191	Dickie Thon	.08	.06	.03
192	Bob Boone	.10	.08	.04
193	Britt Burns	.06	.05	.02
194	Jeff Reardon	.12	.09	.05
195	Jon Matlack	.08	.06	.03
196	Don Slaught	.20	.15	.08
197	Fred Stanley	.06	.05	.02
198	Rick Manning	.06	.05	.02
199	Dave Righetti	.25	.20	.10
200	Dave Stapleton	.06	.05	.02
201	Steve Yeager	.06	.05	.02
202	Enos Cabell	.06	.05	.02
203	Sammy Stewart	.06	.05	.02
204	Moose Haas	.06	.05	.02
205	Lenn Sakata	.06	.05	.02
206	Charlie Moore	.06	.05	.02
207	Alan Trammell	.40	.30	.15
208	Jim Rice	.40	.30	.15
209	Roy Smalley	.08	.06	.03
210	Bill Russell	.08	.06	.03
211	Andre Thornton	.10	.08	.04
212	Willie Aikens	.06	.05	.02
213	Dave McKay	.06	.05	.02
214	Tim Blackwell	.06	.05	.02
215	Buddy Bell	.15	.11	.06
216	Doug DeCinces	.10	.08	.04
217	Tom Herr	.10	.08	.04
218	Frank LaCorte	.06	.05	.02
219	Steve Carlton	.40	.30	.15
220	Terry Kennedy	.08	.06	.03
221	Mike Easler	.08	.06	.03
222	Jack Clark	.25	.20	.10
223	Gene Garber	.06	.05	.02
224	Scott Holman	.06	.05	.02
225	Mike Proly	.06	.05	.02
226	Terry Bulling	.06	.05	.02
227	Jerry Garvin	.06	.05	.02
228	Ron Davis	.06	.05	.02
229	Tom Hume	.06	.05	.02
230	Marc Hill	.06	.05	.02
231	Dennis Martinez	.08	.06	.03
232	Jim Gantner	.08	.06	.03
233	Larry Pashnick	.06	.05	.02
234	Dave Collins	.08	.06	.03
235	Tom Burgmeier	.06	.05	.02
236	Ken Landreaux	.08	.06	.03
237	John Denny	.08	.06	.03
238	Hal McRae	.12	.09	.05
239	Matt Keough	.06	.05	.02
240	Doug Flynn	.06	.05	.02
241	Fred Lynn	.20	.15	.08
242	Billy Sample	.06	.05	.02
243	Tom Paciorek	.06	.05	.02
244	Joe Sambito	.06	.05	.02
245	Sid Monge	.06	.05	.02
246	Ken Oberkfell	.08	.06	.03
247	Joe Pittman (photo actually Juan Eichelberger)	.06	.05	.02
248	Mario Soto	.10	.08	.04
249	Claudell Washington	.08	.06	.03
250	Rick Rhoden	.10	.08	.04
251	Darrell Evans	.15	.11	.06
252	Steve Henderson	.06	.05	.02
253	Manny Castillo	.06	.05	.02
254	Craig Swan	.06	.05	.02
255	Joey McLaughlin	.06	.05	.02
256	Pete Redfern	.06	.05	.02
257	Ken Singleton	.10	.08	.04
258	Robin Yount	.40	.30	.15
259	Elias Sosa	.06	.05	.02
260	Bob Ojeda	.15	.11	.06
261	Bobby Murcer	.10	.08	.04
262	Candy Maldonado	.75	.60	.30
263	Rick Waits	.06	.05	.02
264	Greg Pryor	.06	.05	.02
265	Bob Owchinko	.06	.05	.02
266	Chris Speier	.06	.05	.02
267	Bruce Kison	.06	.05	.02

		MT	NR MT	EX
268	Mark Wagner	.06	.05	.02
269	Steve Kemp	.10	.08	.04
270	Phil Garner	.08	.06	.03
271	Gene Richards	.06	.05	.02
272	Renie Martin	.06	.05	.02
273	Dave Roberts	.06	.05	.02
274	Dan Driessen	.08	.06	.03
275	Rufino Linares	.06	.05	.02
276	Lee Lacy	.08	.06	.03
277	Ryne Sandberg	3.50	2.75	1.50
278	Darrell Porter	.08	.06	.03
279	Cal Ripken	1.00	.70	.40
280	Jamie Easterly	.06	.05	.02
281	Bill Fahey	.06	.05	.02
282	Glenn Hoffman	.06	.05	.02
283	Willie Randolph	.10	.08	.04
284	Fernando Valenzuela	.30	.25	.12
285	Alan Bannister	.06	.05	.02
286	Paul Splittorff	.08	.06	.03
287	Joe Rudi	.10	.08	.04
288	Bill Gullickson	.08	.06	.03
289	Danny Darwin	.08	.06	.03
290	Andy Hassler	.06	.05	.02
291	Ernesto Escarrega	.06	.05	.02
292	Steve Mura	.06	.05	.02
293	Tony Scott	.06	.05	.02
294	Manny Trillo	.08	.06	.03
295	Greg Harris	.08	.06	.03
296	Luis DeLeon	.06	.05	.02
297	Kent Tekulve	.08	.06	.03
298	Atlee Hammaker	.12	.09	.05
299	Bruce Benedict	.06	.05	.02
300	Fergie Jenkins	.15	.11	.06
301	Dave Kingman	.15	.11	.06
302	Bill Caudill	.06	.05	.02
303	John Castino	.06	.05	.02
304	Ernie Whitt	.08	.06	.03
305	Randy Johnson	.06	.05	.02
306	Garth Iorg	.06	.05	.02
307	Gaylord Perry	.30	.25	.12
308	Ed Lynch	.06	.05	.02
309	Keith Moreland	.08	.06	.03
310	Rafael Ramirez	.08	.06	.03
311	Bill Madlock	.15	.11	.06
312	Milt May	.06	.05	.02
313	John Montefusco	.06	.05	.02
314	Wayne Krenchicki	.06	.05	.02
315	George Vukovich	.06	.05	.02
316	Joaquin Andujar	.10	.08	.04
317	Craig Reynolds	.06	.05	.02
318	Rick Burleson	.08	.06	.03
319	Richard Dotson	.10	.08	.04
320	Steve Rogers	.08	.06	.03
321	Dave Schmidt	.10	.08	.04
322	Bud Black	.20	.15	.08
323	Jeff Burroughs	.08	.06	.03
324	Von Hayes	.20	.15	.08
325	Butch Wynegar	.08	.06	.03
326	Carl Yastrzemski	.70	.50	.30
327	Ron Roenicke	.06	.05	.02
328	Howard Johnson	1.50	1.25	.60
329	Rick Dempsey	.08	.06	.03
330a	Jim Slaton (one yellow box on back)			
		.70	.50	.30
330b	Jim Slaton (two yellow boxes on back)			
		.08	.06	.03
331	Benny Ayala	.06	.05	.02
332	Ted Simmons	.15	.11	.06
333	Lou Whitaker	.30	.25	.12
334	Chuck Rainey	.06	.05	.02
335	Lou Piniella	.15	.11	.06
336	Steve Sax	.25	.20	.10
337	Toby Harrah	.08	.06	.03
338	George Brett	.70	.50	.30
339	Davey Lopes	.10	.08	.04
340	Gary Carter	.40	.30	.15
341	John Grubb	.06	.05	.02
342	Tim Foli	.06	.05	.02
343	Jim Kaat	.15	.11	.06
344	Mike LaCoss	.08	.06	.03
345	Larry Christenson	.06	.05	.02
346	Juan Bonilla	.06	.05	.02
347	Omar Moreno	.06	.05	.02
348	Charles Davis	.20	.15	.08
349	Tommy Boggs	.06	.05	.02
350	Rusty Staub	.12	.09	.05
351	Bump Wills	.06	.05	.02
352	Rick Sweet	.06	.05	.02
353	Jim Gott	.15	.11	.06
354	Terry Felton	.06	.05	.02
355	Jim Kern	.06	.05	.02
356	Bill Almon	.06	.05	.02
357	Tippy Martinez	.06	.05	.02
358	Roy Howell	.06	.05	.02
359	Dan Petry	.10	.08	.04
360	Jerry Mumphrey	.08	.06	.03
361	Mark Clear	.08	.06	.03
362	Mike Marshall	.20	.15	.08
363	Lary Sorensen	.06	.05	.02
364	Amos Otis	.08	.06	.03
365	Rick Langford	.06	.05	.02
366	Brad Mills	.06	.05	.02
367	Brian Downing	.10	.08	.04
368	Mike Richardt	.06	.05	.02
369	Aurelio Rodriguez	.08	.06	.03
370	Dave Smith	.08	.06	.03
371	Tug McGraw	.12	.09	.05
372	Doug Bair	.06	.05	.02
373	Ruppert Jones	.06	.05	.02
374	Alex Trevino	.06	.05	.02
375	Ken Dayley	.06	.05	.02
376	Rod Scurry	.06	.05	.02
377	Bob Brenly	.15	.11	.06
378	Scot Thompson	.06	.05	.02
379	Julio Cruz	.06	.05	.02
380	John Stearns	.06	.05	.02
381	Dale Murray	.06	.05	.02
382	Frank Viola	.90	.70	.35
383	Al Bumbry	.08	.06	.03
384	Ben Oglivie	.08	.06	.03
385	Dave Tobik	.06	.05	.02
386	Bob Stanley	.08	.06	.03
387	Andre Robertson	.06	.05	.02
388	Jorge Orta	.06	.05	.02
389	Ed Whitson	.08	.06	.03
390	Don Hood	.06	.05	.02
391	Tom Underwood	.06	.05	.02
392	Tim Wallach	.20	.15	.08
393	Steve Renko	.06	.05	.02
394	Mickey Rivers	.10	.08	.04
395	Greg Luzinski	.12	.09	.05
396	Art Howe	.06	.05	.02
397	Alan Wiggins	.15	.11	.06
398	Jim Barr	.06	.05	.02
399	Ivan DeJesus	.06	.05	.02
400	Tom Lawless	.08	.06	.03
401	Bob Walk	.06	.05	.02
402	Jimmy Smith	.06	.05	.02
403	Lee Smith	.15	.11	.06
404	George Hendrick	.08	.06	.03
405	Eddie Murray	.60	.45	.25
406	Marshall Edwards	.06	.05	.02
407	Lance Parrish	.35	.25	.14
408	Carney Lansford	.08	.06	.03
409	Dave Winfield	.40	.30	.15
410	Bob Welch	.10	.08	.04
411	Larry Milbourne	.06	.05	.02
412	Dennis Leonard	.08	.06	.03
413	Dan Meyer	.06	.05	.02
414	Charlie Lea	.06	.05	.02
415	Rick Honeycutt	.08	.06	.03
416	Mike Witt	.20	.15	.08
417	Steve Trout	.08	.06	.03
418	Glenn Brummer	.06	.05	.02
419	Denny Walling	.06	.05	.02
420	Gary Matthews	.10	.08	.04
421	Charlie Liebrandt (Leibrandt)	.08	.06	.03
422	Juan Eichelberger	.06	.05	.02
423	Matt Guante	.12	.09	.05
424	Bill Laskey	.06	.05	.02
425	Jerry Royster	.06	.05	.02
426	Dickie Noles	.06	.05	.02
427	George Foster	.15	.11	.06
428	Mike Moore	.20	.15	.08
429	Gary Ward	.08	.06	.03
430	Barry Bonnell	.06	.05	.02
431	Ron Washington	.06	.05	.02
432	Rance Mulliniks	.06	.05	.02
433	Mike Stanton	.06	.05	.02
434	Jesse Orosco	.10	.08	.04
435	Larry Bowa	.15	.11	.06
436	Biff Pocoroba	.06	.05	.02
437	Johnny Ray	.15	.11	.06
438	Joe Morgan	.30	.25	.12
439	Eric Show	.20	.15	.08
440	Larry Biittner	.06	.05	.02
441	Greg Gross	.06	.05	.02
442	Gene Tenace	.08	.06	.03
443	Danny Heep	.06	.05	.02
444	Bobby Clark	.06	.05	.02
445	Kevin Hickey	.06	.05	.02
446	Scott Sanderson	.08	.06	.03

#	Player	MT	NR MT	EX
447	Frank Tanana	.10	.08	.04
448	Cesar Geronimo	.06	.05	.02
449	Jimmy Sexton	.06	.05	.02
450	Mike Hargrove	.08	.06	.03
451	Doyle Alexander	.12	.09	.05
452	Dwight Evans	.15	.11	.06
453	Terry Forster	.08	.06	.03
454	Tom Brookens	.06	.05	.02
455	Rich Dauer	.06	.05	.02
456	Rob Picciolo	.06	.05	.02
457	Terry Crowley	.06	.05	.02
458	Ned Yost	.06	.05	.02
459	Kirk Gibson	.30	.25	.12
460	Reid Nichols	.06	.05	.02
461	Oscar Gamble	.08	.06	.03
462	Dusty Baker	.10	.08	.04
463	Jack Perconte	.06	.05	.02
464	Frank White	.10	.08	.04
465	Mickey Klutts	.06	.05	.02
466	Warren Cromartie	.06	.05	.02
467	Larry Parrish	.10	.08	.04
468	Bobby Grich	.10	.08	.04
469	Dane Iorg	.06	.05	.02
470	Joe Niekro	.12	.09	.05
471	Ed Farmer	.06	.05	.02
472	Tim Flannery	.06	.05	.02
473	Dave Parker	.30	.25	.12
474	Jeff Leonard	.10	.08	.04
475	Al Hrabosky	.08	.06	.03
476	Ron Hodges	.06	.05	.02
477	Leon Durham	.10	.08	.04
478	Jim Essian	.06	.05	.02
479	Roy Lee Jackson	.06	.05	.02
480	Brad Havens	.06	.05	.02
481	Joe Price	.06	.05	.02
482	Tony Bernazard	.08	.06	.03
483	Scott McGregor	.10	.08	.04
484	Paul Molitor	.20	.15	.08
485	Mike Ivie	.06	.05	.02
486	Ken Griffey	.12	.09	.05
487	Dennis Eckersley	.10	.08	.04
488	Steve Garvey	.40	.30	.15
489	Mike Fischlin	.06	.05	.02
490	U.L. Washington	.06	.05	.02
491	Steve McCatty	.06	.05	.02
492	Roy Johnson	.06	.05	.02
493	Don Baylor	.15	.11	.06
494	Bobby Johnson	.06	.05	.02
495	Mike Squires	.06	.05	.02
496	Bert Roberge	.06	.05	.02
497	Dick Ruthven	.06	.05	.02
498	Tito Landrum	.06	.05	.02
499	Sixto Lezcano	.06	.05	.02
500	Johnny Bench	.40	.30	.15
501	Larry Whisenton	.06	.05	.02
502	Manny Sarmiento	.06	.05	.02
503	Fred Breining	.06	.05	.02
504	Bill Campbell	.06	.05	.02
505	Todd Cruz	.06	.05	.02
506	Bob Bailor	.06	.05	.02
507	Dave Stieb	.12	.09	.05
508	Al Williams	.06	.05	.02
509	Dan Ford	.06	.05	.02
510	Gorman Thomas	.12	.09	.05
511	Chet Lemon	.08	.06	.03
512	Mike Torrez	.08	.06	.03
513	Shane Rawley	.10	.08	.04
514	Mark Belanger	.08	.06	.03
515	Rodney Craig	.06	.05	.02
516	Onix Concepcion	.08	.06	.03
517	Mike Heath	.06	.05	.02
518	Andre Dawson	.35	.25	.14
519	Luis Sanchez	.06	.05	.02
520	Terry Bogener	.06	.05	.02
521	Rudy Law	.06	.05	.02
522	Ray Knight	.10	.08	.04
523	Joe Lefebvre	.06	.05	.02
524	Jim Wohlford	.06	.05	.02
525	Julio Franco	1.00	.70	.40
526	Ron Oester	.06	.05	.02
527	Rick Mahler	.08	.06	.03
528	Steve Nicosia	.06	.05	.02
529	Junior Kennedy	.06	.05	.02
530a	Whitey Herzog (one yellow box on back)	.70	.50	.30
530b	Whitey Herzog (two yellow boxes on back)	.10	.08	.04
531a	Don Sutton (blue frame around photo)	1.00	.70	.40
531b	Don Sutton (green frame around photo)	.30	.25	.12

#	Player	MT	NR MT	EX
532	Mark Brouhard	.06	.05	.02
533a	Sparky Anderson (one yellow box on back)	.70	.50	.30
533b	Sparky Anderson (two yellow boxes on back)	.10	.08	.04
534	Roger LaFrancois	.06	.05	.02
535	George Frazier	.06	.05	.02
536	Tom Niedenfuer	.08	.06	.03
537	Ed Glynn	.06	.05	.02
538	Lee May	.08	.06	.03
539	Bob Kearney	.06	.05	.02
540	Tim Raines	.35	.25	.14
541	Paul Mirabella	.06	.05	.02
542	Luis Tiant	.12	.09	.05
543	Ron LeFlore	.08	.06	.03
544	Dave LaPoint	.15	.11	.06
545	Randy Moffitt	.06	.05	.02
546	Luis Aguayo	.06	.05	.02
547	Brad Lesley	.06	.05	.02
548	Luis Salazar	.06	.05	.02
549	John Candelaria	.10	.08	.04
550	Dave Bergman	.06	.05	.02
551	Bob Watson	.08	.06	.03
552	Pat Tabler	.10	.08	.04
553	Brent Gaff	.06	.05	.02
554	Al Cowens	.06	.05	.02
555	Tom Brunansky	.25	.20	.10
556	Lloyd Moseby	.12	.09	.05
557a	Pascual Perez (Twins)	.90	.70	.35
557b	Pascual Perez (Braves)	.15	.11	.06
558	Willie Upshaw	.08	.06	.03
559	Richie Zisk	.08	.06	.03
560	Pat Zachry	.06	.05	.02
561	Jay Johnstone	.10	.08	.04
562	Carlos Diaz	.06	.05	.02
563	John Tudor	.10	.08	.04
564	Frank Robinson	.12	.09	.05
565	Dave Edwards	.06	.05	.02
566	Paul Householder	.06	.05	.02
567	Ron Reed	.08	.06	.03
568	Mike Ramsey	.06	.05	.02
569	Kiko Garcia	.06	.05	.02
570	Tommy John	.20	.15	.08
571	Tony LaRussa	.08	.06	.03
572	Joel Youngblood	.06	.05	.02
573	Wayne Tolleson	.15	.11	.06
574	Keith Creel	.06	.05	.02
575	Billy Martin	.12	.09	.05
576	Jerry Dybzinski	.06	.05	.02
577	Rick Cerone	.08	.06	.03
578	Tony Perez	.20	.15	.08
579	Greg Brock	.50	.40	.20
580	Glen Wilson (Glenn)	.60	.45	.25
581	Tim Stoddard	.06	.05	.02
582	Bob McClure	.06	.05	.02
583	Jim Dwyer	.06	.05	.02
584	Ed Romero	.06	.05	.02
585	Larry Herndon	.08	.06	.03
586	Wade Boggs	17.00	12.50	6.75
587	Jay Howell	.15	.11	.06
588	Dave Stewart	.12	.09	.05
589	Bert Blyleven	.15	.11	.06
590	Dick Howser	.08	.06	.03
591	Wayne Gross	.06	.05	.02
592	Terry Francona	.06	.05	.02
593	Don Werner	.06	.05	.02
594	Bill Stein	.06	.05	.02
595	Jesse Barfield	.70	.50	.30
596	Bobby Molinaro	.06	.05	.02
597	Mike Vail	.06	.05	.02
598	Tony Gwynn	8.00	6.00	3.25
599	Gary Rajsich	.06	.05	.02
600	Jerry Ujdur	.06	.05	.02
601	Cliff Johnson	.06	.05	.02
602	Jerry White	.06	.05	.02
603	Bryan Clark	.06	.05	.02
604	Joe Ferguson	.06	.05	.02
605	Guy Sularz	.06	.05	.02
606a	Ozzie Virgil (green frame around photo)	.90	.70	.35
606b	Ozzie Virgil (orange frame around photo)	.15	.11	.06
607	Terry Harper	.10	.08	.04
608	Harvey Kuenn	.08	.06	.03
609	Jim Sundberg	.08	.06	.03
610	Willie Stargell	.30	.25	.12
611	Reggie Smith	.10	.08	.04
612	Rob Wilfong	.06	.05	.02
613	Niekro Brothers (Joe Niekro, Phil Niekro)	.15	.11	.06
614	Lee Elia	.06	.05	.02

		MT	NR MT	EX
615	Mickey Hatcher	.08	.06	.03
616	Jerry Hairston	.06	.05	.02
617	John Martin	.06	.05	.02
618	Wally Backman	.15	.11	.06
619	Storm Davis	.30	.25	.12
620	Alan Knicely	.06	.05	.02
621	John Stuper	.10	.08	.04
622	Matt Sinatro	.06	.05	.02
623	Gene Petralli	.15	.11	.06
624	Duane Walker	.06	.05	.02
625	Dick Williams	.08	.06	.03
626	Pat Corrales	.08	.06	.03
627	Vern Ruhle	.06	.05	.02
628	Joe Torre	.08	.06	.03
629	Anthony Johnson	.06	.05	.02
630	Steve Howe	.08	.06	.03
631	Gary Woods	.06	.05	.02
632	Lamarr Hoyt (LaMarr)	.08	.06	.03
633	Steve Swisher	.06	.05	.02
634	Terry Leach	.10	.08	.04
635	Jeff Newman	.06	.05	.02
636	Brett Butler	.10	.08	.04
637	Gary Gray	.06	.05	.02
638	Lee Mazzilli	.08	.06	.03
639a	Ron Jackson (A's)	9.00	6.75	3.50
639b	Ron Jackson (Angels - green frame around photo)	.90	.70	.35
639c	Ron Jackson (Angels - red frame around photo)	.20	.15	.08
640	Juan Beniquez	.06	.05	.02
641	Dave Rucker	.06	.05	.02
642	Luis Pujols	.06	.05	.02
643	Rick Monday	.10	.08	.04
644	Hosken Powell	.06	.05	.02
645	San Diego Chicken	.20	.15	.08
646	Dave Engle	.06	.05	.02
647	Dick Davis	.06	.05	.02
648	MVP's (Vida Blue, Joe Morgan, Frank Robinson)	.15	.11	.06
649	Al Chambers	.06	.05	.02
650	Jesus Vega	.06	.05	.02
651	Jeff Jones	.06	.05	.02
652	Marvis Foley	.06	.05	.02
653	Ty Cobb Puzzle	.06	.05	.02
---a	Dick Perez/DK Checklist (no word "Checklist" on back)	.70	.50	.30
---b	Dick Perez/DK Checklist (word "Checklist" on back)	.08	.06	.03
---	Checklist 27-130	.06	.05	.02
---	Checklist 131-234	.06	.05	.02
---	Checklist 235-338	.06	.05	.02
---	Checklist 339-442	.06	.05	.02
---	Checklist 443-546	.06	.05	.02
---	Checklist 547-653	.06	.05	.02

1983 Donruss
Action All-Stars

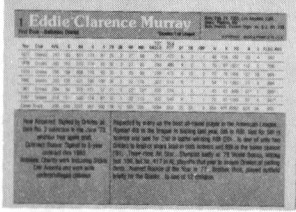

The cards in this 60-card set were designed on a horizontal format and contain a large close-up photo of the player on the left and a smaller action photo on the right. The cards, which measure 3½'' by 5'', have deep red borders and contain the Donruss logo and the year of issue. The card backs have black print on red and white and contain various statistical and biographical information. The cards were sold with puzzle pieces (three pieces on one card per pack) that features Mickey Mantle.

		MT	NR MT	EX
	Complete Set:	6.00	4.50	2.50
	Common Player:	.09	.07	.04
1	Eddie Murray	.40	.30	.15
2	Dwight Evans	.15	.11	.06
3a	Reggie Jackson (red covers part of statistics on back)	.30	.25	.12
3b	Reggie Jackson (red does not cover any statistics on back)	.30	.25	.12
4	Greg Luzinski	.12	.09	.05
5	Larry Herndon	.09	.07	.04
6	Al Oliver	.12	.09	.05
7	Bill Buckner	.09	.07	.04
8	Jason Thompson	.09	.07	.04
9	Andre Dawson	.20	.15	.08
10	Greg Minton	.09	.07	.04
11	Terry Kennedy	.09	.07	.04
12	Phil Niekro	.20	.15	.08
13	Willie Wilson	.12	.09	.05
14	Johnny Bench	.30	.25	.12
15	Ron Guidry	.20	.15	.08
16	Hal McRae	.09	.07	.04
17	Damaso Garcia	.09	.07	.04
18	Gary Ward	.09	.07	.04
19	Cecil Cooper	.12	.09	.05
20	Keith Hernandez	.30	.25	.12
21	Ron Cey	.12	.09	.05
22	Rickey Henderson	.35	.25	.14
23	Nolan Ryan	.30	.25	.12
24	Steve Carlton	.30	.25	.12
25	John Stearns	.09	.07	.04
26	Jim Sundberg	.09	.07	.04
27	Joaquin Andujar	.09	.07	.04
28	Gaylord Perry	.15	.11	.06
29	Jack Clark	.15	.11	.06
30	Bill Madlock	.12	.09	.05
31	Pete Rose	.50	.40	.20
32	Mookie Wilson	.12	.09	.05
33	Rollie Fingers	.15	.11	.06
34	Lonnie Smith	.09	.07	.04
35	Tony Pena	.12	.09	.05
36	Dave Winfield	.30	.25	.12
37	Tim Lollar	.09	.07	.04
38	Rod Carew	.30	.25	.12
39	Toby Harrah	.09	.07	.04
40	Buddy Bell	.12	.09	.05
41	Bruce Sutter	.12	.09	.05
42	George Brett	.40	.30	.15
43	Carlton Fisk	.15	.11	.06
44	Carl Yastrzemski	.40	.30	.15
45	Dale Murphy	.40	.30	.15
46	Bob Horner	.15	.11	.06
47	Dave Concepcion	.12	.09	.05
48	Dave Stieb	.12	.09	.05
49	Kent Hrbek	.20	.15	.08
50	Lance Parrish	.20	.15	.08
51	Joe Niekro	.12	.09	.05
52	Cal Ripken Jr.	.35	.25	.14
53	Fernando Valenzuela	.25	.20	.10
54	Rickie Zisk	.09	.07	.04
55	Leon Durham	.12	.09	.05
56	Robin Yount	.25	.20	.10
57	Mike Schmidt	.40	.30	.15
58	Gary Carter	.30	.25	.12
59	Fred Lynn	.15	.11	.06
60	Checklist	.12	.09	.05

1983 Donruss
Hall of Fame Heroes

The artwork of Dick Perez was featured in the 44-card Donruss Hall of Fame Heroes set issued in 1983. The standard-size cards (2½'' by 3½'') were available in wax packs that contained eight cards plus a Mickey Mantle puzzle piece card (three pieces on one card

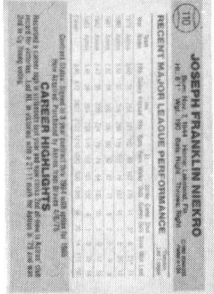

per pack). The backs, which display red and blue print on white stock, contain a short player biographical sketch derived from the Hall of Fame yearbook. The numbered set consists of 44 player cards, a Mantle puzzle card, and a checklist.

		MT	NR MT	EX
Complete Set:		4.50	3.50	1.75
Common Player:		.05	.04	.02
1	Ty Cobb	.30	.25	.12
2	Walter Johnson	.15	.11	.06
3	Christy Mathewson	.15	.11	.06
4	Josh Gibson	.10	.08	.04
5	Honus Wagner	.15	.11	.06
6	Jackie Robinson	.20	.15	.08
7	Mickey Mantle	.60	.45	.25
8	Luke Appling	.05	.04	.02
9	Ted Williams	.30	.25	.12
10	Johnny Mize	.09	.07	.04
11	Satchel Paige	.15	.11	.06
12	Lou Boudreau	.09	.07	.04
13	Jimmie Foxx	.15	.11	.06
14	Duke Snider	.20	.15	.08
15	Monte Irvin	.09	.07	.04
16	Hank Greenberg	.15	.11	.06
17	Roberto Clemente	.20	.15	.08
18	Al Kaline	.15	.11	.06
19	Frank Robinson	.15	.11	.06
20	Joe Cronin	.09	.07	.04
21	Burleigh Grimes	.05	.04	.02
22	The Waner Brothers (Lloyd Waner, Paul Waner)	.09	.07	.04
23	Grover Alexander	.09	.07	.04
24	Yogi Berra	.15	.11	.06
25	James Bell	.05	.04	.02
26	Bill Dickey	.09	.07	.04
27	Cy Young	.15	.11	.06
28	Charlie Gehringer	.09	.07	.04
29	Dizzy Dean	.15	.11	.06
30	Bob Lemon	.09	.07	.04
31	Red Ruffing	.05	.04	.02
32	Stan Musial	.25	.20	.10
33	Carl Hubbell	.15	.11	.06
34	Hank Aaron	.25	.20	.10
35	John McGraw	.09	.07	.04
36	Bob Feller	.15	.11	.06
37	Casey Stengel	.15	.11	.06
38	Ralph Kiner	.09	.07	.04
39	Roy Campanella	.15	.11	.06
40	Mel Ott	.09	.07	.04
41	Robin Roberts	.09	.07	.04
42	Early Wynn	.09	.07	.04
43	Mickey Mantle Puzzle	.09	.07	.04
---	Checklist	.09	.07	.04

1984 Donruss

The 1984 Donruss set consists of 651 numbered cards, seven unnumbered checklists and two "Living Legends" cards (designated A and B). The A and B cards were issued only in wax packs and not available to hobby dealers purchasing vending sets. The card fronts differ in style from the previous years, however the Donruss logo and year of issue are still included. The card backs have black print on green and white

and are identical in format to the preceding year. The standard-size cards (2½" by 3½") were issued with a 63-piece puzzle of Duke Snider. A limited print run of the issue by Donruss caused the set to escalate in price in recent years. The complete set price in the checklist that follows does not include the higher priced variations. Cards marked with a (DK) or a (RR) in the checklist refer to the Diamond Kings and Rated Rookies subsets.

		MT	NR MT	EX
Complete Set:		200.00	150.00	80.00
Common Player:		.10	.08	.04
1a	Robin Yount (DK) (Perez-Steel on back)	.80	.60	.30
1b	Robin Yount (DK) (Perez-Steele on back)	1.50	1.25	.60
2a	Dave Concepcion (DK) (Perez-Steel on back)	.30	.25	.12
2b	Dave Concepcion (DK) (Perez-Steele on back)	.60	.45	.25
3a	Dwayne Murphy (DK) (Perez-Steel on back)	.25	.20	.10
3b	Dwayne Murphy (DK) (Perez-Steele on back)	.60	.45	.25
4a	John Castino (DK) (Perez-Steel on back)	.20	.15	.08
4b	John Castino (DK) (Perez-Steele on back)	.60	.45	.25
5a	Leon Durham (DK) (Perez-Steel on back)	.35	.25	.14
5b	Leon Durham (DK) (Perez-Steele on back)	.70	.50	.30
6a	Rusty Staub (DK) (Perez-Steel on back)	.30	.25	.12
6b	Rusty Staub (DK) (Perez-Steel on back)	.60	.45	.25
7a	Jack Clark (DK) (Perez-Steel on back)	.40	.30	.15
7b	Jack Clark (DK) (Perez-Steel on back)	.80	.60	.30
8a	Dave Dravecky (DK) (Perez-Steel on back)	.25	.20	.10
8b	Dave Dravecky (DK) (Perez-Steele on back)	.60	.45	.25
9a	Al Oliver (DK) (Perez-Steel on back)	.35	.25	.14
9b	Al Oliver (DK) (Perez-Steele on back)	.70	.50	.30
10a	Dave Righetti (DK) (Perez-Steel on back)	.40	.30	.15
10b	Dave Righetti (DK) (Perez-Steele on back)	.80	.60	.30
11a	Hal McRae (DK) (Perez-Steel on back)	.30	.25	.12
11b	Hal McRae (DK) (Perez-Steele on back)	.60	.45	.25
12a	Ray Knight (DK) (Perez-Steel on back)	.25	.20	.10
12b	Ray Knight (DK) (Perez-Steele on back)	.60	.45	.25
13a	Bruce Sutter (DK) (Perez-Steel on back)	.35	.25	.14
13b	Bruce Sutter (DK) (Perez-Steele on back)	.70	.50	.30
14a	Bob Horner (DK) (Perez-Steel on back)	.50	.40	.20

		MT	NR MT	EX
14b	Bob Horner (DK) (Perez-Steele on back)			
		1.00	.70	.40
15a	Lance Parrish (DK) (Perez-Steel on back)			
		.60	.45	.25
15b	Lance Parrish (DK) (Perez-Steele on back)			
		1.25	.90	.50
16a	Matt Young (DK) (Perez-Steel on back)			
		.25	.20	.10
16b	Matt Young (DK) (Perez-Steele on back)			
		.60	.45	.25
17a	Fred Lynn (DK) (Perez-Steel on back)			
		.35	.25	.14
17b	Fred Lynn (DK) (Perez-Steele on back)			
		.70	.50	.30
18a	Ron Kittle (DK) (Perez-Steel on back)			
		.35	.25	.14
18b	Ron Kittle (DK) (Perez-Steele on back)			
		.70	.50	.30
19a	Jim Clancy (DK) (Perez-Steel on back)			
		.25	.20	.10
19b	Jim Clancy (DK) (Perez-Steele on back)			
		.60	.45	.25
20a	Bill Madlock (DK) (Perez-Steel on back)			
		.35	.25	.14
20b	Bill Madlock (DK) (Perez-Steele on back)			
		.70	.50	.30
21a	Larry Parrish (DK) (Perez-Steel on back)			
		.30	.25	.12
21b	Larry Parrish (DK) (Perez-Steele on back)			
		.60	.45	.25
22a	Eddie Murray (DK) (Perez-Steel on back)			
		1.25	.90	.50
22b	Eddie Murray (DK) (Perez-Steele on back)			
		2.50	2.00	1.00
23a	Mike Schmidt (DK) (Perez-Steel on back)			
		1.25	.90	.50
23b	Mike Schmidt (DK) (Perez-Steele on back)			
		2.50	2.00	1.00
24a	Pedro Guerrero (DK) (Perez-Steel on back)			
		.50	.40	.20
24b	Pedro Guerrero (DK) (Perez-Steele on back)			
		1.00	.70	.40
25a	Andre Thornton (DK) (Perez-Steel on back)			
		.30	.25	.12
25b	Andre Thornton (DK) (Perez-Steele on back)			
		.60	.45	.25
26a	Wade Boggs (DK) (Perez-Steel on back)			
		3.75	2.75	1.50
26b	Wade Boggs (DK) (Perez-Steel on back)			
		5.00	3.75	2.00
27	Joel Skinner (RR)	.25	.20	.10
28	Tom Dunbar (RR)	.10	.08	.04
29a	Mike Stenhouse (RR) (no number on back)			
		.15	.11	.06
29b	Mike Stenhouse (RR) (29 on back)			
		3.00	2.25	1.25
30a	Ron Darling (no number on back)	6.00	4.50	2.50
30b	Ron Darling (30 on back)	12.00	9.00	4.75
31	Dion James (RR)	1.50	1.25	.60
32	Tony Fernandez (RR)	7.00	5.25	2.75
33	Angel Salazar (RR)	.20	.15	.08
34	Kevin McReynolds (RR)	6.00	4.50	2.50
35	Dick Schofield (RR)	.60	.45	.25
36	Brad Komminsk (RR)	.15	.11	.06
37	Tim Teufel (RR)	.50	.40	.20
38	Doug Frobel (RR)	.10	.08	.04
39	Greg Gagne (RR)	.75	.60	.30
40	Mike Fuentes (RR)	.10	.08	.04
41	Joe Carter (RR)	7.00	5.25	2.75
42	Mike Brown (RR)	.07	.05	.03
43	Mike Jeffcoat (RR)	7.00	5.25	2.75
44	Sid Fernandez (RR)	4.50	3.50	1.75
45	Brian Dayett (RR)	.12	.09	.05
46	Chris Smith (RR)	.10	.08	.04
47	Eddie Murray	1.25	.90	.50
48	Robin Yount	.70	.50	.30
49	Lance Parrish	.50	.40	.20
50	Jim Rice	.90	.70	.35
51	Dave Winfield	.90	.70	.35
52	Fernando Valenzuela	.70	.50	.30
53	George Brett	1.50	1.25	.60
54	Rickey Henderson	1.25	.90	.50
55	Gary Carter	.90	.70	.35
56	Buddy Bell	.25	.20	.10
57	Reggie Jackson	1.25	.90	.50
58	Harold Baines	.25	.20	.10
59	Ozzie Smith	.25	.20	.10
60	Nolan Ryan	.90	.70	.35
61	Pete Rose	2.50	2.00	1.00
62	Ron Oester	.10	.08	.04
63	Steve Garvey	.90	.70	.35

		MT	NR MT	EX
64	Jason Thompson	.10	.08	.04
65	Jack Clark	.35	.25	.14
66	Dale Murphy	1.50	1.25	.60
67	Leon Durham	.20	.15	.08
68	Darryl Strawberry	15.00	11.00	6.00
69	Richie Zisk	.12	.09	.05
70	Kent Hrbek	.60	.45	.25
71	Dave Stieb	.25	.20	.10
72	Ken Schrom	.10	.08	.04
73	George Bell	2.25	1.75	.90
74	John Moses	.10	.08	.04
75	Ed Lynch	.10	.08	.04
76	Chuck Rainey	.10	.08	.04
77	Biff Pocoroba	.10	.08	.04
78	Cecilio Guante	.10	.08	.04
79	Jim Barr	.10	.08	.04
80	Kurt Bevacqua	.10	.08	.04
81	Tom Foley	.10	.08	.04
82	Joe Lefebvre	.10	.08	.04
83	Andy Van Slyke	1.25	.90	.50
84	Bob Lillis	.10	.08	.04
85	Rick Adams	.10	.08	.04
86	Jerry Hairston	.10	.08	.04
87	Bob James	.30	.25	.12
88	Joe Altobelli	.10	.08	.04
89	Ed Romero	.10	.08	.04
90	John Grubb	.10	.08	.04
91	John Henry Johnson	.10	.08	.04
92	Juan Espino	.10	.08	.04
93	Candy Maldonado	.25	.20	.10
94	Andre Thornton	.20	.15	.08
95	Onix Concepcion	.10	.08	.04
96	Don Hill	.20	.15	.08
97	Andre Dawson	.60	.45	.25
98	Frank Tanana	.15	.11	.06
99	Curt Wilkerson	.20	.15	.08
100	Larry Gura	.12	.09	.05
101	Dwayne Murphy	.15	.11	.06
102	Tom Brennan	.10	.08	.04
103	Dave Righetti	.40	.30	.15
104	Steve Sax	.30	.25	.12
105	Dan Petry	.12	.09	.05
106	Cal Ripken	1.25	.90	.50
107	Paul Molitor	.35	.25	.14
108	Fred Lynn	.35	.25	.14
109	Neil Allen	.10	.08	.04
110	Joe Niekro	.20	.15	.08
111	Steve Carlton	.90	.70	.35
112	Terry Kennedy	.12	.09	.05
113	Bill Madlock	.30	.25	.12
114	Chili Davis	.15	.11	.06
115	Jim Gantner	.12	.09	.05
116	Tom Seaver	.90	.70	.35
117	Bill Buckner	.20	.15	.08
118	Bill Caudill	.10	.08	.04
119	Jim Clancy	.20	.15	.08
120	John Castino	.10	.08	.04
121	Dave Concepcion	.25	.20	.10
122	Greg Luzinski	.20	.15	.08
123	Mike Boddicker	.30	.25	.12
124	Pete Ladd	.10	.08	.04
125	Juan Berenguer	.10	.08	.04
126	John Montefusco	.10	.08	.04
127	Ed Jurak	.10	.08	.04
128	Tom Niedenfuer	.12	.09	.05
129	Bert Blyleven	.30	.25	.12
130	Bud Black	.15	.11	.06
131	Gorman Heimueller	.10	.08	.04
132	Dan Schatzeder	.10	.08	.04
133	Ron Jackson	.10	.08	.04
134	Tom Henke	.80	.60	.30
135	Kevin Hickey	.10	.08	.04
136	Mike Scott	.30	.25	.12
137	Bo Diaz	.12	.09	.05
138	Glenn Brummer	.10	.08	.04
139	Sid Monge	.10	.08	.04
140	Rich Gale	.10	.08	.04
141	Brett Butler	.15	.11	.06
142	Brian Harper	.10	.08	.04
143	John Rabb	.10	.08	.04
144	Gary Woods	.10	.08	.04
145	Pat Putnam	.10	.08	.04
146	Jim Acker	.25	.20	.10
147	Mickey Hatcher	.12	.09	.05
148	Todd Cruz	.10	.08	.04
149	Tom Tellmann	.10	.08	.04
150	John Wockenfuss	.10	.08	.04
151	Wade Boggs	10.00	7.50	4.00
152	Don Baylor	.25	.20	.10
153	Bob Welch	.20	.15	.08
154	Alan Bannister	.10	.08	.04

		MT	NR MT	EX
155	Willie Aikens	.10	.08	.04
156	Jeff Burroughs	.12	.09	.05
157	Bryan Little	.10	.08	.04
158	Bob Boone	.15	.11	.06
159	Dave Hostetler	.10	.08	.04
160	Jerry Dybzinski	.10	.08	.04
161	Mike Madden	.15	.11	.06
162	Luis DeLeon	.10	.08	.04
163	Willie Hernandez	.20	.15	.08
164	Frank Pastore	.10	.08	.04
165	Rick Camp	.10	.08	.04
166	Lee Mazzilli	.12	.09	.05
167	Scot Thompson	.10	.08	.04
168	Bob Forsch	.12	.09	.05
169	Mike Flanagan	.20	.15	.08
170	Rick Manning	.10	.08	.04
171	Chet Lemon	.15	.11	.06
172	Jerry Remy	.10	.08	.04
173	Ron Guidry	.40	.30	.15
174	Pedro Guerrero	.50	.40	.20
175	Willie Wilson	.25	.20	.10
176	Carney Lansford	.15	.11	.06
177	Al Oliver	.30	.25	.12
178	Jim Sundberg	.12	.09	.05
179	Bobby Grich	.20	.15	.08
180	Richard Dotson	.20	.15	.08
181	Joaquin Andujar	.20	.15	.08
182	Jose Cruz	.20	.15	.08
183	Mike Schmidt	1.50	1.25	.60
184	Gary Redus	.40	.30	.15
185	Garry Templeton	.20	.15	.08
186	Tony Pena	.20	.15	.08
187	Greg Minton	.10	.08	.04
188	Phil Niekro	.50	.40	.20
189	Ferguson Jenkins	.30	.25	.12
190	Mookie Wilson	.15	.11	.06
191	Jim Beattie	.10	.08	.04
192	Gary Ward	.12	.09	.05
193	Jesse Barfield	.50	.40	.20
194	Pete Filson	.10	.08	.04
195	Roy Lee Jackson	.10	.08	.04
196	Rick Sweet	.10	.08	.04
197	Jesse Orosco	.15	.11	.06
198	Steve Lake	.12	.09	.05
199	Ken Dayley	.10	.08	.04
200	Manny Sarmiento	.10	.08	.04
201	Mark Davis	.20	.15	.08
202	Tim Flannery	.10	.08	.04
203	Bill Scherrer	.10	.08	.04
204	Al Holland	.10	.08	.04
205	David Von Ohlen	.10	.08	.04
206	Mike LaCoss	.15	.11	.06
207	Juan Beniquez	.10	.08	.04
208	Juan Agosto	.15	.11	.06
209	Bobby Ramos	.10	.08	.04
210	Al Bumbry	.12	.09	.05
211	Mark Brouhard	.10	.08	.04
212	Howard Bailey	.10	.08	.04
213	Bruce Hurst	.20	.15	.08
214	Bob Shirley	.10	.08	.04
215	Pat Zachry	.10	.08	.04
216	Julio Franco	.25	.20	.10
217	Mike Armstrong	.10	.08	.04
218	Dave Beard	.10	.08	.04
219	Steve Rogers	.12	.09	.05
220	John Butcher	.10	.08	.04
221	Mike Smithson	.15	.11	.06
222	Frank White	.20	.15	.08
223	Mike Heath	.10	.08	.04
224	Chris Bando	.10	.08	.04
225	Roy Smalley	.12	.09	.05
226	Dusty Baker	.20	.15	.08
227	Lou Whitaker	.50	.40	.20
228	John Lowenstein	.10	.08	.04
229	Ben Oglivie	.15	.11	.06
230	Doug DeCinces	.20	.15	.08
231	Lonnie Smith	.12	.09	.05
232	Ray Knight	.20	.15	.08
233	Gary Matthews	.20	.15	.08
234	Juan Bonilla	.10	.08	.04
235	Rod Scurry	.10	.08	.04
236	Atlee Hammaker	.12	.09	.05
237	Mike Caldwell	.10	.08	.04
238	Keith Hernandez	.80	.60	.30
239	Larry Bowa	.25	.20	.10
240	Tony Bernazard	.12	.09	.05
241	Damaso Garcia	.12	.09	.05
242	Tom Brunansky	.35	.25	.14
243	Dan Driessen	.12	.09	.05
244	Ron Kittle	.30	.25	.12
245	Tim Stoddard	.10	.08	.04

		MT	NR MT	EX
246	Bob Gibson	.10	.08	.04
247	Marty Castillo	.10	.08	.04
248	Don Mattingly	65.00	49.00	26.00
249	Jeff Newman	.10	.08	.04
250	Alejandro Pena	.20	.15	.08
251	Toby Harrah	.12	.09	.05
252	Cesar Geronimo	.10	.08	.04
253	Tom Underwood	.10	.08	.04
254	Doug Flynn	.10	.08	.04
255	Andy Hassler	.10	.08	.04
256	Odell Jones	.10	.08	.04
257	Rudy Law	.10	.08	.04
258	Harry Spilman	.10	.08	.04
259	Marty Bystrom	.10	.08	.04
260	Dave Rucker	.10	.08	.04
261	Ruppert Jones	.10	.08	.04
262	Jeff Jones	.10	.08	.04
263	Gerald Perry	.50	.40	.20
264	Gene Tenace	.12	.09	.05
265	Brad Wellman	.10	.08	.04
266	Dickie Noles	.10	.08	.04
267	Jamie Allen	.10	.08	.04
268	Jim Gott	.10	.08	.04
269	Ron Davis	.10	.08	.04
270	Benny Ayala	.10	.08	.04
271	Ned Yost	.10	.08	.04
272	Dave Rozema	.10	.08	.04
273	Dave Stapleton	.10	.08	.04
274	Lou Piniella	.25	.20	.10
275	Jose Morales	.10	.08	.04
276	Brod Perkins	.10	.08	.04
277	Butch Davis	.10	.08	.04
278	Tony Phillips	.20	.15	.08
279	Jeff Reardon	.25	.20	.10
280	Ken Forsch	.12	.09	.05
281	Pete O'Brien	1.50	1.25	.60
282	Tom Paciorek	.10	.08	.04
283	Frank LaCorte	.10	.08	.04
284	Tim Lollar	.10	.08	.04
285	Greg Gross	.10	.08	.04
286	Alex Trevino	.10	.08	.04
287	Gene Garber	.10	.08	.04
288	Dave Parker	.50	.40	.20
289	Lee Smith	.20	.15	.08
290	Dave LaPoint	.10	.08	.04
291	John Shelby	.30	.25	.12
292	Charlie Moore	.10	.08	.04
293	Alan Trammell	.60	.45	.25
294	Tony Armas	.20	.15	.08
295	Shane Rawley	.20	.15	.08
296	Greg Brock	.25	.20	.10
297	Hal McRae	.20	.15	.08
298	Mike Davis	.15	.11	.06
299	Tim Raines	.80	.60	.30
300	Bucky Dent	.20	.15	.08
301	Tommy John	.40	.30	.15
302	Carlton Fisk	.40	.30	.15
303	Darrell Porter	.12	.09	.05
304	Dickie Thon	.12	.09	.05
305	Garry Maddox	.15	.11	.06
306	Cesar Cedeno	.20	.15	.08
307	Gary Lucas	.10	.08	.04
308	Johnny Ray	.25	.20	.10
309	Andy McGaffigan	.10	.08	.04
310	Claudell Washington	.12	.09	.05
311	Ryne Sandberg	2.00	1.50	.80
312	George Foster	.30	.25	.12
313	Spike Owen	.30	.25	.12
314	Gary Gaetti	.70	.50	.30
315	Willie Upshaw	.20	.15	.08
316	Al Williams	.10	.08	.04
317	Jorge Orta	.10	.08	.04
318	Orlando Mercado	.10	.08	.04
319	Junior Ortiz	.15	.11	.06
320	Mike Proly	.10	.08	.04
321	Randy Johnson	.10	.08	.04
322	Jim Morrison	.10	.08	.04
323	Max Venable	.10	.08	.04
324	Tony Gwynn	3.00	2.25	1.25
325	Duane Walker	.10	.08	.04
326	Ozzie Virgil	.12	.09	.05
327	Jeff Lahti	.10	.08	.04
328	Bill Dawley	.20	.15	.08
329	Rob Wilfong	.10	.08	.04
330	Marc Hill	.10	.08	.04
331	Ray Burris	.10	.08	.04
332	Allan Ramirez	.10	.08	.04
333	Chuck Porter	.10	.08	.04
334	Wayne Krenchicki	.10	.08	.04
335	Gary Allenson	.10	.08	.04
336	Bob Meacham	.25	.20	.10

#	Player	MT	NR MT	EX		#	Player	MT	NR MT	EX
337	Joe Beckwith	.10	.08	.04		428	Mario Soto	.15	.11	.06
338	Rick Sutcliffe	.25	.20	.10		429	Gene Richards	.10	.08	.04
339	Mark Huismann	.15	.11	.06		430	Dale Berra	.10	.08	.04
340	Tim Conroy	.20	.15	.08		431	Darrell Evans	.25	.20	.10
341	Scott Sanderson	.12	.09	.05		432	Glenn Hubbard	.12	.09	.05
342	Larry Biittner	.10	.08	.04		433	Jody Davis	.20	.15	.08
343	Dave Stewart	.20	.15	.08		434	Danny Heep	.10	.08	.04
344	Darryl Motley	.10	.08	.04		435	Ed Nunez	.30	.25	.12
345	Chris Codiroli	.15	.11	.06		436	Bobby Castillo	.10	.08	.04
346	Rick Behenna	.10	.08	.04		437	Ernie Whitt	.15	.11	.06
347	Andre Robertson	.10	.08	.04		438	Scott Ullger	.10	.08	.04
348	Mike Marshall	.20	.15	.08		439	Doyle Alexander	.20	.15	.08
349	Larry Herndon	.12	.09	.05		440	Domingo Ramos	.10	.08	.04
350	Rich Dauer	.10	.08	.04		441	Craig Swan	.10	.08	.04
351	Cecil Cooper	.25	.20	.10		442	Warren Brusstar	.10	.08	.04
352	Rod Carew	.90	.70	.35		443	Len Barker	.12	.09	.05
353	Willie McGee	.40	.30	.15		444	Mike Easler	.15	.11	.06
354	Phil Garner	.12	.09	.05		445	Renie Martin	.10	.08	.04
355	Joe Morgan	.50	.40	.20		446	Dennis Rasmussen	.50	.40	.20
356	Luis Salazar	.10	.08	.04		447	Ted Power	.15	.11	.06
357	John Candelaria	.20	.15	.08		448	Charlie Hudson	.35	.25	.14
358	Bill Laskey	.10	.08	.04		449	Danny Cox	1.25	.90	.50
359	Bob McClure	.10	.08	.04		450	Kevin Bass	.30	.25	.12
360	Dave Kingman	.30	.25	.12		451	Daryl Sconiers	.10	.08	.04
361	Ron Cey	.20	.15	.08		452	Scott Fletcher	.12	.09	.05
362	Matt Young	.25	.20	.10		453	Bryn Smith	.12	.09	.05
363	Lloyd Moseby	.25	.20	.10		454	Jim Dwyer	.10	.08	.04
364	Frank Viola	.35	.25	.14		455	Rob Picciolo	.10	.08	.04
365	Eddie Milner	.10	.08	.04		456	Enos Cabell	.10	.08	.04
366	Floyd Bannister	.20	.15	.08		457	Dennis "Oil Can" Boyd	.50	.40	.20
367	Dan Ford	.10	.08	.04		458	Butch Wynegar	.12	.09	.05
368	Moose Haas	.10	.08	.04		459	Burt Hooton	.12	.09	.05
369	Doug Bair	.10	.08	.04		460	Ron Hassey	.10	.08	.04
370	Ray Fontenot	.15	.11	.06		461	Danny Jackson	.60	.45	.25
371	Luis Aponte	.10	.08	.04		462	Bob Kearney	.10	.08	.04
372	Jack Fimple	.10	.08	.04		463	Terry Francona	.10	.08	.04
373	Neal Heaton	.30	.25	.12		464	Wayne Tolleson	.10	.08	.04
374	Greg Pryor	.10	.08	.04		465	Mickey Rivers	.15	.11	.06
375	Wayne Gross	.10	.08	.04		466	John Wathan	.12	.09	.05
376	Charlie Lea	.10	.08	.04		467	Bill Almon	.10	.08	.04
377	Steve Lubratich	.10	.08	.04		468	George Vukovich	.10	.08	.04
378	Jon Matlack	.12	.09	.05		469	Steve Kemp	.15	.11	.06
379	Julio Cruz	.10	.08	.04		470	Ken Landreaux	.12	.09	.05
380	John Mizerock	.10	.08	.04		471	Milt Wilcox	.12	.09	.05
381	Kevin Gross	.40	.30	.15		472	Tippy Martinez	.10	.08	.04
382	Mike Ramsey	.10	.08	.04		473	Ted Simmons	.25	.20	.10
383	Doug Gwosdz	.10	.08	.04		474	Tim Foli	.10	.08	.04
384	Kelly Paris	.10	.08	.04		475	George Hendrick	.15	.11	.06
385	Pete Falcone	.10	.08	.04		476	Terry Puhl	.10	.08	.04
386	Milt May	.10	.08	.04		477	Von Hayes	.30	.25	.12
387	Fred Breining	.10	.08	.04		478	Bobby Brown	.10	.08	.04
388	Craig Lefferts	.30	.25	.12		479	Lee Lacy	.12	.09	.05
389	Steve Henderson	.10	.08	.04		480	Joel Youngblood	.10	.08	.04
390	Randy Moffitt	.10	.08	.04		481	Jim Slaton	.10	.08	.04
391	Ron Washington	.10	.08	.04		482	Mike Fitzgerald	.25	.20	.10
392	Gary Roenicke	.10	.08	.04		483	Keith Moreland	.15	.11	.06
393	Tom Candiotti	.30	.25	.12		484	Ron Roenicke	.10	.08	.04
394	Larry Pashnick	.10	.08	.04		485	Luis Leal	.10	.08	.04
395	Dwight Evans	.30	.25	.12		486	Bryan Oelkers	.10	.08	.04
396	Goose Gossage	.40	.30	.15		487	Bruce Berenyi	.10	.08	.04
397	Derrel Thomas	.10	.08	.04		488	LaMarr Hoyt	.12	.09	.05
398	Juan Eichelberger	.10	.08	.04		489	Joe Nolan	.10	.08	.04
399	Leon Roberts	.10	.08	.04		490	Marshall Edwards	.10	.08	.04
400	Davey Lopes	.15	.11	.06		491	Mike Laga	.12	.09	.05
401	Bill Gullickson	.15	.11	.06		492	Rick Cerone	.12	.09	.05
402	Geoff Zahn	.10	.08	.04		493	Mike Miller (Rick)	.10	.08	.04
403	Billy Sample	.10	.08	.04		494	Rick Honeycutt	.15	.11	.06
404	Mike Squires	.10	.08	.04		495	Mike Hargrove	.12	.09	.05
405	Craig Reynolds	.10	.08	.04		496	Joe Simpson	.10	.08	.04
406	Eric Show	.12	.09	.05		497	Keith Atherton	.30	.25	.12
407	John Denny	.12	.09	.05		498	Chris Welsh	.10	.08	.04
408	Dann Bilardello	.10	.08	.04		499	Bruce Kison	.10	.08	.04
409	Bruce Benedict	.10	.08	.04		500	Bob Johnson	.10	.08	.04
410	Kent Tekulve	.15	.11	.06		501	Jerry Koosman	.20	.15	.08
411	Mel Hall	.20	.15	.08		502	Frank DiPino	.10	.08	.04
412	John Stuper	.10	.08	.04		503	Tony Perez	.40	.30	.15
413	Rick Dempsey	.12	.09	.05		504	Ken Oberkfell	.15	.11	.06
414	Don Sutton	.50	.40	.20		505	Mark Thurmond	.20	.15	.08
415	Jack Morris	.50	.40	.20		506	Joe Price	.10	.08	.04
416	John Tudor	.20	.15	.08		507	Pascual Perez	.15	.11	.06
417	Willie Randolph	.20	.15	.08		508	Marvell Wynne	.20	.15	.08
418	Jerry Reuss	.15	.11	.06		509	Mike Krukow	.12	.09	.05
419	Don Slaught	.10	.08	.04		510	Dick Ruthven	.10	.08	.04
420	Steve McCatty	.10	.08	.04		511	Al Cowens	.10	.08	.04
421	Tim Wallach	.25	.20	.10		512	Cliff Johnson	.10	.08	.04
422	Larry Parrish	.20	.15	.08		513	Randy Bush	.20	.15	.08
423	Brian Downing	.20	.15	.08		514	Sammy Stewart	.10	.08	.04
424	Britt Burns	.10	.08	.04		515	Bill Schroeder	.30	.25	.12
425	David Green	.10	.08	.04		516	Aurelio Lopez	.10	.08	.04
426	Jerry Mumphrey	.12	.09	.05		517	Mike Brown	.10	.08	.04
427	Ivan DeJesus	.10	.08	.04		518	Graig Nettles	.35	.25	.14

		MT	NR MT	EX
519	Dave Sax	.12	.09	.05
520	Gerry Willard	.12	.09	.05
521	Paul Splittorff	.12	.09	.05
522	Tom Burgmeier	.10	.08	.04
523	Chris Speier	.10	.08	.04
524	Bobby Clark	.10	.08	.04
525	George Wright	.10	.08	.04
526	Dennis Lamp	.10	.08	.04
527	Tony Scott	.10	.08	.04
528	Ed Whitson	.10	.08	.04
529	Ron Reed	.12	.09	.05
530	Charlie Puleo	.10	.08	.04
531	Jerry Royster	.10	.08	.04
532	Don Robinson	.12	.09	.05
533	Steve Trout	.15	.11	.06
534	Bruce Sutter	.30	.25	.12
535	Bob Horner	.50	.40	.20
536	Pat Tabler	.20	.15	.08
537	Chris Chambliss	.15	.11	.06
538	Bob Ojeda	.20	.15	.08
539	Alan Ashby	.10	.08	.04
540	Jay Johnstone	.15	.11	.06
541	Bob Dernier	.12	.09	.05
542	Brook Jacoby	1.50	1.25	.60
543	U.L. Washington	.10	.08	.04
544	Danny Darwin	.12	.09	.05
545	Kiko Garcia	.10	.08	.04
546	Vance Law	.12	.09	.05
547	Tug McGraw	.25	.20	.10
548	Dave Smith	.15	.11	.06
549	Len Matuszek	.10	.08	.04
550	Tom Hume	.10	.08	.04
551	Dave Dravecky	.15	.11	.06
552	Rick Rhoden	.20	.15	.08
553	Duane Kuiper	.10	.08	.04
554	Rusty Staub	.20	.15	.08
555	Bill Campbell	.10	.08	.04
556	Mike Torrez	.12	.09	.05
557	Dave Henderson	.10	.08	.04
558	Len Whitehouse	.10	.08	.04
559	Barry Bonnell	.10	.08	.04
560	Rick Lysander	.10	.08	.04
561	Garth Iorg	.10	.08	.04
562	Bryan Clark	.10	.08	.04
563	Brian Giles	.10	.08	.04
564	Vern Ruhle	.10	.08	.04
565	Steve Bedrosian	.25	.20	.10
566	Larry McWilliams	.10	.08	.04
567	Jeff Leonard	.20	.15	.08
568	Alan Wiggins	.10	.08	.04
569	Jeff Russell	.15	.11	.06
570	Salome Barojas	.10	.08	.04
571	Dane Iorg	.10	.08	.04
572	Bob Knepper	.15	.11	.06
573	Gary Lavelle	.10	.08	.04
574	Gorman Thomas	.20	.15	.08
575	Manny Trillo	.12	.09	.05
576	Jim Palmer	.70	.50	.30
577	Dale Murray	.10	.08	.04
578	Tom Brookens	.10	.08	.04
579	Rich Gedman	.15	.11	.06
580	Bill Doran	1.25	.90	.50
581	Steve Yeager	.10	.08	.04
582	Dan Spillner	.10	.08	.04
583	Dan Quisenberry	.35	.25	.14
584	Rance Mulliniks	.10	.08	.04
585	Storm Davis	.15	.11	.06
586	Dave Schmidt	.12	.09	.05
587	Bill Russell	.12	.09	.05
588	Pat Sheridan	.20	.15	.08
589	Rafael Ramirez	.12	.09	.05
590	Bud Anderson	.10	.08	.04
591	George Frazier	.10	.08	.04
592	Lee Tunnell	.15	.11	.06
593	Kirk Gibson	.50	.40	.20
594	Scott McGregor	.20	.15	.08
595	Bob Bailor	.10	.08	.04
596	Tom Herr	.20	.15	.08
597	Luis Sanchez	.10	.08	.04
598	Dave Engle	.10	.08	.04
599	Craig McMurtry	.15	.11	.06
600	Carlos Diaz	.10	.08	.04
601	Tom O'Malley	.10	.08	.04
602	Nick Esasky	.40	.30	.15
603	Ron Hodges	.10	.08	.04
604	Ed Vande Berg	.10	.08	.04
605	Alfredo Griffin	.12	.09	.05
606	Glenn Hoffman	.10	.08	.04
607	Hubie Brooks	.20	.15	.08
608	Richard Barnes (photo actually Neal Heaton)	.10	.08	.04

		MT	NR MT	EX
609	Greg Walker	.90	.70	.35
610	Ken Singleton	.20	.15	.08
611	Mark Clear	.12	.09	.05
612	Buck Martinez	.10	.08	.04
613	Ken Griffey	.20	.15	.08
614	Reid Nichols	.10	.08	.04
615	Doug Sisk	.15	.11	.06
616	Bob Brenly	.10	.08	.04
617	Joey McLaughlin	.10	.08	.04
618	Glenn Wilson	.20	.15	.08
619	Bob Stoddard	.10	.08	.04
620	Len Sakata (Lenn)	.10	.08	.04
621	Mike Young	.50	.40	.20
622	John Stefero	.12	.09	.05
623	Carmelo Martinez	.30	.25	.12
624	Dave Bergman	.10	.08	.04
625	Runnin' Reds (David Green, Willie McGee, Lonnie Smith, Ozzie Smith)	.30	.25	.12
626	Rudy May	.12	.09	.05
627	Matt Keough	.10	.08	.04
628	Jose DeLeon	.30	.25	.12
629	Jim Essian	.10	.08	.04
630	Darnell Coles	.50	.40	.20
631	Mike Warren	.15	.11	.06
632	Del Crandall	.10	.08	.04
633	Dennis Martinez	.12	.09	.05
634	Mike Moore	.10	.08	.04
635	Lary Sorensen	.10	.08	.04
636	Ricky Nelson	.10	.08	.04
637	Omar Moreno	.10	.08	.04
638	Charlie Hough	.15	.11	.06
639	Dennis Eckersley	.15	.11	.06
640	Walt Terrell	.70	.50	.30
641	Denny Walling	.10	.08	.04
642	Dave Anderson	.20	.15	.08
643	Jose Oquendo	.25	.20	.10
644	Bob Stanley	.12	.09	.05
645	Dave Geisel	.10	.08	.04
646	Scott Garrelts	.40	.30	.15
647	Gary Pettis	.60	.45	.25
648	Duke Snider Puzzle Card	.10	.08	.04
649	Johnnie LeMaster	.10	.08	.04
650	Dave Collins	.12	.09	.05
651	San Diego Chicken	.25	.20	.10
---a	Checklist 1-26 DK (Perez-Steel on back)	.12	.09	.05
---b	Checklist 1-26 DK (Perez-Steele on back)	.40	.30	.15
---	Checklist 27-130	.10	.08	.04
---	Checklist 131-234	.10	.08	.04
---	Checklist 235-338	.10	.08	.04
---	Checklist 339-442	.10	.08	.04
---	Checklist 443-546	.10	.08	.04
---	Checklist 547-651	.10	.08	.04
---A	Living Legends (Rollie Fingers, Gaylord Perry)	2.75	2.00	1.00
---B	Living Legends (Johnny Bench, Carl Yastrzemski)	3.75	2.75	1.50

1984 Donruss
Action All-Stars

Full-color photos on the card fronts and backs make the 1984 Donruss Action All-Stars set somewhat unusual. The fronts contain a large action photo plus the Donruss logo and year of issue inside a deep red border. The top half of the card backs feature a close-up photo with the bottom portion containing biographical and statistical information. The cards, which measure 3½'' by 5'', were sold with Ted Williams puzzle pieces.

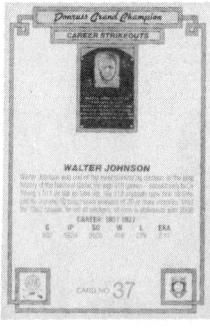

		MT	NR MT	EX
Complete Set:		6.00	4.50	2.50
Common Player:		.09	.07	.04
1	Gary Lavelle	.12	.09	.05
2	Willie McGee	.15	.11	.06
3	Tony Pena	.12	.09	.05
4	Lou Whitaker	.15	.11	.06
5	Robin Yount	.25	.20	.10
6	Doug DeCinces	.09	.07	.04
7	John Castino	.09	.07	.04
8	Terry Kennedy	.09	.07	.04
9	Rickey Henderson	.35	.25	.14
10	Bob Horner	.15	.11	.06
11	Harold Baines	.15	.11	.06
12	Buddy Bell	.12	.09	.05
13	Fernando Valenzuela	.25	.20	.10
14	Nolan Ryan	.30	.25	.12
15	Andre Thornton	.09	.07	.04
16	Gary Redus	.09	.07	.04
17	Pedro Guerrero	.20	.15	.08
18	Andre Dawson	.20	.15	.08
19	Dave Stieb	.12	.09	.05
20	Cal Ripken	.35	.25	.14
21	Ken Griffey	.12	.09	.05
22	Wade Boggs	.75	.60	.30
23	Keith Hernandez	.30	.25	.12
24	Steve Carlton	.30	.25	.12
25	Hal McRae	.12	.09	.05
26	John Lowenstein	.09	.07	.04
27	Fred Lynn	.15	.11	.06
28	Bill Buckner	.09	.07	.04
29	Chris Chambliss	.09	.07	.04
30	Richie Zisk	.09	.07	.04
31	Jack Clark	.15	.11	.06
32	George Hendrick	.09	.07	.04
33	Bill Madlock	.12	.09	.05
34	Lance Parrish	.20	.15	.08
35	Paul Molitor	.15	.11	.06
36	Reggie Jackson	.30	.25	.12
37	Kent Hrbek	.20	.15	.08
38	Steve Garvey	.30	.25	.12
39	Carney Lansford	.09	.07	.04
40	Dale Murphy	.40	.30	.15
41	Greg Luzinski	.12	.09	.05
42	Larry Parrish	.09	.07	.04
43	Ryne Sandberg	.30	.25	.12
44	Dickie Thon	.09	.07	.04
45	Bert Blyleven	.12	.09	.05
46	Ron Oester	.09	.07	.04
47	Dusty Baker	.09	.07	.04
48	Steve Rogers	.09	.07	.04
49	Jim Clancy	.09	.07	.04
50	Eddie Murray	.30	.25	.12
51	Ron Guidry	.20	.15	.08
52	Jim Rice	.30	.25	.12
53	Tom Seaver	.30	.25	.12
54	Pete Rose	.50	.40	.20
55	George Brett	.40	.30	.15
56	Dan Quisenberry	.15	.11	.06
57	Mike Schmidt	.40	.30	.15
58	Ted Simmons	.12	.09	.05
59	Dave Righetti	.15	.11	.06
60	Checklist	.12	.09	.05

1984 Donruss Champions

The 60-card Donruss Champions set includes ten Hall of Famers, forty-nine current players and one numbered checklist. The ten Hall of Famers' cards (called Grand Champions) feature the artwork of Dick Perez, while cards of the current players (called Champions) are color photos. The cards measure 3½'' by 5''. The Grand Champions represent hallmarks of excellence in various statistical categories, while the Champions are the leaders among active players in each category. The ten Grand Champion cards are #'s 1, 8, 14, 20, 26, 31, 37, 43, 50 and 55. The cards were issued with Duke Snider puzzle pieces.

		MT	NR MT	EX
Complete Set:		5.00	3.75	2.00
Common Player:		.07	.05	.03
1	Babe Ruth	.50	.40	.20
2	George Foster	.10	.08	.04
3	Dave Kingman	.10	.08	.04
4	Jim Rice	.25	.20	.10
5	Gorman Thomas	.10	.08	.04
6	Ben Oglivie	.07	.05	.03
7	Jeff Burroughs	.07	.05	.03
8	Hank Aaron	.35	.25	.14
9	Reggie Jackson	.30	.25	.12
10	Carl Yastrzemski	.35	.25	.14
11	Mike Schmidt	.35	.25	.14
12	Graig Nettles	.14	.11	.06
13	Greg Luzinski	.10	.08	.04
14	Ted Williams	.35	.25	.14
15	George Brett	.35	.25	.14
16	Wade Boggs	.45	.35	.20
17	Hal McRae	.10	.08	.04
18	Bill Buckner	.10	.08	.04
19	Eddie Murray	.30	.25	.12
20	Rogers Hornsby	.14	.11	.06
21	Rod Carew	.30	.25	.12
22	Bill Madlock	.10	.08	.04
23	Lonnie Smith	.07	.05	.03
24	Cecil Cooper	.10	.08	.04
25	Ken Griffey	.10	.08	.04
26	Ty Cobb	.35	.25	.14
27	Pete Rose	.40	.30	.15
28	Rusty Staub	.10	.08	.04
29	Tony Perez	.10	.08	.04
30	Al Oliver	.10	.08	.04
31	Cy Young	.14	.11	.06
32	Gaylord Perry	.14	.11	.06
33	Ferguson Jenkins	.10	.08	.04
34	Phil Niekro	.14	.11	.06
35	Jim Palmer	.14	.11	.06
36	Tommy John	.10	.08	.04
37	Walter Johnson	.20	.15	.08
38	Steve Carlton	.25	.20	.10
39	Nolan Ryan	.25	.20	.10
40	Tom Seaver	.25	.20	.10
41	Don Sutton	.14	.11	.06
42	Bert Blyleven	.10	.08	.04
43	Frank Robinson	.20	.15	.08
44	Joe Morgan	.14	.11	.06
45	Rollie Fingers	.14	.11	.06
46	Keith Hernandez	.25	.20	.10
47	Robin Yount	.20	.15	.08
48	Cal Ripken	.25	.20	.10
49	Dale Murphy	.35	.25	.14
50	Mickey Mantle	.70	.50	.30
51	Johnny Bench	.25	.20	.10
52	Carlton Fisk	.14	.11	.06
53	Tug McGraw	.10	.08	.04
54	Paul Molitor	.10	.08	.04
55	Carl Hubbell	.14	.11	.06
56	Steve Garvey	.25	.20	.10
57	Dave Parker	.14	.11	.06
58	Gary Carter	.20	.15	.08
59	Fred Lynn	.14	.11	.06
60	Checklist	.10	.08	.04

Definitions for grading conditions are located in the Introduction of this price guide.

1985 Donruss

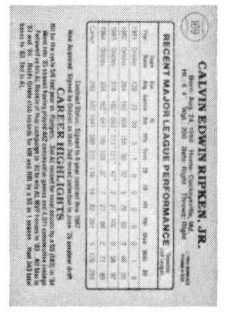

The black-bordered 1985 Donruss set included 653 numbered cards and seven unnumbered checklists. Displaying the artwork of Dick Perez for the fourth consecutive year, card #'s 1-26 featured the Diamond King series. Donruss, realizing the hobby craze over rookie cards, included a Rated Rookies subset (card #'s 27-46). The cards, which are the standard size of 2½'' by 3½'', were issued with a Lou Gehrig puzzle. The backs of the cards have black print on yellow and white. The complete set price does not include the higher priced variations. (DK) and (RR) refer to the Diamond Kings and Rated Rookies subsets.

		MT	NR MT	EX
Complete Set:		120.00	90.00	48.00
Common Player:		.08	.06	.03

		MT	NR MT	EX
1	Ryne Sandberg (DK)	.60	.45	.25
2	Doug DeCinces (DK)	.12	.09	.05
3	Rich Dotson (DK)	.12	.09	.05
4	Bert Blyleven (DK)	.15	.11	.06
5	Lou Whitaker (DK)	.25	.20	.10
6	Dan Quisenberry (DK)	.20	.15	.08
7	Don Mattingly (DK)	5.00	3.75	2.00
8	Carney Lansford (DK)	.10	.08	.04
9	Frank Tanana (DK)	.12	.09	.05
10	Willie Upshaw (DK)	.10	.08	.04
11	Claudell Washington (DK)	.10	.08	.04
12	Mike Marshall (DK)	.15	.11	.06
13	Joaquin Andujar (DK)	.12	.09	.05
14	Cal Ripken, Jr. (DK)	.60	.45	.25
15	Jim Rice (DK)	.50	.40	.20
16	Don Sutton (DK)	.25	.20	.10
17	Frank Viola (DK)	.15	.11	.06
18	Alvin Davis (DK)	.60	.45	.25
19	Mario Soto (DK)	.12	.09	.05
20	Jose Cruz (DK)	.12	.09	.05
21	Charlie Lea (DK)	.10	.08	.04
22	Jesse Orosco (DK)	.10	.08	.04
23	Juan Samuel (DK)	.50	.40	.20
24	Tony Pena (DK)	.12	.09	.05
25	Tony Gwynn (DK)	.50	.40	.20
26	Bob Brenly (DK)	.10	.08	.04
27	Danny Tartabull (RR)	6.00	4.50	2.50
28	Mike Bielecki (RR)	.20	.15	.08
29	Steve Lyons (RR)	.20	.15	.08
30	Jeff Reed (RR)	.15	.11	.06
31	Tony Brewer (RR)	.08	.06	.03
32	John Morris (RR)	.15	.11	.06
33	Daryl Boston (RR)	.25	.20	.10
34	Alfonso Pulido (RR)	.08	.06	.03
35	Steve Kiefer (RR)	.15	.11	.06
36	Larry Sheets (RR)	2.00	1.50	.80
37	Scott Bradley (RR)	.25	.20	.10
38	Calvin Schiraldi (RR)	.40	.30	.15
39	Shawon Dunston (RR)	1.25	.90	.50
40	Charlie Mitchell (RR)	.08	.06	.03
41	Billy Hatcher (RR)	.90	.70	.35
42	Russ Stephans (RR)	.08	.06	.03
43	Alejandro Sanchez (RR)	.08	.06	.03
44	Steve Jeltz (RR)	.15	.11	.06
45	Jim Traber (RR)	.50	.40	.20
46	Doug Loman (RR)	.08	.06	.03
47	Eddie Murray	.60	.45	.25
48	Robin Yount	.40	.30	.15
49	Lance Parrish	.30	.25	.12

		MT	NR MT	EX
50	Jim Rice	.50	.40	.20
51	Dave Winfield	.50	.40	.20
52	Fernando Valenzuela	.40	.30	.15
53	George Brett	.70	.50	.30
54	Dave Kingman	.15	.11	.06
55	Gary Carter	.50	.40	.20
56	Buddy Bell	.12	.09	.05
57	Reggie Jackson	.60	.45	.25
58	Harold Baines	.20	.15	.08
59	Ozzie Smith	.20	.15	.08
60	Nolan Ryan	.50	.40	.20
61	Mike Schmidt	.60	.45	.25
62	Dave Parker	.35	.25	.14
63	Tony Gwynn	.60	.45	.25
64	Tony Pena	.12	.09	.05
65	Jack Clark	.25	.20	.10
66	Dale Murphy	.80	.60	.30
67	Ryne Sandberg	.50	.40	.20
68	Keith Hernandez	.40	.30	.15
69	Alvin Davis	1.50	1.25	.60
70	Kent Hrbek	.30	.25	.12
71	Willie Upshaw	.10	.08	.04
72	Dave Engle	.08	.06	.03
73	Alfredo Griffin	.10	.08	.04
74a	Jack Perconte (last line of highlights begins "Batted .346...")	.10	.08	.04
74b	Jack Perconte (last line of highlights begins "Led the...")	1.25	.90	.50
75	Jesse Orosco	.12	.09	.05
76	Jody Davis	.12	.09	.05
77	Bob Horner	.25	.20	.10
78	Larry McWilliams	.08	.06	.03
79	Joel Youngblood	.08	.06	.03
80	Alan Wiggins	.08	.06	.03
81	Ron Oester	.08	.06	.03
82	Ozzie Virgil	.10	.08	.04
83	Ricky Horton	.35	.25	.14
84	Bill Doran	.12	.09	.05
85	Rod Carew	.50	.40	.20
86	LaMarr Hoyt	.10	.08	.04
87	Tim Wallach	.15	.11	.06
88	Mike Flanagan	.12	.09	.05
89	Jim Sundberg	.10	.08	.04
90	Chet Lemon	.10	.08	.04
91	Bob Stanley	.10	.08	.04
92	Willie Randolph	.12	.09	.05
93	Bill Russell	.10	.08	.04
94	Julio Franco	.15	.11	.06
95	Dan Quisenberry	.20	.15	.08
96	Bill Caudill	.08	.06	.03
97	Bill Gullickson	.12	.09	.05
98	Danny Darwin	.10	.08	.04
99	Curtis Wilkerson	.08	.06	.03
100	Bud Black	.08	.06	.03
101	Tony Phillips	.08	.06	.03
102	Tony Bernazard	.10	.08	.04
103	Jay Howell	.10	.08	.04
104	Burt Hooton	.10	.08	.04
105	Milt Wilcox	.10	.08	.04
106	Rich Dauer	.08	.06	.03
107	Don Sutton	.35	.25	.14
108	Mike Witt	.15	.11	.06
109	Bruce Sutter	.20	.15	.08
110	Enos Cabell	.08	.06	.03
111	John Denny	.08	.06	.03
112	Dave Dravecky	.12	.09	.05
113	Marvell Wynne	.08	.06	.03
114	Johnnie LeMaster	.08	.06	.03
115	Chuck Porter	.08	.06	.03
116	John Gibbons	.08	.06	.03
117	Keith Moreland	.10	.08	.04
118	Darnell Coles	.12	.09	.05
119	Dennis Lamp	.08	.06	.03
120	Ron Davis	.08	.06	.03
121	Nick Esasky	.10	.08	.04
122	Vance Law	.10	.08	.04
123	Gary Roenicke	.08	.06	.03
124	Bill Schroeder	.08	.06	.03
125	Dave Rozema	.08	.06	.03
126	Bobby Meacham	.08	.06	.03
127	Marty Barrett	.25	.20	.10
128	R.J. Reynolds	.35	.25	.14
129	Ernie Camacho	.08	.06	.03
130	Jorge Orta	.08	.06	.03
131	Lary Sorensen	.08	.06	.03
132	Terry Francona	.08	.06	.03
133	Fred Lynn	.25	.20	.10
134	Bobby Jones	.08	.06	.03
135	Jerry Hairston	.08	.06	.03
136	Kevin Bass	.12	.09	.05
137	Garry Maddox	.10	.08	.04

#	Player	MT	NR MT	EX
138	Dave LaPoint	.08	.06	.03
139	Kevin McReynolds	.60	.45	.25
140	Wayne Krenchicki	.08	.06	.03
141	Rafael Ramirez	.08	.06	.03
142	Rod Scurry	.08	.06	.03
143	Greg Minton	.08	.06	.03
144	Tim Stoddard	.08	.06	.03
145	Steve Henderson	.08	.06	.03
146	George Bell	.80	.60	.30
147	Dave Meier	.08	.06	.03
148	Sammy Stewart	.08	.06	.03
149	Mark Brouhard	.08	.06	.03
150	Larry Herndon	.10	.08	.04
151	Oil Can Boyd	.12	.09	.05
152	Brian Dayett	.08	.06	.03
153	Tom Niedenfuer	.10	.08	.04
154	Brook Jacoby	.15	.11	.06
155	Onix Concepcion	.08	.06	.03
156	Tim Conroy	.08	.06	.03
157	Joe Hesketh	.20	.15	.08
158	Brian Downing	.12	.09	.05
159	Tommy Dunbar	.08	.06	.03
160	Marc Hill	.08	.06	.03
161	Phil Garner	.10	.08	.04
162	Jerry Davis	.08	.06	.03
163	Bill Campbell	.08	.06	.03
164	John Franco	.60	.45	.25
165	Len Barker	.10	.08	.04
166	Benny Distefano	.10	.08	.04
167	George Frazier	.08	.06	.03
168	Tito Landrum	.08	.06	.03
169	Cal Ripken	.60	.45	.25
170	Cecil Cooper	.15	.11	.06
171	Alan Trammell	.40	.30	.15
172	Wade Boggs	5.50	4.25	2.25
173	Don Baylor	.15	.11	.06
174	Pedro Guerrero	.25	.20	.10
175	Frank White	.12	.09	.05
176	Rickey Henderson	.60	.45	.25
177	Charlie Lea	.08	.06	.03
178	Pete O'Brien	.20	.15	.08
179	Doug DeCinces	.12	.09	.05
180	Ron Kittle	.12	.09	.05
181	George Hendrick	.10	.08	.04
182	Joe Niekro	.12	.09	.05
183	Juan Samuel	.60	.45	.25
184	Mario Soto	.10	.08	.04
185	Goose Gossage	.25	.20	.10
186	Johnny Ray	.15	.11	.06
187	Bob Brenly	.08	.06	.03
188	Craig McMurtry	.08	.06	.03
189	Leon Durham	.12	.09	.05
190	Dwight Gooden	10.00	7.50	4.00
191	Barry Bonnell	.08	.06	.03
192	Tim Teufel	.10	.08	.04
193	Dave Stieb	.15	.11	.06
194	Mickey Hatcher	.08	.06	.03
195	Jesse Barfield	.30	.25	.12
196	Al Cowens	.08	.06	.03
197	Hubie Brooks	.12	.09	.05
198	Steve Trout	.10	.08	.04
199	Glenn Hubbard	.08	.06	.03
200	Bill Madlock	.15	.11	.06
201	Jeff Robinson	.25	.20	.10
202	Eric Show	.08	.06	.03
203	Dave Concepcion	.15	.11	.06
204	Ivan DeJesus	.08	.06	.03
205	Neil Allen	.08	.06	.03
206	Jerry Mumphrey	.10	.08	.04
207	Mike Brown	.08	.06	.03
208	Carlton Fisk	.30	.25	.12
209	Bryn Smith	.10	.08	.04
210	Tippy Martinez	.08	.06	.03
211	Dion James	.15	.11	.06
212	Willie Hernandez	.12	.09	.05
213	Mike Easler	.10	.08	.04
214	Ron Guidry	.30	.25	.12
215	Rick Honeycutt	.10	.08	.04
216	Brett Butler	.12	.09	.05
217	Larry Gura	.10	.08	.04
218	Ray Burris	.08	.06	.03
219	Steve Rogers	.10	.08	.04
220	Frank Tanana	.12	.09	.05
221	Ned Yost	.08	.06	.03
222	Bret Saberhagen	4.50	3.50	1.75
223	Mike Davis	.10	.08	.04
224	Bert Blyleven	.15	.11	.06
225	Steve Kemp	.10	.08	.04
226	Jerry Reuss	.10	.08	.04
227	Darrell Evans	.15	.11	.06
228	Wayne Gross	.08	.06	.03
229	Jim Gantner	.10	.08	.04
230	Bob Boone	.10	.08	.04
231	Lonnie Smith	.10	.08	.04
232	Frank DiPino	.08	.06	.03
233	Jerry Koosman	.12	.09	.05
234	Graig Nettles	.20	.15	.08
235	John Tudor	.12	.09	.05
236	John Rabb	.08	.06	.03
237	Rick Manning	.08	.06	.03
238	Mike Fitzgerald	.08	.06	.03
239	Gary Matthews	.12	.09	.05
240	Jim Presley	1.50	1.25	.60
241	Dave Collins	.10	.08	.04
242	Gary Gaetti	.30	.25	.12
243	Dann Bilardello	.08	.06	.03
244	Rudy Law	.08	.06	.03
245	John Lowenstein	.08	.06	.03
246	Tom Tellmann	.08	.06	.03
247	Howard Johnson	.25	.20	.10
248	Ray Fontenot	.08	.06	.03
249	Tony Armas	.12	.09	.05
250	Candy Maldonado	.12	.09	.05
251	Mike Jeffcoat	.08	.06	.03
252	Dane Iorg	.08	.06	.03
253	Bruce Bochte	.08	.06	.03
254	Pete Rose	1.25	.90	.50
255	Don Aase	.10	.08	.04
256	George Wright	.08	.06	.03
257	Britt Burns	.08	.06	.03
258	Mike Scott	.20	.15	.08
259	Len Matuszek	.08	.06	.03
260	Dave Rucker	.08	.06	.03
261	Craig Lefferts	.10	.08	.04
262	Jay Tibbs	.20	.15	.08
263	Bruce Benedict	.08	.06	.03
264	Don Robinson	.10	.08	.04
265	Gary Lavelle	.08	.06	.03
266	Scott Sanderson	.10	.08	.04
267	Matt Young	.10	.08	.04
268	Ernie Whitt	.10	.08	.04
269	Houston Jimenez	.08	.06	.03
270	Ken Dixon	.20	.15	.08
271	Peter Ladd	.08	.06	.03
272	Juan Berenguer	.08	.06	.03
273	Roger Clemens	12.00	9.00	4.75
274	Rick Cerone	.10	.08	.04
275	Dave Anderson	.08	.06	.03
276	George Vukovich	.08	.06	.03
277	Greg Pryor	.08	.06	.03
278	Mike Warren	.08	.06	.03
279	Bob James	.08	.06	.03
280	Bobby Grich	.12	.09	.05
281	Mike Mason	.15	.11	.06
282	Ron Reed	.08	.06	.03
283	Alan Ashby	.08	.06	.03
284	Mark Thurmond	.08	.06	.03
285	Joe Lefebvre	.08	.06	.03
286	Ted Power	.10	.08	.04
287	Chris Chambliss	.10	.08	.04
288	Lee Tunnell	.08	.06	.03
289	Rich Bordi	.08	.06	.03
290	Glenn Brummer	.08	.06	.03
291	Mike Boddicker	.15	.11	.06
292	Rollie Fingers	.25	.20	.10
293	Lou Whitaker	.30	.25	.12
294	Dwight Evans	.15	.11	.06
295	Don Mattingly	16.00	12.00	6.50
296	Mike Marshall	.15	.11	.06
297	Willie Wilson	.15	.11	.06
298	Mike Heath	.08	.06	.03
299	Tim Raines	.50	.40	.20
300	Larry Parrish	.12	.09	.05
301	Geoff Zahn	.08	.06	.03
302	Rich Dotson	.12	.09	.05
303	David Green	.08	.06	.03
304	Jose Cruz	.12	.09	.05
305	Steve Carlton	.50	.40	.20
306	Gary Redus	.10	.08	.04
307	Steve Garvey	.50	.40	.20
308	Jose DeLeon	.10	.08	.04
309	Randy Lerch	.08	.06	.03
310	Claudell Washington	.10	.08	.04
311	Lee Smith	.12	.09	.05
312	Darryl Strawberry	2.75	2.00	1.00
313	Jim Beattie	.08	.06	.03
314	John Butcher	.08	.06	.03
315	Damaso Garcia	.10	.08	.04
316	Mike Smithson	.08	.06	.03
317	Luis Leal	.08	.06	.03
318	Ken Phelps	.25	.20	.10
319	Wally Backman	.10	.08	.04

		MT	NR MT	EX
320	Ron Cey	.12	.09	.05
321	Brad Komminsk	.08	.06	.03
322	Jason Thompson	.08	.06	.03
323	Frank Williams	.25	.20	.10
324	Tim Lollar	.08	.06	.03
325	Eric Davis	25.00	18.50	10.00
326	Von Hayes	.15	.11	.06
327	Andy Van Slyke	.20	.15	.08
328	Craig Reynolds	.08	.06	.03
329	Dick Schofield	.10	.08	.04
330	Scott Fletcher	.10	.08	.04
331	Jeff Reardon	.20	.15	.08
332	Rick Dempsey	.10	.08	.04
333	Ben Oglivie	.10	.08	.04
334	Dan Petry	.12	.09	.05
335	Jackie Gutierrez	.08	.06	.03
336	Dave Righetti	.25	.20	.10
337	Alejandro Pena	.08	.06	.03
338	Mel Hall	.12	.09	.05
339	Pat Sheridan	.08	.06	.03
340	Keith Atherton	.10	.08	.04
341	David Palmer	.10	.08	.04
342	Gary Ward	.10	.08	.04
343	Dave Stewart	.12	.09	.05
344	Mark Gubicza	.30	.25	.12
345	Carney Lansford	.10	.08	.04
346	Jerry Willard	.08	.06	.03
347	Ken Griffey	.12	.09	.05
348	Franklin Stubbs	.70	.50	.30
349	Aurelio Lopez	.08	.06	.03
350	Al Bumbry	.10	.08	.04
351	Charlie Moore	.08	.06	.03
352	Luis Sanchez	.08	.06	.03
353	Darrell Porter	.10	.08	.04
354	Bill Dawley	.08	.06	.03
355	Charlie Hudson	.10	.08	.04
356	Garry Templeton	.12	.09	.05
357	Cecilio Guante	.08	.06	.03
358	Jeff Leonard	.12	.09	.05
359	Paul Molitor	.20	.15	.08
360	Ron Gardenhire	.08	.06	.03
361	Larry Bowa	.12	.09	.05
362	Bob Kearney	.08	.06	.03
363	Garth Iorg	.08	.06	.03
364	Tom Brunansky	.15	.11	.06
365	Brad Gulden	.08	.06	.03
366	Greg Walker	.15	.11	.06
367	Mike Young	.12	.09	.05
368	Rick Waits	.08	.06	.03
369	Doug Bair	.08	.06	.03
370	Bob Shirley	.08	.06	.03
371	Bob Ojeda	.12	.09	.05
372	Bob Welch	.12	.09	.05
373	Neal Heaton	.12	.09	.05
374	Danny Jackson (photo actually Steve Farr)	.12	.09	.05
375	Donnie Hill	.08	.06	.03
376	Mike Stenhouse	.08	.06	.03
377	Bruce Kison	.08	.06	.03
378	Wayne Tolleson	.08	.06	.03
379	Floyd Bannister	.12	.09	.05
380	Vern Ruhle	.08	.06	.03
381	Tim Corcoran	.08	.06	.03
382	Kurt Kepshire	.08	.06	.03
383	Bobby Brown	.08	.06	.03
384	Dave Van Gorder	.08	.06	.03
385	Rick Mahler	.08	.06	.03
386	Lee Mazzilli	.10	.08	.04
387	Bill Laskey	.08	.06	.03
388	Thad Bosley	.08	.06	.03
389	Al Chambers	.08	.06	.03
390	Tony Fernandez	.50	.40	.20
391	Ron Washington	.08	.06	.03
392	Bill Swaggerty	.08	.06	.03
393	Bob Gibson	.08	.06	.03
394	Marty Castillo	.08	.06	.03
395	Steve Crawford	.08	.06	.03
396	Clay Christiansen	.08	.06	.03
397	Bob Bailor	.08	.06	.03
398	Mike Hargrove	.10	.08	.04
399	Charlie Leibrandt	.10	.08	.04
400	Tom Burgmeier	.08	.06	.03
401	Razor Shines	.08	.06	.03
402	Rob Wilfong	.08	.06	.03
403	Tom Henke	.15	.11	.06
404	Al Jones	.08	.06	.03
405	Mike LaCoss	.10	.08	.04
406	Luis DeLeon	.08	.06	.03
407	Greg Gross	.08	.06	.03
408	Tom Hume	.08	.06	.03
409	Rick Camp	.08	.06	.03

		MT	NR MT	EX
410	Milt May	.08	.06	.03
411	Henry Cotto	.15	.11	.06
412	Dave Von Ohlen	.08	.06	.03
413	Scott McGregor	.12	.09	.05
414	Ted Simmons	.15	.11	.06
415	Jack Morris	.30	.25	.12
416	Bill Buckner	.15	.11	.06
417	Butch Wynegar	.10	.08	.04
418	Steve Sax	.25	.20	.10
419	Steve Balboni	.10	.08	.04
420	Dwayne Murphy	.10	.08	.04
421	Andre Dawson	.30	.25	.12
422	Charlie Hough	.10	.08	.04
423	Tommy John	.25	.20	.10
424a	Tom Seaver (Floyd Bannister photo - throwing left)	.80	.60	.30
424b	Tom Seaver (correct photo - throwing right)	5.00	3.75	2.00
425	Tom Herr	.12	.09	.05
426	Terry Puhl	.08	.06	.03
427	Al Holland	.08	.06	.03
428	Eddie Milner	.08	.06	.03
429	Terry Kennedy	.10	.08	.04
430	John Candelaria	.12	.09	.05
431	Manny Trillo	.10	.08	.04
432	Ken Oberkfell	.10	.08	.04
433	Rick Sutcliffe	.15	.11	.06
434	Ron Darling	.50	.40	.20
435	Spike Owen	.08	.06	.03
436	Frank Viola	.15	.11	.06
437	Lloyd Moseby	.12	.09	.05
438	Kirby Puckett	10.00	7.50	4.00
439	Jim Clancy	.12	.09	.05
440	Mike Moore	.08	.06	.03
441	Doug Sisk	.08	.06	.03
442	Dennis Eckersley	.10	.08	.04
443	Gerald Perry	.12	.09	.05
444	Dale Berra	.08	.06	.03
445	Dusty Baker	.10	.08	.04
446	Ed Whitson	.08	.06	.03
447	Cesar Cedeno	.12	.09	.05
448	Rick Schu	.20	.15	.08
449	Joaquin Andujar	.12	.09	.05
450	Mark Bailey	.15	.11	.06
451	Ron Romanick	.15	.11	.06
452	Julio Cruz	.08	.06	.03
453	Miguel Dilone	.08	.06	.03
454	Storm Davis	.10	.08	.04
455	Jaime Cocanower	.08	.06	.03
456	Barbaro Garbey	.08	.06	.03
457	Rich Gedman	.12	.09	.05
458	Phil Niekro	.30	.25	.12
459	Mike Scioscia	.08	.06	.03
460	Pat Tabler	.12	.09	.05
461	Darryl Motley	.08	.06	.03
462	Chris Codoroli (Codiroli)	.08	.06	.03
463	Doug Flynn	.08	.06	.03
464	Billy Sample	.08	.06	.03
465	Mickey Rivers	.10	.08	.04
466	John Wathan	.10	.08	.04
467	Bill Krueger	.08	.06	.03
468	Andre Thornton	.12	.09	.05
469	Rex Hudler	.08	.06	.03
470	Sid Bream	.50	.40	.20
471	Kirk Gibson	.35	.25	.14
472	John Shelby	.12	.09	.05
473	Moose Haas	.08	.06	.03
474	Doug Corbett	.08	.06	.03
475	Willie McGee	.35	.25	.14
476	Bob Knepper	.10	.08	.04
477	Kevin Gross	.12	.09	.05
478	Carmelo Martinez	.12	.09	.05
479	Kent Tekulve	.10	.08	.04
480	Chili Davis	.12	.09	.05
481	Bobby Clark	.08	.06	.03
482	Mookie Wilson	.12	.09	.05
483	Dave Owen	.08	.06	.03
484	Ed Nunez	.10	.08	.04
485	Rance Mulliniks	.08	.06	.03
486	Ken Schrom	.08	.06	.03
487	Jeff Russell	.08	.06	.03
488	Tom Paciorek	.08	.06	.03
489	Dan Ford	.08	.06	.03
490	Mike Caldwell	.08	.06	.03
491	Scottie Earl	.08	.06	.03
492	Jose Rijo	.25	.20	.10
493	Bruce Hurst	.12	.09	.05
494	Ken Landreaux	.10	.08	.04
495	Mike Fischlin	.08	.06	.03
496	Don Slaught	.08	.06	.03
497	Steve McCatty	.08	.06	.03

	MT	NR MT	EX
498 Gary Lucas	.08	.06	.03
499 Gary Pettis	.12	.09	.05
500 Marvis Foley	.08	.06	.03
501 Mike Squires	.08	.06	.03
502 Jim Pankovitz	.15	.11	.06
503 Luis Aguayo	.08	.06	.03
504 Ralph Citarella	.08	.06	.03
505 Bruce Bochy	.08	.06	.03
506 Bob Owchinko	.08	.06	.03
507 Pascual Perez	.10	.08	.04
508 Lee Lacy	.10	.08	.04
509 Atlee Hammaker	.08	.06	.03
510 Bob Dernier	.08	.06	.03
511 Ed Vande Berg	.08	.06	.03
512 Cliff Johnson	.08	.06	.03
513 Len Whitehouse	.08	.06	.03
514 Dennis Martinez	.08	.06	.03
515 Ed Romero	.08	.06	.03
516 Rusty Kuntz	.08	.06	.03
517 Rick Miller	.08	.06	.03
518 Dennis Rasmussen	.12	.09	.05
519 Steve Yeager	.08	.06	.03
520 Chris Bando	.08	.06	.03
521 U.L. Washington	.08	.06	.03
522 Curt Young	.60	.45	.25
523 Angel Salazar	.08	.06	.03
524 Curt Kaufman	.08	.06	.03
525 Odell Jones	.08	.06	.03
526 Juan Agosto	.08	.06	.03
527 Denny Walling	.08	.06	.03
528 Andy Hawkins	.08	.06	.03
529 Sixto Lezcano	.08	.06	.03
530 Skeeter Barnes	.08	.06	.03
531 Randy Johnson	.08	.06	.03
532 Jim Morrison	.08	.06	.03
533 Warren Brusstar	.08	.06	.03
534a Jeff Pendelton (first name incorrect)	.85	.60	.35
534b Terry Pendleton (first name correct)	2.50	2.00	1.00
535 Vic Rodriguez	.08	.06	.03
536 Bob McClure	.08	.06	.03
537 Dave Bergman	.08	.06	.03
538 Mark Clear	.10	.08	.04
539 Mike Pagliarulo	3.00	2.25	1.25
540 Terry Whitfield	.08	.06	.03
541 Joe Beckwith	.08	.06	.03
542 Jeff Burroughs	.10	.08	.04
543 Dan Schatzeder	.08	.06	.03
544 Donnie Scott	.08	.06	.03
545 Jim Slaton	.08	.06	.03
546 Greg Luzinski	.12	.09	.05
547 Mark Salas	.25	.20	.10
548 Dave Smith	.10	.08	.04
549 John Wockenfuss	.08	.06	.03
550 Frank Pastore	.08	.06	.03
551 Tim Flannery	.08	.06	.03
552 Rick Rhoden	.12	.09	.05
553 Mark Davis	.08	.06	.03
554 Jeff Dedmon	.15	.11	.06
555 Gary Woods	.08	.06	.03
556 Danny Heep	.08	.06	.03
557 Mark Langston	.80	.60	.30
558 Darrell Brown	.08	.06	.03
559 Jimmy Key	1.00	.70	.40
560 Rick Lysander	.08	.06	.03
561 Doyle Alexander	.12	.09	.05
562 Mike Stanton	.08	.06	.03
563 Sid Fernandez	.40	.30	.15
564 Richie Hebner	.08	.06	.03
565 Alex Trevino	.08	.06	.03
566 Brian Harper	.08	.06	.03
567 Dan Gladden	.50	.40	.20
568 Luis Salazar	.08	.06	.03
569 Tom Foley	.08	.06	.03
570 Larry Andersen	.08	.06	.03
571 Danny Cox	.12	.09	.05
572 Joe Sambito	.08	.06	.03
573 Juan Beniquez	.08	.06	.03
574 Joel Skinner	.08	.06	.03
575 Randy St. Claire	.15	.11	.06
576 Floyd Rayford	.08	.06	.03
577 Roy Howell	.08	.06	.03
578 John Grubb	.08	.06	.03
579 Ed Jurak	.08	.06	.03
580 John Montefusco	.08	.06	.03
581 Orel Hershiser	2.00	1.50	.80
582 Tom Waddell	.15	.11	.06
583 Mark Huismann	.08	.06	.03
584 Joe Morgan	.25	.20	.10
585 Jim Wohlford	.08	.06	.03

	MT	NR MT	EX
586 Dave Schmidt	.10	.08	.04
587 Jeff Kunkel	.12	.09	.05
588 Hal McRae	.12	.09	.05
589 Bill Almon	.08	.06	.03
590 Carmen Castillo	.10	.08	.04
591 Omar Moreno	.08	.06	.03
592 Ken Howell	.20	.15	.08
593 Tom Brookens	.08	.06	.03
594 Joe Nolan	.08	.06	.03
595 Willie Lozado	.08	.06	.03
596 Tom Nieto	.12	.09	.05
597 Walt Terrell	.15	.11	.06
598 Al Oliver	.15	.11	.06
599 Shane Rawley	.12	.09	.05
600 Denny Gonzalez	.10	.08	.04
601 Mark Grant	.15	.11	.06
602 Mike Armstrong	.08	.06	.03
603 George Foster	.15	.11	.06
604 Davey Lopes	.10	.08	.04
605 Salome Barojas	.08	.06	.03
606 Roy Lee Jackson	.08	.06	.03
607 Pete Filson	.08	.06	.03
608 Duane Walker	.08	.06	.03
609 Glenn Wilson	.12	.09	.05
610 Rafael Santana	.20	.15	.08
611 Roy Smith	.08	.06	.03
612 Ruppert Jones	.08	.06	.03
613 Joe Cowley	.10	.08	.04
614 Al Nipper	.25	.20	.10
615 Gene Nelson	.08	.06	.03
616 Joe Carter	.50	.40	.20
617 Ray Knight	.12	.09	.05
618 Chuck Rainey	.08	.06	.03
619 Dan Driessen	.10	.08	.04
620 Daryl Sconiers	.08	.06	.03
621 Bill Stein	.08	.06	.03
622 Roy Smalley	.08	.06	.03
623 Ed Lynch	.08	.06	.03
624 Jeff Stone	.25	.20	.10
625 Bruce Berenyi	.08	.06	.03
626 Kelvin Chapman	.08	.06	.03
627 Joe Price	.08	.06	.03
628 Steve Bedrosian	.12	.09	.05
629 Vic Mata	.08	.06	.03
630 Mike Krukow	.10	.08	.04
631 Phil Bradley	1.50	1.25	.60
632 Jim Gott	.08	.06	.03
633 Randy Bush	.08	.06	.03
634 Tom Browning	.50	.40	.20
635 Lou Gehrig Puzzle Card	.08	.06	.03
636 Reid Nichols	.08	.06	.03
637 Dan Pasqua	2.00	1.50	.80
638 German Rivera	.08	.06	.03
639 Don Schulze	.12	.09	.05
640a Mike Jones (last line of highlights begins "Was 11-7...")	.10	.08	.04
640b Mike Jones (last line of highlights begins "Spent some ...")	1.25	.90	.50
641 Pete Rose	1.25	.90	.50
642 Wade Rowdon	.10	.08	.04
643 Jerry Narron	.08	.06	.03
644 Darrell Miller	.20	.15	.08
645 Tim Hulett	.20	.15	.08
646 Andy McGaffigan	.08	.06	.03
647 Kurt Bevacqua	.08	.06	.03
648 John Russell	.20	.15	.08
649 Ron Robinson	.25	.20	.10
650 Donnie Moore	.12	.09	.05
651a Two for the Title (Don Mattingly, Dave Winfield) (player names in yellow)	2.50	2.00	1.00
651b Two for the Title (Don Mattingly, Dave Winfield) (player names in white)	5.00	3.75	2.00
652 Tim Laudner	.08	.06	.03
653 Steve Farr	.20	.15	.08
--- Checklist 1-26 DK	.08	.06	.03
--- Checklist 27-130	.08	.06	.03
--- Checklist 131-234	.08	.06	.03
--- Checklist 235-338	.08	.06	.03
--- Checklist 339-442	.08	.06	.03
--- Checklist 443-546	.08	.06	.03
--- Checklist 547-653	.08	.06	.03

Definitions for grading conditions are located in the Introduction of this price guide.

1985 Donruss Action All-Stars

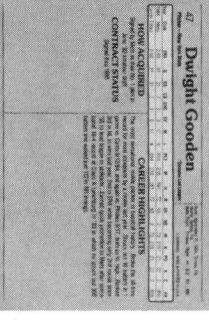

		MT	NR MT	EX
54	Jody Davis	.12	.09	.05
55	Steve Carlton	.30	.25	.12
56	Juan Samuel	.20	.15	.08
57	Gary Carter	.30	.25	.12
58	Harold Baines	.15	.11	.06
59	Eric Show	.09	.07	.04
60	Checklist	.12	.09	.05

1985 Donruss Box Panels

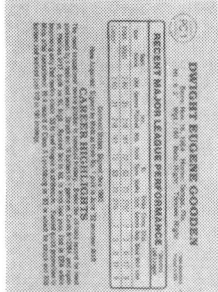

In 1985, Donruss placed on the bottoms of their wax pack boxes a four-card panel which included three player cards and a Lou Gehrig puzzle card. The player cards, numbered PC 1 through PC 3, have backs identical to the regular 1985 Donruss issue. The card fronts are identical in design to the regular issue, but carry different picture poses.

		MT	NR MT	EX
Complete Panel Set:		7.50	5.75	3.00
Complete Singles Set:		3.00	2.25	1.25
Common Single Player:		.15	.11	.06
Panel		7.50	5.75	3.00
1	Dwight Gooden	3.50	2.75	1.50
2	Ryne Sanberg	.30	.25	.12
3	Ron Kittle	.12	.09	.05
---	Gehrig Puzzle Card	.05	.04	.02

1985 Donruss Diamond Kings Supers

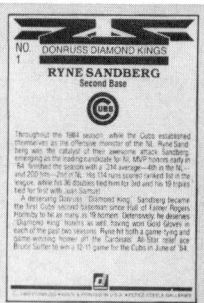

The 1985 Donruss Diamond Kings Supers are enlarged versions of the Diamond Kings cards (#'s 1-26) in the regular 1985 Donruss set. The cards measure 4 15/16'' by 6 3/4''. The Diamond King series features the artwork of Dick Perez. Twenty-eight cards make up the set - twenty-six DK cards, an unnumbered checklist, and an unnumbered Dick Perez card. The back of the Perez card contains a brief history of Dick Perez and the Perez-Steele Gal-

In 1985, Donruss isssued an Action All-Stars set for the third consecutive year. The card fronts feature an action photo with an inset head-shot of the player inside a black border with grey boxes through it. The card backs have black print on blue and white and include statistical and biographical information. The cards were issued with a Lou Gehrig puzzle.

		MT	NR MT	EX
Complete Set:		6.00	4.50	2.50
Common Player:		.09	.07	.04
1	Tim Raines	.35	.25	.14
2	Jim Gantner	.09	.07	.04
3	Mario Soto	.09	.07	.04
4	Spike Owen	.09	.07	.04
5	Lloyd Moseby	.12	.09	.05
6	Damaso Garcia	.09	.07	.04
7	Cal Ripken	.35	.25	.14
8	Dan Quisenberry	.15	.11	.06
9	Eddie Murray	.30	.25	.12
10	Tony Pena	.12	.09	.05
11	Buddy Bell	.12	.09	.05
12	Dave Winfield	.30	.25	.12
13	Ron Kittle	.12	.09	.05
14	Rich Gossage	.12	.09	.05
15	Dwight Evans	.15	.11	.06
16	Al Davis	.15	.11	.06
17	Mike Schmidt	.40	.30	.15
18	Pascual Perez	.09	.07	.04
19	Tony Gwynn	.30	.25	.12
20	Nolan Ryan	.30	.25	.12
21	Robin Yount	.25	.20	.10
22	Mike Marshall	.12	.09	.05
23	Brett Butler	.09	.07	.04
24	Ryne Sandberg	.30	.25	.12
25	Dale Murphy	.40	.30	.15
26	George Brett	.40	.30	.15
27	Jim Rice	.30	.25	.12
28	Ozzie Smith	.15	.11	.06
29	Larry Parrish	.09	.07	.04
30	Jack Clark	.15	.11	.06
31	Manny Trillo	.09	.07	.04
32	Dave Kingman	.12	.09	.05
33	Geoff Zahn	.09	.07	.04
34	Pedro Guerrero	.20	.15	.08
35	Dave Parker	.20	.15	.08
36	Rollie Fingers	.15	.11	.06
37	Fernando Valenzuela	.25	.20	.10
38	Wade Boggs	.75	.60	.30
39	Reggie Jackson	.30	.25	.12
40	Kent Hrbek	.20	.15	.08
41	Keith Hernandez	.30	.25	.12
42	Lou Whitaker	.15	.11	.06
43	Tom Herr	.12	.09	.05
44	Alan Trammell	.20	.15	.08
45	Butch Wynegar	.09	.07	.04
46	Leon Durham	.12	.09	.05
47	Dwight Gooden	.75	.60	.30
48	Don Mattingly	2.00	1.50	.80
49	Phil Niekro	.20	.15	.08
50	Johnny Ray	.12	.09	.05
51	Doug DeCinces	.09	.07	.04
52	Willie Upshaw	.09	.07	.04
53	Lance Parrish	.20	.15	.08

leries. The set could be obtained through a write-in offer found on the wrappers of the regular issue wax packs.

	MT	NR MT	EX
Complete Set:	11.00	8.25	4.50
Common Player:	.20	.15	.08
1 Ryne Sandberg	.60	.45	.25
2 Doug DeCinces	.20	.15	.08
3 Richard Dotson	.20	.15	.08
4 Bert Blyleven	.25	.20	.10
5 Lou Whitaker	.30	.25	.12
6 Dan Quisenberry	.25	.20	.10
7 Don Mattingly	2.50	2.00	1.00
8 Carney Lansford	.20	.15	.08
9 Frank Tanana	.20	.15	.08
10 Willie Upshaw	.20	.15	.08
11 Claudell Washington	.20	.15	.08
12 Mike Marshall	.25	.20	.10
13 Joaquin Andujar	.20	.15	.08
14 Cal Ripken, Jr.	.70	.50	.30
15 Jim Rice	.60	.45	.25
16 Don Sutton	.30	.25	.12
17 Frank Viola	.25	.20	.10
18 Alvin Davis	.30	.25	.12
19 Mario Soto	.20	.15	.08
20 Jose Cruz	.20	.15	.08
21 Charlie Lea	.20	.15	.08
22 Jesse Orosco	.25	.20	.10
23 Juan Samuel	.35	.25	.14
24 Tony Pena	.25	.20	.10
25 Tony Gwynn	.60	.45	.25
26 Bob Brenly	.20	.15	.08
--- Checklist	.12	.09	.05
--- Dick Perez (DK artist)	.12	.09	.05

1985 Donruss Highlights

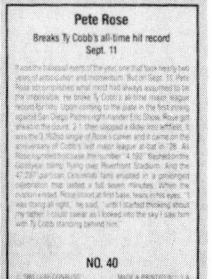

Designed in the style of the regular 1985 Donruss set, this issue features the pitchers and players for each month in the major leagues plus highlight cards of special baseball events and milestones that occurred during the 1985 season. Fifty-six cards, including an unnumbered checklist, comprise the set which was available only through hobby dealers. The cards measure 2½'' by 3½'' and have glossy fronts. The last two cards in the set feature Donruss' picks for the A.L. and N.L. Rookies of the Year. The set was issued in a specially designed box.

	MT	NR MT	EX
Complete Set:	24.00	18.00	9.50
Common Player:	.12	.09	.05
1 Sets Opening Day Record (Tom Seaver)	.40	.30	.15
2 Establishes A.L. Save Mark (Rollie Fingers)	.15	.11	.06
3 A.L. Player of the Month - April (Mike Davis)	.12	.09	.05
4 A.L. Pitcher of the Month - April (Charlie Leibrandt)	.12	.09	.05
5 N.L. Player of the Month - April (Dale Murphy)	1.00	.70	.40
6 N.L. Pitcher of the Month - April (Fernando Valenzuela)	.35	.25	.14

	MT	NR MT	EX
7 N.L. Shortstop Record (Larry Bowa)	.12	.09	.05
8 Joins Reds 2000 Hit Club (Dave Concepcion)	.12	.09	.05
9 Eldest Grand Slammer (Tony Perez)	.15	.11	.06
10 N.L. Career Run Leader (Pete Rose)	1.75	1.25	.70
11 A.L. Player of the Month - May (George Brett)	.90	.70	.35
12 A.L. Pitcher of the Month - May (Dave Stieb)	.12	.09	.05
13 N.L. Player of the Month - May (Dave Parker)	.20	.15	.08
14 N.L. Pitcher of the Month - May (Andy Hawkins)	.12	.09	.05
15 Records 11th Straight Win (Andy Hawkins)	.12	.09	.05
16 Two Homers In First Inning (Von Hayes)	.15	.11	.06
17 A.L. Player of the Month - June (Rickey Henderson)	.80	.60	.30
18 A.L. Pitcher of the Month - June (Jay Howell)	.12	.09	.05
19 N.L. Player of the Month - June (Pedro Guerrero)	.20	.15	.08
20 N.L. Pitcher of the Month - June (John Tudor)	.12	.09	.05
21 Marathon Game Iron Men (Gary Carter, Keith Hernandez)	.35	.25	.14
22 Records 4000th K (Nolan Ryan)	.35	.25	.14
23 All-Star Game MVP (LaMarr Hoyt)	.12	.09	.05
24 1st Ranger To Hit For Cycle (Oddibe McDowell)	.80	.60	.30
25 A.L. Player of the Month - July (George Brett)	.90	.70	.35
26 A.L. Pitcher of the Month - July (Bret Saberhagen)	.20	.15	.08
27 N.L. Player of the Month - July (Keith Hernandez)	.35	.25	.14
28 N.L. Pitcher of the Month - July (Fernando Valenzuela)	.35	.25	.14
29 Record Setting Base Stealers (Vince Coleman, Willie McGee)	.80	.60	.30
30 Notches 300th Career Win (Tom Seaver)	.35	.25	.14
31 Strokes 3000th Hit (Rod Carew)	.40	.30	.15
32 Establishes Met Record (Dwight Gooden)	2.25	1.75	.90
33 Achieves Strikeout Milestone (Dwight Gooden)	2.25	1.75	.90
34 Explodes For 9 RBI (Eddie Murray)	.70	.50	.30
35 A.L. Career Hbp Leader (Don Baylor)	.15	.11	.06
36 A.L. Player of the Month - August (Don Mattingly)	3.25	2.50	1.25
37 A.L. Pitcher of the Month - August (Dave Righetti)	.20	.15	.08
38 N.L. Player of the Month (Willie McGee)	.20	.15	.08
39 N.L. Pitcher of the Month - August (Shane Rawley)	.12	.09	.05
40 Ty-Breaking Hit (Pete Rose)	1.75	1.25	.70
41 Hits 3 Hrs Drives In 8 Runs (Andre Dawson)	.20	.15	.08
42 Sets Yankee Theft Mark (Rickey Henderson)	.80	.60	.30
43 20 Wins In Rookie Season (Tom Browning)	.20	.15	.08
44 Yankee Milestone For Hits (Don Mattingly)	3.25	2.50	1.25
45 A.L. Player of the Month - September (Don Mattingly)	3.25	2.50	1.25
46 A.L. Pitcher of the Month - September (Charlie Leibrandt)	.12	.09	.05
47 N.L. Player of the Month - September (Gary Carter)	.30	.25	.12
48 N.L. Pitcher of the Month - September (Dwight Gooden)	2.25	1.75	.90
49 Major League Record Setter (Wade Boggs)	1.75	1.25	.70
50 Hurls Shutout For 300th Win (Phil Niekro)	.30	.25	.12
51 Venerable HR King (Darrell Evans)	.15	.11	.06
52 N.L. Switch-hitting Record (Willie McGee)	.20	.15	.08
53 Equals DiMaggio Feat (Dave Winfield)	.50	.40	.20
54 Donruss N.L. Rookie of the Year (Vince Coleman)	2.25	1.75	.90

		MT	NR MT	EX
55	Donruss A.L. Rookie of the Year (Ozzie Guillen)	.70	.50	.30
---	Checklist	.20	.15	.08

1985 Donruss Sluggers of the Hall of Fame

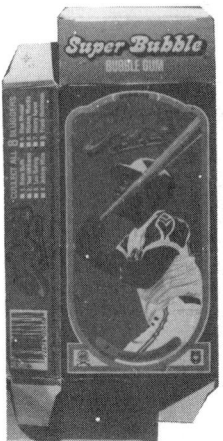

In much the same manner as the first Bazooka cards were issued in 1959, this eight-player set from Donruss consists of cards which formed the bottom panel of a box of bubblegum. When cut off the box, cards measure 3½'' by 6½,'' with blank backs. Players are pictured on the cards in paintings done by Dick Perez.

		MT	NR MT	EX
Complete Set:		8.00	6.00	3.25
Common Player:		.60	.45	.25
1	Babe Ruth	1.50	1.25	.60
2	Ted Williams	1.00	.70	.40
3	Lou Gehrig	1.00	.70	.40
4	Johnny Mize	.60	.45	.25
5	Stan Musial	1.00	.70	.40
6	Mickey Mantle	2.50	2.00	1.00
7	Hank Aaron	1.00	.70	.40
8	Frank Robinson	.70	.50	.30

1986 Donruss

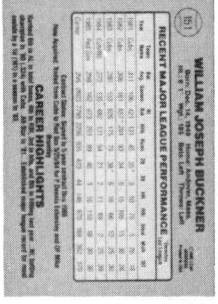

In 1986, Donruss issued a 660-card set which included 653 numbered cards and seven unnumbered checklists. The cards, which measure 2½'' by 3½'', have fronts that feature blue borders and backs that have black print on blue and white. For the fifth year

in a row, the first 26 cards in the set are Diamond Kings. The Rated Rookies subset (card #'s 27-46) appears once again. The cards were distributed with a Hank Aaron puzzle. The complete set price does not include the higher priced variations. In the checklist that follows, (DK) and (RR) refer to the Diamond Kings and Rated Rookies series.

		MT	NR MT	EX
Complete Set:		65.00	49.00	26.00
Common Player:		.06	.05	.02
1	Kirk Gibson (DK)	.25	.20	.10
2	Goose Gossage (DK)	.20	.15	.08
3	Willie McGee (DK)	.15	.11	.06
4	George Bell (DK)	.40	.30	.15
5	Tony Armas (DK)	.10	.08	.04
6	Chili Davis (DK)	.12	.09	.05
7	Cecil Cooper (DK)	.12	.09	.05
8	Mike Boddicker (DK)	.10	.08	.04
9	Davey Lopes (DK)	.10	.08	.04
10	Bill Doran (DK)	.12	.09	.05
11	Bret Saberhagen (DK)	.35	.25	.14
12	Brett Butler (DK)	.10	.08	.04
13	Harold Baines (DK)	.15	.11	.06
14	Mike Davis (DK)	.10	.08	.04
15	Tony Perez (DK)	.15	.11	.06
16	Willie Randolph (DK)	.12	.09	.05
17	Bob Boone (DK)	.10	.08	.04
18	Orel Hershiser (DK)	.30	.25	.12
19	Johnny Ray (DK)	.12	.09	.05
20	Gary Ward (DK)	.10	.08	.04
21	Rick Mahler (DK)	.08	.06	.03
22	Phil Bradley (DK)	.20	.15	.08
23	Jerry Koosman (DK)	.12	.09	.05
24	Tom Brunansky (DK)	.15	.11	.06
25	Andre Dawson (DK)	.30	.25	.12
26	Dwight Gooden (DK)	1.00	.70	.40
27	Kal Daniels (RR)	4.50	3.50	1.75
28	Fred McGriff (RR)	1.00	.70	.40
29	Cory Snyder (RR)	3.50	2.75	1.50
30	Jose Guzman (RR)	.35	.25	.14
31	Ty Gainey (RR)	.12	.09	.05
32	Johnny Abrego (RR)	.08	.06	.03
33a	Andres Galarraga (RR) (no accent mark above "e" in Andres on back)	1.50	1.25	.60
33b	Andres Galarraga (RR) (accent mark above "e" in Andres on back)	2.50	2.00	1.00
34	Dave Shipanoff (RR)	.08	.06	.03
35	Mark McLemore (RR)	.20	.15	.08
36	Marty Clary (RR)	.08	.06	.03
37	Paul O'Neill (RR)	.25	.20	.10
38	Danny Tartabull (RR)	.70	.50	.30
39	Jose Canseco (RR)	11.00	8.25	4.50
40	Juan Nieves (RR)	.80	.60	.30
41	Lance McCullers (RR)	.25	.20	.10
42	Rick Surhoff (RR)	.08	.06	.03
43	Todd Worrell (RR)	1.25	.90	.50
44	Bob Kipper (RR)	.20	.15	.08
45	John Habyan (RR)	.20	.15	.08
46	Mike Woodard (RR)	.12	.09	.05
47	Mike Boddicker	.12	.09	.05
48	Robin Yount	.35	.25	.14
49	Lou Whitaker	.25	.20	.10
50	"Oil Can" Boyd	.10	.08	.04
51	Rickey Henderson	.40	.30	.15
52	Mike Marshall	.12	.09	.05
53	George Brett	.50	.40	.20
54	Dave Kingman	.15	.11	.06
55	Hubie Brooks	.10	.08	.04
56	Oddibe McDowell	.60	.45	.25
57	Doug DeCinces	.10	.08	.04
58	Britt Burns	.06	.05	.02
59	Ozzie Smith	.15	.11	.06
60	Jose Cruz	.10	.08	.04
61	Mike Schmidt	.50	.40	.20
62	Pete Rose	.80	.60	.30
63	Steve Garvey	.40	.30	.15
64	Tony Pena	.10	.08	.04
65	Chili Davis	.10	.08	.04
66	Dale Murphy	.60	.45	.25
67	Ryne Sandberg	.35	.25	.14
68	Gary Carter	.40	.30	.15
69	Alvin Davis	.20	.15	.08
70	Kent Hrbek	.25	.20	.10
71	George Bell	.35	.25	.14
72	Kirby Puckett	1.50	1.25	.60
73	Lloyd Moseby	.10	.08	.04
74	Bob Kearney	.06	.05	.02
75	Dwight Gooden	2.50	2.00	1.00

		MT	NR MT	EX			MT	NR MT	EX
76	Gary Matthews	.10	.08	.04	167	Keith Moreland	.08	.06	.03
77	Rick Mahler	.06	.05	.02	168	Jack Clark	.20	.15	.08
78	Benny Distefano	.06	.05	.02	169	Storm Davis	.06	.05	.02
79	Jeff Leonard	.10	.08	.04	170	Cecil Cooper	.12	.09	.05
80	Kevin McReynolds	.20	.15	.08	171	Alan Trammell	.35	.25	.14
81	Ron Oester	.06	.05	.02	172	Roger Clemens	4.00	3.00	1.50
82	John Russell	.08	.06	.03	173	Don Mattingly	6.00	4.50	2.50
83	Tommy Herr	.10	.08	.04	174	Pedro Guerrero	.20	.15	.08
84	Jerry Mumphrey	.08	.06	.03	175	Willie Wilson	.12	.09	.05
85	Ron Romanick	.06	.05	.02	176	Dwayne Murphy	.08	.06	.03
86	Daryl Boston	.08	.06	.03	177	Tim Raines	.40	.30	.15
87	Andre Dawson	.30	.25	.12	178	Larry Parrish	.10	.08	.04
88	Eddie Murray	.40	.30	.15	179	Mike Witt	.12	.09	.05
89	Dion James	.12	.09	.05	180	Harold Baines	.15	.11	.06
90	Chet Lemon	.08	.06	.03	181	Vince Coleman	2.00	1.50	.80
91	Bob Stanley	.08	.06	.03	182	Jeff Heathcock	.12	.09	.05
92	Willie Randolph	.10	.08	.04	183	Steve Carlton	.40	.30	.15
93	Mike Scioscia	.06	.05	.02	184	Mario Soto	.08	.06	.03
94	Tom Waddell	.06	.05	.02	185	Goose Gossage	.20	.15	.08
95	Danny Jackson	.10	.08	.04	186	Johnny Ray	.12	.09	.05
96	Mike Davis	.08	.06	.03	187	Dan Gladden	.10	.08	.04
97	Mike Fitzgerald	.06	.05	.02	188	Bob Horner	.25	.20	.10
98	Gary Ward	.08	.06	.03	189	Rick Sutcliffe	.15	.11	.06
99	Pete O'Brien	.10	.08	.04	190	Keith Hernandez	.35	.25	.14
100	Bret Saberhagen	.60	.45	.25	191	Phil Bradley	.20	.15	.08
101	Alfredo Griffin	.08	.06	.03	192	Tom Brunansky	.12	.09	.05
102	Brett Butler	.08	.06	.03	193	Jesse Barfield	.25	.20	.10
103	Ron Guidry	.25	.20	.10	194	Frank Viola	.12	.09	.05
104	Jerry Reuss	.08	.06	.03	195	Willie Upshaw	.08	.06	.03
105	Jack Morris	.30	.25	.12	196	Jim Beattie	.06	.05	.02
106	Rick Dempsey	.08	.06	.03	197	Darryl Strawberry	.60	.45	.25
107	Ray Burris	.06	.05	.02	198	Ron Cey	.10	.08	.04
108	Brian Downing	.10	.08	.04	199	Steve Bedrosian	.12	.09	.05
109	Willie McGee	.15	.11	.06	200	Steve Kemp	.08	.06	.03
110	Bill Doran	.10	.08	.04	201	Manny Trillo	.08	.06	.03
111	Kent Tekulve	.08	.06	.03	202	Garry Templeton	.10	.08	.04
112	Tony Gwynn	.40	.30	.15	203	Dave Parker	.25	.20	.10
113	Marvell Wynne	.06	.05	.02	204	John Denny	.06	.05	.02
114	David Green	.06	.05	.02	205	Terry Pendleton	.15	.11	.06
115	Jim Gantner	.08	.06	.03	206	Terry Puhl	.06	.05	.02
116	George Foster	.12	.09	.05	207	Bobby Grich	.10	.08	.04
117	Steve Trout	.08	.06	.03	208	Ozzie Guillen	.40	.30	.15
118	Mark Langston	.15	.11	.06	209	Jeff Reardon	.15	.11	.06
119	Tony Fernandez	.20	.15	.08	210	Cal Ripken Jr.	.50	.40	.20
120	John Butcher	.06	.05	.02	211	Bill Schroeder	.06	.05	.02
121	Ron Robinson	.08	.06	.03	212	Dan Petry	.10	.08	.04
122	Dan Spillner	.06	.05	.02	213	Jim Rice	.40	.30	.15
123	Mike Young	.08	.06	.03	214	Dave Righetti	.20	.15	.08
124	Paul Molitor	.15	.11	.06	215	Fernando Valenzuela	.35	.25	.14
125	Kirk Gibson	.35	.25	.14	216	Julio Franco	.12	.09	.05
126	Ken Griffey	.12	.09	.05	217	Darryl Motley	.06	.05	.02
127	Tony Armas	.10	.08	.04	218	Dave Collins	.08	.06	.03
128	Mariano Duncan	.20	.15	.08	219	Tim Wallach	.12	.09	.05
129	Pat Tabler	.10	.08	.04	220	George Wright	.06	.05	.02
130	Frank White	.10	.08	.04	221	Tommy Dunbar	.06	.05	.02
131	Carney Lansford	.08	.06	.03	222	Steve Balboni	.08	.06	.03
132	Vance Law	.08	.06	.03	223	Jay Howell	.08	.06	.03
133	Dick Schofield	.06	.05	.02	224	Joe Carter	.25	.20	.10
134	Wayne Tolleson	.06	.05	.02	225	Ed Whitson	.06	.05	.02
135	Greg Walker	.10	.08	.04	226	Orel Hershiser	.35	.25	.14
136	Denny Walling	.06	.05	.02	227	Willie Hernandez	.08	.06	.03
137	Ozzie Virgil	.08	.06	.03	228	Lee Lacy	.08	.06	.03
138	Ricky Horton	.10	.08	.04	229	Rollie Fingers	.20	.15	.08
139	LaMarr Hoyt	.08	.06	.03	230	Bob Boone	.08	.06	.03
140	Wayne Krenchicki	.06	.05	.02	231	Joaquin Andujar	.08	.06	.03
141	Glenn Hubbard	.06	.05	.02	232	Craig Reynolds	.06	.05	.02
142	Cecilio Guante	.06	.05	.02	233	Shane Rawley	.10	.08	.04
143	Mike Krukow	.08	.06	.03	234	Eric Show	.06	.05	.02
144	Lee Smith	.10	.08	.04	235	Jose DeLeon	.08	.06	.03
145	Edwin Nunez	.06	.05	.02	236	Jose Uribe	.25	.20	.10
146	Dave Stieb	.12	.09	.05	237	Moose Haas	.06	.05	.02
147	Mike Smithson	.06	.05	.02	238	Wally Backman	.08	.06	.03
148	Ken Dixon	.08	.06	.03	239	Dennis Eckersley	.08	.06	.03
149	Danny Darwin	.08	.06	.03	240	Mike Moore	.06	.05	.02
150	Chris Pittaro	.12	.09	.05	241	Damaso Garcia	.08	.06	.03
151	Bill Buckner	.12	.09	.05	242	Tim Teufel	.08	.06	.03
152	Mike Pagliarulo	.30	.25	.12	243	Dave Concepcion	.12	.09	.05
153	Bill Russell	.08	.06	.03	244	Floyd Bannister	.10	.08	.04
154	Brook Jacoby	.10	.08	.04	245	Fred Lynn	.20	.15	.08
155	Pat Sheridan	.06	.05	.02	246	Charlie Moore	.06	.05	.02
156	Mike Gallego	.10	.08	.04	247	Walt Terrell	.08	.06	.03
157	Jim Wohlford	.06	.05	.02	248	Dave Winfield	.40	.30	.15
158	Gary Pettis	.08	.06	.03	249	Dwight Evans	.12	.09	.05
159	Toby Harrah	.08	.06	.03	250	Dennis Powell	.15	.11	.06
160	Richard Dotson	.10	.08	.04	251	Andre Thornton	.10	.08	.04
161	Bob Knepper	.08	.06	.03	252	Onix Concepcion	.06	.05	.02
162	Dave Dravecky	.08	.06	.03	253	Mike Heath	.06	.05	.02
163	Greg Gross	.06	.05	.02	254a	David Palmer (2B on front)	.08	.06	.03
164	Eric Davis	5.00	3.75	2.00	254b	David Palmer (P on front)	1.00	.70	.40
165	Gerald Perry	.08	.06	.03	255	Donnie Moore	.06	.05	.02
166	Rick Rhoden	.10	.08	.04	256	Curtis Wilkerson	.06	.05	.02

#	Player	MT	NR MT	EX
257	Julio Cruz	.06	.05	.02
258	Nolan Ryan	.40	.30	.15
259	Jeff Stone	.08	.06	.03
260a	John Tudor (1981 Games is .18)	.10	.08	.04
260b	John Tudor (1981 Games is 18)	1.00	.70	.40
261	Mark Thurmond	.06	.05	.02
262	Jay Tibbs	.06	.05	.02
263	Rafael Ramirez	.06	.05	.02
264	Larry McWilliams	.06	.05	.02
265	Mark Davis	.06	.05	.02
266	Bob Dernier	.06	.05	.02
267	Matt Young	.06	.05	.02
268	Jim Clancy	.10	.08	.04
269	Mickey Hatcher	.06	.05	.02
270	Sammy Stewart	.06	.05	.02
271	Bob Gibson	.06	.05	.02
272	Nelson Simmons	.10	.08	.04
273	Rich Gedman	.10	.08	.04
274	Butch Wynegar	.08	.06	.03
275	Ken Howell	.08	.06	.03
276	Mel Hall	.08	.06	.03
277	Jim Sundberg	.08	.06	.03
278	Chris Codiroli	.06	.05	.02
279	Herman Winningham	.20	.15	.08
280	Rod Carew	.40	.30	.15
281	Don Slaught	.06	.05	.02
282	Scott Fletcher	.08	.06	.03
283	Bill Dawley	.06	.05	.02
284	Andy Hawkins	.06	.05	.02
285	Glenn Wilson	.10	.08	.04
286	Nick Esasky	.06	.05	.02
287	Claudell Washington	.08	.06	.03
288	Lee Mazzilli	.08	.06	.03
289	Jody Davis	.10	.08	.04
290	Darrell Porter	.08	.06	.03
291	Scott McGregor	.10	.08	.04
292	Ted Simmons	.12	.09	.05
293	Aurelio Lopez	.06	.05	.02
294	Marty Barrett	.10	.08	.04
295	Dale Berra	.06	.05	.02
296	Greg Brock	.10	.08	.04
297	Charlie Leibrandt	.08	.06	.03
298	Bill Krueger	.06	.05	.02
299	Bryn Smith	.08	.06	.03
300	Burt Hooton	.08	.06	.03
301	Stu Cliburn	.08	.06	.03
302	Luis Salazar	.06	.05	.02
303	Ken Dayley	.06	.05	.02
304	Frank DiPino	.06	.05	.02
305	Von Hayes	.12	.09	.05
306a	Gary Redus (1983 2B is .20)	.08	.06	.03
306b	Gary Redus (1983 2B is 20)	1.00	.70	.40
307	Craig Lefferts	.06	.05	.02
308	Sam Khalifa	.08	.06	.03
309	Scott Garrelts	.08	.06	.03
310	Rick Cerone	.06	.05	.02
311	Shawon Dunston	.20	.15	.08
312	Howard Johnson	.12	.09	.05
313	Jim Presley	.30	.25	.12
314	Gary Gaetti	.25	.20	.10
315	Luis Leal	.06	.05	.02
316	Mark Salas	.08	.06	.03
317	Bill Caudill	.06	.05	.02
318	Dave Henderson	.06	.05	.02
319	Rafael Santana	.06	.05	.02
320	Leon Durham	.10	.08	.04
321	Bruce Sutter	.15	.11	.06
322	Jason Thompson	.06	.05	.02
323	Bob Brenly	.06	.05	.02
324	Carmelo Martinez	.08	.06	.03
325	Eddie Milner	.06	.05	.02
326	Juan Samuel	.15	.11	.06
327	Tom Nieto	.06	.05	.02
328	Dave Smith	.08	.06	.03
329	Urbano Lugo	.08	.06	.03
330	Joel Skinner	.06	.05	.02
331	Bill Gullickson	.08	.06	.03
332	Floyd Rayford	.06	.05	.02
333	Ben Oglivie	.08	.06	.03
334	Lance Parrish	.30	.25	.12
335	Jackie Gutierrez	.06	.05	.02
336	Dennis Rasmussen	.08	.06	.03
337	Terry Whitfield	.06	.05	.02
338	Neal Heaton	.08	.06	.03
339	Jorge Orta	.06	.05	.02
340	Donnie Hill	.06	.05	.02
341	Joe Hesketh	.08	.06	.03
342	Charlie Hough	.10	.08	.04
343	Dave Rozema	.06	.05	.02
344	Greg Pryor	.06	.05	.02
345	Mickey Tettleton	.10	.08	.04
346	George Vukovich	.06	.05	.02
347	Don Baylor	.12	.09	.05
348	Carlos Diaz	.06	.05	.02
349	Barbaro Garbey	.06	.05	.02
350	Larry Sheets	.20	.15	.08
351	Ted Higuera	1.50	1.25	.60
352	Juan Beniquez	.06	.05	.02
353	Bob Forsch	.08	.06	.03
354	Mark Bailey	.06	.05	.02
355	Larry Andersen	.06	.05	.02
356	Terry Kennedy	.08	.06	.03
357	Don Robinson	.08	.06	.03
358	Jim Gott	.06	.05	.02
359	Earnest Riles	.30	.25	.12
360	John Christensen	.10	.08	.04
361	Ray Fontenot	.06	.05	.02
362	Spike Owen	.06	.05	.02
363	Jim Acker	.06	.05	.02
364a	Ron Davis (last line in highlights ends with "...in May.")	.08	.06	.03
364b	Ron Davis (last line in highlights ends with "...relievers (9).")	1.00	.70	.40
365	Tom Hume	.06	.05	.02
366	Carlton Fisk	.25	.20	.10
367	Nate Snell	.08	.06	.03
368	Rick Manning	.06	.05	.02
369	Darrell Evans	.15	.11	.06
370	Ron Hassey	.06	.05	.02
371	Wade Boggs	2.50	2.00	1.00
372	Rick Honeycutt	.08	.06	.03
373	Chris Bando	.06	.05	.02
374	Bud Black	.06	.05	.02
375	Steve Henderson	.06	.05	.02
376	Charlie Lea	.06	.05	.02
377	Reggie Jackson	.40	.30	.15
378	Dave Schmidt	.08	.06	.03
379	Bob James	.06	.05	.02
380	Glenn Davis	1.50	1.25	.60
381	Tim Corcoran	.06	.05	.02
382	Danny Cox	.10	.08	.04
383	Tim Flannery	.06	.05	.02
384	Tom Browning	.15	.11	.06
385	Rick Camp	.06	.05	.02
386	Jim Morrison	.06	.05	.02
387	Dave LaPoint	.06	.05	.02
388	Davey Lopes	.08	.06	.03
389	Al Cowens	.06	.05	.02
390	Doyle Alexander	.10	.08	.04
391	Tim Laudner	.06	.05	.02
392	Don Aase	.08	.06	.03
393	Jaime Cocanower	.06	.05	.02
394	Randy O'Neal	.10	.08	.04
395	Mike Easler	.08	.06	.03
396	Scott Bradley	.08	.06	.03
397	Tom Niedenfuer	.08	.06	.03
398	Jerry Willard	.06	.05	.02
399	Lonnie Smith	.08	.06	.03
400	Bruce Bochte	.06	.05	.02
401	Terry Francona	.06	.05	.02
402	Jim Slaton	.06	.05	.02
403	Bill Stein	.06	.05	.02
404	Tim Hulett	.08	.06	.03
405	Alan Ashby	.06	.05	.02
406	Tim Stoddard	.06	.05	.02
407	Garry Maddox	.08	.06	.03
408	Ted Power	.08	.06	.03
409	Len Barker	.08	.06	.03
410	Denny Gonzalez	.06	.05	.02
411	George Frazier	.06	.05	.02
412	Andy Van Slyke	.10	.08	.04
413	Jim Dwyer	.06	.05	.02
414	Paul Householder	.06	.05	.02
415	Alejandro Sanchez	.06	.05	.02
416	Steve Crawford	.06	.05	.02
417	Dan Pasqua	.30	.25	.12
418	Enos Cabell	.06	.05	.02
419	Mike Jones	.06	.05	.02
420	Steve Kiefer	.06	.05	.02
421	Tim Burke	.30	.25	.12
422	Mike Mason	.06	.05	.02
423	Ruppert Jones	.06	.05	.02
424	Jerry Hairston	.06	.05	.02
425	Tito Landrum	.06	.05	.02
426	Jeff Calhoun	.06	.05	.02
427	Don Carman	.30	.25	.12
428	Tony Perez	.15	.11	.06
429	Jerry Davis	.06	.05	.02
430	Bob Walk	.06	.05	.02
431	Brad Wellman	.06	.05	.02
432	Terry Forster	.08	.06	.03
433	Billy Hatcher	.15	.11	.06

		MT	NR MT	EX
434	Clint Hurdle	.06	.05	.02
435	Ivan Calderon	.60	.45	.25
436	Pete Filson	.06	.05	.02
437	Tom Henke	.10	.08	.04
438	Dave Engle	.06	.05	.02
439	Tom Filer	.06	.05	.02
440	Gorman Thomas	.12	.09	.05
441	Rick Aguilera	.35	.25	.14
442	Scott Sanderson	.08	.06	.03
443	Jeff Dedmon	.06	.05	.02
444	Joe Orsulak	.12	.09	.05
445	Atlee Hammaker	.06	.05	.02
446	Jerry Royster	.06	.05	.02
447	Buddy Bell	.12	.09	.05
448	Dave Rucker	.06	.05	.02
449	Ivan DeJesus	.06	.05	.02
450	Jim Pankovits	.06	.05	.02
451	Jerry Narron	.06	.05	.02
452	Bryan Little	.06	.05	.02
453	Gary Lucas	.06	.05	.02
454	Dennis Martinez	.06	.05	.02
455	Ed Romero	.06	.05	.02
456	Bob Melvin	.12	.09	.05
457	Glenn Hoffman	.06	.05	.02
458	Bob Shirley	.06	.05	.02
459	Bob Welch	.10	.08	.04
460	Carmen Castillo	.06	.05	.02
461	Dave Leeper	.08	.06	.03
462	Tim Birtsas	.10	.08	.04
463	Randy St. Claire	.06	.05	.02
464	Chris Welsh	.06	.05	.02
465	Greg Harris	.06	.05	.02
466	Lynn Jones	.06	.05	.02
467	Dusty Baker	.08	.06	.03
468	Roy Smith	.06	.05	.02
469	Andre Robertson	.06	.05	.02
470	Ken Landreaux	.08	.06	.03
471	Dave Bergman	.06	.05	.02
472	Gary Roenicke	.06	.05	.02
473	Pete Vuckovich	.08	.06	.03
474	Kirk McCaskill	.35	.25	.14
475	Jeff Lahti	.06	.05	.02
476	Mike Scott	.20	.15	.08
477	Darren Daulton	.15	.11	.06
478	Graig Nettles	.15	.11	.06
479	Bill Almon	.06	.05	.02
480	Greg Minton	.06	.05	.02
481	Randy Ready	.08	.06	.03
482	Lenny Dykstra	.80	.60	.30
483	Thad Bosley	.06	.05	.02
484	Harold Reynolds	.30	.25	.12
485	Al Oliver	.12	.09	.05
486	Roy Smalley	.06	.05	.02
487	John Franco	.10	.08	.04
488	Juan Agosto	.06	.05	.02
489	Al Pardo	.06	.05	.02
490	Bill Wegman	.25	.20	.10
491	Frank Tanana	.10	.08	.04
492	Brian Fisher	.35	.25	.14
493	Mark Clear	.08	.06	.03
494	Len Matuszek	.06	.05	.02
495	Ramon Romero	.06	.05	.02
496	John Wathan	.08	.06	.03
497	Rob Picciolo	.06	.05	.02
498	U.L. Washington	.06	.05	.02
499	John Candelaria	.10	.08	.04
500	Duane Walker	.06	.05	.02
501	Gene Nelson	.06	.05	.02
502	John Mizerock	.06	.05	.02
503	Luis Aguayo	.06	.05	.02
504	Kurt Kepshire	.06	.05	.02
505	Ed Wojna	.10	.08	.04
506	Joe Price	.06	.05	.02
507	Milt Thompson	.50	.40	.20
508	Junior Ortiz	.06	.05	.02
509	Vida Blue	.10	.08	.04
510	Steve Engel	.06	.05	.02
511	Karl Best	.08	.06	.03
512	Cecil Fielder	.25	.20	.10
513	Frank Eufemia	.06	.05	.02
514	Tippy Martinez	.06	.05	.02
515	Billy Robidoux	.15	.11	.06
516	Bill Scherrer	.06	.05	.02
517	Bruce Hurst	.10	.08	.04
518	Rich Bordi	.06	.05	.02
519	Steve Yeager	.06	.05	.02
520	Tony Bernazard	.08	.06	.03
521	Hal McRae	.12	.09	.05
522	Jose Rijo	.08	.06	.03
523	Mitch Webster	.50	.40	.20
524	Jack Howell	.60	.45	.25

		MT	NR MT	EX
525	Alan Bannister	.06	.05	.02
526	Ron Kittle	.10	.08	.04
527	Phil Garner	.08	.06	.03
528	Kurt Bevacqua	.06	.05	.02
529	Kevin Gross	.08	.06	.03
530	Bo Diaz	.08	.06	.03
531	Ken Oberkfell	.08	.06	.03
532	Rick Reuschel	.10	.08	.04
533	Ron Meridith	.10	.08	.04
534	Steve Braun	.06	.05	.02
535	Wayne Gross	.06	.05	.02
536	Ray Searage	.06	.05	.02
537	Tom Brookens	.06	.05	.02
538	Al Nipper	.10	.08	.04
539	Billy Sample	.06	.05	.02
540	Steve Sax	.20	.15	.08
541	Dan Quisenberry	.15	.11	.06
542	Tony Phillips	.06	.05	.02
543	Floyd Youmans	.70	.50	.30
544	Steve Buechele	.25	.20	.10
545	Craig Gerber	.06	.05	.02
546	Joe DeSa	.06	.05	.02
547	Brian Harper	.06	.05	.02
548	Kevin Bass	.10	.08	.04
549	Tom Foley	.06	.05	.02
550	Dave Van Gorder	.06	.05	.02
551	Bruce Bochy	.06	.05	.02
552	R.J. Reynolds	.10	.08	.04
553	Chris Brown	.90	.70	.35
554	Bruce Benedict	.06	.05	.02
555	Warren Brusstar	.06	.05	.02
556	Danny Heep	.06	.05	.02
557	Darnell Coles	.08	.06	.03
558	Greg Gagne	.12	.09	.05
559	Ernie Whitt	.08	.06	.03
560	Ron Washington	.06	.05	.02
561	Jimmy Key	.15	.11	.06
562	Billy Swift	.08	.06	.03
563	Ron Darling	.15	.11	.06
564	Dick Ruthven	.06	.05	.02
565	Zane Smith	.25	.20	.10
566	Sid Bream	.10	.08	.04
567a	Joel Youngblood (P on front)	.08	.06	.03
567b	Joel Youngblood (IF on front)	1.00	.70	.40
568	Mario Ramirez	.06	.05	.02
569	Tom Runnells	.06	.05	.02
570	Rick Schu	.06	.05	.02
571	Bill Campbell	.06	.05	.02
572	Dickie Thon	.08	.06	.03
573	Al Holland	.06	.05	.02
574	Reid Nichols	.06	.05	.02
575	Bert Roberge	.06	.05	.02
576	Mike Flanagan	.10	.08	.04
577	Tim Leary	.08	.06	.03
578	Mike Laga	.06	.05	.02
579	Steve Lyons	.06	.05	.02
580	Phil Niekro	.30	.25	.12
581	Gilberto Reyes	.08	.06	.03
582	Jamie Easterly	.06	.05	.02
583	Mark Gubicza	.08	.06	.03
584	Stan Javier	.10	.08	.04
585	Bill Laskey	.06	.05	.02
586	Jeff Russell	.06	.05	.02
587	Dickie Noles	.06	.05	.02
588	Steve Farr	.08	.06	.03
589	Steve Ontiveros	.20	.15	.08
590	Mike Hargrove	.08	.06	.03
591	Marty Bystrom	.06	.05	.02
592	Franklin Stubbs	.15	.11	.06
593	Larry Herndon	.08	.06	.03
594	Bill Swaggerty	.06	.05	.02
595	Carlos Ponce	.06	.05	.02
596	Pat Perry	.15	.11	.06
597	Ray Knight	.10	.08	.04
598	Steve Lombardozzi	.35	.25	.14
599	Brad Havens	.06	.05	.02
600	Pat Clements	.15	.11	.06
601	Joe Niekro	.10	.08	.04
602	Hank Aaron Puzzle Card	.06	.05	.02
603	Dwayne Henry	.10	.08	.04
604	Mookie Wilson	.10	.08	.04
605	Buddy Biancalana	.06	.05	.02
606	Rance Mulliniks	.06	.05	.02
607	Alan Wiggins	.06	.05	.02
608	Joe Cowley	.06	.05	.02
609a	Tom Seaver (green stripes around name)			
		.40	.30	.15
609b	Tom Seaver (yellow stripes around name)			
		1.25	.90	.50
610	Neil Allen	.06	.05	.02
611	Don Sutton	.30	.25	.12

		MT	NR MT	EX
612	Fred Toliver	.10	.08	.04
613	Jay Baller	.10	.08	.04
614	Marc Sullivan	.10	.08	.04
615	John Grubb	.06	.05	.02
616	Bruce Kison	.06	.05	.02
617	Bill Madlock	.12	.09	.05
618	Chris Chambliss	.08	.06	.03
619	Dave Stewart	.10	.08	.04
620	Tim Lollar	.06	.05	.02
621	Gary Lavelle	.06	.05	.02
622	Charles Hudson	.06	.05	.02
623	Joel Davis	.12	.09	.05
624	Joe Johnson	.12	.09	.05
625	Sid Fernandez	.12	.09	.05
626	Dennis Lamp	.06	.05	.02
627	Terry Harper	.06	.05	.02
628	Jack Lazorko	.06	.05	.02
629	Roger McDowell	.50	.40	.20
630	Mark Funderburk	.06	.05	.02
631	Ed Lynch	.06	.05	.02
632	Rudy Law	.06	.05	.02
633	Roger Mason	.10	.08	.04
634	Mike Felder	.15	.11	.06
635	Ken Schrom	.06	.05	.02
636	Bob Ojeda	.10	.08	.04
637	Ed Vande Berg	.06	.05	.02
638	Bobby Meacham	.06	.05	.02
639	Cliff Johnson	.06	.05	.02
640	Garth Iorg	.06	.05	.02
641	Dan Driessen	.08	.06	.03
642	Mike Brown	.06	.05	.02
643	John Shelby	.08	.06	.03
644	Ty-Breaking Hit (Pete Rose)	.50	.40	.20
645	Knuckle Brothers (Joe Niekro, Phil Niekro)	.15	.11	.06
646	Jesse Orosco	.08	.06	.03
647	Billy Beane	.10	.08	.04
648	Cesar Cedeno	.10	.08	.04
649	Bert Blyleven	.15	.11	.06
650	Max Venable	.06	.05	.02
651	Fleet Feet (Vince Coleman, Willie McGee)	.35	.25	.14
652	Calvin Schiraldi	.12	.09	.05
653	King of Kings (Pete Rose)	.70	.50	.30
---	Checklist 1-26 DK	.06	.05	.02
---a	Checklist 27-130 (45 is Beane)	.08	.06	.03
---b	Checklist 27-130 (45 is Habyan)	.60	.45	.25
---	Checklist 131-234	.06	.05	.02
---	Checklist 235-338	.06	.05	.02
---	Checklist 339-442	.06	.05	.02
---	Checklist 443-546	.06	.05	.02
---	Checklist 547-653	.06	.05	.02

		MT	NR MT	EX
1	Tony Gwynn	.30	.25	.12
2	Tommy Herr	.12	.09	.05
3	Steve Garvey	.30	.25	.12
4	Dale Murphy	.40	.30	.15
5	Darryl Strawberry	.35	.25	.14
6	Graig Nettles	.12	.09	.05
7	Terry Kennedy	.09	.07	.04
8	Ozzie Smith	.15	.11	.06
9	LaMarr Hoyt	.09	.07	.04
10	Rickey Henderson	.30	.25	.12
11	Lou Whitaker	.15	.11	.06
12	George Brett	.40	.30	.15
13	Eddie Murray	.30	.25	.12
14	Cal Ripken, Jr.	.35	.25	.14
15	Dave Winfield	.25	.20	.10
16	Jim Rice	.25	.20	.10
17	Carlton Fisk	.15	.11	.06
18	Jack Morris	.15	.11	.06
19	Jose Cruz	.09	.07	.04
20	Tim Raines	.25	.20	.10
21	Nolan Ryan	.25	.20	.10
22	Tony Pena	.12	.09	.05
23	Jack Clark	.15	.11	.06
24	Dave Parker	.20	.15	.08
25	Tim Wallach	.12	.09	.05
26	Ozzie Virgil	.09	.07	.04
27	Fernando Valenzuela	.25	.20	.10
28	Dwight Gooden	.75	.60	.30
29	Glenn Wilson	.09	.07	.04
30	Garry Templeton	.12	.09	.05
31	Goose Gossage	.12	.09	.05
32	Ryne Sandberg	.25	.20	.10
33	Jeff Reardon	.12	.09	.05
34	Pete Rose	.50	.40	.20
35	Scott Garrelts	.09	.07	.04
36	Willie McGee	.12	.09	.05
37	Ron Darling	.12	.09	.05
38	Dick Williams	.09	.07	.04
39	Paul Molitor	.15	.11	.06
40	Damaso Garcia	.09	.07	.04
41	Phil Bradley	.20	.15	.08
42	Dan Petry	.09	.07	.04
43	Willie Hernandez	.09	.07	.04
44	Tom Brunansky	.12	.09	.05
45	Alan Trammell	.20	.15	.08
46	Donnie Moore	.09	.07	.04
47	Wade Boggs	.75	.60	.30
48	Ernie Whitt	.09	.07	.04
49	Harold Baines	.15	.11	.06
50	Don Mattingly	1.75	1.25	.70
51	Gary Ward	.09	.07	.04
52	Bert Blyleven	.12	.09	.05
53	Jimmy Key	.12	.09	.05
54	Cecil Cooper	.12	.09	.05
55	Dave Stieb	.12	.09	.05
56	Rich Gedman	.09	.07	.04
57	Jay Howell	.09	.07	.04
58	Sparky Anderson	.09	.07	.04
59	Minneapolis Metrodome	.09	.07	.04
---	Checklist	.12	.09	.05

1986 Donruss All-Stars

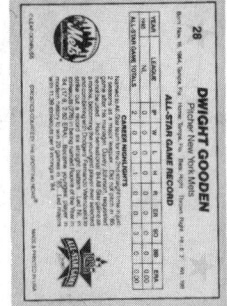

Issued in conjunction with the 1986 Donruss Pop-Up set, the Donruss All-Star consists of 60 cards that measure 3½'' by 5''. Fifty-nine players involved in the 1985 All-Star game plus an unnumbered checklist comprise the set. The card fronts have the same blue border found on the regular 1986 Donruss issue. Retail packs included one Pop-Up card, three All-Star cards and one Hank Aaron puzzle card.

	MT	NR MT	EX
Complete Set:	6.00	4.50	2.50
Common Player:	.09	.07	.04

1986 Donruss Box Panels

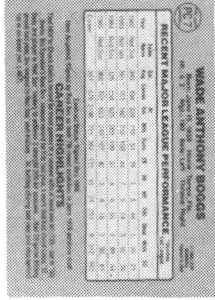

For the second year in a row, Donruss placed baseball cards on the bottom of their wax and cello pack boxes. The cards, which come four to a panel, are the standard 2½'' by 3½'' in size. With numbering that begins where Donruss left off in 1985, cards PC 4

through PC 6 were found on boxes of regular Donruss issue wax packs. Cards PC 7 through PC 9 were found on boxes of the 1986 All-Star/Pop-Up packs. An unnumbered Hank Aaron puzzle card was included on each box.

		MT	NR MT	EX
Complete Panel Set:		6.00	4.50	2.50
Complete Singles Set:		2.50	2.00	1.00
Common Single Player:		.15	.11	.06
Panel		1.75	1.25	.70
4	Kirk Gibson	.30	.25	.12
5	Willie Hernandez	.15	.11	.06
6	Doug DeCinces	.15	.11	.06
---	Aaron Puzzle Card	.04	.03	.02
Panel		2.75	2.00	1.00
7	Wade Boggs	.75	.60	.30
8	Lee Smith	.15	.11	.06
9	Cecil Cooper	.20	.15	.08
---	Aaron Puzzle Card	.04	.03	.02

1986 Donruss Diamond Kings Supers

Donruss produced a set of giant size Diamond Kings in 1986 for the second year in a row. The cards, which measure 4 11/16'' by 6 3/4'', are enlarged versions of the 26 Diamond Kings cards found in the regular 1986 Donruss set. Featuring the artwork of Dick Perez, the set consists of 28 cards - 26 DK's, an unnumbered checklist and an unnumbered Pete Rose ''King of Kings'' card.

		MT	NR MT	EX
Complete Set:		10.00	7.50	4.00
Common Player:		.20	.15	.08
1	Kirk Gibson	.50	.40	.20
2	Goose Gossage	.30	.25	.12
3	Willie McGee	.30	.25	.12
4	George Bell	.50	.40	.20
5	Tony Armas	.20	.15	.08
6	Chili Davis	.25	.20	.10
7	Cecil Cooper	.25	.20	.10
8	Mike Boddicker	.25	.20	.10
9	Davey Lopes	.20	.15	.08
10	Bill Doran	.25	.20	.10
11	Bret Saberhagen	.40	.30	.15
12	Brett Butler	.20	.15	.08
13	Harold Baines	.30	.25	.12
14	Mike Davis	.20	.15	.08
15	Tony Perez	.25	.20	.10
16	Willie Randolph	.25	.20	.10
18	Orel Hershiser	.35	.25	.14
19	Johnny Ray	.25	.20	.10
20	Gary Ward	.20	.15	.08
21	Rick Mahler	.20	.15	.08
22	Phil Bradley	.35	.25	.14
23	Jerry Koosman	.25	.20	.10
24	Tom Brunansky	.25	.20	.10
25	Andre Dawson	.35	.25	.14
26	Dwight Gooden	1.00	.70	.40
---	Checklist	.15	.11	.06
---	King of Kings (Pete Rose)	1.50	1.25	.60

1986 Donruss Highlights

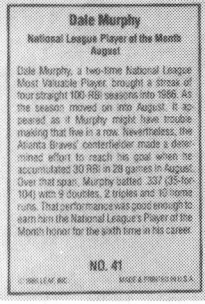

Donruss, for the second year in a row, issued a 56-card highlights set which featured cards of the A.L. and N.L. pitchers and players of each month plus significant events that took place during the 1986 season. The cards, which measure 2½'' by 3½'' in size, are similar in design to the regular 1986 Donruss set but have a gold border instead of blue. A ''Highlights'' logo appears in the lower left corner of each card front. The card backs are designed on a vertical format and feature black print on a yellow background. As in 1985, the set includes Donruss' picks for the Rookies of the Year awards. A new feature was three cards honoring the 1986 Hall of Fame inductees. The set, available only through hobby dealers, was issued in a specially designed box.

		MT	NR MT	EX
Complete Set:		9.00	6.75	3.50
Common Player:		.10	.08	.04
1	Homers In First At-Bat (Will Clark)	.70	.50	.30
2	Oakland Milestone For Strikeouts (Jose Rijo)	.10	.08	.04
3	Royals' All-Time Hit Man (George Brett)	.40	.30	.15
4	Phillies RBI Leader (Mike Schmidt)	.30	.25	.12
5	KKKKKKKKKKKKKKKKKKKK (Roger Clemens)	.80	.60	.30
6	A.L. Pitcher of the Month-April (Roger Clemens)	.80	.60	.30
7	A.L. Player of the Month-April (Kirby Puckett)	.25	.20	.10
8	N.L. Pitcher of the Month-April (Dwight Gooden)	.50	.40	.20
9	N.L. Player of the Month-April (Johnny Ray)	.10	.08	.04
10	Eclipses Mantle HR Record (Reggie Jackson)	.25	.20	.10
11	First Five Hit Game of Career (Wade Boggs)	.60	.45	.25
12	A.L. Pitcher of the Month-May (Don Aase)	.10	.08	.04
13	A.L. Player of the Month-May (Wade Boggs)	.60	.45	.25
14	N.L. Pitcher of the Month-May (Jeff Reardon)	.15	.11	.06
15	N.L. Player of the Month-May (Hubie Brooks)	.15	.11	.06
16	Notches 300th Career Win (Don Sutton)	.20	.15	.08
17	Starts Season 14-0 (Roger Clemens)	.80	.60	.30
18	A.L. Pitcher of the Month-June (Roger Clemens)	.80	.60	.30
19	A.L. Player of the Month-June (Kent Hrbek)	.20	.15	.08
20	N.L. Pitcher of the Month-June (Rick Rhoden)	.10	.08	.04
21	N.L. Player of the Month-June (Kevin Bass)	.10	.08	.04
22	Blasts 4 HRS in 1 Game (Bob Horner)	.15	.11	.06
23	Starting All Star Rookie (Wally Joyner)	1.50	1.25	.60
24	Starts 3rd Straight All Star Game (Darryl Strawberry)	.30	.25	.12

		MT	NR MT	EX
25	Ties All Star Game Record (Fernando Valenzuela)	.20	.15	.08
26	All Star Game MVP (Roger Clemens)	.80	.60	.30
27	A.L. Pitcher of the Month-July (Jack Morris)	.20	.15	.08
28	A.L. Player of the Month-July (Scott Fletcher)	.10	.08	.04
29	N.L. Pitcher of the Month-July (Todd Worrell)	.40	.30	.15
30	N.L. PLayer of the Month-July (Eric Davis)	.70	.50	.30
31	Records 3000th Strikeout (Bert Blyleven)	.15	.11	.06
32	1986 Hall of Fame Inductee (Bobby Doerr)	.15	.11	.06
33	1986 Hall of Fame Inductee (Ernie Lombardi)	.15	.11	.06
34	1986 Hall of Fame Inductee (Willie McCovey)	.20	.15	.08
35	Notches 4000th K (Steve Carlton)	.25	.20	.10
36	Surpasses DiMaggio Record (Mike Schmidt)	.30	.25	.12
37	Records 3rd "Quadruple Double" (Juan Samuel)	.15	.11	.06
38	A.L. Pitcher of the Month-August (Mike Witt)	.15	.11	.06
39	A.L. Player of the Month-August (Doug DeCinces)	.10	.08	.04
40	N.L. Pitcher of the Month-August (Bill Gullickson)	.10	.08	.04
41	N.L. Player of the Month-August (Dale Murphy)	.40	.30	.15
42	Sets Tribe Offensive Record (Joe Carter)	.15	.11	.06
43	Longest HR In Royals Stadium (Bo Jackson)	1.00	.70	.40
44	Majors 1st No-Hitter In 2 Years (Joe Cowley)	.10	.08	.04
45	Sets M.L. Strikeout Record (Jim Deshaies)	.15	.11	.06
46	No Hitter Clinches Division (Mike Scott)	.15	.11	.06
47	A.L. Pitcher of the Month-September (Bruce Hurst)	.10	.08	.04
48	A.L. Player of the Month-September (Don Mattingly)	1.00	.70	.40
49	N.L. Pitcher of the Month-September (Mike Krukow)	.10	.08	.04
50	N.L. Player of the Month-September (Steve Sax)	.20	.15	.08
51	A.L. Record For Steals By A Rookie (John Cangelosi)	.15	.11	.06
52	Shatters M.L. Save Mark (Dave Righetti)	.15	.11	.06
53	Yankee Record For Hits & Doubles (Don Mattingly)	1.00	.70	.40
54	Donruss N.L. Rookie of the Year (Todd Worrell)	.40	.30	.15
55	Donruss A.L. Rookie of the Year (Jose Canseco)	1.50	1.25	.60
56	Highlight Checklist	.10	.08	.04

1986 Donruss Pop-Ups

Issued in conjunction with the 1986 Donruss All-Star set, the Donruss Pop-Ups (18 unnumbered cards) feature the 1985 All-Star Game starting line-ups. The cards, which measure 2½'' by 5'', are die-cut and fold out to form a three-dimensional stand-up card. The background for the cards is the Minneapolis Metrodome, site of the '85 All-Star Game. Retail packs included one Pop-Up card, three All-Star cards and one Hank Aaron puzzle card.

		MT	NR MT	EX
	Complete Set:	6.00	4.50	2.50
	Common Player:	.20	.15	.08
(1)	George Brett	.60	.45	.25
(2)	Carlton Fisk	.30	.25	.12
(3)	Steve Garvey	.50	.40	.20
(4)	Tony Gwynn	.50	.40	.20
(5)	Rickey Henderson	.50	.40	.20
(6)	Tommy Herr	.20	.15	.08
(7)	LaMarr Hoyt	.20	.15	.08
(8)	Terry Kennedy	.20	.15	.08
(9)	Jack Morris	.30	.25	.12
(10)	Dale Murphy	.60	.45	.25
(11)	Eddie Murray	.50	.40	.20
(12)	Graig Nettles	.30	.25	.12
(13)	Jim Rice	.50	.40	.20
(14)	Cal Ripken Jr.	.50	.40	.20
(15)	Ozzie Smith	.30	.25	.12
(16)	Darryl Strawberry	.60	.45	.25
(17)	Lou Whitaker	.30	.25	.12
(18)	Dave Winfield	.50	.40	.20

1986 Donruss Rookies

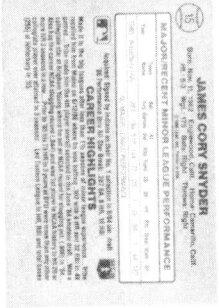

Entitled "The Rookies", this 56-card set includes the top 55 rookies of 1986 plus an unnumbered checklist. The cards, which measure 2½'' by 3½'', are similar to the format used for the 1986 Donruss regular issue, except that the borders are green, rather than blue. Several of the rookies who had cards in the regular '86 Donruss set appear again in "The Rookies" set. The sets, which were only available through hobby dealers, came in a specially designed box.

		MT	NR MT	EX
	Complete Set:	17.00	12.50	6.75
	Common Player:	.15	.11	.06
1	Wally Joyner	4.75	3.50	2.00
2	Tracy Jones	.75	.60	.30
3	Allan Anderson	.15	.11	.06
4	Ed Correa	.45	.35	.20
5	Reggie Williams	.20	.15	.08
6	Charlie Kerfeld	.35	.25	.14
7	Andres Galarraga	.60	.45	.25
8	Bob Tewksbury	.30	.25	.12
9	Al Newman	.15	.11	.06
10	Andres Thomas	.40	.30	.15
11	Barry Bonds	1.25	.90	.50
12	Juan Nieves	.40	.30	.15
13	Mark Eichhorn	.60	.45	.25
14	Dan Plesac	.60	.45	.25
15	Cory Snyder	3.00	2.25	1.25
16	Kelly Gruber	.15	.11	.06

		MT	NR MT	EX
17	Kevin Mitchell	1.00	.70	.40
18	Steve Lombardozzi	.20	.15	.08
19	Mitch Williams	.40	.30	.15
20	John Cerutti	.40	.30	.15
21	Todd Worrell	.60	.45	.25
22	Jose Canseco	4.75	3.50	2.00
23	Pete Incaviglia	2.50	2.00	1.00
24	Jose Guzman	.20	.15	.08
25	Scott Bailes	.40	.30	.15
26	Greg Mathews	.60	.45	.25
27	Eric King	.30	.25	.12
28	Paul Assenmacher	.20	.15	.08
29	Jeff Sellers	.20	.15	.08
30	Bobby Bonilla	.40	.30	.15
31	Doug Drabek	.40	.30	.15
32	Will Clark	3.25	2.50	1.25
33	Bip Roberts	.15	.11	.06
34	Jim Deshaies	.50	.40	.20
35	Mike Lavalliere (LaValliere)	.30	.25	.12
36	Scott Bankhead	.30	.25	.12
37	Dale Sveum	.50	.40	.20
38	Bo Jackson	3.50	2.75	1.50
39	Rob Thompson	.60	.45	.25
40	Eric Plunk	.15	.11	.06
41	Bill Bathe	.15	.11	.06
42	John Kruk	1.50	1.25	.60
43	Andy Allanson	.30	.25	.12
44	Mark Portugal	.15	.11	.06
45	Danny Tartabull	1.25	.90	.50
46	Bob Kipper	.20	.15	.08
47	Gene Walter	.15	.11	.06
48	Rey Quinonez	.15	.11	.06
49	Bobby Witt	.60	.45	.25
50	Bill Mooneyham	.15	.11	.06
51	John Cangelosi	.40	.30	.15
52	Ruben Sierra	1.50	1.25	.60
53	Rob Woodward	.15	.11	.06
54	Ed Hearn	.15	.11	.06
55	Joel McKeon	.15	.11	.06
56	Checklist 1-56	.05	.04	.02

1987 Donruss

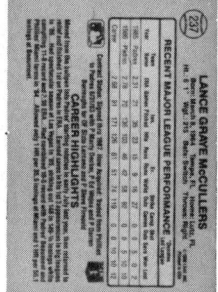

The 1987 Donruss set consists of 660 numbered cards, each measuring 2½'' by 3½'' in size. Full-color photos are surrounded by a bold black border separated by two narrow bands of yellow which enclose a brown area filled with baseballs. The player's name, team and team logo appear on the card fronts along with the words ''Donruss '87.'' The card backs are designed on a horizontal format and contain black print on a yellow and white background. The backs are very similar to those in previous years' sets. Backs on cards issued in wax and rack packs face to the left when turned over, while those issued in vending sets face to the right.

		MT	NR MT	EX
Complete Set:		32.00	24.00	13.00
Common Player:		.05	.04	.02
1	Wally Joyner (DK)	1.25	.90	.50
2	Roger Clemens (DK)	.70	.50	.30
3	Dale Murphy (DK)	.40	.30	.15
4	Darryl Strawberry (DK)	.35	.25	.14
5	Ozzie Smith (DK)	.12	.09	.05
6	Jose Canseco (DK)	1.00	.70	.40

		MT	NR MT	EX
7	Charlie Hough (DK)	.07	.05	.03
8	Brook Jacoby (DK)	.10	.08	.04
9	Fred Lynn (DK)	.15	.11	.06
10	Rick Rhoden (DK)	.10	.08	.04
11	Chris Brown (DK)	.15	.11	.06
12	Von Hayes (DK)	.10	.08	.04
13	Jack Morris (DK)	.20	.15	.08
14a	Kevin McReynolds (DK) ("Donruss Diamond Kings" in white band on back)			
		1.25	.90	.50
14b	Kevin McReynolds (DK) ("Donruss Diamond Kings" in yellow band on back)			
		.15	.11	.06
15	George Brett (DK)	.40	.30	.15
16	Ted Higuera (DK)	.20	.15	.08
17	Hubie Brooks (DK)	.10	.08	.04
18	Mike Scott (DK)	.12	.09	.05
19	Kirby Puckett (DK)	.25	.20	.10
20	Dave Winfield (DK)	.25	.20	.10
21	Lloyd Moseby (DK)	.10	.08	.04
22a	Eric Davis (DK) ("Donruss Diamond Kings" in white band on back)	3.00	2.25	1.25
22b	Eric Davis (DK) ("Donruss Diamond Kings" in yellow band on back)	1.00	.70	.40
23	Jim Presley (DK)	.12	.09	.05
24	Keith Moreland (DK)	.07	.05	.03
25a	Greg Walker (DK) ("Donruss Diamond Kings" in white band on back)	1.25	.90	.50
25b	Greg Walker (DK) ("Donruss Diamond Kings" in yellow band on back)	.10	.08	.04
26	Steve Sax (DK)	.12	.09	.05
27	Checklist 1-27	.05	.04	.02
28	B.J. Surhoff (RR)	1.25	.90	.50
29	Randy Myers (RR)	.25	.20	.10
30	Ken Gerhart (RR)	.40	.30	.15
31	Benito Santiago (RR)	2.00	1.50	.80
32	Greg Swindell (RR)	.50	.40	.20
33	Mike Birkbeck (RR)	.12	.09	.05
34	Terry Steinbach (RR)	.50	.40	.20
35	Bo Jackson (RR)	1.75	1.25	.70
36	Greg Maddux (RR)	.20	.15	.08
37	Jim Lindeman (RR)	.35	.25	.14
38	Devon White (RR)	1.25	.90	.50
39	Eric Bell (RR)	.25	.20	.10
40	Will Fraser (RR)	.25	.20	.10
41	Jerry Browne (RR)	.20	.15	.08
42	Chris James (RR)	.80	.60	.30
43	Rafael Palmeiro (RR)	.50	.40	.20
44	Pat Dodson (RR)	.15	.11	.06
45	Duane Ward (RR)	.12	.09	.05
46	Mark McGwire (RR)	7.00	5.25	2.75
47	Bruce Fields (RR) (photo actually Darnell Coles)	.12	.09	.05
48	Eddie Murray	.35	.25	.14
49	Ted Higuera	.20	.15	.08
50	Kirk Gibson	.25	.20	.10
51	Oil Can Boyd	.07	.05	.03
52	Don Mattingly	2.50	2.00	1.00
53	Pedro Guerrero	.15	.11	.06
54	George Brett	.40	.30	.15
55	Jose Rijo	.05	.04	.02
56	Tim Raines	.30	.25	.12
57	Ed Correa	.25	.20	.10
58	Mike Witt	.12	.09	.05
59	Greg Walker	.10	.08	.04
60	Ozzie Smith	.15	.11	.06
61	Glenn Davis	.30	.25	.12
62	Glenn Wilson	.10	.08	.04
63	Tom Browning	.07	.05	.03
64	Tony Gwynn	.35	.25	.14
65	R.J. Reynolds	.07	.05	.03
66	Will Clark	1.75	1.25	.70
67	Ozzie Virgil	.07	.05	.03
68	Rick Sutcliffe	.12	.09	.05
69	Gary Carter	.30	.25	.12
70	Mike Moore	.05	.04	.02
71	Bert Blyleven	.15	.11	.06
72	Tony Fernandez	.12	.09	.05
73	Kent Hrbek	.15	.11	.06
74	Lloyd Moseby	.10	.08	.04
75	Alvin Davis	.12	.09	.05
76	Keith Hernandez	.25	.20	.10
77	Ryne Sandberg	.25	.20	.10
78	Dale Murphy	.40	.30	.15
79	Sid Bream	.07	.05	.03
80	Chris Brown	.15	.11	.06
81	Steve Garvey	.25	.20	.10
82	Mario Soto	.07	.05	.03
83	Shane Rawley	.07	.05	.03
84	Willie McGee	.12	.09	.05
85	Jose Cruz	.10	.08	.04

		MT	NR MT	EX			MT	NR MT	EX
86	Brian Downing	.07	.05	.03	177	Dan Quisenberry	.12	.09	.05
87	Ozzie Guillen	.12	.09	.05	178	Eric Plunk	.07	.05	.03
88	Hubie Brooks	.10	.08	.04	179	Tim Wallach	.12	.09	.05
89	Cal Ripken	.35	.25	.14	180	Steve Buechele	.07	.05	.03
90	Juan Nieves	.12	.09	.05	181	Don Sutton	.20	.15	.08
91	Lance Parrish	.20	.15	.08	182	Dave Schmidt	.07	.05	.03
92	Jim Rice	.30	.25	.12	183	Terry Pendleton	.10	.08	.04
93	Ron Giudry	.20	.15	.08	184	Jim Deshaies	.30	.25	.12
94	Fernando Valenzuela	.25	.20	.10	185	Steve Bedrosian	.12	.09	.05
95	Andy Allanson	.15	.11	.06	186	Pete Rose	.60	.45	.25
96	Willie Wilson	.12	.09	.05	187	Dave Dravecky	.07	.05	.03
97	Jose Canseco	2.00	1.50	.80	188	Rick Reuschel	.10	.08	.04
98	Jeff Reardon	.12	.09	.05	189	Dan Gladden	.07	.05	.03
99	Bobby Witt	.35	.25	.14	190	Rick Mahler	.05	.04	.02
100	Checklist 28-133	.05	.04	.02	191	Thad Bosley	.05	.04	.02
101	Jose Guzman	.10	.08	.04	192	Ron Darling	.15	.11	.06
102	Steve Balboni	.07	.05	.03	193	Matt Young	.05	.04	.02
103	Tony Phillips	.05	.04	.02	194	Tom Brunansky	.10	.08	.04
104	Brook Jacoby	.10	.08	.04	195	Dave Stieb	.12	.09	.05
105	Dave Winfield	.30	.25	.12	196	Frank Viola	.12	.09	.05
106	Orel Hershiser	.12	.09	.05	197	Tom Henke	.07	.05	.03
107	Lou Whitaker	.20	.15	.08	198	Karl Best	.05	.04	.02
108	Fred Lynn	.15	.11	.06	199	Dwight Gooden	.90	.70	.35
109	Bill Wegman	.07	.05	.03	200	Checklist 134-239	.05	.04	.02
110	Donnie Moore	.05	.04	.02	201	Steve Trout	.07	.05	.03
111	Jack Clark	.15	.11	.06	202	Rafael Ramirez	.05	.04	.02
112	Bob Knepper	.07	.05	.03	203	Bob Walk	.05	.04	.02
113	Von Hayes	.10	.08	.04	204	Roger Mason	.05	.04	.02
114	Leon "Bip" Roberts	.10	.08	.04	205	Terry Kennedy	.07	.05	.03
115	Tony Pena	.10	.08	.04	206	Ron Oester	.05	.04	.02
116	Scott Garrelts	.05	.04	.02	207	John Russell	.05	.04	.02
117	Paul Molitor	.15	.11	.06	208	Greg Mathews	.30	.25	.12
118	Darryl Strawberry	.40	.30	.15	209	Charlie Kerfeld	.10	.08	.04
119	Shawon Dunston	.10	.08	.04	210	Reggie Jackson	.35	.25	.14
120	Jim Presley	.12	.09	.05	211	Floyd Bannister	.10	.08	.04
121	Jesse Barfield	.20	.15	.08	212	Vance Law	.07	.05	.03
122	Gary Gaetti	.12	.09	.05	213	Rich Bordi	.05	.04	.02
123	Kurt Stillwell	.40	.30	.15	214	Dan Plesac	.40	.30	.15
124	Joel Davis	.05	.04	.02	215	Dave Collins	.07	.05	.03
125	Mike Boddicker	.10	.08	.04	216	Bob Stanley	.07	.05	.03
126	Robin Yount	.25	.20	.10	217	Joe Niekro	.10	.08	.04
127	Alan Trammell	.25	.20	.10	218	Tom Niedenfuer	.07	.05	.03
128	Dave Righetti	.15	.11	.06	219	Brett Butler	.07	.05	.03
129	Dwight Evans	.12	.09	.05	220	Charlie Leibrandt	.07	.05	.03
130	Mike Scioscia	.05	.04	.02	221	Steve Ontiveros	.07	.05	.03
131	Julio Franco	.10	.08	.04	222	Tim Burke	.07	.05	.03
132	Bret Saberhagen	.20	.15	.08	223	Curtis Wilkerson	.05	.04	.02
133	Mike Davis	.07	.05	.03	224	Pete Incaviglia	1.25	.90	.50
134	Joe Hesketh	.05	.04	.02	225	Lonnie Smith	.07	.05	.03
135	Wally Joyner	2.50	2.00	1.00	226	Chris Codiroli	.05	.04	.02
136	Don Slaught	.05	.04	.02	227	Scott Bailes	.20	.15	.08
137	Daryl Boston	.05	.04	.02	228	Rickey Henderson	.35	.25	.14
138	Nolan Ryan	.30	.25	.12	229	Ken Howell	.05	.04	.02
139	Mike Schmidt	.40	.30	.15	230	Darnell Coles	.07	.05	.03
140	Tommy Herr	.10	.08	.04	231	Don Aase	.07	.05	.03
141	Garry Templeton	.10	.08	.04	232	Tim Leary	.05	.04	.02
142	Kal Daniels	.80	.60	.30	233	Bob Boone	.07	.05	.03
143	Billy Sample	.05	.04	.02	234	Ricky Horton	.07	.05	.03
144	Johnny Ray	.10	.08	.04	235	Mark Bailey	.05	.04	.02
145	Rob Thompson	.40	.30	.15	236	Kevin Gross	.07	.05	.03
146	Bob Dernier	.05	.04	.02	237	Lance McCullers	.07	.05	.03
147	Danny Tartabull	.25	.20	.10	238	Cecilio Guante	.05	.04	.02
148	Ernie Whitt	.07	.05	.03	239	Bob Melvin	.05	.04	.02
149	Kirby Puckett	.35	.25	.14	240	Billy Jo Robidoux	.05	.04	.02
150	Mike Young	.07	.05	.03	241	Roger McDowell	.12	.09	.05
151	Ernest Riles	.10	.08	.04	242	Leon Durham	.10	.08	.04
152	Frank Tanana	.07	.05	.03	243	Ed Nunez	.05	.04	.02
153	Rich Gedman	.10	.08	.04	244	Jimmy Key	.12	.09	.05
154	Willie Randolph	.10	.08	.04	245	Mike Smithson	.05	.04	.02
155	Bill Madlock	.12	.09	.05	246	Bo Diaz	.05	.04	.02
156	Joe Carter	.15	.11	.06	247	Carlton Fisk	.15	.11	.06
157	Danny Jackson	.07	.05	.03	248	Larry Sheets	.10	.08	.04
158	Carney Lansford	.07	.05	.03	249	Juan Castillo	.12	.09	.05
159	Bryn Smith	.07	.05	.03	250	Eric King	.25	.20	.10
160	Gary Pettis	.07	.05	.03	251	Doug Drabek	.30	.25	.12
161	Oddibe McDowell	.12	.09	.05	252	Wade Boggs	1.50	1.25	.60
162	John Cangelosi	.20	.15	.08	253	Mariano Duncan	.07	.05	.03
163	Mike Scott	.15	.11	.06	254	Pat Tabler	.07	.05	.03
164	Eric Show	.05	.04	.02	255	Frank White	.10	.08	.04
165	Juan Samuel	.12	.09	.05	256	Alfredo Griffin	.07	.05	.03
166	Nick Esasky	.05	.04	.02	257	Floyd Youmans	.12	.09	.05
167	Zane Smith	.10	.08	.04	258	Rob Wilfong	.05	.04	.02
168	Mike Brown	.05	.04	.02	259	Pete O'Brien	.10	.08	.04
169	Keith Moreland	.07	.05	.03	260	Tim Hulett	.05	.04	.02
170	John Tudor	.10	.08	.04	261	Dickie Thon	.07	.05	.03
171	Ken Dixon	.05	.04	.02	262	Darren Daulton	.05	.04	.02
172	Jim Gantner	.07	.05	.03	263	Vince Coleman	.25	.20	.10
173	Jack Morris	.20	.15	.08	264	Andy Hawkins	.05	.04	.02
174	Bruce Hurst	.10	.08	.04	265	Eric Davis	2.25	1.75	.90
175	Dennis Rasmussen	.07	.05	.03	266	Andres Thomas	.20	.15	.08
176	Mike Marshall	.10	.08	.04	267	Mike Diaz	.30	.25	.12

#	Player	MT	NR MT	EX
268	Chili Davis	.10	.08	.04
269	Jody Davis	.10	.08	.04
270	Phil Bradley	.12	.09	.05
271	George Bell	.30	.25	.12
272	Keith Atherton	.05	.04	.02
273	Storm Davis	.05	.04	.02
274	Rob Deer	.25	.20	.10
275	Walt Terrell	.07	.05	.03
276	Roger Clemens	1.00	.70	.40
277	Mike Easler	.07	.05	.03
278	Steve Sax	.15	.11	.06
279	Andre Thornton	.07	.05	.03
280	Jim Sundberg	.07	.05	.03
281	Bill Bathe	.10	.08	.04
282	Jay Tibbs	.05	.04	.02
283	Dick Schofield	.05	.04	.02
284	Mike Mason	.05	.04	.02
285	Jerry Hairston	.05	.04	.02
286	Bill Doran	.10	.08	.04
287	Tim Flannery	.05	.04	.02
288	Gary Redus	.07	.05	.03
289	John Franco	.07	.05	.03
290	Paul Assenmacher	.15	.11	.06
291	Joe Orsulak	.07	.05	.03
292	Lee Smith	.10	.08	.04
293	Mike Laga	.05	.04	.02
294	Rick Dempsey	.07	.05	.03
295	Mike Felder	.07	.05	.03
296	Tom Brookens	.05	.04	.02
297	Al Nipper	.05	.04	.02
298	Mike Pagliarulo	.12	.09	.05
299	Franklin Stubbs	.10	.08	.04
300	Checklist 240-345	.05	.04	.02
301	Steve Farr	.05	.04	.02
302	Bill Mooneyham	.10	.08	.04
303	Andres Galarraga	.15	.11	.06
304	Scott Fletcher	.07	.05	.03
305	Jack Howell	.10	.08	.04
306	Russ Morman	.12	.09	.05
307	Todd Worrell	.20	.15	.08
308	Dave Smith	.07	.05	.03
309	Jeff Stone	.05	.04	.02
310	Ron Robinson	.05	.04	.02
311	Bruce Bochy	.05	.04	.02
312	Jim Winn	.05	.04	.02
313	Mark Davis	.05	.04	.02
314	Jeff Dedmon	.05	.04	.02
315	Jamie Moyer	.20	.15	.08
316	Wally Backman	.07	.05	.03
317	Ken Phelps	.07	.05	.03
318	Steve Lombardozzi	.10	.08	.04
319	Rance Mulliniks	.05	.04	.02
320	Tim Laudner	.05	.04	.02
321	Mark Eichhorn	.30	.25	.12
322	Lee Guetterman	.25	.20	.10
323	Sid Fernandez	.12	.09	.05
324	Jerry Mumphrey	.07	.05	.03
325	David Palmer	.07	.05	.03
326	Bill Almon	.05	.04	.02
327	Candy Maldonado	.10	.08	.04
328	John Kruk	1.00	.70	.40
329	John Denny	.05	.04	.02
330	Milt Thompson	.10	.08	.04
331	Mike LaValliere	.25	.20	.10
332	Alan Ashby	.05	.04	.02
333	Doug Corbett	.05	.04	.02
334	Ron Karkovice	.15	.11	.06
335	Mitch Webster	.10	.08	.04
336	Lee Lacy	.07	.05	.03
337	Glenn Braggs	.50	.40	.20
338	Dwight Lowry	.12	.09	.05
339	Don Baylor	.12	.09	.05
340	Brian Fisher	.10	.08	.04
341	Reggie Williams	.15	.11	.06
342	Tom Candiotti	.05	.04	.02
343	Rudy Law	.05	.04	.02
344	Curt Young	.10	.08	.04
345	Mike Fitzgerald	.05	.04	.02
346	Ruben Sierra	1.50	1.25	.60
347	Mitch Williams	.25	.20	.10
348	Jorge Orta	.05	.04	.02
349	Mickey Tettleton	.05	.04	.02
350	Ernie Camacho	.05	.04	.02
351	Ron Kittle	.10	.08	.04
352	Ken Landreaux	.07	.05	.03
353	Chet Lemon	.07	.05	.03
354	John Shelby	.07	.05	.03
355	Mark Clear	.07	.05	.03
356	Doug DeCinces	.10	.08	.04
357	Ken Dayley	.05	.04	.02
358	Phil Garner	.07	.05	.03
359	Steve Jeltz	.05	.04	.02
360	Ed Whitson	.05	.04	.02
361	Barry Bonds	.60	.45	.25
362	Vida Blue	.10	.08	.04
363	Cecil Cooper	.12	.09	.05
364	Bob Ojeda	.10	.08	.04
365	Dennis Eckersley	.07	.05	.03
366	Mike Morgan	.05	.04	.02
367	Willie Upshaw	.07	.05	.03
368	Allan Anderson	.10	.08	.04
369	Bill Gullickson	.07	.05	.03
370	Bobby Thigpen	.25	.20	.10
371	Juan Beniquez	.05	.04	.02
372	Charlie Moore	.05	.04	.02
373	Dan Petry	.07	.05	.03
374	Rod Scurry	.05	.04	.02
375	Tom Seaver	.30	.25	.12
376	Ed Vande Berg	.05	.04	.02
377	Tony Bernazard	.07	.05	.03
378	Greg Pryor	.05	.04	.02
379	Dwayne Murphy	.07	.05	.03
380	Andy McGaffigan	.05	.04	.02
381	Kirk McCaskill	.10	.08	.04
382	Greg Harris	.05	.04	.02
383	Rich Dotson	.10	.08	.04
384	Craig Reynolds	.05	.04	.02
385	Greg Gross	.05	.04	.02
386	Tito Landrum	.05	.04	.02
387	Craig Lefferts	.05	.04	.02
388	Dave Parker	.20	.15	.08
389	Bob Horner	.15	.11	.06
390	Pat Clements	.07	.05	.03
391	Jeff Leonard	.10	.08	.04
392	Chris Speier	.05	.04	.02
393	John Moses	.05	.04	.02
394	Garth Iorg	.05	.04	.02
395	Greg Gagne	.10	.08	.04
396	Nate Snell	.05	.04	.02
397	Bryan Clutterbuck	.10	.08	.04
398	Darrell Evans	.12	.09	.05
399	Steve Crawford	.05	.04	.02
400	Checklist 346-451	.05	.04	.02
401	Phil Lombardi	.12	.09	.05
402	Rick Honeycutt	.07	.05	.03
403	Ken Schrom	.05	.04	.02
404	Bud Black	.05	.04	.02
405	Donnie Hill	.05	.04	.02
406	Wayne Krenchicki	.05	.04	.02
407	Chuck Finley	.12	.09	.05
408	Toby Harrah	.07	.05	.03
409	Steve Lyons	.05	.04	.02
410	Kevin Bass	.10	.08	.04
411	Marvell Wynne	.05	.04	.02
412	Ron Roenicke	.05	.04	.02
413	Tracy Jones	.50	.40	.20
414	Gene Garber	.05	.04	.02
415	Mike Bielecki	.05	.04	.02
416	Frank DiPino	.05	.04	.02
417	Andy Van Slyke	.10	.08	.04
418	Jim Dwyer	.05	.04	.02
419	Ben Oglivie	.07	.05	.03
420	Dave Bergman	.05	.04	.02
421	Joe Sambito	.05	.04	.02
422	Bob Tewksbury	.15	.11	.06
423	Len Matuszek	.05	.04	.02
424	Mike Kingery	.20	.15	.08
425	Dave Kingman	.12	.09	.05
426	Al Newman	.12	.09	.05
427	Gary Ward	.07	.05	.03
428	Ruppert Jones	.05	.04	.02
429	Harold Baines	.15	.11	.06
430	Pat Perry	.07	.05	.03
431	Terry Puhl	.05	.04	.02
432	Don Carman	.10	.08	.04
433	Eddie Milner	.05	.04	.02
434	LaMarr Hoyt	.07	.05	.03
435	Rick Rhoden	.10	.08	.04
436	Jose Uribe	.07	.05	.03
437	Ken Oberkfell	.07	.05	.03
438	Ron Davis	.05	.04	.02
439	Jesse Orosco	.07	.05	.03
440	Scott Bradley	.05	.04	.02
441	Randy Bush	.05	.04	.02
442	John Cerutti	.30	.25	.12
443	Roy Smalley	.05	.04	.02
444	Kelly Gruber	.10	.08	.04
445	Bob Kearney	.05	.04	.02
446	Ed Hearn	.12	.09	.05
447	Scott Sanderson	.07	.05	.03
448	Bruce Benedict	.05	.04	.02
449	Junior Ortiz	.05	.04	.02

		MT	NR MT	EX
450	Mike Aldrete	.40	.30	.15
451	Kevin McReynolds	.12	.09	.05
452	Rob Murphy	.20	.15	.08
453	Kent Tekulve	.07	.05	.03
454	Curt Ford	.10	.08	.04
455	Davey Lopes	.07	.05	.03
456	Bobby Grich	.10	.08	.04
457	Jose DeLeon	.07	.05	.03
458	Andre Dawson	.20	.15	.08
459	Mike Flanagan	.10	.08	.04
460	Joey Meyer	.20	.15	.08
461	Chuck Cary	.12	.09	.05
462	Bill Buckner	.10	.08	.04
463	Bob Shirley	.05	.04	.02
464	Jeff Hamilton	.20	.15	.08
465	Phil Niekro	.20	.15	.08
466	Mark Gubicza	.07	.05	.03
467	Jerry Willard	.05	.04	.02
468	Bob Sebra	.15	.11	.06
469	Larry Parrish	.10	.08	.04
470	Charlie Hough	.07	.05	.03
471	Hal McRae	.10	.08	.04
472	Dave Leiper	.15	.11	.06
473	Mel Hall	.07	.05	.03
474	Dan Pasqua	.12	.09	.05
475	Bob Welch	.10	.08	.04
476	Johnny Grubb	.05	.04	.02
477	Jim Traber	.10	.08	.04
478	Chris Bosio	.20	.15	.08
479	Mark McLemore	.07	.05	.03
480	John Morris	.05	.04	.02
481	Billy Hatcher	.07	.05	.03
482	Dan Schatzeder	.05	.04	.02
483	Rich Gossage	.15	.11	.06
484	Jim Morrison	.05	.04	.02
485	Bob Brenly	.05	.04	.02
486	Bill Schroeder	.05	.04	.02
487	Mookie Wilson	.10	.08	.04
488	Dave Martinez	.30	.25	.12
489	Harold Reynolds	.10	.08	.04
490	Jeff Hearron	.10	.08	.04
491	Mickey Hatcher	.05	.04	.02
492	Barry Larkin	.70	.50	.30
493	Bob James	.05	.04	.02
494	John Habyan	.05	.04	.02
495	Jim Adduci	.07	.05	.03
496	Mike Heath	.05	.04	.02
497	Tim Stoddard	.05	.04	.02
498	Tony Armas	.07	.05	.03
499	Dennis Powell	.05	.04	.02
500	Checklist 452-557	.05	.04	.02
501	Chris Bando	.05	.04	.02
502	David Cone	.15	.11	.06
503	Jay Howell	.07	.05	.03
504	Tom Foley	.05	.04	.02
505	Ray Chadwick	.10	.08	.04
506	Mike Loynd	.20	.15	.08
507	Neil Allen	.05	.04	.02
508	Danny Darwin	.07	.05	.03
509	Rick Schu	.05	.04	.02
510	Jose Oquendo	.05	.04	.02
511	Gene Walter	.05	.04	.02
512	Terry McGriff	.12	.09	.05
513	Ken Griffey	.10	.08	.04
514	Benny Distefano	.05	.04	.02
515	Terry Mulholland	.10	.08	.04
516	Ed Lynch	.05	.04	.02
517	Bill Swift	.05	.04	.02
518	Manny Lee	.07	.05	.03
519	Andre David	.05	.04	.02
520	Scott McGregor	.07	.05	.03
521	Rick Manning	.05	.04	.02
522	Willie Hernandez	.07	.05	.03
523	Marty Barrett	.10	.08	.04
524	Wayne Tolleson	.05	.04	.02
525	Jose Gonzalez	.20	.15	.08
526	Cory Snyder	1.25	.90	.50
527	Buddy Biancalana	.05	.04	.02
528	Moose Haas	.05	.04	.02
529	Wilfredo Tejada	.12	.09	.05
530	Stu Cliburn	.05	.04	.02
531	Dale Mohorcic	.25	.20	.10
532	Ron Hassey	.05	.04	.02
533	Ty Gainey	.05	.04	.02
534	Jerry Royster	.05	.04	.02
535	Mike Maddux	.20	.15	.08
536	Ted Power	.07	.05	.03
537	Ted Simmons	.12	.09	.05
538	Rafael Belliard	.12	.09	.05
539	Chico Walker	.12	.09	.05
540	Bob Forsch	.07	.05	.03
541	John Stefero	.05	.04	.02
542	Dale Sveum	.35	.25	.14
543	Mark Thurmond	.05	.04	.02
544	Jeff Sellers	.20	.15	.08
545	Joel Skinner	.05	.04	.02
546	Alex Trevino	.05	.04	.02
547	Randy Kutcher	.12	.09	.05
548	Joaquin Andujar	.07	.05	.03
549	Casey Candaele	.20	.15	.08
550	Jeff Russell	.05	.04	.02
551	John Candelaria	.10	.08	.04
552	Joe Cowley	.05	.04	.02
553	Danny Cox	.10	.08	.04
554	Denny Walling	.05	.04	.02
555	Bruce Ruffin	.30	.25	.12
556	Buddy Bell	.10	.08	.04
557	Jimmy Jones	.20	.15	.08
558	Bobby Bonilla	.35	.25	.14
559	Jeff Robinson	.07	.05	.03
560	Ed Olwine	.10	.08	.04
561	Glenallen Hill	.12	.09	.05
562	Lee Mazzilli	.07	.05	.03
563	Mike Brown	.05	.04	.02
564	George Frazier	.05	.04	.02
565	Mike Sharperson	.12	.09	.05
566	Mark Portugal	.12	.09	.05
567	Rick Leach	.05	.04	.02
568	Mark Langston	.10	.08	.04
569	Rafael Santana	.05	.04	.02
570	Manny Trillo	.07	.05	.03
571	Cliff Speck	.05	.04	.02
572	Bob Kipper	.07	.05	.03
573	Kelly Downs	.30	.25	.12
574	Randy Asadoor	.12	.09	.05
575	Dave Magadan	.80	.60	.30
576	Marvin Freeman	.12	.09	.05
577	Jeff Lahti	.05	.04	.02
578	Jeff Calhoun	.05	.04	.02
579	Gus Polidor	.07	.05	.03
580	Gene Nelson	.05	.04	.02
581	Tim Teufel	.05	.04	.02
582	Odell Jones	.05	.04	.02
583	Mark Ryal	.10	.08	.04
584	Randy O'Neal	.05	.04	.02
585	Mike Greenwell	1.50	1.25	.60
586	Ray Knight	.10	.08	.04
587	Ralph Bryant	.20	.15	.08
588	Carmen Castillo	.05	.04	.02
589	Ed Wojna	.05	.04	.02
590	Stan Javier	.05	.04	.02
591	Jeff Musselman	.30	.25	.12
592	Mike Stanley	.35	.25	.14
593	Darrell Porter	.07	.05	.03
594	Drew Hall	.20	.15	.08
595	Rob Nelson	.12	.09	.05
596	Bryan Oelkers	.05	.04	.02
597	Scott Nielsen	.15	.11	.06
598	Brian Holton	.20	.15	.08
599	Kevin Mitchell	.50	.40	.20
600	Checklist 558-660	.05	.04	.02
601	Jackie Gutierrez	.05	.04	.02
602	Barry Jones	.15	.11	.06
603	Jerry Narron	.05	.04	.02
604	Steve Lake	.05	.04	.02
605	Jim Pankovits	.05	.04	.02
606	Ed Romero	.05	.04	.02
607	Dave LaPoint	.05	.04	.02
608	Don Robinson	.07	.05	.03
609	Mike Krukow	.07	.05	.03
610	Dave Valle	.15	.11	.06
611	Len Dykstra	.15	.11	.06
612	Roberto Clemente Puzzle Card	.05	.04	.02
613	Mike Trujillo	.07	.05	.03
614	Damaso Garcia	.07	.05	.03
615	Neal Heaton	.07	.05	.03
616	Juan Berenguer	.05	.04	.02
617	Steve Carlton	.25	.20	.10
618	Gary Lucas	.05	.04	.02
619	Geno Petralli	.05	.04	.02
620	Rick Aguilera	.10	.08	.04
621	Fred McGriff	.12	.09	.05
622	Dave Henderson	.05	.04	.02
623	Dave Clark	.25	.20	.10
624	Angel Salazar	.05	.04	.02
625	Randy Hunt	.05	.04	.02
626	John Gibbons	.05	.04	.02
627	Kevin Brown	.10	.08	.04
628	Bill Dawley	.05	.04	.02
629	Aurelio Lopez	.05	.04	.02
630	Charlie Hudson	.05	.04	.02
631	Ray Soff	.10	.08	.04

		MT	NR MT	EX
632	Ray Hayward	.12	.09	.05
633	Spike Owen	.05	.04	.02
634	Glenn Hubbard	.05	.04	.02
635	Kevin Elster	.30	.25	.12
636	Mike LaCoss	.07	.05	.03
637	Dwayne Henry	.05	.04	.02
638	Rey Quinones (Quinonez)	.20	.15	.08
639	Jim Clancy	.10	.08	.04
640	Larry Andersen	.05	.04	.02
641	Calvin Schiraldi	.07	.05	.03
642	Stan Jefferson	.40	.30	.15
643	Marc Sullivan	.05	.04	.02
644	Mark Grant	.05	.04	.02
645	Cliff Johnson	.05	.04	.02
646	Howard Johnson	.12	.09	.05
647	Dave Sax	.05	.04	.02
648	Dave Stewart	.10	.08	.04
649	Danny Heep	.05	.04	.02
650	Joe Johnson	.05	.04	.02
651	Bob Brower	.25	.20	.10
652	Rob Woodward	.07	.05	.03
653	John Mizerock	.05	.04	.02
654	Tim Pyznarski	.12	.09	.05
655	Luis Aquino	.12	.09	.05
656	Mickey Brantley	.10	.08	.04
657	Doyle Alexander	.10	.08	.04
658	Sammy Stewart	.05	.04	.02
659	Jim Acker	.05	.04	.02
660	Pete Ladd	.05	.04	.02

		MT	NR MT	EX
19	Gary Carter	.30	.25	.12
20	Whitey Herzog	.09	.07	.04
21	Jose Canseco	1.00	.70	.40
22	John Franco	.09	.07	.04
23	Jesse Barfield	.15	.11	.06
24	Rick Rhoden	.09	.07	.04
25	Harold Baines	.15	.11	.06
26	Sid Fernandez	.12	.09	.05
27	George Brett	.40	.30	.15
28	Steve Sax	.15	.11	.06
29	Jim Presley	.12	.09	.05
30	Dave Smith	.09	.07	.04
31	Eddie Murray	.30	.25	.12
32	Mike Scott	.12	.09	.05
33	Don Mattingly	1.75	1.25	.70
34	Dave Parker	.20	.15	.08
35	Tony Fernandez	.15	.11	.06
36	Tim Raines	.25	.20	.10
37	Brook Jacoby	.12	.09	.05
38	Chili Davis	.12	.09	.05
39	Rich Gedman	.09	.07	.04
40	Kevin Bass	.09	.07	.04
41	Frank White	.09	.07	.04
42	Glenn Davis	.15	.11	.06
43	Willie Hernandez	.09	.07	.04
44	Chris Brown	.12	.09	.05
45	Jim Rice	.25	.20	.10
46	Tony Pena	.09	.07	.04
47	Don Aase	.09	.07	.04
48	Hubie Brooks	.12	.09	.05
49	Charlie Hough	.09	.07	.04
50	Jody Davis	.12	.09	.05
51	Mike Witt	.12	.09	.05
52	Jeff Reardon	.12	.09	.05
53	Ken Schrom	.09	.07	.04
54	Fernando Valenzuela	.25	.20	.10
55	Dave Righetti	.20	.15	.08
56	Shane Rawley	.09	.07	.04
57	Ted Higuera	.12	.09	.05
58	Mike Krukow	.09	.07	.04
59	Lloyd Moseby	.12	.09	.05
60	Checklist	.09	.07	.04

1987 Donruss All-Stars

Issued in conjunction with the Donruss Pop-Ups set for the second consecutive year, the 1987 Donruss All-Stars set consists of 59 players (plus a checklist) who were selected to the 1986 All-Star Game. Measuring 3½'' by 5'' in size, the card fronts feature black borders and American or National logos. Included on the backs are the player's career highlights and All-Star game statistics. Retail packs included one Pop-Up card, three All-Star cards and one Roberto Clemente puzzle.

		MT	NR MT	EX
Complete Set:		6.00	4.50	2.50
Common Player:		.09	.07	.04
1	Wally Joyner	1.00	.70	.40
2	Dave Winfield	.25	.20	.10
3	Lou Whitaker	.15	.11	.06
4	Kirby Puckett	.30	.25	.12
5	Cal Ripken, Jr.	.35	.25	.14
6	Rickey Henderson	.30	.25	.12
7	Wade Boggs	.70	.50	.30
8	Roger Clemens	.50	.40	.20
9	Lance Parrish	.15	.11	.06
10	Dick Howser	.09	.07	.04
11	Keith Hernandez	.20	.15	.08
12	Darryl Strawberry	.35	.25	.14
13	Ryne Sandberg	.25	.20	.10
14	Dale Murphy	.40	.30	.15
15	Ozzie Smith	.15	.11	.06
16	Tony Gwynn	.30	.25	.12
17	Mike Schmidt	.40	.30	.15
18	Dwight Gooden	.60	.45	.25

1987 Donruss Box Panels

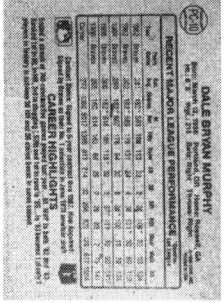

Continuing with an idea they initiated in 1985, Donruss once again placed baseball cards on the bottoms of their retail boxes. The cards, which are 2½'' by 3½'' in size, come four to a panel with each panel containing an unnumbered Roberto Clemente puzzle card. With numbering that begins where Donruss left off in 1986, cards PC 10 through PC 12 were found on boxes of Donruss regular issue wax packs. Cards PC 13 through PC 15 were located on boxes of the 1987 All-Star/Pop-Up packs.

		MT	NR MT	EX
Complete Panel Set:		6.00	4.50	2.50
Complete Singles Set:		2.50	2.00	1.00
Common Single Player:		.15	.11	.06
Panel		3.50	2.75	1.50
10	Dale Murphy	.50	.40	.20
11	Jeff Reardon	.20	.15	.08
12	Jose Canseco	.80	.60	.30
---	Clemente Puzzle Card	.04	.03	.02

Panel		MT	NR MT	EX
		2.50	2.00	1.00
13	Mike Scott	.20	.15	.08
14	Roger Clemens	.70	.50	.30
15	Mike Krukow	.15	.11	.06
---	Clemente Puzzle Card	.04	.03	.02

1987 Donruss Diamond Kings Supers

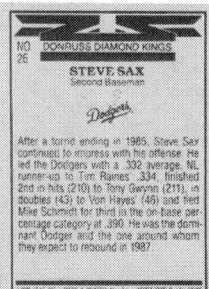

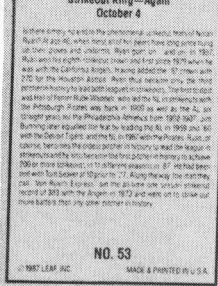

For a third straight baseball card season, Donruss produced a set of enlarged size Diamond Kings. The cards, which measure 4 11/16'' by 6 3/4'', are giant versions of the Diamond Kings subset found in the regular 1987 Donruss set. The 28-card set, which features the artwork of Dick Perez, contains 26 player cards, a checklist and a Roberto Clemente puzzle card. The set was available through a mail-in offer for $9.50 plus three wrappers.

		MT	NR MT	EX
Complete Set:		10.00	7.50	4.00
Common Player:		.20	.15	.08
1	Wally Joyner	1.25	.90	.50
2	Roger Clemens	.80	.60	.30
3	Dale Murphy	.70	.50	.30
4	Darryl Strawberry	.70	.50	.30
5	Ozzie Smith	.30	.25	.12
6	Jose Canseco	1.25	.90	.50
7	Charlie Hough	.20	.15	.08
8	Brook Jacoby	.25	.20	.10
9	Fred Lynn	.30	.25	.12
10	Rick Rhoden	.20	.15	.08
11	Chris Brown	.25	.20	.10
12	Von Hayes	.25	.20	.10
13	Jack Morris	.40	.30	.15
14	Kevin McReynolds	.30	.25	.12
15	George Brett	.70	.50	.30
16	Ted Higuera	.30	.25	.12
17	Hubie Brooks	.25	.20	.10
18	Mike Scott	.30	.25	.12
19	Kirby Puckett	.50	.40	.20
20	Dave Winfield	.50	.40	.20
21	Lloyd Moseby	.25	.20	.10
22	Eric Davis	1.25	.90	.50
23	Jim Presley	.25	.20	.10
24	Keith Moreland	.20	.15	.08
25	Greg Walker	.25	.20	.10
26	Steve Sax	.30	.25	.12
27	Checklist	.15	.11	.06
---	Clemente Puzzle Card	.15	.11	.06

1987 Donruss Highlights

For a third consecutive year, Donruss produced a 56-card set which highlighted the special events of the 1987 baseball season. The cards, which measure 2½'' by 3½'', have a front design similar to the regular 1987 Donruss set. A blue border and the ''Highlights'' logo are the significant differences. The card backs feature black print on a white background and include the date the event took place plus the particulars about it. As in the past, the set includes Donruss' picks for the A.L. and N.L. Rookies of the Year. The set was issued in a specially designed box and was available only through hobby dealers.

		MT	NR MT	EX
Complete Set:		9.00	6.75	3.50
Common Player:		.10	.08	.04
1	First No-Hitter For Brewers (Juan Nieves)	.15	.11	.06
2	Hits 500th Homer (Mike Schmidt)	.30	.25	.12
3	N.L. Player of the Month - April (Eric Davis)	.60	.45	.25
4	N.L. Pitcher of the Month - April (Sid Fernandez)	.15	.11	.06
5	A.L. Player of the Month - April (Brian Downing)	.10	.08	.04
6	A.L. Pitcher of the Month - April (Bret Saberhagen)	.20	.15	.08
7	Free Agent Holdout Returns (Tim Raines)	.25	.20	.10
8	N.L. Player of the Month - May (Eric Davis)	.60	.45	.25
9	N.L. Pitcher of the Month - May (Steve Bedrosian)	.15	.11	.06
10	A.L. Player of the Month - May (Larry Parrish)	.10	.08	.04
11	A.L. Pitcher of the Month - May (Jim Clancy)	.10	.08	.04
12	N.L. Player of the Month - June (Tony Gwynn)	.25	.20	.10
13	N.L. Pitcher of the Month - June (Orel Hershiser)	.15	.11	.06
14	A.L. Player of the Month - June (Wade Boggs)	.50	.40	.20
15	A.L. Pitcher of the Month - June (Steve Ontiveros)	.10	.08	.04
16	All Star Game Hero (Tim Raines)	.25	.20	.10
17	Consecutive Game Homer Streak (Don Mattingly)	1.00	.70	.40
18	1987 Hall of Fame Inductee (Jim "Catfish" Hunter)	.20	.15	.08
19	1987 Hall of Fame Inductee (Ray Dandridge)	.10	.08	.04
20	1987 Hall of Fame Inductee (Billy Williams)	.20	.15	.08
21	N.L. Player of the Month - July (Bo Diaz)	.10	.08	.04
22	N.L. Pitcher of the Month - July (Floyd Youmans)	.15	.11	.06
23	A.L. Player of the Month - July (Don Mattingly)	1.00	.70	.40
24	A.L. Pitcher of the Month - July (Frank Viola)	.15	.11	.06
25	Strikes Out 4 Batters In 1 Inning (Bobby Witt)	.15	.11	.06
26	Ties A.L. 9-Inning Game Hit Mark (Kevin Seitzer)	1.50	1.25	.60
27	Sets Rookie Home Run Record (Mark McGwire)	1.50	1.25	.60
28	Sets Cubs' 1st Year Homer Mark (Andre Dawson)	.20	.15	.08
29	Hits In 39 Straight Games (Paul Molitor)	.15	.11	.06
30	Record Weekend (Kirby Puckett)	.25	.20	.10
31	N.L. Player of the Month - August (Andre Dawson)	.20	.15	.08

	MT	NR MT	EX
32 N.L. Pitcher of the Month - August (Doug Drabek)	.10	.08	.04
33 A.L. Player of the Month - August (Dwight Evans)	.15	.11	.06
34 A.L. Pitcher of the Month - August (Mark Langston)	.15	.11	.06
35 100 RBI In 1st 2 Major League Seasons (Wally Joyner)	.70	.50	.30
36 100 SB In 1st 3 Major League Seasons (Vince Coleman)	.20	.15	.08
37 Orioles' All Time Homer King (Eddie Murray)	.25	.20	.10
38 Ends Consecutive Innings Streak (Cal Ripken)	.25	.20	.10
39 Blue Jays Hit Record 10 Homers In 1 Gamek (Ernie Whitt, Fred McGriff, Rob Ducey)	.15	.11	.06
40 Equal A's RBI Marks (Jose Canseco, Mark McGwire)	1.50	1.25	.60
41 Sets All-Time Catching Record (Bob Boone)	.10	.08	.04
42 Sets Mets' One-Season HR Mark (Darryl Strawberry)	.30	.25	.12
43 N.L.'s All-Time Switch Hit HR King (Howard Johnson)	.15	.11	.06
44 Five Straight 200-Hit Seasons (Wade Boggs)	.60	.45	.25
45 Eclipses Rookie Game Hitting Streak (Benito Santiago)	.80	.60	.30
46 Eclipses Jackson's A's HR Record (Mark McGwire)	1.50	1.25	.60
47 13th Rookie To Collect 200 Hits (Kevin Seitzer)	1.50	1.25	.60
48 Sets Slam Record (Don Mattingly)	1.00	.70	.40
49 N.L. Player of the Month - September (Darryl Strawberry)	.30	.25	.12
50 N.L. Pitcher of the Month - September (Pascual Perez)	.10	.08	.04
51 A.L. Player of the Month - September (Alan Trammell)	.20	.15	.08
52 A.L. Pitcher of the Month - September (Doyle Alexander)	.10	.08	.04
53 Strikeout King - Again (Nolan Ryan)	.20	.15	.08
54 Donruss A.L. Rookie of the Year (Mark McGwire)	1.50	1.25	.60
55 Donruss N.L. Rookie of the Year (Benito Santiago)	.80	.60	.30
56 Highlight Checklist	.10	.08	.04

1987 Donruss Opening Day

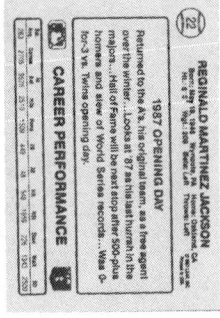

	MT	NR MT	EX
Complete Set:	18.00	13.50	7.25
Common Player:	.05	.04	.02
1 Doug DeCinces	.07	.05	.03
2 Mike Witt	.12	.09	.05
3 George Hendrick	.07	.05	.03
4 Dick Schofield	.05	.04	.02
5 Devon White	.80	.60	.30
6 Butch Wynegar	.05	.04	.02
7 Wally Joyner	1.25	.90	.50
8 Mark McLemore	.05	.04	.02
9 Brian Downing	.07	.05	.03
10 Gary Pettis	.05	.04	.02
11 Bill Doran	.07	.05	.03
12 Phil Garner	.05	.04	.02
13 Jose Cruz	.10	.08	.04
14 Kevin Bass	.07	.05	.03
15 Mike Scott	.12	.09	.05
16 Glenn Davis	.15	.11	.06
17 Alan Ashby	.05	.04	.02
18 Billy Hatcher	.07	.05	.03
19 Craig Reynolds	.05	.04	.02
20 Carney Lansford	.07	.05	.03
21 Mike Davis	.07	.05	.03
22 Reggie Jackson	.30	.25	.12
23 Mickey Tettleton	.07	.05	.03
24 Jose Canseco	1.25	.90	.50
25 Rob Nelson	.05	.04	.02
26 Tony Phillips	.05	.04	.02
27 Dwayne Murphy	.05	.04	.02
28 Alfredo Griffin	.07	.05	.03
29 Curt Young	.05	.04	.02
30 Willie Upshaw	.05	.04	.02
31 Mike Sharperson	.08	.06	.03
32 Rance Mulliniks	.05	.04	.02
33 Ernie Whitt	.08	.06	.03
34 Jesse Barfield	.15	.11	.06
35 Tony Fernandez	.12	.09	.05
36 Lloyd Moseby	.10	.08	.04
37 Jimmy Key	.10	.08	.04
38 Fred McGriff	.10	.08	.04
39 George Bell	.30	.25	.12
40 Dale Murphy	.40	.30	.15
41 Rick Mahler	.05	.04	.02
42 Ken Griffey	.10	.08	.04
43 Andres Thomas	.10	.08	.04
44 Dion James	.08	.06	.03
45 Ozzie Virgil	.08	.06	.03
46 Ken Oberkfell	.05	.04	.02
47 Gary Roenicke	.05	.04	.02
48 Glenn Hubbard	.05	.04	.02
49 Bill Schroeder	.05	.04	.02
50 Greg Brock	.08	.06	.03
51 Billy Jo Robidoux	.05	.04	.02
52 Glenn Braggs	.30	.25	.12
53 Jim Gantner	.05	.04	.02
54 Paul Molitor	.12	.09	.05
55 Dale Sveum	.15	.11	.06
56 Ted Higuera	.12	.09	.05
57 Rob Deer	.08	.06	.03
58 Robin Yount	.25	.20	.10
59 Jim Lindeman	.12	.09	.05
60 Vince Coleman	.15	.11	.06
61 Tommy Herr	.08	.06	.03
62 Terry Pendleton	.08	.06	.03
63 John Tudor	.10	.08	.04
64 Tony Pena	.10	.08	.04
65 Ozzie Smith	.12	.09	.05
66 Tito Landrum	.05	.04	.02
67 Jack Clark	.15	.11	.06
68 Bob Dernier	.05	.04	.02
69 Rick Sutcliffe	.12	.09	.05
70 Andre Dawson	.20	.15	.08
71 Keith Moreland	.08	.06	.03
72 Jody Davis	.08	.06	.03
73 Brian Dayett	.05	.04	.02
74 Leon Durham	.10	.08	.04
75 Ryne Sandberg	.25	.20	.10
76 Shawon Dunston	.10	.08	.04
77 Mike Marshall	.10	.08	.04
78 Bill Madlock	.10	.08	.04
79 Orel Hershiser	.12	.09	.05
80 Mike Ramsey	.05	.04	.02
81 Ken Landreaux	.05	.04	.02
82 Mike Scioscia	.05	.04	.02
83 Franklin Stubbs	.08	.06	.03
84 Mariano Duncan	.05	.04	.02
85 Steve Sax	.15	.11	.06
86 Mitch Webster	.08	.06	.03
87 Reid Nichols	.05	.04	.02
88 Tim Wallach	.10	.08	.04

The Donruss Opening Day set includes all players in major league baseball's starting lineups on the opening day of the 1987 baseball season. Cards in the 272-piece set measure 2½" by 3½" and have a glossy coating. The card fronts are identical in design to the regular Donruss set, but new photos were utilized and the fronts contain maroon borders as opposed to black. The backs carry black printing on white and yellow and carry a brief player biography plus the player's career statistics. The set was packaged in a sturdy 15" by 5" by 2" box with a clear acetate lid and was available only through hobby dealers.

#	Player	MT	NR MT	EX
89	Floyd Youmans	.10	.08	.04
90	Andres Galarraga	.10	.08	.04
91	Hubie Brooks	.10	.08	.04
92	Jeff Reed	.05	.04	.02
93	Alonzo Powell	.05	.04	.02
94	Vance Law	.05	.04	.02
95	Bob Brenly	.05	.04	.02
96	Will Clark	.90	.70	.35
97	Chili Davis	.10	.08	.04
98	Mike Krukow	.10	.08	.04
99	Jose Uribe	.05	.04	.02
100	Chris Brown	.10	.08	.04
101	Rob Thompson	.10	.08	.04
102	Candy Maldonado	.08	.06	.03
103	Jeff Leonard	.08	.06	.03
104	Tom Candiotti	.05	.04	.02
105	Chris Bando	.05	.04	.02
106	Cory Snyder	.40	.30	.15
107	Pat Tabler	.08	.06	.03
108	Andre Thornton	.08	.06	.03
109	Joe Carter	.12	.09	.05
110	Tony Bernazard	.05	.04	.02
111	Julio Franco	.10	.08	.04
112	Brook Jacoby	.10	.08	.04
113	Brett Butler	.08	.06	.03
114	Donnell Nixon	.10	.08	.04
115	Alvin Davis	.12	.09	.05
116	Mark Langston	.10	.08	.04
117	Harold Reynolds	.08	.06	.03
118	Ken Phelps	.08	.06	.03
119	Mike Kingery	.10	.08	.04
120	Dave Valle	.08	.06	.03
121	Rey Quinones	.08	.06	.03
122	Phil Bradley	.12	.09	.05
123	Jim Presley	.12	.09	.05
124	Keith Hernandez	.25	.20	.10
125	Kevin McReynolds	.12	.09	.05
126	Rafael Santana	.05	.04	.02
127	Bob Ojeda	.10	.08	.04
128	Darryl Strawberry	.40	.30	.15
129	Mookie Wilson	.08	.06	.03
130	Gary Carter	.30	.25	.12
131	Tim Teufel	.05	.04	.02
132	Howard Johnson	.10	.08	.04
133	Cal Ripken	.30	.25	.12
134	Rick Burleson	.08	.06	.03
135	Fred Lynn	.12	.09	.05
136	Eddie Murray	.30	.25	.12
137	Ray Knight	.08	.06	.03
138	Alan Wiggins	.05	.04	.02
139	John Shelby	.05	.04	.02
140	Mike Boddicker	.08	.06	.03
141	Ken Gerhart	.10	.08	.04
142	Terry Kennedy	.08	.06	.03
143	Steve Garvey	.25	.20	.10
144	Marvell Wynne	.05	.04	.02
145	Kevin Mitchell	.10	.08	.04
146	Tony Gwynn	.30	.25	.12
147	Joey Cora	.10	.08	.04
148	Benito Santiago	.60	.45	.25
149	Eric Show	.05	.04	.02
150	Garry Templeton	.08	.06	.03
151	Carmelo Martinez	.05	.04	.02
152	Von Hayes	.10	.08	.04
153	Lance Parrish	.15	.11	.06
154	Milt Thompson	.08	.06	.03
155	Mike Easler	.08	.06	.03
156	Juan Samuel	.12	.09	.05
157	Steve Jeltz	.05	.04	.02
158	Glenn Wilson	.08	.06	.03
159	Shane Rawley	.08	.06	.03
160	Mike Schmidt	.30	.25	.12
161	Andy Van Slyke	.08	.06	.03
162	Johnny Ray	.08	.06	.03
163a	Barry Bonds (dark jersey, photo actually Johnny Ray)	10.00	7.50	4.00
163b	Barry Bonds (white jersey, correct photo)	.12	.09	.05
164	Junior Ortiz	.05	.04	.02
165	Rafael Belliard	.05	.04	.02
166	Bob Patterson	.08	.06	.03
167	Bobby Bonilla	.10	.08	.04
168	Sid Bream	.08	.06	.03
169	Jim Morrison	.05	.04	.02
170	Jerry Browne	.10	.08	.04
171	Scott Fletcher	.08	.06	.03
172	Ruben Sierra	.80	.60	.30
173	Larry Parrish	.08	.06	.03
174	Pete O'Brien	.08	.06	.03
175	Pete Incaviglia	.80	.60	.30
176	Don Slaught	.05	.04	.02
177	Oddibe McDowell	.10	.08	.04
178	Charlie Hough	.08	.06	.03
179	Steve Buechele	.05	.04	.02
180	Bob Stanley	.05	.04	.02
181	Wade Boggs	.70	.50	.30
182	Jim Rice	.25	.20	.10
183	Bill Buckner	.10	.08	.04
184	Dwight Evans	.12	.09	.05
185	Spike Owen	.05	.04	.02
186	Don Baylor	.10	.08	.04
187	Marc Sullivan	.05	.04	.02
188	Marty Barrett	.08	.06	.03
189	Dave Henderson	.05	.04	.02
190	Bo Diaz	.05	.04	.02
191	Barry Larkin	.40	.30	.15
192	Kal Daniels	.40	.30	.15
193	Terry Francona	.05	.04	.02
194	Tom Browning	.08	.06	.03
195	Ron Oester	.05	.04	.02
196	Buddy Bell	.10	.08	.04
197	Eric Davis	.90	.70	.35
198	Dave Parker	.15	.11	.06
199	Steve Balboni	.05	.04	.02
200	Danny Tartabull	.20	.15	.08
201	Ed Hearn	.05	.04	.02
202	Buddy Biancalana	.05	.04	.02
203	Danny Jackson	.05	.04	.02
204	Frank White	.08	.06	.03
205	Bo Jackson	.70	.50	.30
206	George Brett	.40	.30	.15
207	Kevin Seitzer	1.50	1.25	.60
208	Willie Wilson	.10	.08	.04
209	Orlando Mercado	.05	.04	.02
210	Darrell Evans	.10	.08	.04
211	Larry Herndon	.05	.04	.02
212	Jack Morris	.15	.11	.06
213	Chet Lemon	.08	.06	.03
214	Mike Heath	.05	.04	.02
215	Darnell Coles	.08	.06	.03
216	Alan Trammell	.20	.15	.08
217	Terry Harper	.05	.04	.02
218	Lou Whitaker	.15	.11	.06
219	Gary Gaetti	.15	.11	.06
220	Tom Nieto	.05	.04	.02
221	Kirby Puckett	.25	.20	.10
222	Tom Brunansky	.10	.08	.04
223	Greg Gagne	.08	.06	.03
224	Dan Gladden	.08	.06	.03
225	Mark Davidson	.08	.06	.03
226	Bert Blyleven	.12	.09	.05
227	Steve Lombardozzi	.08	.06	.03
228	Kent Hrbek	.15	.11	.06
229	Gary Redus	.08	.06	.03
230	Ivan Calderon	.10	.08	.04
231	Tim Hulett	.05	.04	.02
232	Carlton Fisk	.15	.11	.06
233	Greg Walker	.10	.08	.04
234	Ron Karkovice	.08	.06	.03
235	Ozzie Guillen	.10	.08	.04
236	Harold Baines	.12	.09	.05
237	Donnie Hill	.05	.04	.02
238	Rich Dotson	.08	.06	.03
239	Mike Pagliarulo	.10	.08	.04
240	Joel Skinner	.05	.04	.02
241	Don Mattingly	1.00	.70	.40
242	Gary Ward	.08	.06	.03
243	Dave Winfield	.25	.20	.10
244	Dan Pasqua	.10	.08	.04
245	Wayne Tolleson	.05	.04	.02
246	Willie Randolph	.08	.06	.03
247	Dennis Rasmussen	.08	.06	.03
248	Rickey Henderson	.25	.20	.10
249	Angels Logo/Checklist	.05	.04	.02
250	Astros Logo/Checklist	.05	.04	.02
251	Athletics Logo/Checklist	.05	.04	.02
252	Blue Jays Logo/Checklist	.05	.04	.02
253	Braves Logo/Checklist	.05	.04	.02
254	Brewers Logo/Checklist	.05	.04	.02
255	Cardinals Logo/Checklist	.05	.04	.02
256	Dodgers Logo/Checklist	.05	.04	.02
257	Expos Logo/Checklist	.05	.04	.02
258	Giants Logo/Checklist	.05	.04	.02
259	Indians Logo/Checklist	.05	.04	.02
260	Mariners Logo/Checklist	.05	.04	.02
261	Orioles Logo/Checklist	.05	.04	.02
262	Padres Logo/Checklist	.05	.04	.02
263	Phillies Logo/Checklist	.05	.04	.02
264	Pirates Logo/Checklist	.05	.04	.02
265	Rangers Logo/Checklist	.05	.04	.02
266	Red Sox Logo/Checklist	.05	.04	.02
267	Reds Logo/Checklist	.05	.04	.02

		MT	NR MT	EX
268	Royals Logo/Checklist	.05	.04	.02
269	Tigers Logo/Checklist	.05	.04	.02
270	Twins Logo/Checklist	.05	.04	.02
271	White Sox-Cubs Logos/Checklist	.05	.04	.02
272	Yankees-Mets Logos/Checklist	.05	.04	.02

1987 Donruss Pop-Ups

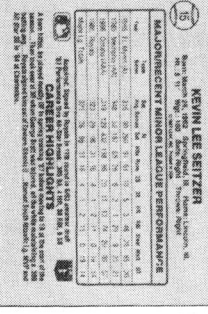

card. The set came housed in a specially designed box and was available only through hobby dealers.

For the second straight year, Donruss released in conjunction with its All-Stars issue a set of cards designed to fold out to form a three-dimensional stand-up card. Consisting of 20 cards as opposed to the previous year's 18, the 1987 Donruss Pop-Ups set contains players selected to the 1986 All-Star Game. Background for the 2½" by 5" cards is the Houston Astrodome, site of the 1986 mid-summer classic. Retail packs included one Pop-Up card, three All-Star cards and one Roberto Clemente puzzle card.

		MT	NR MT	EX
Complete Set:		6.00	4.50	2.50
Common Player:		.20	.15	.08
(1)	Wade Boggs	.80	.60	.30
(2)	Gary Carter	.50	.40	.20
(3)	Roger Clemens	.60	.45	.25
(4)	Dwight Gooden	.60	.45	.25
(5)	Tony Gwynn	.50	.40	.20
(6)	Rickey Henderson	.50	.40	.20
(7)	Keith Hernandez	.40	.30	.15
(8)	Whitey Herzog	.20	.15	.08
(9)	Dick Howser	.20	.15	.08
(10)	Wally Joyner	1.00	.70	.40
(11)	Dale Murphy	.60	.45	.25
(12)	Lance Parrish	.30	.25	.12
(13)	Kirby Puckett	.50	.40	.20
(14)	Cal Ripken	.50	.40	.20
(15)	Ryne Sandberg	.40	.30	.15
(16)	Mike Schmidt	.60	.45	.25
(17)	Ozzie Smith	.30	.25	.12
(18)	Darryl Strawberry	.60	.45	.25
(19)	Lou Whitaker	.30	.25	.12
(20)	Dave Winfield	.50	.40	.20

1987 Donruss Rookies

As they did in 1986, Donruss issued a 56-card set highlighting the major league's most promising rookies. The cards are the standard 2½" by 3½" size and and are identical in design to the regular Donruss issue. The card fronts have green borders as opposed to black found in the regular issue and carry the words "The Rookies" in the lower left portion of the

		MT	NR MT	EX
Complete Set:		10.00	7.50	4.00
Common Player:		.10	.08	.04
1	Mark McGwire	2.00	1.50	.80
2	Eric Bell	.25	.20	.10
3	Mark Williamson	.25	.20	.10
4	Mike Greenwell	.60	.45	.25
5	Ellis Burks	1.75	1 25	.70
6	DeWayne Buice	.20	.15	.08
7	Mark Mclemore (McLemore)	.10	.08	.04
8	Devon White	.40	.30	.15
9	Willie Fraser	.25	.20	.10
10	Lester Lancaster	.25	.20	.10
11	Ken Williams	.25	.20	.10
12	Matt Nokes	2.25	1.75	.90
13	Jeff Robinson	.20	.15	.08
14	Bo Jackson	1.00	.70	.40
15	Kevin Seitzer	2.75	2.00	1.00
16	Billy Ripken	.50	.40	.20
17	B.J. Surhoff	.40	.30	.15
18	Chuck Crim	.15	.11	.06
19	Mike Birbeck	.10	.08	.04
20	Chris Bosio	.15	.11	.06
21	Les Straker	.30	.25	.12
22	Mark Davidson	.15	.11	.06
23	Gene Larkin	.15	.11	.06
24	Ken Gerhart	.20	.15	.08
25	Luis Polonia	.35	.25	.14
26	Terry Steinbach	.25	.20	.10
27	Mickey Brantley	.10	.08	.04
28	Mike Stanley	.25	.20	.10
29	Jerry Browne	.15	.11	.06
30	Todd Benzinger	.65	.50	.25
31	Fred McGriff	.10	.08	.04
32	Mike Henneman	.35	.25	.14
33	Casey Candaele	.15	.11	.06
34	Dave Magadan	.40	.30	.15
35	David Cone	.15	.11	.06
36	Mike Jackson	.20	.15	.08
37	John Mitchell	.20	.15	.08
38	Mike Dunne	.40	.30	.15
39	John Smiley	.20	.15	.08
40	Joe Magrane	.55	.40	.20
41	Jim Lindeman	.25	.20	.10
42	Shane Mack	.45	.35	.20
43	Stan Jefferson	.15	.11	.06
44	Benito Santiago	.40	.30	.15
45	Matt Williams	.40	.30	.15
46	Dave Meads	.20	.15	.08
47	Rafael Palmeiro	.25	.20	.10
48	Bill Long	.25	.20	.10
49	Bob Brower	.15	.11	.06
50	James Steels	.20	.15	.08
51	Paul Noce	.20	.15	.08
52	Greg Maddux	.15	.11	.06
53	Jeff Musselman	.15	.11	.06
54	Brian Holton	.15	.11	.06
55	Chuck Jackson	.20	.15	.08
56	Checklist 1-56	.10	.08	.04

Definitions for grading conditions are located in the Introduction of this price guide.

1988 Donruss

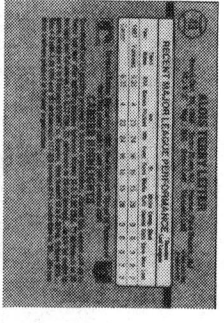

The 1988 Donruss set consists of 660 cards, each measuring 2½'' by 3½'' in size. The card fronts feature a full color photo surrounded by a colorful border — alternating stripes of black, red, black, blue, black, blue, black, red and black (in that order), separated by soft-focus edges and airbrushed fades. The player name and position appears in a red band at the bottom of the card. The Donruss logo is situated in the upper left corner of the card, while the team logo is located in the lower right corner. For the seventh consecutive season, Donruss included a subset of ''Diamond Kings'' cards (#'s 1-27) in the issue. And for the fifth straight year, Donruss incorporated their highly popular ''Rated Rookies'' (card #'s 28-47) with the set.

		MT	NR MT	EX
Complete Set:		25.00	18.50	10.00
Common Player:		.05	.04	.02
1	Mark McGwire (DK)	1.00	.70	.40
2	Tim Raines (DK)	.25	.20	.10
3	Benito Santiago (DK)	.70	.50	.30
4	Alan Trammell (DK)	.25	.20	.10
5	Danny Tartabull (DK)	.20	.15	.08
6	Ron Darling (DK)	.12	.09	.05
7	Paul Molitor (DK)	.12	.09	.05
8	Devon White (DK)	.30	.25	.12
9	Andre Dawson (DK)	.20	.15	.08
10	Julio Franco (DK)	.10	.08	.04
11	Scott Fletcher (DK)	.07	.05	.03
12	Tony Fernandez (DK)	.12	.09	.05
13	Shane Rawley (DK)	.07	.05	.03
14	Kal Daniels (DK)	.20	.15	.08
15	Jack Clark (DK)	.15	.11	.06
16	Dwight Evans (DK)	.12	.09	.05
17	Tommy John (DK)	.15	.11	.06
18	Andy Van Slyke (DK)	.10	.08	.04
19	Gary Gaetti (DK)	.12	.09	.05
20	Mark Langston (DK)	.10	.08	.04
21	Will Clark (DK)	.60	.45	.25
22	Glenn Hubbard (DK)	.07	.05	.03
23	Billy Hatcher (DK)	.07	.05	.03
24	Bob Welch (DK)	.10	.08	.04
25	Ivan Calderon (DK)	.10	.08	.04
26	Cal Ripken (DK)	.35	.25	.14
27	Checklist 1-27	.05	.04	.02
28	Mackey Sasser (RR)	.30	.25	.12
29	Jeff Treadway (RR)	.40	.30	.15
30	Mike Campbell (RR)	.30	.25	.12
31	Lance Johnson (RR)	.30	.25	.12
32	Nelson Liriano (RR)	.25	.20	.10
33	Shawn Abner (RR)	.30	.25	.12
34	Roberto Alomar (RR)	.30	.25	.12
35	Shawn Hillegas (RR)	.25	.20	.10
36	Joey Meyer (RR)	.07	.05	.03
37	Kevin Elster (RR)	.15	.11	.06
38	Jose Lind (RR)	.35	.25	.14
39	Kirt Manwaring (RR)	.40	.30	.15
40	Mark Grace (RR)	.30	.25	.12
41	Jody Reed (RR)	.30	.25	.12
42	John Farrell (RR)	.30	.25	.12
43	Al Leiter (RR)	.35	.25	.14
44	Gary Thurman (RR)	.35	.25	.14
45	Vicente Palacios (RR)	.30	.25	.12

		MT	NR MT	EX
46	Eddie Williams (RR)	.30	.25	.12
47	Jack McDowell (RR)	.30	.25	.12
48	Ken Dixon	.05	.04	.02
49	Mike Birkbeck	.05	.04	.02
50	Eric King	.10	.08	.04
51	Roger Clemens	.60	.45	.25
52	Pat Clements	.05	.04	.02
53	Fernando Valenzuela	.25	.20	.10
54	Mark Gubicza	.07	.05	.03
55	Jay Howell	.07	.05	.03
56	Floyd Youmans	.10	.08	.04
57	Ed Correa	.10	.08	.04
58	DeWayne Buice	.20	.15	.08
59	Jose DeLeon	.05	.04	.02
60	Danny Cox	.10	.08	.04
61	Nolan Ryan	.30	.25	.12
62	Steve Bedrosian	.12	.09	.05
63	Tom Browning	.07	.05	.03
64	Mark Davis	.05	.04	.02
65	R.J. Reynolds	.07	.05	.03
66	Kevin Mitchell	.10	.08	.04
67	Ken Oberkfell	.05	.04	.02
68	Rick Sutcliffe	.12	.09	.05
69	Dwight Gooden	.60	.45	.25
70	Scott Bankhead	.05	.04	.02
71	Bert Blyleven	.15	.11	.06
72	Jimmy Key	.10	.08	.04
73	Les Straker	.20	.15	.08
74	Jim Clancy	.07	.05	.03
75	Mike Moore	.05	.04	.02
76	Ron Darling	.12	.09	.05
77	Ed Lynch	.05	.04	.02
78	Dale Murphy	.40	.30	.15
79	Doug Drabek	.07	.05	.03
80	Scott Garretts	.05	.04	.02
81	Ed Whitson	.05	.04	.02
82	Rob Murphy	.07	.05	.03
83	Shane Rawley	.07	.05	.03
84	Greg Mathews	.10	.08	.04
85	Jim Deshaies	.10	.08	.04
86	Mike Witt	.12	.09	.05
87	Donnie Hill	.05	.04	.02
88	Jeff Reed	.05	.04	.02
89	Mike Boddicker	.10	.08	.04
90	Ted Higuera	.10	.08	.04
91	Walt Terrell	.07	.05	.03
92	Bob Stanley	.05	.04	.02
93	Dave Righetti	.15	.11	.06
94	Orel Hershiser	.12	.09	.05
95	Chris Bando	.05	.04	.02
96	Bret Saberhagen	.20	.15	.08
97	Curt Young	.07	.05	.03
98	Tim Burke	.07	.05	.03
99	Charlie Hough	.07	.05	.03
100	Checklist 28-133	.05	.04	.02
101	Bobby Witt	.10	.08	.04
102	George Brett	.40	.30	.15
103	Mickey Tettleton	.05	.04	.02
104	Scott Bailes	.07	.05	.03
105	Mike Pagliarulo	.10	.08	.04
106	Mike Scioscia	.05	.04	.02
107	Tom Brookens	.05	.04	.02
108	Ray Knight	.07	.05	.03
109	Dan Plesac	.12	.09	.05
110	Wally Joyner	.80	.60	.30
111	Bob Forsch	.05	.04	.02
112	Mike Scott	.12	.09	.05
113	Kevin Gross	.07	.05	.03
114	Benito Santiago	.70	.50	.30
115	Bob Kipper	.05	.04	.02
116	Mike Krukow	.07	.05	.03
117	Chris Bosio	.07	.05	.03
118	Sid Fernandez	.10	.08	.04
119	Jody Davis	.07	.05	.03
120	Mike Morgan	.05	.04	.02
121	Mark Eichhorn	.10	.08	.04
122	Jeff Reardon	.12	.09	.05
123	John Franco	.07	.05	.03
124	Richard Dotson	.07	.05	.03
125	Eric Bell	.07	.05	.03
126	Juan Nieves	.10	.08	.04
127	Jack Morris	.20	.15	.08
128	Rick Rhoden	.10	.08	.04
129	Rich Gedman	.07	.05	.03
130	Ken Howell	.05	.04	.02
131	Brook Jacoby	.10	.08	.04
132	Danny Jackson	.07	.05	.03
133	Gene Nelson	.05	.04	.02
134	Neal Heaton	.07	.05	.03
135	Willie Fraser	.07	.05	.03
136	Jose Guzman	.07	.05	.03

 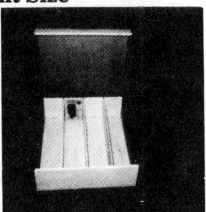

#	Name	MT	NR MT	EX
137	Ozzie Guillen	.10	.08	.04
138	Bob Knepper	.07	.05	.03
139	Mike Jackson	.20	.15	.08
140	Joe Magrane	.50	.40	.20
141	Jimmy Jones	.07	.05	.03
142	Ted Power	.07	.05	.03
143	Ozzie Virgil	.07	.05	.03
144	Felix Fermin	.15	.11	.06
145	Kelly Downs	.10	.08	.04
146	Shawon Dunston	.10	.08	.04
147	Scott Bradley	.05	.04	.02
148	Dave Stieb	.10	.08	.04
149	Frank Viola	.12	.09	.05
150	Terry Kennedy	.07	.05	.03
151	Bill Wegman	.05	.04	.02
152	Matt Nokes	1.50	1.25	.60
153	Wade Boggs	1.00	.70	.40
154	Wayne Tolleson	.05	.04	.02
155	Mariano Duncan	.05	.04	.02
156	Julio Franco	.10	.08	.04
157	Charlie Leibrandt	.07	.05	.03
158	Terry Steinbach	.12	.09	.05
159	Mike Fitzgerald	.05	.04	.02
160	Jack Lazorko	.05	.04	.02
161	Mitch Williams	.07	.05	.03
162	Greg Walker	.07	.05	.03
163	Alan Ashby	.05	.04	.02
164	Tony Gwynn	.35	.25	.14
165	Bruce Ruffin	.10	.08	.04
166	Ron Robinson	.05	.04	.02
167	Zane Smith	.10	.08	.04
168	Junior Ortiz	.05	.04	.02
169	Jamie Moyer	.07	.05	.03
170	Tony Pena	.10	.08	.04
171	Cal Ripken	.35	.25	.14
172	B.J. Surhoff	.25	.20	.10
173	Lou Whitaker	.20	.15	.08
174	Ellis Burks	1.75	1.25	.70
175	Ron Guidry	.20	.15	.08
176	Steve Sax	.15	.11	.06
177	Danny Tartabull	.20	.15	.08
178	Carney Lansford	.07	.05	.03
179	Casey Candaele	.07	.05	.03
180	Scott Fletcher	.07	.05	.03
181	Mark McLemore	.05	.04	.02
182	Ivan Calderon	.10	.08	.04
183	Jack Clark	.15	.11	.06
184	Glenn Davis	.15	.11	.06
185	Luis Aguayo	.05	.04	.02
186	Bo Diaz	.05	.04	.02
187	Stan Jefferson	.10	.08	.04
188	Sid Bream	.07	.05	.03
189	Bob Brenly	.05	.04	.02
190	Dion James	.07	.05	.03
191	Leon Durham	.10	.08	.04
192	Jesse Orosco	.07	.05	.03
193	Alvin Davis	.12	.09	.05
194	Gary Gaetti	.12	.09	.05
195	Fred McGriff	.10	.08	.04
196	Steve Lombardozzi	.07	.05	.03
197	Rance Mulliniks	.05	.04	.02
198	Rey Quinones	.07	.05	.03
199	Gary Carter	.30	.25	.12
200	Checklist 134-239	.05	.04	.02
201	Keith Moreland	.07	.05	.03
202	Ken Griffey	.10	.08	.04
203	Tommy Gregg	.15	.11	.06
204	Will Clark	.70	.50	.30
205	John Kruk	.30	.25	.12
206	Buddy Bell	.10	.08	.04
207	Von Hayes	.10	.08	.04
208	Tommy Herr	.07	.05	.03
209	Craig Reynolds	.05	.04	.02
210	Gary Pettis	.05	.04	.02
211	Harold Baines	.12	.09	.05
212	Vance Law	.05	.04	.02
213	Ken Gerhart	.10	.08	.04
214	Jim Gantner	.05	.04	.02
215	Chet Lemon	.07	.05	.03
216	Dwight Evans	.12	.09	.05
217	Don Mattingly	1.50	1.25	.60
218	Franklin Stubbs	.07	.05	.03
219	Pat Tabler	.07	.05	.03
220	Bo Jackson	.50	.40	.20
221	Tony Phillips	.05	.04	.02
222	Tim Wallach	.10	.08	.04
223	Ruben Sierra	.35	.25	.14
224	Steve Buechele	.05	.04	.02
225	Frank White	.07	.05	.03
226	Alfredo Griffin	.07	.05	.03
227	Greg Swindell	.12	.09	.05
228	Willie Randolph	.07	.05	.03
229	Mike Marshall	.10	.08	.04
230	Alan Trammell	.25	.20	.10
231	Eddie Murray	.35	.25	.14
232	Dale Sveum	.10	.08	.04
233	Dick Schofield	.05	.04	.02
234	Jose Oquendo	.05	.04	.02
235	Bill Doran	.07	.05	.03
236	Milt Thompson	.07	.05	.03
237	Marvell Wynne	.05	.04	.02
238	Bobby Bonilla	.10	.08	.04
239	Chris Speier	.05	.04	.02
240	Glenn Braggs	.12	.09	.05
241	Wally Backman	.07	.05	.03
242	Ryne Sandberg	.25	.20	.10
243	Phil Bradley	.12	.09	.05
244	Kelly Gruber	.05	.04	.02
245	Tom Brunansky	.10	.08	.04
246	Ron Oester	.05	.04	.02
247	Bobby Thigpen	.07	.05	.03
248	Fred Lynn	.15	.11	.06
249	Paul Molitor	.12	.09	.05
250	Darrell Evans	.10	.08	.04
251	Gary Ward	.07	.05	.03
252	Bruce Hurst	.10	.08	.04
253	Bob Welch	.10	.08	.04
254	Joe Carter	.12	.09	.05
255	Willie Wilson	.10	.08	.04
256	Mark McGwire	1.25	.90	.50
257	Mitch Webster	.07	.05	.03
258	Brian Downing	.07	.05	.03
259	Mike Stanley	.10	.08	.04
260	Carlton Fisk	.15	.11	.06
261	Billy Hatcher	.07	.05	.03
262	Glenn Wilson	.07	.05	.03
263	Ozzie Smith	.12	.09	.05
264	Randy Ready	.05	.04	.02
265	Kurt Stillwell	.12	.09	.05
266	David Palmer	.05	.04	.02
267	Mike Diaz	.10	.08	.04
268	Rob Thompson	.10	.08	.04
269	Andre Dawson	.20	.15	.08
270	Lee Guetterman	.07	.05	.03
271	Willie Upshaw	.07	.05	.03
272	Randy Bush	.05	.04	.02
273	Larry Sheets	.10	.08	.04
274	Rob Deer	.10	.08	.04
275	Kirk Gibson	.25	.20	.10
276	Marty Barrett	.07	.05	.03
277	Rickey Henderson	.35	.25	.14
278	Pedro Guerrero	.15	.11	.06
279	Brett Butler	.07	.05	.03
280	Kevin Seitzer	1.25	.90	.50
281	Mike Davis	.07	.05	.03
282	Andres Galarraga	.10	.08	.04
283	Devon White	.30	.25	.12
284	Pete O'Brien	.07	.05	.03
285	Jerry Hairston	.05	.04	.02
286	Kevin Bass	.07	.05	.03
287	Carmelo Martinez	.05	.04	.02
288	Juan Samuel	.10	.08	.04
289	Kal Daniels	.20	.15	.08
290	Andy Hall	.05	.04	.02
291	Andy Van Slyke	.10	.08	.04
292	Lee Smith	.10	.08	.04
293	Vince Coleman	.20	.15	.08
294	Tom Niedenfuer	.05	.04	.02
295	Robin Yount	.25	.20	.10
296	Jeff Robinson	.25	.20	.10
297	Todd Benzinger	.70	.50	.30
298	Dave Winfield	.30	.25	.12
299	Mickey Hatcher	.05	.04	.02
300	Checklist 240-345	.05	.04	.02
301	Bud Black	.05	.04	.02
302	Jose Canseco	.70	.50	.30
303	Tom Foley	.05	.04	.02
304	Pete Incaviglia	.35	.25	.14
305	Bob Boone	.07	.05	.03
306	Bill Long	.25	.20	.10
307	Willie McGee	.12	.09	.05
308	Ken Caminiti	.35	.25	.14
309	Darren Daulton	.05	.04	.02
310	Tracy Jones	.12	.09	.05
311	Greg Booker	.05	.04	.02
312	Mike LaValliere	.07	.05	.03
313	Chili Davis	.10	.08	.04
314	Glenn Hubbard	.05	.04	.02
315	Paul Noce	.20	.15	.08
316	Keith Hernandez	.25	.20	.10
317	Mark Langston	.10	.08	.04
318	Keith Atherton	.05	.04	.02

	MT	NR MT	EX			MT	NR MT	EX
319	Tony Fernandez	.12	.09	.05	410	Dave Smith	.07	.05	.03
320	Kent Hrbek	.15	.11	.06	411	Shane Mack	.30	.25	.12
321	John Cerutti	.10	.08	.04	412	Greg Gross	.05	.04	.02
322	Mike Kingery	.07	.05	.03	413	Nick Esasky	.05	.04	.02
323	Dave Magadan	.20	.15	.08	414	Damaso Garcia	.07	.05	.03
324	Rafael Palmeiro	.12	.09	.05	415	Brian Fisher	.07	.05	.03
325	Jeff Dedmon	.05	.04	.02	416	Brian Dayett	.05	.04	.02
326	Barry Bonds	.12	.09	.05	417	Curt Ford	.05	.04	.02
327	Jeffrey Leonard	.05	.04	.02	418	Mark Williamson	.20	.15	.08
328	Tim Flannery	.05	.04	.02	419	Bill Schroeder	.05	.04	.02
329	Dave Concepcion	.10	.08	.04	420	Mike Henneman	.25	.20	.10
330	Mike Schmidt	.40	.30	.15	421	John Marzano	.60	.45	.25
331	Bill Dawley	.05	.04	.02	422	Ron Kittle	.07	.05	.03
332	Larry Andersen	.05	.04	.02	423	Matt Young	.05	.04	.02
333	Jack Howell	.07	.05	.03	424	Steve Balboni	.05	.04	.02
334	Ken Williams	.25	.20	.10	425	Luis Polonia	.25	.20	.10
335	Bryn Smith	.07	.05	.03	426	Randy St. Claire	.05	.04	.02
336	Billy Ripken	.35	.25	.14	427	Greg Harris	.05	.04	.02
337	Greg Brock	.07	.05	.03	428	Johnny Ray	.10	.08	.04
338	Mike Heath	.05	.04	.02	429	Ray Searage	.05	.04	.02
339	Mike Greenwell	.70	.50	.30	430	Ricky Horton	.07	.05	.03
340	Claudell Washington	.07	.05	.03	431	Gerald Young	.35	.25	.14
341	Jose Gonzalez	.05	.04	.02	432	**Rick Schu**	.05	.04	.02
342	Mel Hall	.07	.05	.03	433	Paul O'Neill	.07	.05	.03
343	Jim Eisenreich	.10	.08	.04	434	Rich Gossage	.15	.11	.06
344	Tony Bernazard	.05	.04	.02	435	John Cangelosi	.07	.05	.03
345	Tim Raines	.25	.20	.10	436	Mike LaCoss	.05	.04	.02
346	Bob Brower	.07	.05	.03	437	Gerald Perry	.07	.05	.03
347	Larry Parrish	.07	.05	.03	438	Dave Martinez	.12	.09	.05
348	Thad Bosley	.05	.04	.02	439	Darryl Strawberry	.35	.25	.14
349	Dennis Eckersley	.07	.05	.03	440	John Moses	.05	.04	.02
350	Cory Snyder	.20	.15	.08	441	Greg Gagne	.07	.05	.03
351	Rick Cerone	.05	.04	.02	442	Jesse Barfield	.15	.11	.06
352	John Shelby	.05	.04	.02	443	George Frazier	.05	.04	.02
353	Larry Herndon	.05	.04	.02	444	Garth Iorg	.05	.04	.02
354	John Habyan	.05	.04	.02	445	Ed Nunez	.05	.04	.02
355	Chuck Crim	.15	.11	.06	446	Rick Aguilera	.07	.05	.03
356	Gus Polidor	.05	.04	.02	447	Jerry Mumphrey	.07	.05	.03
357	Ken Dayley	.05	.04	.02	448	Rafael Ramirez	.05	.04	.02
358	Danny Darwin	.05	.04	.02	449	John Smiley	.25	.20	.10
359	Lance Parrish	.15	.11	.06	450	Atlee Hammaker	.05	.04	.02
360	James Steels	.15	.11	.06	451	Lance McCullers	.07	.05	.03
361	Al Pedrique	.20	.15	.08	452	Guy Hoffman	.07	.05	.03
362	Mike Aldrete	.12	.09	.05	453	Chris James	.12	.09	.05
363	Juan Castillo	.05	.04	.02	454	Terry Pendleton	.07	.05	.03
364	Len Dykstra	.10	.08	.04	455	Dave Meads	.20	.15	.08
365	Luis Quinones	.05	.04	.02	456	Bill Buckner	.10	.08	.04
366	Jim Presley	.12	.09	.05	457	John Pawlowski	.15	.11	.06
367	Lloyd Moseby	.10	.08	.04	458	Bob Sebra	.07	.05	.03
368	Kirby Puckett	.35	.25	.14	459	Jim Dwyer	.05	.04	.02
369	Eric Davis	1.00	.70	.40	460	Jay Aldrich	.15	.11	.06
370	Gary Redus	.07	.05	.03	461	Frank Tanana	.07	.05	.03
371	Dave Schmidt	.05	.04	.02	462	Oil Can Boyd	.07	.05	.03
372	Mark Clear	.05	.04	.02	463	Dan Pasqua	.10	.08	.04
373	Dave Bergman	.05	.04	.02	464	Tim Crews	.30	.25	.12
374	Charles Hudson	.05	.04	.02	465	Andy Allanson	.07	.05	.03
375	Calvin Schiraldi	.05	.04	.02	466	Bill Pecota	.20	.15	.08
376	Alex Trevino	.05	.04	.02	467	Steve Ontiveros	.05	.04	.02
377	Tom Candiotti	.05	.04	.02	468	Hubie Brooks	.10	.08	.04
378	Steve Farr	.05	.04	.02	469	Paul Kilgus	.20	.15	.08
379	Mike Gallego	.05	.04	.02	470	Dale Mohorcic	.07	.05	.03
380	Andy McGaffigan	.05	.04	.02	471	Dan Quisenberry	.12	.09	.05
381	Kirk McCaskill	.07	.05	.03	472	Dave Stewart	.07	.05	.03
382	Oddibe McDowell	.10	.08	.04	473	Dave Clark	.07	.05	.03
383	Floyd Bannister	.07	.05	.03	474	Joel Skinner	.05	.04	.02
384	Denny Walling	.05	.04	.02	475	Dave Anderson	.05	.04	.02
385	Don Carman	.10	.08	.04	476	Dan Petry	.07	.05	.03
386	Todd Worrell	.12	.09	.05	477	Carl Nichols	.20	.15	.08
387	Eric Show	.05	.04	.02	478	Ernest Riles	.05	.04	.02
388	Dave Parker	.20	.15	.08	479	George Hendrick	.07	.05	.03
389	Rick Mahler	.05	.04	.02	480	John Morris	.05	.04	.02
390	Mike Dunne	.35	.25	.14	481	Manny Hernandez	.20	.15	.08
391	Candy Maldonado	.07	.05	.03	482	Jeff Stone	.05	.04	.02
392	Bob Dernier	.05	.04	.02	483	Chris Brown	.10	.08	.04
393	Dave Valle	.05	.04	.02	484	Mike Bielecki	.05	.04	.02
394	Ernie Whitt	.07	.05	.03	485	Dave Dravecky	.07	.05	.03
395	Juan Berenguer	.05	.04	.02	486	Rick Manning	.05	.04	.02
396	Mike Young	.07	.05	.03	487	Bill Almon	.05	.04	.02
397	Mike Felder	.05	.04	.02	488	Jim Sundberg	.05	.04	.02
398	Willie Hernandez	.07	.05	.03	489	Ken Phelps	.07	.05	.03
399	Jim Rice	.30	.25	.12	490	Tom Henke	.07	.05	.03
400	Checklist 346-451	.05	.04	.02	491	Dan Gladden	.07	.05	.03
401	Tommy John	.15	.11	.06	492	Barry Larkin	.12	.09	.05
402	Brian Holton	.05	.04	.02	493	Fred Manrique	.25	.20	.10
403	Carmen Castillo	.05	.04	.02	494	Mike Griffin	.05	.04	.02
404	Jamie Quirk	.05	.04	.02	495	Mark Knudson	.15	.11	.06
405	Dwayne Murphy	.05	.04	.02	496	Bill Madlock	.12	.09	.05
406	Jeff Parrett	.20	.15	.08	497	Tim Stoddard	.05	.04	.02
407	Don Sutton	.20	.15	.08	498	Sam Horn	1.00	.70	.40
408	Jerry Browne	.07	.05	.03	499	Tracy Woodson	.25	.20	.10
409	Jim Winn	.05	.04	.02	500	Checklist 452-557	.05	.04	.02

		MT	NR MT	EX
501	Ken Schrom	.05	.04	.02
502	Angel Salazar	.05	.04	.02
503	Eric Plunk	.05	.04	.02
504	Joe Hesketh	.05	.04	.02
505	Greg Minton	.05	.04	.02
506	Geno Petralli	.05	.04	.02
507	Bob James	.05	.04	.02
508	Robbie Wine	.25	.20	.10
509	Jeff Calhoun	.05	.04	.02
510	Steve Lake	.05	.04	.02
511	Mark Grant	.05	.04	.02
512	Frank Williams	.05	.04	.02
513	Jeff Blauser	.25	.20	.10
514	Bob Walk	.05	.04	.02
515	Craig Lefferts	.05	.04	.02
516	Manny Trillo	.07	.05	.03
517	Jerry Reed	.05	.04	.02
518	Rick Leach	.05	.04	.02
519	Mark Davidson	.15	.11	.06
520	Jeff Ballard	.20	.15	.08
521	Dave Stapleton	.30	.25	.12
522	Pat Sheridan	.05	.04	.02
523	Al Nipper	.05	.04	.02
524	Steve Trout	.07	.05	.03
525	Jeff Hamilton	.07	.05	.03
526	Tommy Hinzo	.20	.15	.08
527	Lonnie Smith	.05	.04	.02
528	Greg Cadaret	.20	.15	.08
529	Rob McClure (Bob)	.05	.04	.02
530	Chuck Finley	.05	.04	.02
531	Jeff Russell	.05	.04	.02
532	Steve Lyons	.05	.04	.02
533	Terry Puhl	.05	.04	.02
534	Eric Nolte	.20	.15	.08
535	Kent Tekulve	.07	.05	.03
536	Pat Pacillo	.25	.20	.10
537	Charlie Puleo	.05	.04	.02
538	Tom Prince	.25	.20	.10
539	Greg Maddux	.07	.05	.03
540	Jim Lindeman	.10	.08	.04
541	Pete Stanicek	.30	.25	.12
542	Steve Kiefer	.05	.04	.02
543	Jim Morrison	.05	.04	.02
544	Spike Owen	.05	.04	.02
545	Jay Buhner	.35	.25	.14
546	Mike Devereaux	.35	.25	.14
547	Jerry Don Gleaton	.05	.04	.02
548	Jose Rijo	.05	.04	.02
549	Dennis Martinez	.05	.04	.02
550	Mike Loynd	.07	.05	.03
551	Darrell Miller	.05	.04	.02
552	Dave LaPoint	.05	.04	.02
553	John Tudor	.10	.08	.04
554	Rocky Childress	.20	.15	.08
555	Wally Ritchie	.20	.15	.08
556	Terry McGriff	.05	.04	.02
557	Dave Leiper	.05	.04	.02
558	Jeff Robinson	.07	.05	.03
559	Jose Uribe	.05	.04	.02
560	Ted Simmons	.12	.09	.05
561	Lester Lancaster	.25	.20	.10
562	Keith Miller	.30	.25	.12
563	Harold Reynolds	.07	.05	.03
564	Gene Larkin	.15	.11	.06
565	Cecil Fielder	.07	.05	.03
566	Roy Smalley	.05	.04	.02
567	Duane Ward	.05	.04	.02
568	Bill Wilkinson	.20	.15	.08
569	Howard Johnson	.10	.08	.04
570	Frank DiPino	.05	.04	.02
571	Pete Smith	.20	.15	.08
572	Darnell Coles	.07	.05	.03
573	Don Robinson	.05	.04	.02
574	Rob Nelson	.05	.04	.02
575	Dennis Rasmussen	.07	.05	.03
576	Steve Jeltz	.05	.04	.02
577	Tom Pagnozzi	.20	.15	.08
578	Ty Gainey	.05	.04	.02
579	Gary Lucas	.05	.04	.02
580	Ron Hassey	.05	.04	.02
581	Herm Winningham	.05	.04	.02
582	Rene Gonzales	.20	.15	.08
583	Brad Komminsk	.05	.04	.02
584	Doyle Alexander	.10	.08	.04
585	Jeff Sellers	.07	.05	.03
586	Bill Gullickson	.07	.05	.03
587	Tim Belcher	.15	.11	.06
588	Doug Jones	.20	.15	.08
589	Melido Perez	.20	.15	.08
590	Rick Honeycutt	.05	.04	.02
591	Pascual Perez	.07	.05	.03

		MT	NR MT	EX
592	Curt Wilkerson	.05	.04	.02
593	Steve Howe	.07	.05	.03
594	John Davis	.25	.20	.10
595	Storm Davis	.05	.04	.02
596	Sammy Stewart	.05	.04	.02
597	Neil Allen	.05	.04	.02
598	Alejandro Pena	.05	.04	.02
599	Mark Thurmond	.05	.04	.02
600	Checklist 558-660	.05	.04	.02
601	Jose Mesa	.20	.15	.08
602	Don August	.20	.15	.08
603	Terry Leach	.07	.05	.03
604	Tom Newell	.20	.15	.08
605	Randall Byers	.20	.15	.08
606	Jim Gott	.05	.04	.02
607	Harry Spilman	.05	.04	.02
608	John Candelaria	.07	.05	.03
609	Mike Brumley	.20	.15	.08
610	Mickey Brantley	.05	.04	.02
611	Jose Nunez	.25	.20	.10
612	Tom Nieto	.05	.04	.02
613	Rick Reuschel	.10	.08	.04
614	Lee Mazzilli	.07	.05	.03
615	Scott Lusader	.30	.25	.12
616	Bobby Meacham	.05	.04	.02
617	Kevin McReynolds	.10	.08	.04
618	Gene Garber	.05	.04	.02
619	Barry Lyons	.20	.15	.08
620	Randy Myers	.07	.05	.03
621	Donnie Moore	.05	.04	.02
622	Domingo Ramos	.05	.04	.02
623	Ed Romero	.05	.04	.02
624	Greg Myers	.20	.15	.08
625	Ripken Baseball Family (Billy Ripken, Cal Ripken, Jr., Cal Ripken, Sr.)	.25	.20	.10
626	Pat Perry	.05	.04	.02
627	Andres Thomas	.10	.08	.04
628	Matt Williams	.35	.25	.14
629	Dave Hengel	.20	.15	.08
630	Jeff Musselman	.07	.05	.03
631	Tim Laudner	.05	.04	.02
632	Bob Ojeda	.10	.08	.04
633	Rafael Santana	.05	.04	.02
634	Wes Gardner	.20	.15	.08
635	Roberto Kelly	.30	.25	.12
636	Mike Flanagan	.07	.05	.03
637	Jay Bell	.20	.15	.08
638	Bob Melvin	.05	.04	.02
639	Damon Berryhill	.25	.20	.10
640	David Wells	.20	.15	.08
641	Stan Musial Puzzle Card	.05	.04	.02
642	Doug Sisk	.05	.04	.02
643	Keith Hughes	.20	.15	.08
644	Tom Glavine	.35	.25	.14
645	Al Newman	.05	.04	.02
646	Scott Sanderson	.05	.04	.02
647	Scott Terry	.05	.04	.02
648	Tim Teufel	.05	.04	.02
649	Garry Templeton	.07	.05	.03
650	Manny Lee	.05	.04	.02
651	Roger McDowell	.07	.05	.03
652	Mookie Wilson	.07	.05	.03
653	David Cone	.07	.05	.03
654	Ron Gant	.25	.20	.10
655	Joe Price	.05	.04	.02
656	George Bell	.30	.25	.12
657	Gregg Jefferies	1.00	.70	.40
658	Todd Stottlemyre	.35	.25	.14
659	Geronimo Berroa	.20	.15	.08
660	Jerry Royster	.05	.04	.02

1986 Dorman's Cheese

Found in specially-marked packages of Dorman's American Cheese Singles, the Dorman's set consists of ten two-card panels of baseball superstars. Labelled as a "Super Star Limited Edition" set, the panels measure 1½" by 2" each and have a perforation line in the center. The fronts contain a color photo along with the Dorman's logo and the player's name, team and position. Due to a lack of proper licensing, all team insignias have been airbrushed from the players' caps. The backs of the cards contain brief player statistics.

or horizontal format. The last fifty cards are the scarcest of the set. Cards cut to form two single cards have little value.

	MT	NR MT	EX
Complete Panel Set:	30.00	22.00	12.00
Complete Singles Set:	12.00	9.00	4.75
Common Panel:	1.25	.90	.50
Common Single Player:	.15	.11	.06
Panel	2.00	1.50	.80
(1) George Brett	.50	.40	.20
(2) Jack Morris	.15	.11	.06
Panel	2.00	1.50	.80
(3) Gary Carter	.40	.30	.15
(4) Cal Ripken	.40	.30	.15
Panel	2.00	1.50	.80
(5) Dwight Gooden	.60	.45	.25
(6) Kent Hrbek	.20	.15	.08
Panel	2.00	1.50	.80
(7) Rickey Henderson	.40	.30	.15
(8) Mike Schmidt	.50	.40	.20
Panel	2.00	1.50	.80
(9) Keith Hernandez	.30	.25	.12
(10) Dale Murphy	.50	.40	.20
Panel	2.00	1.50	.80
(11) Reggie Jackson	.40	.30	.15
(12) Eddie Murray	.40	.30	.15
Panel	3.25	2.50	1.25
(13) Don Mattingly	.80	.60	.30
(14) Ryne Sandberg	.30	.25	.12
Panel	1.25	.90	.50
(15) Willie McGee	.15	.11	.06
(16) Robin Yount	.20	.15	.08
Panel	2.00	1.50	.80
(17) Rick Sutcliff (Sutcliffe)	.15	.11	.06
(18) Wade Boggs	.70	.50	.30
Panel	1.75	1.25	.70
(19) Dave Winfield	.40	.30	.15
(20) Jim Rice	.35	.25	.14

1941 Double Play

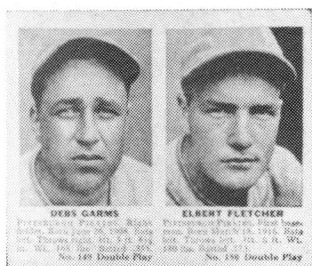

Issued by Gum, Inc., this set includes 75 numbered cards (two consecutive numbers per card) featuring 150 baseball players. The cards, which are blank-backed and measure 2½'' by 3⅛'', contain sepia tone photos of two players. Action and portrait poses are found in the set with card designs on either a vertical

		NR MT	EX	VG
Complete Set:		2600.00	1300.00	780.00
Common Player: 1-100		15.00	7.50	4.50
Common Player: 101-150		25.00	12.50	7.50
1	Larry French			
2	Vance Page	30.00	10.00	4.50
3	Billy Herman			
4	Stanley Hack	25.00	12.50	7.50
5	Linus Frey			
6	John Vander Meer	20.00	10.00	6.00
7	Paul Derringer			
8	Bucky Walters	15.00	7.50	4.50
9	Frank McCormick			
10	Bill Werber	15.00	7.50	4.50
11	Jimmy Ripple			
12	Ernie Lombardi	25.00	12.50	7.50
13	Alex Kampouris			
14	John Wyatt	18.00	9.00	5.50
15	Mickey Owen			
16	Paul Waner	25.00	12.50	7.50
17	Harry Lavagetto			
18	Harold Reiser	20.00	10.00	6.00
19	Jimmy Wasdell			
20	Dolph Camilli	20.00	10.00	6.00
21	Dixie Walker			
22	Ducky Medwick	25.00	12.50	7.50
23	Harold Reese			
24	Kirby Higbe	75.00	37.00	22.00
25	Harry Danning			
26	Cliff Melton	15.00	7.50	4.50
27	Harry Gumbert			
28	Burgess Whitehead	15.00	7.50	4.50
29	Joe Orengo			
30	Joe Moore	15.00	7.50	4.50
31	Mel Ott			
32	Babe Young	35.00	17.50	10.50
33	Lee Handley			
34	Arky Vaughan	25.00	12.50	7.50
35	Bob Klinger			
36	Stanley Brown	15.00	7.50	4.50
37	Terry Moore			
38	Gus Mancuso	15.00	7.50	4.50
39	Johnny Mize			
40	Enos Slaughter	45.00	22.00	13.50
41	John Cooney			
42	Sibby Sisti	15.00	7.50	4.50
43	Max West			
44	Carvel Rowell	15.00	7.50	4.50
45	Dan Litwhiler			
46	Merrill May	15.00	7.50	4.50
47	Frank Hayes			
48	Al Brancato	15.00	7.50	4.50
49	Bob Johnson			
50	Bill Nagel	15.00	7.50	4.50
51	Buck Newsom			
52	Hank Greenberg	30.00	15.00	9.00
53	Barney McCosky			
54	Charley Gehringer	30.00	15.00	9.00
55	Pinky Higgins			
56	Dick Bartell	15.00	7.50	4.50
57	Ted Williams			
58	Jim Tabor	150.00	75.00	45.00
59	Joe Cronin			
60	Jimmy Foxx	65.00	32.00	19.50
61	Lefty Gomez			
62	Phil Rizzuto	100.00	50.00	30.00
63	Joe DiMaggio			
64	Charley Keller	200.00	100.00	60.00
65	Red Rolfe			
66	Bill Dickey	45.00	22.00	13.50
67	Joe Gordon			
68	Red Ruffing	30.00	15.00	9.00
69	Mike Tresh			
70	Luke Appling	25.00	12.50	7.50
71	Moose Solters			
72	John Rigney	15.00	7.50	4.50
73	Buddy Meyer			
74	Ben Chapman	15.00	7.50	4.50
75	Cecil Travis			
76	George Case	15.00	7.50	4.50
77	Joe Krakauskas			
78	Bob Feller	65.00	32.00	19.50
79	Ken Keltner			
80	Hal Trosky	20.00	10.00	6.00
81	Ted Williams			
82	Joe Cronin	175.00	87.00	52.00

		NR MT	EX	VG
83	Joe Gordon			
84	Charley Keller	20.00	10.00	6.00
85	Hank Greenberg			
86	Red Ruffing	35.00	17.50	10.50
87	Hal Trosky			
88	George Case	15.00	7.50	4.50
89	Mel Ott			
90	Burgess Whitehead	35.00	17.50	10.50
91	Harry Danning			
92	Harry Gumbert	15.00	7.50	4.50
93	Babe Young			
94	Cliff Melton	15.00	7.50	4.50
95	Jimmy Ripple			
96	Bucky Walters	15.00	7.50	4.50
97	Stanley Hack			
98	Bob Klinger	15.00	7.50	4.50
99	Johnny Mize			
100	Dan Litwhiler	25.00	12.50	7.50
101	Dominic Dallessandro			
102	Augie Galan	25.00	12.50	7.50
103	Bill Lee			
104	Phil Cavarretta	25.00	12.50	7.50
105	Lefty Grove			
106	Bobby Doerr	60.00	30.00	18.00
107	Frank Pytlak			
108	Dom DiMaggio	30.00	15.00	9.00
109	Gerald Priddy			
110	John Murphy	30.00	15.00	9.00
111	Tommy Henrich			
112	Marius Russo	35.00	17.50	10.50
113	Frank Crosetti			
114	John Sturm	35.00	17.50	10.50
115	Ival Goodman			
116	Myron McCormick	25.00	12.50	7.50
117	Eddie Joost			
118	Ernest Koy	25.00	12.50	7.50
119	Lloyd Waner			
120	Henry Majeski	35.00	17.50	10.50
121	Buddy Hassett			
122	Eugene Moore	25.00	12.50	7.50
123	Nick Etten			
124	John Rizzo	25.00	12.50	7.50
125	Sam Chapman			
126	Wally Moses	25.00	12.50	7.50
127	John Babich			
128	Richard Siebert	25.00	12.50	7.50
129	Nelson Potter			
130	Benny McCoy	25.00	12.50	7.50
131	Clarence Campbell			
132	Louis Boudreau	35.00	17.50	10.50
133	Rolly Hemsley			
134	Mel Harder	25.00	12.50	7.50
135	Gerald Walker			
136	Joe Heving	25.00	12.50	7.50
137	John Rucker			
138	Ace Adams	25.00	12.50	7.50
139	Morris Arnovich			
140	Carl Hubbell	50.00	25.00	15.00
141	Lew Riggs			
142	Leo Durocher	35.00	17.50	10.50
143	Fred Fitzsimmons			
144	Joe Vosmik	25.00	12.50	7.50
145	Frank Crespi			
146	Jim Brown	25.00	12.50	7.50
147	Don Heffner			
148	Harland Clift (Harlond)	25.00	12.50	7.50
149	Debs Garms			
150	Elbert Fletcher	35.00	17.50	7.50

1950 Drake's

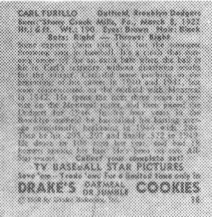

Entitled "TV Baseball Series", the 1950 Drake's Bakeries set pictures 36 different players on a televi-

sion screen format. The cards, which measure 2½" by 2½", contain black and white photos surrounded by a black border. The card backs carry a player biography plus an advertisement advising collectors to look for the cards in packages of Oatmeal or Jumble cookies. The ACC designation for the set is D358.

		NR MT	EX	VG
Complete Set:		2300.00	1150.00	690.00
Common Player:		35.00	17.50	10.50
1	Elwin "Preacher" Roe	75.00	37.00	22.00
2	Clint Hartung	35.00	17.50	10.50
3	Earl Torgeson	35.00	17.50	10.50
4	Leland "Lou" Brissie	35.00	17.50	10.50
5	Edwin "Duke" Snider	175.00	87.00	52.00
6	Roy Campanella	200.00	100.00	60.00
7	Sheldon "Available" Jones	35.00	17.50	10.50
8	Carroll "Whitey" Lockman	35.00	17.50	10.50
9	Bobby Thomson	40.00	20.00	12.00
10	Dick Sisler	35.00	17.50	10.50
11	Gil Hodges	100.00	50.00	30.00
12	Eddie Waitkus	35.00	17.50	10.50
13	Bobby Doerr	50.00	25.00	15.00
14	Warren Spahn	100.00	50.00	30.00
15	John "Buddy" Kerr	35.00	17.50	10.50
16	Sid Gordon	35.00	17.50	10.50
17	Willard Marshall	35.00	17.50	10.50
18	Carl Furillo	45.00	22.00	13.50
19	Harold "Pee Wee" Reese	125.00	62.00	37.00
20	Alvin Dark	40.00	20.00	12.00
21	Del Ennis	35.00	17.50	10.50
22	Ed Stanky	40.00	20.00	12.00
23	Tommy "Old Reliable" Henrich	50.00	25.00	15.00
24	Larry "Yogi" Berra	150.00	75.00	45.00
25	Phil "Scooter" Rizzuto	100.00	50.00	30.00
26	Jerry Coleman	45.00	22.00	13.50
27	Joe Page	45.00	22.00	13.50
28	Allie Reynolds	50.00	25.00	15.00
29	Ray Scarborough	35.00	17.50	10.50
30	George "Birdie" Tebbetts	35.00	17.50	10.50
31	Maurice "Lefty" McDermott	35.00	17.50	10.50
32	Johnny Pesky	40.00	20.00	12.00
33	Dom "Little Professor" DiMaggio	45.00	22.00	13.50
34	Vern "Junior" Stephens	35.00	17.50	10.50
35	Bob Elliott	35.00	17.50	10.50
36	Enos "Country" Slaughter	100.00	50.00	30.00

1981 Drake's

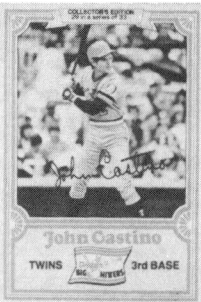
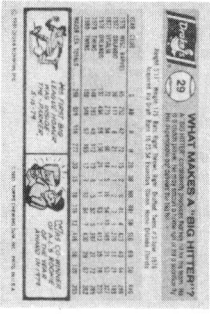

Producing their first baseball card set since 1950, Drake Bakeries, in conjunction with Topps, issued a 33-card set entitled "Big Hitters". The cards, which are the standard 2½" by 3½" in size, feature nineteen American League and fourteen National League sluggers. Full color photos, containing a facsimile autograph, are positioned in red frames for A.L. players and blue frames for N.L. hitters. The player's name, team, position, and the Drake's logo are also included on the card fronts. The card backs, which are similar to the regular 1981 Topps issue, contain the card number (1-33), statistical and biographical information, and the Drake's logo.

		MT	NR MT	EX
	Complete Set:	7.00	5.25	2.75
	Common Player:	.12	.09	.05
1	Carl Yastrzemski	.70	.50	.30
2	Rod Carew	.50	.40	.20
3	Pete Rose	.90	.70	.35
4	Dave Parker	.25	.20	.10
5	George Brett	.70	.50	.30
6	Eddie Murray	.60	.45	.25
7	Mike Schmidt	.70	.50	.30
8	Jim Rice	.45	.35	.20
9	Fred Lynn	.25	.20	.10
10	Reggie Jackson	.60	.45	.25
11	Steve Garvey	.45	.35	.20
12	Ken Singleton	.12	.09	.05
13	Bill Buckner	.12	.09	.05
14	Dave Winfield	.50	.40	.20
15	Jack Clark	.25	.20	.10
16	Cecil Cooper	.20	.15	.08
17	Bob Horner	.25	.20	.10
18	George Foster	.20	.15	.08
19	Dave Kingman	.20	.15	.08
20	Cesar Cedeno	.12	.09	.05
21	Joe Charboneau	.12	.09	.05
22	George Hendrick	.12	.09	.05
23	Gary Carter	.45	.35	.20
24	Al Oliver	.20	.15	.08
25	Bruce Bochte	.12	.09	.05
26	Jerry Mumphrey	.12	.09	.05
27	Steve Kemp	.12	.09	.05
28	Bob Watson	.20	.15	.08
29	John Castino	.12	.09	.05
30	Tony Armas	.12	.09	.05
31	John Mayberry	.12	.09	.05
32	Carlton Fisk	.30	.25	.12
33	Lee Mazzilli	.12	.09	.05

		MT	NR MT	EX
9	Cecil Cooper	.20	.15	.08
10	Jose Cruz	.12	.09	.05
11	Dwight Evans	.25	.20	.10
12	Carlton Fisk	.30	.25	.12
13	George Foster	.20	.15	.08
14	Steve Garvey	.45	.35	.20
15	Kirk Gibson	.40	.30	.15
16	Mike Hargrove	.12	.09	.05
17	George Hendrick	.12	.09	.05
18	Bob Horner	.25	.20	.10
19	Reggie Jackson	.60	.45	.25
20	Terry Kennedy	.12	.09	.05
21	Dave Kingman	.20	.15	.08
22	Greg Luzinski	.20	.15	.08
23	Bill Madlock	.20	.15	.08
24	John Mayberry	.12	.09	.05
25	Eddie Murray	.60	.45	.25
26	Graig Nettles	.20	.15	.08
27	Jim Rice	.45	.35	.20
28	Pete Rose	.90	.70	.35
29	Mike Schmidt	.70	.50	.30
30	Ken Singleton	.12	.09	.05
31	Dave Winfield	.50	.40	.20
32	Butch Wynegar	.12	.09	.05
33	Richie Zisk	.12	.09	.05

1982 Drake's

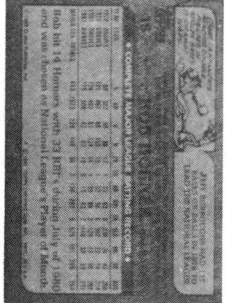

Drake Bakeries produced, in conjunction with Topps, a "2nd Annual Collectors' Edition" in 1982. Thirty-three standard-size cards (2½" by 3½") make up the set. Like the previous year, the set was entitled "Big Hitters" and was comprised of nineteen American League players and thirteen from the National League. The card fronts have a mounted photo appearance and contain a facsimile autograph. The player's name, team, position, and the Drake's logo also are located on the fronts. The card backs, other than being numbered 1-33 and containing a Drake's copyright line, are identical to the regular 1982 Topps issue.

		MT	NR MT	EX
	Complete Set:	9.00	6.75	3.50
	Common Player:	.12	.09	.05
1	Tony Armas	.12	.09	.05
2	Buddy Bell	.20	.15	.08
3	Johnny Bench	.50	.40	.20
4	George Brett	.70	.50	.30
5	Bill Buckner	.12	.09	.05
6	Rod Carew	.50	.40	.20
7	Gary Carter	.45	.35	.20
8	Jack Clark	.25	.20	.10

1983 Drake's

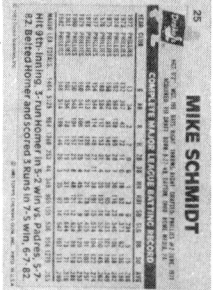

Seventeen American League and sixteen National League "Big Hitters" make up the 33-card "3rd Annual Collectors' Edition" set issued by Drake Bakeries in 1983. The Topps-produced set contains 33 cards which measure 2½" by 3½" in size. The card fronts are somewhat similar in design to the previous year's set. The backs are identical to the 1983 Topps regular issue except for being numbered 1-33 and containing a Drake's logo and copyright line.

		MT	NR MT	EX
	Complete Set:	5.00	3.75	2.00
	Common Player:	.12	.09	.05
1	Don Baylor	.20	.15	.08
2	Bill Buckner	.12	.09	.05
3	Rod Carew	.45	.35	.20
4	Gary Carter	.45	.35	.20
5	Jack Clark	.25	.20	.10
6	Cecil Cooper	.20	.15	.08
7	Dwight Evans	.25	.20	.10
8	George Foster	.20	.15	.08
9	Pedro Guerrero	.30	.25	.12
10	George Hendrick	.12	.09	.05
11	Bob Horner	.25	.20	.10
12	Reggie Jackson	.60	.45	.25
13	Steve Kemp	.12	.09	.05
14	Dave Kingman	.20	.15	.08
15	Bill Madlock	.20	.15	.08
16	Gary Matthews	.12	.09	.05
17	Hal McRae	.12	.09	.05
18	Dale Murphy	.70	.50	.30
19	Eddie Murray	.60	.45	.25
20	Ben Oglivie	.12	.09	.05
21	Al Oliver	.20	.15	.08
22	Jim Rice	.45	.35	.20
23	Cal Ripken	.60	.45	.25
24	Pete Rose	.90	.70	.35
25	Mike Schmidt	.70	.50	.30

		MT	NR MT	EX
26	Ken Singleton	.12	.09	.05
27	Gorman Thomas	.12	.09	.05
28	Jason Thompson	.12	.09	.05
29	Mookie Wilson	.20	.15	.08
30	Willie Wilson	.20	.15	.08
31	Dave Winfield	.50	.40	.20
32	Carl Yastrzemski	.70	.50	.30
33	Robin Yount	.40	.30	.15

1984 Drake's

 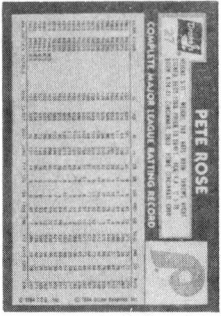

For the fourth year in a row, Drake Bakeries issued a 33-card "Big Hitters" set. The 1984 edition, produced again by Topps, includes 17 National League players and 16 from the American League. As in all previous years, the card fronts feature the player in a batting pose. The backs are identical to the 1984 Topps regular issue except for being numbered 1-33 and carrying the Drake's logo and copyright line. The cards are the standard size 2½" by 3½".

		MT	NR MT	EX
Complete Set:		5.00	3.75	2.00
Complete Set:		.12	.09	.05
1	Don Baylor	.20	.15	.08
2	Wade Boggs	1.25	.90	.50
3	George Brett	.70	.50	.30
4	Bill Buckner	.12	.09	.05
5	Rod Carew	.50	.40	.20
6	Gary Carter	.45	.35	.20
7	Ron Cey	.12	.09	.07
8	Cecil Cooper	.20	.15	.08
9	Andre Dawson	.35	.25	.14
10	Steve Garvey	.45	.35	.20
11	Pedro Guerrero	.30	.25	.12
12	George Hendrick	.12	.09	.05
13	Keith Hernandez	.45	.35	.20
14	Bob Horner	.25	.20	.10
15	Reggie Jackson	.60	.45	.25
16	Steve Kemp	.12	.09	.05
17	Ron Kittle	.20	.15	.08
18	Greg Luzinski	.20	.15	.08
19	Fred Lynn	.20	.15	.08
20	Bill Madlock	.20	.15	.08
21	Gary Matthews	.12	.09	.05
22	Dale Murphy	.70	.50	.30
23	Eddie Murray	.60	.45	.25
24	Al Oliver	.20	.15	.08
25	Jim Rice	.45	.35	.20
26	Cal Ripken	.60	.45	.25
27	Pete Rose	.90	.70	.35
28	Mike Schmidt	.70	.50	.30
29	Darryl Strawberry	1.25	.90	.50
30	Alan Trammell	.25	.20	.10
31	Mookie Wilson	.20	.15	.08
32	Dave Winfield	.50	.40	.20
33	Robin Yount	.40	.30	.15

1985 Drake's

The "5th Annual Collectors' Edition" set produced by Topps for Drake Bakeries consists of 33 "Big Hit-

 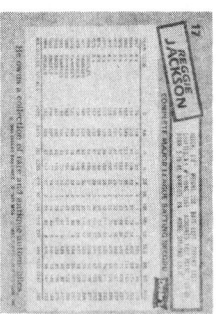

ters" and 11 "Super Pitchers". The new "Super Pitchers" feature increased the set's size from the usual 33 cards to 44. The cards, which measure 2½" by 3½", show the player in either a batting or pitching pose. The backs differ only from the regular 1985 Topps issue in that they are numbered 1-44 and carry the Drake's logo.

		MT	NR MT	EX
Complete Set:		9.00	6.75	3.50
Commmon Player:		.12	.09	.05
1	Tony Armas	.12	.09	.05
2	Harold Baines	.20	.15	.08
3	Don Baylor	.20	.15	.08
4	George Brett	.60	.45	.25
5	Gary Carter	.40	.30	.15
6	Ron Cey	.12	.09	.05
7	Jose Cruz	.12	.09	.05
8	Alvin Davis	.20	.15	.08
9	Chili Davis	.12	.09	.05
10	Dwight Evans	.25	.20	.10
11	Steve Garvey	.40	.30	.15
12	Kirk Gibson	.30	.25	.12
13	Pedro Guerrero	.25	.20	.10
14	Tony Gwynn	.40	.30	.15
15	Keith Hernandez	.35	.25	.14
16	Kent Hrbek	.30	.25	.12
17	Reggie Jackson	.40	.30	.15
18	Gary Matthews	.12	.09	.05
19	Don Mattingly	2.25	1.75	.90
20	Dale Murphy	.60	.45	.25
21	Eddie Murray	.50	.40	.20
22	Dave Parker	.20	.15	.08
23	Lance Parrish	.25	.20	.10
24	Tim Raines	.35	.25	.14
25	Jim Rice	.40	.30	.15
26	Cal Ripken	.50	.40	.20
27	Juan Samuel	.20	.15	.08
28	Ryne Sandberg	.30	.25	.12
29	Mike Schmidt	.50	.40	.20
30	Darryl Strawberry	.40	.30	.15
31	Alan Trammell	.20	.15	.08
32	Dave Winfield	.35	.25	.14
33	Robin Yount	.25	.20	.10
34	Mike Boddicker	.12	.09	.05
35	Steve Carlton	.30	.25	.12
36	Dwight Gooden	1.50	1.25	.60
37	Willie Hernandez	.12	.09	.05
38	Mark Langston	.20	.15	.08
39	Dan Quisenberry	.12	.09	.05
40	Dave Righetti	.20	.15	.08
41	Tom Seaver	.30	.25	.12
42	Bob Stanley	.12	.09	.05
43	Rick Sutcliffe	.20	.15	.08
44	Bruce Sutter	.20	.15	.08

1986 Drake's

For the sixth year in a row, Drake Bakeries issued a baseball card set. Produced for Drake's by Topps in the past, the '86 set was not and was available only by buying the actual products the cards were printed on. The cards, which measure 2½" by 3½", were issued in either two-, three- or four-card panels. Fourteen panels, consisting of 37 different players, comprise

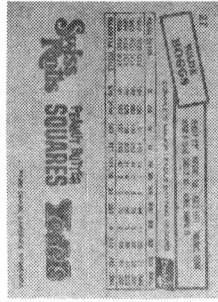

1987 Drake's

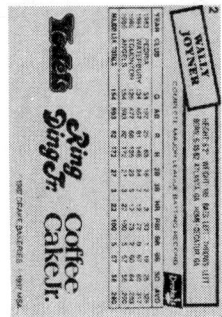

the set. The players who make up the set are tabbed as either "Big Hitters" or "Super Pitchers." Logos of various Drake's products can be found on the panel backs. The value of the set is higher when collected in either panel or complete box form.

		MT	NR MT	EX
Complete Panel Set:		40.00	30.00	16.00
Complete Singles Set:		25.00	18.50	10.00
Common Panel:		1.75	1.25	.70
Common Single Player:		.20	.15	.08
Panel		1.75	1.25	.70
1	Gary Carter	.50	.40	.20
2	Dwight Evans	.25	.20	.10
Panel		1.75	1.25	.70
3	Reggie Jackson	.50	.40	.20
4	Dave Parker	.25	.20	.10
Panel		1.75	1.25	.70
5	Rickey Henderson	.50	.40	.20
6	Pedro Guerrero	.30	.25	.12
Panel		4.50	3.50	1.75
7	Don Mattingly	1.75	1.25	.70
8	Mike Marshall	.25	.20	.10
9	Keith Moreland	.25	.20	.10
Panel		1.75	1.25	.70
10	Keith Hernandez	.35	.25	.14
11	Cal Ripken	.40	.30	.15
Panel		2.25	1.75	.90
12	Dale Murphy	.60	.45	.25
13	Jim Rice	.50	.40	.20
Panel		2.25	1.75	.90
14	George Brett	.60	.45	.25
15	Tim Raines	.50	.40	.20
Panel		1.75	1.25	.70
16	Darryl Strawberry	.60	.45	.25
17	Bill Buckner	.25	.20	.10
Panel		2.75	2.00	1.00
18	Dave Winfield	.50	.40	.20
19	Ryne Sandberg	.35	.25	.14
20	Steve Balboni	.25	.20	.10
21	Tom Herr	.25	.20	.10
Panel		3.50	2.75	1.50
22	Pete Rose	.70	.50	.30
23	Willie McGee	.25	.20	.10
24	Harold Baines	.25	.20	.10
25	Eddie Murray	.50	.40	.20
Panel		4.00	3.00	1.50
26	Mike Schmidt	.60	.45	.25
27	Wade Boggs	1.00	.70	.40
28	Kirk Gibson	.35	.25	.14
Panel		1.75	1.25	.70
29	Bret Saberhagen	.35	.25	.14
30	John Tudor	.20	.15	.08
31	Orel Hershiser	.35	.25	.14
Panel		2.00	1.50	.80
32	Ron Guidry	.25	.20	.10
33	Nolan Ryan	.35	.25	.14
34	Dave Stieb	.25	.20	.10
Panel		2.50	2.00	1.00
35	Dwight Gooden	.70	.50	.30
36	Fernando Valenzuela	.35	.25	.14
37	Tom Browning	.25	.20	.10

Definitions for grading conditions are located in the Introduction of this price guide.

For the seventh consecutive season, Drake Bakeries produced a baseball card set. The cards, which measure 2½" by 3½", were included in either two-, three-, or four-card panels on boxes of various Drake's products distributed in the eastern United States. The set is comprised of 33 cards, with 25 players branded as "Big Hitters" and 8 as "Super Pitchers." The card fronts carry a full-color photo and the Drake's logo surrounded by a brown and yellow border. The backs contain the player's complete major league record.

		MT	NR MT	EX
Complete Panel Set:		40.00	30.00	16.00
Complete Singles Set:		25.00	18.50	10.00
Common Panel:		1.75	1.25	.70
Common Single Player:		.20	.15	.08
Panel		4.25	3.25	1.75
1	Darryl Strawberry	.60	.45	.25
2	Wally Joyner	1.50	1.25	.60
Panel		3.50	2.75	1.50
3	Von Hayes	.25	.20	.10
4	Jose Canseco	1.50	1.25	.60
Panel		2.00	1.50	.80
5	Dave Winfield	.50	.40	.20
6	Cal Ripken	.50	.40	.20
Panel		4.50	3.50	1.75
7	Keith Moreland	.20	.15	.08
8	Don Mattingly	1.75	1.25	.70
9	Willie McGee	.25	.20	.10
Panel		1.75	1.25	.70
10	Keith Hernandez	.35	.25	.14
11	Tony Gwynn	.50	.40	.20
Panel		4.50	3.50	1.75
12	Rickey Henderson	.50	.40	.20
13	Dale Murphy	.60	.45	.25
14	George Brett	.60	.45	.25
15	Jim Rice	.50	.40	.20
Panel		3.75	2.75	1.50
16	Wade Boggs	1.00	.70	.40
17	Kevin Bass	.20	.15	.08
18	Dave Parker	.25	.20	.10
19	Kirby Puckett	.40	.30	.15
Panel		2.00	1.50	.80
20	Gary Carter	.50	.40	.20
21	Ryne Sandberg	.35	.25	.14
22	Harold Baines	.25	.20	.10
Panel		2.75	2.00	1.00
23	Mike Schmidt	.60	.45	.25
24	Eddie Murray	.50	.40	.20
25	Steve Sax	.25	.20	.10
Panel		1.75	1.25	.70
26	Dwight Gooden	.60	.45	.25
27	Jack Morris	.25	.20	.10
Panel		1.75	1.25	.70
28	Ron Darling	.25	.20	.10
29	Fernando Valenzuela	.35	.25	.14
30	John Tudor	.20	.15	.08
Panel		2.50	2.00	1.00
31	Roger Clemens	.70	.50	.30
32	Nolan Ryan	.35	.25	.14
33	Mike Scott	.25	.20	.10

1909-11 E90-1

 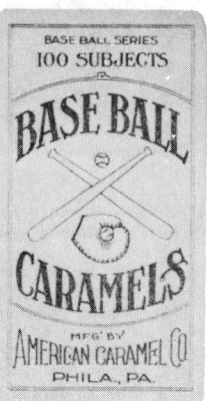

Davis, 1b Phila. Amer.

The E90-1 set was issued by the American Caramel Co. from 1909 through 1911, with the bulk of the set being produced in the first year. The cards, which measure 1½'' by 2¾'' in size and were issued with sticks of caramel candy, are color art reproductions of actual photographs. The card backs state that 100 subjects are included in the set though more actually do exist. There are several levels of scarcity in the set, those levels being mostly determined by the year the cards were issued. Mitchell (Cincinnati), Clarke (Pittsburg), Graham, and Sweeney (Boston) are the most difficult cards in the set to obtain. For the collector's convenience, the players' first names have been added in the checklist that follows.

		NR MT	EX	VG
	Complete Set:	16000.00	8000.00	4000.
	Common Player:	35.00	17.50	10.50
(1)	Bill Bailey	35.00	17.50	10.50
(2)	Home Run Baker	90.00	45.00	27.00
(3)	Jack Barry	35.00	17.50	10.50
(4)	George Bell	35.00	17.50	10.50
(5)	Harry Bemis	70.00	35.00	21.00
(6)	Chief Bender	80.00	40.00	24.00
(7)	Bob Bescher	65.00	32.00	19.50
(8)	Cliff Blankenship	35.00	17.50	10.50
(9)	John Bliss	35.00	17.50	10.50
(10)	Bill Bradley	35.00	17.50	10.50
(11)	Kitty Bransfield ("P" on shirt)	35.00	17.50	10.50
(12)	Kitty Bransfield (no "P" on shirt)	65.00	32.00	19.50
(13)	Roger Bresnahan	80.00	40.00	24.00
(14)	Al Bridwell	35.00	17.50	10.50
(15)	Buster Brown (Boston)	35.00	17.50	10.50
(16)	Mordecai Brown (Chicago)	125.00	62.00	37.00
(17)	Donie Bush	35.00	17.50	10.50
(18)	John Butler	35.00	17.50	10.50
(19)	Howie Camnitz	35.00	17.50	10.50
(20)	Frank Chance	90.00	45.00	27.00
(21)	Hal Chase	45.00	22.00	13.50
(22a)	Fred Clarke (Philadelphia)	70.00	35.00	21.00
(22b)	Fred Clarke (Pittsburgh)	550.00	275.00	165.00
(23)	Wally Clement	65.00	32.00	19.50
(24)	Ty Cobb	600.00	300.00	180.00
(25)	Eddie Collins	90.00	45.00	27.00
(26)	Sam Crawford	80.00	40.00	24.00
(27)	Frank Corridon	35.00	17.50	10.50
(28)	Lou Criger	35.00	17.50	10.50
(29)	George Davis	35.00	17.50	10.50
(30)	Harry Davis	35.00	17.50	10.50
(31)	Ray Demmitt	65.00	32.00	19.50
(32)	Mike Donlin	35.00	17.50	10.50

		NR MT	EX	VG
(33)	Wild Bill Donovan	35.00	17.50	10.50
(34)	Red Dooin	35.00	17.50	10.50
(35)	Patsy Dougherty	65.00	32.00	19.50
(36)	Hugh Duffy	600.00	300.00	180.00
(37)	Jimmy Dygert	35.00	17.50	10.50
(38)	Rube Ellis	35.00	17.50	10.50
(39)	Clyde Engle	35.00	17.50	10.50
(40)	Art Fromme	80.00	40.00	24.00
(41)	George Gibson (back view)	125.00	62.00	37.00
(42)	George Gibson (front view)	35.00	17.50	10.50
(43)	Peaches Graham	800.00	400.00	240.00
(44)	Eddie Grant	35.00	17.50	10.50
(45)	Dolly Gray	35.00	17.50	10.50
(46)	Bob Groom	35.00	17.50	10.50
(47)	Charley Hall	35.00	17.50	10.50
(48)	Roy Hartzell (fielding)	35.00	17.50	10.50
(49)	Roy Hartzell (batting)	35.00	17.50	10.50
(50)	Heinie Heitmuller	35.00	17.50	10.50
(51)	Harry Howell (follow thru)	35.00	17.50	10.50
(52)	Harry Howell (windup)	65.00	32.00	19.50
(53)	Tex Irwin (Erwin)	35.00	17.50	10.50
(54)	Frank Isbell	35.00	17.50	10.50
(55)	Shoeless Joe Jackson	800.00	400.00	240.00
(56)	Hughie Jennings	80.00	40.00	24.00
(57)	Buck Jordon (Jordan)	35.00	17.50	10.50
(58)	Addie Joss (portrait)	80.00	40.00	24.00
(59)	Addie Joss (pitching)	550.00	275.00	165.00
(60)	Ed Karger	550.00	275.00	165.00
(61a)	Willie Keeler (portrait, pink background)			
		80.00	40.00	24.00
(61b)	Willie Keeler (portrait, red background)			
		175.00	87.00	52.00
(62)	Willie Keeler (fielding)	600.00	300.00	180.00
(63)	John Knight	35.00	17.50	10.50
(64)	Harry Krause	35.00	17.50	10.50
(65)	Nap Lajoie	200.00	100.00	60.00
(66)	Tommy Leach (throwing)	35.00	17.50	10.50
(67)	Tommy Leach (batting)	35.00	17.50	10.50
(68)	Sam Leever	35.00	17.50	10.50
(69)	Hans Lobert	65.00	32.00	19.50
(70)	Harry Lumley	35.00	17.50	10.50
(71)	Rube Marquard	80.00	40.00	24.00
(72)	Christy Matthewson (Mathewson)			
		275.00	137.00	82.00
(73)	Stuffy McInnes (McInnis)	35.00	17.50	10.50
(74)	Harry McIntyre	35.00	17.50	10.50
(75)	Larry McLean	65.00	32.00	19.50
(76)	George McQuillan	35.00	17.50	10.50
(77)	Dots Miller	35.00	17.50	10.50
(78)	Fred Mitchell (New York)	35.00	17.50	10.50
(79)	Mike Mitchell (Cincinnati)	2000.00	1000.00	600.00
(80)	George Mullin	35.00	17.50	10.50
(81)	Rebel Oakes	35.00	17.50	10.50
(82)	Paddy O'Connor	35.00	17.50	10.50
(83)	Charley O'Leary	35.00	17.50	10.50
(84)	Orval Overall	65.00	32.00	19.50
(85)	Jim Pastorius	35.00	17.50	10.50
(86)	Ed Phelps	35.00	17.50	10.50
(87)	Eddie Plank	150.00	75.00	45.00
(88)	Lew Richie	35.00	17.50	10.50
(89)	Germany Schaefer	35.00	17.50	10.50
(90)	Biff Schlitzer	65.00	32.00	19.50
(91)	Johnny Seigle (Siegle)	65.00	32.00	19.50
(92)	Dave Shean	65.00	32.00	19.50
(93)	Jimmy Sheckard	65.00	32.00	19.50
(94)	Tris Speaker	500.00	250.00	150.00
(95)	Jake Stahl	550.00	275.00	165.00
(96)	Oscar Stanage	35.00	17.50	10.50
(97)	George Stone (no hands visible)	35.00	17.50	10.50
(98)	George Stone (left hand visible)	35.00	17.50	10.50
(99)	George Stovall	35.00	17.50	10.50
(100)	Ed Summers	35.00	17.50	10.50
(101)	Bill Sweeney (Boston)	800.00	400.00	240.00
(102)	Jeff Sweeney (New York)	35.00	17.50	10.50
(103)	Jesse Tannehill (Chicago A.L.)	35.00	17.50	10.50
(104)	Lee Tannehill (Chicago N.L.)	35.00	17.50	10.50
(105)	Fred Tenney	35.00	17.50	10.50
(106)	Ira Thomas (Philadelphia)	35.00	17.50	10.50
(107)	Roy Thomas (Boston)	35.00	17.50	10.50
(108)	Joe Tinker	80.00	40.00	24.00
(109)	Bob Unglaub	35.00	17.50	10.50
(110)	Jerry Upp	35.00	17.50	10.50
(111)	Honus Wagner (batting)	250.00	125.00	75.00
(112)	Honus Wagner (throwing)	250.00	125.00	75.00
(113)	Bobby Wallace	90.00	45.00	27.00
(114)	Ed Walsh	550.00	275.00	165.00
(115)	Vic Willis	35.00	17.50	10.50
(116)	Hooks Wiltse	65.00	32.00	19.50
(117)	Cy Young (Cleveland)	250.00	125.00	75.00
(118)	Cy Young (Boston)	150.00	75.00	45.00

1922 E120

BOSTON AMERICANS
"RED SOX"
MANAGER—HUGH DUFFY

HERB PENNOCK	PITCHER
ELMER MYERS	PITCHER
JACK QUINN	PITCHER
BEN KARR	PITCHER
HAROLD (MUDDY) RUEL	CATCHER
AL WALTERS	CATCHER
GEORGE BURNS	FIRST B. AND O. F.
DERRILL PRATT	SECOND BASE
CLARK PITTENGER	THIRD BASE
JOE DUGAN	INFIELD
NEMO LEIBOLD	OUTFIELD
ELMER SMITH	OUTFIELD
MIKE MENOSKY	OUTFIELD
JOHN (SHANO) COLLINS	UTILITY
JOE HARRIS	INFIELD AND OUTFIELD

THIS PICTURE IS ONE OF A SERIES OF 240 PICTURES OF BASEBALL STARS—15 PLAYERS IN EACH OF THE 16 MAJOR LEAGUE TEAMS. WE SUPPLY HANDSOME BLANK ALBUMS TO HOLD 120 PICTURES—ONE FOR AMERICAN LEAGUE, ONE FOR NATIONAL LEAGUE—FOR 16 CENTS EACH POSTPAID.

AMERICAN CARAMEL CO.
LANCASTER, PA.   YORK, PA.

JOHN (SHANO) COLLINS
UTILITY, BOSTON AMERICANS

One of the most popular of the "E" issues, the 1922 E120 set was produced by the American Caramel Co. in 1922 and distributed with sticks of caramel candy. The unnumbered cards measure 2'' by 3½'' in size. Cards depicting players from the American League are printed in brown ink on yellow, while the National Leaguers are printed in green on a blue-green background. The card reverses carry team checklists. Many of the E120 photos were used in other sets such as E121, W572, W573 and V61.

		NR MT	EX	VG
Complete Set:		7000.00	3500.00	2100.
Common Player:		20.00	10.00	6.00
(1)	Charles (Babe) Adams	20.00	10.00	6.00
(2)	Eddie Ainsmith	20.00	10.00	6.00
(3)	Vic Aldridge	20.00	10.00	6.00
(4)	Grover C. Alexander	45.00	22.00	13.50
(5)	Jim Bagby	20.00	10.00	6.00
(6)	Frank (Home Run) Baker	40.00	20.00	12.00
(7)	Dave (Beauty) Bancroft	40.00	20.00	12.00
(8)	Walt Barbare	20.00	10.00	6.00
(9)	Turner Barber	20.00	10.00	6.00
(10)	Jess Barnes	20.00	10.00	6.00
(11)	Clyde Barnhart	20.00	10.00	6.00
(12)	John Bassler	20.00	10.00	6.00
(13)	Will Bayne	20.00	10.00	6.00
(14)	Walter (Huck) Betts	20.00	10.00	6.00
(15)	Carson Bigbee	20.00	10.00	6.00
(16)	Lu Blue	20.00	10.00	6.00
(17)	Norman Boeckel	20.00	10.00	6.00
(18)	Sammy Bohne	20.00	10.00	6.00
(19)	George Burns	20.00	10.00	6.00
(20)	George Burns	20.00	10.00	6.00
(21)	"Bullet Joe" Bush	28.00	14.00	8.50
(22)	Leon Cadore	24.00	12.00	7.25
(23)	Marty Callaghan	20.00	10.00	6.00
(24)	Frank Calloway (Callaway)	20.00	10.00	6.00
(25)	Max Carey	40.00	20.00	12.00
(26)	Jimmy Caveney	20.00	10.00	6.00
(27)	Virgil Cheeves	20.00	10.00	6.00
(28)	Vern Clemons	20.00	10.00	6.00
(29)	Ty Cob (Cobb)	500.00	250.00	150.00
(30)	Bert Cole	20.00	10.00	6.00
(31)	Eddie Collins	50.00	25.00	15.00
(32)	John (Shano) Collins	20.00	10.00	6.00
(33)	T.P. (Pat) Collins	20.00	10.00	6.00
(34)	Wilbur Cooper	20.00	10.00	6.00
(35)	Harry Courtney	20.00	10.00	6.00
(36)	Stanley Coveleskie (Coveleski)	40.00	20.00	12.00
(37)	Elmer Cox	20.00	10.00	6.00
(38)	Sam Crane	20.00	10.00	6.00
(39)	Walton Cruise	20.00	10.00	6.00
(40)	Bill Cunningham	20.00	10.00	6.00
(41)	George Cutshaw	20.00	10.00	6.00
(42)	Dave Danforth	20.00	10.00	6.00
(43)	Jake Daubert	24.00	12.00	7.25
(44)	George Dauss	20.00	10.00	6.00
(45)	Frank (Dixie) Davis	20.00	10.00	6.00
(46)	Hank DeBerry	20.00	10.00	6.00
(47)	Albert (Lou) Devormer (DeVormer)			
		24.00	12.00	7.25
(48)	Bill Doak	20.00	10.00	6.00

		NR MT	EX	VG
(49)	Pete Donohue	20.00	10.00	6.00
(50)	"Shufflin" Phil Douglas	24.00	12.00	7.25
(51)	Joe Dugan	24.00	12.00	7.25
(52)	Louis (Pat) Duncan	20.00	10.00	6.00
(53)	Jimmy Dykes	24.00	12.00	7.25
(54)	Howard Ehmke	24.00	12.00	7.25
(55)	Frank Ellerbe	20.00	10.00	6.00
(56)	Urban (Red) Faber	40.00	20.00	12.00
(57)	Bib Falk (Bibb)	20.00	10.00	6.00
(58)	Dana Fillingim	20.00	10.00	6.00
(59)	Max Flack	20.00	10.00	6.00
(60)	Ira Flagstead	20.00	10.00	6.00
(61)	Art Fletcher	20.00	10.00	6.00
(62)	Horace Ford	20.00	10.00	6.00
(63)	Jack Fournier	20.00	10.00	6.00
(64)	Frank Frisch	50.00	25.00	15.00
(65)	Ollie Fuhrman	20.00	10.00	6.00
(66)	Clarence Galloway	20.00	10.00	6.00
(67)	Larry Gardner	20.00	10.00	6.00
(68)	Walter Gerber	20.00	10.00	6.00
(69)	Ed Gharrity	20.00	10.00	6.00
(70)	John Gillespie	20.00	10.00	6.00
(71)	Chas. (Whitey) Glazner	20.00	10.00	6.00
(72)	Johnny Gooch	20.00	10.00	6.00
(73)	Leon Goslin	40.00	20.00	12.00
(74)	Hank Gowdy	24.00	12.00	7.25
(75)	John Graney	20.00	10.00	6.00
(76)	Tom Griffith	20.00	10.00	6.00
(77)	Burleigh Grimes	40.00	20.00	12.00
(78)	Oscar Ray Grimes	20.00	10.00	6.00
(79)	Charlie Grimm	28.00	14.00	8.50
(80)	Heinie Groh	24.00	12.00	7.25
(81)	Jesse Haines	40.00	20.00	12.00
(82)	Earl Hamilton	20.00	10.00	6.00
(83)	Gene (Bubbles) Hargrave	20.00	10.00	6.00
(84)	Bryan Harris (Harriss)	20.00	10.00	6.00
(85)	Joe Harris	20.00	10.00	6.00
(86)	Stanley Harris	20.00	10.00	6.00
(87)	Chas. (Dowdy) Hartnett	40.00	20.00	12.00
(88)	Bob Hasty	20.00	10.00	6.00
(89)	Joe Hauser	24.00	12.00	7.25
(90)	Clif Heathcote (Cliff)	20.00	10.00	6.00
(91)	Harry Heilmann	40.00	20.00	12.00
(92)	Walter (Butch) Henline	20.00	10.00	6.00
(93)	Clarence (Shovel) Hodge	20.00	10.00	6.00
(94)	Walter Holke	20.00	10.00	6.00
(95)	Charles Hollocher	20.00	10.00	6.00
(96)	Harry Hooper	40.00	20.00	12.00
(97)	Rogers Hornsby	125.00	62.00	37.00
(98)	Waite Hoyt	40.00	20.00	12.00
(99)	Wilbur Hubbell (Wilbert)	20.00	10.00	6.00
(100)	Bernard (Bud) Hungling	20.00	10.00	6.00
(101)	Will Jacobson	20.00	10.00	6.00
(102)	Charlie Jamieson	20.00	10.00	6.00
(103)	Ernie Johnson	20.00	10.00	6.00
(104)	Sylvester Johnson	20.00	10.00	6.00
(105)	Walter Johnson	150.00	75.00	45.00
(106)	Jimmy Johnston	20.00	10.00	6.00
(107)	W.R. (Doc) Johnston	20.00	10.00	6.00
(108)	"Deacon" Sam Jones	24.00	12.00	7.25
(109)	Bob Jones	20.00	10.00	6.00
(110)	Percy Jones	20.00	10.00	6.00
(111)	Joe Judge	20.00	10.00	6.00
(112)	Ben Karr	20.00	10.00	6.00
(113)	Johnny Kelleher	20.00	10.00	6.00
(114)	George Kelly	40.00	20.00	12.00
(115)	Lee King	20.00	10.00	6.00
(116)	Wm (Larry) Kopff (Kopf)	20.00	10.00	6.00
(117)	Marty Krug	20.00	10.00	6.00
(118)	Johnny Lavan	20.00	10.00	6.00
(119)	Nemo Leibold	20.00	10.00	6.00
(120)	Roy Leslie	20.00	10.00	6.00
(121)	George Leverette (Leverett)	20.00	10.00	6.00
(122)	Adolfo Luque	20.00	10.00	6.00
(123)	Walter Mails	20.00	10.00	6.00
(124)	Al Mamaux	20.00	10.00	6.00
(125)	"Rabbit" Maranville	40.00	20.00	12.00
(126)	Cliff Markle	20.00	10.00	6.00
(127)	Richard (Rube) Marquard	40.00	20.00	12.00
(128)	Carl Mays	30.00	15.00	9.00
(129)	Hervey McClellan (Harvey)	20.00	10.00	6.00
(130)	Austin McHenry	20.00	10.00	6.00
(131)	"Stuffy" McInnis	24.00	12.00	7.25
(132)	Martin McManus	20.00	10.00	6.00
(133)	Mike McNally	24.00	12.00	7.25
(134)	Hugh McQuillan	20.00	10.00	6.00
(135)	Lee Meadows	20.00	10.00	6.00
(136)	Mike Menosky	20.00	10.00	6.00
(137)	Bob (Dutch) Meusel	30.00	15.00	9.00
(138)	Emil (Irish) Meusel	24.00	12.00	7.25
(139)	Clyde Milan	20.00	10.00	6.00

	NR MT	EX	VG
(140) Edmund (Bing) Miller	20.00	10.00	6.00
(141) Elmer Miller	24.00	12.00	7.25
(142) Lawrence (Hack) Miller	20.00	10.00	6.00
(143) Clarence Mitchell	20.00	10.00	6.00
(144) George Mogridge	20.00	10.00	6.00
(145) Roy Moore	20.00	10.00	6.00
(146) John L. Mokan	20.00	10.00	6.00
(147) John Morrison	20.00	10.00	6.00
(148) Johnny Mostil	20.00	10.00	6.00
(149) Elmer Myers	20.00	10.00	6.00
(150) Hy Myers	20.00	10.00	6.00
(151) Roliene Naylor (Roleine)	20.00	10.00	6.00
(152) Earl (Greasy) Neale	30.00	15.00	9.00
(153) Art Nehf	20.00	10.00	6.00
(154) Les Nunamaker	20.00	10.00	6.00
(155) Joe Oeschger	24.00	12.00	7.25
(156) Bob O'Farrell	20.00	10.00	6.00
(157) Ivan Olson	20.00	10.00	6.00
(158) George O'Neil	20.00	10.00	6.00
(159) Steve O'Neill	20.00	10.00	6.00
(160) Frank Parkinson	20.00	10.00	6.00
(161) Roger Peckinpaugh	24.00	12.00	7.25
(162) Herb Pennock	40.00	20.00	12.00
(163) Ralph (Cy) Perkins	20.00	10.00	6.00
(164) Will Pertica	20.00	10.00	6.00
(165) Jack Peters	20.00	10.00	6.00
(166) Tom Phillips	20.00	10.00	6.00
(167) Val Picinich	20.00	10.00	6.00
(168) Herman Pillette	20.00	10.00	6.00
(169) Ralph Pinelli	24.00	12.00	7.25
(170) Wallie Pipp	30.00	15.00	9.00
(171) Clark Pittenger (Clarke)	20.00	10.00	6.00
(172) Raymond Powell	20.00	10.00	6.00
(173) Derrill Pratt	20.00	10.00	6.00
(174) Jack Quinn	20.00	10.00	6.00
(175) Joe (Goldie) Rapp	20.00	10.00	6.00
(176) John Rawlings	20.00	10.00	6.00
(177) Walter (Dutch) Reuther (Ruether)			
	20.00	10.00	6.00
(178) Sam Rice	40.00	20.00	12.00
(179) Emory Rigney	20.00	10.00	6.00
(180) Jimmy Ring	20.00	10.00	6.00
(181) Eppa Rixey	40.00	20.00	12.00
(182) Charles Robertson	20.00	10.00	6.00
(183) Ed Rommel	24.00	12.00	7.25
(184) Eddie Roush	40.00	20.00	12.00
(185) Harold (Muddy) Ruel	20.00	10.00	6.00
(186) Babe Ruth	650.00	325.00	195.00
(187) Ray Schalk	40.00	20.00	12.00
(188) Wallie Schang	24.00	12.00	7.25
(189) Ray Schmandt	20.00	10.00	6.00
(190) Walter Schmidt	20.00	10.00	6.00
(191) Joe Schultz	20.00	10.00	6.00
(192) Everett Scott	24.00	12.00	7.25
(193) Henry Severeid	20.00	10.00	6.00
(194) Joe Sewell	40.00	20.00	12.00
(195) Howard Shanks	20.00	10.00	6.00
(196) Bob Shawkey	24.00	12.00	7.25
(197) Earl Sheely	20.00	10.00	6.00
(198) Will Sherdel	20.00	10.00	6.00
(199) Ralph Shinners	20.00	10.00	6.00
(200) Urban Shocker	20.00	10.00	6.00
(201) Charles (Chick) Shorten	20.00	10.00	6.00
(202) George Sisler	50.00	25.00	15.00
(203) Earl Smith	20.00	10.00	6.00
(204) Earl Smith	20.00	10.00	6.00
(205) Elmer Smith	20.00	10.00	6.00
(206) Jack Smith	20.00	10.00	6.00
(207) Sherrod Smith	20.00	10.00	6.00
(208) Colonel Snover	20.00	10.00	6.00
(209) Frank Snyder	20.00	10.00	6.00
(210) Al Sothoron	20.00	10.00	6.00
(211) Bill Southworth	24.00	12.00	7.25
(212) Tris Speaker	75.00	37.00	22.00
(213) Arnold Statz	20.00	10.00	6.00
(214) Milton Stock	20.00	10.00	6.00
(215) Amos Strunk	20.00	10.00	6.00
(216) Jim Tierney	20.00	10.00	6.00
(217) John Tobin	20.00	10.00	6.00
(218) Fred Toney	20.00	10.00	6.00
(219) George Toporcer	20.00	10.00	6.00
(220) Harold (Pie) Traynor	50.00	25.00	15.00
(221) George Uhle	20.00	10.00	6.00
(222) Elam Vangilder	20.00	10.00	6.00
(223) Bob Veach	20.00	10.00	6.00
(224) Clarence (Tillie) Walker	20.00	10.00	6.00
(225) Curtis Walker	20.00	10.00	6.00
(226) Al Walters	20.00	10.00	6.00
(227) Bill Wambsganss	28.00	14.00	8.50
(228) Aaron (Erin) Ward	24.00	12.00	7.25
(229) John Watson	20.00	10.00	6.00

	NR MT	EX	VG
(230) Frank Welch	20.00	10.00	6.00
(231) Zach Wheat	40.00	20.00	12.00
(232) Fred (Cy) Williams	24.00	12.00	7.25
(233) Kenneth Williams	24.00	12.00	7.25
(234) Ivy Wingo	20.00	10.00	6.00
(235) Joe Wood	30.00	15.00	9.00
(236) Lawrence Woodall	20.00	10.00	6.00
(237) Russell Wrightstone	20.00	10.00	6.00
(238) Everett Yaryan	20.00	10.00	6.00
(239) Ross Young (Youngs)	40.00	20.00	12.00
(240) J.T. Zachary	20.00	10.00	6.00

1921 E121 Series of 80

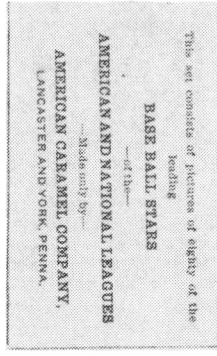

Issued circa 1921, the E121 Series of 80 is designated as such because of the card reverses which indicate the player pictured is just one of 80 baseball stars in the set. The figure of 80 supplied by the American Caramel Co. is incorrect as over 100 different pictures do exist. The unnumbered cards, which measure 2'' by 3½'', feature black and white photos. Two different backs exist for the Series of 80. The common back variation has the first line ending with the word "the", while the scarcer version ends with the word "eighty".

		NR MT	EX	VG
Complete Set:		4700.00	2350.00	1410.
Commmon Player:		20.00	10.00	6.00
(1)	G.C. Alexander (arms above head)			
		65.00	32.00	19.50
(2)	Grover Alexander	45.00	22.00	13.50
(3)	Jim Bagby	20.00	10.00	6.00
(4a)	J. Franklin Baker	40.00	20.00	12.00
(4b)	Frank Baker	40.00	20.00	12.00
(5)	Dave Bancroft (batting)	40.00	20.00	12.00
(6)	Dave Bancroft (leaping)	40.00	20.00	12.00
(7)	Ping Bodie	24.00	12.00	7.25
(8)	George Burns	20.00	10.00	6.00
(9)	Geo. J. Burns	20.00	10.00	6.00
(10)	Owen Bush	20.00	10.00	6.00
(11)	Max Carey (batting)	40.00	20.00	12.00
(12)	Max Carey (hands at hips)	40.00	20.00	12.00
(13)	Cecil Causey	20.00	10.00	6.00
(14)	Ty Cobb (throwing, looking front)			
		325.00	162.00	97.00
(15)	Ty Cobb (throwing, looking right)			
		325.00	162.00	97.00
(16)	Eddie Collins	40.00	20.00	12.00
(17)	"Rip" Collins	24.00	12.00	7.25
(18)	Jake Daubert	24.00	12.00	7.25
(19)	George Dauss	20.00	10.00	6.00
(20)	Charles Deal (dark uniform)	20.00	10.00	6.00
(21)	Charles Deal (white uniform)	20.00	10.00	6.00
(22)	William Doak	20.00	10.00	6.00
(23)	Bill Donovan	20.00	10.00	6.00
(24)	"Phil" Douglas	30.00	15.00	9.00
(25a)	Johnny Evers (Manager)	40.00	20.00	12.00
(25b)	Johnny Evers (Mgr.)	40.00	20.00	12.00
(26)	Urban Faber (dark uniform)	40.00	20.00	12.00
(27)	Urban Faber (white uniform)	40.00	20.00	12.00
(28)	William Fewster (first name actually			
	Wilson)	24.00	12.00	7.25

		NR MT	EX	VG
(29)	Eddie Foster	20.00	10.00	6.00
(30)	Frank Frisch	45.00	22.00	13.50
(31)	W.L. Gardner	20.00	10.00	6.00
(32)	Alexander Gaston	20.00	10.00	6.00
(33)	"Kid" Gleason	20.00	10.00	6.00
(34)	"Mike" Gonzalez	20.00	10.00	6.00
(35)	Hank Gowdy	24.00	12.00	7.25
(36)	John Graney	20.00	10.00	6.00
(37)	Tom Griffith	20.00	10.00	6.00
(38)	Heinie Groh	24.00	12.00	7.25
(39)	Harry Harper	24.00	12.00	7.25
(40)	Harry Heilman (Heilmann)	40.00	20.00	12.00
(41)	Walter Holke (portrait)	20.00	10.00	6.00
(42)	Walter Holke (throwing)	20.00	10.00	6.00
(43)	Charles Hollacher (Hollocher)	20.00	10.00	6.00
(44)	Harry Hooper	40.00	20.00	12.00
(45)	Rogers Hornsby	75.00	37.00	22.00
(46)	Waite Hoyt	40.00	20.00	12.00
(47)	Miller Huggins	40.00	20.00	12.00
(48)	Wm. C. Jacobson	20.00	10.00	6.00
(49)	Hugh Jennings	40.00	20.00	12.00
(50)	Walter Johnson (throwing)	100.00	50.00	30.00
(51)	Walter Johnson (hands at chest)	100.00	50.00	30.00
(52)	James Johnston	20.00	10.00	6.00
(53)	Joe Judge	20.00	10.00	6.00
(54)	George Kelly	40.00	20.00	12.00
(55)	Dick Kerr	20.00	10.00	6.00
(56)	P.J. Kilduff	20.00	10.00	6.00
(57a)	Bill Killifer (incorrect name)	30.00	15.00	9.00
(57b)	Bill Killefer (correct name)	24.00	12.00	7.25
(58)	John Lavan	20.00	10.00	6.00
(59)	"Nemo" Leibold	20.00	10.00	6.00
(60)	Duffy Lewis	24.00	12.00	7.25
(61)	Al Mamaux	20.00	10.00	6.00
(62)	"Rabbit" Maranville	40.00	20.00	12.00
(63a)	Carl May (incorrect name)	40.00	20.00	12.00
(63b)	Carl Mays (correct name)	30.00	15.00	9.00
(64)	John McGraw	45.00	22.00	13.50
(65)	Jack McInnis	24.00	12.00	7.25
(66)	M.J. McNally	24.00	12.00	7.25
(67)	Emil Muesel (Photo actually Lou DeVormer)	24.00	12.00	7.25
(68)	R. Meusel	30.00	15.00	9.00
(69)	Clyde Milan	20.00	10.00	6.00
(70)	Elmer Miller	24.00	12.00	7.25
(71)	Otto Miller	20.00	10.00	6.00
(72)	Guy Morton	20.00	10.00	6.00
(73)	Eddie Murphy	20.00	10.00	6.00
(74)	"Hy" Myers	20.00	10.00	6.00
(75)	Arthur Nehf	20.00	10.00	6.00
(76)	Steve O'Neill	20.00	10.00	6.00
(77a)	Roger Peckinbaugh (incorrect name)	24.00	12.00	7.25
(77b)	Roger Peckinpaugh (correct name)	30.00	15.00	9.00
(78a)	Jeff Pfeffer (Brooklyn)	24.00	12.00	7.25
(78b)	Jeff Pfeffer (St. Louis)	24.00	12.00	7.25
(79)	Walter Pipp	30.00	15.00	9.00
(80)	Jack Quinn	24.00	12.00	7.25
(81)	John Rawlings	20.00	10.00	6.00
(82)	E.C. Rice	40.00	20.00	12.00
(83)	Eppa Rixey, Jr.	40.00	20.00	12.00
(84)	Robert Roth	24.00	12.00	7.25
(85a)	Ed. Roush (C.F.)	40.00	20.00	12.00
(85b)	Ed. Roush (L.F.)	50.00	25.00	15.00
(86a)	Babe Ruth	550.00	275.00	165.00
(86b)	"Babe" Ruth	650.00	325.00	195.00
(86c)	George Ruth	650.00	275.00	165.00
(87)	"Bill" Ryan	20.00	10.00	6.00
(88)	"Slim" Sallee (glove showing)	20.00	10.00	6.00
(89)	"Slim" Sallee (no glove showing)	20.00	10.00	6.00
(90)	Ray Schalk	40.00	20.00	12.00
(91)	Walter Schang	24.00	12.00	7.25
(92a)	Fred Schupp (name incorrect)	30.00	15.00	9.00
(92b)	Ferd Schupp (name correct)	24.00	12.00	7.25
(93)	Everett Scott	20.00	10.00	6.00
(94)	Hank Severeid	20.00	10.00	6.00
(95)	Robert Shawkey	24.00	12.00	7.25
(96a)	Pat Shea ( )	30.00	15.00	9.00
(96b)	"Pat" Shea	24.00	12.00	7.25
(97)	George Sisler (batting)	45.00	22.00	13.50
(98)	George Sisler (throwing)	45.00	22.00	13.50
(99)	Earl Smith	20.00	10.00	6.00
(100)	Frank Snyder	20.00	10.00	6.00
(101a)	Tris Speaker (Mgr.)	60.00	30.00	18.00
(101b)	Tris Speaker (Manager - large projection)	60.00	30.00	18.00
(101c)	Tris Speaker (Manager - small projection)	75.00	37.00	22.00
(102)	Milton Stock	20.00	10.00	6.00

		NR MT	EX	VG
(103)	Amos Strunk	20.00	10.00	6.00
(104)	Zeb Terry	20.00	10.00	6.00
(105)	Chester Thomas	20.00	10.00	6.00
(106)	Fred Toney (trees in background)	20.00	10.00	6.00
(107)	Fred Toney (no trees in background)	20.00	10.00	6.00
(108)	George Tyler	20.00	10.00	6.00
(109)	Jim Vaughn (dark hat)	20.00	10.00	6.00
(110)	Jim Vaughn (white hat)	20.00	10.00	6.00
(111)	Bob Veach (glove in air)	20.00	10.00	6.00
(112)	Bob Veach (arms crossed)	20.00	10.00	6.00
(113)	Oscar Vitt	20.00	10.00	6.00
(114)	W. Wambsganss (photo actually Fred Coumbe)	24.00	12.00	7.25
(115)	Aaron Ward	24.00	12.00	7.25
(116)	Zach Wheat	40.00	20.00	12.00
(117)	George Whitted	20.00	10.00	6.00
(118)	Fred Williams	24.00	12.00	7.25
(119)	Ivy B. Wingo	20.00	10.00	6.00
(120)	Joe Wood	24.00	12.00	7.25
(121)	"Pep" Young	20.00	10.00	6.00

1922 E121 Series of 120

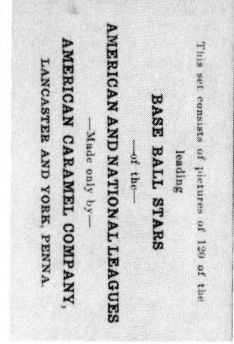

Produced by the American Caramel Co. circa 1922, the E121 Series of 120 is labelled as such by the company's claim that the set contained 120 subjects. Identical in design to the E121 Series of 80 set except for the card backs, the cards measure 2" by 3½" in size. Numerous variations are found in the set, most involving a change in the player's name, team or position.

		NR MT	EX	VG
	Complete Set:	5800.00	2900.00	1740.
	Common Player:	20.00	10.00	6.00
(1)	Chas. "Babe" Adams	20.00	10.00	6.00
(2)	G.C. Alexander	45.00	22.00	13.50
(3)	Jim Bagby	20.00	10.00	6.00
(4)	Dave Bancroft	40.00	20.00	12.00
(5)	Turner Barber	20.00	10.00	6.00
(6a)	Carlson Bigbee (correct name Carson L. Bigbee)	30.00	15.00	9.00
(6b)	Carlson L. Bigbee	24.00	12.00	7.25
(6c)	Corson L. Bigbee	30.00	15.00	9.00
(6d)	L. Bigbee	24.00	12.00	7.25
(7)	"Bullet Joe" Bush	24.00	12.00	7.25
(8)	Max Carey	40.00	20.00	12.00
(9)	Cecil Causey	20.00	10.00	6.00
(10)	Ty Cobb (batting)	325.00	162.00	97.00
(11)	Ty Cobb (throwing)	325.00	162.00	97.00
(12)	Eddie Collins	40.00	20.00	12.00
(13)	A. Wilbur Cooper	20.00	10.00	6.00
(14)	Stanley Coveleskie (Coveleski)	40.00	20.00	12.00
(15)	Dave Danforth	20.00	10.00	6.00
(16)	Jake Daubert	24.00	12.00	7.25
(17)	George Dauss	20.00	10.00	6.00
(18)	"Dixie" Davis	20.00	10.00	6.00
(19)	Lou DeVormer	24.00	12.00	7.25
(20)	William Doak	20.00	10.00	6.00
(21)	Phil Douglas	24.00	12.00	7.25
(22)	Urban Faber	40.00	20.00	12.00

		NR MT	EX	VG
(23)	Bib Falk (Bibb)	20.00	10.00	6.00
(24)	Wm: Fewster (first name actually Wilson)			
		24.00	12.00	7.25
(25)	Max Flack	20.00	10.00	6.00
(26)	Ira Falgstead (Flagstead)	20.00	10.00	6.00
(27)	Frank Frisch	45.00	22.00	13.50
(28)	W.L. Gardner	20.00	10.00	6.00
(29)	Alexander Gaston	20.00	10.00	6.00
(30)	E.P. Gharrity	20.00	10.00	6.00
(31)	George Gibson	20.00	10.00	6.00
(32)	Chas. "Whitey" Glazner	20.00	10.00	6.00
(33)	"Kid" Gleason	20.00	10.00	6.00
(34)	Hank Gowdy	24.00	12.00	7.25
(35)	John Graney	20.00	10.00	6.00
(36)	Tom Griffith	20.00	10.00	6.00
(37)	Chas. Grimm	30.00	15.00	9.00
(38)	Heine Groh	24.00	12.00	7.25
(39)	Jess Haines	40.00	20.00	12.00
(40)	Harry Harper	24.00	12.00	7.25
(41a)	Harry Heilman (name incorrect)	50.00	25.00	15.00
(41b)	Harry Heilmann (name correct)	40.00	20.00	12.00
(42)	Clarence Hodge	20.00	10.00	6.00
(43)	Walter Holke (portrait)	30.00	15.00	9.00
(44)	Walter Holke (throwing)	20.00	10.00	6.00
(45)	Charles Hollocher	20.00	10.00	6.00
(46)	Harry Hooper	40.00	20.00	12.00
(47a)	Rogers Hornsby (2B.)	75.00	37.00	22.00
(47b)	Rogers Hornsby (O.F.)	90.00	45.00	27.00
(48)	Waite Hoyt	40.00	20.00	12.00
(49)	Miller Huggins	40.00	20.00	12.00
(50)	Walter Johnson	100.00	50.00	30.00
(51)	Joe Judge	20.00	10.00	6.00
(52)	George Kelly	40.00	20.00	12.00
(53)	Dick Kerr	20.00	10.00	6.00
(54)	P.J. Kilduff	20.00	10.00	6.00
(55)	Bill Killifer (Killefer) (batting)	20.00	10.00	6.00
(56)	Bill Killifer (Killefer) (throwing)	20.00	10.00	6.00
(57)	John Lavan	20.00	10.00	6.00
(58)	Walter Mails	20.00	10.00	6.00
(59)	"Rabbit" Maranville	40.00	20.00	12.00
(60)	Elwood Martin	20.00	10.00	6.00
(61)	Carl Mays	30.00	15.00	9.00
(62)	John J. McGraw	45.00	22.00	13.50
(63)	Jack McInnis	20.00	10.00	6.00
(64)	M.J. McNally	24.00	12.00	7.25
(65)	Emil Meusel (photo actually Lou DeVormer)	24.00	12.00	7.25
(66)	R. Meusel	30.00	15.00	9.00
(67)	Clyde Milan	20.00	10.00	6.00
(68)	Elmer Miller	24.00	12.00	7.25
(69)	Otto Miller	20.00	10.00	6.00
(70)	Johnny Mostil	20.00	10.00	6.00
(71)	Eddie Mulligan	20.00	10.00	6.00
(72a)	Hy Myers	24.00	12.00	7.25
(72b)	"Hy" Myers	30.00	15.00	9.00
(73)	Earl Neale	30.00	15.00	9.00
(74)	Arthur Nehf	20.00	10.00	6.00
(75)	Leslie Nunamaker	20.00	10.00	6.00
(76)	Joe Oeschger	24.00	12.00	7.25
(77)	Chas. O'Leary	30.00	15.00	9.00
(78)	Steve O'Neill	20.00	10.00	6.00
(79)	D.B. Pratt	20.00	10.00	6.00
(80a)	John Rawlings (2B.)	24.00	12.00	7.25
(80b)	John Rawlings (Utl.)	24.00	12.00	7.25
(81)	E.S. Rice (intials actually E.C.)	40.00	20.00	12.00
(82)	Eppa J. Rixey	40.00	20.00	12.00
(83)	Eppa Rixey, Jr.	40.00	20.00	12.00
(84)	Wilbert Robinson	40.00	20.00	12.00
(85)	Tom Rogers	24.00	12.00	7.25
(86a)	Ed Rounnel	24.00	12.00	7.25
(86b)	Ed. Rommel	24.00	12.00	7.25
(87)	Ed Roush	40.00	20.00	12.00
(88)	"Muddy" Ruel	20.00	10.00	6.00
(89)	Walter Ruether	20.00	10.00	6.00
(90a)	Babe Ruth (photo montage)	650.00	325.00	195.00
(90b)	"Babe" Ruth (photo montage)	550.00	275.00	165.00
(91a)	Babe Ruth (holding bird)	650.00	325.00	195.00
(91b)	"Babe" Ruth (holding bird)	550.00	275.00	165.00
(92)	"Babe" Ruth (holding ball)	550.00	275.00	165.00
(93)	Bill Ryan	20.00	10.00	6.00
(94)	Ray Schalk (catching)	40.00	20.00	12.00
(95)	Ray Schalk (batting)	40.00	20.00	12.00
(96)	Wally Schang	24.00	12.00	7.25
(97)	Ferd Schupp	30.00	15.00	9.00
(98)	Everett Scott	24.00	12.00	7.25
(99)	Joe Sewell	40.00	20.00	12.00
(100)	Robert Shawkey	24.00	12.00	7.25
(101)	Pat Shea	20.00	10.00	6.00
(102)	Earl Sheely	20.00	10.00	6.00
(103)	Urban Schocker	20.00	10.00	6.00
(104)	George Sisler (batting)	45.00	22.00	13.50

		NR MT	EX	VG
(105)	George Sisler (throwing)	60.00	30.00	18.00
(106)	Earl Smith	20.00	10.00	6.00
(107)	Elmer Smith	20.00	10.00	6.00
(108)	Frank Snyder	20.00	10.00	6.00
(109)	Bill Southworth	24.00	12.00	7.25
(110a)	Tris Speaker (large projection)	75.00	37.00	22.00
(110b)	Tris Speaker (small projection)	65.00	32.00	19.50
(111a)	Milton Stock	30.00	15.00	9.00
(111b)	Milton J. Stock	24.00	12.00	7.25
(112)	Amos Strunk	20.00	10.00	6.00
(113)	Zeb Terry	20.00	10.00	6.00
(114)	Fred Toney	20.00	10.00	6.00
(115)	George Topocer (Toporcer)	20.00	10.00	6.00
(116)	Bob Veach	20.00	10.00	6.00
(117)	Oscar Vitt	20.00	10.00	6.00
(118)	Curtis Walker	20.00	10.00	6.00
(119)	W. Wambsganss (photo actually Fred Coumbe)	24.00	12.00	7.25
(120)	Aaron Ward	24.00	12.00	7.25
(121)	Zach Wheat	40.00	20.00	12.00
(122a)	George Whitted (Pittsburgh)	24.00	12.00	7.25
(122b)	George Whitted (Brooklyn)	24.00	12.00	7.25
(123)	Fred Williams	24.00	12.00	7.25
(124)	Ivy B. Wingo	20.00	10.00	6.00
(125)	Ross Young (Youngs)	40.00	20.00	12.00

1916 E135

Produced by the Collins-McCarthy Candy Co. of San Francisco, the 200-card, black and white set represents the company's only venture into issuing non-Pacific Coast League players. The cards, which are numbered alphabetically, measure 2'' by 3¼'' in size and are printed on thin stock. Though the set is entitled "Baseball's Hall of Fame", many nondescript players appear in the issue.

		NR MT	EX	VG
Complete Set:		8500.00	4250.00	2550.
Common Player:		25.00	12.50	7.50
1	Sam Agnew	75.00	25.00	7.50
2	Grover Alexander	90.00	45.00	27.00
3	W.S. Alexander (initials actually W.E.)	25.00	12.50	7.50
4	Leon Ames	25.00	12.50	7.50
5	Fred Anderson	25.00	12.50	7.50
6	Ed Appleton	25.00	12.50	7.50
7	Jimmy Archer	25.00	12.50	7.50
8	Jimmy Austin	25.00	12.50	7.50
9	Jim Bagby	25.00	12.50	7.50
10	H.D. Baird	25.00	12.50	7.50
11	J. Franklin Baker	65.00	32.00	19.50
12	Dave Bancroft	65.00	32.00	19.50
13	Jack Barry	25.00	12.50	7.50
14	Joe Benz	25.00	12.50	7.50
15	Al Betzel	25.00	12.50	7.50
16	Ping Bodie	25.00	12.50	7.50
17	Joe Boehling	25.00	12.50	7.50
18	Eddie Burns	25.00	12.50	7.50
19	George Burns	25.00	12.50	7.50
20	Geo. J. Burns	28.00	14.00	8.50
21	Joe Bush	28.00	14.00	8.50
22	Owen Bush	25.00	12.50	7.50

No.	Name	NR MT	EX	VG
23	Bobby Byrne	25.00	12.50	7.50
24	Forrest Cady	25.00	12.50	7.50
25	Max Carey	65.00	32.00	19.50
26	Ray Chapman	40.00	20.00	12.00
27	Larry Cheney	25.00	12.50	7.50
28	Eddie Cicotte	35.00	17.50	10.50
29	Tom Clarke	25.00	12.50	7.50
30	Ty Cobb	500.00	250.00	150.00
31	Eddie Collins	65.00	32.00	19.50
32	"Shauno" Collins (Shano)	25.00	12.50	7.50
33	Fred Coumbe	25.00	12.50	7.50
34	Harry Coveleskie (Coveleski)	28.00	14.00	8.50
35	Gavvy Cravath	28.00	14.00	8.50
36	Sam Crawford	65.00	32.00	19.50
37	Geo. Cutshaw	25.00	12.50	7.50
38	Jake Daubert	28.00	14.00	8.50
39	Geo. Dauss	25.00	12.50	7.50
40	Charles Deal	25.00	12.50	7.50
41	"Wheezer" Dell	25.00	12.50	7.50
42	William Doak	25.00	12.50	7.50
43	Bill Donovan	28.00	14.00	8.50
44	Larry Doyle	28.00	14.00	8.50
45	Johnny Evers	65.00	32.00	19.50
46	Urban Faber	65.00	32.00	19.50
47	"Hap" Felsch	35.00	17.50	10.50
48	Bill Fischer	25.00	12.50	7.50
49	Ray Fisher	28.00	14.00	8.50
50	Art Fletcher	25.00	12.50	7.50
51	Eddie Foster	25.00	12.50	7.50
52	Jacques Fournier	25.00	12.50	7.50
53	Del Gainer (Gainor)	25.00	12.50	7.50
54	Bert Gallia	25.00	12.50	7.50
55	"Chic" Gandil (Chick)	35.00	17.50	10.50
56	Larry Gardner	25.00	12.50	7.50
57	Joe Gedeon	25.00	12.50	7.50
58	Gus Getz	25.00	12.50	7.50
59	Frank Gilhooley	25.00	12.50	7.50
60	Wm. Gleason	25.00	12.50	7.50
61	M.A. Gonzales (Gonzalez)	25.00	12.50	7.50
62	Hank Gowdy	28.00	14.00	8.50
63	John Graney	25.00	12.50	7.50
64	Tom Griffith	25.00	12.50	7.50
65	Heinie Groh	28.00	14.00	8.50
66	Bob Groom	25.00	12.50	7.50
67	Louis Guisto	25.00	12.50	7.50
68	Earl Hamilton	25.00	12.50	7.50
69	Harry Harper	25.00	12.50	7.50
70	Grover Hartley	25.00	12.50	7.50
71	Harry Heilmann	65.00	32.00	19.50
72	Claude Hendrix	25.00	12.50	7.50
73	Olaf Henriksen	25.00	12.50	7.50
74	John Henry	25.00	12.50	7.50
75	"Buck" Herzog	25.00	12.50	7.50
76a	Hugh High (white stockings, photo actually Claude Williams)	65.00	32.00	19.50
76b	Hugh High (black stockings, correct photo)	28.00	14.00	8.50
77	Dick Hoblitzell	25.00	12.50	7.50
78	Walter Holke	25.00	12.50	7.50
79	Harry Hooper	65.00	32.00	19.50
80	Rogers Hornsby	125.00	62.00	37.00
81	Ivan Howard	25.00	12.50	7.50
82	Joe Jackson	500.00	250.00	150.00
83	Harold Janvrin	25.00	12.50	7.50
84	William James	25.00	12.50	7.50
85	C. Jamieson	25.00	12.50	7.50
86	Hugh Jennings	65.00	32.00	19.50
87	Walter Johnson	150.00	75.00	45.00
88	James Johnston	25.00	12.50	7.50
89	Fielder Jones	25.00	12.50	7.50
90a	Joe Judge (bat on right shoulder, photo actually Ray Morgan)	65.00	32.00	19.50
90b	Joe Judge (bat on left shoulder, correct photo)	28.00	14.00	8.50
91	Hans Lobert	25.00	12.50	7.50
92	Benny Kauff	25.00	12.50	7.50
93	Wm. Killefer Jr.	25.00	12.50	7.50
94	Ed. Konetchy	25.00	12.50	7.50
95	John Lavan	25.00	12.50	7.50
96	Jimmy Lavender	25.00	12.50	7.50
97	"Nemo" Leibold	25.00	12.50	7.50
98	H.B. Leonard	25.00	12.50	7.50
99	Duffy Lewis	28.00	14.00	8.50
100	Tom Long	25.00	12.50	7.50
101	Wm. Louden	25.00	12.50	7.50
102	Fred Luderus	25.00	12.50	7.50
103	Lee Magee	25.00	12.50	7.50
104	Sherwood Magee	28.00	14.00	8.50
105	Al Mamaux	25.00	12.50	7.50
106	Leslie Mann	25.00	12.50	7.50
107	"Rabbit" Maranville	65.00	32.00	19.50
108	Rube Marquard	65.00	32.00	19.50
109	Armando Marsans	25.00	12.50	7.50
110	J. Erskine Mayer	25.00	12.50	7.50
111	George McBride	25.00	12.50	7.50
112	Lew McCarty	25.00	12.50	7.50
113	John J. McGraw	75.00	37.00	22.00
114	Jack McInnis	25.00	12.50	7.50
115	Lee Meadows	25.00	12.50	7.50
116	Fred Merkle	28.00	14.00	8.50
117	"Chief" Meyers	25.00	12.50	7.50
118	Clyde Milan	25.00	12.50	7.50
119	Otto Miller	25.00	12.50	7.50
120	Clarence Mitchell	25.00	12.50	7.50
121a	Ray Morgan (bat on right shoulder, photo actually Joe Judge)	65.00	32.00	19.50
121b	Ray Morgan (bat on left shoulder, correct photo)	28.00	14.00	8.50
122	Guy Morton	25.00	12.50	7.50
123	"Mike" Mowrey	25.00	12.50	7.50
124	Elmer Myers	25.00	12.50	7.50
125	"Hy" Myers	25.00	12.50	7.50
126	A.E. Neale	40.00	20.00	12.00
127	Arthur Nehf	25.00	12.50	7.50
128	J.A. Niehoff	25.00	12.50	7.50
129	Steve O'Neill	25.00	12.50	7.50
130	"Dode" Paskert	25.00	12.50	7.50
131	Roger Peckinpaugh	28.00	14.00	8.50
132	"Pol" Perritt	25.00	12.50	7.50
133	"Jeff" Pfeffer	25.00	12.50	7.50
134	Walter Pipp	40.00	20.00	12.00
135	Derril Pratt (Derrill)	25.00	12.50	7.50
136	Bill Rariden	25.00	12.50	7.50
137	E.C. Rice	65.00	32.00	19.50
138	Wm. A. Ritter (actually Wm. H.)	25.00	12.50	7.50
139	Eppa Rixey	65.00	32.00	19.50
140	Davey Robertson	25.00	12.50	7.50
141	"Bob" Roth	25.00	12.50	7.50
142	Ed. Roush	65.00	32.00	19.50
143	Clarence Rowland	25.00	12.50	7.50
144	Dick Rudolph	25.00	12.50	7.50
145	William Rumler	25.00	12.50	7.50
146a	Reb Russell (pitching follow-thru, photo actually Mellie Wolfgang)	65.00	32.00	19.50
146b	Reb Russell (hands at side, correct photo)	28.00	14.00	8.50
147	"Babe" Ruth	700.00	350.00	210.00
148	Vic Saier	25.00	12.50	7.50
149	"Slim" Sallee	25.00	12.50	7.50
150	Ray Schalk	65.00	32.00	19.50
151	Walter Schang	25.00	12.50	7.50
152	Frank Schulte	25.00	12.50	7.50
153	Ferd Schupp	25.00	12.50	7.50
154	Everett Scott	25.00	12.50	7.50
155	Hank Severeid	25.00	12.50	7.50
156	Howard Shanks	25.00	12.50	7.50
157	Bob Shawkey	28.00	14.00	8.50
158	Jas. Sheckard	25.00	12.50	7.50
159	Ernie Shore	25.00	12.50	7.50
160	C.H. Shorten	25.00	12.50	7.50
161	Burt Shotton	28.00	14.00	8.50
162	Geo. Sisler	75.00	37.00	22.00
163	Elmer Smith	25.00	12.50	7.50
164	J. Carlisle Smith	25.00	12.50	7.50
165	Fred Snodgrass	28.00	14.00	8.50
166	Tris Speaker	100.00	50.00	30.00
167	Oscar Stanage	25.00	12.50	7.50
168	Charles Stengel	150.00	75.00	45.00
169	Milton Stock	25.00	12.50	7.50
170	Amos Strunk	25.00	12.50	7.50
171	"Zeb" Terry	25.00	12.50	7.50
172	"Jeff" Tesreau	25.00	12.50	7.50
173	Chester Thomas	25.00	12.50	7.50
174	Fred Toney	25.00	12.50	7.50
175	Terry Turner	25.00	12.50	7.50
176	George Tyler	25.00	12.50	7.50
177	Jim Vaughn	25.00	12.50	7.50
178	Bob Veach	25.00	12.50	7.50
179	Oscar Vitt	25.00	12.50	7.50
180	Hans Wagner	200.00	100.00	60.00
181	Clarence Walker	25.00	12.50	7.50
182	Jim Walsh	25.00	12.50	7.50
183	Al Walters	25.00	12.50	7.50
184	W. Wambsganss	28.00	14.00	8.50
185	Buck Weaver	35.00	17.50	10.50
186	Carl Weilman	25.00	12.50	7.50
187	Zack Wheat	65.00	32.00	19.50
188	Geo. Whitted	25.00	12.50	7.50
189	Joe Wilhoit	25.00	12.50	7.50
190a	Claude Williams (black stockings, photo actually Hugh High)	65.00	32.00	19.50

		NR MT	EX	VG
190b	Claude Williams (white stockings, correct photo)	35.00	17.50	10.50
191	Fred Williams	28.00	14.00	8.50
192	Art Wilson	25.00	12.50	7.50
193	Lawton Witt	25.00	12.50	7.50
194	Joe Wood	35.00	17.50	10.50
195	William Wortman	25.00	12.50	7.50
196	Steve Yerkes	25.00	12.50	7.50
197	Earl Yingling	25.00	12.50	7.50
198	"Pep" Young (photo actually Ralph Young)	25.00	12.50	7.50
199	Rollie Zeider	25.00	12.50	7.50
200	Henry Zimmerman	75.00	20.00	7.50

1966 East Hill Pirates

Stores in the East Hills Shopping Center, a large mall located in suburban Pittsburgh, distributed cards from this 25-card full-color set in 1966. The cards, which measure 3¼'' by 4¼'', are blank-backed and are numbered by the players' uniform numbers. The numbers appear in the lower right corners of the cards.

		NR MT	EX	VG
	Complete Set:	30.00	15.00	9.00
	Common Player:	.50	.25	.15
3	Harry Walker	.70	.35	.20
7	Bob Bailey	.50	.25	.15
8	Willie Stargell	5.00	2.50	1.50
9	Bill Mazeroski	1.50	.70	.45
10	Jim Pagliaroni	.50	.25	.15
11	Jose Pagan	.50	.25	.15
12	Jerry May	.50	.25	.15
14	Gene Alley	.60	.30	.20
15	Manny Mota	.80	.40	.25
16	Andy Rodgers	.50	.25	.15
17	Donn Clendenon	.60	.30	.20
18	Matty Alou	.80	.40	.25
19	Pete Mikkelsen	.50	.25	.15
20	Jesse Gonder	.50	.25	.15
21	Bob Clemente	10.00	5.00	3.00
22	Woody Fryman	.60	.30	.20
24	Jerry Lynch	.50	.25	.15
25	Tommie Sisk	.50	.25	.15
26	Roy Face	1.25	.60	.40
28	Steve Blass	.60	.30	.20
32	Vernon Law	1.25	.60	.40
34	Al McBean	.50	.25	.15
39	Bob Veale	.60	.30	.20
43	Don Cardwell	.50	.25	.15
45	Gene Michael	.60	.30	.20

1954 Esskay Hot Dogs Orioles

Measuring 2¼'' by 3½'', the 1954 Esskay Hot Dogs set features the Baltimore Orioles. The unnumbered, color cards were issued in panels of two on packages of hot dogs and are usually found with grease stains. The cards have waxed fronts with blank backs on a

white stock. Complete boxes of Esskay Hot Dogs are scarce and command a price of 2-3 times greater than the single card values.

		NR MT	EX	VG
	Complete Set:	3100.00	1550.00	930.00
	Common Player:	80.00	40.00	24.00
(1)	Neil Berry	80.00	40.00	24.00
(2)	Michael Blyzka	80.00	40.00	24.00
(3)	Harry Brecheen	90.00	45.00	27.00
(4)	Gil Coan	80.00	40.00	24.00
(5)	Joe Coleman	80.00	40.00	24.00
(6)	Clinton Courtney	80.00	40.00	24.00
(7)	Charles E. Diering	80.00	40.00	24.00
(8)	Jimmie Dykes	90.00	45.00	27.00
(9)	Frank J. Fanovich	80.00	40.00	24.00
(10)	Howard Fox	80.00	40.00	24.00
(11)	Jim Fridley	80.00	40.00	24.00
(12)	Vinicio "Chico" Garcia	80.00	40.00	24.00
(13)	Jehosie Heard	80.00	40.00	24.00
(14)	Darrell Johnson	80.00	40.00	24.00
(15)	Bob Kennedy	80.00	40.00	24.00
(16)	Dick Kokos	80.00	40.00	24.00
(17)	Dave Koslo	80.00	40.00	24.00
(18)	Lou Kretlow	80.00	40.00	24.00
(19)	Richard D. Kryhoski	80.00	40.00	24.00
(20)	Don Larsen	125.00	62.00	37.00
(21)	Donald E. Lenhardt	80.00	40.00	24.00
(22)	Richard Littlefield	80.00	40.00	24.00
(23)	Sam Mele	80.00	40.00	24.00
(24)	Les Moss	80.00	40.00	24.00
(25)	Ray L. Murray	80.00	40.00	24.00
(26a)	"Bobo" Newsom (no stadium lights in background)	125.00	62.00	37.00
(26b)	"Bobo" Newson (stadium lights in background)	125.00	62.00	37.00
(27)	Tom Oliver	80.00	40.00	24.00
(28)	Duane Pillette	80.00	40.00	24.00
(29)	Francis M. Skaff	80.00	40.00	24.00
(30)	Marlin Stuart	80.00	40.00	24.00
(31)	Robert L. Turley	125.00	62.00	37.00
(32)	Eddie Waitkus	80.00	40.00	24.00
(33)	Vic Wertz	100.00	50.00	30.00
(34)	Robert G. Young	80.00	40.00	24.00

1955 Esskay Hot Dogs Orioles

For the second consecutive year, Esskay Meats placed two baseball cards of Orioles players on their boxes of hot dogs. The unnumbered, color cards measure 2¼'' by 3½'' and can be distinguished from the previous year by unwaxed fronts and grey backs. Many of the same photos from 1954 were used with only minor picture-cropping differences.

NOTE: A card number in parentheses ( ) indicates the set is unnumbered.

HARRY BYRD, Pitcher

		NR MT	EX	VG
	Complete Set:	2300.00	1150.00	690.00
	Common Player:	80.00	40.00	24.00
(1)	Cal Abrams	80.00	40.00	24.00
(2)	Robert S. Alexander	80.00	40.00	24.00
(3)	Harry Byrd	80.00	40.00	24.00
(4)	Gil Coan	80.00	40.00	24.00
(5)	Joseph P. Coleman	80.00	40.00	24.00
(6)	William R. Cox	80.00	40.00	24.00
(7)	Charles E. Diering	80.00	40.00	24.00
(8)	Walter A. Evers	80.00	40.00	24.00
(9)	Don Johnson	80.00	40.00	24.00
(10)	Robert D. Kennedy	80.00	40.00	24.00
(11)	Lou Kretlow	80.00	40.00	24.00
(12)	Robert L. Kuzava	80.00	40.00	24.00
(13)	Fred Marsh	80.00	40.00	24.00
(14)	Charles Maxwell	80.00	40.00	24.00
(15)	Jimmie McDonald	80.00	40.00	24.00
(16)	Bill Miller	80.00	40.00	24.00
(17)	Willy Miranda	80.00	40.00	24.00
(18)	Raymond L. Moore	80.00	40.00	24.00
(19)	John Lester Moss	80.00	40.00	24.00
(20)	"Bobo" Newsom	90.00	45.00	27.00
(21)	Duane Pillette	80.00	40.00	24.00
(22)	Edward S. Waitkus	80.00	40.00	24.00
(23)	Harold W. Smith	80.00	40.00	24.00
(24)	Gus Triandos	100.00	50.00	30.00
(25)	Eugene R. Woodling	100.00	50.00	30.00
(26)	Robert G. Young	80.00	40.00	24.00

1939-1946 Salutation Exhibits

Referred to as "Exhibits" because they were issued by the Exhibit Supply Co. of Chicago, Ill., this group was produced over an 8-year span. They are frequently called "Salutations" because of the personalized greeting found on the card. The black and white cards, which measure 3⅜" by 5⅜", are unnumbered and blank-backed. Most exhibits were sold through vending machines for a penny.

	NR MT	EX	VG
Complete Set:	2400.00	1200.00	720.00
Common Player:	2.50	1.25	.70

		NR MT	EX	VG
(1a)	Luke Appling ("Made In U.S.A." in left corner)	6.50	3.25	2.00
(1b)	Luke Appling ("Made In U.S.A." in right corner)	3.50	1.75	1.00
(2)	Earl Averill	250.00	125.00	75.00
(3)	Charles "Red" Barrett	2.50	1.25	.70
(4)	Henry "Hank" Borowy	2.50	1.25	.70
(5)	Lou Boudreau	4.00	2.00	1.25
(6)	Adolf Camilli	11.00	5.50	3.25
(7)	Phil Cavarretta	3.50	1.75	1.00
(8)	Harland Clift (Harland)	9.00	4.50	2.75
(9)	Tony Cuccinello	11.00	5.50	3.25
(10)	Dizzy Dean	45.00	22.00	13.50
(11)	Paul Derringer	2.50	1.25	.70
(12a)	Bill Dickey ("Made In U.S.A." in left corner)	16.00	8.00	4.75
(12b)	Bill Dickey ("Made In U.S.A." in right corner)	16.00	8.00	4.75
(13)	Joe DiMaggio	15.00	7.50	4.50
(14)	Bob Elliott	2.50	1.25	.70
(15)	Bob Feller (portrait)	60.00	30.00	18.00
(16)	Bob Feller (pitching)	13.00	6.50	4.00
(17)	Dave Ferriss	2.50	1.25	.70
(18)	Jimmy Foxx	60.00	30.00	18.00
(19)	Lou Gehrig	300.00	150.00	90.00
(20)	Charlie Gehringer	90.00	45.00	27.00
(21)	Vernon Gomez	125.00	62.00	37.00
(22a)	Joe Gordon (Cleveland)	16.00	8.00	4.75
(22b)	Joe Gordon (New York)	3.50	1.75	1.00
(23)	Hank Greenberg (Truly yours)	13.00	6.50	4.00
(24)	Hank Greenberg (Very truly yours)	60.00	30.00	18.00
(25)	Robert Grove	50.00	25.00	15.00
(26)	Gabby Hartnett	200.00	100.00	60.00
(27)	Buddy Hassett	9.00	4.50	2.75
(28a)	Jeff Heath (large projection)	16.00	8.00	4.75
(28b)	Jeff Heath (small projection)	2.50	1.25	.70
(29)	Kirby Higbe	9.00	4.50	2.75
(30a)	Tommy Holmes (Yours truly)	2.50	1.25	.70
(30b)	Tommy Holmes (Sincerely yours)	90.00	45.00	27.00
(31)	Carl Hubbell	20.00	10.00	6.00
(32)	Bob Johnson	9.00	4.50	2.75
(33)	Charles Keller	2.50	1.25	.70
(34)	Ken Keltner	16.00	8.00	4.75
(35)	Chuck Klein	125.00	62.00	37.00
(36)	Mike Kreevich	60.00	30.00	18.00
(37)	Joe Kuhel	16.00	8.00	4.75
(38)	Bill Lee	16.00	8.00	4.75
(39)	Ernie Lombardi (Cordially)	150.00	75.00	45.00
(40)	Ernie Lombardi (Cordially yours)	3.50	1.75	1.00
(41a)	Martin Marion ("Made in U.S.A." in left corner)	2.50	1.25	.70
(41b)	Martin Marion ("Made in U.S.A." in right corner)	2.50	1.25	.70
(42)	Merrill May	16.00	8.00	4.75
(43a)	Frank McCormick ("Made In U.S.A." in left corner)	11.00	5.50	3.25
(43b)	Frank McCormick ("Made In U.S.A." in right corner)	3.50	1.75	1.00
(44a)	George McQuinn ("Made In U.S.A." in left corner)	16.00	8.00	4.75
(44b)	George McQuinn ("Made In U.S.A." in right corner)	3.50	1.75	1.00
(45)	Joe Medwick	12.00	6.00	3.50
(46a)	Johnny Mize ("Made In U.S.A." in left corner)	16.00	8.00	4.75
(46b)	Johnny Mize ("Made In U.S.A." in right corner)	10.00	5.00	3.00
(47)	Hugh Mulcahy	60.00	30.00	18.00
(48)	Hal Newhouser	2.50	1.25	.70
(49)	Buck Newson (Newsom)	90.00	45.00	27.00
(50)	Louis (Buck) Newsom	2.50	1.25	.70
(51a)	Mel Ott ("Made In U.S.A." in left corner)	25.00	12.50	7.50
(51b)	Mel Ott ("Made In U.S.A." in right corner)	12.00	6.00	3.50
(52a)	Andy Pafko ("C" on cap)	2.50	1.25	.70
(52b)	Andy Pafko (plain cap)	2.50	1.25	.70
(53)	Claude Passeau	3.50	1.75	1.00
(54a)	Howard Pollet ("Made In U.S.A." in left corner)	11.00	5.50	3.25
(54b)	Howard Pollet ("Made In U.S.A." in right corner)	2.50	1.25	.70
(55a)	Pete Reiser ("Made In U.S.A." in left corner)	60.00	30.00	18.00
(55b)	Pete Reiser ("Made In U.S.A." in right corner)	2.50	1.25	.70
(56)	Johnny Rizzo	60.00	30.00	18.00
(57)	Glenn Russell	60.00	30.00	18.00
(58)	George Stirnweiss	2.50	1.25	.70

		NR MT	EX	VG
(59)	Cecil Travis	10.00	5.00	3.00
(60)	Paul Trout	2.50	1.25	.70
(61)	Johnny Vander Meer	30.00	15.00	9.00
(62)	Arky Vaughn (Vaughan)	10.00	5.00	3.00
(63a)	Fred "Dixie" Walker ("D" on cap)	2.50	1.25	.70
(63b)	Fred "Dixie" Walker ("D" blanked out)			
		17.00	8.50	5.00
(64)	"Bucky" Walters	2.50	1.25	.70
(65)	Lon Warneke	6.50	3.25	2.00
(66)	Ted Williams (#9 shows)	150.00	75.00	45.00
(67)	Ted Williams (#9 not showing)	10.00	5.00	3.00
(68)	Rudy York	2.50	1.25	.70

1947-1966 Exhibits

Called "Exhibits" as they were produced by the Exhibit Supply Co. of Chicago, Ill., this group covers a span of twenty years. Each unnumbered, black and white card, printed on heavy stock, measures 3⅜" by 5⅜" and is blank-backed. The Exhibit Supply Co. issued new sets each year, with many players being repeated year after year. Other players appeared in only one or two years, thereby creating levels of scarcity. Many variations off the same basic pose are found in the group. Those cards are listed in the checklist that follows with an "a", "b", etc. following the assigned card number.

		NR MT	EX	VG
Complete Set:		2600.00	1300.00	780.00
Common Player:		1.25	.60	.40
(1)	Hank Aaron	8.50	4.25	2.50
(2a)	Joe Adcock (script signature)	2.50	1.25	.70
(2b)	Joe Adcock (plain signature)	3.50	1.75	1.00
(3)	Max Alvis	15.00	7.50	4.50
(4)	Johnny Antonelli (Braves)	1.25	.60	.40
(5)	Johnny Antonelli (Giants)	3.50	1.75	1.00
(6)	Luis Aparicio (portrait)	5.00	2.50	1.50
(7)	Luis Aparicio (batting)	15.00	7.50	4.50
(8)	Luke Appling	5.00	2.50	1.50
(9a)	Ritchie Ashburn (Phillies, first name incorrect)	3.50	1.75	1.00
(9b)	Richie Ashburn (Phillies, first name correct)	5.00	2.50	1.50
(10)	Richie Ashburn (Cubs)	10.00	5.00	3.00
(11)	Bob Aspromonte	2.50	1.25	.70
(12)	Toby Atwell	2.50	1.25	.70
(13)	Ed Bailey (with cap)	3.50	1.75	1.00
(14)	Ed Bailey (no cap)	1.25	.60	.40
(15)	Gene Baker	1.25	.60	.40
(16a)	Ernie Banks (bat on shoulder, script signature)	10.00	5.00	3.00
(16b)	Ernie Banks (bat on shoulder, plain signature)	6.00	3.00	1.75
(17)	Ernie Banks (portrait)	12.00	6.00	3.50
(18)	Steve Barber	2.50	1.25	.70
(19)	Earl Battey	3.50	1.75	1.00
(20)	Matt Batts	2.50	1.25	.70
(21a)	Hank Bauer (N.Y. cap)	3.50	1.75	1.00
(21b)	Hank Bauer (plain cap)	5.00	2.50	1.50
(22)	Frank Baumholtz	2.50	1.25	.70
(23)	Gene Bearden	2.50	1.25	.70

		NR MT	EX	VG
(24)	Joe Beggs	8.50	4.25	2.50
(25)	Larry "Yogi" Berra	15.00	7.50	4.50
(26)	Yogi Berra	6.00	3.00	1.75
(27)	Steve Bilko	3.50	1.75	1.00
(28)	Ewell Blackwell (pitching)	5.00	2.50	1.50
(29)	Ewell Blackwell (portrait)	2.50	1.25	.70
(30a)	Don Blasingame (St. Louis cap)	2.50	1.25	.70
(30b)	Don Blasingame (plain cap)	6.00	3.00	1.75
(31)	Ken Boyer	5.00	2.50	1.50
(32)	Ralph Branca	5.00	2.50	1.50
(33)	Jackie Brandt	35.00	17.50	10.50
(34)	Harry Brecheen	1.25	.60	.40
(35)	Tom Brewer	8.50	4.25	2.50
(36)	Lou Brissie	3.50	1.75	1.00
(37)	Bill Bruton	1.25	.60	.40
(38)	Lew Burdette (pitching, side view)			
		2.50	1.25	.70
(39)	Lew Burdette (pitching, front view)			
		6.00	3.00	1.75
(40)	Johnny Callison	5.00	2.50	1.50
(41)	Roy Campanella	10.00	5.00	3.00
(42)	Chico Carrasquel (portrait)	10.00	5.00	3.00
(43)	Chico Carrasquel (leaping)	1.25	.60	.40
(44)	George Case	8.50	4.25	2.50
(45)	Hugh Casey	3.50	1.75	1.00
(46)	Norm Cash	5.00	2.50	1.50
(47)	Orlando Cepeda (portrait)	5.00	2.50	1.50
(48)	Orlando Cepeda (batting)	5.00	2.50	1.50
(49a)	Bob Cerv (A's cap)	5.00	2.50	1.50
(49b)	Bob Cerv (plain cap)	16.00	8.00	4.75
(50)	Dean Chance	2.50	1.25	.70
(51)	Spud Chandler	8.50	4.25	2.50
(52)	Tom Cheney	2.50	1.25	.70
(53)	Bubba Church	3.50	1.75	1.00
(54)	Roberto Clemente	12.00	6.00	3.50
(55)	Rocky Colavito (portrait)	20.00	10.00	6.00
(56)	Rocky Colavito (batting)	5.00	2.50	1.50
(57)	Choo Choo Coleman	10.00	5.00	3.00
(58)	Gordy Coleman	15.00	7.50	4.50
(59)	Jerry Coleman	3.50	1.75	1.00
(60)	Mort Cooper	5.00	2.50	1.50
(61)	Walker Cooper	1.25	.60	.40
(62)	Roger Craig	8.50	4.25	2.50
(63)	Delmar Crandall	1.25	.60	.40
(64)	Joe Cunningham (batting)	20.00	10.00	6.00
(65)	Joe Cunningham (portrait)	5.00	2.50	1.50
(66)	Guy Curtwright (Curtright)	3.50	1.75	1.00
(67)	Bud Daley	25.00	12.50	7.50
(68a)	Alvin Dark (Braves)	5.00	2.50	1.50
(68b)	Alvin Dark (Giants)	3.50	1.75	1.00
(69)	Alvin Dark (Cubs)	5.00	2.50	1.50
(70)	Murray Dickson (Murry)	3.50	1.75	1.00
(71)	Bob Dillinger	5.00	2.50	1.50
(72)	Dom DiMaggio	10.00	5.00	3.00
(73)	Joe Dobson	5.00	2.50	1.50
(74)	Larry Doby	2.50	1.25	.70
(75)	Bobby Doerr	8.50	4.25	2.50
(76)	Dick Donovan (plain cap)	5.00	2.50	1.50
(77)	Dick Donovan (Sox cap)	4.00	2.00	1.25
(78)	Walter Dropo	1.25	.60	.40
(79)	Don Drysdale (glove at waist)	20.00	10.00	6.00
(80)	Don Drysdale (portrait)	20.00	10.00	6.00
(81)	Luke Easter	3.50	1.75	1.00
(82)	Bruce Edwards	3.50	1.75	1.00
(83)	Del Ennis	1.25	.60	.40
(84)	Al Evans	4.50	2.25	1.25
(85)	Walter Evers	1.25	.60	.40
(86)	Ferris Fain (fielding)	5.00	2.50	1.50
(87)	Ferris Fain (portrait)	2.50	1.25	.70
(88)	Dick Farrell	2.50	1.25	.70
(89)	Ed "Whitey" Ford	10.00	5.00	3.00
(90)	Whitey Ford (pitching)	5.00	2.50	1.50
(91)	Whitey Ford (portrait)	40.00	20.00	12.00
(92)	Dick Fowler	5.00	2.50	1.50
(93)	Nelson Fox	3.50	1.75	1.00
(94)	Tito Francona	2.50	1.25	.70
(95)	Bob Friend	2.50	1.25	.70
(96)	Carl Furillo	5.00	2.50	1.50
(97)	Augie Galan	5.00	2.50	1.50
(98)	Jim Gentile	2.50	1.25	.70
(99)	Tony Gonzalez	2.50	1.25	.70
(100)	Billy Goodman (leaping)	2.50	1.25	.70
(101)	Billy Goodman (batting)	5.00	2.50	1.50
(102)	Ted Greengrass (Jim)	2.50	1.25	.70
(103)	Dick Groat	5.00	2.50	1.50
(104)	Steve Gromek	2.50	1.25	.70
(105)	Johnny Groth	1.25	.60	.40
(106)	Orval Grove	10.00	5.00	3.00
(107a)	Frank Gustine (Pirates uniform)	3.50	1.75	1.00
(107b)	Frank Gustine (plain uniform)	3.50	1.75	1.00
(108)	Berthold Haas	10.00	5.00	3.00

	NR MT	EX	VG
(109) Grady Hatton	3.50	1.75	1.00
(110) Jim Hegan	1.25	.60	.40
(111) Tom Henrich	5.00	2.50	1.50
(112) Ray Herbert	15.00	7.50	4.50
(113) Gene Hermanski	4.50	2.25	1.25
(114) Whitey Herzog	3.50	1.75	1.00
(115) Kirby Higbe	10.00	5.00	3.00
(116) Chuck Hinton	2.50	1.25	.70
(117) Don Hoak	10.00	5.00	3.00
(118a) Gil Hodges ("B" on cap)	5.00	2.50	1.50
(118b) Gil Hodges ("LA" on cap)	5.00	2.50	1.50
(119) Johnny Hopp	5.00	2.50	1.50
(120) Elston Howard	2.50	1.25	.70
(121) Frank Howard	5.00	2.50	1.50
(122) Ken Hubbs	20.00	10.00	6.00
(123) Tex Hughson	5.00	2.50	1.50
(124) Fred Hutchinson	4.50	2.25	1.25
(125) Monty Irvin	5.00	2.50	1.50
(126) Joey Jay	2.50	1.25	.70
(127) Jackie Jensen	20.00	10.00	6.00
(128) Sam Jethroe	3.50	1.75	1.00
(129) Bill Johnson	3.50	1.75	1.00
(130) Walter Judnich	5.00	2.50	1.50
(131) Al Kaline (kneeling)	12.00	6.00	3.50
(132) Al Kaline (portrait)	12.00	6.00	3.50
(133) George Kell	5.00	2.50	1.50
(134) Charley Keller	4.50	2.25	1.25
(135) Alex Kellner	1.25	.60	.40
(136) Kenn Keltner (Ken)	3.50	1.75	1.00
(137) Harmon Killebrew (batting)	12.00	6.00	3.50
(138) Harmon Killebrew (throwing)	12.00	6.00	3.50
(139) Harmon Killibrew (Killebrew) (portrait)	20.00	10.00	6.00
(140) Ellis Kinder	2.50	1.25	.70
(141) Ralph Kiner	6.00	3.00	1.75
(142) Billy Klaus	15.00	7.50	4.50
(143) Ted Kluzewski (Kluszewski) (batting)	3.50	1.75	1.00
(144a) Ted Kluzewski (Kluszewski) (Pirates uniform)	3.50	1.75	1.00
(144b) Ted Kluzewski (Kluszewski) (plain uniform)	10.00	5.00	3.00
(145) Don Kolloway	5.00	2.50	1.50
(146) Jim Konstanty	3.50	1.75	1.00
(147) Sandy Koufax	12.00	6.00	3.50
(148) Ed Kranepool	40.00	20.00	12.00
(149a) Tony Kubek (light background)	5.00	2.50	1.50
(149b) Tony Kubek (dark background)	3.50	1.75	1.00
(150a) Harvey Kuenn ("D" on cap)	8.50	4.25	2.50
(150b) Harvey Kuenn (plain cap)	10.00	5.00	3.00
(151) Harvey Kuenn ("SF" on cap)	5.00	2.50	1.50
(152) Kurowski (Whitey)	4.50	2.25	1.25
(153) Eddie Lake	3.50	1.75	1.00
(154) Jim Landis	2.50	1.25	.70
(155) Don Larsen	2.50	1.25	.70
(156) Bob Lemon (glove not visible)	5.00	2.50	1.50
(157) Bob Lemon (glove partially visible)	20.00	10.00	6.00
(158) Buddy Lewis	4.50	2.25	1.25
(159) Johnny Lindell	20.00	10.00	6.00
(160) Phil Linz	15.00	7.50	4.50
(161) Don Lock	15.00	7.50	4.50
(162) Whitey Lockman	2.50	1.25	.70
(163) Johnny Logan	1.25	.60	.40
(164) Dale Long ("P" on cap)	1.25	.60	.40
(165) Dale Long ("C" on cap)	5.00	2.50	1.50
(166) Ed Lopat	3.50	1.75	1.00
(167a) Harry Lowery (name misspelled)	3.50	1.75	1.00
(167b) Harry Lowrey (name correct)	3.50	1.75	1.00
(168) Sal Maglie	2.50	1.25	.70
(169) Art Mahaffey	3.50	1.75	1.00
(170) Hank Majeski	1.25	.60	.40
(171) Frank Malzone	2.50	1.25	.70
(172) Mickey Mantle (batting, pinstriped uniform)	30.00	15.00	9.00
(173a) Mickey Mantle (batting, no pinstripes, first name outlined in white)	20.00	10.00	6.00
(173b) Mickey Mantle (batting, no pinstripes, first name not outlined in white)	20.00	10.00	6.00
(174) Mickey Mantle (portrait)	150.00	75.00	45.00
(175) Martin Marion	5.00	2.50	1.50
(176) Roger Maris	12.00	6.00	3.50
(177) Willard Marshall	3.50	1.75	1.00
(178a) Eddie Matthews (name incorrect)	8.50	4.25	2.50
(178b) Eddie Mathews (name correct)	10.00	5.00	3.00
(179) Ed Mayo	3.50	1.75	1.00
(180) Willie Mays (batting)	10.00	5.00	3.00
(181) Willie Mays (portrait)	12.00	6.00	3.50
(182) Bill Mazeroski (portrait)	5.00	2.50	1.50
(183) Bill Mazeroski (batting)	5.00	2.50	1.50
(184) Ken McBride	2.50	1.25	.70
(185a) Barney McCaskey (McCosky)	10.00	5.00	3.00
(185b) Barney McCoskey (McCosky)	90.00	45.00	27.00
(186) Lindy McDaniel	2.50	1.25	.70
(187) Gil McDougald	2.50	1.25	.70
(188) Albert Mele	10.00	5.00	3.00
(189) Sam Mele	3.50	1.75	1.00
(190) Orestes Minoso ("C" on cap)	5.00	2.50	1.50
(191) Orestes Minoso (Sox on cap)	2.50	1.25	.70
(192) Dale Mitchell	1.25	.60	.40
(193) Wally Moon	5.00	2.50	1.50
(194) Don Mueller	3.50	1.75	1.00
(195) Stan Musial (kneeling)	8.50	4.25	2.50
(196) Stan Musial (batting)	20.00	10.00	6.00
(197) Charley Neal	12.00	6.00	3.50
(198) Don Newcombe (shaking hands)	5.00	2.50	1.50
(199a) Don Newcombe (Dodgers on jacket)	3.50	1.75	1.00
(199b) Don Newcombe (plain jacket)	3.50	1.75	1.00
(200) Hal Newhouser	2.50	1.25	.70
(201) Ron Northey	5.00	2.50	1.50
(202) Bill O'Dell	2.50	1.25	.70
(203) Joe Page	8.50	4.25	2.50
(204) Satchel Paige	16.00	8.00	4.75
(205) Milt Pappas	2.50	1.25	.70
(206) Camilo Pascual	2.50	1.25	.70
(207) Albie Pearson	15.00	7.50	4.50
(208) Johnny Pesky	1.25	.60	.40
(209) Gary Peters	15.00	7.50	4.50
(210) Dave Philley	2.50	1.25	.70
(211) Billy Pierce	2.50	1.25	.70
(212) Jimmy Piersall	16.00	8.00	4.75
(213) Vada Pinson	5.00	2.50	1.50
(214) Bob Porterfield	2.50	1.25	.70
(215) John "Boog" Powell	16.00	8.00	4.75
(216) Vic Raschi	4.50	2.25	1.25
(217a) Harold "Peewee" Reese (fielding, ball partially visible)	6.00	3.00	1.75
(217b) Harold "Peewee" Reese (fielding, ball not visible)	6.00	3.00	1.75
(218) Del Rice	1.25	.60	.40
(219) Bobby Richardson	40.00	20.00	12.00
(220) Phil Rizzuto	6.00	3.00	1.75
(221a) Robin Roberts (script signature)	8.50	4.25	2.50
(221b) Robin Roberts (plain signature)	6.00	3.00	1.75
(222) Brooks Robinson	20.00	10.00	6.00
(223) Eddie Robinson	2.50	1.25	.70
(224) Floyd Robinson	15.00	7.50	4.50
(225) Frankie Robinson	12.00	6.00	3.50
(226) Jackie Robinson	12.00	6.00	3.50
(227) Preacher Roe	4.50	2.25	1.25
(228) Bob Rogers (Rodgers)	15.00	7.50	4.50
(229) Richard Rollins	15.00	7.50	4.50
(230) Pete Runnels	8.50	4.25	2.50
(231) John Sain	3.50	1.75	1.00
(232) Ron Santo	6.00	3.00	1.75
(233) Henry Sauer	3.50	1.75	1.00
(234a) Carl Sawatski ("M" on cap)	2.50	1.25	.70
(234b) Carl Sawatski ("P" on cap)	2.50	1.25	.70
(234c) Carl Sawatski (plain cap)	10.00	5.00	3.00
(235) Johnny Schmitz	3.50	1.75	1.00
(236a) Red Schoendinst (Schoendienst) (fielding, name in white)	3.50	1.75	1.00
(236b) Red Schoendinst (Schoendienst) (fielding, name in red-brown)	5.00	2.50	1.50
(237) Red Schoendinst (Schoendienst) (batting)	2.50	1.25	.70
(238a) Herb Score ("C" on cap)	3.50	1.75	1.00
(238b) Herb Score (plain cap)	8.50	4.25	2.50
(239) Andy Seminick	2.50	1.25	.70
(240) Rip Sewell	5.00	2.50	1.50
(241) Norm Siebern	2.50	1.25	.70
(242) Roy Sievers (batting)	3.50	1.75	1.00
(243a) Roy Sievers (portrait, "W" on cap, light background)	5.00	2.50	1.50
(243b) Roy Sievers (portrait, "W" on cap, dark background)	3.50	1.75	1.00
(243c) Roy Sievers (portrait, plain cap)	4.50	2.25	1.25
(244) Curt Simmons	3.50	1.75	1.00
(245) Dick Sisler	3.50	1.75	1.00
(246) Bill Skowron	3.50	1.75	1.00
(247) Bill "Moose" Skowron	35.00	17.50	10.50
(248) Enos Slaughter	5.00	2.50	1.50
(249a) Duke Snider ("B" on cap)	8.50	4.25	2.50
(249b) Duke Snider ("LA" on cap)	12.00	6.00	3.50
(250a) Warren Spahn ("B" on cap)	6.00	3.00	1.75
(250b) Warren Spahn ("M" on cap)	8.50	4.25	2.50
(251) Stanley Spence	10.00	5.00	3.00
(252) Ed Stanky (plain uniform)	3.50	1.75	1.00
(253) Ed Stanky (Giants uniform)	3.50	1.75	1.00
(254) Vern Stephens (batting)	3.50	1.75	1.00
(255) Vern Stephens (portrait)	3.50	1.75	1.00

	NR MT	EX	VG
(256) Ed Stewart	3.50	1.75	1.00
(257) Snuffy Stirnweiss	10.00	5.00	3.00
(258) George "Birdie" Tebbetts	4.50	2.25	1.25
(259) Frankie Thomas (photo actually Bob Skinner)	20.00	10.00	6.00
(260) Frank Thomas (portrait)	10.00	5.00	3.00
(261) Lee Thomas	2.50	1.25	.70
(262) Bobby Thomson	5.00	2.50	1.50
(263a)Earl Torgeson (Braves uniform)	1.25	.60	.40
(263b)Earl Torgeson (plain uniform)	3.50	1.75	1.00
(264) Gus Triandos	5.00	2.50	1.50
(265) Virgil Trucks	2.50	1.25	.70
(266) Johnny Vandermeer (Vander Meer)	10.00	5.00	3.00
(267) Emil Verban	5.00	2.50	1.50
(268) Mickey Vernon (throwing)	2.50	1.25	.70
(269) Mickey Vernon (batting)	2.50	1.25	.70
(270) Bill Voiselle	5.00	2.50	1.50
(271) Leon Wagner	2.50	1.25	.70
(272a)Eddie Waitkus (throwing, Chicago uniform)	5.00	2.50	1.50
(272b)Eddie Waitkus (throwing, plain uniform)	3.50	1.75	1.00
(273) Eddie Waitkus (portrait)	10.00	5.00	3.00
(274) Dick Wakefield	3.50	1.75	1.00
(275) Harry Walker	5.00	2.50	1.50
(276) Bucky Walters	4.50	2.25	1.25
(277) Pete Ward	20.00	10.00	6.00
(278) Herman Wehmeier	3.50	1.75	1.00
(279) Vic Wertz (batting)	2.50	1.25	.70
(280) Vic Wertz (portrait)	2.50	1.25	.70
(281) Wally Westlake	3.50	1.75	1.00
(282) Wes Westrum	10.00	5.00	3.00
(283) Billy Williams	8.50	4.25	2.50
(284) Maurice Wills	8.50	4.25	2.50
(285a)Gene Woodling (script signature)	2.50	1.25	.70
(285b)Gene Woodling (plain signature)	5.00	2.50	1.50
(286) Taffy Wright	3.50	1.75	1.00
(287) Carl Yastrazemski (Yastrzemski)	110.00	55.00	33.00
(288) Al Zarilla	3.50	1.75	1.00
(289a)Gus Zernial (script signature)	2.50	1.25	.70
(289b)Gus Zernial (plain signature)	5.00	2.50	1.50
(290) Braves Team - 1948	12.00	6.00	3.50
(291) Dodgers Team - 1949	14.00	7.00	4.25
(292) Dodgers Team - 1952	14.00	7.00	4.25
(293) Dodgers Team - 1955	14.00	7.00	4.25
(294) Dodgers Team - 1956	14.00	7.00	4.25
(295) Giants Team - 1951	12.00	6.00	3.50
(296) Giants Team - 1954	12.00	6.00	3.50
(297) Indians Team - 1948	12.00	6.00	3.50
(298) Indians Team - 1954	12.00	6.00	3.50
(299) Phillies Team - 1950	12.00	6.00	3.50
(300) Yankees Team - 1949	15.00	7.50	4.50
(301) Yankees Team - 1950	15.00	7.50	4.50
(302) Yankees Team - 1951	15.00	7.50	4.50
(303) Yankees Team - 1952	15.00	7.50	4.50
(304) Yankees Team - 1955	15.00	7.50	4.50
(305) Yankees Team - 1956	15.00	7.50	4.50

1962 Exhibit Statistic Backs

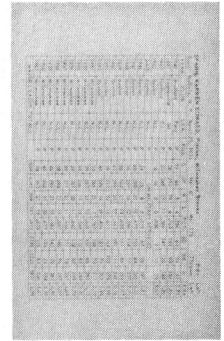

In 1962, the Exhibit Supply Co. added career statistics to the yearly set they produced. The black and white, unnumbered cards measure 3⅜" by 5⅜". The statistics found on the back are printed in black. The set is comprised of 32 cards.

		NR MT	EX	VG
Complete Set:		200.00	100.00	60.00
Common Player:		1.25	.60	.40
(1)	Hank Aaron	12.00	6.00	3.50
(2)	Luis Aparicio	3.50	1.75	1.00
(3)	Ernie Banks	6.50	3.25	2.00
(4)	Larry "Yogi" Berra	8.00	4.00	2.50
(5)	Ken Boyer	2.00	1.00	.60
(6)	Lew Burdette	1.50	.70	.45
(7)	Norm Cash	1.50	.70	.45
(8)	Orlando Cepeda	2.50	1.25	.70
(9)	Roberto Clemente	10.00	5.00	3.00
(10)	Rocky Colavito	2.00	1.00	.60
(11)	Ed "Whitey" Ford	6.50	3.25	2.00
(12)	Nelson Fox	2.50	1.25	.70
(13)	Tito Francona	1.25	.60	.40
(14)	Jim Gentile	1.25	.60	.40
(15)	Dick Groat	1.50	.70	.45
(16)	Don Hoak	1.50	.70	.45
(17)	Al Kaline	6.50	3.25	2.00
(18)	Harmon Killebrew	6.50	3.25	2.00
(19)	Sandy Koufax	10.00	5.00	3.00
(20)	Jim Landis	1.25	.60	.40
(21)	Art Mahaffey	1.25	.60	.40
(22)	Frank Malzone	1.25	.60	.40
(23)	Mickey Mantle	40.00	20.00	12.00
(24)	Roger Maris	6.50	3.25	2.00
(25)	Eddie Mathews	4.50	2.25	1.25
(26)	Willie Mays	12.00	6.00	3.50
(27)	Wally Moon	1.50	.70	.45
(28)	Stan Musial	12.00	6.00	3.50
(29)	Milt Pappas	1.50	.70	.45
(30)	Vada Pinson	2.00	1.00	.60
(31)	Norm Siebern	1.25	.60	.40
(32)	Warren Spahn	4.50	2.25	1.25

1963 Exhibit Statistic Backs

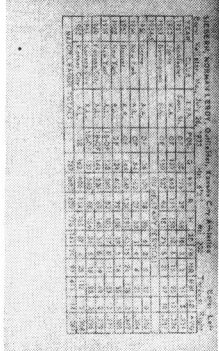

The Exhibit Supply Co. issued a 64-card set with career statistics on the backs of the cards in 1963. The unnumbered, black and white cards are printed on thick cardboard and measure 3⅜" by 5⅜" in size. Cards can be found with the statistics printed in either black or red.

		NR MT	EX	VG
Complete Set:		250.00	125.00	75.00
Common Player:		1.25	.60	.40
(1)	Hank Aaron	12.00	6.00	3.50
(2)	Luis Aparicio	3.50	1.75	1.00
(3)	Bob Aspromonte	1.25	.60	.40
(4)	Ernie Banks	6.50	3.25	2.00
(5)	Steve Barber	1.25	.60	.40
(6)	Earl Battey	1.25	.60	.40
(7)	Larry "Yogi" Berra	8.00	4.00	2.50
(8)	Ken Boyer	2.00	1.00	.60
(9)	Lew Burdette	1.50	.70	.45
(10)	Johnny Callison	1.50	.70	.45
(11)	Norm Cash	1.50	.70	.45
(12)	Orlando Cepeda	2.50	1.25	.70

		NR MT	EX	VG
(13)	Dean Chance	1.25	.60	.40
(14)	Tom Cheney	1.25	.60	.40
(15)	Roberto Clemente	10.00	5.00	3.00
(16)	Rocky Colavito	2.00	1.00	.60
(17)	Choo Choo Coleman	1.25	.60	.40
(18)	Roger Craig	1.50	.70	.45
(19)	Joe Cunningham	1.25	.60	.40
(20)	Don Drysdale	4.50	2.25	1.25
(21)	Dick Farrell	1.25	.60	.40
(22)	Ed "Whitey" Ford	6.50	3.25	2.00
(23)	Nelson Fox	2.50	1.25	.70
(24)	Tito Francona	1.25	.60	.40
(25)	Jim Gentile	1.25	.60	.40
(26)	Tony Gonzalez	1.25	.60	.40
(27)	Dick Groat	1.50	.70	.45
(28)	Ray Herbert	1.25	.60	.40
(29)	Chuck Hinton	1.25	.60	.40
(30)	Don Hoak	1.50	.70	.45
(31)	Frank Howard	2.00	1.00	.60
(32)	Ken Hubbs	1.50	.70	.45
(33)	Joey Jay	1.25	.60	.40
(34)	Al Kaline	6.50	3.25	2.00
(35)	Harmon Killebrew	6.50	3.25	2.00
(36)	Sandy Koufax	10.00	5.00	3.00
(37)	Harvey Kuenn	2.00	1.00	.60
(38)	Jim Landis	1.25	.60	.40
(39)	Art Mahaffey	1.25	.60	.40
(40)	Frank Malzone	1.25	.60	.40
(41)	Mickey Mantle	40.00	20.00	12.00
(42)	Roger Maris	6.50	3.25	2.00
(43)	Eddie Mathews	4.50	2.25	1.25
(44)	Willie Mays	12.00	6.00	3.50
(45)	Bill Mazeroski	2.00	1.00	.60
(46)	Ken McBride	1.25	.60	.40
(47)	Wally Moon	1.50	.70	.45
(48)	Stan Musial	12.00	6.00	3.50
(49)	Charlie Neal	1.25	.60	.40
(50)	Bill O'Dell	1.25	.60	.40
(51)	Milt Pappas	1.50	.70	.45
(52)	Camilo Pascual	1.50	.70	.45
(53)	Jimmy Piersall	2.00	1.00	.60
(54)	Vada Pinson	2.00	1.00	.60
(55)	Brooks Robinson	6.50	3.25	2.00
(56)	Frankie Robinson	6.50	3.25	2.00
(57)	Pete Runnels	1.50	.70	.45
(58)	Ron Santo	2.00	1.00	.60
(59)	Norm Siebern	1.25	.60	.40
(60)	Warren Spahn	4.50	2.25	1.25
(61)	Lee Thomas	1.25	.60	.40
(62)	Leon Wagner	1.25	.60	.40
(63)	Billy Williams	2.50	1.25	.70
(64)	Maurice Wills	2.50	1.25	.70

1987 Farmland Dairies Mets

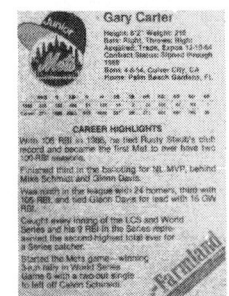

The New York Mets and Farmland Dairies produced a nine-card panel of baseball cards for members of the Junior Mets Club. Members of the club, kids 14 years of age and younger, received the perforated panel as part of a package featuring gifts and special privileges. The cards are the standard 2½" by 3½" with fronts containing a full-color photo encompassed by a blue border. The backs are designed on a vertical format and have player statistics and career highlights. The Farmland Dairies and Junior Mets Club logos are also carried on the cards backs.

		MT	NR MT	EX
Complete Panel Set:		12.00	9.00	4.75
Complete Singles Set:		4.00	3.00	1.50
Common Single Player:		.25	.20	.10
Panel		12.00	9.00	4.75
1	Mookie Wilson	.25	.20	.10
4	Len Dykstra	.30	.25	.12
8	Gary Carter	.70	.50	.30
12	Ron Darling	.40	.30	.15
18	Darryl Strawberry	.70	.50	.30
19	Bob Ojeda	.25	.20	.10
22	Kevin McReynolds	.40	.30	.15
42	Roger McDowell	.25	.20	.10
---	Team Card	.25	.20	.10

1959 Fleer Ted Williams

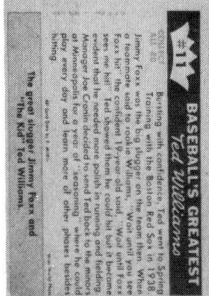

The 80-card 1959 Fleer set tells of the life of baseball great Ted Williams, from his childhood years up to 1958. The full-color cards measure 2½" by 3½" in size and make use of both horizontal and vertical formats. The card backs, all designed horizontally, contain a continuing biography of Williams. Card #68 was withdrawn from the set early in production and is scarce. Counterfeit cards of #68 have been produced and can be distinguished by a cross-hatch pattern which appears over the photo on the card fronts.

		NR MT	EX	VG
Complete Set:		275.00	137.00	82.00
Common Player:		1.25	.60	.40
1	The Early Years	6.00	3.00	1.75
2	Ted's Idol - Babe Ruth	5.00	2.50	1.50
3	Practice Makes Perfect	1.25	.60	.40
4	1934 - Ted Learns The Fine Points			
		1.25	.60	.40
5	Ted's Fame Spreads - 1935-36	1.25	.60	.40
6	Ted Turns Professional	1.25	.60	.40
7	1936 - From Mound To Plate	1.25	.60	.40
8	1937 - First Full Season	1.25	.60	.40
9	1937 - First Step To The Majors	1.25	.60	.40
10	1938 - Gunning As A Pastime	1.25	.60	.40
11	1938 - First Spring Training	2.00	1.00	.60
12	1939 - Burning Up The Minors	1.25	.60	.40
13	1939 - Ted Shows He Will Stay	1.25	.60	.40
14	Outstanding Rookie of 1939	1.25	.60	.40
15	1940 - Williams Licks Sophomore Jinx			
		1.25	.60	.40
16	1941 - Williams' Greatest Year	1.25	.60	.40
17	1941 - How Ted Hit .400	1.25	.60	.40
18	1941 - All-Star Hero	1.25	.60	.40
19	1942 - Ted Wins Triple Crown	1.25	.60	.40
20	1942 - On To Naval Training	1.25	.60	.40
21	1943 - Honors For Williams	1.25	.60	.40
22	1944 - Ted Solos	1.25	.60	.40

		NR MT	EX	VG
23	1944 - Williams Wins His Wings	1.25	.60	.40
24	1945 - Sharpshooter	1.25	.60	.40
25	1945 - Ted Is Discharged	1.25	.60	.40
26	1946 - Off To A Flying Start	1.25	.60	.40
27	July 9, 1946 - One Man Show	1.25	.60	.40
28	July 14, 1946 - The Williams Shift	1.25	.60	.40
29	July 21, 1946, Ted Hits For The Cycle	1.25	.60	.40
30	1946 - Beating The Williams Shift	1.25	.60	.40
31	Oct. 1946 - Sox Lose The Series	1.25	.60	.40
32	1946 - Most Valuable Player	1.25	.60	.40
33	1947 - Another Triple Crown For Ted	1.25	.60	.40
34	1947 - Ted Sets Runs-Scored Record	1.25	.60	.40
35	1948 - The Sox Miss The Pennant	1.25	.60	.40
36	1948 - Banner Year For Ted	1.25	.60	.40
37	1949 - Sox Miss Out Again	1.25	.60	.40
38	1949 - Power Rampage	1.25	.60	.40
39	1950 - Great Start	1.50	.70	.45
40	July 11, 1950 - Ted Crashes Into Wall	1.25	.60	.40
41	1950 - Ted Recovers	1.25	.60	.40
42	1951 - Williams Slowed By Injury	1.25	.60	.40
43	1951 - Leads Outfielders In Double Plays	1.25	.60	.40
44	1952 - Back To The Marines	1.25	.60	.40
45	1952 - Farewell To Baseball?	1.25	.60	.40
46	1952 - Ready For Combat	1.25	.60	.40
47	1953 - Ted Crash Lands Jet	1.25	.60	.40
48	July 14, 1953 - Ted Returns	1.25	.60	.40
49	1953 - Smash Return	1.25	.60	.40
50	March 1954 - Spring Injury	1.25	.60	.40
51	May 16, 1954 - Ted Is Patched Up	1.25	.60	.40
52	1954 - Ted's Comeback	1.25	.60	.40
53	1954 - Ted's Comeback Is A Sucess	1.25	.60	.40
54 One	Dec. 1954, Fisherman Ted Hooks a Big	1.25	.60	.40
55	1955 - Ted Decides Retirement Is "No Go"	1.25	.60	.40
56	1956 - Ted Reaches 400th Homer,	1.25	.60	.40
58	1957 - Williams Hits .388	1.25	.60	.40
59	1957 - Hot September For Ted	1.25	.60	.40
60	1957 - More Records For Ted	1.25	.60	.40
61	1957 - Outfielder Ted	1.25	.60	.40
62	1958 - 6th Batting Title For Ted	1.25	.60	.40
63	Ted's All-Star Record	1.25	.60	.40
64	1958 - Daughter And Famous Daddy	1.25	.60	.40
65	August 30, 1958	1.25	.60	.40
66	1958 - Powerhouse	1.25	.60	.40
67	Two Famous Fisherman	1.50	.70	.45
68	Jan. 23, 1959 - Ted Signs For 1959	150 00	75.00	45.00
69	A Future Ted Williams?	1.25	.60	.40
70	Ted Williams & Jim Thorpe	1.50	.70	.45
71	Ted's Hitting Fundamentals #1	1.25	.60	.40
72	Ted's Hitting Fundamentals #2	1.25	.60	.40
73	Ted's Hitting Fundamentals #3	1.25	.60	.40
74	Here's How!	1.25	.60	.40
75	Williams' Value To Red Sox	4.00	2.00	1.25
76	Ted's Remarkable "On Base" Record	1.25	.60	.40
77	Ted Relaxes	1.25	.60	.40
78	Honors For Williams	1.25	.60	.40
79	Where Ted Stands	1.25	.60	.40
80	Ted's Goals For 1959	2.50	1.25	.70

1960 Fleer

The 1960 Fleer Baseball Greats set consists of 79 cards of the game's top players from the past. (The set does include a card of Ted Williams, who was in his final major league season). The cards are standard size (2½'' by 3½'') and feature color photos inside blue, green, red or yellow borders. The card backs carry a short player biography plus career hitting or pitching statistics. Cards with a Pepper Martin back (#80) but with another player pictured on the front are in existence.

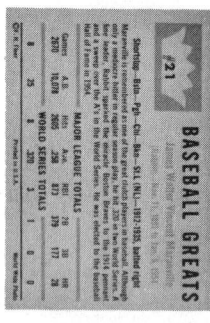

		NR MT	EX	VG
	Complete Set:	125.00	62.00	37.00
	Common Player:	.80	.40	.25
1	Nap Lajoie	3.50	1.75	1.00
2	Christy Mathewson	2.00	1.00	.60
3	Babe Ruth	10.00	5.00	3.00
4	Carl Hubbell	1.25	.60	.40
5	Grover Cleveland Alexander	1.25	.60	.40
6	Walter Johnson	2.50	1.25	.70
7	Chief Bender	.80	.40	.25
8	Roger Bresnahan	.80	.40	.25
9	Mordecai Brown	.80	.40	.25
10	Tris Speaker	2.00	1.00	.60
11	Arky Vaughan	.80	.40	.25
12	Zack Wheat	.80	.40	.25
13	George Sisler	1.25	.60	.40
14	Connie Mack	2.00	1.00	.60
15	Clark Griffith	.80	.40	.25
16	Lou Boudreau	.80	.40	.25
17	Ernie Lombardi	.80	.40	.25
18	Heinie Manush	.80	.40	.25
19	Marty Marion	.80	.40	.25
20	Eddie Collins	.90	.45	.25
21	Rabbit Maranville	.80	.40	.25
22	Joe Medwick	.80	.40	.25
23	Ed Barrow	.80	.40	.25
24	Mickey Cochrane	1.25	.60	.40
25	Jimmy Collins	.80	.40	.25
26	Bob Feller	3.50	1.75	1.00
27	Luke Appling	.80	.40	.25
28	Lou Gehrig	7.00	3.50	2.00
29	Gabby Hartnett	.80	.40	.25
30	Chuck Klein	.80	.40	.25
31	Tony Lazzeri	.80	.40	.25
32	Al Simmons	.80	.40	.25
33	Wilbert Robinson	.80	.40	.25
34	Sam Rice	.80	.40	.25
35	Herb Pennock	.80	.40	.25
36	Mel Ott	1.50	.70	.45
37	Lefty O'Doul	.80	.40	.25
38	Johnny Mize	.90	.45	.25
39	Bing Miller	.80	.40	.25
40	Joe Tinker	.80	.40	.25
41	Frank Baker	.80	.40	.25
42	Ty Cobb	8.00	4.00	2.50
43	Paul Derringer	.80	.40	.25
44	Cap Anson	1.25	.60	.40
45	Jim Bottomley	.80	.40	.25
46	Eddie Plank	.80	.40	.25
47	Cy Young	2.00	1.00	.60
48	Hack Wilson	.80	.40	.25
49	Ed Walsh	.80	.40	.25
50	Frank Chance	.80	.40	.25
51	Dazzy Vance	.80	.40	.25
52	Bill Terry	.90	.45	.25
53	Jimmy Foxx	1.50	.70	.45
54	Lefty Gomez	.90	.45	.25
55	Branch Rickey	.80	.40	.25
56	Ray Schalk	.80	.40	.25
57	Johnny Evers	.80	.40	.25
58	Charlie Gehringer	.90	.45	.25
59	Burleigh Grimes	.80	.40	.25
60	Lefty Grove	1.50	.70	.45
61	Rube Waddell	.80	.40	.25
62	Honus Wagner	2.50	1.25	.70
63	Red Ruffing	.80	.40	.25
64	Judge Landis	.80	.40	.25
65	Harry Heilmann	.80	.40	.25
66	John McGraw	1.25	.60	.40
67	Hughie Jennings	.80	.40	.25
68	Hal Newhouser	.80	.40	.25

		NR MT	EX	VG
69	Waite Hoyt	.80	.40	.25
70	Bobo Newsom	.80	.40	.25
71	Earl Averill	.80	.40	.25
72	Ted Williams	9.00	4.50	2.75
73	Warren Giles	.80	.40	.25
74	Ford Frick	.80	.40	.25
75	Ki Ki Cuyler	.80	.40	.25
76	Paul Waner	.80	.40	.25
77	Pie Traynor	.80	.40	.25
78	Lloyd Waner	.80	.40	.25
79	Ralph Kiner	2.50	1.25	.70

1961 Fleer

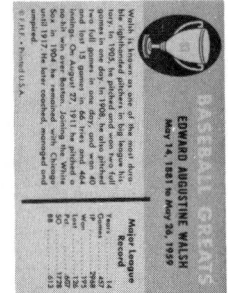

In 1962, Fleer issued another set utilizing the Baseball Greats theme. The 154-card set was issued in two series and features a color player portrait against a color background. The player's name is located in a pennant set at the bottom of the card. The card backs feature orange and black on white stock and contain player biographical and statistical information. The cards measure 2½'' by 3½'' in size. The players in each series are listed alphabetically, with numbers 89-154 being the most difficult to obtain.

		NR MT	EX	VG
Complete Set:		325.00	162.00	97.00
Common Player: 1-88		.80	.40	.25
Common Player: 89-154		2.50	1.25	.70
1	Baker, Cobb, Wheat/Checklist	6.50	3.25	2.00
2	G.C. Alexander	1.25	.60	.40
3	Nick Altrock	.80	.40	.25
4	Cap Anson	1.25	.60	.40
5	Earl Averill	.80	.40	.25
6	Home Run Baker	.80	.40	.25
7	Dave Bancroft	.80	.40	.25
8	Chief Bender	.80	.40	.25
9	Jim Bottomley	.80	.40	.25
10	Roger Bresnahan	.80	.40	.25
11	Mordecai Brown	.80	.40	.25
12	Max Carey	.80	.40	.25
13	Jack Chesbro	.80	.40	.25
14	Ty Cobb	8.00	4.00	2.50
15	Mickey Cochrane	.90	.45	.25
16	Eddie Collins	.80	.40	.25
17	Earle Combs	.80	.40	.25
18	Charles Comiskey	.80	.40	.25
19	Ki Ki Cuyler	.80	.40	.25
20	Paul Derringer	.80	.40	.25
21	Howard Ehmke	.80	.40	.25
22	Billy Evans	.80	.40	.25
23	Johnny Evers	.80	.40	.25
24	Red Faber	.80	.40	.25
25	Bob Feller	3.50	1.75	1.00
26	Wes Ferrell	.80	.40	.25
27	Lew Fonseca	.80	.40	.25
28	Jimmy Foxx	1.50	.70	.45
29	Ford Frick	.80	.40	.25
30	Frankie Frisch	.90	.45	.25
31	Lou Gehrig	7.00	3.50	2.00
32	Charlie Gehringer	.90	.45	.25
33	Warren Giles	.80	.40	.25
34	Lefty Gomez	.90	.45	.25
35	Goose Goslin	.80	.40	.25
36	Clark Griffith	.80	.40	.25
37	Burleigh Grimes	.80	.40	.25
38	Lefty Grove	1.25	.60	.40
39	Chick Hafey	.80	.40	.25
40	Jesse Haines	.80	.40	.25
41	Gabby Hartnett	.80	.40	.25
42	Harry Heilmann	.80	.40	.25
43	Rogers Hornsby	1.25	.60	.40
44	Waite Hoyt	.80	.40	.25
45	Carl Hubbell	1.25	.60	.40
46	Miller Huggins	.80	.40	.25
47	Hughie Jennings	.80	.40	.25
48	Ban Johnson	.80	.40	.25
49	Walter Johnson	2.50	1.25	.70
50	Ralph Kiner	.90	.45	.25
51	Chuck Klein	.80	.40	.25
52	Johnny Kling	.80	.40	.25
53	Judge Landis	.80	.40	.25
54	Tony Lazzeri	.80	.40	.25
55	Ernie Lombardi	.80	.40	.25
56	Dolf Luque	.80	.40	.25
57	Heinie Manush	.80	.40	.25
58	Marty Marion	.80	.40	.25
59	Christy Mathewson	2.00	1.00	.60
60	John McGraw	1.25	.60	.40
61	Joe Medwick	.80	.40	.25
62	Bing Miller	.80	.40	.25
63	Johnny Mize	.90	.45	.25
64	Johnny Mostil	.80	.40	.25
65	Art Nehf	.80	.40	.25
66	Hal Newhouser	.80	.40	.25
67	Bobo Newsom	.80	.40	.25
68	Mel Ott	1.25	.60	.40
69	Allie Reynolds	.80	.40	.25
70	Sam Rice	.80	.40	.25
71	Eppa Rixey	.80	.40	.25
72	Edd Roush	.80	.40	.25
73	Schoolboy Rowe	.80	.40	.25
74	Red Ruffing	.80	.40	.25
75	Babe Ruth	10.00	5.00	3.00
76	Joe Sewell	.80	.40	.25
77	Al Simmons	.80	.40	.25
78	George Sisler	.90	.45	.25
79	Tris Speaker	1.25	.60	.40
80	Fred Toney	.80	.40	.25
81	Dazzy Vance	.80	.40	.25
82	Jim Vaughn	.80	.40	.25
83	Big Ed Walsh	.80	.40	.25
84	Lloyd Waner	.80	.40	.25
85	Paul Waner	.80	.40	.25
86	Zach Wheat	.80	.40	.25
87	Hack Wilson	.80	.40	.25
88	Jimmy Wilson	.80	.40	.25
89	Sisler & Traynor/Checklist	6.50	3.25	2.00
90	Babe Adams	2.50	1.25	.70
91	Dale Alexander	2.50	1.25	.70
92	Jim Bagby	2.50	1.25	.70
93	Ossie Bluege	2.50	1.25	.70
94	Lou Boudreau	3.50	1.75	1.00
95	Tommy Bridges	2.50	1.25	.70
96	Donnie Bush (Donie)	2.50	1.25	.70
97	Dolph Camilli	2.50	1.25	.70
98	Frank Chance	3.50	1.75	1.00
99	Jimmy Collins	2.75	1.50	.80
100	Stanley Coveleskie (Coveleski)	2.75	1.50	.80
101	Hughie Critz	2.50	1.25	.70
102	General Crowder	2.50	1.25	.70
103	Joe Dugan	2.50	1.25	.70
104	Bibb Falk	2.50	1.25	.70
105	Rick Ferrell	2.75	1.50	.80
106	Art Fletcher	2.50	1.25	.70
107	Dennis Galehouse	2.50	1.25	.70
108	Chick Galloway	2.50	1.25	.70
109	Mule Haas	2.50	1.25	.70
110	Stan Hack	2.50	1.25	.70
111	Bump Hadley	2.50	1.25	.70
112	Billy Hamilton	2.75	1.50	.80
113	Joe Hauser	2.50	1.25	.70
114	Babe Herman	2.50	1.25	.70
115	Travis Jackson	2.75	1.50	.80
116	Eddie Joost	2.50	1.25	.70
117	Addie Joss	2.75	1.50	.80
118	Joe Judge	2.50	1.25	.70
119	Joe Kuhel	2.50	1.25	.70
120	Nap Lajoie	4.00	2.00	1.25
121	Dutch Leonard	2.50	1.25	.70
122	Ted Lyons	2.75	1.50	.80
123	Connie Mack	5.00	2.50	1.50
124	Rabbit Maranville	2.75	1.50	.80
125	Fred Marberry	2.50	1.25	.70
126	Iron Man McGinnity	2.75	1.50	.80
127	Oscar Melillo	2.50	1.25	.70

		NR MT	EX	VG
128	Ray Mueller	2.50	1.25	.70
129	Kid Nichols	2.75	1.50	.80
130	Lefty O'Doul	2.50	1.25	.70
131	Bob O'Farrell	2.50	1.25	.70
132	Roger Peckinpaugh	2.50	1.25	.70
133	Herb Pennock	2.75	1.50	.80
134	George Pipgras	2.50	1.25	.70
135	Eddie Plank	2.75	1.50	.80
136	Ray Schalk	2.75	1.50	.80
137	Hal Schumacher	2.50	1.25	.70
138	Luke Sewell	2.50	1.25	.70
139	Bob Shawkey	2.50	1.25	.70
140	Riggs Stephenson	2.50	1.25	.70
141	Billy Sullivan	2.50	1.25	.70
142	Bill Terry	4.00	2.00	1.25
143	Joe Tinker	2.75	1.50	.80
144	Pie Traynor	3.50	1.75	1.00
145	George Uhle	2.50	1.25	.70
146	Hal Troskey (Trosky)	2.50	1.25	.70
147	Arky Vaughan	2.75	1.50	.80
148	Johnny Vander Meer	2.50	1.25	.70
149	Rube Waddell	2.75	1.50	.80
150	Honus Wagner	8.00	4.00	2.50
151	Dixie Walker	2.50	1.25	.70
152	Ted Williams	13.00	6.50	4.00
153	Cy Young	5.00	2.50	1.50
154	Ross Young (Youngs)	4.50	2.25	1.25

		NR MT	EX	VG
22	Jim Kaat	4.00	2.00	1.25
23	Vic Power	1.25	.60	.40
24	Rich Rollins	1.25	.60	.40
25	Bobby Richardson	3.00	1.50	.90
26	Ralph Terry	2.00	1.00	.60
27	Tom Cheney	1.25	.60	.40
28	Chuck Cottier	1.25	.60	.40
29	Jimmy Piersall	2.00	1.00	.60
30	Dave Stenhouse	1.25	.60	.40
31	Glen Hobbie	1.25	.60	.40
32	Ron Santo	2.00	1.00	.60
33	Gene Freese	1.25	.60	.40
34	Vada Pinson	2.00	1.00	.60
35	Bob Purkey	1.25	.60	.40
36	Joe Amalfitano	1.25	.60	.40
37	Bob Aspromonte	1.25	.60	.40
38	Dick Farrell	1.25	.60	.40
39	Al Spangler	1.25	.60	.40
40	Tommy Davis	2.00	1.00	.60
41	Don Drysdale	8.50	4.25	2.50
42	Sandy Koufax	21.00	10.50	6.25
43	Maury Wills	19.00	9.50	5.75
44	Frank Bolling	1.25	.60	.40
45	Warren Spahn	8.50	4.25	2.50
46	Joe Adcock	54.00	27.00	16.00
47	Roger Craig	2.00	1.00	.60
48	Al Jackson	1.50	.70	.45
49	Rod Kanehl	1.50	.70	.45
50	Ruben Amaro	1.25	.60	.40
51	John Callison	1.50	.70	.45
52	Clay Dalrymple	1.25	.60	.40
53	Don Demeter	1.25	.60	.40
54	Art Mahaffey	1.25	.60	.40
55	"Smoky" Burgess	1.50	.70	.45
56	Roberto Clemente	21.00	10.50	6.25
57	Elroy Face	1.50	.70	.45
58	Vernon Law	1.50	.70	.45
59	Bill Mazeroski	2.00	1.00	.60
60	Ken Boyer	2.00	1.00	.60
61	Bob Gibson	8.50	4.25	2.50
62	Gene Oliver	1.25	.60	.40
63	Bill White	1.50	.70	.45
64	Orlando Cepeda	2.50	1.25	.70
65	Jimmy Davenport	1.25	.60	.40
66	Billy O'Dell	2.50	1.25	.70
---	Checklist 1-66	80.00	40.00	24.00

1963 Fleer

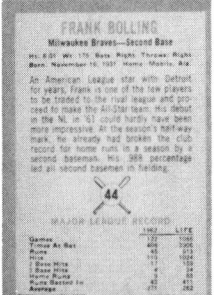

FRANK BOLLING
Milwaukee Braves—2nd Base

A lawsuit by Topps stopped Fleer's 1963 set at one series of 66 cards. Issued with a cookie rather than gum, the set features color photos of current players. The card backs include statistical information for 1962 and career plus a brief player biography. The cards, which measure 2½" by 3½", are numbered 1-66. An unnumbered checklist was issued with the set and is included in the complete set price in the checklist that follows. The checklist and #46 Adcock are scarce.

		NR MT	EX	VG
Complete Set:		400.00	150.00	80.00
Common Player:		1.25	.60	.40
1	Steve Barber	3.50	1.75	1.00
2	Ron Hansen	1.25	.60	.40
3	Milt Pappas	1.50	.70	.45
4	Brooks Robinson	11.50	5.75	3.50
5	Willie Mays	21.00	10.50	6.25
6	Lou Clinton	1.25	.60	.40
7	Bill Monbouquette	1.25	.60	.40
8	Carl Yastrzemski	23.00	11.50	7.00
9	Ray Herbert	1.25	.60	.40
10	Jim Landis	1.25	.60	.40
11	Dick Donovan	1.25	.60	.40
12	Tito Francona	1.25	.60	.40
13	Jerry Kindall	1.25	.60	.40
14	Frank Lary	1.25	.60	.40
15	Dick Howser	2.00	1.00	.60
16	Jerry Lumpe	1.25	.60	.40
17	Norm Siebern	1.25	.60	.40
18	Don Lee	1.25	.60	.40
19	Albie Pearson	1.25	.60	.40
20	Bob Rodgers	1.50	.70	.45
21	Leon Wagner	1.25	.60	.40

1981 Fleer

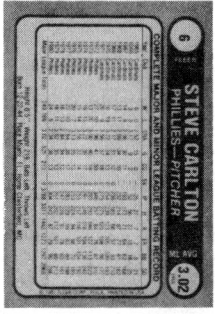

STEVE CARLTON
PITCHER OF THE YEAR

For the first time in 18 years, Fleer issued a baseball card set featuring current players. Fleer's 660-card effort included numerous errors in the first printing run which were subsequently corrected in additional runs. The cards, which measure 2½" by 3½", are numbered alphabetically by team. The card fronts feature a full color photo inside a border which is color-coded by team. The card backs have black, grey and yellow ink on white stock and carry player statistical information. The player's batting average or earned run average is located in a circle in the upper right corner of the card. The complete set price in the checklist that follows does not include the higher priced variations.

	MT	NR MT	EX
Complete Set:	20.00	15.00	8.00
Common Player:	.06	.05	.02
1 Pete Rose	1.75	1.25	.70
2 Larry Bowa	.15	.11	.06
3 Manny Trillo	.08	.06	.03
4 Bob Boone	.10	.08	.04
5a Mike Schmidt (portrait)	.90	.70	.35
5b Mike Schmidt (batting)	.70	.50	.30
6a Steve Carlton ("Lefty" on front)	.80	.60	.30
6b Steve Carlton (Pitcher of the Year on front, date 1066 on back)	.60	.45	.25
6c Steve Carlton (Pitcher of the Year on front, date 1966 on back)	2.00	1.50	.80
7a Tug McGraw (Game Saver on front)	.50	.40	.20
7b Tug McGraw (Pitcher on front)	.12	.09	.05
8 Larry Christenson	.06	.05	.02
9 Bake McBride	.06	.05	.02
10 Greg Luzinski	.15	.11	.06
11 Ron Reed	.08	.06	.03
12 Dickie Noles	.06	.05	.02
13 Keith Moreland	.40	.30	.15
14 Bob Walk	.10	.08	.04
15 Lonnie Smith	.08	.06	.03
16 Dick Ruthven	.06	.05	.02
17 Sparky Lyle	.10	.08	.04
18 Greg Gross	.06	.05	.02
19 Garry Maddox	.10	.08	.04
20 Nino Espinosa	.06	.05	.02
21 George Vukovich	.06	.05	.02
22 John Vukovich	.06	.05	.02
23 Ramon Aviles	.06	.05	.02
24a Kevin Saucier (Ken Saucier on back)	.15	.11	.06
24b Kevin Saucier (Kevin Saucier on back)	.70	.50	.30
25 Randy Lerch	.06	.05	.02
26 Del Unser	.06	.05	.02
27 Tim McCarver	.15	.11	.06
28a George Brett (batting)	1.25	.90	.50
28b George Brett (portrait)	.90	.70	.35
29a Willie Wilson (portrait)	.70	.50	.30
29b Willie Wilson (batting)	.15	.11	.06
30 Paul Splittorff	.08	.06	.03
31 Dan Quisenberry	.20	.15	.08
32a Amos Otis (batting)	.50	.40	.20
32b Amos Otis (portrait)	.10	.08	.04
33 Steve Busby	.08	.06	.03
34 U.L. Washington	.06	.05	.02
35 Dave Chalk	.06	.05	.02
36 Darrell Porter	.08	.06	.03
37 Marty Pattin	.06	.05	.02
38 Larry Gura	.08	.06	.03
39 Renie Martin	.06	.05	.02
40 Rich Gale	.06	.05	.02
41a Hal McRae (dark blue "Royals" on front)	.40	.30	.15
41b Hal McRae (light blue "Royals" on front)	.12	.09	.05
42 Dennis Leonard	.08	.06	.03
43 Willie Aikens	.06	.05	.02
44 Frank White	.10	.08	.04
45 Clint Hurdle	.06	.05	.02
46 John Wathan	.08	.06	.03
47 Pete LaCock	.06	.05	.02
48 Rance Mulliniks	.06	.05	.02
49 Jeff Twitty	.06	.05	.02
50 Jamie Quirk	.06	.05	.02
51 Art Howe	.06	.05	.02
52 Ken Forsch	.08	.06	.03
53 Vern Ruhle	.06	.05	.02
54 Joe Niekro	.12	.09	.05
55 Frank LaCorte	.06	.05	.02
56 J.R. Richard	.10	.08	.04
57 Nolan Ryan	.50	.40	.20
58 Enos Cabell	.08	.06	.03
59 Cesar Cedeno	.12	.09	.05
60 Jose Cruz	.12	.09	.05
61 Bill Virdon	.08	.06	.03
62 Terry Puhl	.06	.05	.02
63 Joaquin Andujar	.10	.08	.04
64 Alan Ashby	.06	.05	.02
65 Joe Sambito	.06	.05	.02
66 Denny Walling	.06	.05	.02
67 Jeff Leonard	.12	.09	.05
68 Luis Pujols	.06	.05	.02
69 Bruce Bochy	.06	.05	.02
70 Rafael Landestoy	.06	.05	.02
71 Dave Smith	.25	.20	.10
72 Danny Heep	.10	.08	.04

	MT	NR MT	EX
73 Julio Gonzalez	.06	.05	.02
74 Craig Reynolds	.06	.05	.02
75 Gary Woods	.06	.05	.02
76 Dave Bergman	.06	.05	.02
77 Randy Niemann	.06	.05	.02
78 Joe Morgan	.30	.25	.12
79a Reggie Jackson (portrait)	1.00	.70	.40
79b Reggie Jackson (batting)	.75	.60	.30
80 Bucky Dent	.10	.08	.04
81 Tommy John	.20	.15	.08
82 Luis Tiant	.12	.09	.05
83 Rick Cerone	.08	.06	.03
84 Dick Howser	.08	.06	.03
85 Lou Piniella	.15	.11	.06
86 Ron Davis	.08	.06	.03
87a Graig Nettles (Craig on back)	12.00	9.00	4.75
87b Graig Nettles (Graig on back)	.30	.25	.12
88 Ron Guidry	.25	.20	.10
89 Rich Gossage	.20	.15	.08
90 Rudy May	.08	.06	.03
91 Gaylord Perry	.30	.25	.12
92 Eric Soderholm	.06	.05	.02
93 Bob Watson	.08	.06	.03
94 Bobby Murcer	.10	.08	.04
95 Bobby Brown	.06	.05	.02
96 Jim Spencer	.06	.05	.02
97 Tom Underwood	.06	.05	.02
98 Oscar Gamble	.08	.06	.03
99 Johnny Oates	.06	.05	.02
100 Fred Stanley	.06	.05	.02
101 Ruppert Jones	.06	.05	.02
102 Dennis Werth	.06	.05	.02
103 Joe Lefebvre	.10	.08	.04
104 Brian Doyle	.06	.05	.02
105 Aurelio Rodriguez	.08	.06	.03
106 Doug Bird	.06	.05	.02
107 Mike Griffin	.06	.05	.02
108 Tim Lollar	.10	.08	.04
109 Willie Randolph	.10	.08	.04
110 Steve Garvey	.50	.40	.20
111 Reggie Smith	.10	.08	.04
112 Don Sutton	.30	.25	.12
113 Burt Hooton	.08	.06	.03
114a Davy Lopes (Davey) (no finger on back)	.10	.08	.04
114b Davy Lopes (Davey) (small finger on back)	1.00	.70	.40
115 Dusty Baker	.10	.08	.04
116 Tom Lasorda	.10	.08	.04
117 Bill Russell	.08	.06	.03
118 Jerry Reuss	.10	.08	.04
119 Terry Forster	.08	.06	.03
120a Robert Welch (Bob Welch on back)	.20	.15	.08
120b Robert Welch (Robert Welch on back)	1.00	.70	.40
121 Don Stanhouse	.06	.05	.02
122 Rick Monday	.10	.08	.04
123 Derrel Thomas	.06	.05	.02
124 Joe Ferguson	.06	.05	.02
125 Rick Sutcliffe	.25	.20	.10
126a Ron Cey (no finger on back)	.12	.09	.05
126b Ron Cey (small finger on back)	1.00	.70	.40
127 Dave Goltz	.08	.06	.03
128 Jay Johnstone	.10	.08	.04
129 Steve Yeager	.06	.05	.02
130 Gary Weiss	.06	.05	.02
131 Mike Scioscia	.20	.15	.08
132 Vic Davalillo	.08	.06	.03
133 Doug Rau	.06	.05	.02
134 Pepe Frias	.06	.05	.02
135 Mickey Hatcher	.08	.06	.03
136 Steve Howe	.15	.11	.06
137 Robert Castillo	.06	.05	.02
138 Gary Thomasson	.06	.05	.02
139 Rudy Law	.06	.05	.02
140 Fernand Valenzuela (Fernando)	4.50	3.50	1.75
141 Manny Mota	.10	.08	.04
142 Gary Carter	.50	.40	.20
143 Steve Rogers	.08	.06	.03
144 Warren Cromartie	.06	.05	.02
145 Andre Dawson	.35	.25	.14
146 Larry Parrish	.10	.08	.04
147 Rowland Office	.06	.05	.02
148 Ellis Valentine	.06	.05	.02
149 Dick Williams	.08	.06	.03
150 Bill Gullickson	.30	.25	.12
151 Elias Sosa	.06	.05	.02
152 John Tamargo	.06	.05	.02
153 Chris Speier	.08	.06	.03
154 Ron LeFlore	.08	.06	.03
155 Rodney Scott	.06	.05	.02

		MT	NR MT	EX
156	Stan Bahnsen	.06	.05	.02
157	Bill Lee	.08	.06	.03
158	Fred Norman	.06	.05	.02
159	Woodie Fryman	.08	.06	.03
160	Dave Palmer	.08	.06	.03
161	Jerry White	.06	.05	.02
162	Roberto Ramos	.06	.05	.02
163	John D'Acquisto	.06	.05	.02
164	Tommy Hutton	.06	.05	.02
165	Charlie Lea	.12	.09	.05
166	Scott Sanderson	.08	.06	.03
167	Ken Macha	.06	.05	.02
168	Tony Bernazard	.08	.06	.03
169	Jim Palmer	.40	.30	.15
170	Steve Stone	.08	.06	.03
171	Mike Flanagan	.10	.08	.04
172	Al Bumbry	.08	.06	.03
173	Doug DeCinces	.10	.08	.04
174	Scott McGregor	.10	.08	.04
175	Mark Belanger	.08	.06	.03
176	Tim Stoddard	.06	.05	.02
177a	Rick Dempsey (no finger on front)	.10	.08	.04
177b	Rick Dempsey (small finger on front)			
		1.00	.70	.40
178	Earl Weaver	.10	.08	.04
179	Tippy Martinez	.06	.05	.02
180	Dennis Martinez	.08	.06	.03
181	Sammy Stewart	.06	.05	.02
182	Rich Dauer	.06	.05	.02
183	Lee May	.08	.06	.03
184	Eddie Murray	.70	.50	.30
185	Benny Ayala	.06	.05	.02
186	John Lowenstein	.06	.05	.02
187	Gary Roenicke	.08	.06	.03
188	Ken Singleton	.10	.08	.04
189	Dan Graham	.06	.05	.02
190	Terry Crowley	.06	.05	.02
191	Kiko Garcia	.06	.05	.02
192	Dave Ford	.06	.05	.02
193	Mark Corey	.06	.05	.02
194	Lenn Sakata	.06	.05	.02
195	Doug DeCinces	.10	.08	.04
196	Johnny Bench	.50	.40	.20
197	Dave Concepcion	.15	.11	.06
198	Ray Knight	.10	.08	.04
199	Ken Griffey	.12	.09	.05
200	Tom Seaver	.50	.40	.20
201	Dave Collins	.08	.06	.03
202	George Foster	.20	.15	.08
203	Junior Kennedy	.06	.05	.02
204	Frank Pastore	.06	.05	.02
205	Dan Driessen	.08	.06	.03
206	Hector Cruz	.06	.05	.02
207	Paul Moskau	.06	.05	.02
208	Charlie Leibrandt	.40	.30	.15
209	Harry Spilman	.06	.05	.02
210	Joe Price	.12	.09	.05
211	Tom Hume	.06	.05	.02
212	Joe Nolan	.06	.05	.02
213	Doug Bair	.06	.05	.02
214	Mario Soto	.10	.08	.04
215a	Bill Bonham (no finger on back)	.08	.06	.03
215b	Bill Bonham (small finger on back)			
		1.00	.70	.40
216a	George Foster (Slugger on front)	.25	.20	.10
216b	George Foster (Outfield on front)	.20	.15	.08
217	Paul Householder	.06	.05	.02
218	Ron Oester	.06	.05	.02
219	Sam Mejias	.06	.05	.02
220	Sheldon Burnside	.06	.05	.02
221	Carl Yastrzemski	.80	.60	.30
222	Jim Rice	.50	.40	.20
223	Fred Lynn	.20	.15	.08
224	Carlton Fisk	.20	.15	.08
225	Rick Burleson	.08	.06	.03
226	Dennis Eckersley	.10	.08	.04
227	Butch Hobson	.06	.05	.02
228	Tom Burgmeier	.06	.05	.02
229	Garry Hancock	.06	.05	.02
230	Don Zimmer	.06	.05	.02
231	Steve Renko	.06	.05	.02
232	Dwight Evans	.15	.11	.06
233	Mike Torrez	.08	.06	.03
234	Bob Stanley	.08	.06	.03
235	Jim Dwyer	.06	.05	.02
236	Dave Stapleton	.10	.08	.04
237	Glenn Hoffman	.08	.06	.03
238	Jerry Remy	.06	.05	.02
239	Dick Drago	.06	.05	.02
240	Bill Campbell	.06	.05	.02
241	Tony Perez	.20	.15	.08

		MT	NR MT	EX
242	Phil Niekro	.30	.25	.12
243	Dale Murphy	.90	.70	.35
244	Bob Horner	.30	.25	.12
245	Jeff Burroughs	.08	.06	.03
246	Rick Camp	.06	.05	.02
247	Bob Cox	.06	.05	.02
248	Bruce Benedict	.06	.05	.02
249	Gene Garber	.06	.05	.02
250	Jerry Royster	.06	.05	.02
251a	Gary Matthews (no finger on back)	.12	.09	.05
251b	Gary Matthews (small finger on back)			
		1.00	.70	.40
252	Chris Chambliss	.08	.06	.03
253	Luis Gomez	.06	.05	.02
254	Bill Nahorodny	.06	.05	.02
255	Doyle Alexander	.12	.09	.05
256	Brian Asselstine	.06	.05	.02
257	Biff Pocoroba	.06	.05	.02
258	Mike Lum	.06	.05	.02
259	Charlie Spikes	.06	.05	.02
260	Glenn Hubbard	.08	.06	.03
261	Tommy Boggs	.06	.05	.02
262	Al Hrabosky	.08	.06	.03
263	Rick Matula	.06	.05	.02
264	Preston Hanna	.06	.05	.02
265	Larry Bradford	.06	.05	.02
266	Rafael Ramirez	.20	.15	.08
267	Larry McWilliams	.06	.05	.02
268	Rod Carew	.60	.45	.25
269	Bobby Grich	.10	.08	.04
270	Carney Lansford	.10	.08	.04
271	Don Baylor	.15	.11	.06
272	Joe Rudi	.10	.08	.04
273	Dan Ford	.06	.05	.02
274	Jim Fregosi	.08	.06	.03
275	Dave Frost	.06	.05	.02
276	Frank Tanana	.10	.08	.04
277	Dickie Thon	.08	.06	.03
278	Jason Thompson	.08	.06	.03
279	Rick Miller	.06	.05	.02
280	Bert Campaneris	.10	.08	.04
281	Tom Donohue	.06	.05	.02
282	Brian Downing	.10	.08	.04
283	Fred Patek	.06	.05	.02
284	Bruce Kison	.06	.05	.02
285	Dave LaRoche	.06	.05	.02
286	Don Aase	.08	.06	.03
287	Jim Barr	.06	.05	.02
288	Alfredo Martinez	.06	.05	.02
289	Larry Harlow	.06	.05	.02
290	Andy Hassler	.06	.05	.02
291	Dave Kingman	.15	.11	.06
292	Bill Buckner	.12	.09	.05
293	Rick Reuschel	.10	.08	.04
294	Bruce Sutter	.15	.11	.06
295	Jerry Martin	.06	.05	.02
296	Scot Thompson	.06	.05	.02
297	Ivan DeJesus	.06	.05	.02
298	Steve Dillard	.06	.05	.02
299	Dick Tidrow	.06	.05	.02
300	Randy Martz	.06	.05	.02
301	Lenny Randle	.06	.05	.02
302	Lynn McGlothen	.06	.05	.02
303	Cliff Johnson	.06	.05	.02
304	Tim Blackwell	.06	.05	.02
305	Dennis Lamp	.06	.05	.02
306	Bill Caudill	.06	.05	.02
307	Carlos Lezcano	.06	.05	.02
308	Jim Tracy	.06	.05	.02
309	Doug Capilla	.06	.05	.02
310	Willie Hernandez	.10	.08	.04
311	Mike Vail	.06	.05	.02
312	Mike Krukow	.08	.06	.03
313	Barry Foote	.06	.05	.02
314	Larry Biittner	.06	.05	.02
315	Mike Tyson	.06	.05	.02
316	Lee Mazzilli	.08	.06	.03
317	John Stearns	.06	.05	.02
318	Alex Trevino	.06	.05	.02
319	Craig Swan	.06	.05	.02
320	Frank Taveras	.06	.05	.02
321	Steve Henderson	.06	.05	.02
322	Neil Allen	.08	.06	.03
323	Mark Bomback	.06	.05	.02
324	Mike Jorgensen	.06	.05	.02
325	Joe Torre	.08	.06	.03
326	Elliott Maddox	.06	.05	.02
327	Pete Falcone	.06	.05	.02
328	Ray Burris	.06	.05	.02
329	Claudell Washington	.08	.06	.03
330	Doug Flynn	.06	.05	.02

#	Player	MT	NR MT	EX
331	Joel Youngblood	.06	.05	.02
332	Bill Almon	.06	.05	.02
333	Tom Hausman	.06	.05	.02
334	Pat Zachry	.06	.05	.02
335	Jeff Reardon	.75	.60	.30
336	Wally Backman	.40	.30	.15
337	Dan Norman	.06	.05	.02
338	Jerry Morales	.06	.05	.02
339	Ed Farmer	.06	.05	.02
340	Bob Molinaro	.06	.05	.02
341	Todd Cruz	.06	.05	.02
342a	Britt Burns (no finger on front)	.20	.15	.08
342b	Britt Burns (small finger on front)	1.00	.70	.40
343	Kevin Bell	.06	.05	.02
344	Tony LaRussa	.08	.06	.03
345	Steve Trout	.08	.06	.03
346	Harold Baines	1.25	.90	.50
347	Richard Wortham	.06	.05	.02
348	Wayne Nordhagen	.06	.05	.02
349	Mike Squires	.06	.05	.02
350	Lamar Johnson	.06	.05	.02
351	Rickey Henderson	.70	.50	.30
352	Francisco Barrios	.06	.05	.02
353	Thad Bosley	.06	.05	.02
354	Chet Lemon	.08	.06	.03
355	Bruce Kimm	.06	.05	.02
356	Richard Dotson	.20	.15	.08
357	Jim Morrison	.06	.05	.02
358	Mike Proly	.06	.05	.02
359	Greg Pryor	.06	.05	.02
360	Dave Parker	.30	.25	.12
361	Omar Moreno	.06	.05	.02
362a	Kent Tekulve (1071 Waterbury on back)	.15	.11	.06
362b	Kent Tekulve (1971 Waterbury on back)	.70	.50	.30
363	Willie Stargell	.40	.30	.15
364	Phil Garner	.08	.06	.03
365	Ed Ott	.06	.05	.02
366	Don Robinson	.08	.06	.03
367	Chuck Tanner	.08	.06	.03
368	Jim Rooker	.06	.05	.02
369	Dale Berra	.06	.05	.02
370	Jim Bibby	.06	.05	.02
371	Steve Nicosia	.06	.05	.02
372	Mike Easler	.10	.08	.04
373	Bill Robinson	.06	.05	.02
374	Lee Lacy	.08	.06	.03
375	John Candelaria	.10	.08	.04
376	Manny Sanguillen	.06	.05	.02
377	Rick Rhoden	.12	.09	.05
378	Grant Jackson	.06	.05	.02
379	Tim Foli	.06	.05	.02
380	Rod Scurry	.10	.08	.04
381	Bill Madlock	.15	.11	.06
382a	Kurt Bevacqua (photo reversed, backwards "P" on cap)	.15	.11	.06
382b	Kurt Bevacqua (correct photo)	.70	.50	.30
383	Bert Blyleven	.15	.11	.06
384	Eddie Solomon	.06	.05	.02
385	Enrique Romo	.06	.05	.02
386	John Milner	.06	.05	.02
387	Mike Hargrove	.08	.06	.03
388	Jorge Orta	.06	.05	.02
389	Toby Harrah	.08	.06	.03
390	Tom Veryzer	.06	.05	.02
391	Miguel Dilone	.06	.05	.02
392	Dan Spillner	.06	.05	.02
393	Jack Brohamer	.06	.05	.02
394	Wayne Garland	.06	.05	.02
395	Sid Monge	.06	.05	.02
396	Rick Waits	.06	.05	.02
397	Joe Charboneau	.12	.09	.05
398	Gary Alexander	.06	.05	.02
399	Jerry Dybzinski	.06	.05	.02
400	Mike Stanton	.06	.05	.02
401	Mike Paxton	.06	.05	.02
402	Gary Gray	.06	.05	.02
403	Rick Manning	.06	.05	.02
404	Bo Diaz	.08	.06	.03
405	Ron Hassey	.06	.05	.02
406	Ross Grimsley	.08	.06	.03
407	Victor Cruz	.06	.05	.02
408	Len Barker	.08	.06	.03
409	Bob Bailor	.06	.05	.02
410	410 (Otto Velez)	.06	.05	.02
411	Ernie Whitt	.08	.06	.03
412	Jim Clancy	.10	.08	.04
413	Barry Bonnell	.06	.05	.02
414	Dave Stieb	.20	.15	.08
415	Damaso Garcia	.20	.15	.08
416	John Mayberry	.08	.06	.03
417	Roy Howell	.06	.05	.02
418	Dan Ainge	.30	.25	.12
419a	Jesse Jefferson (Pirates on back)	.10	.08	.04
419b	Jesse Jefferson (Blue Jays on back)	.50	.40	.20
420	Joey McLaughlin	.06	.05	.02
421	Lloyd Moseby	.90	.70	.35
422	Al Woods	.06	.05	.02
423	Garth Iorg	.06	.05	.02
424	Doug Ault	.06	.05	.02
425	Ken Schrom	.20	.15	.08
426	Mike Willis	.06	.05	.02
427	Steve Braun	.06	.05	.02
428	Bob Davis	.06	.05	.02
429	Jerry Garvin	.06	.05	.02
430	Alfredo Griffin	.08	.06	.03
431	Bob Mattick	.06	.05	.02
432	Vida Blue	.12	.09	.05
433	Jack Clark	.25	.20	.10
434	Willie McCovey	.40	.30	.15
435	Mike Ivie	.06	.05	.02
436a	Darrel Evans (Darrel on front)	.15	.11	.06
436b	Darrell Evans (Darrell on front)	.70	.50	.30
437	Terry Whitfield	.06	.05	.02
438	Rennie Stennett	.06	.05	.02
439	John Montefusco	.08	.06	.03
440	Jim Wohlford	.06	.05	.02
441	Bill North	.06	.05	.02
442	Milt May	.06	.05	.02
443	Max Venable	.06	.05	.02
444	Ed Whitson	.08	.06	.03
445	Al Holland	.10	.08	.04
446	Randy Moffitt	.06	.05	.02
447	Bob Knepper	.08	.06	.03
448	Gary Lavelle	.06	.05	.02
449	Greg Minton	.06	.05	.02
450	Johnnie LeMaster	.06	.05	.02
451	Larry Herndon	.08	.06	.03
452	Rich Murray	.06	.05	.02
453	Joe Pettini	.06	.05	.02
454	Allen Ripley	.06	.05	.02
455	Dennis Littlejohn	.06	.05	.02
456	Tom Griffin	.06	.05	.02
457	Alan Hargesheimer	.06	.05	.02
458	Joe Strain	.06	.05	.02
459	Steve Kemp	.08	.06	.03
460	Sparky Anderson	.10	.08	.04
461	Alan Trammell	.40	.30	.15
462	Mark Fidrych	.08	.06	.03
463	Lou Whitaker	.30	.25	.12
464	Dave Rozema	.06	.05	.02
465	Milt Wilcox	.08	.06	.03
466	Champ Summers	.06	.05	.02
467	Lance Parrish	.35	.25	.14
468	Dan Petry	.10	.08	.04
469	Pat Underwood	.06	.05	.02
470	Rick Peters	.06	.05	.02
471	Al Cowens	.06	.05	.02
472	John Wockenfuss	.06	.05	.02
473	Tom Brookens	.08	.06	.03
474	Richie Hebner	.06	.05	.02
475	Jack Morris	.30	.25	.12
476	Jim Lentine	.06	.05	.02
477	Bruce Robbins	.06	.05	.02
478	Mark Wagner	.06	.05	.02
479	Tim Corcoran	.06	.05	.02
480a	Stan Papi (Pitcher on front)	.15	.11	.06
480b	Stan Papi (Shortstop on front)	.70	.50	.30
481	Kirk Gibson	2.00	1.50	.80
482	Dan Schatzeder	.06	.05	.02
483	Amos Otis	.70	.50	.30
484	Dave Winfield	.40	.30	.15
485	Rollie Fingers	.25	.20	.10
486	Gene Richards	.06	.05	.02
487	Randy Jones	.08	.06	.03
488	Ozzie Smith	.30	.25	.12
489	Gene Tenace	.08	.06	.03
490	Bill Fahey	.06	.05	.02
491	John Curtis	.06	.05	.02
492	Dave Cash	.06	.05	.02
493a	Tim Flannery (photo reversed, batting righty)	.15	.11	.06
493b	Tim Flannery (photo correct, batting lefty)	.70	.50	.30
494	Jerry Mumphrey	.08	.06	.03
495	Bob Shirley	.06	.05	.02
496	Steve Mura	.06	.05	.02
497	Eric Rasmussen	.06	.05	.02
498	Broderick Perkins	.06	.05	.02
499	Barry Evans	.06	.05	.02

		MT	NR MT	EX
500	Chuck Baker	.06	.05	.02
501	Luis Salazar	.10	.08	.04
502	Gary Lucas	.10	.08	.04
503	Mike Armstrong	.06	.05	.02
504	Jerry Turner	.06	.05	.02
505	Dennis Kinney	.06	.05	.02
506	Willy Montanez (Willie)	.06	.05	.02
507	Gorman Thomas	.12	.09	.05
508	Ben Oglivie	.08	.06	.03
509	Larry Hisle	.08	.06	.03
510	Sal Bando	.10	.08	.04
511	Robin Yount	.40	.30	.15
512	Mike Caldwell	.06	.05	.02
513	Sixto Lezcano	.06	.05	.02
514a	Jerry Augustine (Billy Travers photo)			
		.15	.11	.06
514b	Billy Travers (correct name with photo)			
		.70	.50	.30
515	Paul Molitor	.20	.15	.08
516	Moose Haas	.06	.05	.02
517	Bill Castro	.06	.05	.02
518	Jim Slaton	.06	.05	.02
519	Lary Sorensen	.06	.05	.02
520	Bob McClure	.06	.05	.02
521	Charlie Moore	.06	.05	.02
522	Jim Gantner	.08	.06	.03
523	Reggie Cleveland	.06	.05	.02
524	Don Money	.08	.06	.03
525	Billy Travers	.06	.05	.02
526	Buck Martinez	.06	.05	.02
527	Dick Davis	.06	.05	.02
528	Ted Simmons	.15	.11	.06
529	Garry Templeton	.10	.08	.04
530	Ken Reitz	.06	.05	.02
531	Tony Scott	.06	.05	.02
532	Ken Oberkfell	.08	.06	.03
533	Bob Sykes	.06	.05	.02
534	Keith Smith	.06	.05	.02
535	John Littlefield	.06	.05	.02
536	Jim Kaat	.15	.11	.06
537	Bob Forsch	.08	.06	.03
538	Mike Phillips	.06	.05	.02
539	Terry Landrum	.10	.08	.04
540	Leon Durham	.70	.50	.30
541	Terry Kennedy	.08	.06	.03
542	George Hendrick	.08	.06	.03
543	Dane Iorg	.06	.05	.02
544	Mark Littell (photo actually Jeff Little)			
		.06	.05	.02
545	Keith Hernandez	.40	.30	.15
546	Silvio Martinez	.06	.05	.02
547a	Pete Vuckovich (photo actually Don Hood)	.15	.11	.06
547b	Don Hood (correct name with photo)			
		.70	.50	.30
548	Bobby Bonds	.10	.08	.04
549	Mike Ramsey	.06	.05	.02
550	Tom Herr	.10	.08	.04
551	Roy Smalley	.08	.06	.03
552	Jerry Koosman	.12	.09	.05
553	Ken Landreaux	.08	.06	.03
554	John Castino	.06	.05	.02
555	Doug Corbett	.06	.05	.02
556	Bombo Rivera	.06	.05	.02
557	Ron Jackson	.06	.05	.02
558	Butch Wynegar	.08	.06	.03
559	Hosken Powell	.06	.05	.02
560	Pete Redfern	.06	.05	.02
561	Roger Erickson	.06	.05	.02
562	Glenn Adams	.06	.05	.02
563	Rick Sofield	.06	.05	.02
564	Geoff Zahn	.06	.05	.02
565	Pete Mackanin	.06	.05	.02
566	Mike Cubbage	.06	.05	.02
567	Darrell Jackson	.06	.05	.02
568	Dave Edwards	.06	.05	.02
569	Rob Wilfong	.06	.05	.02
570	Sal Butera	.06	.05	.02
571	Jose Morales	.06	.05	.02
572	Rick Langford	.06	.05	.02
573	Mike Norris	.06	.05	.02
574	Rickey Henderson	.70	.50	.30
575	Tony Armas	.10	.08	.04
576	Dave Revering	.06	.05	.02
577	Jeff Newman	.06	.05	.02
578	Bob Lacey	.06	.05	.02
579	Brian Kingman (photo actually Alan Wirth)			
		.06	.05	.02
580	Mitchell Page	.06	.05	.02
581	Billy Martin	.12	.09	.05
582	Rob Picciolo	.06	.05	.02

		MT	NR MT	EX
583	Mike Heath	.06	.05	.02
584	Mickey Klutts	.06	.05	.02
585	Orlando Gonzalez	.06	.05	.02
586	Mike Davis	.30	.25	.12
587	Wayne Gross	.06	.05	.02
588	Matt Keough	.06	.05	.02
589	Steve McCatty	.06	.05	.02
590	Dwayne Murphy	.08	.06	.03
591	Mario Guerrero	.06	.05	.02
592	Dave McKay	.06	.05	.02
593	Jim Essian	.06	.05	.02
594	Dave Heaverlo	.06	.05	.02
595	Maury Wills	.10	.08	.04
596	Juan Beniquez	.06	.05	.02
597	Rodney Craig	.06	.05	.02
598	Jim Anderson	.06	.05	.02
599	Floyd Bannister	.10	.08	.04
600	Bruce Bochte	.06	.05	.02
601	Julio Cruz	.06	.05	.02
602	Ted Cox	.06	.05	.02
603	Dan Meyer	.06	.05	.02
604	Larry Cox	.06	.05	.02
605	Bill Stein	.06	.05	.02
606	Steve Garvey	.50	.40	.20
607	Dave Roberts	.06	.05	.02
608	Leon Roberts	.06	.05	.02
609	Reggie Walton	.06	.05	.02
610	Dave Edler	.06	.05	.02
611	Larry Milbourne	.06	.05	.02
612	Kim Allen	.06	.05	.02
613	Mario Mendoza	.06	.05	.02
614	Tom Paciorek	.08	.06	.03
615	Glenn Abbott	.06	.05	.02
616	Joe Simpson	.06	.05	.02
617	Mickey Rivers	.08	.06	.03
618	Jim Kern	.06	.05	.02
619	Jim Sundberg	.08	.06	.03
620	Richie Zisk	.08	.06	.03
621	Jon Matlack	.08	.06	.03
622	Ferguson Jenkins	.20	.15	.08
623	Pat Corrales	.08	.06	.03
624	Ed Figueroa	.06	.05	.02
625	Buddy Bell	.15	.11	.06
626	Al Oliver	.15	.11	.06
627	Doc Medich	.06	.05	.02
628	Bump Wills	.06	.05	.02
629	Rusty Staub	.12	.09	.05
630	Pat Putnam	.06	.05	.02
631	John Grubb	.06	.05	.02
632	Danny Darwin	.08	.06	.03
633	Ken Clay	.06	.05	.02
634	Jim Norris	.06	.05	.02
635	John Butcher	.06	.05	.02
636	Dave Roberts	.06	.05	.02
637	Billy Sample	.06	.05	.02
638	Carl Yastrzemski	.80	.60	.30
639	Cecil Cooper	.15	.11	.06
640	Mike Schmidt	1.50	1.25	.60
641a	Checklist 1-50 (41 Hal McRae)	.10	.08	.04
641b	Checklist 1-50 (41 Hal McRae Double Threat)	.40	.30	.15
642	Checklist 51-109	.06	.05	.02
643	Checklist 110-168	.06	.05	.02
644a	Checklist 169-220 (202 George Foster)	.10	.08	.04
644b	Checklist 169-220 (202 George Foster "Slugger")	.40	.30	.15
645a	Triple Threat (Larry Bowa, Pete Rose, Mike Schmidt) (no number on back)	1.00	.70	.40
645b	Triple Threat (Larry Bowa, Pete Rose, Mike Schmidt) (645 on back)	2.00	1.50	.80
646	Checklist 221-267	.06	.05	.02
647	Checklist 268-315	.06	.05	.02
648	Checklist 316-359	.06	.05	.02
649	Checklist 360-408	.06	.05	.02
650	Reggie Jackson	1.50	1.25	.60
651	Checklist 409-458	.06	.05	.02
652a	Checklist 459-506 (483 Aurelio Lopez)	.10	.08	.04
652b	Checklist 459-506 (no 483)	.40	.30	.15
653	Willie Wilson	1.00	.70	.40
654a	Checklist 507-550 (514 Jerry Augustine)	.10	.08	.04
654b	Checklist 507-550 (514 Billy Travers)	.40	.30	.15
655	George Brett	2.00	1.50	.80
656	Checklist 551-593	.06	.05	.02
657	Tug McGraw	1.00	.70	.40
658	Checklist 594-637	.06	.05	.02
659a	Checklist 640-660 (last number on front is 551)	.10	.08	.04

		MT	NR MT	EX
659b	Checklist 640-660 (last number on front is 483)	.40	.30	.15
660a	Steve Carlton (date 1066 on back)	1.00	.70	.40
660b	Steve Carlton (date 1966 on back)	2.00	1.50	.80

1981 Fleer Star Stickers

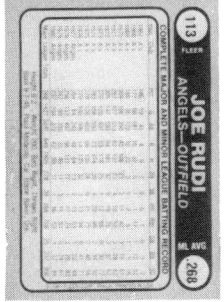

The 128-card 1981 Fleer Star Sticker set was designed for the card fronts to be peeled away from the cardboard backs. The card obverses feature color photos with blue and yellow trim. The card backs are identical in design to the regular 1981 Fleer set except for color and numbering. The set contains three unnumbered checklist cards whose fronts depict Reggie Jackson (#'s 1-42), George Brett (#'s 43-83) and Mike Schmidt (#'s 84-125). The cards, which are the standard 2½'' by 3½'', were issued in gum wax packs.

		MT	NR MT	EX
Complete Set		38.00	28.00	15.00
Common Player		.10	.08	.04
1	Steve Garvey	1.25	.90	.50
2	Ron LeFlore	.15	.11	.06
3	Ron Cey	.35	.25	.14
4	Dave Revering	.10	.08	.04
5	Tony Armas	.35	.25	.14
6	Mike Norris	.10	.08	.04
7	Steve Kemp	.20	.15	.08
8	Bruce Bochte	.10	.08	.04
9	Mike Schmidt	1.75	1.25	.70
10	Scott McGregor	.20	.15	.08
11	Buddy Bell	.35	.25	.14
12	Carney Lansford	.20	.15	.08
13	Carl Yastrzemski	2.50	2.00	1.00
14	Ben Oglivie	.15	.11	.06
15	Willie Stargell	.80	.60	.30
16	Cecil Cooper	.45	.35	.20
17	Gene Richards	.10	.08	.04
18	Jim Kern	.10	.08	.04
19	Jerry Koosman	.35	.25	.14
20	Larry Bowa	.35	.25	.14
21	Kent Tekulve	.20	.15	.08
22	Dan Driessen	.15	.11	.06
23	Phil Niekro	.80	.60	.30
24	Dan Quisenberry	.60	.45	.25
25	Dave Winfield	1.25	.90	.50
26	Dave Parker	.80	.60	.30
27	Rick Langford	.10	.08	.04
28	Amos Otis	.20	.15	.08
29	Bill Buckner	.45	.35	.20
30	Al Bumbry	.10	.08	.04
31	Bake McBride	.10	.08	.04
32	Mickey Rivers	.15	.11	.06
33	Rick Burleson	.15	.11	.06
34	Dennis Eckersley	.20	.15	.08
35	Cesar Cedeno	.20	.15	.08
36	Enos Cabell	.10	.08	.04
37	Johnny Bench	1.25	.90	.50
38	Robin Yount	1.00	.70	.40
39	Mark Belanger	.15	.11	.06
40	Rod Carew	1.50	1.25	.60
41	George Foster	.45	.35	.20
42	Lee Mazzilli	.20	.15	.08
43	Triple Threat (Larry Bowa, Pete Rose, Mike Schmidt)	2.00	1.50	.80
44	J.R. Richard	.20	.15	.08
45	Lou Piniella	.35	.25	.14
46	Ken Landreaux	.15	.11	.06
47	Rollie Fingers	.80	.60	.30
48	Joaquin Andujar	.20	.15	.08
49	Tom Seaver	1.50	1.25	.60
50	Bobby Grich	.20	.15	.08
51	Jon Matlack	.10	.08	.04
52	Jack Clark	.60	.45	.25
53	Jim Rice	1.25	.90	.50
54	Rickey Henderson	1.50	1.25	.60
55	Roy Smalley	.10	.08	.04
56	Mike Flanagan	.20	.15	.08
57	Steve Rogers	.10	.08	.04
58	Carlton Fisk	.60	.45	.25
59	Don Sutton	.80	.60	.30
60	Ken Griffey	.35	.25	.14
61	Burt Hooton	.10	.08	.04
62	Dusty Baker	.20	.15	.08
63	Vida Blue	.35	.25	.14
64	Al Oliver	.35	.25	.14
65	Jim Bibby	.10	.08	.04
66	Tony Perez	.60	.45	.25
67	Davy Lopes (Davey)	.20	.15	.08
68	Bill Russell	.20	.15	.08
69	Larry Parrish	.20	.15	.08
70	Garry Maddox	.15	.11	.06
71	Phil Garner	.15	.11	.06
72	Graig Nettles	.45	.35	.20
73	Gary Carter	1.25	.90	.50
74	Pete Rose	3.00	2.25	1.25
75	Greg Luzinski	.35	.25	.14
76	Ron Guidry	.60	.45	.25
77	Gorman Thomas	.20	.15	.08
78	Jose Cruz	.35	.25	.14
79	Bob Boone	.20	.15	.08
80	Bruce Sutter	.35	.25	.14
81	Chris Chambliss	.15	.11	.06
82	Paul Molitor	.45	.35	.20
83	Tug McGraw	.35	.25	.14
84	Ferguson Jenkins	.45	.35	.20
85	Steve Carlton	1.25	.90	.50
86	Miguel Dilone	.10	.08	.04
87	Reggie Smith	.20	.15	.08
88	Rick Cerone	.10	.08	.04
89	Alan Trammell	1.00	.70	.40
90	Doug DeCinces	.20	.15	.08
91	Sparky Lyle	.20	.15	.08
92	Warren Cromartie	.10	.08	.04
93	Rick Reuschel	.20	.15	.08
94	Larry Hisle	.10	.08	.04
95	Paul Splittorff	.10	.08	.04
96	Manny Trillo	.15	.11	.06
97	Frank White	.20	.15	.08
98	Fred Lynn	.60	.45	.25
99	Bob Horner	.60	.45	.25
100	Omar Moreno	.10	.08	.04
101	Dave Concepcion	.35	.25	.14
102	Larry Gura	.10	.08	.04
103	Ken Singleton	.20	.15	.08
104	Steve Stone	.15	.11	.06
105	Richie Zisk	.15	.11	.06
106	Willie Wilson	.45	.35	.20
107	Willie Randolph	.35	.25	.14
108	Nolan Ryan	1.25	.90	.50
109	Joe Morgan	.80	.60	.30
110	Bucky Dent	.20	.15	.08
111	Dave Kingman	.45	.35	.20
112	John Castino	.10	.08	.04
113	Joe Rudi	.20	.15	.08
114	Ed Farmer	.10	.08	.04
115	Reggie Jackson	1.50	1.25	.60
116	George Brett	1.75	1.25	.70
117	Eddie Murray	1.75	1.25	.70
118	Rich Gossage	.45	.35	.20
119	Dale Murphy	2.00	1.50	.80
120	Ted Simmons	.45	.35	.20
121	Tommy John	.60	.45	.25
122	Don Baylor	.35	.25	.14
123	Andre Dawson	.80	.60	.30
124	Jim Palmer	1.00	.70	.40
125	Garry Templeton	.35	.25	.14
---	Reggie Jackson/Checklist 1-42	1.50	1.25	.60
---	George Brett/Checklist 43-83	1.75	1.25	.70
---	Mike Schmidt/Checklist 84-125	1.75	1.25	.70

1982 Fleer

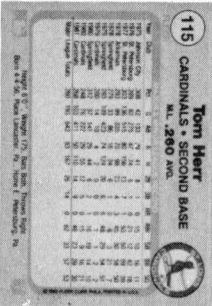

Fleer's 1982 set did not match the quality of the previous year's effort. Many of the photos in the set are blurred and have muddied backgrounds. The cards, which measure 2½'' by 3½'', feature color photos surrounded by a border frame which is colorcoded by team. The card backs are blue, white, and yellow and contain the player's team logo plus the logos of Major League Baseball and the Major League Baseball Players Association. Due to a lawsuit by Topps, Fleer was forced to issue the set with team logo stickers rather than gum. The complete set price does not include the higher priced variations.

		MT	NR MT	EX
Complete Set:		20.00	15.00	8.00
Common Player:		.06	.05	.02
1	Dusty Baker	.10	.08	.04
2	Robert Castillo	.06	.05	.02
3	Ron Cey	.12	.09	.05
4	Terry Forster	.08	.06	.03
5	Steve Garvey	.50	.40	.20
6	Dave Goltz	.08	.06	.03
7	Pedro Guerrero	.40	.30	.15
8	Burt Hooton	.08	.06	.03
9	Steve Howe	.08	.06	.03
10	Jay Johnstone	.10	.08	.04
11	Ken Landreaux	.08	.06	.03
12	Davey Lopes	.10	.08	.04
13	Mike Marshall	1.00	.70	.40
14	Bobby Mitchell	.06	.05	.02
15	Rick Monday	.10	.08	.04
16	Tom Niedenfuer	.35	.25	.14
17	Ted Power	.30	.25	.12
18	Jerry Reuss	.10	.08	.04
19	Ron Roenicke	.06	.05	.02
20	Bill Russell	.08	.06	.03
21	Steve Sax	1.25	.90	.50
22	Mike Scioscia	.06	.05	.02
23	Reggie Smith	.10	.08	.04
24	Dave Stewart	.40	.30	.15
25	Rick Sutcliffe	.15	.11	.06
26	Derrel Thomas	.06	.05	.02
27	Fernando Valenzuela	.60	.45	.25
28	Bob Welch	.10	.08	.04
29	Steve Yeager	.06	.05	.02
30	Bobby Brown	.06	.05	.02
31	Rick Cerone	.08	.06	.03
32	Ron Davis	.06	.05	.02
33	Bucky Dent	.10	.08	.04
34	Barry Foote	.06	.05	.02
35	George Frazier	.06	.05	.02
36	Oscar Gamble	.08	.06	.03
37	Rich Gossage	.20	.15	.08
38	Ron Guidry	.25	.20	.10
39	Reggie Jackson	.60	.45	.25
40	Tommy John	.20	.15	.08
41	Rudy May	.08	.06	.03
42	Larry Milbourne	.06	.05	.02
43	Jerry Mumphrey	.08	.06	.03
44	Bobby Murcer	.10	.08	.04
45	Gene Nelson	.12	.09	.05
46	Graig Nettles	.15	.11	.06
47	Johnny Oates	.06	.05	.02
48	Lou Piniella	.15	.11	.06
49	Willie Randolph	.10	.08	.04
50	Rick Reuschel	.10	.08	.04

		MT	NR MT	EX
51	Dave Revering	.06	.05	.02
52	Dave Righetti	1.50	1.25	.60
53	Aurelio Rodriguez	.08	.06	.03
54	Bob Watson	.08	.06	.03
55	Dennis Werth	.06	.05	.02
56	Dave Winfield	.40	.30	.15
57	Johnny Bench	.50	.40	.20
58	Bruce Berenyi	.06	.05	.02
59	Larry Biittner	.06	.05	.02
60	Scott Brown	.06	.05	.02
61	Dave Collins	.08	.06	.03
62	Geoff Combe	.06	.05	.02
63	Dave Concepcion	.15	.11	.06
64	Dan Driessen	.08	.06	.03
65	Joe Edelen	.06	.05	.02
66	George Foster	.20	.15	.08
67	Ken Griffey	.12	.09	.05
68	Paul Householder	.06	.05	.02
69	Tom Hume	.06	.05	.02
70	Junior Kennedy	.06	.05	.02
71	Ray Knight	.10	.08	.04
72	Mike LaCoss	.08	.06	.03
73	Rafael Landestoy	.06	.05	.02
74	Charlie Leibrandt	.10	.08	.04
75	Sam Mejias	.06	.05	.02
76	Paul Moskau	.06	.05	.02
77	Joe Nolan	.06	.05	.02
78	Mike O'Berry	.06	.05	.02
79	Ron Oester	.06	.05	.02
80	Frank Pastore	.06	.05	.02
81	Joe Price	.06	.05	.02
82	Tom Seaver	.50	.40	.20
83	Mario Soto	.10	.08	.04
84	Mike Vail	.06	.05	.02
85	Tony Armas	.10	.08	.04
86	Shooty Babitt	.06	.05	.02
87	Dave Beard	.06	.05	.02
88	Rick Bosetti	.06	.05	.02
89	Keith Drumright	.06	.05	.02
90	Wayne Gross	.06	.05	.02
91	Mike Heath	.06	.05	.02
92	Rickey Henderson	.60	.45	.25
93	Cliff Johnson	.06	.05	.02
94	Jeff Jones	.06	.05	.02
95	Matt Keough	.06	.05	.02
96	Brian Kingman	.06	.05	.02
97	Mickey Klutts	.06	.05	.02
98	Rick Langford	.06	.05	.02
99	Steve McCatty	.06	.05	.02
100	Dave McKay	.06	.05	.02
101	Dwayne Murphy	.08	.06	.03
102	Jeff Newman	.06	.05	.02
103	Mike Norris	.06	.05	.02
104	Bob Owchinko	.06	.05	.02
105	Mitchell Page	.06	.05	.02
106	Rob Picciolo	.06	.05	.02
107	Jim Spencer	.06	.05	.02
108	Fred Stanley	.06	.05	.02
109	Tom Underwood	.06	.05	.02
110	Joaquin Andujar	.10	.08	.04
111	Steve Braun	.06	.05	.02
112	Bob Forsch	.08	.06	.03
113	George Hendrick	.08	.06	.03
114	Keith Hernandez	.40	.30	.15
115	Tom Herr	.10	.08	.04
116	Dane Iorg	.06	.05	.02
117	Jim Kaat	.15	.11	.06
118	Tito Landrum	.06	.05	.02
119	Sixto Lezcano	.06	.05	.02
120	Mark Littell	.06	.05	.02
121	John Martin	.06	.05	.02
122	Silvio Martinez	.06	.05	.02
123	Ken Oberkfell	.08	.06	.03
124	Darrell Porter	.08	.06	.03
125	Mike Ramsey	.06	.05	.02
126	Orlando Sanchez	.06	.05	.02
127	Bob Shirley	.06	.05	.02
128	Lary Sorensen	.06	.05	.02
129	Bruce Sutter	.15	.11	.06
130	Bob Sykes	.06	.05	.02
131	Garry Templeton	.10	.08	.04
132	Gene Tenace	.08	.06	.03
133	Jerry Augustine	.06	.05	.02
134	Sal Bando	.08	.06	.03
135	Mark Brouhard	.06	.05	.02
136	Mike Caldwell	.06	.05	.02
137	Reggie Cleveland	.06	.05	.02
138	Cecil Cooper	.15	.11	.06
139	Jamie Easterly	.06	.05	.02
140	Marshall Edwards	.06	.05	.02
141	Rollie Fingers	.20	.15	.08

		MT	NR MT	EX			MT	NR MT	EX
142	Jim Gantner	.08	.06	.03	232	Dave Smith	.10	.08	.04
143	Moose Haas	.06	.05	.02	233	Harry Spilman	.06	.05	.02
144	Larry Hisle	.08	.06	.03	234	Don Sutton	.30	.25	.12
145	Roy Howell	.06	.05	.02	235	Dickie Thon	.08	.06	.03
146	Rickey Keeton	.06	.05	.02	236	Denny Walling	.06	.05	.02
147	Randy Lerch	.06	.05	.02	237	Gary Woods	.06	.05	.02
148	Paul Molitor	.20	.15	.08	238	Luis Aguayo	.10	.08	.04
149	Don Money	.08	.06	.03	239	Ramon Aviles	.06	.05	.02
150	Charlie Moore	.06	.05	.02	240	Bob Boone	.10	.08	.04
151	Ben Oglivie	.08	.06	.03	241	Larry Bowa	.15	.11	.06
152	Ted Simmons	.15	.11	.06	242	Warren Brusstar	.06	.05	.02
153	Jim Slaton	.06	.05	.02	243	Steve Carlton	.50	.40	.20
154	Gorman Thomas	.12	.09	.05	244	Larry Christenson	.06	.05	.02
155	Robin Yount	.40	.30	.15	245	Dick Davis	.06	.05	.02
156	Pete Vukovich	.08	.06	.03	246	Greg Gross	.06	.05	.02
157	Benny Ayala	.06	.05	.02	247	Sparky Lyle	.10	.08	.04
158	Mark Belanger	.08	.06	.03	248	Garry Maddox	.10	.08	.04
159	Al Bumbry	.08	.06	.03	249	Gary Matthews	.10	.08	.04
160	Terry Crowley	.06	.05	.02	250	Bake McBride	.06	.05	.02
161	Rich Dauer	.06	.05	.02	251	Tug McGraw	.12	.09	.05
162	Doug DeCinces	.10	.08	.04	252	Keith Moreland	.12	.09	.05
163	Rick Dempsey	.08	.06	.03	253	Dickie Noles	.06	.05	.02
164	Jim Dwyer	.06	.05	.02	254	Mike Proly	.06	.05	.02
165	Mike Flanagan	.10	.08	.04	255	Ron Reed	.08	.06	.03
166	Dave Ford	.06	.05	.02	256	Pete Rose	1.00	.70	.40
167	Dan Graham	.06	.05	.02	257	Dick Ruthven	.06	.05	.02
168	Wayne Krenchicki	.06	.05	.02	258	Mike Schmidt	.80	.60	.30
169	John Lowenstein	.06	.05	.02	259	Lonnie Smith	.08	.06	.03
170	Dennis Martinez	.08	.06	.03	260	Manny Trillo	.08	.06	.03
171	Tippy Martinez	.06	.05	.02	261	Del Unser	.06	.05	.02
172	Scott McGregor	.10	.08	.04	262	George Vukovich	.06	.05	.02
173	Jose Morales	.06	.05	.02	263	Tom Brookens	.06	.05	.02
174	Eddie Murray	.60	.45	.25	264	George Cappuzzello	.06	.05	.02
175	Jim Palmer	.40	.30	.15	265	Marty Castillo	.06	.05	.02
176	Cal Ripken, Jr.	8.00	6.00	3.25	266	Al Cowens	.06	.05	.02
177	Gary Roenicke	.08	.06	.03	267	Kirk Gibson	.35	.25	.14
178	Lenn Sakata	.06	.05	.02	268	Richie Hebner	.06	.05	.02
179	Ken Singleton	.10	.08	.04	269	Ron Jackson	.06	.05	.02
180	Sammy Stewart	.06	.05	.02	270	Lynn Jones	.06	.05	.02
181	Tim Stoddard	.06	.05	.02	271	Steve Kemp	.08	.06	.03
182	Steve Stone	.08	.06	.03	272	Rick Leach	.12	.09	.05
183	Stan Bahnsen	.06	.05	.02	273	Aurelio Lopez	.06	.05	.02
184	Ray Burris	.06	.05	.02	274	Jack Morris	.30	.25	.12
185	Gary Carter	.40	.30	.15	275	Kevin Saucier	.06	.05	.02
186	Warren Cromartie	.06	.05	.02	276	Lance Parrish	.35	.25	.14
187	Andre Dawson	.35	.25	.14	277	Rick Peters	.06	.05	.02
188	Terry Francona	.12	.09	.05	278	Dan Petry	.10	.08	.04
189	Woodie Fryman	.08	.06	.03	279	David Rozema	.06	.05	.02
190	Bill Gullickson	.12	.09	.05	280	Stan Papi	.06	.05	.02
191	Grant Jackson	.06	.05	.02	281	Dan Schatzeder	.06	.05	.02
192	Wallace Johnson	.06	.05	.02	282	Champ Summers	.06	.05	.02
193	Charlie Lea	.06	.05	.02	283	Alan Trammell	.40	.30	.15
194	Bill Lee	.08	.06	.03	284	Lou Whitaker	.30	.25	.12
195	Jerry Manuel	.06	.05	.02	285	Milt Wilcox	.08	.06	.03
196	Brad Mills	.06	.05	.02	286	John Wockenfuss	.06	.05	.02
197	John Milner	.06	.05	.02	287	Gary Allenson	.06	.05	.02
198	Rowland Office	.06	.05	.02	288	Tom Burgmeier	.06	.05	.02
199	David Palmer	.08	.06	.03	289	Bill Campbell	.06	.05	.02
200	Larry Parrish	.10	.08	.04	290	Mark Clear	.08	.06	.03
201	Mike Phillips	.06	.05	.02	291	Steve Crawford	.06	.05	.02
202	Tim Raines	.90	.70	.35	292	Dennis Eckersley	.10	.08	.04
203	Bobby Ramos	.06	.05	.02	293	Dwight Evans	.15	.11	.06
204	Jeff Reardon	.20	.15	.08	294	Rich Gedman	.40	.30	.15
205	Steve Rogers	.08	.06	.03	295	Garry Hancock	.06	.05	.02
206	Scott Sanderson	.08	.06	.03	296	Glenn Hoffman	.06	.05	.02
207	Rodney Scott (photo actually Tim Raines)				297	Bruce Hurst	.25	.20	.10
		.10	.08	.04	298	Carney Lansford	.08	.06	.03
208	Elias Sosa	.06	.05	.02	299	Rick Miller	.06	.05	.02
209	Chris Speier	.08	.06	.03	300	Reid Nichols	.06	.05	.02
210	Tim Wallach	1.25	.90	.50	301	Bob Ojeda	.60	.45	.25
211	Jerry White	.06	.05	.02	302	Tony Perez	.20	.15	.08
212	Alan Ashby	.06	.05	.02	303	Chuck Rainey	.06	.05	.02
213	Cesar Cedeno	.12	.09	.05	304	Jerry Remy	.06	.05	.02
214	Jose Cruz	.12	.09	.05	305	Jim Rice	.40	.30	.15
215	Kiko Garcia	.06	.05	.02	306	Joe Rudi	.10	.08	.04
216	Phil Garner	.08	.06	.03	307	Bob Stanley	.08	.06	.03
217	Danny Heep	.06	.05	.02	308	Dave Stapleton	.06	.05	.02
218	Art Howe	.06	.05	.02	309	Frank Tanana	.10	.08	.04
219	Bob Knepper	.08	.06	.03	310	Mike Torrez	.08	.06	.03
220	Frank LaCorte	.06	.05	.02	311	John Tudor	.25	.20	.10
221	Joe Niekro	.12	.09	.05	312	Carl Yastrzemski	.80	.60	.30
222	Joe Pittman	.06	.05	.02	313	Buddy Bell	.15	.11	.06
223	Terry Puhl	.06	.05	.02	314	Steve Comer	.06	.05	.02
224	Luis Pujols	.06	.05	.02	315	Danny Darwin	.08	.06	.03
225	Craig Reynolds	.06	.05	.02	316	John Ellis	.06	.05	.02
226	J.R. Richard	.10	.08	.04	317	John Grubb	.06	.05	.02
227	Dave Roberts	.06	.05	.02	318	Rick Honeycutt	.08	.06	.03
228	Vern Ruhle	.06	.05	.02	319	Charlie Hough	.10	.08	.04
229	Nolan Ryan	.50	.40	.20	320	Ferguson Jenkins	.15	.11	.06
230	Joe Sambito	.06	.05	.02	321	John Henry Johnson	.06	.05	.02
231	Tony Scott	.06	.05	.02	322	Jim Kern	.06	.05	.02

		MT	NR MT	EX
323	Jon Matlack	.08	.06	.03
324	Doc Medich	.06	.05	.02
325	Mario Mendoza	.06	.05	.02
326	Al Oliver	.15	.11	.06
327	Pat Putnam	.06	.05	.02
328	Mickey Rivers	.08	.06	.03
329	Leon Roberts	.06	.05	.02
330	Billy Sample	.06	.05	.02
331	Bill Stein	.06	.05	.02
332	Jim Sundberg	.08	.06	.03
333	Mark Wagner	.06	.05	.02
334	Bump Wills	.06	.05	.02
335	Bill Almon	.06	.05	.02
336	Harold Baines	.30	.25	.12
337	Ross Baumgarten	.06	.05	.02
338	Tony Bernazard	.08	.06	.03
339	Britt Burns	.08	.06	.03
340	Richard Dotson	.10	.08	.04
341	Jim Essian	.06	.05	.02
342	Ed Farmer	.06	.05	.02
343	Carlton Fisk	.20	.15	.08
344	Kevin Hickey	.06	.05	.02
345	Lamarr Hoyt (LaMarr)	.08	.06	.03
346	Lamar Johnson	.06	.05	.02
347	Jerry Koosman	.12	.09	.05
348	Rusty Kuntz	.06	.05	.02
349	Dennis Lamp	.06	.05	.02
350	Ron LeFlore	.08	.06	.03
351	Chet Lemon	.08	.06	.03
352	Greg Luzinski	.15	.11	.06
353	Bob Molinaro	.06	.05	.02
354	Jim Morrison	.06	.05	.02
355	Wayne Nordhagen	.06	.05	.02
356	Greg Pryor	.06	.05	.02
357	Mike Squires	.06	.05	.02
358	Steve Trout	.08	.06	.03
359	Alan Bannister	.06	.05	.02
360	Len Barker	.08	.06	.03
361	Bert Blyleven	.15	.11	.06
362	Joe Charboneau	.08	.06	.03
363	John Denny	.08	.06	.03
364	Bo Diaz	.08	.06	.03
365	Miguel Dilone	.06	.05	.02
366	Jerry Dybzinski	.06	.05	.02
367	Wayne Garland	.06	.05	.02
368	Mike Hargrove	.08	.06	.03
369	Toby Harrah	.08	.06	.03
370	Ron Hassey	.06	.05	.02
371	Von Hayes	.90	.70	.35
372	Pat Kelly	.06	.05	.02
373	Duane Kuiper	.06	.05	.02
374	Rick Manning	.06	.05	.02
375	Sid Monge	.06	.05	.02
376	Jorge Orta	.06	.05	.02
377	Dave Rosello	.06	.05	.02
378	Dan Spillner	.06	.05	.02
379	Mike Stanton	.06	.05	.02
380	Andre Thornton	.10	.08	.04
381	Tom Veryzer	.06	.05	.02
382	Rick Waits	.06	.05	.02
383	Doyle Alexander	.12	.09	.05
384	Vida Blue	.12	.09	.05
385	Fred Breining	.06	.05	.02
386	Enos Cabell	.08	.06	.03
387	Jack Clark	.25	.20	.10
388	Darrell Evans	.15	.11	.06
389	Tom Griffin	.06	.05	.02
390	Larry Herndon	.08	.06	.03
391	Al Holland	.08	.06	.03
392	Gary Lavelle	.06	.05	.02
393	Johnnie LeMaster	.06	.05	.02
394	Jerry Martin	.06	.05	.02
395	Milt May	.06	.05	.02
396	Greg Minton	.06	.05	.02
397	Joe Morgan	.30	.25	.12
398	Joe Pettini	.06	.05	.02
399	Alan Ripley	.06	.05	.02
400	Billy Smith	.06	.05	.02
401	Rennie Stennett	.06	.05	.02
402	Ed Whitson	.08	.06	.03
403	Jim Wohlford	.06	.05	.02
404	Willie Aikens	.06	.05	.02
405	George Brett	.70	.50	.30
406	Ken Brett	.08	.06	.03
407	Dave Chalk	.06	.05	.02
408	Rich Gale	.06	.05	.02
409	Cesar Geronimo	.06	.05	.02
410	Larry Gura	.08	.06	.03
411	Clint Hurdle	.06	.05	.02
412	Mike Jones	.06	.05	.02
413	Dennis Leonard	.08	.06	.03

		MT	NR MT	EX
414	Renie Martin	.06	.05	.02
415	Lee May	.08	.06	.03
416	Hal McRae	.12	.09	.05
417	Darryl Motley	.06	.05	.02
418	Rance Mulliniks	.06	.05	.02
419	Amos Otis	.08	.06	.03
420	Ken Phelps	.40	.30	.15
421	Jamie Quirk	.06	.05	.02
422	Dan Quisenberry	.20	.15	.08
423	Paul Splittorff	.08	.06	.03
424	U.L. Washington	.06	.05	.02
425	John Wathan	.08	.06	.03
426	Frank White	.10	.08	.04
427	Willie Wilson	.15	.11	.06
428	Brian Asselstine	.06	.05	.02
429	Bruce Benedict	.06	.05	.02
430	Tom Boggs	.06	.05	.02
431	Larry Bradford	.06	.05	.02
432	Rick Camp	.06	.05	.02
433	Chris Chambliss	.08	.06	.03
434	Gene Garber	.06	.05	.02
435	Preston Hanna	.06	.05	.02
436	Bob Horner	.30	.25	.12
437	Glenn Hubbard	.08	.06	.03
438a	Al Hrabosky (All Hrabosky, 5'1" on back)			
		18.00	13.50	7.25
438b	Al Hrabosky (Al Hrabosky, 5'1" on back)			
		1.25	.90	.50
438c	Al Hrabosky (Al Hrabosky, 5'10" on back)			
		.35	.25	.14
439	Rufino Linares	.06	.05	.02
440	Rick Mahler	.25	.20	.10
441	Ed Miller	.06	.05	.02
442	John Montefusco	.08	.06	.03
443	Dale Murphy	.90	.70	.35
444	Phil Niekro	.30	.25	.12
445	Gaylord Perry	.30	.25	.12
446	Biff Pocoroba	.06	.05	.02
447	Rafael Ramirez	.08	.06	.03
448	Jerry Royster	.06	.05	.02
449	Claudell Washington	.08	.06	.03
450	Don Aase	.08	.06	.03
451	Don Baylor	.15	.11	.06
452	Juan Beniquez	.06	.05	.02
453	Rick Burleson	.08	.06	.03
454	Bert Campaneris	.10	.08	.04
455	Rod Carew	.50	.40	.20
456	Bob Clark	.06	.05	.02
457	Brian Downing	.10	.08	.04
458	Dan Ford	.06	.05	.02
459	Ken Forsch	.08	.06	.03
460	Dave Frost	.06	.05	.02
461	Bobby Grich	.10	.08	.04
462	Larry Harlow	.06	.05	.02
463	John Harris	.06	.05	.02
464	Andy Hassler	.06	.05	.02
465	Butch Hobson	.06	.05	.02
466	Jesse Jefferson	.06	.05	.02
467	Bruce Kison	.06	.05	.02
468	Fred Lynn	.20	.15	.08
469	Angel Moreno	.06	.05	.02
470	Ed Ott	.06	.05	.02
471	Fred Patek	.06	.05	.02
472	Steve Renko	.06	.05	.02
473	Mike Witt	.90	.70	.35
474	Geoff Zahn	.06	.05	.02
475	Gary Alexander	.06	.05	.02
476	Dale Berra	.06	.05	.02
477	Kurt Bevacqua	.06	.05	.02
478	Jim Bibby	.06	.05	.02
479	John Candelaria	.10	.08	.04
480	Victor Cruz	.06	.05	.02
481	Mike Easler	.10	.08	.04
482	Tim Foli	.06	.05	.02
483	Lee Lacy	.08	.06	.03
484	Vance Law	.12	.09	.05
485	Bill Madlock	.15	.11	.06
486	Willie Montanez	.06	.05	.02
487	Omar Moreno	.06	.05	.02
488	Steve Nicosia	.06	.05	.02
489	Dave Parker	.30	.25	.12
490	Tony Pena	.25	.20	.10
491	Pascual Perez	.15	.11	.06
492	Johnny Ray	.80	.60	.30
493	Rick Rhoden	.10	.08	.04
494	Bill Robinson	.06	.05	.02
495	Don Robinson	.08	.06	.03
496	Enrique Romo	.06	.05	.02
497	Rod Scurry	.06	.05	.02
498	Eddie Solomon	.06	.05	.02
499	Willie Stargell	.30	.25	.12

		MT	NR MT	EX
500	Kent Tekulve	.08	.06	.03
501	Jason Thompson	.06	.05	.02
502	Glenn Abbott	.06	.05	.02
503	Jim Anderson	.06	.05	.02
504	Floyd Bannister	.10	.08	.04
505	Bruce Bochte	.06	.05	.02
506	Jeff Burroughs	.08	.06	.03
507	Bryan Clark	.10	.08	.04
508	Ken Clay	.06	.05	.02
509	Julio Cruz	.06	.05	.02
510	Dick Drago	.06	.05	.02
511	Gary Gray	.06	.05	.02
512	Dan Meyer	.06	.05	.02
513	Jerry Narron	.06	.05	.02
514	Tom Paciorek	.06	.05	.02
515	Casey Parsons	.06	.05	.02
516	Lenny Randle	.06	.05	.02
517	Shane Rawley	.10	.08	.04
518	Joe Simpson	.06	.05	.02
519	Richie Zisk	.08	.06	.03
520	Neil Allen	.06	.05	.02
521	Bob Bailor	.06	.05	.02
522	Hubie Brooks	.25	.20	.10
523	Mike Cubbage	.06	.05	.02
524	Pete Falcone	.06	.05	.02
525	Doug Flynn	.06	.05	.02
526	Tom Hausman	.06	.05	.02
527	Ron Hodges	.06	.05	.02
528	Randy Jones	.08	.06	.03
529	Mike Jorgensen	.06	.05	.02
530	Dave Kingman	.15	.11	.06
531	Ed Lynch	.10	.08	.04
532	Mike Marshall	.10	.08	.04
533	Lee Mazzilli	.08	.06	.03
534	Dyar Miller	.06	.05	.02
535	Mike Scott	.35	.25	.14
536	Rusty Staub	.12	.09	.05
537	John Stearns	.06	.05	.02
538	Craig Swan	.06	.05	.02
539	Frank Taveras	.06	.05	.02
540	Alex Trevino	.06	.05	.02
541	Ellis Valentine	.06	.05	.02
542	Mookie Wilson	.20	.15	.08
543	Joel Youngblood	.06	.05	.02
544	Pat Zachry	.06	.05	.02
545	Glenn Adams	.06	.05	.02
546	Fernando Arroyo	.06	.05	.02
547	John Verhoeven	.06	.05	.02
548	Sal Butera	.06	.05	.02
549	John Castino	.06	.05	.02
550	Don Cooper	.06	.05	.02
551	Doug Corbett	.06	.05	.02
552	Dave Engle	.06	.05	.02
553	Roger Erickson	.06	.05	.02
554	Danny Goodwin	.06	.05	.02
555a	Darrell Jackson (black cap)	1.00	.70	.40
555b	Darrell Jackson (red cap with emblem)	.10	.08	.04
555c	Darrell Jackson (red cap, no emblem)	.25	.20	.10
556	Pete Mackanin	.06	.05	.02
557	Jack O'Connor	.06	.05	.02
558	Hosken Powell	.06	.05	.02
559	Pete Redfern	.06	.05	.02
560	Roy Smalley	.08	.06	.03
561	Chuck Baker	.06	.05	.02
562	Gary Ward	.08	.06	.03
563	Rob Wilfong	.06	.05	.02
564	Al Williams	.06	.05	.02
565	Butch Wynegar	.08	.06	.03
566	Randy Bass	.06	.05	.02
567	Juan Bonilla	.10	.08	.04
568	Danny Boone	.06	.05	.02
569	John Curtis	.06	.05	.02
570	Juan Eichelberger	.06	.05	.02
571	Barry Evans	.06	.05	.02
572	Tim Flannery	.06	.05	.02
573	Ruppert Jones	.08	.06	.03
574	Terry Kennedy	.08	.06	.03
575	Joe Lefebvre	.06	.05	.02
576a	John Littlefield (pitching lefty)	70.00	52.00	28.00
576b	John Littlefield (pitching righty)	.08	.06	.03
577	Gary Lucas	.06	.05	.02
578	Steve Mura	.06	.05	.02
579	Broderick Perkins	.06	.05	.02
580	Gene Richards	.06	.05	.02
581	Luis Salazar	.06	.05	.02
582	Ozzie Smith	.15	.11	.06
583	John Urrea	.06	.05	.02
584	Chris Welsh	.06	.05	.02
585	Rick Wise	.08	.06	.03

		MT	NR MT	EX
586	Doug Bird	.06	.05	.02
587	Tim Blackwell	.06	.05	.02
588	Bobby Bonds	.10	.08	.04
589	Bill Buckner	.12	.09	.05
590	Bill Caudill	.06	.05	.02
591	Hector Cruz	.06	.05	.02
592	Jody Davis	.50	.40	.20
593	Ivan DeJesus	.06	.05	.02
594	Steve Dillard	.06	.05	.02
595	Leon Durham	.15	.11	.06
596	Rawly Eastwick	.06	.05	.02
597	Steve Henderson	.06	.05	.02
598	Mike Krukow	.08	.06	.03
599	Mike Lum	.06	.05	.02
600	Randy Martz	.06	.05	.02
601	Jerry Morales	.06	.05	.02
602	Ken Reitz	.06	.05	.02
603a	Lee Smith (Cubs logo reversed on back)	1.00	.70	.40
603b	Lee Smith (Cubs logo correct)	.60	.45	.25
604	Dick Tidrow	.06	.05	.02
605	Jim Tracy	.06	.05	.02
606	Mike Tyson	.06	.05	.02
607	Ty Waller	.06	.05	.02
608	Danny Ainge	.12	.09	.05
609	Jorge Bell	8.00	6.00	3.25
610	Mark Bomback	.06	.05	.02
611	Barry Bonnell	.06	.05	.02
612	Jim Clancy	.10	.08	.04
613	Damaso Garcia	.08	.06	.03
614	Jerry Garvin	.06	.05	.02
615	Alfredo Griffin	.08	.06	.03
616	Garth Iorg	.06	.05	.02
617	Luis Leal	.06	.05	.02
618	Ken Macha	.06	.05	.02
619	John Mayberry	.08	.06	.03
620	Joey McLaughlin	.06	.05	.02
621	Lloyd Moseby	.15	.11	.06
622	Dave Stieb	.12	.09	.05
623	Jackson Todd	.06	.05	.02
624	Willie Upshaw	.15	.11	.06
625	Otto Velez	.06	.05	.02
626	Ernie Whitt	.08	.06	.03
627	Al Woods	.06	.05	.02
628	1981 All-Star Game	.08	.06	.03
629	All-Star Infielders (Bucky Dent, Frank White)	.10	.08	.04
630	Big Red Machine (Dave Concepcion, Dan Driessen, George Foster)	.15	.11	.06
631	Top N.L. Relief Pitcher (Bruce Sutter)	.15	.11	.06
632	Steve & Carlton (Steve Carlton, Carlton Fisk)	.25	.20	.10
633	3000th Game, May 25, 1981 (Carl Yastrzemski)	.35	.25	.14
634	Dynamic Duo (Johnny Bench, Tom Seaver)	.30	.25	.12
635	West Meets East (Gary Carter, Fernando Valenzuela)	.30	.25	.12
636a	N.L. Strikeout King (Fernando Valenzuela) ("...led he National League...")	1.00	.70	.40
636b	N.L. Strikeout King (Fernando Valenzuela) ("...led the National League...")	.50	.40	.20
637	1981 Home Run King (Mike Schmidt)	.40	.30	.15
638	N.L. All-Stars (Gary Carter, Dave Parker)	.25	.20	.10
639	Perfect Game! (Len Barker, Bo Diaz)	.08	.06	.03
640	Pete & Re-Pete (Pete Rose, Pete Rose, Jr.)	.90	.70	.35
641	Phillies' Finest (Steve Carlton, Mike Schmidt, Lonnie Smith)	.35	.25	.14
642	Red Sox Reunion (Dwight Evans, Fred Lynn)	.15	.11	.06
643	1981 Most Hits, Most Runs (Rickey Henderson)	.35	.25	.14
644	Most Saves 1981 A.L. (Rollie Fingers)	.15	.11	.06
645	Most 1981 Wins (Tom Seaver)	.25	.20	.10
646a	Yankee Powerhouse (Reggie Jackson, Dave Winfield) (comma after "outfielder" on back)	1.00	.70	.40
646b	Yankee Powerhouse (Reggie Jackson, Dave Winfield) (no comma after "oufielder")	.50	.40	.20
647	Checklist 1-56	.06	.05	.02
648	Checklist 57-109	.06	.05	.02
649	Checklist 110-156	.06	.05	.02
650	Checklist 157-211	.06	.05	.02
651	Checklist 212-262	.06	.05	.02

		MT	NR MT	EX
652	Checklist 263-312	.06	.05	.02
653	Checklist 313-358	.06	.05	.02
654	Checklist 359-403	.06	.05	.02
655	Checklist 404-449	.06	.05	.02
656	Checklist 450-501	.06	.05	.02
657	Checklist 502-544	.06	.05	.02
658	Checklist 545-585	.06	.05	.02
659	Checklist 586-627	.06	.05	.02
660	Checklist 628-646	.06	.05	.02

1983 Fleer

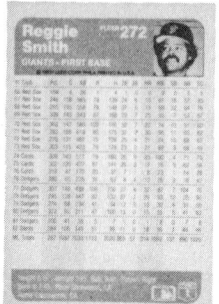

Reggie Smith
FIRST BASE

The 1983 Fleer set features color photos set inside a light brown border. The cards are the standard size of 2½'' by 3½''. A team logo is located at the card bottom and the word ''Fleer'' is found at the top. The card backs are designed on a vertical format and include a small black and white photo of the player along with biographical and statistical information. The reverses are done in two shades of brown on white stock. The set was issued with team logo stickers.

		MT	NR MT	EX
Complete Set:		34.00	25.00	13.50
Common Player:		.06	.05	.02
1	Joaquin Andujar	.10	.08	.04
2	Doug Bair	.06	.05	.02
3	Steve Braun	.06	.05	.02
4	Glenn Brummer	.06	.05	.02
5	Bob Forsch	.08	.06	.03
6	David Green	.10	.08	.04
7	George Hendrick	.08	.06	.03
8	Keith Hernandez	.40	.30	.15
9	Tom Herr	.10	.08	.04
10	Dane Iorg	.06	.05	.02
11	Jim Kaat	.15	.11	.06
12	Jeff Lahti	.06	.05	.02
13	Tito Landrum	.06	.05	.02
14	Dave LaPoint	.15	.11	.06
15	Willie McGee	1.75	1.25	.70
16	Steve Mura	.06	.05	.02
17	Ken Oberkfell	.08	.06	.03
18	Darrell Porter	.08	.06	.03
19	Mike Ramsey	.06	.05	.02
20	Gene Roof	.06	.05	.02
21	Lonnie Smith	.08	.06	.03
22	Ozzie Smith	.15	.11	.06
23	John Stuper	.10	.08	.04
24	Bruce Sutter	.15	.11	.06
25	Gene Tenace	.08	.06	.03
26	Jerry Augustine	.06	.05	.02
27	Dwight Bernard	.06	.05	.02
28	Mark Brouhard	.06	.05	.02
29	Mike Caldwell	.06	.05	.02
30	Cecil Cooper	.15	.11	.06
31	Jamie Easterly	.06	.05	.02
32	Marshall Edwards	.06	.05	.02
33	Rollie Fingers	.20	.15	.08
34	Jim Gantner	.08	.06	.03
35	Moose Haas	.06	.05	.02
36	Roy Howell	.06	.05	.02
37	Peter Ladd	.06	.05	.02
38	Bob McClure	.06	.05	.02
39	Doc Medich	.06	.05	.02

		MT	NR MT	EX
40	Paul Molitor	.20	.15	.08
41	Don Money	.08	.06	.03
42	Charlie Moore	.06	.05	.02
43	Ben Oglivie	.08	.06	.03
44	Ed Romero	.06	.05	.02
45	Ted Simmons	.15	.11	.06
46	Jim Slaton	.06	.05	.02
47	Don Sutton	.30	.25	.12
48	Gorman Thomas	.12	.09	.05
49	Pete Vuckovich	.08	.06	.03
50	Ned Yost	.06	.05	.02
51	Robin Yount	.40	.30	.15
52	Benny Ayala	.06	.05	.02
53	Bob Bonner	.06	.05	.02
54	Al Bumbry	.08	.06	.03
55	Terry Crowley	.06	.05	.02
56	Storm Davis	.30	.25	.12
57	Rich Dauer	.06	.05	.02
58	Rick Dempsey	.08	.06	.03
59	Jim Dwyer	.06	.05	.02
60	Mike Flanagan	.10	.08	.04
61	Dan Ford	.06	.05	.02
62	Glenn Gulliver	.06	.05	.02
63	John Lowenstein	.06	.05	.02
64	Dennis Martinez	.08	.06	.03
65	Tippy Martinez	.06	.05	.02
66	Scott McGregor	.10	.08	.04
67	Eddie Murray	.60	.45	.25
68	Joe Nolan	.06	.05	.02
69	Jim Palmer	.40	.30	.15
70	Cal Ripken, Jr.	1.00	.70	.40
71	Gary Roenicke	.08	.06	.03
72	Lenn Sakata	.06	.05	.02
73	Ken Singleton	.10	.08	.04
74	Sammy Stewart	.06	.05	.02
75	Tim Stoddard	.06	.05	.02
76	Don Aase	.08	.06	.03
77	Don Baylor	.15	.11	.06
78	Juan Beniquez	.06	.05	.02
79	Bob Boone	.10	.08	.04
80	Rick Burleson	.08	.06	.03
81	Rod Carew	.50	.40	.20
82	Bobby Clark	.06	.05	.02
83	Doug Corbett	.06	.05	.02
84	John Curtis	.06	.05	.02
85	Doug DeCinces	.10	.08	.04
86	Brian Downing	.10	.08	.04
87	Joe Ferguson	.06	.05	.02
88	Tim Foli	.06	.05	.02
89	Ken Forsch	.08	.06	.03
90	Dave Goltz	.08	.06	.03
91	Bobby Grich	.10	.08	.04
92	Andy Hassler	.06	.05	.02
93	Reggie Jackson	.50	.40	.20
94	Ron Jackson	.06	.05	.02
95	Tommy John	.20	.15	.08
96	Bruce Kison	.06	.05	.02
97	Fred Lynn	.20	.15	.08
98	Ed Ott	.06	.05	.02
99	Steve Renko	.06	.05	.02
100	Luis Sanchez	.06	.05	.02
101	Rob Wilfong	.06	.05	.02
102	Mike Witt	.20	.15	.08
103	Geoff Zahn	.06	.05	.02
104	Willie Aikens	.06	.05	.02
105	Mike Armstrong	.06	.05	.02
106	Vida Blue	.12	.09	.05
107	Bud Black	.20	.15	.08
108	George Brett	.70	.50	.30
109	Bill Castro	.06	.05	.02
110	Onix Concepcion	.08	.06	.03
111	Dave Frost	.06	.05	.02
112	Cesar Geronimo	.06	.05	.02
113	Larry Gura	.08	.06	.03
114	Steve Hammond	.06	.05	.02
115	Don Hood	.06	.05	.02
116	Dennis Leonard	.08	.06	.03
117	Jerry Martin	.06	.05	.02
118	Lee May	.08	.06	.03
119	Hal McRae	.12	.09	.05
120	Amos Otis	.08	.06	.03
121	Greg Pryor	.06	.05	.02
122	Dan Quisenberry	.20	.15	.08
123	Don Slaught	.20	.15	.08
124	Paul Splittorff	.08	.06	.03
125	U.L. Washington	.06	.05	.02
126	John Wathan	.08	.06	.03
127	Frank White	.10	.08	.04
128	Willie Wilson	.15	.11	.06
129	Steve Bedrosian	.35	.25	.14
130	Bruce Benedict	.06	.05	.02

#	Name	MT	NR MT	EX	#	Name	MT	NR MT	EX
131	Tommy Boggs	.06	.05	.02	222	Dave Stewart	.12	.09	.05
132	Brett Butler	.15	.11	.06	223	Derrel Thomas	.06	.05	.02
133	Rick Camp	.06	.05	.02	224	Fernando Valenzuela	.30	.25	.12
134	Chris Chambliss	.08	.06	.03	225	Bob Welch	.10	.08	.04
135	Ken Dayley	.10	.08	.04	226	Ricky Wright	.06	.05	.02
136	Gene Garber	.06	.05	.02	227	Steve Yeager	.06	.05	.02
137	Terry Harper	.06	.05	.02	228	Bill Almon	.06	.05	.02
138	Bob Horner	.30	.25	.12	229	Harold Baines	.15	.11	.06
139	Glenn Hubbard	.08	.06	.03	230	Salome Barojas	.06	.05	.02
140	Rufino Linares	.06	.05	.02	231	Tony Bernazard	.08	.06	.03
141	Rick Mahler	.08	.06	.03	232	Britt Burns	.06	.05	.02
142	Dale Murphy	.90	.70	.35	233	Richard Dotson	.10	.08	.04
143	Phil Niekro	.30	.25	.12	234	Ernesto Escarrega	.06	.05	.02
144	Pascual Perez	.08	.06	.03	235	Carlton Fisk	.20	.15	.08
145	Biff Pocoroba	.06	.05	.02	236	Jerry Hairston	.06	.05	.02
146	Rafael Ramirez	.08	.06	.03	237	Kevin Hickey	.06	.05	.02
147	Jerry Royster	.06	.05	.02	238	LaMarr Hoyt	.08	.06	.03
148	Ken Smith	.06	.05	.02	239	Steve Kemp	.10	.08	.04
149	Bob Walk	.06	.05	.02	240	Jim Kern	.06	.05	.02
150	Claudell Washington	.08	.06	.03	241	Ron Kittle	.70	.50	.30
151	Bob Watson	.08	.06	.03	242	Jerry Koosman	.12	.09	.05
152	Larry Whisenton	.06	.05	.02	243	Dennis Lamp	.06	.05	.02
153	Porfirio Altamirano	.06	.05	.02	244	Rudy Law	.06	.05	.02
154	Marty Bystrom	.06	.05	.02	245	Vance Law	.08	.06	.03
155	Steve Carlton	.40	.30	.15	246	Ron LeFlore	.08	.06	.03
156	Larry Christenson	.06	.05	.02	247	Greg Luzinski	.12	.09	.05
157	Ivan DeJesus	.06	.05	.02	248	Tom Paciorek	.06	.05	.02
158	John Denny	.08	.06	.03	249	Aurelio Rodriguez	.08	.06	.03
159	Bob Dernier	.15	.11	.06	250	Mike Squires	.06	.05	.02
160	Bo Diaz	.08	.06	.03	251	Steve Trout	.08	.06	.03
161	Ed Farmer	.06	.05	.02	252	Jim Barr	.06	.05	.02
162	Greg Gross	.06	.05	.02	253	Dave Bergman	.06	.05	.02
163	Mike Krukow	.08	.06	.03	254	Fred Breining	.06	.05	.02
164	Garry Maddox	.10	.08	.04	255	Bob Brenly	.15	.11	.06
165	Gary Matthews	.10	.08	.04	256	Jack Clark	.25	.20	.10
166	Tug McGraw	.12	.09	.05	257	Chili Davis	.20	.15	.08
167	Bob Molinaro	.06	.05	.02	258	Darrell Evans	.15	.11	.06
168	Sid Monge	.06	.05	.02	259	Alan Fowlkes	.06	.05	.02
169	Ron Reed	.08	.06	.03	260	Rich Gale	.06	.05	.02
170	Bill Robinson	.06	.05	.02	261	Atlee Hammaker	.12	.09	.05
171	Pete Rose	1.00	.70	.40	262	Al Holland	.06	.05	.02
172	Dick Ruthven	.06	.05	.02	263	Duane Kuiper	.06	.05	.02
173	Mike Schmidt	.60	.45	.25	264	Bill Laskey	.06	.05	.02
174	Manny Trillo	.08	.06	.03	265	Gary Lavelle	.06	.05	.02
175	Ozzie Virgil	.15	.11	.06	266	Johnnie LeMaster	.06	.05	.02
176	George Vukovich	.06	.05	.02	267	Renie Martin	.06	.05	.02
177	Gary Allenson	.06	.05	.02	268	Milt May	.06	.05	.02
178	Luis Aponte	.06	.05	.02	269	Greg Minton	.06	.05	.02
179	Wade Boggs	17.00	12.50	6.75	270	Joe Morgan	.30	.25	.12
180	Tom Burgmeier	.06	.05	.02	271	Tom O'Malley	.06	.05	.02
181	Mark Clear	.08	.06	.03	272	Reggie Smith	.10	.08	.04
182	Dennis Eckersley	.10	.08	.04	273	Guy Sularz	.06	.05	.02
183	Dwight Evans	.15	.11	.06	274	Champ Summers	.06	.05	.02
184	Rich Gedman	.10	.08	.04	275	Max Venable	.06	.05	.02
185	Glenn Hoffman	.06	.05	.02	276	Jim Wohlford	.06	.05	.02
186	Bruce Hurst	.10	.08	.04	277	Ray Burris	.06	.05	.02
187	Carney Lansford	.08	.06	.03	278	Gary Carter	.40	.30	.15
188	Rick Miller	.06	.05	.02	279	Warren Cromartie	.06	.05	.02
189	Reid Nichols	.06	.05	.02	280	Andre Dawson	.35	.25	.14
190	Bob Ojeda	.15	.11	.06	281	Terry Francona	.06	.05	.02
191	Tony Perez	.20	.15	.08	282	Doug Flynn	.06	.05	.02
192	Chuck Rainey	.06	.05	.02	283	Woody Fryman	.08	.06	.03
193	Jerry Remy	.06	.05	.02	284	Bill Gullickson	.08	.06	.03
194	Jim Rice	.40	.30	.15	285	Wallace Johnson	.06	.05	.02
195	Bob Stanley	.08	.06	.03	286	Charlie Lea	.06	.05	.02
196	Dave Stapleton	.06	.05	.02	287	Randy Lerch	.06	.05	.02
197	Mike Torrez	.08	.06	.03	288	Brad Mills	.06	.05	.02
198	John Tudor	.10	.08	.04	289	Dan Norman	.06	.05	.02
199	Julio Valdez	.06	.05	.02	290	Al Oliver	.15	.11	.06
200	Carl Yastrzemski	.70	.50	.30	291	David Palmer	.08	.06	.03
201	Dusty Baker	.10	.08	.04	292	Tim Raines	.35	.25	.14
202	Joe Beckwith	.06	.05	.02	293	Jeff Reardon	.12	.09	.05
203	Greg Brock	.50	.40	.20	294	Steve Rogers	.08	.06	.03
204	Ron Cey	.12	.09	.05	295	Scott Sanderson	.08	.06	.03
205	Terry Forster	.08	.06	.03	296	Dan Schatzeder	.06	.05	.02
206	Steve Garvey	.40	.30	.15	297	Bryn Smith	.08	.06	.03
207	Pedro Guerrero	.25	.20	.10	298	Chris Speier	.06	.05	.02
208	Burt Hooton	.08	.06	.03	299	Tim Wallach	.20	.15	.08
209	Steve Howe	.08	.06	.03	300	Jerry White	.06	.05	.02
210	Ken Landreaux	.08	.06	.03	301	Joel Youngblood	.06	.05	.02
211	Mike Marshall	.20	.15	.08	302	Ross Baumgarten	.06	.05	.02
212	Candy Maldonado	.70	.50	.30	303	Dale Berra	.06	.05	.02
213	Rick Monday	.10	.08	.04	304	John Candelaria	.10	.08	.04
214	Tom Niedenfuer	.10	.08	.04	305	Dick Davis	.06	.05	.02
215	Jorge Orta	.06	.05	.02	306	Mike Easler	.08	.06	.03
216	Jerry Reuss	.10	.08	.04	307	Richie Hebner	.06	.05	.02
217	Ron Roenicke	.06	.05	.02	308	Lee Lacy	.08	.06	.03
218	Vicente Romo	.06	.05	.02	309	Bill Madlock	.15	.11	.06
219	Bill Russell	.08	.06	.03	310	Larry McWilliams	.06	.05	.02
220	Steve Sax	.25	.20	.10	311	John Milner	.06	.05	.02
221	Mike Scioscia	.06	.05	.02	312	Omar Moreno	.06	.05	.02

#	Player	MT	NR MT	EX
313	Jim Morrison	.06	.05	.02
314	Steve Nicosia	.06	.05	.02
315	Dave Parker	.30	.25	.12
316	Tony Pena	.10	.08	.04
317	Johnny Ray	.15	.11	.06
318	Rick Rhoden	.10	.08	.04
319	Don Robinson	.08	.06	.03
320	Enrique Romo	.06	.05	.02
321	Manny Sarmiento	.06	.05	.02
322	Rod Scurry	.06	.05	.02
323	Jim Smith	.06	.05	.02
324	Willie Stargell	.30	.25	.12
325	Jason Thompson	.06	.05	.02
326	Kent Tekulve	.08	.06	.03
327a	Tom Brookens (narrow (1/4") brown box at bottom on back)	.30	.25	.12
327b	Tom Brookens (wide (1 1/4") brown box at bottom on back)	.08	.06	.03
328	Enos Cabell	.06	.05	.02
329	Kirk Gibson	.30	.25	.12
330	Larry Herndon	.08	.06	.03
331	Mike Ivie	.06	.05	.02
332	Howard Johnson	1.50	1.25	.60
333	Lynn Jones	.06	.05	.02
334	Rick Leach	.06	.05	.02
335	Chet Lemon	.08	.06	.03
336	Jack Morris	.30	.25	.12
337	Lance Parrish	.35	.25	.14
338	Larry Pashnick	.06	.05	.02
339	Dan Petry	.10	.08	.04
340	Dave Rozema	.06	.05	.02
341	Dave Rucker	.06	.05	.02
342	Elias Sosa	.06	.05	.02
343	Dave Tobik	.06	.05	.02
344	Alan Trammell	.40	.30	.15
345	Jerry Turner	.06	.05	.02
346	Jerry Ujdur	.06	.05	.02
347	Pat Underwood	.06	.05	.02
348	Lou Whitaker	.30	.25	.12
349	Milt Wilcox	.08	.06	.03
350	Glenn Wilson	.60	.45	.25
351	John Wockenfuss	.06	.05	.02
352	Kurt Bevacqua	.06	.05	.02
353	Juan Bonilla	.06	.05	.02
354	Floyd Chiffer	.06	.05	.02
355	Luis DeLeon	.06	.05	.02
356	Dave Dravecky	.40	.30	.15
357	Dave Edwards	.06	.05	.02
358	Juan Eichelberger	.06	.05	.02
359	Tim Flannery	.06	.05	.02
360	Tony Gwynn	8.00	6.00	3.25
361	Ruppert Jones	.06	.05	.02
362	Terry Kennedy	.08	.06	.03
363	Joe Lefebvre	.06	.05	.02
364	Sixto Lezcano	.06	.05	.02
365	Tim Lollar	.06	.05	.02
366	Gary Lucas	.06	.05	.02
367	John Montefusco	.06	.05	.02
368	Broderick Perkins	.06	.05	.02
369	Joe Pittman	.06	.05	.02
370	Gene Richards	.06	.05	.02
371	Luis Salazar	.06	.05	.02
372	Eric Show	.20	.15	.08
373	Garry Templeton	.10	.08	.04
374	Chris Welsh	.06	.05	.02
375	Alan Wiggins	.15	.11	.06
376	Rick Cerone	.08	.06	.03
377	Dave Collins	.08	.06	.03
378	Roger Erickson	.06	.05	.02
379	George Frazier	.06	.05	.02
380	Oscar Gamble	.08	.06	.03
381	Goose Gossage	.20	.15	.08
382	Ken Griffey	.12	.09	.05
383	Ron Guidry	.25	.20	.10
384	Dave LaRoche	.06	.05	.02
385	Rudy May	.08	.06	.03
386	John Mayberry	.08	.06	.03
387	Lee Mazzilli	.08	.06	.03
388	Mike Morgan	.10	.08	.04
389	Jerry Mumphrey	.08	.06	.03
390	Bobby Murcer	.10	.08	.04
391	Graig Nettles	.15	.11	.06
392	Lou Piniella	.15	.11	.06
393	Willie Randolph	.10	.08	.04
394	Shane Rawley	.10	.08	.04
395	Dave Righetti	.25	.20	.10
396	Andre Robertson	.06	.05	.02
397	Roy Smalley	.08	.06	.03
398	Dave Winfield	.40	.30	.15
399	Butch Wynegar	.08	.06	.03
400	Chris Bando	.06	.05	.02
401	Alan Bannister	.06	.05	.02
402	Len Barker	.08	.06	.03
403	Tom Brennan	.06	.05	.02
404	Carmelo Castillo	.12	.09	.05
405	Miguel Dilone	.06	.05	.02
406	Jerry Dybzinski	.06	.05	.02
407	Mike Fischlin	.06	.05	.02
408	Ed Glynn (photo actually Bud Anderson)	.06	.05	.02
409	Mike Hargrove	.08	.06	.03
410	Toby Harrah	.08	.06	.03
411	Ron Hassey	.06	.05	.02
412	Von Hayes	.20	.15	.08
413	Rick Manning	.06	.05	.02
414	Bake McBride	.06	.05	.02
415	Larry Milbourne	.06	.05	.02
416	Bill Nahorodny	.06	.05	.02
417	Jack Perconte	.06	.05	.02
418	Lary Sorensen	.06	.05	.02
419	Dan Spillner	.06	.05	.02
420	Rick Sutcliffe	.12	.09	.05
421	Andre Thornton	.10	.08	.04
422	Rick Waits	.06	.05	.02
423	Eddie Whitson	.08	.06	.03
424	Jesse Barfield	.70	.50	.30
425	Barry Bonnell	.06	.05	.02
426	Jim Clancy	.10	.08	.04
427	Damaso Garcia	.08	.06	.03
428	Jerry Garvin	.06	.05	.02
429	Alfredo Griffin	.08	.06	.03
430	Garth Iorg	.06	.05	.02
431	Roy Lee Jackson	.06	.05	.02
432	Luis Leal	.06	.05	.02
433	Buck Martinez	.06	.05	.02
434	Joey McLaughlin	.06	.05	.02
435	Lloyd Moseby	.12	.09	.05
436	Rance Mulliniks	.06	.05	.02
437	Dale Murray	.06	.05	.02
438	Wayne Nordhagen	.06	.05	.02
439	Gene Petralli	.15	.11	.06
440	Hosken Powell	.06	.05	.02
441	Dave Stieb	.12	.09	.05
442	Willie Upshaw	.08	.06	.03
443	Ernie Whitt	.08	.06	.03
444	Al Woods	.06	.05	.02
445	Alan Ashby	.06	.05	.02
446	Jose Cruz	.12	.09	.05
447	Kiko Garcia	.06	.05	.02
448	Phil Garner	.08	.06	.03
449	Danny Heep	.06	.05	.02
450	Art Howe	.06	.05	.02
451	Bob Knepper	.08	.06	.03
452	Alan Knicely	.06	.05	.02
453	Ray Knight	.10	.08	.04
454	Frank LaCorte	.06	.05	.02
455	Mike LaCoss	.08	.06	.03
456	Randy Moffitt	.06	.05	.02
457	Joe Niekro	.12	.09	.05
458	Terry Puhl	.06	.05	.02
459	Luis Pujols	.06	.05	.02
460	Craig Reynolds	.06	.05	.02
461	Bert Roberge	.06	.05	.02
462	Vern Ruhle	.06	.05	.02
463	Nolan Ryan	.40	.30	.15
464	Joe Sambito	.06	.05	.02
465	Tony Scott	.06	.05	.02
466	Dave Smith	.08	.06	.03
467	Harry Spilman	.06	.05	.02
468	Dickie Thon	.08	.06	.03
469	Denny Walling	.06	.05	.02
470	Larry Andersen	.06	.05	.02
471	Floyd Bannister	.10	.08	.04
472	Jim Beattie	.06	.05	.02
473	Bruce Bochte	.06	.05	.02
474	Manny Castillo	.06	.05	.02
475	Bill Caudill	.06	.05	.02
476	Bryan Clark	.06	.05	.02
477	Al Cowens	.06	.05	.02
478	Julio Cruz	.06	.05	.02
479	Todd Cruz	.06	.05	.02
480	Gary Gray	.06	.05	.02
481	Dave Henderson	.08	.06	.03
482	Mike Moore	.20	.15	.08
483	Gaylord Perry	.30	.25	.12
484	Dave Revering	.06	.05	.02
485	Joe Simpson	.06	.05	.02
486	Mike Stanton	.06	.05	.02
487	Rick Sweet	.06	.05	.02
488	Ed Vande Berg	.10	.08	.04
489	Richie Zisk	.08	.06	.03
490	Doug Bird	.06	.05	.02

		MT	NR MT	EX
491	Larry Bowa	.15	.11	.06
492	Bill Buckner	.12	.09	.05
493	Bill Campbell	.06	.05	.02
494	Jody Davis	.12	.09	.05
495	Leon Durham	.10	.08	.04
496	Steve Henderson	.06	.05	.02
497	Willie Hernandez	.08	.06	.03
498	Ferguson Jenkins	.15	.11	.06
499	Jay Johnstone	.10	.08	.04
500	Junior Kennedy	.06	.05	.02
501	Randy Martz	.06	.05	.02
502	Jerry Morales	.06	.05	.02
503	Keith Moreland	.08	.06	.03
504	Dickie Noles	.06	.05	.02
505	Mike Proly	.06	.05	.02
506	Allen Ripley	.06	.05	.02
507	Ryne Sandberg	3.50	2.75	1.50
508	Lee Smith	.15	.11	.06
509	Pat Tabler	.15	.11	.06
510	Dick Tidrow	.06	.05	.02
511	Bump Wills	.06	.05	.02
512	Gary Woods	.06	.05	.02
513	Tony Armas	.10	.08	.04
514	Dave Beard	.06	.05	.02
515	Jeff Burroughs	.08	.06	.03
516	John D'Acquisto	.06	.05	.02
517	Wayne Gross	.06	.05	.02
518	Mike Heath	.06	.05	.02
519	Rickey Henderson	.60	.45	.25
520	Cliff Johnson	.06	.05	.02
521	Matt Keough	.06	.05	.02
522	Brian Kingman	.06	.05	.02
523	Rick Langford	.06	.05	.02
524	Davey Lopes	.10	.08	.04
525	Steve McCatty	.06	.05	.02
526	Dave McKay	.06	.05	.02
527	Dan Meyer	.06	.05	.02
528	Dwayne Murphy	.08	.06	.03
529	Jeff Newman	.06	.05	.02
530	Mike Norris	.06	.05	.02
531	Bob Owchinko	.06	.05	.02
532	Joe Rudi	.10	.08	.04
533	Jimmy Sexton	.06	.05	.02
534	Fred Stanley	.06	.05	.02
535	Tom Underwood	.06	.05	.02
536	Neil Allen	.06	.05	.02
537	Wally Backman	.08	.06	.03
538	Bob Bailor	.06	.05	.02
539	Hubie Brooks	.12	.09	.05
540	Carlos Diaz	.06	.05	.02
541	Pete Falcone	.06	.05	.02
542	George Foster	.15	.11	.06
543	Ron Gardenhire	.06	.05	.02
544	Brian Giles	.06	.05	.02
545	Ron Hodges	.06	.05	.02
546	Randy Jones	.08	.06	.03
547	Mike Jorgensen	.06	.05	.02
548	Dave Kingman	.15	.11	.06
549	Ed Lynch	.06	.05	.02
550	Jesse Orosco	.20	.15	.08
551	Rick Ownbey	.06	.05	.02
552	Charlie Puleo	.12	.09	.05
553	Gary Rajsich	.06	.05	.02
554	Mike Scott	.15	.11	.06
555	Rusty Staub	.12	.09	.05
556	John Stearns	.06	.05	.02
557	Craig Swan	.06	.05	.02
558	Ellis Valentine	.06	.05	.02
559	Tom Veryzer	.06	.05	.02
560	Mookie Wilson	.10	.08	.04
561	Pat Zachry	.06	.05	.02
562	Buddy Bell	.15	.11	.06
563	John Butcher	.06	.05	.02
564	Steve Comer	.06	.05	.02
565	Danny Darwin	.08	.06	.03
566	Bucky Dent	.10	.08	.04
567	John Grubb	.06	.05	.02
568	Rick Honeycutt	.08	.06	.03
569	Dave Hostetler	.06	.05	.02
570	Charlie Hough	.10	.08	.04
571	Lamar Johnson	.06	.05	.02
572	Jon Matlack	.08	.06	.03
573	Paul Mirabella	.06	.05	.02
574	Larry Parrish	.10	.08	.04
575	Mike Richardt	.06	.05	.02
576	Mickey Rivers	.10	.08	.04
577	Billy Sample	.06	.05	.02
578	Dave Schmidt	.10	.08	.04
579	Bill Stein	.06	.05	.02
580	Jim Sundberg	.08	.06	.03
581	Frank Tanana	.10	.08	.04

		MT	NR MT	EX
582	Mark Wagner	.06	.05	.02
583	George Wright	.06	.05	.02
584	Johnny Bench	.40	.30	.15
585	Bruce Berenyi	.06	.05	.02
586	Larry Biittner	.06	.05	.02
587	Cesar Cedeno	.12	.09	.05
588	Dave Concepcion	.15	.11	.06
589	Dan Driessen	.08	.06	.03
590	Greg Harris	.08	.06	.03
591	Ben Hayes	.06	.05	.02
592	Paul Householder	.06	.05	.02
593	Tom Hume	.06	.05	.02
594	Wayne Krenchicki	.06	.05	.02
595	Rafael Landestoy	.06	.05	.02
596	Charlie Leibrandt	.08	.06	.03
597	Eddie Milner	.15	.11	.06
598	Ron Oester	.06	.05	.02
599	Frank Pastore	.06	.05	.02
600	Joe Price	.06	.05	.02
601	Tom Seaver	.40	.30	.15
602	Bob Shirley	.06	.05	.02
603	Mario Soto	.10	.08	.04
604	Alex Trevino	.06	.05	.02
605	Mike Vail	.06	.05	.02
606	Duane Walker	.06	.05	.02
607	Tom Brunansky	.25	.20	.10
608	Bobby Castillo	.06	.05	.02
609	John Castino	.06	.05	.02
610	Ron Davis	.06	.05	.02
611	Lenny Faedo	.06	.05	.02
612	Terry Felton	.06	.05	.02
613	Gary Gaetti	1.50	1.25	.60
614	Mickey Hatcher	.08	.06	.03
615	Brad Havens	.06	.05	.02
616	Kent Hrbek	.50	.40	.20
617	Randy Johnson	.06	.05	.02
618	Tim Laudner	.12	.09	.05
619	Jeff Little	.06	.05	.02
620	Bob Mitchell	.06	.05	.02
621	Jack O'Connor	.06	.05	.02
622	John Pacella	.06	.05	.02
623	Pete Redfern	.06	.05	.02
624	Jesus Vega	.06	.05	.02
625	Frank Viola	.90	.70	.35
626	Ron Washington	.06	.05	.02
627	Gary Ward	.08	.06	.03
628	Al Williams	.06	.05	.02
629	Red Sox All-Stars (Mark Clear, Dennis Eckersley, Carl Yastrzemski)	.25	.20	.10
630	300 Career Wins (Terry Bulling, Gaylord Perry)	.15	.11	.06
631	Pride of Venezuela (Dave Concepcion, Manny Trillo)	.10	.08	.04
632	All-Star Infielders (Buddy Bell, Robin Yount)	.15	.11	.06
633	Mr. Vet & Mr. Rookie (Kent Hrbek, Dave Winfield)	.25	.20	.10
634	Fountain of Youth (Pete Rose, Willie Stargell)	.40	.30	.15
635	Big Chiefs (Toby Harrah, Andre Thornton)	.08	.06	.03
636	"Smith Bros." (Lonnie Smith, Ozzie Smith)	.10	.08	.04
637	Base Stealers' Threat (Gary Carter, Bo Diaz)	.15	.11	.06
638	All-Star Catchers (Gary Carter, Carlton Fisk)	.20	.15	.08
639	The Silver Shoe (Rickey Henderson)	.30	.25	.12
640	Home Run Threats (Reggie Jackson, Ben Oglivie)	.25	.20	.10
641	Two Teams - Same Day (Joel Youngblood)	.08	.06	.03
642	Last Perfect Game (Len Barker, Ron Hassey)	.08	.06	.03
643	Blue (Vida Blue)	.10	.08	.04
644	Black & (Bud Black)	.10	.08	.04
645	Power (Reggie Jackson)	.30	.25	.12
646	Speed & (Rickey Henderson)	.30	.25	.12
647	Checklist 1-51	.06	.05	.02
648	Checklist 52-103	.06	.05	.02
649	Checklist 104-152	.06	.05	.02
650	Checklist 153-200	.06	.05	.02
651	Checklist 201-251	.06	.05	.02
652	Checklist 252-301	.06	.05	.02
653	Checklist 302-351	.06	.05	.02
654	Checklist 352-399	.06	.05	.02
655	Checklist 400-444	.06	.05	.02
656	Checklist 445-489	.06	.05	.02
657	Checklist 490-535	.06	.05	.02
658	Checklist 536-583	.06	.05	.02

		MT	NR MT	EX
659	Checklist 584-628	.06	.05	.02
660	Checklist 629-646	.06	.05	.02

1984 Fleer

 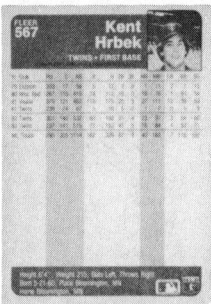

The 1984 Fleer set contained 660 cards for the fourth consecutive year. The cards, which measure 2½" by 3½", feature a color photo surrounded by four white borders and two blue stripes. The top stripe contains the word "Fleer" with the lower carrying the player's name. The card backs contain a small black and white photo of the player and are done in blue ink on white stock. The set was issued with team logo stickers.

		MT	NR MT	EX
Complete Set:		75.00	56.00	30.00
Common Player:		.08	.06	.03
1	Mike Boddicker	.20	.15	.08
2	Al Bumbry	.10	.08	.04
3	Todd Cruz	.08	.06	.03
4	Rich Dauer	.08	.06	.03
5	Storm Davis	.10	.08	.04
6	Rick Dempsey	.10	.08	.04
7	Jim Dwyer	.08	.06	.03
8	Mike Flanagan	.12	.09	.05
9	Dan Ford	.08	.06	.03
10	John Lowenstein	.08	.06	.03
11	Dennis Martinez	.10	.08	.04
12	Tippy Martinez	.08	.06	.03
13	Scott McGregor	.12	.09	.05
14	Eddie Murray	.60	.45	.25
15	Joe Nolan	.08	.06	.03
16	Jim Palmer	.40	.30	.15
17	Cal Ripken, Jr.	.60	.45	.25
18	Gary Roenicke	.08	.06	.03
19	Lenn Sakata	.08	.06	.03
20	John Shelby	.20	.15	.08
21	Ken Singleton	.12	.09	.05
22	Sammy Stewart	.08	.06	.03
23	Tim Stoddard	.08	.06	.03
24	Marty Bystrom	.08	.06	.03
25	Steve Carlton	.50	.40	.20
26	Ivan DeJesus	.08	.06	.03
27	John Denny	.10	.08	.04
28	Bob Dernier	.10	.08	.04
29	Bo Diaz	.10	.08	.04
30	Kiko Garcia	.08	.06	.03
31	Greg Gross	.08	.06	.03
32	Kevin Gross	.35	.25	.14
33	Von Hayes	.20	.15	.08
34	Willie Hernandez	.12	.09	.05
35	Al Holland	.08	.06	.03
36	Charles Hudson	.30	.25	.12
37	Joe Lefebvre	.08	.06	.03
38	Sixto Lezcano	.08	.06	.03
39	Garry Maddox	.12	.09	.05
40	Gary Matthews	.12	.09	.05
41	Len Matuszek	.08	.06	.03
42	Tug McGraw	.15	.11	.06
43	Joe Morgan	.30	.25	.12
44	Tony Perez	.20	.15	.08
45	Ron Reed	.10	.08	.04
46	Pete Rose	1.00	.70	.40
47	Juan Samuel	3.00	2.25	1.25

		MT	NR MT	EX
48	Mike Schmidt	.70	.50	.30
49	Ozzie Virgil	.10	.08	.04
50	Juan Agosto	.12	.09	.05
51	Harold Baines	.25	.20	.10
52	Floyd Bannister	.12	.09	.05
53	Salome Barojas	.08	.06	.03
54	Britt Burns	.08	.06	.03
55	Julio Cruz	.08	.06	.03
56	Richard Dotson	.12	.09	.05
57	Jerry Dybzinski	.08	.06	.03
58	Carlton Fisk	.20	.15	.08
59	Scott Fletcher	.15	.11	.06
60	Jerry Hairston	.08	.06	.03
61	Kevin Hickey	.08	.06	.03
62	Marc Hill	.08	.06	.03
63	LaMarr Hoyt	.10	.08	.04
64	Ron Kittle	.15	.11	.06
65	Jerry Koosman	.12	.09	.05
66	Dennis Lamp	.08	.06	.03
67	Rudy Law	.08	.06	.03
68	Vance Law	.10	.08	.04
69	Greg Luzinski	.12	.09	.05
70	Tom Paciorek	.08	.06	.03
71	Mike Squires	.08	.06	.03
72	Dick Tidrow	.08	.06	.03
73	Greg Walker	.70	.50	.30
74	Glenn Abbott	.08	.06	.03
75	Howard Bailey	.08	.06	.03
76	Doug Bair	.08	.06	.03
77	Juan Berenguer	.08	.06	.03
78	Tom Brookens	.08	.06	.03
79	Enos Cabell	.08	.06	.03
80	Kirk Gibson	.35	.25	.14
81	John Grubb	.08	.06	.03
82	Larry Herndon	.10	.08	.04
83	Wayne Krenchicki	.08	.06	.03
84	Rick Leach	.08	.06	.03
85	Chet Lemon	.10	.08	.04
86	Aurelio Lopez	.08	.06	.03
87	Jack Morris	.30	.25	.12
88	Lance Parrish	.35	.25	.14
89	Dan Petry	.10	.08	.04
90	Dave Rozema	.08	.06	.03
91	Alan Trammell	.40	.30	.15
92	Lou Whitaker	.30	.25	.12
93	Milt Wilcox	.10	.08	.04
94	Glenn Wilson	.12	.09	.05
95	John Wockenfuss	.08	.06	.03
96	Dusty Baker	.12	.09	.05
97	Joe Beckwith	.08	.06	.03
98	Greg Brock	.12	.09	.05
99	Jack Fimple	.08	.06	.03
100	Pedro Guerrero	.35	.25	.14
101	Rick Honeycutt	.10	.08	.04
102	Burt Hooton	.10	.08	.04
103	Steve Howe	.10	.08	.04
104	Ken Landreaux	.10	.08	.04
105	Mike Marshall	.15	.11	.06
106	Rick Monday	.10	.08	.04
107	Jose Morales	.08	.06	.03
108	Tom Niedenfuer	.10	.08	.04
109	Alejandro Pena	.15	.11	.06
110	Jerry Reuss	.12	.09	.05
111	Bill Russell	.10	.08	.04
112	Steve Sax	.20	.15	.08
113	Mike Scioscia	.08	.06	.03
114	Derrel Thomas	.08	.06	.03
115	Fernando Valenzuela	.40	.30	.15
116	Bob Welch	.12	.09	.05
117	Steve Yeager	.08	.06	.03
118	Pat Zachry	.08	.06	.03
119	Don Baylor	.15	.11	.06
120	Bert Campaneris	.12	.09	.05
121	Rick Cerone	.10	.08	.04
122	Ray Fontenot	.12	.09	.05
123	George Frazier	.08	.06	.03
124	Oscar Gamble	.10	.08	.04
125	Goose Gossage	.25	.20	.10
126	Ken Griffey	.15	.11	.06
127	Ron Guidry	.30	.25	.12
128	Jay Howell	.15	.11	.06
129	Steve Kemp	.10	.08	.04
130	Matt Keough	.08	.06	.03
131	Don Mattingly	30.00	22.00	12.00
132	John Montefusco	.08	.06	.03
133	Omar Moreno	.08	.06	.03
134	Dale Murray	.08	.06	.03
135	Graig Nettles	.20	.15	.08
136	Lou Piniella	.15	.11	.06
137	Willie Randolph	.12	.09	.05
138	Shane Rawley	.12	.09	.05

	MT	NR MT	EX			MT	NR MT	EX
139 Dave Righetti	.25	.20	.10	230 Frank LaCorte	.08	.06	.03
140 Andre Robertson	.08	.06	.03	231 Mike LaCoss	.10	.08	.04
141 Bob Shirley	.08	.06	.03	232 Mike Madden	.10	.08	.04
142 Roy Smalley	.10	.08	.04	233 Jerry Mumphrey	.10	.08	.04
143 Dave Winfield	.40	.30	.15	235 Terry Puhl	.08	.06	.03
144 Butch Wynegar	.10	.08	.04	236 Luis Pujols	.08	.06	.03
145 Jim Acker	.15	.11	.06	237 Craig Reynolds	.08	.06	.03
146 Doyle Alexander	.15	.11	.06	238 Vern Ruhle	.08	.06	.03
147 Jesse Barfield	.35	.25	.14	239 Nolan Ryan	.40	.30	.15
148 Jorge Bell	1.50	1.25	.60	240 Mike Scott	.20	.15	.08
149 Barry Bonnell	.08	.06	.03	241 Tony Scott	.08	.06	.03
150 Jim Clancy	.12	.09	.05	242 Dave Smith	.10	.08	.04
151 Dave Collins	.10	.08	.04	243 Dickie Thon	.10	.08	.04
152 Tony Fernandez	4.50	3.50	1.75	244 Denny Walling	.08	.06	.03
153 Damaso Garcia	.10	.08	.04	245 Dale Berra	.08	.06	.03
154 Dave Geisel	.08	.06	.03	246 Jim Bibby	.08	.06	.03
155 Jim Gott	.12	.09	.05	247 John Candelaria	.12	.09	.05
156 Alfredo Griffin	.10	.08	.04	248 Jose DeLeon	.25	.20	.10
157 Garth Iorg	.08	.06	.03	249 Mike Easler	.10	.08	.04
158 Roy Lee Jackson	.08	.06	.03	250 Cecilio Guante	.10	.08	.04
159 Cliff Johnson	.08	.06	.03	251 Richie Hebner	.08	.06	.03
160 Luis Leal	.08	.06	.03	252 Lee Lacy	.10	.08	.04
161 Buck Martinez	.08	.06	.03	253 Bill Madlock	.15	.11	.06
162 Joey McLaughlin	.08	.06	.03	254 Milt May	.08	.06	.03
163 Randy Moffitt	.08	.06	.03	255 Lee Mazzilli	.10	.08	.04
164 Lloyd Moseby	.15	.11	.06	256 Larry McWilliams	.08	.06	.03
165 Rance Mulliniks	.08	.06	.03	257 Jim Morrison	.08	.06	.03
166 Jorge Orta	.08	.06	.03	258 Dave Parker	.30	.25	.12
167 Dave Stieb	.15	.11	.06	259 Tony Pena	.15	.11	.06
168 Willie Upshaw	.12	.09	.05	260 Johnny Ray	.15	.11	.06
169 Ernie Whitt	.10	.08	.04	261 Rick Rhoden	.12	.09	.05
170 Len Barker	.10	.08	.04	262 Don Robinson	.10	.08	.04
171 Steve Bedrosian	.12	.09	.05	263 Manny Sarmiento	.08	.06	.03
172 Bruce Benedict	.08	.06	.03	264 Rod Scurry	.08	.06	.03
173 Brett Butler	.10	.08	.04	265 Kent Tekulve	.10	.08	.04
174 Rick Camp	.08	.06	.03	266 Gene Tenace	.10	.08	.04
175 Chris Chambliss	.10	.08	.04	267 Jason Thompson	.08	.06	.03
176 Ken Dayley	.08	.06	.03	268 Lee Tunnell	.12	.09	.05
177 Pete Falcone	.08	.06	.03	269 Marvell Wynne	.15	.11	.06
178 Terry Forster	.10	.08	.04	270 Ray Burris	.08	.06	.03
179 Gene Garber	.08	.06	.03	271 Gary Carter	.50	.40	.20
180 Terry Harper	.08	.06	.03	272 Warren Cromartie	.08	.06	.03
181 Bob Horner	.30	.25	.12	273 Andre Dawson	.35	.25	.14
182 Glenn Hubbard	.10	.08	.04	274 Doug Flynn	.08	.06	.03
183 Randy Johnson	.08	.06	.03	275 Terry Francona	.08	.06	.03
184 Craig McMurtry	.10	.08	.04	276 Bill Gullickson	.10	.08	.04
185 Donnie Moore	.15	.11	.06	277 Bob James	.20	.15	.08
186 Dale Murphy	1.00	.70	.40	278 Charlie Lea	.08	.06	.03
187 Phil Niekro	.30	.25	.12	279 Bryan Little	.08	.06	.03
188 Pascual Perez	.10	.08	.04	280 Al Oliver	.20	.15	.08
189 Biff Pocoroba	.08	.06	.03	281 Tim Raines	.40	.30	.15
190 Rafael Ramirez	.10	.08	.04	282 Bobby Ramos	.08	.06	.03
191 Jerry Royster	.08	.06	.03	283 Jeff Reardon	.15	.11	.06
192 Claudell Washington	.10	.08	.04	284 Steve Rogers	.10	.08	.04
193 Bob Watson	.10	.08	.04	285 Scott Sanderson	.10	.08	.04
194 Jerry Augustine	.08	.06	.03	286 Dan Schatzeder	.08	.06	.03
195 Mark Brouhard	.08	.06	.03	287 Bryn Smith	.10	.08	.04
196 Mike Caldwell	.08	.06	.03	288 Chris Speier	.08	.06	.03
197 Tom Candiotti	.20	.15	.08	289 Manny Trillo	.10	.08	.04
198 Cecil Cooper	.15	.11	.06	290 Mike Vail	.08	.06	.03
199 Rollie Fingers	.25	.20	.10	291 Tim Wallach	.15	.11	.06
200 Jim Gantner	.10	.08	.04	292 Chris Welsh	.08	.06	.03
201 Bob Gibson	.08	.06	.03	293 Jim Wohlford	.08	.06	.03
202 Moose Haas	.08	.06	.03	294 Kurt Bevacqua	.08	.06	.03
203 Roy Howell	.08	.06	.03	295 Juan Bonilla	.08	.06	.03
204 Pete Ladd	.08	.06	.03	296 Bobby Brown	.08	.06	.03
205 Rick Manning	.08	.06	.03	297 Luis DeLeon	.08	.06	.03
206 Bob McClure	.08	.06	.03	298 Dave Dravecky	.12	.09	.05
207 Paul Molitor	.20	.15	.08	299 Tim Flannery	.08	.06	.03
208 Don Money	.10	.08	.04	300 Steve Garvey	.50	.40	.20
209 Charlie Moore	.08	.06	.03	301 Tony Gwynn	1.75	1.25	.70
210 Ben Oglivie	.10	.08	.04	302 Andy Hawkins	.20	.15	.08
211 Chuck Porter	.08	.06	.03	303 Ruppert Jones	.08	.06	.03
212 Ed Romero	.08	.06	.03	304 Terry Kennedy	.10	.08	.04
213 Ted Simmons	.15	.11	.06	305 Tim Lollar	.08	.06	.03
214 Jim Slaton	.08	.06	.03	306 Gary Lucas	.08	.06	.03
215 Don Sutton	.30	.25	.12	307 Kevin McReynolds	3.50	2.75	1.50
216 Tom Tellmann	.08	.06	.03	308 Sid Monge	.08	.06	.03
217 Pete Vuckovich	.10	.08	.04	309 Mario Ramirez	.08	.06	.03
218 Ned Yost	.08	.06	.03	310 Gene Richards	.08	.06	.03
219 Robin Yount	.40	.30	.15	311 Luis Salazar	.08	.06	.03
220 Alan Ashby	.08	.06	.03	312 Eric Show	.10	.08	.04
221 Kevin Bass	.20	.15	.08	313 Elias Sosa	.08	.06	.03
222 Jose Cruz	.12	.09	.05	314 Garry Templeton	.12	.09	.05
223 Bill Dawley	.15	.11	.06	315 Mark Thurmond	.15	.11	.06
224 Frank DiPino	.08	.06	.03	316 Ed Whitson	.08	.06	.03
225 Bill Doran	.80	.60	.30	317 Alan Wiggins	.08	.06	.03
226 Phil Garner	.10	.08	.04	318 Neil Allen	.08	.06	.03
227 Art Howe	.08	.06	.03	319 Joaquin Andujar	.12	.09	.05
228 Bob Knepper	.10	.08	.04	320 Steve Braun	.08	.06	.03
229 Ray Knight	.12	.09	.05	321 Glenn Brummer	.08	.06	.03

		MT	NR MT	EX
322	Bob Forsch	.10	.08	.04
323	David Green	.08	.06	.03
324	George Hendrick	.10	.08	.04
325	Tom Herr	.12	.09	.05
326	Dane Iorg	.08	.06	.03
327	Jeff Lahti	.08	.06	.03
328	Dave LaPoint	.08	.06	.03
329	Willie McGee	.35	.25	.14
330	Ken Oberkfell	.10	.08	.04
331	Darrell Porter	.10	.08	.04
332	Jamie Quirk	.08	.06	.03
333	Mike Ramsey	.08	.06	.03
334	Floyd Rayford	.08	.06	.03
335	Lonnie Smith	.10	.08	.04
336	Ozzie Smith	.15	.11	.06
337	John Stuper	.08	.06	.03
338	Bruce Sutter	.20	.15	.08
339	Andy Van Slyke	.90	.70	.35
340	Dave Von Ohlen	.08	.06	.03
341	Willie Aikens	.08	.06	.03
342	Mike Armstrong	.08	.06	.03
343	Bud Black	.10	.08	.04
344	George Brett	.70	.50	.30
345	Onix Concepcion	.08	.06	.03
346	Keith Creel	.08	.06	.03
347	Larry Gura	.10	.08	.04
348	Don Hood	.08	.06	.03
349	Dennis Leonard	.10	.08	.04
350	Hal McRae	.12	.09	.05
351	Amos Otis	.10	.08	.04
352	Gaylord Perry	.30	.25	.12
353	Greg Pryor	.08	.06	.03
354	Dan Quisenberry	.20	.15	.08
355	Steve Renko	.08	.06	.03
356	Leon Roberts	.08	.06	.03
357	Pat Sheridan	.15	.11	.06
358	Joe Simpson	.08	.06	.03
359	Don Slaught	.08	.06	.03
360	Paul Splittorff	.10	.08	.04
361	U.L. Washington	.08	.06	.03
362	John Wathan	.10	.08	.04
363	Frank White	.12	.09	.05
364	Willie Wilson	.15	.11	.06
365	Jim Barr	.08	.06	.03
366	Dave Bergman	.08	.06	.03
367	Fred Breining	.08	.06	.03
368	Bob Brenly	.08	.06	.03
369	Jack Clark	.25	.20	.10
370	Chili Davis	.15	.11	.06
371	Mark Davis	.12	.09	.05
372	Darrell Evans	.15	.11	.06
373	Atlee Hammaker	.10	.08	.04
374	Mike Krukow	.10	.08	.04
375	Duane Kuiper	.08	.06	.03
376	Bill Laskey	.08	.06	.03
377	Gary Lavelle	.08	.06	.03
378	Johnnie LeMaster	.08	.06	.03
379	Jeff Leonard	.12	.09	.05
380	Randy Lerch	.08	.06	.03
381	Renie Martin	.08	.06	.03
382	Andy McGaffigan	.08	.06	.03
383	Greg Minton	.08	.06	.03
384	Tom O'Malley	.08	.06	.03
385	Max Venable	.08	.06	.03
386	Brad Wellman	.08	.06	.03
387	Joel Youngblood	.08	.06	.03
388	Gary Allenson	.08	.06	.03
389	Luis Aponte	.08	.06	.03
390	Tony Armas	.12	.09	.05
391	Doug Bird	.08	.06	.03
392	Wade Boggs	7.00	5.25	2.75
393	Dennis Boyd	.35	.25	.14
394	Mike Brown	.08	.06	.03
395	Mark Clear	.10	.08	.04
396	Dennis Eckersley	.12	.09	.05
397	Dwight Evans	.20	.15	.08
398	Rich Gedman	.12	.09	.05
399	Glenn Hoffman	.08	.06	.03
400	Bruce Hurst	.12	.09	.05
401	John Henry Johnson	.08	.06	.03
402	Ed Jurak	.08	.06	.03
403	Rick Miller	.08	.06	.03
404	Jeff Newman	.08	.06	.03
405	Reid Nichols	.08	.06	.03
406	Bob Ojeda	.12	.09	.05
407	Jerry Remy	.08	.06	.03
408	Jim Rice	.40	.30	.15
409	Bob Stanley	.10	.08	.04
410	Dave Stapleton	.08	.06	.03
411	John Tudor	.12	.09	.05
412	Carl Yastrzemski	.80	.60	.30

		MT	NR MT	EX
413	Buddy Bell	.15	.11	.06
414	Larry Biittner	.08	.06	.03
415	John Butcher	.08	.06	.03
416	Danny Darwin	.10	.08	.04
417	Bucky Dent	.12	.09	.05
418	Dave Hostetler	.08	.06	.03
419	Charlie Hough	.12	.09	.05
420	Bobby Johnson	.08	.06	.03
421	Odell Jones	.08	.06	.03
422	Jon Matlack	.10	.08	.04
423	Pete O'Brien	1.00	.70	.40
424	Larry Parrish	.12	.09	.05
425	Mickey Rivers	.10	.08	.04
426	Billy Sample	.08	.06	.03
427	Dave Schmidt	.10	.08	.04
428	Mike Smithson	.12	.09	.05
429	Bill Stein	.08	.06	.03
430	Dave Stewart	.12	.09	.05
431	Jim Sundberg	.10	.08	.04
432	Frank Tanana	.12	.09	.05
433	Dave Tobik	.08	.06	.03
434	Wayne Tolleson	.12	.09	.05
435	George Wright	.08	.06	.03
436	Bill Almon	.08	.06	.03
437	Keith Atherton	.20	.15	.08
438	Dave Beard	.08	.06	.03
439	Tom Burgmeier	.08	.06	.03
440	Jeff Burroughs	.10	.08	.04
441	Chris Codiroli	.12	.09	.05
442	Tim Conroy	.12	.09	.05
443	Mike Davis	.10	.08	.04
444	Wayne Gross	.08	.06	.03
445	Garry Hancock	.08	.06	.03
446	Mike Heath	.08	.06	.03
447	Rickey Henderson	.60	.45	.25
448	Don Hill	.15	.11	.06
449	Bob Kearney	.08	.06	.03
450	Bill Krueger	.10	.08	.04
451	Rick Langford	.08	.06	.03
452	Carney Lansford	.10	.08	.04
453	Davey Lopes	.10	.08	.04
454	Steve McCatty	.08	.06	.03
455	Dan Meyer	.08	.06	.03
456	Dwayne Murphy	.10	.08	.04
457	Mike Norris	.08	.06	.03
458	Ricky Peters	.08	.06	.03
459	Tony Phillips	.15	.11	.06
460	Tom Underwood	.08	.06	.03
461	Mike Warren	.10	.08	.04
462	Johnny Bench	.40	.30	.15
463	Bruce Berenyi	.08	.06	.03
464	Dann Bilardello	.08	.06	.03
465	Cesar Cedeno	.12	.09	.05
466	Dave Concepcion	.15	.11	.06
467	Dan Driessen	.10	.08	.04
468	Nick Esasky	.35	.25	.14
469	Rich Gale	.08	.06	.03
470	Ben Hayes	.08	.06	.03
471	Paul Householder	.08	.06	.03
472	Tom Hume	.08	.06	.03
473	Alan Knicely	.08	.06	.03
474	Eddie Milner	.08	.06	.03
475	Ron Oester	.08	.06	.03
476	Kelly Paris	.08	.06	.03
477	Frank Pastore	.08	.06	.03
478	Ted Power	.10	.08	.04
479	Joe Price	.08	.06	.03
480	Charlie Puleo	.08	.06	.03
481	Gary Redus	.30	.25	.12
482	Bill Scherrer	.08	.06	.03
483	Mario Soto	.10	.08	.04
484	Alex Trevino	.08	.06	.03
485	Duane Walker	.08	.06	.03
486	Larry Bowa	.15	.11	.06
487	Warren Brusstar	.08	.06	.03
488	Bill Buckner	.15	.11	.06
489	Bill Campbell	.08	.06	.03
490	Ron Cey	.12	.09	.05
491	Jody Davis	.12	.09	.05
492	Leon Durham	.15	.11	.06
493	Mel Hall	.20	.15	.08
494	Ferguson Jenkins	.20	.15	.08
495	Jay Johnstone	.10	.08	.04
496	Craig Lefferts	.20	.15	.08
497	Carmelo Martinez	.25	.20	.10
498	Jerry Morales	.08	.06	.03
499	Keith Moreland	.10	.08	.04
500	Dickie Noles	.08	.06	.03
501	Mike Proly	.08	.06	.03
502	Chuck Rainey	.08	.06	.03
503	Dick Ruthven	.08	.06	.03

		MT	NR MT	EX
504	Ryne Sandberg	1.25	.90	.50
505	Lee Smith	.15	.11	.06
506	Steve Trout	.10	.08	.04
507	Gary Woods	.08	.06	.03
508	Juan Beniquez	.08	.06	.03
509	Bob Boone	.12	.09	.05
510	Rick Burleson	.10	.08	.04
511	Rod Carew	.50	.40	.20
512	Bobby Clark	.08	.06	.03
513	John Curtis	.08	.06	.03
514	Doug DeCinces	.12	.09	.05
515	Brian Downing	.12	.09	.05
516	Tim Foli	.08	.06	.03
517	Ken Forsch	.10	.08	.04
518	Bobby Grich	.12	.09	.05
519	Andy Hassler	.08	.06	.03
520	Reggie Jackson	.60	.45	.25
521	Ron Jackson	.08	.06	.03
522	Tommy John	.25	.20	.10
523	Bruce Kison	.08	.06	.03
524	Steve Lubratich	.08	.06	.03
525	Fred Lynn	.25	.20	.10
526	Gary Pettis	.40	.30	.15
527	Luis Sanchez	.08	.06	.03
528	Daryl Sconiers	.08	.06	.03
529	Ellis Valentine	.08	.06	.03
530	Rob Wilfong	.08	.06	.03
531	Mike Witt	.15	.11	.06
532	Geoff Zahn	.08	.06	.03
533	Bud Anderson	.08	.06	.03
534	Chris Bando	.08	.06	.03
535	Alan Bannister	.08	.06	.03
536	Bert Blyleven	.20	.15	.08
537	Tom Brennan	.08	.06	.03
538	Jamie Easterly	.08	.06	.03
539	Juan Eichelberger	.08	.06	.03
540	Jim Essian	.08	.06	.03
541	Mike Fischlin	.08	.06	.03
542	Julio Franco	.40	.30	.15
543	Mike Hargrove	.10	.08	.04
544	Toby Harrah	.10	.08	.04
545	Ron Hassey	.08	.06	.03
546	Neal Heaton	.25	.20	.10
547	Bake McBride	.08	.06	.03
548	Broderick Perkins	.08	.06	.03
549	Lary Sorensen	.08	.06	.03
550	Dan Spillner	.08	.06	.03
551	Rick Sutcliffe	.15	.11	.06
552	Pat Tabler	.10	.08	.04
553	Gorman Thomas	.12	.09	.05
554	Andre Thornton	.12	.09	.05
555	George Vukovich	.08	.06	.03
556	Darrell Brown	.08	.06	.03
557	Tom Brunansky	.20	.15	.08
558	Randy Bush	.15	.11	.06
559	Bobby Castillo	.08	.06	.03
560	John Castino	.08	.06	.03
561	Ron Davis	.08	.06	.03
562	Dave Engle	.08	.06	.03
563	Lenny Faedo	.08	.06	.03
564	Pete Filson	.08	.06	.03
565	Gary Gaetti	.50	.40	.20
566	Mickey Hatcher	.10	.08	.04
567	Kent Hrbek	.40	.30	.15
568	Rusty Kuntz	.08	.06	.03
569	Tim Laudner	.08	.06	.03
570	Rick Lysander	.08	.06	.03
571	Bobby Mitchell	.08	.06	.03
572	Ken Schrom	.08	.06	.03
573	Ray Smith	.08	.06	.03
574	Tim Teufel	.30	.25	.12
575	Frank Viola	.30	.25	.12
576	Gary Ward	.10	.08	.04
577	Ron Washington	.08	.06	.03
578	Len Whitehouse	.08	.06	.03
579	Al Williams	.08	.06	.03
580	Bob Bailor	.08	.06	.03
581	Mark Bradley	.08	.06	.03
582	Hubie Brooks	.15	.11	.06
583	Carlos Diaz	.08	.06	.03
584	George Foster	.20	.15	.08
585	Brian Giles	.08	.06	.03
586	Danny Heep	.08	.06	.03
587	Keith Hernandez	.40	.30	.15
588	Ron Hodges	.08	.06	.03
589	Scott Holman	.08	.06	.03
590	Dave Kingman	.15	.11	.06
591	Ed Lynch	.08	.06	.03
592	Jose Oquendo	.15	.11	.06
593	Jesse Orosco	.10	.08	.04
594	Junior Ortiz	.08	.06	.03

		MT	NR MT	EX
595	Tom Seaver	.40	.30	.15
596	Doug Sisk	.12	.09	.05
597	Rusty Staub	.12	.09	.05
598	John Stearns	.08	.06	.03
599	Darryl Strawberry	9.00	6.75	3.50
600	Craig Swan	.08	.06	.03
601	Walt Terrell	.50	.40	.20
602	Mike Torrez	.10	.08	.04
603	Mookie Wilson	.12	.09	.05
604	Jamie Allen	.08	.06	.03
605	Jim Beattie	.08	.06	.03
606	Tony Bernazard	.10	.08	.04
607	Manny Castillo	.08	.06	.03
608	Bill Caudill	.08	.06	.03
609	Bryan Clark	.08	.06	.03
610	Al Cowens	.08	.06	.03
611	Dave Henderson	.08	.06	.03
612	Steve Henderson	.08	.06	.03
613	Orlando Mercado	.08	.06	.03
614	Mike Moore	.08	.06	.03
615	Ricky Nelson	.08	.06	.03
616	Spike Owen	.20	.15	.08
617	Pat Putnam	.08	.06	.03
618	Ron Roenicke	.08	.06	.03
619	Mike Stanton	.08	.06	.03
620	Bob Stoddard	.08	.06	.03
621	Rick Sweet	.08	.06	.03
622	Roy Thomas	.08	.06	.03
623	Ed Vande Berg	.08	.06	.03
624	Matt Young	.15	.11	.06
625	Richie Zisk	.10	.08	.04
626	'83 All-Star Game Record Breaker (Fred Lynn)	.12	.09	.05
627	'83 All-Star Game Record Breaker (Manny Trillo)	.10	.08	.04
628	N.L. Iron Man (Steve Garvey)	.20	.15	.08
629	A.L. Batting Runner-Up (Rod Carew)	.25	.20	.10
630	A.L. Batting Champion (Wade Boggs)	.60	.45	.25
631	Letting Go Of The Raines (Tim Raines)	.20	.15	.08
632	Double Trouble (Al Oliver)	.10	.08	.04
633	All-Star Second Base (Steve Sax)	.15	.11	.06
634	All-Star Shortstop (Dickie Thon)	.10	.08	.04
635	Ace Firemen (Tippy Martinez, Dan Quisenberry)	.10	.08	.04
636	Reds Reunited (Joe Morgan, Tony Perez, Pete Rose)	.50	.40	.20
637	Backstop Stars (Bob Boone, Lance Parrish)	.15	.11	.06
638	The Pine Tar Incident, 7/24/83 (George Brett, Gaylord Perry)	.30	.25	.12
639	1983 No-Hitters (Bob Forsch, Dave Righetti, Mike Warren)	.10	.08	.04
640	Retiring Superstars (Johnny Bench, Carl Yastrzemski)	.35	.25	.14
641	Going Out In Style (Gaylord Perry)	.15	.11	.06
642	300 Club & Strikeout Record (Steve Carlton)	.20	.15	.08
643	The Managers (Joe Altobelli, Paul Owens)	.10	.08	.04
644	The MVP (Rick Dempsey)	.10	.08	.04
645	The Rookie Winner (Mike Boddicker)	.12	.09	.05
646	The Clincher (Scott McGregor)	.10	.08	.04
647	Checklist: Orioles/Royals (Joe Altobelli)	.08	.06	.03
648	Checklist: Phillies/Giants (Paul Owens)	.08	.06	.03
649	Checklist: White Sox/Red Sox (Tony LaRussa)	.08	.06	.03
650	Checklist: Tigers/Rangers (Sparky Anderson)	.08	.06	.03
651	Checklist: Dodgers/A's (Tom Lasorda)	.08	.06	.03
652	Checklist: Yankees/Reds (Billy Martin)	.08	.06	.03
653	Checklist: Blue Jays/Cubs (Bobby Cox)	.08	.06	.03
654	Checklist: Braves/Angels (Joe Torre)	.08	.06	.03
655	Checklist: Brewers/Indians (Rene Lachemann)	.08	.06	.03
656	Checklist: Astros/Twins (Bob Lillis)	.08	.06	.03
657	Checklist: Pirates/Mets (Chuck Tanner)	.08	.06	.03
658	Checklist: Expos/Mariners (Bill Virdon)	.08	.06	.03
659	Checklist: Padres/Specials (Dick Williams)	.08	.06	.03

		MT	NR MT	EX
660	Checklist: Cardinals/Specials (Whitey Herzog)	.08	.06	.03

1984 Fleer Update

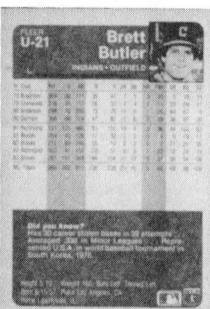

Following the lead of Topps, Fleer issued near the end of the baseball season a 132-card set to update player trades and include rookies not depicted in the regular issue. The cards, which measure 2½" by 3½", are identical in design to the regular issue but numbered U-1 through U-132. Available to the collecting public only through hobby dealers, the set was printed in limited quantities and has escalated in price quite rapidly the past several years. The set was issued with team logo stickers in a specially designed box.

		MT	NR MT	EX
	Complete Set:	225.00	169.00	90.00
	Common Player:	.15	.11	.06
1	Willie Aikens	.15	.11	.06
2	Luis Aponte	.15	.11	.06
3	Mark Bailey	.30	.25	.12
4	Bob Bailor	.15	.11	.06
5	Dusty Baker	.30	.25	.12
6	Steve Balboni	.50	.40	.20
7	Alan Bannister	.15	.11	.06
8	Marty Barrett	3.00	2.25	1.25
9	Dave Beard	.15	.11	.06
10	Joe Beckwith	.15	.11	.06
11	Dave Bergman	.15	.11	.06
12	Tony Bernazard	.20	.15	.08
13	Bruce Bochte	.15	.11	.06
14	Barry Bonnell	.15	.11	.06
15	Phil Bradley	6.00	4.50	2.50
16	Fred Breining	.15	.11	.06
17	Mike Brown	.15	.11	.06
18	Bill Buckner	.60	.45	.25
19	Ray Burris	.15	.11	.06
20	John Butcher	.15	.11	.06
21	Brett Butler	.30	.25	.12
22	Enos Cabell	.15	.11	.06
23	Bill Campbell	.15	.11	.06
24	Bill Caudill	.15	.11	.06
25	Bobby Clark	.15	.11	.06
26	Bryan Clark	.15	.11	.06
27	Roger Clemens	75.00	56.00	30.00
28	Jaime Cocanower	.15	.11	.06
29	Ron Darling	12.00	9.00	4.75
30	Alvin Davis	6.00	4.50	2.50
31	Bob Dernier	.15	.11	.06
32	Carlos Diaz	.15	.11	.06
33	Mike Easler	.30	.25	.12
34	Dennis Eckersley	.30	.25	.12
35	Jim Essian	.15	.11	.06
36	Darrell Evans	.70	.50	.30
37	Mike Fitzgerald	.30	.25	.12
38	Tim Foli	.15	.11	.06
39	John Franco	1.50	1.25	.60
40	George Frazier	.15	.11	.06
41	Rich Gale	.15	.11	.06
42	Barbaro Garbey	.15	.11	.06
43	Dwight Gooden	65.00	49.00	26.00
44	Goose Gossage	1.00	.70	.40
45	Wayne Gross	.15	.11	.06
46	Mark Gubicza	1.00	.70	.40
47	Jackie Gutierrez	.15	.11	.06
48	Toby Harrah	.20	.15	.08
49	Ron Hassey	.15	.11	.06
50	Richie Hebner	.15	.11	.06
51	Willie Hernandez	.50	.40	.20
52	Ed Hodge	.15	.11	.06
53	Ricky Horton	1.00	.70	.40
54	Art Howe	.15	.11	.06
55	Dane Iorg	.15	.11	.06
56	Brook Jacoby	3.50	2.75	1.50
57	Dion James	1.25	.90	.50
58	Mike Jeffcoat	.20	.15	.08
59	Ruppert Jones	.15	.11	.06
60	Bob Kearney	.15	.11	.06
61	Jimmy Key	6.00	4.50	2.50
62	Dave Kingman	.70	.50	.30
63	Brad Komminsk	.20	.15	.08
64	Jerry Koosman	.60	.45	.25
65	Wayne Krenchicki	.15	.11	.06
66	Rusty Kuntz	.15	.11	.06
67	Frank LaCorte	.15	.11	.06
68	Dennis Lamp	.15	.11	.06
69	Tito Landrum	.15	.11	.06
70	Mark Langston	5.00	3.75	2.00
71	Rick Leach	.15	.11	.06
72	Craig Lefferts	.30	.25	.12
73	Gary Lucas	.15	.11	.06
74	Jerry Martin	.15	.11	.06
75	Carmelo Martinez	.30	.25	.12
76	Mike Mason	.40	.30	.15
77	Gary Matthews	.30	.25	.12
78	Andy McGaffigan	.15	.11	.06
79	Joey McLaughlin	.15	.11	.06
80	Joe Morgan	2.00	1.50	.80
81	Darryl Motley	.15	.11	.06
82	Graig Nettles	1.50	1.25	.60
83	Phil Niekro	2.50	2.00	1.00
84	Ken Oberkfell	.20	.15	.08
85	Al Oliver	1.00	.70	.40
86	Jorge Orta	.15	.11	.06
87	Amos Otis	.30	.25	.12
88	Bob Owchinko	.15	.11	.06
89	Dave Parker	2.00	1.50	.80
90	Jack Perconte	.15	.11	.06
91	Tony Perez	1.50	1.25	.60
92	Gerald Perry	1.25	.90	.50
93	Kirby Puckett	60.00	45.00	24.00
94	Shane Rawley	.40	.30	.15
95	Floyd Rayford	.15	.11	.06
96	Ron Reed	.20	.15	.08
97	R.J. Reynolds	1.25	.90	.50
98	Gene Richards	.15	.11	.06
99	Jose Rijo	.90	.70	.35
100	Jeff Robinson	.70	.50	.30
101	Ron Romanick	.40	.30	.15
102	Pete Rose	25.00	18.50	10.00
103	Bret Saberhagen	20.00	15.00	8.00
104	Scott Sanderson	.20	.15	.08
105	Dick Schofield	.40	.30	.15
106	Tom Seaver	7.00	5.25	2.75
107	Jim Slaton	.15	.11	.06
108	Mike Smithson	.20	.15	.08
109	Lary Sorensen	.15	.11	.06
110	Tim Stoddard	.15	.11	.06
111	Jeff Stone	.70	.50	.30
112	Champ Summers	.15	.11	.06
113	Jim Sundberg	.20	.15	.08
114	Rick Sutcliffe	1.00	.70	.40
115	Craig Swan	.15	.11	.06
116	Derrel Thomas	.15	.11	.06
117	Gorman Thomas	.40	.30	.15
118	Alex Trevino	.15	.11	.06
119	Manny Trillo	.20	.15	.08
120	John Tudor	.30	.25	.12
121	Tom Underwood	.15	.11	.06
122	Mike Vail	.15	.11	.06
123	Tom Waddell	.20	.15	.08
124	Gary Ward	.20	.15	.08
125	Terry Whitfield	.15	.11	.06
126	Curtis Wilkerson	.15	.11	.06
127	Frank Williams	.40	.30	.15
128	Glenn Wilson	.40	.30	.15
129	John Wockenfuss	.15	.11	.06
130	Ned Yost	.15	.11	.06
131	Mike Young	1.00	.70	.40
132	Checklist 1-132	.15	.11	.06

1985 Fleer

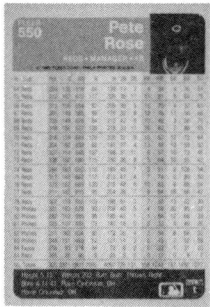

The 1985 Fleer set consists of 660 cards, each measuring 2½" by 3½" in size. The card fronts feature a color photo plus the player's team logo and the word "Fleer". The photos have a color-coded frame which corresponds to the player's team. A grey border surrounds the color-coded frame. The card backs are similar in design to the previous two years, but have two shades of red and black ink on white stock. For the fourth consecutive year, Fleer included special cards and team checklists in the set. Also incorporated in a set for the first time were ten "Major League Prospects" cards, each featuring two rookie hopefuls. The set was issued with team logo stickers.

	MT	NR MT	EX
Complete Set:	75.00	56.00	30.00
Common Player:	.06	.05	.02

		MT	NR MT	EX
1	Doug Bair	.06	.05	.02
2	Juan Berenguer	.06	.05	.02
3	Dave Bergman	.06	.05	.02
4	Tom Brookens	.06	.05	.02
5	Marty Castillo	.06	.05	.02
6	Darrell Evans	.12	.09	.05
7	Barbaro Garbey	.06	.05	.02
8	Kirk Gibson	.30	.25	.12
9	John Grubb	.06	.05	.02
10	Willie Hernandez	.08	.06	.03
11	Larry Herndon	.08	.06	.03
12	Howard Johnson	.25	.20	.10
13	Ruppert Jones	.06	.05	.02
14	Rusty Kuntz	.06	.05	.02
15	Chet Lemon	.08	.06	.03
16	Aurelio Lopez	.06	.05	.02
17	Sid Monge	.06	.05	.02
18	Jack Morris	.25	.20	.10
19	Lance Parrish	.30	.25	.12
20	Dan Petry	.10	.08	.04
21	Dave Rozema	.06	.05	.02
22	Bill Scherrer	.06	.05	.02
23	Alan Trammell	.35	.25	.14
24	Lou Whitaker	.25	.20	.10
25	Milt Wilcox	.08	.06	.03
26	Kurt Bevacqua	.06	.05	.02
27	Greg Booker	.12	.09	.05
28	Bobby Brown	.06	.05	.02
29	Luis DeLeon	.06	.05	.02
30	Dave Dravecky	.08	.06	.03
31	Tim Flannery	.06	.05	.02
32	Steve Garvey	.40	.30	.15
33	Goose Gossage	.20	.15	.08
34	Tony Gwynn	.60	.45	.25
35	Greg Harris	.06	.05	.02
36	Andy Hawkins	.06	.05	.02
37	Terry Kennedy	.08	.06	.03
38	Craig Lefferts	.08	.06	.03
39	Tim Lollar	.06	.05	.02
40	Carmelo Martinez	.10	.08	.04
41	Kevin McReynolds	.50	.40	.20
42	Graig Nettles	.15	.11	.06
43	Luis Salazar	.06	.05	.02
44	Eric Show	.06	.05	.02
45	Garry Templeton	.10	.08	.04
46	Mark Thurmond	.06	.05	.02
47	Ed Whitson	.06	.05	.02
48	Alan Wiggins	.06	.05	.02
49	Rich Bordi	.06	.05	.02
50	Larry Bowa	.12	.09	.05
51	Warren Brusstar	.06	.05	.02
52	Ron Cey	.10	.08	.04
53	Henry Cotto	.12	.09	.05
54	Jody Davis	.10	.08	.04
55	Bob Dernier	.06	.05	.02
56	Leon Durham	.10	.08	.04
57	Dennis Eckersley	.08	.06	.03
58	George Frazier	.06	.05	.02
59	Richie Hebner	.06	.05	.02
60	Dave Lopes	.08	.06	.03
61	Gary Matthews	.10	.08	.04
62	Keith Moreland	.08	.06	.03
63	Rick Reuschel	.10	.08	.04
64	Dick Ruthven	.06	.05	.02
65	Ryne Sandberg	.40	.30	.15
66	Scott Sanderson	.08	.06	.03
67	Lee Smith	.10	.08	.04
68	Tim Stoddard	.06	.05	.02
69	Rick Sutcliffe	.12	.09	.05
70	Steve Trout	.08	.06	.03
71	Gary Woods	.06	.05	.02
72	Wally Backman	.08	.06	.03
73	Bruce Berenyi	.06	.05	.02
74	Hubie Brooks	.10	.08	.04
75	Kelvin Chapman	.06	.05	.02
76	Ron Darling	1.00	.70	.40
77	Sid Fernandez	.90	.70	.35
78	Mike Fitzgerald	.08	.06	.03
79	George Foster	.15	.11	.06
80	Brent Gaff	.06	.05	.02
81	Ron Gardenhire	.06	.05	.02
82	Dwight Gooden	7.00	5.25	2.75
83	Tom Gorman	.06	.05	.02
84	Danny Heep	.06	.05	.02
85	Keith Hernandez	.30	.25	.12
86	Ray Knight	.10	.08	.04
87	Ed Lynch	.06	.05	.02
88	Jose Oquendo	.08	.06	.03
89	Jesse Orosco	.08	.06	.03
90	Rafael Santana	.20	.15	.08
91	Doug Sisk	.06	.05	.02
92	Rusty Staub	.12	.09	.05
93	Darryl Strawberry	1.75	1.25	.70
94	Walt Terrell	.12	.09	.05
95	Mookie Wilson	.10	.08	.04
96	Jim Acker	.06	.05	.02
97	Willie Aikens	.06	.05	.02
98	Doyle Alexander	.10	.08	.04
99	Jesse Barfield	.25	.20	.10
100	George Bell	.60	.45	.25
101	Jim Clancy	.10	.08	.04
102	Dave Collins	.08	.06	.03
103	Tony Fernandez	.35	.25	.14
104	Damaso Garcia	.08	.06	.03
105	Jim Gott	.06	.05	.02
106	Alfredo Griffin	.08	.06	.03
107	Garth Iorg	.06	.05	.02
108	Roy Lee Jackson	.06	.05	.02
109	Cliff Johnson	.06	.05	.02
110	Jimmy Key	.70	.50	.30
111	Dennis Lamp	.06	.05	.02
112	Rick Leach	.06	.05	.02
113	Luis Leal	.06	.05	.02
114	Buck Martinez	.06	.05	.02
115	Lloyd Moseby	.10	.08	.04
116	Rance Mulliniks	.06	.05	.02
117	Dave Stieb	.12	.09	.05
118	Willie Upshaw	.08	.06	.03
119	Ernie Whitt	.08	.06	.03
120	Mike Armstrong	.06	.05	.02
121	Don Baylor	.12	.09	.05
122	Marty Bystrom	.06	.05	.02
123	Rick Cerone	.08	.06	.03
124	Joe Cowley	.08	.06	.03
125	Brian Dayett	.08	.06	.03
126	Tim Foli	.06	.05	.02
127	Ray Fontenot	.06	.05	.02
128	Ken Griffey	.10	.08	.04
129	Ron Guidry	.25	.20	.10
130	Toby Harrah	.08	.06	.03
131	Jay Howell	.08	.06	.03
132	Steve Kemp	.08	.06	.03
133	Don Mattingly	8.00	6.00	3.25
134	Bobby Meacham	.06	.05	.02
135	John Montefusco	.06	.05	.02
136	Omar Moreno	.06	.05	.02
137	Dale Murray	.06	.05	.02
138	Phil Niekro	.25	.20	.10

#	Player	MT	NR MT	EX
139	Mike Pagliarulo	2.25	1.75	.90
140	Willie Randolph	.10	.08	.04
141	Dennis Rasmussen	.12	.09	.05
142	Dave Righetti	.20	.15	.08
143	Jose Rijo	.20	.15	.08
144	Andre Robertson	.06	.05	.02
145	Bob Shirley	.06	.05	.02
146	Dave Winfield	.35	.25	.14
147	Butch Wynegar	.08	.06	.03
148	Gary Allenson	.06	.05	.02
149	Tony Armas	.10	.08	.04
150	Marty Barrett	.20	.15	.08
151	Wade Boggs	3.00	2.25	1.25
152	Dennis Boyd	.10	.08	.04
153	Bill Buckner	.12	.09	.05
154	Mark Clear	.08	.06	.03
155	Roger Clemens	8.00	6.00	3.25
156	Steve Crawford	.06	.05	.02
157	Mike Easler	.08	.06	.03
158	Dwight Evans	.12	.09	.05
159	Rich Gedman	.10	.08	.04
160	Jackie Gutierrez	.06	.05	.02
161	Bruce Hurst	.10	.08	.04
162	John Henry Johnson	.06	.05	.02
163	Rick Miller	.06	.05	.02
164	Reid Nichols	.06	.05	.02
165	Al Nipper	.25	.20	.10
166	Bob Ojeda	.10	.08	.04
167	Jerry Remy	.06	.05	.02
168	Jim Rice	.35	.25	.14
169	Bob Stanley	.08	.06	.03
170	Mike Boddicker	.12	.09	.05
171	Al Bumbry	.08	.06	.03
172	Todd Cruz	.06	.05	.02
173	Rich Dauer	.06	.05	.02
174	Storm Davis	.08	.06	.03
175	Rick Dempsey	.08	.06	.03
176	Jim Dwyer	.06	.05	.02
177	Mike Flanagan	.10	.08	.04
178	Dan Ford	.06	.05	.02
179	Wayne Gross	.06	.05	.02
180	John Lowenstein	.06	.05	.02
181	Dennis Martinez	.06	.05	.02
182	Tippy Martinez	.06	.05	.02
183	Scott McGregor	.10	.08	.04
184	Eddie Murray	.50	.40	.20
185	Joe Nolan	.06	.05	.02
186	Floyd Rayford	.06	.05	.02
187	Cal Ripken, Jr.	.50	.40	.20
188	Gary Roenicke	.06	.05	.02
189	Lenn Sakata	.06	.05	.02
190	John Shelby	.08	.06	.03
191	Ken Singleton	.08	.06	.03
192	Sammy Stewart	.06	.05	.02
193	Bill Swaggerty	.06	.05	.02
194	Tom Underwood	.06	.05	.02
195	Mike Young	.15	.11	.06
196	Steve Balboni	.08	.06	.03
197	Joe Beckwith	.06	.05	.02
198	Bud Black	.06	.05	.02
199	George Brett	.50	.40	.20
200	Onix Concepcion	.06	.05	.02
201	Mark Gubicza	.30	.25	.12
202	Larry Gura	.08	.06	.03
203	Mark Huismann	.08	.06	.03
204	Dane Iorg	.06	.05	.02
205	Danny Jackson	.15	.11	.06
206	Charlie Leibrandt	.08	.06	.03
207	Hal McRae	.10	.08	.04
208	Darryl Motley	.06	.05	.02
209	Jorge Orta	.06	.05	.02
210	Greg Pryor	.06	.05	.02
211	Dan Quisenberry	.15	.11	.06
212	Bret Saberhagen	3.25	2.50	1.25
213	Pat Sheridan	.06	.05	.02
214	Don Slaught	.06	.05	.02
215	U.L. Washington	.06	.05	.02
216	John Wathan	.08	.06	.03
217	Frank White	.10	.08	.04
218	Willie Wilson	.12	.09	.05
219	Neil Allen	.06	.05	.02
220	Joaquin Andujar	.08	.06	.03
221	Steve Braun	.06	.05	.02
222	Danny Cox	.35	.25	.14
223	Bob Forsch	.08	.06	.03
224	David Green	.06	.05	.02
225	George Hendrick	.08	.06	.03
226	Tom Herr	.10	.08	.04
227	Ricky Horton	.30	.25	.12
228	Art Howe	.06	.05	.02
229	Mike Jorgensen	.06	.05	.02
230	Kurt Kepshire	.06	.05	.02
231	Jeff Lahti	.06	.05	.02
232	Tito Landrum	.06	.05	.02
233	Dave LaPoint	.06	.05	.02
234	Willie McGee	.30	.25	.12
235	Tom Nieto	.12	.09	.05
236	Terry Pendleton	.70	.50	.30
237	Darrell Porter	.08	.06	.03
238	Dave Rucker	.06	.05	.02
239	Lonnie Smith	.08	.06	.03
240	Ozzie Smith	.15	.11	.06
241	Bruce Sutter	.15	.11	.06
242	Andy Van Slyke	.15	.11	.06
243	Dave Von Ohlen	.06	.05	.02
244	Larry Andersen	.06	.05	.02
245	Bill Campbell	.06	.05	.02
246	Steve Carlton	.40	.30	.15
247	Tim Corcoran	.06	.05	.02
248	Ivan DeJesus	.06	.05	.02
249	John Denny	.06	.05	.02
250	Bo Diaz	.08	.06	.03
251	Greg Gross	.06	.05	.02
252	Kevin Gross	.10	.08	.04
253	Von Hayes	.12	.09	.05
254	Al Holland	.06	.05	.02
255	Charles Hudson	.08	.06	.03
256	Jerry Koosman	.10	.08	.04
257	Joe Lefebvre	.06	.05	.02
258	Sixto Lezcano	.06	.05	.02
259	Garry Maddox	.08	.06	.03
260	Len Matuszek	.06	.05	.02
261	Tug McGraw	.10	.08	.04
262	Al Oliver	.12	.09	.05
263	Shane Rawley	.10	.08	.04
264	Juan Samuel	.30	.25	.12
265	Mike Schmidt	.50	.40	.20
266	Jeff Stone	.20	.15	.08
267	Ozzie Virgil	.08	.06	.03
268	Glenn Wilson	.10	.08	.04
269	John Wockenfuss	.06	.05	.02
270	Darrell Brown	.06	.05	.02
271	Tom Brunansky	.12	.09	.05
272	Randy Bush	.06	.05	.02
273	John Butcher	.06	.05	.02
274	Bobby Castillo	.06	.05	.02
275	Ron Davis	.06	.05	.02
276	Dave Engle	.06	.05	.02
277	Pete Filson	.06	.05	.02
278	Gary Gaetti	.20	.15	.08
279	Mickey Hatcher	.06	.05	.02
280	Ed Hodge	.06	.05	.02
281	Kent Hrbek	.25	.20	.10
282	Houston Jimenez	.06	.05	.02
283	Tim Laudner	.06	.05	.02
284	Rick Lysander	.06	.05	.02
285	Dave Meier	.06	.05	.02
286	Kirby Puckett	9.00	6.75	3.50
287	Pat Putnam	.06	.05	.02
288	Ken Schrom	.06	.05	.02
289	Mike Smithson	.06	.05	.02
290	Tim Teufel	.08	.06	.03
291	Frank Viola	.12	.09	.05
292	Ron Washington	.06	.05	.02
293	Don Aase	.08	.06	.03
294	Juan Beniquez	.06	.05	.02
295	Bob Boone	.08	.06	.03
296	Mike Brown	.06	.05	.02
297	Rod Carew	.40	.30	.15
298	Doug Corbett	.06	.05	.02
299	Doug DeCinces	.10	.08	.04
300	Brian Downing	.10	.08	.04
301	Ken Forsch	.08	.06	.03
302	Bobby Grich	.10	.08	.04
303	Reggie Jackson	.40	.30	.15
304	Tommy John	.20	.15	.08
305	Curt Kaufman	.06	.05	.02
306	Bruce Kison	.06	.05	.02
307	Fred Lynn	.20	.15	.08
308	Gary Pettis	.10	.08	.04
309	Ron Romanick	.15	.11	.06
310	Luis Sanchez	.06	.05	.02
311	Dick Schofield	.10	.08	.04
312	Daryl Sconiers	.06	.05	.02
313	Jim Slaton	.06	.05	.02
314	Derrel Thomas	.06	.05	.02
315	Rob Wilfong	.06	.05	.02
316	Mike Witt	.12	.09	.05
317	Geoff Zahn	.06	.05	.02
318	Len Barker	.08	.06	.03
319	Steve Bedrosian	.12	.09	.05
320	Bruce Benedict	.06	.05	.02

#	Player	MT	NR MT	EX		#	Player	MT	NR MT	EX
321	Rick Camp	.06	.05	.02		412	Tim Wallach	.12	.09	.05
322	Chris Chambliss	.08	.06	.03		413	Jim Wohlford	.06	.05	.02
323	Jeff Dedmon	.12	.09	.05		414	Bill Almon	.06	.05	.02
324	Terry Forster	.08	.06	.03		415	Keith Atherton	.08	.06	.03
325	Gene Garber	.06	.05	.02		416	Bruce Bochte	.06	.05	.02
326	Albert Hall	.20	.15	.08		417	Tom Burgmeier	.06	.05	.02
327	Terry Harper	.06	.05	.02		418	Ray Burris	.06	.05	.02
328	Bob Horner	.25	.20	.10		419	Bill Caudill	.06	.05	.02
329	Glenn Hubbard	.06	.05	.02		420	Chris Codiroli	.06	.05	.02
330	Randy Johnson	.06	.05	.02		421	Tim Conroy	.06	.05	.02
331	Brad Komminsk	.08	.06	.03		422	Mike Davis	.08	.06	.03
332	Rick Mahler	.06	.05	.02		423	Jim Essian	.06	.05	.02
333	Craig McMurtry	.06	.05	.02		424	Mike Heath	.06	.05	.02
334	Donnie Moore	.06	.05	.02		425	Rickey Henderson	.40	.30	.15
335	Dale Murphy	.60	.45	.25		426	Donnie Hill	.06	.05	.02
336	Ken Oberkfell	.08	.06	.03		427	Dave Kingman	.15	.11	.06
337	Pascual Perez	.08	.06	.03		428	Bill Krueger	.06	.05	.02
338	Gerald Perry	.12	.09	.05		429	Carney Lansford	.08	.06	.03
339	Rafael Ramirez	.06	.05	.02		430	Steve McCatty	.06	.05	.02
340	Jerry Royster	.06	.05	.02		431	Joe Morgan	.20	.15	.08
341	Alex Trevino	.06	.05	.02		432	Dwayne Murphy	.08	.06	.03
342	Claudell Washington	.08	.06	.03		433	Tony Phillips	.06	.05	.02
343	Alan Ashby	.06	.05	.02		434	Lary Sorensen	.06	.05	.02
344	Mark Bailey	.12	.09	.05		435	Mike Warren	.06	.05	.02
345	Kevin Bass	.12	.09	.05		436	Curt Young	.50	.40	.20
346	Enos Cabell	.06	.05	.02		437	Luis Aponte	.06	.05	.02
347	Jose Cruz	.10	.08	.04		438	Chris Bando	.06	.05	.02
348	Bill Dawley	.06	.05	.02		439	Tony Bernazard	.08	.06	.03
349	Frank DiPino	.06	.05	.02		440	Bert Blyleven	.15	.11	.06
350	Bill Doran	.12	.09	.05		441	Brett Butler	.10	.08	.04
351	Phil Garner	.08	.06	.03		442	Ernie Camacho	.06	.05	.02
352	Bob Knepper	.08	.06	.03		443	Joe Carter	1.25	.90	.50
353	Mike LaCoss	.08	.06	.03		444	Carmelo Castillo	.06	.05	.02
354	Jerry Mumphrey	.08	.06	.03		445	Jamie Easterly	.06	.05	.02
355	Joe Niekro	.10	.08	.04		446	Steve Farr	.20	.15	.08
356	Terry Puhl	.06	.05	.02		447	Mike Fischlin	.06	.05	.02
357	Craig Reynolds	.06	.05	.02		448	Julio Franco	.12	.09	.05
358	Vern Ruhle	.06	.05	.02		449	Mel Hall	.08	.06	.03
359	Nolan Ryan	.40	.30	.15		450	Mike Hargrove	.08	.06	.03
360	Joe Sambito	.06	.05	.02		451	Neal Heaton	.10	.08	.04
361	Mike Scott	.15	.11	.06		452	Brook Jacoby	.30	.25	.12
362	Dave Smith	.08	.06	.03		453	Mike Jeffcoat	.06	.05	.02
363	Julio Solano	.10	.08	.04		454	Don Schulze	.10	.08	.04
364	Dickie Thon	.08	.06	.03		455	Roy Smith	.06	.05	.02
365	Denny Walling	.06	.05	.02		456	Pat Tabler	.08	.06	.03
366	Dave Anderson	.06	.05	.02		457	Andre Thornton	.10	.08	.04
367	Bob Bailor	.06	.05	.02		458	George Vukovich	.06	.05	.02
368	Greg Brock	.10	.08	.04		459	Tom Waddell	.10	.08	.04
369	Carlos Diaz	.06	.05	.02		460	Jerry Willard	.06	.05	.02
370	Pedro Guerrero	.25	.20	.10		461	Dale Berra	.06	.05	.02
371	Orel Hershiser	1.75	1.25	.70		462	John Candelaria	.10	.08	.04
372	Rick Honeycutt	.08	.06	.03		463	Jose DeLeon	.08	.06	.03
373	Burt Hooton	.08	.06	.03		464	Doug Frobel	.06	.05	.02
374	Ken Howell	.20	.15	.08		465	Cecilio Guante	.06	.05	.02
375	Ken Landreaux	.08	.06	.03		466	Brian Harper	.06	.05	.02
376	Candy Maldonado	.10	.08	.04		467	Lee Lacy	.08	.06	.03
377	Mike Marshall	.12	.09	.05		468	Bill Madlock	.12	.09	.05
378	Tom Niedenfuer	.08	.06	.03		469	Lee Mazzilli	.08	.06	.03
379	Alejandro Pena	.06	.05	.02		470	Larry McWilliams	.06	.05	.02
380	Jerry Reuss	.08	.06	.03		471	Jim Morrison	.06	.05	.02
381	R.J. Reynolds	.35	.25	.14		472	Tony Pena	.10	.08	.04
382	German Rivera	.06	.05	.02		473	Johnny Ray	.12	.09	.05
383	Bill Russell	.08	.06	.03		474	Rick Rhoden	.10	.08	.04
384	Steve Sax	.20	.15	.08		475	Don Robinson	.08	.06	.03
385	Mike Scioscia	.06	.05	.02		476	Rod Scurry	.06	.05	.02
386	Franklin Stubbs	.60	.45	.25		477	Kent Tekulve	.08	.06	.03
387	Fernando Valenzuela	.35	.25	.14		478	Jason Thompson	.06	.05	.02
388	Bob Welch	.10	.08	.04		479	John Tudor	.10	.08	.04
389	Terry Whitfield	.06	.05	.02		480	Lee Tunnell	.06	.05	.02
390	Steve Yeager	.06	.05	.02		481	Marvell Wynne	.06	.05	.02
391	Pat Zachry	.06	.05	.02		482	Salome Barojas	.06	.05	.02
392	Fred Breining	.06	.05	.02		483	Dave Beard	.06	.05	.02
393	Gary Carter	.40	.30	.15		484	Jim Beattie	.06	.05	.02
394	Andre Dawson	.30	.25	.12		485	Barry Bonnell	.06	.05	.02
395	Miguel Dilone	.06	.05	.02		486	Phil Bradley	1.50	1.25	.60
396	Dan Driessen	.08	.06	.03		487	Al Cowens	.06	.05	.02
397	Doug Flynn	.06	.05	.02		488	Alvin Davis	1.50	1.25	.60
398	Terry Francona	.06	.05	.02		489	Dave Henderson	.06	.05	.02
399	Bill Gullickson	.08	.06	.03		490	Steve Henderson	.06	.05	.02
400	Bob James	.06	.05	.02		491	Bob Kearney	.06	.05	.02
401	Charlie Lea	.06	.05	.02		492	Mark Langston	.70	.50	.30
402	Bryan Little	.06	.05	.02		493	Larry Milbourne	.06	.05	.02
403	Gary Lucas	.06	.05	.02		494	Paul Mirabella	.06	.05	.02
404	David Palmer	.08	.06	.03		495	Mike Moore	.06	.05	.02
405	Tim Raines	.35	.25	.14		496	Edwin Nunez	.15	.11	.06
406	Mike Ramsey	.06	.05	.02		497	Spike Owen	.06	.05	.02
407	Jeff Reardon	.15	.11	.06		498	Jack Perconte	.06	.05	.02
408	Steve Rogers	.08	.06	.03		499	Ken Phelps	.10	.08	.04
409	Dan Schatzeder	.06	.05	.02		500	Jim Presley	1.50	1.25	.60
410	Bryn Smith	.08	.06	.03		501	Mike Stanton	.06	.05	.02
411	Mike Stenhouse	.06	.05	.02		502	Bob Stoddard	.06	.05	.02

#	Player	MT	NR MT	EX		#	Player	MT	NR MT	EX
503	Gorman Thomas	.12	.09	.05		591	Chuck Porter	.06	.05	.02
504	Ed Vande Berg	.06	.05	.02		592	Randy Ready	.15	.11	.06
505	Matt Young	.08	.06	.03		593	Ed Romero	.06	.05	.02
506	Juan Agosto	.06	.05	.02		594	Bill Schroeder	.12	.09	.05
507	Harold Baines	.15	.11	.06		595	Ray Searage	.06	.05	.02
508	Floyd Bannister	.10	.08	.04		596	Ted Simmons	.12	.09	.05
509	Britt Burns	.06	.05	.02		597	Jim Sundberg	.08	.06	.03
510	Julio Cruz	.06	.05	.02		598	Don Sutton	.30	.25	.12
511	Richard Dotson	.10	.08	.04		599	Tom Tellmann	.06	.05	.02
512	Jerry Dybzinski	.06	.05	.02		600	Rick Waits	.06	.05	.02
513	Carlton Fisk	.20	.15	.08		601	Robin Yount	.35	.25	.14
514	Scott Fletcher	.08	.06	.03		602	Dusty Baker	.08	.06	.03
515	Jerry Hairston	.06	.05	.02		603	Bob Brenly	.06	.05	.02
516	Marc Hill	.06	.05	.02		604	Jack Clark	.20	.15	.08
517	LaMarr Hoyt	.08	.06	.03		605	Chili Davis	.10	.08	.04
518	Ron Kittle	.10	.08	.04		606	Mark Davis	.06	.05	.02
519	Rudy Law	.06	.05	.02		607	Dan Gladden	.40	.30	.15
520	Vance Law	.08	.06	.03		608	Atlee Hammaker	.06	.05	.02
521	Greg Luzinski	.10	.08	.04		609	Mike Krukow	.08	.06	.03
522	Gene Nelson	.06	.05	.02		610	Duane Kuiper	.06	.05	.02
523	Tom Paciorek	.06	.05	.02		611	Bob Lacey	.06	.05	.02
524	Ron Reed	.06	.05	.02		612	Bill Laskey	.06	.05	.02
525	Bert Roberge	.06	.05	.02		613	Gary Lavelle	.06	.05	.02
526	Tom Seaver	.30	.25	.12		614	Johnnie LeMaster	.06	.05	.02
527	Roy Smalley	.06	.05	.02		615	Jeff Leonard	.10	.08	.04
528	Dan Spillner	.06	.05	.02		616	Randy Lerch	.06	.05	.02
529	Mike Squires	.06	.05	.02		617	Greg Minton	.06	.05	.02
530	Greg Walker	.12	.09	.05		618	Steve Nicosia	.06	.05	.02
531	Cesar Cedeno	.10	.08	.04		619	Gene Richards	.06	.05	.02
532	Dave Concepcion	.12	.09	.05		620	Jeff Robinson	.25	.20	.10
533	Eric Davis	17.00	12.50	6.75		621	Scot Thompson	.06	.05	.02
534	Nick Esasky	.08	.06	.03		622	Manny Trillo	.08	.06	.03
535	Tom Foley	.06	.05	.02		623	Brad Wellman	.06	.05	.02
536	John Franco	.50	.40	.20		624	Frank Williams	.20	.15	.08
537	Brad Gulden	.06	.05	.02		625	Joel Youngblood	.06	.05	.02
538	Tom Hume	.06	.05	.02		626	Ripken-In-Action (Cal Ripken)	.30	.25	.12
539	Wayne Krenchicki	.06	.05	.02		627	Schmidt-In-Action (Mike Schmidt)	.30	.25	.12
540	Andy McGaffigan	.06	.05	.02		628	Giving the Signs (Sparky Anderson)	.08	.06	.03
541	Eddie Milner	.06	.05	.02		629	A.L. Pitcher's Nightmare (Rickey Henderson, Dave Winfield)	.30	.25	.12
542	Ron Oester	.06	.05	.02		630	N.L. Pitcher's Nightmare (Ryne Sandberg, Mike Schmidt)	.30	.25	.12
543	Bob Owchinko	.06	.05	.02		631	N.L. All-Stars (Gary Carter, Steve Garvey, Ozzie Smith, Darryl Strawberry)	.30	.25	.12
544	Dave Parker	.25	.20	.10		632	All-Star Game Winning Battery (Gary Carter, Charlie Lea)	.15	.11	.06
545	Frank Pastore	.06	.05	.02		633	N.L. Pennant Clinchers (Steve Garvey, Goose Gossage)	.20	.15	.08
546	Tony Perez	.15	.11	.06		634	N.L. Rookie Phenoms (Dwight Gooden, Juan Samuel)	1.00	.70	.40
547	Ted Power	.08	.06	.03		635	Toronto's Big Guns (Willie Upshaw)	.08	.06	.03
548	Joe Price	.06	.05	.02		636	Toronto's Big Guns (Lloyd Moseby)	.08	.06	.03
549	Gary Redus	.10	.08	.04		637	Holland (Al Holland)	.08	.06	.03
550	Pete Rose	1.00	.70	.40		638	Tunnell (Lee Tunnell)	.08	.06	.03
551	Jeff Russell	.08	.06	.03		639	500th Homer (Reggie Jackson)	.30	.25	.12
552	Mario Soto	.08	.06	.03		640	4,000th Hit (Pete Rose)	.50	.40	.20
553	Jay Tibbs	.15	.11	.06		641	Father & Son (Cal Ripken, Jr., Cal Ripken, Sr.)	.30	.25	.12
554	Duane Walker	.06	.05	.02		642	Cubs Team	.08	.06	.03
555	Alan Bannister	.06	.05	.02		643	1984's Two Perfect Games & One No Hitter (Jack Morris, David Palmer, Mike Witt)	.15	.11	.06
556	Buddy Bell	.12	.09	.05		644	Major League Prospect (Willie Lozado, Vic Mata)	.06	.05	.02
557	Danny Darwin	.08	.06	.03		645	Major League Prospect (Kelly Gruber, Randy O'Neal)	.30	.25	.12
558	Charlie Hough	.08	.06	.03		646	Major League Prospect (Jose Roman, Joel Skinner)	.12	.09	.05
559	Bobby Jones	.06	.05	.02		647	Major League Prospect (Steve Kiefer, Danny Tartabull)	4.25	3.25	1.75
560	Odell Jones	.06	.05	.02		648	Major League Prospect (Rob Deer, Alejandro Sanchez)	1.75	1.25	.70
561	Jeff Kunkel	.12	.09	.05		649	Major League Prospect (Shawon Dunston, Bill Hatcher)	1.25	.90	.50
562	Mike Mason	.10	.08	.04		650	Major League Prospect (Mike Bielecki, Ron Robinson)	.30	.25	.12
563	Pete O'Brien	.20	.15	.08		651	Major League Prospect (Zane Smith, Paul Zuvella)	.40	.30	.15
564	Larry Parrish	.10	.08	.04		652	Major League Prospect (Glenn Davis, Joe Hesketh)	4.00	3.00	1.50
565	Mickey Rivers	.08	.06	.03		653	Major League Prospect (Steve Jeltz, John Russell)	.20	.15	.08
566	Billy Sample	.06	.05	.02		654	Checklist 1-95	.06	.05	.02
567	Dave Schmidt	.08	.06	.03		655	Checklist 96-195	.06	.05	.02
568	Donnie Scott	.06	.05	.02		656	Checklist 196-292	.06	.05	.02
569	Dave Stewart	.10	.08	.04		657	Checklist 293-391	.06	.05	.02
570	Frank Tanana	.10	.08	.04		658	Checklist 392-481	.06	.05	.02
571	Wayne Tolleson	.06	.05	.02		659	Checklist 482-575	.06	.05	.02
572	Gary Ward	.08	.06	.03		660	Checklist 576-660	.06	.05	.02
573	Curtis Wilkerson	.06	.05	.02						
574	George Wright	.06	.05	.02						
575	Ned Yost	.06	.05	.02						
576	Mark Brouhard	.06	.05	.02						
577	Mike Caldwell	.06	.05	.02						
578	Bobby Clark	.06	.05	.02						
579	Jaime Cocanower	.06	.05	.02						
580	Cecil Cooper	.15	.11	.06						
581	Rollie Fingers	.20	.15	.08						
582	Jim Gantner	.08	.06	.03						
583	Moose Haas	.06	.05	.02						
584	Dion James	.20	.15	.08						
585	Pete Ladd	.06	.05	.02						
586	Rick Manning	.06	.05	.02						
587	Bob McClure	.06	.05	.02						
588	Paul Molitor	.15	.11	.06						
589	Charlie Moore	.06	.05	.02						
590	Ben Oglivie	.08	.06	.03						

1985 Fleer Limited Edition

1985 Fleer Update

 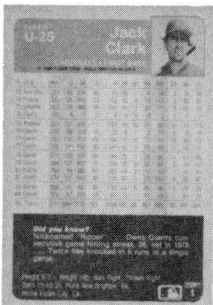

The 1985 Fleer Limited Edition 44-card set was distributed through McCrory's, J.J. Newbury, McClellan, Kress, YDC, and Green stores. The cards, which are the standard 2½'' by 3½'' size, have full color photos inside a red and yellow frame. The card backs are set in black type against two different shades of yellow and contain the player's personal and statisical information. The set was issued in a specially designed box which carried the complete checklist for the set on the back. Six team logo stickers were also included with the set.

For the second straight year, Fleer issued a 132-card update set. The cards, which measure 2½'' by 3½'', portrays players on their new teams and also includes rookies not depicted in the regular issue. The cards are identical in design to the 1985 Fleer set but are numbered U-1 through U-132. The set was issued with team logo stickers in a specially designed box and was available only through hobby dealers.

		MT	NR MT	EX
Complete Set:		5.00	3.75	2.00
Common Player:		.05	.04	.02
1	Buddy Bell	.10	.08	.04
2	Bert Blyleven	.12	.09	.05
3	Wade Boggs	.60	.45	.25
4	George Brett	.30	.25	.12
5	Rod Carew	.25	.20	.10
6	Steve Carlton	.20	.15	.08
7	Alvin Davis	.20	.15	.08
8	Andre Dawson	.15	.11	.06
9	Steve Garvey	.20	.15	.08
10	Goose Gossage	.12	.09	.05
11	Tony Gwynn	.25	.20	.10
12	Keith Hernandez	.20	.15	.08
13	Kent Hrbek	.15	.11	.06
14	Reggie Jackson	.25	.20	.10
15	Dave Kingman	.12	.09	.05
16	Ron Kittle	.07	.05	.03
17	Mark Langston	.10	.08	.04
18	Jeff Leonard	.05	.04	.02
19	Bill Madlock	.10	.08	.04
20	Don Mattingly	1.50	1.25	.60
21	Jack Morris	.15	.11	.06
22	Dale Murphy	.30	.25	.12
23	Eddie Murray	.25	.20	.10
24	Tony Pena	.07	.05	.03
25	Dan Quisenberry	.10	.08	.04
26	Tim Raines	.20	.15	.08
27	Jim Rice	.20	.15	.08
28	Cal Ripken, Jr.	.25	.20	.10
29	Pete Rose	.60	.45	.25
30	Nolan Ryan	.20	.15	.08
31	Ryne Sandberg	.20	.15	.08
32	Steve Sax	.15	.11	.06
33	Mike Schmidt	.30	.25	.12
34	Tom Seaver	.20	.15	.08
35	Ozzie Smith	.12	.09	.05
36	Mario Soto	.05	.04	.02
37	Dave Stieb	.07	.05	.03
38	Darryl Strawberry	.30	.25	.12
39	Rick Sutcliffe	.10	.08	.04
40	Alan Trammell	.20	.15	.08
41	Willie Upshaw	.07	.05	.03
42	Fernando Valenzuela	.20	.15	.08
43	Dave Winfield	.20	.15	.08
44	Robin Yount	.20	.15	.08

		MT	NR MT	EX
Complete Set:		16.00	12.00	6.50
Common Player:		.10	.08	.04
1	Don Aase	.15	.11	.06
2	Bill Almon	.10	.08	.04
3	Dusty Baker	.15	.11	.06
4	Dale Berra	.10	.08	.04
5	Karl Best	.15	.11	.06
6	Tim Birtsas	.20	.15	.08
7	Vida Blue	.20	.15	.08
8	Rich Bordi	.10	.08	.04
9	Daryl Boston	.20	.15	.08
10	Hubie Brooks	.20	.15	.08
11	Chris Brown	1.75	1.25	.70
12	Tom Browning	.40	.30	.15
13	Al Bumbry	.10	.08	.04
14	Tim Burke	.50	.40	.20
15	Ray Burris	.10	.08	.04
16	Jeff Burroughs	.15	.11	.06
17	Ivan Calderon	.80	.60	.30
18	Jeff Calhoun	.10	.08	.04
19	Bill Campbell	.10	.08	.04
20	Don Carman	.40	.30	.15
21	Gary Carter	.80	.60	.30
22	Bobby Castillo	.10	.08	.04
23	Bill Caudill	.10	.08	.04
24	Rick Cerone	.10	.08	.04
25	Jack Clark	.35	.25	.14
26	Pat Clements	.20	.15	.08
27	Stewart Cliburn	.15	.11	.06
28	Vince Coleman	4.00	3.00	1.50
29	Dave Collins	.15	.11	.06
30	Fritz Connally	.10	.08	.04
31	Henry Cotto	.15	.11	.06
32	Danny Darwin	.15	.11	.06
33	Darren Daulton	.20	.15	.08
34	Jerry Davis	.10	.08	.04
35	Brian Dayett	.10	.08	.04
36	Ken Dixon	.20	.15	.08
37	Tommy Dunbar	.10	.08	.04
38	Mariano Duncan	.25	.20	.10
39	Bob Fallon	.10	.08	.04
40	Brian Fisher	.40	.30	.15
41	Mike Fitzgerald	.10	.08	.04
42	Ray Fontenot	.10	.08	.04
43	Greg Gagne	.60	.45	.25
44	Oscar Gamble	.15	.11	.06
45	Jim Gott	.10	.08	.04
46	David Green	.10	.08	.04
47	Alfredo Griffin	.15	.11	.06
48	Ozzie Guillen	.80	.60	.30
49	Toby Harrah	.15	.11	.06
50	Ron Hassey	.10	.08	.04
51	Rickey Henderson	1.00	.70	.40
52	Steve Henderson	.10	.08	.04
53	George Hendrick	.15	.11	.06
54	Teddy Higuera	2.50	2.00	1.00

		MT	NR MT	EX
55	Al Holland	.10	.08	.04
56	Burt Hooton	.15	.11	.06
57	Jay Howell	.15	.11	.06
58	LaMarr Hoyt	.15	.11	.06
59	Tim Hulett	.20	.15	.08
60	Bob James	.12	.09	.05
61	Cliff Johnson	.10	.08	.04
62	Howard Johnson	.90	.70	.35
63	Ruppert Jones	.10	.08	.04
64	Steve Kemp	.15	.11	.06
65	Bruce Kison	.10	.08	.04
66	Mike LaCoss	.15	.11	.06
67	Lee Lacy	.15	.11	.06
68	Dave LaPoint	.10	.08	.04
69	Gary Lavelle	.10	.08	.04
70	Vance Law	.15	.11	.06
71	Manny Lee	.15	.11	.06
72	Sixto Lezcano	.10	.08	.04
73	Tim Lollar	.10	.08	.04
74	Urbano Lugo	.15	.11	.06
75	Fred Lynn	.30	.25	.12
76	Steve Lyons	.15	.11	.06
77	Mickey Mahler	.10	.08	.04
78	Ron Mathis	.15	.11	.06
79	Len Matuszek	.10	.08	.04
80	Oddibe McDowell	1.00	.70	.40
81	Roger McDowell	.90	.70	.35
82	Donnie Moore	.10	.08	.04
83	Ron Musselman	.10	.08	.04
84	Al Oliver	.25	.20	.10
85	Joe Orsulak	.25	.20	.10
86	Dan Pasqua	1.25	.90	.50
87	Chris Pittaro	.15	.11	.06
88	Rick Reuschel	.20	.15	.08
89	Earnie Riles	.40	.30	.15
90	Jerry Royster	.10	.08	.04
91	Dave Rozema	.10	.08	.04
92	Dave Rucker	.10	.08	.04
93	Vern Ruhle	.10	.08	.04
94	Mark Salas	.20	.15	.08
95	Luis Salazar	.10	.08	.04
96	Joe Sambito	.10	.08	.04
97	Billy Sample	.10	.08	.04
98	Alex Sanchez	.10	.08	.04
99	Calvin Schiraldi	.30	.25	.12
100	Rick Schu	.25	.20	.10
101	Larry Sheets	1.25	.90	.50
102	Ron Shepherd	.10	.08	.04
103	Nelson Simmons	.15	.11	.06
104	Don Slaught	.10	.08	.04
105	Roy Smalley	.15	.11	.06
106	Lonnie Smith	.15	.11	.06
107	Nate Snell	.15	.11	.06
108	Lary Sorensen	.10	.08	.04
109	Chris Speier	.10	.08	.04
110	Mike Stenhouse	.10	.08	.04
111	Tim Stoddard	.10	.08	.04
112	John Stuper	.10	.08	.04
113	Jim Sundberg	.15	.11	.06
114	Bruce Sutter	.25	.20	.10
115	Don Sutton	.60	.45	.25
116	Bruce Tanner	.15	.11	.06
117	Kent Tekulve	.15	.11	.06
118	Walt Terrell	.15	.11	.06
119	Mickey Tettleton	.15	.11	.06
120	Rich Thompson	.10	.08	.04
121	Louis Thornton	.15	.11	.06
122	Alex Trevino	.10	.08	.04
123	John Tudor	.20	.15	.08
124	Jose Uribe	.25	.20	.10
125	Dave Valle	.15	.11	.06
126	Dave Von Ohlen	.10	.08	.04
127	Curt Wardle	.10	.08	.04
128	U.L. Washington	.10	.08	.04
129	Ed Whitson	.10	.08	.04
130	Herm Winningham	.20	.15	.08
131	Rich Yett	.15	.11	.06
132	Checklist	.10	.08	.04

1986 Fleer

The 1986 Fleer set contains 660 color photos, with each card measuring 2½'' by 3½'' in size. The card fronts include the word ''Fleer'', the player's team logo, and a player picture enclosed by a dark blue border. The card reverses are minus the black and white photo that was included in past Fleer efforts. Player

biographical and statistical information appear in black and yellow ink on white stock. As in 1985, Fleer devoted ten cards, entitled ''Major League Prospects'', to twenty promising rookie players. The 1986 set, as in the previous four years, was issued with team logo stickers.

		MT	NR MT	EX
Complete Set:		35.00	26.00	14.00
Common Player:		.05	.04	.02
1	Steve Balboni	.07	.05	.03
2	Joe Beckwith	.05	.04	.02
3	Buddy Biancalana	.05	.04	.02
4	Bud Black	.05	.04	.02
5	George Brett	.50	.40	.20
6	Onix Concepcion	.05	.04	.02
7	Steve Farr	.07	.05	.03
8	Mark Gubicza	.07	.05	.03
9	Dane Iorg	.05	.04	.02
10	Danny Jackson	.07	.05	.03
11	Lynn Jones	.05	.04	.02
12	Mike Jones	.05	.04	.02
13	Charlie Leibrandt	.07	.05	.03
14	Hal McRae	.10	.08	.04
15	Omar Moreno	.05	.04	.02
16	Darryl Motley	.05	.04	.02
17	Jorge Orta	.05	.04	.02
18	Dan Quisenberry	.12	.09	.05
19	Bret Saberhagen	.50	.40	.20
20	Pat Sheridan	.05	.04	.02
21	Lonnie Smith	.07	.05	.03
22	Jim Sundberg	.07	.05	.03
23	John Wathan	.07	.05	.03
24	Frank White	.10	.08	.04
25	Willie Wilson	.12	.09	.05
26	Joaquin Andujar	.07	.05	.03
27	Steve Braun	.05	.04	.02
28	Bill Campbell	.05	.04	.02
29	Cesar Cedeno	.10	.08	.04
30	Jack Clark	.20	.15	.08
31	Vince Coleman	1.75	1.25	.70
32	Danny Cox	.10	.08	.04
33	Ken Dayley	.05	.04	.02
34	Ivan DeJesus	.05	.04	.02
35	Bob Forsch	.07	.05	.03
36	Brian Harper	.05	.04	.02
37	Tom Herr	.10	.08	.04
38	Ricky Horton	.07	.05	.03
39	Kurt Kepshire	.05	.04	.02
40	Jeff Lahti	.05	.04	.02
41	Tito Landrum	.05	.04	.02
42	Willie McGee	.15	.11	.06
43	Tom Nieto	.05	.04	.02
44	Terry Pendleton	.15	.11	.06
45	Darrell Porter	.07	.05	.03
46	Ozzie Smith	.15	.11	.06
47	John Tudor	.10	.08	.04
48	Andy Van Slyke	.10	.08	.04
49	Todd Worrell	1.00	.70	.40
50	Jim Acker	.05	.04	.02
51	Doyle Alexander	.10	.08	.04
52	Jesse Barfield	.25	.20	.10
53	George Bell	.35	.25	.14
54	Jeff Burroughs	.07	.05	.03
55	Bill Caudill	.05	.04	.02
56	Jim Clancy	.10	.08	.04
57	Tony Fernandez	.20	.15	.08
58	Tom Filer	.05	.04	.02
59	Damaso Garcia	.07	.05	.03

		MT	NR MT	EX				MT	NR MT	EX
60	Tom Henke	.10	.08	.04	151	Rod Carew		.30	.25	.12
61	Garth Iorg	.05	.04	.02	152	Stewart Cliburn		.07	.05	.03
62	Cliff Johnson	.05	.04	.02	153	Doug DeCinces		.10	.08	.04
63	Jimmy Key	.15	.11	.06	154	Brian Downing		.07	.05	.03
64	Dennis Lamp	.05	.04	.02	155	Ken Forsch		.05	.04	.02
65	Gary Lavelle	.05	.04	.02	156	Craig Gerber		.05	.04	.02
66	Buck Martinez	.05	.04	.02	157	Bobby Grich		.10	.08	.04
67	Lloyd Moseby	.10	.08	.04	158	George Hendrick		.07	.05	.03
68	Rance Mulliniks	.05	.04	.02	159	Al Holland		.05	.04	.02
69	Al Oliver	.10	.08	.04	160	Reggie Jackson		.35	.25	.14
70	Dave Stieb	.12	.09	.05	161	Ruppert Jones		.05	.04	.02
71	Louis Thornton	.12	.09	.05	162	Urbano Lugo		.07	.05	.03
72	Willie Upshaw	.07	.05	.03	163	Kirk McCaskill		.35	.25	.14
73	Ernie Whitt	.07	.05	.03	164	Donnie Moore		.05	.04	.02
74	Rick Aguilera	.35	.25	.14	165	Gary Pettis		.07	.05	.03
75	Wally Backman	.07	.05	.03	166	Ron Romanick		.05	.04	.02
76	Gary Carter	.30	.25	.12	167	Dick Schofield		.05	.04	.02
77	Ron Darling	.15	.11	.06	168	Daryl Sconiers		.05	.04	.02
78	Len Dykstra	.70	.50	.30	169	Jim Slaton		.05	.04	.02
79	Sid Fernandez	.12	.09	.05	170	Don Sutton		.25	.20	.10
80	George Foster	.15	.11	.06	171	Mike Witt		.12	.09	.05
81	Dwight Gooden	2.00	1.50	.80	172	Buddy Bell		.10	.08	.04
82	Tom Gorman	.05	.04	.02	173	Tom Browning		.12	.09	.05
83	Danny Heep	.05	.04	.02	174	Dave Concepcion		.12	.09	.05
84	Keith Hernandez	.30	.25	.12	175	Eric Davis		4.00	3.00	1.50
85	Howard Johnson	.12	.09	.05	176	Bo Diaz		.07	.05	.03
86	Ray Knight	.10	.08	.04	177	Nick Esasky		.05	.04	.02
87	Terry Leach	.07	.05	.03	178	John Franco		.10	.08	.04
88	Ed Lynch	.05	.04	.02	179	Tom Hume		.05	.04	.02
89	Roger McDowell	.40	.30	.15	180	Wayne Krenchicki		.05	.04	.02
90	Jesse Orosco	.07	.05	.03	181	Andy McGaffigan		.05	.04	.02
91	Tom Paciorek	.05	.04	.02	182	Eddie Milner		.05	.04	.02
92	Ronn Reynolds	.10	.08	.04	183	Ron Oester		.05	.04	.02
93	Rafael Santana	.05	.04	.02	184	Dave Parker		.20	.15	.08
94	Doug Sisk	.05	.04	.02	185	Frank Pastore		.05	.04	.02
95	Rusty Staub	.10	.08	.04	186	Tony Perez		.15	.11	.06
96	Darryl Strawberry	.50	.40	.20	187	Ted Power		.07	.05	.03
97	Mookie Wilson	.10	.08	.04	188	Joe Price		.05	.04	.02
98	Neil Allen	.05	.04	.02	189	Gary Redus		.07	.05	.03
99	Don Baylor	.12	.09	.05	190	Ron Robinson		.07	.05	.03
100	Dale Berra	.05	.04	.02	191	Pete Rose		.70	.50	.30
101	Rich Bordi	.05	.04	.02	192	Mario Soto		.07	.05	.03
102	Marty Bystrom	.05	.04	.02	193	John Stuper		.05	.04	.02
103	Joe Cowley	.05	.04	.02	194	Jay Tibbs		.05	.04	.02
104	Brian Fisher	.35	.25	.14	195	Dave Van Gorder		.05	.04	.02
105	Ken Griffey	.10	.08	.04	196	Max Venable		.05	.04	.02
106	Ron Guidry	.20	.15	.08	197	Juan Agosto		.05	.04	.02
107	Ron Hassey	.05	.04	.02	198	Harold Baines		.15	.11	.06
108	Rickey Henderson	.40	.30	.15	199	Floyd Bannister		.10	.08	.04
109	Don Mattingly	3.75	2.75	1.50	200	Britt Burns		.05	.04	.02
110	Bobby Meacham	.05	.04	.02	201	Julio Cruz		.05	.04	.02
111	John Montefusco	.05	.04	.02	202	Joel Davis		.12	.09	.05
112	Phil Niekro	.25	.20	.10	203	Richard Dotson		.10	.08	.04
113	Mike Pagliarulo	.25	.20	.10	204	Carlton Fisk		.20	.15	.08
114	Dan Pasqua	.20	.15	.08	205	Scott Fletcher		.07	.05	.03
115	Willie Randolph	.10	.08	.04	206	Ozzie Guillen		.40	.30	.15
116	Dave Righetti	.20	.15	.08	207	Jerry Hairston		.05	.04	.02
117	Andre Robertson	.05	.04	.02	208	Tim Hulett		.07	.05	.03
118	Billy Sample	.05	.04	.02	209	Bob James		.05	.04	.02
119	Bob Shirley	.05	.04	.02	210	Ron Kittle		.10	.08	.04
120	Ed Whitson	.05	.04	.02	211	Rudy Law		.05	.04	.02
121	Dave Winfield	.30	.25	.12	212	Bryan Little		.05	.04	.02
122	Butch Wynegar	.07	.05	.03	213	Gene Nelson		.05	.04	.02
123	Dave Anderson	.05	.04	.02	214	Reid Nichols		.05	.04	.02
124	Bob Bailor	.05	.04	.02	215	Luis Salazar		.05	.04	.02
125	Greg Brock	.10	.08	.04	216	Tom Seaver		.30	.25	.12
126	Enos Cabell	.05	.04	.02	217	Dan Spillner		.05	.04	.02
127	Bobby Castillo	.05	.04	.02	218	Bruce Tanner		.10	.08	.04
128	Carlos Diaz	.05	.04	.02	219	Greg Walker		.10	.08	.04
129	Mariano Duncan	.20	.15	.08	220	Dave Wehrmeister		.05	.04	.02
130	Pedro Guerrero	.20	.15	.08	221	Juan Berenguer		.05	.04	.02
131	Orel Hershiser	.35	.25	.14	222	Dave Bergman		.05	.04	.02
132	Rick Honeycutt	.07	.05	.03	223	Tom Brookens		.05	.04	.02
133	Ken Howell	.07	.05	.03	224	Darrell Evans		.12	.09	.05
134	Ken Landreaux	.07	.05	.03	225	Barbaro Garbey		.05	.04	.02
135	Bill Madlock	.12	.09	.05	226	Kirk Gibson		.25	.20	.10
136	Candy Maldonado	.10	.08	.04	227	John Grubb		.05	.04	.02
137	Mike Marshall	.10	.08	.04	228	Willie Hernandez		.07	.05	.03
138	Len Matuszek	.05	.04	.02	229	Larry Herndon		.07	.05	.03
139	Tom Niedenfuer	.07	.05	.03	230	Chet Lemon		.07	.05	.03
140	Alejandro Pena	.05	.04	.02	231	Aurelio Lopez		.05	.04	.02
141	Jerry Reuss	.07	.05	.03	232	Jack Morris		.20	.15	.08
142	Bill Russell	.07	.05	.03	233	Randy O'Neal		.05	.04	.02
143	Steve Sax	.15	.11	.06	234	Lance Parrish		.20	.15	.08
144	Mike Scioscia	.05	.04	.02	235	Dan Petry		.10	.08	.04
145	Fernando Valenzuela	.30	.25	.12	236	Alex Sanchez		.05	.04	.02
146	Bob Welch	.10	.08	.04	237	Bill Scherrer		.05	.04	.02
147	Terry Whitfield	.05	.04	.02	238	Nelson Simmons		.10	.08	.04
148	Juan Beniquez	.05	.04	.02	239	Frank Tanana		.10	.08	.04
149	Bob Boone	.07	.05	.03	240	Walt Terrell		.07	.05	.03
150	John Candelaria	.10	.08	.04	241	Alan Trammell		.30	.25	.12

		MT	NR MT	EX
242	Lou Whitaker	.20	.15	.08
243	Milt Wilcox	.07	.05	.03
244	Hubie Brooks	.10	.08	.04
245	Tim Burke	.30	.25	.12
246	Andre Dawson	.20	.15	.08
247	Mike Fitzgerald	.05	.04	.02
248	Terry Francona	.05	.04	.02
249	Bill Gullickson	.07	.05	.03
250	Joe Hesketh	.07	.05	.03
251	Bill Laskey	.05	.04	.02
252	Vance Law	.07	.05	.03
253	Charlie Lea	.05	.04	.02
254	Gary Lucas	.05	.04	.02
255	David Palmer	.07	.05	.03
256	Tim Raines	.30	.25	.12
257	Jeff Reardon	.15	.11	.06
258	Bert Roberge	.05	.04	.02
259	Dan Schatzeder	.05	.04	.02
260	Bryn Smith	.07	.05	.03
261	Randy St. Claire	.07	.05	.03
262	Scot Thompson	.05	.04	.02
263	Tim Wallach	.12	.09	.05
264	U.L. Washington	.05	.04	.02
265	Mitch Webster	.40	.30	.15
266	Herm Winningham	.20	.15	.08
267	Floyd Youmans	.60	.45	.25
268	Don Aase	.07	.05	.03
269	Mike Boddicker	.10	.08	.04
270	Rich Dauer	.05	.04	.02
271	Storm Davis	.05	.04	.02
272	Rick Dempsey	.07	.05	.03
273	Ken Dixon	.07	.05	.03
274	Jim Dwyer	.05	.04	.02
275	Mike Flanagan	.10	.08	.04
276	Wayne Gross	.05	.04	.02
277	Lee Lacy	.07	.05	.03
278	Fred Lynn	.20	.15	.08
279	Tippy Martinez	.05	.04	.02
280	Dennis Martinez	.05	.04	.02
281	Scott McGregor	.07	.05	.03
282	Eddie Murray	.40	.30	.15
283	Floyd Rayford	.05	.04	.02
284	Cal Ripken, Jr.	.40	.30	.15
285	Gary Roenicke	.05	.04	.02
286	Larry Sheets	.30	.25	.12
287	John Shelby	.07	.05	.03
288	Nate Snell	.07	.05	.03
289	Sammy Stewart	.05	.04	.02
290	Alan Wiggins	.05	.04	.02
291	Mike Young	.07	.05	.03
292	Alan Ashby	.05	.04	.02
293	Mark Bailey	.05	.04	.02
294	Kevin Bass	.10	.08	.04
295	Jeff Calhoun	.05	.04	.02
296	Jose Cruz	.10	.08	.04
297	Glenn Davis	.70	.50	.30
298	Bill Dawley	.05	.04	.02
299	Frank DiPino	.05	.04	.02
300	Bill Doran	.10	.08	.04
301	Phil Garner	.07	.05	.03
302	Jeff Heathcock	.12	.09	.05
303	Charlie Kerfeld	.30	.25	.12
304	Bob Knepper	.07	.05	.03
305	Ron Mathis	.10	.08	.04
306	Jerry Mumphrey	.07	.05	.03
307	Jim Pankovits	.05	.04	.02
308	Terry Puhl	.05	.04	.02
309	Craig Reynolds	.05	.04	.02
310	Nolan Ryan	.30	.25	.12
311	Mike Scott	.15	.11	.06
312	Dave Smith	.07	.05	.03
313	Dickie Thon	.07	.05	.03
314	Denny Walling	.05	.04	.02
315	Kurt Bevacqua	.05	.04	.02
316	Al Bumbry	.05	.04	.02
317	Jerry Davis	.05	.04	.02
318	Luis DeLeon	.05	.04	.02
319	Dave Dravecky	.07	.05	.03
320	Tim Flannery	.05	.04	.02
321	Steve Garvey	.30	.25	.12
322	Goose Gossage	.20	.15	.08
323	Tony Gwynn	.40	.30	.15
324	Andy Hawkins	.05	.04	.02
325	LaMarr Hoyt	.07	.05	.03
326	Roy Lee Jackson	.05	.04	.02
327	Terry Kennedy	.07	.05	.03
328	Craig Lefferts	.05	.04	.02
329	Carmelo Martinez	.07	.05	.03
330	Lance McCullers	.20	.15	.08
331	Kevin McReynolds	.15	.11	.06
332	Graig Nettles	.15	.11	.06

		MT	NR MT	EX
333	Jerry Royster	.05	.04	.02
334	Eric Show	.05	.04	.02
335	Tim Stoddard	.05	.04	.02
336	Garry Templeton	.10	.08	.04
337	Mark Thurmond	.05	.04	.02
338	Ed Wojna	.10	.08	.04
339	Tony Armas	.10	.08	.04
340	Marty Barrett	.10	.08	.04
341	Wade Boggs	2.25	1.75	.90
342	Dennis Boyd	.07	.05	.03
343	Bill Buckner	.12	.09	.05
344	Mark Clear	.07	.05	.03
345	Roger Clemens	3.00	2.25	1.25
346	Steve Crawford	.05	.04	.02
347	Mike Easler	.07	.05	.03
348	Dwight Evans	.12	.09	.05
349	Rich Gedman	.10	.08	.04
350	Jackie Gutierrez	.05	.04	.02
351	Glenn Hoffman	.05	.04	.02
352	Bruce Hurst	.10	.08	.04
353	Bruce Kison	.05	.04	.02
354	Tim Lollar	.05	.04	.02
355	Steve Lyons	.07	.05	.03
356	Al Nipper	.07	.05	.03
357	Bob Ojeda	.10	.08	.04
358	Jim Rice	.30	.25	.12
359	Bob Stanley	.07	.05	.03
360	Mike Trujillo	.12	.09	.05
361	Thad Bosley	.05	.04	.02
362	Warren Brusstar	.05	.04	.02
363	Ron Cey	.10	.08	.04
364	Jody Davis	.10	.08	.04
365	Bob Dernier	.05	.04	.02
366	Shawon Dunston	.20	.15	.08
367	Leon Durham	.10	.08	.04
368	Dennis Eckersley	.07	.05	.03
369	Ray Fontenot	.05	.04	.02
370	George Frazier	.05	.04	.02
371	Bill Hatcher	.15	.11	.06
372	Dave Lopes	.07	.05	.03
373	Gary Matthews	.10	.08	.04
374	Ron Meredith	.10	.08	.04
375	Keith Moreland	.07	.05	.03
376	Reggie Patterson	.05	.04	.02
377	Dick Ruthven	.05	.04	.02
378	Ryne Sandberg	.30	.25	.12
379	Scott Sanderson	.07	.05	.03
380	Lee Smith	.10	.08	.04
381	Lary Sorensen	.05	.04	.02
382	Chris Speier	.05	.04	.02
383	Rick Sutcliffe	.12	.09	.05
384	Steve Trout	.07	.05	.03
385	Gary Woods	.05	.04	.02
386	Bert Blyleven	.15	.11	.06
387	Tom Brunansky	.12	.09	.05
388	Randy Bush	.05	.04	.02
389	John Butcher	.05	.04	.02
390	Ron Davis	.05	.04	.02
391	Dave Engle	.05	.04	.02
392	Frank Eufemia	.05	.04	.02
393	Pete Filson	.05	.04	.02
394	Gary Gaetti	.20	.15	.08
395	Greg Gagne	.20	.15	.08
396	Mickey Hatcher	.05	.04	.02
397	Kent Hrbek	.20	.15	.08
398	Tim Laudner	.05	.04	.02
399	Rick Lysander	.05	.04	.02
400	Dave Meier	.05	.04	.02
401	Kirby Puckett	1.25	.90	.50
402	Mark Salas	.07	.05	.03
403	Ken Schrom	.05	.04	.02
404	Roy Smalley	.05	.04	.02
405	Mike Smithson	.05	.04	.02
406	Mike Stenhouse	.05	.04	.02
407	Tim Teufel	.07	.05	.03
408	Frank Viola	.12	.09	.05
409	Ron Washington	.05	.04	.02
410	Keith Atherton	.05	.04	.02
411	Dusty Baker	.07	.05	.03
412	Tim Birtsas	.10	.08	.04
413	Bruce Bochte	.05	.04	.02
414	Chris Codiroli	.05	.04	.02
415	Dave Collins	.07	.05	.03
416	Mike Davis	.07	.05	.03
417	Alfredo Griffin	.07	.05	.03
418	Mike Heath	.05	.04	.02
419	Steve Henderson	.05	.04	.02
420	Donnie Hill	.05	.04	.02
421	Jay Howell	.07	.05	.03
422	Tommy John	.20	.15	.08
423	Dave Kingman	.15	.11	.06

		MT	NR MT	EX			MT	NR MT	EX
424	Bill Krueger	.05	.04	.02	515	Gene Garber	.05	.04	.02
425	Rick Langford	.05	.04	.02	516	Terry Harper	.05	.04	.02
426	Carney Lansford	.07	.05	.03	517	Bob Horner	.20	.15	.08
427	Steve McCatty	.05	.04	.02	518	Glenn Hubbard	.05	.04	.02
428	Dwayne Murphy	.07	.05	.03	519	Joe Johnson	.12	.09	.05
429	Steve Ontiveros	.20	.15	.08	520	Brad Komminsk	.05	.04	.02
430	Tony Phillips	.05	.04	.02	521	Rick Mahler	.05	.04	.02
431	Jose Rijo	.07	.05	.03	522	Dale Murphy	.50	.40	.20
432	Mickey Tettleton	.10	.08	.04	523	Ken Oberkfell	.07	.05	.03
433	Luis Aguayo	.05	.04	.02	524	Pascual Perez	.07	.05	.03
434	Larry Andersen	.05	.04	.02	525	Gerald Perry	.07	.05	.03
435	Steve Carlton	.30	.25	.12	526	Rafael Ramirez	.05	.04	.02
436	Don Carman	.30	.25	.12	527	Steve Shields	.10	.08	.04
437	Tim Corcoran	.05	.04	.02	528	Zane Smith	.10	.08	.04
438	Darren Daulton	.15	.11	.06	529	Bruce Sutter	.15	.11	.06
439	John Denny	.05	.04	.02	530	Milt Thompson	.40	.30	.15
440	Tom Foley	.05	.04	.02	531	Claudell Washington	.07	.05	.03
441	Greg Gross	.05	.04	.02	532	Paul Zuvella	.05	.04	.02
442	Kevin Gross	.07	.05	.03	533	Vida Blue	.10	.08	.04
443	Von Hayes	.12	.09	.05	534	Bob Brenly	.05	.04	.02
444	Charles Hudson	.07	.05	.03	535	Chris Brown	.80	.60	.30
445	Garry Maddox	.07	.05	.03	536	Chili Davis	.10	.08	.04
446	Shane Rawley	.10	.08	.04	537	Mark Davis	.05	.04	.02
447	Dave Rucker	.05	.04	.02	538	Rob Deer	.12	.09	.05
448	John Russell	.07	.05	.03	539	Dan Driessen	.07	.05	.03
449	Juan Samuel	.12	.09	.05	540	Scott Garrelts	.07	.05	.03
450	Mike Schmidt	.40	.30	.15	541	Dan Gladden	.10	.08	.04
451	Rick Schu	.07	.05	.03	542	Jim Gott	.05	.04	.02
452	Dave Shipanoff	.07	.05	.03	543	David Green	.05	.04	.02
453	Dave Stewart	.10	.08	.04	544	Atlee Hammaker	.05	.04	.02
454	Jeff Stone	.07	.05	.03	545	Mike Jeffcoat	.05	.04	.02
455	Kent Tekulve	.07	.05	.03	546	Mike Krukow	.07	.05	.03
456	Ozzie Virgil	.07	.05	.03	547	Dave LaPoint	.05	.04	.02
457	Glenn Wilson	.10	.08	.04	548	Jeff Leonard	.10	.08	.04
458	Jim Beattie	.05	.04	.02	549	Greg Minton	.05	.04	.02
459	Karl Best	.07	.05	.03	550	Alex Trevino	.05	.04	.02
460	Barry Bonnell	.05	.04	.02	551	Manny Trillo	.07	.05	.03
461	Phil Bradley	.20	.15	.08	552	Jose Uribe	.25	.20	.10
462	Ivan Calderon	.50	.40	.20	553	Brad Wellman	.05	.04	.02
463	Al Cowens	.05	.04	.02	554	Frank Williams	.07	.05	.03
464	Alvin Davis	.20	.15	.08	555	Joel Youngblood	.05	.04	.02
465	Dave Henderson	.05	.04	.02	556	Alan Bannister	.05	.04	.02
466	Bob Kearney	.05	.04	.02	557	Glenn Brummer	.05	.04	.02
467	Mark Langston	.12	.09	.05	558	Steve Buechele	.20	.15	.08
468	Bob Long	.05	.04	.02	559	Jose Guzman	.30	.25	.12
469	Mike Moore	.05	.04	.02	560	Toby Harrah	.07	.05	.03
470	Edwin Nunez	.05	.04	.02	561	Greg Harris	.05	.04	.02
471	Spike Owen	.05	.04	.02	562	Dwayne Henry	.10	.08	.04
472	Jack Perconte	.05	.04	.02	563	Burt Hooton	.07	.05	.03
473	Jim Presley	.20	.15	.08	564	Charlie Hough	.10	.08	.04
474	Donnie Scott	.05	.04	.02	565	Mike Mason	.05	.04	.02
475	Bill Swift	.07	.05	.03	566	Oddibe McDowell	.40	.30	.15
476	Danny Tartabull	.50	.40	.20	567	Dickie Noles	.05	.04	.02
477	Gorman Thomas	.10	.08	.04	568	Pete O'Brien	.10	.08	.04
478	Roy Thomas	.05	.04	.02	569	Larry Parrish	.10	.08	.04
479	Ed Vande Berg	.05	.04	.02	570	Dave Rozema	.05	.04	.02
480	Frank Wills	.05	.04	.02	571	Dave Schmidt	.07	.05	.03
481	Matt Young	.05	.04	.02	572	Don Slaught	.05	.04	.02
482	Ray Burris	.05	.04	.02	573	Wayne Tolleson	.05	.04	.02
483	Jaime Cocanower	.05	.04	.02	574	Duane Walker	.05	.04	.02
484	Cecil Cooper	.12	.09	.05	575	Gary Ward	.07	.05	.03
485	Danny Darwin	.07	.05	.03	576	Chris Welsh	.05	.04	.02
486	Rollie Fingers	.20	.15	.08	577	Curtis Wilkerson	.05	.04	.02
487	Jim Gantner	.07	.05	.03	578	George Wright	.05	.04	.02
488	Bob Gibson	.05	.04	.02	579	Chris Bando	.05	.04	.02
489	Moose Haas	.05	.04	.02	580	Tony Bernazard	.07	.05	.03
490	Teddy Higuera	1.25	.90	.50	581	Brett Butler	.07	.05	.03
491	Paul Householder	.05	.04	.02	582	Ernie Camacho	.05	.04	.02
492	Pete Ladd	.05	.04	.02	583	Joe Carter	.20	.15	.08
493	Rick Manning	.05	.04	.02	584	Carmello Castillo (Carmelo)	.05	.04	.02
494	Bob McClure	.05	.04	.02	585	Jamie Easterly	.05	.04	.02
495	Paul Molitor	.15	.11	.06	586	Julio Franco	.10	.08	.04
496	Charlie Moore	.05	.04	.02	587	Mel Hall	.07	.05	.03
497	Ben Oglivie	.07	.05	.03	588	Mike Hargrove	.07	.05	.03
498	Randy Ready	.05	.04	.02	589	Neal Heaton	.07	.05	.03
499	Earnie Riles	.30	.25	.12	590	Brook Jacoby	.10	.08	.04
500	Ed Romero	.05	.04	.02	591	Otis Nixon	.10	.08	.04
501	Bill Schroeder	.05	.04	.02	592	Jerry Reed	.10	.08	.04
502	Ray Searage	.05	.04	.02	593	Vern Ruhle	.05	.04	.02
503	Ted Simmons	.12	.09	.05	594	Pat Tabler	.07	.05	.03
504	Pete Vuckovich	.07	.05	.03	595	Rich Thompson	.05	.04	.02
505	Rick Waits	.05	.04	.02	596	Andre Thornton	.07	.05	.03
506	Robin Yount	.30	.25	.12	597	Dave Von Ohlen	.05	.04	.02
507	Len Barker	.07	.05	.03	598	George Vukovich	.05	.04	.02
508	Steve Bedrosian	.12	.09	.05	599	Tom Waddell	.05	.04	.02
509	Bruce Benedict	.05	.04	.02	600	Curt Wardle	.05	.04	.02
510	Rick Camp	.05	.04	.02	601	Jerry Willard	.05	.04	.02
511	Rick Cerone	.05	.04	.02	602	Bill Almon	.05	.04	.02
512	Chris Chambliss	.07	.05	.03	603	Mike Bielecki	.07	.05	.03
513	Jeff Dedmon	.05	.04	.02	604	Sid Bream	.10	.08	.04
514	Terry Forster	.07	.05	.03	605	Mike Brown	.05	.04	.02

		MT	NR MT	EX
606	Pat Clements	.15	.11	.06
607	Jose DeLeon	.07	.05	.03
608	Denny Gonzalez	.05	.04	.02
609	Cecilio Guante	.05	.04	.02
610	Steve Kemp	.07	.05	.03
611	Sam Khalifa	.07	.05	.03
612	Lee Mazzilli	.07	.05	.03
613	Larry McWilliams	.05	.04	.02
614	Jim Morrison	.05	.04	.02
615	Joe Orsulak	.12	.09	.05
616	Tony Pena	.10	.08	.04
617	Johnny Ray	.10	.08	.04
618	Rick Reuschel	.10	.08	.04
619	R.J. Reynolds	.10	.08	.04
620	Rick Rhoden	.10	.08	.04
621	Don Robinson	.07	.05	.03
622	Jason Thompson	.05	.04	.02
623	Lee Tunnell	.05	.04	.02
624	Jim Winn	.05	.04	.02
625	Marvell Wynne	.05	.04	.02
626	Gooden In Action (Dwight Gooden)	.50	.40	.20
627	Mattingly In Action (Don Mattingly)	1.25	.90	.50
628	4,192! (Pete Rose)	.50	.40	.20
629	3,000 Career Hits (Rod Carew)	.20	.15	.08
630	300 Career Wins (Phil Niekro, Tom Seaver)	.20	.15	.08
631	Ouch! (Don Baylor)	.07	.05	.03
632	Instant Offense (Tim Raines, Darryl Strawberry)	.30	.25	.12
633	Shortstops Supreme (Cal Ripken, Jr., Alan Trammell)	.30	.25	.12
634	Boggs & "Hero" (Wade Boggs, George Brett)	.60	.45	.25
635	Braves Dynamic Duo (Bob Horner, Dale Murphy)	.30	.25	.12
636	Cardinal Ignitors (Vince Coleman, Willie McGee)	.35	.25	.14
637	Terror on the Basepaths (Vince Coleman)	.35	.25	.14
638	Charlie Hustle & Dr. K (Dwight Gooden, Pete Rose)	.70	.50	.30
639	1984 and 1985 A.L. Batting Champs (Wade Boggs, Don Mattingly)	1.50	1.25	.60
640	N.L. West Sluggers (Steve Garvey, Dale Murphy, Dave Parker)	.30	.25	.12
641	Staff Aces (Dwight Gooden, Fernando Valenzuela)	.40	.30	.15
642	Blue Jay Stoppers (Jimmy Key, Dave Stieb)	.10	.08	.04
643	A.L. All-Star Backstops (Carlton Fisk, Rich Gedman)	.10	.08	.04
644	Major League Prospect (Benito Santiago, Gene Walter)	5.00	3.75	2.00
645	Major League Prospects (Colin Ward, Mike Woodard)	.12	.09	.05
646	Major League Prospects (Kal Daniels, Paul O'Neill)	3.75	2.75	1.50
647	Major League Prospects (Andres Galarraga, Fred Toliver)	1.25	.90	.50
648	Major League Prospects (Curt Ford, Bob Kipper)	.25	.20	.10
649	Major League Prospects (Jose Canseco, Eric Plunk)	8.00	6.00	3.25
650	Major League Prospects (Mark McLemore, Gus Polidor)	.20	.15	.08
651	Major League Prospects (Mickey Brantley, Rob Woodward)	.30	.25	.12
652	Major League Prospects (Mark Funderburk, Billy Joe Robidoux)	.15	.11	.06
653	Major League Prospects (Cecil Fielder, Cory Snyder)	3.50	2.75	1.50
654	Checklist 1-97	.05	.04	.02
655	Checklist 98-196	.05	.04	.02
656	Checklist 197-291	.05	.04	.02
657	Checklist 292-385	.05	.04	.02
658	Checklist 386-482	.05	.04	.02
659	Checklist 482-578	.05	.04	.02
660	Checklist 579-660	.05	.04	.02

1986 Fleer All Star Team

Fleer's choices for a major league All-Star team make up this 12-card set. The cards, which measure 2½'' by 3½'', were randomly inserted in 35¢ wax packs and 59¢ cello packs. The card fronts have a color photo set against a bright red background for

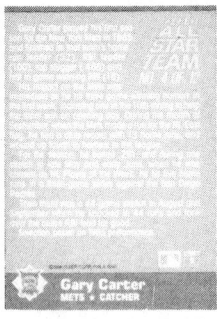

A.L. players or a bright blue background for N.L. players. The card backs feature the player's career highlights set in white type against a red and blue background.

		MT	NR MT	EX
	Complete Set:	20.00	15.00	8.00
	Common Player:	.60	.45	.25
1	Don Mattingly	7.50	5.75	3.00
2	Tom Herr	.60	.45	.25
3	George Brett	2.00	1.50	.80
4	Gary Carter	1.00	.70	.40
5	Cal Ripken, Jr.	1.50	1.25	.60
6	Dave Parker	.75	.60	.30
7	Rickey Henderson	1.50	1.25	.60
8	Pedro Guerrero	.75	.60	.30
9	Dan Quisenberry	.60	.45	.25
10	Dwight Gooden	3.00	2.25	1.25
11	Gorman Thomas	.60	.45	.25
12	John Tudor	.60	.45	.25

1986 Fleer Baseball's Best

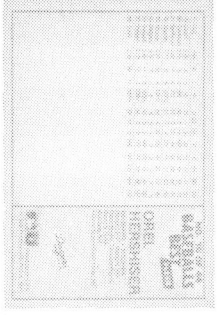

The 1986 Fleer Baseball's Best set consists of 44 cards and was produced for McCrory's store chain and their affiliated stores. Subtitled "Sluggers vs. Pitchers", the set contains 22 each of the game's best hitters and pitchers. The cards, which measure 2½'' by 3½'', have color photos depicting an action pose. The backs are done in blue and red ink on white stock and carry the player's personal and statistical information. The sets were issued in a specially designed box with six team logo stickers.

		MT	NR MT	EX
	Complete Set:	6.00	6.00	3.25
	Common Player:	.05	.07	.04
1	Bert Blyleven	.12	.09	.05
2	Wade Boggs	.60	.70	.35
3	George Brett	.30	.45	.25
4	Tom Browning	.10	.07	.04
5	Jose Canseco	1.00	1.75	.90
6	Will Clark	.70	.90	.50

		MT	NR MT	EX
7	Roger Clemens	.70	1.25	.60
8	Alvin Davis	.10	.15	.08
9	Julio Franco	.10	.09	.05
10	Kirk Gibson	.20	.20	.10
11	Dwight Gooden	.70	.70	.35
12	Goose Gossage	.12	.09	.05
13	Pedro Guerrero	.15	.15	.08
14	Ron Guidry	.15	.09	.05
15	Tony Gwynn	.25	.25	.14
16	Orel Hershiser	.15	.15	.08
17	Kent Hrbek	.15	.15	.08
18	Reggie Jackson	.25	.35	.20
19	Wally Joyner	1.50	1.75	.90
20	Charlie Leibrandt	.05	.07	.04
21	Don Mattingly	1.50	1.25	.60
22	Willie McGee	.12	.15	.08
23	Jack Morris	.15	.15	.08
24	Dale Murphy	.30	.45	.25
25	Eddie Murray	.25	.35	.20
26	Jeff Reardon	.12	.09	.05
27	Rick Reuschel	.07	.07	.04
28	Cal Ripken, Jr	.25	.35	.20
29	Pete Rose	.60	.60	.30
30	Nolan Ryan	.20	.25	.12
31	Bret Saberhagen	.20	.15	.08
32	Ryne Sandberg	.20	.25	.12
33	Mike Schmidt	.30	.45	.25
34	Tom Seaver	.20	.20	.10
35	Bryn Smith	.05	.07	.04
36	Mario Soto	.05	.07	.04
37	Dave Stieb	.07	.09	.05
38	Darryl Strawberry	.30	.35	.20
39	Rick Sutcliffe	.10	.09	.05
40	John Tudor	.07	.07	.04
41	Fernando Valenzuela	.20	.20	.10
42	Bobby Witt	.20	.35	.20
43	Mike Witt	.10	.09	.05
44	Robin Yount	.20	.15	.08

1986 Fleer Box Panels

Picking up on a Donruss idea, Fleer issued eight cards in panels of four on the bottoms of their wax and cello pack boxes. The cards are numbered C-1 through C-8 and are 2½'' by 3½'', with a complete panel measuring 5'' by 7⅛'' in size. Included in the eight cards are six player cards and two team logo/checklist cards.

		MT	NR MT	EX
Complete Panel Set:		4.00	3.00	1.50
Complete Singles Set:		1.75	1.25	.70
Common Single Player:		.20	.15	.08
Panel		2.75	2.00	1.00
1	Royals Logo/Checklist	.05	.04	.02
2	George Brett	.60	.45	.25
3	Ozzie Guillen	.40	.30	.15
4	Dale Murphy	.60	.45	.25
Panel		1.50	1.25	.60
5	Cardinals Logo/Checklist	.05	.04	.02
6	Tom Browning	.20	.15	.08
7	Gary Carter	.35	.25	.14
8	Carlton Fisk	.20	.15	.08

1986 Fleer Future Hall of Famers

 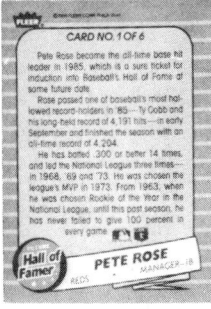

The 1986 Fleer Future Hall of Famers set is comprised of six players Fleer felt would gain eventual entrance into the Baseball Hall of Fame. The cards are the standard 2½'' by 3½'' in size and were randomly inserted in 3-pack cello packs. The card fronts feature a player photo set against a blue background with horizontal light blue stripes. The card backs are printed in black on a blue background and feature player highlights in paragraph form.

		MT	NR MT	EX
Complete Set:		8.00	6.00	3.25
Common Player:		1.25	.90	.50
1	Pete Rose	2.00	1.50	.80
2	Steve Carlton	1.25	.90	.50
3	Tom Seaver	1.25	.90	.50
4	Rod Carew	1.25	.90	.50
5	Nolan Ryan	1.25	.90	.50
6	Reggie Jackson	1.25	.90	.50

1986 Fleer League Leaders

 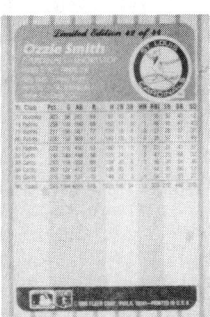

Fleer's 1986 "League Leaders" set features 44 of the game's top players and was issued through the Walgreens drug store chain. The card fronts contain a color photo and feature the player's name, team and position in a blue band near the bottom of the card. The words "League Leaders" appear in a red band at the top of the card. The background for the card fronts is alternating blue and white stripes. The cards backs are printed in blue, red and white and carry the player's statistical information and team logo. The cards are the standard 2½'' by 3½'' size. The set was issued in a special cardboard box, along with six team logo stickers.

	MT	NR MT	EX
Complete Set:	6.00	4.50	2.50
Common Player:	.05	.04	.02

		MT	NR MT	EX
1	Wade Boggs	.60	.45	.25
2	George Brett	.30	.25	.12
3	Jose Canseco	1.50	1.25	.60
4	Rod Carew	.25	.20	.10
5	Gary Carter	.20	.15	.08
6	Jack Clark	.12	.09	.05
7	Vince Coleman	.80	.60	.30
8	Jose Cruz	.07	.05	.03
9	Alvin Davis	.10	.08	.04
10	Mariano Duncan	.07	.05	.03
11	Leon Durham	.07	.05	.03
12	Carlton Fisk	.15	.11	.06
13	Julio Franco	.10	.08	.04
14	Scott Garrelts	.05	.04	.02
15	Steve Garvey	.20	.15	.08
16	Dwight Gooden	.60	.45	.25
17	Ozzie Guillen	.15	.11	.06
18	Willie Hernandez	.07	.05	.03
19	Bob Horner	.10	.08	.04
20	Kent Hrbek	.15	.11	.06
21	Charlie Leibrandt	.05	.04	.02
22	Don Mattingly	1.50	1.25	.60
23	Oddibe McDowell	.15	.11	.06
24	Willie McGee	.10	.08	.04
25	Keith Moreland	.05	.04	.02
26	Lloyd Moseby	.07	.05	.03
27	Dale Murphy	.30	.25	.12
28	Phil Niekro	.15	.11	.06
29	Joe Orsulak	.07	.05	.03
30	Dave Parker	.15	.11	.06
31	Lance Parrish	.15	.11	.06
32	Kirby Puckett	.25	.20	.10
33	Tim Raines	.25	.20	.10
34	Earnie Riles	.10	.08	.04
35	Cal Ripken, Jr.	.25	.20	.10
36	Pete Rose	.60	.45	.25
37	Bret Saberhagen	.15	.11	.06
38	Juan Samuel	.10	.08	.04
39	Ryne Sandberg	.20	.15	.08
40	Tom Seaver	.20	.15	.08
41	Lee Smith	.07	.05	.03
42	Ozzie Smith	.12	.09	.05
43	Dave Stieb	.07	.05	.03
44	Robin Yount	.20	.15	.08

		MT	NR MT	EX
8	Chris Brown	.25	.20	.10
9	Tom Brunansky	.10	.08	.04
10	Gary Carter	.20	.15	.08
11	Vince Coleman	.60	.45	.25
12	Cecil Cooper	.10	.08	.04
13	Jose Cruz	.07	.05	.03
14	Mike Davis	.05	.04	.02
15	Carlton Fisk	.15	.11	.06
16	Julio Franco	.10	.08	.04
17	Damaso Garcia	.05	.04	.02
18	Rich Gedman	.05	.04	.02
19	Kirk Gibson	.20	.15	.08
20	Dwight Gooden	.70	.50	.30
21	Pedro Guerrero	.15	.11	.06
22	Tony Gwynn	.25	.20	.10
23	Rickey Henderson	.25	.20	.10
24	Orel Hershiser	.12	.09	.05
25	LaMarr Hoyt	.05	.04	.02
26	Reggie Jackson	.25	.20	.10
27	Don Mattingly	1.50	1.25	.60
28	Oddibe McDowell	.15	.11	.06
29	Willie McGee	.10	.08	.04
30	Paul Molitor	.10	.08	.04
31	Dale Murphy	.30	.25	.12
32	Eddie Murray	.25	.20	.10
33	Dave Parker	.15	.11	.06
34	Tony Pena	.07	.05	.03
35	Jeff Reardon	.10	.08	.04
36	Cal Ripken, Jr.	.25	.20	.10
37	Pete Rose	.60	.45	.25
38	Bret Saberhagen	.15	.11	.06
39	Juan Samuel	.12	.09	.05
40	Ryne Sandberg	.20	.15	.08
41	Mike Schmidt	.30	.25	.12
42	Lee Smith	.07	.05	.03
43	Don Sutton	.15	.11	.06
44	Lou Whitaker	.15	.11	.06

1986 Fleer Limited Edition

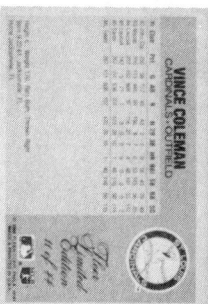

Produced for the McCrory's store chain and their affiliates for the second year in a row, the 1986 Fleer Limited Edition set contains 44 cards. The cards, which are the standard 2½'' by 3½'' size, have color photos enclosed by green, red and yellow trim. The card backs carry black print on two shades of red. The set was issued in a special cardboard box, along with six team logo stickers.

		MT	NR MT	EX
Complete Set:		5.00	3.75	2.00
Common Player:		.06	.05	.02
1	Doyle Alexander	.07	.05	.03
2	Joaquin Andujar	.05	.04	.02
3	Harold Baines	.12	.09	.05
4	Wade Boggs	.60	.45	.25
5	Phil Bradley	.10	.08	.04
6	George Brett	.30	.25	.12
7	Hubie Brooks	.07	.05	.03

1986 Fleer Mini

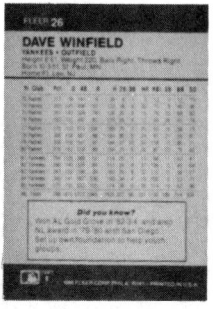

Fleer's 1986 ''Classic Miniatures'' set contains 120 cards that measure 1 13/16'' by 2 9/16'' in size. The design of the high-gloss cards is identical to the regular 1986 Fleer set but the player photos are entirely different. The set, which was issued in a specially designed box along with 18 team logo stickers, was available to the collecting public only through hobby dealers.

		MT	NR MT	EX
Complete Set:		8.00	6.00	3.25
Common Player:		.05	.04	.02
1	George Brett	.30	.25	.12
2	Dan Quisenberry	.10	.08	.04
3	Bret Saberhagen	.15	.11	.06
4	Lonnie Smith	.05	.04	.02
5	Willie Wilson	.10	.08	.04
6	Jack Clark	.12	.09	.05
7	Vince Coleman	.50	.40	.20
8	Tom Herr	.07	.05	.03
9	Willie McGee	.10	.08	.04
10	Ozzie Smith	.12	.09	.05
11	John Tudor	.07	.05	.03
12	Jesse Barfield	.12	.09	.05
13	George Bell	.20	.15	.08
14	Tony Fernandez	.10	.08	.04

		MT	NR MT	EX
15	Damaso Garcia	.05	.04	.02
16	Dave Stieb	.07	.05	.03
17	Gary Carter	.20	.15	.08
18	Ron Darling	.10	.08	.04
19	Dwight Gooden	.60	.45	.25
20	Keith Hernandez	.20	.15	.08
21	Darryl Strawberry	.30	.25	.12
22	Ron Guidry	.15	.11	.06
23	Rickey Henderson	.25	.20	.10
24	Don Mattingly	1.50	1.25	.60
25	Dave Righetti	.12	.09	.05
26	Dave Winfield	.20	.15	.08
27	Mariano Duncan	.07	.05	.03
28	Pedro Guerrero	.12	.09	.05
29	Bill Madlock	.10	.08	.04
30	Mike Marshall	.10	.08	.04
31	Fernando Valenzuela	.20	.15	.08
32	Reggie Jackson	.30	.25	.12
33	Gary Pettis	.05	.04	.02
34	Ron Romanick	.05	.04	.02
35	Don Sutton	.15	.11	.06
36	Mike Witt	.10	.08	.04
37	Buddy Bell	.07	.05	.03
38	Tom Browning	.07	.05	.03
39	Dave Parker	.12	.09	.05
40	Pete Rose	.60	.45	.25
41	Mario Soto	.05	.04	.02
42	Harold Baines	.10	.08	.04
43	Carlton Fisk	.15	.11	.06
44	Ozzie Guillen	.15	.11	.06
45	Ron Kittle	.07	.05	.03
46	Tom Seaver	.20	.15	.08
47	Kirk Gibson	.20	.15	.08
48	Jack Morris	.15	.11	.06
49	Lance Parrish	.15	.11	.06
50	Alan Trammell	.20	.15	.08
51	Lou Whitaker	.15	.11	.06
52	Hubie Brooks	.07	.05	.03
53	Andre Dawson	.15	.11	.06
54	Tim Raines	.20	.15	.08
55	Bryn Smith	.05	.04	.02
56	Tim Wallach	.10	.08	.04
57	Mike Boddicker	.07	.05	.03
58	Eddie Murray	.25	.20	.10
59	Cal Ripken	.25	.20	.10
60	John Shelby	.05	.04	.02
61	Mike Young	.07	.05	.03
62	Jose Cruz	.07	.05	.03
63	Glenn Davis	.15	.11	.06
64	Phil Garner	.05	.04	.02
65	Nolan Ryan	.20	.15	.08
66	Mike Scott	.12	.09	.05
67	Steve Garvey	.20	.15	.08
68	Goose Gossage	.12	.09	.05
69	Tony Gwynn	.25	.20	.10
70	Andy Hawkins	.05	.04	.02
71	Garry Templeton	.07	.05	.03
72	Wade Boggs	.60	.45	.25
73	Roger Clemens	.60	.45	.25
74	Dwight Evans	.12	.09	.05
75	Rich Gedman	.05	.04	.02
76	Jim Rice	.20	.15	.08
77	Shawon Dunston	.10	.08	.04
78	Leon Durham	.10	.08	.04
79	Keith Moreland	.05	.04	.02
80	Ryne Sandberg	.20	.15	.08
81	Rick Sutcliffe	.10	.08	.04
82	Bert Blyleven	.12	.09	.05
83	Tom Brunansky	.10	.08	.04
84	Kent Hrbek	.15	.11	.06
85	Kirby Puckett	.20	.15	.08
86	Bruce Bochte	.05	.04	.02
87	Jose Canseco	1.50	1.25	.60
88	Mike Davis	.05	.04	.02
89	Jay Howell	.05	.04	.02
90	Dwayne Murphy	.05	.04	.02
91	Steve Carlton	.20	.15	.08
92	Von Hayes	.07	.05	.03
93	Juan Samuel	.12	.09	.05
94	Mike Schmidt	.30	.25	.12
95	Glenn Wilson	.07	.05	.03
96	Phil Bradley	.10	.08	.04
97	Alvin Davis	.10	.08	.04
98	Jim Presley	.10	.08	.04
99	Danny Tartabull	.15	.11	.06
100	Cecil Cooper	.10	.08	.04
101	Paul Molitor	.12	.09	.05
102	Earnie Riles	.10	.08	.04
103	Robin Yount	.20	.15	.08
104	Bob Horner	.10	.08	.04
105	Dale Murphy	.30	.25	.12

		MT	NR MT	EX
106	Bruce Sutter	.10	.08	.04
107	Claudell Washington	.05	.04	.02
108	Chris Brown	.20	.15	.08
109	Chili Davis	.07	.05	.03
110	Scott Garrelts	.05	.04	.02
111	Oddibe McDowell	.15	.11	.06
112	Pete O'Brien	.07	.05	.03
113	Gary Ward	.05	.04	.02
114	Brett Butler	.05	.04	.02
115	Julio Franco	.10	.08	.04
116	Brook Jacoby	.10	.08	.04
117	Mike Brown	.05	.04	.02
118	Joe Orsulak	.07	.05	.03
119	Tony Pena	.07	.05	.03
120	R.J. Reynolds	.05	.04	.02

1986 Fleer Star Stickers

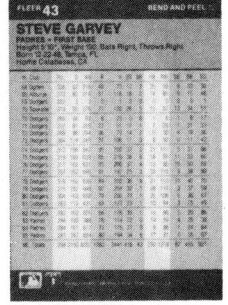

After a five-year layoff, Fleer once again produced a Star Sticker set. The cards, which measure 2½'' by 3½'', have color photos inside dark maroon borders. The card backs are identical to the 1986 regular issue except for the 1-132 numbering system and blue ink instead of yellow. The words ''Bend and Peel'' are found in the upper right corner of the card backs. Card #132 is a multi-player card featuring Dwight Gooden and Dale Murphy on the front and a complete checklist for the set on the reverse. The cards were sold in wax packs with team logo stickers.

		MT	NR MT	EX
Complete Set		24.00	18.00	9.50
Common Player		.05	.04	.02
1	Harold Baines	.20	.15	.08
2	Jesse Barfield	.25	.20	.10
3	Don Baylor	.12	.09	.05
4	Juan Beniquez	.05	.04	.02
5	Tim Birtsas	.08	.06	.03
6	Bert Blyleven	.15	.11	.06
7	Bruce Bochte	.05	.04	.02
8	Wade Boggs	1.50	1.25	.60
9	Dennis Boyd	.12	.09	.05
10	Phil Bradley	.20	.15	.08
11	George Brett	.70	.50	.30
12	Hubie Brooks	.12	.09	.05
13	Chris Brown	.45	.35	.20
14	Tom Browning	.12	.09	.05
15	Tom Brunansky	.15	.11	.06
16	Bill Buckner	.10	.08	.04
17	Britt Burns	.05	.04	.02
18	Brett Butler	.08	.06	.03
19	Jose Canseco	3.50	2.75	1.50
20	Rod Carew	.45	.35	.20
21	Steve Carlton	.40	.30	.15
22	Don Carman	.25	.20	.10
23	Gary Carter	.40	.30	.15
24	Jack Clark	.20	.15	.08
25	Vince Coleman	1.00	.70	.40
26	Cecil Cooper	.15	.11	.06
27	Jose Cruz	.10	.08	.04
28	Ron Darling	.20	.15	.08
29	Alvin Davis	.20	.15	.08
30	Jody Davis	.10	.08	.04
31	Mike Davis	.08	.06	.03
32	Andre Dawson	.25	.20	.10

		MT	NR MT	EX
33	Mariano Duncan	.12	.09	.05
34	Shawon Dunston	.15	.11	.06
35	Leon Durham	.12	.09	.05
36	Darrell Evans	.15	.11	.06
37	Tony Fernandez	.15	.11	.06
38	Carlton Fisk	.20	.15	.08
39	John Franco	.08	.06	.03
40	Julio Franco	.20	.15	.08
41	Damaso Garcia	.05	.04	.02
42	Scott Garrelts	.08	.06	.03
43	Steve Garvey	.40	.30	.15
44	Rich Gedman	.10	.08	.04
45	Kirk Gibson	.30	.25	.12
46	Dwight Gooden	.90	.70	.35
47	Pedro Guerrero	.25	.20	.10
48	Ron Guidry	.20	.15	.08
49	Ozzie Guillen	.35	.25	.14
50	Tony Gwynn	.40	.30	.15
51	Andy Hawkins	.05	.04	.02
52	Von Hayes	.20	.15	.08
53	Rickey Henderson	.60	.45	.25
54	Tom Henke	.12	.09	.05
55	Keith Hernandez	.35	.25	.14
56	Willie Hernandez	.10	.08	.04
57	Tom Herr	.10	.08	.04
58	Orel Hershiser	.20	.15	.08
59	Teddy Higuera	.60	.45	.25
60	Bob Horner	.25	.20	.10
61	Charlie Hough	.08	.06	.03
62	Jay Howell	.08	.06	.03
63	LaMarr Hoyt	.05	.04	.02
64	Kent Hrbek	.30	.25	.12
65	Reggie Jackson	.45	.35	.20
66	Bob James	.05	.04	.02
67	Dave Kingman	.12	.09	.05
68	Ron Kittle	.12	.09	.05
69	Charlie Leibrandt	.08	.06	.03
70	Fred Lynn	.25	.20	.10
71	Mike Marshall	.20	.15	.08
72	Don Mattingly	2.75	2.00	1.00
73	Oddibe McDowell	.25	.20	.10
74	Willie McGee	.25	.20	.10
75	Scott McGregor	.08	.06	.03
76	Paul Molitor	.15	.11	.06
77	Donnie Moore	.05	.04	.02
78	Keith Moreland	.08	.06	.03
79	Jack Morris	.25	.20	.10
80	Dale Murphy	.80	.60	.30
81	Eddie Murray	.50	.40	.20
82	Phil Niekro	.25	.20	.10
83	Joe Orsulak	.15	.11	.06
84	Dave Parker	.25	.20	.10
85	Lance Parrish	.30	.25	.12
86	Larry Parrish	.08	.06	.03
87	Tony Pena	.12	.09	.05
88	Gary Pettis	.12	.09	.05
89	Jim Presley	.20	.15	.08
90	Kirby Puckett	.40	.30	.15
91	Dan Quisenberry	.20	.15	.08
92	Tim Raines	.35	.25	.14
93	Johnny Ray	.12	.09	.05
94	Jeff Reardon	.12	.09	.05
95	Rick Reuschel	.08	.06	.03
96	Jim Rice	.40	.30	.15
97	Dave Righetti	.25	.20	.10
98	Earnie Riles	.20	.15	.08
99	Cal Ripken, Jr.	.60	.45	.25
100	Ron Romanick	.05	.04	.02
101	Pete Rose	1.00	.70	.40
102	Nolan Ryan	.35	.25	.14
103	Bret Saberhagen	.25	.20	.10
104	Mark Salas	.05	.04	.02
105	Juan Samuel	.20	.15	.08
106	Ryne Sandberg	.35	.25	.14
107	Mike Schmidt	.70	.50	.30
108	Mike Scott	.20	.15	.08
109	Tom Seaver	.30	.25	.12
110	Bryn Smith	.05	.04	.02
111	Dave Smith	.08	.06	.03
112	Lee Smith	.10	.08	.04
113	Ozzie Smith	.20	.15	.08
114	Mario Soto	.05	.04	.02
115	Dave Stieb	.12	.09	.05
116	Darryl Strawberry	.50	.40	.20
117	Bruce Sutter	.10	.08	.04
118	Garry Templeton	.12	.09	.05
119	Gorman Thomas	.12	.09	.05
120	Andre Thornton	.12	.09	.05
121	Allan Trammell	.30	.25	.12
122	John Tudor	.10	.08	.04
123	Fernando Valenzuela	.35	.25	.14

		MT	NR MT	EX
124	Frank Viola	.15	.11	.06
125	Gary Ward	.05	.04	.02
126	Lou Whitaker	.25	.20	.10
127	Frank White	.10	.08	.04
128	Glenn Wilson	.12	.09	.05
129	Willie Wilson	.15	.11	.06
130	Dave Winfield	.40	.30	.15
131	Robin Yount	.30	.25	.12
132	Dwight Gooden, Dale Murphy/Checklist	1.25	.90	.50

1986 Fleer Star Stickers Box Panel

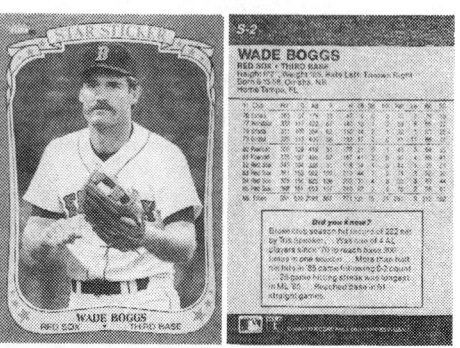

	MT	NR MT	EX
Complete Panel Set:	3.00	2.25	1.25
Complete Singles Set:	1.25	.90	.50
Common Single Player:	.40	.30	.15

		MT	NR MT	EX
Panel		3.00	2.25	1.25
1	Dodgers Logo	.05	.04	.02
2	Wade Boggs	.80	.60	.30
3	Steve Garvey	.30	.25	.12
4	Dave Winfield	.30	.25	.12

1986 Fleer Update

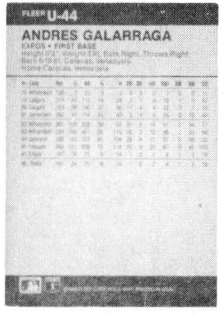

Issued near the end of the baseball season, the 1986 Fleer Update set consists of 132 cards numbered U-1 through U-132. The cards, which measure 2½'' by 3½'' in size, are identical in design to the regular 1986 Fleer set. The purpose of the set is to update player trades and include new players not depicted in the regular issue. The set was issued with team logo stickers in a specially designed box and was available only through hobby dealers.

	MT	NR MT	EX
Complete Set:	16.00	12.00	6.50
Common Player:	.08	.06	.03

		MT	NR MT	EX
1	Mike Aldrete	.50	.40	.20
2	Andy Allanson	.20	.15	.08
3	Neil Allen	.08	.06	.03
4	Joaquin Andujar	.10	.08	.04
5	Paul Assenmacher	.25	.20	.10
6	Scott Bailes	.25	.20	.10
7	Jay Baller	.15	.11	.06
8	Scott Bankhead	.25	.20	.10
9	Bill Bathe	.12	.09	.05
10	Don Baylor	.15	.11	.06
11	Billy Beane	.12	.09	.05
12	Steve Bedrosian	.15	.11	.06
13	Juan Beniquez	.08	.06	.03
14	Barry Bonds	.80	.60	.30
15	Bobby Bonilla	.40	.30	.15
16	Rich Bordi	.08	.06	.03
17	Bill Campbell	.08	.06	.03
18	Tom Candiotti	.08	.06	.03
19	John Cangelosi	.30	.25	.12
20	Jose Canseco	4.00	3.00	1.50
21	Chuck Cary	.20	.15	.08
22	Juan Castillo	.15	.11	.06
23	Rick Cerone	.08	.06	.03
24	John Cerutti	.35	.25	.14
25	Will Clark	3.00	2.25	1.25
26	Mark Clear	.12	.09	.05
27	Darnell Coles	.30	.25	.12
28	Dave Collins	.12	.09	.05
29	Tim Conroy	.08	.06	.03
30	Ed Correa	.30	.25	.12
31	Joe Cowley	.08	.06	.03
32	Bill Dawley	.08	.06	.03
33	Rob Deer	.20	.15	.08
34	John Denny	.08	.06	.03
35	Jim DeShaies (Deshaies)	.35	.25	.14
36	Doug Drabek	.35	.25	.14
37	Mike Easler	.12	.09	.05
38	Mark Eichhorn	.35	.25	.14
39	Dave Engle	.08	.06	.03
40	Mike Fischlin	.08	.06	.03
41	Scott Fletcher	.12	.09	.05
42	Terry Forster	.12	.09	.05
43	Terry Francona	.08	.06	.03
44	Andres Galarraga	.80	.60	.30
45	Lee Guetterman	.30	.25	.12
46	Bill Gullickson	.12	.09	.05
47	Jackie Gutierrez	.08	.06	.03
48	Moose Haas	.08	.06	.03
49	Billy Hatcher	.15	.11	.06
50	Mike Heath	.08	.06	.03
51	Guy Hoffman	.12	.09	.05
52	Tom Hume	.08	.06	.03
53	Pete Incaviglia	2.00	1.50	.80
54	Dane Iorg	.08	.06	.03
55	Chris James	1.00	.70	.40
56	Stan Javier	.12	.09	.05
57	Tommy John	.20	.15	.08
58	Tracy Jones	.70	.50	.30
59	Wally Joyner	3.75	2.75	1.50
60	Wayne Krenchicki	.08	.06	.03
61	John Kruk	1.25	.90	.50
62	Mike LaCoss	.12	.09	.05
63	Pete Ladd	.08	.06	.03
64	Dave LaPoint	.08	.06	.03
65	Mike LaValliere	.12	.09	.05
66	Rudy Law	.08	.06	.03
67	Dennis Leonard	.12	.09	.05
68	Steve Lombardozzi	.30	.25	.12
69	Aurelio Lopez	.08	.06	.03
70	Mickey Mahler	.08	.06	.03
71	Candy Maldonado	.15	.11	.06
72	Roger Mason	.12	.09	.05
73	Greg Mathews	.35	.25	.14
74	Andy McGaffigan	.08	.06	.03
75	Joel McKeon	.15	.11	.06
76	Kevin Mitchell	.60	.45	.25
77	Bill Mooneyham	.15	.11	.06
78	Omar Moreno	.08	.06	.03
79	Jerry Mumphrey	.12	.09	.05
80	Al Newman	.15	.11	.06
81	Phil Niekro	.40	.30	.15
82	Randy Niemann	.08	.06	.03
83	Juan Nieves	.40	.30	.15
84	Bob Ojeda	.15	.11	.06
85	Rick Ownbey	.08	.06	.03
86	Tom Paciorek	.08	.06	.03
87	David Palmer	.12	.09	.05
88	Jeff Parrett	.30	.25	.12
89	Pat Perry	.15	.11	.06
90	Dan Plesac	.40	.30	.15
91	Darrell Porter	.12	.09	.05

		MT	NR MT	EX
92	Luis Quinones	.15	.11	.06
93	Rey Quinonez	.25	.20	.10
94	Gary Redus	.12	.09	.05
95	Jeff Reed	.12	.09	.05
96	Bip Roberts	.12	.09	.05
97	Billy Joe Robidoux	.12	.09	.05
98	Gary Roenicke	.08	.06	.03
99	Ron Roenicke	.08	.06	.03
100	Angel Salazar	.08	.06	.03
101	Joe Sambito	.08	.06	.03
102	Billy Sample	.08	.06	.03
103	Dave Schmidt	.12	.09	.05
104	Ken Schrom	.08	.06	.03
105	Ruben Sierra	2.00	1.50	.80
106	Ted Simmons	.20	.15	.08
107	Sammy Stewart	.08	.06	.03
108	Kurt Stillwell	.50	.40	.20
109	Dale Sveum	.50	.40	.20
110	Tim Teufel	.08	.06	.03
111	Bob Tewksbury	.25	.20	.10
112	Andres Thomas	.25	.20	.10
113	Jason Thompson	.08	.06	.03
114	Milt Thompson	.12	.09	.05
115	Rob Thompson	.35	.25	.14
116	Jay Tibbs	.08	.06	.03
117	Fred Toliver	.12	.09	.05
118	Wayne Tolleson	.08	.06	.03
119	Alex Trevino	.08	.06	.03
120	Manny Trillo	.12	.09	.05
121	Ed Vande Berg	.08	.06	.03
122	Ozzie Virgil	.12	.09	.05
123	Tony Walker	.15	.11	.06
124	Gene Walter	.12	.09	.05
125	Duane Ward	.20	.15	.08
126	Jerry Willard	.08	.06	.03
127	Mitch Williams	.30	.25	.12
128	Reggie Williams	.20	.15	.08
129	Bobby Witt	.40	.30	.15
130	Marvell Wynne	.08	.06	.03
131	Steve Yeager	.08	.06	.03
132	Checklist	.08	.06	.03

1987 Fleer

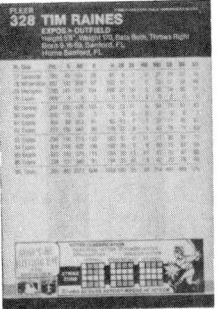

The 1987 Fleer set consists of 660 cards, each measuring 2½'' by 3½''. The card fronts feature an attractive blue and white border. The player's name and position appears in the upper left corner of the card. The player's team logo is located in the lower right corner. The card backs are done in blue, red and white and contain an innovative "Pro Scouts Report" feature which lists the hitter's or pitcher's batting and pitching strengths. For the third year in a row, Fleer included its "Major League Prospects" subset. Fleer produced a glossy-finish Collectors Edition set which came housed in a specially-designed tin box. It was speculated that 100,000 of the glossy sets were produced. After a experiencing a dramatic drop in price during 1987, the glossy set now sells for only a few dollars more than the regular issue.

	MT	NR MT	EX
Complete Set:	36.00	27.00	14.50
Common Player:	.05	.04	.02

#	Player	MT	NR MT	EX
1	Rick Aguilera	.10	.08	.04
2	Richard Anderson	.07	.05	.03
3	Wally Backman	.07	.05	.03
4	Gary Carter	.30	.25	.12
5	Ron Darling	.15	.11	.06
6	Len Dykstra	.15	.11	.06
7	Kevin Elster	.30	.25	.12
8	Sid Fernandez	.12	.09	.05
9	Dwight Gooden	.90	.70	.35
10	Ed Hearn	.12	.09	.05
11	Danny Heep	.05	.04	.02
12	Keith Hernandez	.25	.20	.10
13	Howard Johnson	.12	.09	.05
14	Ray Knight	.10	.08	.04
15	Lee Mazzilli	.07	.05	.03
16	Roger McDowell	.12	.09	.05
17	Kevin Mitchell	.50	.40	.20
18	Randy Niemann	.05	.04	.02
19	Bob Ojeda	.10	.08	.04
20	Jesse Orosco	.07	.05	.03
21	Rafael Santana	.05	.04	.02
22	Doug Sisk	.05	.04	.02
23	Darryl Strawberry	.40	.30	.15
24	Tim Teufel	.05	.04	.02
25	Mookie Wilson	.10	.08	.04
26	Tony Armas	.07	.05	.03
27	Marty Barrett	.10	.08	.04
28	Don Baylor	.12	.09	.05
29	Wade Boggs	1.50	1.25	.60
30	Oil Can Boyd	.07	.05	.03
31	Bill Buckner	.10	.08	.04
32	Roger Clemens	1.00	.70	.40
33	Steve Crawford	.05	.04	.02
34	Dwight Evans	.12	.09	.05
35	Rich Gedman	.10	.08	.04
36	Dave Henderson	.05	.04	.02
37	Bruce Hurst	.10	.08	.04
38	Tim Lollar	.05	.04	.02
39	Al Nipper	.05	.04	.02
40	Spike Owen	.05	.04	.02
41	Jim Rice	.30	.25	.12
42	Ed Romero	.05	.04	.02
43	Joe Sambito	.05	.04	.02
44	Calvin Schiraldi	.15	.11	.06
45	Tom Seaver	.30	.25	.12
46	Jeff Sellers	.20	.15	.08
47	Bob Stanley	.07	.05	.03
48	Sammy Stewart	.05	.04	.02
49	Larry Andersen	.05	.04	.02
50	Alan Ashby	.05	.04	.02
51	Kevin Bass	.10	.08	.04
52	Jeff Calhoun	.05	.04	.02
53	Jose Cruz	.10	.08	.04
54	Danny Darwin	.07	.05	.03
55	Glenn Davis	.30	.25	.12
56	Jim Deshaies	.30	.25	.12
57	Bill Doran	.10	.08	.04
58	Phil Garner	.07	.05	.03
59	Billy Hatcher	.07	.05	.03
60	Charlie Kerfeld	.07	.05	.03
61	Bob Knepper	.07	.05	.03
62	Dave Lopes	.07	.05	.03
63	Aurelio Lopez	.05	.04	.02
64	Jim Pankovits	.05	.04	.02
65	Terry Puhl	.05	.04	.02
66	Craig Reynolds	.05	.04	.02
67	Nolan Ryan	.30	.25	.12
68	Mike Scott	.15	.11	.06
69	Dave Smith	.07	.05	.03
70	Dickie Thon	.07	.05	.03
71	Tony Walker	.12	.09	.05
72	Denny Walling	.05	.04	.02
73	Bob Boone	.07	.05	.03
74	Rick Burleson	.07	.05	.03
75	John Candelaria	.10	.08	.04
76	Doug Corbett	.05	.04	.02
77	Doug DeCinces	.07	.05	.03
78	Brian Downing	.07	.05	.03
79	Chuck Finley	.12	.09	.05
80	Terry Forster	.07	.05	.03
81	Bobby Grich	.10	.08	.04
82	George Hendrick	.07	.05	.03
83	Jack Howell	.20	.15	.08
84	Reggie Jackson	.35	.25	.14
85	Ruppert Jones	.05	.04	.02
86	Wally Joyner	2.50	2.00	1.00
87	Gary Lucas	.05	.04	.02
88	Kirk McCaskill	.10	.08	.04
89	Donnie Moore	.05	.04	.02
90	Gary Pettis	.07	.05	.03
91	Vern Ruhle	.05	.04	.02
92	Dick Schofield	.05	.04	.02
93	Don Sutton	.20	.15	.08
94	Rob Wilfong	.05	.04	.02
95	Mike Witt	.12	.09	.05
96	Doug Drabek	.30	.25	.12
97	Mike Easler	.07	.05	.03
98	Mike Fischlin	.05	.04	.02
99	Brian Fisher	.10	.08	.04
100	Ron Guidry	.20	.15	.08
101	Rickey Henderson	.35	.25	.14
102	Tommy John	.20	.15	.08
103	Ron Kittle	.10	.08	.04
104	Don Mattingly	2.50	2.00	1.00
105	Bobby Meacham	.05	.04	.02
106	Joe Niekro	.10	.08	.04
107	Mike Pagliarulo	.12	.09	.05
108	Dan Pasqua	.12	.09	.05
109	Willie Randolph	.10	.08	.04
110	Dennis Rasmussen	.07	.05	.03
111	Dave Righetti	.15	.11	.06
112	Gary Roenicke	.05	.04	.02
113	Rod Scurry	.05	.04	.02
114	Bob Shirley	.05	.04	.02
115	Joel Skinner	.05	.04	.02
116	Tim Stoddard	.05	.04	.02
117	Bob Tewksbury	.15	.11	.06
118	Wayne Tolleson	.05	.04	.02
119	Claudell Washington	.07	.05	.03
120	Dave Winfield	.30	.25	.12
121	Steve Buechele	.07	.05	.03
122	Ed Correa	.25	.20	.10
123	Scott Fletcher	.07	.05	.03
124	Jose Guzman	.10	.08	.04
125	Toby Harrah	.07	.05	.03
126	Greg Harris	.05	.04	.02
127	Charlie Hough	.07	.05	.03
128	Pete Incaviglia	1.25	.90	.50
129	Mike Mason	.05	.04	.02
130	Oddibe McDowell	.12	.09	.05
131	Dale Mohorcic	.25	.20	.10
132	Pete O'Brien	.10	.08	.04
133	Tom Paciorek	.05	.04	.02
134	Larry Parrish	.10	.08	.04
135	Geno Petralli	.05	.04	.02
136	Darrell Porter	.07	.05	.03
137	Jeff Russell	.05	.04	.02
138	Ruben Sierra	1.50	1.25	.60
139	Don Slaught	.05	.04	.02
140	Gary Ward	.07	.05	.03
141	Curtis Wilkerson	.05	.04	.02
142	Mitch Williams	.25	.20	.10
143	Bobby Witt	.35	.25	.14
144	Dave Bergman	.05	.04	.02
145	Tom Brookens	.05	.04	.02
146	Bill Campbell	.05	.04	.02
147	Chuck Cary	.12	.09	.05
148	Darnell Coles	.07	.05	.03
149	Dave Collins	.07	.05	.03
150	Darrell Evans	.12	.09	.05
151	Kirk Gibson	.25	.20	.10
152	John Grubb	.05	.04	.02
153	Willie Hernandez	.07	.05	.03
154	Larry Herndon	.07	.05	.03
155	Eric King	.25	.20	.10
156	Chet Lemon	.07	.05	.03
157	Dwight Lowry	.12	.09	.05
158	Jack Morris	.20	.15	.08
159	Randy O'Neal	.05	.04	.02
160	Lance Parrish	.20	.15	.08
161	Dan Petry	.07	.05	.03
162	Pat Sheridan	.05	.04	.02
163	Jim Slaton	.05	.04	.02
164	Frank Tanana	.07	.05	.03
165	Walt Terrell	.07	.05	.03
166	Mark Thurmond	.05	.04	.02
167	Alan Trammell	.25	.20	.10
168	Lou Whitaker	.20	.15	.08
169	Luis Aguayo	.05	.04	.02
170	Steve Bedrosian	.12	.09	.05
171	Don Carman	.10	.08	.04
172	Darren Daulton	.05	.04	.02
173	Greg Gross	.05	.04	.02
174	Kevin Gross	.07	.05	.03
175	Von Hayes	.10	.08	.04
176	Charles Hudson	.05	.04	.02
177	Tom Hume	.05	.04	.02
178	Steve Jeltz	.05	.04	.02
179	Mike Maddux	.20	.15	.08
180	Shane Rawley	.07	.05	.03
181	Gary Redus	.07	.05	.03
182	Ron Roenicke	.05	.04	.02

	MT	NR MT	EX			MT	NR MT	EX
183 Bruce Ruffin	.30	.25	.12	274 Dan Gladden	.07	.05	.03
184 John Russell	.05	.04	.02	275 Mike Krukow	.07	.05	.03
185 Juan Samuel	.12	.09	.05	276 Randy Kutcher	.12	.09	.05
186 Dan Schatzeder	.05	.04	.02	277 Mike LaCoss	.07	.05	.03
187 Mike Schmidt	.40	.30	.15	278 Jeff Leonard	.10	.08	.04
188 Rick Schu	.05	.04	.02	279 Candy Maldonado	.10	.08	.04
189 Jeff Stone	.05	.04	.02	280 Roger Mason	.05	.04	.02
190 Kent Tekulve	.07	.05	.03	281 Bob Melvin	.07	.05	.03
191 Milt Thompson	.10	.08	.04	282 Greg Minton	.05	.04	.02
192 Glenn Wilson	.10	.08	.04	283 Jeff Robinson	.07	.05	.03
193 Buddy Bell	.10	.08	.04	284 Harry Spilman	.05	.04	.02
194 Tom Browning	.07	.05	.03	285 Rob Thompson	.40	.30	.15
195 Sal Butera	.05	.04	.02	286 Jose Uribe	.07	.05	.03
196 Dave Concepcion	.12	.09	.05	287 Frank Williams	.05	.04	.02
197 Kal Daniels	.80	.60	.30	288 Joel Youngblood	.05	.04	.02
198 Eric Davis	2.25	1.75	.90	289 Jack Clark	.15	.11	.06
199 John Denny	.05	.04	.02	290 Vince Coleman	.25	.20	.10
200 Bo Diaz	.05	.04	.02	291 Tim Conroy	.05	.04	.02
201 Nick Esasky	.05	.04	.02	292 Danny Cox	.10	.08	.04
202 John Franco	.07	.05	.03	293 Ken Dayley	.05	.04	.02
203 Bill Gullickson	.07	.05	.03	294 Curt Ford	.07	.05	.03
204 Barry Larkin	.70	.50	.30	295 Bob Forsch	.07	.05	.03
205 Eddie Milner	.05	.04	.02	296 Tom Herr	.10	.08	.04
206 Rob Murphy	.20	.15	.08	297 Ricky Horton	.07	.05	.03
207 Ron Oester	.05	.04	.02	298 Clint Hurdle	.05	.04	.02
208 Dave Parker	.20	.15	.08	299 Jeff Lahti	.05	.04	.02
209 Tony Perez	.15	.11	.06	300 Steve Lake	.05	.04	.02
210 Ted Power	.07	.05	.03	301 Tito Landrum	.05	.04	.02
211 Joe Price	.05	.04	.02	302 Mike LaValliere	.25	.20	.10
212 Ron Robinson	.05	.04	.02	303 Greg Mathews	.30	.25	.12
213 Pete Rose	.60	.45	.25	304 Willie McGee	.12	.09	.05
214 Mario Soto	.07	.05	.03	305 Jose Oquendo	.05	.04	.02
215 Kurt Stillwell	.40	.30	.15	306 Terry Pendleton	.10	.08	.04
216 Max Venable	.05	.04	.02	307 Pat Perry	.07	.05	.03
217 Chris Welsh	.05	.04	.02	308 Ozzie Smith	.15	.11	.06
218 Carl Willis	.10	.08	.04	309 Ray Soff	.10	.08	.04
219 Jesse Barfield	.20	.15	.08	310 John Tudor	.10	.08	.04
220 George Bell	.30	.25	.12	311 Andy Van Slyke	.10	.08	.04
221 Bill Caudill	.05	.04	.02	312 Todd Worrell	.20	.15	.08
222 John Cerutti	.30	.25	.12	313 Dann Bilardello	.05	.04	.02
223 Jim Clancy	.10	.08	.04	314 Hubie Brooks	.10	.08	.04
224 Mark Eichhorn	.30	.25	.12	315 Tim Burke	.07	.05	.03
225 Tony Fernandez	.12	.09	.05	316 Andre Dawson	.20	.15	.08
226 Damaso Garcia	.07	.05	.03	317 Mike Fitzgerald	.05	.04	.02
227 Kelly Gruber	.05	.04	.02	318 Tom Foley	.05	.04	.02
228 Tom Henke	.07	.05	.03	319 Andres Galarraga	.15	.11	.06
229 Garth Iorg	.05	.04	.02	320 Joe Hesketh	.05	.04	.02
230 Cliff Johnson	.05	.04	.02	321 Wallace Johnson	.05	.04	.02
231 Joe Johnson	.05	.04	.02	322 Wayne Krenchicki	.05	.04	.02
232 Jimmy Key	.12	.09	.05	323 Vance Law	.07	.05	.03
233 Dennis Lamp	.05	.04	.02	324 Dennis Martinez	.05	.04	.02
234 Rick Leach	.05	.04	.02	325 Bob McClure	.05	.04	.02
235 Buck Martinez	.05	.04	.02	326 Andy McGaffigan	.05	.04	.02
236 Lloyd Moseby	.10	.08	.04	327 Al Newman	.12	.09	.05
237 Rance Mulliniks	.05	.04	.02	328 Tim Raines	.30	.25	.12
238 Dave Stieb	.12	.09	.05	329 Jeff Reardon	.12	.09	.05
239 Willie Upshaw	.07	.05	.03	330 Luis Rivera	.10	.08	.04
240 Ernie Whitt	.07	.05	.03	331 Bob Sebra	.15	.11	.06
241 Andy Allanson	.15	.11	.06	332 Bryn Smith	.07	.05	.03
242 Scott Bailes	.20	.15	.08	333 Jay Tibbs	.05	.04	.02
243 Chris Bando	.05	.04	.02	334 Tim Wallach	.12	.09	.05
244 Tony Bernazard	.07	.05	.03	335 Mitch Webster	.10	.08	.04
245 John Butcher	.05	.04	.02	336 Jim Wohlford	.05	.04	.02
246 Brett Butler	.07	.05	.03	337 Floyd Youmans	.12	.09	.05
247 Ernie Camacho	.05	.04	.02	338 Chris Bosio	.20	.15	.08
248 Tom Candiotti	.05	.04	.02	339 Glenn Braggs	.50	.40	.20
249 Joe Carter	.15	.11	.06	340 Rick Cerone	.05	.04	.02
250 Carmen Castillo	.05	.04	.02	341 Mark Clear	.07	.05	.03
251 Julio Franco	.10	.08	.04	342 Bryan Clutterbuck	.10	.08	.04
252 Mel Hall	.07	.05	.03	343 Cecil Cooper	.12	.09	.05
253 Brook Jacoby	.10	.08	.04	344 Rob Deer	.12	.09	.05
254 Phil Niekro	.20	.15	.08	345 Jim Gantner	.07	.05	.03
255 Otis Nixon	.05	.04	.02	346 Ted Higuera	.20	.15	.08
256 Dickie Noles	.05	.04	.02	347 John Henry Johnson	.05	.04	.02
257 Bryan Oelkers	.05	.04	.02	348 Tim Leary	.07	.05	.03
258 Ken Schrom	.05	.04	.02	349 Rick Manning	.05	.04	.02
259 Don Schulze	.05	.04	.02	350 Paul Molitor	.15	.11	.06
260 Cory Snyder	1.00	.70	.40	351 Charlie Moore	.05	.04	.02
261 Pat Tabler	.07	.05	.03	352 Juan Nieves	.12	.09	.05
262 Andre Thornton	.07	.05	.03	353 Ben Oglivie	.07	.05	.03
263 Rich Yett	.12	.09	.05	354 Dan Plesac	.40	.30	.15
264 Mike Aldrete	.40	.30	.15	355 Ernest Riles	.07	.05	.03
265 Juan Berenguer	.05	.04	.02	356 Billy Joe Robidoux	.05	.04	.02
266 Vida Blue	.10	.08	.04	357 Bill Schroeder	.05	.04	.02
267 Bob Brenly	.05	.04	.02	358 Dale Sveum	.35	.25	.14
268 Chris Brown	.15	.11	.06	359 Gorman Thomas	.10	.08	.04
269 Will Clark	1.75	1.25	.70	360 Bill Wegman	.10	.08	.04
270 Chili Davis	.10	.08	.04	361 Robin Yount	.25	.20	.10
271 Mark Davis	.05	.04	.02	362 Steve Balboni	.07	.05	.03
272 Kelly Downs	.30	.25	.12	363 Scott Bankhead	.20	.15	.08
273 Scott Garrelts	.05	.04	.02	364 Buddy Biancalana	.05	.04	.02

#	Player	MT	NR MT	EX
365	Bud Black	.05	.04	.02
366	George Brett	.40	.30	.15
367	Steve Farr	.05	.04	.02
368	Mark Gubicza	.07	.05	.03
369	Bo Jackson	1.75	1.25	.70
370	Danny Jackson	.07	.05	.03
371	Mike Kingery	.20	.15	.08
372	Rudy Law	.05	.04	.02
373	Charlie Leibrandt	.07	.05	.03
374	Dennis Leonard	.07	.05	.03
375	Hal McRae	.10	.08	.04
376	Jorge Orta	.05	.04	.02
377	Jamie Quirk	.05	.04	.02
378	Dan Quisenberry	.12	.09	.05
379	Bret Saberhagen	.20	.15	.08
380	Angel Salazar	.05	.04	.02
381	Lonnie Smith	.07	.05	.03
382	Jim Sundberg	.07	.05	.03
383	Frank White	.10	.08	.04
384	Willie Wilson	.12	.09	.05
385	Joaquin Andujar	.07	.05	.03
386	Doug Bair	.05	.04	.02
387	Dusty Baker	.07	.05	.03
388	Bruce Bochte	.05	.04	.02
389	Jose Canseco	2.00	1.50	.80
390	Chris Codiroli	.05	.04	.02
391	Mike Davis	.07	.05	.03
392	Alfredo Griffin	.07	.05	.03
393	Moose Haas	.05	.04	.02
394	Donnie Hill	.05	.04	.02
395	Jay Howell	.07	.05	.03
396	Dave Kingman	.12	.09	.05
397	Carney Lansford	.07	.05	.03
398	David Leiper	.15	.11	.06
399	Bill Mooneyham	.10	.08	.04
400	Dwayne Murphy	.07	.05	.03
401	Steve Ontiveros	.07	.05	.03
402	Tony Phillips	.05	.04	.02
403	Eric Plunk	.05	.04	.02
404	Jose Rijo	.05	.04	.02
405	Terry Steinbach	.50	.40	.20
406	Dave Stewart	.10	.08	.04
407	Mickey Tettleton	.05	.04	.02
408	Dave Von Ohlen	.05	.04	.02
409	Jerry Willard	.05	.04	.02
410	Curt Young	.10	.08	.04
411	Bruce Bochy	.05	.04	.02
412	Dave Dravecky	.07	.05	.03
413	Tim Flannery	.05	.04	.02
414	Steve Garvey	.25	.20	.10
415	Goose Gossage	.15	.11	.06
416	Tony Gwynn	.35	.25	.14
417	Andy Hawkins	.05	.04	.02
418	LaMarr Hoyt	.07	.05	.03
419	Terry Kennedy	.07	.05	.03
420	John Kruk	1.00	.70	.40
421	Dave LaPoint	.05	.04	.02
422	Craig Lefferts	.05	.04	.02
423	Carmelo Martinez	.07	.05	.03
424	Lance McCullers	.07	.05	.03
425	Kevin McReynolds	.12	.09	.05
426	Graig Nettles	.12	.09	.05
427	Bip Roberts	.10	.08	.04
428	Jerry Royster	.05	.04	.02
429	Benito Santiago	.80	.60	.30
430	Eric Show	.05	.04	.02
431	Bob Stoddard	.05	.04	.02
432	Garry Templeton	.10	.08	.04
433	Gene Walter	.05	.04	.02
434	Ed Whitson	.05	.04	.02
435	Marvell Wynne	.05	.04	.02
436	Dave Anderson	.05	.04	.02
437	Greg Brock	.10	.08	.04
438	Enos Cabell	.05	.04	.02
439	Mariano Duncan	.07	.05	.03
440	Pedro Guerrero	.15	.11	.06
441	Orel Hershiser	.12	.09	.05
442	Rick Honeycutt	.07	.05	.03
443	Ken Howell	.05	.04	.02
444	Ken Landreaux	.07	.05	.03
445	Bill Madlock	.12	.09	.05
446	Mike Marshall	.10	.08	.04
447	Len Matuszek	.05	.04	.02
448	Tom Niedenfuer	.07	.05	.03
449	Alejandro Pena	.05	.04	.02
450	Dennis Powell	.07	.05	.03
451	Jerry Reuss	.07	.05	.03
452	Bill Russell	.07	.05	.03
453	Steve Sax	.15	.11	.06
454	Mike Scioscia	.05	.04	.02
455	Franklin Stubbs	.10	.08	.04
456	Alex Trevino	.05	.04	.02
457	Fernando Valenzuela	.25	.20	.10
458	Ed Vande Berg	.05	.04	.02
459	Bob Welch	.10	.08	.04
460	Reggie Williams	.15	.11	.06
461	Don Aase	.07	.05	.03
462	Juan Beniquez	.05	.04	.02
463	Mike Boddicker	.10	.08	.04
464	Juan Bonilla	.05	.04	.02
465	Rich Bordi	.05	.04	.02
466	Storm Davis	.05	.04	.02
467	Rick Dempsey	.07	.05	.03
468	Ken Dixon	.05	.04	.02
469	Jim Dwyer	.05	.04	.02
470	Mike Flanagan	.10	.08	.04
471	Jackie Gutierrez	.05	.04	.02
472	Brad Havens	.05	.04	.02
473	Lee Lacy	.07	.05	.03
474	Fred Lynn	.15	.11	.06
475	Scott McGregor	.07	.05	.03
476	Eddie Murray	.35	.25	.14
477	Tom O'Malley	.05	.04	.02
478	Cal Ripken, Jr.	.35	.25	.14
479	Larry Sheets	.10	.08	.04
480	John Shelby	.07	.05	.03
481	Nate Snell	.05	.04	.02
482	Jim Traber	.15	.11	.06
483	Mike Young	.07	.05	.03
484	Neil Allen	.05	.04	.02
485	Harold Baines	.15	.11	.06
486	Floyd Bannister	.10	.08	.04
487	Daryl Boston	.05	.04	.02
488	Ivan Calderon	.10	.08	.04
489	John Cangelosi	.20	.15	.08
490	Steve Carlton	.25	.20	.10
491	Joe Cowley	.05	.04	.02
492	Julio Cruz	.05	.04	.02
493	Bill Dawley	.05	.04	.02
494	Jose DeLeon	.07	.05	.03
495	Richard Dotson	.10	.08	.04
496	Carlton Fisk	.15	.11	.06
497	Ozzie Guillen	.12	.09	.05
498	Jerry Hairston	.05	.04	.02
499	Ron Hassey	.05	.04	.02
500	Tim Hulett	.05	.04	.02
501	Bob James	.05	.04	.02
502	Steve Lyons	.05	.04	.02
503	Joel McKeon	.12	.09	.05
504	Gene Nelson	.05	.04	.02
505	Dave Schmidt	.07	.05	.03
506	Ray Searage	.05	.04	.02
507	Bobby Thigpen	.25	.20	.10
508	Greg Walker	.10	.08	.04
509	Jim Acker	.05	.04	.02
510	Doyle Alexander	.10	.08	.04
511	Paul Assenmacher	.15	.11	.06
512	Bruce Benedict	.05	.04	.02
513	Chris Chambliss	.07	.05	.03
514	Jeff Dedmon	.05	.04	.02
515	Gene Garber	.05	.04	.02
516	Ken Griffey	.10	.08	.04
517	Terry Harper	.05	.04	.02
518	Bob Horner	.15	.11	.06
519	Glenn Hubbard	.05	.04	.02
520	Rick Mahler	.05	.04	.02
521	Omar Moreno	.05	.04	.02
522	Dale Murphy	.40	.30	.15
523	Ken Oberkfell	.07	.05	.03
524	Ed Olwine	.10	.08	.04
525	David Palmer	.07	.05	.03
526	Rafael Ramirez	.05	.04	.02
527	Billy Sample	.05	.04	.02
528	Ted Simmons	.12	.09	.05
529	Zane Smith	.10	.08	.04
530	Bruce Sutter	.12	.09	.05
531	Andres Thomas	.20	.15	.08
532	Ozzie Virgil	.07	.05	.03
533	Allan Anderson	.10	.08	.04
534	Keith Atherton	.05	.04	.02
535	Billy Beane	.05	.04	.02
536	Bert Blyleven	.15	.11	.06
537	Tom Brunansky	.10	.08	.04
538	Randy Bush	.05	.04	.02
539	George Frazier	.05	.04	.02
540	Gary Gaetti	.12	.09	.05
541	Greg Gagne	.10	.08	.04
542	Mickey Hatcher	.05	.04	.02
543	Neal Heaton	.07	.05	.03
544	Kent Hrbek	.15	.11	.06
545	Roy Lee Jackson	.05	.04	.02
546	Tim Laudner	.05	.04	.02

	MT	NR MT	EX
547 Steve Lombardozzi	.10	.08	.04
548 Mark Portugal	.12	.09	.05
549 Kirby Puckett	.35	.25	.14
550 Jeff Reed	.05	.04	.02
551 Mark Salas	.05	.04	.02
552 Roy Smalley	.05	.04	.02
553 Mike Smithson	.05	.04	.02
554 Frank Viola	.12	.09	.05
555 Thad Bosley	.05	.04	.02
556 Ron Cey	.10	.08	.04
557 Jody Davis	.10	.08	.04
558 Ron Davis	.05	.04	.02
559 Bob Dernier	.05	.04	.02
560 Frank DiPino	.05	.04	.02
561 Shawon Dunston	.10	.08	.04
562 Leon Durham	.10	.08	.04
563 Dennis Eckersley	.07	.05	.03
564 Terry Francona	.05	.04	.02
565 Dave Gumpert	.05	.04	.02
566 Guy Hoffman	.07	.05	.03
567 Ed Lynch	.05	.04	.02
568 Gary Matthews	.10	.08	.04
569 Keith Moreland	.07	.05	.03
570 Jamie Moyer	.20	.15	.08
571 Jerry Mumphrey	.07	.05	.03
572 Ryne Sandberg	.25	.20	.10
573 Scott Sanderson	.07	.05	.03
574 Lee Smith	.10	.08	.04
575 Chris Speier	.05	.04	.02
576 Rick Sutcliffe	.12	.09	.05
577 Manny Trillo	.07	.05	.03
578 Steve Trout	.07	.05	.03
579 Karl Best	.05	.04	.02
580 Phil Bradley	.12	.09	.05
581 Scott Bradley	.07	.05	.03
582 Mickey Brantley	.10	.08	.04
583 Mike Brown	.05	.04	.02
584 Alvin Davis	.12	.09	.05
585 Lee Guetterman	.25	.20	.10
586 Mark Huismann	.05	.04	.02
587 Bob Kearney	.05	.04	.02
588 Pete Ladd	.05	.04	.02
589 Mark Langston	.10	.08	.04
590 Mike Moore	.05	.04	.02
591 Mike Morgan	.05	.04	.02
592 John Moses	.05	.04	.02
593 Ken Phelps	.07	.05	.03
594 Jim Presley	.12	.09	.05
595 Rey Quinonez	.20	.15	.08
596 Harold Reynolds	.10	.08	.04
597 Billy Swift	.05	.04	.02
598 Danny Tartabull	.25	.20	.10
599 Steve Yeager	.05	.04	.02
600 Matt Young	.05	.04	.02
601 Bill Almon	.05	.04	.02
602 Rafael Belliard	.12	.09	.05
603 Mike Bielecki	.05	.04	.02
604 Barry Bonds	.60	.45	.25
605 Bobby Bonilla	.35	.25	.14
606 Sid Bream	.07	.05	.03
607 Mike Brown	.05	.04	.02
608 Pat Clements	.07	.05	.03
609 Mike Diaz	.30	.25	.12
610 Cecilio Guante	.05	.04	.02
611 Barry Jones	.15	.11	.06
612 Bob Kipper	.05	.04	.02
613 Larry McWilliams	.05	.04	.02
614 Jim Morrison	.05	.04	.02
615 Joe Orsulak	.07	.05	.03
616 Junior Ortiz	.05	.04	.02
617 Tony Pena	.10	.08	.04
618 Johnny Ray	.10	.08	.04
619 Rick Reuschel	.10	.08	.04
620 R.J. Reynolds	.07	.05	.03
621 Rick Rhoden	.10	.08	.04
622 Don Robinson	.07	.05	.03
623 Bob Walk	.05	.04	.02
624 Jim Winn	.05	.04	.02
625 Youthful Power (Jose Canseco, Pete Incaviglia)	.60	.45	.25
626 300 Game Winners (Phil Niekro, Don Sutton)	.12	.09	.05
627 A.L. Firemen (Don Aase, Dave Righetti)	.07	.05	.03
628 Rookie All-Stars (Jose Canseco, Wally Joyner)	1.25	.90	.50
629 Magic Mets (Gary Carter, Sid Fernandez, Dwight Gooden, Keith Hernandez, Darryl Strawberry)	.60	.45	.25
630 N.L. Best Righties (Mike Krukow, Mike Scott)	.07	.05	.03

	MT	NR MT	EX
631 Sensational Southpaws (John Franco, Fernando Valenzuela)	.10	.08	.04
632 Count 'Em (Bob Horner)	.07	.05	.03
633 A.L. Pitcher's Nightmare (Jose Canseco, Kirby Puckett, Jim Rice)	.50	.40	.20
634 All Star Battery (Gary Carter, Roger Clemens)	.25	.20	.10
635 4,000 Strikeouts (Steve Carlton)	.12	.09	.05
636 Big Bats At First Sack (Glenn Davis, Eddie Murray)	.20	.15	.08
637 On Base (Wade Boggs, Keith Hernandez)	.35	.25	.14
638 Sluggers From Left Side (Don Mattingly, Darryl Strawberry)	.90	.70	.35
639 Former MVP's (Dave Parker, Ryne Sandberg)	.12	.09	.05
640 Dr. K. & Super K (Roger Clemens, Dwight Gooden)	.50	.40	.20
641 A.L. West Stoppers (Charlie Hough, Mike Witt)	.07	.05	.03
642 Doubles & Triples (Tim Raines, Juan Samuel)	.12	.09	.05
643 Outfielders With Punch (Harold Baines, Jesse Barfield)	.10	.08	.04
644 Major League Prospects (Dave Clark, Greg Swindell)	.50	.40	.20
645 Major League Prospects (Ron Karkovice, Russ Morman)	.15	.11	.06
646 Major League Prospects (Willie Fraser, Devon White)	1.25	.90	.50
647 Major League Prospects (Jerry Browne, Mike Stanley)	.35	.25	.14
648 Major League Prospects (Phil Lombardi, Dave Magadan)	.70	.50	.30
649 Major League Prospects (Ralph Bryant, Jose Gonzalez)	.20	.15	.08
650 Major League Prospects (Randy Asadoor, Jimmy Jones)	.25	.20	.10
651 Major League Prospects (Marvin Freeman, Tracy Jones)	.60	.45	.25
652 Major League Prospects (Kevin Seitzer, John Stefero)	7.00	5.25	2.75
653 Major League Prospects (Steve Fireovid, Rob Nelson)	.15	.11	.06
654 Checklist 1-95	.05	.04	.02
655 Checklist 96-192	.05	.04	.02
656 Checklist 193-288	.05	.04	.02
657 Checklist 289-384	.05	.04	.02
658 Checklist 385-483	.05	.04	.02
659 Checklist 484-578	.05	.04	.02
660 Checklist 579-660	.05	.04	.02

1987 Fleer All Star Team

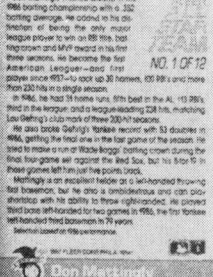

As in 1986, Fleer All Star Team cards were randomly inserted in Fleer wax and cello packs. Twelve cards, each measuring the standard 2½'' by 3½'', comprise the set. The card fronts feature a full-color player photo set against a gray background for American League players and a black background for National Leaguers. Card backs are printed in black, red and white and feature a lengthy player biography. Fleer's choices for a major league All-Star team is once again the theme for the set.

		MT	NR MT	EX
Complete Set:		18.00	13.50	7.25
Common Player:		.60	.45	.25
1	Don Mattingly	7.00	5.25	2.75
2	Gary Carter	1.00	.70	.40
3	Tony Fernandez	.75	.60	.30
4	Steve Sax	.75	.60	.30
5	Kirby Puckett	1.00	.70	.40
6	Mike Schmidt	2.00	1.50	.80
7	Mike Easler	.60	.45	.25
8	Todd Worrell	.75	.60	.30
9	George Bell	1.00	.70	.40
10	Fernando Valenzuela	1.00	.70	.40
11	Roger Clemens	2.00	1.50	.80
12	Tim Raines	1.00	.70	.40

		MT	NR MT	EX
30	Kirby Puckett	.20	.15	.08
31	Johnny Ray	.07	.05	.03
32	Dave Righetti	.12	.09	.05
33	Cal Ripken, Jr.	.25	.20	.10
34	Bret Saberhagen	.15	.11	.06
35	Ryne Sandberg	.20	.15	.08
36	Mike Schmidt	.30	.25	.12
37	Mike Scott	.12	.09	.05
38	Ozzie Smith	.12	.09	.05
39	Robbie Thompson	.10	.08	.04
40	Fernando Valenzuela	.20	.15	.08
41	Mitch Webster	.07	.05	.03
42	Frank White	.07	.05	.03
43	Mike Witt	.10	.08	.04
44	Todd Worrell	.15	.11	.06

1987 Fleer Award Winners

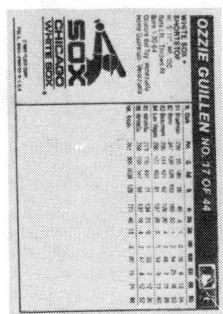

1987 Fleer Baseball All Stars

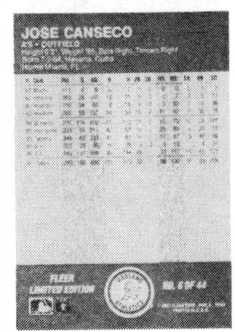

The 1987 Fleer Award Winners boxed set was prepared by Fleer for distribution by 7-Eleven stores. The cards, which measure 2½" by 3½", feature players who have won various major league awards during their careers. The card fronts contain full-color photos surrounded by a yellow border. The name of the award the player won is printed at the bottom of the card in a oval-shaped band designed to resemble a metal nameplate on a trophy. Card backs, printed in black, yellow and white, include lifetime major and minor league statistics along with typical personal information. Each boxed set contained six team logo stickers.

Produced by Fleer for exclusive distribution through Ben Franklin stores, the "Baseball All Stars" set is comprised of 44 cards which are the standard 2½" by 3½" size. The cards have full-color photos surrounded by a bright red border with white pin-stripes at the top and bottom. The card backs are printed in blue, white and dark red and include complete major and minor league statistics. The set was issued in a special cardboard box.

		MT	NR MT	EX
Complete Set:		5.00	3.75	2.00
Common Player:		.05	.04	.02
1	Marty Barrett	.07	.05	.03
2	George Bell	.20	.15	.08
3	Bert Blyleven	.12	.09	.05
4	Bob Boone	.05	.04	.02
5	John Candelaria	.07	.05	.03
6	Jose Canseco	.70	.50	.30
7	Gary Carter	.20	.15	.08
8	Joe Carter	.10	.08	.04
9	Roger Clemens	.40	.30	.15
10	Cecil Cooper	.10	.08	.04
11	Eric Davis	.80	.60	.30
12	Tony Fernandez	.10	.08	.04
13	Scott Fletcher	.05	.04	.02
14	Bob Forsch	.05	.04	.02
15	Dwight Gooden	.40	.30	.15
16	Ron Guidry	.15	.11	.06
17	Ozzie Guillen	.07	.05	.03
18	Bill Gullickson	.05	.04	.02
19	Tony Gwynn	.25	.20	.10
20	Bob Knepper	.05	.04	.02
21	Ray Knight	.05	.04	.02
22	Mark Langston	.07	.05	.03
23	Candy Maldonado	.07	.05	.03
24	Don Mattingly	1.50	1.25	.60
25	Roger McDowell	.07	.05	.03
26	Dale Murphy	.30	.25	.12
27	Dave Parker	.15	.11	.06
28	Lance Parrish	.15	.11	.06
29	Gary Pettis	.05	.04	.02

		MT	NR MT	EX
Complete Set:		5.00	3.75	2.00
Common Player:		.05	.04	.02
1	Harold Baines	.10	.08	.04
2	Jesse Barfield	.12	.09	.05
3	Wade Boggs	.60	.45	.25
4	Dennis "Oil Can" Boyd	.05	.04	.02
5	Scott Bradley	.05	.04	.02
6	Jose Canseco	.70	.50	.30
7	Gary Carter	.20	.15	.08
8	Joe Carter	.10	.08	.04
9	Mark Clear	.05	.04	.02
10	Roger Clemens	.40	.30	.15
11	Jose Cruz	.05	.04	.02
12	Chili Davis	.07	.05	.03
13	Jody Davis	.05	.04	.02
14	Rob Deer	.05	.04	.02
15	Brian Downing	.05	.04	.02
16	Sid Fernandez	.10	.08	.04
17	John Franco	.07	.05	.03
18	Andres Galarraga	.10	.08	.04
19	Dwight Gooden	.40	.30	.15
20	Tony Gwynn	.25	.20	.10
21	Charlie Hough	.05	.04	.02
22	Bruce Hurst	.07	.05	.03
23	Wally Joyner	.70	.50	.30
24	Carney Lansford	.05	.04	.02
25	Fred Lynn	.12	.09	.05
26	Don Mattingly	1.50	1.25	.60
27	Willie McGee	.10	.08	.04
28	Jack Morris	.15	.11	.06
29	Dale Murphy	.30	.25	.12
30	Bob Ojeda	.07	.05	.03
31	Tony Pena	.07	.05	.03
32	Kirby Puckett	.20	.15	.08
33	Dan Quisenberry	.10	.08	.04
34	Tim Raines	.20	.15	.08

		MT	NR MT	EX
35	Willie Randolph	.07	.05	.03
36	Cal Ripken, Jr.	.25	.20	.10
37	Pete Rose	.40	.30	.15
38	Nolan Ryan	.20	.15	.08
39	Juan Samuel	.12	.09	.05
40	Mike Schmidt	.30	.25	.12
41	Ozzie Smith	.12	.09	.05
42	Andres Thomas	.10	.08	.04
43	Fernando Valenzuela	.20	.15	.08
44	Mike Witt	.10	.08	.04

		MT	NR MT	EX
41	Rick Sutcliffe	.10	.08	.04
42	Pat Tabler	.07	.05	.03
43	Fernando Valenzuela	.20	.15	.08
44	Mike Witt	.10	.08	.04

1987 Fleer Baseball's Best

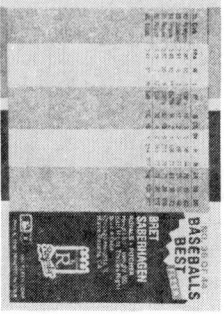

For a second straight baseball card season, Fleer produced for McCrory's stores and their affiliates a 44-card "Baseball's Best" set. Subtitled "Sluggers vs. Pitchers", 28 everyday players and 16 pitchers are featured. The card design is nearly identical to the previous year's effort. The cards, which measure 2½'' by 3½'', were housed in a specially designed box along with six team logo stickers.

		MT	NR MT	EX
	Complete Set:	5.00	3.75	2.00
	Common Player:	.05	.04	.02
1	Kevin Bass	.07	.05	.03
2	Jesse Barfield	.12	.09	.05
3	George Bell	.20	.15	.08
4	Wade Boggs	.60	.45	.25
5	Sid Bream	.05	.04	.02
6	George Brett	.30	.25	.12
7	Ivan Calderon	.07	.05	.03
8	Jose Canseco	.70	.50	.30
9	Jack Clark	.12	.09	.05
10	Roger Clemens	.40	.30	.15
11	Eric Davis	.80	.60	.30
12	Andre Dawson	.15	.11	.06
13	Sid Fernandez	.10	.08	.04
14	John Franco	.07	.05	.03
15	Dwight Gooden	.40	.30	.15
16	Pedro Guerrero	.15	.11	.06
17	Tony Gwynn	.25	.20	.10
18	Rickey Henderson	.25	.20	.10
19	Tom Henke	.07	.05	.03
20	Ted Higuera	.10	.08	.04
21	Pete Incaviglia	.40	.30	.15
22	Wally Joyner	.80	.60	.30
23	Jeff Leonard	.05	.04	.02
24	Joe Magrane	.25	.20	.10
25	Don Mattingly	1.50	1.25	.60
26	Mark McGwire	1.50	1.25	.60
27	Jack Morris	.15	.11	.06
28	Dale Murphy	.30	.25	.12
29	Dave Parker	.15	.11	.06
30	Ken Phelps	.05	.04	.02
31	Kirby Puckett	.20	.15	.08
32	Tim Raines	.20	.15	.08
33	Jeff Reardon	.10	.08	.04
34	Dave Righetti	.12	.09	.05
35	Cal Ripken, Jr.	.25	.20	.10
36	Bret Saberhagen	.15	.11	.06
37	Mike Schmidt	.30	.25	.12
38	Mike Scott	.12	.09	.05
39	Kevin Seitzer	1.50	1.25	.60
40	Darryl Strawberry	.30	.25	.12

1987 Fleer Baseball's Exciting Stars

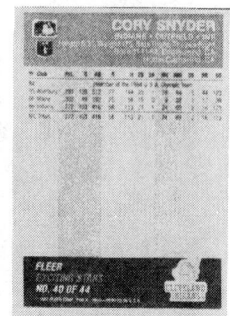

Another entry into the Fleer lineup of individual boxed sets, the "Baseball's Exciting Stars" set was produced by Fleer for Cumberland Farms stores. The card fronts feature a red, white and blue border with the words "Exciting Stars" printed in yellow at the top. The backs are printed in red and blue and carry complete major and minor league statistics. Included with the boxed set of 44 cards were six team logo stickers.

		MT	NR MT	EX
	Complete Set:	5.00	3.75	2.00
	Common Player:	.05	.04	.02
1	Don Aase	.05	.04	.02
2	Rick Aguilera	.07	.05	.03
3	Jesse Barfield	.12	.09	.05
4	Wade Boggs	.60	.45	.25
5	Dennis "Oil Can" Boyd	.05	.04	.02
6	Sid Bream	.05	.04	.02
7	Jose Canseco	.70	.50	.30
8	Steve Carlton	.20	.15	.08
9	Gary Carter	.20	.15	.08
10	Will Clark	.60	.45	.25
11	Roger Clemens	.40	.30	.15
12	Danny Cox	.07	.05	.03
13	Alvin Davis	.10	.08	.04
14	Eric Davis	.80	.60	.30
15	Rob Deer	.07	.05	.03
16	Brian Downing	.05	.04	.02
17	Gene Garber	.05	.04	.02
18	Steve Garvey	.20	.15	.08
19	Dwight Gooden	.40	.30	.15
20	Mark Gubicza	.05	.04	.02
21	Mel Hall	.05	.04	.02
22	Terry Harper	.05	.04	.02
23	Von Hayes	.07	.05	.03
24	Rickey Henderson	.25	.20	.10
25	Tom Henke	.07	.05	.03
26	Willie Hernandez	.07	.05	.03
27	Ted Higuera	.10	.08	.04
28	Rick Honeycutt	.05	.04	.02
29	Kent Hrbek	.15	.11	.06
30	Wally Joyner	.80	.60	.30
31	Charlie Kerfeld	.05	.04	.02
32	Fred Lynn	.12	.09	.05
33	Don Mattingly	1.50	1.25	.60
34	Tim Raines	.20	.15	.08
35	Dennis Rasmussen	.07	.05	.03
36	Johnny Ray	.07	.05	.03
37	Jim Rice	.20	.15	.08
38	Pete Rose	.40	.30	.15
39	Lee Smith	.07	.05	.03
40	Cory Snyder	.20	.15	.08
41	Darryl Strawberry	.30	.25	.12
42	Kent Tekulve	.05	.04	.02

		MT	NR MT	EX
43	Willie Wilson	.10	.08	.04
44	Bobby Witt	.20	.15	.08

1987 Fleer
Baseball's Game Winners

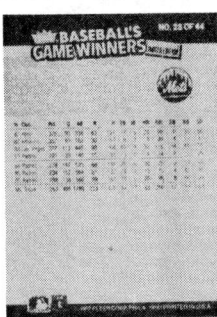

The 1987 Fleer "Baseball's Game Winners" boxed set of 44 cards were produced for distribution through Bi-Mart Discount Drug, Pay'n-Save, Mott's 5 & 10, M.E. Moses, and Winn's stores. The cards, which measure 2½" by 3½", have a light blue border with the player's name and game winning RBI or games won statistics in a yellow oval band at the top of the card. Below the full-color player photo is the name of the set in blue, yellow and red. Included with the boxed set were six team logo stickers.

		MT	NR MT	EX
Complete Set:		5.00	3.75	2.00
Common Player:		.05	.04	.02
1	Harold Baines	.10	.08	.04
2	Don Baylor			
3	George Bell	.20	.15	.08
4	Tony Bernazard	.05	.04	.02
5	Wade Boggs	.60	.45	.25
6	George Brett	.40	.30	.15
7	Hubie Brooks	.07	.05	.03
8	Jose Canseco	.70	.50	.30
9	Gary Carter	.20	.15	.08
10	Roger Clemens	.40	.30	.15
11	Eric Davis	.80	.60	.30
12	Glenn Davis	.15	.11	.06
13	Shawon Dunston	.07	.05	.03
14	Mark Eichhorn	.12	.09	.05
15	Gary Gaetti	.10	.08	.04
16	Steve Garvey	.20	.15	.08
17	Kirk Gibson	.20	.15	.08
18	Dwight Gooden	.40	.30	.15
19	Von Hayes	.07	.05	.03
20	Willie Hernandez	.07	.05	.03
21	Ted Higuera	.10	.08	.04
22	Wally Joyner	.80	.60	.30
23	Bob Knepper	.05	.04	.02
24	Mike Krukow	.05	.04	.02
25	Jeff Leonard	.05	.04	.02
26	Don Mattingly	1.50	1.25	.60
27	Kirk McCaskill	.07	.05	.03
28	Kevin McReynolds	.07	.05	.03
29	Jim Morrison	.05	.04	.02
30	Dale Murphy	.30	.25	.12
31	Pete O'Brien	.07	.05	.03
32	Bob Ojeda	.07	.05	.03
33	Larry Parrish	.07	.05	.03
34	Ken Phelps	.05	.04	.02
35	Dennis Rasmussen	.07	.05	.03
36	Ernest Riles	.07	.05	.03
37	Cal Ripken, Jr.	.25	.20	.10
38	Ron Robinson	.05	.04	.02
39	Steve Sax	.15	.11	.06
40	Mike Schmidt	.30	.25	.12
41	John Tudor	.07	.05	.03
42	Fernando Valenzuela	.20	.15	.08
43	Mike Witt	.10	.08	.04
44	Curt Young	.05	.04	.02

1987 Fleer
Baseball's Hottest Stars

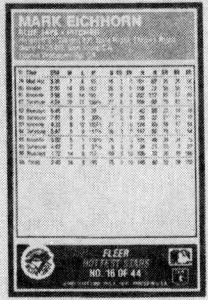

The "Baseball's Hottest Stars" 44-card set was produced by Fleer for the Revco Drug Store chain. Measuring the standard 2½" by 3½", the cards feature full-color photos surrounded by a red, white and blue border. The player's name, position and team appear in a blue band at the bottom of the card. Card backs are printed in red, white and black and contain the player's lifetime professional statistics. The set was housed in a special cardboard box with six team logo stickers.

		MT	NR MT	EX
Complete Set:		5.00	3.75	2.00
Common Player:		.05	.04	.02
1	Joaquin Andujar	.05	.04	.02
2	Harold Baines	.10	.08	.04
3	Kevin Bass	.07	.05	.03
4	Don Baylor	.10	.08	.04
5	Barry Bonds	.20	.15	.08
6	George Brett	.30	.25	.12
7	Tom Brunansky	.10	.08	.04
8	Brett Butler	.05	.04	.02
9	Jose Canseco	.70	.50	.30
10	Roger Clemens	.40	.30	.15
11	Ron Darling	.10	.08	.04
12	Eric Davis	.80	.60	.30
13	Andre Dawson	.15	.11	.06
14	Doug DeCinces	.05	.04	.02
15	Leon Durham	.07	.05	.03
16	Mark Eichhorn	.10	.08	.04
17	Scott Garrelts	.05	.04	.02
18	Dwight Gooden	.40	.30	.15
19	Dave Henderson	.05	.04	.02
20	Rickey Henderson	.25	.20	.10
21	Keith Hernandez	.15	.11	.06
22	Ted Higuera	.10	.08	.04
23	Bob Horner	.10	.08	.04
24	Pete Incaviglia	.40	.30	.15
25	Wally Joyner	.80	.60	.30
26	Mark Langston	.07	.05	.03
27	Don Mattingly	1.50	1.25	.60
28	Dale Murphy	.30	.25	.12
29	Kirk McCaskill	.07	.05	.03
30	Willie McGee	.10	.08	.04
31	Dave Righetti	.12	.09	.05
32	Pete Rose	.40	.30	.15
33	Bruce Ruffin	.15	.11	.06
34	Steve Sax	.15	.11	.06
35	Mike Schmidt	.30	.25	.12
36	Larry Sheets	.10	.08	.04
37	Eric Show	.05	.04	.02
38	Dave Smith	.05	.04	.02
39	Cory Snyder	.20	.15	.08
40	Frank Tanana	.05	.04	.02
41	Alan Trammell	.20	.15	.08
42	Reggie Williams	.10	.08	.04
43	Mookie Wilson	.07	.05	.03
44	Todd Worrell	.15	.11	.06

Definitions for grading conditions are located in the Introduction of this price guide.

1987 Fleer Box Panels

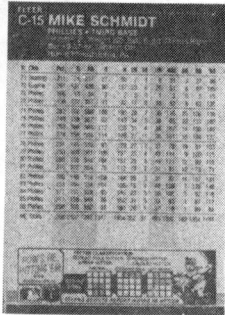

either horizontal or vertical formats. The fronts are bordered in red, white and blue stars and stripes with a thin gold frame around the photo. The backs are printed in red and blue ink on white stock and include information regarding the photo on the card fronts.

		MT	NR MT	EX
	Complete Set:	4.00	3.00	1.50
	Common Player:	.30	.25	.12
1	Left-Hand Finesse Beats Mets (Bruce Hurst)	.30	.25	.12
2	Hernandez And Boggs (Wade Boggs, Keith Hernandez)	1.00	.70	.40
3	Roger Clemens	.70	.50	.30
4	Clutch Hitting (Gary Carter)	.50	.40	.20
5	Darling Picks Up The Slack (Ron Darling)	.30	.25	.12
6	.433 Series Batting Average (Marty Barrett)	.30	.25	.12
7	Dwight Gooden	.70	.50	.30
8	Strategy At Work	.30	.25	.12
9	Dewey! (Dwight Evans)	.30	.25	.12
10	One Strike From Boston Victory (Dave Henderson, Spike Owen)	.30	.25	.12
11	Series Home Run Duo (Ray Knight, Darryl Strawberry)	.60	.45	.25
12	Series M V.P. (Ray Knight)	.30	.25	.12

For the second staright year, Fleer produced a special set of cards designed to stimulate sales of their wax and cello pack boxes. In 1987, Fleer issued 16 cards in panels of four on the bottoms of retail boxes. The cards are numbered C-1 through C-16 and are 2½" by 3½" in size. The cards have the same design as the regular issue set with the player photos and card numbers being different.

		MT	NR MT	EX
	Complete Panel Set:	8.00	6.00	3.25
	Complete Singles Set:	3.50	2.75	1.50
	Common Panel:	2.25	1.75	.90
	Common Single Player:	.20	.15	.08
	Panel	2.50	2.00	1.00
1	Mets Logo	.05	.04	.02
6	Keith Hernandez	.30	.25	.12
8	Dale Murphy	.60	.45	.25
14	Ryne Sandberg	.30	.25	.12
	Panel	2.25	1.75	.90
2	Jesse Barfield	.20	.15	.08
3	George Brett	.60	.45	.25
5	Red Sox Logo	.05	.04	.02
11	Kirby Puckett	.30	.25	.12
	Panel	2.75	2.00	1.00
4	Dwight Gooden	.60	.45	.25
9	Astros Logo	.05	.04	.02
10	Dave Parker	.25	.20	.10
15	Mike Schmidt	.60	.45	.25
	Panel	2.75	2.00	1.00
7	Wally Joyner	1.00	.70	.40
12	Dave Righetti	.20	.15	.08
13	Angels Logo	.05	.04	.02
16	Robin Yount	.25	.20	.10

1987 Fleer Headliners

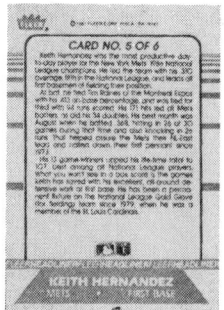

A continuation of the 1986 Future Hall of Famers idea, Fleer encountered legal problems with using the Hall of Fame name and abated them by entitling the set "Headliners." The cards, which are the standard 2½" by 3½" size, were randomly inserted in 3-pack cello packs. Card fronts feature a player photo set against a beige background with bright red stripes. The card backs are printed in black, red and gray and offer a brief biography with an emphasis on the player's performance during the 1986 season.

		MT	NR MT	EX
	Complete Set:	8.00	6.00	3.25
	Common Player:	1.25	.90	.50
1	Wade Boggs	2.00	1.50	.80
2	Jose Canseco	2.00	1.50	.80
3	Dwight Gooden	1.50	1.25	.60
4	Rickey Henderson	1.25	.90	.50
5	Keith Hernandez	1.25	.90	.50
6	Jim Rice	1.25	.90	.50

1987 Fleer '86 World Series

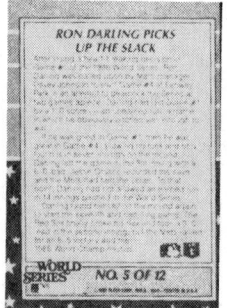

Fleer issued a set of 12 cards highlighting the 1986 World Series between the Boston Red Sox and New York Mets. The sets were available only with Fleer factory-packaged sets of 660 regular issue cards. The cards, which are the standard 2½" by 3½" size, have

1987 Fleer League Leaders

For the second year in a row, Fleer produced a 44-card "League Leaders" set for Walgreens. The card fronts feature a border style which is identical to that used in 1986. However, an elliptical shaped full-color player photo is placed diagonally on the front. "1987 Fleer League Leaders" appears in the upper left cor-

 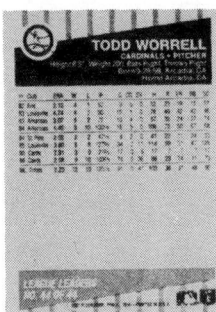  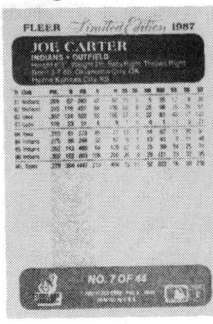

ner of the front although nowhere on the card does it state in which pitching, hitting or fielding department was the player a league leader. The card backs are printed in red and blue on white stock. The cards in the boxed set are the standard 2½'' by 3½'' size.

		MT	NR MT	EX
	Complete Set:	5.00	3.75	2.00
	Common Player:	.05	.04	.02
1	Jesse Barfield	.12	.09	.05
2	Mike Boddicker	.07	.05	.03
3	Wade Boggs	.60	.45	.25
4	Phil Bradley	.10	.08	.04
5	George Brett	.30	.25	.12
6	Hubie Brooks	.07	.05	.03
7	Chris Brown	.10	.08	.04
8	Jose Canseco	.70	.50	.30
9	Joe Carter	.10	.08	.04
10	Roger Clemens	.40	.30	.15
11	Vince Coleman	.15	.11	.06
12	Joe Cowley	.05	.04	.02
13	Kal Daniels	.15	.11	.06
14	Glenn Davis	.15	.11	.06
15	Jody Davis	.07	.05	.03
16	Darrell Evans	.07	.05	.03
17	Dwight Evans	.10	.08	.04
18	John Franco	.07	.05	.03
19	Julio Franco	.10	.08	.04
20	Dwight Gooden	.40	.30	.15
21	Goose Gossage	.12	.09	.05
22	Tom Herr	.07	.05	.03
23	Ted Higuera	.10	.08	.04
24	Bob Horner	.10	.08	.04
25	Pete Incaviglia	.40	.30	.15
26	Wally Joyner	.80	.60	.30
27	Dave Kingman	.12	.09	.05
28	Don Mattingly	1.50	1.25	.60
29	Willie McGee	.10	.08	.04
30	Donnie Moore	.05	.04	.02
31	Keith Moreland	.05	.04	.02
32	Eddie Murray	.25	.20	.10
33	Mike Pagliarulo	.10	.08	.04
34	Larry Parrish	.07	.05	.03
35	Tony Pena	.07	.05	.03
36	Kirby Puckett	.20	.15	.08
37	Pete Rose	.40	.30	.15
38	Juan Samuel	.12	.09	.05
39	Ryne Sandberg	.20	.15	.08
40	Mike Schmidt	.30	.25	.12
41	Darryl Strawberry	.30	.25	.12
42	Greg Walker	.07	.05	.03
43	Bob Welch	.07	.05	.03
44	Todd Worrell	.12	.09	.05

1987 Fleer Limited Edition

For the third straight year, Fleer produced a Limited Edition set for the McCrory's store chain and their affiliates. The cards are the standard 2½'' by 3½'' size and feature light blue borders at the top and bottom and a diagonal red and white border running along both sides. The set was issued in a specially prepared cardboard box, along with six team logo stickers.

		MT	NR MT	EX
	Complete Set:	5.00	3.75	2.00
	Common Player:	.05	.04	.02
1	Floyd Bannister	.05	.04	.02
2	Marty Barrett	.07	.05	.03
3	Steve Bedrosian	.10	.08	.04
4	George Bell	.20	.15	.08
5	George Brett	.30	.25	.12
6	Jose Canseco	.70	.50	.30
7	Joe Carter	.10	.08	.04
8	Will Clark	.50	.40	.20
9	Roger Clemens	.40	.30	.15
10	Vince Coleman	.15	.11	.06
11	Glenn Davis	.15	.11	.06
12	Mike Davis	.05	.04	.02
13	Len Dykstra	.07	.05	.03
14	John Franco	.07	.05	.03
15	Julio Franco	.10	.08	.04
16	Steve Garvey	.20	.15	.08
17	Kirk Gibson	.20	.15	.08
18	Dwight Gooden	.40	.30	.15
19	Tony Gwynn	.25	.20	.10
20	Keith Hernandez	.20	.15	.08
21	Teddy Higuera	.10	.08	.04
22	Kent Hrbek	.15	.11	.06
23	Wally Joyner	.80	.60	.30
24	Mike Krukow	.05	.04	.02
25	Mike Marshall	.10	.08	.04
26	Don Mattingly	1.50	1.25	.60
27	Oddibe McDowell	.10	.08	.04
28	Jack Morris	.15	.11	.06
29	Lloyd Moseby	.07	.05	.03
30	Dale Murphy	.30	.25	.12
31	Eddie Murray	.25	.20	.10
32	Tony Pena	.07	.05	.03
33	Jim Presley	.10	.08	.04
34	Jeff Reardon	.10	.08	.04
35	Jim Rice	.20	.15	.08
36	Pete Rose	.40	.30	.15
37	Mike Schmidt	.30	.25	.12
38	Mike Scott	.12	.09	.05
39	Lee Smith	.07	.05	.03
40	Lonnie Smith	.05	.04	.02
41	Gary Ward	.05	.04	.02
42	Dave Winfield	.20	.15	.08
43	Todd Worrell	.12	.09	.05
44	Robin Yount	.20	.15	.08

1987 Fleer Mini

 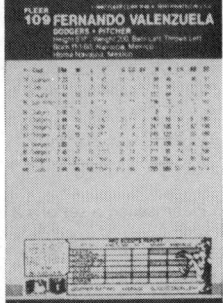

Continuing with an idea originated the previous year, the Fleer "Classic Miniatures" set consists of 120 cards that measure 1 13/16" by 2 9/16" in size. The cards are identical in design to the regular issue set produced by Fleer, but use completely different photos. The set was issued in a specially prepared collectors box along with 18 team logo stickers. The Fleer Mini set was available only through hobby dealers.

		MT	NR MT	EX
Complete Set:		7.00	5.25	2.75
Common Player:		.05	.04	.02
1	Don Aase	.05	.04	.02
2	Joaquin Andujar			
3	Harold Baines	.10	.08	.04
4	Jesse Barfield	.12	.09	.05
5	Kevin Bass	.05	.04	.02
6	Don Baylor	.10	.08	.04
7	George Bell	.20	.15	.08
8	Tony Bernazard	.05	.04	.02
9	Bert Blyleven	.12	.09	.05
10	Wade Boggs	.60	.45	.25
11	Phil Bradley	.10	.08	.04
12	Sid Bream	.05	.04	.02
13	George Brett	.30	.25	.12
14	Hubie Brooks	.07	.05	.03
15	Chris Brown	.10	.08	.04
16	Tom Candiotti	.05	.04	.02
17	Jose Canseco	.70	.50	.30
18	Gary Carter	.20	.15	.08
19	Joe Carter	.10	.08	.04
20	Roger Clemens	.40	.30	.15
21	Vince Coleman	.15	.11	.06
22	Cecil Cooper	.10	.08	.04
23	Ron Darling	.10	.08	.04
24	Alvin Davis	.10	.08	.04
25	Chili Davis	.07	.05	.03
26	Eric Davis	.80	.60	.30
27	Glenn Davis	.15	.11	.06
28	Mike Davis	.05	.04	.02
29	Doug DeCinces	.05	.04	.02
30	Rob Deer	.07	.05	.03
31	Jim Deshaies	.10	.08	.04
32	Bo Diaz	.05	.04	.02
33	Richard Dotson	.07	.05	.03
34	Brian Downing	.05	.04	.02
35	Shawon Dunston	.07	.05	.03
36	Mark Eichhorn	.10	.08	.04
37	Dwight Evans	.12	.09	.05
38	Tony Fernandez	.10	.08	.04
39	Julio Franco	.10	.08	.04
40	Gary Gaetti	.10	.08	.04
41	Andres Galarraga	.10	.08	.04
42	Scott Garrelts	.05	.04	.02
43	Steve Garvey	.20	.15	.08
44	Kirk Gibson	.20	.15	.08
45	Dwight Gooden	.40	.30	.15
46	Ken Griffey	.10	.08	.04
47	Mark Gubicza	.05	.04	.02
48	Ozzie Guillen	.07	.05	.03
49	Bill Gullickson	.05	.04	.02
50	Tony Gwynn	.25	.20	.10
51	Von Hayes	.07	.05	.03
52	Rickey Henderson	.25	.20	.10
53	Keith Hernandez	.15	.11	.06
54	Willie Hernandez	.07	.05	.03
55	Ted Higuera	.10	.08	.04
56	Charlie Hough	.05	.04	.02
57	Kent Hrbek	.15	.11	.06
58	Pete Incaviglia	.40	.30	.15
59	Wally Joyner	.80	.60	.30
60	Bob Knepper	.05	.04	.02
61	Mike Krukow	.05	.04	.02
62	Mark Langston	.10	.08	.04
63	Carney Lansford	.07	.05	.03
64	Jim Lindeman	.12	.09	.05
65	Bill Madlock	.10	.08	.04
66	Don Mattingly	1.50	1.25	.60
67	Kirk McCaskill	.07	.05	.03
68	Lance McCullers	.10	.08	.04
69	Keith Moreland	.05	.04	.02
70	Jack Morris	.15	.11	.06
71	Jim Morrison	.05	.04	.02
72	Lloyd Moseby	.07	.05	.03
73	Jerry Mumphrey	.05	.04	.02
74	Dale Murphy	.30	.25	.12
75	Eddie Murray	.25	.20	.10
76	Pete O'Brien	.07	.05	.03

		MT	NR MT	EX
77	Bob Ojeda	.07	.05	.03
78	Jesse Orosco	.05	.04	.02
79	Dan Pasqua	.10	.08	.04
80	Dave Parker	.12	.09	.05
81	Larry Parrish	.07	.05	.03
82	Jim Presley	.10	.08	.04
83	Kirby Puckett	.20	.15	.08
84	Dan Quisenberry	.10	.08	.04
85	Tim Raines	.20	.15	.08
86	Dennis Rasmussen	.07	.05	.03
87	Johnny Ray	.07	.05	.03
88	Jeff Reardon	.10	.08	.04
89	Jim Rice	.20	.15	.08
90	Dave Righetti	.12	.09	.05
91	Earnest Riles	.07	.05	.03
92	Cal Ripken, Jr.	.25	.20	.10
93	Ron Robinson	.05	.04	.02
94	Juan Samuel	.12	.09	.05
95	Ryne Sandberg	.20	.15	.08
96	Steve Sax	.15	.11	.06
97	Mike Schmidt	.30	.25	.12
98	Ken Schrom	.05	.04	.02
99	Mike Scott	.12	.09	.05
100	Ruben Sierra	.40	.30	.15
101	Lee Smith	.07	.05	.03
102	Ozzie Smith	.12	.09	.05
103	Cory Snyder	.20	.15	.08
104	Kent Tekulve	.05	.04	.02
105	Andres Thomas	.10	.08	.04
106	Rob Thompson	.10	.08	.04
107	Alan Trammell	.20	.15	.08
108	John Tudor	.07	.05	.03
109	Fernando Valenzuela	.20	.15	.08
110	Greg Walker	.07	.05	.03
111	Mitch Webster	.07	.05	.03
112	Lou Whitaker	.15	.11	.06
113	Frank White	.07	.05	.03
114	Reggie Williams	.10	.08	.04
115	Glenn Wilson	.07	.05	.03
116	Willie Wilson	.10	.08	.04
117	Dave Winfield	.20	.15	.08
118	Mike Witt	.10	.08	.04
119	Todd Worrell	.12	.09	.05
120	Floyd Youmans	.07	.05	.03

1987 Fleer Record Setters

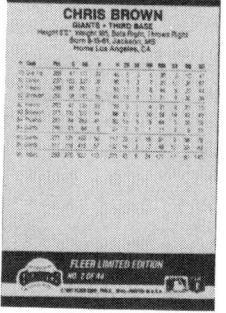

Produced by Fleer for the Eckerd Drug chain, the 1987 Fleer Record Setters set contains 44 cards that measure the standard 2½" by 3½" size. Although the set is titled "Record Setters", the actual records the players have set is not specified anywhere on the cards. Given that several players included in the set were young prospects, a better title for those cards might have been "Possible Record Setters". The set came housed in a special cardboard box with six team logo stickers.

	MT	NR MT	EX
Complete Set:	5.00	3.75	2.00
Common Player:	.05	.04	.02

		MT	NR MT	EX
1	George Brett	.30	.25	.12
2	Chris Brown	.10	.08	.04
3	Jose Canseco	.70	.50	.30
4	Roger Clemens	.40	.30	.15
5	Alvin Davis	.10	.08	.04
6	Shawon Dunston	.07	.05	.03
7	Tony Fernandez	.10	.08	.04
8	Carlton Fisk	.12	.09	.05
9	Gary Gaetti	.10	.08	.04
10	Gene Garber	.05	.04	.02
11	Rich Gedman	.05	.04	.02
12	Dwight Gooden	.40	.30	.15
13	Ozzie Guillen	.07	.05	.03
14	Bill Gullickson	.05	.04	.02
15	Billy Hatcher	.07	.05	.03
16	Orel Hershiser	.10	.08	.04
17	Wally Joyner	.70	.50	.30
18	Ray Knight	.05	.04	.02
19	Craig Lefferts	.05	.04	.02
20	Don Mattingly	1.50	1.25	.60
21	Kevin Mitchell	.12	.09	.05
22	Lloyd Moseby	.07	.05	.03
23	Dale Murphy	.30	.25	.12
24	Eddie Murray	.25	.20	.10
25	Phil Niekro	.15	.11	.06
26	Ben Oglivie	.05	.04	.02
27	Jesse Orosco	.05	.04	.02
28	Joe Orsulak	.05	.04	.02
29	Larry Parrish	.07	.05	.03
30	Tim Raines	.20	.15	.08
31	Shane Rawley	.07	.05	.03
32	Dave Righetti	.12	.09	.05
33	Pete Rose	.40	.30	.15
34	Steve Sax	.15	.11	.06
35	Mike Schmidt	.30	.25	.12
36	Mike Scott	.12	.09	.05
37	Don Sutton	.15	.11	.06
38	Alan Trammell	.20	.15	.08
39	John Tudor	.07	.05	.03
40	Gary Ward	.05	.04	.02
41	Lou Whitaker	.15	.11	.06
42	Willie Wilson	.10	.08	.04
43	Todd Worrell	.15	.11	.06
44	Floyd Youmans	.10	.08	.04

1987 Fleer Star Stickers

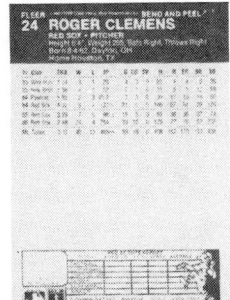

The 1987 Fleer Star Stickers set contains 132 cards which become stickers if the back is bent and peeled off. As in the previous year, the card backs are identical, save the numbering system, to the regular issue cards. The cards measure 2½'' by 3½'' and were sold in wax packs with team logo stickers. The fronts have a green border with a red and white banner wrapped across the upper left corner and the sides. The backs are printed in green and yellow.

		MT	NR MT	EX
Complete Set:		24.00	18.00	9.50
Common Player:		.05	.04	.02
1	Don Aase	.05	.04	.02
2	Harold Baines	.20	.15	.08
3	Floyd Bannister	.08	.06	.03
4	Jesse Barfield	.25	.20	.10

		MT	NR MT	EX
5	Marty Barrett	.10	.08	.04
6	Kevin Bass	.10	.08	.04
7	Don Baylor	.12	.09	.05
8	Steve Bedrosian	.15	.11	.06
9	George Bell	.35	.25	.14
10	Bert Blyleven	.15	.11	.06
11	Mike Boddicker	.10	.08	.04
12	Wade Boggs	1.50	1.25	.60
13	Phil Bradley	.20	.15	.08
14	Sid Bream	.08	.06	.03
15	George Brett	.70	.50	.30
16	Hubie Brooks	.12	.09	.05
17	Tom Brunansky	.15	.11	.06
18	Tom Candiotti	.05	.04	.02
19	Jose Canseco	1.75	1.25	.70
20	Gary Carter	.40	.30	.15
21	Joe Carter	.20	.15	.08
22	Will Clark	1.00	.70	.40
23	Mark Clear	.05	.04	.02
24	Roger Clemens	.80	.60	.30
25	Vince Coleman	.25	.20	.10
26	Jose Cruz	.10	.08	.04
27	Ron Darling	.20	.15	.08
28	Alvin Davis	.20	.15	.08
29	Chili Davis	.12	.09	.05
30	Eric Davis	2.00	1.50	.80
31	Glenn Davis	.25	.20	.10
32	Mike Davis	.05	.04	.02
33	Andre Dawson	.25	.20	.10
34	Doug DeCinces	.08	.06	.03
35	Brian Downing	.08	.06	.03
36	Shawon Dunston	.12	.09	.05
37	Mark Eichhorn	.15	.11	.06
38	Dwight Evans	.20	.15	.08
39	Tony Fernandez	.15	.11	.06
40	Bob Forsch	.05	.04	.02
41	John Franco	.08	.06	.03
42	Julio Franco	.20	.15	.08
43	Gary Gaetti	.20	.15	.08
44	Gene Garber	.05	.04	.02
45	Scott Garrelts	.08	.06	.03
46	Steve Garvey	.40	.30	.15
47	Kirk Gibson	.30	.25	.12
48	Dwight Gooden	.80	.60	.30
49	Ken Griffey	.15	.11	.06
50	Ozzie Guillen	.15	.11	.06
51	Bill Gullickson	.05	.04	.02
52	Tony Gwynn	.40	.30	.15
53	Mel Hall	.08	.06	.03
54	Greg Harris	.05	.04	.02
55	Von Hayes	.20	.15	.08
56	Rickey Henderson	.60	.45	.25
57	Tom Henke	.12	.09	.05
58	Keith Hernandez	.35	.25	.14
59	Willie Hernandez	.10	.08	.04
60	Ted Higuera	.20	.15	.08
61	Bob Horner	.20	.15	.08
62	Charlie Hough	.08	.06	.03
63	Jay Howell	.08	.06	.03
64	Kent Hrbek	.30	.25	.12
65	Bruce Hurst	.12	.09	.05
66	Pete Incaviglia	.70	.50	.30
67	Bob James	.05	.04	.02
68	Wally Joyner	2.00	1.50	.80
69	Mike Krukow	.05	.04	.02
70	Mark Langston	.15	.11	.06
71	Carney Lansford	.08	.06	.03
72	Fred Lynn	.25	.20	.10
73	Bill Madlock	.20	.15	.08
74	Don Mattingly	2.50	2.00	1.00
75	Kirk McCaskill	.10	.08	.04
76	Lance McCullers	.12	.09	.05
77	Oddibe McDowell	.15	.11	.06
78	Paul Molitor	.20	.15	.08
79	Keith Moreland	.08	.06	.03
80	Jack Morris	.25	.20	.10
81	Jim Morrison	.05	.04	.02
82	Jerry Mumphrey	.05	.04	.02
83	Dale Murphy	.80	.60	.30
84	Eddie Murray	.50	.40	.20
85	Ben Oglivie	.05	.04	.02
86	Bob Ojeda	.15	.11	.06
87	Jesse Orosco	.10	.08	.04
88	Dave Parker	.25	.20	.10
89	Larry Parrish	.08	.06	.03
90	Tony Pena	.12	.09	.05
91	Jim Presley	.20	.15	.08
92	Kirby Puckett	.40	.30	.15
93	Dan Quisenberry	.20	.15	.08
94	Tim Raines	.35	.25	.14
95	Dennis Rasmussen	.10	.08	.04

		MT	NR MT	EX
96	Shane Rawley	.10	.08	.04
97	Johnny Ray	.12	.09	.05
98	Jeff Reardon	.12	.09	.05
99	Jim Rice	.40	.30	.15
100	Dave Righetti	.25	.20	.10
101	Cal Ripken, Jr.	.60	.45	.25
102	Pete Rose	1.00	.70	.40
103	Nolan Ryan	.35	.25	.14
104	Juan Samuel	.20	.15	.08
105	Ryne Sandberg	.35	.25	.14
106	Steve Sax	.25	.20	.10
107	Mike Schmidt	.70	.50	.30
108	Mike Scott	.20	.15	.08
109	Dave Smith	.08	.06	.03
110	Lee Smith	.10	.08	.04
111	Lonnie Smith	.05	.04	.02
112	Ozzie Smith	.20	.15	.08
113	Cory Snyder	.50	.40	.20
114	Darryl Strawberry	.50	.40	.20
115	Don Sutton	.25	.20	.10
116	Kent Tekulve	.08	.06	.03
117	Gorman Thomas	.10	.08	.04
118	Alan Trammell	.30	.25	.12
119	John Tudor	.10	.08	.04
120	Fernando Valenzuela	.35	.25	.14
121	Bob Welch	.12	.09	.05
122	Lou Whitaker	.25	.20	.10
123	Frank White	.10	.08	.04
124	Reggie Williams	.12	.09	.05
125	Willie Wilson	.15	.11	.06
126	Dave Winfield	.40	.30	.15
127	Mike Witt	.15	.11	.06
128	Todd Worrell	.25	.20	.10
129	Curt Young	.05	.04	.02
130	Robin Yount	.30	.25	.12
131	Jose Canseco, Don Mattingly/Checklist	1.50	1.25	.60
132	Eric Davis, Bo Jackson/Checklist	1.25	.90	.50

1987 Fleer Star Stickers Box Panels

 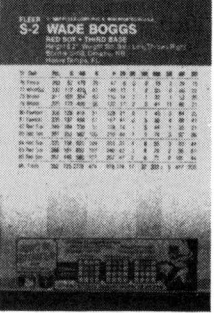

Fleer issued on the bottoms of their Fleer Star Stickers wax pack boxes six player cards plus two team logo/checklist cards. The cards, which measure 2½'' by 3½'', are numbered S-1 through S-8. The cards are identical in design to the Star Stickers.

		MT	NR MT	EX
Complete Panel Set:		6.50	5.00	2.50
Complete Singles Set:		2.75	2.00	1.00
Common Single Player:		.15	.11	.06
Panel		5.75	4.25	2.25
2	Wade Boggs	.80	.60	.30
3	Bert Blyleven	.20	.15	.08
6	Phillies Logo	.05	.04	.02
8	Don Mattingly	1.75	1.25	.70
Panel		1.00	.70	.40
1	Tigers Logo	.05	.04	.02
4	Jose Cruz	.15	.11	.06
5	Glenn Davis	.20	.15	.08
7	Bob Horner	.20	.15	.08

1987 Fleer Update

 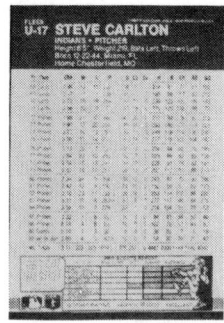

Fleer followed suit on a Topps idea in 1984 and began producing "Update" sets. The 1987 edition brings the regular Fleer set to date by including traded players and hot rookies. The cards measure 2½'' by 3½'' and are housed in a specially designed box with 25 team logo stickers. As a companion to the glossy-coated Fleer Collectors Edition set, Fleer produced a special edition Update set in its own tin box. Values of the glossy-coated cards is only a few dollars more than the regular Update cards.

		MT	NR MT	EX
Complete Set:		9.50	7.25	3.75
Common Player:		.06	.05	.02
1	Scott Bankhead	.08	.06	.03
2	Eric Bell	.20	.15	.08
3	Juan Beniquez	.06	.05	.02
4	Juan Berenguer	.06	.05	.02
5	Mike Birkbeck	.15	.11	.06
6	Randy Bockus	.15	.11	.06
7	Rod Booker	.15	.11	.06
8	Thad Bosley	.06	.05	.02
9	Greg Brock	.10	.08	.04
10	Bob Brower	.20	.15	.08
11	Chris Brown	.15	.11	.06
12	Jerry Browne	.12	.09	.05
13	Ralph Bryant	.10	.08	.04
14	DeWayne Buice	.20	.15	.08
15	Ellis Burks	1.50	1.25	.60
16	Casey Candaele	.20	.15	.08
17	Steve Carlton	.30	.25	.12
18	Juan Castillo	.08	.06	.03
19	Chuck Crim	.15	.11	.06
20	Mark Davidson	.20	.15	.08
21	Mark Davis	.06	.05	.02
22	Storm Davis	.06	.05	.02
23	Bill Dawley	.06	.05	.02
24	Andre Dawson	.40	.30	.15
25	Brian Dayett	.06	.05	.02
26	Rick Dempsey	.08	.06	.03
27	Ken Dowell	.20	.15	.08
28	Dave Dravecky	.10	.08	.04
29	Mike Dunne	.50	.40	.20
30	Dennis Eckersley	.10	.08	.04
31	Cecil Fielder	.08	.06	.03
32	Brian Fisher	.10	.08	.04
33	Willie Fraser	.12	.09	.05
34	Ken Gerhart	.30	.25	.12
35	Jim Gott	.06	.05	.02
36	Dan Gladden	.08	.06	.03
37	Mike Greenwell	1.25	.90	.50
38	Cecilio Guante	.06	.05	.02
39	Albert Hall	.06	.05	.02
40	Atlee Hammaker	.06	.05	.02
41	Mickey Hatcher	.06	.05	.02
42	Mike Heath	.06	.05	.02
43	Neal Heaton	.08	.06	.03
44	Mike Henneman	.35	.25	.14
45	Guy Hoffman	.06	.05	.02
46	Charles Hudson	.08	.06	.03
47	Chuck Jackson	.20	.15	.08
48	Mike Jackson	.20	.15	.08
49	Reggie Jackson	.40	.30	.15
50	Chris James	.50	.40	.20
51	Dion James	.12	.09	.05

		MT	NR MT	EX
52	Stan Javier	.06	.05	.02
53	Stan Jefferson	.30	.25	.12
54	Jimmy Jones	.12	.09	.05
55	Tracy Jones	.25	.20	.10
56	Terry Kennedy	.08	.06	.03
57	Mike Kingery	.10	.08	.04
58	Ray Knight	.10	.08	.04
59	Gene Larkin	.20	.15	.08
60	Mike LaValliere	.08	.06	.03
61	Jack Lazorko	.08	.06	.03
62	Terry Leach	.12	.09	.05
63	Rick Leach	.06	.05	.02
64	Craig Lefferts	.06	.05	.02
65	Jim Lindeman	.30	.25	.12
66	Bill Long	.20	.15	.08
67	Mike Loynd	.15	.11	.06
68	Greg Maddux	.15	.11	.06
69	Bill Madlock	.15	.11	.06
70	Dave Magadan	.50	.40	.20
71	Joe Magrane	.80	.60	.30
72	Fred Manrique	.25	.20	.10
73	Mike Mason	.06	.05	.02
74	Lloyd McClendon	.20	.15	.08
75	Fred McGriff	.40	.30	.15
76	Mark McGwire	3.50	2.75	1.50
77	Mark McLemore	.06	.05	.02
78	Kevin McReynolds	.25	.20	.10
79	Dave Meads	.20	.15	.08
80	Greg Minton	.06	.05	.02
81	John Mitchell	.20	.15	.08
82	Kevin Mitchell	.15	.11	.06
83	John Morris	.06	.05	.02
84	Jeff Musselman	.20	.15	.08
85	Randy Myers	.20	.15	.08
86	Gene Nelson	.06	.05	.02
87	Joe Niekro	.12	.09	.05
88	Tom Nieto	.06	.05	.02
89	Reid Nichols	.06	.05	.02
90	Matt Nokes	2.00	1.50	.80
91	Dickie Noles	.06	.05	.02
92	Edwin Nunez	.06	.05	.02
93	Jose Nunez	.25	.20	.10
94	Paul O'Neill	.10	.08	.04
95	Jim Paciorek	.10	.08	.04
96	Lance Parrish	.20	.15	.08
97	Bill Pecota	.25	.20	.10
98	Tony Pena	.12	.09	.05
99	Luis Polonia	.35	.25	.14
100	Randy Ready	.06	.05	.02
101	Jeff Reardon	.15	.11	.06
102	Gary Redus	.08	.06	.03
103	Rick Rhoden	.10	.08	.04
104	Wally Ritchie	.20	.15	.08
105	Jeff Robinson	.25	.20	.10
106	Mark Salas	.06	.05	.02
107	Dave Schmidt	.08	.06	.03
108	Kevin Seitzer	1.75	1.25	.70
109	John Shelby	.08	.06	.03
110	John Smiley	.30	.25	.12
111	Lary Sorenson	.06	.05	.02
112	Chris Speier	.06	.05	.02
113	Randy St. Claire	.06	.05	.02
114	Jim Sundberg	.08	.06	.03
115	B.J. Surhoff	1.00	.70	.40
116	Greg Swindell	.25	.20	.10
117	Danny Tartabull	.35	.25	.14
118	Dorn Taylor	.15	.11	.06
119	Lee Tunnell	.06	.05	.02
120	Ed Vande Berg	.06	.05	.02
121	Andy Van Slyke	.10	.08	.04
122	Gary Ward	.08	.06	.03
123	Devon White	.70	.50	.30
124	Alan Wiggins	.06	.05	.02
125	Bill Wilkinson	.20	.15	.08
126	Jim Winn	.06	.05	.02
127	Frank Williams	.08	.06	.03
128	Ken Williams	.25	.20	.10
129	Matt Williams	.35	.25	.14
130	Herm Winningham	.08	.06	.03
131	Matt Young	.06	.05	.02
132	Checklist 1-132	.06	.05	.02

1988 Fleer

A clean, uncluttered look was the trademark of the 660-card 1988 Fleer set. The cards, which are the standard 2½'' by 3½'', feature blue and red diagonal lines set inside a white border. The player name and

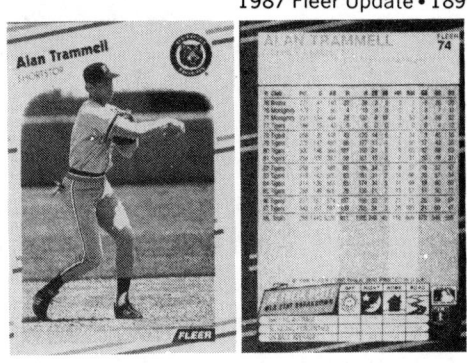

position are located on a slant in the upper left corner of the card. The player's team logo appears in the upper right corner. Below the player photo a blue and red band with the word "Fleer" appears. The backs of the cards include the card number, player personal and career statistics, plus a new feature called "At Their Best." This feature graphically shows a player's pitching or hitting statistics for home and road games and how he fared during day games as opposed to night contests. The set includes 19 special cards (#'s 622-640) and 13 "Major League Prospects" cards (#'s 641-653).

		MT	NR MT	EX
Complete Set:		25.00	18.50	10.00
Common Player:		.05	.04	.02
1	Keith Atherton	.05	.04	.02
2	Don Baylor	.10	.08	.04
3	Juan Berenguer	.05	.04	.02
4	Bert Blyleven	.15	.11	.06
5	Tom Brunansky	.10	.08	.04
6	Randy Bush	.05	.04	.02
7	Steve Carlton	.25	.20	.10
8	Mark Davidson	.15	.11	.06
9	George Frazier	.05	.04	.02
10	Gary Gaetti	.12	.09	.05
11	Greg Gagne	.07	.05	.03
12	Dan Gladden	.07	.05	.03
13	Kent Hrbek	.15	.11	.06
14	Gene Larkin	.15	.11	.06
15	Tim Laudner	.05	.04	.02
16	Steve Lombardozzi	.07	.05	.03
17	Al Newman	.05	.04	.02
18	Joe Niekro	.10	.08	.04
19	Kirby Puckett	.35	.25	.14
20	Jeff Reardon	.12	.09	.05
21	Dan Schatzader (Schatzeder)	.05	.04	.02
22	Roy Smalley	.05	.04	.02
23	Mike Smithson	.05	.04	.02
24	Les Straker	.20	.15	.08
25	Frank Viola	.12	.09	.05
26	Jack Clark	.15	.11	.06
27	Vince Coleman	.20	.15	.08
28	Danny Cox	.10	.08	.04
29	Bill Dawley	.05	.04	.02
30	Ken Dayley	.05	.04	.02
31	Doug DeCinces	.07	.05	.03
32	Curt Ford	.05	.04	.02
33	Bob Forsch	.05	.04	.02
34	David Green	.05	.04	.02
35	Tom Herr	.07	.05	.03
36	Ricky Horton	.07	.05	.03
37	Lance Johnson	.30	.25	.12
38	Steve Lake	.05	.04	.02
39	Jim Lindeman	.12	.09	.05
40	Joe Magrane	.50	.40	.20
41	Greg Mathews	.10	.08	.04
42	Willie McGee	.12	.09	.05
43	John Morris	.05	.04	.02
44	Jose Oquendo	.05	.04	.02
45	Tony Pena	.10	.08	.04
46	Terry Pendleton	.07	.05	.03
47	Ozzie Smith	.12	.09	.05
48	John Tudor	.10	.08	.04
49	Lee Tunnell	.05	.04	.02
50	Todd Worrell	.12	.09	.05
51	Doyle Alexander	.10	.08	.04

#	Player	MT	NR MT	EX
52	Dave Bergman	.05	.04	.02
53	Tom Brookens	.05	.04	.02
54	Darrell Evans	.10	.08	.04
55	Kirk Gibson	.25	.20	.10
56	Mike Heath	.05	.04	.02
57	Mike Henneman	.25	.20	.10
58	Willie Hernandez	.07	.05	.03
59	Larry Herndon	.05	.04	.02
60	Eric King	.10	.08	.04
61	Chet Lemon	.07	.05	.03
62	Scott Lusader	.30	.25	.12
63	Bill Madlock	.12	.09	.05
64	Jack Morris	.20	.15	.08
65	Jim Morrison	.05	.04	.02
66	Matt Nokes	1.50	1.25	.60
67	Dan Petry	.07	.05	.03
68	Jeff Robinson	.25	.20	.10
69	Pat Sheridan	.05	.04	.02
70	Nate Snell	.05	.04	.02
71	Frank Tanana	.07	.05	.03
72	Walt Terrell	.07	.05	.03
73	Mark Thurmond	.05	.04	.02
74	Alan Trammell	.25	.20	.10
75	Lou Whitaker	.20	.15	.08
76	Mike Aldrete	.12	.09	.05
77	Bob Brenly	.05	.04	.02
78	Will Clark	.70	.50	.30
79	Chili Davis	.10	.08	.04
80	Kelly Downs	.10	.08	.04
81	Dave Dravecky	.07	.05	.03
82	Scott Garrelts	.05	.04	.02
83	Atlee Hammaker	.05	.04	.02
84	Dave Henderson	.05	.04	.02
85	Mike Krukow	.07	.05	.03
86	Mike LaCoss	.05	.04	.02
87	Craig Lefferts	.05	.04	.02
88	Jeff Leonard	.07	.05	.03
89	Candy Maldonado	.07	.05	.03
90	Bob Melvin	.05	.04	.02
91	Ed Milner	.05	.04	.02
92	Kevin Mitchell	.10	.08	.04
93	Jon Perlman	.20	.15	.08
94	Rick Reuschel	.10	.08	.04
95	Don Robinson	.05	.04	.02
96	Chris Speier	.05	.04	.02
97	Harry Spilman	.05	.04	.02
98	Robbie Thompson	.10	.08	.04
99	Jose Uribe	.05	.04	.02
100	Mark Wasinger	.25	.20	.10
101	Matt Williams	.35	.25	.14
102	Jesse Barfield	.15	.11	.06
103	George Bell	.30	.25	.12
104	Juan Beniquez	.05	.04	.02
105	John Cerutti	.10	.08	.04
106	Jim Clancy	.07	.05	.03
107	Rob Ducey	.20	.15	.08
108	Mark Eichhorn	.10	.08	.04
109	Tony Fernandez	.12	.09	.05
110	Cecil Fielder	.07	.05	.03
111	Kelly Gruber	.05	.04	.02
112	Tom Henke	.07	.05	.03
113	Garth lorq (lorg)	.05	.04	.02
114	Jimmy Key	.10	.08	.04
115	Rick Leach	.05	.04	.02
116	Manny Lee	.05	.04	.02
117	Nelson Liriano	.25	.20	.10
118	Fred McGriff	.10	.08	.04
119	Lloyd Moseby	.10	.08	.04
120	Rance Mulliniks	.05	.04	.02
121	Jeff Musselman	.07	.05	.03
122	Jose Nunez	.25	.20	.10
123	Dave Stieb	.10	.08	.04
124	Willie Upshaw	.07	.05	.03
125	Duane Ward	.07	.05	.03
126	Ernie Whitt	.07	.05	.03
127	Rick Aguilera	.07	.05	.03
128	Luis Aguayo	.05	.04	.02
129	Mark Carreon	.20	.15	.08
130	Gary Carter	.30	.25	.12
131	David Cone	.10	.08	.04
132	Ron Darling	.12	.09	.05
133	Len Dykstra	.10	.08	.04
134	Sid Fernandez	.10	.08	.04
135	Dwight Gooden	.60	.45	.25
136	Keith Hernandez	.25	.20	.10
137	Gregg Jefferies	1.00	.70	.40
138	Howard Johnson	.10	.08	.04
139	Terry Leach	.07	.05	.03
140	Barry Lyons	.20	.15	.08
141	Dave Magadan	.20	.15	.08
142	Roger McDowell	.07	.05	.03
143	Kevin McReynolds	.10	.08	.04
144	Keith Miller	.30	.25	.12
145	John Mitchell	.25	.20	.10
146	Randy Myers	.07	.05	.03
147	Bob Ojeda	.10	.08	.04
148	Jesse Orosco	.07	.05	.03
149	Rafael Santana	.05	.04	.02
150	Doug Sisk	.05	.04	.02
151	Darryl Strawberry	.35	.25	.14
152	Tim Teufel	.05	.04	.02
153	Gene Walter	.05	.04	.02
154	Mookie Wilson	.07	.05	.03
155	Jay Aldrich	.15	.11	.06
156	Chris Bosio	.07	.05	.03
157	Glenn Braggs	.12	.09	.05
158	Greg Brock	.07	.05	.03
159	Juan Castillo	.05	.04	.02
160	Mark Clear	.05	.04	.02
161	Cecil Cooper	.10	.08	.04
162	Chuck Crim	.15	.11	.06
163	Rob Deer	.10	.08	.04
164	Mike Felder	.05	.04	.02
165	Jim Gantner	.05	.04	.02
166	Ted Higuera	.10	.08	.04
167	Steve Kiefer	.05	.04	.02
168	Rick Manning	.05	.04	.02
169	Paul Molitor	.12	.09	.05
170	Juan Nieves	.10	.08	.04
171	Dan Plesac	.12	.09	.05
172	Earnest Riles	.05	.04	.02
173	Bill Schroeder	.05	.04	.02
174	Steve Stanicek	.20	.15	.08
175	B.J. Surhoff	.25	.20	.10
176	Dale Sveum	.10	.08	.04
177	Bill Wegman	.05	.04	.02
178	Robin Yount	.25	.20	.10
179	Hubie Brooks	.10	.08	.04
180	Tim Burke	.07	.05	.03
181	Casey Candaele	.07	.05	.03
182	Mike Fitzgerald	.05	.04	.02
183	Tom Foley	.05	.04	.02
184	Andres Galarraga	.10	.08	.04
185	Neal Heaton	.07	.05	.03
186	Wallace Johnson	.05	.04	.02
187	Vance Law	.05	.04	.02
188	Dennis Martinez	.05	.04	.02
189	Bob McClure	.05	.04	.02
190	Andy McGaffigan	.05	.04	.02
191	Reid Nichols	.05	.04	.02
192	Pascual Perez	.07	.05	.03
193	Tim Raines	.25	.20	.10
194	Jeff Reed	.05	.04	.02
195	Bob Sebra	.07	.05	.03
196	Bryn Smith	.07	.05	.03
197	Randy St. Claire	.05	.04	.02
198	Tim Wallach	.10	.08	.04
199	Mitch Webster	.07	.05	.03
200	Herm Winningham	.05	.04	.02
201	Floyd Youmans	.10	.08	.04
202	Brad Arnsberg	.25	.20	.10
203	Rick Cerone	.05	.04	.02
204	Pat Clements	.05	.04	.02
205	Henry Cotto	.05	.04	.02
206	Mike Easler	.07	.05	.03
207	Ron Guidry	.20	.15	.08
208	Bill Gullickson	.07	.05	.03
209	Rickey Henderson	.35	.25	.14
210	Charles Hudson	.05	.04	.02
211	Tommy John	.15	.11	.06
212	Roberto Kelly	.30	.25	.12
213	Ron Kittle	.07	.05	.03
214	Don Mattingly	1.50	1.25	.60
215	Bobby Meacham	.05	.04	.02
216	Mike Pagliarulo	.10	.08	.04
217	Dan Pasqua	.10	.08	.04
218	Willie Randolph	.07	.05	.03
219	Rick Rhoden	.10	.08	.04
220	Dave Righetti	.15	.11	.06
221	Jerry Royster	.05	.04	.02
222	Tim Stoddard	.05	.04	.02
223	Wayne Tolleson	.05	.04	.02
224	Gary Ward	.07	.05	.03
225	Claudell Washington	.07	.05	.03
226	Dave Winfield	.30	.25	.12
227	Buddy Bell	.10	.08	.04
228	Tom Browning	.07	.05	.03
229	Dave Concepcion	.10	.08	.04
230	Kal Daniels	.20	.15	.08
231	Eric Davis	1.00	.70	.40
232	Bo Diaz	.05	.04	.02
233	Nick Esasky	.05	.04	.02

#	Player	MT	NR MT	EX
234	John Franco	.07	.05	.03
235	Guy Hoffman	.05	.04	.02
236	Tom Hume	.05	.04	.02
237	Tracy Jones	.12	.09	.05
238	Bill Landrum	.15	.11	.06
239	Barry Larkin	.12	.09	.05
240	Terry McGriff	.07	.05	.03
241	Rob Murphy	.07	.05	.03
242	Ron Oester	.05	.04	.02
243	Dave Parker	.20	.15	.08
244	Pat Perry	.05	.04	.02
245	Ted Power	.07	.05	.03
246	Dennis Rasmussen	.07	.05	.03
247	Ron Robinson	.05	.04	.02
248	Kurt Stillwell	.12	.09	.05
249	Jeff Treadway	.40	.30	.15
250	Frank Williams	.05	.04	.02
251	Steve Balboni	.05	.04	.02
252	Bud Black	.05	.04	.02
253	Thad Bosley	.05	.04	.02
254	George Brett	.40	.30	.15
255	John Davis	.25	.20	.10
256	Steve Farr	.05	.04	.02
257	Gene Garber	.05	.04	.02
258	Jerry Gleaton	.05	.04	.02
259	Mark Gubicza	.07	.05	.03
260	Bo Jackson	.50	.40	.20
261	Danny Jackson	.07	.05	.03
262	Ross Jones	.20	.15	.08
263	Charlie Leibrandt	.07	.05	.03
264	Bill Pecota	.25	.20	.10
265	Melido Perez	.20	.15	.08
266	Jamie Quirk	.05	.04	.02
267	Dan Quisenberry	.12	.09	.05
268	Bret Saberhagen	.20	.15	.08
269	Angel Salazar	.05	.04	.02
270	Kevin Seitzer	1.00	.70	.40
271	Danny Tartabull	.20	.15	.08
272	Gary Thurman	.35	.25	.14
273	Frank White	.07	.05	.03
274	Willie Wilson	.10	.08	.04
275	Tony Bernazard	.05	.04	.02
276	Jose Canseco	.70	.50	.30
277	Mike Davis	.07	.05	.03
278	Storm Davis	.05	.04	.02
279	Dennis Eckersley	.07	.05	.03
280	Alfredo Griffin	.07	.05	.03
281	Rick Honeycutt	.05	.04	.02
282	Jay Howell	.07	.05	.03
283	Reggie Jackson	.35	.25	.14
284	Dennis Lamp	.05	.04	.02
285	Carney Lansford	.07	.05	.03
286	Mark McGwire	1.50	1.25	.60
287	Dwayne Murphy	.05	.04	.02
288	Gene Nelson	.05	.04	.02
289	Steve Ontiveros	.05	.04	.02
290	Tony Phillips	.05	.04	.02
291	Eric Plunk	.05	.04	.02
292	Luis Polonia	.25	.20	.10
293	Rick Rodriguez	.20	.15	.08
294	Terry Steinbach	.12	.09	.05
295	Dave Stewart	.07	.05	.03
296	Curt Young	.07	.05	.03
297	Luis Aguayo			
298	Steve Bedrosian	.12	.09	.05
299	Jeff Calhoun	.05	.04	.02
300	Don Carman	.10	.08	.04
301	Todd Frohwirth	.30	.25	.12
302	Greg Gross	.05	.04	.02
303	Kevin Gross	.07	.05	.03
304	Von Hayes	.10	.08	.04
305	Keith Hughes	.20	.15	.08
306	Mike Jackson	.20	.15	.08
307	Chris James	.12	.09	.05
308	Steve Jeltz	.05	.04	.02
309	Mike Maddux	.10	.08	.04
310	Lance Parrish	.15	.11	.06
311	Shane Rawley	.07	.05	.03
312	Wally Ritchie	.20	.15	.08
313	Bruce Ruffin	.10	.08	.04
314	Juan Samuel	.10	.08	.04
315	Mike Schmidt	.40	.30	.15
316	Rick Schu	.05	.04	.02
317	Jeff Stone	.05	.04	.02
318	Kent Tekulve	.07	.05	.03
319	Milt Thompson	.07	.05	.03
320	Glenn Wilson	.07	.05	.03
321	Rafael Belliard	.05	.04	.02
322	Barry Bonds	.12	.09	.05
323	Bobby Bonilla	.10	.08	.04
324	Sid Bream	.07	.05	.03

#	Player	MT	NR MT	EX
325	John Cangelosi	.07	.05	.03
326	Mike Diaz	.10	.08	.04
327	Doug Drabek	.07	.05	.03
328	Mike Dunne	.35	.25	.14
329	Brian Fisher	.07	.05	.03
330	Brett Gideon	.20	.15	.08
331	Terry Harper	.05	.04	.02
332	Bob Kipper	.05	.04	.02
333	Mike LaValliere	.07	.05	.03
334	Jose Lind	.35	.25	.14
335	Junior Ortiz	.05	.04	.02
336	**Vicente Palacios**	.30	.25	.12
337	Bob Patterson	.20	.15	.08
338	Al Pedrique	.20	.15	.08
339	R.J. Reynolds	.07	.05	.03
340	John Smiley	.25	.20	.10
341	Andy Van Slyke	.10	.08	.04
342	Bob Walk	.05	.04	.02
343	Marty Barrett	.07	.05	.03
344	Todd Benzinger	.70	.50	.30
345	Wade Boggs	1.00	.70	.40
346	Tom Bolton	.20	.15	.08
347	Oil Can Boyd	.07	.05	.03
348	Ellis Burks	1.75	1.25	.70
349	Roger Clemens	.60	.45	.25
350	Steve Crawford	.05	.04	.02
351	Dwight Evans	.12	.09	.05
352	Wes Gardner	.20	.15	.08
353	Rich Gedman	.07	.05	.03
354	Mike Greenwell	.80	.60	.30
355	Sam Horn	1.00	.70	.40
356	Bruce Hurst	.10	.08	.04
357	John Marzano	.60	.45	.25
358	Al Nipper	.05	.04	.02
359	Spike Owen	.05	.04	.02
360	Jody Reed	.30	.25	.12
361	Jim Rice	.30	.25	.12
362	Ed Romero	.05	.04	.02
363	Kevin Romine	.10	.08	.04
364	Joe Sambito	.05	.04	.02
365	Calvin Schiraldi	.05	.04	.02
366	Jeff Sellers	.07	.05	.03
367	Bob Stanley	.05	.04	.02
368	Scott Bankhead	.05	.04	.02
369	Phil Bradley	.12	.09	.05
370	Scott Bradley	.05	.04	.02
371	Mickey Brantley	.05	.04	.02
372	Mike Campbell	.30	.25	.12
373	Alvin Davis	.12	.09	.05
374	Lee Guetterman	.07	.05	.03
375	Dave Hengel	.20	.15	.08
376	Mike Kingery	.07	.05	.03
377	Mark Langston	.10	.08	.04
378	Edgar Martinez	.20	.15	.08
379	Mike Moore	.05	.04	.02
380	Mike Morgan	.05	.04	.02
381	John Moses	.05	.04	.02
382	Donnell Nixon	.20	.15	.08
383	Edwin Nunez	.05	.04	.02
384	Ken Phelps	.07	.05	.03
385	Jim Presley	.12	.09	.05
386	Rey Quinones	.07	.05	.03
387	Jerry Reed	.05	.04	.02
388	Harold Reynolds	.07	.05	.03
389	Dave Valle	.05	.04	.02
390	Bill Wilkinson	.20	.15	.08
391	Harold Baines	.12	.09	.05
392	Floyd Bannister	.07	.05	.03
393	Daryl Boston	.05	.04	.02
394	Ivan Calderon	.10	.08	.04
395	Jose DeLeon	.05	.04	.02
396	Richard Dotson	.07	.05	.03
397	Carlton Fisk	.15	.11	.06
398	Ozzie Guillen	.10	.08	.04
399	Ron Hassey	.05	.04	.02
400	Donnie Hill	.05	.04	.02
401	Bob James	.05	.04	.02
402	Dave LaPoint	.05	.04	.02
403	Bill Lindsey	.15	.11	.06
404	Bill Long	.25	.20	.10
405	Steve Lyons	.05	.04	.02
406	Fred Manrique	.25	.20	.10
407	Jack McDowell	.30	.25	.12
408	Gary Redus	.07	.05	.03
409	Ray Searage	.05	.04	.02
410	Bobby Thigpen	.07	.05	.03
411	Greg Walker	.07	.05	.03
412	Jerry Browne (photo actually Bob Brower)	.07	.05	.03
413	Jim Winn	.05	.04	.02
414	Jody Davis	.07	.05	.03

#	Player	MT	NR MT	EX
415	Andre Dawson	.20	.15	.08
416	Brian Dayett	.05	.04	.02
417	Bob Dernier	.05	.04	.02
418	Frank DiPino	.05	.04	.02
419	Shawon Dunston	.10	.08	.04
420	Leon Durham	.10	.08	.04
421	Les Lancaster	.25	.20	.10
422	Ed Lynch	.05	.04	.02
423	Greg Maddux	.07	.05	.03
424	Dave Martinez	.12	.09	.05
425	Keith Moreland (photo actually Jody Davis)	.07	.05	.03
426	Jamie Moyer	.07	.05	.03
427	Jerry Mumphrey	.07	.05	.03
428	Paul Noce	.20	.15	.08
429	Rafael Palmeiro	.12	.09	.05
430	Wade Rowdon	.10	.08	.04
431	Ryne Sandberg	.25	.20	.10
432	Scott Sanderson	.05	.04	.02
433	Lee Smith	.10	.08	.04
434	Jim Sundberg	.05	.04	.02
435	Rick Sutcliffe	.12	.09	.05
436	Manny Trillo	.07	.05	.03
437	Juan Agosto	.05	.04	.02
438	Larry Andersen	.05	.04	.02
439	Alan Ashby	.05	.04	.02
440	Kevin Bass	.07	.05	.03
441	Ken Caminiti	.35	.25	.14
442	Rocky Childress	.20	.15	.08
443	Jose Cruz	.10	.08	.04
444	Danny Darwin	.05	.04	.02
445	Glenn Davis	.15	.11	.06
446	Jim Deshaies	.10	.08	.04
447	Bill Doran	.07	.05	.03
448	Ty Gainey	.05	.04	.02
449	Billy Hatcher	.07	.05	.03
450	Jeff Heathcock	.05	.04	.02
451	Bob Knepper	.07	.05	.03
452	Rob Mallicoat	.20	.15	.08
453	Dave Meads	.20	.15	.08
454	Craig Reynolds	.05	.04	.02
455	Nolan Ryan	.30	.25	.12
456	Mike Scott	.12	.09	.05
457	Dave Smith	.07	.05	.03
458	Denny Walling	.05	.04	.02
459	Robbie Wine	.25	.20	.10
460	Gerald Young	.35	.25	.14
461	Bob Brower	.07	.05	.03
462	Jerry Browne	.07	.05	.03
463	Steve Buechele	.05	.04	.02
464	Edwin Correa	.10	.08	.04
465	Cecil Espy	.20	.15	.08
466	Scott Fletcher	.07	.05	.03
467	Jose Guzman	.07	.05	.03
468	Greg Harris	.05	.04	.02
469	Charlie Hough	.07	.05	.03
470	Pete Incaviglia	.35	.25	.14
471	Paul Kilgus	.20	.15	.08
472	Mike Loynd	.07	.05	.03
473	Oddibe McDowell	.10	.08	.04
474	Dale Mohorcic	.07	.05	.03
475	Pete O'Brien	.07	.05	.03
476	Larry Parrish	.07	.05	.03
477	Geno Petralli	.05	.04	.02
478	Jeff Russell	.05	.04	.02
479	Ruben Sierra	.35	.25	.14
480	Mike Stanley	.10	.08	.04
481	Curtis Wilkerson	.05	.04	.02
482	Mitch Williams	.07	.05	.03
483	Bobby Witt	.10	.08	.04
484	Tony Armas	.07	.05	.03
485	Bob Boone	.07	.05	.03
486	Bill Buckner	.10	.08	.04
487	DeWayne Buice	.20	.15	.08
488	Brian Downing	.07	.05	.03
489	Chuck Finley	.05	.04	.02
490	Willie Fraser	.07	.05	.03
491	Jack Howell	.07	.05	.03
492	Ruppert Jones	.05	.04	.02
493	Wally Joyner	.80	.60	.30
494	Jack Lazorko	.05	.04	.02
495	Gary Lucas	.05	.04	.02
496	Kirk McCaskill	.07	.05	.03
497	Mark McLemore	.05	.04	.02
498	Darrell Miller	.05	.04	.02
499	Greg Minton	.05	.04	.02
500	Donnie Moore	.05	.04	.02
501	Gus Polidor	.05	.04	.02
502	Johnny Ray	.10	.08	.04
503	Mark Ryal	.07	.05	.03
504	Dick Schofield	.05	.04	.02
505	Don Sutton	.20	.15	.08
506	Devon White	.30	.25	.12
507	Mike Witt	.12	.09	.05
508	Dave Anderson	.05	.04	.02
509	Tim Belcher	.15	.11	.06
510	Ralph Bryant	.07	.05	.03
511	Tim Crews	.30	.25	.12
512	Mike Devereaux	.35	.25	.14
513	Mariano Duncan	.05	.04	.02
514	Pedro Guerrero	.15	.11	.06
515	Jeff Hamilton	.10	.08	.04
516	Mickey Hatcher	.05	.04	.02
517	Brad Havens	.05	.04	.02
518	Orel Hershiser	.12	.09	.05
519	Shawn Hillegas	.25	.20	.10
520	Ken Howell	.05	.04	.02
521	Tim Leary	.05	.04	.02
522	Mike Marshall	.10	.08	.04
523	Steve Sax	.15	.11	.06
524	Mike Scioscia	.05	.04	.02
525	Mike Sharperson	.07	.05	.03
526	John Shelby	.05	.04	.02
527	Franklin Stubbs	.07	.05	.03
528	Fernando Valenzuela	.25	.20	.10
529	Bob Welch	.10	.08	.04
530	Matt Young	.05	.04	.02
531	Jim Acker	.05	.04	.02
532	Paul Assenmacher	.07	.05	.03
533	Jeff Blauser	.25	.20	.10
534	Joe Boever	.15	.11	.06
535	Martin Clary	.07	.05	.03
536	Kevin Coffman	.20	.15	.08
537	Jeff Dedmon	.05	.04	.02
538	Ron Gant	.25	.20	.10
539	Tom Glavine	.35	.25	.14
540	Ken Griffey	.10	.08	.04
541	Al Hall	.05	.04	.02
542	Glenn Hubbard	.05	.04	.02
543	Dion James	.07	.05	.03
544	Dale Murphy	.40	.30	.15
545	Ken Oberkfell	.05	.04	.02
546	David Palmer	.05	.04	.02
547	Gerald Perry	.07	.05	.03
548	Charlie Puleo	.05	.04	.02
549	Ted Simmons	.12	.09	.05
550	Zane Smith	.10	.08	.04
551	Andres Thomas	.10	.08	.04
552	Ozzie Virgil	.07	.05	.03
553	Don Aase	.05	.04	.02
554	Jeff Ballard	.20	.15	.08
555	Eric Bell	.10	.08	.04
556	Mike Boddicker	.10	.08	.04
557	Ken Dixon	.05	.04	.02
558	Jim Dwyer	.05	.04	.02
559	Ken Gerhart	.10	.08	.04
560	Rene Gonzales	.20	.15	.08
561	Mike Griffin	.05	.04	.02
562	John Hayban	.05	.04	.02
563	Terry Kennedy	.07	.05	.03
564	Ray Knight	.07	.05	.03
565	Lee Lacy	.05	.04	.02
566	Fred Lynn	.15	.11	.06
567	Eddie Murray	.35	.25	.14
568	Tom Niedenfuer	.05	.04	.02
569	Bill Ripken	.35	.25	.14
570	Cal Ripken, Jr.	.35	.25	.14
571	Dave Schmidt	.05	.04	.02
572	Larry Sheets	.10	.08	.04
573	Pete Stanicek	.30	.25	.12
574	Mark Williamson	.20	.15	.08
575	Mike Young	.07	.05	.03
576	Shawn Abner	.30	.25	.12
577	Greg Booker	.05	.04	.02
578	Chris Brown	.10	.08	.04
579	Keith Comstock	.20	.15	.08
580	Joey Cora	.20	.15	.08
581	Mark Davis	.05	.04	.02
582	Tim Flannery	.05	.04	.02
583	Goose Gossage	.15	.11	.06
584	Mark Grant	.05	.04	.02
585	Tony Gwynn	.35	.25	.14
586	Andy Hawkins	.05	.04	.02
587	Stan Jefferson	.10	.08	.04
588	Jimmy Jones	.07	.05	.03
589	John Kruk	.30	.25	.12
590	Shane Mack	.30	.25	.12
591	Carmelo Martinez	.05	.04	.02
592	Lance McCullers	.07	.05	.03
593	Eric Nolte	.20	.15	.08
594	Randy Ready	.05	.04	.02
595	Luis Salazar	.05	.04	.02

		MT	NR MT	EX
596	Benito Santiago	.70	.50	.30
597	Eric Show	.05	.04	.02
598	Garry Templeton	.07	.05	.03
599	Ed Whitson	.05	.04	.02
600	Scott Bailes	.07	.05	.03
601	Chris Bando	.05	.04	.02
602	Jay Bell	.20	.15	.08
603	Brett Butler	.07	.05	.03
604	Tom Candiotti	.05	.04	.02
605	Joe Carter	.12	.09	.05
606	Carmen Castillo	.05	.04	.02
607	Brian Dorsett	.20	.15	.08
608	John Farrell	.30	.25	.12
609	Julio Franco	.10	.08	.04
610	Mel Hall	.07	.05	.03
611	Tommy Hinzo	.20	.15	.08
612	Brook Jacoby	.10	.08	.04
613	Doug Jones	.20	.15	.08
614	Ken Schrom	.05	.04	.02
615	Cory Snyder	.20	.15	.08
616	Sammy Stewart	.05	.04	.02
617	Greg Swindell	.12	.09	.05
618	Pat Tabler	.07	.05	.03
619	Ed Vande Berg	.05	.04	.02
620	Eddie Williams	.30	.25	.12
621	Rich Yett	.05	.04	.02
622	Slugging Sophomores (Wally Joyner, Cory Snyder)	.60	.45	.25
623	Dominican Dynamite (George Bell, Pedro Guerrero)	.12	.09	.05
624	Oakland's Power Team (Jose Canseco, Mark McGwire)	1.25	.90	.50
625	Classic Relief (Dan Plesac, Dave Righetti)	.10	.08	.04
626	All Star Righties (Jack Morris, Bret Saberhagen, Mike Witt)	.10	.08	.04
627	Game Closers (Steve Bedrosian, John Franco)	.07	.05	.03
628	Masters of the Double Play (Ryne Sandberg, Ozzie Smith)	.12	.09	.05
629	Rookie Record Setter (Mark McGwire)	1.00	.70	.40
630	Changing the Guard in Boston (Todd Benzinger, Ellis Burks, Mike Greenwell)	1.00	.70	.40
631	N.L. Batting Champs (Tony Gwynn, Tim Raines)	.15	.11	.06
632	Pitching Magic (Orel Hershiser, Mike Scott)	.07	.05	.03
633	Big Bats At First (Mark McGwire, Pat Tabler)	.60	.45	.25
634	Hitting King and the Thief (Vince Coleman, Tony Gwynn)	.12	.09	.05
635	A.L. Slugging Shortstops (Tony Fernandez, Cal Ripken, Jr., Alan Trammell)	.15	.11	.06
636	Tried and True Sluggers (Gary Carter, Mike Schmidt)	.20	.15	.08
637	Crunch Time (Eric Davis, Darryl Strawberry)	.70	.50	.30
638	A.L. All Stars (Matt Nokes, Kirby Puckett)	.40	.30	.15
639	N.L. All Stars (Keith Hernandez, Dale Murphy)	.20	.15	.08
640	The "O's" Brothers (Bill Ripken, Cal Ripken, Jr.)	.20	.15	.08
641	Major League Prospects (Mark Grace, Darrin Jackson)	.35	.25	.14
642	Major League Prospects (Damon Berryhill, Jeff Montgomery)	.35	.25	.14
643	Major League Prospects (Felix Fermin, Jessie Reid)	.30	.25	.12
644	Major League Prospects (Greg Myers, Greg Tabor)	.35	.25	.14
645	Major League Prospects (Jim Eppard, Joey Meyer)	.25	.20	.10
646	Major League Prospects (Adam Peterson, Randy Velarde)	.30	.25	.12
647	Major League Prospects (Chris Gwynn, Peter Smith)	.40	.30	.15
648	Major League Prospects (Greg Jelks, Tom Newell)	.35	.25	.14
649	Major League Prospects (Mario Diaz, Clay Parker)	.30	.25	.12
650	Major League Prospects (Jack Savage, Todd Simmons)	.35	.25	.14
651	Major League Prospects (John Burkett, Kirt Manwaring)	.40	.30	.15
652	Major League Prospects (Dave Otto, Walt Weiss)	.35	.25	.14
653	Major League Prospects (Randell Byers, Jeff King)	.30	.25	.12
654	Checklist 1-101	.05	.04	.02
655	Checklist 102-201	.05	.04	.02
656	Checklist 202-296	.05	.04	.02
657	Checklist 297-390	.05	.04	.02
658	Checklist 391-483	.05	.04	.02
659	Checklist 484-575	.05	.04	.02
660	Checklist 576-660	.05	.04	.02

1987 French/Bray Orioles

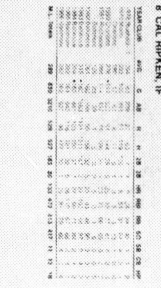

8 CAL RIPKEN, IF
Compliments of
FRENCH/BRAY, INC.

The Baltimore Orioles and French/Bray, Inc. issued a baseball card set to be handed out to fans in attendance at Memorial Stadium on July 26th. Thirty perforated, detachable cards were printed within a 3-panel fold-out piece measuring 9½" by 11¼". The card fronts feature full-color player photos surrounded by an orange border. The French/Bray logo appears on the card front. The backs are of simple design, containing only the player's name, uniform number, position and professional record.

		MT	NR MT	EX
	Complete Set:	10.00	7.50	4.00
	Common Player:	.15	.11	.06
2	Alan Wiggins	.15	.11	.06
3	Bill Ripken	1.00	.70	.40
6	Floyd Rayford	.15	.11	.06
7	Cal Ripken, Sr.	.30	.25	.12
8	Cal Ripken	1.50	1.25	.60
9	Jim Dwyer	.15	.11	.06
10	Terry Crowley	.15	.11	.06
15	Terry Kennedy	.20	.15	.08
16	Scott McGregor	.20	.15	.08
18	Larry Sheets	.70	.50	.30
19	Fred Lynn	.50	.40	.20
20	Frank Robinson	.50	.40	.20
24	Dave Schmidt	.15	.11	.06
25	Ray Knight	.20	.15	.08
27	Lee Lacy	.20	.15	.08
31	Mark Wiley	.15	.11	.06
32	Mark Williamson	.30	.25	.12
33	Eddie Murray	1.50	1.25	.60
38	Ken Gerhart	.80	.60	.30
39	Ken Dixon	.15	.11	.06
40	Jimmy Williams	.15	.11	.06
42	Mike Griffin	.15	.11	.06
43	Mike Young	.40	.30	.15
44	Elrod Hendricks	.15	.11	.06
45	Eric Bell	.40	.30	.15
46	Mike Flanagan	.25	.20	.10
49	Tom Niedenfuer	.20	.15	.08
52	Mike Boddicker	.30	.25	.12
54	John Habyan	.15	.11	.06
57	Tony Arnold	.15	.11	.06

1928 Fro-joy

Capitalizing on the extreme popularity of Babe Ruth, the six-card set was given away with Fro-joy Cones during the August 6-11, 1928 Fro-joy Cone

George Herman ("Babe") Ruth

"The Sultan of Swat," who holds the world's record for home-run hits in a single season with 60 circuit clouts during the regular playing season of 1927, topped by 2 more against Pittsburgh during the World's Series games last year.

Boys—Girls:

Fro-joy Ice Cream, in *Fro-joy* Cones, builds bone and strength. Eat one every day.

Chock-full of

"YOUTH UNITS"

PICTURE NO. 1

This is the first in a series of six pictures of "Babe" Ruth being given free with Fro-joy Cones during Fro-joy Cone Week, August 6th-11th, 1928. The complete set can be exchanged for a large reproduction of "Babe" Ruth's autographed photo. Ask your dealer for a FREE circular giving full details.

Week. The cards, which measure 2 1/16'' by 4'' in size, contain black and white photos designed on either a horizontal or vertical format. The card fronts also contain a caption with a few sentences explaining the photo. The card backs contain advertising for Fro-joy Ice Cream and Cones.

	NR MT	EX	VG
Complete Set:	750.00	375.00	225.00
Common Player:	90.00	45.00	27.00
1	George Herman ("Babe") Ruth	150.00	75.00	45.00
2	Look Out, Mr. Pitcher!	110.00	55.00	33.00
3	"Babe" Ruth's Grip!	90.00	45.00	27.00
4	Ruth is a Crack Fielder	110.00	55.00	33.00
5	Bang! The Babe Lines Out!	110.00	55.00	33.00
6	When The "Babe" Comes Home	125.00	62.00	37.00

1985 Fun Food Buttons

Fun Foods of Little Silver, N.J. issued a set of 133 full-color metal pins in 1985. The buttons, which are 1¼'' in diameter and have a "safety pin" back, have bright borders which correspond to the player's team colors. The button backs are numbered and contain the player's 1984 batting or earned run average. The buttons were available as complete sets through hobby dealers and were also distributed in packs (three buttons per pack) through retail stores.

	MT	NR MT	EX
Complete Set:	16.00	12.00	6.50
Common Player:	.10	.08	.04
1	Dave Winfield	.40	.30	.15
2	Lance Parrish	.25	.20	.10
3	Gary Carter	.35	.25	.14
4	Pete Rose	1.50	1.25	.60
5	Jim Rice	.35	.25	.14
6	George Brett	.60	.45	.25
7	Fernando Valenzuela	.30	.25	.12
8	Darryl Strawberry	.60	.45	.25
9	Steve Garvey	.35	.25	.14

		MT	NR MT	EX
10	Rollie Fingers	.20	.15	.08
11	Mike Schmidt	.60	.45	.25
12	Kent Tekulve	.10	.08	.04
13	Ryne Sandberg	.40	.30	.15
14	Bruce Sutter	.15	.11	.06
15	Tom Seaver	.30	.25	.12
16	Reggie Jackson	.45	.35	.20
17	Rickey Henderson	.50	.40	.20
18	Mark Langston	.35	.25	.14
19	Jack Clark	.20	.15	.08
20	Willie Randolph	.15	.11	.06
21	Kirk Gibson	.30	.25	.12
22	Andre Dawson	.30	.25	.12
23	Dave Concepcion	.15	.11	.06
24	Tony Armas	.10	.08	.04
25	Dan Quisenberry	.15	.11	.06
26	Pedro Guerrero	.25	.20	.10
27	Dwight Gooden	2.25	1.75	.90
28	Tony Gwynn	.40	.30	.15
29	Robin Yount	.30	.25	.12
30	Steve Carlton	.30	.25	.12
31	Bill Madlock	.15	.11	.06
32	Rick Sutcliffe	.15	.11	.06
33	Willie McGee	.25	.20	.10
34	Greg Luzinski	.15	.11	.06
35	Rod Carew	.40	.30	.15
36	Dave Kingman	.15	.11	.06
37	Alvin Davis	.40	.30	.15
38	Chili Davis	.15	.11	.06
39	Don Baylor	.15	.11	.06
40	Alan Trammell	.30	.25	.12
41	Tim Raines	.35	.25	.14
42	Cesar Cedeno	.15	.11	.06
43	Wade Boggs	1.75	1.25	.70
44	Frank White	.15	.11	.06
45	Steve Sax	.25	.20	.10
46	George Foster	.15	.11	.06
47	Terry Kennedy	.15	.11	.06
48	Cecil Cooper	.15	.11	.06
49	John Denny	.10	.08	.04
50	John Candelaria	.10	.08	.04
51	Jody Davis	.15	.11	.06
52	George Hendrick	.10	.08	.04
53	Ron Kittle	.15	.11	.06
54	Fred Lynn	.20	.15	.08
55	Carney Lansford	.10	.08	.04
56	Gorman Thomas	.10	.08	.04
57	Manny Trillo	.10	.08	.04
58	Steve Kemp	.10	.08	.04
59	Jack Morris	.25	.20	.10
60	Dan Petry	.10	.08	.04
61	Mario Soto	.10	.08	.04
62	Dwight Evans	.20	.15	.08
63	Hal McRae	.10	.08	.04
64	Mike Marshall	.15	.11	.06
65	Mookie Wilson	.15	.11	.06
66	Graig Nettles	.15	.11	.06
67	Ben Oglivie	.10	.08	.04
68	Juan Samuel	.25	.20	.10
69	Johnny Ray	.15	.11	.06
70	Gary Matthews	.15	.11	.06
71	Ozzie Smith	.20	.15	.08
72	Carlton Fisk	.20	.15	.08
73	Doug DeCinces	.15	.11	.06
74	Joe Morgan	.20	.15	.08
75	Dave Stieb	.15	.11	.06
76	Buddy Bell	.15	.11	.06
77	Don Mattingly	2.50	2.00	1.00
78	Lou Whitaker	.25	.20	.10
79	Willie Hernandez	.15	.11	.06
80	Dave Parker	.20	.15	.08
81	Bob Stanley	.10	.08	.04
82	Willie Wilson	.15	.11	.06
83	Orel Hershiser	.50	.40	.20
84	Rusty Staub	.15	.11	.06
85	Goose Gossage	.20	.15	.08
86	Don Sutton	.25	.20	.10
87	Al Holland	.10	.08	.04
88	Tony Pena	.15	.11	.06
89	Ron Cey	.15	.11	.06
90	Joaquin Andujar	.10	.08	.04
91	LaMarr Hoyt	.10	.08	.04
92	Tommy John	.20	.15	.08
93	Dwayne Murphy	.10	.08	.04
94	Willie Upshaw	.10	.08	.04
95	Gary Ward	.10	.08	.04
96	Ron Guidry	.20	.15	.08
97	Chet Lemon	.15	.11	.06
98	Aurelio Lopez	.10	.08	.04
99	Tony Perez	.20	.15	.08
100	Bill Buckner	.15	.11	.06

		MT	NR MT	EX
101	Mike Hargrove	.10	.08	.04
102	Scott McGregor	.10	.08	.04
103	Dale Murphy	.70	.50	.30
104	Keith Hernandez	.35	.25	.14
105	Paul Molitor	.20	.15	.08
106	Bert Blyleven	.15	.11	.06
107	Leon Durham	.15	.11	.06
108	Lee Smith	.15	.11	.06
109	Nolan Ryan	.35	.25	.14
110	Harold Baines	.15	.11	.06
111	Kent Hrbek	.25	.20	.10
112	Ron Davis	.10	.08	.04
113	George Bell	.35	.25	.14
114	Charlie Hough	.10	.08	.04
115	Phil Niekro	.25	.20	.10
116	Dave Righetti	.20	.15	.08
117	Darrell Evans	.15	.11	.06
118	Cal Ripken, Jr.	.60	.45	.25
119	Eddie Murray	.50	.40	.20
120	Storm Davis	.10	.08	.04
121	Mike Boddicker	.10	.08	.04
122	Bob Horner	.20	.15	.08
123	Chris Chambliss	.10	.08	.04
124	Ted Simmons	.15	.11	.06
125	Andre Thornton	.15	.11	.06
126	Larry Bowa	.15	.11	.06
127	Bob Dernier	.10	.08	.04
128	Joe Niekro	.15	.11	.06
129	Jose Cruz	.15	.11	.06
130	Tom Brunansky	.20	.15	.08
131	Gary Gaetti	.25	.20	.10
132	Lloyd Moseby	.15	.11	.06
133	Frank Tanana	.10	.08	.04

1983 Gardner's Brewers

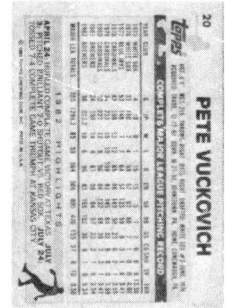

Topps produced in 1983 for Gardner's Bakery of Madison, Wisconsin a 22 card set featuring the American League champion Milwaukee Brewers. The cards, which measure 2½" by 3½", have colorful fronts which contain the player's name, team and position plus the Brewers and Gardner's logos. The card backs are identical to the regular Topps issue but are numbered 1-22. The cards were inserted in specially-marked packages of Gardner's bread products and were susceptible to grease stains.

		MT	NR MT	EX
Complete Set		25.00	18.50	10.00
Common Player		.50	.40	.20
1	Harvey Kuenn	.70	.50	.30
2	Dwight Bernard	.50	.40	.20
3	Mark Brouhard	.50	.40	.20
4	Mike Caldwell	.50	.40	.20

		MT	NR MT	EX
5	Cecil Cooper	1.25	.90	.50
6	Marshall Edwards	.50	.40	.20
7	Rollie Fingers	1.50	1.25	.60
8	Jim Gantner	.70	.50	.30
9	Moose Haas	.50	.40	.20
10	Bob McClure	.50	.40	.20
11	Paul Molitor	2.00	1.50	.80
12	Don Money	.50	.40	.20
13	Charlie Moore	.50	.40	.20
14	Ben Oglivie	.60	.45	.25
15	Ed Romero	.50	.40	.20
16	Ted Simmons	.90	.70	.35
17	Jim Slaton	.50	.40	.20
18	Don Sutton	1.50	1.25	.60
19	Gorman Thomas	.70	.50	.30
20	Pete Vuckovich	.70	.50	.30
21	Ned Yost	.50	.40	.20
22	Robin Yount	2.50	2.00	1.00

1984 Gardner's Brewers

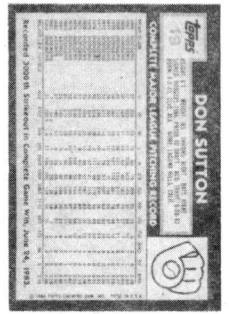

For the second straight year, Gardner's Bakery inserted baseball cards featuring the Milwaukee Brewers with their bread products. The 22-card set, entitled "1984 Series II", have multi-colored fronts that include the Brewers and Gardner's logos. The card backs are identical to the regular 1984 Topps issue except for the 1-22 numbering system. The Topps-produced cards are the standard 2½" by 3½" size. The cards are sometimes found with grease stains, resulting from contact with the bread.

		MT	NR MT	EX
Complete Set:		20.00	15.00	8.00
Common Player:		.50	.40	.20
1	Rene Lachemann	.50	.40	.20
2	Mark Brouhard	.50	.40	.20
3	Mike Caldwell	.50	.40	.20
4	Bobby Clark	.50	.40	.20
5	Cecil Cooper	1.00	.70	.40
6	Rollie Fingers	1.25	.90	.50
7	Jim Gantner	.70	.50	.30
8	Moose Haas	.50	.40	.20
9	Roy Howell	.50	.40	.20
10	Pete Ladd	.50	.40	.20
11	Rick Manning	.50	.40	.20
12	Bob McClure	.50	.40	.20
13	Paul Molitor	1.75	1.25	.70
14	Charlie Moore	.50	.40	.20
15	Ben Oglivie	.60	.45	.25
16	Ed Romero	.50	.40	.20
17	Ted Simmons	.80	.60	.30
18	Jim Sundberg	.50	.40	.20
19	Don Sutton	1.25	.90	.50
20	Tom Tellmann	.50	.40	.20
21	Pete Vuckovich	.60	.45	.25
22	Robin Yount	2.25	1.75	.90

1985 Gardner's Brewers

Gardner's Bakery issued a 22-card set featuring the Milwaukee Brewers for the third consecutive year in

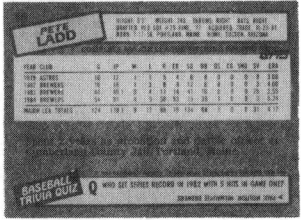

1985. The set was produced by Topps and is designed in a horizontal format. The card fronts feature color photos inside blue, red and yellow frames. The player's name and position are placed in orange boxes to the right of the photo and are accompanied by the Brewers and Gardner's logos. The card backs are identical in design to the regular 1985 Topps set but are blue rather than green and are numbered 1-22. The cards, which were inserted in specially-marked bread products, are often found with grease stains.

		MT	NR MT	EX
Complete Set:		14.00	10.50	5.50
Common Player:		.35	.25	.14
1	George Bamberger	.35	.25	.14
2	Mark Brouhard	.35	.25	.14
3	Bob Clark	.35	.25	.14
4	Jaime Cocanower	.35	.25	.14
5	Cecil Cooper	.90	.70	.35
6	Rollie Fingers	1.25	.90	.50
7	Jim Gantner	.50	.40	.20
8	Moose Haas	.35	.25	.14
9	Dion James	.80	.60	.30
10	Pete Ladd	.35	.25	.14
11	Rick Manning	.35	.25	.14
12	Bob McClure	.35	.25	.14
13	Paul Molitor	1.50	1.25	.60
14	Charlie Moore	.35	.25	.14
15	Ben Oglivie	.50	.40	.20
16	Chuck Porter	.35	.25	.14
17	Ed Romero	.35	.25	.14
18	Bill Schroeder	.35	.25	.14
19	Ted Simmons	.70	.50	.30
20	Tom Tellmann	.35	.25	.14
21	Pete Vuckovich	.50	.40	.20
22	Robin Yount	2.00	1.50	.80

1986 Gatorade Cubs

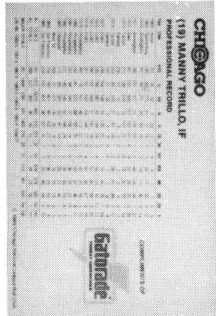

(19) MANNY TRILLO, IF

Gatorade sponsored this 28-card set which was given away at the July 17, 1986 Cubs game. The

cards measure 2⅞'' by 4¼'' and feature color photos set inside red and white frames. The Cubs logo appears at the top of the card in blue and red. The card backs include statistical information and the Gatorade logo. This set marked the fifth consecutive year the Cubs had held a baseball card giveaway promotion.

		MT	NR MT	EX
Complete Set:		9.00	6.75	3.50
Common Player:		.10	.08	.04
4	Gene Michael	.15	.11	.06
6	Keith Moreland	.35	.25	.14
7	Jody Davis	.35	.25	.14
10	Leon Durham	.50	.40	.20
11	Ron Cey	.25	.20	.10
12	Shawon Dunston	.80	.60	.30
15	Davey Lopes	.25	.20	.10
16	Terry Francona	.10	.08	.04
18	Steve Christmas	.10	.08	.04
19	Manny Trillo	.15	.11	.06
20	Bob Dernier	.15	.11	.06
21	Scott Sanderson	.10	.08	.04
22	Jerry Mumphrey	.15	.11	.06
23	Ryne Sandberg	2.00	1.50	.80
27	Thad Bosley	.10	.08	.04
28	Chris Speier	.10	.08	.04
29	Steve Lake	.10	.08	.04
31	Ray Fontenot	.10	.08	.04
34	Steve Trout	.25	.20	.10
36	Gary Matthews	.25	.20	.10
39	George Frazier	.10	.08	.04
40	Rick Sutcliffe	.70	.50	.30
43	Dennis Eckersley	.25	.20	.10
46	Lee Smith	.35	.25	.14
48	Jay Baller	.20	.15	.08
49	Jamie Moyer	.35	.25	.14
50	Guy Hoffman	.10	.08	.04
---	The Coaching Staff (Ruben Amaro, Billy Connors, Johnny Oates, John Vuckovich, Billy Williams)	.15	.11	.06

1987 Gatorade Indians

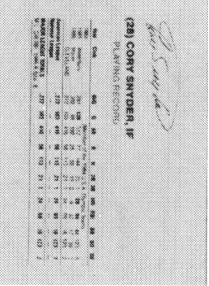

(28) CORY SNYDER, IF
COMPLIMENTS OF Gatorade

For the second year in a row, the Cleveland Indians gave out a perforated set of baseball cards to fans attending the Team Photo/Baseball Card Day promotion. Sponsored by Gatorade, the individual cards measure 2⅛'' by 3⅛''. The fronts contain a full-color photo surrounded by a red frame inside a white border. The player's name, uniform number and the Gatorade logo are also on the fronts. The card backs are printed in black, blue and red and carry a facsimile autograph and the player's playing record.

		MT	NR MT	EX
Complete Set:		6.50	5.00	2.50
Common Player:		.06	.05	.02
2	Brett Butler	.30	.25	.12
4	Tony Bernazard	.12	.09	.05
6	Andy Allanson	.12	.09	.05
7	Pat Corrales	.12	.09	.05
8	Carmen Castillo	.06	.05	.02
10	Pat Tabler	.25	.20	.10
11	Jamie Easterly	.06	.05	.02
12	Dave Clark	.20	.15	.08
13	Ernie Camacho	.06	.05	.02
14	Julio Franco	.40	.30	.15
17	Junior Noboa	.20	.15	.08

		MT	NR MT	EX
18	Ken Schrom	.10	.08	.04
20	Otis Nixon	.06	.05	.02
21	Greg Swindell	.60	.45	.25
22	Frank Wills	.06	.05	.02
23	Chris Bando	.06	.05	.02
24	Rick Dempsey	.12	.09	.05
26	Brook Jacoby	.40	.30	.15
27	Mel Hall	.30	.25	.12
28	Cory Snyder	.90	.70	.35
29	Andre Thornton	.30	.25	.12
30	Joe Carter	.60	.45	.25
35	Phil Niekro	.40	.30	.15
36	Ed Vande Berg	.06	.05	.02
42	Rich Yett	.06	.05	.02
43	Scott Bailes	.40	.30	.15
46	Doug Jones	.20	.15	.08
49	Tom Candiotti	.12	.09	.05
54	Tom Waddell	.06	.05	.02
---	Manager and Coaching Staff (Jack Aker, Bobby Bonds, Pat Corrales, Doc Edwards, Johnny Goryl)	.06	.05	.02

1985 General Mills Stickers

General Mills of Canada inserted a panel of two baseball stickers, in a cellophane wrapper, in each box of Cheerios in 1985. The full-color sticker panels, which measure 2⅜" by 3¾" in size, feature 30 popular players. The stickers are blank-backed and unnumbered and contain the player's name, team and position in both English and French. The General Mills logo appears at the top of each sticker. Curiously, all team insignias on the players' uniforms and hats have been airbrushed off.

		MT	NR MT	EX
Complete Set:		15.00	11.00	6.00
Common Panel:		.60	.45	.25
Panel		.80	.60	.30
(1)	Gary Carter			
(2)	Tom Brunansky			
Panel		.80	.60	.30
(3)	Gary Carter			
(4)	Dave Stieb			
Panel		1.25	.90	.50
(5)	Andre Dawson			
(6)	Alvin Davis			
Panel		1.50	1.25	.60
(7)	Steve Garvey			
(8)	George Bell			
Panel		1.00	.70	.40
(9)	Steve Garvey			
(10)	Jim Rice			
Panel		.80	.60	.30
(11)	Jeff Leonard			
(12)	Eddie Murray			
Panel		1.50	1.25	.60
(13)	Dale Murphy			
(14)	Robin Yount			
Panel		.90	.70	.35
(15)	Terry Puhl			
(16)	Reggie Jackson			
Panel		.60	.45	.25
(17)	Johnny Ray			
(18)	Lou Whitaker			
Panel		.90	.70	.35
(19)	Ryne Sandberg			
(20)	Mike Hargrove			
Panel		1.75	1.25	.70
(21)	Mike Schmidt			
(22)	George Brett			

		MT	NR MT	EX
Panel		1.00	.70	.40
(23)	Ozzie Smith			
(24)	Dave Winfield			
Panel		.60	.45	.25
(25)	Mario Soto			
(26)	Carlton Fisk			
Panel		.80	.60	.30
(27)	Fernando Valenzuela			
(28)	Dwayne Murphy			

1986 General Mills Booklets

In 1986, General Mills of Canada inserted six different "Baseball Players Booklets" in specially marked boxes of Cheerios. Ten different players are featured in each booklet, with statistics for the 1985 season being in both English and French. The booklet, when opened fully, measures 3¾" by 15". Also included in the booklet is a contest sponsored by Petro-Canada service stations to win a day with a major league player at his 1987 spring training site in Florida. Team insignias have been airbrushed off the players' uniforms and caps.

	MT	NR MT	EX
Complete Set:	15.00	11.00	6.00
Common Booklet:	1.50	1.25	.60

1	A.L. East (Wade Boggs, Kirk Gibson, Rickey Henderson, Don Mattingly, Jack Morris, Lance Parrish, Jim Rice, Dave Righetti, Cal Ripken, Lou Whitaker)	3.50	2.75	1.50
2	A.L. West (Harold Baines, Phil Bradley, George Brett, Carlton Fisk, Ozzie Guillen, Kent Hrbek, Reggie Jackson, Dan Quisenberry, Bret Saberhagen, Frank White)	2.25	1.75	.90
3	Toronto Blue Jays (Jesse Barfield, George Bell, Bill Caudill, Tony Fernandez, Damaso Garcia, Lloyd Moseby, Rance Mulliniks, Dave Stieb, Willie Upshaw, Ernie Whitt)	2.00	1.50	.80
4	N.L. East (Gary Carter, Jack Clark, George Foster, Dwight Gooden, Gary Matthews, Willie McGee, Ryne Sandberg, Mike Schmidt, Lee Smith, Ozzie Smith)	3.50	2.75	1.50
5	N.L. West (Dave Concepcion, Pedro Guerrero, Terry Kennedy, Dale Murphy, Graig Nettles, Dave Parker, Tony Perez, Steve Sax, Bruce Sutter, Fernando Valenzuela)	2.25	1.75	.90
6	Montreal Expos (Hubie Brooks, Andre Dawson, Mike Fitzgerald, Vance Law, Tim Raines, Jeff Reardon, Bryn Smith, Jason Thompson, Tim Wallach, Mitch Webster)	1.50	1.25	.60

1987 General Mills Booklets

For a second straight year, General Mills of Canada inserted one of six different "Baseball Super-Stars Booklets" in specially marked boxes of Cheerios and Honey Nut Cheerios cereal. Each booklet contains ten

full-color photos for a total of 60 players. The booklets, when completely unfolded, measure 15'' by 3¾''. Written in both English and French, the set was produced by Mike Schecter and Associates. All team insignias have been airbrushed away.

		MT	NR MT	EX
Complete Set:		15.00	11.00	6.00
Common Booklet:		1.50	1.25	.60
1	Toronto Blue Jays (Jesse Barfield, George Bell, Tony Fernandez, Kelly Gruber, Tom Henke, Jimmy Key, Lloyd Moseby, Dave Stieb, Willie Upshaw, Ernie Whitt)	2.00	1.50	.80
2	A.L. East (Wade Boggs, Roger Clemens, Kirk Gibson, Rickey Henderson, Don Mattingly, Jack Morris, Eddie Murray, Pat Tabler, Dave Winfield, Robin Yount)	3.50	2.75	1.50
3	A.L. West (Phil Bradley, George Brett, Jose Canseco, Carlton Fisk, Reggie Jackson, Wally Joyner, Kirk McCaskill, Larry Parrish, Kirby Puckett, Dan Quisenberry)	3.25	2.50	1.25
4	Montreal Expos (Hubie Brooks, Mike Fitzgerald, Andres Galarraga, Vance Law, Andy McGaffigan, Bryn Smith, Jason Thompson, Tim Wallach, Mitch Webster, Floyd Youmans)	1.00	.70	.40
5	N.L. East (Gary Carter, Dwight Gooden, Keith Hernandez, Willie McGee, Tim Raines, R.J. Reynolds, Ryne Sandberg, Mike Schmidt, Ozzie Smith, Darryl Strawberry)	3.25	2.50	1.25
6	N.L. West (Kevin Bass, Chili Davis, Bill Doran, Pedro Guerrero, Tony Gwynn, Dale Murphy, Dave Parker, Steve Sax, Mike Scott, Fernando Valenzuela)	3.25	2.50	1.25

1933 George C. Miller

The George C. Miller & Co. of Boston, Mass. issued a 32-card set in 1933. The set, which received limited distribution, consists of 16 National League and 16 American League players. The cards are color art reproductions of actual photographs and measure 2⅜'' by 2⅞'' in size. Two distinct variations can be found for each card in the set. Two different typefaces were used, one being much smaller than the

other. The most substantial difference is ''R'' and ''L'' being used for the ''Bats/Throws'' information on one version, while the other spells out ''Right'' and ''Left.'' Collectors were advised on the card backs to collect all 32 cards and return them for prizes. The cards, with a cancellation at the bottom, were returned to the collector with the prize. Two forms of cancellation were used; one involved the complete trimming of the bottom one-quarter of the card, the other a series of diamond-shaped punch holes. Cancelled cards have a significantly decreased value.

		NR MT	EX	VG
Complete Set:		11500.00	5750.00	3450.
Common Player:		225.00	112.00	67.00
(1)	Dale Alexander	225.00	112.00	67.00
(2)	"Ivy" Paul Andrews	1300.00	650.00	390.00
(3)	Earl Averill	325.00	162.00	97.00
(4)	Dick Bartell	225.00	112.00	67.00
(5)	Walter Berger	225.00	112.00	67.00
(6)	Jim Bottomley	325.00	162.00	97.00
(7)	Joe Cronin	375.00	187.00	112.00
(8)	Jerome "Dizzy" Dean	600.00	300.00	180.00
(9)	William Dickey	500.00	250.00	150.00
(10)	Jimmy Dykes	225.00	112.00	67.00
(11)	Wesley Ferrell	225.00	112.00	67.00
(12)	Jimmy Foxx	550.00	275.00	165.00
(13)	Frank Frisch	375.00	187.00	112.00
(14)	Charlie Gehringer	375.00	187.00	112.00
(15)	Leon "Goose" Goslin	325.00	162.00	97.00
(16)	Charlie Grimm	225.00	112.00	67.00
(17)	Bob "Lefty" Grove	400.00	200.00	120.00
(18)	Charles "Chick" Hafey	325.00	162.00	97.00
(19)	Ray Hayworth	225.00	112.00	67.00
(20)	Charles "Chuck" Klein	325.00	162.00	97.00
(21)	Walter "Rabbit" Maranville	325.00	162.00	97.00
(22)	Oscar Melillo	225.00	112.00	67.00
(23)	Frank "Lefty" O'Doul	225.00	112.00	67.00
(24)	Melvin Ott	400.00	200.00	120.00
(25)	Carl Reynolds	225.00	112.00	67.00
(26)	Charles Ruffing	325.00	162.00	97.00
(27)	Al Simmons	325.00	162.00	97.00
(28)	Joe Stripp	225.00	112.00	67.00
(29)	Bill Terry	375.00	187.00	112.00
(30)	Lloyd Waner	325.00	162.00	97.00
(31)	Paul Waner	325.00	162.00	97.00
(32)	Lonnie Warneke	225.00	112.00	67.00

1953 Glendale Hot Dogs Tigers

Glendale Meats issued these unnumbered, full color cards (2⅝'' by 3¾'') in packages of hot dogs. Featuring Detroit Tigers players, the card fronts contain a player picture plus the player's name, a facsimile autograph, and the Tigers logo. The card reverses carry player statistical and biographical information plus an offer for a trip for two to the World Series. Collectors were advised to mail all the cards they had saved to Glendale Meats. The World Series trip plus 150 other prizes were to be given to the individuals sending in the most cards. As with most cards issued with food products, quality-condition cards are tough to find because of the cards' susceptibility to stains. The Houtteman card is extremely scarce.

		NR MT	EX	VG
Complete Set:		4000.00	2000.00	1200.
Common Player:		60.00	30.00	18.00
(1)	Matt Batts	60.00	30.00	18.00
(2)	Johnny Bucha	60.00	30.00	18.00
(3)	Frank Carswell	60.00	30.00	18.00
(4)	Jim Delsing	60.00	30.00	18.00
(5)	Walt Dropo	60.00	30.00	18.00
(6)	Hal Erickson	60.00	30.00	18.00
(7)	Paul Foytack	60.00	30.00	18.00
(8)	Owen Friend	90.00	45.00	27.00
(9)	Ned Garver	60.00	30.00	18.00
(10)	Joe Ginsberg	300.00	150.00	90.00
(11)	Ted Gray	60.00	30.00	18.00
(12)	Fred Hatfield	60.00	30.00	18.00
(13)	Ray Herbert	90.00	45.00	27.00
(14)	Bill Hitchcock	60.00	30.00	18.00
(15)	Bill Hoeft	225.00	112.00	67.00
(16)	Art Houtteman	1750.00	875.00	525.00
(17)	Milt Jordan	125.00	62.00	37.00
(18)	Harvey Kuenn	175.00	87.00	52.00
(19)	Don Lund	60.00	30.00	18.00
(20)	Dave Madison	60.00	30.00	18.00
(21)	Dick Marlowe	60.00	30.00	18.00
(22)	Pat Mullin	60.00	30.00	18.00
(23)	Bob Neiman	60.00	30.00	18.00
(24)	Johnny Pesky	75.00	37.00	22.00
(25)	Jerry Priddy	60.00	30.00	18.00
(26)	Steve Souchock	60.00	30.00	18.00
(27)	Russ Sullivan	60.00	30.00	18.00
(28)	Bill Wight	125.00	62.00	37.00

1961 Golden Press

 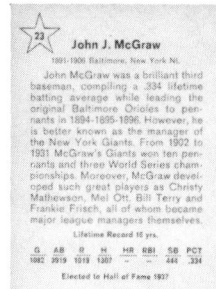

The 1961 Golden Press set features 33 players, all enshrined in the Baseball Hall of Fame. The full color cards measure 2½" by 3½" and came in a booklet with perforations so that they could be easily removed. Full books with the cards intact would command a 50% premium over the set price in the checklist that follows. Card numbers 1-3 and 28-33 are slightly higher in price as they were located on the book's front and back covers, making them more susceptible to scuffing and wear.

		NR MT	EX	VG
Complete Set:		45.00	22.00	13.50
Common Player:		.50	.25	.15
1	Mel Ott	1.50	.70	.45
2	Grover Cleveland Alexander	1.50	.70	.45
3	Babe Ruth	9.00	4.50	2.75
4	Hank Greenberg	.75	.40	.25
5	Bill Terry	.75	.40	.25
6	Carl Hubbell	.75	.40	.25
7	Rogers Hornsby	1.50	.70	.45
8	Dizzy Dean	2.00	1.00	.60
9	Joe DiMaggio	5.00	2.50	1.50
10	Charlie Gehringer	.75	.40	.25
11	Gabby Hartnett	.50	.25	.15
12	Mickey Cochrane	.75	.40	.25

		NR MT	EX	VG
13	George Sisler	.75	.40	.25
14	Joe Cronin	.75	.40	.25
15	Pie Traynor	.50	.25	.15
16	Lou Gehrig	5.00	2.50	1.50
17	Lefty Grove	.90	.45	.25
18	Chief Bender	.50	.25	.15
19	Frankie Frisch	.75	.40	.25
20	Al Simmons	.50	.25	.15
21	Home Run Baker	.50	.25	.15
22	Jimmy Foxx	1.50	.70	.45
23	John McGraw	.90	.45	.25
24	Christy Mathewson	2.50	1.25	.70
25	Ty Cobb	5.00	2.50	1.50
26	Dazzy Vance	.50	.25	.15
27	Bill Dickey	.90	.45	.25
28	Eddie Collins	.75	.40	.25
29	Walter Johnson	3.00	1.50	.90
30	Tris Speaker	1.50	.70	.45
31	Nap Lajoie	1.50	.70	.45
32	Honus Wagner	3.00	1.50	.90
33	Cy Young	3.00	1.50	.90

1933 Goudey

 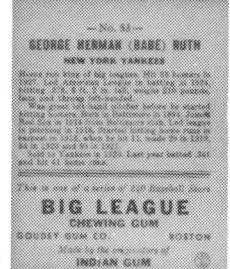

Goudey Gum Co.'s first baseball card issue was their 240 card effort in 1933. The cards are color art reproductions of either portrait or action photos. The numbered cards measure 2⅜" by 2⅞" in size and carry a short player biography on the reverses. Card #106 Napoleon Lajoie is listed in the set though it was not actually issued until 1934. The card is very scarce and is unique in that it carries a 1934 design obverse and a 1933 reverse. The ACC designation for the set is R319.

		NR MT	EX	VG
Complete Set w/o Lajoie:		18000.00	7200.00	4500.
Common Player: 1-40		35.00	17.50	10.50
Common Player: 41-44		30.00	15.00	9.00
Common Player: 45-52		35.00	17.50	10.50
Common Player: 53-240		30.00	15.00	9.00
1	Benny Bengough	600.00	20.00	10.50
2	Arthur (Dazzy) Vance	60.00	30.00	18.00
3	Hugh Critz	35.00	17.50	10.50
4	Henry "Heinie" Schuble	35.00	17.50	10.50
5	Floyd (Babe) Herman	40.00	20.00	12.00
6a	Jimmy Dykes (age is 26 in bio)	40.00	20.00	12.00
6b	Jimmy Dykes (age is 36 in bio)	40.00	20.00	12.00
7	Ted Lyons	60.00	30.00	18.00
8	Roy Johnson	35.00	17.50	10.50
9	Dave Harris	35.00	17.50	10.50
10	Glenn Myatt	35.00	17.50	10.50
11	Billy Rogell	35.00	17.50	10.50
12	George Pipgras	55.00	27.00	16.50
13	Lafayette Thompson	40.00	20.00	12.00
14	Henry Johnson	35.00	17.50	10.50
15	Victor Sorrell	35.00	17.50	10.50
16	George Blaeholder	35.00	17.50	10.50
17	Watson Clark	35.00	17.50	10.50
18	Herold (Muddy) Ruel	35.00	17.50	10.50
19	Bill Dickey	125.00	62.00	37.00
20	Bill Terry	90.00	45.00	27.00
21	Phil Collins	35.00	17.50	10.50
22	Harold (Pie) Traynor	60.00	30.00	18.00
23	Hazen (Ki-Ki) Cuyler	60.00	30.00	18.00
24	Horace Ford	35.00	17.50	10.50
25	Paul Waner	60.00	30.00	18.00

#	Player	NR MT	EX	VG
26	Chalmer Cissell	35.00	17.50	10.50
27	George Connally	35.00	17.50	10.50
28	Dick Bartell	35.00	17.50	10.50
29	Jimmy Foxx	160.00	80.00	48.00
30	Frank Hogan	35.00	17.50	10.50
31	Tony Lazzeri	60.00	30.00	18.00
32	John (Bud) Clancy	35.00	17.50	10.50
33	Ralph Kress	35.00	17.50	10.50
34	Bob O'Farrell	35.00	17.50	10.50
35	Al Simmons	60.00	30.00	18.00
36	Tommy Thevenow	35.00	17.50	10.50
37	Jimmy Wilson	35.00	17.50	10.50
38	Fred Brickell	35.00	17.50	10.50
39	Mark Koenig	35.00	17.50	10.50
40	Taylor Douthit	35.00	17.50	10.50
41	Gus Mancuso	30.00	15.00	9.00
42	Eddie Collins	60.00	30.00	18.00
43	Lew Fonseca	35.00	17.50	10.50
44	Jim Bottomley	55.00	27.00	16.50
45	Larry Benton	35.00	17.50	10.50
46	Ethan Allen	35.00	17.50	10.50
47	Henry "Heinie" Manush	60.00	30.00	18.00
48	Marty McManus	35.00	17.50	10.50
49	Frank Frisch	90.00	45.00	27.00
50	Ed Brandt	35.00	17.50	10.50
51	Charlie Grimm	40.00	20.00	12.00
52	Andy Cohen	35.00	17.50	10.50
53	George Herman (Babe) Ruth	2800.00	1120.00	560.00
54	Ray Kremer	30.00	15.00	9.00
55	Perce (Pat) Malone	30.00	15.00	9.00
56	Charlie Ruffing	55.00	27.00	16.50
57	Earl Clark	30.00	15.00	9.00
58	Frank (Lefty) O'Doul	35.00	17.50	10.50
59	Edmund (Bing) Miller	30.00	15.00	9.00
60	Waite Hoyt	55.00	27.00	16.50
61	Max Bishop	30.00	15.00	9.00
62	"Pepper" Martin	35.00	17.50	10.50
63	Joe Cronin	60.00	30.00	18.00
64	Burleigh Grimes	55.00	27.00	16.50
65	Milton Gaston	30.00	15.00	9.00
66	George Grantham	30.00	15.00	9.00
67	Guy Bush	30.00	15.00	9.00
68	Horace Lisenbee	30.00	15.00	9.00
69	Randy Moore	30.00	15.00	9.00
70	Floyd (Pete) Scott	30.00	15.00	9.00
71	Robert J. Burke	30.00	15.00	9.00
72	Owen Carroll	30.00	15.00	9.00
73	Jesse Haines	55.00	27.00	16.50
74	Eppa Rixey	55.00	27.00	16.50
75	Willie Kamm	30.00	15.00	9.00
76	Gordon (Mickey) Cochrane	80.00	40.00	24.00
77	Adam Comorosky	30.00	15.00	9.00
78	Jack Quinn	30.00	15.00	9.00
79	Urban (Red) Faber	55.00	27.00	16.50
80	Clyde Manion	30.00	15.00	9.00
81	Sam Jones	30.00	15.00	9.00
82	Dibrell Williams	30.00	15.00	9.00
83	Pete Jablonowski	40.00	20.00	12.00
84	Glenn Spencer	30.00	15.00	9.00
85	John Henry "Heinie" Sand	30.00	15.00	9.00
86	Phil Todt	30.00	15.00	9.00
87	Frank O'Rourke	30.00	15.00	9.00
88	Russell Rollings	30.00	15.00	9.00
89	Tris Speaker	150.00	75.00	45.00
90	Jess Petty	30.00	15.00	9.00
91	Tom Zachary	30.00	15.00	9.00
92	Lou Gehrig	1700.00	680.00	340.00
93	John Welch	30.00	15.00	9.00
94	Bill Walker	30.00	15.00	9.00
95	Alvin Crowder	30.00	15.00	9.00
96	Willis Hudlin	30.00	15.00	9.00
97	Joe Morrissey	30.00	15.00	9.00
98	Walter Berger	30.00	15.00	9.00
99	Tony Cuccinello	30.00	15.00	9.00
100	George Uhle	30.00	15.00	9.00
101	Richard Coffman	30.00	15.00	9.00
102	Travis C. Jackson	55.00	27.00	16.50
103	Earl Combs (Earle)	55.00	27.00	16.50
104	Fred Marberry	30.00	15.00	9.00
105	Bernie Friberg	30.00	15.00	9.00
106	Napoleon (Larry) Lajoie	9000.00	4500.00	2700.
107	Henry (Heinie) Manush	55.00	27.00	16.50
108	Joe Kuhel	30.00	15.00	9.00
109	Joe Cronin	60.00	30.00	18.00
110	Leon "Goose" Goslin	55.00	27.00	16.50
111	Monte Weaver	30.00	15.00	9.00
112	Fred Schulte	30.00	15.00	9.00
113	Oswald Bluege	30.00	15.00	9.00
114	Luke Sewell	30.00	15.00	9.00
115	Cliff Heathcote	30.00	15.00	9.00
116	Eddie Morgan	30.00	15.00	9.00
117	Walter (Rabbit) Maranville	55.00	27.00	16.50
118	Valentine J. (Val) Picinich	30.00	15.00	9.00
119	Rogers Hornsby	150.00	75.00	45.00
120	Carl Reynolds	30.00	15.00	9.00
121	Walter Stewart	30.00	15.00	9.00
122	Alvin Crowder	30.00	15.00	9.00
123	Jack Russell	30.00	15.00	9.00
124	Earl Whitehill	30.00	15.00	9.00
125	Bill Terry	80.00	40.00	24.00
126	Joe Moore	30.00	15.00	9.00
127	Melvin Ott	30.00	15.00	9.00
128	Charles (Chuck) Klein	55.00	27.00	16.50
129	Harold Schumacher	35.00	17.50	10.50
130	Fred Fitzsimmons	30.00	15.00	9.00
131	Fred Frankhouse	30.00	15.00	9.00
132	Jim Elliott	30.00	15.00	9.00
133	Fred Lindstrom	55.00	27.00	16.50
134	Edgar (Sam) Rice	55.00	27.00	16.50
135	Elwood (Woody) English	30.00	15.00	9.00
136	Flint Rhem	30.00	15.00	9.00
137	Fred (Red) Lucas	30.00	15.00	9.00
138	Herb Pennock	55.00	27.00	16.50
139	Ben Cantwell	30.00	15.00	9.00
140	Irving (Bump) Hadley	30.00	15.00	9.00
141	Ray Benge	30.00	15.00	9.00
142	Paul Richards	40.00	20.00	12.00
143	Glenn Wright	35.00	17.50	10.50
144	George Herman (Babe) Ruth	2500.00	1000.00	500.00
145	George Walberg	30.00	15.00	9.00
146	Walter Stewart	30.00	15.00	9.00
147	Leo Durocher	55.00	27.00	16.50
148	Eddie Farrell	29.00	14.50	8.75
149	George Herman (Babe) Ruth	2800.00	1120.00	560.00
150	Ray Kolp	30.00	15.00	9.00
151	D'Arcy (Jake) Flowers	30.00	15.00	9.00
152	James (Zack) Taylor	30.00	15.00	9.00
153	Charles (Buddy) Myer	30.00	15.00	9.00
154	Jimmy Foxx	140.00	70.00	42.00
155	Joe Judge	30.00	15.00	9.00
156	Danny Macfayden (MacFayden)	40.00	20.00	12.00
157	Sam Byrd	40.00	20.00	12.00
158	Morris (Moe) Berg	35.00	17.50	10.50
159	Oswald Bluege	30.00	15.00	9.00
160	Lou Gehrig	1700.00	680.00	340.00
161	Al Spohrer	30.00	15.00	9.00
162	Leo Mangum	30.00	15.00	9.00
163	Luke Sewell	30.00	15.00	9.00
164	Lloyd Waner	55.00	27.00	16.50
165	Joe Sewell	55.00	27.00	16.50
166	Sam West	30.00	15.00	9.00
167	Jack Russell	30.00	15.00	9.00
168	Leon (Goose) Goslin	55.00	27.00	16.50
169	Al Thomas	30.00	15.00	9.00
170	Harry McCurdy	30.00	15.00	9.00
171	Charley Jamieson	30.00	15.00	9.00
172	Billy Hargrave	30.00	15.00	9.00
173	Roscoe Holm	30.00	15.00	9.00
174	Warren (Curley) Ogden	30.00	15.00	9.00
175	Dan Howley	30.00	15.00	9.00
176	John Ogden	30.00	15.00	9.00
177	Walter French	30.00	15.00	9.00
178	Jackie Warner	30.00	15.00	9.00
179	Fred Leach	30.00	15.00	9.00
180	Eddie Moore	30.00	15.00	9.00
181	George Herman (Babe) Ruth	3000.00	1200.00	600.00
182	Andy High	30.00	15.00	9.00
183	George Walberg	30.00	15.00	9.00
184	Charley Berry	30.00	15.00	9.00
185	Bob Smith	30.00	15.00	9.00
186	John Schulte	30.00	15.00	9.00
187	Henry (Heinie) Manush	55.00	27.00	16.50
188	Rogers Hornsby	150.00	75.00	45.00
189	Joe Cronin	60.00	30.00	18.00
190	Fred Schulte	30.00	15.00	9.00
191	Ben Chapman	40.00	20.00	12.00
192	Walter Brown	40.00	20.00	12.00
193	Lynford Lary	40.00	20.00	12.00
194	Earl Averill	55.00	27.00	16.50
195	Evar Swanson	30.00	15.00	9.00
196	Leroy Mahaffey	30.00	15.00	9.00
197	Richard (Rick) Ferrell	55.00	27.00	16.50
198	Irving (Jack) Burns	30.00	15.00	9.00
199	Tom Bridges	35.00	17.50	10.50
200	Bill Hallahan	30.00	15.00	9.00
201	Ernie Orsatti	30.00	15.00	9.00
202	Charles Leo (Gabby) Hartnett	55.00	27.00	16.50
203	Lonnie Warneke	30.00	15.00	9.00
204	Jackson Riggs Stephenson	35.00	17.50	10.50
205	Henry (Heinie) Meine	30.00	15.00	9.00
206	Gus Suhr	30.00	15.00	9.00
207	Melvin Ott	90.00	45.00	27.00

		NR MT	EX	VG
208	Byrne (Bernie) James	30.00	15.00	9.00
209	Adolfo Luque	30.00	15.00	9.00
210	Virgil Davis	30.00	15.00	9.00
211	Lewis (Hack) Wilson	55.00	27.00	16.50
212	Billy Urbanski	30.00	15.00	9.00
213	Earl Adams	30.00	15.00	9.00
214	John Kerr	30.00	15.00	9.00
215	Russell Van Atta	40.00	20.00	12.00
216	Vernon Gomez	90.00	45.00	27.00
217	Frank Crosetti	55.00	27.00	16.50
218	Wesley Ferrell	30.00	15.00	9.00
219	George (Mule) Haas	30.00	15.00	9.00
220	Robert (Lefty) Grove	150.00	75.00	45.00
221	Dale Alexander	30.00	15.00	9.00
222	Charley Gehringer	90.00	45.00	27.00
223	Jerome (Dizzy) Dean	350.00	175.00	105.00
224	Frank Demaree	30.00	15.00	9.00
225	Bill Jurges	30.00	15.00	9.00
226	Charley Root	30.00	15.00	9.00
227	Bill Herman	55.00	27.00	16.50
228	Tony Piet	30.00	15.00	9.00
229	Floyd Vaughan	55.00	27.00	16.50
230	Carl Hubbell	90.00	45.00	27.00
231	Joe Moore	30.00	15.00	9.00
232	Frank (Lefty) O'Doul	35.00	17.50	10.50
233	Johnny Vergez	30.00	15.00	9.00
234	Carl Hubbell	90.00	45.00	27.00
235	Fred Fitzsimmons	30.00	15.00	9.00
236	George Davis	30.00	15.00	9.00
237	Gus Mancuso	30.00	15.00	9.00
238	Hugh Critz	30.00	15.00	9.00
239	Leroy Parmelee	40.00	15.00	12.00
240	Harold Schumacher	175.00	20.00	11.00

1934 Goudey

 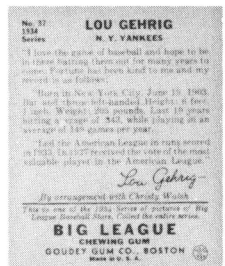

The 1934 Goudey set contains 96 cards (2⅜'' by 2⅞'') that feature color art reproductions of actual photographs. The card fronts have two different designs; one featuring a small head-shot photo of Lou Gehrig with the words "Lou Gehrig says..." inside a blue band, while the other design carries a ""Chuck" Klein says..." and also has his photo. The card backs contain a short player biography that appears to have been written by Gehrig or Klein. The ACC designation for the set is R320.

		NR MT	EX	VG
Complete Set:		10000.00	4000.00	2500.
Common Player:		35.00	17.50	10.50
Common Player: 49-72		40.00	20.00	12.00
Common Player: 73-96		100.00	50.00	30.00

		NR MT	EX	VG
1	Jimmy Foxx	400.00	90.00	40.00
2	Gordon (Mickey) Cochrane	80.00	40.00	20.00
3	Charlie Grimm	40.00	20.00	12.00
4	Elwood (Woody) English	35.00	17.50	10.50
5	Ed Brandt	35.00	17.50	10.50
6	Jerome (Dizzy) Dean	275.00	137.00	82.00
7	Leo Durocher	60.00	30.00	18.00
8	Tony Piet	35.00	17.50	10.50
9	Ben Chapman	45.00	22.00	13.50
10	Charles (Chuck) Klein	60.00	30.00	18.00
11	Paul Waner	60.00	30.00	18.00
12	Carl Hubbell	80.00	40.00	24.00
13	Frank Frisch	70.00	35.00	21.00
14	Willie Kamm	35.00	17.50	10.50
15	Alvin Crowder	35.00	17.50	10.50

		NR MT	EX	VG
16	Joe Kuhel	35.00	17.50	10.50
17	Hugh Critz	35.00	17.50	10.50
18	Henry (Heinie) Manush	60.00	30.00	18.00
19	Robert (Lefty) Grove	125.00	62.00	37.00
20	Frank Hogan	35.00	17.50	10.50
21	Bill Terry	80.00	40.00	24.00
22	Floyd Vaughan	60.00	30.00	18.00
23	Charley Gehringer	70.00	35.00	21.00
24	Ray Benge	35.00	17.50	10.50
25	Roger Cramer	35.00	17.50	10.50
26	Gerald Walker	35.00	17.50	10.50
27	Luke Appling	60.00	30.00	18.00
28	Ed. Coleman	35.00	17.50	10.50
29	Larry French	35.00	17.50	10.50
30	Julius Solters	35.00	17.50	10.50
31	Baxter Jordan	35.00	17.50	10.50
32	John (Blondy) Ryan	35.00	17.50	10.50
33	Frank (Don) Hurst	35.00	17.50	10.50
34	Charles (Chick) Hafey	60.00	30.00	18.00
35	Ernie Lombardi	60.00	30.00	18.00
36	Walter (Huck) Betts	35.00	17.50	10.50
37	Lou Gehrig	1800.00	720.00	360.00
38	Oral Hildebrand	35.00	17.50	10.50
39	Fred Walker	45.00	22.00	13.50
40	John Stone	35.00	17.50	10.50
41	George Earnshaw	35.00	17.50	10.50
42	John Allen	45.00	22.00	13.50
43	Dick Porter	35.00	17.50	10.50
44	Tom Bridges	40.00	20.00	12.00
45	Oscar Melillo	35.00	17.50	10.50
46	Joe Stripp	35.00	17.50	10.50
47	John Frederick	35.00	17.50	10.50
48	James (Tex) Carleton	35.00	17.50	10.50
49	Sam Leslie	40.00	20.00	12.00
50	Walter Beck	40.00	20.00	12.00
51	Jim (Rip) Collins	40.00	20.00	12.00
52	Herman Bell	40.00	20.00	12.00
53	George Watkins	40.00	20.00	12.00
54	Wesley Schulmerich	40.00	20.00	12.00
55	Ed Holley	40.00	20.00	12.00
56	Mark Koenig	40.00	20.00	12.00
57	Bill Swift	40.00	20.00	12.00
58	Earl Grace	40.00	20.00	12.00
59	Joe Mowry	40.00	20.00	12.00
60	Lynn Nelson	40.00	20.00	12.00
61	Lou Gehrig	1800.00	720.00	360.00
62	Henry Greenberg	110.00	55.00	33.00
63	Minter Hayes	40.00	20.00	12.00
64	Frank Grube	40.00	20.00	12.00
65	Cliff Bolton	40.00	20.00	12.00
66	Mel Harder	40.00	20.00	12.00
67	Bob Weiland	40.00	20.00	12.00
68	Bob Johnson	40.00	20.00	12.00
69	John Marcum	40.00	20.00	12.00
70	Ervin (Pete) Fox	40.00	20.00	12.00
71	Lyle Tinning	40.00	20.00	12.00
72	Arndt Jorgens	45.00	22.00	13.50
73	Ed Wells	100.00	50.00	30.00
74	Bob Boken	100.00	50.00	30.00
75	Bill Werber	100.00	50.00	30.00
76	Hal Trosky	100.00	50.00	30.00
77	Joe Vosmik	100.00	50.00	30.00
78	Frank (Pinkey) Higgins	100.00	50.00	30.00
79	Eddie Durham	100.00	50.00	30.00
80	Marty McManus	100.00	50.00	30.00
81	Bob Brown	100.00	50.00	30.00
82	Bill Hallahan	100.00	50.00	30.00
83	Jim Mooney	100.00	50.00	30.00
84	Paul Derringer	110.00	55.00	33.00
85	Adam Comorosky	100.00	50.00	30.00
86	Lloyd Johnson	100.00	50.00	30.00
87	George Darrow	100.00	50.00	30.00
88	Homer Peel	100.00	50.00	30.00
89	Linus Frey	100.00	50.00	30.00
90	Hazen (Ki-Ki) Cuyler	150.00	75.00	45.00
91	Dolph Camilli	110.00	55.00	33.00
92	Steve Larkin	100.00	50.00	30.00
93	Fred Ostermueller	100.00	50.00	30.00
94	Robert A. (Red) Rolfe	125.00	62.00	37.00
95	Myril Hoag	125.00	62.00	37.00
96	Jim DeShong	225.00	70.00	37.00

1935 Goudey

The 1935 Goudey set features four players from the same team on one card. Thirty-six card fronts make up the set with numerous front/back combina-

		NR MT	EX	VG
(31)	Jimmie Foxx, Pinky Higgins, Roy Mahaffey, Dib Williams	85.00	42.00	25.00
(32)	Bump Hadley, Lyn Lary, Heinie Manush, Monte Weaver	35.00	17.50	10.50
(33)	Mel Harder, Bill Knickerbocker, Lefty Stewart, Joe Vosmik	30.00	15.00	9.00
(34)	Travis Jackson, Gus Mancuso, Hal Schumacher, Bill Terry	65.00	32.00	19.50
(35)	Joe Kuhel, Buddy Meyer (Myer), John Stone, Earl Whitehill	30.00	15.00	9.00
(36)	Red Lucas, Tommy Thevenow, Pie Traynor, Glenn Wright	35.00	17.50	10.50

1936 Goudey

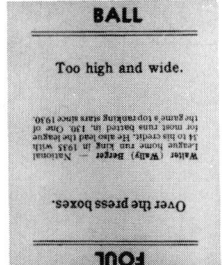

The 1936 Goudey set consists of 25 black and white cards, each measuring 2⅜'' by 2⅞''. A facsimile autograph was positioned on the card fronts. The card backs contain a brief player biography and were to be used by collectors to play a baseball game. Different game situations (out, single, double, etc.) were given on each card. Numerous front/back combinations exist in the set. The ACC designation for the set is R322.

		NR MT	EX	VG
Complete Set:		1200.00	600.00	360.00
Common Player:		30.00	15.00	9.00
(1)	Walter Berger	30.00	15.00	9.00
(2)	Henry Bonura	30.00	15.00	9.00
(3)	Stan Bordagaray	30.00	15.00	9.00
(4)	Bill Brubaker	30.00	15.00	9.00
(5)	Dolph Camilli	35.00	17.50	10.50
(6)	Clydell Castleman	30.00	15.00	9.00
(7)	"Mickey" Cochrane	75.00	37.00	22.00
(8)	Joe Coscarart	30.00	15.00	9.00
(9)	Frank Crosetti	40.00	20.00	12.00
(10)	"Kiki" Cuyler	60.00	30.00	18.00
(11)	Paul Derringer	35.00	17.50	10.50
(12)	Jimmy Dykes	35.00	17.50	10.50
(13)	"Rick" Ferrell	60.00	30.00	18.00
(14)	"Lefty" Gomez	100.00	50.00	30.00
(15)	Hank Greenberg	100.00	50.00	30.00
(16)	"Bucky" Harris	60.00	30.00	18.00
(17)	"Rolly" Hemsley	30.00	15.00	9.00
(18)	Frank Higgins	30.00	15.00	9.00
(19)	Oral Hildebrand	30.00	15.00	9.00
(20)	"Chuck" Klein	60.00	30.00	18.00
(21)	"Pepper" Martin	35.00	17.50	10.50
(22)	"Buck" Newsom	35.00	17.50	10.50
(23)	Joe Vosmik	30.00	15.00	9.00
(24)	Paul Waner	60.00	30.00	18.00
(25)	Bill Werber	30.00	15.00	9.00

1938 Goudey

Sometimes referred to as the Goudey Heads-Up set, this issue begins numbering (#241) where the 1933 Goudey set left off. On the card fronts, a photo is used for the player's head with the body being a cartoon drawing. Twenty-four different players are pictured twice in the set. Card #'s 241-264 feature

---

tions existing. The card backs form nine different puzzles: 1) Tigers Team, 2) Chuck Klein, 3) Frankie Frisch, 4) Mickey Cochrane, 5) Joe Cronin, 6) Jimmy Foxx, 7) Al Simmons, 8) Indians Team, and 9) Senators Team. The cards, which measure 2⅜'' by 2⅞'', have an ACC designation of R321.

		NR MT	EX	VG
Complete Set:		2000.00	1000.00	600.00
Common Player:		30.00	15.00	9.00
(1)	Sparky Adams, Jim Bottomley, Adam Comorosky, Tony Piet	35.00	17.50	10.50
(2)	Ethan Allen, Fred Brickell, Bubber Jonnard, Hack Wilson	35.00	17.50	10.50
(3)	Johnny Allen, Jimmie Deshong (DeShong), Red Rolfe, Dixie Walker	26.00	13.00	7.75
(4)	Luke Appling, Jimmie Dykes, George Earnshaw, Luke Sewell	35.00	17.50	10.50
(5)	Earl Averill, Oral Hildebrand, Willie Kamm, Hal Trosky	35.00	17.50	10.50
(6)	Dick Bartell, Hughie Critz, Gus Mancuso, Mel Ott	50.00	25.00	15.00
(7)	Ray Benge, Fred Fitzsimmons, Mark Koenig, Tom Zachary	26.00	13.00	7.75
(8)	Larry Benton, Ben Cantwell, Flint Rhem, Al Spohrer	30.00	15.00	9.00
(9)	Charlie Berry, Bobby Burke, Red Kress, Dazzy Vance	35.00	17.50	10.50
(10)	Max Bishop, Bill Cissell, Joe Cronin, Carl Reynolds	45.00	22.00	13.50
(11)	George Blaeholder, Dick Coffman, Oscar Melillo, Sammy West	30.00	15.00	9.00
(12)	Cy Blanton, Babe Herman, Tom Padden, Gus Suhr	26.00	13.00	7.75
(13)	Zeke Bonura, Mule Haas, Jackie Hayes, Ted Lyons	35.00	17.50	10.50
(14)	Jim Bottomley, Adam Comorosky, Willis Hudlin, Glenn Myatt	35.00	17.50	10.50
(15)	Ed Brandt, Fred Frankhouse, Shanty Hogan, Gene Moore	30.00	15.00	9.00
(16)	Ed Brandt, Rabbit Maranville, Marty McManus, Babe Ruth	350.00	175.00	105.00
(17)	Tommy Bridges, Mickey Cochrane, Charlie Gehringer, Billy Rogell	65.00	32.00	19.50
(18)	Jack Burns, Frank Grube, Rollie Hemsley, Bob Weiland	30.00	15.00	9.00
(19)	Guy Bush, Waite Hoyt, Lloyd Waner, Paul Waner	50.00	25.00	15.00
(20)	Sammy Byrd, Danny MacFayden, Pepper Martin, Bob O'Farrell	26.00	13.00	7.75
(21)	Gilly Campbell, Ival Goodman, Alex Kampouris, Billy Meyers (Myers)	30.00	15.00	9.00
(22)	Tex Carleton, Dizzy Dean, Frankie Frisch, Ernie Orsatti	110.00	55.00	33.00
(23)	Watty Clark, Lonny Frey, Sam Leslie, Joe Stripp	26.00	13.00	7.75
(24)	Mickey Cochrane, Willie Kamm, Muddy Ruel, Al Simmons	50.00	25.00	15.00
(25)	Ed Coleman, Doc Cramer, Bob Johnson, Johnny Marcum	30.00	15.00	9.00
(26)	General Crowder, Goose Goslin, Firpo Marberry, Heinie Schuble	35.00	17.50	10.50
(27)	Kiki Cuyler, Woody English, Burleigh Grimes, Chuck Klein	50.00	25.00	15.00
(28)	Bill Dickey, Tony Lazzeri, Pat Malone, Red Ruffing	85.00	42.00	25.00
(29)	Rick Ferrell, Wes Ferrell, Fritz Ostermueller, Bill Werber	35.00	17.50	10.50
(30)	Pete Fox, Hank Greenberg, Schoolboy Rowe, Gee Walker	50.00	25.00	15.00

JOE DI MAGGIO, Yankees

plain backgrounds on the card fronts. Card #'s 265-288 contain the same basic design and photo but include small drawings and comments within the background. The card backs contain player statistical and biographical information. The ACC designation for the issue is R323.

		NR MT	EX	VG
Complete Set:		7000.00	3500.00	2100.
Common Player: 241-264		60.00	30.00	18.00
Common Player: 265-288		70.00	35.00	21.00
241	Charlie Gehringer	175.00	87.00	52.00
242	Ervin Fox	60.00	30.00	18.00
243	Joe Kuhel	60.00	30.00	18.00
244	Frank DeMaree	60.00	30.00	18.00
245	Frank Pytlak	60.00	30.00	18.00
246	Ernie Lombardi	90.00	45.00	27.00
247	Joe Vosmik	60.00	30.00	18.00
248	Dick Bartell	60.00	30.00	18.00
249	Jimmy Foxx	250.00	125.00	75.00
250	Joe DiMaggio	800.00	400.00	240.00
251	Bump Hadley	65.00	32.00	19.50
252	Zeke Bonura	60.00	30.00	18.00
253	Hank Greenberg	175.00	87.00	52.00
254	Van Lingle Mungo	70.00	35.00	21.00
255	Julius Solters	60.00	30.00	18.00
256	Vernon Kennedy	60.00	30.00	18.00
257	Al Lopez	100.00	50.00	30.00
258	Bobby Doerr	100.00	50.00	30.00
259	Bill Werber	60.00	30.00	18.00
260	Rudy York	65.00	32.00	19.50
261	Rip Radcliff	60.00	30.00	18.00
262	Joe Ducky Medwick	110.00	55.00	33.00
263	Marvin Owen	60.00	30.00	18.00
264	Bob Feller	300.00	150.00	90.00
265	Charlie Gehringer	200.00	100.00	60.00
266	Ervin Fox	70.00	35.00	21.00
267	Joe Kuhel	70.00	35.00	21.00
268	Frank DeMaree	70.00	35.00	21.00
269	Frank Pytlak	70.00	35.00	21.00
270	Ernie Lombardi	100.00	50.00	30.00
271	Joe Vosmik	70.00	35.00	21.00
272	Dick Bartell	70.00	35.00	21.00
273	Jimmy Foxx	275.00	137.00	82.00
274	Joe DiMaggio	875.00	437.00	262.00
275	Bump Hadley	75.00	37.00	22.00
276	Zeke Bonura	70.00	35.00	21.00
277	Hank Greenberg	200.00	100.00	60.00
278	Van Lingle Mungo	80.00	40.00	24.00
279	Julius Solters	70.00	35.00	21.00
280	Vernon Kennedy	70.00	35.00	21.00
281	Al Lopez	110.00	55.00	33.00
282	Bobby Doerr	110.00	55.00	33.00
283	Bill Werber	70.00	35.00	21.00
284	Rudy York	75.00	37.00	22.00
285	Rip Radcliff	70.00	35.00	21.00
286	Joe Ducky Medwick	125.00	62.00	37.00
287	Marvin Owen	70.00	35.00	21.00
288	Bob Feller	350.00	175.00	105.00

1941 Goudey

Goudey Gum Co.'s last set was issued in 1941. The cards, which measure 2⅜'' by 2⅞'' in size, contain black and white photos set against blue, green, red or yellow backgrounds. The player's name, team and position plus the card number are situated in a box at

the bottom of the card. The card reverses are blank. The ACC designation for the set is R324.

		NR MT	EX	VG
Complete Set:		2200.00	1100.00	660.00
Common Player:		32.00	16.00	9.50
1	Hugh Mulcahy	75.00	20.00	9.50
2	Harlond Clift	32.00	16.00	9.50
3	Louis Chiozza	32.00	16.00	9.50
4	Warren (Buddy) Rosar	36.00	18.00	11.00
5	George McQuinn	32.00	16.00	9.50
6	Emerson Dickman	32.00	16.00	9.50
7	Wayne Ambler	32.00	16.00	9.50
8	Bob Muncrief	32.00	16.00	9.50
9	Bill Deitrich	32.00	16.00	9.50
10	Taft Wright	32.00	16.00	9.50
11	Don Heffner	32.00	16.00	9.50
12	Fritz Ostermueller	32.00	16.00	9.50
13	Frank Hayes	32.00	16.00	9.50
14	John (Jack) Kramer	32.00	16.00	9.50
15	Dario Lodigiani	32.00	16.00	9.50
16	George Case	32.00	16.00	9.50
17	Vito Tamulis	32.00	16.00	9.50
18	Whitlow Wyatt	32.00	16.00	9.50
19	Bill Posedel	32.00	16.00	9.50
20	Carl Hubbell	110.00	55.00	33.00
21	Harold Warstler	125.00	62.00	37.00
22	Joe Sullivan	200.00	100.00	60.00
23	Norman (Babe) Young	125.00	62.00	37.00
24	Stanley Andrews	200.00	100.00	60.00
25	Morris Arnovich	125.00	62.00	37.00
26	Elburt Fletcher	32.00	16.00	9.50
27	Bill Crouch	32.00	16.00	9.50
28	Al Todd	32.00	16.00	9.50
29	Debs Garms	32.00	16.00	9.50
30	Jim Tobin	32.00	16.00	9.50
31	Chester Ross	32.00	16.00	9.50
32	George Coffman	32.00	16.00	9.50
33	Mel Ott	200.00	62.00	60.00

1981 Granny Goose Potato Chips A's

Michael Kelvin Norris
17 Pitcher
Height: 6'2''
Weight: 172
Bats: Right
Throws: Right

Mike is one of the top pitchers in baseball, finishing the 1980 season with a 22-9 record, with a 2.53 ERA. He was voted second in the American League Cy Young competition in 1980.

The 1981 Granny Goose set features the Oakland A's. The cards, which measure 2½'' by 3½'' in size, were issued in bags of potato chips and are sometimes found with grease stains. The cards have full color fronts with the print done in the team's green and yellow colors. The backs contain the A's logo and a short player biography. The Revering card was withdrawn from the set shortly after he was traded and is in shorter supply than the rest of the cards in the set. The cards are numbered in the checklist that follows by the player's uniform number.

		MT	NR MT	EX
Complete Set:		90.00	67.00	36.00
Common Player:		2.00	1.50	.80
1	Billy Martin	10.00	7.50	4.00
2	Mike Heath	2.00	1.50	.80
5	Jeff Newman	2.00	1.50	.80
6	Mitchell Page	2.00	1.50	.80
8	Rob Picciolo	2.00	1.50	.80
10	Wayne Gross	5.00	3.75	2.00
13	Dave Revering	45.00	34.00	18.00
17	Mike Norris	2.00	1.50	.80
20	Tony Armas	4.00	3.00	1.50
21	Dwayne Murphy	6.00	4.50	2.50
22	Rick Langford	2.00	1.50	.80
27	Matt Keough	2.00	1.50	.80
35	Rickey Henderson	20.00	15.00	8.00
39	Dave McKay	2.00	1.50	.80
54	Steve McCatty	2.00	1.50	.80

1982 Granny Goose Potato Chips A's

 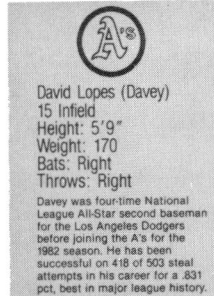

Granny Goose repeated its promotion from the previous year and issued another set featuring the Oakland A's. The cards, which measure 2½'' by 3½'', were distributed in two fashions: in bags of potato chips and at Fan Appreciation Day at Oakland-Alameda Coliseum. The cards are identical in design to the 1981 set and can be distinguished from it by the date on the copyright on the bottom of the card reverse. The cards are numbered in the checklist that follows by the player's uniform number.

		MT	NR MT	EX
Complete Set:		15.00	11.00	6.00
Common Player:		.40	.30	.15
1	Billy Martin	2.00	1.50	.80
2	Mike Heath	.40	.30	.15
5	Jeff Newman	.40	.30	.15
8	Rob Picciolo	.40	.30	.15
10	Wayne Gross	.40	.30	.15
11	Fred Stanley	.40	.30	.15
15	Davey Lopes	.80	.60	.30
17	Mike Norris	.40	.30	.15
20	Tony Armas	1.00	.70	.40
21	Dwayne Murphy	1.00	.70	.40
22	Rick Langford	.40	.30	.15
27	Matt Keough	.40	.30	.15
35	Rickey Henderson	7.00	5.25	2.75
44	Cliff Johnson, Jr.	.40	.30	.15
54	Steve McCatty	.40	.30	.15

1983 Granny Goose Potato Chips A's

 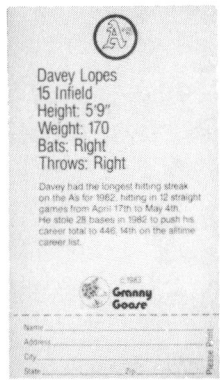

For the third consecutive year, Granny Goose issued a set of baseball cards featuring the Oakland A's. The cards were issued with or without a detachable coupon found at the bottom of each card. Issued in bags of potato chips were the coupon cards, which contained a scratch-off section offering prizes. The cards without the coupon section were given away to fans at Oakland-Alameda Coliseum on July 3, 1983. Cards with the detachable coupon command a 50% premium over the coupon-less variety. The cards in the following checklist are numbered by the player's uniform number.

		MT	NR MT	EX
Complete Set		12.00	9.00	4.75
Common Player		.40	.30	.15
2	Mike Heath	.40	.30	.15
4	Carney Lansford	1.00	.70	.40
10	Wayne Gross	.40	.30	.15
14	Steve Boros	.40	.30	.15
15	Davey Lopes	.80	.60	.30
16	Mike Davis	.80	.60	.30
17	Mike Norris	.40	.30	.15
21	Dwayne Murphy	1.00	.70	.40
22	Rick Langford	.40	.30	.15
27	Matt Keough	.40	.30	.15
31	Tom Underwood	.40	.30	.15
33	Dave Beard	.40	.30	.15
35	Rickey Henderson	7.00	5.25	2.75
39	Tom Burgmeier	.40	.30	.15
54	Steve McCatty	.40	.30	.15

1958 Hire's Root Beer Test Set

Among the scarcest of the regional issues of the late 1950s is the eight-card test issue which preceded the Hire's Root Beer set of 66 cards. Probably issued in a very limited area in the Northeast, the test differ from the regular issue in that they have sepia-toned, rather than color pictures, which are set against plain yellow or orange backgrounds (much like the 1958 Topps!), instead of viewed through a knothole. Like the regular Hire's cards, the 2-5/16'' by 3½'' cards were issued with an attached wedge-shaped tab of

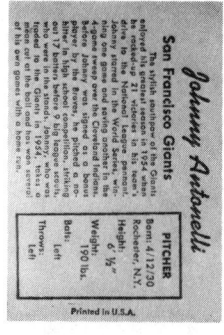

PITCHER—SAN FRANCISCO GIANTS

like size. The tab offered membership in Hire's baseball fan club, and served to hold the card into the carton of bottled root beer with which it was given away. Values quoted here are for cards with tabs. Cards without tabs would be valued approximately 50% lower.

		NR MT	EX	VG
Complete Set:		1200.00	600.00	360.00
Common Player:		100.00	50.00	30.00
(1)	Johnny Antonelli	125.00	62.00	37.00
(2)	Jim Busby	100.00	50.00	30.00
(3)	Chico Fernandez	100.00	50.00	30.00
(4)	Bob Friend	125.00	62.00	37.00
(5)	Vern Law	125.00	62.00	37.00
(6)	Stan Lopata	100.00	50.00	30.00
(7)	Willie Mays	375.00	187.00	112.00
(8)	Al Pilarcik	100.00	50.00	30.00

1958 Hire's Root Beer

TED KLUSZEWSKI
INFIELD—PITTSBURGH PIRATES

Like most baseball cards issued with a tab in the 1950s, the Hire's cards are extremely scarce today in their original form. The basic card was attached to a wedge-shaped tab that served the dual purpose of offering a fan club membership and of holding the card into the cardboard carton of soda bottles with which it was distributed. The card itself measures 2-5/16" by 3½." The tab extends for another 3½". Numbering of the Hire's set begins at 10 and goes through 76, with card #69 never issued, making a set complete at 66 cards. Values given below are for cards with tabs. Cards without tabs would be valued approximately 50% lower.

		NR MT	EX	VG
Complete Set:		1800.00	900.00	540.00
Common Player:		15.00	7.50	4.50
10	Richie Ashburn	110.00	55.00	33.00
11	Chico Carrasquel	15.00	7.50	4.50
12	Dave Philley	15.00	7.50	4.50
13	Don Newcombe	20.00	10.00	6.00
14	Wally Post	15.00	7.50	4.50

		NR MT	EX	VG
15	Rip Repulski	15.00	7.50	4.50
16	Chico Fernandez	15.00	7.50	4.50
17	Larry Doby	20.00	10.00	6.00
18	Hector Brown	15.00	7.50	4.50
19	Danny O'Connell	15.00	7.50	4.50
20	Granny Hamner	15.00	7.50	4.50
21	Dick Groat	17.50	8.75	5.25
22	Ray Narleski	15.00	7.50	4.50
23	Pee Wee Reese	75.00	37.00	22.00
24	Bob Friend	17.50	8.75	5.25
25	Willie Mays	160.00	80.00	48.00
26	Bob Nieman	15.00	7.50	4.50
27	Frank Thomas	15.00	7.50	4.50
28	Curt Simmons	17.50	8.75	5.25
29	Stan Lopata	15.00	7.50	4.50
30	Bob Skinner	15.00	7.50	4.50
31	Ron Kline	15.00	7.50	4.50
32	Willie Miranda	15.00	7.50	4.50
33	Bob Avila	15.00	7.50	4.50
34	Clem Labine	17.50	8.75	5.25
35	Ray Jablonski	15.00	7.50	4.50
36	Bill Mazeroski	20.00	10.00	6.00
37	Billy Gardner	15.00	7.50	4.50
38	Pete Runnels	17.50	8.75	5.25
39	Jack Sanford	15.00	7.50	4.50
40	Dave Sisler	15.00	7.50	4.50
41	Don Zimmer	17.50	8.75	5.25
42	Johnny Podres	20.00	10.00	6.00
43	Dick Farrell	15.00	7.50	4.50
44	Hank Aaron	160.00	80.00	48.00
45	Bill Virdon	17.50	8.75	5.25
46	Bobby Thomson	17.50	8.75	5.25
47	Willard Nixon	15.00	7.50	4.50
48	Billy Loes	15.00	7.50	4.50
49	Hank Sauer	15.00	7.50	4.50
50	Johnny Antonelli	17.50	8.75	5.25
51	Daryl Spencer	15.00	7.50	4.50
52	Ken Lehman	15.00	7.50	4.50
53	Sammy White	15.00	7.50	4.50
54	Charley Neal	15.00	7.50	4.50
55	Don Drysdale	75.00	37.00	22.00
56	Jack Jensen	20.00	10.00	6.00
57	Ray Katt	15.00	7.50	4.50
58	Franklin Sullivan	15.00	7.50	4.50
59	Roy Face	17.50	8.75	5.25
60	Willie Jones	15.00	7.50	4.50
61	Duke Snider	110.00	55.00	33.00
62	Whitey Lockman	15.00	7.50	4.50
63	Gino Cimoli	17.50	8.75	5.25
64	Marv Grissom	15.00	7.50	4.50
65	Gene Baker	15.00	7.50	4.50
66	George Zuverink	15.00	7.50	4.50
67	Ted Kluszewski	20.00	10.00	6.00
68	Jim Busby	15.00	7.50	4.50
69	Not Issued			
70	Curt Barclay	15.00	7.50	4.50
71	Hank Foiles	15.00	7.50	4.50
72	Gene Stephens	15.00	7.50	4.50
73	Al Worthington	15.00	7.50	4.50
74	Al Walker	15.00	7.50	4.50
75	Bob Boyd	15.00	7.50	4.50
76	Al Pilarcik	30.00	15.00	9.00

1975 Hostess

RENNIE STENNETT
INFIELD
Pittsburgh PIRATES

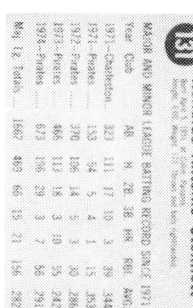

The first of what would become five annual issues, the 1975 Hostess set consists of 50 three-card panels which formed the bottom of boxes of family-size snack cake products. Unlike many similar issues, the Hostess cards do not share common borders, so it was possible to cut them neatly and evenly from the box. Well-cut single cards measure 2¼'' by 3¼'', while a three-card panel measures 7¼'' by 3¼''. Because some of the panels were issued on packages of less popular snack cakes, they are somewhat scarcer today. Since the hobby was quite well developed when the Hostess cards were first issued, there is no lack of complete panels. Even unused complete boxes are available today. Some of the photos in this issue also appear on Topps cards of the era.

		NR MT	EX	VG
Complete Panel Set:		325.00	162.00	97.00
Complete Singles Set:		125.00	62.00	37.00
Common Panel:		2.50	1.25	.70
Common Single Player:		.40	.20	.12
Panel 1		2.50	1.25	.70
1	Bobby Tolan	.40	.20	.12
2	Cookie Rojas	.40	.20	.12
3	Darrell Evans	.60	.30	.20
Panel 2		5.00	2.50	1.50
4	Sal Bando	.50	.25	.15
5	Joe Morgan	1.50	.70	.45
6	Mickey Lolich	.50	.25	.15
Panel 3		3.50	1.75	1.00
7	Don Sutton	.90	.45	.25
8	Bill Melton	.40	.20	.12
9	Tim Foli	.40	.20	.12
Panel 4		5.00	2.50	1.50
10	Joe Lahoud	.40	.20	.12
11a	Bert Hooten (incorrect spelling)	1.50	.70	.45
11b	Burt Hooton (correct spelling)	1.50	.70	.45
12	Paul Blair	.40	.20	.12
Panel 5		2.50	1.25	.70
13	Jim Barr	.40	.20	.12
14	Toby Harrah	.50	.25	.15
15	John Milner	.40	.20	.12
Panel 6		3.50	1.75	1.00
16	Ken Holtzman	.50	.25	.15
17	Cesar Cedeno	.50	.25	.15
18	Dwight Evans	.90	.45	.25
Panel 7		6.50	3.25	2.00
19	Willie McCovey	2.50	1.25	.70
20	Tony Oliva	.50	.25	.15
21	Manny Sanguillen	.40	.20	.12
Panel 8		7.50	3.75	2.25
22	Mickey Rivers	.50	.25	.15
23	Lou Brock	2.50	1.25	.70
24	Craig Nettles	.90	.45	.25
Panel 9		3.00	1.50	.90
25	Jimmy Wynn	.50	.25	.15
26	George Scott	.50	.25	.15
27	Greg Luzinski	.50	.25	.15
Panel 10		20.00	10.00	6.00
28	Bert Campaneris	.50	.25	.15
29	Pete Rose	8.00	4.00	2.50
30	Buddy Bell	.50	.25	.15
Panel 11		2.50	1.25	.70
31	Gary Matthews	.50	.25	.15
32	Fred Patek	.40	.20	.12
33	Mike Lum	.40	.20	.12
Panel 12		2.50	1.25	.70
34	Ellie Rodriguez	.40	.20	.12
35	Milt May	.40	.20	.12
36	Willie Horton	.50	.25	.15
Panel 13		9.50	4.75	2.75
37	Dave Winfield	4.00	2.00	1.25
38	Tom Grieve	.40	.20	.12
39	Barry Foote	.40	.20	.12
Panel 14		2.50	1.25	.70
40	Joe Rudi	.50	.25	.15
41	Bake McBride	.40	.20	.12
42	Mike Cuellar	.50	.25	.15
Panel 15		2.50	1.25	.70
43	Garry Maddox	.50	.25	.15
44	Carlos May	.40	.20	.12
45	Bud Harrelson	.40	.20	.12
Panel 16		15.00	7.50	4.50
46	Dave Chalk	.40	.20	.12
47	Dave Concepcion	.50	.25	.15
48	Carl Yastrzemski	6.50	3.25	2.00

		NR MT	EX	VG
Panel 17		8.50	4.25	2.50
49	Steve Garvey	3.50	1.75	1.00
50	Amos Otis	.50	.25	.15
51	Rickey Reuschel	.50	.25	.15
Panel 18		3.50	1.75	1.00
52	Rollie Fingers	.90	.45	.25
53	Bob Watson	.40	.20	.12
54	John Ellis	.40	.20	.12
Panel 19		9.50	4.75	2.75
55	Bob Bailey	.40	.20	.12
56	Rod Carew	4.00	2.00	1.25
57	Richie Hebner	.40	.20	.12
Panel 20		9.50	4.75	2.75
58	Nolan Ryan	3.50	1.75	1.00
59	Reggie Smith	.50	.25	.15
60	Joe Coleman	.40	.20	.12
Panel 21		10.00	5.00	3.00
61	Ron Cey	.50	.25	.15
62	Darrell Porter	.50	.25	.15
63	Steve Carlton	4.00	2.00	1.25
Panel 22		2.50	1.25	.70
64	Gene Tenace	.40	.20	.12
65	Jose Cardenal	.40	.20	.12
66	Bill Lee	.40	.20	.12
Panel 23		2.50	1.25	.70
67	Dave Lopes	.50	.25	.15
68	Wilbur Wood	.50	.25	.15
69	Steve Renko	.40	.20	.12
Panel 24		3.00	1.50	.90
70	Joe Torre	.50	.25	.15
71	Ted Sizemore	.40	.20	.12
72	Bobby Grich	.50	.25	.15
Panel 25		11.00	5.50	3.25
73	Chris Speier	.40	.20	.12
74	Bert Blyleven	.70	.35	.20
75	Tom Seaver	4.00	2.00	1.25
Panel 26		2.50	1.25	.70
76	Nate Colbert	.40	.20	.12
77	Don Kessinger	.40	.20	.12
78	George Medich	.40	.20	.12
Panel 27		23.00	11.50	7.00
79	Andy Messersmith	.70	.35	.20
80	Robin Yount	9.00	4.50	2.75
81	Al Oliver	2.00	1.00	.60
Panel 28		18.00	9.00	5.50
82	Bill Singer	.50	.25	.15
83	Johnny Bench	6.00	3.00	1.75
84	Gaylord Perry	3.00	1.50	.90
Panel 29		5.00	2.50	1.50
85	Dave Kingman	1.25	.60	.40
86	Ed Herrmann	.50	.25	.15
87	Ralph Garr	.60	.30	.20
Panel 30		23.00	11.50	7.00
88	Reggie Jackson	9.00	4.50	2.75
89a	Doug Radar (incorrect spelling)	2.00	1.00	.60
89b	Doug Rader (correct spelling)	2.00	1.00	.60
90	Elliott Maddox	.50	.25	.15
Panel 31		3.50	1.75	1.00
91	Bill Russell	.60	.30	.20
92	John Mayberry	.50	.25	.15
93	Dave Cash	.50	.25	.15
Panel 32		5.00	2.50	1.50
94	Jeff Burroughs	.60	.30	.20
95	Ted Simmons	1.25	.60	.40
96	Joe Decker	.50	.25	.15
Panel 33		10.00	5.00	3.00
97	Bill Buckner	1.25	.60	.40
98	Bobby Darwin	.50	.25	.15
99	Phil Niekro	3.50	1.75	1.00
Panel 34		3.00	1.50	.90
100	Mike Sundberg (Jim)	.50	.25	.15
101	Greg Gross	.40	.20	.12
102	Luis Tiant	.70	.35	.20
Panel 35		2.50	1.25	.70
103	Glenn Beckert	.40	.20	.12
104	Hal McRae	.50	.25	.15
105	Mike Jorgensen	.40	.20	.12
Panel 36		2.50	1.25	.70
106	Mike Hargrove	.40	.20	.12
107	Don Gullett	.40	.20	.12
108	Tito Fuentes	.40	.20	.12
Panel 37		3.50	1.75	1.00
109	John Grubb	.40	.20	.12
110	Jim Kaat	.80	.40	.25
111	Felix Millan	.40	.20	.12
Panel 38		2.50	1.25	.70
112	Don Money	.40	.20	.12
113	Rick Monday	.50	.25	.15
114	Dick Bosman	.40	.20	.12

		NR MT	EX	VG
Panel 39		3.50	1.75	1.00
115	Roger Metzger	.40	.20	.12
116	Fergie Jenkins	.80	.40	.25
117	Dusky Baker	.50	.25	.15
Panel 40		10.00	5.00	3.00
118	Billy Champion	.50	.25	.15
119	Bob Gibson	3.50	1.75	1.00
120	Bill Freehan	.80	.40	.25
Panel 41		2.50	1.25	.70
121	Cesar Geronimo	.40	.20	.12
122	Jorge Orta	.40	.20	.12
123	Cleon Jones	.40	.20	.12
Panel 42		11.00	5.50	3.25
124	Steve Busby	.40	.20	.12
125a	Bill Madlock (Pitcher)	2.50	1.25	.70
125b	Bill Madlock (Third Base)	2.50	1.25	.70
126	Jim Palmer	2.50	1.25	.70
Panel 43		4.00	2.00	1.25
127	Tony Perez	.80	.40	.25
128	Larry Hisle	.40	.20	.12
129	Rusty Staub	.80	.40	.25
Panel 44		20.00	10.00	6.00
130	Hank Aaron	9.00	4.50	2.75
131	Rennie Stennett	.50	.25	.15
132	Rico Petrocelli	.70	.35	.20
Panel 45		13.00	6.50	4.00
133	Mike Schmidt	4.00	2.00	1.25
134	Sparky Lyle	.50	.25	.15
135	Willie Stargell	2.00	1.00	.60
Panel 46		7.00	3.50	2.00
136	Ken Henderson	.40	.20	.12
137	Willie Montanez	.40	.20	.12
138	Thurman Munson	2.50	1.25	.70
Panel 47		2.50	1.25	.70
139	Richie Zisk	.40	.20	.12
140	Geo. Hendricks (Hendrick)	.50	.25	.15
141	Bobby Murcer	.50	.25	.15
Panel 48		9.00	4.50	2.75
142	Lee May	.50	.25	.15
143	Carlton Fisk	.90	.45	.25
144	Brooks Robinson	3.00	1.50	.90
Panel 49		2.50	1.25	.70
145	Bobby Bonds	.50	.25	.15
146	Gary Sutherland	.40	.20	.12
147	Oscar Gamble	.40	.20	.12
Panel 50		4.50	2.25	1.25
148	Jim Hunt	1.25	.60	.40
149	Tub McGraw	.50	.25	.15
150	Dave McNally	.50	.25	.15

1975 Hostess Twinkie

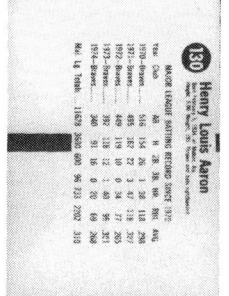

HANK AARON
DESIGNATED HITTER
Milwaukee BREWERS

Believed to have been issued only in the Western states, and on a limited basis at that, the 1975 Hostess Twinkie set features 60 of the cards from the "regular" Hostess set of that year. The cards were issued one per pack with the popular snack cake. Cards 1-36 are a direct pick-up from the Hostess set, while the remaining 24 cards in the set were selected from the more popular names in the remainder of the Hostess issue — with an emphasis on West Coast players. Thus, after card #36, the '75 Twinkie cards are skip-numbered from 40-136. In identical 2¼" by 3¼" size, the Twinkie cards differ from the Hostess issue only in the presence of small black bars at top

and bottom center of the back of the card. Value quoted are for full bottom panels.

		NR MT	EX	VG
Complete Set:		175.00	87.00	52.00
Common Player:		.90	.45	.25
1	Bobby Tolan	.90	.45	.25
2	Cookie Rojas	.90	.45	.25
3	Darrell Evans	2.00	1.00	.60
4	Sal Bando	1.25	.60	.40
5	Joe Morgan	4.00	2.00	1.25
6	Mickey Lolich	2.00	1.00	.60
7	Don Sutton	4.00	2.00	1.25
8	Bill Melton	.90	.45	.25
9	Tim Foli	.90	.45	.25
10	Joe Lahoud	.90	.45	.25
11	Bert Hooten (Burt Hooton)	1.25	.60	.40
12	Paul Blair	.90	.45	.25
13	Jim Barr	.90	.45	.25
14	Toby Harrah	.90	.45	.25
15	John Milner	.90	.45	.25
16	Ken Holtzman	.90	.45	.25
17	Cesar Cedeno	1.25	.60	.40
18	Dwight Evans	3.00	1.50	.90
19	Willie McCovey	6.50	3.25	2.00
20	Tony Oliva	2.00	1.00	.60
21	Manny Sanguillen	.90	.45	.25
22	Mickey Rivers	1.25	.60	.40
23	Lou Brock	6.50	3.25	2.00
24	Graig Nettles	3.00	1.50	.90
25	Jim Wynn	.90	.45	.25
26	George Scott	.90	.45	.25
27	Greg Luzinski	1.25	.60	.40
28	Bert Campaneris	1.25	.60	.40
29	Pete Rose	20.00	10.00	6.00
30	Buddy Bell	2.00	1.00	.60
31	Gary Matthews	1.25	.60	.40
32	Fred Patek	.90	.45	.25
33	Mike Lum	.90	.45	.25
34	Ellie Rodriguez	.90	.45	.25
35	Milt May (photo actually Lee May)			
		1.25	.60	.40
36	Willie Horton	.90	.45	.25
40	Joe Rudi	.90	.45	.25
43	Garry Maddox	.90	.45	.25
46	Dave Chalk	.90	.45	.25
49	Steve Garvey	10.00	5.00	3.00
52	Rollie Fingers	3.50	1.75	1.00
58	Nolan Ryan	9.00	4.50	2.75
61	Ron Cey	1.50	.70	.45
64	Gene Tenace	.90	.45	.25
65	Jose Cardenal	.90	.45	.25
67	Dave Lopes	1.25	.60	.40
68	Wilbur Wood	.90	.45	.25
73	Chris Speier	.90	.45	.25
77	Don Kessinger	.90	.45	.25
79	Andy Messersmith	.90	.45	.25
80	Robin Yount	14.00	7.00	4.25
82	Bill Singer	.90	.45	.25
103	Glenn Beckert	.90	.45	.25
110	Jim Kaat	2.50	1.25	.70
112	Don Money	.90	.45	.25
113	Rick Monday	1.25	.60	.40
122	Jorge Orta	.90	.45	.25
125	Bill Madlock	2.50	1.25	.70
130	Hank Aaron	14.00	7.00	4.25
136	Ken Henderson	.90	.45	.25

1976 Hostess

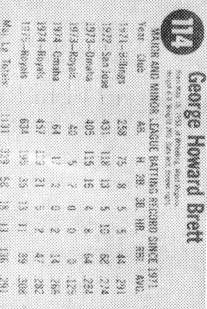

GEORGE BRETT
Kansas City ROYALS
THIRD BASE

The second of five annual Hostess issues, the 1976 cards carried a "Bicentennial" color theme, with red, white and blue stripes at the bottom of the 2¼" by 3¼" cards. Like other Hostess issues, the cards were printed in panels of three as the bottom of family-size boxes of snack cake products. This leads to a degree of scarcity for some of the 150 cards in the set; those which were found on less-popular brands. A well-trimmed three-card panel measures 7¼" by 3¼." Some of the photos used in the 1976 Hostess set will also be found on Topps issues of the era.

		NR MT	EX	VG
Complete Panel Set:		325.00	162.00	97.00
Complete Singles Set:		200.00	100.00	60.00
Common Panel:		2.50	1.25	.70
Common Single Player:		.40	.20	.12
Panel 1		11.00	5.50	3.25
1	Fred Lynn	1.50	.70	.45
2	Joe Morgan	1.50	.70	.45
3	Phil Niekro	2.00	1.00	.60
Panel 2		4.50	2.25	1.25
4	Gaylord Perry	1.25	.60	.40
5	Bob Watson	.40	.20	.12
6	Bill Freehan	.50	.25	.15
Panel 3		6.00	3.00	1.75
7	Lou Brock	2.50	1.25	.70
8	Al Fitzmorris	.40	.20	.12
9	Rennie Stennett	.40	.20	.12
Panel 4		8.00	4.00	2.50
10	Tony Oliva	.50	.25	.15
11	Robin Yount	3.00	1.50	.90
12	Rick Manning	.40	.20	.12
Panel 5		3.50	1.75	1.00
13	Bobby Grich	.50	.25	.15
14	Terry Forster	.40	.20	.12
15	Dave Kingman	.80	.40	.25
Panel 6		7.00	3.50	2.00
16	Thurman Munson	2.50	1.25	.70
17	Rick Reuschel	.50	.25	.15
18	Bobby Bonds	.50	.25	.15
Panel 7		9.00	4.50	2.75
19	Steve Garvey	3.50	1.75	1.00
20	Vida Blue	.50	.25	.15
21	Dave Rader	.40	.20	.12
Panel 8		8.50	4.25	2.50
22	Johnny Bench	3.50	1.75	1.00
23	Luis Tiant	.50	.25	.15
24	Darrell Evans	.60	.30	.20
Panel 9		2.50	1.25	.70
25	Larry Dierker	.40	.20	.12
26	Willie Horton	.50	.25	.15
27	John Ellis	.40	.20	.12
Panel 10		3.00	1.50	.90
28	Al Cowens	.40	.20	.12
29	Jerry Reuss	.50	.25	.15
30	Reggie Smith	.50	.25	.15
Panel 11		13.00	6.50	4.00
31	Bobby Darwin	.50	.25	.15
32	Fritz Peterson	.50	.25	.15
33	Rod Carew	6.00	3.00	1.75
Panel 12		21.00	10.50	6.25
34	Carlos May	.50	.25	.15
35	Tom Seaver	6.00	3.00	1.75
36	Brooks Robinson	4.50	2.25	1.25
Panel 13		2.50	1.25	.70
37	Jose Cardenal	.40	.20	.12
38	Ron Blomberg	.40	.20	.12
39	Lee Stanton	.40	.20	.12
Panel 14		2.50	1.25	.70
40	Dave Cash	.40	.20	.12
41	John Montefusco	.40	.20	.12
42	Bob Tolan	.40	.20	.12
Panel 15		2.50	1.25	.70
43	Carl Morton	.40	.20	.12
44	Rick Burleson	.50	.25	.15
45	Don Gullett	.40	.20	.12
Panel 16		2.50	1.25	.70
46	Vern Ruhle	.40	.20	.12
47	Cesar Cedeno	.50	.25	.15
48	Toby Harrah	.50	.25	.15
Panel 17		5.50	2.75	1.75
49	Willie Stargell	2.00	1.00	.60
50	Al Hrabosky	.40	.20	.12
51	Amos Otis	.50	.25	.15
Panel 18		2.50	1.25	.70
52	Bud Harrelson	.50	.25	.15
53	Jim Hughes	.40	.20	.12
54	George Scott	.50	.25	.15
Panel 19		9.00	4.50	2.75
55	Mike Vail	.50	.25	.15
56	Jim Palmer	3.50	1.75	1.00
57	Jorge Orta	.80	.40	.25
Panel 20		3.50	1.75	1.00
58	Chris Chambliss	.80	.40	.25
59	Dave Chalk	.50	.25	.15
60	Ray Burris	.50	.25	.15
Panel 21		12.00	6.00	3.50
61	Bert Campaneris	.80	.40	.25
62	Gary Carter	4.00	2.00	1.25
63	Ron Cey	.90	.45	.25
Panel 22		26.00	13.00	7.75
64	Carlton Fisk	2.00	1.00	.60
65	Marty Perez	.50	.25	.15
66	Pete Rose	8.00	4.00	2.50
Panel 23		3.50	1.75	1.00
67	Roger Metzger	.50	.25	.15
68	Jim Sundberg	.60	.30	.20
69	Ron LeFlore	.60	.30	.20
Panel 24		3.50	1.75	1.00
70	Ted Sizemore	.50	.25	.15
71	Steve Busby	.50	.25	.15
72	Manny Sanguillen	.50	.25	.15
Panel 25		5.00	2.50	1.50
73	Larry Hisle	.60	.30	.20
74	Pete Broberg	.50	.25	.15
75	Boog Powell	1.25	.60	.40
Panel 26		6.50	3.25	2.00
76	Ken Singleton	.80	.40	.25
77	Rich Gossage	2.00	1.00	.60
78	Jerry Grote	.50	.25	.15
Panel 27		15.00	7.50	4.50
79	Nolan Ryan	5.00	2.50	1.50
80	Rick Monday	.70	.35	.20
81	Graig Nettles	1.25	.60	.40
Panel 28		16.00	8.00	4.75
82	Chris Speier	.40	.20	.12
83	Dave Winfield	3.50	1.75	1.00
84	Mike Schmidt	4.00	2.00	1.25
Panel 29		4.00	2.00	1.25
85	Buzz Capra	.40	.20	.12
86	Tony Perez	.80	.40	.25
87	Dwight Evans	.90	.45	.25
Panel 30		2.50	1.25	.70
88	Mike Hargrove	.40	.20	.12
89	Joe Coleman	.40	.20	.12
90	Greg Gross	.40	.20	.12
Panel 31		2.50	1.25	.70
91	John Mayberry	.40	.20	.12
92	John Candelaria	.50	.25	.15
93	Bake McBride	.40	.20	.12
Panel 32		13.00	6.50	4.00
94	Hank Aaron	5.00	2.50	1.50
95	Buddy Bell	.50	.25	.15
96	Steve Braun	.40	.20	.12
Panel 33		2.50	1.25	.70
97	Jon Matlack	.40	.20	.12
98	Lee May	.50	.25	.15
99	Wilbur Wood	.50	.25	.15
Panel 34		4.00	2.00	1.25
100	Bill Madlock	.90	.45	.25
101	Frank Tanana	.50	.25	.15
102	Mickey Rivers	.50	.25	.15
Panel 35		3.50	1.75	1.00
103	Mike Ivie	.40	.20	.12
104	Rollie Fingers	.90	.45	.25
105	Dave Lopes	.50	.25	.15
Panel 36		3.50	1.75	1.00
106	George Foster	.90	.45	.25
107	Denny Doyle	.40	.20	.12
108	Earl Williams	.40	.20	.12
Panel 37		2.50	1.25	.70
109	Tom Veryzer	.40	.20	.12
110	J.R. Richard	.50	.25	.15
111	Jeff Burroughs	.40	.20	.12
Panel 38		14.00	7.00	4.25
112	Al Oliver	.90	.45	.25
113	Ted Simmons	.80	.40	.25
114	Geroge Brett	5.00	2.50	1.50
Panel 39		3.00	1.50	.90
115	Frank Duffy	.40	.20	.12
116	Bert Blyleven	.70	.35	.20
117	Darrell Porter	.50	.25	.15
Panel 40		2.50	1.25	.70
118	Don Baylor	.60	.30	.20
119	Bucky Dent	.50	.25	.15
120	Felix Millan	.40	.20	.12
Panel 41		2.50	1.25	.70
121	Mike Cuellar	.50	.25	.15
122	Gene Tenace	.40	.20	.12

		NR MT	EX	VG
123	Bobby Murcer	.50	.25	.15
Panel 42		6.50	3.25	2.00
124	Willie McCovey	2.50	1.25	.70
125	Greg Luzinski	.50	.25	.15
126	Larry Parrish	.50	.25	.15
Panel 43		10.00	5.00	3.00
127	Jim Rice	.40	.20	.12
128	Dave Concepcion	.50	.25	.15
129	Jim Wynn	.50	.25	.15
Panel 44		2.50	1.25	.70
130	Tom Grieve	.40	.20	.12
131	Mike Cosgrove	.40	.20	.12
132	Dan Meyer	.40	.20	.12
Panel 45		5.00	2.50	1.50
133	Dave Parker	1.50	.70	.45
134	Don Kessinger	.40	.20	.12
135	Hal McRae	.50	.25	.15
Panel 46		3.50	1.75	1.00
136	Don Money	.40	.20	.12
137	Dennis Eckersley	.50	.25	.15
138	Fergie Jenkins	.80	.40	.25
Panel 47		4.00	2.00	1.25
139	Mike Torrez	.40	.20	.12
140	Jerry Morales	.40	.20	.12
141	Jim Hunter	1.25	.60	.40
Panel 48		2.50	1.25	.70
142	Gary Matthews	.50	.25	.15
143	Randy Jones	.40	.20	.12
144	Mike Jorgensen	.40	.20	.12
Panel 49		13.00	6.50	4.00
145	Larry Bowa	.60	.30	.20
146	Reggie Jackson	5.00	2.50	1.50
147	Steve Yeager	.40	.20	.12
Panel 50		15.00	7.50	4.50
148	Dave May	.40	.20	.12
149	Carl Yastrzemski	6.50	3.25	2.00
150	Cesar Geronimo	.40	.20	.12

		NR MT	EX	VG
13	Bobby Grich	1.25	.60	.40
14	Terry Forster	.90	.45	.25
15	Dave Kingman	2.00	1.00	.60
16	Thurman Munson	6.50	3.25	2.00
17	Rick Reuschel	1.25	.60	.40
18	Bobby Bonds	1.25	.60	.40
19	Steve Garvey	10.00	5.00	3.00
20	Vida Blue	2.00	1.00	.60
21	Dave Rader	.90	.45	.25
22	Johnny Bench	9.00	4.50	2.75
23	Luis Tiant	1.50	.70	.45
24	Darrell Evans	2.00	1.00	.60
25	Larry Dierker	.90	.45	.25
26	Willie Horton	.90	.45	.25
27	John Ellis	.90	.45	.25
28	Al Cowens	.90	.45	.25
29	Jerry Reuss	1.25	.60	.40
30	Reggie Smith	1.25	.60	.40
31	Bobby Darwin	.90	.45	.25
32	Fritz Peterson	.90	.45	.25
33	Rod Carew	10.00	5.00	3.00
34	Carlos May	.90	.45	.25
35	Tom Seaver	10.00	5.00	3.00
36	Brooks Robinson	9.00	4.50	2.75
37	Jose Cardenal	.90	.45	.25
38	Ron Blomberg	.90	.45	.25
39	Lee Stanton	.90	.45	.25
40	Dave Cash	.90	.45	.25
41	John Montefusco	.90	.45	.25
42	Bob Tolan	.90	.45	.25
43	Carl Morton	.90	.45	.25
44	Rick Burleson	1.25	.60	.40
45	Don Gullett	.90	.45	.25
46	Vern Ruhle	.90	.45	.25
47	Cesar Cedeno	1.25	.60	.40
48	Toby Harrah	.90	.45	.25
49	Willie Stargell	5.00	2.50	1.50
50	Al Hrabosky	.90	.45	.25
51	Amos Otis	.90	.45	.25
52	Bud Harrelson	.90	.45	.25
53	Jim Hughes	.90	.45	.25
54	George Scott	.90	.45	.25
55	Mike Vail	.90	.45	.25
56	Jim Palmer	6.50	3.25	2.00
57	Jorge Orta	.90	.45	.25
58	Chris Chambliss	1.25	.60	.40
59	Dave Chalk	.90	.45	.25
60	Ray Burris	.90	.45	.25

1976 Hostess Twinkie

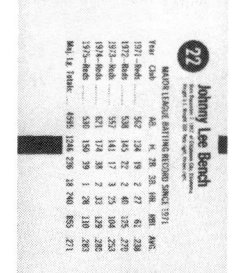

The 60 cards in this regionally-issued (West Coast only) set closely paralleled the first 60 cards in the numerical sequence of the "regular" 1976 Hostess issue. The singular difference is the appearance on the back of a black band toward the center of the card at top and bottom. Also unlike the three-card panels of the regular Hostess issue, the 2¼" by 3¼" Twinkie cards were issued singly, as the cardboard stiffener for the cellophane-wrapped snack cakes. Values quoted are for complete bottom panels.

		NR MT	EX	VG
Complete Set:		175.00	87.00	52.00
Common Player:		.90	.45	.25
1	Fred Lynn	3.00	1.50	.90
2	Joe Morgan	4.00	2.00	1.25
3	Phil Niekro	4.00	2.00	1.25
4	Gaylord Perry	4.50	2.25	1.25
5	Bob Watson	.90	.45	.25
6	Bill Freehan	1.25	.60	.40
7	Lou Brock	6.50	3.25	2.00
8	Al Fitzmorris	.90	.45	.25
9	Rennie Stennett	.90	.45	.25
10	Tony Oliva	2.00	1.00	.60
11	Robin Yount	6.50	3.25	2.00
12	Rick Manning	.90	.45	.25

1977 Hostess

The third of five consecutive annual issues, the 1977 Hostess cards retained the same card size — 2¼" by 3¼," set size — 150 cards, and mode of issue — three cards on a 7¼" by 3¼" panel, as the previous two efforts. Because they were issued as the bottom panel of snack cake boxes, and because some brands of Hostess products were more popular than others, certain cards in the set are scarcer than others.

	NR MT	EX	VG
Complete Panel Set:	300.00	150.00	90.00
Complete Singles Set:	175.00	87.00	52.00
Common Panel:	2.50	1.25	.70
Common Single Player:	.40	.20	.12

#	Player	NR MT	EX	VG
Panel 1		18.00	9.00	5.50
1	Jim Palmer	2.50	1.25	.70
2	Joe Morgan	1.50	.70	.45
3	Reggie Jackson	5.00	2.50	1.50
Panel 2		23.00	11.50	7.00
4	Carl Yastrzemski	6.00	3.00	1.75
5	Thurman Munson	2.50	1.25	.70
6	Johnny Bench	3.50	1.75	1.00
Panel 3		32.00	16.00	9.50
7	Tom Seaver	3.00	1.50	.90
8	Pete Rose	8.00	4.00	2.50
9	Rod Carew	4.00	2.00	1.25
Panel 4		2.50	1.25	.70
10	Luis Tiant	.50	.25	.15
11	Phil Garner	.50	.25	.15
12	Sixto Lezcano	.40	.20	.12
Panel 5		2.50	1.25	.70
13	Mike Torrez	.40	.20	.12
14	Dave Lopes	.50	.25	.15
15	Doug DeCinces	.50	.25	.15
Panel 6		2.50	1.25	.70
16	Jim Spencer	.40	.20	.12
17	Hal McRae	.50	.25	.15
18	Mike Hargrove	.40	.20	.12
Panel 7		4.50	2.25	1.25
19	Willie Montanez	.50	.25	.15
20	Roger Metzger	.50	.25	.15
21	Dwight Evans	1.50	.70	.45
Panel 8		10.00	5.00	3.00
22	Steve Rogers	.50	.25	.15
23	Jim Rice	4.00	2.00	1.25
24	Pete Falcone	.50	.25	.15
Panel 9		9.00	4.50	2.75
25	Greg Luzinski	.90	.45	.25
26	Randy Jones	.50	.25	.15
27	Willie Stargell	3.00	1.50	.90
Panel 10		3.50	1.75	1.00
28	John Hiller	.50	.25	.15
29	Bobby Murcer	.70	.35	.20
30	Rick Monday	.70	.35	.20
Panel 11		9.00	4.50	2.75
31	John Montefusco	.50	.25	.15
32	Lou Brock	3.50	1.75	1.00
33	Bill North	.50	.25	.15
Panel 12		32.00	16.00	9.50
34	Robin Yount	3.50	1.75	1.00
35	Steve Garvey	5.00	2.50	1.50
36	George Brett	8.00	4.00	2.50
Panel 13		3.50	1.75	1.00
37	Toby Harrah	.70	.35	.20
38	Jerry Royster	.50	.25	.15
39	Bob Watson	.60	.30	.20
Panel 14		9.00	4.50	2.75
40	George Foster	.90	.45	.25
41	Gary Carter	3.00	1.50	.90
42	John Denny	.40	.20	.12
Panel 15		17.00	8.50	5.00
43	Mike Schmidt	4.00	2.00	1.25
44	Dave Winfield	3.50	1.75	1.00
45	Al Oliver	.90	.45	.25
Panel 16		3.00	1.50	.90
46	Mark Fidrych	.70	.35	.20
47	Larry Herndon	.50	.25	.15
48	Dave Goltz	.40	.20	.12
Panel 17		3.50	1.75	1.00
49	Jerry Morales	.40	.20	.12
50	Ron LeFlore	.50	.25	.15
51	Fred Lynn	.90	.45	.25
Panel 18		3.50	1.75	1.00
52	Vida Blue	.50	.25	.15
53	Rick Manning	.40	.20	.12
54	Bill Buckner	.70	.35	.20
Panel 19		2.50	1.25	.70
55	Lee May	.50	.25	.15
56	John Mayberry	.40	.20	.12
57	Darrel Chaney	.40	.20	.12
Panel 20		3.50	1.75	1.00
58	Cesar Cedeno	.50	.25	.15
59	Ken Griffey	.50	.25	.15
60	Dave Kingman	.80	.40	.25
Panel 21		3.50	1.75	1.00
61	Ted Simmons	.80	.40	.25
62	Larry Bowa	.50	.25	.15
63	Frank Tanana	.50	.25	.15
Panel 22		2.50	1.25	.70
64	Jason Thompson	.40	.20	.12
65	Ken Brett	.40	.20	.12
66	Roy Smalley	.40	.20	.12
Panel 23		2.50	1.25	.70
67	Ray Burris	.40	.20	.12
68	Rick Burleson	.50	.25	.15

#	Player	NR MT	EX	VG
69	Buddy Bell	.50	.25	.15
Panel 24		5.00	2.50	1.50
70	Don Sutton	1.50	.70	.45
71	Mark Belanger	.40	.20	.12
72	Dennis Leonard	.40	.20	.12
Panel 25		5.00	2.50	1.50
73	Gaylord Perry	1.50	.70	.45
74	Dick Ruthven	.40	.20	.12
75	Jose Cruz	.50	.25	.15
Panel 26		4.50	2.25	1.25
76	Cesar Geronimo	.40	.20	.12
77	Jerry Koosman	.50	.25	.15
78	Garry Templeton	1.25	.60	.40
Panel 27		9.50	4.75	2.75
79	Jim Hunter	1.25	.60	.40
80	John Candelaria	.50	.25	.15
81	Nolan Ryan	3.00	1.50	.90
Panel 28		2.50	1.25	.70
82	Rusty Staub	.50	.25	.15
83	Jim Barr	.40	.20	.12
84	Butch Wynegar	.50	.25	.15
Panel 29		2.50	1.25	.70
85	Jose Cardenal	.40	.20	.12
86	Claudell Washington	.50	.25	.15
87	Bill Travers	.40	.20	.12
Panel 30		2.50	1.25	.70
88	Rick Waits	.40	.20	.12
89	Ron Cey	.50	.25	.15
90	Al Bumbry	.40	.20	.12
Panel 31		2.50	1.25	.70
91	Bucky Dent	.50	.25	.15
92	Amos Otis	.50	.25	.15
93	Tom Grieve	.40	.20	.12
Panel 32		2.50	1.25	.70
94	Enos Cabell	.40	.20	.12
95	Dave Concepcion	.50	.25	.15
96	Felix Millan	.40	.20	.12
Panel 33		2.50	1.25	.70
97	Bake McBride	.40	.20	.12
98	Chris Chambliss	.50	.25	.15
99	Butch Metzger	.40	.20	.12
Panel 34		2.50	1.25	.70
100	Rennie Stennett	.40	.20	.12
101	Dave Roberts	.40	.20	.12
102	Lyman Bostock	.50	.25	.15
Panel 35		3.50	1.75	1.00
103	Rick Reuschel	.40	.20	.12
104	Carlton Fisk	.90	.45	.25
105	Jim Slaton	.40	.20	.12
Panel 36		2.50	1.25	.70
106	Dennis Eckersley	.50	.25	.15
107	Ken Singleton	.50	.25	.15
108	Ralph Garr	.40	.20	.12
Panel 37		8.00	4.00	2.50
109	Freddie Patek	.50	.25	.15
110	Jim Sundberg	.60	.30	.20
111	Phil Niekro	3.00	1.50	.90
Panel 38		3.50	1.75	1.00
112	J.R. Richard	.70	.35	.20
113	Gary Nolan	.50	.25	.15
114	Jon Matlack	.60	.30	.20
Panel 39		20.00	10.00	6.00
115	Keith Hernandez	3.50	1.75	1.00
116	Graig Nettles	.70	.35	.20
117	Steve Carlton	4.50	2.25	1.25
Panel 40		6.50	3.25	2.00
118	Bill Madlock	2.00	1.00	.60
119	Jerry Reuss	.80	.40	.25
120	Aurelio Rodriguez	.50	.25	.15
Panel 41		3.50	1.75	1.00
121	Dan Ford	.50	.25	.15
122	Ray Fosse	.50	.25	.15
123	George Hendrick	.70	.35	.20
Panel 42		2.50	1.25	.70
124	Alan Ashby	.40	.20	.12
125	Joe Lis	.40	.20	.12
126	Sal Bando	.50	.25	.15
Panel 43		4.00	2.00	1.25
127	Richie Zisk	.50	.25	.15
128	Rich Gossage	.90	.45	.25
129	Don Baylor	.50	.25	.15
Panel 44		2.50	1.25	.70
130	Dave McKay	.40	.20	.12
131	Bob Grich	.50	.25	.15
132	Dave Pagan	.40	.20	.12
Panel 45		2.50	1.25	.70
133	Dave Cash	.40	.20	.12
134	Steve Braun	.40	.20	.12
135	Dan Meyer	.40	.20	.12
Panel 46		4.00	2.00	1.25
136	Bill Stein	.40	.20	.12

		NR MT	EX	VG
137	Rollie Fingers	1.25	.60	.40
138	Brian Downing	.50	.25	.15
Panel 47		2.50	1.25	.70
139	Bill Singer	.40	.20	.12
140	Doyle Alexander	.50	.25	.15
141	Gene Tenace	.40	.20	.12
Panel 48		2.50	1.25	.70
142	Gary Matthews	.50	.25	.15
143	Don Gullett	.40	.20	.12
144	Wayne Garland	.40	.20	.12
Panel 49		2.50	1.25	.70
145	Pete Broberg	.40	.20	.12
146	Joe Rudi	.50	.25	.15
147	Glenn Abbott	.40	.20	.12
Panel 50		2.50	1.25	.70
148	George Scott	.50	.25	.15
149	Bert Campaneris	.50	.25	.15
150	Andy Messersmith	.50	.25	.15

1977 Hostess Twinkie

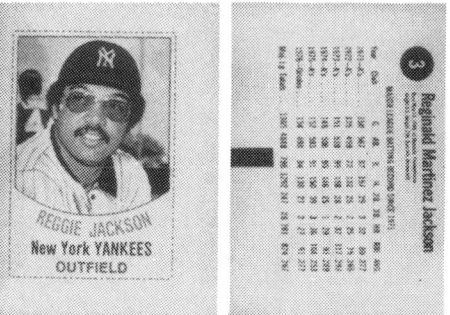

REGGIE JACKSON
New York YANKEES
OUTFIELD

Reginald Martinez Jackson

The 1977 Hostess Twinkie issue, at 150 different cards, is the largest of the single-panel Twinkie sets. It is also the most obscure. The cards, which measure 2¼'' by 3¼'', but are part of a larger panel, were found not only with Twinkies, but with Hostess Cupcakes as well. Card #'s 1-30 and 111-150 are Twinkies panels and #'s 31-135 are Cupcakes panels. Complete Cupcakes panels are approximately 2¼'' by 4½'' in size, while complete Twinkies panels measure 3⅛'' by 4¼''. The photos used in the set are identical to those in the 1977 Hostess three-card panel set. The main difference is the appearance of a black band at the center of the card back. The values quoted in the checklist that follows are for complete bottom panels.

		NR MT	EX	VG
Complete Set:		325.00	162.00	97.50
Common Player:		.80	.40	.25
1	Jim Palmer	5.00	2.50	1.50
2	Joe Morgan	3.00	1.50	.90
3	Reggie Jackson	10.00	5.00	3.00
4	Carl Yastrzemski	12.00	6.00	3.50
5	Thurman Munson	5.00	2.50	1.50
6	Johnny Bench	7.00	3.50	2.00
7	Tom Seaver	6.00	3.00	1.75
8	Pete Rose	15.00	7.50	4.50
9	Rod Carew	8.00	4.00	2.50
10	Luis Tiant	1.00	.50	.30
11	Phil Garner	.80	.40	.25
12	Sixto Lezcano	.80	.40	.25
13	Mike Torrez	.80	.40	.25
14	Dave Lopes	1.00	.50	.30
15	Doug DeCinces	1.00	.50	.30
16	Jim Spencer	.80	.40	.25
17	Hal McRae	1.00	.50	.30
18	Mike Hargrove	.80	.40	.25
19	Willie Montanez	.80	.40	.25
20	Roger Metzger	.80	.40	.25
21	Dwight Evans	2.00	1.00	.60
22	Steve Rogers	.80	.40	.25
23	Jim Rice	5.00	2.50	1.50

		NR MT	EX	VG
24	Pete Falcone	.80	.40	.25
25	Greg Luzinski	1.50	.70	.45
26	Randy Jones	.80	.40	.25
27	Willie Stargell	5.00	2.50	1.50
28	John Hiller	.80	.40	.25
29	Bobby Murcer	1.25	.60	.40
30	Rick Monday	1.00	.50	.30
31	John Montefusco	.80	.40	.25
32	Lou Brock	6.00	3.00	1.75
33	Bill North	.80	.40	.25
34	Robin Yount	5.00	2.50	1.50
35	Steve Garvey	6.00	3.00	1.75
36	George Brett	10.00	5.00	3.00
37	Toby Harrah	.80	.40	.25
38	Jerry Royster	.80	.40	.25
39	Bob Watson	1.00	.50	.30
40	George Foster	1.75	.90	.50
41	Gary Carter	6.00	3.00	1.75
42	John Denny	.80	.40	.25
43	Mike Schmidt	8.00	4.00	2.50
44	Dave Winfield	7.00	3.50	2.00
45	Al Oliver	1.75	.90	.50
46	Mark Fidrych	1.50	.70	.45
47	Larry Herndon	1.00	.50	.30
48	Dave Goltz	.80	.40	.25
49	Jerry Morales	.80	.40	.25
50	Ron LeFlore	1.00	.50	.30
51	Fred Lynn	1.75	.90	.50
52	Vida Blue	1.00	.50	.30
53	Rick Manning	.80	.40	.25
54	Bill Buckner	1.50	.70	.45
55	Lee May	1.00	.50	.30
56	John Mayberry	.80	.40	.25
57	Darrel Chaney	.80	.40	.25
58	Cesar Cedeno	1.25	.60	.40
59	Ken Griffey	1.25	.60	.40
60	Dave Kingman	1.75	.90	.50
61	Ted Simmons	1.50	.70	.45
62	Larry Bowa	1.25	.60	.40
63	Frank Tanana	1.00	.50	.30
64	Jason Thompson	.80	.40	.25
65	Ken Brett	.80	.40	.25
66	Roy Smalley	.80	.40	.25
67	Ray Burris	.80	.40	.25
68	Rick Burleson	1.00	.50	.30
69	Buddy Bell	1.25	.60	.40
70	Don Sutton	3.00	1.50	.90
71	Mark Belanger	.80	.40	.25
72	Dennis Leonard	.80	.40	.25
73	Gaylord Perry	3.50	1.75	1.00
74	Dick Ruthven	.80	.40	.25
75	Jose Cruz	1.25	.60	.40
76	Cesar Geronimo	.80	.40	.25
77	Jerry Koosman	1.25	.60	.40
78	Garry Templeton	2.50	1.25	.70
79	Jim Hunter	3.00	1.50	.90
80	John Candelaria	1.00	.50	.30
81	Nolan Ryan	6.00	3.00	1.75
82	Rusty Staub	1.50	.70	.45
83	Jim Barr	.80	.40	.25
84	Butch Wynegar	1.00	.50	.30
85	Jose Cardenal	.80	.40	.25
86	Claudell Washington	1.00	.50	.30
87	Bill Travers	.80	.40	.25
88	Rick Waits	.80	.40	.25
89	Ron Cey	1.25	.60	.40
90	Al Bumbry	.80	.40	.25
91	Bucky Dent	1.00	.50	.30
92	Amos Otis	1.00	.50	.30
93	Tom Grieve	.80	.40	.25
94	Enos Cabell	.80	.40	.25
95	Dave Concepcion	1.25	.60	.40
96	Felix Millan	.80	.40	.25
97	Bake McBride	.80	.40	.25
98	Chris Chambliss	1.00	.50	.30
99	Butch Metzger	.80	.40	.25
100	Rennie Stennett	.80	.40	.25
101	Dave Roberts	.80	.40	.25
102	Lyman Bostock	1.00	.50	.30
103	Rick Reuschel	1.00	.50	.30
104	Carlton Fisk	2.00	1.00	.60
105	Jim Slaton	.80	.40	.25
106	Dennis Eckersley	1.00	.50	.30
107	Ken Singleton	1.00	.50	.30
108	Ralph Garr	.80	.40	.25
109	Freddie Patek	.80	.40	.25
110	Jim Sundberg	.80	.40	.25
111	Phil Niekro	3.00	1.50	.90
112	J. R. Richard	1.00	.50	.30
113	Gary Nolan	.80	.40	.25
114	Jon Matlack	.80	.40	.25

		NR MT	EX	VG
115	Keith Hernandez	4.00	2.00	1.25
116	Graig Nettles	2.00	1.00	.60
117	Steve Carlton	6.00	3.00	1.75
118	Bill Madlock	1.50	.70	.45
119	Jerry Reuss	1.00	.50	.30
120	Aurelio Rodriguez	.80	.40	.25
121	Dan Ford	.80	.40	.25
122	Ray Fosse	.80	.40	.25
123	George Hendrick	1.00	.50	.30
124	Alan Ashby	.80	.40	.25
125	Joe Lis	.80	.40	.25
126	Sal Bando	1.00	.50	.30
127	Richie Zisk	1.00	.50	.30
128	Rich Gossage	1.75	.90	.50
129	Don Baylor	1.25	.60	.40
130	Dave McKay	.80	.40	.25
131	Bob Grich	1.00	.50	.30
132	Dave Pagan	.80	.40	.25
133	Dave Cash	.80	.40	.25
134	Steve Braun	.80	.4C	.25
135	Dan Meyer	.80	.40	.25
136	Bill Stein	.80	.40	.25
137	Rollie Fingers	2.50	1.25	.70
138	Brian Downing	1.00	.50	.30
139	Bill Singer	.80	.40	.25
140	Doyle Alexander	1.00	.50	.30
141	Gene Tenace	1.00	.50	.30
142	Gary Matthews	1.00	.50	.30
143	Don Gullett	.80	.40	.25
144	Wayne Garland	.80	.40	.25
145	Pete Broberg	.80	.40	.25
146	Joe Rudi	1.00	.50	.30
147	Glenn Abbott	.80	.40	.25
148	George Scott	1.00	.50	.30
149	Bert Campaneris	1.25	.60	.40
150	Andy Messersmith	1.00	.50	.30

1978 Hostess

 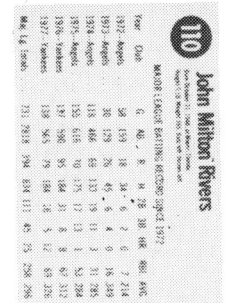

MICKEY RIVERS
NEW YORK YANKEES

Other than the design on the front of the card, there was little different about the 1978 Hostess cards from the three years' issues which had preceded it, or the one which followed. The 2¼'' by 3¼'' cards were printed in panels of three (7¼'' by 3¼'') as the bottom of family-size boxes of snack cakes. The 1978 set was again complete at 150 cards. Like other years of Hostess issues, there are scarcities within the 1978 set that were the result of those panels having been issued with less-popular brands of snack cakes.

		NR MT	EX	VG
Complete Panel:		275.00	137.00	82.00
Complete Singles Set:		150.00	75.00	45.00
Common Panel:		2.50	1.25	.70
Common Single Player:		.40	.20	.12
Panel 1		4.00	2.00	1.25
1	Butch Hobson	.40	.20	.12
2	George Foster	1.25	.60	.40
3	Bob Forsch	.50	.25	.15
Panel 2		5.00	2.50	1.50
4	Tony Perez	.90	.45	.25
5	Bruce Sutter	.90	.45	.25
6	Hal McRae	.50	.25	.15

		NR MT	EX	VG
Panel 3		6.00	3.00	1.75
7	Tommy John	1.50	.70	.45
8	Greg Luzinski	.90	.45	.25
9	Enos Cabell	.40	.20	.12
Panel 4		.50	.25	.15
10	Doug DeCinces	.50	.25	.15
11	Willie Stargell	1.50	.70	.45
12	Ed Halicki	.40	.20	.12
Panel 5		2.50	1.25	.70
13	Larry Hisle	.40	.20	.12
14	Jim Slaton	.40	.20	.12
15	Buddy Bell	.50	.25	.15
Panel 6		2.50	1.25	.70
16	Earl Williams	.40	.20	.12
17	Glenn Abbott	.40	.20	.12
18	Dan Ford	.40	.20	.12
Panel 7		2.50	1.25	.70
19	Gary Mathews	.50	.25	.15
20	Eric Soderholm	.40	.20	.12
21	Bump Wills	.40	.20	.12
Panel 8		7.00	3.50	2.00
22	Keith Hernandez	2.50	1.25	.70
23	Dave Cash	.40	.20	.12
24	George Scott	.50	.25	.15
Panel 9		15.00	7.50	4.50
25	Ron Guidry	1.50	.70	.45
26	Dave Kingman	.80	.40	.25
27	George Brett	5.00	2.50	1.50
Panel 10		3.50	1.75	1.00
28	Bob Watson	.50	.25	.15
29	Bob Boone	.70	.35	.20
30	Reggie Smith	.70	.35	.20
Panel 11		20.00	10.00	6.00
31	Eddie Murray	12.00	6.00	3.50
32	Gary Lavelle	.50	.25	.15
33	Rennie Stennett	.50	.25	.15
Panel 12		3.50	1.75	1.00
34	Duane Kuiper	.50	.25	.15
35	Sixto Lezcano	.50	.25	.15
36	Dave Rozema	.50	.25	.15
Panel 13		3.50	1.75	1.00
37	Butch Wynegar	.50	.25	.15
38	Mitchell Page	.50	.25	.15
39	Bill Stein	.50	.25	.15
Panel 14		2.50	1.25	.70
40	Elliott Maddox	.40	.20	.12
41	Mike Hargrove	.40	.20	.12
42	Bobby Bonds	.50	.25	.15
Panel 15		14.50	7.25	4.25
43	Garry Templeton	.80	.40	.25
44	Johnny Bench	3.50	1.75	1.00
45	Jim Rice	4.00	2.00	1.25
Panel 16		13.00	6.50	4.00
46	Bill Buckner	.80	.40	.25
47	Reggie Jackson	5.00	2.50	1.50
48	Freddie Patek	.40	.20	.12
Panel 17		8.50	4.25	2.50
49	Steve Carlton	3.50	1.75	1.00
50	Cesar Cedeno	.50	.25	.15
51	Steve Yeager	.40	.20	.12
Panel 18		3.50	1.75	1.00
52	Phil Garner	.50	.25	.15
53	Lee May	.50	.25	.15
54	Darrell Evans	.70	.35	.20
Panel 19		2.50	1.25	.70
55	Steve Kemp	.50	.25	.15
56	Dusty Baker	.50	.25	.15
57	Ray Fosse	.40	.20	.12
Panel 20		2.50	1.25	.70
58	Manny Sanguillen	.40	.20	.12
59	Tom Johnson	.40	.20	.12
60	Lee Stanton	.40	.20	.12
Panel 21		10.00	5.00	3.00
61	Jeff Burroughs	.40	.20	.12
62	Bobby Grich	.50	.25	.15
63	Dave Winfield	4.00	2.00	1.25
Panel 22		3.50	1.75	1.00
64	Dan Driessen	.50	.25	.15
65	Ted Simmons	.80	.40	.25
66	Jerry Remy	.40	.20	.12
Panel 23		2.50	1.25	.70
67	Al Cowens	.40	.20	.12
68	Sparky Lyle	.50	.25	.15
69	Manny Trillo	.50	.25	.15
Panel 24		5.00	2.50	1.50
70	Don Sutton	1.50	.70	.45
71	Larry Bowa	.50	.25	.15
72	Jose Cruz	.50	.25	.15
Panel 25		8.00	4.00	2.50
73	Willie McCovey	3.00	1.50	.90
74	Bert Blyleven	.70	.35	.20

		NR MT	EX	VG
75	Ken Singleton	.50	.25	.15
Panel 26		2.50	1.25	.70
76	Bill North	.40	.20	.12
77	Jason Thompson	.40	.20	.12
78	Dennis Eckersley	.50	.25	.15
Panel 27		2.50	1.25	.70
79	Jim Sundberg	.50	.25	.15
80	Jerry Koosman	.50	.25	.15
81	Bruce Bochte	.40	.20	.12
Panel 28		8.00	4.00	2.50
82	George Hendrick	.50	.25	.15
83	Nolan Ryan	3.00	1.50	.90
84	Roy Howell	.40	.20	.12
Panel 29		5.00	2.50	1.50
85	Butch Metzger	.40	.20	.12
86	George Medich	.40	.20	.12
87	Joe Morgan	1.50	.70	.45
Panel 30		3.00	1.50	.90
88	Dennis Leonard	.50	.25	.15
89	Willie Randolph	.50	.25	.15
90	Bobby Murcer	.50	.25	.15
Panel 31		3.00	1.50	.90
91	Rick Manning	.40	.20	.12
92	J.R. Richard	.50	.25	.15
93	Ron Cey	.70	.35	.20
Panel 32		2.50	1.25	.70
94	Sal Bando	.50	.25	.15
95	Ron LeFlore	.50	.25	.15
96	Dave Goltz	.40	.20	.12
Panel 33		2.50	1.25	.70
97	Dan Meyer	.40	.20	.12
98	Chris Chambliss	.50	.25	.15
99	Biff Pocoroba	.40	.20	.12
Panel 34		2.50	1.25	.70
100	Oscar Gamble	.40	.20	.12
101	Frank Tanana	.50	.25	.15
102	Lenny Randle	.40	.20	.12
Panel 35		2.50	1.25	.70
103	Tommy Hutton	.40	.20	.12
104	John Candelaria	.50	.25	.15
105	Jorge Orta	.40	.20	.12
Panel 36		3.00	1.50	.90
106	Ken Reitz	.40	.20	.12
107	Bill Campbell	.40	.20	.12
108	Dave Concepcion	.70	.35	.20
Panel 37		2.50	1.25	.70
109	Joe Ferguson	.40	.20	.12
110	Mickey Rivers	.50	.25	.15
111	Paul Splittorff	.40	.20	.12
Panel 38		11.00	5.50	3.25
112	Davey Lopes	.50	.25	.15
113	Mike Schmidt	4.00	2.00	1.25
114	Joe Rudi	.50	.25	.15
Panel 39		7.00	3.50	2.00
115	Milt May	.40	.20	.12
116	Jim Palmer	2.50	1.25	.70
117	Bill Madlock	.90	.45	.25
Panel 40		2.50	1.25	.70
118	Roy Smalley	.40	.20	.12
119	Cecil Cooper	.50	.25	.15
120	Rick Langford	.40	.20	.12
Panel 41		5.50	2.75	1.75
121	Ruppert Jones	.40	.20	.12
122	Phil Niekro	2.00	1.00	.60
123	Toby Harrah	.50	.25	.15
Panel 42		2.50	1.25	.70
124	Chet Lemon	.50	.25	.15
125	Gene Tenace	.40	.20	.12
126	Steve Henderson	.40	.20	.12
Panel 43		20.00	10.00	6.00
127	Mike Torrez	.40	.20	.12
128	Pete Rose	8.00	4.00	2.50
129	John Denny	.50	.25	.15
Panel 44		4.00	2.00	1.25
130	Darrell Porter	.50	.25	.15
131	Rick Reuschel	.50	.25	.15
132	Graig Nettles	.90	.45	.25
Panel 45		4.50	2.25	1.25
133	Garry Maddox	.50	.25	.15
134	Mike Flanagan	.50	.25	.15
135	Dave Parker	1.25	.60	.40
Panel 46		7.50	3.75	2.25
136	Terry Whitfield	.40	.20	.12
137	Wayne Garland	.40	.20	.12
138	Robin Yount	3.00	1.50	.90
Panel 47		12.00	6.00	3.50
139	Gaylord Perry	2.00	1.00	.60
140	Rod Carew	4.00	2.00	1.25
141	Wayne Gross	.40	.20	.12
Panel 48		5.00	2.50	1.50
142	Barry Bonnell	.40	.20	.12

		NR MT	EX	VG
143	Willie Montanez	.40	.20	.12
144	Rollie Fingers	1.50	.70	.45
Panel 49		11.50	5.75	3.50
145	Bob Bailor	.40	.20	.12
146	Tom Seaver	3.00	1.50	.90
147	Thurman Munson	2.50	1.25	.70
Panel 50		7.50	3.75	2.25
148	Lyman Bostock	.50	.25	.15
149	Gary Carter	3.00	1.50	.90
150	Ron Blomberg	.40	.20	.12

1979 Hostess

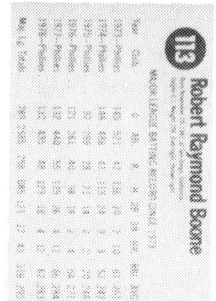

The last of five consecutive annual issues, the 1979 Hostess set retained the 150-card set size, 2¼'' by 3¼'' single-card size and 7¼'' by 3¼'' three-card panel format from the previous years. The cards were printed as the bottom panel on family-size boxes of Hostess snack cakes. Some panels, which were printed on less-popular brands, are somewhat scarcer today than the rest of the set. Like all Hostess issues, because the hobby was in a well-developed state at the time of issue, the 1979s survive today in complete panels and complete unused boxes, for collectors who like original packaging.

	NR MT	EX	VG
Complete Panel Set:	300.00	150.00	90.00
Complete Singles Set:	175.00	87.00	52.00
Common Panel:	2.50	1.25	.70
Common Single Player:	.40	.20	.12

		NR MT	EX	VG
Panel 1		9.50	4.75	2.75
1	John Denny	.40	.20	.12
2	Jim Rice	4.00	2.00	1.25
3	Doug Bair	.40	.20	.12
Panel 2		2.50	1.25	.70
4	Darrell Porter	.50	.25	.15
5	Ross Grimsley	.40	.20	.12
6	Bobby Murcer	.50	.25	.15
Panel 3		17.00	8.50	5.00
7	Lee Mazzilli	.50	.25	.15
8	Steve Garvey	4.00	2.00	1.25
9	Mike Schmidt	4.00	2.00	1.25
Panel 4		6.00	3.00	1.75
10	Terry Whitfield	.40	.20	.12
11	Jim Palmer	2.50	1.25	.70
12	Omar Moreno	.40	.20	.12
Panel 5		2.50	1.25	.70
13	Duane Kuiper	.40	.20	.12
14	Mike Caldwell	.40	.20	.12
15	Steve Kemp	.50	.25	.15
Panel 6		2.50	1.25	.70
16	Dave Goltz	.40	.20	.12
17	Mitchell Page	.40	.20	.12
18	Bill Stein	.40	.20	.12
Panel 7		2.50	1.25	.70
19	Gene Tenace	.40	.20	.12
20	Jeff Burroughs	.40	.20	.12
21	Francisco Barrios	.40	.20	.12
Panel 8		7.50	3.75	2.25
22	Mike Torrez	.40	.20	.12
23	Ken Reitz	.40	.20	.12
24	Gary Carter	3.00	1.50	.90

		NR MT	EX	VG
Panel 9		8.00	4.00	2.50
25	Al Hrabosky	.50	.25	.15
26	Thurman Munson	2.50	1.25	.70
27	Bill Buckner	.80	.40	.25
Panel 10		6.00	3.00	1.75
28	Ron Cey	.90	.45	.25
29	J.R. Richard	.70	.35	.20
30	Greg Luzinski	1.25	.60	.40
Panel 11		4.00	2.00	1.25
31	Ed Ott	.50	.25	.15
32	Denny Martinez	.50	.25	.15
33	Darrell Evans	.90	.45	.25
Panel 12		2.50	1.25	.70
34	Ron LeFlore	.50	.25	.15
35	Rick Waits	.40	.20	.12
36	Cecil Cooper	.50	.25	.15
Panel 13		9.50	4.75	2.75
37	Leon Roberts	.40	.20	.12
38	Rod Carew	4.00	2.00	1.25
39	John Henry Johnson	.40	.20	.12
Panel 14		2.50	1.25	.70
40	Chet Lemon	.50	.25	.15
41	Craig Swan	.40	.20	.12
42	Gary Matthews	.50	.25	.15
Panel 15		3.50	1.75	1.00
43	Lamar Johnson	.40	.20	.12
44	Ted Simmons	.80	.40	.25
45	Ken Griffey	.50	.25	.15
Panel 16		4.00	2.00	1.25
46	Freddie Patek	.40	.20	.12
47	Frank Tanana	.50	.25	.15
48	Rich Gossage	1.25	.60	.40
Panel 17		2.50	1.25	.70
49	Burt Hooton	.40	.20	.12
50	Ellis Valentine	.40	.20	.12
51	Ken Forsch	.40	.20	.12
Panel 18		5.00	2.50	1.50
52	Bob Knepper	.50	.25	.15
53	Dave Parker	1.50	.70	.45
54	Doug DeCinces	.50	.25	.15
Panel 19		8.00	4.00	2.50
55	Robin Yount	3.00	1.50	.90
56	Rusty Staub	.80	.40	.25
57	Gary Alexander	.40	.20	.12
Panel 20		2.50	1.25	.70
58	Julio Cruz	.40	.20	.12
59	Matt Keough	.40	.20	.12
60	Roy Smalley	.40	.20	.12
Panel 21		9.00	4.50	2.75
61	Joe Morgan	1.50	.70	.45
62	Phil Niekro	2.00	1.00	.60
63	Don Baylor	.80	.40	.25
Panel 22		9.00	4.50	2.75
64	Dwight Evans	.90	.45	.25
65	Tom Seaver	3.00	1.50	.90
66	George Hendrick	.50	.25	.15
Panel 23		13.00	6.50	4.00
67	Rick Reuschel	.50	.25	.15
68	Geroge Brett	5.00	2.50	1.50
69	Lou Piniella	.80	.40	.25
Panel 24		8.50	4.25	2.50
70	Enos Cabell	.40	.20	.12
71	Steve Carlton	3.50	1.75	1.00
72	Reggie Smith	.50	.25	.15
Panel 25		4.00	2.00	1.25
73	Rick Dempsey	.50	.25	.15
74	Vida Blue	.80	.40	.25
75	Phil Garner	.70	.35	.20
Panel 26		3.50	1.75	1.00
76	Rick Manning	.50	.25	.15
77	Mark Fidrych	.80	.40	.25
78	Mario Guerrero	.50	.25	.15
Panel 27		5.00	2.50	1.50
79	Bob Stinson	.50	.25	.15
80	Al Oliver	1.25	.60	.40
81	Doug Flynn	.50	.25	.15
Panel 28		5.50	2.75	1.75
82	John Mayberry	.40	.20	.12
83	Gaylord Perry	2.00	1.00	.60
84	Joe Rudi	.50	.25	.15
Panel 29		3.50	1.75	1.00
85	Dave Concepcion	.70	.35	.20
86	John Candelaria	.50	.25	.15
87	Pete Vuckovich	.50	.25	.15
Panel 30		5.00	2.50	1.50
88	Ivan DeJesus	.40	.20	.12
89	Ron Guidry	1.50	.70	.45
90	Hal McRae	.50	.25	.15

		NR MT	EX	VG
Panel 31		5.00	2.50	1.50
91	Cesar Cedeno	.50	.25	.15
92	Don Sutton	1.50	.70	.45
93	Andre Thornton	.50	.25	.15
Panel 32		2.50	1.25	.70
94	Roger Erickson	.40	.20	.12
95	Larry Hisle	.40	.20	.12
96	Jason Thompson	.40	.20	.12
Panel 33		7.50	3.75	2.25
97	Jim Sundberg	.50	.25	.15
98	Bob Horner	3.00	1.50	.90
99	Ruppert Jones	.40	.20	.12
Panel 34		8.00	4.00	2.50
100	Willie Montanez	.40	.20	.12
101	Nolan Ryan	3.00	1.50	.90
102	Ozzie Smith	.70	.35	.20
Panel 35		6.00	3.00	1.75
103	Eric Soderholm	.40	.20	.12
104	Willie Stargell	1.50	.70	.45
105	Bob Bailor	.40	.20	.12
Panel 36		11.00	5.50	3.25
106	Carlton Fisk	2.00	1.00	.60
107	George Foster	.90	.45	.25
108	Keith Hernandez	2.50	1.25	.70
Panel 37		4.00	2.00	1.25
109	Dennis Leonard	.50	.25	.15
110	Graig Nettles	.90	.45	.25
111	Jose Cruz	.50	.25	.15
Panel 38		3.50	1.75	1.00
112	Bobby Grich	.50	.25	.15
113	Bob Boone	.50	.25	.15
114	Dave Lopes	.50	.25	.15
Panel 39		15.00	7.50	4.50
115	Eddie Murray	4.50	2.25	1.25
116	Jack Clark	.90	.45	.25
117	Lou Whitaker	.50	.25	.15
Panel 40		10.00	5.00	3.00
118	Miguel Dilone	.40	.20	.12
119	Sal Bando	.50	.25	.15
120	Reggie Jackson	4.50	2.25	1.25
Panel 41		12.50	6.25	3.75
121	Dale Murphy	5.50	2.75	1.75
122	Jon Matlack	.40	.20	.12
123	Bruce Bochte	.40	.20	.12
Panel 42		9.00	4.50	2.75
124	John Stearns	.40	.20	.12
125	Dave Winfield	3.50	1.75	1.00
126	Jorge Orta	.40	.20	.12
Panel 43		8.50	4.25	2.50
127	Garry Templeton	.70	.35	.20
128	Johnny Bench	3.50	1.75	1.00
129	Butch Hobson	.40	.20	.12
Panel 44		4.50	2.25	1.25
130	Bruce Sutter	1.25	.60	.40
131	Bucky Dent	.50	.25	.15
132	Amos Otis	.50	.25	.15
Panel 45		3.50	1.75	1.00
133	Bert Blyleven	.70	.35	.20
134	Larry Bowa	.50	.25	.15
135	Ken Singleton	.50	.25	.15
Panel 46		3.50	1.75	1.00
136	Sixto Lezcano	.40	.20	.12
137	Roy Howell	.40	.20	.12
138	Bill Madlock	.90	.45	.25
Panel 47		2.50	1.25	.70
139	Dave Revering	.40	.20	.12
140	Richie Zisk	.50	.25	.15
141	Butch Wynegar	.50	.25	.15
Panel 48		18.00	9.00	5.50
142	Alan Ashby	.40	.20	.12
143	Sparky Lyle	.50	.25	.15
144	Pete Rose	7.50	3.75	2.25
Panel 49		4.00	2.00	1.25
145	Dennis Eckersley	.50	.25	.15
146	Dave Kingman	.80	.40	.25
147	Buddy Bell	.70	.35	.20
Panel 50		2.50	1.25	.70
148	Mike Hargrove	.40	.20	.12
149	Jerry Koosman	.50	.25	.15
150	Toby Harrah	.50	.25	.15

1985 Hostess Braves

After a five-year hiatus, Hostess returned to the production of baseball cards in 1985 with an Atlanta Braves team set. The 22 cards in the set were printed by Topps and inserted into packages of snack cake

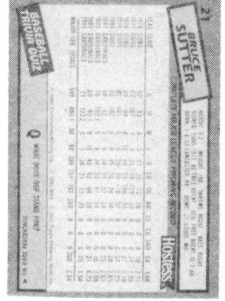

products, three cello-wrapped player cards and a header card per box. The 2½'' by 3½'' cards share a common back design with the regular-issue Topps cards of 1985.

		MT	NR MT	EX
Complete Set:		10.00	7.50	4.00
Common Player:		.35	.25	.14
1	Eddie Haas	.35	.25	.14
2	Len Barker	.35	.25	.14
3	Steve Bedrosian	.90	.70	.35
4	Bruce Benedict	.35	.25	.14
5	Rick Camp	.35	.25	.14
6	Rick Cerone	.35	.25	.14
7	Chris Chambliss	.40	.30	.15
8	Terry Forster	.40	.30	.15
9	Gene Garber	.35	.25	.14
10	Albert Hall	.50	.40	.20
11	Bob Horner	.70	.50	.30
12	Glenn Hubbard	.35	.25	.14
13	Brad Komminsk	.35	.25	.14
14	Rick Mahler	.40	.30	.15
15	Craig McMurtry	.35	.25	.14
16	Dale Murphy	2.00	1.50	.80
17	Ken Oberkfell	.40	.30	.15
18	Pascual Perez	.40	.30	.15
19	Gerald Perry	.50	.40	.20
20	Rafael Ramirez	.35	.25	.14
21	Bruce Sutter	.50	.40	.20
22	Claudell Washington	.40	.30	.15
---	Header Card	.10	.08	.04

1987 Hostess Stickers

Hostess of Canada issued a 30-card set of stickers in specially marked bags of potato chips. One sticker, measuring 1¾'' by 1⅜'' in size, was found in each bag. The stickers have full-color fronts with the player's name appearing in black type in a white band. The Hostess logo and the sticker number are also included on the fronts. The backs are written in both English and French and contain the player's name, position and team.

		MT	NR MT	EX
Complete Set:		25.00	18.50	10.00
Common Player:		.20	.15	.08

		MT	NR MT	EX
1	Jesse Barfield	.60	.45	.25
2	Ernie Whitt	.20	.15	.08
3	George Bell	1.00	.70	.40
4	Hubie Brooks	.20	.15	.08
5	Tim Wallach	.35	.25	.14
6	Floyd Youmans	.35	.25	.14
7	Dale Murphy	1.50	1.25	.60
8	Ryne Sandberg	1.00	.70	.40
9	Eric Davis	2.00	1.50	.80
10	Mike Scott	.35	.25	.14
11	Fernando Valenzuela	.75	.60	.30
12	Gary Carter	1.00	.70	.40
13	Mike Schmidt	1.50	1.25	.60
14	Tony Pena	.20	.15	.08
15	Ozzie Smith	.60	.45	.25
16	Tony Gwynn	1.25	.90	.50
17	Mike Krukow	.20	.15	.08
18	Eddie Murray	1.25	.90	.50
19	Wade Boggs	1.75	1.25	.70
20	Wally Joyner	2.00	1.50	.80
21	Harold Baines	.35	.25	.14
22	Brook Jacoby	.35	.25	.14
23	Lou Whitaker	.75	.60	.30
24	George Brett	1.50	1.25	.60
25	Robin Yount	.75	.60	.30
26	Kirby Puckett	1.00	.70	.40
27	Don Mattingly	2.50	2.00	1.00
28	Jose Canseco	2.00	1.50	.80
29	Phil Bradley	.35	.25	.14
30	Pete O'Brien	.20	.15	.08

1953 Hunter Wieners Cardinals

From the great era of the regionally-issued hot dog cards in the mid-1950s, the 1953 Hunter wieners set of St. Louis Cardinals is certainly among the rarest today. Originally issued in two-card panels, the cards are most often found as 2¼'' by 3¼'' singles today — when they can be found at all. The cards feature a light blue facsimile autograph printed over the stat box at the bottom. They are blank-backed.

		NR MT	EX	VG
Complete Set:		3000.00	1500.00	900.00
Common Player:		80.00	40.00	24.00
(1)	Steve Bilko	80.00	40.00	24.00
(2)	Alpha Brazle	80.00	40.00	24.00
(3)	Cloyd Boyer	80.00	40.00	24.00
(4)	Cliff Chambers	80.00	40.00	24.00
(5)	Michael Clark	80.00	40.00	24.00
(6)	Jack Crimian	80.00	40.00	24.00
(7)	Lester Fusselman	80.00	40.00	24.00
(8)	Harvey Haddix	100.00	50.00	30.00
(9)	Solly Hemus	80.00	40.00	24.00
(10)	Ray Jablonski	80.00	40.00	24.00
(11)	William Johnson	80.00	40.00	24.00
(12)	Harry Lowrey	80.00	40.00	24.00
(13)	Lawrence Miggins	80.00	40.00	24.00
(14)	Stuart Miller	80.00	40.00	24.00
(15)	Wilmer Mizell	80.00	40.00	24.00
(16)	Stanley Musial	750.00	375.00	225.00

		NR MT	EX	VG
(17)	Joseph Presko	80.00	40.00	24.00
(18)	Delbert Rice	80.00	40.00	24.00
(19)	Harold Rice	80.00	40.00	24.00
(20)	Willard Schmidt	80.00	40.00	24.00
(21)	Albert Schoendienst	125.00	62.00	37.00
(22)	Richard Sisler	80.00	40.00	24.00
(23)	Enos Slaughter	175.00	87.00	52.00
(24)	Gerald Staley	80.00	40.00	24.00
(25)	Edward Stanky	100.00	50.00	30.00
(26)	John Yuhas	80.00	40.00	24.00

1954 Hunter Wieners Cardinals

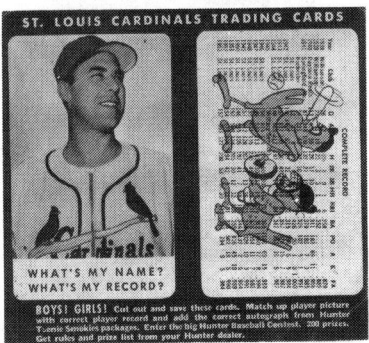

A nearly impossible set to complete today by virtue of the method of its issue, the 1954 Hunter hot dog set essentially features what would traditionally be the front and back of a normal baseball card on two different cards. The "front," containing a color photo of one of 30 St. Louis Cardinals has a box at bottom challenging the collector to name him and quote his stats. The "back" features cartoon Cardinals in action, and contains the answers. However, because both parts were printed on a single panel, and because most of the back (non-picture) panels were thrown away years ago, it is an impossible challenge to complete a '54 Hunter set today. There is no back printing on the 2¼'' by 3½'' cards.

		NR MT	EX	VG
Complete Set:		3800.00	1900.00	1140.
Common Player:		80.00	40.00	24.00
(1)	Tom Alston	80.00	40.00	24.00
(2)	Steve Bilko	80.00	40.00	24.00
(3)	Al Brazle	80.00	40.00	24.00
(4)	Tom Burgess	80.00	40.00	24.00
(5)	Cot Deal	80.00	40.00	24.00
(6)	Alex Grammas	80.00	40.00	24.00
(7)	Harvey Haddix	100.00	50.00	30.00
(8)	Solly Hemus	80.00	40.00	24.00
(9)	Ray Jablonski	80.00	40.00	24.00
(10)	Royce Lint	80.00	40.00	24.00
(11)	Peanuts Lowrey	80.00	40.00	24.00
(12)	Memo Luna	80.00	40.00	24.00
(13)	Stu Miller	80.00	40.00	24.00
(14)	Stan Musial	750.00	375.00	225.00
(15)	Tom Poholsky	80.00	40.00	24.00
(16)	Bill Posedel	80.00	40.00	24.00
(17)	Joe Presko	80.00	40.00	24.00
(18)	Vic Raschi	80.00	40.00	24.00
(19)	Dick Rand	80.00	40.00	24.00
(20)	Rip Repulski	80.00	40.00	24.00
(21)	Del Rice	80.00	40.00	24.00
(22)	John Riddle	80.00	40.00	24.00
(23)	Mike Ryba	80.00	40.00	24.00
(24)	Red Schoendienst	125.00	62.00	37.00
(25)	Dick Schofield	90.00	45.00	27.00
(26)	Eddie Stanky	100.00	50.00	30.00
(27)	Enos Slaughter	175.00	87.00	52.00
(28)	Gerry Staley	80.00	40.00	24.00
(29)	Ed Yuhas	80.00	40.00	24.00
(30)	Sal Yvars	80.00	40.00	24.00

1955 Hunter Wieners Cardinals

The 1955 team set of St. Louis Cardinals included-with packages of Hunter hot dogs featured the third-format change in three years of issue. For 1955, the cards were printed in a tall, narrow 2'' by 4¾'' format, two to a panel. The cards featured both a posed action photo and a portrait photo, along with a fac-simile autograph and brief biographical data on the front. There is no back printing, as the cards were part of the wrapping for packages of hot dogs.

		NR MT	EX	VG
Complete Set:		3700.00	1850.00	1110.
Common Player:		90.00	45.00	27.00
(1)	Thomás Edison Alston	90.00	45.00	27.00
(2)	Kenton Lloyd Boyer	200.00	100.00	60.00
(3)	Harry Lewis Elliott	90.00	45.00	27.00
(4)	John Edward Faszholz	90.00	45.00	27.00
(5)	Joseph Filmore Frazier	90.00	45.00	27.00
(6)	Alexander Pete Grammas	90.00	45.00	27.00
(7)	Harvey Haddix	110.00	55.00	33.00
(8)	Solly Joseph Hemus	90.00	45.00	27.00
(9)	Lawrence Curtis Jackson	90.00	45.00	27.00
(10)	Tony R. Jacobs	90.00	45.00	27.00
(11)	Gordon Bassett Jones	90.00	45.00	27.00
(12)	Paul Edmore LaPalme	90.00	45.00	27.00
(13)	Brooks Ulysses Lawrence	90.00	45.00	27.00
(14)	Wallace Wade Moon	100.00	50.00	30.00
(15)	Stanley Frank Musial	900.00	450.00	270.00
(16)	Thomas George Poholsky	90.00	45.00	27.00
(17)	William John Posedel	90.00	45.00	27.00
(18)	Victor Angelo John Raschi	90.00	45.00	27.00
(19)	Eldon John Repulski	90.00	45.00	27.00
(20)	Delbert Rice	90.00	45.00	27.00
(21)	John Ludy Riddle	90.00	45.00	27.00
(22)	William F. Sarni	90.00	45.00	27.00
(23)	Albert Fred Schoendienst	150.00	75.00	45.00
(24)	Richard John Schofield (actually John Richard)	90.00	45.00	27.00
(25)	Frank Thomas Smith	90.00	45.00	27.00
(26)	Edward R. Stanky	110.00	55.00	33.00
(27)	Bobby Gene Tiefenauer	90.00	45.00	27.00
(28)	William Charles Virdon	150.00	75.00	45.00
(29)	Frederick E. Walker	90.00	45.00	27.00
(30)	Floyd Lewis Woolridge	90.00	45.00	27.00

1982 Hygrade Meats Expos

This 24-card Montreal Expos team set was the object of intense collector speculation when it was

Gary Carter 8

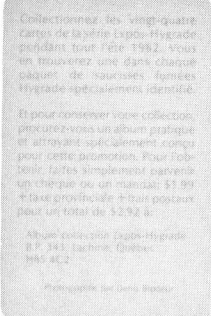

Billy Sample No. 5 OF

first issued. Single cello-wrapped cards were included in packages of Hygrade luncheon meat in the Province of Quebec only. Until a mail-in offer for the complete set appeared later in the season, the set was selling for as high as $45-50. It remains a relatively scarce issue today. The 2'' by 3'' cards are printed on heavy paper, with round corners. Backs are printed only in French, and contain an offer for an album to house the set.

		MT	NR MT	EX
Complete Set:		40.00	30.00	16.00
Common Player:		1.00	.70	.40
0	Al Oliver	2.50	2.00	1.00
4	Chris Speier	1.00	.70	.40
5	John Milner	1.00	.70	.40
6	Jim Fanning	1.00	.70	.40
8	Gary Carter	7.00	5.25	2.75
10	Andre Dawson	5.00	3.75	2.00
11	Frank Tavaras (Taveras)	1.00	.70	.40
16	Terry Francona	1.50	1.25	.60
17	Tim Blackwell	1.00	.70	.40
18	Jerry White	1.00	.70	.40
20	Bob James	1.50	1.25	.60
21	Scott Sanderson	1.00	.70	.40
24	Brad Mills	1.00	.70	.40
29	Tim Wallach	3.00	2.25	1.25
30	Tim Raines	7.00	5.25	2.75
34	Bill Gullickson	1.50	1.25	.60
35	Woodie Fryman	1.00	.70	.40
38	Bryn Smith	1.50	1.25	.60
41	Jeff Reardon	2.00	1.50	.80
44	Dan Norman	1.00	.70	.40
45	Steve Rogers	1.50	1.25	.60
48	Ray Burris	1.00	.70	.40
49	Warren Cromartie	1.00	.70	.40
53	Charlie Lea	1.00	.70	.40

1984 Jarvis Press Rangers

For its second annual "Baseball Card Day" game promotional set, the Rangers picked up a new sponsor, Jarvis Press of Dallas. The 30 cards in the set include 27 players, the manager, trainer and a group card of the coaches. Cards measure 2⅜'' by 3½.'' Color game-action photos make up the card fronts. Backs, printed in black and white, include a portrait photo of the player. A source close to the promotion indicated 10,000 sets were produced.

		MT	NR MT	EX
Complete Set:		6.00	4.50	2.50
Common Player:		.12	.09	.05
1	Bill Stein	.12	.09	.05
2	Alan Bannister	.12	.09	.05
3	Wayne Tolleson	.12	.09	.05
5	Billy Sample	.12	.09	.05
6	Bobby Jones	.12	.09	.05
7	Ned Yost	.12	.09	.05
9	Pete O'Brien	.60	.45	.25
11	Doug Rader	.12	.09	.05
13	Tommy Dunbar	.12	.09	.05
14	Jim Anderson	.12	.09	.05
15	Larry Parrish	.30	.25	.12
16	Mike Mason	.15	.11	.06
17	Mickey Rivers	.20	.15	.08
19	Curtis Wilkerson	.12	.09	.05
20	Jeff Kunkel	.15	.11	.06
21	Odell Jones	.12	.09	.05
24	Dave Schmidt	.15	.11	.06
25	Buddy Bell	.50	.40	.20
26	George Wright	.12	.09	.05
28	Frank Tanana	.15	.11	.06
30	Marv Foley	.12	.09	.05
31	Dave Stewart	.25	.20	.10
32	Gary Ward	.20	.15	.08
36	Dickie Noles	.12	.09	.05
43	Donnie Scott	.12	.09	.05
44	Danny Darwin	.20	.15	.08
49	Charlie Hough	.25	.20	.10
53	Joey McLaughlin	.12	.09	.05
---	Coaching Staff (Rich Donnelly, Glenn Ezell, Merv Rettenmund, Dick Such, Wayne Terwilliger)	.12	.09	.05
---	Trainer (Bill Zeigler)	.12	.09	.05

1986 Jays Potato Chips

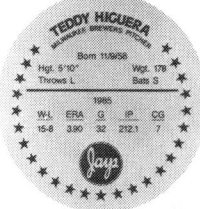

One of a handful of round baseball cards produced for inclusion in boxes of potato chips on a regional basis in 1986, the Jays set of 2⅞'' discs is believed to be the scarcest of the type. The 20 cards in the issue include the most popular Milwaukee Brewers and Chicago Cubs and White Sox players; the set having been distributed in the southern Wisconsin-northern Illinois area. Like many of the recent sets produced by Mike Schecter Associates, the '86 Jays cards feature player photos on which the team logos have been airbrushed off the caps.

		MT	NR MT	EX
Complete Set:		20.00	15.00	8.00
Common Player:		.60	.45	.25
(1)	Harold Baines	1.00	.70	.40
(2)	Cecil Cooper	1.00	.70	.40
(3)	Jody Davis	.80	.60	.30
(4)	Bob Dernier	.60	.45	.25
(5)	Richard Dotson	.70	.50	.30
(6)	Shawon Dunston	1.00	.70	.40
(7)	Carlton Fisk	1.25	.90	.50
(8)	Jim Gantner	.60	.45	.25
(9)	Ozzie Guillen	.80	.60	.30
(10)	Teddy Higuera	1.50	1.25	.60
(11)	Ron Kittle	.80	.60	.30
(12)	Paul Molitor	1.25	.90	.50
(13)	Keith Moreland	.70	.50	.30
(14)	Ernie Riles	.80	.60	.30
(15)	Ryne Sandberg	2.00	1.50	.80
(16)	Tom Seaver	1.50	1.25	.60
(17)	Lee Smith	.70	.50	.30
(18)	Rick Sutcliffe	.80	.60	.30
(19)	Greg Walker	.80	.60	.30
(20)	Robin Yount	1.75	1.25	.70

1962 Jell-O

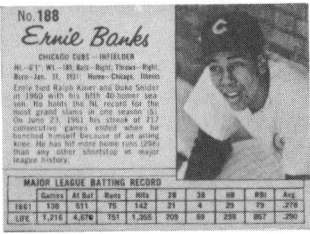

Virtually identical in content to the 1962 Post cereal cards, the '62 Jell-O set of 197 was only issued in the Midwest. Players and card numbers are identical in the two sets, except Brooks Robinson (#29), Ted Kluszewski (#82) and Smoky Burgess (#176) were not issued in the Jell-O version. The Jell-O cards are easy to distinguish from the Posts of that year by the absence of the red oval Post logo and red or blue border around the stat box. Cards which have been neatly trimmed from the box on which they were printed will measure 3½'' by 2½''.

		NR MT	EX	VG
Complete Set:		3600.00	1800.00	1080.
Common Player:		6.00	3.00	1.75
1	Bill Skowron	18.00	9.00	5.50
2	Bobby Richardson	18.00	9.00	5.50
3	Cletis Boyer	10.00	5.00	3.00
4	Tony Kubek	13.00	6.50	4.00
5	Mickey Mantle	300.00	150.00	90.00
6	Roger Maris	32.00	16.00	9.50
7	Yogi Berra	32.00	16.00	9.50
8	Elston Howard	13.00	6.50	4.00
9	Whitey Ford	25.00	12.50	7.50
10	Ralph Terry	10.00	5.00	3.00
11	John Blanchard	7.00	3.50	2.00
12	Luis Arroyo	7.00	3.50	2.00
13	Bill Stafford	18.00	9.00	5.50
14	Norm Cash	10.00	5.00	3.00
15	Jake Wood	6.00	3.00	1.75
16	Steve Boros	6.00	3.00	1.75
17	Chico Fernandez	6.00	3.00	1.75
18	Billy Bruton	6.00	3.00	1.75
19	Ken Aspromonte	6.00	3.00	1.75
20	Al Kaline	32.00	16.00	9.50
21	Dick Brown	6.00	3.00	1.75
22	Frank Lary	7.00	3.50	2.00
23	Don Mossi	7.00	3.50	2.00
24	Phil Regan	6.00	3.00	1.75
25	Charley Maxwell	6.00	3.00	1.75
26	Jim Bunning	13.00	6.50	4.00
27	Jim Gentile	7.00	3.50	2.00
28	Marv Breeding	6.00	3.00	1.75
29	Not Issued			

		NR MT	EX	VG
30	Ron Hansen	6.00	3.00	1.75
31	Jackie Brandt	18.00	9.00	5.50
32	Dick Williams	7.00	3.50	2.00
33	Gus Triandos	7.00	3.50	2.00
34	Milt Pappas	7.00	3.50	2.00
35	Hoyt Wilhelm	18.00	9.00	5.50
36	Chuck Estrada	6.00	3.00	1.75
37	Vic Power	6.00	3.00	1.75
38	Johnny Temple	6.00	3.00	1.75
39	Bubba Phillips	18.00	9.00	5.50
40	Tito Francona	7.00	3.50	2.00
41	Willie Kirkland	6.00	3.00	1.75
42	John Romano	6.00	3.00	1.75
43	Jim Perry	10.00	5.00	3.00
44	Woodie Held	6.00	3.00	1.75
45	Chuck Essegian	6.00	3.00	1.75
46	Roy Sievers	7.00	3.50	2.00
47	Nellie Fox	13.00	6.50	4.00
48	Al Smith	6.00	3.00	1.75
49	Luis Aparicio	18.00	9.00	5.50
50	Jim Landis	6.00	3.00	1.75
51	Minnie Minoso	10.00	5.00	3.00
52	Andy Carey	18.00	9.00	5.50
53	Sherman Lollar	7.00	3.50	2.00
54	Bill Pierce	7.00	3.50	2.00
55	Early Wynn	18.00	9.00	5.50
56	Chuck Schilling	18.00	9.00	5.50
57	Pete Runnels	7.00	3.50	2.00
58	Frank Malzone	7.00	3.50	2.00
59	Don Buddin	10.00	5.00	3.00
60	Gary Geiger	6.00	3.00	1.75
61	Carl Yastrzemski	160.00	80.00	48.00
62	Jackie Jensen	18.00	9.00	5.50
63	Jim Pagliaroni	18.00	9.00	5.50
64	Don Schwall	6.00	3.00	1.75
65	Dale Long	7.00	3.50	2.00
66	Chuck Cottier	10.00	5.00	3.00
67	Billy Klaus	18.00	9.00	5.50
68	Coot Veal	6.00	3.00	1.75
69	Marty Keough	32.00	16.00	9.50
70	Willie Tasby	32.00	16.00	9.50
71	Gene Woodling	7.00	3.50	2.00
72	Gene Green	32.00	16.00	9.50
73	Dick Donovan	10.00	5.00	3.00
74	Steve Bilko	10.00	5.00	3.00
75	Rocky Bridges	18.00	9.00	5.50
76	Eddie Yost	10.00	5.00	3.00
77	Leon Wagner	10.00	5.00	3.00
78	Albie Pearson	10.00	5.00	3.00
79	Ken Hunt	10.00	5.00	3.00
80	Earl Averill	32.00	16.00	9.50
81	Ryne Duren	10.00	5.00	3.00
82	Not Issued			
83	Bob Allison	7.00	3.50	2.00
84	Billy Martin	13.00	6.50	4.00
85	Harmon Killebrew	26.00	13.00	7.75
86	Zorro Versalles	7.00	3.50	2.00
87	Lennie Green	18.00	9.00	5.50
88	Bill Tuttle	6.00	3.00	1.75
89	Jim Lemon	7.00	3.50	2.00
90	Earl Battey	18.00	9.00	5.50
91	Camilo Pascual	7.00	3.50	2.00
92	Norm Siebern	10.00	5.00	3.00
93	Jerry Lumpe	10.00	5.00	3.00
94	Dick Howser	10.00	5.00	3.00
95	Gene Stephens	32.00	16.00	9.50
96	Leo Posada	10.00	5.00	3.00
97	Joe Pignatano	10.00	5.00	3.00
98	Jim Archer	10.00	5.00	3.00
99	Haywood Sullivan	18.00	9.00	5.50
100	Art Ditmar	10.00	5.00	3.00
101	Gil Hodges	25.00	12.50	7.50
102	Charlie Neal	10.00	5.00	3.00
103	Daryl Spencer	10.00	5.00	3.00
104	Maury Wills	18.00	9.00	5.50
105	Tommy Davis	10.00	5.00	3.00
106	Willie Davis	10.00	5.00	3.00
107	John Roseboro	32.00	16.00	9.50
108	John Podres	10.00	5.00	3.00
109	Sandy Koufax	60.00	30.00	18.00
110	Don Drysdale	32.00	16.00	9.50
111	Larry Sherry	18.00	9.00	5.50
112	Jim Gilliam	18.00	9.00	5.50
113	Norm Larker	32.00	16.00	9.50
114	Duke Snider	60.00	30.00	18.00
115	Stan Williams	18.00	9.00	5.50
116	Gordon Coleman	60.00	30.00	18.00
117	Don Blasingame	18.00	9.00	5.50
118	Gene Freese	32.00	16.00	9.50
119	Ed Kasko	32.00	16.00	9.50
120	Gus Bell	18.00	9.00	5.50

		NR MT	EX	VG
121	Vada Pinson	10.00	5.00	3.00
122	Frank Robinson	25.00	12.50	7.50
123	Bob Purkey	10.00	5.00	3.00
124	Joey Jay	10.00	5.00	3.00
125	Jim Brosnan	10.00	5.00	3.00
126	Jim O'Toole	10.00	5.00	3.00
127	Jerry Lynch	10.00	5.00	3.00
128	Wally Post	10.00	5.00	3.00
129	Ken Hunt	10.00	5.00	3.00
130	Jerry Zimmerman	10.00	5.00	3.00
131	Willie McCovey	25.00	12.50	7.50
132	Jose Pagan	18.00	9.00	5.50
133	Felipe Alou	10.00	5.00	3.00
134	Jim Davenport	10.00	5.00	3.00
135	Harvey Kuenn	10.00	5.00	3.00
136	Orlando Cepeda	13.00	6.50	4.00
137	Ed Bailey	10.00	5.00	3.00
138	Sam Jones	10.00	5.00	3.00
139	Mike McCormick	10.00	5.00	3.00
140	Juan Marichal	32.00	16.00	9.50
141	Jack Sanford	10.00	5.00	3.00
142	Willie Mays	100.00	50.00	30.00
143	Stu Miller	60.00	30.00	18.00
144	Joe Amalfitano	10.00	5.00	3.00
145	Joe Adcock	10.00	5.00	3.00
146	Frank Bolling	6.00	3.00	1.75
147	Ed Mathews	25.00	12.50	7.50
148	Roy McMillan	7.00	3.50	2.00
149	Hank Aaron	100.00	50.00	30.00
150	Gino Cimoli	18.00	9.00	5.50
151	Frank Thomas	7.00	3.50	2.00
152	Joe Torre	10.00	5.00	3.00
153	Lou Burdette	10.00	5.00	3.00
154	Bob Buhl	7.00	3.50	2.00
155	Carlton Willey	6.00	3.00	1.75
156	Lee Maye	18.00	9.00	5.50
157	Al Spangler	32.00	16.00	9.50
158	Bill White	32.00	16.00	9.50
159	Ken Boyer	13.00	6.50	4.00
160	Joe Cunningham	10.00	5.00	3.00
161	Carl Warwick	10.00	5.00	3.00
162	Carl Sawatski	6.00	3.00	1.75
163	Lindy McDaniel	6.00	3.00	1.75
164	Ernie Broglio	10.00	5.00	3.00
165	Larry Jackson	6.00	3.00	1.75
166	Curt Flood	13.00	6.50	4.00
167	Curt Simmons	32.00	16.00	9.50
168	Alex Grammas	18.00	9.00	5.50
169	Dick Stuart	7.00	3.50	2.00
170	Bill Mazeroski	18.00	9.00	5.50
171	Don Hoak	10.00	5.00	3.00
172	Dick Groat	10.00	5.00	3.00
173	Roberto Clemente	100.00	50.00	30.00
174	Bob Skinner	18.00	9.00	5.50
175	Bill Virdon	32.00	16.00	9.50
176	Not Issued			
177	Elroy Face	10.00	5.00	3.00
178	Bob Friend	7.00	3.50	2.00
179	Vernon Law	18.00	9.00	5.50
180	Harvey Haddix	32.00	16.00	9.50
181	Hal Smith	18.00	9.00	5.50
182	Ed Bouchee	18.00	9.00	5.50
183	Don Zimmer	7.00	3.50	2.00
184	Ron Santo	10.00	5.00	3.00
185	Andre Rodgers	6.00	3.00	1.75
186	Richie Ashburn	13.00	6.50	4.00
187	George Altman	6.00	3.00	1.75
188	Ernie Banks	25.00	12.50	7.50
189	Sam Taylor	6.00	3.00	1.75
190	Don Elston	6.00	3.00	1.75
191	Jerry Kindall	18.00	9.00	5.50
192	Pancho Herrera	6.00	3.00	1.75
193	Tony Taylor	6.00	3.00	1.75
194	Ruben Amaro	18.00	9.00	5.50
195	Don Demeter	6.00	3.00	1.75
196	Bobby Gene Smith	6.00	3.00	1.75
197	Clay Dalrymple	6.00	3.00	1.75
198	Robin Roberts	18.00	9.00	5.50
199	Art Mahaffey	6.00	3.00	1.75
200	John Buzhardt	6.00	3.00	1.75

1963 Jell-O

Like the other Post and Jell-O issues of the era, the '63 Jell-O set includes many scarce cards; primarily those which were printed as the backs of less popular brands and sizes of the gelatin dessert. Slightly

smaller than the virtually identical Post cereal cards of the same year, the 200 cards in the Jell-O issue measure 3⅜'' by 2½.'' The easiest way to distinguish 1963 Jell-O cards from Post cards is by the red line that separates the 1962 stats from the lifetime stats. On Post cards, the line extends almost all the way to the side borders, on the Jell-O cards, the line begins and ends much closer to the stats.

		NR MT	EX	VG
Complete Set:		2300.00	1150.00	690.00
Common Player:		1.25	.60	.40
1	Vic Power	1.50	.70	.45
2	Bernie Allen	18.00	9.00	5.50
3	Zoilo Versalles	18.00	9.00	5.50
4	Rich Rollins	1.25	.60	.40
5	Harmon Killebrew	6.50	3.25	2.00
6	Lenny Green	18.00	9.00	5.50
7	Bob Allison	2.00	1.00	.60
8	Earl Battey	13.00	6.50	4.00
9	Camilo Pascual	1.50	.70	.45
10	Jim Kaat	32.00	16.00	9.50
11	Jack Kralick	1.25	.60	.40
12	Bill Skowron	18.00	9.00	5.50
13	Bobby Richardson	3.50	1.75	1.00
14	Cletis Boyer	2.00	1.00	.60
15	Mickey Mantle	150.00	75.00	45.00
16	Roger Maris	13.00	6.50	4.00
17	Yogi Berra	13.00	6.50	4.00
18	Elston Howard	18.00	9.00	5.50
19	Whitey Ford	6.50	3.25	2.00
20	Ralph Terry	1.50	.70	.45
21	John Blanchard	13.00	6.50	4.00
22	Bill Stafford	18.00	9.00	5.50
23	Tom Tresh	2.00	1.00	.60
24	Steve Bilko	1.25	.60	.40
25	Bill Moran	1.25	.60	.40
26	Joe Koppe	1.25	.60	.40
27	Felix Torres	1.25	.60	.40
28	Leon Wagner	1.50	.70	.45
29	Albie Pearson	1.25	.60	.40
30	Lee Thomas	1.25	.60	.40
31	Bob Rodgers	18.00	9.00	5.50
32	Dean Chance	1.50	.70	.45
33	Ken McBride	18.00	9.00	5.50
34	George Thomas	18.00	9.00	5.50
35	Joe Cunningham	18.00	9.00	5.50
36	Nelson Fox	3.50	1.75	1.00
37	Luis Aparicio	4.50	2.25	1.25
38	Al Smith	1.25	.60	.40
39	Floyd Robinson	1.25	.60	.40
40	Jim Landis	1.25	.60	.40
41	Charlie Maxwell	1.25	.60	.40
42	Sherman Lollar	1.50	.70	.45
43	Early Wynn	4.50	2.25	1.25
44	Juan Pizarro	18.00	9.00	5.50
45	Ray Herbert	18.00	9.00	5.50
46	Norm Cash	2.50	1.25	.70
47	Steve Boros	18.00	9.00	5.50
48	Dick McAuliffe	1.50	.70	.45
49	Bill Bruton	1.50	.70	.45
50	Rocky Colavito	3.50	1.75	1.00
51	Al Kaline	10.00	5.00	3.00
52	Dick Brown	18.00	9.00	5.50
53	Jim Bunning	3.50	1.75	1.00
54	Hank Aguirre	1.25	.60	.40
55	Frank Lary	18.00	9.00	5.50
56	Don Mossi	18.00	9.00	5.50
57	Jim Gentile	1.50	.70	.45
58	Jackie Brandt	1.25	.60	.40
59	Brooks Robinson	10.00	5.00	3.00
60	Ron Hansen	1.25	.60	.40
61	Jerry Adair	45.00	22.00	13.50

		NR MT	EX	VG
62	John Powell	2.50	1.25	.70
63	Russ Snyder	18.00	9.00	5.50
64	Steve Barber	1.25	.60	.40
65	Milt Pappas	18.00	9.00	5.50
66	Robin Roberts	4.50	2.25	1.25
67	Tito Francona	1.50	.70	.45
68	Jerry Kindall	18.00	9.00	5.50
69	Woodie Held	1.50	.70	.45
70	Bubba Phillips	1.25	.60	.40
71	Chuck Essegian	1.25	.60	.40
72	Willie Kirkland	18.00	9.00	5.50
73	Al Luplow	1.25	.60	.40
74	Ty Cline	18.00	9.00	5.50
75	Dick Donovan	1.25	.60	.40
76	John Romano	1.25	.60	.40
77	Pete Runnels	1.50	.70	.45
78	Ed Bressoud	18.00	9.00	5.50
79	Frank Malzone	1.50	.70	.45
80	Carl Yastrzemski	65.00	32.00	19.50
81	Gary Geiger	1.25	.60	.40
82	Lou Clinton	18.00	9.00	5.50
83	Earl Wilson	1.50	.70	.45
84	Bill Monbouquette	1.50	.70	.45
85	Norm Siebern	1.50	.70	.45
86	Jerry Lumpe	1.50	.70	.45
87	Manny Jimenez	1.25	.60	.40
88	Gino Cimoli	1.25	.60	.40
89	Ed Charles	45.00	22.00	13.50
90	Ed Rakow	1.25	.60	.40
91	Bob Del Greco	18.00	9.00	5.50
92	Haywood Sullivan	18.00	9.00	5.50
93	Chuck Hinton	1.25	.60	.40
94	Ken Retzer	18.00	9.00	5.50
95	Harry Bright	18.00	9.00	5.50
96	Bob Johnson	1.25	.60	.40
97	Dave Stenhouse	18.00	9.00	5.50
98	Chuck Cottier	1.50	.70	.45
99	Tom Cheney	1.25	.60	.40
100	Claude Osteen	18.00	9.00	5.50
101	Orlando Cepeda	3.50	1.75	1.00
102	Charley Hiller	18.00	9.00	5.50
103	Jose Pagan	18.00	9.00	5.50
104	Jim Davenport	1.25	.60	.40
105	Harvey Kuenn	2.50	1.25	.70
106	Willie Mays	50.00	25.00	15.00
107	Felipe Alou	2.00	1.00	.60
108	Tom Haller	1.50	.70	.45
109	Juan Marichal	4.50	2.25	1.25
110	Jack Sanford	1.50	.70	.45
111	Bill O'Dell	1.25	.60	.40
112	Willie McCovey	65.00	32.00	19.50
113	Lee Walls	18.00	9.00	5.50
114	Jim Gilliam	18.00	9.00	5.50
115	Maury Wills	3.50	1.75	1.00
116	Ron Fairly	1.50	.70	.45
117	Tommy Davis	2.50	1.25	.70
118	Duke Snider	6.50	3.25	2.00
119	Willie Davis	2.00	1.00	.60
120	John Roseboro	1.50	.70	.45
121	Sandy Koufax	13.00	6.50	4.00
122	Stan Williams	18.00	9.00	5.50
123	Don Drysdale	6.50	3.25	2.00
124	Daryl Spencer	1.25	.60	.40
125	Gordy Coleman	1.25	.60	.40
126	Don Blasingame	18.00	9.00	5.50
127	Leo Cardenas	1.50	.70	.45
128	Eddie Kasko	18.00	9.00	5.50
129	Jerry Lynch	1.50	.70	.45
130	Vada Pinson	3.50	1.75	1.00
131	Frank Robinson	6.50	3.25	2.00
132	John Edwards	18.00	9.00	5.50
133	Joey Jay	1.25	.60	.40
134	Bob Purkey	1.50	.70	.45
135	Marty Keough	45.00	22.00	13.50
136	Jim O'Toole	18.00	9.00	5.50
137	Dick Stuart	1.50	.70	.45
138	Bill Mazeroski	2.50	1.25	.70
139	Dick Groat	2.00	1.00	.60
140	Don Hoak	1.50	.70	.45
141	Bob Skinner	1.50	.70	.45
142	Bill Virdon	2.00	1.00	.60
143	Roberto Clemente	40.00	20.00	12.00
144	Smoky Burgess	2.00	1.00	.60
145	Bob Friend	1.50	.70	.45
146	Al McBean	18.00	9.00	5.50
147	ElRoy Face	2.00	1.00	.60
148	Joe Adcock	2.50	1.25	.70
149	Frank Bolling	1.25	.60	.40
150	Roy McMillan	1.50	.70	.45
151	Eddie Mathews	6.50	3.25	2.00
152	Hank Aaron	50.00	25.00	15.00

		NR MT	EX	VG
153	Del Crandall	18.00	9.00	5.50
154	Bob Shaw	1.25	.60	.40
155	Lew Burdette	2.50	1.25	.70
156	Joe Torre	18.00	9.00	5.50
157	Tony Cloninger	32.00	16.00	9.50
158	Bill White	1.50	.70	.45
159	Julian Javier	18.00	9.00	5.50
160	Ken Boyer	2.50	1.25	.70
161	Julio Gotay	18.00	9.00	5.50
162	Curt Flood	2.00	1.00	.60
163	Charlie James	32.00	16.00	9.50
164	Gene Oliver	18.00	9.00	5.50
165	Ernie Broglio	1.25	.60	.40
166	Bob Gibson	45.00	22.00	13.50
167	Lindy McDaniel	18.00	9.00	5.50
168	Ray Washburn	1.25	.60	.40
169	Ernie Banks	10.00	5.00	3.00
170	Ron Santo	2.00	1.00	.60
171	George Altman	1.25	.60	.40
172	Billy Williams	40.00	20.00	12.00
173	Andre Rodgers	18.00	9.00	5.50
174	Ken Hubbs	2.00	1.00	.60
175	Don Landrum	18.00	9.00	5.50
176	Dick Bertell	18.00	9.00	5.50
177	Roy Sievers	1.50	.70	.45
178	Tony Taylor	18.00	9.00	5.50
179	John Callison	1.50	.70	.45
180	Don Demeter	1.25	.60	.40
181	Tony Gonzalez	18.00	9.00	5.50
182	Wes Covington	18.00	9.00	5.50
183	Art Mahaffey	1.25	.60	.40
184	Clay Dalrymple	1.25	.60	.40
185	Al Spangler	1.25	.60	.40
186	Roman Mejias	1.25	.60	.40
187	Bob Aspromonte	40.00	20.00	12.00
188	Norm Larker	1.25	.60	.40
189	Johnny Temple	1.25	.60	.40
190	Carl Warwick	18.00	9.00	5.50
191	Bob Lillis	18.00	9.00	5.50
192	Dick Farrell	40.00	20.00	12.00
193	Gil Hodges	4.50	2.25	1.25
194	Marv Throneberry	2.00	1.00	.60
195	Charlie Neal	18.00	9.00	5.50
196	Frank Thomas	1.50	.70	.45
197	Richie Ashburn	3.50	1.75	1.00
198	Felix Mantilla	18.00	9.00	5.50
199	Rod Kanehl	18.00	9.00	5.50
200	Roger Craig	18.00	9.00	5.50

1986 Jiffy Pop

One of the scarcer of the 1986 "regionals," the 20 card Jiffy Pop issue was inserted in packages of heat-and-eat popcorn. A production of Mike Schecter Associates, the 2⅞" round discs feature 20 popular stars, many in the same pictures found in other '86 regionals. Like other MSA issues, caps have had the team logos erased, allowing Jiffy Pop to avoid having to pay a licensing fee to the teams.

		MT	NR MT	EX
Complete Set:		40.00	30.00	16.00
Common Player:		1.00	.70	.40
1	Jim Rice	2.00	1.50	.80
2	Wade Boggs	3.50	2.75	1.50
3	Lance Parrish	1.00	.70	.40
4	George Brett	2.50	2.00	1.00
5	Robin Yount	2.00	1.50	.80
6	Don Mattingly	5.00	3.75	2.00
7	Dave Winfield	2.00	1.50	.80

		MT	NR MT	EX
8	Reggie Jackson	2.25	1.75	.90
9	Cal Ripken	2.25	1.75	.90
10	Eddie Murray	2.25	1.75	.90
11	Pete Rose	3.00	2.25	1.25
12	Ryne Sandberg	2.00	1.50	.80
13	Nolan Ryan	1.25	.90	.50
14	Fernando Valenzuela	1.25	.90	.50
15	Willie McGee	1.00	.70	.40
16	Dale Murphy	2.50	2.00	1.00
17	Mike Schmidt	2.50	2.00	1.00
18	Steve Garvey	2.00	1.50	.80
19	Gary Carter	2.00	1.50	.80
20	Dwight Gooden	2.50	2.00	1.00

1987 Jiffy Pop

For the second year in a row, Jiffy Pop inserted baseball discs in their packages of popcorn. The full-color discs measure 2⅞'' in diameter and were produced by Mike Schecter Associates of Cos Cob, Conn. Titled ''2nd Annual Collectors' Edition'', the card fronts feature player photos with all team insignias airbrushed away. Information on the backs of the discs are printed in bright red on white stock. Die-cut press sheets containing all 20 discs were available via a mail-in offer.

		MT	NR MT	EX
Complete Set:		40.00	30.00	16.00
Common Player:		1.00	.70	.40
1	Ryne Sandberg	2.00	1.50	.80
2	Dale Murphy	2.50	2.00	1.00
3	Jack Morris	1.00	.70	.40
4	Keith Hernandez	1.75	1.25	.70
5	George Brett	2.50	2.00	1.00
6	Don Mattingly	5.00	3.75	2.00
7	Ozzie Smith	1.00	.70	.40
8	Cal Ripken	2.25	1.75	.90
9	Dwight Gooden	3.00	2.25	1.25
10	Pedro Guerrero	1.00	.70	.40
11	Lou Whitaker	1.00	.70	.40
12	Roger Clemens	2.25	1.75	.90
13	Lance Parrish	1.00	.70	.40
14	Rickey Henderson	2.25	1.75	.90
15	Fernando Valenzuela	1.25	.90	.50
16	Mike Schmidt	2.50	2.00	1.00
17	Darryl Strawberry	2.50	2.00	1.00
18	Mike Scott	1.00	.70	.40
19	Jim Rice	2.00	1.50	.80
20	Wade Boggs	3.50	2.75	1.50

1953 Johnston's Cookies Braves

The first and most common of three annual issues, the '53 Johnston's were inserted into boxes of cookies on a regional basis. Complete sets were also available from the company, whose factory sits in the shadow of Milwaukee County Stadium. While at first glance appearing to be color photos, the pictures on the 25 cards in the set are actually well-done colorizations of black and white photos. Cards measure 2-9/16'' by 3-5/8.'' Write-ups on the backs were ''borrowed'' from the Braves' 1953 yearbook.

 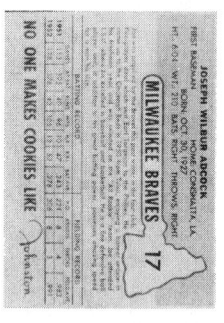

		NR MT	EX	VG
Complete Set:		200.00	80.00	40.00
Common Player:		5.00	2.95	1.50
1	Charlie Grimm	8.00	4.50	2.75
2	John Antonelli	7.00	4.00	2.50
3	Vern Bickford	5.00	2.50	1.50
4	Bob Buhl	7.00	4.00	2.50
5	Lew Burdette	9.00	4.50	2.75
6	Dave Cole	5.00	2.50	1.50
7	Ernie Johnson	5.00	3.25	2.00
8	Dave Jolly	5.00	2.50	1.50
9	Don Liddle	5.00	2.50	1.50
10	Warren Spahn	25.00	13.50	8.00
11	Max Surkont	5.00	2.50	1.50
12	Jim Wilson	5.00	2.50	1.50
13	Sibby Sisti	5.00	2.50	1.50
14	Walker Cooper	5.00	3.25	2.00
15	Del Crandall	9.00	4.50	2.75
16	Ebba St. Claire	5.00	2.50	1.50
17	Joe Adcock	9.00	4.50	2.75
18	George Crowe	5.00	3.25	2.00
19	Jack Dittmer	5.00	2.50	1.50
20	Johnny Logan	7.00	4.00	2.50
21	Ed Mathews	25.00	13.50	8.00
22	Bill Bruton	7.00	4.00	2.50
23	Sid Gordon	5.00	3.25	2.00
24	Andy Pafko	7.00	4.50	2.75
25	Jim Pendleton	5.00	2.50	1.50

1954 Johnston's Cookies Braves

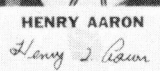
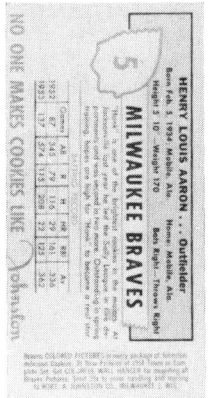

In its second of three annual issues, Johnston's increased the number of cards in its 1954 Braves issue to 35, and switched to an unusual size, a narrow format, 2'' by 3⅞.'' Besides the players and managers, the '54 set also included unnumbered cards of the team trainer and equipment manager. Other cards are numbered by uniform number. After his early-season injury (which gave Hank Aaron a chance to play regularly), Bobby Thomson's card was withdrawn, accounting for its scarcity and high value. A cardboard wall-hanging display into which cards could be inserted was available as a premium offer.

		NR MT	EX	VG
Complete Set:		650.00	275.00	140.00
Common Player:		8.00	4.55	2.30
1	Del Crandall	12.00	6.25	3.75
3	Jim Pendleton	8.00	4.00	2.50
4	Danny O'Connell	8.00	4.00	2.50
5	Henry Aaron	175.00	91.00	55.00
6	Jack Dittmer	8.00	4.00	2.50
9	Joe Adcock	12.00	6.25	3.75
10	Robert Buhl	10.00	5.25	3.25
11	Phillip Paine (Phillips)	8.00	4.00	2.50
12	Ben Johnson	8.00	4.00	2.50
13	Sibby Sisti	8.00	4.00	2.50
15	Charles Gorin	8.00	4.00	2.50
16	Chet Nichols	8.00	4.00	2.50
17	Dave Jolly	8.00	4.00	2.50
19	Jim Wilson	8.00	4.00	2.50
20	Ray Crone	8.00	4.00	2.50
21	Warren Spahn	35.00	17.50	10.50
22	Gene Conley	9.00	5.00	3.00
23	Johnny Logan	10.00	5.25	3.25
24	Charlie White	8.00	4.00	2.50
27	George Metkovich	8.00	4.00	2.50
28	John Cooney	8.00	4.00	2.50
29	Paul Burris	8.00	4.00	2.50
31	Wm. Walters	8.00	4.00	2.50
32	Ernest T. Johnson	8.00	5.00	3.00
33	Lew Burdette	12.00	6.25	3.75
34	Bob Thomson	175.00	81.00	49.00
35	Robert Keely	8.00	4.00	2.50
38	Billy Bruton	10.00	5.25	3.25
40	Charles Grimm	10.00	6.25	3.75
41	Ed Mathews	35.00	17.50	10.50
42	Sam Calderone	8.00	4.00	2.50
47	Joey Jay	8.00	5.00	3.00
48	Andy Pafko	10.00	6.25	3.75
---	Dr. Charles Lacks (trainer)	8.00	4.00	2.50
---	Joseph F. Taylor (asst. trainer)	8.00	4.00	2.50

1955 Johnston's Cookies Braves

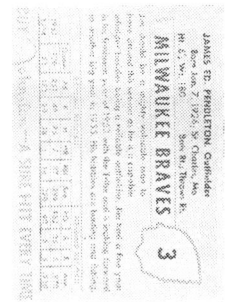

JIM PENDLETON

A third change in size and format was undertaken in the third and final year of Braves set production by Johnston's. The 35 cards in the 1955 set were issued in six fold-out panels of six cards each (Andy Pafko was double-printed). As in 1954, cards are numbered by uniform number, except those of the team equipment manager, trainer and road secretary (former Boston star Duffy Lewis). Single cards measure 2⅞'' by 4.'' Besides including panels in boxes of cookies, the '55 Johnston's could be ordered for 5¢ per panel by mail. The scarcest of the Johnston's issues, the 1955 set can be found today still in complete panels, or as single cards.

	NR MT	EX	VG
Complete Folder Set:	925.00	462.00	277.00
Complete Singles Set:	550.00	275.00	165.00
Common Player:	12.00	6.00	3.50
Common Folder:	110.00	55.00	33.00

		NR MT	EX	VG
1	Del Crandall	16.00	8.00	4.75
3	Jim Pendleton	12.00	6.00	3.50
4	Danny O'Connell	12.00	6.00	3.50
6	Jack Dittmer	12.00	6.00	3.50
9	Joe Adcock	16.00	8.00	4.75
10	Bob Buhl	14.00	7.00	4.25
11	Phil Paine	12.00	6.00	3.50
12	Ray Crone	12.00	6.00	3.50
15	Charlie Gorin	12.00	6.00	3.50
16	Dave Jolly	12.00	6.00	3.50
17	Chet Nichols	12.00	6.00	3.50
18	Chuck Tanner	18.00	9.00	5.50
19	Jim Wilson	12.00	6.00	3.50
20	Dave Koslo	12.00	6.00	3.50
21	Warren Spahn	35.00	17.50	10.50
22	Gene Conley	14.00	7.00	4.25
23	John Logan	14.00	7.00	4.25
24	Charlie White	12.00	6.00	3.50
28	Johnny Cooney	12.00	6.00	3.50
30	Roy Smalley	12.00	6.00	3.50
31	Bucky Walters	12.00	6.00	3.50
32	Ernie Johnson	12.00	6.00	3.50
33	Lew Burdette	18.00	9.00	5.50
34	Bobby Thomson	18.00	9.00	5.50
35	Bob Keely	12.00	6.00	3.50
38	Billy Bruton	14.00	7.00	4.25
39	George Crowe	12.00	6.00	3.50
40	Charlie Grimm	14.00	7.00	4.25
41	Eddie Mathews	35.00	17.50	10.50
44	Hank Aaron	150.00	75.00	45.00
47	Joe Jay	12.00	6.00	3.50
48	Andy Pakfo	14.00	7.00	4.25
---	Dr. Charles K. Lacks	12.00	6.00	3.50
---	Duffy Lewis	12.00	6.00	3.50
---	Joe Taylor	12.00	6.00	3.50
---	Series 1 Folder (Hank Aaron, Lew Burdette, Del Crandall, Charlie Gorin, Bob Keely, Danny O'Connell)	300.00	150.00	90.00
---	Series 2 Folder (Joe Adcock, Joe Jay, Dr. Charles K. Lacks, Chet Nichols, Andy Pafko, Charlie White)	100.00	50.00	30.00
---	Series 3 Folder (Gene Conley, George Crowe, Jim Pendleton, Roy Smalley, Warren Spahn, Joe Taylor)	150.00	75.00	45.00
---	Series 4 Folder (Billy Bruton, John Cooney, Dave Jolly, Dave Koslo, Johnny Logan, Andy Pafko)	100.00	50.00	30.00
---	Series 5 Folder (Ray Crone, Ernie Johnson, Duffy Lewis, Eddie Mathews, Phil Paine, Chuck Tanner)	160.00	80.00	48.00
---	Series 6 Folder (Bob Buhl, Jack Dittmer, Charlie Grimm, Bobby Thomson, Bucky Walters, Jim Wilson)	125.00	62.00	37.00

HOW TO ORDER TRADING CARDS

✓ ◊ CHECK THE SERIES you want and send in

◊ 5¢ IN COIN along with

◊ A LABEL, WRAPPER or BOX END from any Johnston COOKIE or CRACKER package or the label from any 'bake home' can of Johnston HOT FUDGE, BUTTERSCOTCH, or CHOCOLATE SYRUP SUNDAE TOPPINGS.

◊ ADDRESS YOUR ORDER TO:
BRAVES TRADING CARDS, 56 JOHNSTON, MILWAUKEE 1, WIS.

PLEASE SEND ME SERIES (Check One) 1 ☐ 2 ☐ 3 ☐ 4 ☐ 5 ☐ 6 ☐
Name
Address
City _____ State _____

- - - - - - CUT HERE - - - - - -

LIST OF PLAYERS BY SERIES

Series 1	Series 2	Series 3
DEL CRANDALL	JOE ADCOCK	WARREN SPAHN
HANK AARON	CHARLIE WHITE	JIM PENDLETON
LEW BURDETTE	JOE JAY	GENE CONLEY
CHARLIE GORIN	ANDY PAFKO	JOE TAYLOR
BOB KEELY	DR. CHARLES K. LACKS	ROY SMALLEY
DANNY O'CONNELL	CHET NICHOLS	GEORGE CROWE

Series 4	Series 5	Series 6
JOHNNY LOGAN	EDDIE MATHEWS	BOBBY THOMSON
BILLY BRUTON	RAY CRONE	BOB BUHL
DAVE JOLLY	ERNIE JOHNSON	JIM WILSON
DAVE KOSLO	PHIL PAINE	BUCKY WALTERS
JOHN COONEY	DUFFY LEWIS	CHARLIE GRIMM
ANDY PAFKO	CHUCK TANNER	JACK DITTMER

SEND 5¢ AND LABEL, WRAPPER OR BOX END FOR EACH SERIES YOU WANT

CUT CARDS APART — OR KEEP IN SERIES

		MT	NR MT	EX
38	George Brett	.07	.05	.03
39	Mike Schmidt	.07	.05	.03
40	Rollie Fingers	.05	.04	.02
41	Mike Schmidt	.07	.05	.03
42	Don Drysdale	.05	.04	.02
43	Hank Aaron	.07	.05	.03
44	Pete Rose	.10	.08	.04

1982 K-Mart

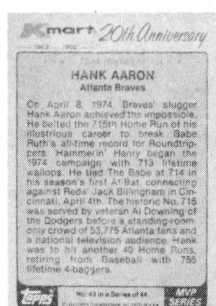

The first of what became dozens of boxed sets specially produced for retail chain stores by the major card producers, the 1982 K-Mart set has not enjoyed any collector popularity. The theme of the set is Most Valuable Players and selected record-breaking performances of the 1962-1981 seasons. The design used miniature reproductions of Topps cards of the era, except in a few cases where designs had to be created because original cards were never issued — 1962 Maury Wills, 1975 Fred Lynn. Originally sold for about $2 per boxed set of 44, large quantities were bought up by speculators who got burned when over-production and lack of demand caused the set to drop as low as 10¢. The 2½'' by 3½'' cards were printed by Topps.

		MT	NR MT	EX
Complete Set:		1.25	.90	.50
Common Player:		.03	.02	.01
1	Mickey Mantle	.25	.20	.10
2	Maury Wills	.05	.04	.02
3	Elston Howard	.03	.02	.01
4	Sandy Koufax	.07	.05	.03
5	Brooks Robinson	.05	.04	.02
6	Ken Boyer	.03	.02	.01
7	Zoilo Versalles	.03	.02	.01
8	Willie Mays	.07	.05	.03
9	Frank Robinson	.05	.04	.02
10	Bob Clemente	.07	.05	.03
11	Carl Yastrzemski	.07	.05	.03
12	Orlando Cepeda	.03	.02	.01
13	Denny McLain	.03	.02	.01
14	Bob Gibson	.05	.04	.02
15	Harmon Killebrew	.05	.04	.02
16	Willie McCovey	.05	.04	.02
17	Boog Powell	.03	.02	.01
18	Johnny Bench	.07	.05	.03
19	Vida Blue	.03	.02	.01
20	Joe Torre	.03	.02	.01
21	Rich Allen	.03	.02	.01
22	Johnny Bench	.07	.05	.03
23	Reggie Jackson	.07	.05	.03
24	Pete Rose	.10	.08	.04
25	Jeff Burroughs	.03	.02	.01
26	Steve Garvey	.07	.05	.03
27	Fred Lynn	.03	.02	.01
28	Joe Morgan	.05	.04	.02
29	Thurman Munson	.05	.04	.02
30	Joe Morgan	.05	.04	.02
31	Rod Carew	.07	.05	.03
32	George Foster	.03	.02	.01
33	Jim Rice	.05	.04	.02
34	Dave Parker	.05	.04	.02
35	Don Baylor	.03	.02	.01
36	Keith Hernandez	.03	.02	.01
37	Willie Stargell	.05	.04	.02

1987 K-Mart

Produced by Topps for K-Mart, the 1987 K-Mart set was distributed by the department stores to celebrate their 25th anniversary. Entitled "Baseball's Stars of the Decades", the 33-card set was issued in a special cardboard box with one stick of bubblegum. The card fronts feature a full-color photo set diagonally against a red background. The backs contain career highlights plus pitching or batting statistics for the decade in which the player enjoyed his greatest success. Cards are the standard 2½'' by 3½'' size.

		MT	NR MT	EX
Complete Set:		5.00	3.75	2.00
Common Player:		.10	.08	.04
1	Hank Aaron	.50	.40	.20
2	Roberto Clemente	.40	.30	.15
3	Bob Gibson	.10	.08	.04
4	Harmon Killebrew	.10	.08	.04
5	Mickey Mantle	.70	.50	.30
6	Juan Marichal	.10	.08	.04
7	Roger Maris	.20	.15	.08
8	Willie Mays	.50	.40	.20
9	Brooks Robinson	.30	.25	.12
10	Frank Robinson	.20	.15	.08
11	Carl Yastrzemski	.50	.40	.20
12	Johnny Bench	.30	.25	.12
13	Lou Brock	.20	.15	.08
14	Rod Carew	.30	.25	.12
15	Steve Carlton	.20	.15	.08
16	Reggie Jackson	.30	.25	.12
17	Jim Palmer	.10	.08	.04
18	Jim Rice	.10	.08	.04
19	Pete Rose	.60	.45	.25
20	Nolan Ryan	.20	.15	.08
21	Tom Seaver	.20	.15	.08
22	Willie Stargell	.10	.08	.04
23	Wade Boggs	.60	.45	.25
24	George Brett	.40	.30	.15
25	Gary Carter	.20	.15	.08
26	Dwight Gooden	.50	.40	.20
27	Rickey Henderson	.20	.15	.08
28	Don Mattingly	.70	.50	.30
29	Dale Murphy	.40	.30	.15
30	Eddie Murray	.20	.15	.08
31	Mike Schmidt	.30	.25	.12
32	Darryl Strawberry	.40	.30	.15
33	Fernando Valenzuela	.10	.08	.04

Definitions for grading conditions are located in the Introduction of this price guide.

1955 Kahn's Wieners Reds

Compliments of Kahn's Wieners
"THE WIENER THE WORLD AWAITED"

The first of what would become 15 successive years of baseball card issues by the Kahn's meat company of Cincinnati is also the rarest. The set consists of six Cincinnati Redlegs player cards, 3¼'' by 4.'' Printed in black and white, with blank backs, the '55 Kahn's cards were distributed at a one-day promotional event at a Cincinnati amusement park, where the featured players were on hand to sign autographs. Like the other Kahn's issues through 1963, the '55 cards have a ½'' white panel containing an advertising message below the player photo. These cards are sometimes found with this portion cut off, greatly reducing the value of the card.

		NR MT	EX	VG
Complete Set:		2000.00	1000.00	600.00
Common Player:		250.00	125.00	75.00
(1)	Gus Bell	450.00	225.00	135.00
(2)	Ted Kluszewski	300.00	150.00	90.00
(3)	Roy McMillan	250.00	125.00	75.00
(4)	Joe Nuxhall	275.00	137.00	82.00
(5)	Wally Post	250.00	125.00	75.00
(6)	Johnny Temple	250.00	125.00	75.00

1956 Kahn's Wieners Reds

Compliments of Kahn's Wieners
"THE WIENER THE WORLD AWAITED"

In 1956, Kahn's expanded its baseball card program to include 15 Redlegs players, and began issuing the cards one per pack in packages of hot dogs. Because the cards were packaged in direct contact with the meat, they are often found today in stained condition. In 3¼'' by 4'' format, black and white with blank back, the '56 Kahn's can be distinguished from later issues by the presence of full stadium photographic backgrounds behind the player photos. Like all Kahn's issues, the 1956 set is unnumbered; the checklists are arranged alphabetically for convenience. The set features the first-ever baseball card of Hall of Famer Frank Robinson.

		NR MT	EX	VG
Complete Set:		1000.00	500.00	300.00
Common Player:		50.00	25.00	15.00
(1)	Ed Bailey	50.00	25.00	15.00
(2)	Gus Bell	55.00	27.00	16.50
(3)	Joe Black	55.00	27.00	16.50
(4)	"Smokey" Burgess	55.00	27.00	16.50
(5)	Art Fowler	50.00	25.00	15.00
(6)	Hershell Freeman	50.00	25.00	15.00
(7)	Ray Jablonski	50.00	25.00	15.00
(8)	John Klippstein	50.00	25.00	15.00
(9)	Ted Kluszewski	90.00	45.00	27.00
(10)	Brooks Lawrence	50.00	25.00	15.00
(11)	Roy McMillan	50.00	25.00	15.00
(12)	Joe Nuxhall	60.00	30.00	18.00
(13)	Wally Post	50.00	25.00	15.00
(14)	Frank Robinson	200.00	100.00	60.00
(15)	Johnny Temple	50.00	25.00	15.00

1957 Kahn's Wieners

Compliments of Kahn's Wieners
"THE WIENER THE WORLD AWAITED"

In its third season of baseball card issue, Kahn's kept the basic 3¼'' by 4'' format, with black and white photos and blank backs. The issue was expanded to 28 players, all Pirates or Reds. The last of the blank-back Kahn's sets, the 1957 Reds players can be distinguished from the 1956 issue by the general lack of background photo detail, in favor of a neutral light gray background. The Dick Groat card appears with two name variations, a facsimile autograph, "Richard Groat," and a printed "Dick Groat."

		NR MT	EX	VG
Complete Set		1600.00	800.00	480.00
Common Player		35.00	17.50	10.50
(1)	Tom Acker	35.00	17.50	10.50
(2)	Ed Bailey	35.00	17.50	10.50
(3)	Gus Bell	45.00	22.00	13.50
(4)	Smokey Burgess	45.00	22.00	13.50
(5)	Roberto Clemente	300.00	150.00	90.00
(6)	George Crowe	35.00	17.50	10.50
(7)	Elroy Face	45.00	22.00	13.50
(8)	Hershell Freeman	35.00	17.50	10.50
(9)	Robert Friend	45.00	22.00	13.50
(10)	Don Gross	35.00	17.50	10.50
(11a)	Dick Groat	50.00	25.00	15.00
(11b)	Richard Groat	100.00	50.00	30.00
(12)	Warren Hacker	35.00	17.50	10.50
(13)	Don Hoak	40.00	20.00	12.00
(14)	Hal Jeffcoat	35.00	17.50	10.50
(15)	Ron Kline	35.00	17.50	10.50
(16)	John Klippstein	35.00	17.50	10.50
(17)	Ted Kluszewski	65.00	32.00	19.50
(18)	Brooks Lawrence	35.00	17.50	10.50
(19)	Dale Long	35.00	17.50	10.50
(20)	Wm. Mazeroski	50.00	25.00	15.00
(21)	Roy McMillan	35.00	17.50	10.50
(22)	Joe Nuxhall	45.00	22.00	13.50
(23)	Wally Post	35.00	17.50	10.50

		NR MT	EX	VG
(24)	Frank Robinson	150.00	75.00	45.00
(25)	Johnny Temple	35.00	17.50	10.50
(26)	Frank Thomas	35.00	17.50	10.50
(27)	Bob Thurman	35.00	17.50	10.50
(28)	Lee Walls	35.00	17.50	10.50

1958 Kahn's Wieners

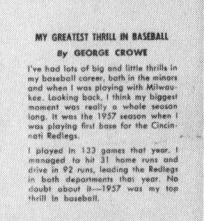

Compliments of Kahn's Wieners
"THE WIENER THE WORLD AWAITED"

Long-time Cincinnati favorite Wally Post became the only Philadelphia Phillies ballplayer to appear in the 15-year run of Kahn's issues when he was traded in 1958, but included as part of the otherwise exclusively Pirates-Reds set. Like previous years, the '58 Kahn's were 3¼'' by 4,'' with black and white player photos. Unlike previous years, however, the cards had printing on the back, a story by the pictured player, titled ''My Greatest Thrill in Baseball.'' Quite similar to the 1959 issue, the '58 Kahn's can be distinguished by the fact that the top line of the advertising panel at bottom has the word ''Wieners'' in 1958, but not in 1959.

		NR MT	EX	VG
Complete Set:		2000.00	1000.00	600.00
Common Player:		35.00	17.50	10.50
(1)	Ed Bailey	35.00	17.50	10.50
(2)	Gene Baker	45.00	22.00	13.50
(3)	Gus Bell	45.00	22.00	13.50
(4)	Smokey Burgess	45.00	22.00	13.50
(5)	Roberto Clemente	300.00	150.00	90.00
(6)	George Crowe	35.00	17.50	10.50
(7)	Elroy Face	45.00	22.00	13.50
(8)	Henry Foiles	35.00	17.50	10.50
(9)	Dee Fondy	35.00	17.50	10.50
(10)	Robert Friend	45.00	22.00	13.50
(11)	Richard Groat	50.00	25.00	15.00
(12)	Harvey Haddix	45.00	22.00	13.50
(13)	Don Hoak	40.00	20.00	12.00
(14)	Hal Jeffcoat	45.00	22.00	13.50
(15)	Ronald L. Kline	45.00	22.00	13.50
(16)	Ted Kluszewski	65.00	32.00	19.50
(17)	Vernon Law	45.00	22.00	13.50
(18)	Brooks Lawrence	35.00	17.50	10.50
(19)	William Mazeroski	50.00	25.00	15.00
(20)	Roy McMillan	35.00	17.50	10.50
(21)	Joe Nuxhall	45.00	22.00	13.50
(22)	Wally Post	125.00	62.00	37.00
(23)	John Powers	35.00	17.50	10.50
(24)	Robert T. Purkey	35.00	17.50	10.50
(25)	Charles Rabe	125.00	62.00	37.00
(26)	Frank Robinson	150.00	75.00	45.00
(27)	Robert Skinner	35.00	17.50	10.50
(28)	Johnny Temple	35.00	17.50	10.50
(29)	Frank Thomas	125.00	62.00	37.00

1959 Kahn's Wieners

A third team was added to the Kahn's lineup in 1959, the Cleveland Indians joining the Pirates and Reds, bringing the number of cards in the set to 38. Again printed black and white in the 3¼'' by 4'' size, the 1959 Kahn's cards can be differentiated from the previous issue by the lack of the word ''Wieners'' on the top line of the advertising panel at bottom. Backs

Compliments of Kahn's
"THE WIENER THE WORLD AWAITED"

again featured a story written by the pictured player, titled ''The Toughest Play I Had to Make,'' ''My Most Difficult Moment in Baseball,'' or ''The Toughest Batters I Have to Face.''

		NR MT	EX	VG
Complete Set:		3300.00	1650.00	990.00
Common Player:		35.00	17.50	10.50
(1)	Ed Bailey	35.00	17.50	10.50
(2)	Gary Bell	35.00	17.50	10.50
(3)	Gus Bell	45.00	22.00	13.50
(4)	Richard Brodowski	350.00	175.00	105.00
(5)	Forrest Burgess	45.00	22.00	13.50
(6)	Roberto Clemente	300.00	150.00	90.00
(7)	Rocky Colavito	65.00	32.00	19.50
(8)	ElRoy Face	45.00	22.00	13.50
(9)	Robert Friend	45.00	22.00	13.50
(10)	Joe Gordon	45.00	22.00	13.50
(11)	Jim Grant	35.00	17.50	10.50
(12)	Richard M. Groat	50.00	25.00	15.00
(13)	Harvey Haddix	325.00	162.00	97.00
(14)	Woodie Held	325.00	162.00	97.00
(15)	Don Hoak	40.00	20.00	12.00
(16)	Ronald Kline	35.00	17.50	10.50
(17)	Ted Kluszewski	65.00	32.00	19.50
(18)	Vernon Law	45.00	22.00	13.50
(19)	Jerry Lynch	35.00	17.50	10.50
(20)	Billy Martin	65.00	32.00	19.50
(21)	William Mazeroski	50.00	25.00	15.00
(22)	Cal McLish	325.00	162.00	97.00
(23)	Roy McMillan	35.00	17.50	10.50
(24)	Minnie Minoso	50.00	25.00	15.00
(25)	Russell Nixon	35.00	17.50	10.50
(26)	Joe Nuxhall	45.00	22.00	13.50
(27)	Jim Perry	45.00	22.00	13.50
(28)	Vada Pinson	50.00	25.00	15.00
(29)	Vic Power	35.00	17.50	10.50
(30)	Robert Purkey	35.00	17.50	10.50
(31)	Frank Robinson	150.00	75.00	45.00
(32)	Herb Score	45.00	22.00	13.50
(33)	Robert Skinner	35.00	17.50	10.50
(34)	George Strickland	35.00	17.50	10.50
(35)	Richard L. Stuart	40.00	20.00	12.00
(36)	John Temple	35.00	17.50	10.50
(37)	Frank Thomas	40.00	20.00	12.00
(38)	George A. Witt	35.00	17.50	10.50

1960 Kahn's Wieners

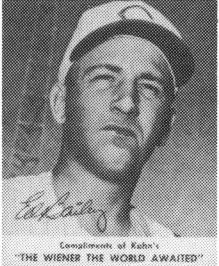

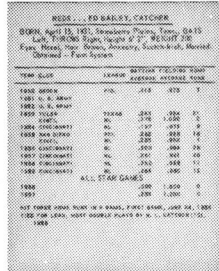

Compliments of Kahn's
"THE WIENER THE WORLD AWAITED"

Three more teams joined the Kahn's roster in 1960, the Chicago Cubs, Chicago White Sox and St. Louis Cardinals. A total of 42 different players are represented in the set. Again 3¼'' by 4'' with black and white photos, the 1960 Kahn's cards featured for the first time player stats and personal data on the back ... except Harvey Kuenn, which was issued with blank back, probably because of the lateness of his trade to the Indians.

		NR MT	EX	VG
Complete Set:		1500.00	750.00	450.00
Common Player:		22.00	11.00	6.50
(1)	Ed Bailey	22.00	11.00	6.50
(2)	Gary Bell	22.00	11.00	6.50
(3)	Gus Bell	27.00	13.50	8.00
(4)	Forrest Burgess	27.00	13.50	8.00
(5)	Gino N. Cimoli	22.00	11.00	6.50
(6)	Roberto Clemente	150.00	75.00	45.00
(7)	ElRoy Face	27.00	13.50	8.00
(8)	Tito Francona	27.00	13.50	8.00
(9)	Robert Friend	27.00	13.50	8.00
(10)	Jim Grant	22.00	11.00	6.50
(11)	Richard Groat	32.00	16.00	9.50
(12)	Harvey Haddix	27.00	13.50	8.00
(13)	Woodie Held	22.00	11.00	6.50
(14)	Bill Henry	22.00	11.00	6.50
(15)	Don Hoak	27.00	13.50	8.00
(16)	Jay Hook	22.00	11.00	6.50
(17)	Eddie Kasko	22.00	11.00	6.50
(18)	Ronnie Kline	32.00	16.00	9.50
(19)	Ted Kluszewski	40.00	20.00	12.00
(20)	Harvey Kuenn	200.00	100.00	60.00
(21)	Vernon S. Law	27.00	13.50	8.00
(22)	Brooks Lawrence	22.00	11.00	6.50
(23)	Jerry Lynch	22.00	11.00	6.50
(24)	Billy Martin	45.00	22.00	13.50
(25)	William Mazeroski	32.00	16.00	9.50
(26)	Cal McLish	22.00	11.00	6.50
(27)	Roy McMillan	22.00	11.00	6.50
(28)	Don Newcombe	27.00	13.50	8.00
(29)	Russ Nixon	22.00	11.00	6.50
(30)	Joe Nuxhall	27.00	13.50	8.00
(31)	James J. O'Toole	22.00	11.00	6.50
(32)	Jim Perry	27.00	13.50	8.00
(33)	Vada Pinson	32.00	16.00	9.50
(34)	Vic Power	22.00	11.00	6.50
(35)	Robert T. Purkey	22.00	11.00	6.50
(36)	Frank Robinson	100.00	50.00	30.00
(37)	Herb Score	27.00	13.50	8.00
(38)	Robert R. Skinner	22.00	11.00	6.50
(39)	Richard L. Stuart	27.00	13.50	8.00
(40)	John Temple	22.00	11.00	6.50
(41)	Frank Thomas	32.00	16.00	9.50
(42)	Lee Walls	27.00	13.50	8.00

1961 Kahn's Wieners

Compliments of Kahn's
"THE WIENER THE WORLD AWAITED"

After a single season, the Chicago and St. Louis teams dropped out of the Kahn's program, but the 1961 set was larger than ever, at 43 cards. The same basic format — 3¼'' by 4'' size, black and white photos and statistical information on the back — was retained. For the first time in '61, the meat company made complete sets of the Kahn's cards available to collectors via a mail-in offer. This makes the 1961 and later Kahn's cards considerably easier to obtain than the earlier issues.

		NR MT	EX	VG
Complete Set:		900.00	450.00	270.00
Common Player:		10.00	5.00	3.00
(1)	John A. Antonelli	15.00	7.50	4.50
(2)	Ed Bailey	13.00	6.50	4.00
(3)	Gary Bell	13.00	6.50	4.00
(4)	Gus Bell	15.00	7.50	4.50
(5)	James P. Brosnan	13.00	6.50	4.00
(6)	Forrest Burgess	15.00	7.50	4.50
(7)	Gino Cimoli	13.00	6.50	4.00
(8)	Roberto Clemente	150.00	75.00	45.00
(9)	Gordon Coleman	13.00	6.50	4.00
(10)	Jimmie Dykes	15.00	7.50	4.50
(11)	ElRoy Face	17.50	8.75	5.25
(12)	Tito Francona	15.00	7.50	4.50
(13)	Robert Friend	15.00	7.50	4.50
(14)	Gene L. Freese	13.00	6.50	4.00
(15)	Jim Grant	13.00	6.50	4.00
(16)	Richard M. Groat	20.00	10.00	6.00
(17)	Harvey Haddix	15.00	7.50	4.50
(18)	Woodie Held	13.00	6.50	4.00
(19)	Don Hoak	15.00	7.50	4.50
(20)	Jay Hook	13.00	6.50	4.00
(21)	Joe Jay	13.00	6.50	4.00
(22)	Eddie Kasko	13.00	6.50	4.00
(23)	Willie Kirkland	13.00	6.50	4.00
(24)	Vernon S. Law	17.50	8.75	5.25
(25)	Jerry Lynch	13.00	6.50	4.00
(26)	Jim Maloney	17.50	8.75	5.25
(27)	William Mazeroski	20.00	10.00	6.00
(28)	Wilmer D. Mizell	15.00	7.50	4.50
(29)	Glenn R. Nelson	13.00	6.50	4.00
(30)	James J. O'Toole	13.00	6.50	4.00
(31)	Jim Perry	15.00	7.50	4.50
(32)	John M. Phillips	13.00	6.50	4.00
(33)	Vada E. Pinson Jr.	20.00	10.00	6.00
(34)	Wally Post	13.00	6.50	4.00
(35)	Vic Power	13.00	6.50	4.00
(36)	Robert T. Purkey	13.00	6.50	4.00
(37)	Frank Robinson	100.00	50.00	30.00
(38)	John A. Romano Jr.	13.00	6.50	4.00
(39)	Dick Schofield	13.00	6.50	4.00
(40)	Robert Skinner	13.00	6.50	4.00
(41)	Hal Smith	13.00	6.50	4.00
(42)	Richard Stuart	15.00	7.50	4.50
(43)	John E. Temple	13.00	6.50	4.00

1962 Kahn's Wieners

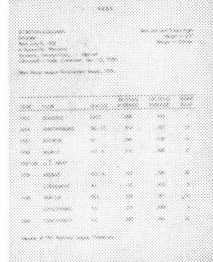

Compliments of Kahn's
"THE WIENER THE WORLD AWAITED"

Besides the familiar Reds, Pirates and Indians players in the 1962 Kahn's set, a fourth team was added, the Minnesota Twins, though the overall size of the set was decreased from the previous year, to 38 players in 1962. The cards retained the 3¼'' by 4'' black and white format of previous years. The '62 Kahn's set is awash in variations. Besides the photo and front design variations on the Bell, Purkey and Power cards, each Cleveland player can be found with two back variations, listing the team either as "Cleveland" or "Cleveland Indians." The complete set values listed below do not include the scarcer variations.

	NR MT	EX	VG
Complete Set:	900.00	450.00	270.00
Common Player:	10.00	5.00	3.00
(1a) Gary Bell (fat man in background)			
	100.00	50.00	30.00

		NR MT	EX	VG
(1b)	Gary Bell (no fat man)	32.00	16.00	9.50
(2)	James P. Brosnan	10.00	5.00	3.00
(3)	Forrest Burgess	15.00	7.50	4.50
(4)	Leonardo Cardenas	10.00	5.00	3.00
(5)	Roberto Clemente	110.00	55.00	33.00
(6a)	Ty Cline (Cleveland Indians back)			
		65.00	32.00	19.50
(6b)	Ty Cline (Cleveland back)	20.00	10.00	6.00
(7)	Gordon Coleman	10.00	5.00	3.00
(8)	Dick Donovan	20.00	10.00	6.00
(9)	John Edwards	10.00	5.00	3.00
(10a)	Tito Francona (Cleveland Indians back)			
		65.00	32.00	19.50
(10b)	Tito Francona (Cleveland back)	20.00	10.00	6.00
(11)	Gene Freese	10.00	5.00	3.00
(12)	Robert B. Friend	15.00	7.50	4.50
(13)	Joe Gibbon	75.00	37.00	22.00
(14a)	Jim Grant (Cleveland Indians back)			
		65.00	32.00	19.50
(14b)	Jim Grant (Cleveland back)	20.00	10.00	6.00
(15)	Richard M. Groat	17.50	8.75	5.25
(16)	Harvey Haddix	15.00	7.50	4.50
(17a)	Woodie Held (Cleveland Indians back)			
		65.00	32.00	19.50
(17b)	Woodie Held (Cleveland back)	20.00	10.00	6.00
(18)	Bill Henry	10.00	5.00	3.00
(19)	Don Hoak	15.00	7.50	4.50
(20)	Ken Hunt	10.00	5.00	3.00
(21)	Joseph R. Jay	10.00	5.00	3.00
(22)	Eddie Kasko	10.00	5.00	3.00
(23a)	Willie Kirkland (Cleveland Indians back)			
		65.00	32.00	19.50
(23b)	Willie Kirkland (Cleveland back)	20.00	10.00	6.00
(24a)	Barry Latman (Cleveland Indians back)			
		65.00	32.00	19.50
(24b)	Barry Latman (Cleveland back)	20.00	10.00	6.00
(25)	Jerry Lynch	10.00	5.00	3.00
(26)	Jim Maloney	15.00	7.50	4.50
(27)	William Mazeroski	17.50	8.75	5.25
(28)	Jim O'Toole	10.00	5.00	3.00
(29a)	Jim Perry (Cleveland Indians back)			
		70.00	35.00	21.00
(29b)	Jim Perry (Cleveland back)	25.00	12.50	7.50
(30a)	John M. Phillips (Cleveland Indians back)			
		65.00	32.00	19.50
(30b)	John M. Phillips (Cleveland back)			
		20.00	10.00	6.00
(31)	Vada E. Pinson	17.50	8.75	5.25
(32)	Wally Post	10.00	5.00	3.00
(33a)	Vic Power (Cleveland Indians back)			
		65.00	32.00	19.50
(33b)	Vic Power (Cleveland back)	20.00	10.00	6.00
(33c)	Vic Power (Minnesota Twins back)			
		110.00	55.00	33.00
(34a)	Robert T. Purkey (no autograph)			
		100.00	50.00	30.00
(34b)	Robert T. Purkey (with autograph)			
		32.00	16.00	9.50
(35)	Frank Robinson	65.00	32.00	19.50
(36a)	John Romano (Cleveland Indians back)			
		65.00	32.00	19.50
(36b)	John Romano (Cleveland back)	20.00	10.00	6.00
(37)	Dick Stuart	15.00	7.50	4.50
(38)	Bill Virdon	15.00	7.50	4.50

1962 Kahn's Wieners
Atlanta Crackers

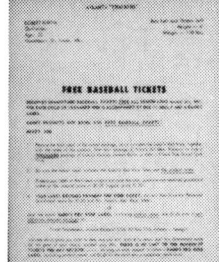

Compliments of Kahn's
"THE WIENER THE WORLD AWAITED"

Kahn's made a single foray into the minor league

market in 1962 with a separate 24-card set of Atlanta Crackers. The cards feature the same basic format, 3¼'' by 4,'' borderless black and white photos with a Kahn's ad message in a white panel below the picture, as the major league issue. The backs are slightly different, having a free ticket offer in place of the player stats. Atlanta was the top farm club of the St. Louis Cardinals in 1962. The most famous alumnus in the set is Tim McCarver.

		NR MT	EX	VG
Complete Set:		400.00	200.00	120.00
Common Player:		13.00	6.50	4.00
(1)	James (Jimmy) Edward Beauchamp			
		13.00	6.50	4.00
(2)	Gerald Peter Buchek	13.00	6.50	4.00
(3)	Robert Burda	13.00	6.50	4.00
(4)	Hal Deitz	13.00	6.50	4.00
(5)	Robert John Duliba	13.00	6.50	4.00
(6)	Harry Michael Fanok	13.00	6.50	4.00
(7)	Phil Gagliano	13.00	6.50	4.00
(8)	John Glenn	13.00	6.50	4.00
(9)	Leroy Gregory	13.00	6.50	4.00
(10)	Richard (Dick) Henry Hughes	13.00	6.50	4.00
(11)	John Charles Kucks, Jr.	13.00	6.50	4.00
(12)	Johnny Joe Lewis	13.00	6.50	4.00
(13)	James (Mac - Timmie) Timothy McCarver			
		30.00	15.00	9.00
(14)	Robert F. Milliken	13.00	6.50	4.00
(15)	Joe Morgan	13.00	6.50	4.00
(16)	Ronald Charles Plaza	13.00	6.50	4.00
(17)	Bob Sadowski	13.00	6.50	4.00
(18)	Jim Saul	13.00	6.50	4.00
(19)	Willard Schmidt	13.00	6.50	4.00
(20)	Joe Schultz	13.00	6.50	4.00
(21)	Thomas Michael (Mike) Shannon			
		17.50	8.75	5.25
(22)	Paul Louis Toth	13.00	6.50	4.00
(23)	Andrew Lou Vickery	13.00	6.50	4.00
(24)	Fred Dwight Whitfield	13.00	6.50	4.00

1963 Kahn's Wieners

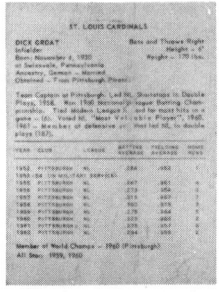

Compliments of Kahn's
"THE WIENER THE WORLD AWAITED"

In 1963, for the first time since Kahn's began issuing baseball cards in 1955, the design underwent a significant change, white borders were added to the top and sides of the player photo. Also, the card size was changed to 3-3/16'' by 4¼.'' Statistical and personal data continued to be printed on the card backs. Joining traditional Reds, Pirates and Indians personnel in the 30-card 1963 set were a handful of N.Y. Yankees and Dick Groat, in his new identity as a St. Louis Cardinal.

		NR MT	EX	VG
Complete Set:		600.00	300.00	180.00
Common Player:		10.00	5.00	3.00
(1)	Robert Bailey	10.00	5.00	3.00
(2)	Don Blasingame	10.00	5.00	3.00
(3)	Clete Boyer	17.50	8.75	5.25
(4)	Forrest Burgess	15.00	7.50	4.50
(5)	Leonardo Cardenas	10.00	5.00	3.00
(6)	Roberto Clemente	110.00	55.00	33.00
(7)	Don Clendennon (Donn Clendenon)			
		10.00	5.00	3.00

		NR MT	EX	VG
(8)	Gordon Coleman	10.00	5.00	3.00
(9)	John A. Edwards	10.00	5.00	3.00
(10)	Gene Freese	10.00	5.00	3.00
(11)	Robert B. Friend	15.00	7.50	4.50
(12)	Joe Gibbon	10.00	5.00	3.00
(13)	Dick Groat	17.50	8.75	5.25
(14)	Harvey Haddix	15.00	7.50	4.50
(15)	Elston Howard	20.00	10.00	6.00
(16)	Joey Jay	10.00	5.00	3.00
(17)	Eddie Kasko	10.00	5.00	3.00
(18)	Tony Kubek	20.00	10.00	6.00
(19)	Jerry Lynch	10.00	5.00	3.00
(20)	Jim Maloney	15.00	7.50	4.50
(21)	William Mazeroski	17.50	8.75	5.25
(22)	Joe Nuxhall	15.00	7.50	4.50
(23)	Jim O'Toole	10.00	5.00	3.00
(24)	Vada E. Pinson	17.50	8.75	5.25
(25)	Robert T. Purkey	10.00	5.00	3.00
(26)	Bob Richardson	20.00	10.00	6.00
(27)	Frank Robinson	60.00	30.00	18.00
(28)	Bill Stafford	15.00	7.50	4.50
(29)	Ralph W. Terry	17.50	8.75	5.25
(30)	Bill Virdon	15.00	7.50	4.50

		NR MT	EX	VG
(28)	Robert A. Veale Jr.	9.00	4.50	2.75
(29)	Bill Virdon	12.00	6.00	3.50
(30)	Leon Wagner	9.00	4.50	2.75
(31)	Fred Whitfield	9.00	4.50	2.75

1965 Kahn's Wieners

 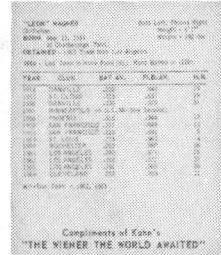

There was little change for the Kahn's issue in 1965 beyond the addition of Milwaukee Braves players to the Reds, Pirates and Indians traditionally included in the set. At 45 players, the 1965 issue was the largest of the Kahn's sets. Once again in 3'' by 3½'' size, the '65s retained the borderless color photo design of the previous season. A look at the stats on the back will confirm the year of issue, however, since the last years of statistics is the year prior to the card's issue.

1964 Kahn's Wieners

After nearly a decade of virtually identical card issues, the 1964 Kahn's issue was an abrupt change. In a new size, 3'' by 3½,'' the nearly square cards featured a borderless color photo. The only other design element on the front of the card was a facsimile autograph. The advertising slogan which had traditionally appeared on the front of the card was moved to the back, where it joined the player's stats and personal data. The teams in the 1964 issue once again reverted to the Reds, Pirates and Indians, to a total of 31 cards.

		NR MT	EX	VG
Complete Set:		800.00	400.00	240.00
Common Player:		9.00	4.50	2.75
(1)	Max Alvis	9.00	4.50	2.75
(2)	Bob Bailey	9.00	4.50	2.75
(3)	Leonardo Cardenas	9.00	4.50	2.75
(4)	Roberto Clemente	110.00	55.00	33.00
(5)	Donn A. Clendenon	9.00	4.50	2.75
(6)	Victor Davalillo	9.00	4.50	2.75
(7)	Dick Donovan	9.00	4.50	2.75
(8)	John A. Edwards	9.00	4.50	2.75
(9)	Robert Friend	12.00	6.00	3.50
(10)	Jim Grant	9.00	4.50	2.75
(11)	Tommy Harper	9.00	4.50	2.75
(12)	Woodie Held	9.00	4.50	2.75
(13)	Joey Jay	9.00	4.50	2.75
(14)	Jack Kralick	9.00	4.50	2.75
(15)	Jerry Lynch	9.00	4.50	2.75
(16)	Jim Maloney	12.00	6.00	3.50
(17)	William S. Mazeroski	15.00	7.50	4.50
(18)	Alvin McBean	9.00	4.50	2.75
(19)	Joe Nuxhall	12.00	6.00	3.50
(20)	Jim Pagliaroni	9.00	4.50	2.75
(21)	Vada E. Pinson Jr.	15.00	7.50	4.50
(22)	Robert T. Purkey	9.00	4.50	2.75
(23)	Pedro Ramos	9.00	4.50	2.75
(24)	Frank Robinson	60.00	30.00	18.00
(25)	John Romano	9.00	4.50	2.75
(26)	Pete Rose	325.00	162.00	97.00
(27)	John Tsitouris	9.00	4.50	2.75

		NR MT	EX	VG
Complete Set:		900.00	450.00	270.00
Common Player:		9.00	4.50	2.75
(1)	Hank Aaron	100.00	50.00	30.00
(2)	Max Alvis	9.00	4.50	2.75
(3)	Jose Azcue	9.00	4.50	2.75
(4)	Bob Bailey	9.00	4.50	2.75
(5)	Frank Bolling	9.00	4.50	2.75
(6)	Leonardo Cardenas	9.00	4.50	2.75
(7)	Rico Ricardo Carty	12.00	6.00	3.50
(8)	Donn A. Clendenon	9.00	4.50	2.75
(9)	Tony Cloninger	9.00	4.50	2.75
(10)	Gordon Coleman	9.00	4.50	2.75
(11)	Victor Davalillo	9.00	4.50	2.75
(12)	John A. Edwards	9.00	4.50	2.75
(13)	Sam Ellis	9.00	4.50	2.75
(14)	Robert Friend	12.00	6.00	3.50
(15)	Tommy Harper	9.00	4.50	2.75
(16)	Chuck Hinton	9.00	4.50	2.75
(17)	Dick Howser	12.00	6.00	3.50
(18)	Joey Jay	9.00	4.50	2.75
(19)	Deron Johnson	9.00	4.50	2.75
(20)	Jack Kralick	9.00	4.50	2.75
(21)	Denny Lemaster	9.00	4.50	2.75
(22)	Jerry Lynch	9.00	4.50	2.75
(23)	Jim Maloney	12.00	6.00	3.50
(24)	Lee Maye	9.00	4.50	2.75
(25)	Williams S. Mazeroski	15.00	7.50	4.50
(26)	Alvin McBean	9.00	4.50	2.75
(27)	Bill McCool	9.00	4.50	2.75
(28)	Sam McDowell	12.00	6.00	3.50
(29)	Donald McMahon	9.00	4.50	2.75
(30)	Denis Menke	9.00	4.50	2.75
(31)	Joe Nuxhall	12.00	6.00	3.50
(32)	Gene Oliver	9.00	4.50	2.75
(33)	Jim O'Toole	9.00	4.50	2.75
(34)	Jim Pagliaroni	9.00	4.50	2.75
(35)	Vada E. Pinson Jr.	15.00	7.50	4.50
(36)	Frank Robinson	60.00	30.00	18.00
(37)	Pete Rose	225.00	112.00	67.00
(38)	Willie Stargell	50.00	25.00	15.00
(39)	Ralph W. Terry	9.00	4.50	2.75
(40)	Luis Tiant	15.00	7.50	4.50
(41)	Joe Torre	17.50	8.75	5.25
(42)	John Tsitouris	9.00	4.50	2.75
(43)	Robert A. Veale Jr.	9.00	4.50	2.75
(44)	Bill Virdon	12.00	6.00	3.50
(45)	Leon Wagner	9.00	4.50	2.75

1966 Kahn's Wieners

1967 Kahn's Wieners

The fourth new format in five years greeted collector's with the introduction of Kahn's 1966 issue of 32 cards. Design consisted of a color photo bordered by white and yellow vertical stripes. The player's name was printed above the photo, and a facsimile autograph appeared across the photo. As printed, the cards were 2-13/16'' by 4'' in size. However, the top portion consisted of a 2-13/16'' by 1-3/8'' advertising panel with a red rose logo and the word ''Kahn's,'' separated from the player portion of the card by a black dotted line. Naturally, many of the cards are found today with the top portion cut off. Values listed here are for cards with the top portion intact. Players from the Cincinnati Reds, Pittsburgh Pirates, Cleveland Indians and Atlanta Braves were included in the set. Since the cards are blank-backed, collectors must learn to differentiate player poses to determine year of issue for some cards.

Retaining the basic format of the 1966 set (see listing for description), the '67 Kahn's set was expanded to 41 players through the addition of several N.Y. Mets players to the previous season's lineup of Reds, Pirates, Indians and Braves. Making the 1967 set especially challenging for collectors is the fact that some cards are found in a smaller size and/or with different colored stripes bordering the color player photo. On the majority of cards, the size remained 2-13/16'' by 4'' (with ad at top; 2-13/16'' by 2-5/8'' without ad at top). However, because of packing in different products, the Ellis, Helms and Torre cards can be found in 2-13/16'' by 3-1/4'' size (with ad; 2-13/16'' by 2-1/8'' without ad). The handful of known border stripe variations are listed below. Values quoted are for cards with the top ad panel intact. The more expensive variation cards are not included in the valuations given below for complete sets.

		NR MT	EX	VG
Complete Set:		1000.00	500.00	300.00
Common Player:		13.00	6.50	4.00
(1)	Henry Aaron	110.00	55.00	33.00
(2)	Felipe Alou	17.50	8.75	5.25
(3)	Max Alvis	13.00	6.50	4.00
(4)	Robert Bailey	13.00	6.50	4.00
(5)	Wade Blasingame	13.00	6.50	4.00
(6)	Frank Bolling	13.00	6.50	4.00
(7)	Leo Cardenas	13.00	6.50	4.00
(8)	Roberto Clemente	100.00	50.00	30.00
(9)	Tony Cloninger	13.00	6.50	4.00
(10)	Vic Davalillo	13.00	6.50	4.00
(11)	John Edwards	13.00	6.50	4.00
(12)	Sam Ellis	13.00	6.50	4.00
(13)	Pedro Gonzalez	13.00	6.50	4.00
(14)	Tommy Harper	13.00	6.50	4.00
(15)	Deron Johnson	13.00	6.50	4.00
(16)	Mack Jones	13.00	6.50	4.00
(17)	Denny Lemaster	13.00	6.50	4.00
(18)	Jim Maloney	17.50	8.75	5.25
(19)	William Mazeroski	20.00	10.00	6.00
(20)	Bill McCool	13.00	6.50	4.00
(21)	Sam McDowell	17.50	8.75	5.25
(22)	Denis Menke	13.00	6.50	4.00
(23)	Joe Nuxhall	17.50	8.75	5.25
(24)	Jim Pagliaroni	13.00	6.50	4.00
(25)	Milt Pappas	17.50	8.75	5.25
(26)	Vada Pinson	20.00	10.00	6.00
(27)	Pete Rose	225.00	112.00	67.00
(28)	Sonny Siebert	13.00	6.50	4.00
(29)	Willie Stargell	70.00	35.00	21.00
(30)	Joe Torre	20.00	10.00	6.00
(31)	Bob Veale	13.00	6.50	4.00
(32)	Fred Whitfield	13.00	6.50	4.00

		NR MT	EX	VG
Complete Set:		1000.00	500.00	300.00
Common Player:		13.00	6.50	4.00
(1)	Henry Aaron	110.00	55.00	33.00
(2)	Gene Alley	13.00	6.50	4.00
(3)	Felipe Alou	17.50	8.75	5.25
(4a)	Matty Alou (yellow & white striped border)	17.50	8.75	5.25
(4b)	Matty Alou (red & white striped border)	20.00	10.00	6.00
(5)	Max Alvis	13.00	6.50	4.00
(6)	Ken Boyer	20.00	10.00	6.00
(7)	Leo Cardenas	13.00	6.50	4.00
(8)	Rico Carty	17.50	8.75	5.25
(9)	Tony Cloninger	13.00	6.50	4.00
(10)	Tommy Davis	17.50	8.75	5.25
(11)	John Edwards	13.00	6.50	4.00
(12a)	Sam Ellis (large size)	13.00	6.50	4.00
(12b)	Sam Ellis (small size)	20.00	10.00	6.00
(13)	Jack Fisher	13.00	6.50	4.00
(14)	Steve Hargan	13.00	6.50	4.00
(15)	Tom Harper	13.00	6.50	4.00
(16a)	Tom Helms (large size)	13.00	6.50	4.00
(16b)	Tom Helms (small size)	20.00	10.00	6.00
(17)	Deron Johnson	13.00	6.50	4.00
(18)	Ken Johnson	13.00	6.50	4.00
(19)	Cleon Jones	13.00	6.50	4.00
(20)	Ed Kranepool	13.00	6.50	4.00
(21a)	James Maloney (yellow & white striped border)	17.50	8.75	5.25
(21b)	James Maloney (red & white striped border)	20.00	10.00	6.00
(22)	Lee May	17.50	8.75	5.25
(23)	Wm. Mazeroski	20.00	10.00	6.00
(24)	Wm. McCool	13.00	6.50	4.00
(25)	Sam McDowell	17.50	8.75	5.25
(26)	Dennis Menke (Denis)	13.00	6.50	4.00
(27)	Jim Pagliaroni	13.00	6.50	4.00

		NR MT	EX	VG
(28)	Don Pavletich	13.00	6.50	4.00
(29)	Tony Perez	25.00	12.50	7.50
(30)	Vada Pinson	20.00	10.00	6.00
(31)	Dennis Ribant	13.00	6.50	4.00
(32)	Pete Rose	175.00	87.00	52.00
(33)	Art Shamsky	13.00	6.50	4.00
(34)	Bob Shaw	13.00	6.50	4.00
(35)	Sonny Siebert	13.00	6.50	4.00
(36)	Wm. Stargell (first name actually Wilver)	70.00	35.00	21.00
(37a)	Joe Torre (large size)	20.00	10.00	6.00
(37b)	Joe Torre (small size)	25.00	12.50	7.50
(38)	Bob Veale	13.00	6.50	4.00
(39)	Leon Wagner	13.00	6.50	4.00
(40)	Fred Whitfield	13.00	6.50	4.00
(41)	Woody Woodward	13.00	6.50	4.00

1968 Kahn's Wieners

EARL WILSON

The number of card size and stripe color variations increased with the 1968 Kahn's issue (see 1967 listing), though the basic card design was retained from the previous two seasons: 2-13/16'' by 4'' size (with ad panel at top; 2-13/16'' by 2-5/8'' with ad panel cut off), color photo bordered by yellow and white vertical stripes. In addition to the basic issue, a number of the cards appear in a smaller, 2-13/16'' by 3-1/4,'' size, while some of them, and others, appears with variations in the color of border stripes. One card, Maloney, can be found with a top portion advertising Blue Mountain brand meats, as well as Kahn's. All in all, quite a challenge for the specialist. The 1968 set featured the largest number of teams represented in any Kahn's issue: Atlanta Braves, Chicago Cubs and White Sox, Cincinnati Reds, Cleveland Indians, Detroit Tigers, N.Y. Mets and Pittsburgh Pirates. Values quoted below are for cards with the ad panel at top; complete set prices do not include the scarcer variations.

		NR MT	EX	VG
Complete Set:		1000.00	500.00	300.00
Common Player:		13.00	6.50	4.00
(1a)	Hank Aaron (large size)	110.00	55.00	33.00
(1b)	Hank Aaron (small size)	125.00	62.00	37.00
(2)	Tommy Agee	13.00	6.50	4.00
(3a)	Gene Alley (large size)	13.00	6.50	4.00
(3b)	Gene Alley (small size)	17.50	8.75	5.25
(4)	Felipe Alou	17.50	8.75	5.25
(5a)	Matty Alou (yellow striped border)	17.50	8.75	5.25
(5b)	Matty Alou (red striped border)	20.00	10.00	6.00
(6a)	Max Alvis (large size)	13.00	6.50	4.00
(6b)	Max Alvis (small size)	17.50	8.75	5.25
(7)	Gerry Arrigo	13.00	6.50	4.00
(8)	John Bench	225.00	112.00	67.00

		NR MT	EX	VG
(9a)	Clete Boyer (large size)	13.00	6.50	4.00
(9b)	Clete Boyer (small size)	17.50	8.75	5.25
(10)	Larry Brown	13.00	6.50	4.00
(11a)	Leo Cardenas (large size)	13.00	6.50	4.00
(11b)	Leo Cardenas (small size)	17.50	8.75	5.25
(12a)	Bill Freehan (large size)	17.50	8.75	5.25
(12b)	Bill Freehan (small size)	20.00	10.00	6.00
(13)	Steve Hargan	13.00	6.50	4.00
(14)	Joel Horlen	13.00	6.50	4.00
(15)	Tony Horton	17.50	8.75	5.25
(16)	Willie Horton	17.50	8.75	5.25
(17)	Ferguson Jenkins	25.00	12.50	7.50
(18)	Deron Johnson	13.00	6.50	4.00
(19)	Mack Jones	13.00	6.50	4.00
(20)	Bob Lee	13.00	6.50	4.00
(21a)	Jim Maloney (large size, rose logo)	17.50	8.75	5.25
(21b)	Jim Maloney (large size, blue mountain logo)	20.00	10.00	6.00
(21c)	Jim Maloney (small size, yellow & white striped border)	20.00	10.00	6.00
(21d)	Jim Maloney (small size, yellow, white & green striped border)	20.00	10.00	6.00
(22a)	Lee May (large size)	17.50	8.75	5.25
(22b)	Lee May (small size)	20.00	10.00	6.00
(23a)	Wm. Mazeroski (large size)	17.50	8.75	5.25
(23b)	Wm. Mazeroski (small size)	20.00	10.00	6.00
(24)	Dick McAuliffe	13.00	6.50	4.00
(25)	Bill McCool	13.00	6.50	4.00
(26a)	Sam McDowell (yellow striped border)	17.50	8.75	5.25
(26b)	Sam McDowell (red striped border)	20.00	10.00	6.00
(27a)	Tony Perez (yellow striped border)	25.00	12.50	7.50
(27b)	Tony Perez (red striped border)	30.00	15.00	9.00
(28)	Gary Peters	13.00	6.50	4.00
(29a)	Vada Pinson (large size)	17.50	8.75	5.25
(29b)	Vada Pinson (small size)	20.00	10.00	6.00
(30)	Chico Ruiz	13.00	6.50	4.00
(31a)	Ron Santo (yellow striped border)	17.50	8.75	5.25
(31b)	Ron Santo (red striped border)	20.00	10.00	6.00
(32)	Art Shamsky	13.00	6.50	4.00
(33)	Luis Tiant	17.50	8.75	5.25
(34a)	Joe Torre (large size)	20.00	10.00	6.00
(34b)	Joe Torre (small size)	25.00	12.50	7.50
(35a)	Bob Veale (large size)	13.00	6.50	4.00
(35b)	Bob Veale (small size)	17.50	8.75	5.25
(36)	Leon Wagner	13.00	6.50	4.00
(37)	Billy Williams	40.00	20.00	12.00
(38)	Earl Wilson	13.00	6.50	4.00

1969 Kahn's Wieners

BILLY WILLIAMS

In its 15th and final year of baseball card issue, Kahn's continued the basic format adopted in 1966. The basic card issue of 22 players was printed in 2-13/16'' by 4'' size (with ad panel at top; 2-13/16'' by 2-5/8'' without panel), blank-backed. Teams represented in the set included the Braves, Cubs, White Sox, Reds, Cardinals, Indians and Pirates. The cards featured a color photo and facsimile autograph bordered by yellow and white vertical stripes. At top was an ad panel consisting of the Kahn's red rose logo. However, because some cards were produced for inclusion of packages other than the standard hot dogs, a number of variations in card size and stripe color were created, as noted in the listings below. The smaller size cards, 2-13/16'' by 3-1/4'' with ad, 2-13/16'' by 2-1/8'' without ad, were created by more closely cropping the player photo at top and bottom. Values quoted below are for cards with the top logo panel intact. Complete set values do not include the scarcer variations.

		NR MT	EX	VG
Complete Set:		525.00	262.00	157.00
Common Player:		13.00	6.50	4.00
(1a)	Hank Aaron (large size)	110.00	55.00	33.00
(1b)	Hank Aaron (small size)	125.00	62.00	37.00
(2)	Matty Alou	17.50	8.75	5.25
(3)	Max Alvis	13.00	6.50	4.00
(4)	Gerry Arrigo	13.00	6.50	4.00
(5)	Steve Blass	13.00	6.50	4.00
(6)	Clay Carroll	13.00	6.50	4.00
(7)	Tony Cloninger	13.00	6.50	4.00
(8)	George Culver	13.00	6.50	4.00
(9)	Joel Horlen	13.00	6.50	4.00
(10)	Tony Horton	17.50	8.75	5.25
(11)	Alex Johnson	13.00	6.50	4.00
(12a)	Jim Maloney (large size)	17.50	8.75	5.25
(12b)	Jim Maloney (small size)	20.00	10.00	6.00
(13a)	Lee May (yellow striped border)	17.50	8.75	5.25
(13b)	Lee May (red striped border)	20.00	10.00	6.00
(14a)	Wm. Mazeroski (yellow striped border)	17.50	8.75	5.25
(14b)	Wm. Mazeroski (red striped border)	20.00	10.00	6.00
(15a)	Sam McDowell (yellow striped border)	17.50	8.75	5.25
(15b)	Sam McDowell (red striped border)	20.00	10.00	6.00
(16a)	Tony Perez (large size)	25.00	12.50	7.50
(16b)	Tony Perez (small size)	30.00	15.00	9.00
(17)	Gary Peters	13.00	6.50	4.00
(18a)	Ron Santo (yellow striped border)	17.50	8.75	5.25
(18b)	Ron Santo (red striped border)	20.00	10.00	6.00
(19)	Luis Tiant	17.50	8.75	5.25
(20)	Joe Torre	20.00	10.00	6.00
(21)	Bob Veale	13.00	6.50	4.00
(22)	Billy Williams	40.00	20.00	12.00

1987 Kahn's Wieners Reds

 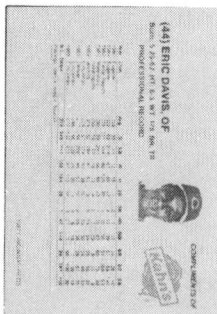

(44) ERIC DAVIS, OF

After a nearly 20-year layoff, Kahn's Wieners produced a baseball card set. Kahn's, who produced card sets between 1955 and 1968, sponsored a 28-card set that was distributed to fans attending the August 2nd game at Riverfront Stadium. The cards are the standard 2½'' by 3½'' size. The fronts offer a full-color player photo bordered in red and white. The

backs carry the Kahn's logo and a head shot of the player.

		MT	NR MT	EX
Complete Set:		12.00	9.00	4.75
Common Player:		.20	.15	.08
6	Bo Diaz	.25	.20	.10
10	Terry Francona	.20	.15	.08
11	Kurt Stillwell	.50	.40	.20
12	Nick Esasky	.30	.25	.12
13	Dave Concepcion	.40	.30	.15
15	Barry Larkin	.70	.50	.30
16	Ron Oester	.20	.15	.08
21	Paul O'Neill	.35	.25	.14
23	Lloyd McClendon	.25	.20	.10
25	Buddy Bell	.40	.30	.15
28	Kal Daniels	1.00	.70	.40
29	Tracy Jones	.60	.45	.25
30	Guy Hoffman	.20	.15	.08
31	John Franco	.40	.30	.15
32	Tom Browning	.30	.25	.12
33	Ron Robinson	.25	.20	.10
34	Bill Gullickson	.25	.20	.10
35	Pat Pacillo	.30	.25	.12
39	Dave Parker	.60	.45	.25
43	Bill Landrum	.25	.20	.10
44	Eric Davis	2.00	1.50	.80
46	Rob Murphy	.30	.25	.12
47	Frank Williams	.25	.20	.10
48	Ted Power	.25	.20	.10

1986 Kas Potato Chips Cardinals

One of a handful of 2⅞'' round baseball card ''discs'' created by Mike Schecter Associates for inclusion regionally in boxes of potato chips, the 20-card Kas set features players of the defending National League Champion St. Louis Cardinals. Fronts feature color photos on which the team logos have been removed from the caps by airbrushing the photos, indicating Kas did not license with the Cardinals for use of its uniform logos. Card backs have minimal personal data and 1985 stats.

		MT	NR MT	EX
Complete Set:		16.00	12.00	6.50
Common Player:		.70	.50	.30
1	Vince Coleman	2.00	1.50	.80
2	Ken Dayley	.70	.50	.30
3	Tito Landrum	.70	.50	.30
4	Steve Braun	.70	.50	.30
5	Danny Cox	1.25	.90	.50
6	Bob Forsch	.80	.60	.30
7	Ozzie Smith	1.50	1.25	.60
8	Brian Harper	.70	.50	.30
9	Jack Clark	1.50	1.25	.60
10	Todd Worrell	2.50	2.00	1.00
11	Joaquin Andujar	.70	.50	.30
12	Tom Nieto	.70	.50	.30
13	Kurt Kepshire	.70	.50	.30
14	Terry Pendleton	1.00	.70	.40
15	Tom Herr	1.00	.70	.40
16	Darrell Porter	.70	.50	.30
17	John Tudor	.90	.70	.35
18	Jeff Lahti	.70	.50	.30
19	Andy Van Slyke	.90	.70	.35
20	Willie McGee	1.50	1.25	.60

1986 Kay Bee

 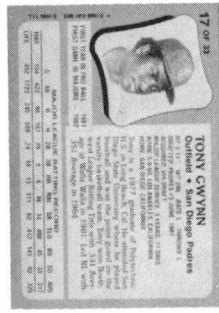

 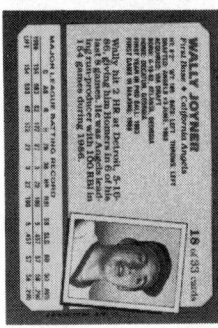

One of the most-widely distributed of the specialty boxed sets of 1986, the Kay Bee toy store chain sets of "Young Superstars of Baseball" was produced by Topps. The 2½" by 3½" cards are printed on white stock with a glossy surface finish. Backs, printed in red and black, are strongly reminiscent of the 1971 Topps cards. While the set concentrated on "young" stars of the game, few of the year's top rookies were included.

		MT	NR MT	EX
Complete Set:		5.00	3.75	2.00
Common Player:		.05	.04	.02
1	Rick Aguilera	.12	.09	.05
2	Chris Brown	.20	.15	.08
3	Tom Browning	.07	.05	.03
4	Tom Brunansky	.07	.05	.03
5	Vince Coleman	.50	.40	.20
6	Ron Darling	.10	.08	.04
7	Alvin Davis	.10	.08	.04
8	Mariano Duncan	.07	.05	.03
9	Shawon Dunston	.07	.05	.03
10	Sid Fernandez	.10	.08	.04
11	Tony Fernandez	.10	.08	.04
12	Brian Fisher	.10	.08	.04
13	John Franco	.07	.05	.03
14	Julio Franco	.10	.08	.04
15	Dwight Gooden	.50	.40	.20
16	Ozzie Guillen	.15	.11	.06
17	Tony Gwynn	.30	.25	.12
18	Jimmy Key	.10	.08	.04
19	Don Mattingly	1.25	.90	.50
20	Oddibe McDowell	.15	.11	.06
21	Roger McDowell	.15	.11	.06
22	Dan Pasqua	.10	.08	.04
23	Terry Pendleton	.07	.05	.03
24	Jim Presley	.10	.08	.04
25	Kirby Puckett	.25	.20	.10
26	Earnie Riles	.10	.08	.04
27	Bret Saberhagen	.15	.11	.06
28	Mark Salas	.05	.04	.02
29	Juan Samuel	.12	.09	.05
30	Jeff Stone	.05	.04	.02
31	Darryl Strawberry	.40	.30	.15
32	Andy Van Slyke	.07	.05	.03
33	Frank Viola	.10	.08	.04

1987 Kay Bee

For a second straight year, Topps produced a 33-card set for the Kay Bee toy store chain. Called "Superstars of Baseball", the cards in the set measure the standard 2½" by 3½" size. The glossy-coated card fronts carry a full-color player photo plus the Kay Bee logo. The card backs, reminiscent of those found in the 1971 Topps set, offer a black and white head shot of the player along with his name, position, personal information, playing record and a brief biography. The set was packaged in a specially designed box.

		MT	NR MT	EX
Complete Set:		4.00	3.00	1.50
Common Player:		.08	.06	.03
1	Harold Baines	.12	.09	.05
2	Jesse Barfield	.12	.09	.05
3	Don Baylor	.08	.06	.03
4	Wade Boggs	.50	.40	.20
5	George Brett	.30	.25	.12
6	Hubie Brooks	.08	.06	.03
7	Jose Canseco	.50	.40	.20
8	Gary Carter	.20	.15	.08
9	Joe Carter	.12	.09	.05
10	Roger Clemens	.30	.25	.12
11	Vince Coleman	.15	.11	.06
12	Glenn Davis	.15	.11	.06
13	Dwight Gooden	.30	.25	.12
14	Pedro Guerrero	.12	.09	.05
15	Tony Gwynn	.25	.20	.10
16	Rickey Henderson	.25	.20	.10
17	Keith Hernandez	.20	.15	.08
18	Wally Joyner	.50	.40	.20
19	Don Mattingly	.70	.50	.30
20	Jack Morris	.15	.11	.06
21	Dale Murphy	.30	.25	.12
22	Eddie Murray	.25	.20	.10
23	Dave Parker	.15	.11	.06
24	Kirby Puckett	.20	.15	.08
25	Tim Raines	.20	.15	.08
26	Jim Rice	.20	.15	.08
27	Dave Righetti	.12	.09	.05
28	Ryne Sandberg	.20	.15	.08
29	Mike Schmidt	.30	.25	.12
30	Mike Scott	.12	.09	.05
31	Darryl Strawberry	.30	.25	.12
32	Fernando Valenzuela	.20	.15	.08
33	Dave Winfield	.20	.15	.08

1986 Keller's Butter Phillies

It's a good thing the Keller's Butter set of six Philadelphia Phillies players is downright unattractive or their value would be sky high. One card was printed on the box of each one pound package of butter. At more than $2 per box, that already makes an expensive set. The 2½" by 2¾" cards feature crude drawings of the players.

		MT	NR MT	EX
Complete Set:		10.00	7.50	4.00
Common Player:		1.00	.70	.40
(1)	Steve Carlton	2.50	2.00	1.00

		MT	NR MT	EX
(2)	Von Hayes	1.75	1.25	.70
(3)	Gary Redus	1.00	.70	.40
(4)	Juan Samuel	1.75	1.25	.70
(5)	Mike Schmidt	5.00	3.75	2.00
(6)	Glenn Wilson	1.50	1.25	.60

1970 Kellogg's

For 14 years in the 1970s and early 1980s, the Kellogg's cereal company provided Topps with virtually the only meaningful national competition in the baseball card market. Kellogg's kicked off its baseball card program in 1970 with a 75-player set of simulated 3-D cards. Single cards were available in selected brands of the company's cereal, while a mail-in program offered complete sets. The 3-D effect was achieved by the sandwiching of a clear color player photo between a purposely blurred stadium background scene and a layer of ribbed plastic. The relatively narrow dimensions of the card, 2¼" by 3½," and the nature of the plastic overlay seem to conspire to cause the cards to curl, often cracking the plastic layer, if not stored properly. Cards with major cracks in the plastic can be considered in Fair condition, at best.

		NR MT	EX	VG
Complete Set:		100.00	50.00	20.00
Common Player: 1-15		.80	.40	.15
Common Player: 16-30		.90	.45	.20
Common Player: 31-75		.80	.40	.15
1	Ed Kranepool	1.50	.40	.15
2	Pete Rose	20.00	10.00	4.00
3	Cleon Jones	.80	.40	.15
4	Willie McCovey	3.50	1.75	.70
5	Mel Stottlemyre	1.00	.50	.20
6	Frank Howard	1.25	.60	.25
7	Tom Seaver	4.00	2.00	.80
8	Don Sutton	2.50	1.25	.50
9	Jim Wynn	.80	.40	.15
10	Jim Maloney	.80	.40	.15
11	Tommie Agee	.80	.40	.15
12	Willie Mays	6.50	3.25	1.25
13	Juan Marichal	3.00	1.50	.60
14	Dave McNally	.90	.45	.20
15	Frank Robinson	3.50	1.75	.70
16	Carlos May	.90	.45	.20
17	Bill Singer	.90	.45	.20
18	Rick Reichardt	.90	.45	.20
19	Boog Powell	1.50	.70	.30
20	Gaylord Perry	3.50	1.75	.70
21	Brooks Robinson	5.00	2.50	1.00
22	Luis Aparicio	3.50	1.75	.70
23	Joel Horlen	.90	.45	.20
24	Mike Epstein	.90	.45	.20
25	Tom Haller	.90	.45	.20
26	Willie Crawford	.90	.45	.20
27	Roberto Clemente	8.00	4.00	1.50
28	Matty Alou	1.25	.60	.25
29	Willie Stargell	4.00	2.00	.80
30	Tim Cullen	.90	.45	.20
31	Randy Hundley	.80	.40	.15

		NR MT	EX	VG
32	Reggie Jackson	6.50	3.25	1.25
33	Rich Allen	1.25	.60	.25
34	Tim McCarver	1.00	.50	.20
35	Ray Culp	.80	.40	.15
36	Jim Fregosi	.90	.45	.20
37	Billy Williams	3.00	1.50	.60
38	Johnny Odom	.80	.40	.15
39	Bert Campaneris	.90	.45	.20
40	Ernie Banks	3.50	1.75	.70
41	Chris Short	.80	.40	.15
42	Ron Santo	.90	.45	.20
43	Glenn Beckert	.80	.40	.15
44	Lou Brock	3.50	1.75	.70
45	Larry Hisle	.80	.40	.15
46	Reggie Smith	.90	.45	.20
47	Rod Carew	4.00	2.00	.80
48	Curt Flood	.90	.45	.20
49	Jim Lonborg	.80	.40	.15
50	Sam McDowell	.90	.45	.20
51	Sal Bando	.90	.45	.20
52	Al Kaline	3.50	1.75	.70
53	Gary Nolan	.80	.40	.15
54	Rico Petrocelli	.80	.40	.15
55	Ollie Brown	.80	.40	.15
56	Luis Tiant	1.25	.60	.25
57	Bill Freehan	.90	.45	.20
58	Johnny Bench	4.00	2.00	.80
59	Joe Pepitone	1.00	.50	.20
60	Bobby Murcer	1.25	.60	.25
61	Harmon Killebrew	3.50	1.75	.70
62	Don Wilson	.80	.40	.15
63	Tony Oliva	1.25	.60	.25
64	Jim Perry	.90	.45	.20
65	Mickey Lolich	1.25	.60	.25
66	Coco Laboy	.80	.40	.15
67	Dean Chance	.80	.40	.15
68	Ken Harrelson	.90	.45	.20
69	Willie Horton	.90	.45	.20
70	Wally Bunker	.80	.40	.15
71a	Bob Gibson (1959 IP blank)	5.00	2.50	1.00
71b	Bob Gibson (1959 IP 76)	3.00	1.50	.60
72	Joe Morgan	3.00	1.50	.60
73	Denny McLain	1.25	.60	.25
74	Tommy Harper	.80	.40	.15
75	Don Mincher	1.25	.40	.15

1971 Kellogg's

 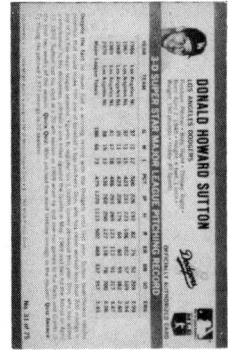

The scarcest and most valuable of the Kellogg's editions, the 75-card 1971 set was the only one not offered by the company on a mail-in basis; the only way to complete it was to buy . . . and buy and buy . . . boxes of cereal. Kellogg's again used the simulated 3-D effect in the cards' design, with the same result being many of the 2¼" by 3½" cards are found today with cracks resulting from the cards' curling. A number of scarcer back variations are checklisted below. In addition, all 75 cards can be found with and without the 1970 date before the "Xograph" copyright line on the back; though there is no difference in value.

	NR MT	EX	VG
Complete Set:	650.00	325.00	130.00
Common Player:	7.00	3.50	1.50
1a Wayne Simpson (SO 120)	15.00	5.00	2.00
1b Wayne Simpson (SO 119)	10.00	3.50	1.50
2 Tom Seaver	20.00	10.00	4.00
3a Jim Perry (IP 2238)	12.00	6.00	2.50
3b Jim Perry (IP 2239)	8.50	4.25	1.75
4a Bob Robertson (RBI 94)	10.00	5.00	2.00
4b Bob Robertson (RBI 95)	7.00	3.50	1.50
5 Roberto Clemente	25.00	12.50	5.00
6a Gaylord Perry (IP 2014)	18.00	9.00	3.50
6b Gaylord Perry (IP 2015)	12.50	6.25	2.50
7a Felipe Alou (1970 Oakland NL)	12.00	6.00	2.50
7b Felipe Alou (1970 Oakland AL)	8.50	4.25	1.75
8 Denis Menke	7.00	3.50	1.50
9a Don Kessinger (Hits 849)	12.00	6.00	2.50
9b Don Kessinger (Hits 850)	8.50	4.25	1.75
10 Willie Mays	25.00	12.50	5.00
11 Jim Hickman	7.00	3.50	1.50
12 Tony Oliva	10.00	5.00	2.00
13 Manny Sanguillen	7.00	3.50	1.50
14a Frank Howard (1968 Washington NL)			
	15.00	7.50	3.00
14b Frank Howard (1968 Washington AL)			
	10.00	5.00	2.00
15 Frank Robinson	17.50	8.75	3.50
16 Willie Davis	8.50	4.25	1.75
17 Lou Brock	15.00	7.50	3.00
18 Cesar Tovar	7.00	3.50	1.50
19 Luis Aparicio	12.50	6.25	2.50
20 Boog Powell	10.00	5.00	2.00
21a Dick Selma (SO 584)	10.00	5.00	2.00
21b Dick Selma (SO 587)	7.00	3.50	1.50
22 Danny Walton	7.00	3.50	1.50
23 Carl Morton	7.00	3.50	1.50
24a Sonny Siebert (SO 1054)	10.00	5.00	2.00
24b Sonny Siebert (SO 1055)	7.00	3.50	1.50
25 Jim Merritt	7.00	3.50	1.50
26a Jose Cardenal (Hits 828)	10.00	5.00	2.00
26b Jose Cardenal (Hits 829)	7.00	3.50	1.50
27 Don Mincher	7.00	3.50	1.50
28a Clyde Wright (California state logo)			
	7.00	3.50	1.50
28b Clyde Wright (Angels crest logo)	10.00	5.00	2.00
29 Les Cain	7.00	3.50	1.50
30 Danny Cater	7.00	3.50	1.50
31 Don Sutton	12.50	6.25	2.50
32 Chuck Dobson	7.00	3.50	1.50
33 Willie McCovey	15.00	7.50	3.00
34 Mike Epstein	7.00	3.50	1.50
35a Paul Blair (Runs 386)	10.00	5.00	2.00
35b Paul Blair (Runs 385)	7.00	3.50	1.50
36 Gary Nolan	7.00	3.50	1.50
37 Sam McDowell	8.50	4.25	1.75
38 Amos Otis	8.50	4.25	1.75
39a Ray Fosse (RBI 69)	10.00	5.00	2.00
39b Ray Fosse (RBI 70)	7.00	3.50	1.50
40 Mel Stottlemyre	8.50	4.25	1.75
41 Cito Gaston	7.00	3.50	1.50
42 Dick Dietz	7.00	3.50	1.50
43 Roy White	8.50	4.25	1.75
44 Al Kaline	17.50	8.75	3.50
45 Carlos May	7.00	3.50	1.50
46a Tommie Agee (RBI 313)	10.00	5.00	2.00
46b Tommie Agee (RBI 314)	7.00	3.50	1.50
47 Tommy Harper	7.00	3.50	1.50
48 Larry Dierker	7.00	3.50	1.50
49 Mike Cuellar	8.50	4.25	1.75
50 Ernie Banks	15.00	7.50	3.00
51 Bob Gibson	15.00	7.50	3.00
52 Reggie Smith	8.50	4.25	1.75
53a Matty Alou (RBI 273)	12.00	6.00	2.50
53b Matty Alou (RBI 274)	8.50	4.25	1.75
54a Alex Johnson (California state logo)			
	7.00	3.50	1.50
54b Alex Johnson (Angels crest logo)	10.00	5.00	2.00
55 Harmon Killebrew	15.00	7.50	3.00
56 Billy Grabarkewitz	7.00	3.50	1.50
57 Rich Allen	10.00	5.00	2.00
58 Tony Perez	10.00	5.00	2.00
59a Dave McNally (SO 1065)	12.00	6.00	2.50
59b Dave McNally (SO 1067)	8.50	4.25	1.75
60a Jim Palmer (SO 564)	18.00	9.00	3.50
60b Jim Palmer (SO 567)	12.50	6.25	2.50
61 Billy Williams	12.50	6.25	2.50
62 Joe Torre	10.00	5.00	2.00
63a Jim Northrup (AB 2773)	10.00	5.00	2.00
63b Jim Northrup (AB 2772)	7.00	3.50	1.50
64a Jim Fregosi (Calif. state logo - Hits 1326)			
	10.00	5.00	2.00

	NR MT	EX	VG
64b Jim Fregosi (Calif. state logo - Hits 1327)			
	7.00	3.50	1.50
64c Jim Fregosi (Angels crest logo)	10.00	5.00	2.00
65 Pete Rose	60.00	30.00	12.00
66a Bud Harrelson	10.00	5.00	2.00
66b Bud Harrelson	7.00	3.50	1.50
67 Tony Taylor	7.00	3.50	1.50
68 Willie Stargell	12.50	6.25	2.50
69 Tony Horton	8.50	4.25	1.75
70a Claude Osteen (no number)	15.00	7.50	3.00
70b Claude Osteen (#70 on back)	7.00	3.50	1.50
71 Glenn Beckert	8.50	4.25	1.75
72 Nate Colbert	7.00	3.50	1.50
73a Rick Monday (AB 1705)	12.00	6.00	2.50
73b Rick Monday (AB 1704)	8.50	4.25	1.75
74a Tommy John (BB 444)	18.00	9.00	3.50
74b Tommy John (BB 443)	13.00	6.50	2.50
75 Chris Short	10.00	3.50	1.50

1972 Kellogg's

 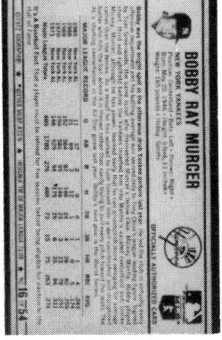

For 1972, Kellogg's reduced both the number of cards in its set and the dimensions of each card, moving to a 2⅛'' by 3¼'' size and fixing the set at 54 cards. Once again, the cards were produced to simulate a 3-D effect (see description for 1970 Kellogg's). Because the cereal company again offered the cards in complete sets via a mail-in offer, the 1972 issue is considerably easier to complete than earlier years. The checklist below includes a considerable number of variations which resulted from the correction of erroneous statistics on the backs of some cards. The complete set values quoted do not include the scarcer variations.

	NR MT	EX	VG
Complete Set:	55.00	28.00	11.00
Common Player:	.70	.35	.14
1a Tom Seaver (1970 ERA 2.85)	9.00	2.25	.90
1b Tom Seaver (1970 ERA 2.81)	6.50	1.75	.70
2 Amos Otis	.80	.40	.15
3a Willie Davis (Runs 842)	1.25	.60	.25
3b Willie Davis (Runs 841)	.80	.40	.15
4 Wilbur Wood	.80	.40	.15
5 Bill Parsons	.70	.35	.14
6 Pete Rose	20.00	10.00	4.00
7a Willie McCovey (HR 360)	5.00	2.50	1.00
7b Willie McCovey (HR 370)	3.50	1.75	.70
8 Fergie Jenkins	1.25	.60	.25
9a Vida Blue (ERA 2.35)	1.50	.70	.30
9b Vida Blue (ERA 2.31)	.90	.45	.20
10 Joe Torre	.90	.45	.20
11 Merv Rettenmund	.70	.35	.14
12 Bill Melton	.70	.35	.14
13a Jim Palmer (Games 170)	4.75	2.50	.90
13b Jim Palmer (Games 168)	3.00	1.50	.60
14 Doug Rader	.70	.35	.14
15a Dave Roberts (...Seaver, the NL leader...)			
	1.25	.60	.25
15b Dave Roberts (...Seaver, the league leader...)			
	.70	.35	.14
16 Bobby Murcer	.90	.45	.20
17 Wes Parker	.80	.40	.15

		NR MT	EX	VG
18a	Joe Coleman (BB 394)	1.25	.60	.25
18b	Joe Coleman (BB 393)	.70	.35	.14
19	Manny Sanguillen	.70	.35	.14
20	Reggie Jackson	4.50	2.25	.90
21	Ralph Garr	.70	.35	.14
22	Jim "Catfish" Hunter	2.50	1.25	.50
23	Rick Wise	.70	.35	.14
24	Glenn Beckert	.70	.35	.14
25	Tony Oliva	.90	.45	.20
26a	Bob Gibson (SO 2577)	4.75	2.50	.90
26b	Bob Gibson (SO 2578)	3.00	1.50	.60
27a	Mike Cuellar (1971 ERA 3.80)	1.25	.60	.25
27b	Mike Cuellar (1971 ERA 3.08)	.80	.40	.15
28	Chris Speier	.70	.35	.14
29a	Dave McNally (ERA 3.18)	1.25	.60	.25
29b	Dave McNally (ERA 3.15)	.80	.40	.15
30	Chico Cardenas	.70	.35	.14
31a	Bill Freehan (AVG. .263)	1.25	.60	.25
31b	Bill Freehan (AVG. .262)	.80	.40	.15
32a	Bud Harrelson (Hits 634)	1.25	.60	.25
32b	Bud Harrelson (Hits 624)	.70	.35	.14
33a	Sam McDowell (...less than 200 innings...)	1.25	.60	.25
33b	Sam McDowell (...less than 225 innings...)	.80	.40	.15
34a	Claude Osteen (1971 ERA 3.25)	1.25	.60	.25
34b	Claude Osteen (1971 ERA 3.51)	.80	.40	.15
35	Reggie Smith	.80	.40	.15
36	Sonny Siebert	.70	.35	.14
37	Lee May	.80	.40	.15
38	Mickey Lolich	.90	.45	.20
39a	Cookie Rojas (2B 149)	1.25	.60	.25
39b	Cookie Rojas (2B 150)	.70	.35	.14
40	Dick Drago	.70	.35	.14
41	Nate Colbert	.70	.35	.14
42	Andy Messersmith	.80	.40	.15
43a	Dave Johnson (AVG. .262)	1.50	.70	.30
43b	Dave Johnson (AVG. .264)	.90	.45	.20
44	Steve Blass	.70	.35	.14
45	Bob Robertson	.70	.35	.14
46a	Billy Williams (...missed only one last season...)	4.75	2.50	.90
46b	Billy Williams (phrase omitted)	3.00	1.50	.60
47	Juan Marichal	3.00	1.50	.60
48	Lou Brock	3.50	1.75	.70
49	Roberto Clemente	6.50	3.25	1.25
50	Mel Stottlemyre	.90	.45	.20
51	Don Wilson	.70	.35	.14
52a	Sal Bando (RBI 355)	1.25	.60	.25
52b	Sal Bando (RBI 356)	.80	.40	.15
53a	Willie Stargell (2B 197)	4.25	2.25	.80
53b	Willie Stargell (2B 196)	2.50	1.25	.50
54a	Willie Mays (RBI 1855)	12.00	4.25	1.75
54b	Willie Mays (RBI 1856)	8.50	3.25	1.30

1972 Kellogg's All-Time Greats

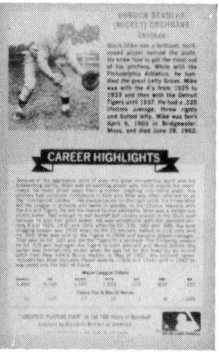

Kellogg's issued a second baseball card set in 1972, inserted into packages of breakfast rolls. The 2¼" by 3½" cards also featured a simulated 3-D effect, but the 15 players in the set were "All-Time Baseball Greats," rather than current players. The '72 Kellogg's ATG set is virtually identical to a Rold Gold pretzel issue of 1970; the only difference being the 1972 copyright date on the back of the Kellogg's cards,

while the pretzel issue bears a 1970 date. The pretzel cards are considerably scarcer than the Kellogg's.

		NR MT	EX	VG
	Complete Set:	14.00	7.00	4.25
	Common Player:	.50	.25	.15
1	Walter Johnson	1.25	.60	.40
2	Rogers Hornsby	.80	.40	.25
3	John McGraw	.50	.25	.15
4	Mickey Cochrane	.50	.25	.15
5	George Sisler	.50	.25	.15
6	Babe Ruth	3.50	1.75	1.00
7	Robert "Lefty" Grove	.70	.35	.20
8	Harold "Pie" Traynor	.50	.25	.15
9	Honus Wagner	.90	.45	.25
10	Eddie Collins	.50	.25	.15
11	Tris Speaker	.70	.35	.20
12	Cy Young	.80	.40	.25
13	Lou Gehrig	2.00	1.00	.60
14	Babe Ruth	3.50	1.75	1.00
15	Ty Cobb	2.00	1.00	.60

1973 Kellogg's

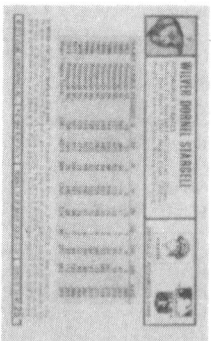

The lone exception to Kellogg's long run of simulated 3-D effect cards came in 1973, when the cereal company's 54-card set was produced by "normal" printing methods. In 2¼" by 3½" size, the design was otherwise quite compatible with the issues which preceded and succeeded it. Because it was available via a mail-in offer, it is not as scarce as some other Kellogg's issues.

		NR MT	EX	VG
	Complete Set:	45.00	22.00	13.50
	Common Player:	.50	.25	.15
1	Amos Otis	.80	.25	.15
2	Ellie Rodriguez	.50	.25	.15
3	Mickey Lolich	.80	.40	.25
4	Tony Oliva	.80	.40	.25
5	Don Sutton	1.25	.60	.40
6	Pete Rose	11.00	5.50	3.25
7	Steve Carlton	4.00	2.00	1.25
8	Bobby Bonds	.70	.35	.20
9	Wilbur Wood	.70	.35	.20
10	Billy Williams	2.50	1.25	.70
11	Steve Blass	.50	.25	.15
12	Jon Matlack	.50	.25	.15
13	Cesar Cedeno	.70	.35	.20
14	Bob Gibson	2.50	1.25	.70
15	Sparky Lyle	.80	.40	.25
16	Nolan Ryan	3.50	1.75	1.00
17	Jim Palmer	2.50	1.25	.70
18	Ray Fosse	.50	.25	.15
19	Bobby Murcer	.80	.40	.25
20	Jim "Catfish" Hunter	2.50	1.25	.70
21	Tug McGraw	.90	.45	.25
22	Reggie Jackson	4.50	2.25	1.25
23	Bill Stoneman	.50	.25	.15
24	Lou Piniella	.90	.45	.25
25	Willie Stargell	2.50	1.25	.70
26	Dick Allen	.90	.45	.25
27	Carlton Fisk	1.25	.60	.40

		NR MT	EX	VG
28	Fergie Jenkins	.90	.45	.25
29	Phil Niekro	1.50	.70	.45
30	Gary Nolan	.50	.25	.15
31	Joe Torre	.90	.45	.25
32	Bobby Tolan	.50	.25	.15
33	Nate Colbert	.50	.25	.15
34	Joe Morgan	2.50	1.25	.70
35	Bert Blyleven	.90	.45	.25
36	Joe Rudi	.70	.35	.20
37	Ralph Garr	.50	.25	.15
38	Gaylord Perry	2.00	1.00	.60
39	Bobby Grich	.80	.40	.25
40	Lou Brock	2.50	1.25	.70
41	Pete Broberg	.50	.25	.15
42	Manny Sanguillen	.50	.25	.15
43	Willie Davis	.70	.35	.20
44	Dave Kingman	.90	.45	.25
45	Carlos May	.50	.25	.15
46	Tom Seaver	4.00	2.00	1.25
47	Mike Cuellar	.70	.35	.20
48	Joe Coleman	.50	.25	.15
49	Claude Osteen	.70	.35	.20
50	Steve Kline	.50	.25	.15
51	Rod Carew	4.00	2.00	1.25
52	Al Kaline	3.50	1.75	1.00
53	Larry Dieker	.50	.25	.15
54	Ron Santo	.90	.45	.25

		NR MT	EX	VG
24	Orlando Cepeda	1.25	.60	.25
25	Ron Hunt	.50	.25	.10
26	Wayne Twitchell	.50	.25	.10
27	Ron Fairly	.70	.35	.14
28	Johnny Bench	3.50	1.75	.70
29	John Mayberry	.50	.25	.10
30	Rod Carew	3.50	1.75	.70
31	Ken Holtzman	.70	.35	.14
32	Billy Williams	2.50	1.25	.50
33	Dick Allen	.80	.40	.15
34a	Wilbur Wood (SO 959)	1.25	.60	.25
34b	Wilbur Wood (SO 960)	.70	.35	.14
35	Danny Thompson	.50	.25	.10
36	Joe Morgan	2.50	1.25	.50
37	Willie Stargell	2.50	1.25	.50
38	Pete Rose	13.00	6.50	2.50
39	Bobby Bonds	.70	.35	.14
40	Chris Speier	.50	.25	.10
41	Sparky Lyle	.80	.40	.15
42	Cookie Rojas	.50	.25	.10
43	Tommy Davis	.70	.35	.14
44	Jim "Catfish" Hunter	2.50	1.25	.50
45	Willie Davis	.70	.35	.14
46	Bert Blyleven	.90	.45	.20
47	Pat Kelly	.50	.25	.10
48	Ken Singleton	.70	.35	.14
49	Manny Mota	.70	.35	.14
50	Dave Johnson	.90	.45	.20
51	Sal Bando	.70	.35	.14
52	Tom Seaver	3.50	1.75	.70
53	Felix Millan	.50	.25	.10
54	Ron Blomberg	.80	.35	.14

1974 Kellogg's

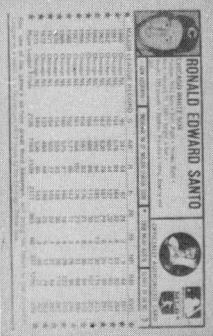

For 1974, Kellogg's returned to the use of simulated 3-D for its 54-player baseball card issue (see 1970 Kellogg's listing for description). In 2⅛" by 3¼" size, the cards were available as a complete set via a mail-in offer.

		NR MT	EX	VG
Complete Set:		40.00	20.00	8.00
Common Player:		.50	.25	.10
1	Bob Gibson	3.50	1.50	.60
2	Rick Monday	.70	.35	.14
3	Joe Coleman	.50	.25	.10
4	Bert Campaneris	.80	.40	.15
5	Carlton Fisk	1.25	.60	.25
6	Jim Palmer	2.50	1.25	.50
7a	Ron Santo (Chicago Cubs)	1.50	.70	.30
7b	Ron Santo (Chicago White Sox)	.80	.40	.15
8	Nolan Ryan	3.50	1.75	.70
9	Greg Luzinski	.80	.40	.15
10a	Buddy Bell (Runs 134)	1.50	.70	.30
10b	Buddy Bell (Runs 135)	.90	.45	.20
11	Bob Watson	.50	.25	.10
12	Bill Singer	.50	.25	.10
13	Dave May	.50	.25	.10
14	Jim Brewer	.50	.25	.10
15	Manny Sanguillen	.50	.25	.10
16	Jeff Burroughs	.50	.25	.10
17	Amos Otis	.50	.25	.10
18	Ed Goodson	.50	.25	.10
19	Nate Colbert	.50	.25	.10
20	Reggie Jackson	4.00	2.00	.80
21	Ted Simmons	.90	.45	.20
22	Bobby Murcer	.80	.40	.15
23	Willie Horton	.70	.35	.14

1975 Kellogg's

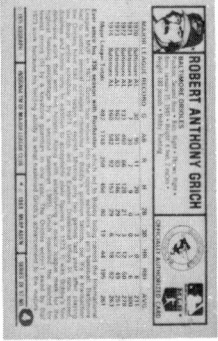

While the card size remained static at 2⅛" by 3¼," the size of the 1975 Kellogg's "3-D" set was increased by three, to 57 cards. Despite the fact cards could be obtained by a mail-in offer, as well as in cereal boxes, the '75 Kellogg's are noticeably scarcer than the company's other issues, with the exception of the 1971 set. Also helping to raise the value of the cards is the presence of an unusually large number of current and future Hall of Famers.

		NR MT	EX	VG
Complete Set:		120.00	60.00	24.00
Common Player:		2.00	1.00	.40
1	Roy White	3.50	1.25	.50
2	Ross Grimsley	2.00	1.00	.40
3	Reggie Smith	2.50	1.25	.50
4a	Bob Grich ("...1973 work..." in last line)	4.00	2.00	.80
4b	Bob Grich (no "...1973 work...")	2.50	1.25	.50
5	Greg Gross	2.00	1.00	.40
6	Bob Watson	2.00	1.00	.40
7	Johnny Bench	11.00	5.50	2.25
8	Jeff Burroughs	2.00	1.00	.40
9	Elliott Maddox	2.00	1.00	.40
10	Jon Matlack	2.00	1.00	.40
11	Pete Rose	23.00	11.50	4.50
12	Leroy Stanton	2.00	1.00	.40
13	Bake McBride	2.00	1.00	.40
14	Jorge Orta	2.00	1.00	.40

		NR MT	EX	VG
15	Al Oliver	2.50	1.25	.50
16	John Briggs	2.00	1.00	.40
17	Steve Garvey	9.00	4.50	1.75
18	Brooks Robinson	9.00	4.50	1.75
19	John Hiller	2.00	1.00	.40
20	Lynn McGlothen	2.00	1.00	.40
21	Cleon Jones	2.00	1.00	.40
22	Fergie Jenkins	2.50	1.25	.50
23	Bill North	2.00	1.00	.40
24	Steve Busby	2.00	1.00	.40
25	Richie Zisk	2.00	1.00	.40
26	Nolan Ryan	10.00	5.00	2.00
27	Joe Morgan	6.50	3.25	1.25
28	Joe Rudi	2.50	1.25	.50
29	Jose Cardenal	2.00	1.00	.40
30	Andy Messersmith	2.00	1.00	.40
31	Willie Montanez	2.00	1.00	.40
32	Bill Buckner	2.50	1.25	.50
33	Rod Carew	10.00	5.00	2.00
34	Lou Piniella	2.50	1.25	.50
35	Ralph Garr	2.00	1.00	.40
36	Mike Marshall	2.00	1.00	.40
37	Garry Maddox	2.00	1.00	.40
38	Dwight Evans	2.50	1.25	.50
39	Lou Brock	9.00	4.50	1.75
40	Ken Singleton	2.50	1.25	.50
41	Steve Braun	2.00	1.00	.40
42	Dick Allen	2.50	1.25	.50
43	Johnny Grubb	2.00	1.00	.40
44a	Jim Hunter (Oakland)	12.00	6.00	2.50
44b	Jim Hunter (New York)	8.00	4.00	1.50
45	Gaylord Perry	6.50	3.25	1.25
46	George Hendrick	2.50	1.25	.50
47	Sparky Lyle	2.50	1.25	.50
48	Dave Cash	2.00	1.00	.40
49	Luis Tiant	2.50	1.25	.50
50	Cesar Geronimo	2.00	1.00	.40
51	Carl Yastrzemski	17.00	8.50	3.50
52	Ken Brett	2.00	1.00	.40
53	Hal McRae	2.50	1.25	.50
54	Reggie Jackson	11.00	5.50	2.25
55	Rollie Fingers	3.50	1.75	.70
56	Mike Schmidt	13.00	6.50	2.50
57	Richie Hebner	2.50	1.00	.40

		NR MT	EX	VG
6a	Clay Carroll (Cincinnati)	2.75	1.50	.80
6b	Clay Carroll (Chicago)	1.50	.70	.45
7	Joe Rudi	1.50	.70	.45
8	Reggie Jackson	10.00	5.00	3.00
9	Felix Millan	1.25	.60	.40
10	Jim Rice	9.00	4.50	2.75
11	Bert Blyleven	2.50	1.25	.70
12	Ken Singleton	1.50	.70	.45
13	Don Sutton	2.50	1.25	.70
14	Joe Morgan	5.00	2.50	1.50
15	Dave Parker	5.00	2.50	1.50
16	Dave Cash	1.25	.60	.40
17	Ron LeFlore	1.25	.60	.40
18	Greg Luzinski	2.00	1.00	.60
19	Dennis Eckersley	2.00	1.00	.60
20	Bill Madlock	2.50	1.25	.70
21	George Scott	1.25	.60	.40
22	Willie Stargell	4.50	2.25	1.25
23	Al Hrabosky	1.25	.60	.40
24	Carl Yastrzemski	13.00	6.50	4.00
25	Jim Kaat	2.50	1.25	.70
26	Marty Perez	1.25	.60	.40
27	Bob Watson	1.25	.60	.40
28	Eric Soderholm	1.25	.60	.40
29	Bill Lee	1.25	.60	.40
30a	Frank Tanana (1975 ERA 2.63)	2.50	1.25	.70
30b	Frank Tanana (1975 ERA 2.62)	1.50	.70	.45
31	Fred Lynn	3.50	1.75	1.00
32a	Tom Seaver (1967 PCT. 552)	10.00	5.00	3.00
32b	Tom Seaver (1967 Pct. .552)	8.00	4.00	2.50
33	Steve Busby	1.25	.60	.40
34	Gary Carter	10.00	5.00	3.00
35	Rick Wise	1.25	.60	.40
36	Johnny Bench	10.00	5.00	3.00
37	Jim Palmer	8.00	4.00	2.50
38	Bobby Murcer	2.00	1.00	.60
39	Von Joshua	1.25	.60	.40
40	Lou Brock	8.00	4.00	2.50
41a	Mickey Rivers (last line begins "In three...")	2.50	1.25	.70
41b	Mickey Rivers (last line begins "The Yankees...")	1.50	.70	.45
42	Manny Sanguillen	1.25	.60	.40
43	Jerry Reuss	1.50	.70	.45
44	Ken Griffey	1.50	.70	.45
45a	Jorge Orta (AB 1616)	2.25	1.25	.70
45b	Jorge Orta (AB 1615)	1.25	.60	.40
46	John Mayberry	1.25	.60	.40
47a	Vida Blue (2nd line reads "...pitched more innings...")	3.00	1.50	.90
47b	Vida Blue (2nd line reads "...struck out more...")	2.00	1.00	.60
48	Rod Carew	10.00	5.00	3.00
49a	Jon Matlack (1975 ER 87)	2.25	1.25	.70
49b	Jon Matlack (1975 ER 86)	1.25	.60	.40
50	Boog Powell	2.50	1.25	.70
51a	Mike Hargrove (AB 935)	2.25	1.25	.70
51b	Mike Hargrove (AB 934)	1.25	.60	.40
52a	Paul Lindblad (1975 ERA 2.72)	2.25	1.25	.70
52b	Paul Lindblad (1975 ERA 2.73)	1.25	.60	.40
53	Thurman Munson	6.50	3.25	2.00
54	Steve Garvey	8.00	4.00	2.50
55	Pete Rose	18.00	9.00	5.50
56a	Greg Gross (Games 302)	2.25	1.25	.70
56b	Greg Gross (Games 334)	1.25	.60	.40
57	Ted Simmons	2.50	1.00	.40

1976 Kellogg's

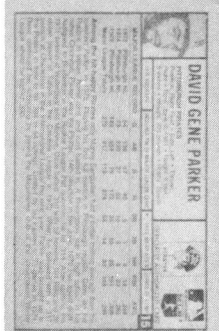

A sizeable list of corrected errors and other variation cards dots the checklist for the 57-card 1976 Kellogg's 3-D set. Again containing 57 cards, the first three cards in the set are found far less often than cards #4-57, indicating they were short-printed in relation to the rest of the set. The complete set values quoted below do not include the scarcer variation cards. Card size remained at 2⅛" by 3¼."

		NR MT	EX	VG
Complete Set:		65.00	32.00	19.50
Common Player:		1.25	.60	.40
1	Steve Hargan	10.00	5.00	3.00
2	Claudell Washington	10.00	5.00	3.00
3	Don Gullett	10.00	5.00	3.00
4	Randy Jones	1.25	.60	.40
5	Jim "Catfish" Hunter	6.50	3.25	2.00

1977 Kellogg's

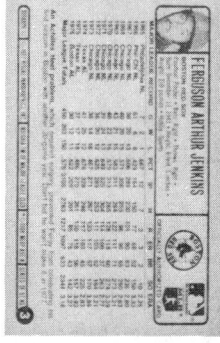

Other than another innovative card design to complement the simulated 3-D effect, there was little change in the 1977 Kellogg's issue. Set size remained at 57 cards, the cards remained in the 2⅛'' by 3¼'' format, and the cards were available either individually in boxes of cereal, or as a complete set via a mail-in box top offer. The 1977 set is the last in which Kellogg's used a player portrait photo on the back of the card.

		NR MT	EX	VG
	Complete Set:	40.00	20.00	8.00
	Common Player:	.40	.20	.08
1	George Foster	.90	.40	.15
2	Bert Campaneris	.70	.35	.14
3	Fergie Jenkins	.90	.45	.20
4	Dock Ellis	.40	.20	.08
5	John Montefusco	.40	.20	.08
6	George Brett	8.50	4.25	1.75
7	John Candelaria	.50	.25	.10
8	Fred Norman	.40	.20	.08
9	Bill Travers	.40	.20	.08
10	Hal McRae	.70	.35	.14
11	Doug Rau	.40	.20	.08
12	Greg Luzinski	.70	.35	.14
13	Ralph Garr	.40	.20	.08
14	Steve Garvey	4.50	2.25	.90
15	Rick Manning	.40	.20	.08
16	Lyman Bostock	.50	.25	.10
17	Randy Jones	.40	.20	.08
18a	Ron Cey (58 homers in first sentence)			
		1.25	.60	.25
18b	Ron Cey (48 homers in first sentence)			
		.80	.40	.15
19	Dave Parker	1.25	.60	.25
20	Pete Rose	11.00	5.50	2.25
21a	Wayne Garland (last line begins "Prior to...")			
		.90	.45	.20
21b	Wayne Garland (last line begins "There he...")			
		.40	.20	.08
22	Bill North	.40	.20	.08
23	Thurman Munson	2.50	1.25	.50
24	Tom Poquette	.40	.20	.08
25	Ron LeFlore	.50	.25	.10
26	Mark Fidrych	.50	.25	.10
27	Sixto Lezcano	.40	.20	.08
28	Dave Winfield	4.00	2.00	.80
29	Jerry Koosman	.70	.35	.14
30	Mike Hargrove	.40	.20	.08
31	Willie Montanez	.40	.20	.08
32	Don Stanhouse	.40	.20	.08
33	Jay Johnstone	.50	.25	.10
34	Bake McBride	.40	.20	.08
35	Dave Kingman	.90	.45	.20
36	Freddie Patek	.40	.20	.08
37	Garry Maddox	.50	.25	.10
38a	Ken Reitz (last line begins "The previous...")			
		.90	.45	.20
38b	Ken Reitz (last line begins "In late...")			
		.40	.20	.08
39	Bobby Grich	.70	.35	.14
40	Cesar Geronimo	.40	.20	.08
41	Jim Lonborg	.40	.20	.08
42	Ed Figueroa	.40	.20	.08
43	Bill Madlock	.90	.45	.20
44	Jerry Remy	.40	.20	.08
45	Frank Tanana	.50	.25	.10
46	Al Oliver	.90	.45	.20
47	Charlie Hough	.50	.25	.10
48	Lou Piniella	.80	.40	.15
49	Ken Griffey	.70	.35	.14
50	Jose Cruz	.70	.35	.14
51	Rollie Fingers	1.25	.60	.25
52	Chris Chambliss	.50	.25	.10
53	Rod Carew	4.00	2.00	.80
54	Andy Messersmith	.40	.20	.08
55	Mickey Rivers	.50	.25	.10
56	Butch Wynegar	.50	.25	.10
57	Steve Carlton	5.00	1.75	.70

1978 Kellogg's

Besides the substitution of a Tony the Tiger drawing for a player portrait photo on the back of the card,

the 1978 Kellogg's set offered no major changes from the previous few years issues. Cards were once again in the 2⅛'' by 3¼'' format, with 57 cards comprising a complete set. Single cards were available in selected brands of the company's cereal, while complete sets could be obtained by a mail-in offer.

		NR MT	EX	VG
	Complete Set:	40.00	20.00	8.00
	Common Player:	.40	.20	.08
1	Steve Carlton	4.00	1.50	.60
2	Bucky Dent	.70	.35	.14
3	Mike Schmidt	4.00	2.00	.80
4	Ken Griffey	.50	.25	.10
5	Al Cowens	.40	.20	.08
6	George Brett	5.00	2.50	1.00
7	Lou Brock	3.00	1.50	.60
8	Rich Gossage	1.25	.60	.25
9	Tom Johnson	.40	.20	.08
10	George Foster	.80	.40	.15
11	Dave Winfield	3.50	1.75	.70
12	Dan Meyer	.40	.20	.08
13	Chris Chambliss	.50	.25	.10
14	Paul Dade	.40	.20	.08
15	Jeff Burroughs	.40	.20	.08
16	Jose Cruz	.70	.35	.14
17	Mickey Rivers	.50	.25	.10
18	John Candelaria	.50	.25	.10
19	Ellis Valentine	.40	.20	.08
20	Hal McRae	.70	.35	.14
21	Dave Rozema	.40	.20	.08
22	Lenny Randle	.40	.20	.08
23	Willie McCovey	3.00	1.50	.60
24	Ron Cey	.70	.35	.14
25	Eddie Murray	12.00	6.00	2.50
26	Larry Bowa	.70	.35	.14
27	Tom Seaver	3.50	1.75	.70
28	Garry Maddox	.50	.25	.10
29	Rod Carew	4.00	2.00	.80
30	Thurman Munson	2.50	1.25	.50
31	Garry Templeton	.70	.35	.14
32	Eric Soderholm	.40	.20	.08
33	Greg Luzinski	.70	.35	.14
34	Reggie Smith	.50	.25	.10
35	Dave Goltz	.40	.20	.08
36	Tommy John	1.25	.60	.25
37	Ralph Garr	.40	.20	.08
38	Alan Bannister	.40	.20	.08
39	Bob Bailor	.40	.20	.08
40	Reggie Jackson	4.00	2.00	.80
41	Cecil Cooper	.80	.40	.15
42	Burt Hooton	.40	.20	.08
43	Sparky Lyle	.70	.35	.14
44	Steve Ontiveros	.40	.20	.08
45	Rick Reuschel	.50	.25	.10
46	Lyman Bostock	.50	.25	.10
47	Mitchell Page	.40	.20	.08
48	Bruce Sutter	.80	.40	.15
49	Jim Rice	3.50	1.75	.70
50	Bob Forsch	.50	.25	.10
51	Nolan Ryan	3.50	1.75	.70
52	Dave Parker	1.25	.60	.25
53	Bert Blyleven	.90	.45	.20
54	Frank Tanana	.50	.25	.10
55	Ken Singleton	.50	.25	.10
56	Mike Hargrove	.40	.20	.08
57	Don Sutton	2.50	.75	.30

1979 Kellogg's

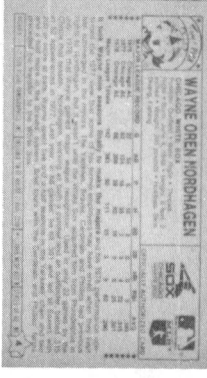

For its 1979 3-D issue, Kellogg's increased the size of the set to 60 cards, but reduced the width of the cards to 1 15/16.'' Depth stayed the same as in previous years, 3¼.'' The narrower card format seems to have compounded the problem of curling and subsequent cracking of the ribbed plastic surface which helps give the card a 3-D effect. Cards with major cracks can be graded no higher than VG. The complete set price in the checklist that follows does not include the scarcer variations. Numerous minor variations featuring copyright and trademark logos can be found in the set.

		NR MT	EX	VG
	Complete Set:	30.00	15.00	6.00
	Common Player:	.30	.15	.06
1	Bruce Sutter	.80	.35	.14
2	Ted Simmons	.70	.35	.14
3	Ross Grimsley	.30	.15	.06
4	Wayne Nordhagen	.30	.15	.06
5a	Jim Palmer (PCT. .649)	2.25	1.25	.45
5b	Jim Palmer (PCT. .650)	1.50	.70	.30
6	John Henry Johnson	.30	.15	.06
7	Jason Thompson	.30	.15	.06
8	Pat Zachry	.30	.15	.06
9	Dennis Eckersley	.50	.25	.10
10a	Paul Splittorff (IP 1665)	.60	.30	.12
10b	Paul Splittorff (IP 1666)	.30	.15	.06
11a	Ron Guidry (Hits 397)	2.00	1.00	.40
11b	Ron Guidry (Hits 396)	1.25	.60	.25
12	Jeff Burroughs	.30	.15	.06
13	Rod Carew	2.50	1.25	.50
14a	Buddy Bell (no trade line in bio)	1.25	.60	.25
14b	Buddy Bell (trade line in bio)	.70	.35	.14
15	Jim Rice	2.50	1.25	.50
16	Garry Maddox	.50	.25	.10
17	Willie McCovey	2.50	1.25	.50
18	Steve Carlton	2.50	1.25	.50
19a	J. R. Richard (stats begin with 1972)			
		.60	.30	.12
19b	J. R. Richard (stats begin with 1971)			
		.30	.15	.06
20	Paul Molitor	.90	.45	.20
21a	Dave Parker (AVG. .281)	2.00	1.00	.40
21b	Dave Parker (AVG. .318)	1.25	.60	.25
22	Pete Rose	8.00	4.00	1.50
23a	Vida Blue (Runs 819)	1.25	.60	.25
23b	Vida Blue (Runs 818)	.70	.35	.14
24	Richie Zisk	.30	.15	.06
25a	Darrell Porter (2B 101)	.90	.45	.20
25b	Darrell Porter (2B 111)	.50	.25	.10
26a	Dan Driessen (Games 642)	.90	.45	.20
26b	Dan Driessen (Games 742)	.50	.25	.10
27	Geoff Zahn	.30	.15	.06
28	Phil Niekro	1.25	.60	.25
29	Tom Seaver	2.50	1.25	.50
30	Fred Lynn	1.00	.50	.20
31	Bill Bonham	.30	.15	.06
32	George Foster	.80	.40	.15
33a	Terry Puhl (last line of bio begins "Terry...")			
		.60	.30	.12

		NR MT	EX	VG
33b	Terry Puhl (last line of bio begins "His...")			
		.30	.15	.06
34a	John Candelaria (age is 24)	.90	.45	.20
34b	John Candelaria (age is 25)	.50	.25	.10
35	Bob Knepper	.50	.25	.10
36	Freddie Patek	.30	.15	.06
37	Chris Chambliss	.50	.25	.10
38a	Bob Forsch (1977 Games 86)	.90	.45	.20
38b	Bob Forsch (1977 Games 35)	.50	.25	.10
39a	Ken Griffey (1978 AB 674)	.90	.45	.20
39b	Ken Griffey (1978 AB 614)	.50	.25	.10
40	Jack Clark	.90	.45	.20
41	Dwight Evans	.90	.45	.20
42	Lee Mazzilli	.50	.25	.10
43	Mario Guerrero	.30	.15	.06
44	Larry Bowa	.50	.25	.10
45a	Carl Yastrzemski (Games 9930)	6.00	3.00	1.25
45b	Carl Yastrzemski (Games 9929)	4.00	2.00	.80
46a	Reggie Jackson (1978 Games 162)			
		5.00	2.50	1.00
46b	Reggie Jackson (1978 Games 139)			
		3.00	1.50	.60
47	Rick Reuschel	.50	.25	.10
48a	Mike Flanagan (1976 SO 57)	.90	.45	.20
48b	Mike Flanagan (1976 SO 56)	.50	.25	.10
49	Gaylord Perry	1.25	.60	.25
50	George Brett	3.50	1.75	.70
51a	Craig Reynolds (last line of bio begins "He spent...")			
		.60	.30	.12
51b	Craig Reynolds (last line of bio begins "In those...")			
		.30	.15	.06
52	Davey Lopes	.50	.25	.10
53a	Bill Almon (2B 31)	.60	.30	.12
53b	Bill Almon (2B 41)	.30	.15	.06
54	Roy Howell	.30	.15	.06
55	Frank Tanana	.50	.25	.10
56a	Doug Rau (1978 PCT. .577)	.60	.30	.12
56b	Doug Rau (1978 PCT. .625)	.30	.15	.06
57a	Rick Monday (1976 Runs 197)	.90	.45	.20
57b	Rick Monday (1976 Runs 107)	.50	.25	.10
58	Jon Matlack	.30	.15	.06
59a	Ron Jackson (last line of bio begins "His best...")			
		.60	.30	.12
59b	Ron Jackson (last line of bio begins "The Twins...")			
		.30	.15	.06
60	Jim Sundberg	.50	.20	.08

1980 Kellogg's

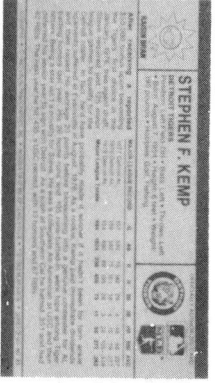

The 1980 cereal company issue featured the narrowest format of any Kellogg's card, 1⅞'' by 3¼.'' For the second straight year, set size remained at 60 cards, available either singly in boxes of cereal, or as complete sets by a mail-in offer.

		NR MT	EX	VG
	Complete Set:	20.00	10.00	4.00
	Common Player:	.30	.15	.06
1	Ross Grimsley	.30	.15	.06
2	Mike Schmidt	2.50	1.25	.50
3	Mike Flanagan	.40	.20	.08
4	Ron Guidry	.90	.45	.20

		NR MT	EX	VG
5	Bert Blyleven	.80	.40	.15
6	Dave Kingman	.80	.40	.15
7	Jeff Newman	.30	.15	.06
8	Steve Rogers	.30	.15	.06
9	George Brett	3.00	1.50	.60
10	Bruce Sutter	.70	.35	.14
11	Gorman Thomas	.50	.25	.10
12	Darrell Porter	.40	.20	.08
13	Roy Smalley	.30	.15	.06
14	Steve Carlton	1.50	.70	.30
15	Jim Palmer	1.25	.60	.25
16	Bob Bailor	.30	.15	.06
17	Jason Thompson	.30	.15	.06
18	Graig Nettles	.80	.40	.15
19	Ron Cey	.50	.25	.10
20	Nolan Ryan	1.50	.70	.30
21	Ellis Valentine	.30	.15	.06
22	Larry Hisle	.30	.15	.06
23	Dave Parker	.90	.45	.20
24	Eddie Murray	3.00	1.50	.60
25	Willie Stargell	1.25	.60	.25
26	Reggie Jackson	2.50	1.25	.50
27	Carl Yastrzemski	3.50	1.75	.70
28	Andre Thornton	.40	.20	.08
29	Davey Lopes	.40	.20	.08
30	Ken Singleton	.40	.20	.08
31	Steve Garvey	2.50	1.25	.50
32	Dave Winfield	2.50	1.25	.50
33	Steve Kemp	.40	.20	.08
34	Claudell Washington	.40	.20	.08
35	Pete Rose	6.50	3.25	1.25
36	Cesar Cedeno	.40	.20	.08
37	John Stearns	.30	.15	.06
38	Lee Mazzilli	.30	.15	.06
39	Larry Bowa	.40	.20	.08
40	Fred Lynn	.80	.40	.15
41	Carlton Fisk	.90	.45	.20
42	Vida Blue	.50	.25	.10
43	Keith Hernandez	1.25	.60	.25
44	Jim Rice	2.00	1.00	.40
45	Ted Simmons	.80	.40	.15
46	Chet Lemon	.30	.15	.06
47	Fergie Jenkins	.50	.25	.10
48	Gary Matthews	.40	.20	.08
49	Tom Seaver	2.50	1.25	.50
50	George Foster	.70	.35	.14
51	Phil Niekro	1.25	.60	.25
52	Johnny Bench	2.50	1.25	.50
53	Buddy Bell	.80	.40	.15
54	Lance Parrish	.90	.45	.20
55	Joaquin Andujar	.30	.15	.06
56	Don Baylor	.50	.25	.10
57	Jack Clark	.80	.40	.15
58	J.R. Richard	.30	.15	.06
59	Bruce Bochte	.30	.15	.06
60	Rod Carew	3.00	1.50	.60

		MT	NR MT	EX
Complete Set:		10.00	5.00	2.50
Common Player:		.08	.04	.02
1	George Foster	.15	.08	.04
2	Jim Palmer	.30	.15	.08
3	Reggie Jackson	.70	.35	.20
4	Al Oliver	.15	.08	.04
5	Mike Schmidt	.70	.35	.20
6	Nolan Ryan	.40	.20	.10
7	Bucky Dent	.10	.05	.03
8	George Brett	.70	.35	.20
9	Jim Rice	.40	.20	.10
10	Steve Garvey	.40	.20	.10
11	Willie Stargell	.30	.15	.08
12	Phil Niekro	.25	.13	.06
13	Dave Parker	.25	.13	.06
14	Cesar Cedeno	.10	.05	.03
15	Don Baylor	.10	.05	.03
16	J.R. Richard	.08	.04	.02
17	Tony Perez	.15	.08	.04
18	Eddie Murray	.70	.35	.20
19	Chet Lemon	.08	.04	.02
20	Ben Oglivie	.08	.04	.02
21	Dave Winfield	.45	.25	.11
22	Joe Morgan	.20	.10	.05
23	Vida Blue	.10	.05	.03
24	Willie Wilson	.15	.08	.04
25	Steve Henderson	.08	.04	.02
26	Rod Carew	.50	.25	.13
27	Garry Templeton	.10	.05	.03
28	Dave Concepcion	.10	.05	.03
29	Davey Lopes	.10	.05	.03
30	Ken Landreaux	.08	.04	.02
31	Keith Hernandez	.40	.20	.10
32	Cecil Cooper	.10	.05	.03
33	Rickey Henderson	.60	.30	.15
34	Frank White	.10	.05	.03
35	George Hendrick	.08	.04	.02
36	Reggie Smith	.10	.05	.03
37	Tug McGraw	.15	.08	.04
38	Tom Seaver	.45	.25	.11
39	Ken Singleton	.10	.05	.03
40	Fred Lynn	.20	.10	.05
41	Rich "Goose" Gossage	.20	.10	.05
42	Terry Puhl	.08	.04	.02
43	Larry Bowa	.10	.05	.03
44	Phil Garner	.08	.04	.02
45	Ron Guidry	.25	.13	.06
46	Lee Mazzilli	.08	.04	.02
47	Dave Kingman	.15	.08	.04
48	Carl Yastrzemski	.80	.40	.20
49	Rick Burleson	.08	.04	.02
50	Steve Carlton	.45	.25	.11
51	Alan Trammell	.30	.15	.08
52	Tommy John	.25	.13	.06
53	Paul Molitor	.20	.10	.05
54	Joe Charboneau	.08	.04	.02
55	Rick Langford	.08	.04	.02
56	Bruce Sutter	.10	.05	.03
57	Robin Yount	.35	.20	.09
58	Steve Stone	.08	.04	.02
59	Larry Gura	.08	.04	.02
60	Mike Flanagan	.10	.05	.03
61	Bob Horner	.20	.10	.05
62	Bruce Bochte	.08	.04	.02
63	Pete Rose	1.00	.50	.25
64	Buddy Bell	.15	.08	.04
65	Johnny Bench	.50	.25	.13
66	Mike Hargrove	.08	.04	.02

1981 Kellogg's

"Bigger" is the word to best describe Kellogg's 1981 card set. Not only were the cards themselves larger than ever before (or since) at 2½" by 3½," but the size of the set was increased to 66, the largest since the 75-card issues of 1970-1971. The '81 Kellogg's set was available only as complete sets by mail. It is thought that the wider format of the '81s may help prevent the problems of curling and cracking from which other years of Kellogg's issues suffer.

1982 Kellogg's

For the second straight year in 1982, Kellogg's cards were not inserted into cereal boxes, but had to be obtained by sending cash and box tops to the company for complete sets. The '82 cards were downsized both in number of cards in the set — 64 — and in physical dimensions, 2⅛" by 3¼."

Definitions for grading conditions are located in the Introduction of this price guide.

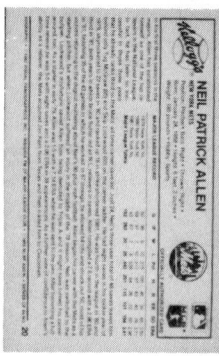

	MT	NR MT	EX
Complete Set:	12.00	6.00	3.00
Common Player:	.12	.06	.03

		MT	NR MT	EX
1	Richie Zisk	.12	.06	.03
2	Bill Buckner	.12	.06	.03
3	George Brett	.90	.45	.25
4	Rickey Henderson	.70	.35	.20
5	Jack Morris	.30	.15	.08
6	Ozzie Smith	.25	.13	.06
7	Rollie Fingers	.25	.13	.06
8	Tom Seaver	.50	.25	.13
9	Fernando Valenzuela	.60	.30	.15
10	Hubie Brooks	.12	.06	.03
11	Nolan Ryan	.50	.25	.13
12	Dave Winfield	.60	.30	.15
13	Bob Horner	.25	.13	.06
14	Reggie Jackson	.90	.45	.25
15	Burt Hooton	.12	.06	.03
16	Mike Schmidt	.90	.45	.25
17	Bruce Sutter	.20	.10	.05
18	Pete Rose	1.50	.70	.40
19	Dave Kingman	.20	.10	.05
20	Neil Allen	.12	.06	.03
21	Don Sutton	.25	.13	.06
22	Dave Concepcion	.20	.10	.05
23	Keith Hernandez	.50	.25	.13
24	Gary Carter	.70	.35	.20
25	Carlton Fisk	.30	.15	.08
26	Ron Guidry	.25	.13	.06
27	Steve Carlton	.50	.25	.13
28	Robin Yount	.40	.20	.10
29	John Castino	.12	.06	.03
30	Johnny Bench	.70	.35	.20
31	Bob Knepper	.12	.06	.03
32	Rich "Goose" Gossage	.20	.10	.05
33	Buddy Bell	.20	.10	.05
34	Art Howe	.12	.06	.03
35	Tony Armas	.12	.06	.03
36	Phil Niekro	.30	.15	.08
37	Len Barker	.12	.06	.03
38	Bobby Grich	.20	.10	.05
39	Steve Kemp	.12	.06	.03
40	Kirk Gibson	.35	.20	.09
41	Carney Lansford	.20	.10	.05
42	Jim Palmer	.40	.20	.10
43	Carl Yastrzemski	1.00	.50	.25
44	Rick Burleson	.12	.06	.03
45	Dwight Evans	.25	.13	.06
46	Ron Cey	.20	.10	.05
47	Steve Garvey	.70	.35	.20
48	Dave Parker	.30	.15	.08
49	Mike Easler	.12	.06	.03
50	Dusty Baker	.12	.06	.03
51	Rod Carew	.70	.35	.20
52	Chris Chambliss	.12	.06	.03
53	Tim Raines	.60	.30	.15
54	Chet Lemon	.12	.06	.03
55	Bill Madlock	.20	.10	.05
56	George Foster	.20	.10	.05
57	Dwayne Murphy	.12	.06	.03
58	Ken Singleton	.20	.10	.05
59	Mike Norris	.12	.06	.03
60	Cecil Cooper	.20	.10	.05
61	Al Oliver	.20	.10	.05
62	Willie Wilson	.25	.13	.06
63	Vida Blue	.20	.10	.05
64	Eddie Murray	.90	.45	.25

1983 Kellogg's

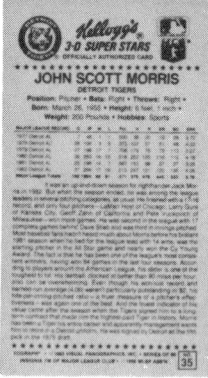

In its 14th and final year of baseball card issue, Kellogg's returned to the policy of inserting single cards into cereal boxes, as well as offering complete sets by a mail-in box top redemption offer. The 3-D cards themselves returned to a narrow — 1⅞" by 3¼" — format, while the set size was reduced to 60 cards.

	MT	NR MT	EX
Complete Set:	12.00	6.00	3.00
Common Player:	.10	.05	.03

		MT	NR MT	EX
1	Rod Carew	.50	.25	.13
2	Rollie Fingers	.20	.10	.05
3	Reggie Jackson	.50	.25	.13
4	George Brett	.70	.35	.20
5	Hal McRae	.15	.08	.04
6	Pete Rose	1.25	.60	.30
7	Fernando Valenzuela	.35	.20	.09
8	Rickey Henderson	.45	.25	.11
9	Carl Yastrzemski	.70	.35	.20
10	Rich "Goose" Gossage	.20	.10	.05
11	Eddie Murray	.50	.25	.13
12	Buddy Bell	.15	.08	.04
13	Jim Rice	.40	.20	.10
14	Robin Yount	.35	.20	.09
15	Dave Winfield	.45	.25	.11
16	Harold Baines	.20	.10	.05
17	Garry Templeton	.15	.08	.04
18	Bill Madlock	.20	.10	.05
19	Pete Vuckovich	.10	.05	.03
20	Pedro Guerrero	.25	.13	.06
21	Ozzie Smith	.20	.10	.05
22	George Foster	.20	.10	.05
23	Willie Wilson	.20	.10	.05
24	Johnny Ray	.15	.08	.04
25	George Hendrick	.10	.05	.03
26	Andre Thornton	.10	.05	.03
27	Leon Durham	.15	.08	.04
28	Cecil Cooper	.15	.08	.04
29	Don Baylor	.15	.08	.04
30	Lonnie Smith	.10	.05	.03
31	Nolan Ryan	.40	.20	.10
32	Dan Quisenberry (Quisenberry)	.20	.10	.05
33	Len Barker	.10	.05	.03
34	Neil Allen	.10	.05	.03
35	Jack Morris	.30	.15	.08
36	Dave Stieb	.15	.08	.04
37	Bruce Sutter	.15	.08	.04
38	Jim Sundberg	.10	.05	.03
39	Jim Palmer	.35	.20	.09
40	Lance Parrish	.35	.20	.09
41	Floyd Bannister	.15	.08	.04
42	Larry Gura	.10	.05	.03
43	Britt Burns	.10	.05	.03
44	Toby Harrah	.10	.05	.03
45	Steve Carlton	.45	.25	.11
46	Greg Minton	.10	.05	.03
47	Gorman Thomas	.15	.08	.04
48	Jack Clark	.25	.13	.06
49	Keith Hernandez	.40	.20	.10
50	Greg Luzinski	.15	.08	.04
51	Fred Lynn	.25	.13	.06
52	Dale Murphy	.70	.35	.20

		MT	NR MT	EX
53	Kent Hrbek	.35	.20	.09
54	Bob Horner	.20	.10	.05
55	Gary Carter	.50	.25	.13
56	Carlton Fisk	.25	.13	.06
57	Dave Concepcion	.15	.08	.04
58	Mike Schmidt	.50	.25	.13
59	Bill Buckner	.10	.05	.03
60	Bobby Grich	.15	.08	.04

1986 Kitty Clover Potato Chips Royals

Twenty players of the 1985 World's Champion Kansas City Royals were featured in a round card set inserted into packages of potato chips in the K.C. area. The 2⅞'' discs were similar to a handful of snack issues produced by Mike Schecter Associates in that team logos have been airbrushed off the players' caps, and the photos of some of the players can be found on other regional issues of 1986.

		MT	NR MT	EX
Complete Set:		20.00	15.00	8.00
Common Player:		.70	.50	.30
1	Lonnie Smith	.70	.50	.30
2	Buddy Biancalana	.70	.50	.30
3	Bret Saberhagen	1.75	1.25	.70
4	Hal McRae	.80	.60	.30
5	Onix Concepcion	.70	.50	.30
6	Jorge Orta	.70	.50	.30
7	Bud Black	.80	.60	.30
8	Dan Quisenberry	1.00	.70	.40
9	Dane Iorg	.70	.50	.30
10	Charlie Leibrandt	.80	.60	.30
11	Pat Sheridan	.70	.50	.30
12	John Wathan	.80	.60	.30
13	Frank White	.90	.70	.35
14	Darryl Motley	.70	.50	.30
15	Willie Wilson	1.00	.70	.40
16	Danny Jackson	.80	.60	.30
17	Steve Balboni	.80	.60	.30
18	Jim Sundberg	.70	.50	.30
19	Mark Gubicza	.80	.60	.30
20	George Brett	3.00	2.25	1.25

1987 Kraft

Kraft Foods, Inc. issued a 48-card set on specially marked packages of their Macaroni & Cheese Dinners. Titled ''Home Plate Heroes'', 24 two-card panels measuring 3½'' by 7⅛'' make up the set. Individual cards measure 2¼'' by 3½'' and are numbered 1 through 48. Different two-card panel combinations were produced. The blank-backed cards feature fronts with full-color photos, although all team insignias have been erased. In conjunction with the card set, Kraft offered a contest to ''Win A Day With A Major Leaguer.'' Mike Schecter Associates produced the set for Kraft.

		MT	NR MT	EX
Complete Set:		30.00	22.00	12.00
Common Player:		.20	.15	.08
1	Eddie Murray	.75	.60	.30
2	Dale Murphy	1.00	.70	.40
3	Cal Ripken	.75	.60	.30
4	Mike Scott	.35	.25	.14
5	Jim Rice	.60	.45	.25
6	Jody Davis	.20	.15	.08
7	Wade Boggs	1.50	1.25	.60
8	Ryne Sandberg	.60	.45	.25
9	Wally Joyner	1.50	1.25	.60
10	Eric Davis	1.25	.90	.50
11	Ozzie Guillen	.20	.15	.08
12	Tony Pena	.20	.15	.08
13	Harold Baines	.35	.25	.14
14	Johnny Ray	.20	.15	.08
15	Joe Carter	.35	.25	.14
16	Ozzie Smith	.35	.25	.14
17	Cory Snyder	.75	.60	.30
18	Vince Coleman	.35	.25	.14
19	Kirk Gibson	.60	.45	.25
20	Steve Garvey	.75	.60	.30
21	George Brett	1.00	.70	.40
22	John Tudor	.20	.15	.08
23	Robin Yount	.60	.45	.25
24	Von Hayes	.35	.25	.14
25	Kent Hrbek	.35	.25	.14
26	Darryl Strawberry	1.00	.70	.40
27	Kirby Puckett	.60	.45	.25
28	Ron Darling	.35	.25	.14
29	Don Mattingly	2.00	1.50	.80
30	Mike Schmidt	1.00	.70	.40
31	Rickey Henderson	.75	.60	.30
32	Fernando Valenzuela	.60	.45	.25
33	Dave Winfield	.60	.45	.25
34	Pete Rose	1.25	.90	.50
35	Jose Canseco	1.50	1.25	.60
36	Glenn Davis	.35	.25	.14
37	Alvin Davis	.35	.25	.14
38	Steve Sax	.35	.25	.14
39	Pete Incaviglia	1.00	.70	.40
40	Jeff Reardon	.35	.25	.14
41	Jesse Barfield	.35	.25	.14
42	Hubie Brooks	.20	.15	.08
43	George Bell	.60	.45	.25
44	Tony Gwynn	.75	.60	.30
45	Roger Clemens	.75	.60	.30
46	Chili Davis	.20	.15	.08
47	Mike Witt	.35	.25	.14
48	Nolan Ryan	.60	.45	.25

1960 Lake to Lake Dairy Braves

This 28-card set of unnumbered 2½'' by 3¼'' cards offers a special challenge for the condition-conscious collector. Originally issued by being stapled to milk cartons, the cards were redeemable for prizes ranging from pen and pencil sets to Braves tickets. When sent in for redemption, the cards had a hole punched in the corner. Naturally, collectors most desire cards without the staple or punch holes. Cards are printed in blue ink on front, red ink on back. Because he was traded in May, and his card withdrawn, the Ray Boone card is scarce; the Billy Bruton card is unaccountably scarcer still.

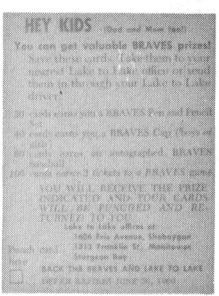

RED SCHOENDIENST
Second Base

		NR MT	EX	VG
	Complete Set:	950.00	475.00	285.00
	Common Player:	12.00	6.00	3.50
(1)	Henry Aaron	175.00	87.00	52.00
(2)	Joe Adcock	17.50	8.75	5.25
(3)	Ray Boone	125.00	62.00	37.00
(4)	Bill Bruton	175.00	87.00	52.00
(5)	Bob Buhl	17.50	8.75	5.25
(6)	Lou Burdette	20.00	10.00	6.00
(7)	Chuck Cottier	12.00	6.00	3.50
(8)	Wes Covington	15.00	7.50	4.50
(9)	Del Crandall	17.50	8.75	5.25
(10)	Charlie Dressen	15.00	7.50	4.50
(11)	Bob Giggie	12.00	6.00	3.50
(12)	Joey Jay	12.00	6.00	3.50
(13)	Johnny Logan	15.00	7.50	4.50
(14)	Felix Mantilla	12.00	6.00	3.50
(15)	Lee Maye	12.00	6.00	3.50
(16)	Don McMahon	12.00	6.00	3.50
(17)	George Myatt	12.00	6.00	3.50
(18)	Andy Pafko	15.00	7.50	4.50
(19)	Juan Pizarro	12.00	6.00	3.50
(20)	Mel Roach	12.00	6.00	3.50
(21)	Bob Rush	12.00	6.00	3.50
(22)	Bob Scheffing	12.00	6.00	3.50
(23)	Red Schoendienst	20.00	10.00	6.00
(24)	Warren Spahn	40.00	20.00	12.00
(25)	Al Spangler	12.00	6.00	3.50
(26)	Frank Torre	12.00	6.00	3.50
(27)	Carl Willey	12.00	6.00	3.50
(28)	Whitlow Wyatt	12.00	6.00	3.50

1948-1949 Leaf

76---TED (The Kid) WILLIAMS

ALL-STAR BASEBALL GUM

TED WILLIAMS

The first color baseball cards of the post-World War II era were the 98-card, 2⅜" by 2⅞," set produced by Chicago's Leaf Gum Company in 1948-1949. The color was crude, probably helping to make the set less popular than the Bowman issues of the same era. One of the toughest post-war sets to complete, exactly half of the Leaf issue — 49 of the cards — are significantly harder to find than the other 49. Probably intended to confound bubblegum buyers of the

day, the set is skip-numbered between 1-168. Card backs contain offers of felt pennants, an album for the cards or 5½" by 7½" premium photos of Hall of Famers.

		NR MT	EX	VG
	Complete Set:	13000.00	6500.00	3900.
	Common Player:	12.00	6.00	3.50
	Common Scarce Player:	160.00	80.00	48.00
1	Joe DiMaggio	500.00	225.00	140.00
3	Babe Ruth	500.00	250.00	150.00
4	Stan Musial	200.00	100.00	60.00
5	Virgil Trucks	160.00	80.00	48.00
8	Leroy Paige	800.00	400.00	240.00
10	Paul Trout	12.00	6.00	3.50
11	Phil Rizzuto	65.00	32.00	19.50
13	Casimer Michaels	160.00	80.00	48.00
14	Billy Johnson	17.50	8.75	5.25
17	Frank Overmire	12.00	6.00	3.50
19	John Wyrostek	160.00	80.00	48.00
20	Hank Sauer	160.00	80.00	48.00
22	Al Evans	12.00	6.00	3.50
26	Sam Chapman	12.00	6.00	3.50
27	Mickey Harris	12.00	6.00	3.50
28	Jim Hegan	12.00	6.00	3.50
29	Elmer Valo	12.00	6.00	3.50
30	Bill Goodman	160.00	80.00	48.00
31	Lou Brissie	12.00	6.00	3.50
32	Warren Spahn	65.00	32.00	19.50
33	Harry Lowrey	160.00	80.00	48.00
36	Al Zarilla	160.00	80.00	48.00
38	Ted Kluszewski	30.00	15.00	9.00
39	Ewell Blackwell	17.50	8.75	5.25
42	Kent Peterson	12.00	6.00	3.50
43	Eddie Stevens	160.00	80.00	48.00
45	Ken Keltner	160.00	80.00	48.00
46	Johnny Mize	50.00	25.00	15.00
47	George Vico	12.00	6.00	3.50
48	Johnny Schmitz	160.00	80.00	48.00
49	Del Ennis	12.00	6.00	3.50
50	Dick Wakefield	12.00	6.00	3.50
51	Alvin Dark	200.00	100.00	60.00
53	John Vandermeer (Vander Meer)	17.50	8.75	5.25
54	Bobby Adams	160.00	80.00	48.00
55	Tommy Henrich	200.00	100.00	60.00
56	Larry Jensen (Jansen)	12.00	6.00	3.50
57	Bob McCall	12.00	6.00	3.50
59	Lucius Appling	45.00	22.00	13.50
61	Jake Early	12.00	6.00	3.50
62	Eddie Joost	160.00	80.00	48.00
63	Barney McCosky	160.00	80.00	48.00
65	Bob Elliot (Elliott)	12.00	6.00	3.50
66	Orval Grove	160.00	80.00	48.00
68	Ed Miller	160.00	80.00	48.00
70	John Wagner	150.00	75.00	45.00
72	Hank Edwards	12.00	6.00	3.50
73	Pat Seerey	12.00	6.00	3.50
75	Dom DiMaggio	200.00	100.00	60.00
76	Ted Williams	275.00	137.00	82.00
77	Roy Smalley	12.00	6.00	3.50
78	Walter Evers	160.00	80.00	48.00
79	Jackie Robinson	225.00	112.00	67.00
81	George Kurowski	160.00	80.00	48.00
82	Johnny Lindell	17.50	8.75	5.25
83	Bobby Doerr	45.00	22.00	13.50
84	Sid Hudson	12.00	6.00	3.50
85	Dave Philley	160.00	80.00	48.00
86	Ralph Weigel	12.00	6.00	3.50
88	Frank Gustine	160.00	80.00	48.00
91	Ralph Kiner	50.00	25.00	15.00
93	Bob Feller	550.00	275.00	165.00
95	George Stirnweiss	17.50	8.75	5.25
97	Martin Marion	17.50	8.75	5.25
98	Hal Newhouser	175.00	87.00	52.00
102a	Gene Hermansk (incorrect spelling)	160.00	80.00	48.00
102b	Gene Hermanski (correct spelling)	17.50	8.75	5.25
104	Edward Stewart	160.00	80.00	48.00
106	Lou Boudreau	45.00	22.00	13.50
108	Matthew Batts	160.00	80.00	48.00
111	Gerald Priddy	12.00	6.00	3.50
113	Emil Leonard	160.00	80.00	48.00
117	Joe Gordon	17.50	8.75	5.25
120	George Kell	325.00	162.00	97.00
121	John Pesky	160.00	80.00	48.00
123	Clifford Fannin	160.00	80.00	48.00
125	Andy Pafko	17.50	8.75	5.25
127	Enos Slaughter	325.00	162.00	97.00

		NR MT	EX	VG
128	Warren Rosar	12.00	6.00	3.50
129	Kirby Higbe	160.00	80.00	48.00
131	Sid Gordon	160.00	80.00	48.00
133	Tommy Holmes	160.00	80.00	48.00
136a	Cliff Aberson (full sleeve)	12.00	6.00	3.50
136b	Cliff Aberson (short sleeve)	65.00	32.00	19.50
137	Harry Walker	160.00	80.00	48.00
138	Larry Doby	225.00	112.00	67.00
139	Johnny Hopp	12.00	6.00	3.50
142	Danny Murtaugh	160.00	80.00	48.00
143	Dick Sisler	160.00	80.00	48.00
144	Bob Dillinger	160.00	80.00	48.00
146	Harold Reiser	175.00	87.00	52.00
149	Henry Majeski	160.00	80.00	48.00
153	Floyd Baker	160.00	80.00	48.00
158	Harry Brecheen	160.00	80.00	48.00
159	Mizell Platt	12.00	6.00	3.50
160	Bob Scheffing	160.00	80.00	48.00
161	Vernon Stephens	160.00	80.00	48.00
163	Freddy Hutchinson	175.00	87.00	52.00
165	Dale Mitchell	160.00	80.00	48.00
168	Phil Cavaretta (Cavarretta)	200.00	87.00	52.00

1960 Leaf

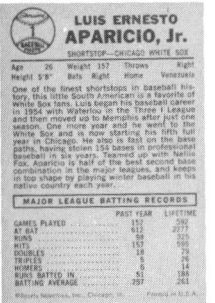

While known to the hobby as "Leaf" cards, this set of 144 cards carries the copyright of Sports Novelties Inc., Chicago. The 2½" by 3½" cards feature black-and-white player portrait photos, with backgrounds airbrushed away. Cards were sold in 5¢ wax packs with a marble, rather than a piece of bubblegum. The second half of the set, cards #73-144, are very scarce and make the set a real challenge for the collector. Even more rare are a handful of photo variations, generally extreme close-ups, within the first 72 cards. It is thought that these variations were never actually issued. Back variations also exist, on which certain lines of the biographies have been erased. Card #25, Jim Grant, is found in two versions, with his own picture (black cap) and with a photo of Brooks Lawrence (white cap). It is thought that the scarce "face only" variations may be an early test issue by Leaf as only a handful are known to exist. Complete set prices quoted here do not include the scarcer variations.

		NR MT	EX	VG
Complete Set:		1100.00	550.00	330.00
Common Player: 1-72		.70	.35	.20
Common Player: 73-144		8.00	4.00	2.50
1a	Luis Aparicio (face only photo)	40.00	20.00	12.00
1b	Luis Aparicio (cap to chest photo)	9.00	3.00	1.50
2	Woody Held	.70	.35	.20
3	Frank Lary	.80	.40	.25
4	Camilo Pascual	.80	.40	.25
5	Frank Herrera	.70	.35	.20
6	Felipe Alou	.90	.45	.25
7	Bennie Daniels	.70	.35	.20
8	Roger Craig	.90	.45	.25
9	Eddie Kasko	.70	.35	.20
10	Bob Grim	.70	.35	.20
11	Jim Busby	.70	.35	.20
12a	Ken Boyer (face only photo)	35.00	17.50	10.50
12b	Ken Boyer (cap to chest photo)	2.00	1.00	.60
13	Bob Boyd	.70	.35	.20

		NR MT	EX	VG
14	Sam Jones	.70	.35	.20
15	Larry Jackson	.70	.35	.20
16	Roy Face	1.25	.60	.40
17a	Walt Moryn (face only photo)	30.00	15.00	9.00
17b	Walt Moryn (cap to chest photo)	.70	.35	.20
18	Jim Gilliam	2.00	1.00	.60
19	Don Newcombe	.90	.45	.25
20	Glen Hobbie	.70	.35	.20
21	Pedro Ramos	.70	.35	.20
22	Ryne Duren	1.50	.70	.45
23a	Joe Jay (face only photo)	30.00	15.00	9.00
23b	Joe Jay (cap to chest photo)	.70	.35	.20
24	Lou Berberet	.70	.35	.20
25a	Jim Grant (white cap, photo actually Brooks Lawrence)	10.00	5.00	3.00
25b	Jim Grant (dark cap, correct photo)	30.00	15.00	9.00
26	Tom Borland	.70	.35	.20
27	Brooks Robinson	12.00	6.00	3.50
28	Jerry Adair	.80	.40	.25
29	Ron Jackson	.70	.35	.20
30	George Strickland	.70	.35	.20
31	Rocky Bridges	.70	.35	.20
32	Bill Tuttle	.70	.35	.20
33	Ken Hunt	1.25	.60	.40
34	Hal Griggs	.70	.35	.20
35a	Jim Coates (face only photo)	30.00	15.00	9.00
35b	Jim Coates (cap to chest photo)	1.25	.60	.40
36	Brooks Lawrence	.70	.35	.20
37	Duke Snider	10.00	5.00	3.00
38	Al Spangler	.70	.35	.20
39	Jim Owens	.70	.35	.20
40	Bill Virdon	1.50	.70	.45
41	Ernie Broglio	.70	.35	.20
42	Andre Rodgers	.70	.35	.20
43	Julio Becquer	.70	.35	.20
44	Tony Taylor	.70	.35	.20
45	Jerry Lynch	.80	.40	.25
46	Cletis Boyer	1.50	.70	.45
47	Jerry Lumpe	.80	.40	.25
48	Charlie Maxwell	.70	.35	.20
49	Jim Perry	.90	.45	.25
50	Danny McDevitt	.70	.35	.20
51	Juan Pizarro	.70	.35	.20
52	Dallas Green	1.25	.60	.40
53	Bob Friend	1.25	.60	.40
54	Jack Sanford	.80	.40	.25
55	Jim Rivera	.70	.35	.20
56	Ted Wills	.70	.35	.20
57	Milt Pappas	.80	.40	.25
58a	Hal Smith (face only photo, team & position on back)	30.00	15.00	9.00
58b	Hal Smith (cap to chest photo, team & position on back)	.70	.35	.20
58c	Hal Smith (cap to chest photo, team blacked out on back)	20.00	10.00	6.00
58d	Hal Smith (cap to chest photo, team missing on back)	20.00	10.00	6.00
59	Bob Avila	.70	.35	.20
60	Clem Labine	.80	.40	.25
61a	Vic Rehm (face only photo)	30.00	15.00	9.00
61b	Vic Rehm (cap to chest photo)	.80	.40	.25
62	John Gabler	1.25	.60	.40
63	John Tsitouris	.70	.35	.20
64	Dave Sisler	.70	.35	.20
65	Vic Power	.80	.40	.25
66	Earl Battey	.80	.40	.25
67	Bob Purkey	.80	.40	.25
68	Moe Drabowsky	.70	.35	.20
69	Hoyt Wilhelm	4.50	2.25	1.25
70	Humberto Robinson	.70	.35	.20
71	Whitey Herzog	1.75	.90	.50
72a	Dick Donovan (face only photo)	30.00	15.00	9.00
72b	Dick Donovan (cap to chest photo)	.80	.40	.25
73	Gordon Jones	8.00	4.00	2.50
74	Joe Hicks	8.00	4.00	2.50
75	Ray Culp	9.00	4.50	2.75
76	Dick Drott	8.00	4.00	2.50
77	Bob Duliba	8.00	4.00	2.50
78	Art Ditmar	11.00	5.50	3.25
79	Steve Korcheck	8.00	4.00	2.50
80	Henry Mason	8.00	4.00	2.50
81	Harry Simpson	8.00	4.00	2.50
82	Gene Green	8.00	4.00	2.50
83	Bob Shaw	8.00	4.00	2.50
84	Howard Reed	8.00	4.00	2.50
85	Dick Stigman	8.00	4.00	2.50
86	Rip Repulski	8.00	4.00	2.50
87	Seth Morehead	8.00	4.00	2.50
88	Camilo Carreon	8.00	4.00	2.50
89	John Blanchard	11.00	5.50	3.25

		NR MT	EX	VG
90	Billy Hoeft	8.00	4.00	2.50
91	Fred Hopke	9.00	4.50	2.75
92	Joe Martin	8.00	4.00	2.50
93	Wally Shannon	9.00	4.50	2.75
94	Baseball's Two Hal Smiths (Harold Raymond Smith, Harold Wayne Smith)	15.00	7.50	4.50
95	Al Schroll	8.00	4.00	2.50
96	John Kucks	8.00	4.00	2.50
97	Tom Morgan	8.00	4.00	2.50
98	Willie Jones	8.00	4.00	2.50
99	Marshall Renfroe	9.00	4.50	2.75
100	Willie Tasby	8.00	4.00	2.50
101	Irv Noren	8.00	4.00	2.50
102	Russ Snyder	8.00	4.00	2.50
103	Bob Turley	15.00	7.50	4.50
104	Jim Woods	8.00	4.00	2.50
105	Ronnie Kline	8.00	4.00	2.50
106	Steve Bilko	8.00	4.00	2.50
107	Elmer Valo	11.00	5.50	3.25
108	Tom McAvoy	9.00	4.50	2.75
109	Stan Williams	8.00	4.00	2.50
110	Earl Averill	8.00	4.00	2.50
111	Lee Walls	8.00	4.00	2.50
112	Paul Richards	9.00	4.50	2.75
113	Ed Sadowski	8.00	4.00	2.50
114	Stover McIlwain	9.00	4.50	2.75
115	Chuck Tanner (photo actually Ken Kuhn)	15.00	7.50	4.50
116	Lou Klimchock	8.00	4.00	2.50
117	Neil Chrisley	8.00	4.00	2.50
118	John Callison	15.00	7.50	4.50
119	Hal Smith	8.00	4.00	2.50
120	Carl Sawatski	8.00	4.00	2.50
121	Frank Leja	11.00	5.50	3.25
122	Earl Torgeson	8.00	4.00	2.50
123	Art Schult	8.00	4.00	2.50
124	Jim Brosnan	9.00	4.50	2.75
125	George Anderson	20.00	10.00	6.00
126	Joe Pignatano	8.00	4.00	2.50
127	Rocky Nelson	8.00	4.00	2.50
128	Orlando Cepeda	20.00	10.00	6.00
129	Daryl Spencer	8.00	4.00	2.50
130	Ralph Lumenti	8.00	4.00	2.50
131	Sam Taylor	8.00	4.00	2.50
132	Harry Brecheen	9.00	4.50	2.75
133	Johnny Groth	8.00	4.00	2.50
134	Wayne Terwilliger	8.00	4.00	2.50
135	Kent Hadley	11.00	5.50	3.25
136	Faye Throneberry	8.00	4.00	2.50
137	Jack Meyer	8.00	4.00	2.50
138	Chuck Cottier	8.00	4.00	2.50
139	Joe DeMaestri	11.00	5.50	3.25
140	Gene Freese	8.00	4.00	2.50
141	Curt Flood	15.00	7.50	4.50
142	Gino Cimoli	8.00	4.00	2.50
143	Clay Dalrymple	8.00	4.00	2.50
144	Jim Bunning	30.00	9.00	4.50

1985 Leaf-Donruss

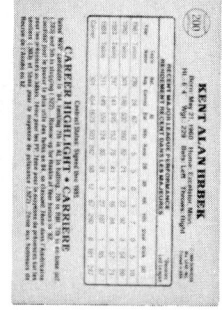

In an attempt to share in the Canadian baseball card market Donruss in 1985 issued a 264-card version of its regular set to be sold in Canada. Fronts of the 2½'' by 3½'' cards are virtually identical to the regular '85 Donruss cards of the same players, except that a green stylized leaf has been added to the logo in the upper-left. On back, player biographies have been re-written to accomodate both English and French versions, and new card numbers have been assigned. The 264 cards in this shortened set concentrate on star-caliber players, as well as those of Canada's two major league teams. A special two-card subset, ''Canadian Greats,'' featured paintings of Dave Steib and Tim Raines. The Donruss-Leaf cards were widely distributed in the U.S. through hobby dealers.

		MT	NR MT	EX
Complete Set:		26.00	19.50	10.50
Common Player:		.05	.04	.02
1	Ryne Sandberg (DK)	.30	.25	.12
2	Doug DeCinces (DK)	.10	.08	.04
3	Rich Dotson (DK)	.07	.05	.03
4	Bert Blyleven (DK)	.12	.09	.05
5	Lou Whitaker (DK)	.20	.15	.08
6	Dan Quisenberry (DK)	.12	.09	.05
7	Don Mattingly (DK)	1.50		
8	Carney Lansford (DK)	.07	.05	.03
9	Frank Tanana (DK)	.07	.05	.03
10	Willie Upshaw (DK)	.07	.05	.03
11	Claudell Washington (DK)	.07	.05	.03
12	Mike Marshall (DK)	.12	.09	.05
13	Joaquin Andujar (DK)	.07	.05	.03
14	Cal Ripken, Jr. (DK)	.40	.30	.15
15	Jim Rice (DK)	.30	.25	.12
16	Don Sutton (DK)	.20	.15	.08
17	Frank Viola (DK)	.10	.08	.04
18	Alvin Davis (DK)	.20	.15	.08
19	Mario Soto (DK)	.07	.05	.03
20	Jose Cruz (DK)	.07	.05	.03
21	Charlie Lea (DK)	.07	.05	.03
22	Jesse Orosco (DK)	.07	.05	.03
23	Juan Samuel (DK)	.20	.15	.08
24	Tony Pena (DK)	.07	.05	.03
25	Tony Gwynn (DK)	.30	.25	.12
26	Bob Brenly (DK)	.07	.05	.03
27	Steve Kiefer (RR)	.10	.08	.04
28	Joe Morgan	.20	.15	.08
29	Luis Leal	.05	.04	.02
30	Dan Gladden	.20	.15	.08
31	Shane Rawley	.07	.05	.03
32	Mark Clear	.05	.04	.02
33	Terry Kennedy	.07	.05	.03
34	Hal McRae	.07	.05	.03
35	Mickey Rivers	.05	.04	.02
36	Tom Brunansky	.10	.08	.04
37	LaMarr Hoyt	.05	.04	.02
38	Orel Hershiser	.90	.70	.35
39	Chris Bando	.05	.04	.02
40	Lee Lacy	.05	.04	.02
41	Lance Parrish	.25	.20	.10
42	George Foster	.12	.09	.05
43	Kevin McReynolds	.20	.15	.08
44	Robin Yount	.30	.25	.12
45	Craig McMurtry	.05	.04	.02
46	Mike Witt	.10	.08	.04
47	Gary Redus	.07	.05	.03
48	Dennis Rasmussen	.07	.05	.03
49	Gary Woods	.05	.04	.02
50	Phil Bradley	.60	.45	.25
51	Steve Bedrosian	.10	.08	.04
52	Duane Walker	.05	.04	.02
53	Geoff Zahn	.05	.04	.02
54	Dave Stieb	.10	.08	.04
55	Pascual Perez	.07	.05	.03
56	Mark Langston	.30	.25	.12
57	Bob Dernier	.05	.04	.02
58	Joe Cowley	.05	.04	.02
59	Dan Schatzeder	.05	.04	.02
60	Ozzie Smith	.12	.09	.05
61	Bob Knepper	.05	.04	.02
62	Keith Hernandez	.30	.25	.12
63	Rick Rhoden	.07	.05	.03
64	Alejandro Pena	.05	.04	.02
65	Damaso Garcia	.07	.05	.03
66	Chili Davis	.10	.08	.04
67	Al Oliver	.10	.08	.04
68	Alan Wiggins	.05	.04	.02
69	Darryl Motley	.05	.04	.02
70	Gary Ward	.05	.04	.02
71	John Butcher	.05	.04	.02
72	Scott McGregor	.07	.05	.03
73	Bruce Hurst	.07	.05	.03
74	Dwayne Murphy	.05	.04	.02
75	Greg Luzinski	.10	.08	.04
76	Pat Tabler	.07	.05	.03

		MT	NR MT	EX
77	Chet Lemon	.07	.05	.03
78	Jim Sundberg	.05	.04	.02
79	Wally Backman	.07	.05	.03
80	Terry Puhl	.05	.04	.02
81	Storm Davis	.05	.04	.02
82	Jim Wohlford	.05	.04	.02
83	Willie Randolph	.07	.05	.03
84	Ron Cey	.07	.05	.03
85	Jim Beattie	.05	.04	.02
86	Rafael Ramirez	.05	.04	.02
87	Cesar Cedeno	.07	.05	.03
88	Bobby Grich	.07	.05	.03
89	Jason Thompson	.05	.04	.02
90	Steve Sax	.15	.11	.06
91	Tony Fernandez	.15	.11	.06
92	Jeff Leonard	.07	.05	.03
93	Von Hayes	.10	.08	.04
94	Steve Garvey	.30	.25	.12
95	Steve Balboni	.05	.04	.02
96	Larry Parrish	.07	.05	.03
97	Tim Teufel	.05	.04	.02
98	Sammy Stewart	.05	.04	.02
99	Roger Clemens	4.00	3.00	1.50
100	Steve Kemp	.07	.05	.03
101	Tom Seaver	.30	.25	.12
102	Andre Thornton	.07	.05	.03
103	Kirk Gibson	.20	.15	.08
104	Ted Simmons	.10	.08	.04
105	David Palmer	.07	.05	.03
106	Roy Lee Jackson	.05	.04	.02
107	Kirby Puckett	3.00	2.25	1.25
108	Charlie Hough	.07	.05	.03
109	Mike Boddicker	.07	.05	.03
110	Willie Wilson	.10	.08	.04
111	Tim Lollar	.05	.04	.02
112	Tony Armas	.07	.05	.03
113	Steve Carlton	.30	.25	.12
114	Gary Lavelle	.05	.04	.02
115	Cliff Johnson	.05	.04	.02
116	Ray Burris	.05	.04	.02
117	Rudy Law	.05	.04	.02
118	Mike Scioscia	.05	.04	.02
119	Kent Tekulve	.07	.05	.03
120	George Vukovich	.05	.04	.02
121	Barbaro Garbey	.05	.04	.02
122	Mookie Wilson	.07	.05	.03
123	Ben Oglivie	.05	.04	.02
124	Jerry Mumphrey	.05	.04	.02
125	Willie McGee	.20	.15	.08
126	Jeff Reardon	.10	.08	.04
127	Dave Winfield	.30	.25	.12
128	Lee Smith	.07	.05	.03
129	Ken Phelps	.07	.05	.03
130	Rick Camp	.05	.04	.02
131	Dave Concepcion	.10	.08	.04
132	Rod Carew	.35	.25	.14
133	Andre Dawson	.20	.15	.08
134	Doyle Alexander	.10	.08	.04
135	Miguel Dilone	.05	.04	.02
136	Jim Gott	.05	.04	.02
137	Eric Show	.05	.04	.02
138	Phil Niekro	.20	.15	.08
139	Rick Sutcliffe	.10	.08	.04
140	Two For The Tittle (Don Mattingly, Dave Winfield)	1.25	.90	.50
141	Ken Oberkfell	.05	.04	.02
142	Jack Morris	.15	.11	.06
143	Lloyd Moseby	.10	.08	.04
144	Pete Rose	.60	.45	.25
145	Gary Gaetti	.10	.08	.04
146	Don Baylor	.10	.08	.04
147	Bobby Meacham	.05	.04	.02
148	Frank White	.07	.05	.03
149	Mark Thurmond	.05	.04	.02
150	Dwight Evans	.10	.08	.04
151	Al Holland	.05	.04	.02
152	Joel Youngblood	.05	.04	.02
153	Rance Mulliniks	.05	.04	.02
154	Bill Caudill	.05	.04	.02
155	Carlton Fisk	.15	.11	.06
156	Rick Honeycutt	.05	.04	.02
157	John Candelaria	.07	.05	.03
158	Alan Trammell	.25	.20	.10
159	Darryl Strawberry	.80	.60	.30
160	Aurelio Lopez	.05	.04	.02
161	Enos Cabell	.05	.04	.02
162	Dion James	.07	.05	.03
163	Bruce Sutter	.12	.09	.05
164	Razor Shines	.05	.04	.02
165	Butch Wynegar	.05	.04	.02
166	Rich Bordi	.05	.04	.02

		MT	NR MT	EX
167	Spike Owen	.05	.04	.02
168	Chris Chambliss	.07	.05	.03
169	Dave Parker	.20	.15	.08
170	Reggie Jackson	.35	.25	.14
171	Bryn Smith	.07	.05	.03
172	Dave Collins	.05	.04	.02
173	Dave Engle	.05	.04	.02
174	Buddy Bell	.07	.05	.03
175	Mike Flanagan	.07	.05	.03
176	George Brett	.40	.30	.15
177	Graig Nettles	.10	.08	.04
178	Jerry Koosman	.07	.05	.03
179	Wade Boggs	1.00	.70	.40
180	Jody Davis	.07	.05	.03
181	Ernie Whitt	.05	.04	.02
182	Dave Kingman	.10	.08	.04
183	Vance Law	.05	.04	.02
184	Fernando Valenzuela	.25	.20	.10
185	Bill Madlock	.10	.08	.04
186	Brett Butler	.07	.05	.03
187	Doug Sisk	.05	.04	.02
188	Dan Petry	.07	.05	.03
189	Joe Niekro	.07	.05	.03
190	Rollie Fingers	.12	.09	.05
191	David Green	.05	.04	.02
192	Steve Rogers	.05	.04	.02
193	Ken Griffey	.07	.05	.03
194	Scott Sanderson	.05	.04	.02
195	Barry Bonnell	.05	.04	.02
196	Bruce Benedict	.05	.04	.02
197	Keith Moreland	.07	.05	.03
198	Fred Lynn	.12	.09	.05
199	Tim Wallach	.10	.08	.04
200	Kent Hrbek	.15	.11	.06
201	Pete O'Brien	.07	.05	.03
202	Bud Black	.05	.04	.02
203	Eddie Murray	.35	.25	.14
204	Goose Gossage	.15	.11	.06
205	Mike Schmidt	.35	.25	.14
206	Mike Easler	.07	.05	.03
207	Jack Clark	.12	.09	.05
208	Rickey Henderson	.35	.25	.14
209	Jesse Barfield	.15	.11	.06
210	Ron Kittle	.07	.05	.03
211	Pedro Guerrero	.15	.11	.06
212	Johnny Ray	.07	.05	.03
213	Julio Franco	.10	.08	.04
214	Hubie Brooks	.07	.05	.03
215	Darrell Evans	.10	.08	.04
216	Nolan Ryan	.30	.25	.12
217	Jim Gantner	.05	.04	.02
218	Tim Raines	.30	.25	.12
219	Dave Righetti	.15	.11	.06
220	Gary Matthews	.07	.05	.03
221	Jack Perconte	.05	.04	.02
222	Dale Murphy	.40	.30	.15
223	Brian Downing	.07	.05	.03
224	Mickey Hatcher	.05	.04	.02
225	Lonnie Smith	.05	.04	.02
226	Jorge Orta	.05	.04	.02
227	Milt Wilcox	.05	.04	.02
228	John Denny	.05	.04	.02
229	Marty Barrett	.07	.05	.03
230	Alfredo Griffin	.07	.05	.03
231	Harold Baines	.12	.09	.05
232	Bill Russell	.07	.05	.03
233	Marvell Wynne	.05	.04	.02
234	Dwight Gooden	4.00	3.00	1.50
235	Willie Hernandez	.07	.05	.03
236	Bill Gullickson	.05	.04	.02
237	Ron Guidry	.15	.11	.06
238	Leon Durham	.07	.05	.03
239	Al Cowens	.05	.04	.02
240	Bob Horner	.12	.09	.05
241	Gary Carter	.30	.25	.12
242	Glenn Hubbard	.05	.04	.02
243	Steve Trout	.05	.04	.02
244	Jay Howell	.07	.05	.03
245	Terry Francona	.05	.04	.02
246	Cecil Cooper	.10	.08	.04
247	Larry McWilliams	.05	.04	.02
248	George Bell	.25	.20	.10
249	Larry Herndon	.05	.04	.02
250	Ozzie Virgil	.05	.04	.02
251	Canadian Great (Dave Stieb)	.50	.40	.20
252	Canadian Great (Tim Raines)	.80	.60	.30
253	Ricky Horton	.12	.09	.05
254	Bill Buckner	.10	.08	.04
255	Dan Driessen	.05	.04	.02
256	Ron Darling	.15	.11	.06
257	Doug Flynn	.05	.04	.02

		MT	NR MT	EX
258	Darrell Porter	.05	.04	.02
259	George Hendrick	.05	.04	.02
653	Lou Gehrig Puzzle Card	.05	.04	.02
---	Checklist 1-26 DK	.05	.04	.02
---	Checklist 27-102	.05	.04	.02
---	Checklist 103-178	.05	.04	.02
---	Checklist 179-259	.05	.04	.02

1986 Leaf

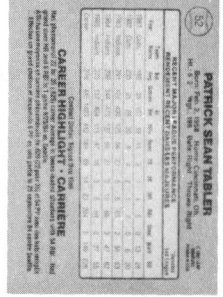

For its second Canadian card set, in 1986, the Donruss name was removed from the front of the company's 264-card issue, identifying the cards as "Leaf '86." Again concentrating on big-name stars and players from the Expos and Blue Jays, the 2½" by 3½" cards feature a design virtually identical to the 1986 Donruss cards. Backs were altered to allow the publication of career highlights in both English and French, and card numbers were changed. The "Canadian Greats" cards in the 1986 Leaf set, painted portraits rather than photos, were Jesse Barfield and Jeff Reardon. Besides being sold in its intended market in Canada, the set was widely distributed in the U.S. through hobby vendors.

		MT	NR MT	EX
Complete Set:		18.00	13.50	7.20
Common Player:		.05	.04	.02

		MT	NR MT	EX
1	Kirk Gibson (DK)	.15	.11	.06
2	Goose Gossage (DK)	.12	.09	.05
3	Willie McGee (DK)	.10	.08	.04
4	George Bell (DK)	.30	.25	.12
5	Tony Armas (DK)	.07	.05	.03
6	Chili Davis (DK)	.10	.08	.04
7	Cecil Cooper (DK)	.10	.08	.04
8	Mike Boddicker (DK)	.07	.05	.03
9	Davey Lopes (DK)	.07	.05	.03
10	Bill Doran (DK)	.10	.08	.04
11	Bret Saberhagen (DK)	.25	.20	.10
12	Brett Butler (DK)	.07	.05	.03
13	Harold Baines (DK)	.10	.08	.04
14	Mike Davis (DK)	.07	.05	.03
15	Tony Perez (DK)	.10	.08	.04
16	Willie Randolph (DK)	.07	.05	.03
17	Bob Boone (DK)	.07	.05	.03
18	Orel Hershiser (DK)	.20	.15	.08
19	Johnny Ray (DK)	.10	.08	.04
20	Gary Ward (DK)	.07	.05	.03
21	Rick Mahler (DK)	.07	.05	.03
22	Phil Bradley (DK)	.12	.09	.05
23	Jerry Koosman (DK)	.07	.05	.03
24	Tom Brunansky (DK)	.10	.08	.04
25	Andre Dawson (DK)	.20	.15	.08
26	Dwight Gooden (DK)	.80	.60	.30
27	Andres Galarraga (RR)	.60	.45	.25
28	Fred McGriff (RR)	.60	.45	.25
29	Dave Shipanoff (RR)	.05	.04	.02
30	Danny Jackson	.05	.04	.02
31	Robin Yount	.25	.20	.10
32	Mike Fitzgerald	.05	.04	.02
33	Lou Whitaker	.15	.11	.06
34	Alfredo Griffin	.07	.05	.03
35	"Oil Can" Boyd	.07	.05	.03
36	Ron Guidry	.15	.11	.06
37	Rickey Henderson	.30	.25	.12

		MT	NR MT	EX
38	Jack Morris	.15	.11	.06
39	Brian Downing	.07	.05	.03
40	Mike Marshall	.10	.08	.04
41	Tony Gwynn	.30	.25	.12
42	George Brett	.40	.30	.15
43	Jim Gantner	.05	.04	.02
44	Hubie Brooks	.07	.05	.03
45	Tony Fernandez	.15	.11	.06
46	Oddibe McDowell	.25	.20	.10
47	Ozzie Smith	.12	.09	.05
48	Ken Griffey	.07	.05	.03
49	Jose Cruz	.07	.05	.03
50	Mariano Duncan	.10	.08	.04
51	Mike Schmidt	.30		
52	Pat Tabler	.07	.05	.03
53	Pete Rose	.70	.50	.30
54	Frank White	.07	.05	.03
55	Carney Lansford	.07	.05	.03
56	Steve Garvey	.30	.25	.12
57	Vance Law	.05	.04	.02
58	Tony Pena	.07	.05	.03
59	Wayne Tolleson	.05	.04	.02
60	Dale Murphy	.50	.40	.20
61	LaMarr Hoyt	.05	.04	.02
62	Ryne Sandberg	.25	.20	.10
63	Gary Carter	.30	.25	.12
64	Lee Smith	.07	.05	.03
65	Alvin Davis	.15	.11	.06
66	Edwin Nunez	.07	.05	.03
67	Kent Hrbek	.20	.15	.08
68	Dave Stieb	.10	.08	.04
69	Kirby Puckett	.80	.60	.30
70	Paul Molitor	.12	.09	.05
71	Glenn Hubbard	.05	.04	.02
72	Lloyd Moseby	.10	.08	.04
73	Mike Smithson	.05	.04	.02
74	Jeff Leonard	.07	.05	.03
75	Danny Darwin	.05	.04	.02
76	Kevin McReynolds	.12	.09	.05
77	Bill Buckner	.07	.05	.03
78	Ron Oester	.05	.04	.02
79	Tommy Herr	.07	.05	.03
80	Mike Pagliarulo	.20	.15	.08
81	Ron Romanick	.05	.04	.02
82	Brook Jacoby	.10	.08	.04
83	Eddie Murray	.30	.25	.12
84	Gary Pettis	.05	.04	.02
85	Chet Lemon	.07	.05	.03
86	Toby Harrah	.07	.05	.03
87	Mike Scioscia	.05	.04	.02
88	Bert Blyleven	.12	.09	.05
89	Dave Righetti	.15	.11	.06
90	Bob Knepper	.07	.05	.03
91	Fernando Valenzuela	.25	.20	.10
92	Dave Dravecky	.07	.05	.03
93	Julio Franco	.10	.08	.04
94	Keith Moreland	.07	.05	.03
95	Darryl Motley	.05	.04	.02
96	Jack Clark	.12	.09	.05
97	Tim Wallach	.10	.08	.04
98	Steve Balboni	.05	.04	.02
99	Storm Davis	.05	.04	.02
100	Jay Howell	.07	.05	.03
101	Alan Trammell	.25	.20	.10
102	Willie Hernandez	.07	.05	.03
103	Don Mattingly	2.50	2.00	1.00
104	Lee Lacy	.05	.04	.02
105	Pedro Guerrero	.15	.11	.06
106	Willie Wilson	.10	.08	.04
107	Craig Reynolds	.05	.04	.02
108	Tim Raines	.30	.25	.12
109	Shane Rawley	.07	.05	.03
110	Larry Parrish	.07	.05	.03
111	Eric Show	.05	.04	.02
112	Mike Witt	.10	.08	.04
113	Dennis Eckersley	.07	.05	.03
114	Mike Moore	.05	.04	.02
115	Vince Coleman	1.00	.70	.40
116	Damaso Garcia	.07	.05	.03
117	Steve Carlton	.30	.25	.12
118	Floyd Bannister	.07	.05	.03
119	Mario Soto	.05	.04	.02
120	Fred Lynn	.15	.11	.06
121	Bob Horner	.15	.11	.06
122	Rick Sutcliffe	.10	.08	.04
123	Walt Terrell	.07	.05	.03
124	Keith Hernandez	.25	.20	.10
125	Dave Winfield	.30	.25	.12
126	Frank Viola	.10	.08	.04
127	Dwight Evans	.12	.09	.05
128	Willie Upshaw	.07	.05	.03

		MT	NR MT	EX
129	Andre Thornton	.07	.05	.03
130	Donnie Moore	.05	.04	.02
131	Darryl Strawberry	.50	.40	.20
132	Nolan Ryan	.30	.25	.12
133	Garry Templeton	.07	.05	.03
134	John Tudor	.07	.05	.03
135	Dave Parker	.15	.11	.06
136	Larry McWilliams	.05	.04	.02
137	Terry Pendleton	.07	.05	.03
138	Terry Puhl	.05	.04	.02
139	Bob Dernier	.05	.04	.02
140	Ozzie Guillen	.25	.20	.10
141	Jim Clancy	.07	.05	.03
142	Cal Ripken, Jr.	.40	.30	.15
143	Mickey Hatcher	.05	.04	.02
144	Dan Petry	.07	.05	.03
145	Rich Gedman	.07	.05	.03
146	Jim Rice	.30	.25	.12
147	Butch Wynegar	.05	.04	.02
148	Donnie Hill	.05	.04	.02
149	Jim Sundberg	.05	.04	.02
150	Joe Hesketh	.07	.05	.03
151	Chris Codiroli	.05	.04	.02
152	Charlie Hough	.07	.05	.03
153	Herman Winningham	.12	.09	.05
154	Dave Rozema	.05	.04	.02
155	Don Slaught	.05	.04	.02
156	Juan Beniquez	.05	.04	.02
157	Ted Higuera	.60	.45	.25
158	Andy Hawkins	.05	.04	.02
159	Don Robinson	.05	.04	.02
160	Glenn Wilson	.07	.05	.03
161	Earnest Riles	.15	.11	.06
162	Nick Esasky	.05	.04	.02
163	Carlton Fisk	.15	.11	.06
164	Claudell Washington	.07	.05	.03
165	Scott McGregor	.07	.05	.03
166	Nate Snell	.05	.04	.02
167	Ted Simmons	.10	.08	.04
168	Wade Boggs	1.25	.90	.50
169	Marty Barrett	.07	.05	.03
170	Bud Black	.05	.04	.02
171	Charlie Leibrandt	.07	.05	.03
172	Charlie Lea	.05	.04	.02
173	Reggie Jackson	.30	.25	.12
174	Bryn Smith	.07	.05	.03
175	Glenn Davis	.60	.45	.25
176	Von Hayes	.10	.08	.04
177	Danny Cox	.07	.05	.03
178	Sam Khalifa	.05	.04	.02
179	Tom Browning	.10	.08	.04
180	Scott Garrelts	.07	.05	.03
181	Shawon Dunston	.10	.08	.04
182	Doyle Alexander	.10	.08	.04
183	Jim Presley	.20	.15	.08
184	Al Cowens	.05	.04	.02
185	Mark Salas	.05	.04	.02
186	Tom Niedenfuer	.05	.04	.02
187	Dave Henderson	.05	.04	.02
188	Lonnie Smith	.05	.04	.02
189	Bruce Bochte	.05	.04	.02
190	Leon Durham	.07	.05	.03
191	Terry Francona	.05	.04	.02
192	Bruce Sutter	.10	.08	.04
193	Steve Crawford	.05	.04	.02
194	Bob Brenly	.05	.04	.02
195	Dan Pasqua	.20	.15	.08
196	Juan Samuel	.12	.09	.05
197	Floyd Rayford	.05	.04	.02
198	Tim Burke	.15	.11	.06
199	Ben Oglivie	.05	.04	.02
200	Don Carman	.15	.11	.06
201	Lance Parrish	.20	.15	.08
202	Terry Forster	.05	.04	.02
203	Neal Heaton	.07	.05	.03
204	Ivan Calderon	.25	.20	.10
205	Jorge Orta	.05	.04	.02
206	Tom Henke	.10	.08	.04
207	Rick Reuschel	.10	.08	.04
208	Dan Quisenberry	.12	.09	.05
209	Ty-Breaking Hit (Pete Rose)	.30	.25	.12
210	Floyd Youmans	.40	.30	.15
211	Tom Filer	.05	.04	.02
212	R.J. Reynolds	.07	.05	.03
213	Gorman Thomas	.10	.08	.04
214	Canadian Great (Jeff Reardon)	.40	.30	.15
215	Chris Brown	.40	.30	.15
216	Rick Aguilera	.15	.11	.06
217	Ernie Whitt	.05	.04	.02
218	Joe Orsulak	.07	.05	.03
219	Jimmy Key	.10	.08	.04

		MT	NR MT	EX
220	Atlee Hammaker	.05	.04	.02
221	Ron Darling	.10	.08	.04
222	Zane Smith	.12	.09	.05
223	Bob Welch	.07	.05	.03
224	Reid Nichols	.05	.04	.02
225	Fleet Feet (Vince Coleman, Willie McGee)	.15	.11	.06
226	Mark Gubicza	.07	.05	.03
227	Tim Birtsas	.05	.04	.02
228	Mike Hargrove	.05	.04	.02
229	Randy St. Claire	.05	.04	.02
230	Larry Herndon	.05	.04	.02
231	Dusty Baker	.07	.05	.03
232	Mookie Wilson	.07	.05	.03
233	Jeff Lahti	.05	.04	.02
234	Tom Seaver	.30	.25	.12
235	Mike Scott	.12	.09	.05
236	Don Sutton	.20	.15	.08
237	Roy Smalley	.05	.04	.02
238	Bill Madlock	.10	.08	.04
239	Charles Hudson	.07	.05	.03
240	John Franco	.07	.05	.03
241	Frank Tanana	.07	.05	.03
242	Sid Fernandez	.10	.08	.04
243	Knuckle Brothers (Joe Niekro, Phil Niekro)	.10	.08	.04
244	Dennis Lamp	.05	.04	.02
245	Gene Nelson	.05	.04	.02
246	Terry Harper	.05	.04	.02
247	Vida Blue	.07	.05	.03
248	Roger McDowell	.20	.15	.08
249	Tony Bernazard	.05	.04	.02
250	Cliff Johnson	.05	.04	.02
251	Hal McRae	.07	.05	.03
252	Garth Iorg	.05	.04	.02
253	Mitch Webster	.20	.15	.08
254	Canadian Great (Jesse Barfield)	.70	.50	.30
255	Dan Driessen	.05	.04	.02
256	Mike Brown	.05	.04	.02
257	Ron Kittle	.07	.05	.03
258	Bo Diaz	.05	.04	.02
259	Hank Aaron Puzzle Card	.05	.04	.02
260	King of Kings (Pete Rose)	.50	.40	.20
---	Checklist 1-26 DK	.05	.04	.02
---	Checklist 27-106	.05	.04	.02
---	Checklist 107-186	.05	.04	.02
---	Checklist 187-260	.05	.04	.02

1987 Leaf

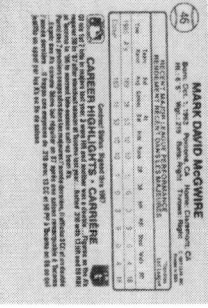

For the third consecutive season, Leaf-Donruss issued a Canadian baseball card set. The Canadian cards are nearly identical to the American set except for the name "Leaf" which appears on the front in place of "Donruss". The set contains 264 cards, each measuring the standard 2½" by 3½", with a special emphasis being placed on players from the Montreal and Toronto teams. The card backs feature career highlights written in both English and French. As in the previous years, two "Canadian Greats" cards appear in the set. These painted portraits feature Mark Eichhorn and Floyd Youmans.

	MT	NR MT	EX
Complete Set:	15.00	11.00	6.00
Common Player:	.04	.03	.02

		MT	**NR MT**	**EX**
1	Wally Joyner (DK)	.80	.60	.30
2	Roger Clemens (DK)	.50	.40	.20
3	Dale Murphy (DK)	.30	.25	.12
4	Darryl Strawberry (DK)	.25	.20	.10
5	Ozzie Smith (DK)	.10	.08	.04
6	Jose Canseco (DK)	.70	.50	.30
7	Charlie Hough (DK)	.06	.05	.02
8	Brook Jacoby (DK)	.08	.06	.03
9	Fred Lynn (DK)	.10	.08	.04
10	Rick Rhoden (DK)	.06	.05	.02
11	Chris Brown (DK)	.10	.08	.04
12	Von Hayes (DK)	.08	.06	.03
13	Jack Morris (DK)	.15	.11	.06
14	Kevin McReynolds (DK)	.10	.08	.04
15	George Brett (DK)	.30	.25	.12
16	Ted Higuera (DK)	.12	.09	.05
17	Hubie Brooks (DK)	.06	.05	.02
18	Mike Scott (DK)	.08	.06	.03
19	Kirby Puckett (DK)	.20	.15	.08
20	Dave Winfield (DK)	.20	.15	.08
21	Lloyd Moseby (DK)	.08	.06	.03
22	Eric Davis (DK)	.70	.50	.30
23	Jim Presley (DK)	.10	.08	.04
24	Keith Moreland (DK)	.06	.05	.02
25	Greg Walker (DK)	.08	.06	.03
26	Steve Sax (DK)	.10	.08	.04
27	Checklist 1-27	.04	.03	.02
28	B.J. Surhoff (RR)	.60	.45	.25
29	Randy Myers (RR)	.15	.11	.06
30	Ken Gerhart (RR)	.20	.15	.08
31	Benito Santiago (RR)	.80	.60	.30
32	Greg Swindell (RR)	.20	.15	.08
33	Mike Birkbeck (RR)	.08	.06	.03
34	Terry Steinbach (RR)	.20	.15	.08
35	Bo Jackson (RR)	.80	.60	.30
36	Greg Maddux (RR)	.10	.08	.04
37	Jim Lindeman (RR)	.15	.11	.06
38	Devon White (RR)	.60	.45	.25
39	Eric Bell (RR)	.12	.09	.05
40	Will Fraser (RR)	.12	.09	.05
41	Jerry Browne (RR)	.10	.08	.04
42	Chris James (RR)	.40	.30	.15
43	Rafael Palmeiro (RR)	.25	.20	.10
44	Pat Dodson (RR)	.08	.06	.03
45	Duane Ward (RR)	.08	.06	.03
46	Mark McGwire (RR)	2.50	2.00	1.00
47	Bruce Fields (RR) (photo actually Darnell Coles)	.08	.06	.03
48	Jody Davis	.08	.06	.03
49	Roger McDowell	.10	.08	.04
50	Jose Guzman	.08	.06	.03
51	Oddibe McDowell	.08	.06	.03
52	Harold Baines	.10	.08	.04
53	Dave Righetti	.12	.09	.05
54	Moose Haas	.04	.03	.02
55	Mark Langston	.08	.06	.03
56	Kirby Puckett	.25	.20	.10
57	Dwight Evans	.10	.08	.04
58	Willie Randolph	.06	.05	.02
59	Wally Backman	.06	.05	.02
60	Bryn Smith	.06	.05	.02
61	Tim Wallach	.08	.06	.03
62	Joe Hesketh	.06	.05	.02
63	Garry Templeton	.06	.05	.02
64	Rob Thompson	.10	.08	.04
65	Canadian Greats (Floyd Youmans)	.40	.30	.15
66	Ernest Riles	.08	.06	.03
67	Robin Yount	.20	.15	.08
68	Darryl Strawberry	.30	.25	.12
69	Ernie Whitt	.05	.04	.02
70	Dave Winfield	.20	.15	.08
71	Paul Molitor	.12	.09	.05
72	Dave Stieb	.10	.08	.04
73	Tom Henke	.08	.06	.03
74	Frank Viola	.10	.08	.04
75	Scott Garrelts	.06	.05	.02
76	Mike Boddicker	.06	.05	.02
77	Keith Moreland	.06	.05	.02
78	Lou Whitaker	.15	.11	.06
79	Dave Parker	.15	.11	.06
80	Lee Smith	.06	.05	.02
81	Tom Candiotti	.04	.03	.02
82	Greg Harris	.04	.03	.02
83	Fred Lynn	.12	.09	.05
84	Dwight Gooden	.40	.30	.15
85	Ron Darling	.08	.06	.03
86	Mike Krukow	.04	.03	.02
87	Spike Owen	.04	.03	.02
88	Len Dykstra	.10	.08	.04
89	Rick Aguilera	.10	.08	.04
90	Jim Clancy	.06	.05	.02

		MT	**NR MT**	**EX**
91	Joe Johnson	.04	.03	.02
92	Damaso Garcia	.06	.05	.02
93	Sid Fernandez	.08	.06	.03
94	Bob Ojeda	.08	.06	.03
95	Ted Higuera	.10	.08	.04
96	George Brett	.30	.25	.12
97	Willie Wilson	.08	.06	.03
98	Cal Ripken	.25	.20	.10
99	Kent Hrbek	.12	.09	.05
100	Bert Blyleven	.10	.08	.04
101	Ron Guidry	.12	.09	.05
102	Andy Allanson	.08	.06	.03
103	Dave Henderson	.05	.04	.02
104	Kirk Gibson	.20	.15	.08
105	Lloyd Moseby	.08	.06	.03
106	Tony Fernandez	.10	.08	.04
107	Lance Parrish	.15	.11	.06
108	Ozzie Smith	.10	.08	.04
109	Gary Carter	.20	.15	.08
110	Eddie Murray	.25	.20	.10
111	Mike Witt	.08	.06	.03
112	Bobby Witt	.12	.09	.05
113	Willie McGee	.12	.09	.05
114	Steve Garvey	.20	.15	.08
115	Glenn Davis	.12	.09	.05
116	Jose Cruz	.06	.05	.02
117	Ozzie Guillen	.06	.05	.02
118	Alvin Davis	.08	.06	.03
119	Jose Rijo	.04	.03	.02
120	Bill Madlock	.08	.06	.03
121	Tommy Herr	.06	.05	.02
122	Mike Schmidt	.30	.25	.12
123	Mike Scioscia	.04	.03	.02
124	Terry Pendleton	.06	.05	.02
125	Leon Durham	.06	.05	.02
126	Alan Trammell	.20	.15	.08
127	Jesse Barfield	.12	.09	.05
128	Shawon Dunston	.06	.05	.02
129	Pete Rose	.40	.30	.15
130	Von Hayes	.08	.06	.03
131	Julio Franco	.08	.06	.03
132	Juan Samuel	.10	.08	.04
133	Joe Carter	.10	.08	.04
134	Brook Jacoby	.08	.06	.03
135	Jack Morris	.15	.11	.06
136	Bob Horner	.10	.08	.04
137	Calvin Schiraldi	.04	.03	.02
138	Tom Browning	.06	.05	.02
139	Shane Rawley	.06	.05	.02
140	Mario Soto	.04	.03	.02
141	Dale Murphy	.30	.25	.12
142	Hubie Brooks	.06	.05	.02
143	Jeff Reardon	.10	.08	.04
144	Will Clark	.80	.60	.30
145	Ed Correa	.10	.08	.04
146	Glenn Wilson	.06	.05	.02
147	Johnny Ray	.06	.05	.02
148	Fernando Valenzuela	.20	.15	.08
149	Tim Raines	.20	.15	.08
150	Don Mattingly	1.25	.90	.50
151	Jose Canseco	1.00	.70	.40
152	Gary Pettis	.04	.03	.02
153	Don Sutton	.15	.11	.06
154	Jim Presley	.08	.06	.03
155	Checklist 28-105	.04	.03	.02
156	Dale Sveum	.12	.09	.05
157	Cory Snyder	.50	.40	.20
158	Jeff Sellers	.08	.06	.03
159	Denny Walling	.04	.03	.02
160	Danny Cox	.06	.05	.02
161	Bob Forsch	.04	.03	.02
162	Joaquin Andujar	.04	.03	.02
163	Roberto Clemente Puzzle Card	.04	.03	.02
164	Paul Assenmacher	.08	.06	.03
165	Marty Barrett	.06	.05	.02
166	Ray Knight	.06	.05	.02
167	Rafael Santana	.04	.03	.02
168	Bruce Ruffin	.10	.08	.04
169	Buddy Bell	.06	.05	.02
170	Kevin Mitchell	.20	.15	.08
171	Ken Oberkfell	.04	.03	.02
172	Gene Garber	.04	.03	.02
173	Canadian Greats (Mark Eichhorn)	.40	.30	.15
174	Don Carman	.06	.05	.02
175	Jesse Orosco	.06	.05	.02
176	Mookie Wilson	.06	.05	.02
177	Gary Ward	.04	.03	.02
178	John Franco	.06	.05	.02
179	Eric Davis	1.25	.90	.50
180	Walt Terrell	.06	.05	.02
181	Phil Niekro	.15	.11	.06

		MT	NR MT	EX
182	Pat Tabler	.06	.05	.02
183	Brett Butler	.06	.05	.02
184	George Bell	.20	.15	.08
185	Pete Incaviglia	.50	.40	.20
186	Pete O'Brien	.06	.05	.02
187	Jimmy Key	.08	.06	.03
188	Frank White	.06	.05	.02
189	Mike Pagliarulo	.08	.06	.03
190	Roger Clemens	.50	.40	.20
191	Rickey Henderson	.25	.20	.10
192	Mike Easler	.06	.05	.02
193	Wade Boggs	.70	.50	.30
194	Vince Coleman	.15	.11	.06
195	Charlie Kerfeld	.06	.05	.02
196	Dickie Thon	.04	.03	.02
197	Bill Doran	.06	.05	.02
198	Alfredo Griffin	.06	.05	.02
199	Carlton Fisk	.12	.09	.05
200	Phil Bradley	.08	.06	.03
201	Reggie Jackson	.25	.20	.10
202	Bob Boone	.04	.03	.02
203	Steve Sax	.10	.08	.04
204	Tom Niedenfuer	.04	.03	.02
205	Tim Burke	.06	.05	.02
206	Floyd Youmans	.12	.09	.05
207	Jay Tibbs	.04	.03	.02
208	Chili Davis	.06	.05	.02
209	Larry Parrish	.06	.05	.02
210	John Cerutti	.12	.09	.05
211	Kevin Bass	.06	.05	.02
212	Andre Dawson	.12	.09	.05
213	Bob Sebra	.12	.09	.05
214	Kevin McReynolds	.08	.06	.03
215	Jim Morrison	.04	.03	.02
216	Candy Maldonado	.06	.05	.02
217	John Kruk	.40	.30	.15
218	Todd Worrell	.12	.09	.05
219	Barry Bonds	.25	.20	.10
220	Andy McGaffigan	.04	.03	.02
221	Andres Galarraga	.08	.06	.03
222	Mike Fitzgerald	.04	.03	.02
223	Kirk McCaskill	.06	.05	.02
224	Dave Smith	.04	.03	.02
225	Ruben Sierra	.50	.40	.20
226	Scott Fletcher	.04	.03	.02
227	Chet Lemon	.06	.05	.02
228	Dan Petry	.06	.05	.02
229	Mark Eichhorn	.10	.08	.04
230	Cecil Cooper	.08	.06	.03
231	Willie Upshaw	.06	.05	.02
232	Don Baylor	.08	.06	.03
233	Keith Hernandez	.20	.15	.08
234	Ryne Sandberg	.20	.15	.08
235	Tony Gwynn	.25	.20	.10
236	Chris Brown	.08	.06	.03
237	Pedro Guerrero	.10	.08	.04
238	Mark Gubicza	.06	.05	.02
239	Sid Bream	.06	.05	.02
240	Joe Cowley	.04	.03	.02
241	Bill Buckner	.08	.06	.03
242	John Candelaria	.06	.05	.02
243	Scott McGregor	.06	.05	.02
244	Tom Brunansky	.08	.06	.03
245	Gary Gaetti	.10	.08	.04
246	Orel Hershiser	.10	.08	.04
247	Jim Rice	.20	.15	.08
248	Oil Can Boyd	.06	.05	.02
249	Bob Knepper	.04	.03	.02
250	Danny Tartabull	.20	.15	.08
251	John Cangelosi	.10	.08	.04
252	Wally Joyner	1.25	.90	.50
253	Bruce Hurst	.06	.05	.02
254	Rich Gedman	.06	.05	.02
255	Jim Deshaies	.12	.09	.05
256	Tony Pena	.06	.05	.02
257	Nolan Ryan	.20	.15	.08
258	Mike Scott	.10	.08	.04
259	Checklist 106-183	.04	.03	.02
260	Dennis Rasmussen	.06	.05	.02
261	Bret Saberhagen	.15	.11	.06
262	Steve Balboni	.04	.03	.02
263	Tom Seaver	.20	.15	.08
264	Checklist 184-264	.04	.03	.02

Definitions for grading conditions are located in the Introduction of this price guide.

1987 Leaf Candy City Team

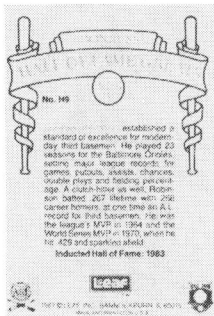

As part of their endorsement for the Seventh International Special Olympics Summer Games, Leaf produced an 18-card set of trading cards. Twelve of the 18 cards feature Baseball Hall of Fame greats. These cards measure 2½'' by 3½'' and are numbered H1 through H12. The remaining six cards in the set are numbered S1-S6 and feature unnamed Special Olympics champions. All cards feature the artwork of Dick Perez. The cards were available through a mail-in offer advertised at special store displays. Only the baseball-related subjects are listed in the checklist that follows.

		MT	NR MT	EX
	Complete Set:	2.50	2.00	1.00
	Common Player:	.10	.08	.04
1	Mickey Mantle	.60	.45	.25
2	Yogi Berra	.25	.20	.10
3	Roy Campanella	.25	.20	.10
4	Stan Musial	.35	.25	.14
5	Ted Williams	.35	.25	.14
6	Duke Snider	.25	.20	.10
7	Hank Aaron	.35	.25	.14
8	Pee Wee Reese	.20	.15	.08
9	Brooks Robinson	.20	.15	.08
10	Al Kaline	.20	.15	.08
11	Willie McCovey	.15	.11	.06
12	Cool Papa Bell	.10	.08	.04

1986 Lite Beer Astros

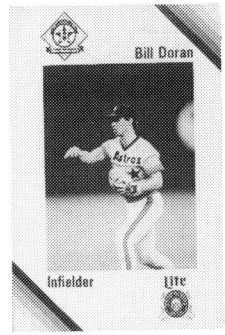
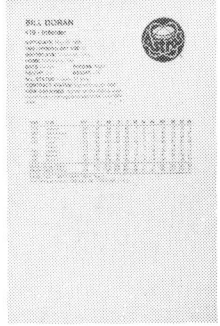

		MT	NR MT	EX
	Complete Set:	60.00	45.00	24.00
	Common Player:	1.50	1.25	.60
3	Phil Garner	1.50	1.25	.60
6	Mark Bailey	1.50	1.25	.60
10	Dickie Thon	2.00	1.50	.80
11	Frank DiPino	1.50	1.25	.60
12	Craig Reynolds	1.50	1.25	.60
14	Alan Ashby	1.50	1.25	.60
17	Kevin Bass	3.00	2.25	1.25

		MT	NR MT	EX
19	Bill Doran	3.00	2.25	1.25
20	Jim Pankovits	1.50	1.25	.60
21	Terry Puhl	1.50	1.25	.60
22	Hal Lanier	2.00	1.50	.80
25	Jose Cruz	3.00	2.25	1.25
27	Glenn Davis	6.00	4.50	2.50
28	Billy Hatcher	2.50	2.00	1.00
29	Denny Walling	1.50	1.25	.60
33	Mike Scott	3.00	2.25	1.25
34	Nolan Ryan	5.00	3.75	2.00
37	Charlie Kerfeld	3.00	2.25	1.25
39	Bob Knepper	2.00	1.50	.80
43	Jim Deshaies	3.50	2.75	1.50
45	Dave Smith	2.00	1.50	.80
53	Mike Madden	1.50	1.25	.60

1986 Lite Beer Rangers

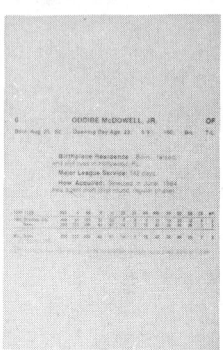

#0 ODDIBE McDOWELL
Outfielder

		MT	NR MT	EX
Complete Set:		60.00	45.00	24.00
Common Player:		1.50	1.25	.60
0	Oddibe McDowell	4.00	3.00	1.50
1	Scott Fletcher	2.00	1.50	.80
2	Bobby Valentine	2.00	1.50	.80
4	Don Slaught	1.50	1.25	.60
5	Pete Incaviglia	7.00	5.25	2.75
9	Pete O'Brien	3.00	2.25	1.25
10	Art Howe	1.50	1.25	.60
11	Toby Harrah	2.00	1.50	.80
12	Geno Petralli	1.50	1.25	.60
13	Joe Ferguson	1.50	1.25	.60
14	Tim Foli	1.50	1.25	.60
15	Larry Parrish	3.00	2.25	1.25
16	Mike Mason	1.50	1.25	.60
17	Darrell Porter	2.00	1.50	.80
18	Ed Correa	4.00	3.00	1.50
19	Curtis Wilkerson	1.50	1.25	.60
22	Steve Buechele	3.00	2.25	1.25
23	Jose Guzman	4.00	3.00	1.50
24	Ricky Wright	1.50	1.25	.60
27	Greg Harris	1.50	1.25	.60
31	Tom Robson	1.50	1.25	.60
32	Gary Ward	2.00	1.50	.80
35	Tom House	1.50	1.25	.60
44	Tom Paciorek	1.50	1.25	.60
45	Dwayne Henry	3.00	2.25	1.25
48	Bobby Witt	4.00	3.00	1.50
49	Charlie Hough	3.00	2.25	1.25
---	Arlington Stadium	1.50	1.25	.60

Definitions for grading conditions are located in the Introduction of this price guide.

1916 M101-4
The Sporting News

JOSH DEVORE
R. F.—Philadelphia Nationals
46

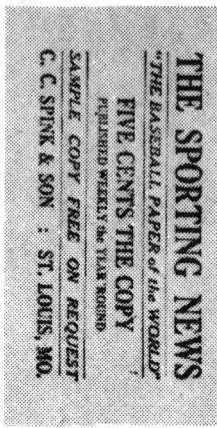

This 200-card set was issued as a premium by *The Sporting News* and was also used by Weil Baking, the Globe Stores, and several other regional advertisers. The 1⅝'' by 3'' cards contain bordered black-and-white photos on the fronts, with player name, position and team, as well as a card number. Card backs are in a horizontal format and show an advertisement for the sponsoring sports weekly. Most of the day's top players and many Hall of Famers are included in the set, with the Ty Cobb and Babe Ruth cards carrying the highest values.

		NR MT	EX	VG
Complete Set:		7000.00	2800.00	1400.
Common Player:		18.00	9.00	5.50
1	Babe Adams	30.00	9.00	5.50
2	Sam Agnew	20.00	9.00	5.50
3	Eddie Ainsmith	18.00	9.00	5.50
4	Grover Alexander	65.00	32.00	19.50
5	Leon Ames	18.00	9.00	5.50
6	Jimmy Archer	18.00	9.00	5.50
7	Jimmy Austin	18.00	9.00	5.50
8	H.D. Baird	25.00	12.50	7.50
9	J. Franklin Baker	45.00	22.00	13.50
10	Dave Bancroft	45.00	22.00	13.50
11	Jack Barry	18.00	9.00	5.50
12	Zinn Beck	18.00	9.00	5.50
13	"Chief" Bender	50.00	25.00	15.00
14	Joe Benz	18.00	9.00	5.50
15	Bob Bescher	18.00	9.00	5.50
16	Al Betzel	18.00	9.00	5.50
17	Mordecai Brown	45.00	22.00	13.50
18	Eddie Burns	18.00	9.00	5.50
19	George Burns	25.00	12.50	7.50
20	Geo. J. Burns	18.00	9.00	5.50
21	Joe Bush	25.00	12.50	7.50
22	"Donie" Bush	20.00	10.00	6.00
23	Art Butler	18.00	9.00	5.50
24	Bobbie Byrne	18.00	9.00	5.50
25	Forrest Cady	25.00	12.50	7.50
26	Jimmy Callahan	18.00	9.00	5.50
27	Ray Caldwell	18.00	9.00	5.50
28	Max Carey	45.00	22.00	13.50
29	George Chalmers	18.00	9.00	5.50
30,	Ray Chapman	25.00	12.50	7.50
31	Larry Cheney	18.00	9.00	5.50
32	Eddie Cicotte	25.00	12.50	7.50
33	Tom Clarke	18.00	9.00	5.50

		NR MT	EX	VG
34	Eddie Collins	45.00	22.00	13.50
35	"Shauno" Collins	18.00	9.00	5.50
36	Charles Comiskey	45.00	22.00	13.50
37	Joe Connolly	18.00	9.00	5.50
38	Ty Cobb	600.00	240.00	150.00
39	Harry Coveleskie (Coveleski)	18.00	9.00	5.50
40	Gavvy Cravath	25.00	12.50	7.50
41	Sam Crawford	45.00	22.00	13.50
42	Jean Dale	18.00	9.00	5.50
43	Jake Daubert	25.00	12.50	7.50
44	Charles Deal	18.00	9.00	5.50
45	Al Demaree	18.00	9.00	5.50
46	Josh Devore	25.00	12.50	7.50
47	William Doak	18.00	9.00	5.50
48	Bill Donovan	18.00	9.00	5.50
49	Charles Dooin	18.00	9.00	5.50
50	Mike Doolan	18.00	9.00	5.50
51	Larry Doyle	20.00	10.00	6.00
52	Jean Dubuc	18.00	9.00	5.50
53	Oscar Dugey	18.00	9.00	5.50
54	Johnny Evers	45.00	22.00	13.50
55	Urban Faber	45.00	22.00	13.50
56	"Hap" Felsch	25.00	12.50	7.50
57	Bill Fischer	18.00	9.00	5.50
58	Ray Fisher	25.00	12.50	7.50
59	Max Flack	18.00	9.00	5.50
60	Art Fletcher	18.00	9.00	5.50
61	Eddie Foster	18.00	9.00	5.50
62	Jacques Fournier	18.00	9.00	5.50
63	Del Gainer (Gainor)	18.00	9.00	5.50
64	"Chic" Gandil	25.00	12.50	7.50
65	Larry Gardner	18.00	9.00	5.50
66	Joe Gedeon	18.00	9.00	5.50
67	Gus Getz	18.00	9.00	5.50
68	Geo. Gibson	18.00	9.00	5.50
69	Wilbur Good	18.00	9.00	5.50
70	Hank Gowdy	20.00	10.00	6.00
71	John Graney	18.00	9.00	5.50
72	Clark Griffith	50.00	25.00	15.00
73	Tom Griffith	18.00	9.00	5.50
74	Heinie Groh	20.00	10.00	6.00
75	Earl Hamilton	18.00	9.00	5.50
76	Bob Harmon	18.00	9.00	5.50
77	Roy Hartzell	18.00	9.00	5.50
78	Claude Hendrix	18.00	9.00	5.50
79	Olaf Henrikson	18.00	9.00	5.50
80	John Henry	18.00	9.00	5.50
81	"Buck" Herzog	18.00	9.00	5.50
82	Hugh High	18.00	9.00	5.50
83	Dick Hoblitzell	18.00	9.00	5.50
84	Harry Hooper	45.00	22.00	13.50
85	Ivan Howard	18.00	9.00	5.50
86	Miller Huggins	45.00	22.00	13.50
87	Joe Jackson	500.00	200.00	125.00
88	William James	18.00	9.00	5.50
89	Harold Janvrin	18.00	9.00	5.50
90	Hugh Jennings	45.00	22.00	13.50
91	Walter Johnson	250.00	100.00	63.00
92	Fielder Jones	18.00	9.00	5.50
93	Joe Judge	25.00	12.50	7.50
94	Bennie Kauff	18.00	9.00	5.50
95	Wm. Killefer Jr.	18.00	9.00	5.50
96	Ed. Konetchy	18.00	9.00	5.50
97	Napoleon Lajoie	130.00	52.00	33.00
98	Jack Lapp	18.00	9.00	5.50
99	John Lavan	18.00	9.00	5.50
100	Jimmy Lavender	18.00	9.00	5.50
101	"Nemo" Leibold	18.00	9.00	5.50
102	H.B. Leonard	18.00	9.00	5.50
103	Duffy Lewis	20.00	10.00	6.00
104	Hans Lobert	18.00	9.00	5.50
105	Tom Long	18.00	9.00	5.50
106	Fred Luderus	18.00	9.00	5.50
107	Connie Mack	75.00	37.00	22.00
108	Lee Magee	18.00	9.00	5.50
109	Sherwood Magee	25.00	12.50	7.50
110	Al. Mamaux	18.00	9.00	5.50
111	Leslie Mann	18.00	9.00	5.50
112	"Rabbit" Maranville	45.00	22.00	13.50
113	Rube Marquard	45.00	22.00	13.50
114	J. Erskine Mayer	18.00	9.00	5.50
115	George McBride	18.00	9.00	5.50
116	John J. McGraw	55.00	27.00	16.50
117	Jack McInnis	20.00	10.00	6.00
118	Fred Merkle	20.00	10.00	6.00
119	Chief Meyers	18.00	9.00	5.50
120	Clyde Milan	18.00	9.00	5.50
121	John Miller	25.00	12.50	7.50
122	Otto Miller	18.00	9.00	5.50
123	Willie Mitchell	18.00	9.00	5.50
124	Fred Mollwitz	18.00	9.00	5.50

		NR MT	EX	VG
125	Pat Moran	18.00	9.00	5.50
126	Ray Morgan	18.00	9.00	5.50
127	Geo. Moriarty	18.00	9.00	5.50
128	Guy Morton	18.00	9.00	5.50
129	Mike Mowrey	25.00	12.50	7.50
130	Ed. Murphy	25.00	12.50	7.50
131	"Hy" Myers	18.00	9.00	5.50
132	J.A. Niehoff	18.00	9.00	5.50
133	Rube Oldring	18.00	9.00	5.50
134	Oliver O'Mara	18.00	9.00	5.50
135	Steve O'Neill	18.00	9.00	5.50
136	"Dode" Paskert	18.00	9.00	5.50
137	Roger Peckinpaugh	25.00	12.50	7.50
138	Walter Pipp	25.00	12.50	7.50
139	Derril Pratt (Derrill)	18.00	9.00	5.50
140	Pat Ragan	25.00	12.50	7.50
141	Bill Rariden	18.00	9.00	5.50
142	Eppa Rixey	45.00	22.00	13.50
143	Davey Robertson	18.00	9.00	5.50
144	Wilbert Robinson	45.00	22.00	13.50
145	Bob Roth	18.00	9.00	5.50
146	Ed. Roush	45.00	22.00	13.50
147	Clarence Rowland	18.00	9.00	5.50
148	"Nap" Rucker	18.00	9.00	5.50
149	Dick Rudolph	18.00	9.00	5.50
150	Reb Russell	18.00	9.00	5.50
151	Babe Ruth	1000.00	400.00	250.00
152	Vic Saier	18.00	9.00	5.50
153	"Slim" Sallee	18.00	9.00	5.50
154	Ray Schalk	45.00	22.00	13.50
155	Walter Schang	18.00	9.00	5.50
156	Frank Schulte	18.00	9.00	5.50
157	Everett Scott	18.00	9.00	5.50
158	Jim Scott	18.00	9.00	5.50
159	Tom Seaton	18.00	9.00	5.50
160	Howard Shanks	18.00	9.00	5.50
161	Bob Shawkey	25.00	12.50	7.50
162	Ernie Shore	20.00	10.00	6.00
163	Burt Shotton	20.00	10.00	6.00
164	Geo. Sisler	50.00	25.00	15.00
165	J. Carlisle Smith	18.00	9.00	5.50
166	Fred Snodgrass	18.00	9.00	5.50
167	Geo. Stallings	18.00	9.00	5.50
168a	Oscar Stanage (catching)	25.00	12.50	7.50
168b	Oscar Stanage (portrait to waist)	25.00	12.50	7.50
169	Charles Stengel	200.00	80.00	50.00
170	Milton Stock	18.00	9.00	5.50
171	Amos Strunk	25.00	12.50	7.50
172	Billy Sullivan	18.00	9.00	5.50
173	"Jeff" Tesreau	18.00	9.00	5.50
174	Joe Tinker	45.00	22.00	13.50
175	Fred Toney	18.00	9.00	5.50
176	Terry Turner	18.00	9.00	5.50
177	George Tyler	25.00	12.50	7.50
178	Jim Vaughn	18.00	9.00	5.50
179	Bob Veach	18.00	9.00	5.50
180	James Viox	18.00	9.00	5.50
181	Oscar Vitt	18.00	9.00	5.50
182	Hans Wagner	225.00	90.00	56.00
183	Clarence Walker	25.00	12.50	7.50
184	Ed. Walsh	45.00	22.00	13.50
185	W. Wambsganss (photo actually Fritz Coumbe)	25.00	12.50	7.50
186	Buck Weaver	25.00	12.50	7.50
187	Carl Weilman	18.00	9.00	5.50
188	Zach Wheat	45.00	22.00	13.50
189	Geo. Whitted	18.00	9.00	5.50
190	Fred Williams	20.00	10.00	6.00
191	Art Wilson	18.00	9.00	5.50
192	J. Owen Wilson	18.00	9.00	5.50
193	Ivy Wingo	18.00	9.00	5.50
194	"Mel" Wolfgang	18.00	9.00	5.50
195	Joe Wood	30.00	15.00	9.00
196	Steve Yerkes	18.00	9.00	5.50
197	"Pep" Young	25.00	12.50	7.50
198	Rollie Zeider	18.00	9.00	5.50
199	Heiny Zimmerman	20.00	9.00	5.50
200	Ed. Zwilling	30.00	9.00	5.50

1915 M101-5
The Sporting News

This set, which is quite similar to the M101-5 Sporting News issue, was also issued as a promotional premium by *The Sporting News*. The 200 black-and-white cards once again are printed with player photo,

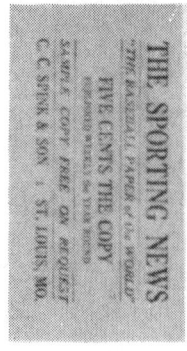

name, position, team and card number on the fronts and advertising on the backs. The set checklist is the same as for sets issued by Morehouse Baking and Standard Baking. Most of the players included in the 1⅝" by 3" set also appear in the prior *Sporting News* edition.

		NR MT	EX	VG
Complete Set:		7000.00	2800.00	1400.
Common Player:		18.00	9.10	4.60
1	Babe Adams	30.00	9.00	5.50
2	Sam Agnew	20.00	9.00	5.50
3	Eddie Ainsmith	18.00	9.00	5.50
4	Grover Alexander	65.00	32.00	19.50
5	Leon Ames	18.00	9.00	5.50
6	Jimmy Archer	18.00	9.00	5.50
7	Jimmy Austin	18.00	9.00	5.50
8	J. Franklin Baker	45.00	22.00	13.50
9	Dave Bancroft	45.00	22.00	13.50
10	Jack Barry	18.00	10.00	6.00
11	Zinn Beck	18.00	9.00	5.50
12	Lute Boone	25.00	12.50	7.50
13	Joe Benz	18.00	9.00	5.50
14	Bob Bescher	18.00	9.00	5.50
15	Al Betzel	18.00	9.00	5.50
16	Roger Bresnahan	50.00	26.00	15.50
17	Eddie Burns	18.00	9.00	5.50
18	Geo. J. Burns	18.00	10.00	6.00
19	Joe Bush	20.00	10.00	6.00
20	Owen Bush	18.00	9.00	5.50
21	Art Butler	18.00	9.00	5.50
22	Bobbie Byrne	18.00	9.00	5.50
23a	Forrest Cady	65.00	32.00	19.50
23b	Mordecai Brown	50.00	26.00	15.50
24	Jimmy Callahan	18.00	9.00	5.50
25	Ray Caldwell	18.00	10.00	6.00
26	Max Carey	45.00	22.00	13.50
27	George Chalmers	18.00	9.00	5.50
28	Frank Chance	65.00	32.00	19.50
29	Ray Chapman	20.00	12.50	7.50
30	Larry Cheney	18.00	10.00	6.00
31	Eddie Cicotte	25.00	12.50	7.50
32	Tom Clarke	18.00	9.00	5.50
33	Eddie Collins	45.00	22.00	13.50
34	"Shauno" Collins	18.00	9.00	5.50
35	Charles Comisky (Comiskey)	45.00	22.00	13.50
36	Joe Connolly	18.00	9.00	5.50
37	Luther Cook	25.00	12.50	7.50
38	Jack Coombs	25.00	12.50	7.50
39	Dan Costello	25.00	12.50	7.50
40	Harry Coveleskie (Coveleski)	18.00	10.00	6.00
41	Gavvy Cravath	25.00	12.50	7.50
42	Sam Crawford	45.00	22.00	13.50
43	Jean Dale	18.00	9.00	5.50
44	Jake Daubert	25.00	12.50	7.50
45	Geo. A. Davis Jr.	25.00	12.50	7.50
46	Charles Deal	18.00	9.00	5.50
47	Al Demaree	18.00	9.00	5.50
48	William Doak	18.00	9.00	5.50
49	Bill Donovan	18.00	10.00	6.00
50	Charles Dooin	18.00	10.00	6.00
51	Mike Doolan	18.00	9.00	5.50
52	Larry Doyle	20.00	10.00	6.00
53	Jean Dubuc	18.00	9.00	5.50
54	Oscar Dugey	18.00	9.00	5.50
55	Johnny Evers	45.00	22.00	13.50
56	Urban Faber	45.00	22.00	13.50
57	"Hap" Felsch	25.00	12.50	7.50

		NR MT	EX	VG
58	Bill Fischer	18.00	9.00	5.50
59	Ray Fisher	25.00	12.50	7.50
60	Max Flack	18.00	9.00	5.50
61	Art Fletcher	18.00	10.00	6.00
62	Eddie Foster	18.00	9.00	5.50
63	Jacques Fournier	18.00	9.00	5.50
64	Del Gainer (Gainor)	18.00	9.00	5.50
65	Larry Gardner	18.00	9.00	5.50
66	Joe Gedeon	18.00	10.00	6.00
67	Gus Getz	18.00	10.00	6.00
68	Geo. Gibson	18.00	9.00	5.50
69	Wilbur Good	18.00	9.00	5.50
70	Hank Gowdy	20.00	10.00	6.00
71	John Graney	18.00	9.00	5.50
72	Tom Griffith	18.00	9.00	5.50
73	Heinie Groh	20.00	10.00	6.00
74	Earl Hamilton	18.00	9.00	5.50
75	Bob Harmon	18.00	9.00	5.50
76	Roy Hartzell	18.00	10.00	6.00
77	Claude Hendrix	18.00	9.00	5.50
78	Olaf Henriksen	18.00	9.00	5.50
79	John Henry	18.00	9.00	5.50
80	"Buck" Herzog	18.00	9.00	5.50
81	Hugh High	18.00	10.00	6.00
82	Dick Hoblitzell	18.00	9.00	5.50
83	Harry Hooper	45.00	22.00	13.50
84	Ivan Howard	18.00	9.00	5.50
85	Miller Huggins	45.00	22.00	13.50
86	Joe Jackson	500.00	200.00	125.00
87	William James	18.00	9.00	5.50
88	Harold Janvrin	18.00	9.00	5.50
89	Hugh Jennings	45.00	22.00	13.50
90	Walter Johnson	250.00	100.00	63.00
91	Fielder Jones	18.00	9.00	5.50
92	Bennie Kauff	18.00	10.00	6.00
93	Wm. Killefer Jr.	18.00	9.00	5.50
94	Ed. Konetchy	18.00	9.00	5.50
95	Napoleon Lajoie	130.00	52.00	33.00
96	Jack Lapp	18.00	9.00	5.50
97a	John Lavan (correct spelling)	25.00	12.50	7.50
97b	John Lavin (incorrect spelling)	25.00	12.50	7.50
98	Jimmy Lavender	18.00	9.00	5.50
99	"Nemo" Leibold	18.00	9.00	5.50
100	H.B. Leonard	18.00	9.00	5.50
101	Duffy Lewis	20.00	10.00	6.00
102	Hans Lobert	18.00	10.00	6.00
103	Tom Long	18.00	9.00	5.50
104	Fred Luderus	18.00	9.00	5.50
105	Connie Mack	75.00	36.00	22.00
106	Lee Magee	18.00	10.00	6.00
107	Al. Mamaux	18.00	9.00	5.50
108	Leslie Mann	18.00	9.00	5.50
109	"Rabbit" Maranville	45.00	22.00	13.50
110	Rube Marquard	45.00	22.00	13.50
111	Armando Marsans	25.00	12.50	7.50
112	J. Erskine Mayer	18.00	9.00	5.50
113	George McBride	18.00	9.00	5.50
114	John J. McGraw	55.00	27.00	16.00
115	Jack McInnis	18.00	10.00	6.00
116	Fred Merkle	20.00	10.00	6.00
117	Chief Meyers	18.00	10.00	6.00
118	Clyde Milan	18.00	9.00	5.50
119	Otto Miller	18.00	10.00	6.00
120	Willie Mitchel (Mitchell)	18.00	9.00	5.50
121	Fred Mollwitz	18.00	9.00	5.50
122	J. Herbert Moran	25.00	12.50	7.50
123	Pat Moran	18.00	9.00	5.50
124	Ray Morgan	18.00	9.00	5.50
125	Geo. Moriarty	18.00	9.00	5.50
126	Guy Morton	18.00	9.00	5.50
127	Ed. Murphy (photo actually Danny Murphy)	25.00	12.50	7.50
128	John Murray	25.00	12.50	7.50
129	"Hy" Myers	18.00	10.00	6.00
130	J.A. Niehoff	18.00	9.00	5.50
131	Leslie Nunamaker	25.00	12.50	7.50
132	Rube Oldring	18.00	9.00	5.50
133	Oliver O'Mara	18.00	10.00	6.00
134	Steve O'Neill	18.00	9.00	5.50
135	"Dode" Paskert	18.00	9.00	5.50
136	Roger Peckinpaugh (photo actually Gavvy Cravath)	25.00	12.50	7.50
137	E.J. Pfeffer (photo actually Jeff Pfeffer)	25.00	12.50	7.50
138	Geo. Pierce (Pearce)	25.00	12.50	7.50
139	Walter Pipp	25.00	12.50	7.50
140	Derril Pratt (Derrill)	18.00	9.00	5.50
141	Bill Rariden	18.00	10.00	6.00
142	Eppa Rixey	45.00	22.00	13.50
143	Davey Robertson	18.00	10.00	6.00
144	Wilbert Robertson	45.00	22.00	13.50

		NR MT	EX	VG
145	Bob Roth	18.00	9.00	5.50
146	Ed. Roush	45.00	22.00	13.50
147	Clarence Rowland	18.00	9.00	5.50
148	"Nap" Rucker	18.00	10.00	6.00
149	Dick Rudolph	18.00	9.00	5.50
150	Reb Russell	18.00	9.00	5.50
151	Babe Ruth	1000.00	400.00	250.00
152	Vic Saier	18.00	9.00	5.50
153	"Slim" Sallee	18.00	9.00	5.50
154	"Germany" Schaefer	25.00	12.50	7.50
155	Ray Schalk	45.00	22.00	13.50
156	Walter Schang	18.00	9.00	5.50
157	Chas. Schmidt	25.00	12.50	7.50
158	Frank Schulte	18.00	9.00	5.50
159	Jim Scott	18.00	9.00	5.50
160	Everett Scott	18.00	9.00	5.50
161	Tom Seaton	18.00	9.00	5.50
162	Howard Shanks	18.00	9.00	5.50
163	Bob Shawkey (photo actually Jack McInnis)	25.00	12.50	7.50
164	Ernie Shore	20.00	10.00	6.00
165	Burt Shotton	20.00	10.00	6.00
166	George Sisler	50.00	26.00	15.50
167	J. Carlisle Smith	18.00	9.00	5.50
168	Fred Snodgrass	18.00	9.00	5.50
169	Geo. Stallings	18.00	9.00	5.50
170	Oscar Stanage (photo actually Chas. Schmidt)	18.00	9.00	5.50
171	Charles Stengel	200.00	80.00	50.00
172	Milton Stock	18.00	9.00	5.50
173	Amos Strunk (photo actually Olaf Henriksen)	25.00	12.50	7.50
174	Billy Sullivan	18.00	9.00	5.50
175	Chas. Tesreau	25.00	12.50	7.50
176	Jim Thorpe	500.00	200.00	125.00
177	Joe Tinker	45.00	22.00	13.50
178	Fred Toney	18.00	9.00	5.50
179	Terry Turner	18.00	9.00	5.50
180	Jim Vaughn	18.00	9.00	5.50
181	Bob Veach	18.00	9.00	5.50
182	James Voix	18.00	9.00	5.50
183	Oscar Vitt	18.00	9.00	5.50
184	Hans Wagner	225.00	90.00	56.00
185	Clarence Walker (photo not Walker)	25.00	12.50	7.50
186	Zach Wheat	45.00	22.00	13.50
187	Ed. Walsh	45.00	22.00	13.50
188	Buck Weaver	25.00	12.50	7.50
189	Carl Weilman	18.00	9.00	5.50
190	Geo. Whitted	18.00	9.00	5.50
191	Fred Williams	20.00	10.00	6.00
192	Art Wilson	18.00	9.00	5.50
193	J. Owen Wilson	18.00	9.00	5.50
194	Ivy Wingo	18.00	9.00	5.50
195	"Mel" Wolfgang	18.00	9.00	5.50
196	Joe Wood	30.00	15.00	9.00
197	Steve Yerkes	18.00	9.00	5.50
198	Rollie Zeider	18.00	9.00	5.50
199	Heiny Zimmerman	20.00	9.00	5.50
200	Ed. Zwilling	30.00	9.00	5.50

1911 M116 Sporting Life

Livingstone, Philadelphia Amer.

This set of 1½'' by 2¾'' cards was offered to subscribers of *Sporting Life*, a major competitor of *The Sporting News* in the early part of the century. The cards were issued in 24 series of 12 cards each. Specialists consider the set complete at 310 different cards, including variations on which the background is in blue, rather than pastel colors. Each of the 16 major league teams are represented by 13 to 21 players, with nine minor leaguers also included. Card fronts are black and white photos that have been hand colored and carry the player's name and team. Card backs show various ads for the magazine. The last 72 cards issued are scarcer than the earlier series.

		NR MT	EX	VG
	Complete Set:	12000.00	4800.00	2400.
	Common Player:	22.00	11.00	6.50
1	Ed Abbaticchio	22.00	11.00	6.50
2	Babe Adams	45.00	22.00	13.50
3	Red Ames	45.00	22.00	13.50
4	Jimmy Archer	45.00	22.00	13.50
5	Frank Arrelanes (Arellanes)	22.00	11.00	6.50
6	Tommy Atkins	45.00	22.00	13.50
7	Jimmy Austin	45.00	22.00	13.50
8	Les Bachman (Backman)	22.00	11.00	6.50
9	Bill Bailey	22.00	11.00	6.50
10	Home Run Baker	75.00	37.00	22.00
11	Cy Barger	25.00	12.50	7.50
12	Jack Barry	25.00	12.50	7.50
13	Johnny Bates	22.00	11.00	6.50
14	Ginger Beaumont	22.00	11.00	6.50
15	Fred Beck	22.00	11.00	6.50
16	Heinie Beckendorf	22.00	11.00	6.50
17	Fred Beebe	22.00	11.00	6.50
18	George Bell	25.00	12.50	7.50
19	Harry Bemis	22.00	11.00	6.50
20a	Chief Bender (blue background)	95.00	47.00	28.00
20b	Chief Bender (pastel background)	75.00	37.00	22.00
21	Bill Bergen	25.00	12.50	7.50
22	Heinie Berger	22.00	11.00	6.50
23	Bob Bescher	22.00	11.00	6.50
24	Joe Birmingham	22.00	11.00	6.50
25	Lena Blackburn (Blackburne)	22.00	11.00	6.50
26	John Bliss	45.00	22.00	13.50
27	Bruno Block	45.00	22.00	13.50
28	Bill Bradley	22.00	11.00	6.50
29	Kitty Bransfield	22.00	11.00	6.50
30	Roger Bresnahan	65.00	32.00	19.50
31	Al Bridwell	25.00	12.50	7.50
32	Buster Brown (Boston N.L.)	22.00	11.00	6.50
33a	Mordecai Brown (blue background, Chicago N.L.)	95.00	47.00	28.00
33b	Mordecai Brown (pastel background, Chicago N.L.)	75.00	37.00	22.00
34	Al Burch	25.00	12.50	7.50
35	Donie Bush	25.00	12.50	7.50
36	Bobby Byrne	22.00	11.00	6.50
37	Howie Camnitz	22.00	11.00	6.50
38	Vin Campbell	45.00	22.00	13.50
39	Bill Carrigan	22.00	11.00	6.50
40a	Frank Chance (blue background)	95.00	47.00	28.00
40b	Frank Chance (pastel background)	75.00	37.00	22.00
41	Chappy Charles	22.00	11.00	6.50
42a	Hal Chase (blue background)	50.00	25.00	15.00
42b	Hal Chase (pastel background)	32.00	16.00	9.50
43	Ed Cicotte	30.00	15.00	9.00
44	Fred Clarke (Pittsburgh)	65.00	32.00	19.50
45	Nig Clarke (Cleveland)	22.00	11.00	6.50
46	Tommy Clarke (Cincinnati)	45.00	22.00	13.50
47a	Ty Cobb (blue background)	800.00	320.00	200.00
47b	Ty Cobb (pastel background)	600.00	240.00	150.00
48a	Eddie Collins (blue background)	95.00	47.00	28.00
48b	Eddie Collins (pastel background)	75.00	37.00	22.00
49	Ray Collins	45.00	22.00	13.50
50	Wid Conroy	22.00	11.00	6.50
51	Jack Coombs	30.00	15.00	9.00
52	Frank Corridon	22.00	11.00	6.50

Complete set prices do not include the higher priced variations, unless noted otherwise.

		NR MT	EX	VG
53	Harry Coveleskie (Coveleski)	95.00	47.00	28.00
54	Doc Crandall	25.00	12.50	7.50
55a	Sam Crawford (blue background)	95.00	47.00	28.00
55b	Sam Crawford (pastel background)	75.00	37.00	22.00
56	Birdie Cree	25.00	12.50	7.50
57	Lou Criger	25.00	12.50	7.50
58	Dode Criss	45.00	22.00	13.50
59	Cliff Curtis	45.00	22.00	13.50
60	Bill Dahlen	25.00	12.50	7.50
61	Bill Davidson	45.00	22.00	13.50
62a	Harry Davis (blue background)	45.00	22.00	13.50
62b	Harry Davis (pastel background)	25.00	12.50	7.50
63	Jim Delehanty (Delahanty)	22.00	11.00	6.50
64	Ray Demmitt	45.00	22.00	13.50
65	Rube Dessau	45.00	22.00	13.50
66	Art Devlin	25.00	12.50	7.50
67	Josh Devore	45.00	22.00	13.50
68	Pat Donahue	22.00	11.00	6.50
69	Patsy Donovan	45.00	22.00	13.50
70	Wild Bill Donovan	22.00	11.00	6.50
71a	Red Dooin (blue background)	45.00	22.00	13.50
71b	Red Dooin (pastel background)	25.00	12.50	7.50
72	Mickey Doolan	22.00	11.00	6.50
73	Patsy Dougherty	22.00	11.00	6.50
74	Tom Downey	22.00	11.00	6.50
75	Jim Doyle	22.00	11.00	6.50
76a	Larry Doyle (blue background)	45.00	22.00	13.50
76b	Larry Doyle (pastel background)	25.00	12.50	7.50
77	Hugh Duffy	75.00	37.00	22.00
78	Jimmy Dygert	22.00	11.00	6.50
79	Dick Eagan (Egan)	22.00	11.00	6.50
80	Kid Elberfeld	22.00	11.00	6.50
81	Rube Ellis	22.00	11.00	6.50
82	Clyde Engle	22.00	11.00	6.50
83	Tex Erwin	45.00	22.00	13.50
84	Steve Evans	45.00	22.00	13.50
85	Johnny Evers	65.00	32.00	19.50
86	Bob Ewing	22.00	11.00	6.50
87	Cy Falkenberg	22.00	11.00	6.50
88	George Ferguson	22.00	11.00	6.50
89	Art Fletcher	45.00	22.00	13.50
90	Elmer Flick	65.00	32.00	19.50
91	John Flynn	45.00	22.00	13.50
92	Russ Ford	45.00	22.00	13.50
93	Eddie Foster	75.00	37.00	22.00
94	Bill Foxen	22.00	11.00	6.50
95	John Frill	75.00	37.00	22.00
96	Sam Frock	45.00	22.00	13.50
97	Art Fromme	22.00	11.00	6.50
98	Earl Gardner (New York A.L.)	45.00	22.00	13.50
99	Larry Gardner (Boston A.L.)	45.00	22.00	13.50
100	Harry Gaspar	45.00	22.00	13.50
101	Doc Gessler	22.00	11.00	6.50
102a	George Gibson (blue background)	45.00	22.00	13.50
102b	George Gibson (pastel background)	25.00	12.50	7.50
103	Bill Graham (St. Louis A.L.)	22.00	11.00	6.50
104	Peaches Graham (Boston N.L.)	22.00	11.00	6.50
105	Eddie Grant	22.00	11.00	6.50
106	Clark Griffith	65.00	32.00	19.50
107	Ed Hahn	22.00	11.00	6.50
108	Charley Hall	22.00	11.00	6.50
109	Bob Harmon	45.00	22.00	13.50
110	Topsy Hartsel	22.00	11.00	6.50
111	Roy Hartzell	22.00	11.00	6.50
112	Heinie Heitmuller	22.00	11.00	6.50
113	Buck Herzog	22.00	11.00	6.50
114	Dick Hoblitzel (Hoblitzell)	22.00	11.00	6.50
115	Danny Hoffman	22.00	11.00	6.50
116	Solly Hofman	22.00	11.00	6.50
117	Harry Hooper	95.00	47.00	28.00
118	Harry Howell	22.00	11.00	6.50
119	Miller Huggins	75.00	37.00	22.00
120	Long Tom Hughes	75.00	37.00	22.00
121	Rudy Hulswitt	22.00	11.00	6.50
122	John Hummel	25.00	12.50	7.50
123	George Hunter	25.00	12.50	7.50
124	Ham Hyatt	22.00	11.00	6.50
125	Fred Jacklitsch	22.00	11.00	6.50
126a	Hughie Jennings (blue background)	95.00	47.00	28.00
126b	Hughie Jennings (pastel background)	75.00	37.00	22.00
127	Walter Johnson	250.00	100.00	63.00
128	Davy Jones	22.00	11.00	6.50
129	Tom Jones	22.00	11.00	6.50
130a	Tim Jordan (blue background)	45.00	22.00	13.50
130b	Tim Jordan (pastel background)	25.00	12.50	7.50

		NR MT	EX	VG
131	Addie Joss	75.00	37.00	22.00
132	Johnny Kane	22.00	11.00	6.50
133	Ed Karger	22.00	11.00	6.50
134	Red Killifer (Killefer)	45.00	22.00	13.50
135	Johnny Kling	22.00	11.00	6.50
136	Otto Knabe	22.00	11.00	6.50
137	John Knight	45.00	22.00	13.50
138	Ed Konetchy	22.00	11.00	6.50
139	Harry Krause	22.00	11.00	6.50
140	Rube Kroh	22.00	11.00	6.50
141	Art Krueger	75.00	37.00	22.00
142a	Nap Lajoie (blue background)	130.00	65.00	39.00
142b	Nap Lajoie (pastel background)	100.00	50.00	30.00
143	Fred Lake (Boston N.L.)	22.00	11.00	6.50
144	Joe Lake (St. Louis A.L.)	45.00	22.00	13.50
145	Frank LaPorte	25.00	12.50	7.50
146	Jack Lapp	45.00	22.00	13.50
147	Chick Lathers	45.00	22.00	13.50
148a	Tommy Leach (blue background)	45.00	22.00	13.50
148b	Tommy Leach (pastel background)	25.00	12.50	7.50
149	Sam Leever	22.00	11.00	6.50
150	Lefty Leifield	22.00	11.00	6.50
151	Ed Lennox	25.00	12.50	7.50
152	Fred Linke (Link)	45.00	22.00	13.50
153	Paddy Livingstone (Livingston)	22.00	11.00	6.50
154	Hans Lobert	22.00	11.00	6.50
155	Bris Lord (Cleveland)	22.00	11.00	6.50
156a	Harry Lord (blue background, Boston A.L.)	45.00	22.00	13.50
156b	Harry Lord (pastel background, Boston A.L.)	25.00	12.50	7.50
157	Johnny Lush	22.00	11.00	6.50
158	Connie Mack	100.00	50.00	30.00
159	Tom Madden	45.00	22.00	13.50
160	Nick Maddox	22.00	11.00	6.50
161	Sherry Magee	25.00	12.50	7.50
162	Christy Mathewson	225.00	90.00	56.00
163	Al Mattern	22.00	11.00	6.50
164	Jimmy McAleer	22.00	11.00	6.50
165	George McBride	45.00	22.00	13.50
166a	Amby McConnell (Boston A.L.)	22.00	11.00	6.50
166b	Amby McConnell (Chicago A.L.)	600.00	240.00	150.00
167	Pryor McElveen	25.00	12.50	7.50
168	John McGraw	90.00	45.00	27.00
169	Deacon McGuire	22.00	11.00	6.50
170	Stuffy McInnes (McInnis)	45.00	22.00	13.50
171	Harry McIntire (McIntyre)	22.00	11.00	6.50
172	Matty McIntyre	22.00	11.00	6.50
173	Larry McLean	22.00	11.00	6.50
174	Tommy McMillan	22.00	11.00	6.50
175a	George McQuillan (blue background, Philadelphia N.L.)	45.00	22.00	13.50
175b	George McQuillan (pastel background, Philadelphia N.L.)	25.00	12.50	7.50
175c	George McQuillan (Cincinnati)	600.00	240.00	150.00
176	Paul Meloan	45.00	22.00	13.50
177	Fred Merkle	25.00	12.50	7.50
178	Clyde Milan	22.00	11.00	6.50
179	Dots Miller (Pittsburgh)	22.00	11.00	6.50
180	Warren Miller (Washington)	45.00	22.00	13.50
181	Fred Mitchell	75.00	37.00	22.00
182	Mike Mitchell	22.00	11.00	6.50
183	Earl Moore	22.00	11.00	6.50
184	Pat Moran	22.00	11.00	6.50
185	Lew Moren	22.00	11.00	6.50
186	Cy Morgan	22.00	11.00	6.50
187	George Moriarty	22.00	11.00	6.50
188	Mike Mowrey	45.00	22.00	13.50
189	George Mullin	22.00	11.00	6.50
190	Danny Murphy	22.00	11.00	6.50
191	Red Murray	25.00	12.50	7.50
192	Chief Myers (Meyers)	45.00	22.00	13.50
193	Tom Needham	22.00	11.00	6.50
194	Harry Niles	22.00	11.00	6.50
195	Rebel Oakes	45.00	22.00	13.50
196	Jack O'Connor	22.00	11.00	6.50
197	Paddy O'Connor	22.00	11.00	6.50
198	Bill O'Hara	75.00	37.00	22.00
199	Rube Oldring	22.00	11.00	6.50
200	Charley O'Leary	22.00	11.00	6.50
201	Orval Overall	22.00	11.00	6.50
202	Freddy Parent	22.00	11.00	6.50
203	Dode Paskert	45.00	22.00	13.50
204	Fred Payne	45.00	22.00	13.50
205	Barney Pelty	22.00	11.00	6.50
206	Hub Pernoll	45.00	22.00	13.50
207	George Perring	75.00	37.00	22.00
208	Big Jeff Pfeffer	45.00	22.00	13.50

		NR MT	EX	VG
209	Jack Pfiester	22.00	11.00	6.50
210	Art Phelan	45.00	22.00	13.50
211	Ed Phelps	22.00	11.00	6.50
212	Deacon Phillippe	22.00	11.00	6.50
213	Eddie Plank	85.00	42.00	25.00
214	Jack Powell	22.00	11.00	6.50
215	Billy Purtell	22.00	11.00	6.50
216	Farmer Ray	75.00	37.00	22.00
217	Bugs Raymond	25.00	12.50	7.50
218	Doc Reisling	22.00	11.00	6.50
219	Ed Reulbach	22.00	11.00	6.50
220	Lew Richie	22.00	11.00	6.50
221	Jack Rowan	22.00	11.00	6.50
222	Nap Rucker	25.00	12.50	7.50
223	Slim Sallee	22.00	11.00	6.50
224	Doc Scanlon	25.00	12.50	7.50
225	Germany Schaefer	22.00	11.00	6.50
226	Lou Schettler	45.00	22.00	13.50
227	Admiral Schlei	25.00	12.50	7.50
228	Boss Schmidt	22.00	11.00	6.50
229	Wildfire Schulte	22.00	11.00	6.50
230	Al Schweitzer	22.00	11.00	6.50
231	Jim Scott	45.00	22.00	13.50
232	Cy Seymour	25.00	12.50	7.50
233	Tillie Shafer	25.00	12.50	7.50
234	Bud Sharpe	45.00	22.00	13.50
235	Dave Shean	45.00	22.00	13.50
236	Jimmy Sheckard	22.00	11.00	6.50
237	Mike Simon	45.00	22.00	13.50
238	Charlie Smith (Boston N.L.)	45.00	22.00	13.50
239	Frank Smith (Chicago A.L.)	22.00	11.00	6.50
240	Harry Smith (Boston N.L.)	22.00	11.00	6.50
241	Fred Snodgrass	25.00	12.50	7.50
242	Bob Spade	22.00	11.00	6.50
243	Tully Sparks	22.00	11.00	6.50
244	Tris Speaker	250.00	100.00	63.00
245	Jake Stahl	22.00	11.00	6.50
246	George Stallings	25.00	12.50	7.50
247	Oscar Stanage	22.00	11.00	6.50
248	Harry Steinfeldt	30.00	15.00	9.00
249	Jim Stephens	22.00	11.00	6.50
250	George Stone	22.00	11.00	6.50
251	George Stovall	22.00	11.00	6.50
252	Gabby Street	22.00	11.00	6.50
253	Sailor Stroud	45.00	22.00	13.50
254	Amos Strunk	45.00	22.00	13.50
255	George Suggs	22.00	11.00	6.50
256	Billy Sullivan	22.00	11.00	6.50
257	Ed Summers	22.00	11.00	6.50
258	Bill Sweeney (Boston N.L.)	22.00	11.00	6.50
259	Jeff Sweeney (New York A.L.)	45.00	22.00	13.50
260	Lee Tannehill	22.00	11.00	6.50
261a	Fred Tenney (blue background)	45.00	22.00	13.50
261b	Fred Tenney (pastel background)	25.00	12.50	7.50
262a	Ira Thomas (blue background)	45.00	22.00	13.50
262b	Ira Thomas (pastel background)	25.00	12.50	7.50
263	Jack Thoney	22.00	11.00	6.50
264	Joe Tinker	65.00	32.00	19.50
265	John Titus	45.00	22.00	13.50
266	Terry Turner	22.00	11.00	6.50
267	Bob Unglaub	22.00	11.00	6.50
268	Rube Waddell	75.00	37.00	22.00
269a	Hans Wagner (blue background, Pittsburgh)	375.00	150.00	94.00
269b	Hans Wagner (pastel background, Pittsburgh)	250.00	100.00	63.00
270	Heinie Wagner (Boston A.L.)	22.00	11.00	6.50
271	Bobby Wallace	65.00	32.00	19.50
272	Ed Walsh (Chicago A.L.)	75.00	37.00	22.00
273a	Jimmy Walsh (grey background)	75.00	37.00	22.00
273b	Jimmy Walsh (white background)	75.00	37.00	22.00
274	Doc White	22.00	11.00	6.50
275	Kaiser Wilhelm	25.00	12.50	7.50
276	Ed Willett	22.00	11.00	6.50
277	Vic Willis	22.00	11.00	6.50
278	Art Wilson (New York N.L.)	25.00	12.50	7.50
279	Owen Wilson (Pittsburgh)	22.00	11.00	6.50
280	Hooks Wiltse	25.00	12.50	7.50
281	Harry Wolter	25.00	12.50	7.50
282	Smoky Joe Wood	55.00	27.00	16.50
283	Ralph Works	22.00	11.00	6.50
284	Cy Young (Cleveland)	100.00	50.00	30.00
285	Irv Young (Chicago A.L.)	22.00	11.00	6.50
286	Heinie Zimmerman	45.00	22.00	13.50
287	Dutch Zwilling	45.00	22.00	13.50

1987 M&M's

 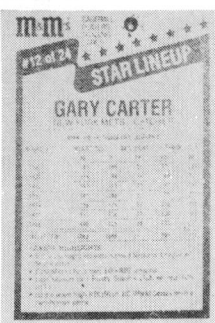

The M&M's "Star Lineup" set consists of 12 two-card panels inserted in specially marked packages of large M&M's candy. The two-card panels measure 5" by 3½" with individual cards measuring 2½" by 3½" in size. The full-color photos are enclosed by a wavy blue frame and a white border. Card backs are printed in red ink on white stock and carry the player's career statistics and highlights. All team insignias have been airbrushed away. The set was designed and produced by Mike Schecter and Associates.

		MT	NR MT	EX
Complete Panel Set:		15.00	11.00	6.00
Complete Singles Set:		6.00	4.50	2.50
Common Panel:		1.00	.70	.40
Common Single Player:		.10	.08	.04
Panel		1.50	1.25	.60
1	Wally Joyner	.50	.40	.20
2	Tony Pena	.10	.08	.04
Panel		1.50	1.25	.60
3	Mike Schmidt	.30	.25	.12
4	Ryne Sandberg	.20	.15	.08
Panel		1.50	1.25	.60
5	Wade Boggs	.40	.30	.15
6	Jack Morris	.20	.15	.08
Panel		1.25	.90	.50
7	Roger Clemens	.30	.25	.12
8	Harold Baines	.15	.11	.06
Panel		1.75	1.25	.70
9	Dale Murphy	.30	.25	.12
10	Jose Canseco	.40	.30	.15
Panel		2.25	1.75	.90
11	Don Mattingly	.70	.50	.30
12	Gary Carter	.20	.15	.08
Panel		1.50	1.25	.60
13	Cal Ripken, Jr.	.25	.20	.10
14	George Brett	.30	.25	.12
Panel		1.00	.70	.40
15	Kirby Puckett	.20	.15	.08
16	Joe Carter	.15	.11	.06
Panel		1.00	.70	.40
17	Mike Witt	.15	.11	.06
18	Mike Scott	.15	.11	.06
Panel		1.25	.90	.50
19	Fernando Valenzuela	.20	.15	.08
20	Steve Garvey	.20	.15	.08
Panel		1.00	.70	.40
21	Steve Sax	.15	.11	.06
22	Nolan Ryan	.20	.15	.08
Panel		1.25	.90	.50
23	Tony Gwynn	.25	.20	.10
24	Ozzie Smith	.15	.11	.06

1986 Meadow Gold
Blank Back Set of 16

This was the second set to be distributed by Meadow Gold Dairy (Beatrice Foods) in 1986. It was issued on Double Play ice cream cartons, one card per package. Full-color player photos have team logos and insignias airbrushed away. This 16-card set is very similar to the Meadow Gold popsicle set, but the

photos are different in some instances. The cards measure 2⅜'' by 3½.'' The Willie McGee card is reportedly tougher to find than other cards in the set.

		MT	NR MT	EX
Complete Set:		80.00	60.00	44.00
Common Player:		4.00	2.95	2.20
(1)	George Brett	7.00	5.25	3.75
(2)	Wade Boggs	7.00	5.25	3.75
(3)	Carlton Fisk	4.00	3.00	2.25
(4)	Steve Garvey	6.00	4.50	3.25
(5)	Dwight Gooden	7.50	5.75	4.25
(6)	Pedro Guerrero	4.00	3.00	2.25
(7)	Reggie Jackson	6.50	5.00	3.50
(8)	Don Mattingly	10.00	7.50	5.50
(9)	Willie McGee	4.00	3.00	2.25
(10)	Dale Murphy	7.00	5.25	3.75
(11)	Cal Ripken	6.50	5.00	3.50
(12)	Pete Rose	8.00	6.00	4.50
(13)	Ryne Sandberg	6.00	4.50	3.25
(14)	Mike Schmidt	7.00	5.25	3.75
(15)	Fernando Valenzuela	6.00	4.50	3.25
(16)	Dave Winfield	6.50	5.00	3.50

1986 Meadow Gold
Statistic Back Set of 20

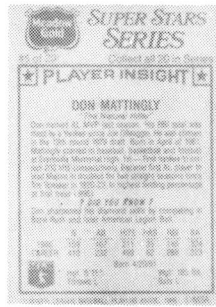

Beatrice Foods produced this set of 20 cards on specially marked boxes of Meadow Gold Double Play popsicles, fudgesicles and bubblegum coolers. They came in two-card panels and have full-color player pictures with player name, team and position printed below the photo. Card backs are printed in red ink and feature player career highlights. The cards measure 2⅜'' by 3½'' and were distributed in the West and Midwest. It is considered one of the toughest 1986 regional sets to complete.

	MT	NR MT	EX
Complete Panel Set:	35.00	41.00	27.00
Complete Singles Set:	15.00	18.00	12.50
Common Panel:	2.00	3.00	2.00
Common Single Player:	.30	.45	.30
Panel 1	5.00	5.25	3.75

		MT	NR MT	EX
1	George Brett	1.50	1.50	1.00
2	Fernando Valenzuela	.70	.70	.50
Panel 2		6.50	5.75	4.25
3	Dwight Gooden	2.00	2.00	1.50
4	Dale Murphy	1.50	1.50	1.00
Panel 3		8.00	6.75	5.00
5	Don Mattingly	3.00	2.25	1.75
6	Reggie Jackson	1.25	1.25	.80
Panel 4		6.50	5.75	4.25
7	Dave Winfield	1.00	1.25	.80
8	Pete Rose	2.00	2.00	1.50
Panel 5		5.00	5.25	3.75
9	Wade Boggs	2.00	1.50	1.00
10	Willie McGee	.50	.45	.35
Panel 6		5.50	5.00	3.50
11	Cal Ripkin (Ripken)	1.25	1.25	.80
12	Ryne Sandberg	1.00	.70	.50
Panel 7		5.00	5.00	3.50
13	Carlton Fisk	.50	.45	.35
14	Jim Rice	1.00	.70	.50
Panel 8		7.00	5.25	3.75
15	Steve Garvey	1.00	.70	.50
16	Mike Schmidt	2.00	1.50	1.00
Panel 9		4.00	3.00	2.25
17	Bruce Sutter	.60	.45	.35
18	Pedro Guerrero	.60	.45	.35
Panel 10		4.00	3.00	2.25
19	Rick Sutcliff (Sutcliffe)	.60	.45	.35
20	Rich Gossage	.60	.45	.35

1986 Meadow Gold Milk

The third set from Meadow Gold from 1986 came on milk cartons; on pint, quart and half-gallon size containers. The cards measure 2½'' by 3½'' and feature drawings instead of photographs. Different dairies distributed the cards in various colors of ink. The cards can be found printed in red, brown or black ink. The crude drawings have prevented this rare set from being higher in price.

		MT	NR MT	EX
Complete Set:		50.00	37.00	20.00
Common Player:		2.00	1.50	.80
(1)	Pete Rose	7.00	5.25	2.75
(2)	George Brett	4.00	3.00	1.50
(3)	Willie McGee	2.00	1.50	.80
(4)	Wade Boggs	5.00	3.75	2.00
(5)	Steve Carlton	2.00	1.50	.80
(6)	Mike Schmidt	3.00	2.25	1.25
(7)	Dale Murphy	4.00	3.00	1.50
(8)	Cal Ripken, Jr.	3.00	2.25	1.25
(9)	Dwight Gooden	9.00	6.75	3.50
(10)	Fernando Valenzuela	2.00	1.50	.80
(11)	Ryne Sandberg	2.00	1.50	.80
(12)	Don Mattingly	12.00	9.00	4.75

1971 Milk Duds

These cards were issued on the backs of five-cent packages of Milk Duds candy. Most collectors prefer to collect complete boxes, rather than cut-out cards,

		NR MT	EX	VG
16c	Mel Stottlemyer (Stottlemyre)	8.00	4.00	2.50
17a	Tommy Harper	7.00	3.50	2.00
17b	Frank Robinson	25.00	12.50	7.50
17c	Reggie Smith	9.00	4.50	2.75
18a	Orlando Cepeda	13.00	6.50	4.00
18b	Rico Petrocelli	8.00	4.00	2.50
18c	Brooks Robinson	25.00	12.50	7.50
19a	Tony Oliva	11.00	5.50	3.25
19b	Milt Pappas	8.00	4.00	2.50
19c	Bobby Tolan	7.00	3.50	2.00
20a	Ernie Banks	20.00	10.00	6.00
20b	Don Kessinger	8.00	4.00	2.50
20c	Joe Torre	9.00	4.50	2.75
21a	Fergie Jenkins	13.00	6.50	4.00
21b	Jim Palmer	16.00	8.00	4.75
21c	Ron Santo	9.00	4.50	2.75
22a	Randy Hundley	7.00	3.50	2.00
22b	Dennis Menke (Denis)	7.00	3.50	2.00
22c	Boog Powell	11.00	5.50	3.25
23a	Dick Dietz	7.00	3.50	2.00
23b	Tommy John	13.00	6.50	4.00
23c	Brooks Robinson	25.00	12.50	7.50
24a	Danny Cater	7.00	3.50	2.00
24b	Harmon Killebrew	25.00	12.50	7.50
24c	Jim Perry	8.00	4.00	2.50

which measure approximately 1-13/16'' by 2-5/8''
when trimmed tightly. Values quoted below are for
complete boxes. The set includes 37 National League
and 32 American League players. Card numbers
appear on the box flap, with each number from 1
through 24 being shared by three different players. A
suffix (a, b, and c) has been added for the collector's
convenience. Harmon Killebrew, Brooks Robinson
and Pete Rose were double-printed.

		NR MT	EX	VG
Complete Set:		900.00	450.00	270.00
Common Player:		7.00	3.50	2.00
1a	Frank Howard	11.00	5.50	3.25
1b	Fritz Peterson	7.00	3.50	2.00
1c	Pete Rose	78.00	39.00	23.00
2a	Johnny Bench	25.00	12.50	7.50
2b	Rico Carty	9.00	4.50	2.75
2c	Pete Rose	78.00	39.00	23.00
3a	Ken Holtzman	8.00	4.00	2.50
3b	Willie Mays	35.00	17.50	10.50
3c	Cesar Tovar	7.00	3.50	2.00
4a	Willie Davis	9.00	4.50	2.75
4b	Harmon Killebrew	25.00	12.50	7.50
4c	Felix Millan	7.00	3.50	2.00
5a	Billy Grabarkewitz	7.00	3.50	2.00
5b	Andy Messersmith	8.00	4.00	2.50
5c	Thurman Munson	20.00	10.00	6.00
6a	Luis Aparicio	16.00	8.00	4.75
6b	Lou Brock	20.00	10.00	6.00
6c	Bill Melton	7.00	3.50	2.00
7a	Ray Culp	7.00	3.50	2.00
7b	Willie McCovey	20.00	10.00	6.00
7c	Luke Walker	7.00	3.50	2.00
8a	Roberto Clemente	35.00	17.50	10.50
8b	Jim Merritt	7.00	3.50	2.00
8c	Claud Osteen (Claude)	8.00	4.00	2.50
9a	Stan Bahnsen	7.00	3.50	2.00
9b	Sam McDowell	9.00	4.50	2.75
9c	Billy Williams	16.00	8.00	4.75
10a	Jim Hickman	7.00	3.50	2.00
10b	Dave McNally	9.00	4.50	2.75
10c	Tony Perez	13.00	6.50	4.00
11a	Hank Aaron	35.00	17.50	10.50
11b	Glen Beckert (Glenn)	8.00	4.00	2.50
11c	Ray Fosse	7.00	3.50	2.00
12a	Alex Johnson	7.00	3.50	2.00
12b	Gaylord Perry	16.00	8.00	4.75
12c	Wayne Simpson	7.00	3.50	2.00
13a	Dave Johnson	9.00	4.50	2.75
13b	George Scott	8.00	4.00	2.50
13c	Tom Seaver	25.00	12.50	7.50
14a	Bill Freehan	9.00	4.50	2.75
14b	Bud Harrelson	8.00	4.00	2.50
14c	Manny Sanguillen	7.00	3.50	2.00
15a	Bob Gibson	20.00	10.00	6.00
15b	Rusty Staub	11.00	5.50	3.25
15c	Roy White	8.00	4.00	2.50
16a	Jim Fregosi	9.00	4.50	2.75
16b	Jim Hunter	16.00	8.00	4.75

1984 Milton Bradley

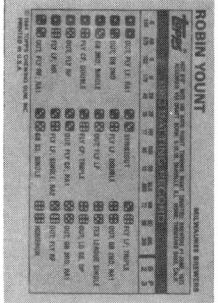

In 1984 Milton Bradley printed their baseball game
cards in full-color and adopted the standard baseball
card size of 2½'' by 3½.'' A total of 30 cards were in
the set. The card fronts show the player photos with
the team insignias and logos airbrushed away. The
game is called Championship Baseball. Card backs
varied in style; some had player statistics plus game
information, and others only game information.

		MT	NR MT	EX
Complete Set:		10.00	7.50	4.00
Common Player:		.25	.20	.10
(1)	Wade Boggs	1.25	.90	.50
(2)	George Brett	.80	.60	.30
(3)	Rod Carew	.50	.40	.20
(4)	Steve Carlton	.40	.30	.15
(5)	Gary Carter	.50	.40	.20
(6)	Dave Concepcion	.25	.20	.10
(7)	Cecil Cooper	.25	.20	.10
(8)	Andre Dawson	.35	.25	.14
(9)	Carlton Fisk	.35	.25	.14
(10)	Steve Garvey	.50	.40	.20
(11)	Pedro Guerrero	.35	.25	.14
(12)	Ron Guidry	.35	.25	.14
(13)	Rickey Henderson	.60	.45	.25
(14)	Reggie Jackson	.50	.40	.20
(15)	Ron Kittle	.25	.20	.10
(16)	Bill Madlock	.25	.20	.10
(17)	Dale Murphy	.80	.60	.30
(18)	Al Oliver	.25	.20	.10
(19)	Darrell Porter	.25	.20	.10
(20)	Cal Ripken	.60	.45	.25
(21)	Pete Rose	1.25	.90	.50
(22)	Steve Sax	.35	.25	.14
(23)	Mike Schmidt	.70	.50	.30
(24)	Ted Simmons	.25	.20	.10
(25)	Ozzie Smith	.30	.25	.12
(26)	Dave Stieb	.25	.20	.10

		MT	NR MT	EX
(27)	Fernando Valenzuela	.40	.30	.15
(28)	Lou Whitaker	.35	.25	.14
(29)	Dave Winfield	.50	.40	.20
(30)	Robin Yount	.40	.30	.15

1986 Minnesota Twins Team Issue

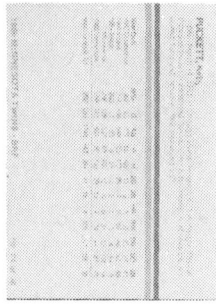

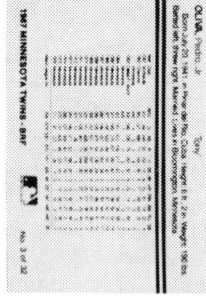

fronts are borderless, containing only the player photo. The backs are printed in blue and red on white card stock and carry the player's personal data and career record. The Twins also produced a post card set which was similar in design to the standard-size card set, but utilized different photos.

		MT	NR MT	EX
Complete Set:		6.00	4.50	2.50
Common Player:		.08	.06	.03
1	Stephen Paul Lombardozzi	.25	.20	.10
2	Roy Frederick Smalley III	.10	.08	.04
3	Pedro Oliva, Jr.	.15	.11	.06
4	Gregory Carpenter Gagne	.20	.15	.08
5	Gary Joseph Gaetti	.35	.25	.14
6	Jay Thomas Kelly	.15	.11	.06
7	Thomas Andrew Nieto	.08	.06	.03
8	Mark Bruce Salas	.08	.06	.03
9	Kent Alan Hrbek	.50	.40	.20
10	Timothy Jon Laudner	.15	.11	.06
11	Frank John Viola, Jr.	.30	.25	.12
12	Lester Paul Straker	.20	.15	.08
13	George Allen Frazier	.08	.06	.03
14	Keith Rowe Atherton	.10	.08	.04
15	Thomas Andrew Brunansky	.35	.25	.14
16	Robert Randall Bush	.08	.06	.03
17	Albert Dwayne Newman	.10	.08	.04
18	John Mark Davidson	.08	.06	.03
19	Rik Aalbert Blyleven	.25	.20	.10
20	Clinton Daniel Gladden III	.20	.15	.08
21	Kirby Puckett	.80	.60	.30
22	Mark Steven Portugal	.10	.08	.04
23	Juan Bautista Berenguer	.15	.11	.06
24	Jeffrey James Reardon	.30	.25	.12
25	Richard Stanley Such	.08	.06	.03
26	Richard Francis Stelmaszek	.08	.06	.03
27	Warren Richard Renick	.08	.06	.03
28	Willard Wayne Terwilliger	.08	.06	.03
29	Joseph Charles Klink	.08	.06	.03
30	Billy Mike Smithson	.08	.06	.03
31	Team Photo	.08	.06	.03
32	Twins Logo/Checklist	.08	.06	.03

This team-issued set contains 36 2-9/16'' by 3-1/2'' full color cards. Fronts feature the Twins 25th anniversary logo and a jersey at the bottom of each card with the player's uniform number. All cards, except an action shot of Bert Blyleven, are posed photos, with a facsimile autograph on each. The set also includes a checklist and a team photo.

		MT	NR MT	EX
Complete Set:		6.00	4.50	2.50
Common Player:		.08	.06	.03
1	Christopher Francis Pittaro	.08	.06	.03
2	Stephen Paul Lombardozzi	.20	.15	.08
3	Roy Frederick Smalley, III	.10	.08	.04
4	Pedro Oliva, Jr.	.15	.11	.06
5	Gary Joseph Gaetti	.35	.25	.14
6	Michael Vaughn Hatcher	.08	.06	.03
7	Jeffrey Scott Reed	.08	.06	.03
8	Mark Bruce Salas	.08	.06	.03
9	Kent Alan Hrbek	.50	.40	.20
10	Timothy Jon Laudner	.15	.11	.06
11	Frank John Viola, Jr.	.30	.25	.12
12	Dennis Allen Burtt	.10	.08	.04
13	Alejandro Sanchez	.08	.06	.03
14	LeRoy Purdy Smith, III	.08	.06	.03
15	William Lamar Beane, III	.10	.08	.04
16	William Peter Filson	.08	.06	.03
17	Thomas Andrew Brunansky	.35	.25	.14
18	Robert Randall Bush	.08	.06	.03
19	Frank Anthony Eufemia, III	.08	.06	.03
20	John Mark Davidson	.15	.11	.06
21	Rik Aalbert Blyleven	.25	.20	.10
22	Gregory Carpenter Gagne	.20	.15	.08
23	John Daniel Butcher	.08	.06	.03
24	Kirby Puckett	.80	.60	.30
25	William Carol Latham, Jr.	.10	.08	.04
26	Ronald Washington	.08	.06	.03
27	Ronald Gene Davis	.08	.06	.03
28	Jay Thomas Kelly	.15	.11	.06
29	Richard Stanley Such	.08	.06	.03
30	Richard Francis Stelmaszek	.08	.06	.03
31	Raymond Robert Miller	.08	.06	.03
32	Willard Wayne Terwilliger	.08	.06	.03
33	Billy Mike Smithson	.08	.06	.03
34	Alvis Woods	.08	.06	.03
35	Team Photo	.08	.06	.03
36	Twins Logo/Checklist	.08	.06	.03

1987 Minnesota Twins Team Issue

The Minnesota Twins produced a 32-card set of 2½'' by 3½'' full-color baseball cards to be sold at the ballpark and through their souvenir catalog. The card

1959 Morrell Meats Dodgers

This popular set of Los Angeles Dodgers player cards was the first issue of a three-year run for the Southern California meat company. The 12 cards in

this 2½'' by 3½'' set are unnumbered and feature full-frame, unbordered color photos. Card backs feature a company ad and list only the player's name, birthdate and birthplace. Two interesting errors exist in the set, as the cards for Clem Labine and Norm Larker show photos of Stan Williams and Joe Pignatano, respectively. Dodger greats Sandy Koufax and Duke Snider are key cards in the set.

		NR MT	EX	VG
Complete Set:		675.00	337.00	202.00
Common Player:		35.00	17.50	10.50
(1)	Don Drysdale	75.00	37.00	22.00
(2)	Carl Furillo	50.00	25.00	15.00
(3)	Jim Gilliam	50.00	25.00	15.00
(4)	Gil Hodges	70.00	35.00	21.00
(5)	Sandy Koufax	110.00	55.00	33.00
(6)	Clem Labine (photo actually Stan Williams)	35.00	17.50	10.50
(7)	Norm Larker (photo actually Joe Pignatano)	35.00	17.50	10.50
(8)	Charlie Neal	35.00	17.50	10.50
(9)	Johnny Podres	50.00	25.00	15.00
(10)	John Roseboro	35.00	17.50	10.50
(11)	Duke Snider	85.00	42.00	25.00
(12)	Don Zimmer	35.00	17.50	10.50

1960 Morrell Meats Dodgers

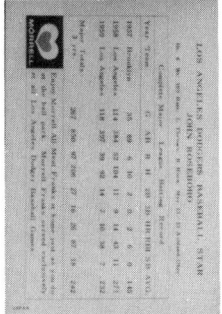

This 12-card set is the same 2½'' by 3½'' size as the 1959 set, and again features unbordered color card fronts. Five of the players included are new to the Morrell's sets. Card backs in 1960 list player statistics and brief personal data on each player. Cards for Gil Hodges, Carl Furillo and Duke Snider are apparently more scarce than others in the set. The 1960 set is again unnumbered.

		NR MT	EX	VG
Complete Set		475.00	237.00	142.00
Common Player		10.00	5.00	3.00
(1)	Walt Alston	15.00	7.50	4.50
(2)	Roger Craig	10.00	5.00	3.00
(3)	Don Drysdale	25.00	12.50	7.50
(4)	Carl Furillo	45.00	22.00	13.50
(5)	Gil Hodges	65.00	32.00	19.50
(6)	Sandy Koufax	50.00	25.00	15.00
(7)	Wally Moon	10.00	5.00	3.00
(8)	Charlie Neal	10.00	5.00	3.00
(9)	Johnny Podres	15.00	7.50	4.50
(10)	John Roseboro	10.00	5.00	3.00
(11)	Larry Sherry	10.00	5.00	3.00
(12)	Duke Snider	80.00	40.00	24.00

1961 Morrell Meats Dodgers

The Morrell set shrunk to just six cards in 1961, with a format almost identical to the 1960 cards. Card fronts are again full-color, unbordered photos, with player statistics on the backs. The unnumbered

cards measure a slightly smaller 2¼'' by 3¼,'' and comparison of statistical information can also distinguish the cards from the 1960 version. Top cards in the set are Don Drysdale and Sandy Koufax, who are also the only two players to appear in all three years of the Morrell Meats sets.

		NR MT	EX	VG
Complete Set:		125.00	62.00	37.00
Common Player:		10.00	5.00	3.00
(1)	Tommy Davis	12.00	6.00	3.50
(2)	Don Drysdale	25.00	12.50	7.50
(3)	Frank Howard	12.00	6.00	3.50
(4)	Sandy Koufax	45.00	22.00	13.50
(5)	Norm Larker	10.00	5.00	3.00
(6)	Maury Wills	15.00	7.50	4.50

1952 Mother's Cookies

This is one of the most popular regional minor league sets ever issued. Cards of Pacific Coast League players were included in packages of cookies. Distribution was limited to the West Coast. The 64 cards feature full color photos on a colored background, with player name and team. The cards measure 2-13/16'' by 3-1/2,'' though the cards' rounded corners cause some variation in listed size. Card backs feature a very brief player statistic, card numbers and an offer for purchasing postage stamps. Five cards (11, 16, 29, 37 and 43) are considered scarce, while card #4 (Chuck Connors) is the most popular.

		NR MT	EX	VG
Complete Set:		1200.00	600.00	360.00
Common Player:		12.00	6.00	3.50
1	Johnny Lindell	18.00	9.00	5.50
2	Jim Davis	12.00	6.00	3.50
3	Al Gettle (Gettel)	12.00	6.00	3.50
4	Chuck Connors	110.00	55.00	33.00
5	Joe Grace	12.00	6.00	3.50
6	Eddie Basinski	12.00	6.00	3.50
7	Gene Handley	12.00	6.00	3.50

		NR MT	EX	VG
8	Walt Judnich	12.00	6.00	3.50
9	Jim Marshall	12.00	6.00	3.50
10	Max West	12.00	6.00	3.50
11	Bill MacCawley	30.00	15.00	9.00
12	Moreno Peiretti	12.00	6.00	3.50
13	Fred Haney	18.00	9.00	5.50
14	Earl Johnson	12.00	6.00	3.50
15	Dave Dahle	12.00	6.00	3.50
16	Bob Talbot	30.00	15.00	9.00
17	Smokey Singleton	12.00	6.00	3.50
18	Frank Austin	12.00	6.00	3.50
19	Joe Gordon	18.00	9.00	5.50
20	Joe Marty	12.00	6.00	3.50
21	Bob Gillespie	12.00	6.00	3.50
22	Red Embree	12.00	6.00	3.50
23	Lefty Olsen	12.00	6.00	3.50
24	Whitey Wietelmann	12.00	6.00	3.50
25	Frank O'Doul	18.00	9.00	5.50
26	Memo Luna	12.00	6.00	3.50
27	John Davis	12.00	6.00	3.50
28	Dick Faber	12.00	6.00	3.50
29	Buddy Peterson	90.00	45.00	27.00
30	Hank Schenz	12.00	6.00	3.50
31	Tookie Gilbert	12.00	6.00	3.50
32	Mel Ott	60.00	30.00	18.00
33	Sam Chapman	12.00	6.00	3.50
34	Dick Cole	12.00	6.00	3.50
35	John Ragni	12.00	6.00	3.50
36	Tom Saffell	12.00	6.00	3.50
37	Roy Welmaker	30.00	15.00	9.00
38	Lou Stringer	12.00	6.00	3.50
39	Artie Wilson	12.00	6.00	3.50
40	Chuck Stevens	12.00	6.00	3.50
41	Charlie Schanz	12.00	6.00	3.50
42	Al Lyons	12.00	6.00	3.50
43	Joe Erautt	90.00	45.00	27.00
44	Clarence Maddern	12.00	6.00	3.50
45	Gene Baker	12.00	6.00	3.50
46	Tom Heath	12.00	6.00	3.50
47	Al Lien	12.00	6.00	3.50
48	Bill Reeder	12.00	6.00	3.50
49	Bob Thurman	12.00	6.00	3.50
50	Ray Orteig	12.00	6.00	3.50
51	Joe Brovia	12.00	6.00	3.50
52	Jim Russell	12.00	6.00	3.50
53	Fred Sanford	12.00	6.00	3.50
54	Jim Gladd	12.00	6.00	3.50
55	Clay Hopper	12.00	6.00	3.50
56	Bill Glynn	12.00	6.00	3.50
57	Mike McCormick	12.00	6.00	3.50
58	Richie Myers	12.00	6.00	3.50
59	Vinnie Smith	12.00	6.00	3.50
60	Stan Hack	18.00	9.00	5.50
61	Bob Spicer	12.00	6.00	3.50
62	Jack Hollis	12.00	6.00	3.50
63	Ed Chandler	12.00	6.00	3.50
64	Bill Moisan	18.00	9.00	5.50

1953 Mother's Cookies

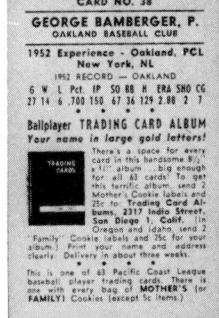

CARD NO. 38

GEORGE BAMBERGER, P.
OAKLAND BASEBALL CLUB

1952 Experience - Oakland, PCL
New York, NL

1952 RECORD — OAKLAND

G   W   L   Pct.   IP   SO   BB   H   ERA   SHO   CG
27   14   6   .700   150   67   36   129   2.88   2   7

Ballplayer TRADING CARD ALBUM
Your name in large gold letters!

There's a space for every card in this handsome 8½" x 11" album . . . big enough for all 63 cards! To get this terrific album, send 2 Mother's Cookie labels and 25c to Trading Card Album, 3217 India Street, San Diego 3, Calif. (in Oregon and Idaho send 2 "Family" Cookie labels and 25c for your album.) Print your name and address clearly. Delivery in about three weeks.

This is one of 63 Pacific Coast League baseball player trading cards. There is one with every bag of MOTHER'S (or FAMILY) Cookies (except 5c items).

The 1953 Mother's Cookies cards are again 2-3/16'' by 3-1/2'', with rounded corners. There are 63 players from Pacific Coast League teams included. The full-color fronts have facsimile autographs rather than printed player names, and card backs offer a trading card album. Cards are generally more plentiful

than in the 1952 set, with 11 of the cards apparently double printed.

		NR MT	EX	VG
Complete Set:		425.00	213.00	128.00
Common Player:		6.00	3.00	1.75
1	Lee Winter	9.00	4.50	2.75
2	Joe Ostrowski	6.00	3.00	1.75
3	Will Ramsdell	6.00	3.00	1.75
4	Bobby Bragan	9.00	4.50	2.75
5	Fletcher Robbe	6.00	3.00	1.75
6	Aaron Robinson	6.00	3.00	1.75
7	Augie Galan	6.00	3.00	1.75
8	Buddy Peterson	6.00	3.00	1.75
9	Frank Lefty O'Doul	12.00	6.00	3.50
10	Walt Pocekay	6.00	3.00	1.75
11	Nini Tornay	6.00	3.00	1.75
12	Jim Moran	6.00	3.00	1.75
13	George Schmees	6.00	3.00	1.75
14	Al Widmar	6.00	3.00	1.75
15	Ritchie Myers	6.00	3.00	1.75
16	Bill Howerton	6.00	3.00	1.75
17	Chuck Stevens	6.00	3.00	1.75
18	Joe Brovia	6.00	3.00	1.75
19	Max West	6.00	3.00	1.75
20	Eddie Malone	6.00	3.00	1.75
21	Gene Handley	6.00	3.00	1.75
22	William D. McCawley	6.00	3.00	1.75
23	Bill Sweeney	6.00	3.00	1.75
24	Tom Alston	6.00	3.00	1.75
25	George Vico	6.00	3.00	1.75
26	Hank Arft	6.00	3.00	1.75
27	Al Benton	6.00	3.00	1.75
28	"Pete" Milne	6.00	3.00	1.75
29	Jim Gladd	6.00	3.00	1.75
30	Earl Rapp	6.00	3.00	1.75
31	Ray Orteig	6.00	3.00	1.75
32	Eddie Basinski	6.00	3.00	1.75
33	Reno Cheso	6.00	3.00	1.75
34	Clarence Maddern	6.00	3.00	1.75
35	Marino Pieretti	6.00	3.00	1.75
36	Bill Raimondi	6.00	3.00	1.75
37	Frank Kelleher	6.00	3.00	1.75
38	George Bamberger	12.00	6.00	3.50
39	Dick Smith	6.00	3.00	1.75
40	Charley Schanz	6.00	3.00	1.75
41	John Van Cuyk	6.00	3.00	1.75
42	Lloyd Hittle	6.00	3.00	1.75
43	Tommy Heath	6.00	3.00	1.75
44	Frank Kalin	6.00	3.00	1.75
45	Jack Tobin	6.00	3.00	1.75
46	Jim Davis	6.00	3.00	1.75
47	Claude Christie	6.00	3.00	1.75
48	Elvin Tappe	6.00	3.00	1.75
49	Stan Hack	9.00	4.50	2.75
50	Fred Richards	6.00	3.00	1.75
51	Clay Hopper	6.00	3.00	1.75
52	Roy Welmaker	6.00	3.00	1.75
53	Red Adams	6.00	3.00	1.75
54	Piper Davis	6.00	3.00	1.75
55	Spider Jorgensen	6.00	3.00	1.75
56	Lee Walls	6.00	3.00	1.75
57	Jack Phillips	6.00	3.00	1.75
58	Red Lynn	6.00	3.00	1.75
59	Eddie Beckman	6.00	3.00	1.75
60	Gene Desautels	6.00	3.00	1.75
61	Bob Dillinger	6.00	3.00	1.75
62	Al Federoff	6.00	3.00	1.75
63	Bill Boemler	6.00	3.00	1.75

1983 Mother's Cookies Giants

After putting out PCL sets in 1952 and 1953, Mother's Cookies distributed this full-color set of 20 San Francisco Giants cards three decades later. The 2½'' by 3½'' cards were produced by Barry Colla and included the Giants logo and player's name on the attractive card fronts. Card backs are numbered and contain biographical information, the Mother's Cookies logo, and a space for the player's autograph. Fifteen cards were given to every fan at the August 7, 1983 Giants game, with each fan also receiving a coupon good for five additional cards.

		MT	NR MT	EX
1	Steve Boros	.50	.40	.20
2	Rickey Henderson	2.50	2.00	1.00
3	Joe Morgan	1.25	.90	.50
4	Dwayne Murphy	.70	.50	.30
5	Mike Davis	.70	.50	.30
6	Bruce Bochte	.50	.40	.20
7	Carney Lansford	.70	.50	.30
8	Steve McCatty	.50	.40	.20
9	Mike Heath	.50	.40	.20
10	Chris Codiroli	.60	.45	.25
11	Bill Almon	.50	.40	.20
12	Bill Caudill	.50	.40	.20
13	Donnie Hill	.50	.40	.20
14	Lary Sorenson	.50	.40	.20
15	Dave Kingman	.80	.60	.30
16	Garry Hancock	.50	.40	.20
17	Jeff Burroughs	.60	.45	.25
18	Tom Burgmeier	.50	.40	.20
19	Jim Essian	.50	.40	.20
20	Mike Warren	.60	.45	.25
21	Davey Lopes	.60	.45	.25
22	Ray Burris	.50	.40	.20
23	Tony Phillips	.50	.40	.20
24	Tim Conroy	.50	.40	.20
25	Jeff Bettendorf	.50	.40	.20
26	Keith Atherton	.60	.45	.25
27	A's Coaches (Clete Boyer, Bob Didier, Jackie Moore, Ron Schueler, Billy Williams)	.50	.40	.20
28	Oakland Coliseum/Checklist	.50	.40	.20

		MT	NR MT	EX
Complete Set:		15.00	11.00	6.00
Common Player:		.50	.40	.20
1	Frank Robinson	1.00	.70	.40
2	Jack Clark	1.75	1.25	.70
3	Chili Davis	1.50	1.25	.60
4	Johnnie LeMaster	.50	.40	.20
5	Greg Minton	.50	.40	.20
6	Bob Brenly	.70	.50	.30
7	Fred Breining	.50	.40	.20
8	Jeff Leonard	1.00	.70	.40
9	Darrell Evans	1.25	.90	.50
10	Tom O'Malley	.50	.40	.20
11	Duane Kuiper	.50	.40	.20
12	Mike Krukow	.60	.45	.25
13	Atlee Hammaker	.50	.40	.20
14	Gary Lavelle	.50	.40	.20
15	Bill Laskey	.50	.40	.20
16	Max Venable	.50	.40	.20
17	Joel Youngblood	.50	.40	.20
18	Dave Bergman	.50	.40	.20
19	Mike Vail	.50	.40	.20
20	Andy McGaffigan	.50	.40	.20

1984 Mother's Cookies Astros

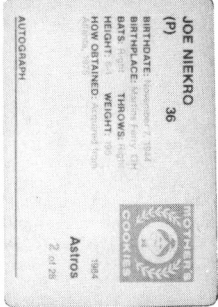

Mother's Cookies also issued a full-color team set for the Houston Astros in 1984. The Astros set measures 2½'' by 3½,'' and card fronts feature unbordered color photos with rounded corners. Card backs are quite similar in format to the 1983 Mother's Cookies Giants, with brief biographical information, card numbers, Mother's Cookies logo and space for player autograph. There are 28 cards in the Astros set, with 20 of the cards distributed during a stadium promotion. Fans also received a coupon redeemable for eight additional cards. Since these additional cards do not necessarily complete collectors' sets, Mother's Cookies cards became very popular among card traders. The Astros set includes one card for the coaches and a checklist.

		MT	NR MT	EX
Complete Set:		15.00	11.00	6.00
Common Player:		.50	.40	.20
1	Nolan Ryan	1.50	1.25	.60
2	Joe Niekro	.60	.45	.25
3	Alan Ashby	.50	.40	.20
4	Bill Doran	1.25	.90	.50
5	Phil Garner	.60	.45	.25
6	Ray Knight	.60	.45	.25
7	Dickie Thon	.60	.45	.25
8	Jose Cruz	.70	.50	.30
9	Jerry Mumphrey	.50	.40	.20
10	Terry Puhl	.50	.40	.20
11	Enos Cabell	.50	.40	.20
12	Harry Spilman	.50	.40	.20
13	Dave Smith	.60	.45	.25

1984 Mother's Cookies A's

Following the success of their one set in 1983, Mother's Cookies issued five more team sets of cards in 1984. The A's set measures 2½'' by 3½,'' and card fronts feature unbordered color photos with rounded corners. Card backs are quite similar in format to the 1983 Mother's Cookies Giants, with brief biographical information, card numbers, Mother's Cookies logo and space for player autograph. There are 28 cards in the A's set, with 20 of the cards distributed during a stadium promotion. Fans also received a coupon redeemable for eight additional cards. Since these additional cards do not necessarily complete collectors' sets, Mother's Cookies cards became very popular among card traders. The A's set includes cards for the manager, coaches and a checklist.

	MT	NR MT	EX
Complete Set:	15.00	11.00	6.00
Common Player:	.50	.40	.20

		MT	NR MT	EX
14	Mike Scott	.90	.70	.35
15	Bob Lillis	.50	.40	.20
16	Bob Knepper	.60	.45	.25
17	Frank DiPino	.50	.40	.20
18	Tom Wieghaus	.50	.40	.20
19	Denny Walling	.50	.40	.20
20	Tony Scott	.50	.40	.20
21	Alan Bannister	.50	.40	.20
22	Bill Dawley	.50	.40	.20
23	Vern Ruhle	.50	.40	.20
24	Mike LaCoss	.50	.40	.20
25	Mike Madden	.50	.40	.20
26	Craig Reynolds	.50	.40	.20
27	Astros Coaches (Cot Deal, Don Leppert, Denis Menke, Les Moss, Jerry Walker)	.50	.40	.20
28	Astros Logo/Checklist	.50	.40	.20

1984 Mother's Cookies Giants

Mother's Cookies issued a second annual full-color card set for the San Francisco Giants in 1984. The Giants set measures 2½'' by 3½,'' and the round-cornered cards feature drawings of former Giant All-Star team selections. Card backs are quite similar in format to the 1983 Mother's Cookies Giants, with brief biographical information, card numbers and Mother's Cookies logo. No autograph space is included. There are 28 cards in the Giants set, with 20 of the cards distributed during a stadium promotion. Fans also received a coupon redeemable for eight additional cards. Since these additional cards do not necessarily complete collectors' sets, Mother's Coookies cards became very popular among card traders. Card number 28 is a checklist chart.

		MT	NR MT	EX
	Complete Set:	15.00	11.00	6.00
	Common Player:	.50	.40	.20
1	Willie Mays	1.50	1.25	.60
2	Willie McCovey	1.25	.90	.50
3	Juan Marichal	1.25	.90	.50
4	Gaylord Perry	1.25	.90	.50
5	Tom Haller	.60	.45	.25
6	Jim Davenport	.50	.40	.20
7	Jack Clark	.80	.60	.30
8	Greg Minton	.50	.40	.20
9	Atlee Hammaker	.50	.40	.20
10	Gary Lavelle	.50	.40	.20
11	Orlando Cepeda	1.00	.70	.40
12	Bobby Bonds	.80	.60	.30
13	John Antonelli	.60	.45	.25
14	Bob Schmidt	.50	.40	.20
15	Sam Jones	.50	.40	.20
16	Mike McCormick	.60	.45	.25
17	Ed Bailey	.50	.40	.20
18	Stu Miller	.50	.40	.20
19	Felipe Alou	.70	.50	.30
20	Jim Hart	.60	.45	.25
21	Dick Dietz	.50	.40	.20
22	Chris Speier	.50	.40	.20
23	Bobby Murcer	.70	.50	.30
24	John Montefusco	.50	.40	.20
25	Vida Blue	.70	.50	.30
26	Ed Whitson	.50	.40	.20
27	Darrell Evans	.60	.45	.25
28	All-Star Game Logo/Checklist	.50	.40	.20

1984 Mother's Cookies Mariners

 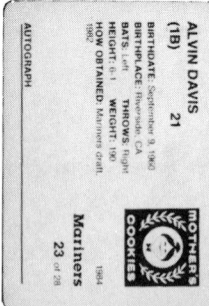

Mother's Cookies also issued a full-color set for the Seattle Mariners in 1984. The Mariners set measures 2½'' by 3½,'' and card fronts feature unbordered color photos with rounded corners. Card backs are quite similar in format to the 1983 Mother's Cookies Giants, with brief biographical information, card numbers, Mother's Cookies logo and space for player autograph. There are 28 cards in the Mariners set, with 20 of the cards distributed during a stadium promotion. Fans also received a coupon redeemable for eight additional cards. Since these additional cards do not necessarily complete collectors' sets, Mother's Cookies cards became very popular among card traders. The Mariners set includes one card each for the manager, coaches and a checklist.

		MT	NR MT	EX
	Complete Set:	16.00	12.00	6.50
	Common Player:	.50	.40	.20
1	Del Crandall	.60	.45	.25
2	Barry Bonnell	.50	.40	.20
3	Dave Henderson	.50	.40	.20
4	Bob Kearney	.50	.40	.20
5	Mike Moore	.50	.40	.20
6	Spike Owen	.70	.50	.30
7	Gorman Thomas	.70	.50	.30
8	Ed Vande Berg	.50	.40	.20
9	Matt Young	.70	.50	.30
10	Larry Milbourne	.50	.40	.20
11	Dave Beard	.50	.40	.20
12	Jim Beattie	.50	.40	.20
13	Mark Langston	1.25	.90	.50
14	Orlando Mercado	.50	.40	.20
15	Jack Perconte	.50	.40	.20
16	Pat Putnam	.50	.40	.20
17	Paul Mirabella	.50	.40	.20
18	Domingo Ramos	.50	.40	.20
19	Al Cowens	.50	.40	.20
20	Mike Stanton	.50	.40	.20
21	Steve Henderson	.50	.40	.20
22	Bob Stoddard	.50	.40	.20
23	Alvin Davis	1.75	1.25	.70
24	Phil Bradley	1.75	1.25	.70
25	Roy Thomas	.50	.40	.20
26	Darnell Coles	.80	.60	.30
27	Mariners Coaches (Chuck Cottier, Frank Funk, Ben Hines, Phil Roof, Rick Sweet)	.50	.40	.20
28	Seattle Kingdome/Checklist	.50	.40	.20

1984 Mother's Cookies Padres

Mother's Cookies also issued a full-color set for the San Diego Padres in 1984. The Padres set measures 2½'' by 3½,'' and card fronts feature unbordered color photos with rounded corners. Card backs are quite similar in format to the 1983 Mother's Cookies Giants, with brief biographical information, card numbers, Mother's Cookies logo and space for player autograph. There are 28 cards in the Padres set, with

color photos with rounded corners. Card backs are quite similar in format to the 1984 Mother's Cookies A's, with brief biographical information, card numbers, Mother's Cookies logo and space for player autograph. Card backs are dated 1985. There are 28 cards in the A's set, which was distributed in its entirety during a stadium promotion. The A's set includes one card each for the manager, coaches and a checklist.

		MT	NR MT	EX
Complete Set:		12.00	9.00	4.75
Common Player:		.40	.30	.15
1	Jackie Moore	.40	.30	.15
2	Dave Kingman	.70	.50	.30
3	Don Sutton	.90	.70	.35
4	Mike Heath	.40	.30	.15
5	Alfredo Griffin	.60	.45	.25
6	Dwayne Murphy	.60	.45	.25
7	Mike Davis	.60	.45	.25
8	Carney Lansford	.60	.45	.25
9	Chris Codiroli	.40	.30	.15
10	Bruce Bochte	.40	.30	.15
11	Mickey Tettleton	.50	.40	.20
12	Donnie Hill	.40	.30	.15
13	Rob Picciolo	.40	.30	.15
14	Dave Collins	.50	.40	.20
15	Dusty Baker	.60	.45	.25
16	Tim Conroy	.40	.30	.15
17	Keith Atherton	.40	.30	.15
18	Jay Howell	.50	.40	.20
19	Mike Warren	.40	.30	.15
20	Steve McCatty	.40	.30	.15
21	Bill Krueger	.40	.30	.15
22	Curt Young	.80	.60	.30
23	Dan Meyer	.40	.30	.15
24	Mike Gallego	.50	.40	.20
25	Jeff Kaiser	.40	.30	.15
26	Steve Henderson	.40	.30	.15
27	A's Coaches (Clete Boyer, Bob Didier, Dave McKay, Wes Stock, Billy Williams)			
		.40	.30	.15
28	Oakland Coliseum/Checklist	.40	.30	.15

20 of the cards distributed during a stadium promotion. Fans also received a coupon redeemable for eight additional cards. Since these additional cards do not necessarily complete collectors' sets, Mother's Cookies cards became very popular among card traders. The Padres set includes one card each for the manager, coaches and a checklist.

		MT	NR MT	EX
Complete Set:		18.00	13.50	7.25
Common Player:		.50	.40	.20
1	Dick Williams	.60	.45	.25
2	Rich Gossage	1.00	.70	.40
3	Tim Lollar	.50	.40	.20
4	Eric Show	.60	.45	.25
5	Terry Kennedy	.60	.45	.25
6	Kurt Bevacqua	.50	.40	.20
7	Steve Garvey	1.75	1.25	.70
8	Garry Templeton	.70	.50	.30
9	Tony Gwynn	2.50	2.00	1.00
10	Alan Wiggins	.50	.40	.20
11	Dave Dravecky	.60	.45	.25
12	Tim Flannery	.50	.40	.20
13	Kevin McReynolds	1.50	1.25	.60
14	Bobby Brown	.50	.40	.20
15	Ed Whitson	.50	.40	.20
16	Doug Gwosdz	.50	.40	.20
17	Luis DeLeon	.50	.40	.20
18	Andy Hawkins	.60	.45	.25
19	Craig Lefferts	.60	.45	.25
20	Carmelo Martinez	.70	.50	.30
21	Sid Monge	.50	.40	.20
22	Graig Nettles	.80	.60	.30
23	Mario Ramirez	.50	.40	.20
24	Luis Salazar	.50	.40	.20
25	Champ Summers	.50	.40	.20
26	Mark Thurmond	.50	.40	.20
27	Padres Coaches (Harry Dunlop, Deacon Jones, Jack Krol, Norm Sherry, Ozzie Virgil)			
		.50	.40	.20
28	Jack Murphy Stadium/Checklist	.50	.40	.20

1985 Mother's Cookies A's

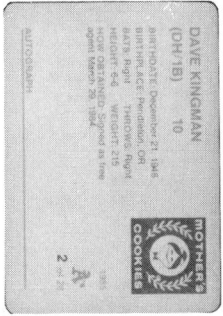

Mother's Cookies again issued five full-color sets for Major League teams in 1985. The A's set measures 2½'' by 3½,'' and card fronts feature unbordered

1985 Mother's Cookies Astros

Mother's Cookies issued a second annual full-color set for the Houston Astros in 1985. The Astros set measures 2½'' by 3½,'' and card fronts feature unbordered color photos with rounded corners. Card backs are quite similar in format to the 1984 Mother's Cookies Astros, with brief biographical information, card numbers, Mother's Cookies logo and space for player autograph. Card backs are dated 1985. There are 28 cards in the Astros set, which was distributed in its entirety during a stadium promotion. The Astros set includes one card each for the manager, coaches and a checklist.

		MT	NR MT	EX
Complete Set:		12.00	9.00	4.75
Complete Player:		.40	.30	.15
1	Bob Lillis	.40	.30	.15

		MT	NR MT	EX
2	Nolan Ryan	1.50	1.25	.60
3	Phil Garner	.50	.40	.20
4	Jose Cruz	.60	.45	.25
5	Denny Walling	.40	.30	.15
6	Joe Niekro	.60	.45	.25
7	Terry Puhl	.40	.30	.15
8	Bill Doran	.60	.45	.25
9	Dickie Thon	.40	.30	.15
10	Enos Cabell	.40	.30	.15
11	Frank Dipino (DiPino)	.40	.30	.15
12	Julio Solano	.40	.30	.15
13	Alan Ashby	.40	.30	.15
14	Craig Reynolds	.40	.30	.15
15	Jerry Mumphrey	.40	.30	.15
16	Bill Dawley	.40	.30	.15
17	Mark Bailey	.40	.30	.15
18	Mike Scott	.80	.60	.30
19	Harry Spilman	.40	.30	.15
20	Bob Knepper	.50	.40	.20
21	Dave Smith	.50	.40	.20
22	Kevin Bass	.60	.45	.25
23	Tim Tolman	.40	.30	.15
24	Jeff Calhoun	.40	.30	.15
25	Jim Pankovits	.40	.30	.15
26	Ron Mathis	.40	.30	.15
27	Astros Coaches (Cot Deal, Matt Galante, Don Leppert, Denis Menke, Jerry Walker)	.40	.30	.15
28	Astros Logo/Checklist	.40	.30	.15

1985 Mother's Cookies Giants

Mother's Cookies issued a third annual full-color set for the San Francisco Giants in 1985. The Giants set measures 2½'' by 3½,'' and card fronts feature unbordered color photos of current players with rounded corners. Card backs are quite similar in format to the 1983 Mother's Cookies Giants, with brief biographical information, card numbers, Mother's Cookies logo and space for player autograph. Card backs are dated 1985. There are 28 cards in the Giants set, which was distributed in its entirety during a stadium promotion. The Giants set includes one card each for the manager, coaches and a checklist.

		MT	NR MT	EX
Complete Set:		12.00	9.00	4.75
Common Player:		.40	.30	.15
1	Jim Davenport	.40	.30	.15
2	Chili Davis	.60	.45	.25
3	Dan Gladden	.60	.45	.25
4	Jeff Leonard	.60	.45	.25
5	Manny Trillo	.50	.40	.20
6	Atlee Hammaker	.40	.30	.15
7	Bob Brenly	.40	.30	.15
8	Greg Minton	.40	.30	.15
9	Bill Laskey	.40	.30	.15
10	Vida Blue	.60	.45	.25
11	Mike Krukow	.50	.40	.20
12	Frank Williams	.60	.45	.25
13	Jose Uribe	.50	.40	.20
14	Johnnie LeMaster	.40	.30	.15
15	Scot Thompson	.40	.30	.15
16	Dave LaPoint	.40	.30	.15
17	David Green	.40	.30	.15

		MT	NR MT	EX
18	Chris Brown	1.50	1.25	.60
19	Joel Younglood	.40	.30	.15
20	Mark Davis	.40	.30	.15
21	Jim Gott	.40	.30	.15
22	Doug Gwosdz	.40	.30	.15
23	Scott Garrelts	.50	.40	.20
24	Gary Rajsich	.40	.30	.15
25	Rob Deer	1.25	.90	.50
26	Brad Wellman	.40	.30	.15
27	Coaches (Rocky Bridges, Chuck Hiller, Tom McCraw, Bob Miller, Jack Mull)	.40	.30	.15
28	Candlestick Park/Checklist	.40	.30	.15

1985 Mother's Cookies Mariners

 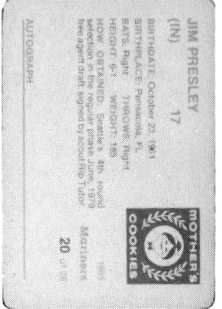

Mother's Cookies issued a second annual full-color set for the Seattle Mariners in 1985. The Mariners set measures 2½'' by 3½,'' and card fronts feature unbordered color photos with rounded corners. Card backs are quite similar in format to the 1984 Mother's Cookies Mariners, with brief biographical information, card numbers, Mother's Cookies logo and space for player autograph. Card backs are dated 1985. There are 28 cards in the Mariners set, which was distributed in its entirety during a stadium promotion. The Mariners set includes one card each for the manager, coaches and a checklist.

		MT	NR MT	EX
Complete Set		14.00	10.50	5.50
Common Player		.40	.30	.15
1	Chuck Cottier	.40	.30	.15
2	Alvin Davis	1.00	.70	.40
3	Mark Langston	.70	.50	.30
4	Dave Henderson	.40	.30	.15
5	Ed Vande Berg	.40	.30	.15
6	Al Cowens	.40	.30	.15
7	Spike Owen	.40	.30	.15
8	Mike Moore	.40	.30	.15
9	Gorman Thomas	.60	.45	.25
10	Barry Bonnell	.40	.30	.15
11	Jack Perconte	.40	.30	.15
12	Domingo Ramos	.40	.30	.15
13	Bob Kearney	.40	.30	.15
14	Matt Young	.40	.30	.15
15	Jim Beattie	.40	.30	.15
16	Mike Stanton	.40	.30	.15
17	David Valle	.50	.40	.20
18	Ken Phelps	.60	.45	.25
19	Salome Barojas	.40	.30	.15
20	Jim Presley	2.00	1.50	.80
21	Phil Bradley	1.00	.70	.40
22	Dave Geisel	.40	.30	.15
23	Harold Reynolds	.70	.50	.30
24	Edwin Nunez	.60	.45	.25
25	Mike Morgan	.40	.30	.15
26	Ivan Calderon	.80	.60	.30
27	Mariners Coaches (Deron Johnson, Jim Mahoney, Marty Martinez, Phil Regan, Phil Roof)	.40	.30	.15
28	Seattle Kingdome/Checklist	.40	.30	.15

1985 Mother's Cookies Padres

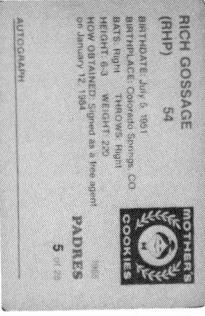

Mother's Cookies issued a second annual full-color set for the San Diego Padres in 1985. The Padres set measures 2½'' by 3½,'' and card fronts feature unbordered color photos with rounded corners. Card backs are quite similar in format to the 1984 Mother's Cookies Padres, with brief biographical information, card numbers, Mother's Cookies logo and space for player autograph. Card backs are dated 1985. There are 28 cards in the Padres set, which was distributed in its entirety during a stadium promotion. The Padres set includes one card each for the manager, coaches and a checklist.

		MT	NR MT	EX
Complete Set:		12.00	9.00	4.75
Common Player:		.40	.30	.15
1	Dick Williams	.50	.40	.20
2	Tony Gwynn	2.50	2.00	1.00
3	Kevin McReynolds	.80	.60	.30
4	Graig Nettles	.70	.50	.30
5	Rich Gossage	.90	.70	.35
6	Steve Garvey	1.75	1.25	.70
7	Garry Templeton	.50	.40	.20
8	Dave Dravecky	.50	.40	.20
9	Eric Show	.50	.40	.20
10	Terry Kennedy	.50	.40	.20
11	Luis DeLeon	.40	.30	.15
12	Bruce Bochy	.40	.30	.15
13	Andy Hawkins	.40	.30	.15
14	Kurt Bevacqua	.40	.30	.15
15	Craig Lefferts	.40	.30	.15
16	Mario Ramirez	.40	.30	.15
17	LaMarr Hoyt	.40	.30	.15
18	Jerry Royster	.40	.30	.15
19	Tim Stoddard	.40	.30	.15
20	Tim Flannery	.40	.30	.15
21	Mark Thurmond	.40	.30	.15
22	Greg Booker	.50	.40	.20
23	Bobby Brown	.40	.30	.15
24	Carmelo Martinez	.50	.40	.20
25	Al Bumbry	.40	.30	.15
26	Jerry Davis	.40	.30	.15
27	Padres Coaches (Galen Cisco, Harry Dunlop, Deacon Jones, Jack Krol, Ozzie Virgil)	.40	.30	.15
28	Jack Murphy Stadium/Checklist	.40	.30	.15

1986 Mother's Cookies A's

Mother's Cookies produced four more full-color team card sets in 1986, with only the San Diego Padres not repeating from the 1985 group. The third annual set for the Oakland A's measures 2½'' by 3½,'' and card fronts feature unbordered color photos with rounded corners. Card backs are quite similar in format to previous years, with brief biographical information, card numbers and Mother's Cookies logo. Card backs are dated 1986. There are 28 cards in the A's set, with 20 of the cards distributed during a stadium promotion. Each fan also received a coupon redeemable for eight additional cards. The A's set includes one card each for the manager, coaches and a checklist.

		MT	NR MT	EX
Complete Set:		15.00	11.00	6.00
Common Player:		.35	.25	.14
1	Jackie Moore	.30	.25	.12
2	Dave Kingman	.60	.45	.25
3	Dusty Baker	.40	.30	.15
4	Joaquin Andujar	.40	.30	.15
5	Alfredo Griffin	.40	.30	.15
6	Dwayne Murphy	.40	.30	.15
7	Mike Davis	.40	.30	.15
8	Carney Lansford	.40	.30	.15
9	Jose Canseco	9.00	6.75	3.50
10	Bruce Bochte	.30	.25	.12
11	Mickey Tettleton	.30	.25	.12
12	Donnie Hill	.30	.25	.12
13	Jose Rijo	.30	.25	.12
14	Rick Langford	.30	.25	.12
15	Chris Codiroli	.30	.25	.12
16	Moose Haas	.30	.25	.12
17	Keith Atherton	.30	.25	.12
18	Jay Howell	.40	.30	.15
19	Tony Phillips	.30	.25	.12
20	Steve Henderson	.30	.25	.12
21	Bill Krueger	.30	.25	.12
22	Steve Ontiveros	.40	.30	.15
23	Bill Bathe	.30	.25	.12
24	Rickey Peters	.30	.25	.12
25	Tim Birtsas	.30	.25	.12
26	Trainers Card (Frank Ciensczyk, Larry Davis, Steve Vucinich, Barry Weinberg)	.30	.25	.12
27	Coaches Card (Bob Didier, Dave McKay, Jeff Newman, Ron Plaza, Wes Stock, Bob Watson)	.30	.25	.12
28	Oakland Coliseum/Checklist	.30	.25	.12

1986 Mother's Cookies Astros

Mother's Cookies produced a third annual set for the Houston Astros in 1985. The set measures 2½'' by 3½,'' and card fronts feature unbordered color paintings of all-time Houston All-Star Game performers. The round-cornered cards have backs quite similar in format to previous years, with brief biographical information, card numbers and Mother's Cookies logo. Card backs are dated 1986. There are 28 cards in the Astros set, with 20 of the cards distributed during a stadium promotion. Each fan also received a coupon redeemable for eight additional cards. The Astros set also includes a checklist card.

		MT	NR MT	EX
Complete Set:		10.00	7.50	4.00
Common Player:		.35	.25	.14
1	Dick Farrell	.35	.25	.14
2	Hal Woodeschick (Woodeshick)	.35	.25	.14
3	Joe Morgan	.80	.60	.30
4	Claude Raymond	.35	.25	.14
5	Mike Cuellar	.40	.30	.15
6	Rusty Staub	.60	.45	.25
7	Jimmy Wynn	.40	.30	.15
8	Larry Dierker	.40	.30	.15
9	Denis Menke	.35	.25	.14
10	Don Wilson	.35	.25	.14
11	Cesar Cedeno	.50	.40	.20
12	Lee May	.40	.30	.15
13	Bob Watson	.40	.30	.15
14	Ken Forsch	.40	.30	.15
15	Joaquin Andujar	.40	.30	.15
16	Terry Puhl	.35	.25	.14
17	Joe Niekro	.40	.30	.15
18	Craig Reynolds	.35	.25	.14
19	Joe Sambito	.35	.25	.14
20	Jose Cruz	.60	.45	.25
21	J.R. Richard	.40	.30	.15
22	Bob Knepper	.40	.30	.15
23	Nolan Ryan	1.00	.70	.40
24	Ray Knight	.40	.30	.15
25	Bill Dawley	.35	.25	.14
26	Dickie Thon	.40	.30	.15
27	Jerry Mumphrey	.35	.25	.14
28	Astros Logo/Checklist	.35	.25	.14

1986 Mother's Cookies Giants

Mother's Cookies produced a fourth annual set for the San Francisco Giants in 1985. The set measures 2½'' by 3½,'' and card fronts feature unbordered color photos with rounded corners. Card backs are quite similar in format to previous years, with brief biographical information, card numbers and Mother's Cookies logo. Card backs are dated 1986. There are 28 cards in the Giants set, with 20 of the cards distributed during a stadium promotion. Each fan also received a coupon redeemable for eight additional cards. The Giants set also includes a card for the manager and a checklist.

		MT	NR MT	EX
Complete Set:		10.00	7.50	4.00
Common Player:		.35	.25	.14
1	Roger Craig	.40	.30	.15
2	Chili Davis	.60	.45	.25
3	Dan Gladden	.40	.30	.15
4	Jeff Leonard	.60	.45	.25
5	Bob Brenly	.35	.25	.14
6	Atlee Hammaker	.35	.25	.14
7	Will Clark	2.50	2.00	1.00

		MT	NR MT	EX
8	Greg Minton	.35	.25	.14
9	Candy Maldonado	.40	.30	.15
10	Vida Blue	.50	.40	.20
11	Mike Krukow	.40	.30	.15
12	Bob Melvin	.40	.30	.15
13	Jose Uribe	.35	.25	.14
14	Dan Driessen	.35	.25	.14
15	Jeff Robinson	.40	.30	.15
16	Rob Thompson	.70	.50	.30
17	Mike LaCoss	.35	.25	.14
18	Chris Brown	.60	.45	.25
19	Scott Garrelts	.35	.25	.14
20	Mark Davis	.35	.25	.14
21	Jim Gott	.35	.25	.14
22	Brad Wellman	.35	.25	.14
23	Roger Mason	.35	.25	.14
24	Bill Laskey	.35	.25	.14
25	Brad Gulden	.35	.25	.14
26	Joel Youngblood	.35	.25	.14
27	Juan Berenguer	.35	.25	.14
28	Coaches/Checklist (Bill Fahey, Bob Lillis, Gordy MacKenzie, Jose Morales, Norm Sherry)	.35	.25	.14

1986 Mother's Cookies Mariners

Mother's Cookies produced a third annual set for the Seattle Mariners in 1985. The set measures 2½'' by 3½,'' and card fronts feature unbordered color photos with rounded corners. Card backs are quite similar in format to previous years, with brief biographical information, card numbers and Mother's Cookies logo. Card backs are dated 1986. There are 28 cards in the Mariners set, with 20 of the cards distributed during a stadium promotion. Each fan also received a coupon redeemable for eight additional cards. The Mariners set also includes a card for the manager and a checklist.

		MT	NR MT	EX
Complete Set		8.00	6.00	3.25
Common Player		.35	.25	.14
1	Dick Williams	.40	.30	.15
2	Alvin Davis	.70	.50	.30
3	Mark Langston	.60	.45	.25
4	Dave Henderson	.35	.25	.14
5	Steve Yeager	.35	.25	.14
6	Al Cowens	.35	.25	.14
7	Jim Presley	.80	.60	.30
8	Phil Bradley	.70	.50	.30
9	Gorman Thomas	.50	.40	.20
10	Barry Bonnell	.35	.25	.14
11	Milt Wilcox	.35	.25	.14
12	Domingo Ramos	.35	.25	.14
13	Paul Mirabella	.35	.25	.14
14	Matt Young	.35	.25	.14
15	Ivan Calderon	.50	.40	.20
16	Bill Swift	.40	.30	.15
17	Pete Ladd	.35	.25	.14
18	Ken Phelps	.40	.30	.15
19	Karl Best	.35	.25	.14
20	Spike Owen	.35	.25	.14
21	Mike Moore	.35	.25	.14

		MT	NR MT	EX
22	Danny Tartabull	1.50	1.25	.60
23	Bob Kearney	.35	.25	.14
24	Edwin Nunez	.35	.25	.14
25	Mike Morgan	.35	.25	.14
26	Roy Thomas	.35	.25	.14
27	Jim Beattie	.35	.25	.14
28	Coaches/Checklist (Deron Johnson, Marty Martinez, Phil Regan, Phil Roof, Ozzie Virgil)	.35	.25	.14

1987 Mother's Cookies A's

Continuing with a tradition of producing beautiful baseball cards, Mother's Cookies of Oakland, Calif. issued a 28-card set featuring every Oakland A's player to have been elected to the All-Star Game since 1968. The full-color photos came from the private collection of nationally known photographer Doug McWilliams. Twenty of the 28 cards were given out to fans attending the A's game of July 5th. An additional 8 cards were available by redeeming a mail-in certificate. The cards, which measure 2½" by 3½", feature rounded corners. The card backs carry the player's All-Star Game statistics.

		MT	NR MT	EX
	Complete Set:	15.00	11.00	6.00
	Common Player:	.30	.25	.12
1	Bert Campaneris	.40	.30	.15
2	Rick Monday	.40	.30	.15
3	John Odom	.30	.25	.12
4	Sal Bando	.40	.30	.15
5	Reggie Jackson	1.00	.70	.40
6	Jim Hunter	.70	.50	.30
7	Vida Blue	.50	.40	.20
8	Dave Duncan	.30	.25	.12
9	Joe Rudi	.40	.30	.15
10	Rollie Fingers	.60	.45	.25
11	Ken Holtzman	.40	.30	.15
12	Dick Williams	.40	.30	.15
13	Alvin Dark	.30	.25	.12
14	Gene Tenace	.40	.30	.15
15	Claudell Washington	.30	.25	.12
16	Phil Garner	.30	.25	.12
17	Wayne Gross	.30	.25	.12
18	Matt Keough	.30	.25	.12
19	Jeff Newman	.30	.25	.12
20	Rickey Henderson	1.00	.70	.40
21	Tony Armas	.40	.30	.15
22	Mike Norris	.30	.25	.12
23	Billy Martin	.50	.40	.20
24	Bill Caudill	.30	.25	.12
25	Jay Howell	.40	.30	.15
26	Jose Canseco	2.00	1.50	.80
27	Jose and Reggie (Jose Canseco, Reggie Jackson)	1.50	1.25	.60
28	A's Logo/Checklist	.30	.25	.12

Definitions for grading conditions are located in the Introduction of this price guide.

1987 Mother's Cookies Astros

Twenty of 28 cards featuring Astros players were given out to the first 25,000 fans attending the July 17th game at the Astrodome. An additional 8 cards (though not necessarily the exact 8 needed to complete a set) were available from the card producer, Mother's Cookies, by redeeming a mail-in certificate. The cards have rounded corners and measure the standard 2½" by 3½". The backs are printed in purple and orange and contain personal player information, the Mother's Cookies logo, the card number and a spot for the player's autograph.

		MT	NR MT	EX
	Complete Set:	10.00	7.50	4.00
	Common Player:	.30	.25	.12
1	Hal Lanier	.40	.30	.15
2	Mike Scott	.80	.60	.30
3	Jose Cruz	.50	.40	.20
4	Bill Doran	.50	.40	.20
5	Bob Knepper	.40	.30	.15
6	Phil Garner	.40	.30	.15
7	Terry Puhl	.30	.25	.12
8	Nolan Ryan	1.50	1.25	.60
9	Kevin Bass	.50	.40	.20
10	Glenn Davis	.80	.60	.30
11	Alan Ashby	.30	.25	.12
12	Charlie Kerfeld	.30	.25	.12
13	Denny Walling	.30	.25	.12
14	Danny Darwin	.30	.25	.12
15	Mark Bailey	.30	.25	.12
16	Davey Lopes	.40	.30	.15
17	Dave Meads	.40	.30	.15
18	Aurelio Lopez	.30	.25	.12
19	Craig Reynolds	.30	.25	.12
20	Dave Smith	.40	.30	.15
21	Larry Anderson (Andersen)	.30	.25	.12
22	Jim Pankovits	.30	.25	.12
23	Jim Deshaies	.50	.40	.20
24	Bert Pena	.40	.30	.15
25	Dickie Thon	.30	.25	.12
26	Billy Hatcher	.50	.40	.20
27	Astros Coaches (Yogi Berra, Matt Galante, Denis Menke, Les Moss, Gene Tenace)	.30	.25	.12
28	Houston Astrodome/Checklist	.30	.25	.12

1987 Mother's Cookies Dodgers

Mother's Cookies produced for the first time in 1987 a baseball card set featuring the Los Angeles Dodgers. Twenty of the 28 cards in the set were given out to youngsters 14 and under at Dodger Stadium on August 9th. An additional 8 cards were available from Mother's Cookies via a mail-in coupon card. The borderless, full-color cards measure 2½" by 3½" and have rounded corners. A special album designed to house the set was available for $3.95 through a mail-in offer.

		MT	NR MT	EX
Complete Set:		10.00	7.50	4.00
Common Player:		.30	.25	.12
1	Tom Lasorda	.40	.30	.15
2	Pedro Guerrero	.80	.60	.30
3	Steve Sax	.80	.60	.30
4	Fernando Valenzuela	1.25	.90	.50
5	Mike Marshall	.50	.40	.20
6	Orel Hershiser	.60	.45	.25
7	Mariano Duncan	.30	.25	.12
8	Bill Madlock	.40	.30	.15
9	Bob Welch	.40	.30	.15
10	Mike Scioscia	.30	.25	.12
11	Mike Ramsey	.30	.25	.12
12	Matt Young	.30	.25	.12
13	Franklin Stubbs	.40	.30	.15
14	Tom Niedenfuer	.30	.25	.12
15	Reggie Williams	.40	.30	.15
16	Rick Honeycutt	.30	.25	.12
17	Dave Anderson	.30	.25	.12
18	Alejandro Pena	.30	.25	.12
19	Ken Howell	.30	.25	.12
20	Len Matuszek	.30	.25	.12
21	Tim Leary	.30	.25	.12
22	Tracy Woodson	.40	.30	.15
23	Alex Trevino	.30	.25	.12
24	Ken Landreaux	.30	.25	.12
25	Mickey Hatcher	.30	.25	.12
26	Brian Holton	.40	.30	.15
27	Dodgers' Coaches (Joey Amalfitano, Mark Cresse, Don McMahon, Manny Mota, Ron Perranoski, Bill Russell)	.30	.25	.12
28	Dodger Stadium/Checklist	.30	.25	.12

1987 Mother's Cookies Giants

Distribution of the 1987 Mother's Cookies Giants cards took place at Candlestick Park for the Giants' June 27th game. Twenty of the 28 cards in the set were given to the first 25,000 fans entering the park. The starter packet of 20 cards contained a mail-in coupon card which was good for an additional 8 cards. The cards, which measure 2½" by 3½" in size, have rounded corners. The card backs are printed in red and purple and contain personal and statistical information along with the Mother's Cookies logo.

		MT	NR MT	EX
Complete Set:		10.00	7.50	4.00
Common Player:		.30	.25	.12
1	Roger Craig	.40	.30	.15
2	Will Clark	1.25	.90	.50
3	Chili Davis	.50	.40	.20
4	Bob Brenly	.30	.25	.12
5	Chris Brown	.60	.45	.25
6	Mike Krukow	.40	.30	.15
7	Candy Maldonado	.40	.30	.15
8	Jeffrey Leonard	.50	.40	.20
9	Greg Minton	.30	.25	.12
10	Robby Thompson	.40	.30	.15
11	Scott Garrelts	.30	.25	.12
12	Bob Melvin	.30	.25	.12
13	Jose Uribe	.30	.25	.12
14	Mark Davis	.30	.25	.12
15	Eddie Milner	.30	.25	.12
16	Harry Spilman	.30	.25	.12
17	Kelly Downs	.60	.45	.25
18	Chris Speier	.30	.25	.12
19	Jim Gott	.30	.25	.12
20	Joel Youngblood	.30	.25	.12
21	Mike LaCoss	.30	.25	.12
22	Matt Williams	.70	.50	.30
23	Roger Mason	.30	.25	.12
24	Mike Aldrete	.70	.50	.30
25	Jeff Robinson	.30	.25	.12
26	Mark Grant	.30	.25	.12
27	Coaches (Bill Fahey, Bob Lillis, Gordon MacKenzie, Jose Morales, Norm Sherry, Don Zimmer)	.30	.25	.12
28	Candlestick Park/Checklist	.30	.25	.12

1987 Mother's Cookies Mariners

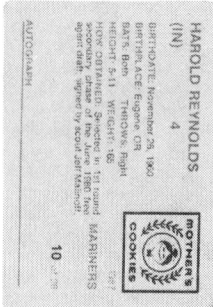

For the fourth consecutive year, Mother's Cookies issued a baseball card set featuring the Seattle Mariners. Twenty of the 28 cards in the set were distributed to the first 20,000 fans entering the Kingdome on August 9th. An additional cards (though not necessarily the 8 cards needed to complete the set) were available by redeeming a mail-in certificate. Collectors were encouraged to trade to complete a set. The 2½" by 3½" full-color cards feature glossy finishes and rounded corners. A specially designed album to house the set was available.

		MT	NR MT	EX
Complete Set:		8.00	6.00	3.25
Common Player:		.30	.25	.12
1	Dick Williams	.40	.30	.15
2	Alvin Davis	.60	.45	.25
3	Mike Moore	.30	.25	.12
4	Jim Presley	.60	.45	.25
5	Mark Langston	.50	.40	.20
6	Phil Bradley	.60	.45	.25
7	Ken Phelps	.40	.30	.15
8	Mike Morgan	.30	.25	.12
9	David Valle	.30	.25	.12
10	Harold Reynolds	.40	.30	.15
11	Edwin Nunez	.30	.25	.12
12	Bob Kearney	.30	.25	.12

		MT	NR MT	EX
13	Scott Bankhead	.40	.30	.15
14	Scott Bradley	.30	.25	.12
15	Mickey Brantley	.40	.30	.15
16	Mark Huismann	.30	.25	.12
17	Mike Kingery	.40	.30	.15
18	John Moses	.30	.25	.12
19	Donell Nixon	.40	.30	.15
20	Rey Quinones	.40	.30	.15
21	Domingo Ramos	.30	.25	.12
22	Jerry Reed	.30	.25	.12
23	Rich Renteria	.40	.30	.15
24	Rich Monteleone	.40	.30	.15
25	Mike Trujillo	.30	.25	.12
26	Bill Wilkinson	.40	.30	.15
27	John Christensen	.30	.25	.12
28	Coaches/Checklist (Billy Connors, Frank Howard, Phil Roof, Bobby Tolan, Ozzie Virgil)	.30	.25	.12

1987 Mother's Cookies Rangers

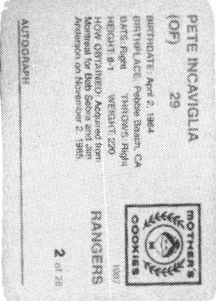

While Mother's Cookies of Oakland, Calif. had been producing high-quality baseball card sets of various teams, the Texas Rangers were highlighted for the first time in 1987. Twenty cards from the 28-card set were handed out to the first 25,000 fans entering Arlington Stadium on July 17th. An additional 8 cards (though not necessarily the 8 needed to complete a set) were available by redeeming a mail-in certificate. The cards, which measure 2½'' by 3½'', have rounded corners and glossy finishes like all Mother's Cookies issued in 1987.

		MT	NR MT	EX
	Complete Set:	10.00	7.50	4.00
	Complete Set:	.30	.25	.12
1	Bobby Valentine	.40	.30	.15
2	Pete Incaviglia	1.75	1.25	.70
3	Charlie Hough	.40	.30	.15
4	Oddibe McDowell	.70	.50	.30
5	Larry Parrish	.50	.40	.20
6	Scott Fletcher	.40	.30	.15
7	Steve Buechele	.30	.25	.12
8	Tom Paciorek	.30	.25	.12
9	Pete O'Brien	.70	.50	.30
10	Darrell Porter	.30	.25	.12
11	Greg Harris	.30	.25	.12
12	Don Slaught	.30	.25	.12
13	Ruben Sierra	1.75	1.25	.70
14	Curtis Wilkerson	.30	.25	.12
15	Dale Mohorcic	.40	.30	.15
16	Ron Meredith	.30	.25	.12
17	Mitch Williams	.40	.30	.15
18	Bob Brower	.40	.30	.15
19	Edwin Correa	.50	.40	.20
20	Geno Petralli	.30	.25	.12
21	Mike Loynd	.40	.30	.15
22	Jerry Browne	.40	.30	.15
23	Jose Guzman	.40	.30	.15
24	Jeff Kunkel	.30	.25	.12
25	Bobby Witt	.60	.45	.25
26	Jeff Russell	.30	.25	.12
27	Trainers (Danny Wheat, Bill Zeigler)	.30	.25	.12

		MT	NR MT	EX
28	Rangers' Coaches/Checklist (Joe Ferguson, Tim Foli, Tom House, Art Howe, Dave Oliver, Tom Robson)	.30	.25	.12

1987 Mother's Cookies Mark McGwire

A four-card set featuring outstanding rookie Mark McGwire of the Oakland Athletics was produced by Mother's Cookies of Oakland, Calif. Cards are 2½'' by 3½'' and have rounded corners and glossy finishes like other Mother's issues. The four-card set was obtainable by two methods. A complete set could be received by sending in eight proof of purchase seals. Also, sets could be secured at the National Sports Collectors Convention held July 9-12 in San Francisco. Convention goers received one card as a bonus for each Mother's Cookies baseball card album purchased.

		MT	NR MT	EX
	Complete Set:	10.00	7.50	4.00
	Common Player:	2.00	1.50	.80
1	Mark McGwire (portrait)	2.00	1.50	.80
2	Mark McGwire (leaning on bat rack)	2.00	1.50	.80
3	Mark McGwire (beginning batting swing)	2.00	1.50	.80
4	Mark McGwire (batting follow-through)	2.00	1.50	.80

1887 N28 Allen & Ginter

Generally considered the first of the tobacco card issues, this 50-card set was titled "The World Champions" and included 10 baseball players and 40 other sports personalities such as John L. Sullivan and Buffalo Bill Cody. The 1½'' by 2¾'' cards were inserted in boxes of Allen & Ginter cigarettes. The card fronts are color lithographs on white card stock, and are considered among the most attractive cards ever produced. All card backs have a complete checklist for this unnumbered set, which includes six eventual Hall of Famers (Cap Anson, John Clarkson, Charles Comiskey, Timothy Keefe, Mike Kelly and John Ward). Eight of the 10 players shown are from the National League and the other two from the American Association, then also considered a major league.

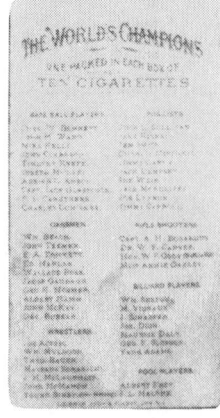

CHARLES COMISKEY.

	NR MT	EX	VG
Complete Set:	2700.00	1350.00	810.00
Common Player:	150.00	75.00	45.00
(1) Adrian C. Anson	800.00	400.00	240.00
(2) Chas. W. Bennett	150.00	75.00	45.00
(3) R.L. Caruthers	150.00	75.00	45.00
(4) John Clarkson	275.00	137.00	82.00
(5) Charles Comiskey	275.00	137.00	82.00
(6) Capt. John Glasscock	150.00	75.00	45.00
(7) Timothy Keefe	275.00	137.00	82.00
(8) Mike Kelly	325.00	162.00	97.00
(9) Joseph Mulvey	150.00	75.00	45.00
(10) John M. Ward	275.00	137.00	82.00

1888 N29 Allen & Ginter

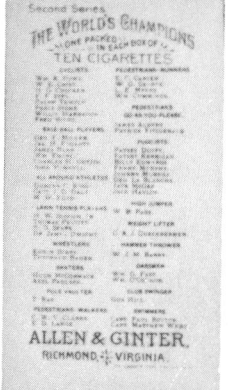

JAMES RYAN.
CENTRE FIELDER · CHICAGO.

After their 1887 first series of tobacco cards proved a success, Allen & Ginter issued a second series of "World Champions" in 1888. Once again, 50 of these 1½" by 2¾" color cards were produced, in virtually the same style as the year before. Only six baseball players are included in this set, with New York Giants catcher Buck Ewing the only player of note. The most obvious difference from the 1887 cards is the absence of the Allen & Ginter name on the card fronts. All six baseball players are from National League teams.

	NR MT	EX	VG
Complete Set:	3100.00	1550.00	930.00
Common Player:	450.00	225.00	135.00
(1) Wm. Ewing	775.00	387.00	232.00
(2) Jas. H. Fogarty (middle initial actually G.)			
	450.00	225.00	135.00

	NR MT	EX	VG
(3) Charles H. Getzin (Getzein)	450.00	225.00	135.00
(4) Geo. F. Miller	450.00	225.00	135.00
(5) John Morrell (Morrill)	450.00	225.00	135.00
(6) James Ryan	450.00	225.00	135.00

1887-1890 N172 Old Judge

GOODWIN & CO. New York.

This is one of the most fascinating of all card sets, as the number of cards issued will probably never be finally determined. These cards were issued by the Goodwin & Co. tobacco firm in their Old Judge and, to a lesser extent, Gypsy Queen cigarettes. Players from more than 40 major and minor league teams are pictured on the approximately 1½" by 2½" cards, with some 518 different players known to exist. Up to 17 different pose and team variations exist for some players, and the cards were issued both with and without dates on the card fronts, numbered and unnumbered, and with both handwritten and machine-printed names. Known variations number over 2,340. The cards themselves are sepia-toned photographs pasted onto thick cardboard. They are blank backed.

The N172 Goodwin listings are based on the recording in The Cartophilic Society's World Index, Part IV, compiled by E.C. Wharton-Tigar with the help of many collectors, especially Donald J. McPherson of California and Lew Lipset of New York.

	NR MT	EX	VG
Common Player:	65.00	32.00	19.50
Brown's Champions	120.00	60.00	36.00
Dotted Ties	300.00	150.00	90.00
1 Gus Albert (Alberts)	65.00	32.00	19.50
2 Alcott	65.00	32.00	19.50
3 Alexander	65.00	32.00	19.50
4 Myron Allen (Kansas City)	65.00	32.00	19.50
5 Bob Allen (Pittsburgh, Philadelphia)			
	65.00	32.00	19.50
6 Uncle Bill Alvord	65.00	32.00	19.50
7 Varney Anderson	65.00	32.00	19.50
8 Wally Andrews (Omaha)	65.00	32.00	19.50
9 Ed Andrews (Philadelphia)	65.00	32.00	19.50
9-6 Ed Andrews, Buster Hoover	100.00	50.00	30.00
10 Bill Annis	65.00	32.00	19.50
11 Cap Anson	725.00	363.00	218.00
12 Old Hoss Ardner	65.00	32.00	19.50
13 Tug Arundel	65.00	32.00	19.50
14 Jersey Bakley (Bakely)	65.00	32.00	19.50
15 Fido Baldwin (Chicago, Columbus)			
	65.00	32.00	19.50
16 Kid Baldwin (Cincinnati)	65.00	32.00	19.50
17 Lady Baldwin (Detroit, Cincinnati)			
	65.00	32.00	19.50
18 James Banning	65.00	32.00	19.50
19 Samuel Barkley	65.00	32.00	19.50
20 John Barnes	65.00	32.00	19.50
21 Bald Billy Barnie	90.00	45.00	27.00

		NR MT	EX	VG
22	Charles Bassett	65.00	32.00	19.50
23	Charles Bastian	65.00	32.00	19.50
23-6	Charles Bastian, Pop Schriver	100.00	50.00	30.00
24	Ed Beatin	65.00	32.00	19.50
25	Eagle Eye Beckley	225.00	112.00	67.00
26	Stephen Behel (dotted tie)	300.00	150.00	90.00
27	Charles Bennett	100.00	50.00	30.00
28	Louis Bierbauer	65.00	32.00	19.50
28-5	Louis Bierbauer, Bob Gamble	100.00	50.00	30.00
29	Bill Bishop	65.00	32.00	19.50
30	Bill Blair	65.00	32.00	19.50
31	Ned Bligh	65.00	32.00	19.50
32	Bogart	65.00	32.00	19.50
33	Boyce	65.00	32.00	19.50
34	Boyd	100.00	50.00	30.00
35	Honest John Boyle (St. Louis, Chicago)	65.00	32.00	19.50
36	Handsome Boyle (Indianapolis, New York)	65.00	32.00	19.50
37	Nick Bradley (Kansas City, Worcester)	65.00	32.00	19.50
38	Grin Bradley (Sioux City)	65.00	32.00	19.50
39	Stephen Brady (dotted tie)	300.00	150.00	90.00
40	Breckenridge	160.00	80.00	48.00
41	Timothy Brosnam	65.00	32.00	19.50
42	Cal Broughton	65.00	32.00	19.50
43	Big Dan Brouthers	225.00	112.00	67.00
44	Thomas Brown (Pittsburgh, Boston)	65.00	32.00	19.50
45	California Brown (New York)	65.00	32.00	19.50
46	Pete Browning	100.00	50.00	30.00
47	Charles Brynan	65.00	32.00	19.50
48	Al Buckenberger	65.00	32.00	19.50
49	Dick Buckley	65.00	32.00	19.50
50	Charles Buffinton	65.00	32.00	19.50
51	Ernest Burch	65.00	32.00	19.50
52	Bill Burdick	65.00	32.00	19.50
53	Black Jack Burdock	65.00	32.00	19.50
54	Robert Burks (Burk)	80.00	40.00	24.00
55	Watch Burnham	100.00	50.00	30.00
56	James Burns (Kansas City, Omaha)	65.00	32.00	19.50
57	No World Index listing			
58	Oyster Burns (Baltimore, Brooklyn)	65.00	32.00	19.50
59	Thomas Burns (Chicago)	65.00	32.00	19.50
60	Doc Bushong (Brooklyn)	65.00	32.00	19.50
60-1	Doc Bushong (Brown's Champions)	120.00	60.00	36.00
61	Patsy Cahill	65.00	32.00	19.50
62	Count Campau	65.00	32.00	19.50
63	Jimmy Canavan	65.00	32.00	19.50
64	Bart Cantz	65.00	32.00	19.50
65	Handsome Jack Carney	65.00	32.00	19.50
66	Hick Carpenter	65.00	32.00	19.50
67	Cliff Carroll (Washington)	80.00	40.00	24.00
68	Scrappy Carroll (St. Paul, Chicago)	65.00	32.00	19.50
69	Frederick Carroll (Pittsburgh)	65.00	32.00	19.50
70	Jumbo Cartwright	65.00	32.00	19.50
71	Parisian Bob Caruthers (Brooklyn)	80.00	40.00	24.00
71-1	Parisian Bob Caruthers (Brown's Champions)	120.00	60.00	36.00
72	Daniel Casey	100.00	50.00	30.00
73	Icebox Chamberlain	65.00	32.00	19.50
74	Cupid Childs	65.00	32.00	19.50
75	Spider Clark (Washington)	65.00	32.00	19.50
76	Bob Clark (Brooklyn)	65.00	32.00	19.50
76-6	Bob Clark, Mickey Hughes	100.00	50.00	30.00
77	Dad Clarke	65.00	32.00	19.50
78	John Clarkson	225.00	112.00	67.00
79	Jack Clements	65.00	32.00	19.50
80	Elmer Cleveland	65.00	32.00	19.50
81	Monk Cline	65.00	32.00	19.50
82	Cody	65.00	32.00	19.50
83	John Coleman	65.00	32.00	19.50
84	Bill Collins (New York, Newark)	65.00	32.00	19.50
85	Hub Collins (Louisville, Brooklyn)	65.00	32.00	19.50
86	Commy Comiskey (St. Louis, Chicago)	260.00	130.00	78.00
86-1	Commy Comiskey (Brown's Champions)	300.00	150.00	90.00
87	Pete Connell	100.00	50.00	30.00
88	Roger Connor	225.00	112.00	67.00
89	Dick Conway (Boston, Worcester)	65.00	32.00	19.50
90	Pete Conway (Detroit, Pittsburgh, Indianapolis)	65.00	32.00	19.50
91	Jim Conway (Kansas City)	65.00	32.00	19.50

		NR MT	EX	VG
92	Paul Cook	65.00	32.00	19.50
93	Jimmy Cooney	80.00	40.00	24.00
94	Larry Corcoran	65.00	32.00	19.50
95	Pop Corkhill	65.00	32.00	19.50
96	Cannon Ball Crane (New York)	65.00	32.00	19.50
97	Samuel Crane (Washington)	65.00	32.00	19.50
98	Jack Crogan (Croghan)	100.00	50.00	30.00
99	John Crooks	65.00	32.00	19.50
100	Lave Cross	100.00	50.00	30.00
101	N.C. Crossley	65.00	32.00	19.50
102	Joe Crotty (Sioux City)	65.00	32.00	19.50
102-1	Joe Crotty (dotted tie)	260.00	130.00	78.00
103	Billy Crowell	65.00	32.00	19.50
104	Jim Cudworth	65.00	32.00	19.50
105	Bert Cunningham	65.00	32.00	19.50
106	Tacks Curtis	65.00	32.00	19.50
107	Ed Cushman (dotted tie)	300.00	150.00	90.00
107-2	Ed Cushman (Toledo)	160.00	80.00	48.00
108	Tony Cusick	65.00	32.00	19.50
109	Dailey (Oakland)	160.00	80.00	48.00
110	Edward Dailey (Daily) (Philadelphia, Washington, Columbus)	65.00	32.00	19.50
111	Bill Daley (Boston)	65.00	32.00	19.50
112	Con Daley (Daily) (Boston, Indianapolis)	65.00	32.00	19.50
113	Abner Dalrymple	65.00	32.00	19.50
114	Tido Daly (Chicago, Washington)	65.00	32.00	19.50
115	Sun Daly (Minneapolis)	65.00	32.00	19.50
116	Law Daniels	65.00	32.00	19.50
117	Dell Darling	65.00	32.00	19.50
118	William Darnbrough	65.00	32.00	19.50
118.5	Davin	160.00	80.00	48.00
119	Jumbo Davis	65.00	32.00	19.50
120	Pat Dealey	65.00	32.00	19.50
121	Tom Deasley	65.00	32.00	19.50
122	Harry Decker	65.00	32.00	19.50
123	Big Ed Delahanty	325.00	163.00	98.00
124	Jerry Denny	65.00	32.00	19.50
125	Jim Devlin	65.00	32.00	19.50
126	Tom Dolan	65.00	32.00	19.50
127	Jack Donahue (San Francisco)	160.00	80.00	48.00
128	Jim Donahue (Kansas City)	65.00	32.00	19.50
128-1	Jim Donohue (Donahue) (dotted tie)	290.00	145.00	87.00
129	Jim Donnelly	65.00	32.00	19.50
130	Dooley	160.00	80.00	48.00
131	Doran	100.00	50.00	30.00
132	Mike Dorgan	65.00	32.00	19.50
133	Doyle	160.00	80.00	48.00
134	Home Run Duffe (Duffee)	65.00	32.00	19.50
135	Hugh Duffy	225.00	112.00	67.00
136	Dan Dugdale	100.00	50.00	30.00
137	Duck Duke	65.00	32.00	19.50
138	Sure Shot Dunlap	65.00	32.00	19.50
139	Dunn	100.00	50.00	30.00
140	Jesse Duryea	65.00	32.00	19.50
141	Frank Dwyer	65.00	32.00	19.50
142	Billy Earle	65.00	32.00	19.50
143	Buck Ebright	65.00	32.00	19.50
144	Red Ehret	65.00	32.00	19.50
145	R. Emmerke	65.00	32.00	19.50
146	Dude Esterbrook	65.00	32.00	19.50
147	Henry Esterday	65.00	32.00	19.50
148	Long John Ewing (Louisville)	65.00	32.00	19.50
149	Buck Ewing (New York)	225.00	112.00	67.00
149-11	Willie Breslin-mascot, Buck Ewing	200.00	100.00	60.00
150	Jay Faatz	65.00	32.00	19.50
151	Bill Fagan	65.00	32.00	19.50
152	Bill Farmer	65.00	32.00	19.50
153	Sid Farrar	65.00	32.00	19.50
154	Jack Farrell (Washington, Baltimore)	65.00	32.00	19.50
155	Duke Farrell (Chicago)	65.00	32.00	19.50
156	Frank Fennelly	65.00	32.00	19.50
157	Charlie Ferguson	65.00	32.00	19.50
158	Alex Ferson	65.00	32.00	19.50
159	Wallace Fessenden (umpire)	120.00	60.00	36.00
160	Jocko Fields	65.00	32.00	19.50
161	Fischer	100.00	50.00	30.00
162	Thomas Flanigan (Flanagan)	65.00	32.00	19.50
163	Silver Flint	65.00	32.00	19.50
164	Thomas Flood	65.00	32.00	19.50
164.5	Jocko Flynn	160.00	80.00	48.00
165	Jim Fogarty	65.00	32.00	19.50
166	Frank Foreman	65.00	32.00	19.50
167	Tom Forster (Hartford)	160.00	80.00	48.00
167-2	Tom Forster (dotted tie, incorrect name (F.W. Foster) on front)	300.00	150.00	90.00
168	Elmer Foster (New York, Minneapolis)	65.00	32.00	19.50

		NR MT	EX	VG
168-1	Elmer Foster (dotted tie)	300.00	150.00	90.00
169	No World Index listing			
170	Dave Foutz (Brooklyn)	65.00	32.00	19.50
170-1	Dave Foutz (Brown's Champions)	120.00	60.00	36.00
171	Julie Freeman	65.00	32.00	19.50
172	Will Fry	65.00	32.00	19.50
172.5	Fudger	160.00	80.00	48.00
173	William Fuller (Milwaukee)	65.00	32.00	19.50
174	Shorty Fuller (St. Louis)	65.00	32.00	19.50
175	Chris Fulmer	65.00	32.00	19.50
175-6	Chris Fulmer, Foghorn Tucker	100.00	50.00	30.00
176	Honest John Gaffney	100.00	50.00	30.00
177	Pud Galvin	225.00	112.00	67.00
178	Bob Gamble	80.00	40.00	24.00
179	Charlie Ganzel	65.00	32.00	19.50
180	Gid Gardner	65.00	32.00	19.50
180-5	Gid Gardner, Miah Murray	100.00	50.00	30.00
181	Hank Gastreich	65.00	32.00	19.50
182	Emil Geiss	65.00	32.00	19.50
183	Frenchy Genins	65.00	32.00	19.50
184	Bill George	65.00	32.00	19.50
185	Joe Gerhardt	65.00	32.00	19.50
186	Charlie Getzein	65.00	32.00	19.50
187	Bobby Gilks	65.00	32.00	19.50
188	Pete Gillespie	65.00	32.00	19.50
189	Barney Gilligan	65.00	32.00	19.50
190	Frank Gilmore	65.00	32.00	19.50
191	Pebbly Jack Glasscock	100.00	50.00	30.00
192	Kid Gleason (Philadelphia)	80.00	40.00	24.00
193	Will Gleason (Athletics)	65.00	32.00	19.50
193-1	Will Gleason (Brown's Champions)	120.00	60.00	36.00
194	Mouse Glenn	65.00	32.00	19.50
195	Mike Goodfellow	65.00	32.00	19.50
196	Piano Legs Gore	65.00	32.00	19.50
197	Frank Graves	65.00	32.00	19.50
198	Bill Greenwood	65.00	32.00	19.50
199	Ed Greer	65.00	32.00	19.50
200	Mike Griffin	65.00	32.00	19.50
201	Old Fox Griffith	300.00	150.00	90.00
202	Henry Gruber	65.00	32.00	19.50
203	Ad Gumbert	65.00	32.00	19.50
204	Tom Gunning	65.00	32.00	19.50
205	Joe Gunson	65.00	32.00	19.50
206	Gentleman George Haddock	65.00	32.00	19.50
207	Bill Hafner (Hoffner)	65.00	32.00	19.50
208	Willie Hahm (mascot)	100.00	50.00	30.00
209	Bill Hallman	65.00	32.00	19.50
210	Sliding Billy Hamilton	300.00	150.00	90.00
211	Frank Hankinson (dotted tie)	300.00	150.00	90.00
212	Ned Hanlon	80.00	40.00	24.00
213	William Hanrahan	65.00	32.00	19.50
213.5	Hapeman	160.00	80.00	48.00
214	Pa Harkins	65.00	32.00	19.50
215	Bill Hart	65.00	32.00	19.50
216	William Hasamdear	80.00	40.00	24.00
217	Gill Hatfield	65.00	32.00	19.50
218	Egyptian Healey (Healy)	65.00	32.00	19.50
219	Healy	65.00	32.00	19.50
220	Guy Hecker	100.00	50.00	30.00
221	Tony Hellman	65.00	32.00	19.50
222	Hardie Henderson	65.00	32.00	19.50
222-10	Ed Greer, Hardie Henderson	100.00	50.00	30.00
223	Moxie Hengle	65.00	32.00	19.50
224	John Henry	65.00	32.00	19.50
225	Ed Herr	65.00	32.00	19.50
226	Hunkey Hines (St. Louis Whites)	65.00	32.00	19.50
227	Paul Hines (Washington, Indianapolis)	65.00	32.00	19.50
228	Texas Wonder Hoffman	65.00	32.00	19.50
229	Eddie Hogan	65.00	32.00	19.50
230	Bill Holbert	65.00	32.00	19.50
230-1	Bill Holbert (dotted tie)	300.00	150.00	90.00
231	Bug Holliday	65.00	32.00	19.50
232	Charles Hoover (Chicago, Kansas City)	65.00	32.00	19.50
233	Buster Hoover (Philadelphia)	65.00	32.00	19.50
234	Jack Horner	65.00	32.00	19.50
234-3	Jack Horner, E.H. Warner	100.00	50.00	30.00
235	Joe Hornung	65.00	32.00	19.50
236	Pete Hotaling	65.00	32.00	19.50
237	Bill Howes (Hawes)	65.00	32.00	19.50
238	Dummy Hoy	120.00	60.00	36.00
239	Nat Hudson (St. Louis)	65.00	32.00	19.50
239-1	Nat Hudson (Brown's Champions)	120.00	60.00	36.00
240	Mickey Hughes	65.00	32.00	19.50
241	Hungler	65.00	32.00	19.50
242	Wild Bill Hutchinson	65.00	32.00	19.50
243	John Irwin (Washington)	65.00	32.00	19.50

		NR MT	EX	VG
244	Cutrate Irwin (Philadelphia)	65.00	32.00	19.50
245	A.C. Jantzen	65.00	32.00	19.50
246	Frederick Jevne	65.00	32.00	19.50
247	Spud Johnson	65.00	32.00	19.50
248	Dick Johnston	65.00	32.00	19.50
249	Jordan	65.00	32.00	19.50
250	Heinie Kappell (Kappel)	65.00	32.00	19.50
251	Tim Keefe (New York)	225.00	112.00	67.00
251-8	Tim Keefe, Danny Richardson	200.00	100.00	60.00
252	George Keefe (Washington)	65.00	32.00	19.50
253	Jim Keenan	65.00	32.00	19.50
254	King Kelly (Boston)	300.00	150.00	90.00
255	Honest John Kelly (Louisville)	100.00	50.00	30.00
255-3	Honest John Kelly (umpire)	100.00	50.00	30.00
255-4	Honest John Kelly, Jim Powell	100.00	50.00	30.00
256	No World Index listing			
257	Charles Kelly (Philadelphia)	65.00	32.00	19.50
258	Rudy Kemmler (St. Paul)	100.00	50.00	30.00
258-1	Rudy Kemler (Kemmler) (Brown's Champions)	120.00	60.00	36.00
259	Theodore Kennedy	65.00	32.00	19.50
260	J.J. Kenyon	65.00	32.00	19.50
261	John Kerins	65.00	32.00	19.50
262	Matt Kilroy	65.00	32.00	19.50
263	Silver King	65.00	32.00	19.50
264	August Kloff (Klopf)	65.00	32.00	19.50
265	William Klusman	65.00	32.00	19.50
266	Philip Knell	65.00	32.00	19.50
267	Fred Knouff	65.00	32.00	19.50
268	Charles Kremmeyer (Krehmeyer)	160.00	80.00	48.00
269	Bill Krieg	65.00	32.00	19.50
269-10	August Kloff, Bill Kreig	100.00	50.00	30.00
270	Gus Krock	65.00	32.00	19.50
271	Willie Kuehne	65.00	32.00	19.50
272	Fred Lange	100.00	50.00	30.00
273	Ted Larkin	65.00	32.00	19.50
274	Arlie Latham (St. Louis)	100.00	50.00	30.00
274-1	Arlie Latham (Brown's Champions)	160.00	80.00	48.00
275	Chuck Lauer (Laver)	65.00	32.00	19.50
276	John Leighton	65.00	32.00	19.50
276.5	Levy	160.00	80.00	48.00
277	Tom Loftus	65.00	32.00	19.50
278	Germany Long (Kansas City, Chicago Maroons)	80.00	40.00	24.00
279	Danny Long (Oakland)	160.00	80.00	48.00
280	Tom Lovett	65.00	32.00	19.50
281	Bobby Lowe	100.00	50.00	30.00
282	Jack Lynch	65.00	32.00	19.50
282-1	Jack Lynch (dotted tie)	300.00	150.00	90.00
283	Denny Lyons (Athletics)	65.00	32.00	19.50
284	Harry Lyons (St. Louis)	65.00	32.00	19.50
285	Connie Mack (Washington)	525.00	263.00	158.00
286	Reddie Mack (Louisville, Baltimore)	65.00	32.00	19.50
287	Little Mac Macullar	65.00	32.00	19.50
288	Kid Madden	65.00	32.00	19.50
289	Danny Mahoney	100.00	50.00	30.00
290	Grasshopper Maines (Mains)	65.00	32.00	19.50
291	Fred Mann	65.00	32.00	19.50
292	Jimmy Manning	65.00	32.00	19.50
293	Lefty Marr	65.00	32.00	19.50
294	Willie Breslin (mascot)	100.00	50.00	30.00
295	Leech Maskrey	65.00	32.00	19.50
296	Bobby Mathews	80.00	40.00	24.00
297	Mike Mattimore	65.00	32.00	19.50
298	Smiling Al Maul	65.00	32.00	19.50
299	Al Mays (Columbus)	65.00	32.00	19.50
299-1	Al Mays (dotted tie)	300.00	150.00	90.00
300	Jimmy McAleer	80.00	40.00	24.00
301	Tommy McCarthy (Philadelphia, St. Louis)	225.00	112.00	67.00
302	John McCarthy (McCarty) (Kansas City)	80.00	40.00	24.00
303	Jim McCauley	100.00	50.00	30.00
304	Bill McClellan	65.00	32.00	19.50
305	Jerry McCormack (McCormick)	65.00	32.00	19.50
306	Jim McCormick	80.00	40.00	24.00
307	McCreachery (photo actually Deacon White)	100.00	50.00	30.00
308	Thomas McCullum (McCallum)	65.00	32.00	19.50
308.5	McDonald	160.00	80.00	48.00
309	Chippy McGarr	65.00	32.00	19.50
310	Jack McGeachy	65.00	32.00	19.50
311	John McGlone	65.00	32.00	19.50
312	Deacon McGuire	80.00	40.00	24.00
313	Bill McGunnigle	100.00	50.00	30.00
314	Ed McKean	65.00	32.00	19.50
315	Alex McKinnon	65.00	32.00	19.50
316	Tom McLaughlin	300.00	150.00	90.00

		NR MT	EX	VG
317	Bid McPhee	65.00	32.00	19.50
318	James McQuaid (Denver)	65.00	32.00	19.50
319	John McQuaid (umpire)	100.00	50.00	30.00
320	Jim McTamany	65.00	32.00	19.50
321	George McVey	65.00	32.00	19.50
321.5	Steady Pete Meegan	160.00	80.00	48.00
322	John Messitt	65.00	32.00	19.50
323	Doggie Miller (Pittsburgh)	65.00	32.00	19.50
324	Joseph Miller (Omaha, Minneapolis)			
		65.00	32.00	19.50
325	Jocko Milligan	65.00	32.00	19.50
326	E.L. Mills	65.00	32.00	19.50
327	Daniel Minnehan (Minahan)	65.00	32.00	19.50
328	Sam Moffet	65.00	32.00	19.50
329	Honest John Morrill	65.00	32.00	19.50
330	Ed Morris	65.00	32.00	19.50
331	Count Mullane	100.00	50.00	30.00
332	Joseph Mulvey	80.00	40.00	24.00
333	P.L. Murphy (St. Paul)	65.00	32.00	19.50
334	Pat Murphy (New York)	65.00	32.00	19.50
335	Miah Murray	65.00	32.00	19.50
336	Truthful Jim Mutrie	65.00	32.00	19.50
337	George Myers (Indianapolis)	65.00	32.00	19.50
338	Al Myers (Washington, Philadelphia)			
		65.00	32.00	19.50
339	Tom Nagle	65.00	32.00	19.50
340	Billy Nash	65.00	32.00	19.50
341	Candy Nelson (dotted tie)	300.00	150.00	90.00
342	Kid Nichols (Omaha)	360.00	180.00	108.00
343	Samuel Nichols (Nichol) (Pittsburgh)			
		65.00	32.00	19.50
344	J.W. Nicholson (Chicago Maroons)			
		100.00	50.00	30.00
345	Parson Nicholson (St. Louis, Cleveland)			
		65.00	32.00	19.50
346	Little Nick Nicol (Cincinnati)	65.00	32.00	19.50
346-1	Little Nick Nicoll (Nicol) (Brown's Champions)	120.00	60.00	36.00
346-8	Little Nick Nicol, Big John Reilly			
		100.00	50.00	30.00
347	Frederick Nyce	65.00	32.00	19.50
348	Doc Oberlander	65.00	32.00	19.50
349	Jack O'Brien (Brooklyn, Baltimore)			
		65.00	32.00	19.50
350	Billy O'Brien (Washington)	65.00	32.00	19.50
351	Darby O'Brien (Brooklyn)	65.00	32.00	19.50
352	John O'Brien (Cleveland)	65.00	32.00	19.50
353	P.J. O'Connell	65.00	32.00	19.50
354	Rowdy Jack O'Connor	65.00	32.00	19.50
355	Hank O'Day	80.00	40.00	24.00
356	Tip O'Neil (O'Neill) (St. Louis)	80.00	40.00	24.00
356-6	Tip O'Neil (O'Neill) (Brown's Champions)			
		120.00	60.00	36.00
357	Tip O'Neill (photo actually Deacon White, St. Louis)	80.00	40.00	24.00
357.5	O'Neill (Oakland)	160.00	80.00	48.00
358	Orator Jim O'Rourke (New York)			
		225.00	112.00	67.00
359	Tom O'Rourke (Boston)	65.00	32.00	19.50
360	Dave Orr	65.00	32.00	19.50
360-1	Dave Orr (dotted tie)	300.00	150.00	90.00
361	Charles Parsons	65.00	32.00	19.50
362	Owen Patton	65.00	32.00	19.50
363	Jimmy Peeples (Peoples)	65.00	32.00	19.50
363-3	Hardie Henderson, Jimmy Peeples			
		100.00	50.00	30.00
364	Hip Perrier	300.00	150.00	90.00
365	Patrick Pettee	65.00	32.00	19.50
365-5	Bobby Lowe, Patrick Pettee	100.00	50.00	30.00
366	Fred Pfeffer	65.00	32.00	19.50
367	Dick Phelan	65.00	32.00	19.50
368	Bill Phillips	65.00	32.00	19.50
369	Jack Pickett	65.00	32.00	19.50
370	George Pinkney	65.00	32.00	19.50
371	Tom Poorman	65.00	32.00	19.50
372	Henry Porter	65.00	32.00	19.50
373	Jim Powell	65.00	32.00	19.50
373.5	Thomas Powers	160.00	80.00	48.00
374	Blondie Purcell	65.00	32.00	19.50
375	Tom Quinn (Baltimore)	65.00	32.00	19.50
376	Joe Quinn (Boston, Des Moines)	65.00	32.00	19.50
377	Old Hoss Radbourn	225.00	112.00	67.00
378	Shorty Radford	65.00	32.00	19.50
379	Toad Ramsey	65.00	32.00	19.50
380	Rehse	65.00	32.00	19.50
381	Long John Reilly (Cincinnati)	65.00	32.00	19.50
382	Princeton Charlie Reilly (St. Paul)			
		65.00	32.00	19.50
383	Charlie Reynolds	65.00	32.00	19.50
384	Hardy Richardson (Detroit, Boston)			
		65.00	32.00	19.50

		NR MT	EX	VG
385	Danny Richardson (New York)	65.00	32.00	19.50
386	Charles Ripslager (dotted tie)	300.00	150.00	90.00
387	John Roach	65.00	32.00	19.50
388	Uncle Robbie Robinson (Athletics)			
		300.00	150.00	90.00
389	M.C. Robinson (Minneapolis)	65.00	32.00	19.50
390	Yank Robinson (St. Louis)	65.00	32.00	19.50
390-6	Yank Robinson (Brown's Champions)			
		120.00	60.00	36.00
391	George Rooks	100.00	50.00	30.00
392	Chief Roseman (dotted tie)	300.00	150.00	90.00
393	Dave Rowe (Kansas City)	65.00	32.00	19.50
394	Jack Rowe (Detroit)	65.00	32.00	19.50
395	Amos Rusie	360.00	180.00	108.00
396	Jimmy Ryan	100.00	50.00	30.00
397	Doc Sage	65.00	32.00	19.50
397-4	Doc Sage, Bill Van Dyke	100.00	50.00	30.00
398	Ben Sanders	65.00	32.00	19.50
399	Frank Scheibeck	65.00	32.00	19.50
400	Al Schellhase (Schellhasse)	65.00	32.00	19.50
401	William Schenkel	65.00	32.00	19.50
402	Schildknecht	65.00	32.00	19.50
403	Gus Schmelz	65.00	32.00	19.50
404	Jumbo Schoeneck	65.00	32.00	19.50
405	Pop Schriver	65.00	32.00	19.50
406	Emmett Seery	65.00	32.00	19.50
407	Billy Serad	65.00	32.00	19.50
408	Ed Seward	65.00	32.00	19.50
409	Orator Shafer (Shaffer) (Des Moines)			
		65.00	32.00	19.50
410	Taylor Shafer (Shaffer) (St. Paul)			
		65.00	32.00	19.50
411	Daniel Shannon	65.00	32.00	19.50
412	William Sharsig	100.00	50.00	30.00
413	Samuel Shaw (Baltimore, Newark)			
		65.00	32.00	19.50
414	John Shaw (Minneapolis)	65.00	32.00	19.50
415	Bill Shindle	65.00	32.00	19.50
416	George Shoch	65.00	32.00	19.50
417	Otto Shomberg (Schomberg)	65.00	32.00	19.50
418	Lev Shreve	65.00	32.00	19.50
419	Ed Silch	65.00	32.00	19.50
420	Mike Slattery	65.00	32.00	19.50
421	Skyrocket Smith (Louisville)	65.00	32.00	19.50
422	Phenomenal Smith (Baltimore, Athletics)			
		100.00	50.00	30.00
423	Mike Smith (Cincinnati)	65.00	32.00	19.50
424	Sam Smith (Des Moines)	65.00	32.00	19.50
425	Germany Smith (Brooklyn)	65.00	32.00	19.50
426	Pap Smith (Pittsburgh, Boston)	65.00	32.00	19.50
427	Nick Smith (St. Joseph)	65.00	32.00	19.50
428	P.T. Somers	65.00	32.00	19.50
429	Joe Sommer	65.00	32.00	19.50
430	Pete Sommers	65.00	32.00	19.50
431	Little Bill Sowders (Boston)	65.00	32.00	19.50
432	John Sowders (St. Paul, Kansas City)			
		65.00	32.00	19.50
433	Charlie Sprague	65.00	32.00	19.50
434	Ed Sproat	65.00	32.00	19.50
435	Harry Staley	65.00	32.00	19.50
436	Dan Stearns	65.00	32.00	19.50
437	Cannonball Stemmyer (Stemmeyer)			
		65.00	32.00	19.50
438	B.F. Stephens	80.00	40.00	24.00
439	John Sterling	65.00	32.00	19.50
439.5	Stockwell	160.00	80.00	48.00
440	Harry Stovey	120.00	60.00	36.00
441	Scott Stratton	65.00	32.00	19.50
442	Joe Straus (Strauss)	65.00	32.00	19.50
443	Cub Stricker	65.00	32.00	19.50
444	Marty Sullivan (Chicago, Indianapolis)			
		65.00	32.00	19.50
445	Mike Sullivan (Athletics)	80.00	40.00	24.00
446	Billy Sunday	160.00	80.00	48.00
447	Sy Sutcliffe	65.00	32.00	19.50
448	Ezra Sutton	65.00	32.00	19.50
449	Ed Swartwood	65.00	32.00	19.50
450	Park Swartzel	65.00	32.00	19.50
451	Pete Sweeney	65.00	32.00	19.50
451.5	Louis Sylvester	160.00	80.00	48.00
452	Pop Tate	65.00	32.00	19.50
453	Patsy Tebeau	65.00	32.00	19.50
454	John Tener	100.00	50.00	30.00
455	Adonis Terry	80.00	40.00	24.00
456	Big Sam Thompson	225.00	112.00	67.00
457	Silent Mike Tiernan	65.00	32.00	19.50
458	Cannonball Titcomb	65.00	32.00	19.50
459	Buster Tomney	65.00	32.00	19.50
460	Stephen Toole	65.00	32.00	19.50
461	Sleepy Townsend	65.00	32.00	19.50
462	Bill Traffley	65.00	32.00	19.50

		NR MT	EX	VG
463	George Treadway	65.00	32.00	19.50
464	Sam Trott	65.00	32.00	19.50
464-6	Oyster Burns, Sam Trott	100.00	50.00	30.00
465	Foghorn Tucker	65.00	32.00	19.50
466	A.M. Tuckerman	65.00	32.00	19.50
467	George Turner	65.00	32.00	19.50
468	Larry Twitchell	65.00	32.00	19.50
469	Jim Tyng	65.00	32.00	19.50
470	Bill Van Dyke	80.00	40.00	24.00
471	Rip Van Haltren	80.00	40.00	24.00
472	Farmer Vaughn	65.00	32.00	19.50
472.5	Veach	160.00	80.00	48.00
473	Lee Viau	65.00	32.00	19.50
474	Bill Vinton	65.00	32.00	19.50
475	Joe Visner	65.00	32.00	19.50
476	Christian Von Der Ahe (Brown's Champions)	225.00	112.00	67.00
477	Reddy Walsh	65.00	32.00	19.50
478	Monte Ward	225.00	112.00	67.00
479	E.H. Warner	100.00	50.00	30.00
480	Bill Watkins	65.00	32.00	19.50
481	Farmer Weaver	65.00	32.00	19.50
482	Count Weber	65.00	32.00	19.50
483	Stump Weidman	65.00	32.00	19.50
484	Wild Bill Weidner (Widner)	65.00	32.00	19.50
485	Curt Welch, Curt Welch (Brown's Champions)	120.00	60.00	36.00
485-7	Will Gleason, Curt Welch	100.00	50.00	30.00
486	Smiling Mickey Welch (New York)	225.00	112.00	67.00
487	Jake Wells (Kansas City)	100.00	50.00	30.00
488	Frank Wells (Milwaukee)	100.00	50.00	30.00
489	Joe Werrick	65.00	32.00	19.50
490	Buck West	65.00	32.00	19.50
491	A.C. "Cannonball" Weyhing	65.00	32.00	19.50
492	John Weyhing	65.00	32.00	19.50
493	Bobby Wheelock	65.00	32.00	19.50
494	Pat Whitacre (Whitaker)	80.00	40.00	24.00
495	Pat Whitaker	65.00	32.00	19.50
496	Deacon White (Detroit, Pittsburgh)	80.00	40.00	24.00
497	Bill White (Louisville)	65.00	32.00	19.50
498	Grasshopper Whitney (Washington, Indianapolis)	65.00	32.00	19.50
499	Art Whitney (Pittsburgh, New York)	65.00	32.00	19.50
500	G. Whitney (St. Joseph)	65.00	32.00	19.50
501	James Williams	100.00	50.00	30.00
502	Ned Williamson	100.00	50.00	30.00
502-7	Willie Hahm - mascot, Ned Williamson	160.00	80.00	48.00
503	C.H. Willis	65.00	32.00	19.50
504	Watt Wilmot	65.00	32.00	19.50
505	George Winkleman (Winkelman)	65.00	32.00	19.50
506	Medoc Wise	65.00	32.00	19.50
507	Chicken Wolf	65.00	32.00	19.50
508	George "Dandy" Wood	65.00	32.00	19.50
509	Pete Wood	65.00	32.00	19.50
510	Harry Wright	500.00	250.00	150.00
511	Chief Zimmer	65.00	32.00	19.50
512	Frank Zinn	65.00	32.00	19.50

1887 N284 Buchner Gold Coin

Isssued circa 1887, the N284 issue was produced by D. Buchner & Company for its Gold Coin brand of chewing tobacco. Actually, the series was not comprised only of baseball players — actors, jockeys, firemen and policemen were also included. The cards, which measure 1¾'' by 3'', are color drawings. The set is not a popular one among collectors as the drawings do not represent the players designated on the cards. In most instances, players at a given position share the same drawing depicted on the card front. Three different card backs are found, all advising collectors to save the valuable chewing tobacco wrappers. Wrappers could be redeemed for various prizes.

		NR MT	EX	VG
	Complete Set:	18000.00	9000.00	5400.
	Common Player:	90.00	45.00	27.00
(1)	Ed Andrews (hands at neck)	90.00	45.00	27.00
(2)	Ed Andrews (hands waist high)	110.00	55.00	33.00
(3)	Cap Anson (hands outstretched)	300.00	150.00	90.00
(4)	Cap Anson (left hand on hip)	325.00	162.00	97.00
(5)	Tug Arundel	90.00	45.00	27.00
(6)	Sam Barkley (Pittsburgh)	90.00	45.00	27.00
(7)	Sam Barkley (St. Louis)	120.00	60.00	36.00
(8)	Charley Bassett	90.00	45.00	27.00
(9)	Charlie Bastian	90.00	45.00	27.00
(10)	Ed Beecher	90.00	45.00	27.00
(11)	Charlie Bennett	90.00	45.00	27.00
(12)	Handsome Henry Boyle	110.00	55.00	33.00
(13)	Dan Brouthers (hands outstretched)	200.00	100.00	60.00
(14)	Dan Brouthers (with bat)	230.00	115.00	69.00
(15)	Tom Brown	90.00	45.00	27.00
(16)	Jack Burdock	90.00	45.00	27.00
(17)	Oyster Burns (Baltimore)	110.00	55.00	33.00
(18)	Tom Burns (Chicago)	90.00	45.00	27.00
(19)	Doc Bushong	120.00	60.00	36.00
(20)	John Cahill	110.00	55.00	33.00
(21)	Cliff Carroll (Washington)	90.00	45.00	27.00
(22)	Fred Carroll (Pittsburgh)	90.00	45.00	27.00
(23)	Parisian Bob Carruthers (Caruthers)	130.00	65.00	39.00
(24)	Dan Casey	120.00	60.00	36.00
(25)	John Clarkson (ball at chest)	200.00	100.00	60.00
(26)	John Clarkson (arm oustretched)	230.00	115.00	69.00
(27)	Jack Clements	90.00	45.00	27.00
(28)	John Coleman	90.00	45.00	27.00
(29)	Charles Comiskey	300.00	150.00	90.00
(30)	Roger Connor (hands outstretched)	200.00	100.00	60.00
(31)	Roger Connor (hands oustreched, face level)	230.00	115.00	69.00
(32)	Corbett	110.00	55.00	33.00
(33)	Sam Craig (Crane)	110.00	55.00	33.00
(34)	Sam Crane	110.00	55.00	33.00
(35)	Crowley	110.00	55.00	33.00
(36)	Ed Cushmann (Cushman)	110.00	55.00	33.00
(37)	Ed Dailey (Daily)	90.00	45.00	27.00
(38)	Con Daley (Daily)	90.00	45.00	27.00
(39)	Pat Deasley	110.00	55.00	33.00
(40)	Jerry Denny (hands on knees)	90.00	45.00	27.00
(41)	Jerry Denny (hands on thighs)	110.00	55.00	33.00
(42)	Jim Donnelly	90.00	45.00	27.00
(43)	Jim Donohue (Donahue)	110.00	55.00	33.00
(44)	Mike Dorgan (right field)	90.00	45.00	27.00
(45)	Mike Dorgan (batter)	110.00	55.00	33.00
(46)	Sure Shot Dunlap	90.00	45.00	27.00
(47)	Dude Esterbrook	110.00	55.00	33.00
(48)	Buck Ewing (ready to tag)	200.00	100.00	60.00
(49)	Buck Ewing (hands at neck)	230.00	115.00	69.00
(50)	Sid Farrar	90.00	45.00	27.00
(51)	Jack Farrell (ready to tag)	90.00	45.00	27.00
(52)	Jack Farrell (hands at knees)	110.00	55.00	33.00
(53)	Charlie Ferguson	90.00	45.00	27.00
(54)	Silver Flint	90.00	45.00	27.00
(55)	Jim Fogerty (Fogarty)	90.00	45.00	27.00
(56)	Tom Forster	110.00	55.00	33.00
(57)	Dave Foutz	130.00	65.00	39.00
(58)	Chris Fulmer	110.00	55.00	33.00
(59)	Joe Gerhardt	110.00	55.00	33.00
(60)	Charlie Getzein	90.00	45.00	27.00
(61)	Pete Gillespie (left field)	90.00	45.00	27.00
(62)	Pete Gillespie (batter)	110.00	55.00	33.00
(63)	Barney Gilligan	90.00	45.00	27.00
(64)	Pebbly Jack Glasscock (fielding grounder)	110.00	55.00	33.00
(65)	Pebbly Jack Glasscock (hands on knees)	120.00	60.00	36.00

		NR MT	EX	VG
(66)	Will Gleason	120.00	60.00	36.00
(67)	Piano Legs Gore	90.00	45.00	27.00
(68)	Frank Hankinson	110.00	55.00	33.00
(69)	Ned Hanlon	90.00	45.00	27.00
(70)	Hart	110.00	55.00	33.00
(71)	Egyptian Healy	90.00	45.00	27.00
(72)	Paul Hines (centre field)	90.00	45.00	27.00
(73)	Paul Hines (batter)	110.00	55.00	33.00
(74)	Joe Hornung	90.00	45.00	27.00
(75)	Cutrate Irwin	90.00	45.00	27.00
(76)	Dick Johnston	90.00	45.00	27.00
(77)	Tim Keefe (right arm outstretched)	200.00	100.00	60.00
(78)	Tim Keefe (arm outstretched)	230.00	115.00	69.00
(79)	King Kelly (right field)	230.00	115.00	69.00
(80)	King Kelly (catcher)	260.00	130.00	78.00
(81)	Kennedy	110.00	55.00	33.00
(82)	Matt Kilroy	110.00	55.00	33.00
(83)	Arlie Latham	130.00	65.00	39.00
(84)	Jimmy Manning	90.00	45.00	27.00
(85)	Bill McClellan (existence not confirmed)			
(86)	Jim McCormick	110.00	55.00	33.00
(87)	Jack McGeachy	90.00	45.00	27.00
(88)	Jumbo McGinnis	120.00	60.00	36.00
(89)	George Meyers (Myers)	110.00	55.00	33.00
(90)	Doggie Miller	90.00	45.00	27.00
(91)	Honest John Morrill (hands outstretched)	90.00	45.00	27.00
(92)	Honest John Morrill (hands at neck)	110.00	55.00	33.00
(93)	Tom Morrissy (Morrissey)	110.00	55.00	33.00
(94)	Joe Mulvey (hands on knees)	90.00	45.00	27.00
(95)	Joe Mulvey (hands above head)	110.00	55.00	33.00
(96)	Al Myers	90.00	45.00	27.00
(97)	Candy Nelson	110.00	55.00	33.00
(98)	Little Nick Nichol	120.00	60.00	36.00
(99)	Billy O'Brien	90.00	45.00	27.00
(100)	Tip O'Neil (O'Neill)	130.00	65.00	39.00
(101)	Orator Jim O'Rourke (hands cupped)	200.00	100.00	60.00
(102)	Orator Jim O'Rourke (hands on thighs)	230.00	115.00	69.00
(103)	Dave Orr	110.00	55.00	33.00
(104)	Jimmy Peoples	90.00	45.00	27.00
(105)	Fred Pfeffer	90.00	45.00	27.00
(106)	Bill Phillips	90.00	45.00	27.00
(107)	Mark Polhemus	90.00	45.00	27.00
(108)	Henry Porter	90.00	45.00	27.00
(109)	Blondie Purcell	110.00	55.00	33.00
(110)	Old Hoss Radbourn (hands at chest)	200.00	100.00	60.00
(111)	Old Hoss Radbourn (hands above waist)	230.00	115.00	69.00
(112)	Danny Richardson (New York, hands at knees)	90.00	45.00	27.00
(113)	Danny Richardson (New York, foot on base)	110.00	55.00	33.00
(114)	Hardy Richardson (Detroit, hands at right shoulder)	90.00	45.00	27.00
(115)	Hardy Richardson (Detroit, hands above head)	110.00	55.00	33.00
(116)	Yank Robinson	120.00	60.00	36.00
(117)	George Rooks	110.00	55.00	33.00
(118)	Chief Rosemann (Roseman)	110.00	55.00	33.00
(119)	Jimmy Ryan	110.00	55.00	33.00
(120)	Emmett Seery (hands at right shoulder)	90.00	45.00	27.00
(121)	Emmett Seery (hands outstretched)	110.00	55.00	33.00
(122)	Otto Shomberg (Schomberg)	90.00	45.00	27.00
(123)	Pap Smith	90.00	45.00	27.00
(124)	Joe Strauss	110.00	55.00	33.00
(125)	Danny Sullivan	120.00	60.00	36.00
(126)	Marty Sullivan	90.00	45.00	27.00
(127)	Billy Sunday	120.00	60.00	36.00
(128)	Ezra Sutton	90.00	45.00	27.00
(129)	Big Sam Thompson (hand at belt)	200.00	100.00	60.00
(130)	Big Sam Thompson (hands chest high)	230.00	115.00	69.00
(131)	Chris Von Der Ahe	260.00	130.00	78.00
(132)	Monte Ward (fielding grounder)	200.00	100.00	60.00
(133)	Monte Ward (hands by knee)	230.00	115.00	69.00
(134)	Monte Ward (hands on knees)	230.00	115.00	69.00
(135)	Curt Welch	120.00	60.00	36.00
(136)	Deacon White	110.00	55.00	33.00
(137)	Art Whitney (Pittsburgh)	90.00	45.00	27.00
(138)	Grasshopper Whitney (Washington)	90.00	45.00	27.00

		NR MT	EX	VG
(139)	Ned Williamson (fielding grounder)	120.00	60.00	36.00
(140)	Ned Williamson (hands at chest)	130.00	65.00	39.00
(141)	Medoc Wise	90.00	45.00	27.00
(142)	Dandy Wood (hands at right shoulder)	90.00	45.00	27.00
(143)	Dandy Wood (stealing base)	110.00	55.00	33.00

1895 N300 Mayo's Cut Plug

These 1⅝'' by 2⅞'' cards were issued by the Mayo Tobacco Works of Richmond, Virginia. There are 48 cards in the set, with 40 different players pictured. Twenty-eight of the players are pictured in uniform and 12 are shown in street clothes. Eight players appear both ways. Eight of the uniformed players also appear in two variations, creating the 48-card total. Card fronts are black and white or sepia portraits on black cardboard, with a Mayo's Cut Plug ad at the bottom of each card. Cards are unnumbered.

		NR MT	EX	VG
	Complete Set:	9000.00	4500.00	2700.
	Common Player:	130.00	65.00	39.00
(1)	Charlie Abbey	130.00	65.00	39.00
(2)	Cap Anson	650.00	325.00	195.00
(3)	Jimmy Bannon	130.00	65.00	39.00
(4a)	Dan Brouthers (Baltimore on shirt)	325.00	162.00	97.00
(4b)	Dan Brouthers (Louisville on shirt)	400.00	200.00	120.00
(5)	Ed Cartwright	130.00	65.00	39.00
(6)	John Clarkson	325.00	162.00	97.00
(7)	Tommy Corcoran	130.00	65.00	39.00
(8)	Lave Cross	150.00	75.00	45.00
(9)	Bill Dahlen	130.00	65.00	39.00
(10)	Tom Daly	130.00	65.00	39.00
(11)	Ed Delehanty (Delahanty)	325.00	162.00	97.00
(12)	Hugh Duffy	325.00	162.00	97.00
(13a)	Buck Ewing (Cleveland on shirt)	325.00	162.00	97.00
(13b)	Buck Ewing (Cincinnati on shirt)	400.00	200.00	120.00
(14)	Dave Foutz	150.00	75.00	45.00
(15)	Charlie Ganzel	130.00	65.00	39.00
(16a)	Jack Glasscock (Pittsburg on shirt)	150.00	75.00	45.00
(16b)	Jack Glasscock (Louisville on shirt)	165.00	82.00	49.00
(17)	Mike Griffin	130.00	65.00	39.00
(18a)	George Haddock (no team on shirt)	165.00	82.00	49.00
(18b)	George Haddock (Philadelphia on shirt)	130.00	65.00	39.00
(19)	Bill Hallman	130.00	65.00	39.00
(20)	Billy Hamilton	325.00	162.00	97.00
(21)	Bill Joyce	130.00	65.00	39.00
(22)	Brickyard Kennedy	130.00	65.00	39.00
(23a)	Tom Kinslow (no team on shirt)	165.00	82.00	49.00

	NR MT	EX	VG
(23b) Tom Kinslow (Pittsburg on shirt)			
	130.00	65.00	39.00
(24) Arlie Latham	150.00	75.00	45.00
(25) Herman Long	150.00	75.00	45.00
(26) Tom Lovett	130.00	65.00	39.00
(27) Bobby Lowe	150.00	75.00	45.00
(28) Tommy McCarthy	325.00	162.00	97.00
(29) Yale Murphy	130.00	65.00	39.00
(30) Billy Nash	130.00	65.00	39.00
(31) Kid Nichols	325.00	162.00	97.00
(32a) Fred Pfeffer (2nd Base)	130.00	65.00	39.00
(32b) Fred Pfeffer (Retired)	165.00	82.00	49.00
(33) Wilbert Robinson	400.00	200.00	120.00
(34a) Amos Russie (incorrect spelling)			
	425.00	212.00	127.00
(34b) Amos Rusie (correct spelling)	325.00	162.00	97.00
(35) Jimmy Ryan	150.00	75.00	45.00
(36) Bill Shindle	130.00	65.00	39.00
(37) Germany Smith	130.00	65.00	39.00
(38) Otis Stocksdale (Stockdale)	130.00	65.00	39.00
(39) Tommy Tucker	130.00	65.00	39.00
(40a) Monte Ward (2nd Base)	325.00	162.00	97.00
(40b) Monte Ward (Retired)	400.00	200.00	120.00

1969 Nabisco Team Flakes

Frank Robinson—OF
Baltimore Orioles

This set of cards is seen in two different sizes: 1-15/16'' by 3'' and 1-3/4'' by 2-15/16.'' This is explained by the varying widths of the card borders on the backs of Nabisco cereal packages. Cards are action color photos bordered in yellow. Twenty-four of the top players in the game are included in the set, which was issued in three series of eight cards each. No team insignias are visible on any of the cards. Packages described the cards as ''Mini Posters.''

		NR MT	EX	VG
Complete Set:		400.00	200.00	120.00
Common Player:		4.00	2.00	1.25
(1)	Hank Aaron	40.00	20.00	12.00
(2)	Richie Allen	7.00	3.50	2.00
(3)	Lou Brock	25.00	12.50	7.50
(4)	Paul Casanova	4.00	2.00	1.25
(5)	Roberto Clemente	40.00	20.00	12.00
(6)	Al Ferrara	4.00	2.00	1.25
(7)	Bill Freehan	5.00	2.50	1.50
(8)	Jim Fregosi	5.00	2.50	1.50
(9)	Bob Gibson	20.00	10.00	6.00
(10)	Tony Horton	5.00	2.50	1.50
(11)	Tommy John	10.00	5.00	3.00
(12)	Al Kaline	25.00	12.50	7.50
(13)	Jim Lonborg	4.00	2.00	1.25
(14)	Juan Marichal	20.00	10.00	6.00
(15)	Willie Mays	40.00	20.00	12.00
(16)	Rick Monday	5.00	2.50	1.50
(17)	Tony Oliva	6.00	3.00	1.75
(18)	Brooks Robinson	30.00	15.00	9.00
(19)	Frank Robinson	25.00	12.50	7.50
(20)	Pete Rose	65.00	32.00	19.50
(21)	Ron Santo	6.00	3.00	1.75
(22)	Tom Seaver	30.00	15.00	9.00
(23)	Rusty Staub	6.00	3.00	1.75
(24)	Mel Stottlemyre	5.00	2.50	1.50

1983 Nalley Potato Chips Mariners

These large (8-11/16'' by 10-11/16'') photo cards were issued only in the area of Washington state by Nalley Potato Chips. The six Seattle Mariners are pictured in full color on the entire back panel of each box. On the side panels, detailed player stats and biographies are listed on one side, with a Mariner schedule and ticket discount offer on the other side.

		MT	NR MT	EX
Complete Set:		25.00	18.50	10.00
Common Player:		2.50	2.00	1.00
8	Rick Sweet	6.00	4.50	2.50
16	Al Cowens	2.50	2.00	1.00
21	Todd Cruz	2.50	2.00	1.00
22	Richie Zisk	3.50	2.75	1.50
36	Gaylord Perry	8.00	6.00	3.25
37	Bill Caudill	2.50	2.00	1.00

1986 National Photo Royals

(5) GEORGE BRETT, 3B

These 2⅞'' by 4¼'' cards were a team-issue produced in conjunction with National Photo. The 24-card set includes 21 players, manager Dick Howser, a card commemorating the Royals' 1985 World Championship and a discount offer card from National Photo. Card fronts feature full-color action photos, with a blue ''Kansas City Royals'' at the top of each card. Each player's name, number and position are also included. Card backs list complete professional career statistics, along with the National Photo logo.

		MT	NR MT	EX
Complete Set:		10.00	7.50	4.00
Common Player:		.25	.20	.10
1	Buddy Biancalana	.25	.20	.10
3	Jorge Orta	.25	.20	.10
4	Greg Pryor	.25	.20	.10
5	George Brett	2.00	1.50	.80
6	Willie Wilson	.70	.50	.30

		MT	NR MT	EX
8	Jim Sundberg	.35	.25	.14
10	Dick Howser	.35	.25	.14
11	Hal McRae	.50	.40	.20
20	Frank White	.50	.40	.20
21	Lonnie Smith	.35	.25	.14
22	Dennis Leonard	.35	.25	.14
23	Mark Gubicza	.40	.30	.15
24	Darryl Motley	.25	.20	.10
25	Danny Jackson	.35	.25	.14
26	Steve Farr	.35	.25	.14
29	Dan Quisenberry	.50	.40	.20
31	Bret Saberhagen	1.25	.90	.50
35	Lynn Jones	.25	.20	.10
37	Charlie Leibrandt	.35	.25	.14
38	Mark Huismann	.25	.20	.10
40	Buddy Black	.35	.25	.14
45	Steve Balboni	.35	.25	.14
---	Header Card	.25	.20	.10
---	Discount Card	.25	.20	.10

1984 Nestle

 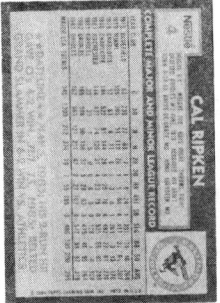

This set was issued by the Nestle candy company in conjunction with Topps. Cards are in standard 2½" by 3½" size and feature the top 22 players of 1984 — 11 from each league. This full-color "Dream Team" includes one player at each position, plus right- and left-handed starting pitchers and one reliever. Card fronts have a Nestle logo in the upper-right corner and card backs have the candy company logo in the upper left, along with a new checklist number for this 22-card set.

		MT	NR MT	EX
Complete Set:		20.00	15.00	8.00
Common Player:		.60	.45	.25
1	Eddie Murray	1.75	1.25	.70
2	Lou Whitaker	.80	.60	.30
3	George Brett	2.25	1.75	.90
4	Cal Ripken	1.75	1.25	.70
5	Jim Rice	1.25	.90	.50
6	Dave Winfield	1.50	1.25	.60
7	Lloyd Moseby	.60	.45	.25
8	Lance Parrish	.80	.60	.30
9	LaMarr Hoyt	.60	.45	.25
10	Ron Guidry	.70	.50	.30
11	Dan Quisenberry	.70	.50	.30
12	Steve Garvey	1.50	1.25	.60
13	Johnny Ray	.60	.45	.25
14	Mike Schmidt	2.00	1.50	.80
15	Ozzie Smith	.80	.60	.30
16	Andre Dawson	1.00	.70	.40
17	Tim Raines	1.50	1.25	.60
18	Dale Murphy	2.25	1.75	.90
19	Tony Pena	.60	.45	.25
20	John Denny	.60	.45	.25
21	Steve Carlton	1.25	.90	.50
22	Al Holland	.60	.45	.25
---	Checklist	.30	.25	.12

Definitions for grading conditions are located in the Introduction of this price guide.

1987 Nestle

 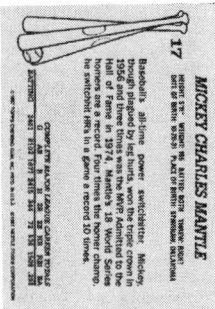

Nestle, in conjunction with Topps, issued a 33-card set in 1987. Card #'s 1-11 feature black and white photos of players from the "Golden Era." Cards #'s 12-33 features full-color photos of American (12-22) and National League (23-33) players from the "Modern Era" of baseball. Interestingly, the Feller card is not a photo but rather a color rendering of his 1953 Topps card. The cards measure 2½" by 3½" and have all team emblems airbrushed away. Three cards were inserted in specially marked six-packs of various Nestle candy bars. Two complete sets were available through a mail-in offer for $1.50 and three proof of purchase seals.

		MT	NR MT	EX
Complete Set:		8.00	6.00	3.25
Common Player:		.09	.07	.04
1	Lou Gehrig	.50	.40	.20
2	Rogers Hornsby	.20	.15	.08
3	Pie Traynor	.09	.07	.04
4	Honus Wagner	.30	.25	.12
5	Babe Ruth	.80	.60	.30
6	Tris Speaker	.15	.11	.06
7	Ty Cobb	.60	.45	.25
8	Mickey Cochrane	.09	.07	.04
9	Walter Johnson	.30	.25	.12
10	Carl Hubbell	.09	.07	.04
11	Jimmie Foxx	.20	.15	.08
12	Rod Carew	.30	.25	.12
13	Nellie Fox	.09	.07	.04
14	Brooks Robinson	.30	.25	.12
15	Luis Aparicio	.15	.11	.06
16	Frank Robinson	.20	.15	.08
17	Mickey Mantle	1.00	.70	.40
18	Ted Williams	.50	.40	.20
19	Yogi Berra	.30	.25	.12
20	Bob Feller	.20	.15	.08
21	Whitey Ford	.20	.15	.08
22	Harmon Killebrew	.20	.15	.08
23	Stan Musial	.50	.40	.20
24	Jackie Robinson	.40	.30	.15
25	Eddie Mathews	.20	.15	.08
26	Ernie Banks	.20	.15	.08
27	Roberto Clemente	.40	.30	.15
28	Willie Mays	.50	.40	.20
29	Hank Aaron	.50	.40	.20
30	Johnny Bench	.30	.25	.12
31	Bob Gibson	.20	.15	.08
32	Warren Spahn	.20	.15	.08
33	Duke Snider	.20	.15	.08

1985 Nike

Nike, the athletic shoe company, has produced posters and counter-display cards of its posters for several years, but in 1985 issued a five-card set of postcard-size cards. The cards are borderless, color miniature versions (3-1/16" by 5-1/16") of the Nike posters. Backs feature personal data and career highlights, along with the warning, "Promotional Use Only/Not For Resale." The five-card set includes two baseball players.

DWIGHT GOODEN

Height: 6'2" Born: November 16, 1964 Team: NEW YORK METS
Tampa, Florida (National League)

Weight: 190 Position: Pitcher

Career Highlights:
1984 Established major league record for most strikeouts by rookie season (276).
1984 Tied rookie, major league for most strikeouts, two consecutive games (32, 16? 9).
1984 Established National League record for most strikeouts, three consecutive games (43), September 7, 12, 17.
1984 Tied for National League lead in wins with 1.
1984 Selected National League Rookie of the Year by The Sporting News.
1984 Named National League Rookie of the Year by Baseball Writers' Association of America.
1985 Selected to New York Mets organization to seek award distinguishes selected all free-agent draft, June 7.

Presented at Use only. Not For Resale.

		MT	NR MT	EX
Complete Set:		6.00	4.50	2.50
Common Player:		.35	.25	.14
(1)	Dwight Gooden (baseball)	2.50	2.00	1.00
(2)	Michael Jordan (basketball)	1.00	.70	.40
(3)	James Lofton (football)	.60	.45	.25
(4)	John McEnroe (tennis)	.35	.25	.14
(5)	Lance Parrish (baseball)	1.25	.90	.50

1954 N.Y. Journal-American

DODGERS AT HOME
1954

April 15	Pittsburgh
April 17, 18*	New York
April 21 (N)	Philadelphia
May 11 (N), 12	Milwaukee
May 13, 14 (N), 15	St. Louis
May 16* (2)	Cincinnati
May 18 (N), 19	Chicago
May 31 (N), 22, 23* (2), 24 (N)	Pittsburgh
May 25, 26 (N), 27	Philadelphia
June 15 (N), 16 (N), 17	Milwaukee
June 18 (N), 19, 20* (2)	Chicago
June 22, 23 (N), 24	Cincinnati
June 25 (N), 26, 27*	St. Louis
July 6 (N), 7 (N), 8	New York
July 9 (N), 10, 11* (2)	Philadelphia
July 27, 28 (N), 29	Chicago
July 30 (N), 31, Aug. 1*, 2 (N)	Milwaukee
Aug. 3 (N), 4 (N), 5	St. Louis
Aug. 6 (N), 7, 8*	Cincinnati
Aug. 13 (N), 14, 15*	New York
Aug. 20 (N), 21, 22*	Philadelphia
Sept. 4* (2)	Pittsburgh
Sept. 8 (N), 9	St. Louis
Sept. 10 (N), 11	Milwaukee
Sept. 12* (2)	Chicago
Sept. 14 (N), 15, 16	Cincinnati
Sept. 20 (N), 21, 22	New York
Sept. 24, 25, 26*	Pittsburgh

*Sunday, Holiday   (N) Night Game
(2) Double Header

Issued during the golden age of baseball in New York City, this 59-card set features only players from the three New York teams of the day — the Giants, Yankees and Dodgers. The 2'' by 4'' cards were issued at newsstands with the purchase of this now-extinct newspaper. Card fronts have promotional copy and a contest serial number in addition to the player's name and photo. Cards are black and white and unnumbered. Many of the game's top stars are included, such as Mickey Mantle, Willie Mays, Gil Hodges, Duke Snider, Jackie Robinson and Yogi Berra. Card backs featured team schedules.

		NR MT	EX	VG
Complete Set:		1400.00	700.00	420.00
Common Player:		10.00	5.00	3.00
(1)	Johnny Antonelli	12.00	6.00	3.50
(2)	Hank Bauer	18.00	9.00	5.50
(3)	Yogi Berra	50.00	25.00	15.00
(4)	Joe Black	12.00	6.00	3.50

		NR MT	EX	VG
(5)	Harry Byrd	10.00	5.00	3.00
(6)	Roy Campanella	50.00	25.00	15.00
(7)	Andy Carey	10.00	5.00	3.00
(8)	Jerry Coleman	10.00	5.00	3.00
(9)	Joe Collins	10.00	5.00	3.00
(10)	Billy Cox	10.00	5.00	3.00
(11)	Al Dark	12.00	6.00	3.50
(12)	Carl Erskine	18.00	9.00	5.50
(13)	Whitey Ford	30.00	15.00	9.00
(14)	Carl Furillo	18.00	9.00	5.50
(15)	Junior Gilliam	18.00	9.00	5.50
(16)	Ruben Gomez	10.00	5.00	3.00
(17)	Marv Grissom	10.00	5.00	3.00
(18)	Jim Hearn	10.00	5.00	3.00
(19)	Gil Hodges	30.00	15.00	9.00
(20)	Bobby Hofman	10.00	5.00	3.00
(21)	Jim Hughes	10.00	5.00	3.00
(22)	Monte Irvin	20.00	10.00	6.00
(23)	Larry Jansen	10.00	5.00	3.00
(24)	Ray Katt	10.00	5.00	3.00
(25)	Steve Kraly	10.00	5.00	3.00
(26)	Bob Kuzava	10.00	5.00	3.00
(27)	Clem Labine	12.00	6.00	3.50
(28)	Frank Leja	10.00	5.00	3.00
(29)	Don Liddle	10.00	5.00	3.00
(30)	Whitey Lockman	10.00	5.00	3.00
(31)	Billy Loes	10.00	5.00	3.00
(32)	Eddie Lopat	18.00	9.00	5.50
(33)	Gil McDougald	18.00	9.00	5.50
(34)	Sal Maglie	12.00	6.00	3.50
(35)	Mickey Mantle	300.00	150.00	90.00
(36)	Willie Mays	125.00	62.00	37.00
(37)	Russ Meyer	10.00	5.00	3.00
(38)	Bill Miller	10.00	5.00	3.00
(39)	Tom Morgan	10.00	5.00	3.00
(40)	Don Mueller	10.00	5.00	3.00
(41)	Don Newcombe	18.00	9.00	5.50
(42)	Irv Noren	10.00	5.00	3.00
(43)	Erv Palica	10.00	5.00	3.00
(44)	PeeWee Reese	35.00	17.50	10.50
(45)	Allie Reynolds	18.00	9.00	5.50
(46)	Dusty Rhodes	10.00	5.00	3.00
(47)	Phil Rizzuto	25.00	12.50	7.50
(48)	Ed Robinson	10.00	5.00	3.00
(49)	Jackie Robinson	90.00	45.00	27.00
(50)	Preacher Roe	18.00	9.00	5.50
(51)	George Shuba	10.00	5.00	3.00
(52)	Duke Snider	65.00	32.00	19.50
(53)	Hank Thompson	10.00	5.00	3.00
(54)	Wes Westrum	10.00	5.00	3.00
(55)	Hoyt Wilhelm	25.00	12.50	7.50
(56)	Davey Williams	10.00	5.00	3.00
(57)	Dick Williams	12.00	6.00	3.50
(58)	Gene Woodling	12.00	6.00	3.50
(59)	Al Worthington	10.00	5.00	3.00

1986 N.Y. Mets Super Fan Club

This special nine-card panel was issued by the fan club of the 1986 World Champion Mets, along with other souvenir items gained with membership in the club. Included in the full-color set are eight top Mets players, with a promotional card in the center of the panel. Individual cards measure 2½'' by 3½,'' and are perforated at the edges to facilitate separation. The full panel measures 7½'' by 10½.'' Card fronts feature posed photos of each player, along with name, position and team logo. Backs feature career and personal data, and are printed in the team's blue and orange colors.

	MT	NR MT	EX
Complete Panel Set:	12.00	9.00	4.75
Complete Singles Set:	4.00	3.00	1.50
Common Player:	.15	.11	.06
Panel	12.00	9.00	4.75
1 Wally Backman	.15	.11	.06
2 Gary Carter	.70	.50	.30
3 Ron Darling	.40	.30	.15
4 Dwight Gooden	.90	.70	.35
5 Keith Hernandez	.60	.45	.25
6 Howard Johnson	.30	.25	.12
7 Roger McDowell	.40	.30	.15
8 Darryl Strawberry	.70	.50	.30
--- Membership Card	.05	.04	.02

1960 Nu-Card
Baseball Hi-Lites

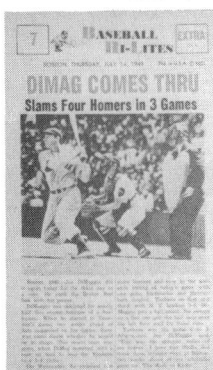

These large, 3¼'' by 5⅜,'' cards are printed in a mock newspaper format, with a headline, picture and story describing one of baseball's greatest events. There are 72 events featured in the set, which is printed in red and black. Each card is numbered in the upper left corner. The card backs offer a quiz question and answer. Certain cards in the set can be found with the fronts printed entirely in black. These cards may command a slight premium.

	NR MT	EX	VG
Complete Set:	125.00	62.00	37.00
Common Player:	.60	.30	.20
1 Babe Hits 3 Homers In A Series Game	10.00	3.00	1.75
2 Podres Pitching Wins Series	.75	.40	.25
3 Bevans Pitches No Hitter, Almost	.75	.40	.25
4 Box Score Devised By Reporter	.60	.30	.20
5 VanderMeer Pitches 2 No Hitters	1.00	.50	.30
6 Indians Take Bums	.60	.30	.20
7 DiMag Comes Thru	5.00	2.50	1.50
8 Mathewson Pitches 3 W.S. Shutouts	1.75	.90	.50
9 Haddix Pitches 12 Perfect Innings	.75	.40	.25
10 Thomson's Homer Sinks Dodgers	1.50	.70	.45
11 Hubbell Strikes Out 5 A.L. Stars	1.50	.70	.45
12 Pickoff Ends Series (Marty Marion)	.75	.40	.25
13 Cards Take Series From Yanks (Grover Cleveland Alexander)	1.50	.70	.45
14 Dizzy And Daffy Win Series	3.50	1.75	1.00
15 Owen Drops 3rd Strike	.75	.40	.25
16 Ruth Calls His Shot	8.00	4.00	2.50
17 Merkle Pulls Boner	.75	.40	.25
18 Larsen Hurls Perfect World Series Game	1.50	.70	.45

	NR MT	EX	VG
19 Bean Ball Ends Career Of Mickey Cochrane	1.25	.60	.40
20 Banks Belts 47 Homers, Earns MVP Honors	1.75	.90	.50
21 Stan Musial Hits 5 Homers In 1 Day	3.50	1.75	1.00
22 Mickey Mantle Hits Longest Homer	10.00	5.00	3.00
23 Sievers Captures Home Run Title	.75	.40	.25
24 Gehrig Consecutive Game Record Ends	5.00	2.50	1.50
25 Red Schoendienst Key Player In Victory	.75	.40	.25
26 Midget Pinch-Hits For St. Louis Browns (Eddie Gaedel)	1.25	.60	.40
27 Willie Mays Makes Greatest Catch	3.50	1.75	1.00
28 Homer By Berra Puts Yanks In 1st Place	2.25	1.25	.70
29 Campy National League's MVP	2.25	1.25	.70
30 Bob Turley Hurls Yanks To Championship	.75	.40	.25
31 Dodgers Take Series From Sox In Six	.75	.40	.25
32 Furillo Hero As Dodgers Beat Chicago	.75	.40	.25
33 Adcock Gets Four Homers And A Double	.75	.40	.25
34 Dickey Chosen All Star Catcher	1.25	.60	.40
35 Burdette Beats Yanks In 3 Series Games	1.00	.50	.30
36 Umpires Clear White Sox Bench	.60	.30	.20
37 Reese Honored As Greatest Dodger S.S.	1.75	.90	.50
38 Joe DiMaggio Hits In 56 Straight Games	5.00	2.50	1.50
39 Ted Williams Hits .406 For Season	5.00	2.50	1.50
40 Johnson Pitches 56 Scoreless Innings	2.25	1.25	.70
41 Hodges Hits 4 Home Runs In Nite Game	1.75	.90	.50
42 Greenberg Returns To Tigers From Army	1.25	.60	.40
43 Ty Cobb Named Best Player Of All Time	5.00	2.50	1.50
44 Robin Roberts Wins 28 Games	1.25	.60	.40
45 Rizzuto's 2 Runs Save 1st Place	1.50	.70	.45
46 Tigers Beat Out Senators For Pennant (Hal Newhouser)	.75	.40	.25
47 Babe Ruth Hits 60th Home Run	8.50	4.25	2.50
48 Cy Young Honored	1.75	.90	.50
49 Killebrew Starts Spring Training	1.75	.90	.50
50 Mantle Hits Longest Homer At Stadium	10.00	5.00	3.00
51 Braves Take Pennant (Hank Aaron)	3.50	1.75	1.00
52 Ted Williams Hero Of All Star Game	5.00	2.50	1.50
53 Robinson Saves Dodgers For Playoffs (Jackie Robinson)	3.50	1.75	1.00
54 Snodgrass Muffs A Fly Ball	.75	.40	.25
55 Snider Belts 2 Homers	2.25	1.25	.70
56 New York Giants Win 26 Straight Games (Christy Mathewson)	1.75	.90	.50
57 Ted Kluszewski Stars In 1st Game Win	.75	.40	.25
58 Ott Walks 5 Times In A Single Game (Mel Ott)	1.25	.60	.40
59 Harvey Kuenn Takes Batting Title	.75	.40	.25
60 Bob Feller Hurls 3rd No-Hitter Of Career	2.25	1.25	.70
61 Yanks Champs Again! (Casey Stengel)	1.50	.70	.45
62 Aaron's Bat Beats Yankees In Series	3.50	1.75	1.00
63 Warren Spahn Beats Yanks in World Series	1.50	.70	.45
64 Ump's Wrong Call Helps Dodgers	.75	.40	.25
65 Kaline Hits 3 Homers, 2 In Same Inning	1.75	.90	.50
66 Bob Allison Named A.L. Rookie of Year	.75	.40	.25
67 McCovey Blasts Way Into Giant Lineup	1.75	.90	.50
68 Colavito Hits Four Homers In One Game	1.00	.50	.30
69 Erskine Sets Strike Out Record In W.S.	.75	.40	.25
70 Sal Maglie Pitches No-Hit Game	.75	.40	.25
71 Early Wynn Victory Crushes Yanks	1.25	.60	.40

		NR MT	EX	VG
72	Nellie Fox American League's M.V.P.			
		3.00	.60	.40

1961 Nu-Card Baseball Scoops

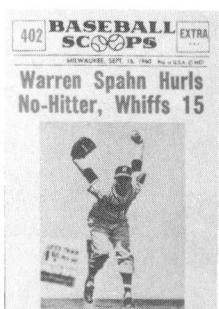
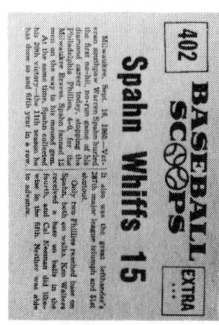

Very similar in style to their set of the year before, the Nu-Card Baseball Scoops were issued in a smaller 2½" by 3½" size, but still featured the mock newspaper card front. This 80-card set is numbered from 401 to 480, with cards shown on both the card front and back. These cards, which commemorate great moments in individual players' careers, included only the headline and black-and-white photo on the fronts, with the descriptive story on the card backs. Cards are again printed in red and black. It appears the set may have been counterfeited, though when is not known. These cards can be determined by examining the card photo for unusual blurring and fuzziness.

		NR MT	EX	VG
	Complete Set:	80.00	40.00	24.00
	Common Player:	.30	.15	.09
401	Gentile Powers Birds Into 1st	1.00	.50	.30
402	Warren Spahn Hurls No-Hitter, Whiffs 15	1.00	.50	.30
403	Mazeroski's Homer Wins Series For Bucs	.75	.40	.25
404	Willie Mays' 3 Triples Paces Giants	2.25	1.25	.70
405	Woodie Held Slugs 2 Homers, 6 RBIs	.30	.15	.09
406	Vern Law Winner Of Cy Young Award	.40	.20	.12
407	Runnels Makes 9 Hits in Twin-Bill	.30	.15	.09
408	Braves' Lew Burdette Wins No-Hitter, 1-0	.70	.35	.20
409	Dick Stuart Hits 3 Homers, Single	.30	.15	.09
410	Don Cardwell Of Cubs Pitches No-Hit Game	.30	.15	.09
411	Camilo Pascual Strikes Out 15 Bosox	.30	.15	.09
412	Eddie Mathews Blasts 300th Big League HR	1.00	.50	.30
413	Groat, NL Bat King, Named Loop's MVP	.70	.35	.20
414	AL Votes To Expand To 10 Teams (Gene Autry)	1.25	.60	.40
415	Bobby Richardson Sets Series Mark	.75	.40	.25
416	Maris Nips Mantle For AL MVP Award	2.50	1.25	.70
417	Merkle Pulls Boner	.30	.15	.09
418	Larsen Hurls Perefect World Series Game	.75	.40	.25
419	Bean Ball Ends Career Of Mickey Cochrane	.70	.35	.20
420	Banks Belts 47 Homers, Earns MVP Award	1.50	.70	.45
421	Stan Musial Hits 5 Homers In 1 Day	2.50	1.25	.70
422	Mickey Mantle Hits Longest Homer	8.00	4.00	2.50
423	Sievers Captures Home Run Title	.30	.15	.09
424	Gehrig Consecutive Game Record Ends	4.00	2.00	1.25

		NR MT	EX	VG
425	Red Schoendienst Key Player In Victory	.70	.35	.20
426	Midget Pinch-Hits For St. Louis Browns (Eddie Gaedel)	.75	.40	.25
427	Willie Mays Makes Greatest Catch	2.50	1.25	.70
428	Robinson Saves Dodgers For Playoffs	2.50	1.25	.70
429	Campy Most Valuable Player	2.50	1.25	.70
430	Turley Hurls Yanks To Championship	.40	.20	.12
431	Dodgers Take Series From Sox In Six (Larry Sherry)	.30	.15	.09
432	Furillo Hero In 3rd World Series Game	.70	.35	.20
433	Adcock Gets Four Homers, Double	.70	.35	.20
434	Dickey Chosen All Star Catcher	1.00	.50	.30
435	Burdette Beats Yanks In 3 Series Games	.75	.40	.25
436	Umpires Clear White Sox Bench	.30	.15	.09
437	Reese Honored As Greatest Dodgers S.S.	1.50	.70	.45
438	Joe DiMaggio Hits In 56 Straight Games	4.00	2.00	1.25
439	Ted Williams Hits .406 For Season	4.00	2.00	1.25
440	Johnson Pitches 56 Scoreless Innings	2.50	1.25	.70
441	Hodges Hits 4 Home Runs In Nite Game	1.50	.70	.45
442	Greenberg Returns To Tigers From Army	1.00	.50	.30
443	Ty Cobb Named Best Player Of All Time	4.00	2.00	1.25
444	Robin Roberts Wins 28 Games	1.00	.50	.30
445	Rizzuto's 2 Runs Save 1st Place	1.25	.60	.40
446	Tigers Beat Out Senators For Pennant (Hal Newhouser)	.30	.15	.09
447	Babe Ruth Hits 60th Home Run	5.00	2.50	1.50
448	Cy Young Honored	1.50	.70	.45
449	Killebrew Starts Spring Training	1.25	.60	.40
450	Mantle Hits Longest Homer At Stadium	8.00	4.00	2.50
451	Braves Take Pennant	.30	.15	.09
452	Ted Williams Hero Of All Star Game	2.50	1.25	.70
453	Homer By Berra Puts Yanks In 1st Place	2.50	1.25	.70
454	Snodgrass Muffs A Fly Ball	.30	.15	.09
455	Babe Hits 3 Homers In A Series Game	5.00	2.50	1.50
456	New York Wins 26 Straight Games	.30	.15	.09
457	Ted Kluszewski Stars In 1st Series Win	.40	.20	.12
458	Ott Walks 5 Times In A Single Game	1.00	.50	.30
459	Harvey Kuenn Takes Batting Title	.40	.20	.12
460	Bob Feller Hurls 3rd No-Hitter Of Career	2.50	1.25	.70
461	Yanks Champs Again! (Casey Stengel)	1.50	.70	.45
462	Aaron's Bat Beats Yankees In Series	2.50	1.25	.70
463	Warren Spahn Beats Yanks In World Series	1.00	.50	.30
464	Ump's Wrong Call Helps Dodgers	.30	.15	.09
465	Kaline Hits 3 Homers, 2 In Same Inning	1.50	.70	.45
466	Bob Allison Named A.L. Rookie Of Year	.40	.20	.12
467	DiMag Comes Thru	4.00	2.00	1.25
468	Colavito Hits Four Homers In One Game	.70	.35	.20
469	Erskine Sets Strike Out Record In W.S.	.70	.35	.20
470	Sal Maglie Pitches No-Hit Game	.70	.35	.20
471	Early Wynn Victory Crushes Yanks	1.00	.50	.30
472	Nellie Fox American League's MVP	.75	.40	.25
473	Pickoff Ends Series (Marty Marion)	.40	.20	.12
474	Podres Pitching Wins Series	.80	.40	.25
475	Owen Drops 3rd Strike	.30	.15	.09
476	Dizzy And Daffy Win Series	2.50	1.25	.70
477	Mathewson Pitches 3 W.S. Shutouts	1.50	.70	.45
478	Haddix Pitches 12 Perfect Innings	.40	.20	.12
479	Hubbell Strike Out 5 A.L. Stars	1.00	.50	.30
480	Homer Sinks Dodgers (Bobby Thomson)	1.25	.60	.40

1965 Old London Coins

1986 Oh Henry! Indians

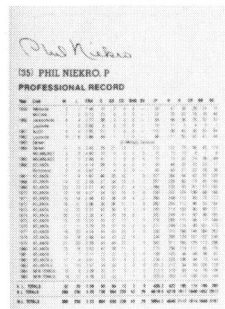

This 30-card set of Cleveland Indians players was distributed by the team at a special Photo/Baseball Card Day at Municipal Stadium. The cards were printed within a special 3-panel perforated fold-out piece which featured four action shots of the Indians on the cover. Unfolded, there are two panels containing the baseball cards and a third which contains a team photo. Cards measure 2¼'' by 3⅛'' and are full-color studio portraits. Photos are framed in blue with a white border and list player name, number and position. Card fronts also include a picture of the sponsoring candy bar. Card backs include facsimile autograph and professional records. Each card is perforated for separation.

		MT	NR MT	EX
Complete Set:		6.50	5.00	2.50
Common Player:		.06	.05	.02
2	Brett Butler	.30	.25	.12
4	Tony Bernazard	.12	.09	.05
6	Andy Allanson	.20	.15	.08
7	Pat Corrales	.12	.09	.05
8	Carmen Castillo	.06	.05	.02
10	Pat Tabler	.30	.25	.12
13	Ernie Camacho	.06	.05	.02
14	Julio Franco	.40	.30	.15
15	Dan Rohn	.06	.05	.02
18	Ken Schrom	.10	.08	.04
20	Otis Nixon	.12	.09	.05
22	Fran Mullins	.12	.09	.05
23	Chris Bando	.06	.05	.02
24	Ed Williams	.20	.15	.08
26	Brook Jacoby	.40	.30	.15
27	Mel Hall	.30	.25	.12
29	Andre Thornton	.30	.25	.12
30	Joe Carter	.50	.40	.20
35	Phil Niekro	.40	.30	.15
36	Jamie Easterly	.06	.05	.02
37	Don Schulze	.06	.05	.02
42	Rich Yett	.12	.09	.05
43	Scott Bailes	.30	.25	.12
44	Neal Heaton	.20	.15	.08
46	Jim Kern	.06	.05	.02
48	Dickie Noles	.06	.05	.02
49	Tom Candiotti	.10	.08	.04
53	Reggie Ritter	.12	.09	.05
54	Tom Waddell	.06	.05	.02
---	Coaching Staff (Jack Aker, Bobby Bonds, Doc Edwards, Johnny Goryl)	.06	.05	.02

These 1½'' diameter metal coins were included in Old London snack food packages. The 40 coins in this set feature two players from each of the Major Leagues' then 20 teams, with the exception of St. Louis (3) and the New York Mets (1). Coin fronts have color photos and player names, while the silver-colored coin backs give brief biographies of each player. An Old London logo is also displayed on each coin back. Space Magic, Ltd. produced the coins. This is the same company which produced similar sets for Topps in 1964 and 1971.

		NR MT	EX	VG
Complete Set:		500.00	250.00	150.00
Common Player:		2.50	1.25	.70
(1)	Henry Aaron	45.00	22.00	13.50
(2)	Richie Allen	5.00	2.50	1.50
(3)	Bob Allison	3.00	1.50	.90
(4)	Ernie Banks	25.00	12.50	7.50
(5)	Ken Boyer	5.00	2.50	1.50
(6)	Jim Bunning	8.00	4.00	2.50
(7)	Orlando Cepeda	8.00	4.00	2.50
(8)	Dean Chance	2.50	1.25	.70
(9)	Rocky Colavito	5.00	2.50	1.50
(10)	Vic Davalillo	2.50	1.25	.70
(11)	Tommy Davis	5.00	2.50	1.50
(12)	Ron Fairly	3.00	1.50	.90
(13)	Dick Farrell	2.50	1.25	.70
(14)	Jim Fregosi	4.00	2.00	1.25
(15)	Bob Friend	4.00	2.00	1.25
(16)	Dick Groat	5.00	2.50	1.50
(17)	Ron Hunt	2.50	1.25	.70
(18)	Chuck Hinton	2.50	1.25	.70
(19)	Ken Johnson	2.50	1.25	.70
(20)	Al Kaline	25.00	12.50	7.50
(21)	Harmon Killebrew	20.00	10.00	6.00
(22)	Don Lock	2.50	1.25	.70
(23)	Mickey Mantle	90.00	45.00	27.00
(24)	Roger Maris	25.00	12.50	7.50
(25)	Willie Mays	45.00	22.00	13.50
(26)	Bill Mazeroski	6.50	3.25	2.00
(27)	Gary Peters	2.50	1.25	.70
(28)	Vada Pinson	5.00	2.50	1.50
(29)	John Powell	5.00	2.50	1.50
(30)	Dick Radatz	2.50	1.25	.70
(31)	Brooks Robinson	25.00	12.50	7.50
(32)	Frank Robinson	25.00	12.50	7.50
(33)	Tracy Stallard	2.50	1.25	.70
(34)	Joe Torre	6.50	3.25	2.00
(35)	Leon Wagner	2.50	1.25	.70
(36)	Pete Ward	2.50	1.25	.70
(37)	Dave Wickersham	2.50	1.25	.70
(38)	Billy Williams	18.00	9.00	5.50
(39)	John Wyatt	2.50	1.25	.70
(40)	Carl Yastrzemski	50.00	25.00	15.00

1986 O-Pee-Chee

As usual, the 1986 O-Pee-Chee set was issued in close simulation of the Topps cards for the same year. The 396 cards in the set are 2½'' by 3½'' and use almost all of the same pictures as the Topps set. The O-Pee-Chee cards, being a Canadian issue, list player information in both English and French. There is an abundance of players from the two Canadian teams — Toronto and Montreal. As the O-Pee-Chee set was issued later in the year than the Topps regular

RAZOR SHINES

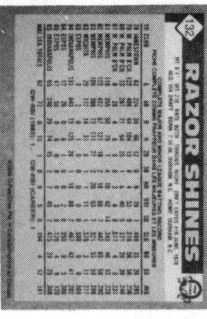

issue, players who changed teams after the printing date are noted with a traded line at the bottom of the player photo. O-Pee-Chee's logo appears in the upper-right of each card front.

		MT	NR MT	EX
Complete Set:		16.00	12.00	6.50
Common Player:		.05	.04	.02
1	Pete Rose	.70	.50	.30
2	Ken Landreaux	.05	.04	.02
3	Rob Picciolo	.05	.04	.02
4	Steve Garvey	.25	.20	.10
5	Andy Hawkins	.05	.04	.02
6	Rudy Law	.05	.04	.02
7	Lonnie Smith	.25	.20	.10
8	Dwayne Murphy	.25	.20	.10
9	Moose Haas	.05	.04	.02
10	Tony Gwynn	.35	.25	.14
11	Bob Ojeda	.07	.05	.03
12	Jose Uribe	.12	.09	.05
13	Bob Kearney	.05	.04	.02
14	Julio Cruz	.05	.04	.02
15	Eddie Whitson	.05	.04	.02
16	Rick Schu	.07	.05	.03
17	Mike Stenhouse	.05	.04	.02
18	Lou Thornton	.10	.08	.04
19	Ryne Sandberg	.25	.20	.10
20	Lou Whitaker	.15	.11	.06
21	Mark Brouhard	.05	.04	.02
22	Gary Lavelle	.05	.04	.02
23	Manny Lee	.10	.08	.04
24	Don Slaught	.05	.04	.02
25	Willie Wilson	.10	.08	.04
26	Mike Marshall	.10	.08	.04
27	Ray Knight	.07	.05	.03
28	Mario Soto	.07	.05	.03
29	Dave Anderson	.05	.04	.02
30	Eddie Murray	.35	.25	.14
31	Dusty Baker	.07	.05	.03
32	Steve Yeager	.05	.04	.02
33	Andy Van Slyke	.10	.08	.04
34	Dave Righetti	.15	.11	.06
35	Jeff Reardon	.10	.08	.04
36	Burt Hooton	.05	.04	.02
37	Johnny Ray	.07	.05	.03
38	Glenn Hoffman	.05	.04	.02
39	Rick Mahler	.05	.04	.02
40	Ken Griffey	.07	.05	.03
41	Brad Wellman	.05	.04	.02
42	Joe Hesketh	.07	.05	.03
43	Mark Salas	.05	.04	.02
44	Jorge Orta	.05	.04	.02
45	Damaso Garcia	.07	.05	.03
46	Jim Acker	.05	.04	.02
47	Bill Madlock	.12	.09	.05
48	Bill Almon	.05	.04	.02
49	Rick Manning	.05	.04	.02
50	Dan Quisenberry	.12	.09	.05
51	Jim Gantner	.05	.04	.02
52	Kevin Bass	.07	.05	.03
53	Len Dykstra	.40	.30	.15
54	John Franco	.07	.05	.03
55	Fred Lynn	.12	.09	.05
56	Jim Morrison	.05	.04	.02
57	Bill Doran	.07	.05	.03
58	Leon Durham	.07	.05	.03
59	Andre Thornton	.07	.05	.03
60	Dwight Evans	.10	.08	.04
61	Larry Herndon	.05	.04	.02
62	Bob Boone	.05	.04	.02

		MT	NR MT	EX
63	Kent Hrbek	.15	.11	.06
64	Floyd Bannister	.07	.05	.03
65	Harold Baines	.10	.08	.04
66	Pat Tabler	.07	.05	.03
67	Carmelo Martinez	.07	.05	.03
68	Ed Lynch	.05	.04	.02
69	George Foster	.10	.08	.04
70	Dave Winfield	.25	.20	.10
71	Ken Schrom	.05	.04	.02
72	Toby Harrah	.05	.04	.02
73	Jackie Gutierrez	.05	.04	.02
74	Rance Mulliniks	.05	.04	.02
75	Jose DeLeon	.05	.04	.02
76	Ron Romanick	.05	.04	.02
77	Charlie Leibrandt	.07	.05	.03
78	Bruce Benedict	.05	.04	.02
79	Dave Schmidt	.05	.04	.02
80	Darryl Strawberry	.40	.30	.15
81	Wayne Krenchicki	.05	.04	.02
82	Tippy Martinez	.05	.04	.02
83	Phil Garner	.05	.04	.02
84	Darrell Porter	.05	.04	.02
85	Tony Perez	.10	.08	.04
86	Tom Waddell	.05	.04	.02
87	Tim Hulett	.05	.04	.02
88	Barbaro Garbey	.05	.04	.02
89	Randy St. Claire	.05	.04	.02
90	Garry Templeton	.07	.05	.03
91	Tim Teufel	.05	.04	.02
92	Al Cowens	.05	.04	.02
93	Scot Thompson	.05	.04	.02
94	Tom Herr	.07	.05	.03
95	Ozzie Virgil	.05	.04	.02
96	Jose Cruz	.07	.05	.03
97	Gary Gaetti	.12	.09	.05
98	Roger Clemens	1.25	.90	.50
99	Vance Law	.05	.04	.02
100	Nolan Ryan	.25	.20	.10
101	Mike Smithson	.05	.04	.02
102	Rafael Santana	.05	.04	.02
103	Darrell Evans	.10	.08	.04
104	Rich Gossage	.15	.11	.06
105	Gary Ward	.07	.05	.03
106	Jim Gott	.05	.04	.02
107	Rafael Ramirez	.05	.04	.02
108	Ted Power	.07	.05	.03
109	Ron Guidry	.15	.11	.06
110	Scott McGregor	.07	.05	.03
111	Mike Scioscia	.05	.04	.02
112	Glenn Hubbard	.05	.04	.02
113	U.L. Washington	.05	.04	.02
114	Al Oliver	.10	.08	.04
115	Jay Howell	.07	.05	.03
116	Brook Jacoby	.10	.08	.04
117	Willie McGee	.12	.09	.05
118	Jerry Royster	.05	.04	.02
119	Barry Bonnell	.05	.04	.02
120	Steve Carlton	.25	.20	.10
121	Alfredo Griffin	.07	.05	.03
122	David Green	.05	.04	.02
123	Greg Walker	.07	.05	.03
124	Frank Tanana	.07	.05	.03
125	Dave Lopes	.07	.05	.03
126	Mike Krukow	.07	.05	.03
127	Jack Howell	.25	.20	.10
128	Greg Harris	.05	.04	.02
129	Herm Winningham	.10	.08	.04
130	Alan Trammell	.25	.20	.10
131	Checklist 1-132	.05	.04	.02
132	Razor Shines	.05	.04	.02
133	Bruce Sutter	.10	.08	.04
134	Carney Lansford	.07	.05	.03
135	Joe Niekro	.07	.05	.03
136	Ernie Whitt	.07	.05	.03
137	Charlie Moore	.05	.04	.02
138	Mel Hall	.07	.05	.03
139	Roger McDowell	.25	.20	.10
140	John Candelaria	.07	.05	.03
141	Bob Rodgers	.05	.04	.02
142	Manny Trillo	.07	.05	.03
143	Dave Palmer	.05	.04	.02
144	Robin Yount	.25	.20	.10
145	Pedro Guerrero	.15	.11	.06
146	Von Hayes	.10	.08	.04
147	Lance Parrish	.15	.11	.06
148	Mike Heath	.05	.04	.02
149	Brett Butler	.07	.05	.03
150	Joaquin Andujar	.07	.05	.03
151	Graig Nettles	.10	.08	.04
152	Pete Vuckovich	.05	.04	.02
153	Jason Thompson	.05	.04	.02

		MT	NR MT	EX
154	Bert Roberge	.05	.04	.02
155	Bob Grich	.07	.05	.03
156	Roy Smalley	.05	.04	.02
157	Ron Hassey	.05	.04	.02
158	Bob Stanley	.05	.04	.02
159	Orel Hershiser	.25	.20	.10
160	Chet Lemon	.07	.05	.03
161	Terry Puhl	.05	.04	.02
162	Dave LaPoint	.05	.04	.02
163	Onix Concepcion	.05	.04	.02
164	Steve Balboni	.05	.04	.02
165	Mike Davis	.07	.05	.03
166	Dickie Thon	.05	.04	.02
167	Zane Smith	.10	.08	.04
168	Jeff Burroughs	.05	.04	.02
169	Alex Trevino	.05	.04	.02
170	Gary Carter	.25	.20	.10
171	Tito Landrum	.05	.04	.02
172	Sammy Stewart	.05	.04	.02
173	Wayne Gross	.05	.04	.02
174	Britt Burns	.05	.04	.02
175	Steve Sax	.15	.11	.06
176	Jody Davis	.07	.05	.03
177	Joel Youngblood	.05	.04	.02
178	Fernando Valenzuela	.25	.20	.10
179	Storm Davis	.05	.04	.02
180	Don Mattingly	1.75	1.25	.70
181	Steve Bedrosian	.10	.08	.04
182	Jesse Orosco	.07	.05	.03
183	Gary Roenicke	.05	.04	.02
184	Don Baylor	.10	.08	.04
185	Rollie Fingers	.15	.11	.06
186	Ruppert Jones	.05	.04	.02
187	Scott Fletcher	.05	.04	.02
188	Bob Dernier	.05	.04	.02
189	Mike Mason	.05	.04	.02
190	George Hendrick	.05	.04	.02
191	Wally Backman	.07	.05	.03
192	Oddibe McDowell	.20	.15	.08
193	Bruce Hurst	.07	.05	.03
194	Ron Cey	.07	.05	.03
195	Dave Concepcion	.10	.08	.04
196	Doyle Alexander	.10	.08	.04
197	Dale Murray	.05	.04	.02
198	Mark Langston	.10	.08	.04
199	Dennis Eckersley	.07	.05	.03
200	Mike Schmidt	.35	.25	.14
201	Nick Esasky	.05	.04	.02
202	Ken Dayley	.05	.04	.02
203	Rick Cerone	.05	.04	.02
204	Larry McWilliams	.05	.04	.02
205	Brian Downing	.07	.05	.03
206	Danny Darwin	.05	.04	.02
207	Bill Caudill	.05	.04	.02
208	Dave Rozema	.05	.04	.02
209	Eric Show	.05	.04	.02
210	Brad Komminsk	.05	.04	.02
211	Chris Bando	.05	.04	.02
212	Chris Speier	.05	.04	.02
213	Jim Clancy	.07	.05	.03
214	Randy Bush	.05	.04	.02
215	Frank White	.07	.05	.03
216	Dan Petry	.07	.05	.03
217	Tim Wallach	.10	.08	.04
218	Mitch Webster	.25	.20	.10
219	Dennis Lamp	.05	.04	.02
220	Bob Horner	.15	.11	.06
221	Dave Henderson	.05	.04	.02
222	Dave Smith	.07	.05	.03
223	Willie Upshaw	.07	.05	.03
224	Cesar Cedeno	.07	.05	.03
225	Ron Darling	.12	.09	.05
226	Lee Lacy	.05	.04	.02
227	John Tudor	.07	.05	.03
228	Jim Presley	.25	.20	.10
229	Bill Gullickson	.07	.05	.03
230	Terry Kennedy	.07	.05	.03
231	Bob Knepper	.07	.05	.03
232	Rick Rhoden	.10	.08	.04
233	Richard Dotson	.07	.05	.03
234	Jesse Barfield	.20	.15	.08
235	Butch Wynegar	.05	.04	.02
236	Jerry Reuss	.07	.05	.03
237	Juan Samuel	.12	.09	.05
238	Larry Parrish	.07	.05	.03
239	Bill Buckner	.07	.05	.03
240	Pat Sheridan	.05	.04	.02
241	Tony Fernandez	.12	.09	.05
242	Rich Thompson	.05	.04	.02
243	Rickey Henderson	.35	.25	.14
244	Craig Lefferts	.05	.04	.02

		MT	NR MT	EX
245	Jim Sundberg	.05	.04	.02
246	Phil Niekro	.20	.15	.08
247	Terry Harper	.05	.04	.02
248	Spike Owen	.05	.04	.02
249	Bret Saberhagen	.25	.20	.10
250	Dwight Gooden	1.00	.70	.40
251	Rich Dauer	.05	.04	.02
252	Keith Hernandez	.25	.20	.10
253	Bo Diaz	.05	.04	.02
254	Ozzie Guillen	.25	.20	.10
255	Tony Armas	.07	.05	.03
256	Andre Dawson	.15	.11	.06
257	Doug DeCinces	.07	.05	.03
258	Tim Burke	.20	.15	.08
259	Dennis Boyd	.07	.05	.03
260	Tony Pena	.07	.05	.03
261	Sal Butera	.05	.04	.02
262	Wade Boggs	1.25	.90	.50
263	Checklist 133-254	.05	.04	.02
264	Ron Oester	.05	.04	.02
265	Ron Davis	.05	.04	.02
266	Keith Moreland	.07	.05	.03
267	Paul Molitor	.12	.09	.05
268	John Denny	.05	.04	.02
269	Frank Viola	.10	.08	.04
270	Jack Morris	.15	.11	.06
271	Dave Collins	.05	.04	.02
272	Bert Blyleven	.12	.09	.05
273	Jerry Willard	.05	.04	.02
274	Matt Young	.05	.04	.02
275	Charlie Hough	.07	.05	.03
276	Dave Dravecky	.07	.05	.03
277	Garth Iorg	.05	.04	.02
278	Hal McRae	.10	.08	.04
279	Curt Wilkerson	.05	.04	.02
280	Tim Raines	.25	.20	.10
281	Bill Laskey	.05	.04	.02
282	Jerry Mumphrey	.05	.04	.02
283	Pat Clements	.05	.04	.02
284	Bob James	.05	.04	.02
285	Buddy Bell	.10	.08	.04
286	Tom Brookens	.05	.04	.02
287	Dave Parker	.15	.11	.06
288	Ron Kittle	.07	.05	.03
289	Johnnie LeMaster	.05	.04	.02
290	Carlton Fisk	.15	.11	.06
291	Jimmy Key	.10	.08	.04
292	Gary Matthews	.07	.05	.03
293	Marvell Wynne	.05	.04	.02
294	Danny Cox	.07	.05	.03
295	Kirk Gibson	.20	.15	.08
296	Mariano Duncan	.10	.08	.04
297	Ozzie Smith	.12	.09	.05
298	Craig Reynolds	.05	.04	.02
299	Bryn Smith	.07	.05	.03
300	George Brett	.40	.30	.15
301	Walt Terrell	.07	.05	.03
302	Greg Gross	.05	.04	.02
303	Claudell Washington	.07	.05	.03
304	Howard Johnson	.12	.09	.05
305	Phil Bradley	.12	.09	.05
306	R.J. Reynolds	.07	.05	.03
307	Bob Brenly	.05	.04	.02
308	Hubie Brooks	.07	.05	.03
309	Alvin Davis	.12	.09	.05
310	Donnie Hill	.05	.04	.02
311	Dick Schofield	.05	.04	.02
312	Tom Filer	.05	.04	.02
313	Mike Fitzgerald	.05	.04	.02
314	Marty Barrett	.07	.05	.03
315	Mookie Wilson	.07	.05	.03
316	Alan Knicely	.05	.04	.02
317	Ed Romero	.05	.04	.02
318	Glenn Wilson	.07	.05	.03
319	Bud Black	.05	.04	.02
320	Jim Rice	.25	.20	.10
321	Terry Pendleton	.07	.05	.03
322	Dave Kingman	.12	.09	.05
323	Gary Pettis	.05	.04	.02
324	Dan Schatzeder	.05	.04	.02
325	Juan Beniquez	.05	.04	.02
326	Kent Tekulve	.07	.05	.03
327	Mike Pagliarulo	.20	.15	.08
328	Pete O'Brien	.07	.05	.03
329	Kirby Puckett	.60	.45	.25
330	Rick Sutcliffe	.10	.08	.04
331	Alan Ashby	.05	.04	.02
332	Willie Randolph	.07	.05	.03
333	Tom Henke	.07	.05	.03
334	Ken Oberkfell	.05	.04	.02
335	Don Sutton	.20	.15	.08

		MT	NR MT	EX
336	Dan Gladden	.07	.05	.03
337	George Vuckovich	.05	.04	.02
338	Jorge Bell	.30	.25	.12
339	Jim Dwyer	.05	.04	.02
340	Cal Ripken	.35	.25	.14
341	Willie Hernandez	.07	.05	.03
342	Gary Redus	.07	.05	.03
343	Jerry Koosman	.07	.05	.03
344	Jim Wohlford	.05	.04	.02
345	Donnie Moore	.05	.04	.02
346	Floyd Youmans	.40	.30	.15
347	Gorman Thomas	.07	.05	.03
348	Cliff Johnson	.05	.04	.02
349	Ken Howell	.05	.04	.02
350	Jack Clark	.12	.09	.05
351	Gary Lucas	.05	.04	.02
352	Bob Clark	.05	.04	.02
353	Dave Stieb	.10	.08	.04
354	Tony Bernazard	.05	.04	.02
355	Lee Smith	.07	.05	.03
356	Mickey Hatcher	.05	.04	.02
357	Ed Vande Berg	.05	.04	.02
358	Rick Dempsey	.05	.04	.02
359	Bobby Cox	.05	.04	.02
360	Lloyd Moseby	.10	.08	.04
361	Shane Rawley	.07	.05	.03
362	Garry Maddox	.07	.05	.03
363	Buck Martinez	.05	.04	.02
364	Ed Nunez	.07	.05	.03
365	Luis Leal	.05	.04	.02
366	Dale Berra	.05	.04	.02
367	Mike Boddicker	.07	.05	.03
368	Greg Brock	.07	.05	.03
369	Al Holland	.05	.04	.02
370	Vince Coleman	1.00	.70	.40
371	Rod Carew	.25	.20	.10
372	Ben Oglivie	.05	.04	.02
373	Lee Mazzilli	.07	.05	.03
374	Terry Francona	.05	.04	.02
375	Rich Gedman	.07	.05	.03
376	Charlie Lea	.05	.04	.02
377	Joe Carter	.15	.11	.06
378	Bruce Bochte	.05	.04	.02
379	Bobby Meacham	.05	.04	.02
380	LaMarr Hoyt	.05	.04	.02
381	Jeff Leonard	.07	.05	.03
382	Ivan Calderon	.25	.20	.10
383	Chris Brown	.50	.40	.20
384	Steve Trout	.07	.05	.03
385	Cecil Cooper	.10	.08	.04
386	Cecil Fielder	.10	.08	.04
387	Tim Flannery	.05	.04	.02
388	Chris Codiroli	.05	.04	.02
389	Glenn Davis	.50	.40	.20
390	Tom Seaver	.25	.20	.10
391	Julio Franco	.10	.08	.04
392	Tom Brunansky	.10	.08	.04
393	Rob Wilfong	.05	.04	.02
394	Reggie Jackson	.30	.25	.12
395	Scott Garrelts	.05	.04	.02
396	Checklist 255-396	.05	.04	.02

1986 O-Pee-Chee Box Panels

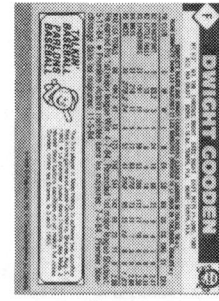

The Canadian card company licensed by Topps to distribute cards in Canada is O-Pee-Chee. In 1986 O-Pee-Chee issued wax pack boxes with baseball cards printed on the box bottom. Four cards appear on four different boxes making a complete set of 16. The cards are identical to the 1986 Topps wax box issue with the exception of the O-Pee-Chee logo replacing Topps and the addition of French on the card backs. These bilingual cards were issued in Canada but are readily available in the USA. The cards are the standard 2½'' by 3½'' size, printed in full-color with black and red card backs. The panel cards are not numbered but instead are lettered from A through P, and are designated as sets #1-4.

		MT	NR MT	EX
Complete Set:		10.00	7.50	4.00
Complete Singles Set:		6.00	4.50	2.50
Common Panel:		3.00	2.25	1.25
Common Single Player:		.20	.15	.08
Panel		3.25	2.50	1.25
A	Jorge Bell	.35	.25	.14
B	Wade Boggs	.70	.50	.30
C	George Brett	.50	.40	.20
D	Vince Coleman	.50	.40	.20
Panel		2.75	2.00	1.00
E	Carlton Fisk	.20	.15	.08
F	Dwight Gooden	.70	.50	.30
G	Pedro Guerrero	.20	.15	.08
H	Ron Guidry	.20	.15	.08
Panel		3.50	2.75	1.50
I	Reggie Jackson	.40	.30	.15
J	Don Mattingly	.90	.70	.35
K	Oddibe McDowell	.20	.15	.08
L	Willie McGee	.20	.15	.08
Panel		3.25	2.50	1.25
M	Dale Murphy	.50	.40	.20
N	Pete Rose	.70	.50	.30
O	Bret Saberhagen	.20	.15	.08
P	Fernando Valenzuela	.30	.25	.12

1987 O-Pee-Chee

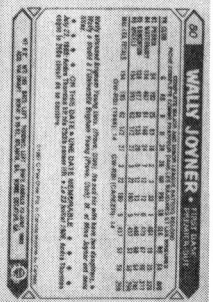

O-Pee-Chee of London, Ont., under license from the Topps Chewing Gum Co., continued a practice started in 1965 by issuing a baseball card set for 1987. The 396-card set is identical in design to the regular Topps set, save the name ''O-Pee-Chee'' replacing ''Topps'' in the lower right corner. Because the set is issued after its American counterpart, several cards appear with trade notations and corrected logos on the fronts. The cards, which are printed on white stock and are the standard 2½'' by 3½'', feature backs written in both English and French.

		MT	NR MT	EX
Complete Set:		.04	.03	.02
Common Player:		.04	.03	.02
1	Ken Oberkfell	.04	.03	.02
2	Jack Howell	.10	.08	.04
3	Hubie Brooks	.07	.05	.03
4	Bob Grich	.07	.05	.03
5	Rick Leach	.04	.03	.02
6	Phil Niekro	.15	.11	.06
7	Rickey Henderson	.25	.20	.10
8	Terry Pendleton	.07	.05	.03
9	Jay Tibbs	.04	.03	.02
10	Cecil Cooper	.10	.08	.04
11	Mario Soto	.07	.05	.03

		MT	NR MT	EX				MT	NR MT	EX
12	George Bell	.25	.20	.10		103	Rick Aguilera	.07	.05	.03
13	Nick Esasky	.04	.03	.02		104	Buddy Bell	.07	.05	.03
14	Larry McWilliams	.04	.03	.02		105	Floyd Youmans	.10	.08	.04
15	Dan Quisenberry	.10	.08	.04		106	Lou Whitaker	.15	.11	.06
16	Ed Lynch	.04	.03	.02		107	Ozzie Smith	.10	.08	.04
17	Pete O'Brien	.07	.05	.03		108	Jim Gantner	.04	.03	.02
18	Luis Aguayo	.04	.03	.02		109	R.J. Reynolds	.07	.05	.03
19	Matt Young	.04	.03	.02		110	John Tudor	.07	.05	.03
20	Gary Carter	.20	.15	.08		111	Alfredo Griffin	.07	.05	.03
21	Tom Paciorek	.04	.03	.02		112	Mike Flanagan	.07	.05	.03
22	Doug DeCinces	.07	.05	.03		113	Neil Allen	.04	.03	.02
23	Lee Smith	.07	.05	.03		114	Ken Griffey	.07	.05	.03
24	Jesse Barfield	.12	.09	.05		115	Donnie Moore	.04	.03	.02
25	Bert Blyleven	.10	.08	.04		116	Bob Horner	.12	.09	.05
26	Greg Brock	.07	.05	.03		117	Ron Shepherd	.04	.03	.02
27	Dan Petry	.07	.05	.03		118	Cliff Johnson	.04	.03	.02
28	Rick Dempsey	.04	.03	.02		119	Vince Coleman	.15	.11	.06
29	Jimmy Key	.10	.08	.04		120	Eddie Murray	.25	.20	.10
30	Tim Raines	.20	.15	.08		121	Dwayne Murphy	.04	.03	.02
31	Bruce Hurst	.07	.05	.03		122	Jim Clancy	.07	.05	.03
32	Manny Trillo	.07	.05	.03		123	Ken Landreaux	.04	.03	.02
33	Andy Van Slyke	.07	.05	.03		124	Tom Nieto	.04	.03	.02
34	Ed Vande Berg	.04	.03	.02		125	Bob Brenly	.04	.03	.02
35	Sid Bream	.07	.05	.03		126	George Brett	.30	.25	.12
36	Dave Winfield	.20	.15	.08		127	Vance Law	.04	.03	.02
37	Scott Garrelts	.04	.03	.02		128	Checklist 1-132	.04	.03	.02
38	Dennis Leonard	.04	.03	.02		129	Bob Knepper	.07	.05	.03
39	Marty Barrett	.07	.05	.03		130	Dwight Gooden	.50	.40	.20
40	Dave Righetti	.12	.09	.05		131	Juan Bonilla	.04	.03	.02
41	Bo Diaz	.04	.03	.02		132	Tim Burke	.07	.05	.03
42	Gary Redus	.07	.05	.03		133	Bob McClure	.04	.03	.02
43	Tom Niedenfuer	.04	.03	.02		134	Scott Bailes	.10	.08	.04
44	Greg Harris	.04	.03	.02		135	Mike Easler	.07	.05	.03
45	Jim Presley	.10	.08	.04		136	Ron Romanick	.04	.03	.02
46	Danny Gladden	.07	.05	.03		137	Rich Gedman	.07	.05	.03
47	Ron Smalley	.04	.03	.02		138	Bob Dernier	.04	.03	.02
48	Wally Backman	.07	.05	.03		139	John Denny	.04	.03	.02
49	Tom Seaver	.20	.15	.08		140	Bret Saberhagen	.15	.11	.06
50	Dave Smith	.07	.05	.03		141	Herm Winningham	.04	.03	.02
51	Mel Hall	.07	.05	.03		142	Rick Sutcliffe	.10	.08	.04
52	Tim Flannery	.04	.03	.02		143	Ryne Sandberg	.20	.15	.08
53	Julio Cruz	.04	.03	.02		144	Mike Scioscia	.04	.03	.02
54	Dick Schofield	.04	.03	.02		145	Charlie Kerfeld	.04	.03	.02
55	Tim Wallach	.10	.08	.04		146	Jim Rice	.20	.15	.08
56	Glenn Davis	.15	.11	.06		147	Steve Trout	.07	.05	.03
57	Darren Daulton	.04	.03	.02		148	Jesse Orosco	.07	.05	.03
58	Chico Walker	.04	.03	.02		149	Mike Boddicker	.07	.05	.03
59	Garth Iorg	.04	.03	.02		150	Wade Boggs	.70	.50	.30
60	Tony Pena	.07	.05	.03		151	Dane Iorg	.04	.03	.02
61	Ron Hassey	.04	.03	.02		152	Rick Burleson	.07	.05	.03
62	Dave Dravecky	.07	.05	.03		153	Duane Ward	.04	.03	.02
63	Jorge Orta	.04	.03	.02		154	Rick Reuschel	.07	.05	.03
64	Al Nipper	.04	.03	.02		155	Nolan Ryan	.20	.15	.08
65	Tom Browning	.07	.05	.03		156	Bill Caudill	.04	.03	.02
66	Marc Sullivan	.04	.03	.02		157	Danny Darwin	.04	.03	.02
67	Todd Worrell	.15	.11	.06		158	Ed Romero	.04	.03	.02
68	Glenn Hubbard	.04	.03	.02		159	Bill Almon	.04	.03	.02
69	Carney Lansford	.07	.05	.03		160	Julio Franco	.10	.08	.04
70	Charlie Hough	.07	.05	.03		161	Kent Hrbek	.15	.11	.06
71	Lance McCullers	.10	.08	.04		162	Chill Davis	.07	.05	.03
72	Walt Terrell	.07	.05	.03		163	Kevin Gross	.07	.05	.03
73	Bob Kearney	.04	.03	.02		164	Carlton Fisk	.12	.09	.05
74	Dan Pasqua	.10	.08	.04		165	Jeff Reardon	.10	.08	.04
75	Ron Darling	.10	.08	.04		166	Bob Boone	.04	.03	.02
76	Robin Yount	.20	.15	.08		167	Rick Honeycutt	.04	.03	.02
77	Pat Tabler	.07	.05	.03		168	Dan Schatzeder	.04	.03	.02
78	Tom Foley	.04	.03	.02		169	Jim Wohlford	.04	.03	.02
79	Juan Nieves	.12	.09	.05		170	Phil Bradley	.10	.08	.04
80	Wally Joyner	1.25	.90	.50		171	Ken Schrom	.04	.03	.02
81	Wayne Krenchicki	.04	.03	.02		172	Ron Oester	.04	.03	.02
82	Kirby Puckett	.25	.20	.10		173	Juan Beniquez	.04	.03	.02
83	Bob Ojeda	.07	.05	.03		174	Tony Armas	.07	.05	.03
84	Mookie Wilson	.07	.05	.03		175	Bob Stanley	.04	.03	.02
85	Kevin Bass	.07	.05	.03		176	Steve Buechele	.04	.03	.02
86	Kent Tekulve	.07	.05	.03		177	Keith Moreland	.07	.05	.03
87	Mark Salas	.04	.03	.02		178	Cecil Fielder	.07	.05	.03
88	Brian Downing	.07	.05	.03		179	Gary Gaetti	.12	.09	.05
89	Ozzie Guillen	.10	.08	.04		180	Chris Brown	.10	.08	.04
90	Dave Stieb	.10	.08	.04		181	Tom Herr	.07	.05	.03
91	Rance Mulliniks	.04	.03	.02		182	Lee Lacy	.04	.03	.02
92	Mike Witt	.10	.08	.04		183	Ozzie Virgil	.04	.03	.02
93	Charlie Moore	.04	.03	.02		184	Paul Molitor	.12	.09	.05
94	Jose Uribe	.04	.03	.02		185	Roger McDowell	.10	.08	.04
95	Oddibe McDowell	.10	.08	.04		186	Mike Marshall	.10	.08	.04
96	Ray Soff	.04	.03	.02		187	Ken Howell	.04	.03	.02
97	Glenn Wilson	.07	.05	.03		188	Rob Deer	.10	.08	.04
98	Brook Jacoby	.10	.08	.04		189	Joe Hesketh	.07	.05	.03
99	Darryl Motley	.04	.03	.02		190	Jim Sundberg	.04	.03	.02
100	Steve Garvey	.20	.15	.08		191	Kelly Gruber	.04	.03	.02
101	Frank White	.07	.05	.03		192	Cory Snyder	.60	.45	.25
102	Mike Moore	.04	.03	.02		193	Dave Concepcion	.07	.05	.03

		MT	NR MT	EX				MT	NR MT	EX
194	Kirk McCaskill	.10	.08	.04		285	Dennis Boyd	.07	.05	.03
195	Mike Pagliarulo	.12	.09	.05		286	Tim Hulett	.04	.03	.02
196	Rick Manning	.04	.03	.02		287	Craig Lefferts	.04	.03	.02
197	Brett Butler	.07	.05	.03		288	Tito Landrum	.04	.03	.02
198	Tony Gwynn	.30	.25	.12		289	Manny Lee	.04	.03	.02
199	Mariano Duncan	.04	.03	.02		290	Leon Durham	.07	.05	.03
200	Pete Rose	.50	.40	.20		291	Johnny Ray	.07	.05	.03
201	John Cangelosi	.12	.09	.05		292	Franklin Stubbs	.07	.05	.03
202	Danny Cox	.07	.05	.03		293	Bob Rodgers	.04	.03	.02
203	Butch Wynegar	.04	.03	.02		294	Terry Francona	.04	.03	.02
204	Chris Chambliss	.07	.05	.03		295	Len Dykstra	.10	.08	.04
205	Graig Nettles	.10	.08	.04		296	Tom Candiotti	.04	.03	.02
206	Chet Lemon	.07	.05	.03		297	Frank DiPino	.04	.03	.02
207	Don Aase	.04	.03	.02		298	Craig Reynolds	.04	.03	.02
208	Mike Mason	.04	.03	.02		299	Jerry Hairston	.04	.03	.02
209	Alan Trammell	.20	.15	.08		300	Reggie Jackson	.25	.20	.10
210	Lloyd Moseby	.10	.08	.04		301	Luis Aquino	.07	.05	.03
211	Richard Dotson	.07	.05	.03		302	Greg Walker	.07	.05	.03
212	Mike Fitzgerald	.04	.03	.02		303	Terry Kennedy	.07	.05	.03
213	Darrell Porter	.04	.03	.02		304	Phil Garner	.04	.03	.02
214	Checklist 133-264	.04	.03	.02		305	John Franco	.07	.05	.03
215	Mark Langston	.10	.08	.04		306	Bill Buckner	.07	.05	.03
216	Steve Farr	.04	.03	.02		307	Kevin Mitchell	.25	.20	.10
217	Dann Bilardello	.04	.03	.02		308	Don Slaught	.04	.03	.02
218	Gary Ward	.07	.05	.03		309	Harold Baines	.10	.08	.04
219	Cecilio Guante	.04	.03	.02		310	Frank Viola	.10	.08	.04
220	Joe Carter	.10	.08	.04		311	Dave Lopes	.07	.05	.03
221	Ernie Whitt	.07	.05	.03		312	Cal Ripken	.25	.20	.10
222	Denny Walling	.04	.03	.02		313	John Candelaria	.07	.05	.03
223	Charlie Leibrandt	.07	.05	.03		314	Bob Sebra	.10	.08	.04
224	Wayne Tolleson	.04	.03	.02		315	Bud Black	.04	.03	.02
225	Mike Smithson	.04	.03	.02		316	Brian Fisher	.07	.05	.03
226	Zane Smith	.07	.05	.03		317	Clint Hurdle	.04	.03	.02
227	Terry Puhl	.04	.03	.02		318	Ernie Riles	.07	.05	.03
228	Eric Davis	1.25	.90	.50		319	Dave LaPoint	.04	.03	.02
229	Don Mattingly	1.50	1.25	.60		320	Barry Bonds	.35	.25	.14
230	Don Baylor	.14	.11	.06		321	Tim Stoddard	.04	.03	.02
231	Frank Tanana	.07	.05	.03		322	Ron Cey	.07	.05	.03
232	Tom Brookens	.04	.03	.02		323	Al Newman	.07	.05	.03
233	Steve Bedrosian	.10	.08	.04		324	Jerry Royster	.04	.03	.02
234	Wallace Johnson	.04	.03	.02		325	Garry Templeton	.07	.05	.03
235	Alvin Davis	.10	.08	.04		326	Mark Gubicza	.07	.05	.03
236	Tommy John	.15	.11	.06		327	Andre Thornton	.07	.05	.03
237	Jim Morrison	.04	.03	.02		328	Bob Welch	.07	.05	.03
238	Ricky Horton	.07	.05	.03		329	Tony Fernandez	.12	.09	.05
239	Shane Rawley	.07	.05	.03		330	Mike Scott	.12	.09	.05
240	Steve Balboni	.04	.03	.02		331	Jack Clark	.12	.09	.05
241	Mike Krukow	.07	.05	.03		332	Danny Tartabull	.60	.45	.25
242	Rick Mahler	.04	.03	.02		333	Greg Minton	.04	.03	.02
243	Bill Doran	.07	.05	.03		334	Ed Correa	.15	.11	.06
244	Mark Clear	.04	.03	.02		335	Candy Maldonado	.07	.05	.03
245	Willie Upshaw	.07	.05	.03		336	Dennis Lamp	.04	.03	.02
246	Hal McRae	.10	.08	.04		337	Sid Fernandez	.10	.08	.04
247	Jose Canseco	1.25	.90	.50		338	Greg Gross	.04	.03	.02
248	George Hendrick	.04	.03	.02		339	Willie Hernandez	.07	.05	.03
249	Doyle Alexander	.07	.05	.03		340	Roger Clemens	.60	.45	.25
250	Teddy Higuera	.12	.09	.05		341	Mickey Hatcher	.04	.03	.02
251	Tom Hume	.04	.03	.02		342	Bob James	.04	.03	.02
252	Denny Martinez	.04	.03	.02		343	Jose Cruz	.07	.05	.03
253	Eddie Milner	.04	.03	.02		344	Bruce Sutter	.10	.08	.04
254	Steve Sax	.15	.11	.06		345	Andre Dawson	.15	.11	.06
255	Juan Samuel	.12	.09	.05		346	Shawon Dunston	.07	.05	.03
256	Dave Bergman	.04	.03	.02		347	Scott McGregor	.07	.05	.03
257	Bob Forsch	.04	.03	.02		348	Carmelo Martinez	.04	.03	.02
258	Steve Yeager	.04	.03	.02		349	Storm Davis	.04	.03	.02
259	Don Sutton	.15	.11	.06		350	Keith Hernandez	.20	.15	.08
260	Vida Blue	.07	.05	.03		351	Andy McGaffigan	.04	.03	.02
261	Tom Brunansky	.10	.08	.04		352	Dave Parker	.15	.11	.06
262	Joe Sambito	.04	.03	.02		353	Ernie Camacho	.04	.03	.02
263	Mitch Webster	.10	.08	.04		354	Eric Show	.04	.03	.02
264	Checklist 265-396	.04	.03	.02		355	Don Carman	.15	.11	.06
265	Darrell Evans	.10	.08	.04		356	Floyd Bannister	.07	.05	.03
266	Dave Kingman	.12	.09	.05		357	Willie McGee	.12	.09	.05
267	Howard Johnson	.10	.08	.04		358	Atlee Hammaker	.04	.03	.02
268	Greg Pryor	.04	.03	.02		359	Dale Murphy	.35	.25	.14
269	Tippy Martinez	.04	.03	.02		360	Pedro Guerrero	.15	.11	.06
270	Jody Davis	.07	.05	.03		361	Will Clark	.80	.60	.30
271	Steve Carlton	.20	.15	.08		362	Bill Campbell	.04	.03	.02
272	Andres Galarraga	.12	.09	.05		363	Alejandro Pena	.04	.03	.02
273	Fernando Valenzuela	.20	.15	.08		364	Dennis Rasmussen	.07	.05	.03
274	Jeff Hearron	.04	.03	.02		365	Rick Rhoden	.07	.05	.03
275	Ray Knight	.07	.05	.03		366	Randy St. Claire	.04	.03	.02
276	Bill Madlock	.10	.08	.04		367	Willie Wilson	.10	.08	.04
277	Tom Henke	.07	.05	.03		368	Dwight Evans	.10	.08	.04
278	Gary Pettis	.04	.03	.02		369	Moose Haas	.04	.03	.02
279	Jimy Williams	.04	.03	.02		370	Fred Lynn	.12	.09	.05
280	Jeffrey Leonard	.07	.05	.03		371	Mark Eichhorn	.12	.09	.05
281	Bryn Smith	.07	.05	.03		372	Dave Schmidt	.04	.03	.02
282	John Cerutti	.12	.09	.05		373	Jerry Reuss	.07	.05	.03
283	Gary Roenicke	.04	.03	.02		374	Lance Parrish	.15	.11	.06
284	Joaquin Andujar	.07	.05	.03		375	Ron Guidry	.15	.11	.06

		MT	NR MT	EX
376	Jack Morris	.15	.11	.06
377	Willie Randolph	.07	.05	.03
378	Joel Youngblood	.04	.03	.02
379	Darryl Strawberry	.30	.25	.12
380	Rich Gossage	.12	.09	.05
381	Dennis Eckersley	.07	.05	.03
382	Gary Lucas	.04	.03	.02
383	Ron Davis	.04	.03	.02
384	Pete Incaviglia	.70	.50	.30
385	Orel Hershiser	.10	.08	.04
386	Kirk Gibson	.20	.15	.08
387	Don Robinson	.04	.03	.02
388	Darnell Coles	.07	.05	.03
389	Von Hayes	.10	.08	.04
390	Gary Matthews	.07	.05	.03
391	Jay Howell	.07	.05	.03
392	Tim Laudner	.04	.03	.02
393	Rod Scurry	.04	.03	.02
394	Tony Bernazard	.04	.03	.02
395	Damasco Garcia	.07	.05	.03
396	Mike Schmidt	.30	.25	.12

1987 O-Pee-Chee Box Panels

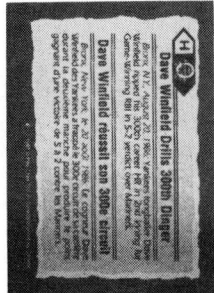

For the second consecutive year, O-Pee-Chee placed baseball cards on the bottoms of their retail wax pack boxes. The 2⅛" by 3" cards were issued in panels of four and are slightly smaller in size than the regular issue O-Pee-Chee cards. The card fronts are identical in design to the regular issue, while the backs contain a newspaper-type commentary written in both French and English. Collectors may note the 1987 Topps wax box cards were issued on side panels as opposed to box bottoms. Because the O-Pee-Chee wax boxes are smaller in size than their U.S. counterparts, printing cards on side panels could not be accomplished.

		MT	NR MT	EX
Complete Panel Set:		6.00	4.50	2.50
Complete Singles Set:		2.50	2.00	1.00
Common Single Player:		.15	.11	.06
Panel		1.75	1.25	.70
A	Don Baylor	.15	.11	.06
B	Steve Carlton	.30	.25	.12
C	Ron Cey	.15	.11	.06
D	Cecil Cooper	.15	.11	.06
Panel		2.75	2.00	1.00
E	Rickey Henderson	.35	.25	.14
F	Jim Rice	.30	.25	.12
G	Don Sutton	.20	.15	.08
H	Dave Winfield	.30	.25	.12

Definitions for grading conditions are located in the Introduction of this price guide.

1963 Pepsi-Cola Colt .45's

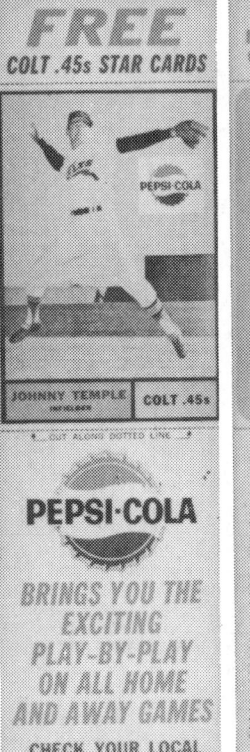
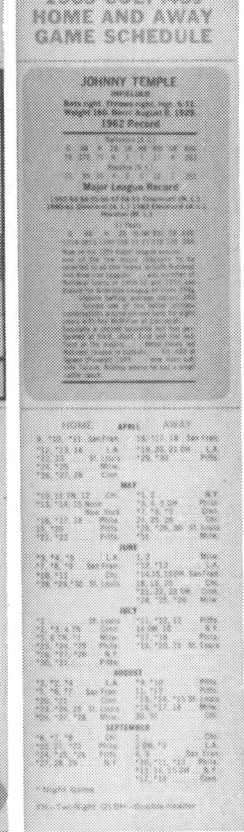

This 16-card set was distributed regionally in Texas in bottled six-packs of Pepsi. The cards were issued on panels 2⅜" by 9⅛", which were fit in between the bottles in each carton. Values quoted in the checklist below are for complete panels. A standard 2⅜" by 3¾" card was printed on each panel, which also included promos for Pepsi and the Colt .45's, as well as a team schedule. Card fronts were black and white posed action photos with blue and red trim. Player name and position and Pepsi logo are also included. Card backs offer player statistics and career highlights. The John Bateman card, which was apparently never distributed publicly, is among the rarest collectible baseball cards of the 1960s.

		NR MT	EX	VG
Complete Set w/o Bateman:		150.00	75.00	45.50
Common Player:		5.00	2.50	1.50
1	Bob Aspromonte	5.00	2.50	1.50
2	John Bateman	400.00	200.00	120.00
3	Bob Bruce	5.00	2.50	1.50
4	Jim Campbell	5.00	2.50	1.50

		NR MT	EX	VG
5	Dick Farrell	5.00	2.50	1.50
6	Ernie Fazio	5.00	2.50	1.50
7	Carroll Hardy	5.00	2.50	1.50
8	J.C. Hartman	5.00	2.50	1.50
9	Ken Johnson	5.00	2.50	1.50
10	Bob Lillis	5.00	2.50	1.50
11	Don McMahon	5.00	2.50	1.50
12	Pete Runnels	8.00	4.00	2.50
13	Al Spangler	5.00	2.50	1.50
14	Rusty Staub	15.00	7.50	4.50
15	Johnny Temple	5.00	2.50	1.50
16	Carl Warwick	60.00	30.00	18.00

1985 Performance Printing Rangers

 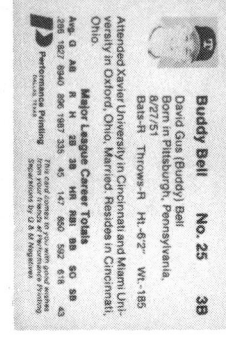

A local printing company sponsored this 28-card set of the Texas Rangers. The 2⅜" by 3½" cards are in full color and are numbered on the back by uniform number. Card fronts feature full-color game-action photos. The 25 players on the Rangers' active roster at press time are included, along with manager Bobby Valentine and unnumbered coaches and trainer cards. The black-and-white card backs have a smaller portrait photo of each player, as well as biographical information and career statistics.

		MT	NR MT	EX
	Complete Set:	6.00	4.50	2.50
	Common Player:	.12	.09	.05
0	Oddibe McDowell	1.00	.70	.40
1	Bill Stein	.12	.09	.05
2	Bobby Valentine	.15	.11	.06
3	Wayne Tolleson	.12	.09	.05
4	Don Slaught	.12	.09	.05
5	Alan Bannister	.12	.09	.05
6	Bobby Jones	.12	.09	.05
7	Glenn Brummer	.12	.09	.05
8	Luis Pujols	.12	.09	.05
9	Pete O'Brien	.50	.40	.20
11	Toby Harrah	.25	.20	.10
13	Tommy Dunbar	.12	.09	.05
15	Larry Parrish	.30	.25	.12
16	Mike Mason	.15	.11	.06
19	Curtis Wilkerson	.12	.09	.05
24	Dave Schmidt	.15	.11	.06
25	Buddy Bell	.50	.40	.20
27	Greg Harris	.12	.09	.05
30	Dave Rozema	.12	.09	.05
32	Gary Ward	.25	.20	.10
36	Dickie Noles	.12	.09	.05
41	Chris Welsh	.12	.09	.05
44	Cliff Johnson	.12	.09	.05
46	Burt Hooton	.20	.15	.08
48	Dave Stewart	.30	.25	.12
49	Charlie Hough	.30	.25	.12
---	Trainers (Danny Wheat, Bill Zeigler)			
		.12	.09	.05
---	Rangers Coaches (Rich Donnelly, Glenn Ezell, Tom House, Art Howe, Wayne Terwilliger)			
		.12	.09	.05

1986 Performance Printing Rangers

For the second time, the Texas Rangers issued a full-color card set in conjunction with this local printing company. Fronts of the 28-card set include player name, position and team logo beneath the color photo. Backs of the 2⅜" by 3½" cards are in black-and-white, with a small portrait photo of each player along with personal and professional statistics. Cards were distributed at the Aug. 23 Rangers home game, and the set includes all of the Rangers' fine rookies such as Bobby Witt, Pete Incaviglia, Edwin Correa and Ruben Sierra.

		MT	NR MT	EX
	Complete Set:	7.00	5.25	2.75
	Common Player:	.10	.08	.04
0	Oddibe McDowell	.50	.40	.20
1	Scott Fletcher	.20	.15	.08
2	Bobby Valentine	.15	.11	.06
3	Ruben Sierra	1.50	1.25	.60
4	Don Slaught	.10	.08	.04
9	Pete O'Brien	.40	.30	.15
11	Toby Harrah	.20	.15	.08
12	Geno Petralli	.10	.08	.04
15	Larry Parrish	.25	.20	.10
16	Mike Mason	.10	.08	.04
17	Darrell Porter	.15	.11	.06
18	Edwin Correa	.50	.40	.20
19	Curtis Wilkerson	.10	.08	.04
22	Steve Buechele	.30	.25	.12
23	Jose Guzman	.40	.30	.15
24	Ricky Wright	.10	.08	.04
27	Greg Harris	.10	.08	.04
28	Mitch Williams	.30	.25	.12
29	Pete Incaviglia	1.25	.90	.50
32	Gary Ward	.15	.11	.06
34	Dale Mohorcic	.30	.25	.12
40	Jeff Russell	.10	.08	.04
44	Tom Paciorek	.10	.08	.04
46	Mike Loynd	.30	.25	.12
48	Bobby Witt	.60	.45	.25
49	Charlie Hough	.20	.15	.08
---	Coaching Staff (Joe Ferguson, Tim Foli, Tom House, Art Howe, Tom Robson)	.10	.08	.04
---	Trainers (Danny Wheat, Bill Zeigler)			
		.10	.08	.04

1961 Peters Meats Twins

This set, featuring the first-year 1961 Minnesota Twins, is in a large, 4⅝" by 3½," format. Cards are on thick cardboard and heavily waxed, as they were used as partial packaging for the company's meat products. Card fronts feature full-color photos, team and Peters logos, and biographical information. The cards are blank backed.

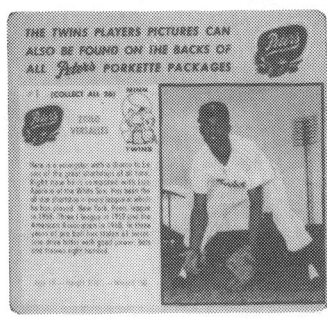

	NR MT	EX	VG
Complete Set:	5500.00	2750.00	1650.
Common Player: 1-115	8.00	4.00	2.50
Common Player: 116-162	40.00	20.00	12.00
1 Alvin Jacob Powell	45.00	8.00	3.50
2a Lee Theo Grissom (name in upper case letters)	10.00	4.00	2.50
2b Lee Theo Grissom (name in upper and lower case)	12.00	5.00	3.00
3a Charles Herbert Ruffing (name in upper case letters)	45.00	22.00	13.50
3b Charles Herbert Ruffing (name in upper and lower case)	50.00	25.00	15.00
4a Eldon LeRoy Auker (name in upper case letters)	8.00	4.00	2.50
4b Eldon LeRoy Auker (name in upper and lower case)	10.00	5.00	3.00
5a James Luther Sewell (name in upper case letters)	10.00	5.00	3.00
5b James Luther Sewell (name in upper and lower case)	12.00	6.00	3.50
6a Leo Ernest Durocher (name in upper case letters)	40.00	20.00	12.00
6b Leo Ernest Durocher (name in upper and lower case)	45.00	22.00	13.50
7a Robert Pershing Doerr (name in upper case letters)	35.00	17.50	10.50
7b Robert Pershing Doerr (name in upper and lower case)	40.00	20.00	12.00
8 Henry Pippen	8.00	4.00	2.50
9a James Tobin (name in upper case letters)	8.00	4.00	2.50
9b James Tobin (name in upper and lower case)	10.00	5.00	3.00
10 James Brooklyn DeShong	8.00	4.00	2.50
11 John Costa Rizzo	8.00	4.00	2.50
12 Hershel Ray Martin (Herschel)	8.00	4.00	2.50
13a Luke Daniel Hamlin (name in upper case letters)	8.00	4.00	2.50
13b Luke Daniel Hamlin (name in upper and lower case)	10.00	5.00	3.00
14a James R. Tabor ("...Tabor batted .295,...")	8.00	4.00	2.50
14b James R. Tabor ("...Tabor batted 295,...")	10.00	5.00	3.00
15a Paul Derringer (name in upper case letters)	10.00	5.00	3.00
15b Paul Derringer (name in upper and lower case)	12.00	6.00	3.50
16 John Peacock	8.00	4.00	2.50
17 Emerson Dickman	8.00	4.00	2.50
18a Harry Danning (name in upper case letters)	8.00	4.00	2.50
18b Harry Danning (name in upper and lower case)	10.00	5.00	3.00
19 Paul Dean	15.00	7.50	4.50
20 Joseph Heving	8.00	4.00	2.50
21a Emil Leonard (name in upper case letters)	8.00	4.00	2.50
21b Emil Leonard (name in upper and lower case)	10.00	5.00	3.00
22a William Henry Walters (name in upper case letters)	10.00	5.00	3.00
22b William Henry Walters (name in upper and lower case)	12.00	6.00	3.50
23 Burgess U. Whitehead	8.00	4.00	2.50
24a Richard S. Coffman (S. Richard) ("...Senators the same year.")	8.00	4.00	2.50
24b Richard S. Coffman (S. Richard) ("...Browns the same year.")	15.00	7.50	4.50
25a George Alexander Selkirk (name in upper case letters)	15.00	7.50	4.50
25b George Alexander Selkirk (name in upper and lower case)	20.00	7.50	4.50
26a Joseph Paul DiMaggio ("...206 hits in 1938 games...")	700.00	350.00	210.00
26b Joseph Paul DiMaggio ("...206 hits in 138 games...")	800.00	400.00	240.00
27a Fred Ray Ostermueller (name in upper case letters)	8.00	4.00	2.50
27b Fred Ray Ostermueller (name in upper and lower case)	10.00	5.00	3.00
28 Sylvester Johnson	8.00	4.00	2.50
29a John Francis Wilson (name in upper case letters)	8.00	4.00	2.50
29b John Francis Wilson (name in upper and lower case)	10.00	5.00	3.00
30a William Malcolm Dickey (name in upper case letters)	75.00	37.00	22.00
30b William Malcolm Dickey (name in upper and lower case)	80.00	40.00	24.00

	NR MT	EX	VG
Complete Set:	550.00	275.00	165.00
Common Player:	12.00	6.00	3.50
1 Zoilo Versalles	18.00	9.00	5.50
2 Eddie Lopat	18.00	9.00	5.50
3 Pedro Ramos	12.00	6.00	3.50
4 Charles "Chuck" Stobbs	12.00	6.00	3.50
5 Don Mincher	18.00	9.00	5.50
6 Jack Kralick	12.00	6.00	3.50
7 Jim Kaat	40.00	20.00	12.00
8 Hal Naragon	12.00	6.00	3.50
9 Don Lee	12.00	6.00	3.50
10 Harry "Cookie" Lavagetto	14.00	7.00	4.25
11 Tom "Pete" Whisenant	12.00	6.00	3.50
12 Elmer Valo	12.00	6.00	3.50
13 Ray Moore	12.00	6.00	3.50
14 Billy Gardner	12.00	6.00	3.50
15 Lenny Green	12.00	6.00	3.50
16 Sam Mele	12.00	6.00	3.50
17 Jim Lemon	14.00	7.00	4.25
18 Harmon "Killer" Killebrew	125.00	62.00	37.00
19 Paul Giel	14.00	7.00	4.25
20 Reno Bertoia	12.00	6.00	3.50
21 Clyde McCullough	12.00	6.00	3.50
22 Earl Battey	18.00	9.00	5.50
23 Camilo Pascual	18.00	9.00	5.50
24 Dan Dobbek	12.00	6.00	3.50
25 Joe "Valvy" Valdivielso	12.00	6.00	3.50
26 Billy Consolo	12.00	6.00	3.50

1939 Play Ball

With the issuance of this card set by Gum Incorporated, a new era of baseball cards was born. Although the cards were black-and-white, the full-frame, actual photos on the card fronts were of better quality than previously seen, and the 2½'' by 3¼'' size was larger and more popular than the smaller tobacco and caramel cards of the early 20th Century. Card backs featured player names and extensive biographies. There are 162 cards in the set, including superstars Joe DiMaggio and Ted Williams. Card number 126 was never issued.

Complete set prices do not include the higher priced variations, unless noted otherwise.

		NR MT	EX	VG
31a	Samuel West (name in upper case letters)	8.00	4.00	2.50
31b	Samuel West (name in upper and lower case)	10.00	5.00	3.00
32	Robert I. Seeds	8.00	4.00	2.50
33	Del Howard Young (name actually Del Edward)	8.00	4.00	2.50
34a	Frank Joseph Demaree (Joseph Franklin) (name in upper case letters)	8.00	4.00	2.50
34b	Frank Joseph Demaree (Joseph Franklin) (name in upper and lower case)	10.00	5.00	3.00
35a	William Frederick Jurges (name in upper case letters)	10.00	5.00	3.00
35b	William Frederick Jurges (name in upper and lower case)	12.00	6.00	3.50
36a	Frank Andrew McCormick (name in upper case letters)	8.00	4.00	2.50
36b	Frank Andrew McCormick (name in upper and lower case)	10.00	5.00	3.00
37	Virgil Lawrence Davis	8.00	4.00	2.50
38a	William Harrison Myers (name in upper case letters)	8.00	4.00	2.50
38b	William Harrison Myers (name in upper and lower case)	10.00	5.00	3.00
39a	Richard Benjamin Ferrell (name in upper case letters)	40.00	20.00	12.00
39b	Richard Benjamin Ferrell (name in upper and lower case)	45.00	22.00	13.50
40	James Charles Bagby Jr.	8.00	4.00	2.50
41a	Lonnie Warneke ("...the earned run department...")	8.00	4.00	2.50
41b	Lonnie Warneke ("...the earned-run department...")	10.00	5.00	3.00
42	Arndt Jorgens	12.00	6.00	3.50
43	Melo Almada	8.00	4.00	2.50
44	Donald Henry Heffner	8.00	4.00	2.50
45a	Merrill May (name in upper case letters)	8.00	4.00	2.50
45b	Merrill May (name in upper and lower case)	10.00	5.00	3.00
46a	Morris Arnovich (name in upper case letters)	8.00	4.00	2.50
46b	Morris Arnovich (name in upper and lower case)	10.00	5.00	3.00
47a	John Kelly Lewis, Jr. (name in upper case letters)	8.00	4.00	2.50
47b	John Kelly Lewis, Jr. (name in upper and lower case)	10.00	5.00	3.00
48a	Vernon Gomez (name in upper case letters)	75.00	37.00	22.00
48b	Vernon Gomez (name in upper and lower case)	80.00	40.00	32.00
49	Edward Miller	8.00	4.00	2.50
50a	Charles Len Gehringer (name actually Charles Leonard) (name in upper case letters)	75.00	37.00	22.00
50b	Charles Len Gehringer (name actually Charles Leonard) (name in upper & lower case)	80.00	40.00	24.00
51a	Melvin Thomas Ott (name in upper case)	85.00	42.00	25.00
51b	Melvin Thomas Ott (name in upper and lower case)	90.00	45.00	27.00
52a	Thomas D. Henrich (name in upper case letters)	25.00	12.50	7.50
52b	Thomas D. Henrich (name in upper and lower case)	30.00	15.00	9.00
53a	Carl Owen Hubbell (name in upper case letters)	75.00	37.00	22.00
53b	Carl Owen Hubbell (name in upper and lower case)	80.00	40.00	24.00
54a	Harry Edward Gumbert (name in upper case letters)	8.00	4.00	2.50
54b	Harry Edward Gumbert (name in upper and lower case)	10.00	5.00	3.00
55a	Floyd E. Vaughan (Joseph Floyd) (name in upper case letters)	40.00	20.00	12.00
55b	Floyd E. Vaughan (Joseph Floyd) (name in upper and lower case)	45.00	22.00	13.50
56a	Henry Greenberg (name in upper case letters)	85.00	42.00	25.00
56b	Henry Greenberg (name in upper and lower case)	90.00	45.00	27.00
57a	John A. Hassett (name in upper case letters)	8.00	4.00	2.50
57b	John A. Hassett (name in upper and lower case)	10.00	5.00	3.00
58	Louis Peo Chiozza	8.00	4.00	2.50
59	Kendall Chase	8.00	4.00	2.50
60a	Lynwood Thomas Rowe (name in upper case letters)	10.00	5.00	3.00
60b	Lynwood Thomas Rowe (name in upper and lower case)	12.00	6.00	3.50
61a	Anthony F. Cuccinello (name in upper case letters)	8.00	4.00	2.50
61b	Anthony F. Cuccinello (name in upper and lower case)	10.00	5.00	3.00
62	Thomas Carey	8.00	4.00	2.50
63	Emmett Mueller	8.00	4.00	2.50
64a	Wallace Moses, Jr. (name in upper case letters)	8.00	4.00	2.50
64b	Wallace Moses, Jr. (name in upper and lower case)	10.00	5.00	3.00
65a	Harry Francis Craft (name in upper case letters)	8.00	4.00	2.50
65b	Harry Francis Craft (name in upper and lower case)	10.00	5.00	3.00
66	James A. Ripple	8.00	4.00	2.50
67	Edwin Joost	8.00	4.00	2.50
68	Fred Singleton	8.00	4.00	2.50
69	Elbert Preston Fletcher (Elburt)	8.00	4.00	2.50
70	Fred Maloy Frankhouse (Meloy)	8.00	4.00	2.50
71a	Marcellus Monte Pearson (name actually Montgomery Marcellus) (name in upper case)	12.00	6.00	3.50
71b	Marcellus Monte Pearson (name actually Montgomery Marcellus) (name in upper & lower)	15.00	7.50	4.50
72a	Debs Garms (Born: Bango, Tex.)	8.00	4.00	2.50
72b	Debs Garms (Born: Bangs, Tex.)	15.00	7.50	4.50
73a	Harold H. Schumacher (Born: Dolgville, N.Y.)	10.00	5.00	3.00
73b	Harold H. Schumacher (Born: Dolgeville, N.Y.)	20.00	10.00	6.00
74a	Harry A. Lavagetto (name in upper case letters)	12.00	6.00	3.50
74b	Harry A. Lavagetto (name in upper and lower case)	15.00	7.50	4.50
75a	Stanley Bordagaray (name in upper case letters)	8.00	4.00	2.50
75b	Stanley Bordagaray (name in upper and lower case)	10.00	5.00	3.00
76	Goodwin George Rosen	8.00	4.00	2.50
77	Lewis Sidney Riggs	8.00	4.00	2.50
78a	Julius Joseph Solters (name in upper case letters)	8.00	4.00	2.50
78b	Julius Joseph Solters (name in upper and lower case)	10.00	5.00	3.00
79a	Joseph Gregg Moore (given name is Joe) (Weight: 157 lbs.)	8.00	4.00	2.50
79b	Joseph Gregg Moore (given name is Joe) (Weight: 175 lbs.)	15.00	7.50	4.50
80a	Irwin Fox (Ervin) (Weight: 165 lbs.)	8.00	4.00	2.50
80b	Irwin Fox (Ervin) (Weight: 157 lbs.)	15.00	7.50	4.50
81a	Ellsworth Dahlgren (name in upper case letters)	12.00	6.00	3.50
81b	Ellsworth Dahlgren (name in upper and lower case)	15.00	7.50	4.50
82a	Charles Herbert Klein (name in upper case letters)	60.00	30.00	18.00
82b	Charles Herbert Klein (name in upper and lower case)	65.00	32.00	19.50
83a	August Richard Suhr (name in upper case letters)	8.00	4.00	2.50
83b	August Richard Suhr (name in upper and lower case)	10.00	5.00	3.00
84	Lamar Newsome	8.00	4.00	2.50
85	John Walter Cooney	8.00	4.00	2.50
86a	Adolph Camilli (Adolf) ("...start of the 1928 season,...")	10.00	5.00	3.00
86b	Adolph Camilli (Adolf) ("...start of the 1938 season,...")	20.00	10.00	6.00
87	Milburn G. Shoffner (middle initial actually J.)	8.00	4.00	2.50
88	Charles Keller	20.00	10.00	6.00
89a	Lloyd James Waner (name in upper case letters)	45.00	22.00	13.50
89b	Lloyd James Waner (name in upper and lower case)	50.00	25.00	15.00
90a	Robert H. Klinger (name in upper case letters)	8.00	4.00	2.50
90b	Robert H. Klinger (name in upper and lower case)	10.00	5.00	3.00
91a	John H. Knott (name in upper case letters)	8.00	4.00	2.50
91b	John H. Knott (name in upper and lower case)	10.00	5.00	3.00
92a	Ted Williams (name in upper case letters)	650.00	325.00	195.00

		NR MT	EX	VG
92b	Ted Williams (name in upper and lower			
	case)	675.00	337.00	202.00
93	Charles M. Gelbert	8.00	4.00	2.50
94	Henry E. Manush	40.00	20.00	12.00
95a	Whitlow Wyatt (name in upper case			
	letters)	10.00	5.00	3.00
95b	Whitlow Wyatt (name in upper and lower			
	case)	12.00	6.00	3.50
96a	Ernest Gordon Phelps (name in upper			
	case letters)	10.00	5.00	3.00
96b	Ernest Gordon Phelps (name in upper and			
	lower case)	12.00	6.00	3.50
97a	Robert Lee Johnson (name in upper case			
	letters)	8.00	4.00	2.50
97b	Robert Lee Johnson (name in upper and			
	lower case)	10.00	5.00	3.00
98	Arthur Carter Whitney	8.00	4.00	2.50
99a	Walter Anton Berger (name in upper case			
	letters)	10.00	5.00	3.00
99b	Walter Anton Berger (name in upper and			
	lower case)	12.00	6.00	3.50
100a	Charles Solomon Myer (name in upper			
	case letters)	8.00	4.00	2.50
100b	Charles Solomon Myer (name in upper			
	and lower case)	10.00	5.00	3.00
101a	Roger M. Cramer ("...the Martinburg			
	Club...")	8.00	4.00	2.50
101b	Roger M. Cramer ("...the Martinsburg			
	Club...")	15.00	7.50	4.50
102a	Lemuel Floyd Young (name in upper case			
	letters)	8.00	4.00	2.50
102b	Lemuel Floyd Young (name in upper and			
	lower case)	10.00	5.00	3.00
103	Morris Berg	10.00	5.00	3.00
104a	Thomas Davis Bridges ("...280 games,			
	winning 283,...")	10.00	5.00	3.00
104b	Thomas Davis Bridges ("...280 games,			
	winning 133,...")	20.00	10.00	6.00
105a	Donald Eric McNair (name in upper case			
	letters)	8.00	4.00	2.50
105b	Donald Eric McNair (name in upper and			
	lower case)	10.00	5.00	3.00
106	Albert Stark	8.00	4.00	2.50
107	Joseph Franklin Vosmik	8.00	4.00	2.50
108a	Frank Witman Hayes (name in upper case			
	letters)	8.00	4.00	2.50
108b	Frank Witman Hayes (name in upper and			
	lower case)	10.00	5.00	3.00
109a	Myril Hoag (name in upper case letters)			
		8.00	4.00	2.50
109b	Myril Hoag (name in upper and lower			
	case)	10.00	5.00	3.00
110	Fred L. Fitzsimmons	10.00	5.00	3.00
111a	Van Lingle Mungo (name in upper case			
	letters)	15.00	7.50	4.50
111b	Van Lingle Mungo (name in upper and			
	lower case)	20.00	10.00	6.00
112a	Paul Glee Waner ("...Waner, the older...")			
		45.00	22.00	13.50
112b	Paul Glee Waner ("...Waner, the elder...")			
		60.00	30.00	18.00
113	Al Schacht	12.00	6.00	3.50
114a	Cecil Travis (name in upper case letters)			
		8.00	4.00	2.50
114b	Cecil Travis (name in upper and lower			
	case)	10.00	5.00	3.00
115a	Ralph Kress (name in upper case letters)			
		8.00	4.00	2.50
115b	Ralph Kress (name in upper and lower			
	case)	10.00	5.00	3.00
116	Eugene A. Desautels	40.00	20.00	12.00
117	Wayne Ambler	40.00	20.00	12.00
118	Lynn Nelson	40.00	20.00	12.00
119	Willard McKee Hershberger	40.00	20.00	12.00
120	Harold Benton Warstler (middle name			
	actually Burton)	40.00	20.00	12.00
121	William J. Posedel	40.00	20.00	12.00
122	George Hartley McQuinn	40.00	20.00	12.00
123	Ray T. Davis	40.00	20.00	12.00
124	Walter George Brown	40.00	20.00	12.00
125	Clifford George Melton	40.00	20.00	12.00
126	Not Issued			
127	Gilbert Herman Brack	40.00	20.00	12.00
128	Joseph Emil Bowman	40.00	20.00	12.00
129	William Swift	40.00	20.00	12.00
130	Wilbur Lee Brubaker	40.00	20.00	12.00
131	Morton Cecil Cooper	40.00	20.00	12.00
132	James Roberson Brown	40.00	20.00	12.00
133	Lynn Myers	40.00	20.00	12.00
134	Forrest Pressnell	40.00	20.00	12.00
135	Arnold Malcolm Owen	40.00	20.00	12.00

		NR MT	EX	VG
136	Roy Chester Bell	40.00	20.00	12.00
137	Peter William Appleton	40.00	20.00	12.00
138	George Washington Case Jr.	40.00	20.00	12.00
139	Vitautas C. Tamulis	40.00	20.00	12.00
140	Raymond Hall Hayworth	40.00	20.00	12.00
141	Peter Coscarart	40.00	20.00	12.00
142	Ira Kendall Hutchinson	40.00	20.00	12.00
143	Howard Earl Averill	100.00	50.00	30.00
144	Henry J. Bonura	40.00	20.00	12.00
145	Hugh Noyes Mulcahy	40.00	20.00	12.00
146	Thomas Sunkel	40.00	20.00	12.00
147	George D. Coffman	40.00	20.00	12.00
148	William Trotter	40.00	20.00	12.00
149	Max Edward West	40.00	20.00	12.00
150	James Elton Walkup	40.00	20.00	12.00
151	Hugh Thomas Casey	45.00	22.00	13.50
152	Roy Weatherly	40.00	20.00	12.00
153	Paul H. Trout	45.00	22.00	13.50
154	John W. Hudson	40.00	20.00	12.00
155	James Paul Outlaw (middle name actually			
	Paulus)	40.00	20.00	12.00
156	Raymond Berres	40.00	20.00	12.00
157	Donald Willard Padgett (middle name			
	actually Wilson)	40.00	20.00	12.00
158	Luther Baxter Thomas	40.00	20.00	12.00
159	Russell E. Evans	40.00	20.00	12.00
160	Eugene Moore Jr.	40.00	20.00	12.00
161	Linus Reinhard Frey	40.00	20.00	12.00
162	Lloyd Albert Moore	75.00	20.00	12.00

1940 Play Ball

 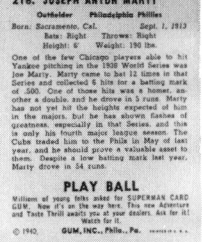

Following the success of their initial effort in 1939, Gum Incorporated issued a bigger and better set in 1940. The 240 black-and-white cards were once again in the 2½'' by 3⅛'' size, but the photos on the card fronts were enclosed by a frame which listed the player's name. Card backs again offer extensive biographies. Backs were also dated. A number of old timers were issued along with the current day's players, and many Hall of Famers are included. The final 60 cards of the set are more difficult to obtain.

		NR MT	EX	VG
Complete Set:		9500.00	4750.00	2850.
Common Player: 1-120		8.00	4.00	2.50
Common Player: 121-180		9.00	4.50	2.75
Common Player: 181-240		35.00	17.50	10.50
1	Joe DiMaggio	900.00	450.00	270.00
2	"Art" Jorgens	12.00	6.00	3.50
3	"Babe" Dahlgren	12.00	6.00	3.50
4	"Tommy" Henrich	25.00	12.50	7.50
5	"Monte" Pearson	12.00	6.00	3.50
6	"Lefty" Gomez	90.00	45.00	27.00
7	"Bill" Dickey	90.00	45.00	27.00
8	"Twinkletoes" Selkirk	12.00	6.00	3.50
9	"Charley" Keller	25.00	12.50	7.50
10	"Red" Ruffing	50.00	25.00	15.00
11	"Jake" Powell	12.00	6.00	3.50
12	"Johnny" Schulte	12.00	6.00	3.50
13	"Jack" Knott	8.00	4.00	2.50
14	"Rabbit" McNair	8.00	4.00	2.50
15	George Case	8.00	4.00	2.50
16	Cecil Travis	8.00	4.00	2.50
17	"Buddy" Myer	8.00	4.00	2.50
18	"Charley" Gelbert	8.00	4.00	2.50
19	"Ken" Chase	8.00	4.00	2.50
20	"Buddy" Lewis	8.00	4.00	2.50

#	Player	NR MT	EX	VG
21	"Rick" Ferrell	45.00	22.00	13.50
22	"Sammy" West	8.00	4.00	2.50
23	"Dutch" Leonard	8.00	4.00	2.50
24	Frank "Blimp" Hayes	8.00	4.00	2.50
25	"Cherokee" Bob Johnson	8.00	4.00	2.50
26	"Wally" Moses	8.00	4.00	2.50
27	"Ted" Williams	650.00	325.00	195.00
28	"Gene" Desautels	8.00	4.00	2.50
29	"Doc" Cramer	8.00	4.00	2.50
30	"Moe" Berg	10.00	5.00	3.00
31	"Jack" Wilson	8.00	4.00	2.50
32	"Jim" Bagby	8.00	4.00	2.50
33	"Fritz" Ostermueller	8.00	4.00	2.50
34	John Peacock	8.00	4.00	2.50
35	"Joe" Heving	8.00	4.00	2.50
36	"Jim" Tabor	8.00	4.00	2.50
37	Emerson Dickman	8.00	4.00	2.50
38	"Bobby" Doerr	35.00	17.50	10.50
39	"Tom" Carey	8.00	4.00	2.50
40	"Hank" Greenberg	100.00	50.00	30.00
41	"Charley" Gehringer	80.00	40.00	24.00
42	"Bud" Thomas	8.00	4.00	2.50
43	Pete Fox	8.00	4.00	2.50
44	"Dizzy" Trout	10.00	5.00	3.00
45	"Red" Kress	8.00	4.00	2.50
46	Earl Averill	50.00	25.00	15.00
47	"Old Os" Vitt	8.00	4.00	2.50
48	"Luke" Sewell	10.00	5.00	3.00
49	"Stormy Weather" Weatherly	8.00	4.00	2.50
50	"Hal" Trosky	8.00	4.00	2.50
51	"Don" Heffner	8.00	4.00	2.50
52	Myril Hoag	8.00	4.00	2.50
53	"Mac" McQuinn	8.00	4.00	2.50
54	"Bill" Trotter	8.00	4.00	2.50
55	"Slick" Coffman	8.00	4.00	2.50
56	"Eddie" Miller	8.00	4.00	2.50
57	Max West	8.00	4.00	2.50
58	"Bill" Posedel	8.00	4.00	2.50
59	"Rabbit" Warstler	8.00	4.00	2.50
60	John Cooney	8.00	4.00	2.50
61	"Tony" Cuccinello	8.00	4.00	2.50
62	"Buddy" Hassett	8.00	4.00	2.50
63	"Pete" Cascarart	8.00	4.00	2.50
64	"Van" Mungo	20.00	10.00	6.00
65	"Fitz" Fitzsimmons	10.00	5.00	3.00
66	"Babe" Phelps	10.00	5.00	3.00
67	"Whit" Wyatt	10.00	5.00	3.00
68	"Dolph" Camilli	12.00	6.00	3.50
69	"Cookie" Lavagetto	12.00	6.00	3.50
70	"Hot Potato" Hamlin	8.00	4.00	2.50
71	"Mel" Almada	8.00	4.00	2.50
72	"Chuck" Dressen	12.00	6.00	3.50
73	"Bucky" Walters	10.00	5.00	3.00
74	"Duke" Derringer	10.00	5.00	3.00
75	"Buck" McCormick	8.00	4.00	2.50
76	"Lonny" Frey	8.00	4.00	2.50
77	"Bill" Hershberger	8.00	4.00	2.50
78	"Lew" Riggs	8.00	4.00	2.50
79	"Wildfire" Craft	8.00	4.00	2.50
80	"Bill" Myers	8.00	4.00	2.50
81	"Wally" Berger	10.00	5.00	3.00
82	"Hank" Gowdy	8.00	4.00	2.50
83	"Clif" Melton (Cliff)	8.00	4.00	2.50
84	"Jo-Jo" Moore	8.00	4.00	2.50
85	"Hal" Schumacher	12.00	6.00	3.50
86	Harry Gumbert	8.00	4.00	2.50
87	Carl Hubbell	85.00	42.00	25.00
88	"Mel" Ott	90.00	45.00	27.00
89	"Bill" Jurges	10.00	5.00	3.00
90	Frank Demaree	8.00	4.00	2.50
91	Bob "Suitcase" Seeds	8.00	4.00	2.50
92	"Whitey" Whitehead	8.00	4.00	2.50
93	Harry "The Horse" Danning	8.00	4.00	2.50
94	"Gus" Suhr	8.00	4.00	2.50
95	"Mul" Mulcahy	8.00	4.00	2.50
96	"Heinie" Mueller	8.00	4.00	2.50
97	"Morry" Arnovich	8.00	4.00	2.50
98	"Pinky" May	8.00	4.00	2.50
99	"Syl" Johnson	8.00	4.00	2.50
100	"Hersh" Martin	8.00	4.00	2.50
101	"Del" Young	8.00	4.00	2.50
102	"Chuck" Klein	75.00	37.00	22.00
103	"Elbie" Fletcher	8.00	4.00	2.50
104	"Big Poison" Waner	60.00	30.00	18.00
105	"Little Poison" Waner	60.00	30.00	18.00
106	"Pep" Young	8.00	4.00	2.50
107	"Arky" Vaughan	45.00	22.00	13.50
108	"Johnny" Rizzo	8.00	4.00	2.50
109	"Don" Padgett	8.00	4.00	2.50
110	"Tom" Sunkel	8.00	4.00	2.50
111	"Mickey" Owen	8.00	4.00	2.50
112	"Jimmy" Brown	8.00	4.00	2.50
113	"Mort" Cooper	8.00	4.00	2.50
114	"Lon" Warneke	8.00	4.00	2.50
115	"Mike" Gonzales (Gonzalez)	8.00	4.00	2.50
116	"Al" Schacht	12.00	6.00	3.50
117	"Dolly" Stark	8.00	4.00	2.50
118	"Schoolboy" Hoyt	50.00	25.00	15.00
119	"Ol Pete" Alexander	85.00	42.00	25.00
120	Walter "Big Train" Johnson	110.00	55.00	33.00
121	Atley Donald	15.00	7.50	4.50
122	"Sandy" Sundra	15.00	7.50	4.50
123	"Hildy" Hildebrand	15.00	7.50	4.50
124	"Colonel" Combs	70.00	35.00	21.00
125	"Art" Fletcher	15.00	7.50	4.50
126	"Jake" Solters	9.00	4.50	2.75
127	"Muddy" Ruel	9.00	4.50	2.75
128	"Pete" Appleton	9.00	4.50	2.75
129	"Bucky" Harris	50.00	25.00	15.00
130	"Deerfoot" Milan	9.00	4.50	2.75
131	"Zeke" Bonura	9.00	4.50	2.75
132	Connie Mack	90.00	45.00	27.00
133	"Jimmie" Foxx	125.00	62.00	37.00
134	"Joe" Cronin	80.00	40.00	24.00
135	"Line Drive" Nelson	9.00	4.50	2.75
136	"Cotton" Pippen	9.00	4.50	2.75
137	"Bing" Miller	9.00	4.50	2.75
138	"Beau" Bell	9.00	4.50	2.75
139	Elden Auker (Eldon)	9.00	4.50	2.75
140	"Dick" Coffman	9.00	4.50	2.75
141	"Casey" Stengel	120.00	60.00	36.00
142	"Highpockets" Kelly	50.00	25.00	15.00
143	"Gene" Moore	9.00	4.50	2.75
144	"Joe" Vosmik	9.00	4.50	2.75
145	"Vito" Tamulis	9.00	4.50	2.75
146	"Tot" Pressnell	9.00	4.50	2.75
147	"Johnny" Hudson	9.00	4.50	2.75
148	"Hugh" Casey	12.00	6.00	3.50
149	"Pinky" Shoffner	9.00	4.50	2.75
150	"Whitey" Moore	9.00	4.50	2.75
151	Edwin Joost	9.00	4.50	2.75
152	"Jimmy" Wilson	9.00	4.50	2.75
153	"Bill" McKechnie	45.00	22.00	13.50
154	"Jumbo" Brown	9.00	4.50	2.75
155	"Ray" Hayworth	9.00	4.50	2.75
156	"Daffy" Dean	20.00	10.00	6.00
157	"Lou" Chiozza	9.00	4.50	2.75
158	"Stonewall" Jackson	50.00	25.00	15.00
159	"Pancho" Snyder	9.00	4.50	2.75
160	"Hans" Lobert	9.00	4.50	2.75
161	"Debs" Garms	9.00	4.50	2.75
162	"Joe" Bowman	9.00	4.50	2.75
163	"Spud" Davis	9.00	4.50	2.75
164	"Ray" Berres	9.00	4.50	2.75
165	"Bob" Klinger	9.00	4.50	2.75
166	"Bill" Brubaker	9.00	4.50	2.75
167	"Frankie" Frisch	60.00	30.00	18.00
168	"Honus" Wagner	125.00	62.00	37.00
169	"Gabby" Street	9.00	4.50	2.75
170	"Tris" Speaker	100.00	50.00	30.00
171	Harry Heilmann	50.00	25.00	15.00
172	"Chief" Bender	50.00	25.00	15.00
173	"Larry" Lajoie	110.00	55.00	33.00
174	"Johnny" Evers	50.00	25.00	15.00
175	"Christy" Mathewson	125.00	62.00	37.00
176	"Heinie" Manush	50.00	25.00	15.00
177	Frank "Homerun" Baker	55.00	27.00	16.50
178	Max Carey	55.00	27.00	16.50
179	George Sisler	70.00	35.00	21.00
180	"Mickey" Cochrane	75.00	37.00	22.00
181	"Spud" Chandler	40.00	20.00	12.00
182	"Knick" Knickerbocker	40.00	20.00	12.00
183	Marvin Breuer	40.00	20.00	12.00
184	"Mule" Haas	35.00	17.50	10.50
185	"Joe" Kuhel	35.00	17.50	10.50
186	Taft Wright	35.00	17.50	10.50
187	"Jimmy" Dykes	40.00	20.00	12.00
188	"Joe" Krakauskas	35.00	17.50	10.50
189	"Jim" Bloodworth	35.00	17.50	10.50
190	"Charley" Berry	35.00	17.50	10.50
191	John Babich	35.00	17.50	10.50
192	"Dick" Siebert	35.00	17.50	10.50
193	"Chubby" Dean	35.00	17.50	10.50
194	"Sam" Chapman	35.00	17.50	10.50
195	"Dee" Miles	35.00	17.50	10.50
196	"Nonny" Nonnenkamp	35.00	17.50	10.50
197	"Lou" Finney	35.00	17.50	10.50
198	"Denny" Galehouse	35.00	17.50	10.50
199	"Pinky" Higgins	35.00	17.50	10.50
200	"Soupy" Campbell	35.00	17.50	10.50
201	Barney McCosky	35.00	17.50	10.50
202	"Al" Milnar	35.00	17.50	10.50

		NR MT	EX	VG
203	"Bad News" Hale	35.00	17.50	10.50
204	Harry Eisenstat	35.00	17.50	10.50
205	"Rollie" Hemsley	35.00	17.50	10.50
206	"Chet" Laabs	35.00	17.50	10.50
207	"Gus" Mancuso	35.00	17.50	10.50
208	Lee Gamble	35.00	17.50	10.50
209	"Hy" Vandenberg	35.00	17.50	10.50
210	"Bill" Lohrman	35.00	17.50	10.50
211	"Pop" Joiner	35.00	17.50	10.50
212	"Babe" Young	35.00	17.50	10.50
213	John Rucker	35.00	17.50	10.50
214	"Ken" O'Dea	35.00	17.50	10.50
215	"Johnnie" McCarthy	35.00	17.50	10.50
216	"Joe" Marty	35.00	17.50	10.50
217	Walter Beck	35.00	17.50	10.50
218	"Wally" Millies	35.00	17.50	10.50
219	"Russ" Bauers	35.00	17.50	10.50
220	Mace Brown	35.00	17.50	10.50
221	Lee Handley	35.00	17.50	10.50
222	"Max" Butcher	35.00	17.50	10.50
223	Hugh "Ee-Yah" Jennings	75.00	37.00	22.00
224	"Pie" Traynor	100.00	50.00	30.00
225	"Shoeless Joe" Jackson	450.00	225.00	135.00
226	Harry Hooper	75.00	37.00	22.00
227	"Pop" Haines	75.00	37.00	22.00
228	"Charley" Grimm	45.00	22.00	13.50
229	"Buck" Herzog	35.00	17.50	10.50
230	"Red" Faber	75.00	37.00	22.00
231	"Dolf" Luque	35.00	17.50	10.50
232	"Goose" Goslin	75.00	37.00	22.00
233	"Moose" Earnshaw	35.00	17.50	10.50
234	Frank "Husk" Chance	90.00	45.00	27.00
235	John J. McGraw	100.00	50.00	30.00
236	"Sunny Jim" Bottomley	75.00	37.00	22.00
237	"Wee Willie" Keeler	90.00	45.00	27.00
238	"Poosh 'Em Up Tony" Lazzeri	50.00	25.00	15.00
239	George Uhle	40.00	17.50	10.50
240	"Bill" Atwood	75.00	17.50	10.50

1941 Play Ball

"DUKE" DERRINGER

4. **PAUL DERRINGER**
Pitcher Cincinnati Reds

Born: Springfield, Ky. October 17, 1906
Bats: Right Throws: Right
Height: 6' 4" Weight: 205 lbs.

It was Paul Derringer, unsuccessful in two previous World Series, who came through last year for the Cincinnati Reds to outpitch Buck Newsom in that seventh and deciding game of the 1940 classic. Paul won two of those important four games necessary for the world's title and it was his great pitching during the season that helped bring the Reds to their second straight pennant. For the third consecutive year, Derringer won 20 or more games—20 in 1940—while yielding only 48 bases on balls in 297 innings in game pitched. Again that he is one of the greatest control pitchers in baseball. It was also Paul who was credited with the National League triumph over the American in the 1940 All-Star game, allowing only 1 hit in two innings and striking out three.

PLAY BALL
Sports Hall of Fame
Also ask for BLONY Super Bubble Gum, "the twist that lasts longer."

GUM, INC., Phila., Pa.

While the card backs are quite similar to the black-and-white cards Gum Incorporated issued in 1940, the card fronts in the 1941 set were printed in color. Many of card photos, however, are just color versions of the player's 1940 card. The cards are still in the 2½'' by 3⅛'' size, but only 72 cards are included in the set. Joe DiMaggio and Ted Williams continue to be the key players in the set, while cards 49-72 are rarer than the lower-numbered cards. The cards were printed in sheets, and can still be found that way, or in paper strips, lacking the cardboard backing.

		NR MT	EX	VG
Complete Set:		5000.00	2500.00	1500.
Common Player: 1-48		25.00	12.50	7.50
Common Player: 49-72		30.00	12.50	9.00
1	"Eddie" Miller	60.00	15.00	7.50
2	Max West	30.00	12.50	7.50
3	"Bucky" Walters	25.00	12.50	7.50
4	"Duke" Derringer	30.00	15.00	9.00
5	"Buck" McCormick	25.00	12.50	7.50
6	Carl Hubbell	90.00	45.00	27.00
7	"The Horse" Danning	25.00	12.50	7.50
8	"Mel" Ott	100.00	50.00	30.00
9	"Pinky" May	25.00	12.50	7.50
10	"Arky" Vaughan	50.00	25.00	15.00
11	Debs Garms	25.00	12.50	7.50

		NR MT	EX	VG
12	"Jimmy" Brown	25.00	12.50	7.50
13	"Jimmie" Foxx	150.00	75.00	45.00
14	"Ted" Williams	600.00	300.00	180.00
15	"Joe" Cronin	65.00	32.00	19.50
16	"Hal" Trosky	25.00	12.50	7.50
17	"Stormy" Weatherly	25.00	12.50	7.50
18	"Hank" Greenberg	125.00	62.00	37.00
19	"Charley" Gehringer	90.00	45.00	27.00
20	"Red" Ruffing	70.00	35.00	21.00
21	"Charlie" Keller	40.00	20.00	12.00
22	"Indian Bob" Johnson	25.00	12.50	7.50
23	"Mac" McQuinn	25.00	12.50	7.50
24	"Dutch" Leonard	25.00	12.50	7.50
25	"Gene" Moore	25.00	12.50	7.50
26	Harry "Gunboat" Gumbert	25.00	12.50	7.50
27	"Babe" Young	25.00	12.50	7.50
28	"Joe" Marty	25.00	12.50	7.50
29	"Jack" Wilson	25.00	12.50	7.50
30	"Lou" Finney	25.00	12.50	7.50
31	"Joe" Kuhel	25.00	12.50	7.50
32	Taft Wright	25.00	12.50	7.50
33	"Happy" Milnar	25.00	12.50	7.50
34	"Rollie" Hemsley	25.00	12.50	7.50
35	"Pinky" Higgins	25.00	12.50	7.50
36	Barney McCosky	25.00	12.50	7.50
37	"Soupy" Campbell	25.00	12.50	7.50
38	Atley Donald	30.00	15.00	9.00
39	"Tommy" Henrich	40.00	20.00	12.00
40	"Johnny" Babich	25.00	12.50	7.50
41	Frank "Blimp" Hayes	25.00	12.50	7.50
42	"Wally" Moses	25.00	12.50	7.50
43	Albert "Bronk" Brancato	25.00	12.50	7.50
44	"Sam" Chapman	25.00	12.50	7.50
45	Elden Auker (Eldon)	25.00	12.50	7.50
46	"Sid" Hudson	25.00	12.50	7.50
47	"Buddy" Lewis	25.00	12.50	7.50
48	Cecil Travis	25.00	12.50	7.50
49	"Babe" Dahlgren	30.00	15.00	9.00
50	"Johnny" Cooney	30.00	15.00	9.00
51	"Dolph" Camilli	35.00	17.50	10.50
52	Kirby Higbe	35.00	17.50	10.50
53	Luke "Hot Potato" Hamlin	30.00	15.00	9.00
54	"Pee Wee" Reese	250.00	125.00	75.00
55	"Whit" Wyatt	35.00	17.50	10.50
56	"Vandy" Vander Meer	40.00	20.00	12.00
57	"Moe" Arnovich	30.00	15.00	9.00
58	"Frank" Demaree	30.00	15.00	9.00
59	"Bill" Jurges	30.00	15.00	9.00
60	"Chuck" Klein	80.00	40.00	24.00
61	"Vince" DiMaggio	80.00	40.00	24.00
62	"Elbie" Fletcher	30.00	15.00	9.00
63	"Dom" DiMaggio	80.00	40.00	24.00
64	"Bobby" Doerr	80.00	40.00	24.00
65	"Tommy" Bridges	35.00	17.50	10.50
66	Harland Clift (Harlond)	30.00	15.00	9.00
67	"Walt" Judnich	30.00	15.00	9.00
68	"Jack" Knott	30.00	15.00	9.00
69	George Case	30.00	15.00	9.00
70	"Bill" Dickey	225.00	112.00	67.00
71	"Joe" DiMaggio	850.00	425.00	255.00
72	"Lefty" Gomez	225.00	112.00	67.00

1985 Polaroid/J.C. Penney Indians

Polaroid
JCPenney

JOE
CARTER
Outfielder

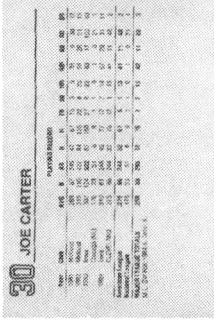

JOE CARTER

30

While the Cleveland Indians continued its four-year tradition of baseball card promotional game issues in

1985, the sponsor changed from Wheaties to Polaroid/JC Penney. The 32-card set features 30 player cards, a manager card and a group card of the coaching staff. Though produced in the "safety set" format — slightly oversize (2-13/16" by 4-1/8"), with wide white borders — the Indians cards carry no safety message. Backs, once again numbered by uniform number, contain major and minor league stats.

		MT	NR MT	EX
Complete Set:		8.00	6.00	3.25
Common Player:		.15	.11	.06
2	Brett Butler	.35	.25	.14
4	Tony Bernazard	.20	.15	.08
8	Carmen Castillo	.15	.11	.06
10	Pat Tabler	.40	.30	.15
12	Benny Ayala	.15	.11	.06
13	Ernie Camacho	.15	.11	.06
14	Julio Franco	.60	.45	.25
16	Jerry Willard	.15	.11	.06
18	Pat Corrales	.20	.15	.08
20	Otis Nixon	.20	.15	.08
21	Mike Hargrove	.25	.20	.10
22	Mike Fischlin	.15	.11	.06
23	Chris Bando	.15	.11	.06
24	George Vukovich	.15	.11	.06
26	Brook Jacoby	.70	.50	.30
27	Mel Hall	.35	.25	.14
28	Bert Blyleven	.50	.40	.20
29	Andre Thornton	.35	.25	.14
30	Joe Carter	.70	.50	.30
32	Rick Behenna	.15	.11	.06
33	Roy Smith	.15	.11	.06
35	Jerry Reed	.20	.15	.08
36	Jamie Easterly	.15	.11	.06
38	Dave Von Ohlen	.15	.11	.06
41	Rich Thompson	.15	.11	.06
43	Bryan Clark	.15	.11	.06
44	Neal Heaton	.30	.25	.12
48	Vern Ruhle	.15	11	.06
49	Jeff Barkley	.15	.11	.06
50	Ramon Romero	.15	.11	.06
54	Tom Waddell	.20	.15	.08
---	Tribe Coaching Staff (Bobby Bonds, Johnny Goryl, Don McMahon, Ed Napolean, Dennis Sommers)	.20	.15	.08

1979 Police/Fire Safety Giants

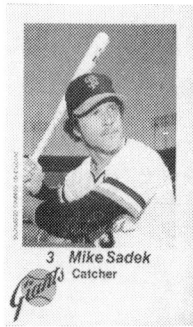

3 Mike Sadek
Catcher

Tips from
the Giants

Balk

Each of the full-color cards measures 2⅝" by 4⅛" and is numbered by player uniform number. The set includes 20 Giants players and coaches. The player's name, position and facsimile autograph are the card fronts, along with the Giants logo. Card backs have a "Tip from the Giants" and sponsor logos for the Giants and radio station KNBR, all printed in the Giants' orange and black colors. Half of the set was distributed at a ballpark promotion during the 1979 season, while the other cards were available only from police agencies in several San Francisco Bay area counties.

		NR MT	EX	VG
Complete Set		14.00	7.00	4.25
Common Player		.30	.15	.09
1	Dave Bristol	.30	.15	.09
2	Marc Hill	.30	.15	.09
3	Mike Sadek	.50	.25	.15
5	Tom Haller	.30	.15	.09
6	Joe Altobelli	.50	.25	.15
8	Larry Shepard	.50	.25	.15
9	Heity Cruz	.30	.15	.09
10	Johnnie LeMaster	.30	.15	.09
12	Jim Davenport	.30	.15	.09
14	Vida Blue	.90	.45	.25
15	Mike Ivie	.30	.15	.09
16	Roger Metzger	.30	.15	.09
17	Randy Moffitt	.30	.15	.09
18	Bill Madlock	1.25	.60	.40
21	Rob Andrews	.50	.25	.15
22	Jack Clark	2.00	1.00	.60
25	Dave Roberts	.30	.15	.09
26	John Montefusco	.50	.25	.15
28	Ed Halicki	.50	.25	.15
30	John Tamargo	.30	.15	.09
31	Larry Herndon	.50	.25	.15
36	Bill North	.50	.25	.15
39	Bob Knepper	.70	.35	.20
40	John Curtis	.50	.25	.15
41	Darrell Evans	1.25	.60	.40
43	Tom Griffin	.50	.25	.15
44	Willie McCovey	3.00	1.50	.90
46	Gary Lavelle	.50	.25	.15
49	Max Venable	.50	.25	.15

1980 Police/Fire Safety Columbus Clippers

Columbus Clippers
LH Pitcher
DAVE RIGHETTI—24

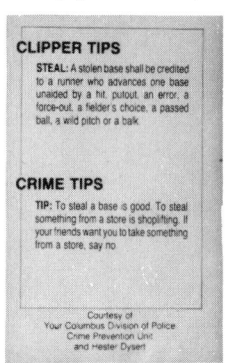

CLIPPER TIPS

STEAL: A stolen base shall be credited to a runner who advances one base unaided by a hit, putout, an error, a force-out, a fielder's choice, a passed ball, a wild pitch or a balk.

CRIME TIPS

TIP: To steal a base is good. To steal something from a store is shoplifting. If your friends want you to take something from a store, say no.

Courtesy of
Your Columbus Division of Police
Crime Prevention Unit
and Hester Dysert

This minor league police safety set was issued by the Columbus, Ohio, Police Department. The Columbus Clippers were then affiliated with the New York Yankees. This set contains 25 cards including one of Dave Righetti. The cards are printed with full-color fronts and player statistics on the back along with a safety message. The cards are 2⅜" by 3¾" size. Complete sets can still be found with moderate effort.

		NR MT	EX	VG
Complete Set		25.00	12.50	7.50
Common Player		.70	.35	.20
2	Brian Doyle	.80	.40	.25
11	Roger Holt	.70	.35	.20
12	Dennis Sherrill	.70	.35	.20
14	Joe Lefebvre	.80	.40	.25
15	Garry Smith	.70	.35	.20
16	Joe Altibelli (Altobelli) (manager)	.90	.45	.25
17	Dave Coleman	.70	.35	.20
18	Roger Slagle	.70	.35	.20
20	Brad Gulden	.70	.35	.20
21	Jim Lewis	.70	.35	.20
22	Marv Thompson	.70	.35	.20
23	Tim Lollar	.90	.45	.25
24	Dave Righetti	6.50	3.25	2.00

		NR MT	EX	VG
25	Roy Staiger	.70	.35	.20
26	Bruce Robinson	.70	.35	.20
27	Greg Cochran	.70	.35	.20
28	Jim Nettles	.70	.35	.20
29	Bob Kammeyer	.70	.35	.20
30	Dave Wehrmeister	.70	.35	.20
31	Jim McDonald	.70	.35	.20
33	Marshall Brandt (Brant)	.70	.35	.20
34	Chris Welsh	.70	.35	.20
36	Ken Clay	.70	.35	.20
---	George H. Sisler Jr. (general manager)	.70	.35	.20
---	Coaches/Trainer Card (Sammy Ellis, Mark Letendre, Jerry McNertney)	.70	.35	.20

1980 Police/Fire Safety Dodgers

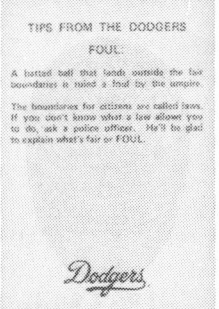

Producers of one of the most popular police and safety sets in baseball, the Los Angeles Dodgers began this successful promotion in 1980. The 2-13/16'' by 4-1/8'' cards feature attractive, full-color photos on the card fronts, along with brief personal statistics. Card backs include "Tips from the Dodgers" along with the team and Los Angeles Police Department logos. The 30 cards are numbered by player uniform number, with an unnumbered team card also included in the set.

		NR MT	EX	VG
	Complete Set:	8.00	4.00	2.50
	Common Player:	.30	.15	.09
5	Johnny Oates	.30	.15	.09
6	Steve Garvey	1.50	.70	.45
7	Steve Yeager	.30	.15	.09
8	Reggie Smith	.50	.25	.15
9	Gary Thomasson	.30	.15	.09
10	Ron Cey	.50	.25	.15
12	Dusty Baker	.50	.25	.15
13	Joe Ferguson	.30	.15	.09
15	Davey Lopes	.50	.25	.15
16	Rick Monday	.50	.25	.15
18	Bill Russell	.40	.20	.12
20	Don Sutton	.80	.40	.25
21	Jay Johnstone	.40	.20	.12
23	Teddy Martinez	.30	.15	.09
27	Joe Beckwith	.30	.15	.09
28	Pedro Guerrero	1.00	.50	.30
29	Don Stanhouse	.30	.15	.09
30	Derrel Thomas	.30	.15	.09
31	Doug Rau	.30	.15	.09
34	Ken Brett	.30	.15	.09
35	Bob Welch	.50	.25	.15
37	Robert Castillo	.30	.15	.09
38	Dave Goltz	.40	.20	.12
41	Jerry Reuss	.50	.25	.15
43	Rick Sutcliffe	.50	.25	.15
44	Mickey Hatcher	.30	.15	.09
46	Burt Hooton	.40	.20	.12
49	Charlie Hough	.40	.20	.12
51	Terry Forster	.40	.20	.12
---	Team Photo	.30	.15	.09

1980 Police/Fire Safety Giants

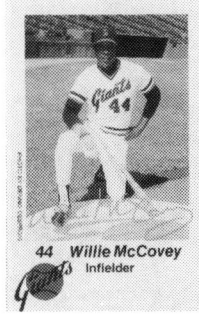

The 1980 Giants police set is virtually identical in format to its 1979 forerunner. Card design and colors are the same on both front and back, with radio station KNBR and the S.F. Police Department once again co-sponsors. The 2⅝'' by 4⅛'' cards again feature fronts with full-color photos and facsimile autographs, while backs are in the team's orange and black colors. The set numbers 31 players and coaches, with each card numbered by uniform number. As in 1979, half the cards were distributed at a stadium promotion, with the remainder available only from police officers.

		NR MT	EX	VG
	Complete Set:	9.00	4.50	2.75
	Common Player:	.30	.15	.09
1	Dave Bristol	.30	.15	.09
2	Marc Hill	.30	.15	.09
3	Mike Sadek	.30	.15	.09
5	Jim Lefebvre	.30	.15	.09
6	Rennie Stennett	.30	.15	.09
7	Milt May	.30	.15	.09
8	Vern Benson	.30	.15	.09
9	Jim Wohlford	.30	.15	.09
10	Johnnie LeMaster	.30	.15	.09
12	Jim Davenport	.30	.15	.09
14	Vida Blue	.90	.45	.25
15	Mike Ivie	.30	.15	.09
16	Roger Metzger	.30	.15	.09
17	Randy Moffitt	.30	.15	.09
19	Al Holland	.30	.15	.09
20	Joe Strain	.30	.15	.09
22	Jack Clark	1.50	.70	.45
26	John Montefusco	.40	.20	.12
28	Ed Halicki	.30	.15	.09
31	Larry Herndon	.50	.25	.15
32	Ed Whitson	.40	.20	.12
36	Bill North	.40	.20	.12
38	Greg Minton	.40	.20	.12
39	Bob Knepper	.50	.25	.15
41	Darrell Evans	.90	.45	.25
42	John Van Ornum	.30	.15	.09
43	Tom Griffin	.30	.15	.09
44	Willie McCovey	2.50	1.25	.70
45	Terry Whitfield	.30	.15	.09
46	Gary Lavelle	.40	.20	.12
47	Don McMahon	.30	.15	.09

1981 Police/Fire Safety Braves

The first Atlanta Braves police set was a cooperative effort of the team, Hostess, Coca-Cola and the Atlanta Police Department. Card fronts feature full-color photos of 27 different Braves and manager Bobby Cox. Police and team logos are on the card backs. Card backs offer capsule biographies of the players, along with a tip for youngsters. The 2⅝'' by 4⅛'' cards are numbered by uniform number. Terry

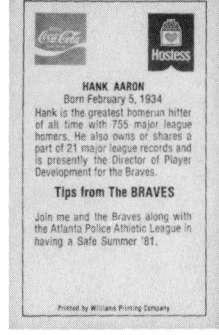

HANK AARON
Born February 5, 1934
Hank is the greatest homerun hitter of all time with 755 major league homers. He also owns or shares a part of 21 major league records and is presently the Director of Player Development for the Braves.

Tips from The BRAVES

Join me and the Braves along with the Atlanta Police Athletic League in having a Safe Summer '81.

Printed by Williams Printing Company

Hank Aaron
Outfield
6-0—189

Harper, #19, appears to be somewhat scarcer than the other cards in the set. Reportedly, 33,000 sets were printed.

		MT	NR MT	EX
Complete Set:		12.00	9.00	4.75
Common Player:		.30	.25	.12
1	Jerry Royster	.30	.25	.12
3	Dale Murphy	2.25	1.75	.90
4	Biff Pocoroba	.30	.25	.12
5	Bob Horner	1.00	.70	.40
6	Bob Cox	.30	.25	.12
9	Luis Gomez	.30	.25	.12
10	Chris Chambliss	.40	.30	.15
15	Bill Nahorodny	.30	.25	.12
16	Rafael Ramirez	.35	.25	.14
17	Glenn Hubbard	.35	.25	.14
18	Claudell Washington	.40	.30	.15
19	Terry Harper	.70	.50	.30
20	Bruce Benedict	.30	.25	.12
24	John Montefusco	.30	.25	.12
25	Rufino Linares	.30	.25	.12
26	Gene Garber	.30	.25	.12
30	Brian Asselstine	.30	.25	.12
34	Larry Bradford	.30	.25	.12
35	Phil Niekro	1.25	.90	.50
37	Rick Camp	.30	.25	.12
39	Al Hrabosky	.35	.25	.14
40	Tommy Boggs	.30	.25	.12
42	Rick Mahler	.40	.30	.15
45	Ed Miller	.30	.25	.12
46	Gaylord Perry	1.25	.90	.50
49	Preston Hanna	.30	.25	.12
---	Hank Aaron	2.25	1.75	.90

1981 Police/Fire Safety Columbus Clippers

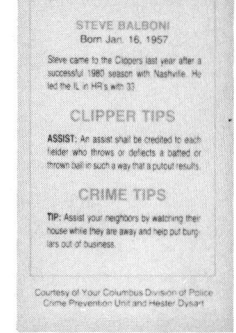

STEVE BALBONI
Born Jan. 16, 1957

Steve came to the Clippers last year after a successful 1980 season with Nashville. He led the IL in HR's with 33.

CLIPPER TIPS

ASSIST: An assist shall be credited to each fielder who throws or deflects a batted or thrown ball in such a way that a putout results.

CRIME TIPS

TIP: Assist your neighbors by watching their house while they are away and help put burglars out of business.

1981 Columbus Clippers
Infielder
STEVE BALBONI—37

Courtesy of Your Columbus Division of Police Crime Prevention Unit and Hester Dysart

The Columbus Clippers minor league team (then affiliated with the New York Yankees) are featured for the second consecutive year. The set contained 25 full-color cards in the 2⅜'' by 3¾'' size. Card backs feature player biographies and a safety tip. The set, sponsored by the Columbus Police Department, is not too difficult to find.

		MT	NR MT	EX
Complete Set		14.00	10.50	5.50
Common Player		.30	.25	.12
2	Andre Robertson	.50	.40	.20
6	Dan Schmitz	.30	.25	.12
11	Buck Showalter	.30	.25	.12
12	Tucker Ashford	.30	.25	.12
13	Garry Smith	.30	.25	.12
15	Rick Stenholm	.30	.25	.12
17	Dave Coleman	.30	.25	.12
21	Jim Lewis	.30	.25	.12
22	Wayne Harer	.30	.25	.12
23	Pat Callahan	.30	.25	.12
24	Dave Righetti	3.00	2.25	1.25
25	Pat Tabler	2.00	1.50	.80
26	Frank Verdi (manager)	.30	.25	.12
27	Greg Cochran	.30	.25	.12
28	Dave Wehrmeister	.30	.25	.12
29	Juan Espino	.35	.25	.14
30	John Pacella	.30	.25	.12
31	Paul Boris	.30	.25	.12
33	Marshall Brant	.30	.25	.12
35	Brian Ryder	.30	.25	.12
36	Mike Griffin	.40	.30	.15
37	Steve Balboni	1.25	.90	.50
---	Sgt. Dick Hoover (policeman)	.30	.25	.12
---	George H. Sisler Jr. (general manager)	.30	.25	.12
---	Coaches/Trainer Card (Sammy Ellis, Mark Letendre, Jerry McNertney)	.30	.25	.12

1981 Police/Fire Safety Dodgers

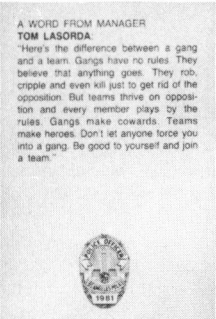

A WORD FROM MANAGER TOM LASORDA

"Here's the difference between a gang and a team. Gangs have no rules. They believe that anything goes. They rob, cripple and even kill just to get rid of the opposition. Gangs make cowards. Teams make heroes. Don't let anyone force you into a gang. Be good to yourself and join a team."

TOM LASORDA
No. 2 — Manager
LAPD SALUTES THE 1981
Dodgers

Very similar in format to their successful set of the year before, the Los Angeles Dodgers 1981 police set grew to 32 cards (from 30). This was due to the acquisitions of Ken Landreaux and Dave Stewart shortly before printing of the sets. These two cards may even have been added after the initial printing run, making them slightly more difficult to obtain. The full-color cards are again 2-13/16'' by 4-1/8'', with a safety tip on the card back. Each card front has the line "LAPD Salutes the 1981 Dodgers."

		MT	NR MT	EX
Complete Set		9.00	6.75	3.50
Common Player		.20	.15	.08
2	Tom Lasorda	.40	.30	.15
3	Rudy Law	.20	.15	.08
6	Steve Garvey	1.00	.70	.40
7	Steve Yeager	.20	.15	.08
8	Reggie Smith	.40	.30	.15
10	Ron Cey	.40	.30	.15
12	Dusty Baker	.35	.25	.14
13	Joe Ferguson	.20	.15	.08
14	Mike Scioscia	.25	.20	.10

		MT	NR MT	EX
15	Davey Lopes	.35	.25	.14
16	Rick Monday	.35	.25	.14
18	Bill Russell	.30	.25	.12
21	Jay Johnstone	.25	.20	.10
26	Don Stanhouse	.20	.15	.08
27	Joe Beckwith	.20	.15	.08
28	Pete Guerrero	.70	.50	.30
30	Derrel Thomas	.20	.15	.08
34	Fernando Valenzuela	2.00	1.50	.80
35	Bob Welch	.35	.25	.14
36	Pepe Frias	.20	.15	.08
37	Robert Castillo	.20	.15	.08
38	Dave Goltz	.25	.20	.10
41	Jerry Reuss	.35	.25	.14
43	Rick Sutcliffe	.50	.40	.20
44a	Mickey Hatcher	.25	.20	.10
44b	Ken Landreaux	.70	.50	.30
46	Burt Hooton	.25	.20	.10
48	Dave Stewart	1.00	.70	.40
51	Terry Forster	.25	.20	.10
57	Steve Howe	.30	.25	.12
---	Coaching Staff (Monty Basgall, Mark Cresse, Tom Lasorda, Manny Mota, Danny Ozark, Ron Perranoski)	.20	.15	.08
---	Team Photo/Checklist	.20	.15	.08

1981 Police/Fire Safety Mariners

These 2⅝'' by 4⅛'' cards were co-sponsored by the Washington State Crime Prevention Assoc., Coca-Cola, Kiwanis and Ernst Home Centers. There are 16 players featured in this full-color set, with each card numbered in the lower-left of the card back. Card fronts list player name and position and have a team logo. Card backs are printed in blue and red and offer a "Tip from the Mariners" along with the four sponsor logos.

		MT	NR MT	EX
	Complete Set:	5.00	3.75	2.00
	Common Player:	.25	.20	.10
1	Jeff Burroughs	.40	.30	.15
2	Floyd Bannister	.60	.45	.25
3	Glenn Abbott	.25	.20	.10
4	Jim Anderson	.25	.20	.10
5	Danny Meyer	.25	.20	.10
6	Dave Edler	.25	.20	.10
7	Julio Cruz	.30	.25	.12
8	Kenny Clay	.25	.20	.10
9	Lenny Randle	.25	.20	.10
10	Mike Parrott	.25	.20	.10
11	Tom Paciorek	.40	.30	.15
12	Jerry Narron	.25	.20	.10
13	Richie Zisk	.50	.40	.20
14	Maury Wills	.50	.40	.20
15	Joe Simpson	.25	.20	.10
16	Shane Rawley	.60	.45	.25

NOTE: A card number in parentheses ( ) indicates the set is unnumbered.

1981 Police/Fire Safety Royals

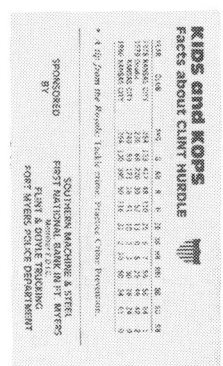

Ten of the most popular 1981 Kansas City players are featured in this 2½'' by 4⅛'' card set. Card fronts feature full-color photos with player name, position, facsimile autograph and team logo. Backs include player statistics, a tip from the Royals and list the four sponsoring organizations. Surprisingly, the set was issued by the Ft. Myers, Fla., police department, near the Royals' spring training headquarters.

		MT	NR MT	EX
	Complete Set:	24.00	18.00	9.50
	Common Player:	.35	.25	.14
(1)	Willie Mays Aikens	.35	.25	.14
(2)	George Brett	15.00	11.00	6.00
(3)	Rich Gale	.35	.25	.14
(4)	Clint Hurdle	.35	.25	.14
(5)	Dennis Leonard	1.00	.70	.40
(6)	Hal McRae	1.25	.90	.50
(7)	Amos Otis	1.00	.70	.40
(8)	U.L. Washington	.35	.25	.14
(9)	Frank White	1.25	.90	.50
(10)	Willie Wilson	2.00	1.50	.80

1982 Police/Fire Safety Braves

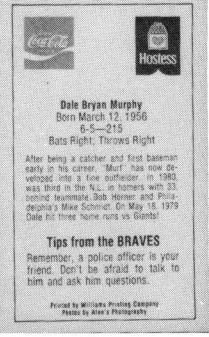

After their successful debut in 1981, the Atlanta Braves, the Atlanta Police Department, Coca-Cola and Hostess issued another card set in '82. This 30-card set is extremely close in format to the 1981 set and again measures 2⅝'' by 4⅛.'' The full-color player photos are outstanding, and each card front also bears a statement marking the '82 Braves record-breaking, 13-game, season-opening win streak.

Card backs offer short biographies and "Tips from the Braves." Sponsors logos are also included. Reportedly, only 8,000 of these sets were printed.

		MT	NR MT	EX
Complete Set:		18.00	13.50	7.25
Common Player:		.30	.25	.12
1	Jerry Royster	.30	.25	.12
3	Dale Murphy	2.50	2.00	1.00
4	Biff Pocoroba	.30	.25	.12
5	Bob Horner	1.25	.90	.50
6	Randy Johnson	.30	.25	.12
8	Bob Watson	2.00	1.50	.80
9	Joe Torre	.40	.30	.15
10	Chris Chambliss	.40	.30	.15
15	C. Washington	.40	.30	.15
16	Rafael Ramirez	.35	.25	.14
17	Glenn Hubbard	.35	.25	.14
20	Bruce Benedict	.30	.25	.12
22	Brett Butler	.70	.50	.30
23	Tommie Aaron	.40	.30	.15
25	Rufino Linares	.30	.25	.12
26	Gene Garber	.30	.25	.12
27	Larry McWilliams	.30	.25	.12
28	Larry Whisenton	.30	.25	.12
32	Steve Bedrosian	1.00	.70	.40
35	Phil Niekro	1.25	.90	.50
37	Rick Camp	.30	.25	.12
38	Joe Cowley	.35	.25	.14
39	Al Hrabosky	.35	.25	.14
42	Rick Mahler	.40	.30	.15
43	Bob Walk	.30	.25	.12
45	Bob Gibson	1.25	.90	.50
49	Preston Hanna	.30	.25	.12
52	Joe Pignatano	.30	.25	.12
53	Dal Maxvill	.30	.25	.12
54	Rube Walker	.30	.25	.12

1982 Police/Fire Safety Brewers

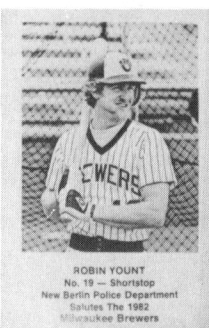
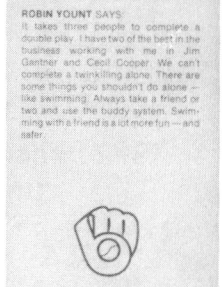

ROBIN YOUNT SAYS:
It takes three people to complete a double play. I have two of the best in the business working with me in Jim Gantner and Cecil Cooper. We can't complete a twinkilling alone. There are some things you shouldn't do alone — like swimming. Always take a friend or two and use the buddy system. Swimming with a friend is a lot more fun — and safer.

ROBIN YOUNT
No. 19 — Shortstop
New Berlin Police Department
Salutes The 1982
Milwaukee Brewers

The inaugural Milwaukee Brewers police set contains 30 cards in a 2-13/16" by 4-1/8" format. There are 26 players included in the set, which is numbered by player uniform number. Unnumbered cards were also issued for general manager Harry Dalton, manager Buck Rodgers, the coaches and a team card with checklist. The full-color photos are especially attractive, printed on the cards' crisp white stock. Several variations exist, as a number of Milwaukee area law enforcement agencies distributed the cards, and credit lines on the card fronts were changed accord-

		MT	NR MT	EX
Complete Set:		8.00	6.00	3.25
Common Player:		.20	.15	.08
4	Paul Molitor	.70	.50	.30
5	Ned Yost	.20	.15	.08
7	Don Money	.25	.20	.10
9	Larry Hisle	.25	.20	.10
10	Bob McClure	.20	.15	.08
11	Ed Romero	.20	.15	.08

		MT	NR MT	EX
13	Roy Howell	.20	.15	.08
15	Cecil Cooper	.50	.40	.20
17	Jim Gantner	.30	.25	.12
19	Robin Yount	1.00	.70	.40
20	Gorman Thomas	.40	.30	.15
22	Charlie Moore	.20	.15	.08
23	Ted Simmons	.50	.40	.20
24	Ben Oglivie	.30	.25	.12
26	Kevin Bass	.60	.45	.25
28	Jamie Easterly	.20	.15	.08
29	Mark Brouhard	.20	.15	.08
30	Moose Haas	.20	.15	.08
34	Rollie Fingers	.60	.45	.25
35	Randy Lerch	.20	.15	.08
37	Buck Rodgers	.20	.15	.08
41	Jim Slaton	.20	.15	.08
45	Doug Jones	.20	.15	.08
46	Jerry Augustine	.20	.15	.08
47	Dwight Bernard	.20	.15	.08
48	Mike Caldwell	.25	.20	.10
50	Pete Vuckovich	.30	.25	.12
---	Team Photo/Checklist	.20	.15	.08
---	Harry Dalton (general mgr.)	.20	.15	.08
---	Coaches Card (Pat Dobson, Larry Haney, Ron Hansen, Cal McLish, Buck Rodgers, Harry Warner)	.20	.15	.08

1982 Police/Fire Safety Columbus Clippers

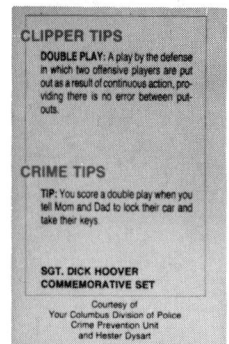

CLIPPER TIPS

DOUBLE PLAY: A play by the defense in which two offensive players are put out as a result of continuous action, providing there is no error between putouts.

CRIME TIPS

TIP: You score a double play when you tell Mom and Dad to lock their car and take their keys.

SGT. DICK HOOVER
COMMEMORATIVE SET
Courtesy of
Your Columbus Division of Police
Crime Prevention Unit
and Hester Dysart

1982 Columbus Clippers
STEVE BALBONI
First Base — No. 35
6 3″ 225 lbs.

The most valuable of all the Columbus Clipper sets, this 1982 issue (2⅜" by 3¾") contains Don Mattingly card. A complete set consists of 25 cards with full-color fronts and player biographies on the back. The Columbus Clipper card sets were issued in conjunction with the Columbus, Ohio, Police Department and distributed by the team at the Clippers ballpark and by police officers in the community.

		MT	NR MT	EX
Complete Set		32.00	24.00	13.00
Common Player		.30	.25	.12
2	Andre Robertson	.40	.30	.15
6	Dan Schmitz	.30	.25	.12
11	Scott Patterson	.30	.25	.12
12	Tucker Ashford	.30	.25	.12
13	Garry Smith	.30	.25	.12
14	Mike Patterson	.30	.25	.12
15	Jamie Werly	.30	.25	.12
17	John Pacella	.30	.25	.12
19	Don Mattingly	24.00	18.00	9.50
21	Jim Lewis	.30	.25	.12
22	Wayne Harer	.30	.25	.12
23	Dave Stegman	.30	.25	.12
24	Curt Kaufman	.30	.25	.12
25	Mike Bruhert	.30	.25	.12
26	Frank Verdi (manager)	.30	.25	.12
27	Greg Cochran	.30	.25	.12
28	Dave Wehrmeister	.30	.25	.12
29	Juan Espino	.30	.25	.12
30	Pete Filson	.35	.25	.14
31	Bobby Ramos	.30	.25	.12

		MT	NR MT	EX
33	Marshall Brant	.30	.25	.12
35	Steve Balboni	.70	.50	.30
38	Bob Sykes	.30	.25	.12
---	George H. Sisler Jr. (general manager)	.30	.25	.12
---	Coaches/Trainer Card (Steve Donohue, Sammy Ellis, Jerry McNertney)	.30	.25	.12

1982 Police/Fire Safety Dodgers

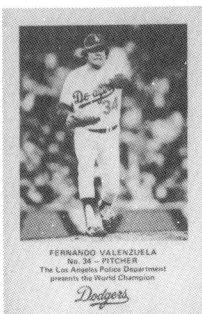
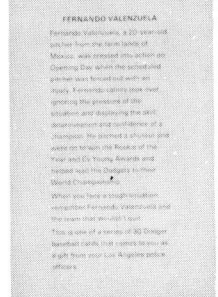

Again issued in the same 2-13/16'' by 4-1/8'' size of the '80 and '81 sets, the 1982 Los Angeles set commemorates the team's 1981 World Championship. In addition to the 26 cards numbered by uniform for players and manager Tom Lasorda, there are four unnumbered cards which feature the team winning the division, league and World Series titles, plus one of the World Series trophy. The full-color card photos are once again vivid portraits on a clean white card stock. Card backs offer brief biographies and stadium information in addition to a safety tip.

		MT	NR MT	EX
Complete Set		6.00	4.50	2.50
Common Player		.15	.11	.06
2	Tom Lasorda	.30	.25	.12
6	Steve Garvey	1.00	.70	.40
7	Steve Yeager	.15	.11	.06
8	Mark Belanger	.20	.15	.08
10	Ron Cey	.30	.25	.12
12	Dusty Baker	.25	.20	.10
14	Mike Scioscia	.20	.15	.08
16	Rick Monday	.25	.20	.10
18	Bill Russell	.20	.15	.08
21	Jay Johnstone	.20	.15	.08
26	Alejandro Pena	.30	.25	.12
28	Pedro Guerrero	.70	.50	.30
30	Derrel Thomas	.15	.11	.06
31	Jorge Orta	.15	.11	.06
34	Fernando Valenzuela	1.00	.70	.40
35	Bob Welch	.25	.20	.10
38	Dave Goltz	.20	.15	.08
40	Ron Roenicke	.15	.11	.06
41	Jerry Reuss	.25	.20	.10
44	Ken Landreaux	.20	.15	.08
46	Burt Hooton	.20	.15	.08
48	Dave Stewart	.25	.20	.10
49	Tom Niedenfuer	.40	.30	.15
51	Terry Forster	.20	.15	.08
52	Steve Sax	.90	.70	.35
57	Steve Howe	.20	.15	.08
---	Division Championship	.15	.11	.06
---	League Championship	.15	.11	.06
---	World Series Championship	.15	.11	.06
---	Trophy Card/Checklist	.15	.11	.06

Definitions for grading conditions are located in the Introduction of this price guide.

1983 Police/Fire Safety Braves

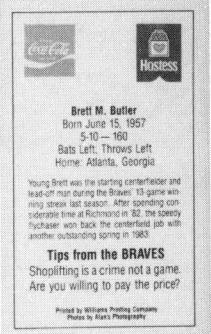

An almost exact replica of their 1982 set, the 1983 Atlanta police set includes 30 cards numbered by uniform. Sponsors Hostess, Coca-Cola and the Atlanta Police Department returned for the third year. The cards are again 2⅝'' by 4⅛,'' with full-color photos and police and team logos on the card fronts. A statement noting the team's 1982 National League Western Division title in the upper right corner is the key difference on the card fronts. As in 1982, 8,000 sets were reportedly printed.

		MT	NR MT	EX
Complete Set:		12.00	9.00	4.75
Common Player:		.25	.20	.10
1	Jerry Royster	.30	.25	.12
3	Dale Murphy	2.25	1.75	.90
4	Biff Pocoroba	.30	.25	.12
5	Bob Horner	1.00	.70	.40
6	Randy Johnson	.30	.25	.12
8	Bob Watson	.35	.25	.14
9	Joe Torre	.40	.30	.15
10	Chris Chambliss	.40	.30	.15
11	Ken Smith	.30	.25	.12
15	Claudell Washington	.40	.30	.15
16	Rafael Ramirez	.35	.25	.14
17	Glenn Hubbard	.35	.25	.14
19	Terry Harper	.30	.25	.12
20	Bruce Benedict	.30	.25	.12
22	Brett Butler	.40	.30	.15
24	Larry Owen	.30	.25	.12
26	Gene Garber	.30	.25	.12
27	Pascual Perez	.30	.25	.12
29	Craig McMurtry	.35	.25	.14
32	Steve Bedrosian	.60	.45	.25
33	Pete Falcone	.30	.25	.12
35	Phil Niekro	1.25	.90	.50
36	Sonny Jackson	.30	.25	.12
37	Rick Camp	.30	.25	.12
45	Bob Gibson	1.25	.90	.50
49	Rick Behenna	.30	.25	.12
51	Terry Forster	.35	.25	.14
52	Joe Pignatano	.30	.25	.12
53	Dal Maxvill	.30	.25	.12
54	Rube Walker	.30	.25	.12

1983 Police/Fire Safety Brewers

Similar to 1982, a number of issuer variations exist for the 1983 Brewers police set, as law enforcement agencies throughout the state distributed the set with their own credit lines on the cards. At least 28 variations are known to exist, with those issued by smaller agencies being scarcest. Prices quoted below are the most common variations, generally the Milwaukee P.D. and a few small-town departments whose entire supply of police cards seem to have fallen into

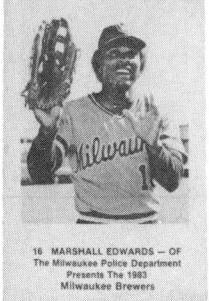

MARSHALL EDWARDS SAYS
Outfielders use judgement to play the game properly. We must judge fly balls and line drives and react quickly. Use good judgement when choosing your friends. Follow people who set a good example, someone you can learn from. If you get involved with bad friends, react quickly, get away from them before they get you in trouble.

16 MARSHALL EDWARDS — OF
The Milwaukee Police Department
Presents The 1983
Milwaukee Brewers

dealers' hands. Some specialists are willing to pay a premium for the scarcer departments' issues. The 30 2-13/16'' by 4-1/8'' cards include 29 players and coaches, along with a team card (with checklist back). The team card and group coaches' card are unnumbered, while the others are numbered by uniform number.

		MT	NR MT	EX
Complete Set:		6.50	5.00	2.50
Common Player:		.20	.15	.08
4	Paul Molitor	.70	.50	.30
5	Ned Yost	.20	.15	.08
7	Don Money	.25	.20	.10
8	Rob Picciolo	.20	.15	.08
10	Bob McClure	.20	.15	.08
11	Ed Romero	.20	.15	.08
13	Roy Howell	.20	.15	.08
15	Cecil Cooper	.50	.40	.20
16	Marshall Edwards	.20	.15	.08
17	Jim Gantner	.30	.25	.12
19	Robin Yount	1.00	.70	.40
20	Gorman Thomas	.40	.30	.15
21	Don Sutton	.60	.45	.25
22	Charlie Moore	.20	.15	.08
23	Ted Simmons	.50	.40	.20
24	Ben Oglivie	.30	.25	.12
26	Bob Skube	.20	.15	.08
27	Pete Ladd	.20	.15	.08
28	Jamie Easterly	.20	.15	.08
30	Moose Haas	.20	.15	.08
32	Harvey Kuenn	.30	.25	.12
34	Rollie Fingers	.60	.45	.25
40	Bob Gibson	.20	.15	.08
41	Jim Slaton	.20	.15	.08
42	Tom Tellmann	.20	.15	.08
46	Jerry Augustine	.20	.15	.08
48	Mike Caldwell	.25	.20	.10
50	Pete Vuckovich	.30	.25	.12
---	Team Photo/Checklist	.20	.15	.08
---	Coaches Card (Pat Dobson, Dave Garcia, Larry Haney, Ron Hansen)	.20	.15	.08

1983 Police/Fire Safety Dodgers

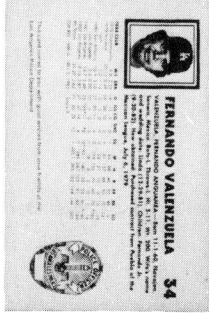

While these full-color cards remained 2-13/16'' by 4-1/8'' and card fronts were similar to those of previous years, the card backs are quite different. Card backs are in a horizontal design for the first time, and include a small head portrait photo of the player in the upper-left corner. Fairly complete player statistics are included but there is no safety tip. The 30 cards are numbered by uniform number, with an unnumbered coaches card also included. Fronts include the year, team logo, player name and number.

		MT	NR MT	EX
Complete Set		6.00	4.50	2.50
Common Player		.15	.11	.06
2	Tom Lasorda	.30	.25	.12
3	Steve Sax	.50	.40	.20
5	Mike Marshall	.60	.45	.25
7	Steve Yeager	.15	.11	.06
12	Dusty Baker	.25	.20	.10
14	Mike Scioscia	.20	.15	.08
16	Rick Monday	.25	.20	.10
17	Greg Brock	.40	.30	.15
18	Bill Russell	.20	.15	.08
20	Candy Maldonado	.40	.30	.15
21	Ricky Wright	.15	.11	.06
22	Mark Bradley	.15	.11	.06
23	Dave Sax	.15	.11	.06
26	Alejandro Pena	.20	.15	.08
27	Joe Beckwith	.15	.11	.06
28	Pedro Guerrero	.60	.45	.25
30	Derrel Thomas	.15	.11	.06
34	Fernando Valenzuela	.70	.50	.30
35	Bob Welch	.25	.20	.10
38	Pat Zachry	.15	.11	.06
40	Ron Roenicke	.15	.11	.06
41	Jerry Reuss	.25	.20	.10
43	Jose Morales	.15	.11	.06
44	Ken Landreaux	.20	.15	.08
46	Burt Hooton	.20	.15	.08
47	Larry White	.15	.11	.06
48	Dave Stewart	.25	.20	.10
49	Tom Niedenfuer	.25	.20	.10
57	Steve Howe	.35	.25	.14
---	Coaches Card (Joe Amalfitano, Monty Basgall, Mark Cresse, Manny Mota, Ron Perranoski)	.15	.11	.06

1983 Police/Fire Safety Royals

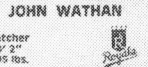

JOHN WATHAN
Catcher
6' 2''
205 lbs.

After skipping the 1982 season, the Ft. Myers, Fla., police department issued a Royals safety set in 1983 that was almost identical to their set of 1981. The set was again 2½'' by 4⅛'' and numbered just 10 players. Cards are unnumbered, with vertical fronts and horizontal backs. Card fronts have team logos, player name and postion and facsimile autographs. Backs list the four sponsoring organizations, a "Tip from the Royals" and a "Kids and Cops Fact" about each player.

		MT	NR MT	EX
	Complete Set:	24.00	18.00	9.50
	Common Player:	.35	.25	.14
(1)	Willie Mays Aikens	.35	.25	.14
(2)	George Brett	15.00	11.00	6.00
(3)	Dennis Leonard	1.00	.70	.40
(4)	Hal McRae	1.25	.90	.50
(5)	Amos Otis	1.00	.70	.40
(6)	Dan Quisenberry	2.00	1.50	.80
(7)	U.L. Washington	.35	.25	.14
(8)	John Wathan	.50	.40	.20
(9)	Frank White	1.25	.90	.50
(10)	Willie Wilson	2.00	1.50	.80

		MT	NR MT	EX
53	Dennis Lamp	.20	.15	.08
---	Team Logo/Checklist	.20	.15	.08

1984 Police/Fire Safety Blue Jays

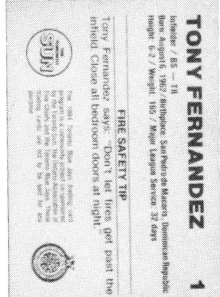

This 35-card set was issued in conjuction with the *Toronto Sun* newspaper and various Ontario area fire departments. The cards feature full-color action photos on the fronts, along with player name, number and position. Rather than the customary wide white border on front, the Blue Jays fire safety set features bright blue borders. The card backs include brief player biographies and a fire safety tip. The 2½'' by 3½'' cards were distributed five at a time at two-week intervals during the summer of 1984.

		MT	NR MT	EX
	Complete Set:	10.00	7.50	4.00
	Common Player:	.20	.15	.08
1	Tony Fernandez	1.00	.70	.40
3	Jimy Williams	.20	.15	.08
4	Alfredo Griffin	.30	.25	.12
5	Rance Mulliniks	.20	.15	.08
6	Bobby Cox	.20	.15	.08
7	Damaso Garcia	.30	.25	.12
8	John Sullivan	.20	.15	.08
9	Rick Leach	.20	.15	.08
10	Dave Collins	.25	.20	.10
11	George Bell	1.00	.70	.40
12	Ernie Whitt	.30	.25	.12
13	Buck Martinez	.20	.15	.08
15	Lloyd Moseby	.60	.45	.25
16	Garth Iorg	.20	.15	.08
17	Kelly Gruber	.25	.20	.10
18	Jim Clancy	.30	.25	.12
23	Mitch Webster	.60	.45	.25
24	Willie Aikens	.20	.15	.08
25	Roy Lee Jackson	.20	.15	.08
26	Willie Upshaw	.40	.30	.15
27	Jimmy Key	1.00	.70	.40
29	Jesse Barfield	.80	.60	.30
31	Jim Acker	.20	.15	.08
33	Doyle Alexander	.30	.25	.12
34	Stan Clarke	.20	.15	.08
35	Bryan Clark	.20	.15	.08
37	Dave Stieb	.60	.45	.25
38	Jim Gott	.20	.15	.08
41	Al Widmar	.20	.15	.08
42	Billy Smith	.20	.15	.08
43	Cito Gaston	.20	.15	.08
44	Cliff Johnson	.20	.15	.08
48	Luis Leal	.20	.15	.08

1984 Police/Fire Safety Braves

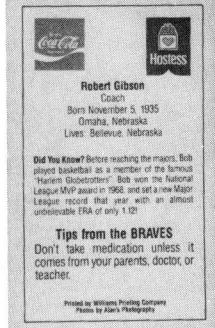

A fourth annual effort by the Braves, the Atlanta Police Department, Coca-Cola and Hostess. This 30-card set continued to be printed in a 2⅝'' by 4⅛'' format, with full-color photos plus team and police logos on the card fronts. For the first time, the cards also have a large logo and date in the upper right corner. Hostess and Coke logos again are on the card backs, with brief player information and a safety tip. Two cards in the set (Pascual Perez and Rafael Ramirez) were issued in Spanish. Cards were distributed two per week by Atlanta police officers. As in 1982 and 1983, a reported 8,000 sets were printed.

		MT	NR MT	EX
	Complete Set:	11.00	8.25	4.50
	Common Player:	.25	.20	.10
1	Jerry Royster	.25	.20	.10
3	Dale Murphy	2.25	1.75	.90
5	Bob Horner	1.00	.70	.40
6	Randy Johnson	.25	.20	.10
8	Bob Watson	.30	.25	.12
9	Joe Torre	.40	.30	.15
10	Chris Chambliss	.40	.30	.15
11	Mike Jorgensen	.25	.20	.10
15	Claudell Washington	.40	.30	.15
16	Rafael Ramirez	.30	.25	.12
17	Glenn Hubbard	.30	.25	.12
19	Terry Harper	.25	.20	.10
20	Bruce Benedict	.25	.20	.10
25	Alex Trevino	.25	.20	.10
26	Gene Garber	.25	.20	.10
27	Pascual Perez	.30	.25	.12
28	Gerald Perry	.70	.50	.30
29	Craig McMurtry	.25	.20	.10
31	Donnie Moore	.25	.20	.10
32	Steve Bedrosian	.60	.45	.25
33	Pete Falcone	.25	.20	.10
37	Rick Camp	.25	.20	.10
39	Len Barker	.30	.25	.12
42	Rick Mahler	.40	.30	.15
45	Bob Gibson	1.00	.70	.40
51	Terry Forster	.30	.25	.12
52	Joe Pignatano	.25	.20	.10
53	Dal Maxvill	.25	.20	.10
54	Rube Walker	.25	.20	.10
55	Luke Appling	.60	.45	.25

1984 Police/Fire Safety Brewers

The king of the variations again in 1984, the Milwaukee Brewers set has been found with more than 50

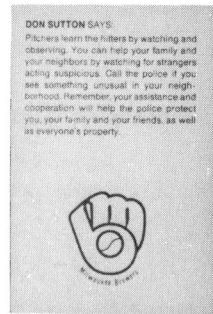

DON SUTTON SAYS:
Pitchers learn the hitters by watching and observing. You can help your family and your neighbors by watching for strangers acting suspicious. Call the police if you see something unusual in your neighborhood. Remember, your assistance and cooperation will help the police protect you, your family and your friends, as well as everyone's property.

20 DON SUTTON — P
The Winneconne Police Department Presents the 1984
MILWAUKEE BREWERS

different police agencies' credit lines on the front of the cards. Once again, statewide law enforcement agencies participated in distributing the sets. Some departments also include a badge of the participating agency on the card backs. The full-color cards measure 2-13/16'' by 4-1/8.'' There are 28 numbered player and manager cards, along with an unnumbered coaches card and a team card. Player names, uniform numbers and positions are listed on each card front. Prices listed are for the most common variety (Milwaukee P.D.); sets issued by smaller departments may be worth a premium to specialists.

		MT	NR MT	EX
Complete Set		6.00	4.50	2.50
Common Player		.15	.11	.06
2	Randy Ready	.30	.25	.12
4	Paul Molitor	.60	.45	.25
8	Jim Sundberg	.15	.11	.06
9	Rene Lachemann	.15	.11	.06
10	Bob McClure	.15	.11	.06
11	Ed Romero	.15	.11	.06
13	Roy Howell	.15	.11	.06
14	Dion James	.50	.40	.20
15	Cecil Cooper	.40	.30	.15
17	Jim Gantner	.25	.20	.10
19	Robin Yount	.90	.70	.35
20	Don Sutton	.50	.40	.20
21	Bill Schroeder	.40	.30	.15
22	Charlie Moore	.15	.11	.06
23	Ted Simmons	.40	.30	.15
24	Ben Oglivie	.25	.20	.10
25	Bobby Clark	.15	.11	.06
27	Pete Ladd	.15	.11	.06
28	Rick Manning	.15	.11	.06
29	Mark Brouhard	.15	.11	.06
30	Moose Haas	.15	.11	.06
34	Rollie Fingers	.50	.40	.20
42	Tom Tellmann	.15	.11	.06
43	Chuck Porter	.15	.11	.06
46	Jerry Augustine	.15	.11	.06
47	Jaime Cocanower	.15	.11	.06
48	Mike Caldwell	.20	.15	.08
50	Pete Vuckovich	.25	.20	.10
---	Team Photo/Checklist	.15	.11	.06
---	Coaches Card (Pat Dobson, Dave Garcia, Larry Haney, Tom Trebelhorn)	.15	.11	.06

1984 Police/Fire Safety Columbus Clippers

The Columbus Clippers, in conjunction with the Columbus, Ohio, Police Department, issued this, their fourth card set after skipping 1983. The cards are distributed each season at the Clippers ballpark and at local police departments. The 1984 set contained 25 cards with full-color fronts and player biographies on the back. The cards measure 2-3/8'' by 3-3/4.''

Definitions for grading conditions are located in the Introduction of this price guide.

BUTCH HOBSON
Born Aug. 17, 1951

1984 Columbus Clippers
BUTCH HOBSON

CLIPPER TIPS

UMPIRE: Responsible for the conduct of the game in accordance to the rules and for maintaining discipline and order.

CRIME TIPS

		MT	NR MT	EX
Complete Set		8.00	6.00	3.25
Common Player		.20	.15	.08
2	Andre Robertson	.30	.25	.12
4	Kelly Heath	.20	.15	.08
12	Rex Hudler	.20	.15	.08
14	Victor Mata	.40	.30	.15
15	Mike O'Berry	.20	.15	.08
17	Butch Hobson	.30	.25	.12
19	Kelly Scott	.20	.15	.08
20	Curt Brown	.20	.15	.08
21	Brian Dayett	.25	.20	.10
23	Dan Briggs	.20	.15	.08
24	Mike Pagliarulo	3.00	2.25	1.25
25	Don Fowler	.20	.15	.08
27	Don Cooper	.20	.15	.08
29	Pat Rooney	.20	.15	.08
31	Scott Patterson	.20	.15	.08
32	Matt Winters	.20	.15	.08
34	George Cappuzzello	.20	.15	.08
36	Joe Cowley	.30	.25	.12
38	Clay Christiansen	.20	.15	.08
39	Dennis Rasmussen	.80	.60	.30
40	Scott Bradley	.50	.40	.20
42	Pete Dalena	.20	.15	.08
---	"Stump" Merrill (manager)	.20	.15	.08
---	George H. Sisler Jr. (general manager)	.20	.15	.08
---	Coaches/Trainer Card (Mark Connor, Steve Donohue, Gil Patterson, Mickey Vernon)	.20	.15	.08

1984 Police/Fire Safety Dodgers

Dodgers MIKE MARSHALL 1984 5

MIKE MARSHALL

This was the fifth yearly effort of the Dodgers and the Los Angeles Police Department. There are 30 cards in the set, which remains 2-13/16'' by 4-1/8.'' Card fronts are designed somewhat differently than previous years, with more posed photos, bolder player names and numbers and a different team logo. Card backs again feature a small portrait photo in the upper-left corner, along with brief biographical information and an anti-drug tip. Card backs are in Dodger blue. Cards are numbered by uniform number, with an unnumbered coaches card also included.

		MT	NR MT	EX
	Common Player	.15	.11	.06
2	Complete Set, Tom Lasorda	.30	.25	.12
3	Steve Sax	.50	.40	.20
5	Mike Marshall	.40	.30	.15
7	Steve Yeager	.15	.11	.06
9	Greg Brock	.30	.25	.12
10	Dave Anderson	.20	.15	.08
14	Mike Scioscia	.20	.15	.08
16	Rick Monday	.25	.20	.10
17	Rafael Landestoy	.15	.11	.06
18	Bill Russell	.20	.15	.08
20	Candy Maldonado	.30	.25	.12
21	Bob Bailor	.15	.11	.06
25	German Rivera	.15	.11	.06
26	Alejandro Pena	.20	.15	.08
27	Carlos Diaz	.15	.11	.06
28	Pedro Guerrero	.60	.45	.25
31	Jack Fimple	.15	.11	.06
34	Fernando Valenzuela	.70	.50	.30
35	Bob Welch	.25	.20	.10
38	Pat Zachry	.15	.11	.06
40	Rick Honeycutt	.20	.15	.08
41	Jerry Reuss	.25	.20	.10
43	Jose Morales	.15	.11	.06
44	Ken Landreaux	.20	.15	.08
45	Terry Whitfield	.15	.11	.06
46	Burt Hooton	.20	.15	.08
49	Tom Niedenfuer	.25	.20	.10
55	Orel Hershiser	1.00	.70	.40
56	Richard Rodas	.15	.11	.06
---	Coaches Card (Joe Amalfitano, Monty Basgall, Mark Cresse, Manny Mota, Ron Perranoski)	.15	.11	.06

1985 Police/Fire Safety Blue Jays

The Toronto Blue Jays issued a 35-card fire safety set for the second year in a row in 1985. Cards feature players, coaches, manager, checklist and team picture. The full-color photos are on the card fronts with a blue border. The backs feature player stats and a safety tip. The cards measure 2½'' by 3½'' and were distributed throughout the Province of Ontario, Canada.

		MT	NR MT	EX
	Complete Set:	8.00	6.00	3.25
	Common Player:	.20	.15	.08
1	Tony Fernandez	.50	.40	.20
3	Jimy Williams	.20	.15	.08
4	Manny Lee	.25	.20	.10
5	Rance Mulliniks	.20	.15	.08
6	Bobby Cox	.20	.15	.08
7	Damaso Garcia	.30	.25	.12
8	John Sullivan	.20	.15	.08
11	George Bell	1.00	.70	.40
12	Ernie Whitt	.30	.25	.12
13	Buck Martinez	.20	.15	.08
15	Lloyd Moseby	.40	.30	.15

		MT	NR MT	EX
16	Garth Iorg	.20	.15	.08
17	Kelly Gruber	.20	.15	.08
18	Jim Clancy	.30	.25	.12
22	Jimmy Key	.50	.40	.20
23	Mitch Webster	.30	.25	.12
24	Willie Aikens	.20	.15	.08
25	Len Matuszek	.20	.15	.08
26	Willie Upshaw	.30	.25	.12
28	Lou Thornton	.25	.20	.10
29	Jesse Barfield	.80	.60	.30
30	Ron Musselman	.20	.15	.08
31	Jim Acker	.20	.15	.08
33	Doyle Alexander	.30	.25	.12
36	Bill Caudill	.20	.15	.08
37	Dave Stieb	.50	.40	.20
41	Al Widmar	.20	.15	.08
42	Billy Smith	.20	.15	.08
43	Cito Gaston	.20	.15	.08
44	Jeff Burroughs	.20	.15	.08
46	Gary Lavelle	.20	.15	.08
48	Luis Leal	.20	.15	.08
50	Tom Henke	.40	.30	.15
53	Dennis Lamp	.20	.15	.08
---	Team Logo/Checklist	.20	.15	.08
---	Team Photo/Schedule	.20	.15	.08

1985 Police/Fire Safety Braves

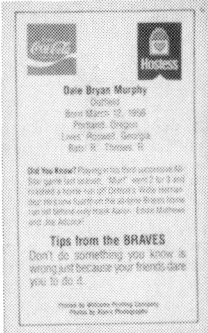

There are again 30 full-color cards in this fifth annual set. Hostess, Coca-Cola and the Atlanta Police Department joined the team as sponsors again for the 2⅝'' by 4⅛'' set. Card backs are similar to previous years, with the only difference on the fronts being a swap in position for the year and team logo. The cards are checklisted by uniform number.

		MT	NR MT	EX
	Complete Set	11.00	8.25	4.50
	Common Player	.25	.20	.10
2	Albert Hall	.40	.30	.15
3	Dale Murphy	2.25	1.75	.90
5	Rick Cerone	.25	.20	.10
7	Bobby Wine	.25	.20	.10
10	Chris Chambliss	.35	.25	.14
11	Bob Horner	1.00	.70	.40
12	Paul Runge	.30	.25	.12
15	Claudell Washington	.35	.25	.14
16	Rafael Ramirez	.30	.25	.12
17	Glenn Hubbard	.30	.25	.12
18	Paul Zuvella	.30	.25	.12
19	Terry Harper	.25	.20	.10
20	Bruce Benedict	.25	.20	.10
22	Eddie Haas	.25	.20	.10
24	Ken Oberkfell	.30	.25	.12
26	Gene Garber	.25	.20	.10
27	Pascual Perez	.30	.25	.12
28	Gerald Perry	.40	.30	.15
29	Craig McMurtry	.25	.20	.10
32	Steve Bedrosian	.50	.40	.20
33	Johnny Sain	.35	.25	.14
34	Zane Smith	.60	.45	.25
36	Brad Komminsk	.30	.25	.12

		MT	NR MT	EX
37	Rick Camp	.25	.20	.10
39	Len Barker	.30	.25	.12
40	Bruce Sutter	.70	.50	.30
42	Rick Mahler	.35	.25	.14
51	Terry Forster	.30	.25	.12
52	Leo Mazzone	.25	.20	.10
53	Bobby Dews	.25	.20	.10

1985 Police/Fire Safety Brewers

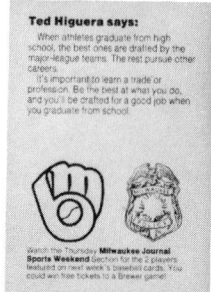

Ted Higuera says: When athletes graduate from high school, the best ones are drafted by the major-league teams. The rest pursue other careers.

It's important to learn a trade or profession. Be the best at what you do, and you'll be drafted for a good job when you graduate from school.

49 **Ted Higuera** P
The Milwaukee Police Department and The Milwaukee Journal present the 1985 **Milwaukee Brewers**

Watch the Thursday **Milwaukee Journal Sports Weekend** section for the 2 players featured on next week's baseball cards. You could win free tickets to a Brewer game!

The Brewers changed the size of their annual police set in 1985, but almost imperceptibly. The full-color cards are 2¾" by 4⅛," a slight 1/16" narrower than the four previous efforts. Player and team name on the card fronts are much bolder than in previous years. Once again, numerous area police groups distributed the sets, leading to nearly 60 variations, as each agency put their own credit line on the cards. Card backs include the Brewers logo, a safety tip and, in some cases, a badge of the participating law enforcement group. There are 27 numbered playercards (by uniform number) and three unnumbered cards — team roster, coaches and a newspaper carrier card. Prices are for the most common departments.

		MT	NR MT	EX
	Complete Set	6.00	4.50	2.50
	Common Player	.15	.11	.06
2	Randy Ready	.15	.11	.06
4	Paul Molitor	.60	.45	.25
5	Doug Loman	.15	.11	.06
7	Paul Householder	.15	.11	.06
10	Bob McClure	.15	.11	.06
11	Ed Romero	.15	.11	.06
14	Dion James	.30	.25	.12
15	Cecil Cooper	.40	.30	.15
17	Jim Gantner	.25	.20	.10
18	Danny Darwin	.20	.15	.08
19	Robin Yount	.90	.70	.35
21	Bill Schroeder	.20	.15	.08
22	Charlie Moore	.15	.11	.06
23	Ted Simmons	.40	.30	.15
24	Ben Oglivie	.25	.20	.10
26	Brian Giles	.15	.11	.06
27	Pete Ladd	.15	.11	.06
28	Rick Manning	.15	.11	.06
29	Mark Brouhard	.15	.11	.06
30	Moose Haas	.15	.11	.06
31	George Bamberger	.15	.11	.06
34	Rollie Fingers	.50	.40	.20
40	Bob Gibson	.15	.11	.06
41	Ray Searage	.15	.11	.06
47	Jaime Cocanower	.15	.11	.06
48	Ray Burris	.15	.11	.06
49	Ted Higuera	1.00	.70	.40
50	Pete Vuckovich	.25	.20	.10
---	Coaches Card (Andy Etchebarren, Larry Haney, Frank Howard, Tony Muser, Herm Starrette)	.15	.11	.06
---	Team Photo	.15	.11	.06

1985 Police/Fire Safety Columbus Clippers

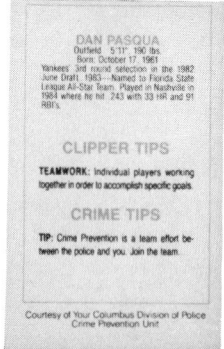

DAN PASQUA
Outfield 5'11" 190 lbs
Born: October 17, 1961
Yankees' 3rd round selection in the 1982 June Draft, 1983 — Named to Florida State League All-Star Team. Played in Nashville in 1984 where he hit .243 with 33 HR and 91 RBI's

CLIPPER TIPS

TEAMWORK: Individual players working together in order to accomplish specific goals.

CRIME TIPS

TIP: Crime Prevention is a team effort between the police and you. Join the team.

1985 Columbus Clippers
DAN PASQUA
Outfielder—No. 21
6'0" 203 lbs.

Courtesy of Your Columbus Division of Police
Crime Prevention Unit

The 1985 edition of this minor league team issue was, once again, 25 cards. The Columbus Clippers were affiliated with the New York Yankees and had issued sets each year (except 1983) since 1980. The cards are 2⅜" by 3¾." They have a full-color player picture on the front and a brief biography with a safety tip on the back.

		MT	NR MT	EX
	Complete Set	7.00	5.25	2.75
	Common Player	.20	.15	.08
1	Kelly Heath	.20	.15	.08
3	Tom Barrett	.20	.15	.08
5	Kelly Scott	.20	.15	.08
11	Alphonso Pulido (Alfonso)	.25	.20	.10
12	Rex Hudler	.20	.15	.08
14	Pete Dalena	.20	.15	.08
15	Tim Knight	.20	.15	.08
16	Bert Bradley	.20	.15	.08
17	Butch Hobson	.30	.25	.12
18	Matt Winters	.20	.15	.08
19	Keith Smith	.20	.15	.08
20	Curt Brown	.20	.15	.08
21	Dan Pasqua	2.00	1.50	.80
23	Dan Briggs	.20	.15	.08
26	Al Williams	.20	.15	.08
27	Don Cooper	.20	.15	.08
29	Juan Espino	.20	.15	.08
37	Brian Fisher	.80	.60	.30
38	Jim Deshaies	.80	.60	.30
39	Clay Christiansen	.20	.15	.08
42	Mark Silva	.20	.15	.08
44	Kelly Faulk	.20	.15	.08
---	Carl "Stump" Merrill (manager)	.20	.15	.08
---	Coaches/Trainer Card (Steve Donohue, Q.V. Lowe, Jerry McNertney, Mickey Vernon)	.20	.15	.08
---	George H. Sisler Jr. (general manager)	.20	.15	.08

1985 Police/Fire Safety Phillies

This is a brilliantly colored 2⅝" by 4⅛" set, co-sponsored by the Phillies and Cigna Corporation. Card fronts include player name, number, position and team logo. The 16 cards are numbered on the back, and include biographical information and a safety tip. The cards were distributed by several Philadelphia area police departments.

Definitions for grading conditions are located in the Introduction of this price guide.

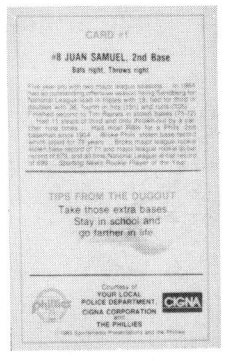

		MT	NR MT	EX
6	Hal Lanier	.25	.20	.10
7	Denny Walling	.20	.15	.08
8	Alan Ashby	.20	.15	.08
9	Phil Garner	.25	.20	.10
10	Charlie Kerfeld	.40	.30	.15
11	Dave Smith	.30	.25	.12
12	Jose Cruz	.40	.30	.15
13	Craig Reynolds	.20	.15	.08
14	Mark Bailey	.20	.15	.08
15	Bob Knepper	.30	.25	.12
16	Julio Solano	.20	.15	.08
17	Dickie Thon	.25	.20	.10
18	Mike Madden	.20	.15	.08
19	Jeff Calhoun	.20	.15	.08
20	Tony Walker	.25	.20	.10
21	Terry Puhl	.20	.15	.08
22	Glenn Davis	1.00	.70	.40
23	Billy Hatcher	.40	.30	.15
24	Jim Deshaies	.50	.40	.20
25	Frank DiPino	.20	.15	.08
26	Coaching Staff (Yogi Berra, Matt Galante, Denis Menke, Les Moss, Gene Tenace)	.20	.15	.08

1986 Police/Fire Safety Blue Jays

This was the third consecutive year the Toronto Blue Jays issued a team fire safety set of 36 baseball cards. Over four million cards were reportedly printed and given out at every fire station in Ontario, Canada. The cards are printed in full color and include players and other personnel. The set was co-sponsored by the local fire departments, Bubble Yum and the *Toronto Star*. The cards measure 2½'' by 3½.''

		MT	NR MT	EX
Complete Set:		8.00	6.00	3.25
Common Player:		.20	.15	.08
1	Tony Fernandez	.50	.40	.20
3	Jimy Williams	.20	.15	.08
5	Rance Mulliniks	.20	.15	.08
7	Damaso Garcia	.30	.25	.12
8	John Sullivan	.20	.15	.08
9	Rick Leach	.20	.15	.08
11	George Bell	1.00	.70	.40
12	Ernie Whitt	.30	.25	.12
13	Buck Martinez	.20	.15	.08
15	Lloyd Moseby	.40	.30	.15
16	Garth Iorg	.20	.15	.08
17	Kelly Gruber	.20	.15	.08
18	Jim Clancy	.30	.25	.12
22	Jimmy Key	.50	.40	.20
23	Cecil Fielder	.30	.25	.12
24	John McLaren	.15	.11	.06
25	Steve Davis	.20	.15	.08
26	Willie Upshaw	.30	.25	.12
29	Jesse Barfield	.80	.60	.30
31	Jim Acker	.20	.15	.08
33	Doyle Alexander	.30	.25	.12
36	Bill Caudill	.20	.15	.08
37	Dave Stieb	.50	.40	.20
38	Mark Eichhorn	.50	.40	.20
39	Don Gordon	.25	.20	.10
41	Al Widmar	.20	.15	.08

		MT	NR MT	EX
Complete Set:		6.00	4.50	2.50
Common Player:		.15	.11	.06
1	Juan Samuel	.50	.40	.20
2	Von Hayes	.40	.30	.15
3	Ozzie Virgil	.20	.15	.08
4	Mike Schmidt	1.00	.70	.40
5	Greg Gross	.15	.11	.06
6	Tim Corcoran	.15	.11	.06
7	Jerry Koosman	.25	.20	.10
8	Jeff Stone	.25	.20	.10
9	Glenn Wilson	.30	.25	.12
10	Steve Jeltz	.25	.20	.10
11	Garry Maddox	.20	.15	.08
12	Steve Carlton	.70	.50	.30
13	John Denny	.20	.15	.08
14	Kevin Gross	.30	.25	.12
15	Shane Rawley	.30	.25	.12
16	Charlie Hudson	.30	.25	.12

1986 Police/Fire Safety Astros

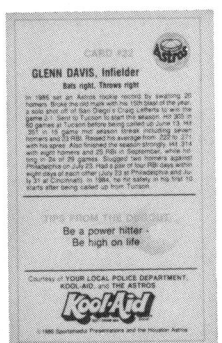

This full-color police safety set for the 1986 Houston Astros was issued by the Houston Police Department and sponsored by Kool-Aid. The 26-card set was distributed at the Astrodome on June 14, when 15,000 sets of the first 12 cards were given away. The balance of the set was distributed throughout the summer by the Houston police. The cards feature player photos on the front and a safety tip on the card back. The cards measure 4⅛'' by 2⅝.''

		MT	NR MT	EX
Complete Set:		8.00	6.00	3.25
Common Player:		.20	.15	.08
1	Jim Pankovits	.20	.15	.08
2	Nolan Ryan	1.00	.70	.40
3	Mike Scott	.60	.45	.25
4	Kevin Bass	.40	.30	.15
5	Bill Doran	.40	.30	.15

		MT	NR MT	EX
42	Billy Smith	.20	.15	.08
43	Cito Gaston	.20	.15	.08
44	Cliff Johnson	.20	.15	.08
46	Gary Lavelle	.20	.15	.08
49	Tom Filer	.20	.15	.08
50	Tom Henke	.40	.30	.15
53	Dennis Lamp	.20	.15	.08
54	Jeff Hearron	.20	.15	.08
---	Team Photo	.20	.15	.08
---	10th Anniversary Logo Card	.20	.15	.08

1986 Police/Fire Safety Braves

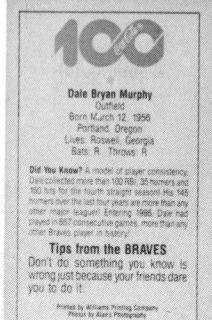

The Police Athletic League of Atlanta issued a 30-card full-color set featuring the Atlanta Braves players and personnel. The cards measure 2⅝'' by 4⅛.'' Card fronts include player photos with name, uniform number and position below the photo. The cards backs offer the 100th Anniversary Coca-Cola logo, player information, statistics and a safety related tip. This is the sixth consecutive year that the Braves issued a safety set. The cards were available from police officers in Atlanta.

		MT	NR MT	EX
	Complete Set	11.00	8.25	4.50
	Common Player	.25	.20	.10
2	Russ Nixon	.25	.20	.10
3	Dale Murphy	2.00	1.50	.80
4	Bob Skinner	.25	.20	.10
5	Billy Sample	.25	.20	.10
7	Chuck Tanner	.35	.25	.14
8	Willie Stargell	.80	.60	.30
9	Ozzie Virgil	.35	.25	.14
10	Chris Chambliss	.35	.25	.14
11	Bob Horner	1.00	.70	.40
14	Andres Thomas	.50	.40	.20
15	Claudell Washington	.35	.25	.14
16	Rafael Ramirez	.30	.25	.12
17	Glenn Hubbard	.30	.25	.12
18	Omar Moreno	.25	.20	.10
19	Terry Harper	.25	.20	.10
20	Bruce Benedict	.25	.20	.10
23	Ted Simmons	.50	.40	.20
24	Ken Oberkfell	.30	.25	.12
26	Gene Garber	.25	.20	.10
29	Craig McMurtry	.25	.20	.10
30	Paul Assenmacher	.40	.30	.15
33	Johnny Sain	.30	.25	.12
34	Zane Smith	.40	.30	.15
38	Joe Johnson	.30	.25	.12
40	Bruce Sutter	.60	.45	.25
42	Rick Mahler	.35	.25	.14
46	David Palmer	.30	.25	.12
48	Duane Ward	.30	.25	.12
49	Jeff Dedmon	.25	.20	.10
52	Al Monchak	.25	.20	.10

1986 Police/Fire Safety Brewers

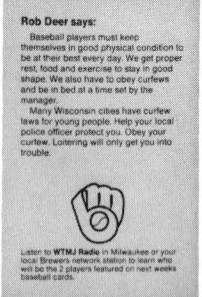

The Milwaukee Brewers, in conjunction with the Milwaukee Police Department, WTMJ Radio and Kinney Shoes, produced this attractive police safety set of 30 cards. The cards measure 2-13/16'' by 4-1/2.'' A thin black border encloses a full-color player photo on the front. The card backs give a safety tip and promos for the sponsor. The cards were distributed throughout the state of Wisconsin by numerous police departments; those of the smaller departments generally being scarcer than those issued in the big cities. Prices quoted below are for the most common departments' issues.

		MT	NR MT	EX
	Complete Set:	6.00	4.50	2.50
	Common Player:	.15	.11	.06
1	Ernest Riles	.50	.40	.20
2	Randy Ready	.15	.11	.06
3	Juan Castillo	.25	.20	.10
4	Paul Molitor	.60	.45	.25
7	Paul Householder	.15	.11	.06
10	Bob McClure	.15	.11	.06
11	Rick Cerone	.15	.11	.06
13	Billy Jo Robidoux	.40	.30	.15
15	Cecil Cooper	.40	.30	.15
16	Mike Felder	.30	.25	.12
17	Jim Gantner	.25	.20	.10
18	Danny Darwin	.20	.15	.08
19	Robin Yount	.90	.70	.35
20	Juan Nieves	.80	.60	.30
21	Bill Schroeder	.20	.15	.08
22	Charlie Moore	.15	.11	.06
24	Ben Oglivie	.25	.20	.10
25	Mark Clear	.15	.11	.06
28	Rick Manning	.15	.11	.06
31	George Bamberger	.15	.11	.06
37	Dan Plesac	.80	.60	.30
39	Tim Leary	.15	.11	.06
41	Ray Searage	.15	.11	.06
43	Chuck Porter	.15	.11	.06
45	Rob Deer	.50	.40	.20
46	Bill Wegman	.40	.30	.15
47	Jamie Cocanower	.15	.11	.06
49	Ted Higuera	.50	.40	.20
---	Coaches Card (Andy Etchebarren, Larry Haney, Frank Howard, Tony Muser, Herm Starrette)	.15	.11	.06
---	Team Photo/Roster	.15	.11	.06

1986 Police/Fire Safety Columbus Clippers

This was the sixth year that the Columbus Clippers issued a baseball card set, and the 1986 edition celebrated the Clippers 10th Anniversary. The 25-card set features full-color player photos on the card front with player name, position, height, weight and club logos. The card backs have player biographies and safety tip. The cards were printed courtesy of the

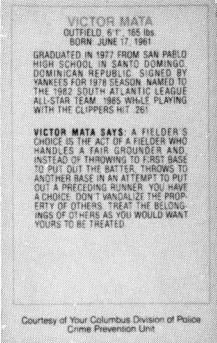

Columbus Police Crime Prevention Unit. The Clippers were affiliated with the New York Yankees. Cards measure 2⅜" by 3¾."

		MT	NR MT	EX
Complete Set:		6.00	4.50	2.50
Common Player:		.20	.15	.08
(1)	Mike Armstrong	.20	.15	.08
(2)	Brad Arnsberg	.50	.40	.20
(3)	Clay Christiansen	.20	.15	.08
(4)	Pete Dalena	.20	.15	.08
(5)	Orestes Destrade	.70	.50	.30
(6)	Doug Drabek	.70	.50	.30
(7)	Juan Espino	.20	.15	.08
(8)	Kelly Faulk	.20	.15	.08
(9)	Randy Graham	.20	.15	.08
(10)	Leo Hernandez	.20	.15	.08
(11)	Al Holland	.25	.20	.10
(12)	Phil Lombardi	.50	.40	.20
(13)	Victor Mata	.30	.25	.12
(14)	Derwin McNealy	.20	.15	.08
(15)	Dan Pasqua	.80	.60	.30
(16)	Scott Patterson	.20	.15	.08
(17)	Jeff Pries	.20	.15	.08
(18)	Alfonso Pulido	.25	.20	.10
(19)	Andre Robertson	.30	.25	.12
(20)	Mark Silva	.20	.15	.08
(21)	Keith Smith	.20	.15	.08
(22)	Mike Soper	.20	.15	.08
(23)	Dave Stegman	.20	.15	.08
(24)	Coaches/Trainer Card (Brian Butterfield, Dave LaRoche, Kevin Rand)	.20	.15	.08
(25)	Managers Card (Barry Clinton "Barry" Foote, George H. Sisler Jr.)	.20	.15	.08

1986 Police/Fire Safety Dodgers

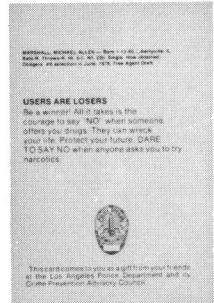

After skipping the 1985 season the Los Angeles Dodgers once again issued baseball cards related to police safety. The club had issued sets from 1980-84. The 1986 set features 30 full-color glossy cards measuring 2¼" by 4⅛." The cards are numbered accord-

ing to player uniforms. The backs feature brief player data and a safety tip from the Los Angeles Police Department. The sets were given away May 18 during Baseball Card Day at Dodger Stadium.

		MT	NR MT	EX
Complete Set		5.00	3.75	2.00
Common Player		.15	.11	.06
2	Tom Lasorda	.25	.20	.10
3	Steve Sax	.40	.30	.15
5	Mike Marshall	.35	.25	.14
9	Greg Brock	.30	.25	.12
10	Dave Anderson	.15	.11	.06
12	Bill Madlock	.35	.25	.14
14	Mike Scioscia	.20	.15	.08
17	Len Matuszek	.15	.11	.06
18	Bill Russell	.20	.15	.08
22	Franklin Stubbs	.40	.30	.15
23	Enos Cabell	.15	.11	.06
25	Mariano Duncan	.30	.25	.12
26	Alejandro Pena	.20	.15	.08
27	Carlos Diaz	.15	.11	.06
28	Pedro Guerrero	.50	.40	.20
29	Alex Trevino	.15	.11	.06
31	Ed Vande Berg	.15	.11	.06
34	Fernando Valenzuela	.60	.45	.25
35	Bob Welch	.25	.20	.10
40	Rick Honeycutt	.20	.15	.08
41	Jerry Reuss	.25	.20	.10
43	Ken Howell	.20	.15	.08
44	Ken Landreaux	.20	.15	.08
45	Terry Whitfield	.15	.11	.06
48	Dennis Powell	.20	.15	.08
49	Tom Niedenfuer	.25	.20	.10
51	Reggie Williams	.30	.25	.12
55	Orel Hershiser	.35	.25	.14
---	Team Photo/Checklist	.15	.11	.06
---	Coaching Staff (Joe Amalfitano, Monty Basgall, Mark Cresse, Ben Hines, Don McMahon, Manny Mota, Ron Perranoski)	.15	.11	.06

1986 Police/Fire Safety Phillies

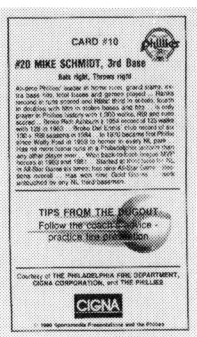

For the second straight year, the Philadelphia Phillies issued a 16-card safety set. However, in 1986 the set was issued was issued in conjunction with the Philadelphia Fire Department rather than the police. Cigna Corporation remained a sponsor. The cards, which measure 2⅝" by 4⅛" in size, feature full color photos. Along with other pertinent information, the card backs contain a short player biography and a "Tips From The Dugout" fire safety hint.

		MT	NR MT	EX
Complete Set		6.00	4.50	2.50
Common Player		.15	.11	.06
1	Juan Samuel	.50	.40	.20
2	Don Carman	.35	.25	.14
3	Von Hayes	.30	.25	.12
4	Kent Tekulve	.20	.15	.08

		MT	NR MT	EX
5	Greg Gross	.15	.11	.06
6	Shane Rawley	.25	.20	.10
7	Darren Daulton	.20	.15	.08
8	Kevin Gross	.25	.20	.10
9	Steve Jeltz	.15	.11	.06
10	Mike Schmidt	1.00	.70	.40
11	Steve Bedrosian	.35	.25	.14
12	Gary Redus	.20	.15	.08
13	Charles Hudson	.20	.15	.08
14	John Russell	.20	.15	.08
15	Fred Toliver	.20	.15	.08
16	Glenn Wilson	.25	.20	.10

1987 Police/Fire Safety Astros

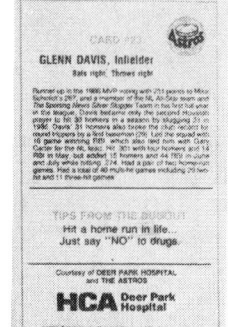

The 1987 Houston Astros safety set was produced through the combined efforts of the Astros, Deer Park Hospital and Sportsmedia Presentations. Card #'s 1-12 were handed out to youngsters 14 and under at the Astrodome on July 14th. The balance of the distribution was handled by Deer Park Hospital. The cards, which measure 2⅝" by 4⅛", contain full-color photos. The backs offer a brief team/player history and a "Tips From The Dugout" anti-drug message.

		MT	NR MT	EX
	Complete Set:	8.00	6.00	3.25
	Common Player:	.20	.15	.08
1	Larry Andersen	.20	.15	.08
2	Mark Bailey	.20	.15	.08
3	Jose Cruz	.40	.30	.15
4	Danny Darwin	.25	.20	.10
5	Bill Doran	.40	.30	.15
6	Billy Hatcher	.40	.30	.15
7	Hal Lanier	.25	.20	.10
8	Davey Lopes	.30	.25	.12
9	Dave Meads	.30	.25	.12
10	Craig Reynolds	.20	.15	.08
11	Mike Scott	.60	.45	.25
12	Denny Walling	.20	.15	.08
13	Aurelio Lopez	.20	.15	.08
14	Dickie Thon	.25	.20	.10
15	Terry Puhl	.20	.15	.08
16	Nolan Ryan	1.00	.70	.40
17	Dave Smith	.30	.25	.12
18	Julio Solano	.20	.15	.08
19	Jim Deshaies	.30	.25	.12
20	Bob Knepper	.30	.25	.12
21	Alan Ashby	.20	.15	.08
22	Kevin Bass	.40	.30	.15
23	Glenn Davis	1.00	.70	.40
24	Phil Garner	.25	.20	.10
25	Jim Pankovits	.20	.15	.08
26	Coaching Staff (Yogi Berra, Matt Galante, Denis Menke, Les Moss, Gene Tenace)	.20	.15	.08

Definitions for grading conditions are located in the Introduction of this price guide.

1987 Police/Fire Safety Blue Jays

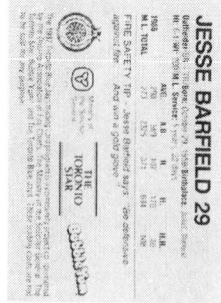

JESSE BARFIELD
29
outfielder

For the fourth consecutive year, the Toronto Blue Jays issued a fire safety set of 36 cards. As in 1986, the set was sponsored by the local fire departments and governing agencies, Bubble Yum and the *Toronto Star*. The card fronts feature a full-color photo surrounded by a white border. The backs carry a fire safety tip and logos of all sponsors, plus player personal data and statistics. Produced on thin stock, cards in the set are the standard 2½" by 3½" size.

		MT	NR MT	EX
	Complete Set:	7.00	5.25	2.75
	Common Player:	.15	.11	.06
1	Tony Fernandez	.40	.30	.15
3	Jimy Williams	.15	.11	.06
5	Rance Mulliniks	.15	.11	.06
8	John Sullivan	.15	.11	.06
9	Rick Leach	.15	.11	.06
10	Mike Sharperson	.20	.15	.08
11	George Bell	.90	.70	.35
12	Ernie Whitt	.25	.20	.10
15	Lloyd Moseby	.35	.25	.14
16	Garth Iorg	.15	.11	.06
17	Kelly Gruber	.15	.11	.06
18	Jim Clancy	.25	.20	.10
19	Fred McGriff	.70	.50	.30
22	Jimmy Key	.40	.30	.15
23	Cecil Fielder	.20	.15	.08
24	John McLaren	.15	.11	.06
26	Willie Upshaw	.25	.20	.10
29	Jesse Barfield	.60	.45	.25
31	Duane Ward	.20	.15	.08
33	Joe Johnson	.15	.11	.06
35	Jeff Musselman	.35	.25	.14
37	Dave Stieb	.40	.30	.15
38	Mark Eichhorn	.25	.20	.10
40	Rob Ducey	.25	.20	.10
41	Al Widmar	.15	.11	.06
42	Billy Smith	.15	.11	.06
43	Cito Gaston	.15	.11	.06
45	Jose Nunez	.40	.30	.15
46	Gary Lavelle	.15	.11	.06
47	Matt Stark	.15	.11	.06
48	Craig McMurtry	.15	.11	.06
50	Tom Henke	.25	.20	.10
54	Jeff Hearron	.15	.11	.06
55	John Cerutti	.25	.20	.10
---	Logo/Won-Loss Record	.15	.11	.06
---	Team Photo/Checklist	.15	.11	.06

1987 Police/Fire Safety Brewers

The Milwaukee Brewers issued a safety set in 1987 for the sixth consecutive year. As in the past, many local police departments throughout Wisconsin participated in the giveaway program. The Milwaukee version was sponsored by Kinney Shoe Stores and WTMJ Radio and were handed out to youngsters attending

Dan Plesac says:

"Major League Baseball selects their players by drafting athletes after they graduate from high school. Only a few make it in the big leagues, the rest pursue other careers.

Whatever career path you choose, if you study and work hard, you'll be the best at it, and you'll be drafted for a good job when you graduate. It's important to learn a trade or profession."

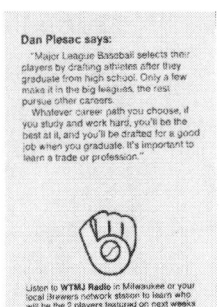

37   Dan Plesac   P
Iola, Manawa & Marion Police Departments
and Wisconsin Power and Light
present the 1987
Milwaukee Brewers

Listen to WTMJ Radio in Milwaukee or your local Brewers network station to learn who will be the 2 players featured on next weeks baseball cards.

the Baseball Card Day at County Stadium on May 9th. The cards, which measure 2¼" by 4⅛", feature full-color photos plus a safety tip on the backs. Chris Bosio can be found with a uniform number of 26 or 29. The card was corrected to #29 in later printings.

		MT	NR MT	EX
Complete Set:		6.00	4.50	2.50
Common Player:		.15	.11	.06
1	Ernest Riles	.20	.15	.08
2	Edgar Diaz	.20	.15	.08
3	Juan Castillo	.15	.11	.06
4	Paul Molitor	.50	.40	.20
5	B.J. Surhoff	1.00	.70	.40
7	Dale Sveum	.60	.45	.25
9	Greg Brock	.25	.20	.10
13	Billy Jo Robidoux	.15	.11	.06
14	Jim Paciorek	.15	.11	.06
15	Cecil Cooper	.30	.25	.12
16	Mike Felder	.15	.11	.06
17	Jim Gantner	.20	.15	.08
19	Robin Yount	.80	.60	.30
20	Juan Nieves	.30	.25	.12
21	Bill Schroeder	.20	.15	.08
25	Mark Clear	.15	.11	.06
26a	Glenn Braggs	.60	.45	.25
26b	Chris Bosio	1.00	.70	.40
28	Rick Manning	.15	.11	.06
29	Chris Bosio	.40	.30	.15
32	Chuck Crim	.30	.25	.12
34	Mark Ciardi	.25	.20	.10
37	Dan Plesac	.40	.30	.15
38	John Henry Johnson	.15	.11	.06
40	Mike Birbeck	.25	.20	.10
42	Tom Trebelhorn	.20	.15	.08
45	Rob Deer	.30	.25	.12
46	Bill Wegman	.20	.15	.08
49	Ted Higuera	.40	.30	.15
---	Coaches Card (Andy Etchebarren, Larry Haney, Chuck Hartenstein, Dave Hilton, Tony Muser)	.15	.11	.06
---	Team Photo/Roster	.15	.11	.06

1987 Police/Fire Safety Columbus Clippers

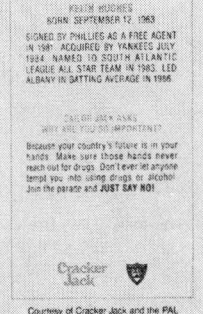

A popular police set because many of the players included in the issue have major league experience, the 1987 Columbus Clippers police set was sponsored by Cracker Jack. Twenty-five cards, each measuring 2⅜" by 3¾", comprise the set. The card fronts feature a full-color photo surrounded by a Cracker Jack border. Card backs contain the player's name, birth date and a brief biography plus a safety tip. The 1987 edition marked the seventh time in eight years the Clippers issued a police set.

		MT	NR MT	EX
Complete Set:		6.00	4.50	2.50
Common Player:		.20	.15	.08
(1)	Mike Armstrong	.20	.15	.08
(2)	Brad Arnsberg	.35	.25	.14
(3)	Rich Bordi	.25	.20	.10
(4)	Jay Buhner	.70	.50	.30
(5)	Pete Dalena	.20	.15	.08
(6)	Bucky Dent (manager)	.40	.30	.15
(7)	Orestes Destrade	.50	.40	.20
(8)	Juan Espino	.20	.15	.08
(9)	Pete Filson	.25	.20	.10
(10)	Bill Fulton	.20	.15	.08
(11)	Randy Graham	.20	.15	.08
(12)	Al Holland	.25	.20	.10
(13)	Keith Hughes	.40	.30	.15
(14)	Roberto Kelly	.70	.50	.30
(15)	Al Leiter	.70	.50	.30
(16)	Bryan Little	.20	.15	.08
(17)	Phil Lombardi	.30	.25	.12
(18)	Mitch Lyden	.20	.15	.08
(19)	Bobby Meacham	.30	.25	.12
(20)	Alfonso Pulido	.25	.20	.10
(21)	Ron Romanick	.30	.25	.12
(22)	Glenn Sherlock	.20	.15	.08
(23)	George Sisler (general manager)	.20	.15	.08
(24)	Shane Turner	.20	.15	.08
(25)	Coaches (Clete Boyer, Jerry McNertney, Ken Rowe, John "Champ" Summers)	.20	.15	.08

1987 Police/Fire Safety Dodgers

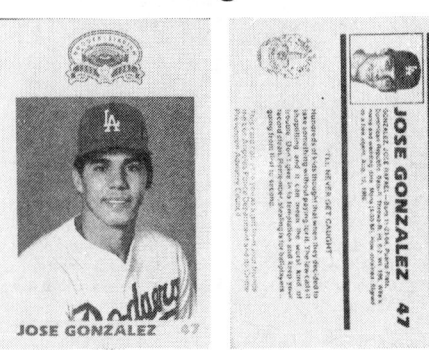

JOSE GONZALEZ

Producing a police set for the seventh time in eight years, the 1987 edition contains 30 cards which measure 2 13/16" by 4 1/8". The set includes a special Dodger Stadium 25th Anniversary card. The card fronts contain a full-color photo plus the Dodger Stadium 25th Anniversary logo. The photos are a mix of action and posed shots. The backs contain personal player data plus a police safety tip. The cards were given out April 24th at Dodger Stadium and were distributed by the LAPD at a rate of two cards per week.

		MT	NR MT	EX
Complete Set:		5.00	3.75	2.00
Common Player:		.15	.11	.06
2	Tom Lasorda	.25	.20	.10
3	Steve Sax	.40	.30	.15
5	Mike Marshall	.35	.25	.14

		MT	NR MT	EX
10	Dave Anderson	.15	.11	.06
12	Bill Madlock	.30	.25	.12
14	Mike Scioscia	.20	.15	.08
15	Gilberto Reyes	.25	.20	.10
17	Len Matuszek	.15	.11	.06
21	Reggie Williams	.25	.20	.10
22	Franklin Stubbs	.25	.20	.10
23	Tim Leary	.15	.11	.06
25	Mariano Duncan	.20	.15	.08
26	Alejandro Pena	.20	.15	.08
28	Pedro Guerrero	.50	.40	.20
29	Alex Trevino	.15	.11	.06
33	Jeff Hamilton	.30	.25	.12
34	Fernando Valenzuela	.60	.45	.25
35	Bob Welch	.25	.20	.10
36	Matt Young	.15	.11	.06
40	Rick Honeycutt	.20	.15	.08
41	Jerry Reuss	.25	.20	.10
43	Ken Howell	.15	.11	.06
44	Ken Landreaux	.20	.15	.08
46	Ralph Bryant	.30	.25	.12
47	Jose Gonzalez	.30	.25	.12
49	Tom Niedenfuer	.25	.20	.10
51	Brian Holton	.30	.25	.12
55	Orel Hershiser	.35	.25	.14
---	Coaching Staff (Joe Amalfitano, Mark Cresse, Tom Lasorda, Don McMahon, Manny Mota, Ron Perranoski, Bill Russell)	.15	.11	.06
---	Dodger Stadium/Checklist	.15	.11	.06

1960 Post Cereal

These cards were issued on the backs of Grape Nuts cereal and measure an oversized 7'' by 8¾.'' The nine cards in the set include five baseball players (Al Kaline, Mickey Mantle, Don Drysdale, Harmon Killebrew and Ed Mathews) as well as two football and two basketball players. The full-color photos were placed on a color background and bordered by a wood frame design. The cards covered the entire back of the cereal box and were blank backed. Card fronts also include the player's name and team and a facsimile autograph. A panel on the side of the box contained player biographical information. A scarce set, cards are very difficult to obtain in mint condition.

		NR MT	EX	VG
	Complete Set:	2100.00	1050.00	630.00
	Common Player:	75.00	37.00	22.00
(1)	Bob Cousy	75.00	37.00	22.00
(2)	Don Drysdale	175.00	87.00	52.00
(3)	Frank Gifford	150.00	75.00	45.00
(4)	Al Kaline	200.00	100.00	60.00
(5)	Harmon Killebrew	175.00	87.00	52.00
(6)	Ed Mathews	175.00	87.00	52.00
(7)	Mickey Mantle	900.00	450.00	270.00
(8)	Bob Pettit	75.00	37.00	22.00
(9)	John Unitas	150.00	75.00	45.00

1961 Post Cereal

Two hundred different players are included in this set, but with variations the number of different cards exceeds 350. This was the first large-scale card set by the cereal company and it proved very popular with fans. Cards were issued both singly and in various panel sizes on the thick cardboard stock of cereal boxes, as well on thinner stock, in team sheets issued directly by Post via a mail-in offer. About 10 cards in the set were issued in significantly smaller quantities, making their prices much higher than other comparable players in the set. Individual cards measure 3½'' by 2½,'' and all cards are numbered in the upper-left corner. Card fronts have full-color portrait photos of the player, along with biographical information and 1960 and career statistics. Card backs are blank.

		NR MT	EX	VG
	Complete Set:	950.00	475.00	285.00
	Common Player:	.90	.45	.25
1a	Yogi Berra (box)	15.00	7.50	4.50
1b	Yogi Berra (company)	10.00	5.00	3.00
2a	Elston Howard (box)	4.00	2.00	1.25
2b	Elston Howard (company)	2.50	1.25	.70
3a	Bill Skowron (box)	2.00	1.00	.60
3b	Bill Skowron (company)	2.00	1.00	.60
4a	Mickey Mantle (box)	40.00	20.00	12.00
5	Bob Turley (company)	8.00	4.00	2.50
6a	Whitey Ford (box)	5.00	2.50	1.50
6b	Whitey Ford (company)	5.00	2.50	1.50
7a	Roger Maris (box)	8.00	4.00	2.50
7b	Roger Maris (company)	8.00	4.00	2.50
8a	Bobby Richardson (box)	2.50	1.25	.70
8b	Bobby Richardson (company)	2.50	1.25	.70
9a	Tony Kubek (box)	2.50	1.25	.70
9b	Tony Kubek (company)	2.50	1.25	.70
10	Gil McDougald (box)	20.00	10.00	6.00
11	Cletis Boyer (box)	1.50	.70	.45
12a	Hector Lopez (box)	1.50	.70	.45
12b	Hector Lopez (company)	1.50	.70	.45
13	Bob Cerv (box)	1.50	.70	.45
14	Ryne Duren (box)	1.50	.70	.45
15	Bobby Shantz (box)	1.50	.70	.45
16	Art Ditmar (box)	1.50	.70	.45
17	Jim Coates (box)	1.50	.70	.45
18	John Blanchard (box)	1.50	.70	.45
19a	Luis Aparicio (box)	3.50	1.75	1.00
19b	Luis Aparicio (company)	3.50	1.75	1.00
20a	Nelson Fox (box)	3.00	1.50	.90
20b	Nelson Fox (company)	3.00	1.50	.90
21a	Bill Pierce (box)	5.00	2.50	1.50
21b	Bill Pierce (company)	3.00	1.50	.90
22a	Early Wynn (box)	5.00	2.50	1.50
22b	Early Wynn (company)	10.00	5.00	3.00
23	Bob Shaw (box)	60.00	30.00	18.00
24a	Al Smith (box)	2.50	1.25	.70
24b	Al Smith (company)	.90	.45	.25
25a	Minnie Minoso (box)	2.00	1.00	.60
25b	Minnie Minoso (company)	2.00	1.00	.60
26a	Roy Sievers (box)	1.25	.60	.40
26b	Roy Sievers (company)	1.25	.60	.40
27a	Jim Landis (box)	1.50	.70	.45
27b	Jim Landis (company)	.90	.45	.25
28a	Sherman Lollar (box)	2.50	1.25	.70

Complete set prices do not include the higher priced variations, unless noted otherwise.

		NR MT	EX	VG
28b	Sherman Lollar (company)	1.00	.50	.30
29	Gerry Staley (box)	.90	.45	.25
30a	Gene Freese (box, White Sox)	.90	.45	.25
30b	Gene Freese (company, Reds)	5.00	2.50	1.50
31	Ted Kluszewski (box)	2.50	1.25	.70
32	Turk Lown (box)	.90	.45	.25
33a	Jim Rivera (box)	.90	.45	.25
33b	Jim Rivera (company)	.90	.45	.25
34	Frank Baumann (box)	.90	.45	.25
35a	Al Kaline (box)	9.00	4.50	2.75
35b	Al Kaline (company)	7.00	3.50	2.00
36a	Rocky Colavito (box)	5.00	2.50	1.50
36b	Rocky Colavito (company)	3.00	1.50	.90
37a	Charley Maxwell (box)	3.50	1.75	1.00
37b	Charley Maxwell (company)	.90	.45	.25
38a	Frank Lary (box)	1.00	.50	.30
38b	Frank Lary (company)	1.00	.50	.30
39a	Jim Bunning (box)	2.50	1.25	.70
39b	Jim Bunning (company)	2.50	1.25	.70
40a	Norm Cash (box)	1.50	.70	.45
40b	Norm Cash (company)	1.50	.70	.45
41a	Frank Bolling (box, Tigers)	7.00	3.50	2.00
41b	Frank Bolling (company, Braves)	4.00	2.00	1.25
42a	Don Mossi (box)	1.00	.50	.30
42b	Don Mossi (company)	1.00	.50	.30
43a	Lou Berberet (box)	.90	.45	.25
43b	Lou Berberet (company)	.90	.45	.25
44	Dave Sisler (box)	.90	.45	.25
45	Ed Yost (box)	1.00	.50	.30
46	Pete Burnside (box)	.90	.45	.25
47a	Pete Runnels (box)	2.50	1.25	.70
47b	Pete Runnnels (company)	1.25	.60	.40
48a	Frank Malzone (box)	1.00	.50	.30
48b	Frank Malzone (company)	1.00	.50	.30
49a	Vic Wertz (box)	4.00	2.00	1.25
49b	Vic Wertz (company)	2.50	1.25	.70
50a	Tom Brewer (box)	2.00	1.00	.60
50b	Tom Brewer (company)	.90	.45	.25
51a	Willie Tasby (box, no sold line)	7.00	3.50	2.00
51b	Willie Tasby (company, sold line)	.90	.45	.25
52a	Russ Nixon (box)	.90	.45	.25
52b	Russ Nixon (company)	.90	.45	.25
53a	Don Buddin (box)	.90	.45	.25
53b	Don Buddin (company)	.90	.45	.25
54a	Bill Monbouquette (box)	1.00	.50	.30
54b	Bill Monbouquette (company)	1.00	.50	.30
55a	Frank Sullivan (box, Red Sox)	.90	.45	.25
55b	Frank Sullivan (company, Phillies)	13.00	6.50	4.00
56a	Haywood Sullivan (box)	1.00	.50	.30
56b	Haywood Sullivan (company)	1.00	.50	.30
57a	Harvey Kuenn (box, Indians)	2.50	1.25	.70
57b	Harvey Kuenn (company, Giants)	5.00	2.50	1.50
58a	Gary Bell (box)	4.00	2.00	1.25
58b	Gary Bell (company)	1.25	.60	.40
59a	Jim Perry (box)	1.25	.60	.40
59b	Jim Perry (company)	1.25	.60	.40
60a	Jim Grant (box)	2.50	1.25	.70
60b	Jim Grant (company)	1.25	.60	.40
61a	Johnny Temple (box)	.90	.45	.25
61b	Johnny Temple (company)	.90	.45	.25
62a	Paul Foytack (box)	.90	.45	.25
62b	Paul Foytack (company)	.90	.45	.25
63a	Vic Power (box)	1.00	.50	.30
63b	Vic Power (company)	1.00	.50	.30
64a	Tito Francona (box)	1.00	.50	.30
64b	Tito Francona (company)	1.00	.50	.30
65a	Ken Aspromonte (box, no sold line)	5.00	2.50	1.50
65b	Ken Aspromonte (company, sold line)	5.00	2.50	1.50
66	Bob Wilson (box)	.90	.45	.25
67a	John Romano (box)	.90	.45	.25
67b	John Romano (company)	.90	.45	.25
68a	Jim Gentile (box)	2.00	1.00	.60
68b	Jim Gentile (company)	1.00	.50	.30
69a	Gus Triandos (box)	2.50	1.25	.70
69b	Gus Triandos (company)	1.00	.50	.30
70	Gene Woodling (box)	12.00	6.00	3.50
71a	Milt Pappas (box)	2.50	1.25	.70
71b	Milt Pappas (company)	1.00	.50	.30
72a	Ron Hansen (box)	2.50	1.25	.70
72b	Ron Hansen (company)	.90	.45	.25
73	Chuck Estrada (company)	60.00	30.00	18.00
74a	Steve Barber (box)	.90	.45	.25
74b	Steve Barber (company)	.90	.45	.25
75a	Brooks Robinson (box)	10.00	5.00	3.00
75b	Brooks Robinson (company)	8.00	4.00	2.50
76a	Jackie Brandt (box)	.90	.45	.25
76b	Jackie Brandt (company)	.90	.45	.25
77a	Marv Breeding (box)	.90	.45	.25
77b	Marv Breedding (company)	.90	.45	.25
78	Hal Brown (box)	.90	.45	.25
79	Billy Klaus (box)	.90	.45	.25
80a	Hoyt Wilhelm (box)	3.50	1.75	1.00
80b	Hoyt Wilhelm (company)	4.00	2.00	1.25
81a	Jerry Lumpe (box)	5.00	2.50	1.50
81b	Jerry Lumpe (company)	3.50	1.75	1.00
82a	Norm Siebern (box)	1.00	.50	.30
82b	Norm Siebern (company)	1.00	.50	.30
83a	Bud Daley (box)	1.25	.60	.40
83b	Bud Daley (company)	2.00	1.00	.60
84a	Bill Tuttle (box)	.90	.45	.25
84b	Bill Tuttle (company)	.90	.45	.25
85a	Marv Throneberry (box)	2.00	1.00	.60
85b	Marv Throneberry (company)	2.00	1.00	.60
86a	Dick Williams (box)	1.25	.60	.40
86b	Dick Williams (company)	1.25	.60	.40
87a	Ray Herbert (box)	.90	.45	.25
87b	Ray Herbert (company)	.90	.45	.25
88a	Whitey Herzog (box)	1.50	.70	.45
88b	Whitey Herzog (company)	1.50	.70	.45
89a	Ken Hamlin (box, no sold line)	.90	.45	.25
89b	Ken Hamlin (company, sold line)	8.00	4.00	2.50
90a	Hank Bauer (box)	1.50	.70	.45
90b	Hank Bauer (company)	1.50	.70	.45
91a	Bob Allison (box, Minneapolis)	3.50	1.75	1.00
91b	Bob Allison (company, Minnesota)	4.00	2.00	1.25
92a	Harmon Killebrew (box, Minneapolis)	9.00	4.50	2.75
92b	Harmon Killebrew (company, Minnesota)	8.00	4.00	2.50
93a	Jim Lemon (box, Minneapolis)	25.00	12.50	7.50
93b	Jim Lemon (company, Minnesota)	5.00	2.50	1.50
94	Chuck Stobbs (company)	90.00	45.00	27.00
95a	Reno Bertoia (box, Minneapolis)	.90	.45	.25
95b	Reno Bertoia (company, Minnesota)	3.50	1.75	1.00
96a	Billy Gardner (box, Minneapolis)	1.00	.50	.30
96b	Billy Gardner (company, Minnesota)	3.50	1.75	1.00
97a	Earl Battey (box, Minneapolis)	3.50	1.75	1.00
97b	Earl Battey (company, Minnesota)	3.50	1.75	1.00
98a	Pedro Ramos (box, Minneapolis)	.90	.45	.25
98b	Pedro Ramos (company, Minnesota)	3.50	1.75	1.00
99a	Camilio Pascual (Camilo) (box, Minneapolis)	1.00	.50	.30
99b	Camilio Pascual (Camilo) (company, Minnesota)	3.50	1.75	1.00
100a	Billy Consolo (box, Minneapolis)	.90	.45	.25
100b	Billy Consolo (company, Minnesota)	3.50	1.75	1.00
101a	Warren Spahn (box)	12.00	6.00	3.50
101b	Warren Spahn (company)	7.00	3.50	2.00
102a	Lew Burdette (box)	2.00	1.00	.60
102b	Lew Burdette (company)	2.00	1.00	.60
103a	Bob Buhl (box)	1.00	.50	.30
103b	Bob Buhl (company)	1.00	.50	.30
104a	Joe Adcock (box)	3.50	1.75	1.00
104b	Joe Adcock (company)	2.00	1.00	.60
105a	John Logan (box)	3.50	1.75	1.00
105b	John Logan (company)	1.25	.60	.40
106	Ed Mathews (company)	20.00	10.00	6.00
107a	Hank Aaron (box)	15.00	7.50	4.50
107b	Hank Aaron (company)	15.00	7.50	4.50
108a	Wes Covington (box)	1.00	.50	.30
108b	Wes Covington (company)	1.00	.50	.30
109a	Bill Bruton (box, Braves)	5.00	2.50	1.50
109b	Bill Bruton (company, Tigers)	5.00	2.50	1.50
110a	Del Crandall (box)	3.50	1.75	1.00
110b	Del Crandall (company)	1.25	.60	.40
111	Red Schoendienst (box)	1.50	.70	.45
112	Juan Pizarro (box)	.90	.45	.25
113	Chuck Cottier (box)	5.00	2.50	1.50
114	Al Spangler (box)	.90	.45	.25
115a	Dick Farrell (box)	5.00	2.50	1.50
115b	Dick Farrell (company)	3.50	1.75	1.00
116a	Jim Owens (box)	5.00	2.50	1.50
116b	Jim Owens (company)	3.50	1.75	1.00
117a	Robin Roberts (box)	4.00	2.00	1.25
117b	Robin Roberts (company)	4.00	2.00	1.25
118a	Tony Taylor (box)	.90	.45	.25
118b	Tony Taylor (company)	.90	.45	.25
119a	Lee Walls (box)	.90	.45	.25
119b	Lee Walls (company)	.90	.45	.25
120a	Tony Curry (box)	.90	.45	.25
120b	Tony Curry (company)	.90	.45	.25
121a	Pancho Herrera (box)	.90	.45	.25

		NR MT	EX	VG
121b	Pancho Herrera (company)	.90	.45	.25
122a	Ken Walters (box)	.90	.45	.25
122b	Ken Walters (company)	.90	.45	.25
123a	John Callison (box)	1.00	.50	.30
123b	John Callison (company)	1.00	.50	.30
124a	Gene Conley (box, Phillies)	1.00	.50	.30
124b	Gene Conley (company, Red Sox)	10.00	5.00	3.00
125a	Bob Friend (box)	3.50	1.75	1.00
125b	Bob Friend (company)	1.50	.70	.45
126a	Vernon Law (box)	3.50	1.75	1.00
126b	Vernon Law (company)	1.50	.70	.45
127a	Dick Stuart (box)	1.00	.50	.30
127b	Dick Stuart (company)	1.00	.50	.30
128a	Bill Mazeroski (box)	2.00	1.00	.60
128b	Bill Mazeroski (company)	2.00	1.00	.60
129a	Dick Groat (box)	2.50	1.25	.70
129b	Dick Groat (company)	1.50	.70	.45
130a	Don Hoak (box)	1.00	.50	.30
130b	Don Hoak (company)	1.00	.50	.30
131a	Bob Skinner (box)	1.00	.50	.30
131b	Bob Skinner (company)	1.00	.50	.30
132a	Bob Clemente (box)	20.00	10.00	6.00
132b	Bob Clemente (company)	15.00	7.50	4.50
133	Roy Face (box)	2.50	1.25	.70
134	Harvey Haddix (box)	1.25	.60	.40
135	Bill Virdon (box)	20.00	10.00	6.00
136a	Gino Cimoli (box)	.90	.45	.25
136b	Gino Cimoli (company)	.90	.45	.25
137	Rocky Nelson (box)	.90	.45	.25
138a	Smoky Burgess (box)	1.25	.60	.40
138b	Smoky Burgess (company)	1.25	.60	.40
139	Hal Smith (box)	.90	.45	.25
140	Wilmer Mizell (box)	.90	.45	.25
141a	Mike McCormick (box)	1.00	.50	.30
141b	Mike McCormick (company)	1.00	.50	.30
142a	John Antonelli (box, Giants)	2.50	1.25	.70
142b	John Antonelli (company, Indians)	3.50	1.75	1.00
143a	Sam Jones (box)	3.50	1.75	1.00
143b	Sam Jones (company)	1.50	.70	.45
144a	Orlando Cepeda (box)	4.00	2.00	1.25
144b	Orlando Cepeda (company)	3.50	1.75	1.00
145a	Willie Mays (box)	15.00	7.50	4.50
145b	Willie Mays (company)	15.00	7.50	4.50
146a	Willie Kirkland (box, Giants)	4.00	2.00	1.25
146b	Willie Kirkland (company, Indians)	4.00	2.00	1.25
147a	Willie McCovey (box)	5.00	2.50	1.50
147b	Willie McCovey (company)	7.00	3.50	2.00
148a	Don Blasingame (box)	.90	.45	.25
148b	Don Blasingame (company)	.90	.45	.25
149a	Jim Davenport (box)	.90	.45	.25
149b	Jim Davenport (company)	.90	.45	.25
150a	Hobie Landrith (box)	.90	.45	.25
150b	Hobie Landrith (company)	.90	.45	.25
151	Bob Schmidt (box)	.90	.45	.25
152a	Ed Bressoud (box)	.90	.45	.25
152b	Ed Bressoud (company)	.90	.45	.25
153a	Andre Rodgers (box, no traded line)	5.00	2.50	1.50
153b	Andre Rodgers (box, traded line)	.90	.45	.25
154	Jack Sanford (box)	1.00	.50	.30
155	Billy O'Dell (box)	.90	.45	.25
156a	Norm Larker (box)	2.00	1.00	.60
156b	Norm Larker (company)	2.00	1.00	.60
157a	Charlie Neal (box)	.90	.45	.25
157b	Charlie Neal (company)	.90	.45	.25
158a	Jim Gilliam (box)	3.50	1.75	1.00
158b	Jim Gilliam (company)	2.00	1.00	.60
159a	Wally Moon (box)	1.00	.50	.30
159b	Wally Moon (company)	1.00	.50	.30
160a	Don Drysdale (box)	5.00	2.50	1.50
160b	Don Drysdale (company)	5.00	2.50	1.50
161a	Larry Sherry (box)	1.00	.50	.30
161b	Larry Sherry (company)	1.00	.50	.30
162	Stan Williams (box)	4.00	2.00	1.25
163	Mel Roach (box)	25.00	12.50	7.50
164a	Maury Wills (box)	3.50	1.75	1.00
164b	Maury Wills (company)	3.50	1.75	1.00
165	Tom Davis (box)	1.50	.70	.45
166a	John Roseboro (box)	1.00	.50	.30
166b	John Roseboro (company)	1.00	.50	.30
167a	Duke Snider (box)	7.00	3.50	2.00
167b	Duke Snider (company)	8.00	4.00	2.50
168a	Gil Hodges (boxes)	4.50	2.25	1.25
168b	Gil Hodges (company)	5.00	2.50	1.50
169	John Podres (box)	2.00	1.00	.60
170	Ed Roebuck (box)	.90	.45	.25
171a	Ken Boyer (box)	4.00	2.00	1.25
171b	Ken Boyer (company)	3.50	1.75	1.00
172a	Joe Cunningham (box)	.90	.45	.25

		NR MT	EX	VG
172b	Joe Cunningham (company)	.90	.45	.25
173a	Daryl Spencer (box)	.90	.45	.25
173b	Daryl Spencer (company)	.90	.45	.25
174a	Larry Jackson (box)	.90	.45	.25
174b	Larry Jackson (company)	.90	.45	.25
175a	Lindy McDaniel (box)	.90	.45	.25
175b	Lindy McDaniel (company)	.90	.45	.25
176a	Bill White (box)	1.25	.60	.40
176b	Bill White (company)	1.25	.60	.40
177a	Alex Grammas (box)	.90	.45	.25
177b	Alex Grammas (company)	.90	.45	.25
178a	Curt Flood (box)	1.50	.70	.45
178b	Curt Flood (company)	1.50	.70	.45
179a	Ernie Broglio (box)	.90	.45	.25
179b	Ernie Broglio (company)	.90	.45	.25
180a	Hal Smith (box)	.90	.45	.25
180b	Hal Smith (company)	.90	.45	.25
181a	Vada Pinson (box)	2.00	1.00	.60
181b	Vada Pinson (company)	2.00	1.00	.60
182a	Frank Robinson (box)	12.00	6.00	3.50
182b	Frank Robinson (company)	12.00	6.00	3.50
183	Roy McMillan (box)	40.00	20.00	12.00
184a	Bob Purkey (box)	1.00	.50	.30
184b	Bob Purkey (company)	1.00	.50	.30
185a	Ed Kasko (box)	.90	.45	.25
185b	Ed Kasko (company)	.90	.45	.25
186a	Gus Bell (box)	1.00	.50	.30
186b	Gus Bell (company)	1.00	.50	.30
187a	Jerry Lynch (box)	.90	.45	.25
187b	Jerry Lynch (company)	.90	.45	.25
188a	Ed Bailey (box)	.90	.45	.25
188b	Ed Bailey (company)	.90	.45	.25
189a	Jim O'Toole (box)	.90	.45	.25
189b	Jim O'Toole (company)	.90	.45	.25
190a	Billy Martin (box, no sold line)	2.50	1.25	.70
190b	Billy Martin (company, sold line)	8.00	4.00	2.50
191a	Ernie Banks (box)	9.00	4.50	2.75
191b	Ernie Banks (company)	6.00	3.00	1.75
192a	Richie Ashburn (box)	2.50	1.25	.70
192b	Richie Ashburn (company)	2.50	1.25	.70
193a	Frank Thomas (box)	20.00	10.00	6.00
193b	Frank Thomas (company)	5.00	2.50	1.50
194a	Don Cardwell (box)	.90	.45	.25
194b	Don Cardwell (company)	.90	.45	.25
195a	George Altman (box)	.90	.45	.25
195b	George Altman (company)	.90	.45	.25
196a	Ron Santo (box)	2.50	1.25	.70
196b	Ron Santo (company)	2.50	1.25	.70
197a	Glen Hobbie (box)	.90	.45	.25
198a	Sam Taylor (box)	.90	.45	.25
198b	Sam Taylor (company)	.90	.45	.25
199a	Jerry Kindall (box)	.90	.45	.25
199b	Jerry Kindall (company)	.90	.45	.25
200a	Don Elston (box)	2.50	1.25	.70
200b	Don Elston (company)	2.50	1.25	.70

1962 Post Cereal

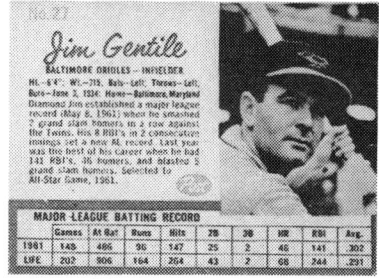

Like the 1961 Post set, there are 200 players pictured in the set of 3½'' by 2½'' cards. Differences include a Post logo on the card fronts and the player's name in script lettering. Cards are again blank backed and were issued in panels of five to seven cards on cereal boxes. American League players were numbered 1-100 and National League players 101-200. With variations there are approximately 210 of the full-color cards known. A handful of the '62 cards were also issued in smaller quantities. The cards of Mickey Mantle and Roger Maris were reproduced in a special two-card panel for a magazine insert. Stock for this insert is slightly thinner, with white margins. The 1962 Post Canadian and Jello sets have virtually the same checklist as this set.

		NR MT	EX	VG
	Complete Set:	900.00	450.00	270.00
	Common Player:	.90	.45	.25
1	Bill Skowron	4.00	2.00	1.25
2	Bobby Richardson	2.50	1.25	.70
3	Cletis Boyer	1.50	.70	.45
4	Tony Kubek	2.50	1.25	.70
5a	Mickey Mantle (from box, no printing on back)	35.00	17.50	10.50
5b	Mickey Mantle (from ad, printing on back)	35.00	17.50	10.50
6a	Roger Maris (from box, no printing on back)	8.00	4.00	2.50
6b	Roger Maris (from ad, printing on back)	8.00	4.00	2.50
7	Yogi Berra	8.00	4.00	2.50
8	Elston Howard	2.50	1.25	.70
9	Whitey Ford	5.00	2.50	1.50
10	Ralph Terry	1.50	.70	.45
11	John Blanchard	1.50	.70	.45
12	Luis Arroyo	1.50	.70	.45
13	Bill Stafford	1.50	.70	.45
14a	Norm Cash (Throws: Right)	1.50	.70	.45
14b	Norm Cash (Throws: Left)	4.00	2.00	1.25
15	Jake Wood	.90	.45	.25
16	Steve Boros	1.00	.50	.30
17	Chico Fernandez	.90	.45	.25
18	Bill Bruton	1.00	.50	.30
19	Rocky Colavito	2.50	1.25	.70
20	Al Kaline	7.00	3.50	2.00
21	Dick Brown	.90	.45	.25
22	Frank Lary	1.00	.50	.30
23	Don Mossi	1.00	.50	.30
24	Phil Regan	.90	.45	.25
25	Charley Maxwell	.90	.45	.25
26	Jim Bunning	2.50	1.25	.70
27a	Jim Gentile (Home: Baltimore)	1.00	.50	.30
27b	Jim Gentile (Home: San Lorenzo)	4.00	2.00	1.25
28	Marv Breeding	.90	.45	.25
29	Brooks Robinson	7.00	3.50	2.00
30	Ron Hansen	.90	.45	.25
31	Jackie Brandt	.90	.45	.25
32	Dick Williams	1.25	.60	.40
33	Gus Triandos	1.00	.50	.30
34	Milt Pappas	1.00	.50	.30
35	Hoyt Wilhelm	3.50	1.75	1.00
36	Chuck Estrada	4.00	2.00	1.25
37	Vic Power	1.00	.50	.30
38	Johnny Temple	.90	.45	.25
39	Bubba Phillips	.90	.45	.25
40	Tito Francona	1.00	.50	.30
41	Willie Kirkland	.90	.45	.25
42	John Romano	.90	.45	.25
43	Jim Perry	1.25	.60	.40
44	Woodie Held	1.00	.50	.30
45	Chuck Essegian	.90	.45	.25
46	Roy Sievers	1.25	.60	.40
47	Nellie Fox	3.00	1.50	.90
48	Al Smith	.90	.45	.25
49	Luis Aparicio	3.50	1.75	1.00
50	Jim Landis	.90	.45	.25
51	Minnie Minoso	1.50	.70	.45
52	Andy Carey	.90	.45	.25
53	Sherman Lollar	1.00	.50	.30
54	Bill Pierce	1.25	.60	.40
55	Early Wynn	20.00	10.00	6.00
56	Chuck Schilling	.90	.45	.25
57	Pete Runnels	1.00	.50	.30
58	Frank Malzone	1.00	.50	.30
59	Don Buddin	.90	.45	.25
60	Gary Geiger	.90	.45	.25
61	Carl Yastrzemski	25.00	12.50	7.50
62	Jackie Jensen	1.50	.70	.45
63	Jim Pagliaroni	.90	.45	.25
64	Don Schwall	.90	.45	.25
65	Dale Long	1.00	.50	.30
66	Chuck Cottier	.90	.45	.25
67	Billy Klaus	.90	.45	.25
68	Coot Veal	.90	.45	.25
69	Marty Keough	20.00	10.00	6.00
70	Willie Tasby	.90	.45	.25
71	Gene Woodling	1.00	.50	.30
72	Gene Green	.90	.45	.25
73	Dick Donovan	.90	.45	.25
74	Steve Bilko	.90	.45	.25

		NR MT	EX	VG
75	Rocky Bridges	.90	.45	.25
76	Eddie Yost	1.00	.50	.30
77	Leon Wagner	1.00	.50	.30
78	Albie Pearson	.90	.45	.25
79	Ken Hunt	.90	.45	.25
80	Earl Averill	.90	.45	.25
81	Ryne Duren	1.00	.50	.30
82	Ted Kluszewski	2.00	1.00	.60
83	Bob Allison	15.50	7.75	4.75
84	Billy Martin	3.00	1.50	.90
85	Harmon Killebrew	5.00	2.50	1.50
86	Zoilo Versalles	1.00	.50	.30
87	Lenny Green	.90	.45	.25
88	Bill Tuttle	.90	.45	.25
89	Jim Lemon	1.00	.50	.30
90	Earl Battey	1.00	.50	.30
91	Camilo Pascual	1.00	.50	.30
92	Norm Siebern	40.00	20.00	12.00
93	Jerry Lumpe	1.00	.50	.30
94	Dick Howser	1.50	.70	.45
95a	Gene Stephens (Born: Jan. 5)	1.00	.50	.30
95b	Gene Stephens (Born: Jan. 20)	4.00	2.00	1.25
96	Leo Posada	.90	.45	.25
97	Joe Pignatano	.90	.45	.25
98	Jim Archer	.90	.45	.25
99	Haywood Sullivan	1.00	.50	.30
100	Art Ditmar	.90	.45	.25
101	Gil Hodges	40.00	20.00	12.00
102	Charlie Neal	.90	.45	.25
103	Daryl Spencer	10.00	5.00	3.00
104	Maury Wills	4.00	2.00	1.25
105	Tommy Davis	1.50	.70	.45
106	Willie Davis	1.25	.60	.40
107	John Roseboro	1.00	.50	.30
108	John Podres	2.00	1.00	.60
109a	Sandy Koufax (blue lines around stats)	15.00	7.50	4.50
109b	Sandy Koufax (red lines around stats)	10.00	5.00	3.00
110	Don Drysdale	5.00	2.50	1.50
111	Larry Sherry	1.00	.50	.30
112	Jim Gilliam	2.00	1.00	.60
113	Norm Larker	20.00	10.00	6.00
114	Duke Snider	6.00	3.00	1.75
115	Stan Williams	.90	.45	.25
116	Gordy Coleman	50.00	25.00	15.00
117	Don Blasingame	.90	.45	.25
118	Gene Freese	.90	.45	.25
119	Ed Kasko	.90	.45	.25
120	Gus Bell	1.00	.50	.30
121	Vada Pinson	2.00	1.00	.60
122	Frank Robinson	12.00	6.00	3.50
123	Bob Purkey	1.00	.50	.30
124a	Joey Jay (blue lines around stats)	6.00	3.00	1.75
124b	Joey Jay (red lines around stats)	1.00	.50	.30
125	Jim Brosnan	1.00	.50	.30
126	Jim O'Toole	.90	.45	.25
127	Jerry Lynch	40.00	20.00	12.00
128	Wally Post	1.00	.50	.30
129	Ken Hunt	.90	.45	.25
130	Jerry Zimmerman	.90	.45	.25
131	Willie McCovey	50.00	25.00	15.00
132	Jose Pagan	.90	.45	.25
133	Felipe Alou	1.25	.60	.40
134	Jim Davenport	.90	.45	.25
135	Harvey Kuenn	1.50	.70	.45
136	Orlando Cepeda	3.00	1.50	.90
137	Ed Bailey	.90	.45	.25
138	Sam Jones	.90	.45	.25
139	Mike McCormick	1.00	.50	.30
140	Juan Marichal	50.00	25.00	15.00
141	Jack Sanford	1.00	.50	.30
142	Willie Mays	20.00	10.00	6.00
143	Stu Miller (photo actually Chuck Hiller)	4.00	2.00	1.25
144	Joe Amalfitano	6.00	3.00	1.75
145a	Joe Adock (name incorrect)	15.00	7.50	4.50
145b	Joe Adcock (name correct)	1.50	.70	.45
146	Frank Bolling	.90	.45	.25
147	Ed Mathews	5.00	2.50	1.50
148	Roy McMillan	1.00	.50	.30
149	Hank Aaron	15.00	7.50	4.50
150	Gino Cimoli	.90	.45	.25
151	Frank Thomas	1.00	.50	.30

Complete set prices do not include the higher priced variations, unless noted otherwise.

		NR MT	EX	VG
152	Joe Torre	2.50	1.25	.70
153	Lou Burdette	2.00	1.00	.60
154	Bob Buhl	1.00	.50	.30
155	Carlton Willey	.90	.45	.25
156	Lee Maye	.90	.45	.25
157	Al Spangler	.90	.45	.25
158	Bill White	20.00	10.00	6.00
159	Ken Boyer	2.50	1.25	.70
160	Joe Cunningham	.90	.45	.25
161	Carl Warwick	.90	.45	.25
162	Carl Sawatski	.90	.45	.25
163	Lindy McDaniel	.90	.45	.25
164	Ernie Broglio	.90	.45	.25
165	Larry Jackson	.90	.45	.25
166	Curt Flood	1.50	.70	.45
167	Curt Simmons	1.00	.50	.30
168	Alex Grammas	.90	.45	.25
169	Dick Stuart	1.00	.50	.30
170	Bill Mazeroski	2.00	1.00	.60
171	Don Hoak	1.00	.50	.30
172	Dick Groat	1.50	.70	.45
173a	Roberto Clemente (blue lines around stats)	15.00	7.50	4.50
173b	Roberto Clemente (red lines around stats)	12.00	6.00	3.50
174	Bob Skinner	1.00	.50	.30
175	Bill Virdon	1.25	.60	.40
176	Smoky Burgess	1.25	.60	.40
177	Elroy Face	1.25	.60	.40
178	Bob Friend	1.00	.50	.30
179	Vernon Law	1.00	.50	.30
180	Harvey Haddix	1.00	.50	.30
181	Hal Smith	.90	.45	.25
182	Ed Bouchee	.90	.45	.25
183	Don Zimmer	1.00	.50	.30
184	Ron Santo	2.00	1.00	.60
185	Andre Rodgers	.90	.45	.25
186	Richie Ashburn	2.50	1.25	.70
187a	George Altman (last line is "…1955).)	1.00	.50	.30
187b	George Altman (last line is "…1955."	2.50	1.25	.70
188	Ernie Banks	6.00	3.00	1.75
189	Sam Taylor	.90	.45	.25
190	Don Elston	.90	.45	.25
191	Jerry Kindall	.90	.45	.25
192	Pancho Herrera	.90	.45	.25
193	Tony Taylor	.90	.45	.25
194	Ruben Amaro	.90	.45	.25
195	Don Demeter	.90	.45	.25
196	Bobby Gene Smith	.90	.45	.25
197	Clay Dalrymple	.90	.45	.25
198	Robin Roberts	4.00	2.00	1.25
199	Art Mahaffey	.90	.45	.25
200	John Buzhardt	2.00	1.00	.60

1963 Post Cereal

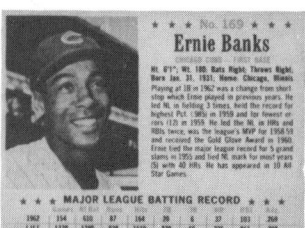

Another 200-player, 3½'' by 2½'' set that, with variations, total more than 205 cards. Numerous color variations also exist due to the different cereal boxes on which the cards were printed. As many as 25 cards in the set are considered scarce, making it much more difficult to complete than the other major Post sets. Star cards also command higher prices than in the '61 or '62 Post cards. The 1963 Post cards are almost identical to the '63 Jello set, which is a slight ¼'' narrower. Cards are still blank backed, with color player photo, bios, and statistics on the numbered card fronts. No Post logo appears on the '63 cards.

		NR MT	EX	VG
	Complete Set:	2800.00	1400.00	840.00
	Common Player:	.90	.49	.25
1	Vic Power	3.50	1.75	1.00
2	Bernie Allen	.90	.45	.25
3	Zoilo Versalles	1.00	.50	.30
4	Rich Rollins	.90	.45	.25
5	Harmon Killebrew	10.00	5.25	3.25
6	Lenny Green	30.00	16.00	9.50
7	Bob Allison	1.25	.60	.35
8	Earl Battey	1.00	.50	.30
9	Camilo Pascual	1.00	.50	.30
10	Jim Kaat	3.00	1.50	.90
11	Jack Kralick	.90	.45	.25
12	Bill Skowron	1.50	.80	.50
13	Bobby Richardson	2.50	1.25	.70
14	Cletis Boyer	1.50	.80	.50
15	Mickey Mantle	200.00	97.00	58.00
16	Roger Maris	125.00	65.00	39.00
17	Yogi Berra	10.00	5.00	3.00
18	Elston Howard	2.50	1.25	.70
19	Whitey Ford	5.00	2.50	1.50
20	Ralph Terry	1.50	.80	.50
21	John Blanchard	1.50	.60	.35
22	Bill Stafford	1.50	.60	.35
23	Tom Tresh	1.50	.80	.50
24	Steve Bilko	.90	.45	.25
25	Bill Moran	.90	.45	.25
26a	Joe Koppe (1962 Avg. is .277)	1.00	.45	.25
26b	Joe Koppe (1962 Avg. is .227)	9.00	4.50	2.75
27	Felix Torres	.90	.45	.25
28a	Leon Wagner (lifetime Avg. is .278)	1.00	.50	.30
28b	Leon Wagner (lifetime Avg. is .272)	9.00	4.50	2.75
29	Albie Pearson	.90	.45	.25
30	Lee Thomas (photo actually George Thomas)	60.00	32.00	19.00
31	Bob Rodgers	1.00	.50	.30
32	Dean Chance	1.00	.50	.30
33	Ken McBride	.90	.45	.25
34	George Thomas (photo actually Lee Thomas)	.90	.45	.25
35	Joe Cunningham	.90	.45	.25
36	Nelson Fox	3.00	1.50	.90
37	Luis Aparicio	4.00	2.00	1.25
38	Al Smith	25.00	13.00	7.75
39	Floyd Robinson	75.00	39.00	23.00
40	Jim Landis	.90	.45	.25
41	Charlie Maxwell	.90	.45	.25
42	Sherman Lollar	1.00	.50	.30
43	Early Wynn	4.00	2.00	1.25
44	Juan Pizarro	.90	.45	.25
45	Ray Herbert	.90	.45	.25
46	Norm Cash	1.50	.80	.50
47	Steve Boros	1.00	.50	.30
48	Dick McAuliffe	20.00	9.75	5.75
49	Bill Bruton	1.00	.50	.30
50	Rocky Colavito	2.50	1.25	.70
51	Al Kaline	7.00	3.25	2.00
52	Dick Brown	.90	.45	.25
53	Jim Bunning	75.00	39.00	23.00
54	Hank Aguirre	.90	.45	.25
55	Frank Lary	1.00	.50	.30
56	Don Mossi	1.00	.50	.30
57	Jim Gentile	1.00	.50	.30
58	Jackie Brandt	.90	.45	.25
59	Brooks Robinson	8.00	4.00	2.50
60	Ron Hansen	.90	.45	.25
61	Jerry Adair	125.00	65.00	39.00
62	John Powell	3.00	1.50	.90
63	Russ Snyder	.90	.45	.25
64	Steve Barber	.90	.45	.25
65	Milt Pappas	1.00	.50	.30
66	Robin Roberts	4.00	2.00	1.25
67	Tito Francona	1.00	.50	.30
68	Jerry Kindall	.90	.45	.25
69	Woodie Held	1.00	.50	.30
70	Bubba Phillips	10.00	5.25	3.25
71	Chuck Essegian	.90	.45	.25
72	Willie Kirkland	.90	.45	.25
73	Al Luplow	.90	.45	.25
74	Ty Cline	.90	.45	.25
75	Dick Donovan	.90	.45	.25
76	John Romano	.90	.45	.25
77	Pete Runnels	1.00	.50	.30
78	Ed Bressoud	.90	.45	.25
79	Frank Malzone	.90	.45	.25
80	Carl Yastrzemski	200.00	114.00	68.00
81	Gary Geiger	.90	.45	.25
82	Lou Clinton	.90	.45	.25

		NR MT	EX	VG
83	Earl Wilson	.90	.45	.25
84	Bill Monbouquette	1.00	.50	.30
85	Norm Siebern	1.00	.50	.30
86	Jerry Lumpe	75.00	39.00	23.00
87	Manny Jimenez	75.00	39.00	23.00
88	Gino Cimoli	.90	.45	.25
89	Ed Charles	.90	.45	.25
90	Ed Rakow	.90	.45	.25
91	Bob Del Greco	.90	.45	.25
92	Haywood Sullivan	1.00	.50	.30
93	Chuck Hinton	.90	.45	.25
94	Ken Retzer	.90	.45	.25
95	Harry Bright	.90	.45	.25
96	Bob Johnson	.90	.45	.25
97	Dave Stenhouse	10.00	5.25	3.25
98	Chuck Cottier	20.00	9.75	5.75
99	Tom Cheney	.90	.45	.25
100	Claude Osteen	10.00	5.25	3.25
101	Orlando Cepeda	3.00	1.50	.90
102	Charley Hiller	.90	.45	.25
103	Jose Pagan	.90	.45	.25
104	Jim Davenport	.90	.45	.25
105	Harvey Kuenn	1.50	.80	.50
106	Willie Mays	20.00	9.75	5.75
107	Felipe Alou	1.25	.60	.35
108	Tom Haller	75.00	39.00	23.00
109	Juan Marichal	4.00	2.00	1.25
110	Jack Sanford	1.00	.50	.30
111	Bill O'Dell	.90	.45	.25
112	Willie McCovey	5.00	2.50	1.50
113	Lee Walls	.90	.45	.25
114	Jim Gilliam	2.50	1.25	.70
115	Maury Wills	2.50	1.25	.70
116	Ron Fairly	1.00	.50	.30
117	Tommy Davis	1.50	.80	.50
118	Duke Snider	6.00	3.25	2.00
119	Willie Davis	125.00	65.00	39.00
120	John Roseboro	1.00	.50	.30
121	Sandy Koufax	12.00	5.75	3.50
122	Stan Williams	.90	.45	.25
123	Don Drysdale	5.00	2.50	1.50
124a	Daryl Spencer (no arm showing)	1.00	.45	.25
124b	Daryl Spencer (part of arm showing)	9.00	4.50	2.75
125	Gordy Coleman	.90	.45	.25
126	Don Blasingame	.90	.45	.25
127	Leo Cardenas	1.00	.50	.30
128	Eddie Kasko	125.00	65.00	39.00
129	Jerry Lynch	10.00	5.25	3.25
130	Vada Pinson	2.00	1.00	.60
131a	Frank Robinson (no stripes on hat)	6.00	3.25	2.00
131b	Frank Robinson (stripes on hat)	9.00	4.50	2.75
132	John Edwards	.90	.45	.25
133	Joey Jay	.90	.45	.25
134	Bob Purkey	1.00	.50	.30
135	Marty Keough	10.00	5.25	3.25
136	Jim O'Toole	.90	.45	.25
137	Dick Stuart	1.00	.50	.30
138	Bill Mazeroski	2.00	1.00	.60
139	Dick Groat	1.50	.80	.50
140	Don Hoak	25.00	13.00	7.75
141	Bob Skinner	10.00	5.25	3.25
142	Bill Virdon	1.50	.80	.50
143	Roberto Clemente	12.00	5.75	3.50
144	Smoky Burgess	1.25	.60	.35
145	Bob Friend	1.00	.50	.30
146	Al McBean	.90	.45	.25
147	El Roy Face (Elroy)	1.50	.80	.50
148	Joe Adcock	1.50	.80	.50
149	Frank Bolling	.90	.45	.25
150	Roy McMillan	1.00	.50	.30
151	Eddie Mathews	6.00	3.25	2.00
152	Hank Aaron	50.00	26.00	15.50
153	Del Crandall	25.00	13.00	7.75
154a	Bob Shaw (third sentence has "In 1959" twice)	9.00	4.50	2.75
154b	Bob Shaw (third sentence has "In 1959" once)	1.00	.45	.25
155	Lew Burdette	2.00	1.00	.60
156	Joe Torre	2.50	1.25	.70
157	Tony Cloninger	.90	.45	.25
158	Bill White	1.50	.80	.50
159	Julian Javier	1.00	.50	.30
160	Ken Boyer	2.50	1.25	.70
161	Julio Gotay	.90	.45	.25
162	Curt Flood	75.00	39.00	23.00
163	Charlie James	.90	.45	.25
164	Gene Oliver	.90	.45	.25
165	Ernie Broglio	.90	.45	.25
166	Bob Gibson	5.00	2.50	1.50

		NR MT	EX	VG
167a	Lindy McDaniel (before trade line)	1.00	.45	.25
167b	Lindy McDaniel (no before trade line)	4.00	2.00	1.25
168	Ray Washburn	.90	.45	.25
169	Ernie Banks	6.00	3.25	2.00
170	Ron Santo	2.00	1.00	.60
171	George Altman	.90	.45	.25
172	Billy Williams	75.00	39.00	23.00
173	Andre Rodgers	6.00	3.25	2.00
174	Ken Hubbs	12.00	6.50	4.00
175	Don Landrum	.90	.45	.25
176	Dick Bertell	10.00	5.25	3.25
177	Roy Sievers	1.25	.60	.35
178	Tony Taylor	.90	.45	.25
179	John Callison	1.25	.60	.35
180	Don Demeter	.90	.45	.25
181	Tony Gonzalez	.90	.45	.25
182	Wes Covington	12.00	6.50	4.00
183	Art Mahaffey	.90	.45	.25
184	Clay Dalrymple	.90	.45	.25
185	Al Spangler	.90	.45	.25
186	Roman Mejias	.90	.45	.25
187	Bob Aspromonte	225.00	114.00	68.00
188	Norm Larker	25.00	13.00	7.75
189	Johnny Temple	.90	.45	.25
190	Carl Warwick	.90	.45	.25
191	Bob Lillis	.90	.45	.25
192	Dick Farrell	.90	.45	.25
193	Gil Hodges	5.00	2.50	1.50
194	Marv Throneberry	2.50	1.25	.70
195	Charlie Neal	6.00	3.25	2.00
196	Frank Thomas	125.00	65.00	39.00
197	Richie Ashburn	13.00	6.50	4.00
198	Felix Mantilla	.90	.45	.25
199	Rod Kanehl	12.00	6.50	4.00
200	Roger Craig	2.50	1.25	.70

1962 Post Cereal Canadian

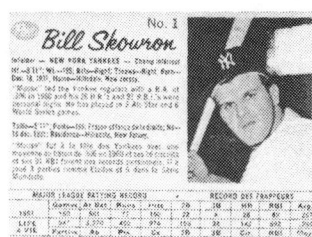

This Canadian set of cards is scarce due to the much more limited distribution in Canada. The cards were printed on the back of the cereal box itself and contained a full-color player photo with biography and statistics given in both French and English. The card backs were blank. Cards measure 3½'' by 2½.'' This 200-card set is very similar to the Post Cereal cards printed in the U.S. The Post logo appears at the upper-left corner in the Canadian issue. Several cards are scarce because of limited distribution and there are two Whitey Ford cards, the corrected card being the most scarce.

		NR MT	EX	VG
Complete Set:		1550.00	775.00	465.00
Common Player:		2.00	1.00	.60
1	Bill Skowron	8.00	4.00	2.50
2	Bobby Richardson	6.00	3.00	1.75
3	Cletis Boyer	3.50	1.75	1.00
4	Tony Kubek	6.00	3.00	1.75
5a	Mickey Mantle (script name large)	90.00	45.00	27.00
5b	Mickey Mantle (script name small)	60.00	30.00	18.00
6	Roger Maris	12.00	6.00	3.50
7	Yogi Berra	12.00	6.00	3.50
8	Elston Howard	4.00	2.00	1.25
9a	Whitey Ford (Dodgers)	20.00	10.00	6.00
9b	Whitey Ford (Yankees)	30.00	15.00	9.00
10	Ralph Terry	20.00	10.00	6.00
11	John Blanchard	3.00	1.50	.90
12	Luis Arroyo	3.00	1.50	.90

		NR MT	EX	VG			NR MT	EX	VG
13	Bill Stafford	3.00	1.50	.90	99	Haywood Sullivan	20.00	10.00	6.00
14	Norm Cash	4.00	2.00	1.25	100	Art Ditmar	20.00	10.00	6.00
15	Jake Wood	2.00	1.00	.60	101	Gil Hodges	10.00	5.00	3.00
16	Steve Boros	2.00	1.00	.60	102	Charlie Neal	2.00	1.00	.60
17	Chico Fernandez	2.00	1.00	.60	103	Daryl Spencer	2.00	1.00	.60
18	Bill Bruton	2.00	1.00	.60	104	Maury Wills	5.00	2.50	1.50
19a	Rocky Colavito (script name large)				105	Tommy Davis	8.00	4.00	2.50
		5.00	2.50	1.50	106	Willie Davis	4.00	2.00	1.25
19b	Rocky Colavito (script name small)				107	John Roseboro	3.00	1.50	.90
		5.00	2.50	1.50	108	John Podres	4.00	2.00	1.25
20	Al Kaline	12.00	6.00	3.50	109	Sandy Koufax	25.00	12.50	7.50
21	Dick Brown	6.00	3.00	1.75	110	Don Drysdale	12.00	6.00	3.50
22a	Frank Lary (French bio variation)	6.00	3.00	1.75	111	Larry Sherry	20.00	10.00	6.00
22b	Frank Lary (French bio variation)	6.00	3.00	1.75	112	Jim Gilliam	20.00	10.00	6.00
23	Don Mossi	2.00	1.00	.60	113	Norm Larker	2.00	1.00	.60
24	Phil Regan	2.00	1.00	.60	114	Duke Snider	20.00	10.00	6.00
25	Charley Maxwell	2.00	1.00	.60	115	Stan Williams	2.00	1.00	.60
26	Jim Bunning	5.00	2.50	1.50	116	Gordy Coleman	2.00	1.00	.60
27a	Jim Gentile (French bio variation)	4.00	2.00	1.25	117	Don Blasingame	20.00	10.00	6.00
27b	Jim Gentile (French bio variation)	4.00	2.00	1.25	118	Gene Freese	6.00	3.00	1.75
28	Marv Breeding	2.00	1.00	.60	119	Ed Kasko	2.00	1.00	.60
29	Brooks Robinson	20.00	10.00	6.00	120	Gus Bell	2.00	1.00	.60
30	Ron Hansen	2.00	1.00	.60	121	Vada Pinson	4.50	2.25	1.25
31	Jackie Brandt	2.00	1.00	.60	122	Frank Robinson	12.00	6.00	3.50
32	Dick Williams	20.00	10.00	6.00	123	Bob Purkey	20.00	10.00	6.00
33	Gus Triandos	2.00	1.00	.60	124	Joey Jay	2.00	1.00	.60
34	Milt Pappas	3.00	1.50	.90	125	Jim Brosnan	3.00	1.50	.90
35	Hoyt Wilhelm	12.00	6.00	3.50	126	Jim O'Toole	2.00	1.00	.60
36	Chuck Estrada	2.00	1.00	.60	127	Jerry Lynch	2.00	1.00	.60
37	Vic Power	2.00	1.00	.60	128	Wally Post	45.00	22.00	13.50
38	Johnny Temple	2.00	1.00	.60	129	Ken Hunt	2.00	1.00	.60
39	Bubba Phillips	20.00	10.00	6.00	130	Jerry Zimmerman	2.00	1.00	.60
40	Tito Francona	2.00	1.00	.60	131	Willie McCovey	12.00	6.00	3.50
41	Willie Kirkland	6.00	3.00	1.75	132	Jose Pagan	2.00	1.00	.60
42	John Romano	6.00	3.00	1.75	133	Felipe Alou	3.50	1.75	1.00
43	Jim Perry	4.00	2.00	1.25	134	Jim Davenport	2.00	1.00	.60
44	Woodie Held	2.00	1.00	.60	135	Harvey Kuenn	4.00	2.00	1.25
45	Chuck Essegian	2.00	1.00	.60	136	Orlando Cepeda	6.00	3.00	1.75
46	Roy Sievers	3.50	1.75	1.00	137	Ed Bailey	20.00	10.00	6.00
47	Nellie Fox	5.00	2.50	1.50	138	Sam Jones	20.00	10.00	6.00
48	Al Smith	2.00	1.00	.60	139	Mike McCormick	2.00	1.00	.60
49	Luis Aparicio	12.00	6.00	3.50	140	Juan Marichal	12.00	6.00	3.50
50	Jim Landis	2.00	1.00	.60	141	Jack Sanford	2.00	1.00	.60
51	Minnie Minoso	20.00	10.00	6.00	142a	Willie Mays (big head)	30.00	15.00	9.00
52	Andy Carey	6.00	3.00	1.75	142b	Willie Mays (small head)	40.00	20.00	12.00
53	Sherman Lollar	2.00	1.00	.60	143	Stu Miller	2.00	1.00	.60
54	Bill Pierce	3.50	1.75	1.00	144	Joe Amalfitano	20.00	10.00	6.00
55	Early Wynn	9.00	4.50	2.75	145	Joe Adcock	4.00	2.00	1.25
56	Chuck Schilling	2.00	1.00	.60	146	Frank Bolling	2.00	1.00	.60
57	Pete Runnels	3.00	1.50	.90	147	Ed Mathews	10.00	5.00	3.00
58	Frank Malzone	2.00	1.00	.60	148	Roy McMillan	2.00	1.00	.60
59	Don Buddin	6.00	3.00	1.75	149a	Hank Aaron (script name large)	30.00	15.00	9.00
60	Gary Geiger	2.00	1.00	.60	149b	Hank Aaron (script name small)	30.00	15.00	9.00
61	Carl Yastrzemski	35.00	17.50	10.50	150	Gino Cimoli	2.00	1.00	.60
62	Jackie Jensen	8.00	4.00	2.50	151	Frank Thomas	2.00	1.00	.60
63	Jim Pagliaroni	2.00	1.00	.60	152	Joe Torre	4.50	2.25	1.25
64	Don Schwall	2.00	1.00	.60	153	Lou Burdette	4.50	2.25	1.25
65	Dale Long	2.00	1.00	.60	154	Bob Buhl	3.00	1.50	.90
66	Chuck Cottier	2.00	1.00	.60	155	Carlton Willey	2.00	1.00	.60
67	Billy Klaus	2.00	1.00	.60	156	Lee Maye	2.00	1.00	.60
68	Coot Veal	2.00	1.00	.60	157	Al Spangler	2.00	1.00	.60
69	Marty Keough	2.00	1.00	.60	158	Bill White	3.50	1.75	1.00
70	Willie Tasby	20.00	10.00	6.00	159	Ken Boyer	25.00	12.50	7.50
71	Gene Woodling (photo reversed)	3.00	1.50	.90	160	Joe Cunningham	2.00	1.00	.60
72	Gene Green	2.00	1.00	.60	161	Carl Warwick	6.00	3.00	1.75
73	Dick Donovan	2.00	1.00	.60	162	Carl Sawatski	2.00	1.00	.60
74	Steve Bilko	2.00	1.00	.60	163	Lindy McDaniel	2.00	1.00	.60
75	Rocky Bridges	6.00	3.00	1.75	164	Ernie Broglio	2.00	1.00	.60
76	Eddie Yost	2.00	1.00	.60	165	Larry Jackson	2.00	1.00	.60
77	Leon Wagner	20.00	10.00	6.00	166	Curt Flood	4.00	2.00	1.25
78	Albie Pearson	6.00	3.00	1.75	167	Curt Simmons	7.00	3.50	2.00
79	Ken Hunt	2.00	1.00	.60	168	Alex Grammas	2.00	1.00	.60
80	Earl Averill	2.00	1.00	.60	169	Dick Stuart	3.00	1.50	.90
81	Ryne Duren	4.00	2.00	1.25	170	Bill Mazeroski	20.00	10.00	6.00
82	Ted Kluszewski	4.00	2.00	1.25	171	Don Hoak	2.00	1.00	.60
83	Bob Allison	3.00	1.50	.90	172	Dick Groat	8.00	4.00	2.50
84	Billy Martin	5.00	2.50	1.50	173	Roberto Clemente	25.00	12.50	7.50
85	Harmon Killebrew	10.00	5.00	3.00	174	Bob Skinner	2.00	1.00	.60
86	Zoilo Versalles	2.00	1.00	.60	175	Bill Virdon	4.00	2.00	1.25
87	Lenny Green	2.00	1.00	.60	176	Smoky Burgess	7.00	3.50	2.00
88	Bill Tuttle	2.00	1.00	.60	177	Elroy Face	7.00	3.50	2.00
89	Jim Lemon	2.00	1.00	.60	178	Bob Friend	3.00	1.50	.90
90	Earl Battey	2.00	1.00	.60	179	Vernon Law	3.50	1.75	1.00
91	Camilo Pascual	3.00	1.50	.90	180	Harvey Haddix	3.00	1.50	.90
92	Norm Siebern	2.00	1.00	.60	181	Hal Smith	20.00	10.00	6.00
93	Jerry Lumpe	2.00	1.00	.60	182	Ed Bouchee	2.00	1.00	.60
94	Dick Howser	20.00	10.00	6.00	183	Don Zimmer	4.00	2.00	1.25
95	Gene Stephens	2.00	1.00	.60	184	Ron Santo	4.50	2.25	1.25
96	Leo Posada	2.00	1.00	.60	185	Andre Rodgers	2.00	1.00	.60
97	Joe Pignatano	2.00	1.00	.60	186	Richie Ashburn	5.00	2.50	1.50
98	Jim Archer	2.00	1.00	.60	187	George Altman	2.00	1.00	.60

		NR MT	EX	VG
188	Ernie Banks	20.00	10.00	6.00
189	Sam Taylor	2.00	1.00	.60
190	Don Elston	2.00	1.00	.60
191	Jerry Kindall	2.00	1.00	.60
192	Pancho Herrera	2.00	1.00	.60
193	Tony Taylor	2.00	1.00	.60
194	Ruben Amaro	2.00	1.00	.60
195	Don Demeter	20.00	10.00	6.00
196	Bobby Gene Smith	2.00	1.00	.60
197	Clay Dalrymple	2.00	1.00	.60
198	Robin Roberts	10.00	5.00	3.00
199	Art Mahaffey	2.00	1.00	.60
200	John Buzhardt	5.00	2.50	1.50

1986 Provigo Expos

 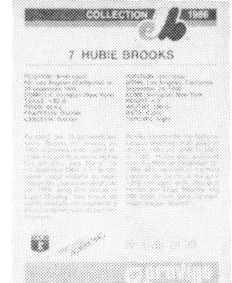

This 28-card set was issued in three-card panels of 7½'' by 3⅜.'' Each card measures 2½'' by 3⅜,'' and each panel includes two players and an advertising card. Panels are perforated to allow for separation, if desired. Card fronts have high quality game-action color photos with the player's name, uniform number and Expos and Provigo logos. Card backs include biographical information in both French and English and list the card's number within the set. There are 24 player, one manager and two coaches cards, along with a card of the Expos mascot, Youppi.

		MT	NR MT	EX
Complete Panel Set:		8.00	6.00	3.25
Complete Singles Set:		2.50	2.00	1.00
Common Panel:		.35	.25	.14
Common Single Player:		.06	.05	.02
Panel 1		.50	.40	.20
1	Hubie Brooks	.10	.08	.04
2	Dann Bilardello	.06	.05	.02
---	Checklist	.03	.02	.01
Panel 2		.35	.25	.14
3	Buck Rodgers	.06	.05	.02
4	Andy McGaffigan	.06	.05	.02
---	Album Offer	.03	.02	.01
Panel 3		.70	.50	.30
5	Mitch Webster	.20	.15	.08
6	Jim Wohlford	.06	.05	.02
---	Album Offer	.03	.02	.01
Panel 4		.90	.70	.35
7	Tim Raines	1.25	.90	.50
8	Jay Tibbs	.06	.05	.02
---	Album Offer	.03	.02	.01
Panel 5		1.50	1.25	.60
9	Andre Dawson	.30	.25	.12
10	Andres Galarraga	.25	.20	.10
---	Album Offer	.03	.02	.01
Panel 6		.50	.40	.20
11	Tim Wallach	.15	.11	.06
12	Dan Schatzeder	.06	.05	.02
---	Checklist	.03	.02	.01
Panel 7		.50	.40	.20
13	Jeff Reardon	.12	.09	.05
14	Expos' Coaching Staff (Larry Bearnarth, Joe Kerrigan, Bobby Winkles)	.06	.05	.02
---	Album Offer	.03	.02	.01
Panel 8		.35	.25	.14
15	Jason Thompson	.06	.05	.02
16	Bert Roberge	.06	.05	.02
---	$1 Expos Ticket Coupon	.03	.02	.01

		MT	NR MT	EX
Panel 9		.50	.40	.20
17	Al Newman	.10	.08	.04
18	Tim Burke	.10	.08	.04
---	Album Offer	.03	.02	.01
Panel 10		.35	.25	.14
19	Bryn Smith	.08	.06	.03
20	Wayne Krenchicki	.06	.05	.02
---	Album Offer	.03	.02	.01
Panel 11		.50	.40	.20
21	Joe Hesketh	.10	.08	.04
22	Herman Winningham	.10	.08	.04
---	Album Offer	.03	.02	.01
Panel 12		1.00	.70	.40
23	Vance Law	.06	.05	.02
24	Floyd Youmans	.35	.25	.14
---	Album Offer	.03	.02	.01
Panel 13		.50	.40	.20
25	Jeff Parrett	.12	.09	.05
26	Mike Fitzgerald	.06	.05	.02
---	Album Offer	.03	.02	.01
Panel 14		.35	.25	.14
27	Youppi (Team Mascot)	.06	.05	.02
28	Expos' Coaching Staff (Ron Hansen, Ken Macha, Rick Renick)	.06	.05	.02
---	Album Offer	.03	.02	.01

1986 Quaker Oats

The Quaker Company, in conjunction with Topps, produced this 33-card set of current baseball stars for packaging in groups of three in Chewy Granola Bars packages. The cards are noted as the ''1st Annual Collectors Edition.'' They are numbered and measure 2½'' by 3½.'' Card fronts feature full-color player photos with product name at the top and player name, team and position below the photo. The complete set was offered via mail order by the Quaker Company.

		MT	NR MT	EX
Complete Set:		8.00	6.00	3.25
Common Player:		.15	.11	.06
1	Willie McGee	.15	.11	.06
2	Dwight Gooden	.60	.45	.25
3	Vince Coleman	.30	.25	.12
4	Gary Carter	.25	.20	.10
5	Jack Clark	.15	.11	.06
6	Steve Garvey	.25	.20	.10
7	Tony Gwynn	.35	.25	.14
8	Dale Murphy	.40	.30	.15
9	Dave Parker	.15	.11	.06
10	Tim Raines	.25	.20	.10
11	Pete Rose	.60	.45	.25
12	Nolan Ryan	.25	.20	.10

		MT	NR MT	EX
13	Ryne Sandberg	.20	.15	.08
14	Mike Schmidt	.35	.25	.14
15	Ozzie Smith	.15	.11	.06
16	Darryl Strawberry	.35	.25	.14
17	Fernando Valenzuela	.20	.15	.08
18	Don Mattingly	1.25	.90	.50
19	Bret Saberhagen	.20	.15	.08
20	Ozzie Guillen	.20	.15	.08
21	Bert Blyleven	.15	.11	.06
22	Wade Boggs	.80	.60	.30
23	George Brett	.40	.30	.15
24	Darrell Evans	.15	.11	.06
25	Rickey Henderson	.35	.25	.14
26	Reggie Jackson	.30	.25	.12
27	Eddie Murray	.30	.25	.12
28	Phil Niekro	.20	.15	.08
29	Dan Quisenberry	.15	.11	.06
30	Jim Rice	.25	.20	.10
31	Cal Ripken	.30	.25	.12
32	Tom Seaver	.25	.20	.10
33	Dave Winfield	.25	.20	.10
---	Offer Card	.03	.02	.01

		MT	NR MT	EX
13	George Brett	.35	.25	.14
14	Nolan Ryan	.20	.15	.08
15	Rickey Henderson	.30	.25	.12
16	Steve Carlton	.25	.20	.10
17	Rod Carew	.25	.20	.10
18	Steve Garvey	.25	.20	.10
19	Reggie Jackson	.25	.20	.10
20	Dave Concepcion	.10	.08	.04
21	Robin Yount	.20	.15	.08
22	Mike Schmidt	.35	.25	.14
23	Jim Palmer	.20	.15	.08
24	Bruce Sutter	.10	.08	.04
25	Dan Quisenberry	.10	.08	.04
26	Bill Madlock	.10	.08	.04
27	Cecil Cooper	.10	.08	.04
28	Gary Carter	.25	.20	.10
29	Fred Lynn	.15	.11	.06
30	Pedro Guerrero	.15	.11	.06
31	Ron Guidry	.15	.11	.06
32	Keith Hernandez	.20	.15	.08
33	Carlton Fisk	.15	.11	.06

1984 Ralston Purina

This set, produced in conjunction with Topps, has 33 of the game's top players, and is titled "1st Annual Collector's Edition." The full-color photos on the 2½" by 3½" cards are all close-up poses. Topps' logo appears only on the card fronts, and the backs are completely different from Topps' regular issue of 1984. Card backs feature a checkerboard look, coinciding with the well known Ralston Purina logo. Cards are numbered 1-33, with odd numbers American Leaguers and even numbered cards for National League players. Four cards were packed in boxes of Cookie Crisp and Donkey Kong Junior brand cereals, and the complete set was available via a mail-in offer.

		MT	NR MT	EX
Complete Set:		4.00	3.00	1.50
Common Player:		.10	.08	.04
1	Eddie Murray	.30	.25	.12
2	Ozzie Smith	.10	.08	.04
3	Ted Simmons	.10	.08	.04
4	Pete Rose	.50	.40	.20
5	Greg Luzinski	.10	.08	.04
6	Andre Dawson	.15	.11	.06
7	Dave Winfield	.25	.20	.10
8	Tom Seaver	.25	.20	.10
9	Jim Rice	.25	.20	.10
10	Fernando Valenzuela	.20	.15	.08
11	Wade Boggs	.60	.45	.25
12	Dale Murphy	.35	.25	.14

1987 Ralston Purina

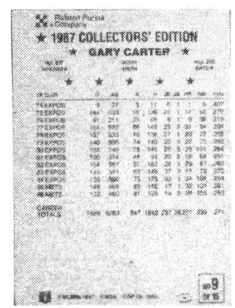

The Ralston Purina Company, in conjunction with Mike Schecter Associates, issued a 15-card set in specially marked boxes of Cookie Crisp and Honey Graham Chex brands of cereal. Three different cards, each measuring 2½" by 3½" and wrapped in cellophane, were inserted in each box. The card fronts contain a full-color photo with the team insignia airbrushed away. Above the photo are two yellow crossed bats and a star, with the player's uniform number inside the star. The card backs are grey with red printing and contain the set name, card number, player's name, personal information and career major league statistics. As part of the Ralston Purina promotion, the company advertised an uncut sheet of cards which was available by finding an "instant-winner" game card or sending $1 plus two non-winning cards. Cards on the uncut sheet are identical in design to the single cards, save the omission of the words "1987 Collectors Edition" in the upper right corner. A complete uncut sheet in Mint condition is valued at $10.

		MT	NR MT	EX
Complete Set:		15.00	11.00	6.00
Common Player:		1.00	.70	.40
1	Nolan Ryan	1.25	.90	.50
2	Steve Garvey	1.25	.90	.50
3	Wade Boggs	2.00	1.50	.80
4	Dave Winfield	1.25	.90	.50
5	Don Mattingly	2.75	2.00	1.00
6	Don Sutton	1.00	.70	.40
7	Dave Parker	1.00	.70	.40
8	Eddie Murray	1.25	.90	.50
9	Gary Carter	1.25	.90	.50
10	Roger Clemens	1.50	1.25	.60
11	Fernando Valenzuela	1.25	.90	.50
12	Cal Ripken Jr.	1.25	.90	.50
13	Ozzie Smith	1.00	.70	.40
14	Mike Schmidt	1.50	1.25	.60
15	Ryne Sandberg	1.25	.90	.50

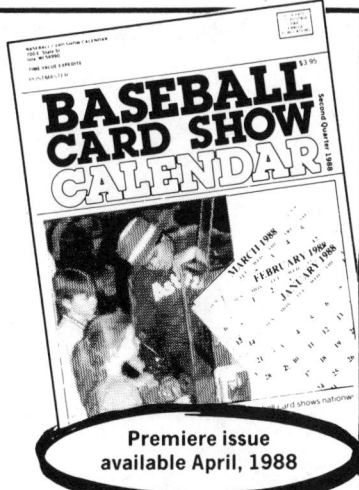

1954 Red Heart Dog Food

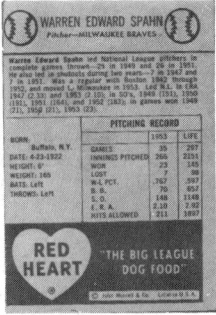

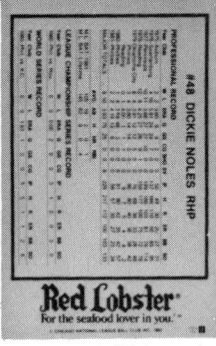

This set of 33 cards was issued in three color-coded series by the Red Heart Dog Food Co. Card fronts feature hand-colored photos on either a blue, green or red background. The 11 red-background cards are scarcer than the 11-card blue or green series. Backs of the 2⅝'' by 3¾'' cards contain biographical and statistical information along with a Red Heart ad. Each 11-card series was available via a mail-in offer. As late as the early 1970s, the company was still sending cards to collectors who requested them.

		NR MT	EX	VG
Complete Set:		1000.00	500.00	300.00
Common Player:		14.00	7.00	4.25
(1)	Richie Ashburn	25.00	12.50	7.50
(2)	Frankie Baumholtz	17.00	8.50	5.00
(3)	Gus Bell	14.00	7.00	4.25
(4)	Billy Cox	17.00	8.50	5.00
(5)	Alvin Dark	17.00	8.50	5.00
(6)	Carl Erskine	20.00	10.00	6.00
(7)	Ferris Fain	14.00	7.00	4.25
(8)	Dee Fondy	14.00	7.00	4.25
(9)	Nelson Fox	20.00	10.00	6.00
(10)	Jim Gilliam	20.00	10.00	6.00
(11)	Jim Hegan	17.00	8.50	5.00
(12)	George Kell	25.00	12.50	7.50
(13)	Ted Kluszewski	20.00	10.00	6.00
(14)	Ralph Kiner	30.00	15.00	9.00
(15)	Harvey Kuenn	17.00	8.50	5.00
(16)	Bob Lemon	30.00	15.00	9.00
(17)	Sherman Lollar	14.00	7.00	4.25
(18)	Mickey Mantle	200.00	100.00	60.00
(19)	Billy Martin	30.00	15.00	9.00
(20)	Gil McDougald	20.00	10.00	6.00
(21)	Roy McMillan	14.00	7.00	4.25
(22)	Minnie Minoso	17.00	8.50	5.00
(23)	Stan Musial	125.00	62.00	37.00
(24)	Billy Pierce	17.00	8.50	5.00
(25)	Al Rosen	20.00	10.00	6.00
(26)	Hank Sauer	13.50	6.75	4.00
(27)	Red Schoendienst	20.00	10.00	6.00
(28)	Enos Slaughter	25.00	12.50	7.50
(29)	Duke Snider	50.00	25.00	15.00
(30)	Warren Spahn	30.00	15.00	9.00
(31)	Sammy White	14.00	7.00	4.25
(32)	Eddie Yost	14.00	7.00	4.25
(33)	Gus Zernial	14.00	7.00	4.25

1982 Red Lobster Cubs

This 28-card set was co-sponsored by the team and a seafood restaurant chain for distribution at a 1982 Cubs promotional game. Card fronts are unbordered color photos, with player name, number, position and facimile autograph superimposed. The set includes 25 players on the 2¼'' by 3½'' cards, along with a card for manager Lee Elia, an unnumbered card for the coaching staff and a team picture. Card backs have very complete player statistics and a Red Lobster ad.

		MT	NR MT	EX
Complete Set:		9.00	6.75	3.50
Common Player:		.20	.15	.08
1	Larry Bowa	.40	.30	.15
4	Lee Elia	.20	.15	.08
6	Keith Moreland	.40	.30	.15
7	Jody Davis	.40	.30	.15
10	Leon Durham	.50	.40	.20
15	Junior Kennedy	.20	.15	.08
17	Bump Wills	.20	.15	.08
18	Scot Thompson	.20	.15	.08
21	Jay Johnstone	.25	.20	.10
22	Bill Buckner	.40	.30	.15
23	Ryne Sandberg	2.50	2.00	1.00
24	Jerry Morales	.20	.15	.08
25	Gary Woods	.20	.15	.08
28	Steve Henderson	.20	.15	.08
29	Bob Molinaro	.20	.15	.08
31	Fergie Jenkins	.70	.50	.30
33	Al Ripley	.20	.15	.08
34	Randy Martz	.20	.15	.08
36	Mike Proly	.20	.15	.08
37	Ken Kravec	.20	.15	.08
38	Willie Hernandez	.40	.30	.15
39	Bill Campbell	.20	.15	.08
41	Dick Tidrow	.20	.15	.08
46	Lee Smith	.50	.40	.20
47	Doug Bird	.20	.15	.08
48	Dickie Noles	.20	.15	.08
---	Team Photo	.20	.15	.08
---	Coaching Staff (Billy Connors, Tom Harmon, Gordy MacKenzie, John Vuckovich, Billy Williams)	.20	.15	.08

1952 Red Man Tobacco

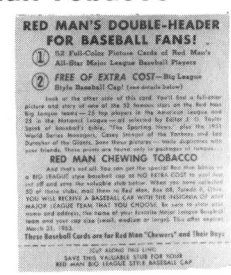

This was the first national set of tobacco cards produced since the golden days of tobacco sets in the early part of the century. There are 52 cards in the set, with 25 top players and one manager from each league. Player selection was made by Editor J.G. Taylor Spink of The Sporting News. Cards measure 3½'' by 4'', including a ½'' tab at the bottom of each card. These tabs were redeemable for a free baseball cap from Red Man. Cards are harder to find with tabs intact, and thus more valuable in that form. Values quoted here are for cards with tabs, cards with the tabs removed would be valued about 50% of the

Baseball Card Collectors . . . Get a
FREE ISSUE
of Sports Collectors Digest

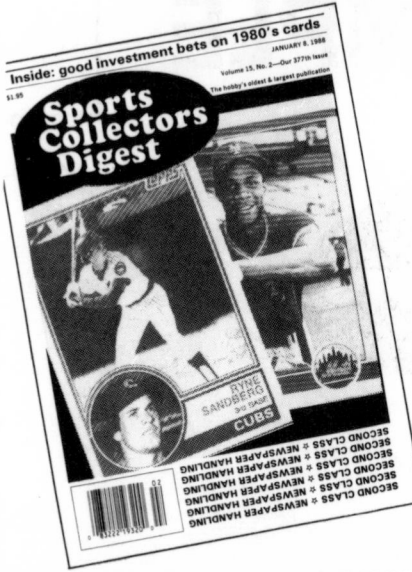

Here's just a sampling of what SPORTS COLLECTORS DIGEST has to offer collectors like you every week . . .

- **Tens of thousands of baseball cards** and other sports collectibles for sale from all eras.

- **Price Guide** to more than 27,000 baseball cards produced since 1948.

- **Articles, columns, and news** about cards, teams, and players from all eras.

- **Show calendar** listing hundreds of upcoming baseball card shows you can visit.

- **Weekly frequency** puts you on top of the action 52 times a year.

Send for your FREE SAMPLE COPY or subscribe today. Get in on the fun of baseball card collecting with the help of the hobby's #1 publication. Complete and mail the postcard below.

Use the postcard below to order your

FREE SAMPLE

of

Sports Collectors Digest

different teams. Complete set prices quoted below do not include the scarcer of the variation pairs. Cards still measure 3½'' by 4'' with tabs intact. Cards without tabs are worth about 50% of the values quoted below. Formats for the cards remain virtually unchanged, with card numbers included within the player information boxes well as on the tabs.

		NR MT	EX	VG
	Complete Set:	950.00	475.00	285.00
	Common Player:	10.00	5.00	3.00
A	Bobby Avila	10.00	5.00	3.00
N	Richie Ashburn	20.00	10.00	6.00
A	Jim Busby	10.00	5.00	3.00
N	Billy Cox	14.00	7.00	4.25
A	Nelson Fox	20.00	10.00	6.00
N	Del Crandall	14.00	7.00	4.25
Aa	George Kell (Boston)	45.00	22.00	13.50
Ab	George Kell (Chicago)	60.00	30.00	18.00
N	Carl Erskine	18.00	9.00	5.50
A	Sherman Lollar	10.00	5.00	3.00
N	Monte Irvin	30.00	15.00	9.00
Aa	Sam Mele (Baltimore)	30.00	15.00	9.00
Ab	Sam Mele (Chicago)	50.00	25.00	15.00
N	Ted Kluszewski	18.00	9.00	5.50
A	Orestes Minoso	14.00	7.00	4.25
N	Don Mueller	10.00	5.00	3.00
A	Mel Parnell	10.00	5.00	3.00
N	Andy Pafko	14.00	7.00	4.25
Aa	Dave Philley (Cleveland)	30.00	15.00	9.00
Ab	Dave Philley (Philadelphia)	50.00	25.00	15.00
N	Del Rice	10.00	5.00	3.00
0A	Billy Pierce	14.00	7.00	4.25
0N	Al Schoendienst	18.00	9.00	5.50
1A	Jim Piersall	14.00	7.00	4.25
1N	Warren Spahn	39.00	19.50	11.50
2A	Al Rosen	18.00	9.00	5.50
2N	Curt Simmons	14.00	7.00	4.25
3A	"Mickey" Vernon	14.00	7.00	4.25
3N	Roy Campanella	75.00	37.00	22.00
4A	Sammy White	10.00	5.00	3.00
4N	Jim Gilliam	18.00	9.00	5.50
5A	Gene Woodling	14.00	7.00	4.25
5N	"Pee Wee" Reese	45.00	22.00	13.50
6A	Ed "Whitey" Ford	45.00	22.00	13.50
6N	Edwin "Duke" Snider	75.00	37.00	22.00
7A	Phil Rizzuto	39.00	19.50	11.50
7N	Rip Repulski	10.00	5.00	3.00
8A	Bob Porterfield	10.00	5.00	3.00
8N	Robin Roberts	30.00	15.00	9.00
9A	Al "Chico" Carrasquel	10.00	5.00	3.00
9Na	Enos Slaughter	75.00	37.00	22.00
9Nb	Gus Bell	75.00	37.00	22.00
20A	Larry "Yogi" Berra	55.00	27.00	16.50
20N	Johnny Logan	10.00	5.00	3.00
1A	Bob Lemon	30.00	15.00	9.00
21N	Johnny Antonelli	14.00	7.00	4.25
22A	Ferris Fain	14.00	7.00	4.25
22N	Gil Hodges	45.00	22.00	13.50
23A	Hank Bauer	14.00	7.00	4.25
23N	Eddie Mathews	39.00	19.50	11.50
24A	Jim Delsing	10.00	5.00	3.00
24N	Lew Burdette	18.00	9.00	5.50
25A	Gil McDougald	18.00	9.00	5.50
25N	Willie Mays	100.00	50.00	30.00

from each league, with no known var... all Red Man sets, those cards comp... redeemable tabs are more valuable. ... below are for cards with tabs; cards w... removed are worth about 50% of those fi...

		NR MT		Co...
	Complete Set:	950.00	47...	Co...
	Common Player:	10.00		
1A	Ray Boone	10.00	5...	
1N	Richie Ashburn	20.00	10...	
2A	Jim Busby	10.00	5...	
2N	Del Crandall	14.00	7.0...	
3A	Ed "Whitey" Ford	45.00	22.00	
3N	Gil Hodges	45.00	22.00	
4A	Nelson Fox	20.00	10.00	
4N	Brooks Lawrence	10.00	5.00	
5A	Bob Grim	10.00	5.00	
5N	Johnny Logan	10.00	5.00	
6A	Jack Harshman	10.00	5.00	
6N	Sal Maglie	14.00	7.00	4...
7A	Jim Hegan	10.00	5.00	3...
7N	Willie Mays	100.00	50.00	30.0
8A	Bob Lemon	30.00	15.00	9.0...
8N	Don Mueller	10.00	5.00	3.00
9A	Irv Noren	10.00	5.00	3.00
9N	Bill Sarni	10.00	5.00	3.00
10A	Bob Porterfield	10.00	5.00	3.00
10N	Warren Spahn	39.00	19.50	11.50
11A	Al Rosen	18.00	9.00	5.50
11N	Henry Thompson	10.00	5.00	3.00
12A	"Mickey" Vernon	14.00	7.00	4.25
12N	Hoyt Wilhelm	30.00	15.00	9.00
13A	Vic Wertz	10.00	5.00	3.00
13N	Johnny Antonelli	14.00	7.00	4.25
14A	Early Wynn	30.00	15.00	9.00
14N	Carl Erskine	18.00	9.00	5.50
15A	Bobby Avila	10.00	5.00	3.00
15N	Granny Hamner	10.00	5.00	3.00
16A	Larry "Yogi" Berra	55.00	27.00	16.50
16N	Ted Kluszewski	18.00	9.00	5.50
17A	Joe Coleman	10.00	5.00	3.00
17N	Pee Wee Reese	45.00	22.00	13.50
18A	Larry Doby	18.00	9.00	5.50
18N	Al Schoendienst	18.00	9.00	5.50
19A	Jackie Jensen	14.00	7.00	4.25
19N	Duke Snider	75.00	37.00	22.00
20A	Pete Runnels	10.00	5.00	3.00
20N	Frank Thomas	10.00	5.00	3.00
21A	Jim Piersall	14.00	7.00	4.25
21N	Ray Jablonski	10.00	5.00	3.00
22A	Hank Bauer	14.00	7.00	4.25
22N	James "Dusty" Rhodes	10.00	5.00	3.00
23A	"Chico" Carrasquel	10.00	5.00	3.00
23N	Gus Bell	10.00	5.00	3.00
24A	Orestes Minoso	14.00	7.00	4.25
24N	Curt Simmons	14.00	7.00	4.25
25A	Sandy Consuegra	10.00	5.00	3.00
25N	Marvin Grissom	10.00	5.00	3.00

1955 Rodeo Meats Athletics

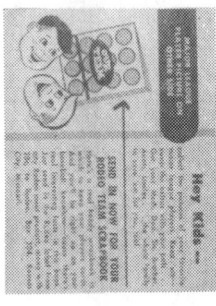

Cloyd Boyer

This set of 2½'' by 3½'' color cards was issued by a local meat company to commemorate the first year of the Athletics in Kansas City. There are 38 different players included in the set, with nine players known to appear in two different variations for a total of 47 cards in the set. Most variations are in background colors, although Bobby Shantz is also listed incorrectly as "Schantz" on one variation. The cards are

1955 Red Man Tobacco

These 50 cards are quite similar to the 1954 edition, with card fronts virtually unchanged except for data in the biographical box on the color picture area. This set of the 3½'' by 4'' cards includes 25 players

d figures. Card fronts are full-color paintings of player, with biographical information inset in the ait area. Card backs contain company advertis- Cards are numbered and dated only on the tabs.

	NR MT	EX	VG
plete Set:	950.00	475.00	285.00
mon Player:	10.00	5.00	3.00
Casey Stengel	45.00	22.00	13.50
Leo Durocher	30.00	15.00	9.00
Roberto Avila	10.00	5.00	3.00
Richie Ashburn	20.00	10.00	6.00
Larry "Yogi" Berra	55.00	27.00	16.50
Ewell Blackwell	14.00	7.00	4.25
Gil Coan	10.00	5.00	3.00
Cliff Chambers	10.00	5.00	3.00
Dom DiMaggio	18.00	9.00	5.50
Murry Dickson	10.00	5.00	3.00
Larry Doby	18.00	9.00	5.50
Sid Gordon	10.00	5.00	3.00
Ferris Fain	14.00	7.00	4.25
Granny Hamner	10.00	5.00	3.00
Bob Feller	55.00	27.00	16.50
Jim Hearn	10.00	5.00	3.00
Nelson Fox	20.00	10.00	6.00
Monte Irvin	30.00	15.00	9.00
Johnny Groth	10.00	5.00	3.00
Larry Jansen	10.00	5.00	3.00
Jim Hegan	10.00	5.00	3.00
Willie Jones	10.00	5.00	3.00
Eddie Joost	10.00	5.00	3.00
Ralph Kiner	30.00	15.00	9.00
George Kell	32.00	16.00	9.50
Whitey Lockman	10.00	5.00	3.00
Gil McDougald	18.00	9.00	5.50
Sal Maglie	14.00	7.00	4.25
Orestes Minoso	14.00	7.00	4.25
Willie Mays	100.00	50.00	30.00
Bill Pierce	14.00	7.00	4.25
Stan Musial	100.00	50.00	30.00
Bob Porterfield	10.00	5.00	3.00
Pee Wee Reese	45.00	22.00	13.50
Eddie Robinson	10.00	5.00	3.00
Robin Roberts	32.00	16.00	9.50
Saul Rogovin	10.00	5.00	3.00
Al Schoendienst	18.00	9.00	5.50
Bobby Shantz	14.00	7.00	4.25
Enos Slaughter	32.00	16.00	9.50
Vern Stephens	10.00	5.00	3.00
Duke Snider	70.00	35.00	21.00
Vic Wertz	10.00	5.00	3.00
Warren Spahn	35.00	17.50	10.50
Ted Williams	130.00	65.00	39.00
Eddie Stanky	14.00	7.00	4.25
Early Wynn	32.00	16.00	9.50
Bobby Thomson	18.00	9.00	5.50
Eddie Yost	10.00	5.00	3.00
Earl Torgeson	10.00	5.00	3.00
Gus Zernial	10.00	5.00	3.00
Wes Westrum	10.00	5.00	3.00

are more valuable. Prices below are for cards tabs; cards with tabs removed are worth about of the stated values. Each league is represented I players and a manager on the full-color cards, a of 52.

		NR MT	EX
Complete Set:		950.00	475.00
Common Player:		10.00	5.00
1A	Casey Stengel	45.00	22.00
1N	Charlie Dressen	14.00	7.00
2A	Hank Bauer	14.00	7.00
2N	Bobby Adams	10.00	5.00
3A	Larry "Yogi" Berra	55.00	27.00
3N	Richie Ashburn	20.00	10.00
4A	Walt Dropo	10.00	5.00
4N	Joe Black	14.00	7.00
5A	Nelson Fox	20.00	10.00
5N	Roy Campanella	75.00	37.00
6A	Jackie Jensen	14.00	7.00
6N	Ted Kluszewski	18.00	9.00
7A	Eddie Joost	10.00	5.00
7N	Whitey Lockman	10.00	5.00
8A	George Kell	32.00	16.00
8N	Sal Maglie	14.00	7.00
9A	Dale Mitchell	10.00	5.00
9N	Andy Pafko	14.00	7.00
10A	Phil Rizzuto	35.00	17.50
10N	Pee Wee Reese	45.00	22.00
11A	Eddie Robinson	10.00	5.00
11N	Robin Roberts	32.00	16.00
12A	Gene Woodling	14.00	7.00
12N	Al Schoendienst	18.00	9.00
13A	Gus Zernial	10.00	5.00
13N	Enos Slaughter	32.00	16.00
14A	Early Wynn	32.00	16.00
14N	Edwin "Duke" Snider	75.00	37.00
15A	Joe Dobson	10.00	5.00
15N	Ralph Kiner	32.00	16.00
16A	Billy Pierce	14.00	7.00
16N	Hank Sauer	10.00	5.00
17A	Bob Lemon	32.00	16.00
17N	Del Ennis	10.00	5.00
18A	Johnny Mize	32.00	16.00
18N	Granny Hamner	10.00	5.00
19A	Bob Porterfield	10.00	5.00
19N	Warren Spahn	35.00	17.50
20A	Bobby Shantz	14.00	7.00
20N	Wes Westrum	10.00	5.00
21A	"Mickey" Vernon	14.00	7.00
21N	Hoyt Wilhelm	32.00	16.00
22A	Dom DiMaggio	18.00	9.00
22N	Murry Dickson	10.00	5.00
23A	Gil McDougald	18.00	9.00
23N	Warren Hacker	10.00	5.00
24A	Al Rosen	18.00	9.00
24N	Gerry Staley	10.00	5.00
25A	Mel Parnell	10.00	5.00
25N	Bobby Thomson	14.00	7.00
26A	Roberto Avila	10.00	5.00
26N	Stan Musial	116.00	58.00

1953 Red Man Tobacco

This was the chewing tobacco company's second annual set of 3½'' by 4'' cards, including the tabs at the bottom of the cards. Formats for both the fronts and backs are similar to the '52 edition. The 1953 Red Man cards, however, include card numbers within the player biographical section, and the card backs are headlined ''New for '53.'' Once again, cards with intact tabs (which were redeemable for a free cap)

1954 Red Man Tobacco

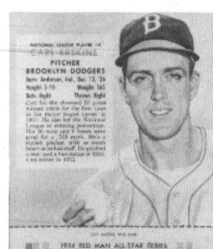

In 1954 the Red Man set eliminated manager c from the set, and issued only 25 player cards for league. There are, however, four variations w bring the total set size to 54 full-color cards. National league #19s are known (Gus Bell and Slaughter), while American Leaguers George Sam Mele and Dave Philley are each shown with unnumbered, with Rodeo logo and player name on the fronts, and an ad for a scrapbook album listed on the backs.

		NR MT	EX	VG
	Complete Set:	2500.00	1250.00	750.00
	Common Player:	40.00	20.00	12.00
(1)	Joe Astroth	40.00	20.00	12.00
(2)	Harold Bevan	65.00	32.00	19.50
(3)	Charles Bishop	65.00	32.00	19.50
(4)	Don Bollweg	65.00	32.00	19.50
(5)	Lou Boudreau	90.00	45.00	27.00
(6)	Cloyd Boyer (blue background)	65.00	32.00	19.50
(7)	Cloyd Boyer (pink background)	40.00	20.00	12.00
(8)	Ed Burtschy	65.00	32.00	19.50
(9)	Art Ceccarelli	40.00	20.00	12.00
(10)	Joe DeMaestri (pea green background)	65.00	32.00	19.50
(11)	Joe DeMaestri (light green background)	40.00	20.00	12.00
(12)	Art Ditmar	40.00	20.00	12.00
(13)	John Dixon	65.00	32.00	19.50
(14)	Jim Finigan	40.00	20.00	12.00
(15)	Marion Fricano	65.00	32.00	19.50
(16)	John Gray	65.00	32.00	19.50
(17)	Tom Gorman	40.00	20.00	12.00
(18)	Ray Herbert	40.00	20.00	12.00
(19)	Forest "Spook" Jacobs (Forrest)	65.00	32.00	19.50
(20)	Alex Kellner	65.00	32.00	19.50
(21)	Harry Kraft (Craft)	40.00	20.00	12.00
(22)	Jack Littrell	40.00	20.00	12.00
(23)	Hector Lopez	50.00	25.00	15.00
(24)	Oscar Melillo	40.00	20.00	12.00
(25)	Arnold Portocarrero (purple background)	65.00	32.00	19.50
(26)	Arnold Portocarrero (grey background)	40.00	20.00	12.00
(27)	Vic Power (pink background)	75.00	37.00	22.00
(28)	Vic Power (yellow background)	50.00	25.00	15.00
(29)	Vic Raschi	65.00	32.00	19.50
(30)	Bill Renna (dark pink background)	65.00	32.00	19.50
(31)	Bill Renna (light pink background)	40.00	20.00	12.00
(32)	Al Robertson	65.00	32.00	19.50
(33)	Johnny Sain	75.00	37.00	22.00
(34a)	Bobby Schantz (incorrect spelling)	100.00	50.00	30.00
(34b)	Bobby Shantz (correct spelling)	75.00	37.00	22.00
(35)	Wilmer Shantz (orange background)	65.00	32.00	19.50
(36)	Wilmer Shantz (purple background)	40.00	20.00	12.00
(37)	Harry Simpson	40.00	20.00	12.00
(38)	Enos Slaughter	125.00	62.00	37.00
(39)	Lou Sleater	40.00	20.00	12.00
(40)	George Susce	40.00	20.00	12.00
(41)	Bob Trice	65.00	32.00	19.50
(42)	Elmer Valo (yellow background)	65.00	32.00	19.50
(43)	Elmer Valo (green background)	40.00	20.00	12.00
(44)	Bill Wilson (yellow background)	65.00	32.00	19.50
(45)	Bill Wilson (purple background)	40.00	20.00	12.00
(46)	Gus Zernial	50.00	25.00	15.00

1956 Rodeo Meats Athletics

Gus Zernial

Rodeo Meats issued another Kansas City Athletics set in 1956, but this one was a much smaller 13-card set. The 2½" by 3½" cards are again unnumbered, with player name and Rodeo logo on the fronts. Card

backs feature some of the same graphics and copy as the 1955 cards, but the album offer is omitted. The full-color cards were only available in packages of Rodeo hot dogs.

		NR MT	EX	VG
	Complete Set:	650.00	325.00	195.00
	Common Player:	40.00	20.00	12.00
(1)	Joe Astroth	40.00	20.00	12.00
(2)	Lou Boudreau	90.00	45.00	27.00
(3)	Joe DeMaestri	40.00	20.00	12.00
(4)	Art Ditmar	40.00	20.00	12.00
(5)	Jim Finigan	40.00	20.00	12.00
(6)	Hector Lopez	50.00	25.00	15.00
(7)	Vic Power	50.00	25.00	15.00
(8)	Bobby Shantz	75.00	37.00	22.00
(9)	Harry Simpson	40.00	20.00	12.00
(10)	Enos Slaughter	100.00	50.00	30.00
(11)	Elmer Valo	40.00	20.00	12.00
(12)	Gus Zernial	50.00	25.00	15.00

1970 Rold Gold Pretzels All-Time Baseball Greats

The 1970 Rold Gold Pretzels set of 15 cards honors the "Greatest Players Ever" in the first 100 years of baseball as chosen by the Baseball Writers of America. The cards, which measure 2¼" by 3½" in size, feature a simulated 3-D effect. The set was re-released in 1972 by Kellogg's in packages of Dan-ish-Go-Rounds. Rold Gold cards can be differentiated from the Kellogg's cards of 1972 by the 1970 copyright date found on the card reverse.

		NR MT	EX	VG
	Complete Set:	28.00	14.00	8.50
	Common Player:	1.00	.50	.30
1	Walter Johnson	2.50	1.25	.70
2	Rogers Hornsby	1.50	.70	.45
3	John McGraw	1.00	.50	.30
4	Mickey Cochrane	1.00	.50	.30
5	George Sisler	1.00	.50	.30
6	Babe Ruth	7.00	3.50	2.00
7	Robert "Lefty" Grove	1.50	.70	.45
8	Harold "Pie" Traynor	1.00	.50	.30
9	Honus Wagner	1.75	.90	.50
10	Eddie Collins	1.00	.50	.30
11	Tris Speaker	1.50	.70	.45
12	Cy Young	1.00	.50	.30
13	Lou Gehrig	4.00	2.00	1.25
14	Babe Ruth	7.00	3.50	2.00
15	Ty Cobb	4.00	2.00	1.25

1950-52 Royal Desserts

This set of 24 cards was issued one per box on the backs of various Royal Dessert products over a period of three years. The basic set contains 24 players, however a number of variations create the much higher total for the set. In 1950 Royal issued cards with two different tints — black and white with red, or

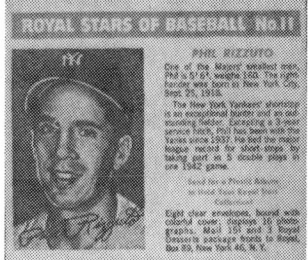

blue and white with red. Over the next two years, various of the cards' biographies were updated up to three times in some cases. Some players from the set left the majors after 1950 and others were apparently never updated, but the 23 biography updates that do exist, added to the original 24 cards issued in 1950, give the set total of 47 cards. The 2½'' by 3½'' cards are blank backed, with personal and playing biographies alongside the card front photos.

	NR MT	EX	VG
Complete Set:	850.00	425.00	255.00
Common Player:	13.00	6.50	4.00
1a Stan Musial (2nd paragraph begins "Musial's 207...")	110.00	55.00	33.00
1b Stan Musial (2nd paragraph begins "Musial batted...")	110.00	55.00	33.00
2a Pee Wee Reese (2nd paragraph begins "Pee Wee's...")	55.00	27.00	16.50
2b Pee Wee Reese (2nd paragraph begins "Captain...")	55.00	27.00	16.50
3a George Kell (2nd paragraph ends "...in 1945, '46.")	30.00	15.00	9.00
3b George Kell (2nd paragraph ends "...two base hits, 56.")	30.00	15.00	9.00
4a Dom DiMaggio (2nd paragraph ends "...during 1947.")	30.00	15.00	9.00
4b Dom DiMaggio (2nd paragraph ends "...with 11.")	30.00	15.00	9.00
5a Warren Spahn (2nd paragraph ends "...shutouts 7.")	50.00	25.00	15.00
5b Warren Spahn (2nd paragraph ends "...with 191.")	50.00	25.00	15.00
6a Andy Pafko (2nd paragraph ends "...7 games.")	25.00	12.50	7.50
6b Andy Pafko (2nd paragraph ends "...National League.")	25.00	12.50	7.50
6c Andy Pafko (2nd paragraph ends "...weighs 190.")	25.00	12.50	7.50
7a Andy Seminick (2nd paragraph ends "...as outfield.")	20.00	10.00	6.00
7b Andy Seminick (2nd paragraph ends "...since 1916.")	20.00	10.00	6.00
7c Andy Seminick (2nd paragraph ends "...in the outfield.")	20.00	10.00	6.00
7d Andy Seminick (2nd paragraph ends "...right handed.")	20.00	10.00	6.00
8a Lou Brissie (2nd paragraph ends "...when pitching.")	20.00	10.00	6.00
8b Lou Brissie (2nd paragraph ends "...weighs 215.")	20.00	10.00	6.00
9a Ewell Blackwell (2nd paragraph begins "Despite recent illness...")	25.00	12.50	7.50
9b Ewell Blackwell (2nd paragraph begins "Blackwell's...")	25.00	12.50	7.50
10a Bobby Thomson (2nd paragraph begins "In 1949...")	25.00	12.50	7.50
10b Bobby Thomson (2nd paragraph begins "Thomson is...")	25.00	12.50	7.50
11a Phil Rizzuto (2nd paragraph ends "...one 1942 game.")	50.00	25.00	15.00
11b Phil Rizzuto (2nd paragraph ends "...Most Valuable Player.")	50.00	25.00	15.00
12 Tommy Henrich	30.00	15.00	9.00
13 Joe Gordon	25.00	12.50	7.50
14a Ray Scarborough (Senators)	20.00	10.00	6.00
14b Ray Scarborough (White Sox, 2nd paragraph ends "...military service.")	20.00	10.00	6.00
14c Ray Scarborough (White Sox, 2nd paragraph ends "...the season.")	20.00	10.00	6.00
14d Ray Scarborough (Red Sox)	20.00	10.00	6.00

	NR MT	EX	VG
15a Stan Rojek (Pirates)	20.00	10.00	6.00
15b Stan Rojek (Browns)	20.00	10.00	6.00
16 Luke Appling	30.00	15.00	9.00
17 Willard Marshall	20.00	10.00	6.00
18 Alvin Dark	30.00	15.00	9.00
19a Dick Sisler (2nd paragraph ends "...service record.")	20.00	10.00	6.00
19b Dick Sisler (2nd paragraph ends "...National League flag.")	20.00	10.00	6.00
19c Dick Sisler (2nd paragraph ends "...Nov. 2, 1920.")	20.00	10.00	6.00
19d Dick Sisler (2nd paragraph ends "...from '46 to '48.")	20.00	10.00	6.00
20 Johnny Ostrowski	20.00	10.00	6.00
21a Virgil Trucks (2nd paragraph ends "...in military service.")	25.00	12.50	7.50
21b Virgil Trucks (2nd paragraph ends "...that year.")	25.00	12.50	7.50
21c Virgil Trucks (2nd paragraph ends "...for military service.")	25.00	12.50	7.50
22 Eddie Robinson	20.00	10.00	6.00
23 Nanny Fernandez	20.00	10.00	6.00
24 Ferris Fain	25.00	12.50	7.50

1976 SSPC Set

 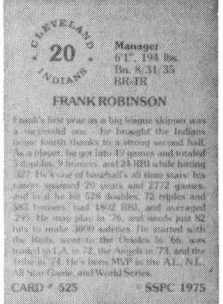

This set, issued by the Sport Star Publishing Company in 1976 as a collectors' issue, was withdrawn from the market because of legal entanglements. Because SSPC agreed never to reprint the issue, some collectors feel it has an air of legitimacy. The complete set contains 630 full-color cards, each 2½'' by 3½'' in size. The cards look similar to the 1953 Bowmans, with only the player picture (no identification) on the fronts. Card backs are in a vertical format, with personal stats, brief biographies and card numbers.

	NR MT	EX	VG
Complete Set:	48.00	24.00	14.50
Common Player:	.05	.03	.02
1 Lee William (Buzz) Capra	.10	.05	.03
2 Thomas Ross House	.05	.03	.02
3 Maximino Leon	.05	.03	.02
4 Carl Wendle Morton	.05	.03	.02
5 Philip Henry Niekro	.70	.35	.20
6 Michael Wayne Thompson	.05	.03	.02
7 Elias Sosa (Martinez)	.05	.03	.02
8 Larvell Blanks	.05	.03	.02
9 Darrell Wayne Evans	.20	.10	.06
10 Rodney Joe Gilbreath	.05	.03	.02
11 Michael Ken-Wai Lum	.05	.03	.02
12 Craig George Robinson	.05	.03	.02
13 Earl Craig Williams, Jr.	.05	.03	.02
14 Victor Crosby Correll	.05	.03	.02

#	Player	NR MT	EX	VG		#	Player	NR MT	EX	VG
15	Biff Pocoroba	.05	.03	.02		105	Chris Edward Speier	.07	.04	.02
16	Johnny B. (Dusty) Baker, Jr.	.10	.05	.03		106	Derrel Osbon Thomas	.05	.03	.02
17	Ralph Allen Garr	.07	.04	.02		107	Gary Leah Thomasson	.05	.03	.02
18	Clarence Edward (Cito) Gaston	.05	.03	.02		108	Glenn Charles Adams	.05	.03	.02
19	David LaFrance May	.05	.03	.02		109	Von Everett Joshua	.05	.03	.02
20	Rowland Johnnie Office	.05	.03	.02		110	Gary Nathaniel Matthews	.10	.05	.03
21	Robert Brooks Beall	.05	.03	.02		111	Bobby Ray Murcer	.12	.06	.04
22	George Lee (Sparky) Anderson	.10	.05	.03		112	Horace Arthur Speed III	.05	.03	.02
23	John Eugene Billingham	.05	.03	.02		113	Wesley Noreen Westrum	.05	.03	.02
24	Pedro Rodriguez Borbon	.05	.03	.02		114	Richard Nevin Folkers	.05	.03	.02
25	Clay Palmer Carroll	.07	.04	.02		115	Alan Benton Foster	.05	.03	.02
26	Patrick Leonard Darcy	.05	.03	.02		116	David James Freisleben	.05	.03	.02
27	Donald Edward Gullett	.07	.04	.02		117	Daniel Vincent Frisella	.05	.03	.02
28	Clayton Laws Kirby	.05	.03	.02		118	Randall Leo Jones	.07	.04	.02
29	Gary Lynn Nolan	.05	.03	.02		119	Daniel Ray Spillner	.05	.03	.02
30	Fredie Hubert Norman	.05	.03	.02		120	Howard Lawrence (Larry) Hardy	.05	.03	.02
31	Johnny Lee Bench	1.50	.70	.45		121	Cecil Randolph (Randy) Hundley	.05	.03	.02
32	William Francis Plummer	.05	.03	.02		122	Fred Lyn Kendall	.05	.03	.02
33	Darrel Lee Chaney	.05	.03	.02		123	John Francis McNamara	.05	.03	.02
34	David Ismael Concepcion	.15	.08	.05		124	Rigoberto (Tito) Fuentes	.05	.03	.02
35	Terrence Michael Crowley	.05	.03	.02		125	Enzo Octavio Hernandez	.05	.03	.02
36	Daniel Driessen	.07	.04	.02		126	Stephen Michael Huntz	.05	.03	.02
37	Robert Douglas Flynn, Jr.	.05	.03	.02		127	Michael Wilson Ivie	.05	.03	.02
38	Joe Leonard Morgan	.70	.35	.20		128	Hector Epitacio Torres	.05	.03	.02
39	Atanasio Rigal (Tony) Perez	.40	.20	.12		129	Theodore Rodger Kubiak	.05	.03	.02
40	George Kenneth (Ken) Griffey	.15	.08	.05		130	John Maywood Grubb, Jr.	.05	.03	.02
41	Peter Edward Rose	5.00	2.50	1.50		131	John Henry Scott	.05	.03	.02
42	Edison Rosanda Armbrister	.05	.03	.02		132	Robert Tolan	.07	.04	.02
43	John Christopher Vukovich	.05	.03	.02		133	David Mark Winfield	1.50	.70	.45
44	George Arthur Foster	.20	.10	.06		134	William Joseph Gogolewski	.05	.03	.02
45	Cesar Francisco Geronimo	.05	.03	.02		135	Danny L. Osborn	.05	.03	.02
46	Mervin Weldon Rettenmund	.05	.03	.02		136	James Lee Kaat	.25	.13	.08
47	James Frederick Crawford	.05	.03	.02		137	Claude Wilson Osteen	.07	.04	.02
48	Kenneth Roth Forsch	.05	.03	.02		138	Cecil Lee Upshaw, Jr.	.05	.03	.02
49	Douglas James Konieczny	.05	.03	.02		139	Wilbur Forrester Wood, Jr.	.07	.04	.02
50	Joseph Franklin Niekro	.12	.06	.04		140	Lloyd Cecil Allen	.05	.03	.02
51	Clifford Johnson	.05	.03	.02		141	Brian Jay Downing	.10	.05	.03
52	Alfred Henry (Skip) Jutze	.05	.03	.02		142	James Sarkis Essian, Jr.	.05	.03	.02
53	Milton Scott May	.05	.03	.02		143	Russell Earl (Bucky) Dent	.12	.06	.04
54	Robert Patrick Andrews	.05	.03	.02		144	Jorge Orta	.05	.03	.02
55	Kenneth George Boswell	.05	.03	.02		145	Lee Edward Richard	.05	.03	.02
56	Tommy Vann Helms	.05	.03	.02		146	William Allen Stein	.05	.03	.02
57	Roger Henry Metzger	.05	.03	.02		147	Kenneth Joseph Henderson	.05	.03	.02
58	Lawrence William Milbourne	.05	.03	.02		148	Carlos May	.07	.04	.02
59	Douglas Lee Rader	.05	.03	.02		149	Nyls Wallace Rex Nyman	.05	.03	.02
60	Robert Jose Watson	.07	.04	.02		150	Robert Pasquali Coluccio, Jr.	.05	.03	.02
61	Enos Milton Cabell, Jr.	.05	.03	.02		151	Charles William Tanner, Jr.	.10	.05	.03
62	Jose Delan Cruz	.15	.08	.05		152	Harold Patrick (Pat) Kelly	.05	.03	.02
63	Cesar Cedeno	.15	.08	.05		153	Jerry Wayne Hairston	.05	.03	.02
64	Gregory Eugene Gross	.05	.03	.02		154	Richard Fred (Pete) Varney, Jr.	.05	.03	.02
65	Wilbur Leon Howard	.05	.03	.02		155	William Edwin Melton	.07	.04	.02
66	Alphonso Erwin Downing	.05	.03	.02		156	Richard Michael Gossage	.50	.25	.15
67	Burt Carlton Hooton	.07	.04	.02		157	Terry Jay Forster	.07	.04	.02
68	Charles Oliver Hough	.10	.05	.03		158	Richard Michael Hinton	.05	.03	.02
69	Thomas Edward John	.40	.20	.12		159	Nelson Kelley Briles	.05	.03	.02
70	John Alexander Messersmith	.07	.04	.02		160	Alan James Fitzmorris	.05	.03	.02
71	Douglas James Rau	.05	.03	.02		161	Stephen Bernard Mingori	.05	.03	.02
72	Richard Alan Rhoden	.12	.06	.04		162	Martin William Pattin	.05	.03	.02
73	Donald Howard Sutton	.60	.30	.20		163	Paul William Splittorff, Jr.	.07	.04	.02
74	Frederick Steven Auerbach	.05	.03	.02		164	Dennis Patrick Leonard	.07	.04	.02
75	Ronald Charles Cey	.12	.06	.04		165	John Albert (Buck) Martinez	.05	.03	.02
76	Ivan De Jesus	.05	.03	.02		166	Gorrell Robert (Bob) Stinson III	.05	.03	.02
77	Steven Patrick Garvey	1.50	.70	.45		167	George Howard Brett	3.50	1.75	1.00
78	Leonadus Lacy	.07	.04	.02		168	Harmon Clayton Killebrew, Jr.	1.50	.70	.45
79	David Earl Lopes	.10	.05	.03		169	John Claiborn Mayberry	.07	.04	.02
80	Kenneth Lee McMullen	.05	.03	.02		170	Freddie Joe Patek	.05	.03	.02
81	Joseph Vance Ferguson	.05	.03	.02		171	Octavio (Cookie) Rojas	.05	.03	.02
82	Paul Ray Powell	.05	.03	.02		172	Rodney Darrell Scott	.05	.03	.02
83	Stephen Wayne Yeager	.05	.03	.02		173	Tolia (Tony) Solaita	.05	.03	.02
84	Willie Murphy Crawford	.05	.03	.02		174	Frank White, Jr.	.10	.05	.03
85	Henry Cruz	.05	.03	.02		175	Alfred Edward Cowens, Jr.	.05	.03	.02
86	Charles Fuqua Manuel	.05	.03	.02		176	Harold Abraham McRae	.12	.06	.04
87	Manuel Mota	.10	.05	.03		177	Amos Joseph Otis	.07	.04	.02
88	Thomas Marian Paciorek	.05	.03	.02		178	Vada Edward Pinson, Jr.	.20	.10	.06
89	James Sherman Wynn	.10	.05	.03		179	James Eugene Wohlford	.05	.03	.02
90	Walter Emmons Alston	.30	.15	.09		180	James Douglas Bird	.05	.03	.02
91	William Joseph Buckner	.15	.08	.05		181	Mark Alan Littell	.05	.03	.02
92	James Leland Barr	.05	.03	.02		182	Robert McClure	.05	.03	.02
93	Ralph Michael (Mike) Caldwell	.05	.03	.02		183	Steven Lee Busby	.07	.04	.02
94	John Francis D'Acquisto	.05	.03	.02		184	Francis Xavier Healy	.05	.03	.02
95	David Wallace Heaverlo	.05	.03	.02		185	Dorrel Norman Elvert (Whitey) Herzog	.10	.05	.03
96	Gary Robert Lavelle	.05	.03	.02		186	Andrew Earl Hassler	.05	.03	.02
97	John Joseph Montefusco, Jr.	.05	.03	.02		187	Lynn Nolan Ryan, Jr.	1.50	.70	.45
98	Charles Prosek Williams	.05	.03	.02		188	William Robert Singer	.05	.03	.02
99	Christopher Paul Arnold	.05	.03	.02		189	Frank Daryl Tanana	.10	.05	.03
100	Mark Kevin Hill (Marc)	.05	.03	.02		190	Eduardo Figueroa	.05	.03	.02
101	David Martin Rader	.05	.03	.02		191	David S. Collins	.07	.04	.02
102	Charles Bruce Miller	.05	.03	.02		192	Richard Hirshfeld Williams	.07	.04	.02
103	Guillermo Naranjo (Willie) Montanez	.07	.04	.02		193	Eliseo Rodriguez	.05	.03	.02
104	Steven Robert Ontiveros	.05	.03	.02		194	David Lee Chalk	.05	.03	.02

		NR MT	EX	VG			NR MT	EX	VG
195	Winston Enriquillo Llenas	.05	.03	.02	283	Michael Ray Tyson	.05	.03	.02
196	Rudolph Bart Meoli	.05	.03	.02	284	Ted Crawford Sizemore	.05	.03	.02
197	Orlando Ramirez	.05	.03	.02	285	Mario Miguel Guerrero	.05	.03	.02
198	Gerald Peter Remy	.05	.03	.02	286	Larry Lintz	.05	.03	.02
199	Billy Edward Smith	.05	.03	.02	287	Kenneth Victor Rudolph	.05	.03	.02
200	Bruce Anton Bochte	.05	.03	.02	288	Richard Arlin Billings	.05	.03	.02
201	Joseph Michael Lahoud, Jr.	.05	.03	.02	289	Jerry Wayne Mumphrey	.10	.05	.03
202	Morris Nettles, Jr.	.05	.03	.02	290	Michael Sherman Wallace	.05	.03	.02
203	John Milton (Mickey) Rivers	.07	.04	.02	291	Alan Thomas Hrabosky	.07	.04	.02
204	Leroy Bobby Stanton	.05	.03	.02	292	Kenneth Lee Reynolds	.05	.03	.02
205	Victor Albury	.05	.03	.02	293	Michael Douglas Garman	.05	.03	.02
206	Thomas Henry Burgmeier	.05	.03	.02	294	Robert Herbert Forsch	.10	.05	.03
207	William Franklin Butler	.05	.03	.02	295	John Allen Denny	.07	.04	.02
208	William Richard Campbell	.05	.03	.02	296	Harold R. Rasmussen	.05	.03	.02
209	Alton Ray Corbin	.05	.03	.02	297	Lynn Everratt McGlothen (Everett)	.05	.03	.02
210	George Henry (Joe) Decker, Jr.	.05	.03	.02	298	Michael Roswell Barlow	.05	.03	.02
211	James Michael Hughes	.05	.03	.02	299	Gregory John Terlecky	.05	.03	.02
212	Edward Norman Bane (photo actually Mike Pazik)	.05	.03	.02	300	Albert Fred (Red) Schoendienst	.10	.05	.03
213	Glenn Dennis Borgmann	.05	.03	.02	301	Ricky Eugene Reuschel	.12	.06	.04
214	Rodney Cline Carew	1.75	.90	.50	302	Steven Michael Stone	.07	.04	.02
215	Stephen Robert Brye	.05	.03	.02	303	William Gordon Bonham	.05	.03	.02
216	Darnell Glenn (Dan) Ford	.05	.03	.02	304	Oscar Joseph Zamora	.05	.03	.02
217	Antonio Oliva	.25	.13	.08	305	Kenneth Douglas Frailing	.05	.03	.02
218	David Allan Goltz	.07	.04	.02	306	Milton Edward Wilcox	.07	.04	.02
219	Rikalbert Blyleven	.30	.15	.09	307	Darold Duane Knowles	.05	.03	.02
220	Larry Eugene Hisle	.07	.04	.02	308	Rufus James (Jim) Marshall	.05	.03	.02
221	Stephen Russell Braun, III	.05	.03	.02	309	Bill Madlock, Jr.	.25	.13	.08
222	Jerry Wayne Terrell	.05	.03	.02	310	Jose Domec Cardenal	.07	.04	.02
223	Eric Thane Soderholm	.05	.03	.02	311	Robert James (Rick) Monday, Jr.	.10	.05	.03
224	Philip Anthony Roof	.05	.03	.02	312	Julio Ruben (Jerry) Morales	.05	.03	.02
225	Danny Leon Thompson	.05	.03	.02	313	Timothy Kenneth Hosley	.05	.03	.02
226	James William Colborn	.05	.03	.02	314	Gene Taylor Hiser	.05	.03	.02
227	Thomas Andrew Murphy	.05	.03	.02	315	Donald Eulon Kessinger	.07	.04	.02
228	Eduardo Rodriguez	.05	.03	.02	316	Jesus Manuel (Manny) Trillo	.10	.05	.03
229	James Michael Slaton	.05	.03	.02	317	Ralph Pierre (Pete) LaCock, Jr.	.05	.03	.02
230	Edward Nelson Sprague	.05	.03	.02	318	George Eugene Mitterwald	.05	.03	.02
231	Charles William Moore, Jr.	.05	.03	.02	319	Steven Eugene Swisher	.05	.03	.02
232	Darrell Ray Porter	.07	.04	.02	320	Robert Walter Sperring	.05	.03	.02
233	Kurt Anthony Bevacqua	.05	.03	.02	321	Victor Lanier Harris	.05	.03	.02
234	Pedro Garcia	.05	.03	.02	322	Ronald Ray Dunn	.05	.03	.02
235	James Michael (Mike) Hegan	.05	.03	.02	323	Jose Manuel Morales	.05	.03	.02
236	Donald Wayne Money	.07	.04	.02	324	Peter MacKanin, Jr.	.05	.03	.02
237	George C. Scott, Jr.	.07	.04	.02	325	James Charles Cox	.05	.03	.02
238	Robin R. Yount	1.25	.60	.40	326	Larry Alton Parrish	.12	.06	.04
239	Henry Louis Aaron	3.00	1.50	.90	327	Michael Jorgensen	.05	.03	.02
240	Robert Walker Ellis	.05	.03	.02	328	Timothy John Foli	.05	.03	.02
241	Sixto Lezcano	.05	.03	.02	329	Harold Noel Breeden	.05	.03	.02
242	Robert Vance Mitchell	.05	.03	.02	330	Nathan Colbert, Jr.	.05	.03	.02
243	James Gorman Thomas, III	.10	.05	.03	331	Jesus Maria (Pepe) Frias	.05	.03	.02
244	William Edward Travers	.05	.03	.02	332	James Patrick (Pat) Scanlon	.05	.03	.02
245	Peter Sven Broberg	.05	.03	.02	333	Robert Sherwood Bailey	.05	.03	.02
246	William Howard Sharp	.05	.03	.02	334	Gary Edmund Carter	1.50	.70	.45
247	Arthur Bobby Lee Darwin	.05	.03	.02	335	Jose Mauei (Pepe) Mangual	.05	.03	.02
248	Rick Gerald Austin (photo actually Larry Anderson)	.05	.03	.02	336	Lawrence David Biittner	.05	.03	.02
249	Lawrence Dennis Anderson (photo actually Rick Austin)	.05	.03	.02	337	James Lawrence Lyttle, Jr.	.05	.03	.02
250	Thomas Antony Bianco	.05	.03	.02	338	Gary Roenicke	.07	.04	.02
251	DeLancy LaFayette Currence	.05	.03	.02	339	Anthony Scott	.05	.03	.02
252	Steven Raymond Foucault	.05	.03	.02	340	Jerome Cardell White	.05	.03	.02
253	William Alfred Hands, Jr.	.05	.03	.02	341	James Edward Dwyer	.05	.03	.02
254	Steven Lowell Hargan	.05	.03	.02	342	Ellis Clarence Valentine	.05	.03	.02
255	Ferguson Arthur Jenkins	.30	.15	.09	343	Frederick John Scherman, Jr.	.05	.03	.02
256	Bob Mitchell Sheldon	.05	.03	.02	344	Dennis Herman Blair	.05	.03	.02
257	James Umbarger	.05	.03	.02	345	Woodrow Thompson Fryman	.07	.04	.02
258	Clyde Wright	.05	.03	.02	346	Charles Gilbert Taylor	.05	.03	.02
259	William Roger Fahey	.05	.03	.02	347	Daniel Dean Warthen	.05	.03	.02
260	James Howard Sundberg	.07	.04	.02	348	Donald George Carrithers	.05	.03	.02
261	Leonardo Alfonso Cardenas	.05	.03	.02	349	Stephen Douglas Rogers	.07	.04	.02
262	James Louis Fregosi	.10	.05	.03	350	Dale Albert Murray	.05	.03	.02
263	Dudley Michael (Mike) Hargrove	.07	.04	.02	351	Edwin Donald (Duke) Snider	1.00	.50	.30
264	Colbert Dale (Toby) Harrah	.10	.05	.03	352	Ralph George Houk	.07	.04	.02
265	Roy Lee Howell	.05	.03	.02	353	John Frederick Hiller	.07	.04	.02
266	Leonard Shenoff Randle	.05	.03	.02	354	Michael Stephen Lolich	.20	.10	.06
267	Roy Frederick Smalley III	.07	.04	.02	355	David Lawrence Lemanczyk	.05	.03	.02
268	James Lloyd Spencer	.05	.03	.02	356	Lerrin Harris LaGrow	.05	.03	.02
269	Jeffrey Alan Burroughs	.07	.04	.02	357	Fred Arroyo	.05	.03	.02
270	Thomas Alan Grieve	.05	.03	.02	358	Joseph Howard Coleman	.05	.03	.02
271	Joseph Lovitto, Jr.	.05	.03	.02	359	Benjamin A. Oglivie	.07	.04	.02
272	Frank Joseph Lucchesi	.05	.03	.02	360	Willie Wattison Horton	.10	.05	.03
273	David Earl Nelson	.05	.03	.02	361	John Clinton Knox	.05	.03	.02
274	Ted Lyle Simmons	.20	.10	.06	362	Leon Kauffman Roberts	.05	.03	.02
275	Louis Clark Brock	1.50	.70	.45	363	Ronald LeFlore	.10	.05	.03
276	Ronald Ray Fairly	.07	.04	.02	364	Gary Lynn Sutherland	.05	.03	.02
277	Arnold Ray (Bake) McBride	.05	.03	.02	365	Daniel Thomas Meyer	.05	.03	.02
278	Carl Reginald (Reggie) Smith	.12	.06	.04	366	Aurelio Rodriguez	.07	.04	.02
279	William Henry Davis	.10	.05	.03	367	Thomas Martin Veryzer	.05	.03	.02
280	Kenneth John Reitz	.05	.03	.02	368	Lavern Jack Pierce	.05	.03	.02
281	Charles William (Buddy) Bradford	.05	.03	.02	369	Eugene Richard Michael	.05	.03	.02
282	Luis Antonio Melendez	.05	.03	.02	370	Robert (Billy) Baldwin	.05	.03	.02
					371	William James Gates Brown	.05	.03	.02
					372	Mitchell Jack (Mickey) Stanley	.07	.04	.02
					373	Terryal Gene Humphrey	.05	.03	.02

	NR MT	EX	VG
374 Doyle Lafayette Alexander	.12	.06	.04
375 Miguel Angel (Mike) Cuellar	.10	.05	.03
376 Marcus Wayne Garland	.05	.03	.02
377 Ross Albert Grimsley III	.07	.04	.02
378 Grant Dwight Jackson	.05	.03	.02
379 Dyar K. Miller	.05	.03	.02
380 James Alvin Palmer	1.25	.60	.40
381 Michael Augustine Torrez	.07	.04	.02
382 Michael Henry Willis	.05	.03	.02
383 David Edwin Duncan	.05	.03	.02
384 Elrod Jerome Hendricks	.05	.03	.02
385 James Neamon Hutto Jr.	.05	.03	.02
386 Robert Michael Bailor	.05	.03	.02
387 Douglas Vernon DeCinces	.10	.05	.03
388 Robert Anthony Grich	.10	.05	.03
389 Lee Andrew May	.07	.04	.02
390 Anthony Joseph Muser	.05	.03	.02
391 Timothy C. Nordbrook	.05	.03	.02
392 Brooks Calbert Robinson, Jr.	1.75	.90	.50
393 Royle Stillman	.05	.03	.02
394 Don Edward Baylor	.15	.08	.05
395 Paul L.D. Blair	.07	.04	.02
396 Alonza Benjamin Bumbry	.07	.04	.02
397 Larry Duane Harlow	.05	.03	.02
398 Herman Thomas (Tommy) Davis, Jr.			
	.10	.05	.03
399 James Thomas Northrup	.07	.04	.02
400 Kenneth Wayne Singleton	.12	.06	.04
401 Thomas Michael Shopay	.05	.03	.02
402 Fredrick Michael Lynn	.40	.20	.12
403 Carlton Ernest Fisk	.50	.25	.15
404 Cecil Celester Cooper	.20	.10	.06
405 James Edward Rice	1.50	.70	.45
406 Juan Jose Beniquez	.05	.03	.02
407 Robert Dennis Doyle	.05	.03	.02
408 Dwight Michael Evans	.20	.10	.06
409 Carl Michael Yastrzemski	3.00	1.50	.90
410 Richard Paul Burleson	.07	.04	.02
411 Bernardo Carbo	.05	.03	.02
412 Douglas Lee Griffin, Jr.	.05	.03	.02
413 Americo P. Petrocelli	.07	.04	.02
414 Robert Edward Montgomery	.05	.03	.02
415 Timothy P. Blackwell	.05	.03	.02
416 Richard Alan Miller	.05	.03	.02
417 Darrell Dean Johnson	.05	.03	.02
418 Jim Scott Burton	.05	.03	.02
419 James Arthur Willoughby	.05	.03	.02
420 Rogelio (Roger) Moret	.05	.03	.02
421 William Francis Lee, III	.07	.04	.02
422 Richard Anthony Drago	.05	.03	.02
423 Diego Pablo Segui	.05	.03	.02
424 Luis Clemente Tiant	.15	.08	.05
425 James Augustus (Catfish) Hunter	1.00	.50	.30
426 Richard Clyde Sawyer	.05	.03	.02
427 Rudolph May Jr.	.07	.04	.02
428 Richard William Tidrow	.05	.03	.02
429 Albert Walter (Sparky) Lyle	.12	.06	.04
430 George Francis (Doc) Medich	.05	.03	.02
431 Patrick Edward Dobson, Jr.	.07	.04	.02
432 David Percy Pagan	.05	.03	.02
433 Thurman Lee Munson	1.50	.70	.45
434 Carroll Christopher Chambliss	.10	.05	.03
435 Roy Hilton White	.12	.06	.04
436 Walter Allen Williams	.05	.03	.02
437 Graig Nettles	.30	.15	.09
438 John Rikard (Rick) Dempsey	.07	.04	.02
439 Bobby Lee Bonds	.12	.06	.04
440 Edward Martin Hermann (Herrmann)			
	.05	.03	.02
441 Santos Alomar	.05	.03	.02
442 Frederick Blair Stanley	.05	.03	.02
443 Terry Bertland Whitfield	.05	.03	.02
444 Richard Alan Bladt	.05	.03	.02
445 Louis Victor Piniella	.12	.06	.04
446 Richard Allen Coggins	.05	.03	.02
447 Edwin Albert Brinkman	.07	.04	.02
448 James Percy Mason	.05	.03	.02
449 Larry Murray	.05	.03	.02
450 Ronald Mark Blomberg	.07	.04	.02
451 Elliott Maddox	.05	.03	.02
452 Kerry Dineen	.05	.03	.02
453 Alfred Manuel (Billy) Martin	.15	.08	.05
454 Dave Bergman	.05	.03	.02
455 Otoniel Velez	.05	.03	.02
456 Joseph Walter Hoerner	.05	.03	.02
457 Frank Edwin (Tug) McGraw, Jr.	.12	.06	.04
458 Henry Eugene (Gene) Garber	.05	.03	.02
459 Steven Norman Carlton	1.50	.70	.45
460 Larry Richard Christenson	.05	.03	.02
461 Thomas Gerald Underwood	.05	.03	.02
462 James Reynold Lonborg	.07	.04	.02

	NR MT	EX	VG
463 John William (Jay) Johnstone, Jr.	.07	.04	.02
464 Lawrence Robert Bowa	.12	.06	.04
465 David Cash, Jr.	.05	.03	.02
466 Ollie Lee Brown	.05	.03	.02
467 Gregory Michael Luzinski	.12	.06	.04
468 Johnny Lane Oates	.05	.03	.02
469 Michael Allen Anderson	.05	.03	.02
470 Michael Jack Schmidt	2.75	1.50	.80
471 Robert Raymond Boone	.07	.04	.02
472 Thomas George Hutton	.05	.03	.02
473 Richard Anthony Allen	.15	.08	.05
474 Antonio Taylor	.05	.03	.02
475 Jerry Lindsey Martin	.05	.03	.02
476 Daniel Leonard Ozark	.05	.03	.02
477 Richard David Ruthven	.05	.03	.02
478 James Richard Todd, Jr.	.05	.03	.02
479 Paul Aaron Lindblad	.05	.03	.02
480 Roland Glen Fingers	.50	.25	.15
481 Vida Blue, Jr.	.15	.08	.05
482 Kenneth Dale Holtzman	.07	.04	.02
483 Richard Allen Bosman	.05	.03	.02
484 Wilfred Charles (Sonny) Siebert	.05	.03	.02
485 William Glenn Abbott	.05	.03	.02
486 Stanley Raymond Bahnsen	.05	.03	.02
487 Michael Norris	.05	.03	.02
488 Alvin Ralph Dark	.07	.04	.02
489 Claudell Washington	.10	.05	.03
490 Joseph Oden Rudi	.10	.05	.03
491 William Alex North	.05	.03	.02
492 Dagoberto Blanco (Bert) Campaneris			
	.12	.06	.04
493 Fury Gene Tenace	.07	.04	.02
494 Reginald Martinez Jackson	2.50	1.25	.70
495 Philip Mason Garner	.07	.04	.02
496 Billy Leo Williams	1.00	.50	.30
497 Salvatore Leonard Bando	.10	.05	.03
498 James William Holt	.05	.03	.02
499 Teodoro Noel Martinez	.05	.03	.02
500 Raymond Earl Fosse	.05	.03	.02
501 Matthew Alexander	.05	.03	.02
502 Wallace Larry Haney	.05	.03	.02
503 Angel Luis Mangual	.05	.03	.02
504 Fred Ray Beene	.05	.03	.02
505 Thomas William Buskey	.05	.03	.02
506 Dennis Lee Eckersley	.10	.05	.03
507 Roric Edward Harrison	.05	.03	.02
508 Donald Harris Hood	.05	.03	.02
509 James Lester Kern	.05	.03	.02
510 David Eugene LaRoche	.05	.03	.02
511 Fred Ingels (Fritz) Peterson	.05	.03	.02
512 James Michael Strickland	.05	.03	.02
513 Michael Richard (Rick) Waits	.05	.03	.02
514 Alan Dean Ashby	.05	.03	.02
515 John Charles Ellis	.05	.03	.02
516 Rick Cerone	.07	.04	.02
517 David Gus (Buddy) Bell	.15	.08	.05
518 John Anthony Brohamer, Jr.	.05	.03	.02
519 Ricardo Adolfo Jacobo Carty	.10	.05	.03
520 Edward Carlton Crosby	.05	.03	.02
521 Frank Thomas Duffy	.05	.03	.02
522 Duane Eugene Kuiper (photo actually Rick Manning)	.05	.03	.02
523 Joseph Anthony Lis	.05	.03	.02
524 John Wesley (Boog) Powell	.25	.13	.08
525 Frank Robinson	1.50	.70	.45
526 Oscar Charles Gamble	.07	.04	.02
527 George Andrew Hendrick	.07	.04	.02
528 John Lee Lowenstein	.05	.03	.02
529 Richard Eugene Manning (photo actually Duane Kuiper)	.05	.03	.02
530 Tommy Alexander Smith	.05	.03	.02
531 Leslie Charles (Charlie) Spikes	.05	.03	.02
532 Steve Jack Kline	.05	.03	.02
533 Edward Emil Kranepool	.07	.04	.02
534 Michael Vail	.05	.03	.02
535 Delbert Bernard Unser	.05	.03	.02
536 Felix Bernardo Martinez Millan	.05	.03	.02
537 Daniel Joseph (Rusty) Staub	.20	.10	.06
538 Jesus Maria Rojas Alou	.07	.04	.02
539 Ronald Wayne Garrett	.05	.03	.02
540 Michael Dwaine Phillips	.05	.03	.02
541 Joseph Paul Torre	.20	.10	.06
542 David Arthur Kingman	.30	.15	.09
543 Eugene Anthony Clines	.05	.03	.02
544 Jack Seale Heidemann	.05	.03	.02
545 Derrel McKinley (Bud) Harrelson	.07	.04	.02
546 John Hardin Stearns	.05	.03	.02
547 John David Milner	.05	.03	.02
548 Robert John Apodaca	.05	.03	.02
549 Claude Edward (Skip) Lockwood Jr.			
	.05	.03	.02

		NR MT	EX	VG
550	Kenneth George Sanders	.05	.03	.02
551	George Thomas (Tom) Seaver	1.75	.90	.50
552	Ricky Alan Baldwin	.05	.03	.02
553	Jonathan Trumpbour Matlack	.07	.04	.02
554	Henry Gaylon Webb	.05	.03	.02
555	Randall Lee Tate	.05	.03	.02
556	Tom Edward Hall	.05	.03	.02
557	George Heard Stone Jr.	.05	.03	.02
558	Craig Steven Swan	.05	.03	.02
559	Gerald Allen Cram	.05	.03	.02
560	Roy J. Staiger	.05	.03	.02
561	Kenton C. Tekulve	.10	.05	.03
562	Jerry Reuss	.10	.05	.03
563	John R. Candelaria	.12	.06	.04
564	Lawrence C. Demery	.05	.03	.02
565	David John Giusti Jr.	.05	.03	.02
566	James Phillip Rooker	.05	.03	.02
567	Ramon Gonzalez Hernandez	.05	.03	.02
568	Bruce Eugene Kison	.05	.03	.02
569	Kenneth Alven Brett (Alvin)	.07	.04	.02
570	Robert Ralph Moose Jr.	.05	.03	.02
571	Manuel Jesus Sanguillen	.07	.04	.02
572	David Gene Parker	1.00	.50	.30
573	Wilver Dornel Stargell	1.25	.60	.40
574	Richard Walter Zisk	.07	.04	.02
575	Renaldo Antonio Stennett	.05	.03	.02
576	Albert Oliver Jr.	.30	.15	.09
577	William Henry Robinson Jr.	.05	.03	.02
578	Robert Eugene Robertson	.05	.03	.02
579	Richard Joseph Hebner	.05	.03	.02
580	Edgar Leon Kirkpatrick	.05	.03	.02
581	Don Robert (Duffy) Dyer	.05	.03	.02
582	Craig Reynolds	.05	.03	.02
583	Franklin Fabian Taveras	.05	.03	.02
584	William Larry Randolph	.20	.10	.06
585	Arthur H. Howe	.05	.03	.02
586	Daniel Edward Murtaugh	.07	.04	.02
587	Charles Richard (Rich) McKinney	.05	.03	.02
588	James Edward Goodson	.05	.03	.02
589	George Brett, Al Cowans/Checklist	.80	.40	.25
590	Keith Hernandez, Lou Brock/Checklist	.80	.40	.25
591	Jerry Koosman, Duke Snider/Checklist	.30	.15	.09
592	John Knox, Maury Wills/Checklist	.10	.05	.03
593a	Catfish Hunter, Noland Ryan/Checklist	20.00	10.00	6.00
593b	Catfish Hunter, Nolan Ryan/Checklist	.50	.25	.15
594	Ralph Branca, Carl Erskine, Pee Wee Reese/Checklist	.25	.13	.08
595	Willie Mays, Herb Score/Checklist	.70	.35	.20
596	Larry Eugene Cox	.05	.03	.02
597	Eugene William Mauch	.07	.04	.02
598	William Frederick (Whitey) Wietelmann	.05	.03	.02
599	Wayne Kirby Simpson	.05	.03	.02
600	Melvin Erskine Thomason	.05	.03	.02
601	Issac Bernard (Ike) Hampton	.05	.03	.02
602	Kenneth S. Crosby	.05	.03	.02
603	Ralph Emanuel Rowe	.05	.03	.02
604	James Vernon Tyrone	.05	.03	.02
605	Michael Dennis Kelleher	.05	.03	.02
606	Mario Mendoza	.05	.03	.02
607	Michael George Rogodzinski	.05	.03	.02
608	Robert Collins Gallagher	.05	.03	.02
609	Jerry Martin Koosman	.12	.06	.04
610	Joseph Filmore Frazier	.05	.03	.02
611	Karl Kuehl	.05	.03	.02
612	Frank J. LaCorte	.05	.03	.02
613	Raymond Douglas Bare	.05	.03	.02
614	Billy Arnold Muffett	.05	.03	.02
615	William Harry Laxton	.05	.03	.02
616	Willie Howard Mays	2.00	1.00	.60
617	Philip Joseph Cavaretta (Cavarretta)	.07	.04	.02
618	Theodore Bernard Kluszewski	.15	.08	.05
619	Elston Gene Howard	.15	.08	.05
620	Alexander Peter Grammas	.05	.03	.02
621	James Barton (Mickey) Vernon	.07	.04	.02
622	Richard Allan Sisler	.05	.03	.02
623	Harvey Haddix, Jr.	.07	.04	.02
624	Bobby Brooks Winkles	.05	.03	.02
625	John Michael Pesky	.07	.04	.02
626	James Houston Davenport	.05	.03	.02
627	David Allen Tomlin	.05	.03	.02
628	Roger Lee Craig	.07	.04	.02
629	John Joseph Amalfitano	.05	.03	.02
630	James Harrison Reese	.05	.03	.02

1962 Salada Tea-Junket Dessert Coins

These 1⅜" diameter plastic coins were issued in packages of Salada Tea and Junket Pudding mix. There are 221 different players available, with variations bringing the total of different coins to 261. Each coin has a paper color photo inserted in the front which contains the player's name and position plus the coin number. The plastic rims come in six different colors, all color coded per team. (For example, the Yankees are found with light blue rims). Production began with 180 coins, but the addition of the Mets and Colt .45's to the National League allowed the company to expand the set's size. Twenty expansion players were added along with 21 other players. Several players' coins were dropped after the initial "180" run, causing some scarcities. A Gary Geiger coin with a "BO", instead of a "B", on his cap is sometimes found on collectors' want lists. Most Salada experts do not consider this coin to be a legitimate variation. The mark, which somewhat resembles an "O", is merely a printing smear and not an intended cap emblem. It has also been decided by Salada experts that a Jim Lemon coin with red shirt buttons does not exist.

		NR MT	EX	VG
Complete Set w/o variations:		2200.00	1100.00	660.00
Complete Set with variations:		5500.00	2750.00	1650.
Common Player:		2.00	1.00	.60
1	Jim Gentile	2.50	1.25	.70
2	Bill Pierce	110.00	55.00	33.00
3	Chico Fernandez	2.00	1.00	.60
4	Tom Brewer	30.00	15.00	9.00
5	Woody Held	2.50	1.25	.70
6	Ray Herbert	30.00	15.00	9.00
7a	Ken Aspromonte (Angels)	7.00	3.50	2.00
7b	Ken Aspromonte (Indians)	3.50	1.75	1.00
8	Whitey Ford	23.00	11.50	7.00
9	Jim Lemon	2.50	1.25	.70
10	Billy Klaus	2.00	1.00	.60
11	Steve Barber	30.00	15.00	9.00
12	Nellie Fox	7.00	3.50	2.00
13	Jim Bunning	6.00	3.00	1.75
14	Frank Malzone	2.50	1.25	.70
15	Tito Francona	2.50	1.25	.70
16	Bobby Del Greco	2.00	1.00	.60
17a	Steve Bilko (red shirt buttons)	6.00	3.00	1.75
17b	Steve Bilko (white shirt buttons)	3.00	1.50	.90
18	Tony Kubek	45.00	22.00	13.50
19	Earl Battey	2.50	1.25	.70
20	Chuck Cottier	2.50	1.25	.70
21	Willie Tasby	2.00	1.00	.60
22	Bob Allison	3.00	1.50	.90
23	Roger Maris	20.00	10.00	6.00
24a	Earl Averill (red shirt buttons)	6.00	3.00	1.75
24b	Earl Averill (white shirt buttons)	3.00	1.50	.90
25	Jerry Lumpe	2.50	1.25	.70
26	Jim Grant	30.00	15.00	9.00
27	Carl Yastrzemski	78.00	39.00	23.00
28	Rocky Colavito	3.50	1.75	1.00
29	Al Smith	2.00	1.00	.60
30	Jim Busby	30.00	15.00	9.00
31	Dick Howser	3.00	1.50	.90
32	Jim Perry	3.00	1.50	.90
33	Yogi Berra	30.00	15.00	9.00
34a	Ken Hamlin (red shirt buttons)	6.00	3.00	1.75
34b	Ken Hamlin (white shirt buttons)	3.00	1.50	.90

#	Name	NR MT	EX	VG
35	Dale Long	2.50	1.25	.70
36	Harmon Killebrew	20.00	10.00	6.00
37	Dick Brown	2.00	1.00	.60
38	Gary Geiger	2.00	1.00	.60
39a	Minnie Minoso (White Sox)	35.00	17.50	10.50
39b	Minnie Minoso (Cardinals)	18.00	9.00	5.50
40	Brooks Robinson	39.00	19.50	11.50
41	Mickey Mantle	90.00	45.00	27.00
42	Bennie Daniels	2.00	1.00	.60
43	Billy Martin	5.00	2.50	1.50
44	Vic Power	2.50	1.25	.70
45	Joe Pignatano	2.00	1.00	.60
46a	Ryne Duren (red shirt buttons)	6.00	3.00	1.75
46b	Ryne Duren (white shirt buttons)	3.50	1.75	1.00
47a	Pete Runnels (2B)	7.00	3.50	2.00
47b	Pete Runnels (1B)	3.50	1.75	1.00
48a	Dick Williams (name on right)	1000.00	500.00	300.00
48b	Dick Williams (name on left)	3.50	1.75	1.00
49	Jim Landis	2.00	1.00	.60
50	Steve Boros	2.50	1.25	.70
51a	Zoilo Versalles (red shirt buttons)	6.00	3.00	1.75
51b	Zoilo Versalles (white shirt buttons)	3.00	1.50	.90
52a	Johnny Temple (Indians)	7.00	3.50	2.00
52b	Johnny Temple (Orioles)	3.50	1.75	1.00
53a	Jackie Brandt (Oriole)	3.50	1.75	1.00
53b	Jackie Brandt (Orioles)	800.00	400.00	240.00
54	Joe McClain	2.00	1.00	.60
55	Sherm Lollar	2.50	1.25	.70
56	Gene Stephens	2.00	1.00	.60
57a	Leon Wagner (red shirt buttons)	6.00	3.00	1.75
57b	Leon Wagner (white shirt buttons)	3.00	1.50	.90
58	Frank Lary	2.50	1.25	.70
59	Bill Skowron	3.50	1.75	1.00
60	Vic Wertz	2.50	1.25	.70
61	Willie Kirkland	2.00	1.00	.60
62	Leo Posada	2.00	1.00	.60
63a	Albie Pearson (red shirt buttons)	6.00	3.00	1.75
63b	Albie Pearson (white shirt buttons)	3.00	1.50	.90
64	Bobby Richardson	6.00	3.00	1.75
65a	Marv Breeding (SS)	7.00	3.50	2.00
65b	Marv Breeding (2B)	3.50	1.75	1.00
66	Roy Sievers	80.00	40.00	24.00
67	Al Kaline	30.00	15.00	9.00
68a	Don Buddin (Red Sox)	7.00	3.50	2.00
68b	Don Buddin (Colts)	3.50	1.75	1.00
69a	Lenny Green (red shirt buttons)	6.00	3.00	1.75
69B	Lenny Green (white shirt buttons)	3.00	1.50	.90
70	Gene Green	30.00	15.00	9.00
71	Luis Aparicio	13.00	6.50	4.00
72	Norm Cash	3.00	1.50	.90
73	Jackie Jensen	35.00	17.50	10.50
74	Bubba Phillips	2.00	1.00	.60
75	Jim Archer	2.00	1.00	.60
76a	Ken Hunt (red shirt buttons)	6.00	3.00	1.75
76b	Ken Hunt (white shirt buttons)	3.00	1.50	.90
77	Ralph Terry	3.00	1.50	.90
78	Camilo Pascual	2.50	1.25	.70
79	Marty Keough	30.00	15.00	9.00
80	Cletis Boyer	3.00	1.50	.90
81	Jim Pagliaroni	2.00	1.00	.60
82a	Gene Leek (red shirt buttons)	6.00	3.00	1.75
82b	Gene Leek (white shirt buttons)	3.00	1.50	.90
83	Jake Wood	2.00	1.00	.60
84	Coot Veal	30.00	15.00	9.00
85	Norm Siebern	2.50	1.25	.70
86a	Andy Carey (White Sox)	30.00	15.00	9.00
86b	Andy Carey (Phillies)	3.50	1.75	1.00
87a	Bill Tuttle (red shirt buttons)	6.00	3.00	1.75
87b	Bill Tuttle (white shirt buttons)	3.00	1.50	.90
88a	Jimmy Piersall (Indians)	7.00	3.50	2.00
88b	Jimmy Piersall (Senators)	3.50	1.75	1.00
89	Ron Hansen	30.00	15.00	9.00
90a	Chuck Stobbs (red shirt buttons)	6.00	3.00	1.75
90b	Chuck Stobbs (white shirt buttons)	3.00	1.50	.90
91a	Ken McBride (red shirt buttons)	6.00	3.00	1.75
91b	Ken McBride (white shirt buttons)	3.00	1.50	.90
92	Bill Bruton	2.50	1.25	.70
93	Gus Triandos	2.50	1.25	.70
94	John Romano	2.00	1.00	.60
95	Elston Howard	5.00	2.50	1.50
96	Gene Woodling	2.50	1.25	.70
97a	Early Wynn (pitching pose)	45.00	22.00	13.50
97b	Early Wynn (portrait)	25.00	12.50	7.50
98	Milt Pappas	2.50	1.25	.70
99	Bill Monbouquette	2.50	1.25	.70
100	Wayne Causey	2.00	1.00	.60
101	Don Elston	2.00	1.00	.60
102a	Charlie Neal (Dodgers)	7.00	3.50	2.00
102b	Charlie Neal (Mets)	3.50	1.75	1.00
103	Don Blasingame	2.00	1.00	.60
104	Frank Thomas	30.00	15.00	9.00
105	Wes Covington	2.50	1.25	.70
106	Chuck Hiller	2.00	1.00	.60
107	Don Hoak	2.50	1.25	.70
108a	Bob Lillis (Cardinals)	18.00	9.00	5.50
108b	Bob Lillis (Colts)	3.50	1.75	1.00
109	Sandy Koufax	35.00	17.50	10.50
110	Gordy Coleman	2.00	1.00	.60
111	Ed Matthews (Mathews)	18.00	9.00	5.50
112	Art Mahaffey	2.00	1.00	.60
113a	Ed Bailey (red period above "i" in Giants)	7.00	3.50	2.00
113b	Ed Bailey (white period)	3.00	1.50	.90
114	Smoky Burgess	3.00	1.50	.90
115	Bill White	3.00	1.50	.90
116	Ed Bouchee	30.00	15.00	9.00
117	Bob Buhl	2.50	1.25	.70
118	Vada Pinson	3.50	1.75	1.00
119	Carl Sawatski	2.00	1.00	.60
120	Dick Stuart	2.50	1.25	.70
121	Harvey Kuenn	45.00	22.00	13.50
122	Pancho Herrera	2.00	1.00	.60
123a	Don Zimmer (Cubs)	7.00	3.50	2.00
123b	Don Zimmer (Mets)	4.50	2.25	1.25
124	Wally Moon	2.50	1.25	.70
125	Joe Adcock	3.00	1.50	.90
126	Joey Jay	2.00	1.00	.60
127a	Maury Wills (blue "3" on shirt)	15.50	7.75	4.75
127b	Maury Wills (red "3" on shirt)	7.00	3.50	2.00
128	George Altman	2.00	1.00	.60
129a	John Buzhardt (Phillies)	7.00	3.50	2.00
129b	John Buzhardt (White Sox)	6.00	3.00	1.75
130	Felipe Alou	3.00	1.50	.90
131	Bill Mazeroski	3.50	1.75	1.00
132	Ernie Broglio	2.00	1.00	.60
133	John Roseboro	2.50	1.25	.70
134	Mike McCormick	2.50	1.25	.70
135a	Chuck Smith (Phillies)	7.00	3.50	2.00
135b	Chuck Smith (White Sox)	6.00	3.00	1.75
136	Ron Santo	3.50	1.75	1.00
137	Gene Freese	2.00	1.00	.60
138	Dick Groat	3.50	1.75	1.00
139	Curt Flood	3.50	1.75	1.00
140	Frank Bolling	2.00	1.00	.60
141	Clay Dalrymple	2.00	1.00	.60
142	Willie McCovey	30.00	15.00	9.00
143	Bob Skinner	2.50	1.25	.70
144	Lindy McDaniel	2.00	1.00	.60
145	Glen Hobbie	2.00	1.00	.60
146a	Gil Hodges (Dodgers)	50.00	25.00	15.00
146b	Gil Hodges (Mets)	25.00	12.50	7.50
147	Eddie Kasko	2.00	1.00	.60
148	Gino Cimoli	30.00	15.00	9.00
149	Willie Mays	65.00	32.00	19.50
150	Roberto Clemente	45.00	22.00	13.50
151	Red Schoendienst	5.00	2.50	1.50
152	Joe Torre	3.50	1.75	1.00
153	Bob Purkey	2.50	1.25	.70
154a	Tommy Davis (3B)	7.00	3.50	2.00
154b	Tommy Davis (OF)	5.00	2.50	1.50
155a	Andre Rogers (incorrect spelling)	7.00	3.50	2.00
155b	Andre Rodgers (correct spelling)	3.50	1.75	1.00
156	Tony Taylor	2.00	1.00	.60
157	Bob Friend	3.00	1.50	.90
158a	Gus Bell (Redlegs)	7.00	3.50	2.00
158b	Gus Bell (Mets)	4.50	2.25	1.25
159	Roy McMillan	2.50	1.25	.70
160	Carl Warwick	2.00	1.00	.60
161	Willie Davis	3.00	1.50	.90
162	Sam Jones	45.00	22.00	13.50
163	Ruben Amaro	2.00	1.00	.60
164	Sam Taylor	2.00	1.00	.60
165	Frank Robinson	30.00	15.00	9.00
166	Lou Burdette	3.00	1.50	.90
167	Ken Boyer	3.50	1.75	1.00
168	Bill Virdon	3.00	1.50	.90
169	Jim Davenport	2.00	1.00	.60
170	Don Demeter	2.00	1.00	.60
171	Richie Ashburn	35.00	17.50	10.50
172	John Podres	3.50	1.75	1.00
173a	Joe Cunningham (Cardinals)	45.00	22.00	13.50
173b	Joe Cunningham (White Sox)	25.00	12.50	7.50
174	ElRoy Face	3.00	1.50	.90
175	Orlando Cepeda	6.00	3.00	1.75
176a	Bobby Gene Smith (Phillies)	7.00	3.50	2.00
176b	Bobby Gene Smith (Mets)	3.50	1.75	1.00
177a	Ernie Banks (OF)	40.00	20.00	12.00
177b	Ernie Banks (SS)	20.00	10.00	6.00

		NR MT	EX	VG
178a	Daryl Spencer (3B)	7.00	3.50	2.00
178b	Daryl Spencer (1B)	3.50	1.75	1.00
179	Bob Schmidt	30.00	15.00	9.00
180	Hank Aaron	60.00	30.00	18.00
181	Hobie Landrith	3.50	1.75	1.00
182a	Ed Broussard	400.00	200.00	120.00
182b	Ed Bressoud	25.00	12.50	7.50
183	Felix Mantilla	3.50	1.75	1.00
184	Dick Farrell	3.50	1.75	1.00
185	Bob Miller	3.50	1.75	1.00
186	Don Taussig	3.50	1.75	1.00
187	Pumpsie Green	3.50	1.75	1.00
188	Bobby Shantz	6.00	3.00	1.75
189	Roger Craig	6.00	3.00	1.75
190	Hal Smith	3.50	1.75	1.00
191	John Edwards	3.50	1.75	1.00
192	John DeMerit	3.50	1.75	1.00
193	Joe Amalfitano	3.50	1.75	1.00
194	Norm Larker	3.50	1.75	1.00
195	Al Heist	3.50	1.75	1.00
196	Al Spangler	3.50	1.75	1.00
197	Alex Grammas	3.50	1.75	1.00
198	Gerry Lynch	3.50	1.75	1.00
199	Jim McKnight	3.50	1.75	1.00
200	Jose Pagen (Pagan)	3.50	1.75	1.00
201	Junior Gilliam	18.00	9.00	5.50
202	Art Ditmar	3.50	1.75	1.00
203	Pete Daley	3.50	1.75	1.00
204	Johnny Callison	5.00	2.50	1.50
205	Stu Miller	3.50	1.75	1.00
206	Russ Snyder	3.50	1.75	1.00
207	Billy Williams	30.00	15.00	9.00
208	Walter Bond	3.50	1.75	1.00
209	Joe Koppe	3.50	1.75	1.00
210	Don Schwall	13.00	6.50	4.00
211	Billy Gardner	5.00	2.50	1.50
212	Chuck Estrada	3.50	1.75	1.00
213	Gary Bell	3.50	1.75	1.00
214	Floyd Robinson	3.50	1.75	1.00
215	Duke Snider	45.00	22.00	13.50
216	Lee Maye	3.50	1.75	1.00
217	Howie Bedell	3.50	1.75	1.00
218	Bob Will	3.50	1.75	1.00
219	Dallas Green	6.00	3.00	1.75
220	Carroll Hardy	3.50	1.75	1.00
221	Danny O'Connell	3.50	1.75	1.00

		NR MT	EX	VG
5	Juan Marichal	15.00	7.50	4.50
6	Bob Purkey	3.00	1.50	.90
7	Bob Shaw	3.00	1.50	.90
8	Warren Spahn	18.00	9.00	5.50
9	Johnny Podres	5.00	2.50	1.50
10	Art Mahaffey	3.00	1.50	.90
11	Del Crandall	4.00	2.00	1.25
12	John Roseboro	4.00	2.00	1.25
13	Orlando Cepeda	6.00	3.00	1.75
14	Bill Mazeroski	5.00	2.50	1.50
15	Ken Boyer	5.00	2.50	1.50
16	Dick Groat	5.00	2.50	1.50
17	Ernie Banks	18.00	9.00	5.50
18	Frank Bolling	3.00	1.50	.90
19	Jim Davenport	3.00	1.50	.90
20	Maury Wills	6.00	3.00	1.75
21	Tommy Davis	4.00	2.00	1.25
22	Willie Mays	40.00	20.00	12.00
23	Roberto Clemente	40.00	20.00	12.00
24	Henry Aaron	40.00	20.00	12.00
25	Felipe Alou	4.00	2.00	1.25
26	Johnny Callison	4.00	2.00	1.25
27	Richie Ashburn	8.00	4.00	2.50
28	Eddie Mathews	15.00	7.50	4.50
29	Frank Robinson	18.00	9.00	5.50
30	Billy Williams	15.00	7.50	4.50
31	George Altman	3.00	1.50	.90
32	Hank Aguirre	3.00	1.50	.90
33	Jim Bunning	5.00	2.50	1.50
34	Dick Donovan	3.00	1.50	.90
35	Bill Monbouquette	3.00	1.50	.90
36	Camilo Pascual	4.00	2.00	1.25
37	David Stenhouse	3.00	1.50	.90
38	Ralph Terry	4.00	2.00	1.25
39	Hoyt Wilhelm	12.00	6.00	3.50
40	Jim Kaat	8.00	4.00	2.50
41	Ken McBride	3.00	1.50	.90
42	Ray Herbert	3.00	1.50	.90
43	Milt Pappas	4.00	2.00	1.25
44	Earl Battey	3.00	1.50	.90
45	Elston Howard	5.00	2.50	1.50
46	John Romano	3.00	1.50	.90
47	Jim Gentile	3.00	1.50	.90
48	Billy Moran	3.00	1.50	.90
49	Rich Rollins	3.00	1.50	.90
50	Luis Aparicio	12.00	6.00	3.50
51	Norm Siebern	3.00	1.50	.90
52	Bobby Richardson	6.00	3.00	1.75
53	Brooks Robinson	25.00	12.50	7.50
54	Tom Tresh	4.00	2.00	1.25
55	Leon Wagner	3.00	1.50	.90
56	Mickey Mantle	90.00	45.00	27.00
57	Roger Maris	18.00	9.00	5.50
58	Rocky Colavito	5.00	2.50	1.50
59	Lee Thomas	3.00	1.50	.90
60	Jim Landis	3.00	1.50	.90
61	Pete Runnels	4.00	2.00	1.25
62	Yogi Berra	25.00	12.50	7.50
63	Al Kaline	25.00	12.50	7.50

1963 Salada Tea-Junket Dessert Coins

A much smaller set of baseball coins was issued by Salada/Junket in 1963. The 63 coins issued were called "All-Star Baseball Coins" and included most of the top players of the day. Unlike 1962, the coins were made of metal and measured a slightly larger 1½" diameter. American League players have blue rims on their coins, while National Leaguers are rimmed in red. Coin fronts contain no printing on the full-color player photos, while backs list coin number, player name, team and position, along with brief statistics and the sponsors' logos.

		NR MT	EX	VG
Complete Set:		675.00	337.00	202.00
Common Player:		3.00	1.50	.90
1	Don Drysdale	15.00	7.50	4.50
2	Dick Farrell	3.00	1.50	.90
3	Bob Gibson	15.00	7.50	4.50
4	Sandy Koufax	30.00	15.00	9.00

1986 Schnucks Milk Cardinals

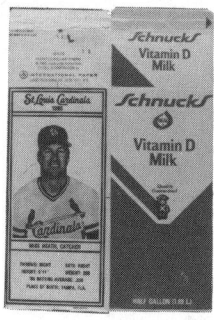

These milk carton panels were issued by Schnucks supermarkets in the St. Louis and southwestern Illinois areas. The 3¾" by 7½" blank-back panels feature black and white photos of 24 different St. Louis players along with personal information and 1985

playing statistics. A mascot and schedule card were also included in the set.

		MT	NR MT	EX
Complete Set:		28.00	21.00	11.00
Common Player:		.60	.45	.25
(1)	Jack Clark	2.50	2.00	1.00
(2)	Vince Coleman	3.50	2.75	1.50
(3)	Tim Conroy	.60	.45	.25
(4)	Danny Cox	1.25	.90	.50
(5)	Ken Dayley	.60	.45	.25
(6)	Bob Forsch	.90	.70	.35
(7)	Mike Heath	.60	.45	.25
(8)	Tom Herr	1.25	.90	.50
(9)	Rick Horton	.90	.70	.35
(10)	Clint Hurdle	.60	.45	.25
(11)	Kurt Kepshire	.60	.45	.25
(12)	Jeff Lahti	.60	.45	.25
(13)	Tito Landrum	.60	.45	.25
(14)	Mike Lavalliere	.60	.45	.25
(15)	Tom Lawless	.60	.45	.25
(16)	Willie McGee	2.50	2.00	1.00
(17)	Jose Oquendo	.60	.45	.25
(18)	Rick Ownbey	.60	.45	.25
(19)	Terry Pendleton	1.25	.90	.50
(20)	Pat Perry	.60	.45	.25
(21)	Ozzie Smith	2.50	2.00	1.00
(22)	John Tudor	1.50	1.25	.60
(23)	Andy Van Slyke	.90	.70	.35
(24)	Todd Worrell	3.50	2.75	1.50
(25)	Fred Bird (mascot)	.60	.45	.25
(26)	1986 Cardinals Schedule	.60	.45	.25

1988 Score

A fifth member joined the group of nationally distributed baseball cards in 1988. Titled ''Score,'' the new cards are characterized by extremely sharp and excellent full-color photography and printing. Card backs are full-color also and carry a player head-shot, along with a brief biography and player personal and statistical information. The 660 cards in the set each measure 2½'' by 3½'' in size. The fronts come with one of six different border colors — blue, red, green, purple, orange and gold — which are equally divided at 110 cards per color. The Score set was produced by Major League Marketing, the same company that markets the ''triple-action'' Sportflics card sets.

		MT	NR MT	EX
Complete Set:		18.00	13.50	7.25
Common Player:		.03	.02	.01
1	Don Mattingly	1.25	.90	.50
2	Wade Boggs	.80	.60	.30
3	Tim Raines	.20	.15	.08
4	Andre Dawson	.15	.11	.06
5	Mark McGwire	1.00	.70	.40
6	Kevin Seitzer	1.25	.90	.50
7	Wally Joyner	.70	.50	.30
8	Jesse Barfield	.10	.08	.04
9	Pedro Guerrero	.12	.09	.05
10	Eric Davis	.80	.60	.30
11	George Brett	.30	.25	.12
12	Ozzie Smith	.10	.08	.04

		MT	NR MT	EX
13	Rickey Henderson	.25	.20	.10
14	Jim Rice	.20	.15	.08
15	Matt Nokes	1.25	.90	.50
16	Mike Schmidt	.30	.25	.12
17	Dave Parker	.12	.09	.05
18	Eddie Murray	.25	.20	.10
19	Andres Galarraga '	.08	.06	.03
20	Tony Fernandez	.10	.08	.04
21	Kevin McReynolds	.08	.06	.03
22	B.J. Surhoff	.20	.15	.08
23	Pat Tabler	.06	.05	.02
24	Kirby Puckett	.25	.20	.10
25	Benny Santiago	.50	.40	.20
26	Ryne Sandberg	.15	.11	.06
27	Kelly Downs	.08	.06	.03
28	Jose Cruz	.06	.05	.02
29	Pete O'Brien	.06	.05	.02
30	Mark Langston	.08	.06	.03
31	Lee Smith	.08	.06	.03
32	Juan Samuel	.10	.08	.04
33	Kevin Bass	.06	.05	.02
34	R.J. Reynolds	.06	.05	.02
35	Steve Sax	.12	.09	.05
36	John Kruk	.20	.15	.08
37	Alan Trammell	.15	.11	.06
38	Chris Bosio	.06	.05	.02
39	Brook Jacoby	.08	.06	.03
40	Willie McGee	.10	.08	.04
41	Dave Magadan	.15	.11	.06
42	Fred Lynn	.10	.08	.04
43	Kent Hrbek	.12	.09	.05
44	Brian Downing	.06	.05	.02
45	Jose Canseco	.60	.45	.25
46	Jim Presley	.08	.06	.03
47	Mike Stanley	.08	.06	.03
48	Tony Pena	.06	.05	.02
49	David Cone	.06	.05	.02
50	Rick Sutcliffe	.10	.08	.04
51	Doug Drabek	.06	.05	.02
52	Bill Doran	.06	.05	.02
53	Mike Scioscia	.03	.02	.01
54	Candy Maldonado	.06	.05	.02
55	Dave Winfield	.20	.15	.08
56	Lou Whitaker	.12	.09	.05
57	Tom Henke	.06	.05	.02
58	Ken Gerhart	.08	.06	.03
59	Glenn Braggs	.10	.08	.04
60	Julio Franco	.08	.06	.03
61	Charlie Leibrandt	.06	.05	.02
62	Gary Gaetti	.10	.08	.04
63	Bob Boone	.06	.05	.02
64	Luis Polonia	.20	.15	.08
65	Dwight Evans	.10	.08	.04
66	Phil Bradley	.10	.08	.04
67	Mike Boddicker	.06	.05	.02
68	Vince Coleman	.15	.11	.06
69	Howard Johnson	.08	.06	.03
70	Tim Wallach	.08	.06	.03
71	Keith Moreland	.06	.05	.02
72	Barry Larkin	.10	.08	.04
73	Alan Ashby	.03	.02	.01
74	Rick Rhoden	.06	.05	.02
75	Darrell Evans	.08	.06	.03
76	Dave Stieb	.08	.06	.03
77	Dan Plesac	.10	.08	.04
78	Jack Clark	.12	.09	.05
79	Frank White	.06	.05	.02
80	Joe Carter	.10	.08	.04
81	Mike Witt	.08	.06	.03
82	Terry Steinbach	.10	.08	.04
83	Alvin Davis	.10	.08	.04
84	Tom Herr	.06	.05	.02
85	Vance Law	.03	.02	.01
86	Kal Daniels	.15	.11	.06
87	Rick Honeycutt	.03	.02	.01
88	Alfredo Griffin	.06	.05	.02
89	Bret Saberhagen	.15	.11	.06
90	Bert Blyleven	.10	.08	.04
91	Jeff Reardon	.10	.08	.04
92	Cory Snyder	.15	.11	.06
93	Greg Walker	.06	.05	.02
94	Joe Magrane	.35	.25	.14
95	Rob Deer	.08	.06	.03
96	Ray Knight	.06	.05	.02
97	Casey Candaele	.06	.05	.02
98	John Cerutti	.08	.06	.03
99	Eric Bell	.06	.05	.02
100	Will Clark	.60	.45	.25
101	Buddy Bell	.08	.06	.03
102	Willie Wilson	.08	.06	.03
103	Dave Schmidt	.03	.02	.01

		MT	NR MT	EX			MT	NR MT	EX
104	Dennis Eckersley	.06	.05	.02	195	Donnie Moore	.03	.02	.01
105	Don Sutton	.12	.09	.05	196	Dan Pasqua	.08	.06	.03
106	Danny Tartabull	.15	.11	.06	197	Jim Gantner	.03	.02	.01
107	Fred McGriff	.08	.06	.03	198	Mark Eichhorn	.08	.06	.03
108	Les Straker	.15	.11	.06	199	John Grubb	.03	.02	.01
109	Lloyd Moseby	.08	.06	.03	200	Bill Ripken	.30	.25	.12
110	Roger Clemens	.50	.40	.20	201	Sam Horn	.90	.70	.35
111	Glenn Hubbard	.03	.02	.01	202	Todd Worrell	.10	.08	.04
112	Ken Williams	.20	.15	.08	203	Terry Leach	.06	.05	.02
113	Ruben Sierra	.35	.25	.14	204	Garth Iorg	.03	.02	.01
114	Stan Jefferson	.08	.06	.03	205	Brian Dayett	.03	.02	.01
115	Milt Thompson	.06	.05	.02	206	Bo Diaz	.03	.02	.01
116	Bobby Bonilla	.08	.06	.03	207	Craig Reynolds	.03	.02	.01
117	Wayne Tolleson	.03	.02	.01	208	Brian Holton	.03	.02	.01
118	Matt Williams	.30	.25	.12	209	Marvelle Wynne (Marvell)	.03	.02	.01
119	Chet Lemon	.06	.05	.02	210	Dave Concepcion	.06	.05	.02
120	Dale Sveum	.08	.06	.03	211	Mike Davis	.06	.05	.02
121	Dennis Boyd	.06	.05	.02	212	Devon White	.25	.20	.10
122	Brett Butler	.06	.05	.02	213	Mickey Brantley	.03	.02	.01
123	Terry Kennedy	.06	.05	.02	214	Greg Gagne	.06	.05	.02
124	Jack Howell	.06	.05	.02	215	Oddibe McDowell	.08	.06	.03
125	Curt Young	.06	.05	.02	216	Jimmy Key	.08	.06	.03
126	Dave Valle	.03	.02	.01	217	Dave Bergman	.03	.02	.01
127	Curt Wilkerson	.03	.02	.01	218	Calvin Schiraldi	.03	.02	.01
128	Tim Teufel	.03	.02	.01	219	Larry Sheets	.08	.06	.03
129	Ozzie Virgil	.06	.05	.02	220	Mike Easler	.06	.05	.02
130	Brian Fisher	.06	.05	.02	221	Kurt Stillwell	.10	.08	.04
131	Lance Parrish	.12	.09	.05	222	Chuck Jackson	.20	.15	.08
132	Tom Browning	.06	.05	.02	223	Dave Martinez	.12	.09	.05
133	Larry Andersen	.03	.02	.01	224	Tim Leary	.03	.02	.01
134	Bob Brenley (Brenly)	.03	.02	.01	225	Steve Garvey	.20	.15	.08
135	Mike Marshall	.08	.06	.03	226	Greg Mathews	.08	.06	.03
136	Gerald Perry	.06	.05	.02	227	Doug Sisk	.03	.02	.01
137	Bobby Meacham	.03	.02	.01	228	Dave Henderson	.03	.02	.01
138	Larry Herndon	.03	.02	.01	229	Jimmy Dwyer	.03	.02	.01
139	Fred Manrique	.20	.15	.08	230	Larry Owen	.03	.02	.01
140	Charlie Hough	.06	.05	.02	231	Andre Thornton	.06	.05	.02
141	Ron Darling	.10	.08	.04	232	Mark Salas	.03	.02	.01
142	Herm Winningham	.03	.02	.01	233	Tom Brookens	.03	.02	.01
143	Mike Diaz	.08	.06	.03	234	Greg Brock	.06	.05	.02
144	Mike Jackson	.15	.11	.06	235	Rance Mulliniks	.03	.02	.01
145	Denny Walling	.03	.02	.01	236	Bob Brower	.06	.05	.02
146	Rob Thompson	.08	.06	.03	237	Joe Niekro	.06	.05	.02
147	Franklin Stubbs	.06	.05	.02	238	Scott Bankhead	.03	.02	.01
148	Albert Hall	.03	.02	.01	239	Doug DeCinces	.06	.05	.02
149	Bobby Witt	.08	.06	.03	240	Tommy John	.12	.09	.05
150	Lance McCullers	.06	.05	.02	241	Rich Gedman	.06	.05	.02
151	Scott Bradley	.03	.02	.01	242	Ted Power	.06	.05	.02
152	Mark McLemore	.03	.02	.01	243	Dave Meads	.15	.11	.06
153	Tim Laudner	.03	.02	.01	244	Jim Sundberg	.03	.02	.01
154	Greg Swindell	.10	.08	.04	245	Ken Oberkfell	.03	.02	.01
155	Marty Barrett	.06	.05	.02	246	Jimmy Jones	.06	.05	.02
156	Mike Heath	.03	.02	.01	247	Ken Landreaux	.03	.02	.01
157	Gary Ward	.06	.05	.02	248	Jose Oquendo	.03	.02	.01
158	Lee Mazilli (Mazzilli)	.06	.05	.02	249	John Mitchell	.20	.15	.08
159	Tom Foley	.03	.02	.01	250	Don Baylor	.08	.06	.03
160	Robin Yount	.15	.11	.06	251	Scott Fletcher	.06	.05	.02
161	Steve Bedrosian	.10	.08	.04	252	Al Newman	.03	.02	.01
162	Bob Walk	.03	.02	.01	253	Carney Lansford	.06	.05	.02
163	Nick Esasky	.03	.02	.01	254	Johnny Ray	.06	.05	.02
164	Ken Caminiti	.30	.25	.12	255	Gary Pettis	.03	.02	.01
165	Jose Uribe	.03	.02	.01	256	Ken Phelps	.06	.05	.02
166	Dave Anderson	.03	.02	.01	257	Tim Stoddard	.03	.02	.01
167	Ed Whitson	.03	.02	.01	258	Rick Leach	.03	.02	.01
168	Ernie Whitt	.06	.05	.02	259	Ed Romero	.03	.02	.01
169	Cecil Cooper	.08	.06	.03	260	Sid Bream	.06	.05	.02
170	Mike Pagliarulo	.08	.06	.03	261	Tom Niedenfuer	.03	.02	.01
171	Pat Sheridan	.03	.02	.01	262	Rick Dempsey	.03	.02	.01
172	Chris Bando	.03	.02	.01	263	Lonnie Smith	.03	.02	.01
173	Lee Lacy	.03	.02	.01	264	Bob Forsch	.03	.02	.01
174	Steve Lombardozzi	.06	.05	.02	265	Barry Bonds	.10	.08	.04
175	Mike Greenwell	.60	.45	.25	266	Willie Randolph	.06	.05	.02
176	Greg Minton	.03	.02	.01	267	Mike Ramsey	.03	.02	.01
177	Moose Haas	.03	.02	.01	268	Don Slaught	.03	.02	.01
178	Mike Kingery	.06	.05	.02	269	Mickey Tettleton	.03	.02	.01
179	Greg Harris	.03	.02	.01	270	Jerry Reuss	.06	.05	.02
180	Bo Jackson	.30	.25	.12	271	Marc Sullivan	.03	.02	.01
181	Carmelo Martinez	.03	.02	.01	272	Jim Morrison	.03	.02	.01
182	Alex Trevino	.03	.02	.01	273	Steve Balboni	.03	.02	.01
183	Ron Oester	.03	.02	.01	274	Dick Schofield	.03	.02	.01
184	Danny Darwin	.03	.02	.01	275	John Tudor	.06	.05	.02
185	Mike Krukow	.06	.05	.02	276	Gene Larkin	.12	.09	.05
186	Rafael Palmeiro	.10	.08	.04	277	Harold Reynolds	.06	.05	.02
187	Tim Burke	.06	.05	.02	278	Jerry Browne	.06	.05	.02
188	Roger McDowell	.08	.06	.03	279	Willie Upshaw	.06	.05	.02
189	Garry Templeton	.06	.05	.02	280	Ted Higuera	.08	.06	.03
190	Terry Pendleton	.06	.05	.02	281	Terry McGriff	.03	.02	.01
191	Larry Parrish	.06	.05	.02	282	Terry Puhl	.03	.02	.01
192	Rey Quinones	.06	.05	.02	283	Mark Wasinger	.20	.15	.08
193	Joaquin Andujar	.06	.05	.02	284	Luis Salazar	.03	.02	.01
194	Tom Brunansky	.08	.06	.03	285	Ted Simmons	.08	.06	.03

#	Name	MT	NR MT	EX
286	John Shelby	.03	.02	.01
287	John Smiley	.20	.15	.08
288	Curt Ford	.03	.02	.01
289	Steve Crawford	.03	.02	.01
290	Dan Quisenberry	.08	.06	.03
291	Alan Wiggins	.03	.02	.01
292	Randy Bush	.03	.02	.01
293	John Candelaria	.06	.05	.02
294	Tony Phillips	.03	.02	.01
295	Mike Morgan	.03	.02	.01
296	Bill Wegman	.03	.02	.01
297	Terry Francona	.03	.02	.01
298	Mickey Hatcher	.03	.02	.01
299	Andres Thomas	.08	.06	.03
300	Bob Stanley	.03	.02	.01
301	Alfredo Pedrique	.15	.11	.06
302	Jim Lindeman	.10	.08	.04
303	Wally Backman	.06	.05	.02
304	Paul O'Neill	.06	.05	.02
305	Hubie Brooks	.08	.06	.03
306	Steve Buechele	.03	.02	.01
307	Bobby Thigpen	.06	.05	.02
308	George Hendrick	.06	.05	.02
309	John Moses	.03	.02	.01
310	Ron Guidry	.12	.09	.05
311	Bill Schroeder	.03	.02	.01
312	Jose Nunez	.20	.15	.08
313	Bud Black	.03	.02	.01
314	Joe Sambito	.03	.02	.01
315	Scott McGregor	.06	.05	.02
316	Rafael Santana	.03	.02	.01
317	Frank Williams	.03	.02	.01
318	Mike Fitzgerald	.03	.02	.01
319	Rick Mahler	.03	.02	.01
320	Jim Gott	.03	.02	.01
321	Mariano Duncan	.03	.02	.01
322	Jose Guzman	.06	.05	.02
323	Lee Guetterman	.06	.05	.02
324	Dan Gladden	.06	.05	.02
325	Gary Carter	.20	.15	.08
326	Tracy Jones	.10	.08	.04
327	Floyd Youmans	.08	.06	.03
328	Bill Dawley	.03	.02	.01
329	Paul Noce	.15	.11	.06
330	Angel Salazar	.03	.02	.01
331	Goose Gossage	.12	.09	.05
332	George Frazier	.03	.02	.01
333	Ruppert Jones	.03	.02	.01
334	Billy Jo Robidoux	.03	.02	.01
335	Mike Scott	.10	.08	.04
336	Randy Myers	.06	.05	.02
337	Bob Sebra	.06	.05	.02
338	Eric Show	.03	.02	.01
339	Mitch Williams	.06	.05	.02
340	Paul Molitor	.10	.08	.04
341	Gus Polidor	.03	.02	.01
342	Steve Trout	.06	.05	.02
343	Jerry Don Gleaton	.03	.02	.01
344	Bob Knepper	.06	.05	.02
345	Mitch Webster	.06	.05	.02
346	John Morris	.03	.02	.01
347	Andy Hawkins	.03	.02	.01
348	Dave Leiper	.03	.02	.01
349	Ernest Riles	.03	.02	.01
350	Dwight Gooden	.40	.30	.15
351	Dave Righetti	.12	.09	.05
352	Pat Dodson	.06	.05	.02
353	John Habyan	.03	.02	.01
354	Jim Deshaies	.08	.06	.03
355	Butch Wynegar	.03	.02	.01
356	Bryn Smith	.06	.05	.02
357	Matt Young	.03	.02	.01
358	Tom Pagnozzi	.15	.11	.06
359	Floyd Rayford	.03	.02	.01
360	Darryl Strawberry	.30	.25	.12
361	Sal Butera	.03	.02	.01
362	Domingo Ramos	.03	.02	.01
363	Chris Brown	.08	.06	.03
364	Jose Gonzalez	.03	.02	.01
365	Dave Smith	.06	.05	.02
366	Andy McGaffigan	.03	.02	.01
367	Stan Javier	.03	.02	.01
368	Henry Cotto	.03	.02	.01
369	Mike Birkbeck	.03	.02	.01
370	Len Dykstra	.08	.06	.03
371	Dave Collins	.03	.02	.01
372	Spike Owen	.03	.02	.01
373	Geno Petralli	.03	.02	.01
374	Ron Karkovice	.06	.05	.02
375	Shane Rawley	.06	.05	.02
376	DeWayne Buice	.15	.11	.06

#	Name	MT	NR MT	EX
377	Bill Pecota	.15	.11	.06
378	Leon Durham	.06	.05	.02
379	Ed Olwine	.03	.02	.01
380	Bruce Hurst	.06	.05	.02
381	Bob McClure	.03	.02	.01
382	Mark Thurmond	.03	.02	.01
383	Buddy Biancalana	.03	.02	.01
384	Tim Conroy	.03	.02	.01
385	Tony Gwynn	.25	.20	.10
386	Greg Gross	.03	.02	.01
387	Barry Lyons	.15	.11	.06
388	Mike Felder	.03	.02	.01
389	Pat Clements	.03	.02	.01
390	Ken Griffey	.06	.05	.02
391	Mark Davis	.03	.02	.01
392	Jose Rijo	.03	.02	.01
393	Mike Young	.06	.05	.02
394	Willie Fraser	.06	.05	.02
395	Dion James	.06	.05	.02
396	Steve Shields	.12	.09	.05
397	Randy St. Claire	.03	.02	.01
398	Danny Jackson	.06	.05	.02
399	Cecil Fielder	.06	.05	.02
400	Keith Hernandez	.15	.11	.06
401	Don Carman	.08	.06	.03
402	Chuck Crim	.12	.09	.05
403	Rob Woodward	.03	.02	.01
404	Junior Ortiz	.03	.02	.01
405	Glenn Wilson	.06	.05	.02
406	Ken Howell	.03	.02	.01
407	Jeff Kunkel	.03	.02	.01
408	Jeff Reed	.03	.02	.01
409	Chris James	.10	.08	.04
410	Zane Smith	.06	.05	.02
411	Ken Dixon	.03	.02	.01
412	Ricky Horton	.06	.05	.02
413	Frank DiPino	.03	.02	.01
414	Shane Mack	.25	.20	.10
415	Danny Cox	.08	.06	.03
416	Andy Van Slyke	.06	.05	.02
417	Danny Heep	.03	.02	.01
418	John Cangelosi	.06	.05	.02
419	John Christensen	.03	.02	.01
420	Joey Cora	.15	.11	.06
421	Mike LaValliere	.06	.05	.02
422	Kelly Gruber	.03	.02	.01
423	Bruce Benedict	.03	.02	.01
424	Len Matuszek	.03	.02	.01
425	Kent Tekulve	.06	.05	.02
426	Rafael Ramirez	.03	.02	.01
427	Mike Flanagan	.06	.05	.02
428	Mike Gallego	.03	.02	.01
429	Juan Castillo	.03	.02	.01
430	Neal Heaton	.06	.05	.02
431	Phil Garner	.03	.02	.01
432	Mike Dunne	.30	.25	.12
433	Wallace Johnson	.03	.02	.01
434	Jack O'Connor	.03	.02	.01
435	Steve Jeltz	.03	.02	.01
436	Donnell Nixon	.15	.11	.06
437	Jack Lazorko	.03	.02	.01
438	Keith Comstock	.15	.11	.06
439	Jeff Robinson	.03	.02	.01
440	Graig Nettles	.08	.06	.03
441	Mel Hall	.06	.05	.02
442	Gerald Young	.30	.25	.12
443	Gary Redus	.06	.05	.02
444	Charlie Moore	.03	.02	.01
445	Bill Madlock	.08	.06	.03
446	Mark Clear	.03	.02	.01
447	Greg Booker	.03	.02	.01
448	Rick Schu	.03	.02	.01
449	Ron Kittle	.06	.05	.02
450	Dale Murphy	.30	.25	.12
451	Bob Dernier	.03	.02	.01
452	Dale Mohorcic	.06	.05	.02
453	Rafael Belliard	.03	.02	.01
454	Charlie Puleo	.03	.02	.01
455	Dwayne Murphy	.03	.02	.01
456	Jim Eisenreich	.08	.06	.03
457	David Palmer	.03	.02	.01
458	Dave Stewart	.06	.05	.02
459	Pasqual Perez	.06	.05	.02
460	Glenn Davis	.12	.09	.05
461	Dan Petry	.06	.05	.02
462	Jim Winn	.03	.02	.01
463	Darrell Miller	.03	.02	.01
464	Mike Moore	.03	.02	.01
465	Mike LaCoss	.03	.02	.01
466	Steve Farr	.03	.02	.01
467	Jerry Mumphrey	.06	.05	.02

#	Player	MT	NR MT	EX
468	Kevin Gross	.06	.05	.02
469	Bruce Bochy	.03	.02	.01
470	Orel Hershiser	.08	.06	.03
471	Eric King	.08	.06	.03
472	Ellis Burks	1.50	1.25	.60
473	Darren Daulton	.03	.02	.01
474	Mookie Wilson	.06	.05	.02
475	Frank Viola	.08	.06	.03
476	Ron Robinson	.03	.02	.01
477	Bob Melvin	.03	.02	.01
478	Jeff Musselman	.06	.05	.02
479	Charlie Kerfeld	.03	.02	.01
480	Richard Dotson	.06	.05	.02
481	Kevin Mitchell	.08	.06	.03
482	Gary Roenicke	.03	.02	.01
483	Tim Flannery	.03	.02	.01
484	Rich Yett	.03	.02	.01
485	Pete Incaviglia	.25	.20	.10
486	Rick Cerone	.03	.02	.01
487	Tony Armas	.06	.05	.02
488	Jerry Reed	.03	.02	.01
489	Davey Lopes	.06	.05	.02
490	Frank Tanana	.06	.05	.02
491	Mike Loynd	.06	.05	.02
492	Bruce Ruffin	.08	.06	.03
493	Chris Speier	.03	.02	.01
494	Tom Hume	.03	.02	.01
495	Jesse Orosco	.06	.05	.02
496	Robbie Wine, Jr.	.20	.15	.08
497	Jeff Montgomery	.20	.15	.08
498	Jeff Dedmon	.03	.02	.01
499	Luis Aguayo	.03	.02	.01
500	Reggie Jackson (1968-75 Oakland Athletics)	.20	.15	.08
501	Reggie Jackson (1976 Baltimore Orioles)	.20	.15	.08
502	Reggie Jackson (1977-81 New York Yankees)	.20	.15	.08
503	Reggie Jackson (1982-86 California Angels)	.20	.15	.08
504	Reggie Jackson (1987 Oakland Athletics)	.20	.15	.08
505	Billy Hatcher	.06	.05	.02
506	Ed Lynch	.03	.02	.01
507	Willie Hernandez	.06	.05	.02
508	Jose DeLeon	.03	.02	.01
509	Joel Youngblood	.03	.02	.01
510	Bob Welch	.06	.05	.02
511	Steve Ontiveros	.03	.02	.01
512	Randy Ready	.03	.02	.01
513	Juan Nieves	.08	.06	.03
514	Jeff Russell	.03	.02	.01
515	Von Hayes	.08	.06	.03
516	Mark Gubicza	.06	.05	.02
517	Ken Dayley	.03	.02	.01
518	Don Aase	.03	.02	.01
519	Rick Reuschel	.08	.06	.03
520	Mike Henneman	.20	.15	.08
521	Rick Aguilera	.06	.05	.02
522	Jay Howell	.06	.05	.02
523	Ed Correa	.08	.06	.03
524	Manny Trillo	.06	.05	.02
525	Kirk Gibson	.15	.11	.06
526	Wally Ritchie	.15	.11	.06
527	Al Nipper	.03	.02	.01
528	Atlee Hammaker	.03	.02	.01
529	Shawon Dunston	.08	.06	.03
530	Jim Clancy	.06	.05	.02
531	Tom Paciorek	.03	.02	.01
532	Joel Skinner	.03	.02	.01
533	Scott Garrelts	.03	.02	.01
534	Tom O'Malley	.03	.02	.01
535	John Franco	.06	.05	.02
536	Paul Kilgus	.15	.11	.06
537	Darrell Porter	.03	.02	.01
538	Walt Terrell	.06	.05	.02
539	Bill Long	.20	.15	.08
540	George Bell	.20	.15	.08
541	Jeff Sellers	.06	.05	.02
542	Joe Boever	.12	.09	.05
543	Steve Howe	.06	.05	.02
544	Scott Sanderson	.03	.02	.01
545	Jack Morris	.15	.11	.06
546	Todd Benzinger	.60	.45	.25
547	Steve Henderson	.03	.02	.01
548	Eddie Milner	.03	.02	.01
549	Jeff Robinson	.20	.15	.08
550	Cal Ripken, Jr.	.25	.20	.10
551	Jody Davis	.06	.05	.02
552	Kirk McCaskill	.06	.05	.02
553	Craig Lefferts	.03	.02	.01
554	Darnell Coles	.06	.05	.02
555	Phil Niekro	.15	.11	.06
556	Mike Aldrete	.10	.08	.04
557	Pat Perry	.03	.02	.01
558	Juan Agosto	.03	.02	.01
559	Rob Murphy	.06	.05	.02
560	Dennis Rasmussen	.06	.05	.02
561	Manny Lee	.03	.02	.01
562	Jeff Blauser	.20	.15	.08
563	Bob Ojeda	.06	.05	.02
564	Dave Dravecky	.06	.05	.02
565	Gene Garber	.03	.02	.01
566	Ron Roenicke	.03	.02	.01
567	Tommy Hinzo	.15	.11	.06
568	Eric Nolte	.15	.11	.06
569	Ed Hearn	.03	.02	.01
570	Mark Davidson	.12	.09	.05
571	Jim Walewander	.15	.11	.06
572	Donnie Hill	.03	.02	.01
573	Jamie Moyer	.06	.05	.02
574	Ken Schrom	.03	.02	.01
575	Nolan Ryan	.20	.15	.08
576	Jim Acker	.03	.02	.01
577	Jamie Quirk	.03	.02	.01
578	Jay Aldrich	.12	.09	.05
579	Claudell Washington	.06	.05	.02
580	Jeff Leonard	.06	.05	.02
581	Carmen Castillo	.03	.02	.01
582	Daryl Boston	.03	.02	.01
583	Jeff DeWillis	.15	.11	.06
584	John Marzano	.50	.40	.20
585	Bill Gullickson	.06	.05	.02
586	Andy Allanson	.06	.05	.02
587	Lee Tunnell	.03	.02	.01
588	Gene Nelson	.03	.02	.01
589	Dave LaPoint	.03	.02	.01
590	Harold Baines	.10	.08	.04
591	Bill Buckner	.08	.06	.03
592	Carlton Fisk	.12	.09	.05
593	Rick Manning	.03	.02	.01
594	Doug Jones	.15	.11	.06
595	Tom Candiotti	.03	.02	.01
596	Steve Lake	.03	.02	.01
597	Jose Lind	.30	.25	.12
598	Ross Jones	.15	.11	.06
599	Gary Matthews	.06	.05	.02
600	Fernando Valezuela	.15	.11	.06
601	Dennis Martinez	.03	.02	.01
602	Les Lancaster	.20	.15	.08
603	Ozzie Guillen	.08	.06	.03
604	Tony Bernazard	.03	.02	.01
605	Chili Davis	.06	.05	.02
606	Roy Smalley	.03	.02	.01
607	Ivan Calderon	.08	.06	.03
608	Jay Tibbs	.03	.02	.01
609	Guy Hoffman	.03	.02	.01
610	Doyle Alexander	.08	.06	.03
611	Mike Bielecki	.03	.02	.01
612	Shawn Hillegas	.20	.15	.08
613	Keith Atherton	.03	.02	.01
614	Eric Plunk	.03	.02	.01
615	Sid Fernandez	.08	.06	.03
616	Dennis Lamp	.03	.02	.01
617	Dave Engle	.03	.02	.01
618	Harry Spilman	.03	.02	.01
619	Don Robinson	.03	.02	.01
620	John Farrell	.25	.20	.10
621	Nelson Liriano	.20	.15	.08
622	Floyd Bannister	.06	.05	.02
623	Rookie Prospect (Randy Milligan)	.30	.25	.12
624	Rookie Prospect (Kevin Elster)	.12	.09	.05
625	Rookie Prospect (Jody Reed)	.25	.20	.10
626	Rookie Prospect (Shawn Abner)	.25	.20	.10
627	Rookie Prospect (Kirt Manwaring)	.35	.25	.14
628	Rookie Prospect (Pete Stanicek)	.25	.20	.10
629	Rookie Prospect (Rob Ducey)	.15	.11	.06
630	Rookie Prospect (Steve Kiefer)	.03	.02	.01
631	Rookie Prospect (Gary Thurman)	.30	.25	.12
632	Rookie Prospect (Darrel Akerfelds)	.20	.15	.08
633	Rookie Prospect (Dave Clark)	.08	.06	.03
634	Rookie Prospect (Roberto Kelly)	.30	.25	.12
635	Rookie Prospect (Keith Hughes)	.30	.25	.12
636	Rookie Prospect (John Davis)	.25	.20	.10
637	Rookie Prospect (Mike Devereaux)	.30	.25	.12
638	Rookie Prospect (Tom Glavine)	.30	.25	.12
639	Rookie Prospect (Keith Miller)	.25	.20	.10
640	Rookie Prospect (Chris Gwynn)	.30	.25	.12
641	Rookie Prospect (Tim Crews)	.25	.20	.10
642	Rookie Prospect (Mackey Sasser)	.25	.20	.10
643	Rookie Prospect (Vicente Palacios)	.25	.20	.10
644	Rookie Prospect (Kevin Romine)	.08	.06	.03

		MT	NR MT	EX
645	Rookie Prospect (Gregg Jefferies)	.80	.60	.30
646	Rookie Prospect (Jeff Treadway)	.35	.25	.14
647	Rookie Prospect (Ronnie Gant)	.20	.15	.08
648	Rookie Sluggers (Mark McGwire, Matt Nokes)	.70	.50	.30
649	Speed and Power (Eric Davis, Tim Raines)	.25	.20	.10
650	Game Breakers (Jack Clark, Don Mattingly)	.60	.45	.25
651	Super Shortstops (Tony Fernandez, Cal Ripken, Jr., Alan Trammell)	.15	.11	.06
652	1987 Highlights (Vince Coleman)	.08	.06	.03
653	1987 Highlights (Kirby Puckett)	.12	.09	.05
654	1987 Highlights (Benito Santiago)	.20	.15	.08
655	1987 Highlights (Juan Nieves)	.06	.05	.02
656	1987 Highlights (Steve Bedrosian)	.06	.05	.02
657	1987 Highlights (Mike Schmidt)	.15	.11	.06
658	1987 Highlights (Don Mattingly)	.60	.45	.25
659	1987 Highlights (Mark McGwire)	.60	.45	.25
660	1987 Highlights (Paul Molitor)	.08	.06	.03

1983 7-11 Slurpee Coins

This first production of player coins by 7-11 stores was distributed only in the Los Angeles area. The test promotion, which awarded a coin to every purchaser of a large Slurpee drink, must have proved successful, as it was expanded nationally in subsequent years. Six California Angels and six Los Angeles Dodgers are included in the full-color set, with Angels players in red backgrounds and the Dodgers in blue. The 1¾'' inch diameter plastic coins feature both an action and a portrait photo of the player, which can be alternately seen by moving the coin slightly from side to side. The 12 coin backs are numbered and include brief statistics and the company logo.

		MT	NR MT	EX
	Complete Set:	16.00	12.00	6.50
	Common Player:	.70	.50	.30
1	Rod Carew	1.75	1.25	.70
2	Steve Sax	1.25	.90	.50
3	Fred Lynn	1.00	.70	.40
4	Pedro Guerrero	1.25	.90	.50
5	Reggie Jackson	2.00	1.50	.80
6	Dusty Baker	.70	.50	.30
7	Doug DeCinces	.70	.50	.30
8	Fernando Valenzuela	1.75	1.25	.70
9	Tommy John	1.00	.70	.40
10	Rick Monday	.70	.50	.30
11	Bobby Grich	.70	.50	.30
12	Greg Brock	.70	.50	.30

1984 7-11 Slurpee Coins

The 7-11 coins were distributed nationally in 1984, with 60 different players displayed on 72 total coins. The coins, called ''Slurpee Discs,'' were issued in three different regional sets of 24 coins each. East, West and Central regional series were distributed, with players on teams in those areas of the country dominating the region's set. George Brett, Andre Dawson, Dale Murphy, Eddie Murray, Mike Schmidt and Robin Yount appear in all three of the full-color sets. At least one player appears from every Major

 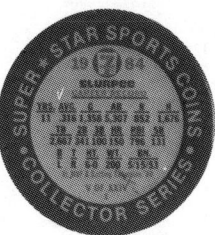

League team. Formats are very similar to the 1983 coins, with double-image photos on the fronts and statistics and coin numbers on the backs.

	MT	NR MT	EX
Complete Set:	50.00	37.00	20.00
Common Player:	.70	.50	.30

Eastern Region

		MT	NR MT	EX
1	Andre Dawson	.90	.70	.35
2	Robin Yount	1.00	.70	.40
3	Dale Murphy	1.25	.90	.50
4	Mike Schmidt	1.25	.90	.50
5	George Brett	1.25	.90	.50
6	Eddie Murray	1.25	.90	.50
7	Dave Winfield	1.00	.70	.40
8	Tom Seaver	1.00	.70	.40
9	Mike Boddicker	.60	.45	.25
10	Wade Boggs	2.00	1.50	.80
11	Bill Madlock	.70	.50	.30
12	Steve Carlton	1.00	.70	.40
13	Dave Stieb	.60	.45	.25
14	Cal Ripken, Jr.	1.25	.90	.50
15	Jim Rice	1.00	.70	.40
16	Ron Guidry	.80	.60	.30
17	Darryl Strawberry	2.00	1.50	.80
18	Tony Pena	.60	.45	.25
19	John Denny	.60	.45	.25
20	Tim Raines	1.00	.70	.40
21	Rick Dempsey	.60	.45	.25
22	Rich Gossage	.80	.60	.30
23	Gary Matthews	.60	.45	.25
24	Keith Hernandez	1.00	.70	.40

Central Region

		MT	NR MT	EX
1	Andre Dawson	.90	.70	.35
2	Robin Yount	1.00	.70	.40
3	Dale Murphy	1.25	.90	.50
4	Mike Schmidt	1.25	.90	.50
5	George Brett	1.25	.90	.50
6	Eddie Murray	1.25	.90	.50
7	Bruce Sutter	.70	.50	.30
8	Cecil Cooper	.70	.50	.30
9	Willie McGee	.80	.60	.30
10	Mike Hargrove	.60	.45	.25
11	Kent Hrbek	1.00	.70	.40
12	Carlton Fisk	.80	.60	.30
13	Mario Soto	.60	.45	.25
14	Lonnie Smith	.60	.45	.25
15	Gary Carter	1.00	.70	.40
16	Lou Whitaker	.90	.70	.35
17	Ron Kittle	.60	.45	.25
18	Paul Molitor	.80	.60	.30
19	Ozzie Smith	.80	.60	.30
20	Fergie Jenkins	.70	.50	.30
21	Ted Simmons	.70	.50	.30
22	Pete Rose	2.00	1.50	.80
23	LaMarr Hoyt	.60	.45	.25
24	Dan Quisenberry	.70	.50	.30

Western Region

		MT	NR MT	EX
1	Andre Dawson	.90	.70	.35
2	Robin Yount	1.00	.70	.40
3	Dale Murphy	1.25	.90	.50
4	Mike Schmidt	1.25	.90	.50
5	George Brett	1.25	.90	.50
6	Eddie Murray	1.25	.90	.50
7	Steve Garvey	1.00	.70	.40
8	Rod Carew	1.25	.90	.50
9	Fernando Valenzuela	1.00	.70	.40

		MT	NR MT	EX
10	Bob Horner	.70	.50	.30
11	Buddy Bell	.60	.45	.25
12	Reggie Jackson	1.25	.90	.50
13	Nolan Ryan	1.00	.70	.40
14	Pedro Guerrero	.80	.60	.30
15	Atlee Hammaker	.60	.45	.25
16	Fred Lynn	.80	.60	.30
17	Terry Kennedy	.60	.45	.25
18	Dusty Baker	.60	.45	.25
19	Jose Cruz	.60	.45	.25
20	Steve Rogers	.60	.45	.25
21	Rickey Henderson	1.25	.90	.50
22	Steve Sax	.80	.60	.30
23	Dickie Thon	.60	.45	.25
24	Matt Young	.60	.45	.25

1985 7-11 Slurpee Coins

In 1985 the "Slurpee Disc" promotion was further expanded to a total of 94 full-color coins. Formats were very similar to the previous two years, but there were six different regional sets. Five of these regional series contain 16 coins, with a Detroit series totaling 14. The other five regions are : East, West, Great Lakes, Central and Southeast. The coins are again 1¼'' in diameter, printed on plastic, with double-image photos. All coins are numbered. No player appears in all regions, although several are in two or more.

	MT	NR MT	EX
Complete Set:	70.00	52.00	28.00
Common Player:	.60	.45	.25

Eastern Region

		MT	NR MT	EX
1	Eddie Murray	1.00	.70	.40
2	George Brett	1.25	.90	.50
3	Steve Carlton	1.00	.70	.40
4	Jim Rice	1.00	.70	.40
5	Dave Winfield	1.00	.70	.40
6	Mike Boddicker	.40	.30	.15
7	Wade Boggs	1.75	1.25	.70
8	Dwight Evans	.60	.45	.25
9	Dwight Gooden	2.00	1.50	.80
10	Keith Hernandez	.90	.70	.35
11	Bill Madlock	.50	.40	.20
12	Don Mattingly	2.50	2.00	1.00
13	Dave Righetti	.70	.50	.30
14	Cal Ripken, Jr.	1.00	.70	.40
15	Juan Samuel	.70	.50	.30
16	Mike Schmidt	1.25	.90	.50

Southeastern Region

		MT	NR MT	EX
1	Dale Murphy	1.25	.90	.50
2	Steve Carlton	1.00	.70	.40
3	Nolan Ryan	1.00	.70	.40
4	Bruce Sutter	.50	.40	.20
5	Dave Winfield	1.00	.70	.40
6	Steve Bedrosian	.50	.40	.20
7	Andre Dawson	.70	.50	.30
8	Kirk Gibson	.80	.60	.30
9	Fred Lynn	.60	.45	.25
10	Gary Matthews	.40	.30	.15
11	Phil Niekro	.70	.50	.30
12	Tim Raines	1.00	.70	.40
13	Darryl Strawberry	1.50	1.25	.60

		MT	NR MT	EX
14	Dave Stieb	.40	.30	.15
15	Willie Upshaw	.40	.30	.15
16	Lou Whitaker	.70	.50	.30

Great Lakes Region

		MT	NR MT	EX
1	Willie Hernandez	.40	.30	.15
2	George Brett	1.25	.90	.50
3	Dave Winfield	1.00	.70	.40
4	Eddie Murray	1.00	.70	.40
5	Bruce Sutter	.50	.40	.20
6	Harold Baines	.60	.45	.25
7	Bert Blyleven	.60	.45	.25
8	Leon Durham	.50	.40	.20
9	Chet Lemon	.40	.30	.15
10	Pete Rose	2.00	1.50	.80
11	Ryne Sandberg	1.00	.70	.40
12	Tom Seaver	1.00	.70	.40
13	Mario Soto	.40	.30	.15
14	Rick Sutcliffe	.50	.40	.20
15	Alan Trammell	.90	.70	.35
16	Robin Yount	1.00	.70	.40

Southwest/Central Region

		MT	NR MT	EX
1	Nolan Ryan	1.00	.70	.40
2	George Brett	1.25	.90	.50
3	Dave Winfield	1.00	.70	.40
4	Mike Schmidt	1.25	.90	.50
5	Bruce Sutter	.50	.40	.20
6	Joaquin Andujar	.40	.30	.15
7	Willie Hernandez	.40	.30	.15
8	Wade Boggs	1.75	1.25	.70
9	Gary Carter	1.00	.70	.40
10	Jose Cruz	.40	.30	.15
11	Kent Hrbek	.70	.50	.30
12	Reggie Jackson	1.00	.70	.40
13	Lance Parrish	.70	.50	.30
14	Terry Puhl	.40	.30	.15
15	Dan Quisenberry	.50	.40	.20
16	Ozzie Smith	.60	.45	.25

Western Region

		MT	NR MT	EX
1	Mike Schmidt	1.25	.90	.50
2	Jim Rice	1.00	.70	.40
3	Dale Murphy	1.25	.90	.50
4	Eddie Murray	1.00	.70	.40
5	Dave Winfield	1.00	.70	.40
6	Rod Carew	1.00	.70	.40
7	Alvin Davis	.70	.50	.30
8	Steve Garvey	1.00	.70	.40
9	Rich Gossage	.60	.45	.25
10	Pedro Guerrero	.70	.50	.30
11	Tony Gwynn	1.00	.70	.40
12	Rickey Henderson	1.00	.70	.40
13	Reggie Jackson	1.00	.70	.40
14	Jeff Leonard	.40	.30	.15
15	Alejandro Pena	.40	.30	.15
16	Fernando Valenzuela	.90	.70	.35

Detroit Tigers

		MT	NR MT	EX
1	Sparky Anderson	.60	.45	.25
2	Darrell Evans	.80	.60	.30
3	Kirk Gibson	1.25	.90	.50
4	Willie Hernandez	.50	.40	.20
5	Larry Herndon	.50	.40	.20
6	Chet Lemon	.50	.40	.20
7	Aurelio Lopez	.40	.30	.15
8	Jack Morris	1.00	.70	.40
9	Lance Parrish	1.00	.70	.40
10	Dan Petry	.50	.40	.20
11	Dave Rozema	.40	.30	.15
12	Alan Trammell	1.25	.90	.50
13	Lou Whitaker	1.00	.70	.40
14	Milt Wilcox	.40	.30	.15

1986 7-11 Slurpee Coins

This marked the fourth year of production for these coins, issued with the purchase of a large Slurpee drink at 7-11 stores. Once again there are different regional issues, with 16 coins issued for four different

		MT	NR MT	EX
15	Home Run Hitters (Tom Brunansky, Cecil Cooper, Darrell Evans)	.40	.30	.15
16	Big Hitters (Kirk Gibson, Paul Molitor, Greg Walker)	.60	.45	.25

Midwestern Region

		MT	NR MT	EX
1	Dwight Gooden	1.50	1.25	.60
2	Batting Champs (Wade Boggs, George Brett, Pete Rose)	2.00	1.50	.80
3	MVP's (Keith Hernandez, Don Mattingly, Cal Ripken, Jr.)	1.75	1.25	.70
4	Slugging Champs (Harold Baines, Pedro Guerrero, Dave Parker)	.60	.45	.25
5	Home Run Champs (Dale Murphy, Jim Rice, Mike Schmidt)	1.25	.90	.50
6	Cy Young Winners (Ron Guidry, Bret Saberhagen, Fernando Valenzuela)	.70	.50	.30
7	Bullpen Aces (Rich Gossage, Dan Quisenberry, Bruce Sutter)	.50	.40	.20
8	Strikeout Kings (Steve Carlton, Nolan Ryan, Tom Seaver)	1.25	.90	.50
9	1985 Rookies (Vince Coleman, Glenn Davis, Oddibe McDowell)	1.25	.90	.50
10	Gold Glovers (Buddy Bell, Ozzie Smith, Lou Whitaker)	.60	.45	.25
11	Ace Pitchers (Mike Scott, Mario Soto, John Tudor)	.40	.30	.15
12	Bullpen Aces (Jeff Lahti, Ted Power, Dave Smith)	.40	.30	.15
13	Big Hitters (Jack Clark, Jose Cruz, Bob Horner)	.60	.45	.25
14	Star Second Basemen (Bill Doran, Tommy Herr, Ron Oester)	.40	.30	.15
15	1985 Rookie Pitchers (Tom Browning, Joe Hesketh, Todd Worrell)	.60	.45	.25
16	Top Switch-Hitters (Willie McGee, Jerry Mumphrey, Pete Rose)	1.00	.70	.40

Western Region

		MT	NR MT	EX
1	Dwight Gooden	1.50	1.25	.60
2	Batting Champs (Wade Boggs, George Brett, Pete Rose)	2.00	1.50	.80
3	MVP's (Keith Hernandez, Don Mattingly, Cal Ripken, Jr.)	1.75	1.25	.70
4	Slugging Champs (Harold Baines, Pedro Guerrero, Dave Parker)	.60	.45	.25
5	Home Run Champs (Dale Murphy, Jim Rice, Mike Schmidt)	1.25	.90	.50
6	Cy Young Winners (Ron Guidry, Bret Saberhagen, Fernando Valenzuela)	.70	.50	.30
7	Bullpen Aces (Rich Gossage, Dan Quisenberry, Bruce Sutter)	.50	.40	.20
8	Strikeout Kings (Steve Carlton, Nolan Ryan, Tom Seaver)	1.25	.90	.50
9	Home Run Champs (Reggie Jackson, Dave Kingman, Gorman Thomas)	.80	.60	.30
10	Batting Champs (Rod Carew, Tony Gwynn, Carney Lansford)	.90	.70	.35
11	Sluggers (Phil Bradley, Mike Marshall, Graig Nettles)	.50	.40	.20
12	Ace Pitchers (Andy Hawkins, Orel Hershiser, Mike Witt)	.50	.40	.20
13	1985 Rookies (Chris Brown, Ivan Calderon, Mariano Duncan)	.70	.50	.30
14	Big Hitters (Steve Garvey, Bill Madlock, Jim Presley)	.70	.50	.30
15	Bullpen Aces (Jay Howell, Donnie Moore, Ed Nunez)	.40	.30	.15
16	1985 Bullpen Rookies (Karl Best, Stewart Cliburn, Steve Ontiveros)	.40	.30	.15

1987 7-11 Slurpee Coins

Continuing with a tradition started in 1983, 7-Eleven stores offered a free "Super Star Sports Coin" with the purchase of a Slurpee drink. Five different regional sets of Slurpee coins were issued for 1987, a total of 75 coins. Each coin measures 1¾'' in diameter and features a multiple image effect which allows three different pictures to be seen, depending on how the coin is tilted. The coin reverses contain career records and personal player information.

---

regions in 1986. The 1¾'' diameter plastic coins each feature three different players' pictures, which can be seen alternately by tilting from side to side. Eight of the coins are the same in every region. Each coin is numbered on the back, along with brief player information.

	MT	NR MT	EX
Complete Set:	50.00	37.00	20.00
Common Player:	.40	.30	.15

Eastern Region

		MT	NR MT	EX
1	Dwight Gooden	1.50	1.25	.60
2	Batting Champs (Wade Boggs, George Brett, Pete Rose)	2.00	1.50	.80
3	MVP's (Keith Hernandez, Don Mattingly, Cal Ripken, Jr.)	1.75	1.25	.70
4	Slugging Champs (Harold Baines, Pedro Guerrero, Dave Parker)	.60	.45	.25
5	Home Run Champs (Dale Murphy, Jim Rice, Mike Schmidt)	1.25	.90	.50
6	Cy Young Winners (Ron Guidry, Bret Saberhagen, Fernando Valenzuela)	.70	.50	.30
7	Bullpen Aces (Rich Gossage, Dan Quisenberry, Bruce Sutter)	.50	.40	.20
8	Strikeout Kings (Steve Carlton, Nolan Ryan, Tom Seaver)	1.25	.90	.50
9	1985 Rookies (Steve Lyons, Rick Schu, Larry Sheets)	.50	.40	.20
10	Bullpen Aces (Jeff Reardon, Dave Righetti, Bob Stanley)	.50	.40	.20
11	Power Hitters (George Bell, Darryl Strawberry, Dave Winfield)	1.00	.70	.40
12	Base Stealers (Rickey Henderson, Tim Raines, Juan Samuel)	1.00	.70	.40
13	Home Run Hitters (Andre Dawson, Dwight Evans, Eddie Murray)	.80	.60	.30
14	Ace Pitchers (Mike Boddicker, Ron Darling, Dave Stieb)	.40	.30	.15
15	1985 Bullpen Rookies (Tim Burke, Brian Fisher, Roger McDowell)	.50	.40	.20
16	Sluggers (Jesse Barfield, Gary Carter, Fred Lynn)	.70	.50	.30

Mideastern Region

		MT	NR MT	EX
1	Dwight Gooden	1.50	1.25	.60
2	Batting Champs (Wade Boggs, George Brett, Pete Rose)	2.00	1.50	.80
3	MVP's (Keith Hernandez, Don Mattingly, Cal Ripken)	1.75	1.25	.70
4	Slugging Champs (Harold Baines, Pedro Guerrero, Dave Parker)	.60	.45	.25
5	Home Run Champs (Dale Murphy, Jim Rice, Mike Schmidt)	1.25	.90	.50
6	Cy Young Winners (Ron Guidry, Bret Saberhagen, Fernando Valenzuela)	.70	.50	.30
7	Bullpen Aces (Rich Gossage, Dan Quisenberry, Bruce Sutter)	.50	.40	.20
8	Strikeout Kings (Steve Carlton, Nolan Ryan, Tom Seaver)	1.25	.90	.50
9	MVP's (Willie Hernandez, Ryne Sandberg, Robin Yount)	.70	.50	.30
10	Ace Pitchers (Bert Blyleven, Jack Morris, Rick Sutcliffe)	.50	.40	.20
11	Bullpen Aces (Rollie Fingers, Bob James, Lee Smith)	.40	.30	.15
12	All-Star Catchers (Carlton Fisk, Lance Parrish, Tony Pena)	.60	.45	.25
13	1985 Rookies (Shawon Dunston, Ozzie Guillen, Ernest Riles)	.50	.40	.20
14	Star Outfielders (Brett Butler, Chet Lemon, Willie Wilson)	.40	.30	.15

		MT	NR MT	EX
	Complete Set:	40.00	30.00	16.00
	Common Player:	.40	.30	.15

Eastern Region

		MT	NR MT	EX
1	Gary Carter	1.00	.70	.40
2	Don Baylor	.50	.40	.20
3	Rickey Henderson	1.00	.70	.40
4	Lenny Dykstra	.50	.40	.20
5	Wade Boggs	1.75	1.25	.70
6	Mike Pagliarulo	.60	.45	.25
7	Dwight Gooden	1.25	.90	.50
8	Roger Clemens	1.25	.90	.50
9	Dave Righetti	.70	.50	.30
10	Keith Hernandez	.90	.70	.35
11	Pat Dodson	.50	.40	.20
12	Don Mattingly	2.25	1.75	.90
13	Darryl Strawberry	1.25	.90	.50
14	Jim Rice	1.00	.70	.40
15	Dave Winfield	1.00	.70	.40

Mideastern Region

		MT	NR MT	EX
1	Gary Carter	1.00	.70	.40
2	Marty Barrett	.50	.40	.20
3	Jody Davis	.50	.40	.20
4	Don Aase	.40	.30	.15
5	Lenny Dykstra	.50	.40	.20
6	Wade Boggs	1.75	1.25	.70
7	Keith Moreland	.50	.40	.20
8	Mike Boddicker	.40	.30	.15
9	Dwight Gooden	1.25	.90	.50
10	Roger Clemens	1.25	.90	.50
11	Ryne Sandberg	1.00	.70	.40
12	Eddie Murray	1.00	.70	.40
13	Keith Hernandez	.90	.70	.35
14	Jim Rice	1.00	.70	.40
15	Lee Smith	.50	.40	.20
16	Cal Ripken, Jr.	1.00	.70	.40

Great Lakes Region

		MT	NR MT	EX
1	Harold Baines	.60	.45	.25
2	Jody Davis	.50	.40	.20
3	John Cangelosi	.50	.40	.20
4	Shawon Dunston	.50	.40	.20
5	Dave Cochrane	.40	.30	.15
6	Leon Durham	.50	.40	.20
7	Carlton Fisk	.70	.50	.30
8	Dennis Eckersley	.40	.30	.15
9	Ozzie Guillen	.50	.40	.20
10	Gary Matthews	.50	.40	.20
11	Ron Karkovice	.50	.40	.20
12	Keith Moreland	.50	.40	.20
13	Bobby Thigpen	.50	.40	.20
14	Ryne Sandberg	1.00	.70	.40
15	Greg Walker	.50	.40	.20
16	Lee Smith	.50	.40	.20

Western Region

		MT	NR MT	EX
1	Doug DeCinces	.50	.40	.20
2	Mariano Duncan	.40	.30	.15
3	Wally Joyner	1.75	1.25	.70
4	Pedro Guerrero	.70	.50	.30
5	Kirk McCaskill	.40	.30	.15
6	Orel Hershiser	.60	.45	.25
7	Gary Pettis	.40	.30	.15
8	Mike Marshall	.60	.45	.25
9	Dick Schofield	.40	.30	.15
10	Steve Sax	.80	.60	.30
11	Don Sutton	.80	.60	.30
12	Mike Scioscia	.40	.30	.15
13	Devon White	1.25	.90	.50
14	Franklin Stubbs	.50	.40	.20
15	Mike Witt	.50	.40	.20
16	Fernando Valenzuela	1.00	.70	.40

Detroit Tigers

		MT	NR MT	EX
1	Darnell Coles	.40	.30	.15
2	Darrell Evans	.60	.45	.25
3	Kirk Gibson	1.00	.70	.40
4	Willie Hernandez	.50	.40	.20
5	Larry Herndon	.50	.40	.20
6	Chet Lemon	.50	.40	.20
7	Dwight Lowry	.40	.30	.15
8	Jack Morris	.90	.70	.35
9	Dan Petry	.50	.40	.20
10	Frank Tanana	.40	.30	.15
11	Alan Trammell	1.00	.70	.40
12	Lou Whitaker	.90	.70	.35

1985 7-11 Twins

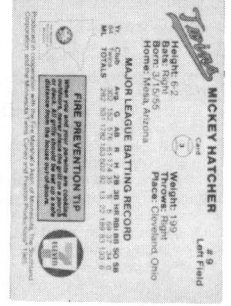

The Minnesota Twins, in co-operation with 7-11 and the Fire Marshall's Association, issued this set of 13 baseball fire safety cards. The card fronts feature full-color pictures of Twins players. A fire safety tip and short player history appear on the back. The cards were given out at all 7-11 stores in the state and at the Twins June 3 baseball game. Each fan received one baseball card with a poster which told how to collect the other cards in the set. Twelve cards feature players and the 13th card has an artist's rendering of Twins players on the front and a checklist of the set on the back. A group of 50,000 cards was distributed to fifth graders throughout the state by the fire departments.

		MT	NR MT	EX
	Complete Set:	5.00	3.75	2.00
	Common Player:	.20	.15	.08
1	Kirby Puckett	1.25	.90	.50
2	Frank Viola	.60	.45	.25
3	Mickey Hatcher	.20	.15	.08
4	Kent Hrbek	1.00	.70	.40
5	John Butcher	.20	.15	.08
6	Roy Smalley	.20	.15	.08
7	Tom Brunansky	.80	.60	.30
8	Ron Davis	.20	.15	.08
9	Gary Gaetti	.90	.70	.35
10	Tim Teufel	.30	.25	.12
11	Mike Smithson	.20	.15	.08
12	Tim Laudner	.30	.25	.12
—	Checklist	.10	.08	.04

1984 7-Up Cubs

The Chicago Cubs and 7-Up issued this 28-card set featuring full-color game-action photos on a 2¼'' by 3½'' borderless front. The backs have the player's

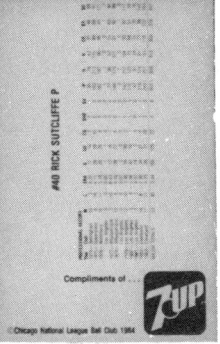

stats and personal information. This is the third consecutive year the Cubs issued this type of set as a give-away at a ''Baseball Card Day'' promotional game.

		MT	NR MT	EX
Complete Set:		12.00	9.00	4.75
Common Player:		.20	.15	.08
1	Larry Bowa	.40	.30	.15
6	Keith Moreland	.60	.45	.25
7	Jody Davis	.60	.45	.25
10	Leon Durham	.60	.45	.25
11	Ron Cey	.40	.30	.15
15	Ron Hassey	.20	.15	.08
18	Richie Hebner	.20	.15	.08
19	Dave Owen	.20	.15	.08
20	Bob Dernier	.30	.25	.12
21	Jay Johnstone	.30	.25	.12
23	Ryne Sandberg	3.00	2.25	1.25
24	Scott Sanderson	.30	.25	.12
25	Gary Woods	.20	.15	.08
27	Thad Bosley	.20	.15	.08
28	Henry Cotto	.40	.30	.15
34	Steve Trout	.40	.30	.15
36	Gary Matthews	.40	.30	.15
39	George Frazier	.20	.15	.08
40	Rick Sutcliffe	.80	.60	.30
41	Warren Brusstar	.20	.15	.08
42	Rich Bordi	.20	.15	.08
43	Dennis Eckersley	.30	.25	.12
44	Dick Ruthven	.20	.15	.08
46	Lee Smith	.60	.45	.25
47	Rick Reuschel	.50	.40	.20
49	Tim Stoddard	.20	.15	.08
---	Jim Frey	.20	.15	.08
---	Cubs Coaches (Ruben Amaro, Billy Connors, Johnny Oates, John Vukovich, Don Zimmer)	.20	.15	.08

1985 7-Up Cubs

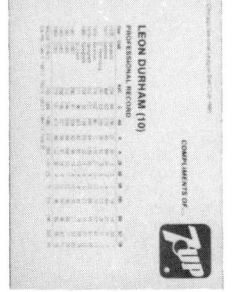

(10) LEON DURHAM IF

This is the second year a Chicago Cubs card set was released with 7-Up as the sponsor. The set has 28 unnumbered cards in the standard 2½'' by 3½'' size.

They were distributed to fans attending the Cubs game on August 14 at Wrigley Field. They feature full-color game-action photos of the players. Card backs contain the player's professional stats.

		MT	NR MT	EX
Complete Set:		7.00	5.25	2.75
Common Player:		.10	.08	.04
1	Larry Bowa	.25	.20	.10
6	Keith Moreland	.40	.30	.15
7	Jody Davis	.40	.30	.15
10	Leon Durham	.40	.30	.15
11	Ron Cey	.30	.25	.12
15	Davey Lopes	.25	.20	.10
16	Steve Lake	.10	.08	.04
18	Richie Hebner	.10	.08	.04
20	Bob Dernier	.15	.11	.06
21	Scott Sanderson	.15	.11	.06
22	Billy Hatcher	.30	.25	.12
23	Ryne Sandberg	2.00	1.50	.80
24	Brian Dayett	.10	.08	.04
25	Gary Woods	.10	.08	.04
27	Thad Bosley	.10	.08	.04
28	Chris Speier	.10	.08	.04
31	Ray Fontenot	.10	.08	.04
34	Steve Trout	.25	.20	.10
36	Gary Matthews	.30	.25	.12
39	George Frazier	.10	.08	.04
40	Rick Sutcliffe	.60	.45	.25
41	Warren Brusstar	.10	.08	.04
42	Lary Sorensen	.10	.08	.04
43	Dennis Eckersley	.25	.20	.10
44	Dick Ruthven	.10	.08	.04
46	Lee Smith	.40	.30	.15
---	Jim Frey	.10	.08	.04
---	Coaching Staff (Ruben Amaro, Billy Connors, Johnny Oates, John Vukovich, Don Zimmer)	.10	.08	.04

1984 Smokey Bear Angels

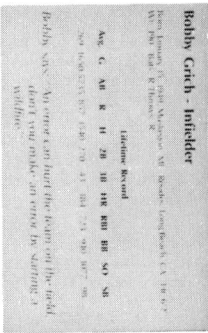

This 32-card set was distributed at a June home game to fans 14 and under. Cards measure 2½'' by 3½.'' The full-color card fronts list player name along with team logo, and Forestry service logos commemorating the 40th birthday of Smokey the Bear. The black-and-white card backs list tips for preventing forest fires.

		MT	NR MT	EX
Complete Set:		8.00	6.00	3.25
Common Player:		.20	.15	.08
(1)	Don Aase	.30	.25	.12
(2)	Juan Beniquez	.20	.15	.08
(3)	Bob Boone	.30	.25	.12
(4)	Rick Burleson	.30	.25	.12
(5)	Rod Carew	1.00	.70	.40
(6)	John Curtis	.20	.15	.08
(7)	Doug DeCinces	.30	.25	.12
(8)	Brian Downing	.30	.25	.12
(9)	Ken Forsch	.20	.15	.08
(10)	Bobby Grich	.30	.25	.12
(11)	Reggie Jackson	1.00	.70	.40

		MT	NR MT	EX
(12)	Ron Jackson	.20	.15	.08
(13)	Tommy John	.60	.45	.25
(14)	Curt Kaufman	.20	.15	.08
(15)	Bruce Kison	.20	.15	.08
(16)	Frank LaCorte	.20	.15	.08
(17)	Fred Lynn	.60	.45	.25
(18)	John McNamara	.20	.15	.08
(19)	Jerry Narron	.20	.15	.08
(20)	Gary Pettis	.50	.40	.20
(21)	Robert Picciolo	.20	.15	.08
(22)	Ron Romanick	.30	.25	.12
(23)	Luis Sanchez	.20	.15	.08
(24)	Dick Schofield	.40	.30	.15
(25)	Daryl Sconiers	.20	.15	.08
(26)	Jim Slaton	.20	.15	.08
(27)	Ellis Valentine	.20	.15	.08
(28)	Robert Wilfong	.20	.15	.08
(29)	Mike Witt	.60	.45	.25
(30)	Geoff Zahn	.20	.15	.08
---	Forestry Dept. Logo Card	.10	.08	.04
---	Smokey Logo Card	.10	.08	.04

1984 Smokey Bear Dodgers

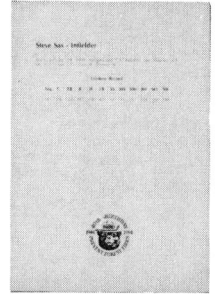

Unlike the California Angels and San Diego Padres sets issued in conjunction with the Forestry Service in 1984, the Los Angeles Dodgers set contains only three players, pictured on much larger , 5'' by 7'' cards. Ken Landreaux, Tom Niedenfuer and Steve Sax (plus a Smokey the Bear card) are pictured on the cards. Each player is pictured in a forest scene on the full-color fronts. Backs of the unnumbered cards have brief biographical information and lifetime statistics. The cards were distributed at a Dodgers home game.

		MT	NR MT	EX
Complete Set:		10.00	7.50	4.00
Common Player:		2.50	2.00	1.00
(1)	Ken Landreaux	2.50	2.00	1.00
(2)	Tom Niedenfuer	2.50	2.00	1.00
(3)	Steve Sax	5.00	3.75	2.00
(4)	Smokey Bear	.50	.40	.20

1984 Smokey Bear Jackson Mets In Majors

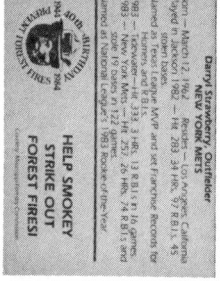

This set, issued in conjuction with the Mississippi Forestry Commission, features big leaguers who played for the Mets' Double-A farm club. The 15 3'' by 4'' cards have a black-and-white portrait photo on the front, with name, position and major league team shown in blue. Smokey the Bear logo is also included. Card backs feature player information and careeer highlights.

		MT	NR MT	EX
Complete Set:		20.00	15.00	8.00
Common Player:		.70	.50	.30
(1)	Neil Allen	.90	.70	.35
(2)	Wally Backman	1.25	.90	.50
(3)	Hubie Brooks	1.50	1.25	.60
(4)	Jody Davis	1.50	1.25	.60
(5)	Brian Giles	.70	.50	.30
(6)	Dave Johnson	1.50	1.25	.60
(7)	Tim Leary	.75	.60	.30
(8)	Lee Mazzilli	1.25	.90	.50
(9)	Jesse Orosco	1.25	.90	.50
(10)	Jeff Reardon	1.75	1.25	.70
(11)	Doug Sisk	.75	.60	.30
(12)	Darryl Strawberry	7.00	5.25	2.75
(13)	Mookie Wilson	1.50	1.25	.60
(14)	Marvel Wynne (Marvell)	.70	.50	.30
(15)	Ned Yost	.70	.50	.30

1984 Smokey Bear Padres

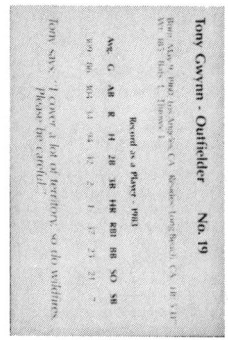

This set of 28 full-color cards is very similar in format to the Angels set of the same year. San Diego Padres players are posed in photos with Smokey the Bear. Foresty Department and team logos are also pictured on the card fronts. The Padres cards feature players, coaches, broadcasters and the The Famous Chicken all posing with Smokey. Backs of the cards, which were distributed at a Padres home game, offer brief player information and a fire prevention tip.

		MT	NR MT	EX
Complete Set:		10.00	7.50	4.00
Common Player:		.25	.20	.10
1	Garry Templeton	.50	.40	.20
2	Alan Wiggins	.25	.20	.10
4	Luis Salazar	.25	.20	.10
6	Steve Garvey	1.00	.70	.40
7	Kurt Bevacqua	.25	.20	.10
10	Doug Gwosdz	.25	.20	.10
11	Tim Flannery	.25	.20	.10
16	Terry Kennedy	.40	.30	.15
18	Kevin McReynolds	1.00	.70	.40
19	Tony Gwynn	1.50	1.25	.60
20	Bobby Brown	.25	.20	.10
30	Eric Show	.40	.30	.15
31	Ed Whitson	.25	.20	.10
35	Luis DeLeon	.25	.20	.10
38	Mark Thurmond	.25	.20	.10
42	Sid Monge	.25	.20	.10
43	Dave Dravecky	.40	.30	.15
48	Tim Lollar	.25	.20	.10
---	Smokey Logo Card	.25	.20	.10

		MT	NR MT	EX
---	The Chicken (mascot)	.35	.25	.14
---	Dave Campbell (broadcaster)	.25	.20	.10
---	Jerry Coleman (broadcaster)	.25	.20	.10
---	Harry Dunlop (coach)	.25	.20	.10
---	Harold (Doug) Harvey (umpire)	.25	.20	.10
---	Jack Krol (coach)	.25	.20	.10
---	Jack McKeon (vice-president)	.25	.20	.10
---	Norm Sherry (coach)	.25	.20	.10
---	Ozzie Virgil (coach)	.25	.20	.10
---	Dick Williams (manager)	.35	.25	.14

1985 Smokey Bear Angels

The California Forestry Service and the California Angels gave this full-color set of oversized baseball cards to fans attending the July 14 game at Anaheim Stadium. The 24 cards feature player photos on the fronts with their last name at the top of the cards above the picture. On the card bottom are the logos for Smokey Bear, the Angels, the State Forestry Service and the U.S. Forestry Service. The cards measure 4¼'' by 6.'' On the card backs, printed in black and white, are personal data, limited playing stats and a wildfire safety tip from Smokey the Bear.

		MT	NR MT	EX
	Complete Set:	7.00	5.25	2.75
	Complete Set:	.20	.15	.08
1	Mike Witt	.60	.45	.25
2	Reggie Jackson	1.00	.70	.40
3	Bob Boone	.30	.25	.12
4	Mike Brown	.20	.15	.08
5	Rod Carew	1.00	.70	.40
6	Doug DeCinces	.30	.25	.12
7	Brian Downing	.30	.25	.12
8	Ken Forsch	.20	.15	.08
9	Gary Pettis	.30	.25	.12
10	Jerry Narron	.20	.15	.08
11	Ron Romanick	.20	.15	.08
12	Bobby Grich	.30	.25	.12
13	Dick Schofield	.30	.25	.12
14	Juan Beniquez	.20	.15	.08
15	Geoff Zahn	.20	.15	.08
16	Luis Sanchez	.20	.15	.08
17	Jim Slaton	.20	.15	.08
18	Doug Corbett	.20	.15	.08
19	Ruppert Jones	.20	.15	.08
20	Rob Wilfong	.20	.15	.08
21	Donnie Moore	.20	.15	.08
22	Pat Clements	.30	.25	.12
23	Tommy John	.60	.45	.25
24	Gene Mauch	.30	.25	.12

1986 Smokey Bear Angels

The California Angels, in conjuction with the Forestry Service, issued this 24-card set of Wildfire Prevention baseball cards. The cards measure 4¼'' by 6'' and offer a full-color front with the player's picture placed in an oval frame. The card backs have player

stats with a drawing and slogan for fire prevention. The sets were given out on August 9 at the Angels game in Anaheim Stadium.

		MT	NR MT	EX
	Complete Set:	8.00	6.00	3.25
	Common Player:	.20	.15	.08
1	Mike Witt	.60	.45	.25
2	Reggie Jackson	1.00	.70	.40
3	Bob Boone	.30	.25	.12
4	Don Sutton	.60	.45	.25
5	Kirk McCaskill	.50	.40	.20
6	Doug DeCinces	.30	.25	.12
7	Brian Downing	.30	.25	.12
8	Doug Corbett	.20	.15	.08
9	Gary Pettis	.30	.25	.12
10	Jerry Narron	.20	.15	.08
11	Ron Romanick	.20	.15	.08
12	Bobby Grich	.30	.25	.12
13	Dick Schofield	.30	.25	.12
14	George Hendrick	.30	.25	.12
15	Rick Burleson	.30	.25	.12
16	John Candelaria	.30	.25	.12
17	Jim Slaton	.20	.15	.08
18	Darrell Miller	.30	.25	.12
19	Ruppert Jones	.20	.15	.08
20	Rob Wilfong	.20	.15	.08
21	Donnie Moore	.20	.15	.08
22	Wally Joyner	2.50	2.00	1.00
23	Terry Forster	.30	.25	.12
24	Gene Mauch	.30	.25	.12

1987 Smokey Bear

The U.S. Forestry Service and Major League Baseball united in an effort to promote National Smokey the Bear Day. Two perforated sheets of baseball cards, one each for the American and National Leagues, were produced by the Forestry Service. The sheet of American Leaguers measures 18'' by 24'' and contains 16 full-color cards. The National League sheet measures 20'' by 18'' and contains 15 cards. Each individual card is 4'' by 6'' and contains a fire prevention tip on the back. An average number of

25,000 sets was sent to all teams.

		MT	NR MT	EX
Complete Set:		8.00	6.00	3.25
Common Player:		.20	.15	.08
1A	Jose Canseco	1.00	.70	.40
1N	Steve Sax	.40	.30	.15
2A	Dennis "Oil Can" Boyd	.20	.15	.08
2N	Dale Murphy	.80	.60	.30
3A	John Candelaria	.20	.15	.08
3N	Jody Davis	.25	.20	.10
4A	Harold Baines	.30	.25	.12
4N	Bill Gullickson	.20	.15	.08
5A	Joe Carter	.30	.25	.12
5N	Mike Scott	.30	.25	.12
6A	Jack Morris	.50	.40	.20
6N	Roger McDowell	.25	.20	.10
7A	Buddy Biancalana	.20	.15	.08
7N	Steve Bedrosian	.30	.25	.12
8A	Kirby Puckett	.70	.50	.30
8N	Johnny Ray	.25	.20	.10
9A	Mike Pagliarulo	.30	.25	.12
9N	Ozzie Smith	.30	.25	.12
10A	Larry Sheets	.25	.20	.10
10N	Steve Garvey	.60	.45	.25
11A	Mike Moore	.20	.15	.08
11N	Smokey Bear Logo Card	.05	.04	.02
12A	Charlie Hough	.20	.15	.08
12N	Mike Krukow	.20	.15	.08
13A	Smokey Bear Logo Card	.05	.04	.02
13N	Smokey Bear	.05	.04	.02
14A	Tom Henke	.20	.15	.08
14N	Mike Fitzgerald	.20	.15	.08
15A	Jim Gantner	.20	.15	.08
15N	National League Logo Card	.05	.04	.02
16A	American League Logo Card	.05	.04	.02

1987 Smokey Bear A's

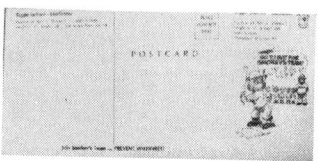

The 1987 Smokey Bear A's set is not comparable to any other Smokey Bear issue produced in 1987 or before. The twelve cards in the set are bound together in a book titled "Smokey Bear's Fire Prevention Color-Grams." The Color-Gram cards feature two cards in one. A near-standard size (2½" by 3¾") black and white card is attached to a large perforated (3¾" by 6") card, also black and white. The large card, which has a postcard back, features a caricature photo of the player and is intended to be colored and then mailed. The card backs contain personal and statistical information and carry a Smokey the Bear cartoon message. The books were distributed at an Oakland A's game during the 1987 season.

		MT	NR MT	EX
Complete Book:		6.00	4.50	2.50
Complete Singles Set:		3.00	2.25	1.25
Common Single Player:		.15	.11	.06
(1)	Joaquin Andujar	.20	.15	.08
(2)	Jose Canseco	1.00	.70	.40
(3)	Mike Davis	.30	.25	.12
(4)	Alfredo Griffin	.25	.20	.10

		MT	NR MT	EX
(5)	Moose Haas	.15	.11	.06
(6)	Jay Howell	.25	.20	.10
(7)	Reggie Jackson	.70	.50	.30
(8)	Carney Lansford	.30	.25	.12
(9)	Dwayne Murphy	.30	.25	.12
(10)	Tony Phillips	.15	.11	.06
(11)	Dave Stewart	.40	.30	.15
(12)	Curt Young	.30	.25	.12

1987 Smokey Bear Angels

A 24-card set featuring the California Angels and produced by the U.S. Forestry Service was distributed to 25,000 fans in attendance at Anaheim Stadium on August 1st. The full-color cards measure 4" by 6". The card fronts carry a unique design with baseballs and bats framing the player photo. Only the player's last name is given on the card fronts. The backs contain the player's name, position and personal statistics along with a Smokey Bear cartoon and a fire prevention tip.

		MT	NR MT	EX
Complete Set:		8.00	6.00	3.25
Common Player:		.20	.15	.08
1	John Candelaria	.30	.25	.12
2	Don Sutton	.60	.45	.25
3	Mike Witt	.60	.45	.25
4	Gary Lucas	.20	.15	.08
5	Kirk McCaskill	.30	.25	.12
6	Chuck Finley	.25	.20	.10
7	Willie Fraser	.50	.40	.20
8	Donnie Moore	.20	.15	.08
9	Urbano Lugo	.20	.15	.08
10	Butch Wynegar	.25	.20	.10
11	Darrell Miller	.20	.15	.08
12	Wally Joyner	2.00	1.50	.80
13	Mark McLemore	.25	.20	.10
14	Mark Ryal	.25	.20	.10
15	Dick Schofield	.25	.20	.10
16	Jack Howell	.30	.25	.12
17	Doug DeCinces	.30	.25	.12
18	Gus Polidor	.25	.20	.10
19	Brian Downing	.30	.25	.12
20	Gary Pettis	.30	.25	.12
21	Ruppert Jones	.20	.15	.08
22	George Hendrick	.25	.20	.10
23	Devon White	1.50	1.25	.60
---	Smokey Bear Logo Card/Checklist	.10	.08	.04

1987 Smokey Bear Braves

Cards from the 1987 Smokey Bear Atlanta Braves set were given out at several different Braves games, with about 25,000 sets in all being distributed. The 4" by 6" cards feature Atlanta players in an oval frame, bordered in red, white and blue. Only the player's last name is listed on the card fronts. Card backs contain the player's name, position and personal data plus a Smokey Bear cartoon with a fire safety message.

		MT	NR MT	EX
	Complete Set:	8.00	6.00	3.25
	Common Player:	.20	.15	.08
1	Zane Smith	.50	.40	.20
2	Charlie Puleo	.20	.15	.08
3	Randy O'Neal	.20	.15	.08
4	David Palmer	.30	.25	.12
5	Rick Mahler	.30	.25	.12
6	Ed Olwine	.20	.15	.08
7	Jeff Dedmon	.20	.15	.08
8	Paul Assenmacher	.30	.25	.12
9	Gene Garber	.20	.15	.08
10	Jim Acker	.20	.15	.08
11	Bruce Benedict	.20	.15	.08
12	Ozzie Virgil	.30	.25	.12
13	Ted Simmons	.40	.30	.15
14	Dale Murphy	1.25	.90	.50
15	Graig Nettles	.40	.30	.15
16	Ken Oberkfell	.30	.25	.12
17	Gerald Perry	.40	.30	.15
18	Rafael Ramirez	.25	.20	.10
19	Ken Griffey	.30	.25	.12
20	Andres Thomas	.40	.30	.15
21	Glenn Hubbard	.25	.20	.10
22	Damaso Garcia	.25	.20	.10
23	Gary Roenicke	.20	.15	.08
24	Dion James	.40	.30	.15
25	Albert Hall	.20	.15	.08
26	Chuck Tanner	.25	.20	.10
—	Smokey Bear Logo Card/Checklist	.10	.08	.04

1987 Smokey Bear Cardinals

Approximately 25,000 fans in attendance at Busch Stadium on August 24th received a 25-card set featuring the St. Louis Cardinals. Produced by the U.S. Forestry Service, the cards measure 4'' by 6''. The card fronts feature a full-color photo set inside an oval frame. Only the player's last name appears on the front. The card reverse carries the player's name, position and personal data plus a Smokey Bear cartoon with a fire prevention message.

	MT	NR MT	EX
Complete Set:	8.00	6.00	3.25
Common Player:	.20	.15	.08

		MT	NR MT	EX
1	Ray Soff	.20	.15	.08
2	Todd Worrell	.70	.50	.30
3	John Tudor	.40	.30	.15
4	Pat Perry	.20	.15	.08
5	Rick Horton	.30	.25	.12
6	Dan Cox	.40	.30	.15
7	Bob Forsch	.30	.25	.12
8	Greg Mathews	.50	.40	.20
9	Bill Dawley	.20	.15	.08
10	Steve Lake	.20	.15	.08
11	Tony Pena	.40	.30	.15
12	Tom Pagnozzi	.30	.25	.12
13	Jack Clark	.70	.50	.30
14	Jim Lindeman	.60	.45	.25
15	Mike Laga	.20	.15	.08
16	Terry Pendleton	.40	.30	.15
17	Ozzie Smith	.70	.50	.30
18	Jose Oquendo	.20	.15	.08
19	Tom Lawless	.20	.15	.08
20	Tom Herr	.40	.30	.15
21	Curt Ford	.20	.15	.08
22	Willie McGee	.70	.50	.30
23	Tito Landrum	.20	.15	.08
24	Vince Coleman	.80	.60	.30
25	Whitey Herzog	.30	.25	.12

1987 Smokey Bear Dodgers

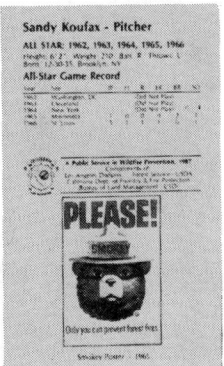

The 40-card Smokey Bear Dodgers set features "25 Years of Dodger All-Stars." The cards, which measure 2½'' by 3¾'', were given out to fans 14 years of age and younger at the September 18th game at Dodger Stadium. The card fronts contain full-color photos set in the shape of Dodger Stadium and have attractive silver borders. The backs carry the player's All-Star Game record plus a fire prevention message. Many of the photos used in the set were from team-issued picture packs sold by the Dodgers in the past.

		MT	NR MT	EX
	Complete Set:	10.00	7.50	4.00
	Common Player:	.20	.15	.08
(1)	Walt Alston	.40	.30	.15
(2)	Dusty Baker	.20	.15	.08
(3)	Jim Brewer	.20	.15	.08
(4)	Ron Cey	.30	.25	.12
(5)	Tommy Davis	.25	.20	.10
(6)	Willie Davis	.25	.20	.10
(7)	Don Drysdale	.80	.60	.30
(8)	Steve Garvey	.80	.60	.30
(9)	Bill Grabarkewitz	.20	.15	.08
(10)	Pedro Guerrero	.50	.40	.20
(11)	Tom Haller	.20	.15	.08
(12)	Orel Hershiser	.40	.30	.15
(13)	Burt Hooton	.20	.15	.08
(14)	Steve Howe	.20	.15	.08
(15)	Tommy John	.50	.40	.20
(16)	Sandy Koufax	1.25	.90	.50
(17)	Tom Lasorda	.30	.25	.12
(18)	Jim Lefebvre	.20	.15	.08
(19)	Davey Lopes	.30	.25	.12
(20)	Mike Marshall (outfielder)	.40	.30	.15

		MT	NR MT	EX
(21)	Mike Marshall (pitcher)	.25	.20	.10
(22)	Andy Messersmith	.20	.15	.08
(23)	Rick Monday	.25	.20	.10
(24)	Manny Mota	.25	.20	.10
(25)	Claude Osteen	.20	.15	.08
(26)	Johnny Podres	.30	.25	.12
(27)	Phil Regan	.20	.15	.08
(28)	Jerry Reuss	.25	.20	.10
(29)	Rick Rhoden	.25	.20	.10
(30)	John Roseboro	.25	.20	.10
(31)	Bill Russell	.25	.20	.10
(32)	Steve Sax	.40	.30	.15
(33)	Bill Singer	.20	.15	.08
(34)	Reggie Smith	.30	.25	.12
(35)	Don Sutton	.60	.45	.25
(36)	Fernando Valenzuela	.80	.60	.30
(37)	Bob Welch	.30	.25	.12
(38)	Maury Wills	.40	.30	.15
(39)	Jim Wynn	.20	.15	.08
(40)	Logo Card/Checklist	.10	.08	.04

1987 Smokey Bear Rangers

 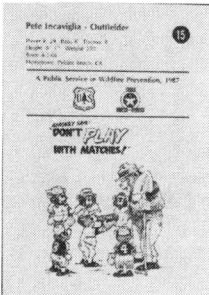

The 1987 Smokey Bear Rangers set is made up of 18 full-color cards. Co-sponsored by the Texas Rangers, U.S. Forest Service and Texas Forest Service, the set was given out to fans at special promotions at Arlington Stadium. The cards measure 4¼'' by 6'' and feature full-color photos on the fronts. The backs contain brief player personal information, along with the card number and a Smokey the Bear cartoon message. Card #4 Mike Mason was withdrawn from the sets given out by the Rangers after he was traded.

		MT	NR MT	EX
	Complete Set:	25.00	18.50	10.00
	Common Player:	.30	.25	.12
1	Charlie Hough	.60	.45	.25
2	Greg Harris	.30	.25	.12
3	Jose Guzman	.60	.45	.25
4	Mike Mason	10.00	7.50	4.00
5	Dale Mohorcic	.60	.45	.25
6	Bobby Witt	.80	.60	.30
7	Mitch Williams	.60	.45	.25
8	Geno Petralli	.30	.25	.12
9	Don Slaught	.30	.25	.12
10	Darrell Porter	.30	.25	.12
11	Steve Beuchele	.40	.80	.15
12	Pete O'Brien	.80	.60	.30
13	Scott Fletcher	.40	.30	.15
14	Tom Paciorek	.40	.30	.15
15	Pete Incaviglia	1.50	1.25	.60
16	Oddibe McDowell	.80	.60	.30
17	Ruben Sierra	1.50	1.25	.60
18	Larry Parrish	.60	.45	.25

1933 Sport Kings

This 48-card set was issued by the Goudey Gum Company. Participants in 18 different sports are included in the set, which honors the top sports fig-

ures of the era. Three baseball players are pictured on the 2⅜'' by 2⅞'' cards (only the baseball players are checklisted here). Card fronts are color portraits and include the player's name and silhouette representations of the respective sport. Card backs are numbered and list biographical information and a company ad.

		NR MT	EX	VG
	Complete Set:	3200.00	1280.00	800.00
1	Ty Cobb	600.00	240.00	150.00
2	Babe Ruth	1200.00	480.00	300.00
42	Carl Hubbell	175.00	88.00	52.00

1948 Sport Thrills

 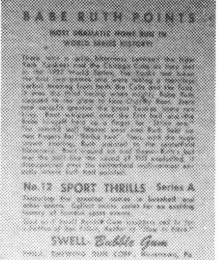

This is a set of black-and-white cards which depict memorable events in baseball history. Cards measure 2½'' by 3'' and have a picture frame border and event title on the card fronts. Card backs describe the event in detail. Twenty cards were produced in this set by the Swell Gum Company of Philadelphia. Each card is numbered, and card numbers 9, 11, 16 and 20 are considered more difficult to obtain.

		NR MT	EX	VG
	Complete Set:	675.00	337.00	202.00
	Common Player:	12.00	6.00	3.50
1	Greatest Single Inning (Mickey Cochrane, Jimmy Foxx, George Haas, Bing Miller, Al Simmons)	25.00	12.50	7.50
2	Amazing Record (Pete Reiser)	12.00	6.00	3.50
3	Dramatic Debut (Jackie Robinson)	60.00	30.00	18.00
4	Greatest Pitcher (Walter Johnson)	30.00	15.00	9.00
5	Three Strikes Not Out! (Tommy Henrich, Mickey Owen)	12.00	6.00	3.50
6	Home Run Wins Series (Bill Dickey)	18.00	9.00	5.50
7	Never Say Die Pitcher (Hal Schumacher)	12.00	6.00	3.50
8	Five Strikeouts! (Carl Hubbell)	18.00	9.00	5.50
9	Greatest Catch! (Al Gionfriddo)	25.00	12.50	7.50
10	No Hits! No Runs! (Johnny Vander Meer)	12.00	6.00	3.50
11	Bases Loaded! (Tony Lazzeri, Bob O'Farrell)	25.00	12.50	7.50

		NR MT	EX	VG
12	Most Dramatic Home Run (Lou Gehrig, Babe Ruth)	90.00	45.00	27.00
13	Winning Run (Tommy Bridges, Mickey Cochrane, Goose Goslin)	12.00	6.00	3.50
14	Great Slugging (Lou Gehrig)	75.00	37.00	22.00
15	Four Men to Stop Him! (Jim Bagby, Al Smith)	12.00	6.00	3.50
16	Three Run Homer in Ninth! (Joe DiMaggio, Joe Gordon, Ted Williams)	90.00	45.00	27.00
17	Football Block! (Whitey Kurowski, Johnny Lindell)	12.00	6.00	3.50
18	Home Run to Fame (Pee Wee Reese)	25.00	12.50	7.50
19	Strikout Record! (Bob Feller)	30.00	15.00	9.00
20	Rifle Arm! (Carl Furillo)	30.00	15.00	9.00

1986 Sportflics

 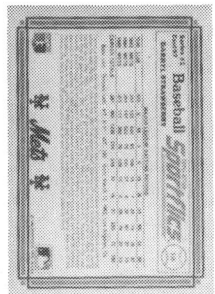

The premiere issue from Sportflics was distributed nationally by Amurol Division of Wrigley Gum Company. These high quality, 3-phase "Magic Motion" cards depict three different photos per card, with each visible separately as the card is tilted. The 1986 issue featured 200 full-color baseball cards plus 133 trivia cards. The cards come in the standard 2½" by 3½" size with the backs containing player stats and personal information. There are three different types of picture cards: 1) Tri-Star cards, 50 cards which feature three players on one card; 2) Big Six cards, 10 cards which have six players in special categories; and 3) the Big Twelve card of 12 World Series players from the Royals. The trivia cards are 1¾" by 2" and do not have player photos.

		MT	NR MT	EX
	Complete Set:	32.00	24.00	13.00
	Common Player:	.10	.08	.04
1	George Brett	1.00	.70	.40
2	Don Mattingly	4.00	3.00	1.50
3	Wade Boggs	2.00	1.50	.80
4	Eddie Murray	.60	.45	.25
5	Dale Murphy	1.00	.70	.40
6	Rickey Henderson	.70	.50	.30
7	Harold Baines	.20	.15	.08
8	Cal Ripken, Jr.	.60	.45	.25
9	Orel Hershiser	.30	.25	.12
10	Bret Saberhagen	.30	.25	.12
11	Tim Raines	.40	.30	.15
12	Fernando Valenzuela	.35	.25	.14
13	Tony Gwynn	.60	.45	.25
14	Pedro Guerrero	.25	.20	.10
15	Keith Hernandez	.35	.25	.14
16	Ernest Riles	.35	.25	.14
17	Jim Rice	.40	.30	.15
18	Ron Guidry	.25	.20	.10
19	Willie McGee	.25	.20	.10
20	Ryne Sandberg	.40	.30	.15
21	Kirk Gibson	.30	.25	.12
22	Ozzie Guillen	.50	.40	.20
23	Dave Parker	.25	.20	.10
24	Vince Coleman	2.00	1.50	.80
25	Tom Seaver	.35	.25	.14
26	Brett Butler	.10	.08	.04
27	Steve Carlton	.35	.25	.14

		MT	NR MT	EX
28	Gary Carter	.35	.25	.14
29	Cecil Cooper	.15	.11	.06
30	Jose Cruz	.10	.08	.04
31	Alvin Davis	.20	.15	.08
32	Dwight Evans	.15	.11	.06
33	Julio Franco	.15	.11	.06
34	Damaso Garcia	.10	.08	.04
35	Steve Garvey	.35	.25	.14
36	Kent Hrbek	.20	.15	.08
37	Reggie Jackson	.50	.40	.20
38	Fred Lynn	.20	.15	.08
39	Paul Molitor	.15	.11	.06
40	Jim Presley	.20	.15	.08
41	Dave Righetti	.20	.15	.08
42	Robin Yount	.35	.25	.14
43	Nolan Ryan	.35	.25	.14
44	Mike Schmidt	.80	.60	.30
45	Lee Smith	.10	.08	.04
46	Rick Sutcliffe	.15	.11	.06
47	Bruce Sutter	.15	.11	.06
48	Lou Whitaker	.25	.20	.10
49	Dave Winfield	.50	.40	.20
50	Pete Rose	1.50	1.25	.60
51	National League MVPs (Steve Garvey, Pete Rose, Ryne Sandberg)	.70	.50	.30
52	Slugging Stars (Harold Baines, George Brett, Jim Rice)	.50	.40	.20
53	No-Hitters (Phil Niekro, Jerry Reuss, Mike Witt)	.15	.11	.06
54	Big Hitters (Don Mattingly, Cal Ripken, Jr., Robin Yount)	1.25	.90	.50
55	Bullpen Aces (Goose Gossage, Dan Quisenberry, Lee Smith)	.10	.08	.04
56	Rookies of the Year (Pete Rose, Steve Sax, Darryl Strawberry)	.80	.60	.30
57	American League MVPs (Don Baylor, Reggie Jackson, Cal Ripken, Jr.)	.25	.20	.10
58	Repeat Batting Champs (Bill Madlock, Dave Parker, Pete Rose)	.60	.45	.25
59	Cy Young Winners (Mike Flanagan, Ron Guidry, LaMarr Hoyt)	.10	.08	.04
60	Double Award Winners (Tom Seaver, Rick Sutcliffe, Fernando Valenzuela)	.20	.15	.08
61	Home Run Champs (Tony Armas, Reggie Jackson, Jim Rice)	.25	.20	.10
62	National League MVPs (Keith Hernandez, Dale Murphy, Mike Schmidt)	.50	.40	.20
63	American League MVPs (George Brett, Fred Lynn, Robin Yount)	.30	.25	.12
64	Comeback Players (Bert Blyleven, John Denny, Jerry Koosman)	.10	.08	.04
65	Cy Young Relievers (Rollie Fingers, Willie Hernandez, Bruce Sutter)	.15	.11	.06
66	Rookies Of The Year (Andre Dawson, Bob Horner, Gary Matthews)	.15	.11	.06
67	Rookies Of The Year (Carlton Fisk, Ron Kittle, Tom Seaver)	.15	.11	.06
68	Home Run Champs (George Foster, Dave Kingman, Mike Schmidt)	.30	.25	.12
69	Double Award Winners (Rod Carew, Cal Ripken, Jr., Pete Rose)	.70	.50	.30
70	Cy Young Winners (Steve Carlton, Tom Seaver, Rick Sutcliffe)	.25	.20	.10
71	Top Sluggers (Reggie Jackson, Fred Lynn, Robin Yount)	.20	.15	.08
72	Rookies of the Year (Dave Righetti, Rick Sutcliffe, Fernando Valenzuela)	.15	.11	.06
73	Rookies Of The Year (Fred Lynn, Eddie Murray, Cal Ripken, Jr.)	.25	.20	.10
74	Rookies Of The Year (Rod Carew, Alvin Davis, Lou Whitaker)	.20	.15	.08
75	Batting Champs (Wade Boggs, Carney Lansford, Don Mattingly)	1.50	1.25	.60
76	Jesse Barfield	.20	.15	.08
77	Phil Bradley	.20	.15	.08
78	Chris Brown	.80	.60	.30
79	Tom Browning	.15	.11	.06
80	Tom Brunansky	.15	.11	.06
81	Bill Buckner	.10	.08	.04
82	Chili Davis	.15	.11	.06
83	Mike Davis	.10	.08	.04
84	Rich Gedman	.10	.08	.04
85	Willie Hernandez	.10	.08	.04
86	Ron Kittle	.10	.08	.04
87	Lee Lacy	.10	.08	.04
88	Bill Madlock	.15	.11	.06
89	Mike Marshall	.15	.11	.06
90	Keith Moreland	.10	.08	.04
91	Graig Nettles	.15	.11	.06
92	Lance Parrish	.20	.15	.08
93	Kirby Puckett	.40	.30	.15

#	Name	MT	NR MT	EX
94	Juan Samuel	.20	.15	.08
95	Steve Sax	.20	.15	.08
96	Dave Stieb	.10	.08	.04
97	Darryl Strawberry	.80	.60	.30
98	Willie Upshaw	.10	.08	.04
99	Frank Viola	.15	.11	.06
100	Dwight Gooden	1.50	1.25	.60
101	Joaquin Andujar	.10	.08	.04
102	George Bell	.60	.45	.25
103	Bert Blyleven	.15	.11	.06
104	Mike Boddicker	.10	.08	.04
105	Britt Burns	.10	.08	.04
106	Rod Carew	.40	.30	.15
107	Jack Clark	.20	.15	.08
108	Danny Cox	.10	.08	.04
109	Ron Darling	.15	.11	.06
110	Andre Dawson	.25	.20	.10
111	Leon Durham	.10	.08	.04
112	Tony Fernandez	.15	.11	.06
113	Tom Herr	.10	.08	.04
114	Teddy Higuera	1.00	.70	.40
115	Bob Horner	.20	.15	.08
116	Dave Kingman	.15	.11	.06
117	Jack Morris	.25	.20	.10
118	Dan Quisenberry	.20	.15	.08
119	Jeff Reardon	.15	.11	.06
120	Bryn Smith	.10	.08	.04
121	Ozzie Smith	.25	.20	.10
122	John Tudor	.15	.11	.06
123	Tim Wallach	.15	.11	.06
124	Willie Wilson	.15	.11	.06
125	Carlton Fisk	.25	.20	.10
126	RBI Sluggers (Gary Carter, George Foster, Al Oliver)	.15	.11	.06
127	Run Scorers (Keith Hernandez, Tim Raines, Ryne Sandberg)	.25	.20	.10
128	Run Scorers (Paul Molitor, Cal Ripken, Jr., Willie Wilson)	.15	.11	.06
129	No-Hitters (John Candelaria, Dennis Eckersley, Bob Forsch)	.10	.08	.04
130	World Series MVPs (Ron Cey, Rollie Fingers, Pete Rose)	.50	.40	.20
131	All-Star Game MVPs (Dave Concepcion, George Foster, Bill Madlock)	.10	.08	.04
132	Cy Young Winners (Vida Blue, John Denny, Fernando Valenzuela)	.15	.11	.06
133	Comeback Players (Doyle Alexander, Joaquin Andujar, Richard Dotson)	.10	.08	.04
134	Big Winners (John Denny, Tom Seaver, Rick Sutcliffe)	.15	.11	.06
135	Veteran Pitchers (Phil Niekro, Tom Seaver, Don Sutton)	.25	.20	.10
136	Rookies Of The Year (Vince Coleman, Dwight Gooden, Alfredo Griffin)	1.00	.70	.40
137	All-Star Game MVPs (Gary Carter, Steve Garvey, Fred Lynn)	.20	.15	.08
138	Veteran Hitters (Tony Perez, Pete Rose, Rusty Staub)	.50	.40	.20
139	Power Hitters (George Foster, Jim Rice, Mike Schmidt)	.30	.25	.12
140	Batting Champs (Bill Buckner, Tony Gwynn, Al Oliver)	.20	.15	.08
141	No-Hitters (Jack Morris, Dave Righetti, Nolan Ryan)	.20	.15	.08
142	No-Hitters (Vida Blue, Bert Blyleven, Tom Seaver)	.15	.11	.06
143	Strikeout Kings (Dwight Gooden, Nolan Ryan, Fernando Valenzuela)	.60	.45	.25
144	Base Stealers (Dave Lopes, Tim Raines, Willie Wilson)	.15	.11	.06
145	RBI Sluggers (Tony Armas, Cecil Cooper, Eddie Murray)	.20	.15	.08
146	American League MVPs (Rod Carew, Rollie Fingers, Jim Rice)	.25	.20	.10
147	World Series MVPs (Rick Dempsey, Reggie Jackson, Alan Trammell)	.25	.20	.10
148	World Series MVPs (Pedro Guerrero, Darrell Porter, Mike Schmidt)	.20	.15	.08
149	ERA Leaders (Mike Boddicker, Ron Guidry, Rick Sutcliffe)	.10	.08	.04
150	Comeback Players (Reggie Jackson, Dave Kingman, Fred Lynn)	.20	.15	.08
151	Buddy Bell	.15	.11	.06
152	Dennis Boyd	.10	.08	.04
153	Dave Concepcion	.15	.11	.06
154	Brian Downing	.10	.08	.04
155	Shawon Dunston	.15	.11	.06
156	John Franco	.10	.08	.04
157	Scott Garrelts	.10	.08	.04
158	Bob James	.10	.08	.04
159	Charlie Leibrandt	.10	.08	.04
160	Oddibe McDowell	.70	.50	.30
161	Roger McDowell	.50	.40	.20
162	Mike Moore	.10	.08	.04
163	Phil Niekro	.25	.20	.10
164	Al Oliver	.15	.11	.06
165	Tony Pena	.10	.08	.04
166	Ted Power	.10	.08	.04
167	Mike Scioscia	.10	.08	.04
168	Mario Soto	.10	.08	.04
169	Bob Stanley	.10	.08	.04
170	Garry Templeton	.10	.08	.04
171	Andre Thornton	.10	.08	.04
172	Alan Trammell	.30	.25	.12
173	Doug DeCinces	.10	.08	.04
174	Greg Walker	.10	.08	.04
175	Don Sutton	.25	.20	.10
176	1985 Award Winners (Vince Coleman, Dwight Gooden, Ozzie Guillen, Don Mattingly, Willie McGee, Bret Saberhagen)	1.25	.90	.50
177	1985 Hot Rookies (Stewart Cliburn, Brian Fisher, Joe Hesketh, Joe Orsulak, Mark Salas, Larry Sheets)	.50	.40	.20
178	Future Stars (Jose Canseco, Mark Funderburk, Mike Greenwell, Steve Lombardozzi, Billy Joe Robidoux, Dan Tartabull)	5.00	3.75	2.00
179	1985 Gold Glovers (George Brett, Ron Guidry, Keith Hernandez, Don Mattingly, Willie McGee, Dale Murphy)	1.25	.90	.50
180	Active .300 Hitters (Wade Boggs, George Brett, Rod Carew, Cecil Cooper, Don Mattingly, Willie Wilson)	1.25	.90	.50
181	Active .300 Hitters (Pedro Guerrero, Tony Gwynn, Keith Hernandez, Bill Madlock, Dave Parker, Pete Rose)	.70	.50	.30
182	1985 Milestones (Rod Carew, Phil Niekro, Pete Rose, Nolan Ryan, Tom Seaver, Matt Tallman)	1.25	.90	.50
183	1985 Triple Crown (Wade Boggs, Darrell Evans, Don Mattingly, Willie McGee, Dale Murphy, Dave Parker)	1.25	.90	.50
184	1985 Highlights (Wade Boggs, Dwight Gooden, Rickey Henderson, Don Mattingly, Willie McGee, John Tudor)	1.50	1.25	.60
185	1985 20-Game Winners (Joaquin Andujar, Tom Browning, Dwight Gooden, Ron Guidry, Bret Saberhagen, John Tudor)	.60	.45	.25
186	Kansas City Royals (Steve Balboni, George Brett, Dane Iorg, Danny Jackson, Charlie Leibrandt, Darryl Motley, Dan Quisenberry, Bret Saberhagen, Lonnie Smith, Jim Sundberg, Frank White, Willie Wilson)	.40	.30	.15
187	Hubie Brooks	.10	.08	.04
188	Glenn Davis	.50	.40	.20
189	Darrell Evans	.10	.08	.04
190	Rich Gossage	.20	.15	.08
191	Andy Hawkins	.10	.08	.04
192	Jay Howell	.10	.08	.04
193	LaMarr Hoyt	.10	.08	.04
194	Davey Lopes	.10	.08	.04
195	Mike Scott	.15	.11	.06
196	Ted Simmons	.15	.11	.06
197	Gary Ward	.10	.08	.04
198	Bob Welch	.15	.11	.06
199	Mike Young	.10	.08	.04
200	Buddy Biancalana	.10	.08	.04

1986 Sportflics Decade Greats

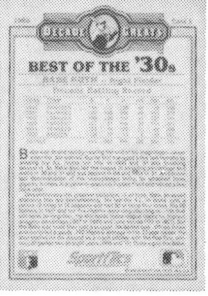

This set produced by Sportflics featured outstanding players, by position, from the 1930s to the 1980s, by decades. Card fronts are printed in sepia-toned photos or full-color with the Sportflics 3-phase "Magic Motion" animation. The complete set contains 75 cards with 59 single player cards and 16 multi-player cards. Biographies appear on the card backs which are printed in full-color and color-coded by decade. The set was distributed only through hobby dealers and is in the popular 2½" by 3½" size.

		MT	NR MT	EX
	Complete Set:	12.00	9.00	4.75
	Common Player:	.15	.11	.06
1	Babe Ruth	2.00	1.50	.80
2	Jimmie Foxx	.40	.30	.15
3	Lefty Grove	.30	.25	.12
4	Hank Greenberg	.30	.25	.12
5	Al Simmons	.15	.11	.06
6	Carl Hubbell	.30	.25	.12
7	Joe Cronin	.25	.20	.10
8	Mel Ott	.30	.25	.12
9	Lefty Gomez	.30	.25	.12
10	Lou Gehrig	1.50	1.25	.60
11	Pie Traynor	.15	.11	.06
12	Charlie Gehringer	.30	.25	.12
13	Catchers (Mickey Cochrane, Bill Dickey, Gabby Hartnett)	.30	.25	.12
14	Pitchers (Dizzy Dean, Paul Derringer, Red Ruffing)	.30	.25	.12
15	Outfielders (Earl Averill, Joe Medwick, Paul Waner)	.15	.11	.06
16	Bob Feller	.60	.45	.25
17	Lou Boudreau	.15	.11	.06
18	Enos Slaughter	.25	.20	.10
19	Hal Newhouser	.15	.11	.06
20	Joe DiMaggio	1.50	1.25	.60
21	Pee Wee Reese	.40	.30	.15
22	Phil Rizzuto	.30	.25	.12
23	Ernie Lombardi	.15	.11	.06
24	Infielders (Joe Cronin, George Kell, Johnny Mize)	.15	.11	.06
25	Ted Williams	1.50	1.25	.60
26	Mickey Mantle	3.00	2.25	1.25
27	Warren Spahn	.30	.25	.12
28	Jackie Robinson	1.00	.70	.40
29	Ernie Banks	.30	.25	.12
30	Stan Musial	1.00	.70	.40
31	Yogi Berra	.60	.45	.25
32	Duke Snider	.70	.50	.30
33	Roy Campanella	.70	.50	.30
34	Eddie Mathews	.30	.25	.12
35	Ralph Kiner	.30	.25	.12
36	Early Wynn	.25	.20	.10
37	Double Play Duo (Luis Aparicio, Nellie Fox)	.25	.20	.10
38	First Basemen (Gil Hodges, Ted Kluszewski, Mickey Vernon)	.25	.20	.10
40	Henry Aaron	1.00	.70	.40
41	Frank Robinson	.30	.25	.12
42	Bob Gibson	.30	.25	.12
43	Roberto Clemente	1.00	.70	.40
44	Whitey Ford	.40	.30	.15
45	Brooks Robinson	.50	.40	.20
46	Juan Marichal	.25	.20	.10
47	Carl Yastrzemski	1.00	.70	.40
48	First Basemen (Orlando Cepeda, Harmon Killebrew, Willie McCovey)	.30	.25	.12
49	Catchers (Bill Freehan, Elston Howard, Joe Torre)	.15	.11	.06
50	Willie Mays	1.00	.70	.40
51	Outfielders (Al Kaline, Tony Oliva, Billy Williams)	.30	.25	.12
52	Tom Seaver	.60	.45	.25
53	Reggie Jackson	.70	.50	.30
54	Steve Carlton	.40	.30	.15
55	Mike Schmidt	.70	.50	.30
56	Joe Morgan	.25	.20	.10
57	Jim Rice	.40	.30	.15
58	Jim Palmer	.30	.25	.12
59	Lou Brock	.30	.25	.12
60	Pete Rose	1.25	.90	.50
61	Steve Garvey	.40	.30	.15
62	Catchers (Carlton Fisk, Thurman Munson, Ted Simmons)	.25	.20	.10
63	Pitchers (Vida Blue, Catfish Hunter, Nolan Ryan)	.30	.25	.12
64	George Brett	.80	.60	.30
65	Don Mattingly	2.00	1.50	.80

		MT	NR MT	EX
66	Fernando Valenzuela	.30	.25	.12
67	Dale Murphy	.80	.60	.30
68	Wade Boggs	1.25	.90	.50
69	Rickey Henderson	.60	.45	.25
70	Eddie Murray	.60	.45	.25
71	Ron Guidry	.25	.20	.10
72	Catchers (Gary Carter, Lance Parrish, Tony Pena)	.30	.25	.12
73	Infielders (Cal Ripken, Jr., Lou Whitaker, Robin Yount)	.30	.25	.12
74	Outfielders (Pedro Guerrero, Tim Raines, Dave Winfield)	.30	.25	.12
75	Dwight Gooden	1.00	.70	.40

1986 Sportflics Rookies

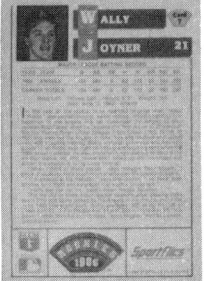

The 1986 Rookies set issued by Sportflics offered 50 cards and featured 47 individual rookie players. In addition there were two Tri-Star cards; one highlights former Rookies of the Year and the other features three prominent players. There is one "Big Six" card featuring six superstars. The full-color photos on the 2½" by 3½" cards use Sportflics 3-phase "Magic Motion" animation. The set was packaged in an attractive collector box which also contained 34 trivia cards that measure 1¾" by 2." The set was distributed only by hobby dealers.

		MT	NR MT	EX
	Complete Set:	14.00	10.50	5.50
	Common Player:	.20	.15	.08
1	John Kruk	1.00	.70	.40
2	Edwin Correa	.30	.25	.12
3	Pete Incaviglia	1.25	.90	.50
4	Dale Sveum	.40	.30	.15
5	Juan Nieves	.30	.25	.12
6	Will Clark	1.75	1.25	.70
7	Wally Joyner	2.50	2.00	1.00
8	Lance McCullers	.20	.15	.08
9	Scott Bailes	.20	.15	.08
10	Dan Plesac	.40	.30	.15
11	Jose Canseco	2.50	2.00	1.00
12	Bobby Witt	.30	.25	.12
13	Barry Bonds	.70	.50	.30
14	Andres Thomas	.20	.15	.08
15	Jim Deshaies	.30	.25	.12
16	Ruben Sierra	1.50	1.25	.60
17	Steve Lombardozzi	.20	.15	.08
18	Cory Snyder	1.75	1.25	.70
19	Reggie Williams	.20	.15	.08
20	Mitch Williams	.20	.15	.08
21	Glenn Braggs	.50	.40	.20
22	Danny Tartabull	.50	.40	.20
23	Charlie Kerfeld	.20	.15	.08
24	Paul Assenmacher	.20	.15	.08
25	Robby Thompson	.30	.25	.12
26	Bobby Bonilla	.30	.25	.12
27	Andres Galarraga	.30	.25	.12
28	Billy Jo Robidoux	.20	.15	.08
29	Bruce Ruffin	.30	.25	.12
30	Greg Swindell	.40	.30	.15
31	John Cangelosi	.20	.15	.08
32	Jim Traber	.20	.15	.08
33	Russ Morman	.20	.15	.08
34	Barry Larkin	.60	.45	.25
35	Todd Worrell	.40	.30	.15
36	John Cerutti	.30	.25	.12

		MT	NR MT	EX
37	Mike Kingery	.20	.15	.08
38	Mark Eichhorn	.30	.25	.12
39	Scott Bankhead	.20	.15	.08
40	Bo Jackson	1.75	1.25	.70
41	Greg Mathews	.30	.25	.12
42	Eric King	.30	.25	.12
43	Kal Daniels	.40	.30	.15
44	Calvin Schiraldi	.20	.15	.08
45	Mickey Brantley	.20	.15	.08
46	Outstanding Rookie Seasons (Fred Lynn, Willie Mays, Pete Rose)	.80	.60	.30
47	Outstanding Rookie Seasons (Dwight Gooden, Tom Seaver, Fernando Valenzuela)	.80	.60	.30
48	Outstanding Rookie Seasons (Eddie Murray, Dave Righetti, Cal Ripken, Jr., Steve Sax, Darryl Strawberry, Lou Whitaker)	.60	.45	.25
49	Kevin Mitchell	.40	.30	.15
50	Mike Diaz	.30	.25	.12

1987 Sportflics

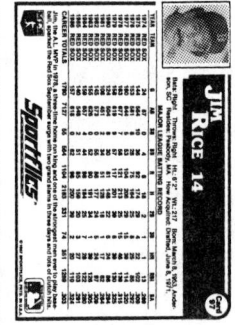

For its second season in the national baseball card market, Sportflics' basic issue was again a 200-card set of 2½'' by 3½'' ''Magic Motion'' cards, which offer three different photos on the same card, each visible in turn as the card is moved from top to bottom or side to side. Besides single-player cards, the '87 Sportflics set includes several three- and six-player cards, though not as many as in the 1986 set. Card backs feature a small player portrait photo on the single-player cards, an innovation for 1987.

		MT	NR MT	EX
Complete Set:		32.00	24.00	13.00
Common Player:		.10	.08	.04
1	Don Mattingly	3.00	2.25	1.25
2	Wade Boggs	1.75	1.25	.70
3	Dale Murphy	.70	.50	.30
4	Rickey Henderson	.60	.45	.25
5	George Brett	.70	.50	.30
6	Eddie Murray	.50	.40	.20
7	Kirby Puckett	.40	.30	.15
8	Ryne Sandberg	.35	.25	.14
9	Cal Ripken Jr.	.50	.40	.20
10	Roger Clemens	.80	.60	.30
11	Ted Higuera	.20	.15	.08
12	Steve Sax	.20	.15	.08
13	Chris Brown	.15	.11	.06
14	Jesse Barfield	.15	.11	.06
15	Kent Hrbek	.20	.15	.08
16	Robin Yount	.30	.25	.12
17	Glenn Davis	.30	.25	.12
18	Hubie Brooks	.10	.08	.04
19	Mike Scott	.15	.11	.06
20	Darryl Strawberry	.60	.45	.25
21	Alvin Davis	.15	.11	.06
22	Eric Davis	1.50	1.25	.60
23	Danny Tartabull	.40	.30	.15
24a	Cory Snyder (1986 copyright; Pat Tabler photo on back)	1.50	1.25	.60
24b	Cory Snyder (1987 copyright; Snyder photo on back)	1.00	.70	.40
25	Pete Rose	1.25	.90	.50

		MT	NR MT	EX
26	Wally Joyner	2.50	2.00	1.00
27	Pedro Guerrero	.20	.15	.08
28	Tom Seaver	.35	.25	.14
29	Bob Knepper	.10	.08	.04
30	Mike Schmidt	.60	.45	.25
31	Tony Gwynn	.50	.40	.20
32	Don Slaught	.10	.08	.04
33	Todd Worrell	.40	.30	.15
34	Tim Raines	.40	.30	.15
35	Dave Parker	.20	.15	.08
36	Bob Ojeda	.10	.08	.04
37	Pete Incaviglia	1.00	.70	.40
38	Bruce Hurst	.10	.08	.04
39	Bobby Witt	.35	.25	.14
40	Steve Garvey	.40	.30	.15
41	Dave Winfield	.40	.30	.15
42	Jose Cruz	.10	.08	.04
43	Orel Hershiser	.20	.15	.08
44	Reggie Jackson	.40	.30	.15
45	Chili Davis	.15	.11	.06
46	Robby Thompson	.35	.25	.14
47	Dennis Boyd	.10	.08	.04
48	Kirk Gibson	.25	.20	.10
49	Fred Lynn	.20	.15	.08
50	Gary Carter	.35	.25	.14
51	George Bell	.50	.40	.20
52	Pete O'Brien	.15	.11	.06
53	Ron Darling	.15	.11	.06
54	Paul Molitor	.15	.11	.06
55	Mike Pagliarulo	.20	.15	.08
56	Mike Boddicker	.10	.08	.04
57	Dave Righetti	.20	.15	.08
58	Len Dykstra	.25	.20	.10
59	Mike Witt	.15	.11	.06
60	Tony Bernazard	.10	.08	.04
61	John Kruk	.80	.60	.30
62	Mike Krukow	.10	.08	.04
63	Sid Fernandez	.15	.11	.06
64	Gary Gaetti	.20	.15	.08
65	Vince Coleman	.35	.25	.14
66	Pat Tabler	.10	.08	.04
67	Mike Scioscia	.10	.08	.04
68	Scott Garrelts	.10	.08	.04
69	Brett Butler	.10	.08	.04
70	Bill Buckner	.10	.08	.04
71a	Dennis Rasmussen (1986 copyright; John Montefusco photo on back)	.25	.20	.10
71b	Dennis Rasmussen (1987 copyright; Rasmussen photo on back)			
72	Tim Wallach	.15	.11	.06
73	Bob Horner	.20	.15	.08
74	Willie McGee	.15	.11	.06
75	American League First Basemen (Wally Joyner, Don Mattingly, Eddie Murray)	1.50	1.25	.60
76	Jesse Orosco	.10	.08	.04
77	National League Relief Pitchers (Jeff Reardon, Dave Smith, Todd Worrell)	.20	.15	.08
78	Candy Maldonado	.10	.08	.04
79	National League Shortstops (Hubie Brooks, Shawon Dunston, Ozzie Smith)	.15	.11	.06
80	American League Left Fielders (George Bell, Jose Canseco, Jim Rice)	1.25	.90	.50
81	Bert Blyleven	.15	.11	.06
82	Mike Marshall	.15	.11	.06
83	Ron Guidry	.20	.15	.08
84	Julio Franco	.10	.08	.04
85	Willie Wilson	.15	.11	.06
86	Lee Lacy	.10	.08	.04
87	Jack Morris	.20	.15	.08
88	Ray Knight	.10	.08	.04
89	Phil Bradley	.15	.11	.06
90	Jose Canseco	2.00	1.50	.80
91	Gary Ward	.10	.08	.04
92	Mike Easler	.10	.08	.04
93	Tony Pena	.10	.08	.04
94	Dave Smith	.10	.08	.04
95	Will Clark	1.50	1.25	.60
96	Lloyd Moseby	.10	.08	.04
97	Jim Rice	.40	.30	.15
98	Shawon Dunston	.10	.08	.04
99	Don Sutton	.25	.20	.10
100	Dwight Gooden	1.00	.70	.40
101	Lance Parrish	.20	.15	.08
102	Mark Langston	.15	.11	.06
103	Floyd Youmans	.25	.20	.10
104	Lee Smith	.10	.08	.04
105	Willie Hernandez	.10	.08	.04
106	Doug DeCinces	.10	.08	.04
107	Ken Schrom	.10	.08	.04

		MT	NR MT	EX
108	Don Carman	.15	.11	.06
109	Brook Jacoby	.15	.11	.06
110	Steve Bedrosian	.15	.11	.06
111	American League Pitchers (Roger Clemens, Teddy Higuera, Jack Morris)	.50	.40	.20
112	American League Second Basemen (Marty Barrett, Tony Bernazard, Lou Whitaker)	.15	.11	.06
113	American League Shortstops (Tony Fernandez, Scott Fletcher, Cal Ripken)	.25	.20	.10
114	American League Third Basemen (Wade Boggs, Geroge Brett, Gary Gaetti)	.70	.50	.30
115	National League Third Basemen (Chris Brown, Mike Schmidt, Tim Wallach)	.35	.25	.14
116	National League Second Basemen (Bill Doran, Johnny Ray, Ryne Sandberg)	.20	.15	.08
117	National League Right Fielders (Kevin Bass, Tony Gwynn, Dave Parker)	.25	.20	.10
118	Hot Rookie Prospects (David Clark, Pat Dodson, Ty Gainey, Phil Lombardi, Benito Santiago, Terry Steinbach)	1.25	.90	.50
119	1986 Season Highlights (Dave Righetti, Mike Scott, Fernando Valenzuela)	.15	.11	.06
120	National League Pitchers (Dwight Gooden, Mike Scott, Fernando Valenzuela)	.40	.30	.15
121	Johnny Ray	.10	.08	.04
122	Keith Moreland	.10	.08	.04
123	Juan Samuel	.15	.11	.06
124	Wally Backman	.10	.08	.04
125	Nolan Ryan	.30	.25	.12
126	Greg Harris	.10	.08	.04
127	Kirk McCaskill	.15	.11	.06
128	Dwight Evans	.15	.11	.06
129	Rick Rhoden	.10	.08	.04
130	Bill Madlock	.15	.11	.06
131	Oddibe McDowell	.15	.11	.06
132	Darrell Evans	.10	.08	.04
133	Keith Hernandez	.30	.25	.12
134	Tom Brunansky	.15	.11	.06
135	Kevin McReynolds	.15	.11	.06
136	Scott Fletcher	.10	.08	.04
137	Lou Whitaker	.20	.15	.08
138	Carney Lansford	.10	.08	.04
139	Andre Dawson	.25	.20	.10
140	Carlton Fisk	.20	.15	.08
141	Buddy Bell	.15	.11	.06
142	Ozzie Smith	.20	.15	.08
143	Dan Pasqua	.15	.11	.06
144	Kevin Mitchell	.60	.45	.25
145	Bret Saberhagen	.25	.20	.10
146	Charlie Kerfeld	.15	.11	.06
147	Phil Niekro	.25	.20	.10
148	John Candelaria	.10	.08	.04
149	Rich Gedman	.10	.08	.04
150	Fernando Valenzuela	.30	.25	.12
151	National League Catchers (Gary Carter, Tony Pena, Mike Scioscia)	.15	.11	.06
152	National League Left Fielders (Vince Coleman, Jose Cruz, Tim Raines)	.20	.15	.08
153	American League Right Fielders (Harold Baines, Jesse Barfield, Dave Winfield)	.25	.20	.10
154	American League Catchers (Rich Gedman, Lance Parrish, Don Slaught)	.15	.11	.06
155	National League Center Fielders (Eric Davis, Kevin McReynolds, Dale Murphy)	.80	.60	.30
156	1986 Season Highlights (Jim Deshaies, Mike Schmidt, Don Sutton)	.30	.25	.12
157	American League Speedburners (John Cangelosi, Rickey Henderson, Gary Pettis)	.25	.20	.10
158	Hot Rookie Prospects (Randy Asadoor, Casey Candaele, Dave Cochrane, Rafael Palmeiro, Tim Pyznarski, Kevin Seitzer)	2.50	2.00	1.00
159	The Best of the Best (Roger Clemens, Dwight Gooden, Rickey Henderson, Don Mattingly, Dale Murphy, Eddie Murray)	1.25	.90	.50
160	Roger McDowell	.15	.11	.06
161	Brian Downing	.10	.08	.04
162	Bill Doran	.15	.11	.06
163	Don Baylor	.15	.11	.06
164	Alfredo Griffin	.10	.08	.04
165	Don Aase	.10	.08	.04
166	Glenn Wilson	.10	.08	.04
167	Dan Quisenberry	.15	.11	.06
168	Frank White	.10	.08	.04
169	Cecil Cooper	.15	.11	.06

		MT	NR MT	EX
170	Jody Davis	.10	.08	.04
171	Harold Baines	.20	.15	.08
172	Rob Deer	.15	.11	.06
173	John Tudor	.15	.11	.06
174	Larry Parrish	.10	.08	.04
175	Kevin Bass	.10	.08	.04
176	Joe Carter	.15	.11	.06
177	Mitch Webster	.15	.11	.06
178	Dave Kingman	.15	.11	.06
179	Jim Presley	.15	.11	.06
180	Mel Hall	.10	.08	.04
181	Shane Rawley	.10	.08	.04
182	Marty Barrett	.10	.08	.04
183	Damaso Garcia	.10	.08	.04
184	Bobby Grich	.10	.08	.04
185	Leon Durham	.10	.08	.04
186	Ozzie Guillen	.15	.11	.06
187	Tony Fernandez	.15	.11	.06
188	Alan Trammell	.30	.25	.12
189	Jim Clancy	.10	.08	.04
190	Bo Jackson	1.75	1.25	.70
191	Bob Forsch	.10	.08	.04
192	John Franco	.10	.08	.04
193	Von Hayes	.15	.11	.06
194	American League Relief Pitchers (Don Aase, Mark Eichhorn, Dave Righetti)	.15	.11	.06
195	National League First Basemen (Will Clark, Glenn Davis, Keith Hernandez)	.50	.40	.20
196	1986 Season Highlights (Roger Clemens, Joe Cowley, Bob Horner)	.35	.25	.14
197	The Best of the Best (Wade Boggs, George Brett, Hubie Brooks, Tony Gwynn, Tim Raines, Ryne Sandberg)	.80	.60	.30
198	American League Center Fielders (Rickey Henderson, Fred Lynn, Kirby Puckett)	.25	.20	.10
199	National League Speedburners (Vince Coleman, Eric Davis, Tim Raines)	.70	.50	.30
200	Steve Carlton	.35	.25	.14

1987 Sportflics
Hot Rookie Prospects

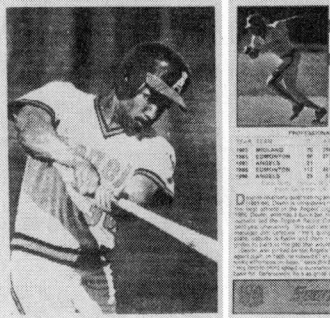

The 1987 Sportflics Rookie Prospects set consists of 10 cards that are the standard 2½" by 3½" size. The card fronts feature Sportflics' "Magic Motion" process. Card backs contain a player photo plus a short biography and player personal and statistical information. The set was offered in two separately wrapped mylar packs of five cards to hobby dealers purchasing cases of Sportflics' Team Preview set. Twenty-four packs of "Rookie Prospects" cards were included with each case.

		MT	NR MT	EX
Complete Set:		10.00	7.50	4.00
Common Player:		.50	.40	.20
1	Terry Steinbach	.75	.60	.30
2	Rafael Palmeiro	1.00	.70	.40
3	Dave Magadan	1.25	.90	.50
4	Marvin Freeman	.50	.40	.20
5	Brick Smith	.50	.40	.20
6	B.J. Surhoff	1.50	1.25	.60
7	John Smiley	.50	.40	.20
8	Alonzo Powell	.50	.40	.20
9	Benny Santiago	1.75	1.25	.70
10	Devon White	1.75	1.25	.70

1987 Sportflics Rookie Discs

The 1987 Sportflics Rookie Discs set consists of seven discs which measure 4" in diameter. The front of the discs offer three "Magic Motion" photos in full color, encompassed by a blue border. The disc backs are printed in red, blue, yellow and green and includes the team logo, player statistics, player biography and the disc number. The set was issued with Cooperstown Timeless Trivia Cards.

		MT	NR MT	EX
Complete Set:		15.00	11.00	6.00
Common Player:		.50	.40	.20
1	Casey Candaele	.50	.40	.20
2	Mark McGwire	2.50	2.00	1.00
3	Kevin Seitzer	2.00	1.50	.80
4	Joe Magrane	1.00	.70	.40
5	Benito Santiago	1.50	1.25	.60
6	Dave Magadan	1.25	1.25	.60
7	Devon White	1.50	1.25	.60

		MT	NR MT	EX
6	Casey Candaele	.20	.15	.08
7	Joey Cora	.20	.15	.08
8	Ken Gerhart	.40	.30	.15
9	Mike Greenwell	1.50	1.25	.60
10	Stan Jefferson	.30	.25	.12
11	Dave Magadan	.80	.60	.30
12	Joe Magrane	.50	.40	.20
13	Fred McGriff	.30	.25	.12
14	Mark McGwire	1.50	1.25	.60
15	Mark McLemore	.20	.15	.08
16	Jeff Musselman	.20	.15	.08
17	Matt Nokes	1.75	1.25	.70
18	Paul O'Neill	.20	.15	.08
19	Luis Polonia	.30	.25	.12
20	Benny Santiago	1.25	.90	.50
21	Kevin Seitzer	1.50	1.25	.60
22	Terry Steinbach	.30	.25	.12
23	B.J. Surhoff	.80	.60	.30
24	Devon White	1.25	.90	.50
25	Matt Williams	.40	.30	.15
26	DeWayne Buice	.20	.15	.08
27	Willie Fraser	.20	.15	.08
28	Bill Ripken	.40	.30	.15
29	Mike Henneman	.30	.25	.12
30	Shawn Hillegas	.30	.25	.12
31	Shane Mack	.30	.25	.12
32	Rafael Palmeiro	.60	.45	.25
33	Mike Jackson	.30	.25	.12
34	Gene Larkin	.20	.15	.08
35	Jimmy Jones	.20	.15	.08
36	Gerald Young	.40	.30	.15
37	Ken Caminiti	.40	.30	.15
38	Sam Horn	1.25	.90	.50
39	David Cone	.20	.15	.08
40	Mike Dunne	.50	.40	.20
41	Ken Williams	.30	.25	.12
42	John Morris	.20	.15	.08
43	Jim Lindeman	.40	.30	.15
44	Todd Benzinger	1.25	.90	.50
45	Mike Stanley	.30	.25	.12
46	Les Straker	.30	.25	.12
47	Jeff Robinson	.30	.25	.12
48	Jeff Blauser	.30	.25	.12
49	John Marzano	.80	.60	.30
50	Keith Miller	.50	.40	.20

1987 Sportflics Rookies

The 1987 Sportflics Rookies set was issued in two series of 25 cards. The first was released in July with the second series following in October. The cards, which are the standard 2½" by 3½", feature Sportflics' special Magic Motion process. The card fronts contain a full-color photo and present three different pictures, depending on how the card is held. The backs also contain a full-color photo along with player statistics and a biography.

		MT	NR MT	EX
Complete Set:		14.00	10.50	5.50
Common Player:		.20	.15	.08
1	Eric Bell	.20	.15	.08
2	Chris Bosio	.20	.15	.08
3	Bob Brower	.20	.15	.08
4	Jerry Browne	.20	.15	.08
5	Ellis Burks	2.00	1.50	.80

1987 Sportflics Superstar Discs

Released in three series of six discs and numbered 1 through 18, the 1987 Sportflics Superstar Disc set features the special "Magic Motion" process. Each disc, which measures 4½" in diameter, contains three different player photos, depending on which way it is tilted. A red border, containing eleven stars, the player's name and uniform number, surrounds the photo. The backs have a turquoise border which carries the words "Superstar Disc Collector Series." The backs also include the team logo, player statistics, player biography and the disc number. The discs were issued with eighteen 1¾" by 2½" Cooperstown Timeless Trivia Cards.

		MT	NR MT	EX
Complete Set:		35.00	26.00	14.00
Common Player:		1.00	.70	.40
1	Jose Canseco	3.00	2.25	1.25
2	Mike Scott	1.00	.70	.40
3	Ryne Sandberg	1.50	1.25	.60

		MT	NR MT	EX
4	Mike Schmidt	2.25	1.75	.90
5	Dale Murphy	2.25	1.75	.90
6	Fernando Valenzuela	1.50	1.25	.60
7	Tony Gwynn	2.00	1.50	.80
8	Cal Ripken	2.00	1.50	.80
9	Gary Carter	1.75	1.25	.70
10	Cory Snyder	1.75	1.25	.70
11	Kirby Puckett	1.75	1.25	.70
12	George Brett	2.25	1.75	.90
13	Keith Hernandez	1.50	1.25	.60
14	Rickey Henderson	2.00	1.50	.80
15	Tim Raines	1.75	1.25	.70
16	Bo Jackson	2.00	1.50	.80
17	Pete Rose	2.50	2.00	1.00
18	Eric Davis	3.00	2.25	1.25

1987 Sportflics Team Preview

 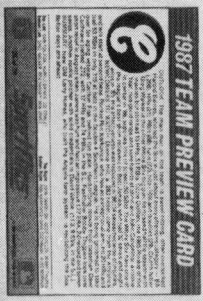

The 1987 Sportflics Team Preview set appeared to be a good idea, but never caught on with collectors. The intent of the set is to provide a pre-season look at each of the 26 major league clubs. The card backs contain three categories of the team preview — Outlook, Newcomers to Watch and Summary. Using the Magic Motion process, 12 different players are featured on the card fronts. Four of the different player photos can be made visible at once. The cards, which measure 2½'' by 3½,'' were issued with team logo/trivia cards in a specially designed box.

		MT	NR MT	EX
Complete Set:		10.00	7.50	4.00
Common Team:		.40	.30	.15
1	Texas Rangers (Scott Fletcher, Greg Harris, Charlie Hough, Pete Incaviglia, Mike Loynd, Oddibe McDowell, Pete O'Brien, Larry Parrish, Ruben Sierra, Don Slaught, Mitch Williams, Bobby Witt)	.50	.40	.20
2	New York Mets (Wally Backman, Gary Carter, Ron Darling, Lenny Dykstra, Sid Fernandez, Dwight Gooden, Keith Hernandez, Dave Magadan, Kevin McReynolds, Randy Myers, Bob Ojeda, Darryl Strawberry)	.70	.50	.30
3	Cleveland Indians (Tony Bernazard, Brett Butler, Tom Candiotti, Joe Carter, Julio Franco, Mel Hall, Brook Jacoby, Phil Niekro, Ken Schrom, Cory Snyder, Greg Swindell, Pat Tabler)	.50	.40	.20
4	Cincinnati Reds (Buddy Bell, Tom Browning, Kal Daniels, Eric Davis, John Franco, Bill Gullickson, Tracy Jones, Barry Larkin, Rob Murphy, Paul O'Neill, Dave Parker, Pete Rose)	.60	.45	.25
5	Toronto Blue Jays (Jesse Barfield, George Bell, John Cerutti, Mark Eichhorn, Tony Fernandez, Tom Henke, Glenallen Hill, Jimmy Key, Fred McGriff, Lloyd Moseby, Dave Stieb, Willie Upshaw)	.50	.40	.20
6	Philadelphia Phillies (Steve Bedrosian, Don Carman, Marvin Freeman, Kevin Gross, Von Hayes, Shane Rawley, Bruce Ruffin, Juan Samuel, Mike Schmidt, Kent Tekulve, Milt Thompson, Glenn Wilson)	.50	.40	.20

		MT	NR MT	EX
7	New York Yankees (Rickey Henderson, Phil Lombardi, Don Mattingly, Mike Pagliarulo, Dan Pasqua, Willie Randolph, Dennis Rasmussen, Rick Rhoden, Dave Righetti, Joel Skinner, Bob Tewksbury, Dave Winfield)	.70	.50	.30
8	Houston Astros (Kevin Bass, Jose Cruz, Glenn Davis, Jim Deshaies, Bill Doran, Ty Gainey, Charlie Kerfeld, Bob Knepper, Nolan Ryan, Mike Scott, Dave Smith, Robby Wine)	.40	.30	.15
9	Boston Red Sox (Marty Barrett, Don Baylor, Wade Boggs, Dennis Boyd, Roger Clemens, Pat Dodson, Dwight Evans, Mike Greenwell, Dave Henderson, Bruce Hurst, Jim Rice, Calvin Schiraldi)	.60	.45	.25
10	San Francisco Giants (Bob Brenly, Chris Brown, Will Clark, Chili Davis, Kelly Downs, Scott Garrelts, Mark Grant, Mike Krukow, Jeff Leonard, Candy Maldonado, Terry Mulholland, Robby Thompson)	.50	.40	.20
11	California Angels (John Candelaria, Doug DeCinces, Brian Downing, Ruppert Jones, Wally Joyner, Kirk McCaskill, Darrell Miller, Donnie Moore, Gary Pettis, Don Sutton, Devon White, Mike Witt)	.50	.40	.20
12	St. Louis Cardinals (Jack Clark, Vince Coleman, Danny Cox, Bob Forsch, Tom Herr, Joe Magrane, Willie McGee, Terry Pendleton, Ozzie Smith, John Tudor, Andy Van Slyke, Todd Worrell)	.60	.45	.25
13	Kansas City Royals (George Brett, Mark Gubicza, Bo Jackson, Charlie Leibrandt, Hal McRae, Dan Quisenberry, Bret Saberhagen, Kevin Seitzer, Lonnie Smith, Danny Tartabull, Frank White, Willie Wilson)	.50	.40	.20
14	Los Angeles Dodgers (Ralph Bryant, Mariano Duncan, Jose Gonzalez, Pedro Guerrero, Orel Hershiser, Mike Marshall, Steve Sax, Mike Scioscia, Franklin Stubbs, Fernando Valenzuela, Reggie Williams, Matt Young)	.50	.40	.20
15	Detroit Tigers (Darnell Coles, Darrell Evans, Kirk Gibson, Willie Hernandez, Eric King, Chet Lemon, Dwight Lowry, Jack Morris, Dan Petry, Frank Tanana, Alan Trammell, Lou Whitaker)	.60	.45	.25
16	San Diego Padres (Randy Asadoor, Steve Garvey, Tony Gwynn, Andy Hawkins, Jim Jones, John Kruk, Craig Lefferts, Shane Mack, Lance McCullers, Kevin Mitchell, Benny Santiago, Ed Wojna)	.50	.40	.20
17	Minnesota Twins (Bert Blyleven, Tom Brunansky, Gary Gaetti, Kent Hrbek, Joe Klink, Steve Lombardozzi, Kirby Puckett, Jeff Reardon, Mark Salas, Roy Smalley, Frank Viola)	.60	.45	.25
18	Pittsburgh Pirates (Barry Bonds, Bobby Bonilla, Sid Bream, Mike Diaz, Brian Fisher, Jim Morrison, Joe Orsulak, Bob Patterson, Tony Pena, Johnny Ray, R.J. Reynolds, John Smiley)	.50	.40	.20
19	Milwaukee Brewers (Glenn Braggs, Rob Deer, Teddy Higuera, Paul Molitor, Juan Nieves, Dan Plesac, Tim Pyznarski, Ernest Riles, Billy Jo Robidoux, B.J. Surhoff, Dale Sveum, Robin Yount)	.50	.40	.20
20	Montreal Expos (Hubie Brooks, Tim Burke, Casey Candaele, Dave Collins, Mike Fitzgerald, Andres Galarraga, Billy Moore, Alonzo Powell, Randy St. Claire, Tim Wallach, Mitch Webster, Floyd Youmans)	.50	.40	.20
21	Baltimore Orioles (Don Aase, Eric Bell, Mike Boddicker, Ken Gerhardt, Terry Kennedy, Ray Knight, Lee Lacy, Fred Lynn, Eddie Murray, Cal Ripken, Jr., Larry Sheets, Jim Traber)	.50	.40	.20
22	Chicago Cubs (Jody Davis, Shawon Dunston, Leon Durham, Dennis Eckersley, Greg Maddux, Dave Martinez, Keith Moreland, Jerry Mumphrey, Rafael Palmeiro, Ryne Sandberg, Scott Sanderson, Lee Smith)	.40	.30	.15
23	Oakland Athletics (Jose Canseco, Mike Davis, Alfredo Griffin, Reggie Jackson, Carney Lansford, Mark McGwire, Dwayne Murphy, Rob Nelson, Tony Phillips, Jose Rijo, Terry Steinbach, Curt Young)	.60	.45	.25
24	Atlanta Braves (Paul Assenmacher, Gene Garber, Tom Glavine, Ken Griffey, Glenn Hubbard, Dion James, Rick Mahler, Dale			

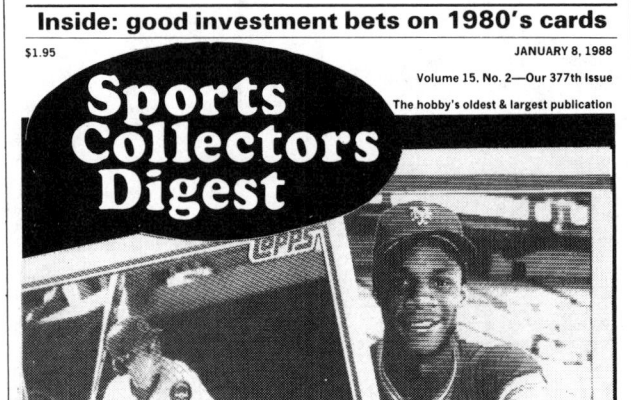

		MT	NR MT	EX
	Murphy, Ken Oberkfell, David Palmer, Zane Smith, Andres Thomas)	.50	.40	.20
25	Seattle Mariners (Scott Bankhead, Phil Bradley, Scott Bradley, Mickey Brantley, Alvin Davis, Steve Fireovid, Mark Langston, Mike Moore, Donell Nixon, Ken Phelps, Jim Presley, Dave Valle)	.50	.40	.20
26	Chicago White Sox (Harold Baines, John Cangelosi, Dave Cochrane, Joe Cowley, Carlton Fisk, Ozzie Guillen, Ron Hassey, Bob James, Ron Karkovice, Russ Mormon, Bobby Thigpen, Greg Walker)	.40	.30	.15

1988 Sportflics

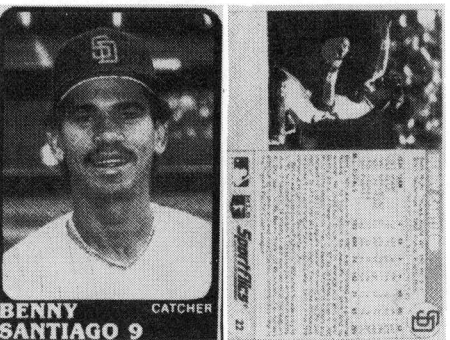

BENNY SANTIAGO 9 — CATCHER

The design of the 1988 Sportflics set differs greatly from the previous two years. Besides increasing the number of cards in the set to 225, Sportflics included the player name, team and uniform number on the card front. The triple-action color photos are surrounded by a red border. The backs are redesigned, also. Full-color action photos, plus extensive statistics and informative biographies are utilized. Three highlights cards and three rookie prospects cards are also included in the set. The cards are the standard 2½" by 3½".

		MT	NR MT	EX
	Complete Set:	30.00	22.00	12.00
	Common Player:	.10	.08	.04
1	Don Mattingly	3.00	2.25	1.25
2	Tim Raines	.35	.25	.14
3	Andre Dawson	.25	.20	.10
4	George Bell	.40	.30	.15
5	Joe Carter	.15	.11	.06
6	Matt Nokes	1.50	1.25	.60
7	Dave Winfield	.35	.25	.14
8	Kirby Puckett	.35	.25	.14
9	Will Clark	.60	.45	.25
10	Eric Davis	1.00	.70	.40
11	Rickey Henderson	.50	.40	.20
12	Ryne Sandberg	.25	.20	.10
13	Jesse Barfield	.15	.11	.06
14	Ozzie Guillen	.10	.08	.04
15	Bret Saberhagen	.20	.15	.08
16	Tony Gwynn	.40	.30	.15
17	Kevin Seitzer	1.25	.90	.50
18	Jack Clark	.15	.11	.06
19	Danny Tartabull	.30	.25	.12
20	Ted Higuera	.15	.11	.06
21	Charlie Leibrandt, Jr.	.10	.08	.04
22	Benny Santiago	.80	.60	.30
23	Fred Lynn	.15	.11	.06
24	Rob Thompson	.10	.08	.04
25	Alan Trammell	.25	.20	.10
26	Tony Fernandez	.15	.11	.06
27	Rick Sutcliffe	.15	.11	.06
28	Gary Carter	.30	.25	.12
29	Cory Snyder	.30	.25	.12
30	Lou Whitaker	.20	.15	.08
31	Keith Hernandez	.25	.20	.10
32	Mike Witt	.15	.11	.06
33	Harold Baines	.15	.11	.06
34	Robin Yount	.25	.20	.10

		MT	NR MT	EX
35	Mike Schmidt	.60	.45	.25
36	Dion James	.10	.08	.04
37	Tom Candiotti	.10	.08	.04
38	Tracy Jones	.20	.15	.08
39	Nolan Ryan	.25	.20	.10
40	Fernando Valenzuela	.25	.20	.10
41	Vance Law	.10	.08	04
42	Roger McDowell	.10	.08	.04
43	Carlton Fisk	.15	.11	.06
44	Scott Garrelts	.10	.08	.04
45	Lee Guetterman	.10	.08	.04
46	Mark Langston	.15	.11	.06
47	Willie Randolph	.10	.08	.04
48	Bill Doran	.10	.08	.04
49	Larry Parrish	.10	.08	.04
50	Wade Boggs	1.75	1.25	.70
51	Shane Rawley	.10	.08	.04
52	Alvin Davis	.10	.08	.04
53	Jeff Reardon	.15	.11	.06
54	Jim Presley	.10	.08	.04
55	Kevin Bass	.10	.08	.04
56	Kevin McReynolds	.10	.08	.04
57	B.J. Surhoff	.20	.15	.08
58	Julio Franco	.10	.08	.04
59	Eddie Murray	.40	.30	.15
60	Jody Davis	.10	.08	.04
61	Todd Worrell	.15	.11	.06
62	Von Hayes	.10	.08	.04
63	Billy Hatcher	.10	.08	.04
64	John Kruk	.25	.20	.10
65	Tom Henke	.10	.08	.04
66	Mike Scott	.15	.11	.06
67	Vince Coleman	.20	.15	.08
68	Ozzie Smith	.15	.11	.06
69	Ken Williams	.30	.25	.12
70	Steve Bedrosian	.15	.11	.06
71	Luis Polonia	.25	.20	.10
72	Brook Jacoby	.15	.11	.06
73	Ron Darling	.15	.11	.06
74	Lloyd Moseby	.10	.08	.04
75	Wally Joyner	.70	.50	.30
76	Dan Quisenberry	.15	.11	.06
77	Scott Fletcher	.10	.08	.04
78	Kirk McCaskill	.10	.08	.04
79	Paul Molitor	.15	.11	.06
80	Mike Aldrete	.15	.11	.06
81	Neal Heaton	.10	.08	.04
82	Jeffrey Leonard	.10	.08	.04
83	Dave Magadan	.20	.15	.08
84	Danny Cox	.10	.08	.04
85	Lance McCullers	.10	.08	.04
86	Jay Howell	.10	.08	.04
87	Charlie Hough	.10	.08	.04
88	Gene Garber	.10	.08	.04
89	Jesse Orosco	.10	.08	.04
90	Don Robinson	.10	.08	.04
91	Willie McGee	.15	.11	.06
92	Bert Blyleven	.15	.11	.06
93	Phil Bradley	.10	.08	.04
94	Terry Kennedy	.10	.08	.04
95	Kent Hrbek	.20	.15	.08
96	Juan Samuel	.15	.11	.06
97	Pedro Guerrero	.20	.15	.08
98	Sid Bream	.10	.08	.04
99	Devon White	.50	.40	.20
100	Mark McGwire	1.00	.70	.40
101	Dave Parker	.15	.11	.06
102	Glenn Davis	.15	.11	.06
103	Greg Walker	.10	.08	.04
104	Rick Rhoden	.10	.08	.04
105	Mitch Webster	.10	.08	.04
106	Lenny Dykstra	.10	.08	.04
107	Gene Larkin	.15	.11	.06
108	Floyd Youmans	.10	.08	.04
109	Andy Van Slyke	.10	.08	.04
110	Mike Scioscia	.10	.08	.04
111	Kirk Gibson	.25	.20	.10
112	Kal Daniels	.30	.25	.12
113	Ruben Sierra	.60	.45	.25
114	Sam Horn	1.25	.90	.50
115	Ray Knight	.10	.08	.04
116	Jimmy Key	.10	.08	.04
117	Bo Diaz	.10	.08	.04
118	Mike Greenwell	.60	.45	.25
119	Barry Bonds	.15	.11	.06
120	Reggie Jackson	.40	.30	.15
121	Mike Pagliarulo	.15	.11	.06
122	Tommy John	.20	.15	.08
123	Bill Madlock	.15	.11	.06
124	Ken Caminiti	.40	.30	.15
125	Gary Ward	.10	.08	.04

		MT	NR MT	EX
126	Candy Maldonado	.10	.08	.04
127	Harold Reynolds	.10	.08	.04
128	Joe Magrane	.30	.25	.12
129	Mike Henneman	.25	.20	.10
130	Jim Gantner	.10	.08	.04
131	Bobby Bonilla	.10	.08	.04
132	John Farrell	.35	.25	.14
133	Frank Tanana	.10	.08	.04
134	Zane Smith	.10	.08	.04
135	Dave Righetti	.20	.15	.08
136	Rick Reuschel	.10	.08	.04
137	Dwight Evans	.15	.11	.06
138	Howard Johnson	.10	.08	.04
139	Terry Leach	.10	.08	.04
140	Casey Candaele	.10	.08	.04
141	Tom Herr	.10	.08	.04
142	Tony Pena	.10	.08	.04
143	Lance Parrish	.20	.15	.08
144	Ellis Burks	1.75	1.25	.70
145	Pete O'Brien	.10	.08	.04
146	Mike Boddicker	.10	.08	.04
147	Buddy Bell	.10	.08	.04
148	Bo Jackson	.40	.30	.15
149	Frank White	.10	.08	.04
150	George Brett	.60	.45	.25
151	Tim Wallach	.10	.08	.04
152	Cal Ripken, Jr.	.40	.30	.15
153	Brett Butler	.10	.08	.04
154	Gary Gaetti	.15	.11	.06
155	Darryl Strawberry	.50	.40	.20
156	Alfredo Griffin	.10	.08	.04
157	Marty Barrett	.10	.08	.04
158	Jim Rice	.35	.25	.14
159	Terry Pendleton	.10	.08	.04
160	Orel Hershiser	.15	.11	.06
161	Larry Sheets	.10	.08	.04
162	Dave Stewart	.10	.08	.04
163	Shawon Dunston	.10	.08	.04
164	Keith Moreland	.10	.08	.04
165	Ken Oberkfell	.10	.08	.04
166	Ivan Calderon	.15	.11	.06
167	Bob Welch	.10	.08	.04
168	Fred McGriff	.15	.11	.06
169	Pete Incaviglia	.35	.25	.14
170	Dale Murphy	.60	.45	.25
171	Mike Dunne	.35	.25	.14
172	Chili Davis	.10	.08	.04
173	Milt Thompson	.10	.08	.04
174	Terry Steinbach	.15	.11	.06
175	Oddibe McDowell	.15	.11	.06
176	Jack Morris	.20	.15	.08
177	Sid Fernandez	.10	.08	.04
178	Ken Griffey	.10	.08	.04
179	Lee Smith	.10	.08	.04
180	1987 Highlights (Juan Nieves, Kirby Puckett, Mike Schmidt)	.25	.20	.10
181	Brian Downing	.10	.08	.04
182	Andres Galarraga	.15	.11	.06
183	Rob Deer	.10	.08	.04
184	Greg Brock	.10	.08	.04
185	Doug DeCinces	.10	.08	.04
186	Johnny Ray	.10	.08	.04
187	Hubie Brooks	.10	.08	.04
188	Darrell Evans	.10	.08	.04
189	Mel Hall	.10	.08	.04
190	Jim Deshaies	.10	.08	.04
191	Dan Plesac	.15	.11	.06
192	Willie Wilson	.15	.11	.06
193	Mike LaValliere	.10	.08	.04
194	Tom Brunansky	.15	.11	.06
195	John Franco	.10	.08	.04
196	Frank Viola	.15	.11	.06
197	Bruce Hurst	.10	.08	.04
198	John Tudor	.10	.08	.04
199	Bob Forsch	.10	.08	.04
200	Dwight Gooden	.60	.45	.25
201	Jose Canseco	.70	.50	.30
202	Carney Lansford	.10	.08	.04
203	Kelly Downs	.10	.08	.04
204	Glenn Wilson	.10	.08	.04
205	Pat Tabler	.10	.08	.04
206	Mike Davis	.10	.08	.04
207	Roger Clemens	.50	.40	.20
208	Dave Smith	.10	.08	.04
209	Curt Young	.10	.08	.04
210	Mark Eichhorn	.10	.08	.04
211	Juan Nieves	.10	.08	.04
212	Bob Boone	.10	.08	.04
213	Don Sutton	.20	.15	.08
214	Willie Upshaw	.10	.08	.04
215	Jim Clancy	.10	.08	.04

		MT	NR MT	EX
216	Bill Ripken	.40	.30	.15
217	Ozzie Virgil	.10	.08	.04
218	Dave Concepcion	.10	.08	.04
219	Alan Ashby	.10	.08	.04
220	Mike Marshall	.15	.11	.06
221	1987 Highlights (Vince Coleman, Mark McGwire, Paul Molitor)	.50	.40	.20
222	1987 Highlights (Steve Bedrosian, Don Mattingly, Benito Santiago)	.80	.60	.30
223	Hot Rookie Prospects (Shawn Abner, Jay Buhner, Gary Thurman)	.40	.30	.15
224	Hot Rookie Prospects (Tim Crews, John Davis, Vincente Palacios)	.40	.30	.15
225	Hot Rookie Prospects (Keith Miller, Jody Reed, Jeff Treadway)	.50	.40	.20

1981 Squirt

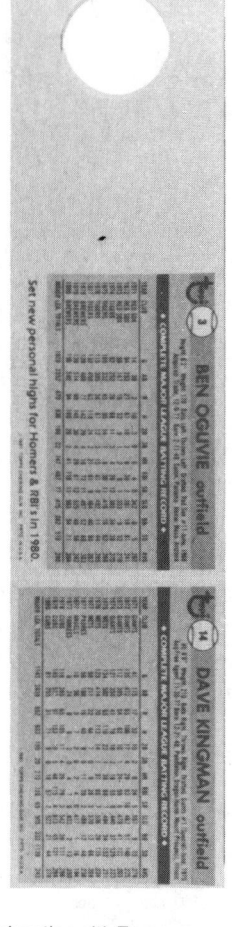

These cards, issued in conjunction with Topps, were issued as two-card panels in eight-pack cartons of the soft drink. Individual cards measure the standard 2½" by 3½," while the vertical panels measure 2½" by 10½," with a promotional card reading "FREE Topps 1981 Baseball Cards" attached. The promotional card is blank backed, while the player card backs are similar to Topps' regular issue, though re-numbered for inclusion in this 33-card set. Most of the game's top players are included. There are only 22 different two-card panels, as card numbers 1-11 appear in two different bottom panel combinations. Card fronts feature a color player portrait photo within a baseball design, team and position designations, and the Squirt logo.

		MT	NR MT	EX
Complete Panel Set:		16.00	12.00	6.50
Complete Singles Set:		7.00	5.25	2.75
Common Panel:		.30	.25	.12
Common Single Player:		.07	.05	.03
Panel 1		.80	.60	.30
1	George Brett	.30	.25	.12
12	Garry Templeton	.10	.08	.04
Panel 2		.80	.60	.30
1	George Brett	.30	.25	.12
23	Jerry Mumphrey	.10	.08	.04
Panel 3		.30	.25	.12
2	George Foster	.10	.08	.04
13	Rick Burleson	.10	.08	.04
Panel 4		.30	.25	.12
2	George Foster	.10	.08	.04
24	Tony Armas	.10	.08	.04
Panel 5		.30	.25	.12
3	Ben Oglivie	.07	.05	.03
14	Dave Kingman	.15	.11	.06
Panel 6		.35	.25	.14
3	Ben Oglivie	.07	.05	.03
25	Fred Lynn	.15	.11	.06
Panel 7		1.25	.90	.50
4	Steve Garvey	.20	.15	.08
15	Eddie Murray	.45	.35	.20
Panel 8		.60	.45	.25
4	Steve Garvey	.20	.15	.08
26	Ron LeFlore	.10	.08	.04
Panel 9		1.25	.90	.50
5	Reggie Jackson	.25	.20	.10
16	Don Sutton	.30	.25	.12
Panel 10		.90	.70	.35
5	Reggie Jackson	.25	.20	.10
27	Steve Kemp	.15	.11	.06
Panel 11		.20	.15	.08
6	Bill Buckner	.07	.05	.03
17	Dusty Baker	.10	.08	.04
Panel 12		.70	.50	.30
6	Bill Buckner	.07	.05	.03
28	Rickey Henderson	.45	.35	.20
Panel 13		.60	.45	.25
7	Jim Rice	.15	.11	.06
18	Jack Clark	.15	.11	.06
Panel 14		.50	.40	.20
7	Jim Rice	.15	.11	.06
29	John Castino	.10	.08	.04
Panel 15		1.25	.90	.50
8	Mike Schmidt	.25	.20	.10
19	Dave Winfield	.45	.35	.20
Panel 16		.80	.60	.30
8	Mike Schmidt	.25	.20	.10
30	Cecil Cooper	.20	.15	.08
Panel 17		1.25	.90	.50
9	Rod Carew	.20	.15	.08
20	Johnny Bench	.45	.35	.20
Panel 18		.80	.60	.30
9	Rod Carew	.20	.15	.08
31	Bruce Bochte	.10	.08	.04
Panel 19		.35	.25	.14
10	Dave Parker	.10	.08	.04
21	Lee Mazzilli	.10	.08	.04
Panel 20		.35	.25	.14
10	Dave Parker	.10	.08	.04
32	Joe Charboneau	.10	.08	.04
Panel 21		1.25	.90	.50
11	Pete Rose	.50	.40	.20
22	Al Oliver	.20	.15	.08
Panel 22		1.25	.90	.50
11	Pete Rose	.50	.40	.20
33	Chet Lemon	.10	.08	.04

of the positions on the three-card panels. Card backs are numbered and list player statistics.

		MT	NR MT	EX
Complete Set:		7.00	5.25	2.75
Common Player:		.15	.11	.06
1	Cecil Cooper	.25	.20	.10
2	Jerry Remy	.15	.11	.06
3	George Brett	.80	.60	.30
4	Alan Trammell	.35	.25	.14
5	Reggie Jackson	.60	.45	.25
6	Kirk Gibson	.35	.25	.14
7	Dave Winfield	.50	.40	.20
8	Carlton Fisk	.30	.25	.12
9	Ron Guidry	.30	.25	.12
10	Dennis Leonard	.15	.11	.06
11	Rollie Fingers	.30	.25	.12
12	Pete Rose	1.00	.70	.40
13	Phil Garner	.15	.11	.06
14	Mike Schmidt	80	.60	.30
15	Dave Concepcion	.20	.15	.08
16	George Hendrick	.15	.11	.06
17	Andre Dawson	.35	.25	.14
18	George Foster	.20	.15	.08
19	Gary Carter	.50	.40	.20
20	Fernando Valenzuela	.40	.30	.15
21	Tom Seaver	.50	.40	.20
22	Bruce Sutter	.25	.20	.10

1982 Squirt

This set was again prepared in conjunction with Topps, but in 1982 the Squirt cards are completely different from Topps' regular issue. Only 22 players are included in the full-color set, with the 2½'' by 3½'' player cards available on one- or two-player panels. Card panels come in four variations, with free grocery contest and scratch-off game cards taking one or two

1953 Stahl-Meyer Franks

These nine cards, issued in packages of hot dogs by a New York area meat company, featured three players from each of the New York teams of the day — Dodgers, Giants and Yankees — pictured on the 3¼'' by 4½'' cards. Card fronts in this unnumbered set feature color photos with player name and facsimile autograph. Card backs list both biographical and sta-

tistical information on half the card and a ticket offer promotion on the other half. Card corners are cut diagonally, although some cards (apparently cut from sheets) with square corners have been seen. Cards are white-bordered.

		NR MT	EX	VG
	Complete Set:	3200.00	1600.00	960.00
	Common Player:	100.00	50.00	30.00
(1)	Hank Bauer	125.00	62.00	37.00
(2)	Roy Campanella	450.00	225.00	135.00
(3)	Gil Hodges	200.00	100.00	60.00
(4)	Monte Irvin	150.00	75.00	45.00
(5)	Whitey Lockman	100.00	50.00	30.00
(6)	Mickey Mantle	1400.00	700.00	420.00
(7)	Phil Rizzuto	200.00	100.00	60.00
(8)	Duke Snider	400.00	200.00	120.00
(9)	Bobby Thompson	125.00	62.00	37.00

1954 Stahl-Meyer Franks

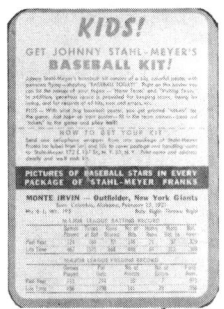

		NR MT	EX	VG
	Complete Set:	3800.00	1900.00	1140.
	Common Player:	100.00	50.00	30.00
(1)	Hank Bauer	125.00	62.00	37.00
(2)	Carl Erskine	125.00	62.00	37.00
(3)	Gil Hodges	200.00	100.00	60.00
(4)	Monte Irvin	150.00	75.00	45.00
(5)	Whitey Lockman	100.00	50.00	30.00
(6)	Gil McDougald	125.00	62.00	37.00
(7)	Mickey Mantle	1400.00	700.00	420.00
(8)	Willie Mays	750.00	375.00	225.00
(9)	Don Mueller	100.00	50.00	30.00
(10)	Don Newcombe	125.00	62.00	37.00
(11)	Phil Rizzuto	200.00	100.00	60.00
(12)	Duke Snider	400.00	200.00	120.00

1955 Stahl-Meyer Franks

Eleven of the 12 players in the 1955 set are the same as those featured in 1954. The exception is the New York Giants Dusty Rhodes, who replaced Willie Mays on the 3¼'' by 4½'' cards. Card fronts are again full-color photos bordered in yellow with diagonal cor-

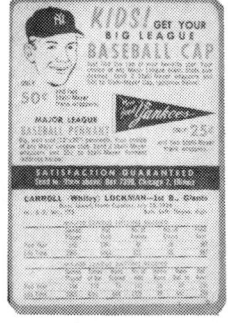

ners, and four players from each of the three New York teams are featured. Card backs offer a new promotion, with a drawing of Mickey Mantle and advertisements selling pennants and caps. Player statistics are still included on the vertical card backs, and they remain unnumbered.

		NR MT	EX	VG
	Complete Set:	3200.00	1600.00	960.00
	Common Player:	100.00	50.00	30.00
(1)	Hank Bauer	125.00	62.00	37.00
(2)	Carl Erskine	125.00	62.00	37.00
(3)	Gil Hodges	200.00	100.00	60.00
(4)	Monte Irvin	150.00	75.00	45.00
(5)	Whitey Lockman	100.00	50.00	30.00
(6)	Mickey Mantle	1400.00	700.00	420.00
(7)	Gil McDougald	125.00	62.00	37.00
(8)	Don Mueller	100.00	50.00	30.00
(9)	Don Newcombe	125.00	62.00	37.00
(10)	Jim Rhodes	100.00	50.00	30.00
(11)	Phil Rizzuto	200.00	100.00	60.00
(12)	Duke Snider	400.00	200.00	120.00

1983 Stuart Expos

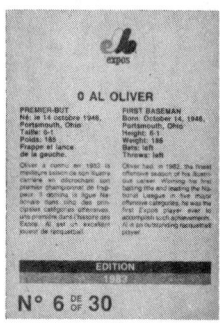

This set of Montreal Expos players and coaches was issued by a Montreal area baking company, for inclusion in packages of snack cakes. The 30 cards feature full-color player photos, with player name, number and team logo also on the card fronts. Card backs list brief player biographies, in both English and French. Twenty-five players, are pictured on the 2½'' by 3½'' cards.

		MT	NR MT	EX
	Complete Set:	8.00	6.00	3.25
	Common Player:	.20	.15	.08
1	Bill Virdon	.30	.25	.12
2	Woodie Fryman	.25	.20	.10
3	Vern Rapp	.20	.15	.08
4	Andre Dawson	.80	.60	.30
5	Jeff Reardon	.50	.40	.20
6	Al Oliver	.40	.30	.15
7	Doug Flynn	.20	.15	.08

		MT	NR MT	EX
8	Gary Carter	1.00	.70	.40
9	Tim Raines	1.50	1.25	.60
10	Steve Rogers	.30	.25	.12
11	Billy DeMars	.20	.15	.08
12	Tim Wallach	.50	.40	.20
13	Galen Cisco	.20	.15	.08
14	Terry Francona	.20	.15	.08
15	Bill Gullickson	.30	.25	.12
16	Ray Burris	.20	.15	.08
17	Scott Sanderson	.25	.20	.10
18	Warren Cromartie	.25	.20	.10
19	Jerry White	.20	.15	.08
20	Bobby Ramos	.20	.15	.08
21	Jim Wolhford	.20	.15	.08
22	Dan Schatzeder	.20	.15	.08
23	Charlie Lea	.25	.20	.10
24	Bryan Little	.20	.15	.08
25	Mel Wright	.20	.15	.08
26	Tim Blackwell	.20	.15	.08
27	Chris Speier	.20	.15	.08
28	Randy Lerch	.20	.15	.08
29	Bryn Smith	.30	.25	.12
30	Brad Mills	.20	.15	.08

		MT	NR MT	EX
27	Chris Speier	.40	.30	.15
28	Derrel Thomas	.40	.30	.15
29	Doug Flynn	.40	.30	.15
30	Bryan Little	.40	.30	.15
31	Argenis Salazar	.40	.30	.15
32	Mike Fuentes	.40	.30	.15
33	Joe Kerrigan	.40	.30	.15
34	Andy McGaffigan	.45	.35	.20
35	Fred Breining	.40	.30	.15
36	Expos 1983 All-Stars (Gary Carter, Andre Dawson, Tim Raines, Steve Rogers)	1.75	1.25	.70
37	Co-Players Of The Year (Andre Dawson, Tim Raines)	1.75	1.25	.70
38	Expos' Coaching Staff (Felipe Alou, Galen Cisco, Billy DeMars, Joe Kerrigan, Russ Nixon, Bill Virdon)	.40	.30	.15
39	Team Photo	.40	.30	.15
40	Checklist	.40	.30	.15

1987 Stuart

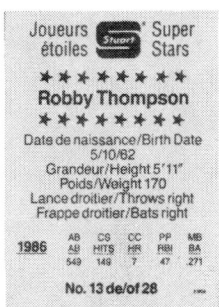

Twenty-eight four-part folding panels make up the 1987 Stuart Super Stars set, which was issued only in Canada. Three player cards and a sweepstakes entry form card comprise each panel. All 26 major league teams are included with the Montreal Expos and Toronto Blue Jays being represented twice. The cards, which are full color and measure 2½'' by 3½'', are written in both English and French. The card backs contain the player's previous year's statistics. All team insignias have been airbrushed away.

1984 Stuart Expos

For the second year in a row, Stuart Cakes issued a full-color card set of the Montreal Expos. The 2½'' by 3½'' cards again list player name and number along with team and company logos on the card fronts. Card backs are bilingual, with biographical information in both English and French. The 40-card set was issued in two series. Cards #21-40, issued late in the summer, are more difficult to find than the first 20 cards. The 40 cards include players, the manager, coaches and team mascot.

		MT	NR MT	EX
	Complete Set:	32.00	24.00	13.00
	Common Player: 1-20	.20	.15	.08
	Common Player: 21-40	.40	.30	.15
1	Youppi! (mascot)	.20	.15	.08
2	Bill Virdon	.40	.30	.15
3	Billy DeMars	.20	.15	.08
4	Galen Cisco	.20	.15	.08
5	Russ Nixon	.20	.15	.08
6	Felipe Alou	.25	.20	.10
7	Dan Schatzeder	.20	.15	.08
8	Charlie Lea	.30	.25	.12
9	Bobby Ramos	.20	.15	.08
10	Bob James	.40	.30	.15
11	Andre Dawson	1.00	.70	.40
12	Gary Lucas	.20	.15	.08
13	Jeff Reardon	.70	.50	.30
14	Tim Wallach	.70	.50	.30
15	Gary Carter	1.25	.90	.50
16	Bill Gullickson	.40	.30	.15
17	Pete Rose	2.25	1.75	.90
18	Terry Francona	.20	.15	.08
20	Tim Raines	1.50	1.25	.60
21	Bryn Smith	.60	.45	.25
22	Greg Harris	.40	.30	.15
23	David Palmer	.50	.40	.20
24	Jim Wolhford	.40	.30	.15
25	Miguel Dilone	.40	.30	.15
26	Mike Stenhouse	.40	.30	.15

		MT	NR MT	EX
	Complete Panel Set:	45.00	34.00	18.00
	Complete Singles Set:	18.00	13.50	7.25
	Common Panel:	1.25	.90	.50
	Common Single Player:	.10	.08	.04
	Panel (New York Mets)	4.00	3.00	1.50
1	Gary Carter, Keith Hernandez, Darryl Strawberry	.60	.45	.25
	Panel (Atlanta Braves)	2.25	1.75	.90
2	Bruce Benedict, Ken Griffey, Dale Murphy	.60	.45	.25
	Panel (Chicago Cubs)	1.75	1.25	.70
3	Jody Davis, Andre Dawson, Leon Durham	.20	.15	.08
	Panel (Cincinnati Reds)	3.25	2.50	1.25
4	Buddy Bell, Eric Davis, Dave Parker	.30	.25	.12
	Panel (Houston Astros)	2.25	1.75	.90
5	Glenn Davis, Nolan Ryan, Mike Scott	.25	.20	.10
	Panel (Los Angeles Dodgers)	2.25	1.75	.90
6	Pedro Guerrero, Mike Marshall, Fernando Valenzuela	.40	.30	.15
	Panel (Montreal Expos)	2.00	1.50	.80
7	Tim Raines, Tim Wallach, Mitch Webster	.15	.11	.06
	Panel (Montreal Expos)	1.25	.90	.50
8	Hubie Brooks, Bryn Smith, Floyd Youmans	.20	.15	.08
	Panel (Philadelphia Phillies)	2.50	2.00	1.00
9	Shane Rawley, Juan Samuel, Mike Schmidt	.60	.45	.25
	Panel (Pittsburgh Pirates)	1.25	.90	.50
10	Jim Morrison, Johnny Ray, R.J. Reynolds	.15	.11	.06

		MT	NR MT	EX
	Panel (St. Louis Cardinals)	2.00	1.50	.80
11	Jack Clark, Vince Coleman, Ozzie Smith			
		.25	.20	.10
	Panel (San Diego Padres)	3.25	2.50	1.25
12	Steve Garvey, Tony Gwynn, John Kruk			
		.40	.30	.15
	Panel (San Francisco Giants)	1.50	1.25	.60
13	Chili Davis, Jeffrey Leonard, Robbie Thompson			
		.20	.15	.08
	Panel (Baltimore Orioles)	3.25	2.50	1.25
14	Fred Lynn, Eddie Murray, Cal Ripken			
		.50	.40	.20
	Panel (Boston Red Sox)	4.00	3.00	1.50
15	Don Baylor, Wade Boggs, Roger Clemens			
		.60	.45	.25
	Panel	3.00	2.25	1.25
16	Doug DeCinces, Wally Joyner, Mike Witt			
		.20	.15	.08
	Panel (Chicago White Sox)	2.00	1.50	.80
17	Harold Baines, Carlton Fisk, Ozzie Guillen			
		.20	.15	.08
	Panel (Cleveland Indians)	1.75	1.25	.70
18	Joe Carter, Julio Franco, Pat Tabler			
		.20	.15	.08
	Panel (Detroit Tigers)	2.75	2.00	1.00
19	Kirk Gibson, Jack Morris, Alan Trammell			
		.40	.30	.15
	Panel (Kansas City Royals)	2.75	2.00	1.00
20	George Brett, Bret Saberhagen, Willie Wilson			
		.20	.15	.08
	Panel (Milwaukee Brewers)	2.25	1.75	.90
21	Cecil Cooper, Paul Molitor, Robin Yount			
		.40	.30	.15
	Panel (Minnesota Twins)	2.50	2.00	1.00
22	Tom Brunansky, Kent Hrbek, Kirby Puckett			
		.50	.40	.20
	Panel (New York Yankees)	5.00	3.75	2.00
23	Rickey Henderson, Don Mattingly, Dave Winfield			
		.50	.40	.20
	Panel (Oakland A's)	2.50	2.00	1.00
24	Jose Canseco, Alfredo Griffin, Carney Lansford			
		.10	.08	.04
	Panel 25 (Seattle Mariners)	1.50	1.25	.60
25	Phil Bradley, Alvin Davis, Mark Langston			
		.20	.15	.08
	Panel (Texas Rangers)	2.00	1.50	.80
26	Pete Incaviglia, Pete O'Brien, Larry Parrish			
		.15	.11	.06
	Panel (Toronto Blue Jays)	2.50	2.00	1.00
27	Jesse Barfield, George Bell, Tony Fernandez			
		.25	.20	.10
	Panel (Toronto Blue Jays)	1.25	.90	.50
28	Lloyd Moseby, Dave Stieb, Ernie Whitt			
		.10	.08	.04

The Sugardale Meats set of black-and-white cards measures 5⅛'' by 3¾.'' The 22-card set includes 18 Cleveland Indians and four Pittsburgh Pirates. Indians cards are numbered from 1-19 with card #6 not issued. Pirates cards are lettered from A to D. Card fronts contain a relatively small player photo, with biographical information and Sugardale logo. Card backs are printed in red and offer playing tips and another company logo. Card #10 (Bob Nieman) is considerably more scarce than other cards in the set.

		NR MT	EX	VG
	Complete Set:	1000.00	500.00	300.00
	Common Player:	40.00	20.00	12.00
A	Dick Groat	65.00	32.00	19.50
B	Roberto Clemente	350.00	175.00	105.00
C	Don Hoak	50.00	25.00	15.00
D	Dick Stuart	50.00	25.00	15.00
1	Barry Latman	40.00	20.00	12.00
2	Gary Bell	45.00	22.00	13.50
3	Dick Donovan	40.00	20.00	12.00
4	Frank Funk	40.00	20.00	12.00
5	Jim Perry	55.00	27.00	16.50
6	Not issued			
7	Johnny Romano	40.00	20.00	12.00
8	Ty Cline	40.00	20.00	12.00
9	Tito Francona	45.00	22.00	13.50
10	Bob Nieman	200.00	100.00	60.00
11	Willie Kirkland	40.00	20.00	12.00
12	Woodie Held	45.00	22.00	13.50
13	Jerry Kindall	40.00	20.00	12.00
14	Bubba Phillips	40.00	20.00	12.00
15	Mel Harder	45.00	22.00	13.50
16	Salty Parker	40.00	20.00	12.00
17	Ray Katt	40.00	20.00	12.00
18	Mel McGaha	40.00	20.00	12.00
19	Pedro Ramos	40.00	20.00	12.00

1963 Sugardale Weiners

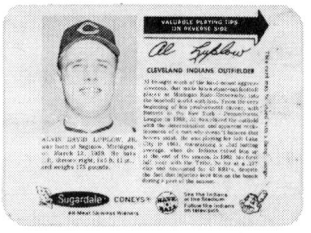

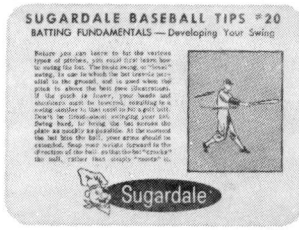

1962 Sugardale Weiners

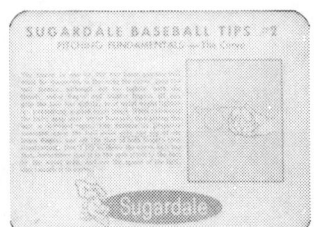

Sugardale Meats again featured Cleveland and Pittsburgh players in its '63 set, which grew to 31 cards. The black and white cards again measured 5⅛'' by 3¾,'' and consisted of 28 Indians and five Pirates. Card formats are virtually identical to the 1962 cards, with the only real difference being the information included in the player biographies. Cards are numbered 1-38, with cards #6, 29-32 not issued. Cards for Bob Skinner (#35) and Jim Perry (#5) are scarce, as these two players were traded during the season and their cards withdrawn from distribution. The red card backs again offer playing tips.

		NR MT	EX	VG
	Complete Set:	1300.00	650.00	390.00
A	Don Cardwell	40.00	20.00	12.00
B	Robert R. Skinner	110.00	55.00	33.00
C	Donald B. Schwall	40.00	20.00	12.00
D	Jim Pagliaroni	40.00	20.00	12.00
E	Dick Schofield	45.00	22.00	13.50
1	Barry Latman	40.00	20.00	12.00
2	Gary Bell	45.00	22.00	13.50
3	Dick Donovan	40.00	20.00	12.00
4	Joe Adcock	60.00	30.00	18.00
5	Jim Perry	120.00	60.00	36.00
6	Not issued			
7	Johnny Romano	40.00	20.00	12.00
8	Mike De La Hoz	40.00	20.00	12.00
9	Tito Francona	45.00	22.00	13.50
10	Gene Green	40.00	20.00	12.00
11	Willie Kirkland	40.00	20.00	12.00
12	Woodie Held	45.00	22.00	13.50
13	Jerry Kindall	40.00	20.00	12.00
14	Max Alvis	45.00	22.00	13.50
15	Mel Harder	45.00	22.00	13.50
16	George Strickland	40.00	20.00	12.00
17	Elmer Valo	40.00	20.00	12.00
18	Birdie Tebbetts	45.00	22.00	13.50
19	Pedro Ramos	40.00	20.00	12.00
20	Al Luplow	40.00	20.00	12.00
21	Not issued			
22	Not issued			
23	Jim Grant	45.00	22.00	13.50
24	Victor Davalillo	45.00	22.00	13.50
25	Jerry Walker	40.00	20.00	12.00
26	Sam McDowell	60.00	30.00	18.00
27	Fred Whitfield	40.00	20.00	12.00
28	Jack Kralick	40.00	20.00	12.00
29	Not issued			
30	Not issued			
31	Not issued			
32	Not issued			
33	Bob Allen	40.00	20.00	12.00

1911 T3 Turkey Reds

Turkey Reds are the only cabinet cards the average collector can have a realistic chance to complete. Obtained by mailing in coupons found in Turkey Red, Fez and Old Mill brand cigarettes, the Turkey Reds measure 5¾'' by 8,'' a size known to collectors as ''cabinet cards.'' Turkey Reds feature full color lithograph fronts with wide gray frames. Backs carried either a numbered ordering list or an ad for Turkey Red cigarettes. The Turkey Red series consists of 25 boxers and 100 baseball players. Despite their cost, Turkey Reds remain very popular today as the most attractive of the old cabinet sets.

		NR MT	EX	VG
	Complete Set:	20000.00	10000.	6000.
	Common Player: 1-50	125.00	62.00	37.00
	Common Player: 77-126	150.00	75.00	45.00
1	Mordecai Brown	225.00	112.00	67.00
2	Bill Bergen	125.00	62.00	37.00
3	Tommy Leach	125.00	62.00	37.00
4	Roger Bresnahan	225.00	112.00	67.00
5	Sam Crawford	225.00	112.00	67.00
6	Hal Chase	150.00	75.00	45.00
7	Howie Camnitz	125.00	62.00	37.00
8	Fred Clarke	225.00	112.00	67.00
9	Ty Cobb	2800.00	1000.00	400.00
10	Art Devlin	125.00	62.00	37.00
11	Bill Dahlen	125.00	62.00	37.00
12	Wil Bill Donovan	125.00	62.00	37.00
13	Larry Doyle	125.00	62.00	37.00
14	Red Dooin	125.00	62.00	37.00
15	Kid Elberfeld	125.00	62.00	37.00
16	Johnny Evers	225.00	112.00	67.00
17	Clark Griffith	225.00	112.00	67.00
18	Hughie Jennings	225.00	112.00	67.00
19	Addie Joss	250.00	125.00	75.00
20	Tim Jordan	125.00	62.00	37.00
21	Red Kleinow	125.00	62.00	37.00
22	Harry Krause	125.00	62.00	37.00
23	Nap Lajoie	450.00	225.00	135.00
24	Mike Mitchell	125.00	62.00	37.00
25	Matty McIntyre	125.00	62.00	37.00
26	John McGraw	300.00	150.00	90.00
27	Christy Mathewson	600.00	300.00	180.00
28a	Harry McIntyre (Brooklyn)	125.00	62.00	37.00
28b	Harry McIntyre (Brooklyn and Chicago)			
		225.00	112.00	67.00
29	Amby McConnell	125.00	62.00	37.00
30	George Mullin	125.00	62.00	37.00
31	Sherry Magee	125.00	62.00	37.00
32	Orval Overall	125.00	62.00	37.00
33	Jake Pfeister	125.00	62.00	37.00
34	Nap Rucker	125.00	62.00	37.00
35	Joe Tinker	225.00	112.00	67.00
36	Tris Speaker	450.00	225.00	135.00
37	Slim Sallee	125.00	62.00	37.00
38	Jake Stahl	125.00	62.00	37.00
39	Rube Waddell	225.00	112.00	67.00
40a	Vic Willis (Pittsburg)	125.00	62.00	37.00
40b	Vic Willis (Pittsburg and St. Louis)			
		225.00	112.00	67.00
41	Hooks Wiltse	125.00	62.00	37.00
42	Cy Young	500.00	250.00	150.00
43	Out At Third	150.00	75.00	45.00
44	Trying To Catch Him Napping	150.00	75.00	45.00
45	Jordan & Herzog At First	150.00	75.00	45.00
46	Safe At Third	150.00	75.00	45.00
47	Frank Chance At Bat	250.00	125.00	75.00
48	Jack Murray At Bat	150.00	75.00	45.00
49	A Close Play At Second	150.00	75.00	45.00
50	Chief Myers At Bat	150.00	75.00	45.00
51	Jem Driscoll	125.00	62.00	37.00
52	Abe Attell	125.00	62.00	37.00
53	Ad Wolgast	125.00	62.00	37.00
54	Johnny Coulon	125.00	62.00	37.00
55	James Jeffries	125.00	62.00	37.00
56	"Twin" (Jack Sullivan)	125.00	62.00	37.00
57	Battling Nelson	125.00	62.00	37.00
58	Packey Mc Farland	125.00	62.00	37.00
59	Tommy Murphy	125.00	62.00	37.00
60	Owen Moran	125.00	62.00	37.00
61	Johnny Marto	125.00	62.00	37.00
62	Jimmie Gardner	125.00	62.00	37.00
63	Harry Lewis	125.00	62.00	37.00
64	Wm Papke	125.00	62.00	37.00
65	Sam Langford	125.00	62.00	37.00
66	Knock-Out Brown	125.00	62.00	37.00
67	Stanley Ketchel	125.00	62.00	37.00
68	Joe Jeannette	125.00	62.00	37.00
69	Leach Cross	125.00	62.00	37.00
70	Phil Mc Govern	125.00	62.00	37.00
71	Battling Hurley	125.00	62.00	37.00
72	Honey Mellody	125.00	62.00	37.00
73	Al Kaufman	125.00	62.00	37.00
74	Willie Lewis	125.00	62.00	37.00
75	"Philadelphia" (Jack O'Brien)	125.00	62.00	37.00
76	Jack Johnson	125.00	62.00	37.00
77	Red Ames	150.00	75.00	45.00
78	Home Run Baker	250.00	125.00	75.00
79	George Bell	150.00	75.00	45.00
80	Chief Bender	250.00	125.00	75.00
81	Bob Bescher	150.00	75.00	45.00
82	Kitty Bransfield	150.00	75.00	45.00
83	Al Bridwell	150.00	75.00	45.00

		NR MT	EX	VG
84	George Browne	150.00	75.00	45.00
85	Bill Burns	150.00	75.00	45.00
86	Bill Carrigan	150.00	75.00	45.00
87	Eddie Collins	275.00	137.00	82.00
88	Harry Coveleski	150.00	75.00	45.00
89	Lou Criger	150.00	75.00	45.00
90a	Mickey Doolin (name incorrect)	275.00	137.00	82.00
90b	Mickey Doolan (name correct)	150.00	75.00	45.00
91	Tom Downey	150.00	75.00	45.00
92	Jimmy Dygert	150.00	75.00	45.00
93	Art Fromme	150.00	75.00	45.00
94	George Gibson	150.00	75.00	45.00
95	Peaches Graham	150.00	75.00	45.00
96	Bob Groom	150.00	75.00	45.00
97	Dick Hoblitzell	150.00	75.00	45.00
98	Solly Hofman	150.00	75.00	45.00
99	Walter Johnson	800.00	400.00	240.00
100	Davy Jones	150.00	75.00	45.00
101	Wee Willie Keeler	325.00	162.00	97.00
102	Johnny Kling	150.00	75.00	45.00
103	Ed Konetchy	150.00	75.00	45.00
104	Ed Lennox	150.00	75.00	45.00
105	Hans Lobert	150.00	75.00	45.00
106	Harry Lord	150.00	75.00	45.00
107	Rube Manning	150.00	75.00	45.00
108	Fred Merkle	150.00	75.00	45.00
109	Pat Moran	150.00	75.00	45.00
110	George McBride	150.00	75.00	45.00
111	Harry Niles	150.00	75.00	45.00
112a	Dode Paskert (Cincinnati)	275.00	137.00	82.00
112b	Dode Paskert (Cincinnati and Philadelphia)	150.00	75.00	45.00
113	Bugs Raymond	150.00	75.00	45.00
114	Bob Rhoades (Rhoads)	300.00	150.00	90.00
115	Admiral Schlei	150.00	75.00	45.00
116	Boss Schmidt	150.00	75.00	45.00
117	Wildfire Schulte	150.00	75.00	45.00
118	Frank Smith	150.00	75.00	45.00
119	George Stone	150.00	75.00	45.00
120	Gabby Street	150.00	75.00	45.00
121	Billy Sullivan	150.00	75.00	45.00
122a	Fred Tenney (New York)	275.00	137.00	82.00
122b	Fred Tenney (New York and Boston)	150.00	75.00	45.00
123	Ira Thomas	150.00	75.00	45.00
124	Bobby Wallace	275.00	137.00	82.00
125	Ed Walsh	300.00	150.00	90.00
126	Owen Wilson	150.00	75.00	45.00

1913 T200 Fatima Team Cards

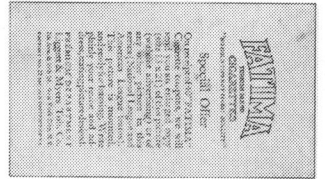

Issued by the Ligget & Myers Tobacco Co. in 1913 with Fatima brand cigarettes, the T200 set consists of eight National and eight American League team cards. The cards measure 2⅝'' by 4¾'' and are glossy photographs on paper stock. Although it is unknown why, several of the cards are more difficult to obtain than others. The team cards feature 369 different players, managers and mascots. The card backs contain an offer for an enlarged copy (13'' by 21'') of a team card, minus the advertising on front, in exchange for 40 Fatima cigarette coupons. These large T200 premiums are very rare and have a value of 12-15 times greater than a common T200 card.

		NR MT	EX	VG
Complete Set:		2000.00	1000.00	600.00
Common Team:		80.00	37.00	22.00
(1)	Boston Nationals	125.00	62.00	37.00
(2)	Brooklyn Nationals	80.00	37.00	22.00
(3)	Chicago Nationals	80.00	37.00	22.00
(4)	Cincinnati Nationals	80.00	37.00	22.00
(5)	New York Nationals	100.00	37.00	22.00
(6)	Philadelphia Nationals	80.00	37.00	22.00
(7)	Pittsburgh Nationals	80.00	37.00	22.00
(8)	St. Louis Nationals	125.00	62.00	37.00
(9)	Boston Americans	80.00	37.00	22.00
(10)	Chicago Americans	80.00	37.00	22.00
(11)	Cleveland Americans	80.00	37.00	22.00
(12)	Detroit Americans	175.00	87.00	52.00
(13)	New York Americans	250.00	125.00	75.00
(14)	Philadelphia Americans	80.00	37.00	22.00
(15)	St. Louis Americans	225.00	112.00	67.00
(16)	Washington Americans	80.00	37.00	22.00

1911 T201
Mecca Double Folders

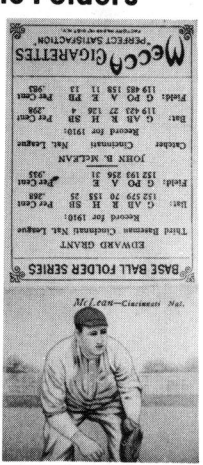

These cards found in packages of Mecca cigarettes featured one player when the card was open, and another when the card was folded; two players sharing the same pair of legs. Mecca Double Folders measured 2-1/4'' by 4-11/16.'' The fronts were color litographs with the player's name appearing in black script in the upper left. Backs were printed in red and contained an innovation in the form of player statistics. The 50-card set contains 100 different players including a number of Hall of Famers. Relatively inexpensive today, Mecca Double Folders with two players (Topps ''borrowed'' the idea in 1955) and statistics were one of the most innovative series of the tobacco card era.

		NR MT	EX	VG
Complete Set:		2600.00	1300.00	780.00
Common Player:		25.00	12.50	7.50
(1)	Abstein, Butler	25.00	12.50	7.50
(2)	Baker, Collins	80.00	40.00	24.00
(3)	Baker, Downie (Downey)	25.00	12.50	7.50
(4)	Barrett, McGlynn	25.00	12.50	7.50
(5)	Barry, Lapp	25.00	12.50	7.50
(6)	Bender, Oldring	50.00	25.00	15.00
(7)	Bergen, Wheat	50.00	25.00	15.00
(8)	Blair, Hartzell	30.00	15.00	9.00
(9)	Bresnahan, Huggins	80.00	40.00	24.00
(10)	Bridwell, Matthewson (Mathewson)	125.00	62.00	37.00
(11)	Brown, Hofman	50.00	25.00	15.00
(12)	Byrne, Clarke	40.00	20.00	12.00

		NR MT	EX	VG
(13)	Chance, Evers	100.00	50.00	30.00
(14)	Chase, Sweeney	35.00	17.50	10.50
(15)	Cicotte, Thoney	30.00	15.00	9.00
(16)	Clarke, Gaspar	25.00	12.50	7.50
(17)	Cobb, Crawford	400.00	200.00	120.00
(18)	Cole, Kling	25.00	12.50	7.50
(19)	Coombs, Thomas	25.00	12.50	7.50
(20)	Daubert, Rucker	35.00	17.50	10.50
(21)	Donovan, Stroud	25.00	12.50	7.50
(22)	Dooin, Titus	25.00	12.50	7.50
(23)	Dougherty, Lord	250.00	125.00	75.00
(24)	Downs, Odwell	25.00	12.50	7.50
(25)	Doyle, Meyers	30.00	15.00	9.00
(26)	Dygert, Seymour	25.00	12.50	7.50
(27)	Elberfeld, McBride	25.00	12.50	7.50
(28)	Falkenberg, Lajoie	80.00	40.00	24.00
(29)	Fitzpatrick, Killian	25.00	12.50	7.50
(30)	Ford, Johnson	30.00	15.00	9.00
(31)	Foster, Ward	25.00	12.50	7.50
(32)	Gardner, Speaker	80.00	40.00	24.00
(33)	Gibson, Leach	25.00	12.50	7.50
(34)	Graham, Mattern	25.00	12.50	7.50
(35)	Grant, McLean	25.00	12.50	7.50
(36)	Hauser, Lush	25.00	12.50	7.50
(37)	Herzog, Miller	25.00	12.50	7.50
(38)	Hickman, Hinchman	25.00	12.50	7.50
(39)	Jennings, Summers	50.00	25.00	15.00
(40)	Johnson, Street	175.00	87.00	52.00
(41)	LaPorte, Stephens	25.00	12.50	7.50
(42)	Lake, Wallace	40.00	20.00	12.00
(43)	Leifield, Simon	25.00	12.50	7.50
(44)	Lobert, Moore	25.00	12.50	7.50
(45)	McCabe, Starr	25.00	12.50	7.50
(46)	McCarty, McGinnity	50.00	25.00	15.00
(47)	Merkle, Wiltse	30.00	15.00	9.00
(48)	Payne, Walsh	50.00	25.00	15.00
(49)	Stovall, Turner	25.00	12.50	7.50
(50)	Williams, Woodruff	25.00	12.50	7.50

1912 T202 Hassan Triple Folders

Measuring 5½'' by 2¼'', Hassan cigarette cards carried the concept of multiple-player cards even further than the innovative Mecca set of the previous year. Scored so that the two end cards — which are full color and very close to exact duplicates of T-205 "Gold Borders" — can fold over the black and white center panel, the Hassan Triple Folder appears like a booklet when closed. The two end cards are individual player cards, while the larger center panel contains an action scene. Usually the two player cards are not related to the action scene. The unique Hassan Triple Folders feature player biographies on the back of the two individual cards with a description of the action on the back of the center panel. Values depend on the player featured in the center panel, as well as the players featured on the end cards.

	NR MT	EX	VG
Complete Set of 132:	14000.00	7000.00	4200.
Common Player:	60.00	30.00	18.00

		NR MT	EX	VG
(1a)	A Close Play At The Home Plate (LaPorte, Wallace)	80.00	40.00	24.00
(1b)	A Close Play At The Home Plate (Pelty, Wallace)	80.00	40.00	24.00

		NR MT	EX	VG
(2)	A Desperate Slide For Third (Ty Cobb, O'Leary)	600.00	300.00	180.00
(3a)	A Great Batsman (Barger, Bergen)	60.00	30.00	18.00
(3b)	A Great Batsman (Bergen, Rucker)	60.00	30.00	18.00
(4)	Ambrose McConnell At Bat (Blair, Quinn)	60.00	30.00	18.00
(5)	A Wide Throw Saves Crawford (Mullin, Stanage)	60.00	30.00	18.00
(6)	Baker Gets His Man (Baker, Collins)	150.00	75.00	45.00
(7)	Birmingham Gets To Third (Johnson, Street)	175.00	87.00	52.00
(8)	Birmingham's Home Run (Birmingham, Turner)	275.00	137.00	82.00
(9)	Bush Just Misses Austin (Magee, Moran)	60.00	30.00	18.00
(10a)	Carrigan Blocks His Man (Gaspar, McLean)	60.00	30.00	18.00
(10b)	Carrigan Blocks His Man (Carrigan, Wagner)	60.00	30.00	18.00
(11)	Catching Him Napping (Bresnahan, Oakes)	80.00	40.00	24.00
(12)	Caught Asleep Off First (Bresnahan, Harmon)	80.00	40.00	24.00
(13a)	Chance Beats Out A Hit (Chance, Foxen)	100.00	50.00	30.00
(13b)	Chance Beats Out A Hit (Archer, McIntyre)	75.00	37.00	22.00
(13c)	Chance Beats Out A Hit (Archer, Overall)	75.00	37.00	22.00
(13d)	Chance Beats Out A Hit (Archer, Rowan)	75.00	37.00	22.00
(13e)	Chance Beats Out A Hit (Chance, Shean)	100.00	50.00	30.00
(14a)	Chase Dives Into Third (Chase, Wolter)	70.00	35.00	21.00
(14b)	Chase Dives Into Third (Clarke, Gibson)	80.00	40.00	24.00
(14c)	Chase Dives Into Third (Gibson, Phillippe)	60.00	30.00	18.00
(15a)	Chase Gets Ball Too Late (Egan, Mitchell)	60.00	30.00	18.00
(15b)	Chase Gets Ball Too Late (Chase, Wolter)	70.00	35.00	21.00
(16a)	Chase Guarding First (Chase, Wolter)	70.00	35.00	21.00
(16b)	Chase Guarding First (Clarke, Gibson)	80.00	40.00	24.00
(16c)	Chase Guarding First (Gibson, Leifield)	60.00	30.00	18.00
(17)	Chase Ready For The Squeeze Play (Magee, Paskert)	60.00	30.00	18.00
(18)	Chase Safe At Third (Baker, Barry)	80.00	40.00	24.00
(19)	Chief Bender Waiting For A Good One (Bender, Thomas)	80.00	40.00	24.00
(20)	Clarke Hikes For Home (Bridwell, Kling)	60.00	30.00	18.00
(21)	Close At First (Ball, Stovall)	60.00	30.00	18.00
(22a)	Close At The Plate (Payne, Walsh)	80.00	40.00	24.00
(22b)	Close At The Plate (Payne, White)	60.00	30.00	18.00
(23)	Close At Third - Speaker (Speaker, Wood)	110.00	55.00	33.00
(24)	Close At Third - Wagner (Carrigan, Wagner)	60.00	30.00	18.00
(25a)	Collins Easily Safe (Byrne, Clarke)	80.00	40.00	24.00
(25b)	Collins Easily Safe (Baker, Collins)	150.00	75.00	45.00
(25c)	Collins Easily Safe (Collins, Murphy)	100.00	50.00	30.00
(26)	Crawford About To Smash One (Stanage, Summers)	60.00	30.00	18.00
(27)	Cree Rolls Home (Daubert, Hummel)	70.00	35.00	21.00
(28)	Davy Jones' Great Slide (Delahanty, Jones)	60.00	30.00	18.00
(29a)	Devlin Gets His Man (Devlin (Giants), Mathewson)	275.00	137.00	82.00
(29b)	Devlin Gets His Man (Devlin (Rustlers), Mathewson)	125.00	62.00	37.00
(29c)	Devlin Gets His Man (Fletcher, Mathewson)	110.00	55.00	33.00
(29d)	Devlin Gets His Man (Mathewson, Meyers)	110.00	55.00	33.00
(30a)	Donlin Out At First (Camnitz, Gibson)	60.00	30.00	18.00

	NR MT	EX	VG
(30b) Donlin Out At First (Doyle, Merkle)	60.00	30.00	18.00
(30c) Donlin Out At First (Leach, Wilson)	60.00	30.00	18.00
(30d) Donlin Out At First (Dooin, Magee)	60.00	30.00	18.00
(30e) Donlin Out At First (Gibson, Phillippe)	60.00	30.00	18.00
(31a) Dooin Gets His Man (Dooin, Doolan)	60.00	30.00	18.00
(31b) Dooin Gets His Man (Dooin, Lobert)	60.00	30.00	18.00
(31c) Dooin Gets His Man (Dooin, Titus)	60.00	30.00	18.00
(32) Easy For Larry (Doyle, Merkle)	60.00	30.00	18.00
(33) Elberfeld Beats The Throw (Elberfeld, Milan)	60.00	30.00	18.00
(34) Elberfeld Gets His Man (Elberfeld, Milan)	60.00	30.00	18.00
(35) Engle In A Close Play (Engle, Speaker)	100.00	50.00	30.00
(36a) Evers Makes A Safe Slide (Archer, Evers)	80.00	40.00	24.00
(36b) Evers Makes A Safe Slide (Chance, Evers)	110.00	55.00	33.00
(36c) Evers Makes A Safe Slide (Archer, Overall)	60.00	30.00	18.00
(36d) Evers Makes A Safe Slide (Archer, Reulbach)	60.00	30.00	18.00
(36e) Evers Makes A Safe Slide (Chance, Tinker)	110.00	55.00	33.00
(37) Fast Work At Third (Cobb, O'Leary)	600.00	300.00	180.00
(38a) Ford Putting Over A Spitter (Ford, Vaughn)	60.00	30.00	18.00
(38b) Ford Putting Over A Spitter (Sweeney)	60.00	30.00	18.00
(39) Good Play At Third (Cobb, Moriarity)	600.00	300.00	180.00
(40) Grant Gets His Man (Grant, Hoblitzell)	60.00	30.00	18.00
(41a) Hal Chase Too Late (McConnell, McIntyre)	60.00	30.00	18.00
(41b) Hal Chase Too Late (McLean, Suggs)	60.00	30.00	18.00
(42) Harry Lord At Third (Lennox, Tinker)	80.00	40.00	24.00
(43) Hartzell Covering Third (Dahlen, Scanlan)	60.00	30.00	18.00
(44) Hartsel Strikes Out (Gray, Groom)	60.00	30.00	18.00
(45) Held At Third (Lord, Tannehill)	60.00	30.00	18.00
(46) Jake Stahl Guarding First (Cicotte, Stahl)	70.00	35.00	21.00
(47) Jim Delahanty At Bat (Delahanty, Jones)	60.00	30.00	18.00
(48a) Just Before The Battle (Ames, Meyers)	60.00	30.00	18.00
(48b) Just Before The Battle (Bresnahan, McGraw)	110.00	55.00	33.00
(48c) Just Before The Battle (Crandall, Meyers)	60.00	30.00	18.00
(48d) Just Before The Battle (Becker, Devore)	60.00	30.00	18.00
(48e) Just Before The Battle (Fletcher, Mathewson)	110.00	55.00	33.00
(48f) Just Before The Battle (Marquard, Meyers)	80.00	40.00	24.00
(48g) Just Before The Battle (Jennings, McGraw)	110.00	55.00	33.00
(48h) Just Before The Battle (Mathewson, Meyers)	110.00	55.00	33.00
(48i) Just Before The Battle (Murray, Snodgrass)	60.00	30.00	18.00
(48j) Just Before The Battle (Meyers, Wiltse)	60.00	30.00	18.00
(49) Knight Catches A Runner (Johnson, Knight)	125.00	62.00	37.00
(50a) Lobert Almost Caught (Bridwell, Kling)	60.00	30.00	18.00
(50b) Lobert Almost Caught (Kling, Young)	100.00	50.00	30.00
(50c) Lobert Almost Caught (Kling, Mattern)	60.00	30.00	18.00
(50d) Lobert Almost Caught (Kling, Steinfeldt)	60.00	30.00	18.00
(51) Lobert Gets Tenney (Dooin, Lobert)	60.00	30.00	18.00
(52) Lord Catches His Man (Lord, Tannehil)	60.00	30.00	18.00

	NR MT	EX	VG
(53) McConnell Caught (Needham, Richie)	60.00	30.00	18.00
(54) McIntyre At Bat (McConnell, McIntyre)	60.00	30.00	18.00
(55) Moriarty Spiked (Stanage, Willett)	60.00	30.00	18.00
(56) Nearly Caught (Bates, Bescher)	60.00	30.00	18.00
(57) Oldring Almost Home (Lord, Oldring)	60.00	30.00	18.00
(58) Schaefer On First (McBride, Milan)	60.00	30.00	18.00
(59) Schaefer Steals Second (Clark Griffith, McBride)	80.00	40.00	24.00
(60) Scoring From Second (Lord, Oldring)	60.00	30.00	18.00
(61a) Scrambling Back To First (Barger, Bergen)	60.00	30.00	18.00
(61b) Scrambling Back To First (Chase, Wolter)	70.00	35.00	21.00
(62) Speaker Almost Caught (Clarke, Miller)	80.00	40.00	24.00
(63) Speaker Rounding Third (Speaker, Wood)	110.00	55.00	33.00
(64) Speaker Scores (Engle, Speaker)	110.00	55.00	33.00
(65) Stahl Safe (Austin, Stovall)	60.00	30.00	18.00
(66) Stone About To Swing (Schulte, Sheckard)	60.00	30.00	18.00
(67a) Sullivan Puts Up A High One (Evans, Huggins)	80.00	40.00	24.00
(67b) Sullivan Puts Up A High One (Gray, Groom)	60.00	30.00	18.00
(68a) Sweeney Gets Stahl (Ford, Vaughn)	60.00	30.00	18.00
(68b) Sweeney Gets Stahl (Ford, Sweeney)	60.00	30.00	18.00
(69) Tenney Lands Safely (Latham, Raymond)	60.00	30.00	18.00
(70a) The Athletic Infield (Baker, Barry)	80.00	40.00	24.00
(70b) The Athletic Infield (Brown, Graham)	80.00	40.00	24.00
(70c) The Athletic Infield (Hauser, Konetchy)	60.00	30.00	18.00
(70d) The Athletic Infield (Krause, Thomas)	60.00	30.00	18.00
(71) The Pinch Hitter (Egan, Hoblitzell)	60.00	30.00	18.00
(72) The Scissors Slide (Birmingham, Turner)	60.00	30.00	18.00
(73a) Tom Jones At Bat (Fromme, McLean)	60.00	30.00	18.00
(73b) Tom Jones At Bat (Gaspar, McLean)	60.00	30.00	18.00
(74a) Too Late For Devlin (Ames, Meyers)	60.00	30.00	18.00
(74b) Too Late For Devlin (Crandall, Meyers)	60.00	30.00	18.00
(74c) Too Late For Devlin (Devlin (Giants), Mathewson)	275.00	137.00	82.00
(74d) Too Late For Devlin (Devlin (Rustlers), Mathewson)	125.00	62.00	37.00
(74e) Too Late For Devlin (Marquard, Meyers)	80.00	40.00	24.00
(74f) Too Late For Devlin (Meyers, Wiltse)	60.00	30.00	18.00
(75a) Ty Cobb Steals Third (Cobb, Jennings)	650.00	325.00	195.00
(75b) Ty Cobb Steals Third (Cobb, Moriarty)	600.00	300.00	180.00
(75c) Ty Cobb Steals Third (Austin, Stovall)	550.00	275.00	165.00
(76) Wheat Strikes Out (Dahlen, Wheat)	80.00	40.00	24.00

1909 T204 Ramly

While issued with both Ramly and T.T.T. brand Turkish tobacco cigarettes, the 121 cards in this set take their name from the more common of the two brands. By any name, the set is one of the more interesting and attractive of the early 20th Century. The 2½'' by 2½'' cards carry black and white oval photographic portraits with impressive gold embossed frames and borders on the front. Toward the bottom appears the player's last name, position,

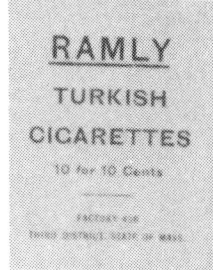

RAMLY

TURKISH

CIGARETTES

10 for 10 Cents

FACTORY 418
THIRD DISTRICT, STATE OF MASS.

POWELL
Pitcher, St. Louis A. L.

team and league. Backs carry only the most basic information on the cigarette company. Due to their scarcity, the Ramly set is not widely collected.

	NR MT	EX	VG
Complete Set:	18000.00	9000.00	5400.
Common Player:	125.00	62.00	37.00
(1) Whitey Alperman	125.00	62.00	37.00
(2) John Anderson	125.00	62.00	37.00
(3) Jimmy Archer	125.00	62.00	37.00
(4) Frank Arrelanes (Arellanes)	125.00	62.00	37.00
(5) Jim Ball	125.00	62.00	37.00
(6) Neal Ball	125.00	62.00	37.00
(7a) Frank C. Bancroft (photo inside oval frame)	125.00	62.00	37.00
(7b) Frank C. Bancroft (photo inside square frame)	250.00	125.00	75.00
(8) Johnny Bates	125.00	62.00	37.00
(9) Fred Beebe	125.00	62.00	37.00
(10) George Bell	125.00	62.00	37.00
(11) Chief Bender	300.00	150.00	90.00
(12) Walter Blair	125.00	62.00	37.00
(13) Cliff Blankenship	125.00	62.00	37.00
(14) Frank Bowerman	125.00	62.00	37.00
(15a) Wm. Bransfield (photo inside oval frame)	125.00	62.00	37.00
(15b) Wm. Bransfield (photo inside square frame)	250.00	125.00	75.00
(16) Roger Bresnahan	300.00	150.00	90.00
(17) Al Bridwell	125.00	62.00	37.00
(18) Mordecai Brown	300.00	150.00	90.00
(19) Fred Burchell	125.00	62.00	37.00
(20a) Jesse C. Burkett (photo inside oval frame)	300.00	150.00	90.00
(20b) Jesse C. Burkett (photo inside square frame)	450.00	225.00	135.00
(21) Bobby Byrnes (Byrne)	125.00	62.00	37.00
(22) Bill Carrigan	125.00	62.00	37.00
(23) Frank Chance	350.00	175.00	105.00
(24) Charlie Chech	125.00	62.00	37.00
(25) Ed Cicolte (Cicotte)	135.00	67.00	40.00
(26) Bill Clymer	125.00	62.00	37.00
(27) Andy Coakley	125.00	62.00	37.00
(28) Jimmy Collins	325.00	162.00	97.00
(29) Ed. Collins	325.00	162.00	97.00
(30) Wid Conroy	125.00	62.00	37.00
(31) Jack Coombs	125.00	62.00	37.00
(32) Doc Crandall	125.00	62.00	37.00
(33) Lou Criger	125.00	62.00	37.00
(34) Harry Davis	125.00	62.00	37.00
(35) Art Devlin	125.00	62.00	37.00
(36a) Wm. H. Dineen (Dinneen) (photo inside oval frame)	125.00	62.00	37.00
(36b) Wm. H. Dineen (Dinneen) (photo inside square frame)	250.00	125.00	75.00
(37) Jiggs Donahue	125.00	62.00	37.00
(38) Mike Donlin	125.00	62.00	37.00
(39) Wild Bill Donovan	125.00	62.00	37.00
(40) Gus Dorner	125.00	62.00	37.00
(41) Joe Dunn	125.00	62.00	37.00
(42) Kid Elberfield (Elberfeld)	125.00	62.00	37.00
(43) Johnny Evers	300.00	150.00	90.00
(44) Bob Ewing	125.00	62.00	37.00
(45) Cecil Ferguson	125.00	62.00	37.00
(46) Hobe Ferris	125.00	62.00	37.00
(47) Jerry Freeman	125.00	62.00	37.00
(48) Art Fromme	125.00	62.00	37.00
(49) Bob Ganley	125.00	62.00	37.00
(50) Doc Gessler	125.00	62.00	37.00
(51) Peaches Graham	125.00	62.00	37.00
(52) Clark Griffith	300.00	150.00	90.00
(53) Roy Hartzell	125.00	62.00	37.00

	NR MT	EX	VG
(54) Charlie Hemphill	125.00	62.00	37.00
(55) Dick Hoblitzel (Hoblitzell)	125.00	62.00	37.00
(56) Geo. Howard	125.00	62.00	37.00
(57) Harry Howell	125.00	62.00	37.00
(58) Miller Huggins	300.00	150.00	90.00
(59) John Hummell (Hummel)	125.00	62.00	37.00
(60) Walter Johnson	800.00	400.00	240.00
(61) Thos. Jones	125.00	62.00	37.00
(62) Mike Kahoe	125.00	62.00	37.00
(63) Ed Kargar	125.00	62.00	37.00
(64) Wee Willie Keeler	400.00	200.00	120.00
(65) Red Kleinon (Kleinow)	125.00	62.00	37.00
(66) Jack Knight	125.00	62.00	37.00
(67) Ed Konetchey (Konetchy)	125.00	62.00	37.00
(68) Vive Lindaman	125.00	62.00	37.00
(69) Hans Loebert (Lobert)	125.00	62.00	37.00
(70) Harry Lord	125.00	62.00	37.00
(71) Harry Lumley	125.00	62.00	37.00
(72) Johnny Lush	125.00	62.00	37.00
(73) Rube Manning	125.00	62.00	37.00
(74) Jimmy McAleer	125.00	62.00	37.00
(75) Amby McConnell	125.00	62.00	37.00
(76) Moose McCormick	125.00	62.00	37.00
(77) Harry McIntyre	125.00	62.00	37.00
(78) Larry McLean	125.00	62.00	37.00
(79) Fred Merkle	125.00	62.00	37.00
(80) Clyde Milan	125.00	62.00	37.00
(81) Mike Mitchell	125.00	62.00	37.00
(82a) Pat Moran (photo inside oval frame)	125.00	62.00	37.00
(82b) Pat Moran (photo inside square frame)	250.00	125.00	75.00
(83) Cy Morgan	125.00	62.00	37.00
(84) Tim Murname (Murnane)	125.00	62.00	37.00
(85) Danny Murphy	125.00	62.00	37.00
(86) Red Murray	125.00	62.00	37.00
(87) Doc Newton	125.00	62.00	37.00
(88) Simon Nichols (Nicholls)	125.00	62.00	37.00
(89) Harry Niles	125.00	62.00	37.00
(90) Bill O'Hare (O'Hara)	125.00	62.00	37.00
(91) Charley O'Leary	125.00	62.00	37.00
(92) Dode Paskert	125.00	62.00	37.00
(93) Barney Pelty	125.00	62.00	37.00
(94) Jake Pfeister	125.00	62.00	37.00
(95) Ed Plank	450.00	225.00	135.00
(96) Jack Powell	125.00	62.00	37.00
(97) Bugs Raymond	125.00	62.00	37.00
(98) Tom Reilly	125.00	62.00	37.00
(99) Claude Ritchey	125.00	62.00	37.00
(100) Nap Rucker	125.00	62.00	37.00
(101) Ed Ruelbach (Reulbach)	125.00	62.00	37.00
(102) Slim Sallee	125.00	62.00	37.00
(103) Germany Schaefer	125.00	62.00	37.00
(104) Jimmy Schekard (Sheckard)	125.00	62.00	37.00
(105) Admiral Schlei	125.00	62.00	37.00
(106) Wildfire Schulte	125.00	62.00	37.00
(107) Jimmy Sebring	125.00	62.00	37.00
(108) Bill Shipke	125.00	62.00	37.00
(109) Charlie Smith	125.00	62.00	37.00
(110) Tubby Spencer	125.00	62.00	37.00
(111) Jake Stahl	125.00	62.00	37.00
(112) Jim Stephens	125.00	62.00	37.00
(113) Harry Stienfeldt (Steinfeldt)	125.00	62.00	37.00
(114) Gabby Street	125.00	62.00	37.00
(115) Bill Sweeney	125.00	62.00	37.00
(116) Fred Tenney	125.00	62.00	37.00
(117) Ira Thomas	125.00	62.00	37.00
(118) Joe Tinker	300.00	150.00	90.00
(119) Bob Unclane (Unglaub)	125.00	62.00	37.00
(120) Heinie Wagner	125.00	62.00	37.00
(121) Bobby Wallace	300.00	150.00	90.00

1911 T205 Gold Border

Taking their hobby nickname from their border color, these cards were issued in a number of different cigarette brands. Cards measure 1½'' by 2⅝.'' American League cards feature a color lithograph of the player inside a stylized baseball diamond. National League cards have head-and-shoulders portraits and a plain background, plus the first-ever use of a facsimile autograph in a major card set. The 12 minor league players in the set feature three-quarter length portraits or action pictures in an elaborate frame of columns and other devices. Major League backs carry the player's full name (a first) and statistics. Minor League backs lack the statistics.

 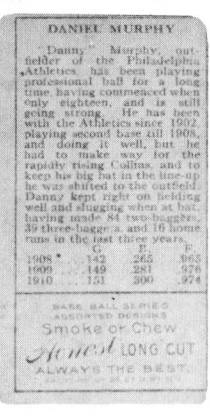

	NR MT	EX	VG
Complete Set:	17000.00	8500.00	5100.
Common Player:	40.00	20.00	12.00
(1) Edward J. Abbaticchio	40.00	20.00	12.00
(2) Doc Adkins	100.00	50.00	30.00
(3) Leon K. Ames	40.00	20.00	12.00
(4) Jas. P. Archer	40.00	20.00	12.00
(5) Jimmy Austin	40.00	20.00	12.00
(6) Bill Bailey	40.00	20.00	12.00
(7) Home Run Baker	125.00	62.00	37.00
(8) Neal Ball	40.00	20.00	12.00
(9) E.B. Barger (full "B" on cap)	40.00	20.00	12.00
(10) E.B. Barger (partial "B" on cap)	150.00	75.00	45.00
(11) Jack Barry	40.00	20.00	12.00
(12) Emil Batch	100.00	50.00	30.00
(13) John W. Bates	40.00	20.00	12.00
(14) Fred Beck	40.00	20.00	12.00
(15) B. Becker	40.00	20.00	12.00
(16) George G. Bell	40.00	20.00	12.00
(17) Chas. Bender	125.00	62.00	37.00
(18) William Bergen	40.00	20.00	12.00
(19) Bob Bescher	40.00	20.00	12.00
(20) Joe Birmingham	40.00	20.00	12.00
(21) Lena Blackburne	40.00	20.00	12.00
(22) William E. Bransfield	40.00	20.00	12.00
(23) Roger P. Bresnahan (mouth closed)	125.00	62.00	37.00
(24) Roger P. Bresnahan (mouth open)	175.00	87.00	52.00
(25) A.H. Bridwell	40.00	20.00	12.00
(26) Mordecai Brown	125.00	62.00	37.00
(27) Robert Byrne	40.00	20.00	12.00
(28) Hick Cady	100.00	50.00	30.00
(29) H. Camnitz	40.00	20.00	12.00
(30) Bill Carrigan	40.00	20.00	12.00
(31) Frank J. Chance	150.00	75.00	45.00
(32a) Hal Chase (both ears show, gold diamond frame extends below shoulders)	60.00	30.00	18.00
(32b) Hal Chase (both ears show, gold diamond frame ends at shoulders)	60.00	30.00	18.00
(33) Hal Chase (only left ear shows)	175.00	87.00	52.00
(34) Ed Cicotte	50.00	25.00	15.00
(35) Fred C. Clarke	110.00	55.00	33.00
(36) Ty Cobb	900.00	450.00	270.00
(37) Eddie Collins (mouth closed)	125.00	62.00	37.00
(38) Eddie Collins (mouth open)	175.00	87.00	52.00
(39) Jimmy Collins	200.00	100.00	60.00
(40) Frank J. Corridon	40.00	20.00	12.00
(41a) Otis Crandall ("t" not crossed in name)	40.00	20.00	12.00
(41b) Otis Crandall ("t" crossed in name)	40.00	20.00	12.00
(42) Lou Criger	40.00	20.00	12.00
(43) W.F. Dahlen	125.00	62.00	37.00
(44) Jake Daubert	50.00	25.00	15.00
(45) Jim Delahanty	40.00	20.00	12.00
(46) Arthur Devlin	40.00	20.00	12.00
(47) Josh Devore	40.00	20.00	12.00
(48) W.R. Dickson	40.00	20.00	12.00
(49) Jiggs Donohue (Donahue)	125.00	62.00	37.00
(50) Chas. S. Dooin	40.00	20.00	12.00
(51) Michael J. Doolan	40.00	20.00	12.00
(52a) Patsy Dougherty (red sock for team emblem)	40.00	20.00	12.00
(52b) Patsy Dougherty (white sock for team emblem)	125.00	62.00	37.00

	NR MT	EX	VG
(53) Thomas Downey	40.00	20.00	12.00
(54) Larry Doyle	40.00	20.00	12.00
(55) Hugh Duffy	125.00	62.00	37.00
(56) Jack Dunn	100.00	50.00	30.00
(57) Jimmy Dygert	40.00	20.00	12.00
(58) R. Egan	40.00	20.00	12.00
(59) Kid Elberfeld	40.00	20.00	12.00
(60) Clyde Engle	40.00	20.00	12.00
(61) Louis Evans	40.00	20.00	12.00
(62) John J. Evers	125.00	62.00	37.00
(63) Robert Ewing	40.00	20.00	12.00
(64) G.C. Ferguson	40.00	20.00	12.00
(65) Ray Fisher	125.00	62.00	37.00
(66) Arthur Fletcher	40.00	20.00	12.00
(67) John A. Flynn	40.00	20.00	12.00
(68) Russ Ford (black cap)	40.00	20.00	12.00
(69) Russ Ford (white cap)	150.00	75.00	45.00
(70) Wm. A. Foxen	40.00	20.00	12.00
(71) Jimmy Frick	100.00	50.00	30.00
(72) Arthur Fromme	40.00	20.00	12.00
(73) Earl Gardner	40.00	20.00	12.00
(74) H.L. Gaspar	40.00	20.00	12.00
(75) George Gibson	40.00	20.00	12.00
(76) Wilbur Goode	40.00	20.00	12.00
(77) George F. Graham (Rustlers)	40.00	20.00	12.00
(78) George F. Graham (Cubs)	175.00	87.00	52.00
(79) Edward L. Grant	150.00	75.00	45.00
(80a) Dolly Gray (no stats on back)	40.00	20.00	12.00
(80b) Dolly Gray (stats on back)	100.00	50.00	30.00
(81) Clark Griffith	110.00	55.00	33.00
(82) Bob Groom	40.00	20.00	12.00
(83) Charlie Hanford	100.00	50.00	30.00
(84) Bob Harmon (both ears show)	40.00	20.00	12.00
(85) Bob Harmon (only left ear shows)	150.00	75.00	45.00
(86) Topsy Hartsel	40.00	20.00	12.00
(87) Arnold J. Hauser	40.00	20.00	12.00
(88) Charlie Hemphill	40.00	20.00	12.00
(89) C.L. Herzog	40.00	20.00	12.00
(90a) R. Hoblitzell (no stats on back)	300.00	150.00	90.00
(90b) R. Hoblitzell ("Cin." after 2nd 1908 in stats)	75.00	37.00	22.00
(90c) R. Hoblitzel (name incorrect, no "Cin." after 1908 in stats)	40.00	20.00	12.00
(90d) R. Hoblitzell (name correct, no "Cin." after 1908 in stats)	75.00	37.00	22.00
(91) Danny Hoffman	40.00	20.00	12.00
(92) Miller J. Huggins	110.00	55.00	33.00
(93) John E. Hummel	40.00	20.00	12.00
(94) Fred Jacklitsch	40.00	20.00	12.00
(95) Hughie Jennings	110.00	55.00	33.00
(96) Walter Johnson	300.00	150.00	90.00
(97) D. Jones	40.00	20.00	12.00
(98) Tom Jones	40.00	20.00	12.00
(99) Addie Joss	175.00	87.00	52.00
(100) Ed Karger	125.00	62.00	37.00
(101) Ed Killian	40.00	20.00	12.00
(102) Red Kleinow	125.00	62.00	37.00
(103) John G. Kling	40.00	20.00	12.00
(104) Jack Knight	40.00	20.00	12.00
(105) Ed Konetchy	40.00	20.00	12.00
(106) Harry Krause	40.00	20.00	12.00
(107) Floyd M. Kroh	40.00	20.00	12.00
(108) Frank LaPorte	40.00	20.00	12.00
(109) Frank Lang (Lange)	40.00	20.00	12.00
(110a) A. Latham (A. Latham on back)	40.00	20.00	12.00
(110b) A. Latham (W.A. Latham on back)	40.00	20.00	12.00
(111) Thomas W. Leach	40.00	20.00	12.00
(112) Watty Lee	100.00	50.00	30.00
(113) Sam Leever	40.00	20.00	12.00
(114a) A. Leifield (initial "A." on front)	40.00	20.00	12.00
(114b) A.P. Leifield (initials "A.P." on front)	40.00	20.00	12.00
(115) Edgar Lennox	40.00	20.00	12.00
(116) Paddy Livingston	40.00	20.00	12.00
(117) John B. Lobert	40.00	20.00	12.00
(118) Bris Lord (Athletics)	40.00	20.00	12.00
(119) Harry Lord (White Sox)	40.00	20.00	12.00
(120) Jno. C. Lush	40.00	20.00	12.00
(121) Nick Maddox	40.00	20.00	12.00
(122) Sherwood R. Magee	50.00	25.00	15.00
(123) R.W. Marquard	125.00	62.00	37.00
(124) C. Mathewson	300.00	150.00	90.00
(125) A.A. Mattern	40.00	20.00	12.00
(126) Sport McAllister	100.00	50.00	30.00
(127) George McBride	40.00	20.00	12.00
(128) Amby McConnell	40.00	20.00	12.00
(129) P.M. McElveen	40.00	20.00	12.00
(130) J.J. McGraw	150.00	75.00	45.00
(131) Harry McIntyre (Cubs)	40.00	20.00	12.00

		NR MT	EX	VG
(132)	Matty McIntyre (White Sox)	40.00	20.00	12.00
(133)	M.A. McLean (initials actually J.B.)			
		40.00	20.00	12.00
(134)	Fred Merkle	50.00	25.00	15.00
(135)	George Merritt	100.00	50.00	30.00
(136)	J.T. Meyers	40.00	20.00	12.00
(137)	Clyde Milan	40.00	20.00	12.00
(138)	J.D. Miller	40.00	20.00	12.00
(139)	M.F. Mitchell	40.00	20.00	12.00
(140a)	P.J. Moran (stray line of type below stats)			
		40.00	20.00	12.00
(140b)	P.J. Moran (no stray line)	40.00	20.00	12.00
(141)	George Moriarty	40.00	20.00	12.00
(142)	George Mullin	40.00	20.00	12.00
(143)	Danny Murphy	40.00	20.00	12.00
(144)	Jack Murray	40.00	20.00	12.00
(145)	John Nee	100.00	50.00	30.00
(146)	Thomas J. Needham	40.00	20.00	12.00
(147)	Rebel Oakes	40.00	20.00	12.00
(148)	Rube Oldring	40.00	20.00	12.00
(149)	Charley O'Leary	40.00	20.00	12.00
(150)	Fred Olmstead	40.00	20.00	12.00
(151)	Orval Overall	40.00	20.00	12.00
(152)	Freddy Parent	40.00	20.00	12.00
(153)	George Paskert	40.00	20.00	12.00
(154)	Billy Payne	40.00	20.00	12.00
(155)	Barney Pelty	40.00	20.00	12.00
(156)	John Pfeister	40.00	20.00	12.00
(157)	Jimmy Phelan	100.00	50.00	30.00
(158)	E.J. Phelps	40.00	20.00	12.00
(159)	C. Phillippe	40.00	20.00	12.00
(160)	Jack Quinn	40.00	20.00	12.00
(161)	A.L. Raymond	150.00	75.00	45.00
(162)	E.M. Reulbach	40.00	20.00	12.00
(163)	Lewis Richie	40.00	20.00	12.00
(164)	John A. Rowan	150.00	75.00	45.00
(165)	George N. Rucker	40.00	20.00	12.00
(166)	W.D. Scanlan	125.00	62.00	37.00
(167)	Germany Schaefer	40.00	20.00	12.00
(168)	George Schlei	40.00	20.00	12.00
(169)	Boss Schmidt	40.00	20.00	12.00
(170)	F.M. Schulte	40.00	20.00	12.00
(171)	Jim Scott	40.00	20.00	12.00
(172)	B.H. Sharpe	40.00	20.00	12.00
(173)	David Shean (Rustlers)	40.00	20.00	12.00
(174)	David Shean (Cubs)	175.00	87.00	52.00
(175)	Jas. T. Sheckard	40.00	20.00	12.00
(176)	Hack Simmons	40.00	20.00	12.00
(177)	Tony Smith	40.00	20.00	12.00
(178)	Fred C. Snodgrass	40.00	20.00	12.00
(179)	Tris Speaker	225.00	112.00	67.00
(180)	Jake Stahl	40.00	20.00	12.00
(181)	Oscar Stanage	40.00	20.00	12.00
(182)	Harry Steinfeldt	50.00	25.00	15.00
(183)	George Stone	40.00	20.00	12.00
(184)	George Stovall	40.00	20.00	12.00
(185)	Gabby Street	40.00	20.00	12.00
(186)	George F. Suggs	125.00	62.00	37.00
(187)	Ed Summers	40.00	20.00	12.00
(188)	Jeff Sweeney	125.00	62.00	37.00
(189)	Lee Tannehill	40.00	20.00	12.00
(190)	Ira Thomas	40.00	20.00	12.00
(191)	Joe Tinker	125.00	62.00	37.00
(192)	John Titus	40.00	20.00	12.00
(193)	Terry Turner	150.00	75.00	45.00
(194)	James Vaughn	40.00	20.00	12.00
(195)	Heinie Wagner	125.00	62.00	37.00
(196)	Bobby Wallace (with cap)	125.00	62.00	37.00
(197a)	Bobby Wallace (no cap, one line of 1910 stats)	175.00	87.00	52.00
(197b)	Bobby Wallace (no cap, two lines of 1910 stats)	225.00	112.00	67.00
(198)	Ed Walsh	150.00	75.00	45.00
(199)	Z.D. Wheat	125.00	62.00	37.00
(200)	Doc White (White Sox)	40.00	20.00	12.00
(201)	Kirb. White (Pirates)	150.00	75.00	45.00
(202)	Irvin K. Wilhelm	150.00	75.00	45.00
(203)	Ed Willett	40.00	20.00	12.00
(204)	J. Owen Wilson	40.00	20.00	12.00
(205)	George R. Wiltse (both ears show)			
		40.00	20.00	12.00
(206)	George R. Wiltse (only right ear shows)			
		150.00	75.00	45.00
(207)	Harry Wolter	40.00	20.00	12.00
(208)	Cy Young	225.00	112.00	67.00

NOTE: A card number in parentheses ( ) indicates the set is unnumbered.

1909-11 T206 White Border

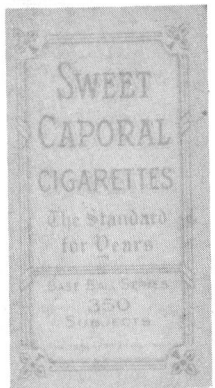

The nearly 525 cards which make up the T-206 set are the most popular of the early tobacco card issues. Players are depicted in a color lithograph against a variety of colorful backgrounds, surrounded by a white border. Player names on the 1½'' by 2⅝'' cards appear at the bottom with the city and league, when a city had more than one team. Backs contain an ad for one of 16 brands of cigarettes. There are 389 major leaguer cards and 134 minor leaguer cards in the set, but with front/back varieties the number of potentially different cards runs into the thousands. The set features many expensive cards including a number of pose and/or team variations, along with the very scarce Eddie Plank card and the ''King of Baseball Cards,'' the T206 Honus Wagner, the most avidly sought of all baseball cards.

		NR MT	EX	VG
Complete Set w/o Big 4:		20000.00	10000.	6000.
Common Player:		30.00	15.00	9.00
Common Minor Leaguer:		32.00	16.00	9.50
Common Southern Leaguer:		75.00	37.00	22.00
(1)	Ed Abbaticchio (blue sleeves)	35.00	17.50	10.50
(2)	Ed Abbaticchio (brown sleeves)	30.00	15.00	9.00
(3)	Fred Abbott	32.00	16.00	9.50
(4)	Bill Abstein	30.00	15.00	9.00
(5)	Doc Adkins	32.00	16.00	9.50
(6)	Whitey Alperman	35.00	17.50	10.50
(7)	Red Ames (hands at chest)	35.00	17.50	10.50
(8)	Red Ames (hands above head)	35.00	17.50	10.50
(9)	Red Ames (portrait)	30.00	15.00	9.00
(10)	John Anderson	32.00	16.00	9.50
(11)	Frank Arellanes	30.00	15.00	9.00
(12)	Herman Armbruster	32.00	16.00	9.50
(13)	Harry Arndt	32.00	16.00	9.50
(14)	Jake Atz	30.00	15.00	9.00
(15)	Home Run Baker	100.00	50.00	30.00
(16)	Neal Ball (New York)	35.00	17.50	10.50
(17)	Neal Ball (Cleveland)	30.00	15.00	9.00
(18)	Jap Barbeau	35.00	17.50	10.50
(19)	Cy Barger	32.00	16.00	9.50
(20)	Jack Barry (Philadelphia)	30.00	15.00	9.00
(21)	Shad Barry (Milwaukee)	32.00	16.00	9.50
(22)	Jack Bastian	75.00	37.00	22.00
(23)	Emil Batch	32.00	16.00	9.50
(24)	Johnny Bates	35.00	17.50	10.50
(25)	Harry Bay	75.00	37.00	22.00
(26)	Ginger Beaumont	35.00	17.50	10.50
(27)	Fred Beck	30.00	15.00	9.00
(28)	Beals Becker	30.00	15.00	9.00
(29)	Jake Beckley	100.00	50.00	30.00
(30)	George Bell (hands above head)	35.00	17.50	10.50
(31)	George Bell (pitching follow thru)			
		30.00	15.00	9.00
(32)	Chief Bender (pitching, no trees in background)	80.00	40.00	24.00
(33)	Chief Bender (pitching, trees in background)	80.00	40.00	24.00
(34)	Chief Bender (portrait)	100.00	50.00	30.00

		NR MT	EX	VG
(35)	Bill Bergen (batting)	35.00	17.50	10.50
(36)	Bill Bergen (catching)	32.00	16.00	9.50
(37)	Heinie Berger	30.00	15.00	9.00
(38)	Bill Bernhard	75.00	37.00	22.00
(39)	Bob Bescher (hands in air)	30.00	15.00	9.00
(40)	Bob Bescher (portrait)	30.00	15.00	9.00
(41)	Joe Birmingham	35.00	17.50	10.50
(42)	Lena Blackburne	32.00	16.00	9.50
(43)	Jack Bliss	30.00	15.00	9.00
(44)	Frank Bowerman	35.00	17.50	10.50
(45)	Bill Bradley (portrait)	35.00	17.50	10.50
(46)	Bill Bradley (with bat)	30.00	15.00	9.00
(47)	Dave Brain	32.00	16.00	9.50
(48)	Kitty Bransfield	35.00	17.50	10.50
(49)	Roy Brashear	32.00	16.00	9.50
(50)	Ted Breitenstein	75.00	37.00	22.00
(51)	Roger Bresnahan (portrait)	125.00	62.00	37.00
(52)	Roger Bresnahan (with bat)	90.00	45.00	27.00
(53)	Al Bridwell (portrait, no cap)	30.00	15.00	9.00
(54)	Al Bridwell (portrait, with cap)	35.00	17.50	10.50
(55a)	George Brown (Browne) (Chicago)			
		35.00	17.50	10.50
(55b)	George Brown (Browne) (Washington)			
		300.00	150.00	90.00
(56)	Mordecai Brown (Chicago on shirt)			
		80.00	40.00	24.00
(57)	Mordecai Brown (Cubs on shirt)			
		125.00	62.00	37.00
(58)	Mordecai Brown (portrait)	125.00	62.00	37.00
(59)	Al Burch (batting)	80.00	40.00	24.00
(60)	Al Burch (fielding)	30.00	15.00	9.00
(61)	Fred Burchell	32.00	16.00	9.50
(62)	Jimmy Burke	32.00	16.00	9.50
(63)	Bill Burns	30.00	15.00	9.00
(64)	Donie Bush	30.00	15.00	9.00
(65)	John Butler	32.00	16.00	9.50
(66)	Bobby Byrne	30.00	15.00	9.00
(67)	Howie Camnitz (arm at side)	30.00	15.00	9.00
(68)	Howie Camnitz (arms folded)	35.00	17.50	10.50
(69)	Harry Camnitz (hands above head)			
		30.00	15.00	9.00
(70)	Billy Campbell	30.00	15.00	9.00
(71)	Scoops Carey	75.00	37.00	22.00
(72)	Charley Carr	32.00	16.00	9.50
(73)	Bill Carrigan	30.00	15.00	9.00
(74)	Doc Casey	32.00	16.00	9.50
(75)	Peter Cassidy	32.00	16.00	9.50
(76)	Frank Chance (batting)	100.00	50.00	30.00
(77)	Frank Chance (portrait, red background)			
		125.00	62.00	37.00
(78)	Frank Chance (portrait, yellow background)			
		100.00	50.00	30.00
(79)	Bill Chappelle	32.00	16.00	9.50
(80)	Chappie Charles	30.00	15.00	9.00
(81)	Hal Chase (holding trophy)	40.00	20.00	12.00
(82)	Hal Chase (portrait, blue background)			
		40.00	20.00	12.00
(83)	Hal Chase (portrait, pink background)			
		80.00	40.00	24.00
(84)	Hal Chase (throwing, dark cap)	40.00	20.00	12.00
(85)	Hal Chase (throwing, white cap)			
		125.00	62.00	37.00
(86)	Jack Chesbro	125.00	62.00	37.00
(87)	Ed Cicotte	40.00	20.00	12.00
(88)	Bill Clancy (Clancey)	32.00	16.00	9.50
(89)	Josh Clark (Clarke) (Columbus)	32.00	16.00	9.50
(90)	Fred Clarke (Pittsburg, holding bat)			
		110.00	55.00	33.00
(91)	Fred Clarke (Pittsburg, portrait)			
		110.00	55.00	33.00
(92)	Nig Clarke (Cleveland)	35.00	17.50	10.50
(93)	Bill Clymer	32.00	16.00	9.50
(94)	Ty Cobb (portrait, green background)			
		1000.00	500.00	300.00
(95)	Ty Cobb (portrait, red background)			
		700.00	350.00	210.00
(96)	Ty Cobb (with bat off shoulder)	800.00	400.00	240.00
(97)	Ty Cobb (with bat on shoulder)	900.00	450.00	270.00
(98)	Cad Coles	75.00	37.00	22.00
(99)	Eddie Collins (Philadelphia)	100.00	50.00	30.00
(100)	Jimmy Collins (Minneapolis)	100.00	50.00	30.00
(101)	Bunk Congalton	32.00	16.00	9.50
(102)	Wid Conroy (fielding)	35.00	17.50	10.50
(103)	Wid Conroy (with bat)	30.00	15.00	9.00
(104)	Harry Covaleski (Coveleski)	35.00	17.50	10.50
(105)	Doc Crandall (portrait, no cap)	35.00	17.50	10.50
(106)	Doc Crandall (portrait, with cap)	30.00	15.00	9.00
(107)	Bill Cranston	75.00	37.00	22.00
(108)	Gavvy Cravath	40.00	20.00	12.00
(109)	Sam Crawford (throwing)	125.00	62.00	37.00
(110)	Sam Crawford (with bat)	100.00	50.00	30.00

		NR MT	EX	VG
(111)	Birdie Cree	30.00	15.00	9.00
(112)	Lou Criger	35.00	17.50	10.50
(113)	Dode Criss	35.00	17.50	10.50
(114)	Monte Cross	32.00	16.00	9.50
(115a)	Bill Dahlen (Boston)	35.00	17.50	10.50
(115b)	Bill Dahlen (Brooklyn)	125.00	62.00	37.00
(116)	Paul Davidson	32.00	16.00	9.50
(117)	George Davis (Chicago)	35.00	17.50	10.50
(118)	Harry Davis (Philadelphia, Davis on front)			
		30.00	15.00	9.00
(119)	Harry Davis (Philadelphia, H. Davis on front)			
		35.00	17.50	10.50
(120)	Frank Delehanty (Delahanty) (Louisville)			
		32.00	16.00	9.50
(121)	Jim Delehanty (Delahanty) (Washington)			
		35.00	17.50	10.50
(122a)	Ray Demmitt (New York)	30.00	15.00	9.00
(122b)	Ray Demmitt (St. Louis)	1800.00	900.00	540.00
(123)	Rube Dessau	32.00	16.00	9.50
(124)	Art Devlin	35.00	17.50	10.50
(125)	Josh Devore	30.00	15.00	9.00
(126)	Bill Dineen (Dinneen)	30.00	15.00	9.00
(127)	Mike Donlin (fielding)	80.00	40.00	24.00
(128)	Mike Donlin (seated)	35.00	17.50	10.50
(129)	Mike Donlin (with bat)	30.00	15.00	9.00
(130)	Jiggs Donahue (Donahue)	35.00	17.50	10.50
(131)	Wild Bill Donovan (portrait)	35.00	17.50	10.50
(132)	Wild Bill Donovan (throwing)	30.00	15.00	9.00
(133)	Red Dooin	35.00	17.50	10.50
(134)	Mickey Doolan (batting)	30.00	15.00	9.00
(135)	Mickey Doolan (fielding)	30.00	15.00	9.00
(136)	Mickey Doolin (Doolan)	35.00	17.50	10.50
(137)	Gus Dorner	32.00	16.00	9.50
(138)	Patsy Dougherty (arm in air)	30.00	15.00	9.00
(139)	Patsy Dougherty (portrait)	35.00	17.50	10.50
(140)	Tom Downey (batting)	30.00	15.00	9.00
(141)	Tom Downey (fielding)	30.00	15.00	9.00
(142)	Jerry Downs	32.00	16.00	9.50
(143a)	Joe Doyle (N.Y. Natl., hands above head)			
		10000.00	5000.00	3000.
(143b)	Joe Doyle (N.Y., hands above head)			
		30.00	15.00	9.00
(144)	Larry Doyle (N.Y. Nat'l., portrait)			
		35.00	17.50	10.50
(145)	Larry Doyle (N.Y. Nat'l., throwing)			
		40.00	20.00	12.00
(146)	Larry Doyle (N.Y. Nat'l., with bat)			
		35.00	17.50	10.50
(147)	Jean Dubuc	30.00	15.00	9.00
(148)	Hugh Duffy	90.00	45.00	27.00
(149)	Jack Dunn (Baltimore)	32.00	16.00	9.50
(150)	Joe Dunn (Brooklyn)	32.00	16.00	9.50
(151)	Bull Durham	35.00	17.50	10.50
(152)	Jimmy Dygert	30.00	15.00	9.00
(153)	Ted Easterly	30.00	15.00	9.00
(154)	Dick Egan	30.00	15.00	9.00
(155a)	Kid Elberfeld (New York)	35.00	17.50	10.50
(155b)	Kid Elberfeld (Washington, portrait)			
		700.00	350.00	210.00
(156)	Kid Elberfeld (Washington, fielding)			
		30.00	15.00	9.00
(157)	Roy Ellam	75.00	37.00	22.00
(158)	Clyde Engle	30.00	15.00	9.00
(159)	Steve Evans	30.00	15.00	9.00
(160)	Johnny Evers (portrait)	125.00	62.00	37.00
(161)	Johnny Evers (with bat, Chicago on shirt)			
		80.00	40.00	24.00
(162)	Johnny Evers (with bat, Cubs on shirt)			
		150.00	75.00	45.00
(163)	Bob Ewing	35.00	17.50	10.50
(164)	Cecil Ferguson	30.00	15.00	9.00
(165)	Hobe Ferris	35.00	17.50	10.50
(166)	Lou Fiene (portrait)	30.00	15.00	9.00
(167)	Lou Fiene (throwing)	30.00	15.00	9.00
(168)	Steamer Flanagan	32.00	16.00	9.50
(169)	Art Fletcher	30.00	15.00	9.00
(170)	Elmer Flick	125.00	62.00	37.00
(171)	Russ Ford	30.00	15.00	9.00
(172)	Ed Foster	75.00	37.00	22.00
(173)	Jerry Freeman	32.00	16.00	9.50
(174)	John Frill	30.00	15.00	9.00
(175)	Charlie Fritz	75.00	37.00	22.00
(176)	Art Fromme	30.00	15.00	9.00
(177)	Chick Gandil	35.00	17.50	10.50
(178)	Bob Ganley	35.00	17.50	10.50
(179)	John Ganzel	32.00	16.00	9.50
(180)	Harry Gasper	30.00	15.00	9.00
(181)	Rube Geyer	30.00	15.00	9.00
(182)	George Gibson	35.00	17.50	10.50
(183)	Billy Gilbert	35.00	17.50	10.50
(184)	Wilbur Goode (Good)	35.00	17.50	10.50

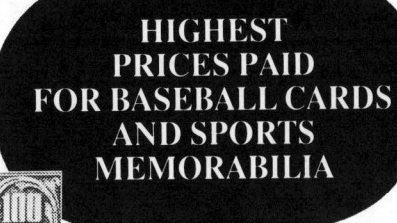

	NR MT	EX	VG
(185) Bill Graham (St. Louis)	30.00	15.00	9.00
(186) Peaches Graham (Boston)	30.00	15.00	9.00
(187) Dolly Gray	30.00	15.00	9.00
(188) Ed Greminger	75.00	37.00	22.00
(189) Clark Griffith (batting)	100.00	50.00	30.00
(190) Clark Griffith (portrait)	125.00	62.00	37.00
(191) Moose Grimshaw	32.00	16.00	9.50
(192) Bob Groom	30.00	15.00	9.00
(193) Guiheen	75.00	37.00	22.00
(194) Ed Hahn	35.00	17.50	10.50
(195) Bob Hall	32.00	16.00	9.50
(196) Bill Hallman	32.00	16.00	9.50
(197) Jack Hannifan (Hannifin)	32.00	16.00	9.50
(198) Bill Hart (Little Rock)	75.00	37.00	22.00
(199) Jimmy Hart (Montgomery)	75.00	37.00	22.00
(200) Topsy Hartsel	30.00	15.00	9.00
(201) Jack Hayden	32.00	16.00	9.50
(202) J. Ross Helm	75.00	37.00	22.00
(203) Charlie Hemphill	35.00	17.50	10.50
(204) Buck Herzog (Boston)	30.00	15.00	9.00
(205) Buck Herzog (New York)	35.00	17.50	10.50
(206) Gordon Hickman	75.00	37.00	22.00
(207) Bill Hinchman (Cleveland)	35.00	17.50	10.50
(208) Harry Hinchman (Toledo)	32.00	16.00	9.50
(209) Dick Hoblitzell	30.00	15.00	9.00
(210) Danny Hoffman (St. Louis)	30.00	15.00	9.00
(211) Izzy Hoffman (Providence)	32.00	16.00	9.50
(212) Solly Hofman	30.00	15.00	9.00
(213) Bock Hooker	75.00	37.00	22.00
(214) Del Howard (Chicago)	30.00	15.00	9.00
(215) Ernie Howard (Savannah)	75.00	37.00	22.00
(216) Harry Howell (hand at waist)	30.00	15.00	9.00
(217) Harry Howell (portrait)	30.00	15.00	9.00
(218) Miller Huggins (hands at mouth)	80.00	40.00	24.00
(219) Miller Huggins (portrait)	90.00	45.00	27.00
(220) Rudy Hulswitt	30.00	15.00	9.00
(221) John Hummel	30.00	15.00	9.00
(222) George Hunter	30.00	15.00	9.00
(223) Frank Isbell	35.00	17.50	10.50
(224) Fred Jacklitsch	35.00	17.50	10.50
(225) Jimmy Jackson	32.00	16.00	9.50
(226) Hughie Jennings (one hand showing)	80.00	40.00	24.00
(227) Hughie Jennings (both hands showing)	80.00	40.00	24.00
(228) Hughie Jennings (portrait)	100.00	50.00	30.00
(229) Walter Johnson (hands at chest)	250.00	125.00	75.00
(230) Walter Johnson (portrait)	300.00	150.00	90.00
(231) Fielder Jones (Chicago, hands at hips)	35.00	17.50	10.50
(232) Fielder Jones (Chicago, portrait)	35.00	17.50	10.50
(233) Davy Jones (Detroit)	30.00	15.00	9.00
(234) Tom Jones (St. Louis)	35.00	17.50	10.50
(235) Dutch Jordan (Atlanta)	75.00	37.00	22.00
(236) Tim Jordan (Brooklyn, batting)	30.00	15.00	9.00
(237) Tim Jordan (Brooklyn, portrait)	35.00	17.50	10.50
(238) Addie Joss (hands at chest)	100.00	50.00	30.00
(239) Addie Joss (portrait)	125.00	62.00	37.00
(240) Ed Karger	35.00	17.50	10.50
(241) Willie Keeler (portrait)	150.00	75.00	45.00
(242) Willie Keeler (with bat)	150.00	75.00	45.00
(243) Joe Kelley	110.00	55.00	33.00
(244) J.F. Kiernan	75.00	37.00	22.00
(245) Ed Killian (hands at chest)	30.00	15.00	9.00
(246) Ed Killian (portrait)	35.00	17.50	10.50
(247) Frank King	75.00	37.00	22.00
(248) Rube Kisinger (Kissinger)	32.00	16.00	9.50
(249a)Red Kleinow (Boston)	250.00	125.00	75.00
(249b)Red Kleinow (New York, catching)	30.00	15.00	9.00
(250) Red Kleinow (New York, with bat)	35.00	17.50	10.50
(251) Johnny Kling	35.00	17.50	10.50
(252) Otto Knabe	30.00	15.00	9.00
(253) Jack Knight (portrait)	30.00	15.00	9.00
(254) Jack Knight (with bat)	30.00	15.00	9.00
(255) Ed Konetchy (glove above head)	35.00	17.50	10.50
(256) Ed Konetchy (glove near ground)	30.00	15.00	9.00
(257) Harry Krause (pitching)	30.00	15.00	9.00
(258) Harry Krause (portrait)	30.00	15.00	9.00
(259) Rube Kroh	30.00	15.00	9.00
(260) Otto Kruger (Krueger)	32.00	16.00	9.50
(261) James Lafitte	75.00	37.00	22.00
(262) Nap Lajoie (portrait)	200.00	100.00	60.00
(263) Nap Lajoie (throwing)	200.00	100.00	60.00
(264) Nap Lajoie (with bat)	175.00	87.00	52.00
(265) Joe Lake (New York)	35.00	17.50	10.50
(266) Joe Lake (St. Louis, ball in hand)	30.00	15.00	9.00

	NR MT	EX	VG
(267) Joe Lake (St. Louis, no ball in hand)	30.00	15.00	9.00
(268) Frank LaPorte	30.00	15.00	9.00
(269) Arlie Latham	30.00	15.00	9.00
(270) Bill Lattimore	32.00	16.00	9.50
(271) Jimmy Lavender	32.00	16.00	9.50
(272) Tommy Leach (bending over)	30.00	15.00	9.00
(273) Tommy Leach (portrait)	35.00	17.50	10.50
(274) Lefty Leifield (batting)	30.00	15.00	9.00
(275) Lefty Leifield (pitching)	35.00	17.50	10.50
(276) Ed Lennox	30.00	15.00	9.00
(277) Harry Lentz (Sentz)	75.00	37.00	22.00
(278) Glenn Liebhardt	35.00	17.50	10.50
(279) Vive Lindaman	35.00	17.50	10.50
(280) Perry Lipe	75.00	37.00	22.00
(281) Paddy Livingstone (Livingston)	30.00	15.00	9.00
(282) Hans Lobert	35.00	17.50	10.50
(283) Harry Lord	30.00	15.00	9.00
(284) Harry Lumley	35.00	17.50	10.50
(285a)Carl Lundgren (Chicago)	225.00	112.00	67.00
(285b)Carl Lundgren (Kansas City)	32.00	16.00	9.50
(286) Nick Maddox	30.00	15.00	9.00
(287a)Sherry Magie (Magee)	5500.00	2750.00	1650.
(287b)Sherry Magee (portrait)	40.00	20.00	12.00
(288) Sherry Magee (with bat)	35.00	17.50	10.50
(289) Bill Malarkey	32.00	16.00	9.50
(290) Billy Maloney	32.00	16.00	9.50
(291) George Manion	75.00	37.00	22.00
(292) Rube Manning (batting)	35.00	17.50	10.50
(293) Rube Manning (pitching)	30.00	15.00	9.00
(294) Rube Marquard (hands at thighs)	125.00	62.00	37.00
(295) Rube Marquard (pitching follow thru)	100.00	50.00	30.00
(296) Rube Marquard (portrait)	100.00	50.00	30.00
(297) Doc Marshall	30.00	15.00	9.00
(298) Christy Mathewson (dark cap)	275.00	137.00	82.00
(299) Christy Mathewson (portrait)	325.00	162.00	97.00
(300) Christy Mathewson (white cap)	300.00	150.00	90.00
(301) Al Mattern	30.00	15.00	9.00
(302) John McAleese	30.00	15.00	9.00
(303) George McBride	30.00	15.00	9.00
(304) Pat McCauley	75.00	37.00	22.00
(305) Moose McCormick	30.00	15.00	9.00
(306) Pryor McElveen	30.00	15.00	9.00
(307) Dan McGann	32.00	16.00	9.50
(308) Jim McGinley	32.00	16.00	9.50
(309) Iron Man McGinnity	100.00	50.00	30.00
(310) Stoney McGlynn	32.00	16.00	9.50
(311) John McGraw (finger in air)	125.00	62.00	37.00
(312) John McGraw (glove at hip)	100.00	50.00	30.00
(313) John McGraw (portrait, no cap)	125.00	62.00	37.00
(314) John McGraw (portrait, with cap)	100.00	50.00	30.00
(315) Harry McIntyre (Brooklyn)	35.00	17.50	10.50
(316) Harry McIntyre (Brooklyn & Chicago)	30.00	15.00	9.00
(317) Matty McIntyre (Detroit)	30.00	15.00	9.00
(318) Larry McLean	30.00	15.00	9.00
(319) George McQuillan (ball in hand)	35.00	17.50	10.50
(320) George McQuillan (with bat)	30.00	15.00	9.00
(321) Fred Merkle (portrait)	40.00	20.00	12.00
(322) Fred Merkle (throwing)	35.00	17.50	10.50
(323) George Merritt	32.00	16.00	9.50
(324) Chief Meyers	30.00	15.00	9.00
(325) Clyde Milan	30.00	15.00	9.00
(326) Dots Miller (Pittsburg)	30.00	15.00	9.00
(327) Molly Miller (Dallas)	75.00	37.00	22.00
(328) Bill Milligan	32.00	16.00	9.50
(329) Fred Mitchell (Toronto)	32.00	16.00	9.50
(330) Mike Mitchell (Cincinnati)	30.00	15.00	9.00
(331) Dan Moeller	32.00	16.00	9.50
(332) Carlton Molesworth	75.00	37.00	22.00
(333) Herbie Moran (Providence)	32.00	16.00	9.50
(334) Pat Moran (Chicago)	30.00	15.00	9.00
(335) George Moriarty	30.00	15.00	9.00
(336) Mike Mowrey	30.00	15.00	9.00
(337) Dom Mullaney	75.00	37.00	22.00
(338) George Mullen (Mullin)	30.00	15.00	9.00
(339) George Mullin (throwing)	35.00	17.50	10.50
(340) George Mullin (with bat)	30.00	15.00	9.00
(341) Danny Murphy (batting)	30.00	15.00	9.00
(342) Danny Murphy (throwing)	35.00	17.50	10.50
(343) Red Murray (batting)	30.00	15.00	9.00
(344) Red Murray (portrait)	30.00	15.00	9.00
(345) Chief Myers (Meyers) (batting)	30.00	15.00	9.00
(346) Chief Myers (Meyers) (fielding)	30.00	15.00	9.00
(347) Billy Nattress	32.00	16.00	9.50
(348) Tom Needham	30.00	15.00	9.00
(349) Simon Nicholls (hands on knees)	35.00	17.50	10.50

	NR MT	EX	VG
(350) Simon Nichols (Nicholls) (batting)			
	30.00	15.00	9.00
(351) Harry Niles	35.00	17.50	10.50
(352) Rebel Oakes	30.00	15.00	9.00
(353) Frank Oberlin	32.00	16.00	9.50
(354) Peter O'Brien	32.00	16.00	9.50
(355a) Bill O'Hara (New York)	30.00	15.00	9.00
(355b) Bill O'Hara (St. Louis)	1400.00	700.00	420.00
(356) Rube Oldring (batting)	30.00	15.00	9.00
(357) Rube Oldring (fielding)	35.00	17.50	10.50
(358) Charley O'Leary (hands on knees)			
	30.00	15.00	9.00
(359) Charley O'Leary (portrait)	35.00	17.50	10.50
(360) William J. O'Neil	32.00	16.00	9.50
(361) Al Orth	75.00	37.00	22.00
(362) William Otey	75.00	37.00	22.00
(363) Orval Overall (hand face level)	30.00	15.00	9.00
(364) Orval Overall (hands waist level)	30.00	15.00	9.00
(365) Orval Overall (portrait)	35.00	17.50	10.50
(366) Frank Owen	35.00	17.50	10.50
(367) George Paige	75.00	37.00	22.00
(368) Fred Parent	35.00	17.50	10.50
(369) Dode Paskert	30.00	15.00	9.00
(370) Jim Pastorius	35.00	17.50	10.50
(371) Harry Pattee	80.00	40.00	24.00
(372) Billy Payne	30.00	15.00	9.00
(373) Barney Pelty (horizontal photo)	80.00	40.00	24.00
(374) Barney Pelty (vertical photo)	30.00	15.00	9.00
(375) Hub Perdue	75.00	37.00	22.00
(376) George Perring	30.00	15.00	9.00
(377) Arch Persons	75.00	37.00	22.00
(378) Francis (Big Jeff) Pfeffer	30.00	15.00	9.00
(379) Jake Pfeister (seated)	30.00	15.00	9.00
(380) Jake Pfeister (throwing)	30.00	15.00	9.00
(381) Jimmy Phelan	32.00	16.00	9.50
(382) Eddie Phelps	30.00	15.00	9.00
(383) Deacon Phillippe	30.00	15.00	9.00
(384) Ollie Pickering	32.00	16.00	9.50
(385) Eddie Plank	8000.00	4000.00	2400.
(386) Phil Poland	32.00	16.00	9.50
(387) Jack Powell	35.00	17.50	10.50
(388) Mike Powers	80.00	40.00	24.00
(389) Billy Purtell	30.00	15.00	9.00
(390) Ambrose Puttman (Puttmann)	32.00	16.00	9.50
(391) Lee Quillen (Quillin)	32.00	16.00	9.50
(392) Jack Quinn	30.00	15.00	9.00
(393) Newt Randall	32.00	16.00	9.50
(394) Bugs Raymond	30.00	15.00	9.00
(395) Ed Reagan	75.00	37.00	22.00
(396) Ed Reulbach (glove showing)	80.00	40.00	24.00
(397) Ed Reulbach (no glove showing)	30.00	15.00	9.00
(398) Dutch Revelle	75.00	37.00	22.00
(399) Bob Rhoades (Rhoads) (hands at chest)			
	30.00	15.00	9.00
(400) Bob Rhoades (Rhoads) (right arm extended)			
	30.00	15.00	9.00
(401) Charlie Rhodes	30.00	15.00	9.00
(402) Claude Ritchey	35.00	17.50	10.50
(403) Lou Ritter	32.00	16.00	9.50
(404) Ike Rockenfeld	75.00	37.00	22.00
(405) Claude Rossman	30.00	15.00	9.00
(406) Nap Rucker (portrait)	35.00	17.50	10.50
(407) Nap Rucker (throwing)	30.00	15.00	9.00
(408) Dick Rudolph	32.00	16.00	9.50
(409) Ray Ryan	75.00	37.00	22.00
(410) Germany Schaefer (Detroit)	35.00	17.50	10.50
(411) Germany Schaefer (Washington)			
	30.00	15.00	9.00
(412) George Schirm	32.00	16.00	9.50
(413) Larry Schlafly	32.00	16.00	9.50
(414) Admiral Schlei (batting)	30.00	15.00	9.00
(415) Admiral Schlei (catching)	35.00	17.50	10.50
(416) Admiral Schlei (portrait)	30.00	15.00	9.00
(417) Boss Schmidt (portrait)	30.00	15.00	9.00
(418) Boss Schmidt (throwing)	35.00	17.50	10.50
(419) Ossee Schreck (Schreckengost)	32.00	16.00	9.50
(420) Wildfire Schulte (front view)	35.00	17.50	10.50
(421) Wildfire Schulte (back view)	30.00	15.00	9.00
(422) Jim Scott	30.00	15.00	9.00
(423) Charles Seitz	75.00	37.00	22.00
(424) Cy Seymour (batting)	35.00	17.50	10.50
(425) Cy Seymour (portrait)	30.00	15.00	9.00
(426) Cy Seymour (throwing)	30.00	15.00	9.00
(427) Spike Shannon	32.00	16.00	9.50
(428) Bud Sharpe	32.00	16.00	9.50
(429) Shag Shaughnessy	75.00	37.00	22.00
(430) Al Shaw (St. Louis)	35.00	17.50	10.50
(431) Hunky Shaw (Providence)	32.00	16.00	9.50
(432) Jimmy Sheckard (glove showing)			
	30.00	15.00	9.00
(433) Jimmy Sheckard (no glove showing)			
	35.00	17.50	10.50
(434) Bill Shipke	35.00	17.50	10.50
(435) Jimmy Slagle	32.00	16.00	9.50
(436) Carlos Smith (Shreveport)	75.00	37.00	22.00
(437) Frank Smith (Chicago, F. Smith on front)			
	75.00	37.00	22.00
(438a) Frank Smith (Chicago, white cap)			
	30.00	15.00	9.00
(438b) Frank Smith (Chicago & Boston)			
	275.00	137.00	82.00
(439) "Happy" Smith (Brooklyn)	30.00	15.00	9.00
(440) Heinie Smith (Buffalo)	32.00	16.00	9.50
(441) Sid Smith (Atlanta)	75.00	37.00	22.00
(442) Fred Snodgrass (batting)	35.00	17.50	10.50
(443) Fred Snodgrass (catching)	35.00	17.50	10.50
(444) Bob Spade	30.00	15.00	9.00
(445) Tris Speaker	175.00	87.00	52.00
(446) Tubby Spencer	35.00	17.50	10.50
(447) Jake Stahl (glove shows)	30.00	15.00	9.00
(448) Jake Stahl (no glove shows)	35.00	17.50	10.50
(449) Oscar Stanage	30.00	15.00	9.00
(450) Dolly Stark	75.00	37.00	22.00
(451) Charlie Starr	30.00	15.00	9.00
(452) Harry Steinfeldt (portrait)	40.00	20.00	12.00
(453) Harry Steinfeldt (with bat)	35.00	17.50	10.50
(454) Jim Stephens	30.00	15.00	9.00
(455) George Stone	35.00	17.50	10.50
(456) George Stovall (batting)	30.00	15.00	9.00
(457) George Stovall (portrait)	35.00	17.50	10.50
(458) Sam Strang	32.00	16.00	9.50
(459) Gabby Street (catching)	30.00	15.00	9.00
(460) Gabby Street (portrait)	30.00	15.00	9.00
(461) Billy Sullivan	35.00	17.50	10.50
(462) Ed Summers	30.00	15.00	9.00
(463) Bill Sweeney (Boston)	30.00	15.00	9.00
(464) Jeff Sweeney (New York)	30.00	15.00	9.00
(465) Jesse Tannehill (Washington)	30.00	15.00	9.00
(466) Lee Tannehill (Chicago, L. Tannehill on front)			
	35.00	17.50	10.50
(467) Lee Tannehill (Chicago, Tannehill on front)			
	30.00	15.00	9.00
(468) Dummy Taylor	32.00	16.00	9.50
(469) Fred Tenney	35.00	17.50	10.50
(470) Tony Thebo	75.00	37.00	22.00
(471) Jake Thielman	32.00	16.00	9.50
(472) Ira Thomas	30.00	15.00	9.00
(473) Woodie Thornton	75.00	37.00	22.00
(474) Joe Tinker (bat off shoulder)	100.00	50.00	30.00
(475) Joe Tinker (bat on shoulder)	100.00	50.00	30.00
(476) Joe Tinker (hands on knees)	125.00	62.00	37.00
(477) Joe Tinker (portrait)	125.00	62.00	37.00
(478) John Titus	30.00	15.00	9.00
(479) Terry Turner	35.00	17.50	10.50
(480) Bob Unglaub	30.00	15.00	9.00
(481) Juan Violat (Viola)	75.00	37.00	22.00
(482) Rube Waddell (portrait)	125.00	62.00	37.00
(483) Rube Waddell (throwing)	125.00	62.00	37.00
(484) Heinie Wagner (bat on left shoulder)			
	60.00	30.00	18.00
(485) Heinie Wagner (bat on right shoulder)			
	30.00	15.00	9.00
(486) Honus Wagner	36000.00	18000.	10800.
(487) Bobby Wallace	100.00	50.00	30.00
(488) Ed Walsh	100.00	50.00	30.00
(489) Jack Warhop	30.00	15.00	9.00
(490) Jake Weimer	35.00	17.50	10.50
(491) James Westlake	75.00	37.00	22.00
(492) Zack Wheat	90.00	45.00	27.00
(493) Doc White (Chicago, pitching)	30.00	15.00	9.00
(494) Doc White (Chicago, portrait)	35.00	17.50	10.50
(495) Foley White (Houston)	75.00	37.00	22.00
(496) Jack White (Buffalo)	32.00	16.00	9.50
(497) Kaiser Wilhelm (hands at chest)	35.00	17.50	10.50
(498) Kaiser Wilhelm (with bat)	30.00	15.00	9.00
(499) Ed Willett	30.00	15.00	9.00
(500) Ed Willetts (Willett)	30.00	15.00	9.00
(501) Jimmy Williams	35.00	17.50	10.50
(502) Vic Willis (Pittsburg)	60.00	30.00	18.00
(503) Vic Willis (St. Louis, throwing)	30.00	15.00	9.00
(504) Vic Willis (St. Louis, with bat)	30.00	15.00	9.00
(505) Owen Wilson	30.00	15.00	9.00
(506) Hooks Wiltse (pitching)	32.00	16.00	9.50
(507) Hooks Wiltse (portrait, no cap)	35.00	17.50	10.50
(508) Hooks Wiltse (portrait, with cap)	30.00	15.00	9.00
(509) Lucky Wright	32.00	16.00	9.50
(510) Cy Young (Cleveland, glove shows)			
	125.00	62.00	37.00
(511) Cy Young (Cleveland, bare hand shows)			
	150.00	75.00	45.00
(512) Cy Young (portrait)	150.00	75.00	45.00

	NR MT	EX	VG
(513) Irv Young (Minneapolis)	32.00	16.00	9.50
(514) Heinie Zimmerman	30.00	15.00	9.00

1912 T207 Brown Background

Harry Lord

Harry Lord, the brilliant White Sox third baseman, came to Chicago in one of the queerest baseball deals ever recorded. Lord, first achieved success in the New England League, where, in 1908, he was lifted to the Boston Americans. Although rated as a wonderful ball player, he fell out with the club management, and was traded to Comiskey, who secured a star. Lord played wonderful ball in 1911 and is rated by many as the greatest third baseman now playing—a worthy successor to Bradley and Collins. Last season he batted .321, fielded .941 and led his club with stolen bases.

RECRUIT
LITTLE CIGARS

LORD-CHICAGO-AMER.

These 1½'' by 2⅝'' cards take their name from the background color which frames the rather drab sepia and white player drawings. They have tan borders making them less colorful then the more popular issues of their era. Player pictures are also on the dull side, with a white strip containing the player's last name, team and league. Card backs have the player's full name, a baseball biography and an ad for one of several brands of cigarettes. The set features 200 players including stars and three classic rarities: Irving Lewis (Boston-Nat.), Ward Miller (Chicago-Nat.) and Louis Lowdermilk (St. Louis-Nat.). There are a number of other scarce cards in the set including a higher than usual number of obscure players.

	NR MT	EX	VG
Complete Set:	20000.00	10000.00	6000.
Common Player:	40.00	20.00	12.00
(1) John B. Adams	100.00	50.00	30.00
(2) Edward Ainsmith	40.00	20.00	12.00
(3) Rafael Almeida	100.00	50.00	30.00
(4a) James Austin (insignia on shirt)	50.00	25.00	15.00
(4b) James Austin (no insignia on shirt)			
	100.00	50.00	30.00
(5) Neal Ball	40.00	20.00	12.00
(6) Eros Barger	40.00	20.00	12.00
(7) Jack Barry	40.00	20.00	12.00
(8) Charles Bauman	125.00	62.00	37.00
(9) Beals Becker	40.00	20.00	12.00
(10) Chief (Albert) Bender	125.00	62.00	37.00
(11) Joseph Benz	100.00	50.00	30.00
(12) Robert Bescher	40.00	20.00	12.00
(13) Joe Birmingham	100.00	50.00	30.00
(14) Russell Blackburne	100.00	50.00	30.00
(15) Fred Blanding	100.00	50.00	30.00
(16) Jimmy Block	40.00	20.00	12.00
(17) Ping Bodie	40.00	20.00	12.00
(18) Hugh Bradley	40.00	20.00	12.00
(19) Roger Bresnahan	125.00	62.00	37.00
(20) J.F. Bushelman	100.00	50.00	30.00
(21) Henry (Hank) Butcher	100.00	50.00	30.00
(22) Robert M. Byrne	40.00	20.00	12.00
(23) John James Callahan	40.00	20.00	12.00
(24) Howard Camnitz	40.00	20.00	12.00
(25) Max Carey	125.00	62.00	37.00
(26) William Carrigan	40.00	20.00	12.00
(27) George Chalmers	40.00	20.00	12.00
(28) Frank Leroy Chance	150.00	75.00	45.00
(29) Edward Cicotte	50.00	25.00	15.00
(30) Tom Clarke	40.00	20.00	12.00
(31) Leonard Cole	40.00	20.00	12.00
(32) John Collins	80.00	40.00	24.00
(33) Robert Coulson	40.00	20.00	12.00

	NR MT	EX	VG
(34) Tex Covington	40.00	20.00	12.00
(35) Otis Crandall	40.00	20.00	12.00
(36) William Cunningham	100.00	50.00	30.00
(37) Dave Danforth	40.00	20.00	12.00
(38) Bert Daniels	40.00	20.00	12.00
(39) John Daubert	50.00	25.00	15.00
(40a) Harry Davis (brown "C" on cap)	50.00	25.00	15.00
(40b) Harry Davis (blue "C" on cap)	50.00	25.00	15.00
(41) Jim Delehanty	40.00	20.00	12.00
(42) Claude Derrick	40.00	20.00	12.00
(43) Arthur Devlin	40.00	20.00	12.00
(44) Joshua Devore	40.00	20.00	12.00
(45) Mike Donlin	100.00	50.00	30.00
(46) Edward Donnelly	100.00	50.00	30.00
(47) Charles Dooin	40.00	20.00	12.00
(48) Tom Downey	100.00	50.00	30.00
(49) Lawrence Doyle	40.00	20.00	12.00
(50) Del Drake	40.00	20.00	12.00
(51) Ted Easterly	40.00	20.00	12.00
(52) George Ellis	40.00	20.00	12.00
(53) Clyde Engle	40.00	20.00	12.00
(54) R.E. Erwin	40.00	20.00	12.00
(55) Louis Evans	40.00	20.00	12.00
(56) John Ferry	40.00	20.00	12.00
(57a) Ray Fisher (blue cap)	50.00	25.00	15.00
(57b) Ray Fisher (white cap)	50.00	25.00	15.00
(58) Arthur Fletcher	40.00	20.00	12.00
(59) Jacques Fournier	100.00	50.00	30.00
(60) Arthur Fromme	40.00	20.00	12.00
(61) Del Gainor	40.00	20.00	12.00
(62) William Lawrence Gardner	40.00	20.00	12.00
(63) Lefty George	40.00	20.00	12.00
(64) Roy Golden	40.00	20.00	12.00
(65) Harry Gowdy	40.00	20.00	12.00
(66) George Graham	80.00	40.00	24.00
(67) J.G. Graney	40.00	20.00	12.00
(68) Vean Gregg	100.00	50.00	30.00
(69) Casey Hageman	40.00	20.00	12.00
(70) Charlie Hall	40.00	20.00	12.00
(71) E.S. Hallinan	40.00	20.00	12.00
(72) Earl Hamilton	40.00	20.00	12.00
(73) Robert Harmon	40.00	20.00	12.00
(74) Grover Hartley	100.00	50.00	30.00
(75) Olaf Henriksen	40.00	20.00	12.00
(76) John Henry	80.00	40.00	24.00
(77) Charles Herzog	100.00	50.00	30.00
(78) Robert Higgins	40.00	20.00	12.00
(79) Chester Hoff	100.00	50.00	30.00
(80) William Hogan	40.00	20.00	12.00
(81) Harry Hooper	175.00	87.00	52.00
(82) Ben Houser	100.00	50.00	30.00
(83) Hamilton Hyatt	100.00	50.00	30.00
(84) Walter Johnson	350.00	175.00	105.00
(85) George Kaler	40.00	20.00	12.00
(86) William Kelly	100.00	50.00	30.00
(87) Jay Kirke	100.00	50.00	30.00
(88) John Kling	40.00	20.00	12.00
(89) Otto Knabe	40.00	20.00	12.00
(90) Elmer Knetzer	40.00	20.00	12.00
(91) Edward Konetchy	40.00	20.00	12.00
(92) Harry Krause	40.00	20.00	12.00
(93) "Red" Kuhn	100.00	50.00	30.00
(94) Joseph Kutina	100.00	50.00	30.00
(95) F.H. (Bill) Lange	100.00	50.00	30.00
(96) Jack Lapp	40.00	20.00	12.00
(97) W. Arlington Latham	40.00	20.00	12.00
(98) Thomas W. Leach	40.00	20.00	12.00
(99) Albert Leifield	40.00	20.00	12.00
(100) Edgar Lennox	40.00	20.00	12.00
(101) Duffy Lewis	40.00	20.00	12.00
(102a) Irving Lewis (no emblem on sleeve)			
	1700.00	850.00	510.00
(102b) Irving Lewis (emblem on sleeve)			
	1700.00	850.00	510.00
(103) Jack Lively	40.00	20.00	12.00
(104a) Paddy Livingston ("A" on shirt)	150.00	75.00	45.00
(104b) Paddy Livingston (big "C" on shirt)			
	150.00	75.00	45.00
(104c) Paddy Livingston (little "C" on shirt)			
	50.00	25.00	15.00
(105) Briscoe Lord (Philadelphia)	40.00	20.00	12.00
(106) Harry Lord (Chicago)	40.00	20.00	12.00
(107) Louis Lowdermilk	1700.00	850.00	510.00
(108) Richard Marquard	125.00	62.00	37.00
(109) Armando Marsans	40.00	20.00	12.00
(110) George McBride	40.00	20.00	12.00
(111) Alexander McCarthy	125.00	62.00	37.00
(112) Edward McDonald	40.00	20.00	12.00
(113) John J. McGraw	175.00	87.00	52.00
(114) Harry McIntire (McIntyre)	40.00	20.00	12.00
(115) Matthew McIntyre	40.00	20.00	12.00

	NR MT	EX	VG
(116) William McKechnie	175.00	87.00	52.00
(117) Larry McLean	40.00	20.00	12.00
(118) Clyde Milan	40.00	20.00	12.00
(119) John B. Miller (Pittsburg)	40.00	20.00	12.00
(120) Otto Miller (Brooklyn)	100.00	50.00	30.00
(121) Roy Miller (Boston)	100.00	50.00	30.00
(122) Ward Miller (Chicago)	1700.00	850.00	510.00
(123) Mike Mitchell (Cleveland, front depicts Willie Mitchell)	80.00	40.00	24.00
(124) Mike Mitchell (Cincinnati)	40.00	20.00	12.00
(125) Geo. Mogridge	100.00	50.00	30.00
(126) Earl Moore	100.00	50.00	30.00
(127) Patrick J. Moran	40.00	20.00	12.00
(128) Cy Morgan (Philadelphia)	40.00	20.00	12.00
(129) Ray Morgan (Washington)	40.00	20.00	12.00
(130) George Moriarty	100.00	50.00	30.00
(131a) George Mullin ("D" on cap)	50.00	25.00	15.00
(131b) George Mullin (no "D" on cap)	50.00	25.00	15.00
(132) Thomas Needham	40.00	20.00	12.00
(133) Red Nelson	100.00	50.00	30.00
(134) Herbert Northen	40.00	20.00	12.00
(135) Leslie Nunamaker	40.00	20.00	12.00
(136) Rebel Oakes	40.00	20.00	12.00
(137) Buck O'Brien	40.00	20.00	12.00
(138) Rube Oldring	40.00	20.00	12.00
(139) Ivan Olson	40.00	20.00	12.00
(140) Martin J. O'Toole	40.00	20.00	12.00
(141) George Paskart (Paskert)	40.00	20.00	12.00
(142) Barney Pelty	100.00	50.00	30.00
(143) Herbert Perdue	40.00	20.00	12.00
(144) O.C. Peters	100.00	50.00	30.00
(145) Arthur Phelan	100.00	50.00	30.00
(146) Jack Quinn	40.00	20.00	12.00
(147) Don Carlos Ragan	350.00	175.00	105.00
(148) Arthur Rasmussen	275.00	137.00	82.00
(149) Morris Rath	100.00	50.00	30.00
(150) Edward Reulbach	40.00	20.00	12.00
(151) Napoleon Rucker	40.00	20.00	12.00
(152) J.B. Ryan	100.00	50.00	30.00
(153) Victor Saier	400.00	200.00	120.00
(154) William Scanlon	40.00	20.00	12.00
(155) Germany Schaefer	40.00	20.00	12.00
(156) Wilbur Schardt	40.00	20.00	12.00
(157) Frank Schulte	40.00	20.00	12.00
(158) Jim Scott	40.00	20.00	12.00
(159) Henry Severoid (Severeid)	40.00	20.00	12.00
(160) Mike Simon	40.00	20.00	12.00
(161) Frank E. Smith (Cincinnati)	40.00	20.00	12.00
(162) Wallace Smith (St. Louis)	40.00	20.00	12.00
(163) Fred Snodgrass	40.00	20.00	12.00
(164) Tristam Speaker	450.00	225.00	135.00
(165) Harry Lee Spratt	40.00	20.00	12.00
(166) Edward Stack	40.00	20.00	12.00
(167) Oscar Stanage	40.00	20.00	12.00
(168) William Steele	40.00	20.00	12.00
(169) Harry Steinfeldt	40.00	20.00	12.00
(170) George Stovall	40.00	20.00	12.00
(171) Charles (Gabby) Street	40.00	20.00	12.00
(172) Amos Strunk	40.00	20.00	12.00
(173) William Sullivan	40.00	20.00	12.00
(174) William J. Sweeney	100.00	50.00	30.00
(175) Leeford Tannehill	40.00	20.00	12.00
(176) C.D. Thomas	40.00	20.00	12.00
(177) Joseph Tinker	125.00	62.00	37.00
(178) Bert Tooley	40.00	20.00	12.00
(179) Terence Turner (Terrence)	40.00	20.00	12.00
(180) George Tyler	400.00	200.00	120.00
(181) Jim Vaughn	40.00	20.00	12.00
(182) Chas. (Heinie) Wagner	40.00	20.00	12.00
(183) Ed (Dixie) Walker	40.00	20.00	12.00
(184) Robert Wallace	125.00	62.00	37.00
(185) John Warhop	40.00	20.00	12.00
(186) George Weaver	100.00	50.00	30.00
(187) Zach Wheat	125.00	62.00	37.00
(188) G. Harris White	100.00	50.00	30.00
(189) Ernest Wilie	100.00	50.00	30.00
(190) Bob Williams	40.00	20.00	12.00
(191) Arthur Wilson (New York)	100.00	50.00	30.00
(192) Owen Wilson (Pittsburg)	40.00	20.00	12.00
(193) George Wiltse	40.00	20.00	12.00
(194) Ivey Wingo	40.00	20.00	12.00
(195) Harry Wolverton	40.00	20.00	12.00
(196) Joe Wood	80.00	40.00	24.00
(197) Eugene Woodburn	100.00	50.00	30.00
(198) Ralph Works	225.00	112.00	67.00
(199) Stanley Yerkes	40.00	20.00	12.00
(200) Rollie Zeider	80.00	40.00	24.00

NOTE: A card number in parentheses ( ) indicates the set is unnumbered.

1986 Tastykake Phillies

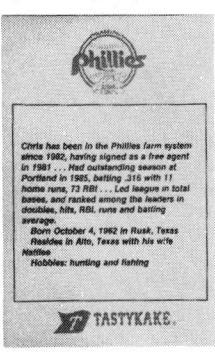

#26   CHRIS JAMES   OF

The 1986 Tastykake Phillies set consists of 49 cards that measure 3½'' by 5¼'' in size. The cards were given at the Phillies' annual baseball card day promotion. The card fronts feature a full-color photo along with the player's name, uniform number and position. The card backs are printed in red and black and carry a brief player biography. Five cards commemorating past Phillies' pennants were included in the set.

	MT	NR MT	EX
Complete Set:	8.00	6.00	3.25
Common Player:	.15	.11	.06
2 Jim Davenport	.15	.11	.06
3 Claude Osteen	.15	.11	.06
4 Lee Elia	.15	.11	.06
5 Mike Ryan	.15	.11	.06
6 John Russell	.20	.15	.08
7 John Felske	.15	.11	.06
8 Juan Samuel	.50	.40	.20
9 Von Hayes	.35	.25	.14
10 Darren Daulton	.15	.11	.06
11 Tom Foley	.15	.11	.06
12 Glenn Wilson	.30	.25	.12
14 Jeff Stone	.20	.15	.08
15 Rick Schu	.20	.15	.08
16 Luis Aguayo	.15	.11	.06
20 Mike Schmidt	1.00	.70	.40
21 Greg Gross	.15	.11	.06
22 Gary Redus	.25	.20	.10
23 Joe Lefebvre	.15	.11	.06
24 Milt Thompson	.30	.25	.12
25 Del Unser	.15	.11	.06
26 Chris James	1.00	.70	.40
27 Kent Tekulve	.25	.20	.10
28 Shane Rawley	.30	.25	.12
29 Ronn Reynolds	.15	.11	.06
30 Steve Jeltz	.15	.11	.06
31 Garry Maddox	.25	.20	.10
32 Steve Carlton	.70	.50	.30
33 Dave Shipanoff	.20	.15	.08
35 Randy Lerch	.15	.11	.06
36 Robin Roberts	.60	.45	.25
39 Dave Rucker	.15	.11	.06
40 Steve Bedrosian	.40	.30	.15
41 Tom Hume	.15	.11	.06
42 Don Carman	.50	.40	.20
43 Fred Toliver	.20	.15	.08
46 Kevin Gross	.30	.25	.12
47 Larry Andersen	.15	.11	.06
48 Dave Stewart	.30	.25	.12
49 Charles Hudson	.20	.15	.08
50 Rocky Childress	.25	.20	.10
--- Future Phillies (Ramon Caraballo, Joe Cipolloni)	.20	.15	.08
--- Future Phillies (Arturo Gonzalez, Mike Maddux)	.40	.30	.15
--- Future Phillies (Ricky Jordan, Francisco Melendez)	.30	.25	.12
--- Future Phillies (Randy Day, Kevin Ward)	.20	.15	.08
--- The 1915 Phillies	.15	.11	.06
--- The 1950 Phillies	.15	.11	.06
--- The 1980 Phillies	.15	.11	.06
--- The 1983 Phillies	.15	.11	.06
--- June 11, 1985 - A Night To Remember	.15	.11	.06

1987 Tastykake Phillies

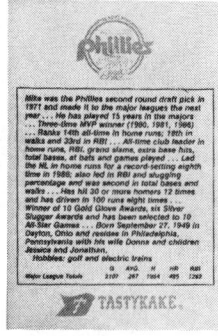

A 46-card set featuring the Philadelphia Phillies and sponsored by Tastykake was given out to fans present at Veterans Stadium for the Phillies' April 12th baseball card day promotion. The cards measure 3½'' by 5¼'' with fronts that feature a full-color player photo framed with a white border. The player's name, number and position appear below the photo. Card backs are printed in red and black and contain a brief biography. The set was available for $4 via a mail-in offer to the Phillies ball club.

		MT	NR MT	EX
Complete Set:		8.00	6.00	3.25
Common Player:		.15	.11	.06
6	John Russell	.20	.15	.08
7	John Felske	.15	.11	.06
8	Juan Samuel	.50	.40	.20
10	Darren Daulton	.15	.11	.06
11	Greg Legg	.20	.15	.08
12	Glenn Wilson	.30	.25	.12
13	Lance Parrish	.50	.40	.20
14	Jeff Stone	.20	.15	.08
15	Rick Schu	.20	.15	.08
16	Luis Aguayo	.15	.11	.06
17	Ron Roenicke	.15	.11	.06
18	Chris James	1.00	.70	.40
20	Mike Schmidt	1.00	.70	.40
21	Greg Gross	.15	.11	.06
23	Joe Cipolloni	.20	.15	.08
24	Milt Thompson	.30	.25	.12
27	Kent Tekulve	.25	.20	.10
28	Shane Rawley	.30	.25	.12
29	Ronn Reynolds	.15	.11	.06
30	Steve Jeltz	.15	.11	.06
33	Mike Jackson	.40	.30	.15
34	Mike Easler	.25	.20	.10
35	Dan Schatzeder	.15	.11	.06
37	Ken Dowell	.20	.15	.08
38	Jim Olander	.20	.15	.08
39a	Joe Cowley	.15	.11	.06
39b	Bob Scanlan	.20	.15	.08
40	Steve Bedrosian	.40	.30	.15
41	Tom Hume	.15	.11	.06
42	Don Carman	.30	.25	.12
43	Freddie Toliver	.15	.11	.06
44	Mike Maddux	.30	.25	.12
45	Greg Jelks	.40	.30	.15
46	Kevin Gross	.25	.20	.10
47	Bruce Ruffin	.40	.30	.15
48	Marvin Freeman	.30	.25	.12
49	Len Watts	.20	.15	.08
50	Tom Newell	.20	.15	.08
51	Ken Jackson	.30	.25	.12
52	Todd Frohwirth	.30	.25	.12
58	Doug Bair	.15	.11	.06
---	Shawn Burton, Rick Lundblade	.20	.15	.08
---	Jeff Kaye, Darren Loy	.20	.15	.08
---	Phillies Coaches (Jim Davenport, Lee Elia, Claude Osteen, Mike Ryan, Del Unser)	.15	.11	.06
---	Phillie Phanatic	.15	.11	.06
---	Team Photo	.15	.11	.06

1933 Tatoo Orbit

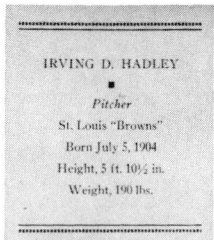

Found in 1¢ packages of Tattoo gum these 2'' by 2¼'' cards were produced by the Orbit Gum Company of Chicago, Illinois. Fronts feature a photograph which is tinted to give skin some color. Stylized baseball park backgrounds are separated from the photograph by a black line. The rest of the background is printed in vivid red, yellow and green. Card backs have the player's name, team, position, birth date, height and weight. The 60-card set is not common, but their interesting format does not seem to have struck a responsive chord in today's collectors. Cards of Bump Hadley and George Blaeholder are the most elusive, followed by those of Ivy Andrews and Rogers Hornsby.

		NR MT	EX	VG
Complete Set:		2500.00	1250.00	750.00
Common Player:		25.00	12.50	7.50
(1)	Dale Alexander	25.00	12.50	7.50
(2)	Ivy Paul Andrews	95.00	47.00	28.00
(3)	Earl Averill	45.00	22.00	13.50
(4)	Richard Bartell	25.00	12.50	7.50
(5)	Walter Berger	25.00	12.50	7.50
(6)	George F. Blaeholder	125.00	62.00	37.00
(7)	Irving J. Burns	25.00	12.50	7.50
(8)	Guy T. Bush	25.00	12.50	7.50
(9)	Bruce D. Campbell	25.00	12.50	7.50
(10)	William Cissell	25.00	12.50	7.50
(11)	Lefty Clark	25.00	12.50	7.50
(12)	Mickey Cochrane	60.00	30.00	18.00
(13)	Phil Collins	25.00	12.50	7.50
(14)	Hazen Kiki Cuyler	45.00	22.00	13.50
(15)	Dizzy Dean	140.00	70.00	42.00
(16)	Jimmy Dykes	30.00	15.00	9.00
(17)	George L. Earnshaw	25.00	12.50	7.50
(18)	Woody English	25.00	12.50	7.50
(19)	Lewis A. Fonseca	30.00	15.00	9.00
(20)	Jimmy Foxx	100.00	50.00	30.00
(21)	Burleigh A. Grimes	45.00	22.00	13.50
(22)	Charles John Grimm	30.00	15.00	9.00
(23)	Robert M. Grove	60.00	30.00	18.00
(24)	Frank Grube	25.00	12.50	7.50
(25)	George W. Haas	25.00	12.50	7.50
(26)	Irving D. Hadley	125.00	62.00	37.00
(27)	Chick Hafey	45.00	22.00	13.50
(28)	Jesse Joseph Haines	45.00	22.00	13.50
(29)	William Hallahan	25.00	12.50	7.50
(30)	Melvin Harder	25.00	12.50	7.50
(31)	Gabby Hartnett	45.00	22.00	13.50
(32)	Babe Herman	30.00	15.00	9.00
(33)	William Herman	45.00	22.00	13.50
(34)	Rogers Hornsby	150.00	75.00	45.00
(35)	Roy C. Johnson	25.00	12.50	7.50
(36)	J. Smead Jolley	25.00	12.50	7.50
(37)	William Jurges	25.00	12.50	7.50
(38)	William Kamm	25.00	12.50	7.50
(39)	Mark A. Koenig	25.00	12.50	7.50
(40)	James J. Levey	25.00	12.50	7.50
(41)	Ernie Lombardi	45.00	22.00	13.50
(42)	Red Lucas	25.00	12.50	7.50
(43)	Ted Lyons	45.00	22.00	13.50
(44)	Connie Mack	75.00	37.00	22.00
(45)	Pat Malone	25.00	12.50	7.50
(46)	Pepper Martin	30.00	15.00	9.00
(47)	Marty McManus	25.00	12.50	7.50
(48)	Frank J. O'Doul	30.00	15.00	9.00
(49)	Richard Porter	25.00	12.50	7.50
(50)	Carl N. Reynolds	25.00	12.50	7.50
(51)	Charles Henrt Root	25.00	12.50	7.50

		NR MT	EX	VG
(52)	Robert Seeds	25.00	12.50	7.50
(53)	Al H. Simmons	45.00	22.00	13.50
(54)	Jackson Riggs Stepheson	30.00	15.00	9.00
(55)	Bud Tinning	25.00	12.50	7.50
(56)	Joe Vosmik	25.00	12.50	7.50
(57)	Rube Walberg	25.00	12.50	7.50
(58)	Paul Waner	45.00	22.00	13.50
(59)	Lonnie Warneke	25.00	12.50	7.50
(60)	Arthur C. Whitney	25.00	12.50	7.50

1986 Texas Gold
Ice Cream Reds

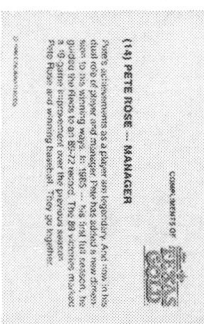

(14) PETE ROSE MANAGER

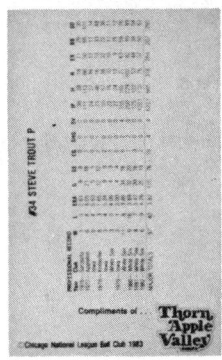

#24 STEVE TROUT P

One of the last regional baseball cards sets produced during the 1986 season was a 28-card team set sponsored by a Cincinnati-area ice cream company and given to fans attending a Sept. 19 game. Photos on the 2½'' by 3½'' cards are game action shots, and include three different cards of playing manager Pete Rose. The set is also notable for the inclusion of first cards of some of the Reds' young stars.

		MT	NR MT	EX
	Complete Set:	20.00	15.00	8.00
	Common Player:	.25	.20	.10
6	Bo Diaz	.35	.25	.14
9	Max Venable	.25	.20	.10
11	Kurt Stillwell	.80	.60	.30
12	Nick Esasky	.35	.25	.14
13	Dave Concepcion	.50	.40	.20
14a	Pete Rose (commemorative)	1.25	.90	.50
14b	Pete Rose (infield)	1.50	1.25	.60
14c	Pete Rose (manager)	1.50	1.25	.60
16	Ron Oester	.25	.20	.10
20	Eddie Milner	.25	.20	.10
22	Sal Butera	.25	.20	.10
24	Tony Perez	.70	.50	.30
25	Buddy Bell	.50	.40	.20
28	Kal Daniels	1.50	1.25	.60
29	Tracy Jones	.80	.60	.30
31	John Franco	.50	.40	.20
32	Tom Browning	.40	.30	.15
33	Ron Robinson	.35	.25	.14
34	Bill Gullickson	.30	.25	.12
36	Mario Soto	.35	.25	.14
39	Dave Parker	.80	.60	.30
40	John Denny	.25	.20	.10
44	Eric Davis	2.50	2.00	1.00
45	Chris Welsh	.25	.20	.10
48	Ted Power	.30	.25	.12
49	Joe Price	.25	.20	.10
---	Coaches Card (Scott Breeden, Billy DeMars, Tommy Helms, Bruce Kimm, Jim Lett, George Scherger)	.30	.25	.12
---	Logo/Coupon Card	.10	.08	.04

1983 Thorn Apple Valley Cubs

This set of 27 cards was issued in conjunction with a ''Baseball Card Day'' promotion at Wrigley Field in 1983. Thorn Apple Valley was the meat company which produced the hot dogs sold at the ballpark.

The cards feature borderless color photos with the player's name, uniform number (also the card's number in the checklist) and an abbreviation for their position. Card backs feature annual statistics. Of the 27 cards, which measure 2¼'' by 3½'', 25 feature players, one is a team card, and one features the manager and coaches.

		MT	NR MT	EX
	Complete Set:	10.00	7.50	4.00
	Common Player:	.20	.15	.08
1	Larry Bowa	.35	.25	.14
6	Keith Moreland	.35	.25	.14
7	Jody Davis	.40	.30	.15
10	Leon Durham	.40	.30	.15
11	Ron Cey	.30	.25	.12
16	Steve Lake	.20	.15	.08
20	Thad Bosley	.20	.15	.08
21	Jay Johnstone	.25	.20	.10
22	Bill Buckner	.40	.30	.15
23	Ryne Sandberg	3.00	2.25	1.25
24	Jerry Morales	.20	.15	.08
25	Gary Woods	.20	.15	.08
27	Mel Hall	.30	.25	.12
29	Tom Veryzer	.20	.15	.08
30	Chuck Rainey	.20	.15	.08
31	Fergie Jenkins	.50	.40	.20
32	Craig Lefferts	.30	.25	.12
33	Joe Carter	2.00	1.50	.80
34	Steve Trout	.30	.25	.12
36	Mike Proly	.20	.15	.08
39	Bill Campbell	.20	.15	.08
41	Warren Brusstar	.20	.15	.08
44	Dick Ruthven	.20	.15	.08
46	Lee Smith	.40	.30	.15
48	Dickie Noles	.20	.15	.08
---	Coaching Staff (Ruben Amaro, Billy Connors, Duffy Dyer, Lee Elia, Fred Koenig, John Vukovich)	.20	.15	.08
---	Team Photo	.20	.15	.08

1947 Tip Top Bread

ENOS SLAUGHTER
Outfield, St. Louis, N.L.

This 163-card set actually consists of a group of regional issues, some of which are more scarce then others. The 2¼'' by 3'' cards are borderless with a black and white player photo below which is a white strip containing the player's name, position, city name and league. Backs carry an advertisement. The set is known for a quantity of obscure players, many of whom played during the talent-lean World War II seasons. Overall it is a scarce set, with a number of interesting cards including first-issues of Yogi Berra and Joe Garagiola.

		NR MT	EX	VG
	Complete Set:	9000.00	4500.00	2700.00
	Common Player:	35.00	17.50	10.50
(1)	Bill Ayers	35.00	17.50	10.50
(2)	Floyd Baker	50.00	25.00	15.00
(3)	Charles Barrett	50.00	25.00	15.00
(4)	Eddie Basinski	35.00	17.50	10.50
(5)	John Berardino	50.00	25.00	15.00
(6)	Larry Berra	150.00	75.00	45.00
(7)	Bill Bevens	50.00	25.00	15.00
(8)	Robert Blattner	35.00	17.50	10.50
(9)	Ernie Bonham	35.00	17.50	10.50
(10)	Bob Bragan	45.00	22.00	13.50
(11)	Ralph Branca	70.00	35.00	21.00
(12)	Alpha Brazle	35.00	17.50	10.50
(13)	Bobbie Brown	60.00	30.00	18.00
(14)	Mike Budnick	35.00	17.50	10.50
(15)	Ken Burkhart	35.00	17.50	10.50
(16)	Thomas Byrne	50.00	25.00	15.00
(17)	Earl Caldwell	50.00	25.00	15.00
(18)	"Hank" Camelli	50.00	25.00	15.00
(19)	Hugh Casey	45.00	22.00	13.50
(20)	Phil Cavarretta	65.00	32.00	19.50
(21)	Bob Chipman	50.00	25.00	15.00
(22)	Lloyd Christopher	50.00	25.00	15.00
(23)	Bill Cox	35.00	17.50	10.50
(24)	Bernard Creger	35.00	17.50	10.50
(25)	Frank Crosetti	65.00	32.00	19.50
(26)	Joffre Cross	35.00	17.50	10.50
(27)	Leon Culberson	50.00	25.00	15.00
(28)	Dick Culler	50.00	25.00	15.00
(29)	Dom DiMaggio	100.00	50.00	30.00
(30)	George Dickey	60.00	30.00	18.00
(31)	Chas. E. Diering	35.00	17.50	10.50
(32)	Joseph Dobson	50.00	25.00	15.00
(33)	Bob Doerr	125.00	62.00	37.00
(34)	Ervin Dusak	35.00	17.50	10.50
(35)	Bruce Edwards	40.00	20.00	12.00
(36)	Walter "Hoot" Evers	50.00	25.00	15.00
(37)	Clifford Fannin	35.00	17.50	10.50
(38)	"Nanny" Fernandez	50.00	25.00	15.00
(39)	Dave "Boo" Ferriss	50.00	25.00	15.00
(40)	Elbie Fletcher	35.00	17.50	10.50
(41)	Dennis Galehouse	35.00	17.50	10.50
(42)	Joe Garagiola	100.00	50.00	30.00
(43)	Sid Gordon	35.00	17.50	10.50
(44)	John Gorsica	50.00	25.00	15.00
(45)	Hal Gregg	40.00	20.00	12.00
(46)	Frank Gustine	35.00	17.50	10.50
(47)	Stanley Hack	65.00	32.00	19.50
(48)	Mickey Harris	50.00	25.00	15.00
(49)	Clinton Hartung	35.00	17.50	10.50
(50)	Joe Hatten	40.00	20.00	12.00
(51)	Frank Hayes	50.00	25.00	15.00
(52)	"Jeff" Heath	35.00	17.50	10.50
(53)	Tom Henrich	70.00	35.00	21.00
(54)	Gene Hermanski	40.00	20.00	12.00
(55)	Kirby Higbe	35.00	17.50	10.50
(56)	Ralph Hodgin	50.00	25.00	15.00
(57)	Tex Hughson	50.00	25.00	15.00
(58)	Fred Hutchinson	70.00	35.00	21.00
(59)	LeRoy Jarvis	35.00	17.50	10.50
(60)	"Si" Johnson	50.00	25.00	15.00
(61)	Don Johnson	50.00	25.00	15.00
(62)	Earl Johnson	50.00	25.00	15.00
(63)	John Jorgenson	40.00	20.00	12.00
(64)	Walter Judnick (Judnich)	35.00	17.50	10.50
(65)	Tony Kaufmann	35.00	17.50	10.50
(66)	George Kell	125.00	62.00	37.00
(67)	Charlie Keller	65.00	32.00	19.50
(68)	Bob Kennedy	50.00	25.00	15.00
(69)	Montia Kennedy	35.00	17.50	10.50
(70)	Ralph Kiner	80.00	40.00	24.00
(71)	Dave Koslo	35.00	17.50	10.50
(72)	Jack Kramer	35.00	17.50	10.50
(73)	Joe Kuhel	50.00	25.00	15.00
(74)	George Kurowski	35.00	17.50	10.50
(75)	Emil Kush	50.00	25.00	15.00
(76)	"Eddie" Lake	50.00	25.00	15.00
(77)	Harry Lavagetto	45.00	22.00	13.50
(78)	Bill Lee	50.00	25.00	15.00
(79)	Thornton Lee	50.00	25.00	15.00
(80)	Paul Lehner	35.00	17.50	10.50
(81)	John Lindell	50.00	25.00	15.00
(82)	Danny Litwhiler	50.00	25.00	15.00
(83)	"Mickey" Livingston	50.00	25.00	15.00
(84)	Carroll Lockman	35.00	17.50	10.50
(85)	Jack Lohrke	35.00	17.50	10.50
(86)	Ernie Lombardi	80.00	40.00	24.00
(87)	Vic Lombardi	40.00	20.00	12.00
(88)	Edmund Lopat	65.00	32.00	19.50
(89)	Harry Lowrey	50.00	25.00	15.00
(90)	Marty Marion	50.00	25.00	15.00
(91)	Willard Marshall	35.00	17.50	10.50
(92)	Phil Masi	50.00	25.00	15.00
(93)	Edward J. Mayo	50.00	25.00	15.00
(94)	Clyde McCullough	50.00	25.00	15.00
(95)	Frank Melton	40.00	20.00	12.00
(96)	Cass Michaels	50.00	25.00	15.00
(97)	Ed Miksis	40.00	20.00	12.00
(98)	Arthur Mills	50.00	25.00	15.00
(99)	Johnny Mize	80.00	40.00	24.00
(100)	Lester Moss	35.00	17.50	10.50
(101)	"Pat" Mullin	50.00	25.00	15.00
(102)	"Bob" Muncrief	35.00	17.50	10.50
(103)	George Munger	35.00	17.50	10.50
(104)	Fritz Ostermueller	35.00	17.50	10.50
(105)	James P. Outlaw	50.00	25.00	15.00
(106)	Frank "Stub" Overmire	50.00	25.00	15.00
(107)	Andy Pafko	60.00	30.00	18.00
(108)	Joe Page	50.00	25.00	15.00
(109)	Roy Partee	50.00	25.00	15.00
(110)	Johnny Pesky	60.00	30.00	18.00
(111)	Nelson Potter	35.00	17.50	10.50
(112)	Mel Queen	50.00	25.00	15.00
(113)	Marion Rackley	40.00	20.00	12.00
(114)	Al Reynolds	70.00	35.00	21.00
(115)	Del Rice	35.00	17.50	10.50
(116)	Marv Rickert	50.00	25.00	15.00
(117)	John Rigney	50.00	25.00	15.00
(118)	Aaron Robinson	50.00	25.00	15.00
(119)	"Preacher" Roe	45.00	22.00	13.50
(120)	Carvel Rowell	50.00	25.00	15.00
(121)	Jim Russell	35.00	17.50	10.50
(122)	Rip Russell	50.00	25.00	15.00
(123)	Phil Rizzuto	100.00	50.00	30.00
(124)	Connie Ryan	50.00	25.00	15.00
(125)	John Sain	90.00	45.00	27.00
(126)	Ray Sanders	50.00	25.00	15.00
(127)	Fred Sanford	35.00	17.50	10.50
(128)	Johnny Schmitz	50.00	25.00	15.00
(129)	Joe Schultz	35.00	17.50	10.50
(130)	"Rip" Sewell	35.00	17.50	10.50
(131)	Dick Sisler	35.00	17.50	10.50
(132)	"Sibby" Sisti	50.00	25.00	15.00
(133)	Enos Slaughter	80.00	40.00	24.00
(134)	"Billy" Southworth	50.00	25.00	15.00
(135)	Warren Spahn	150.00	75.00	45.00
(136)	Verne Stephens (Vern)	35.00	17.50	10.50
(137)	George Sternweiss (Stirnweiss)	50.00	25.00	15.00
(138)	Ed Stevens	40.00	20.00	12.00
(139)	Nick Strincevich	35.00	17.50	10.50
(140)	"Bobby" Sturgeon	50.00	25.00	15.00
(141)	Robt. "Bob" Swift	50.00	25.00	15.00
(142)	Geo. "Birdie" Tibbetts (Tebbetts)	55.00	27.00	16.50
(143)	"Mike" Tresh	55.00	27.00	16.50
(144)	Ken Trinkle	35.00	17.50	10.50
(145)	Paul "Diz" Trout	55.00	27.00	16.50
(146)	Virgil "Fire" Trucks	55.00	27.00	16.50
(147)	Thurman Tucker	50.00	25.00	15.00
(148)	Bill Voiselle	35.00	17.50	10.50
(149)	Hal Wagner	50.00	25.00	15.00
(150)	Honus Wagner	100.00	50.00	30.00
(151)	Eddy Waitkus	50.00	25.00	15.00
(152)	Richard "Dick" Wakefield	50.00	25.00	15.00
(153)	Jack Wallaesa	50.00	25.00	15.00
(154)	Charles Wensloff	50.00	25.00	15.00
(155)	Ted Wilks	35.00	17.50	10.50
(156)	Mickey Witek	35.00	17.50	10.50
(157)	"Jerry" Witte	35.00	17.50	10.50
(158)	Ed Wright	50.00	25.00	15.00
(159)	Taft Wright	35.00	17.50	10.50
(160)	Henry Wyse	50.00	25.00	15.00
(161)	"Rudy" York	55.00	27.00	16.50
(162)	Al Zarilla	35.00	17.50	10.50
(163)	Bill Zuber	50.00	25.00	15.00

1948 Topps Magic Photos

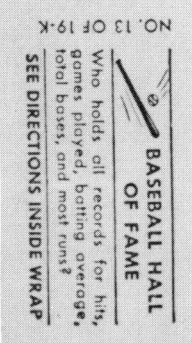

The first Topps baseball cards appeared as a subset of 19 cards from an issue of 252 "Magic Photos." The set takes its name from the self-developing nature of the cards. The cards were blank on the front when first taken from the wrapper. By spitting on the wrapper and holding it to the card while exposing it to light, the black and white photo appeared. Measuring ⅞" by 1½," the cards are very similar to Topps 1956 "Hocus Focus" issue.

		NR MT	EX	VG
	Complete Set:	600.00	300.00	180.00
	Common Player:	10.00	5.00	3.00
1	Lou Boudreau	20.00	10.00	6.00
2	Cleveland Indians	10.00	5.00	3.00
3	Bob Eliott	15.00	7.50	4.50
4	Cleveland Indians 4-3	10.00	5.00	3.00
5	Cleveland Indians 4-1 (Lou Boudreau Scoring)	20.00	10.00	6.00
6	"Babe" Ruth 714	150.00	75.00	45.00
7	Tris Speaker 793	25.00	12.50	7.50
8	Rogers Hornsby	30.00	15.00	9.00
9	Connie Mack	30.00	15.00	9.00
10	Christy Mathewson	35.00	17.50	10.50
11	Hans Wagner	35.00	17.50	10.50
12	Grover Alexander	30.00	15.00	9.00
13	Ty Cobb	90.00	45.00	27.00
14	Lou Gehrig	90.00	45.00	27.00
15	Walter Johnson	35.00	17.50	10.50
16	Cy Young	25.00	12.50	7.50
17	George Sisler 257	20.00	10.00	6.00
18	Tinker and Evers	20.00	10.00	6.00
19	Third Base Cleveland Indians	10.00	5.00	3.00

1951 Topps Blue Backs

Sold two cards in a package with a piece of candy for 1¢, the Topps Blue Backs are more scarce then their Red Back counterparts. The 2" by 2⅝" cards carry a black and white player photograph on a red, white, yellow and green background along with the player's name and other information including their 1950 record on the front. The back is printed in blue on a white background. The 52-card set has varied baseball situations on them making the playing of a rather elementary game of baseball possible. Although scarce, Blue Backs were printed on thick cardboard and have survived quite well over the years. There are, however, few stars (Johnny Mize and Enos Slaughter are two) in the set. Despite being a Topps product, Blue Backs do not currently enjoy great popularity.

		NR MT	EX	VG
	Complete Set:	1250.00	625.00	375.00
	Common Player:	20.00	10.00	6.00
1	Eddie Yost	20.00	10.00	6.00
2	Henry (Hank) Majeski	20.00	10.00	6.00
3	Richie Ashburn	40.00	20.00	12.00
4	Del Ennis	20.00	10.00	6.00
5	Johnny Pesky	25.00	12.50	7.50
6	Albert (Red) Schoendienst	30.00	15.00	9.00
7	Gerald Staley	20.00	10.00	6.00
8	Dick Sisler	20.00	10.00	6.00
9	Johnny Sain	30.00	15.00	9.00
10	Joe Page	30.00	15.00	9.00
11	Johnny Groth	20.00	10.00	6.00
12	Sam Jethroe	20.00	10.00	6.00
13	James (Mickey) Vernon	25.00	12.50	7.50
14	George Munger	20.00	10.00	6.00
15	Eddie Joost	20.00	10.00	6.00
16	Murry Dickson	20.00	10.00	6.00
17	Roy Smalley	20.00	10.00	6.00
18	Ned Garver	20.00	10.00	6.00
19	Phil Masi	20.00	10.00	6.00
20	Ralph Branca	25.00	12.50	7.50
21	Billy Johnson	20.00	10.00	6.00
22	Bob Kuzava	20.00	10.00	6.00
23	Paul (Dizzy) Trout	20.00	10.00	6.00
24	Sherman Lollar	20.00	10.00	6.00
25	Sam Mele	20.00	10.00	6.00
26	Chico Carresquel (Carrasquel)	20.00	10.00	6.00
27	Andy Pafko	25.00	12.50	7.50
28	Harry (The Cat) Brecheen	20.00	10.00	6.00
29	Granville Hamner	20.00	10.00	6.00
30	Enos (Country) Slaughter	40.00	20.00	12.00
31	Lou Brissie	20.00	10.00	6.00
32	Bob Elliott	20.00	10.00	6.00
33	Don Lenhardt	20.00	10.00	6.00
34	Earl Torgeson	20.00	10.00	6.00
35	Tommy Byrne	30.00	15.00	9.00
36	Cliff Fannin	20.00	10.00	6.00
37	Bobby Doerr	40.00	20.00	12.00
38	Irv Noren	20.00	10.00	6.00
39	Ed Lopat	30.00	15.00	9.00
40	Vic Wertz	25.00	12.50	7.50
41	Johnny Schmitz	20.00	10.00	6.00
42	Bruce Edwards	20.00	10.00	6.00
43	Willie (Puddin' Head) Jones	20.00	10.00	6.00
44	Johnny Wyrostek	20.00	10.00	6.00
45	Bill Pierce	25.00	12.50	7.50
46	Gerry Priddy	20.00	10.00	6.00
47	Herman Wehmeier	20.00	10.00	6.00
48	Billy Cox	20.00	10.00	6.00
49	Henry (Hank) Sauer	20.00	10.00	6.00
50	Johnny Mize	50.00	25.00	15.00
51	Eddie Waitkus	20.00	10.00	6.00
52	Sam Chapman	20.00	10.00	6.00

1951 Topps Red Backs

Like the Blue Backs, the Topps Red Backs which were sold at the same time, came two to a package for 1¢. Their black and white photographs appeared on a red, white, blue and yellow background. The back printing was red on white. Their 2'' by 2⅝'' size is the same as Blue Backs. Also identical are the set size (52 cards) and the game situations to be found on the fronts of the cards, for use in playing a card game of baseball. Red Backs are more common than the Blue Backs by virtue of a recent discovery of a large hoard of unopened boxes.

		NR MT	EX	VG
Complete Set:		500.00	250.00	150.00
Common Player:		6.00	3.00	1.75
1	Larry (Yogi) Berra	50.00	25.00	15.00
2	Sid Gordon	5.00	2.50	1.50
3	Ferris Fain	6.00	3.00	1.75
4	Verne Stephens (Vern)	6.00	3.00	1.75
5	Phil Rizzuto	20.00	10.00	6.00
6	Allie Reynolds	10.00	5.00	3.00
7	Howie Pollet	5.00	2.50	1.50
8	Early Wynn	20.00	10.00	6.00
9	Roy Sievers	6.00	3.00	1.75
10	Mel Parnell	6.00	3.00	1.75
11	Gene Hermanski	5.00	2.50	1.50
12	Jim Hegan	5.00	2.50	1.50
13	Dale Mitchell	5.00	2.50	1.50
14	Wayne Terwilliger	5.00	2.50	1.50
15	Ralph Kiner	20.00	10.00	6.00
16	Preacher Roe	8.00	4.00	2.50
17	Dave Bell	8.00	4.00	2.50
18	Gerry Coleman	8.00	4.00	2.50
19	Dick Kokos	5.00	2.50	1.50
20	Dominick DiMaggio (Dominic)	10.00	5.00	3.00
21	Larry Jansen	5.00	2.50	1.50
22	Bob Feller	25.00	12.50	7.50
23	Ray Boone	6.00	3.00	1.75
24	Hank Bauer	10.00	5.00	3.00
25	Cliff Chambers	5.00	2.50	1.50
26	Luke Easter	6.00	3.00	1.75
27	Wally Westlake	5.00	2.50	1.50
28	Elmer Valo	5.00	2.50	1.50
29	Bob Kennedy	5.00	2.50	1.50
30	Warren Spahn	20.00	10.00	6.00
31	Gil Hodges	20.00	10.00	6.00
32	Henry Thompson	5.00	2.50	1.50
33	William Werle	5.00	2.50	1.50
34	Grady Hatton	5.00	2.50	1.50
35	Al Rosen	10.00	5.00	3.00
36a	Gus Zernial (Chicago in bio)	20.00	10.00	6.00
36b	Gus Zernial (Philadelphia in bio)	10.00	5.00	3.00
37	Wes Westrum	6.00	3.00	1.75
38	Ed (Duke) Snider	40.00	20.00	12.00
39	Ted Kluszewski	10.00	5.00	3.00
40	Mike Garcia	6.00	3.00	1.75
41	Whitey Lockman	5.00	2.50	1.50
42	Ray Scarborough	5.00	2.50	1.50
43	Maurice McDermott	5.00	2.50	1.50
44	Sid Hudson	5.00	2.50	1.50
45	Andy Seminick	5.00	2.50	1.50
46	Billy Goodman	5.00	2.50	1.50
47	Tommy Glaviano	5.00	2.50	1.50
48	Eddie Stanky	6.00	3.00	1.75
49	Al Zarilla	5.00	2.50	1.50
50	Monte Irvin	15.00	7.50	4.50
51	Eddie Robinson	5.00	2.50	1.50
52a	Tommy Holmes (Boston in bio)	20.00	10.00	6.00
52b	Tommy Holmes (Hartford in bio)	10.00	5.00	3.00

1951 Topps Connie Mack All-Stars

A set of die-cut, 2-1/16'' by 5-1/4'' cards, all eleven players are Hall of Famers. The cards featured a black and white photograph of the player printed on a red background with a red, white, blue, yellow and black plaque underneath. Like the "Current All-Stars," with which they were issued, the background could be removed making it possible for the card to stand up. This practice, however, resulted in the card's mutilation and lowered it's condition in the eyes of today's collectors. Connie Mack All-Stars are

scarce today and despite being relatively expensive, retain a certain popularity as one of Topps first issues.

		NR MT	EX	VG
Complete Set:		4000.00	2000.00	1200.
Common Player:		125.00	62.00	37.00
(1)	Grover Cleveland Alexander	300.00	150.00	90.00
(2)	Gordon Stanley Cochrane	225.00	112.00	67.00
(3)	Edward Trowbridge Collins	150.00	75.00	45.00
(4)	James J. Collins	125.00	62.00	37.00
(5)	Henry Louis Gehrig	750.00	375.00	225.00
(6)	Walter Johnson	325.00	162.00	97.00
(7)	Connie Mack	225.00	112.00	67.00
(8)	Christopher Mathewson	300.00	150.00	90.00
(9)	George Herman Ruth	1100.00	550.00	330.00
(10)	Tristram Speaker	150.00	75.00	45.00
(11)	John Peter Wagner	300.00	150.00	90.00

1951 Topps Current All-Stars

The Topps Current All-Stars are very similar to the Connie Mack All-Stars of the same year. The 2-1/16 by 5-1/4'' cards have a black and white photograph on a red die-cut background. Most of the background could be folded over or removed so that the card would stand up. A plaque at the base carried brief biographical information. The set was to contain 11 cards, but only eight were actually issued in gum packs. Those of Jim Konstanty, Robin Roberts and Eddie Stanky were not released and are very rare. A big problem with the set is that if the card was used as it was intended it was folded and, thus, damaged from a collector's viewpoint. That makes top quality examples of any players difficult to find and quite expensive.

		NR MT	EX	VG
Complete Set:		16000.00	1175.00	590.00
Common Player:		150.00	81.25	41.25
(1)	Lawrence (Yogi) Berra	525.00	260.00	156.00
(2)	Lawrence Eugene Doby	225.00	114.00	68.00
(3)	Walter Dropo	225.00	114.00	68.00
(4)	Walter (Hoot) Evers	150.00	81.00	49.00
(5)	George Clyde Kell	300.00	146.00	88.00

		NR MT	EX	VG
(6)	Ralph McPherran Kiner	325.00	162.00	97.00
(7)	James Casimir Konstanty	4500.00	2275.00	1365.
(8)	Robert G. Lemon	325.00	162.00	97.00
(9)	Phillip Rizzuto	350.00	179.00	107.00
(10)	Robin Evan Roberts	4500.00	2275.00	1365.
(11)	Edward Raymond Stanky	4500.00	2275.00	1365.

1951 Topps Teams

An innovative issue for 1951, the Topps team cards were a nine-card set, 5-1/4" by 2-1/16," which carried a black-and-white picture of a major league team surrounded by a yellow border on the front. The back identifies team members with red printing on white cardboard. There are two versions of each card, with and without the date "1950" in the banner that carries the team name. Undated versions are valued slightly higher than the cards with dates. Strangely, only nine teams were issued. Scarcity varies, with the Cardinals and Red Sox being the most difficult to obtain.

		NR MT	EX	VG
Complete Set:		950.00	475.00	285.00
Common Team:		90.00	45.00	27.00
(1a)	Boston Red Sox (1950)	110.00	55.00	33.00
(1b)	Boston Red Sox (without 1950)			
		125.00	62.00	37.00
(2a)	Brooklyn Dodgers (1950)	150.00	75.00	45.00
(2b)	Brooklyn Dodgers (without 1950)			
		175.00	87.00	52.00
(3a)	Chicago White Sox (1950)	90.00	45.00	27.00
(3b)	Chicago White Sox (without 1950)			
		100.00	50.00	30.00
(4a)	Cincinnati Reds (1950)	90.00	45.00	27.00
(4b)	Cincinnati Reds (without 1950)	100.00	50.00	30.00
(5a)	New York Giants (1950)	110.00	55.00	33.00
(5b)	New York Giants (without 1950)			
		125.00	62.00	37.00
(6a)	Philadelphia Athletics (1950)	90.00	45.00	27.00
(6b)	Philadelphia Athletics (without 1950)			
		100.00	50.00	30.00
(7a)	Philadelphia Phillies (1950)	90.00	45.00	27.00
(7b)	Philadelphia Phillies (without 1950)			
		100.00	50.00	30.00
(8a)	St. Louis Cardinals (1950)	90.00	45.00	27.00
(8b)	St. Louis Cardinals (without 1950)			
		100.00	50.00	30.00
(9a)	Washington Senators (1950)	90.00	45.00	27.00
(9b)	Washington Senators (without 1950)			
		100.00	50.00	30.00

1952 Topps

At 407 cards, the 1952 Topps set was the largest set of its day, both in number of cards and physical

---

Complete set prices do not include the higher priced variations, unless noted otherwise.

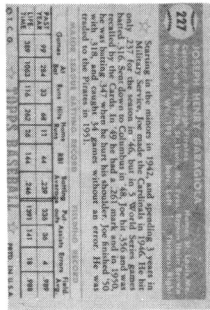

dimensions of the cards. Cards are 2⅝" by 3¾" with a hand-colored black and white photo on front. Major baseball card innovations presented in the set include the first-ever use of color team logos as part of the design, and the inclusion of stats for the previous season and overall career on the backs. A major variety in the set is that first 80 cards can be found with backs printed entirely in black or black and red. Backs entirely in black command a $5-10 premium. Card numbers 311-407 were printed in limited supplies and are extremely rare.

		NR MT	EX	VG
Complete Set:		36000.00	12600.00	7200.
Common Player: 1-80		55.00	11.00	5.50
Common Player: 81-250		20.00	6.00	3.00
Common Player: 251-280		40.00	12.00	6.00
Common Player: 281-300		50.00	15.00	7.50
Common Player: 301-310		40.00	12.00	6.00
Common Player: 311-407		140.00	70.00	42.00
1	Andy Pafko	550.00	16.00	8.00
2	James E. Runnels	80.00	12.00	6.00
3	Hank Thompson	55.00	11.00	5.50
4	Don Lenhardt	55.00	11.00	5.50
5	Larry Jansen	55.00	11.00	5.50
6	Grady Hatton	55.00	11.00	5.50
7	Wayne Terwilliger	60.00	12.00	6.00
8	Fred Marsh	55.00	11.00	5.50
9	Bobby Hogue	65.00	13.00	6.50
10	Al Rosen	80.00	16.00	8.00
11	Phil Rizzuto	125.00	25.00	12.50
12	Monty Basgall	55.00	11.00	5.50
13	Johnny Wyrostek	55.00	11.00	5.50
14	Bob Elliott	55.00	11.00	5.50
15	Johnny Pesky	60.00	12.00	6.00
16	Gene Hermanski	55.00	11.00	5.50
17	Jim Hegan	55.00	11.00	5.50
18	Merrill Combs	55.00	11.00	5.50
19	Johnny Bucha	55.00	11.00	5.50
20	Billy Loes	80.00	16.00	8.00
21	Ferris Fain	60.00	12.00	6.00
22	Dom DiMaggio	80.00	16.00	8.00
23	Billy Goodman	55.00	11.00	5.50
24	Luke Easter	60.00	12.00	6.00
25	Johnny Groth	55.00	11.00	5.50
26	Monty Irvin	90.00	18.00	9.00
27	Sam Jethroe	55.00	11.00	5.50
28	Jerry Priddy	55.00	11.00	5.50
29	Ted Kluszewski	80.00	16.00	8.00
30	Mel Parnell	60.00	12.00	6.00
31	Gus Zernial	60.00	12.00	6.00
32	Eddie Robinson	55.00	11.00	5.50
33	Warren Spahn	125.00	25.00	12.50
34	Elmer Valo	55.00	11.00	5.50
35	Hank Sauer	60.00	12.00	6.00
36	Gil Hodges	110.00	22.00	11.00
37	Duke Snider	175.00	35.00	17.50
38	Wally Westlake	55.00	11.00	5.50
39	"Dizzy" Trout	60.00	12.00	6.00
40	Irv Noren	55.00	11.00	5.50
41	Bob Wellman	55.00	11.00	5.50
42	Lou Kretlow	55.00	11.00	5.50
43	Ray Scarborough	55.00	11.00	5.50
44	Con Dempsey	55.00	11.00	5.50
45	Eddie Joost	55.00	11.00	5.50
46	Gordon Goldsberry	55.00	11.00	5.50
47	Willie Jones	55.00	11.00	5.50

		NR MT	EX	VG			NR MT	EX	VG
48a	Joe Page (Johnny Sain bio)	200.00	40.00	20.00	137	Roy McMillan	25.00	7.50	3.75
48b	Joe Page (correct bio)	80.00	16.00	8.00	138	Bill MacDonald	20.00	6.00	3.00
49a	Johnny Sain (Joe Page bio)	200.00	40.00	20.00	139	Ken Wood	20.00	6.00	3.00
49b	Johnny Sain (correct bio)	80.00	16.00	8.00	140	John Antonelli	25.00	7.50	3.75
50	Marv Rickert	55.00	11.00	5.50	141	Clint Hartung	20.00	6.00	3.00
51	Jim Russell	60.00	12.00	6.00	142	Harry Perkowski	20.00	6.00	3.00
52	Don Mueller	55.00	11.00	5.50	143	Les Moss	20.00	6.00	3.00
53	Chris Van Cuyk	60.00	12.00	6.00	144	Ed Blake	20.00	6.00	3.00
54	Leo Kiely	55.00	11.00	5.50	145	Joe Haynes	20.00	6.00	3.00
55	Ray Boone	60.00	12.00	6.00	146	Frank House	20.00	6.00	3.00
56	Tommy Glaviano	55.00	11.00	5.50	147	Bob Young	20.00	6.00	3.00
57	Ed Lopat	80.00	16.00	8.00	148	Johnny Klippstein	20.00	6.00	3.00
58	Bob Mahoney	55.00	11.00	5.50	149	Dick Kryhoski	20.00	6.00	3.00
59	Robin Roberts	100.00	20.00	10.00	150	Ted Beard	20.00	6.00	3.00
60	Sid Hudson	55.00	11.00	5.50	151	Wally Post	20.00	6.00	3.00
61	"Tookie" Gilbert	55.00	11.00	5.50	152	Al Evans	20.00	6.00	3.00
62	Chuck Stobbs	55.00	11.00	5.50	153	Bob Rush	20.00	6.00	3.00
63	Howie Pollet	55.00	11.00	5.50	154	Joe Muir	20.00	6.00	3.00
64	Roy Sievers	65.00	13.00	6.50	155	Frank Overmire	30.00	9.00	4.50
65	Enos Slaughter	100.00	20.00	10.00	156	Frank Hiller	20.00	6.00	3.00
66	"Preacher" Roe	80.00	16.00	8.00	157	Bob Usher	20.00	6.00	3.00
67	Allie Reynolds	80.00	16.00	8.00	158	Eddie Waitkus	20.00	6.00	3.00
68	Cliff Chambers	55.00	11.00	5.50	159	Saul Rogovin	20.00	6.00	3.00
69	Virgil Stallcup	55.00	11.00	5.50	160	Owen Friend	20.00	6.00	3.00
70	Al Zarilla	55.00	11.00	5.50	161	Bud Byerly	20.00	6.00	3.00
71	Tom Upton	55.00	11.00	5.50	162	Del Crandall	25.00	7.50	3.75
72	Karl Olson	55.00	11.00	5.50	163	Stan Rojek	20.00	6.00	3.00
73	William Werle	55.00	11.00	5.50	164	Walt Dubiel	20.00	6.00	3.00
74	Andy Hansen	55.00	11.00	5.50	165	Eddie Kazak	20.00	6.00	3.00
75	Wes Westrum	60.00	12.00	6.00	166	Paul LaPalme	20.00	6.00	3.00
76	Eddie Stanky	65.00	13.00	6.50	167	Bill Howerton	20.00	6.00	3.00
77	Bob Kennedy	55.00	11.00	5.50	168	Charlie Silvera	30.00	9.00	4.50
78	Ellis Kinder	55.00	11.00	5.50	169	Howie Judson	20.00	6.00	3.00
79	Gerald Staley	55.00	11.00	5.50	170	Gus Bell	25.00	7.50	3.75
80	Herman Wehmeier	55.00	11.00	5.50	171	Ed Erautt	20.00	6.00	3.00
81	Vernon Law	25.00	7.50	3.75	172	Eddie Miksis	20.00	6.00	3.00
82	Duane Pillette	20.00	6.00	3.00	173	Roy Smalley	20.00	6.00	3.00
83	Billy Johnson	20.00	6.00	3.00	174	Clarence Marshall	20.00	6.00	3.00
84	Vern Stephens	20.00	6.00	3.00	175	Billy Martin	175.00	53.00	26.00
85	Bob Kuzava	30.00	9.00	4.50	176	Hank Edwards	20.00	6.00	3.00
86	Ted Gray	20.00	6.00	3.00	177	Bill Wight	20.00	6.00	3.00
87	Dale Coogan	20.00	6.00	3.00	178	Cass Michaels	20.00	6.00	3.00
88	Bob Feller	100.00	30.00	15.00	179	Frank Smith	20.00	6.00	3.00
89	Johnny Lipon	20.00	6.00	3.00	180	Charley Maxwell	25.00	7.50	3.75
90	Mickey Grasso	20.00	6.00	3.00	181	Bob Swift	20.00	6.00	3.00
91	Al Schoendienst	30.00	9.00	4.50	182	Billy Hitchcock	20.00	6.00	3.00
92	Dale Mitchell	20.00	6.00	3.00	183	Erv Dusak	20.00	6.00	3.00
93	Al Sima	20.00	6.00	3.00	184	Bob Ramazzotti	20.00	6.00	3.00
94	Sam Mele	20.00	6.00	3.00	185	Bill Nicholson	20.00	6.00	3.00
95	Ken Holcombe	20.00	6.00	3.00	186	Walt Masterson	20.00	6.00	3.00
96	Willard Marshall	20.00	6.00	3.00	187	Bob Miller	20.00	6.00	3.00
97	Earl Torgeson	20.00	6.00	3.00	188	Clarence Podbielan	25.00	7.50	3.75
98	Bill Pierce	25.00	7.50	3.75	189	Pete Reiser	25.00	7.50	3.75
99	Gene Woodling	40.00	12.00	6.00	190	Don Johnson	20.00	6.00	3.00
100	Del Rice	20.00	6.00	3.00	191	Yogi Berra	200.00	60.00	30.00
101	Max Lanier	20.00	6.00	3.00	192	Myron Ginsberg	20.00	6.00	3.00
102	Bill Kennedy	20.00	6.00	3.00	193	Harry Simpson	20.00	6.00	3.00
103	Cliff Mapes	20.00	6.00	3.00	194	Joe Hatten	20.00	6.00	3.00
104	Don Kolloway	20.00	6.00	3.00	195	Orestes Minoso	30.00	9.00	4.50
105	John Pramesa	20.00	6.00	3.00	196	Solly Hemus	20.00	6.00	3.00
106	Mickey Vernon	25.00	7.50	3.75	197	George Strickland	20.00	6.00	3.00
107	Connie Ryan	20.00	6.00	3.00	198	Phil Haugstad	25.00	7.50	3.75
108	Jim Konstanty	25.00	7.50	3.75	199	George Zuverink	20.00	6.00	3.00
109	Ted Wilks	20.00	6.00	3.00	200	Ralph Houk	50.00	15.00	7.50
110	Dutch Leonard	20.00	6.00	3.00	201	Alex Kellner	20.00	6.00	3.00
111	Harry Lowrey	20.00	6.00	3.00	202	Joe Collins	30.00	9.00	4.50
112	Henry Majeski	20.00	6.00	3.00	203	Curt Simmons	25.00	7.50	3.75
113	Dick Sisler	20.00	6.00	3.00	204	Ron Northey	20.00	6.00	3.00
114	Willard Ramsdell	20.00	6.00	3.00	205	Clyde King	25.00	7.50	3.75
115	George Munger	20.00	6.00	3.00	206	Joe Ostrowski	30.00	9.00	4.50
116	Carl Scheib	20.00	6.00	3.00	207	Mickey Harris	20.00	6.00	3.00
117	Sherman Lollar	25.00	7.50	3.75	208	Marlin Stuart	20.00	6.00	3.00
118	Ken Raffensberger	20.00	6.00	3.00	209	Howie Fox	20.00	6.00	3.00
119	Maurice McDermott	20.00	6.00	3.00	210	Dick Fowler	20.00	6.00	3.00
120	Bob Chakales	20.00	6.00	3.00	211	Ray Coleman	20.00	6.00	3.00
121	Gus Niarhos	20.00	6.00	3.00	212	Ned Garver	20.00	6.00	3.00
122	Jack Jensen	40.00	12.00	6.00	213	Nippy Jones	20.00	6.00	3.00
123	Eddie Yost	25.00	7.50	3.75	214	Johnny Hopp	30.00	9.00	4.50
124	Monte Kennedy	20.00	6.00	3.00	215	Hank Bauer	40.00	12.00	6.00
125	Bill Rigney	25.00	7.50	3.75	216	Richie Ashburn	40.00	12.00	6.00
126	Fred Hutchinson	25.00	7.50	3.75	217	George Stirnweiss	20.00	6.00	3.00
127	Paul Minner	20.00	6.00	3.00	218	Clyde McCullough	20.00	6.00	3.00
128	Don Bollweg	30.00	9.00	4.50	219	Bobby Shantz	25.00	7.50	3.75
129	Johnny Mize	60.00	18.00	9.00	220	Joe Presko	20.00	6.00	3.00
130	Sheldon Jones	20.00	6.00	3.00	221	Granny Hamner	20.00	6.00	3.00
131	Morrie Martin	20.00	6.00	3.00	222	"Hoot" Evers	20.00	6.00	3.00
132	Clyde Kluttz	20.00	6.00	3.00	223	Del Ennis	25.00	7.50	3.75
133	Al Widmar	20.00	6.00	3.00	224	Bruce Edwards	20.00	6.00	3.00
134	Joe Tipton	20.00	6.00	3.00	225	Frank Baumholtz	20.00	6.00	3.00
135	Dixie Howell	20.00	6.00	3.00	226	Dave Philley	25.00	7.50	3.75
136	Johnny Schmitz	25.00	7.50	3.75	227	Joe Garagiola	60.00	18.00	9.00

		NR MT	EX	VG
228	Al Brazle	20.00	6.00	3.00
229	Gene Bearden	20.00	6.00	3.00
230	Matt Batts	20.00	6.00	3.00
231	Sam Zoldak	20.00	6.00	3.00
232	Billy Cox	30.00	9.00	4.50
233	Bob Friend	25.00	7.50	3.75
234	Steve Souchock	20.00	6.00	3.00
235	Walt Dropo	25.00	7.50	3.75
236	Ed Fitz Gerald	20.00	6.00	3.00
237	Jerry Coleman	30.00	9.00	4.50
238	Art Houtteman	20.00	6.00	3.00
239	Rocky Bridges	25.00	7.50	3.75
240	Jack Phillips	20.00	6.00	3.00
241	Tommy Byrne	20.00	6.00	3.00
242	Tom Poholsky	20.00	6.00	3.00
243	Larry Doby	30.00	9.00	4.50
244	Vic Wertz	25.00	7.50	3.75
245	Sherry Robertson	20.00	6.00	3.00
246	George Kell	50.00	15.00	7.50
247	Randy Gumpert	20.00	6.00	3.00
248	Frank Shea	20.00	6.00	3.00
249	Bobby Adams	20.00	6.00	3.00
250	Carl Erskine	40.00	12.00	6.00
251	Chico Carrasquel	40.00	12.00	6.00
252	Vern Bickford	40.00	12.00	6.00
253	Johnny Berardino	50.00	15.00	7.50
254	Joe Dobson	40.00	12.00	6.00
255	Clyde Vollmer	40.00	12.00	6.00
256	Pete Suder	40.00	12.00	6.00
257	Bobby Avila	40.00	12.00	6.00
258	Steve Gromek	40.00	12.00	6.00
259	Bob Addis	40.00	12.00	6.00
260	Pete Castiglione	40.00	12.00	6.00
261	Willie Mays	750.00	195.00	97.00
262	Virgil Trucks	45.00	13.50	6.75
263	Harry Brecheen	45.00	13.50	6.75
264	Roy Hartsfield	40.00	12.00	6.00
265	Chuck Diering	40.00	12.00	6.00
266	Murry Dickson	40.00	12.00	6.00
267	Sid Gordon	40.00	12.00	6.00
268	Bob Lemon	140.00	42.00	21.00
269	Willard Nixon	40.00	12.00	6.00
270	Lou Brissie	40.00	12.00	6.00
271	Jim Delsing	40.00	12.00	6.00
272	Mike Garcia	45.00	13.50	6.75
273	Erv Palica	45.00	13.50	6.75
274	Ralph Branca	60.00	18.00	9.00
275	Pat Mullin	40.00	12.00	6.00
276	Jim Wilson	40.00	12.00	6.00
277	Early Wynn	140.00	42.00	21.00
278	Al Clark	40.00	12.00	6.00
279	Ed Stewart	40.00	12.00	6.00
280	Cloyd Boyer	40.00	12.00	6.00
281	Tommy Brown	50.00	15.00	7.50
282	Birdie Tebbetts	50.00	15.00	7.50
283	Phil Masi	50.00	15.00	7.50
284	Hank Arft	50.00	15.00	7.50
285	Cliff Fannin	50.00	15.00	7.50
286	Joe DeMaestri	50.00	15.00	7.50
287	Steve Bilko	50.00	15.00	7.50
288	Chet Nichols	50.00	15.00	7.50
289	Tommy Holmes	55.00	16.50	8.25
290	Joe Astroth	50.00	15.00	7.50
291	Gil Coan	50.00	15.00	7.50
292	Floyd Baker	50.00	15.00	7.50
293	Sibby Sisti	50.00	15.00	7.50
294	Walker Cooper	50.00	15.00	7.50
295	Phil Cavarretta	55.00	16.50	8.25
296	"Red" Rolfe	50.00	15.00	7.50
297	Andy Seminick	50.00	15.00	7.50
298	Bob Ross	50.00	15.00	7.50
299	Ray Murray	50.00	15.00	7.50
300	Barney McCosky	50.00	15.00	7.50
301	Bob Porterfield	40.00	12.00	6.00
302	Max Surkont	40.00	12.00	6.00
303	Harry Dorish	40.00	12.00	6.00
304	Sam Dente	40.00	12.00	6.00
305	Paul Richards	45.00	13.50	6.75
306	Lou Sleator	40.00	12.00	6.00
307	Frank Campos	40.00	12.00	6.00
308	Luis Aloma	40.00	12.00	6.00
309	Jim Busby	40.00	12.00	6.00
310	George Metkovich	40.00	12.00	6.00
311	Mickey Mantle	6500.00	2275.00	1300.
312	Jackie Robinson	600.00	300.00	180.00
313	Bobby Thomson	160.00	80.00	48.00
314	Roy Campanella	775.00	387.00	232.00
315	Leo Durocher	200.00	100.00	60.00
316	Davey Williams	140.00	70.00	42.00
317	Connie Marrero	140.00	70.00	42.00
318	Hal Gregg	140.00	70.00	42.00

		NR MT	EX	VG
319	Al Walker	140.00	70.00	42.00
320	John Rutherford	140.00	70.00	42.00
321	Joe Black	175.00	87.00	52.00
322	Randy Jackson	140.00	70.00	42.00
323	Bubba Church	140.00	70.00	42.00
324	Warren Hacker	140.00	70.00	42.00
325	Bill Serena	140.00	70.00	42.00
326	George Shuba	140.00	70.00	42.00
327	Archie Wilson	140.00	70.00	42.00
328	Bob Borkowski	140.00	70.00	42.00
329	Ivan Delock	140.00	70.00	42.00
330	Turk Lown	140.00	70.00	42.00
331	Tom Morgan	160.00	80.00	48.00
332	Tony Bartirome	140.00	70.00	42.00
333	Pee Wee Reese	450.00	225.00	135.00
334	Wilmer Mizell	140.00	70.00	42.00
335	Ted Lepcio	140.00	70.00	42.00
336	Dave Koslo	140.00	70.00	42.00
337	Jim Hearn	140.00	70.00	42.00
338	Sal Yvars	140.00	70.00	42.00
339	Russ Meyer	140.00	70.00	42.00
340	Bob Hooper	140.00	70.00	42.00
341	Hal Jeffcoat	140.00	70.00	42.00
342	Clem Labine	175.00	87.00	52.00
343	Dick Gernert	140.00	70.00	42.00
344	Ewell Blackwell	160.00	80.00	48.00
345	Sam White	140.00	70.00	42.00
346	George Spencer	140.00	70.00	42.00
347	Joe Adcock	160.00	80.00	48.00
348	Bob Kelly	140.00	70.00	42.00
349	Bob Cain	140.00	70.00	42.00
350	Cal Abrams	140.00	70.00	42.00
351	Al Dark	175.00	87.00	52.00
352	Karl Drews	140.00	70.00	42.00
353	Bob Del Greco	140.00	70.00	42.00
354	Fred Hatfield	140.00	70.00	42.00
355	Bobby Morgan	140.00	70.00	42.00
356	Toby Atwell	140.00	70.00	42.00
357	Smoky Burgess	160.00	80.00	48.00
358	John Kucab	140.00	70.00	42.00
359	Dee Fondy	140.00	70.00	42.00
360	George Crowe	140.00	70.00	42.00
361	Bill Posedel	140.00	70.00	42.00
362	Ken Heintzelman	140.00	70.00	42.00
363	Dick Rozek	140.00	70.00	42.00
364	Clyde Sukeforth	140.00	70.00	42.00
365	"Cookie" Lavagetto	150.00	75.00	45.00
366	Dave Madison	140.00	70.00	42.00
367	Bob Thorpe	140.00	70.00	42.00
368	Ed Wright	140.00	70.00	42.00
369	Dick Groat	200.00	100.00	60.00
370	Billy Hoeft	140.00	70.00	42.00
371	Bob Hofman	140.00	70.00	42.00
372	Gil McDougald	225.00	112.00	67.00
373	Jim Turner	160.00	80.00	48.00
374	Al Benton	140.00	70.00	42.00
375	Jack Merson	140.00	70.00	42.00
376	Faye Throneberry	140.00	70.00	42.00
377	Chuck Dressen	175.00	87.00	52.00
378	Les Fusselman	140.00	70.00	42.00
379	Joe Rossi	140.00	70.00	42.00
380	Clem Koshorek	140.00	70.00	42.00
381	Milton Stock	140.00	70.00	42.00
382	Sam Jones	140.00	70.00	42.00
383	Del Wilber	140.00	70.00	42.00
384	Frank Crosetti	225.00	112.00	67.00
385	Herman Franks	140.00	70.00	42.00
386	Eddie Yuhas	140.00	70.00	42.00
387	Billy Meyer	140.00	70.00	42.00
388	Bob Chipman	140.00	70.00	42.00
389	Ben Wade	140.00	70.00	42.00
390	Glenn Nelson	140.00	70.00	42.00
391	Ben Chapman (photo actually Sam Chapman)	140.00	70.00	42.00
392	Hoyt Wilhelm	375.00	187.00	112.00
393	Ebba St. Claire	140.00	70.00	42.00
394	Billy Herman	175.00	87.00	52.00
395	Jake Pitler	140.00	70.00	42.00
396	Dick Williams	175.00	87.00	52.00
397	Forrest Main	140.00	70.00	42.00
398	Hal Rice	140.00	70.00	42.00
399	Jim Fridley	140.00	70.00	42.00
400	Bill Dickey	450.00	225.00	135.00
401	Bob Schultz	140.00	70.00	42.00
402	Earl Harrist	140.00	70.00	42.00
403	Bill Miller	160.00	80.00	48.00
404	Dick Brodowski	140.00	70.00	42.00
405	Eddie Pellagrini	140.00	70.00	42.00
406	Joe Nuxhall	175.00	87.00	52.00
407	Ed Mathews	1400.00	250.00	135.00

1953 Topps

The 1953 Topps set reflects the company's continuing legal battles with Bowman. The set, originally intended to consist of 280 cards, is lacking six numbers (#'s 253, 261, 267, 268, 271 and 275) which probably represent players whose contracts were lost to the competition. The 2⅝'' by 3¾'' cards feature painted player pictures. A color team logo appears at a bottom panel (red for American League and black for National.) Card backs contain the first baseball trivia questions along with brief statistics and player biographies. In the red panel at the top which lists the player's personal data, cards from the 2nd series (#'s 86-165 plus 10, 44, 61, 72 and 81) can be found with that data printed in either black or white, black being the scarcer variety. Cards #221-280 are the scarce high numbers.

	NR MT	EX	VG
Complete Set:	8000.00	2800.00	1600.
Common Player: 1-165	9.00	4.50	2.75
Common Player: 166-220	7.00	3.50	2.00
Common Player: 221-280	32.00	16.00	9.50

		NR MT	EX	VG
1	Jackie Robinson	300.00	80.00	45.00
2	Luke Easter	15.00	5.00	3.00
3	George Crowe	15.00	7.50	4.50
4	Ben Wade	15.00	7.50	4.50
5	Joe Dobson	15.00	7.50	4.50
6	Sam Jones	15.00	7.50	4.50
7	Bob Borkowski	9.00	4.50	2.75
8	Clem Koshorek	9.00	4.50	2.75
9	Joe Collins	20.00	10.00	6.00
10	Smoky Burgess	20.00	10.00	6.00
11	Sal Yvars	15.00	7.50	4.50
12	Howie Judson	9.00	4.50	2.75
13	Connie Marrero	9.00	4.50	2.75
14	Clem Labine	12.00	6.00	3.50
15	Bobo Newsom	10.00	5.00	3.00
16	Harry Lowrey	9.00	4.50	2.75
17	Billy Hitchcock	15.00	7.50	4.50
18	Ted Lepcio	9.00	4.50	2.75
19	Mel Parnell	10.00	5.00	3.00
20	Hank Thompson	15.00	7.50	4.50
21	Billy Johnson	15.00	7.50	4.50
22	Howie Fox	15.00	7.50	4.50
23	Toby Atwell	9.00	4.50	2.75
24	Ferris Fain	15.00	7.50	4.50
25	Ray Boone	15.00	7.50	4.50
26	Dale Mitchell	9.00	4.50	2.75
27	Roy Campanella	110.00	44.00	28.00
28	Eddie Pellagrini	15.00	7.50	4.50
29	Hal Jeffcoat	15.00	7.50	4.50
30	Willard Nixon	15.00	7.50	4.50
31	Ewell Blackwell	25.00	12.50	7.50
32	Clyde Vollmer	15.00	7.50	4.50
33	Bob Kennedy	9.00	4.50	2.75
34	George Shuba	15.00	7.50	4.50
35	Irv Noren	15.00	7.50	4.50
36	Johnny Groth	9.00	4.50	2.75
37	Ed Mathews	40.00	20.00	12.00
38	Jim Hearn	9.00	4.50	2.75
39	Eddie Miksis	15.00	7.50	4.50
40	John Lipon	15.00	7.50	4.50
41	Enos Slaughter	40.00	20.00	12.00
42	Gus Zernial	10.00	5.00	3.00
43	Gil McDougald	25.00	12.50	7.50
44	Ellis Kinder	20.00	10.00	6.00
45	Grady Hatton	9.00	4.50	2.75
46	Johnny Klippstein	9.00	4.50	2.75
47	Bubba Church	9.00	4.50	2.75
48	Bob Del Greco	9.00	4.50	2.75
49	Faye Throneberry	9.00	4.50	2.75
50	Chuck Dressen	12.00	6.00	3.50
51	Frank Campos	9.00	4.50	2.75
52	Ted Gray	9.00	4.50	2.75
53	Sherman Lollar	10.00	5.00	3.00
54	Bob Feller	50.00	25.00	15.00
55	Maurice McDermott	9.00	4.50	2.75
56	Gerald Staley	9.00	4.50	2.75
57	Carl Scheib	15.00	7.50	4.50
58	George Metkovich	15.00	7.50	4.50
59	Karl Drews	9.00	4.50	2.75
60	Cloyd Boyer	9.00	4.50	2.75
61	Early Wynn	50.00	25.00	15.00
62	Monte Irvin	25.00	12.50	7.50
63	Gus Niarhos	9.00	4.50	2.75
64	Dave Philley	15.00	7.50	4.50
65	Earl Harrist	15.00	7.50	4.50
66	Orestes Minoso	20.00	10.00	6.00
67	Roy Sievers	12.00	6.00	3.50
68	Del Rice	15.00	7.50	4.50
69	Dick Brodowski	15.00	7.50	4.50
70	Ed Yuhas	15.00	7.50	4.50
71	Tony Bartirome	15.00	7.50	4.50
72	Fred Hutchinson	12.00	6.00	3.50
73	Eddie Robinson	15.00	7.50	4.50
74	Joe Rossi	15.00	7.50	4.50
75	Mike Garcia	15.00	7.50	4.50
76	Pee Wee Reese	60.00	30.00	18.00
77	John Mize	30.00	15.00	9.00
78	Al Schoendienst	20.00	10.00	6.00
79	Johnny Wyrostek	15.00	7.50	4.50
80	Jim Hegan	15.00	7.50	4.50
81	Joe Black	25.00	12.50	7.50
82	Mickey Mantle	1200.00	420.00	240.00
83	Howie Pollet	15.00	7.50	4.50
84	Bob Hooper	9.00	4.50	2.75
85	Bobby Morgan	10.00	5.00	3.00
86	Billy Martin	40.00	20.00	12.00
87	Ed Lopat	15.00	7.50	4.50
88	Willie Jones	9.00	4.50	2.75
89	Chuck Stobbs	9.00	4.50	2.75
90	Hank Edwards	9.00	4.50	2.75
91	Ebba St. Claire	9.00	4.50	2.75
92	Paul Minner	9.00	4.50	2.75
93	Hal Rice	9.00	4.50	2.75
94	William Kennedy	9.00	4.50	2.75
95	Willard Marshall	9.00	4.50	2.75
96	Virgil Trucks	10.00	5.00	3.00
97	Don Kolloway	9.00	4.50	2.75
98	Cal Abrams	9.00	4.50	2.75
99	Dave Madison	9.00	4.50	2.75
100	Bill Miller	15.00	7.50	4.50
101	Ted Wilks	9.00	4.50	2.75
102	Connie Ryan	9.00	4.50	2.75
103	Joe Astroth	9.00	4.50	2.75
104	Yogi Berra	90.00	36.00	23.00
105	Joe Nuxhall	12.00	6.00	3.50
106	Johnny Antonelli	10.00	5.00	3.00
107	Danny O'Connell	9.00	4.50	2.75
108	Bob Porterfield	9.00	4.50	2.75
109	Alvin Dark	15.00	7.50	4.50
110	Herman Wehmeier	9.00	4.50	2.75
111	Hank Sauer	8.00	4.00	2.50
112	Ned Garver	9.00	4.50	2.75
113	Jerry Priddy	9.00	4.50	2.75
114	Phil Rizzuto	45.00	22.00	13.50
115	George Spencer	9.00	4.50	2.75
116	Frank Smith	9.00	4.50	2.75
117	Sid Gordon	9.00	4.50	2.75
118	Gus Bell	10.00	5.00	3.00
119	John Sain	20.00	10.00	6.00
120	Davey Williams	9.00	4.50	2.75
121	Walt Dropo	9.00	4.50	2.75
122	Elmer Valo	9.00	4.50	2.75
123	Tommy Byrne	9.00	4.50	2.75
124	Sibby Sisti	9.00	4.50	2.75
125	Dick Williams	15.00	7.50	4.50
126	Bill Connelly	9.00	4.50	2.75
127	Clint Courtney	9.00	4.50	2.75
128	Wilmer Mizell	9.00	4.50	2.75
129	Keith Thomas	9.00	4.50	2.75
130	Turk Lown	9.00	4.50	2.75
131	Harry Byrd	9.00	4.50	2.75
132	Tom Morgan	15.00	7.50	4.50
133	Gil Coan	9.00	4.50	2.75
134	Rube Walker	10.00	5.00	3.00

		NR MT	EX	VG
135	Al Rosen	20.00	10.00	6.00
136	Ken Heintzelman	9.00	4.50	2.75
137	John Rutherford	10.00	5.00	3.00
138	George Kell	25.00	12.50	7.50
139	Sammy White	9.00	4.50	2.75
140	Tommy Glaviano	9.00	4.50	2.75
141	Allie Reynolds	20.00	10.00	6.00
142	Vic Wertz	10.00	5.00	3.00
143	Billy Pierce	10.00	5.00	3.00
144	Bob Schultz	9.00	4.50	2.75
145	Harry Dorish	9.00	4.50	2.75
146	Granville Hamner	9.00	4.50	2.75
147	Warren Spahn	50.00	25.00	15.00
148	Mickey Grasso	9.00	4.50	2.75
149	Dom DiMaggio	20.00	10.00	6.00
150	Harry Simpson	9.00	4.50	2.75
151	Hoyt Wilhelm	25.00	12.50	7.50
152	Bob Adams	9.00	4.50	2.75
153	Andy Seminick	9.00	4.50	2.75
154	Dick Groat	15.00	7.50	4.50
155	Dutch Leonard	9.00	4.50	2.75
156	Jim Rivera	9.00	4.50	2.75
157	Bob Addis	9.00	4.50	2.75
158	John Logan	10.00	5.00	3.00
159	Wayne Terwilliger	9.00	4.50	2.75
160	Bob Young	9.00	4.50	2.75
161	Vern Bickford	9.00	4.50	2.75
162	Ted Kluszewski	20.00	10.00	6.00
163	Fred Hatfield	9.00	4.50	2.75
164	Frank Shea	9.00	4.50	2.75
165	Billy Hoeft	7.00	3.50	2.00
166	Bill Hunter	7.00	3.50	2.00
167	Art Schult	12.00	6.00	3.50
168	Willard Schmidt	7.00	3.50	2.00
169	Dizzy Trout	8.00	4.00	2.50
170	Bill Werle	7.00	3.50	2.00
171	Bill Glynn	7.00	3.50	2.00
172	Rip Repulski	7.00	3.50	2.00
173	Preston Ward	7.00	3.50	2.00
174	Billy Loes	10.00	5.00	3.00
175	Ron Kline	7.00	3.50	2.00
176	Don Hoak	10.00	5.00	3.00
177	Jim Dyck	7.00	3.50	2.00
178	Jim Waugh	7.00	3.50	2.00
179	Gene Hermanski	7.00	3.50	2.00
180	Virgil Stallcup	7.00	3.50	2.00
181	Al Zarilla	7.00	3.50	2.00
182	Bob Hofman	7.00	3.50	2.00
183	Stu Miller	8.00	4.00	2.50
184	Hal Brown	8.00	4.00	2.50
185	Jim Pendleton	7.00	3.50	2.00
186	Charlie Bishop	7.00	3.50	2.00
187	Jim Fridley	7.00	3.50	2.00
188	Andy Carey	12.00	6.00	3.50
189	Ray Jablonski	7.00	3.50	2.00
190	Dixie Walker	8.00	4.00	2.50
191	Ralph Kiner	25.00	12.50	7.50
192	Wally Westlake	7.00	3.50	2.00
193	Mike Clark	7.00	3.50	2.00
194	Eddie Kazak	7.00	3.50	2.00
195	Ed McGhee	7.00	3.50	2.00
196	Bob Keegan	7.00	3.50	2.00
197	Del Crandall	10.00	5.00	3.00
198	Forrest Main	7.00	3.50	2.00
199	Marion Fricano	7.00	3.50	2.00
200	Gordon Goldsberry	7.00	3.50	2.00
201	Paul LaPalme	7.00	3.50	2.00
202	Carl Sawatski	7.00	3.50	2.00
203	Cliff Fannin	7.00	3.50	2.00
204	Dick Bokelmann	7.00	3.50	2.00
205	Vern Benson	7.00	3.50	2.00
206	Ed Bailey	8.00	4.00	2.50
207	Whitey Ford	40.00	20.00	12.00
208	Jim Wilson	7.00	3.50	2.00
209	Jim Greengrass	7.00	3.50	2.00
210	Bob Cerv	12.00	6.00	3.50
211	J.W. Porter	7.00	3.50	2.00
212	Jack Dittmer	7.00	3.50	2.00
213	Ray Scarborough	12.00	6.00	3.50
214	Bill Bruton	8.00	4.00	2.50
215	Gene Conley	8.00	4.00	2.50
216	Jim Hughes	8.00	4.00	2.50
217	Murray Wall	7.00	3.50	2.00
218	Les Fusselman	7.00	3.50	2.00
219	Pete Runnels (photo actually Don Johnson)	8.00	4.00	2.50
220	Satchell Paige	200.00	80.00	50.00
221	Bob Milliken	35.00	17.50	10.50
222	Vic Janowicz	35.00	17.50	10.50
223	John O'Brien	32.00	16.00	9.50
224	Lou Sleater	32.00	16.00	9.50

		NR MT	EX	VG
225	Bobby Shantz	40.00	20.00	12.00
226	Ed Erautt	32.00	16.00	9.50
227	Morris Martin	32.00	16.00	9.50
228	Hal Newhouser	40.00	20.00	12.00
229	Rocky Krsnich	32.00	16.00	9.50
230	Johnny Lindell	32.00	16.00	9.50
231	Solly Hemus	32.00	16.00	9.50
232	Dick Kokos	32.00	16.00	9.50
233	Al Aber	32.00	16.00	9.50
234	Ray Murray	32.00	16.00	9.50
235	John Hetki	32.00	16.00	9.50
236	Harry Perkowski	32.00	16.00	9.50
237	Clarence Podbielan	32.00	16.00	9.50
238	Cal Hogue	32.00	16.00	9.50
239	Jim Delsing	32.00	16.00	9.50
240	Freddie Marsh	32.00	16.00	9.50
241	Al Sima	32.00	16.00	9.50
242	Charlie Silvera	40.00	20.00	12.00
243	Carlos Bernier	32.00	16.00	9.50
244	Willie Mays	850.00	340.00	213.00
245	Bill Norman	32.00	16.00	9.50
246	Roy Face	50.00	25.00	15.00
247	Mike Sandlock	32.00	16.00	9.50
248	Gene Stephens	32.00	16.00	9.50
249	Ed O'Brien	32.00	16.00	9.50
250	Bob Wilson	32.00	16.00	9.50
251	Sid Hudson	32.00	16.00	9.50
252	Henry Foiles	32.00	16.00	9.50
253	Not Issued			
254	Preacher Roe	45.00	23.00	13.50
255	Dixie Howell	35.00	17.50	10.50
256	Les Peden	32.00	16.00	9.50
257	Bob Boyd	32.00	16.00	9.50
258	Jim Gilliam	175.00	70.00	44.00
259	Roy McMillan	32.00	16.00	9.50
260	Sam Calderone	32.00	16.00	9.50
261	Not Issued			
262	Bob Oldis	32.00	16.00	9.50
263	John Podres	175.00	70.00	44.00
264	Gene Woodling	45.00	22.00	13.50
265	Jackie Jensen	45.00	22.00	13.50
266	Bob Cain	32.00	16.00	9.50
267	Not Issued			
268	Not Issued			
269	Duane Pillette	32.00	16.00	9.50
270	Vern Stephens	32.00	16.00	9.50
271	Not Issued			
272	Bill Antonello	35.00	17.50	10.50
273	Harvey Haddix	45.00	22.00	13.50
274	John Riddle	32.00	16.00	9.50
275	Not Issued			
276	Ken Raffensberger	32.00	16.00	9.50
277	Don Lund	32.00	16.00	9.50
278	Willie Miranda	32.00	16.00	9.50
279	Joe Coleman	35.00	16.00	9.50
280	Milt Bolling	200.00	25.00	9.50

1954 Topps

The first issue to use two player pictures on the front, the 1954 Topps set is very popular today. Solid color backgrounds frame both color head-and-shoulders and black-and-white action pictures of the player. The player's name, position team and team logo appear at the top. Backs include an "Inside Baseball" cartoon regarding the player as well as statistics and biography. The 250-card, 2⅝" by 3¾," set included manager and coaches cards, and the first

use of two players together on a modern card; the players were, appropriately, the O'Brien twins.

		NR MT	EX	VG
Complete Set:		4800.00	1675.00	950.00
Common Player: 1-50		7.00	3.50	2.00
Common Player: 51-75		6.00	3.00	1.75
Common Player: 76-250		7.00	3.50	2.00
1	Ted Williams	300.00	63.00	38.00
2	Gus Zernial	10.00	4.00	2.00
3	Monte Irvin	17.50	8.75	5.25
4	Hank Sauer	7.00	3.50	2.00
5	Ed Lopat	15.00	7.50	4.50
6	Pete Runnels	8.00	4.00	2.50
7	Ted Kluszewski	12.00	6.00	3.50
8	Bobby Young	7.00	3.50	2.00
9	Harvey Haddix	8.00	4.00	2.50
10	Jackie Robinson	100.00	40.00	25.00
11	Paul Smith	7.00	3.50	2.00
12	Del Crandall	8.00	4.00	2.50
13	Billy Martin	35.00	17.50	10.50
14	Preacher Roe	12.00	6.00	3.50
15	Al Rosen	12.00	6.00	3.50
16	Vic Janowicz	7.00	3.50	2.00
17	Phil Rizzuto	35.00	17.50	10.50
18	Walt Dropo	7.00	3.50	2.00
19	Johnny Lipon	7.00	3.50	2.00
20	Warren Spahn	35.00	17.50	10.50
21	Bobby Shantz	10.00	5.00	3.00
22	Jim Greengrass	7.00	3.50	2.00
23	Luke Easter	8.00	4.00	2.50
24	Granny Hamner	7.00	3.50	2.00
25	Harvey Kuenn	15.00	7.50	4.50
26	Ray Jablonski	7.00	3.50	2.00
27	Ferris Fain	8.00	4.00	2.50
28	Paul Minner	7.00	3.50	2.00
29	Jim Hegan	7.00	3.50	2.00
30	Ed Mathews	35.00	17.50	10.50
31	Johnny Klippstein	7.00	3.50	2.00
32	Duke Snider	60.00	30.00	18.00
33	Johnny Schmitz	7.00	3.50	2.00
34	Jim Rivera	7.00	3.50	2.00
35	Junior Gilliam	15.00	7.50	4.50
36	Hoyt Wilhelm	20.00	10.00	6.00
37	Whitey Ford	40.00	20.00	12.00
38	Eddie Stanky	8.00	4.00	2.50
39	Sherm Lollar	8.00	4.00	2.50
40	Mel Parnell	8.00	4.00	2.50
41	Willie Jones	7.00	3.50	2.00
42	Don Mueller	7.00	3.50	2.00
43	Dick Groat	10.00	5.00	3.00
44	Ned Garver	7.00	3.50	2.00
45	Richie Ashburn	15.00	7.50	4.50
46	Ken Raffensberger	7.00	3.50	2.00
47	Ellis Kinder	7.00	3.50	2.00
48	Billy Hunter	7.00	3.50	2.00
49	Ray Murray	7.00	3.50	2.00
50	Yogi Berra	90.00	36.00	23.00
51	Johnny Lindell	15.00	7.50	4.50
52	Vic Power	15.00	7.50	4.50
53	Jack Dittmer	15.00	7.50	4.50
54	Vern Stephens	15.00	7.50	4.50
55	Phil Cavarretta	17.50	8.75	5.25
56	Willie Miranda	20.00	10.00	6.00
57	Luis Aloma	15.00	7.50	4.50
58	Bob Wilson	15.00	7.50	4.50
59	Gene Conley	17.50	8.75	5.25
60	Frank Baumholtz	15.00	7.50	4.50
61	Bob Cain	15.00	7.50	4.50
62	Eddie Robinson	20.00	10.00	6.00
63	Johnny Pesky	17.50	8.75	5.25
64	Hank Thompson	15.00	7.50	4.50
65	Bob Swift	15.00	7.50	4.50
66	Ted Lepcio	15.00	7.50	4.50
67	Jim Willis	15.00	7.50	4.50
68	Sammy Calderone	15.00	7.50	4.50
69	Bud Podbielan	15.00	7.50	4.50
70	Larry Doby	25.00	12.50	7.50
71	Frank Smith	15.00	7.50	4.50
72	Preston Ward	15.00	7.50	4.50
73	Wayne Terwilliger	15.00	7.50	4.50
74	Bill Taylor	15.00	7.50	4.50
75	Fred Haney	15.00	7.50	4.50
76	Bob Scheffing	7.00	3.50	2.00
77	Ray Boone	8.00	4.00	2.50
78	Ted Kazanski	7.00	3.50	2.00
79	Andy Pafko	10.00	5.00	3.00
80	Jackie Jensen	12.00	6.00	3.50
81	Dave Hoskins	7.00	3.50	2.00
82	Milt Bolling	7.00	3.50	2.00
83	Joe Collins	12.00	6.00	3.50
84	Dick Cole	7.00	3.50	2.00
85	Bob Turley	12.00	6.00	3.50
86	Billy Herman	15.00	7.50	4.50
87	Roy Face	10.00	5.00	3.00
88	Matt Batts	7.00	3.50	2.00
89	Howie Pollet	7.00	3.50	2.00
90	Willie Mays	175.00	87.00	52.00
91	Bob Oldis	7.00	3.50	2.00
92	Wally Westlake	7.00	3.50	2.00
93	Sid Hudson	7.00	3.50	2.00
94	Ernie Banks	275.00	110.00	69.00
95	Hal Rice	7.00	3.50	2.00
96	Charlie Silvera	12.00	6.00	3.50
97	Jerry Lane	7.00	3.50	2.00
98	Joe Black	10.00	5.00	3.00
99	Bob Hofman	7.00	3.50	2.00
100	Bob Keegan	7.00	3.50	2.00
101	Gene Woodling	15.00	7.50	4.50
102	Gil Hodges	30.00	15.00	9.00
103	Jim Lemon	8.00	4.00	2.50
104	Mike Sandlock	7.00	3.50	2.00
105	Andy Carey	12.00	6.00	3.50
106	Dick Kokos	7.00	3.50	2.00
107	Duane Pillette	7.00	3.50	2.00
108	Thornton Kipper	7.00	3.50	2.00
109	Bill Bruton	8.00	4.00	2.50
110	Harry Dorish	7.00	3.50	2.00
111	Jim Delsing	7.00	3.50	2.00
112	Bill Renna	7.00	3.50	2.00
113	Bob Boyd	7.00	3.50	2.00
114	Dean Stone	7.00	3.50	2.00
115	"Rip" Repulski	7.00	3.50	2.00
116	Steve Bilko	7.00	3.50	2.00
117	Solly Hemus	7.00	3.50	2.00
118	Carl Scheib	7.00	3.50	2.00
119	Johnny Antonelli	8.00	4.00	2.50
120	Roy McMillan	7.00	3.50	2.00
121	Clem Labine	10.00	5.00	3.00
122	Johnny Logan	8.00	4.00	2.50
123	Bobby Adams	7.00	3.50	2.00
124	Marion Fricano	7.00	3.50	2.00
125	Harry Perkowski	7.00	3.50	2.00
126	Ben Wade	8.00	4.00	2.50
127	Steve O'Neill	7.00	3.50	2.00
128	Henry Aaron	500.00	200.00	125.00
129	Forrest Jacobs	7.00	3.50	2.00
130	Hank Bauer	15.00	7.50	4.50
131	Reno Bertoia	7.00	3.50	2.00
132	Tom Lasorda	90.00	36.00	23.00
133	Del Baker	7.00	3.50	2.00
134	Cal Hogue	7.00	3.50	2.00
135	Joe Presko	7.00	3.50	2.00
136	Connie Ryan	7.00	3.50	2.00
137	Wally Moon	12.00	6.00	3.50
138	Bob Borkowski	7.00	3.50	2.00
139	Ed & Johnny O'Brien	20.00	10.00	6.00
140	Tom Wright	7.00	3.50	2.00
141	Joe Jay	8.00	4.00	2.50
142	Tom Poholsky	7.00	3.50	2.00
143	Rollie Hemsley	7.00	3.50	2.00
144	Bill Werle	7.00	3.50	2.00
145	Elmer Valo	7.00	3.50	2.00
146	Don Johnson	7.00	3.50	2.00
147	John Riddle	7.00	3.50	2.00
148	Bob Trice	7.00	3.50	2.00
149	Jim Robertson	7.00	3.50	2.00
150	Dick Kryhoski	7.00	3.50	2.00
151	Alex Grammas	7.00	3.50	2.00
152	Mike Blyzka	7.00	3.50	2.00
153	"Rube" Walker	8.00	4.00	2.50
154	Mike Fornieles	7.00	3.50	2.00
155	Bob Kennedy	7.00	3.50	2.00
156	Joe Coleman	7.00	3.50	2.00
157	Don Lenhardt	7.00	3.50	2.00
158	"Peanuts" Lowrey	7.00	3.50	2.00
159	Dave Philley	7.00	3.50	2.00
160	"Red" Kress	7.00	3.50	2.00
161	John Hetki	7.00	3.50	2.00
162	Herman Wehmeier	7.00	3.50	2.00
163	Frank House	7.00	3.50	2.00
164	Stu Miller	7.00	3.50	2.00
165	Jim Pendleton	7.00	3.50	2.00
166	Johnny Podres	15.00	7.50	4.50
167	Don Lund	7.00	3.50	2.00
168	Morrie Martin	7.00	3.50	2.00
169	Jim Hughes	8.00	4.00	2.50
170	Jim Rhodes	8.00	4.00	2.50
171	Leo Kiely	7.00	3.50	2.00
172	Hal Brown	7.00	3.50	2.00
173	Jack Harshman	7.00	3.50	2.00

		NR MT	EX	VG
174	Tom Qualters	7.00	3.50	2.00
175	Frank Leja	12.00	6.00	3.50
176	Bob Keely	7.00	3.50	2.00
177	Bob Milliken	8.00	4.00	2.50
178	Bill Gylnn (Glynn)	7.00	3.50	2.00
179	Gair Allie	7.00	3.50	2.00
180	Wes Westrum	8.00	4.00	2.50
181	Mel Roach	7.00	3.50	2.00
182	Chuck Harmon	7.00	3.50	2.00
183	Earle Combs	12.00	6.00	3.50
184	Ed Bailey	7.00	3.50	2.00
185	Chuck Stobbs	7.00	3.50	2.00
186	Karl Olson	7.00	3.50	2.00
187	"Heinie" Manush	12.00	6.00	3.50
188	Dave Jolly	7.00	3.50	2.00
189	Bob Ross	7.00	3.50	2.00
190	Ray Herbert	7.00	3.50	2.00
191	Dick Schofield	10.00	5.00	3.00
192	"Cot" Deal	7.00	3.50	2.00
193	Johnny Hopp	7.00	3.50	2.00
194	Bill Sarni	7.00	3.50	2.00
195	Bill Consolo	7.00	3.50	2.00
196	Stan Jok	7.00	3.50	2.00
197	"Schoolboy" Rowe	8.00	4.00	2.50
198	Carl Sawatski	7.00	3.50	2.00
199	"Rocky" Nelson	7.00	3.50	2.00
200	Larry Jansen	7.00	3.50	2.00
201	Al Kaline	275.00	110.00	69.00
202	Bob Purkey	8.00	4.00	2.50
203	Harry Brecheen	8.00	4.00	2.50
204	Angel Scull	7.00	3.50	2.00
205	Johnny Sain	15.00	7.50	4.50
206	Ray Crone	7.00	3.50	2.00
207	Tom Oliver	7.00	3.50	2.00
208	Grady Hatton	7.00	3.50	2.00
209	Charlie Thompson	8.00	4.00	2.50
210	Bob Buhl	10.00	5.00	3.00
211	Don Hoak	10.00	5.00	3.00
212	Mickey Micelotta	7.00	3.50	2.00
213	John Fitzpatrick	7.00	3.50	2.00
214	Arnold Portocarrero	7.00	3.50	2.00
215	Ed McGhee	7.00	3.50	2.00
216	Al Sima	7.00	3.50	2.00
217	Paul Schreiber	7.00	3.50	2.00
218	Fred Marsh	7.00	3.50	2.00
219	Charlie Kress	7.00	3.50	2.00
220	Ruben Gomez	7.00	3.50	2.00
221	Dick Brodowski	7.00	3.50	2.00
222	Bill Wilson	7.00	3.50	2.00
223	Joe Haynes	7.00	3.50	2.00
224	Dick Weik	7.00	3.50	2.00
225	Don Liddle	7.00	3.50	2.00
226	Jehosie Heard	7.00	3.50	2.00
227	Buster Mills	7.00	3.50	2.00
228	Gene Hermanski	7.00	3.50	2.00
229	Bob Talbot	7.00	3.50	2.00
230	Bob Kuzava	12.00	6.00	3.50
231	Roy Smalley	7.00	3.50	2.00
232	Lou Limmer	7.00	3.50	2.00
233	Augie Galan	7.00	3.50	2.00
234	Jerry Lynch	10.00	5.00	3.00
235	Vern Law	10.00	5.00	3.00
236	Paul Penson	7.00	3.50	2.00
237	Mike Ryba	7.00	3.50	2.00
238	Al Aber	7.00	3.50	2.00
239	Bill Skowron	20.00	10.00	6.00
240	Sam Mele	7.00	3.50	2.00
241	Bob Miller	7.00	3.50	2.00
242	Curt Roberts	7.00	3.50	2.00
243	Ray Blades	7.00	3.50	2.00
244	Leroy Wheat	7.00	3.50	2.00
245	Roy Sievers	10.00	5.00	3.00
246	Howie Fox	7.00	3.50	2.00
247	Eddie Mayo	7.00	3.50	2.00
248	Al Smith	8.00	4.00	2.50
249	Wilmer Mizell	7.00	3.50	2.00
250	Ted Williams	300.00	63.00	38.00

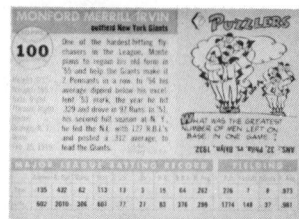

1955 Topps

The 1955 Topps set was numerically the smallest of the regular issue Topps sets. The 3¾'' by 2⅝'' cards mark the first time that Topps used a horizontal format. While that format was new, the design was not; they were very similar to the 1954 cards to the point many pictures appeared in both years. Although it was slated for a 210-card set, the 1955 Topps set

turned out to be only 206 cards with numbers 175, 186, 203 and 209 never being released. The scarce high numbers in this set begin with #161.

		NR MT	EX	VG
Complete Set:		3500.00	1225.00	700.00
Common Player: 1-160		5.00	2.50	1.50
Common Player: 151-160		7.00	3.50	2.00
Common Player: 161-210		9.00	4.50	2.75
1	"Dusty" Rhodes	15.00	6.00	1.50
2	Ted Williams	150.00	60.00	38.00
3	Art Fowler	5.00	2.50	1.50
4	Al Kaline	40.00	20.00	12.00
5	Jim Gilliam	9.00	4.50	2.75
6	Stan Hack	6.00	3.00	1.75
7	Jim Hegan	5.00	2.50	1.50
8	Hal Smith	5.00	2.50	1.50
9	Bob Miller	5.00	2.50	1.50
10	Bob Keegan	5.00	2.50	1.50
11	Ferris Fain	6.00	3.00	1.75
12	"Jake" Thies	5.00	2.50	1.50
13	Fred Marsh	5.00	2.50	1.50
14	Jim Finigan	5.00	2.50	1.50
15	Jim Pendleton	5.00	2.50	1.50
16	Roy Sievers	7.00	3.50	2.00
17	Bobby Hofman	5.00	2.50	1.50
18	Russ Kemmerer	5.00	2.50	1.50
19	Billy Herman	9.00	4.50	2.75
20	Andy Carey	9.00	4.50	2.75
21	Alex Grammas	5.00	2.50	1.50
22	Bill Skowron	12.00	6.00	3.50
23	Jack Parks	5.00	2.50	1.50
24	Hal Newhouser	6.00	3.00	1.75
25	Johnny Podres	9.00	4.50	2.75
26	Dick Groat	7.00	3.50	2.00
27	Billy Gardner	5.00	2.50	1.50
28	Ernie Banks	40.00	20.00	12.00
29	Herman Wehmeier	5.00	2.50	1.50
30	Vic Power	5.00	2.50	1.50
31	Warren Spahn	30.00	15.00	9.00
32	Ed McGhee	5.00	2.50	1.50
33	Tom Qualters	5.00	2.50	1.50
34	Wayne Terwilliger	5.00	2.50	1.50
35	Dave Jolly	5.00	2.50	1.50
36	Leo Kiely	5.00	2.50	1.50
37	Joe Cunningham	7.00	3.50	2.00
38	Bob Turley	12.00	6.00	3.50
39	Bill Glynn	5.00	2.50	1.50
40	Don Hoak	7.00	3.50	2.00
41	Chuck Stobbs	5.00	2.50	1.50
42	"Windy" McCall	5.00	2.50	1.50
43	Harvey Haddix	6.00	3.00	1.75
44	"Corky" Valentine	5.00	2.50	1.50
45	Hank Sauer	5.00	2.50	1.50
46	Ted Kazanski	5.00	2.50	1.50
47	Hank Aaron	125.00	50.00	32.00
48	Bob Kennedy	5.00	2.50	1.50
49	J.W. Porter	5.00	2.50	1.50
50	Jackie Robinson	70.00	35.00	21.00
51	Jim Hughes	6.00	3.00	1.75
52	Bill Tremel	5.00	2.50	1.50
53	Bill Taylor	5.00	2.50	1.50

		NR MT	EX	VG
54	Lou Limmer	5.00	2.50	1.50
55	"Rip" Repulski	5.00	2.50	1.50
56	Ray Jablonski	5.00	2.50	1.50
57	Billy O'Dell	6.00	3.00	1.75
58	Jim Rivera	5.00	2.50	1.50
59	Gair Allie	5.00	2.50	1.50
60	Dean Stone	5.00	2.50	1.50
61	"Spook" Jacobs	5.00	2.50	1.50
62	Thornton Kipper	5.00	2.50	1.50
63	Joe Collins	9.00	4.50	2.75
64	Gus Triandos	7.00	3.50	2.00
65	Ray Boone	6.00	3.00	1.75
66	Ron Jackson	5.00	2.50	1.50
67	Wally Moon	6.00	3.00	1.75
68	Jim Davis	5.00	2.50	1.50
69	Ed Bailey	5.00	2.50	1.50
70	Al Rosen	12.00	6.00	3.50
71	Ruben Gomez	5.00	2.50	1.50
72	Karl Olson	5.00	2.50	1.50
73	Jack Shepard	5.00	2.50	1.50
74	Bob Borkowski	5.00	2.50	1.50
75	Sandy Amoros	6.00	3.00	1.75
76	Howie Pollet	5.00	2.50	1.50
77	Arnold Portocarrero	5.00	2.50	1.50
78	Gordon Jones	5.00	2.50	1.50
79	Danny Schell	5.00	2.50	1.50
80	Bob Grim	9.00	4.50	2.75
81	Gene Conley	6.00	3.00	1.75
82	Chuck Harmon	5.00	2.50	1.50
83	Tom Brewer	5.00	2.50	1.50
84	Camilo Pascual	7.00	3.50	2.00
85	Don Mossi	7.00	3.50	2.00
86	Bill Wilson	5.00	2.50	1.50
87	Frank House	5.00	2.50	1.50
88	Bob Skinner	7.00	3.50	2.00
89	Joe Frazier	5.00	2.50	1.50
90	Karl Spooner	9.00	4.50	2.75
91	Milt Bolling	5.00	2.50	1.50
92	Don Zimmer	12.00	6.00	3.50
93	Steve Bilko	5.00	2.50	1.50
94	Reno Bertoia	5.00	2.50	1.50
95	Preston Ward	5.00	2.50	1.50
96	Charlie Bishop	5.00	2.50	1.50
97	Carlos Paula	5.00	2.50	1.50
98	Johnny Riddle	5.00	2.50	1.50
99	Frank Leja	9.00	4.50	2.75
100	Monte Irvin	17.50	8.75	5.25
101	Johnny Gray	5.00	2.50	1.50
102	Wally Westlake	5.00	2.50	1.50
103	Charlie White	5.00	2.50	1.50
104	Jack Harshman	5.00	2.50	1.50
105	Chuck Diering	5.00	2.50	1.50
106	Frank Sullivan	6.00	3.00	1.75
107	Curt Roberts	5.00	2.50	1.50
108	"Rube" Walker	6.00	3.00	1.75
109	Ed Lopat	12.00	6.00	3.50
110	Gus Zernial	6.00	3.00	1.75
111	Bob Milliken	6.00	3.00	1.75
112	Nelson King	5.00	2.50	1.50
113	Harry Brecheen	6.00	3.00	1.75
114	Lou Ortiz	5.00	2.50	1.50
115	Ellis Kinder	5.00	2.50	1.50
116	Tom Hurd	5.00	2.50	1.50
117	Mel Roach	5.00	2.50	1.50
118	Bob Purkey	5.00	2.50	1.50
119	Bob Lennon	5.00	2.50	1.50
120	Ted Kluszewski	12.00	6.00	3.50
121	Bill Renna	5.00	2.50	1.50
122	Carl Sawatski	5.00	2.50	1.50
123	Sandy Koufax	250.00	100.00	63.00
124	Harmon Killebrew	90.00	36.00	23.00
125	Ken Boyer	17.50	8.75	5.25
126	Dick Hall	6.00	3.00	1.75
127	Dale Long	6.00	3.00	1.75
128	Ted Lepcio	5.00	2.50	1.50
129	Elvin Tappe	5.00	2.50	1.50
130	Mayo Smith	5.00	2.50	1.50
131	Grady Hatton	5.00	2.50	1.50
132	Bob Trice	5.00	2.50	1.50
133	Dave Hoskins	5.00	2.50	1.50
134	Joe Jay	5.00	2.50	1.50
135	Johnny O'Brien	5.00	2.50	1.50
136	"Bunky" Stewart	5.00	2.50	1.50
137	Harry Elliott	5.00	2.50	1.50
138	Ray Herbert	5.00	2.50	1.50
139	Steve Kraly	9.00	4.50	2.75
140	Mel Parnell	6.00	3.00	1.75
141	Tom Wright	5.00	2.50	1.50
142	Jerry Lynch	5.00	2.50	1.50
143	Dick Schofield	5.00	2.50	1.50
144	Joe Amalfitano	5.00	2.50	1.50

		NR MT	EX	VG
145	Elmer Valo	5.00	2.50	1.50
146	Dick Donovan	6.00	3.00	1.75
147	Laurin Pepper	5.00	2.50	1.50
148	Hal Brown	5.00	2.50	1.50
149	Ray Crone	5.00	2.50	1.50
150	Mike Higgins	5.00	2.50	1.50
151	"Red" Kress	7.00	3.50	2.00
152	Harry Agganis	25.00	12.50	7.50
153	"Bud" Podbielan	7.00	3.50	2.00
154	Willie Miranda	7.00	3.50	2.00
155	Ed Mathews	45.00	23.00	13.50
156	Joe Black	15.00	7.50	4.50
157	Bob Miller	7.00	3.50	2.00
158	Tom Carroll	15.00	7.50	4.50
159	Johnny Schmitz	7.00	3.50	2.00
160	Ray Narleski	7.00	3.50	2.00
161	Chuck Tanner	17.50	8.75	5.25
162	Joe Coleman	9.00	4.50	2.75
163	Faye Throneberry	9.00	4.50	2.75
164	Roberto Clemente	325.00	130.00	81.00
165	Don Johnson	9.00	4.50	2.75
166	Hank Bauer	17.50	8.75	5.25
167	Tom Casagrande	9.00	4.50	2.75
168	Duane Pillette	9.00	4.50	2.75
169	Bob Oldis	9.00	4.50	2.75
170	Jim Pearce	9.00	4.50	2.75
171	Dick Brodowski	9.00	4.50	2.75
172	Frank Baumholtz	9.00	4.50	2.75
173	Bob Kline	9.00	4.50	2.75
174	Rudy Minarcin	9.00	4.50	2.75
175	Not Issued			
176	Norm Zauchin		4.50	2.75
177	Jim Robertson	9.00	4.50	2.75
178	Bobby Adams	9.00	4.50	2.75
179	Jim Bolger	9.00	4.50	2.75
180	Clem Labine	12.00	6.00	3.50
181	Roy McMillan	9.00	4.50	2.75
182	Humberto Robinson	9.00	4.50	2.75
183	Tony Jacobs	9.00	4.50	2.75
184	Harry Perkowski	9.00	4.50	2.75
185	Don Ferrarese	9.00	4.50	2.75
186	Not Issued			
187	Gil Hodges	90.00	45.00	27.00
188	Charlie Silvera	12.00	6.00	3.50
189	Phil Rizzuto	90.00	45.00	27.00
190	Gene Woodling	10.00	5.00	3.00
191	Ed Stanky	10.00	5.00	3.00
192	Jim Delsing	9.00	4.50	2.75
193	Johnny Sain	15.00	7.50	4.50
194	Willie Mays	275.00	110.00	69.00
195	Ed Roebuck	10.00	5.00	3.00
196	Gale Wade	9.00	4.50	2.75
197	Al Smith	9.00	4.50	2.75
198	Yogi Berra	125.00	63.00	38.00
199	Bert Hamric	10.00	5.00	3.00
200	Jack Jensen	15.00	7.50	4.50
201	Sherm Lollar	10.00	5.00	3.00
202	Jim Owens	9.00	4.50	2.75
203	Not Issued			
204	Frank Smith	9.00	4.50	2.75
205	Gene Freese	9.00	4.50	2.75
206	Pete Daley	9.00	4.50	2.75
207	Bill Consolo	9.00	4.50	2.75
208	Ray Moore	9.00	4.50	2.75
209	Not Issued			
210	Duke Snider	275.00	88.00	53.00

1955 Topps Double Headers

This set is a throwback to the 1911 Mecca Double Folders. The cards were perforated allowing them to be folded. Open, there is a color painting of a player set against a ballpark background. When folded you get a different stadium and player, although both share the same lower legs and feet. Backs gave abbreviated career histories. Placed side by side in reverse numerical order, the backgrounds form a continuous stadium scene. When open, the cards measure 2-1/16'' by 4-7/8.'' The 66 cards in the set mean 132 total players, all of whom also appeared in the lower number regular 1955 Topps set.

Definitions for grading conditions are located in the Introduction of this price guide.

		NR MT	EX	VG
	Complete Set:	2000.00	1000.00	600.00
	Common Player:	18.00	9.00	5.50
1	Al Rosen			
2	Chuck Diering	25.00	12.50	7.50
3	Monte Irvin			
4	Russ Kemmerer	25.00	12.50	7.50
5	Ted Kazanski			
6	Gordon Jones	18.00	9.00	5.50
7	Bill Taylor			
8	Billy O'Dell	18.00	9.00	5.50
9	J.W. Porter			
10	Thornton Kipper	18.00	9.00	5.50
11	Curt Roberts			
12	Arnie Portocarrero	18.00	9.00	5.50
13	Wally Westlake			
14	Frank House	18.00	9.00	5.50
15	"Rube" Walker			
16	Lou Limmer	18.00	9.00	5.50
17	Dean Stone			
18	Charlie White	18.00	9.00	5.50
19	Karl Spooner			
20	Jim Hughes	25.00	12.50	7.50
21	Bill Skowron			
22	Frank Sullivan	25.00	12.50	7.50
23	Jack Shepard			
24	Stan Hack	25.00	12.50	7.50
25	Jackie Robinson			
26	Don Hoak	100.00	50.00	30.00
27	"Dusty" Rhodes			
28	Jim Davis	18.00	9.00	5.50
29	Vic Power			
30	Ed Bailey	18.00	9.00	5.50
31	Howie Pollet			
32	Ernie Banks	80.00	40.00	24.00
33	Jim Pendleton			
34	Gene Conley	18.00	9.00	5.50
35	Karl Olson	18.00	9.00	5.50
36	Andy Carey	18.00	9.00	5.50
37	Wally Moon	18.00	9.00	5.50
38	Joe Cunningham	18.00	9.00	5.50
39	Fred Marsh			
40	"Jake" Thies	18.00	9.00	5.50
41	Ed Lopat			
42	Harvey Haddix	25.00	12.50	7.50
43	Leo Kiely			
44	Chuck Stobbs	18.00	9.00	5.50
45	Al Kaline			
46	"Corky" Valentine	80.00	40.00	24.00
47	"Spook" Jacobs			
48	Johnny Gray	18.00	9.00	5.50
49	Ron Jackson			
50	Jim Finigan	18.00	9.00	5.50
51	Ray Jablonski			
52	Bob Keegan	18.00	9.00	5.50
53	Billy Herman			
54	Sandy Amoros	25.00	12.50	7.50

		NR MT	EX	VG
55	Chuck Harmon			
56	Bob Skinner	18.00	9.00	5.50
57	Dick Hall			
58	Bob Grim	18.00	9.00	5.50
59	Billy Glynn			
60	Bob Miller	18.00	9.00	5.50
61	Billy Gardner			
62	John Hetki	18.00	9.00	5.50
63	Bob Borkowski			
64	Bob Turley	25.00	12.50	7.50
65	Joe Collins			
66	Jack Harshman	18.00	9.00	5.50
67	Jim Hegan			
68	Jack Parks	18.00	9.00	5.50
69	Ted Williams			
70	Hal Smith	160.00	80.00	48.00
71	Gair Allie			
72	Grady Hatton	18.00	9.00	5.50
73	Jerry Lynch			
74	Harry Brecheen	18.00	9.00	5.50
75	Tom Wright			
76	"Bunky" Stewart	18.00	9.00	5.50
77	Dave Hoskins			
78	Ed McGhee	18.00	9.00	5.50
79	Roy Sievers			
80	Art Fowler	18.00	9.00	5.50
81	Danny Schell			
82	Gus Triandos	18.00	9.00	5.50
83	Joe Frazier			
84	Don Mossi	18.00	9.00	5.50
85	Elmer Valo			
86	Hal Brown	18.00	9.00	5.50
87	Bob Kennedy			
88	"Windy" McCall	18.00	9.00	5.50
89	Ruben Gomez			
90	Jim Rivera	18.00	9.00	5.50
91	Lou Ortiz			
92	Milt Bolling	18.00	9.00	5.50
93	Carl Sawatski			
94	Elvin Tappe	18.00	9.00	5.50
95	Dave Jolly			
96	Bobby Hofman	18.00	9.00	5.50
97	Preston Ward			
98	Don Zimmer	18.00	9.00	5.50
99	Bill Renna			
100	Dick Groat	25.00	12.50	7.50
101	Bill Wilson			
102	Bill Tremel	18.00	9.00	5.50
103	Hank Sauer			
104	Camilo Pascual	25.00	12.50	7.50
105	Hank Aaron			
106	Ray Herbert	175.00	87.00	52.00
107	Alex Grammas			
108	Tom Qualters	18.00	9.00	5.50
109	Hal Newhouser			
110	Charlie Bishop	25.00	12.50	7.50
111	Harmon Killebrew			
112	John Podres	80.00	40.00	24.00
113	Ray Boone			
114	Bob Purkey	18.00	9.00	5.50
115	Dale Long			
116	Ferris Fain	18.00	9.00	5.50
117	Steve Bilko			
118	Bob Milliken	18.00	9.00	5.50
119	Mel Parnell			
120	Tom Hurd	18.00	9.00	5.50
121	Ted Kluszewski			
122	Jim Owens	25.00	12.50	7.50
123	Gus Zernial			
124	Bob Trice	18.00	9.00	5.50
125	"Rip" Repulski			
126	Ted Lepcio	18.00	9.00	5.50
127	Warren Spahn			
128	Tom Brewer	65.00	32.00	19.50
129	Jim Gilliam			
130	Ellis Kinder	25.00	12.50	7.50
131	Herm Wehmeier			
132	Wayne Terwilliger	18.00	9.00	5.50

1956 Topps

This 340-card set is quite similar in design to the 1955 Topps set, again using both a portrait and an "action" picture. Some portraits are the same as those used in 1955 (and even 1954.) Innovations found in the 1956 Topps set of 2⅝'' by 3¾'' cards include team cards introduced as part of a regular

set. Additionally, there are two unnumbered checklist cards (the complete set price quoted below does not include the checklist cards.) Finally, there are cards of the two league presidents, William Harridge and Warren Giles. On the backs, a three-panel cartoon depicts big moments from the player's career while biographical information appears above the cartoon and statistics below. Card backs for #'s 1-180 can be found with either white or grey cardboard. Some dealers charge a premium for grey backs (#'s 1-100) and white backs (#'s 101-180).

		NR MT	EX	VG
Complete Set:		3600.00	1260.00	720.00
Common Player: 1-100		3.00	1.50	.90
Common Player: 101-180		5.00	2.50	1.50
Common Player: 181-260		6.00	3.00	1.75
Common Player: 261-340		5.00	2.50	1.50
1	William Harridge	60.00	3.00	1.25
2	Warren Giles	7.00	2.00	1.25
3	Elmer Valo	3.00	1.50	.90
4	Carlos Paula	3.00	1.50	.90
5	Ted Williams	125.00	50.00	32.00
6	Ray Boone	4.00	2.00	1.25
7	Ron Negray	3.00	1.50	.90
8	Walter Alston	11.00	5.50	3.25
9	Ruben Gomez	3.00	1.50	.90
10	Warren Spahn	20.00	10.00	6.00
11a	Cubs Team (with date)	25.00	12.50	7.50
11b	Cubs Team (no date, name centered)			
		7.00	3.50	2.00
11c	Cubs Team (no date, name at left)			
		10.00	5.00	3.00
12	Andy Carey	5.00	2.50	1.50
13	Roy Face	5.00	2.50	1.50
14	Ken Boyer	7.00	3.50	2.00
15	Ernie Banks	25.00	12.50	7.50
16	Hector Lopez	5.00	2.50	1.50
17	Gene Conley	4.00	2.00	1.25
18	Dick Donovan	3.00	1.50	.90
19	Chuck Diering	3.00	1.50	.90
20	Al Kaline	30.00	15.00	9.00
21	Joe Collins	5.00	2.50	1.50
22	Jim Finigan	3.00	1.50	.90
23	Freddie Marsh	3.00	1.50	.90
24	Dick Groat	5.00	2.50	1.50
25	Ted Kluszewski	7.00	3.50	2.00
26	Grady Hatton	3.00	1.50	.90
27	Nelson Burbrink	3.00	1.50	.90
28	Bobby Hofman	3.00	1.50	.90
29	Jack Harshman	3.00	1.50	.90
30	Jackie Robinson	70.00	35.00	21.00
31	Hank Aaron	80.00	40.00	24.00
32	Frank House	3.00	1.50	.90
33	Roberto Clemente	100.00	40.00	25.00
34	Tom Brewer	3.00	1.50	.90
35	Al Rosen	7.00	3.50	2.00
36	Rudy Minarcin	3.00	1.50	.90
37	Alex Grammas	3.00	1.50	.90
38	Bob Kennedy	3.00	1.50	.90
39	Don Mossi	4.00	2.00	1.25

		NR MT	EX	VG
40	Bob Turley	7.00	3.50	2.00
41	Hank Sauer	3.00	1.50	.90
42	Sandy Amoros	4.00	2.00	1.25
43	Ray Moore	3.00	1.50	.90
44	"Windy" McCall	3.00	1.50	.90
45	Gus Zernial	4.00	2.00	1.25
46	Gene Freese	3.00	1.50	.90
47	Art Fowler	3.00	1.50	.90
48	Jim Hegan	3.00	1.50	.90
49	Pedro Ramos	4.00	2.00	1.25
50	"Dusty" Rhodes	4.00	2.00	1.25
51	Ernie Oravetz	3.00	1.50	.90
52	Bob Grim	5.00	2.50	1.50
53	Arnold Portocarrero	3.00	1.50	.90
54	Bob Keegan	3.00	1.50	.90
55	Wally Moon	4.00	2.00	1.25
56	Dale Long	4.00	2.00	1.25
57	"Duke" Maas	3.00	1.50	.90
58	Ed Roebuck	4.00	2.00	1.25
59	Jose Santiago	3.00	1.50	.90
60	Mayo Smith	3.00	1.50	.90
61	Bill Skowron	7.00	3.50	2.00
62	Hal Smith	3.00	1.50	.90
63	Roger Craig	10.00	5.00	3.00
64	Luis Arroyo	3.00	1.50	.90
65	Johnny O'Brien	3.00	1.50	.90
66	Bob Speake	3.00	1.50	.90
67	Vic Power	3.00	1.50	.90
68	Chuck Stobbs	3.00	1.50	.90
69	Chuck Tanner	5.00	2.50	1.50
70	Jim Rivera	3.00	1.50	.90
71	Frank Sullivan	3.00	1.50	.90
72a	Phillies Team (with date)	25.00	12.50	7.50
72b	Phillies Team (no date, name centered)			
		7.00	3.50	2.00
72c	Philadelphia Phillies (no date, name at left)			
		10.00	5.00	3.00
73	Wayne Terwilliger	3.00	1.50	.90
74	Jim King	3.00	1.50	.90
75	Roy Sievers	4.00	2.00	1.25
76	Ray Crone	3.00	1.50	.90
77	Harvey Haddix	4.00	2.00	1.25
78	Herman Wehmeier	3.00	1.50	.90
79	Sandy Koufax	90.00	36.00	23.00
80	Gus Triandos	4.00	2.00	1.25
81	Wally Westlake	3.00	1.50	.90
82	Bill Renna	3.00	1.50	.90
83	Karl Spooner	4.00	2.00	1.25
84	"Babe" Birrer	3.00	1.50	.90
85a	Indians Team (with date)	25.00	12.50	7.50
85b	Indians Team (no date, name centered)			
		7.00	3.50	2.00
85c	Indians Team (no date, name at left)			
		10.00	5.00	3.00
86	Ray Jablonski	3.00	1.50	.90
87	Dean Stone	3.00	1.50	.90
88	Johnny Kucks	5.00	2.50	1.50
89	Norm Zauchin	3.00	1.50	.90
90a	Redlegs Team (with date)	25.00	12.50	7.50
90b	Redlegs Team (no date, name centered)			
		7.00	3.50	2.00
90c	Redlegs Team (no date, name at left)			
		10.00	5.00	3.00
91	Gail Harris	3.00	1.50	.90
92	"Red" Wilson	3.00	1.50	.90
93	George Susce, Jr.	3.00	1.50	.90
94	Ronnie Kline	3.00	1.50	.90
95a	Braves Team (with date)	25.00	12.50	7.50
95b	Braves Team (no date, name centered)			
		7.00	3.50	2.00
95c	Braves Team (no date, name at left)			
		10.00	5.00	3.00
96	Bill Tremel	3.00	1.50	.90
97	Jerry Lynch	3.00	1.50	.90
98	Camilo Pascual	4.00	2.00	1.25
99	Don Zimmer	7.00	3.50	2.00
100a	Orioles Team (with date)	25.00	12.50	7.50
100b	Orioles Team (no date, name centered)			
		7.00	3.50	2.00
100c	Orioles Team (no date, name at left)			
		10.00	5.00	3.00
101	Roy Campanella	70.00	35.00	21.00
102	Jim Davis	5.00	2.50	1.50
103	Willie Miranda	5.00	2.50	1.50
104	Bob Lennon	5.00	2.50	1.50
105	Al Smith	5.00	2.50	1.50
106	Joe Astroth	5.00	2.50	1.50
107	Ed Mathews	25.00	12.50	7.50
108	Laurin Pepper	5.00	2.50	1.50
109	Enos Slaughter	18.00	9.00	5.50
110	Yogi Berra	55.00	27.00	16.50

		NR MT	EX	VG			NR MT	EX	VG
111	Red Sox Team	8.00	4.00	2.50	202	Jim Hearn	6.00	3.00	1.75
112	Dee Fondy	5.00	2.50	1.50	203	Bill Tuttle	6.00	3.00	1.75
113	Phil Rizzuto	25.00	12.50	7.50	204	Art Swanson	6.00	3.00	1.75
114	Jim Owens	5.00	2.50	1.50	205	"Whitey" Lockman	6.00	3.00	1.75
115	Jackie Jensen	8.00	4.00	2.50	206	Erv Palica	6.00	3.00	1.75
116	Eddie O'Brien	5.00	2.50	1.50	207	Jim Small	6.00	3.00	1.75
117	Virgil Trucks	6.00	3.00	1.75	208	Elston Howard	15.00	7.50	4.50
118	"Nellie" Fox	12.00	6.00	3.50	209	Max Surkont	6.00	3.00	1.75
119	Larry Jackson	6.00	3.00	1.75	210	Mike Garcia	7.00	3.50	2.00
120	Richie Ashburn	12.00	6.00	3.50	211	Murry Dickson	6.00	3.00	1.75
121	Pirates Team	7.00	3.50	2.00	212	Johnny Temple	6.00	3.00	1.75
122	Willard Nixon	5.00	2.50	1.50	213	Tigers Team	12.00	6.00	3.50
123	Roy McMillan	5.00	2.50	1.50	214	Bob Rush	6.00	3.00	1.75
124	Don Kaiser	5.00	2.50	1.50	215	Tommy Byrne	9.00	4.50	2.75
125	"Minnie" Minoso	8.00	4.00	2.50	216	Jerry Schoonmaker	6.00	3.00	1.75
126	Jim Brady	5.00	2.50	1.50	217	Billy Klaus	6.00	3.00	1.75
127	Willie Jones	5.00	2.50	1.50	218	Joe Nuxall (Nuxhall)	6.00	3.00	1.75
128	Eddie Yost	5.00	2.50	1.50	219	Lew Burdette	8.00	4.00	2.50
129	"Jake" Martin	5.00	2.50	1.50	220	Del Ennis	6.00	3.00	1.75
130	Willie Mays	100.00	40.00	25.00	221	Bob Friend	7.00	3.50	2.00
131	Bob Roselli	5.00	2.50	1.50	222	Dave Philley	6.00	3.00	1.75
132	Bobby Avila	5.00	2.50	1.50	223	Randy Jackson	7.00	3.50	2.00
133	Ray Narleski	5.00	2.50	1.50	224	"Bud" Podbielan	6.00	3.00	1.75
134	Cardinals Team	7.00	3.50	2.00	225	Gil McDougald	12.00	6.00	3.50
135	Mickey Mantle	500.00	200.00	125.00	226	Giants Team	30.00	15.00	9.00
136	Johnny Logan	6.00	3.00	1.75	227	Russ Meyer	6.00	3.00	1.75
137	Al Silvera	5.00	2.50	1.50	228	"Mickey" Vernon	7.00	3.50	2.00
138	Johnny Antonelli	6.00	3.00	1.75	229	Harry Brecheen	7.00	3.50	2.00
139	Tommy Carroll	8.00	4.00	2.50	230	"Chico" Carrasquel	6.00	3.00	1.75
140	Herb Score	10.00	5.00	3.00	231	Bob Hale	6.00	3.00	1.75
141	Joe Frazier	5.00	2.50	1.50	232	"Toby" Atwell	6.00	3.00	1.75
142	Gene Baker	5.00	2.50	1.50	233	Carl Erskine	12.00	6.00	3.50
143	Jim Piersall	8.00	4.00	2.50	234	"Pete" Runnels	7.00	3.50	2.00
144	Leroy Powell	5.00	2.50	1.50	235	Don Newcombe	12.00	6.00	3.50
145	Gil Hodges	25.00	12.50	7.50	236	Athletics Team	8.00	4.00	2.50
146	Senators Team	7.00	3.50	2.00	237	Jose Valdivielso	6.00	3.00	1.75
147	Earl Torgeson	5.00	2.50	1.50	238	Walt Dropo	6.00	3.00	1.75
148	Alvin Dark	8.00	4.00	2.50	239	Harry Simpson	6.00	3.00	1.75
149	"Dixie" Howell	5.00	2.50	1.50	240	"Whitey" Ford	50.00	25.00	15.00
150	"Duke" Snider	50.00	25.00	15.00	241	Don Mueller	6.00	3.00	1.75
151	"Spook" Jacobs	5.00	2.50	1.50	242	Hershell Freeman	6.00	3.00	1.75
152	Billy Hoeft	5.00	2.50	1.50	243	Sherm Lollar	7.00	3.50	2.00
153	Frank Thomas	5.00	2.50	1.50	244	Bob Buhl	7.00	3.50	2.00
154	Dave Pope	5.00	2.50	1.50	245	Billy Goodman	6.00	3.00	1.75
155	Harvey Kuenn	7.00	3.50	2.00	246	Tom Gorman	6.00	3.00	1.75
156	Wes Westrum	6.00	3.00	1.75	247	Bill Sarni	6.00	3.00	1.75
157	Dick Brodowski	5.00	2.50	1.50	248	Bob Porterfield	6.00	3.00	1.75
158	Wally Post	5.00	2.50	1.50	249	Johnny Klippstein	6.00	3.00	1.75
159	Clint Courtney	5.00	2.50	1.50	250	Larry Doby	10.00	5.00	3.00
160	Billy Pierce	7.00	3.50	2.00	251	Yankees Team	60.00	30.00	18.00
161	Joe DeMaestri	5.00	2.50	1.50	252	Vernon Law	7.00	3.50	2.00
162	"Gus" Bell	6.00	3.00	1.75	253	Irv Noren	9.00	4.50	2.75
163	Gene Woodling	6.00	3.00	1.75	254	George Crowe	6.00	3.00	1.75
164	Harmon Killebrew	40.00	20.00	12.00	255	Bob Lemon	20.00	10.00	6.00
165	"Red" Schoendienst	8.00	4.00	2.50	256	Tom Hurd	6.00	3.00	1.75
166	Dodgers Team	65.00	32.00	19.50	257	Bobby Thomson	8.00	4.00	2.50
167	Harry Dorish	5.00	2.50	1.50	258	Art Ditmar	6.00	3.00	1.75
168	Sammy White	5.00	2.50	1.50	259	Sam Jones	6.00	3.00	1.75
169	Bob Nelson	5.00	2.50	1.50	260	"Pee Wee" Reese	65.00	32.00	19.50
170	Bill Virdon	7.00	3.50	2.00	261	Bobby Shantz	6.00	3.00	1.75
171	Jim Wilson	5.00	2.50	1.50	262	Howie Pollet	4.00	2.00	1.25
172	Frank Torre	6.00	3.00	1.75	263	Bob Miller	4.00	2.00	1.25
173	Johnny Podres	10.00	5.00	3.00	264	Ray Monzant	4.00	2.00	1.25
174	Glen Gorbous	5.00	2.50	1.50	265	Sandy Consuegra	4.00	2.00	1.25
175	Del Crandall	7.00	3.50	2.00	266	Don Ferrarese	4.00	2.00	1.25
176	Alex Kellner	5.00	2.50	1.50	267	Bob Nieman	5.00	2.50	1.50
177	Hank Bauer	12.00	6.00	3.50	268	Dale Mitchell	4.00	2.00	1.25
178	Joe Black	6.00	3.00	1.75	269	Jack Meyer	4.00	2.00	1.25
179	Harry Chiti	5.00	2.50	1.50	270	Billy Loes	6.00	3.00	1.75
180	Robin Roberts	20.00	10.00	6.00	271	Foster Castleman	4.00	2.00	1.25
181	Billy Martin	35.00	17.50	10.50	272	Danny O'Connell	4.00	2.00	1.25
182	Paul Minner	6.00	3.00	1.75	273	Walker Cooper	4.00	2.00	1.25
183	Stan Lopata	6.00	3.00	1.75	274	Frank Baumholtz	4.00	2.00	1.25
184	Don Bessent	7.00	3.50	2.00	275	Jim Greengrass	4.00	2.00	1.25
185	Bill Bruton	7.00	3.50	2.00	276	George Zuverink	4.00	2.00	1.25
186	Ron Jackson	6.00	3.00	1.75	277	Daryl Spencer	4.00	2.00	1.25
187	Early Wynn	20.00	10.00	6.00	278	Chet Nichols	4.00	2.00	1.25
188	White Sox Team	8.00	4.00	2.50	279	Johnny Groth	4.00	2.00	1.25
189	Ned Garver	6.00	3.00	1.75	280	Jim Gilliam	8.00	4.00	2.50
190	Carl Furillo	12.00	6.00	3.50	281	Art Houtteman	4.00	2.00	1.25
191	Frank Lary	7.00	3.50	2.00	282	Warren Hacker	4.00	2.00	1.25
192	"Smoky" Burgess	8.00	4.00	2.50	283	Hal Smith	4.00	2.00	1.25
193	Wilmer Mizell	6.00	3.00	1.75	284	Ike Delock	4.00	2.00	1.25
194	Monte Irvin	15.00	7.50	4.50	285	Eddie Miksis	4.00	2.00	1.25
195	George Kell	18.00	9.00	5.50	286	Bill Wight	4.00	2.00	1.25
196	Tom Poholsky	6.00	3.00	1.75	287	Bobby Adams	4.00	2.00	1.25
197	Granny Hamner	6.00	3.00	1.75	288	Bob Cerv	8.00	4.00	2.50
198	Ed Fitzgerald (Fitz Gerald)	6.00	3.00	1.75	289	Hal Jeffcoat	4.00	2.00	1.25
199	Hank Thompson	6.00	3.00	1.75	290	Curt Simmons	5.00	2.50	1.50
200	Bob Feller	40.00	20.00	12.00	291	Frank Kellert	4.00	2.00	1.25
201	"Rip" Repulski	6.00	3.00	1.75	292	Luis Aparicio	35.00	17.50	10.50

		NR MT	EX	VG
293	Stu Miller	4.00	2.00	1.25
294	Ernie Johnson	4.00	2.00	1.25
295	Clem Labine	6.00	3.00	1.75
296	Andy Seminick	4.00	2.00	1.25
297	Bob Skinner	5.00	2.50	1.50
298	Johnny Schmitz	4.00	2.00	1.25
299	Charley Neal	7.00	3.50	2.00
300	Vic Wertz	5.00	2.50	1.50
301	Marv Grissom	4.00	2.00	1.25
302	Eddie Robinson	7.00	3.50	2.00
303	Jim Dyck	4.00	2.00	1.25
304	Frank Malzone	5.00	2.50	1.50
305	Brooks Lawrence	4.00	2.00	1.25
306	Curt Roberts	4.00	2.00	1.25
307	Hoyt Wilhelm	18.00	9.00	5.50
308	"Chuck" Harmon	4.00	2.00	1.25
309	Don Blasingame	5.00	2.50	1.50
310	Steve Gromek	4.00	2.00	1.25
311	Hal Naragon	4.00	2.00	1.25
312	Andy Pafko	6.00	3.00	1.75
313	Gene Stephens	4.00	2.00	1.25
314	Hobie Landrith	4.00	2.00	1.25
315	Milt Bolling	4.00	2.00	1.25
316	Jerry Coleman	8.00	4.00	2.50
317	Al Aber	4.00	2.00	1.25
318	Fred Hatfield	4.00	2.00	1.25
319	Jack Crimian	4.00	2.00	1.25
320	Joe Adcock	6.00	3.00	1.75
321	Jim Konstanty	7.00	3.50	2.00
322	Karl Olson	4.00	2.00	1.25
323	Willard Schmidt	4.00	2.00	1.25
324	"Rocky" Bridges	4.00	2.00	1.25
325	Don Liddle	4.00	2.00	1.25
326	Connie Johnson	4.00	2.00	1.25
327	Bob Wiesler	4.00	2.00	1.25
328	Preston Ward	4.00	2.00	1.25
329	Lou Berberet	4.00	2.00	1.25
330	Jim Busby	4.00	2.00	1.25
331	Dick Hall	4.00	2.00	1.25
332	Don Larsen	10.00	5.00	3.00
333	Rube Walker	5.00	2.50	1.50
334	Bob Miller	4.00	2.00	1.25
335	Don Hoak	5.00	2.50	1.50
336	Ellis Kinder	4.00	2.00	1.25
337	Bobby Morgan	4.00	2.00	1.25
338	Jim Delsing	4.00	2.00	1.25
339	Rance Pless	4.00	2.00	1.25
340	Mickey McDermott	15.00	4.00	2.00
---	Checklist 1/3	125.00	50.00	32.00
---	Checklist 2/4	125.00	50.00	32.00

1956 Topps Hocus Focus

A direct descendant of the 1948 Topps "Magic Photo" issue. Again, the baseball players were part of a larger overall series covering several topical areas. There were two distinct issues of Hocus Focus cards in 1956. The "large" cards, measuring 1" by 1⅝," consists of 18 players. The "small" cards, ⅞" by 1⅜," state on the back that they were a series of 23, though only 11 are known. Besides players on the cards themselves, the easiest way to distinguish Hocus Focus cards of 1956 from the Magic Photos series of 1948 is to remember that the 1956 cards actually have the words "Hocus Focus" on the back.

The photos on these cards were developed by wetting the card's surface and exposing to light. Prices below are for cards with well-developed pictures. Cards with poorly developed photos are worth significantly less.

1956 Hocus Focus Large

		NR MT	EX	VG
Complete Set:		525.00	262.00	157.00
Common Player:		10.00	5.00	3.00
1	Dick Groat	25.00	12.50	7.50
2	Ed Lopat	25.00	12.50	7.50
3	Hank Sauer	10.00	5.00	3.00
4	"Dusty" Rhodes	10.00	5.00	3.00
5	Ted Williams	125.00	62.00	37.00
6	Harvey Haddix	10.00	5.00	3.00
7	Ray Boone	10.00	5.00	3.00
8	Al Rosen	25.00	12.50	7.50
9	Mayo Smith	10.00	5.00	3.00
10	Warren Spahn	70.00	35.00	21.00
11	Jim Rivera	10.00	5.00	3.00
12	Ted Kluszewski	25.00	12.50	7.50
13	Gus Zernial	10.00	5.00	3.00
14	Jackie Robinson	100.00	50.00	30.00
15	Hal Smith	10.00	5.00	3.00
16	Johnny Schmitz	10.00	5.00	3.00
17	"Spook" Jacobs	10.00	5.00	3.00
18	Mel Parnell	10.00	5.00	3.00

1956 Hocus Focus Small

		NR MT	EX	VG
Complete Set:		575.00	287.00	172.00
Common Player: 1-23		10.00	5.00	3.00
1	Babe Ruth	175.00	87.00	52.00
2	Unknown			
3	Dick Groat	15.00	7.50	4.50
4	Unknown			
5	Unknown			
6	"Dusty" Rhodes	10.00	5.00	3.00
7	Ted Williams	125.00	62.00	37.00
8	Harvey Haddix	10.00	5.00	3.00
9	Ray Boone	10.00	5.00	3.00
10	Unknown			
11	Unknown			
12	Warren Spahn	70.00	35.00	21.00
13	Jim Rivera	10.00	5.00	3.00
14	Ted Kluszewski	25.00	12.50	7.50
15	Gus Zernial	10.00	5.00	3.00
16	Unknown			
17	Unknown			
18	Johnny Schmitz	10.00	5.00	3.00
19	Unknown			
20	Karl Spooner	15.00	7.50	4.50
21	Ed Mathews	70.00	35.00	21.00
22	Unknown			
23	Unknown			

1956 Topps Pins

One of Topps first specialty issues, the 60-pin set of ballplayers issued in 1956 contains a high percentage of big-name stars which, combined with the scarcity of the pins, makes collecting a complete set extremely challenging. Compounding the situation is the fact that some pins are seen far less often than others, though the reason is unknown. Chuck Stobbs, Hector Lopez and Chuck Diering are unaccountably scarce. Measuring 1⅛'' in diameter, the pins utilize the same portraits found on 1956 Topps baseball cards, set against a solid color background.

		NR MT	EX	VG
	Complete Set:	1800.00	900.00	540.00
	Common Player:	10.00	5.00	3.00
(1)	Hank Aaron	80.00	40.00	24.00
(2)	Sandy Amoros	10.00	5.00	3.00
(3)	Luis Arroyo	10.00	5.00	3.00
(4)	Ernie Banks	50.00	25.00	15.00
(5)	Yogi Berra	60.00	30.00	18.00
(6)	Joe Black	15.00	7.50	4.50
(7)	Ray Boone	15.00	7.50	4.50
(8)	Ken Boyer	20.00	10.00	6.00
(9)	Joe Collins	10.00	5.00	3.00
(10)	Gene Conley	10.00	5.00	3.00
(11)	Chuck Diering	175.00	87.00	52.00
(12)	Dick Donovan	10.00	5.00	3.00
(13)	Jim Finigan	10.00	5.00	3.00
(14)	Art Fowler	10.00	5.00	3.00
(15)	Ruben Gomez	10.00	5.00	3.00
(16)	Dick Groat	20.00	10.00	6.00
(17)	Harvey Haddix	15.00	7.50	4.50
(18)	Jack Harshman	10.00	5.00	3.00
(19)	Grady Hatton	10.00	5.00	3.00
(20)	Jim Hegan	10.00	5.00	3.00
(21)	Gil Hodges	40.00	20.00	12.00
(22)	Bobby Hofman	10.00	5.00	3.00
(23)	Frank House	10.00	5.00	3.00
(24)	Jackie Jensen	20.00	10.00	6.00
(25)	Al Kaline	50.00	25.00	15.00
(26)	Bob Kennedy	10.00	5.00	3.00
(27)	Ted Kluszewski	25.00	12.50	7.50
(28)	Dale Long	10.00	5.00	3.00
(29)	Hector Lopez	175.00	87.00	52.00
(30)	Ed Mathews	40.00	20.00	12.00
(31)	Willie Mays	80.00	40.00	24.00
(32)	Roy McMillan	10.00	5.00	3.00
(33)	Willie Miranda	10.00	5.00	3.00
(34)	Wally Moon	15.00	7.50	4.50
(35)	Don Mossi	10.00	5.00	3.00
(36)	Ron Negray	10.00	5.00	3.00
(37)	Johnny O'Brien	10.00	5.00	3.00
(38)	Carlos Paula	10.00	5.00	3.00
(39)	Vic Power	10.00	5.00	3.00
(40)	Jim Rivera	10.00	5.00	3.00
(41)	Phil Rizzuto	40.00	20.00	12.00
(42)	Jackie Robinson	80.00	40.00	24.00
(43)	Al Rosen	25.00	12.50	7.50
(44)	Hank Sauer	15.00	7.50	4.50
(45)	Roy Sievers	15.00	7.50	4.50
(46)	Bill Skowron	20.00	10.00	6.00
(47)	Al Smith	10.00	5.00	3.00
(48)	Hal Smith	10.00	5.00	3.00
(49)	Mayo Smith	10.00	5.00	3.00
(50)	Duke Snider	60.00	30.00	18.00
(51)	Warren Spahn	40.00	20.00	12.00
(52)	Karl Spooner	15.00	7.50	4.50
(53)	Chuck Stobbs	150.00	75.00	45.00
(54)	Frank Sullivan	10.00	5.00	3.00
(55)	Bill Tremel	10.00	5.00	3.00
(56)	Gus Triandos	10.00	5.00	3.00
(57)	Bob Turley	20.00	10.00	6.00
(58)	Herman Wehmeier	10.00	5.00	3.00
(59)	Ted Williams	100.00	50.00	30.00
(60)	Gus Zernial	10.00	5.00	3.00

1957 Topps

For 1957, Topps reduced the size of its cards to the now-standard 2½'' by 3½.'' Set size was increased to 407 cards. Another change came in the form of the use of real color photographs as opposed to the hand-colored black-and-whites of previous years. For the first time since 1954, there were also cards with more than one player. The two, ''Dodger Sluggers'' and ''Yankees' Power Hitters'' began a trend toward the increased use of multiple-player cards. Another innovation was found on the backs, where, for the first time, complete player statistics were found. The scarce cards in the set are not the highest numbers, but rather #265-#352. Four unnumbered checklist

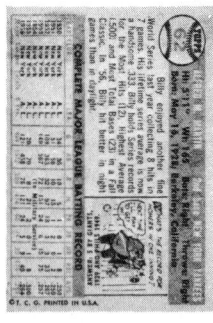

cards were issued along with the set. They are quite expensive and are not included in the complete set prices quoted below.

		NR MT	EX	VG
	Complete Set:	4500.00	1575.00	900.00
	Common Player: 1-264	2.50	1.25	.70
	Common Player: 265-352	10.00	5.00	3.00
	Common Player: 353-407	2.50	1.25	.70
1	Ted Williams	250.00	40.00	24.00
2	Yogi Berra	50.00	25.00	15.00
3	Dale Long	3.00	1.50	.90
4	Johnny Logan	3.00	1.50	.90
5	Sal Maglie	5.00	2.50	1.50
6	Hector Lopez	2.50	1.25	.70
7	Luis Aparicio	12.00	6.00	3.50
8	Don Mossi	3.00	1.50	.90
9	Johnny Temple	2.50	1.25	.70
10	Willie Mays	80.00	40.00	24.00
11	George Zuverink	2.50	1.25	.70
12	Dick Groat	4.00	2.00	1.25
13	Wally Burnette	2.50	1.25	.70
14	Bob Nieman	2.50	1.25	.70
15	Robin Roberts	12.00	6.00	3.50
16	Walt Moryn	2.50	1.25	.70
17	Billy Gardner	2.50	1.25	.70
18	Don Drysdale	65.00	32.00	19.50
19	Bob Wilson	2.50	1.25	.70
20	Hank Aaron (photo reversed)	80.00	40.00	24.00
21	Frank Sullivan	2.50	1.25	.70
22	Jerry Snyder (photo actually Ed Fitz Gerald)	2.50	1.25	.70
23	Sherm Lollar	3.00	1.50	.90
24	Bill Mazeroski	8.00	4.00	2.50
25	Whitey Ford	30.00	15.00	9.00
26	Bob Boyd	2.50	1.25	.70
27	Ted Kazanski	2.50	1.25	.70
28	Gene Conley	3.00	1.50	.90
29	Whitey Herzog	10.00	5.00	3.00
30	Pee Wee Reese	30.00	15.00	9.00
31	Ron Northey	2.50	1.25	.70
32	Hersh Freeman	2.50	1.25	.70
33	Jim Small	2.50	1.25	.70
34	Tom Sturdivant	4.00	2.00	1.25
35	Frank Robinson	90.00	36.00	23.00
36	Bob Grim	4.00	2.00	1.25
37	Frank Torre	2.50	1.25	.70
38	Nellie Fox	8.00	4.00	2.50
39	Al Worthington	2.50	1.25	.70
40	Early Wynn	12.00	6.00	3.50
41	Hal Smith	2.50	1.25	.70
42	Dee Fondy	2.50	1.25	.70
43	Connie Johnson	2.50	1.25	.70
44	Joe DeMaestri	2.50	1.25	.70
45	Carl Furillo	5.00	2.50	1.50
46	Bob Miller	2.50	1.25	.70
47	Don Blasingame	2.50	1.25	.70
48	Bill Bruton	3.00	1.50	.90
49	Daryl Spencer	2.50	1.25	.70
50	Herb Score	4.00	2.00	1.25
51	Clint Courtney	2.50	1.25	.70
52	Lee Walls	2.50	1.25	.70
53	Clem Labine	3.50	1.75	1.00
54	Elmer Valo	2.50	1.25	.70
55	Ernie Banks	35.00	17.50	10.50
56	Dave Sisler	2.50	1.25	.70
57	Jim Lemon	2.50	1.25	.70
58	Ruben Gomez	2.50	1.25	.70
59	Dick Williams	4.00	2.00	1.25
60	Billy Hoeft	2.50	1.25	.70

		NR MT	EX	VG
61	Dusty Rhodes	3.00	1.50	.90
62	Billy Martin	30.00	15.00	9.00
63	Ike Delock	2.50	1.25	.70
64	Pete Runnels	3.00	1.50	.90
65	Wally Moon	3.00	1.50	.90
66	Brooks Lawrence	2.50	1.25	.70
67	Chico Carrasquel	2.50	1.25	.70
68	Ray Crone	2.50	1.25	.70
69	Roy McMillan	2.50	1.25	.70
70	Richie Ashburn	8.00	4.00	2.50
71	Murry Dickson	2.50	1.25	.70
72	Bill Tuttle	2.50	1.25	.70
73	George Crowe	2.50	1.25	.70
74	Vito Valentinetti	2.50	1.25	.70
75	Jim Piersall	4.00	2.00	1.25
76	Bob Clemente	75.00	37.00	22.00
77	Paul Foytack	2.50	1.25	.70
78	Vic Wertz	3.50	1.75	1.00
79	Lindy McDaniel	3.50	1.75	1.00
80	Gil Hodges	25.00	12.50	7.50
81	Herm Wehmeier	2.50	1.25	.70
82	Elston Howard	8.00	4.00	2.50
83	Lou Skizas	2.50	1.25	.70
84	Moe Drabowsky	2.50	1.25	.70
85	Larry Doby	5.00	2.50	1.50
86	Bill Sarni	2.50	1.25	.70
87	Tom Gorman	2.50	1.25	.70
88	Harvey Kuenn	4.00	2.00	1.25
89	Roy Sievers	3.50	1.75	1.00
90	Warren Spahn	30.00	15.00	9.00
91	Mack Burk	2.50	1.25	.70
92	Mickey Vernon	3.00	1.50	.90
93	Hal Jeffcoat	2.50	1.25	.70
94	Bobby Del Greco	2.50	1.25	.70
95	Mickey Mantle	500.00	200.00	125.00
96	Hank Aguirre	3.50	1.75	1.00
97	Yankees Team	18.00	9.00	5.50
98	Al Dark	5.00	2.50	1.50
99	Bob Keegan	2.50	1.25	.70
100	League Presidents (Warren Giles, William Harridge)	4.00	2.00	1.25
101	Chuck Stobbs	2.50	1.25	.70
102	Ray Boone	3.00	1.50	.90
103	Joe Nuxhall	3.00	1.50	.90
104	Hank Foiles	2.50	1.25	.70
105	Johnny Antonelli	3.00	1.50	.90
106	Ray Moore	2.50	1.25	.70
107	Jim Rivera	2.50	1.25	.70
108	Tommy Byrne	4.00	2.00	1.25
109	Hank Thompson	2.50	1.25	.70
110	Bill Virdon	4.00	2.00	1.25
111	Hal Smith	2.50	1.25	.70
112	Tom Brewer	2.50	1.25	.70
113	Wilmer Mizell	2.50	1.25	.70
114	Braves Team	8.00	4.00	2.50
115	Jim Gilliam	5.00	2.50	1.50
116	Mike Fornieles	2.50	1.25	.70
117	Joe Adcock	4.00	2.00	1.25
118	Bob Porterfield	2.50	1.25	.70
119	Stan Lopata	2.50	1.25	.70
120	Bob Lemon	12.00	6.00	3.50
121	Cletis Boyer	6.00	3.00	1.75
122	Ken Boyer	5.00	2.50	1.50
123	Steve Ridzik	2.50	1.25	.70
124	Dave Philley	3.00	1.50	.90
125	Al Kaline	35.00	17.50	10.50
126	Bob Wiesler	2.50	1.25	.70
127	Bob Buhl	3.00	1.50	.90
128	Ed Bailey	2.50	1.25	.70
129	Saul Rogovin	2.50	1.25	.70
130	Don Newcombe	5.00	2.50	1.50
131	Milt Bolling	2.50	1.25	.70
132	Art Ditmar	4.00	2.00	1.25
133	Del Crandall	4.00	2.00	1.25
134	Don Kaiser	2.50	1.25	.70
135	Bill Skowron	8.00	4.00	2.50
136	Jim Hegan	2.50	1.25	.70
137	Bob Rush	2.50	1.25	.70
138	Minnie Minoso	5.00	2.50	1.50
139	Lou Kretlow	2.50	1.25	.70
140	Frank Thomas	2.50	1.25	.70
141	Al Aber	2.50	1.25	.70
142	Charley Thompson	2.50	1.25	.70
143	Andy Pafko	3.50	1.75	1.00
144	Ray Narleski	2.50	1.25	.70
145	Al Smith	2.50	1.25	.70
146	Don Ferrarese	2.50	1.25	.70
147	Al Walker	3.00	1.50	.90
148	Don Mueller	2.50	1.25	.70
149	Bob Kennedy	2.50	1.25	.70
150	Bob Friend	3.50	1.75	1.00

		NR MT	EX	VG
151	Willie Miranda	2.50	1.25	.70
152	Jack Harshman	2.50	1.25	.70
153	Karl Olson	2.50	1.25	.70
154	Red Schoendienst	5.00	2.50	1.50
155	Jim Brosnan	3.00	1.50	.90
156	Gus Triandos	3.00	1.50	.90
157	Wally Post	2.50	1.25	.70
158	Curt Simmons	3.50	1.75	1.00
159	Solly Drake	2.50	1.25	.70
160	Billy Pierce	4.00	2.00	1.25
161	Pirates Team	5.00	2.50	1.50
162	Jack Meyer	2.50	1.25	.70
163	Sammy White	2.50	1.25	.70
164	Tommy Carroll	4.00	2.00	1.25
165	Ted Kluszewski	8.00	4.00	2.50
166	Roy Face	3.50	1.75	1.00
167	Vic Power	2.50	1.25	.70
168	Frank Lary	3.00	1.50	.90
169	Herb Plews	2.50	1.25	.70
170	Duke Snider	50.00	25.00	15.00
171	Red Sox Team	7.00	3.50	2.00
172	Gene Woodling	3.00	1.50	.90
173	Roger Craig	5.00	2.50	1.50
174	Willie Jones	2.50	1.25	.70
175	Don Larsen	5.00	2.50	1.50
176	Gene Baker	2.50	1.25	.70
177	Eddie Yost	2.50	1.25	.70
178	Don Bessent	3.00	1.50	.90
179	Ernie Oravetz	2.50	1.25	.70
180	Gus Bell	3.00	1.50	.90
181	Dick Donovan	2.50	1.25	.70
182	Hobie Landrith	2.50	1.25	.70
183	Cubs Team	6.00	3.00	1.75
184	Tito Francona	3.50	1.75	1.00
185	Johnny Kucks	4.00	2.00	1.25
186	Jim King	2.50	1.25	.70
187	Virgil Trucks	3.00	1.50	.90
188	Felix Mantilla	2.50	1.25	.70
189	Willard Nixon	2.50	1.25	.70
190	Randy Jackson	3.00	1.50	.90
191	Joe Margoneri	2.50	1.25	.70
192	Jerry Coleman	4.00	2.00	1.25
193	Del Rice	2.50	1.25	.70
194	Hal Brown	2.50	1.25	.70
195	Bobby Avila	2.50	1.25	.70
196	Larry Jackson	2.50	1.25	.70
197	Hank Sauer	3.00	1.50	.90
198	Tigers Team	7.00	3.50	2.00
199	Vernon Law	3.50	1.75	1.00
200	Gil McDougald	8.00	4.00	2.50
201	Sandy Amoros	3.00	1.50	.90
202	Dick Gernert	2.50	1.25	.70
203	Hoyt Wilhelm	10.00	5.00	3.00
204	Athletics Team	5.00	2.50	1.50
205	Charley Maxwell	2.50	1.25	.70
206	Willard Schmidt	2.50	1.25	.70
207	Billy Hunter	2.50	1.25	.70
208	Lew Burdette	4.00	2.00	1.25
209	Bob Skinner	3.00	1.50	.90
210	Roy Campanella	50.00	25.00	15.00
211	Camilo Pascual	3.00	1.50	.90
212	Rocco Colavito	12.00	6.00	3.50
213	Les Moss	2.50	1.25	.70
214	Phillies Team	5.00	2.50	1.50
215	Enos Slaughter	12.00	6.00	3.50
216	Marv Grissom	2.50	1.25	.70
217	Gene Stephens	2.50	1.25	.70
218	Ray Jablonski	2.50	1.25	.70
219	Tom Acker	2.50	1.25	.70
220	Jackie Jensen	4.00	2.00	1.25
221	Dixie Howell	2.50	1.25	.70
222	Alex Grammas	2.50	1.25	.70
223	Frank House	2.50	1.25	.70
224	Marv Blaylock	2.50	1.25	.70
225	Harry Simpson	2.50	1.25	.70
226	Preston Ward	2.50	1.25	.70
227	Jerry Staley	2.50	1.25	.70
228	Smoky Burgess	3.50	1.75	1.00
229	George Susce	2.50	1.25	.70
230	George Kell	10.00	5.00	3.00
231	Solly Hemus	2.50	1.25	.70
232	Whitey Lockman	2.50	1.25	.70
233	Art Fowler	2.50	1.25	.70
234	Dick Cole	2.50	1.25	.70
235	Tom Poholsky	2.50	1.25	.70
236	Joe Ginsberg	2.50	1.25	.70
237	Foster Castleman	2.50	1.25	.70
238	Eddie Robinson	2.50	1.25	.70
239	Tom Morgan	2.50	1.25	.70
240	Hank Bauer	8.00	4.00	2.50
241	Joe Lonnett	2.50	1.25	.70

		NR MT	EX	VG
242	Charley Neal	3.50	1.75	1.00
243	Cardinals Team	6.00	3.00	1.75
244	Billy Loes	2.50	1.25	.70
245	Rip Repulski	2.50	1.25	.70
246	Jose Valdivielso	2.50	1.25	.70
247	Turk Lown	2.50	1.25	.70
248	Jim Finigan	2.50	1.25	.70
249	Dave Pope	2.50	1.25	.70
250	Ed Mathews	15.00	7.50	4.50
251	Orioles Team	5.00	2.50	1.50
252	Carl Erskine	5.00	2.50	1.50
253	Gus Zernial	3.00	1.50	.90
254	Ron Negray	2.50	1.25	.70
255	Charlie Silvera	2.50	1.25	.70
256	Ronnie Kline	2.50	1.25	.70
257	Walt Dropo	3.00	1.50	.90
258	Steve Gromek	2.50	1.25	.70
259	Eddie O'Brien	2.50	1.25	.70
260	Del Ennis	3.00	1.50	.90
261	Bob Chakales	2.50	1.25	.70
262	Bobby Thomson	4.00	2.00	1.25
263	George Strickland	2.50	1.25	.70
264	Bob Turley	6.00	3.00	1.75
265	Harvey Haddix	15.00	7.50	4.50
266	Ken Kuhn	10.00	5.00	3.00
267	Danny Kravitz	10.00	5.00	3.00
268	Jackie Collum	10.00	5.00	3.00
269	Bob Cerv	10.00	5.00	3.00
270	Senators Team	15.00	7.50	4.50
271	Danny O'Connell	10.00	5.00	3.00
272	Bobby Shantz	20.00	10.00	6.00
273	Jim Davis	10.00	5.00	3.00
274	Don Hoak	12.00	6.00	3.50
275	Indians Team	15.00	7.50	4.50
276	Jim Pyburn	10.00	5.00	3.00
277	Johnny Podres	30.00	15.00	9.00
278	Fred Hatfield	10.00	5.00	3.00
279	Bob Thurman	10.00	5.00	3.00
280	Alex Kellner	10.00	5.00	3.00
281	Gail Harris	10.00	5.00	3.00
282	Jack Dittmer	10.00	5.00	3.00
283	Wes Covington	12.00	6.00	3.50
284	Don Zimmer	15.00	7.50	4.50
285	Ned Garver	10.00	5.00	3.00
286	Bobby Richardson	50.00	25.00	15.00
287	Sam Jones	10.00	5.00	3.00
288	Ted Lepcio	10.00	5.00	3.00
289	Jim Bolger	10.00	5.00	3.00
290	Andy Carey	15.00	7.50	4.50
291	Windy McCall	10.00	5.00	3.00
292	Billy Klaus	10.00	5.00	3.00
293	Ted Abernathy	10.00	5.00	3.00
294	Rocky Bridges	10.00	5.00	3.00
295	Joe Collins	10.00	5.00	3.00
296	Johnny Klippstein	10.00	5.00	3.00
297	Jack Crimian	10.00	5.00	3.00
298	Irv Noren	10.00	5.00	3.00
299	Chuck Harmon	10.00	5.00	3.00
300	Mike Garcia	12.00	6.00	3.50
301	Sam Esposito	10.00	5.00	3.00
302	Sandy Koufax	200.00	80.00	50.00
303	Billy Goodman	10.00	5.00	3.00
304	Joe Cunningham	12.00	6.00	3.50
305	Chico Fernandez	10.00	5.00	3.00
306	Darrell Johnson	15.00	7.50	4.50
307	Jack Phillips	10.00	5.00	3.00
308	Dick Hall	10.00	5.00	3.00
309	Jim Busby	10.00	5.00	3.00
310	Max Surkont	10.00	5.00	3.00
311	Al Pilarcik	10.00	5.00	3.00
312	Tony Kubek	50.00	25.00	15.00
313	Mel Parnell	12.00	6.00	3.50
314	Ed Bouchee	10.00	5.00	3.00
315	Lou Berberet	10.00	5.00	3.00
316	Billy O'Dell	10.00	5.00	3.00
317	Giants Team	25.00	12.50	7.50
318	Mickey McDermott	10.00	5.00	3.00
319	Gino Cimoli	12.00	6.00	3.50
320	Neil Chrisley	10.00	5.00	3.00
321	Red Murff	10.00	5.00	3.00
322	Redlegs Team	25.00	12.50	7.50
323	Wes Westrum	12.00	6.00	3.50
324	Dodgers Team	50.00	25.00	15.00
325	Frank Bolling	10.00	5.00	3.00
326	Pedro Ramos	10.00	5.00	3.00
327	Jim Pendleton	10.00	5.00	3.00
328	Brooks Robinson	200.00	80.00	50.00
329	White Sox Team	15.00	7.50	4.50
330	Jim Wilson	10.00	5.00	3.00
331	Ray Katt	10.00	5.00	3.00
332	Bob Bowman	10.00	5.00	3.00

		NR MT	EX	VG
333	Ernie Johnson	10.00	5.00	3.00
334	Jerry Schoonmaker	10.00	5.00	3.00
335	Granny Hamner	10.00	5.00	3.00
336	Haywood Sullivan	12.00	6.00	3.50
337	Rene Valdes	12.00	6.00	3.50
338	Jim Bunning	50.00	25.00	15.00
339	Bob Speake	10.00	5.00	3.00
340	Bill Wight	10.00	5.00	3.00
341	Don Gross	10.00	5.00	3.00
342	Gene Mauch	15.00	7.50	4.50
343	Taylor Phillips	10.00	5.00	3.00
344	Paul LaPalme	10.00	5.00	3.00
345	Paul Smith	10.00	5.00	3.00
346	Dick Littlefield	10.00	5.00	3.00
347	Hal Naragon	10.00	5.00	3.00
348	Jim Hearn	10.00	5.00	3.00
349	Nelson King	10.00	5.00	3.00
350	Eddie Miksis	10.00	5.00	3.00
351	Dave Hillman	10.00	5.00	3.00
352	Ellis Kinder	10.00	5.00	3.00
353	Cal Neeman	2.50	1.25	.70
354	Rip Coleman	2.50	1.25	.70
355	Frank Malzone	3.00	1.50	.90
356	Faye Throneberry	2.50	1.25	.70
357	Earl Torgeson	2.50	1.25	.70
358	Jerry Lynch	2.50	1.25	.70
359	Tom Cheney	2.50	1.25	.70
360	Johnny Groth	2.50	1.25	.70
361	Curt Barclay	2.50	1.25	.70
362	Roman Mejias	2.50	1.25	.70
363	Eddie Kasko	2.50	1.25	.70
364	Cal McLish	2.50	1.25	.70
365	Ossie Virgil	2.50	1.25	.70
366	Ken Lehman	3.00	1.50	.90
367	Ed Fitz Gerald	2.50	1.25	.70
368	Bob Purkey	2.50	1.25	.70
369	Milt Graff	2.50	1.25	.70
370	Warren Hacker	2.50	1.25	.70
371	Bob Lennon	2.50	1.25	.70
372	Norm Zauchin	2.50	1.25	.70
373	Pete Whisenant	2.50	1.25	.70
374	Don Cardwell	2.50	1.25	.70
375	Jim Landis	3.00	1.50	.90
376	Don Elston	3.00	1.50	.90
377	Andre Rodgers	2.50	1.25	.70
378	Elmer Singleton	2.50	1.25	.70
379	Don Lee	2.50	1.25	.70
380	Walker Cooper	2.50	1.25	.70
381	Dean Stone	2.50	1.25	.70
382	Jim Brideweser	2.50	1.25	.70
383	Juan Pizarro	3.00	1.50	.90
384	Bobby Gene Smith	2.50	1.25	.70
385	Art Houtteman	2.50	1.25	.70
386	Lyle Luttrell	2.50	1.25	.70
387	Jack Sanford	3.00	1.50	.90
388	Pete Daley	2.50	1.25	.70
389	Dave Jolly	2.50	1.25	.70
390	Reno Bertoia	2.50	1.25	.70
391	Ralph Terry	6.00	3.00	1.75
392	Chuck Tanner	4.00	2.00	1.25
393	Raul Sanchez	2.50	1.25	.70
394	Luis Arroyo	2.50	1.25	.70
395	Bubba Phillips	2.50	1.25	.70
396	Casey Wise	2.50	1.25	.70
397	Roy Smalley	2.50	1.25	.70
398	Al Cicotte	4.00	2.00	1.25
399	Billy Consolo	2.50	1.25	.70
400	Dodgers' Sluggers (Roy Campanella, Carl Furillo, Gil Hodges, Duke Snider)	100.00	40.00	25.00
401	Earl Battey	3.50	1.75	1.00
402	Jim Pisoni	2.50	1.25	.70
403	Dick Hyde	2.50	1.25	.70
404	Harry Anderson	2.50	1.25	.70
405	Duke Maas	2.50	1.25	.70
406	Bob Hale	2.50	1.25	.70
407	Yankees' Power Hitters (Yogi Berra, Mickey Mantle)	175.00	50.00	32.00
---	Checklist Series 1-2	70.00	35.00	21.00
---	Checklist Series 2-3	100.00	40.00	25.00
---	Checklist Series 3-4	150.00	60.00	38.00
---	Checklist Series 4-5	200.00	80.00	50.00
---	Contest Card (Saturday, May 4th)	15.00	7.50	4.50
---	Contest Card (Saturday, May 25th)	15.00	7.50	4.50

Definitions for grading conditions are located in the Introduction of this price guide.

1958 Topps

Topps continued to expand its set size in 1958 with the release of a 494-card set. One card, #145, was not issued after Ed Bouchee was suspended. Cards retained the 2½'' by 3½'' size. There are a number of variations including yellow or white lettering on 33 cards between #2 and #108 (higher priced yellow letter variations checklisted below are not included in the complete set prices). The number of multiple player cards was increased. A major innovation was the addition of 20 "All Star" cards. For the first time, checklists were incorporated into the numbered series, as the backs of team cards.

		NR MT	EX	VG
Complete Set:		2800.00	975.00	550.00
Common Player: 1-110		2.50	1.25	.70
Common Player: 111-440		2.00	1.00	.60
Common Player: 441-495		1.25	.60	.40
1	Ted Williams	225.00	35.00	21.00
2a	Bob Lemon (yellow team letters)			
		25.00	10.00	6.00
2b	Bob Lemon (white team letters)	15.00	6.00	3.50
3	Alex Kellner	2.50	1.25	.70
4	Hank Foiles	2.50	1.25	.70
5	Willie Mays	70.00	35.00	21.00
6	George Zuverink	2.50	1.25	.70
7	Dale Long	3.00	1.50	.90
8a	Eddie Kasko (yellow name letters)			
		10.00	5.00	3.00
8b	Eddie Kasko (white name letters)	3.00	1.50	.90
9	Hank Bauer	6.00	3.00	1.75
10	Lou Burdette	4.00	2.00	1.25
11a	Jim Rivera (yellow team letters)	10.00	5.00	3.00
11b	Jim Rivera (white team letters)	3.00	1.50	.90
12	George Crowe	2.50	1.25	.70
13a	Billy Hoeft (yellow name letters)	10.00	5.00	3.00
13b	Billy Hoeft (white name, orange triangle by foot)	4.00	2.00	1.25
13c	Billy Hoeft (white name, red triangle by foot)	3.00	1.50	.90
14	Rip Repulski	2.50	1.25	.70
15	Jim Lemon	2.50	1.25	.70
16	Charley Neal	2.50	1.25	.70
17	Felix Mantilla	2.50	1.25	.70
18	Frank Sullivan	2.50	1.25	.70
19	Giants Team/Checklist 1-88	8.00	4.00	2.50
20a	Gil McDougald (yellow name letters)			
		20.00	10.00	6.00
20b	Gil McDougald (white name letters)			
		6.00	3.00	1.75
21	Curt Barclay	2.50	1.25	.70
22	Hal Naragon	2.50	1.25	.70
23a	Bill Tuttle (yellow name letters)	10.00	5.00	3.00
23b	Bill Tuttle (white name letters)	3.00	1.50	.90
24a	Hobie Landrith (yellow name letters)			
		10.00	5.00	3.00
24b	Hobie Landrith (white name letters)			
		3.00	1.50	.90
25	Don Drysdale	20.00	10.00	6.00
26	Ron Jackson	2.50	1.25	.70
27	Bud Freeman	2.50	1.25	.70

Definitions for grading conditions are located in the Introduction of this price guide.

		NR MT	EX	VG
28	Jim Busby	2.50	1.25	.70
29	Ted Lepcio	2.50	1.25	.70
30a	Hank Aaron (yellow name letters)			
		100.00	50.00	30.00
30b	Hank Aaron (white name letters)	65.00	32.00	19.50
31	Tex Clevenger	2.50	1.25	.70
32a	J.W. Porter (yellow name letters)			
		10.00	5.00	3.00
32b	J.W. Porter (white name letters)	3.00	1.50	.90
33a	Cal Neeman (yellow team letters)			
		10.00	5.00	3.00
33b	Cal Neeman (white team letters)	3.00	1.50	.90
34	Bob Thurman	2.50	1.25	.70
35a	Don Mossi (yellow team letters)	10.00	5.00	3.00
35b	Don Mossi (white team letters)	3.00	1.50	.90
36	Ted Kazanski	2.50	1.25	.70
37	Mike McCormick (photo actually Ray Monzant)	3.50	1.75	1.00
38	Dick Gernert	2.50	1.25	.70
39	Bob Martyn	2.50	1.25	.70
40	George Kell	9.00	4.50	2.75
41	Dave Hillman	2.50	1.25	.70
42	John Roseboro	3.50	1.75	1.00
43	Sal Maglie	5.00	2.50	1.50
44	Senators Team/Checklist 1-88	8.00	4.00	2.50
45	Dick Groat	3.50	1.75	1.00
46a	Lou Sleater (yellow name letters)			
		10.00	5.00	3.00
46b	Lou Sleater (white name letters)	3.00	1.50	.90
47	Roger Maris	175.00	70.00	44.00
48	Chuck Harmon	2.50	1.25	.70
49	Smoky Burgess	3.50	1.75	1.00
50a	Billy Pierce (yellow team letters)	12.00	6.00	3.50
50b	Billy Pierce (white team letters)	4.00	2.00	1.25
51	Del Rice	2.50	1.25	.70
52a	Bob Clemente (yellow team letters)			
		75.00	37.00	22.00
52b	Bob Clemente (white team letters)			
		40.00	20.00	12.00
53a	Morrie Martin (yellow name letters)			
		10.00	5.00	3.00
53b	Morrie Martin (white name letters)			
		3.00	1.50	.90
54	Norm Siebern	5.00	2.50	1.50
55	Chico Carrasquel	2.50	1.25	.70
56	Bill Fischer	2.50	1.25	.70
57a	Tim Thompson (yellow name letters)			
		10.00	5.00	3.00
57b	Tim Thompson (white name letters)			
		3.00	1.50	.90
58a	Art Schult (yellow team letters)	10.00	5.00	3.00
58b	Art Schult (white team letters)	3.00	1.50	.90
59	Dave Sisler	2.50	1.25	.70
60a	Del Ennis (yellow name letters)	10.00	5.00	3.00
60b	Del Ennis (white name letters)	3.00	1.50	.90
61a	Darrell Johnson (yellow name letters)			
		12.00	6.00	3.50
61b	Darrell Johnson (white name letters)			
		4.00	2.00	1.25
62	Joe DeMaestri	2.50	1.25	.70
63	Joe Nuxhall	3.00	1.50	.90
64	Joe Lonnett	2.50	1.25	.70
65a	Von McDaniel (yellow name letters)			
		10.00	5.00	3.00
65b	Von McDaniel (white name letters)			
		3.00	1.50	.90
66	Lee Walls	2.50	1.25	.70
67	Joe Ginsberg	2.50	1.25	.70
68	Daryl Spencer	2.50	1.25	.70
69	Wally Burnette	2.50	1.25	.70
70a	Al Kaline (yellow name letters)	60.00	30.00	18.00
70b	Al Kaline (white name letters)	20.00	10.00	6.00
71	Dodgers Team/Checklist 1-88	10.00	5.00	3.00
72	Bud Byerly	2.50	1.25	.70
73	Pete Daley	2.50	1.25	.70
74	Roy Face	3.50	1.75	1.00
75	Gus Bell	3.00	1.50	.90
76a	Dick Farrell (yellow name letters)			
		10.00	5.00	3.00
76b	Dick Farrell (white team letters)	3.00	1.50	.90
77a	Don Zimmer (yellow name letters)			
		12.00	6.00	3.50
77b	Don Zimmer (white team letters)	4.00	2.00	1.25
78a	Ernie Johnson (yellow name letters)			
		10.00	5.00	3.00
78b	Ernie Johnson (white name letters)			
		3.00	1.50	.90
79a	Dick Williams (yellow name letters)			
		12.00	6.00	3.50
79b	Dick Williams (white team letters)	4.00	2.00	1.25
80	Dick Drott	2.50	1.25	.70

		NR MT	EX	VG
81a	Steve Boros (yellow team letters)			
		12.00	6.00	3.50
81b	Steve Boros (white team letters)	3.00	1.50	.90
82	Ronnie Kline	2.50	1.25	.70
83	Bob Hazle	2.50	1.25	.70
84	Billy O'Dell	2.50	1.25	.70
85a	Luis Aparicio (yellow team letters)			
		20.00	10.00	6.00
85b	Luis Aparicio (white team letters)			
		10.00	5.00	3.00
86	Valmy Thomas	2.50	1.25	.70
87	Johnny Kucks	4.00	2.00	1.25
88	Duke Snider	25.00	12.50	7.50
89	Billy Klaus	2.50	1.25	.70
90	Robin Roberts	12.00	6.00	3.50
91	Chuck Tanner	4.00	2.00	1.25
92a	Clint Courtney (yellow name letters)			
		10.00	5.00	3.00
92b	Clint Courtney (white name letters)			
		3.00	1.50	.90
93	Sandy Amoros	2.50	1.25	.70
94	Bob Skinner	3.00	1.50	.90
95	Frank Bolling	2.50	1.25	.70
96	Joe Durham	2.50	1.25	.70
97a	Larry Jackson (yellow name letters)			
		10.00	5.00	3.00
97b	Larry Jackson (white name letters)			
		3.00	1.50	.90
98a	Billy Hunter (yellow name letters)			
		10.00	5.00	3.00
98b	Billy Hunter (white name letters)	3.00	1.50	.90
99	Bobby Adams	2.50	1.25	.70
100a	Early Wynn (yellow team letters)	20.00	10.00	6.00
100b	Early Wynn (white team letters)	12.00	6.00	3.50
101a	Bobby Richardson (yellow name letters)			
		20.00	10.00	6.00
101b	Bobby Richardson (white name letters)			
		8.00	4.00	2.50
102	George Strickland	2.50	1.25	.70
103	Jerry Lynch	2.50	1.25	.70
104	Jim Pendleton	2.50	1.25	.70
105	Billy Gardner	2.50	1.25	.70
106	Dick Schofield	2.50	1.25	.70
107	Ossie Virgil	2.50	1.25	.70
108a	Jim Landis (yellow team letters)	10.00	5.00	3.00
108b	Jim Landis (white team letters)	3.00	1.50	.90
109	Herb Plews	2.50	1.25	.70
110	Johnny Logan	3.00	1.50	.90
111	Stu Miller	2.00	1.00	.60
112	Gus Zernial	2.50	1.25	.70
113	Jerry Walker	2.00	1.00	.60
114	Irv Noren	2.00	1.00	.60
115	Jim Bunning	6.00	3.00	1.75
116	Dave Philley	2.50	1.25	.70
117	Frank Torre	2.00	1.00	.60
118	Harvey Haddix	2.00	1.00	.60
119	Harry Chiti	2.00	1.00	.60
120	Johnny Podres	4.00	2.00	1.25
121	Eddie Miksis	2.00	1.00	.60
122	Walt Moryn	2.00	1.00	.60
123	Dick Tomanek	2.00	1.00	.60
124	Bobby Usher	2.00	1.00	.60
125	Al Dark	3.50	1.75	1.00
126	Stan Palys	2.00	1.00	.60
127	Tom Sturdivant	3.50	1.75	1.00
128	Willie Kirkland	2.50	1.25	.70
129	Jim Derrington	2.00	1.00	.60
130	Jackie Jensen	3.50	1.75	1.00
131	Bob Henrich	2.00	1.00	.60
132	Vernon Law	3.00	1.50	.90
133	Russ Nixon	2.00	1.00	.60
134	Phillies Team/Checklist 89-176	7.00	3.50	2.00
135	Mike Drabowsky	2.00	1.00	.60
136	Jim Finingan	2.00	1.00	.60
137	Russ Kemmerer	2.00	1.00	.60
138	Earl Torgeson	2.00	1.00	.60
139	George Brunet	2.00	1.00	.60
140	Wes Covington	2.50	1.25	.70
141	Ken Lehman	2.00	1.00	.60
142	Enos Slaughter	10.00	5.00	3.00
143	Billy Muffett	2.00	1.00	.60
144	Bobby Morgan	2.00	1.00	.60
145	Not Issued			
146	Dick Gray	2.00	1.00	.60
147	Don McMahon	3.00	1.50	.90
148	Billy Consolo	2.00	1.00	.60
149	Tom Acker	2.00	1.00	.60
150	Mickey Mantle	325.00	130.00	80.00
151	Buddy Pritchard	2.00	1.00	.60
152	Johnny Antonelli	3.00	1.50	.90
153	Les Moss	2.00	1.00	.60
154	Harry Byrd	2.00	1.00	.60
155	Hector Lopez	2.00	1.00	.60
156	Dick Hyde	2.00	1.00	.60
157	Dee Fondy	2.00	1.00	.60
158	Indians Team/Checklist 177-264	7.00	3.50	2.00
159	Taylor Phillips	2.00	1.00	.60
160	Don Hoak	2.50	1.25	.70
161	Don Larsen	4.00	2.00	1.25
162	Gil Hodges	15.00	7.50	4.50
163	Jim Wilson	2.00	1.00	.60
164	Bob Taylor	2.00	1.00	.60
165	Bob Nieman	2.00	1.00	.60
166	Danny O'Connell	2.00	1.00	.60
167	Frank Baumann	2.00	1.00	.60
168	Joe Cunningham	2.50	1.25	.70
169	Ralph Terry	2.50	1.25	.70
170	Vic Wertz	3.00	1.50	.90
171	Harry Anderson	2.00	1.00	.60
172	Don Gross	2.00	1.00	.60
173	Eddie Yost	2.50	1.25	.70
174	A's Team/Checklist 89-176	7.00	3.50	2.00
175	Marv Throneberry	5.00	2.50	1.50
176	Bob Buhl	2.50	1.25	.70
177	Al Smith	2.00	1.00	.60
178	Ted Kluszewski	5.00	2.50	1.50
179	Willy Miranda	2.00	1.00	.60
180	Lindy McDaniel	2.00	1.00	.60
181	Willie Jones	2.00	1.00	.60
182	Joe Caffie	2.00	1.00	.60
183	Dave Jolly	2.00	1.00	.60
184	Elvin Tappe	2.00	1.00	.60
185	Ray Boone	2.50	1.25	.70
186	Jack Meyer	2.00	1.00	.60
187	Sandy Koufax	55.00	28.00	17.00
188	Milt Bolling (photo actually Lou Berberet)			
		2.00	1.00	.60
189	George Susce	2.00	1.00	.60
190	Red Schoendienst	4.00	2.00	1.25
191	Art Ceccarelli	2.00	1.00	.60
192	Milt Graff	2.00	1.00	.60
193	Jerry Lumpe	4.00	2.00	1.25
194	Roger Craig	3.00	1.50	.90
195	Whitey Lockman	2.00	1.00	.60
196	Mike Garcia	2.50	1.25	.70
197	Haywood Sullivan	2.50	1.25	.70
198	Bill Virdon	3.00	1.50	.90
199	Don Blasingame	2.00	1.00	.60
200	Bob Keegan	2.00	1.00	.60
201	Jim Bolger	2.00	1.00	.60
202	Woody Held	3.00	1.50	.90
203	Al Walker	2.00	1.00	.60
204	Leo Kiely	2.00	1.00	.60
205	Johnny Temple	2.00	1.00	.60
206	Bob Shaw	3.00	1.50	.90
207	Solly Hemus	2.00	1.00	.60
208	Cal McLish	2.00	1.00	.60
209	Bob Anderson	2.00	1.00	.60
210	Wally Moon	2.50	1.25	.70
211	Pete Burnside	2.00	1.00	.60
212	Bubba Phillips	2.00	1.00	.60
213	Red Wilson	2.00	1.00	.60
214	Willard Schmidt	2.00	1.00	.60
215	Jim Gilliam	3.50	1.75	1.00
216	Cards Team/Checklist 177-264	7.00	3.50	2.00
217	Jack Harshman	2.00	1.00	.60
218	Dick Rand	2.00	1.00	.60
219	Camilo Pascual	2.50	1.25	.70
220	Tom Brewer	2.00	1.00	.60
221	Jerry Kindall	2.00	1.00	.60
222	Bud Daley	2.00	1.00	.60
223	Andy Pafko	3.00	1.50	.90
224	Bob Grim	3.50	1.75	1.00
225	Billy Goodman	2.00	1.00	.60
226	Bob Smith (photo actually Bobby Gene Smith)	2.00	1.00	.60
227	Gene Stephens	2.00	1.00	.60
228	Duke Maas	2.00	1.00	.60
229	Frank Zupo	2.00	1.00	.60
230	Richie Ashburn	6.00	3.00	1.75
231	Lloyd Merritt	2.00	1.00	.60
232	Reno Bertoia	2.00	1.00	.60
233	Mickey Vernon	2.50	1.25	.70
234	Carl Sawatski	2.00	1.00	.60
235	Tom Gorman	2.00	1.00	.60
236	Ed Fitz Gerald	2.00	1.00	.60
237	Bill Wight	2.00	1.00	.60
238	Bill Mazeroski	4.00	2.00	1.25
239	Chuck Stobbs	2.00	1.00	.60
240	Moose Skowron	6.00	3.00	1.75
241	Dick Littlefield	2.00	1.00	.60
242	Johnny Klippstein	2.00	1.00	.60

		NR MT	EX	VG
243	Larry Raines	2.00	1.00	.60
244	Don Demeter	2.50	1.25	.70
245	Frank Lary	2.50	1.25	.70
246	Yankees Team/Checklist 177-264			
		15.00	7.50	4.50
247	Casey Wise	2.00	1.00	.60
248	Herm Wehmeier	2.00	1.00	.60
249	Ray Moore	2.00	1.00	.60
250	Roy Sievers	3.00	1.50	.90
251	Warren Hacker	2.00	1.00	.60
252	Bob Trowbridge	2.00	1.00	.60
253	Don Mueller	2.00	1.00	.60
254	Alex Grammas	2.00	1.00	.60
255	Bob Turley	5.00	2.50	1.50
256	W. Sox Team/Checklist 265-352			
		7.00	3.50	2.00
257	Hal Smith	2.00	1.00	.60
258	Carl Erskine	4.00	2.00	1.25
259	Al Pilarcik	2.00	1.00	.60
260	Frank Malzone	2.50	1.25	.70
261	Turk Lown	2.00	1.00	.60
262	Johnny Groth	2.00	1.00	.60
263	Eddie Bressoud	2.50	1.25	.70
264	Jack Sanford	2.50	1.25	.70
265	Pete Runnels	2.50	1.25	.70
266	Connie Johnson	2.00	1.00	.60
267	Sherm Lollar	2.50	1.25	.70
268	Granny Hamner	2.00	1.00	.60
269	Paul Smith	2.00	1.00	.60
270	Warren Spahn	15.00	7.50	4.50
271	Billy Martin	6.00	3.00	1.75
272	Ray Crone	2.00	1.00	.60
273	Hal Smith	2.00	1.00	.60
274	Rocky Bridges	2.00	1.00	.60
275	Elston Howard	6.00	3.00	1.75
276	Bobby Avila	2.00	1.00	.60
277	Virgil Trucks	2.50	1.25	.70
278	Mack Burk	2.00	1.00	.60
279	Bob Boyd	2.00	1.00	.60
280	Jim Piersall	3.00	1.50	.90
281	Sam Taylor	2.00	1.00	.60
282	Paul Foytack	2.00	1.00	.60
283	Ray Shearer	2.00	1.00	.60
284	Ray Katt	2.00	1.00	.60
285	Frank Robinson	25.00	12.50	7.50
286	Gino Cimoli	2.00	1.00	.60
287	Sam Jones	2.00	1.00	.60
288	Harmon Killebrew	20.00	10.00	6.00
289	Series Hurling Rivals (Lou Burdette, Bobby Shantz)			
		3.50	1.75	1.00
290	Dick Donovan	2.00	1.00	.60
291	Don Landrum	2.00	1.00	.60
292	Ned Garver	2.00	1.00	.60
293	Gene Freese	2.00	1.00	.60
294	Hal Jeffcoat	2.00	1.00	.60
295	Minnie Minoso	3.50	1.75	1.00
296	Ryne Duren	5.00	2.50	1.50
297	Don Buddin	2.00	1.00	.60
298	Jim Hearn	2.00	1.00	.60
299	Harry Simpson	3.50	1.75	1.00
300	League Presidents (Warren Giles, William Harridge)			
		3.50	1.75	1.00
301	Randy Jackson	2.00	1.00	.60
302	Mike Baxes	2.00	1.00	.60
303	Neil Chrisley	2.00	1.00	.60
304	Tigers' Big Bats (Al Kaline, Harvey Kuenn)			
		5.00	2.50	1.50
305	Clem Labine	2.50	1.25	.70
306	Whammy Douglas	2.00	1.00	.60
307	Brooks Robinson	30.00	15.00	9.00
308	Paul Giel	2.00	1.00	.60
309	Gail Harris	2.00	1.00	.60
310	Ernie Banks	20.00	12.50	7.50
311	Bob Purkey	2.00	1.00	.60
312	Red Sox Team/Checklist 353-440			
		7.00	3.50	2.00
313	Bob Rush	2.00	1.00	.60
314	Dodgers' Boss & Power (Walter Alston, Duke Snider)			
		10.00	5.00	3.00
315	Bob Friend	3.00	1.50	.90
316	Tito Francona	2.50	1.25	.70
317	Albie Pearson	3.00	1.50	.90
318	Frank House	2.00	1.00	.60
319	Lou Skizas	2.00	1.00	.60
320	Whitey Ford	20.00	10.00	6.00
321	Sluggers Supreme (Ted Kluszewski, Ted Williams)			
		10.00	5.00	3.00
322	Harding Peterson	2.00	1.00	.60
323	Elmer Valo	2.00	1.00	.60
324	Hoyt Wilhelm	8.00	4.00	2.50
325	Joe Adcock	3.00	1.50	.90

		NR MT	EX	VG
326	Bob Miller	2.00	1.00	.60
327	Cubs Team/Checklist 265-352	7.00	3.50	2.00
328	Ike Delock	2.00	1.00	.60
329	Bob Cerv	2.00	1.00	.60
330	Ed Bailey	2.00	1.00	.60
331	Pedro Ramos	2.00	1.00	.60
332	Jim King	2.00	1.00	.60
333	Andy Carey	3.50	1.75	1.00
334	Mound Aces (Bob Friend, Billy Pierce)			
		3.00	1.50	.90
335	Ruben Gomez	2.00	1.00	.60
336	Bert Hamric	2.00	1.00	.60
337	Hank Aguirre	2.00	1.00	.60
338	Walt Dropo	2.50	1.25	.70
339	Fred Hatfield	2.00	1.00	.60
340	Don Newcombe	4.00	2.00	1.25
341	Pirates Team/Checklist 265-352	7.00	3.50	2.00
342	Jim Brosnan	2.50	1.25	.70
343	Orlando Cepeda	18.00	9.00	5.50
344	Bob Porterfield	2.00	1.00	.60
345	Jim Hegan	2.00	1.00	.60
346	Steve Bilko	2.00	1.00	.60
347	Don Rudolph	2.00	1.00	.60
348	Chico Fernandez	2.00	1.00	.60
349	Murry Dickson	2.00	1.00	.60
350	Ken Boyer	4.00	2.00	1.25
351	Braves' Fence Busters (Hank Aaron, Joe Adcock, Del Crandall, Ed Mathews)			
		12.00	6.00	3.50
352	Herb Score	3.00	1.50	.90
353	Stan Lopata	2.00	1.00	.60
354	Art Ditmar	3.50	1.75	1.00
355	Bill Bruton	2.50	1.25	.70
356	Bob Malkmus	2.00	1.00	.60
357	Danny McDevitt	2.00	1.00	.60
358	Gene Baker	2.00	1.00	.60
359	Billy Loes	2.00	1.00	.60
360	Roy McMillan	2.00	1.00	.60
361	Mike Fornieles	2.00	1.00	.60
362	Ray Jablonski	2.00	1.00	.60
363	Don Elston	2.00	1.00	.60
364	Earl Battey	2.50	1.25	.70
365	Tom Morgan	2.00	1.00	.60
366	Gene Green	2.00	1.00	.60
367	Jack Urban	2.00	1.00	.60
368	Rocky Colavito	6.00	3.00	1.75
369	Ralph Lumenti	2.00	1.00	.60
370	Yogi Berra	30.00	15.00	9.00
371	Marty Keough	2.00	1.00	.60
372	Don Cardwell	2.00	1.00	.60
373	Joe Pignatano	2.00	1.00	.60
374	Brooks Lawrence	2.00	1.00	.60
375	Pee Wee Reese	25.00	12.50	7.50
376	Charley Rabe	2.00	1.00	.60
377a	Braves Team (alphabetical checklist on back)			
		8.00	4.00	2.50
377b	Braves Team (numerical checklist on back)			
		25.00	12.50	7.50
378	Hank Sauer	2.50	1.25	.70
379	Ray Herbert	2.00	1.00	.60
380	Charley Maxwell	2.00	1.00	.60
381	Hal Brown	2.00	1.00	.60
382	Al Cicotte	3.50	1.75	1.00
383	Lou Berberet	2.00	1.00	.60
384	John Goryl	2.00	1.00	.60
385	Wilmer Mizell	2.00	1.00	.60
386	Birdie's Young Sluggers (Ed Bailey, Frank Robinson, Birdie Tebbetts)			
		6.00	3.00	1.75
387	Wally Post	2.00	1.00	.60
388	Billy Moran	2.00	1.00	.60
389	Bill Taylor	2.00	1.00	.60
390	Del Crandall	3.00	1.50	.90
391	Dave Melton	2.00	1.00	.60
392	Bennie Daniels	2.00	1.00	.60
393	Tony Kubek	8.00	4.00	2.50
394	Jim Grant	3.00	1.50	.90
395	Willard Nixon	2.00	1.00	.60
396	Dutch Dotterer	2.00	1.00	.60
397a	Tigers Team (alphabetical checklist on back)			
		8.00	4.00	2.50
397b	Tigers Team (numerical checklist on back)			
		30.00	15.00	9.00
398	Gene Woodling	2.50	1.25	.70
399	Marv Grissom	2.00	1.00	.60
400	Nellie Fox	6.00	3.00	1.75
401	Don Bessent	2.00	1.00	.60
402	Bobby Gene Smith	2.00	1.00	.60
403	Steve Korcheck	2.00	1.00	.60
404	Curt Simmons	3.00	1.50	.90
405	Ken Aspromonte	2.00	1.00	.60
406	Vic Power	2.00	1.00	.60
407	Carlton Willey	2.00	1.00	.60

		NR MT	EX	VG
408a	Orioles Team (alphabetical checklist on			
	back)	7.00	3.50	2.00
408b	Orioles Team (numerical checklist on			
	back)	25.00	12.50	7.50
409	Frank Thomas	2.00	1.00	.60
410	Murray Wall	2.00	1.00	.60
411	Tony Taylor	2.50	1.25	.70
412	Jerry Staley	2.00	1.00	.60
413	Jim Davenport	2.50	1.25	.70
414	Sammy White	2.00	1.00	.60
415	Bob Bowman	2.00	1.00	.60
416	Foster Castleman	2.00	1.00	.60
417	Carl Furillo	4.00	2.00	1.25
418	World Series Batting Foes (Hank Aaron,			
	Mickey Mantle)	55.00	22.00	15.00
419	Bobby Shantz	4.00	2.00	1.25
420	Vada Pinson	7.00	3.50	2.00
421	Dixie Howell	2.00	1.00	.60
422	Norm Zauchin	2.00	1.00	.60
423	Phil Clark	2.00	1.00	.60
424	Larry Doby	3.50	1.75	1.00
425	Sam Esposito	2.00	1.00	.60
426	Johnny O'Brien	2.00	1.00	.60
427	Al Worthington	2.00	1.00	.60
428a	Redlegs Team (alphabetical checklist on			
	back)	7.00	3.50	2.00
428b	Redlegs Team (numerical checklist on			
	back)	25.00	12.50	7.50
429	Gus Triandos	2.50	1.25	.70
430	Bobby Thomson	3.00	1.50	.90
431	Gene Conley	2.50	1.25	.70
432	John Powers	2.00	1.00	.60
433	Pancho Herrera	2.00	1.00	.60
434	Harvey Kuenn	3.00	1.50	.90
435	Ed Roebuck	2.00	1.00	.60
436	Rival Fence Busters (Willie Mays, Duke			
	Snider)	30.00	15.00	9.00
437	Bob Speake	2.00	1.00	.60
438	Whitey Herzog	3.50	1.75	1.00
439	Ray Narleski	2.00	1.00	.60
440	Ed Mathews	15.00	7.50	4.50
441	Jim Marshall	1.25	.60	.40
442	Phil Paine	1.25	.60	.40
443	Billy Harrell	4.00	2.00	1.25
444	Danny Kravitz	1.25	.60	.40
445	Bob Smith	1.25	.60	.40
446	Carroll Hardy	4.00	2.00	1.25
447	Ray Monzant	1.25	.60	.40
448	Charlie Lau	2.50	1.25	.70
449	Gene Fodge	1.25	.60	.40
450	Preston Ward	4.00	2.00	1.25
451	Joe Taylor	1.25	.60	.40
452	Roman Mejias	1.25	.60	.40
453	Tom Qualters	1.25	.60	.40
454	Harry Hanebrink	1.25	.60	.40
455	Hal Griggs	1.25	.60	.40
456	Dick Brown	1.25	.60	.40
457	Milt Pappas	2.50	1.25	.70
458	Julio Becquer	1.25	.60	.40
459	Ron Blackburn	1.25	.60	.40
460	Chuck Essegian	1.25	.60	.40
461	Ed Mayer	1.25	.60	.40
462	Gary Geiger	4.00	2.00	1.25
463	Vito Valentinetti	1.25	.60	.40
464	Curt Flood	6.00	3.00	1.75
465	Arnie Portocarrero	1.25	.60	.40
466	Pete Whisenant	1.25	.60	.40
467	Glen Hobbie	1.25	.60	.40
468	Bob Schmidt	1.25	.60	.40
469	Don Ferrarese	1.25	.60	.40
470	R.C. Stevens	1.25	.60	.40
471	Lenny Green	1.25	.60	.40
472	Joe Jay	1.25	.60	.40
473	Bill Renna	1.25	.60	.40
474	Roman Semproch	1.25	.60	.40
475	All-Star Managers (Fred Haney, Casey			
	Stengel)	12.00	6.00	3.50
476	Stan Musial AS	15.00	7.50	3.50
477	Bill Skowron AS	3.50	1.75	1.00
478	Johnny Temple AS	2.00	1.00	.60
479	Nellie Fox AS	4.00	2.00	1.25
480	Eddie Mathews AS	7.00	3.50	2.00
481	Frank Malzone AS	2.00	1.00	.60
482	Ernie Banks AS	7.00	3.50	2.00
483	Luis Aparicio AS	5.00	2.50	1.50
484	Frank Robinson AS	7.00	3.50	2.00
485	Ted Williams AS	20.00	10.00	6.00
486	Willie Mays AS	15.00	7.50	4.50
487	Mickey Mantle AS	25.00	10.00	6.25
488	Hank Aaron AS	15.00	7.50	4.50
489	Jackie Jensen AS	3.00	1.50	.90

		NR MT	EX	VG
490	Ed Bailey AS	2.00	1.00	.60
491	Sherm Lollar AS	2.00	1.00	.60
492	Bob Friend AS	3.00	1.50	.90
493	Bob Turley AS	3.50	1.75	1.00
494	Warren Spahn AS	7.00	3.50	2.00
495	Herb Score AS	5.00	1.50	.60
---	Contest Card (All-Star Game, July 8)			
		15.00	7.50	4.50

1959 Topps

 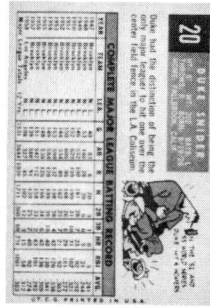

These 2½'' by 3½'' cards had a round photograph at the center of the front with a solid-color background and white border. A facsimile autograph is found across the photo. The 572-card set marks the largest set issued to that time. Card numbers below 507 had red and green printing with the card number in white in a green box. On high number cards, beginning with #507, the printing is black and red and the card number is in a black box. Specialty cards include multiple player cards, team cards with checklists, "All-Star" cards, highlights from the previous season, and 31 "Rookie Stars." There is also a card of the commissioner, Ford Frick, and one of Roy Campanella in a wheelchair. A handful of cards can be found with and without lines added to the biographies on back indicating trades or demotions; those without the added lines are considerably more rare and valuable and are not included in the complete set price. Cards #'s 199-286 can be found with either white or grey backs, with the grey stock being the less common.

		NR MT	EX	VG
Complete Set:		2800.00	975.00	550.00
Common Player: 1-110		2.00	1.00	.60
Common Player: 111-506		1.50	.70	.45
Common Player: 507-572		5.00	2.50	1.50
1	Ford Frick	15.00	2.00	1.00
2	Eddie Yost	3.50	1.25	.70
3	Don McMahon	2.00	1.00	.60
4	Albie Pearson	2.00	1.00	.60
5	Dick Donovan	2.00	1.00	.60
6	Alex Grammas	2.00	1.00	.60
7	Al Pilarcik	2.00	1.00	.60
8	Phillies Team/Checklist 1-88	7.00	3.50	2.00
9	Paul Giel	2.00	1.00	.60
10	Mickey Mantle	250.00	110.00	60.00
11	Billy Hunter	2.00	1.00	.60
12	Vern Law	3.00	1.50	.90
13	Dick Gernert	2.00	1.00	.60
14	Pete Whisenant	2.00	1.00	.60
15	Dick Drott	2.00	1.00	.60
16	Joe Pignatano	2.00	1.00	.60
17	Danny's All-Stars (Ted Kluszewski, Danny			
	Murtaugh, Frank Thomas)	3.00	1.50	.90
18	Jack Urban	2.00	1.00	.60
19	Ed Bressoud	2.00	1.00	.60
20	Duke Snider	25.00	12.50	7.50
21	Connie Johnson	2.00	1.00	.60
22	Al Smith	2.00	1.00	.60
23	Murry Dickson	3.25	1.75	1.00
24	Red Wilson	2.00	1.00	.60
25	Don Hoak	2.50	1.25	.70
26	Chuck Stobbs	2.00	1.00	.60

#	Name	NR MT	EX	VG
27	Andy Pafko	2.50	1.25	.70
28	Red Worthington	2.00	1.00	.60
29	Jim Bolger	2.00	1.00	.60
30	Nellie Fox	6.00	3.00	1.75
31	Ken Lehman	2.00	1.00	.60
32	Don Buddin	2.00	1.00	.60
33	Ed Fitz Gerald	2.00	1.00	.60
34	Pitchers Beware (Al Kaline, Charlie Maxwell)	6.00	3.00	1.75
35	Ted Kluszewski	4.00	2.00	1.25
36	Hank Aguirre	2.00	1.00	.60
37	Gene Green	2.00	1.00	.60
38	Morrie Martin	2.00	1.00	.60
39	Ed Bouchee	2.00	1.00	.60
40	Warren Spahn	18.00	9.00	5.50
41	Bob Martyn	2.00	1.00	.60
42	Murray Wall	2.00	1.00	.60
43	Steve Bilko	2.00	1.00	.60
44	Vito Valentinetti	2.00	1.00	.60
45	Andy Carey	3.25	1.75	1.00
46	Bill Henry	2.00	1.00	.60
47	Jim Finigan	2.00	1.00	.60
48	Orioles Team/Checklist 1-88	7.00	3.50	2.00
49	Bill Hall	2.00	1.00	.60
50	Willie Mays	55.00	27.00	16.50
51	Rip Coleman	2.00	1.00	.60
52	Coot Veal	2.00	1.00	.60
53	Stan Williams	2.00	1.00	.60
54	Mel Roach	2.00	1.00	.60
55	Tom Brewer	2.00	1.00	.60
56	Carl Sawatski	2.00	1.00	.60
57	Al Cicotte	2.00	1.00	.60
58	Eddie Miksis	2.00	1.00	.60
59	Irv Noren	2.00	1.00	.60
60	Bob Turley	4.00	2.00	1.25
61	Dick Brown	2.00	1.00	.60
62	Tony Taylor	2.00	1.00	.60
63	Jim Hearn	2.00	1.00	.60
64	Joe DeMaestri	2.00	1.00	.60
65	Frank Torre	2.00	1.00	.60
66	Joe Ginsberg	2.00	1.00	.60
67	Brooks Lawrence	2.00	1.00	.60
68	Dick Schofield	2.00	1.00	.60
69	Giants Team/Checklist 89-176	7.00	3.50	2.00
70	Harvey Kuenn	3.00	1.50	.90
71	Don Bessent	2.00	1.00	.60
72	Bill Renna	2.00	1.00	.60
73	Ron Jackson	2.00	1.00	.60
74	Directing the Power (Cookie Lavagetto, Jim Lemon, Roy Sievers)	2.50	1.25	.70
75	Sam Jones	2.00	1.00	.60
76	Bobby Richardson	6.00	3.00	1.75
77	John Goryl	2.00	1.00	.60
78	Pedro Ramos	2.00	1.00	.60
79	Harry Chiti	2.00	1.00	.60
80	Minnie Minoso	3.25	1.75	1.00
81	Hal Jeffcoat	2.00	1.00	.60
82	Bob Boyd	2.00	1.00	.60
83	Bob Smith	2.00	1.00	.60
84	Reno Bertoia	2.00	1.00	.60
85	Harry Anderson	2.00	1.00	.60
86	Bob Keegan	2.00	1.00	.60
87	Danny O'Connell	2.00	1.00	.60
88	Herb Score	3.00	1.50	.90
89	Billy Gardner	2.00	1.00	.60
90	Bill Skowron	6.00	3.00	1.75
91	Herb Moford	2.00	1.00	.60
92	Dave Philley	2.50	1.25	.70
93	Julio Becquer	2.00	1.00	.60
94	W. Sox Team/Checklist 89-176	12.00	6.00	3.50
95	Carl Willey	2.00	1.00	.60
96	Lou Berberet	2.00	1.00	.60
97	Jerry Lynch	2.00	1.00	.60
98	Arnie Portocarrero	2.00	1.00	.60
99	Ted Kazanski	2.00	1.00	.60
100	Bob Cerv	2.00	1.00	.60
101	Alex Kellner	2.00	1.00	.60
102	Felipe Alou	6.00	3.00	1.75
103	Billy Goodman	2.00	1.00	.60
104	Del Rice	2.00	1.00	.60
105	Lee Walls	2.00	1.00	.60
106	Hal Woodeshick	2.00	1.00	.60
107	Norm Larker	2.00	1.00	.60
108	Zack Monroe	3.25	1.75	1.00
109	Bob Schmidt	2.00	1.00	.60
110	George Witt	2.00	1.00	.60
111	Redlegs Team/Checklist 89-176	7.00	3.50	2.00
112	Billy Consolo	1.50	.70	.45
113	Taylor Phillips	1.50	.70	.45
114	Earl Battey	2.00	1.00	.60
115	Mickey Vernon	2.00	1.00	.60
116	Bob Allison	4.00	2.00	1.25
117	John Blanchard	3.25	1.75	1.00
118	John Buzhardt	1.50	.70	.45
119	John Callison	4.00	2.00	1.25
120	Chuck Coles	1.50	.70	.45
121	Bob Conley	1.50	.70	.45
122	Bennie Daniels	1.50	.70	.45
123	Don Dillard	1.50	.70	.45
124	Dan Dobbek	1.50	.70	.45
125	Ron Fairly	3.50	1.75	1.00
126	Eddie Haas	1.50	.70	.45
127	Kent Hadley	1.50	.70	.45
128	Bob Hartman	1.50	.70	.45
129	Frank Herrera	1.50	.70	.45
130	Lou Jackson	1.50	.70	.45
131	Deron Johnson	3.25	1.75	1.00
132	Don Lee	1.50	.70	.45
133	Bob Lillis	2.00	1.00	.60
134	Jim McDaniel	1.50	.70	.45
135	Gene Oliver	1.50	.70	.45
136	Jim O'Toole	2.50	1.25	.70
137	Dick Ricketts	1.50	.70	.45
138	John Romano	1.50	.70	.45
139	Ed Sadowski	1.50	.70	.45
140	Charlie Secrest	1.50	.70	.45
141	Joe Shipley	1.50	.70	.45
142	Dick Stigman	1.50	.70	.45
143	Willie Tasby	1.50	.70	.45
144	Jerry Walker	1.50	.70	.45
145	Dom Zanni	1.50	.70	.45
146	Jerry Zimmerman	1.50	.70	.45
147	Cub's Clubbers (Ernie Banks, Dale Long, Walt Moryn)	6.00	3.00	1.75
148	Mike McCormick	2.00	1.00	.60
149	Jim Bunning	6.00	3.00	1.75
150	Stan Musial	40.00	20.00	12.00
151	Bob Malkmus	1.50	.70	.45
152	Johnny Klippstein	1.50	.70	.45
153	Jim Marshall	1.50	.70	.45
154	Ray Herbert	1.50	.70	.45
155	Enos Slaughter	10.00	5.00	3.00
156	Ace Hurlers (Billy Pierce, Robin Roberts)	3.50	1.75	1.00
157	Felix Mantilla	1.50	.70	.45
158	Walt Dropo	2.00	1.00	.60
159	Bob Shaw	1.50	.70	.45
160	Dick Groat	2.50	1.25	.70
161	Frank Baumann	1.50	.70	.45
162	Bobby G. Smith	1.50	.70	.45
163	Sandy Koufax	35.00	17.50	10.50
164	Johnny Groth	1.50	.70	.45
165	Bill Bruton	2.00	1.00	.60
166	Destruction Crew (Rocky Colavito, Larry Doby, Minnie Minoso)	3.00	1.50	.90
167	Duke Maas	3.00	1.50	.90
168	Carroll Hardy	1.50	.70	.45
169	Ted Abernathy	1.50	.70	.45
170	Gene Woodling	2.00	1.00	.60
171	Willard Schmidt	1.50	.70	.45
172	A's Team/Checklist 177-242	6.00	3.00	1.75
173	Bill Monbouquette	2.50	1.25	.70
174	Jim Pendleton	1.50	.70	.45
175	Dick Farrell	1.50	.70	.45
176	Preston Ward	1.50	.70	.45
177	Johnny Briggs	1.50	.70	.45
178	Ruben Amaro	1.50	.70	.45
179	Don Rudolph	1.50	.70	.45
180	Yogi Berra	25.00	12.50	7.50
181	Bob Porterfield	1.50	.70	.45
182	Milt Graff	1.50	.70	.45
183	Stu Miller	1.50	.70	.45
184	Harvey Haddix	2.00	1.00	.60
185	Jim Busby	1.50	.70	.45
186	Mudcat Grant	2.00	1.00	.60
187	Bubba Phillips	1.50	.70	.45
188	Juan Pizarro	1.50	.70	.45
189	Neil Chrisley	1.50	.70	.45
190	Bill Virdon	2.50	1.25	.70
191	Russ Kemmerer	1.50	.70	.45
192	Charley Beamon	1.50	.70	.45
193	Sammy Taylor	1.50	.70	.45
194	Jim Brosnan	2.00	1.00	.60
195	Rip Repulski	1.50	.70	.45
196	Billy Moran	1.50	.70	.45
197	Ray Semproch	1.50	.70	.45
198	Jim Davenport	1.50	.70	.45
199	Leo Kiely	1.50	.70	.45
200	Warren Giles	2.50	1.25	.70
201	Tom Acker	1.50	.70	.45
202	Roger Maris	40.00	20.00	12.00
203	Ozzie Virgil	1.50	.70	.45

		NR MT	EX	VG
204	Casey Wise	1.50	.70	.45
205	Don Larsen	5.00	2.50	1.50
206	Carl Furillo	3.50	1.75	1.00
207	George Strickland	1.50	.70	.45
208	Willie Jones	1.50	.70	.45
209	Lenny Green	1.50	.70	.45
210	Ed Bailey	1.50	.70	.45
211	Bob Blaylock	1.50	.70	.45
212	Fence Busters (Hank Aaron, Eddie Mathews)	15.00	7.50	4.50
213	Jim Rivera	1.50	.70	.45
214	Marcelino Solis	1.50	.70	.45
215	Jim Lemon	1.50	.70	.45
216	Andre Rodgers	1.50	.70	.45
217	Carl Erskine	3.00	1.50	.90
218	Roman Mejias	1.50	.70	.45
219	George Zuverink	1.50	.70	.45
220	Frank Malzone	2.00	1.00	.60
221	Bob Bowman	1.50	.70	.45
222	Bobby Shantz	3.50	1.75	1.00
223	Cards Team/Checklist 265-352	6.00	3.00	1.75
224	Claude Osteen	3.00	1.50	.90
225	Johnny Logan	2.00	1.00	.60
226	Art Ceccarelli	1.50	.70	.45
227	Hal Smith	1.50	.70	.45
228	Don Gross	1.50	.70	.45
229	Vic Power	1.50	.70	.45
230	Bill Fischer	1.50	.70	.45
231	Ellis Burton	1.50	.70	.45
232	Eddie Kasko	1.50	.70	.45
233	Paul Foytack	1.50	.70	.45
234	Chuck Tanner	2.50	1.25	.70
235	Valmy Thomas	1.50	.70	.45
236	Ted Bowsfield	1.50	.70	.45
237	Run Preventers (Gil McDougald, Bobby Richardson, Bob Turley)	3.50	1.75	1.00
238	Gene Baker	1.50	.70	.45
239	Bob Trowbridge	1.50	.70	.45
240	Hank Bauer	5.00	2.50	1.50
241	Billy Muffett	1.50	.70	.45
242	Ron Samford	1.50	.70	.45
243	Marv Grissom	1.50	.70	.45
244	Dick Gray	1.50	.70	.45
245	Ned Garver	1.50	.70	.45
246	J.W. Porter	1.50	.70	.45
247	Don Ferrarese	1.50	.70	.45
248	Red Sox Team/Checklist 177-264	7.00	3.50	2.00
249	Bobby Adams	1.50	.70	.45
250	Billy O'Dell	1.50	.70	.45
251	Cletis Boyer	4.00	2.00	1.25
252	Ray Boone	2.00	1.00	.60
253	Seth Morehead	1.50	.70	.45
254	Zeke Bella	1.50	.70	.45
255	Del Ennis	2.00	1.00	.60
256	Jerry Davie	1.50	.70	.45
257	Leon Wagner	3.00	1.50	.90
258	Fred Kipp	1.50	.70	.45
259	Jim Pisoni	1.50	.70	.45
260	Early Wynn	10.00	5.00	3.00
261	Gene Stephens	1.50	.70	.45
262	Hitters' Foes (Don Drysdale, Clem Labine, Johnny Podres)	4.00	2.00	1.25
263	Buddy Daley	1.50	.70	.45
264	Chico Carrasquel	1.50	.70	.45
265	Ron Kline	1.50	.70	.45
266	Woody Held	2.00	1.00	.60
267	John Romonosky	1.50	.70	.45
268	Tito Francona	2.00	1.00	.60
269	Jack Meyer	1.50	.70	.45
270	Gil Hodges	12.00	6.00	3.50
271	Orlando Pena	2.00	1.00	.60
272	Jerry Lumpe	3.25	1.75	1.00
273	Joe Jay	1.50	.70	.45
274	Jerry Kindall	1.50	.70	.45
275	Jack Sanford	1.50	.70	.45
276	Pete Daley	1.50	.70	.45
277	Turk Lown	1.50	.70	.45
278	Chuck Essegian	1.50	.70	.45
279	Ernie Johnson	1.50	.70	.45
280	Frank Bolling	1.50	.70	.45
281	Walt Craddock	1.50	.70	.45
282	R.C. Stevens	1.50	.70	.45
283	Russ Heman	1.50	.70	.45
284	Steve Korcheck	1.50	.70	.45
285	Joe Cunningham	2.00	1.00	.60
286	Dean Stone	1.50	.70	.45
287	Don Zimmer	2.50	1.25	.70
288	Dutch Dotterer	1.50	.70	.45
289	Johnny Kucks	3.00	1.50	.90
290	Wes Covington	2.00	1.00	.60

		NR MT	EX	VG
291	Pitching Partners (Camilo Pascual, Pedro Ramos)	2.00	1.00	.60
292	Dick Williams	2.50	1.25	.70
293	Ray Moore	1.50	.70	.45
294	Hank Foiles	1.50	.70	.45
295	Billy Martin	4.00	2.00	1.25
296	Ernie Broglio	2.00	1.00	.60
297	Jackie Brandt	2.00	1.00	.60
298	Tex Clevenger	1.50	.70	.45
299	Billy Klaus	1.50	.70	.45
300	Richie Ashburn	6.00	3.00	1.75
301	Earl Averill	1.50	.70	.45
302	Don Mossi	2.00	1.00	.60
303	Marty Keough	1.50	.70	.45
304	Cubs Team/Checklist 265-352	6.00	3.00	1.75
305	Curt Raydon	1.50	.70	.45
306	Jim Gilliam	3.50	1.75	1.00
307	Curt Barclay	1.50	.70	.45
308	Norm Siebern	3.50	1.75	1.00
309	Sal Maglie	3.00	1.50	.90
310	Luis Aparicio	9.00	4.50	2.75
311	Norm Zauchin	1.50	.70	.45
312	Don Newcombe	2.50	1.25	.70
313	Frank House	1.50	.70	.45
314	Don Cardwell	1.50	.70	.45
315	Joe Adcock	2.50	1.25	.70
316a	Ralph Lumenti (without option statement)	35.00	17.50	10.50
316b	Ralph Lumenti (with option statement)	1.50	.70	.45
317	N.L. Hitting Kings (Richie Ashburn, Willie Mays)	12.00	6.00	3.50
318	Rocky Bridges	1.50	.70	.45
319	Dave Hillman	1.50	.70	.45
320	Bob Skinner	2.00	1.00	.60
321a	Bob Giallombardo (without option statement)	35.00	17.50	10.50
321b	Bob Giallombardo (with option statement)	1.50	.70	.45
322a	Harry Hanebrink (without trade statement)	35.00	17.50	10.50
322b	Harry Hanebrink (with trade statement)	1.50	.70	.45
323	Frank Sullivan	1.50	.70	.45
324	Don Demeter	1.50	.70	.45
325	Ken Boyer	3.50	1.75	1.00
326	Marv Throneberry	3.50	1.75	1.00
327	Gary Bell	2.00	1.00	.60
328	Lou Skizas	1.50	.70	.45
329	Tigers Team/Checklist 353-429	7.00	3.50	2.00
330	Gus Triandos	2.00	1.00	.60
331	Steve Boros	2.00	1.00	.60
332	Ray Monzant	1.50	.70	.45
333	Harry Simpson	1.50	.70	.45
334	Glen Hobbie	1.50	.70	.45
335	Johnny Temple	1.50	.70	.45
336a	Billy Loes (without trade statement)	35.00	17.50	10.50
336b	Billy Loes (with trade statement)	1.50	.70	.45
337	George Crowe	1.50	.70	.45
338	George Anderson	9.00	4.50	2.75
339	Roy Face	2.50	1.25	.70
340	Roy Sievers	2.00	1.00	.60
341	Tom Qualters	1.50	.70	.45
342	Ray Jablonski	1.50	.70	.45
343	Billy Hoeft	1.50	.70	.45
344	Russ Nixon	1.50	.70	.45
345	Gil McDougald	4.00	2.00	1.25
346	Batter Bafflers (Tom Brewer, Dave Sisler)	2.00	1.00	.60
347	Bob Buhl	2.00	1.00	.60
348	Ted Lepcio	1.50	.70	.45
349	Hoyt Wilhelm	8.00	4.00	2.50
350	Ernie Banks	20.00	10.00	6.00
351	Earl Torgeson	1.50	.70	.45
352	Robin Roberts	10.00	5.00	3.00
353	Curt Flood	3.00	1.50	.90
354	Pete Burnside	1.50	.70	.45
355	Jim Piersall	2.50	1.25	.70
356	Bob Mabe	1.50	.70	.45
357	Dick Stuart	3.50	1.75	1.00
358	Ralph Terry	2.00	1.00	.60
359	Bill White	4.00	2.00	1.25
360	Al Kaline	20.00	10.00	6.00
361	Willard Nixon	1.50	.70	.45
362a	Dolan Nichols (without option statement)	35.00	17.50	10.50
362b	Dolan Nichols (with option statement)	1.50	.70	.45
363	Bobby Avila	1.50	.70	.45
364	Danny McDevitt	1.50	.70	.45

#	Player	NR MT	EX	VG
365	Gus Bell	2.00	1.00	.60
366	Humberto Robinson	1.50	.70	.45
367	Cal Neeman	1.50	.70	.45
368	Don Mueller	1.50	.70	.45
369	Dick Tomanek	1.50	.70	.45
370	Pete Runnels	2.00	1.00	.60
371	Dick Brodowski	1.50	.70	.45
372	Jim Hegan	1.50	.70	.45
373	Herb Plews	1.50	.70	.45
374	Art Ditmar	3.00	1.50	.90
375	Bob Nieman	1.50	.70	.45
376	Hal Naragon	1.50	.70	.45
377	Johnny Antonelli	2.00	1.00	.60
378	Gail Harris	1.50	.70	.45
379	Bob Miller	1.50	.70	.45
380	Hank Aaron	50.00	25.00	15.00
381	Mike Baxes	1.50	.70	.45
382	Curt Simmons	2.00	1.00	.60
383	Words of Wisdom (Don Larsen, Casey Stengel)	5.00	2.50	1.50
384	Dave Sisler	1.50	.70	.45
385	Sherm Lollar	2.00	1.00	.60
386	Jim Delsing	1.50	.70	.45
387	Don Drysdale	15.00	7.50	4.50
388	Bob Will	1.50	.70	.45
389	Joe Nuxhall	2.00	1.00	.60
390	Orlando Cepeda	6.00	3.00	1.75
391	Milt Pappas	2.00	1.00	.60
392	Whitey Herzog	3.00	1.50	.90
393	Frank Lary	2.00	1.00	.60
394	Randy Jackson	1.50	.70	.45
395	Elston Howard	5.00	2.50	1.50
396	Bob Rush	1.50	.70	.45
397	Senators Team / Checklist 430-495	6.00	3.00	1.75
398	Wally Post	1.50	.70	.45
399	Larry Jackson	1.50	.70	.45
400	Jackie Jensen	3.00	1.50	.90
401	Ron Blackburn	1.50	.70	.45
402	Hector Lopez	1.50	.70	.45
403	Clem Labine	2.00	1.00	.60
404	Hank Sauer	2.00	1.00	.60
405	Roy McMillan	1.50	.70	.45
406	Solly Drake	1.50	.70	.45
407	Moe Drabowsky	1.50	.70	.45
408	Keystone Combo (Luis Aparicio, Nellie Fox)	6.00	3.00	1.75
409	Gus Zernial	2.00	1.00	.60
410	Billy Pierce	2.50	1.25	.70
411	Whitey Lockman	1.50	.70	.45
412	Stan Lopata	1.50	.70	.45
413	Camillo Pascual (Camilo)	2.00	1.00	.60
414	Dale Long	2.00	1.00	.60
415	Bill Mazeroski	3.00	1.50	.90
416	Haywood Sullivan	1.50	.70	.45
417	Virgil Trucks	3.00	1.50	.90
418	Gino Cimoli	1.50	.70	.45
419	Braves Team / Checklist 353-429	7.00	3.50	2.00
420	Rocco Colavito	3.50	1.75	1.00
421	Herm Wehmeier	1.50	.70	.45
422	Hobie Landrith	1.50	.70	.45
423	Bob Grim	1.50	.70	.45
424	Ken Aspromonte	1.50	.70	.45
425	Del Crandall	2.50	1.25	.70
426	Jerry Staley	1.50	.70	.45
427	Charlie Neal	1.50	.70	.45
428	Buc Hill Aces (Roy Face, Bob Friend, Ron Kline, Vern Law)	3.00	1.50	.90
429	Bobby Thomson	2.00	1.00	.60
430	Whitey Ford	20.00	10.00	6.00
431	Whammy Douglas	1.50	.70	.45
432	Smoky Burgess	2.50	1.25	.70
433	Billy Harrell	1.50	.70	.45
434	Hal Griggs	1.50	.70	.45
435	Frank Robinson	20.00	10.00	6.00
436	Granny Hamner	1.50	.70	.45
437	Ike Delock	1.50	.70	.45
438	Sam Esposito	1.50	.70	.45
439	Brooks Robinson	25.00	12.50	7.50
440	Lou Burdette	4.00	2.00	1.25
441	John Roseboro	2.00	1.00	.60
442	Ray Narleski	1.50	.70	.45
443	Daryl Spencer	1.50	.70	.45
444	Ronnie Hansen	2.00	1.00	.60
445	Cal McLish	1.50	.70	.45
446	Rocky Nelson	1.50	.70	.45
447	Bob Anderson	1.50	.70	.45
448	Vada Pinson	3.00	1.50	.90
449	Tom Gorman	1.50	.70	.45
450	Ed Mathews	15.00	7.50	4.50
451	Jimmy Constable	1.50	.70	.45

#	Player	NR MT	EX	VG
452	Chico Fernandez	1.50	.70	.45
453	Les Moss	1.50	.70	.45
454	Phil Clark	1.50	.70	.45
455	Larry Doby	3.00	1.50	.90
456	Jerry Casale	1.50	.70	.45
457	Dodgers Team / Checklist 430-495	12.00	6.00	3.50
458	Gordon Jones	1.50	.70	.45
459	Bill Tuttle	1.50	.70	.45
460	Bob Friend	2.50	1.25	.70
461	Mantle Hits 42nd Homer For Crown	20.00	9.00	5.00
462	Colavito's Great Catch Saves Game	2.50	1.25	.70
463	Kaline Becomes Youngest Bat Champ	6.00	3.00	1.75
464	Mays' Catch Makes Series History	12.00	6.00	3.50
465	Sievers Sets Homer Mark	2.00	1.00	.60
466	Pierce All Star Starter	2.00	1.00	.60
467	Aaron Clubs World Series Homer	12.00	6.00	3.50
468	Snider's Play Brings L.A. Victory	8.00	4.00	2.50
469	Hustler Banks Wins M.V.P. Award	6.00	3.00	1.75
470	Musial Raps Out 3,000th Hit	8.00	4.00	2.50
471	Tom Sturdivant	3.00	1.50	.90
472	Gene Freese	1.50	.70	.45
473	Mike Fornieles	1.50	.70	.45
474	Moe Thacker	1.50	.70	.45
475	Jack Harshman	1.50	.70	.45
476	Indians Team / Checklist 496-572	6.00	3.00	1.75
477	Barry Latman	1.50	.70	.45
478	Bob Clemente	35.00	17.50	10.50
479	Lindy McDaniel	1.50	.70	.45
480	Red Schoendienst	3.00	1.50	.90
481	Charley Maxwell	1.50	.70	.45
482	Russ Meyer	1.50	.70	.45
483	Clint Courtney	1.50	.70	.45
484	Willie Kirkland	1.50	.70	.45
485	Ryne Duren	3.50	1.75	1.00
486	Sammy White	1.50	.70	.45
487	Hal Brown	1.50	.70	.45
488	Walt Moryn	1.50	.70	.45
489	John C. Powers	1.50	.70	.45
490	Frank Thomas	1.50	.70	.45
491	Don Blasingame	1.50	.70	.45
492	Gene Conley	2.00	1.00	.60
493	Jim Landis	1.50	.70	.45
494	Don Pavletich	1.50	.70	.45
495	Johnny Podres	3.00	1.50	.90
496	Wayne Terwilliger	1.50	.70	.45
497	Hal R. Smith	1.50	.70	.45
498	Dick Hyde	1.50	.70	.45
499	Johnny O'Brien	1.50	.70	.45
500	Vic Wertz	2.00	1.00	.60
501	Bobby Tiefenauer	1.50	.70	.45
502	Al Dark	3.00	1.50	.90
503	Jim Owens	1.50	.70	.45
504	Ossie Alvarez	1.50	.70	.45
505	Tony Kubek	6.00	3.00	1.75
506	Bob Purkey	1.50	.70	.45
507	Bob Hale	5.00	2.50	1.50
508	Art Fowler	6.00	3.00	1.75
509	Norm Cash	15.00	7.50	4.50
510	Yankees Team / Checklist 496-572	25.00	12.50	7.50
511	George Susce	6.00	3.00	1.75
512	George Altman	6.00	3.00	1.75
513	Tom Carroll	6.00	3.00	1.75
514	Bob Gibson	100.00	40.00	25.00
515	Harmon Killebrew	35.00	17.50	10.50
516	Mike Garcia	7.00	3.50	2.00
517	Joe Koppe	6.00	3.00	1.75
518	Mike Cueller (Cuellar)	8.00	4.00	2.50
519	Infield Power (Dick Gernert, Frank Malzone, Pete Runnels)	8.00	4.00	2.50
520	Don Elston	6.00	3.00	1.75
521	Gary Geiger	6.00	3.00	1.75
522	Gene Snyder	6.00	3.00	1.75
523	Harry Bright	6.00	3.00	1.75
524	Larry Osborne	6.00	3.00	1.75
525	Jim Coates	8.00	4.00	2.50
526	Bob Speake	6.00	3.00	1.75
527	Solly Hemus	6.00	3.00	1.75
528	Pirates Team / Checklist 496-572	15.00	7.50	4.50
529	George Bamberger	8.00	4.00	2.50
530	Wally Moon	7.00	3.50	2.00
531	Ray Webster	6.00	3.00	1.75
532	Mark Freeman	6.00	3.00	1.75
533	Darrell Johnson	7.00	3.50	2.00
534	Faye Throneberry	6.00	3.00	1.75

		NR MT	EX	VG
535	Ruben Gomez	6.00	3.00	1.75
536	Dan Kravitz	6.00	3.00	1.75
537	Rodolfo Arias	6.00	3.00	1.75
538	Chick King	6.00	3.00	1.75
539	Gary Blaylock	6.00	3.00	1.75
540	Willy Miranda	6.00	3.00	1.75
541	Bob Thurman	6.00	3.00	1.75
542	Jim Perry	10.00	5.00	3.00
543	Corsair Outfield Trio (Bob Clemente, Bob			
	Skinner, Bill Virdon)	25.00	12.50	7.50
544	Lee Tate	6.00	3.00	1.75
545	Tom Morgan	6.00	3.00	1.75
546	Al Schroll	6.00	3.00	1.75
547	Jim Baxes	6.00	3.00	1.75
548	Elmer Singleton	6.00	3.00	1.75
549	Howie Nunn	6.00	3.00	1.75
550	Roy Campanella	50.00	25.00	15.00
551	Fred Haney AS	7.00	3.50	2.00
552	Casey Stengel AS	15.00	7.50	4.50
553	Orlando Cepeda AS	9.00	4.50	2.75
554	Bill Skowron AS	8.00	4.00	2.50
555	Bill Mazeroski AS	8.00	4.00	2.50
556	Nellie Fox AS	9.00	4.50	2.75
557	Ken Boyer AS	8.00	4.00	2.50
558	Frank Malzone AS	7.00	3.50	2.00
559	Ernie Banks AS	18.00	9.00	5.50
560	Luis Aparicio AS	12.00	6.00	3.50
561	Hank Aaron AS	35.00	17.50	10.50
562	Al Kaline AS	18.00	9.00	5.50
563	Willie Mays AS	35.00	17.50	10.50
564	Mickey Mantle AS	90.00	40.00	20.00
565	Wes Covington AS	7.00	3.50	2.00
566	Roy Sievers AS	7.00	3.50	2.00
567	Del Crandall AS	7.00	3.50	2.00
568	Gus Triandos AS	7.00	3.50	2.00
569	Bob Friend AS	7.00	3.50	2.00
570	Bob Turley AS	8.00	4.00	2.50
571	Warren Spahn AS	18.00	7.50	4.50
572	Billy Pierce AS	15.00	4.00	2.00

1960 Topps

GIL HODGES
LOS ANGELES DODGERS   1st BASE

In 1960, Topps returned to a horizontal format (3½" by 2½") with a color portrait and black-and-white "action" photograph on the front. Backs return to the use of just the previous year and lifetime statistics along with a cartoon and short career summary or previous season highlights. Specialty cards in the 572-card set saw the continuation of multi-player cards, managers and coaches cards, and highlights of the 1959 World Series. Two groups of rookie cards are included. The first are #117-148 which are the Sport Magazine rookies. The second group is called "Topps All-Star Rookies." Finally there is a continuation of the All-Star cards to close out the set in the

scarcer high numbers. Card #'s 375-440 can be found with backs printed on either white or grey cardboard, with the white stock being the less common.

		NR MT	EX	VG
Complete Set:		2500.00	875.00	500.00
Common Player: 1-286		1.00	.50	.30
Common Player: 287-440		1.25	.60	.40
Common Player: 441-506		1.75	.90	.50
Common Player: 507-572		4.50	2.25	1.25
1	Early Wynn	12.00	6.00	3.00
2	Roman Mejias	2.00	.50	.30
3	Joe Adcock	2.00	1.00	.60
4	Bob Purkey	1.00	.50	.30
5	Wally Moon	1.50	.70	.45
6	Lou Berberet	1.00	.50	.30
7	Master & Mentor (Willie Mays, Bill Rigney)			
		8.00	4.00	2.50
8	Bud Daley	1.00	.50	.30
9	Faye Throneberry	1.00	.50	.30
10	Ernie Banks	15.00	7.50	4.50
11	Norm Siebern	1.25	.60	.40
12	Milt Pappas	1.25	.60	.40
13	Wally Post	1.00	.50	.30
14	Jim Grant	1.00	.50	.30
15	Pete Runnels	1.25	.60	.40
16	Ernie Broglio	1.00	.50	.30
17	Johnny Callison	1.50	.70	.45
18	Dodgers Team/Checklist 1-88	8.00	4.00	2.50
19	Felix Mantilla	1.00	.50	.30
20	Roy Face	1.75	.90	.50
21	Dutch Dotterer	1.00	.50	.30
22	Rocky Bridges	1.00	.50	.30
23	Eddie Fisher	1.00	.50	.30
24	Dick Gray	1.00	.50	.30
25	Roy Sievers	1.75	.90	.50
26	Wayne Terwilliger	1.00	.50	.30
27	Dick Drott	1.00	.50	.30
28	Brooks Robinson	20.00	10.00	6.00
29	Clem Labine	1.25	.60	.40
30	Tito Francona	1.25	.60	.40
31	Sammy Esposito	1.00	.50	.30
32	Sophomore Stalwarts (Jim O'Toole, Vada			
	Pinson)	1.75	.90	.50
33	Tom Morgan	1.00	.50	.30
34	George Anderson	2.50	1.25	.70
35	Whitey Ford	15.00	7.50	4.50
36	Russ Nixon	1.00	.50	.30
37	Bill Bruton	1.25	.60	.40
38	Jerry Casale	1.00	.50	.30
39	Earl Averill	1.00	.50	.30
40	Joe Cunningham	1.25	.60	.40
41	Barry Latman	1.00	.50	.30
42	Hobie Landrith	1.00	.50	.30
43	Senators Team/Checklist 1-88	5.00	2.50	1.50
44	Bobby Locke	1.00	.50	.30
45	Roy McMillan	1.00	.50	.30
46	Jack Fisher	1.00	.50	.30
47	Don Zimmer	1.75	.90	.50
48	Hal Smith	1.00	.50	.30
49	Curt Raydon	1.00	.50	.30
50	Al Kaline	15.00	7.50	4.50
51	Jim Coates	1.75	.90	.50
52	Dave Philley	1.25	.60	.40
53	Jackie Brandt	1.00	.50	.30
54	Mike Fornieles	1.00	.50	.30
55	Bill Mazeroski	2.50	1.25	.70
56	Steve Korcheck	1.00	.50	.30
57	Win - Savers (Turk Lown, Gerry Staley)			
		1.25	.60	.40
58	Gino Cimoli	1.00	.50	.30
59	Juan Pizarro	1.00	.50	.30
60	Gus Triandos	1.25	.60	.40
61	Eddie Kasko	1.00	.50	.30
62	Roger Craig	1.75	.90	.50
63	George Strickland	1.00	.50	.30
64	Jack Meyer	1.00	.50	.30
65	Elston Howard	3.50	1.75	1.00
66	Bob Trowbridge	1.00	.50	.30
67	Jose Pagan	1.25	.60	.40
68	Dave Hillman	1.00	.50	.30
69	Billy Goodman	1.00	.50	.30
70	Lou Burdette	2.50	1.25	.70
71	Marty Keough	1.00	.50	.30
72	Tigers Team/Checklist 89-176	7.00	3.50	2.00
73	Bob Gibson	15.00	7.50	4.50
74	Walt Moryn	1.00	.50	.30
75	Vic Power	1.00	.50	.30
76	Bill Fischer	1.00	.50	.30

		NR MT	EX	VG			NR MT	EX	VG
77	Hank Foiles	1.00	.50	.30	166	Chuck Essegian	1.00	.50	.30
78	Bob Grim	1.00	.50	.30	167	Valmy Thomas	1.00	.50	.30
79	Walt Dropo	1.25	.60	.40	168	Alex Grammas	1.00	.50	.30
80	Johnny Antonelli	1.50	.70	.45	169	Jake Striker	1.00	.50	.30
81	Russ Snyder	1.00	.50	.30	170	Del Crandall	1.75	.90	.50
82	Ruben Gomez	1.00	.50	.30	171	Johnny Groth	1.00	.50	.30
83	Tony Kubek	3.50	1.75	1.00	172	Willie Kirkland	1.00	.50	.30
84	Hal Smith	1.00	.50	.30	173	Billy Martin	4.50	2.25	1.25
85	Frank Lary	1.25	.60	.40	174	Indians Team/Checklist 89-176	5.00	2.50	1.50
86	Dick Gernert	1.00	.50	.30	175	Pedro Ramos	1.00	.50	.30
87	John Romonosky	1.00	.50	.30	176	Vada Pinson	2.50	1.25	.70
88	John Roseboro	1.25	.60	.40	177	Johnny Kucks	1.00	.50	.30
89	Hal Brown	1.00	.50	.30	178	Woody Held	1.25	.60	.40
90	Bobby Avila	1.00	.50	.30	179	Rip Coleman	1.00	.50	.30
91	Bennie Daniels	1.00	.50	.30	180	Harry Simpson	1.00	.50	.30
92	Whitey Herzog	2.50	1.25	.70	181	Billy Loes	1.00	.50	.30
93	Art Schult	1.00	.50	.30	182	Glen Hobbie	1.00	.50	.30
94	Leo Kiely	1.00	.50	.30	183	Eli Grba	1.75	.90	.50
95	Frank Thomas	1.00	.50	.30	184	Gary Geiger	1.00	.50	.30
96	Ralph Terry	2.25	1.25	.70	185	Jim Owens	1.00	.50	.30
97	Ted Lepcio	1.00	.50	.30	186	Dave Sisler	1.00	.50	.30
98	Gordon Jones	1.00	.50	.30	187	Jay Hook	1.00	.50	.30
99	Lenny Green	1.00	.50	.30	188	Dick Williams	1.75	.90	.50
100	Nellie Fox	4.50	2.25	1.25	189	Don McMahon	1.00	.50	.30
101	Bob Miller	1.00	.50	.30	190	Gene Woodling	1.25	.60	.40
102	Kent Hadley	1.75	.90	.50	191	Johnny Klippstein	1.00	.50	.30
103	Dick Farrell	1.00	.50	.30	192	Danny O'Connell	1.00	.50	.30
104	Dick Schofield	1.00	.50	.30	193	Dick Hyde	1.00	.50	.30
105	Larry Sherry	1.00	.50	.30	194	Bobby Gene Smith	1.00	.50	.30
106	Billy Gardner	1.00	.50	.30	195	Lindy McDaniel	1.00	.50	.30
107	Carl Willey	1.00	.50	.30	196	Andy Carey	1.75	.90	.50
108	Pete Daley	1.00	.50	.30	197	Ron Kline	1.00	.50	.30
109	Cletis Boyer	2.25	1.25	.70	198	Jerry Lynch	1.00	.50	.30
110	Cal McLish	1.00	.50	.30	199	Dick Donovan	1.00	.50	.30
111	Vic Wertz	1.50	.70	.45	200	Willie Mays	45.00	22.00	13.50
112	Jack Harshman	1.00	.50	.30	201	Larry Osborne	1.00	.50	.30
113	Bob Skinner	1.25	.60	.40	202	Fred Kipp	1.00	.50	.30
114	Ken Aspromonte	1.00	.50	.30	203	Sammy White	1.00	.50	.30
115	Fork & Knuckler (Roy Face, Hoyt Wilhelm)				204	Ryne Duren	2.50	1.25	.70
		3.00	1.50	.90	205	Johnny Logan	1.25	.60	.40
116	Jim Rivera	1.00	.50	.30	206	Claude Osteen	1.25	.60	.40
117	Tom Borland	1.00	.50	.30	207	Bob Boyd	1.00	.50	.30
118	Bob Bruce	1.00	.50	.30	208	W. Sox Team/Checklist 177-264	5.00	2.50	1.50
119	Chico Cardenas	1.50	.70	.45	209	Ron Blackburn	1.00	.50	.30
120	Duke Carmel	1.00	.50	.30	210	Harmon Killebrew	15.00	7.50	4.50
121	Camilo Carreon	1.00	.50	.30	211	Taylor Phillips	1.00	.50	.30
122	Don Dillard	1.00	.50	.30	212	Walt Alston	4.50	2.25	1.25
123	Dan Dobbek	1.00	.50	.30	213	Chuck Dressen	1.25	.60	.40
124	Jim Donohue	1.00	.50	.30	214	Jimmie Dykes	1.00	.50	.30
125	Dick Ellsworth	1.50	.70	.45	215	Bob Elliott	1.00	.50	.30
126	Chuck Estrada	1.25	.60	.40	216	Joe Gordon	1.25	.60	.40
127	Ronnie Hansen	1.00	.50	.30	217	Charley Grimm	1.25	.60	.40
128	Bill Harris	1.00	.50	.30	218	Solly Hemus	1.00	.50	.30
129	Bob Hartman	1.00	.50	.30	219	Fred Hutchinson	1.25	.60	.40
130	Frank Herrera	1.00	.50	.30	220	Billy Jurges	1.00	.50	.30
131	Ed Hobaugh	1.00	.50	.30	221	Cookie Lavagetto	1.00	.50	.30
132	Frank Howard	8.00	4.00	2.50	222	Al Lopez	3.50	1.75	1.00
133	Manuel Javier	2.00	1.00	.60	223	Danny Murtaugh	1.50	.70	.45
134	Deron Johnson	1.75	.90	.50	224	Paul Richards	1.25	.60	.40
135	Ken Johnson	1.00	.50	.30	225	Bill Rigney	1.00	.50	.30
136	Jim Kaat	20.00	10.00	6.00	226	Eddie Sawyer	1.00	.50	.30
137	Lou Klimchock	1.00	.50	.30	227	Casey Stengel	10.00	5.00	3.00
138	Art Mahaffey	1.25	.60	.40	228	Ernie Johnson	1.00	.50	.30
139	Carl Mathias	1.00	.50	.30	229	Joe Morgan	1.00	.50	.30
140	Julio Navarro	1.00	.50	.30	230	Mound Magicians (Bob Buhl, Lou			
141	Jim Proctor	1.00	.50	.30		Burdette, Warren Spahn)	5.00	2.50	1.50
142	Bill Short	1.75	.90	.50	231	Hal Naragon	1.00	.50	.30
143	Al Spangler	1.00	.50	.30	232	Jim Busby	1.00	.50	.30
144	Al Stieglitz	1.00	.50	.30	233	Don Elston	1.00	.50	.30
145	Jim Umbricht	1.00	.50	.30	234	Don Demeter	1.00	.50	.30
146	Ted Wieand	1.00	.50	.30	235	Gus Bell	1.25	.60	.40
147	Bob Will	1.00	.50	.30	236	Dick Ricketts	1.00	.50	.30
148	Carl Yastrzemski	150.00	75.00	45.00	237	Elmer Valo	1.75	.90	.50
149	Bob Nieman	1.00	.50	.30	238	Danny Kravitz	1.00	.50	.30
150	Billy Pierce	1.75	.90	.50	239	Joe Shipley	1.00	.50	.30
151	Giants Team/Checklist 177-264	5.00	2.50	1.50	240	Luis Aparicio	9.00	4.50	2.75
152	Gail Harris	1.00	.50	.30	241	Albie Pearson	1.00	.50	.30
153	Bobby Thomson	1.50	.70	.45	242	Cards Team/Checklist 265-352	5.00	2.50	1.50
154	Jim Davenport	1.00	.50	.30	243	Bubba Phillips	1.00	.50	.30
155	Charlie Neal	1.00	.50	.30	244	Hal Griggs	1.00	.50	.30
156	Art Ceccarelli	1.00	.50	.30	245	Eddie Yost	1.25	.60	.40
157	Rocky Nelson	1.00	.50	.30	246	Lee Maye	1.00	.50	.30
158	Wes Covington	1.00	.50	.30	247	Gil McDougald	3.50	1.75	1.00
159	Jim Piersall	1.50	.70	.45	248	Del Rice	1.00	.50	.30
160	Rival All Stars (Ken Boyer, Mickey Mantle)				249	Earl Wilson	1.25	.60	.40
		15.00	6.75	3.75	250	Stan Musial	40.00	20.00	12.00
161	Ray Narleski	1.00	.50	.30	251	Bobby Malkmus	1.00	.50	.30
162	Sammy Taylor	1.00	.50	.30	252	Ray Herbert	1.00	.50	.30
163	Hector Lopez	2.00	1.00	.60	253	Eddie Bressoud	1.00	.50	.30
164	Reds Team/Checklist 89-176	6.00	3.00	1.75	254	Arnie Portocarrero	1.00	.50	.30
165	Jack Sanford	1.00	.50	.30	255	Jim Gilliam	2.50	1.25	.70

		NR MT	EX	VG
256	Dick Brown	1.00	.50	.30
257	Gordy Coleman	1.00	.50	.30
258	Dick Groat	3.50	1.75	1.00
259	George Altman	1.00	.50	.30
260	Power Plus (Rocky Colavito, Tito Francona)	2.50	1.25	.70
261	Pete Burnside	1.00	.50	.30
262	Hank Bauer	1.50	.70	.45
263	Darrell Johnson	1.00	.50	.30
264	Robin Roberts	10.00	5.00	3.00
265	Rip Repulski	1.00	.50	.30
266	Joe Jay	1.00	.50	.30
267	Jim Marshall	1.00	.50	.30
268	Al Worthington	1.00	.50	.30
269	Gene Green	1.00	.50	.30
270	Bob Turley	2.50	1.25	.70
271	Julio Becquer	1.00	.50	.30
272	Fred Green	1.00	.50	.30
273	Neil Chrisley	1.00	.50	.30
274	Tom Acker	1.00	.50	.30
275	Curt Flood	2.00	1.00	.60
276	Ken McBride	1.00	.50	.30
277	Harry Bright	1.00	.50	.30
278	Stan Williams	1.00	.50	.30
279	Chuck Tanner	2.00	1.00	.60
280	Frank Sullivan	1.00	.50	.30
281	Ray Boone	1.25	.60	.40
282	Joe Nuxhall	1.75	.90	.50
283	John Blanchard	1.75	.90	.50
284	Don Gross	1.00	.50	.30
285	Harry Anderson	1.00	.50	.30
286	Ray Semproch	1.00	.50	.30
287	Felipe Alou	2.50	1.25	.70
288	Bob Mabe	1.25	.60	.40
289	Willie Jones	1.25	.60	.40
290	Jerry Lumpe	1.50	.70	.45
291	Bob Keegan	1.25	.60	.40
292	Dodger Backstops (Joe Pignatano, John Roseboro)	2.00	1.00	.60
293	Gene Conley	1.50	.70	.45
294	Tony Taylor	1.00	.50	.30
295	Gil Hodges	12.00	6.00	3.50
296	Nelson Chittum	1.25	.60	.40
297	Reno Bertoia	1.25	.60	.40
298	George Witt	1.25	.60	.40
299	Earl Torgeson	1.25	.60	.40
300	Hank Aaron	50.00	25.00	15.00
301	Jerry Davie	1.25	.60	.40
302	Phillies Team/ Checklist 353-429	6.00	3.00	1.75
303	Billy O'Dell	1.25	.60	.40
304	Joe Ginsberg	1.25	.60	.40
305	Richie Ashburn	5.00	2.50	1.50
306	Frank Baumann	1.25	.60	.40
307	Gene Oliver	1.25	.60	.40
308	Dick Hall	1.25	.60	.40
309	Bob Hale	1.25	.60	.40
310	Frank Malzone	1.50	.70	.45
311	Raul Sanchez	1.25	.60	.40
312	Charlie Lau	1.50	.70	.45
313	Turk Lown	1.25	.60	.40
314	Chico Fernandez	1.25	.60	.40
315	Bobby Shantz	3.00	1.50	.90
316	Willie McCovey	65.00	32.00	19.50
317	Pumpsie Green	1.25	.60	.40
318	Jim Baxes	1.25	.60	.40
319	Joe Koppe	1.25	.60	.40
320	Bob Allison	1.75	.90	.50
321	Ron Fairly	1.50	.70	.45
322	Willie Tasby	1.25	.60	.40
323	Johnny Romano	1.25	.60	.40
324	Jim Perry	2.00	1.00	.60
325	Jim O'Toole	1.50	.70	.45
326	Bob Clemente	40.00	20.00	12.00
327	Ray Sadecki	2.00	1.00	.60
328	Earl Battey	1.50	.70	.45
329	Zack Monroe	2.00	1.00	.60
330	Harvey Kuenn	2.00	1.00	.60
331	Henry Mason	1.25	.60	.40
332	Yankees Team/Checklist 265-352	12.00	6.00	3.50
333	Danny McDevitt	1.25	.60	.40
334	Ted Abernathy	1.25	.60	.40
335	Red Schoendienst	2.50	1.25	.70
336	Ike Delock	1.25	.60	.40
337	Cal Neeman	1.25	.60	.40
338	Ray Monzant	1.25	.60	.40
339	Harry Chiti	1.25	.60	.40
340	Harvey Haddix	2.00	1.00	.60
341	Carroll Hardy	1.25	.60	.40
342	Casey Wise	1.25	.60	.40
343	Sandy Koufax	40.00	20.00	12.00

		NR MT	EX	VG
344	Clint Courtney	1.25	.60	.40
345	Don Newcombe	2.00	1.00	.60
346	J.C. Martin (photo actually Gary Peters)	1.25	.60	.40
347	Ed Bouchee	1.25	.60	.40
348	Barry Shetrone	1.25	.60	.40
349	Moe Drabowsky	1.25	.60	.40
350	Mickey Mantle	250.00	110.00	60.00
351	Don Nottebart	1.25	.60	.40
352	Cincy Clouters (Gus Bell, Jerry Lynch, Frank Robinson)	4.00	2.00	1.25
353	Don Larsen	1.75	.90	.50
354	Bob Lillis	1.50	.70	.45
355	Bill White	2.00	1.00	.60
356	Joe Amalfitano	1.25	.60	.40
357	Al Schroll	1.25	.60	.40
358	Joe DeMaestri	2.00	1.00	.60
359	Buddy Gilbert	1.25	.60	.40
360	Herb Score	2.00	1.00	.60
361	Bob Oldis	1.25	.60	.40
362	Russ Kemmerer	1.25	.60	.40
363	Gene Stephens	1.25	.60	.40
364	Paul Foytack	1.25	.60	.40
365	Minnie Minoso	2.50	1.25	.70
366	Dallas Green	3.00	1.50	.90
367	Bill Tuttle	1.25	.60	.40
368	Daryl Spencer	1.25	.60	.40
369	Billy Hoeft	1.25	.60	.40
370	Bill Skowron	4.00	2.00	1.25
371	Bud Byerly	1.25	.60	.40
372	Frank House	1.25	.60	.40
373	Don Hoak	1.75	.90	.50
374	Bob Buhl	1.50	.70	.45
375	Dale Long	1.50	.70	.45
376	Johnny Briggs	1.25	.60	.40
377	Roger Maris	35.00	17.50	10.50
378	Stu Miller	1.25	.60	.40
379	Red Wilson	1.25	.60	.40
380	Bob Shaw	1.25	.60	.40
381	Braves Team/Checklist 353-429	6.00	3.00	1.75
382	Ted Bowsfield	1.25	.60	.40
383	Leon Wagner	1.25	.60	.40
384	Don Cardwell	1.25	.60	.40
385	World Series Game 1 (Neal Steals Second)	3.00	1.50	.90
386	World Series Game 2 (Neal Belts 2nd Homer)	3.00	1.50	.90
387	World Series Game 3 (Furillo Breaks Up Game)	3.00	1.50	.90
388	World Series Game 4 (Hodges' Winning Homer)	3.50	1.75	1.00
389	World Series Game 5 (Luis Swipes Base)	3.50	1.75	1.00
390	World Series Game 6 (Scrambling After Ball)	3.00	1.50	.90
391	World Series Summary (The Champs Celebrate)	3.00	1.50	.90
392	Tex Clevenger	1.25	.60	.40
393	Smoky Burgess	2.00	1.00	.60
394	Norm Larker	1.25	.60	.40
395	Hoyt Wilhelm	9.00	4.50	2.75
396	Steve Bilko	1.25	.60	.40
397	Don Blasingame	1.25	.60	.40
398	Mike Cuellar	1.75	.90	.50
399	Young Hill Stars (Jack Fisher, Milt Pappas, Jerry Walker)	1.75	.90	.50
400	Rocky Colavito	3.50	1.75	1.00
401	Bob Duliba	1.25	.60	.40
402	Dick Stuart	1.75	.90	.50
403	Ed Sadowski	1.25	.60	.40
404	Bob Rush	1.25	.60	.40
405	Bobby Richardson	4.00	2.00	1.25
406	Billy Klaus	1.25	.60	.40
407	Gary Peters (photo actually J.C. Martin)	2.00	1.00	.60
408	Carl Furillo	3.00	1.50	.90
409	Ron Samford	1.25	.60	.40
410	Sam Jones	1.25	.60	.40
411	Ed Bailey	1.25	.60	.40
412	Bob Anderson	1.25	.60	.40
413	A's Team/Checklist 430-495	6.00	3.00	1.75
414	Don Williams	1.25	.60	.40
415	Bob Cerv	1.25	.60	.40
416	Humberto Robinson	1.25	.60	.40
417	Chuck Cottier	1.50	.70	.45
418	Don Mossi	1.50	.70	.45
419	George Crowe	1.25	.60	.40
420	Ed Mathews	12.00	6.00	3.50
421	Duke Maas	2.00	1.00	.60
422	Johnny Powers	1.25	.60	.40
423	Ed Fitz Gerald	1.25	.60	.40

		NR MT	EX	VG
424	Pete Whisenant	1.25	.60	.40
425	Johnny Podres	2.50	1.25	.70
426	Ron Jackson	1.25	.60	.40
427	Al Grunwald	1.25	.60	.40
428	Al Smith	1.25	.60	.40
429	American League Kings (Nellie Fox, Harvey Kuenn)	3.00	1.50	.90
430	Art Ditmar	2.00	1.00	.60
431	Andre Rodgers	1.25	.60	.40
432	Chuck Stobbs	1.25	.60	.40
433	Irv Noren	1.25	.60	.40
434	Brooks Lawrence	1.25	.60	.40
435	Gene Freese	1.25	.60	.40
436	Marv Throneberry	1.75	.90	.50
437	Bob Friend	2.00	1.00	.60
438	Jim Coker	1.25	.60	.40
439	Tom Brewer	1.25	.60	.40
440	Jim Lemon	1.75	.90	.50
441	Gary Bell	1.75	.90	.50
442	Joe Pignatano	1.75	.90	.50
443	Charlie Maxwell	1.75	.90	.50
444	Jerry Kindall	1.75	.90	.50
445	Warren Spahn	18.00	9.00	5.50
446	Ellis Burton	1.75	.90	.50
447	Ray Moore	1.75	.90	.50
448	Jim Gentile	2.50	1.25	.70
449	Jim Brosnan	2.00	1.00	.60
450	Orlando Cepeda	6.00	3.00	1.75
451	Curt Simmons	2.25	1.25	.70
452	Ray Webster	1.75	.90	.50
453	Vern Law	3.00	1.50	.90
454	Hal Woodeshick	1.75	.90	.50
455	Orioles Coaches (Harry Brecheen, Lum Harris, Eddie Robinson)	2.00	1.00	.60
456	Red Sox Coaches (Del Baker, Billy Herman, Sal Maglie, Rudy York)	2.50	1.25	.70
457	Cubs Coaches (Lou Klein, Charlie Root, Elvin Tappe)	2.00	1.00	.60
458	White Sox Coaches (Ray Berres, Johnny Cooney, Tony Cuccinello, Don Gutteridge)	2.00	1.00	.60
459	Reds Coaches (Cot Deal, Wally Moses, Reggie Otero)	2.00	1.00	.60
460	Indians Coaches (Mel Harder, Red Kress, Bob Lemon, Jo-Jo White)	2.50	1.25	.70
461	Tigers Coaches (Luke Appling, Tom Ferrick, Billy Hitchcock)	2.50	1.25	.70
462	A's Coaches (Walker Cooper, Fred Fitzsimmons, Don Heffner)	2.00	1.00	.60
463	Dodgers Coaches (Joe Becker, Bobby Bragan, Greg Mulleavy, Pete Reiser)	2.50	1.25	.70
464	Braves Coaches (George Myatt, Andy Pafko, Bob Scheffing, Whitlow Wyatt)	2.25	1.25	.70
465	Yankees Coaches (Frank Crosetti, Bill Dickey, Ralph Houk, Ed Lopat)	5.00	2.50	1.50
466	Phillies Coaches (Dick Carter, Andy Cohen, Ken Silvestri)	2.00	1.00	.60
467	Pirates Coaches (Bill Burwell, Sam Narron, Frank Oceak, Mickey Vernon)	2.50	1.25	.70
468	Cardinals Coaches (Ray Katt, Johnny Keane, Howie Pollet, Harry Walker)	2.00	1.00	.60
469	Giants Coaches (Salty Parker, Bill Posedel, Wes Westrum)	2.00	1.00	.60
470	Senators Coaches (Ellis Clary, Sam Mele, Bob Swift)	2.00	1.00	.60
471	Ned Garver	1.75	.90	.50
472	Al Dark	3.00	1.50	.90
473	Al Cicotte	1.75	.90	.50
474	Haywood Sullivan	2.00	1.00	.60
475	Don Drysdale	18.00	9.00	5.50
476	Lou Johnson	1.75	.90	.50
477	Don Ferrarese	1.75	.90	.50
478	Frank Torre	1.75	.90	.50
479	Georges Maranda	1.75	.90	.50
480	Yogi Berra	30.00	15.00	9.00
481	Wes Stock	1.75	.90	.50
482	Frank Bolling	1.75	.90	.50
483	Camilo Pascual	2.00	1.00	.60
484	Pirates Team/Checklist 430-495	10.00	5.00	3.00
485	Ken Boyer	3.00	1.50	.90
486	Bobby Del Greco	1.75	.90	.50
487	Tom Sturdivant	1.75	.90	.50
488	Norm Cash	4.00	2.00	1.25
489	Steve Ridzik	1.75	.90	.50
490	Frank Robinson	20.00	10.00	6.00
491	Mel Roach	1.75	.90	.50
492	Larry Jackson	1.75	.90	.50
493	Duke Snider	25.00	12.50	7.50
494	Orioles Team/Checklist 496-572	6.00	3.00	1.75
495	Sherm Lollar	2.00	1.00	.60
496	Bill Virdon	2.50	1.25	.70
497	John Tsitouris	1.75	.90	.50
498	Al Pilarcik	1.75	.90	.50
499	Johnny James	2.50	1.25	.70
500	Johnny Temple	1.75	.90	.50
501	Bob Schmidt	1.75	.90	.50
502	Jim Bunning	6.00	3.00	1.75
503	Don Lee	1.75	.90	.50
504	Seth Morehead	1.75	.90	.50
505	Ted Kluszewski	3.50	1.75	1.00
506	Lee Walls	1.75	.90	.50
507	Dick Stigman	4.50	2.25	1.25
508	Billy Consolo	4.50	2.25	1.25
509	Tommy Davis	7.00	3.50	2.00
510	Jerry Staley	4.50	2.25	1.25
511	Ken Walters	4.50	2.25	1.25
512	Joe Gibbon	4.50	2.25	1.25
513	Cubs Team/Checklist 496-572	12.00	6.00	3.50
514	Steve Barber	5.00	2.50	1.50
515	Stan Lopata	4.50	2.25	1.25
516	Marty Kutyna	4.50	2.25	1.25
517	Charley James	4.50	2.25	1.25
518	Tony Gonzalez	5.00	2.50	1.50
519	Ed Roebuck	4.50	2.25	1.25
520	Don Buddin	4.50	2.25	1.25
521	Mike Lee	4.50	2.25	1.25
522	Ken Hunt	6.00	3.00	1.75
523	Clay Dalrymple	5.00	2.50	1.50
524	Bill Henry	4.50	2.25	1.25
525	Marv Breeding	4.50	2.25	1.25
526	Paul Giel	4.50	2.25	1.25
527	Jose Valdivielso	4.50	2.25	1.25
528	Ben Johnson	4.50	2.25	1.25
529	Norm Sherry	4.50	2.25	1.25
530	Mike McCormick	5.00	2.50	1.50
531	Sandy Amoros	4.50	2.25	1.25
532	Mike Garcia	6.00	3.00	1.75
533	Lu Clinton	4.50	2.25	1.25
534	Ken MacKenzie	4.50	2.25	1.25
535	Whitey Lockman	4.50	2.25	1.25
536	Wynn Hawkins	4.50	2.25	1.25
537	Red Sox Team/Checklist 496-572	15.00	7.50	4.50
538	Frank Barnes	4.50	2.25	1.25
539	Gene Baker	4.50	2.25	1.25
540	Jerry Walker	4.50	2.25	1.25
541	Tony Curry	4.50	2.25	1.25
542	Ken Hamlin	4.50	2.25	1.25
543	Elio Chacon	4.50	2.25	1.25
544	Bill Monbouquette	5.00	2.50	1.50
545	Carl Sawatski	4.50	2.25	1.25
546	Hank Aguirre	4.50	2.25	1.25
547	Bob Aspromonte	5.00	2.50	1.50
548	Don Mincher	6.00	3.00	1.75
549	John Buzhardt	4.50	2.25	1.25
550	Jim Landis	4.50	2.25	1.25
551	Ed Rakow	4.50	2.25	1.25
552	Walt Bond	4.50	2.25	1.25
553	Bill Skowron AS	8.00	4.00	2.50
554	Willie McCovey AS	30.00	15.00	9.00
555	Nellie Fox AS	10.00	5.00	3.00
556	Charlie Neal AS	5.00	2.50	1.50
557	Frank Malzone AS	6.00	3.00	1.75
558	Eddie Mathews AS	15.00	7.50	4.50
559	Luis Aparicio AS	12.00	6.00	3.50
560	Ernie Banks AS	18.00	9.00	5.50
561	Al Kaline AS	18.00	9.00	5.50
562	Joe Cunningham AS	5.00	2.50	1.50
563	Mickey Mantle AS	95.00	45.00	25.00
564	Willie Mays AS	40.00	20.00	12.00
565	Roger Maris AS	30.00	15.00	9.00
566	Hank Aaron AS	40.00	20.00	12.00
567	Sherm Lollar AS	5.00	2.50	1.50
568	Del Crandall AS	6.00	3.00	1.75
569	Camilo Pascual AS	5.00	2.50	1.50
570	Don Drysdale AS	15.00	7.50	4.50
571	Billy Pierce AS	6.00	3.00	1.75
572	Johnny Antonelli AS	12.00	4.00	1.75

1960 Topps Tattoos

Probably the least popular of all Topps products among parents and teachers, the Topps Tattoos were delightful little items on the reverse of the wrappers of Topps "Tattoo Bubble Gum." The entire wrapper was 1-9/16" by 3-1/2." The happy owner simply moistened his skin and applied the back of the wrap-

		NR MT	EX	VG
(50)	Johnny Temple	6.00	3.00	1.75
(51)	Gus Triandos	6.00	3.00	1.75
(52)	Jerry Walker	6.00	3.00	1.75
(53)	Bill White	10.00	5.00	3.00
(54)	Gene Woodling	10.00	5.00	3.00
(55)	Early Wynn	25.00	12.50	7.50
(56)	Chicago Cubs Logo	6.00	3.00	1.75
(57)	Cincinnati Reds Logo	6.00	3.00	1.75
(58)	Los Angeles Dodgers Logo	6.00	3.00	1.75
(59)	Milwaukee Braves Logo	6.00	3.00	1.75
(60)	Philadelphia Phillies Logo	6.00	3.00	1.75
(61)	Pittsburgh Pirates Logo	10.00	5.00	3.00
(62)	San Francisco Giants Logo	6.00	3.00	1.75
(63)	St. Louis Cardinals Logo	6.00	3.00	1.75
(64)	Baltimore Orioles Logo	6.00	3.00	1.75
(65)	Boston Red Sox Logo	6.00	3.00	1.75
(66)	Chicago White Sox Logo	6.00	3.00	1.75
(67)	Cleveland Indians Logo	6.00	3.00	1.75
(68)	Detroit Tigers Logo	6.00	3.00	1.75
(69)	Kansas City Athletics Logo	6.00	3.00	1.75
(70)	New York Yankees Logo	13.00	6.50	4.00
(71)	Washington Senators Logo	6.00	3.00	1.75
(72)	Autograph (Richie Ashburn)	6.00	3.00	1.75
(73)	Autograph (Rocky Colavito)	6.00	3.00	1.75
(74)	Autograph (Roy Face)	6.00	3.00	1.75
(75)	Autograph (Jackie Jensen)	6.00	3.00	1.75
(76)	Autograph (Harmon Killebrew)	10.00	5.00	3.00
(77)	Autograph (Mickey Mantle)	70.00	35.00	21.00
(78)	Autograph (Willie Mays)	20.00	10.00	6.00
(79)	Autograph (Stan Musial)	20.00	10.00	6.00
(80)	Autograph (Billy Pierce)	6.00	3.00	1.75
(81)	Autograph (Jerry Walker)	6.00	3.00	1.75
(82)	Run-Down	6.00	3.00	1.75
(83)	Out At First	6.00	3.00	1.75
(84)	The Final Word	6.00	3.00	1.75
(85)	Twisting Foul	6.00	3.00	1.75
(86)	Out At Home	6.00	3.00	1.75
(87)	Circus Catch	6.00	3.00	1.75
(88)	Great Catch	6.00	3.00	1.75
(89)	Stolen Base	6.00	3.00	1.75
(90)	Grand Slam Homer	6.00	3.00	1.75
(91)	Double Play	6.00	3.00	1.75
(92)	Right-Handed Follow-Thru (no caption)			
		6.00	3.00	1.75
(93)	Right-Handed High Leg Kick (no caption)			
		6.00	3.00	1.75
(94)	Left-Handed Pitcher (no caption)	6.00	3.00	1.75
(95)	Right-Handed Batter (no caption)	6.00	3.00	1.75
(96)	Left-Handed Batter (no caption)	6.00	3.00	1.75

per to the wet spot. Presto, out came a "tattoo" in color (athough often blurred by running colors). The set offered 96 tattoo possibilities of which 55 were players, 16 teams, 15 action shots and 10 autographed balls. Surviving specimens are very rare today.

		NR MT	EX	VG
Complete Set:		1500.00	750.00	450.00
Common Player:		6.00	3.00	1.75
(1)	Hank Aaron	75.00	37.00	22.00
(2)	Bob Allison	10.00	5.00	3.00
(3)	John Antonelli	10.00	5.00	3.00
(4)	Richie Ashburn	15.00	7.50	4.50
(5)	Ernie Banks	30.00	15.00	9.00
(6)	Yogi Berra	40.00	20.00	12.00
(7)	Lew Burdette	13.00	6.50	4.00
(8)	Orlando Cepeda	15.00	7.50	4.50
(9)	Rocky Colavito	13.00	6.50	4.00
(10)	Joe Cunningham	6.00	3.00	1.75
(11)	Buddy Daley	6.00	3.00	1.75
(12)	Don Drysdale	25.00	12.50	7.50
(13)	Ryne Duren	10.00	5.00	3.00
(14)	Roy Face	10.00	5.00	3.00
(15)	Whitey Ford	30.00	15.00	9.00
(16)	Nellie Fox	15.00	7.50	4.50
(17)	Tito Francona	6.00	3.00	1.75
(18)	Gene Freese	6.00	3.00	1.75
(19)	Jim Gilliam	13.00	6.50	4.00
(20)	Dick Groat	13.00	6.50	4.00
(21)	Ray Herbert	6.00	3.00	1.75
(22)	Glen Hobbie	6.00	3.00	1.75
(23)	Jackie Jensen	13.00	6.50	4.00
(24)	Sam Jones	6.00	3.00	1.75
(25)	Al Kaline	30.00	15.00	9.00
(26)	Harmon Killebrew	25.00	12.50	7.50
(27)	Harvy Kuenn (Harvey)	13.00	6.50	4.00
(28)	Frank Lary	6.00	3.00	1.75
(29)	Vernon Law	10.00	5.00	3.00
(30)	Frank Malzone	6.00	3.00	1.75
(31)	Mickey Mantle	200.00	100.00	60.00
(32)	Roger Maris	30.00	15.00	9.00
(33)	Ed Mathews	25.00	12.50	7.50
(34)	Willie Mays	70.00	35.00	21.00
(35)	Cal Mclish	6.00	3.00	1.75
(36)	Wally Moon	10.00	5.00	3.00
(37)	Walt Moryn	6.00	3.00	1.75
(38)	Don Mossi	6.00	3.00	1.75
(39)	Stan Musial	70.00	35.00	21.00
(40)	Charlie Neal	6.00	3.00	1.75
(41)	Don Newcombe	10.00	5.00	3.00
(42)	Milt Pappas	10.00	5.00	3.00
(43)	Camilo Pascual	10.00	5.00	3.00
(44)	Billie Pierce (Billy)	10.00	5.00	3.00
(45)	Robin Roberts	25.00	12.50	7.50
(46)	Frank Robinson	30.00	15.00	9.00
(47)	Pete Runnels	10.00	5.00	3.00
(48)	Herb Score	10.00	5.00	3.00
(49)	Warren Spahn	25.00	12.50	7.50

1961 Topps

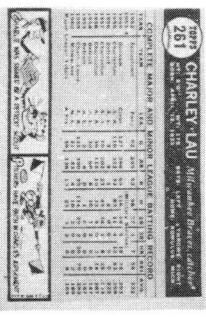

Except for some of the specialty cards, Topps returned to a vertical format with their 1961 cards. The set was numbered through 598, however only 587 cards were printed. No numbers 426, 587 and 588 were issued. Two cards numbered 463 exist (one a Braves team card and one a player card of Jack Fisher). Actually, the Braves team card was checklisted as #426. Designs for 1961 were basically large color portraits; backs returned to extensive statistics. If there weren't enough of them, a three-panel cartoon highlighting the player's career appeared. Innovations included numbered checklists, cards for statistical leaders, and 10 "Baseball Thrills" cards. Scarce high numbers are #523-589.

		NR MT	EX	VG
	Complete Set:	3600.00	1260.00	720.00
	Common Player: 1-370	.90	.45	.25
	Common Player: 371-522	1.25	.60	.40
	Common Player: 523-589	15.00	7.50	4.50
1	Dick Groat	10.00	1.50	.60
2	Roger Maris	35.00	15.00	9.00
3	John Buzhardt	.90	.45	.25
4	Lenny Green	.90	.45	.25
5	Johnny Romano	.90	.45	.25
6	Ed Roebuck	.90	.45	.25
7	White Sox Team	2.50	1.25	.75
8	Dick Williams	1.50	.70	.45
9	Bob Purkey	.90	.45	.25
10	Brooks Robinson	18.00	9.00	5.50
11	Curt Simmons	1.25	.60	.40
12	Moe Thacker	.90	.45	.25
13	Chuck Cottier	.90	.45	.25
14	Don Mossi	1.25	.60	.40
15	Willie Kirkland	.90	.45	.25
16	Billy Muffett	.90	.45	.25
17	Checklist 1-88	5.00	2.50	1.50
18	Jim Grant	.90	.45	.25
19	Cletis Boyer	2.25	1.25	.70
20	Robin Roberts	10.00	5.00	3.00
21	Zorro Versalles	2.00	1.00	.60
22	Clem Labine	1.25	.60	.40
23	Don Demeter	.90	.45	.25
24	Ken Johnson	.90	.45	.25
25	Red's Heavy Artillery (Gus Bell, Vada Pinson, Frank Robinson)	4.00	2.00	1.25
26	Wes Stock	.90	.45	.25
27	Jerry Kindall	.90	.45	.25
28	Hector Lopez	1.50	.70	.45
29	Don Nottebart	.90	.45	.25
30	Nellie Fox	4.00	2.00	1.25
31	Bob Schmidt	.90	.45	.25
32	Ray Sadecki	.90	.45	.25
33	Gary Geiger	.90	.45	.25
34	Wynn Hawkins	.90	.45	.25
35	Ron Santo	6.00	3.00	1.75
36	Jack Kralick	.90	.45	.25
37	Charlie Maxwell	.90	.45	.25
38	Bob Lillis	.90	.45	.25
39	Leo Posada	.90	.45	.25
40	Bob Turley	2.50	1.25	.70
41	N.L. Batting Leaders (Bob Clemente, Dick Groat, Norm Larker, Willie Mays)	4.00	2.00	1.25
42	A.L. Batting Leaders (Minnie Minoso, Pete Runnels, Bill Skowron, Al Smith)	2.50	1.25	.70
43	N.L. Home Run Leaders (Hank Aaron, Ernie Banks, Ken Boyer, Eddie Mathews)	4.00	2.00	1.25
44	A.L. Home Run Leaders (Rocky Colavito, Jim Lemon, Mickey Mantle, Roger Maris)	10.00	4.50	2.50
45	N.L. E.R.A. Leaders (Ernie Broglio, Don Drysdale, Bob Friend, Mike McCormick, Stan Williams)	3.25	1.75	1.00
46	A.L. E.R.A. Leaders (Frank Baumann, Hal Brown, Jim Bunning, Art Ditmar)	2.50	1.25	.70
47	N.L. Pitching Leaders (Ernie Broglio, Lou Burdette, Vern Law, Warren Spahn)	3.25	1.75	1.00
48	A.L. Pitching Leaders (Bud Daley, Art Ditmar, Chuck Estrada, Frank Lary, Milt Pappas, Jim Perry)	2.50	1.25	.70
49	N.L. Strikeout Leaders (Ernie Broglio, Don Drysdale, Sam Jones, Sandy Koufax)	4.00	2.00	1.25
50	A.L. Strikeout Leaders (Jim Bunning, Frank Lary, Pedro Ramos, Early Wynn)	3.00	1.50	.90
51	Tigers Team	3.50	1.75	1.00
52	George Crowe	.90	.45	.25
53	Russ Nixon	.90	.45	.25
54	Earl Francis	.90	.45	.25
55	Jim Davenport	.90	.45	.25
56	Russ Kemmerer	.90	.45	.25
57	Marv Throneberry	1.75	.90	.50
58	Joe Schaffernoth	.90	.45	.25
59	Jim Woods	.90	.45	.25
60	Woodie Held	.90	.45	.25
61	Ron Piche	.90	.45	.25
62	Al Pilarcik	.90	.45	.25
63	Jim Kaat	8.00	4.00	2.50
64	Alex Grammas	.90	.45	.25
65	Ted Kluszewski	3.50	1.75	1.00
66	Bill Henry	.90	.45	.25
67	Ossie Virgil	.90	.45	.25
68	Deron Johnson	1.50	.70	.45
69	Earl Wilson	.90	.45	.25
70	Bill Virdon	2.00	1.00	.60
71	Jerry Adair	1.25	.60	.40
72	Stu Miller	.90	.45	.25
73	Al Spangler	.90	.45	.25
74	Joe Pignatano	.90	.45	.25
75	Lindy Shows Larry (Larry Jackson, Lindy McDaniel)	1.50	.70	.45
76	Harry Anderson	.90	.45	.25
77	Dick Stigman	.90	.45	.25
78	Lee Walls	.90	.45	.25
79	Joe Ginsberg	.90	.45	.25
80	Harmon Killebrew	15.00	7.50	4.50
81	Tracy Stallard	.90	.45	.25
82	Joe Christopher	.90	.45	.25
83	Bob Bruce	.90	.45	.25
84	Lee Maye	.90	.45	.25
85	Jerry Walker	.90	.45	.25
86	Dodgers Team	3.50	1.75	1.00
87	Joe Amalfitano	.90	.45	.25
88	Richie Ashburn	4.00	2.00	1.25
89	Billy Martin	4.00	2.00	1.25
90	Jerry Staley	.90	.45	.25
91	Walt Moryn	.90	.45	.25
92	Hal Naragon	.90	.45	.25
93	Tony Gonzalez	.90	.45	.25
94	Johnny Kucks	.90	.45	.25
95	Norm Cash	3.50	1.75	1.00
96	Billy O'Dell	.90	.45	.25
97	Jerry Lynch	.90	.45	.25
98a	Checklist 89-176 (word "Checklist" in red on front)	7.00	3.50	2.00
98b	Checklist 89-176 ("Checklist" in yellow, 98 on back in black)	5.00	2.50	1.50
98c	Checklist 89-176 ("Checklist" in yellow, 98 on back in white)	7.00	3.50	2.00
99	Don Buddin	.90	.45	.25
100	Harvey Haddix	1.50	.70	.45
101	Bubba Phillips	.90	.45	.25
102	Gene Stephens	.90	.45	.25
103	Ruben Amaro	.90	.45	.25
104	John Blanchard	1.50	.70	.45
105	Carl Willey	.90	.45	.25
106	Whitey Herzog	2.00	1.00	.60
107	Seth Morehead	.90	.45	.25
108	Dan Dobbek	.90	.45	.25
109	Johnny Podres	2.25	1.25	.70
110	Vada Pinson	3.00	1.50	.90
111	Jack Meyer	.90	.45	.25
112	Chico Fernandez	.90	.45	.25
113	Mike Fornieles	.90	.45	.25
114	Hobie Landrith	.90	.45	.25
115	Johnny Antonelli	1.25	.60	.40
116	Joe DeMaestri	1.50	.70	.45
117	Dale Long	1.25	.60	.40
118	Chris Cannizzaro	.90	.45	.25
119	A's Big Armor (Hank Bauer, Jerry Lumpe, Norm Siebern)	1.50	.70	.45
120	Ed Mathews	12.00	6.00	3.50
121	Eli Grba	.90	.45	.25
122	Cubs Team	2.50	1.25	.75
123	Billy Gardner	.90	.45	.25
124	J.C. Martin	.90	.45	.25
125	Steve Barber	.90	.45	.25
126	Dick Stuart	1.25	.60	.40
127	Ron Kline	.90	.45	.25
128	Rip Repulski	.90	.45	.25
129	Ed Hobaugh	.90	.45	.25
130	Norm Larker	.90	.45	.25
131	Paul Richards	1.25	.60	.40
132	Al Lopez	3.00	1.50	.90
133	Ralph Houk	3.00	1.50	.90
134	Mickey Vernon	1.25	.60	.40
135	Fred Hutchinson	1.25	.60	.40
136	Walt Alston	4.00	2.00	1.25
137	Chuck Dressen	1.25	.60	.40
138	Danny Murtaugh	1.25	.60	.40
139	Solly Hemus	.90	.45	.25
140	Gus Triandos	1.25	.60	.40
141	Billy Williams	30.00	15.00	9.00
142	Luis Arroyo	1.50	.70	.45
143	Russ Snyder	.90	.45	.25
144	Jim Coker	.90	.45	.25
145	Bob Buhl	1.25	.60	.40
146	Marty Keough	.90	.45	.25
147	Ed Rakow	.90	.45	.25
148	Julian Javier	1.25	.60	.40
149	Bob Oldis	.90	.45	.25
150	Willie Mays	40.00	20.00	12.00
151	Jim Donohue	.90	.45	.25
152	Earl Torgeson	.90	.45	.25
153	Don Lee	.90	.45	.25
154	Bobby Del Greco	.90	.45	.25

#	Player	NR MT	EX	VG
155	Johnny Temple	.90	.45	.25
156	Ken Hunt	.90	.45	.25
157	Cal McLish	.90	.45	.25
158	Pete Daley	.90	.45	.25
159	Orioles Team	2.50	1.25	.75
160	Whitey Ford	15.00	7.50	4.50
161	Sherman Jones (photo actually Eddie Fisher)	.90	.45	.25
162	Jay Hook	.90	.45	.25
163	Ed Sadowski	.90	.45	.25
164	Felix Mantilla	.90	.45	.25
165	Gino Cimoli	.90	.45	.25
166	Danny Kravitz	.90	.45	.25
167	Giants Team	2.50	1.25	.75
168	Tommy Davis	3.00	1.50	.90
169	Don Elston	.90	.45	.25
170	Al Smith	.90	.45	.25
171	Paul Foytack	.90	.45	.25
172	Don Dillard	.90	.45	.25
173	Beantown Bombers (Jackie Jensen, Frank Malzone, Vic Wertz)	2.00	1.00	.60
174	Ray Semproch	.90	.45	.25
175	Gene Freese	.90	.45	.25
176	Ken Aspromonte	.90	.45	.25
177	Don Larsen	1.50	.70	.45
178	Bob Nieman	.90	.45	.25
179	Joe Koppe	.90	.45	.25
180	Bobby Richardson	4.00	2.00	1.25
181	Fred Green	.90	.45	.25
182	Dave Nicholson	.90	.45	.25
183	Andre Rodgers	.90	.45	.25
184	Steve Bilko	.90	.45	.25
185	Herb Score	1.50	.70	.45
186	Elmer Valo	.90	.45	.25
187	Billy Klaus	.90	.45	.25
188	Jim Marshall	.90	.45	.25
189	Checklist 177-264	5.00	2.50	1.50
190	Stan Williams	.90	.45	.25
191	Mike de la Hoz	.90	.45	.25
192	Dick Brown	.90	.45	.25
193	Gene Conley	1.25	.60	.40
194	Gordy Coleman	.90	.45	.25
195	Jerry Casale	.90	.45	.25
196	Ed Bouchee	.90	.45	.25
197	Dick Hall	.90	.45	.25
198	Carl Sawatski	.90	.45	.25
199	Bob Boyd	.90	.45	.25
200	Warren Spahn	12.00	6.00	3.50
201	Pete Whisenant	.90	.45	.25
202	Al Neiger	.90	.45	.25
203	Eddie Bressoud	.90	.45	.25
204	Bob Skinner	1.25	.60	.40
205	Bill Pierce	1.75	.90	.50
206	Gene Green	.90	.45	.25
207	Dodger Southpaws (Sandy Koufax, Johnny Podres)	8.00	4.00	2.50
208	Larry Osborne	.90	.45	.25
209	Ken McBride	.90	.45	.25
210	Pete Runnels	1.25	.60	.40
211	Bob Gibson	12.00	6.00	3.50
212	Haywood Sullivan	1.25	.60	.40
213	Bill Stafford	2.00	1.00	.60
214	Danny Murphy	.90	.45	.25
215	Gus Bell	1.25	.60	.40
216	Ted Bowsfield	.90	.45	.25
217	Mel Roach	.90	.45	.25
218	Hal Brown	.90	.45	.25
219	Gene Mauch	2.50	1.25	.70
220	Al Dark	1.25	.60	.40
221	Mike Higgins	.90	.45	.25
222	Jimmie Dykes	.90	.45	.25
223	Bob Scheffing	.90	.45	.25
224	Joe Gordon	1.25	.60	.40
225	Bill Rigney	.90	.45	.25
226	Harry Lavagetto	.90	.45	.25
227	Juan Pizarro	.90	.45	.25
228	Yankees Team	8.00	4.00	2.50
229	Rudy Hernandez	.90	.45	.25
230	Don Hoak	1.25	.60	.40
231	Dick Drott	.90	.45	.25
232	Bill White	1.50	.70	.45
233	Joe Jay	.90	.45	.25
234	Ted Lepcio	.90	.45	.25
235	Camilo Pascual	1.25	.60	.40
236	Don Gile	.90	.45	.25
237	Billy Loes	.90	.45	.25
238	Jim Gilliam	2.50	1.25	.70
239	Dave Sisler	.90	.45	.25
240	Ron Hansen	.90	.45	.25
241	Al Cicotte	.90	.45	.25
242	Hal W. Smith	.90	.45	.25
243	Frank Lary	1.25	.60	.40
244	Chico Cardenas	1.25	.60	.40
245	Joe Adcock	2.00	1.00	.60
246	Bob Davis	.90	.45	.25
247	Billy Goodman	.90	.45	.25
248	Ed Keegan	.90	.45	.25
249	Reds Team	4.00	2.00	1.25
250	Buc Hill Aces (Roy Face, Vern Law)	2.00	1.00	.60
251	Bill Bruton	.90	.45	.25
252	Bill Short	1.50	.70	.45
253	Sammy Taylor	.90	.45	.25
254	Ted Sadowski	.90	.45	.25
255	Vic Power	.90	.45	.25
256	Billy Hoeft	.90	.45	.25
257	Carroll Hardy	.90	.45	.25
258	Jack Sanford	.90	.45	.25
259	John Schaive	.90	.45	.25
260	Don Drysdale	12.00	6.00	3.50
261	Charlie Lau	1.25	.60	.40
262	Tony Curry	.90	.45	.25
263	Ken Hamlin	.90	.45	.25
264	Glen Hobbie	.90	.45	.25
265	Tony Kubek	4.00	2.00	1.25
266	Lindy McDaniel	.90	.45	.25
267	Norm Siebern	1.25	.60	.40
268	Ike DeLock (Delock)	.90	.45	.25
269	Harry Chiti	.90	.45	.25
270	Bob Friend	1.50	.70	.45
271	Jim Landis	.90	.45	.25
272	Tom Morgan	.90	.45	.25
273	Checklist 265-352	5.00	2.50	1.50
274	Gary Bell	.90	.45	.25
275	Gene Woodling	1.25	.60	.40
276	Ray Rippelmeyer	.90	.45	.25
277	Hank Foiles	.90	.45	.25
278	Don McMahon	.90	.45	.25
279	Jose Pagan	.90	.45	.25
280	Frank Howard	2.50	1.25	.70
281	Frank Sullivan	.90	.45	.25
282	Faye Throneberry	.90	.45	.25
283	Bob Anderson	.90	.45	.25
284	Dick Gernert	.90	.45	.25
285	Sherm Lollar	1.25	.60	.40
286	George Witt	.90	.45	.25
287	Carl Yastrzemski	85.00	42.00	25.00
288	Albie Pearson	.90	.45	.25
289	Ray Moore	.90	.45	.25
290	Stan Musial	30.00	15.00	9.00
291	Tex Clevenger	.90	.45	.25
292	Jim Baumer	.90	.45	.25
293	Tom Sturdivant	.90	.45	.25
294	Don Blasingame	.90	.45	.25
295	Milt Pappas	1.25	.60	.40
296	Wes Covington	.90	.45	.25
297	Athletics Team	2.50	1.25	.70
298	Jim Golden	.90	.45	.25
299	Clay Dalrymple	.90	.45	.25
300	Mickey Mantle	175.00	80.00	45.00
301	Chet Nichols	.90	.45	.25
302	Al Heist	.90	.45	.25
303	Gary Peters	1.25	.60	.40
304	Rocky Nelson	.90	.45	.25
305	Mike McCormick	1.25	.60	.40
306	World Series Game 1 (Virdon Saves Game)	3.50	1.75	1.00
307	World Series Game 2 (Mantle Slams 2 Homers)	15.00	7.50	4.50
308	World Series Game 3 (Richardson Is Hero)	4.00	2.00	1.25
309	World Series Game 4 (Cimoli Is Safe In Crucial Play)	3.00	1.50	.90
310	World Series Game 5 (Face Saves the Day)	3.50	1.75	1.00
311	World Series Game 6 (Ford Pitches Second Shutout)	5.00	2.50	1.50
312	World Series Game 7 (Mazeroski's Homer Wins It!)	5.00	2.50	1.50
313	World Series Summary (The Winners Celebrate)	3.00	1.50	.90
314	Bob Miller	.90	.45	.25
315	Earl Battey	1.25	.60	.40
316	Bobby Gene Smith	.90	.45	.25
317	Jim Brewer	1.25	.60	.40
318	Danny O'Connell	.90	.45	.25
319	Valmy Thomas	.90	.45	.25
320	Lou Burdette	2.50	1.25	.70
321	Marv Breeding	.90	.45	.25
322	Bill Kunkel	.90	.45	.25
323	Sammy Esposito	.90	.45	.25
324	Hank Aguirre	.90	.45	.25

#	Player	NR MT	EX	VG
325	Wally Moon	1.25	.60	.40
326	Dave Hillman	.90	.45	.25
327	Matty Alou	4.00	2.00	1.25
328	Jim O'Toole	.90	.45	.25
329	Julio Becquer	.90	.45	.25
330	Rocky Colavito	3.00	1.50	.90
331	Ned Garver	.90	.45	.25
332	Dutch Dotterer (photo actually Tommy Dotterer)	.90	.45	.25
333	Fritz Brickell	1.50	.70	.45
334	Walt Bond	.90	.45	.25
335	Frank Bolling	.90	.45	.25
336	Don Mincher	1.25	.60	.40
337	Al's Aces (Al Lopez, Herb Score, Early Wynn)	3.50	1.75	1.00
338	Don Landrum	.90	.45	.25
339	Gene Baker	.90	.45	.25
340	Vic Wertz	1.25	.60	.40
341	Jim Owens	.90	.45	.25
342	Clint Courtney	.90	.45	.25
343	Earl Robinson	.90	.45	.25
344	Sandy Koufax	30.00	15.00	9.00
345	Jim Piersall	2.00	1.00	.60
346	Howie Nunn	.90	.45	.25
347	Cardinals Team	2.50	1.25	.70
348	Steve Boros	1.25	.60	.40
349	Danny McDevitt	1.50	.70	.45
350	Ernie Banks	15.00	7.50	4.50
351	Jim King	.90	.45	.25
352	Bob Shaw	.90	.45	.25
353	Howie Bedell	.90	.45	.25
354	Billy Harrell	.90	.45	.25
355	Bob Allison	1.25	.60	.40
356	Ryne Duren	2.25	1.25	.70
357	Daryl Spencer	.90	.45	.25
358	Earl Averill	.90	.45	.25
359	Dallas Green	1.25	.60	.40
360	Frank Robinson	18.00	9.00	5.50
361a	Checklist 353-429 ("Topps Baseball" in black on front)	5.00	2.50	1.50
361b	Checklist 353-429 ("Topps Baseball" in yellow)	6.00	3.00	1.75
362	Frank Funk	.90	.45	.25
363	John Roseboro	1.25	.60	.40
364	Moe Drabowsky	.90	.45	.25
365	Jerry Lumpe	1.25	.60	.40
366	Eddie Fisher	.90	.45	.25
367	Jim Rivera	.90	.45	.25
368	Bennie Daniels	.90	.45	.25
369	Dave Philley	1.25	.60	.40
370	Roy Face	2.00	1.00	.60
371	Bill Skowron	5.00	2.50	1.50
372	Bob Hendley	1.25	.60	.40
373	Red Sox Team	5.00	2.50	1.50
374	Paul Giel	1.25	.60	.40
375	Ken Boyer	4.00	2.00	1.25
376	Mike Roarke	1.25	.60	.40
377	Ruben Gomez	1.25	.60	.40
378	Wally Post	1.25	.60	.40
379	Bobby Shantz	2.50	1.25	.70
380	Minnie Minoso	3.00	1.50	.90
381	Dave Wickersham	1.25	.60	.40
382	Frank Thomas	1.25	.60	.40
383	Frisco First Liners (Mike McCormick, Billy O'Dell, Jack Sanford)	2.00	1.00	.60
384	Chuck Essegian	1.25	.60	.40
385	Jim Perry	2.50	1.25	.70
386	Joe Hicks	1.25	.60	.40
387	Duke Maas	2.50	1.25	.70
388	Bob Clemente	35.00	17.50	10.50
389	Ralph Terry	3.00	1.50	.90
390	Del Crandall	2.50	1.25	.70
391	Winston Brown	1.25	.60	.40
392	Reno Bertoia	1.25	.60	.40
393	Batter Bafflers (Don Cardwell, Glen Hobbie)	1.50	.70	.45
394	Ken Walters	1.25	.60	.40
395	Chuck Estrada	1.25	.60	.40
396	Bob Aspromonte	1.25	.60	.40
397	Hal Woodeshick	1.25	.60	.40
398	Hank Bauer	2.50	1.25	.70
399	Cliff Cook	1.25	.60	.40
400	Vern Law	2.50	1.25	.70
401	Babe Ruth Hits 60th Homer	10.00	5.00	3.00
402	Larsen Pitches Perfect Game	7.00	3.50	2.00
403	Brooklyn-Boston Play 26-Inning Tie	2.00	1.00	.60
404	Hornsby Tops N.L. With .424 Average	3.50	1.75	1.00
405	Gehrig Benched After 2,130 Games	7.00	3.50	2.00
406	Mantle Blasts 565 ft. Home Run	20.00	9.00	5.00
407	Jack Chesbro Wins 41st Game	2.50	1.25	.70
408	Mathewson Strikes Out 267 Batters	3.50	1.75	1.00
409	Johnson Hurls 3rd Shutout in 4 Days	4.00	2.00	1.25
410	Haddix Pitches 12 Perfect Innings	2.50	1.25	.70
411	Tony Taylor	1.25	.60	.40
412	Larry Sherry	1.25	.60	.40
413	Eddie Yost	1.50	.70	.45
414	Dick Donovan	1.25	.60	.40
415	Hank Aaron	55.00	27.00	16.50
416	Dick Howser	4.00	2.00	1.25
417	Juan Marichal	60.00	30.00	18.00
418	Ed Bailey	1.25	.60	.40
419	Tom Borland	1.25	.60	.40
420	Ernie Broglio	1.25	.60	.40
421	Ty Cline	1.25	.60	.40
422	Bud Daley	1.25	.60	.40
423	Charlie Neal	1.25	.60	.40
424	Turk Lown	1.25	.60	.40
425	Yogi Berra	25.00	12.50	7.50
426	Not Issued			
427	Dick Ellsworth	1.25	.60	.40
428	Ray Barker	1.25	.60	.40
429	Al Kaline	20.00	10.00	6.00
430	Bill Mazeroski	3.50	1.75	1.00
431	Chuck Stobbs	1.25	.60	.40
432	Coot Veal	1.25	.60	.40
433	Art Mahaffey	1.25	.60	.40
434	Tom Brewer	1.25	.60	.40
435	Orlando Cepeda	5.00	2.50	1.50
436	Jim Maloney	2.50	1.25	.70
437	Checklist 430-506	6.00	3.00	1.75
438	Curt Flood	2.50	1.25	.70
439	Phil Regan	1.75	.90	.50
440	Luis Aparicio	10.00	5.00	3.00
441	Dick Bertell	1.25	.60	.40
442	Gordon Jones	1.25	.60	.40
443	Duke Snider	20.00	10.00	6.00
444	Joe Nuxhall	1.75	.90	.50
445	Frank Malzone	1.50	.70	.45
446	Bob "Hawk" Taylor	1.25	.60	.40
447	Harry Bright	1.25	.60	.40
448	Del Rice	1.25	.60	.40
449	Bobby Bolin	1.50	.70	.45
450	Jim Lemon	1.25	.60	.40
451	Power For Ernie (Ernie Broglio, Daryl Spencer, Bill White)	1.75	.90	.50
452	Bob Allen	1.25	.60	.40
453	Dick Schofield	1.25	.60	.40
454	Pumpsie Green	1.25	.60	.40
455	Early Wynn	10.00	5.00	3.00
456	Hal Bevan	1.25	.60	.40
457	Johnny James	1.25	.60	.40
458	Willie Tasby	1.25	.60	.40
459	Terry Fox	1.25	.60	.40
460	Gil Hodges	12.00	6.00	3.50
461	Smoky Burgess	2.50	1.25	.70
462	Lou Klimchock	1.25	.60	.40
463a	Braves Team (should be card #426)	4.00	2.00	1.25
463b	Jack Fisher	1.25	.60	.40
464	Leroy Thomas	1.50	.70	.45
465	Roy McMillan	1.25	.60	.40
466	Ron Moeller	1.25	.60	.40
467	Indians Team	3.50	1.75	1.00
468	Johnny Callison	1.75	.90	.50
469	Ralph Lumenti	1.25	.60	.40
470	Roy Sievers	1.75	.90	.50
471	Phil Rizzuto MVP	8.00	4.00	2.50
472	Yogi Berra MVP	15.00	7.50	4.50
473	Bobby Shantz MVP	3.50	1.75	1.00
474	Al Rosen MVP	3.50	1.75	1.00
475	Mickey Mantle MVP	30.00	13.50	7.50
476	Jackie Jensen MVP	3.50	1.75	1.00
477	Nellie Fox MVP	4.00	2.00	1.25
478	Roger Maris MVP	18.00	9.00	5.50
479	Jim Konstanty MVP	2.50	1.25	.70
480	Roy Campanella MVP	15.00	7.50	4.50
481	Hank Sauer MVP	2.50	1.25	.70
482	Willie Mays MVP	15.00	7.50	4.50
483	Don Newcombe MVP	3.50	1.75	1.00
484	Hank Aaron MVP	15.00	7.50	4.50
485	Ernie Banks MVP	10.00	5.00	3.00
486	Dick Groat MVP	3.50	1.75	1.00
487	Gene Oliver	1.25	.60	.40
488	Joe McClain	1.25	.60	.40
489	Walt Dropo	1.50	.70	.45
490	Jim Bunning	5.00	2.50	1.50
491	Phillies Team	3.50	1.75	1.00

		NR MT	EX	VG
492	Ron Fairly	1.50	.70	.45
493	Don Zimmer	2.00	1.00	.60
494	Tom Cheney	1.25	.60	.40
495	Elston Howard	5.00	2.50	1.50
496	Ken MacKenzie	1.25	.60	.40
497	Willie Jones	1.25	.60	.40
498	Ray Herbert	1.25	.60	.40
499	Chuck Schilling	1.25	.60	.40
500	Harvey Kuenn	3.00	1.50	.90
501	John DeMerit	1.25	.60	.40
502	Clarence Coleman	1.25	.60	.40
503	Tito Francona	1.50	.70	.45
504	Billy Consolo	1.25	.60	.40
505	Red Schoendienst	3.50	1.75	1.00
506	Willie Davis	5.00	2.50	1.50
507	Pete Burnside	1.25	.60	.40
508	Rocky Bridges	1.25	.60	.40
509	Camilo Carreon	1.25	.60	.40
510	Art Ditmar	2.50	1.25	.70
511	Joe Morgan	1.25	.60	.40
512	Bob Will	1.25	.60	.40
513	Jim Brosnan	1.50	.70	.45
514	Jake Wood	1.25	.60	.40
515	Jackie Brandt	1.25	.60	.40
516	Checklist 507-587	6.00	3.00	1.75
517	Willie McCovey	30.00	15.00	9.00
518	Andy Carey	1.25	.60	.40
519	Jim Pagliaroni	1.25	.60	.40
520	Joe Cunningham	1.50	.70	.45
521	Brother Battery (Larry Sherry, Norm Sherry)	2.00	1.00	.60
522	Dick Farrell	1.25	.60	.40
523	Joe Gibbon	15.00	7.50	4.50
524	Johnny Logan	18.00	9.00	5.50
525	Ron Perranoski	20.00	10.00	6.00
526	R.C. Stevens	15.00	7.50	4.50
527	Gene Leek	15.00	7.50	4.50
528	Pedro Ramos	15.00	7.50	4.50
529	Bob Roselli	15.00	7.50	4.50
530	Bobby Malkmus	15.00	7.50	4.50
531	Jim Coates	20.00	10.00	6.00
532	Bob Hale	15.00	7.50	4.50
533	Jack Curtis	15.00	7.50	4.50
534	Eddie Kasko	15.00	7.50	4.50
535	Larry Jackson	15.00	7.50	4.50
536	Bill Tuttle	15.00	7.50	4.50
537	Bobby Locke	15.00	7.50	4.50
538	Chuck Hiller	15.00	7.50	4.50
539	Johnny Klippstein	15.00	7.50	4.50
540	Jackie Jensen	25.00	12.50	7.50
541	Roland Sheldon	20.00	10.00	6.00
542	Twins Team	25.00	12.50	7.50
543	Roger Craig	25.00	12.50	7.50
544	George Thomas	15.00	7.50	4.50
545	Hoyt Wilhelm	40.00	20.00	12.00
546	Marty Kutyna	15.00	7.50	4.50
547	Leon Wagner	18.00	9.00	5.50
548	Ted Wills	15.00	7.50	4.50
549	Hal R. Smith	15.00	7.50	4.50
550	Frank Baumann	15.00	7.50	4.50
551	George Altman	15.00	7.50	4.50
552	Jim Archer	15.00	7.50	4.50
553	Bill Fischer	15.00	7.50	4.50
554	Pirates Team	25.00	12.50	7.50
555	Sam Jones	15.00	7.50	4.50
556	Ken R. Hunt	15.00	7.50	4.50
557	Jose Valdivielso	15.00	7.50	4.50
558	Don Ferrarese	15.00	7.50	4.50
559	Jim Gentile	18.00	9.00	5.50
560	Barry Latman	15.00	7.50	4.50
561	Charley James	15.00	7.50	4.50
562	Bill Monbouquette	18.00	9.00	5.50
563	Bob Cerv	20.00	10.00	6.00
564	Don Cardwell	15.00	7.50	4.50
565	Felipe Alou	20.00	10.00	6.00
566	Paul Richards AS	18.00	9.00	5.50
567	Danny Murtaugh AS	18.00	9.00	5.50
568	Bill Skowron AS	25.00	12.50	7.50
569	Frank Herrera AS	18.00	9.00	5.50
570	Nellie Fox AS	30.00	15.00	9.00
571	Bill Mazeroski AS	25.00	12.50	7.50
572	Brooks Robinson AS	50.00	25.00	15.00
573	Ken Boyer AS	25.00	12.50	7.50
574	Luis Aparicio AS	30.00	15.00	9.00
575	Ernie Banks AS	40.00	20.00	12.00
576	Roger Maris AS	50.00	25.00	15.00
577	Hank Aaron AS	100.00	50.00	30.00
578	Mickey Mantle AS	225.00	100.00	55.00
579	Willie Mays AS	100.00	50.00	30.00
580	Al Kaline AS	40.00	20.00	12.00
581	Frank Robinson AS	40.00	20.00	12.00

		NR MT	EX	VG
582	Earl Battey AS	18.00	9.00	5.50
583	Del Crandall AS	20.00	10.00	6.00
584	Jim Perry AS	20.00	10.00	6.00
585	Bob Friend AS	20.00	10.00	6.00
586	Whitey Ford AS	50.00	20.00	9.00
587	Not Issued			
588	Not Issued			
589	Warren Spahn AS	75.00	25.00	12.00

1961 Topps Dice Game

One of the more obscure Topps test issues that may have never actually been issued is the 1961 Topps Dice Game. Eighteen black and white cards, each measuring 2½'' by 3½'' in size, comprise the set. Interestingly, there are no identifying marks, such as copyrights or trademarks, to indicate the set was produced by Topps. The card backs contain various baseball plays that occur when a certain pitch is called and a specific number of the dice is rolled.

		NR MT	EX	VG
Complete Set:		7000.00	3500.00	2100.
Common Player:		100.00	50.00	30.00
(1)	Earl Battey	100.00	50.00	30.00
(2)	Del Crandall	100.00	50.00	30.00
(3)	Jim Davenport	100.00	50.00	30.00
(4)	Don Drysdale	250.00	125.00	75.00
(5)	Dick Groat	150.00	75.00	45.00
(6)	Al Kaline	400.00	200.00	120.00
(7)	Tony Kubek	150.00	75.00	45.00
(8)	Mickey Mantle	2500.00	1250.00	750.00
(9)	Willie Mays	800.00	400.00	240.00
(10)	Bill Mazeroski	150.00	75.00	45.00
(11)	Stan Musial	800.00	400.00	240.00
(12)	Camilo Pascual	100.00	50.00	30.00
(13)	Bobby Richardson	150.00	75.00	45.00
(14)	Brooks Robinson	400.00	200.00	120.00
(15)	Frank Robinson	300.00	150.00	90.00
(16)	Norm Siebern	100.00	50.00	30.00
(17)	Leon Wagner	100.00	50.00	30.00
(18)	Bill White	100.00	50.00	30.00

1961 Topps Magic Rub Offs

Not too different in concept from the tattoos of the previous year, the Topps Magic Rub Off was designed to leave impressions of team themes or individual players when properly applied. Measuring 2-1/16'' by 3-1/16,'' the Magic Rub Off was not designed specifically for application to the owner's skin. The set of 36 Rub Offs seems to almost be a tongue-in-cheek product as the team themes were a far cry from official logos, and the players seem to have been included for their nicknames. Among the players (one representing each team) the best known and most valuable are Yogi Berra and Ernie Banks.

		NR MT	EX	VG
	Complete Set:	75.00	37.00	22.00
	Common Player:	.75	.40	.25
(1)	Baltimore Orioles Pennant	.80	.40	.25
(2)	Ernie "Bingo" Banks	10.00	5.00	3.00
(3)	Yogi Berra	15.00	7.50	4.50
(4)	Boston Red Sox Pennant	.80	.40	.25
(5)	Jackie "Ozark" Brandt	1.00	.50	.30
(6)	Jim "Professor" Brosnan	1.00	.50	.30
(7)	Chicago Cubs Pennant	.80	.40	.25
(8)	Chicago White Sox Pennant	.80	.40	.25
(9)	Cincinnati Red Legs Pennant	.80	.40	.25
(10)	Cleveland Indians Pennant	.80	.40	.25
(11)	Detroit Tigers Pennant	1.00	.50	.30
(12)	Henry "Dutch" Dotterer	1.00	.50	.30
(13)	Joe "Flash" Gordon	1.25	.60	.40
(14)	Harvey "The Kitten" Haddix	1.25	.60	.40
(15)	Frank "Pancho" Hererra	1.00	.50	.30
(16)	Frank "Tower" Howard	3.00	1.50	.90
(17)	"Sad" Sam Jones	1.00	.50	.30
(18)	Kansas City Athletics Pennant	.80	.40	.25
(19)	Los Angeles Angels Pennant	.80	.40	.25
(20)	Los Angeles Dodgers Pennant	1.00	.50	.30
(21)	Omar "Turk" Lown	1.00	.50	.30
(22)	Billy "The Kid" Martin	5.00	2.50	1.50
(23)	Duane "Duke" Mass (Maas)	1.00	.50	.30
(24)	Charlie "Paw Paw" Maxwell	1.00	.50	.30
(25)	Milwaukee Braves Pennant	.80	.40	.25
(26)	Minnesota Twins Pennant	.80	.40	.25
(27)	"Farmer" Ray Moore	.80	.40	.25
(28)	Walt "Moose" Moryn	.80	.40	.25
(29)	New York Yankees Pennant	2.00	1.00	.60
(30)	Philadelphia Phillies Pennant	.80	.40	.25
(31)	Pittsburgh Pirates Pennant	.80	.40	.25
(32)	John "Honey" Romano	1.00	.50	.30
(33)	"Pistol Pete" Runnels	1.25	.60	.40
(34)	St. Louis Cardinals Pennant	.70	.35	.20
(35)	San Francisco Giants Pennant	.70	.35	.20
(36)	Washington Senators Pennant	.70	.35	.20

1961 Topps Stamps

Issued as an added insert to 1961 Topps packages, these 1-3/8" by 1-3/16" stamps were designed to be collected and placed in an album which could be bought for an additional 10¢. Packs of cards contained two stamps. There are 208 stamps in a com-

plete set which depict 207 different players (Al Kaline appears twice). There were 104 players on brown stamps and 104 on green. While there are many Hall of Famers on the stamps, prices remain low because there is relatively little interest in what is a non-card set.

		NR MT	EX	VG
	Complete Set:	150.00	75.00	45.00
	Stamp Album:	25.00	12.50	7.50
	Common Player:	.25	.13	.08
(1)	Hank Aaron	7.00	3.50	2.00
(2)	Joe Adcock	.35	.20	.11
(3)	Hank Aguirre	.25	.13	.08
(4)	Bob Allison	.30	.15	.09
(5)	George Altman	.25	.13	.08
(6)	Bob Anderson	.25	.13	.08
(7)	Johnny Antonelli	.30	.15	.09
(8)	Luis Aparicio	1.00	.50	.30
(9)	Luis Arroyo	.35	.20	.11
(10)	Richie Ashburn	.80	.40	.25
(11)	Ken Aspromonte	.25	.13	.08
(12)	Ed Bailey	.25	.13	.08
(13)	Ernie Banks	3.00	1.50	.90
(14)	Steve Barber	.25	.13	.08
(15)	Earl Battey	.30	.15	.09
(16)	Hank Bauer	.50	.25	.15
(17)	Gus Bell	.30	.15	.09
(18)	Yogi Berra	5.00	2.50	1.50
(19)	Reno Bertoia	.25	.13	.08
(20)	John Blanchard	.35	.20	.11
(21)	Don Blasingame	.25	.13	.08
(22)	Frank Bolling	.25	.13	.08
(23)	Steve Boros	.25	.13	.08
(24)	Ed Bouchee	.25	.13	.08
(25)	Bob Boyd	.25	.13	.08
(26)	Cletis Boyer	.35	.20	.11
(27)	Ken Boyer	.50	.25	.15
(28)	Jackie Brandt	.25	.13	.08
(29)	Marv Breeding	.25	.13	.08
(30)	Eddie Bressoud	.25	.13	.08
(31)	Jim Brewer	.25	.13	.08
(32)	Tom Brewer	.25	.13	.08
(33)	Jim Brosnan	.30	.15	.09
(34)	Bill Bruton	.25	.13	.08
(35)	Bob Buhl	.30	.15	.09
(36)	Jim Bunning	.80	.40	.25
(37)	Smoky Burgess	.30	.15	.09
(38)	John Buzhardt	.25	.13	.08
(39)	Johnny Callison	.30	.15	.09
(40)	Chico Cardenas	.25	.13	.08
(41)	Andy Carey	.25	.13	.08
(42)	Jerry Casale	.25	.13	.08
(43)	Norm Cash	.50	.25	.15
(44)	Orlando Cepeda	1.00	.50	.30
(45)	Bob Cerv	.25	.13	.08
(46)	Harry Chiti	.25	.13	.08
(47)	Gene Conley	.30	.15	.09
(48)	Wes Covington	.25	.13	.08
(49)	Del Crandall	.35	.20	.11
(50)	Tony Curry	.25	.13	.08
(51)	Bud Daley	.25	.13	.08
(52)	Pete Daley	.25	.13	.08
(53)	Clay Dalrymple	.25	.13	.08
(54)	Jim Davenport	.25	.13	.08
(55)	Tommy Davis	.35	.20	.11
(56)	Bobby Del Greco	.25	.13	.08
(57)	Ike Delock	.25	.13	.08
(58)	Art Ditmar	.35	.20	.11
(59)	Dick Donovan	.25	.13	.08
(60)	Don Drysdale	2.50	1.25	.70
(61)	Dick Ellsworth	.25	.13	.08
(62)	Don Elston	.25	.13	.08
(63)	Chuck Estrada	.25	.13	.08
(64)	Roy Face	.35	.20	.11
(65)	Dick Farrell	.25	.13	.08
(66)	Chico Fernandez	.25	.13	.08
(67)	Curt Flood	.35	.20	.11
(68)	Whitey Ford	3.50	1.75	1.00
(69)	Tito Francona	.25	.13	.08
(70)	Gene Freese	.25	.13	.08
(71)	Bob Friend	.35	.20	.11
(72)	Billy Gardner	.25	.13	.08
(73)	Ned Garver	.25	.13	.08
(74)	Gary Geiger	.25	.13	.08
(75)	Jim Gentile	.25	.13	.08
(76)	Dick Gernert	.25	.13	.08
(77)	Tony Gonzalez	.25	.13	.08
(78)	Alex Grammas	.25	.13	.08
(79)	Jim Grant	.25	.13	.08

		NR MT	EX	VG
(80)	Dick Groat	.35	.20	.11
(81)	Dick Hall	.25	.13	.08
(82)	Ron Hansen	.25	.13	.08
(83)	Bob Hartman	.25	.13	.08
(84)	Woodie Held	.25	.13	.08
(85)	Ray Herbert	.25	.13	.08
(86)	Frank Herrera	.25	.13	.08
(87)	Whitey Herzog	.50	.25	.15
(88)	Don Hoak	.30	.15	.09
(89)	Elston Howard	.80	.40	.25
(90)	Frank Howard	.50	.25	.15
(91)	Ken Hunt	.25	.13	.08
(92)	Larry Jackson	.25	.13	.08
(93)	Julian Javier	.25	.13	.08
(94)	Joe Jay	.25	.13	.08
(95)	Jackie Jensen	.50	.25	.15
(96)	Jim Kaat	.80	.40	.25
(97a)	Al Kaline (green)	3.50	1.75	1.00
(97b)	Al Kaline (brown)	3.50	1.75	1.00
(98)	Eddie Kasko	.25	.13	.08
(99)	Russ Kemmerer	.25	.13	.08
(100)	Harmon Killebrew	3.50	1.75	1.00
(101)	Billy Klaus	.25	.13	.08
(102)	Ron Kline	.25	.13	.08
(103)	Johnny Klippstein	.25	.13	.08
(104)	Ted Kluszewski	.25	.13	.08
(105)	Tony Kubek	.80	.40	.25
(106)	Harvey Kuenn	.50	.25	.15
(107)	Jim Landis	.25	.13	.08
(108)	Hobie Landrith	.25	.13	.08
(109)	Norm Larker	.25	.13	.08
(110)	Frank Lary	.25	.13	.08
(111)	Barry Latman	.25	.13	.08
(112)	Vern Law	.30	.15	.09
(113)	Jim Lemon	.25	.13	.08
(114)	Sherm Lollar	.30	.15	.09
(115)	Dale Long	.30	.15	.09
(116)	Jerry Lumpe	.25	.13	.08
(117)	Jerry Lynch	.25	.13	.08
(118)	Art Mahaffey	.25	.13	.08
(119)	Frank Malzone	.25	.13	.08
(120)	Felix Mantilla	.25	.13	.08
(121)	Mickey Mantle	25.00	12.50	7.50
(122)	Juan Marichal	2.50	1.25	.70
(123)	Roger Maris	7.00	3.50	2.00
(124)	Billy Martin	1.00	.50	.30
(125)	J.C. Martin	.25	.13	.08
(126)	Ed Mathews	2.50	1.25	.70
(127)	Charlie Maxwell	.25	.13	.08
(128)	Willie Mays	7.00	3.50	2.00
(129)	Bill Mazeroski	.50	.25	.15
(130)	Mike McCormick	.25	.13	.08
(131)	Willie McCovey	2.50	1.25	.70
(132)	Lindy McDaniel	.25	.13	.08
(133)	Roy McMillan	.25	.13	.08
(134)	Minnie Minoso	.50	.25	.15
(135)	Bill Monbouquette	.25	.13	.08
(136)	Wally Moon	.30	.15	.09
(137)	Stan Musial	7.00	3.50	2.00
(138)	Charlie Neal	.25	.13	.08
(139)	Rocky Nelson	.25	.13	.08
(140)	Russ Nixon	.25	.13	.08
(141)	Billy O'Dell	.25	.13	.08
(142)	Jim O'Toole	.25	.13	.08
(143)	Milt Pappas	.30	.15	.09
(144)	Camilo Pascual	.30	.15	.09
(145)	Jim Perry	.35	.20	.11
(146)	Bubba Phillips	.25	.13	.08
(147)	Bill Pierce	.35	.20	.11
(148)	Jim Piersall	.35	.20	.11
(149)	Vada Pinson	.50	.25	.15
(150)	Johnny Podres	.35	.20	.11
(151)	Wally Post	.25	.13	.08
(152)	Vic Powers (Power)	.25	.13	.08
(153)	Pedro Ramos	.25	.13	.08
(154)	Robin Roberts	1.50	.70	.45
(155)	Brooks Robinson	3.50	1.75	1.00
(156)	Frank Robinson	3.00	1.50	.90
(157)	Ed Roebuck	.25	.13	.08
(158)	John Romano	.25	.13	.08
(159)	John Roseboro	.30	.15	.09
(160)	Pete Runnels	.30	.15	.09
(161)	Ed Sadowski	.25	.13	.08
(162)	Jack Sanford	.25	.13	.08
(163)	Ron Santo	.35	.20	.11
(164)	Ray Semproch	.25	.13	.08
(165)	Bobby Shantz	.50	.25	.15
(166)	Bob Shaw	.25	.13	.08
(167)	Larry Sherry	.25	.13	.08
(168)	Norm Siebern	.25	.13	.08
(169)	Roy Sievers	.35	.20	.11

		NR MT	EX	VG
(170)	Curt Simmons	.30	.15	.09
(171)	Dave Sisler	.25	.13	.08
(172)	Bob Skinner	.25	.13	.08
(173)	Al Smith	.25	.13	.08
(174)	Hal Smith	.25	.13	.08
(175)	Hal Smith	.25	.13	.08
(176)	Duke Snider	3.50	1.75	1.00
(177)	Warren Spahn	2.50	1.25	.70
(178)	Daryl Spencer	.25	.13	.08
(179)	Bill Stafford	.35	.20	.11
(180)	Jerry Staley	.25	.13	.08
(181)	Gene Stephens	.25	.13	.08
(182)	Chuck Stobbs	.25	.13	.08
(183)	Dick Stuart	.30	.15	.09
(184)	Willie Tasby	.25	.13	.08
(185)	Sammy Taylor	.25	.13	.08
(186)	Tony Taylor	.25	.13	.08
(187)	Johnny Temple	.25	.13	.08
(188)	Marv Throneberry	.50	.25	.15
(189)	Gus Triandos	.30	.15	.09
(190)	Bob Turley	.35	.20	.11
(191)	Bill Tuttle	.25	.13	.08
(192)	Zorro Versalles	.25	.13	.08
(193)	Bill Virdon	.35	.20	.11
(194)	Lee Walls	.25	.13	.08
(195)	Vic Wertz	.30	.15	.09
(196)	Pete Whisenant	.25	.13	.08
(197)	Bill White	.30	.15	.09
(198)	Hoyt Wilhelm	1.50	.70	.45
(199)	Bob Will	.25	.13	.08
(200)	Carl Willey	.25	.13	.08
(201)	Billy Williams	1.50	.70	.45
(202)	Dick Williams	.50	.25	.15
(203)	Stan Williams	.25	.13	.08
(204)	Gene Woodling	.35	.20	.11
(205)	Early Wynn	1.50	.70	.45
(206)	Carl Yastrzemski	12.00	6.00	3.50
(207)	Eddie Yost	.25	.13	.08

1962 Topps

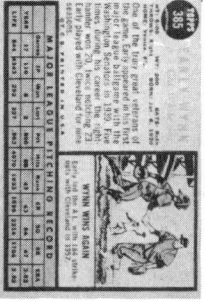

The 1962 Topps set established another plateau for set size with 598 cards. The 2½" by 3½" cards feature a photograph set against a woodgrain background. The lower righthand corner has been made to look like it is curling away. Many established specialty cards dot the set including statistical leaders, multi-player cards, team cards, checklists, World Series cards and All-Stars. Of note is that 1962 was the first year of the multi-player rookie card. There is a 9-card "In Action" subset and a 10-card run of special Babe Ruth cards. Photo variations of several cards in the 2nd Series (#'s 110-196) exist. All cards in the 2nd Series can be found with two distinct printing variations, an early printing with the cards containing a very noticeable greenish tint having been corrected to clear photos in subsequent print runs. The complete set price in the checklist that follows does not include the higher priced variations.

	NR MT	EX	VG
Complete Set:	3200.00	1000.00	550.00
Common Player: 1-370	1.00	.45	.25
Common Player: 371-522	1.75	.80	.45
Common Player: 523-598	7.00	3.25	1.75

		NR MT	EX	VG
1	Roger Maris	100.00	13.50	7.50
2	Jim Brosnan	1.75	.60	.30
3	Pete Runnels	1.25	.60	.30
4	John DeMerit	1.75	.80	.45
5	Sandy Koufax	40.00	18.00	10.00
6	Marv Breeding	1.00	.45	.25
7	Frank Thomas	1.75	.80	.45
8	Ray Herbert	1.00	.45	.25
9	Jim Davenport	1.00	.45	.25
10	Bob Clemente	25.00	11.00	6.25
11	Tom Morgan	1.00	.45	.25
12	Harry Craft	1.00	.45	.25
13	Dick Howser	1.75	.80	.45
14	Bill White	1.25	.60	.30
15	Dick Donovan	1.00	.45	.25
16	Darrell Johnson	1.00	.45	.25
17	Johnny Callison	1.75	.80	.45
18	Managers' Dream (Mickey Mantle, Willie Mays)	45.00	18.00	9.00
19	Ray Washburn	1.25	.60	.30
20	Rocky Colavito	3.00	1.25	.70
21	Jim Kaat	3.00	1.25	.70
22a	Checklist 1-88 (numbers 121 - 176 on back)	5.00	2.25	1.25
22b	Checklist 1-88 (numbers 33-88 on back)	4.00	1.75	1.00
23	Norm Larker	1.00	.45	.25
24	Tigers Team	3.50	1.50	.90
25	Ernie Banks	12.00	5.50	3.00
26	Chris Cannizzaro	1.75	.80	.45
27	Chuck Cottier	1.00	.45	.25
28	Minnie Minoso	2.50	1.25	.60
29	Casey Stengel	12.00	5.50	3.00
30	Ed Mathews	10.00	4.50	2.50
31	Tom Tresh	6.00	2.75	1.50
32	John Roseboro	1.75	.80	.45
33	Don Larsen	1.50	.70	.40
34	Johnny Temple	1.00	.45	.25
35	Don Schwall	1.75	.80	.45
36	Don Leppert	1.00	.45	.25
37	Tribe Hill Trio (Barry Latman, Jim Perry, Dick Stigman)	1.75	.80	.45
38	Gene Stephens	1.00	.45	.25
39	Joe Koppe	1.00	.45	.25
40	Orlando Cepeda	5.00	2.25	1.25
41	Cliff Cook	1.00	.45	.25
42	Jim King	1.00	.45	.25
43	Dodgers Team	3.50	1.50	.90
44	Don Taussig	1.00	.45	.25
45	Brooks Robinson	15.00	6.75	3.75
46	Jack Baldschun	1.25	.60	.30
47	Bob Will	1.00	.45	.25
48	Ralph Terry	2.50	1.25	.60
49	Hal Jones	1.00	.45	.25
50	Stan Musial	35.00	15.50	8.75
51	A.L. Batting Leaders (Norm Cash, Elston Howard, Al Kaline, Jim Piersall)	3.00	1.25	.70
52	N.L. Batting Leaders (Ken Boyer, Bob Clemente, Wally Moon, Vada Pinson)	3.50	1.50	.90
53	A.L. Home Run Leaders (Jim Gentile, Harmon Killebrew, Mickey Mantle, Roger Maris)	10.00	4.50	2.50
54	N.L. Home Run Leaders (Orlando Cepeda, Willie Mays, Frank Robinson)	3.50	1.50	.90
55	A.L. E.R.A. Leaders (Dick Donovan, Don Mossi, Milt Pappas, Bill Stafford)	2.50	1.25	.60
56	N.L. E.R.A. Leaders (Mike McCormick, Jim O'Toole, Curt Simmons, Warren Spahn)	3.00	1.25	.70
57	A.L. Win Leaders (Steve Barber, Jim Bunning, Whitey Ford, Frank Lary)	3.00	1.25	.70
58	N.L. Win Leaders (Joe Jay, Jim O'Toole, Warren Spahn)	3.00	1.25	.70
59	A.L. Strikeout Leaders (Jim Bunning, Whitey Ford, Camilo Pascual, Juan Pizzaro)	3.00	1.25	.70
60	N.L. Strikeout Leaders (Don Drysdale, Sandy Koufax, Jim O'Toole, Stan Williams)	3.50	1.50	.90
61	Cardinals Team	2.50	1.25	.60
62	Steve Boros	1.25	.60	.30
63	Tony Cloninger	2.00	.90	.50
64	Russ Snyder	1.00	.45	.25
65	Bobby Richardson	5.00	2.25	1.25
66	Cuno Barragan (Barragan)	1.00	.45	.25
67	Harvey Haddix	1.50	.70	.40
68	Ken L. Hunt	1.00	.45	.25
69	Phil Ortega	1.00	.45	.25
70	Harmon Killebrew	12.00	5.50	3.00
71	Dick LeMay	1.00	.45	.25

		NR MT	EX	VG
72	Bob's Pupils (Steve Boros, Bob Scheffing, Jake Wood)	1.50	.70	.40
73	Nellie Fox	7.00	3.25	1.75
74	Bob Lillis	1.00	.45	.25
75	Milt Pappas	1.75	.80	.45
76	Howie Bedell	1.00	.45	.25
77	Tony Taylor	1.00	.45	.25
78	Gene Green	1.00	.45	.25
79	Ed Hobaugh	1.00	.45	.25
80	Vada Pinson	2.50	1.25	.60
81	Jim Pagliaroni	1.00	.45	.25
82	Deron Johnson	1.00	.45	.25
83	Larry Jackson	1.00	.45	.25
84	Lenny Green	1.00	.45	.25
85	Gil Hodges	10.00	4.50	2.50
86	Donn Clendenon	1.75	.80	.45
87	Mike Roarke	1.00	.45	.25
88	Ralph Houk	2.50	1.25	.60
89	Barney Schultz	1.00	.45	.25
90	Jim Piersall	2.00	.90	.50
91	J.C. Martin	1.00	.45	.25
92	Sam Jones	1.00	.45	.25
93	John Blanchard	2.00	.90	.50
94	Jay Hook	1.75	.80	.45
95	Don Hoak	1.75	.80	.45
96	Eli Grba	1.00	.45	.25
97	Tito Francona	1.25	.60	.30
98	Checklist 89-176	4.00	1.75	1.00
99	John Powell	8.00	3.50	2.00
100	Warren Spahn	12.00	5.50	3.00
101	Carroll Hardy	1.00	.45	.25
102	Al Schroll	1.00	.45	.25
103	Don Blasingame	1.00	.45	.25
104	Ted Savage	1.00	.45	.25
105	Don Mossi	1.25	.60	.30
106	Carl Sawatski	1.00	.45	.25
107	Mike McCormick	1.25	.60	.30
108	Willie Davis	2.50	1.25	.60
109	Bob Shaw	1.00	.45	.25
110	Bill Skowron	5.00	2.25	1.25
111	Dallas Green	1.75	.80	.45
112	Hank Foiles	1.00	.45	.25
113	White Sox Team	2.50	1.25	.60
114	Howie Koplitz	1.00	.45	.25
115	Bob Skinner	1.25	.60	.30
116	Herb Score	2.00	.90	.50
117	Gary Geiger	1.00	.45	.25
118	Julian Javier	1.25	.60	.30
119	Danny Murphy	1.00	.45	.25
120	Bob Purkey	1.00	.45	.25
121	Billy Hitchcock	1.00	.45	.25
122	Norm Bass	1.00	.45	.25
123	Mike de la Hoz	1.00	.45	.25
124	Bill Pleis	1.00	.45	.25
125	Gene Woodling	1.50	.70	.40
126	Al Cicotte	1.00	.45	.25
127	Pride of the A's (Hank Bauer, Jerry Lumpe, Norm Siebern)	1.75	.80	.45
128	Art Fowler	1.00	.45	.25
129a	Lee Walls (facing left)	8.00	3.50	2.00
129b	Lee Walls (facing right)	1.00	.45	.25
130	Frank Bolling	1.00	.45	.25
131	Pete Richert	1.50	.70	.40
132a	Angels Team (with inset photos)	8.00	3.50	2.00
132b	Angels Team (without inset photos)	3.00	1.25	.70
133	Felipe Alou	1.75	.80	.45
134a	Billy Hoeft (green sky in background)	8.00	3.50	2.00
134b	Billy Hoeft (blue sky in background)	1.00	.45	.25
135	Babe As A Boy	7.00	3.25	1.75
136	Babe Joins Yanks	7.00	3.25	1.75
137	Babe and Mgr. Huggins	7.00	3.25	1.75
138	The Famous Slugger	7.00	3.25	1.75
139a	Hal Reniff (pitching)	35.00	15.50	8.75
139b	Hal Reniff (portrait)	9.00	4.00	2.25
139c	Babe Hits 60	7.00	3.25	1.75
140	Gehrig and Ruth	9.00	4.00	2.25
141	Twilight Years	7.00	3.25	1.75
142	Coaching for the Dodgers	7.00	3.25	1.75
143	Greatest Sports Hero	7.00	3.25	1.75
144	Farewell Speech	7.00	3.25	1.75
145	Barry Latman	1.00	.45	.25
146	Don Demeter	1.00	.45	.25
147a	Bill Kunkel (pitching)	8.00	3.50	2.00
147b	Bill Kunkel (portrait)	1.00	.45	.25
148	Wally Post	1.00	.45	.25
149	Bob Duliba	1.00	.45	.25
150	Al Kaline	12.00	5.50	3.00
151	Johnny Klippstein	1.00	.45	.25

#	Player	NR MT	EX	VG
152	Mickey Vernon	1.25	.60	.30
153	Pumpsie Green	1.00	.45	.25
154	Lee Thomas	1.00	.45	.25
155	Stu Miller	1.00	.45	.25
156	Merritt Ranew	1.00	.45	.25
157	Wes Covington	1.00	.45	.25
158	Braves Team	3.00	1.25	.70
159	Hal Reniff	2.00	.90	.50
160	Dick Stuart	1.25	.60	.30
161	Frank Baumann	1.00	.45	.25
162	Sammy Drake	1.75	.80	.45
163	Hot Corner Guardians (Cletis Boyer, Billy Gardner)	3.00	1.25	.70
164	Hal Naragon	1.00	.45	.25
165	Jackie Brandt	1.00	.45	.25
166	Don Lee	1.00	.45	.25
167	Tim McCarver	6.00	2.75	1.50
168	Leo Posada	1.00	.45	.25
169	Bob Cerv	2.00	.90	.50
170	Ron Santo	3.50	1.50	.90
171	Dave Sisler	1.00	.45	.25
172	Fred Hutchinson	1.25	.60	.30
173	Chico Fernandez	1.00	.45	.25
174a	Carl Willey (with cap)	8.00	3.50	2.00
174b	Carl Willey (no cap)	1.00	.45	.25
175	Frank Howard	3.00	1.25	.70
176a	Eddie Yost (batting)	7.00	3.25	1.75
176b	Eddie Yost (portrait)	1.25	.60	.30
177	Bobby Shantz	1.50	.70	.40
178	Camilo Carreon	1.00	.45	.25
179	Tom Sturdivant	1.00	.45	.25
180	Bob Allison	1.50	.70	.40
181	Paul Brown	1.00	.45	.25
182	Bob Nieman	1.00	.45	.25
183	Roger Craig	3.00	1.25	.70
184	Haywood Sullivan	1.25	.60	.30
185	Roland Sheldon	2.00	.90	.50
186	Mack Jones	1.25	.60	.30
187	Gene Conley	1.25	.60	.30
188	Chuck Hiller	1.00	.45	.25
189	Dick Hall	1.00	.45	.25
190a	Wally Moon (with cap)	9.00	4.00	2.25
190b	Wally Moon (no cap)	1.50	.70	.40
191	Jim Brewer	1.00	.45	.25
192a	Checklist 177-264 (192 is Check List, 3)	6.00	2.75	1.50
192b	Checklist 177-264 (192 is Check List 3)	4.00	1.75	1.00
193	Eddie Kasko	1.00	.45	.25
194	Dean Chance	3.00	1.25	.70
195	Joe Cunningham	1.25	.60	.30
196	Terry Fox	1.00	.45	.25
197	Daryl Spencer	1.00	.45	.25
198	Johnny Keane	1.25	.60	.30
199	Gaylord Perry	50.00	22.00	12.50
200	Mickey Mantle	300.00	120.00	60.00
201	Ike Delock	1.00	.45	.25
202	Carl Warwick	1.00	.45	.25
203	Jack Fisher	1.00	.45	.25
204	Johnny Weekly	1.00	.45	.25
205	Gene Freese	1.00	.45	.25
206	Senators Team	2.50	1.25	.60
207	Pete Burnside	1.00	.45	.25
208	Billy Martin	4.00	1.75	1.00
209	Jim Fregosi	5.00	2.25	1.25
210	Roy Face	1.75	.80	.45
211	Midway Masters (Frank Bolling, Roy McMillan)	1.50	.70	.40
212	Jim Owens	1.00	.45	.25
213	Richie Ashburn	5.00	2.25	1.25
214	Dom Zanni	1.00	.45	.25
215	Woody Held	1.00	.45	.25
216	Ron Kline	1.00	.45	.25
217	Walt Alston	4.00	1.75	1.00
218	Joe Torre	10.00	4.50	2.50
219	Al Downing	4.00	1.75	1.00
220	Roy Sievers	1.50	.70	.40
221	Bill Short	1.00	.45	.25
222	Jerry Zimmerman	1.00	.45	.25
223	Alex Grammas	1.00	.45	.25
224	Don Rudolph	1.00	.45	.25
225	Frank Malzone	1.25	.60	.30
226	Giants Team	4.00	1.75	1.00
227	Bobby Tiefenauer	1.00	.45	.25
228	Dale Long	1.25	.60	.30
229	Jesus McFarlane	1.00	.45	.25
230	Camlio Pascual	1.50	.70	.40
231	Ernie Bowman	1.00	.45	.25
232	World Series Game 1 (Yanks Win Opener)	3.00	1.25	.70
233	World Series Game 2 (Jay Ties It Up)	3.00	1.25	.70
234	World Series Game 3 (Maris Wins It In The 9th)	8.00	3.50	2.00
235	World Series Game 4 (Ford Sets New Mark)	7.00	3.25	1.75
236	World Series Game 5 (Yanks Crush Reds In Finale)	3.00	1.25	.70
237	World Series Summary (The Winners Celebrate)	3.00	1.25	.70
238	Norm Sherry	1.00	.45	.25
239	Cecil Butler	1.00	.45	.25
240	George Altman	1.00	.45	.25
241	Johnny Kucks	1.00	.45	.25
242	Mel McGaha	1.00	.45	.25
243	Robin Roberts	10.00	4.50	2.50
244	Don Gile	1.00	.45	.25
245	Ron Hansen	1.00	.45	.25
246	Art Ditmar	1.00	.45	.25
247	Joe Pignatano	1.00	.45	.25
248	Bob Aspromonte	1.00	.45	.25
249	Ed Keegan	1.00	.45	.25
250	Norm Cash	3.00	1.25	.70
251	Yankees Team	8.00	3.50	2.00
252	Earl Francis	1.00	.45	.25
253	Harry Chiti	1.00	.45	.25
254	Gordon Windhorn	1.00	.45	.25
255	Juan Pizarro	1.00	.45	.25
256	Elio Chacon	1.75	.80	.45
257	Jack Spring	1.00	.45	.25
258	Marty Keough	1.00	.45	.25
259	Lou Klimchock	1.00	.45	.25
260	Bill Pierce	1.75	.80	.45
261	George Alusik	1.00	.45	.25
262	Bob Schmidt	1.00	.45	.25
263	The Right Pitch (Joe Jay, Bob Purkey, Jim Turner)	1.50	.70	.40
264	Dick Ellsworth	1.00	.45	.25
265	Joe Adcock	2.00	.90	.50
266	John Anderson	1.00	.45	.25
267	Dan Dobbek	1.00	.45	.25
268	Ken McBride	1.00	.45	.25
269	Bob Oldis	1.00	.45	.25
270	Dick Groat	2.00	.90	.50
271	Ray Rippelmeyer	1.00	.45	.25
272	Earl Robinson	1.00	.45	.25
273	Gary Bell	1.00	.45	.25
274	Sammy Taylor	1.00	.45	.25
275	Norm Siebern	1.25	.60	.30
276	Hal Kostad	1.00	.45	.25
277	Checklist 265-352	4.00	1.75	1.00
278	Ken Johnson	1.00	.45	.25
279	Hobie Landrith	1.75	.80	.45
280	Johnny Podres	2.50	1.25	.60
281	Jake Gibbs	2.25	1.00	.60
282	Dave Hillman	1.00	.45	.25
283	Charlie Smith	1.00	.45	.25
284	Ruben Amaro	1.00	.45	.25
285	Curt Simmons	1.75	.80	.45
286	Al Lopez	3.00	1.25	.70
287	George Witt	1.00	.45	.25
288	Billy Williams	10.00	4.50	2.50
289	Mike Krsnich	1.00	.45	.25
290	Jim Gentile	1.25	.60	.30
291	Hal Stowe	2.00	.90	.50
292	Jerry Kindall	1.00	.45	.25
293	Bob Miller	1.75	.80	.45
294	Phillies Team	2.50	1.25	.60
295	Vern Law	1.75	.80	.45
296	Ken Hamlin	1.00	.45	.25
297	Ron Perranoski	1.25	.60	.30
298	Bill Tuttle	1.00	.45	.25
299	Don Wert	1.25	.60	.30
300	Willie Mays	55.00	25.00	13.50
301	Galen Cisco	1.00	.45	.25
302	John Edwards	1.25	.60	.30
303	Frank Torre	1.00	.45	.25
304	Dick Farrell	1.00	.45	.25
305	Jerry Lumpe	1.00	.45	.25
306	Redbird Rippers (Larry Jackson, Lindy McDaniel)	1.50	.70	.40
307	Jim Grant	1.00	.45	.25
308	Neil Chrisley	1.75	.80	.45
309	Moe Morhardt	1.00	.45	.25
310	Whitey Ford	15.00	6.75	3.75
311	Kubek Makes The Double Play	3.50	1.50	.90
312	Spahn Shows No-Hit Form	6.00	2.75	1.50
313	Maris Blasts 61st	10.00	4.50	2.50
314	Colavito's Power	3.50	1.50	.90
315	Ford Tosses A Curve	6.00	2.75	1.50
316	Killebrew Sends One Into Orbit	5.00	2.25	1.25

		NR MT	EX	VG
317	Musial Plays 21st Season	8.00	3.50	2.00
318	The Switch Hitter Connects (Mickey Mantle)	25.00	10.00	5.00
319	McCormick Shows His Stuff	1.50	.70	.40
320	Hank Aaron	60.00	27.00	15.00
321	Lee Stange	1.00	.45	.25
322	Al Dark	1.50	.70	.40
323	Don Landrum	1.00	.45	.25
324	Joe McClain	1.00	.45	.25
325	Luis Aparicio	10.00	4.50	2.50
326	Tom Parsons	1.00	.45	.25
327	Ozzie Virgil	1.00	.45	.25
328	Ken Walters	1.00	.45	.25
329	Bob Bolin	1.00	.45	.25
330	Johnny Romano	1.00	.45	.25
331	Moe Drabowsky	1.00	.45	.25
332	Don Buddin	1.00	.45	.25
333	Frank Cipriani	1.00	.45	.25
334	Red Sox Team	3.50	1.50	.90
335	Bill Bruton	1.00	.45	.25
336	Billy Muffett	1.00	.45	.25
337	Jim Marshall	1.75	.80	.45
338	Billy Gardner	2.25	1.00	.60
339	Jose Valdivielso	1.00	.45	.25
340	Don Drysdale	12.00	5.50	3.00
341	Mike Hershberger	1.00	.45	.25
342	Ed Rakow	1.00	.45	.25
343	Albie Pearson	1.00	.45	.25
344	Ed Bauta	1.00	.45	.25
345	Chuck Schilling	1.00	.45	.25
346	Jack Kralick	1.00	.45	.25
347	Chuck Hinton	1.00	.45	.25
348	Larry Burright	1.00	.45	.25
349	Paul Foytack	1.00	.45	.25
350	Frank Robinson	15.00	6.75	3.75
351	Braves' Backstops (Del Crandall, Joe Torre)	3.00	1.25	.70
352	Frank Sullivan	1.00	.45	.25
353	Bill Mazeroski	3.50	1.50	.90
354	Roman Mejias	1.00	.45	.25
355	Steve Barber	1.00	.45	.25
356	Tom Haller	1.75	.80	.45
357	Jerry Walker	1.00	.45	.25
358	Tommy Davis	2.50	1.25	.60
359	Bobby Locke	1.00	.45	.25
360	Yogi Berra	20.00	9.00	5.00
361	Bob Hendley	1.00	.45	.25
362	Ty Cline	1.00	.45	.25
363	Bob Roselli	1.00	.45	.25
364	Ken Hunt	1.00	.45	.25
365	Charley Neal	1.75	.80	.45
366	Phil Regan	1.00	.45	.25
367	Checklist 353-429	4.00	1.75	1.00
368	Bob Tillman	1.00	.45	.25
369	Ted Bowsfield	1.00	.45	.25
370	Ken Boyer	4.00	1.75	1.00
371	Earl Battey	2.00	.90	.50
372	Jack Curtis	1.75	.80	.45
373	Al Heist	1.75	.80	.45
374	Gene Mauch	2.50	1.25	.60
375	Ron Fairly	2.50	1.25	.60
376	Bud Daley	2.75	1.25	.70
377	Johnny Orsino	1.75	.80	.45
378	Bennie Daniels	1.75	.80	.45
379	Chuck Essegian	1.75	.80	.45
380	Lou Burdette	4.00	1.75	1.00
381	Chico Cardenas	2.25	1.00	.60
382	Dick Williams	3.50	1.50	.90
383	Ray Sadecki	2.00	.90	.50
384	Athletics Team	3.50	1.50	.90
385	Early Wynn	10.00	4.50	2.50
386	Don Mincher	2.25	1.00	.60
387	Lou Brock	60.00	27.00	15.00
388	Ryne Duren	2.50	1.25	.60
389	Smoky Burgess	3.00	1.25	.70
390	Orlando Cepeda AS	5.00	2.25	1.25
391	Bill Mazeroski AS	3.50	1.50	.90
392	Ken Boyer AS	3.50	1.50	.90
393	Roy McMillan AS	2.50	1.25	.60
394	Hank Aaron AS	20.00	9.00	5.00
395	Willie Mays AS	20.00	9.00	5.00
396	Frank Robinson AS	12.00	5.50	3.00
397	John Roseboro AS	2.50	1.25	.60
398	Don Drysdale AS	10.00	4.50	2.50
399	Warren Spahn AS	10.00	4.50	2.50
400	Elston Howard	5.00	2.25	1.25
401	AL & NL Homer Kings (Orlando Cepeda, Roger Maris)	12.00	5.50	3.00
402	Gino Cimoli	1.75	.80	.45
403	Chet Nichols	1.75	.80	.45
404	Tim Harkness	1.75	.80	.45

		NR MT	EX	VG
405	Jim Perry	2.75	1.25	.70
406	Bob Taylor	1.75	.80	.45
407	Hank Aguirre	1.75	.80	.45
408	Gus Bell	2.50	1.25	.60
409	Pirates Team	3.50	1.50	.90
410	Al Smith	1.75	.80	.45
411	Danny O'Connell	1.75	.80	.45
412	Charlie James	1.75	.80	.45
413	Matty Alou	3.50	1.50	.90
414	Joe Gaines	1.75	.80	.45
415	Bill Virdon	3.50	1.50	.90
416	Bob Scheffing	1.75	.80	.45
417	Joe Azcue	1.75	.80	.45
418	Andy Carey	1.75	.80	.45
419	Bob Bruce	1.75	.80	.45
420	Gus Triandos	2.00	.90	.50
421	Ken MacKenzie	2.50	1.25	.60
422	Steve Bilko	1.75	.80	.45
423	Rival League Relief Aces (Roy Face, Hoyt Wilhelm)	5.00	2.25	1.25
424	Al McBean	1.75	.80	.45
425	Carl Yastrzemski	125.00	56.00	31.00
426	Bob Farley	1.75	.80	.45
427	Jake Wood	1.75	.80	.45
428	Joe Hicks	1.75	.80	.45
429	Bill O'Dell	1.75	.80	.45
430	Tony Kubek	6.00	2.75	1.50
431	Bob Rodgers	3.00	1.25	.70
432	Jim Pendleton	1.75	.80	.45
433	Jim Archer	1.75	.80	.45
434	Clay Dalrymple	1.75	.80	.45
435	Larry Sherry	1.75	.80	.45
436	Felix Mantilla	2.50	1.25	.60
437	Ray Moore	1.75	.80	.45
438	Dick Brown	1.75	.80	.45
439	Jerry Buchek	1.75	.80	.45
440	Joe Jay	1.75	.80	.45
441	Checklist 430-506	5.00	2.25	1.25
442	Wes Stock	1.75	.80	.45
443	Del Crandall	3.50	1.50	.90
444	Ted Wills	1.75	.80	.45
445	Vic Power	1.75	.80	.45
446	Don Elston	1.75	.80	.45
447	Willie Kirkland	1.75	.80	.45
448	Joe Gibbon	1.75	.80	.45
449	Jerry Adair	1.75	.80	.45
450	Jim O'Toole	1.75	.80	.45
451	Jose Tartabull	2.25	1.00	.60
452	Earl Averill	1.75	.80	.45
453	Cal McLish	1.75	.80	.45
454	Floyd Robinson	1.75	.80	.45
455	Luis Arroyo	3.00	1.25	.70
456	Joe Amalfitano	1.75	.80	.45
457	Lou Clinton	1.75	.80	.45
458a	Bob Buhl ("M" on cap)	2.50	1.25	.60
458b	Bob Buhl (plain cap)	25.00	11.00	6.25
459	Ed Bailey	1.75	.80	.45
460	Jim Bunning	7.00	3.25	1.75
461	Ken Hubbs	6.00	2.75	1.50
462a	Willie Tasby ("W" on cap)	1.75	.80	.45
462b	Willie Tasby (plain cap)	25.00	11.00	6.25
463	Hank Bauer	3.00	1.25	.70
464	Al Jackson	3.50	1.50	.90
465	Reds Team	4.00	1.75	1.00
466	Norm Cash AS	4.00	1.75	1.00
467	Chuck Schilling AS	3.00	1.25	.70
468	Brooks Robinson AS	12.00	5.50	3.00
469	Luis Aparicio AS	8.00	3.50	2.00
470	Al Kaline AS	10.00	4.50	2.50
471	Mickey Mantle AS	35.00	14.00	7.00
472	Rocky Colavito AS	5.00	2.25	1.25
473	Elston Howard AS	5.00	2.25	1.25
474	Frank Lary AS	3.00	1.25	.70
475	Whitey Ford AS	10.00	4.50	2.50
476	Orioles Team	3.50	1.50	.90
477	Andre Rodgers	1.75	.80	.45
478	Don Zimmer	3.50	1.50	.90
479	Joel Horlen	2.75	1.25	.70
480	Harvey Kuenn	3.50	1.50	.90
481	Vic Wertz	2.50	1.25	.60
482	Sam Mele	1.75	.80	.45
483	Don McMahon	1.75	.80	.45
484	Dick Schofield	1.75	.80	.45
485	Pedro Ramos	1.75	.80	.45
486	Jim Gilliam	4.00	1.75	1.00
487	Jerry Lynch	1.75	.80	.45
488	Hal Brown	1.75	.80	.45
489	Julio Gotay	1.75	.80	.45
490	Clete Boyer	4.00	1.75	1.00
491	Leon Wagner	1.75	.80	.45
492	Hal Smith	1.75	.80	.45

		NR MT	EX	VG
493	Danny McDevitt	1.75	.80	.45
494	Sammy White	1.75	.80	.45
495	Don Cardwell	1.75	.80	.45
496	Wayne Causey	1.75	.80	.45
497	Ed Bouchee	2.50	1.25	.60
498	Jim Donohue	1.75	.80	.45
499	Zoilo Versalles	2.25	1.00	.60
500	Duke Snider	20.00	9.00	5.00
501	Claude Osteen	2.50	1.25	.60
502	Hector Lopez	3.00	1.25	.70
503	Danny Murtaugh	2.00	.90	.50
504	Eddie Bressoud	1.75	.80	.45
505	Juan Marichal	20.00	9.00	5.00
506	Charley Maxwell	1.75	.80	.45
507	Ernie Broglio	1.75	.80	.45
508	Gordy Coleman	1.75	.80	.45
509	Dave Giusti	2.25	1.00	.60
510	Jim Lemon	1.75	.80	.45
511	Bubba Phillips	1.75	.80	.45
512	Mike Fornieles	1.75	.80	.45
513	Whitey Herzog	4.00	1.75	1.00
514	Sherm Lollar	2.00	.90	.50
515	Stan Williams	1.75	.80	.45
516	Checklist 507-598	6.00	2.75	1.50
517	Dave Wickersham	1.75	.80	.45
518	Lee Maye	1.75	.80	.45
519	Bob Johnson	1.75	.80	.45
520	Bob Friend	3.00	1.25	.70
521	Jacke Davis	1.75	.80	.45
522	Lindy McDaniel	1.75	.80	.45
523	Russ Nixon	7.00	3.25	1.75
524	Howie Nunn	7.00	3.25	1.75
525	George Thomas	7.00	3.25	1.75
526	Hal Woodeshick	7.00	3.25	1.75
527	Dick McAuliffe	9.00	4.00	2.25
528	Turk Lown	7.00	3.25	1.75
529	John Schaive	7.00	3.25	1.75
530	Bob Gibson	55.00	25.00	13.50
531	Bobby G. Smith	7.00	3.25	1.75
532	Dick Stigman	7.00	3.25	1.75
533	Charley Lau	8.00	3.50	2.00
534	Tony Gonzalez	7.00	3.25	1.75
535	Ed Roebuck	7.00	3.25	1.75
536	Dick Gernert	7.00	3.25	1.75
537	Indians Team	9.00	4.00	2.25
538	Jack Sanford	7.00	3.25	1.75
539	Billy Moran	7.00	3.25	1.75
540	Jim Landis	7.00	3.25	1.75
541	Don Nottebart	7.00	3.25	1.75
542	Dave Philley	8.00	3.50	2.00
543	Bob Allen	7.00	3.25	1.75
544	Willie McCovey	55.00	25.00	13.50
545	Hoyt Wilhelm	25.00	11.00	6.25
546	Moe Thacker	7.00	3.25	1.75
547	Don Ferrarese	7.00	3.25	1.75
548	Bobby Del Greco	7.00	3.25	1.75
549	Bill Rigney	7.00	3.25	1.75
550	Art Mahaffey	7.00	3.25	1.75
551	Harry Bright	7.00	3.25	1.75
552	Cubs Team	12.00	5.50	3.00
553	Jim Coates	10.00	4.50	2.50
554	Bubba Morton	7.00	3.25	1.75
555	John Buzhardt	7.00	3.25	1.75
556	Al Spangler	7.00	3.25	1.75
557	Bob Anderson	7.00	3.25	1.75
558	John Goryl	7.00	3.25	1.75
559	Mike Higgins	7.00	3.25	1.75
560	Chuck Estrada	7.00	3.25	1.75
561	Gene Oliver	7.00	3.25	1.75
562	Bill Henry	7.00	3.25	1.75
563	Ken Aspromonte	7.00	3.25	1.75
564	Bob Grim	7.00	3.25	1.75
565	Jose Pagan	7.00	3.25	1.75
566	Marty Kutyna	7.00	3.25	1.75
567	Tracy Stallard	7.00	3.25	1.75
568	Jim Golden	7.00	3.25	1.75
569	Ed Sadowski	7.00	3.25	1.75
570	Bill Stafford	10.00	4.50	2.50
571	Billy Klaus	7.00	3.25	1.75
572	Bob Miller	8.00	3.50	2.00
573	Johnny Logan	8.00	3.50	2.00
574	Dean Stone	7.00	3.25	1.75
575	Red Schoendienst	12.00	5.50	3.00
576	Russ Kemmerer	7.00	3.25	1.75
577	Dave Nicholson	7.00	3.25	1.75
578	Jim Duffalo	7.00	3.25	1.75
579	Jim Schaffer	7.00	3.25	1.75
580	Bill Monbouquette	8.00	3.50	2.00
581	Mel Roach	7.00	3.25	1.75
582	Ron Piche	7.00	3.25	1.75
583	Larry Osborne	7.00	3.25	1.75

		NR MT	EX	VG
584	Twins Team	12.00	5.50	3.00
585	Glen Hobbie	7.00	3.25	1.75
586	Sammy Esposito	7.00	3.25	1.75
587	Frank Funk	7.00	3.25	1.75
588	Birdie Tebbetts	7.00	3.25	1.75
589	Bob Turley	15.00	6.75	3.75
590	Curt Flood	12.00	5.50	3.00
591	Rookie Parade Pitchers (Sam McDowell, Ron Nischwitz, Art Quirk, Dick Radatz, Ron Taylor)	20.00	9.00	5.00
592	Rookie Parade Pitchers (Bo Belinsky, Joe Bonikowski, Jim Bouton, Dan Pfister, Dave Stenhouse)	25.00	11.00	6.25
593	Rookie Parade Pitchers (Craig Anderson, Jack Hamilton, Jack Lamabe, Bob Moorhead, Bob Veale)	15.00	6.75	3.75
594	Rookie Parade Catchers (Doug Camilli, Doc Edwards, Don Pavletich, Ken Retzer, Bob Uecker)	90.00	36.00	23.00
595	Rookie Parade Infielders (Ed Charles, Marlin Coughtry, Bob Sadowski, Felix Torres)	15.00	6.75	3.75
596	Rookie Parade Infielders (Bernie Allen, Phil Linz, Joe Pepitone, Rich Rollins)	25.00	11.00	6.25
597	Rookie Parade Infielders (Rod Kanehl, Jim McKnight, Denis Menke, Amado Samuel)	15.00	6.75	3.75
598	Rookie Parade Outfielders (Howie Goss, Jim Hickman, Manny Jimenez, Al Luplow, Ed Olivares)	25.00	10.00	5.00

1962 Topps Baseball Bucks

Issued in their own 1¢ package, the 1962 Topps "Baseball Bucks" were another in the growing list of specialty Topps items. The 96 Baseball Bucks in the set measured 4⅛" by 1¾," and were designed to look vaguely like dollar bills. The center player portrait has a banner underneath with the player's name. His home park is shown on the right and there is some biographical information on the left. The back features a large denomination, with the player's league and team logo on either side.

		NR MT	EX	VG
Complete Set:		475.00	237.00	142.00
Common Player:		1.25	.60	.40
(1)	Hank Aaron	20.00	10.00	6.00
(2)	Joe Adcock	2.50	1.25	.70
(3)	George Altman	1.25	.60	.40
(4)	Jim Archer	1.25	.60	.40
(5)	Richie Ashburn	4.50	2.25	1.25
(6)	Ernie Banks	7.00	3.50	2.00
(7)	Earl Battey	2.00	1.00	.60
(8)	Gus Bell	2.00	1.00	.60
(9)	Yogi Berra	10.00	5.00	3.00
(10)	Ken Boyer	2.50	1.25	.70
(11)	Jackie Brandt	1.25	.60	.40
(12)	Jim Bunning	3.50	1.75	1.00
(13)	Lou Burdette	2.50	1.25	.70
(14)	Don Cardwell	1.25	.60	.40
(15)	Norm Cash	2.50	1.25	.70
(16)	Orlando Cepeda	4.00	2.00	1.25
(17)	Bob Clemente	18.00	9.00	5.50
(18)	Rocky Colavito	2.50	1.25	.70
(19)	Chuck Cottier	1.25	.60	.40
(20)	Roger Craig	2.00	1.00	.60

		NR MT	EX	VG
(21)	Bennie Daniels	1.25	.60	.40
(22)	Don Demeter	1.25	.60	.40
(23)	Don Drysdale	6.00	3.00	1.75
(24)	Chuck Estrada	1.25	.60	.40
(25)	Dick Farrell	1.25	.60	.40
(26)	Whitey Ford	7.00	3.50	2.00
(27)	Nellie Fox	4.00	2.00	1.25
(28)	Tito Francona	1.25	.60	.40
(29)	Bob Friend	2.00	1.00	.60
(30)	Jim Gentile	1.25	.60	.40
(31)	Dick Gernert	1.25	.60	.40
(32)	Lenny Green	1.25	.60	.40
(33)	Dick Groat	2.50	1.25	.70
(34)	Woody Held	1.25	.60	.40
(35)	Don Hoak	2.00	1.00	.60
(36)	Gil Hodges	6.00	3.00	1.75
(37)	Frank Howard	2.50	1.25	.70
(38)	Elston Howard	3.50	1.75	1.00
(39)	Dick Howser	2.50	1.25	.70
(40)	Ken Hunt	1.25	.60	.40
(41)	Larry Jackson	1.25	.60	.40
(42)	Joe Jay	3.50	1.75	1.00
(43)	Al Kaline	8.00	4.00	2.50
(44)	Harmon Killebrew	8.00	4.00	2.50
(45)	Sandy Koufax	13.00	6.50	4.00
(46)	Harvey Kuenn	3.50	1.75	1.00
(47)	Jim Landis	1.25	.60	.40
(48)	Norm Larker	1.25	.60	.40
(49)	Frank Lary	1.25	.60	.40
(50)	Jerry Lumpe	1.25	.60	.40
(51)	Art Mahaffey	1.25	.60	.40
(52)	Frank Malzone	1.25	.60	.40
(53)	Felix Mantilla	2.00	1.00	.60
(54)	Mickey Mantle	75.00	37.00	22.00
(55)	Roger Maris	8.00	4.00	2.50
(56)	Ed Mathews	6.00	3.00	1.75
(57)	Willie Mays	20.00	10.00	6.00
(58)	Ken McBride	1.25	.60	.40
(59)	Mike McCormick	1.25	.60	.40
(60)	Minnie Minoso	3.50	1.75	1.00
(61)	Wally Moon	2.00	1.00	.60
(62)	Stu Miller	1.25	.60	.40
(63)	Stan Musial	13.00	6.50	4.00
(64)	Danny O'Connell	1.25	.60	.40
(65)	Jim O'Toole	3.50	1.75	1.00
(66)	Camilo Pascual	2.00	1.00	.60
(67)	Jim Perry	2.50	1.25	.70
(68)	Jimmy Piersall	3.50	1.75	1.00
(69)	Vada Pinson	5.00	2.50	1.50
(70)	Juan Pizarro	1.25	.60	.40
(71)	Johnny Podres	2.50	1.25	.70
(72)	Vic Power	1.25	.60	.40
(73)	Bob Purkey	20.00	10.00	6.00
(74)	Pedro Ramos	1.25	.60	.40
(75)	Brooks Robinson	9.00	4.50	2.75
(76)	Floyd Robinson	1.25	.60	.40
(77)	Frank Robinson	7.00	3.50	2.00
(78)	Johnny Romano	1.25	.60	.40
(79)	Pete Runnels	2.00	1.00	.60
(80)	Don Schwall	1.25	.60	.40
(81)	Bobby Shantz	2.50	1.25	.70
(82)	Norm Siebern	1.25	.60	.40
(83)	Roy Sievers	2.00	1.00	.60
(84)	Hal (W.) Smith	1.25	.60	.40
(85)	Warren Spahn	6.00	3.00	1.75
(86)	Dick Stuart	2.00	1.00	.60
(87)	Tony Taylor	1.25	.60	.40
(88)	Lee Thomas	1.25	.60	.40
(89)	Gus Triandos	2.00	1.00	.60
(90)	Leon Wagner	1.25	.60	.40
(91)	Jerry Walker	1.25	.60	.40
(92)	Bill White	2.00	1.00	.60
(93)	Billy Williams	5.00	2.50	1.50
(94)	Gene Woodling	2.00	1.00	.60
(95)	Early Wynn	5.00	2.50	1.50
(96)	Carl Yastrzemski	35.00	17.50	10.50

the wrong team — Athletics — and was later corrected to the Phillies.

		NR MT	EX	VG
Complete Set:		150.00	75.00	45.00
Stamp Album:		25.00	12.50	7.50
Common Player:		.25	.13	.08
(1)	Hank Aaron	7.00	3.50	2.00
(2)	Jerry Adair	.25	.13	.08
(3)	Joe Adcock	.35	.20	.11
(4)	Bob Allison	.30	.15	.09
(5)	Felipe Alou	.35	.20	.11
(6)	George Altman	.25	.13	.08
(7)	Joe Amalfitano	.25	.13	.08
(8)	Ruben Amaro	.25	.13	.08
(9)	Luis Aparicio	1.00	.50	.30
(10)	Jim Archer	.25	.13	.08
(11)	Bob Aspromonte	.25	.13	.08
(12)	Ed Bailey	.25	.13	.08
(13)	Jack Baldschun	.25	.13	.08
(14)	Ernie Banks	3.00	1.50	.90
(15)	Earl Battey	.30	.15	.09
(16)	Gus Bell	.35	.20	.11
(17)	Yogi Berra	5.00	2.50	1.50
(18)	Dick Bertell	.25	.13	.08
(19)	Steve Bilko	.25	.13	.08
(20)	Frank Bolling	.25	.13	.08
(21)	Steve Boros	.25	.13	.08
(22)	Ted Bowsfield	.25	.13	.08
(23)	Clete Boyer	.35	.20	.11
(24)	Ken Boyer	.50	.25	.15
(25)	Jackie Brandt	.25	.13	.08
(26)	Bill Bruton	.25	.13	.08
(27)	Jim Bunning	.80	.40	.25
(28)	Lou Burdette	.35	.20	.11
(29)	Smoky Burgess	.30	.15	.09
(30)	Johnny Callizon (Callison)	.30	.15	.09
(31)	Don Cardwell	.25	.13	.08
(32)	Camilo Carreon	.25	.13	.08
(33)	Norm Cash	.50	.25	.15
(34)	Orlando Cepeda	1.00	.50	.30
(35)	Bob Clemente	5.00	2.50	1.50
(36)	Ty Cline	.25	.13	.08
(37)	Rocky Colavito	.80	.40	.25
(38)	Gordon Coleman	.25	.13	.08
(39)	Chuck Cottier	.25	.13	.08
(40)	Roger Craig	.35	.20	.11
(41)	Del Crandall	.35	.20	.11
(42)	Pete Daley	.25	.13	.08
(43)	Clay Dalrymple	.25	.13	.08
(44)	Bennie Daniels	.25	.13	.08
(45)	Jim Davenport	.25	.13	.08
(46)	Don Demeter	.25	.13	.08
(47)	Dick Donovan	.25	.13	.08
(48)	Don Drysdale	2.50	1.25	.70
(49)	John Edwards	.25	.13	.08
(50)	Dick Ellsworth	.25	.13	.08
(51)	Chuck Estrada	.25	.13	.08
(52)	Roy Face	.35	.20	.11
(53)	Ron Fairly	.30	.15	.09
(54)	Dick Farrell	.25	.13	.08
(55)	Whitey Ford	3.00	1.50	.90
(56)	Mike Fornieles	.25	.13	.08
(57)	Nellie Fox	.80	.40	.25
(58)	Tito Francona	.25	.13	.08
(59)	Gene Freese	.25	.13	.08
(60)	Bob Friend	.35	.20	.11
(61)	Gary Geiger	.25	.13	.08
(62)	Jim Gentile	.25	.13	.08
(63)	Tony Gonzalez	.25	.13	.08
(64)	Lenny Green	.25	.13	.08

1962 Topps Stamps

An artistic improvement over the somewhat drab Topps stamps of the previous year, the 1962 stamps, 1⅜'' by 1⅞,'' had color player photographs set on red or yellow backgrounds. As in 1961, they were issued in two-stamp panels as insert with Topps baseball cards. A change from 1961 was the inclusion of team emblems in the set. A complete set consists of 201 stamps; Roy Sievers was originally portrayed on

		NR MT	EX	VG
(65)	Dick Groat	.35	.20	.11
(66)	Ron Hansen	.25	.13	.08
(67)	Al Heist	.25	.13	.08
(68)	Woody Held	.25	.13	.08
(69)	Ray Herbert	.25	.13	.08
(70)	Chuck Hinton	.25	.13	.08
(71)	Don Hoak	.30	.15	.09
(72)	Glen Hobbie	.25	.13	.08
(73)	Gil Hodges	2.50	1.25	.70
(74)	Jay Hook	.35	.20	.11
(75)	Elston Howard	.80	.40	.25
(76)	Frank Howard	.50	.25	.15
(77)	Dick Howser	.35	.20	.11
(78)	Ken Hunt	.25	.13	.08
(79)	Larry Jackson	.25	.13	.08
(80)	Julian Javier	.25	.13	.08
(81)	Joe Jay	.25	.13	.08
(82)	Bob Johnson	.25	.13	.08
(83)	Sam Jones	.25	.13	.08
(84)	Al Kaline	3.50	1.75	1.00
(85)	Eddie Kasko	.25	.13	.08
(86)	Harmon Killebrew	3.50	1.75	1.00
(87)	Sandy Koufax	5.00	2.50	1.50
(88)	Jack Kralick	.25	.13	.08
(89)	Tony Kubek	.80	.40	.25
(90)	Harvey Kuenn	.50	.25	.15
(91)	Jim Landis	.25	.13	.08
(92)	Hobie Landrith	.35	.20	.11
(93)	Frank Lary	.25	.13	.08
(94)	Barry Latman	.25	.13	.08
(95)	Jerry Lumpe	.25	.13	.08
(96)	Art Mahaffey	.25	.13	.08
(97)	Frank Malzone	.25	.13	.08
(98)	Felix Mantilla	.35	.20	.11
(99)	Mickey Mantle	20.00	10.00	6.00
(100)	Juan Marichal	2.00	1.00	.60
(101)	Roger Maris	5.00	2.50	1.50
(102)	J.C. Martin	.25	.13	.08
(103)	Ed Mathews	2.50	1.25	.70
(104)	Willie Mays	7.00	3.50	2.00
(105)	Bill Mazeroski	.50	.25	.15
(106)	Ken McBride	.25	.13	.08
(107)	Tim McCarver	.50	.25	.15
(108)	Joe McClain	.25	.13	.08
(109)	Mike McCormick	.25	.13	.08
(110)	Lindy McDaniel	.25	.13	.08
(111)	Roy McMillan	.25	.13	.08
(112)	Bob L. Miller	.35	.20	.11
(113)	Stu Miller	.25	.13	.08
(114)	Minnie Minoso	.50	.25	.15
(115)	Bill Monbouquette	.25	.13	.08
(116)	Wally Moon	.30	.15	.09
(117)	Don Mossi	.30	.15	.09
(118)	Stan Musial	7.00	3.50	2.00
(119)	Russ Nixon	.25	.13	.08
(120)	Danny O'Connell	.25	.13	.08
(121)	Jim O'Toole	.25	.13	.08
(122)	Milt Pappas	.30	.15	.09
(123)	Camilo Pascual	.30	.15	.09
(124)	Albie Pearson	.25	.13	.08
(125)	Jim Perry	.35	.20	.11
(126)	Bubba Phillips	.25	.13	.08
(127)	Jimmy Piersall	.35	.20	.11
(128)	Vada Pinson	.50	.25	.15
(129)	Juan Pizarro	.25	.13	.08
(130)	Johnny Podres	.35	.20	.11
(131)	Leo Posada	.25	.13	.08
(132)	Vic Power	.25	.13	.08
(133)	Bob Purkey	.25	.13	.08
(134)	Pedro Ramos	.25	.13	.08
(135)	Bobby Richardson	.80	.40	.25
(136)	Brooks Robinson	3.50	1.75	1.00
(137)	Floyd Robinson	.25	.13	.08
(138)	Frank Robinson	3.00	1.50	.90
(139)	Bob Rodgers	.30	.15	.09
(140)	Johnny Romano	.25	.13	.08
(141)	John Roseboro	.30	.15	.09
(142)	Pete Runnels	.30	.15	.09
(143)	Ray Sadecki	.25	.13	.08
(144)	Ron Santo	.35	.20	.11
(145)	Chuck Schilling	.25	.13	.08
(146)	Barney Schultz	.25	.13	.08
(147)	Don Schwall	.25	.13	.08
(148)	Bobby Shantz	.35	.20	.11
(149)	Bob Shaw	.25	.13	.08
(150)	Norm Siebern	.25	.13	.08
(151a)	Roy Sievers (Kansas City)	1.00	.50	.30
(151b)	Roy Sievers (Philadelphia)	.30	.15	.09
(152)	Bill Skowron	.50	.25	.15
(153)	Hal (W.) Smith	.25	.13	.08
(154)	Duke Snider	3.50	1.75	1.00

		NR MT	EX	VG
(155)	Warren Spahn	2.50	1.25	.70
(156)	Al Spangler	.25	.13	.08
(157)	Daryl Spencer	.25	.13	.08
(158)	Gene Stephens	.25	.13	.08
(159)	Dick Stuart	.30	.15	.09
(160)	Haywood Sullivan	.25	.13	.08
(161)	Tony Taylor	.25	.13	.08
(162)	George Thomas	.25	.13	.08
(163)	Lee Thomas	.25	.13	.08
(164)	Bob Tiefenauer	.25	.13	.08
(165)	Joe Torre	.50	.25	.15
(166)	Gus Triandos	.30	.15	.09
(167)	Bill Tuttle	.25	.13	.08
(168)	Zoilo Versalles	.25	.13	.08
(169)	Bill Virdon	.35	.20	.11
(170)	Leon Wagner	.25	.13	.08
(171)	Jerry Walker	.25	.13	.08
(172)	Lee Walls	.25	.13	.08
(173)	Bill White	.30	.15	.09
(174)	Hoyt Wilhelm	1.25	.60	.40
(175)	Billy Williams	1.50	.70	.45
(176)	Jake Wood	.25	.13	.08
(177)	Gene Woodling	.35	.20	.11
(178)	Early Wynn	1.25	.60	.40
(179)	Carl Yastrzemski	12.00	6.00	3.50
(180)	Don Zimmer	.35	.20	.11
(181)	Baltimore Orioles Logo	.25	.13	.08
(182)	Boston Red Sox Logo	.25	.13	.08
(183)	Chicago Cubs Logo	.25	.13	.08
(184)	Chicago White Sox Logo	.25	.13	.08
(185)	Cincinnati Reds Logo	.25	.13	.08
(186)	Cleveland Indians Logo	.25	.13	.08
(187)	Detroit Tigers Logo	.25	.13	.08
(188)	Houston Colts Logo	.25	.13	.08
(189)	Kansas City Athletics Logo	.25	.13	.08
(190)	Los Angeles Angels Logo	.25	.13	.08
(191)	Los Angeles Dodgers Logo	.25	.13	.08
(192)	Milwaukee Braves Logo	.25	.13	.08
(193)	Minnesota Twins Logo	.25	.13	.08
(194)	New York Mets Logo	.35	.20	.11
(195)	New York Yankees Logo	.35	.20	.11
(196)	Philadelphia Phillies Logo	.25	.13	.08
(197)	Pittsburgh Pirates Logo	.25	.13	.08
(198)	St. Louis Cardinals Logo	.25	.13	.08
(199)	San Francisco Giants Logo	.25	.13	.08
(200)	Washington Senators Logo	.25	.13	.08

1963 Topps

 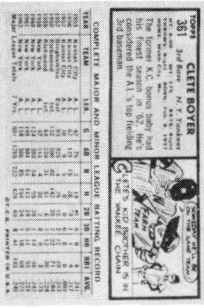

Although the number of cards dropped to 576, the 1963 Topps set is among the most popular of the 1960s. A color photo dominates the 2½'' by 3½'' card, but a colored circle at the bottom carries a black and white portrait, as well. A colored band gives the player's name, team and position. The backs again feature career statistics and a cartoon, career summary and brief biographical details. The set is somewhat unlike those immediately preceding it in that there are fewer specialty cards. The major groupings are statistical leaders, World Series highlights and rookies. It is one rookie which makes the set special: Pete Rose. As one of most avidly sought cards in history and a high number at that, the Rose rookie card accounts for much of the value of a complete set.

		NR MT	EX	VG
	Complete Set:	2700.00	950.00	550.00
	Common Player: 1-283	.50	.25	.15
	Common Player: 284-446	.90	.45	.25
	Common Player: 447-506	4.50	2.25	1.25
	Common Player: 507-576	2.50	1.25	.70
1	N.L. Batting Leaders (Hank Aaron, Tommy Davis, Stan Musial, Frank Robinson, Bill White)	10.00	5.00	3.00
2	A.L. Batting Leaders (Chuck Hinton, Mickey Mantle, Floyd Robinson, Pete Runnels, Norm Siebern)	9.00	4.50	2.50
3	N.L. Home Run Leaders (Hank Aaron, Ernie Banks, Orlando Cepeda, Willie Mays, Frank Robinson)	5.00	2.50	1.50
4	A.L. Home Run Leaders (Norm Cash, Rocky Colavito, Jim Gentile, Harmon Killebrew, Roger Maris, Leon Wagner)	4.00	2.00	1.25
5	N.L. E.R.A. Leaders (Don Drysdale, Bob Gibson, Sandy Koufax, Bob Purkey, Bob Shaw)	4.00	2.00	1.25
6	A.L. E.R.A. Leaders (Hank Aguirre, Dean Chance, Eddie Fisher, Whitey Ford, Robin Roberts)	3.50	1.75	1.00
7	N.L. Pitching Leaders (Don Drysdale, Joe Jay, Art Mahaffey, Billy O'Dell, Bob Purkey, Jack Sanford)	3.50	1.75	1.00
8	A.L. Pitching Leaders (Jim Bunning, Dick Donovan, Ray Herbert, Camilo Pascual, Ralph Terry)	3.00	1.50	.90
9	N.L. Strikeout Leaders (Don Drysdale, Dick Farrell, Bob Gibson, Sandy Koufax, Billy O'Dell)	4.00	2.00	1.25
10	A.L. Strikeout Leaders (Jim Bunning, Jim Kaat, Camilo Pascual, Juan Pizarro, Ralph Terry)	3.00	1.50	.90
11	Lee Walls	.50	.25	.15
12	Steve Barber	.50	.25	.15
13	Phillies Team	2.25	1.25	.70
14	Pedro Ramos	.50	.25	.15
15	Ken Hubbs	2.00	1.00	.60
16	Al Smith	.50	.25	.15
17	Ryne Duren	.90	.45	.25
18	Buc Blasters (Smoky Burgess, Bob Clemente, Bob Skinner, Dick Stuart)	6.00	3.00	1.75
19	Pete Burnside	.50	.25	.15
20	Tony Kubek	4.00	2.00	1.25
21	Marty Keough	.50	.25	.15
22	Curt Simmons	.90	.45	.25
23	Ed Lopat	1.25	.60	.40
24	Bob Bruce	.50	.25	.15
25	Al Kaline	10.00	5.00	3.00
26	Ray Moore	.50	.25	.15
27	Choo Choo Coleman	.90	.45	.25
28	Mike Fornieles	.50	.25	.15
29a	1962 Rookie Stars (John Boozer, Ray Culp, Sammy Ellis, Jesse Gonder)	5.00	2.50	1.50
29b	1963 Rookie Stars (John Boozer, Ray Culp, Sammy Ellis, Jesse Gonder)	1.25	.60	.40
30	Harvey Kuenn	1.50	.70	.45
31	Cal Koonce	.50	.25	.15
32	Tony Gonzalez	.50	.25	.15
33	Bo Belinsky	2.00	1.00	.60
34	Dick Schofield	.50	.25	.15
35	John Buzhardt	.50	.25	.15
36	Jerry Kindall	.50	.25	.15
37	Jerry Lynch	.50	.25	.15
38	Bud Daley	1.00	.50	.30
39	Angels Team	2.25	1.25	.70
40	Vic Power	.50	.25	.15
41	Charlie Lau	.90	.45	.25
42	Stan Williams	1.00	.50	.30
43	Veteran Masters (Casey Stengel, Gene Woodling)	3.50	1.75	1.00
44	Terry Fox	.50	.25	.15
45	Bob Aspromonte	.50	.25	.15
46	Tommie Aaron	1.25	.60	.40
47	Don Lock	.50	.25	.15
48	Birdie Tebbetts	.50	.25	.15
49	Dal Maxvill	1.25	.60	.40
50	Bill Pierce	1.25	.60	.40
51	George Alusik	.50	.25	.15
52	Chuck Schilling	.50	.25	.15
53	Joe Moeller	.50	.25	.15
54a	1962 Rookie Stars (Jack Cullen, Dave DeBusschere, Harry Fanok, Nelson Mathews)	6.50	3.25	2.00
54b	1963 Rookie Stars (Jack Cullen, Dave DeBusschere, Harry Fanok, Nelson Mathews)	2.50	1.25	.70
55	Bill Virdon	1.50	.70	.45
56	Dennis Bennett	.50	.25	.15
57	Billy Moran	.50	.25	.15
58	Bob Will	.50	.25	.15
59	Craig Anderson	.70	.35	.20
60	Elston Howard	4.50	2.25	1.25
61	Ernie Bowman	.50	.25	.15
62	Bob Hendley	.50	.25	.15
63	Reds Team	2.50	1.25	.75
64	Dick McAuliffe	.70	.35	.20
65	Jackie Brandt	.50	.25	.15
66	Mike Joyce	.50	.25	.15
67	Ed Charles	.50	.25	.15
68	Friendly Foes (Gil Hodges, Duke Snider)	6.50	3.25	2.00
69	Bud Zipfel	.50	.25	.15
70	Jim O'Toole	.50	.25	.15
71	Bobby Wine	.90	.45	.25
72	Johnny Romano	.50	.25	.15
73	Bobby Bragan	.70	.35	.20
74	Denver Lemaster	.70	.35	.20
75	Bob Allison	1.25	.60	.40
76	Earl Wilson	.50	.25	.15
77	Al Spangler	.50	.25	.15
78	Marv Throneberry	3.50	1.75	1.00
79	Checklist 1-88	2.50	1.25	.70
80	Jim Gilliam	3.00	1.50	.90
81	Jimmie Schaffer	.50	.25	.15
82	Ed Rakow	.50	.25	.15
83	Charley James	.50	.25	.15
84	Ron Kline	.50	.25	.15
85	Tom Haller	.70	.35	.20
86	Charley Maxwell	.50	.25	.15
87	Bob Veale	.70	.35	.20
88	Ron Hansen	.50	.25	.15
89	Dick Stigman	.50	.25	.15
90	Gordy Coleman	.50	.25	.15
91	Dallas Green	.90	.45	.25
92	Hector Lopez	1.00	.50	.30
93	Galen Cisco	.70	.35	.20
94	Bob Schmidt	.50	.25	.15
95	Larry Jackson	.50	.25	.15
96	Lou Clinton	.50	.25	.15
97	Bob Duliba	.50	.25	.15
98	George Thomas	.50	.25	.15
99	Jim Umbricht	.50	.25	.15
100	Joe Cunningham	.70	.35	.20
101	Joe Gibbon	.50	.25	.15
102a	Checklist 89-176 ("Checklist" in red on front)	3.00	1.50	.90
102b	Checklist 89-176 ("Checklist" in white)	6.00	3.00	1.75
103	Chuck Essegian	.50	.25	.15
104	Lew Krausse	.50	.25	.15
105	Ron Fairly	.90	.45	.25
106	Bob Bolin	.50	.25	.15
107	Jim Hickman	.90	.45	.25
108	Hoyt Wilhelm	6.00	3.00	1.75
109	Lee Maye	.50	.25	.15
110	Rich Rollins	.70	.35	.20
111	Al Jackson	.90	.45	.25
112	Dick Brown	.50	.25	.15
113	Don Landrum (photo actally Ron Santo)	.70	.35	.20
114	Dan Osinski	.50	.25	.15
115	Carl Yastrzemski	50.00	25.00	15.00
116	Jim Brosnan	.70	.35	.20
117	Jacke Davis	.50	.25	.15
118	Sherm Lollar	.90	.45	.25
119	Bob Lillis	.50	.25	.15
120	Roger Maris	20.00	10.00	6.00
121	Jim Hannan	.50	.25	.15
122	Julio Gotay	.50	.25	.15
123	Frank Howard	2.50	1.25	.70
124	Dick Howser	1.50	.70	.45
125	Robin Roberts	6.00	3.00	1.75
126	Bob Uecker	18.00	9.00	5.50
127	Bill Tuttle	.50	.25	.15
128	Matty Alou	.90	.45	.25
129	Gary Bell	.50	.25	.15
130	Dick Groat	1.50	.70	.45
131	Senators Team	2.25	1.25	.70
132	Jack Hamilton	.50	.25	.15
133	Gene Freese	.50	.25	.15
134	Bob Scheffing	.50	.25	.15
135	Richie Ashburn	4.50	2.25	1.25
136	Ike Delock	.50	.25	.15
137	Mack Jones	.50	.25	.15

#	Player	NR MT	EX	VG
138	Pride of N.L. (Willie Mays, Stan Musial)	12.00	6.00	3.50
139	Earl Averill	.50	.25	.15
140	Frank Lary	.70	.35	.20
141	Manny Mota	3.00	1.50	.90
142	World Series Game 1 (Yanks' Ford Wins Series Opener)	3.50	1.75	1.00
143	World Series Game 2 (Sanford Flashes Shutout Magic)	2.25	1.25	.70
144	World Series Game 3 (Maris Sparks Yankee Rally)	4.00	2.00	1.25
145	World Series Game 4 (Hiller Blasts Grand Slammer)	2.25	1.25	.70
146	World Series Game 5 (Tresh's Homer Defeats Giants)	3.00	1.50	.90
147	World Series Game 6 (Pierce Stars In 3 Hit Victory)	3.00	1.50	.90
148	World Series Game 7 (Yanks Celebrate As Terry Wins)	3.00	1.50	.90
149	Marv Breeding	.50	.25	.15
150	Johnny Podres	2.00	1.00	.60
151	Pirates Team	2.25	1.25	.70
152	Ron Nischwitz	.50	.25	.15
153	Hal Smith	.50	.25	.15
154	Walt Alston	3.00	1.50	.90
155	Bill Stafford	1.00	.50	.30
156	Roy McMillan	.50	.25	.15
157	Diego Segui	.70	.35	.20
158	1963 Rookie Stars (Rogelio Alvarez, Tommy Harper, Dave Roberts, Bob Saverine)	.90	.45	.25
159	Jim Pagliaroni	.50	.25	.15
160	Juan Pizarro	.50	.25	.15
161	Frank Torre	.50	.25	.15
162	Twins Team	2.25	1.25	.70
163	Don Larsen	1.25	.60	.40
164	Bubba Morton	.50	.25	.15
165	Jim Kaat	5.00	2.50	1.50
166	Johnny Keane	.50	.25	.15
167	Jim Fregosi	1.50	.70	.45
168	Russ Nixon	.50	.25	.15
169	1963 Rookie Stars (Dick Egan, Julio Navarro, Gaylord Perry, Tommie Sisk)	15.00	7.50	4.50
170	Joe Adcock	1.50	.70	.45
171	Steve Hamilton	.50	.25	.15
172	Gene Oliver	.50	.25	.15
173	Bomber's Best (Mickey Mantle, Bobby Richardson, Tom Tresh)	20.00	9.00	5.00
174	Larry Burright	.70	.35	.20
175	Bob Buhl	.70	.35	.20
176	Jim King	.50	.25	.15
177	Bubba Phillips	.50	.25	.15
178	Johnny Edwards	.50	.25	.15
179	Ron Piche	.50	.25	.15
180	Bill Skowron	1.50	.70	.45
181	Sammy Esposito	.50	.25	.15
182	Albie Pearson	.50	.25	.15
183	Joe Pepitone	4.00	2.00	1.25
184	Vern Law	1.25	.60	.40
185	Chuck Hiller	.50	.25	.15
186	Jerry Zimmerman	.50	.25	.15
187	Willie Kirkland	.50	.25	.15
188	Eddie Bressoud	.50	.25	.15
189	Dave Giusti	.50	.25	.15
190	Minnie Minoso	1.50	.70	.45
191	Checklist 177-264	3.00	1.50	.90
192	Clay Dalrymple	.50	.25	.15
193	Andre Rodgers	.50	.25	.15
194	Joe Nuxhall	.90	.45	.25
195	Manny Jimenez	.50	.25	.15
196	Doug Camilli	.50	.25	.15
197	Roger Craig	2.00	1.00	.60
198	Lenny Green	.50	.25	.15
199	Joe Amalfitano	.50	.25	.15
200	Mickey Mantle	225.00	100.00	55.00
201	Cecil Butler	.50	.25	.15
202	Red Sox Team	2.50	1.25	.75
203	Chico Cardenas	.50	.25	.15
204	Don Nottebart	.50	.25	.15
205	Luis Aparicio	6.00	3.00	1.75
206	Ray Washburn	.50	.25	.15
207	Ken Hunt	.50	.25	.15
208	1963 Rookie Stars (Ron Herbel, John Miller, Ron Taylor, Wally Wolf)	.50	.25	.15
209	Hobie Landrith	.50	.25	.15
210	Sandy Koufax	50.00	25.00	15.00
211	Fred Whitfield	.50	.25	.15
212	Glen Hobbie	.50	.25	.15
213	Billy Hitchcock	.50	.25	.15
214	Orlando Pena	.50	.25	.15
215	Bob Skinner	.70	.35	.20
216	Gene Conley	.70	.35	.20
217	Joe Christopher	.70	.35	.20
218	Tiger Twirlers (Jim Bunning, Frank Lary, Don Mossi)	2.00	1.00	.60
219	Chuck Cottier	.50	.25	.15
220	Camilo Pascual	.90	.45	.25
221	Cookie Rojas	.90	.45	.25
222	Cubs Team	2.25	1.25	.70
223	Eddie Fisher	.50	.25	.15
224	Mike Roarke	.50	.25	.15
225	Joe Jay	.50	.25	.15
226	Julian Javier	.70	.35	.20
227	Jim Grant	.50	.25	.15
228	1963 Rookie Stars (Max Alvis, Bob Bailey, Ed Kranepool, Pedro Oliva)	10.00	5.00	3.00
229	Willie Davis	1.50	.70	.45
230	Pete Runnels	.70	.35	.20
231	Eli Grba (photo actually Ryne Duren)	.70	.35	.20
232	Frank Malzone	.70	.35	.20
233	Casey Stengel	8.00	4.00	2.50
234	Dave Nicholson	.50	.25	.15
235	Billy O'Dell	.50	.25	.15
236	Bill Bryan	.50	.25	.15
237	Jim Coates	1.00	.50	.30
238	Lou Johnson	.50	.25	.15
239	Harvey Haddix	.90	.45	.25
240	Rocky Colavito	3.00	1.50	.90
241	Billy Smith	.50	.25	.15
242	Power Plus (Hank Aaron, Ernie Banks)	10.00	5.00	3.00
243	Don Leppert	.50	.25	.15
244	John Tsitouris	.50	.25	.15
245	Gil Hodges	8.00	4.00	2.50
246	Lee Stange	.50	.25	.15
247	Yankees Team	6.00	3.00	1.75
248	Tito Francona	.70	.35	.20
249	Leo Burke	.50	.25	.15
250	Stan Musial	40.00	20.00	12.00
251	Jack Lamabe	.50	.25	.15
252	Ron Santo	2.00	1.00	.60
253	1963 Rookie Stars (Len Gabrielson, Pete Jernigan, Deacon Jones, John Wojcik)	.50	.25	.15
254	Mike Hershberger	.50	.25	.15
255	Bob Shaw	.50	.25	.15
256	Jerry Lumpe	.70	.35	.20
257	Hank Aguirre	.50	.25	.15
258	Alvin Dark	.90	.45	.25
259	Johnny Logan	.70	.35	.20
260	Jim Gentile	.70	.35	.20
261	Bob Miller	.50	.25	.15
262	Ellis Burton	.50	.25	.15
263	Dave Stenhouse	.50	.25	.15
264	Phil Linz	1.50	.70	.45
265	Vada Pinson	2.50	1.25	.70
266	Bob Allen	.50	.25	.15
267	Carl Sawatski	.50	.25	.15
268	Don Demeter	.50	.25	.15
269	Don Mincher	.70	.35	.20
270	Felipe Alou	.90	.45	.25
271	Dean Stone	.50	.25	.15
272	Danny Murphy	.50	.25	.15
273	Sammy Taylor	.70	.35	.20
274	Checklist 265-352	3.00	1.50	.90
275	Ed Mathews	8.00	4.00	2.50
276	Barry Shetrone	.50	.25	.15
277	Dick Farrell	.50	.25	.15
278	Chico Fernandez	.50	.25	.15
279	Wally Moon	.90	.45	.25
280	Bob Rodgers	.90	.45	.25
281	Tom Sturdivant	.50	.25	.15
282	Bob Del Greco	.50	.25	.15
283	Roy Sievers	.90	.45	.25
284	Dave Sisler	.90	.45	.25
285	Dick Stuart	1.25	.60	.40
286	Stu Miller	.90	.45	.25
287	Dick Bertell	.90	.45	.25
288	White Sox Team	3.00	1.50	.90
289	Hal Brown	2.00	1.00	.60
290	Bill White	1.50	.70	.45
291	Don Rudolph	.90	.45	.25
292	Pumpsie Green	1.25	.60	.40
293	Bill Pleis	.90	.45	.25
294	Bill Rigney	.90	.45	.25
295	Ed Roebuck	.90	.45	.25
296	Doc Edwards	1.25	.60	.40
297	Jim Golden	.90	.45	.25
298	Don Dillard	.90	.45	.25

		NR MT	EX	VG
299	1963 Rookie Stars (Tom Butters, Bob Dustal, Dave Morehead, Dan Schneider)			
		.90	.45	.25
300	Willie Mays	60.00	30.00	18.00
301	Bill Fischer	.90	.45	.25
302	Whitey Herzog	3.00	1.50	.90
303	Earl Francis	.90	.45	.25
304	Harry Bright	.90	.45	.25
305	Don Hoak	1.25	.60	.40
306	Star Receivers (Earl Battey, Elston Howard)			
		3.00	1.50	.90
307	Chet Nichols	.90	.45	.25
308	Camilo Carreon	.90	.45	.25
309	Jim Brewer	.90	.45	.25
310	Tommy Davis	2.25	1.25	.70
311	Joe McClain	.90	.45	.25
312	Colt .45s Team	6.00	3.00	1.75
313	Ernie Broglio	.90	.45	.25
314	John Goryl	.90	.45	.25
315	Ralph Terry	2.50	1.25	.70
316	Norm Sherry	1.25	.60	.40
317	Sam McDowell	2.25	1.25	.70
318	Gene Mauch	1.25	.60	.40
319	Joe Gaines	.90	.45	.25
320	Warren Spahn	12.00	6.00	3.50
321	Gino Cimoli	.90	.45	.25
322	Bob Turley	1.50	.70	.45
323	Bill Mazeroski	3.00	1.50	.90
324	1963 Rookie Stars (Vic Davalillo, Phil Roof, Pete Ward, George Williams)	1.75	.90	.50
325	Jack Sanford	.90	.45	.25
326	Hank Foiles	.90	.45	.25
327	Paul Foytack	.90	.45	.25
328	Dick Williams	2.00	1.00	.60
329	Lindy McDaniel	.90	.45	.25
330	Chuck Hinton	.90	.45	.25
331	Series Foes (Bill Pierce, Bill Stafford)			
		2.25	1.25	.70
332	Joel Horlen	.90	.45	.25
333	Carl Warwick	.90	.45	.25
334	Wynn Hawkins	1.25	.60	.40
335	Leon Wagner	1.25	.60	.40
336	Ed Bauta	.90	.45	.25
337	Dodgers Team	6.00	3.00	1.75
338	Russ Kemmerer	.90	.45	.25
339	Ted Bowsfield	.90	.45	.25
340	Yogi Berra	25.00	12.50	7.50
341	Jack Baldschun	.90	.45	.25
342	Gene Woodling	1.75	.90	.50
343	Johnny Pesky	1.25	.60	.40
344	Don Schwall	.90	.45	.25
345	Brooks Robinson	20.00	10.00	6.00
346	Billy Hoeft	.90	.45	.25
347	Joe Torre	4.50	2.25	1.25
348	Vic Wertz	1.50	.70	.45
349	Zoilo Versalles	1.25	.60	.40
350	Bob Purkey	.90	.45	.25
351	Al Luplow	.90	.45	.25
352	Ken Johnson	.90	.45	.25
353	Billy Williams	8.00	4.00	2.50
354	Dom Zanni	.90	.45	.25
355	Dean Chance	1.25	.60	.40
356	John Schaive	1.00	.50	.30
357	George Altman	1.00	.50	.30
358	Milt Pappas	1.25	.60	.40
359	Haywood Sullivan	1.25	.60	.40
360	Don Drysdale	12.00	6.00	3.50
361	Clete Boyer	3.00	1.50	.90
362	Checklist 353-429	4.00	2.00	1.25
363	Dick Radatz	1.25	.60	.40
364	Howie Goss	.90	.45	.25
365	Jim Bunning	5.00	2.50	1.50
366	Tony Taylor	.90	.45	.25
367	Tony Cloninger	1.25	.60	.40
368	Ed Bailey	.90	.45	.25
369	Jim Lemon	.90	.45	.25
370	Dick Donovan	.90	.45	.25
371	Rod Kanehl	1.25	.60	.40
372	Don Lee	.90	.45	.25
373	Jim Campbell	.90	.45	.25
374	Claude Osteen	1.25	.60	.40
375	Ken Boyer	3.50	1.75	1.00
376	Johnnie Wyatt	.90	.45	.25
377	Orioles Team	3.00	1.50	.90
378	Bill Henry	.90	.45	.25
379	Bob Anderson	.90	.45	.25
380	Ernie Banks	20.00	10.00	6.00
381	Frank Baumann	.90	.45	.25
382	Ralph Houk	3.00	1.50	.90
383	Pete Richert	.90	.45	.25
384	Bob Tillman	.90	.45	.25

		NR MT	EX	VG
385	Art Mahaffey	.90	.45	.25
386	1963 Rookie Stars (John Bateman, Larry Bearnarth, Ed Kirkpatrick, Garry Roggenburk)	1.25	.60	.40
387	Al McBean	.90	.45	.25
388	Jim Davenport	.90	.45	.25
389	Frank Sullivan	.90	.45	.25
390	Hank Aaron	55.00	27.00	16.50
391	Bill Dailey	.90	.45	.25
392	Tribe Thumpers (Tito Francona, Johnny Romano)	1.50	.70	.45
393	Ken MacKenzie	1.25	.60	.40
394	Tim McCarver	3.50	1.75	1.00
395	Don McMahon	.90	.45	.25
396	Joe Koppe	.90	.45	.25
397	Athletics Team	3.00	1.50	.90
398	Boog Powell	4.50	2.25	1.25
399	Dick Ellsworth	.90	.45	.25
400	Frank Robinson	20.00	10.00	6.00
401	Jim Bouton	5.00	2.50	1.50
402	Mickey Vernon	1.25	.60	.40
403	Ron Perranoski	1.25	.60	.40
404	Bob Oldis	.90	.45	.25
405	Floyd Robinson	.90	.45	.25
406	Howie Koplitz	.90	.45	.25
407	1963 Rookie Stars (Larry Elliot, Frank Kostro, Chico Ruiz, Dick Simpson)	.90	.45	.25
408	Billy Gardner	.90	.45	.25
409	Roy Face	2.00	1.00	.60
410	Earl Battey	1.25	.60	.40
411	Jim Constable	.90	.45	.25
412	Dodgers' Big Three (Don Drysdale, Sandy Koufax, Johnny Podres)	15.00	7.50	4.50
413	Jerry Walker	.90	.45	.25
414	Ty Cline	.90	.45	.25
415	Bob Gibson	20.00	10.00	6.00
416	Alex Grammas	.90	.45	.25
417	Giants Team	3.00	1.50	.90
418	Johnny Orsino	.90	.45	.25
419	Tracy Stallard	1.25	.60	.40
420	Bobby Richardson	5.00	2.50	1.50
421	Tom Morgan	.90	.45	.25
422	Fred Hutchinson	1.25	.60	.40
423	Ed Hobaugh	.90	.45	.25
424	Charley Smith	.90	.45	.25
425	Smoky Burgess	1.75	.90	.50
426	Barry Latman	.90	.45	.25
427	Bernie Allen	.90	.45	.25
428	Carl Boles	.90	.45	.25
429	Lou Burdette	2.50	1.25	.70
430	Norm Siebern	1.25	.60	.40
431a	Checklist 430-506 ("Checklist" in black on front)	7.00	3.50	2.00
431b	Checklist 430-506 ("Checklist" in white)	4.50	2.25	1.25
432	Roman Mejias	.90	.45	.25
433	Denis Menke	1.50	.70	.45
434	Johnny Callison	1.75	.90	.50
435	Woody Held	.90	.45	.25
436	Tim Harkness	1.25	.60	.40
437	Bill Bruton	.90	.45	.25
438	Wes Stock	.90	.45	.25
439	Don Zimmer	2.00	1.00	.60
440	Juan Marichal	12.00	6.00	3.50
441	Lee Thomas	.90	.45	.25
442	J.C. Hartman	.90	.45	.25
443	Jim Piersall	2.00	1.00	.60
444	Jim Maloney	1.25	.60	.40
445	Norm Cash	2.50	1.25	.70
446	Whitey Ford	20.00	10.00	6.00
447	Felix Mantilla	4.50	2.25	1.25
448	Jack Kralick	4.50	2.25	1.25
449	Jose Tartabull	4.50	2.25	1.25
450	Bob Friend	6.00	3.00	1.75
451	Indians Team	8.00	4.00	2.50
452	Barney Schultz	4.50	2.25	1.25
453	Jake Wood	4.50	2.25	1.25
454a	Art Fowler (card # on orange background)	7.00	3.50	2.00
454b	Art Fowler (card # on white background)	4.50	2.25	1.25
455	Ruben Amaro	4.50	2.25	1.25
456	Jim Coker	4.50	2.25	1.25
457	Tex Clevenger	6.00	3.00	1.75
458	Al Lopez	8.00	4.00	2.50
459	Dick LeMay	4.50	2.25	1.25
460	Del Crandall	6.00	3.00	1.75
461	Norm Bass	4.50	2.25	1.25
462	Wally Post	4.50	2.25	1.25
463	Joe Schaffernoth	4.50	2.25	1.25
464	Ken Aspromonte	4.50	2.25	1.25

		NR MT	EX	VG
465	Chuck Estrada	4.50	2.25	1.25
466	1963 Rookie Stars (Bill Freehan, Tony Martinez, Nate Oliver, Jerry Robinson)			
		8.50	4.25	2.50
467	Phil Ortega	4.50	2.25	1.25
468	Carroll Hardy	4.50	2.25	1.25
469	Jay Hook	5.00	2.50	1.50
470	Tom Tresh	20.00	10.00	6.00
471	Ken Retzer	4.50	2.25	1.25
472	Lou Brock	65.00	32.00	19.50
473	Mets Team	15.00	7.50	4.50
474	Jack Fisher	4.50	2.25	1.25
475	Gus Triandos	5.00	2.50	1.50
476	Frank Funk	4.50	2.25	1.25
477	Donn Clendenon	5.00	2.50	1.50
478	Paul Brown	4.50	2.25	1.25
479	Ed Brinkman	5.00	2.50	1.50
480	Bill Monbouquette	5.00	2.50	1.50
481	Bob Taylor	4.50	2.25	1.25
482	Felix Torres	4.50	2.25	1.25
483	Jim Owens	4.50	2.25	1.25
484	Dale Long	6.00	3.00	1.75
485	Jim Landis	4.50	2.25	1.25
486	Ray Sadecki	4.50	2.25	1.25
487	John Roseboro	5.00	2.50	1.50
488	Jerry Adair	4.50	2.25	1.25
489	Paul Toth	4.50	2.25	1.25
490	Willie McCovey	45.00	22.00	13.50
491	Harry Craft	4.50	2.25	1.25
492	Dave Wickersham	4.50	2.25	1.25
493	Walt Bond	4.50	2.25	1.25
494	Phil Regan	4.50	2.25	1.25
495	Frank Thomas	5.00	2.50	1.50
496	1963 Rookie Stars (Carl Bouldin, Steve Dalkowski, Fred Newman, Jack Smith)			
		5.00	2.50	1.50
497	Bennie Daniels	4.50	2.25	1.25
498	Eddie Kasko	4.50	2.25	1.25
499	J.C. Martin	4.50	2.25	1.25
500	Harmon Killebrew	30.00	15.00	9.00
501	Joe Azcue	4.50	2.25	1.25
502	Daryl Spencer	4.50	2.25	1.25
503	Braves Team	8.00	4.00	2.50
504	Bob Johnson	4.50	2.25	1.25
505	Curt Flood	10.00	5.00	3.00
506	Gene Green	4.50	2.25	1.25
507	Roland Sheldon	4.00	2.00	1.25
508	Ted Savage	2.50	1.25	.70
509a	Checklist 507-576 (copyright centered)			
		12.00	6.00	3.50
509b	Checklist 509-576 (copyright to right)			
		10.00	5.00	3.00
510	Ken McBride	2.50	1.25	.70
511	Charlie Neal	3.00	1.50	.90
512	Cal McLish	2.50	1.25	.70
513	Gary Geiger	2.50	1.25	.70
514	Larry Osborne	2.50	1.25	.70
515	Don Elston	2.50	1.25	.70
516	Purnal Goldy	2.50	1.25	.70
517	Hal Woodeshick	2.50	1.25	.70
518	Don Blasingame	2.50	1.25	.70
519	Claude Raymond	2.50	1.25	.70
520	Orlando Cepeda	10.00	5.00	3.00
521	Dan Pfister	2.50	1.25	.70
522	1963 Rookie Stars (Mel Nelson, Gary Peters, Art Quirk, Jim Roland)	2.75	1.50	.80
523	Bill Kunkel	4.00	2.00	1.25
524	Cardinals Team	6.00	3.00	1.75
525	Nellie Fox	9.00	4.50	2.75
526	Dick Hall	2.50	1.25	.70
527	Ed Sadowski	2.50	1.25	.70
528	Carl Willey	3.00	1.50	.90
529	Wes Covington	2.50	1.25	.70
530	Don Mossi	2.75	1.50	.80
531	Sam Mele	2.50	1.25	.70
532	Steve Boros	2.50	1.25	.70
533	Bobby Shantz	5.00	2.50	1.50
534	Ken Walters	2.50	1.25	.70
535	Jim Perry	5.00	2.50	1.50
536	Norm Larker	2.50	1.25	.70
537	1963 Rookie Stars (Pedro Gonzalez, Ken McMullen, Pete Rose, Al Weis)	450.00	225.00	135.00
538	George Brunet	2.50	1.25	.70
539	Wayne Causey	2.50	1.25	.70
540	Bob Clemente	90.00	36.00	23.00
541	Ron Moeller	2.50	1.25	.70
542	Lou Klimchock	2.50	1.25	.70
543	Russ Snyder	2.50	1.25	.70
544	1963 Rookie Stars (Duke Carmel, Bill Haas, Dick Phillips, Rusty Staub)	25.00	12.50	7.50
545	Jose Pagan	2.50	1.25	.70

		NR MT	EX	VG
546	Hal Reniff	4.00	2.00	1.25
547	Gus Bell	3.00	1.50	.90
548	Tom Satriano	2.50	1.25	.70
549	1963 Rookie Stars (Marcelino Lopez, Pete Lovrich, Elmo Plaskett, Paul Ratliff)	2.75	1.50	.80
550	Duke Snider	40.00	20.00	12.00
551	Billy Klaus	2.50	1.25	.70
552	Tigers Team	7.00	3.50	2.00
553	1963 Rookie Stars (Brock Davis, Jim Gosger, John Herrnstein, Willie Stargell)			
		90.00	36.00	23.00
554	Hank Fischer	2.50	1.25	.70
555	John Blanchard	4.00	2.00	1.25
556	Al Worthington	2.50	1.25	.70
557	Cuno Barragan	2.50	1.25	.70
558	1963 Rookie Stars (Bill Faul, Ron Hunt, Bob Lipski, Al Moran)	3.50	1.75	1.00
559	Danny Murtaugh	3.00	1.50	.90
560	Ray Herbert	2.50	1.25	.70
561	Mike de la Hoz	2.50	1.25	.70
562	1963 Rookie Stars (Randy Cardinal, Dave McNally, Don Rowe, Ken Rowe)	5.00	2.50	1.50
563	Mike McCormick	2.75	1.50	.80
564	George Banks	2.50	1.25	.70
565	Larry Sherry	2.50	1.25	.70
566	Cliff Cook	3.00	1.50	.90
567	Jim Duffalo	2.50	1.25	.70
568	Bob Sadowski	2.50	1.25	.70
569	Luis Arroyo	4.50	2.25	1.25
570	Frank Bolling	2.50	1.25	.70
571	Johnny Klippstein	2.50	1.25	.70
572	Jack Spring	2.50	1.25	.70
573	Coot Veal	2.50	1.25	.70
574	Hal Kolstad	2.50	1.25	.70
575	Don Cardwell	2.75	1.25	.70
576	Johnny Temple	6.00	1.75	.70

1963 Topps Peel-Offs

BOB CLEMENTE
POTS. PIRATES OUTFIELD

Measuring 1¼" by 2¾," Topps Peel-Offs were an insert with 1963 Topps baseball cards. There are 46 players in the unnumbered set, each pictured in a color photo inside an oval with the player's name, team and position in a band below. The back of the Peel-Off was removable, leaving a sticky surface that made the Peel-Off a popular decorative item among youngsters of the day. Naturally, that makes them quite scarce today, but as a non-card Topps issue, demand is not particularly strong

		NR MT	EX	VG
Complete Set:		150.00	75.00	45.00
Common Player:			.50	.30
(1)	Hank Aaron	10.00	5.00	3.00
(2)	Luis Aparicio	3.00	1.50	.90
(3)	Richie Ashburn	2.00	1.00	.60
(4)	Bob Aspromonte	1.00	.50	.30
(5)	Ernie Banks	5.00	2.50	1.50
(6)	Ken Boyer	1.50	.70	.45
(7)	Jim Bunning	1.75	.90	.50
(8)	Johnny Callison	1.25	.60	.40
(9)	Orlando Cepeda	1.75	.90	.50
(10)	Bob Clemente	8.00	4.00	2.50
(11)	Rocky Colavito	1.75	.90	.50
(12)	Tommy Davis	1.50	.70	.45

		NR MT	EX	VG
(13)	Dick Donovan	1.00	.50	.30
(14)	Don Drysdale	4.00	2.00	1.25
(15)	Dick Farrell	1.00	.50	.30
(16)	Jim Gentile	1.00	.50	.30
(17)	Ray Herbert	1.00	.50	.30
(18)	Chuck Hinton	1.00	.50	.30
(19)	Ken Hubbs	1.50	.70	.45
(20)	Al Jackson	1.00	.50	.30
(21)	Al Kaline	5.00	2.50	1.50
(22)	Harmon Killebrew	5.00	2.50	1.50
(23)	Sandy Koufax	8.00	4.00	2.50
(24)	Jerry Lumpe	1.00	.50	.30
(25)	Art Mahaffey	1.00	.50	.30
(26)	Mickey Mantle	35.00	17.50	10.50
(27)	Willie Mays	10.00	5.00	3.00
(28)	Bill Mazeroski	1.50	.70	.45
(29)	Bill Monbouquette	1.00	.50	.30
(30)	Stan Musial	10.00	5.00	3.00
(31)	Camilo Pascual	1.25	.60	.40
(32)	Bob Purkey	1.00	.50	.30
(33)	Bobby Richardson	1.75	.90	.50
(34)	Brooks Robinson	6.00	3.00	1.75
(35)	Floyd Robinson	1.00	.50	.30
(36)	Frank Robinson	5.00	2.50	1.50
(37)	Bob Rodgers	1.00	.50	.30
(38)	Johnny Romano	1.00	.50	.30
(39)	Jack Sanford	1.00	.50	.30
(40)	Norm Siebern	1.00	.50	.30
(41)	Warren Spahn	5.00	2.50	1.50
(42)	Dave Stenhouse	1.00	.50	.30
(43)	Ralph Terry	1.25	.60	.40
(44)	Lee Thomas	1.00	.50	.30
(45)	Bill White	1.25	.60	.40
(46)	Carl Yastrzemski	12.00	6.00	3.50

1964 Topps

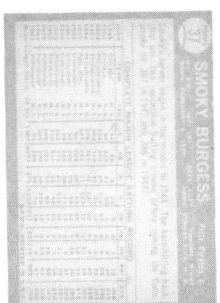

The 1964 Topps set is a 587-card issue of 2½'' by 3½'' cards which is considered by many as being among the company's best efforts. Card fronts feature a large color photo which blends into a top panel which contains the team name, while a panel below the picture carries the player's name and position. An interesting innovation on the back was the baseball quiz question which required the rubbing of a white panel to reveal the answer. As in 1963, specialty cards remained modest in number with a 12-card set of statistical leaders, a few multi-player cards, rookies and World Series highlights. An interesting card is an ''In Memoriam'' card for Ken Hubbs who was killed in an airplane crash.

		NR MT	EX	VG
Complete Set:		1700.00	600.00	350.00
Common Player: 1-370		.50	.25	.15
Common Player: 371-522		.80	.40	.25
Common Player: 523-587		2.50	1.25	.70
1	N.L. E.R.A. Leaders (Dick Ellsworth, Bob Friend, Sandy Koufax)	7.00	2.50	1.25
2	A.L. E.R.A. Leaders (Camilo Pascual, Gary Peters, Juan Pizarro)	3.00	1.50	.90
3	N.L. Pitching Leaders (Sandy Koufax, Jim Maloney, Juan Marichal, Warren Spahn)	5.00	2.50	1.50

		NR MT	EX	VG
4a	A.L. Pitching Leaders (Jim Bouton, Whitey Ford, Camilo Pascual) (apostrophe after "Pitching" on back)	5.00	2.50	1.50
4b	A.L. Pitching Leaders (Jim Bouton, Whitey Ford, Camilo Pascual) (no apostrophe)	3.50	1.75	1.00
5	N.L. Strikeout Leaders (Don Drysdale, Sandy Koufax, Jim Maloney)	4.00	2.00	1.25
6	A.L. Strikeout Leaders (Jim Bunning, Camilo Pascual, Dick Stigman)	3.00	1.50	.90
7	N.L. Batting Leaders (Hank Aaron, Bob Clemente, Tommy Davis, Dick Groat)	5.00	2.50	1.50
8	A.L. Batting Leaders (Al Kaline, Rich Rollins, Carl Yastrzemski)	5.00	2.50	1.50
9	N.L. Home Run Leaders (Hank Aaron, Orlando Cepeda, Willie Mays, Willie McCovey)	5.00	2.50	1.50
10	A.L. Home Run Leaders (Bob Allison, Harmon Killebrew, Dick Stuart)	3.50	1.75	1.00
11	N.L. R.B.I. Leaders (Hank Aaron, Ken Boyer, Bill White)	4.50	2.25	1.25
12	A.L. R.B.I. Leaders (Al Kaline, Harmon Killebrew, Dick Stuart)	4.50	2.25	1.25
13	Hoyt Wilhelm	6.00	3.00	1.75
14	Dodgers Rookies (Dick Nen, Nick Willhite)	.50	.25	.15
15	Zoilo Versalles	.60	.30	.20
16	John Boozer	.50	.25	.15
17	Willie Kirkland	.50	.25	.15
18	Billy O'Dell	.50	.25	.15
19	Don Wert	.50	.25	.15
20	Bob Friend	1.25	.60	.40
21	Yogi Berra	20.00	10.00	6.00
22	Jerry Adair	.50	.25	.15
23	Chris Zachary	.50	.25	.15
24	Carl Sawatski	.50	.25	.15
25	Bill Monbouquette	.60	.30	.20
26	Gino Cimoli	.50	.25	.15
27	Mets Team	3.50	1.75	1.00
28	Claude Osteen	.80	.40	.25
29	Lou Brock	20.00	10.00	6.00
30	Ron Perranoski	.60	.30	.20
31	Dave Nicholson	.50	.25	.15
32	Dean Chance	1.25	.60	.40
33	Reds Rookies (Sammy Ellis, Mel Queen)	.60	.30	.20
34	Jim Perry	1.25	.60	.40
35	Ed Mathews	8.00	4.00	2.50
36	Hal Reniff	1.00	.50	.30
37	Smoky Burgess	1.25	.60	.40
38	Jim Wynn	1.50	.70	.45
39	Hank Aguirre	.50	.25	.15
40	Dick Groat	1.50	.70	.45
41	Friendly Foes (Willie McCovey, Leon Wagner)	3.00	1.50	.90
42	Moe Drabowsky	.50	.25	.15
43	Roy Sievers	.90	.45	.25
44	Duke Carmel	.60	.30	.20
45	Milt Pappas	.90	.45	.25
46	Ed Brinkman	.60	.30	.20
47	Giants Rookies (Jesus Alou, Ron Herbel)	1.25	.60	.40
48	Bob Perry	.50	.25	.15
49	Bill Henry	.50	.25	.15
50	Mickey Mantle	150.00	70.00	50.00
51	Pete Richert	.50	.25	.15
52	Chuck Hinton	.50	.25	.15
53	Denis Menke	.50	.25	.15
54	Sam Mele	.50	.25	.15
55	Ernie Banks	10.00	5.00	3.00
56	Hal Brown	.50	.25	.15
57	Tim Harkness	.60	.30	.20
58	Don Demeter	.50	.25	.15
59	Ernie Broglio	.50	.25	.15
60	Frank Malzone	.60	.30	.20
61	Angel Backstops (Bob Rodgers, Ed Sadowski)	.80	.40	.25
62	Ted Savage	.50	.25	.15
63	Johnny Orsino	.50	.25	.15
64	Ted Abernathy	.50	.25	.15
65	Felipe Alou	1.25	.60	.40
66	Eddie Fisher	.50	.25	.15
67	Tigers Team	3.50	1.75	1.00
68	Willie Davis	1.50	.70	.45
69	Clete Boyer	1.50	.70	.45
70	Joe Torre	2.50	1.25	.70
71	Jack Spring	.50	.25	.15
72	Chico Cardenas	.50	.25	.15
73	Jimmie Hall	.80	.40	.25

		NR MT	EX	VG
74	Pirates Rookies (Tom Butters, Bob Priddy)	.50	.25	.15
75	Wayne Causey	.50	.25	.15
76	Checklist 1-88	3.00	1.50	.90
77	Jerry Walker	.50	.25	.15
78	Merritt Ranew	.50	.25	.15
79	Bob Heffner	.50	.25	.15
80	Vada Pinson	2.50	1.25	.70
81	All-Star Vets (Nellie Fox, Harmon Killebrew)	4.00	2.00	1.25
82	Jim Davenport	.50	.25	.15
83	Gus Triandos	.60	.30	.20
84	Carl Willey	.60	.30	.20
85	Pete Ward	.60	.30	.20
86	Al Downing	1.50	.70	.45
87	Cardinals Team	4.00	2.00	1.25
88	John Roseboro	.80	.40	.25
89	Boog Powell	2.50	1.25	.70
90	Earl Battey	.80	.40	.25
91	Bob Bailey	.60	.30	.20
92	Steve Ridzik	.50	.25	.15
93	Gary Geiger	.50	.25	.15
94	Braves Rookies (Jim Britton, Larry Maxie)	.50	.25	.15
95	George Altman	.60	.30	.20
96	Bob Buhl	.60	.30	.20
97	Jim Fregosi	1.25	.60	.40
98	Bill Bruton	.50	.25	.15
99	Al Stanek	.50	.25	.15
100	Elston Howard	3.50	1.75	1.00
101	Walt Alston	3.00	1.50	.90
102	Checklist 89-176	3.00	1.50	.90
103	Curt Flood	2.00	1.00	.60
104	Art Mahaffey	.50	.25	.15
105	Woody Held	.50	.25	.15
106	Joe Nuxhall	.80	.40	.25
107	White Sox Rookies (Bruce Howard, Frank Kreutzer)	.50	.25	.15
108	John Wyatt	.50	.25	.15
109	Rusty Staub	5.00	2.50	1.50
110	Albie Pearson	.50	.25	.15
111	Don Elston	.50	.25	.15
112	Bob Tillman	.50	.25	.15
113	Grover Powell	.60	.30	.20
114	Don Lock	.50	.25	.15
115	Frank Bolling	.50	.25	.15
116	Twins Rookies (Tony Oliva, Jay Ward)	4.00	2.00	1.25
117	Earl Francis	.50	.25	.15
118	John Blanchard	1.00	.50	.30
119	Gary Kolb	.50	.25	.15
120	Don Drysdale	8.00	4.00	2.50
121	Pete Runnels	.80	.40	.25
122	Don McMahon	.50	.25	.15
123	Jose Pagan	.50	.25	.15
124	Orlando Pena	.50	.25	.15
125	Pete Rose	130.00	65.00	39.00
126	Russ Snyder	.50	.25	.15
127	Angels Rookies (Aubrey Gatewood, Dick Simpson)	.50	.25	.15
128	Mickey Lolich	5.00	2.50	1.50
129	Amado Samuel	.60	.30	.20
130	Gary Peters	.60	.30	.20
131	Steve Boros	.60	.30	.20
132	Braves Team	2.25	1.25	.70
133	Jim Grant	.50	.25	.15
134	Don Zimmer	1.50	.70	.45
135	Johnny Callison	1.50	.70	.45
136	World Series Game 1 (Koufax Strikes Out 15)	5.00	2.50	1.50
137	World Series Game 2 (Davis Sparks Rally)	2.50	1.25	.70
138	World Series Game 3 (L.A. Takes 3rd Straight)	2.50	1.25	.70
139	World Series Game 4 (Sealing Yanks' Doom)	2.50	1.25	.70
140	World Series Summary (The Dodgers Celebrate)	2.50	1.25	.70
141	Danny Murtaugh	.60	.30	.20
142	John Bateman	.50	.25	.15
143	Bubba Phillips	.50	.25	.15
144	Al Worthington	.50	.25	.15
145	Norm Siebern	.60	.30	.20
146	Indians Rookies (Bob Chance, Tommy John)	15.00	7.50	4.50
147	Ray Sadecki	.50	.25	.15
148	J.C. Martin	.50	.25	.15
149	Paul Foytack	.50	.25	.15
150	Willie Mays	30.00	15.00	9.00
151	Athletics Team	2.25	1.25	.70
152	Denver Lemaster	.50	.25	.15

		NR MT	EX	VG
153	Dick Williams	1.50	.70	.45
154	Dick Tracewski	.50	.25	.15
155	Duke Snider	10.00	5.00	3.00
156	Bill Dailey	.50	.25	.15
157	Gene Mauch	.90	.45	.25
158	Ken Johnson	.50	.25	.15
159	Charlie Dees	.50	.25	.15
160	Ken Boyer	4.00	2.00	1.25
161	Dave McNally	1.25	.60	.40
162	Hitting Area (Vada Pinson, Dick Sisler)	1.25	.60	.40
163	Donn Clendenon	.80	.40	.25
164	Bud Daley	1.00	.50	.30
165	Jerry Lumpe	.60	.30	.20
166	Marty Keough	.50	.25	.15
167	Senators Rookies (Mike Brumley, Lou Piniella)	12.00	6.00	3.50
168	Al Weis	.50	.25	.15
169	Del Crandall	1.25	.60	.40
170	Dick Radatz	.60	.30	.20
171	Ty Cline	.50	.25	.15
172	Indians Team	2.25	1.25	.70
173	Ryne Duren	.90	.45	.25
174	Doc Edwards	.60	.30	.20
175	Billy Williams	6.00	3.00	1.75
176	Tracy Stallard	.60	.30	.20
177	Harmon Killebrew	8.00	4.00	2.50
178	Hank Bauer	.90	.45	.25
179	Carl Warwick	.50	.25	.15
180	Tommy Davis	1.50	.70	.45
181	Dave Wickersham	.50	.25	.15
182	Sox Sockers (Chuck Schilling, Carl Yastrzemski)	7.00	3.50	2.00
183	Ron Taylor	.50	.25	.15
184	Al Luplow	.50	.25	.15
185	Jim O'Toole	.50	.25	.15
186	Roman Mejias	.50	.25	.15
187	Ed Roebuck	.50	.25	.15
188	Checklist 177-264	3.00	1.50	.90
189	Bob Hendley	.50	.25	.15
190	Bobby Richardson	4.00	2.00	1.25
191	Clay Dalrymple	.50	.25	.15
192	Cubs Rookies (John Boccabella, Billy Cowan)	.50	.25	.15
193	Jerry Lynch	.50	.25	.15
194	John Goryl	.50	.25	.15
195	Floyd Robinson	.50	.25	.15
196	Jim Gentile	.60	.30	.20
197	Frank Lary	.60	.30	.20
198	Len Gabrielson	.50	.25	.15
199	Joe Azcue	.50	.25	.15
200	Sandy Koufax	30.00	15.00	9.00
201	Orioles Rookies (Sam Bowens, Wally Bunker)	.60	.30	.20
202	Galen Cisco	.60	.30	.20
203	John Kennedy	.50	.25	.15
204	Matty Alou	.90	.45	.25
205	Nellie Fox	4.00	2.00	1.25
206	Steve Hamilton	1.00	.50	.30
207	Fred Hutchinson	.70	.35	.20
208	Wes Covington	.50	.25	.15
209	Bob Allen	.50	.25	.15
210	Carl Yastrzemski	40.00	20.00	12.00
211	Jim Coker	.50	.25	.15
212	Pete Lovrich	.50	.25	.15
213	Angels Team	2.25	1.25	.70
214	Ken McMullen	.60	.30	.20
215	Ray Herbert	.50	.25	.15
216	Mike de la Hoz	.50	.25	.15
217	Jim King	.50	.25	.15
218	Hank Fischer	.50	.25	.15
219	Young Aces (Jim Bouton, Al Downing)	2.00	1.00	.60
220	Dick Ellsworth	.50	.25	.15
221	Bob Saverine	.50	.25	.15
222	Bill Pierce	.90	.45	.25
223	George Banks	.50	.25	.15
224	Tommie Sisk	.50	.25	.15
225	Roger Maris	20.00	10.00	6.00
226	Colts Rookies (Gerald Grote, Larry Yellen)	1.25	.60	.40
227	Barry Latman	.50	.25	.15
228	Felix Mantilla	.50	.25	.15
229	Charley Lau	.80	.40	.25
230	Brooks Robinson	15.00	7.50	4.50
231	Dick Calmus	.50	.25	.15
232	Al Lopez	3.00	1.50	.90
233	Hal Smith	.50	.25	.15
234	Gary Bell	.50	.25	.15
235	Ron Hunt	.80	.40	.25
236	Bill Faul	.50	.25	.15

	NR MT	EX	VG
237 Cubs Team	2.25	1.25	.70
238 Roy McMillan	.50	.25	.15
239 Herm Starrette	.50	.25	.15
240 Bill White	1.50	.70	.45
241 Jim Owens	.50	.25	.15
242 Harvey Kuenn	1.50	.70	.45
243 Phillies Rookies (Richie Allen, John Herrnstein)	8.00	4.00	2.50
244 Tony LaRussa	2.50	1.25	.70
245 Dick Stigman	.50	.25	.15
246 Manny Mota	1.25	.60	.40
247 Dave DeBusschere	2.00	1.00	.60
248 Johnny Pesky	.80	.40	.25
249 Doug Camilli	.50	.25	.15
250 Al Kaline	10.00	5.00	3.00
251 Choo Choo Coleman	.80	.40	.25
252 Ken Aspromonte	.50	.25	.15
253 Wally Post	.50	.25	.15
254 Don Hoak	.70	.35	.20
255 Lee Thomas	.50	.25	.15
256 Johnny Weekly	.50	.25	.15
257 Giants Team	2.25	1.25	.70
258 Garry Roggenburk	.50	.25	.15
259 Harry Bright	1.00	.50	.30
260 Frank Robinson	10.00	5.00	3.00
261 Jim Hannan	.50	.25	.15
262 Cardinals Rookie Stars (Harry Fanok, Mike Shannon)	1.50	.70	.45
263 Chuck Estrada	.50	.25	.15
264 Jim Landis	.50	.25	.15
265 Jim Bunning	4.00	2.00	1.25
266 Gene Freese	.50	.25	.15
267 Wilbur Wood	1.50	.70	.45
268 Bill's Got It (Danny Murtaugh, Bill Virdon)	.90	.45	.25
269 Ellis Burton	.50	.25	.15
270 Rich Rollins	.50	.25	.15
271 Bob Sadowski	.50	.25	.15
272 Jake Wood	.50	.25	.15
273 Mel Nelson	.50	.25	.15
274 Checklist 265-352	3.00	1.50	.90
275 John Tsitouris	.50	.25	.15
276 Jose Tartabull	.50	.25	.15
277 Ken Retzer	.50	.25	.15
278 Bobby Shantz	1.50	.70	.45
279 Joe Koppe	.50	.25	.15
280 Juan Marichal	8.00	4.00	2.50
281 Yankees Rookies (Jake Gibbs, Tom Metcalf)	1.00	.50	.30
282 Bob Bruce	.50	.25	.15
283 Tommy McCraw	.60	.30	.20
284 Dick Schofield	.50	.25	.15
285 Robin Roberts	6.00	3.00	1.75
286 Don Landrum	.50	.25	.15
287 Red Sox Rookies (Tony Conigliaro, Bill Spanswick)	4.00	2.00	1.25
288 Al Moran	.60	.30	.20
289 Frank Funk	.50	.25	.15
290 Bob Allison	.90	.45	.25
291 Phil Ortega	.50	.25	.15
292 Mike Roarke	.50	.25	.15
293 Phillies Team	2.25	1.25	.70
294 Ken Hunt	.50	.25	.15
295 Roger Craig	1.50	.70	.45
296 Ed Kirkpatrick	.50	.25	.15
297 Ken MacKenzie	.50	.25	.15
298 Harry Craft	.50	.25	.15
299 Bill Stafford	1.00	.50	.30
300 Hank Aaron	35.00	17.50	10.50
301 Larry Brown	.50	.25	.15
302 Dan Pfister	.50	.25	.15
303 Jim Campbell	.50	.25	.15
304 Bob Johnson	.50	.25	.15
305 Jack Lamabe	.50	.25	.15
306 Giant Gunners (Orlando Cepeda, Willie Mays)	8.00	4.00	2.50
307 Joe Gibbon	.50	.25	.15
308 Gene Stephens	.50	.25	.15
309 Paul Toth	.50	.25	.15
310 Jim Gilliam	3.00	1.50	.90
311 Tom Brown	.50	.25	.15
312 Tigers Rookies (Fritz Fisher, Fred Gladding)	.50	.25	.15
313 Chuck Hiller	.50	.25	.15
314 Jerry Buchek	.50	.25	.15
315 Bo Belinsky	.90	.45	.25
316 Gene Oliver	.50	.25	.15
317 Al Smith	.50	.25	.15
318 Twins Team	2.25	1.25	.70
319 Paul Brown	.50	.25	.15
320 Rocky Colavito	3.00	1.50	.90

	NR MT	EX	VG
321 Bob Lillis	.50	.25	.15
322 George Brunet	.50	.25	.15
323 John Buzhardt	.50	.25	.15
324 Casey Stengel	8.00	4.00	2.50
325 Hector Lopez	1.00	.50	.30
326 Ron Brand	.50	.25	.15
327 Don Blasingame	.50	.25	.15
328 Bob Shaw	.50	.25	.15
329 Russ Nixon	.50	.25	.15
330 Tommy Harper	.80	.40	.25
331 A.L. Bombers (Norm Cash, Al Kaline, Mickey Mantle, Roger Maris)	35.00	16.00	8.75
332 Ray Washburn	.50	.25	.15
333 Billy Moran	.50	.25	.15
334 Lew Krausse	.50	.25	.15
335 Don Mossi	.60	.30	.20
336 Andre Rodgers	.50	.25	.15
337 Dodgers Rookies (Al Ferrara, Jeff Torborg)	.80	.40	.25
338 Jack Kralick	.50	.25	.15
339 Walt Bond	.50	.25	.15
340 Joe Cunningham	.60	.30	.20
341 Jim Roland	.50	.25	.15
342 Willie Stargell	18.00	9.00	5.50
343 Senators Team	2.25	1.25	.70
344 Phil Linz	1.00	.50	.30
345 Frank Thomas	.60	.30	.20
346 Joe Jay	.50	.25	.15
347 Bobby Wine	.60	.30	.20
348 Ed Lopat	.90	.45	.25
349 Art Fowler	.50	.25	.15
350 Willie McCovey	10.00	5.00	3.00
351 Dan Schneider	.50	.25	.15
352 Eddie Bressoud	.50	.25	.15
353 Wally Moon	.90	.45	.25
354 Dave Giusti	.50	.25	.15
355 Vic Power	.50	.25	.15
356 Reds Rookies (Bill McCool, Chico Ruiz)	.50	.25	.15
357 Charley James	.50	.25	.15
358 Ron Kline	.50	.25	.15
359 Jim Schaffer	.50	.25	.15
360 Joe Pepitone	2.50	1.25	.70
361 Jay Hook	.60	.30	.20
362 Checklist 353-429	3.00	1.50	.90
363 Dick McAuliffe	.60	.30	.20
364 Joe Gaines	.50	.25	.15
365 Cal McLish	.50	.25	.15
366 Nelson Mathews	.50	.25	.15
367 Fred Whitfield	.50	.25	.15
368 White Sox Rookies (Fritz Ackley, Don Buford)	.90	.45	.25
369 Jerry Zimmerman	.50	.25	.15
370 Hal Woodeshick	.50	.25	.15
371 Frank Howard	3.00	1.50	.90
372 Howie Koplitz	.80	.40	.25
373 Pirates Team	3.00	1.50	.90
374 Bobby Bolin	.80	.40	.25
375 Ron Santo	2.50	1.25	.70
376 Dave Morehead	.80	.40	.25
377 Bob Skinner	.90	.45	.25
378 Braves Rookies (Jack Smith, Woody Woodward)	.90	.45	.25
379 Tony Gonzalez	.80	.40	.25
380 Whitey Ford	12.00	6.00	3.50
381 Bob Taylor	.90	.45	.25
382 Wes Stock	.80	.40	.25
383 Bill Rigney	.80	.40	.25
384 Ron Hansen	.80	.40	.25
385 Curt Simmons	1.25	.60	.40
386 Lenny Green	.80	.40	.25
387 Terry Fox	.80	.40	.25
388 Athletics Rookies (John O'Donoghue, George Williams)	.80	.40	.25
389 Jim Umbricht	.80	.40	.25
390 Orlando Cepeda	4.50	2.25	1.25
391 Sam McDowell	1.25	.60	.40
392 Jim Pagliaroni	.80	.40	.25
393 Casey Teaches (Ed Kranepool, Casey Stengel)	3.00	1.50	.90
394 Bob Miller	.80	.40	.25
395 Tom Tresh	3.00	1.50	.90
396 Dennis Bennett	.80	.40	.25
397 Chuck Cottier	.80	.40	.25
398 Mets Rookies (Bill Haas, Dick Smith)	.90	.45	.25
399 Jackie Brandt	.80	.40	.25
400 Warren Spahn	10.00	5.00	3.00
401 Charlie Maxwell	.80	.40	.25
402 Tom Sturdivant	.80	.40	.25
403 Reds Team	3.50	1.75	1.00

		NR MT	EX	VG
404	Tony Martinez	.80	.40	.25
405	Ken McBride	.80	.40	.25
406	Al Spangler	.80	.40	.25
407	Bill Freehan	2.00	1.00	.60
408	Cubs Rookies (Fred Burdette, Jim Stewart)	.80	.40	.25
409	Bill Fischer	.80	.40	.25
410	Dick Stuart	1.25	.60	.40
411	Lee Walls	.80	.40	.25
412	Ray Culp	.80	.40	.25
413	Johnny Keane	.80	.40	.25
414	Jack Sanford	.80	.40	.25
415	Tony Kubek	4.50	2.25	1.25
416	Lee Maye	.80	.40	.25
417	Don Cardwell	.80	.40	.25
418	Orioles Rookies (Darold Knowles, Les Narum)	.90	.45	.25
419	Ken Harrelson	3.00	1.50	.90
420	Jim Maloney	.90	.45	.25
421	Camilo Carreon	.80	.40	.25
422	Jack Fisher	.90	.45	.25
423	Tops In NL (Hank Aaron, Willie Mays)	25.00	12.50	7.50
424	Dick Bertell	.80	.40	.25
425	Norm Cash	2.50	1.25	.70
426	Bob Rodgers	1.25	.60	.40
427	Don Rudolph	.80	.40	.25
428	Red Sox Rookies (Archie Skeen, Pete Smith)	.80	.40	.25
429	Tim McCarver	3.00	1.50	.90
430	Juan Pizarro	.80	.40	.25
431	George Alusik	.80	.40	.25
432	Ruben Amaro	.80	.40	.25
433	Yankees Team	8.00	4.00	2.50
434	Don Nottebart	.80	.40	.25
435	Vic Davalillo	.90	.45	.25
436	Charlie Neal	.80	.40	.25
437	Ed Bailey	.80	.40	.25
438	Checklist 430-506	4.00	2.00	1.25
439	Harvey Haddix	1.50	.70	.45
440	Bob Clemente	30.00	15.00	9.00
441	Bob Duliba	.80	.40	.25
442	Pumpsie Green	.90	.45	.25
443	Chuck Dressen	.90	.45	.25
444	Larry Jackson	.80	.40	.25
445	Bill Skowron	2.50	1.25	.70
446	Julian Javier	.90	.45	.25
447	Ted Bowsfield	.80	.40	.25
448	Cookie Rojas	.90	.45	.25
449	Deron Johnson	.80	.40	.25
450	Steve Barber	.80	.40	.25
451	Joe Amalfitano	.80	.40	.25
452	Giants Rookies (Gil Garrido, Jim Hart)	1.25	.60	.40
453	Frank Baumann	.80	.40	.25
454	Tommie Aaron	1.25	.60	.40
455	Bernie Allen	.80	.40	.25
456	Dodgers Rookies (Wes Parker, John Werhas)	2.00	1.00	.60
457	Jesse Gonder	.90	.45	.25
458	Ralph Terry	2.00	1.00	.60
459	Red Sox Rookies (Pete Charton, Dalton Jones)	.80	.40	.25
460	Bob Gibson	12.00	6.00	3.50
461	George Thomas	.80	.40	.25
462	Birdie Tebbetts	.80	.40	.25
463	Don Leppert	.80	.40	.25
464	Dallas Green	1.25	.60	.40
465	Mike Hershberger	.80	.40	.25
466	Athletics Rookies (Dick Green, Aurelio Monteagudo)	.90	.45	.25
467	Bob Aspromonte	.80	.40	.25
468	Gaylord Perry	15.00	7.50	4.50
469	Cubs Rookies (Fred Norman, Sterling Slaughter)	.80	.40	.25
470	Jim Bouton	3.00	1.50	.90
471	Gates Brown	1.25	.60	.40
472	Vern Law	1.50	.70	.45
473	Orioles Team	3.00	1.50	.90
474	Larry Sherry	.80	.40	.25
475	Ed Charles	.80	.40	.25
476	Braves Rookies (Rico Carty, Dick Kelley)	3.50	1.75	1.00
477	Mike Joyce	.90	.45	.25
478	Dick Howser	2.00	1.00	.60
479	Cardinals Rookies (Dave Bakenhaster, Johnny Lewis)	.80	.40	.25
480	Bob Purkey	.80	.40	.25
481	Chuck Schilling	.80	.40	.25
482	Phillies Rookies (John Briggs, Danny Cater)	.90	.45	.25

		NR MT	EX	VG
483	Fred Valentine	.80	.40	.25
484	Bill Pleis	.80	.40	.25
485	Tom Haller	.90	.45	.25
486	Bob Kennedy	.80	.40	.25
487	Mike McCormick	.90	.45	.25
488	Yankees Rookies (Bob Meyer, Pete Mikkelsen)	1.50	.70	.45
489	Julio Navarro	.80	.40	.25
490	Ron Fairly	1.50	.70	.45
491	Ed Rakow	.80	.40	.25
492	Colts Rookies (Jim Beauchamp, Mike White)	.80	.40	.25
493	Don Lee	.80	.40	.25
494	Al Jackson	.90	.45	.25
495	Bill Virdon	2.00	1.00	.60
496	White Sox Team	3.00	1.50	.90
497	Jeoff Long	.80	.40	.25
498	Dave Stenhouse	.80	.40	.25
499	Indians Rookies (Chico Salmon, Gordon Seyfried)	.80	.40	.25
500	Camilo Pascual	1.25	.60	.40
501	Bob Veale	.90	.45	.25
502	Angels Rookies (Bobby Knoop, Bob Lee)	.90	.45	.25
503	Earl Wilson	.80	.40	.25
504	Claude Raymond	.80	.40	.25
505	Stan Williams	1.50	.70	.45
506	Bobby Bragan	.90	.45	.25
507	John Edwards	.80	.40	.25
508	Diego Segui	.80	.40	.25
509	Pirates Rookies (Gene Alley, Orlando McFarlane)	1.25	.60	.40
510	Lindy McDaniel	.80	.40	.25
511	Lou Jackson	.80	.40	.25
512	Tigers Rookies (Willie Horton, Joe Sparma)	3.00	1.50	.90
513	Don Larsen	1.50	.70	.45
514	Jim Hickman	1.25	.60	.40
515	Johnny Romano	.80	.40	.25
516	Twins Rookies (Jerry Arrigo, Dwight Siebler)	.80	.40	.25
517a	Checklist 507-587 (wrong numbering on back)	7.00	3.50	2.00
517b	Checklist 507-587 (correct numbering on back)	4.50	2.25	1.25
518	Carl Bouldin	.80	.40	.25
519	Charlie Smith	.90	.45	.25
520	Jack Baldschun	.80	.40	.25
521	Tom Satriano	.80	.40	.25
522	Bobby Tiefenauer	.80	.40	.25
523	Lou Burdette	5.00	2.50	1.50
524	Reds Rookies (Jim Dickson, Bobby Klaus)	2.50	1.25	.70
525	Al McBean	2.50	1.25	.70
526	Lou Clinton	2.50	1.25	.70
527	Larry Bearnarth	3.00	1.50	.90
528	Athletics Rookies (Dave Duncan, Tom Reynolds)	3.00	1.50	.90
529	Al Dark	3.50	1.75	1.00
530	Leon Wagner	3.00	1.50	.90
531	Dodgers Team	8.00	4.00	2.50
532	Twins Rookies (Bud Bloomfield, Joe Nossek)	2.50	1.25	.70
533	Johnny Klippstein	2.50	1.25	.70
534	Gus Bell	3.00	1.50	.90
535	Phil Regan	2.50	1.25	.70
536	Mets Rookies (Larry Elliot, John Stephenson)	3.00	1.50	.90
537	Dan Osinski	2.50	1.25	.70
538	Minnie Minoso	5.00	2.50	1.50
539	Roy Face	4.00	2.00	1.25
540	Luis Aparicio	12.00	6.00	3.50
541	Braves Rookies (Phil Niekro, Phil Roof)	55.00	27.00	16.50
542	Don Mincher	3.00	1.50	.90
543	Bob Uecker	30.00	15.00	9.00
544	Colts Rookies (Steve Hertz, Joe Hoerner)	2.50	1.25	.70
545	Max Alvis	3.00	1.50	.90
546	Joe Christopher	3.00	1.50	.90
547	Gil Hodges	8.00	4.00	2.50
548	N.L. Rookies (Wayne Schurr, Paul Speckenbach)	2.50	1.25	.70
549	Joe Moeller	2.50	1.25	.70
550	Ken Hubbs	8.00	4.00	2.50
551	Billy Hoeft	2.50	1.25	.70
552	Indians Rookies (Tom Kelley, Sonny Siebert)	3.00	1.50	.90
553	Jim Brewer	2.50	1.25	.70
554	Hank Foiles	2.50	1.25	.70
555	Lee Stange	2.50	1.25	.70

		NR MT	EX	VG
556	Mets Rookies (Steve Dillon, Ron Locke)			
		3.00	1.50	.90
557	Leo Burke	2.50	1.25	.70
558	Don Schwall	2.50	1.25	.70
559	Dick Phillips	2.50	1.25	.70
560	Dick Farrell	2.50	1.25	.70
561	Phillies Rookies (Dave Bennett, Rick Wise)			
		3.50	1.75	1.00
562	Pedro Ramos	2.50	1.25	.70
563	Dal Maxvill	3.50	1.75	1.00
564	A.L. Rookies (Joe McCabe, Jerry McNertney)			
		2.50	1.25	.70
565	Stu Miller	2.50	1.25	.70
566	Ed Kranepool	4.00	2.00	1.25
567	Jim Kaat	8.00	4.00	2.50
568	N.L. Rookies (Phil Gagliano, Cap Peterson)			
		2.50	1.25	.70
569	Fred Newman	2.50	1.25	.70
570	Bill Mazeroski	5.00	2.50	1.50
571	Gene Conley	3.50	1.75	1.00
572	A.L. Rookies (Dick Egan, Dave Gray)			
		2.50	1.25	.70
573	Jim Duffalo	2.50	1.25	.70
574	Manny Jimenez	2.50	1.25	.70
575	Tony Cloninger	3.00	1.50	.90
576	Mets Rookies (Jerry Hinsley, Bill Wakefield)			
		3.00	1.50	.90
577	Gordy Coleman	2.50	1.25	.70
578	Glen Hobbie	2.50	1.25	.70
579	Red Sox Team	6.00	3.00	1.75
580	Johnny Podres	5.00	2.50	1.50
581	Yankees Rookies (Pedro Gonzalez, Archie Moore)			
		4.00	2.00	1.25
582	Rod Kanehl	3.00	1.50	.90
583	Tito Francona	3.00	1.50	.90
584	Joel Horlen	2.50	1.25	.70
585	Tony Taylor	2.50	1.25	.70
586	Jim Piersall	5.00	2.50	1.50
587	Bennie Daniels	6.00	1.50	.70

1964 Topps Coins

The 164 metal coins in this set were issued by Topps as inserts in the company's baseball card wax packs. The series is divided into two principal types, 120 "regular" coins and 44 All-Star coins. The 1½" diameter coins feature a full color background to the player photos in the "regular" series, while the players in the All-Star series are featured against plain red or blue backgrounds. There are two variations each of the Mantle, Causey and Hinton coins among the All-Star subset.

		NR MT	EX	VG
Complete Set:		575.00	287.00	172.00
Common Player:		.90	.45	.25
1	Don Zimmer	1.00	.50	.30
2	Jim Wynn	1.00	.50	.30
3	Johnny Orsino	.90	.45	.25
4	Jim Bouton	1.25	.60	.40
5	Dick Groat	1.25	.60	.40
6	Leon Wagner	.90	.45	.25
7	Frank Malzone	.90	.45	.25
8	Steve Barber	.90	.45	.25
9	Johnny Romano	.90	.45	.25
10	Tom Tresh	1.25	.60	.40
11	Felipe Alou	1.00	.50	.30
12	Dick Stuart	1.00	.50	.30
13	Claude Osteen	1.00	.50	.30
14	Juan Pizarro	.90	.45	.25

		NR MT	EX	VG
15	Donn Clendenon	.90	.45	.25
16	Jimmie Hall	.90	.45	.25
17	Larry Jackson	.90	.45	.25
18	Brooks Robinson	10.00	5.00	3.00
19	Bob Allison	1.00	.50	.30
20	Ed Roebuck	.90	.45	.25
21	Pete Ward	.90	.45	.25
22	Willie McCovey	8.00	4.00	2.50
23	Elston Howard	1.50	.70	.45
24	Diego Segui	.90	.45	.25
25	Ken Boyer	1.50	.70	.45
26	Carl Yastrzemski	20.00	10.00	6.00
27	Bill Mazeroski	1.50	.70	.45
28	Jerry Lumpe	.90	.45	.25
29	Woody Held	.90	.45	.25
30	Dick Radatz	.90	.45	.25
31	Luis Aparicio	5.00	2.50	1.50
32	Dave Nicholson	.90	.45	.25
33	Ed Mathews	7.50	3.75	2.25
34	Don Drysdale	7.50	3.75	2.25
35	Ray Culp	.90	.45	.25
36	Juan Marichal	7.00	3.50	2.00
37	Frank Robinson	8.00	4.00	2.50
38	Chuck Hinton	.90	.45	.25
39	Floyd Robinson	.90	.45	.25
40	Tommy Harper	.90	.45	.25
41	Ron Hansen	.90	.45	.25
42	Ernie Banks	8.00	4.00	2.50
43	Jesse Gonder	.90	.45	.25
44	Billy Williams	7.00	3.50	2.00
45	Vada Pinson	1.50	.70	.45
46	Rocky Colavito	1.50	.70	.45
47	Bill Monbouquette	.90	.45	.25
48	Max Alvis	.90	.45	.25
49	Norm Siebern	.90	.45	.25
50	John Callison	1.00	.50	.30
51	Rich Rollins	.90	.45	.25
52	Ken McBride	.90	.45	.25
53	Don Lock	.90	.45	.25
54	Ron Fairly	1.00	.50	.30
55	Bob Clemente	15.00	7.50	4.50
56	Dick Ellsworth	.90	.45	.25
57	Tommy Davis	1.25	.60	.40
58	Tony Gonzalez	.90	.45	.25
59	Bob Gibson	7.50	3.75	2.25
60	Jim Maloney	.90	.45	.25
61	Frank Howard	1.50	.70	.45
62	Jim Pagliaroni	.90	.45	.25
63	Orlando Cepeda	2.00	1.00	.60
64	Ron Perranoski	.90	.45	.25
65	Curt Flood	1.25	.60	.40
66	Al McBean	.90	.45	.25
67	Dean Chance	.90	.45	.25
68	Ron Santo	1.25	.60	.40
69	Jack Baldschun	.90	.45	.25
70	Milt Pappas	.90	.45	.25
71	Gary Peters	.90	.45	.25
72	Bobby Richardson	1.50	.70	.45
73	Lee Thomas	.90	.45	.25
74	Hank Aguirre	.90	.45	.25
75	Carl Willey	.90	.45	.25
76	Camilo Pascual	.90	.45	.25
77	Bob Friend	1.00	.50	.30
78	Bill White	1.00	.50	.30
79	Norm Cash	1.25	.60	.40
80	Willie Mays	15.00	7.50	4.50
81	Duke Carmel	.90	.45	.25
82	Pete Rose	30.00	15.00	9.00
83	Hank Aaron	15.00	7.50	4.50
84	Bob Aspromonte	.90	.45	.25
85	Jim O'Toole	.90	.45	.25
86	Vic Davalillo	.90	.45	.25
87	Bill Freehan	1.00	.50	.30
88	Warren Spahn	8.00	4.00	2.50
89	Ron Hunt	.90	.45	.25
90	Denis Menke	.90	.45	.25
91	Turk Farrell	.90	.45	.25
92	Jim Hickman	.90	.45	.25
93	Jim Bunning	2.00	1.00	.60
94	Bob Hendley	.90	.45	.25
95	Ernie Broglio	.90	.45	.25
96	Rusty Staub	1.50	.70	.45
97	Lou Brock	8.00	4.00	2.50
98	Jim Fregosi	1.00	.50	.30
99	Jim Grant	.90	.45	.25
100	Al Kaline	8.00	4.00	2.50
101	Earl Battey	.90	.45	.25
102	Wayne Causey	.90	.45	.25
103	Chuck Schilling	.90	.45	.25
104	Boog Powell	1.50	.70	.45
105	Dave Wickersham	.90	.45	.25

		NR MT	EX	VG
106	Sandy Koufax	12.00	6.00	3.50
107	John Bateman	.90	.45	.25
108	Ed Brinkman	.90	.45	.25
109	Al Downing	1.00	.50	.30
110	Joe Azcue	.90	.45	.25
111	Albie Pearson	.90	.45	.25
112	Harmon Killebrew	8.00	4.00	2.50
113	Tony Taylor	.90	.45	.25
114	Alvin Jackson	.90	.45	.25
115	Billy O'Dell	.90	.45	.25
116	Don Demeter	.90	.45	.25
117	Ed Charles	.90	.45	.25
118	Joe Torre	1.50	.70	.45
119	Don Nottebart	.90	.45	.25
120	Mickey Mantle	40.00	20.00	12.00
121	Joe Pepitone	1.25	.60	.40
122	Dick Stuart	.90	.45	.25
123	Bobby Richardson	1.50	.70	.45
124	Jerry Lumpe	.90	.45	.25
125	Brooks Robinson	10.00	5.00	3.00
126	Frank Malzone	.90	.45	.25
127	Luis Aparicio	5.00	2.50	1.50
128	Jim Fregosi	1.00	.50	.30
129	Al Kaline	8.00	4.00	2.50
130	Leon Wagner	.90	.45	.25
131a	Mickey Mantle (batting lefthanded)			
		40.00	20.00	12.00
131b	Mickey Mantle (batting righthanded)			
		40.00	20.00	12.00
132	Albie Pearson	.90	.45	.25
133	Harmon Killebrew	8.00	4.00	2.50
134	Carl Yastrzemski	20.00	10.00	6.00
135	Elston Howard	1.50	.70	.45
136	Earl Battey	.90	.45	.25
137	Camilo Pascual	.90	.45	.25
138	Jim Bouton	1.25	.60	.40
139	Whitey Ford	8.00	4.00	2.50
140	Gary Peters	.90	.45	.25
141	Bill White	1.00	.50	.30
142	Orlando Cepeda	2.00	1.00	.60
143	Bill Mazeroski	1.50	.70	.45
144	Tony Taylor	.90	.45	.25
145	Ken Boyer	1.50	.70	.45
146	Ron Santo	1.25	.60	.40
147	Dick Groat	1.25	.60	.40
148	Roy McMillan	.90	.45	.25
149	Hank Aaron	15.00	7.50	4.50
150	Bob Clemente	15.00	7.50	4.50
151	Willie Mays	15.00	7.50	4.50
152	Vada Pinson	1.50	.70	.45
153	Tommy Davis	1.25	.60	.40
154	Frank Robinson	8.00	4.00	2.50
155	Joe Torre	1.50	.70	.45
156	Tim McCarver	1.25	.60	.40
157	Juan Marichal	7.00	3.50	2.00
158	Jim Maloney	.90	.45	.25
159	Sandy Koufax	12.00	6.00	3.50
160	Warren Spahn	8.00	4.00	2.50
161a	Wayne Causey (N.L. on back)	15.00	7.50	4.50
161b	Wayne Causey (A.L. on back)	1.00	.50	.30
162a	Chuck Hinton (N.L. on back)	15.00	7.50	4.50
162b	Chuck Hinton (A.L. on back)	1.00	.50	.30
163	Bob Aspromonte	.90	.45	.25
164	Ron Hunt	.90	.45	.25

1964 Topps Giants

Measuring 3⅛'' by 5¼'' the Topps Giants were the company's first postcard-size issue. The cards feature large color photographs surrounded by white borders with a white baseball containing the player's name, position and team. Card backs carry another photo of the player surrounded by a newspaper-style explanation of the depicted career highlight. The 60-card set contains primarily stars which means it's an excellent place to find inexpensive cards of Hall of Famers. The '64 Giants were not printed in equal quantity and seven of the cards, including HOFers Koufax and Mays, are significantly scarcer than the remainder of the set.

		NR MT	EX	VG
Complete Set:		50.00	25.00	15.00
Common Player:		.15	.08	.05
1	Gary Peters	.15	.08	.05
2	Ken Johnson	.15	.08	.05
3	Sandy Koufax	8.00	4.00	2.50
4	Bob Bailey	.15	.08	.05
5	Milt Pappas	.25	.13	.08
6	Ron Hunt	.15	.08	.05
7	Whitey Ford	1.75	.90	.50
8	Roy McMillan	.15	.08	.05
9	Rocky Colavito	.40	.20	.12
10	Jim Bunning	.50	.25	.15
11	Bob Clemente	2.25	1.25	.70
12	Al Kaline	1.50	.70	.45
13	Nellie Fox	.60	.30	.20
14	Tony Gonzalez	.15	.08	.05
15	Jim Gentile	.15	.08	.05
16	Dean Chance	.15	.08	.05
17	Dick Ellsworth	.15	.08	.05
18	Jim Fregosi	.25	.13	.08
19	Dick Groat	.40	.20	.12
20	Chuck Hinton	.15	.08	.05
21	Elston Howard	.50	.25	.15
22	Dick Farrell	.15	.08	.05
23	Albie Pearson	.15	.08	.05
24	Frank Howard	.50	.25	.15
25	Mickey Mantle	10.00	5.00	3.00
26	Joe Torre	.40	.20	.12
27	Ed Brinkman	.15	.08	.05
28	Bob Friend	2.50	1.25	.70
29	Frank Robinson	1.75	.90	.50
30	Bill Freehan	.25	.13	.08
31	Warren Spahn	1.25	.60	.40
32	Camilo Pascual	.15	.08	.05
33	Pete Ward	.15	.08	.05
34	Jim Maloney	.15	.08	.05
35	Dave Wickersham	.15	.08	.05
36	Johnny Callison	.25	.13	.08
37	Juan Marichal	1.25	.60	.40
38	Harmon Killebrew	1.75	.90	.50
39	Luis Aparicio	1.25	.60	.40
40	Dick Radatz	.15	.08	.05
41	Bob Gibson	1.50	.70	.45
42	Dick Stuart	2.50	1.25	.70
43	Tommy Davis	.40	.20	.12
44	Tony Oliva	.50	.25	.15
45	Wayne Causey	2.50	1.25	.70
46	Max Alvis	.15	.08	.05
47	Galen Cisco	2.50	1.25	.70
48	Carl Yastrzemski	3.00	1.50	.90
49	Hank Aaron	2.50	1.25	.70
50	Brooks Robinson	2.00	1.00	.60
51	Willie Mays	8.00	4.00	2.50
52	Billy Williams	1.25	.60	.40
53	Juan Pizarro	.15	.08	.05
54	Leon Wagner	.15	.08	.05
55	Orlando Cepeda	.70	.35	.20
56	Vada Pinson	.50	.25	.15
57	Ken Boyer	.60	.30	.20
58	Ron Santo	.40	.20	.12
59	John Romano	.15	.08	.05
60	Bill Skowron	2.50	1.25	.70

1964 Topps Photo Tatoos

Apparently not content to leave the skin of American children without adornment, Topps jumped back into the tattoo field in 1964 with the release of a new series. Measuring 1-9/16'' by 3-1/2,'' there were 75

		NR MT	EX	VG
(50)	Lee Thomas	2.50	1.25	.70
(51)	Joe Torre	8.00	4.00	2.50
(52)	Pete Ward	2.50	1.25	.70
(53)	C. Willey	2.50	1.25	.70
(54)	B. Williams	20.00	10.00	6.00
(55)	Yastrzemski	70.00	35.00	21.00
(56)	Baltimore Orioles Logo	2.50	1.25	.70
(57)	Boston Red Sox Logo	2.50	1.25	.70
(58)	Chicago Cubs Logo	2.50	1.25	.70
(59)	Chicago White Sox Logo	2.50	1.25	.70
(60)	Cincinnati Reds Logo	2.50	1.25	.70
(61)	Cleveland Indians Logo	2.50	1.25	.70
(62)	Detroit Tigers Logo	3.00	1.50	.90
(63)	Houston Colts Logo	2.50	1.25	.70
(64)	Kansas City Athletics Logo	2.50	1.25	.70
(65)	Los Angeles Angels Logo	2.50	1.25	.70
(66)	Los Angeles Dodgers Logo	3.00	1.50	.90
(67)	Milwaukee Braves Logo	2.50	1.25	.70
(68)	Minnesota Twins Logo	2.50	1.25	.70
(69)	New York Mets Logo	3.00	1.50	.90
(70)	New York Yankees Logo	5.00	2.50	1.50
(71)	Philadelphia Phillies Logo	2.50	1.25	.70
(72)	Pittsburgh Pirates Logo	2.50	1.25	.70
(73)	St. Louis Cardinals Logo	3.00	1.50	.90
(74)	San Francisco Giants Logo	2.50	1.25	.70
(75)	Washington Senators Logo	2.50	1.25	.70

tattoos in a complete set. The picture side for the 20 team tattoos gives the team logo and name. For the player tattoos, the picture side has the player's face, name and team.

		NR MT	EX	VG
Complete Set:		700.00	350.00	225.00
Common Player:		2.50	1.25	.70
(1)	Hank Aaron	40.00	20.00	12.00
(2)	H. Aguirre	2.50	1.25	.70
(3)	Max Alvis	2.50	1.25	.70
(4)	Ernie Banks	25.00	12.50	7.50
(5)	S. Barber	2.50	1.25	.70
(6)	K. Boyer	8.00	4.00	2.50
(7)	J. Callison	5.00	2.50	1.50
(8)	Norm Cash	8.00	4.00	2.50
(9)	W. Causey	2.50	1.25	.70
(10)	O. Cepeda	10.00	5.00	3.00
(11)	R. Colavito	10.00	5.00	3.00
(12)	Ray Culp	2.50	1.25	.70
(13)	Davalillo	2.50	1.25	.70
(14)	Drabowsky	2.50	1.25	.70
(15)	Ellsworth	2.50	1.25	.70
(16)	Curt Flood	8.00	4.00	2.50
(17)	B. Freehan	5.00	2.50	1.50
(18)	J. Fregosi	5.00	2.50	1.50
(19)	Bob Friend	5.00	2.50	1.50
(20)	D. Groat	5.00	2.50	1.50
(21)	Woody Held	2.50	1.25	.70
(22)	F. Howard	8.00	4.00	2.50
(23)	Al Jackson	2.50	1.25	.70
(24)	L. Jackson	2.50	1.25	.70
(25)	K. Johnson	2.50	1.25	.70
(26)	Al Kaline	25.00	12.50	7.50
(27a)	Killebrew (green background)	25.00	12.50	7.50
(27b)	Killebrew (red background)	25.00	12.50	7.50
(28)	S. Koufax	35.00	17.50	10.50
(29)	Lock	2.50	1.25	.70
(30)	F. Malzone	2.50	1.25	.70
(31)	M. Mantle	125.00	62.00	37.00
(32)	E. Mathews	20.00	10.00	6.00
(33a)	Willie Mays (yellow background encompasses entire head)	40.00	20.00	12.00
(33b)	Willie Mays (yellow background covers one-half of head)	40.00	20.00	12.00
(34)	Mazeroski	8.00	4.00	2.50
(35)	K. McBride	2.50	1.25	.70
(36)	Monbouquette	2.50	1.25	.70
(37)	Nicholson	2.50	1.25	.70
(38)	C. Osteen	5.00	2.50	1.50
(39)	M. Pappas	5.00	2.50	1.50
(40)	C. Pascual	5.00	2.50	1.50
(41)	A. Pearson	2.50	1.25	.70
(42)	Perranoski	2.50	1.25	.70
(43)	G. Peters	2.50	1.25	.70
(44)	B. Powell	8.00	4.00	2.50
(45)	F. Robinson	25.00	12.50	7.50
(46)	J. Romano	2.50	1.25	.70
(47)	N. Siebern	2.50	1.25	.70
(48)	W. Spahn	20.00	10.00	6.00
(49)	D. Stuart	5.00	2.50	1.50

1964 Topps Stand-Ups

These 2½'' by 3½'' cards were the first since the All-Star sets of 1951 to be die-cut. This made it possible for a folded card to stand on display. The 77-cards in the set featured color photographs of the player with yellow and green backgrounds. Directions for folding are on the yellow top background, and when folded only the green background remains. Of the 77 cards, 55 were double-printed while 22 were single-printed, making them twice as scarce. Included in the single-printed group are Warren Spahn, Don Drysdale, Juan Marichal, Willie McCovey and Carl Yastrzemski.

		NR MT	EX	VG
Complete Set:		1300.00	650.00	390.00
Common Player:		2.50	1.25	.70
(1)	Hank Aaron	50.00	25.00	15.00
(2)	Hank Aguirre	2.50	1.25	.70
(3)	George Altman	2.50	1.25	.70
(4)	Max Alvis	2.50	1.25	.70
(5)	Bob Aspromonte	2.50	1.25	.70
(6)	Jack Baldschun	12.00	6.00	3.50
(7)	Ernie Banks	20.00	10.00	6.00
(8)	Steve Barber	2.50	1.25	.70
(9)	Earl Battey	2.50	1.25	.70
(10)	Ken Boyer	6.00	3.00	1.75
(11)	Ernie Broglio	2.50	1.25	.70
(12)	Johnny Callison	4.00	2.00	1.25
(13)	Norm Cash	15.00	7.50	4.50
(14)	Wayne Causey	2.50	1.25	.70
(15)	Orlando Cepeda	8.00	4.00	2.50
(16)	Ed Charles	2.50	1.25	.70
(17)	Bob Clemente	50.00	25.00	15.00
(18)	Donn Clendenon	12.00	6.00	3.50
(19)	Rocky Colavito	6.00	3.00	1.75
(20)	Ray Culp	12.00	6.00	3.50

		NR MT	EX	VG
(21)	Tommy Davis	6.00	3.00	1.75
(22)	Don Drysdale	40.00	20.00	12.00
(23)	Dick Ellsworth	2.50	1.25	.70
(24)	Dick Farrell	2.50	1.25	.70
(25)	Jim Fregosi	4.00	2.00	1.25
(26)	Bob Friend	4.00	2.00	1.25
(27)	Jim Gentile	2.50	1.25	.70
(28)	Jesse Gonder	12.00	6.00	3.50
(29)	Tony Gonzalez	12.00	6.00	3.50
(30)	Dick Groat	6.00	3.00	1.75
(31)	Woody Held	2.50	1.25	.70
(32)	Chuck Hinton	2.50	1.25	.70
(33)	Elston Howard	7.00	3.50	2.00
(34)	Frank Howard	15.00	7.50	4.50
(35)	Ron Hunt	2.50	1.25	.70
(36)	Al Jackson	2.50	1.25	.70
(37)	Ken Johnson	2.50	1.25	.70
(38)	Al Kaline	25.00	12.50	.7.50
(39)	Harmon Killebrew	20.00	10.00	6.00
(40)	Sandy Koufax	35.00	17.50	10.50
(41)	Don Lock	12.00	6.00	3.50
(42)	Jerry Lumpe	12.00	6.00	3.50
(43)	Jim Maloney	2.50	1.25	.70
(44)	Frank Malzone	2.50	1.25	.70
(45)	Mickey Mantle	175.00	87.00	52.00
(46)	Juan Marichal	40.00	20.00	12.00
(47)	Ed Mathews	40.00	20.00	12.00
(48)	Willie Mays	50.00	25.00	15.00
(49)	Bill Mazeroski	6.00	3.00	1.75
(50)	Ken McBride	2.50	1.25	.70
(51)	Willie McCovey	40.00	20.00	12.00
(52)	Claude Osteen	2.50	1.25	.70
(53)	Jim O'Toole	2.50	1.25	.70
(54)	Camilo Pascual	2.50	1.25	.70
(55)	Albie Pearson	12.00	6.00	3.50
(56)	Gary Peters	2.50	1.25	.70
(57)	Vada Pinson	6.00	3.00	1.75
(58)	Juan Pizarro	2.50	1.25	.70
(59)	Boog Powell	6.00	3.00	1.75
(60)	Bobby Richardson	7.00	3.50	2.00
(61)	Brooks Robinson	25.00	12.50	7.50
(62)	Floyd Robinson	2.50	1.25	.70
(63)	Frank Robinson	20.00	10.00	6.00
(64)	Ed Roebuck	12.00	6.00	3.50
(65)	Rich Rollins	2.50	1.25	.70
(66)	Johnny Romano	2.50	1.25	.70
(67)	Ron Santo	15.00	7.50	4.50
(68)	Norm Siebern	2.50	1.25	.70
(69)	Warren Spahn	40.00	20.00	12.00
(70)	Dick Stuart	12.00	6.00	3.50
(71)	Lee Thomas	2.50	1.25	.70
(72)	Joe Torre	7.00	3.50	2.00
(73)	Pete Ward	2.50	1.25	.70
(74)	Bill White	12.00	6.00	3.50
(75)	Billy Williams	40.00	20.00	12.00
(76)	Hal Woodeshick	12.00	6.00	3.50
(77)	Carl Yastrzemski	275.00	137.00	82.00

1965 Topps

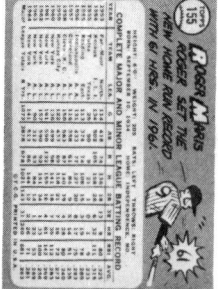

The 1965 Topps set featured a large color photograph of the player which was surrounded by a colored, round-cornered frame and a white border. The bottom of the 2½'' by 3½'' cards include a pennant with a color team logo and name over the left side of a rectangle which features the player's name and position. Backs feature statistics and, if space allowed, a cartoon and headline about the player.

There are no multi-player cards in 1965 other than the usual team cards and World Series highlights. Rookie cards included team, as well as league, groupings of from two to four players per card. Also present in the 598-card set were statistical leaders.

		NR MT	EX	VG
Complete Set:		2000.00	700.00	400.00
Common Player: 1-198		.50	.25	.15
Common Player: 199-446		.70	.35	.20
Common Player: 447-522		.90	.45	.25
Common Player: 523-598		2.50	1.25	.75
1	A.L. Batting Leaders (Elston Howard, Tony Oliva, Brooks Robinson)	6.00	3.00	1.75
2	N.L. Batting Leaders (Hank Aaron, Rico Carty, Bob Clemente)	5.00	2.50	1.50
3	A.L. Home Run Leaders (Harmon Killebrew, Mickey Mantle, Boog Powell)	10.00	4.50	2.50
4	N.L. Home Run Leaders (Johnny Callison, Orlando Cepeda, Jim Hart, Willie Mays, Billy Williams)	4.50	2.25	1.25
5	A.L. RBI Leaders (Harmon Killebrew, Mickey Mantle, Brooks Robinson, Dick Stuart)	10.00	4.50	2.50
6	N.L. RBI Leaders (Ken Boyer, Willie Mays, Ron Santo)	4.50	2.25	1.25
7	A.L. ERA Leaders (Dean Chance, Joel Horlen)	2.50	1.25	.70
8	N.L. ERA Leaders (Don Drysdale, Sandy Koufax)	4.50	2.25	1.25
9	A.L. Pitching Leaders (Wally Bunker, Dean Chance, Gary Peters, Juan Pizarro, Dave Wickersham)	2.50	1.25	.70
10	N.L. Pitching Leaders (Larry Jackson, Juan Marichal, Ray Sadecki)	3.50	1.75	1.00
11	A.L. Strikeout Leaders (Dean Chance, Al Downing, Camilo Pascual)	2.50	1.25	.70
12	N.L. Strikeout Leaders (Don Drysdale, Bob Gibson, Bob Veale)	3.50	1.75	1.00
13	Pedro Ramos	1.00	.50	.30
14	Len Gabrielson	.50	.25	.15
15	Robin Roberts	6.00	3.00	1.75
16	Astros Rookies (Sonny Jackson, Joe Morgan)	30.00	15.00	9.00
17	Johnny Romano	.50	.25	.15
18	Bill McCool	.50	.25	.15
19	Gates Brown	.60	.30	.20
20	Jim Bunning	4.00	2.00	1.25
21	Don Blasingame	.50	.25	.15
22	Charlie Smith	.60	.30	.20
23	Bob Tiefenauer	.50	.25	.15
24	Twins Team	4.00	2.00	1.25
25	Al McBean	.50	.25	.15
26	Bobby Knoop	.50	.25	.15
27	Dick Bertell	.50	.25	.15
28	Barney Schultz	.50	.25	.15
29	Felix Mantilla	.50	.25	.15
30	Jim Bouton	2.50	1.25	.70
31	Mike White	.50	.25	.15
32	Herman Franks	.50	.25	.15
33	Jackie Brandt	.50	.25	.15
34	Cal Koonce	.50	.25	.15
35	Ed Charles	.50	.25	.15
36	Bobby Wine	.60	.30	.20
37	Fred Gladding	.50	.25	.15
38	Jim King	.50	.25	.15
39	Gerry Arrigo	.50	.25	.15
40	Frank Howard	2.50	1.25	.70
41	White Sox Rookies (Bruce Howard, Marv Staehle)	.50	.25	.15
42	Earl Wilson	.50	.25	.15
43	Mike Shannon	.60	.30	.20
44	Wade Blasingame	.50	.25	.15
45	Roy McMillan	.60	.30	.20
46	Bob Lee	.50	.25	.15
47	Tommy Harper	.70	.35	.20
48	Claude Raymond	.60	.30	.20
49	Orioles Rookies (Curt Blefary, John Miller)	.90	.45	.25
50	Juan Marichal	8.00	4.00	2.50
51	Billy Bryan	.50	.25	.15
52	Ed Roebuck	.50	.25	.15
53	Dick McAuliffe	.60	.30	.20
54	Joe Gibbon	.50	.25	.15
55	Tony Conigliaro	2.50	1.25	.70
56	Ron Kline	.50	.25	.15
57	Cardinals Team	2.25	1.25	.70
58	Fred Talbot	.50	.25	.15

		NR MT	EX	VG
59	Nate Oliver	.50	.25	.15
60	Jim O'Toole	.50	.25	.15
61	Chris Cannizzaro	.60	.30	.20
62	Jim Katt (Kaat)	4.00	2.00	1.25
63	Ty Cline	.50	.25	.15
64	Lou Burdette	2.00	1.00	.60
65	Tony Kubek	4.00	2.00	1.25
66	Bill Rigney	.50	.25	.15
67	Harvey Haddix	.90	.45	.25
68	Del Crandall	.90	.45	.25
69	Bill Virdon	1.25	.60	.40
70	Bill Skowron	1.25	.60	.40
71	John O'Donoghue	.50	.25	.15
72	Tony Gonzalez	.50	.25	.15
73	Dennis Ribant	.60	.30	.20
74	Red Sox Rookies (Rico Petrocelli, Jerry Stephenson)	2.50	1.25	.70
75	Deron Johnson	.50	.25	.15
76	Sam McDowell	.90	.45	.25
77	Doug Camilli	.50	.25	.15
78	Dal Maxvill	.60	.30	.20
79a	Checklist 1-88 (61 is C. Cannizzaro)	3.00	1.50	.90
79b	Checklist 1-88 (61 is Cannizzaro)	5.00	2.50	1.50
80	Turk Farrell	.50	.25	.15
81	Don Buford	.60	.30	.20
82	Braves Rookies (Santos Alomar, John Braun)	.60	.30	.20
83	George Thomas	.50	.25	.15
84	Ron Herbel	.50	.25	.15
85	Willie Smith	.50	.25	.15
86	Les Narum	.50	.25	.15
87	Nelson Mathews	.50	.25	.15
88	Jack Lamabe	.50	.25	.15
89	Mike Hershberger	.50	.25	.15
90	Rich Rollins	.50	.25	.15
91	Cubs Team	2.25	1.25	.70
92	Dick Howser	1.25	.60	.40
93	Jack Fisher	.60	.30	.20
94	Charlie Lau	.90	.45	.25
95	Bill Mazeroski	2.50	1.25	.70
96	Sonny Siebert	.60	.30	.20
97	Pedro Gonzalez	1.00	.50	.30
98	Bob Miller	.50	.25	.15
99	Gil Hodges	5.00	2.50	1.50
100	Ken Boyer	2.50	1.25	.70
101	Fred Newman	.50	.25	.15
102	Steve Boros	.60	.30	.20
103	Harvey Kuenn	1.25	.60	.40
104	Checklist 89-176	3.00	1.50	.90
105	Chico Salmon	.50	.25	.15
106	Gene Oliver	.50	.25	.15
107	Phillies Rookies (Pat Corrales, Costen Shockley)	2.00	1.00	.60
108	Don Mincher	.60	.30	.20
109	Walt Bond	.50	.25	.15
110	Ron Santo	1.50	.70	.45
111	Lee Thomas	.50	.25	.15
112	Derrell Griffith	.50	.25	.15
113	Steve Barber	.50	.25	.15
114	Jim Hickman	.80	.40	.25
115	Bobby Richardson	3.50	1.75	1.00
116	Cardinals Rookies (Dave Dowling, Bob Tolan)	1.25	.60	.40
117	Wes Stock	.50	.25	.15
118	Hal Lanier	1.50	.70	.45
119	John Kennedy	.50	.25	.15
120	Frank Robinson	10.00	5.00	3.00
121	Gene Alley	.70	.35	.20
122	Bill Pleis	.50	.25	.15
123	Frank Thomas	.50	.25	.15
124	Tom Satriano	.50	.25	.15
125	Juan Pizarro	.50	.25	.15
126	Dodgers Team	4.00	2.00	1.25
127	Frank Lary	.60	.30	.20
128	Vic Davalillo	.60	.30	.20
129	Bennie Daniels	.50	.25	.15
130	Al Kaline	10.00	5.00	3.00
131	Johnny Keane	1.50	.70	.45
132	World Series Game 1 (Cards Take Opener)	2.50	1.25	.70
133	World Series Game 2 (Stottlemyre Wins)	3.00	1.50	.90
134	World Series Game 3 (Mantle's Clutch HR)	12.00	6.00	3.50
135	World Series Game 4 (Boyer's Grand Slam)	2.50	1.25	.70
136	World Series Game 5 (10th Inning Triumph)	2.50	1.25	.70
137	World Series Game 6 (Bouton Wins Again)	3.00	1.50	.90

		NR MT	EX	VG
138	World Series Game 7 (Gibson Wins Finale)	3.50	1.75	1.00
139	World Series Summary (The Cards Celebrate)	2.50	1.25	.70
140	Dean Chance	.60	.30	.20
141	Charlie James	.50	.25	.15
142	Bill Monbouquette	.60	.30	.20
143	Pirates Rookies (John Gelnar, Jerry May)	.50	.25	.15
144	Ed Kranepool	.90	.45	.25
145	Luis Tiant	5.00	2.50	1.50
146	Ron Hansen	.50	.25	.15
147	Dennis Bennett	.50	.25	.15
148	Willie Kirkland	.50	.25	.15
149	Wayne Schurr	.50	.25	.15
150	Brooks Robinson	12.00	6.00	3.50
151	Athletics Team	2.25	1.25	.70
152	Phil Ortega	.50	.25	.15
153	Norm Cash	2.00	1.00	.60
154	Bob Humphreys	.50	.25	.15
155	Roger Maris	12.00	6.00	3.50
156	Bob Sadowski	.50	.25	.15
157	Zoilo Versalles	1.50	.70	.45
158	Dick Sisler	.50	.25	.15
159	Jim Duffalo	.50	.25	.15
160	Bob Clemente	30.00	15.00	9.00
161	Frank Baumann	.50	.25	.15
162	Russ Nixon	.50	.25	.15
163	John Briggs	.50	.25	.15
164	Al Spangler	.50	.25	.15
165	Dick Ellsworth	.50	.25	.15
166	Indians Rookies (Tommie Agee, George Culver)	1.50	.70	.45
167	Bill Wakefield	.60	.30	.20
168	Dick Green	.60	.30	.20
169	Dave Vineyard	.50	.25	.15
170	Hank Aaron	40.00	20.00	12.00
171	Jim Roland	.50	.25	.15
172	Jim Piersall	1.50	.70	.45
173	Tigers Team	3.25	1.75	1.00
174	Joe Jay	.50	.25	.15
175	Bob Aspromonte	.50	.25	.15
176	Willie McCovey	10.00	5.00	3.00
177	Pete Mikkelsen	1.00	.50	.30
178	Dalton Jones	.50	.25	.15
179	Hal Woodeshick	.50	.25	.15
180	Bob Allison	1.25	.60	.40
181	Senators Rookies (Don Loun, Joe McCabe)	.50	.25	.15
182	Mike de la Hoz	.50	.25	.15
183	Dave Nicholson	.50	.25	.15
184	John Boozer	.50	.25	.15
185	Max Alvis	.50	.25	.15
186	Billy Cowan	.50	.25	.15
187	Casey Stengel	10.00	5.00	3.00
188	Sam Bowens	.50	.25	.15
189	Checklist 177-264	3.00	1.50	.90
190	Bill White	1.25	.60	.40
191	Phil Regan	.50	.25	.15
192	Jim Coker	.50	.25	.15
193	Gaylord Perry	10.00	5.00	3.00
194	Angels Rookies (Bill Kelso, Rick Reichardt)	.60	.30	.20
195	Bob Veale	.60	.30	.20
196	Ron Fairly	.70	.35	.20
197	Diego Segui	.50	.25	.15
198	Smoky Burgess	1.25	.60	.40
199	Bob Heffner	.70	.35	.20
200	Joe Torre	2.50	1.25	.70
201	Twins Rookies (Cesar Tovar, Sandy Valdespino)	1.00	.50	.30
202	Leo Burke	.70	.35	.20
203	Dallas Green	1.25	.60	.40
204	Russ Snyder	.70	.35	.20
205	Warren Spahn	10.00	5.00	3.00
206	Willie Horton	1.25	.60	.40
207	Pete Rose	140.00	70.00	42.00
208	Tommy John	8.00	4.00	2.50
209	Pirates Team	2.50	1.25	.70
210	Jim Fregosi	1.50	.70	.45
211	Steve Ridzik	.70	.35	.20
212	Ron Brand	.70	.35	.20
213	Jim Davenport	.70	.35	.20
214	Bob Purkey	.70	.35	.20
215	Pete Ward	.70	.35	.20
216	Al Worthington	.70	.35	.20
217	Walt Alston	3.50	1.75	1.00
218	Dick Schofield	.70	.35	.20
219	Bob Meyer	.70	.35	.20
220	Billy Williams	7.00	3.50	2.00
221	John Tsitouris	.70	.35	.20

		NR MT	EX	VG
222	Bob Tillman	.70	.35	.20
223	Dan Osinski	.70	.35	.20
224	Bob Chance	.70	.35	.20
225	Bo Belinsky	1.00	.50	.30
226	Yankees Rookies (Jake Gibbs, Elvio Jimenez)	1.50	.70	.45
227	Bobby Klaus	.80	.40	.25
228	Jack Sanford	.70	.35	.20
229	Lou Clinton	.70	.35	.20
230	Ray Sadecki	.70	.35	.20
231	Jerry Adair	.70	.35	.20
232	Steve Blass	1.00	.50	.30
233	Don Zimmer	1.50	.70	.45
234	White Sox Team	2.50	1.25	.70
235	Chuck Hinton	.70	.35	.20
236	Dennis McLain	6.00	3.00	1.75
237	Bernie Allen	.70	.35	.20
238	Joe Moeller	.70	.35	.20
239	Doc Edwards	1.00	.50	.30
240	Bob Bruce	.70	.35	.20
241	Mack Jones	.70	.35	.20
242	George Brunet	.70	.35	.20
243	Reds Rookies (Ted Davidson, Tommy Helms)	1.00	.50	.30
244	Lindy McDaniel	.70	.35	.20
245	Joe Pepitone	3.00	1.50	.90
246	Tom Butters	.70	.35	.20
247	Wally Moon	1.00	.50	.30
248	Gus Triandos	.80	.40	.25
249	Dave McNally	1.25	.60	.40
250	Willie Mays	40.00	20.00	12.00
251	Billy Herman	2.00	1.00	.60
252	Pete Richert	.70	.35	.20
253	Danny Cater	.80	.40	.25
254	Roland Sheldon	1.50	.70	.45
255	Camilo Pascual	1.00	.50	.30
256	Tito Francona	.80	.40	.25
257	Jim Wynn	1.25	.60	.40
258	Larry Bearnarth	.80	.40	.25
259	Tigers Rookies (Jim Northrup, Ray Oyler)	1.25	.60	.40
260	Don Drysdale	10.00	5.00	3.00
261	Duke Carmel	1.50	.70	.45
262	Bud Daley	.70	.35	.20
263	Marty Keough	.70	.35	.20
264	Bob Buhl	.80	.40	.25
265	Jim Pagliaroni	.70	.35	.20
266	Bert Campaneris	3.00	1.50	.90
267	Senators Team	2.50	1.25	.70
268	Ken McBride	.70	.35	.20
269	Frank Bolling	.70	.35	.20
270	Milt Pappas	1.00	.50	.30
271	Don Wert	.70	.35	.20
272	Chuck Schilling	.70	.35	.20
273	Checklist 265-352	3.25	1.75	1.00
274	Lum Harris	.70	.35	.20
275	Dick Groat	1.75	.90	.50
276	Hoyt Wilhelm	6.00	3.00	1.75
277	Johnny Lewis	.80	.40	.25
278	Ken Retzer	.70	.35	.20
279	Dick Tracewski	.70	.35	.20
280	Dick Stuart	.80	.40	.25
281	Bill Stafford	1.50	.70	.45
282	Giants Rookies (Dick Estelle, Masanori Murakami)	1.25	.60	.40
283	Fred Whitfield	.70	.35	.20
284	Nick Willhite	.70	.35	.20
285	Ron Hunt	.80	.40	.25
286	Athletics Rookies (Jim Dickson, Aurelio Monteagudo)	.70	.35	.20
287	Gary Kolb	.70	.35	.20
288	Jack Hamilton	.70	.35	.20
289	Gordy Coleman	.70	.35	.20
290	Wally Bunker	.70	.35	.20
291	Jerry Lynch	.70	.35	.20
292	Larry Yellen	.70	.35	.20
293	Angels Team	2.50	1.25	.70
294	Tim McCarver	2.75	1.50	.80
295	Dick Radatz	.80	.40	.25
296	Tony Taylor	.70	.35	.20
297	Dave DeBusschere	3.50	1.75	1.00
298	Jim Stewart	.70	.35	.20
299	Jerry Zimmerman	.70	.35	.20
300	Sandy Koufax	40.00	20.00	12.00
301	Birdie Tebbetts	.70	.35	.20
302	Al Stanek	.70	.35	.20
303	Johnny Orsino	.70	.35	.20
304	Dave Stenhouse	.70	.35	.20
305	Rico Carty	1.50	.70	.45
306	Bubba Phillips	.70	.35	.20
307	Barry Latman	.70	.35	.20

		NR MT	EX	VG
308	Mets Rookies (Cleon Jones, Tom Parsons)	1.25	.60	.40
309	Steve Hamilton	1.50	.70	.45
310	Johnny Callison	1.25	.60	.40
311	Orlando Pena	.70	.35	.20
312	Joe Nuxhall	1.00	.50	.30
313	Jimmie Schaffer	.70	.35	.20
314	Sterling Slaughter	.70	.35	.20
315	Frank Malzone	.80	.40	.25
316	Reds Team	2.75	1.50	.80
317	Don McMahon	.70	.35	.20
318	Matty Alou	1.00	.50	.30
319	Ken McMullen	.70	.35	.20
320	Bob Gibson	10.00	5.00	3.00
321	Rusty Staub	3.50	1.75	1.00
322	Rick Wise	1.00	.50	.30
323	Hank Bauer	.80	.40	.25
324	Bobby Locke	.70	.35	.20
325	Donn Clendenon	.80	.40	.25
326	Dwight Siebler	.70	.35	.20
327	Denis Menke	.70	.35	.20
328	Eddie Fisher	.70	.35	.20
329	Hawk Taylor	.80	.40	.25
330	Whitey Ford	12.00	6.00	3.50
331	Dodgers Rookies (Al Ferrara, John Purdin)	.80	.40	.25
332	Ted Abernathy	.70	.35	.20
333	Tommie Reynolds	.70	.35	.20
334	Vic Roznovsky	.70	.35	.20
335	Mickey Lolich	3.25	1.75	1.00
336	Woody Held	.70	.35	.20
337	Mike Cuellar	1.50	.70	.45
338	Phillies Team	2.50	1.25	.70
339	Ryne Duren	1.00	.50	.30
340	Tony Oliva	3.50	1.75	1.00
341	Bobby Bolin	.70	.35	.20
342	Bob Rodgers	.80	.40	.25
343	Mike McCormick	.80	.40	.25
344	Wes Parker	.80	.40	.25
345	Floyd Robinson	.80	.40	.25
346	Bobby Bragan	.80	.40	.25
347	Roy Face	1.50	.70	.45
348	George Banks	.70	.35	.20
349	Larry Miller	.80	.40	.25
350	Mickey Mantle	300.00	120.00	60.00
351	Jim Perry	1.25	.60	.40
352	Alex Johnson	1.00	.50	.30
353	Jerry Lumpe	.80	.40	.25
354	Cubs Rookies (Billy Ott, Jack Warner)	.70	.35	.20
355	Vada Pinson	2.50	1.25	.70
356	Bill Spanswick	.70	.35	.20
357	Carl Warwick	.70	.35	.20
358	Albie Pearson	.70	.35	.20
359	Ken Johnson	.70	.35	.20
360	Orlando Cepeda	4.00	2.00	1.25
361	Checklist 353-429	3.25	1.75	1.00
362	Don Schwall	.70	.35	.20
363	Bob Johnson	.70	.35	.20
364	Galen Cisco	.80	.40	.25
365	Jim Gentile	.80	.40	.25
366	Dan Schneider	.70	.35	.20
367	Leon Wagner	.80	.40	.25
368	White Sox Rookies (Ken Berry, Joel Gibson)	.80	.40	.25
369	Phil Linz	1.50	.70	.45
370	Tommy Davis	1.50	.70	.45
371	Frank Kreutzer	.70	.35	.20
372	Clay Dalrymple	.70	.35	.20
373	Curt Simmons	1.00	.50	.30
374	Angels Rookies (Jose Cardenal, Dick Simpson)	1.00	.50	.30
375	Dave Wickersham	.70	.35	.20
376	Jim Landis	.70	.35	.20
377	Willie Stargell	10.00	5.00	3.00
378	Chuck Estrada	.70	.35	.20
379	Giants Team	2.50	1.25	.70
380	Rocky Colavito	3.00	1.50	.90
381	Al Jackson	.80	.40	.25
382	J.C. Martin	.70	.35	.20
383	Felipe Alou	1.00	.50	.30
384	Johnny Klippstein	.70	.35	.20
385	Carl Yastrzemski	50.00	25.00	15.00
386	Cubs Rookies (Paul Jaeckel, Fred Norman)	.70	.35	.20
387	Johnny Podres	2.00	1.00	.60
388	John Blanchard	1.50	.70	.45
389	Don Larsen	1.25	.60	.40
390	Bill Freehan	1.25	.60	.40
391	Mel McGaha	.70	.35	.20
392	Bob Friend	1.50	.70	.45

		NR MT	EX	VG
393	Ed Kirkpatrick	.70	.35	.20
394	Jim Hannan	.70	.35	.20
395	Jim Hart	.80	.40	.25
396	Frank Bertaina	.70	.35	.20
397	Jerry Buchek	.70	.35	.20
398	Reds Rookies (Dan Neville, Art Shamsky)			
		.80	.40	.25
399	Ray Herbert	.70	.35	.20
400	Harmon Killebrew	10.00	5.00	3.00
401	Carl Willey	.80	.40	.25
402	Joe Amalfitano	.70	.35	.20
403	Red Sox Team	3.00	1.50	.90
404	Stan Williams	.70	.35	.20
405	John Roseboro	.80	.40	.25
406	Ralph Terry	.80	.40	.25
407	Lee Maye	.70	.35	.20
408	Larry Sherry	.70	.35	.20
409	Astros Rookies (Jim Beauchamp, Larry Dierker)			
		1.00	.50	.30
410	Luis Aparicio	7.00	3.50	2.00
411	Roger Craig	2.00	1.00	.60
412	Bob Bailey	.70	.35	.20
413	Hal Reniff	1.50	.70	.45
414	Al Lopez	3.00	1.50	.90
415	Curt Flood	1.50	.70	.45
416	Jim Brewer	.70	.35	.20
417	Ed Brinkman	.80	.40	.25
418	Johnny Edwards	.70	.35	.20
419	Ruben Amaro	.70	.35	.20
420	Larry Jackson	.70	.35	.20
421	Twins Rookies (Gary Dotter, Jay Ward)			
		.70	.35	.20
422	Aubrey Gatewood	.70	.35	.20
423	Jesse Gonder	.80	.40	.25
424	Gary Bell	.70	.35	.20
425	Wayne Causey	.70	.35	.20
426	Braves Team	2.50	1.25	.70
427	Bob Saverine	.70	.35	.20
428	Bob Shaw	.70	.35	.20
429	Don Demeter	.70	.35	.20
430	Gary Peters	.80	.40	.25
431	Cardinals Rookies (Nelson Briles, Wayne Spiezio)			
		1.00	.50	.30
432	Jim Grant	.80	.40	.25
433	John Bateman	.70	.35	.20
434	Dave Morehead	.70	.35	.20
435	Willie Davis	1.50	.70	.45
436	Don Elston	.70	.35	.20
437	Chico Cardenas	.70	.35	.20
438	Harry Walker	.80	.40	.25
439	Moe Drabowsky	.70	.35	.20
440	Tom Tresh	2.50	1.25	.70
441	Denver Lemaster	.70	.35	.20
442	Vic Power	.70	.35	.20
443	Checklist 430-506	3.25	1.75	1.00
444	Bob Hendley	.70	.35	.20
445	Don Lock	.70	.35	.20
446	Art Mahaffey	.70	.35	.20
447	Julian Javier	1.00	.50	.30
448	Lee Stange	.90	.45	.25
449	Mets Rookies (Jerry Hinsley, Gary Kroll)			
		1.00	.50	.30
450	Elston Howard	4.50	2.25	1.25
451	Jim Owens	.90	.45	.25
452	Gary Geiger	.90	.45	.25
453	Dodgers Rookies (Willie Crawford, John Werhas)			
		1.00	.50	.30
454	Ed Rakow	.90	.45	.25
455	Norm Siebern	1.00	.50	.30
456	Bill Henry	.90	.45	.25
457	Bob Kennedy	.90	.45	.25
458	John Buzhardt	.90	.45	.25
459	Frank Kostro	.90	.45	.25
460	Richie Allen	4.00	2.00	1.25
461	Braves Rookies (Clay Carroll, Phil Niekro)			
		20.00	10.00	6.00
462	Lew Krausse (photo actually Pete Lovrich)			
		.90	.45	.25
463	Manny Mota	1.25	.60	.40
464	Ron Piche	.90	.45	.25
465	Tom Haller	1.00	.50	.30
466	Senators Rookies (Pete Craig, Dick Nen)			
		.90	.45	.25
467	Ray Washburn	.90	.45	.25
468	Larry Brown	.90	.45	.25
469	Don Nottebart	.90	.45	.25
470	Yogi Berra	20.00	10.00	6.00
471	Billy Hoeft	.90	.45	.25
472	Don Pavletich	.90	.45	.25
473	Orioles Rookies (Paul Blair, Dave Johnson)			
		7.00	3.50	2.00

		NR MT	EX	VG
474	Cookie Rojas	.70	.35	.20
475	Clete Boyer	3.00	1.50	.90
476	Billy O'Dell	.90	.45	.25
477	Cardinals Rookies (Fritz Ackley, Steve Carlton)			
		90.00	45.00	27.00
478	Wilbur Wood	1.00	.50	.30
479	Ken Harrelson	2.50	1.25	.70
480	Joel Horlen	.90	.45	.25
481	Indians Team	3.00	1.50	.90
482	Bob Priddy	.90	.45	.25
483	George Smith	.90	.45	.25
484	Ron Perranoski	1.00	.50	.30
485	Nellie Fox	4.00	2.00	1.25
486	Angels Rookies (Tom Egan, Pat Rogan)			
		.90	.45	.25
487	Woody Woodward	1.00	.50	.30
488	Ted Wills	.90	.45	.25
489	Gene Mauch	1.50	.70	.45
490	Earl Battey	1.00	.50	.30
491	Tracy Stallard	.90	.45	.25
492	Gene Freese	.90	.45	.25
493	Tigers Rookies (Bruce Brubaker, Bill Roman)			
		.90	.45	.25
494	Jay Ritchie	.90	.45	.25
495	Joe Christopher	1.00	.50	.30
496	Joe Cunningham	1.00	.50	.30
497	Giants Rookies (Ken Henderson, Jack Hiatt)			
		1.00	.50	.30
498	Gene Stephens	.90	.45	.25
499	Stu Miller	.90	.45	.25
500	Ed Mathews	12.00	6.00	3.50
501	Indians Rookies (Ralph Gagliano, Jim Rittwage)			
		.90	.45	.25
502	Don Cardwell	.90	.45	.25
503	Phil Gagliano	.90	.45	.25
504	Jerry Grote	1.00	.50	.30
505	Ray Culp	.90	.45	.25
506	Sam Mele	.90	.45	.25
507	Sammy Ellis	.90	.45	.25
508a	Checklist 507-598 (large print on front)			
		6.00	3.00	1.75
508b	Checklist 507-598 (small print on front)			
		4.00	2.00	1.25
509	Red Sox Rookies (Bob Guindon, Gerry Vezendy)			
		.90	.45	.25
510	Ernie Banks	20.00	10.00	6.00
511	Ron Locke	1.00	.50	.30
512	Cap Peterson	.90	.45	.25
513	Yankees Team	8.00	4.00	2.50
514	Joe Azcue	.90	.45	.25
515	Vern Law	2.00	1.00	.60
516	Al Weis	.90	.45	.25
517	Angels Rookies (Paul Schaal, Jack Warner)			
		.90	.45	.25
518	Ken Rowe	.90	.45	.25
519	Bob Uecker	25.00	12.50	7.50
520	Tony Cloninger	1.00	.50	.30
521	Phillies Rookies (Dave Bennett, Morrie Stevens)			
		.90	.45	.25
522	Hank Aguirre	.90	.45	.25
523	Mike Brumley	2.50	1.25	.70
524	Dave Giusti	2.50	1.25	.70
525	Eddie Bressoud	2.50	1.25	.70
526	Athletics Rookies (Jim Hunter, Rene Lachemann, Skip Lockwood, Johnny Odom)			
		35.00	17.50	10.50
527	Jeff Torborg	3.00	1.50	.90
528	George Altman	2.50	1.25	.70
529	Jerry Fosnow	2.50	1.25	.70
530	Jim Maloney	3.00	1.50	.90
531	Chuck Hiller	2.50	1.25	.70
532	Hector Lopez	4.00	2.00	1.25
533	Mets Rookies (Jim Bethke, Tug McGraw, Dan Napolean, Ron Swoboda)			
		10.00	5.00	3.00
534	John Herrnstein	2.50	1.25	.70
535	Jack Kralick	2.50	1.25	.70
536	Andre Rodgers	2.50	1.25	.70
537	Angels Rookies (Marcelino Lopez, Rudy May, Phil Roof)			
		4.00	2.00	1.25
538	Chuck Dressen	3.00	1.50	.90
539	Herm Starrette	2.50	1.25	.70
540	Lou Brock	25.00	12.50	7.50
541	White Sox Rookies (Greg Bollo, Bob Locker)			
		2.50	1.25	.70
542	Lou Klimchock	2.50	1.25	.70
543	Ed Connolly	2.50	1.25	.70
544	Howie Reed	2.50	1.25	.70
545	Jesus Alou	3.00	1.50	.90
546	Indians Rookies (Ray Barker, Bill Davis, Mike Hedlund, Floyd Weaver)			
		2.50	1.25	.70
547	Jake Wood	2.50	1.25	.70

		NR MT	EX	VG
548	Dick Stigman	2.50	1.25	.70
549	Cubs Rookies (Glenn Beckert, Roberto Pena)	4.00	2.00	1.25
550	Mel Stottlemyre	8.00	4.00	2.50
551	Mets Team	8.00	4.00	2.50
552	Julio Gotay	2.50	1.25	.70
553	Astros Rookies (Dan Coombs, Jack McClure, Gene Ratliff)	2.50	1.25	.70
554	Chico Ruiz	2.50	1.25	.70
555	Jack Baldschun	2.50	1.25	.70
556	Red Schoendienst	4.00	2.00	1.25
557	Jose Santiago	2.50	1.25	.70
558	Tommie Sisk	2.50	1.25	.70
559	Ed Bailey	2.50	1.25	.70
560	Boog Powell	6.00	3.00	1.75
561	Dodgers Rookies (Dennis Daboll, Mike Kekich, Jim Lefebvre, Hector Valle)	4.00	2.00	1.25
562	Billy Moran	2.50	1.25	.70
563	Julio Navarro	2.50	1.25	.70
564	Mel Nelson	2.50	1.25	.70
565	Ernie Broglio	2.50	1.25	.70
566	Yankees Rookies (Gil Blanco, Art Lopez, Ross Moschitto)	4.00	2.00	1.25
567	Tommie Aaron	3.00	1.50	.90
568	Ron Taylor	2.50	1.25	.70
569	Gino Cimoli	2.50	1.25	.70
570	Claude Osteen	4.00	2.00	1.25
571	Ossie Virgil	2.50	1.25	.70
572	Orioles Team	6.00	3.00	1.75
573	Red Sox Rookies (Jim Lonborg, Gerry Moses, Mike Ryan, Bill Schlesinger)	5.00	2.50	1.50
574	Roy Sievers	4.00	2.00	1.25
575	Jose Pagan	2.50	1.25	.70
576	Terry Fox	2.50	1.25	.70
577	A.L. Rookies (Jim Buschhorn, Darold Knowles, Richie Scheinblum)	2.50	1.25	.70
578	Camilo Carreon	2.50	1.25	.70
579	Dick Smith	2.50	1.25	.70
580	Jimmie Hall	2.50	1.25	.70
581	N.L. Rookies (Kevin Collins, Tony Perez, Dave Ricketts)	35.00	17.50	10.50
582	Bob Schmidt	4.00	2.00	1.25
583	Wes Covington	2.50	1.25	.70
584	Harry Bright	2.50	1.25	.70
585	Hank Fischer	2.50	1.25	.70
586	Tommy McCraw	2.50	1.25	.70
587	Joe Sparma	2.50	1.25	.70
588	Lenny Green	2.50	1.25	.70
589	Giants Rookies (Frank Linzy, Bob Schroder)	2.50	1.25	.70
590	Johnnie Wyatt	2.50	1.25	.70
591	Bob Skinner	3.00	1.50	.90
592	Frank Bork	2.50	1.25	.70
593	Tigers Rookies (Jackie Moore, John Sullivan)	2.50	1.25	.70
594	Joe Gaines	2.50	1.25	.70
595	Don Lee	2.50	1.25	.70
596	Don Landrum	2.50	1.25	.70
597	Twins Rookies (Joe Nossek, Dick Reese, John Sevcik)	3.00	1.25	.70
598	Al Downing	8.00	3.00	1.75

1965 Topps Embossed

Inserted in regular pack, the 2⅛'' by 3½'' Topps Embossed cards were one of the more fascinating issues of the company. The fronts feature an embossed profile portrait on gold foil-like cardboard (some collectors report finding the cards with silver cardboard). The player's name, team and position are below the portrait — which is good, because most of the embossed portraits are otherwise unrecognizeable. There is a gold border with American League players framed in blue and National Leaguers in red. The set contained 72 cards divided equally between the leagues. The set provides an inexpensive way to add some interesting cards to a collection. Being special cards, almost everyone depicted is a star.

		NR MT	EX	VG
	Complete Set:	55.00	27.00	16.50
	Common Player:	.40	.20	.12
1	Carl Yastrzemski	5.00	2.50	1.50
2	Ron Fairly	.50	.25	.15
3	Max Alvis	.40	.20	.12
4	Jim Ray Hart	.40	.20	.12
5	Bill Skowron	.60	.30	.20
6	Ed Kranepool	.50	.25	.15
7	Tim McCarver	.60	.30	.20
8	Sandy Koufax	3.00	1.50	.90
9	Donn Clendenon	.40	.20	.12
10	John Romano	.40	.20	.12
11	Mickey Mantle	12.00	6.00	3.50
12	Joe Torre	.70	.35	.20
13	Al Kaline	2.00	1.00	.60
14	Al McBean	.40	.20	.12
15	Don Drysdale	1.50	.70	.45
16	Brooks Robinson	2.00	1.00	.60
17	Jim Bunning	1.00	.50	.30
18	Gary Peters	.40	.20	.12
19	Bob Clemente	3.00	1.50	.90
20	Milt Pappas	.50	.25	.15
21	Wayne Causey	.40	.20	.12
22	Frank Robinson	2.00	1.00	.60
23	Bill Mazeroski	.60	.30	.20
24	Diego Segui	.40	.20	.12
25	Jim Bouton	.60	.30	.20
26	Ed Mathews	1.50	.70	.45
27	Willie Mays	3.50	1.75	1.00
28	Ron Santo	.60	.30	.20
29	Boog Powell	.60	.30	.20
30	Ken McBride	.40	.20	.12
31	Leon Wagner	.40	.20	.12
32	John Callison	.50	.25	.15
33	Zoilo Versalles	.40	.20	.12
34	Jack Baldschun	.40	.20	.12
35	Ron Hunt	.40	.20	.12
36	Richie Allen	.70	.35	.20
37	Frank Malzone	.40	.20	.12
38	Bob Allison	.50	.25	.15
39	Jim Fregosi	.60	.30	.20
40	Billy Williams	1.50	.70	.45
41	Bill Freehan	.50	.25	.15
42	Vada Pinson	.70	.35	.20
43	Bill White	.50	.25	.15
44	Roy McMillan	.40	.20	.12
45	Orlando Cepeda	1.00	.50	.30
46	Rocky Colavito	.70	.35	.20
47	Ken Boyer	.70	.35	.20
48	Dick Radatz	.40	.20	.12
49	Tommy Davis	.60	.30	.20
50	Walt Bond	.40	.20	.12
51	John Orsino	.40	.20	.12
52	Joe Christopher	.40	.20	.12
53	Al Spangler	.40	.20	.12
54	Jim King	.40	.20	.12
55	Mickey Lolich	.70	.35	.20
56	Harmon Killebrew	2.00	1.00	.60
57	Bob Shaw	.40	.20	.12
58	Ernie Banks	2.00	1.00	.60
59	Hank Aaron	3.50	1.75	1.00
60	Chuck Hinton	.40	.20	.12
61	Bob Aspromonte	.40	.20	.12
62	Lee Maye	.40	.20	.12
63	Joe Cunningham	.40	.20	.12
64	Pete Ward	.40	.20	.12
65	Bobby Richardson	1.00	.50	.30
66	Dean Chance	.40	.20	.12
67	Dick Ellsworth	.40	.20	.12
68	Jim Maloney	.40	.20	.12
69	Bob Gibson	1.50	.70	.45

SANDY KOUFAX

CARD 8 NUMBER

PRINTED IN U.S.A.

		NR MT	EX	VG
70	Earl Battey	.40	.20	.12
71	Tony Kubek	1.00	.50	.30
72	Jack Kralick	.40	.20	.12

1965 Topps Transfers

Issued as strips of three players each as inserts in 1965, the Topps Transfers were 2'' by 3'' portraits of players. The transfers have blue or red bands at the top and bottom with the team name and position in the top band and the player's name in the bottom. As is so often the case, the superstars in the transfer set can be quite expensive, but like many of Topps non-card products, the transfers are neither terribly expensive or popular today.

	NR MT	EX	VG
Complete Set:	200.00	100.00	60.00
Common Player:	.60	.30	.20

		NR MT	EX	VG
(1)	Hank Aaron	15.00	7.50	4.50
(2)	Richie Allen	.80	.40	.25
(3)	Bob Allison	.70	.35	.20
(4)	Max Alvis	.60	.30	.20
(5)	Luis Aparicio	2.50	1.25	.70
(6)	Bob Aspromonte	.60	.30	.20
(7)	Walt Bond	.60	.30	.20
(8)	Jim Bouton	.80	.40	.25
(9)	Ken Boyer	.80	.40	.25
(10)	Jim Bunning	1.00	.50	.30
(11)	John Callison	.70	.35	.20
(12)	Rico Carty	.70	.35	.20
(13)	Wayne Causey	.60	.30	.20
(14)	Orlando Cepeda	1.00	.50	.30
(15)	Bob Chance	.60	.30	.20
(16)	Dean Chance	.60	.30	.20
(17)	Joe Christopher	.60	.30	.20
(18)	Bob Clemente	15.00	7.50	4.50
(19)	Rocky Colavito	.80	.40	.25
(20)	Tony Conigliaro	.70	.35	.20
(21)	Tommy Davis	.80	.40	.25
(22)	Don Drysdale	4.00	2.00	1.25
(23)	Bill Freehan	.70	.35	.20
(24)	Jim Fregosi	.70	.35	.20
(25)	Bob Gibson	4.00	2.00	1.25
(26)	Dick Groat	.70	.35	.20
(27)	Tom Haller	.60	.30	.20
(28)	Chuck Hinton	.60	.30	.20
(29)	Elston Howard	1.00	.50	.30
(30)	Ron Hunt	.60	.30	.20
(31)	Al Jackson	.60	.30	.20
(32)	Al Kaline	5.00	2.50	1.50
(33)	Harmon Killebrew	5.00	2.50	1.50
(34)	Jim King	.60	.30	.20
(35)	Ron Kline	.60	.30	.20
(36)	Bobby Knoop	.60	.30	.20
(37)	Sandy Koufax	10.00	5.00	3.00
(38)	Ed Kranepool	.60	.30	.20
(39)	Jim Maloney	.60	.30	.20
(40)	Mickey Mantle	50.00	25.00	15.00
(41)	Juan Marichal	4.00	2.00	1.25
(42)	Lee Maye	.60	.30	.20
(43)	Willie Mays	15.00	7.50	4.50
(44)	Bill Mazeroski	.80	.40	.25
(45)	Tony Oliva	.80	.40	.25

		NR MT	EX	VG
(46)	Jim O'Toole	.60	.30	.20
(47)	Milt Pappas	.70	.35	.20
(48)	Camilo Pascual	.70	.35	.20
(49)	Gary Peters	.60	.30	.20
(50)	Vada Pinson	.80	.40	.25
(51)	Juan Pizarro	.60	.30	.20
(52)	Boog Powell	.80	.40	.25
(53)	Dick Radatz	.60	.30	.20
(54)	Bobby Richardson	1.00	.50	.30
(55)	Brooks Robinson	6.00	3.00	1.75
(56)	Frank Robinson	5.00	2.50	1.50
(57)	Bob Rodgers	.70	.35	.20
(58)	John Roseboro	.70	.35	.20
(59)	Ron Santo	.80	.40	.25
(60)	Diego Segui	.60	.30	.20
(61)	Bill Skowron	.70	.35	.20
(62)	Al Spangler	.60	.30	.20
(63)	Dick Stuart	.70	.35	.20
(64)	Luis Tiant	.80	.40	.25
(65)	Joe Torre	.80	.40	.25
(66)	Bob Veale	.60	.30	.20
(67)	Leon Wagner	.60	.30	.20
(68)	Pete Ward	.60	.30	.20
(69)	Bill White	.70	.35	.20
(70)	Dave Wickersham	.60	.30	.20
(71)	Billy Williams	3.00	1.50	.90
(72)	Carl Yastrzemski	25.00	12.50	7.50

1966 Topps

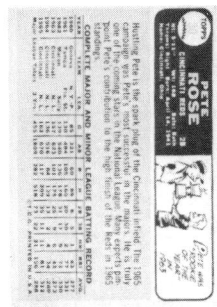

In 1966, Topps produced another 598-card set. This time, the 2½'' by 3½'' cards featured the almost traditional color photograph with a diagonal stripe in the upper left-hand corner carrying the team name. A band at the bottom carried the player's name and position. Multi-player cards returned in 1966 after having had a year's hiatus. The statistical leader cards featured the categorical leader and two runners-up. Most team managers had cards as well. The 1966 set features a handful of cards found with or without a notice of the player's sale or trade to another team. Cards without the notice bring higher prices, but are not included in the complete set prices below.

	NR MT	EX	VG
Complete Set:	2200.00	750.00	425.00
Common Player: 1-110	.40	.20	.12
Common Player: 111-446	.50	.25	.15
Common Player: 447-522	1.50	.75	.45
Common Player: 523-598	6.00	3.00	1.75

		NR MT	EX	VG
1	Willie Mays	100.00	15.00	9.00
2	Ted Abernathy	.60	.20	.12
3	Sam Mele	.40	.20	.12
4	Ray Culp	.40	.20	.12
5	Jim Fregosi	1.00	.50	.30
6	Chuck Schilling	.40	.20	.12
7	Tracy Stallard	.40	.20	.12
8	Floyd Robinson	.40	.20	.12
9	Clete Boyer	1.50	.70	.45
10	Tony Cloninger	.50	.25	.15
11	Senators Rookies (Brant Alyea, Pete Craig)	.40	.20	.12
12	John Tsitouris	.40	.20	.12
13	Lou Johnson	.40	.20	.12
14	Norm Siebern	.50	.25	.15

		NR MT	EX	VG
15	Vern Law	1.00	.50	.30
16	Larry Brown	.50	.25	.15
17	Johnny Stephenson	.50	.25	.15
18	Roland Sheldon	.40	.20	.12
19	Giants Team	2.00	1.00	.60
20	Willie Horton	.80	.40	.25
21	Don Nottebart	.40	.20	.12
22	Joe Nossek	.40	.20	.12
23	Jack Sanford	.40	.20	.12
24	Don Kessinger	1.25	.60	.40
25	Pete Ward	.40	.20	.12
26	Ray Sadecki	.40	.20	.12
27	Orioles Rookies (Andy Etchebarren, Darold Knowles)	.50	.25	.15
28	Phil Niekro	10.00	5.00	3.00
29	Mike Brumley	.40	.20	.12
30	Pete Rose	60.00	30.00	18.00
31	Jack Cullen	.80	.40	.25
32	Adolfo Phillips	.40	.20	.12
33	Jim Pagliaroni	.40	.20	.12
34	Checklist 1-88	2.00	1.00	.60
35	Ron Swoboda	.80	.40	.25
36	Jim Hunter	12.00	6.00	3.50
37	Billy Herman	1.50	.70	.45
38	Ron Nischwitz	.40	.20	.12
39	Ken Henderson	.40	.20	.12
40	Jim Grant	.40	.20	.12
41	Don LeJohn	.40	.20	.12
42	Aubrey Gatewood	.40	.20	.12
43	Don Landrum	.40	.20	.12
44	Indians Rookies (Bill Davis, Tom Kelley)	.40	.20	.12
45	Jim Gentile	.50	.25	.15
46	Howie Koplitz	.40	.20	.12
47	J.C. Martin	.40	.20	.12
48	Paul Blair	.80	.40	.25
49	Woody Woodward	.50	.25	.15
50	Mickey Mantle	150.00	70.00	40.00
51	Gordon Richardson	.50	.25	.15
52	Power Plus (Johnny Callison, Wes Covington)	1.00	.50	.30
53	Bob Duliba	.40	.20	.12
54	Jose Pagan	.40	.20	.12
55	Ken Harrelson	1.50	.70	.45
56	Sandy Valdespino	.40	.20	.12
57	Jim Lefebvre	.50	.25	.15
58	Dave Wickersham	.40	.20	.12
59	Reds Team	2.25	1.25	.70
60	Curt Flood	1.50	.70	.45
61	Bob Bolin	.40	.20	.12
62a	Merritt Ranew (no sold statement)	15.00	7.50	4.50
62b	Merritt Ranew (with sold statement)	.40	.20	.12
63	Jim Stewart	.40	.20	.12
64	Bob Bruce	.40	.20	.12
65	Leon Wagner	.50	.25	.15
66	Al Weis	.40	.20	.12
67	Mets Rookies (Cleon Jones, Dick Selma)	.80	.40	.25
68	Hal Reniff	.80	.40	.25
69	Ken Hamlin	.40	.20	.12
70	Carl Yastrzemski	40.00	20.00	12.00
71	Frank Carpin	.40	.20	.12
72	Tony Perez	8.00	4.00	2.50
73	Jerry Zimmerman	.40	.20	.12
74	Don Mossi	.50	.25	.15
75	Tommy Davis	1.50	.70	.45
76	Red Schoendienst	1.00	.50	.30
77	Johnny Orsino	.40	.20	.12
78	Frank Linzy	.40	.20	.12
79	Joe Pepitone	2.00	1.00	.60
80	Richie Allen	2.50	1.25	.70
81	Ray Oyler	.40	.20	.12
82	Bob Hendley	.40	.20	.12
83	Albie Pearson	.40	.20	.12
84	Braves Rookies (Jim Beauchamp, Dick Kelley)	.40	.20	.12
85	Eddie Fisher	.40	.20	.12
86	John Bateman	.40	.20	.12
87	Dan Napoleon	.50	.25	.15
88	Fred Whitfield	.40	.20	.12
89	Ted Davidson	.40	.20	.12
90	Luis Aparicio	6.00	3.00	1.75
91a	Bob Uecker (no trade statement)	40.00	20.00	12.00
91b	Bob Uecker (with trade statement)	12.00	6.00	3.50
92	Yankees Team	4.00	2.00	1.25
93	Jim Lonborg	1.00	.50	.30
94	Matty Alou	1.00	.50	.30
95	Pete Richert	.40	.20	.12
96	Felipe Alou	1.00	.50	.30
97	Jim Merritt	.40	.20	.12
98	Don Demeter	.40	.20	.12
99	Buc Belters (Donn Clendenon, Willie Stargell)	3.50	1.75	1.00
100	Sandy Koufax	25.00	12.50	7.50
101a	Checklist 89-176 (115 is Spahn)	6.00	3.00	1.75
101b	Checklist 89-176 (115 is Henry)	3.00	1.50	.90
102	Ed Kirkpatrick	.40	.20	.12
103a	Dick Groat (no trade statement)	20.00	10.00	6.00
103b	Dick Groat (with trade statement.)	1.50	.70	.45
104a	Alex Johnson (no trade statement)	15.00	7.50	4.50
104b	Alex Johnson (with trade statement)	.50	.25	.15
105	Milt Pappas	.70	.35	.20
106	Rusty Staub	2.50	1.25	.70
107	Athletics Rookies (Larry Stahl, Ron Tompkins)	.40	.20	.12
108	Bobby Klaus	.50	.25	.15
109	Ralph Terry	.50	.25	.15
110	Ernie Banks	10.00	5.00	3.00
111	Gary Peters	.60	.30	.20
112	Manny Mota	.80	.40	.25
113	Hank Aguirre	.50	.25	.15
114	Jim Gosger	.50	.25	.15
115	Bill Henry	.50	.25	.15
116	Walt Alston	2.50	1.25	.70
117	Jake Gibbs	1.00	.50	.30
118	Mike McCormick	.60	.30	.20
119	Art Shamsky	.50	.25	.15
120	Harmon Killebrew	10.00	5.00	3.00
121	Ray Herbert	.50	.25	.15
122	Joe Gaines	.50	.25	.15
123	Pirates Rookies (Frank Bork, Jerry May)	.50	.25	.15
124	Tug McGraw	3.00	1.50	.90
125	Lou Brock	10.00	5.00	3.00
126	Jim Palmer	45.00	22.00	13.50
127	Ken Berry	.50	.25	.15
128	Jim Landis	.50	.25	.15
129	Jack Kralick	.50	.25	.15
130	Joe Torre	2.25	1.25	.70
131	Angels Team	2.25	1.25	.70
132	Orlando Cepeda	3.50	1.75	1.00
133	Don McMahon	.50	.25	.15
134	Wes Parker	.60	.30	.20
135	Dave Morehead	.50	.25	.15
136	Woody Held	.50	.25	.15
137	Pat Corrales	1.00	.50	.30
138	Roger Repoz	1.00	.50	.30
139	Cubs Rookies (Byron Browne, Don Young)	.50	.25	.15
140	Jim Maloney	.60	.30	.20
141	Tom McCraw	.50	.25	.15
142	Don Dennis	.50	.25	.15
143	Jose Tartabull	.50	.25	.15
144	Don Schwall	.50	.25	.15
145	Bill Freehan	.70	.35	.20
146	George Altman	.50	.25	.15
147	Lum Harris	.50	.25	.15
148	Bob Johnson	.50	.25	.15
149	Dick Nen	.50	.25	.15
150	Rocky Colavito	2.50	1.25	.70
151	Gary Wagner	.50	.25	.15
152	Frank Malzone	.60	.30	.20
153	Rico Carty	1.50	.70	.45
154	Chuck Hiller	.60	.30	.20
155	Marcelino Lopez	.50	.25	.15
156	DP Combo (Hal Lanier, Dick Schofield)	1.00	.50	.30
157	Rene Lachemann	.60	.30	.20
158	Jim Brewer	.50	.25	.15
159	Chico Ruiz	.50	.25	.15
160	Whitey Ford	10.00	5.00	3.00
161	Jerry Lumpe	.60	.30	.20
162	Lee Maye	.50	.25	.15
163	Tito Francona	.60	.30	.20
164	White Sox Rookies (Tommie Agee, Marv Staehle)	.80	.40	.25
165	Don Lock	.50	.25	.15
166	Chris Krug	.50	.25	.15
167	Boog Powell	2.50	1.25	.70
168	Dan Osinski	.50	.25	.15
169	Duke Sims	.50	.25	.15
170	Cookie Rojas	.50	.25	.15
171	Nick Willhite	.50	.25	.15
172	Mets Team	3.00	1.50	.90
173	Al Spangler	.50	.25	.15

		NR MT	EX	VG
174	Ron Taylor	.50	.25	.15
175	Bert Campaneris	1.50	.70	.45
176	Jim Davenport	.50	.25	.15
177	Hector Lopez	1.00	.50	.30
178	Bob Tillman	.50	.25	.15
179	Cardinals Rookies (Dennis Aust, Bob Tolan)	.60	.30	.20
180	Vada Pinson	2.50	1.25	.70
181	Al Worthington	.50	.25	.15
182	Jerry Lynch	.50	.25	.15
183a	Checklist 177-264 (large print on front)	2.50	1.25	.70
183b	Checklist 177-264 (small print on front)	4.00	2.00	1.25
184	Denis Menke	.50	.25	.15
185	Bob Buhl	.60	.30	.20
186	Ruben Amaro	1.00	.50	.30
187	Chuck Dressen	.60	.30	.20
188	Al Luplow	.60	.30	.20
189	John Roseboro	.80	.40	.25
190	Jimmie Hall	.50	.25	.15
191	Darrell Sutherland	.60	.30	.20
192	Vic Power	.50	.25	.15
193	Dave McNally	1.00	.50	.30
194	Senators Team	2.25	1.25	.70
195	Joe Morgan	10.00	5.00	3.00
196	Don Pavletich	.50	.25	.15
197	Sonny Siebert	.60	.30	.20
198	Mickey Stanley	1.00	.50	.30
199	Chisox Clubbers (Floyd Robinson, Johnny Romano, Bill Skowron)	1.00	.50	.30
200	Ed Mathews	7.00	3.50	2.00
201	Jim Dickson	.50	.25	.15
202	Clay Dalrymple	.50	.25	.15
203	Jose Santiago	.50	.25	.15
204	Cubs Team	2.25	1.25	.70
205	Tom Tresh	2.00	1.00	.60
206	Alvin Jackson	.50	.25	.15
207	Frank Quilici	.50	.25	.15
208	Bob Miller	.50	.25	.15
209	Tigers Rookies (Fritz Fisher, John Hiller)	1.25	.60	.40
210	Bill Mazeroski	2.50	1.25	.70
211	Frank Kreutzer	.50	.25	.15
212	Ed Kranepool	1.00	.50	.30
213	Fred Newman	.50	.25	.15
214	Tommy Harper	.60	.30	.20
215	N.L. Batting Leaders (Hank Aaron, Bob Clemente, Willie Mays)	6.00	3.00	1.75
216	A.L. Batting Leaders (Vic Davalillo, Tony Oliva, Carl Yastrzemski)	4.00	2.00	1.25
217	N.L. Home Run Leaders (Willie Mays, Willie McCovey, Billy Williams)	5.00	2.50	1.50
218	A.L. Home Run Leaders (Norm Cash, Tony Conigliaro, Willie Horton)	2.50	1.25	.70
219	N.L. RBI Leaders (Deron Johnson, Willie Mays, Frank Robinson)	4.00	2.00	1.25
220	A.L. RBI Leaders (Rocky Colavito, Willie Horton, Tony Oliva)	2.50	1.25	.70
221	N.L. ERA Leaders (Sandy Koufax, Vern Law, Juan Marichal)	4.00	2.00	1.25
222	A.L. ERA Leaders (Eddie Fisher, Sam McDowell, Sonny Siebert)	2.50	1.25	.70
223	N.L. Pitching Leaders (Tony Cloninger, Don Drysdale, Sandy Koufax)	4.00	2.00	1.25
224	A.L. Pitching Leaders (Jim Grant, Jim Kaat, Mel Stottlemyre)	3.00	1.50	.90
225	N.L. Strikeout Leaders (Bob Gibson, Sandy Koufax, Bob Veale)	4.00	2.00	1.25
226	A.L. Strikeout Leaders (Mickey Lolich, Sam McDowell, Denny McLain, Sonny Siebert)	2.50	1.25	.70
227	Russ Nixon	.50	.25	.15
228	Larry Dierker	.60	.30	.20
229	Hank Bauer	.70	.35	.20
230	Johnny Callison	1.25	.60	.40
231	Floyd Weaver	.50	.25	.15
232	Glenn Beckert	1.00	.50	.30
233	Dom Zanni	.50	.25	.15
234	Yankees Rookies (Rich Beck, Roy White)	3.50	1.75	1.00
235	Don Cardwell	.50	.25	.15
236	Mike Hershberger	.50	.25	.15
237	Billy O'Dell	.50	.25	.15
238	Dodgers Team	3.50	1.75	1.00
239	Orlando Pena	.50	.25	.15
240	Earl Battey	.60	.30	.20
241	Dennis Ribant	.60	.30	.20
242	Jesus Alou	.60	.30	.20
243	Nelson Briles	.60	.30	.20
244	Astros Rookies (Chuck Harrison, Sonny Jackson)	.50	.25	.15
245	John Buzhardt	.50	.25	.15
246	Ed Bailey	.50	.25	.15
247	Carl Warwick	.50	.25	.15
248	Pete Mikkelsen	.50	.25	.15
249	Bill Rigney	.50	.25	.15
250	Sam Ellis	.50	.25	.15
251	Ed Brinkman	.60	.30	.20
252	Denver Lemaster	.50	.25	.15
253	Don Wert	.50	.25	.15
254	Phillies Rookies (Ferguson Jenkins, Bill Sorrell)	15.00	7.50	4.50
255	Willie Stargell	8.00	4.00	2.50
256	Lew Krausse	.50	.25	.15
257	Jeff Torborg	.60	.30	.20
258	Dave Giusti	.50	.25	.15
259	Red Sox Team	2.50	1.25	.70
260	Bob Shaw	.50	.25	.15
261	Ron Hansen	.50	.25	.15
262	Jack Hamilton	.60	.30	.20
263	Tom Egan	.50	.25	.15
264	Twins Rookies (Andy Kosco, Ted Uhlaender)	.50	.25	.15
265	Stu Miller	.50	.25	.15
266	Pedro Gonzalez	.50	.25	.15
267	Joe Sparma	.50	.25	.15
268	John Blanchard	.50	.25	.15
269	Don Heffner	.50	.25	.15
270	Claude Osteen	.80	.40	.25
271	Hal Lanier	1.00	.50	.30
272	Jack Baldschun	.50	.25	.15
273	Astro Aces (Bob Aspromonte, Rusty Staub)	1.50	.70	.45
274	Buster Narum	.50	.25	.15
275	Tim McCarver	2.50	1.25	.70
276	Jim Bouton	2.50	1.25	.70
277	George Thomas	.50	.25	.15
278	Calvin Koonce	.50	.25	.15
279a	Checklist 265-352 (player's cap black)	4.00	2.00	1.25
279b	Checklist 265-352 (player's cap red)	3.00	1.50	.90
280	Bobby Knoop	.50	.25	.15
281	Bruce Howard	.50	.25	.15
282	Johnny Lewis	.60	.30	.20
283	Jim Perry	1.00	.50	.30
284	Bobby Wine	.60	.30	.20
285	Luis Tiant	2.50	1.25	.70
286	Gary Geiger	.50	.25	.15
287	Jack Aker	.50	.25	.15
288	Dodgers Rookies (Bill Singer, Don Sutton)	40.00	20.00	12.00
289	Larry Sherry	.60	.30	.20
290	Ron Santo	2.00	1.00	.60
291	Moe Drabowsky	.50	.25	.15
292	Jim Coker	.50	.25	.15
293	Mike Shannon	.60	.30	.20
294	Steve Ridzik	.50	.25	.15
295	Jim Hart	.60	.30	.20
296	Johnny Keane	1.25	.60	.40
297	Jim Owens	.50	.25	.15
298	Rico Petrocelli	1.25	.60	.40
299	Lou Burdette	2.00	1.00	.60
300	Bob Clemente	30.00	15.00	9.00
301	Greg Bollo	.50	.25	.15
302	Ernie Bowman	.60	.30	.20
303	Indians Team	2.25	1.25	.70
304	John Herrnstein	.50	.25	.15
305	Camilo Pascual	.80	.40	.25
306	Ty Cline	.50	.25	.15
307	Clay Carroll	.60	.30	.20
308	Tom Haller	.60	.30	.20
309	Diego Segui	.50	.25	.15
310	Frank Robinson	15.00	7.50	4.50
311	Reds Rookies (Tommy Helms, Dick Simpson)	.80	.40	.25
312	Bob Saverine	.50	.25	.15
313	Chris Zachary	.50	.25	.15
314	Hector Valle	.50	.25	.15
315	Norm Cash	2.00	1.00	.60
316	Jack Fisher	.60	.30	.20
317	Dalton Jones	.50	.25	.15
318	Harry Walker	.60	.30	.20
319	Gene Freese	.50	.25	.15
320	Bob Gibson	10.00	5.00	3.00
321	Rick Reichardt	.50	.25	.15
322	Bill Faul	.50	.25	.15
323	Ray Barker	1.00	.50	.30
324	John Boozer	.50	.25	.15
325	Vic Davalillo	.60	.30	.20

		NR MT	EX	VG
326	Braves Team	2.25	1.25	.70
327	Bernie Allen	.50	.25	.15
328	Jerry Grote	.80	.40	.25
329	Pete Charton	.50	.25	.15
330	Ron Fairly	.80	.40	.25
331	Ron Herbel	.50	.25	.15
332	Billy Bryan	.50	.25	.15
333	Senators Rookies (Joe Coleman, Jim French)	.80	.40	.25
334	Marty Keough	.50	.25	.15
335	Juan Pizarro	.50	.25	.15
336	Gene Alley	.60	.30	.20
337	Fred Gladding	.50	.25	.15
338	Dal Maxvill	.60	.30	.20
339	Del Crandall	1.00	.50	.30
340	Dean Chance	.60	.30	.20
341	Wes Westrum	.80	.40	.25
342	Bob Humphreys	.50	.25	.15
343	Joe Christopher	.50	.25	.15
344	Steve Blass	.70	.35	.20
345	Bob Allison	1.00	.50	.30
346	Mike de la Hoz	.50	.25	.15
347	Phil Regan	.50	.25	.15
348	Orioles Team	3.50	1.75	1.00
349	Cap Peterson	.50	.25	.15
350	Mel Stottlemyre	3.00	1.50	.90
351	Fred Valentine	.50	.25	.15
352	Bob Aspromonte	.50	.25	.15
353	Al McBean	.50	.25	.15
354	Smoky Burgess	1.00	.50	.30
355	Wade Blasingame	.50	.25	.15
356	Red Sox Rookies (Owen Johnson, Ken Sanders)	.50	.25	.15
357	Gerry Arrigo	.50	.25	.15
358	Charlie Smith	.50	.25	.15
359	Johnny Briggs	.50	.25	.15
360	Ron Hunt	.80	.40	.25
361	Tom Satriano	.50	.25	.15
362	Gates Brown	.50	.25	.15
363	Checklist 353-429	3.00	1.50	.90
364	Nate Oliver	.50	.25	.15
365	Roger Maris	20.00	10.00	6.00
366	Wayne Causey	.50	.25	.15
367	Mel Nelson	.50	.25	.15
368	Charlie Lau	.80	.40	.25
369	Jim King	.50	.25	.15
370	Chico Cardenas	.50	.25	.15
371	Lee Stange	.50	.25	.15
372	Harvey Kuenn	1.50	.70	.45
373	Giants Rookies (Dick Estelle, Jack Hiatt)	.50	.25	.15
374	Bob Locker	.50	.25	.15
375	Donn Clendenon	.60	.30	.20
376	Paul Schaal	.50	.25	.15
377	Turk Farrell	.50	.25	.15
378	Dick Tracewski	.50	.25	.15
379	Cardinals Team	2.25	1.25	.70
380	Tony Conigliaro	2.00	1.00	.60
381	Hank Fischer	.50	.25	.15
382	Phil Roof	.50	.25	.15
383	Jackie Brandt	.50	.25	.15
384	Al Downing	1.50	.70	.45
385	Ken Boyer	2.50	1.25	.70
386	Gil Hodges	5.00	2.50	1.50
387	Howie Reed	.50	.25	.15
388	Don Mincher	.60	.30	.20
389	Jim O'Toole	.50	.25	.15
390	Brooks Robinson	12.00	6.00	3.50
391	Chuck Hinton	.50	.25	.15
392	Cubs Rookies (Bill Hands, Randy Hundley)	.80	.40	.25
393	George Brunet	.50	.25	.15
394	Ron Brand	.50	.25	.15
395	Len Gabrielson	.50	.25	.15
396	Jerry Stephenson	.50	.25	.15
397	Bill White	1.00	.50	.30
398	Danny Cater	.50	.25	.15
399	Ray Washburn	.50	.25	.15
400	Zoilo Versalles	.60	.30	.20
401	Ken McMullen	.50	.25	.15
402	Jim Hickman	.80	.40	.25
403	Fred Talbot	.50	.25	.15
404	Pirates Team	2.25	1.25	.70
405	Elston Howard	3.00	1.50	.90
406	Joe Jay	.50	.25	.15
407	John Kennedy	.50	.25	.15
408	Lee Thomas	.50	.25	.15
409	Billy Hoeft	.50	.25	.15
410	Al Kaline	10.00	5.00	3.00
411	Gene Mauch	.80	.40	.25
412	Sam Bowens	.50	.25	.15
413	John Romano	.50	.25	.15
414	Dan Coombs	.50	.25	.15
415	Max Alvis	.50	.25	.15
416	Phil Ortega	.50	.25	.15
417	Angels Rookies (Jim McGlothlin, Ed Sukla)	.50	.25	.15
418	Phil Gagliano	.50	.25	.15
419	Mike Ryan	.50	.25	.15
420	Juan Marichal	8.00	4.00	2.50
421	Roy McMillan	.60	.30	.20
422	Ed Charles	.50	.25	.15
423	Ernie Broglio	.50	.25	.15
424	Reds Rookies (Lee May, Darrell Osteen)	2.25	1.25	.70
425	Bob Veale	.60	.30	.20
426	White Sox Team	2.25	1.25	.70
427	John Miller	.50	.25	.15
428	Sandy Alomar	.50	.25	.15
429	Bill Monbouquette	.60	.30	.20
430	Don Drysdale	8.00	4.00	2.50
431	Walt Bond	.50	.25	.15
432	Bob Heffner	.50	.25	.15
433	Alvin Dark	.80	.40	.25
434	Willie Kirkland	.50	.25	.15
435	Jim Bunning	4.00	2.00	1.25
436	Julian Javier	.50	.25	.15
437	Al Stanek	.50	.25	.15
438	Willie Smith	.50	.25	.15
439	Pedro Ramos	1.00	.50	.30
440	Deron Johnson	.50	.25	.15
441	Tommie Sisk	.50	.25	.15
442	Orioles Rookies (Ed Barnowski, Eddie Watt)	.50	.25	.15
443	Bill Wakefield	.60	.30	.20
444a	Checklist 430-506 (456 is R. Sox Rookies)	3.00	1.50	.90
444b	Checklist 430-506 (456 is Red Sox Rookies)	5.00	2.50	1.50
445	Jim Kaat	4.00	2.00	1.25
446	Mack Jones	.50	.25	.15
447	Dick Ellsworth (photo actually Ken Hubbs)	1.50	.70	.45
448	Eddie Stanky	1.75	.90	.50
449	Joe Moeller	1.50	.70	.45
450	Tony Oliva	4.50	2.25	1.25
451	Barry Latman	1.50	.70	.45
452	Joe Azcue	1.50	.70	.45
453	Ron Kline	1.50	.70	.45
454	Jerry Buchek	1.50	.70	.45
455	Mickey Lolich	3.50	1.75	1.00
456	Red Sox Rookies (Darrell Brandon, Joe Foy)	1.50	.70	.45
457	Joe Gibbon	1.50	.70	.45
458	Manny Jiminez (Jimenez)	1.50	.70	.45
459	Bill McCool	1.50	.70	.45
460	Curt Blefary	1.50	.70	.45
461	Roy Face	3.00	1.50	.90
462	Bob Rodgers	2.50	1.25	.70
463	Phillies Team	3.75	2.00	1.25
464	Larry Bearnarth	1.75	.90	.50
465	Don Buford	1.75	.90	.50
466	Ken Johnson	1.50	.70	.45
467	Vic Roznovsky	1.50	.70	.45
468	Johnny Podres	3.50	1.75	1.00
469	Yankees Rookies (Bobby Murcer, Dooley Womack)	8.00	4.00	2.50
470	Sam McDowell	2.50	1.25	.70
471	Bob Skinner	1.75	.90	.50
472	Terry Fox	1.50	.70	.45
473	Rich Rollins	1.50	.70	.45
474	Dick Schofield	1.50	.70	.45
475	Dick Radatz	1.75	.90	.50
476	Bobby Bragan	1.75	.90	.50
477	Steve Barber	1.50	.70	.45
478	Tony Gonzalez	1.50	.70	.45
479	Jim Hannan	1.50	.70	.45
480	Dick Stuart	2.25	1.25	.70
481	Bob Lee	1.50	.70	.45
482	Cubs Rookies (John Boccabella, Dave Dowling)	1.50	.70	.45
483	Joe Nuxhall	2.25	1.25	.70
484	Wes Covington	1.50	.70	.45
485	Bob Bailey	1.50	.70	.45
486	Tommy John	7.00	3.50	2.00
487	Al Ferrara	1.50	.70	.45
488	George Banks	1.50	.70	.45
489	Curt Simmons	2.25	1.25	.70
490	Bobby Richardson	6.00	3.00	1.75
491	Dennis Bennett	1.50	.70	.45
492	Athletics Team	3.75	2.00	1.25
493	Johnny Klippstein	1.50	.70	.45

WE LIKE MICKEY MANTLE AND MICKEY MAHLER.

At the Dragon's Den, we know that some people are concerned with baseball card investments. That's why we strive to carry all the hot players and sets at competitive prices.

We also know that plenty of people collect baseball cards just for the fun of it. That's why we have an extensive selection of common cards, in order, from 1952 to 1987, as well as football, hockey and non-sports cards. Whether you need a $50.00 Mickey Mantle or a 5¢ Mickey Mahler, our veteran staff will be happy to help you.

Come and discover why Westchester's largest collector's store is Westchester's best store.

		NR MT	EX	VG
494	Gordon Coleman	1.50	.70	.45
495	Dick McAuliffe	1.75	.90	.50
496	Lindy McDaniel	1.50	.70	.45
497	Chris Cannizzaro	1.50	.70	.45
498	Pirates Rookies (Woody Fryman, Luke Walker)	2.50	1.25	.70
499	Wally Bunker	1.50	.70	.45
500	Hank Aaron	40.00	20.00	12.00
501	John O'Donoghue	1.50	.70	.45
502	Lenny Green	1.50	.70	.45
503	Steve Hamilton	2.25	1.25	.70
504	Grady Hatton	1.50	.70	.45
505	Jose Cardenal	1.75	.90	.50
506	Bo Belinsky	2.00	1.00	.60
507	John Edwards	1.50	.70	.45
508	Steve Hargan	1.75	.90	.50
509	Jake Wood	1.50	.70	.45
510	Hoyt Wilhelm	10.00	5.00	3.00
511	Giants Rookies (Bob Barton, Tito Fuentes)	1.75	.90	.50
512	Dick Stigman	1.50	.70	.45
513	Camilo Carreon	1.50	.70	.45
514	Hal Woodeshick	1.50	.70	.45
515	Frank Howard	4.00	2.00	1.25
516	Eddie Bressoud	1.75	.90	.50
517a	Checklist 507-598 (529 is W. Sox Rookies)	6.00	3.00	1.75
517b	Checklist 506-598 (529 is White Sox Rookies)	8.00	4.00	2.50
518	Braves Rookies (Herb Hippauf, Arnie Umbach)	1.50	.70	.45
519	Bob Friend	3.25	1.75	1.00
520	Jim Wynn	2.50	1.25	.70
521	John Wyatt	1.50	.70	.45
522	Phil Linz	1.50	.70	.45
523	Bob Sadowski	6.00	3.00	1.75
524	Giants Rookies (Ollie Brown, Don Mason)	12.00	6.00	3.50
525	Gary Bell	6.00	3.00	1.75
526	Twins Team	30.00	15.00	9.00
527	Julio Navarro	6.00	3.00	1.75
528	Jesse Gonder	12.00	6.00	3.50
529	White Sox Rookies (Lee Elia, Dennis Higgins, Bill Voss)	6.50	3.25	2.00
530	Robin Roberts	25.00	12.50	7.50
531	Joe Cunningham	6.50	3.25	2.00
532	Aurelio Monteagudo	6.00	3.00	1.75
533	Jerry Adair	6.00	3.00	1.75
534	Mets Rookies (Dave Eilers, Rob Gardner)	6.50	3.25	2.00
535	Willie Davis	10.00	5.00	3.00
536	Dick Egan	6.00	3.00	1.75
537	Herman Franks	6.00	3.00	1.75
538	Bob Allen	6.00	3.00	1.75
539	Astros Rookies (Bill Heath, Carroll Sembera)	6.00	3.00	1.75
540	Denny McLain	20.00	10.00	6.00
541	Gene Oliver	6.00	3.00	1.75
542	George Smith	6.00	3.00	1.75
543	Roger Craig	10.00	5.00	3.00
544	Cardinals Rookies (Joe Hoerner, George Kernek, Jimmy Williams)	12.00	6.00	3.50
545	Dick Green	12.00	6.00	3.50
546	Dwight Siebler	6.00	3.00	1.75
547	Horace Clarke	15.00	7.50	4.50
548	Gary Kroll	12.00	6.00	3.50
549	Senators Rookies (Al Closter, Casey Cox)	6.00	3.00	1.75
550	Willie McCovey	60.00	30.00	18.00
551	Bob Purkey	12.00	6.00	3.50
552	Birdie Tebbetts	6.00	3.00	1.75
553	Major League Rookies (Pat Garrett, Jackie Warner)	6.00	3.00	1.75
554	Jim Northrup	7.00	3.50	2.00
555	Ron Perranoski	7.00	3.50	2.00
556	Mel Queen	12.00	6.00	3.50
557	Felix Mantilla	6.00	3.00	1.75
558	Red Sox Rookies (Guido Grilli, Pete Magrini, George Scott)	10.00	5.00	3.00
559	Roberto Pena	6.00	3.00	1.75
560	Joel Horlen	6.00	3.00	1.75
561	Choo Choo Coleman	12.00	6.00	3.50
562	Russ Snyder	6.00	3.00	1.75
563	Twins Rookies (Pete Cimino, Cesar Tovar)	6.50	3.25	2.00
564	Bob Chance	6.00	3.00	1.75
565	Jimmy Piersall	20.00	10.00	6.00
566	Mike Cuellar	8.00	4.00	2.50
567	Dick Howser	8.00	4.00	2.50
568	Athletics Rookies (Paul Lindblad, Ron Stone)	6.00	3.00	1.75

		NR MT	EX	VG
569	Orlando McFarlane	6.00	3.00	1.75
570	Art Mahaffey	12.00	6.00	3.50
571	Dave Roberts	6.00	3.00	1.75
572	Bob Priddy	6.00	3.00	1.75
573	Derrell Griffith	6.00	3.00	1.75
574	Mets Rookies (Bill Hepler, Bill Murphy)	6.50	3.25	2.00
575	Earl Wilson	6.00	3.00	1.75
576	Dave Nicholson	12.00	6.00	3.50
577	Jack Lamabe	6.00	3.00	1.75
578	Chi Chi Olivo	6.00	3.00	1.75
579	Orioles Rookies (Frank Bertaina, Gene Brabender, Dave Johnson)	12.00	6.00	3.50
580	Billy Williams	25.00	12.50	7.50
581	Tony Martinez	6.00	3.00	1.75
582	Garry Roggenburk	6.00	3.00	1.75
583	Tigers Team	35.00	17.50	10.50
584	Yankees Rookies (Frank Fernandez, Fritz Peterson)	8.00	4.00	2.50
585	Tony Taylor	6.00	3.00	1.75
586	Claude Raymond	6.00	3.00	1.75
587	Dick Bertell	6.00	3.00	1.75
588	Athletics Rookies (Chuck Dobson, Ken Suarez)	6.00	3.00	1.75
589	Lou Klimchock	6.50	3.25	2.00
590	Bill Skowron	20.00	10.00	6.00
591	N.L. Rookies (Grant Jackson, Bart Shirley)	12.00	6.00	3.50
592	Andre Rodgers	6.00	3.00	1.75
593	Doug Camilli	12.00	6.00	3.50
594	Chico Salmon	6.00	3.00	1.75
595	Larry Jackson	6.00	3.00	1.75
596	Astros Rookies (Nate Colbert, Greg Sims)	7.00	3.50	2.00
597	John Sullivan	8.00	3.00	1.75
598	Gaylord Perry	150.00	30.00	15.00

1966 Topps Rub-Offs

Returning to a concept last tried in 1961, Topps tried an expanded version of Rub-offs in 1966. Measuring 2-1/16'' by 3,'' the Rub-offs are in vertical format for the 100 players and horizontal for the 20 team pennants. The player Rub-offs feature a color photo.

		NR MT	EX	VG
Complete Set:		175.00	87.00	52.00
Common Player:		.60	.30	.20
(1)	Hank Aaron	8.00	4.00	2.50
(2)	Jerry Adair	.60	.30	.20
(3)	Richie Allen	1.00	.50	.30
(4)	Jesus Alou	.60	.30	.20
(5)	Max Alvis	.60	.30	.20
(6)	Bob Aspromonte	.60	.30	.20
(7)	Ernie Banks	3.50	1.75	1.00
(8)	Earl Battey	.70	.35	.20
(9)	Curt Blefary	.60	.30	.20
(10)	Ken Boyer	1.00	.50	.30
(11)	Bob Bruce	.60	.30	.20
(12)	Jim Bunning	1.50	.70	.45
(13)	Johnny Callison	.70	.35	.20
(14)	Bert Campaneris	.70	.35	.20
(15)	Jose Cardenal	.60	.30	.20
(16)	Dean Chance	.60	.30	.20

		NR MT	EX	VG
(17)	Ed Charles	.60	.30	.20
(18)	Bob Clemente	7.00	3.50	2.00
(19)	Tony Cloninger	.60	.30	.20
(20)	Rocky Colavito	1.00	.50	.30
(21)	Tony Conigliaro	1.00	.50	.30
(22)	Vic Davilillo	.60	.30	.20
(23)	Willie Davis	.70	.35	.20
(24)	Don Drysdale	3.00	1.50	.90
(25)	Sammy Ellis	.60	.30	.20
(26)	Dick Ellsworth	.60	.30	.20
(27)	Ron Fairly	.70	.35	.20
(28)	Dick Farrell	.60	.30	.20
(29)	Eddie Fisher	.60	.30	.20
(30)	Jack Fisher	.60	.30	.20
(31)	Curt Flood	.70	.35	.20
(32)	Whitey Ford	3.50	1.75	1.00
(33)	Bill Freehan	.70	.35	.20
(34)	Jim Fregosi	.70	.35	.20
(35)	Bob Gibson	3.00	1.50	.90
(36)	Jim Grant	.60	.30	.20
(37)	Jimmie Hall	.60	.30	.20
(38)	Ken Harrelson	.70	.35	.20
(39)	Jim Hart	.60	.30	.20
(40)	Joel Horlen	.60	.30	.20
(41)	Willie Horton	.70	.35	.20
(42)	Frank Howard	1.00	.50	.30
(43)	Deron Johnson	.60	.30	.20
(44)	Al Kaline	4.00	2.00	1.25
(45)	Harmon Killebrew	4.00	2.00	1.25
(46)	Bobby Knoop	.60	.30	.20
(47)	Sandy Koufax	7.00	3.50	2.00
(48)	Ed Kranepool	.60	.30	.20
(49)	Gary Kroll	.60	.30	.20
(50)	Don Landrum	.60	.30	.20
(51)	Vernon Law	.70	.35	.20
(52)	Johnny Lewis	.60	.30	.20
(53)	Don Lock	.60	.30	.20
(54)	Mickey Lolich	1.00	.50	.30
(55)	Jim Maloney	.60	.30	.20
(56)	Felix Mantilla	.60	.30	.20
(57)	Mickey Mantle	35.00	17.50	10.50
(58)	Juan Marichal	3.00	1.50	.90
(59)	Ed Mathews	3.00	1.50	.90
(60)	Willie Mays	8.00	4.00	2.50
(61)	Bill Mazeroski	1.00	.50	.30
(62)	Dick McAuliffe	.60	.30	.20
(63)	Tim McCarver	.70	.35	.20
(64)	Willie McCovey	3.00	1.50	.90
(65)	Sammy McDowell	.70	.35	.20
(66)	Ken McMullen	.60	.30	.20
(67)	Denis Menke	.60	.30	.20
(68)	Bill Monbouquette	.60	.30	.20
(69)	Joe Morgan	2.00	1.00	.60
(70)	Fred Newman	.60	.30	.20
(71)	John O'Donoghue	.60	.30	.20
(72)	Tony Oliva	1.00	.50	.30
(73)	Johnny Orsino	.60	.30	.20
(74)	Phil Ortega	.60	.30	.20
(75)	Milt Pappas	.70	.35	.20
(76)	Dick Radatz	.60	.30	.20
(77)	Bobby Richardson	1.50	.70	.45
(78)	Pete Richert	.60	.30	.20
(79)	Brooks Robinson	4.00	2.00	1.25
(80)	Floyd Robinson	.60	.30	.20
(81)	Frank Robinson	3.50	1.75	1.00
(82)	Cookie Rojas	.60	.30	.20
(83)	Pete Rose	20.00	10.00	6.00
(84)	John Roseboro	.60	.30	.20
(85)	Ron Santo	1.00	.50	.30
(86)	Bill Skowron	.70	.35	.20
(87)	Willie Stargell	3.00	1.50	.90
(88)	Mel Stottlemyre	.70	.35	.20
(89)	Dick Stuart	.60	.30	.20
(90)	Ron Swoboda	.60	.30	.20
(91)	Fred Talbot	.60	.30	.20
(92)	Ralph Terry	.60	.30	.20
(93)	Joe Torre	1.00	.50	.30
(94)	Tom Tresh	.70	.35	.20
(95)	Bob Veale	.60	.30	.20
(96)	Pete Ward	.60	.30	.20
(97)	Bill White	.70	.35	.20
(98)	Billy Williams	2.00	1.00	.60
(99)	Jim Wynn	.70	.35	.20
(100)	Carl Yastrzemski	12.00	6.00	3.50
(101)	Angels Pennant	.60	.30	.20
(102)	Astros Pennant	.60	.30	.20
(103)	Athletics Pennant	.60	.30	.20
(104)	Braves Pennant	.60	.30	.20
(105)	Cards Pennant	.60	.30	.20
(106)	Cubs Pennant	.60	.30	.20
(107)	Dodgers Pennant	.60	.30	.20

		NR MT	EX	VG
(108)	Giants Pennant	.60	.30	.20
(109)	Indians Pennant	.60	.30	.20
(110)	Mets Pennant	.60	.30	.20
(111)	Orioles Pennant	.60	.30	.20
(112)	Phillies Pennant	.60	.30	.20
(113)	Pirates Pennant	.60	.30	.20
(114)	Red Sox Pennant	.60	.30	.20
(115)	Reds Pennant	.60	.30	.20
(116)	Senators Pennant	.60	.30	.20
(117)	Tigers Pennant	.60	.30	.20
(118)	Twins Pennant	.60	.30	.20
(119)	White Sox Pennant	.60	.30	.20
(120)	Yankees Pennant	.60	.30	.20

1967 Topps

 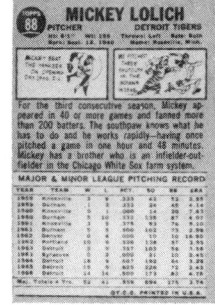

This 609-card set of 2½'' by 3½'' cards marked the largest set up to that time for Topps. Card fronts feature large color photographs bordered by white. The player's name and position are printed at the top with the team at the bottom. Across the front of the card with the exception of #254 (Milt Pappas) there is a facsimile autograph. Backs were the first to be done vertically, although they continued to carry familiar statistical and biographical information. The only sub-sets were statistical leaders and World Series highlights. Rookie cards were done by team or league with two players per card. The high numbers (#534-609) in '67 are quite scarce, and while it is known that some are even scarcer, by virtue of having been short-printed in relation to the rest of the series, there is no general agreement on which cards are involved.

		NR MT	EX	VG
Complete Set:		2400.00	825.00	450.00
Common Player: 1-110		.40	.20	.12
Common Player: 111-370		.50	.25	.15
Common Player: 371-457		.60	.30	.20
Common Player: 458-533		1.50	.70	.45
Common Player: 534-609		4.00	2.00	1.25
1	The Champs (Hank Bauer, Brooks Robinson, Frank Robinson)	8.00	2.50	1.50
2	Jack Hamilton	.60	.25	.15
3	Duke Sims	.40	.20	.12
4	Hal Lanier	.70	.35	.20
5	Whitey Ford	8.00	4.00	2.50
6	Dick Simpson	.40	.20	.12
7	Don McMahon	.40	.20	.12
8	Chuck Harrison	.40	.20	.12
9	Ron Hansen	.40	.20	.12
10	Matty Alou	.80	.40	.25
11	Barry Moore	.40	.20	.12
12	Dodgers Rookies (Jimmy Campanis, Bill Singer)	.50	.25	.15
13	Joe Sparma	.40	.20	.12
14	Phil Linz	.40	.20	.12
15	Earl Battey	.50	.25	.15
16	Bill Hands	.40	.20	.12
17	Jim Gosger	.40	.20	.12
18	Gene Oliver	.40	.20	.12
19	Jim McGlothlin	.40	.20	.12
20	Orlando Cepeda	4.00	2.00	1.25
21	Dave Bristol	.40	.20	.12

		NR MT	EX	VG
22	Gene Brabender	.40	.20	.12
23	Larry Elliot	.50	.25	.15
24	Bob Allen	.40	.20	.12
25	Elston Howard	3.00	1.50	.90
26a	Bob Priddy (no trade statement)	7.00	3.50	2.00
26b	Bob Priddy (with trade statement)	.40	.20	.12
27	Bob Saverine	.40	.20	.12
28	Barry Latman	.40	.20	.12
29	Tommy McCraw	.40	.20	.12
30	Al Kaline	7.00	3.50	2.00
31	Jim Brewer	.40	.20	.12
32	Bob Bailey	.40	.20	.12
33	Athletics Rookies (Sal Bando, Randy Schwartz).	1.75	.90	.50
34	Pete Cimino	.40	.20	.12
35	Rico Carty	1.00	.50	.30
36	Bob Tillman	.40	.20	.12
37	Rick Wise	.50	.25	.15
38	Bob Johnson	.40	.20	.12
39	Curt Simmons	.80	.40	.25
40	Rick Reichardt	.40	.20	.12
41	Joe Hoerner	.40	.20	.12
42	Mets Team	3.00	1.50	.90
43	Chico Salmon	.40	.20	.12
44	Joe Nuxhall	.80	.40	.25
45	Roger Maris	12.00	6.00	3.50
46	Lindy McDaniel	.40	.20	.12
47	Ken McMullen	.40	.20	.12
48	Bill Freehan	.80	.40	.25
49	Roy Face	1.25	.60	.40
50	Tony Oliva	2.50	1.25	.70
51	Astros Rookies (Dave Adlesh, Wes Bales)	.40	.20	.12
52	Dennis Higgins	.40	.20	.12
53	Clay Dalrymple	.40	.20	.12
54	Dick Green	.40	.20	.12
55	Don Drysdale	7.00	3.50	2.00
56	Jose Tartabull	.40	.20	.12
57	Pat Jarvis	.50	.25	.15
58	Paul Schaal	.40	.20	.12
59	Ralph Terry	.60	.30	.20
60	Luis Aparicio	5.00	2.50	1.50
61	Gordy Coleman	.40	.20	.12
62	Checklist 1-109 (Frank Robinson)	3.00	1.50	.90
63	Cards' Clubbers (Lou Brock, Curt Flood)	4.50	2.25	1.25
64	Fred Valentine	.40	.20	.12
65	Tom Haller	.50	.25	.15
66	Manny Mota	.80	.40	.25
67	Ken Berry	.40	.20	.12
68	Bob Buhl	.50	.25	.15
69	Vic Davalillo	.50	.25	.15
70	Ron Santo	1.75	.90	.50
71	Camilo Pascual	.70	.35	.20
72	Tigers Rookies (George Korince, John Matchick)	.40	.20	.12
73	Rusty Staub	2.50	1.25	.70
74	Wes Stock	.40	.20	.12
75	George Scott	1.00	.50	.30
76	Jim Barbieri	.40	.20	.12
77	Dooley Womack	.80	.40	.25
78	Pat Corrales	1.00	.50	.30
79	Bubba Morton	.40	.20	.12
80	Jim Maloney	.50	.25	.15
81	Eddie Stanky	.70	.35	.20
82	Steve Barber	.40	.20	.12
83	Ollie Brown	.40	.20	.12
84	Tommie Sisk	.40	.20	.12
85	Johnny Callison	1.00	.50	.30
86a	Mike McCormick (no trade statement)	8.00	4.00	2.50
86b	Mike McCormick (with trade statement)	.70	.35	.20
87	George Altman	.40	.20	.12
88	Mickey Lolich	2.25	1.25	.70
89	Felix Millan	.80	.40	.25
90	Jim Nash	.40	.20	.12
91	Johnny Lewis	.50	.25	.15
92	Ray Washburn	.40	.20	.12
93	Yankees Rookies (Stan Bahnsen, Bobby Murcer)	2.50	1.25	.70
94	Ron Fairly	.80	.40	.25
95	Sonny Siebert	.50	.25	.15
96	Art Shamsky	.40	.20	.12
97	Mike Cuellar	.80	.40	.25
98	Rich Rollins	.40	.20	.12
99	Lee Stange	.40	.20	.12
100	Frank Robinson	7.00	3.50	2.00
101	Ken Johnson	.40	.20	.12
102	Phillies Team	2.00	1.00	.60

		NR MT	EX	VG
103a	Checklist 110-196 (Mickey Mantle) (170 is D McAuliffe)	8.00	4.00	2.50
103b	Checklist 110-196 (Mickey Mantle) (170 is D. McAuliffe)	6.00	3.00	1.75
104	Minnie Rojas	.40	.20	.12
105	Ken Boyer	2.00	1.00	.60
106	Randy Hundley	.50	.25	.15
107	Joel Horlen	.40	.20	.12
108	Alex Johnson	.40	.20	.12
109	Tribe Thumpers (Rocky Colavito, Leon Wagner)	1.50	.70	.45
110	Jack Aker	.40	.20	.12
111	John Kennedy	.50	.25	.15
112	Dave Wickersham	.50	.25	.15
113	Dave Nicholson	.50	.25	.15
114	Jack Baldschun	.50	.25	.15
115	Paul Casanova	.50	.25	.15
116	Herman Franks	.50	.25	.15
117	Darrell Brandon	.50	.25	.15
118	Bernie Allen	.50	.25	.15
119	Wade Blasingame	.50	.25	.15
120	Floyd Robinson	.50	.25	.15
121	Ed Bressoud	.60	.30	.20
122	George Brunet	.50	.25	.15
123	Pirates Rookies (Jim Price, Luke Walker)	.50	.25	.15
124	Jim Stewart	.50	.25	.15
125	Moe Drabowsky	.50	.25	.15
126	Tony Taylor	.50	.25	.15
127	John O'Donoghue	.50	.25	.15
128	Ed Spiezio	.50	.25	.15
129	Phil Roof	.50	.25	.15
130	Phil Regan	.50	.25	.15
131	Yankees Team	4.00	2.00	1.25
132	Ozzie Virgil	.50	.25	.15
133	Ron Kline	.50	.25	.15
134	Gates Brown	.50	.25	.15
135	Deron Johnson	.50	.25	.15
136	Carroll Sembera	.50	.25	.15
137	Twins Rookies (Ron Clark, Jim Ollom)	.50	.25	.15
138	Dick Kelley	.50	.25	.15
139	Dalton Jones	.50	.25	.15
140	Willie Stargell	7.00	3.50	2.00
141	John Miller	.50	.25	.15
142	Jackie Brandt	.50	.25	.15
143	Sox Sockers (Don Buford, Pete Ward)	.80	.40	.25
144	Bill Hepler	.60	.30	.20
145	Larry Brown	.50	.25	.15
146	Steve Carlton	40.00	20.00	12.00
147	Tom Egan	.50	.25	.15
148	Adolfo Phillips	.50	.25	.15
149	Joe Moeller	.50	.25	.15
150	Mickey Mantle	150.00	70.00	40.00
151	World Series Game 1 (Moe Mows Down 11)	2.00	1.00	.60
152	World Series Game 2 (Palmer Blanks Dodgers)	3.50	1.75	1.00
153	World Series Game 3 (Blair's Homer Defeats L.A.)	2.00	1.00	.60
154	World Series Game 4 (Orioles Win 4th Straight)	2.00	1.00	.60
155	World Series Summary (The Winners Celebrate)	2.00	1.00	.60
156	Ron Herbel	.50	.25	.15
157	Danny Cater	.50	.25	.15
158	Jimmy Coker	.50	.25	.15
159	Bruce Howard	.50	.25	.15
160	Willie Davis	1.25	.60	.40
161	Dick Williams	1.25	.60	.40
162	Billy O'Dell	.50	.25	.15
163	Vic Roznovsky	.50	.25	.15
164	Dwight Siebler	.50	.25	.15
165	Cleon Jones	.80	.40	.25
166	Ed Mathews	7.00	3.50	2.00
167	Senators Rookies (Joe Coleman, Tim Cullen)	.60	.30	.20
168	Ray Culp	.50	.25	.15
169	Horace Clarke	1.00	.50	.30
170	Dick McAuliffe	.60	.30	.20
171	Calvin Koonce	.50	.25	.15
172	Bill Heath	.50	.25	.15
173	Cardinals Team	2.00	1.00	.60
174	Dick Radatz	.60	.30	.20
175	Bobby Knoop	.50	.25	.15
176	Sammy Ellis	.50	.25	.15
177	Tito Fuentes	.50	.25	.15
178	John Buzhardt	.50	.25	.15
179	Braves Rookies (Cecil Upshaw, Chas. Vaughn)	.50	.25	.15

		NR MT	EX	VG
180	Curt Blefary	.50	.25	.15
181	Terry Fox	.50	.25	.15
182	Ed Charles	.50	.25	.15
183	Jim Pagliaroni	.50	.25	.15
184	George Thomas	.50	.25	.15
185	Ken Holtzman	2.75	1.50	.80
186	Mets Maulers (Ed Kranepool, Ron Swoboda)	1.50	.70	.45
187	Pedro Ramos	.50	.25	.15
188	Ken Harrelson	1.50	.70	.45
189	Chuck Hinton	.50	.25	.15
190	Turk Farrell	.50	.25	.15
191a	Checklist 197-283 (Willie Mays) (214 is Dick Kelley)	5.00	2.50	1.50
191b	Checklist 197-283 (Willie Mays) (214 is Tom Kelley)	4.00	2.00	1.25
192	Fred Gladding	.50	.25	.15
193	Jose Cardenal	.60	.30	.20
194	Bob Allison	.80	.40	.25
195	Al Jackson	.50	.25	.15
196	Johnny Romano	.50	.25	.15
197	Ron Perranoski	.60	.30	.20
198	Chuck Hiller	.60	.30	.20
199	Billy Hitchcock	.50	.25	.15
200	Willie Mays	30.00	15.00	9.00
201	Hal Reniff	1.00	.50	.30
202	Johnny Edwards	.50	.25	.15
203	Al McBean	.50	.25	.15
204	Orioles Rookies (Mike Epstein, Tom Phoebus)	.80	.40	.25
205	Dick Groat	1.50	.70	.45
206	Dennis Bennett	.50	.25	.15
207	John Orsino	.50	.25	.15
208	Jack Lamabe	.50	.25	.15
209	Joe Nossek	.50	.25	.15
210	Bob Gibson	10.00	5.00	3.00
211	Twins Team	2.00	1.00	.60
212	Chris Zachary	.50	.25	.15
213	Jay Johnstone	1.75	.90	.50
214	Tom Kelley	.50	.25	.15
215	Ernie Banks	8.00	4.00	2.50
216	Bengal Belters (Norm Cash, Al Kaline)	3.50	1.75	1.00
217	Rob Gardner	.60	.30	.20
218	Wes Parker	.60	.30	.20
219	Clay Carroll	.60	.30	.20
220	Jim Hart	.60	.30	.20
221	Woody Fryman	.60	.30	.20
222	Reds Rookies (Lee May, Darrell Osteen)	1.00	.50	.30
223	Mike Ryan	.50	.25	.15
224	Walt Bond	.50	.25	.15
225	Mel Stottlemyre	2.25	1.25	.70
226	Julian Javier	.60	.30	.20
227	Paul Lindblad	.50	.25	.15
228	Gil Hodges	4.00	2.00	1.25
229	Larry Jackson	.50	.25	.15
230	Boog Powell	2.50	1.25	.70
231	John Bateman	.50	.25	.15
232	Don Buford	.60	.30	.20
233	A.L. ERA Leaders (Steve Hargan, Joel Horlen, Gary Peters)	2.00	1.00	.60
234	N.L. ERA Leaders (Mike Cuellar, Sandy Koufax, Juan Marichal)	4.00	2.00	1.25
235	A.L. Pitching Leaders (Jim Kaat, Denny McLain, Earl Wilson)	2.50	1.25	.70
236	N.L. Pitching Leaders (Bob Gibson, Sandy Koufax, Juan Marichal, Gaylord Perry)	5.00	2.50	1.50
237	A.L. Strikeout Leaders (Jim Kaat, Sam McDowell, Earl Wilson)	2.50	1.25	.70
238	N.L. Strikeout Leaders (Jim Bunning, Sandy Koufax, Bob Veale)	4.00	2.00	1.25
239	AL 1966 Batting Leaders (Al Kaline, Tony Oliva, Frank Robinson)	4.00	2.00	1.25
240	N.L. Batting Leaders (Felipe Alou, Matty Alou, Rico Carty)	2.00	1.00	.60
241	A.L. RBI Leaders (Harmon Killebrew, Boog Powell, Frank Robinson)	3.50	1.75	1.00
242	N.L. RBI Leaders (Hank Aaron, Richie Allen, Bob Clemente)	4.00	2.00	1.25
243	A.L. Home Run Leaders (Harmon Killebrew, Boog Powell, Frank Robinson)	3.50	1.75	1.00
244	N.L. Home Run Leaders (Hank Aaron, Richie Allen, Willie Mays)	4.00	2.00	1.25
245	Curt Flood	1.50	.70	.45
246	Jim Perry	1.00	.50	.30
247	Jerry Lumpe	.60	.30	.20
248	Gene Mauch	.80	.40	.25
249	Nick Willhite	.50	.25	.15
250	Hank Aaron	30.00	15.00	9.00
251	Woody Held	.50	.25	.15
252	Bob Bolin	.50	.25	.15
253	Indians Rookies (Bill Davis, Gus Gil)	.50	.25	.15
254	Milt Pappas	.80	.40	.25
255	Frank Howard	2.50	1.25	.70
256	Bob Hendley	.50	.25	.15
257	Charley Smith	1.00	.50	.30
258	Lee Maye	.50	.25	.15
259	Don Dennis	.50	.25	.15
260	Jim Lefebvre	.60	.30	.20
261	John Wyatt	.50	.25	.15
262	Athletics Team	2.00	1.00	.60
263	Hank Aguirre	.50	.25	.15
264	Ron Swoboda	.80	.40	.25
265	Lou Burdette	1.50	.70	.45
266	Pitt Power (Donn Clendenon, Willie Stargell)	3.50	1.75	1.00
267	Don Schwall	.50	.25	.15
268	John Briggs	.50	.25	.15
269	Don Nottebart	.50	.25	.15
270	Zoilo Versalles	.60	.30	.20
271	Eddie Watt	.50	.25	.15
272	Cubs Rookies (Bill Connors, Dave Dowling)	.50	.25	.15
273	Dick Lines	.50	.25	.15
274	Bob Aspromonte	.50	.25	.15
275	Fred Whitfield	.50	.25	.15
276	Bruce Brubaker	.50	.25	.15
277	Steve Whitaker	1.00	.50	.30
278	Checklist 284-370 (Jim Kaat)	3.00	1.50	.90
279	Frank Linzy	.50	.25	.15
280	Tony Conigliaro	2.00	1.00	.60
281	Bob Rodgers	.70	.35	.20
282	Johnny Odom	.60	.30	.20
283	Gene Alley	.60	.30	.20
284	Johnny Podres	1.50	.70	.45
285	Lou Brock	10.00	5.00	3.00
286	Wayne Causey	.50	.25	.15
287	Mets Rookies (Greg Goossen, Bart Shirley)	.60	.30	.20
288	Denver Lemaster	.50	.25	.15
289	Tom Tresh	1.75	.90	.50
290	Bill White	1.00	.50	.30
291	Jim Hannan	.50	.25	.15
292	Don Pavletich	.50	.25	.15
293	Ed Kirkpatrick	.50	.25	.15
294	Walt Alston	3.00	1.50	.90
295	Sam McDowell	1.00	.50	.30
296	Glenn Beckert	.80	.40	.25
297	Dave Morehead	.50	.25	.15
298	Ron Davis	.50	.25	.15
299	Norm Siebern	.60	.30	.20
300	Jim Kaat	4.00	2.00	1.25
301	Jesse Gonder	.50	.25	.15
302	Orioles Team	2.00	1.00	.60
303	Gil Blanco	.50	.25	.15
304	Phil Gagliano	.50	.25	.15
305	Earl Wilson	.50	.25	.15
306	Bud Harrelson	1.75	.90	.50
307	Jim Beauchamp	.50	.25	.15
308	Al Downing	1.25	.60	.40
309	Hurlers Beware (Richie Allen, Johnny Callison)	2.00	1.00	.60
310	Gary Peters	.60	.30	.20
311	Ed Brinkman	.60	.30	.20
312	Don Mincher	.60	.30	.20
313	Bob Lee	.50	.25	.15
314	Red Sox Rookies (Mike Andrews, Reggie Smith)	3.00	1.50	.90
315	Billy Williams	6.00	3.00	1.75
316	Jack Kralick	.50	.25	.15
317	Cesar Tovar	.50	.25	.15
318	Dave Giusti	.50	.25	.15
319	Paul Blair	.60	.30	.20
320	Gaylord Perry	7.00	3.50	2.00
321	Mayo Smith	.50	.25	.15
322	Jose Pagan	.50	.25	.15
323	Mike Hershberger	.50	.25	.15
324	Hal Woodeshick	.50	.25	.15
325	Chico Cardenas	.50	.25	.15
326	Bob Uecker	10.00	5.00	3.00
327	Angels Team	2.00	1.00	.60
328	Clete Boyer	.80	.40	.25
329	Charlie Lau	.80	.40	.25
330	Claude Osteen	.80	.40	.25
331	Joe Foy	.50	.25	.15
332	Jesus Alou	.50	.25	.15
333	Ferguson Jenkins	5.00	2.50	1.50
334	Twin Terrors (Bob Allison, Harmon Killebrew)	3.50	1.75	1.00

		NR MT	EX	VG
335	Bob Veale	.60	.30	.20
336	Joe Azcue	.50	.25	.15
337	Joe Morgan	5.00	2.50	1.50
338	Bob Locker	.50	.25	.15
339	Chico Ruiz	.50	.25	.15
340	Joe Pepitone	2.00	1.00	.60
341	Giants Rookies (Dick Dietz, Bill Sorrell)			
		.60	.30	.20
342	Hank Fischer	.50	.25	.15
343	Tom Satriano	.50	.25	.15
344	Ossie Chavarria	.50	.25	.15
345	Stu Miller	.50	.25	.15
346	Jim Hickman	.60	.30	.20
347	Grady Hatton	.50	.25	.15
348	Tug McGraw	2.25	1.25	.70
349	Bob Chance	.50	.25	.15
350	Joe Torre	2.00	1.00	.60
351	Vern Law	1.25	.60	.40
352	Ray Oyler	.50	.25	.15
353	Bill McCool	.50	.25	.15
354	Cubs Team	2.00	1.00	.60
355	Carl Yastrzemski	55.00	27.00	16.50
356	Larry Jaster	.50	.25	.15
357	Bill Skowron	1.50	.70	.45
358	Ruben Amaro	1.00	.50	.30
359	Dick Ellsworth	.50	.25	.15
360	Leon Wagner	.60	.30	.20
361	Checklist 371-457 (Bob Clemente)			
		4.50	2.25	1.25
362	Darold Knowles	.50	.25	.15
363	Dave Johnson	2.00	1.00	.60
364	Claude Raymond	.50	.25	.15
365	John Roseboro	.70	.35	.20
366	Andy Kosco	.50	.25	.15
367	Angels Rookies (Bill Kelso, Don Wallace)			
		.50	.25	.15
368	Jack Hiatt	.50	.25	.15
369	Jim Hunter	6.00	3.00	1.75
370	Tommy Davis	1.50	.70	.45
371	Jim Lonborg	1.50	.70	.45
372	Mike de la Hoz	.60	.30	.20
373	White Sox Rookies (Duane Josephson, Fred Klages)			
		.60	.30	.20
374	Mel Queen	.60	.30	.20
375	Jake Gibbs	1.00	.50	.30
376	Don Lock	.60	.30	.20
377	Luis Tiant	2.25	1.25	.70
378	Tigers Team	3.00	1.50	.90
379	Jerry May	.60	.30	.20
380	Dean Chance	.70	.35	.20
381	Dick Schofield	.60	.30	.20
382	Dave McNally	1.00	.50	.30
383	Ken Henderson	.60	.30	.20
384	Cardinals Rookies (Jim Cosman, Dick Hughes)			
		.60	.30	.20
385	Jim Fregosi	1.25	.60	.40
386	Dick Selma	.70	.35	.20
387	Cap Peterson	.60	.30	.20
388	Arnold Earley	.60	.30	.20
389	Al Dark	.80	.40	.25
390	Jim Wynn	1.00	.50	.30
391	Wilbur Wood	.80	.40	.25
392	Tommy Harper	.70	.35	.20
393	Jim Bouton	2.25	1.25	.70
394	Jake Wood	.60	.30	.20
395	Chris Short	1.00	.50	.30
396	Atlanta Aces (Tony Cloninger, Denis Menke)			
		1.00	.50	.30
397	Willie Smith	.60	.30	.20
398	Jeff Torborg	.70	.35	.20
399	Al Worthington	.60	.30	.20
400	Bob Clemente	25.00	12.50	7.50
401	Jim Coates	.60	.30	.20
402	Phillies Rookies (Grant Jackson, Billy Wilson)			
		.60	.30	.20
403	Dick Nen	.60	.30	.20
404	Nelson Briles	.70	.35	.20
405	Russ Snyder	.60	.30	.20
406	Lee Elia	.70	.35	.20
407	Reds Team	2.50	1.25	.70
408	Jim Northrup	.70	.35	.20
409	Ray Sadecki	.60	.30	.20
410	Lou Johnson	.60	.30	.20
411	Dick Howser	1.50	.70	.45
412	Astros Rookies (Norm Miller, Doug Rader)			
		.80	.40	.25
413	Jerry Grote	.80	.40	.25
414	Casey Cox	.60	.30	.20
415	Sonny Jackson	.60	.30	.20
416	Roger Repoz	.60	.30	.20
417	Bob Bruce	.60	.30	.20

		NR MT	EX	VG
418	Sam Mele	.60	.30	.20
419	Don Kessinger	.80	.40	.25
420	Denny McLain	3.00	1.50	.90
421	Dal Maxvill	.70	.35	.20
422	Hoyt Wilhelm	6.00	3.00	1.75
423	Fence Busters (Willie Mays, Willie McCovey)			
		8.00	4.00	2.50
424	Pedro Gonzalez	.60	.30	.20
425	Pete Mikkelsen	.60	.30	.20
426	Lou Clinton	1.00	.50	.30
427	Ruben Gomez	.60	.30	.20
428	Dodgers Rookies (Tom Hutton, Gene Michael)			
		1.00	.50	.30
429	Garry Roggenburk	.60	.30	.20
430	Pete Rose	65.00	32.00	19.50
431	Ted Uhlaender	.60	.30	.20
432	Jimmie Hall	.60	.30	.20
433	Al Luplow	.70	.35	.20
434	Eddie Fisher	.60	.30	.20
435	Mack Jones	.60	.30	.20
436	Pete Ward	.60	.30	.20
437	Senators Team	2.25	1.25	.70
438	Chuck Dobson	.60	.30	.20
439	Byron Browne	.60	.30	.20
440	Steve Hargan	.60	.30	.20
441	Jim Davenport	.60	.30	.20
442	Yankees Rookies (Bill Robinson, Joe Verbanic)			
		1.25	.60	.40
443	Tito Francona	.70	.35	.20
444	George Smith	.60	.30	.20
445	Don Sutton	10.00	5.00	3.00
446	Russ Nixon	.60	.30	.20
447	Bo Belinsky	1.00	.50	.30
448	Harry Walker	.70	.35	.20
449	Orlando Pena	.60	.30	.20
450	Richie Allen	3.00	1.50	.90
451	Fred Newman	.60	.30	.20
452	Ed Kranepool	.80	.40	.25
453	Aurelio Monteagudo	.60	.30	.20
454a	Checklist 458-533 (Juan Marichal) (left ear shows)			
		5.00	2.50	1.50
454b	Checklist 458-533 (Juan Marichal) (no left ear)			
		4.00	2.00	1.25
455	Tommie Agee	.70	.35	.20
456	Phil Niekro	5.00	2.50	1.50
457	Andy Etchebarren	.60	.30	.20
458	Lee Thomas	1.50	.70	.45
459	Senators Rookies (Dick Bosman, Pete Craig)			
		1.75	.90	.50
460	Harmon Killebrew	20.00	10.00	6.00
461	Bob Miller	1.50	.70	.45
462	Bob Barton	1.50	.70	.45
463	Tribe Hill Aces (Sam McDowell, Sonny Siebert)			
		2.50	1.25	.70
464	Dan Coombs	1.50	.70	.45
465	Willie Horton	2.00	1.00	.60
466	Bobby Wine	1.50	.70	.45
467	Jim O'Toole	1.50	.70	.45
468	Ralph Houk	3.00	1.50	.90
469	Len Gabrielson	1.50	.70	.45
470	Bob Shaw	1.50	.70	.45
471	Rene Lachemann	1.50	.70	.45
472	Pirates Rookies (John Gelnar, George Spriggs)			
		1.50	.70	.45
473	Jose Santiago	1.50	.70	.45
474	Bob Tolan	1.75	.90	.50
475	Jim Palmer	25.00	12.50	7.50
476	Tony Perez	30.00	15.00	9.00
477	Braves Team	3.25	1.75	1.00
478	Bob Humphreys	1.50	.70	.45
479	Gary Bell	1.50	.70	.45
480	Willie McCovey	10.00	5.00	3.00
481	Leo Durocher	3.00	1.50	.90
482	Bill Monbouquette	1.75	.90	.50
483	Jim Landis	1.50	.70	.45
484	Jerry Adair	1.50	.70	.45
485	Tim McCarver	3.00	1.50	.90
486	Twins Rookies (Rich Reese, Bill Whitby)			
		1.50	.70	.45
487	Tom Reynolds	1.50	.70	.45
488	Gerry Arrigo	1.50	.70	.45
489	Doug Clemens	1.50	.70	.45
490	Tony Cloninger	1.75	.90	.50
491	Sam Bowens	1.50	.70	.45
492	Pirates Team	3.25	1.75	1.00
493	Phil Ortega	1.50	.70	.45
494	Bill Rigney	1.50	.70	.45
495	Fritz Peterson	2.25	1.25	.70
496	Orlando McFarlane	1.50	.70	.45
497	Ron Campbell	1.50	.70	.45
498	Larry Dierker	1.75	.90	.50

		NR MT	EX	VG
499	Indians Rookies (George Culver, Jose Vidal)	1.50	.70	.45
500	Juan Marichal	8.00	4.00	2.50
501	Jerry Zimmerman	1.50	.70	.45
502	Derrell Griffith	1.50	.70	.45
503	Dodgers Team	4.00	2.00	1.25
504	Orlando Martinez	1.50	.70	.45
505	Tommy Helms	1.50	.70	.45
506	Smoky Burgess	2.50	1.25	.70
507	Orioles Rookies (Ed Barnowski, Larry Haney)	1.50	.70	.45
508	Dick Hall	1.50	.70	.45
509	Jim King	1.50	.70	.45
510	Bill Mazeroski	3.00	1.50	.90
511	Don Wert	1.50	.70	.45
512	Red Schoendienst	2.25	1.25	.70
513	Marcelino Lopez	1.50	.70	.45
514	John Werhas	1.50	.70	.45
515	Bert Campaneris	2.25	1.25	.70
516	Giants Team	3.25	1.75	1.00
517	Fred Talbot	2.00	1.00	.60
518	Denis Menke	1.50	.70	.45
519	Ted Davidson	1.50	.70	.45
520	Max Alvis	1.50	.70	.45
521	Bird Bombers (Curt Blefary, Boog Powell)	3.00	1.50	.90
522	John Stephenson	1.50	.70	.45
523	Jim Merritt	1.50	.70	.45
524	Felix Mantilla	1.50	.70	.45
525	Ron Hunt	1.75	.90	.50
526	Tigers Rookies (Pat Dobson, George Korince)	2.00	1.00	.60
527	Dennis Ribant	1.50	.70	.45
528	Rico Petrocelli	2.00	1.00	.60
529	Gary Wagner	1.50	.70	.45
530	Felipe Alou	2.50	1.25	.70
531	Checklist 534-609 (Brooks Robinson)	5.00	2.50	1.50
532	Jim Hicks	1.50	.70	.45
533	Jack Fisher	1.50	.70	.45
534	Hank Bauer	4.00	2.00	1.25
535	Donn Clendenon	2.50	1.25	.70
536	Cubs Rookies (Joe Niekro, Paul Popovich)	10.00	5.00	3.00
537	Chuck Estrada	4.00	2.00	1.25
538	J.C. Martin	4.00	2.00	1.25
539	Dick Egan	4.00	2.00	1.25
540	Norm Cash	15.00	7.50	4.50
541	Joe Gibbon	4.00	2.00	1.25
542	Athletics Rookies (Rick Monday, Tony Pierce)	5.00	2.50	1.50
543	Dan Schneider	4.00	2.00	1.25
544	Indians Team	7.00	3.50	2.00
545	Jim Grant	4.00	2.00	1.25
546	Woody Woodward	4.50	2.25	1.25
547	Red Sox Rookies (Russ Gibson, Bill Rohr)	4.00	2.00	1.25
548	Tony Gonzalez	4.00	2.00	1.25
549	Jack Sanford	6.00	3.00	1.75
550	Vada Pinson	5.00	2.50	1.50
551	Doug Camilli	4.00	2.00	1.25
552	Ted Savage	4.00	2.00	1.25
553	Yankees Rookies (Mike Hegan, Thad Tillotson)	10.00	5.00	3.00
554	Andre Rodgers	4.00	2.00	1.25
555	Don Cardwell	4.00	2.00	1.25
556	Al Weis	4.00	2.00	1.25
557	Al Ferrara	6.00	3.00	1.75
558	Orioles Rookies (Mark Belanger, Bill Dillman)	7.00	3.50	2.00
559	Dick Tracewski	4.00	2.00	1.25
560	Jim Bunning	25.00	12.50	7.50
561	Sandy Alomar	4.00	2.00	1.25
562	Steve Blass	4.50	2.25	1.25
563	Joe Adcock	10.00	5.00	3.00
564	Astros Rookies (Alonzo Harris, Aaron Pointer)	4.00	2.00	1.25
565	Lew Krausse	4.00	2.00	1.25
566	Gary Geiger	4.00	2.00	1.25
567	Steve Hamilton	5.00	2.50	1.50
568	John Sullivan	4.00	2.00	1.25
569	A.L. Rookies (Hank Allen, Rod Carew)	125.00	62.00	37.00
570	Maury Wills	65.00	32.00	19.50
571	Larry Sherry	6.00	3.00	1.75
572	Don Demeter	6.00	3.00	1.75
573	White Sox Team	8.00	4.00	2.50
574	Jerry Buchek	6.00	3.00	1.75
575	Dave Boswell	6.00	3.00	1.75
576	N.L. Rookies (Norm Gigon, Ramon Hernandez)	6.00	3.00	1.75

		NR MT	EX	VG
577	Bill Short	4.00	2.00	1.25
578	John Boccabella	4.00	2.00	1.25
579	Bill Henry	4.00	2.00	1.25
580	Rocky Colavito	15.00	7.50	4.50
581	Mets Rookies (Bill Denehy, Tom Seaver)	400.00	200.00	120.00
582	Jim Owens	4.00	2.00	1.25
583	Ray Barker	5.00	2.50	1.50
584	Jim Piersall	10.00	5.00	3.00
585	Wally Bunker	4.00	2.00	1.25
586	Manny Jimenez	4.00	2.00	1.25
587	N.L. Rookies (Don Shaw, Gary Sutherland)	10.00	5.00	3.00
588	Johnny Klippstein	4.00	2.00	1.25
589	Dave Ricketts	4.00	2.00	1.25
590	Pete Richert	4.00	2.00	1.25
591	Ty Cline	4.00	2.00	1.25
592	N.L. Rookies (Jim Shellenback, Ron Willis)	6.00	3.00	1.75
593	Wes Westrum	4.50	2.25	1.25
594	Dan Osinski	4.00	2.00	1.25
595	Cookie Rojas	4.00	2.00	1.25
596	Galen Cisco	4.00	2.00	1.25
597	Ted Abernathy	4.00	2.00	1.25
598	White Sox Rookies (Ed Stroud, Walt Williams)	6.00	3.00	1.75
599	Bob Duliba	4.00	2.00	1.25
600	Brooks Robinson	125.00	62.00	37.00
601	Bill Bryan	5.00	2.50	1.50
602	Juan Pizarro	4.00	2.00	1.25
603	Athletics Rookies (Tim Talton, Ramon Webster)	4.00	2.00	1.25
604	Red Sox Team	25.00	12.50	7.50
605	Mike Shannon	5.00	2.50	1.50
606	Ron Taylor	4.00	2.00	1.25
607	Mickey Stanley	5.00	2.50	1.50
608	Cubs Rookies (Rich Nye, John Upham)	5.00	2.00	1.25
609	Tommy John	45.00	12.50	7.50

1967 Topps Pin-Ups

The 5'' by 7'' ''All Star Pin-ups'' were inserts to regular 1967 Topps baseball cards. They featured a full color picture with the player's name, position and team in a circle on the lower left side of the front. Numbered, the set consists of 32 players (generally big names). Even so, they are rather inexpensive. Because the large paper pin-ups had to be folded several times to fit into the wax packs, they are almost never found in true ''Mint'' condition.

		NR MT	EX	VG
Complete Set:		20.00	10.00	6.00
Common Player:		.20	.10	.06
1	Boog Powell	.40	.20	.12
2	Bert Campaneris	.30	.15	.09
3	Brooks Robinson	2.00	1.00	.60
4	Tommie Agee	.20	.10	.06
5	Carl Yastrzemski	3.50	1.75	1.00
6	Mickey Mantle	10.00	5.00	3.00
7	Frank Howard	.50	.25	.15
8	Sam McDowell	.25	.13	.08

		NR MT	EX	VG
9	Orlando Cepeda	.60	.30	.20
10	Chico Cardenas	.20	.10	.06
11	Bob Clemente	3.00	1.50	.90
12	Willie Mays	3.00	1.50	.90
13	Cleon Jones	.20	.10	.06
14	John Callison	.25	.13	.08
15	Hank Aaron	3.00	1.50	.90
16	Don Drysdale	2.00	1.00	.60
17	Bobby Knoop	.20	.10	.06
18	Tony Oliva	.50	.25	.15
19	Frank Robinson	2.00	1.00	.60
20	Denny McLain	.50	.25	.15
21	Al Kaline	2.00	1.00	.60
22	Joe Pepitone	.40	.20	.12
23	Harmon Killebrew	2.00	1.00	.60
24	Leon Wagner	.20	.10	.06
25	Joe Morgan	1.00	.50	.30
26	Ron Santo	.40	.20	.12
27	Joe Torre	.60	.30	.20
28	Juan Marichal	1.50	.70	.45
29	Matty Alou	.25	.13	.08
30	Felipe Alou	.25	.13	.08
31	Ron Hunt	.20	.10	.06
32	Willie McCovey	2.00	1.00	.60

		NR MT	EX	VG
19	Willie Mays	500.00	250.00	150.00
20	Hank Aaron	500.00	250.00	150.00
21	Carl Yastrzemski	600.00	300.00	180.00
22	Ron Santo	75.00	37.00	22.00
23	Jim Hunter	125.00	62.00	37.00
24	Jim Wynn	50.00	25.00	15.00

1967 Topps Giant Stand-Ups

WILLIE MAYS

Never actually issued, no more than a handful of each of these rare test issues has made their way into the hobby market. Designed so that the color photo of the player's head could be popped out of the black background, and the top folded over to create a stand-up display, examples of these 3⅛" by 5¼" cards can be found either die-cut around the portrait or without the cutting. Blank-backed, there are 24 cards in the set, numbered on the front at bottom left. The cards are popular with advanced superstar collectors.

		NR MT	EX	VG
Complete Set:		5000.00	2500.00	1500.
Common Player:		50.00	25.00	15.00
1	Pete Rose	750.00	375.00	225.00
2	Gary Peters	50.00	25.00	15.00
3	Frank Robinson	150.00	75.00	45.00
4	Jim Lonborg	50.00	25.00	15.00
5	Ron Swoboda	50.00	25.00	15.00
6	Harmon Killebrew	150.00	75.00	45.00
7	Bob Clemente	500.00	250.00	150.00
8	Mickey Mantle	1500.00	750.00	450.00
9	Jim Fregosi	75.00	37.00	22.00
10	Al Kaline	175.00	87.00	52.00
11	Don Drysdale	150.00	75.00	45.00
12	Dean Chance	50.00	25.00	15.00
13	Orlando Cepeda	75.00	37.00	22.00
14	Tim McCarver	75.00	37.00	22.00
15	Frank Howard	75.00	37.00	22.00
16	Max Alvis	50.00	25.00	15.00
17	Rusty Staub	75.00	37.00	22.00
18	Richie Allen	75.00	37.00	22.00

1967 Topps Stickers Pirates

JUAN PIZARRO

Considered a "test" issue, this 33-sticker set of 2½" by 3½" stickers is very similar to the Red Sox stickers which were produced the same year. Player stickers have a color picture (often just the player's head) and the player's name in large "comic book" letters. Besides the players, there are other topics such as "I Love the Pirates," "Bob Clemente for Mayor," and a number of similar sentiments. The stickers have blank backs and are rather scarce.

		NR MT	EX	VG
Complete Set:		175.00	87.00	52.00
Common Player:		3.00	1.50	.90
1	Gene Alley	5.00	2.50	1.50
2	Matty Alou	7.00	3.50	2.00
3	Dennis Ribant	3.00	1.50	.90
4	Steve Blass	5.00	2.50	1.50
5	Juan Pizarro	3.00	1.50	.90
6	Bob Clemente	60.00	30.00	18.00
7	Donn Clendenon	5.00	2.50	1.50
8	Roy Face	7.00	3.50	2.00
9	Woody Fryman	3.00	1.50	.90
10	Jesse Gonder	3.00	1.50	.90
11	Vern Law	7.00	3.50	2.00
12	Al McBean	3.00	1.50	.90
13	Jerry May	3.00	1.50	.90
14	Bill Mazeroski	9.00	4.50	2.75
15	Pete Mikkelsen	3.00	1.50	.90
16	Manny Mota	5.00	2.50	1.50
17	Billy O'Dell	3.00	1.50	.90
18	Jose Pagan	3.00	1.50	.90
19	Jim Pagliaroni	3.00	1.50	.90
20	Johnny Pesky	3.00	1.50	.90
21	Tommie Sisk	3.00	1.50	.90
22	Willie Stargell	30.00	15.00	9.00
23	Bob Veale	5.00	2.50	1.50
24	Harry Walker	3.00	1.50	.90
25	I Love The Pirates	3.00	1.50	.90
26	Let's Go Pirates	3.00	1.50	.90
27	Bob Clemente For Mayor	30.00	15.00	9.00
28	National League Batting Champion (Matty Alou)	4.00	2.00	1.25
29	Happiness Is A Pirate Win	3.00	1.50	.90
30	Donn Clendenon Is My Hero	4.00	2.00	1.25
31	Pirates' Home Run Champion (Willie Stargell)	15.00	7.50	4.50
32	Pirates Logo	3.00	1.50	.90
33	Pirates Pennant	3.00	1.50	.90

1967 Topps Stickers Red Sox

Like the 1967 Pirates Stickers, the Red Sox Stickers were part of the same test procedure. The Red Sox Stickers have the same 2½" by 3½" dimensions,

color picture and large player's name on the front. A complete set is 33 stickers. The majority are players, but themes such as "Let's Go Red Sox" are also included.

		NR MT	EX	VG
Complete Set:		160.00	80.00	48.00
Co:nmon Player:		3.00	1.50	.90
1	Dennis Bennett	3.00	1.50	.90
2	Darrell Brandon	3.00	1.50	.90
3	Tony Conigliaro	7.00	3.50	2.00
4	Don Demeter	3.00	1.50	.90
5	Hank Fischer	3.00	1.50	.90
6	Joe Foy	3.00	1.50	.90
7	Mike Andrews	3.00	1.50	.90
8	Dalton Jones	3.00	1.50	.90
9	Jim Lonborg	7.00	3.50	2.00
10	Don McMahon	3.00	1.50	.90
11	Dave Morehead	3.00	1.50	.90
12	George Smith	3.00	1.50	.90
13	Rico Petrocelli	5.00	2.50	1.50
14	Mike Ryan	3.00	1.50	.90
15	Jose Santiago	3.00	1.50	.90
16	George Scott	5.00	2.50	1.50
17	Sal Maglie	5.00	2.50	1.50
18	Reggie Smith	7.00	3.50	2.00
19	Lee Stange	3.00	1.50	.90
20	Jerry Stephenson	3.00	1.50	.90
21	Jose Tartabull	3.00	1.50	.90
22	George Thomas	3.00	1.50	.90
23	Bob Tillman	3.00	1.50	.90
24	Johnnie Wyatt	3.00	1.50	.90
25	Carl Yastrzemski	75.00	37.00	22.00
26	Dick Williams	5.00	2.50	1.50
27	I Love The Red Sox	3.00	1.50	.90
28	Let's Go Red Sox	3.00	1.50	.90
29	Carl Yastrzemski For Mayor	35.00	17.50	10.50
30	Tony Conigliaro Is My Hero	5.00	2.50	1.50
31	Happiness Is A Boston Win	3.00	1.50	.90
32	Red Sox Logo	3.00	1.50	.90
33	Red Sox Pennant	3.00	1.50	.90

1968 Topps

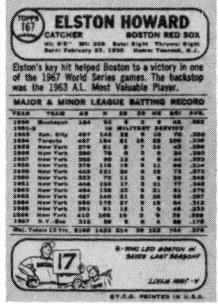

In 1968, Topps returned to a 598-card set of 2½'' by 3½'' cards. It is not, however, more of the same by way of appearance as the cards featured a color

photograph on a background of what appears to be a burlap fabric. The player's name is below the photo, but on the unusual background. A colored circle on the lower right carries the team and position. Backs were also changed. While retaining the vertical format introduced the previous year, with stats in the middle and cartoon at the bottom. The set featured many of the old favorite subsets including statistical leaders, World Series highlights, multi-player cards, checklists, rookie cards and the return of All-Star cards.

		NR MT	EX	VG
Complete Set:		1300.00	450.00	250.00
Common Player: 1-456		.40	.20	.12
Common Player: 457-598		.80	.40	.25
1	N.L. Batting Leaders (Matty Alou, Bob Clemente, Tony Gonzalez)	5.00	2.00	1.00
2	A.L. Batting Leaders (Al Kaline, Frank Robinson, Carl Yastrzemski)	4.00	2.00	1.25
3	N.L. RBI Leaders (Hank Aaron, Orlando Cepeda, Bob Clemente)	4.00	2.00	1.25
4	A.L. RBI Leaders (Harmon Killebrew, Frank Robinson, Carl Yastrzemski)	4.00	2.00	1.25
5	N.L. Home Run Leaders (Hank Aaron, Willie McCovey, Ron Santo, Jim Wynn)	4.00	2.00	1.25
6	A.L. Home Run Leaders (Frank Howard, Harmon Killebrew, Carl Yastrzemski)	4.00	2.00	1.25
7	N.L. ERA Leaders (Jim Bunning, Phil Niekro, Chris Short)	2.50	1.25	.70
8	A.L. ERA Leaders (Joe Horlen, Gary Peters, Sonny Siebert)	1.50	.70	.45
9	N.L. Pitching Leaders (Jim Bunning, Ferguson Jenkins, Mike McCormick, Claude Osteen)	2.50	1.25	.70
10a	A.L. Pitching Leaders (Dean Chance, Jim Lonborg, Earl Wilson) ("Lonborg" on back)	3.50	1.75	1.00
10b	A.L. Pitching Leaders (Dean Chance, Jim Lonborg, Earl Wilson) ("Lonborg" on back)	1.50	.70	.45
11	N.L. Strikeout Leaders (Jim Bunning, Ferguson Jenkins, Gaylord Perry)	3.00	1.50	.90
12	A.L. Strikeout Leaders (Dean Chance, Jim Lonborg, Sam McDowell)	1.50	.70	.45
13	Chuck Hartenstein	.40	.20	.12
14	Jerry McNertney	.40	.20	.12
15	Ron Hunt	.50	.25	.15
16	Indians Rookies (Lou Piniella, Richie Scheinblum)	2.50	1.25	.70
17	Dick Hall	.40	.20	.12
18	Mike Hershberger	.40	.20	.12
19	Juan Pizarro	.40	.20	.12
20	Brooks Robinson	10.00	5.00	3.00
21	Ron Davis	.40	.20	.12
22	Pat Dobson	.50	.25	.15
23	Chico Cardenas	.40	.20	.12
24	Bobby Locke	.40	.20	.12
25	Julian Javier	.50	.25	.15
26	Darrell Brandon	.40	.20	.12
27	Gil Hodges	4.00	2.00	1.25
28	Ted Uhlaender	.40	.20	.12
29	Joe Verbanic	.80	.40	.25
30	Joe Torre	2.00	1.00	.60
31	Ed Stroud	.40	.20	.12
32	Joe Gibbon	.40	.20	.12
33	Pete Ward	.40	.20	.12
34	Al Ferrara	.40	.20	.12
35	Steve Hargan	.40	.20	.12
36	Pirates Rookies (Bob Moose, Bob Robertson)	.70	.35	.20
37	Billy Williams	5.00	2.50	1.50
38	Tony Pierce	.40	.20	.12
39	Cookie Rojas	.40	.20	.12
40	Denny McLain	3.50	1.75	1.00
41	Julio Gotay	.40	.20	.12
42	Larry Haney	.40	.20	.12
43	Gary Bell	.40	.20	.12
44	Frank Kostro	.40	.20	.12
45	Tom Seaver	45.00	22.00	13.50
46	Dave Ricketts	.40	.20	.12
47	Ralph Houk	1.75	.90	.50
48	Ted Davidson	.40	.20	.12
49a	Ed Brinkman (yellow team letters)	20.00	10.00	6.00
49b	Ed Brinkman (white team letters)	.50	.25	.15
50	Willie Mays	25.00	12.50	7.50
51	Bob Locker	.40	.20	.12

		NR MT	EX	VG
52	Hawk Taylor	.40	.20	.12
53	Gene Alley	.50	.25	.15
54	Stan Williams	.40	.20	.12
55	Felipe Alou	1.00	.50	.30
56	Orioles Rookies (Dave Leonhard, Dave May)	.40	.20	.12
57	Dan Schneider	.40	.20	.12
58	Ed Mathews	6.00	3.00	1.75
59	Don Lock	.40	.20	.12
60	Ken Holtzman	1.00	.50	.30
61	Reggie Smith	1.50	.70	.45
62	Chuck Dobson	.40	.20	.12
63	Dick Kenworthy	.50	.25	.15
64	Jim Merritt	.40	.20	.12
65	John Roseboro	.70	.35	.20
66a	Casey Cox (yellow team letters)	20.00	10.00	6.00
66b	Casey Cox (white team letters)	.40	.20	.12
67	Checklist 1-109 (Jim Kaat)	3.00	1.50	.90
68	Ron Willis	.40	.20	.12
69	Tom Tresh	1.75	.90	.50
70	Bob Veale	.50	.25	.15
71	Vern Fuller	.40	.20	.12
72	Tommy John	3.50	1.75	1.00
73	Jim Hart	.50	.25	.15
74	Milt Pappas	.70	.35	.20
75	Don Mincher	.50	.25	.15
76	Braves Rookies (Jim Britton, Ron Reed)	1.00	.50	.30
77	Don Wilson	.70	.35	.20
78	Jim Northrup	.50	.25	.15
79	Ted Kubiak	.40	.20	.12
80	Rod Carew	30.00	15.00	9.00
81	Larry Jackson	.40	.20	.12
82	Sam Bowens	.40	.20	.12
83	John Stephenson	.40	.20	.12
84	Bob Tolan	.50	.25	.15
85	Gaylord Perry	5.00	2.50	1.50
86	Willie Stargell	6.00	3.00	1.75
87	Dick Williams	1.00	.50	.30
88	Phil Regan	.40	.20	.12
89	Jake Gibbs	.80	.40	.25
90	Vada Pinson	2.00	1.00	.60
91	Jim Ollom	.40	.20	.12
92	Ed Kranepool	.80	.40	.25
93	Tony Cloninger	.50	.25	.15
94	Lee Maye	.40	.20	.12
95	Bob Aspromonte	.40	.20	.12
96	Senators Rookies (Frank Coggins, Dick Nold)	.40	.20	.12
97	Tom Phoebus	.40	.20	.12
98	Gary Sutherland	.40	.20	.12
99	Rocky Colavito	2.25	1.25	.70
100	Bob Gibson	8.00	4.00	2.50
101	Glenn Beckert	.70	.35	.20
102	Jose Cardenal	.50	.25	.15
103	Don Sutton	4.00	2.00	1.25
104	Dick Dietz	.40	.20	.12
105	Al Downing	1.25	.60	.40
106	Dalton Jones	.40	.20	.12
107	Checklist 110-196 (Juan Marichal)	3.50	1.75	1.00
108	Don Pavletich	.40	.20	.12
109	Bert Campaneris	1.00	.50	.30
110	Hank Aaron	25.00	12.50	7.50
111	Rich Reese	.40	.20	.12
112	Woody Fryman	.50	.25	.15
113	Tigers Rookies (Tom Matchick, Daryl Patterson)	.40	.20	.12
114	Ron Swoboda	.70	.35	.20
115	Sam McDowell	.70	.35	.20
116	Ken McMullen	.40	.20	.12
117	Larry Jaster	.40	.20	.12
118	Mark Belanger	1.00	.50	.30
119	Ted Savage	.40	.20	.12
120	Mel Stottlemyre	2.00	1.00	.60
121	Jimmie Hall	.40	.20	.12
122	Gene Mauch	.80	.40	.25
123	Jose Santiago	.40	.20	.12
124	Nate Oliver	.40	.20	.12
125	Joe Horlen	.40	.20	.12
126	Bobby Etheridge	.40	.20	.12
127	Paul Lindblad	.40	.20	.12
128	Astros Rookies (Tom Dukes, Alonzo Harris)	.40	.20	.12
129	Mickey Stanley	.50	.25	.15
130	Tony Perez	4.00	2.00	1.25
131	Frank Bertaina	.40	.20	.12
132	Bud Harrelson	1.00	.50	.30
133	Fred Whitfield	.40	.20	.12
134	Pat Jarvis	.40	.20	.12
135	Paul Blair	.50	.25	.15

		NR MT	EX	VG
136	Randy Hundley	.40	.20	.12
137	Twins Team	2.00	1.00	.60
138	Ruben Amaro	.80	.40	.25
139	Chris Short	.70	.35	.20
140	Tony Conigliaro	1.50	.70	.45
141	Dal Maxvill	.50	.25	.15
142	White Sox Rookies (Buddy Bradford, Bill Voss)	.40	.20	.12
143	Pete Cimino	.40	.20	.12
144	Joe Morgan	4.00	2.00	1.25
145	Don Drysdale	7.00	3.50	2.00
146	Sal Bando	1.00	.50	.30
147	Frank Linzy	.40	.20	.12
148	Dave Bristol	.40	.20	.12
149	Bob Saverine	.40	.20	.12
150	Bob Clemente	18.00	9.00	5.50
151	World Series Game 1 (Brock Socks 4-Hits In Opener)	3.50	1.75	1.00
152	World Series Game 2 (Yaz Smashes Two Homers)	5.00	2.50	1.50
153	World Series Game 3 (Briles Cools Off Boston)	2.00	1.00	.60
154	World Series Game 4 (Gibson Hurls Shutout!)	3.50	1.75	1.00
155	World Series Game 5 (Lonborg Wins Again!)	2.50	1.25	.70
156	World Series Game 6 (Petrocelli Socks Two Homers)	2.50	1.25	.70
157	World Series Game 7 (St. Louis Wins It!)	2.00	1.00	.60
158	World Series Summary (The Cardinals Celebrate!)	2.00	1.00	.60
159	Don Kessinger	.70	.35	.20
160	Earl Wilson	.50	.25	.15
161	Norm Miller	.40	.20	.12
162	Cardinals Rookies (Hal Gilson, Mike Torrez)	1.00	.50	.30
163	Gene Brabender	.40	.20	.12
164	Ramon Webster	.40	.20	.12
165	Tony Oliva	2.50	1.25	.70
166	Claude Raymond	.40	.20	.12
167	Elston Howard	2.50	1.25	.70
168	Dodgers Team	2.50	1.25	.70
169	Bob Bolin	.40	.20	.12
170	Jim Fregosi	1.00	.50	.30
171	Don Nottebart	.40	.20	.12
172	Walt Williams	.40	.20	.12
173	John Boozer	.40	.20	.12
174	Bob Tillman	.40	.20	.12
175	Maury Wills	3.50	1.75	1.00
176	Bob Allen	.40	.20	.12
177	Mets Rookies (Jerry Koosman, Nolan Ryan)	125.00	62.00	37.00
178	Don Wert	.50	.25	.15
179	Bill Stoneman	.40	.20	.12
180	Curt Flood	1.50	.70	.45
181	Jerry Zimmerman	.40	.20	.12
182	Dave Giusti	.40	.20	.12
183	Bob Kennedy	.40	.20	.12
184	Lou Johnson	.40	.20	.12
185	Tom Haller	.50	.25	.15
186	Eddie Watt	.40	.20	.12
187	Sonny Jackson	.40	.20	.12
188	Cap Peterson	.40	.20	.12
189	Bill Landis	.40	.20	.12
190	Bill White	1.00	.50	.30
191	Dan Frisella	.50	.25	.15
192a	Checklist 197-283 (Carl Yastrzemski) ("To increase the..." on back)	4.50	2.25	1.25
192b	Checklist 197-283 (Carl Yastrzemski) ("To increase your..." on back)	6.00	3.00	1.75
193	Jack Hamilton	.40	.20	.12
194	Don Buford	.50	.25	.15
195	Joe Pepitone	2.00	1.00	.60
196	Gary Nolan	.40	.20	.12
197	Larry Brown	.40	.20	.12
198	Roy Face	1.25	.60	.40
199	A's Rookies (Darrell Osteen, Roberto Rodriguez)	.40	.20	.12
200	Orlando Cepeda	3.50	1.75	1.00
201	Mike Marshall	1.75	.90	.50
202	Adolfo Phillips	.40	.20	.12
203	Dick Kelley	.40	.20	.12
204	Andy Etchebarren	.40	.20	.12
205	Juan Marichal	6.00	3.00	1.75
206	Cal Ermer	.40	.20	.12
207	Carroll Sembera	.40	.20	.12
208	Willie Davis	1.00	.50	.30
209	Tim Cullen	.40	.20	.12
210	Gary Peters	.50	.25	.15
211	J.C. Martin	.50	.25	.15

		NR MT	EX	VG
212	Dave Morehead	.40	.20	.12
213	Chico Ruiz	.40	.20	.12
214	Yankees Rookies (Stan Bahnsen, Frank Fernandez)	1.00	.50	.30
215	Jim Bunning	3.50	1.75	1.00
216	Bubba Morton	.40	.20	.12
217	Turk Farrell	.40	.20	.12
218	Ken Suarez	.40	.20	.12
219	Rob Gardner	.40	.20	.12
220	Harmon Killebrew	7.00	3.50	2.00
221	Braves Team	2.00	1.00	.60
222	Jim Hardin	.40	.20	.12
223	Ollie Brown	.40	.20	.12
224	Jack Aker	.40	.20	.12
225	Richie Allen	2.25	1.25	.70
226	Jimmie Price	.40	.20	.12
227	Joe Hoerner	.40	.20	.12
228	Dodgers Rookies (Jack Billingham, Jim Fairey)	.60	.30	.20
229	Fred Klages	.40	.20	.12
230	Pete Rose	45.00	22.00	13.50
231	Dave Baldwin	.40	.20	.12
232	Denis Menke	.40	.20	.12
233	George Scott	.80	.40	.25
234	Bill Monbouquette	.80	.40	.25
235	Ron Santo	1.50	.70	.45
236	Tug McGraw	1.75	.90	.50
237	Alvin Dark	.70	.35	.20
238	Tom Satriano	.40	.20	.12
239	Bill Henry	.40	.20	.12
240	Al Kaline	10.00	5.00	3.00
241	Felix Millan	.50	.25	.15
242	Moe Drabowsky	.40	.20	.12
243	Rich Rollins	.40	.20	.12
244	John Donaldson	.40	.20	.12
245	Tony Gonzalez	.40	.20	.12
246	Fritz Peterson	1.00	.50	.30
247	Red Rookies (Johnny Bench, Ron Tompkins)	125.00	62.00	37.00
248	Fred Valentine	.40	.20	.12
249	Bill Singer	.60	.30	.20
250	Carl Yastrzemski	25.00	12.50	7.50
251	Manny Sanguillen	1.25	.60	.40
252	Angels Team	2.00	1.00	.60
253	Dick Hughes	.40	.20	.12
254	Cleon Jones	.80	.40	.25
255	Dean Chance	.50	.25	.15
256	Norm Cash	2.00	1.00	.60
257	Phil Niekro	4.00	2.00	1.25
258	Cubs Rookies (Jose Arcia, Bill Schlesinger)	.40	.20	.12
259	Ken Boyer	1.75	.90	.50
260	Jim Wynn	.80	.40	.25
261	Dave Duncan	.40	.20	.12
262	Rick Wise	.50	.25	.15
263	Horace Clarke	.80	.40	.25
264	Ted Abernathy	.40	.20	.12
265	Tommy Davis	1.50	.70	.45
266	Paul Popovich	.40	.20	.12
267	Herman Franks	.40	.20	.12
268	Bob Humphreys	.40	.20	.12
269	Bob Tiefenauer	.40	.20	.12
270	Matty Alou	1.00	.50	.30
271	Bobby Knoop	.40	.20	.12
272	Ray Culp	.40	.20	.12
273	Dave Johnson	1.75	.90	.50
274	Mike Cuellar	.80	.40	.25
275	Tim McCarver	1.75	.90	.50
276	Jim Roland	.40	.20	.12
277	Jerry Buchek	.50	.25	.15
278a	Checklist 284-370 (Orlando Cepeda) (copyright at right)	3.00	1.50	.90
278b	Checklist 284-370 (Orlando Cepeda) (copyright at left)	5.00	2.50	1.50
279	Bill Hands	.40	.20	.12
280	Mickey Mantle	125.00	55.00	30.00
281	Jim Campanis	.40	.20	.12
282	Rick Monday	1.25	.60	.40
283	Mel Queen	.40	.20	.12
284	John Briggs	.40	.20	.12
285	Dick McAuliffe	.60	.30	.20
286	Cecil Upshaw	.40	.20	.12
287	White Sox Rookies (Mickey Abarbanel, Cisco Carlos)	.40	.20	.12
288	Dave Wickersham	.40	.20	.12
289	Woody Held	.40	.20	.12
290	Willie McCovey	7.00	3.50	2.00
291	Dick Lines	.40	.20	.12
292	Art Shamsky	.60	.30	.20
293	Bruce Howard	.40	.20	.12
294	Red Schoendienst	1.25	.60	.40

		NR MT	EX	VG
295	Sonny Siebert	.40	.20	.12
296	Byron Browne	.40	.20	.12
297	Russ Gibson	.40	.20	.12
298	Jim Brewer	.40	.20	.12
299	Gene Michael	1.00	.50	.30
300	Rusty Staub	2.00	1.00	.60
301	Twins Rookies (George Mitterwald, Rick Renick)	.40	.20	.12
302	Gerry Arrigo	.40	.20	.12
303	Dick Green	.40	.20	.12
304	Sandy Valdespino	.40	.20	.12
305	Minnie Rojas	.40	.20	.12
306	Mike Ryan	.40	.20	.12
307	John Hiller	.70	.35	.20
308	Pirates Team	2.00	1.00	.60
309	Ken Henderson	.40	.20	.12
310	Luis Aparicio	5.00	2.50	1.50
311	Jack Lamabe	.40	.20	.12
312	Curt Blefary	.40	.20	.12
313	Al Weis	.50	.25	.15
314	Red Sox Rookies (Bill Rohr, George Spriggs)	.40	.20	.12
315	Zoilo Versalles	.50	.25	.15
316	Steve Barber	.80	.40	.25
317	Ron Brand	.40	.20	.12
318	Chico Salmon	.40	.20	.12
319	George Culver	.40	.20	.12
320	Frank Howard	2.00	1.00	.60
321	Leo Durocher	2.25	1.25	.70
322	Dave Boswell	.50	.25	.15
323	Deron Johnson	.40	.20	.12
324	Jim Nash	.40	.20	.12
325	Manny Mota	.80	.40	.25
326	Dennis Ribant	.40	.20	.12
327	Tony Taylor	.40	.20	.12
328	Angels Rookies (Chuck Vinson, Jim Weaver)	.40	.20	.12
329	Duane Josephson	.40	.20	.12
330	Roger Maris	10.00	5.00	3.00
331	Dan Osinski	.40	.20	.12
332	Doug Rader	.50	.25	.15
333	Ron Herbel	.40	.20	.12
334	Orioles Team	2.00	1.00	.60
335	Bob Allison	1.00	.50	.30
336	John Purdin	.40	.20	.12
337	Bill Robinson	.80	.40	.25
338	Bob Johnson	.40	.20	.12
339	Rich Nye	.40	.20	.12
340	Max Alvis	.40	.20	.12
341	Jim Lemon	.40	.20	.12
342	Ken Johnson	.40	.20	.12
343	Jim Gosger	.40	.20	.12
344	Donn Clendenon	.50	.25	.15
345	Bob Hendley	.50	.25	.15
346	Jerry Adair	.40	.20	.12
347	George Brunet	.40	.20	.12
348	Phillies Rookies (Larry Colton, Dick Thoenen)	.40	.20	.12
349	Ed Spiezio	.40	.20	.12
350	Hoyt Wilhelm	5.00	2.50	1.50
351	Bob Barton	.40	.20	.12
352	Jackie Hernandez	.40	.20	.12
353	Mack Jones	.40	.20	.12
354	Pete Richert	.40	.20	.12
355	Ernie Banks	7.00	3.50	2.00
356	Checklist 371-457 (Ken Holtzman)	2.50	1.25	.70
357	Len Gabrielson	.40	.20	.12
358	Mike Epstein	.50	.25	.15
359	Joe Moeller	.40	.20	.12
360	Willie Horton	.80	.40	.25
361	Harmon Killebrew AS	4.00	2.00	1.25
362	Orlando Cepeda AS	2.50	1.25	.70
363	Rod Carew AS	6.00	3.00	1.75
364	Joe Morgan AS	2.50	1.25	.70
365	Brooks Robinson AS	5.00	2.50	1.50
366	Ron Santo AS	1.50	.70	.45
367	Jim Fregosi AS	1.00	.50	.30
368	Gene Alley AS	1.00	.50	.30
369	Carl Yastrzemski AS	7.00	3.50	2.00
370	Hank Aaron AS	7.00	3.50	2.00
371	Tony Oliva AS	2.00	1.00	.60
372	Lou Brock AS	4.00	2.00	1.25
373	Frank Robinson AS	4.00	2.00	1.25
374	Bob Clemente AS	7.00	3.50	2.00
375	Bill Freehan AS	1.00	.50	.30
376	Tim McCarver AS	1.50	.70	.45
377	Joe Horlen AS	1.00	.50	.30
378	Bob Gibson AS	4.00	2.00	1.25
379	Gary Peters AS	1.00	.50	.30
380	Ken Holtzman AS	1.00	.50	.30

#	Player	NR MT	EX	VG
381	Boog Powell	2.50	1.25	.70
382	Ramon Hernandez	.40	.20	.12
383	Steve Whitaker	.80	.40	.25
384	Reds Rookies (Bill Henry, Hal McRae)	3.00	1.50	.90
385	Jim Hunter	5.00	2.50	1.50
386	Greg Goossen	.50	.25	.15
387	Joe Foy	.40	.20	.12
388	Ray Washburn	.40	.20	.12
389	Jay Johnstone	.80	.40	.25
390	Bill Mazeroski	1.75	.90	.50
391	Bob Priddy	.40	.20	.12
392	Grady Hatton	.40	.20	.12
393	Jim Perry	1.00	.50	.30
394	Tommie Aaron	.70	.35	.20
395	Camilo Pascual	.70	.35	.20
396	Bobby Wine	.40	.20	.12
397	Vic Davalillo	.50	.25	.15
398	Jim Grant	.40	.20	.12
399	Ray Oyler	.50	.25	.15
400	Mike McCormick	.50	.25	.15
401	Mets Team	3.25	1.75	1.00
402	Mike Hegan	1.00	.50	.30
403	John Buzhardt	.40	.20	.12
404	Floyd Robinson	.40	.20	.12
405	Tommy Helms	.50	.25	.15
406	Dick Ellsworth	.40	.20	.12
407	Gary Kolb	.40	.20	.12
408	Steve Carlton	25.00	12.50	7.50
409	Orioles Rookies (Frank Peters, Ron Stone)	.40	.20	.12
410	Ferguson Jenkins	3.50	1.75	1.00
411	Ron Hansen	.40	.20	.12
412	Clay Carroll	.50	.25	.15
413	Tommy McCraw	.40	.20	.12
414	Mickey Lolich	2.25	1.25	.70
415	Johnny Callison	1.00	.50	.30
416	Bill Rigney	.40	.20	.12
417	Willie Crawford	.40	.20	.12
418	Eddie Fisher	.40	.20	.12
419	Jack Hiatt	.40	.20	.12
420	Cesar Tovar	.40	.20	.12
421	Ron Taylor	.50	.25	.15
422	Rene Lachemann	.40	.20	.12
423	Fred Gladding	.40	.20	.12
424	White Sox Team	2.00	1.00	.60
425	Jim Maloney	.50	.25	.15
426	Hank Allen	.40	.20	.12
427	Dick Calmus	.40	.20	.12
428	Vic Roznovsky	.40	.20	.12
429	Tommie Sisk	.40	.20	.12
430	Rico Petrocelli	.80	.40	.25
431	Dooley Womack	.80	.40	.25
432	Indians Rookies (Bill Davis, Jose Vidal)	.40	.20	.12
433	Bob Rodgers	.70	.35	.20
434	Ricardo Joseph	.40	.20	.12
435	Ron Perranoski	.50	.25	.15
436	Hal Lanier	.80	.40	.25
437	Don Cardwell	.50	.25	.15
438	Lee Thomas	.40	.20	.12
439	Luman Harris	.40	.20	.12
440	Claude Osteen	.70	.35	.20
441	Alex Johnson	.40	.20	.12
442	Dick Bosman	.40	.20	.12
443	Joe Azcue	.40	.20	.12
444	Jack Fisher	.40	.20	.12
445	Mike Shannon	.50	.25	.15
446	Ron Kline	.40	.20	.12
447	Tigers Rookies (George Korince, Fred Lasher)	.40	.20	.12
448	Gary Wagner	.40	.20	.12
449	Gene Oliver	.40	.20	.12
450	Jim Kaat	3.50	1.75	1.00
451	Al Spangler	.40	.20	.12
452	Jesus Alou	.50	.25	.15
453	Sammy Ellis	.40	.20	.12
454	Checklist 458-533 (Frank Robinson)	4.00	2.00	1.25
455	Rico Carty	1.00	.50	.30
456	John O'Donoghue	.40	.20	.12
457	Jim Lefebvre	.50	.25	.15
458	Lew Krausse	.40	.20	.12
459	Dick Simpson	.40	.20	.12
460	Jim Lonborg	1.00	.50	.30
461	Chuck Hiller	.40	.20	.12
462	Barry Moore	.40	.20	.12
463	Jimmie Schaffer	.40	.20	.12
464	Don McMahon	.40	.20	.12
465	Tommie Agee	.80	.40	.25
466	Bill Dillman	.40	.20	.12
467	Dick Howser	1.50	.70	.45
468	Larry Sherry	.40	.20	.12
469	Ty Cline	.40	.20	.12
470	Bill Freehan	1.00	.50	.30
471	Orlando Pena	.40	.20	.12
472	Walt Alston	2.50	1.25	.70
473	Al Worthington	.40	.20	.12
474	Paul Schaal	.40	.20	.12
475	Joe Niekro	2.25	1.25	.70
476	Woody Woodward	.50	.25	.15
477	Phillies Team	2.00	1.00	.60
478	Dave McNally	1.00	.50	.30
479	Phil Gagliano	.40	.20	.12
480	Manager's Dream (Chico Cardenas, Bob Clemente, Tony Oliva)	7.00	3.50	2.00
481	John Wyatt	.40	.20	.12
482	Jose Pagan	.40	.20	.12
483	Darold Knowles	.40	.20	.12
484	Phil Roof	.40	.20	.12
485	Ken Berry	.40	.20	.12
486	Cal Koonce	.50	.25	.15
487	Lee May	1.25	.60	.40
488	Dick Tracewski	.40	.20	.12
489	Wally Bunker	.40	.20	.12
490	Super Stars (Harmon Killebrew, Mickey Mantle, Willie Mays)	25.00	11.50	6.25
491	Denny Lemaster	.40	.20	.12
492	Jeff Torborg	.50	.25	.15
493	Jim McGlothlin	.40	.20	.12
494	Ray Sadecki	.40	.20	.12
495	Leon Wagner	.50	.25	.15
496	Steve Hamilton	.80	.40	.25
497	Cards Team	3.50	1.75	1.00
498	Bill Bryan	.40	.20	.12
499	Steve Blass	.50	.25	.15
500	Frank Robinson	8.00	4.00	2.50
501	John Odom	.50	.25	.15
502	Mike Andrews	.40	.20	.12
503	Al Jackson	.50	.25	.15
504	Russ Snyder	.40	.20	.12
505	Joe Sparma	.50	.25	.15
506	Clarence Jones	.40	.20	.12
507	Wade Blasingame	.40	.20	.12
508	Duke Sims	.40	.20	.12
509	Dennis Higgins	.40	.20	.12
510	Ron Fairly	.80	.40	.25
511	Bill Kelso	.40	.20	.12
512	Grant Jackson	.40	.20	.12
513	Hank Bauer	.70	.35	.20
514	Al McBean	.40	.20	.12
515	Russ Nixon	.40	.20	.12
516	Pete Mikkelsen	.40	.20	.12
517	Diego Segui	.40	.20	.12
518a	Checklist 534-598 (Clete Boyer) (539 is Maj. L. Rookies)	3.00	1.50	.90
518b	Checklist 534-598 (Clete Boyer) (539 is Amer. L. Rookies)	5.00	2.50	1.50
519	Jerry Stephenson	.40	.20	.12
520	Lou Brock	8.00	4.00	2.50
521	Don Shaw	.50	.25	.15
522	Wayne Causey	.40	.20	.12
523	John Tsitouris	.40	.20	.12
524	Andy Kosco	.80	.40	.25
525	Jim Davenport	.40	.20	.12
526	Bill Denehy	.40	.20	.12
527	Tito Francona	.50	.25	.15
528	Tigers Team	5.00	2.50	1.50
529	Bruce Von Hoff	.40	.20	.12
530	Bird Belters (Brooks Robinson, Frank Robinson)	5.00	2.50	1.50
531	Chuck Hinton	.40	.20	.12
532	Luis Tiant	1.75	.90	.50
533	Wes Parker	.70	.35	.20
534	Bob Miller	.80	.40	.25
535	Danny Cater	.80	.40	.25
536	Bill Short	.90	.45	.25
537	Norm Siebern	.90	.45	.25
538	Manny Jimenez	.80	.40	.25
539	Major League Rookies (Mike Ferraro, Jim Ray)	1.25	.60	.40
540	Nelson Briles	.90	.45	.25
541	Sandy Alomar	.80	.40	.25
542	John Boccabella	.80	.40	.25
543	Bob Lee	.80	.40	.25
544	Mayo Smith	.90	.45	.25
545	Lindy McDaniel	.80	.40	.25
546	Roy White	2.50	1.25	.70
547	Dan Coombs	.80	.40	.25
548	Bernie Allen	.80	.40	.25
549	Orioles Rookies (Curt Motton, Roger Nelson)	.80	.40	.25

		NR MT	EX	VG
550	Clete Boyer	1.25	.60	.40
551	Darrell Sutherland	.80	.40	.25
552	Ed Kirkpatrick	.80	.40	.25
553	Hank Aguirre	.80	.40	.25
554	A's Team	3.00	1.50	.90
555	Jose Tartabull	.80	.40	.25
556	Dick Selma	.90	.45	.25
557	Frank Quilici	.80	.40	.25
558	John Edwards	.80	.40	.25
559	Pirates Rookies (Carl Taylor, Luke Walker)			
		.80	.40	.25
560	Paul Casanova	.80	.40	.25
561	Lee Elia	.90	.45	.25
562	Jim Bouton	2.50	1.25	.70
563	Ed Charles	.90	.45	.25
564	Eddie Stanky	1.25	.60	.40
565	Larry Dierker	.90	.45	.25
566	Ken Harrelson	2.00	1.00	.60
567	Clay Dalrymple	.80	.40	.25
568	Willie Smith	.80	.40	.25
569	N.L. Rookies (Ivan Murrell, Les Rohr)			
		.90	.45	.25
570	Rick Reichardt	.80	.40	.25
571	Tony LaRussa	1.75	.90	.50
572	Don Bosch	.90	.45	.25
573	Joe Coleman	.90	.45	.25
574	Reds Team	3.00	1.50	.90
575	Jim Palmer	10.00	5.00	3.00
576	Dave Adlesh	.80	.40	.25
577	Fred Talbot	1.25	.60	.40
578	Orlando Martinez	.80	.40	.25
579	N.L. Rookies (Larry Hisle, Mike Lum)			
		1.75	.90	.50
580	Bob Bailey	.80	.40	.25
581	Garry Roggenburk	.80	.40	.25
582	Jerry Grote	1.25	.60	.40
583	Gates Brown	.90	.45	.25
584	Larry Shepard	.80	.40	.25
585	Wilbur Wood	1.25	.60	.40
586	Jim Pagliaroni	.80	.40	.25
587	Roger Repoz	.80	.40	.25
588	Dick Schofield	.80	.40	.25
589	Twins Rookies (Ron Clark, Moe Ogier)			
		.80	.40	.25
590	Tommy Harper	.90	.45	.25
591	Dick Nen	.80	.40	.25
592	John Bateman	.80	.40	.25
593	Lee Stange	.80	.40	.25
594	Phil Linz	.90	.45	.25
595	Phil Ortega	.80	.40	.25
596	Charlie Smith	1.25	.60	.40
597	Bill McCool	.90	.40	.25
598	Jerry May	2.00	.60	.25

1968 Topps
Action All-Star Stickers

Still another of the many Topps test issues of the late 1960s, the Action All-Star stickers were sold in a strip of three, with bubblegum, for 10¢. The strip was comprised of three 3¼'' by 5¼'' panels, perforated at the joints for separation. The central panel, which was numbered, contained a large color picture of a star player. The top and bottom panels contained smaller pictures of three players each. While there are 16 numbered center panels, only 12 of them are different; panels 13-16 show players previously used. Similarly, the triple-player panels at top and bottom of stickers 13-16 repeat panels from #1-4. Prices below are for stickers which have all three panels still joined. Individual panels are priced significantly lower.

	NR MT	EX	VG
Complete Set:	1250.00	625.00	375.00
Common Player:	18.00	9.00	5.50

		NR MT	EX	VG
1	Orlando Cepeda, Joe Horlen, Al Kaline, Bill Mazeroski, Claude Osteen, Mel Stottlemyre, Carl Yastrzemski	100.00	50.00	30.00
2	Don Drysdale, Harmon Killebrew, Mike McCormick, Tom Phoebus, George Scott, Ron Swoboda, Pete Ward	30.00	15.00	9.00
3	Hank Aaron, Paul Casanova, Jim Maloney, Joe Pepitone, Rick Reichardt, Frank Robinson, Tom Seaver	35.00	17.50	10.50
4	Bob Aspromonte, Johnny Callison, Dean Chance, Jim Lefebvre, Jim Lonborg, Frank Robinson, Ron Santo	25.00	12.50	7.50
5	Bert Campaneris, Al Downing, Willie Horton, Ed Kranepool, Willie Mays, Pete Rose, Ron Santo	200.00	100.00	60.00
6	Max Alvis, Ernie Banks, Al Kaline, Tim McCarver, Rusty Staub, Walt Williams, Carl Yastrzemski	70.00	35.00	21.00
7	Rod Carew, Tony Gonzalez, Steve Hargan, Mickey Mantle, Willie McCovey, Rick Monday, Billy Williams	275.00	137.00	82.00
8	Clete Boyer, Jim Bunning, Tony Conigliaro, Mike Cuellar, Joe Horlen, Ken McMullen, Don Mincher	18.00	9.00	5.50
9	Orlando Cepeda, Bob Clemente, Jim Fregosi, Harmon Killebrew, Willie Mays, Chris Short, Earl Wilson	40.00	20.00	12.00
10	Hank Aaron, Bob Gibson, Bud Harrelson, Jim Hunter, Mickey Mantle, Gary Peters, Vada Pinson	100.00	50.00	30.00

		NR MT	EX	VG
11	Don Drysdale, Bill Freehan, Frank Howard, Ferguson Jenkins, Tony Oliva, Bob Veale, Jim Wynn	30.00	15.00	9.00
12	Richie Allen, Bob Clemente, Sam McDowell, Jim McGlothlin, Tony Perez, Brooks Robinson, Joe Torre	100.00	50.00	30.00
13	Dean Chance, Don Drysdale, Jim Lefebvre, Tom Phoebus, Frank Robinson, George Scott, Carl Yastrzemski	100.00	50.00	30.00
14	Paul Casanova, Orlando Cepeda, Joe Horlen, Harmon Killebrew, Bill Mazeroski, Rick Reichardt, Tom Seaver	35.00	17.50	10.50
15	Bob Aspromonte, Johnny Callison, Jim Lonborg, Mike McCormick, Frank Robinson, Ron Swoboda, Pete Ward	30.00	15.00	9.00
16	Hank Aaron, Al Kaline, Jim Maloney, Claude Osteen, Joe Pepitone, Ron Santo, Mel Stottlemyre	30.00	15.00	9.00

		NR MT	EX	VG
28	Rusty Staub	.70	.35	.20
29	Rod Carew	2.75	1.50	.80
30	Pete Rose	7.50	3.75	2.25
31	Joe Torre	.70	.35	.20
32	Orlando Cepeda	1.00	.50	.30
33	Jim Fregosi	.50	.25	.15

1968 Topps Game

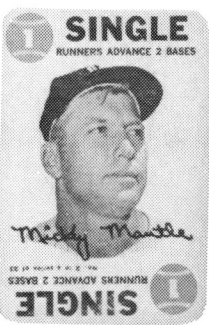 

A throwback to the Red and Blue Back sets of 1951, the 33-cards in the 1968 game series, inserted into packs of regular '68 Topps cards or purchased as a complete boxed set, enable the owner to play a game of baseball based on the game situations on each card. Also on the 2¼'' by 3¼'' cards were a color photograph of a player and his facsimile autograph. One redeeming social value of the set (assuming you're not mesmerized by the game) is that it affords an inexpensive way to get big-name cards as the set is loaded with stars, but not at all popular with collectors.

		NR MT	EX	VG
Complete Set:		40.00	20.00	12.00
Common Player:		.30	.15	.09
1	Mateo Alou	.50	.25	.15
2	Mickey Mantle	10.00	5.00	3.00
3	Carl Yastrzemski	3.25	1.75	1.00
4	Henry Aaron	3.00	1.50	.90
5	Harmon Killebrew	1.75	.90	.50
6	Roberto Clemente	3.00	1.50	.90
7	Frank Robinson	1.75	.90	.50
8	Willie Mays	3.00	1.50	.90
9	Brooks Robinson	2.00	1.00	.60
10	Tommy Davis	.50	.25	.15
11	Bill Freehan	.50	.25	.15
12	Claude Osteen	.40	.20	.12
13	Gary Peters	.30	.15	.09
14	Jim Lonborg	.40	.20	.12
15	Steve Hargan	.30	.15	.09
16	Dean Chance	.40	.20	.12
17	Mike McCormick	.30	.15	.09
18	Tim McCarver	.60	.30	.20
19	Ron Santo	.60	.30	.20
20	Tony Gonzalez	.30	.15	.09
21	Frank Howard	.70	.35	.20
22	George Scott	.40	.20	.12
23	Rich Allen	.70	.35	.20
24	Jim Wynn	.40	.20	.12
25	Gene Alley	.40	.20	.12
26	Rick Monday	.40	.20	.12
27	Al Kaline	2.00	1.00	.60

1968 Topps Plaks

Among the scarcest of the Topps test issues of the late 1960s, the ''All Star Baseball Plaks'' were plastic busts of two dozen stars of the era which came packaged like model airplane parts. The busts had to be snapped off a sprue and could be inserted into a base which carried the player's name. Packed with the plastic plaks was one of two checklist cards which featured six color photos per side. The 2⅛'' by 4'' checklist cards are popular with superstar collectors and are considerably easier to find today than the actual plaks.

		NR MT	EX	VG
Complete Set:		2200.00	1100.00	660.00
Common Player:		20.00	10.00	6.00
1	Max Alvis	20.00	10.00	6.00
2	Frank Howard	30.00	15.00	9.00
3	Dean Chance	20.00	10.00	6.00
4	Jim Hunter	50.00	25.00	15.00
5	Jim Fregosi	25.00	12.50	7.50
6	Al Kaline	60.00	30.00	18.00
7	Harmon Killebrew	60.00	30.00	18.00
8	Gary Peters	20.00	10.00	6.00
9	Jim Lonborg	20.00	10.00	6.00
10	Frank Robinson	60.00	30.00	18.00
11	Mickey Mantle	700.00	350.00	210.00
12	Carl Yastrzemski	175.00	87.00	52.00
13	Hank Aaron	100.00	50.00	30.00

		NR MT	EX	VG
14	Bob Clemente	100.00	50.00	30.00
15	Richie Allen	30.00	15.00	9.00
16	Tommy Davis	25.00	12.50	7.50
17	Orlando Cepeda	30.00	15.00	9.00
18	Don Drysdale	50.00	25.00	15.00
19	Willie Mays	100.00	50.00	30.00
20	Rusty Staub	30.00	15.00	9.00
21	Tim McCarver	30.00	15.00	9.00
22	Pete Rose	250.00	125.00	75.00
23	Ron Santo	30.00	15.00	9.00
24	Jim Wynn	20.00	10.00	6.00
---	Checklist Card 1-12	250.00	125.00	75.00
---	Checklist Card 13-24	250.00	125.00	75.00

		NR MT	EX	VG
20	Willie Mays	20.00	10.00	6.00
21	Ron Santo	7.00	3.50	2.00
22	Rusty Staub	7.00	3.50	2.00
23	Pete Rose	50.00	25.00	15.00
24	Frank Robinson	15.00	7.50	4.50

1968 Topps 3-D

These are very rare pioneer issues on the part of Topps. The cards measure 2¼'' by 3½'' and were specially printed to simulate a three-dimensional effect. Backgrounds are a purposely blurred stadium scene, in front of which was a normally sharp color player photograph. The outer layer is a thin coating of ribbed plastic. The special process gave the picture the illusion of depth when the card was moved or tilted. As this was done two years before Kellogg's began it's 3-D cards, this 12-card test issue really was breaking new ground. Unfortunately, production and distribution were limited making the cards very tough to find.

		NR MT	EX	VG
	Complete Set:	5000.00	2500.00	1500.
	Common Player:	250.00	125.00	75.00
(1)	Bob Clemente	1000.00	500.00	300.00
(2)	Willie Davis	300.00	150.00	90.00
(3)	Ron Fairly	300.00	150.00	90.00
(4)	Curt Flood	300.00	150.00	90.00
(5)	Jim Lonborg	300.00	150.00	90.00
(6)	Jim Maloney	250.00	125.00	75.00
(7)	Tony Perez	400.00	200.00	120.00
(8)	Boog Powell	350.00	175.00	105.00
(9)	Bill Robinson	250.00	125.00	75.00
(10)	Rusty Staub	350.00	175.00	105.00
(11)	Mel Stottlemyre	300.00	150.00	90.00
(12)	Ron Swoboda	250.00	125.00	75.00

1968 Topps Posters

Yet another innovation from the creative minds at Topps appeared in 1968; a set of color player posters. Measuring 9¾'' by 18⅛,'' each poster was sold separately with its own piece of gum, rather than as an insert. The posters feature a large color photograph with a star at the bottom containing the player's name, position and team. There are 24 different posters which were folded numerous times to fit into the package they were sold in.

		NR MT	EX	VG
	Complete Set:	350.00	175.00	105.00
	Common Player:	5.00	2.50	1.50
1	Dean Chance	5.00	2.50	1.50
2	Max Alvis	5.00	2.50	1.50
3	Frank Howard	8.00	4.00	2.50
4	Jim Fregosi	7.00	3.50	2.00
5	Jim Hunter	10.00	5.00	3.00
6	Bob Clemente	20.00	10.00	6.00
7	Don Drysdale	12.00	6.00	3.50
8	Jim Wynn	5.00	2.50	1.50
9	Al Kaline	15.00	7.50	4.50
10	Harmon Killebrew	15.00	7.50	4.50
11	Jim Lonborg	5.00	2.50	1.50
12	Orlando Cepeda	8.00	4.00	2.50
13	Gary Peters	5.00	2.50	1.50
14	Hank Aaron	20.00	10.00	6.00
15	Richie Allen	8.00	4.00	2.50
16	Carl Yastrzemski	25.00	12.50	7.50
17	Ron Swoboda	5.00	2.50	1.50
18	Mickey Mantle	75.00	37.00	22.00
19	Tim McCarver	7.00	3.50	2.00

1969 Topps

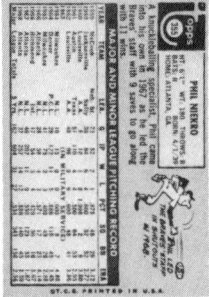

The 1969 Topps set broke yet another record for quantity as the issue was officially a whopping 664

cards. With substantial numbers of variations, the number of possible cards runs closer to 700. Design of the 2½'' by 3½'' set featured a color photo with the team name printed in block letters underneath. A circle contains the player's name and position. Card backs returned to a horizontal format. Despite the size of the set, it contained no team cards. It did, however, have multi-player cards, All-Stars, statistical leaders, and World Series highlights. Most significant among the varieties are white and yellow letter cards from the run of #440-#511. The complete set prices below do not include the scarcer and more expensive ''white letter'' variations.

	NR MT	EX	VG
Complete Set:	1250.00	425.00	250.00
Common Player: 1-218	.40	.20	.12
Common Player: 219-327	.60	.30	.20
Common Player: 328-512	.40	.20	.12
Common Player: 513-664	.50	.25	.15

		NR MT	EX	VG
1	A.L. Batting Leaders (Danny Cater, Tony Oliva, Carl Yastrzemski)	5.00	2.00	1.00
2	N.L. Batting Leaders (Felipe Alou, Matty Alou, Pete Rose)	4.00	2.00	1.25
3	A.L. RBI Leaders (Ken Harrelson, Frank Howard, Jim Northrup)	2.00	1.00	.60
4	N.L. RBI Leaders (Willie McCovey, Ron Santo, Billy Williams)	3.50	1.75	1.00
5	A.L. Home Run Leaders (Ken Harrelson, Willie Horton, Frank Howard)	2.00	1.00	.60
6	N.L. Home Run Leaders (Richie Allen, Ernie Banks, Willie McCovey)	3.50	1.75	1.00
7	A.L. ERA Leaders (Sam McDowell, Dave McNally, Luis Tiant)	2.00	1.00	.60
8	N.L. ERA Leaders (Bobby Bolin, Bob Gibson, Bob Veale)	3.00	1.50	.90
9	A.L. Pitching Leaders (Denny McLain, Dave McNally, Mel Stottlemyre, Luis Tiant)	2.00	1.00	.60
10	N.L. Pitching Leaders (Bob Gibson, Fergie Jenkins, Juan Marichal)	3.50	1.75	1.00
11	A.L. Strikeout Leaders (Sam McDowell, Denny McLain, Luis Tiant)	2.00	1.00	.60
12	N.L. Strikeout Leaders (Bob Gibson, Fergie Jenkins, Bill Singer)	3.00	1.50	.90
13	Mickey Stanley	.50	.25	.15
14	Al McBean	.40	.20	.12
15	Boog Powell	2.50	1.25	.70
16	Giants Rookies (Cesar Gutierrez, Rich Robertson)	.40	.20	.12
17	Mike Marshall	1.25	.60	.40
18	Dick Schofield	.40	.20	.12
19	Ken Suarez	.40	.20	.12
20	Ernie Banks	7.00	3.50	2.00
21	Jose Santiago	.40	.20	.12
22	Jesus Alou	.50	.25	.15
23	Lew Krausse	.40	.20	.12
24	Walt Alston	2.00	1.00	.60
25	Roy White	1.25	.60	.40
26	Clay Carroll	.50	.25	.15
27	Bernie Allen	.40	.20	.12
28	Mike Ryan	.40	.20	.12
29	Dave Morehead	.40	.20	.12
30	Bob Allison	1.00	.50	.30
31	Mets Rookies (Gary Gentry, Amos Otis)	1.25	.60	.40
32	Sammy Ellis	.40	.20	.12
33	Wayne Causey	.40	.20	.12
34	Gary Peters	.50	.25	.15
35	Joe Morgan	4.00	2.00	1.25
36	Luke Walker	.40	.20	.12
37	Curt Motton	.40	.20	.12
38	Zoilo Versalles	.50	.25	.15
39	Dick Hughes	.40	.20	.12
40	Mayo Smith	.40	.20	.12
41	Bob Barton	.40	.20	.12
42	Tommy Harper	1.00	.50	.30
43	Joe Niekro	1.25	.60	.40
44	Danny Cater	.40	.20	.12
45	Maury Wills	2.50	1.25	.70
46	Fritz Peterson	1.00	.50	.30
47a	Paul Popovich (emblem visible thru airbrush)	4.00	2.00	1.25
47b	Paul Popovich (helmet emblem completely airbrushed)	.40	.20	.12
48	Brant Alyea	.40	.20	.12
49a	Royals Rookies (Steve Jones, Eliseo Rodriquez) (Rodriguez on front)	6.00	3.00	1.75

		NR MT	EX	VG
49b	Royals Rookies (Steve Jones, Eliseo Rodriguez) (Rodriguez on front)	.40	.20	.12
50	Bob Clemente	18.00	9.00	5.50
51	Woody Fryman	.50	.25	.15
52	Mike Andrews	.40	.20	.12
53	Sonny Jackson	.40	.20	.12
54	Cisco Carlos	.40	.20	.12
55	Jerry Grote	1.00	.50	.30
56	Rich Reese	.40	.20	.12
57	Checklist 1-109 (Denny McLain)	3.00	1.50	.90
58	Fred Gladding	.40	.20	.12
59	Jay Johnstone	.70	.35	.20
60	Nelson Briles	.40	.20	.12
61	Jimmie Hall	.40	.20	.12
62	Chico Salmon	.80	.40	.25
63	Jim Hickman	.50	.25	.15
64	Bill Monbouquette	.50	.25	.15
65	Willie Davis	1.00	.50	.30
66	Orioles Rookies (Mike Adamson, Merv Rettenmund)	.70	.35	.20
67	Bill Stoneman	.40	.20	.12
68	Dave Duncan	.40	.20	.12
69	Steve Hamilton	.70	.35	.20
70	Tommy Helms	.50	.25	.15
71	Steve Whitaker	.40	.20	.12
72	Ron Taylor	.60	.30	.20
73	Johnny Briggs	.40	.20	.12
74	Preston Gomez	.40	.20	.12
75	Luis Aparicio	5.00	2.50	1.50
76	Norm Miller	.40	.20	.12
77a	Ron Perranoski (LA visible thru airbrush)	4.50	2.25	1.25
77b	Ron Perranoski (cap emblem completely airbrushed)	.50	.25	.15
78	Tom Satriano	.40	.20	.12
79	Milt Pappas	.70	.35	.20
80	Norm Cash	1.75	.90	.50
81	Mel Queen	.40	.20	.12
82	Pirates Rookies (Rich Hebner, Al Oliver)	10.00	5.00	3.00
83	Mike Ferraro	.80	.40	.25
84	Bob Humphreys	.40	.20	.12
85	Lou Brock	8.00	4.00	2.50
86	Pete Richert	.40	.20	.12
87	Horace Clarke	.70	.35	.20
88	Rich Nye	.40	.20	.12
89	Russ Gibson	.40	.20	.12
90	Jerry Koosman	2.50	1.25	.70
91	Al Dark	.70	.35	.20
92	Jack Billingham	.50	.25	.15
93	Joe Foy	.40	.20	.12
94	Hank Aguirre	.40	.20	.12
95	Johnny Bench	40.00	20.00	12.00
96	Denver Lemaster	.40	.20	.12
97	Buddy Bradford	.40	.20	.12
98	Dave Giusti	.40	.20	.12
99a	Twins Rookies (Danny Morris, Graig Nettles) (black loop above "Twins")	15.00	7.50	4.50
99b	Twins Rookies (Danny Morris, Graig Nettles) (no black loop)	10.00	5.00	3.00
100	Hank Aaron	20.00	10.00	6.00
101	Daryl Patterson	.40	.20	.12
102	Jim Davenport	.40	.20	.12
103	Roger Repoz	.40	.20	.12
104	Steve Blass	.50	.25	.15
105	Rick Monday	.80	.40	.25
106	Jim Hannan	.40	.20	.12
107a	Checklist 110-218 (Bob Gibson) (161 is Jim Purdin)	3.00	1.50	.90
107b	Checklist 110-218 (Bob Gibson) (161 is John Purdin)	6.00	3.00	1.75
108	Tony Taylor	.40	.20	.12
109	Jim Lonborg	.80	.40	.25
110	Mike Shannon	.50	.25	.15
111	Johnny Morris	.80	.40	.25
112	J.C. Martin	.70	.35	.20
113	Dave May	.40	.20	.12
114	Yankees Rookies (Alan Closter, John Cumberland)	.70	.35	.20
115	Bill Hands	.40	.20	.12
116	Chuck Harrison	.40	.20	.12
117	Jim Fairey	.40	.20	.12
118	Stan Williams	.40	.20	.12
119	Doug Rader	.50	.25	.15
120	Pete Rose	30.00	15.00	9.00
121	Joe Grzenda	.40	.20	.12
122	Ron Fairly	.80	.40	.25
123	Wilbur Wood	.80	.40	.25
124	Hank Bauer	.80	.40	.25
125	Ray Sadecki	.40	.20	.12
126	Dick Tracewski	.40	.20	.12

		NR MT	EX	VG
127	Kevin Collins	.60	.30	.20
128	Tommie Aaron	.70	.35	.20
129	Bill McCool	.40	.20	.12
130	Carl Yastrzemski	20.00	10.00	6.00
131	Chris Cannizzaro	.40	.20	.12
132	Dave Baldwin	.40	.20	.12
133	Johnny Callison	1.00	.50	.30
134	Jim Weaver	.40	.20	.12
135	Tommy Davis	1.50	.70	.45
136	Cards Rookies (Steve Huntz, Mike Torrez)			
		.50	.25	.15
137	Wally Bunker	.40	.20	.12
138	John Bateman	.40	.20	.12
139	Andy Kosco	.40	.20	.12
140	Jim Lefebvre	.50	.25	.15
141	Bill Dillman	.40	.20	.12
142	Woody Woodward	.50	.25	.15
143	Joe Nossek	.40	.20	.12
144	Bob Hendley	.60	.30	.20
145	Max Alvis	.50	.25	.15
146	Jim Perry	1.00	.50	.30
147	Leo Durocher	2.25	1.25	.70
148	Lee Stange	.40	.20	.12
149	Ollie Brown	.40	.20	.12
150	Denny McLain	3.00	1.50	.90
151a	Clay Dalrymple (Phillies)	6.00	3.00	1.75
151b	Clay Dalrymple (Orioles)	.40	.20	.12
152	Tommie Sisk	.40	.20	.12
153	Ed Brinkman	.50	.25	.15
154	Jim Britton	.40	.20	.12
155	Pete Ward	.40	.20	.12
156	Astros Rookies (Hal Gilson, Leon McFadden)	.40	.20	.12
157	Bob Rodgers	.70	.35	.20
158	Joe Gibbon	.40	.20	.12
159	Jerry Adair	.40	.20	.12
160	Vada Pinson	2.00	1.00	.60
161	John Purdin	.40	.20	.12
162	World Series Game 1 (Gibson Fans 17; Sets New Record)	3.50	1.75	1.00
163	World Series Game 2 (Tiger Homers Deck The Cards)	2.50	1.25	.70
164	World Series Game 3 (McCarver's Homer Puts St. Louis Ahead)	2.50	1.25	.70
165	World Series Game 4 (Brock's Lead-Off Homer Starts Cards' Romp)	3.50	1.75	1.00
166	World Series Game 5 (Kaline's Key Hit Sparks Tiger Rally)	3.50	1.75	1.00
167	World Series Game 6 (Tiger 10-Run Inning Ties Mark)	2.50	1.25	.70
168	World Series Game 7 (Lolich Series Hero, Outduels Gibson)	2.75	1.50	.80
169	World Series Summary (Tigers Celebrate Their Victory)	2.50	1.25	.70
170	Frank Howard	2.00	1.00	.60
171	Glenn Beckert	.80	.40	.25
172	Jerry Stephenson	.40	.20	.12
173	White Sox Rookies (Bob Christian, Gerry Nyman)	.40	.20	.12
174	Grant Jackson	.40	.20	.12
175	Jim Bunning	3.50	1.75	1.00
176	Joe Azcue	.40	.20	.12
177	Ron Reed	.50	.25	.15
178	Ray Oyler	.80	.40	.25
179	Don Pavletich	.40	.20	.12
180	Willie Horton	.80	.40	.25
181	Mel Nelson	.40	.20	.12
182	Bill Rigney	.40	.20	.12
183	Don Shaw	.40	.20	.12
184	Roberto Pena	.40	.20	.12
185	Tom Phoebus	.40	.20	.12
186	John Edwards	.40	.20	.12
187	Leon Wagner	.50	.25	.15
188	Rick Wise	.50	.25	.15
189	Red Sox Rookies (Joe Lahoud, John Thibdeau)	.40	.20	.12
190	Willie Mays	20.00	10.00	6.00
191	Lindy McDaniel	.70	.35	.20
192	Jose Pagan	.40	.20	.12
193	Don Cardwell	.70	.35	.20
194	Ted Uhlaender	.40	.20	.12
195	John Odom	.50	.25	.15
196	Lum Harris	.40	.20	.12
197	Dick Selma	.40	.20	.12
198	Willie Smith	.40	.20	.12
199	Jim French	.40	.20	.12
200	Bob Gibson	7.00	3.50	2.00
201	Russ Snyder	.40	.20	.12
202	Don Wilson	.40	.20	.12
203	Dave Johnson	1.50	.70	.45
204	Jack Hiatt	.40	.20	.12

		NR MT	EX	VG
205	Rick Reichardt	.40	.20	.12
206	Phillies Rookies (Larry Hisle, Barry Lersch)	.80	.40	.25
207	Roy Face	1.25	.60	.40
208a	Donn Clendenon (Expos)	6.00	3.00	1.75
208b	Donn Clendenon (Houston)	.50	.25	.15
209	Larry Haney (photo reversed)	.80	.40	.25
210	Felix Millan	.40	.20	.12
211	Galen Cisco	.40	.20	.12
212	Tom Tresh	1.25	.60	.40
213	Gerry Arrigo	.40	.20	.12
214	Checklist 219-327	2.50	1.25	.70
215	Rico Petrocelli	.80	.40	.25
216	Don Sutton	4.00	2.00	1.25
217	John Donaldson	.40	.20	.12
218	John Roseboro	.60	.30	.20
219	Freddie Patek	1.00	.50	.30
220	Sam McDowell	1.00	.50	.30
221	Art Shamsky	.80	.40	.25
222	Duane Josephson	.50	.25	.15
223	Tom Dukes	.50	.25	.15
224	Angels Rookies (Bill Harrelson, Steve Kealey)	.50	.25	.15
225	Don Kessinger	.80	.40	.25
226	Bruce Howard	.50	.25	.15
227	Frank Johnson	.50	.25	.15
228	Dave Leonhard	.50	.25	.15
229	Don Lock	.50	.25	.15
230	Rusty Staub	2.50	1.25	.70
231	Pat Dobson	.70	.35	.20
232	Dave Ricketts	.50	.25	.15
233	Steve Barber	.80	.40	.25
234	Dave Bristol	.50	.25	.15
235	Jim Hunter	5.00	2.50	1.50
236	Manny Mota	.80	.40	.25
237	Bobby Cox	1.50	.70	.45
238	Ken Johnson	.50	.25	.15
239	Bob Taylor	.50	.25	.15
240	Ken Harrelson	2.00	1.00	.60
241	Jim Brewer	.50	.25	.15
242	Frank Kostro	.50	.25	.15
243	Ron Kline	.50	.25	.15
244	Indians Rookies (Ray Fosse, George Woodson)	1.00	.50	.30
245	Ed Charles	.80	.40	.25
246	Joe Coleman	.60	.30	.20
247	Gene Oliver	.50	.25	.15
248	Bob Priddy	.50	.25	.15
249	Ed Spiezio	.50	.25	.15
250	Frank Robinson	8.00	4.00	2.50
251	Ron Herbel	.50	.25	.15
252	Chuck Cottier	.50	.25	.15
253	Jerry Johnson	.50	.25	.15
254	Joe Schultz	.80	.40	.25
255	Steve Carlton	25.00	12.50	7.50
256	Gates Brown	.50	.25	.15
257	Jim Ray	.50	.25	.15
258	Jackie Hernandez	.50	.25	.15
259	Bill Short	.50	.25	.15
260	Reggie Jackson	200.00	80.00	50.00
261	Bob Johnson	.50	.25	.15
262	Mike Kekich	.80	.40	.25
263	Jerry May	.50	.25	.15
264	Bill Landis	.50	.25	.15
265	Chico Cardenas	.50	.25	.15
266	Dodgers Rookies (Alan Foster, Tom Hutton)	.50	.25	.15
267	Vicente Romo	.50	.25	.15
268	Al Spangler	.50	.25	.15
269	Al Weis	.80	.40	.25
270	Mickey Lolich	2.50	1.25	.70
271	Larry Stahl	.50	.25	.15
272	Ed Stroud	.50	.25	.15
273	Ron Willis	.50	.25	.15
274	Clyde King	.50	.25	.15
275	Vic Davalillo	.60	.30	.20
276	Gary Wagner	.50	.25	.15
277	Rod Hendricks	.60	.30	.20
278	Gary Geiger	.50	.25	.15
279	Roger Nelson	.50	.25	.15
280	Alex Johnson	.50	.25	.15
281	Ted Kubiak	.50	.25	.15
282	Pat Jarvis	.50	.25	.15
283	Sandy Alomar	.50	.25	.15
284	Expos Rookies (Jerry Robertson, Mike Wegener)	.50	.25	.15
285	Don Mincher	1.00	.50	.30
286	Dock Ellis	1.00	.50	.30
287	Jose Tartabull	.50	.25	.15
288	Ken Holtzman	.80	.40	.25
289	Bart Shirley	.50	.25	.15

		NR MT	EX	VG
290	Jim Kaat	3.50	1.75	1.00
291	Vern Fuller	.50	.25	.15
292	Al Downing	1.00	.50	.30
293	Dick Dietz	.50	.25	.15
294	Jim Lemon	.50	.25	.15
295	Tony Perez	3.50	1.75	1.00
296	Andy Messersmith	1.25	.60	.40
297	Deron Johnson	.50	.25	.15
298	Dave Nicholson	.50	.25	.15
299	Mark Belanger	.80	.40	.25
300	Felipe Alou	1.25	.60	.40
301	Darrell Brandon	.80	.40	.25
302	Jim Pagliaroni	.50	.25	.15
303	Cal Koonce	.80	.40	.25
304	Padres Rookies (Bill Davis, Clarence Gaston)	.70	.35	.20
305	Dick McAuliffe	.60	.30	.20
306	Jim Grant	.50	.25	.15
307	Gary Kolb	.50	.25	.15
308	Wade Blasingame	.50	.25	.15
309	Walt Williams	.50	.25	.15
310	Tom Haller	.60	.30	.20
311	Sparky Lyle	2.00	1.00	.60
312	Lee Elia	.60	.30	.20
313	Bill Robinson	.80	.40	.25
314	Checklist 328-425 (Don Drysdale)	3.50	1.75	1.00
315	Eddie Fisher	.50	.25	.15
316	Hal Lanier	.80	.40	.25
317	Bruce Look	.50	.25	.15
318	Jack Fisher	.50	.25	.15
319	Ken McMullen	.50	.25	.15
320	Dal Maxvill	.60	.30	.20
321	Jim McAndrew	.80	.40	.25
322	Jose Vidal	.80	.40	.25
323	Larry Miller	.50	.25	.15
324	Tigers Rookies (Les Cain, Dave Campbell)	.50	.25	.15
325	Jose Cardenal	.60	.30	.20
326	Gary Sutherland	.50	.25	.15
327	Willie Crawford	.50	.25	.15
328	Joe Horlen	.40	.20	.12
329	Rick Joseph	.40	.20	.12
330	Tony Conigliaro	1.50	.70	.45
331	Braves Rookies (Gil Garrido, Tom House)	.50	.25	.15
332	Fred Talbot	.80	.40	.25
333	Ivan Murrell	.40	.20	.12
334	Phil Roof	.40	.20	.12
335	Bill Mazeroski	1.75	.90	.50
336	Jim Roland	.40	.20	.12
337	Marty Martinez	.40	.20	.12
338	Del Unser	.50	.25	.15
339	Reds Rookies (Steve Mingori, Jose Pena)	.40	.20	.12
340	Dave McNally	.80	.40	.25
341	Dave Adlesh	.40	.20	.12
342	Bubba Morton	.40	.20	.12
343	Dan Frisella	.70	.35	.20
344	Tom Matchick	.40	.20	.12
345	Frank Linzy	.40	.20	.12
346	Wayne Comer	.80	.40	.25
347	Randy Hundley	.40	.20	.12
348	Steve Hargan	.40	.20	.12
349	Dick Williams	.80	.40	.25
350	Richie Allen	2.00	1.00	.60
351	Carroll Sembera	.40	.20	.12
352	Paul Schaal	.40	.20	.12
353	Jeff Torborg	.50	.25	.15
354	Nate Oliver	.80	.40	.25
355	Phil Niekro	4.00	2.00	1.25
356	Frank Quilici	.40	.20	.12
357	Carl Taylor	.40	.20	.12
358	Athletics Rookies (George Lauzerique, Roberto Rodriguez)	.40	.20	.12
359	Dick Kelley	.40	.20	.12
360	Jim Wynn	.80	.40	.25
361	Gary Holman	.40	.20	.12
362	Jim Maloney	.50	.25	.15
363	Russ Nixon	.40	.20	.12
364	Tommie Agee	.80	.40	.25
365	Jim Fregosi	1.00	.50	.30
366	Bo Belinsky	1.00	.50	.30
367	Lou Johnson	.40	.20	.12
368	Vic Roznovsky	.40	.20	.12
369	Bob Skinner	.40	.20	.12
370	Juan Marichal	6.00	3.00	1.75
371	Sal Bando	.80	.40	.25
372	Adolfo Phillips	.40	.20	.12
373	Fred Lasher	.40	.20	.12
374	Bob Tillman	.40	.20	.12
375	Harmon Killebrew	9.00	4.50	2.75

		NR MT	EX	VG
376	Royals Rookies (Mike Fiore, Jim Rooker)	.50	.25	.15
377	Gary Bell	.80	.40	.25
378	Jose Herrera	.40	.20	.12
379	Ken Boyer	1.75	.90	.50
380	Stan Bahnsen	.80	.40	.25
381	Ed Kranepool	.80	.40	.25
382	Pat Corrales	.80	.40	.25
383	Casey Cox	.40	.20	.12
384	Larry Shepard	.40	.20	.12
385	Orlando Cepeda	3.50	1.75	1.00
386	Jim McGlothlin	.40	.20	.12
387	Bobby Klaus	.40	.20	.12
388	Tom McCraw	.40	.20	.12
389	Dan Coombs	.40	.20	.12
390	Bill Freehan	.70	.35	.20
391	Ray Culp	.40	.20	.12
392	Bob Burda	.40	.20	.12
393	Gene Brabender	.40	.20	.12
394	Pilots Rookies (Lou Piniella, Marv Staehle)	2.25	1.25	.70
395	Chris Short	.60	.30	.20
396	Jim Campanis	.40	.20	.12
397	Chuck Dobson	.40	.20	.12
398	Tito Francona	.50	.25	.15
399	Bob Bailey	.40	.20	.12
400	Don Drysdale	6.00	3.00	1.75
401	Jake Gibbs	.80	.40	.25
402	Ken Boswell	.70	.35	.20
403	Bob Miller	.40	.20	.12
404	Cubs Rookies (Vic LaRose, Gary Ross)	.40	.20	.12
405	Lee May	1.00	.50	.30
406	Phil Ortega	.40	.20	.12
407	Tom Egan	.40	.20	.12
408	Nate Colbert	.40	.20	.12
409	Bob Moose	.40	.20	.12
410	Al Kaline	7.00	3.50	2.00
411	Larry Dierker	.50	.25	.15
412	Checklist 426-512 (Mickey Mantle)	6.00	3.00	1.75
413	Roland Sheldon	.80	.40	.25
414	Duke Sims	.40	.20	.12
415	Ray Washburn	.40	.20	.12
416	Willie McCovey AS	3.50	1.75	1.00
417	Ken Harrelson AS	1.00	.50	.30
418	Tommy Helms AS	.70	.35	.20
419	Rod Carew AS	4.50	2.25	1.25
420	Ron Santo AS	1.00	.50	.30
421	Brooks Robinson AS	4.00	2.00	1.25
422	Don Kessinger AS	.70	.35	.20
423	Bert Campaneris AS	.80	.40	.25
424	Pete Rose AS	8.00	4.00	2.50
425	Carl Yastrzemski AS	6.00	3.00	1.75
426	Curt Flood AS	1.00	.50	.30
427	Tony Oliva AS	1.50	.70	.45
428	Lou Brock AS	3.50	1.75	1.00
429	Willie Horton AS	.80	.40	.25
430	Johnny Bench AS	4.50	2.25	1.25
431	Bill Freehan AS	.70	.35	.20
432	Bob Gibson AS	3.50	1.75	1.00
433	Denny McLain AS	1.50	.70	.45
434	Jerry Koosman AS	1.00	.50	.30
435	Sam McDowell AS	.80	.40	.25
436	Gene Alley	.70	.35	.20
437	Luis Alcaraz	.40	.20	.12
438	Gary Waslewski	.40	.20	.12
439	White Sox Rookies (Ed Herrmann, Dan Lazar)	.40	.20	.12
440a	Willie McCovey (last name in white)	60.00	30.00	18.00
440b	Willie McCovey (last name in yellow)	9.00	4.50	2.75
441a	Dennis Higgins (last name in white)	10.00	5.00	3.00
441b	Dennis Higgins (last name in yellow)	.40	.20	.12
442	Ty Cline	.40	.20	.12
443	Don Wert	.40	.20	.12
444a	Joe Moeller (last name in white)	10.00	5.00	3.00
444b	Joe Moeller (last name in yellow)	.40	.20	.12
445	Bobby Knoop	.40	.20	.12
446	Claude Raymond	.40	.20	.12
447a	Ralph Houk (last name in white)	15.00	7.50	4.50
447b	Ralph Houk (last name in yellow)	1.50	.70	.45
448	Bob Tolan	.50	.25	.15
449	Paul Lindblad	.40	.20	.12
450	Billy Williams	5.00	2.50	1.50
451a	Rich Rollins (first name in white)	10.00	5.00	3.00
451b	Rich Rollins (first name in yellow)	.80	.40	.25
452a	Al Ferrara (first name in white)	10.00	5.00	3.00

		NR MT	EX	VG
452b	Al Ferrara (first name in yellow)	.40	.20	.12
453	Mike Cuellar	.80	.40	.25
454a	Phillies Rookies (Larry Colton, Don Money) (names in white)	10.00	5.00	3.00
454b	Phillies Rookies (Larry Colton, Don Money) (names in yellow)	.80	.40	.25
455	Sonny Siebert	.40	.20	.12
456	Bud Harrelson	1.00	.50	.30
457	Dalton Jones	.40	.20	.12
458	Curt Blefary	.40	.20	.12
459	Dave Boswell	.40	.20	.12
460	Joe Torre	1.75	.90	.50
461a	Mike Epstein (last name in white)	10.00	5.00	3.00
461b	Mike Epstein (last name in yellow)	.50	.25	.15
462	Red Schoendienst	1.00	.50	.30
463	Dennis Ribant	.40	.20	.12
464a	Dave Marshall (last name in white)	10.00	5.00	3.00
464b	Dave Marshall (last name in yellow)	.40	.20	.12
465	Tommy John	4.00	2.00	1.25
466	John Boccabella	.40	.20	.12
467	Tom Reynolds	.40	.20	.12
468a	Pirates Rookies (Bruce Dal Canton, Bob Robertson) (names in white)	10.00	5.00	3.00
468b	Pirates Rookies (Bruce Dal Canton, Bob Robertson) (names in yellow)	.50	.25	.15
469	Chico Ruiz	.40	.20	.12
470a	Mel Stottlemyre (last name in white)	15.00	7.50	4.50
470b	Mel Stottlemyre (last name in yellow)	1.50	.70	.45
471a	Ted Savage (last name in white)	10.00	5.00	3.00
471b	Ted Savage (last name in yellow)	.40	.20	.12
472	Jim Price	.40	.20	.12
473a	Jose Arcia (first name in white)	10.00	5.00	3.00
473b	Jose Arcia (first name in yellow)	.40	.20	.12
474	Tom Murphy	.40	.20	.12
475	Tim McCarver	1.50	.70	.45
476a	Red Sox Rookies (Ken Brett, Gerry Moses) (names in white)	10.00	5.00	3.00
476b	Red Sox Rookies (Ken Brett, Gerry Moses) (names in yellow)	.50	.25	.15
477	Jeff James	.40	.20	.12
478	Don Buford	.60	.30	.20
479	Richie Scheinblum	.40	.20	.12
480	Tom Seaver	30.00	15.00	9.00
481	Bill Melton	.80	.40	.25
482a	Jim Gosger (first name in white)	10.00	5.00	3.00
482b	Jim Gosger (first name in yellow)	.80	.40	.25
483	Ted Abernathy	.40	.20	.12
484	Joe Gordon	.50	.25	.15
485a	Gaylord Perry (last name in white)	35.00	17.50	10.50
485b	Gaylord Perry (last name in yellow)	5.00	2.50	1.50
486a	Paul Casanova (last name in white)	10.00	5.00	3.00
486b	Paul Casanova (last name in yellow)	.40	.20	.12
487	Denis Menke	.40	.20	.12
488	Joe Sparma	.40	.20	.12
489	Clete Boyer	.80	.40	.25
490	Matty Alou	1.00	.50	.30
491a	Twins Rookies (Jerry Crider, George Mitterwald) (names in white)	10.00	5.00	3.00
491b	Twins Rookies (Jerry Crider, George Mitterwald) (names in yellow)	.40	.20	.12
492	Tony Cloninger	.50	.25	.15
493a	Wes Parker (last name in white)	10.00	5.00	3.00
493b	Wes Parker (last name in yellow)	.70	.35	.20
494	Ken Berry	.40	.20	.12
495	Bert Campaneris	1.25	.60	.40
496	Larry Jaster	.40	.20	.12
497	Julian Javier	.40	.20	.12
498	Juan Pizarro	.40	.20	.12
499	Astros Rookies (Don Bryant, Steve Shea)	.40	.20	.12
500a	Mickey Mantle (last name in white)	275.00	125.00	70.00
500b	Mickey Mantle (last name in yellow)	125.00	55.00	30.00
501a	Tony Gonzalez (first name in white)	10.00	5.00	3.00
501b	Tony Gonzalez (first name in yellow)	.40	.20	.12
502	Minnie Rojas	.40	.20	.12
503	Larry Brown	.40	.20	.12
504	Checklist 513-588 (Brooks Robinson)	4.00	2.00	1.25
505a	Bobby Bolin (last name in white)	10.00	5.00	3.00

		NR MT	EX	VG
505b	Bobby Bolin (last name in yellow)	.40	.20	.12
506	Paul Blair	.50	.25	.15
507	Cookie Rojas	.40	.20	.12
508	Moe Drabowsky	.40	.20	.12
509	Manny Sanguillen	.50	.25	.15
510	Rod Carew	20.00	10.00	6.00
511a	Diego Segui (first name in white)	10.00	5.00	3.00
511b	Diego Segui (first name in yellow)	.80	.40	.25
512	Cleon Jones·	.80	.40	.25
513	Camilo Pascual	.80	.40	.25
514	Mike Lum	.50	.25	.15
515	Dick Green	.50	.25	.15
516	Earl Weaver	3.50	1.75	1.00
517	Mike McCormick	.60	.30	.20
518	Fred Whitfield	.50	.25	.15
519	Yankees Rookies (Len Boehmer, Gerry Kenney)	.80	.40	.25
520	Bob Veale	.60	.30	.20
521	George Thomas	.50	.25	.15
522	Joe Hoerner	.50	.25	.15
523	Bob Chance	.50	.25	.15
524	Expos Rookies (Jose Laboy, Floyd Wicker)	.50	.25	.15
525	Earl Wilson	.50	.25	.15
526	Hector Torres	.50	.25	.15
527	Al Lopez	3.00	1.50	.90
528	Claude Osteen	.80	.40	.25
529	Ed Kirkpatrick	.50	.25	.15
530	Cesar Tovar	.50	.25	.15
531	Dick Farrell	.50	.25	.15
532	Bird Hill Aces (Mike Cuellar, Jim Hardin, Dave McNally, Tom Phoebus)	1.50	.70	.45
533	Nolan Ryan	40.00	20.00	12.00
534	Jerry McNertney	.80	.40	.25
535	Phil Regan	.50	.25	.15
536	Padres Rookies (Danny Breeden, Dave Roberts)	.60	.30	.20
537	Mike Paul	.50	.25	.15
538	Charlie Smith	.50	.25	.15
539	Ted Shows How (Mike Epstein, Ted Williams)	3.25	1.75	1.00
540	Curt Flood	1.50	.70	.45
541	Joe Verbanic	.80	.40	.25
542	Bob Aspromonte	.50	.25	.15
543	Fred Newman	.50	.25	.15
544	Tigers Rookies (Mike Kilkenny, Ron Woods)	.50	.25	.15
545	Willie Stargell	7.00	3.50	2.00
546	Jim Nash	.50	.25	.15
547	Billy Martin	3.25	1.75	1.00
548	Bob Locker	.50	.25	.15
549	Ron Brand	.50	.25	.15
550	Brooks Robinson	9.00	4.50	2.75
551	Wayne Granger	.50	.25	.15
552	Dodgers Rookies (Ted Sizemore, Bill Sudakis)	.70	.35	.20
553	Ron Davis	.50	.25	.15
554	Frank Bertaina	.50	.25	.15
555	Jim Hart	.60	.30	.20
556	A's Stars (Sal Bando, Bert Campaneris, Danny Cater)	1.50	.70	.45
557	Frank Fernandez	.80	.40	.25
558	Tom Burgmeier	.60	.30	.20
559	Cards Rookies (Joe Hague, Jim Hicks)	.50	.25	.15
560	Luis Tiant	1.50	.70	.45
561	Ron Clark	.50	.25	.15
562	Bob Watson	1.00	.50	.30
563	Marty Pattin	.80	.40	.25
564	Gil Hodges	6.00	3.00	1.75
565	Hoyt Wilhelm	5.00	2.50	1.50
566	Ron Hansen	.50	.25	.15
567	Pirates Rookies (Elvio Jimenez, Jim Shellenback)	.50	.25	.15
568	Cecil Upshaw	.50	.25	.15
569	Billy Harris	.50	.25	.15
570	Ron Santo	1.75	.90	.50
571	Cap Peterson	.50	.25	.15
572	Giants Heroes (Juan Marichal, Willie McCovey)	6.00	3.00	1.75
573	Jim Palmer	10.00	5.00	3.00
574	George Scott	.80	.40	.25
575	Bill Singer	.60	.30	.20
576	Phillies Rookies (Ron Stone, Bill Wilson)	.50	.25	.15
577	Mike Hegan	.80	.40	.25
578	Don Bosch	.50	.25	.15
579	Dave Nelson	.60	.30	.20
580	Jim Northrup	.60	.30	.20
581	Gary Nolan	.50	.25	.15

		NR MT	EX	VG
582a	Checklist 589-664 (Tony Oliva) (red circle on back)	3.50	1.75	1.00
582b	Checklist 589-664 (Tony Oliva) (white circle on back)	2.50	1.25	.70
583	Clyde Wright	.70	.35	.20
584	Don Mason	.50	.25	.15
585	Ron Swoboda	.80	.40	.25
586	Tim Cullen	.50	.25	.15
587	Joe Rudi	1.75	.90	.50
588	Bill White	1.00	.50	.30
589	Joe Pepitone	2.00	1.00	.60
590	Rico Carty	1.00	.50	.30
591	Mike Hedlund	.50	.25	.15
592	Padres Rookies (Rafael Robles, Al Santorini)	.50	.25	.15
593	Don Nottebart	.50	.25	.15
594	Dooley Womack	.50	.25	.15
595	Lee Maye	.50	.25	.15
596	Chuck Hartenstein	.50	.25	.15
597	A.L. Rookies (Larry Burchart, Rollie Fingers, Bob Floyd)	12.00	6.00	3.50
598	Ruben Amaro	.50	.25	.15
599	John Boozer	.50	.25	.15
600	Tony Oliva	2.25	1.25	.70
601	Tug McGraw	2.00	1.00	.60
602	Cubs Rookies (Alec Distaso, Jim Qualls, Don Young)	.50	.25	.15
603	Joe Keough	.50	.25	.15
604	Bobby Etheridge	.50	.25	.15
605	Dick Ellsworth	.50	.25	.15
606	Gene Mauch	.80	.40	.25
607	Dick Bosman	.50	.25	.15
608	Dick Simpson	.80	.40	.25
609	Phil Gagliano	.50	.25	.15
610	Jim Hardin	.50	.25	.15
611	Braves Rookies (Bob Didier, Walt Hriniak, Gary Neibauer)	.50	.25	.15
612	Jack Aker	.80	.40	.25
613	Jim Beauchamp	.50	.25	.15
614	Astros Rookies (Tom Griffin, Skip Guinn)	.50	.25	.15
615	Len Gabrielson	.50	.25	.15
616	Don McMahon	.50	.25	.15
617	Jesse Gonder	.50	.25	.15
618	Ramon Webster	.50	.25	.15
619	Royals Rookies (Bill Butler, Pat Kelly, Juan Rios)	.60	.30	.20
620	Dean Chance	.60	.30	.20
621	Bill Voss	.50	.25	.15
622	Dan Osinski	.50	.25	.15
623	Hank Allen	.50	.25	.15
624	N.L. Rookies (Darrel Chaney, Duffy Dyer, Terry Harmon)	.70	.35	.20
625	Mack Jones	.50	.25	.15
626	Gene Michael	1.00	.50	.30
627	George Stone	.50	.25	.15
628	Red Sox Rookies (Bill Conigliaro, Syd O'Brien, Fred Wenz)	.70	.35	.20
629	Jack Hamilton	.50	.25	.15
630	Bobby Bonds	3.00	1.50	.90
631	John Kennedy	.80	.40	.25
632	Jon Warden	.50	.25	.15
633	Harry Walker	.60	.30	.20
634	Andy Etchebarren	.50	.25	.15
635	George Culver	.50	.25	.15
636	Woodie Held	.50	.25	.15
637	Padres Rookies (Jerry DaVanon, Clay Kirby, Frank Reberger)	.60	.30	.20
638	Ed Sprague	.50	.25	.15
639	Barry Moore	.50	.25	.15
640	Fergie Jenkins	3.50	1.75	1.00
641	N.L. Rookies (Bobby Darwin, Tommy Dean, John Miller)	.50	.25	.15
642	John Hiller	.60	.30	.20
643	Billy Cowan	.80	.40	.25
644	Chuck Hinton	.50	.25	.15
645	George Brunet	.50	.25	.15
646	Expos Rookies (Dan McGinn, Carl Morton)	.70	.35	.20
647	Dave Wickersham	.50	.25	.15
648	Bobby Wine	.50	.25	.15
649	Al Jackson	.70	.35	.20
650	Ted Williams	5.00	2.50	1.50
651	Gus Gil	.80	.40	.25
652	Eddie Watt	.50	.25	.15
653	Aurelio Rodriguez (photo actually Leonard Garcia, batboy)	1.25	.60	.40
654	White Sox Rookies (Carlos May, Rich Morales, Don Secrist)	.80	.40	.25
655	Mike Hershberger	.50	.25	.15
656	Dan Schneider	.50	.25	.15

		NR MT	EX	VG
657	Bobby Murcer	2.00	1.00	.60
658	A.L. Rookies (Bill Burbach, Tom Hall, Jim Miles)	.80	.40	.25
659	Johnny Podres	1.50	.70	.45
660	Reggie Smith	1.50	.70	.45
661	Jim Merritt	.50	.25	.15
662	Royals Rookies (Dick Drago, Bob Oliver, George Spriggs)	.60	.30	.20
663	Dick Radatz	.70	.30	.20
664	Ron Hunt	2.00	.35	.20

1969 Topps Decals

Designed as an insert for 1969 regular issue card packs, these decals were virtually identical in format to the '69 cards. The 48 decals in the set measure 1'' by 2½,'' although they are mounted on white paper backing which measures 1¾'' by 2⅛.''

		NR MT	EX	VG
Complete Set:		100.00	50.00	30.00
Common Player:		1.00	.50	.30
(1)	Hank Aaron	12.00	6.00	3.50
(2)	Richie Allen	2.50	1.25	.70
(3)	Felipe Alou	1.75	.90	.50
(4)	Matty Alou	1.75	.90	.50
(5)	Luis Aparicio	4.50	2.25	1.25
(6)	Bob Clemente	12.00	6.00	3.50
(7)	Donn Clendenon	1.00	.50	.30
(8)	Tommy Davis	1.75	.90	.50
(9)	Don Drysdale	6.00	3.00	1.75
(10)	Joe Foy	1.00	.50	.30
(11)	Jim Fregosi	1.75	.90	.50
(12)	Bob Gibson	6.00	3.00	1.75
(13)	Tony Gonzalez	1.00	.50	.30
(14)	Tom Haller	1.00	.50	.30
(15)	Ken Harrelson	1.75	.90	.50
(16)	Tommy Helms	1.00	.50	.30
(17)	Willie Horton	1.75	.90	.50
(18)	Frank Howard	2.50	1.25	.70
(19)	Reggie Jackson	20.00	10.00	6.00
(20)	Fergie Jenkins	3.50	1.75	1.00
(21)	Harmon Killebrew	6.00	3.00	1.75
(22)	Jerry Koosman	1.75	.90	.50
(23)	Mickey Mantle	35.00	17.50	10.50
(24)	Willie Mays	12.00	6.00	3.50
(25)	Tim McCarver	1.75	.90	.50
(26)	Willie McCovey	6.00	3.00	1.75
(27)	Sam McDowell	1.75	.90	.50
(28)	Denny McLain	1.75	.90	.50
(29)	Dave McNally	1.75	.90	.50
(30)	Don Mincher	1.00	.50	.30
(31)	Rick Monday	1.75	.90	.50
(32)	Tony Oliva	2.50	1.25	.70
(33)	Camilo Pascual	1.00	.50	.30
(34)	Rick Reichardt	1.00	.50	.30
(35)	Pete Rose	25.00	12.50	7.50
(36)	Frank Robinson	6.00	3.00	1.75
(37)	Ron Santo	1.75	.90	.50
(38)	Dick Selma	1.00	.50	.30
(39)	Tom Seaver	12.00	6.00	3.50
(40)	Chris Short	1.00	.50	.30
(41)	Rusty Staub	1.75	.90	.50
(42)	Mel Stottlemyre	1.75	.90	.50
(43)	Luis Tiant	1.75	.90	.50
(44)	Pete Ward	1.00	.50	.30
(45)	Hoyt Wilhelm	4.50	2.25	1.25
(46)	Maury Wills	2.50	1.25	.70

		NR MT	EX	VG
(47)	Jim Wynn	1.75	.90	.50
(48)	Carl Yastrzemski	15.00	7.50	4.50

1969 Topps Deckle

PETE ROSE
No. 21 of 33 photos

These 2¼'' by 3¼'' inch cards take their name from their interesting borders which have a scalloped effect. The fronts have a black and white picture of the player along with a blue facsimile autograph. Backs have the player's name and the card number in light blue ink in a small box at the bottom of the card. Technically, there are only 33 numbered cards, but there are actually 35 possible players; both Jim Wynn and Hoyt Wilhelm cards are found as #11 while cards of Joe Foy and Rusty Staub can be found as #22. Most of the players in the set are stars or at least above average.

		NR MT	EX	VG
Complete Set:		40.00	20.00	12.00
Common Player:		.30	.15	.09
1	Brooks Robinson	2.50	1.25	.70
2	Boog Powell	.50	.25	.15
3	Ken Harrelson	.40	.20	.12
4	Carl Yastrzemski	5.00	2.50	1.50
5	Jim Fregosi	.40	.20	.12
6	Luis Aparicio	1.25	.60	.40
7	Luis Tiant	.40	.20	.12
8	Denny McLain	.40	.20	.12
9	Willie Horton	.40	.20	.12
10	Bill Freehan	.40	.20	.12
11a	Hoyt Wilhelm	3.25	1.75	1.00
11b	Jim Wynn	5.00	2.50	1.50
12	Rod Carew	2.50	1.25	.70
13	Mel Stottlemyre	.40	.20	.12
14	Rick Monday	.40	.20	.12
15	Tommy Davis	.40	.20	.12
16	Frank Howard	.50	.25	.15
17	Felipe Alou	.40	.20	.12
18	Don Kessinger	.40	.20	.12
19	Ron Santo	.50	.25	.15
20	Tommy Helms	.30	.15	.09
21	Pete Rose	7.50	3.75	2.25
22a	Rusty Staub	2.25	1.25	.70
22b	Joe Foy	5.00	2.50	1.50
23	Tom Haller	.30	.15	.09
24	Maury Wills	.50	.25	.15
25	Jerry Koosman	.40	.20	.12
26	Richie Allen	.50	.25	.15
27	Bob Clemente	3.50	1.75	1.00
28	Curt Flood	.40	.20	.12
29	Bob Gibson	2.00	1.00	.60
30	Al Ferrara	.30	.15	.09
31	Willie McCovey	2.00	1.00	.60
32	Juan Marichal	2.00	1.00	.60
33	Willie Mays	4.00	2.00	1.25

1969 Topps 4-on-1
Mini Stickers

Another in the long line of Topps tests, the 4-on-1s are 2½'' by 3½'' cards with blank backs featuring a

quartet of miniature stickers in the design of the same cards from the 1969 Topps regular set. There are 25 different cards, for a total of 100 different stickers. As they are not common, Mint cards bring fairly strong prices on today's market. As the set was drawn from 3rd Series of the regular cards, it includes some rookie stickers and World Series highlight stickers.

		NR MT	EX	VG
Complete Set:		925.00	462.00	277.00
Common Player:		15.00	7.50	4.50
(1)	Jerry Adair, Willie Mays, Johnny Morris, Don Wilson	100.00	50.00	30.00
(2)	Tommie Aaron, Jim Britton, Donn Clendenon, Woody Woodward	15.00	7.50	4.50
(3)	World Series Game 4, Tommy Davis, Don Pavletich, Vada Pinson	20.00	10.00	6.00
(4)	Max Alvis, Glenn Beckert, Ron Fairly, Rick Wise	15.00	7.50	4.50
(5)	Johnny Callison, Jim French, Lum Harris, Dick Selma	15.00	7.50	4.50
(6)	World Series Game 3, Bob Gibson, Larry Haney, Rick Reichardt	40.00	20.00	12.00
(7)	Houston Rookie Stars, Wally Bunker, Don Cardwell, Joe Gibbon	15.00	7.50	4.50
(8)	Ollie Brown, Jim Bunning, Andy Kosco, Ron Reed	20.00	10.00	6.00
(9)	Bill Dillman, Jim Lefebvre, John Purdin, John Roseboro	15.00	7.50	4.50
(10)	Bill Hands, Chuck Harrison, Lindy McDaniel, Felix Millan	15.00	7.50	4.50
(11)	Jack Hiatt, Dave Johnson, Mel Nelson, Tommie Sisk	18.00	9.00	5.50
(12)	Clay Dalrymple, Leo Durocher, John Odom, Wilbur Wood	18.00	9.00	5.50
(13)	Hank Bauer, Kevin Collins, Ray Oyler, Russ Snyder	15.00	7.50	4.50
(14)	Red Sox Rookie Stars, World Series Game 7, Gerry Arrigo, Jim Perry	18.00	9.00	5.50
(15)	World Series Game 2, Bill McCool, Roberto Pena, Doug Rader	15.00	7.50	4.50
(16)	Ed Brinkman, Roy Face, Willie Horton, Bob Rodgers	18.00	9.00	5.50
(17)	Dave Baldwin, J.C. Martin, Dave May, Ray Sadecki	15.00	7.50	4.50
(18)	World Series Game 1, Jose Pagan, Tom Phoebus, Mike Shannon	15.00	7.50	4.50
(19)	Pete Rose, Lee Stange, Don Sutton, Ted Uhlaender	275.00	137.00	82.00
(20)	Joe Grzenda, Frank Howard, Dick Tracewski, Jim Weaver	20.00	10.00	6.00
(21)	White Sox Rookie Stars, Joe Azcue, Grant Jackson, Denny McLain	20.00	10.00	6.00
(22)	John Edwards, Jim Fairey, Phillies Rookies, Stan Williams	15.00	7.50	4.50
(23)	World Series Summary, John Bateman, Willie Smith, Leon Wagner	15.00	7.50	4.50
(24)	World Series Game 5, Yankees Rookies, Chris Cannizzaro, Bob Hendley	15.00	7.50	4.50
(25)	Cardinals Rookie Stars, Joe Nossek, Rico Petrocelli, Carl Yastrzemski	175.00	87.00	52.00

Definitions for grading conditions are located in the Introduction of this price guide.

1969 Topps Stamps

Topps continued to refine its efforts at baseball stamps in 1969, with the release of 240 player stamps each measuring 1'' by 1-7/16.'' Each stamp had a color photo along with the player's name, position and team. Unlike prior stamp issues, the 1969 stamps had 24 separate albums (one per team). The stamps were issued in strips of 12.

	NR MT	EX	VG
Complete Sheet Set:	110.00	55.00	33.00
Common Sheet:	1.25	.60	.40
Complete Stamp Album Set:	14.00	7.00	4.25
Single Stamp Album:	.50	.25	.15

(1) Tommie Agee, Sandy Alomar, Jose Cardenal, Dean Chance, Joe Foy, Jim Grant, Don Kessinger, Mickey Mantle, Jerry May, Bob Rodgers, Cookie Rojas, Gary Sutherland 18.00 9.00 5.50
(2) Jesus Alou, Mike Andrews, Larry Brown, Moe Drabowsky, Alex Johnson, Lew Krausse, Jim Lefebvre, Dal Maxvill, John Odom, Claude Osteen, Rick Reichardt, Luis Tiant 1.50 .70 .45
(3) Hank Aaron, Matty Alou, Max Alvis, Nelson Briles, Eddie Fisher, Bud Harrelson, Willie Horton, Randy Hundley, Larry Jaster, Jim Kaat, Gary Peters, Pete Ward 7.00 3.50 2.00
(4) Don Buford, John Callison, Tommy Davis, Jackie Hernandez, Fergie Jenkins, Lee May, Denny McLain, Bob Oliver, Roberto Pena, Tony Perez, Joe Torre, Tom Tresh 3.00 1.50 .90
(5) Jim Bunning, Dean Chance, Joe Foy, Sonny Jackson, Don Kessinger, Rick Monday, Gaylord Perry, Roger Repoz, Cookie Rojas, Mel Stottlemyre, Leon Wagner, Jim Wynn 3.00 1.50 .90
(6) Felipe Alou, Gerry Arrigo, Bob Aspromonte, Gary Bell, Clay Dalrymple, Jim Fregosi, Tony Gonzalez, Duane Josephson, Dick McAuliffe, Tony Oliva, Brooks Robinson, Willie Stargell 6.00 3.00 1.75
(7) Steve Barber, Donn Clendenon, Joe Coleman, Vic Davalillo, Russ Gibson, Jerry Grote, Tom Haller, Andy Kosco, Willie McCovey, Don Mincher, Joe Morgan, Don Wilson 4.00 2.00 1.25
(8) George Brunet, Don Buford, John Callison, Danny Cater, Tommy Davis, Willie Davis, John Edwards, Jim Hart, Mickey Lolich, Willie Mays, Roberto Pena, Mickey Stanley 7.00 3.50 2.00
(9) Ernie Banks, Glenn Beckert, Ken Berry, Horace Clarke, Bob Clemente, Larry Dierker, Len Gabrielson, Jake Gibbs, Jerry Koosman, Sam McDowell, Tom Satriano, Bill Singer 3.50 1.75 1.00
(10) Gene Alley, Lou Brock, Larry Brown, Moe Drabowsky, Frank Howard, Tommie John, Roger Nelson, Claude Osteen, Phil Regan, Rick Reichardt, Tony Taylor, Roy White 4.00 2.00 1.25
(11) Bob Allison, John Bateman, Don Drysdale, Dave Johnson, Harmon Killebrew, Jim Maloney, Bill Mazeroski, Gerry McNertney, Ron Perranoski, Rico Petrocelli, Pete Rose, Billy Williams 18.00 9.00 5.50

	NR MT	EX	VG

(12) Bernie Allen, Jose Arcia, Stan Bahnsen, Sal Bando, Jim Davenport, Tito Francona, Dick Green, Ron Hunt, Mack Jones, Vada Pinson, George Scott, Don Wert 1.50 .70 .45
(13) Gerry Arrigo, Bob Aspromonte, Joe Azcue, Curt Blefary, Orlando Cepeda, Bill Freehan, Jim Fregosi, Dave Giusti, Duane Josephson, Tim McCarver, Jose Santiago, Bob Tolan 2.00 1.00 .60
(14) Jerry Adair, Johnny Bench, Clete Boyer, John Briggs, Bert Campaneris, Woody Fryman, Ron Kline, Bobby Knoop, Ken McMullen, Adolfo Phillips, John Roseboro, Tom Seaver 7.00 3.50 2.00
(15) Norm Cash, Ron Fairly, Bob Gibson, Bill Hands, Cleon Jones, Al Kaline, Paul Schaal, Mike Shannon, Duke Sims, Reggie Smith, Steve Whitaker, Carl Yastrzemski 12.00 6.00 3.50
(16) Steve Barber, Paul Casanova, Dick Dietz, Russ Gibson, Jerry Grote, Tom Haller, Ed Kranepool, Juan Marichal, Denis Menke, Jim Nash, Bill Robinson, Frank Robinson 4.00 2.00 1.25
(17) Bobby Bolin, Ollie Brown, Rod Carew, Mike Epstein, Bud Harrelson, Larry Jaster, Dave McNally, Willie Norton, Milt Pappas, Gary Peters, Paul Popovich, Stan Williams 6.00 3.00 1.75
(18) Ted Abernathy, Bob Allison, Ed Brinkman, Don Drysdale, Jim Hardin, Julian Javier, Hal Lanier, Jim McGlothlin, Ron Perranoski, Rich Rollins, Ron Santo, Billy Williams 3.00 1.50 .90
(19) Richie Allen, Luis Aparicio, Wally Bunker, Curt Flood, Ken Harrelson, Jim Hunter, Denver Lemaster, Felix Millan, Jim Northrop (Northrup), Art Shamsky, Larry Stahl, Ted Uhlaender 3.00 1.50 .90
(20) Bob Bailey, Johnny Bench, Woody Fryman, Jim Hannan, Ron Kline, Al McBean, Camilo Pascual, Joe Pepitone, Doug Rader, Ron Reed, John Roseboro, Sonny Siebert 3.00 1.50 .90
(21) Jack Aker, Tommy Harper, Tommy Helms, Dennis Higgins, Jim Hunter, Don Lock, Lee Maye, Felix Millan, Jim Northrop (Northrup), Larry Stahl, Don Sutton, Zoilo Versalles 3.00 1.50 .90
(22) Norm Cash, Ed Charles, Joe Horlen, Pat Jarvis, Jim Lonborg, Manny Mota, Boog Powell, Dick Selma, Mike Shannon, Duke Sims, Steve Whitaker, Hoyt Wilhelm 3.00 1.50 .90
(23) Bernie Allen, Ray Culp, Al Ferrara, Tito Francona, Dick Green, Ron Hunt, Ray Oyler, Tom Phoebus, Rusty Staub, Bob Veale, Maury Wills, Wilbur Wood 2.00 1.00 .60
(24) Ernie Banks, Mark Belanger, Steve Blass, Horace Clarke, Bob Clemente, Larry Dierker, Dave Duncan, Chico Salmon, Chris Short, Ron Swoboda, Cesar Tovar, Rick Wise 3.50 1.75 1.00

1969 Topps Supers

These 2¼'' by 3¼'' cards were not the bigger ''Super'' cards which would be seen in following years. Rather, what enabled Topps to dub them ''Super Baseball Cards'' was their high-gloss finish which enhanced the bright color photograph used on their fronts. The only other design element on the front was a facsimile autograph. The backs contained a box at the bottom which carried the player's name, team, position, a copyright line and the card number. Another unusual feature was that the cards had rounded corners. The 66-card set saw limited production meaning supplies are tight today. Considering the quality of the cards and the fact that many big names are represented, it's easy to understand why the set is quite expensive and desirable.

		NR MT	EX	VG
Complete Set:		3200.00	1600.00	960.00
Common Player:		9.00	5.85	2.95
1	Dave McNally	15.00	9.75	5.75
2	Frank Robinson	80.00	52.00	31.00
3	Brooks Robinson	100.00	65.00	39.00
4	Ken Harrelson	15.00	9.75	5.75
5	Carl Yastrzemski	250.00	162.00	97.00
6	Ray Culp	9.00	5.75	3.50
7	James Fregosi	12.00	7.75	4.75
8	Rick Reichardt	9.00	5.75	3.50
9	V. Davalillo	9.00	5.75	3.50
10	Luis Aparicio	35.00	19.50	11.50
11	Pete Ward	9.00	5.75	3.50
12	Joe Horlen	9.00	5.75	3.50
13	Luis Tiant	15.00	9.75	5.75
14	Sam McDowell	12.00	7.75	4.75
15	Jose Cardenal	9.00	5.75	3.50
16	Willie Horton	12.00	7.75	4.75
17	Denny McLain	15.00	9.75	5.75
18	Bill Freehan	12.00	7.75	4.75
19	Harmon Killebrew	60.00	39.00	23.00
20	Tony Oliva	20.00	13.00	7.75
21	Dean Chance	9.00	5.75	3.50
22	Joe Foy	9.00	5.75	3.50
23	Roger Nelson	9.00	5.75	3.50
24	Mickey Mantle	600.00	292.00	175.00
25	Mel Stottlemyre	12.00	7.75	4.75
26	Roy White	12.00	7.75	4.75
27	Rick Monday	12.00	7.75	4.75
28	Reginald Jackson	350.00	179.00	107.00
29	Dagoberto Campaneris	12.00	7.75	4.75
30	Frank Howard	20.00	13.00	7.75
31	Camilo Pascual	12.00	7.75	4.75
32	Tommy Davis	15.00	9.75	5.75
33	Don Mincher	9.00	5.75	3.50
34	Henry Aaron	200.00	130.00	78.00
35	Felipe Rojas Alou	12.00	7.75	4.75
36	Joseph Torre	15.00	9.75	5.75
37	Fergie Jenkins	15.00	9.75	5.75
38	Ronald Santo	15.00	9.75	5.75
39	Billy Williams	40.00	23.00	14.00
40	Tommy Helms	9.00	5.75	3.50
41	Pete Rose	450.00	292.00	175.00
42	Joe Morgan	35.00	19.50	11.50
43	Jim Wynn	12.00	7.75	4.75
44	Curt Blefary	9.00	5.75	3.50
45	Willie Davis	12.00	7.75	4.75
46	Donald Drysdale	50.00	26.00	15.50
47	Tom Haller	9.00	5.75	3.50
48	Rusty Staub	20.00	13.00	7.75
49	Maurice Wills	20.00	13.00	7.75
50	Cleon Jones	9.00	5.75	3.50
51	Jerry Koosman	15.00	9.75	5.75
52	Tom Seaver	125.00	65.00	39.00
53	Rich Allen	15.00	9.75	5.75
54	Chris Short	9.00	5.75	3.50
55	Cookie Rojas	9.00	5.75	3.50
56	Mateo Alou	12.00	7.75	4.75
57	Steve Blass	9.00	5.75	3.50
58	Roberto Clemente	200.00	97.00	58.00
59	Curt Flood	15.00	9.75	5.75
60	Robert Gibson	50.00	32.00	19.00
61	Tim McCarver	15.00	9.75	5.75
62	Dick Selma	9.00	5.75	3.50
63	Ollie Brown	9.00	5.75	3.50
64	Juan Marichal	50.00	26.00	15.50
65	Willie Mays	200.00	130.00	78.00
66	Willie McCovey	60.00	39.00	23.00

1969 Topps Team Posters

Picking up where the 1968 posters left off, the 1969 poster was larger at about 12" by 20." The posters, 24 in number like the previous year, were very differ-

ent in style. Each has a team focus with a large pennant carrying the team name, along with nine or ten photos of players. Each of the photos carries a name and a facsimile autograph. Unfortunately, the bigger size of 1969 posters meant they had to be folded to fit in their packages as was the case in 1968. That means that collectors today will have a tough job finding them without fairly heavy creases from the folding.

		NR MT	EX	VG
Complete Set:		750.00	375.00	225.00
Common Poster:		20.00	10.00	6.00
1	Detroit Tigers (Norm Cash, Bill Freehan, Willie Horton, Al Kaline, Mickey Lolich, Dick McAuliffe, Denny McLain, Jim Northrup, Mickey Stanley, Don Wert, Earl Wilson)	40.00	20.00	12.00
2	Atlanta Braves (Hank Aaron, Felipe Alou, Clete Boyer, Rico Carty, Tito Francona, Sonny Jackson, Pat Jarvis, Felix Millan, Phil Niekro, Milt Pappas, Joe Torre)	40.00	20.00	12.00
3	Boston Red Sox (Mike Andrews, Tony Conigliaro, Ray Culp, Russ Gibson, Ken Harrelson, Jim Lonborg, Rico Petrocelli, Jose Santiago, George Scott, Reggie Smith, Carl Yastrzemski)	60.00	30.00	18.00
4	Chicago Cubs (Ernie Banks, Glenn Beckert, Bill Hands, Jim Hickman, Ken Holtzman, Randy Hundley, Fergie Jenkins, Don Kessinger, Adolfo Phillips, Ron Santo, Billy Williams)	30.00	15.00	9.00
5	Baltimore Orioles (Mark Belanger, Paul Blair, Don Buford, Andy Etchebarren, Jim Hardin, Dave Johnson, Tom McNally, Tom Phoebus, Boog Powell, Brooks Robinson, Frank Robinson)	50.00	25.00	15.00
6	Houston Astros (Curt Blefary, Donn Clendenon, Larry Dierker, John Edwards, Denny Lemaster, Denis Menke, Norm Miller, Joe Morgan, Doug Rader, Don Wilson, Jim Wynn)	20.00	10.00	6.00
7	Kansas City Royals (Jerry Adair, Wally Bunker, Mike Fiore, Joe Foy, Jackie Hernandez, Pat Kelly, Dave Morehead, Roger Nelson, Dave Nicholson, Eliseo Rodriguez, Steve Whitaker)	20.00	10.00	6.00
8	Philadelphia Phillies (Richie Allen, Johnny Callison, Woody Fryman, Larry Hisle, Don Money, Cookie Rojas, Mike Ryan, Chris Short, Tony Taylor, Bill White, Rick Wise)	20.00	10.00	6.00
9	Seattle Pilots (Jack Aker, Steve Barber, Gary Bell, Tommy Davis, Jim Gosger, Tommy Harper, Gerry McNertney, Don Mincher, Ray Oyler, Rich Rollins, Chico Salmon)	30.00	15.00	9.00
10	Montreal Expos (Bob Bailey, John Bateman, Jack Billingham, Jim Grant, Larry Jaster, Jim Laboy, Manny Mota, Rusty Staub, Gary Sutherland, Jim Williams, Maury Wills)	20.00	10.00	6.00
11	Chicago White Sox (Sandy Alomar, Luis Aparicio, Ken Berry, Buddy Bradford, Joe Horlen, Tommy John, Duane Josephson, Tom McCraw, Bill Melton, Pete Ward, Wilbur Wood)	20.00	10.00	6.00

		NR MT	EX	VG
12	San Diego Padres (Jose Arcia, Danny Breeden, Ollie Brown, Bill Davis, Ron Davis, Tony Gonzalez, Dick Kelley, Al McBean, Roberto Pena, Dick Selma, Ed Spiezio)	20.00	10.00	6.00
13	Cleveland Indians (Max Alvis, Joe Azcue, Jose Cardenal, Vern Fuller, Lou Johnson, Sam McDowell, Sonny Siebert, Duke Sims, Russ Snyder, Luis Tiant, Zoilo Versalles)	20.00	10.00	6.00
14	San Francisco Giants (Bobby Bolin, Jim Davenport, Dick Dietz, Jim Hart, Ron Hunt, Hal Lanier, Juan Marichal, Willie Mays, Willie McCovey, Gaylord Perry, Charlie Smith)	40.00	20.00	12.00
15	Minnesota Twins (Bob Allison, Chico Cardenas, Rod Carew, Dean Chance, Jim Kaat, Harmon Killebrew, Tony Oliva, Jim Perry, John Roseboro, Cesar Tovar, Ted Uhlaender)	40.00	20.00	12.00
16	Pittsburgh Pirates (Gene Alley, Matty Alou, Steve Blass, Jim Bunning, Bob Clemente, Rich Hebner, Jerry May, Bill Mazeroski, Bob Robertson, Willie Stargell, Bob Veale)	40.00	20.00	12.00
17	California Angels (Ruben Amaro, George Brunet, Bob Chance, Vic Davalillo, Jim Fregosi, Bobby Knoop, Jim McGlothlin, Rick Reichardt, Roger Repoz, Bob Rodgers, Hoyt Wilhelm)	25.00	12.50	7.50
18	St. Louis Cardinals (Nelson Briles, Lou Brock, Orlando Cepeda, Curt Flood, Bob Gibson, Julian Javier, Dal Maxvill, Tim McCarver, Vada Pinson, Mike Shannon, Ray Washburn)	30.00	15.00	9.00
19	New York Yankees (Stan Bahnsen, Horace Clarke, Bobby Cox, Jake Gibbs, Mickey Mantle, Joe Pepitone, Fritz Peterson, Bill Robinson, Mel Stottlemyre, Tom Tresh, Roy White)	90.00	45.00	27.00
20	Cincinnati Reds (Gerry Arrigo, Johnny Bench, Tommy Helms, Alex Johnson, Jim Maloney, Lee May, Gary Nolan, Tony Perez, Pete Rose, Bob Tolan, Woody Woodward)	75.00	37.00	22.00
21	Oakland Athletics (Sal Bando, Bert Campaneris, Danny Cater, Dick Green, Mike Hershberger, Jim Hunter, Reggie Jackson, Rick Monday, Jim Nash, John Odom, Jim Pagliaroni)	60.00	30.00	18.00
22	Los Angeles Dodgers (Willie Crawford, Willie Davis, Don Drysdale, Ron Fairly, Tom Haller, Andy Kosco, Jim Lefebvre, Claude Osteen, Paul Popovich, Bill Singer, Bill Sudakis)	30.00	15.00	9.00
23	Washington Senators (Bernie Allen, Brant Alyea, Ed Brinkman, Paul Casanova, Joe Coleman, Mike Epstein, Jim Hannan, Frank Howard, Ken McMullen, Camilo Pascual, Del Unser)	20.00	10.00	6.00
24	New York Mets (Tommie Agee, Ken Boswell, Ed Charles, Jerry Grote, Bud Harrelson, Cleon Jones, Jerry Koosman, Ed Kranepool, Jim McAndrew, Tom Seaver, Ron Swoboda)	60.00	30.00	18.00

1970 Topps

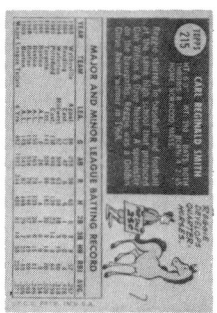

Topps established another set size record by coming out with 720 cards in 1970. The 2½'' by 3½''

Reggie Smith — OUTFIELD

cards had a color photo with a thin white frame. The photo had the player's team overprinted at the top, while the player's name in script and his position were at the bottom. A gray border then surrounded the front. Card back followed the normal design pattern, although they were more readable then some issues of the past. Team cards returned and were joined with many of the usual specialty cards. The World Series highlights were joined by cards with Play-off highlights. Statistical leaders and All-Stars are also included in the set. High number cards provide the most expensive cards in the set.

		NR MT	EX	VG
Complete Set:		900.00	325.00	180.00
Common Player: 1-546		.30	.15	.09
Common Player: 547-633		.50	.25	.15
Common Player: 634-720		1.25	.60	.40
1	World Champions (Mets Team)	5.00	1.25	.70
2	Diego Segui	.60	.25	.15
3	Darrel Chaney	.30	.15	.09
4	Tom Egan	.30	.15	.09
5	Wes Parker	.40	.20	.12
6	Grant Jackson	.30	.15	.09
7	Indians Rookies (Gary Boyd, Russ Nagelson)	.30	.15	.09
8	Jose Martinez	.30	.15	.09
9	Checklist 1-132	2.50	1.25	.70
10	Carl Yastrzemski	18.00	9.00	5.50
11	Nate Colbert	.30	.15	.09
12	John Hiller	.40	.20	.12
13	Jack Hiatt	.30	.15	.09
14	Hank Allen	.30	.15	.09
15	Larry Dierker	.40	.20	.12
16	Charlie Metro	.30	.15	.09
17	Hoyt Wilhelm	3.50	1.75	1.00
18	Carlos May	.50	.25	.15
19	John Boccabella	.30	.15	.09
20	Dave McNally	.60	.30	.20
21	Athletics Rookies (Vida Blue, Gene Tenace)	2.00	1.00	.60
22	Ray Washburn	.30	.15	.09
23	Bill Robinson	.50	.25	.15
24	Dick Selma	.30	.15	.09
25	Cesar Tovar	.30	.15	.09
26	Tug McGraw	1.25	.60	.40
27	Chuck Hinton	.30	.15	.09
28	Billy Wilson	.30	.15	.09
29	Sandy Alomar	.30	.15	.09
30	Matty Alou	.80	.40	.25
31	Marty Pattin	.50	.25	.15
32	Harry Walker	.40	.20	.12
33	Don Wert	.30	.15	.09
34	Willie Crawford	.30	.15	.09
35	Joe Horlen	.30	.15	.09
36	Reds Rookies (Danny Breeden, Bernie Carbo)	.50	.25	.15
37	Dick Drago	.30	.15	.09
38	Mack Jones	.30	.15	.09
39	Mike Nagy	.30	.15	.09
40	Rich Allen	1.50	.70	.45
41	George Lauzerique	.30	.15	.09
42	Tito Fuentes	.30	.15	.09
43	Jack Aker	.50	.25	.15
44	Roberto Pena	.30	.15	.09
45	Dave Johnson	1.00	.50	.30
46	Ken Rudolph	.30	.15	.09
47	Bob Miller	.30	.15	.09
48	Gill Garrido (Gil)	.30	.15	.09
49	Tim Cullen	.30	.15	.09
50	Tommie Agee	.40	.20	.12
51	Bob Christian	.30	.15	.09
52	Bruce Dal Canton	.30	.15	.09
53	John Kennedy	.50	.25	.15
54	Jeff Torborg	.40	.20	.12
55	John Odom	.40	.20	.12
56	Phillies Rookies (Joe Lis, Scott Reid)	.30	.15	.09
57	Pat Kelly	.30	.15	.09
58	Dave Marshall	.30	.15	.09
59	Dick Ellsworth	.30	.15	.09
60	Jim Wynn	.60	.30	.20
61	N.L. Batting Leaders (Bob Clemente, Cleon Jones, Pete Rose)	3.50	1.75	1.00
62	A.L. Batting Leaders (Rod Carew, Tony Oliva, Reggie Smith)	2.50	1.25	.70
63	N.L. RBI Leaders (Willie McCovey, Tony Perez, Ron Santo)	2.50	1.25	.70

		NR MT	EX	VG
64	A.L. RBI Leaders (Reggie Jackson, Harmon Killebrew, Boog Powell)	2.50	1.25	.70
65	N.L. Home Run Leaders (Hank Aaron, Lee May, Willie McCovey)	3.00	1.50	.90
66	A.L. Home Run Leaders (Frank Howard, Reggie Jackson, Harmon Killebrew)	2.50	1.25	.70
67	N.L. ERA Leaders (Steve Carlton, Bob Gibson, Juan Marichal)	3.00	1.50	.90
68	A.L. ERA Leaders (Dick Bosman, Mike Cuellar, Jim Palmer)	2.00	1.00	.60
69	N.L. Pitching Leaders (Fergie Jenkins, Juan Marichal, Phil Niekro, Tom Seaver)	2.50	1.25	.70
70	A.L. Pitching Leaders (Dave Boswell, Mike Cuellar, Dennis McLain, Dave McNally, Jim Perry, Mel Stottlemyre)	2.00	1.00	.60
71	N.L. Strikeout Leaders (Bob Gibson, Fergie Jenkins, Bill Singer)	2.50	1.25	.70
72	A.L. Strikeout Leaders (Mickey Lolich, Sam McDowell, Andy Messersmith)	2.00	1.00	.60
73	Wayne Granger	.30	.15	.09
74	Angels Rookies (Greg Washburn, Wally Wolf)	.30	.15	.09
75	Jim Kaat	2.25	1.25	.70
76	Carl Taylor	.30	.15	.09
77	Frank Linzy	.30	.15	.09
78	Joe Lahoud	.30	.15	.09
79	Clay Kirby	.30	.15	.09
80	Don Kessinger	.40	.20	.12
81	Dave May	.30	.15	.09
82	Frank Fernandez	.50	.25	.15
83	Don Cardwell	.30	.15	.09
84	Paul Casanova	.30	.15	.09
85	Max Alvis	.30	.15	.09
86	Lum Harris	.30	.15	.09
87	Steve Renko	.30	.15	.09
88	Pilots Rookies (Dick Baney, Miguel Fuentes)	.50	.25	.15
89	Juan Rios	.30	.15	.09
90	Tim McCarver	1.00	.50	.30
91	Rich Morales	.30	.15	.09
92	George Culver	.30	.15	.09
93	Rick Renick	.30	.15	.09
94	Fred Patek	.40	.20	.12
95	Earl Wilson	.30	.15	.09
96	Cards Rookies (Leron Lee, Jerry Reuss)	2.00	1.00	.60
97	Joe Moeller	.30	.15	.09
98	Gates Brown	.30	.15	.09
99	Bobby Pfeil	.30	.15	.09
100	Mel Stottlemyre	1.00	.50	.30
101	Bobby Floyd	.30	.15	.09
102	Joe Rudi	.80	.40	.25
103	Frank Reberger	.30	.15	.09
104	Gerry Moses	.30	.15	.09
105	Tony Gonzalez	.30	.15	.09
106	Darold Knowles	.30	.15	.09
107	Bobby Etheridge	.30	.15	.09
108	Tom Burgmeier	.40	.20	.12
109	Expos Rookies (Garry Jestadt, Carl Morton)	.40	.20	.12
110	Bob Moose	.30	.15	.09
111	Mike Hegan	.50	.25	.15
112	Dave Nelson	.30	.15	.09
113	Jim Ray	.30	.15	.09
114	Gene Michael	.60	.30	.20
115	Alex Johnson	.40	.20	.12
116	Sparky Lyle	1.00	.50	.30
117	Don Young	.30	.15	.09
118	George Mitterwald	.30	.15	.09
119	Chuck Taylor	.30	.15	.09
120	Sal Bando	.80	.40	.25
121	Orioles Rookies (Fred Beene, Terry Crowley)	.40	.20	.12
122	George Stone	.30	.15	.09
123	Don Gutteridge	.30	.15	.09
124	Larry Jaster	.30	.15	.09
125	Deron Johnson	.30	.15	.09
126	Marty Martinez	.30	.15	.09
127	Joe Coleman	.40	.20	.12
128a	Checklist 133-263 (226 is R Perranoski)	3.00	1.50	.90
128b	Checklist 133-263 (226 is R. Perranoski)	2.50	1.25	.70
129	Jimmie Price	.30	.15	.09
130	Ollie Brown	.30	.15	.09
131	Dodgers Rookies (Ray Lamb, Bob Stinson)	.30	.15	.09
132	Jim McGlothlin	.30	.15	.09
133	Clay Carroll	.40	.20	.12
134	Danny Walton	.50	.25	.15
135	Dick Dietz	.30	.15	.09
136	Steve Hargan	.30	.15	.09
137	Art Shamsky	.30	.15	.09
138	Joe Foy	.30	.15	.09
139	Rich Nye	.30	.15	.09
140	Reggie Jackson	30.00	15.00	9.00
141	Pirates Rookies (Dave Cash, Johnny Jeter)	.50	.25	.15
142	Fritz Peterson	.50	.25	.15
143	Phil Gagliano	.30	.15	.09
144	Ray Culp	.30	.15	.09
145	Rico Carty	.80	.40	.25
146	Danny Murphy	.30	.15	.09
147	Angel Hermoso	.30	.15	.09
148	Earl Weaver	1.25	.60	.40
149	Billy Champion	.30	.15	.09
150	Harmon Killebrew	5.00	2.50	1.50
151	Dave Roberts	.30	.15	.09
152	Ike Brown	.30	.15	.09
153	Gary Gentry	.30	.15	.09
154	Senators Rookies (Jan Dukes, Jim Miles)	.30	.15	.09
155	Denis Menke	.30	.15	.09
156	Eddie Fisher	.30	.15	.09
157	Manny Mota	.50	.25	.15
158	Jerry McNertney	.50	.25	.15
159	Tommy Helms	.40	.20	.12
160	Phil Niekro	3.50	1.75	1.00
161	Richie Scheinblum	.30	.15	.09
162	Jerry Johnson	.30	.15	.09
163	Syd O'Brien	.30	.15	.09
164	Ty Cline	.30	.15	.09
165	Ed Kirkpatrick	.30	.15	.09
166	Al Oliver	2.50	1.25	.70
167	Bill Burbach	.50	.25	.15
168	Dave Watkins	.30	.15	.09
169	Tom Hall	.30	.15	.09
170	Billy Williams	4.00	2.00	1.25
171	Jim Nash	.30	.15	.09
172	Braves Rookies (Ralph Garr, Garry Hill)	1.00	.50	.30
173	Jim Hicks	.30	.15	.09
174	Ted Sizemore	.30	.15	.09
175	Dick Bosman	.30	.15	.09
176	Jim Hart	.40	.20	.12
177	Jim Northrup	.40	.20	.12
178	Denny Lemaster	.30	.15	.09
179	Ivan Murrell	.30	.15	.09
180	Tommy John	2.50	1.25	.70
181	Sparky Anderson	1.25	.60	.40
182	Dick Hall	.30	.15	.09
183	Jerry Grote	.40	.20	.12
184	Ray Fosse	.40	.20	.12
185	Don Mincher	.50	.25	.15
186	Rick Joseph	.30	.15	.09
187	Mike Hedlund	.30	.15	.09
188	Manny Sanguillen	.40	.20	.12
189	Yankees Rookies (Dave McDonald, Thurman Munson)	30.00	15.00	9.00
190	Joe Torre	1.25	.60	.40
191	Vicente Romo	.30	.15	.09
192	Jim Qualls	.30	.15	.09
193	Mike Wegener	.30	.15	.09
194	Chuck Manuel	.30	.15	.09
195	N.L. Playoff Game 1 (Seaver Wins Opener!)	3.00	1.50	.90
196	N.L. Playoff Game 2 (Mets Show Muscle!)	1.75	.90	.50
197	N.L. Playoff Game 3 (Ryan Saves The Day!)	3.00	1.50	.90
198	N.L. Playoffs Summary (We're Number One!)	1.75	.90	.50
199	A.L. Playoff Game 1 (Orioles Win A Squeaker!)	1.50	.70	.45
200	A.L. Playoff Game 2 (Powell Scores Winning Run!)	1.75	.90	.50
201	A.L. Playoff Game 3 (Birds Wrap It Up!)	1.50	.70	.45
202	A.L. Playoffs Summary (Sweep Twins In Three!)	1.50	.70	.45
203	Rudy May	.40	.20	.12
204	Len Gabrielson	.30	.15	.09
205	Bert Campaneris	.80	.40	.25
206	Clete Boyer	.40	.20	.12
207	Tigers Rookies (Norman McRae, Bob Reed)	.30	.15	.09
208	Fred Gladding	.30	.15	.09
209	Ken Suarez	.30	.15	.09
210	Juan Marichal	4.50	2.25	1.25
211	Ted Williams	5.00	2.50	1.50
212	Al Santorini	.30	.15	.09

		NR MT	EX	VG
213	Andy Etchebarren	.30	.15	.09
214	Ken Boswell	.30	.15	.09
215	Reggie Smith	.60	.30	.20
216	Chuck Hartenstein	.30	.15	.09
217	Ron Hansen	.30	.15	.09
218	Ron Stone	.30	.15	.09
219	Jerry Kenney	.50	.25	.15
220	Steve Carlton	12.00	6.00	3.50
221	Ron Brand	.30	.15	.09
222	Jim Rooker	.30	.15	.09
223	Nate Oliver	.30	.15	.09
224	Steve Barber	.50	.25	.15
225	Lee May	.60	.30	.20
226	Ron Perranoski	.40	.20	.12
227	Astros Rookies (John Mayberry, Bob Watkins)	1.00	.50	.30
228	Aurelio Rodriguez	.40	.20	.12
229	Rich Robertson	.30	.15	.09
230	Brooks Robinson	6.50	3.25	2.00
231	Luis Tiant	1.25	.60	.40
232	Bob Didier	.30	.15	.09
233	Lew Krausse	.30	.15	.09
234	Tommy Dean	.30	.15	.09
235	Mike Epstein	.40	.20	.12
236	Bob Veale	.40	.20	.12
237	Russ Gibson	.30	.15	.09
238	Jose Laboy	.30	.15	.09
239	Ken Berry	.30	.15	.09
240	Fergie Jenkins	2.50	1.25	.70
241	Royals Rookies (Al Fitzmorris, Scott Northey)	.30	.15	.09
242	Walter Alston	1.75	.90	.50
243	Joe Sparma	.30	.15	.09
244a	Checklist 264-372 (red bat on front)	3.00	1.50	.90
244b	Checklist 264-372 (brown bat on front)	2.50	1.25	.70
245	Leo Cardenas	.30	.15	.09
246	Jim McAndrew	.30	.15	.09
247	Lou Klimchock	.30	.15	.09
248	Jesus Alou	.40	.20	.12
249	Bob Locker	.50	.25	.15
250	Willie McCovey	5.50	2.75	1.75
251	Dick Schofield	.30	.15	.09
252	Lowell Palmer	.30	.15	.09
253	Ron Woods	.50	.25	.15
254	Camilo Pascual	.50	.25	.15
255	Jim Spencer	.50	.25	.15
256	Vic Davalillo	.40	.20	.12
257	Dennis Higgins	.30	.15	.09
258	Paul Popovich	.30	.15	.09
259	Tommie Reynolds	.30	.15	.09
260	Claude Osteen	.50	.25	.15
261	Curt Motton	.30	.15	.09
262	Padres Rookies (Jerry Morales, Jim Williams)	.30	.15	.09
263	Duane Josephson	.30	.15	.09
264	Rich Hebner	.40	.20	.12
265	Randy Hundley	.30	.15	.09
266	Wally Bunker	.30	.15	.09
267	Twins Rookies (Herman Hill, Paul Ratliff)	.30	.15	.09
268	Claude Raymond	.30	.15	.09
269	Cesar Gutierrez	.30	.15	.09
270	Chris Short	.40	.20	.12
271	Greg Goossen	.50	.25	.15
272	Hector Torres	.30	.15	.09
273	Ralph Houk	1.00	.50	.30
274	Gerry Arrigo	.30	.15	.09
275	Duke Sims	.30	.15	.09
276	Ron Hunt	.40	.20	.12
277	Paul Doyle	.30	.15	.09
278	Tommie Aaron	.50	.25	.15
279	Bill Lee	.50	.25	.15
280	Donn Clendenon	.40	.20	.12
281	Casey Cox	.30	.15	.09
282	Steve Huntz	.30	.15	.09
283	Angel Bravo	.30	.15	.09
284	Jack Baldschun	.30	.15	.09
285	Paul Blair	.40	.20	.12
286	Dodgers Rookies (Bill Buckner, Jack Jenkins)	5.00	2.50	1.50
287	Fred Talbot	.30	.15	.09
288	Larry Hisle	.40	.20	.12
289	Gene Brabender	.50	.25	.15
290	Rod Carew	12.00	6.00	3.50
291	Leo Durocher	1.25	.60	.40
292	Eddie Leon	.30	.15	.09
293	Bob Bailey	.30	.15	.09
294	Jose Azcue	.30	.15	.09
295	Cecil Upshaw	.30	.15	.09

		NR MT	EX	VG
296	Woody Woodward	.40	.20	.12
297	Curt Blefary	.50	.25	.15
298	Ken Henderson	.30	.15	.09
299	Buddy Bradford	.30	.15	.09
300	Tom Seaver	20.00	10.00	6.00
301	Chico Salmon	.30	.15	.09
302	Jeff James	.30	.15	.09
303	Brant Alyea	.30	.15	.09
304	Bill Russell	1.25	.60	.40
305	World Series Game 1 (Buford Belts Leadoff Homer!)	1.75	.90	.50
306	World Series Game 2 (Clendenon's Homer Breaks Ice!)	1.75	.90	.50
307	World Series Game 3 (Agee's Catch Saves The Day!)	1.75	.90	.50
308	World Series Game 4 (Martin's Bunt Ends Deadlock!)	1.75	.90	.50
309	World Series Game 5 (Koosman Shuts The Door!)	1.75	.90	.50
310	World Series Summary (Mets Whoop It Up!)	1.75	.90	.50
311	Dick Green	.30	.15	.09
312	Mike Torrez	.40	.20	.12
313	Mayo Smith	.30	.15	.09
314	Bill McCool	.30	.15	.09
315	Luis Aparicio	4.50	2.25	1.25
316	Skip Guinn	.30	.15	.09
317	Red Sox Rookies (Luis Alvarado, Billy Conigliaro)	.40	.20	.12
318	Willie Smith	.30	.15	.09
319	Clayton Dalrymple	.30	.15	.09
320	Jim Maloney	.40	.20	.12
321	Lou Piniella	1.50	.70	.45
322	Luke Walker	.30	.15	.09
323	Wayne Comer	.50	.25	.15
324	Tony Taylor	.30	.15	.09
325	Dave Boswell	.30	.15	.09
326	Bill Voss	.30	.15	.09
327	Hal King	.30	.15	.09
328	George Brunet	.30	.15	.09
329	Chris Cannizzaro	.30	.15	.09
330	Lou Brock	5.50	2.75	1.75
331	Chuck Dobson	.30	.15	.09
332	Bobby Wine	.30	.15	.09
333	Bobby Murcer	1.25	.60	.40
334	Phil Regan	.30	.15	.09
335	Bill Freehan	.40	.20	.12
336	Del Unser	.30	.15	.09
337	Mike McCormick	.40	.20	.12
338	Paul Schaal	.30	.15	.09
339	Johnny Edwards	.30	.15	.09
340	Tony Conigliaro	1.25	.60	.40
341	Bill Sudakis	.30	.15	.09
342	Wilbur Wood	.40	.20	.12
343a	Checklist 373-459 (red bat on front)	3.50	1.75	1.00
343b	Checklist 373-459 (brown bat on front)	3.00	1.50	.90
344	Marcelino Lopez	.30	.15	.09
345	Al Ferrara	.30	.15	.09
346	Red Schoendienst	.70	.35	.20
347	Russ Snyder	.30	.15	.09
348	Mets Rookies (Jesse Hudson, Mike Jorgensen)	.40	.20	.12
349	Steve Hamilton	.50	.25	.15
350	Roberto Clemente	18.00	9.00	5.50
351	Tom Murphy	.30	.15	.09
352	Bob Barton	.30	.15	.09
353	Stan Williams	.30	.15	.09
354	Amos Otis	.50	.25	.15
355	Doug Rader	.30	.15	.09
356	Fred Lasher	.30	.15	.09
357	Bob Burda	.30	.15	.09
358	Pedro Borbon	.40	.20	.12
359	Phil Roof	.50	.25	.15
360	Curt Flood	1.00	.50	.30
361	Ray Jarvis	.30	.15	.09
362	Joe Hague	.30	.15	.09
363	Tom Shopay	.30	.15	.09
364	Dan McGinn	.30	.15	.09
365	Zoilo Versalles	.40	.20	.12
366	Barry Moore	.30	.15	.09
367	Mike Lum	.30	.15	.09
368	Ed Herrmann	.30	.15	.09
369	Alan Foster	.30	.15	.09
370	Tommy Harper	.70	.35	.20
371	Rod Gaspar	.30	.15	.09
372	Dave Giusti	.30	.15	.09
373	Roy White	1.00	.50	.30
374	Tommie Sisk	.30	.15	.09
375	Johnny Callison	.80	.40	.25

#	Name	NR MT	EX	VG
376	Lefty Phillips	.30	.15	.09
377	Bill Butler	.30	.15	.09
378	Jim Davenport	.30	.15	.09
379	Tom Tischinski	.30	.15	.09
380	Tony Perez	3.00	1.50	.90
381	Athletics Rookies (Bobby Brooks, Mike Olivo)	.30	.15	.09
382	Jack DiLauro	.30	.15	.09
383	Mickey Stanley	.40	.20	.12
384	Gary Neibauer	.30	.15	.09
385	George Scott	.40	.20	.12
386	Bill Dillman	.30	.15	.09
387	Orioles Team	1.50	.70	.45
388	Byron Browne	.30	.15	.09
389	Jim Shellenback	.30	.15	.09
390	Willie Davis	.80	.40	.25
391	Larry Brown	.30	.15	.09
392	Walt Hriniak	.30	.15	.09
393	John Gelnar	.50	.25	.15
394	Gil Hodges	3.50	1.75	1.00
395	Walt Williams	.30	.15	.09
396	Steve Blass	.40	.20	.12
397	Roger Repoz	.30	.15	.09
398	Bill Stoneman	.30	.15	.09
399	Yankees Team	2.00	1.00	.60
400	Denny McLain	1.50	.70	.45
401	Giants Rookies (John Harrell, Bernie Williams)	.30	.15	.09
402	Ellie Rodriguez	.30	.15	.09
403	Jim Bunning	3.00	1.50	.90
404	Rich Reese	.30	.15	.09
405	Bill Hands	.30	.15	.09
406	Mike Andrews	.30	.15	.09
407	Bob Watson	.40	.20	.12
408	Paul Lindblad	.30	.15	.09
409	Bob Tolan	.40	.20	.12
410	Boog Powell	2.00	1.00	.60
411	Dodgers Team	1.50	.70	.45
412	Larry Burchart	.30	.15	.09
413	Sonny Jackson	.30	.15	.09
414	Paul Edmondson	.30	.15	.09
415	Julian Javier	.30	.15	.09
416	Joe Verbanic	.50	.25	.15
417	John Bateman	.30	.15	.09
418	John Donaldson	.50	.25	.15
419	Ron Taylor	.30	.15	.09
420	Ken McMullen	.30	.15	.09
421	Pat Dobson	.40	.20	.12
422	Royals Team	1.25	.60	.40
423	Jerry May	.30	.15	.09
424	Mike Kilkenny	.30	.15	.09
425	Bobby Bonds	1.25	.60	.40
426	Bill Rigney	.30	.15	.09
427	Fred Norman	.30	.15	.09
428	Don Buford	.40	.20	.12
429	Cubs Rookies (Randy Bobb, Jim Cosman)	.30	.15	.09
430	Andy Messersmith	.50	.25	.15
431	Ron Swoboda	.40	.20	.12
432a	Checklist 460-546 ("Baseball" on front in yellow)	4.00	2.00	1.25
432b	Checklist 460-546 ("Baseball" on front in white)	2.50	1.25	.70
433	Ron Bryant	.30	.15	.09
434	Felipe Alou	.70	.35	.20
435	Nelson Briles	.30	.15	.09
436	Phillies Team	1.25	.60	.40
437	Danny Cater	.50	.25	.15
438	Pat Jarvis	.30	.15	.09
439	Lee Maye	.30	.15	.09
440	Bill Mazeroski	1.00	.50	.30
441	John O'Donoghue	.50	.25	.15
442	Gene Mauch	.70	.35	.20
443	Al Jackson	.30	.15	.09
444	White Sox Rookies (Bill Farmer, John Matias)	.30	.15	.09
445	Vada Pinson	1.25	.60	.40
446	Billy Grabarkewitz	.40	.20	.12
447	Lee Stange	.30	.15	.09
448	Astros Team	1.25	.60	.40
449	Jim Palmer	7.50	3.75	2.25
450	Willie McCovey AS	3.50	1.75	1.00
451	Boog Powell AS	1.00	.50	.30
452	Felix Millan AS	.50	.25	.15
453	Rod Carew AS	4.00	2.00	1.25
454	Ron Santo AS	.80	.40	.25
455	Brooks Robinson AS	3.50	1.75	1.00
456	Don Kessinger AS	.50	.25	.15
457	Rico Petrocelli AS	.50	.25	.15
458	Pete Rose AS	8.00	4.00	2.50
459	Reggie Jackson AS	6.50	3.25	2.00
460	Matty Alou AS	.70	.35	.20
461	Carl Yastrzemski AS	5.00	2.50	1.50
462	Hank Aaron AS	5.50	2.75	1.75
463	Frank Robinson AS	3.50	1.75	1.00
464	Johnny Bench AS	4.50	2.25	1.25
465	Bill Freehan AS	.50	.25	.15
466	Juan Marichal AS	2.75	1.50	.80
467	Denny McLain AS	.80	.40	.25
468	Jerry Koosman AS	.60	.30	.20
469	Sam McDowell AS	.60	.30	.20
470	Willie Stargell	6.00	3.00	1.75
471	Chris Zachary	.30	.15	.09
472	Braves Team	1.25	.60	.40
473	Don Bryant	.50	.25	.15
474	Dick Kelley	.30	.15	.09
475	Dick McAuliffe	.40	.20	.12
476	Don Shaw	.30	.15	.09
477	Orioles Rookies (Roger Freed, Al Severinsen)	.30	.15	.09
478	Bob Heise	.30	.15	.09
479	Dick Woodson	.30	.15	.09
480	Glenn Beckert	.40	.20	.12
481	Jose Tartabull	.30	.15	.09
482	Tom Hilgendorf	.30	.15	.09
483	Gail Hopkins	.30	.15	.09
484	Gary Nolan	.30	.15	.09
485	Jay Johnstone	.50	.25	.15
486	Terry Harmon	.30	.15	.09
487	Cisco Carlos	.30	.15	.09
488	J.C. Martin	.30	.15	.09
489	Eddie Kasko	.30	.15	.09
490	Bill Singer	.40	.20	.12
491	Graig Nettles	4.00	2.00	1.25
492	Astros Rookies (Keith Lampard, Scipio Spinks)	.30	.15	.09
493	Lindy McDaniel	.50	.25	.15
494	Larry Stahl	.30	.15	.09
495	Dave Morehead	.30	.15	.09
496	Steve Whitaker	.30	.15	.09
497	Eddie Watt	.30	.15	.09
498	Al Weis	.30	.15	.09
499	Skip Lockwood	.50	.25	.15
500	Hank Aaron	18.00	9.00	5.50
501	White Sox Team	1.25	.60	.40
502	Rollie Fingers	3.50	1.75	1.00
503	Dal Maxvill	.40	.20	.12
504	Don Pavletich	.30	.15	.09
505	Ken Holtzman	.40	.20	.12
506	Ed Stroud	.30	.15	.09
507	Pat Corrales	.50	.25	.15
508	Joe Niekro	.70	.35	.20
509	Expos Team	1.25	.60	.40
510	Tony Oliva	1.75	.90	.50
511	Joe Hoerner	.30	.15	.09
512	Billy Harris	.30	.15	.09
513	Preston Gomez	.30	.15	.09
514	Steve Hovley	.50	.25	.15
515	Don Wilson	.30	.15	.09
516	Yankees Rookies (John Ellis, Jim Lyttle)	.50	.25	.15
517	Joe Gibbon	.30	.15	.09
518	Bill Melton	.40	.20	.12
519	Don McMahon	.30	.15	.09
520	Willie Horton	.70	.35	.20
521	Cal Koonce	.30	.15	.09
522	Angels Team	1.25	.60	.40
523	Jose Pena	.30	.15	.09
524	Alvin Dark	.60	.30	.20
525	Jerry Adair	.30	.15	.09
526	Ron Herbel	.30	.15	.09
527	Don Bosch	.30	.15	.09
528	Elrod Hendricks	.30	.15	.09
529	Bob Aspromonte	.30	.15	.09
530	Bob Gibson	6.00	3.00	1.75
531	Ron Clark	.30	.15	.09
532	Danny Murtaugh	.50	.25	.15
533	Buzz Stephen	.50	.25	.15
534	Twins Team	1.50	.70	.45
535	Andy Kosco	.30	.15	.09
536	Mike Kekich	.50	.25	.15
537	Joe Morgan	4.00	2.00	1.25
538	Bob Humphreys	.30	.15	.09
539	Phillies Rookies (Larry Bowa, Dennis Doyle)	3.00	1.50	.90
540	Gary Peters	.40	.20	.12
541	Bill Heath	.30	.15	.09
542a	Checklist 547-633 (grey bat on front)	3.50	1.75	1.00
542b	Checklist 547-633 (brown bat on front)	2.50	1.25	.70
543	Clyde Wright	.30	.15	.09

		NR MT	EX	VG
544	Reds Team	1.25	.60	.40
545	Ken Harrelson	1.25	.60	.40
546	Ron Reed	.40	.20	.12
547	Rick Monday	.80	.40	.25
548	Howie Reed	.50	.25	.15
549	Cardinals Team	1.75	.90	.50
550	Frank Howard	2.25	1.25	.70
551	Dock Ellis	.60	.30	.20
552	Royals Rookies (Don O'Riley, Dennis Paepke, Fred Rico)	.50	.25	.15
553	Jim Lefebvre	.60	.30	.20
554	Tom Timmermann	.50	.25	.15
555	Orlando Cepeda	3.25	1.75	1.00
556	Dave Bristol	.70	.35	.20
557	Ed Kranepool	.70	.35	.20
558	Vern Fuller	.50	.25	.15
559	Tommy Davis	1.25	.60	.40
560	Gaylord Perry	5.00	2.50	1.50
561	Tom McCraw	.50	.25	.15
562	Ted Abernathy	.50	.25	.15
563	Red Sox Team	2.00	1.00	.60
564	Johnny Briggs	.50	.25	.15
565	Jim Hunter	5.00	2.50	1.50
566	Gene Alley	.60	.30	.20
567	Bob Oliver	.50	.25	.15
568	Stan Bahnsen	.70	.35	.20
569	Cookie Rojas	.50	.25	.15
570	Jim Fregosi	1.00	.50	.30
571	Jim Brewer	.50	.25	.15
572	Frank Quilici	.50	.25	.15
573	Padres Rookies (Mike Corkins, Rafael Robles, Ron Slocum)	.50	.25	.15
574	Bobby Bolin	.70	.35	.20
575	Cleon Jones	.60	.30	.20
576	Milt Pappas	.60	.30	.20
577	Bernie Allen	.50	.25	.15
578	Tom Griffin	.50	.25	.15
579	Tigers Team	2.25	1.25	.70
580	Pete Rose	70.00	35.00	21.00
581	Tom Satriano	.50	.25	.15
582	Mike Paul	.50	.25	.15
583	Hal Lanier	.70	.35	.20
584	Al Downing	.60	.30	.20
585	Rusty Staub	2.00	1.00	.60
586	Rickey Clark	.50	.25	.15
587	Jose Arcia	.50	.25	.15
588a	Checklist 634-720 (666 is Adolpho Phillips)	4.50	2.25	1.25
588b	Checklist 634-720 (666 is Adolfo Phillips)	3.00	1.50	.90
589	Joe Keough	.50	.25	.15
590	Mike Cuellar	.70	.35	.20
591	Mike Ryan	.50	.25	.15
592	Daryl Patterson	.50	.25	.15
593	Cubs Team	1.75	.90	.50
594	Jake Gibbs	.70	.35	.20
595	Maury Wills	2.50	1.25	.70
596	Mike Hershberger	.70	.35	.20
597	Sonny Siebert	.50	.25	.15
598	Joe Pepitone	1.00	.50	.30
599	Senators Rookies (Gene Martin, Dick Stelmaszek, Dick Such)	.50	.25	.15
600	Willie Mays	24.00	12.00	7.25
601	Pete Richert	.50	.25	.15
602	Ted Savage	.50	.25	.15
603	Ray Oyler	.50	.25	.15
604	Clarence Gaston	.50	.25	.15
605	Rick Wise	.60	.30	.20
606	Chico Ruiz	.50	.25	.15
607	Gary Waslewski	.50	.25	.15
608	Pirates Team	1.75	.90	.50
609	Buck Martinez	.60	.30	.20
610	Jerry Koosman	1.25	.60	.40
611	Norm Cash	1.50	.70	.45
612	Jim Hickman	.60	.30	.20
613	Dave Baldwin	.70	.35	.20
614	Mike Shannon	.60	.30	.20
615	Mark Belanger	.60	.30	.20
616	Jim Merritt	.50	.25	.15
617	Jim French	.50	.25	.15
618	Billy Wynne	.50	.25	.15
619	Norm Miller	.50	.25	.15
620	Jim Perry	1.00	.50	.30
621	Braves Rookies (Darrell Evans, Rick Kester, Mike McQueen)	5.00	2.50	1.50
622	Don Sutton	4.00	2.00	1.25
623	Horace Clarke	.70	.35	.20
624	Clyde King	.50	.25	.15
625	Dean Chance	.60	.30	.20
626	Dave Ricketts	.50	.25	.15
627	Gary Wagner	.50	.25	.15

		NR MT	EX	VG
628	Wayne Garrett	.50	.25	.15
629	Merv Rettenmund	.60	.30	.20
630	Ernie Banks	10.00	5.00	3.00
631	Athletics Team	1.75	.90	.50
632	Gary Sutherland	.50	.25	.15
633	Roger Nelson	.50	.25	.15
634	Bud Harrelson	2.00	1.00	.60
635	Bob Allison	2.00	1.00	.60
636	Jim Stewart	1.25	.60	.40
637	Indians Team	2.50	1.25	.70
638	Frank Bertaina	1.25	.60	.40
639	Dave Campbell	1.25	.60	.40
640	Al Kaline	18.00	9.00	5.50
641	Al McBean	1.25	.60	.40
642	Angels Rookies (Greg Garrett, Gordon Lund, Jarvis Tatum)	1.25	.60	.40
643	Jose Pagan	1.25	.60	.40
644	Gerry Nyman	1.25	.60	.40
645	Don Money	1.50	.70	.45
646	Jim Britton	1.25	.60	.40
647	Tom Matchick	1.25	.60	.40
648	Larry Haney	1.25	.60	.40
649	Jimmie Hall	1.25	.60	.40
650	Sam McDowell	2.00	1.00	.60
651	Jim Gosger	1.25	.60	.40
652	Rich Rollins	1.75	.90	.50
653	Moe Drabowsky	1.25	.60	.40
654	N.L. Rookies (Boots Day, Oscar Gamble, Angel Mangual)	2.25	1.25	.70
655	John Roseboro	1.50	.70	.45
656	Jim Hardin	1.25	.60	.40
657	Padres Team	2.50	1.25	.70
658	Ken Tatum	1.25	.60	.40
659	Pete Ward	1.75	.90	.50
660	Johnny Bench	75.00	37.00	22.00
661	Jerry Robertson	1.25	.60	.40
662	Frank Lucchesi	1.25	.60	.40
663	Tito Francona	1.50	.70	.45
664	Bob Robertson	1.25	.60	.40
665	Jim Lonborg	2.00	1.00	.60
666	Adolfo Phillips	1.25	.60	.40
667	Bob Meyer	1.75	.90	.50
668	Bob Tillman	1.25	.60	.40
669	White Sox Rookies (Bart Johnson, Dan Lazar, Mickey Scott)	1.25	.60	.40
670	Ron Santo	2.50	1.25	.70
671	Jim Campanis	1.25	.60	.40
672	Leon McFadden	1.25	.60	.40
673	Ted Uhlaender	1.25	.60	.40
674	Dave Leonhard	1.25	.60	.40
675	Jose Cardenal	1.50	.70	.45
676	Senators Team	2.50	1.25	.70
677	Woodie Fryman	1.50	.70	.45
678	Dave Duncan	1.25	.60	.40
679	Ray Sadecki	1.25	.60	.40
680	Rico Petrocelli	1.75	.90	.50
681	Bob Garibaldi	1.25	.60	.40
682	Dalton Jones	1.25	.60	.40
683	Reds Rookies (Vern Geishert, Hal McRae, Wayne Simpson)	2.25	1.25	.70
684	Jack Fisher	1.25	.60	.40
685	Tom Haller	1.50	.70	.45
686	Jackie Hernandez	1.25	.60	.40
687	Bob Priddy	1.25	.60	.40
688	Ted Kubiak	1.75	.90	.50
689	Frank Tepedino	1.75	.90	.50
690	Ron Fairly	1.75	.90	.50
691	Joe Grzenda	1.25	.60	.40
692	Duffy Dyer	1.25	.60	.40
693	Bob Johnson	1.25	.60	.40
694	Gary Ross	1.25	.60	.40
695	Bobby Knoop	1.25	.60	.40
696	Giants Team	2.50	1.25	.70
697	Jim Hannan	1.25	.60	.40
698	Tom Tresh	2.00	1.00	.60
699	Hank Aguirre	1.25	.60	.40
700	Frank Robinson	18.00	9.00	5.50
701	Jack Billingham	1.25	.60	.40
702	A.L. Rookies (Bob Johnson, Ron Klimkowski, Bill Zepp)	1.75	.90	.50
703	Lou Marone	1.25	.60	.40
704	Frank Baker	1.25	.60	.40
705	Tony Cloninger	1.50	.70	.45
706	John McNamara	2.00	1.00	.60
707	Kevin Collins	1.25	.60	.40
708	Jose Santiago	1.25	.60	.40
709	Mike Fiore	1.25	.60	.40
710	Felix Millan	1.25	.60	.40
711	Ed Brinkman	1.25	.70	.45
712	Nolan Ryan	40.00	20.00	12.00
713	Pilots Team	8.00	4.00	2.50

		NR MT	EX	VG
714	Al Spangler	1.25	.60	.40
715	Mickey Lolich	3.50	1.75	1.00
716	Cards Rookies (Sal Campisi, Reggie Cleveland, Santiago Guzman)	1.50	.70	.45
717	Tom Phoebus	1.25	.60	.40
718	Ed Spiezio	1.25	.60	.40
719	Jim Roland	1.75	.60	.40
720	Rick Reichardt	4.00	.70	.40

1970 Topps Candy Lids

The 1970 Topps Candy Lids are a test issue that was utilized again in 1973. The set is made up of 24 lids that measure 1⅞'' in diameter and were designed to be the tops of small 1.1 oz. tubs of "Baseball Stars Candy". Unlike the 1973 versions, the 1970 lids have no border surrounding the full-color photos. Frank Howard, Tom Seaver and Carl Yastrzemski photos are found on the bottom (inside) of the candy lid.

		NR MT	EX	VG
Complete Set:		250.00	125.00	75.00
Common Player:		2.00	1.00	.60
(1)	Hank Aaron	30.00	15.00	9.00
(2)	Rich Allen	4.00	2.00	1.25
(3)	Luis Aparicio	12.00	6.00	3.50
(4)	Johnny Bench	20.00	10.00	6.00
(5)	Ollie Brown	2.00	1.00	.60
(6)	Willie Davis	3.00	1.50	.90
(7)	Jim Fregosi	3.00	1.50	.90
(8)	Mike Hegan	2.00	1.00	.60
(9)	Frank Howard	4.00	2.00	1.25
(10)	Reggie Jackson	25.00	12.50	7.50
(11)	Fergie Jenkins	7.00	3.50	2.00
(12)	Harmon Killebrew	15.00	7.50	4.50
(13)	Juan Marichal	15.00	7.50	4.50
(14)	Bill Mazeroski	4.00	2.00	1.25
(15)	Tim McCarver	4.00	2.00	1.25
(16)	Sam McDowell	2.00	1.00	.60
(17)	Denny McLain	3.00	1.50	.90
(18)	Lou Piniella	3.00	1.50	.90
(19)	Frank Robinson	15.00	7.50	4.50
(20)	Tom Seaver	20.00	10.00	6.00
(21)	Rusty Staub	3.00	1.50	.90
(22)	Mel Stottlemyre	3.00	1.50	.90
(23)	Jim Wynn	2.00	1.00	.60
(24)	Carl Yastrzemski	25.00	12.50	7.50

1970 Topps Posters

Helping to ease a price increase, Topps included extremely fragile 8-11/16'' by 9-5/8'' posters in packs of regular cards. The posters feature color portraits and a smaller black and white "action" pose as well as the player's name, team and position at the top. Although there are Hall of Famers in the 24-poster set, all the top names are not represented. Once again, due to folding, heavy creases are a fact of life for the collector today.

		NR MT	EX	VG
Complete Set:		25.00	12.50	7.50
Common Player:		.40	.20	.12
1	Joe Horlen	.40	.20	.12
2	Phil Niekro	1.50	.70	.45
3	Willie Davis	.50	.25	.15
4	Lou Brock	2.00	1.00	.60
5	Ron Santo	.60	.30	.20
6	Ken Harrelson	.50	.25	.15
7	Willie McCovey	2.00	1.00	.60
8	Rick Wise	.40	.20	.12
9	Andy Messersmith	.40	.20	.12
10	Ron Fairly	.50	.25	.15
11	Johnny Bench	3.00	1.50	.90
12	Frank Robinson	2.50	1.25	.70
13	Tommie Agee	.40	.20	.12
14	Roy White	.50	.25	.15
15	Larry Dierker	.40	.20	.12
16	Rod Carew	3.00	1.50	.90
17	Don Mincher	.40	.20	.12
18	Ollie Brown	.40	.20	.12
19	Ed Kirkpatrick	.40	.20	.12
20	Reggie Smith	.50	.25	.15
21	Bob Clemente	5.00	2.50	1.50
22	Frank Howard	.60	.30	.20
23	Bert Campaneris	.50	.25	.15
24	Denny McLain	.60	.30	.20

1970-1971 Topps Scratch-Offs

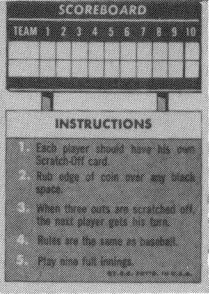

Needing inserts, and having not given up on the idea of a game which could be played with baseball cards, Topps provided a new game, the baseball scratch-off. The set was 24 cards. Unfolded they measured 3⅜'' by 5,'' and revealed a baseball game of sorts which was played by rubbing the black ink off playing squares which then determined the "action." Fronts of the cards had a player picture as "captain," while backs had instructions and a scoreboard. Inserts with white centers were from 1970 while those with red centers were from 1971.

		NR MT	EX	VG
Complete Set:		20.00	10.00	6.00
Common Player:		.30	.15	.09
(1)	Hank Aaron	2.00	1.00	.60
(2)	Rich Allen	.50	.25	.15
(3)	Luis Aparicio	1.00	.50	.30
(4)	Sal Bando	.30	.15	.09
(5)	Glenn Beckert	.30	.15	.09
(6)	Dick Bosman	.30	.15	.09
(7)	Nate Colbert	.30	.15	.09
(8)	Mike Hegan	.30	.15	.09
(9)	Mack Jones	.30	.15	.09

		NR MT	EX	VG
(10)	Al Kaline	1.50	.70	.45
(11)	Harmon Killebrew	1.50	.70	.45
(12)	Juan Marichal	1.25	.60	.40
(13)	Tim McCarver	.40	.20	.12
(14)	Sam McDowell	.30	.15	.09
(15)	Claude Osteen	.30	.15	.09
(16)	Tony Perez	.60	.30	.20
(17)	Lou Piniella	.40	.20	.12
(18)	Boog Powell	.50	.25	.15
(19)	Tom Seaver	2.00	1.00	.60
(20)	Jim Spencer	.30	.15	.09
(21)	Willie Stargell	1.25	.60	.40
(22)	Mel Stottlemyre	.30	.15	.09
(23)	Jim Wynn	.30	.15	.09
(24)	Carl Yastrzemski	2.25	1.25	.70

1970 Topps Story Booklets

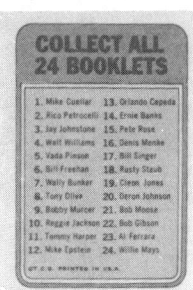

Measuring 2-1/2'' by 3-7/16,'' the Topps Story Booklet was a 1970 regular pack insert. The booklet featured a photo, title and booklet number on the ''cover.'' Inside were six pages of comic book story. The backs gave a checklist of other available booklets. Not every star had a booklet as the set was only 24 in number.

		NR MT	EX	VG
Complete Set:		15.00	7.50	4.50
Common Player:		.30	.15	.09
1	Mike Cuellar	.40	.20	.12
2	Rico Petrocelli	.40	.20	.12
3	Jay Johnstone	.40	.20	.12
4	Walt Williams	.30	.15	.09
5	Vada Pinson	.50	.25	.15
6	Bill Freehan	.40	.20	.12
7	Wally Bunker	.30	.15	.09
8	Tony Oliva	.50	.25	.15
9	Bobby Murcer	.40	.20	.12
10	Reggie Jackson	3.00	1.50	.90
11	Tommy Harper	.30	.15	.09
12	Mike Epstein	.30	.15	.09
13	Orlando Cepeda	.80	.40	.25
14	Ernie Banks	1.50	.70	.45
15	Pete Rose	8.00	4.00	2.50
16	Denis Menke	.30	.15	.09
17	Bill Singer	.30	.15	.09
18	Rusty Staub	.50	.25	.15
19	Cleon Jones	.30	.15	.09
20	Deron Johnson	.30	.15	.09
21	Bob Moose	.30	.15	.09
22	Bob Gibson	1.50	.70	.45
23	Al Ferrara	.30	.15	.09
24	Willie Mays	2.50	1.25	.70

1970 Topps Supers

Representing a refinement of the concept begun in 1969, the 1970 Topps Supers had a new 3⅛'' by 5¼'' postcard size. Printed on heavy stock with rounded corners, card fronts featured a borderless color photograph and facsimile autograph. Card backs were simply an enlarged back from the player's regular

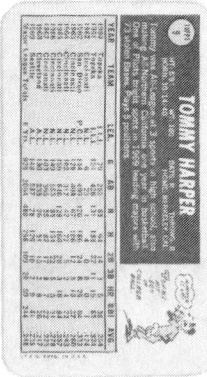

1970 Topps card. The Topps Supers set numbered 42 cards. Probably due to the press sheet configuration, eight of the 42 had smaller printings. The most elusive is card #38 (Boog Powell). The set was more widely produced than was the case in 1969, meaning collectors stand a much better chance of affording it.

		NR MT	EX	VG
Complete Set:		150.00	75.00	45.00
Common Player:		.75	.40	.25
1	Claude Osteen	3.00	1.50	.90
2	Sal Bando	3.50	1.75	1.00
3	Luis Aparicio	2.50	1.25	.70
4	Harmon Killebrew	4.00	2.00	1.25
5	Tom Seaver	20.00	10.00	6.00
6	Larry Dierker	.80	.40	.25
7	Bill Freehan	1.00	.50	.30
8	Johnny Bench	7.00	3.50	2.00
9	Tommy Harper	.80	.40	.25
10	Sam McDowell	1.00	.50	.30
11	Louis Brock	4.00	2.00	1.25
12	Roberto Clemente	9.00	4.50	2.75
13	Willie McCovey	4.00	2.00	1.25
14	Rico Petrocelli	.80	.40	.25
15	Philip Niekro	2.25	1.25	.70
16	Frank Howard	1.50	.70	.45
17	Denny McLain	1.25	.60	.40
18	Willie Mays	9.00	4.50	2.75
19	Wilver Stargell	3.50	1.75	1.00
20	Joe Horlen	.80	.40	.25
21	Ronald Santo	1.00	.50	.30
22	Dick Bosman	.80	.40	.25
23	Tim McCarver	1.00	.50	.30
24	Henry Aaron	9.00	4.50	2.75
25	Andy Messersmith	.80	.40	.25
26	Tony Oliva	1.25	.60	.40
27	Mel Stottlemyre	1.00	.50	.30
28	Reginald M. Jackson	15.00	7.50	4.50
29	Carl Yastrzemski	12.00	6.00	3.50
30	James Fregosi	1.00	.50	.30
31	Vada Pinson	1.25	.60	.40
32	Lou Piniella	1.25	.60	.40
33	Robert Gibson	4.00	2.00	1.25
34	Pete Rose	25.00	12.50	7.50
35	Jim Wynn	1.00	.50	.30
36	Ollie Brown	3.00	1.50	.90
37	Frank Robinson	15.00	7.50	4.50
38	John "Boog" Powell	50.00	25.00	15.00
39	Willie Davis	3.50	1.75	1.00
40	Billy Williams	10.00	5.00	3.00
41	Rusty Staub	1.25	.60	.40
42	Tommie Agee	.80	.40	.25

1971 Topps

In 1971, Topps again increased the size of its set to 752 cards. These well-liked cards, measuring 2½'' by 3½,'' featured a large color photo which had a thin white frame. Above the picture, in the card's overall black border, was the player's name, team and position. A facsimile autograph completed the front.

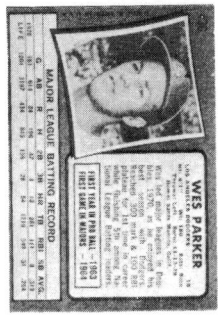

Backs featured a major change as a black-and-white "snapshot" of the player appeared. Abbreviated statistics, a line giving the player's first pro and major league games and a short biography complete the back of these innovative cards. Specialty cards in this issue were limited. There were statistical leaders as well as World Series and Play-Off highlights. High numbers from #644-752 are scarce.

		NR MT	EX	VG
	Complete Set:	1000.00	350.00	200.00
	Common Player: 1-523	.35	.20	.11
	Common Player: 524-643	.70	.35	.20
	Common Player: 644-752	1.50	.70	.45
1	World Champions (Orioles Team)	5.00	1.25	.60
2	Dock Ellis	.50	.20	.12
3	Dick McAuliffe	.40	.20	.12
4	Vic Davalillo	.40	.20	.12
5	Thurman Munson	15.00	7.50	4.50
6	Ed Spiezio	.35	.20	.11
7	Jim Holt	.35	.20	.11
8	Mike McQueen	.35	.20	.11
9	George Scott	.50	.25	.15
10	Claude Osteen	.50	.25	.15
11	Elliott Maddox	.50	.25	.15
12	Johnny Callison	.60	.30	.20
13	White Sox Rookies (Charlie Brinkman, Dick Moloney)	.35	.20	.11
14	Dave Concepcion	4.00	2.00	1.25
15	Andy Messersmith	.40	.20	.12
16	Ken Singleton	1.50	.70	.45
17	Billy Sorrell	.35	.20	.11
18	Norm Miller	.35	.20	.11
19	Skip Pitlock	.35	.20	.11
20	Reggie Jackson	20.00	10.00	6.00
21	Dan McGinn	.35	.20	.11
22	Phil Roof	.35	.20	.11
23	Oscar Gamble	.40	.20	.12
24	Rich Hand	.35	.20	.11
25	Clarence Gaston	.35	.20	.11
26	Bert Blyleven	10.00	5.00	3.00
27	Pirates Rookies (Fred Cambria, Gene Clines)	.35	.20	.11
28	Ron Klimkowski	.40	.20	.12
29	Don Buford	.40	.20	.12
30	Phil Niekro	3.25	1.75	1.00
31	Eddie Kasko	.35	.20	.11
32	Jerry DaVanon	.35	.20	.11
33	Del Unser	.35	.20	.11
34	Sandy Vance	.35	.20	.11
35	Lou Piniella	1.25	.60	.40
36	Dean Chance	.40	.20	.12
37	Rich McKinney	.35	.20	.11
38	Jim Colborn	.40	.20	.12
39	Tigers Rookies (Gene Lamont, Lerrin LaGrow)	.40	.20	.12
40	Lee May	.60	.30	.20
41	Rick Austin	.35	.20	.11
42	Boots Day	.35	.20	.11
43	Steve Kealey	.35	.20	.11
44	Johnny Edwards	.35	.20	.11
45	Jim Hunter	3.50	1.75	1.00
46	Dave Campbell	.35	.20	.11
47	Johnny Jeter	.35	.20	.11
48	Dave Baldwin	.35	.20	.11
49	Don Money	.40	.20	.12
50	Willie McCovey	5.00	2.50	1.50
51	Steve Kline	.40	.20	.12
52	Braves Rookies (Oscar Brown, Earl Williams)	.40	.20	.12
53	Paul Blair	.40	.20	.12
54	Checklist 1-132	2.50	1.25	.70
55	Steve Carlton	10.00	5.00	3.00
56	Duane Josephson	.35	.20	.11
57	Von Joshua	.35	.20	.11
58	Bill Lee	.40	.20	.12
59	Gene Mauch	.60	.30	.20
60	Dick Bosman	.35	.20	.11
61	A.L. Batting Leaders (Alex Johnson, Tony Oliva, Carl Yastrzemski)	2.25	1.25	.70
62	N.L. Batting Leaders (Rico Carty, Manny Sanguillen, Joe Torre)	1.25	.60	.40
63	A.L. RBI Leaders (Tony Conigliaro, Frank Howard, Boog Powell)	1.25	.60	.40
64	N.L. RBI Leaders (Johnny Bench, Tony Perez, Billy Williams)	2.25	1.25	.70
65	A.L. Home Run Leaders (Frank Howard, Harmon Killebrew, Carl Yastrzemski)	2.25	1.25	.70
66	N.L. Home Run Leaders (Johnny Bench, Tony Perez, Billy Williams)	2.25	1.25	.70
67	A.L. ERA Leaders (Jim Palmer, Diego Segui, Clyde Wright)	1.25	.60	.40
68	N.L. ERA Leaders (Tom Seaver, Wayne Simpson, Luke Walker)	1.50	.70	.45
69	A.L. Pitching Leaders (Mike Cuellar, Dave McNally, Jim Perry)	1.25	.60	.40
70	N.L. Pitching Leaders (Bob Gibson, Fergie Jenkins, Gaylord Perry)	2.00	1.00	.60
71	A.L. Strikeout Leaders (Bob Johnson, Mickey Lolich, Sam McDowell)	1.25	.60	.40
72	N.L. Strikeout Leaders (Bob Gibson, Fergie Jenkins, Tom Seaver)	2.25	1.25	.70
73	George Brunet	.35	.20	.11
74	Twins Rookies (Pete Hamm, Jim Nettles)	.35	.20	.11
75	Gary Nolan	.35	.20	.11
76	Ted Savage	.35	.20	.11
77	Mike Compton	.35	.20	.11
78	Jim Spencer	.40	.20	.12
79	Wade Blasingame	.35	.20	.11
80	Bill Melton	.40	.20	.12
81	Felix Millan	.35	.20	.11
82	Casey Cox	.35	.20	.11
83	Mets Rookies (Randy Bobb, Tim Foli)	.50	.25	.15
84	Marcel Lachemann	.35	.20	.11
85	Billy Grabarkewitz	.35	.20	.11
86	Mike Kilkenny	.35	.20	.11
87	Jack Heidemann	.35	.20	.11
88	Hal King	.35	.20	.11
89	Ken Brett	.35	.20	.11
90	Joe Pepitone	.70	.35	.20
91	Bob Lemon	1.25	.60	.40
92	Fred Wenz	.35	.20	.11
93	Senators Rookies (Norm McRae, Denny Riddleberger)	.35	.20	.11
94	Don Hahn	.35	.20	.11
95	Luis Tiant	1.50	.70	.45
96	Joe Hague	.35	.20	.11
97	Floyd Wicker	.35	.20	.11
98	Joe Decker	.35	.20	.11
99	Mark Belanger	.40	.20	.12
100	Pete Rose	45.00	22.00	13.50
101	Les Cain	.35	.20	.11
102	Astros Rookies (Ken Forsch, Larry Howard)	.50	.25	.15
103	Rich Severson	.35	.20	.11
104	Dan Frisella	.35	.20	.11
105	Tony Conigliaro	1.25	.60	.40
106	Tom Dukes	.35	.20	.11
107	Roy Foster	.35	.20	.11
108	John Cumberland	.35	.20	.11
109	Steve Hovley	.35	.20	.11
110	Bill Mazeroski	1.25	.60	.40
111	Yankees Rookies (Loyd Colson, Bobby Mitchell)	.40	.20	.12
112	Manny Mota	.60	.30	.20
113	Jerry Crider	.35	.20	.11
114	Billy Conigliaro	.40	.20	.12
115	Donn Clendenon	.40	.20	.12
116	Ken Sanders	.35	.20	.11
117	Ted Simmons	5.00	2.50	1.50
118	Cookie Rojas	.35	.20	.11
119	Frank Lucchesi	.35	.20	.11
120	Willie Horton	.60	.30	.20
121	1971 Rookie Stars (Jim Dunegan, Roe Skidmore)	.35	.20	.11
122	Eddie Watt	.35	.20	.11
123a	Checklist 133-263 (card # on right, orange helmet)	2.50	1.25	.70

		NR MT	EX	VG
123b	Checklist 133-263 (card # on right, red helmet)	2.50	1.25	.70
123c	Checklist 133-263 (card # centered)	3.50	1.75	1.00
124	Don Gullett	.70	.35	.20
125	Ray Fosse	.35	.20	.11
126	Danny Coombs	.35	.20	.11
127	Danny Thompson	.40	.20	.12
128	Frank Johnson	.35	.20	.11
129	Aurelio Monteagudo	.35	.20	.11
130	Denis Menke	.35	.20	.11
131	Curt Blefary	.40	.20	.12
132	Jose Laboy	.35	.20	.11
133	Mickey Lolich	1.25	.60	.40
134	Jose Arcia	.35	.20	.11
135	Rick Monday	.50	.25	.15
136	Duffy Dyer	.35	.20	.11
137	Marcelino Lopez	.35	.20	.11
138	Phillies Rookies (Joe Lis, Willie Montanez)	.50	.25	.15
139	Paul Casanova	.35	.20	.11
140	Gaylord Perry	4.00	2.00	1.25
141	Frank Quilici	.35	.20	.11
142	Mack Jones	.35	.20	.11
143	Steve Blass	.40	.20	.12
144	Jackie Hernandez	.35	.20	.11
145	Bill Singer	.40	.20	.12
146	Ralph Houk	.80	.40	.25
147	Bob Priddy	.35	.20	.11
148	John Mayberry	.50	.25	.15
149	Mike Hershberger	.35	.20	.11
150	Sam McDowell	.70	.35	.20
151	Tommy Davis	.70	.35	.20
152	Angels Rookies (Lloyd Allen, Winston Llenas)	.35	.20	.11
153	Gary Ross	.35	.20	.11
154	Cesar Gutierrez	.35	.20	.11
155	Ken Henderson	.35	.20	.11
156	Bart Johnson	.35	.20	.11
157	Bob Bailey	.35	.20	.11
158	Jerry Reuss	1.00	.50	.30
159	Jarvis Tatum	.35	.20	.11
160	Tom Seaver	15.00	7.50	4.50
161	Coins Checklist	2.50	1.25	.70
162	Jack Billingham	.35	.20	.11
163	Buck Martinez	.35	.20	.11
164	Reds Rookies (Frank Duffy, Milt Wilcox)	.60	.30	.20
165	Cesar Tovar	.35	.20	.11
166	Joe Hoerner	.35	.20	.11
167	Tom Grieve	.35	.20	.11
168	Bruce Dal Canton	.35	.20	.11
169	Ed Herrmann	.35	.20	.11
170	Mike Cuellar	.60	.30	.20
171	Bobby Wine	.35	.20	.11
172	Duke Sims	.35	.20	.11
173	Gil Garrido	.35	.20	.11
174	Dave LaRoche	.50	.25	.15
175	Jim Hickman	.40	.20	.12
176	Red Sox Rookies (Doug Griffin, Bob Montgomery)	.35	.20	.11
177	Hal McRae	.70	.35	.20
178	Dave Duncan	.35	.20	.11
179	Mike Corkins	.35	.20	.11
180	Al Kaline	6.00	3.00	1.75
181	Hal Lanier	.60	.30	.20
182	Al Downing	.40	.20	.12
183	Gil Hodges	3.50	1.75	1.00
184	Stan Bahnsen	.50	.25	.15
185	Julian Javier	.40	.20	.12
186	Bob Spence	.35	.20	.11
187	Ted Abernathy	.35	.20	.11
188	Dodgers Rookies (Mike Strahler, Bob Valentine)	1.75	.90	.50
189	George Mitterwald	.35	.20	.11
190	Bob Tolan	.40	.20	.12
191	Mike Andrews	.35	.20	.11
192	Billy Wilson	.35	.20	.11
193	Bob Grich	1.75	.90	.50
194	Mike Lum	.35	.20	.11
195	A.L. Playoff Game 1 (Powell Muscles Twins!)	1.25	.60	.40
196	A.L. Playoff Game 2 (McNally Makes It Two Straight!)	1.25	.60	.40
197	A.L. Playoff Game 3 (Palmer Mows 'Em Down!)	1.75	.90	.50
198	A.L. Playoffs Summary (A Team Effort!)	1.25	.60	.40
199	N.L. Playoff Game 1 (Cline Pinch-Triple Decides It!)	1.25	.60	.40
200	N.L. Playoff Game 2 (Tolan Scores For Third Time!)	1.25	.60	.40
201	N.L. Playoff Game 3 (Cline Scores Winning Run!)	1.25	.60	.40
202	N.L. Playoffs Summary (World Series Bound!)	1.25	.60	.40
203	Larry Gura	.70	.35	.20
204	Brewers Rookies (George Kopacz, Bernie Smith)	.35	.20	.11
205	Gerry Moses	.35	.20	.11
206a	Checklist 264-393 (orange helmet)	2.50	1.25	.70
206b	Checklist 264-393 (red helmet)	2.50	1.25	.70
207	Alan Foster	.35	.20	.11
208	Billy Martin	1.75	.90	.50
209	Steve Renko	.35	.20	.11
210	Rod Carew	15.00	7.50	4.50
211	Phil Hennigan	.35	.20	.11
212	Rich Hebner	.40	.20	.12
213	Frank Baker	.40	.20	.12
214	Al Ferrara	.35	.20	.11
215	Diego Segui	.35	.20	.11
216	Cards Rookies (Reggie Cleveland, Luis Melendez)	.35	.20	.11
217	Ed Stroud	.35	.20	.11
218	Tony Cloninger	.40	.20	.12
219	Elrod Hendricks	.35	.20	.11
220	Ron Santo	.80	.40	.25
221	Dave Morehead	.35	.20	.11
222	Bob Watson	.40	.20	.12
223	Cecil Upshaw	.35	.20	.11
224	Alan Gallagher	.35	.20	.11
225	Gary Peters	.40	.20	.12
226	Bill Russell	.60	.30	.20
227	Floyd Weaver	.35	.20	.11
228	Wayne Garrett	.35	.20	.11
229	Jim Hannan	.35	.20	.11
230	Willie Stargell	5.00	2.50	1.50
231	Indians Rookies (Vince Colbert, John Lowenstein)	.50	.25	.15
232	John Strohmayer	.35	.20	.11
233	Larry Bowa	1.75	.90	.50
234	Jim Lyttle	.40	.20	.12
235	Nate Colbert	.35	.20	.11
236	Bob Humphreys	.35	.20	.11
237	Cesar Cedeno	1.50	.70	.45
238	Chuck Dobson	.35	.20	.11
239	Red Schoendienst	.60	.30	.20
240	Clyde Wright	.35	.20	.11
241	Dave Nelson	.35	.20	.11
242	Jim Ray	.35	.20	.11
243	Carlos May	.40	.20	.12
244	Bob Tillman	.35	.20	.11
245	Jim Kaat	2.50	1.25	.70
246	Tony Taylor	.35	.20	.11
247	Royals Rookies (Jerry Cram, Paul Splittorff)	.70	.35	.20
248	Hoyt Wilhelm	3.50	1.75	1.00
249	Chico Salmon	.35	.20	.11
250	Johnny Bench	15.00	7.50	4.50
251	Frank Reberger	.35	.20	.11
252	Eddie Leon	.35	.20	.11
253	Bill Sudakis	.35	.20	.11
254	Cal Koonce	.35	.20	.11
255	Bob Robertson	.35	.20	.11
256	Tony Gonzalez	.35	.20	.11
257	Nelson Briles	.35	.20	.11
258	Dick Green	.35	.20	.11
259	Dave Marshall	.35	.20	.11
260	Tommy Harper	.40	.20	.12
261	Darold Knowles	.35	.20	.11
262	Padres Rookies (Dave Robinson, Jim Williams)	.35	.20	.11
263	John Ellis	.40	.20	.12
264	Joe Morgan	3.50	1.75	1.00
265	Jim Northrup	.40	.20	.12
266	Bill Stoneman	.35	.20	.11
267	Rich Morales	.35	.20	.11
268	Phillies Team	1.25	.60	.40
269	Gail Hopkins	.35	.20	.11
270	Rico Carty	.70	.35	.20
271	Bill Zepp	.35	.20	.11
272	Tommy Helms	.40	.20	.12
273	Pete Richert	.35	.20	.11
274	Ron Slocum	.35	.20	.11
275	Vada Pinson	1.25	.60	.40
276	Giants Rookies (Mike Davison, George Foster)	4.00	2.00	1.25
277	Gary Waslewski	.40	.20	.12
278	Jerry Grote	.50	.25	.15

		NR MT	EX	VG
279	Lefty Phillips	.35	.20	.11
280	Fergie Jenkins	3.00	1.50	.90
281	Danny Walton	.35	.20	.11
282	Jose Pagan	.35	.20	.11
283	Dick Such	.35	.20	.11
284	Jim Gosger	.35	.20	.11
285	Sal Bando	.60	.30	.20
286	Jerry McNertney	.35	.20	.11
287	Mike Fiore	.35	.20	.11
288	Joe Moeller	.35	.20	.11
289	White Sox Team	1.25	.60	.40
290	Tony Oliva	1.50	.70	.45
291	George Culver	.35	.20	.11
292	Jay Johnstone	.60	.30	.20
293	Pat Corrales	.50	.25	.15
294	Steve Dunning	.35	.20	.11
295	Bobby Bonds	1.25	.60	.40
296	Tom Timmermann	.35	.20	.11
297	Johnny Briggs	.35	.20	.11
298	Jim Nelson	.35	.20	.11
299	Ed Kirkpatrick	.35	.20	.11
300	Brooks Robinson	7.00	3.50	2.00
301	Earl Wilson	.35	.20	.11
302	Phil Gagliano	.35	.20	.11
303	Lindy McDaniel	.40	.20	.12
304	Ron Brand	.35	.20	.11
305	Reggie Smith	.60	.30	.20
306	Jim Nash	.35	.20	.11
307	Don Wert	.35	.20	.11
308	Cards Team	1.25	.60	.40
309	Dick Ellsworth	.35	.20	.11
310	Tommie Agee	.40	.20	.12
311	Lee Stange	.35	.20	.11
312	Harry Walker	.40	.20	.12
313	Tom Hall	.35	.20	.11
314	Jeff Torborg	.40	.20	.12
315	Ron Fairly	.50	.25	.15
316	Fred Scherman	.35	.20	.11
317	Athletics Rookies (Jim Driscoll, Angel Mangual)	.35	.20	.11
318	Rudy May	.40	.20	.12
319	Ty Cline	.35	.20	.11
320	Dave McNally	.50	.25	.15
321	Tom Matchick	.35	.20	.11
322	Jim Beauchamp	.35	.20	.11
323	Billy Champion	.35	.20	.11
324	Graig Nettles	2.50	1.25	.70
325	Juan Marichal	5.00	2.50	1.50
326	Richie Scheinblum	.35	.20	.11
327	World Series Game 1 (Powell Homers To Opposite Field!)	.60	.40	
328	World Series Game 2 (Buford Goes 2-For 4!)	1.25	.60	.40
329	World Series Game 3 (F. Robinson Shows Muscle!)	2.00	1.00	.60
330	World Series Game 4 (Reds Stay Alive!)	1.25	.60	.40
331	World Series Game 5 (B. Robinson Commits Robbery!)	2.00	1.00	.60
332	World Series Summary (Clinching Performance!)	1.25	.60	.40
333	Clay Kirby	.35	.20	.11
334	Roberto Pena	.35	.20	.11
335	Jerry Koosman	1.00	.50	.30
336	Tigers Team	1.75	.90	.50
337	Jesus Alou	.40	.20	.12
338	Gene Tenace	.50	.25	.15
339	Wayne Simpson	.35	.20	.11
340	Rico Petrocelli	.50	.25	.15
341	Steve Garvey	55.00	27.00	16.50
342	Frank Tepedino	.40	.20	.12
343	Pirates Rookies (Ed Acosta, Milt May)	.40	.20	.12
344	Ellie Rodriguez	.35	.20	.11
345	Joe Horlen	.35	.20	.11
346	Lum Harris	.35	.20	.11
347	Ted Uhlaender	.35	.20	.11
348	Fred Norman	.35	.20	.11
349	Rich Reese	.35	.20	.11
350	Billy Williams	4.00	2.00	1.25
351	Jim Shellenback	.35	.20	.11
352	Denny Doyle	.35	.20	.11
353	Carl Taylor	.35	.20	.11
354	Don McMahon	.35	.20	.11
355	Bud Harrelson	.40	.20	.12
356	Bob Locker	.35	.20	.11
357	Reds Team	1.25	.60	.40
358	Danny Cater	.40	.20	.12
359	Ron Reed	.40	.20	.12
360	Jim Fregosi	.80	.40	.25
361	Don Sutton	3.50	1.75	1.00

		NR MT	EX	VG
362	Orioles Rookies (Mike Adamson, Roger Freed)	.35	.20	.11
363	Mike Nagy	.35	.20	.11
364	Tommy Dean	.35	.20	.11
365	Bob Johnson	.35	.20	.11
366	Ron Stone	.35	.20	.11
367	Dalton Jones	.35	.20	.11
368	Bob Veale	.40	.20	.12
369a	Checklist 394-523 (orange helmet)	2.50	1.25	.70
369b	Checklist 394-523 (red helmet, black line above ear)	2.50	1.25	.70
369c	Checklist 394-523 (red helmet, no line)	2.50	1.25	.70
370	Joe Torre	2.25	1.25	.70
371	Jack Hiatt	.35	.20	.11
372	Lew Krausse	.35	.20	.11
373	Tom McCraw	.35	.20	.11
374	Clete Boyer	.50	.25	.15
375	Steve Hargan	.35	.20	.11
376	Expos Rookies (Clyde Mashore, Ernie McAnally)	.35	.20	.11
377	Greg Garrett	.35	.20	.11
378	Tito Fuentes	.35	.20	.11
379	Wayne Granger	.35	.20	.11
380	Ted Williams	4.00	2.00	1.25
381	Fred Gladding	.35	.20	.11
382	Jake Gibbs	.40	.20	.12
383	Rod Gaspar	.35	.20	.11
384	Rollie Fingers	2.50	1.25	.70
385	Maury Wills	1.25	.60	.40
386	Red Sox Team	1.50	.70	.45
387	Ron Herbel	.35	.20	.11
388	Al Oliver	2.25	1.25	.70
389	Ed Brinkman	.40	.20	.12
390	Glenn Beckert	.50	.25	.15
391	Twins Rookies (Steve Brye, Cotton Nash)	.35	.20	.11
392	Grant Jackson	.35	.20	.11
393	Merv Rettenmund	.40	.20	.12
394	Clay Carroll	.40	.20	.12
395	Roy White	.70	.35	.20
396	Dick Schofield	.35	.20	.11
397	Alvin Dark	.50	.25	.15
398	Howie Reed	.35	.20	.11
399	Jim French	.35	.20	.11
400	Hank Aaron	15.00	7.50	4.50
401	Tom Murphy	.35	.20	.11
402	Dodgers Team	1.50	.70	.45
403	Joe Coleman	.40	.20	.12
404	Astros Rookies (Buddy Harris, Roger Metzger)	.35	.20	.11
405	Leo Cardenas	.35	.20	.11
406	Ray Sadecki	.35	.20	.11
407	Joe Rudi	.60	.30	.20
408	Rafael Robles	.35	.20	.11
409	Don Pavletich	.35	.20	.11
410	Ken Holtzman	.40	.20	.12
411	George Spriggs	.35	.20	.11
412	Jerry Johnson	.35	.20	.11
413	Pat Kelly	.35	.20	.11
414	Woodie Fryman	.40	.20	.12
415	Mike Hegan	.35	.20	.11
416	Gene Alley	.40	.20	.12
417	Dick Hall	.35	.20	.11
418	Adolfo Phillips	.35	.20	.11
419	Ron Hansen	.40	.20	.12
420	Jim Merritt	.35	.20	.11
421	John Stephenson	.35	.20	.11
422	Frank Bertaina	.35	.20	.11
423	Tigers Rookies (Tim Marting, Dennis Saunders)	.35	.20	.11
424	Roberto Rodriquez (Rodriguez)	.35	.20	.11
425	Doug Rader	.35	.20	.11
426	Chris Cannizzaro	.35	.20	.11
427	Bernie Allen	.35	.20	.11
428	Jim McAndrew	.35	.20	.11
429	Chuck Hinton	.35	.20	.11
430	Wes Parker	.40	.20	.12
431	Tom Burgmeier	.35	.20	.11
432	Bob Didier	.35	.20	.11
433	Skip Lockwood	.35	.20	.11
434	Gary Sutherland	.35	.20	.11
435	Jose Cardenal	.40	.20	.12
436	Wilbur Wood	.50	.25	.15
437	Danny Murtaugh	.40	.20	.12
438	Mike McCormick	.50	.25	.15
439	Phillies Rookies (Greg Luzinski, Scott Reid)	1.75	.90	.50
440	Bert Campaneris	.70	.35	.20
441	Milt Pappas	.40	.20	.12

#	Player	NR MT	EX	VG
442	Angels Team	1.25	.60	.40
443	Rich Robertson	.35	.20	.11
444	Jimmie Price	.35	.20	.11
445	Art Shamsky	.35	.20	.11
446	Bobby Bolin	.35	.20	.11
447	Cesar Geronimo	.60	.30	.20
448	Dave Roberts	.35	.20	.11
449	Brant Alyea	.35	.20	.11
450	Bob Gibson	5.50	2.75	1.75
451	Joe Keough	.35	.20	.11
452	John Boccabella	.35	.20	.11
453	Terry Crowley	.35	.20	.11
454	Mike Paul	.35	.20	.11
455	Don Kessinger	.40	.20	.12
456	Bob Meyer	.35	.20	.11
457	Willie Smith	.35	.20	.11
458	White Sox Rookies (Dave Lemonds, Ron Lolich)	.35	.20	.11
459	Jim Lefebvre	.40	.20	.12
460	Fritz Peterson	.50	.25	.15
461	Jim Hart	.40	.20	.12
462	Senators Team	1.50	.70	.45
463	Tom Kelley	.35	.20	.11
464	Aurelio Rodriguez	.40	.20	.12
465	Tim McCarver	.80	.40	.25
466	Ken Berry	.35	.20	.11
467	Al Santorini	.35	.20	.11
468	Frank Fernandez	.35	.20	.11
469	Bob Aspromonte	.35	.20	.11
470	Bob Oliver	.35	.20	.11
471	Tom Griffin	.35	.20	.11
472	Ken Rudolph	.35	.20	.11
473	Gary Wagner	.35	.20	.11
474	Jim Fairey	.35	.20	.11
475	Ron Perranoski	.40	.20	.12
476	Dal Maxvill	.40	.20	.12
477	Earl Weaver	1.00	.50	.30
478	Bernie Carbo	.40	.20	.12
479	Dennis Higgins	.35	.20	.11
480	Manny Sanguillen	.40	.20	.12
481	Daryl Patterson	.35	.20	.11
482	Padres Team	1.25	.60	.40
483	Gene Michael	.50	.25	.15
484	Don Wilson	.35	.20	.11
485	Ken McMullen	.35	.20	.11
486	Steve Huntz	.35	.20	.11
487	Paul Schaal	.35	.20	.11
488	Jerry Stephenson	.35	.20	.11
489	Luis Alvarado	.35	.20	.11
490	Deron Johnson	.35	.20	.11
491	Jim Hardin	.35	.20	.11
492	Ken Boswell	.35	.20	.11
493	Dave May	.35	.20	.11
494	Braves Rookies (Ralph Garr, Rick Kester)	.50	.25	.15
495	Felipe Alou	.60	.30	.20
496	Woody Woodward	.40	.20	.12
497	Horacio Pina	.35	.20	.11
498	John Kennedy	.35	.20	.11
499	Checklist 524-643	2.50	1.25	.70
500	Jim Perry	.60	.30	.20
501	Andy Etchebarren	.35	.20	.11
502	Cubs Team	1.25	.60	.40
503	Gates Brown	.35	.20	.11
504	Ken Wright	.35	.20	.11
505	Ollie Brown	.35	.20	.11
506	Bobby Knoop	.35	.20	.11
507	George Stone	.35	.20	.11
508	Roger Repoz	.35	.20	.11
509	Jim Grant	.35	.20	.11
510	Ken Harrelson	1.25	.60	.40
511	Chris Short	.40	.20	.12
512	Red Sox Rookies (Mike Garman, Dick Mills)	.35	.20	.11
513	Nolan Ryan	15.00	7.50	4.50
514	Ron Woods	.40	.20	.12
515	Carl Morton	.35	.20	.11
516	Ted Kubiak	.35	.20	.11
517	Charlie Fox	.35	.20	.11
518	Joe Grzenda	.35	.20	.11
519	Willie Crawford	.35	.20	.11
520	Tommy John	3.00	1.50	.90
521	Leron Lee	.35	.20	.11
522	Twins Team	1.25	.60	.40
523	John Odom	.40	.20	.12
524	Mickey Stanley	.80	.40	.25
525	Ernie Banks	10.00	5.00	3.00
526	Ray Jarvis	.70	.35	.20
527	Cleon Jones	.80	.40	.25
528	Wally Bunker	.70	.35	.20

#	Player	NR MT	EX	VG
529	N.L. Rookies (Bill Buckner, Enzo Hernandez, Marty Perez)	2.50	1.25	.70
530	Carl Yastrzemski	24.00	12.00	7.25
531	Mike Torrez	.80	.40	.25
532	Bill Rigney	.70	.35	.20
533	Mike Ryan	.70	.35	.20
534	Luke Walker	.70	.35	.20
535	Curt Flood	1.75	.90	.50
536	Claude Raymond	.70	.35	.20
537	Tom Egan	.70	.35	.20
538	Angel Bravo	.70	.35	.20
539	Larry Brown	.70	.35	.20
540	Larry Dierker	.80	.40	.25
541	Bob Burda	.70	.35	.20
542	Bob Miller	.70	.35	.20
543	Yankees Team	2.75	1.50	.80
544	Vida Blue	2.50	1.25	.70
545	Dick Dietz	.70	.35	.20
546	John Matias	.70	.35	.20
547	Pat Dobson	.80	.40	.25
548	Don Mason	.70	.35	.20
549	Jim Brewer	.70	.35	.20
550	Harmon Killebrew	10.00	5.00	3.00
551	Frank Linzy	.70	.35	.20
552	Buddy Bradford	.70	.35	.20
553	Kevin Collins	.70	.35	.20
554	Lowell Palmer	.70	.35	.20
555	Walt Williams	.70	.35	.20
556	Jim McGlothlin	.70	.35	.20
557	Tom Satriano	.70	.35	.20
558	Hector Torres	.70	.35	.20
559	A.L. Rookies (Terry Cox, Bill Gogolewski, Gary Jones)	.80	.40	.25
560	Rusty Staub	2.25	1.25	.70
561	Syd O'Brien	.70	.35	.20
562	Dave Giusti	.70	.35	.20
563	Giants Team	2.00	1.00	.60
564	Al Fitzmorris	.70	.35	.20
565	Jim Wynn	1.00	.50	.30
566	Tim Cullen	.70	.35	.20
567	Walt Alston	2.50	1.25	.70
568	Sal Campisi	.70	.35	.20
569	Ivan Murrell	.70	.35	.20
570	Jim Palmer	9.00	4.50	2.75
571	Ted Sizemore	.70	.35	.20
572	Jerry Kenney	.80	.40	.25
573	Ed Kranepool	1.00	.50	.30
574	Jim Bunning	3.50	1.75	1.00
575	Bill Freehan	1.00	.50	.30
576	Cubs Rookies (Brock Davis, Adrian Garrett, Garry Jestadt)	.70	.35	.20
577	Jim Lonborg	1.00	.50	.30
578	Ron Hunt	.80	.40	.25
579	Marty Pattin	.70	.35	.20
580	Tony Perez	4.00	2.00	1.25
581	Roger Nelson	.70	.35	.20
582	Dave Cash	.70	.35	.20
583	Ron Cook	.70	.35	.20
584	Indians Team	2.00	1.00	.60
585	Willie Davis	1.50	.70	.45
586	Dick Woodson	.70	.35	.20
587	Sonny Jackson	.70	.35	.20
588	Tom Bradley	.70	.35	.20
589	Bob Barton	.70	.35	.20
590	Alex Johnson	.70	.35	.20
591	Jackie Brown	.70	.35	.20
592	Randy Hundley	.70	.35	.20
593	Jack Aker	.80	.40	.25
594	Cards Rookies (Bob Chlupsa, Al Hrabosky, Bob Stinson)	1.50	.70	.45
595	Dave Johnson	1.75	.90	.50
596	Mike Jorgensen	.70	.35	.20
597	Ken Suarez	.70	.35	.20
598	Rick Wise	.80	.40	.25
599	Norm Cash	2.00	1.00	.60
600	Willie Mays	25.00	12.50	7.50
601	Ken Tatum	.70	.35	.20
602	Marty Martinez	.70	.35	.20
603	Pirates Team	3.00	1.50	.90
604	John Gelnar	.70	.35	.20
605	Orlando Cepeda	3.00	1.50	.90
606	Chuck Taylor	.70	.35	.20
607	Paul Ratliff	.70	.35	.20
608	Mike Wegener	.70	.35	.20
609	Leo Durocher	1.50	.70	.45
610	Amos Otis	1.00	.50	.30
611	Tom Phoebus	.70	.35	.20
612	Indians Rookies (Lou Camilli, Ted Ford, Steve Mingori)	.70	.35	.20
613	Pedro Borbon	.80	.40	.25
614	Billy Cowan	.70	.35	.20

		NR MT	EX	VG
615	Mel Stottlemyre	1.75	.90	.50
616	Larry Hisle	.80	.40	.25
617	Clay Dalrymple	.70	.35	.20
618	Tug McGraw	2.25	1.25	.70
619a	Checklist 644-752 (no copyright on back)			
		4.50	2.25	1.25
619b	Checklist 644-752 (with copyright, no			
	wavy line on helmet brim)	3.00	1.50	.90
619c	Checklist 644-752 (with copyright, wavy			
	line on helmet brim)	3.00	1.50	.90
620	Frank Howard	2.25	1.25	.70
621	Ron Bryant	.70	.35	.20
622	Joe Lahoud	.70	.35	.20
623	Pat Jarvis	.70	.35	.20
624	Athletics Team	2.00	1.00	.60
625	Lou Brock	10.00	5.00	3.00
626	Freddie Patek	.80	.40	.25
627	Steve Hamilton	.70	.35	.20
628	John Bateman	.70	.35	.20
629	John Hiller	.80	.40	.25
630	Roberto Clemente	20.00	10.00	6.00
631	Eddie Fisher	.70	.35	.20
632	Darrel Chaney	.70	.35	.20
633	A.L. Rookies (Bobby Brooks, Pete Koegel,			
	Scott Northey)	.70	.35	.20
634	Phil Regan	.70	.35	.20
635	Bobby Murcer	2.00	1.00	.60
636	Denny Lemaster	.70	.35	.20
637	Dave Bristol	.70	.35	.20
638	Stan Williams	.70	.35	.20
639	Tom Haller	.80	.40	.25
640	Frank Robinson	12.00	6.00	3.50
641	Mets Team	2.50	1.25	.70
642	Jim Roland	.70	.35	.20
643	Rick Reichardt	.70	.35	.20
644	Jim Stewart	1.50	.70	.45
645	Jim Maloney	1.75	.90	.50
646	Bobby Floyd	1.50	.70	.45
647	Juan Pizarro	1.50	.70	.45
648	Mets Rookies (Rich Folkers, Ted Martinez,			
	Jon Matlack)	3.25	1.75	1.00
649	Sparky Lyle	3.00	1.50	.90
650	Rich Allen	6.00	3.00	1.75
651	Jerry Robertson	1.50	.70	.45
652	Braves Team	3.25	1.75	1.00
653	Russ Snyder	1.50	.70	.45
654	Don Shaw	1.50	.70	.45
655	Mike Epstein	1.75	.90	.50
656	Gerry Nyman	1.50	.70	.45
657	Jose Azcue	1.50	.70	.45
658	Paul Lindblad	1.50	.70	.45
659	Byron Browne	1.50	.70	.45
660	Ray Culp	1.50	.70	.45
661	Chuck Tanner	2.50	1.25	.70
662	Mike Hedlund	1.50	.70	.45
663	Marv Staehle	1.50	.70	.45
664	Major League Rookies (Archie Reynolds,			
	Bob Reynolds, Ken Reynolds)	1.50	.70	.45
665	Ron Swoboda	1.50	.70	.45
666	Gene Brabender	1.50	.70	.45
667	Pete Ward	1.75	.90	.50
668	Gary Neibauer	1.50	.70	.45
669	Ike Brown	1.50	.70	.45
670	Bill Hands	1.50	.70	.45
671	Bill Voss	1.50	.70	.45
672	Ed Crosby	1.50	.70	.45
673	Gerry Janeski	1.50	.70	.45
674	Expos Team	3.25	1.75	1.00
675	Dave Boswell	1.50	.70	.45
676	Tommie Reynolds	1.50	.70	.45
677	Jack DiLauro	1.50	.70	.45
678	George Thomas	1.50	.70	.45
679	Don O'Riley	1.50	.70	.45
680	Don Mincher	1.75	.90	.50
681	Bill Butler	1.50	.70	.45
682	Terry Harmon	1.50	.70	.45
683	Bill Burbach	1.75	.90	.50
684	Curt Motton	1.50	.70	.45
685	Moe Drabowsky	1.50	.70	.45
686	Chico Ruiz	1.50	.70	.45
687	Ron Taylor	1.50	.70	.45
688	Sparky Anderson	3.25	1.75	1.00
689	Frank Baker	1.50	.70	.45
690	Bob Moose	1.50	.70	.45
691	Bob Heise	1.50	.70	.45
692	A.L. Rookies (Hal Haydel, Rogelio Moret,			
	Wayne Twitchell)	1.50	.70	.45
693	Jose Pena	1.50	.70	.45
694	Rick Renick	1.50	.70	.45
695	Joe Niekro	3.25	1.75	1.00
696	Jerry Morales	1.50	.70	.45

		NR MT	EX	VG
697	Rickey Clark	1.50	.70	.45
698	Brewers Team	3.50	1.75	1.00
699	Jim Britton	1.50	.70	.45
700	Boog Powell	4.00	2.00	1.25
701	Bob Garibaldi	1.50	.70	.45
702	Milt Ramirez	1.50	.70	.45
703	Mike Kekich	1.75	.90	.50
704	J.C. Martin	1.50	.70	.45
705	Dick Selma	1.50	.70	.45
706	Joe Foy	1.50	.70	.45
707	Fred Lasher	1.50	.70	.45
708	Russ Nagelson	1.50	.70	.45
709	Major League Rookies (Dusty Baker, Don			
	Baylor, Tom Paciorek)	20.00	10.00	6.00
710	Sonny Siebert	1.50	.70	.45
711	Larry Stahl	1.50	.70	.45
712	Jose Martinez	1.50	.70	.45
713	Mike Marshall	2.50	1.25	.70
714	Dick Williams	2.50	1.25	.70
715	Horace Clarke	1.75	.90	.50
716	Dave Leonhard	1.50	.70	.45
717	Tommie Aaron	1.75	.90	.50
718	Billy Wynne	1.50	.70	.45
719	Jerry May	1.50	.70	.45
720	Matty Alou	2.50	1.25	.70
721	John Morris	1.50	.70	.45
722	Astros Team	3.25	1.75	1.00
723	Vicente Romo	1.50	.70	.45
724	Tom Tischinski	1.50	.70	.45
725	Gary Gentry	1.50	.70	.45
726	Paul Popovich	1.50	.70	.45
727	Ray Lamb	1.50	.70	.45
728	N.L. Rookies (Keith Lampard, Wayne			
	Redmond, Bernie Williams)	1.50	.70	.45
729	Dick Billings	1.50	.70	.45
730	Jim Rooker	1.50	.70	.45
731	Jim Qualls	1.50	.70	.45
732	Bob Reed	1.50	.70	.45
733	Lee Maye	1.50	.70	.45
734	Rob Gardner	1.75	.90	.50
735	Mike Shannon	1.75	.90	.50
736	Mel Queen	1.50	.70	.45
737	Preston Gomez	1.50	.70	.45
738	Russ Gibson	1.50	.70	.45
739	Barry Lersch	1.50	.70	.45
740	Luis Aparicio	10.00	5.00	3.00
741	Skip Guinn	1.50	.70	.45
742	Royals Team	3.25	1.75	1.00
743	John O'Donoghue	1.50	.70	.45
744	Chuck Manuel	1.50	.70	.45
745	Sandy Alomar	1.50	.70	.45
746	Andy Kosco	1.50	.70	.45
747	N.L. Rookies (Balor Moore, Al Severinsen,			
	Scipio Spinks)	1.50	.70	.45
748	John Purdin	1.50	.70	.45
749	Ken Szotkiewicz	1.50	.70	.45
750	Denny McLain	4.00	2.00	1.25
751	Al Weis	1.75	.70	.45
752	Dick Drago	3.50	.80	.45

1971 Topps Baseball Tattoos

Topps once again produced baseball tattoos in 1971. This time, the tattoos came in a variety of sizes, shapes and themes. The sheets of tattoos measured 3½'' by 14¼.'' Each sheet contained an assortment of tattoos in two sizes, 1-3/4'' by 2-3/8,'' or 1-3/16''

by 1-3/4.'' There were players, facsimile auto-graphed baseballs, team pennants and assorted base-ball cartoon figures carried on the 16 different sheets. Listings below are for complete sheets; with the exception of the biggest-name stars, individual tat-toos have little or no collector value.

	NR MT	EX	VG
Complete Sheet Set:	125.00	62.00	37.00
Common Sheet:	3.00	1.50	.90

1   Brooks Robinson Autograph, Montreal Expos Pennant, San Francisco Giants Pennant, Sal Bando, Dick Bosman, Nate Colbert, Cleon Jones, Juan Marichal, B. Robinson   9.00   4.50   2.75

2   Boston Red Sox Pennant, CArl Yastrzemski Autograph, New York Mets Pennant, Glenn Beckert, Tommy Harper, Ken Henderson, Fritz Peterson, Bob Robertson, C. Yastrzemski   15.00   7.50   4.50

3   Jim Fregosi Autograph, New York Yankees Pennant, Philadelphia Phillies Pennant, Orlando Cepeda, Jim Fregosi, Randy Hundley, Reggie Jackson, Jerry Koosman, Jim Palmer   13.00   6.50   4.00

4   Kansas City Royals Pennant, Oakland Athletics Pennant, Sam McDowell Autograph, Dick Dietz, C. Gaston, Dave Johnson, Sam McDowell, Gary Nolan, Amos Otis   3.50   1.75   1.00

5   Al Kaline Autograph, Atlanta Braves Pennant, L.A. Dodgers Pennant, B. Grabarkewitz, Al Kaline, Lee May, Tom Murphy, Vada Pinson, M. Sanguillen   9.00   4.50   2.75

6   Chicago Cubs Pennant, Cincinnati Reds Pennant, Harmon Killebrew Autograph, Luis Aparicio, Paul Blair, C. Cannizzaro, D. Clendenon, Larry Dieker, H. Killebrew   9.00   4.50   2.75

7   Boog Powell Autograph, Cleveland Indians Pennant, Milwaukee Brewers Pennant, Rich Allen, B. Campaneris, Don Money, Boog Powell, Ted Savage, Rusty Staub   4.00   2.00   1.25

8   Chicago White Sox Pennant, Frank Howard Autograph, San Diego Padres Pennant, Leo Cardenas, Bill Hands, Frank Howard, Wes Parker, Reggie Smith, W. Stargell   4.00   2.00   1.25

9   Detroit Tigers Pennant, Henry Aaron Autograph, Hank Aaron, Tommy Agee, Jim Hunter, Dick McAuliffe, Tony Perez, Lou Piniella   13.00   6.50   4.00

10   Baltimore Orioles Pennant, Fergie Jenkins Autograph, R. Clemente, T. Conigliaro, Fergie Jenkins, T. Munson, Gary Peters, Joe Torre   11.00   5.50   3.25

11   Johnny Bench Autograph, Washington Senators Pennant, Johnny Bench, Rico Carty, B. Mazeroski, Bob Oliver, R. Petrocelli, F. Robinson   9.00   4.50   2.75

12   Billy Williams Autograph, Houston Astros Pennant, Bill Freehan, Dave McNally, Felix Millan, M. Stottlemyre, Bob Tolan, Billy Williams   4.50   2.25   1.25

13   Pittsburgh Pirates Pennant, Willie McCovey Autograph, Ray Culp, Bud Harrelson, Mickey Lolich, W. McCovey, Ron Santo, Roy White   8.00   4.00   2.50

14   Minnesota Twins Pennant, Tom Seaver Autograph, Bill Melton, Jim Perry, Pete Rose, Tom Seaver, Maury Wills, Clyde Wright   25.00   12.50   7.50

15   Robert Gibson Autograph, St. Louis Cardinals Pennant, Rod Carew, Bob Gibson, Alex Johnson, Don Kessinger, Jim Merritt, Rick Monday   8.00   4.00   2.50

16   California Angels Pennant, Willie Mays Autograph, Larry Bowa, Mike Cuellar, Ray Fosse, Willie Mays, Carl Morton, Tony Oliva   13.00   6.50   4.00

1971 Topps Coins

Measuring 1½'' in diameter, the latest edition of the Topps coins was a 153-piece set. The coins fea-ture a color photograph surrounded by a colored band on the front. The band carried the player's name, team, position and several stars. Backs had a short biography, the coin number and encourage-ment to collect the entire set. Back colors differ with #1-51 having a brass back, #52-102 chrome backs, and the rest have blue backs. Most of the stars of the period are included in the set.

		NR MT	EX	VG
Complete Set:		400.00	200.00	120.00
Common Player:		.90	.45	.25
1	Clarence Gaston	.90	.45	.25
2	Dave Johnson	1.25	.60	.40
3	Jim Bunning	2.00	1.00	.60
4	Jim Spencer	.90	.45	.25
5	Felix Millan	.90	.45	.25
6	Gerry Moses	.90	.45	.25
7	Fergie Jenkins	2.00	1.00	.60
8	Felipe Alou	1.00	.50	.30
9	Jim McGlothlin	.90	.45	.25
10	Dick McAuliffe	.90	.45	.25
11	Joe Torre	1.50	.70	.45
12	Jim Perry	1.25	.60	.40
13	Bobby Bonds	1.25	.60	.40
14	Danny Cater	.90	.45	.25
15	Bill Mazeroski	1.50	.70	.45
16	Luis Aparicio	5.00	2.50	1.50
17	Doug Rader	.90	.45	.25
18	Vada Pinson	1.50	.70	.45
19	John Bateman	.90	.45	.25
20	Lew Krausse	.90	.45	.25
21	Billy Grabarkewitz	.90	.45	.25
22	Frank Howard	1.50	.70	.45
23	Jerry Koosman	1.25	.60	.40
24	Rod Carew	12.00	6.00	3.50
25	Al Ferrara	.90	.45	.25
26	Dave McNally	1.00	.50	.30
27	Jim Hickman	.90	.45	.25
28	Sandy Alomar	.90	.45	.25
29	Lee May	1.00	.50	.30
30	Rico Petrocelli	1.00	.50	.30
31	Don Money	.90	.45	.25
32	Jim Rooker	.90	.45	.25
33	Dick Dietz	.90	.45	.25
34	Roy White	1.00	.50	.30
35	Carl Morton	.90	.45	.25
36	Walt Williams	.90	.45	.25
37	Phil Niekro	3.25	1.75	1.00
38	Bill Freehan	1.00	.50	.30
39	Julian Javier	.90	.45	.25
40	Rick Monday	1.00	.50	.30
41	Don Wilson	.90	.45	.25
42	Ray Fosse	.90	.45	.25
43	Art Shamsky	.90	.45	.25
44	Ted Savage	.90	.45	.25
45	Claude Osteen	1.00	.50	.30
46	Ed Brinkman	.90	.45	.25
47	Matty Alou	1.00	.50	.30
48	Bob Oliver	.90	.45	.25
49	Danny Coombs	.90	.45	.25
50	Frank Robinson	8.00	4.00	2.50
51	Randy Hundley	.90	.45	.25
52	Cesar Tovar	.90	.45	.25
53	Wayne Simpson	.90	.45	.25
54	Bobby Murcer	1.25	.60	.40
55	Tony Taylor	.90	.45	.25
56	Tommy John	2.50	1.25	.70
57	Willie McCovey	7.50	3.75	2.25
58	Carl Yastrzemski	20.00	10.00	6.00
59	Bob Bailey	.90	.45	.25
60	Clyde Wright	.90	.45	.25
61	Orlando Cepeda	2.00	1.00	.60
62	Al Kaline	8.00	4.00	2.50
63	Bob Gibson	7.50	3.75	2.25
64	Bert Campaneris	1.25	.60	.40

		NR MT	EX	VG
65	Ted Sizemore	.90	.45	.25
66	Duke Sims	.90	.45	.25
67	Bud Harrelson	.90	.45	.25
68	Jerry McNertney	.90	.45	.25
69	Jim Wynn	1.00	.50	.30
70	Dick Bosman	.90	.45	.25
71	Roberto Clemente	15.00	7.50	4.50
72	Rich Reese	.90	.45	.25
73	Gaylord Perry	3.50	1.75	1.00
74	Boog Powell	1.50	.70	.45
75	Billy Williams	5.00	2.50	1.50
76	Bill Melton	.90	.45	.25
77	Nate Colbert	.90	.45	.25
78	Reggie Smith	1.25	.60	.40
79	Deron Johnson	.90	.45	.25
80	Jim Hunter	5.00	2.50	1.50
81	Bob Tolan	.90	.45	.25
82	Jim Northrup	.90	.45	.25
83	Ron Fairly	1.00	.50	.30
84	Alex Johnson	.90	.45	.25
85	Pat Jarvis	.90	.45	.25
86	Sam McDowell	1.00	.50	.30
87	Lou Brock	8.00	4.00	2.50
88	Danny Walton	.90	.45	.25
89	Denis Menke	.90	.45	.25
90	Jim Palmer	5.00	2.50	1.50
91	Tommie Agee	.90	.45	.25
92	Duane Josephson	.90	.45	.25
93	Willie Davis	1.00	.50	.30
94	Mel Stottlemyre	1.00	.50	.30
95	Ron Santo	1.25	.60	.40
96	Amos Otis	1.00	.50	.30
97	Ken Henderson	.90	.45	.25
98	George Scott	1.00	.50	.30
99	Dock Ellis	.90	.45	.25
100	Harmon Killebrew	8.00	4.00	2.50
101	Pete Rose	30.00	15.00	9.00
102	Rick Reichardt	.90	.45	.25
103	Cleon Jones	.90	.45	.25
104	Ron Perranoski	.90	.45	.25
105	Tony Perez	2.50	1.25	.70
106	Mickey Lolich	1.25	.60	.40
107	Tim McCarver	1.25	.60	.40
108	Reggie Jackson	12.00	6.00	3.50
109	Chris Cannizzaro	.90	.45	.25
110	Steve Hargan	.90	.45	.25
111	Rusty Staub	2.50	1.25	.70
112	Andy Messersmith	1.00	.50	.30
113	Rico Carty	1.25	.60	.40
114	Brooks Robinson	7.00	3.50	2.00
115	Steve Carlton	7.00	3.50	2.00
116	Mike Hegan	.90	.45	.25
117	Joe Morgan	4.50	2.25	1.25
118	Thurman Munson	5.00	2.50	1.50
119	Don Kessinger	1.00	.50	.30
120	Joe Horlen	.90	.45	.25
121	Wes Parker	1.00	.50	.30
122	Sonny Siebert	.90	.45	.25
123	Willie Stargell	5.00	2.50	1.50
124	Ellie Rodriguez	.90	.45	.25
125	Juan Marichal	7.00	3.50	2.00
126	Mike Epstein	.90	.45	.25
127	Tom Seaver	7.00	3.50	2.00
128	Tony Oliva	2.50	1.25	.70
129	Jim Merritt	.90	.45	.25
130	Willie Horton	1.00	.50	.30
131	Rick Wise	.90	.45	.25
132	Sal Bando	1.00	.50	.30
133	Ollie Brown	.90	.45	.25
134	Ken Harrelson	1.00	.50	.30
135	Mack Jones	.90	.45	.25
136	Jim Fregosi	1.00	.50	.30
137	Hank Aaron	15.00	7.50	4.50
138	Fritz Peterson	.90	.45	.25
139	Joe Hague	.90	.45	.25
140	Tommy Harper	.90	.45	.25
141	Larry Dierker	.90	.45	.25
142	Tony Conigliaro	1.50	.70	.45
143	Glenn Beckert	1.00	.50	.30
144	Carlos May	.90	.45	.25
145	Don Sutton	3.25	1.75	1.00
146	Paul Casanova	.90	.45	.25
147	Bob Moose	.90	.45	.25
148	Leo Cardenas	.90	.45	.25
149	Johnny Bench	7.00	3.50	2.00
150	Mike Cuellar	1.00	.50	.30
151	Donn Clendenon	.90	.45	.25
152	Lou Piniella	1.25	.60	.40
153	Willie Mays	15.00	7.50	4.50

1971 Topps Greatest Moments

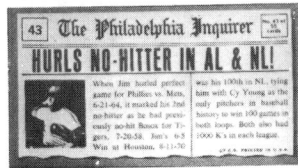

This 55-card set features a great moment from the careers of top players at the time. The front of the 2½'' by x4¾'' cards features a portrait photo of the player at the left and deckle-edge action photo at the right. There is a small headline on the white border of the action photo. The player's name and ''One of Baseball's Greatest Moments'' along with a black border complete the front. The back features a detail from the front photo and the story of the event. The newspaper style presentation includes the name of real newspapers. Relatively scarce, virtually every card in this set is a star or at least an above-average player.

		NR MT	EX	VG
Complete Set:		1100.00	550.00	330.00
Common Player:		4.00	2.00	1.25
1	Thurman Munson	40.00	20.00	12.00
2	Hoyt Wilhelm	25.00	12.50	7.50
3	Rico Carty	12.00	6.00	3.50
4	Carl Morton	4.00	2.00	1.25
5	Sal Bando	5.00	2.50	1.50
6	Bert Campaneris	5.00	2.50	1.50
7	Jim Kaat	20.00	10.00	6.00
8	Harmon Killebrew	50.00	25.00	15.00
9	Brooks Robinson	70.00	35.00	21.00
10	Jim Perry	15.00	7.50	4.50
11	Tony Oliva	18.00	9.00	5.50
12	Vada Pinson	18.00	9.00	5.50
13	Johnny Bench	150.00	75.00	45.00
14	Tony Perez	20.00	10.00	6.00
15	Pete Rose	90.00	45.00	27.00
16	Jim Fregosi	4.00	2.00	1.25
17	Alex Johnson	4.00	2.00	1.25
18	Clyde Wright	4.00	2.00	1.25
19	Al Kaline	25.00	12.50	7.50
20	Denny McLain	18.00	9.00	5.50
21	Jim Northrup	12.00	6.00	3.50
22	Bill Freehan	15.00	7.50	4.50
23	Mickey Lolich	18.00	9.00	5.50
24	Bob Gibson	18.00	9.00	5.50
25	Tim McCarver	5.00	2.50	1.50
26	Orlando Cepeda	7.00	3.50	2.00
27	Lou Brock	18.00	9.00	5.50
28	Nate Colbert	4.00	2.00	1.25
29	Maury Wills	18.00	9.00	5.50
30	Wes Parker	12.00	6.00	3.50
31	Jim Wynn	15.00	7.50	4.50
32	Larry Dierker	12.00	6.00	3.50
33	Bill Melton	12.00	6.00	3.50
34	Joe Morgan	35.00	17.50	10.50
35	Rusty Staub	18.00	9.00	5.50
36	Ernie Banks	25.00	12.50	7.50
37	Billy Williams	30.00	15.00	9.00
38	Lou Piniella	18.00	9.00	5.50
39	Rico Petrocelli	4.00	2.00	1.25
40	Carl Yastrzemski	60.00	30.00	18.00
41	Willie Mays	45.00	22.00	13.50
42	Tommy Harper	12.00	6.00	3.50
43	Jim Bunning	7.00	3.50	2.00
44	Fritz Peterson	12.00	6.00	3.50
45	Roy White	15.00	7.50	4.50
46	Bobby Murcer	15.00	7.50	4.50
47	Reggie Jackson	175.00	87.00	52.00

		NR MT	EX	VG
48	Frank Howard	18.00	9.00	5.50
49	Dick Bosman	12.00	6.00	3.50
50	Sam McDowell	4.00	2.00	1.25
51	Luis Aparicio	12.00	6.00	3.50
52	Willie McCovey	15.00	7.50	4.50
53	Joe Pepitone	15.00	7.50	4.50
54	Jerry Grote	12.00	6.00	3.50
55	Bud Harrelson	12.00	6.00	3.50

1971 Topps Supers

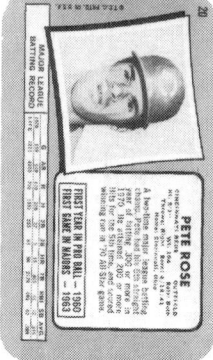

		NR MT	EX	VG
36	Tommie Agee	.70	.35	.20
37	Roberto Clemente	10.00	5.00	3.00
38	Reggie Jackson	15.00	7.50	4.50
39	Clyde Wright	.70	.35	.20
40	Rich Allen	1.50	.70	.45
41	Curt Flood	1.25	.60	.40
42	Fergie Jenkins	1.75	.90	.50
43	Willie Stargell	3.00	1.50	.90
44	Henry Aaron	10.00	5.00	3.00
45	Amos Otis	1.00	.50	.30
46	Willie McCovey	4.50	2.25	1.25
47	William Melton	.70	.35	.20
48	Robert Gibson	3.50	1.75	1.00
49	Carl Yastrzemski	15.00	7.50	4.50
50	Glenn Beckert	1.00	.50	.30
51	Ray Fosse	.70	.35	.20
52	Clarence Gaston	.70	.35	.20
53	Tom Seaver	8.00	4.00	2.50
54	Al Kaline	6.00	3.00	1.75
55	Jim Northrup	.70	.35	.20
56	Willie Mays	10.00	5.00	3.00
57	Sal Bando	1.00	.50	.30
58	Deron Johnson	.70	.35	.20
59	Brooks Robinson	7.00	3.50	2.00
60	Harmon Killebrew	6.00	3.00	1.75
61	Joseph Torre	1.75	.90	.50
62	Lou Piniella	1.25	.60	.40
63	Tommy Harper	.70	.35	.20

Topps continued to produce its special oversized cards in 1971. The cards, measuring 3⅛" by 5¼," carried a large color photograph with a facsimile autograph on the front. Backs were basically enlargements of the player's regular Topps card. The set size was enlarged to 63 cards in 1971, so there were no short-printed cards as in 1970. Again, Topps included almost every major star who was active at the time, so the set of oversized cards with rounded corners remains an interesting source for those seeking the big names of the era.

		NR MT	EX	VG
	Complete Set:	175.00	87.00	52.00
	Common Player:	.70	.35	.20
1	Reggie Smith	1.00	.50	.30
2	Gaylord Perry	3.00	1.50	.90
3	Ted Savage	.70	.35	.20
4	Donn Clendenon	.70	.35	.20
5	John "Boog" Powell	1.25	.60	.40
6	Tony Perez	1.75	.90	.50
7	Dick Bosman	.70	.35	.20
8	Alex Johnson	.70	.35	.20
9	Rusty Staub	1.25	.60	.40
10	Mel Stottlemyre	1.00	.50	.30
11	Tony Oliva	1.50	.70	.45
12	Bill Freehan	1.00	.50	.30
13	Fritz Peterson	.70	.35	.20
14	Wes Parker	.70	.35	.20
15	Cesar Cedeno	1.25	.60	.40
16	Sam McDowell	1.00	.50	.30
17	Frank Howard	1.50	.70	.45
18	Dave McNally	1.00	.50	.30
19	Rico Petrocelli	.70	.35	.20
20	Pete Rose	25.00	12.50	7.50
21	Luke Walker	.70	.35	.20
22	Nate Colbert	.70	.35	.20
23	Luis Aparicio	2.50	1.25	.70
24	Jim Perry	1.00	.50	.30
25	Louis Brock	4.50	2.25	1.25
26	Roy White	1.00	.50	.30
27	Claude Osteen	.70	.35	.20
28	Carl W. Morton	.70	.35	.20
29	Ricardo A. Jacabo Carty	1.00	.50	.30
30	Larry Dierker	.70	.35	.20
31	Dagoberto Campaneris	1.00	.50	.30
32	Johnny Bench	7.00	3.50	2.00
33	Felix Millan	.70	.35	.20
34	Tim McCarver	1.25	.60	.40
35	Ronald Santo	1.25	.60	.40

1972 Topps

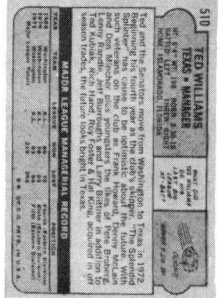

The largest Topps issue of its time appeared in 1972, with the set size reaching the 787 mark. The 2½" by 3½" cards are something special as well. Their fronts have a color photo which is shaped into an arch and surrounded by two different color borders, all of which is inside the overall white border. The player's name is in a white panel below the picture while the team name is above the picture in what might best be described as "superhero" type in a variety of colors. No mention of the player's position appears on the front. Cards backs are tame by comparison featuring statistics and a trivia question. The set featured a record number of speciality cards including more than six dozen "In Action" (shown as "IA" in checklists below) cards featuring action shots of popular players. There are the usual statistical leaders, Play-off and World Series highlights. Other innovations were 16 "Boyhood Photo" cards which depicted scrapbook black-and-whites of 1972's top players, and a group of cards depicting the trophies which comprise baseball's major awards. Finally, a group of seven "Traded" cards was included which featured a large "Traded" across the front of the card.

	NR MT	EX	VG
Complete Set:	900.00	325.00	180.00
Common Player: 1-394	.25	.13	.08
Common Player: 395-525	.30	.15	.09
Common Player: 526-656	.50	.25	.15
Common Player: 657-787	1.25	.60	.40
1　World Champions (Pirates Team)	4.00	.75	.45

		NR MT	EX	VG
2	Ray Culp	.25	.13	.08
3	Bob Tolan	.30	.15	.09
4	Checklist 1-132	2.25	1.25	.70
5	John Bateman	.25	.13	.08
6	Fred Scherman	.25	.13	.08
7	Enzo Hernandez	.25	.13	.08
8	Ron Swoboda	.30	.15	.09
9	Stan Williams	.25	.13	.08
10	Amos Otis	.40	.20	.12
11	Bobby Valentine	.60	.30	.20
12	Jose Cardenal	.30	.15	.09
13	Joe Grzenda	.25	.13	.08
14	Phillies Rookiess (Mike Anderson, Pete Koegel, Wayne Twitchell)	.25	.13	.08
15	Walt Williams	.25	.13	.08
16	Mike Jorgensen	.25	.13	.08
17	Dave Duncan	.25	.13	.08
18a	Juan Pizarro (green under "C" and "S")	3.50	1.75	1.00
18b	Juan Pizarro (yellow under "C" and "S")	.25	.13	.08
19	Billy Cowan	.25	.13	.08
20	Don Wilson	.25	.13	.08
21	Braves Team	.90	.45	.25
22	Rob Gardner	.30	.15	.09
23	Ted Kubiak	.25	.13	.08
24	Ted Ford	.25	.13	.08
25	Bill Singer	.30	.15	.09
26	Andy Etchebarren	.25	.13	.08
27	Bob Johnson	.25	.13	.08
28	Twins Rookies (Steve Brye, Bob Gebhard, Hal Haydel)	.25	.13	.08
29a	Bill Bonham (green under "C" and "S")	3.50	1.75	1.00
29b	Bill Bonham (yellow under "C" and "S")	.30	.15	.09
30	Rico Petrocelli	.50	.25	.15
31	Cleon Jones	.30	.15	.09
32	Cleon Jones IA	.30	.15	.09
33	Billy Martin	1.50	.70	.45
34	Billy Martin IA	.80	.40	.25
35	Jerry Johnson	.25	.13	.08
36	Jerry Johnson IA	.25	.13	.08
37	Carl Yastrzemski	12.00	6.00	3.50
38	Carl Yastrzemski IA	6.00	3.00	1.75
39	Bob Barton	.25	.13	.08
40	Bob Barton IA	.25	.13	.08
41	Tommy Davis	.60	.30	.20
42	Tommy Davis IA	.30	.15	.09
43	Rick Wise	.30	.15	.09
44	Rick Wise IA	.25	.13	.08
45a	Glenn Beckert (green under "C" and "S")	3.50	1.75	1.00
45b	Glenn Beckert (yellow under "C" and "S")	.40	.20	.12
46	Glenn Beckert IA	.30	.15	.09
47	John Ellis	.30	.15	.09
48	John Ellis IA	.30	.15	.09
49	Willie Mays	12.00	6.00	3.50
50	Willie Mays IA	6.00	3.00	1.75
51	Harmon Killebrew	4.00	2.00	1.25
52	Harmon Killebrew IA	2.00	1.00	.60
53	Bud Harrelson	.40	.20	.12
54	Bud Harrelson IA	.30	.15	.09
55	Clyde Wright	.25	.13	.08
56	Rich Chiles	.25	.13	.08
57	Bob Oliver	.25	.13	.08
58	Ernie McAnally	.25	.13	.08
59	Fred Stanley	.40	.20	.12
60	Manny Sanguillen	.30	.15	.09
61	Cubs Rookies (Gene Hiser, Burt Hooton, Earl Stephenson)	1.00	.50	.30
62	Angel Mangual	.25	.13	.08
63	Duke Sims	.25	.13	.08
64	Pete Broberg	.25	.13	.08
65	Cesar Cedeno	.80	.40	.25
66	Ray Corbin	.25	.13	.08
67	Red Schoendienst	.50	.25	.15
68	Jim York	.25	.13	.08
69	Roger Freed	.25	.13	.08
70	Mike Cuellar	.50	.25	.15
71	Angels Team	.90	.45	.25
72	Bruce Kison	.80	.40	.25
73	Steve Huntz	.25	.13	.08
74	Cecil Upshaw	.25	.13	.08
75	Bert Campaneris	.60	.30	.20
76	Don Carrithers	.25	.13	.08
77	Ron Theobald	.25	.13	.08
78	Steve Arlin	.25	.13	.08
79	Red Sox Rookies (Cecil Cooper, Carlton Fisk, Mike Garman)	15.00	7.50	4.50
80	Tony Perez	2.00	1.00	.60
81	Mike Hedlund	.25	.13	.08
82	Ron Woods	.25	.13	.08
83	Dalton Jones	.25	.13	.08
84	Vince Colbert	.25	.13	.08
85	N.L. Batting Leaders (Glenn Beckert, Ralph Garr, Joe Torre)	1.25	.60	.40
86	A.L. Batting Leaders (Bobby Murcer, Tony Oliva, Merv Rettenmund)	1.25	.60	.40
87	N.L. RBI Leaders (Hank Aaron, Willie Stargell, Joe Torre)	2.25	1.25	.70
88	A.L. RBI Leaders (Harmon Killebrew, Frank Robinson, Reggie Smith)	2.25	1.25	.70
89	N.L. Home Run Leaders (Hank Aaron, Lee May, Willie Stargell)	2.25	1.25	.70
90	A.L. Home Run Leaders (Norm Cash, Reggie Jackson, Bill Melton)	.90	.50	.50
91	N.L. ERA Leaders (Dave Roberts, Tom Seaver, Don Wilson)	1.75	.90	.50
92	A.L. ERA Leaders (Vida Blue, Jim Palmer, Wilbur Wood)	1.50	.70	.45
93	N.L. Pitching Leaders (Steve Carlton, Al Downing, Fergie Jenkins, Tom Seaver)	2.00	1.00	.60
94	A.L. Pitching Leaders (Vida Blue, Mickey Lolich, Wilbur Wood)	1.25	.60	.40
95	N.L. Strikeout Leaders (Fergie Jenkins, Tom Seaver, Bill Stoneman)	1.75	.90	.50
96	A.L. Strikeout Leaders (Vida Blue, Joe Coleman, Mickey Lolich)	1.25	.60	.40
97	Tom Kelley	.25	.13	.08
98	Chuck Tanner	.50	.25	.15
99	Ross Grimsley	.60	.30	.20
100	Frank Robinson	4.00	2.00	1.25
101	Astros Rookies (Ray Busse, Bill Grief, J.R. Richard)	1.00	.50	.30
102	Lloyd Allen	.25	.13	.08
103	Checklist 133-263	2.25	1.25	.70
104	Toby Harrah	1.00	.50	.30
105	Gary Gentry	.25	.13	.08
106	Brewers Team	.90	.45	.25
107	Jose Cruz	1.75	.90	.50
108	Gary Waslewski	.30	.15	.09
109	Jerry May	.25	.13	.08
110	Ron Hunt	.30	.15	.09
111	Jim Grant	.25	.13	.08
112	Greg Luzinski	.80	.40	.25
113	Rogelio Moret	.25	.13	.08
114	Bill Buckner	1.25	.60	.40
115	Jim Fregosi	.70	.35	.20
116	Ed Farmer	.30	.15	.09
117a	Cleo James (green under "C" and "S")	3.50	1.75	1.00
117b	Cleo James (yellow under "C" and "S")	.25	.13	.08
118	Skip Lockwood	.25	.13	.08
119	Marty Perez	.25	.13	.08
120	Bill Freehan	.60	.30	.20
121	Ed Sprague	.25	.13	.08
122	Larry Biittner	.25	.13	.08
123	Ed Acosta	.25	.13	.08
124	Yankees (Alan Closter, Roger Hambright, Rusty Torres)	.30	.15	.09
125	Dave Cash	.25	.13	.08
126	Bart Johnson	.25	.13	.08
127	Duffy Dyer	.25	.13	.08
128	Eddie Watt	.25	.13	.08
129	Charlie Fox	.25	.13	.08
130	Bob Gibson	4.00	2.00	1.25
131	Jim Nettles	.25	.13	.08
132	Joe Morgan	2.50	1.25	.70
133	Joe Keough	.25	.13	.08
134	Carl Morton	.25	.13	.08
135	Vada Pinson	.80	.40	.25
136	Darrel Chaney	.25	.13	.08
137	Dick Williams	.50	.25	.15
138	Mike Kekich	.30	.15	.09
139	Tim McCarver	.80	.40	.25
140	Pat Dobson	.30	.15	.09
141	Mets Rookies (Buzz Capra, Jon Matlack, Leroy Stanton)	.40	.20	.12
142	Chris Chambliss	1.50	.70	.45
143	Garry Jestadt	.25	.13	.08
144	Marty Pattin	.25	.13	.08
145	Don Kessinger	.40	.20	.12
146	Steve Kealey	.25	.13	.08
147	Dave Kingman	3.50	1.75	1.00
148	Dick Billings	.25	.13	.08
149	Gary Neibauer	.25	.13	.08
150	Norm Cash	.70	.35	.20
151	Jim Brewer	.25	.13	.08

#	Player	NR MT	EX	VG
152	Gene Clines	.25	.13	.08
153	Rick Auerbach	.25	.13	.08
154	Ted Simmons	1.50	.70	.45
155	Larry Dierker	.30	.15	.09
156	Twins Team	.90	.45	.25
157	Don Gullett	.40	.20	.12
158	Jerry Kenney	.30	.15	.09
159	John Boccabella	.25	.13	.08
160	Andy Messersmith	.40	.20	.12
161	Brock Davis	.25	.13	.08
162	Brewers Rookies (Jerry Bell, Darrell Porter, Bob Reynolds) (Bell & Porter photos transposed)	1.00	.50	.30
163	Tug McGraw	.80	.40	.25
164	Tug McGraw IA	.40	.20	.12
165	Chris Speier	.80	.40	.25
166	Chris Speier IA	.40	.20	.12
167	Deron Johnson	.25	.13	.08
168	Deron Johnson IA	.25	.13	.08
169	Vida Blue	.80	.40	.25
170	Vida Blue IA	.40	.20	.12
171	Darrell Evans	1.50	.70	.45
172	Darrell Evans IA	.80	.40	.25
173	Clay Kirby	.25	.13	.08
174	Clay Kirby IA	.25	.13	.08
175	Tom Haller	.30	.15	.09
176	Tom Haller IA	.25	.13	.08
177	Paul Schaal	.25	.13	.08
178	Paul Schaal IA	.25	.13	.08
179	Dock Ellis	.30	.15	.09
180	Dock Ellis IA	.25	.13	.08
181	Ed Kranepool	.40	.20	.12
182	Ed Kranepool IA	.30	.15	.09
183	Bill Melton	.30	.15	.09
184	Bill Melton IA	.25	.13	.08
185	Ron Bryant	.25	.13	.08
186	Ron Bryant IA	.25	.13	.08
187	Gates Brown	.25	.13	.08
188	Frank Lucchesi	.25	.13	.08
189	Gene Tenace	.40	.20	.12
190	Dave Giusti	.25	.13	.08
191	Jeff Burroughs	.80	.40	.25
192	Cubs Team	.90	.45	.25
193	Kurt Bevacqua	.40	.20	.12
194	Fred Norman	.25	.13	.08
195	Orlando Cepeda	2.00	1.00	.60
196	Mel Queen	.25	.13	.08
197	Johnny Briggs	.25	.13	.08
198	Dodgers Rookies (Charlie Hough, Bob O'Brien, Mike Strahler)	1.50	.70	.45
199	Mike Fiore	.25	.13	.08
200	Lou Brock	4.00	2.00	1.25
201	Phil Roof	.25	.13	.08
202	Scipio Spinks	.25	.13	.08
203	Ron Blomberg	.50	.25	.15
204	Tommy Helms	.25	.13	.08
205	Dick Drago	.25	.13	.08
206	Dal Maxvill	.30	.15	.09
207	Tom Egan	.25	.13	.08
208	Milt Pappas	.40	.20	.12
209	Joe Rudi	.60	.30	.20
210	Denny McLain	1.25	.60	.40
211	Gary Sutherland	.25	.13	.08
212	Grant Jackson	.25	.13	.08
213	Angels Rookies (Art Kusnyer, Billy Parker, Tom Silverio)	.25	.13	.08
214	Mike McQueen	.25	.13	.08
215	Alex Johnson	.25	.13	.08
216	Joe Niekro	.50	.25	.15
217	Roger Metzger	.25	.13	.08
218	Eddie Kasko	.25	.13	.08
219	Rennie Stennett	.40	.20	.12
220	Jim Perry	.60	.30	.20
221	N.L. Playoffs (Bucs Champs!)	1.25	.60	.40
222	A.L. Playoffs (Orioles Champs!)	1.25	.60	.40
223	World Series Game 1	1.25	.60	.40
224	World Series Game 2	1.25	.60	.40
225	World Series Game 3	1.25	.60	.40
226	World Series Game 4	1.50	.70	.45
227	World Series Game 5	1.25	.60	.40
228	World Series Game 6	1.25	.60	.40
229	World Series Game 7	1.25	.60	.40
230	World Series Summary (Series Celebration)	1.25	.60	.40
231	Casey Cox	.25	.13	.08
232	Giants Rookies (Chris Arnold, Jim Barr, Dave Rader)	.30	.15	.09
233	Jay Johnstone	.40	.20	.12
234	Ron Taylor	.25	.13	.08
235	Merv Rettenmund	.30	.15	.09
236	Jim McGlothlin	.25	.13	.08

#	Player	NR MT	EX	VG
237	Yankees Team	1.25	.60	.40
238	Leron Lee	.25	.13	.08
239	Tom Timmermann	.25	.13	.08
240	Rich Allen	1.75	.90	.50
241	Rollie Fingers	2.50	1.25	.70
242	Don Mincher	.30	.15	.09
243	Frank Linzy	.25	.13	.08
244	Steve Braun	.25	.13	.08
245	Tommie Agee	.30	.15	.09
246	Tom Burgmeier	.25	.13	.08
247	Milt May	.25	.13	.08
248	Tom Bradley	.25	.13	.08
249	Harry Walker	.30	.15	.09
250	Boog Powell	1.25	.60	.40
251a	Checklist 264-394 (small print on front)	2.25	1.25	.70
251b	Checklist 264-394 (large print on front)	2.25	1.25	.70
252	Ken Reynolds	.25	.13	.08
253	Sandy Alomar	.25	.13	.08
254	Boots Day	.25	.13	.08
255	Jim Lonborg	.40	.20	.12
256	George Foster	1.50	.70	.45
257	Tigers Rookies (Jim Foor, Tim Hosley, Paul Jata)	.25	.13	.08
258	Randy Hundley	.25	.13	.08
259	Sparky Lyle	.70	.35	.20
260	Ralph Garr	.40	.20	.12
261	Steve Mingori	.25	.13	.08
262	Padres Team	.90	.45	.25
263	Felipe Alou	.50	.25	.15
264	Tommy John	2.00	1.00	.60
265	Wes Parker	.30	.15	.09
266	Bobby Bolin	.25	.13	.08
267	Dave Concepcion	1.75	.90	.50
268	A's Rookies (Dwain Anderson, Chris Floethe)	.25	.13	.08
269	Don Hahn	.25	.13	.08
270	Jim Palmer	4.00	2.00	1.25
271	Ken Rudolph	.25	.13	.08
272	Mickey Rivers	1.00	.50	.30
273	Bobby Floyd	.25	.13	.08
274	Al Severinsen	.25	.13	.08
275	Cesar Tovar	.25	.13	.08
276	Gene Mauch	.50	.25	.15
277	Elliott Maddox	.30	.15	.09
278	Dennis Higgins	.25	.13	.08
279	Larry Brown	.25	.13	.08
280	Willie McCovey	4.00	2.00	1.25
281	Bill Parsons	.25	.13	.08
282	Astros Team	.90	.45	.25
283	Darrell Brandon	.25	.13	.08
284	Ike Brown	.25	.13	.08
285	Gaylord Perry	4.00	2.00	1.25
286	Gene Alley	.30	.15	.09
287	Jim Hardin	.30	.15	.09
288	Johnny Jeter	.25	.13	.08
289	Syd O'Brien	.25	.13	.08
290	Sonny Siebert	.25	.13	.08
291	Hal McRae	.60	.30	.20
292	Hal McRae IA	.30	.15	.09
293	Danny Frisella	.25	.13	.08
294	Danny Frisella IA	.25	.13	.08
295	Dick Dietz	.25	.13	.08
296	Dick Dietz IA	.25	.13	.08
297	Claude Osteen	.40	.20	.12
298	Claude Osteen IA	.30	.15	.09
299	Hank Aaron	12.00	6.00	3.50
300	Hank Aaron IA	6.00	3.00	1.75
301	George Mitterwald	.25	.13	.08
302	George Mitterwald IA	.25	.13	.08
303	Joe Pepitone	.50	.25	.15
304	Joe Pepitone IA	.30	.15	.09
305	Ken Boswell	.25	.13	.08
306	Ken Boswell IA	.25	.13	.08
307	Steve Renko	.25	.13	.08
308	Steve Renko IA	.25	.13	.08
309	Roberto Clemente	12.00	6.00	3.50
310	Roberto Clemente IA	6.00	3.00	1.75
311	Clay Carroll	.30	.15	.09
312	Clay Carroll IA	.25	.13	.08
313	Luis Aparicio	3.00	1.50	.90
314	Luis Aparicio IA	1.50	.70	.45
315	Paul Splittorff	.30	.15	.09
316	Cardinals Rookies (Jim Bibby, Santiago Guzman, Jorge Roque)	.50	.25	.15
317	Rich Hand	.25	.13	.08
318	Sonny Jackson	.25	.13	.08
319	Aurelio Rodriguez	.30	.15	.09
320	Steve Blass	.30	.15	.09
321	Joe Lahoud	.25	.13	.08

		NR MT	EX	VG
322	Jose Pena	.25	.13	.08
323	Earl Weaver	.80	.40	.25
324	Mike Ryan	.25	.13	.08
325	Mel Stottlemyre	.80	.40	.25
326	Pat Kelly	.25	.13	.08
327	Steve Stone	1.00	.50	.30
328	Red Sox Team	1.00	.50	.30
329	Roy Foster	.25	.13	.08
330	Jim Hunter	3.50	1.75	1.00
331	Stan Swanson	.25	.13	.08
332	Buck Martinez	.25	.13	.08
333	Steve Barber	.25	.13	.08
334	Rangers Rookies (Bill Fahey, Jim Mason, Tom Ragland)	.25	.13	.08
335	Bill Hands	.25	.13	.08
336	Marty Martinez	.25	.13	.08
337	Mike Kilkenny	.25	.13	.08
338	Bob Grich	.70	.35	.20
339	Ron Cook	.25	.13	.08
340	Roy White	.70	.35	.20
341	Boyhood Photo (Joe Torre)	.50	.25	.15
342	Boyhood Photo (Wilbur Wood)	.40	.20	.12
343	Boyhood Photo (Willie Stargell)	1.50	.70	.45
344	Boyhood Photo (Dave McNally)	.40	.20	.12
345	Boyhood Photo (Rick Wise)	.30	.15	.09
346	Boyhood Photo (Jim Fregosi)	.40	.20	.12
347	Boyhood Photo (Tom Seaver)	2.00	1.00	.60
348	Boyhood Photo (Sal Bando)	.40	.20	.12
349	Al Fitzmorris	.25	.13	.08
350	Frank Howard	1.25	.60	.40
351	Braves Rookies (Jimmy Britton, Tom House, Rick Kester)	.25	.13	.08
352	Dave LaRoche	.30	.15	.09
353	Art Shamsky	.25	.13	.08
354	Tom Murphy	.25	.13	.08
355	Bob Watson	.30	.15	.09
356	Gerry Moses	.25	.13	.08
357	Woodie Fryman	.30	.15	.09
358	Sparky Anderson	.70	.35	.20
359	Don Pavletich	.25	.13	.08
360	Dave Roberts	.25	.13	.08
361	Mike Andrews	.25	.13	.08
362	Mets Team	1.25	.60	.40
363	Ron Klimkowski	.25	.13	.08
364	Johnny Callison	.50	.25	.15
365	Dick Bosman	.25	.13	.08
366	Jimmy Rosario	.25	.13	.08
367	Ron Perranoski	.30	.15	.09
368	Danny Thompson	.30	.15	.09
369	Jim Lefebvre	.30	.15	.09
370	Don Buford	.30	.15	.09
371	Denny Lemaster	.25	.13	.08
372	Royals Rookies (Lance Clemons, Monty Montgomery)	.25	.13	.08
373	John Mayberry	.40	.20	.12
374	Jack Heidemann	.25	.13	.08
375	Reggie Cleveland	.25	.13	.08
376	Andy Kosco	.25	.13	.08
377	Terry Harmon	.25	.13	.08
378	Checklist 395-525	2.25	1.25	.70
379	Ken Berry	.25	.13	.08
380	Earl Williams	.30	.15	.09
381	White Sox Team	.90	.45	.25
382	Joe Gibbon	.25	.13	.08
383	Brant Alyea	.25	.13	.08
384	Dave Campbell	.25	.13	.08
385	Mickey Stanley	.30	.15	.09
386	Jim Colborn	.25	.13	.08
387	Horace Clarke	.30	.15	.09
388	Charlie Williams	.25	.13	.08
389	Bill Rigney	.25	.13	.08
390	Willie Davis	.50	.25	.15
391	Ken Sanders	.25	.13	.08
392	Pirates Rookies (Fred Cambria, Richie Zisk)	.70	.35	.20
393	Curt Motton	.25	.13	.08
394	Ken Forsch	.30	.15	.09
395	Matty Alou	.60	.30	.20
396	Paul Lindblad	.30	.15	.09
397	Phillies Team	.90	.45	.25
398	Larry Hisle	.40	.20	.12
399	Milt Wilcox	.40	.20	.12
400	Tony Oliva	1.50	.70	.45
401	Jim Nash	.30	.15	.09
402	Bobby Heise	.30	.15	.09
403	John Cumberland	.30	.15	.09
404	Jeff Torborg	.40	.20	.12
405	Ron Fairly	.50	.25	.15
406	George Hendrick	1.00	.50	.30
407	Chuck Taylor	.30	.15	.09
408	Jim Northrup	.40	.20	.12
409	Frank Baker	.40	.20	.12
410	Fergie Jenkins	2.00	1.00	.60
411	Bob Montgomery	.30	.15	.09
412	Dick Kelley	.30	.15	.09
413	White Sox Rookies (Don Eddy, Dave Lemonds)	.30	.15	.09
414	Bob Miller	.30	.15	.09
415	Cookie Rojas	.30	.15	.09
416	Johnny Edwards	.30	.15	.09
417	Tom Hall	.30	.15	.09
418	Tom Shopay	.30	.15	.09
419	Jim Spencer	.30	.15	.09
420	Steve Carlton	15.00	7.50	4.50
421	Ellie Rodriguez	.30	.15	.09
422	Ray Lamb	.30	.15	.09
423	Oscar Gamble	.40	.20	.12
424	Bill Gogolewski	.30	.15	.09
425	Ken Singleton	.70	.35	.20
426	Ken Singleton IA	.40	.20	.12
427	Tito Fuentes	.30	.15	.09
428	Tito Fuentes IA	.30	.15	.09
429	Bob Robertson	.30	.15	.09
430	Bob Robertson IA	.30	.15	.09
431	Clarence Gaston	.30	.15	.09
432	Clarence Gaston IA	.30	.15	.09
433	Johnny Bench	15.00	7.50	4.50
434	Johnny Bench IA	7.00	3.50	2.00
435	Reggie Jackson	15.00	7.50	4.50
436	Reggie Jackson IA	8.00	4.00	2.50
437	Maury Wills	1.50	.70	.45
438	Maury Wills IA	.70	.35	.20
439	Billy Williams	3.50	1.75	1.00
440	Billy Williams IA	1.75	.90	.50
441	Thurman Munson	9.00	4.50	2.75
442	Thurman Munson IA	4.00	2.00	1.25
443	Ken Henderson	.30	.15	.09
444	Ken Henderson IA	.30	.15	.09
445	Tom Seaver	12.00	6.00	3.50
446	Tom Seaver IA	6.00	3.00	1.75
447	Willie Stargell	4.00	2.00	1.25
448	Willie Stargell IA	2.00	1.00	.60
449	Bob Lemon	.90	.45	.25
450	Mickey Lolich	1.25	.60	.40
451	Tony LaRussa	.60	.30	.20
452	Ed Herrmann	.30	.15	.09
453	Barry Lersch	.30	.15	.09
454	A's Team	2.00	1.00	.60
455	Tommy Harper	.40	.20	.12
456	Mark Belanger	.40	.20	.12
457	Padres Rookies (Darcy Fast, Mike Ivie, Derrel Thomas)	.40	.20	.12
458	Aurelio Monteagudo	.30	.15	.09
459	Rick Renick	.30	.15	.09
460	Al Downing	.40	.20	.12
461	Tim Cullen	.30	.15	.09
462	Rickey Clark	.30	.15	.09
463	Bernie Carbo	.30	.15	.09
464	Jim Roland	.30	.15	.09
465	Gil Hodges	2.50	1.25	.70
466	Norm Miller	.30	.15	.09
467	Steve Kline	.40	.20	.12
468	Richie Scheinblum	.30	.15	.09
469	Ron Herbel	.30	.15	.09
470	Ray Fosse	.30	.15	.09
471	Luke Walker	.30	.15	.09
472	Phil Gagliano	.30	.15	.09
473	Dan McGinn	.30	.15	.09
474	Orioles Rookies (Don Baylor, Roric Harrison, Johnny Oates)	3.00	1.50	.90
475	Gary Nolan	.30	.15	.09
476	Lee Richard	.30	.15	.09
477	Tom Phoebus	.30	.15	.09
478a	Checklist 526-656 (small print on front)	2.25	1.25	.70
478b	Checklist 526-656 (large printing on front)	2.25	1.25	.70
479	Don Shaw	.30	.15	.09
480	Lee May	.60	.30	.20
481	Billy Conigliaro	.30	.15	.09
482	Joe Hoerner	.30	.15	.09
483	Ken Suarez	.30	.15	.09
484	Lum Harris	.30	.15	.09
485	Phil Regan	.30	.15	.09
486	John Lowenstein	.30	.15	.09
487	Tigers Team	1.50	.70	.45
488	Mike Nagy	.30	.15	.09
489	Expos Rookies (Terry Humphrey, Keith Lampard)	.30	.15	.09
490	Dave McNally	.50	.25	.15
491	Boyhood Photo (Lou Piniella)	.60	.30	.20
492	Boyhood Photo (Mel Stottlemyre)	.40	.20	.12

		NR MT	EX	VG
493	Boyhood Photo (Bob Bailey)	.30	.15	.09
494	Boyhood Photo (Willie Horton)	.40	.20	.12
495	Boyhood Photo (Bill Melton)	.30	.15	.09
496	Boyhood Photo (Bud Harrelson)	.40	.20	.12
497	Boyhood Photo (Jim Perry)	.40	.20	.12
498	Boyhood Photo (Brooks Robinson)			
		2.00	1.00	.60
499	Vicente Romo	.30	.15	.09
500	Joe Torre	1.25	.60	.40
501	Pete Hamm	.30	.15	.09
502	Jackie Hernandez	.30	.15	.09
503	Gary Peters	.30	.15	.09
504	Ed Spiezio	.30	.15	.09
505	Mike Marshall	.50	.25	.15
506	Indians Rookies (Terry Ley, Jim Moyer, Dick Tidrow)	.60	.30	.20
507	Fred Gladding	.30	.15	.09
508	Ellie Hendricks	.30	.15	.09
509	Don McMahon	.30	.15	.09
510	Ted Williams	4.00	2.00	1.25
511	Tony Taylor	.30	.15	.09
512	Paul Popovich	.30	.15	.09
513	Lindy McDaniel	.40	.20	.12
514	Ted Sizemore	.30	.15	.09
515	Bert Blyleven	3.25	1.75	1.00
516	Oscar Brown	.30	.15	.09
517	Ken Brett	.40	.20	.12
518	Wayne Garrett	.30	.15	.09
519	Ted Abernathy	.30	.15	.09
520	Larry Bowa	1.25	.60	.40
521	Alan Foster	.30	.15	.09
522	Dodgers Team	1.25	.60	.40
523	Chuck Dobson	.30	.15	.09
524	Reds Rookies (Ed Armbrister, Mel Behney)	.30	.15	.09
525	Carlos May	.40	.20	.12
526	Bob Bailey	.70	.35	.20
527	Dave Leonhard	.70	.35	.20
528	Ron Stone	.70	.35	.20
529	Dave Nelson	.70	.35	.20
530	Don Sutton	3.50	1.75	1.00
531	Freddie Patek	.70	.35	.20
532	Fred Kendall	.70	.35	.20
533	Ralph Houk	1.25	.60	.40
534	Jim Hickman	.80	.40	.25
535	Ed Brinkman	.80	.40	.25
536	Doug Rader	.70	.35	.20
537	Bob Locker	.70	.35	.20
538	Charlie Sands	.70	.35	.20
539	Terry Forster	1.25	.60	.40
540	Felix Millan	.70	.35	.20
541	Roger Repoz	.70	.35	.20
542	Jack Billingham	.70	.35	.20
543	Duane Josephson	.70	.35	.20
544	Ted Martinez	.70	.35	.20
545	Wayne Granger	.70	.35	.20
546	Joe Hague	.70	.35	.20
547	Indians Team	1.50	.70	.45
548	Frank Reberger	.70	.35	.20
549	Dave May	.70	.35	.20
550	Brooks Robinson	10.00	5.00	3.00
551	Ollie Brown	.70	.35	.20
552	Ollie Brown IA	.70	.35	.20
553	Wilbur Wood	.90	.45	.25
554	Wilbur Wood IA	.80	.40	.25
555	Ron Santo	1.50	.70	.45
556	Ron Santo IA	.80	.40	.25
557	John Odom	.70	.35	.20
558	John Odom IA	.70	.35	.20
559	Pete Rose	55.00	27.00	16.50
560	Pete Rose IA	25.00	12.50	7.50
561	Leo Cardenas	.70	.35	.20
562	Leo Cardenas IA	.70	.35	.20
563	Ray Sadecki	.70	.35	.20
564	Ray Sadecki IA	.70	.35	.20
565	Reggie Smith	.90	.45	.25
566	Reggie Smith IA	.80	.40	.25
567	Juan Marichal	5.00	2.50	1.50
568	Juan Marichal IA	2.50	1.25	.70
569	Ed Kirkpatrick	.70	.35	.20
570	Ed Kirkpatrick IA	.70	.35	.20
571	Nate Colbert	.70	.35	.20
572	Nate Colbert IA	.70	.35	.20
573	Fritz Peterson	.80	.40	.25
574	Fritz Peterson IA	.80	.40	.25
575	Al Oliver	2.25	1.25	.70
576	Leo Durocher	1.25	.60	.40
577	Mike Paul	.70	.35	.20
578	Billy Grabarkewitz	.70	.35	.20
579	Doyle Alexander	2.50	1.25	.70
580	Lou Piniella	1.75	.90	.50

		NR MT	EX	VG
581	Wade Blasingame	.70	.35	.20
582	Expos Team	1.50	.70	.45
583	Darold Knowles	.70	.35	.20
584	Jerry McNertney	.70	.35	.20
585	George Scott	.80	.40	.25
586	Denis Menke	.70	.35	.20
587	Billy Wilson	.70	.35	.20
588	Jim Holt	.70	.35	.20
589	Hal Lanier	1.00	.50	.30
590	Graig Nettles	2.50	1.25	.70
591	Paul Casanova	.70	.35	.20
592	Lew Krausse	.70	.35	.20
593	Rich Morales	.70	.35	.20
594	Jim Beauchamp	.70	.35	.20
595	Nolan Ryan	15.00	7.50	4.50
596	Manny Mota	.90	.45	.25
597	Jim Magnuson	.80	.40	.25
598	Hal King	.70	.35	.20
599	Billy Champion	.70	.35	.20
600	Al Kaline	10.00	5.00	3.00
601	George Stone	.70	.35	.20
602	Dave Bristol	.70	.35	.20
603	Jim Ray	.70	.35	.20
604a	Checklist 657-787 (copyright on right)			
		3.50	1.75	1.00
604b	Checklist 657-787 (copyright on left)			
		5.00	2.50	1.50
605	Nelson Briles	.70	.35	.20
606	Luis Melendez	.70	.35	.20
607	Frank Duffy	.70	.35	.20
608	Mike Corkins	.70	.35	.20
609	Tom Grieve	.70	.35	.20
610	Bill Stoneman	.70	.35	.20
611	Rich Reese	.70	.35	.20
612	Joe Decker	.70	.35	.20
613	Mike Ferraro	.70	.35	.20
614	Ted Uhlaender	.70	.35	.20
615	Steve Hargan	.70	.35	.20
616	Joe Ferguson	.80	.40	.25
617	Royals Team	1.50	.70	.45
618	Rich Robertson	.70	.35	.20
619	Rich McKinney	.80	.40	.25
620	Phil Niekro	4.00	2.00	1.25
621	Commissioners Award	.90	.45	.25
622	MVP Award	.90	.45	.25
623	Cy Young Award	.90	.45	.25
624	Minor League Player Of The Year Award			
		.90	.45	.25
625	Rookie Of The Year Award	.90	.45	.25
626	Babe Ruth Award	1.00	.50	.30
627	Moe Drabowsky	.70	.35	.20
628	Terry Crowley	.70	.35	.20
629	Paul Doyle	.70	.35	.20
630	Rich Hebner	.80	.40	.25
631	John Strohmayer	.70	.35	.20
632	Mike Hegan	.70	.35	.20
633	Jack Hiatt	.70	.35	.20
634	Dick Woodson	.70	.35	.20
635	Don Money	.80	.40	.25
636	Bill Lee	.90	.45	.25
637	Preston Gomez	.70	.35	.20
638	Ken Wright	.70	.35	.20
639	J.C. Martin	.70	.35	.20
640	Joe Coleman	.80	.40	.25
641	Mike Lum	.70	.35	.20
642	Denny Riddleberger	.70	.35	.20
643	Russ Gibson	.70	.35	.20
644	Bernie Allen	.80	.40	.25
645	Jim Maloney	.80	.40	.25
646	Chico Salmon	.70	.35	.20
647	Bob Moose	.70	.35	.20
648	Jim Lyttle	.70	.35	.20
649	Pete Richert	.70	.35	.20
650	Sal Bando	1.00	.50	.30
651	Reds Team	2.00	1.00	.60
652	Marcelino Lopez	.70	.35	.20
653	Jim Fairey	.70	.35	.20
654	Horacio Pina	.70	.35	.20
655	Jerry Grote	.80	.40	.25
656	Rudy May	.80	.40	.25
657	Bobby Wine	1.50	.70	.45
658	Steve Dunning	1.50	.70	.45
659	Bob Aspromonte	1.50	.70	.45
660	Paul Blair	1.75	.90	.50
661	Bill Virdon	2.00	1.00	.60
662	Stan Bahnsen	1.75	.90	.50
663	Fran Healy	1.50	.70	.45
664	Bobby Knoop	1.50	.70	.45
665	Chris Short	1.75	.90	.50
666	Hector Torres	1.50	.70	.45
667	Ray Newman	1.50	.70	.45

		NR MT	EX	VG
668	Rangers Team	3.25	1.75	1.00
669	Willie Crawford	1.50	.70	.45
670	Ken Holtzman	2.00	1.00	.60
671	Donn Clendenon	1.75	.90	.50
672	Archie Reynolds	1.50	.70	.45
673	Dave Marshall	1.50	.70	.45
674	John Kennedy	1.50	.70	.45
675	Pat Jarvis	1.50	.70	.45
676	Danny Cater	1.50	.70	.45
677	Ivan Murrell	1.50	.70	.45
678	Steve Luebber	1.50	.70	.45
679	Astros Rookies (Bob Fenwick, Bob Stinson)	1.50	.70	.45
680	Dave Johnson	3.50	1.75	1.00
681	Bobby Pfeil	1.50	.70	.45
682	Mike McCormick	1.75	.90	.50
683	Steve Hovley	1.50	.70	.45
684	Hal Breeden	1.50	.70	.45
685	Joe Horlen	1.50	.70	.45
686	Steve Garvey	65.00	32.00	19.50
687	Del Unser	1.50	.70	.45
688	Cardinals Team	3.25	1.75	1.00
689	Eddie Fisher	1.50	.70	.45
690	Willie Montanez	1.75	.90	.50
691	Curt Blefary	1.50	.70	.45
692	Curt Blefary IA	1.50	.70	.45
693	Alan Gallagher	1.50	.70	.45
694	Alan Gallagher IA	1.50	.70	.45
695	Rod Carew	60.00	30.00	18.00
696	Rod Carew IA	25.00	12.50	7.50
697	Jerry Koosman	4.50	2.25	1.25
698	Jerry Koosman IA	2.25	1.25	.70
699	Bobby Murcer	4.00	2.00	1.25
700	Bobby Murcer IA	2.00	1.00	.60
701	Jose Pagan	1.50	.70	.45
702	Jose Pagan IA	1.50	.70	.45
703	Doug Griffin	1.50	.70	.45
704	Doug Griffin IA	1.50	.70	.45
705	Pat Corrales	2.25	1.25	.70
706	Pat Corrales IA	1.75	.90	.50
707	Tim Foli	1.50	.70	.45
708	Tim Foli IA	1.50	.70	.45
709	Jim Kaat	6.00	3.00	1.75
710	Jim Kaat IA	3.00	1.50	.90
711	Bobby Bonds	3.75	2.00	1.25
712	Bobby Bonds IA	2.00	1.00	.60
713	Gene Michael	2.00	1.00	.60
714	Gene Michael IA	1.75	.90	.50
715	Mike Epstein	1.75	.90	.50
716	Jesus Alou	1.75	.90	.50
717	Bruce Dal Canton	1.50	.70	.45
718	Del Rice	1.50	.70	.45
719	Cesar Geronimo	1.75	.90	.50
720	Sam McDowell	2.50	1.25	.70
721	Eddie Leon	1.50	.70	.45
722	Bill Sudakis	1.50	.70	.45
723	Al Santorini	1.50	.70	.45
724	A.L. Rookies (John Curtis, Rich Hinton, Mickey Scott)	1.75	.90	.50
725	Dick McAuliffe	1.75	.90	.50
726	Dick Selma	1.50	.70	.45
727	Jose Laboy	1.50	.70	.45
728	Gail Hopkins	1.50	.70	.45
729	Bob Veale	1.75	.90	.50
730	Rick Monday	2.25	1.25	.70
731	Orioles Team	3.25	1.75	1.00
732	George Culver	1.50	.70	.45
733	Jim Hart	1.75	.90	.50
734	Bob Burda	1.50	.70	.45
735	Diego Segui	1.50	.70	.45
736	Bill Russell	2.50	1.25	.70
737	Lenny Randle	1.75	.90	.50
738	Jim Merritt	1.50	.70	.45
739	Don Mason	1.50	.70	.45
740	Rico Carty	3.00	1.50	.90
741	Major League Rookies (Tom Hutton, Rick Miller, John Milner)	1.75	.90	.50
742	Jim Rooker	1.50	.70	.45
743	Cesar Gutierrez	1.50	.70	.45
744	Jim Slaton	2.00	1.00	.60
745	Julian Javier	1.50	.70	.45
746	Lowell Palmer	1.50	.70	.45
747	Jim Stewart	1.50	.70	.45
748	Phil Hennigan	1.50	.70	.45
749	Walter Alston	4.50	2.25	1.25
750	Willie Horton	2.50	1.25	.70
751	Steve Carlton Traded	30.00	15.00	9.00
752	Joe Morgan Traded	12.00	6.00	3.50
753	Denny McLain Traded	4.50	2.25	1.25
754	Frank Robinson Traded	12.00	6.00	3.50
755	Jim Fregosi Traded	2.50	1.25	.70

		NR MT	EX	VG
756	Rick Wise Traded	2.00	1.00	.60
757	Jose Cardenal Traded	1.75	.90	.50
758	Gil Garrido	1.50	.70	.45
759	Chris Cannizzaro	1.50	.70	.45
760	Bill Mazeroski	3.50	1.75	1.00
761	Major League Rookies (Ron Cey, Ben Oglivie, Bernie Williams)	10.00	5.00	3.00
762	Wayne Simpson	1.50	.70	.45
763	Ron Hansen	1.50	.70	.45
764	Dusty Baker	3.00	1.50	.90
765	Ken McMullen	1.50	.70	.45
766	Steve Hamilton	1.50	.70	.45
767	Tom McCraw	1.50	.70	.45
768	Denny Doyle	1.50	.70	.45
769	Jack Aker	1.75	.90	.50
770	Jim Wynn	2.25	1.25	.70
771	Giants Team	3.25	1.75	1.00
772	Ken Tatum	1.50	.70	.45
773	Ron Brand	1.50	.70	.45
774	Luis Alvarado	1.50	.70	.45
775	Jerry Reuss	3.50	1.75	1.00
776	Bill Voss	1.50	.70	.45
777	Hoyt Wilhelm	8.00	4.00	2.50
778	Twins Rookies (Vic Albury, Rick Dempsey, Jim Strickland)	2.50	1.25	.70
779	Tony Cloninger	1.75	.90	.50
780	Dick Green	1.50	.70	.45
781	Jim McAndrew	1.50	.70	.45
782	Larry Stahl	1.50	.70	.45
783	Les Cain	1.50	.70	.45
784	Ken Aspromonte	1.50	.70	.45
785	Vic Davalillo	1.75	.90	.50
786	Chuck Brinkman	1.75	.70	.45
787	Ron Reed	4.00	.90	.50

1972 Topps Cloth Stickers

Despite the fact they were never actually issued, examples of this test issue can readily be found within the hobby. The set of 33 contains stickers with designs identical to cards found in three contiguous rows of a regular Topps card sheet that year; thus the inclusion of a meaningless checklist card. Sometimes found in complete 33-sticker strips, individual stickers nominally measure 2½'' by 3½,'' though dimensions vary according to the care with which they were cut. Stickers are unnumbered and blank-backed, and do not contain glue.

		NR MT	EX	VG
	Complete Set:	175.00	87.00	52.00
	Common Player:	3.00	1.50	.90
(1)	Hank Aaron	50.00	25.00	15.00
(2)	Luis Aparicio IA	10.00	5.00	3.00
(3)	Ike Brown	3.00	1.50	.90
(4)	Johnny Callison	5.00	2.50	1.50
(5)	Checklist 264-319	3.00	1.50	.90
(6)	Roberto Clemente IA	25.00	12.50	7.50
(7)	Dave Concepcion	8.00	4.00	2.50
(8)	Ron Cook	3.00	1.50	.90
(9)	Willie Davis	5.00	2.50	1.50
(10)	Al Fitzmorris	3.00	1.50	.90
(11)	Bobby Floyd	3.00	1.50	.90
(12)	Roy Foster	3.00	1.50	.90

		NR MT	EX	VG
(13)	Jim Fregosi Boyhood Photo	4.00	2.00	1.25
(14)	Danny Frisella IA	3.00	1.50	.90
(15)	Woody Fryman	3.50	1.75	1.00
(16)	Terry Harmon	3.00	1.50	.90
(17)	Frank Howard	7.00	3.50	2.00
(18)	Ron Klimkowski	3.00	1.50	.90
(19)	Joe Lahoud	3.00	1.50	.90
(20)	Jim Lefebvre	3.50	1.75	1.00
(21)	Elliott Maddox	3.00	1.50	.90
(22)	Marty Martinez	3.00	1.50	.90
(23)	Willie McCovey	25.00	12.50	7.50
(24)	Hal McRae	6.00	3.00	1.75
(25)	Syd O'Brien	3.00	1.50	.90
(26)	Red Sox Team	4.00	2.00	1.25
(27)	Aurelio Rodriguez	3.50	1.75	1.00
(28)	Al Severinsen	3.00	1.50	.90
(29)	Art Shamsky	3.00	1.50	.90
(30)	Steve Stone	4.00	2.00	1.25
(31)	Stan Swanson	3.00	1.50	.90
(32)	Bob Watson	3.50	1.75	1.00
(33)	Roy White	6.00	3.00	1.75

Willie Davis
DODGERS   OUTFIELD

1972 Topps Posters

Issued as a separate set, rather than as a wax pack insert, the 24 9-7/16'' by 18'' 1972 posters featured a borderless full-color picture on the front with the player's name, team and position. Printed on very thin paper, the posters as happened with earlier issues, were folded for packaging causing large creases which cannot be removed. Even so, they are good display items for they feature many of the stars of the period.

		NR MT	EX	VG
	Complete Set:	300.00	150.00	90.00
	Common Player:	5.00	2.50	1.50
1	Dave McNally	5.00	2.50	1.50
2	Carl Yastrzemski	30.00	15.00	9.00
3	Bill Melton	5.00	2.50	1.50
4	Ray Fosse	5.00	2.50	1.50
5	Mickey Lolich	6.00	3.00	1.75
6	Amos Otis	5.00	2.50	1.50
7	Tony Oliva	6.00	3.00	1.75
8	Vida Blue	6.00	3.00	1.75
9	Hank Aaron	20.00	10.00	6.00

		NR MT	EX	VG
10	Fergie Jenkins	8.00	4.00	2.50
11	Pete Rose	50.00	25.00	15.00
12	Willie Davis	6.00	3.00	1.75
13	Tom Seaver	20.00	10.00	6.00
14	Rick Wise	5.00	2.50	1.50
15	Willie Stargell	12.00	6.00	3.50
16	Joe Torre	7.00	3.50	2.00
17	Willie Mays	20.00	10.00	6.00
18	Andy Messersmith	5.00	2.50	1.50
19	Wilbur Wood	5.00	2.50	1.50
20	Harmon Killebrew	15.00	7.50	4.50
21	Billy Williams	12.00	6.00	3.50
22	Bud Harrelson	5.00	2.50	1.50
23	Roberto Clemente	20.00	10.00	6.00
24	Willie McCovey	15.00	7.50	4.50

Valuable Topps Cards

1973 Topps

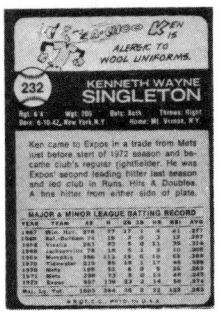

Topps cut back to 660 cards in 1973. The set is interesting for it marks the last time cards were issued by series, a procedure which had produced many a scarce high number card over the years. These 2½'' by 3½'' cards had a color photo, accented by a silhouette of a player on the front, indicative of position. Card backs were vertical for the first time since 1968, with the usual statistical and biographical information. Specialty cards began with #1 which depicted Ruth, Mays and Aaron as the all-time home run leaders. It was followed by statistical leaders, although there were also several all-time leader cards. Also present were Play-off and World Series highlights. From the age and youth department Topps had coaches and managers as well as more "Boyhood Photos."

		NR MT	EX	VG
Complete Set:		525.00	184.00	105.00
Common Player: 1-396		.25	.13	.08
Common Player: 397-528		.40	.20	.12
Common Player: 529-660		1.00	.50	.30
1	All Time Home Run Leaders (Hank Aaron, Willie Mays, Babe Ruth)	9.00	3.00	1.75
2	Rich Hebner	.30	.15	.09
3	Jim Lonborg	.40	.20	.12
4	John Milner	.25	.13	.08
5	Ed Brinkman	.30	.15	.09
6	Mac Scarce	.25	.13	.08
7	Rangers Team	.90	.45	.25
8	Tom Hall	.25	.13	.08
9	Johnny Oates	.25	.13	.08
10	Don Sutton	2.00	1.00	.60
11	Chris Chambliss	.70	.35	.20
12a	Padres Mgr./Coaches (Dave Garcia, Johnny Podres, Bob Skinner, Whitey Wietelmann, Don Zimmer) (Coaches background brown)	.50	.25	.15
12b	Padres Mgr./Coaches (Dave Garcia, Johnny Podres, Bob Skinner, Whitey Wietelmann, Don Zimmer) (Coaches background orange)	.40	.20	.12
13	George Hendrick	.70	.35	.20
14	Sonny Siebert	.25	.13	.08
15	Ralph Garr	.30	.15	.09
16	Steve Braun	.25	.13	.08
17	Fred Gladding	.25	.13	.08
18	Leroy Stanton	.25	.13	.08
19	Tim Foli	.25	.13	.08
20a	Stan Bahnsen (small gap in left border)	.50	.25	.15
20b	Stan Bahnsen (no gap)	.25	.13	.08
21	Randy Hundley	.25	.13	.08
22	Ted Abernathy	.25	.13	.08
23	Dave Kingman	1.25	.60	.40
24	Al Santorini	.25	.13	.08
25	Roy White	.40	.20	.12
26	Pirates Team	.90	.45	.25
27	Bill Gogolewski	.25	.13	.08
28	Hal McRae	.50	.25	.15
29	Tony Taylor	.25	.13	.08
30	Tug McGraw	.60	.30	.20
31	Buddy Bell	3.50	1.75	1.00
32	Fred Norman	.25	.13	.08
33	Jim Breazeale	.25	.13	.08
34	Pat Dobson	.30	.15	.09

		NR MT	EX	VG
35	Willie Davis	.50	.25	.15
36	Steve Barber	.25	.13	.08
37	Bill Robinson	.25	.13	.08
38	Mike Epstein	.30	.15	.09
39	Dave Roberts	.25	.13	.08
40	Reggie Smith	.50	.25	.15
41	Tom Walker	.25	.13	.08
42	Mike Andrews	.25	.13	.08
43	Randy Moffitt	.30	.15	.09
44	Rick Monday	.40	.20	.12
45	Ellie Rodriguez (photo actually John Felske)	.25	.13	.08
46	Lindy McDaniel	.30	.15	.09
47	Luis Melendez	.25	.13	.08
48	Paul Splittorff	.30	.15	.09
49a	Twins Mgr./Coaches (Vern Morgan, Frank Quilici, Bob Rodgers, Ralph Rowe, Al Worthington) (Coaches background brown)	.50	.25	.15
49b	Twins Mgr./Coaches (Vern Morgan, Frank Quilici, Bob Rodgers, Ralph Rowe, Al Worthington) (Coaches background orange)	.30	.15	.09
50	Roberto Clemente	10.00	5.00	3.00
51	Chuck Seelbach	.25	.13	.08
52	Denis Menke	.25	.13	.08
53	Steve Dunning	.25	.13	.08
54	Checklist 1-132	2.00	1.00	.60
55	Jon Matlack	.40	.20	.12
56	Merv Rettenmund	.30	.15	.09
57	Derrel Thomas	.25	.13	.08
58	Mike Paul	.25	.13	.08
59	Steve Yeager	.60	.30	.20
60	Ken Holtzman	.40	.20	.12
61	Batting Leaders (Rod Carew, Billy Williams)	1.75	.90	.50
62	Home Run Leaders (Dick Allen, Johnny Bench)	1.50	.70	.45
63	Runs Batted In Leaders (Dick Allen, Johnny Bench)	1.50	.70	.45
64	Stolen Base Leaders (Lou Brock, Bert Campaneris)	1.25	.60	.40
65	Earned Run Average Leaders (Steve Carlton, Luis Tiant)	1.25	.60	.40
66	Victory Leaders (Steve Carlton, Gaylord Perry, Wilbur Wood)	1.25	.60	.40
67	Strikeout Leaders (Steve Carlton, Nolan Ryan)	2.50	1.25	.70
68	Leading Firemen (Clay Carroll, Sparky Lyle)	.80	.40	.25
69	Phil Gagliano	.25	.13	.08
70	Milt Pappas	.40	.20	.12
71	Johnny Briggs	.25	.13	.08
72	Ron Reed	.30	.15	.09
73	Ed Herrmann	.25	.13	.08
74	Billy Champion	.25	.13	.08
75	Vada Pinson	.80	.40	.25
76	Doug Rader	.25	.13	.08
77	Mike Torrez	.30	.15	.09
78	Richie Scheinblum	.25	.13	.08
79	Jim Willoughby	.25	.13	.08
80	Tony Oliva	1.25	.60	.40
81a	Cubs Mgr./Coaches (Hank Aguirre, Ernie Banks, Larry Jansen, Whitey Lockman, Pete Reiser) (trees in Coaches background)	.70	.35	.20
81b	Cubs Mgr./Coaches (Hank Aguirre, Ernie Banks, Larry Jansen, Whitey Lockman, Pete Reiser) (orange, solid background)	.50	.25	.15
82	Fritz Peterson	.30	.15	.09
83	Leron Lee	.25	.13	.08
84	Rollie Fingers	1.50	.70	.45
85	Ted Simmons	1.25	.60	.40
86	Tom McCraw	.25	.13	.08
87	Ken Boswell	.25	.13	.08
88	Mickey Stanley	.30	.15	.09
89	Jack Billingham	.25	.13	.08
90	Brooks Robinson	4.00	2.00	1.25
91	Dodgers Team	1.00	.50	.30
92	Jerry Bell	.25	.13	.08
93	Jesus Alou	.30	.15	.09
94	Dick Billings	.25	.13	.08
95	Steve Blass	.30	.15	.09
96	Doug Griffin	.25	.13	.08
97	Willie Montanez	.30	.15	.09
98	Dick Woodson	.25	.13	.08
99	Carl Taylor	.25	.13	.08
100	Hank Aaron	12.00	6.00	3.50
101	Ken Henderson	.25	.13	.08
102	Rudy May	.30	.15	.09
103	Celerino Sanchez	.30	.15	.09
104	Reggie Cleveland	.25	.13	.08

		NR MT	EX	VG
105	Carlos May	.30	.15	.09
106	Terry Humphrey	.25	.13	.08
107	Phil Hennigan	.25	.13	.08
108	Bill Russell	.40	.20	.12
109	Doyle Alexander	1.00	.50	.30
110	Bob Watson	.30	.15	.09
111	Dave Nelson	.25	.13	.08
112	Gary Ross	.25	.13	.08
113	Jerry Grote	.30	.15	.09
114	Lynn McGlothen	.25	.13	.08
115	Ron Santo	.80	.40	.25
116a	Yankees Mgr./Coaches (Jim Hegan, Ralph Houk, Elston Howard, Dick Howser, Jim Turner) (Coaches background brown)	1.00	.50	.30
116b	Yankees Mgr./Coaches (Jim Hegan, Ralph Houk, Elston Howard, Dick Howser, Jim Turner) (Coaches background orange)	.70	.35	.20
117	Ramon Hernandez	.25	.13	.08
118	John Mayberry	.40	.20	.12
119	Larry Bowa	.80	.40	.25
120	Joe Coleman	.30	.15	.09
121	Dave Rader	.25	.13	.08
122	Jim Strickland	.25	.13	.08
123	Sandy Alomar	.25	.13	.08
124	Jim Hardin	.25	.13	.08
125	Ron Fairly	.40	.20	.12
126	Jim Brewer	.25	.13	.08
127	Brewers Team	.90	.45	.25
128	Ted Sizemore	.25	.13	.08
129	Terry Forster	.40	.20	.12
130	Pete Rose	20.00	10.00	6.00
131a	Red Sox Mgr./Coaches (Doug Camilli, Eddie Kasko, Don Lenhardt, Eddie Popowski, Lee Stange) (Coaches background brown)	.50	.25	.15
131b	Red Sox Mgr./Coaches (Doug Camilli, Eddie Kasko, Don Lenhardt, Eddie Popowski, Lee Stange) (Coaches background orange)	.30	.15	.09
132	Matty Alou	.60	.30	.20
133	Dave Roberts	.25	.13	.08
134	Milt Wilcox	.30	.15	.09
135	Lee May	.50	.25	.15
136a	Orioles Mgr./Coaches (George Bamberger, Jim Frey, Billy Hunter, George Staller, Earl Weaver) (Coaches background brown)	1.00	.50	.30
136b	Orioles Mgr./Coaches (George Bamberger, Jim Frey, Billy Hunter, George Staller, Earl Weaver) (Coaches background orange)	.70	.35	.20
137	Jim Beauchamp	.25	.13	.08
138	Horacio Pina	.25	.13	.08
139	Carmen Fanzone	.25	.13	.08
140	Lou Piniella	.80	.40	.25
141	Bruce Kison	.30	.15	.09
142	Thurman Munson	5.00	2.50	1.50
143	John Curtis	.25	.13	.08
144	Marty Perez	.25	.13	.08
145	Bobby Bonds	.70	.35	.20
146	Woodie Fryman	.30	.15	.09
147	Mike Anderson	.25	.13	.08
148	Dave Goltz	.60	.30	.20
149	Ron Hunt	.30	.15	.09
150	Wilbur Wood	.40	.20	.12
151	Wes Parker	.30	.15	.09
152	Dave May	.25	.13	.08
153	Al Hrabosky	.40	.20	.12
154	Jeff Torborg	.30	.15	.09
155	Sal Bando	.70	.35	.20
156	Cesar Geronimo	.30	.15	.09
157	Denny Riddleberger	.25	.13	.08
158	Astros Team	.90	.45	.25
159	Clarence Gaston	.25	.13	.08
160	Jim Palmer	4.00	2.00	1.25
161	Ted Martinez	.25	.13	.08
162	Pete Broberg	.25	.13	.08
163	Vic Davalillo	.30	.15	.09
164	Monty Montgomery	.25	.13	.08
165	Luis Aparicio	2.75	1.50	.80
166	Terry Harmon	.25	.13	.08
167	Steve Stone	.50	.25	.15
168	Jim Northrup	.30	.15	.09
169	Ron Schueler	.25	.13	.08
170	Harmon Killebrew	3.50	1.75	1.00
171	Bernie Carbo	.25	.13	.08
172	Steve Kline	.30	.15	.09
173	Hal Breeden	.25	.13	.08
174	Rich Gossage	5.00	2.50	1.50

		NR MT	EX	VG
175	Frank Robinson	3.50	1.75	1.00
176	Chuck Taylor	.25	.13	.08
177	Bill Plummer	.25	.13	.08
178	Don Rose	.25	.13	.08
179a	A's Mgr./Coaches (Jerry Adair, Vern Hoscheit, Irv Noren, Wes Stock, Dick Williams) (Coaches background brown)	.80	.40	.25
179b	A's Mgr./Coaches (Jerry Adair, Vern Hoscheit, Irv Noren, Wes Stock, Dick Williams) (Coaches background orange)	.50	.25	.15
180	Fergie Jenkins	1.50	.70	.45
181	Jack Brohamer	.25	.13	.08
182	Mike Caldwell	.50	.25	.15
183	Don Buford	.30	.15	.09
184	Jerry Koosman	.50	.25	.15
185	Jim Wynn	.40	.20	.12
186	Bill Fahey	.25	.13	.08
187	Luke Walker	.25	.13	.08
188	Cookie Rojas	.25	.13	.08
189	Greg Luzinski	.70	.35	.20
190	Bob Gibson	3.50	1.75	1.00
191	Tigers Team	1.25	.60	.40
192	Pat Jarvis	.25	.13	.08
193	Carlton Fisk	3.50	1.75	1.00
194	Jorge Orta	.50	.25	.15
195	Clay Carroll	.30	.15	.09
196	Ken McMullen	.25	.13	.08
197	Ed Goodson	.25	.13	.08
198	Horace Clarke	.30	.15	.09
199	Bert Blyleven	1.50	.70	.45
200	Billy Williams	2.75	1.50	.80
201	A.L. Playoffs (Hendrick Scores Winning Run.)	1.00	.50	.30
202	N.L. Playoffs (Foster's Run Decides It.)	1.00	.50	.30
203	World Series Game 1 (Tenace The Menace.)	1.00	.50	.30
204	World Series Game 2 (A's Make It Two Straight.)	1.00	.50	.30
205	World Series Game 3 (Reds Win Squeeker.)	1.00	.50	.30
206	World Series Game 4 (Tenace Singles In Ninth.)	1.00	.50	.30
207	World Series Game 5 (Odom Out At Plate.)	1.00	.50	.30
208	World Series Game 6 (Reds' Slugging Ties Series.)	1.00	.50	.30
209	World Series Game 7 (Campy Starts Winning Rally.)	1.00	.50	.30
210	World Series Summary (World Champions.)	1.00	.50	.30
211	Balor Moore	.25	.13	.08
212	Joe Lahoud	.25	.13	.08
213	Steve Garvey	10.00	5.00	3.00
214	Dave Hamilton	.25	.13	.08
215	Dusty Baker	.50	.25	.15
216	Toby Harrah	.40	.20	.12
217	Don Wilson	.25	.13	.08
218	Aurelio Rodriguez	.30	.15	.09
219	Cardinals Team	.90	.45	.25
220	Nolan Ryan	7.00	3.50	2.00
221	Fred Kendall	.25	.13	.08
222	Rob Gardner	.25	.13	.08
223	Bud Harrelson	.30	.15	.09
224	Bill Lee	.30	.15	.09
225	Al Oliver	1.25	.60	.40
226	Ray Fosse	.25	.13	.08
227	Wayne Twitchell	.25	.13	.08
228	Bobby Darwin	.25	.13	.08
229	Roric Harrison	.25	.13	.08
230	Joe Morgan	2.50	1.25	.70
231	Bill Parsons	.25	.13	.08
232	Ken Singleton	.40	.20	.12
233	Ed Kirkpatrick	.25	.13	.08
234	Bill North	.50	.25	.15
235	Jim Hunter	3.00	1.50	.90
236	Tito Fuentes	.25	.13	.08
237a	Braves Mgr./Coaches (Lew Burdette, Jim Busby, Roy Hartsfield, Eddie Mathews, Ken Silvestri) (Coaches background brown)	1.25	.60	.40
237b	Braves Mgr./Coaches (Lew Burdette, Jim Busby, Roy Hartsfield, Eddie Mathews, Ken Silvestri) (Coaches background orange)	1.00	.50	.30
238	Tony Muser	.25	.13	.08
239	Pete Richert	.25	.13	.08
240	Bobby Murcer	.60	.30	.20
241	Dwain Anderson	.25	.13	.08

		NR MT	EX	VG
242	George Culver	.25	.13	.08
243	Angels Team	.90	.45	.25
244	Ed Acosta	.25	.13	.08
245	Carl Yastrzemski	10.00	5.00	3.00
246	Ken Sanders	.25	.13	.08
247	Del Unser	.25	.13	.08
248	Jerry Johnson	.25	.13	.08
249	Larry Biittner	.25	.13	.08
250	Manny Sanguillen	.30	.15	.09
251	Roger Nelson	.25	.13	.08
252a	Giants Mgr./Coaches (Joe Amalfitano, Charlie Fox, Andy Gilbert, Don McMahon, John McNamara) (Coaches background brown)	.50	.25	.15
252b	Giants Mgr./Coaches (Joe Amalfitano, Charlie Fox, Andy Gilbert, Don McMahon, John McNamara) (Coaches background orange)	.30	.15	.09
253	Mark Belanger	.30	.15	.09
254	Bill Stoneman	.25	.13	.08
255	Reggie Jackson	12.00	6.00	3.50
256	Chris Zachary	.25	.13	.08
257a	Mets Mgr./Coaches (Yogi Berra, Roy McMillan, Joe Pignatano, Rube Walker, Eddie Yost) (Coaches background brown)	1.50	.70	.45
257b	Mets Mgr./Coaches (Yogi Berra, Roy McMillan, Joe Pignatano, Rube Walker, Eddie Yost) (Coaches background orange)	1.25	.60	.40
258	Tommy John	1.75	.90	.50
259	Jim Holt	.25	.13	.08
260	Gary Nolan	.25	.13	.08
261	Pat Kelly	.25	.13	.08
262	Jack Aker	.25	.13	.08
263	George Scott	.30	.15	.09
264	Checklist 133-264	2.00	1.00	.60
265	Gene Michael	.40	.20	.12
266	Mike Lum	.25	.13	.08
267	Lloyd Allen	.25	.13	.08
268	Jerry Morales	.25	.13	.08
269	Tim McCarver	.70	.35	.20
270	Luis Tiant	.80	.40	.25
271	Tom Hutton	.25	.13	.08
272	Ed Farmer	.25	.13	.08
273	Chris Speier	.30	.15	.09
274	Darold Knowles	.25	.13	.08
275	Tony Perez	1.25	.60	.40
276	Joe Lovitto	.25	.13	.08
277	Bob Miller	.25	.13	.08
278	Orioles Team	.90	.45	.25
279	Mike Strahler	.25	.13	.08
280	Al Kaline	4.00	2.00	1.25
281	Mike Jorgensen	.25	.13	.08
282	Steve Hovley	.25	.13	.08
283	Ray Sadecki	.25	.13	.08
284	Glenn Borgmann	.25	.13	.08
285	Don Kessinger	.30	.15	.09
286	Frank Linzy	.25	.13	.08
287	Eddie Leon	.25	.13	.08
288	Gary Gentry	.25	.13	.08
289	Bob Oliver	.25	.13	.08
290	Cesar Cedeno	.40	.20	.12
291	Rogelio Moret	.25	.13	.08
292	Jose Cruz	.80	.40	.25
293	Bernie Allen	.30	.15	.09
294	Steve Arlin	.25	.13	.08
295	Bert Campaneris	.60	.30	.20
296	Reds Mgr./Coaches (Sparky Anderson, Alex Grammas, Ted Kluszewski, George Scherger, Larry Shepard)	.70	.35	.20
297	Walt Williams	.25	.13	.08
298	Ron Bryant	.25	.13	.08
299	Ted Ford	.25	.13	.08
300	Steve Carlton	8.00	4.00	2.50
301	Billy Grabarkewitz	.25	.13	.08
302	Terry Crowley	.25	.13	.08
303	Nelson Briles	.25	.13	.08
304	Duke Sims	.25	.13	.08
305	Willie Mays	12.00	6.00	3.50
306	Tom Burgmeier	.25	.13	.08
307	Boots Day	.25	.13	.08
308	Skip Lockwood	.25	.13	.08
309	Paul Popovich	.25	.13	.08
310	Dick Allen	.80	.40	.25
311	Joe Decker	.25	.13	.08
312	Oscar Brown	.25	.13	.08
313	Jim Ray	.25	.13	.08
314	Ron Swoboda	.30	.15	.09
315	John Odom	.30	.15	.09
316	Padres Team	.90	.45	.25
317	Danny Cater	.25	.13	.08
318	Jim McGlothlin	.25	.13	.08
319	Jim Spencer	.25	.13	.08
320	Lou Brock	3.50	1.75	1.00
321	Rich Hinton	.25	.13	.08
322	Garry Maddox	.80	.40	.25
323	Tigers Mgr./Coaches (Art Fowler, Billy Martin, Joe Schultz, Charlie Silvera, Dick Tracewski)	1.00	.50	.30
324	Al Downing	.30	.15	.09
325	Boog Powell	1.00	.50	.30
326	Darrell Brandon	.25	.13	.08
327	John Lowenstein	.25	.13	.08
328	Bill Bonham	.25	.13	.08
329	Ed Kranepool	.30	.15	.09
330	Rod Carew	7.00	3.50	2.00
331	Carl Morton	.25	.13	.08
332	John Felske	.30	.15	.09
333	Gene Clines	.25	.13	.08
334	Freddie Patek	.25	.13	.08
335	Bob Tolan	.30	.15	.09
336	Tom Bradley	.25	.13	.08
337	Dave Duncan	.25	.13	.08
338	Checklist 265-396	2.00	1.00	.60
339	Dick Tidrow	.30	.15	.09
340	Nate Colbert	.30	.15	.09
341	Boyhood Photo (Jim Palmer)	1.25	.60	.40
342	Boyhood Photo (Sam McDowell)	.40	.20	.12
343	Boyhood Photo (Bobby Murcer)	.40	.20	.12
344	Boyhood Photo (Jim Hunter)	1.25	.60	.40
345	Boyhood Photo (Chris Speier)	.30	.15	.09
346	Boyhood Photo (Gaylord Perry)	1.25	.60	.40
347	Royals Team	.90	.45	.25
348	Rennie Stennett	.30	.15	.09
349	Dick McAuliffe	.30	.15	.09
350	Tom Seaver	8.00	4.00	2.50
351	Jimmy Stewart	.25	.13	.08
352	Don Stanhouse	.40	.20	.12
353	Steve Brye	.25	.13	.08
354	Billy Parker	.25	.13	.08
355	Mike Marshall	.40	.20	.12
356	White Sox Mgr./Coaches (Joe Lonnett, Jim Mahoney, Al Monchak, Johnny Sain, Chuck Tanner)	.50	.25	.15
357	Ross Grimsley	.30	.15	.09
358	Jim Nettles	.25	.13	.08
359	Cecil Upshaw	.25	.13	.08
360	Joe Rudi (photo actually Gene Tenace)	.40	.20	.12
361	Fran Healy	.25	.13	.08
362	Eddie Watt	.25	.13	.08
363	Jackie Hernandez	.25	.13	.08
364	Rick Wise	.30	.15	.09
365	Rico Petrocelli	.40	.20	.12
366	Brock Davis	.25	.13	.08
367	Burt Hooton	.40	.20	.12
368	Bill Buckner	.70	.35	.20
369	Lerrin LaGrow	.25	.13	.08
370	Willie Stargell	3.50	1.75	1.00
371	Mike Kekich	.30	.15	.09
372	Oscar Gamble	.30	.15	.09
373	Clyde Wright	.25	.13	.08
374	Darrell Evans	.70	.35	.20
375	Larry Dierker	.30	.15	.09
376	Frank Duffy	.25	.13	.08
377	Expos Mgr./Coaches (Dave Bristol, Larry Doby, Gene Mauch, Cal McLish, Jerry Zimmerman)	.50	.25	.15
378	Lenny Randle	.25	.13	.08
379	Cy Acosta	.25	.13	.08
380	Johnny Bench	8.00	4.00	2.50
381	Vicente Romo	.25	.13	.08
382	Mike Hegan	.25	.13	.08
383	Diego Segui	.25	.13	.08
384	Don Baylor	1.00	.50	.30
385	Jim Perry	.50	.25	.15
386	Don Money	.30	.15	.09
387	Jim Barr	.25	.13	.08
388	Ben Oglivie	.50	.25	.15
389	Mets Team	1.75	.90	.50
390	Mickey Lolich	.70	.35	.20
391	Lee Lacy	.80	.40	.25
392	Dick Drago	.25	.13	.08
393	Jose Cardenal	.30	.15	.09
394	Sparky Lyle	.70	.35	.20
395	Roger Metzger	.25	.13	.08
396	Grant Jackson	.25	.13	.08
397	Dave Cash	.40	.20	.12
398	Rich Hand	.40	.20	.12
399	George Foster	1.50	.70	.45
400	Gaylord Perry	3.00	1.50	.90
401	Clyde Mashore	.40	.20	.12
402	Jack Hiatt	.40	.20	.12

		NR MT	EX	VG
403	Sonny Jackson	.40	.20	.12
404	Chuck Brinkman	.40	.20	.12
405	Cesar Tovar	.40	.20	.12
406	Paul Lindblad	.40	.20	.12
407	Felix Millan	.40	.20	.12
408	Jim Colborn	.40	.20	.12
409	Ivan Murrell	.40	.20	.12
410	Willie McCovey	3.50	1.75	1.00
411	Ray Corbin	.40	.20	.12
412	Manny Mota	.60	.30	.20
413	Tom Timmermann	.40	.20	.12
414	Ken Rudolph	.40	.20	.12
415	Marty Pattin	.40	.20	.12
416	Paul Schaal	.40	.20	.12
417	Scipio Spinks	.40	.20	.12
418	Bobby Grich	.60	.30	.20
419	Casey Cox	.50	.25	.15
420	Tommie Agee	.50	.25	.15
421	Angels Mgr./Coaches (Tom Morgan, Salty Parker, Jimmie Reese, John Roseboro, Bobby Winkles)	.40	.20	.12
422	Bob Robertson	.40	.20	.12
423	Johnny Jeter	.40	.20	.12
424	Denny Doyle	.40	.20	.12
425	Alex Johnson	.40	.20	.12
426	Dave LaRoche	.40	.20	.12
427	Rick Auerbach	.40	.20	.12
428	Wayne Simpson	.40	.20	.12
429	Jim Fairey	.40	.20	.12
430	Vida Blue	.80	.40	.25
431	Gerry Moses	.50	.25	.15
432	Dan Frisella	.40	.20	.12
433	Willie Horton	.60	.30	.20
434	Giants Team	1.00	.50	.30
435	Rico Carty	.60	.30	.20
436	Jim McAndrew	.40	.20	.12
437	John Kennedy	.40	.20	.12
438	Enzo Hernandez	.40	.20	.12
439	Eddie Fisher	.40	.20	.12
440	Glenn Beckert	.50	.25	.15
441	Gail Hopkins	.40	.20	.12
442	Dick Dietz	.40	.20	.12
443	Danny Thompson	.50	.25	.15
444	Ken Brett	.50	.25	.15
445	Ken Berry	.40	.20	.12
446	Jerry Reuss	.60	.30	.20
447	Joe Hague	.40	.20	.12
448	John Hiller	.50	.25	.15
449a	Indians Mgr./Coaches (Ken Aspromonte, Rocky Colavito, Joe Lutz, Warren Spahn) (Spahn's ear pointed)	.50	.25	.15
449b	Indians Mgr./Coaches (Ken Aspromonte, Rocky Colavito, Joe Lutz, Warren Spahn) (Spahn's ear round)	.80	.40	.25
450	Joe Torre	1.00	.50	.30
451	John Vukovich	.40	.20	.12
452	Paul Casanova	.40	.20	.12
453	Checklist 397-528	2.25	1.25	.70
454	Tom Haller	.50	.25	.15
455	Bill Melton	.50	.25	.15
456	Dick Green	.40	.20	.12
457	John Strohmayer	.40	.20	.12
458	Jim Mason	.40	.20	.12
459	Jimmy Howarth	.40	.20	.12
460	Bill Freehan	.60	.30	.20
461	Mike Corkins	.40	.20	.12
462	Ron Blomberg	.50	.25	.15
463	Ken Tatum	.40	.20	.12
464	Cubs Team	1.00	.50	.30
465	Dave Giusti	.40	.20	.12
466	Jose Arcia	.40	.20	.12
467	Mike Ryan	.40	.20	.12
468	Tom Griffin	.40	.20	.12
469	Dan Monzon	.40	.20	.12
470	Mike Cuellar	.60	.30	.20
471	Hit Leader (Ty Cobb)	2.50	1.25	.70
472	Grand Slam Leader (Lou Gehrig)	2.50	1.25	.70
473	Total Base Leader (Hank Aaron)	2.50	1.25	.70
474	R.B.I. Leader (Babe Ruth)	4.00	2.00	1.25
475	Batting Leader (Ty Cobb)	2.50	1.25	.70
476	Shutout Leader (Walter Johnson)	1.25	.60	.40
477	Victory Leader (Cy Young)	1.25	.60	.40
478	Strikeout Leader (Walter Johnson)	1.25	.60	.40
479	Hal Lanier	.60	.30	.20
480	Juan Marichal	3.50	1.75	1.00
481	White Sox Team	1.00	.50	.30
482	Rick Reuschel	1.50	.70	.45
483	Dal Maxvill	.50	.25	.15
484	Ernie McAnally	.40	.20	.12
485	Norm Cash	.80	.40	.25

		NR MT	EX	VG
486a	Phillies Mgr./Coaches (Carroll Berringer, Billy DeMars, Danny Ozark, Ray Rippelmeyer, Bobby Wine) (Coaches background brown red)	.70	.35	.20
486b	Phillies Mgr./Coaches (Carroll Beringer, Billy DeMars, Danny Ozark, Ray Rippelmeyer, Bobby Wine) (Coaches background orange)	.50	.25	.15
487	Bruce Dal Canton	.40	.20	.12
488	Dave Campbell	.40	.20	.12
489	Jeff Burroughs	.60	.30	.20
490	Claude Osteen	.60	.30	.20
491	Bob Montgomery	.40	.20	.12
492	Pedro Borbon	.40	.20	.12
493	Duffy Dyer	.40	.20	.12
494	Rich Morales	.40	.20	.12
495	Tommy Helms	.40	.20	.12
496	Ray Lamb	.40	.20	.12
497	Cardinals Mgr./Coaches (Vern Benson, George Kissell, Red Schoendienst, Barney Schultz)	.70	.35	.20
498	Graig Nettles	2.50	1.25	.70
499	Bob Moose	.40	.20	.12
500	A's Team	1.75	.90	.50
501	Larry Gura	.50	.25	.15
502	Bobby Valentine	.60	.30	.20
503	Phil Niekro	3.00	1.50	.90
504	Earl Williams	.40	.20	.12
505	Bob Bailey	.40	.20	.12
506	Bart Johnson	.40	.20	.12
507	Darrel Chaney	.40	.20	.12
508	Gates Brown	.40	.20	.12
509	Jim Nash	.40	.20	.12
510	Amos Otis	.60	.30	.20
511	Sam McDowell	.60	.30	.20
512	Dalton Jones	.40	.20	.12
513	Dave Marshall	.40	.20	.12
514	Jerry Kenney	.40	.20	.12
515	Andy Messersmith	.50	.25	.15
516	Danny Walton	.40	.20	.12
517a	Pirates Mgr./Coaches (Don Leppert, Bill Mazeroski, Dave Ricketts, Bill Virdon, Mel Wright) (Coaches background brown)	1.00	.50	.30
517b	Pirates Mgr./Coaches (Don Leppert, Bill Mazeroski, Dave Ricketts, Bill Virdon, Mel Wright) (Coaches background orange)	.50	.25	.15
518	Bob Veale	.50	.25	.15
519	John Edwards	.40	.20	.12
520	Mel Stottlemyre	.60	.30	.20
521	Braves Team	1.00	.50	.30
522	Leo Cardenas	.40	.20	.12
523	Wayne Granger	.40	.20	.12
524	Gene Tenace	.40	.20	.12
525	Jim Fregosi	.70	.35	.20
526	Ollie Brown	.40	.20	.12
527	Dan McGinn	.40	.20	.12
528	Paul Blair	.50	.25	.15
529	Milt May	1.00	.50	.30
530	Jim Kaat	3.00	1.50	.90
531	Ron Woods	1.00	.50	.30
532	Steve Mingori	1.00	.50	.30
533	Larry Stahl	1.00	.50	.30
534	Dave Lemonds	1.00	.50	.30
535	John Callison	1.25	.60	.40
536	Phillies Team	2.50	1.25	.70
537	Bill Slayback	1.00	.50	.30
538	Jim Hart	1.25	.60	.40
539	Tom Murphy	1.00	.50	.30
540	Cleon Jones	1.25	.60	.40
541	Bob Bolin	1.00	.50	.30
542	Pat Corrales	1.50	.70	.45
543	Alan Foster	1.00	.50	.30
544	Von Joshua	1.00	.50	.30
545	Orlando Cepeda	3.00	1.50	.90
546	Jim York	1.00	.50	.30
547	Bobby Heise	1.00	.50	.30
548	Don Durham	1.00	.50	.30
549	Rangers Mgr./Coaches (Chuck Estrada, Whitey Herzog, Chuck Hiller, Jackie Moore)	2.00	1.00	.60
550	Dave Johnson	2.75	1.50	.80
551	Mike Kilkenny	1.00	.50	.30
552	J.C. Martin	1.00	.50	.30
553	Mickey Scott	1.00	.50	.30
554	Dave Concepcion	2.50	1.25	.70
555	Bill Hands	1.00	.50	.30
556	Yankees Team	3.50	1.75	1.00
557	Bernie Williams	1.00	.50	.30
558	Jerry May	1.00	.50	.30
559	Barry Lersch	1.00	.50	.30

		NR MT	EX	VG
560	Frank Howard	2.25	1.25	.70
561	Jim Geddes	1.00	.50	.30
562	Wayne Garrett	1.00	.50	.30
563	Larry Haney	1.00	.50	.30
564	Mike Thompson	1.00	.50	.30
565	Jim Hickman	1.25	.60	.40
566	Lew Krausse	1.00	.50	.30
567	Bob Fenwick	1.00	.50	.30
568	Ray Newman	1.00	.50	.30
569	Dodgers Mgr./Coaches (Red Adams, Walt Alston, Monty Basgall, Jim Gillam, Tom Lasorda)	3.00	1.50	.90
570	Bill Singer	1.25	.60	.40
571	Rusty Torres	1.00	.50	.30
572	Gary Sutherland	1.00	.50	.30
573	Fred Beene	1.25	.60	.40
574	Bob Didier	1.00	.50	.30
575	Dock Ellis	1.25	.60	.40
576	Expos Team	2.50	1.25	.70
577	Eric Soderholm	1.25	.60	.40
578	Ken Wright	1.00	.50	.30
579	Tom Grieve	1.00	.50	.30
580	Joe Pepitone	1.75	.90	.50
581	Steve Kealey	1.00	.50	.30
582	Darrell Porter	1.50	.70	.45
583	Bill Greif	1.00	.50	.30
584	Chris Arnold	1.00	.50	.30
585	Joe Niekro	2.00	1.00	.60
586	Bill Sudakis	1.25	.60	.40
587	Rich McKinney	1.00	.50	.30
588	Checklist 529-660	10.00	5.00	3.00
589	Ken Forsch	1.25	.60	.40
590	Deron Johnson	1.00	.50	.30
591	Mike Hedlund	1.00	.50	.30
592	John Boccabella	1.00	.50	.30
593	Royals Mgr./Coaches (Galen Cisco, Harry Dunlop, Charlie Lau, Jack McKeon)	1.25	.60	.40
594	Vic Harris	1.00	.50	.30
595	Don Gullett	1.25	.60	.40
596	Red Sox Team	2.75	1.50	.80
597	Mickey Rivers	1.50	.70	.45
598	Phil Roof	1.00	.50	.30
599	Ed Crosby	1.00	.50	.30
600	Dave McNally	1.50	.70	.45
601	Rookie Catchers (George Pena, Sergio Robles, Rick Stelmaszek)	1.00	.50	.30
602	Rookie Pitchers (Mel Behney, Ralph Garcia, Doug Rau)	1.25	.60	.40
603	Rookie Third Basemen (Terry Hughes, Bill McNulty, Ken Reitz)	1.25	.60	.40
604	Rookie Pitchers (Jesse Jefferson, Dennis O'Toole, Bob Strampe)	1.00	.50	.30
605	Rookie First Basemen (Pat Bourque, Enos Cabell, Gonzalo Marquez)	1.50	.70	.45
606	Rookie Outfielders (Gary Matthews, Tom Paciorek, Jorge Roque)	2.25	1.25	.70
607	Rookie Shortstops (Ray Busse, Pepe Frias, Mario Guerrero)	1.00	.50	.30
608	Rookie Pitchers (Steve Busby, Dick Colpaert, George Medich)	1.25	.60	.40
609	Rookie Second Basemen (Larvell Blanks, Pedro Garcia, Dave Lopes)	2.50	1.25	.70
610	Rookie Pitchers (Jimmy Freeman, Charlie Hough, Hank Webb)	1.50	.70	.45
611	Rookie Outfielders (Rich Coggins, Jim Wohlford, Richie Zisk)	1.25	.60	.40
612	Rookie Pitchers (Steve Lawson, Bob Reynolds, Brent Strom)	1.00	.50	.30
613	Rookie Catchers (Bob Boone, Mike Ivie, Skip Jutze)	3.25	1.75	1.00
614	Rookie Outfielders (Alonza Bumbry, Dwight Evans, Charlie Spikes)	15.00	7.50	4.50
615	Rookie Third Basemen (Ron Cey, John Hilton, Mike Schmidt)	150.00	75.00	45.00
616	Rookie Pitchers (Norm Angelini, Steve Blateric, Mike Garman)	1.25	.60	.40
617	Rich Chiles	1.00	.50	.30
618	Andy Etchebarren	1.00	.50	.30
619	Billy Wilson	1.00	.50	.30
620	Tommy Harper	1.25	.60	.40
621	Joe Ferguson	1.00	.50	.30
622	Larry Hisle	1.25	.60	.40
623	Steve Renko	1.00	.50	.30
624	Astros Mgr./Coaches (Leo Durocher, Preston Gomez, Grady Hatton, Hub Kittle, Jim Owens)	2.00	1.00	.60
625	Angel Mangual	1.00	.50	.30
626	Bob Barton	1.00	.50	.30
627	Luis Alvarado	1.00	.50	.30
628	Jim Slaton	1.25	.60	.40
629	Indians Team	2.50	1.25	.70

		NR MT	EX	VG
630	Denny McLain	2.50	1.25	.70
631	Tom Matchick	1.00	.50	.30
632	Dick Selma	1.00	.50	.30
633	Ike Brown	1.00	.50	.30
634	Alan Closter	1.25	.60	.40
635	Gene Alley	1.25	.60	.40
636	Rick Clark	1.00	.50	.30
637	Norm Niller	1.00	.50	.30
638	Ken Reynolds	1.00	.50	.30
639	Willie Crawford	1.00	.50	.30
640	Dick Bosman	1.00	.50	.30
641	Reds Team	2.75	1.50	.80
642	Jose Laboy	1.00	.50	.30
643	Al Fitzmorris	1.00	.50	.30
644	Jack Heidemann	1.00	.50	.30
645	Bob Locker	1.00	.50	.30
646	Brewers Mgr./Coaches (Del Crandall, Harvey Kuenn, Joe Nossek, Bob Shaw, Jim Walton)	1.50	.70	.45
647	George Stone	1.00	.50	.30
648	Tom Egan	1.00	.50	.30
649	Rich Folkers	1.00	.50	.30
650	Felipe Alou	1.75	.90	.50
651	Don Carrithers	1.00	.50	.30
652	Ted Kubiak	1.00	.50	.30
653	Joe Hoerner	1.00	.50	.30
654	Twins Team	2.50	1.25	.70
655	Clay Kirby	1.00	.50	.30
656	John Ellis	1.00	.50	.30
657	Bob Johnson	1.00	.50	.30
658	Elliott Maddox	1.25	.60	.40
659	Jose Pagan	1.25	.50	.30
660	Fred Scherman	2.00	.60	.40

1973 Topps Candy Lids

A bit out of the ordinary, the Topps Candy Lids were the top of a product called "Baseball Stars Bubble Gum." The bottom (inside) of the lids carry a color photo of a player with a ribbon which contains name, position and team. The lids were 1⅞" in diameter. A total of 55 different lids were made featuring most of the stars of the day.

		NR MT	EX	VG
Complete Set:		400.00	200.00	120.00
Common Player:		2.00	1.00	.60
(1)	Hank Aaron	30.00	15.00	9.00
(2)	Dick Allen	4.00	2.00	1.25
(3)	Dusty Baker	2.00	1.00	.60
(4)	Sal Bando	3.00	1.50	.90
(5)	Johnny Bench	20.00	10.00	6.00
(6)	Bobby Bonds	3.00	1.50	.90
(7)	Dick Bosman	2.00	1.00	.60
(8)	Lou Brock	15.00	7.50	4.50
(9)	Rod Carew	20.00	10.00	6.00
(10)	Steve Carlton	20.00	10.00	6.00
(11)	Nate Colbert	2.00	1.00	.60
(12)	Willie Davis	3.00	1.50	.90
(13)	Larry Dierker	2.00	1.00	.60
(14)	Mike Epstein	2.00	1.00	.60
(15)	Carlton Fisk	7.00	3.50	2.00
(16)	Tim Foli	2.00	1.00	.60
(17)	Ray Fosse	2.00	1.00	.60
(18)	Bill Freehan	3.00	1.50	.90
(19)	Bob Gibson	15.00	7.50	4.50
(20)	Bud Harrelson	2.00	1.00	.60
(21)	Jim Hunter	12.00	6.00	3.50

		NR MT	EX	VG
(22)	Reggie Jackson	25.00	12.50	7.50
(23)	Fergie Jenkins	7.00	3.50	2.00
(24)	Al Kaline	15.00	7.50	4.50
(25)	Harmon Killebrew	15.00	7.50	4.50
(26)	Clay Kirby	2.00	1.00	.60
(27)	Mickey Lolich	4.00	2.00	1.25
(28)	Greg Luzinski	3.00	1.50	.90
(29)	Mike Marshall	2.00	1.00	.60
(30)	Lee May	2.00	1.00	.60
(31)	John Mayberry	2.00	1.00	.60
(32)	Willie Mays	30.00	15.00	9.00
(33)	Willie McCovey	15.00	7.50	4.50
(34)	Thurman Munson	15.00	7.50	4.50
(35)	Bobby Murcer	3.00	1.50	.90
(36)	Gary Nolan	2.00	1.00	.60
(37)	Amos Otis	2.00	1.00	.60
(38)	Jim Palmer	12.00	6.00	3.50
(39)	Gaylord Perry	12.00	6.00	3.50
(40)	Lou Piniella	3.00	1.50	.90
(41)	Brooks Robinson	18.00	9.00	5.50
(42)	Frank Robinson	15.00	7.50	4.50
(43)	Ellie Rodriguez	2.00	1.00	.60
(44)	Pete Rose	65.00	32.00	19.50
(45)	Nolan Ryan	18.00	9.00	5.50
(46)	Manny Sanguillen	2.00	1.00	.60
(47)	George Scott	2.00	1.00	.60
(48)	Tom Seaver	20.00	10.00	6.00
(49)	Chris Speier	2.00	1.00	.60
(50)	Willie Stargell	15.00	7.50	4.50
(51)	Don Sutton	12.00	6.00	3.50
(52)	Joe Torre	4.00	2.00	1.25
(53)	Billy Williams	12.00	6.00	3.50
(54)	Wilbur Wood	2.00	1.00	.60
(55)	Carl Yastrzemski	25.00	12.50	7.50

1973 Topps Comics

Strictly a test issue, if ever publicly distributed at all (most are found without any folding which would have occurred had they actually been used to wrap a piece of bubblegum), the 24 players in the '73 Topps Comics issue appeared on 4-5/8" by 3-7/16" waxed paper wrappers. The inside of the wrapper combined a color photo and facsimile autograph with a comic-style presentation of the player's career highlights. The Comics shared a checklist with the '73 Topps Pin-Ups, virtually all star players.

		NR MT	EX	VG
Complete Set:		1400.00	700.00	420.00
Common Player:		35.00	17.50	10.50
(1)	Hank Aaron	100.00	50.00	30.00
(2)	Dick Allen	40.00	20.00	12.00
(3)	Johnny Bench	80.00	40.00	24.00
(4)	Steve Carlton	65.00	32.00	19.50
(5)	Nate Colbert	35.00	17.50	10.50

		NR MT	EX	VG
(6)	Willie Davis	40.00	20.00	12.00
(7)	Mike Epstein	35.00	17.50	10.50
(8)	Reggie Jackson	100.00	50.00	30.00
(9)	Harmon Killebrew	60.00	30.00	18.00
(10)	Mickey Lolich	40.00	20.00	12.00
(11)	Mike Marshall	35.00	17.50	10.50
(12)	Lee May	35.00	17.50	10.50
(13)	Willie McCovey	60.00	30.00	18.00
(14)	Bobby Murcer	40.00	20.00	12.00
(15)	Gaylord Perry	50.00	25.00	15.00
(16)	Lou Piniella	40.00	20.00	12.00
(17)	Brooks Robinson	60.00	30.00	18.00
(18)	Nolan Ryan	60.00	30.00	18.00
(19)	George Scott	35.00	17.50	10.50
(20)	Tom Seaver	80.00	40.00	24.00
(21)	Willie Stargell	50.00	25.00	15.00
(22)	Joe Torre	40.00	20.00	12.00
(23)	Billy Williams	50.00	25.00	15.00
(24)	Carl Yastrzemski	125.00	62.00	37.00

1973 Topps Pin-Ups

Another test issue of 1973, the 24 Topps Pin-Ups included the same basic format and the same checklist of star-caliber players as the Comics test issue of the same year. The 3-7/16" by 4-5/8" Pin-Ups were actually the inside of a wrapper for a piece of bubble-gum. The color player photo featured a decorative lozenge inserted at bottom with the player's name, team and position. There was also a facsimile autograph. Curiously, neither the Pin-Ups nor the Comics of 1973 bear team logos on the players' caps.

		NR MT	EX	VG
Complete Set:		1250.00	625.00	375.00
Common Player:		30.00	15.00	9.00
(1)	Hank Aaron	90.00	45.00	27.00
(2)	Dick Allen	35.00	17.50	10.50
(3)	Johnny Bench	70.00	35.00	21.00
(4)	Steve Carlton	60.00	30.00	18.00
(5)	Nate Colbert	30.00	15.00	9.00
(6)	Willie Davis	35.00	17.50	10.50
(7)	Mike Epstein	30.00	15.00	9.00
(8)	Reggie Jackson	90.00	45.00	27.00
(9)	Harmon Killebrew	50.00	25.00	15.00
(10)	Mickey Lolich	35.00	17.50	10.50
(11)	Mike Marshall	30.00	15.00	9.00
(12)	Lee May	30.00	15.00	9.00
(13)	Willie McCovey	50.00	25.00	15.00
(14)	Bobby Murcer	35.00	17.50	10.50
(15)	Gaylord Perry	45.00	22.00	13.50
(16)	Lou Piniella	35.00	17.50	10.50
(17)	Brooks Robinson	55.00	27.00	16.50
(18)	Nolan Ryan	55.00	27.00	16.50
(19)	George Scott	30.00	15.00	9.00
(20)	Tom Seaver	75.00	37.00	22.00
(21)	Willie Stargell	45.00	22.00	13.50
(22)	Joe Torre	35.00	17.50	10.50
(23)	Billy Williams	45.00	22.00	13.50
(24)	Carl Yastrzemski	110.00	55.00	33.00

NOTE: A card number in parentheses ( ) indicates the set is unnumbered.

1973 Topps Team Checklists

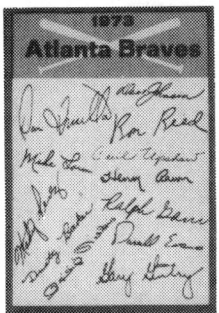

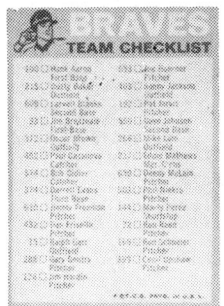

A 24-card unnumbered set of 2½'' by 3½'' cards that is generally believed to have been included among high numbers in 1973, while also being made available in a mail-in offer. The front of the cards has the team name at the top and a white panel with various facsimile autographs takes up the rest of the space except for a blue border. Backs feature the team name and checklist. Relatively scarce, these somewhat mysterious cards are not included by many in their collections despite their obvious relationship to the regular set.

		NR MT	EX	VG
Complete Set:		70.00	35.00	21.00
Common Player:		3.00	1.50	.90
(1)	Atlanta Braves	3.00	1.50	.90
(2)	Baltimore Orioles	3.00	1.50	.90
(3)	Boston Red Sox	3.00	1.50	.90
(4)	California Angels	3.00	1.50	.90
(5)	Chicago Cubs	3.00	1.50	.90
(6)	Chicago White Sox	3.00	1.50	.90
(7)	Cincinnati Reds	3.00	1.50	.90
(8)	Cleveland Indians	3.00	1.50	.90
(9)	Detroit Tigers	3.50	1.75	1.00
(10)	Houston Astros	3.00	1.50	.90
(11)	Kansas City Royals	3.00	1.50	.90
(12)	Los Angeles Dodgers	3.00	1.50	.90
(13)	Milwaukee Brewers	3.00	1.50	.90
(14)	Minnesota Twins	3.00	1.50	.90
(15)	Montreal Expos	3.00	1.50	.90
(16)	New York Mets	3.50	1.75	1.00
(17)	New York Yankees	3.50	1.75	1.00
(18)	Oakland A's	3.50	1.75	1.00
(19)	Philadelphia Phillies	3.00	1.50	.90
(20)	Pittsburgh Pirates	3.00	1.50	.90
(21)	St. Louis Cardinals	3.00	1.50	.90
(22)	San Diego Padres	3.00	1.50	.90
(23)	San Francisco Giants	3.00	1.50	.90
(24)	Texas Rangers	3.00	1.50	.90

1974 Topps

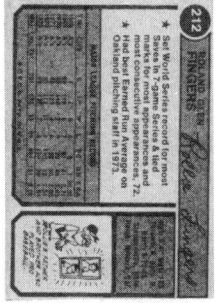

Issued all at once at the beginning of the year, rather than by series throughout the baseball season

as had been done since 1952, this 660-card '74 Topps set features a famous group of error cards. At the time the cards were printed, it was uncertain whether the San Diego Padres would move to Washington, D.C., and by the time a decision was made some Padres cards had appeared with a "Washington, Nat'l League" designation on the front. A total of 15 cards were affected, and those with the Washington team designation bring prices well in excess of regular cards of the same players (the Washington variations are not included in the complete set prices quoted below). The 2½'' by 3½'' cards feature color photos (frequently game-action shots) along with the player's name, team and position. Specialty cards abound, starting with a Hank Aaron tribute and running through the usual managers, statistical leaders, Play-off and World Series highlights multi-player rookie cards and All-Stars.

		NR MT	EX	VG
Complete Set:		350.00	150.00	90.00
Common Player:		.20	.10	.06
1	Hank Aaron	12.00	4.00	2.50
2	Aaron Special 1954-57	3.00	1.50	.90
3	Aaron Special 1958-61	3.00	1.50	.90
4	Aaron Special 1962-65	3.00	1.50	.90
5	Aaron Special 1966-69	3.00	1.50	.90
6	Aaron Special 1970-73	3.00	1.50	.90
7	Jim Hunter	2.50	1.25	.70
8	George Theodore	.20	.10	.06
9	Mickey Lolich	.60	.30	.20
10	Johnny Bench	6.50	.3.25	2.00
11	Jim Bibby	.25	.13	.08
12	Dave May	.20	.10	.06
13	Tom Hilgendorf	.20	.10	.06
14	Paul Popovich	.20	.10	.06
15	Joe Torre	.80	.40	.25
16	Orioles Team	.80	.40	.25
17	Doug Bird	.20	.10	.06
18	Gary Thomasson	.20	.10	.06
19	Gerry Moses	.25	.13	.08
20	Nolan Ryan	5.50	2.75	1.75
21	Bob Gallagher	.20	.10	.06
22	Cy Acosta	.20	.10	.06
23	Craig Robinson	.20	.10	.06
24	John Hiller	.25	.13	.08
25	Ken Singleton	.30	.15	.09
26	Bill Campbell	.40	.20	.12
27	George Scott	.30	.15	.09
28	Manny Sanguillen	.25	.13	.08
29	Phil Niekro	2.00	1.00	.60
30	Bobby Bonds	.50	.25	.15
31	Astros Mgr./Coaches (Roger Craig, Preston Gomez, Grady Hatton, Hub Kittle, Bob Lillis)	.20	.10	.06
32a	John Grubb (Washington)	3.50	1.75	1.00
32b	John Grubb (San Diego)	.25	.13	.08
33	Don Newhauser	.20	.10	.06
34	Andy Kosco	.20	.10	.06
35	Gaylord Perry	2.25	1.25	.70
36	Cardinals Team	.80	.40	.25
37	Dave Sells	.20	.10	.06
38	Don Kessinger	.25	.13	.08
39	Ken Suarez	.20	.10	.06
40	Jim Palmer	3.25	1.75	1.00
41	Bobby Floyd	.20	.10	.06
42	Claude Osteen	.30	.15	.09
43	Jim Wynn	.30	.15	.09
44	Mel Stottlemyre	.40	.20	.12
45	Dave Johnson	.70	.35	.20
46	Pat Kelly	.20	.10	.06
47	Dick Ruthven	.25	.13	.08
48	Dick Sharon	.20	.10	.06
49	Steve Renko	.20	.10	.06
50	Rod Carew	5.50	2.75	1.75
51	Bobby Heise	.20	.10	.06
52	Al Oliver	1.25	.60	.40
53a	Fred Kendall (Washington)	3.50	1.75	1.00
53b	Fred Kendall (San Diego)	.25	.13	.08
54	Elias Sosa	.25	.13	.08
55	Frank Robinson	3.50	1.75	1.00
56	Mets Team	1.00	.50	.30
57	Darold Knowles	.20	.10	.06
58	Charlie Spikes	.20	.10	.06
59	Ross Grimsley	.25	.13	.08
60	Lou Brock	3.50	1.75	1.00
61	Luis Aparicio	2.50	1.25	.70

		NR MT	EX	VG
62	Bob Locker	.20	.10	.06
63	Bill Sudakis	.20	.10	.06
64	Doug Rau	.20	.10	.06
65	Amos Otis	.30	.15	.09
66	Sparky Lyle	.50	.25	.15
67	Tommy Helms	.20	.10	.06
68	Grant Jackson	.20	.10	.06
69	Del Unser	.20	.10	.06
70	Dick Allen	.80	.40	.25
71	Danny Frisella	.20	.10	.06
72	Aurleio Rodriguez	.25	.13	.08
73	Mike Marshall	.70	.35	.20
74	Twins Team	.80	.40	.25
75	Jim Colborn	.20	.10	.06
76	Mickey Rivers	.30	.15	.09
77a	Rich Troedson (Washington)	3.50	1.75	1.00
77b	Rich Troedson (San Diego)	.25	.13	.08
78	Giants Mgr./Coaches (Joe Amalfitano, Charlie Fox, Andy Gilbert, Don McMahon, John McNamara)	.20	.10	.06
79	Gene Tenace	.30	.15	.09
80	Tom Seaver	6.00	3.00	1.75
81	Frank Duffy	.20	.10	.06
82	Dave Giusti	.20	.10	.06
83	Orlando Cepeda	1.00	.50	.30
84	Rick Wise	.25	.13	.08
85	Joe Morgan	2.50	1.25	.70
86	Joe Ferguson	.20	.10	.06
87	Fergie Jenkins	1.25	.60	.40
88	Freddie Patek	.20	.10	.06
89	Jackie Brown	.20	.10	.06
90	Bobby Murcer	.40	.20	.12
91	Ken Forsch	.25	.13	.08
92	Paul Blair	.25	.13	.08
93	Rod Gilbreath	.20	.10	.06
94	Tigers Team	.90	.45	.25
95	Steve Carlton	6.00	3.00	1.75
96	Jerry Hairston	.40	.20	.12
97	Bob Bailey	.20	.10	.06
98	Bert Blyleven	1.00	.50	.30
99	Brewers Mgr./Coaches (Del Crandall, Harvey Kuenn, Joe Nossek, Jim Walton, Al Widmar)	.25	.13	.08
100	Willie Stargell	3.00	1.50	.90
101	Bobby Valentine	.30	.15	.09
102a	Bill Greif (Washington)	3.50	1.75	1.00
102b	Bill Greif (San Diego)	.25	.13	.08
103	Sal Bando	.40	.20	.12
104	Ron Bryant	.20	.10	.06
105	Carlton Fisk	1.50	.70	.45
106	Harry Parker	.20	.10	.06
107	Alex Johnson	.20	.10	.06
108	Al Hrabosky	.25	.13	.08
109	Bob Grich	.40	.20	.12
110	Billy Williams	2.75	1.50	.80
111	Clay Carroll	.25	.13	.08
112	Dave Lopes	.40	.20	.12
113	Dick Drago	.20	.10	.06
114	Angels Team	.80	.40	.25
115	Willie Horton	.30	.15	.09
116	Jerry Reuss	.30	.15	.09
117	Ron Blomberg	.25	.13	.08
118	Bill Lee	.25	.13	.08
119	Phillies Mgr./Coaches (Carroll Beringer, Bill DeMars, Danny Ozark, Ray Ripplemeyer, Bobby Wine)	.25	.13	.08
120	Wilbur Wood	.30	.15	.09
121	Larry Lintz	.20	.10	.06
122	Jim Holt	.20	.10	.06
123	Nelson Briles	.20	.10	.06
124	Bob Coluccio	.20	.10	.06
125a	Nate Colbert (Washington)	3.50	1.75	1.00
125b	Nate Colbert (San Diego)	.30	.15	.09
126	Checklist 1-132	1.50	.70	.45
127	Tom Paciorek	.25	.13	.08
128	John Ellis	.20	.10	.06
129	Chris Speier	.25	.13	.08
130	Reggie Jackson	8.00	4.00	2.50
131	Bob Boone	.50	.25	.15
132	Felix Millan	.20	.10	.06
133	David Clyde	.30	.15	.09
134	Denis Menke	.20	.10	.06
135	Roy White	.40	.20	.12
136	Rick Reuschel	.80	.40	.25
137	Al Bumbry	.25	.13	.08
138	Ed Brinkman	.25	.13	.08
139	Aurelio Monteagudo	.20	.10	.06
140	Darrell Evans	.60	.30	.20
141	Pat Bourque	.20	.10	.06
142	Pedro Garcia	.20	.10	.06
143	Dick Woodson	.20	.10	.06

		NR MT	EX	VG
144	Dodgers Mgr./Coaches (Red Adams, Walter Alston, Monty Basgall, Jim Gilliam, Tom Lasorda)	1.25	.60	.40
145	Dock Ellis	.25	.13	.08
146	Ron Fairly	.30	.15	.09
147	Bart Johnson	.20	.10	.06
148a	Dave Hilton (Washington)	3.50	1.75	1.00
148b	Dave Hilton (San Diego)	.25	.13	.08
149	Mac Scarce	.20	.10	.06
150	John Mayberry	.30	.15	.09
151	Diego Segui	.20	.10	.06
152	Oscar Gamble	.30	.15	.09
153	Jon Matlack	.30	.15	.09
154	Astros Team	.80	.40	.25
155	Bert Campaneris	.40	.20	.12
156	Randy Moffitt	.20	.10	.06
157	Vic Harris	.20	.10	.06
158	Jack Billingham	.20	.10	.06
159	Jim Ray Hart	.25	.13	.08
160	Brooks Robinson	3.50	1.75	1.00
161	Ray Burris	.40	.20	.12
162	Bill Freehan	.40	.20	.12
163	Ken Berry	.20	.10	.06
164	Tom House	.20	.10	.06
165	Willie Davis	.40	.20	.12
166	Royals Mgr./Coaches (Galen Cisco, Harry Dunlop, Charlie Lau, Jack McKeon)	.25	.13	.08
167	Luis Tiant	.50	.25	.15
168	Danny Thompson	.25	.13	.08
169	Steve Rogers	.70	.35	.20
170	Bill Melton	.25	.13	.08
171	Eduardo Rodriguez	.20	.10	.06
172	Gene Clines	.20	.10	.06
173a	Randy Jones (Washington)	4.00	2.00	1.25
173b	Randy Jones (San Diego)	.40	.20	.12
174	Bill Robinson	.20	.10	.06
175	Reggie Cleveland	.20	.10	.06
176	John Lowenstein	.20	.10	.06
177	Dave Roberts	.20	.10	.06
178	Garry Maddox	.40	.20	.12
179	Mets Mgr./Coaches (Yogi Berra, Roy McMillan, Joe Pignatano, Rube Walker, Eddie Yost)	1.25	.60	.40
180	Ken Holtzman	.30	.15	.09
181	Cesar Geronimo	.25	.13	.08
182	Lindy McDaniel	.25	.13	.08
183	Johnny Oates	.20	.10	.06
184	Rangers Team	.80	.40	.25
185	Jose Cardenal	.25	.13	.08
186	Fred Scherman	.20	.10	.06
187	Don Baylor	.70	.35	.20
188	Rudy Meoli	.20	.10	.06
189	Jim Brewer	.20	.10	.06
190	Tony Oliva	.80	.40	.25
191	Al Fitzmorris	.20	.10	.06
192	Mario Guerrero	.20	.10	.06
193	Tom Walker	.20	.10	.06
194	Darrell Porter	.30	.15	.09
195	Carlos May	.25	.13	.08
196	Jim Fregosi	.40	.20	.12
197a	Vicente Romo (Washington)	3.50	1.75	1.00
197b	Vicente Romo (San Diego)	.25	.13	.08
198	Dave Cash	.20	.10	.06
199	Mike Kekich	.20	.10	.06
200	Cesar Cedeno	.40	.20	.12
201	Batting Leaders (Rod Carew, Pete Rose)	3.00	1.50	.90
202	Home Run Leaders (Reggie Jackson, Willie Stargell)	2.00	1.00	.60
203	Runs Batted In Leaders (Reggie Jackson, Willie Stargell)	2.00	1.00	.60
204	Stolen Base Leaders (Lou Brock, Tommy Harper)	1.25	.60	.40
205	Victory Leaders (Ron Bryant, Wilbur Wood)	.50	.25	.15
206	Earned Run Average Leaders (Jim Palmer, Tom Seaver)	2.00	1.00	.60
207	Strikeout Leaders (Nolan Ryan, Tom Seaver)	2.00	1.00	.60
208	Leading Firemen (John Hiller, Mike Marshall)	.50	.25	.15
209	Ted Sizemore	.20	.10	.06
210	Bill Singer	.25	.13	.08
211	Cubs Team	.80	.40	.25
212	Rollie Fingers	1.50	.70	.45
213	Dave Rader	.20	.10	.06
214	Billy Grabarkewitz	.20	.10	.06
215	Al Kaline	3.50	1.75	1.00
216	Ray Sadecki	.20	.10	.06
217	Tim Foli	.20	.10	.06
218	Johnny Briggs	.20	.10	.06

#	Player	NR MT	EX	VG
219	Doug Griffin	.20	.10	.06
220	Don Sutton	2.00	1.00	.60
221	White Sox Mgr./Coaches (Joe Lonnett, Jim Mahoney, Alex Monchak, Johnny Sain, Chuck Tanner)	.30	.15	.09
222	Ramon Hernandez	.20	.10	.06
223	Jeff Burroughs	.50	.25	.15
224	Roger Metzger	.20	.10	.06
225	Paul Splittorff	.25	.13	.08
226a	Washington Nat'l. Team	6.00	3.00	1.75
226b	Padres Team	1.00	.50	.30
227	Mike Lum	.20	.10	.06
228	Ted Kubiak	.20	.10	.06
229	Fritz Peterson	.30	.15	.09
230	Tony Perez	1.25	.60	.40
231	Dick Tidrow	.20	.10	.06
232	Steve Brye	.20	.10	.06
233	Jim Barr	.20	.10	.06
234	John Milner	.20	.10	.06
235	Dave McNally	.30	.15	.09
236	Cardinals Mgr./Coaches (Vern Benson, George Kissell, Johnny Lewis, Red Schoendienst, Barney Schultz)	.30	.15	.09
237	Ken Brett	.25	.13	.08
238	Fran Healy	.20	.10	.06
239	Bill Russell	.30	.15	.09
240	Joe Coleman	.25	.13	.08
241a	Glenn Beckert (Washington)	4.00	2.00	1.25
241b	Glenn Beckert (San Diego)	.30	.15	.09
242	Bill Gogolewski	.20	.10	.06
243	Bob Oliver	.20	.10	.06
244	Carl Morton	.20	.10	.06
245	Cleon Jones	.25	.13	.08
246	A's Team	1.25	.60	.40
247	Rick Miller	.20	.10	.06
248	Tom Hall	.20	.10	.06
249	George Mitterwald	.20	.10	.06
250a	Willie McCovey (Washington)	20.00	10.00	6.00
250b	Willie McCovey (San Diego)	4.00	2.00	1.25
251	Graig Nettles	1.50	.70	.45
252	Dave Parker	15.00	7.50	4.50
253	John Boccabella	.20	.10	.06
254	Stan Bahnsen	.20	.10	.06
255	Larry Bowa	.40	.20	.12
256	Tom Griffin	.20	.10	.06
257	Buddy Bell	1.25	.60	.40
258	Jerry Morales	.20	.10	.06
259	Bob Reynolds	.20	.10	.06
260	Ted Simmons	.80	.40	.25
261	Jerry Bell	.20	.10	.06
262	Ed Kirkpatrick	.20	.10	.06
263	Checklist 133-264	1.50	.70	.45
264	Joe Rudi	.40	.20	.12
265	Tug McGraw	.60	.30	.20
266	Jim Northrup	.25	.13	.08
267	Andy Messersmith	.30	.15	.09
268	Tom Grieve	.20	.10	.06
269	Bob Johnson	.20	.10	.06
270	Ron Santo	.50	.25	.15
271	Bill Hands	.20	.10	.06
272	Paul Casanova	.20	.10	.06
273	Checklist 265-396	1.50	.70	.45
274	Fred Beene	.25	.13	.08
275	Ron Hunt	.25	.13	.08
276	Angels Mgr./Coaches (Tom Morgan, Salty Parker, Jimmie Reese, John Roseboro, Bobby Winkles)	.20	.10	.06
277	Gary Nolan	.20	.10	.06
278	Cookie Rojas	.20	.10	.06
279	Jim Crawford	.20	.10	.06
280	Carl Yastrzemski	8.00	4.00	2.50
281	Giants Team	.80	.40	.25
282	Doyle Alexander	.40	.20	.12
283	Mike Schmidt	35.00	17.50	10.50
284	Dave Duncan	.20	.10	.06
285	Reggie Smith	.40	.20	.12
286	Tony Muser	.20	.10	.06
287	Clay Kirby	.20	.10	.06
288	Gorman Thomas	1.50	.70	.45
289	Rick Auerbach	.20	.10	.06
290	Vida Blue	.60	.30	.20
291	Don Hahn	.20	.10	.06
292	Chuck Seelbach	.20	.10	.06
293	Milt May	.20	.10	.06
294	Steve Foucault	.20	.10	.06
295	Rick Monday	.30	.15	.09
296	Ray Corbin	.20	.10	.06
297	Hal Breeden	.20	.10	.06
298	Roric Harrison	.20	.10	.06
299	Gene Michael	.30	.15	.09
300	Pete Rose	15.00	7.50	4.50
301	Bob Montgomery	.20	.10	.06
302	Rudy May	.25	.13	.08
303	George Hendrick	.30	.15	.09
304	Don Wilson	.20	.10	.06
305	Tito Fuentes	.20	.10	.06
306	Orioles Mgr./Coaches (George Bamberger, Jim Frey, Billy Hunter, George Staller, Earl Weaver)	.70	.35	.20
307	Luis Melendez	.20	.10	.06
308	Bruce Dal Canton	.20	.10	.06
309a	Dave Roberts (Washington)	3.50	1.75	1.00
309b	Dave Roberts (San Diego)	.25	.13	.08
310	Terry Forster	.30	.15	.09
311	Jerry Grote	.25	.13	.08
312	Deron Johnson	.20	.10	.06
313	Berry Lersch	.20	.10	.06
314	Brewers Team	.80	.40	.25
315	Ron Cey	.60	.30	.20
316	Jim Perry	.40	.20	.12
317	Richie Zisk	.30	.15	.09
318	Jim Merritt	.20	.10	.06
319	Randy Hundley	.20	.10	.06
320	Dusty Baker	.40	.20	.12
321	Steve Braun	.20	.10	.06
322	Ernie McAnally	.20	.10	.06
323	Richie Scheinblum	.20	.10	.06
324	Steve Kline	.25	.13	.08
325	Tommy Harper	.25	.13	.08
326	Reds Mgr./Coaches (Sparky Anderson, Alex Grammas, Ted Kluszewski, George Scherger, Larry Shepard)	.50	.25	.15
327	Tom Timmermann	.20	.10	.06
328	Skip Jutze	.20	.10	.06
329	Mark Belanger	.30	.15	.09
330	Juan Marichal	2.75	1.50	.80
331	All Star Catchers (Johnny Bench, Carlton Fisk)	2.00	1.00	.60
332	All Star First Basemen (Hank Aaron, Dick Allen)	2.00	1.00	.60
333	All Star Second Basemen (Rod Carew, Joe Morgan)	2.00	1.00	.60
334	All Star Third Basemen (Brooks Robinson, Ron Santo)	1.25	.60	.40
335	All Star Shortstops (Bert Campaneris, Chris Speier)	.40	.20	.12
336	All Star Left Fielders (Bobby Murcer, Pete Rose)	2.50	1.25	.70
337	All Star Center Fielders (Cesar Cedeno, Amos Otis)	.40	.20	.12
338	All Star Right Fielders (Reggie Jackson, Billy Williams)	2.00	1.00	.60
339	All Star Pitchers (Jim Hunter, Rick Wise)	.80	.40	.25
340	Thurman Munson	4.00	2.00	1.25
341	Dan Driessen	.80	.40	.25
342	Jim Lonborg	.30	.15	.09
343	Royals Team	.80	.40	.25
344	Mike Caldwell	.25	.13	.08
345	Bill North	.25	.13	.08
346	Ron Reed	.25	.13	.08
347	Sandy Alomar	.20	.10	.06
348	Pete Richert	.20	.10	.06
349	John Vukovich	.20	.10	.06
350	Bob Gibson	2.75	1.50	.80
351	Dwight Evans	3.00	1.50	.90
352	Bill Stoneman	.20	.10	.06
353	Rich Coggins	.20	.10	.06
354	Cubs Mgr./Coaches (Hank Aguirre, Whitey Lockman, Jim Marshall, J.C. Martin, Al Spangler)	.20	.10	.06
355	Dave Nelson	.40	.20	.12
356	Jerry Koosman	.40	.20	.12
357	Buddy Bradford	.20	.10	.06
358	Dal Maxvill	.25	.13	.08
359	Brent Strom	.20	.10	.06
360	Greg Luzinski	.70	.35	.20
361	Don Carrithers	.20	.10	.06
362	Hal King	.20	.10	.06
363	Yankees Team	1.25	.60	.40
364a	Clarence Gaston (Washington)	3.50	1.75	1.00
364b	Clarence Gaston (San Diego)	.25	.13	.08
365	Steve Busby	.25	.13	.08
366	Larry Hisle	.25	.13	.08
367	Norm Cash	.50	.25	.15
368	Manny Mota	.40	.20	.12
369	Paul Lindblad	.20	.10	.06
370	Bob Watson	.25	.13	.08
371	Jim Slaton	.20	.10	.06
372	Ken Reitz	.20	.10	.06
373	John Curtis	.20	.10	.06
374	Marty Perez	.20	.10	.06

#	Player	NR MT	EX	VG
375	Earl Williams	.20	.10	.06
376	Jorge Orta	.25	.13	.08
377	Ron Woods	.20	.10	.06
378	Burt Hooton	.30	.15	.09
379	Rangers Mgr./Coaches (Art Fowler, Frank Lucchesi, Billy Martin, Jackie Moore, Charlie Silvera)	.80	.40	.25
380	Bud Harrelson	.25	.13	.08
381	Charlie Sands	.20	.10	.06
382	Bob Moose	.20	.10	.06
383	Phillies Team	.80	.40	.25
384	Chris Chambliss	.40	.20	.12
385	Don Gullett	.25	.13	.08
386	Gary Matthews	.60	.30	.20
387a	Rich Morales (Washington)	3.50	1.75	1.00
387b	Rich Morales (San Diego)	.25	.13	.08
388	Phil Roof	.20	.10	.06
389	Gates Brown	.20	.10	.06
390	Lou Piniella	.70	.35	.20
391	Billy Champion	.20	.10	.06
392	Dick Green	.20	.10	.06
393	Orlando Pena	.20	.10	.06
394	Ken Henderson	.20	.10	.06
395	Doug Rader	.20	.10	.06
396	Tommy Davis	.40	.20	.12
397	George Stone	.20	.10	.06
398	Duke Sims	.25	.13	.08
399	Mike Paul	.20	.10	.06
400	Harmon Killebrew	3.00	1.50	.90
401	Elliott Maddox	.20	.10	.06
402	Jim Rooker	.20	.10	.06
403	Red Sox Mgr./Coaches (Don Bryant, Darrell Johnson, Eddie Popowski, Lee Stange, Don Zimmer)	.25	.13	.08
404	Jim Howarth	.20	.10	.06
405	Ellie Rodriguez	.20	.10	.06
406	Steve Arlin	.20	.10	.06
407	Jim Wohlford	.20	.10	.06
408	Charlie Hough	.40	.20	.12
409	Ike Brown	.20	.10	.06
410	Pedro Borbon	.20	.10	.06
411	Frank Baker	.20	.10	.06
412	Chuck Taylor	.20	.10	.06
413	Don Money	.25	.13	.08
414	Checklist 397-528	1.50	.70	.45
415	Gary Gentry	.20	.10	.06
416	White Sox Team	.80	.40	.25
417	Rich Folkers	.20	.10	.06
418	Walt Williams	.20	.10	.06
419	Wayne Twitchell	.20	.10	.06
420	Ray Fosse	.20	.10	.06
421	Dan Fife	.20	.10	.06
422	Gonzalo Marquez	.20	.10	.06
423	Fred Stanley	.25	.13	.08
424	Jim Beauchamp	.20	.10	.06
425	Pete Broberg	.20	.10	.06
426	Rennie Stennett	.20	.10	.06
427	Bobby Bolin	.20	.10	.06
428	Gary Sutherland	.20	.10	.06
429	Dick Lange	.20	.10	.06
430	Matty Alou	.40	.20	.12
431	Gene Garber	.50	.25	.15
432	Chris Arnold	.20	.10	.06
433	Lerrin LaGrow	.20	.10	.06
434	Ken McMullen	.20	.10	.06
435	Dave Concepcion	.70	.35	.20
436	Don Hood	.20	.10	.06
437	Jim Lyttle	.20	.10	.06
438	Ed Herrmann	.20	.10	.06
439	Norm Miller	.20	.10	.06
440	Jim Kaat	1.25	.60	.40
441	Tom Ragland	.20	.10	.06
442	Alan Foster	.20	.10	.06
443	Tom Hutton	.20	.10	.06
444	Vic Davalillo	.25	.13	.08
445	George Medich	.30	.15	.09
446	Len Randle	.20	.10	.06
447	Twins Mgr./Coaches (Vern Morgan, Frank Quilici, Bob Rodgers, Ralph Rowe)	.20	.10	.06
448	Ron Hodges	.20	.10	.06
449	Tom McCraw	.20	.10	.06
450	Rich Hebner	.25	.13	.08
451	Tommy John	1.50	.70	.45
452	Gene Hiser	.20	.10	.06
453	Balor Moore	.20	.10	.06
454	Kurt Bevacqua	.20	.10	.06
455	Tom Bradley	.20	.10	.06
456	Dave Winfield	25.00	12.50	7.50
457	Chuck Goggin	.20	.10	.06
458	Jim Ray	.20	.10	.06
459	Reds Team	.90	.45	.25
460	Boog Powell	.90	.45	.25
461	John Odom	.25	.13	.08
462	Luis Alvarado	.20	.10	.06
463	Pat Dobson	.30	.15	.09
464	Jose Cruz	.80	.40	.25
465	Dick Bosman	.20	.10	.06
466	Dick Billings	.20	.10	.06
467	Winston Llenas	.20	.10	.06
468	Pepe Frias	.20	.10	.06
469	Joe Decker	.20	.10	.06
470	A.L. Playoffs	2.00	1.00	.60
471	N.L. Playoffs	.80	.40	.25
472	World Series Game 1	.80	.40	.25
473	World Series Game 2	2.00	1.00	.60
474	World Series Game 3	.80	.40	.25
475	World Series Game 4	.80	.40	.25
476	World Series Game 5	.80	.40	.25
477	World Series Game 6	2.00	1.00	.60
478	World Series Game 7	.80	.40	.25
479	World Series Summary	.80	.40	.25
480	Willie Crawford	.20	.10	.06
481	Jerry Terrell	.20	.10	.06
482	Bob Didier	.20	.10	.06
483	Braves Team	.80	.40	.25
484	Carmen Fanzone	.20	.10	.06
485	Felipe Alou	.40	.20	.12
486	Steve Stone	.40	.20	.12
487	Ted Martinez	.20	.10	.06
488	Andy Etchebarren	.20	.10	.06
489	Pirates Mgr./Coaches (Don Leppert, Bill Mazeroski, Danny Murtaugh, Don Osborn, Bob Skinner)	.30	.15	.09
490	Vada Pinson	.70	.35	.20
491	Roger Nelson	.20	.10	.06
492	Mike Rogodzinski	.20	.10	.06
493	Joe Hoerner	.20	.10	.06
494	Ed Goodson	.20	.10	.06
495	Dick McAuliffe	.25	.13	.08
496	Tom Murphy	.20	.10	.06
497	Bobby Mitchell	.20	.10	.06
498	Pat Corrales	.40	.20	.12
499	Rusty Torres	.20	.10	.06
500	Lee May	.40	.20	.12
501	Eddie Leon	.20	.10	.06
502	Dave LaRoche	.20	.10	.06
503	Eric Soderholm	.20	.10	.06
504	Joe Niekro	.40	.20	.12
505	Bill Buckner	.50	.25	.15
506	Ed Farmer	.20	.10	.06
507	Larry Stahl	.20	.10	.06
508	Expos Team	.80	.40	.25
509	Jesse Jefferson	.20	.10	.06
510	Wayne Garrett	.20	.10	.06
511	Toby Harrah	.30	.15	.09
512	Joe Lahoud	.20	.10	.06
513	Jim Campanis	.20	.10	.06
514	Paul Schaal	.20	.10	.06
515	Willie Montanez	.25	.13	.08
516	Horacio Pina	.20	.10	.06
517	Mike Hegan	.25	.13	.08
518	Derrel Thomas	.20	.10	.06
519	Bill Sharp	.20	.10	.06
520	Tim McCarver	.60	.30	.20
521	Indians Mgr./Coaches (Ken Aspromonte, Clay Bryant, Tony Pacheco)	.20	.10	.06
522	J.R. Richard	.30	.15	.09
523	Cecil Cooper	1.50	.70	.45
524	Bill Plummer	.20	.10	.06
525	Clyde Wright	.20	.10	.06
526	Frank Tepedino	.20	.10	.06
527	Bobby Darwin	.20	.10	.06
528	Bill Bonham	.20	.10	.06
529	Horace Clarke	.25	.13	.08
530	Mickey Stanley	.25	.13	.08
531	Expos Mgr./Coaches (Dave Bristol, Larry Doby, Gene Mauch, Cal McLish, Jerry Zimmerman)	.40	.20	.12
532	Skip Lockwood	.20	.10	.06
533	Mike Phillips	.20	.10	.06
534	Eddie Watt	.20	.10	.06
535	Bob Tolan	.25	.13	.08
536	Duffy Dyer	.20	.10	.06
537	Steve Mingori	.20	.10	.06
538	Cesar Tovar	.20	.10	.06
539	Lloyd Allen	.20	.10	.06
540	Bob Robertson	.20	.10	.06
541	Indians Team	.80	.40	.25
542	Rich Gossage	2.00	1.00	.60
543	Danny Cater	.20	.10	.06
544	Ron Schueler	.20	.10	.06
545	Billy Conigliaro	.20	.10	.06

		NR MT	EX	VG
546	Mike Corkins	.20	.10	.06
547	Glenn Borgmann	.20	.10	.06
548	Sonny Siebert	.20	.10	.06
549	Mike Jorgensen	.20	.10	.06
550	Sam McDowell	.40	.20	.12
551	Von Joshua	.20	.10	.06
552	Denny Doyle	.20	.10	.06
553	Jim Willoughby	.20	.10	.06
554	Tim Johnson	.20	.10	.06
555	Woodie Fryman	.25	.13	.08
556	Dave Campbell	.20	.10	.06
557	Jim McGlothlin	.20	.10	.06
558	Bill Fahey	.20	.10	.06
559	Darrel Chaney	.20	.10	.06
560	Mike Cuellar	.40	.20	.12
561	Ed Kranepool	.30	.15	.09
562	Jack Aker	.20	.10	.06
563	Hal McRae	.40	.20	.12
564	Mike Ryan	.20	.10	.06
565	Milt Wilcox	.25	.13	.08
566	Jackie Hernandez	.20	.10	.06
567	Red Sox Team	.90	.45	.25
568	Mike Torrez	.25	.13	.08
569	Rick Dempsey	.40	.20	.12
570	Ralph Garr	.30	.15	.09
571	Rich Hand	.20	.10	.06
572	Enzo Hernandez	.20	.10	.06
573	Mike Adams	.20	.10	.06
574	Bill Parsons	.20	.10	.06
575	Steve Garvey	8.00	4.00	2.50
576	Scipio Spinks	.20	.10	.06
577	Mike Sadek	.20	.10	.06
578	Ralph Houk	.40	.20	.12
579	Cecil Upshaw	.20	.10	.06
580	Jim Spencer	.20	.10	.06
581	Fred Norman	.20	.10	.06
582	Bucky Dent	.90	.45	.25
583	Marty Pattin	.20	.10	.06
584	Ken Rudolph	.20	.10	.06
585	Merv Rettenmund	.25	.13	.08
586	Jack Brohamer	.20	.10	.06
587	Larry Christenson	.25	.13	.08
588	Hal Lanier	.40	.20	.12
589	Boots Day	.20	.10	.06
590	Rogelio Moret	.20	.10	.06
591	Sonny Jackson	.20	.10	.06
592	Ed Bane	.20	.10	.06
593	Steve Yeager	.25	.13	.08
594	Leroy Stanton	.20	.10	.06
595	Steve Blass	.25	.13	.08
596	Rookie Pitchers (Wayne Garland, Fred Holdsworth, Mark Littell, Dick Pole)	.30	.15	.09
597	Rookie Shortstops (Dave Chalk, John Gamble, Pete Mackanin, Manny Trillo)	.80	.40	.25
598	Rookie Outfielders (Dave Augustine, Ken Griffey, Steve Ontiveros, Jim Tyrone)	2.00	1.00	.60
599a	Rookie Pitchers (Ron Diorio, Dave Freisleben, Frank Riccelli, Greg Shanahan) (Freisleben- Washington)	.80	.40	.25
599b	Rookie Pitchers (Ron Diorio, Dave Freisleben, Frank Riccelli, Greg Shanahan) (Freisleben- San Diego large print)	3.50	1.75	1.00
599c	Rookie Pitchers (Ron Diorio, Dave Freisleben, Frank Riccelli, Greg Shanahan) (Freisleben- San Diego small print)	6.00	3.00	1.75
600	Rookie Infielders (Ron Cash, Jim Cox, Bill Madlock, Reggie Sanders)	6.00	3.00	1.75
601	Rookie Outfielders (Ed Armbrister, Rich Bladt, Brian Downing, Bake McBride)	1.50	.70	.45
602	Rookie Pitchers (Glenn Abbott, Rick Henninger, Craig Swan, Dan Vossler)	.20	.10	.06
603	Rookie Catchers (Barry Foote, Tom Lundstedt, Charlie Moore, Sergio Robles)	.30	.15	.09
604	Rookie Infielders (Terry Hughes, John Knox, Andy Thornton, Frank White)	2.00	1.00	.60
605	Rookie Pitchers (Vic Albury, Ken Frailing, Kevin Kobel, Frank Tanana)	1.00	.50	.30
606	Rookie Outfielders (Jim Fuller, Wilbur Howard, Tommy Smith, Otto Velez)	.25	.13	.08
607	Rookie Shortstops (Leo Foster, Tom Heintzelman, Dave Rosello, Frank Taveras)	.25	.13	.08
608a	Rookie Pitchers (Bob Apodaco, Dick Baney, John D'Acquisto, Mike Wallace)	2.50	1.25	.70
608b	Rookie Pitchers (Bob Apodaca, Dick Baney, John D'Acquisto, Mike Wallace)	.25	.13	.08
609	Rico Petrocelli	.30	.15	.09
610	Dave Kingman	.90	.45	.25

		NR MT	EX	VG
611	Rick Stelmaszek	.20	.10	.06
612	Luke Walker	.20	.10	.06
613	Dan Monzon	.20	.10	.06
614	Adrian Devine	.20	.10	.06
615	Johnny Jeter	.20	.10	.06
616	Larry Gura	.25	.13	.08
617	Ted Ford	.20	.10	.06
618	Jim Mason	.20	.10	.06
619	Mike Anderson	.20	.10	.06
620	Al Downing	.25	.13	.08
621	Bernie Carbo	.20	.10	.06
622	Phil Gagliano	.20	.10	.06
623	Celerino Sanchez	.25	.13	.08
624	Bob Miller	.20	.10	.06
625	Ollie Brown	.20	.10	.06
626	Pirates Team	.80	.40	.25
627	Carl Taylor	.20	.10	.06
628	Ivan Murrell	.20	.10	.06
629	Rusty Staub	.70	.35	.20
630	Tommie Agee	.25	.13	.08
631	Steve Barber	.20	.10	.06
632	George Culver	.20	.10	.06
633	Dave Hamilton	.20	.10	.06
634	Braves Mgr./Coaches (Jim Busby, Eddie Mathews, Connie Ryan, Ken Silvestri, Herm Starrette)	.90	.45	.25
635	John Edwards	.20	.10	.06
636	Dave Goltz	.25	.13	.08
637	Checklist 529-660	1.50	.70	.45
638	Ken Sanders	.20	.10	.06
639	Joe Lovitto	.20	.10	.06
640	Milt Pappas	.40	.20	.12
641	Chuck Brinkman	.20	.10	.06
642	Terry Harmon	.20	.10	.06
643	Dodgers Team	.90	.45	.25
644	Wayne Granger	.25	.13	.08
645	Ken Boswell	.20	.10	.06
646	George Foster	1.25	.60	.40
647	Juan Beniquez	.70	.35	.20
648	Terry Crowley	.20	.10	.06
649	Fernando Gonzalez	.20	.10	.06
650	Mike Epstein	.20	.10	.06
651	Leron Lee	.20	.10	.06
652	Gail Hopkins	.20	.10	.06
653	Bob Stinson	.20	.10	.06
654a	Jesus Alou (no position listed)	5.00	2.50	1.50
654b	Jesus Alou (Outfield)	.40	.20	.12
655	Mike Tyson	.20	.10	.06
656	Adrian Garrett	.20	.10	.06
657	Jim Shellenback	.20	.10	.06
658	Lee Lacy	.30	.15	.09
659	Joe Lis	.20	.10	.06
660	Larry Dierker	.50	.13	.08

1974 Topps Deckle

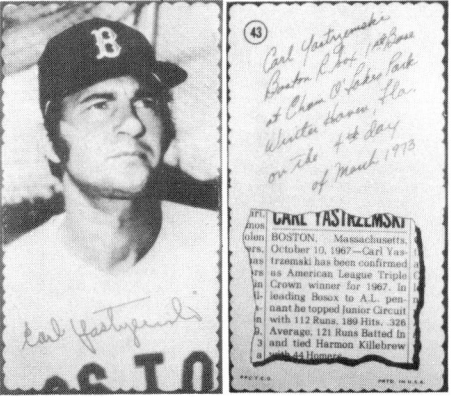

These borderless 2⅞'' by 5'' cards feature a black-and-white photograph with a facsimile autograph on the front. The backs have in handwritten script the player's name, team, position and the date and location of the picture. Below is a mock newspaper clipping providing a detail from the player's career. The cards take their names from their specially-cut edges which give them a scalloped appearance. The 72-card set was a test issue and received rather limited distribution.

		NR MT	EX	VG
Complete Set:		1400.00	700.00	420.00
Common Player:		10.00	5.00	3.00
1	Amos Otis	10.00	5.00	3.00
2	Darrell Evans	15.00	7.50	4.50
3	Robert Gibson	35.00	17.50	10.50
4	David Nelson	10.00	5.00	3.00
5	Steven N. Carlton	60.00	30.00	18.00
6	Jim "Catfish" Hunter	30.00	15.00	9.00
7	Thurman Munson	50.00	25.00	15.00
8	Bob Grich	15.00	7.50	4.50
9	Tom Seaver	60.00	30.00	18.00
10	Ted L. Simmons	20.00	10.00	6.00
11	Robert J. Valentine	10.00	5.00	3.00
12	Don Sutton	25.00	12.50	7.50
13	Wilbur Wood	10.00	5.00	3.00
14	Douglas Lee Rader	10.00	5.00	3.00
15	Chris Chambliss	10.00	5.00	3.00
16	Pete Rose	250.00	125.00	75.00
17	John F. Hiller	10.00	5.00	3.00
18	Burt Hooton	10.00	5.00	3.00
19	Tim Foli	10.00	5.00	3.00
20	Louis Brock	50.00	25.00	15.00
21	Ron Bryant	10.00	5.00	3.00
22	Manuel Sanguillen	10.00	5.00	3.00
23	Bobby Tolan	10.00	5.00	3.00
24	Greg Luzinski	15.00	7.50	4.50
25	Brooks Robinson	60.00	30.00	18.00
26	Felix Millan	10.00	5.00	3.00
27	Luis Tiant	15.00	7.50	4.50
28	Willie McCovey	40.00	20.00	12.00
29	Chris Speier	10.00	5.00	3.00
30	George Scott	10.00	5.00	3.00
31	Willie Stargell	40.00	20.00	12.00
32	Rod Carew	50.00	25.00	15.00
33	Leslie Charles Spikes	10.00	5.00	3.00
34	Nate Colbert	10.00	5.00	3.00
35	Richie Hebner	10.00	5.00	3.00
36	Bobby Lee Bonds	15.00	7.50	4.50
37	Buddy Bell	15.00	7.50	4.50
38	Claude Osteen	10.00	5.00	3.00
39	Richard A. Allen	15.00	7.50	4.50
40	Bill Russell	10.00	5.00	3.00
41	Nolan Ryan	50.00	25.00	15.00
42	Willie Davis	15.00	7.50	4.50
43	Carl Yastrzemski	150.00	75.00	45.00
44	Jonathon T. Matlack	10.00	5.00	3.00
45	Jim Palmer	30.00	15.00	9.00
46	Dagoberto Campaneris	15.00	7.50	4.50
47	Bert Blyleven	20.00	10.00	6.00
48	Jeff Burroughs	10.00	5.00	3.00
49	James W. Colborn	10.00	5.00	3.00
50	Dave Johnson	15.00	7.50	4.50
51	John Mayberry	10.00	5.00	3.00
52	Don Kessinger	10.00	5.00	3.00
53	Joseph H. Coleman	10.00	5.00	3.00
54	Tony Perez	20.00	10.00	6.00
55	Jose Cardenal	10.00	5.00	3.00
56	Paul Splittorff	10.00	5.00	3.00
57	Henry Aaron	125.00	62.00	37.00
58	David May	10.00	5.00	3.00
59	Fergie Jenkins	20.00	10.00	6.00
60	Ron Blomberg	10.00	5.00	3.00
61	Reggie Jackson	125.00	62.00	37.00
62	Tony Oliva	15.00	7.50	4.50
63	Bobby Ray Murcer	15.00	7.50	4.50
64	Carlton Fisk	20.00	10.00	6.00
65	Stephen Rogers	10.00	5.00	3.00
66	Frank Robinson	40.00	20.00	12.00
67	Joe Ferguson	10.00	5.00	3.00
68	Bill Melton	10.00	5.00	3.00
69	Robert Watson	10.00	5.00	3.00
70	Larry Bowa	15.00	7.50	4.50
71	Johnny Bench	70.00	35.00	21.00
72	Willie Horton	10.00	5.00	3.00

1974 Topps Puzzles

One of many test issues by Topps in the mid-1970s, the 12-player jigsaw puzzle set was an innovation which never caught on with collectors. The 40-piece,

4-2/4'' by 7-3/16,'' puzzles featured color photos with a decorative lozenge at bottom naming the player, team and position. Puzzles came in individual wrappers. Puzzle proofs are sometimes available as well, uncut pictures as used on the puzzles, before being glued to the cardboard.

		NR MT	EX	VG
Complete Set:		450.00	225.00	135.00
Common Player:		12.00	6.00	3.50
(1)	Hank Aaron	60.00	30.00	18.00
(2)	Dick Allen	12.00	6.00	3.50
(3)	Johnny Bench	40.00	20.00	12.00
(4)	Bobby Bonds	12.00	6.00	3.50
(5)	Bob Gibson	25.00	12.50	7.50
(6)	Reggie Jackson	60.00	30.00	18.00
(7)	Bobby Murcer	12.00	6.00	3.50
(8)	Jim Palmer	25.00	12.50	7.50
(9)	Nolan Ryan	40.00	20.00	12.00
(10)	Tom Seaver	40.00	20.00	12.00
(11)	Willie Stargell	25.00	12.50	7.50
(12)	Carl Yastrzemski	70.00	35.00	21.00

1974 Topps Stamps

Topps continued to market baseball stamps in 1974 through the release of 240 unnumbered stamps featuring color player portraits. The player's name, team and position are found in an oval at the bottom of the 1'' by 1½'' stamps. The stamps, sold separately, rather than issued as an insert, came in strips of six which were then pasted in an appropriate team album designed to hold 10 stamps.

	NR MT	EX	VG
Complete Sheet Set:	80.00	40.00	24.00
Common Sheet:	.90	.45	.25
Complete Stamp Album Set:	40.00	20.00	12.00
Single Stamp Album:	1.50	.70	.45

(1) Hank Aaron, Luis Aparicio, Bob Bailey, Johnny Bench, Ron Blomberg, Bob Boone, Lou Brock, Bud Harrelson, Randy Jones, Dave Rader, Nolan Ryan, Joe Torre 5.00 2.50 1.50

(2) Buddy Bell, Steve Braun, Jerry Grote, Tommy Helms, Bill Lee, Mike Lum, Dave May, Brooks Robinson, Bill Russell, Del Unser, Wilbur Wood, Carl Yastrzemski 10.00 5.00 3.00

(3) Jerry Bell, Jerry Bell, Jim Colborn, Toby Harrah, Ken Henderson, John Hiller, Randy Hundley, Don Kessinger, Jerry Koosman, Dave Lopes, Felix Millan, Thurman Munson, Ted Simmons 3.00 1.50 .90

(4) Jerry Bell, Bill Buckner, Jim Colborn, Ken Henderson, Don Kessinger, Felix Millan, George Mitterwald, Dave Roberts, Ted Simmons, Jim Slaton, Charlie Spikes, Paul Splittorff .90 .45 .25

(5) Glenn Beckert, Jim Bibby, Bill Buckner, Jim Lonborg, George Mitterwald, Dave Parker, Dave Roberts, Jim Slaton, Reggie Smith, Charlie Spikes, Paul Splittorff, Bob Watson 3.00 1.50 .90

(6) Paul Blair, Bobby Bonds, Ed Brinkman, Norm Cash, Mike Epstein, Tommy Harper, Mike Marshall, Phil Niekro, Cookie Rojas, George Scott, Mel Stottlemyre, Jim Wynn 3.00 1.50 .90

(7) Jack Billingham, Reggie Cleveland, Bobby Darwin, Dave Duncan, Tim Foli, Ed Goodson, Cleon Jones, Mickey Lolich, George Medich, John Milner, Rick Monday, Bobby Murcer .90 .45 .25

(8) Steve Carlton, Orlando Cepeda, Joe Decker, Reggie Jackson, Dave Johnson, John Mayberry, Bill Melton, Roger Metzger, Dave Nelson, Jerry Reuss, Jim Spencer, Bobby Valentine 5.00 2.50 1.50

(9) Dan Driessen, Pedro Garcia, Grant Jackson, Al Kaline, Clay Kirby, Carlos May, Willie Montanez, Rogelio Moret, Jim Palmer, Doug Rader, J. R. Richard, Frank Robinson 3.00 1.50 .90

(10) Pedro Garcia, Ralph Garr, Wayne Garrett, Ron Hunt, Al Kaline, Fred Kendall, Carlos May, Jim Palmer, Doug Rader, Frank Robinson, Rick Wise, Richie Zisk 3.00 1.50 .90

(11) Dusty Baker, Larry Bowa, Steve Busby, Chris Chambliss, Dock Ellis, Cesar Geronimo, Fran Healy, Deron Johnson, Jorge Orta, Joe Rudi, Mickey Stanley, Rennie Stennett 3.00 1.50 .90

(12) Bob Coluccio, Ray Corbin, John Ellis, Oscar Gamble, Dave Giusti, Bill Greif, Alex Johnson, Mike Jorgensen, Andy Messersmith, Elias Sosa, Willie Stargell 3.00 1.50 .90

(13) Ron Bryant, Nate Colbert, Jose Cruz, Dan Driessen, Billy Grabarkewitz, Don Gullett, Willie Horton, Grant Jackson, Clay Kirby, Willie Montanez, Rogelio Moret, J. R. Richard .90 .45 .25

(14) Carlton Fisk, Bill Freehan, Bobby Grich, Vic Harris, George Hendrick, Ed Herrmann, Jim Holt, Ken Holtzman, Fergie Jenkins, Lou Piniella, Steve Rogers, Ken Singleton 3.00 1.50 .90

(15) Stan Bahnsen, Sal Bando, Mark Belanger, David Clyde, Willie Crawford, Burt Hooton, Jon Matlack, Tim McCarver, Joe Morgan, Gene Tenace, Dick Tidrow, Dave Winfield 4.00 2.00 1.25

(16) Hank Aaron, Stan Bahnsen, Bob Bailey, Johnny Bench, Bob Boone, Joe Matlack, Tim McCarver, Joe Morgan, Dave Rader, Gene Tenace, Dick Tidrow, Joe Torre 4.00 2.00 1.25

(17) John Boccabella, Frank Duffy, Darrell Evans, Sparky Lyle, Lee May, Don Money, Bill North, Ted Sizemore, Chris Speier, Wayne Twitchell, Billy Williams, Earl Williams .90 .45 .25

(18) John Boccabella, Bobby Darwin, Frank Duffy, Dave Duncan, Tim Foli, Cleon Jones, Mickey Lolich, Sparky Lyle, Lee May, Rick Monday, Bill North, Billy Williams .90 .45 .25

(19) Don Baylor, Vida Blue, Tom Bradley, Jose Cardenal, Ron Cey, Greg Luzinski, Johnny Oates, Tony Oliva, Al Oliver, Tony Perez, Darrell Porter, Roy White 3.00 1.50 .90

(20) Pedro Borbon, Rod Carew, Roric Harrison, Jim Hunter, Ed Kirkpatrick, Garry Maddox, Gene Michael, Rick Miller, Claude Osteen, Amos Otis, Rich Reuschel, Mike Tyson 4.00 2.00 1.25

(21) Sandy Alomar, Bert Campaneris, Tommy Davis, Joe Ferguson, Tito Fuentes, Jerry Morales, Carl Morton, Gaylord Perry, Vada Pinson, Dave Roberts, Ellie Rodriguez 3.00 1.50 .90

(22) Dick Allen, Jeff Burroughs, Joe Coleman, Terry Forster, Bob Gibson, Harmon Killebrew, Tug McGraw, Bob Oliver, Steve Renko, Pete Rose, Luis Tiant, Otto Velez 13.00 6.50 4.00

(23) Johnny Briggs, Willie Davis, Jim Fregosi, Rich Hebner, Pat Kelly, Dave Kingman, Willie McCovey, Graig Nettles, Freddie Patek, Marty Pattin, Manny Sanguillen, Richie Scheinblum 4.00 2.00 1.25

(24) Bert Blyleven, Nelson Briles, Cesar Cedeno, Ron Fairly, Johnny Grubb, Dave McNally, Aurelio Rodriguez, Ron Santo, Tom Seaver, Bill Singer, Bill Sudakis, Don Sutton 5.00 2.50 1.50

1974 Topps Team Checklists

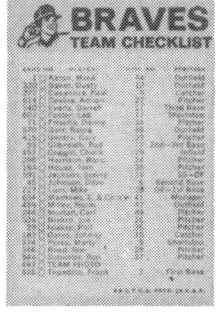

A repeat of the 1973 mystery set in the form of 24 unnumbered 2½″ by 3½″ checklist cards. As with the 1973 set, the '74s feature a team name on the front at the top with a white panel and a number of facsimile autographs below. Backs feature the team name and a checklist. The big difference between the 1973 and 1974 checklists is that the '73s have blue borders while the '74s have a red border. The '74s were inserted into packages of the regular issue Topps cards.

		NR MT	EX	VG
Complete Set:		6.50	3.25	2.00
Common Checklist:		.25	.13	.08
(1)	Atlanta Braves	.25	.13	.08
(2)	Baltimore Orioles	.25	.13	.08
(3)	Boston Red Sox	.25	.13	.08
(4)	California Angels	.25	.13	.08
(5)	Chicago Cubs	.25	.13	.08
(6)	Chicago White Sox	.25	.13	.08
(7)	Cincinnati Reds	.25	.13	.08
(8)	Cleveland Indians	.25	.13	.08
(9)	Detroit Tigers	.35	.20	.11
(10)	Houston Astros	.25	.13	.08
(11)	Kansas City Royals	.25	.13	.08
(12)	Los Angeles Dodgers	.35	.20	.11
(13)	Milwaukee Brewers	.25	.13	.08
(14)	Minnesota Twins	.25	.13	.08
(15)	Montreal Expos	.25	.13	.08
(16)	New York Mets	.35	.20	.11
(17)	New York Yankees	.35	.20	.11
(18)	Oakland A's	.35	.20	.11
(19)	Philadelphia Phillies	.25	.13	.08
(20)	Pittsburgh Pirates	.25	.13	.08
(21)	St. Louis Cardinals	.25	.13	.08
(22)	San Diego Padres	.25	.13	.08
(23)	San Francisco Giants	.25	.13	.08
(24)	Texas Rangers	.25	.13	.08

1974 Topps Traded

 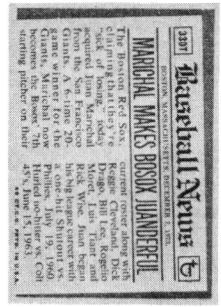

1975 Topps

 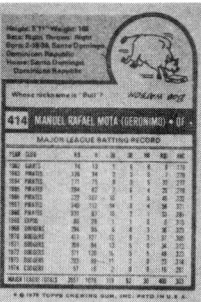

Appearing late in the season, these 2½'' by 3½'' cards were basically the same as the regular issue Topps cards. The major change was that a big red panel with the word ''TRADED'' as added below the player photo. Backs featured a ''Baseball News'' newspaper which contained the details of the trade. Card numbers correspond to the player's regular card number in 1974 except that the suffix ''T'' is added after the number. The set consists of 43 player cards and a checklist. In most cases Topps did not obtain pictures of the players in their new uniforms. Instead, the Topps artists simply provided the needed changes to existing photos.

This year Topps produced another 660-card set, one which collectors either seem to like or despise. The 2½'' by 3½'' cards have a color photo which is framed by a round-cornered white frame. Around that is an eye-catching two-color border in bright colors. The team name appears at the top in bright letters while player name is at the bottom, and his position in a baseball at the lower right. A facsimile autograph runs across the picture. Card backs are vertical and feature normal statistical and biographical information along with a trivia quiz. Specialty cards include a new 24-card series on MVP winners going back to 1951. Other specialty cards include statistical leaders and post-season highlights. The real highlight of the set, however, are the rookie cards which include in their numbers such names as George Brett, Gary Carter, Robin Yount, Jim Rice, Keith Hernandez, Fred Lynn and John Denny. While the set was released at one time, cards number 1-132 were printed in somewhat shorter supply than the remainder of the issue.

		NR MT	EX	VG
Complete Set:		7.00	3.50	2.00
Common Player:		.12	.06	.04

23T	Craig Robinson	.12	.06	.04
42T	Claude Osteen	.15	.08	.05
43T	Jim Wynn	.20	.10	.06
51T	Bobby Heise	.12	.06	.04
59T	Ross Grimsley	.15	.08	.05
62T	Bob Locker	.12	.06	.04
63T	Bill Sudakis	.12	.06	.04
73T	Mike Marshall	.20	.10	.06
123T	Nelson Briles	.12	.06	.04
139T	Aurelio Monteagudo	.12	.06	.04
151T	Diego Segui	.12	.06	.04
165T	Willie Davis	.20	.10	.06
175T	Reggie Cleveland	.12	.06	.04
182T	Lindy McDaniel	.12	.06	.04
186T	Fred Scherman	.12	.06	.04
249T	George Mitterwald	.12	.06	.04
262T	Ed Kirkpatrick	.12	.06	.04
269T	Bob Johnson	.12	.06	.04
270T	Ron Santo	.30	.15	.09
313T	Barry Lersch	.12	.06	.04
319T	Randy Hundley	.12	.06	.04
330T	Juan Marichal	1.25	.60	.40
348T	Pete Richert	.12	.06	.04
373T	John Curtis	.12	.06	.04
390T	Lou Piniella	.50	.25	.15
428T	Gary Sutherland	.12	.06	.04
454T	Kurt Bevacqua	.12	.06	.04
458T	Jim Ray	.12	.06	.04
485T	Felipe Alou	.20	.10	.06
486T	Steve Stone	.15	.08	.05
496T	Tom Murphy	.12	.06	.04
516T	Horacio Pina	.12	.06	.04
534T	Eddie Watt	.12	.06	.04
538T	Cesar Tovar	.12	.06	.04
544T	Ron Schueler	.12	.06	.04
579T	Cecil Upshaw	.12	.06	.04
585T	Merv Rettenmund	.15	.08	.05
612T	Luke Walker	.12	.06	.04
616T	Larry Gura	.15	.08	.05
618T	Jim Mason	.12	.06	.04
630T	Tommie Agee	.15	.08	.05
648T	Terry Crowley	.12	.06	.04
649T	Fernando Gonzalez	.12	.06	.04
---	Traded Checklist	.70	.35	.20

		NR MT	EX	VG
Complete Set:		500.00	225.00	125.00
Common Player: 1-132		.25	.13	.08
Common Player: 133-660		.20	.10	.06

1	'74 Highlights (Hank Aaron)	8.00	2.50	1.25
2	'74 Highlights (Lou Brock)	1.50	.70	.45
3	'74 Highlights (Bob Gibson)	1.50	.70	.45
4	'74 Highlights (Al Kaline)	1.50	.70	.45
5	'74 Highlights (Nolan Ryan)	2.00	1.00	.60
6	'74 Highlights (Mike Marshall)	.40	.20	.12
7	'74 Highlights (Dick Bosman, Steve Busby, Nolan Ryan)	.90	.45	.25
8	Rogelio Moret	.25	.13	.08
9	Frank Tepedino	.25	.13	.08
10	Willie Davis	.30	.15	.09
11	Bill Melton	.30	.15	.09
12	David Clyde	.30	.15	.09
13	Gene Locklear	.25	.13	.08
14	Milt Wilcox	.30	.15	.09
15	Jose Cardenal	.30	.15	.09
16	Frank Tanana	.40	.20	.12
17	Dave Concepcion	.60	.30	.20
18	Tigers Team (Ralph Houk)	.90	.45	.25
19	Jerry Koosman	.40	.20	.12
20	Thurman Munson	4.00	2.00	1.25
21	Rollie Fingers	1.50	.70	.45
22	Dave Cash	.25	.13	.08
23	Bill Russell	.30	.15	.09
24	Al Fitzmorris	.25	.13	.08
25	Lee May	.40	.20	.12
26	Dave McNally	.30	.15	.09
27	Ken Reitz	.25	.13	.08
28	Tom Murphy	.25	.13	.08
29	Dave Parker	5.00	2.50	1.50
30	Bert Blyleven	1.00	.50	.30
31	Dave Rader	.25	.13	.08
32	Reggie Cleveland	.25	.13	.08
33	Dusty Baker	.40	.20	.12
34	Steve Renko	.25	.13	.08
35	Ron Santo	.50	.25	.15
36	Joe Lovitto	.25	.13	.08
37	Dave Freisleben	.25	.13	.08
38	Buddy Bell	1.00	.50	.30

#	Player	NR MT	EX	VG
39	Andy Thornton	.70	.35	.20
40	Bill Singer	.30	.15	.09
41	Cesar Geronimo	.30	.15	.09
42	Joe Coleman	.30	.15	.09
43	Cleon Jones	.30	.15	.09
44	Pat Dobson	.30	.15	.09
45	Joe Rudi	.40	.20	.12
46	Phillies Team (Danny Ozark)	.80	.40	.25
47	Tommy John	1.25	.60	.40
48	Freddie Patek	.25	.13	.08
49	Larry Dierker	.25	.13	.08
50	Brooks Robinson	3.50	1.75	1.00
51	Bob Forsch	.80	.40	.25
52	Darrell Porter	.30	.15	.09
53	Dave Giusti	.25	.13	.08
54	Eric Soderholm	.25	.13	.08
55	Bobby Bonds	.50	.25	.15
56	Rick Wise	.30	.15	.09
57	Dave Johnson	.80	.40	.25
58	Chuck Taylor	.25	.13	.08
59	Ken Henderson	.25	.13	.08
60	Fergie Jenkins	1.25	.60	.40
61	Dave Winfield	7.00	3.50	2.00
62	Fritz Peterson	.25	.13	.08
63	Steve Swisher	.25	.13	.08
64	Dave Chalk	.25	.13	.08
65	Don Gullett	.30	.15	.09
66	Willie Horton	.30	.15	.09
67	Tug McGraw	.50	.25	.15
68	Ron Blomberg	.30	.15	.09
69	John Odom	.30	.15	.09
70	Mike Schmidt	18.00	9.00	5.50
71	Charlie Hough	.30	.15	.09
72	Royals Team (Jack McKeon)	.80	.40	.25
73	J.R. Richard	.30	.15	.09
74	Mark Belanger	.30	.15	.09
75	Ted Simmons	.70	.35	.20
76	Ed Sprague	.25	.13	.08
77	Richie Zisk	.30	.15	.09
78	Ray Corbin	.25	.13	.08
79	Gary Matthews	.40	.20	.12
80	Carlton Fisk	1.50	.70	.45
81	Ron Reed	.30	.15	.09
82	Pat Kelly	.25	.13	.08
83	Jim Merritt	.25	.13	.08
84	Enzo Hernandez	.25	.13	.08
85	Bill Bonham	.25	.13	.08
86	Joe Lis	.25	.13	.08
87	George Foster	1.25	.60	.40
88	Tom Egan	.25	.13	.08
89	Jim Ray	.25	.13	.08
90	Rusty Staub	.60	.30	.20
91	Dick Green	.25	.13	.08
92	Cecil Upshaw	.30	.15	.09
93	Dave Lopes	.40	.20	.12
94	Jim Lonborg	.30	.15	.09
95	John Mayberry	.30	.15	.09
96	Mike Cosgrove	.25	.13	.08
97	Earl Williams	.25	.13	.08
98	Rich Folkers	.25	.13	.08
99	Mike Hegan	.25	.13	.08
100	Willie Stargell	2.50	1.25	.70
101	Expos Team (Gene Mauch)	.80	.40	.25
102	Joe Decker	.25	.13	.08
103	Rick Miller	.25	.13	.08
104	Bill Madlock	1.50	.70	.45
105	Buzz Capra	.25	.13	.08
106	Mike Hargrove	.40	.20	.12
107	Jim Barr	.25	.13	.08
108	Tom Hall	.25	.13	.08
109	George Hendrick	.30	.15	.09
110	Wilbur Wood	.30	.15	.09
111	Wayne Garrett	.25	.13	.08
112	Larry Hardy	.25	.13	.08
113	Elliott Maddox	.30	.15	.09
114	Dick Lange	.25	.13	.08
115	Joe Ferguson	.25	.13	.08
116	Lerrin LaGrow	.25	.13	.08
117	Orioles (Earl Weaver)	.90	.45	.25
118	Mike Anderson	.25	.13	.08
119	Tommy Helms	.25	.13	.08
120	Steve Busby (photo actually Fran Healy)	.30	.15	.09
121	Bill North	.25	.13	.08
122	Al Hrabosky	.30	.15	.09
123	Johnny Briggs	.25	.13	.08
124	Jerry Reuss	.40	.20	.12
125	Ken Singleton	.40	.20	.12
126	Checklist 1-132	1.50	.70	.45
127	Glen Borgmann	.25	.13	.08
128	Bill Lee	.30	.15	.09

#	Player		EX	VG
129	Rick Monday	.30	.15	.09
130	Phil Niekro	2.00	1.00	.60
131	Toby Harrah	.30	.15	.09
132	Randy Moffitt	.25	.13	.08
133	Dan Driessen	.30	.15	.09
134	Ron Hodges	.20	.10	.06
135	Charlie Spikes	.20	.10	.06
136	Jim Mason	.25	.13	.08
137	Terry Forster	.30	.15	.09
138	Del Unser	.20	.10	.06
139	Horacio Pina	.20	.10	.06
140	Steve Garvey	5.00	2.50	1.50
141	Mickey Stanley	.25	.13	.08
142	Bob Reynolds	.20	.10	.06
143	Cliff Johnson	.40	.20	.12
144	Jim Wohlford	.20	.10	.06
145	Ken Holtzman	.30	.15	.09
146	Padres Team (John McNamara)	.80	.40	.25
147	Pedro Garcia	.20	.10	.06
148	Jim Rooker	.20	.10	.06
149	Tim Foli	.20	.10	.06
150	Bob Gibson	2.50	1.25	.70
151	Steve Brye	.20	.10	.06
152	Mario Guerrero	.20	.10	.06
153	Rick Reuschel	.40	.20	.12
154	Mike Lum	.20	.10	.06
155	Jim Bibby	.20	.10	.06
156	Dave Kingman	1.25	.60	.40
157	Pedro Borbon	.20	.10	.06
158	Jerry Grote	.25	.13	.08
159	Steve Arlin	.20	.10	.06
160	Graig Nettles	1.50	.70	.45
161	Stan Bahnsen	.20	.10	.06
162	Willie Montanez	.20	.10	.06
163	Jim Brewer	.20	.10	.06
164	Mickey Rivers	.25	.13	.08
165	Doug Rader	.20	.10	.06
166	Woodie Fryman	.25	.13	.08
167	Rich Coggins	.20	.10	.06
168	Bill Greif	.20	.10	.06
169	Cookie Rojas	.20	.10	.06
170	Bert Campaneris	.40	.20	.12
171	Ed Kirkpatrick	.20	.10	.06
172	Red Sox Team (Darrell Johnson)	1.25	.60	.40
173	Steve Rogers	.30	.15	.09
174	Bake McBride	.25	.13	.08
175	Don Money	.25	.13	.08
176	Burt Hooton	.30	.15	.09
177	Vic Correll	.20	.10	.06
178	Cesar Tovar	.20	.10	.06
179	Tom Bradley	.20	.10	.06
180	Joe Morgan	2.50	1.25	.70
181	Fred Beene	.20	.10	.06
182	Don Hahn	.20	.10	.06
183	Mel Stottlemyre	.40	.20	.12
184	Jorge Orta	.20	.10	.06
185	Steve Carlton	5.00	2.50	1.50
186	Willie Crawford	.20	.10	.06
187	Denny Doyle	.20	.10	.06
188	Tom Griffin	.20	.10	.06
189	1951 - MVPs (Larry (Yogi) Berra, Roy Campanella)	1.50	.70	.45
190	1952 - MVPs (Hank Sauer, Bobby Shantz)	.40	.20	.12
191	1953 - MVPs (Roy Campanella, Al Rosen)	.90	.45	.25
192	1954 - MVPs (Yogi Berra, Willie Mays)	1.50	.70	.45
193	1955 - MVPs (Yogi Berra, Roy Campanella)	1.50	.70	.45
194	1956 - MVPs (Mickey Mantle, Don Newcombe)	3.00	1.50	.90
195	1957 - MVPs (Hank Aaron, Mickey Mantle)	3.50	1.75	1.00
196	1958 - MVPs (Ernie Banks, Jackie Jensen)	.90	.45	.25
197	1959 - MVPs (Ernie Banks, Nellie Fox)	.90	.45	.25
198	1960 - MVPs (Dick Groat, Roger Maris)	1.25	.60	.40
199	1961 - MVPs (Roger Maris, Frank Robinson)	1.50	.70	.45
200	1962 - MVPs (Mickey Mantle, Maury Wills)	3.00	1.50	.90
201	1963 - MVPs (Elston Howard, Sandy Koufax)	1.50	.70	.45
202	1964 - MVPs (Ken Boyer, Brooks Robinson)	1.25	.60	.40
203	1965 - MVPs (Willie Mays, Zoilo Versalles)	1.25	.60	.40

#	Player	NR MT	EX	VG
204	1966 - MVPs (Bob Clemente, Frank Robinson)	1.50	.70	.45
205	1967 - MVPs (Orlando Cepeda, Carl Yastrzemski)	1.25	.60	.40
206	1968 - MVPs (Bob Gibson, Denny McLain)	1.25	.60	.40
207	1969 - MVPs (Harmon Killebrew, Willie McCovey)	1.50	.70	.45
208	1970 - MVPs (Johnny Bench, Boog Powell)	1.25	.60	.40
209	1971 - MVPs (Vida Blue, Joe Torre)	.50	.25	.15
210	1972 - MVPs (Rich Allen, Johnny Bench)	1.25	.60	.40
211	1973 - MVPs (Reggie Jackson, Pete Rose)	2.50	1.25	.70
212	1974 - MVPs (Jeff Burroughs, Steve Garvey)	.90	.45	.25
213	Oscar Gamble	.25	.13	.08
214	Harry Parker	.20	.10	.06
215	Bobby Valentine	.30	.15	.09
216	Giants Team (Wes Westrum)	.80	.40	.25
217	Lou Piniella	.70	.35	.20
218	Jerry Johnson	.20	.10	.06
219	Ed Herrmann	.20	.10	.06
220	Don Sutton	1.50	.70	.45
221	Aurelio Rodriquez (Rodriguez)	.25	.13	.08
222	Dan Spillner	.20	.10	.06
223	Robin Yount	30.00	15.00	9.00
224	Ramon Hernandez	.20	.10	.06
225	Bob Grich	.40	.20	.12
226	Bill Campbell	.25	.13	.08
227	Bob Watson	.25	.13	.08
228	George Brett	50.00	25.00	15.00
229	Barry Foote	.20	.10	.06
230	Jim Hunter	2.00	1.00	.60
231	Mike Tyson	.20	.10	.06
232	Diego Segui	.20	.10	.06
233	Billy Grabarkewitz	.20	.10	.06
234	Tom Grieve	.20	.10	.06
235	Jack Billingham	.20	.10	.06
236	Angels Team (Dick Williams)	.80	.40	.25
237	Carl Morton	.20	.10	.06
238	Dave Duncan	.20	.10	.06
239	George Stone	.20	.10	.06
240	Garry Maddox	.25	.13	.08
241	Dick Tidrow	.25	.13	.08
242	Jay Johnstone	.25	.13	.08
243	Jim Kaat	1.25	.60	.40
244	Bill Buckner	.50	.25	.15
245	Mickey Lolich	.50	.25	.15
246	Cardinals Team (Red Schoendienst)	.80	.40	.25
247	Enos Cabell	.25	.13	.08
248	Randy Jones	.25	.13	.08
249	Danny Thompson	.25	.13	.08
250	Ken Brett	.25	.13	.08
251	Fran Healy	.20	.10	.06
252	Fred Scherman	.20	.10	.06
253	Jesus Alou	.25	.13	.08
254	Mike Torrez	.25	.13	.08
255	Dwight Evans	1.50	.70	.45
256	Billy Champion	.20	.10	.06
257	Checklist 133-264	1.50	.70	.45
258	Dave LaRoche	.20	.10	.06
259	Len Randle	.20	.10	.06
260	Johnny Bench	5.00	2.50	1.50
261	Andy Hassler	.20	.10	.06
262	Rowland Office	.20	.10	.06
263	Jim Perry	.40	.20	.12
264	John Milner	.20	.10	.06
265	Ron Bryant	.20	.10	.06
266	Sandy Alomar	.25	.13	.08
267	Dick Ruthven	.20	.10	.06
268	Hal McRae	.40	.20	.12
269	Doug Rau	.20	.10	.06
270	Ron Fairly	.30	.15	.09
271	Jerry Moses	.20	.10	.06
272	Lynn McGlothen	.20	.10	.06
273	Steve Braun	.20	.10	.06
274	Vicente Romo	.20	.10	.06
275	Paul Blair	.25	.13	.08
276	White Sox Team (Chuck Tanner)	.80	.40	.25
277	Frank Taveras	.20	.10	.06
278	Paul Lindblad	.20	.10	.06
279	Milt May	.20	.10	.06
280	Carl Yastrzemski	6.50	3.25	2.00
281	Jim Slaton	.20	.10	.06
282	Jerry Morales	.20	.10	.06
283	Steve Foucault	.20	.10	.06
284	Ken Griffey	.70	.35	.20
285	Ellie Rodriguez	.20	.10	.06

#	Player	NR MT	EX	VG
286	Mike Jorgensen	.20	.10	.06
287	Roric Harrison	.20	.10	.06
288	Bruce Ellingsen	.20	.10	.06
289	Ken Rudolph	.20	.10	.06
290	Jon Matlack	.25	.13	.08
291	Bill Sudakis	.25	.13	.08
292	Ron Schueler	.20	.10	.06
293	Dick Sharon	.20	.10	.06
294	Geoff Zahn	.40	.20	.12
295	Vada Pinson	.60	.30	.20
296	Alan Foster	.20	.10	.06
297	Craig Kusick	.20	.10	.06
298	Johnny Grubb	.20	.10	.06
299	Bucky Dent	.40	.20	.12
300	Reggie Jackson	7.00	3.50	2.00
301	Dave Roberts	.20	.10	.06
302	Rick Burleson	.50	.25	.15
303	Grant Jackson	.20	.10	.06
304	Pirates Team (Danny Murtaugh)	.80	.40	.25
305	Jim Colborn	.20	.10	.06
306	Batting Leaders (Rod Carew, Ralph Garr)	.80	.40	.25
307	Home Run Leaders (Dick Allen, Mike Schmidt)	.90	.45	.25
308	Runs Batted In Leaders (Johnny Bench, Jeff Burroughs)	.80	.40	.25
309	Stolen Base Leaders (Lou Brock, Bill North)	.80	.40	.25
310	Victory Leaders (Jim Hunter, Fergie Jenkins, Andy Messersmith, Phil Niekro)	.80	.40	.25
311	Earned Run Average Leaders (Buzz Capra, Jim Hunter)	.50	.25	.15
312	Strikeout Leaders (Steve Carlton, Nolan Ryan)	1.75	.90	.50
313	Leading Firemen (Terry Forster, Mike Marshall)	.50	.25	.15
314	Buck Martinez	.20	.10	.06
315	Don Kessinger	.25	.13	.08
316	Jackie Brown	.20	.10	.06
317	Joe Lahoud	.20	.10	.06
318	Ernie McAnally	.20	.10	.06
319	Johnny Oates	.20	.10	.06
320	Pete Rose	15.00	7.50	4.50
321	Rudy May	.25	.13	.08
322	Ed Goodson	.20	.10	.06
323	Fred Holdsworth	.20	.10	.06
324	Ed Kranepool	.30	.15	.09
325	Tony Oliva	.80	.40	.25
326	Wayne Twitchell	.20	.10	.06
327	Jerry Hairston	.20	.10	.06
328	Sonny Siebert	.20	.10	.06
329	Ted Kubiak	.20	.10	.06
330	Mike Marshall	.30	.15	.09
331	Indians Team (Frank Robinson)	.90	.45	.25
332	Fred Kendall	.20	.10	.06
333	Dick Drago	.20	.10	.06
334	Greg Gross	.30	.15	.09
335	Jim Palmer	3.25	1.75	1.00
336	Rennie Stennett	.20	.10	.06
337	Kevin Kobel	.20	.10	.06
338	Rick Stelmaszek	.20	.10	.06
339	Jim Fregosi	.40	.20	.12
340	Paul Splittorff	.25	.13	.08
341	Hal Breeden	.20	.10	.06
342	Leroy Stanton	.20	.10	.06
343	Danny Frisella	.20	.10	.06
344	Ben Oglivie	.30	.15	.09
345	Clay Carroll	.25	.13	.08
346	Bobby Darwin	.20	.10	.06
347	Mike Caldwell	.20	.10	.06
348	Tony Muser	.20	.10	.06
349	Ray Sadecki	.20	.10	.06
350	Bobby Murcer	.40	.20	.12
351	Bob Boone	.40	.20	.12
352	Darold Knowles	.20	.10	.06
353	Luis Melendez	.20	.10	.06
354	Dick Bosman	.20	.10	.06
355	Chris Cannizzaro	.20	.10	.06
356	Rico Petrocelli	.30	.15	.09
357	Ken Forsch	.25	.13	.08
358	Al Bumbry	.25	.13	.08
359	Paul Popovich	.20	.10	.06
360	George Scott	.30	.15	.09
361	Dodgers Team (Walter Alston)	1.00	.50	.30
362	Steve Hargan	.20	.10	.06
363	Carmen Fanzone	.20	.10	.06
364	Doug Bird	.20	.10	.06
365	Bob Bailey	.20	.10	.06
366	Ken Sanders	.20	.10	.06
367	Craig Robinson	.20	.10	.06

		NR MT	EX	VG
368	Vic Albury	.20	.10	.06
369	Merv Rettenmund	.20	.10	.06
370	Tom Seaver	6.00	3.00	1.75
371	Gates Brown	.20	.10	.06
372	John D'Acquisto	.20	.10	.06
373	Bill Sharp	.20	.10	.06
374	Eddie Watt	.20	.10	.06
375	Roy White	.40	.20	.12
376	Steve Yeager	.20	.10	.06
377	Tom Hilgendorf	.20	.10	.06
378	Derrel Thomas	.20	.10	.06
379	Bernie Carbo	.20	.10	.06
380	Sal Bando	.40	.20	.12
381	John Curtis	.20	.10	.06
382	Don Baylor	.60	.30	.20
383	Jim York	.20	.10	.06
384	Brewers Team (Del Crandall)	.80	.40	.25
385	Dock Ellis	.25	.13	.08
386	Checklist 265-396	1.50	.70	.45
387	Jim Spencer	.20	.10	.06
388	Steve Stone	.30	.15	.09
389	Tony Solaita	.20	.10	.06
390	Ron Cey	.40	.20	.12
391	Don DeMola	.20	.10	.06
392	Bruce Bochte	.40	.20	.12
393	Gary Gentry	.20	.10	.06
394	Larvell Blanks	.20	.10	.06
395	Bud Harrelson	.25	.13	.08
396	Fred Norman	.20	.10	.06
397	Bill Freehan	.40	.20	.12
398	Elias Sosa	.20	.10	.06
399	Terry Harmon	.20	.10	.06
400	Dick Allen	.80	.40	.25
401	Mike Wallace	.25	.13	.08
402	Bob Tolan	.25	.13	.08
403	Tom Buskey	.20	.10	.06
404	Ted Sizemore	.20	.10	.06
405	John Montague	.20	.10	.06
406	Bob Gallagher	.20	.10	.06
407	Herb Washington	.30	.15	.09
408	Clyde Wright	.20	.10	.06
409	Bob Robertson	.20	.10	.06
410	Mike Cueller (Cuellar)	.40	.20	.12
411	George Mitterwald	.20	.10	.06
412	Bill Hands	.20	.10	.06
413	Marty Pattin	.20	.10	.06
414	Manny Mota	.30	.15	.09
415	John Hiller	.25	.13	.08
416	Larry Lintz	.20	.10	.06
417	Skip Lockwood	.20	.10	.06
418	Leo Foster	.20	.10	.06
419	Dave Goltz	.25	.13	.08
420	Larry Bowa	.40	.20	.12
421	Mets Team (Yogi Berra)	1.00	.50	.30
422	Brian Downing	.30	.15	.09
423	Clay Kirby	.20	.10	.06
424	John Lowenstein	.20	.10	.06
425	Tito Fuentes	.20	.10	.06
426	George Medich	.25	.13	.08
427	Clarence Gaston	.20	.10	.06
428	Dave Hamilton	.20	.10	.06
429	Jim Dwyer	.30	.15	.09
430	Luis Tiant	.50	.25	.15
431	Rod Gilbreath	.20	.10	.06
432	Ken Berry	.20	.10	.06
433	Larry Demery	.20	.10	.06
434	Bob Locker	.20	.10	.06
435	Dave Nelson	.20	.10	.06
436	Ken Frailing	.20	.10	.06
437	Al Cowens	.40	.20	.12
438	Don Carrithers	.20	.10	.06
439	Ed Brinkman	.25	.13	.08
440	Andy Messersmith	.30	.15	.09
441	Bobby Heise	.20	.10	.06
442	Maximino Leon	.20	.10	.06
443	Twins Team (Frank Quilici)	.80	.40	.25
444	Gene Garber	.25	.13	.08
445	Felix Millan	.20	.10	.06
446	Bart Johnson	.20	.10	.06
447	Terry Crowley	.20	.10	.06
448	Frank Duffy	.20	.10	.06
449	Charlie Williams	.20	.10	.06
450	Willie McCovey	3.00	1.50	.90
451	Rick Dempsey	.40	.20	.12
452	Angel Mangual	.20	.10	.06
453	Claude Osteen	.30	.15	.09
454	Doug Griffin	.20	.10	.06
455	Don Wilson	.20	.10	.06
456	Bob Coluccio	.20	.10	.06
457	Mario Mendoza	.20	.10	.06
458	Ross Grimsley	.25	.13	.08

		NR MT	EX	VG
459	A.L. Championships	.80	.40	.25
460	N.L. Championships	.80	.40	.25
461	World Series Game 1	1.50	.70	.45
462	World Series Game 2	.80	.40	.25
463	World Series Game 3	1.00	.50	.30
464	World Series Game 4	.80	.40	.25
465	World Series Game 5	.80	.40	.25
466	World Series Summary	.80	.40	.25
467	Ed Halicki	.20	.10	.06
468	Bobby Mitchell	.20	.10	.06
469	Tom Dettore	.20	.10	.06
470	Jeff Burroughs	.30	.15	.09
471	Bob Stinson	.20	.10	.06
472	Bruce Dal Canton	.20	.10	.06
473	Ken McMullen	.20	.10	.06
474	Luke Walker	.20	.10	.06
475	Darrell Evans	.60	.30	.20
476	Ed Figueroa	.30	.15	.09
477	Tom Hutton	.20	.10	.06
478	Tom Burgmeier	.20	.10	.06
479	Ken Boswell	.20	.10	.06
480	Carlos May	.25	.13	.08
481	Will McEnaney	.30	.15	.09
482	Tom McCraw	.20	.10	.06
483	Steve Ontiveros	.20	.10	.06
484	Glenn Beckert	.30	.15	.09
485	Sparky Lyle	.40	.20	.12
486	Ray Fosse	.20	.10	.06
487	Astros Team (Preston Gomez)	.80	.40	.25
488	Bill Travers	.20	.10	.06
489	Cecil Cooper	1.00	.50	.30
490	Reggie Smith	.30	.15	.09
491	Doyle Alexander	.40	.20	.12
492	Rich Hebner	.25	.13	.08
493	Don Stanhouse	.20	.10	.06
494	Pete LaCock	.25	.13	.08
495	Nelson Briles	.20	.10	.06
496	Pepe Frias	.20	.10	.06
497	Jim Nettles	.20	.10	.06
498	Al Downing	.25	.13	.08
499	Marty Perez	.20	.10	.06
500	Nolan Ryan	5.00	2.50	1.50
501	Bill Robinson	.20	.10	.06
502	Pat Bourque	.20	.10	.06
503	Fred Stanley	.25	.13	.08
504	Buddy Bradford	.20	.10	.06
505	Chris Speier	.25	.13	.08
506	Leron Lee	.20	.10	.06
507	Tom Carroll	.20	.10	.06
508	Bob Hansen	.20	.10	.06
509	Dave Hilton	.20	.10	.06
510	Vida Blue	.50	.25	.15
511	Rangers Team (Billy Martin)	.90	.45	.25
512	Larry Milbourne	.20	.10	.06
513	Dick Pole	.20	.10	.06
514	Jose Cruz	.50	.25	.15
515	Manny Sanguillen	.25	.13	.08
516	Don Hood	.20	.10	.06
517	Checklist 397-528	1.25	.60	.40
518	Leo Cardenas	.20	.10	.06
519	Jim Todd	.20	.10	.06
520	Amos Otis	.30	.15	.09
521	Dennis Blair	.20	.10	.06
522	Gary Sutherland	.20	.10	.06
523	Tom Paciorek	.25	.13	.08
524	John Doherty	.20	.10	.06
525	Tom House	.20	.10	.06
526	Larry Hisle	.25	.13	.08
527	Mac Scarce	.20	.10	.06
528	Eddie Leon	.20	.10	.06
529	Gary Thomasson	.20	.10	.06
530	Gaylord Perry	2.25	1.25	.70
531	Reds Team (Sparky Anderson)	.90	.45	.25
532	Gorman Thomas	.60	.30	.20
533	Rudy Meoli	.20	.10	.06
534	Alex Johnson	.25	.13	.08
535	Gene Tenace	.25	.13	.08
536	Bob Moose	.20	.10	.06
537	Tommy Harper	.25	.13	.08
538	Duffy Dyer	.20	.10	.06
539	Jesse Jefferson	.20	.10	.06
540	Lou Brock	3.00	1.50	.90
541	Roger Metzger	.20	.10	.06
542	Pete Broberg	.20	.10	.06
543	Larry Biittner	.20	.10	.06
544	Steve Mingori	.20	.10	.06
545	Billy Williams	2.25	1.25	.70
546	John Knox	.20	.10	.06
547	Von Joshua	.20	.10	.06
548	Charlie Sands	.20	.10	.06
549	Bill Butler	.20	.10	.06

		NR MT	EX	VG
550	Ralph Garr	.25	.13	.08
551	Larry Christenson	.20	.10	.06
552	Jack Brohamer	.20	.10	.06
553	John Boccabella	.20	.10	.06
554	Rich Gossage	1.25	.60	.40
555	Al Oliver	1.00	.50	.30
556	Tim Johnson	.20	.10	.06
557	Larry Gura	.25	.13	.08
558	Dave Roberts	.20	.10	.06
559	Bob Montgomery	.20	.10	.06
560	Tony Perez	.80	.40	.25
561	A's Team (Alvin Dark)	.90	.45	.25
562	Gary Nolan	.20	.10	.06
563	Wilbur Howard	.20	.10	.06
564	Tommy Davis	.40	.20	.12
565	Joe Torre	.70	.35	.20
566	Ray Burris	.20	.10	.06
567	Jim Sundberg	.70	.35	.20
568	Dale Murray	.20	.10	.06
569	Frank White	.40	.20	.12
570	Jim Wynn	.30	.15	.09
571	Dave Lemanczyk	.20	.10	.06
572	Roger Nelson	.20	.10	.06
573	Orlando Pena	.20	.10	.06
574	Tony Taylor	.20	.10	.06
575	Gene Clines	.20	.10	.06
576	Phil Roof	.20	.10	.06
577	John Morris	.20	.10	.06
578	Dave Tomlin	.20	.10	.06
579	Skip Pitlock	.20	.10	.06
580	Frank Robinson	3.00	1.50	.90
581	Darrel Chaney	.20	.10	.06
582	Eduardo Rodriguez	.20	.10	.06
583	Andy Etchebarren	.20	.10	.06
584	Mike Garman	.20	.10	.06
585	Chris Chambliss	.40	.20	.12
586	Tim McCarver	.60	.30	.20
587	Chris Ward	.20	.10	.06
588	Rick Auerbach	.20	.10	.06
589	Braves Team (Clyde King)	.80	.40	.25
590	Cesar Cedeno	.40	.20	.12
591	Glenn Abbott	.20	.10	.06
592	Balor Moore	.20	.10	.06
593	Gene Lamont	.20	.10	.06
594	Jim Fuller	.20	.10	.06
595	Joe Niekro	.40	.20	.12
596	Ollie Brown	.20	.10	.06
597	Winston Llenas	.20	.10	.06
598	Bruce Kison	.20	.10	.06
599	Nate Colbert	.20	.10	.06
600	Rod Carew	5.00	2.50	1.50
601	Juan Beniquez	.30	.15	.09
602	John Vukovich	.20	.10	.06
603	Lew Krausse	.20	.10	.06
604	Oscar Zamora	.20	.10	.06
605	John Ellis	.20	.10	.06
606	Bruce Miller	.20	.10	.06
607	Jim Holt	.20	.10	.06
608	Gene Michael	.30	.15	.09
609	Ellie Hendricks	.20	.10	.06
610	Ron Hunt	.25	.13	.08
611	Yankees Team (Bill Virdon)	1.25	.60	.40
612	Terry Hughes	.20	.10	.06
613	Bill Parsons	.20	.10	.06
614	Rookie Pitchers (Jack Kucek, Dyar Miller, Vern Ruhle, Paul Siebert)	.20	.10	.06
615	Rookie Pitchers (Pat Darcy, Dennis Leonard, Tom Underwood, Hank Webb)	.60	.30	.20
616	Rookie Outfielders (Dave Augustine, Pepe Mangual, Jim Rice, John Scott)	40.00	20.00	12.00
617	Rookie Infielders (Mike Cubbage, Doug DeCinces, Reggie Sanders, Manny Trillo)	1.75	.90	.50
618	Rookie Pitchers (Jamie Easterly, Tom Johnson, Scott McGregor, Rick Rhoden)	3.00	1.50	.90
619	Rookie Outfielders (Benny Ayala, Nyls Nyman, Tommy Smith, Jerry Turner)	.20	.10	.06
620	Rookie Catchers-Outfielders (Gary Carter, Marc Hill, Danny Meyer, Leon Roberts)	40.00	20.00	12.00
621	Rookie Pitchers (John Denny, Rawly Eastwick, Jim Kern, Juan Veintidos)	.60	.30	.20
622	Rookie Outfielders (Ed Armbrister, Fred Lynn, Tom Poquette, Terry Whitfield)	10.00	5.00	3.00
623	Rookie Infielders (Phil Garner, Keith Hernandez, Bob Sheldon, Tom Veryzer)	25.00	12.50	7.50

		NR MT	EX	VG
624	Rookie Pitchers (Doug Konieczny, Gary Lavelle, Jim Otten, Eddie Solomon)	.30	.15	.09
625	Boog Powell	.70	.35	.20
626	Larry Haney	.20	.10	.06
627	Tom Walker	.20	.10	.06
628	Ron LeFlore	.80	.40	.25
629	Joe Hoerner	.20	.10	.06
630	Greg Luzinski	.70	.35	.20
631	Lee Lacy	.25	.13	.08
632	Morris Nettles	.20	.10	.06
633	Paul Casanova	.20	.10	.06
634	Cy Acosta	.20	.10	.06
635	Chuck Dobson	.20	.10	.06
636	Charlie Moore	.25	.13	.08
637	Ted Martinez	.20	.10	.06
638	Cubs Team (Jim Marshall)	.80	.40	.25
639	Steve Kline	.20	.10	.06
640	Harmon Killebrew	2.50	1.25	.70
641	Jim Northrup	.25	.13	.08
642	Mike Phillips	.20	.10	.06
643	Brent Strom	.20	.10	.06
644	Bill Fahey	.20	.10	.06
645	Danny Cater	.20	.10	.06
646	Checklist 529-660	1.50	.70	.45
647	Claudell Washington	1.25	.60	.40
648	Dave Pagan	.25	.13	.08
649	Jack Heidemann	.20	.10	.06
650	Dave May	.20	.10	.06
651	John Morlan	.20	.10	.06
652	Lindy McDaniel	.20	.10	.06
653	Lee Richards	.20	.10	.06
654	Jerry Terrell	.20	.10	.06
655	Rico Carty	.40	.20	.12
656	Bill Plummer	.20	.10	.06
657	Bob Oliver	.20	.10	.06
658	Vic Harris	.20	.10	.06
659	Bob Apodaca	.20	.10	.06
660	Hank Aaron	10.00	3.75	2.00

1975 Topps Mini

 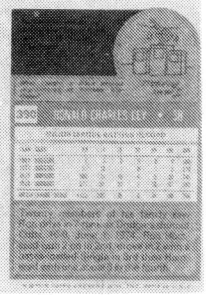

One of the most popular Topps sets of the 1970s is really a test issue. The Topps Minis measure 2¼'' by 3⅛,'' exactly 20% smaller then the regular card size. Other than their size, the Minis are in every way the same as the regular cards. The experiment apparently took place in parts of Michigan and the West Coast, where the Minis were snapped up quickly by collectors.

		NR MT	EX	VG
Complete Set:		800.00	400.00	240.00
Common Player:		.50	.25	.15
1	'74 Highlights (Hank Aaron)	12.00	6.00	3.50
2	'74 Highlights (Lou Brock)	2.25	1.25	.70
3	'74 Highlights (Bob Gibson)	2.25	1.25	.70
4	'74 Highlights (Al Kaline)	2.25	1.25	.70
5	'74 Highlights (Nolan Ryan)	2.25	1.25	.70
6	'74 Highlights (Mike Marshall)	.60	.30	.20
7	'74 Highlights (Dick Bosman, Steve Busby, Nolan Ryan)	1.25	.60	.40
8	Rogelio Moret	.40	.20	.12
9	Frank Tepedino	.40	.20	.12
10	Willie Davis	.60	.30	.20
11	Bill Melton	.40	.20	.12
12	David Clyde	.40	.20	.12
13	Gene Locklear	.40	.20	.12

#	Player	NR MT	EX	VG
14	Milt Wilcox	.40	.20	.12
15	Jose Cardenal	.40	.20	.12
16	Frank Tanana	.60	.30	.20
17	Dave Concepcion	.90	.45	.25
18	Tigers Team (Ralph Houk)	1.25	.60	.40
19	Jerry Koosman	.40	.20	.12
20	Thurman Munson	8.00	4.00	2.50
21	Rollie Fingers	3.00	1.50	.90
22	Dave Cash	.40	.20	.12
23	Bill Russell	.60	.30	.20
24	Al Fitzmorris	.40	.20	.12
25	Lee May	.60	.30	.20
26	Dave McNally	.60	.30	.20
27	Ken Reitz	.40	.20	.12
28	Tom Murphy	.40	.20	.12
29	Dave Parker	10.00	5.00	3.00
30	Bert Blyleven	2.00	1.00	.60
31	Dave Rader	.40	.20	.12
32	Reggie Cleveland	.40	.20	.12
33	Dusty Baker	.60	.30	.20
34	Steve Renko	.40	.20	.12
35	Ron Santo	.80	.40	.25
36	Joe Lovitto	.40	.20	.12
37	Dave Freisleben	.40	.20	.12
38	Buddy Bell	1.50	.70	.45
39	Andy Thornton	1.00	.50	.30
40	Bill Singer	.40	.20	.12
41	Cesar Geronimo	.40	.20	.12
42	Joe Coleman	.40	.20	.12
43	Cleon Jones	.40	.20	.12
44	Pat Dobson	.40	.20	.12
45	Joe Rudi	.60	.30	.20
46	Phillies Team (Danny Ozark)	1.25	.60	.40
47	Tommy John	2.50	1.25	.70
48	Freddie Patek	.40	.20	.12
49	Larry Dierker	.40	.20	.12
50	Brooks Robinson	7.00	3.50	2.00
51	Bob Forsch	1.25	.60	.40
52	Darrell Porter	.60	.30	.20
53	Dave Giusti	.40	.20	.12
54	Eric Soderholm	.40	.20	.12
55	Bobby Bonds	.80	.40	.25
56	Rick Wise	.60	.30	.20
57	Dave Johnson	1.25	.60	.40
58	Chuck Taylor	.40	.20	.12
59	Ken Henderson	.40	.20	.12
60	Fergie Jenkins	1.75	.90	.50
61	Dave Winfield	12.00	6.00	3.50
62	Fritz Peterson	.40	.20	.12
63	Steve Swisher	.40	.20	.12
64	Dave Chalk	.40	.20	.12
65	Don Gullett	.40	.20	.12
66	Willie Horton	.60	.30	.20
67	Tug McGraw	.80	.40	.25
68	Ron Blomberg	.40	.20	.12
69	John Odom	.40	.20	.12
70	Mike Schmidt	50.00	25.00	15.00
71	Charlie Hough	.60	.30	.20
72	Royals Team (Jack McKeon)	1.25	.60	.40
73	J.R. Richard	.60	.30	.20
74	Mark Belanger	.60	.30	.20
75	Ted Simmons	1.00	.50	.30
76	Ed Sprague	.40	.20	.12
77	Richie Zisk	.60	.30	.20
78	Ray Corbin	.40	.20	.12
79	Gary Matthews	.60	.30	.20
80	Carlton Fisk	3.00	1.50	.90
81	Ron Reed	.40	.20	.12
82	Pat Kelly	.40	.20	.12
83	Jim Merritt	.40	.20	.12
84	Enzo Hernandez	.40	.20	.12
85	Bill Bonham	.40	.20	.12
86	Joe Lis	.40	.20	.12
87	George Foster	1.75	.90	.50
88	Tom Egan	.40	.20	.12
89	Jim Ray	.40	.20	.12
90	Rusty Staub	.90	.45	.25
91	Dick Green	.40	.20	.12
92	Cecil Upshaw	.40	.20	.12
93	Dave Lopes	.60	.30	.20
94	Jim Lonborg	.40	.20	.12
95	John Mayberry	.40	.20	.12
96	Mike Cosgrove	.40	.20	.12
97	Earl Williams	.40	.20	.12
98	Rich Folkers	.40	.20	.12
99	Mike Hegan	.40	.20	.12
100	Willie Stargell	5.00	2.50	1.50
101	Expos Team (Gene Mauch)	1.25	.60	.40
102	Joe Decker	.40	.20	.12
103	Rick Miller	.40	.20	.12
104	Bill Madlock	2.25	1.25	.70
105	Buzz Capra	.40	.20	.12
106	Mike Hargrove	.60	.30	.20
107	Jim Barr	.40	.20	.12
108	Tom Hall	.40	.20	.12
109	George Hendrick	.40	.20	.12
110	Wilbur Wood	.40	.20	.12
111	Wayne Garrett	.40	.20	.12
112	Larry Hardy	.40	.20	.12
113	Elliott Maddox	.40	.20	.12
114	Dick Lange	.40	.20	.12
115	Joe Ferguson	.40	.20	.12
116	Lerrin LaGrow	.40	.20	.12
117	Orioles Team (Earl Weaver)	1.25	.60	.40
118	Mike Anderson	.40	.20	.12
119	Tommy Helms	.40	.20	.12
120	Steve Busby (photo actually Fran Healy)	.40	.20	.12
121	Bill North	.40	.20	.12
122	Al Hrabosky	.40	.20	.12
123	Johnny Briggs	.40	.20	.12
124	Jerry Reuss	.60	.30	.20
125	Ken Singleton	.60	.30	.20
126	Checklist 1-132	2.25	1.25	.70
127	Glen Borgmann	.40	.20	.12
128	Bill Lee	.60	.30	.20
129	Rick Monday	.60	.30	.20
130	Phil Niekro	4.00	2.00	1.25
131	Toby Harrah	.40	.20	.12
132	Randy Moffitt	.40	.20	.12
133	Dan Driessen	.60	.30	.20
134	Ron Hodges	.40	.20	.12
135	Charlie Spikes	.40	.20	.12
136	Jim Mason	.40	.20	.12
137	Terry Forster	.40	.20	.12
138	Del Unser	.40	.20	.12
139	Horacio Pina	.40	.20	.12
140	Steve Garvey	10.00	5.00	3.00
141	Mickey Stanley	.40	.20	.12
142	Bob Reynolds	.40	.20	.12
143	Cliff Johnson	.40	.20	.12
144	Jim Wohlford	.40	.20	.12
145	Ken Holtzman	.60	.30	.20
146	Padres Team (John McNamara)	1.25	.60	.40
147	Pedro Garcia	.40	.20	.12
148	Jim Rooker	.40	.20	.12
149	Tim Foli	.40	.20	.12
150	Bob Gibson	5.00	2.50	1.50
151	Steve Brye	.40	.20	.12
152	Mario Guerrero	.40	.20	.12
153	Rick Reuschel	.60	.30	.20
154	Mike Lum	.40	.20	.12
155	Jim Bibby	.40	.20	.12
156	Dave Kingman	1.75	.90	.50
157	Pedro Borbon	.40	.20	.12
158	Jerry Grote	.40	.20	.12
159	Steve Arlin	.40	.20	.12
160	Graig Nettles	2.25	1.25	.70
161	Stan Bahnsen	.40	.20	.12
162	Willie Montanez	.40	.20	.12
163	Jim Brewer	.40	.20	.12
164	Mickey Rivers	.60	.30	.20
165	Doug Rader	.40	.20	.12
166	Woodie Fryman	.40	.20	.12
167	Rich Coggins	.40	.20	.12
168	Bill Greif	.40	.20	.12
169	Cookie Rojas	.40	.20	.12
170	Bert Campaneris	.60	.30	.20
171	Ed Kirkpatrick	.40	.20	.12
172	Red Sox Team (Darrell Johnson)	1.25	.60	.40
173	Steve Rogers	.60	.30	.20
174	Bake McBride	.40	.20	.12
175	Don Money	.40	.20	.12
176	Burt Hooton	.40	.20	.12
177	Vic Correll	.40	.20	.12
178	Cesar Tovar	.40	.20	.12
179	Tom Bradley	.40	.20	.12
180	Joe Morgan	5.00	2.50	1.50
181	Fred Beene	.40	.20	.12
182	Don Hahn	.40	.20	.12
183	Mel Stottlemyre	.60	.30	.20
184	Jorge Orta	.40	.20	.12
185	Steve Carlton	15.00	7.50	4.50
186	Willie Crawford	.40	.20	.12
187	Denny Doyle	.40	.20	.12
188	Tom Griffin	.40	.20	.12
189	1951-MVPs (Larry (Yogi) Berra, Roy Campanella)	2.25	1.25	.70
190	1952-MVPs (Hank Sauer, Bobby Shantz)	.60	.30	.20
191	1953-MVPs (Roy Campanella, Al Rosen)	1.25	.60	.40

		NR MT	EX	VG
192	1954-MVPs (Yogi Berra, Willie Mays)			
		2.25	1.25	.70
193	1955-MVPs (Yogi Berra, Roy Campanella)			
		2.25	1.25	.70
194	1956-MVPs (Mickey Mantle, Don Newcombe)	4.50	2.25	1.25
195	1957-MVPs (Hank Aaron, Mickey Mantle)			
		5.25	2.75	1.50
196	1958-MVPs (Ernie Banks, Jackie Jensen)			
		1.25	.60	.40
197	1959-MVPs (Ernie Banks, Nellie Fox)			
		1.25	.60	.40
198	1960-MVPs (Dick Groat, Roger Maris)			
		1.75	.90	.50
199	1961-MVPs (Roger Maris, Frank Robinson)	2.25	1.25	.70
200	1962-MVPs (Mickey Mantle, Maury Wills)			
		4.50	2.25	1.25
201	1963-MVPs (Elston Howard, Sandy Koufax)	2.25	1.25	.70
202	1964-MVPs (Ken Boyer, Brooks Robinson)	1.75	.90	.50
203	1965-MVPs (Willie Mays, Zoilo Versalles)	1.75	.90	.50
204	1966-MVPs (Bob Clemente, Frank Robinson)	2.25	1.25	.70
205	1967-MVPs (Orlando Cepeda, Carl Yastrzemski)	1.75	.90	.50
206	1968-MVPs (Bob Gibson, Denny McLain)	1.75	.90	.50
207	1969-MVPs (Harmon Killebrew, Willie McCovey)	2.25	1.25	.70
208	1970-MVPs (Johnny Bench, Boog Powell)	1.75	.90	.50
209	1971-MVPs (Vida Blue, Joe Torre)	.80	.40	.25
210	1972-MVPs (Rich Allen, Johnny Bench)	1.75	.90	.50
211	1973-MVPs (Reggie Jackson, Pete Rose)	3.75	2.00	1.25
212	1974-MVPs (Jeff Burroughs, Steve Garvey)	1.25	.60	.40
213	Oscar Gamble	.40	.20	.12
214	Harry Parker	.40	.20	.12
215	Bobby Valentine	.40	.20	.12
216	Giants Team (Wes Westrum)	1.25	.60	.40
217	Lou Piniella	.80	.40	.25
218	Jerry Johnson	.40	.20	.12
219	Ed Herrmann	.40	.20	.12
220	Don Sutton	3.00	1.50	.90
221	Aurelio Rodriquez (Rodriguez)	.40	.20	.12
222	Dan Spillner	.40	.20	.12
223	Robin Yount	45.00	22.00	13.50
224	Ramon Hernandez	.40	.20	.12
225	Bob Grich	.60	.30	.20
226	Bill Campbell	.40	.20	.12
227	Bob Watson	.40	.20	.12
228	George Brett	65.00	32.00	19.50
229	Barry Foote	.40	.20	.12
230	Jim Hunter	4.00	2.00	1.25
231	Mike Tyson	.40	.20	.12
232	Diego Segui	.40	.20	.12
233	Billy Grabarkewitz	.40	.20	.12
234	Tom Grieve	.40	.20	.12
235	Jack Billingham	.40	.20	.12
236	Angels Team (Dick Williams)	1.25	.60	.40
237	Carl Morton	.40	.20	.12
238	Dave Duncan	.40	.20	.12
239	George Stone	.40	.20	.12
240	Garry Maddox	.60	.30	.20
241	Dick Tidrow	.40	.20	.12
242	Jay Johnstone	.60	.30	.20
243	Jim Kaat	2.00	1.00	.60
244	Bill Buckner	.80	.40	.25
245	Mickey Lolich	.80	.40	.25
246	Cardinals Team (Red Schoendienst)	1.25	.60	.40
247	Enos Cabell	.40	.20	.12
248	Randy Jones	.40	.20	.12
249	Danny Thompson	.40	.20	.12
250	Ken Brett	.40	.20	.12
251	Fran Healy	.40	.20	.12
252	Fred Scherman	.40	.20	.12
253	Jesus Alou	.40	.20	.12
254	Mike Torrez	.40	.20	.12
255	Dwight Evans	2.25	1.25	.70
256	Billy Champion	.40	.20	.12
257	Checklist 133-264	2.25	1.25	.70
258	Dave LaRoche	.40	.20	.12
259	Len Randle	.40	.20	.12
260	Johnny Bench	12.00	6.00	3.50
261	Andy Hassler	.40	.20	.12

		NR MT	EX	VG
262	Rowland Office	.40	.20	.12
263	Jim Perry	.60	.30	.20
264	John Milner	.40	.20	.12
265	Ron Bryant	.40	.20	.12
266	Sandy Alomar	.40	.20	.12
267	Dick Ruthven	.40	.20	.12
268	Hal McRae	.60	.30	.20
269	Doug Rau	.40	.20	.12
270	Ron Fairly	.60	.30	.20
271	Jerry Moses	.40	.20	.12
272	Lynn McGlothen	.40	.20	.12
273	Steve Braun	.40	.20	.12
274	Vicente Romo	.40	.20	.12
275	Paul Blair	.60	.30	.20
276	White Sox Team (Chuck Tanner)	1.25	.60	.40
277	Frank Taveras	.40	.20	.12
278	Paul Lindblad	.40	.20	.12
279	Milt May	.40	.20	.12
280	Carl Yastrzemski	15.00	7.50	4.50
281	Jim Slaton	.40	.20	.12
282	Jerry Morales	.40	.20	.12
283	Steve Foucault	.40	.20	.12
284	Ken Griffey	1.00	.50	.30
285	Ellie Rodriguez	.40	.20	.12
286	Mike Jorgensen	.40	.20	.12
287	Roric Harrison	.40	.20	.12
288	Bruce Ellingsen	.40	.20	.12
289	Ken Rudolph	.40	.20	.12
290	Jon Matlack	.40	.20	.12
291	Bill Sudakis	.40	.20	.12
292	Ron Schueler	.40	.20	.12
293	Dick Sharon	.40	.20	.12
294	Geoff Zahn	.40	.20	.12
295	Vada Pinson	.90	.45	.25
296	Alan Foster	.40	.20	.12
297	Craig Kusick	.40	.20	.12
298	Johnny Grubb	.40	.20	.12
299	Bucky Dent	.60	.30	.20
300	Reggie Jackson	20.00	10.00	6.00
301	Dave Roberts	.40	.20	.12
302	Rick Burleson	.80	.40	.25
303	Grant Jackson	.40	.20	.12
304	Pirates Team (Danny Murtaugh)	1.25	.60	.40
305	Jim Colborn	.40	.20	.12
306	Batting Leaders (Rod Carew, Ralph Garr)	1.25	.60	.40
307	Home Run Leaders (Dick Allen, Mike Schmidt)	1.25	.60	.40
308	Runs Batted In Leaders (Johnny Bench, Jeff Burroughs)	1.25	.60	.40
309	Stole Base Leaders (Lou Brock, Bill North)	1.25	.60	.40
310	Victory Leaders (Jim Hunter, Fergie Jenkins, Andy Messersmith, Phil Niekro)	1.25	.60	.40
311	Earned Run Average Leaders (Buzz Capra, Jim Hunter)	.80	.40	.25
312	Strikeout Leaders (Steve Carlton, Nolan Ryan)	2.50	1.25	.70
313	Leading Firemen (Terry Forster, Mike Marshall)	.80	.40	.25
314	Buck Martinez	.40	.20	.12
315	Don Kessinger	.40	.20	.12
316	Jackie Brown	.40	.20	.12
317	Joe Lahoud	.40	.20	.12
318	Ernie McAnally	.40	.20	.12
319	Johnny Oates	.40	.20	.12
320	Pete Rose	40.00	20.00	12.00
321	Rudy May	.40	.20	.12
322	Ed Goodson	.40	.20	.12
323	Fred Holdsworth	.40	.20	.12
324	Ed Kranepool	.40	.20	.12
325	Tony Oliva	1.25	.60	.40
326	Wayne Twitchell	.40	.20	.12
327	Jerry Hairston	.40	.20	.12
328	Sonny Siebert	.40	.20	.12
329	Ted Kubiak	.40	.20	.12
330	Mike Marshall	.60	.30	.20
331	Indians Team (Frank Robinson)	1.25	.60	.40
332	Fred Kendall	.40	.20	.12
333	Dick Drago	.40	.20	.12
334	Greg Gross	.40	.20	.12
335	Jim Palmer	7.00	3.50	2.00
336	Rennie Stennett	.40	.20	.12
337	Kevin Kobel	.40	.20	.12
338	Rick Stelmaszek	.40	.20	.12
339	Jim Fregosi	.60	.30	.20
340	Paul Splittorff	.40	.20	.12
341	Hal Breeden	.40	.20	.12
342	Leroy Stanton	.40	.20	.12
343	Danny Frisella	.40	.20	.12

#	Player	NR MT	EX	VG
344	Ben Oglivie	.60	.30	.20
345	Clay Carroll	.40	.20	.12
346	Bobby Darwin	.40	.20	.12
347	Mike Caldwell	.40	.20	.12
348	Tony Muser	.40	.20	.12
349	Ray Sadecki	.40	.20	.12
350	Bobby Murcer	.60	.30	.20
351	Bob Boone	.60	.30	.20
352	Darold Knowles	.40	.20	.12
353	Luis Melendez	.40	.20	.12
354	Dick Bosman	.40	.20	.12
355	Chris Cannizzaro	.40	.20	.12
356	Rico Petrocelli	.40	.20	.12
357	Ken Forsch	.40	.20	.12
358	Al Bumbry	.40	.20	.12
359	Paul Popovich	.40	.20	.12
360	George Scott	.40	.20	.12
361	Dodgers Team (Walter Alston)	1.50	.70	.45
362	Steve Hargan	.40	.20	.12
363	Carmen Fanzone	.40	.20	.12
364	Doug Bird	.40	.20	.12
365	Bob Bailey	.40	.20	.12
366	Ken Sanders	.40	.20	.12
367	Craig Robinson	.40	.20	.12
368	Vic Albury	.40	.20	.12
369	Merv Rettenmund	.40	.20	.12
370	Tom Seaver	15.00	7.50	4.50
371	Gates Brown	.40	.20	.12
372	John D'Acquisto	.40	.20	.12
373	Bill Sharp	.40	.20	.12
374	Eddie Watt	.40	.20	.12
375	Roy White	.60	.30	.20
376	Steve Yeager	.40	.20	.12
377	Tom Hilgendorf	.40	.20	.12
378	Derrel Thomas	.40	.20	.12
379	Bernie Carbo	.40	.20	.12
380	Sal Bando	.60	.30	.20
381	John Curtis	.40	.20	.12
382	Don Baylor	.90	.45	.25
383	Jim York	.40	.20	.12
384	Brewers Team (Del Crandall)	1.25	.60	.40
385	Dock Ellis	.40	.20	.12
386	Checklist 265-396	2.25	1.25	.70
387	Jim Spencer	.40	.20	.12
388	Steve Stone	.60	.30	.20
389	Tony Solaita	.40	.20	.12
390	Ron Cey	.60	.30	.20
391	Don DeMola	.40	.20	.12
392	Bruce Bochte	.40	.20	.12
393	Gary Gentry	.40	.20	.12
394	Larvell Blanks	.40	.20	.12
395	Bud Harrelson	.40	.20	.12
396	Fred Norman	.40	.20	.12
397	Bill Freehan	.60	.30	.20
398	Elias Sosa	.40	.20	.12
399	Terry Harmon	.40	.20	.12
400	Dick Allen	1.25	.60	.40
401	Mike Wallace	.40	.20	.12
402	Bob Tolan	.40	.20	.12
403	Tom Buskey	.40	.20	.12
404	Ted Sizemore	.40	.20	.12
405	John Montague	.40	.20	.12
406	Bob Gallagher	.40	.20	.12
407	Herb Washington	.40	.20	.12
408	Clyde Wright	.40	.20	.12
409	Bob Robertson	.40	.20	.12
410	Mike Cueller (Cuellar)	.60	.30	.20
411	George Mitterwald	.40	.20	.12
412	Bill Hands	.40	.20	.12
413	Marty Pattin	.40	.20	.12
414	Manny Mota	.60	.30	.20
415	John Hiller	.40	.20	.12
416	Larry Lintz	.40	.20	.12
417	Skip Lockwood	.40	.20	.12
418	Leo Foster	.40	.20	.12
419	Dave Goltz	.40	.20	.12
420	Larry Bowa	.60	.30	.20
421	Mets Team (Yogi Berra)	1.50	.70	.45
422	Brian Downing	.60	.30	.20
423	Clay Kirby	.40	.20	.12
424	John Lowenstein	.40	.20	.12
425	Tito Fuentes	.40	.20	.12
426	George Medich	.40	.20	.12
427	Clarence Gaston	.40	.20	.12
428	Dave Hamilton	.40	.20	.12
429	Jim Dwyer	.40	.20	.12
430	Luis Tiant	.80	.40	.25
431	Rod Gilbreath	.40	.20	.12
432	Ken Berry	.40	.20	.12
433	Larry Demery	.40	.20	.12
434	Bob Locker	.40	.20	.12
435	Dave Nelson	.40	.20	.12
436	Ken Frailing	.40	.20	.12
437	Al Cowens	.40	.20	.12
438	Don Carrithers	.40	.20	.12
439	Ed Brinkman	.40	.20	.12
440	Andy Messersmith	.60	.30	.20
441	Bobby Heise	.40	.20	.12
442	Maximino Leon	.40	.20	.12
443	Twins Team (Frank Quilici)	1.25	.60	.40
444	Gene Garber	.40	.20	.12
445	Felix Millan	.40	.20	.12
446	Bart Johnson	.40	.20	.12
447	Terry Crowley	.40	.20	.12
448	Frank Duffy	.40	.20	.12
449	Charlie Williams	.40	.20	.12
450	Willie McCovey	7.00	3.50	2.00
451	Rick Dempsey	.60	.30	.20
452	Angel Mangual	.40	.20	.12
453	Claude Osteen	.40	.20	.12
454	Doug Griffin	.40	.20	.12
455	Don Wilson	.40	.20	.12
456	Bob Coluccio	.40	.20	.12
457	Mario Mendoza	.40	.20	.12
458	Ross Grimsley	.40	.20	.12
459	A.L. Championships	1.25	.60	.40
460	N.L. Championships	1.25	.60	.40
461	World Series Game 1	2.25	1.25	.70
462	World Series Game 2	1.50	.70	.45
463	World Series Game 3	1.50	.70	.45
464	World Series Game 4	1.25	.60	.40
465	World Series Game 5	1.25	.60	.40
466	World Series Summary	1.25	.60	.40
467	Ed Halicki	.40	.20	.12
468	Bobby Mitchell	.40	.20	.12
469	Tom Dettore	.40	.20	.12
470	Jeff Burroughs	.40	.20	.12
471	Bob Stinson	.40	.20	.12
472	Bruce Dal Canton	.40	.20	.12
473	Ken McMullen	.40	.20	.12
474	Luke Walker	.40	.20	.12
475	Darrell Evans	.90	.45	.25
476	Ed Figueroa	.40	.20	.12
477	Tom Hutton	.40	.20	.12
478	Tom Burgmeier	.40	.20	.12
479	Ken Boswell	.40	.20	.12
480	Carlos May	.40	.20	.12
481	Will McEnaney	.40	.20	.12
482	Tom McCraw	.40	.20	.12
483	Steve Ontiveros	.40	.20	.12
484	Glenn Beckert	.40	.20	.12
485	Sparky Lyle	.60	.30	.20
486	Ray Fosse	.40	.20	.12
487	Astros Team (Preston Gomez)	1.25	.60	.40
488	Bill Travers	.40	.20	.12
489	Cecil Cooper	1.50	.70	.45
490	Reggie Smith	.60	.30	.20
491	Doyle Alexander	.60	.30	.20
492	Rich Hebner	.40	.20	.12
493	Doug Stanhouse	.40	.20	.12
494	Pete LaCock	.40	.20	.12
495	Nelson Briles	.40	.20	.12
496	Pepe Frias	.40	.20	.12
497	Jim Nettles	.40	.20	.12
498	Al Downing	.40	.20	.12
499	Marty Perez	.40	.20	.12
500	Nolan Ryan	12.00	6.00	3.50
501	Bill Robinson	.40	.20	.12
502	Pat Bourque	.40	.20	.12
503	Fred Stanley	.40	.20	.12
504	Buddy Bradford	.40	.20	.12
505	Chris Speier	.40	.20	.12
506	Leron Lee	.40	.20	.12
507	Tom Carroll	.40	.20	.12
508	Bob Hansen	.40	.20	.12
509	Dave Hilton	.40	.20	.12
510	Vida Blue	.80	.40	.25
511	Rangers Team (Billy Martin)	1.25	.60	.40
512	Larry Milbourne	.40	.20	.12
513	Dick Pole	.40	.20	.12
514	Jose Cruz	.80	.40	.25
515	Manny Sanguillen	.40	.20	.12
516	Don Hood	.40	.20	.12
517	Checklist 397-528	2.25	1.25	.70
518	Leo Cardenas	.40	.20	.12
519	Jim Todd	.40	.20	.12
520	Amos Otis	.40	.20	.12
521	Dennis Blair	.40	.20	.12
522	Gary Sutherland	.40	.20	.12
523	Tom Paciorek	.40	.20	.12
524	John Doherty	.40	.20	.12
525	Tom House	.40	.20	.12

		NR MT	EX	VG
526	Larry Hisle	.40	.20	.12
527	Mac Scarce	.40	.20	.12
528	Eddie Leon	.40	.20	.12
529	Gary Thomasson	.40	.20	.12
530	Gaylord Perry	6.00	3.00	1.75
531	Reds Team (Sparky Anderson)	1.25	.60	.40
532	Gorman Thomas	.80	.40	.25
533	Rudy Meoli	.40	.20	.12
534	Alex Johnson	.40	.20	.12
535	Gene Tenace	.40	.20	.12
536	Bob Moose	.40	.20	.12
537	Tommy Harper	.40	.20	.12
538	Duffy Dyer	.40	.20	.12
539	Jesse Jefferson	.40	.20	.12
540	Lou Brock	7.00	3.50	2.00
541	Roger Metzger	.40	.20	.12
542	Pete Broberg	.40	.20	.12
543	Larry Biittner	.40	.20	.12
544	Steve Mingori	.40	.20	.12
545	Billy Williams	6.00	3.00	1.75
546	John Knox	.40	.20	.12
547	Von Joshua	.40	.20	.12
548	Charlie Sands	.40	.20	.12
549	Bill Butler	.40	.20	.12
550	Ralph Garr	.40	.20	.12
551	Larry Christenson	.40	.20	.12
552	Jack Brohamer	.40	.20	.12
553	John Boccabella	.40	.20	.12
554	Rich Gossage	1.75	.90	.50
555	Al Oliver	1.50	.70	.45
556	Tim Johnson	.40	.20	.12
557	Larry Gura	.40	.20	.12
558	Dave Roberts	.40	.20	.12
559	Bob Montgomery	.40	.20	.12
560	Tony Perez	1.25	.60	.40
561	A's Team (Alvin Dark)	1.25	.60	.40
562	Gary Nolan	.40	.20	.12
563	Wilbur Howard	.40	.20	.12
564	Tommy Davis	.60	.30	.20
565	Joe Torre	1.00	.50	.30
566	Ray Burris	.40	.20	.12
567	Jim Sundberg	1.00	.50	.30
568	Dale Murray	.40	.20	.12
569	Frank White	.60	.30	.20
570	Jim Wynn	.60	.30	.20
571	Dave Lemanczyk	.40	.20	.12
572	Roger Nelson	.40	.20	.12
573	Orlando Pena	.40	.20	.12
574	Tony Taylor	.40	.20	.12
575	Gene Clines	.40	.20	.12
576	Phil Roof	.40	.20	.12
577	John Morris	.40	.20	.12
578	Dave Tomlin	.40	.20	.12
579	Skip Pitlock	.40	.20	.12
580	Frank Robinson	7.00	3.50	2.00
581	Darrel Chaney	.40	.20	.12
582	Eduardo Rodriguez	.40	.20	.12
583	Andy Etchebarren	.40	.20	.12
584	Mike Garman	.40	.20	.12
585	Chris Chambliss	.60	.30	.20
586	Tim McCarver	.90	.45	.25
587	Chris Ward	.40	.20	.12
588	Rick Auerbach	.40	.20	.12
589	Braves Team (Clyde King)	1.25	.60	.40
590	Cesar Cedeno	.60	.30	.20
591	Glenn Abbott	.40	.20	.12
592	Balor Moore	.40	.20	.12
593	Gene Lamont	.40	.20	.12
594	Jim Fuller	.40	.20	.12
595	Joe Niekro	.60	.30	.20
596	Ollie Brown	.40	.20	.12
597	Winston Llenas	.40	.20	.12
598	Bruce Kison	.40	.20	.12
599	Nate Colbert	.40	.20	.12
600	Rod Carew	10.00	5.00	3.00
601	Juan Beniquez	.40	.20	.12
602	John Vukovich	.40	.20	.12
603	Lew Krausse	.40	.20	.12
604	Oscar Zamora	.40	.20	.12
605	John Ellis	.40	.20	.12
606	Bruce Miller	.40	.20	.12
607	Jim Holt	.40	.20	.12
608	Gene Michael	.40	.20	.12
609	Ellie Hendricks	.40	.20	.12
610	Ron Hunt	.40	.20	.12
611	Yankees Team (Bill Virdon)	1.75	.90	.50
612	Terry Hughes	.40	.20	.12
613	Bill Parsons	.40	.20	.12
614	Rookie Pitchers (Jack Kucek, Dyar Miller, Vern Ruhle, Paul Siebert)	.40	.20	.12

		NR MT	EX	VG
615	Rookie Pitchers (Pat Darcy, Dennis Leonard, Tom Underwood, Hank Webb)	.90	.45	.25
616	Rookie Outfielders (Dave Augustine, Pepe Mangual, Jim Rice, John Scott)	60.00	30.00	18.00
617	Rookie Infielders (Mike Cubbage, Doug DeCinces, Reggie Sanders, Manny Trillo)	2.50	1.25	.70
618	Rookie Pitchers (Jamie Easterly, Tom Johnson, Scott McGregor, Rick Rhoden)	4.00	2.00	1.25
619	Rookie Outfielders (Benny Ayala, Nyls Nyman, Tommy Smith, Jerry Turner)	.40	.20	.12
620	Rookie Catchers-Outfielders (Gary Carter, Marc Hill, Danny Meyer, Leon Roberts)	60.00	30.00	18.00
621	Rookie Pitchers (John Denny, Rawly Eastwick, Jim Kern, Juan Veintidos)	.90	.45	.25
622	Rookie Outfielders (Ed Armbrister, Fred Lynn, Tom Poquette, Terry Whitfield)	15.00	7.50	4.50
623	Rookie Infielders (Phil Garner, Keith Hernandez, Bob Sheldon, Tom Veryzer)	35.00	17.50	10.50
624	Rookie Pitchers (Doug Konieczny, Gary Lavelle, Jim Otten, Eddie Solomon)	.40	.20	.12
625	Boog Powell	1.00	.50	.30
626	Larry Haney	.40	.20	.12
627	Tom Walker	.40	.20	.12
628	Ron LeFlore	1.25	.60	.40
629	Joe Hoerner	.40	.20	.12
630	Greg Luzinski	1.00	.50	.30
631	Lee Lacy	.40	.20	.12
632	Morris Nettles	.40	.20	.12
633	Paul Casanova	.40	.20	.12
634	Cy Acosta	.40	.20	.12
635	Chuck Dobson	.40	.20	.12
636	Charlie Moore	.40	.20	.12
637	Ted Martinez	.40	.20	.12
638	Cubs Team (Jim Marshall)	1.25	.60	.40
639	Steve Kline	.40	.20	.12
640	Harmon Killebrew	6.00	3.00	1.75
641	Jim Northrup	.40	.20	.12
642	Mike Phillips	.40	.20	.12
643	Brent Strom	.40	.20	.12
644	Bill Fahey	.40	.20	.12
645	Danny Cater	.40	.20	.12
646	Checklist 529-660	2.25	1.25	.70
647	Claudell Washington	1.75	.90	.50
648	Dave Pagan	.40	.20	.12
649	Jack Heidemann	.40	.20	.12
650	Dave May	.40	.20	.12
651	John Morlan	.40	.20	.12
652	Lindy McDaniel	.40	.20	.12
653	Lee Richards	.40	.20	.12
654	Jerry Terrell	.40	.20	.12
655	Rico Carty	.60	.30	.20
656	Bill Plummer	.40	.20	.12
657	Bob Oliver	.40	.20	.12
658	Vic Harris	.40	.20	.12
659	Bob Apodaca	.40	.20	.12
660	Hank Aaron	20.00	10.00	6.00

1976 Topps

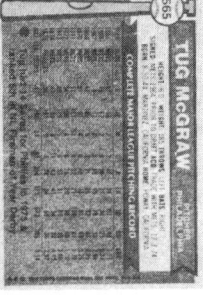

These 2½'' by 3½'' cards begin a design trend for Topps. The focus was more on the photo quality than in past years with a corresponding trend toward simplicity in the borders. The front of the cards has the player's name and team in two strips while his position is in the lower left corner under a drawing of a player representing that position. Backs have a bat and ball with the card number on the left, statistics and personal information and career highlights on the right. The 660-card set featured a number of specialty sets including record-setting performances, statistical leaders, Play-off and World Series highlights, the Sporting News All-Time All-Stars and father and son combinations. Team cards had both regular versions and ones printed on thinner cardboard which were available in uncut sheet form from Topps.

		NR MT	EX	VG
Complete Set:		250.00	110.00	60.00
Commmon Player:		.15	.08	.05
1	'75 Record Breaker (Hank Aaron)	8.00	2.50	1.25
2	'75 Record Breaker (Bobby Bonds)	.40	.20	.12
3	'75 Record Breaker (Mickey Lolich)	.35	.20	.11
4	'75 Record Breaker (Dave Lopes)	.35	.20	.11
5	'75 Record Breaker (Tom Seaver)	1.50	.70	.45
6	'75 Record Breaker (Rennie Stennett)	.30	.15	.09
7	Jim Umbarger	.15	.08	.05
8	Tito Fuentes	.15	.08	.05
9	Paul Lindblad	.15	.08	.05
10	Lou Brock	2.50	1.25	.70
11	Jim Hughes	.15	.08	.05
12	Richie Zisk	.20	.10	.06
13	Johnny Wockenfuss	.15	.08	.05
14	Gene Garber	.20	.10	.06
15	George Scott	.25	.13	.08
16	Bob Apodaca	.15	.08	.05
17	Yankees Team (Billy Martin)	1.25	.60	.40
18	Dale Murray	.15	.08	.05
19	George Brett	12.00	6.00	3.50
20	Bob Watson	.20	.10	.06
21	Dave LaRoche	.15	.08	.05
22	Bill Russell	.20	.10	.06
23	Brian Downing	.25	.13	.08
24	Cesar Geronimo	.20	.10	.06
25	Mike Torrez	.20	.10	.06
26	Andy Thornton	.25	.13	.08
27	Ed Figueroa	.15	.08	.05
28	Dusty Baker	.25	.13	.08
29	Rick Burleson	.30	.15	.09
30	John Montefusco	.35	.20	.11
31	Len Randle	.15	.08	.05
32	Danny Frisella	.15	.08	.05
33	Bill North	.15	.08	.05
34	Mike Garman	.15	.08	.05
35	Tony Oliva	.60	.30	.20
36	Frank Taveras	.15	.08	.05
37	John Hiller	.20	.10	.06
38	Garry Maddox	.20	.10	.06
39	Pete Broberg	.15	.08	.05
40	Dave Kingman	.80	.40	.25
41	Tippy Martinez	.40	.20	.12
42	Barry Foote	.15	.08	.05
43	Paul Splittorff	.20	.10	.06
44	Doug Rader	.15	.08	.05
45	Boog Powell	.60	.30	.20
46	Dodgers Team (Walter Alston)	1.00	.50	.30
47	Jesse Jefferson	.15	.08	.05
48	Dave Concepcion	.40	.20	.12
49	Dave Duncan	.15	.08	.05
50	Fred Lynn	2.25	1.25	.70
51	Ray Burris	.15	.08	.05
52	Dave Chalk	.15	.08	.05
53	Mike Beard	.15	.08	.05
54	Dave Rader	.15	.08	.05
55	Gaylord Perry	2.00	1.00	.60
56	Bob Tolan	.20	.10	.06
57	Phil Garner	.30	.15	.09
58	Ron Reed	.20	.10	.06
59	Larry Hisle	.20	.10	.06
60	Jerry Reuss	.30	.15	.09
61	Ron LeFlore	.30	.15	.09
62	Johnny Oates	.15	.08	.05
63	Bobby Darwin	.15	.08	.05
64	Jerry Koosman	.30	.15	.09
65	Chris Chambliss	.30	.15	.09
66	Father & Son (Buddy Bell, Gus Bell)	.50	.25	.15
67	Father & Son (Bob Boone, Ray Boone)	.40	.20	.12
68	Father & Son (Joe Coleman, Joe Coleman, Jr.)	.20	.10	.06
69	Father & Son (Jim Hegan, Mike Hegan)	.20	.10	.06
70	Father & Son (Roy Smalley, Roy Smalley, Jr.)	.25	.13	.08
71	Steve Rogers	.20	.10	.06
72	Hal McRae	.25	.13	.08
73	Orioles Team (Earl Weaver)	.80	.40	.25
74	Oscar Gamble	.20	.10	.06
75	Larry Dierker	.20	.10	.06
76	Willie Crawford	.15	.08	.05
77	Pedro Borbon	.15	.08	.05
78	Cecil Cooper	1.00	.50	.30
79	Jerry Morales	.15	.08	.05
80	Jim Kaat	.90	.45	.25
81	Darrell Evans	.50	.25	.15
82	Von Joshua	.15	.08	.05
83	Jim Spencer	.15	.08	.05
84	Brent Strom	.15	.08	.05
85	Mickey Rivers	.25	.13	.08
86	Mike Tyson	.15	.08	.05
87	Tom Burgmeier	.15	.08	.05
88	Duffy Dyer	.15	.08	.05
89	Vern Ruhle	.15	.08	.05
90	Sal Bando	.30	.15	.09
91	Tom Hutton	.15	.08	.05
92	Eduardo Rodriguez	.15	.08	.05
93	Mike Phillips	.15	.08	.05
94	Jim Dwyer	.30	.15	.09
95	Brooks Robinson	2.50	1.25	.70
96	Doug Bird	.15	.08	.05
97	Wilbur Howard	.15	.08	.05
98	Dennis Eckersley	1.00	.50	.30
99	Lee Lacy	.20	.10	.06
100	Jim Hunter	2.00	1.00	.60
101	Pete LaCock	.15	.08	.05
102	Jim Willoughby	.15	.08	.05
103	Biff Pocoroba	.15	.08	.05
104	Reds Team (Sparky Anderson)	.90	.45	.25
105	Gary Lavelle	.15	.08	.05
106	Tom Grieve	.15	.08	.05
107	Dave Roberts	.15	.08	.05
108	Don Kirkwood	.15	.08	.05
109	Larry Lintz	.15	.08	.05
110	Carlos May	.20	.10	.06
111	Danny Thompson	.20	.10	.06
112	Kent Tekulve	.80	.40	.25
113	Gary Sutherland	.15	.08	.05
114	Jay Johnstone	.25	.13	.08
115	Ken Holtzman	.25	.13	.08
116	Charlie Moore	.15	.08	.05
117	Mike Jorgensen	.15	.08	.05
118	Red Sox Team (Darrell Johnson)	.90	.45	.25
119	Checklist 1-132	1.25	.60	.40
120	Rusty Staub	.35	.20	.11
121	Tony Solaita	.15	.08	.05
122	Mike Cosgrove	.15	.08	.05
123	Walt Williams	.20	.10	.06
124	Doug Rau	.15	.08	.05
125	Don Baylor	.50	.25	.15
126	Tom Dettore	.15	.08	.05
127	Larvell Blanks	.15	.08	.05
128	Ken Griffey	.35	.20	.11
129	Andy Etchebarren	.15	.08	.05
130	Luis Tiant	.40	.20	.12
131	Bill Stein	.25	.13	.08
132	Don Hood	.15	.08	.05
133	Gary Matthews	.25	.13	.08
134	Mike Ivie	.15	.08	.05
135	Bake McBride	.20	.10	.06
136	Dave Goltz	.20	.10	.06
137	Bill Robinson	.15	.08	.05
138	Lerrin LaGrow	.15	.08	.05
139	Gorman Thomas	.35	.20	.11
140	Vida Blue	.40	.20	.12
141	Larry Parrish	2.00	1.00	.60
142	Dick Drago	.15	.08	.05
143	Jerry Grote	.20	.10	.06
144	Al Fitzmorris	.15	.08	.05
145	Larry Bowa	.35	.20	.11
146	George Medich	.20	.10	.06
147	Astros Team (Bill Virdon)	.80	.40	.25
148	Stan Thomas	.15	.08	.05
149	Tommy Davis	.30	.15	.09
150	Steve Garvey	4.50	2.25	1.25
151	Bill Bonham	.15	.08	.05
152	Leroy Stanton	.15	.08	.05
153	Buzz Capra	.15	.08	.05
154	Bucky Dent	.30	.15	.09
155	Jack Billingham	.15	.08	.05

		NR MT	EX	VG
156	Rico Carty	.25	.13	.08
157	Mike Caldwell	.15	.08	.05
158	Ken Reitz	.15	.08	.05
159	Jerry Terrell	.15	.08	.05
160	Dave Winfield	4.00	2.00	1.25
161	Bruce Kison	.15	.08	.05
162	Jack Pierce	.15	.08	.05
163	Jim Slaton	.15	.08	.05
164	Pepe Mangual	.15	.08	.05
165	Gene Tenace	.20	.10	.06
166	Skip Lockwood	.15	.08	.05
167	Freddie Patek	.15	.08	.05
168	Tom Hilgendorf	.15	.08	.05
169	Graig Nettles	1.00	.50	.30
170	Rick Wise	.20	.10	.06
171	Greg Gross	.15	.08	.05
172	Rangers Team (Frank Lucchesi)	.80	.40	.25
173	Steve Swisher	.15	.08	.05
174	Charlie Hough	.25	.13	.08
175	Ken Singleton	.30	.15	.09
176	Dick Lange	.15	.08	.05
177	Marty Perez	.15	.08	.05
178	Tom Buskey	.15	.08	.05
179	George Foster	1.00	.50	.30
180	Rich Gossage	1.25	.60	.40
181	Willie Montanez	.20	.10	.06
182	Harry Rasmussen	.15	.08	.05
183	Steve Braun	.15	.08	.05
184	Bill Greif	.15	.08	.05
185	Dave Parker	3.00	1.50	.90
186	Tom Walker	.15	.08	.05
187	Pedro Garcia	.15	.08	.05
188	Fred Scherman	.15	.08	.05
189	Claudell Washington	.40	.20	.12
190	Jon Matlack	.25	.13	.08
191	N.L. Batting Leaders (Bill Madlock, Manny Sanguillen, Ted Simmons)	.60	.30	.20
192	A.L. Batting Leaders (Rod Carew, Fred Lynn, Thurman Munson)	1.50	.70	.45
193	N.L. Home Run Leaders (Dave Kingman, Greg Luzinski, Mike Schmidt)	1.25	.60	.40
194	A.L. Home Run Leaders (Reggie Jackson, John Mayberry, George Scott)	1.25	.60	.40
195	N.L. Runs Batted In Ldrs. (Johnny Bench, Greg Luzinski, Tony Perez)	.60	.30	.20
196	A.L. Runs Batted In Ldrs. (Fred Lynn, John Mayberry, George Scott)	.60	.30	.20
197	N.L. Stolen Base Leaders (Lou Brock, Dave Lopes, Joe Morgan)	.90	.45	.25
198	A.L. Stolen Base Leaders (Amos Otis, Mickey Rivers, Claudell Washington)	.50	.25	.15
199	N.L. Victory Leaders (Randy Jones, Andy Messersmith, Tom Seaver)	.80	.40	.25
200	A.L. Victory Leaders (Vida Blue, Jim Hunter, Jim Palmer)	.90	.45	.25
201	N.L. Earned Run Avg. Ldrs. (Randy Jones, Andy Messersmith, Tom Seaver)	.80	.40	.25
202	A.L. Earned Run Avg. Ldrs. (Dennis Eckersley, Jim Hunter, Jim Palmer)	.90	.45	.25
203	N.L. Strikeout Leaders (Andy Messersmith, John Montefusco, Tom Seaver)	.80	.40	.25
204	A.L. Strikeout Leaders (Bert Blyleven, Gaylord Perry, Frank Tanana)	.70	.35	.20
205	Major League Leading Firemen (Rich Gossage, Al Hrabosky)	.50	.25	.15
206	Manny Trillo	.20	.10	.06
207	Andy Hassler	.15	.08	.05
208	Mike Lum	.15	.08	.05
209	Alan Ashby	.35	.20	.11
210	Lee May	.25	.13	.08
211	Clay Carroll	.20	.10	.06
212	Pat Kelly	.15	.08	.05
213	Dave Heaverlo	.15	.08	.05
214	Eric Soderholm	.15	.08	.05
215	Reggie Smith	.25	.13	.08
216	Expos Team (Karl Kuehl)	.80	.40	.25
217	Dave Freisleben	.15	.08	.05
218	John Knox	.15	.08	.05
219	Tom Murphy	.15	.08	.05
220	Manny Sanguillen	.20	.10	.06
221	Jim Todd	.15	.08	.05
222	Wayne Garrett	.15	.08	.05
223	Ollie Brown	.15	.08	.05
224	Jim York	.15	.08	.05
225	Roy White	.25	.13	.08
226	Jim Sundberg	.25	.13	.08
227	Oscar Zamora	.15	.08	.05
228	John Hale	.15	.08	.05
229	Jerry Remy	.30	.15	.09
230	Carl Yastrzemski	6.00	3.00	1.75

		NR MT	EX	VG
231	Tom House	.15	.08	.05
232	Frank Duffy	.15	.08	.05
233	Grant Jackson	.15	.08	.05
234	Mike Sadek	.15	.08	.05
235	Bert Blyleven	1.00	.50	.30
236	Royals Team (Whitey Herzog)	.80	.40	.25
237	Dave Hamilton	.15	.08	.05
238	Larry Biittner	.15	.08	.05
239	John Curtis	.15	.08	.05
240	Pete Rose	15.00	7.50	4.50
241	Hector Torres	.15	.08	.05
242	Dan Meyer	.15	.08	.05
243	Jim Rooker	.15	.08	.05
244	Bill Sharp	.15	.08	.05
245	Felix Millan	.15	.08	.05
246	Cesar Tovar	.15	.08	.05
247	Terry Harmon	.15	.08	.05
248	Dick Tidrow	.20	.10	.06
249	Cliff Johnson	.20	.10	.06
250	Fergie Jenkins	1.00	.50	.30
251	Rick Monday	.30	.15	.09
252	Tim Nordbrook	.15	.08	.05
253	Bill Buckner	.50	.25	.15
254	Rudy Meoli	.15	.08	.05
255	Fritz Peterson	.15	.08	.05
256	Rowland Office	.15	.08	.05
257	Ross Grimsley	.20	.10	.06
258	Nyls Nyman	.15	.08	.05
259	Darrel Chaney	.15	.08	.05
260	Steve Busby	.20	.10	.06
261	Gary Thomasson	.15	.08	.05
262	Checklist 133-264	1.50	.70	.45
263	Lyman Bostock	.80	.40	.25
264	Steve Renko	.15	.08	.05
265	Willie Davis	.30	.15	.09
266	Alan Foster	.15	.08	.05
267	Aurelio Rodriguez	.20	.10	.06
268	Del Unser	.15	.08	.05
269	Rick Austin	.15	.08	.05
270	Willie Stargell	2.75	1.50	.80
271	Jim Lonborg	.20	.10	.06
272	Rick Dempsey	.25	.13	.08
273	Joe Niekro	.30	.15	.09
274	Tommy Harper	.20	.10	.06
275	Rick Manning	.40	.20	.12
276	Mickey Scott	.15	.08	.05
277	Cubs Team (Jim Marshall)	.80	.40	.25
278	Bernie Carbo	.15	.08	.05
279	Roy Howell	.15	.08	.05
280	Burt Hooton	.20	.10	.06
281	Dave May	.15	.08	.05
282	Dan Osborn	.15	.08	.05
283	Merv Rettenmund	.15	.08	.05
284	Steve Ontiveros	.15	.08	.05
285	Mike Cuellar	.25	.13	.08
286	Jim Wohlford	.15	.08	.05
287	Pete Mackanin	.15	.08	.05
288	Bill Campbell	.15	.08	.05
289	Enzo Hernandez	.15	.08	.05
290	Ted Simmons	.60	.30	.20
291	Ken Sanders	.15	.08	.05
292	Leon Roberts	.15	.08	.05
293	Bill Castro	.15	.08	.05
294	Ed Kirkpatrick	.15	.08	.05
295	Dave Cash	.15	.08	.05
296	Pat Dobson	.20	.10	.06
297	Roger Metzger	.15	.08	.05
298	Dick Bosman	.15	.08	.05
299	Champ Summers	.15	.08	.05
300	Johnny Bench	5.00	2.50	1.50
301	Jackie Brown	.15	.08	.05
302	Rick Miller	.15	.08	.05
303	Steve Foucault	.15	.08	.05
304	Angels Team (Dick Williams)	.80	.40	.25
305	Andy Messersmith	.25	.13	.08
306	Rod Gilbreath	.15	.08	.05
307	Al Bumbry	.20	.10	.06
308	Jim Barr	.15	.08	.05
309	Bill Melton	.20	.10	.06
310	Randy Jones	.30	.15	.09
311	Cookie Rojas	.15	.08	.05
312	Don Carrithers	.15	.08	.05
313	Dan Ford	.25	.13	.08
314	Ed Kranepool	.25	.13	.08
315	Al Hrabosky	.20	.10	.06
316	Robin Yount	6.00	3.00	1.75
317	John Candelaria	2.25	1.25	.70
318	Bob Boone	.30	.15	.09
319	Larry Gura	.20	.10	.06
320	Willie Horton	.25	.13	.08
321	Jose Cruz	.35	.20	.11

		NR MT	EX	VG
322	Glenn Abbott	.15	.08	.05
323	Rob Sperring	.15	.08	.05
324	Jim Bibby	.15	.08	.05
325	Tony Perez	.70	.35	.20
326	Dick Pole	.15	.08	.05
327	Dave Moates	.15	.08	.05
328	Carl Morton	.15	.08	.05
329	Joe Ferguson	.15	.08	.05
330	Nolan Ryan	4.50	2.25	1.25
331	Padres Team (John McNamara)	.80	.40	.25
332	Charlie Williams	.15	.08	.05
333	Bob Coluccio	.15	.08	.05
334	Dennis Leonard	.25	.13	.08
335	Bob Grich	.25	.13	.08
336	Vic Albury	.15	.08	.05
337	Bud Harrelson	.20	.10	.06
338	Bob Bailey	.15	.08	.05
339	John Denny	.25	.13	.08
340	Jim Rice	12.00	6.00	3.50
341	All Time All-Stars (Lou Gehrig)	2.50	1.25	.70
342	All Time All-Stars (Rogers Hornsby)	1.25	.60	.40
343	All Time All-Stars (Pie Traynor)	.80	.40	.25
344	All Time All-Stars (Honus Wagner)	1.25	.60	.40
345	All Time All-Stars (Babe Ruth)	4.00	2.00	1.25
346	All Time All-Stars (Ty Cobb)	2.50	1.25	.70
347	All Time All-Stars (Ted Williams)	2.50	1.25	.70
348	All Time All-Stars (Mickey Cochrane)	.80	.40	.25
349	All Time All-Stars (Walter Johnson)	1.25	.60	.40
350	All Time All-Stars (Lefty Grove)	1.00	.50	.30
351	Randy Hundley	.15	.08	.05
352	Dave Giusti	.15	.08	.05
353	Sixto Lezcano	.30	.15	.09
354	Ron Blomberg	.20	.10	.06
355	Steve Carlton	4.50	2.25	1.25
356	Ted Martinez	.15	.08	.05
357	Ken Forsch	.20	.10	.06
358	Buddy Bell	.50	.25	.15
359	Rick Reuschel	.30	.15	.09
360	Jeff Burroughs	.20	.10	.06
361	Tigers Team (Ralph Houk)	1.00	.50	.30
362	Will McEnaney	.15	.08	.05
363	Dave Collins	.70	.35	.20
364	Elias Sosa	.15	.08	.05
365	Carlton Fisk	1.25	.60	.40
366	Bobby Valentine	.30	.15	.09
367	Bruce Miller	.15	.08	.05
368	Wilbur Wood	.25	.13	.08
369	Frank White	.30	.15	.09
370	Ron Cey	.40	.20	.12
371	Ellie Hendricks	.15	.08	.05
372	Rick Baldwin	.15	.08	.05
373	Johnny Briggs	.15	.08	.05
374	Dan Warthen	.15	.08	.05
375	Ron Fairly	.25	.13	.08
376	Rich Hebner	.20	.10	.06
377	Mike Hegan	.15	.08	.05
378	Steve Stone	.25	.13	.08
379	Ken Boswell	.15	.08	.05
380	Bobby Bonds	.35	.20	.11
381	Denny Doyle	.15	.08	.05
382	Matt Alexander	.15	.08	.05
383	John Ellis	.15	.08	.05
384	Phillies Team (Danny Ozark)	.80	.40	.25
385	Mickey Lolich	.40	.20	.12
386	Ed Goodson	.15	.08	.05
387	Mike Miley	.15	.08	.05
388	Stan Perzanowski	.15	.08	.05
389	Glenn Adams	.15	.08	.05
390	Don Gullett	.20	.10	.06
391	Jerry Hairston	.15	.08	.05
392	Checklist 265-396	1.50	.70	.45
393	Paul Mitchell	.15	.08	.05
394	Fran Healy	.15	.08	.05
395	Jim Wynn	.30	.15	.09
396	Bill Lee	.20	.10	.06
397	Tim Foli	.15	.08	.05
398	Dave Tomlin	.15	.08	.05
399	Luis Melendez	.15	.08	.05
400	Rod Carew	4.25	2.25	1.25
401	Ken Brett	.20	.10	.06
402	Don Money	.20	.10	.06
403	Geoff Zahn	.20	.10	.06
404	Enos Cabell	.20	.10	.06
405	Rollie Fingers	1.25	.60	.40
406	Ed Herrmann	.20	.10	.06
407	Tom Underwood	.15	.08	.05
408	Charlie Spikes	.15	.08	.05
409	Dave Lemanczyk	.15	.08	.05
410	Ralph Garr	.20	.10	.06
411	Bill Singer	.20	.10	.06
412	Toby Harrah	.25	.13	.08
413	Pete Varney	.15	.08	.05
414	Wayne Garland	.15	.08	.05
415	Vada Pinson	.50	.25	.15
416	Tommy John	1.25	.60	.40
417	Gene Clines	.15	.08	.05
418	Jose Morales	.15	.08	.05
419	Reggie Cleveland	.15	.08	.05
420	Joe Morgan	3.00	1.50	.90
421	A's Team	.80	.40	.25
422	Johnny Grubb	.15	.08	.05
423	Ed Halicki	.15	.08	.05
424	Phil Roof	.15	.08	.05
425	Rennie Stennett	.15	.08	.05
426	Bob Forsch	.25	.13	.08
427	Kurt Bevacqua	.15	.08	.05
428	Jim Crawford	.15	.08	.05
429	Fred Stanley	.20	.10	.06
430	Jose Cardenal	.20	.10	.06
431	Dick Ruthven	.15	.08	.05
432	Tom Veryzer	.15	.08	.05
433	Rick Waits	.15	.08	.05
434	Morris Nettles	.15	.08	.05
435	Phil Niekro	2.00	1.00	.60
436	Bill Fahey	.15	.08	.05
437	Terry Forster	.25	.13	.08
438	Doug DeCinces	.50	.25	.15
439	Rick Rhoden	.60	.30	.20
440	John Mayberry	.25	.13	.08
441	Gary Carter	12.00	6.00	3.50
442	Hank Webb	.15	.08	.05
443	Giants Team	.80	.40	.25
444	Gary Nolan	.15	.08	.05
445	Rico Petrocelli	.25	.13	.08
446	Larry Haney	.15	.08	.05
447	Gene Locklear	.15	.08	.05
448	Tom Johnson	.15	.08	.05
449	Bob Robertson	.15	.08	.05
450	Jim Palmer	3.50	1.75	1.00
451	Buddy Bradford	.15	.08	.05
452	Tom Hausman	.15	.08	.05
453	Lou Piniella	.60	.30	.20
454	Tom Griffin	.15	.08	.05
455	Dick Allen	.50	.25	.15
456	Joe Coleman	.20	.10	.06
457	Ed Crosby	.15	.08	.05
458	Earl Williams	.15	.08	.05
459	Jim Brewer	.15	.08	.05
460	Cesar Cedeno	.30	.15	.09
461	NL & AL Championships	.80	.40	.25
462	1975 World Series	.80	.40	.25
463	Steve Hargan	.15	.08	.05
464	Ken Henderson	.15	.08	.05
465	Mike Marshall	.30	.15	.09
466	Bob Stinson	.15	.08	.05
467	Woodie Fryman	.20	.10	.06
468	Jesus Alou	.20	.10	.06
469	Rawly Eastwick	.15	.08	.05
470	Bobby Murcer	.35	.20	.11
471	Jim Burton	.15	.08	.05
472	Bob Davis	.15	.08	.05
473	Paul Blair	.20	.10	.06
474	Ray Corbin	.15	.08	.05
475	Joe Rudi	.30	.15	.09
476	Bob Moose	.15	.08	.05
477	Indians Team (Frank Robinson)	.80	.40	.25
478	Lynn McGlothen	.15	.08	.05
479	Bobby Mitchell	.15	.08	.05
480	Mike Schmidt	12.00	6.00	3.50
481	Rudy May	.20	.10	.06
482	Tim Hosley	.15	.08	.05
483	Mickey Stanley	.20	.10	.06
484	Eric Raich	.15	.08	.05
485	Mike Hargrove	.20	.10	.06
486	Bruce Dal Canton	.15	.08	.05
487	Leron Lee	.15	.08	.05
488	Claude Osteen	.20	.10	.06
489	Skip Jutze	.15	.08	.05
490	Frank Tanana	.30	.15	.09
491	Terry Crowley	.15	.08	.05
492	Marty Pattin	.15	.08	.05
493	Derrel Thomas	.15	.08	.05
494	Craig Swan	.15	.08	.05
495	Nate Colbert	.15	.08	.05
496	Juan Beniquez	.20	.10	.06
497	Joe McIntosh	.15	.08	.05
498	Glenn Borgmann	.15	.08	.05
499	Mario Guerrero	.15	.08	.05
500	Reggie Jackson	7.00	3.50	2.00

		NR MT	EX	VG
501	Billy Champion	.15	.08	.05
502	Tim McCarver	.50	.25	.15
503	Elliott Maddox	.20	.10	.06
504	Pirates Team (Danny Murtaugh)	.80	.40	.25
505	Mark Belanger	.20	.10	.06
506	George Mitterwald	.15	.08	.05
507	Ray Bare	.15	.08	.05
508	Duane Kuiper	.20	.10	.06
509	Bill Hands	.15	.08	.05
510	Amos Otis	.25	.13	.08
511	Jamie Easterly	.15	.08	.05
512	Ellie Rodriguez	.15	.08	.05
513	Bart Johnson	.15	.08	.05
514	Dan Driessen	.30	.15	.09
515	Steve Yeager	.15	.08	.05
516	Wayne Granger	.15	.08	.05
517	John Milner	.15	.08	.05
518	Doug Flynn	.20	.10	.06
519	Steve Brye	.15	.08	.05
520	Willie McCovey	2.50	1.25	.70
521	Jim Colborn	.15	.08	.05
522	Ted Sizemore	.15	.08	.05
523	Bob Montgomery	.15	.08	.05
524	Pete Falcone	.15	.08	.05
525	Billy Williams	2.00	1.00	.60
526	Checklist 397-528	1.50	.70	.45
527	Mike Anderson	.15	.08	.05
528	Dock Ellis	.20	.10	.06
529	Deron Johnson	.15	.08	.05
530	Don Sutton	1.50	.70	.45
531	Mets Team (Joe Frazier)	.90	.45	.25
532	Milt May	.15	.08	.05
533	Lee Richard	.15	.08	.05
534	Stan Bahnsen	.15	.08	.05
535	Dave Nelson	.15	.08	.05
536	Mike Thompson	.15	.08	.05
537	Tony Muser	.15	.08	.05
538	Pat Darcy	.15	.08	.05
539	John Balaz	.15	.08	.05
540	Bill Freehan	.25	.13	.08
541	Steve Mingori	.15	.08	.05
542	Keith Hernandez	6.00	3.00	1.75
543	Wayne Twitchell	.15	.08	.05
544	Pepe Frias	.15	.08	.05
545	Sparky Lyle	.35	.20	.11
546	Dave Rosello	.15	.08	.05
547	Roric Harrison	.15	.08	.05
548	Manny Mota	.25	.13	.08
549	Randy Tate	.15	.08	.05
550	Hank Aaron	7.00	3.50	2.00
551	Jerry DaVanon	.15	.08	.05
552	Terry Humphrey	.15	.08	.05
553	Randy Moffitt	.15	.08	.05
554	Ray Fosse	.15	.08	.05
555	Dyar Miller	.15	.08	.05
556	Twins Team (Gene Mauch)	.80	.40	.25
557	Dan Spillner	.15	.08	.05
558	Clarence Gaston	.15	.08	.05
559	Clyde Wright	.15	.08	.05
560	Jorge Orta	.15	.08	.05
561	Tom Carroll	.15	.08	.05
562	Adrian Garrett	.15	.08	.05
563	Larry Demery	.15	.08	.05
564	Bubble Gum Blowing Champ (Kurt Bevacqua)	.30	.15	.09
565	Tug McGraw	.35	.20	.11
566	Ken McMullen	.15	.08	.05
567	George Stone	.15	.08	.05
568	Rob Andrews	.15	.08	.05
569	Nelson Briles	.15	.08	.05
570	George Hendrick	.20	.10	.06
571	Don DeMola	.15	.08	.05
572	Rich Coggins	.20	.10	.06
573	Bill Travers	.15	.08	.05
574	Don Kessinger	.20	.10	.06
575	Dwight Evans	1.00	.50	.30
576	Maximino Leon	.15	.08	.05
577	Marc Hill	.15	.08	.05
578	Ted Kubiak	.15	.08	.05
579	Clay Kirby	.15	.08	.05
580	Bert Campaneris	.30	.15	.09
581	Cardinals Team (Red Schoendienst)	.80	.40	.25
582	Mike Kekich	.15	.08	.05
583	Tommy Helms	.15	.08	.05
584	Stan Wall	.15	.08	.05
585	Joe Torre	.50	.25	.15
586	Ron Schueler	.15	.08	.05

		NR MT	EX	VG
587	Leo Cardenas	.15	.08	.05
588	Kevin Kobel	.15	.08	.05
589	Rookie Pitchers (Santo Alcala, Mike Flanagan, Joe Pactwa, Pablo Torrealba)	1.50	.70	.45
590	Rookie Outfielders (Henry Cruz, Chet Lemon, Ellis Valentine, Terry Whitfield)	1.00	.50	.30
591	Rookie Pitchers (Steve Grilli, Craig Mitchell, Jose Sosa, George Throop)	.15	.08	.05
592	Rookie Infielders (Dave McKay, Willie Randolph, Jerry Royster, Roy Staiger)	2.75	1.50	.80
593	Rookie Pitchers (Larry Anderson, Ken Crosby, Mark Littell, Butch Metzger)	.25	.13	.08
594	Rookie Catchers & Outfielders (Andy Merchant, Ed Ott, Royle Stillman, Jerry White)	.15	.08	.05
595	Rookie Pitchers (Steve Barr, Art DeFilippis, Randy Lerch, Sid Monge)	.15	.08	.05
596	Rookie Infielders (Lamar Johnson, Johnny LeMaster, Jerry Manuel, Craig Reynolds)	.35	.20	.11
597	Rookie Pitchers (Don Aase, Jack Kucek, Frank LaCorte, Mike Pazik)	.50	.25	.15
598	Rookie Outfielders (Hector Cruz, Jamie Quirk, Jerry Turner, Joe Wallis)	.20	.10	.06
599	Rookie Pitchers (Rob Dressler, Ron Guidry, Bob McClure, Pat Zachry)	12.00	6.00	3.50
600	Tom Seaver	4.00	2.00	1.25
601	Ken Rudolph	.15	.08	.05
602	Doug Konieczny	.15	.08	.05
603	Jim Holt	.15	.08	.05
604	Joe Lovitto	.15	.08	.05
605	Al Downing	.20	.10	.06
606	Brewers Team (Alex Grammas)	.80	.40	.25
607	Rich Hinton	.15	.08	.05
608	Vic Correll	.15	.08	.05
609	Fred Norman	.15	.08	.05
610	Greg Luzinski	.40	.20	.12
611	Rich Folkers	.15	.08	.05
612	Joe Lahoud	.15	.08	.05
613	Tim Johnson	.15	.08	.05
614	Fernando Arroyo	.15	.08	.05
615	Mike Cubbage	.15	.08	.05
616	Buck Martinez	.15	.08	.05
617	Darold Knowles	.15	.08	.05
618	Jack Brohamer	.15	.08	.05
619	Bill Butler	.15	.08	.05
620	Al Oliver	.70	.35	.20
621	Tom Hall	.15	.08	.05
622	Rick Auerbach	.15	.08	.05
623	Bob Allietta	.15	.08	.05
624	Tony Taylor	.15	.08	.05
625	J.R. Richard	.25	.13	.08
626	Bob Sheldon	.15	.08	.05
627	Bill Plummer	.15	.08	.05
628	John D'Acquisto	.15	.08	.05
629	Sandy Alomar	.20	.10	.06
630	Chris Speier	.20	.10	.06
631	Braves Team (Dave Bristol)	.80	.40	.25
632	Rogelio Moret	.15	.08	.05
633	John Stearns	.30	.15	.09
634	Larry Christenson	.15	.08	.05
635	Jim Fregosi	.25	.13	.08
636	Joe Decker	.15	.08	.05
637	Bruce Bochte	.20	.10	.06
638	Doyle Alexander	.30	.15	.09
639	Fred Kendall	.15	.08	.05
640	Bill Madlock	1.25	.60	.40
641	Tom Paciorek	.20	.10	.06
642	Dennis Blair	.15	.08	.05
643	Checklist 529-660	1.50	.70	.45
644	Tom Bradley	.15	.08	.05
645	Darrell Porter	.20	.10	.06
646	John Lowenstein	.15	.08	.05
648	Al Cowens	.20	.10	.06
649	Dave Roberts	.15	.08	.05
650	Thurman Munson	4.25	2.25	1.25
651	John Odom	.20	.10	.06
652	Ed Armbrister	.15	.08	.05
653	Mike Norris	.30	.15	.09
654	Doug Griffin	.15	.08	.05
655	Mike Vail	.15	.08	.05
656	White Sox Team (Chuck Tanner)	.80	.40	.25
657	Roy Smalley	.60	.30	.20
658	Jerry Johnson	.15	.08	.05
659	Ben Oglivie	.25	.13	.08
660	Dave Lopes	.90	.13	.08

1976 Topps Traded

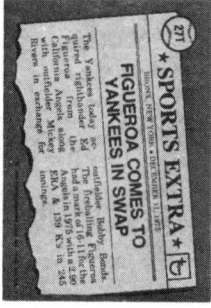

1977 Topps

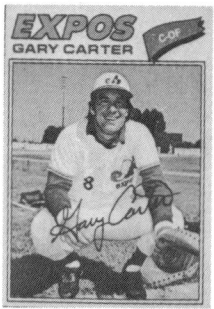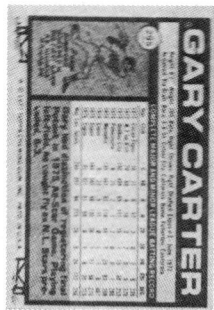

Similar to the Topps Traded set of 1974, the 2½" by 3½" cards featured photos of players traded after the printing deadline. The style of the cards is essentially the same as the regular issue but with a large "Sports Extra" headline announcing the trade and its date. The backs continue in newspaper style to detail the specifics of the trade. There were 43 player cards and one checklist in the set. Numbers remain same as the player's regular card, with the addition of a "T" suffix.

The 1977 Topps Set was a 660-card effort featuring front designs dominated by a color photograph on which there was a facsimile autograph. Above the picture were the player's name, team and position. The backs of the 2½" by 3½" cards included personal and career statistics along with newspaper style highlights and a cartoon. Specialty cards included statistical leaders, record performances, a new "Turn Back The Clock" feature which highlighted great past moments and a "Big League Brothers" feature.

		NR MT	EX	VG
Complete Set:		8.00	4.00	2.50
Common Player:		.15	.08	.05
27T	Ed Figueroa	.20	.10	.06
28T	Dusty Baker	.35	.20	.11
44T	Doug Rader	.15	.08	.05
58T	Ron Reed	.20	.10	.06
74T	Oscar Gamble	.25	.13	.08
80T	Jim Kaat	.60	.30	.20
83T	Jim Spencer	.15	.08	.05
85T	Mickey Rivers	.30	.15	.09
99T	Lee Lacy	.20	.10	.06
120T	Rusty Staub	.50	.25	.15
127T	Larvell Blanks	.15	.08	.05
146T	George Medich	.15	.08	.05
158T	Ken Reitz	.15	.08	.05
208T	Mike Lum	.15	.08	.05
211T	Clay Carroll	.20	.10	.06
231T	Tom House	.15	.08	.05
250T	Fergie Jenkins	.70	.35	.20
259T	Darrel Chaney	.15	.08	.05
292T	Leon Roberts	.15	.08	.05
296T	Pat Dobson	.20	.10	.06
309T	Bill Melton	.20	.10	.06
338T	Bob Bailey	.15	.08	.05
380T	Bobby Bonds	.35	.20	.11
383T	John Ellis	.15	.08	.05
385T	Mickey Lolich	.50	.25	.15
401T	Ken Brett	.20	.10	.06
410T	Ralph Garr	.20	.10	.06
411T	Bill Singer	.20	.10	.06
428T	Jim Crawford	.15	.08	.05
434T	Morris Nettles	.15	.08	.05
464T	Ken Henderson	.15	.08	.05
497T	Joe McIntosh	.15	.08	.05
524T	Pete Falcone	.15	.08	.05
527T	Mike Anderson	.15	.08	.05
528T	Dock Ellis	.20	.10	.06
532T	Milt May	.15	.08	.05
554T	Ray Fosse	.15	.08	.05
579T	Clay Kirby	.15	.08	.05
583T	Tommy Helms	.15	.08	.05
592T	Willie Randolph	.80	.40	.25
618T	Jack Brohamer	.15	.08	.05
632T	Rogelio Moret	.15	.08	.05
649T	Dave Roberts	.15	.08	.05
---	Traded Checklist	.80	.40	.25

Definitions for grading conditions are located in the Introduction of this price guide.

		NR MT	EX	VG
Complete Set:		250.00	110.00	60.00
Common Player:		.15	.08	.05
1	Batting Leaders (George Brett, Bill Madlock)	2.50	.70	.45
2	Home Run Leaders (Graig Nettles, Mike Schmidt)	1.25	.60	.40
3	Runs Batted In Leaders (George Foster, Lee May)	.50	.25	.15
4	Stolen Base Leaders (Dave Lopes, Bill North)	.30	.15	.09
5	Victory Leaders (Randy Jones, Jim Palmer)	.80	.40	.25
6	Strikeout Leaders (Nolan Ryan, Tom Seaver)	1.50	.70	.45
7	Earned Run Avg. Ldrs. (John Denny, Mark Fidrych)	.35	.20	.11
8	Leading Firemen (Bill Campbell, Rawly Eastwick)	.30	.15	.09
9	Doug Rader	.15	.08	.05
10	Reggie Jackson	7.00	3.50	2.00
11	Rob Dressler	.15	.08	.05
12	Larry Haney	.15	.08	.05
13	Luis Gomez	.15	.08	.05
14	Tommy Smith	.15	.08	.05
15	Don Gullett	.20	.10	.06
16	Bob Jones	.15	.08	.05
17	Steve Stone	.25	.13	.08
18	Indians Team (Frank Robinson)	.80	.40	.25
19	John D'Acquisto	.15	.08	.05
20	Graig Nettles	.90	.45	.25
21	Ken Forsch	.20	.10	.06
22	Bill Freehan	.25	.13	.08
23	Dan Driessen	.25	.13	.08
24	Carl Morton	.15	.08	.05
25	Dwight Evans	.90	.45	.25
26	Ray Sadecki	.15	.08	.05
27	Bill Buckner	.35	.20	.11
28	Woodie Fryman	.20	.10	.06
29	Bucky Dent	.25	.13	.08
30	Greg Luzinski	.40	.20	.12
31	Jim Todd	.15	.08	.05
32	Checklist 1-132	1.25	.60	.40
33	Wayne Garland	.15	.08	.05
34	Angels Team (Norm Sherry)	.70	.35	.20
35	Rennie Stennett	.15	.08	.05
36	John Ellis	.15	.08	.05
37	Steve Hargan	.15	.08	.05
38	Craig Kusick	.15	.08	.05
39	Tom Griffin	.15	.08	.05
40	Bobby Murcer	.30	.15	.09
41	Jim Kern	.15	.08	.05
42	Jose Cruz	.30	.15	.09
43	Ray Bare	.15	.08	.05
44	Bud Harrelson	.20	.10	.06

		NR MT	EX	VG
45	Rawly Eastwick	.15	.08	.05
46	Buck Martinez	.15	.08	.05
47	Lynn McGlothen	.15	.08	.05
48	Tom Paciorek	.20	.10	.06
49	Grant Jackson	.15	.08	.05
50	Ron Cey	.35	.20	.11
51	Brewers Team (Alex Grammas)	.70	.35	.20
52	Ellis Valentine	.20	.10	.06
53	Paul Mitchell	.15	.08	.05
54	Sandy Alomar	.20	.10	.06
55	Jeff Burroughs	.25	.13	.08
56	Rudy May	.20	.10	.06
57	Marc Hill	.15	.08	.05
58	Chet Lemon	.30	.15	.09
59	Larry Christenson	.15	.08	.05
60	Jim Rice	6.50	3.25	2.00
61	Manny Sanguillen	.15	.08	.05
62	Eric Raich	.15	.08	.05
63	Tito Fuentes	.15	.08	.05
64	Larry Biittner	.15	.08	.05
65	Skip Lockwood	.15	.08	.05
66	Roy Smalley	.25	.13	.08
67	Joaquin Andujar	.90	.45	.25
68	Bruce Bochte	.20	.10	.06
69	Jim Crawford	.15	.08	.05
70	Johnny Bench	3.50	1.75	1.00
71	Dock Ellis	.20	.10	.06
72	Mike Anderson	.15	.08	.05
73	Charlie Williams	.15	.08	.05
74	A's Team (Jack McKeon)	.70	.35	.20
75	Dennis Leonard	.20	.10	.06
76	Tim Foli	.15	.08	.05
77	Dyar Miller	.15	.08	.05
78	Bob Davis	.15	.08	.05
79	Don Money	.20	.10	.06
80	Andy Messersmith	.25	.13	.08
81	Juan Beniquez	.20	.10	.06
82	Jim Rooker	.15	.08	.05
83	Kevin Bell	.15	.08	.05
84	Ollie Brown	.15	.08	.05
85	Duane Kuiper	.15	.08	.05
86	Pat Zachry	.15	.08	.05
87	Glenn Borgmann	.15	.08	.05
88	Stan Wall	.15	.08	.05
89	Butch Hobson	.25	.13	.08
90	Cesar Cedeno	.30	.15	.09
91	John Verhoeven	.15	.08	.05
92	Dave Rosello	.15	.08	.05
93	Tom Poquette	.15	.08	.05
94	Craig Swan	.15	.08	.05
95	Keith Hernandez	3.00	1.50	.90
96	Lou Piniella	.40	.20	.12
97	Dave Heaverlo	.15	.08	.05
98	Milt May	.15	.08	.05
99	Tom Hausman	.15	.08	.05
100	Joe Morgan	1.50	.70	.45
101	Dick Bosman	.15	.08	.05
102	Jose Morales	.15	.08	.05
103	Mike Bacsik	.15	.08	.05
104	Omar Moreno	.30	.15	.09
105	Steve Yeager	.15	.08	.05
106	Mike Flanagan	.35	.20	.11
107	Bill Melton	.20	.10	.06
108	Alan Foster	.15	.08	.05
109	Jorge Orta	.15	.08	.05
110	Steve Carlton	4.25	2.25	1.25
111	Rico Petrocelli	.25	.13	.08
112	Bill Greif	.15	.08	.05
113	Blue Jays Mgr./Coaches (Roy Hartsfield, Don Leppert, Bob Miller, Jackie Moore, Harry Warner)	.25	.13	.08
114	Bruce Dal Canton	.15	.08	.05
115	Rick Manning	.20	.10	.06
116	Joe Niekro	.30	.15	.09
117	Frank White	.25	.13	.08
118	Rick Jones	.15	.08	.05
119	John Stearns	.20	.10	.06
120	Rod Carew	4.00	2.00	1.25
121	Gary Nolan	.15	.08	.05
122	Ben Oglivie	.20	.10	.06
123	Fred Stanley	.20	.10	.06
124	George Mitterwald	.15	.08	.05
125	Bill Travers	.15	.08	.05
126	Rod Gilbreath	.15	.08	.05
127	Ron Fairly	.25	.13	.08
128	Tommy John	1.25	.60	.40
129	Mike Sadek	.15	.08	.05
130	Al Oliver	.60	.30	.20
131	Orlando Ramirez	.15	.08	.05
132	Chip Lang	.15	.08	.05
133	Ralph Garr	.20	.10	.06

		NR MT	EX	VG
134	Padres Team (John McNamara)	.70	.35	.20
135	Mark Belanger	.20	.10	.06
136	Jerry Mumphrey	.70	.35	.20
137	Jeff Terpko	.15	.08	.05
138	Bob Stinson	.15	.08	.05
139	Fred Norman	.15	.08	.05
140	Mike Schmidt	8.50	4.25	2.50
141	Mark Littell	.15	.08	.05
142	Steve Dillard	.15	.08	.05
143	Ed Herrmann	.15	.08	.05
144	Bruce Sutter	2.00	1.00	.60
145	Tom Veryzer	.15	.08	.05
146	Dusty Baker	.25	.13	.08
147	Jackie Brown	.15	.08	.05
148	Fran Healy	.20	.10	.06
149	Mike Cubbage	.15	.08	.05
150	Tom Seaver	3.50	1.75	1.00
151	Johnnie LeMaster	.15	.08	.05
152	Gaylord Perry	1.75	.90	.50
153	Ron Jackson	.15	.08	.05
154	Dave Giusti	.15	.08	.05
155	Joe Rudi	.25	.13	.08
156	Pete Mackanin	.15	.08	.05
157	Ken Brett	.20	.10	.06
158	Ted Kubiak	.15	.08	.05
159	Bernie Carbo	.15	.08	.05
160	Will McEnaney	.15	.08	.05
161	Garry Templeton	1.00	.50	.30
162	Mike Cuellar	.25	.13	.08
163	Dave Hilton	.15	.08	.05
164	Tug McGraw	.35	.20	.11
165	Jim Wynn	.25	.13	.08
166	Bill Campbell	.15	.08	.05
167	Rich Hebner	.20	.10	.06
168	Charlie Spikes	.15	.08	.05
169	Darold Knowles	.15	.08	.05
170	Thurman Munson	3.25	1.75	1.00
171	Ken Sanders	.15	.08	.05
172	John Milner	.15	.08	.05
173	Chuck Scrivener	.15	.08	.05
174	Nelson Briles	.15	.08	.05
175	Butch Wynegar	.60	.30	.20
176	Bob Robertson	.15	.08	.05
177	Bart Johnson	.15	.08	.05
178	Bombo Rivera	.15	.08	.05
179	Paul Hartzell	.15	.08	.05
180	Dave Lopes	.25	.13	.08
181	Ken McMullen	.15	.08	.05
182	Dan Spillner	.15	.08	.05
183	Cardinals Team (Vern Rapp)	.70	.35	.20
184	Bo McLaughlin	.15	.08	.05
185	Sixto Lezcano	.20	.10	.06
186	Doug Flynn	.15	.08	.05
187	Dick Pole	.15	.08	.05
188	Bob Tolan	.20	.10	.06
189	Rick Dempsey	.20	.10	.06
190	Ray Burris	.15	.08	.05
191	Doug Griffin	.15	.08	.05
192	Clarence Gaston	.15	.08	.05
193	Larry Gura	.20	.10	.06
194	Gary Matthews	.25	.13	.08
195	Ed Figueroa	.20	.10	.06
196	Len Randle	.15	.08	.05
197	Ed Ott	.15	.08	.05
198	Wilbur Wood	.20	.10	.06
199	Pepe Frias	.15	.08	.05
200	Frank Tanana	.30	.15	.09
201	Ed Kranepool	.25	.13	.08
202	Tom Johnson	.15	.08	.05
203	Ed Armbrister	.15	.08	.05
204	Jeff Newman	.15	.08	.05
205	Pete Falcone	.15	.08	.05
206	Boog Powell	.50	.25	.15
207	Glenn Abbott	.15	.08	.05
208	Checklist 133-264	1.25	.60	.40
209	Rob Andrews	.15	.08	.05
210	Fred Lynn	1.50	.70	.45
211	Giants Team (Joe Altobelli)	.70	.35	.20
212	Jim Mason	.15	.08	.05
213	Maximino Leon	.15	.08	.05
214	Darrell Porter	.20	.10	.06
215	Butch Metzger	.15	.08	.05
216	Doug DeCinces	.25	.13	.08
217	Tom Underwood	.15	.08	.05
218	John Wathan	.60	.30	.20
219	Joe Coleman	.20	.10	.06
220	Chris Chambliss	.30	.15	.09
221	Bob Bailey	.15	.08	.05
222	Francisco Barrios	.15	.08	.05
223	Earl Williams	.15	.08	.05
224	Rusty Torres	.15	.08	.05

		NR MT	EX	VG
225	Bob Apodaca	.15	.08	.05
226	Leroy Stanton	.15	.08	.05
227	Joe Sambito	.35	.20	.11
228	Twins Team (Gene Mauch)	.80	.40	.25
229	Don Kessinger	.20	.10	.06
230	Vida Blue	.40	.20	.12
231	Record Breaker (George Brett)	1.75	.90	.50
232	Record Breaker (Minnie Minoso)	.35	.20	.11
233	Record Breaker (Jose Morales)	.20	.10	.06
234	Record Breaker (Nolan Ryan)	1.25	.60	.40
235	Cecil Cooper	.60	.30	.20
236	Tom Buskey	.15	.08	.05
237	Gene Clines	.15	.08	.05
238	Tippy Martinez	.20	.10	.06
239	Bill Plummer	.15	.08	.05
240	Ron LeFlore	.25	.13	.08
241	Dave Tomlin	.15	.08	.05
242	Ken Henderson	.15	.08	.05
243	Ron Reed	.20	.10	.06
244	John Mayberry	.20	.10	.06
245	Rick Rhoden	.30	.15	.09
246	Mike Vail	.15	.08	.05
247	Chris Knapp	.15	.08	.05
248	Wilbur Howard	.15	.08	.05
249	Pete Redfern	.15	.08	.05
250	Bill Madlock	.60	.30	.20
251	Tony Muser	.15	.08	.05
252	Dale Murray	.15	.08	.05
253	John Hale	.15	.08	.05
254	Doyle Alexander	.30	.15	.09
255	George Scott	.20	.10	.06
256	Joe Hoerner	.15	.08	.05
257	Mike Miley	.15	.08	.05
258	Luis Tiant	.35	.20	.11
259	Mets Team (Joe Frazier)	.80	.40	.25
260	J.R. Richard	.25	.13	.08
261	Phil Garner	.20	.10	.06
262	Al Cowens	.20	.10	.06
263	Mike Marshall	.25	.13	.08
264	Tom Hutton	.15	.08	.05
265	Mark Fidrych	.50	.25	.15
266	Derrel Thomas	.15	.08	.05
267	Ray Fosse	.15	.08	.05
268	Rick Sawyer	.15	.08	.05
269	Joe Lis	.15	.08	.05
270	Dave Parker	2.50	1.25	.70
271	Terry Forster	.20	.10	.06
272	Lee Lacy	.20	.10	.06
273	Eric Soderholm	.15	.08	.05
274	Don Stanhouse	.15	.08	.05
275	Mike Hargrove	.20	.10	.06
276	A.L. Championship (Chambliss' Dramatic Homer Decides It)	.70	.35	.20
277	N.L. Championship (Reds Sweep Phillies 3 In Row)	.70	.35	.20
278	Danny Frisella	.15	.08	.05
279	Joe Wallis	.15	.08	.05
280	Jim Hunter	2.00	1.00	.60
281	Roy Staiger	.15	.08	.05
282	Sid Monge	.15	.08	.05
283	Jerry DaVanon	.15	.08	.05
284	Mike Norris	.20	.10	.06
285	Brooks Robinson	2.50	1.25	.70
286	Johnny Grubb	.15	.08	.05
287	Reds Team (Sparky Anderson)	.80	.40	.25
288	Bob Montgomery	.15	.08	.05
289	Gene Garber	.20	.10	.06
290	Amos Otis	.20	.10	.06
291	Jason Thompson	.35	.20	.11
292	Rogelio Moret	.15	.08	.05
293	Jack Brohamer	.15	.08	.05
294	George Medich	.15	.08	.05
295	Gary Carter	6.25	3.25	2.00
296	Don Hood	.15	.08	.05
297	Ken Reitz	.15	.08	.05
298	Charlie Hough	.20	.10	.06
299	Otto Velez	.15	.08	.05
300	Jerry Koosman	.30	.15	.09
301	Toby Harrah	.20	.10	.06
302	Mike Garman	.15	.08	.05
303	Gene Tenace	.20	.10	.06
304	Jim Hughes	.15	.08	.05
305	Mickey Rivers	.25	.13	.08
306	Rick Waits	.15	.08	.05
307	Gary Sutherland	.15	.08	.05
308	Gene Pentz	.15	.08	.05
309	Red Sox Team (Don Zimmer)	.80	.40	.25
310	Larry Bowa	.30	.15	.09
311	Vern Ruhle	.15	.08	.05
312	Rob Belloir	.15	.08	.05
313	Paul Blair	.20	.10	.06

		NR MT	EX	VG
314	Steve Mingori	.15	.08	.05
315	Dave Chalk	.15	.08	.05
316	Steve Rogers	.20	.10	.06
317	Kurt Bevacqua	.15	.08	.05
318	Duffy Dyer	.15	.08	.05
319	Rich Gossage	.90	.45	.25
320	Ken Griffey	.30	.15	.09
321	Dave Goltz	.20	.10	.06
322	Bill Russell	.20	.10	.06
323	Larry Lintz	.15	.08	.05
324	John Curtis	.15	.08	.05
325	Mike Ivie	.15	.08	.05
326	Jesse Jefferson	.15	.08	.05
327	Astros Team (Bill Virdon)	.70	.35	.20
328	Tommy Boggs	.15	.08	.05
329	Ron Hodges	.15	.08	.05
330	George Hendrick	.20	.10	.06
331	Jim Colborn	.15	.08	.05
332	Elliott Maddox	.20	.10	.06
333	Paul Reuschel	.15	.08	.05
334	Bill Stein	.15	.08	.05
335	Bill Robinson	.15	.08	.05
336	Denny Doyle	.15	.08	.05
337	Ron Schueler	.15	.08	.05
338	Dave Duncan	.15	.08	.05
339	Adrian Devine	.15	.08	.05
340	Hal McRae	.30	.15	.09
341	Joe Kerrigan	.15	.08	.05
342	Jerry Remy	.15	.08	.05
343	Ed Halicki	.15	.08	.05
344	Brian Downing	.20	.10	.06
345	Reggie Smith	.25	.13	.08
346	Bill Singer	.20	.10	.06
347	George Foster	1.25	.60	.40
348	Brent Strom	.15	.08	.05
349	Jim Holt	.15	.08	.05
350	Larry Dierker	.20	.10	.06
351	Jim Sundberg	.20	.10	.06
352	Mike Phillips	.15	.08	.05
353	Stan Thomas	.15	.08	.05
354	Pirates Team (Chuck Tanner)	.80	.40	.25
355	Lou Brock	2.25	1.25	.70
356	Checklist 265-396	1.25	.60	.40
357	Tim McCarver	.40	.20	.12
358	Tom House	.15	.08	.05
359	Willie Randolph	.80	.40	.25
360	Rick Monday	.25	.13	.08
361	Eduardo Rodriguez	.15	.08	.05
362	Tommy Davis	.30	.15	.09
363	Dave Roberts	.15	.08	.05
364	Vic Correll	.15	.08	.05
365	Mike Torrez	.20	.10	.06
366	Ted Sizemore	.15	.08	.05
367	Dave Hamilton	.15	.08	.05
368	Mike Jorgensen	.15	.08	.05
369	Terry Humphrey	.15	.08	.05
370	John Montefusco	.20	.10	.06
371	Royals Team (Whitey Herzog)	.80	.40	.25
372	Rich Folkers	.15	.08	.05
373	Bert Campaneris	.30	.15	.09
374	Kent Tekulve	.30	.15	.09
375	Larry Hisle	.20	.10	.06
376	Nino Espinosa	.15	.08	.05
377	Dave McKay	.15	.08	.05
378	Jim Umbarger	.15	.08	.05
379	Larry Cox	.15	.08	.05
380	Lee May	.25	.13	.08
381	Bob Forsch	.20	.10	.06
382	Charlie Moore	.15	.08	.05
383	Stan Bahnsen	.15	.08	.05
384	Darrel Chaney	.15	.08	.05
385	Dave LaRoche	.15	.08	.05
386	Manny Mota	.25	.13	.08
387	Yankees Team (Billy Martin)	1.25	.60	.40
388	Terry Harmon	.15	.08	.05
389	Ken Kravec	.15	.08	.05
390	Dave Winfield	3.25	1.75	1.00
391	Dan Warthen	.15	.08	.05
392	Phil Roof	.15	.08	.05
393	John Lowenstein	.15	.08	.05
394	Bill Laxton	.15	.08	.05
395	Manny Trillo	.20	.10	.06
396	Tom Murphy	.15	.08	.05
397	Larry Herndon	.50	.25	.15
398	Tom Burgmeier	.15	.08	.05
399	Bruce Boisclair	.15	.08	.05
400	Steve Garvey	3.25	1.75	1.00
401	Mickey Scott	.15	.08	.05
402	Tommy Helms	.15	.08	.05
403	Tom Grieve	.15	.08	.05
404	Eric Rasmussen	.15	.08	.05

		NR MT	EX	VG
405	Claudell Washington	.25	.13	.08
406	Tim Johnson	.15	.08	.05
407	Dave Freisleben	.15	.08	.05
408	Cesar Tovar	.20	.10	.06
409	Pete Broberg	.15	.08	.05
410	Willie Montanez	.15	.08	.05
411	World Series Games 1 & 2	.70	.35	.20
412	World Series Games 2 & 3	.70	.35	.20
413	World Series Summary	.70	.35	.20
414	Tommy Harper	.20	.10	.06
415	Jay Johnstone	.20	.10	.06
416	Chuck Hartenstein	.15	.08	.05
417	Wayne Garrett	.15	.08	.05
418	White Sox Team (Bob Lemon)	.80	.40	.25
419	Steve Swisher	.15	.08	.05
420	Rusty Staub	.35	.20	.11
421	Doug Rau	.15	.08	.05
422	Freddie Patek	.15	.08	.05
423	Gary Lavelle	.15	.08	.05
424	Steve Brye	.15	.08	.05
425	Joe Torre	.40	.20	.12
426	Dick Drago	.15	.08	.05
427	Dave Rader	.15	.08	.05
428	Rangers Team (Frank Lucchesi)	.70	.35	.20
429	Ken Boswell	.15	.08	.05
430	Fergie Jenkins	.80	.40	.25
431	Dave Collins	.25	.13	.08
432	Buzz Capra	.15	.08	.05
433	Turn Back The Clock (Nate Colbert)	.20	.10	.06
434	Turn Back The Clock (Carl Yastrzemski)	2.00	1.00	.60
435	Turn Back The Clock (Maury Wills)	.35	.20	.11
436	Turn Back The Clock (Bob Keegan)	.20	.10	.06
437	Turn Back The Clock (Ralph Kiner)	.50	.25	.15
438	Marty Perez	.15	.08	.05
439	Gorman Thomas	.30	.15	.09
440	Jon Matlack	.20	.10	.06
441	Larvell Blanks	.15	.08	.05
442	Braves Team (Dave Bristol)	.70	.35	.20
443	Lamar Johnson	.15	.08	.05
444	Wayne Twitchell	.15	.08	.05
445	Ken Singleton	.25	.13	.08
446	Bill Bonham	.15	.08	.05
447	Jerry Turner	.15	.08	.05
448	Ellie Rodriguez	.15	.08	.05
449	Al Fitzmorris	.15	.08	.05
450	Pete Rose	9.00	4.50	2.75
451	Checklist 397-528	1.25	.60	.40
452	Mike Caldwell	.15	.08	.05
453	Pedro Garcia	.15	.08	.05
454	Andy Etchebarren	.15	.08	.05
455	Rick Wise	.20	.10	.06
456	Leon Roberts	.15	.08	.05
457	Steve Luebber	.15	.08	.05
458	Leo Foster	.15	.08	.05
459	Steve Foucault	.15	.08	.05
460	Willie Stargell	2.50	1.25	.70
461	Dick Tidrow	.20	.10	.06
462	Don Baylor	.35	.20	.11
463	Jamie Quirk	.15	.08	.05
464	Randy Moffitt	.15	.08	.05
465	Rico Carty	.25	.13	.08
466	Fred Holdsworth	.15	.08	.05
467	Phillies Team (Danny Ozark)	.70	.35	.20
468	Ramon Hernandez	.15	.08	.05
469	Pat Kelly	.15	.08	.05
470	Ted Simmons	.60	.30	.20
471	Del Unser	.15	.08	.05
472	Rookie Pitchers (Don Aase, Bob McClure, Gil Patterson, Dave Wehrmeister)	.25	.13	.08
473	Rookie Outfielders (Andre Dawson, Gene Richards, John Scott, Denny Walling)	18.00	9.00	5.50
474	Rookie Shortstops (Bob Bailor, Kiko Garcia, Craig Reynolds, Alex Taveras)	.15	.08	.05
475	Rookie Pitchers (Chris Batton, Rick Camp, Scott McGregor, Manny Sarmiento)	.30	.15	.09
476	Rookie Catchers (Gary Alexander, Rick Cerone, Dale Murphy, Kevin Pasley)	65.00	32.00	19.50
477	Rookie Infielders (Doug Ault, Rich Dauer, Orlando Gonzalez, Phil Mankowski)	.25	.13	.08
478	Rookie Pitchers (Jim Gideon, Leon Hooten, Dave Johnson, Mark Lemongello)	.15	.08	.05
479	Rookie Outfielders (Brian Asselstine, Wayne Gross, Sam Mejias, Alvis Woods)	.25	.13	.08
480	Carl Yastrzemski	4.00	2.00	1.25
481	Roger Metzger	.15	.08	.05
482	Tony Solaita	.15	.08	.05
483	Richie Zisk	.20	.10	.06
484	Burt Hooton	.20	.10	.06
485	Roy White	.30	.15	.09
486	Ed Bane	.15	.08	.05
487	Rookie Pitchers (Larry Anderson, Ed Glynn, Joe Henderson, Greg Terlecky)	.15	.08	.05
488	Rookie Outfielders (Jack Clark, Ruppert Jones, Lee Mazzilli, Dan Thomas)	10.00	5.00	3.00
489	Rookie Pitchers (Len Barker, Randy Lerch, Greg Minton, Mike Overy)	.40	.20	.12
490	Rookie Shortstops (Billy Almon, Mickey Klutts, Tommy McMillan, Mark Wagner)	.25	.13	.08
491	Rookie Pitchers (Mike Dupree, Denny Martinez, Craig Mitchell, Bob Sykes)	.50	.25	.15
492	Rookie Outfielders (Tony Armas, Steve Kemp, Carlos Lopez, Gary Woods)	1.00	.50	.30
493	Rookie Pitchers (Mike Krukow, Jim Otten, Gary Wheelock, Mike Willis)	1.00	.50	.30
494	Rookie Infielders (Juan Bernhardt, Mike Champion, Jim Gantner, Bump Wills)	.50	.25	.15
495	Al Hrabosky	.20	.10	.06
496	Gary Thomasson	.15	.08	.05
497	Clay Carroll	.20	.10	.06
498	Sal Bando	.25	.13	.08
499	Pablo Torrealba	.15	.08	.05
500	Dave Kingman	.60	.30	.20
501	Jim Bibby	.15	.08	.05
502	Randy Hundley	.15	.08	.05
503	Bill Lee	.20	.10	.06
504	Dodgers Team (Tom Lasorda)	1.00	.50	.30
505	Oscar Gamble	.20	.10	.06
506	Steve Grilli	.15	.08	.05
507	Mike Hegan	.15	.08	.05
508	Dave Pagan	.15	.08	.05
509	Cookie Rojas	.15	.08	.05
510	John Candelaria	.60	.30	.20
511	Bill Fahey	.15	.08	.05
512	Jack Billingham	.15	.08	.05
513	Jerry Terrell	.15	.08	.05
514	Cliff Johnson	.15	.08	.05
515	Chris Speier	.15	.08	.05
516	Bake McBride	.15	.08	.05
517	Pete Vuckovich	.50	.25	.15
518	Cubs Team (Herman Franks)	.70	.35	.20
519	Don Kirkwood	.15	.08	.05
520	Garry Maddox	.20	.10	.06
521	Bob Grich	.25	.13	.08
522	Enzo Hernandez	.15	.08	.05
523	Rollie Fingers	1.00	.50	.30
524	Rowland Office	.15	.08	.05
525	Dennis Eckersley	.30	.15	.09
526	Larry Parrish	.40	.20	.12
527	Dan Meyer	.15	.08	.05
528	Bill Castro	.15	.08	.05
529	Jim Essian	.15	.08	.05
530	Rick Reuschel	.30	.15	.09
531	Lyman Bostock	.25	.13	.08
532	Jim Willoughby	.15	.08	.05
533	Mickey Stanley	.20	.10	.06
534	Paul Splittorff	.20	.10	.06
535	Cesar Geronimo	.20	.10	.06
536	Vic Albury	.15	.08	.05
537	Dave Roberts	.15	.08	.05
538	Frank Taveras	.15	.08	.05
539	Mike Wallace	.15	.08	.05
540	Bob Watson	.20	.10	.06
541	John Denny	.20	.10	.06
542	Frank Duffy	.15	.08	.05
543	Ron Blomberg	.20	.10	.06
544	Gary Ross	.15	.08	.05
545	Bob Boone	.25	.13	.08
546	Orioles Team (Earl Weaver)	.80	.40	.25
547	Willie McCovey	2.00	1.00	.60
548	Joel Youngblood	.30	.15	.09
549	Jerry Royster	.15	.08	.05
550	Randy Jones	.20	.10	.06
551	Bill North	.15	.08	.05
552	Pepe Mangual	.15	.08	.05
553	Jack Heidemann	.15	.08	.05
554	Bruce Kimm	.15	.08	.05
555	Dan Ford	.20	.10	.06
556	Doug Bird	.15	.08	.05
557	Jerry White	.15	.08	.05
558	Elias Sosa	.15	.08	.05
559	Alan Bannister	.15	.08	.05
560	Dave Concepcion	.35	.20	.11
561	Pete LaCock	.15	.08	.05
562	Checklist 529-660	1.25	.60	.40
563	Bruce Kison	.15	.08	.05

		NR MT	EX	VG
564	Alan Ashby	.20	.10	.06
565	Mickey Lolich	.40	.20	.12
566	Rick Miller	.15	.08	.05
567	Enos Cabell	.20	.10	.06
568	Carlos May	.20	.10	.06
569	Jim Lonborg	.20	.10	.06
570	Bobby Bonds	.35	.20	.11
571	Darrell Evans	.40	.20	.12
572	Ross Grimsley	.20	.10	.06
573	Joe Ferguson	.15	.08	.05
574	Aurelio Rodriguez	.20	.10	.06
575	Dick Ruthven	.15	.08	.05
576	Fred Kendall	.15	.08	.05
577	Jerry Augustine	.15	.08	.05
578	Bob Randall	.15	.08	.05
579	Don Carrithers	.15	.08	.05
580	George Brett	7.50	3.75	2.25
581	Pedro Borbon	.15	.08	.05
582	Ed Kirkpatrick	.15	.08	.05
583	Paul Lindblad	.15	.08	.05
584	Ed Goodson	.15	.08	.05
585	Rick Burleson	.20	.10	.06
586	Steve Renko	.15	.08	.05
587	Rick Baldwin	.15	.08	.05
588	Dave Moates	.15	.08	.05
589	Mike Cosgrove	.15	.08	.05
590	Buddy Bell	.30	.15	.09
591	Chris Arnold	.15	.08	.05
592	Dan Briggs	.15	.08	.05
593	Dennis Blair	.15	.08	.05
594	Biff Pocoroba	.15	.08	.05
595	John Hiller	.20	.10	.06
596	Jerry Martin	.25	.13	.08
597	Mariners Mgr./Coaches (Don Bryant, Jim Busby, Darrell Johnson, Vada Pinson, Wes Stock)	.25	.13	.08
598	Sparky Lyle	.35	.20	.11
599	Mike Tyson	.15	.08	.05
600	Jim Palmer	2.25	1.25	.70
601	Mike Lum	.15	.08	.05
602	Andy Hassler	.15	.08	.05
603	Willie Davis	.25	.13	.08
604	Jim Slaton	.15	.08	.05
605	Felix Millan	.15	.08	.05
606	Steve Braun	.15	.08	.05
607	Larry Demery	.15	.08	.05
608	Roy Howell	.15	.08	.05
609	Jim Barr	.15	.08	.05
610	Jose Cardenal	.20	.10	.06
611	Dave Lemanczyk	.15	.08	.05
612	Barry Foote	.15	.08	.05
613	Reggie Cleveland	.15	.08	.05
614	Greg Gross	.15	.08	.05
615	Phil Niekro	1.50	.70	.45
616	Tommy Sandt	.15	.08	.05
617	Bobby Darwin	.15	.08	.05
618	Pat Dobson	.20	.10	.06
619	Johnny Oates	.15	.08	.05
620	Don Sutton	1.50	.70	.45
621	Tigers Team (Ralph Houk)	.80	.40	.25
622	Jim Wohlford	.15	.08	.05
623	Jack Kucek	.15	.08	.05
624	Hector Cruz	.15	.08	.05
625	Ken Holtzman	.25	.13	.08
626	Al Bumbry	.20	.10	.06
627	Bob Myrick	.15	.08	.05
628	Mario Guerrero	.15	.08	.05
629	Bobby Valentine	.25	.13	.08
630	Bert Blyleven	.80	.40	.25
631	Big League Brothers (George Brett, Ken Brett)	1.75	.90	.50
632	Big League Brothers (Bob Forsch, Ken Forsch)	.30	.15	.09
633	Big League Brothers (Carlos May, Lee May)	.30	.15	.09
634	Big League Brothers (Paul Reuschel, Rick Reuschel) (names switched)	.30	.15	.09
635	Robin Yount	4.00	2.00	1.25
636	Santo Alcala	.15	.08	.05
637	Alex Johnson	.15	.08	.05
638	Jim Kaat	.80	.40	.25
639	Jerry Morales	.15	.08	.05
640	Carlton Fisk	.90	.45	.25
641	Dan Larson	.15	.08	.05
642	Willie Crawford	.15	.08	.05
643	Mike Pazik	.15	.08	.05
644	Matt Alexander	.15	.08	.05
645	Jerry Reuss	.25	.13	.08
646	Andres Mora	.15	.08	.05
647	Expos Team (Dick Williams)	.80	.40	.25
648	Jim Spencer	.15	.08	.05

		NR MT	EX	VG
649	Dave Cash	.15	.08	.05
650	Nolan Ryan	3.50	1.75	1.00
651	Von Joshua	.15	.08	.05
652	Tom Walker	.15	.08	.05
653	Diego Segui	.15	.08	.05
654	Ron Pruitt	.15	.08	.05
655	Tony Perez	.80	.40	.25
656	Ron Guidry	3.00	1.50	.90
657	Mick Kelleher	.15	.08	.05
658	Marty Pattin	.15	.08	.05
659	Merv Rettenmund	.15	.08	.05
660	Willie Horton	.70	.13	.08

1977 Topps Cloth Stickers

 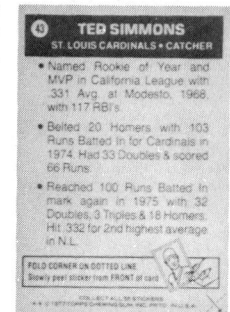

One of the few Topps specialty issues of the late 1970s, the 73-piece set of cloth stickers issued in 1977 included 55 player stickers — which exactly duplicated the players' regular-issue Topps cards of that year — and 18 puzzle cards which could be joined to form a photo of the American League or National League All-Star teams. Issued as a separate issue, the 2½'' by 3½'' stickers had a paper backing which could be removed to allow the cloth to be adhered to a jacket, notebook, etc.

		NR MT	EX	VG
	Complete Set:	50.00	25.00	15.00
	Common Player:	.20	.10	.06
1	Alan Ashby	.20	.10	.06
2	Buddy Bell	1.00	.50	.30
3	Johnny Bench	2.25	1.25	.70
4	Vida Blue	.50	.25	.15
5	Bert Blyleven	1.00	.50	.30
6	Steve Braun	.50	.25	.15
7	George Brett	3.50	1.75	1.00
8	Lou Brock	1.75	.90	.50
9	Jose Cardenal	.20	.10	.06
10	Rod Carew	3.50	1.75	1.00
11	Steve Carlton	2.25	1.25	.70
12	Dave Cash	.20	.10	.06
13	Cesar Cedeno	1.00	.50	.30
14	Ron Cey	.50	.25	.15
15	Mark Fidrych	.50	.25	.15
16	Dan Ford	.20	.10	.06
17	Wayne Garland	.20	.10	.06
18	Ralph Garr	.20	.10	.06
19	Steve Garvey	2.25	1.25	.70
20	Mike Hargrove	.20	.10	.06
21	Jim Hunter	1.25	.60	.40
22	Reggie Jackson	3.25	1.75	1.00
23	Randy Jones	.20	.10	.06
24	Dave Kingman	1.00	.50	.30
25	Bill Madlock	.70	.35	.20
26	Lee May	.50	.25	.15
27	John Mayberry	.20	.10	.06
28	Andy Messersmith	.20	.10	.06
29	Willie Montanez	.20	.10	.06
30	John Montefusco	.50	.25	.15
31	Joe Morgan	1.25	.60	.40
32	Thurman Munson	1.75	.90	.50
33	Bobby Murcer	.50	.25	.15
34	Al Oliver	1.25	.60	.40
35	Dave Pagan	.20	.10	.06
36	Jim Palmer	3.50	1.75	1.00

		NR MT	EX	VG
37	Tony Perez	.70	.35	.20
38	Pete Rose	10.00	5.00	3.00
39	Joe Rudi	.50	.25	.15
40	Nolan Ryan	3.50	1.75	1.00
41	Mike Schmidt	3.25	1.75	1.00
42	Tom Seaver	3.25	1.75	1.00
43	Ted Simmons	.70	.35	.20
44	Bill Singer	.20	.10	.06
45	Willie Stargell	1.50	.70	.45
46	Rusty Staub	.50	.25	.15
47	Don Sutton	1.25	.60	.40
48	Luis Tiant	.70	.35	.20
49	Bill Travers	.20	.10	.06
50	Claudell Washington	.50	.25	.15
51	Bob Watson	.20	.10	.06
52	Dave Winfield	3.00	1.50	.90
53	Carl Yastrzemski	4.50	2.25	1.25
54	Robin Yount	1.75	.90	.50
55	Richie Zisk	.20	.10	.06

1978 Topps

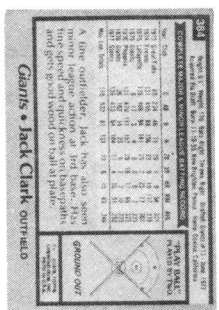

JACK CLARK

At 726 cards, this was the largest issue from Topps since 1972. In design, the color player photo is slightly larger than usual with the player's name and team at the bottom. In the upper right-hand corner of the 2½'' by 3½'' cards there is a small white baseball with the player's position. Most of the starting All-Stars from the previous year had a red, white and blue shield instead of the baseball. Backs feature statistics and a baseball situation which made a card game of baseball possible. Specialty cards include baseball records, statistical leaders and the World Series and Play-offs. As one row of cards per sheet had to be double-printed to accommodate the 726-card set size, some cards are more common, yet that seems to have no serious impact on their prices.

		NR MT	EX	VG
	Complete Set:	200.00	90.00	50.00
	Common Player:	.12	.06	.04
1	Record Breaker (Lou Brock)	2.00	.45	.25
2	Record Breaker (Sparky Lyle)	.25	.13	.08
3	Record Breaker (Willie McCovey)	.70	.35	.20
4	Record Breaker (Brooks Robinson)	.90	.45	.25
5	Record Breaker (Pete Rose)	2.00	1.00	.60
6	Record Breaker (Nolan Ryan)	1.00	.50	.30
7	Record Breaker (Reggie Jackson)	1.50	.70	.45
8	Mike Sadek	.12	.06	.04
9	Doug DeCinces	.25	.13	.08
10	Phil Niekro	1.25	.60	.40
11	Rick Manning	.12	.06	.04
12	Don Aase	.20	.10	.06
13	Art Howe	.12	.06	.04
14	Lerrin LaGrow	.12	.06	.04
15	Tony Perez	.25	.13	.08
16	Roy White	.25	.13	.08
17	Mike Krukow	.25	.13	.08
18	Bob Grich	.25	.13	.08
19	Darrell Porter	.20	.10	.06
20	Pete Rose	3.50	1.75	1.00
21	Steve Kemp	.25	.13	.08
22	Charlie Hough	.20	.10	.06
23	Bump Wills	.12	.06	.04

		NR MT	EX	VG
24	Don Money	.12	.06	.04
25	Jon Matlack	.20	.10	.06
26	Rich Hebner	.12	.06	.04
27	Geoff Zahn	.12	.06	.04
28	Ed Ott	.12	.06	.04
29	Bob Lacey	.12	.06	.04
30	George Hendrick	.20	.10	.06
31	Glenn Abbott	.12	.06	.04
32	Garry Templeton	.40	.20	.12
33	Dave Lemanczyk	.12	.06	.04
34	Willie McCovey	2.00	1.00	.60
35	Sparky Lyle	.30	.15	.09
36	Eddie Murray	35.00	17.50	10.50
37	Rick Waits	.12	.06	.04
38	Willie Montanez	.12	.06	.04
39	Floyd Bannister	.90	.45	.25
40	Carl Yastrzemski	3.00	1.50	.90
41	Burt Hooton	.20	.10	.06
42	Jorge Orta	.12	.06	.04
43	Bill Atkinson	.12	.06	.04
44	Toby Harrah	.20	.10	.06
45	Mark Fidrych	.25	.13	.08
46	Al Cowens	.12	.06	.04
47	Jack Billingham	.12	.06	.04
48	Don Baylor	.35	.20	.11
49	Ed Kranepool	.20	.10	.06
50	Rick Reuschel	.25	.13	.08
51	Charlie Moore	.12	.06	.04
52	Jim Lonborg	.20	.10	.06
53	Phil Garner	.12	.06	.04
54	Tom Johnson	.12	.06	.04
55	Mitchell Page	.12	.06	.04
56	Randy Jones	.20	.10	.06
57	Dan Meyer	.12	.06	.04
58	Bob Forsch	.20	.10	.06
59	Otto Velez	.12	.06	.04
60	Thurman Munson	2.25	1.25	.70
61	Larvell Blanks	.12	.06	.04
62	Jim Barr	.12	.06	.04
63	Don Zimmer	.20	.10	.06
64	Gene Pentz	.12	.06	.04
65	Ken Singleton	.25	.13	.08
66	White Sox Team	.50	.25	.15
67	Claudell Washington	.25	.13	.08
68	Steve Foucault	.12	.06	.04
69	Mike Vail	.12	.06	.04
70	Rich Gossage	.70	.35	.20
71	Terry Humphrey	.12	.06	.04
72	Andre Dawson	4.00	2.00	1.25
73	Andy Hassler	.12	.06	.04
74	Checklist 1-121	.90	.45	.25
75	Dick Ruthven	.12	.06	.04
76	Steve Ontiveros	.12	.06	.04
77	Ed Kirkpatrick	.12	.06	.04
78	Pablo Torrealba	.12	.06	.04
79	Darrell Johnson	.12	.06	.04
80	Ken Griffey	.25	.13	.08
81	Pete Redfern	.12	.06	.04
82	Giants Team	.50	.25	.15
83	Bob Montgomery	.12	.06	.04
84	Kent Tekulve	.25	.13	.08
85	Ron Fairly	.20	.10	.06
86	Dave Tomlin	.12	.06	.04
87	John Lowenstein	.12	.06	.04
88	Mike Phillips	.12	.06	.04
89	Ken Clay	.20	.10	.06
90	Larry Bowa	.30	.15	.09
91	Oscar Zamora	.12	.06	.04
92	Adrian Devine	.12	.06	.04
93	Bobby Cox	.12	.06	.04
94	Chuck Scrivener	.12	.06	.04
95	Jamie Quirk	.12	.06	.04
96	Orioles Team	.50	.25	.15
97	Stan Bahnsen	.12	.06	.04
98	Jim Essian	.12	.06	.04
99	Willie Hernandez	.80	.40	.25
100	George Brett	4.00	2.00	1.25
101	Sid Monge	.12	.06	.04
102	Matt Alexander	.12	.06	.04
103	Tom Murphy	.12	.06	.04
104	Lee Lacy	.20	.10	.06
105	Reggie Cleveland	.12	.06	.04
106	Bill Plummer	.12	.06	.04
107	Ed Halicki	.12	.06	.04
108	Von Joshua	.12	.06	.04
109	Joe Torre	.30	.15	.09
110	Richie Zisk	.20	.10	.06
111	Mike Tyson	.12	.06	.04
112	Astros Team	.50	.25	.15
113	Don Carrithers	.12	.06	.04
114	Paul Blair	.20	.10	.06

		NR MT	EX	VG
115	Gary Nolan	.12	.06	.04
116	Tucker Ashford	.12	.06	.04
117	John Montague	.12	.06	.04
118	Terry Harmon	.12	.06	.04
119	Denny Martinez	.25	.13	.08
120	Gary Carter	3.25	1.75	1.00
121	Alvis Woods	.12	.06	.04
122	Dennis Eckersley	.25	.13	.08
123	Manny Trillo	.20	.10	.06
124	Dave Rozema	.25	.13	.08
125	George Scott	.20	.10	.06
126	Paul Moskau	.12	.06	.04
127	Chet Lemon	.20	.10	.06
128	Bill Russell	.20	.10	.06
129	Jim Colborn	.12	.06	.04
130	Jeff Burroughs	.20	.10	.06
131	Bert Blyleven	.60	.30	.20
132	Enos Cabell	.20	.10	.06
133	Jerry Augustine	.12	.06	.04
134	Steve Henderson	.25	.13	.08
135	Ron Guidry	.90	.45	.25
136	Ted Sizemore	.12	.06	.04
137	Craig Kusick	.12	.06	.04
138	Larry Demery	.12	.06	.04
139	Wayne Gross	.12	.06	.04
140	Rollie Fingers	.70	.35	.20
141	Ruppert Jones	.20	.10	.06
142	John Montefusco	.20	.10	.06
143	Keith Hernandez	2.50	1.25	.70
144	Jesse Jefferson	.12	.06	.04
145	Rick Monday	.20	.10	.06
146	Doyle Alexander	.30	.15	.09
147	Lee Mazzilli	.25	.13	.08
148	Andre Thornton	.25	.13	.08
149	Dale Murray	.12	.06	.04
150	Bobby Bonds	.35	.20	.11
151	Milt Wilcox	.20	.10	.06
152	Ivan DeJesus	.20	.10	.06
153	Steve Stone	.25	.13	.08
154	Cecil Cooper	.20	.10	.06
155	Butch Hobson	.12	.06	.04
156	Andy Messersmith	.20	.10	.06
157	Pete LaCock	.12	.06	.04
158	Joaquin Andujar	.25	.13	.08
159	Lou Piniella	.35	.20	.11
160	Jim Palmer	2.00	1.00	.60
161	Bob Boone	.25	.13	.08
162	Paul Thormodsgard	.12	.06	.04
163	Bill North	.12	.06	.04
164	Bob Owchinko	.12	.06	.04
165	Rennie Stennett	.12	.06	.04
166	Carlos Lopez	.12	.06	.04
167	Tim Foli	.12	.06	.04
168	Reggie Smith	.25	.13	.08
169	Jerry Johnson	.12	.06	.04
170	Lou Brock	2.00	1.00	.60
171	Pat Zachry	.12	.06	.04
172	Mike Hargrove	.20	.10	.06
173	Robin Yount	2.75	1.50	.80
174	Wayne Garland	.12	.06	.04
175	Jerry Morales	.12	.06	.04
176	Milt May	.12	.06	.04
177	Gene Garber	.12	.06	.04
178	Dave Chalk	.12	.06	.04
179	Dick Tidrow	.20	.10	.06
180	Dave Concepcion	.35	.20	.11
181	Ken Forsch	.20	.10	.06
182	Jim Spencer	.12	.06	.04
183	Doug Bird	.12	.06	.04
184	Checklist 122-242	.90	.45	.25
185	Ellis Valentine	.20	.10	.06
186	Bob Stanley	.25	.13	.08
187	Jerry Royster	.12	.06	.04
188	Al Bumbry	.20	.10	.06
189	Tom Lasorda	.30	.15	.09
190	John Candelaria	.25	.13	.08
191	Rodney Scott	.12	.06	.04
192	Padres Team	.50	.25	.15
193	Rich Chiles	.12	.06	.04
194	Derrel Thomas	.12	.06	.04
195	Larry Dierker	.20	.10	.06
196	Bob Bailor	.12	.06	.04
197	Nino Espinosa	.12	.06	.04
198	Ron Pruitt	.12	.06	.04
199	Craig Reynolds	.12	.06	.04
200	Reggie Jackson	3.25	1.75	1.00
201	Batting Leaders (Rod Carew, Dave Parker)	.80	.40	.25
202	Home Run Leaders (George Foster, Jim Rice)	.30	.15	.09
203	Runs Batted In Ldrs. (George Foster, Larry Hisle)	.30	.15	.09
204	Stolen Base Leaders (Freddie Patek, Frank Taveras)	.12	.06	.04
205	Victory Leaders (Steve Carlton, Dave Goltz, Dennis Leonard, Jim Palmer)	.60	.30	.20
206	Strikeout Leaders (Phil Niekro, Nolan Ryan)	.35	.20	.11
207	Earned Run Avg. Ldrs. (John Candelaria, Frank Tanana)	.12	.06	.04
208	Leading Firemen (Bill Campbell, Rollie Fingers)	.35	.20	.11
209	Dock Ellis	.12	.06	.04
210	Jose Cardenal	.12	.06	.04
211	Earl Weaver	.20	.10	.06
212	Mike Caldwell	.12	.06	.04
213	Alan Bannister	.12	.06	.04
214	Angels Team	.50	.25	.15
215	Darrell Evans	.35	.20	.11
216	Mike Paxton	.12	.06	.04
217	Rod Gilbreath	.12	.06	.04
218	Marty Pattin	.12	.06	.04
219	Mike Cubbage	.12	.06	.04
220	Pedro Borbon	.12	.06	.04
221	Chris Speier	.20	.10	.06
222	Jerry Martin	.12	.06	.04
223	Bruce Kison	.12	.06	.04
224	Jerry Tabb	.12	.06	.04
225	Don Gullett	.12	.06	.04
226	Joe Ferguson	.12	.06	.04
227	Al Fitzmorris	.12	.06	.04
228	Manny Mota	.12	.06	.04
229	Leo Foster	.12	.06	.04
230	Al Hrabosky	.20	.10	.06
231	Wayne Nordhagen	.12	.06	.04
232	Mickey Stanley	.20	.10	.06
233	Dick Pole	.12	.06	.04
234	Herman Franks	.12	.06	.04
235	Tim McCarver	.35	.20	.11
236	Terry Whitfield	.12	.06	.04
237	Rich Dauer	.12	.06	.04
238	Juan Beniquez	.20	.10	.06
239	Dyar Miller	.12	.06	.04
240	Gene Tenace	.20	.10	.06
241	Pete Vuckovich	.20	.10	.06
242	Barry Bonnell	.12	.06	.04
243	Bob McClure	.12	.06	.04
244	Expos Team	.20	.10	.06
245	Rick Burleson	.20	.10	.06
246	Dan Driessen	.25	.13	.08
247	Larry Christenson	.12	.06	.04
248	Frank White	.12	.06	.04
249	Dave Goltz	.12	.06	.04
250	Graig Nettles	.30	.15	.09
251	Don Kirkwood	.12	.06	.04
252	Steve Swisher	.12	.06	.04
253	Jim Kern	.12	.06	.04
254	Dave Collins	.20	.10	.06
255	Jerry Reuss	.20	.10	.06
256	Joe Altobelli	.12	.06	.04
257	Hector Cruz	.12	.06	.04
258	John Hiller	.20	.10	.06
259	Dodgers Team	.80	.40	.25
260	Bert Campaneris	.25	.13	.08
261	Tim Hosley	.12	.06	.04
262	Rudy May	.20	.10	.06
263	Danny Walton	.12	.06	.04
264	Jamie Easterly	.12	.06	.04
265	Sal Bando	.12	.06	.04
266	Bob Shirley	.25	.13	.08
267	Doug Ault	.12	.06	.04
268	Gil Flores	.12	.06	.04
269	Wayne Twitchell	.12	.06	.04
270	Carlton Fisk	.90	.45	.25
271	Randy Lerch	.12	.06	.04
272	Royle Stillman	.12	.06	.04
273	Fred Norman	.12	.06	.04
274	Freddie Patek	.12	.06	.04
275	Dan Ford	.12	.06	.04
276	Bill Bonham	.12	.06	.04
277	Bruce Boisclair	.12	.06	.04
278	Enrique Romo	.12	.06	.04
279	Bill Virdon	.20	.10	.06
280	Buddy Bell	.30	.15	.09
281	Eric Rasmussen	.12	.06	.04
282	Yankees Team	1.00	.50	.30
283	Omar Moreno	.12	.06	.04
284	Randy Moffitt	.12	.06	.04
285	Steve Yeager	.12	.06	.04
286	Ben Oglivie	.20	.10	.06
287	Kiko Garcia	.12	.06	.04

		NR MT	EX	VG
288	Dave Hamilton	.12	.06	.04
289	Checklist 243-363	.90	.45	.25
290	Willie Horton	.20	.10	.06
291	Gary Ross	.12	.06	.04
292	Gene Richard	.12	.06	.04
293	Mike Willis	.12	.06	.04
294	Larry Parrish	.25	.13	.08
295	Bill Lee	.20	.10	.06
296	Biff Pocoroba	.12	.06	.04
297	Warren Brusstar	.12	.06	.04
298	Tony Armas	.25	.13	.08
299	Whitey Herzog	.30	.15	.09
300	Joe Morgan	1.50	.70	.45
301	Buddy Schultz	.12	.06	.04
302	Cubs Team	.50	.25	.15
303	Sam Hinds	.12	.06	.04
304	John Milner	.12	.06	.04
305	Rico Carty	.20	.10	.06
306	Joe Niekro	.25	.13	.08
307	Glenn Borgmann	.12	.06	.04
308	Jim Rooker	.12	.06	.04
309	Cliff Johnson	.20	.10	.06
310	Don Sutton	1.25	.60	.40
311	Jose Baez	.12	.06	.04
312	Greg Minton	.12	.06	.04
313	Andy Etchebarren	.12	.06	.04
314	Paul Lindblad	.12	.06	.04
315	Mark Belanger	.20	.10	.06
316	Henry Cruz	.12	.06	.04
317	Dave Johnson	.30	.15	.09
318	Tom Griffin	.12	.06	.04
319	Alan Ashby	.12	.06	.04
320	Fred Lynn	.90	.45	.25
321	Santo Alcala	.12	.06	.04
322	Tom Paciorek	.20	.10	.06
323	Jim Fregosi	.12	.06	.04
324	Vern Rapp	.12	.06	.04
325	Bruce Sutter	.70	.35	.20
326	Mike Lum	.12	.06	.04
327	Rick Langford	.12	.06	.04
328	Brewers Team	.50	.25	.15
329	John Verhoeven	.12	.06	.04
330	Bob Watson	.20	.10	.06
331	Mark Littell	.12	.06	.04
332	Duane Kuiper	.12	.06	.04
333	Jim Todd	.12	.06	.04
334	John Stearns	.12	.06	.04
335	Bucky Dent	.30	.15	.09
336	Steve Busby	.20	.10	.06
337	Tom Grieve	.12	.06	.04
338	Dave Heaverlo	.12	.06	.04
339	Mario Guerrero	.12	.06	.04
340	Bake McBride	.12	.06	.04
341	Mike Flanagan	.25	.13	.08
342	Aurelio Rodriguez	.20	.10	.06
343	John Wathan	.12	.06	.04
344	Sam Ewing	.12	.06	.04
345	Luis Tiant	.35	.20	.11
346	Larry Biittner	.12	.06	.04
347	Terry Forster	.20	.10	.06
348	Del Unser	.12	.06	.04
349	Rick Camp	.12	.06	.04
350	Steve Garvey	2.75	1.50	.80
351	Jeff Torborg	.20	.10	.06
352	Tony Scott	.12	.06	.04
353	Doug Bair	.12	.06	.04
354	Cesar Geronimo	.20	.10	.06
355	Bill Travers	.12	.06	.04
356	Mets Team	.70	.35	.20
357	Tom Poquette	.12	.06	.04
358	Mark Lemongello	.12	.06	.04
359	Marc Hill	.12	.06	.04
360	Mike Schmidt	5.00	2.50	1.50
361	Chris Knapp	.12	.06	.04
362	Dave May	.12	.06	.04
363	Bob Randall	.12	.06	.04
364	Jerry Turner	.12	.06	.04
365	Ed Figueroa	.20	.10	.06
366	Larry Milbourne	.12	.06	.04
367	Rick Dempsey	.20	.10	.06
368	Balor Moore	.12	.06	.04
369	Tim Nordbrook	.12	.06	.04
370	Rusty Staub	.30	.15	.09
371	Ray Burris	.12	.06	.04
372	Brian Asselstine	.12	.06	.04
373	Jim Willoughby	.12	.06	.04
374	Jose Morales	.12	.06	.04
375	Tommy John	.90	.45	.25
376	Jim Wohlford	.12	.06	.04
377	Manny Sarmiento	.12	.06	.04
378	Bobby Winkles	.12	.06	.04
379	Skip Lockwood	.12	.06	.04
380	Ted Simmons	.50	.25	.15
381	Phillies Team	.70	.35	.20
382	Joe Lahoud	.12	.06	.04
383	Mario Mendoza	.12	.06	.04
384	Jack Clark	3.00	1.50	.90
385	Tito Fuentes	.12	.06	.04
386	Bob Gorinski	.12	.06	.04
387	Ken Holtzman	.25	.13	.08
388	Bill Fahey	.12	.06	.04
389	Julio Gonzalez	.12	.06	.04
390	Oscar Gamble	.20	.10	.06
391	Larry Haney	.12	.06	.04
392	Billy Almon	.12	.06	.04
393	Tippy Martinez	.12	.06	.04
394	Roy Howell	.12	.06	.04
395	Jim Hughes	.12	.06	.04
396	Bob Stinson	.12	.06	.04
397	Greg Gross	.12	.06	.04
398	Don Hood	.12	.06	.04
399	Pete Mackanin	.12	.06	.04
400	Nolan Ryan	2.25	1.25	.70
401	Sparky Anderson	.30	.15	.09
402	Dave Campbell	.12	.06	.04
403	Bud Harrelson	.20	.10	.06
404	Tigers Team	.60	.30	.20
405	Rawly Eastwick	.12	.06	.04
406	Mike Jorgensen	.12	.06	.04
407	Odell Jones	.12	.06	.04
408	Joe Zdeb	.12	.06	.04
409	Ron Schueler	.12	.06	.04
410	Bill Madlock	.60	.30	.20
411	A.L. Championships (Yankees Rally To Defeat Royals)	.70	.35	.20
412	N.L. Championships (Dodgers Overpower Phillies In Four)	.50	.25	.15
413	World Series (Reggie & Yankees Reign Supreme)	1.25	.60	.40
414	Darold Knowles	.12	.06	.04
415	Ray Fosse	.12	.06	.04
416	Jack Brohamer	.12	.06	.04
417	Mike Garman	.12	.06	.04
418	Tony Muser	.12	.06	.04
419	Jerry Garvin	.12	.06	.04
420	Greg Luzinski	.35	.20	.11
421	Junior Moore	.12	.06	.04
422	Steve Braun	.12	.06	.04
423	Dave Rosello	.12	.06	.04
424	Red Sox Team	.70	.35	.20
425	Steve Rogers	.12	.06	.04
426	Fred Kendall	.12	.06	.04
427	Mario Soto	.70	.35	.20
428	Joel Youngblood	.20	.10	.06
429	Mike Barlow	.12	.06	.04
430	Al Oliver	.40	.20	.12
431	Butch Metzger	.12	.06	.04
432	Terry Bulling	.12	.06	.04
433	Fernando Gonzalez	.12	.06	.04
434	Mike Norris	.12	.06	.04
435	Checklist 364-484	.90	.45	.25
436	Vic Harris	.12	.06	.04
437	Bo McLaughlin	.12	.06	.04
438	John Ellis	.12	.06	.04
439	Ken Kravec	.12	.06	.04
440	Dave Lopes	.25	.13	.08
441	Larry Gura	.20	.10	.06
442	Elliott Maddox	.12	.06	.04
443	Darrel Chaney	.12	.06	.04
444	Roy Hartsfield	.12	.06	.04
445	Mike Ivie	.12	.06	.04
446	Tug McGraw	.35	.20	.11
447	Leroy Stanton	.12	.06	.04
448	Bill Castro	.12	.06	.04
449	Tim Blackwell	.12	.06	.04
450	Tom Seaver	2.25	1.25	.70
451	Twins Team	.50	.25	.15
452	Jerry Mumphrey	.25	.13	.08
453	Doug Flynn	.12	.06	.04
454	Dave LaRoche	.12	.06	.04
455	Bill Robinson	.12	.06	.04
456	Vern Ruhle	.12	.06	.04
457	Bob Bailey	.12	.06	.04
458	Jeff Newman	.12	.06	.04
459	Charlie Spikes	.12	.06	.04
460	Jim Hunter	1.75	.90	.50
461	Rob Andrews	.12	.06	.04
462	Rogelio Moret	.12	.06	.04
463	Kevin Bell	.12	.06	.04
464	Jerry Grote	.20	.10	.06
465	Hal McRae	.30	.15	.09
466	Dennis Blair	.12	.06	.04

	NR MT	EX	VG			NR MT	EX	VG
467	Alvin Dark	.20	.10	.06	558	Paul Mitchell	.12	.06	.04
468	Warren Cromartie	.20	.10	.06	559	Phil Mankowski	.12	.06	.04
469	Rick Cerone	.20	.10	.06	560	Dave Parker	2.00	1.00	.60
470	J.R. Richard	.25	.13	.08	561	Charlie Williams	.12	.06	.04
471	Roy Smalley	.20	.10	.06	562	Glenn Burke	.12	.06	.04
472	Ron Reed	.20	.10	.06	563	Dave Rader	.12	.06	.04
473	Bill Buckner	.30	.15	.09	564	Mick Kelleher	.12	.06	.04
474	Jim Slaton	.12	.06	.04	565	Jerry Koosman	.25	.13	.08
475	Gary Matthews	.20	.10	.06	566	Merv Rettenmund	.12	.06	.04
476	Bill Stein	.12	.06	.04	567	Dick Drago	.12	.06	.04
477	Doug Capilla	.12	.06	.04	568	Tom Hutton	.12	.06	.04
478	Jerry Remy	.12	.06	.04	569	Lary Sorensen	.20	.10	.06
479	Cardinals Team	.50	.25	.15	570	Dave Kingman	.60	.30	.20
480	Ron LeFlore	.25	.13	.08	571	Buck Martinez	.12	.06	.04
481	Jackson Todd	.12	.06	.04	572	Rick Wise	.20	.10	.06
482	Rick Miller	.12	.06	.04	573	Luis Gomez	.12	.06	.04
483	Ken Macha	.12	.06	.04	574	Bob Lemon	.30	.15	.09
484	Jim Norris	.12	.06	.04	575	Pat Dobson	.20	.10	.06
485	Chris Chambliss	.30	.15	.09	576	Sam Mejias	.12	.06	.04
486	John Curtis	.12	.06	.04	577	A's Team	.50	.25	.15
487	Jim Tyrone	.12	.06	.04	578	Buzz Capra	.12	.06	.04
488	Dan Spillner	.12	.06	.04	579	Rance Mulliniks	.35	.20	.11
489	Rudy Meoli	.12	.06	.04	580	Rod Carew	2.50	1.25	.70
490	Amos Otis	.20	.10	.06	581	Lynn McGlothen	.12	.06	.04
491	Scott McGregor	.25	.13	.08	582	Fran Healy	.20	.10	.06
492	Jim Sundberg	.20	.10	.06	583	George Medich	.12	.06	.04
493	Steve Renko	.12	.06	.04	584	John Hale	.12	.06	.04
494	Chuck Tanner	.20	.10	.06	585	Woodie Fryman	.12	.06	.04
495	Dave Cash	.12	.06	.04	586	Ed Goodson	.12	.06	.04
496	Jim Clancy	.30	.15	.09	587	John Urrea	.12	.06	.04
497	Glenn Adams	.12	.06	.04	588	Jim Mason	.12	.06	.04
498	Joe Sambito	.20	.10	.06	589	Bob Knepper	.80	.40	.25
499	Mariners Team	.50	.25	.15	590	Bobby Murcer	.30	.15	.09
500	George Foster	.70	.35	.20	591	George Zeber	.20	.10	.06
501	Dave Roberts	.12	.06	.04	592	Bob Apodaca	.12	.06	.04
502	Pat Rockett	.12	.06	.04	593	Dave Skaggs	.12	.06	.04
503	Ike Hampton	.12	.06	.04	594	Dave Freisleben	.12	.06	.04
504	Roger Freed	.12	.06	.04	595	Sixto Lezcano	.12	.06	.04
505	Felix Millan	.12	.06	.04	596	Gary Wheelock	.12	.06	.04
506	Ron Blomberg	.12	.06	.04	597	Steve Dillard	.12	.06	.04
507	Willie Crawford	.12	.06	.04	598	Eddie Solomon	.12	.06	.04
508	Johnny Oates	.12	.06	.04	599	Gary Woods	.12	.06	.04
509	Brent Strom	.12	.06	.04	600	Frank Tanana	.25	.13	.08
510	Willie Stargell	1.75	.90	.50	601	Gene Mauch	.25	.13	.08
511	Frank Duffy	.12	.06	.04	602	Eric Soderholm	.12	.06	.04
512	Larry Herndon	.25	.13	.08	603	Will McEnaney	.12	.06	.04
513	Barry Foote	.12	.06	.04	604	Earl Williams	.12	.06	.04
514	Rob Sperring	.12	.06	.04	605	Rick Rhoden	.25	.13	.08
515	Tim Corcoran	.12	.06	.04	606	Pirates Team	.50	.25	.15
516	Gary Beare	.12	.06	.04	607	Fernando Arroyo	.12	.06	.04
517	Andres Mora	.12	.06	.04	608	Johnny Grubb	.12	.06	.04
518	Tommy Boggs	.12	.06	.04	609	John Denny	.20	.10	.06
519	Brian Downing	.25	.13	.08	610	Garry Maddox	.20	.10	.06
520	Larry Hisle	.20	.10	.06	611	Pat Scanlon	.12	.06	.04
521	Steve Staggs	.12	.06	.04	612	Ken Henderson	.12	.06	.04
522	Dick Williams	.20	.10	.06	613	Marty Perez	.12	.06	.04
523	Donnie Moore	.40	.20	.12	614	Joe Wallis	.12	.06	.04
524	Bernie Carbo	.12	.06	.04	615	Clay Carroll	.20	.10	.06
525	Jerry Terrell	.12	.06	.04	616	Pat Kelly	.12	.06	.04
526	Reds Team	.60	.30	.20	617	Joe Nolan	.12	.06	.04
527	Vic Correll	.12	.06	.04	618	Tommy Helms	.12	.06	.04
528	Rob Picciolo	.12	.06	.04	619	Thad Bosley	.20	.10	.06
529	Paul Hartzell	.12	.06	.04	620	Willie Randolph	.30	.15	.09
530	Dave Winfield	2.25	1.25	.70	621	Craig Swan	.12	.06	.04
531	Tom Underwood	.12	.06	.04	622	Champ Summers	.12	.06	.04
532	Skip Jutze	.12	.06	.04	623	Eduardo Rodriguez	.12	.06	.04
533	Sandy Alomar	.12	.06	.04	624	Gary Alexander	.12	.06	.04
534	Wilbur Howard	.12	.06	.04	625	Jose Cruz	.25	.13	.08
535	Checklist 485-605	.90	.45	.25	626	Blue Jays Team	.25	.13	.08
536	Roric Harrison	.12	.06	.04	627	Dave Johnson	.12	.06	.04
537	Bruce Bochte	.20	.10	.06	628	Ralph Garr	.20	.10	.06
538	Johnnie LeMaster	.12	.06	.04	629	Don Stanhouse	.12	.06	.04
539	Vic Davalillo	.12	.06	.04	630	Ron Cey	.25	.13	.08
540	Steve Carlton	2.50	1.25	.70	631	Danny Ozark	.20	.10	.06
541	Larry Cox	.12	.06	.04	632	Rowland Office	.12	.06	.04
542	Tim Johnson	.12	.06	.04	633	Tom Veryzer	.12	.06	.04
543	Larry Harlow	.12	.06	.04	634	Len Barker	.20	.10	.06
544	Len Randle	.12	.06	.04	635	Joe Rudi	.25	.13	.08
545	Bill Campbell	.12	.06	.04	636	Jim Bibby	.12	.06	.04
546	Ted Martinez	.12	.06	.04	637	Duffy Dyer	.12	.06	.04
547	John Scott	.12	.06	.04	638	Paul Splittorff	.20	.10	.06
548	Billy Hunter	.12	.06	.04	639	Gene Clines	.12	.06	.04
549	Joe Kerrigan	.12	.06	.04	640	Lee May	.12	.06	.04
550	John Mayberry	.20	.10	.06	641	Doug Rau	.12	.06	.04
551	Braves Team	.50	.25	.15	642	Denny Doyle	.12	.06	.04
552	Francisco Barrios	.12	.06	.04	643	Tom House	.12	.06	.04
553	Terry Puhl	.35	.20	.11	644	Jim Dwyer	.12	.06	.04
554	Joe Coleman	.20	.10	.06	645	Mike Torrez	.20	.10	.06
555	Butch Wynegar	.20	.10	.06	646	Rick Auerbach	.12	.06	.04
556	Ed Armbrister	.12	.06	.04	647	Steve Dunning	.12	.06	.04
557	Tony Solaita	.12	.06	.04	648	Gary Thomasson	.12	.06	.04

		NR MT	EX	VG
649	Moose Haas	.30	.15	.09
650	Cesar Cedeno	.25	.13	.08
651	Doug Rader	.12	.06	.04
652	Checklist 606-726	.90	.45	.25
653	Ron Hodges	.12	.06	.04
654	Pepe Frias	.12	.06	.04
655	Lyman Bostock	.20	.10	.06
656	Dave Garcia	.12	.06	.04
657	Bombo Rivera	.12	.06	.04
658	Manny Sanguillen	.12	.06	.04
659	Rangers Team	.50	.25	.15
660	Jason Thompson	.20	.10	.06
661	Grant Jackson	.12	.06	.04
662	Paul Dade	.12	.06	.04
663	Paul Reuschel	.12	.06	.04
664	Fred Stanley	.20	.10	.06
665	Dennis Leonard	.20	.10	.06
666	Billy Smith	.12	.06	.04
667	Jeff Byrd	.12	.06	.04
668	Dusty Baker	.25	.13	.08
669	Pete Falcone	.12	.06	.04
670	Jim Rice	3.75	2.00	1.25
671	Gary Lavelle	.12	.06	.04
672	Don Kessinger	.20	.10	.06
673	Steve Brye	.12	.06	.04
674	Ray Knight	.90	.45	.25
675	Jay Johnstone	.20	.10	.06
676	Bob Myrick	.12	.06	.04
677	Ed Herrmann	.12	.06	.04
678	Tom Burgmeier	.12	.06	.04
679	Wayne Garrett	.12	.06	.04
680	Vida Blue	.30	.15	.09
681	Rob Belloir	.12	.06	.04
682	Ken Brett	.20	.10	.06
683	Mike Champion	.12	.06	.04
684	Ralph Houk	.20	.10	.06
685	Frank Taveras	.12	.06	.04
686	Gaylord Perry	1.75	.90	.50
687	Julio Cruz	.25	.13	.08
688	George Mitterwald	.12	.06	.04
689	Indians Team	.50	.25	.15
690	Mickey Rivers	.25	.13	.08
691	Ross Grimsley	.20	.10	.06
692	Ken Reitz	.12	.06	.04
693	Lamar Johnson	.12	.06	.04
694	Elias Sosa	.12	.06	.04
695	Dwight Evans	.60	.30	.20
696	Steve Mingori	.12	.06	.04
697	Roger Metzger	.12	.06	.04
698	Juan Bernhardt	.12	.06	.04
699	Jackie Brown	.12	.06	.04
700	Johnny Bench	2.50	1.25	.70
701	Rookie Pitchers (Tom Hume, Larry Landreth, Steve McCatty, Bruce Taylor)	.25	.13	.08
702	Rookie Catchers (Bill Nahorodny, Kevin Pasley, Rick Sweet, Don Werner)	.12	.06	.04
703	Rookie Pitchers (Larry Andersen, Tim Jones, Mickey Mahler, Jack Morris)	5.00	2.50	1.50
704	Rookie 2nd Basemen (Garth Iorg, Dave Oliver, Sam Perlozzo, Lou Whitaker)	7.00	3.50	2.00
705	Rookie Outfielders (Dave Bergman, Miguel Dilone, Clint Hurdle, Willie Norwood)	.25	.13	.08
706	Rookie 1st Basemen (Wayne Cage, Ted Cox, Pat Putnam, Dave Revering)	.20	.10	.06
707	Rookie Shortstops (Mickey Klutts, Paul Molitor, Alan Trammell, U.L. Washington)	25.00	12.50	7.50
708	Rookie Catchers (Bo Diaz, Dale Murphy, Lance Parrish, Ernie Whitt)	30.00	15.00	9.00
709	Rookie Pitchers (Steve Burke, Matt Keough, Lance Rautzhan, Dan Schatzeder)	.25	.13	.08
710	Rookie Outfielders (Dell Alston, Rick Bosetti, Mike Easler, Keith Smith)	1.25	.60	.40
711	Rookie Pitchers (Cardell Camper, Dennis Lamp, Craig Mitchell, Roy Thomas)	.12	.06	.04
712	Bobby Valentine	.25	.13	.08
713	Bob Davis	.12	.06	.04
714	Mike Anderson	.12	.06	.04
715	Jim Kaat	.60	.30	.20
716	Clarence Gaston	.12	.06	.04
717	Nelson Briles	.12	.06	.04
718	Ron Jackson	.12	.06	.04
719	Randy Elliott	.12	.06	.04
720	Fergie Jenkins	.60	.30	.20
721	Billy Martin	.70	.35	.20
722	Pete Broberg	.12	.06	.04
723	Johnny Wockenfuss	.12	.06	.04
724	Royals Team	.70	.35	.20

		NR MT	EX	VG
725	Kurt Bevacqua	.12	.06	.04
726	Wilbur Wood	.40	.10	.06

1979 Topps

 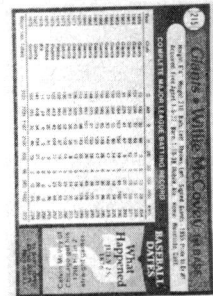

The size of this issue remained the same as in 1978 with 726 cards making their appearance. Actually, the 2½" by 3½" cards had a relatively minor design change from the previous year, as well. The large color photo still dominates the front, with the player's name, team and position below it. The baseball with his position has been moved to the lower left and the position is replaced by a Topps logo. On the back, the printing color was changed and the game situation is replaced by a quiz called "Baseball Dates." Specialty cards include statistical leaders, major league records set during the season and eight cards devoted to career records. For the first time, rookies were arranged by teams under the heading of "Prospects."

		NR MT	EX	VG
	Complete Set:	135.00	60.00	30.00
	Common Player:	.12	.06	.04
1	Batting Leaders (Rod Carew, Dave Parker)	1.50	.40	.25
2	Home Run Leaders (George Foster, Jim Rice)	.60	.30	.20
3	Runs Batted In Leaders (George Foster, Jim Rice)	.60	.30	.20
4	Stolen Base Leaders (Ron LeFlore, Omar Moreno)	.25	.13	.08
5	Victory Leaders (Ron Guidry, Gaylord Perry)	.50	.25	.15
6	Strikeout Leaders (J.R. Richard, Nolan Ryan)	.50	.25	.15
7	Earned Run Avg. Leaders (Ron Guidry, Craig Swan)	.25	.13	.08
8	Leading Firemen (Rollie Fingers, Rich Gossage)	.40	.20	.12
9	Dave Campbell	.12	.06	.04
10	Lee May	.20	.10	.06
11	Marc Hill	.12	.06	.04
12	Dick Drago	.12	.06	.04
13	Paul Dade	.12	.06	.04
14	Rafael Landestoy	.12	.06	.04
15	Ross Grimsley	.20	.10	.06
16	Fred Stanley	.20	.10	.06
17	Donnie Moore	.20	.10	.06
18	Tony Solaita	.12	.06	.04
19	Larry Gura	.12	.06	.04
20	Joe Morgan	.40	.20	.12
21	Kevin Kobel	.12	.06	.04
22	Mike Jorgensen	.12	.06	.04
23	Terry Forster	.20	.10	.06
24	Paul Molitor	2.50	1.25	.70
25	Steve Carlton	2.50	1.25	.70
26	Jamie Quirk	.12	.06	.04
27	Dave Goltz	.20	.10	.06
28	Steve Brye	.12	.06	.04
29	Rick Langford	.12	.06	.04
30	Dave Winfield	2.50	1.25	.70
31	Tom House	.12	.06	.04
32	Jerry Mumphrey	.20	.10	.06
33	Dave Rozema	.12	.06	.04

		NR MT	EX	VG			NR MT	EX	VG
34	Rob Andrews	.12	.06	.04	125	Rick Burleson	.20	.10	.06
35	Ed Figueroa	.20	.10	.06	126	Doug Bair	.12	.06	.04
36	Alan Ashby	.12	.06	.04	127	Thad Bosley	.12	.06	.04
37	Joe Kerrigan	.12	.06	.04	128	Ted Martinez	.12	.06	.04
38	Bernie Carbo	.12	.06	.04	129	Marty Pattin	.12	.06	.04
39	Dale Murphy	8.00	4.00	2.50	130	Bob Watson	.12	.06	.04
40	Dennis Eckersley	.20	.10	.06	131	Jim Clancy	.30	.15	.09
41	Twins Team (Gene Mauch)	.50	.25	.15	132	Rowland Office	.12	.06	.04
42	Ron Blomberg	.12	.06	.04	133	Bill Castro	.12	.06	.04
43	Wayne Twitchell	.12	.06	.04	134	Alan Bannister	.12	.06	.04
44	Kurt Bevacqua	.12	.06	.04	135	Bobby Murcer	.25	.13	.08
45	Al Hrabosky	.20	.10	.06	136	Jim Kaat	.60	.30	.20
46	Ron Hodges	.12	.06	.04	137	Larry Wolfe	.12	.06	.04
47	Fred Norman	.12	.06	.04	138	Mark Lee	.12	.06	.04
48	Merv Rettenmund	.12	.06	.04	139	Luis Pujols	.12	.06	.04
49	Vern Ruhle	.12	.06	.04	140	Don Gullett	.20	.10	.06
50	Steve Garvey	1.25	.60	.40	141	Tom Paciorek	.20	.10	.06
51	Ray Fosse	.12	.06	.04	142	Charlie Williams	.12	.06	.04
52	Randy Lerch	.12	.06	.04	143	Tony Scott	.12	.06	.04
53	Mick Kelleher	.12	.06	.04	144	Sandy Alomar	.12	.06	.04
54	Dell Alston	.12	.06	.04	145	Rick Rhoden	.25	.13	.08
55	Willie Stargell	2.00	1.00	.60	146	Duane Kuiper	.12	.06	.04
56	John Hale	.12	.06	.04	147	Dave Hamilton	.12	.06	.04
57	Eric Rasmussen	.12	.06	.04	148	Bruce Boisclair	.12	.06	.04
58	Bob Randall	.12	.06	.04	149	Manny Sarmiento	.12	.06	.04
59	John Denny	.12	.06	.04	150	Wayne Cage	.12	.06	.04
60	Mickey Rivers	.20	.10	.06	151	John Hiller	.20	.10	.06
61	Bo Diaz	.20	.10	.06	152	Rick Cerone	.20	.10	.06
62	Randy Moffitt	.12	.06	.04	153	Dennis Lamp	.12	.06	.04
63	Jack Brohamer	.12	.06	.04	154	Jim Gantner	.12	.06	.04
64	Tom Underwood	.12	.06	.04	155	Dwight Evans	.50	.25	.15
65	Mark Belanger	.20	.10	.06	156	Buddy Solomon	.12	.06	.04
66	Tigers Team (Les Moss)	.60	.30	.20	157	U.L. Washington	.12	.06	.04
67	Jim Mason	.12	.06	.04	158	Joe Sambito	.12	.06	.04
68	Joe Niekro	.12	.06	.04	159	Roy White	.25	.13	.08
69	Elliott Maddox	.12	.06	.04	160	Mike Flanagan	.30	.15	.09
70	John Candelaria	.25	.13	.08	161	Barry Foote	.12	.06	.04
71	Brian Downing	.20	.10	.06	162	Tom Johnson	.12	.06	.04
72	Steve Mingori	.12	.06	.04	163	Glenn Burke	.12	.06	.04
73	Ken Henderson	.12	.06	.04	164	Mickey Lolich	.35	.20	.11
74	Shane Rawley	1.00	.50	.30	165	Frank Taveras	.12	.06	.04
75	Steve Yeager	.12	.06	.04	166	Leon Roberts	.12	.06	.04
76	Warren Cromartie	.12	.06	.04	167	Roger Metzger	.12	.06	.04
77	Dan Briggs	.12	.06	.04	168	Dave Freisleben	.12	.06	.04
78	Elias Sosa	.12	.06	.04	169	Bill Nahorodny	.12	.06	.04
79	Ted Cox	.12	.06	.04	170	Don Sutton	1.25	.60	.40
80	Jason Thompson	.20	.10	.06	171	Gene Clines	.12	.06	.04
81	Roger Erickson	.12	.06	.04	172	Mike Bruhert	.12	.06	.04
82	Mets Team (Joe Torre)	.60	.30	.20	173	John Lowenstein	.12	.06	.04
83	Fred Kendall	.12	.06	.04	174	Rick Auerbach	.12	.06	.04
84	Greg Minton	.12	.06	.04	175	George Hendrick	.20	.10	.06
85	Gary Matthews	.20	.10	.06	176	Aurelio Rodriguez	.20	.10	.06
86	Rodney Scott	.12	.06	.04	177	Ron Reed	.20	.10	.06
87	Pete Falcone	.12	.06	.04	178	Alvis Woods	.12	.06	.04
88	Bob Molinaro	.12	.06	.04	179	Jim Beattie	.12	.06	.04
89	Dick Tidrow	.20	.10	.06	180	Larry Hisle	.20	.10	.06
90	Bob Boone	.25	.13	.08	181	Mike Garman	.12	.06	.04
91	Terry Crowley	.12	.06	.04	182	Tim Johnson	.12	.06	.04
92	Jim Bibby	.12	.06	.04	183	Paul Splittorff	.20	.10	.06
93	Phil Mankowski	.12	.06	.04	184	Darrel Chaney	.12	.06	.04
94	Len Barker	.20	.10	.06	185	Mike Torrez	.20	.10	.06
95	Robin Yount	2.25	1.25	.70	186	Eric Soderholm	.12	.06	.04
96	Indians Team (Jeff Torborg)	.50	.25	.15	187	Mark Lemongello	.12	.06	.04
97	Sam Mejias	.12	.06	.04	188	Pat Kelly	.12	.06	.04
98	Ray Burris	.12	.06	.04	189	Eddie Whitson	.40	.20	.12
99	John Wathan	.20	.10	.06	190	Ron Cey	.25	.13	.08
100	Tom Seaver	1.25	.60	.40	191	Mike Norris	.12	.06	.04
101	Roy Howell	.12	.06	.04	192	Cardinals Team (Ken Boyer)	.50	.25	.15
102	Mike Anderson	.12	.06	.04	193	Glenn Adams	.12	.06	.04
103	Jim Todd	.12	.06	.04	194	Randy Jones	.20	.10	.06
104	Johnny Oates	.12	.06	.04	195	Bill Madlock	.40	.20	.12
105	Rick Camp	.12	.06	.04	196	Steve Kemp	.12	.06	.04
106	Frank Duffy	.12	.06	.04	197	Bob Apodaca	.12	.06	.04
107	Jesus Alou	.20	.10	.06	198	Johnny Grubb	.12	.06	.04
108	Eduardo Rodriguez	.12	.06	.04	199	Larry Milbourne	.12	.06	.04
109	Joel Youngblood	.20	.10	.06	200	Johnny Bench	1.25	.60	.40
110	Vida Blue	.30	.15	.09	201	Record Breaker (Mike Edwards)	.12	.06	.04
111	Roger Freed	.12	.06	.04	202	Record Breaker (Ron Guidry)	.35	.20	.11
112	Phillies Team (Danny Ozark)	.50	.25	.15	203	Record Breaker (J.R. Richard)	.20	.10	.06
113	Pete Redfern	.12	.06	.04	204	Record Breaker (Pete Rose)	1.50	.70	.45
114	Cliff Johnson	.20	.10	.06	205	Record Breaker (John Stearns)	.12	.06	.04
115	Nolan Ryan	2.25	1.25	.70	206	Record Breaker (Sammy Stewart)	.12	.06	.04
116	Ozzie Smith	7.00	3.50	2.00	207	Dave Lemanczyk	.12	.06	.04
117	Grant Jackson	.12	.06	.04	208	Clarence Gaston	.12	.06	.04
118	Bud Harrelson	.20	.10	.06	209	Reggie Cleveland	.12	.06	.04
119	Don Stanhouse	.12	.06	.04	210	Larry Bowa	.30	.15	.09
120	Jim Sundberg	.20	.10	.06	211	Denny Martinez	.20	.10	.06
121	Checklist 1-121	.25	.13	.08	212	Carney Lansford	1.00	.50	.30
122	Mike Paxton	.12	.06	.04	213	Bill Travers	.12	.06	.04
123	Lou Whitaker	2.00	1.00	.60	214	Red Sox Team (Don Zimmer)	.60	.30	.20
124	Dan Schatzeder	.12	.06	.04	215	Willie McCovey	1.50	.70	.45

#		NR MT	EX	VG		#		NR MT	EX	VG
216	Wilbur Wood	.20	.10	.06		307	Larvell Blanks	.12	.06	.04
217	Steve Dillard	.12	.06	.04		308	Bert Blyleven	.60	.30	.20
218	Dennis Leonard	.20	.10	.06		309	Ralph Garr	.20	.10	.06
219	Roy Smalley	.20	.10	.06		310	Thurman Munson	2.00	1.00	.60
220	Cesar Geronimo	.20	.10	.06		311	Gary Lavelle	.12	.06	.04
221	Jesse Jefferson	.12	.06	.04		312	Bob Robertson	.12	.06	.04
222	Bob Beall	.12	.06	.04		313	Dyar Miller	.12	.06	.04
223	Kent Tekulve	.25	.13	.08		314	Larry Harlow	.12	.06	.04
224	Dave Revering	.12	.06	.04		315	Jon Matlack	.20	.10	.06
225	Rich Gossage	.70	.35	.20		316	Milt May	.12	.06	.04
226	Ron Pruitt	.12	.06	.04		317	Jose Cardenal	.12	.06	.04
227	Steve Stone	.20	.10	.06		318	Bob Welch	1.00	.50	.30
228	Vic Davalillo	.20	.10	.06		319	Wayne Garrett	.12	.06	.04
229	Doug Flynn	.12	.06	.04		320	Carl Yastrzemski	2.50	1.25	.70
230	Bob Forsch	.20	.10	.06		321	Gaylord Perry	1.50	.70	.45
231	Johnny Wockenfuss	.12	.06	.04		322	Danny Goodwin	.12	.06	.04
232	Jimmy Sexton	.12	.06	.04		323	Lynn McGlothen	.12	.06	.04
233	Paul Mitchell	.12	.06	.04		324	Mike Tyson	.12	.06	.04
234	Toby Harrah	.20	.10	.06		325	Cecil Cooper	.40	.20	.12
235	Steve Rogers	.20	.10	.06		326	Pedro Borbon	.12	.06	.04
236	Jim Dwyer	.12	.06	.04		327	Art Howe	.12	.06	.04
237	Billy Smith	.12	.06	.04		328	A's Team (Jack McKeon)	.50	.25	.15
238	Balor Moore	.12	.06	.04		329	Joe Coleman	.20	.10	.06
239	Willie Horton	.20	.10	.06		330	George Brett	3.00	1.50	.90
240	Rick Reuschel	.25	.13	.08		331	Mickey Mahler	.12	.06	.04
241	Checklist 122-242	.25	.13	.08		332	Gary Alexander	.12	.06	.04
242	Pablo Torrealba	.12	.06	.04		333	Chet Lemon	.20	.10	.06
243	Buck Martinez	.12	.06	.04		334	Craig Swan	.12	.06	.04
244	Pirates Team (Chuck Tanner)	.80	.40	.25		335	Chris Chambliss	.25	.13	.08
245	Jeff Burroughs	.20	.10	.06		336	Bobby Thompson	.12	.06	.04
246	Darrell Jackson	.12	.06	.04		337	John Montague	.12	.06	.04
247	Tucker Ashford	.12	.06	.04		338	Vic Harris	.12	.06	.04
248	Pete LaCock	.12	.06	.04		339	Ron Jackson	.12	.06	.04
249	Paul Thormodsgard	.12	.06	.04		340	Jim Palmer	1.50	.70	.45
250	Willie Randolph	.30	.15	.09		341	Willie Upshaw	.80	.40	.25
251	Jack Morris	2.00	1.00	.60		342	Dave Roberts	.12	.06	.04
252	Bob Stinson	.12	.06	.04		343	Ed Glynn	.12	.06	.04
253	Rick Wise	.20	.10	.06		344	Jerry Royster	.12	.06	.04
254	Luis Gomez	.12	.06	.04		345	Tug McGraw	.30	.15	.09
255	Tommy John	.80	.40	.25		346	Bill Buckner	.30	.15	.09
256	Mike Sadek	.12	.06	.04		347	Doug Rau	.12	.06	.04
257	Adrian Devine	.12	.06	.04		348	Andre Dawson	2.50	1.25	.70
258	Mike Phillips	.12	.06	.04		349	Jim Wright	.12	.06	.04
259	Reds Team (Sparky Anderson)	.60	.30	.20		350	Garry Templeton	.25	.13	.08
260	Richie Zisk	.20	.10	.06		351	Wayne Nordhagen	.12	.06	.04
261	Mario Guerrero	.12	.06	.04		352	Steve Renko	.12	.06	.04
262	Nelson Briles	.12	.06	.04		353	Checklist 243-363	.60	.30	.20
263	Oscar Gamble	.20	.10	.06		354	Bill Bonham	.12	.06	.04
264	Don Robinson	.50	.25	.15		355	Lee Mazzilli	.20	.10	.06
265	Don Money	.20	.10	.06		356	Giants Team (Joe Altobelli)	.50	.25	.15
266	Jim Willoughby	.12	.06	.04		357	Jerry Augustine	.12	.06	.04
267	Joe Rudi	.20	.10	.06		358	Alan Trammell	3.25	1.75	1.00
268	Julio Gonzalez	.12	.06	.04		359	Dan Spillner	.12	.06	.04
269	Woodie Fryman	.20	.10	.06		360	Amos Otis	.20	.10	.06
270	Butch Hobson	.12	.06	.04		361	Tom Dixon	.12	.06	.04
271	Rawly Eastwick	.12	.06	.04		362	Mike Cubbage	.12	.06	.04
272	Tim Corcoran	.12	.06	.04		363	Craig Skok	.12	.06	.04
273	Jerry Terrell	.12	.06	.04		364	Gene Richards	.12	.06	.04
274	Willie Norwood	.12	.06	.04		365	Sparky Lyle	.30	.15	.09
275	Junior Moore	.12	.06	.04		366	Juan Bernhardt	.12	.06	.04
276	Jim Colborn	.12	.06	.04		367	Dave Skaggs	.12	.06	.04
277	Tom Grieve	.12	.06	.04		368	Don Aase	.20	.10	.06
278	Andy Messersmith	.25	.13	.08		369a	Bump Wills (Blue Jays)	3.00	1.50	.90
279	Jerry Grote	.12	.06	.04		369b	Bump Wills (Rangers)	4.00	2.00	1.25
280	Andre Thornton	.25	.13	.08		370	Dave Kingman	.35	.20	.11
281	Vic Correll	.12	.06	.04		371	Jeff Holly	.12	.06	.04
282	Blue Jays Team (Roy Hartsfield)	.50	.25	.15		372	Lamar Johnson	.12	.06	.04
283	Ken Kravec	.12	.06	.04		373	Lance Rautzhan	.12	.06	.04
284	Johnnie LeMaster	.12	.06	.04		374	Ed Herrmann	.12	.06	.04
285	Bobby Bonds	.30	.15	.09		375	Bill Campbell	.12	.06	.04
286	Duffy Dyer	.12	.06	.04		376	Gorman Thomas	.25	.13	.08
287	Andres Mora	.12	.06	.04		377	Paul Moskau	.12	.06	.04
288	Milt Wilcox	.20	.10	.06		378	Rob Picciolo	.12	.06	.04
289	Jose Cruz	.25	.13	.08		379	Dale Murray	.12	.06	.04
290	Dave Lopes	.25	.13	.08		380	John Mayberry	.20	.10	.06
291	Tom Griffin	.12	.06	.04		381	Astros Team (Bill Virdon)	.50	.25	.15
292	Don Reynolds	.12	.06	.04		382	Jerry Martin	.12	.06	.04
293	Jerry Garvin	.12	.06	.04		383	Phil Garner	.20	.10	.06
294	Pepe Frias	.12	.06	.04		384	Tommy Boggs	.12	.06	.04
295	Mitchell Page	.12	.06	.04		385	Dan Ford	.12	.06	.04
296	Preston Hanna	.12	.06	.04		386	Francisco Barrios	.12	.06	.04
297	Ted Sizemore	.12	.06	.04		387	Gary Thomasson	.12	.06	.04
298	Rich Gale	.12	.06	.04		388	Jack Billingham	.12	.06	.04
299	Steve Ontiveros	.12	.06	.04		389	Joe Zdeb	.12	.06	.04
300	Rod Carew	2.25	1.25	.70		390	Rollie Fingers	.70	.35	.20
301	Tom Hume	.12	.06	.04		391	Al Oliver	.40	.20	.12
302	Braves Team (Bobby Cox)	.50	.25	.15		392	Doug Ault	.12	.06	.04
303	Lary Sorensen	.12	.06	.04		393	Scott McGregor	.25	.13	.08
304	Steve Swisher	.12	.06	.04		394	Randy Stein	.12	.06	.04
305	Willie Montanez	.12	.06	.04		395	Dave Cash	.12	.06	.04
306	Floyd Bannister	.30	.15	.09		396	Bill Plummer	.12	.06	.04

		NR MT	EX	VG			NR MT	EX	VG
397	Sergio Ferrer	.12	.06	.04	480	Fred Lynn	.70	.35	.20
398	Ivan DeJesus	.12	.06	.04	481	Skip Lockwood	.12	.06	.04
399	David Clyde	.12	.06	.04	482	Craig Reynolds	.12	.06	.04
400	Jim Rice	2.75	1.50	.80	483	Checklist 364-484	.25	.13	.08
401	Ray Knight	.25	.13	.08	484	Rick Waits	.12	.06	.04
402	Paul Hartzell	.12	.06	.04	485	Bucky Dent	.25	.13	.08
403	Tim Foli	.12	.06	.04	486	Bob Knepper	.25	.13	.08
404	White Sox Team (Don Kessinger)	.50	.25	.15	487	Miguel Dilone	.12	.06	.04
405	Butch Wynegar	.20	.10	.06	488	Bob Owchinko	.12	.06	.04
406	Joe Wallis	.12	.06	.04	489	Larry Cox (photo actually Dave Rader)			
407	Pete Vuckovich	.20	.10	.06			.12	.06	.04
408	Charlie Moore	.12	.06	.04	490	Al Cowens	.12	.06	.04
409	Willie Wilson	1.25	.60	.40	491	Tippy Martinez	.12	.06	.04
410	Darrell Evans	.30	.15	.09	492	Bob Bailor	.12	.06	.04
411	Hits Record Holders (Ty Cobb, George Sisler)	.70	.35	.20	493	Larry Christenson	.12	.06	.04
					494	Jerry White	.12	.06	.04
412	Runs Batted In Record Holders (Hank Aaron, Hack Wilson)	.70	.35	.20	495	Tony Perez	.60	.30	.20
					496	Barry Bonnell	.12	.06	.04
413	Home Run Record Holders (Hank Aaron, Roger Maris)	1.00	.50	.30	497	Glenn Abbott	.12	.06	.04
					498	Rich Chiles	.12	.06	.04
414	Batting Avg. Record Holders (Ty Cobb, Roger Hornsby)	.70	.35	.20	499	Rangers Team (Pat Corrales)	.50	.25	.15
					500	Ron Guidry	1.00	.50	.30
415	Stolen Bases Record Holders (Lou Brock)	.70	.35	.20	501	Junior Kennedy	.12	.06	.04
					502	Steve Braun	.12	.06	.04
416	Wins Record Holders (Jack Chesbro, Cy Young)	.40	.20	.12	503	Terry Humphrey	.12	.06	.04
					504	Larry McWilliams	.20	.10	.06
417	Strikeouts Record Holders (Walter Johnson, Nolan Ryan)	.30	.15	.09	505	Ed Kranepool	.20	.10	.06
					506	John D'Acquisto	.12	.06	.04
418	Earned Run Avg. Record Holders (Walter Johnson, Dutch Leonard)	.20	.10	.06	507	Tony Armas	.20	.10	.06
					508	Charlie Hough	.20	.10	.06
419	Dick Ruthven	.12	.06	.04	509	Mario Mendoza	.12	.06	.04
420	Ken Griffey	.25	.13	.08	510	Ted Simmons	.40	.20	.12
421	Doug DeCinces	.25	.13	.08	511	Paul Reuschel	.12	.06	.04
422	Ruppert Jones	.12	.06	.04	512	Jack Clark	1.25	.60	.40
423	Bob Montgomery	.12	.06	.04	513	Dave Johnson	.30	.15	.09
424	Angels Team (Jim Fregosi)	.60	.30	.20	514	Mike Proly	.12	.06	.04
425	Rick Manning	.12	.06	.04	515	Enos Cabell	.12	.06	.04
426	Chris Speier	.20	.10	.06	516	Champ Summers	.12	.06	.04
427	Andy Replogle	.12	.06	.04	517	Al Bumbry	.20	.10	.06
428	Bobby Valentine	.25	.13	.08	518	Jim Umbarger	.12	.06	.04
429	John Urrea	.12	.06	.04	519	Ben Oglivie	.20	.10	.06
430	Dave Parker	1.25	.60	.40	520	Gary Carter	2.75	1.50	.80
431	Glenn Borgmann	.12	.06	.04	521	Sam Ewing	.12	.06	.04
432	Dave Heaverlo	.12	.06	.04	522	Ken Holtzman	.20	.10	.06
433	Larry Biittner	.12	.06	.04	523	John Milner	.12	.06	.04
434	Ken Clay	.20	.10	.06	524	Tom Burgmeier	.12	.06	.04
435	Gene Tenace	.20	.10	.06	525	Freddie Patek	.20	.10	.06
436	Hector Cruz	.12	.06	.04	526	Dodgers Team (Tom Lasorda)	.60	.30	.20
437	Rick Williams	.12	.06	.04	527	Lerrin LaGrow	.12	.06	.04
438	Horace Speed	.12	.06	.04	528	Wayne Gross	.12	.06	.04
439	Frank White	.25	.13	.08	529	Brian Asselstine	.12	.06	.04
440	Rusty Staub	.30	.15	.09	530	Frank Tanana	.25	.13	.08
441	Lee Lacy	.20	.10	.06	531	Fernando Gonzalez	.12	.06	.04
442	Doyle Alexander	.25	.13	.08	532	Buddy Schultz	.12	.06	.04
443	Bruce Bochte	.12	.06	.04	533	Leroy Stanton	.12	.06	.04
444	Aurelio Lopez	.25	.13	.08	534	Ken Forsch	.12	.06	.04
445	Steve Henderson	.12	.06	.04	535	Ellis Valentine	.12	.06	.04
446	Jim Lonborg	.20	.10	.06	536	Jerry Reuss	.20	.10	.06
447	Manny Sanguillen	.12	.06	.04	537	Tom Veryzer	.12	.06	.04
448	Moose Haas	.12	.06	.04	538	Mike Ivie	.12	.06	.04
449	Bombo Rivera	.12	.06	.04	539	John Ellis	.12	.06	.04
450	Dave Concepcion	.30	.15	.09	540	Greg Luzinski	.30	.15	.09
451	Royals Team (Whitey Herzog)	.50	.25	.15	541	Jim Slaton	.12	.06	.04
452	Jerry Morales	.12	.06	.04	542	Rick Bosetti	.12	.06	.04
453	Chris Knapp	.12	.06	.04	543	Kiko Garcia	.12	.06	.04
454	Len Randle	.12	.06	.04	544	Fergie Jenkins	.40	.20	.12
455	Bill Lee	.12	.06	.04	545	John Stearns	.12	.06	.04
456	Chuck Baker	.12	.06	.04	546	Bill Russell	.20	.10	.06
457	Bruce Sutter	.70	.35	.20	547	Clint Hurdle	.12	.06	.04
458	Jim Essian	.12	.06	.04	548	Enrique Romo	.12	.06	.04
459	Sid Monge	.12	.06	.04	549	Bob Bailey	.12	.06	.04
460	Graig Nettles	.50	.25	.15	550	Sal Bando	.20	.10	.06
461	Jim Barr	.12	.06	.04	551	Cubs Team (Herman Franks)	.50	.25	.15
462	Otto Velez	.12	.06	.04	552	Jose Morales	.12	.06	.04
463	Steve Comer	.12	.06	.04	553	Denny Walling	.12	.06	.04
464	Joe Nolan	.12	.06	.04	554	Matt Keough	.12	.06	.04
465	Reggie Smith	.25	.13	.08	555	Biff Pocoroba	.12	.06	.04
466	Mark Littell	.12	.06	.04	556	Mike Lum	.12	.06	.04
467	Don Kessinger	.12	.06	.04	557	Ken Brett	.20	.10	.06
468	Stan Bahnsen	.12	.06	.04	558	Jay Johnstone	.20	.10	.06
469	Lance Parrish	3.50	1.75	1.00	559	Greg Pryor	.12	.06	.04
470	Garry Maddox	.12	.06	.04	560	John Montefusco	.20	.10	.06
471	Joaquin Andujar	.20	.10	.06	561	Ed Ott	.12	.06	.04
472	Craig Kusick	.12	.06	.04	562	Dusty Baker	.25	.13	.08
473	Dave Roberts	.12	.06	.04	563	Roy Thomas	.12	.06	.04
474	Dick Davis	.12	.06	.04	564	Jerry Turner	.12	.06	.04
475	Dan Driessen	.20	.10	.06	565	Rico Carty	.25	.13	.08
476	Tom Poquette	.12	.06	.04	566	Nino Espinosa	.12	.06	.04
477	Bob Grich	.25	.13	.08	567	Rich Hebner	.12	.06	.04
478	Juan Beniquez	.12	.06	.04	568	Carlos Lopez	.12	.06	.04
479	Padres Team (Roger Craig)	.50	.25	.15	569	Bob Sykes	.12	.06	.04

		NR MT	EX	VG
570	Cesar Cedeno	.25	.13	.08
571	Darrell Porter	.20	.10	.06
572	Rod Gilbreath	.12	.06	.04
573	Jim Kern	.12	.06	.04
574	Claudell Washington	.20	.10	.06
575	Luis Tiant	.30	.15	.09
576	Mike Parrott	.12	.06	.04
577	Brewers Team (George Bamberger)			
		.50	.25	.15
578	Pete Broberg	.12	.06	.04
579	Greg Gross	.12	.06	.04
580	Ron Fairly	.20	.10	.06
581	Darold Knowles	.12	.06	.04
582	Paul Blair	.20	.10	.06
583	Julio Cruz	.12	.06	.04
584	Jim Rooker	.12	.06	.04
585	Hal McRae	.25	.13	.08
586	Bob Horner	3.00	1.50	.90
587	Ken Reitz	.12	.06	.04
588	Tom Murphy	.12	.06	.04
589	Terry Whitfield	.12	.06	.04
590	J.R. Richard	.20	.10	.06
591	Mike Hargrove	.20	.10	.06
592	Mike Krukow	.20	.10	.06
593	Rick Dempsey	.20	.10	.06
594	Bob Shirley	.20	.10	.06
595	Phil Niekro	1.25	.60	.40
596	Jim Wohlford	.12	.06	.04
597	Bob Stanley	.20	.10	.06
598	Mark Wagner	.12	.06	.04
599	Jim Spencer	.20	.10	.06
600	George Foster	.70	.35	.20
601	Dave LaRoche	.12	.06	.04
602	Checklist 485-605	.60	.30	.20
603	Rudy May	.12	.06	.04
604	Jeff Newman	.12	.06	.04
605	Rick Monday	.12	.06	.04
606	Expos Team (Dick Williams)	.50	.25	.15
607	Omar Moreno	.12	.06	.04
608	Dave McKay	.12	.06	.04
609	Silvio Martinez	.12	.06	.04
610	Mike Schmidt	4.00	2.00	1.25
611	Jim Norris	.12	.06	.04
612	Rick Honeycutt	.50	.25	.15
613	Mike Edwards	.12	.06	.04
614	Willie Hernandez	.25	.13	.08
615	Ken Singleton	.20	.10	.06
616	Billy Almon	.12	.06	.04
617	Terry Puhl	.12	.06	.04
618	Jerry Remy	.12	.06	.04
619	Ken Landreaux	.35	.20	.11
620	Bert Campaneris	.25	.13	.08
621	Pat Zachry	.12	.06	.04
622	Dave Collins	.20	.10	.06
623	Bob McClure	.12	.06	.04
624	Larry Herndon	.20	.10	.06
625	Mark Fidrych	.25	.13	.08
626	Yankees Team (Bob Lemon)	.80	.40	.25
627	Gary Serum	.12	.06	.04
628	Del Unser	.12	.06	.04
629	Gene Garber	.12	.06	.04
630	Bake McBride	.12	.06	.04
631	Jorge Orta	.12	.06	.04
632	Don Kirkwood	.12	.06	.04
633	Rob Wilfong	.12	.06	.04
634	Paul Lindblad	.20	.10	.06
635	Don Baylor	.50	.25	.15
636	Wayne Garland	.12	.06	.04
637	Bill Robinson	.12	.06	.04
638	Al Fitzmorris	.12	.06	.04
639	Manny Trillo	.20	.10	.06
640	Eddie Murray	5.00	2.50	1.50
641	Bobby Castillo	.20	.10	.06
642	Wilbur Howard	.12	.06	.04
643	Tom Hausman	.12	.06	.04
644	Manny Mota	.20	.10	.06
645	George Scott	.12	.06	.04
646	Rick Sweet	.12	.06	.04
647	Bob Lacey	.12	.06	.04
648	Lou Piniella	.35	.20	.11
649	John Curtis	.12	.06	.04
650	Pete Rose	4.50	2.25	1.25
651	Mike Caldwell	.12	.06	.04
652	Stan Papi	.12	.06	.04
653	Warren Brusstar	.12	.06	.04
654	Rick Miller	.12	.06	.04
655	Jerry Koosman	.30	.15	.09
656	Hosken Powell	.12	.06	.04
657	George Medich	.12	.06	.04
658	Taylor Duncan	.12	.06	.04
659	Mariners Team (Darrell Johnson)	.50	.25	.15

		NR MT	EX	VG
660	Ron LeFlore	.12	.06	.04
661	Bruce Kison	.12	.06	.04
662	Kevin Bell	.12	.06	.04
663	Mike Vail	.12	.06	.04
664	Doug Bird	.12	.06	.04
665	Lou Brock	1.50	.70	.45
666	Rich Dauer	.12	.06	.04
667	Don Hood	.12	.06	.04
668	Bill North	.12	.06	.04
669	Checklist 606-726	.60	.30	.20
670	Jim Hunter	.70	.35	.20
671	Joe Ferguson	.12	.06	.04
672	Ed Halicki	.12	.06	.04
673	Tom Hutton	.12	.06	.04
674	Dave Tomlin	.12	.06	.04
675	Tim McCarver	.30	.15	.09
676	Johnny Sutton	.12	.06	.04
677	Larry Parrish	.25	.13	.08
678	Geoff Zahn	.12	.06	.04
679	Derrel Thomas	.12	.06	.04
680	Carlton Fisk	.80	.40	.25
681	John Henry Johnson	.20	.10	.06
682	Dave Chalk	.12	.06	.04
683	Dan Meyer	.12	.06	.04
684	Jamie Easterly	.12	.06	.04
685	Sixto Lezcano	.12	.06	.04
686	Ron Schueler	.12	.06	.04
687	Rennie Stennett	.12	.06	.04
688	Mike Willis	.12	.06	.04
689	Orioles Team (Earl Weaver)	.70	.35	.20
690	Buddy Bell	.12	.06	.04
691	Dock Ellis	.12	.06	.04
692	Mickey Stanley	.20	.10	.06
693	Dave Rader	.12	.06	.04
694	Burt Hooton	.20	.10	.06
695	Keith Hernandez	2.00	1.00	.60
696	Andy Hassler	.12	.06	.04
697	Dave Bergman	.12	.06	.04
698	Bill Stein	.12	.06	.04
699	Hal Dues	.12	.06	.04
700	Reggie Jackson	1.50	.70	.45
701	Orioles Prospects (Mark Corey, John Flinn, Sammy Stewart)	.20	.10	.06
702	Red Sox Prospects (Joel Finch, Garry Hancock, Allen Ripley)	.12	.06	.04
703	Angels Prospects (Jim Anderson, Dave Frost, Bob Slater)	.12	.06	.04
704	White Sox Prospects (Ross Baumgarten, Mike Colbern, Mike Squires)	.20	.10	.06
705	Indians Prospects (Alfredo Griffin, Tim Norrid, Dave Oliver)	.60	.30	.20
706	Tigers Prospects (Dave Stegman, Dave Tobik, Kip Young)	.12	.06	.04
707	Royals Prospects (Randy Bass, Jim Gaudet, Randy McGilberry)	.12	.06	.04
708	Brewers Prospects (Kevin Bass, Eddie Romero, Ned Yost)	1.25	.60	.40
709	Twins Prospects (Sam Perlozzo, Rick Sofield, Kevin Stanfield)	.12	.06	.04
710	Yankees Prospects (Brian Doyle, Mike Heath, Dave Rajsich)	.30	.15	.09
711	A's Prospects (Dwayne Murphy, Bruce Robinson, Alan Wirth)	.60	.30	.20
712	Mariners Prospects (Bud Anderson, Greg Biercevicz, Byron McLaughlin)	.12	.06	.04
713	Rangers Prospects (Danny Darwin, Pat Putnam, Billy Sample)	.40	.20	.12
714	Blue Jays Prospects (Victor Cruz, Pat Kelly, Ernie Whitt)	.20	.10	.06
715	Braves Prospects (Bruce Benedict, Glenn Hubbard, Larry Whisenton)	.40	.20	.12
716	Cubs Prospects (Dave Geisel, Karl Pagel, Scot Thompson)	.20	.10	.06
717	Reds Prospects (Mike LaCoss, Ron Oester, Harry Spilman)	.40	.20	.12
718	Astros Prospects (Bruce Bochy, Mike Fischlin, Don Pisker)	.12	.06	.04
719	Dodgers Prospects (Pedro Guerrero, Rudy Law, Joe Simpson)	6.00	3.00	1.75
720	Expos Prospects (Jerry Fry, Jerry Pirtle, Scott Sanderson)	.40	.20	.12
721	Mets Prospects (Juan Berenguer, Dwight Bernard, Dan Norman)	.35	.20	.11
722	Phillies Prospects (Jim Morrison, Lonnie Smith, Jim Wright)	.60	.30	.20
723	Pirates Prospects (Dale Berra, Eugenio Cotes, Ben Wiltbank)	.30	.15	.09
724	Cardinals Prospects (Tom Bruno, George Frazier, Terry Kennedy)	.70	.35	.20
725	Padres Prospects (Jim Beswick, Steve Mura, Broderick Perkins)	.12	.06	.04

	NR MT	EX	VG
726 Giants Prospects (Greg Johnston, Joe Strain, John Tamargo)	.25	.06	.04

1979 Topps Comics

Issued as the 3'' by 3¾'' wax wrapper for a piece of bubblegum, this "test" issue was bought up in great quantities by speculators and remains rather common. It is also inexpensive, because the comic-style player representations were not popular with collectors. The set is complete at 33 pieces.

	NR MT	EX	VG
Complete Set:	6.50	3.25	2.00
Common Player:	.10	.05	.03
1 Eddie Murray	.40	.20	.12
2 Jim Rice	.30	.15	.09
3 Carl Yastrzemski	.60	.30	.20
4 Nolan Ryan	.30	.15	.09
5 Chet Lemon	.10	.05	.03
6 Andre Thornton	.10	.05	.03
7 Rusty Staub	.15	.08	.05
8 Ron LeFlore	.10	.05	.03
9 George Brett	.50	.25	.15
10 Larry Hisle	.10	.05	.03
11 Rod Carew	.35	.20	.11
12 Reggie Jackson	.40	.20	.12
13 Ron Guidry	.20	.10	.06
14 Mitchell Page	.10	.05	.03
15 Leon Roberts	.10	.05	.03
16 Al Oliver	.15	.08	.05
17 John Mayberry	.10	.05	.03
18 Bob Horner	.20	.10	.06
19 Phil Niekro	.25	.13	.08
20 Dave Kingman	.15	.08	.05
21 John Bench	.40	.20	.12
22 Tom Seaver	.40	.20	.12
23 J.R. Richard	.10	.05	.03
24 Steve Garvey	.35	.20	.11
25 Reggie Smith	.15	.08	.05
26 Ross Grimsley	.10	.05	.03
27 Craig Swan	.10	.05	.03
28 Pete Rose	.90	.45	.25
29 Dave Parker	.20	.10	.06
30 Ted Simmons	.15	.08	.05
31 Dave Winfield	.30	.15	.09
32 Jack Clark	.20	.10	.06
33 Vida Blue	.15	.08	.05

1980 Topps

Again numbering 726 cards measuring 2½'' by 3½,'' Topps did make some design changes in 1980. Fronts have the usual color picture with a facsimile autograph. The player's name appears above the picture, while his position is on a pennant at the upper left and his team on another pennant the lower right. Backs no longer feature games, returning instead to statistics, personal information, a few headlines and a cartoon about the player. Specialty cards include statistical leaders, and previous season highlights. Many rookies again appeared in team threesomes.

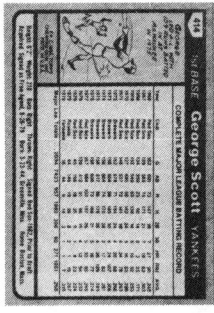

		NR MT	EX	VG
	Complete Set:	135.00	60.00	30.00
	Common Player:	.12	.06	.04
1	1979 Highlights (Lou Brock, Carl Yastrzemski)	1.50	.70	.45
2	1979 Highlights (Willie McCovey)	.80	.40	.25
3	1979 Highlights (Manny Mota)	.20	.10	.06
4	1979 Highlights (Pete Rose)	1.75	.90	.50
5	1979 Highlights (Garry Templeton)	.25	.13	.08
6	1979 Highlights (Del Unser)	.12	.06	.04
7	Mike Lum	.12	.06	.04
8	Craig Swan	.12	.06	.04
9	Steve Braun	.12	.06	.04
10	Denny Martinez	.20	.10	.06
11	Jimmy Sexton	.12	.06	.04
12	John Curtis	.12	.06	.04
13	Ron Pruitt	.12	.06	.04
14	Dave Cash	.12	.06	.04
15	Bill Campbell	.12	.06	.04
16	Jerry Narron	.20	.10	.06
17	Bruce Sutter	.60	.30	.20
18	Ron Jackson	.12	.06	.04
19	Balor Moore	.12	.06	.04
20	Dan Ford	.12	.06	.04
21	Manny Sarmiento	.12	.06	.04
22	Pat Putnam	.12	.06	.04
23	Derrel Thomas	.12	.06	.04
24	Jim Slaton	.12	.06	.04
25	Lee Mazzilli	.20	.10	.06
26	Marty Pattin	.12	.06	.04
27	Del Unser	.12	.06	.04
28	Bruce Kison	.12	.06	.04
29	Mark Wagner	.12	.06	.04
30	Vida Blue	.30	.15	.09
31	Jay Johnstone	.20	.10	.06
32	Julio Cruz	.12	.06	.04
33	Tony Scott	.12	.06	.04
34	Jeff Newman	.12	.06	.04
35	Luis Tiant	.30	.15	.09
36	Rusty Torres	.12	.06	.04
37	Kiko Garcia	.12	.06	.04
38	Dan Spillner	.12	.06	.04
39	Rowland Office	.12	.06	.04
40	Carlton Fisk	.70	.35	.20
41	Rangers Team (Pat Corrales)	.50	.25	.15
42	Dave Palmer	.40	.20	.12
43	Bombo Rivera	.12	.06	.04
44	Bill Fahey	.12	.06	.04
45	Frank White	.25	.13	.08
46	Rico Carty	.20	.10	.06
47	Bill Bonham	.12	.06	.04
48	Rick Miller	.12	.06	.04
49	Mario Guerrero	.12	.06	.04
50	J.R. Richard	.20	.10	.06
51	Joe Ferguson	.12	.06	.04
52	Warren Brusstar	.12	.06	.04
53	Ben Oglivie	.20	.10	.06
54	Dennis Lamp	.12	.06	.04
55	Bill Madlock	.50	.25	.15
56	Bobby Valentine	.20	.10	.06
57	Pete Vuckovich	.20	.10	.06
58	Doug Flynn	.12	.06	.04
59	Eddy Putman	.12	.06	.04
60	Bucky Dent	.25	.13	.08
61	Gary Serum	.12	.06	.04
62	Mike Ivie	.12	.06	.04
63	Bob Stanley	.20	.10	.06
64	Joe Nolan	.12	.06	.04
65	Al Bumbry	.20	.10	.06
66	Royals Team (Jim Frey)	.60	.30	.20
67	Doyle Alexander	.25	.13	.08

#	Player	NR MT	EX	VG
68	Larry Harlow	.12	.06	.04
69	Rick Williams	.12	.06	.04
70	Gary Carter	2.25	1.25	.70
71	John Milner	.12	.06	.04
72	Fred Howard	.12	.06	.04
73	Dave Collins	.20	.10	.06
74	Sid Monge	.12	.06	.04
75	Bill Russell	.20	.10	.06
76	John Stearns	.12	.06	.04
77	Dave Stieb	1.75	.90	.50
78	Ruppert Jones	.12	.06	.04
79	Bob Owchinko	.12	.06	.04
80	Ron LeFlore	.20	.10	.06
81	Ted Sizemore	.12	.06	.04
82	Astros Team (Bill Virdon)	.50	.25	.15
83	Steve Trout	.40	.20	.12
84	Gary Lavelle	.12	.06	.04
85	Ted Simmons	.40	.20	.12
86	Dave Hamilton	.12	.06	.04
87	Pepe Frias	.12	.06	.04
88	Ken Landreaux	.20	.10	.06
89	Don Hood	.20	.10	.06
90	Manny Trillo	.20	.10	.06
91	Rick Dempsey	.20	.10	.06
92	Rick Rhoden	.25	.13	.08
93	Dave Roberts	.12	.06	.04
94	Neil Allen	.30	.15	.09
95	Cecil Cooper	.35	.20	.11
96	A's Team (Jim Marshall)	.50	.25	.15
97	Bill Lee	.20	.10	.06
98	Jerry Terrell	.12	.06	.04
99	Victor Cruz	.12	.06	.04
100	Johnny Bench	2.25	1.25	.70
101	Aurelio Lopez	.12	.06	.04
102	Rich Dauer	.12	.06	.04
103	Bill Caudill	.25	.13	.08
104	Manny Mota	.20	.10	.06
105	Frank Tanana	.20	.10	.06
106	Jeff Leonard	2.25	1.25	.70
107	Francisco Barrios	.12	.06	.04
108	Bob Horner	1.25	.60	.40
109	Bill Travers	.12	.06	.04
110	Fred Lynn	.35	.20	.11
111	Bob Knepper	.20	.10	.06
112	White Sox Team (Tony LaRussa)	.50	.25	.15
113	Geoff Zahn	.12	.06	.04
114	Juan Beniquez	.20	.10	.06
115	Sparky Lyle	.25	.13	.08
116	Larry Cox	.12	.06	.04
117	Dock Ellis	.12	.06	.04
118	Phil Garner	.20	.10	.06
119	Sammy Stewart	.12	.06	.04
120	Greg Luzinski	.30	.15	.09
121	Checklist 1-121	.50	.25	.15
122	Dave Rosello	.12	.06	.04
123	Lynn Jones	.12	.06	.04
124	Dave Lemanczyk	.12	.06	.04
125	Tony Perez	.50	.25	.15
126	Dave Tomlin	.12	.06	.04
127	Gary Thomasson	.12	.06	.04
128	Tom Burgmeier	.12	.06	.04
129	Craig Reynolds	.12	.06	.04
130	Amos Otis	.20	.10	.06
131	Paul Mitchell	.12	.06	.04
132	Biff Pocoroba	.12	.06	.04
133	Jerry Turner	.12	.06	.04
134	Matt Keough	.12	.06	.04
135	Bill Buckner	.30	.15	.09
136	Dick Ruthven	.12	.06	.04
137	John Castino	.20	.10	.06
138	Ross Baumgarten	.12	.06	.04
139	Dane Iorg	.20	.10	.06
140	Rich Gossage	.60	.30	.20
141	Gary Alexander	.12	.06	.04
142	Phil Huffman	.12	.06	.04
143	Bruce Bochte	.12	.06	.04
144	Steve Comer	.12	.06	.04
145	Darrell Evans	.30	.15	.09
146	Bob Welch	.35	.20	.11
147	Terry Puhl	.12	.06	.04
148	Manny Sanguillen	.12	.06	.04
149	Tom Hume	.12	.06	.04
150	Jason Thompson	.20	.10	.06
151	Tom Hausman	.12	.06	.04
152	John Fulgham	.12	.06	.04
153	Tim Blackwell	.12	.06	.04
154	Lary Sorensen	.12	.06	.04
155	Jerry Remy	.12	.06	.04
156	Tony Brizzolara	.12	.06	.04
157	Willie Wilson	.20	.10	.06
158	Rob Picciolo	.12	.06	.04
159	Ken Clay	.20	.10	.06
160	Eddie Murray	3.25	1.75	1.00
161	Larry Christenson	.12	.06	.04
162	Bob Randall	.12	.06	.04
163	Steve Swisher	.12	.06	.04
164	Greg Pryor	.12	.06	.04
165	Omar Moreno	.12	.06	.04
166	Glenn Abbott	.12	.06	.04
167	Jack Clark	1.25	.60	.40
168	Rick Waits	.12	.06	.04
169	Luis Gomez	.12	.06	.04
170	Burt Hooton	.20	.10	.06
171	Fernando Gonzalez	.12	.06	.04
172	Ron Hodges	.12	.06	.04
173	John Henry Johnson	.12	.06	.04
174	Ray Knight	.20	.10	.06
175	Rick Reuschel	.25	.13	.08
176	Champ Summers	.12	.06	.04
177	Dave Heaverlo	.12	.06	.04
178	Tim McCarver	.30	.15	.09
179	Ron Davis	.25	.13	.08
180	Warren Cromartie	.12	.06	.04
181	Moose Haas	.12	.06	.04
182	Ken Reitz	.12	.06	.04
183	Jim Anderson	.12	.06	.04
184	Steve Renko	.12	.06	.04
185	Hal McRae	.25	.13	.08
186	Junior Moore	.12	.06	.04
187	Alan Ashby	.12	.06	.04
188	Terry Crowley	.12	.06	.04
189	Kevin Kobel	.12	.06	.04
190	Buddy Bell	.25	.13	.08
191	Ted Martinez	.12	.06	.04
192	Braves Team (Bobby Cox)	.50	.25	.15
193	Dave Goltz	.20	.10	.06
194	Mike Easler	.30	.15	.09
195	John Montefusco	.20	.10	.06
196	Lance Parrish	1.50	.70	.45
197	Byron McLaughlin	.12	.06	.04
198	Dell Alston	.12	.06	.04
199	Mike LaCoss	.20	.10	.06
200	Jim Rice	2.25	1.25	.70
201	Batting Leaders (Keith Hernandez, Fred Lynn)	.50	.25	.15
202	Home Run Leaders (Dave Kingman, Gorman Thomas)	.25	.13	.08
203	Runs Batted In Leaders (Don Baylor, Dave Winfield)	.50	.25	.15
204	Stolen Base Leaders (Omar Moreno, Willie Wilson)	.20	.10	.06
205	Victory Leaders (Mike Flanagan, Joe Niekro, Phil Niekro)	.40	.20	.12
206	Strikeout Leaders (J.R. Richard, Nolan Ryan)	.50	.25	.15
207	Earned Run Avg. Leaders (Ron Guidry, J.R. Richard)	.25	.13	.08
208	Wayne Cage	.12	.06	.04
209	Von Joshua	.12	.06	.04
210	Steve Carlton	2.25	1.25	.70
211	Dave Skaggs	.12	.06	.04
212	Dave Roberts	.12	.06	.04
213	Mike Jorgensen	.12	.06	.04
214	Angels Team (Jim Fregosi)	.50	.25	.15
215	Sixto Lezcano	.12	.06	.04
216	Phil Mankowski	.12	.06	.04
217	Ed Halicki	.12	.06	.04
218	Jose Morales	.12	.06	.04
219	Steve Mingori	.12	.06	.04
220	Dave Concepcion	.30	.15	.09
221	Joe Cannon	.12	.06	.04
222	Ron Hassey	.25	.13	.08
223	Bob Sykes	.12	.06	.04
224	Willie Montanez	.12	.06	.04
225	Lou Piniella	.30	.15	.09
226	Bill Stein	.12	.06	.04
227	Len Barker	.20	.10	.06
228	Johnny Oates	.12	.06	.04
229	Jim Bibby	.12	.06	.04
230	Dave Winfield	1.75	.90	.50
231	Steve McCatty	.12	.06	.04
232	Alan Trammell	1.50	.70	.45
233	LaRue Washington	.12	.06	.04
234	Vern Ruhle	.12	.06	.04
235	Andre Dawson	1.50	.70	.45
236	Marc Hill	.12	.06	.04
237	Scott McGregor	.20	.10	.06
238	Rob Wilfong	.12	.06	.04
239	Don Aase	.20	.10	.06
240	Dave Kingman	.40	.20	.12
241	Checklist 122-242	.50	.25	.15
242	Lamar Johnson	.12	.06	.04

		NR MT	EX	VG
243	Jerry Augustine	.12	.06	.04
244	Cardinals Team (Ken Boyer)	.50	.25	.15
245	Phil Niekro	.90	.45	.25
246	Tim Foli	.12	.06	.04
247	Frank Riccelli	.12	.06	.04
248	Jamie Quirk	.12	.06	.04
249	Jim Clancy	.25	.13	.08
250	Jim Kaat	.50	.25	.15
251	Kip Young	.12	.06	.04
252	Ted Cox	.12	.06	.04
253	John Montague	.12	.06	.04
254	Paul Dade	.12	.06	.04
255	Dusty Baker	.12	.06	.04
256	Roger Erickson	.12	.06	.04
257	Larry Herndon	.20	.10	.06
258	Paul Moskau	.12	.06	.04
259	Mets Team (Joe Torre)	.60	.30	.20
260	Al Oliver	.35	.20	.11
261	Dave Chalk	.12	.06	.04
262	Benny Ayala	.12	.06	.04
263	Dave LaRoche	.12	.06	.04
264	Bill Robinson	.12	.06	.04
265	Robin Yount	1.75	.90	.50
266	Bernie Carbo	.12	.06	.04
267	Dan Schatzeder	.12	.06	.04
268	Rafael Landestoy	.12	.06	.04
269	Dave Tobik	.12	.06	.04
270	Mike Schmidt	1.50	.70	.45
271	Dick Drago	.12	.06	.04
272	Ralph Garr	.20	.10	.06
273	Eduardo Rodriguez	.12	.06	.04
274	Dale Murphy	5.50	2.75	1.75
275	Jerry Koosman	.25	.13	.08
276	Tom Veryzer	.12	.06	.04
277	Rick Bosetti	.12	.06	.04
278	Jim Spencer	.20	.10	.06
279	Rob Andrews	.12	.06	.04
280	Gaylord Perry	.90	.45	.25
281	Paul Blair	.20	.10	.06
282	Mariners Team (Darrell Johnson)	.50	.25	.15
283	John Ellis	.12	.06	.04
284	Larry Murray	.12	.06	.04
285	Don Baylor	.35	.20	.11
286	Darold Knowles	.12	.06	.04
287	John Lowenstein	.12	.06	.04
288	Dave Rozema	.12	.06	.04
289	Bruce Bochy	.12	.06	.04
290	Steve Garvey	2.00	1.00	.60
291	Randy Scarbery	.12	.06	.04
292	Dale Berra	.20	.10	.06
293	Elias Sosa	.12	.06	.04
294	Charlie Spikes	.12	.06	.04
295	Larry Gura	.20	.10	.06
296	Dave Rader	.12	.06	.04
297	Tim Johnson	.12	.06	.04
298	Ken Holtzman	.20	.10	.06
299	Steve Henderson	.12	.06	.04
300	Ron Guidry	.90	.45	.25
301	Mike Edwards	.12	.06	.04
302	Dodgers Team (Tom Lasorda)	.60	.30	.20
303	Bill Castro	.12	.06	.04
304	Butch Wynegar	.20	.10	.06
305	Randy Jones	.20	.10	.06
306	Denny Walling	.12	.06	.04
307	Rick Honeycutt	.20	.10	.06
308	Mike Hargrove	.20	.10	.06
309	Larry McWilliams	.12	.06	.04
310	Dave Parker	1.00	.50	.30
311	Roger Metzger	.12	.06	.04
312	Mike Barlow	.12	.06	.04
313	Johnny Grubb	.12	.06	.04
314	Tim Stoddard	.20	.10	.06
315	Steve Kemp	.25	.13	.08
316	Bob Lacey	.12	.06	.04
317	Mike Anderson	.12	.06	.04
318	Jerry Reuss	.20	.10	.06
319	Chris Speier	.12	.06	.04
320	Dennis Eckersley	.20	.10	.06
321	Keith Hernandez	1.50	.70	.45
322	Claudell Washington	.20	.10	.06
323	Mick Kelleher	.12	.06	.04
324	Tom Underwood	.12	.06	.04
325	Dan Driessen	.20	.10	.06
326	Bo McLaughlin	.12	.06	.04
327	Ray Fosse	.12	.06	.04
328	Twins Team (Gene Mauch)	.50	.25	.15
329	Bert Roberge	.12	.06	.04
330	Al Cowens	.12	.06	.04
331	Rich Hebner	.12	.06	.04
332	Enrique Romo	.12	.06	.04
333	Jim Norris	.12	.06	.04

		NR MT	EX	VG
334	Jim Beattie	.20	.10	.06
335	Willie McCovey	1.50	.70	.45
336	George Medich	.12	.06	.04
337	Carney Lansford	.25	.13	.08
338	Johnny Wockenfuss	.12	.06	.04
339	John D'Acquisto	.12	.06	.04
340	Ken Singleton	.20	.10	.06
341	Jim Essian	.12	.06	.04
342	Odell Jones	.12	.06	.04
343	Mike Vail	.12	.06	.04
344	Randy Lerch	.12	.06	.04
345	Larry Parrish	.20	.10	.06
346	Buddy Solomon	.12	.06	.04
347	Harry Chappas	.20	.10	.06
348	Checklist 243-363	.50	.25	.15
349	Jack Brohamer	.12	.06	.04
350	George Hendrick	.50	.25	.15
351	Bob Davis	.12	.06	.04
352	Dan Briggs	.12	.06	.04
353	Andy Hassler	.12	.06	.04
354	Rick Auerbach	.12	.06	.04
355	Gary Matthews	.20	.10	.06
356	Padres Team (Jerry Coleman)	.50	.25	.15
357	Bob McClure	.12	.06	.04
358	Lou Whitaker	1.00	.50	.30
359	Randy Moffitt	.12	.06	.04
360	Darrell Porter	.12	.06	.04
361	Wayne Garland	.12	.06	.04
362	Danny Goodwin	.12	.06	.04
363	Wayne Gross	.12	.06	.04
364	Ray Burris	.12	.06	.04
365	Bobby Murcer	.25	.13	.08
366	Rob Dressler	.12	.06	.04
367	Billy Smith	.12	.06	.04
368	Willie Aikens	.20	.10	.06
369	Jim Kern	.12	.06	.04
370	Cesar Cedeno	.25	.13	.08
371	Jack Morris	1.25	.60	.40
372	Joel Youngblood	.12	.06	.04
373	Dan Petry	.60	.30	.20
374	Jim Gantner	.20	.10	.06
375	Ross Grimsley	.12	.06	.04
376	Gary Allenson	.12	.06	.04
377	Junior Kennedy	.12	.06	.04
378	Jerry Mumphrey	.20	.10	.06
379	Kevin Bell	.12	.06	.04
380	Garry Maddox	.20	.10	.06
381	Cubs Team (Preston Gomez)	.50	.25	.15
382	Dave Freisleben	.12	.06	.04
383	Ed Ott	.12	.06	.04
384	Joey McLaughlin	.12	.06	.04
385	Enos Cabell	.12	.06	.04
386	Darrell Jackson	.12	.06	.04
387a	Fred Stanley (name in red)	.20	.10	.06
387b	Fred Stanley (name in yellow)	1.00	.50	.30
388	Mike Paxton	.12	.06	.04
389	Pete LaCock	.12	.06	.04
390	Fergie Jenkins	.40	.20	.12
391	Tony Armas	.12	.06	.04
392	Milt Wilcox	.20	.10	.06
393	Ozzie Smith	1.25	.60	.40
394	Reggie Cleveland	.12	.06	.04
395	Ellis Valentine	.12	.06	.04
396	Dan Meyer	.12	.06	.04
397	Roy Thomas	.12	.06	.04
398	Barry Foote	.12	.06	.04
399	Mike Proly	.12	.06	.04
400	George Foster	.50	.25	.15
401	Pete Falcone	.12	.06	.04
402	Merv Rettenmund	.12	.06	.04
403	Pete Redfern	.12	.06	.04
404	Orioles Team (Earl Weaver)	.60	.30	.20
405	Dwight Evans	.60	.30	.20
406	Paul Molitor	.80	.40	.25
407	Tony Solaita	.12	.06	.04
408	Bill North	.12	.06	.04
409	Paul Splittorff	.20	.10	.06
410	Bobby Bonds	.25	.13	.08
411	Frank LaCorte	.12	.06	.04
412	Thad Bosley	.12	.06	.04
413	Allen Ripley	.12	.06	.04
414	George Scott	.20	.10	.06
415	Bill Atkinson	.12	.06	.04
416	Tom Brookens	.25	.13	.08
417	Craig Chamberlain	.12	.06	.04
418	Roger Freed	.12	.06	.04
419	Vic Correll	.12	.06	.04
420	Butch Hobson	.12	.06	.04
421	Doug Bird	.12	.06	.04
422	Larry Milbourne	.12	.06	.04
423	Dave Frost	.12	.06	.04

		NR MT	EX	VG
424	Yankees Team (Dick Howser)	.70	.35	.20
425	Mark Belanger	.20	.10	.06
426	Grant Jackson	.12	.06	.04
427	Tom Hutton	.12	.06	.04
428	Pat Zachry	.12	.06	.04
429	Duane Kuiper	.12	.06	.04
430	Larry Hisle	.12	.06	.04
431	Mike Krukow	.20	.10	.06
432	Willie Norwood	.12	.06	.04
433	Rich Gale	.12	.06	.04
434	Johnnie LeMaster	.12	.06	.04
435	Don Gullett	.20	.10	.06
436	Billy Almon	.12	.06	.04
437	Joe Niekro	.20	.10	.06
438	Dave Revering	.12	.06	.04
439	Mike Phillips	.12	.06	.04
440	Don Sutton	.90	.45	.25
441	Eric Soderholm	.12	.06	.04
442	Jorge Orta	.12	.06	.04
443	Mike Parrott	.12	.06	.04
444	Alvis Woods	.12	.06	.04
445	Mark Fidrych	.20	.10	.06
446	Duffy Dyer	.12	.06	.04
447	Nino Espinosa	.12	.06	.04
448	Jim Wohlford	.12	.06	.04
449	Doug Bair	.12	.06	.04
450	George Brett	3.50	1.75	1.00
451	Indians Team (Dave Garcia)	.50	.25	.15
452	Steve Dillard	.12	.06	.04
453	Mike Bacsik	.12	.06	.04
454	Tom Donohue	.12	.06	.04
455	Mike Torrez	.20	.10	.06
456	Frank Taveras	.12	.06	.04
457	Bert Blyleven	.50	.25	.15
458	Billy Sample	.12	.06	.04
459	Mickey Lolich	.12	.06	.04
460	Willie Randolph	.25	.13	.08
461	Dwayne Murphy	.20	.10	.06
462	Mike Sadek	.12	.06	.04
463	Jerry Royster	.12	.06	.04
464	John Denny	.12	.06	.04
465	Rick Monday	.20	.10	.06
466	Mike Squires	.12	.06	.04
467	Jesse Jefferson	.12	.06	.04
468	Aurelio Rodriguez	.20	.10	.06
469	Randy Niemann	.12	.06	.04
470	Bob Boone	.20	.10	.06
471	Hosken Powell	.12	.06	.04
472	Willie Hernandez	.20	.10	.06
473	Bump Wills	.12	.06	.04
474	Steve Busby	.12	.06	.04
475	Cesar Geronimo	.12	.06	.04
476	Bob Shirley	.20	.10	.06
477	Buck Martinez	.12	.06	.04
478	Gil Flores	.12	.06	.04
479	Expos Team (Dick Williams)	.50	.25	.15
480	Bob Watson	.20	.10	.06
481	Tom Paciorek	.12	.06	.04
482	Rickey Henderson	28.00	14.00	8.50
483	Bo Diaz	.20	.10	.06
484	Checklist 364-484	.50	.25	.15
485	Mickey Rivers	.20	.10	.06
486	Mike Tyson	.12	.06	.04
487	Wayne Nordhagen	.12	.06	.04
488	Roy Howell	.12	.06	.04
489	Preston Hanna	.12	.06	.04
490	Lee May	.20	.10	.06
491	Steve Mura	.12	.06	.04
492	Todd Cruz	.12	.06	.04
493	Jerry Martin	.12	.06	.04
494	Craig Minetto	.12	.06	.04
495	Bake McBride	.12	.06	.04
496	Silvio Martinez	.12	.06	.04
497	Jim Mason	.12	.06	.04
498	Danny Darwin	.20	.10	.06
499	Giants Team (Dave Bristol)	.50	.25	.15
500	Tom Seaver	1.75	.90	.50
501	Rennie Stennett	.12	.06	.04
502	Rich Wortham	.12	.06	.04
503	Mike Cubbage	.12	.06	.04
504	Gene Garber	.12	.06	.04
505	Bert Campaneris	.20	.10	.06
506	Tom Buskey	.12	.06	.04
507	Leon Roberts	.12	.06	.04
508	U.L. Washington	.12	.06	.04
509	Ed Glynn	.12	.06	.04
510	Ron Cey	.25	.13	.08
511	Eric Wilkins	.12	.06	.04
512	Jose Cardenal	.12	.06	.04
513	Tom Dixon	.12	.06	.04
514	Steve Ontiveros	.12	.06	.04

		NR MT	EX	VG
515	Mike Caldwell	.12	.06	.04
516	Hector Cruz	.12	.06	.04
517	Don Stanhouse	.12	.06	.04
518	Nelson Norman	.12	.06	.04
519	Steve Nicosia	.12	.06	.04
520	Steve Rogers	.20	.10	.06
521	Ken Brett	.12	.06	.04
522	Jim Morrison	.12	.06	.04
523	Ken Henderson	.12	.06	.04
524	Jim Wright	.12	.06	.04
525	Clint Hurdle	.12	.06	.04
526	Phillies Team (Dallas Green)	.70	.35	.20
527	Doug Rau	.12	.06	.04
528	Adrian Devine	.12	.06	.04
529	Jim Barr	.12	.06	.04
530	Jim Sundberg	.12	.06	.04
531	Eric Rasmussen	.12	.06	.04
532	Willie Horton	.20	.10	.06
533	Checklist 485-605	.50	.25	.15
534	Andre Thornton	.25	.13	.08
535	Bob Forsch	.20	.10	.06
536	Lee Lacy	.20	.10	.06
537	Alex Trevino	.20	.10	.06
538	Joe Strain	.12	.06	.04
539	Rudy May	.12	.06	.04
540	Pete Rose	4.00	2.00	1.25
541	Miguel Dilone	.12	.06	.04
542	Joe Coleman	.12	.06	.04
543	Pat Kelly	.12	.06	.04
544	Rick Sutcliffe	3.00	1.50	.90
545	Jeff Burroughs	.20	.10	.06
546	Rick Langford	.12	.06	.04
547	John Wathan	.20	.10	.06
548	Dave Rajsich	.12	.06	.04
549	Larry Wolfe	.12	.06	.04
550	Ken Griffey	.25	.13	.08
551	Pirates Team (Chuck Tanner)	.50	.25	.15
552	Bill Nahorodny	.12	.06	.04
553	Dick Davis	.12	.06	.04
554	Art Howe	.12	.06	.04
555	Ed Figueroa	.20	.10	.06
556	Joe Rudi	.20	.10	.06
557	Mark Lee	.12	.06	.04
558	Alfredo Griffin	.25	.13	.08
559	Dale Murray	.12	.06	.04
560	Dave Lopes	.25	.13	.08
561	Eddie Whitson	.20	.10	.06
562	Joe Wallis	.12	.06	.04
563	Will McEnaney	.12	.06	.04
564	Rick Manning	.12	.06	.04
565	Dennis Leonard	.20	.10	.06
566	Bud Harrelson	.20	.10	.06
567	Skip Lockwood	.12	.06	.04
568	Gary Roenicke	.25	.13	.08
569	Terry Kennedy	.30	.15	.09
570	Roy Smalley	.20	.10	.06
571	Joe Sambito	.12	.06	.04
572	Jerry Morales	.12	.06	.04
573	Kent Tekulve	.20	.10	.06
574	Scot Thompson	.12	.06	.04
575	Ken Kravec	.12	.06	.04
576	Jim Dwyer	.12	.06	.04
577	Blue Jays Team (Bobby Mattick)	.50	.25	.15
578	Scott Sanderson	.20	.10	.06
579	Charlie Moore	.12	.06	.04
580	Nolan Ryan	1.75	.90	.50
581	Bob Bailor	.12	.06	.04
582	Brian Doyle	.20	.10	.06
583	Bob Stinson	.12	.06	.04
584	Kurt Bevacqua	.12	.06	.04
585	Al Hrabosky	.20	.10	.06
586	Mitchell Page	.12	.06	.04
587	Garry Templeton	.25	.13	.08
588	Greg Minton	.12	.06	.04
589	Chet Lemon	.20	.10	.06
590	Jim Palmer	1.25	.60	.40
591	Rick Cerone	.20	.10	.06
592	Jon Matlack	.20	.10	.06
593	Jesus Alou	.12	.06	.04
594	Dick Tidrow	.12	.06	.04
595	Don Money	.20	.10	.06
596	Rick Matula	.12	.06	.04
597	Tom Poquette	.12	.06	.04
598	Fred Kendall	.12	.06	.04
599	Mike Norris	.12	.06	.04
600	Reggie Jackson	2.25	1.25	.70
601	Buddy Schultz	.12	.06	.04
602	Brian Downing	.20	.10	.06
603	Jack Billingham	.12	.06	.04
604	Glenn Adams	.12	.06	.04
605	Terry Forster	.20	.10	.06

		NR MT	EX	VG
606	Reds Team (John McNamara)	.50	.25	.15
607	Woodie Fryman	.20	.10	.06
608	Alan Bannister	.12	.06	.04
609	Ron Reed	.20	.10	.06
610	Willie Stargell	1.50	.70	.45
611	Jerry Garvin	.12	.06	.04
612	Cliff Johnson	.12	.06	.04
613	Randy Stein	.12	.06	.04
614	John Hiller	.20	.10	.06
615	Doug DeCinces	.20	.10	.06
616	Gene Richards	.12	.06	.04
617	Joaquin Andujar	.20	.10	.06
618	Bob Montgomery	.12	.06	.04
619	Sergio Ferrer	.12	.06	.04
620	Richie Zisk	.20	.10	.06
621	Bob Grich	.20	.10	.06
622	Mario Soto	.20	.10	.06
623	Gorman Thomas	.20	.10	.06
624	Lerrin LaGrow	.12	.06	.04
625	Chris Chambliss	.25	.13	.08
626	Tigers Team (Sparky Anderson)	.60	.30	.20
627	Pedro Borbon	.12	.06	.04
628	Doug Capilla	.12	.06	.04
629	Jim Todd	.12	.06	.04
630	Larry Bowa	.25	.13	.08
631	Mark Littell	.12	.06	.04
632	Barry Bonnell	.12	.06	.04
633	Bob Apodaca	.12	.06	.04
634	Glenn Borgmann	.12	.06	.04
635	John Candelaria	.20	.10	.06
636	Toby Harrah	.20	.10	.06
637	Joe Simpson	.12	.06	.04
638	Mark Clear	.35	.20	.11
639	Larry Biittner	.12	.06	.04
640	Mike Flanagan	.25	.13	.08
641	Ed Kranepool	.20	.10	.06
642	Ken Forsch	.12	.06	.04
643	John Mayberry	.20	.10	.06
644	Charlie Hough	.20	.10	.06
645	Rick Burleson	.20	.10	.06
646	Checklist 606-726	.50	.25	.15
647	Milt May	.12	.06	.04
648	Roy White	.20	.10	.06
649	Tom Griffin	.12	.06	.04
650	Joe Morgan	1.00	.50	.30
651	Rollie Fingers	.50	.25	.15
652	Mario Mendoza	.12	.06	.04
653	Stan Bahnsen	.12	.06	.04
654	Bruce Boisclair	.12	.06	.04
655	Tug McGraw	.25	.13	.08
656	Larvell Blanks	.12	.06	.04
657	Dave Edwards	.12	.06	.04
658	Chris Knapp	.12	.06	.04
659	Brewers Team (George Bamberger)	.50	.25	.15
660	Rusty Staub	.30	.15	.09
661	Orioles Future Stars (Mark Corey, Dave Ford, Wayne Krenchicki)	.12	.06	.04
662	Red Sox Future Stars (Joel Finch, Mike O'Berry, Chuck Rainey)	.12	.06	.04
663	Angels Future Stars (Ralph Botting, Bob Clark, Dickie Thon)	.30	.15	.09
664	White Sox Future Stars (Mike Colbern, Guy Hoffman, Dewey Robinson)	.20	.10	.06
665	Indians Future Stars (Larry Andersen, Bobby Cuellar, Sandy Wihtol)	.12	.06	.04
666	Tigers Future Stars (Mike Chris, Al Greene, Bruce Robbins)	.12	.06	.04
667	Royals Future Stars (Renie Martin, Bill Paschall, Dan Quisenberry)	1.50	.70	.45
668	Brewers Future Stars (Danny Boitano, Willie Mueller, Lenn Sakata)	.12	.06	.04
669	Twins Future Stars (Dan Graham, Rick Sofield, Gary Ward)	.60	.30	.20
670	Yankees Future Stars (Bobby Brown, Brad Gulden, Darryl Jones)	.20	.10	.06
671	A's Future Stars (Derek Bryant, Brian Kingman, Mike Morgan)	.20	.10	.06
672	Mariners Future Stars (Charlie Beamon, Rodney Craig, Rafael Vasquez)	.12	.06	.04
673	Rangers Future Stars (Brian Allard, Jerry Don Gleaton, Greg Mahlberg)	.12	.06	.04
674	Blue Jays Future Stars (Butch Edge, Pat Kelly, Ted Wilborn)	.12	.06	.04
675	Braves Future Stars (Bruce Benedict, Larry Bradford, Eddie Miller)	.12	.06	.04
676	Cubs Future Stars (Dave Geisel, Steve Macko, Karl Pagel)	.12	.06	.04
677	Reds Future Stars (Art DeFreites, Frank Pastore, Harry Spilman)	.20	.10	.06

		NR MT	EX	VG
678	Astros Future Stars (Reggie Baldwin, Alan Knicely, Pete Ladd)	.20	.10	.06
679	Dodgers Future Stars (Joe Beckwith, Mickey Hatcher, Dave Patterson)	.30	.15	.09
680	Expos Future Stars (Tony Bernazard, Randy Miller, John Tamargo)	.40	.20	.12
681	Mets Future Stars (Dan Norman, Jesse Orosco, Mike Scott)	6.00	3.00	1.75
682	Phillies Future Stars (Ramon Aviles, Dickie Noles, Kevin Saucier)	.20	.10	.06
683	Pirates Future Stars (Dorian Boyland, Alberto Lois, Harry Saferight)	.12	.06	.04
684	Cardinals Future Stars (George Frazier, Tom Herr, Dan O'Brien)	.70	.35	.20
685	Padres Future Stars (Tim Flannery, Brian Greer, Jim Wilhelm)	.12	.06	.04
686	Giants Future Stars (Greg Johnston, Dennis Littlejohn, Phil Nastu)	.12	.06	.04
687	Mike Heath	.12	.06	.04
688	Steve Stone	.25	.13	.08
689	Red Sox Team (Don Zimmer)	.60	.30	.20
690	Tommy John	.60	.30	.20
691	Ivan DeJesus	.12	.06	.04
692	Rawly Eastwick	.12	.06	.04
693	Craig Kusick	.12	.06	.04
694	Jim Rooker	.12	.06	.04
695	Reggie Smith	.20	.10	.06
696	Julio Gonzalez	.12	.06	.04
697	David Clyde	.12	.06	.04
698	Oscar Gamble	.20	.10	.06
699	Floyd Bannister	.20	.10	.06
700	Rod Carew	1.00	.50	.30
701	Ken Oberkfell	.35	.20	.11
702	Ed Farmer	.12	.06	.04
703	Otto Velez	.12	.06	.04
704	Gene Tenace	.20	.10	.06
705	Freddie Patek	.12	.06	.04
706	Tippy Martinez	.12	.06	.04
707	Elliott Maddox	.12	.06	.04
708	Bob Tolan	.12	.06	.04
709	Pat Underwood	.12	.06	.04
710	Graig Nettles	.35	.20	.11
711	Bob Galasso	.12	.06	.04
712	Rodney Scott	.12	.06	.04
713	Terry Whitfield	.12	.06	.04
714	Fred Norman	.12	.06	.04
715	Sal Bando	.20	.10	.06
716	Lynn McGlothen	.12	.06	.04
717	Mickey Klutts	.12	.06	.04
718	Greg Gross	.12	.06	.04
719	Don Robinson	.20	.10	.06
720	Carl Yastrzemski	1.25	.60	.40
721	Paul Hartzell	.12	.06	.04
722	Jose Cruz	.20	.10	.06
723	Shane Rawley	.20	.10	.06
724	Jerry White	.12	.06	.04
725	Rick Wise	.20	.10	.06
726	Steve Yeager	.20	.06	.04

1980 Topps Superstar 5x7 Photos

In actuality, they measure 4⅞" by 6⅞". These were another Topps "test" issue that was bought up almost entirely by investors. The 60 cards have a color photo on the front and a blue ink facsimile autograph. Backs have the player's name, team position and card number. The issue was printed on different cardboard stocks with the first on thick cardboard with a white back and the second on thinner cardboard with a gray back. Prices below are for the more common gray backs; white backs are valued about three times the figures shown. The issue was distributed in selected geographical areas, but they were hoarded quickly. Those who hoarded them still probably have much of their supply as the set has never taken off, despite the presence of many big-name stars.

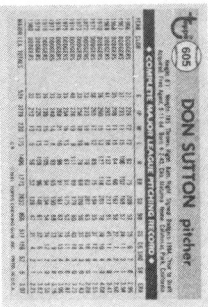

	NR MT	EX	VG
Complete Set:	7.00	3.50	2.00
Common Player:	.10	.05	.03
1	Willie Stargell	.30	.15	.09
2	Mike Schmidt	.30	.15	.09
3	Johnny Bench	.50	.25	.15
4	Jim Palmer	.35	.20	.11
5	Jim Rice	.40	.20	.12
6	Reggie Jackson	.25	.13	.08
7	Ron Guidry	.20	.10	.06
8	Lee Mazzilli	.10	.05	.03
9	Don Baylor	.15	.08	.05
10	Fred Lynn	.20	.10	.06
11	Ken Singleton	.10	.05	.03
12	Rod Carew	.25	.13	.08
13	Steve Garvey	.25	.13	.08
14	George Brett	.30	.15	.09
15	Tom Seaver	.40	.20	.12
16	Dave Kingman	.15	.08	.05
17	Dave Parker	.10	.05	.03
18	Dave Winfield	.40	.20	.12
19	Pete Rose	1.00	.50	.30
20	Nolan Ryan	.40	.20	.12
21	Graig Nettles	.15	.08	.05
22	Carl Yastrzemski	.60	.30	.20
23	Tommy John	.25	.13	.08
24	George Foster	.15	.08	.05
25	James Rodney Richard	.10	.05	.03
26	Keith Hernandez	.30	.15	.09
27	Bob Horner	.20	.10	.06
28	Eddie Murray	.40	.20	.12
29	Steve Kemp	.10	.05	.03
30	Gorman Thomas	.10	.05	.03
31	Sixto Lezcano	.10	.05	.03
32	Bruce Sutter	.15	.08	.05
33	Cecil Cooper	.15	.08	.05
34	Larry Bowa	.10	.05	.03
35	Al Oliver	.15	.08	.05
36	Ted Simmons	.15	.08	.05
37	Garry Templeton	.10	.05	.03
38	Jerry Koosman	.10	.05	.03
39	Darrell Porter	.10	.05	.03
40	Roy Smalley	.10	.05	.03
41	Craig Swan	.10	.05	.03
42	Jason Thompson	.10	.05	.03
43	Andre Thornton	.10	.05	.03
44	Rick Manning	.10	.05	.03
45	Kent Tekulve	.10	.05	.03
46	Phil Niekro	.30	.15	.09
47	Buddy Bell	.15	.08	.05
48	Randy Jones	.10	.05	.03
49	Brian Downing	.10	.05	.03
50	Amos Otis	.10	.05	.03
51	Rick Bosetti	.10	.05	.03
52	Gary Carter	.40	.20	.12
53	Larry Parrish	.15	.08	.05
54	Jack Clark	.20	.10	.06
55	Bruce Bochte	.10	.05	.03
56	Cesar Cedeno	.15	.08	.05
57	Chet Lemon	.10	.05	.03
58	Dave Revering	.10	.05	.03
59	Vida Blue	.15	.08	.05
60	Davey Lopes	.15	.08	.05

1981 Topps

Another 726-card set of 2½'' by 3½'' cards from Topps. The cards had the usual color photo with all cards from the same team sharing the same color borders. The player's name appears under the photo with his team and position appearing on a baseball cap at the lower left. The Topps logo returned in a

small baseball in the lower right corner. Card backs included the usual stats along with a headline and a cartoon if there was room. Specialty cards include previous season record-breakers, highlights of the Play-offs and World Series along with the final appearance of team cards.

		MT	NR MT	EX
Complete Set:		80.00	60.00	32.00
Common Player:		.08	.06	.03
1	Batting Leaders (George Brett, Bill Buckner)	.70	.50	.30
2	Home Run Leaders (Reggie Jackson, Ben Oglivie, Mike Schmidt)	.40	.30	.15
3	Runs Batted In Leaders (Cecil Cooper, Mike Schmidt)	.30	.25	.12
4	Stolen Base Leaders (Rickey Henderson, Ron LeFlore)	.25	.20	.10
5	Victory Leaders (Steve Carlton, Steve Stone)	.20	.15	.08
6	Strikeout Leaders (Len Barker, Steve Carlton)	.20	.15	.08
7	Earned Run Avg. Leaders (Rudy May, Don Sutton)	.15	.11	.06
8	Leading Firemen (Rollie Fingers, Tom Hume, Dan Quisenberry)	.15	.11	.06
9	Pete LaCock	.08	.06	.03
10	Mike Flanagan	.12	.09	.05
11	Jim Wohlford	.08	.06	.03
12	Mark Clear	.12	.09	.05
13	Joe Charboneau	.15	.11	.06
14	John Tudor	1.25	.90	.50
15	Larry Parrish	.15	.11	.06
16	Ron Davis	.10	.08	.04
17	Cliff Johnson	.08	.06	.03
18	Glenn Adams	.08	.06	.03
19	Jim Clancy	.15	.11	.06
20	Jeff Burroughs	.10	.08	.04
21	Ron Oester	.08	.06	.03
22	Danny Darwin	.10	.08	.04
23	Alex Trevino	.08	.06	.03
24	Don Stanhouse	.08	.06	.03
25	Sixto Lezcano	.08	.06	.03
26	U.L. Washington	.08	.06	.03
27	Champ Summers	.08	.06	.03
28	Enrique Romo	.08	.06	.03
29	Gene Tenace	.10	.08	.04
30	Jack Clark	.50	.40	.20
31	Checklist 1-121	.08	.06	.03
32	Ken Oberkfell	.10	.08	.04
33	Rick Honeycutt	.10	.08	.04
34	Aurelio Rodriguez	.10	.08	.04
35	Mitchell Page	.08	.06	.03
36	Ed Farmer	.08	.06	.03
37	Gary Roenicke	.12	.09	.05
38	Win Remmerswaal	.08	.06	.03
39	Tom Veryzer	.08	.06	.03
40	Tug McGraw	.20	.15	.08
41	Rangers Future Stars (Bob Babcock, John Butcher, Jerry Don Gleaton)	.10	.08	.04
42	Jerry White	.08	.06	.03
43	Jose Morales	.08	.06	.03
44	Larry McWilliams	.08	.06	.03
45	Enos Cabell	.10	.08	.04
46	Rick Bosetti	.08	.06	.03
47	Ken Brett	.10	.08	.04
48	Dave Skaggs	.08	.06	.03
49	Bob Shirley	.08	.06	.03
50	Dave Lopes	.15	.11	.06

		MT	NR MT	EX
51	Bill Robinson	.08	.06	.03
52	Hector Cruz	.08	.06	.03
53	Kevin Saucier	.08	.06	.03
54	Ivan DeJesus	.08	.06	.03
55	Mike Norris	.08	.06	.03
56	Buck Martinez	.08	.06	.03
57	Dave Roberts	.08	.06	.03
58	Joel Youngblood	.08	.06	.03
59	Dan Petry	.20	.15	.08
60	Willie Randolph	.15	.11	.06
61	Butch Wynegar	.12	.09	.05
62	Joe Pettini	.08	.06	.03
63	Steve Renko	.08	.06	.03
64	Brian Asselstine	.08	.06	.03
65	Scott McGregor	.12	.09	.05
66	Royals Future Stars (Manny Castillo, Tim Ireland, Mike Jones)	.08	.06	.03
67	Ken Kravec	.08	.06	.03
68	Matt Alexander	.08	.06	.03
69	Ed Halicki	.08	.06	.03
70	Al Oliver	.15	.11	.06
71	Hal Dues	.08	.06	.03
72	Barry Evans	.08	.06	.03
73	Doug Bair	.08	.06	.03
74	Mike Hargrove	.10	.08	.04
75	Reggie Smith	.15	.11	.06
76	Mario Mendoza	.08	.06	.03
77	Mike Barlow	.08	.06	.03
78	Steve Dillard	.08	.06	.03
79	Bruce Robbins	.08	.06	.03
80	Rusty Staub	.20	.15	.08
81	Dave Stapleton	.12	.09	.05
82	Astros Future Stars (Danny Heep, Alan Knicely, Bobby Sprowl)	.08	.06	.03
83	Mike Proly	.08	.06	.03
84	Johnnie LeMaster	.08	.06	.03
85	Mike Caldwell	.10	.08	.04
86	Wayne Gross	.08	.06	.03
87	Rick Camp	.08	.06	.03
88	Joe Lefebvre	.10	.08	.04
89	Darrell Jackson	.08	.06	.03
90	Bake McBride	.08	.06	.03
91	Tim Stoddard	.08	.06	.03
92	Mike Easler	.12	.09	.05
93	Ed Glynn	.08	.06	.03
94	Harry Spilman	.08	.06	.03
95	Jim Sundberg	.10	.08	.04
96	A's Future Stars (Dave Beard, Ernie Camacho, Pat Dempsey)	.15	.11	.06
97	Chris Speier	.10	.08	.04
98	Clint Hurdle	.08	.06	.03
99	Eric Wilkins	.08	.06	.03
100	Rod Carew	1.25	.90	.50
101	Benny Ayala	.08	.06	.03
102	Dave Tobik	.08	.06	.03
103	Jerry Martin	.08	.06	.03
104	Terry Forster	.10	.08	.04
105	Jose Cruz	.15	.11	.06
106	Don Money	.10	.08	.04
107	Rich Wortham	.08	.06	.03
108	Bruce Benedict	.08	.06	.03
109	Mike Scott	.80	.60	.30
110	Carl Yastrzemski	1.50	1.25	.60
111	Greg Minton	.08	.06	.03
112	White Sox Future Stars (Rusty Kuntz, Fran Mullins, Leo Sutherland)	.08	.06	.03
113	Mike Phillips	.08	.06	.03
114	Tom Underwood	.08	.06	.03
115	Roy Smalley	.10	.08	.04
116	Joe Simpson	.08	.06	.03
117	Pete Falcone	.08	.06	.03
118	Kurt Bevacqua	.08	.06	.03
119	Tippy Martinez	.08	.06	.03
120	Larry Bowa	.20	.15	.08
121	Larry Harlow	.08	.06	.03
122	John Denny	.10	.08	.04
123	Al Cowens	.08	.06	.03
124	Jerry Garvin	.08	.06	.03
125	Andre Dawson	.70	.50	.30
126	Charlie Leibrandt	.60	.45	.25
127	Rudy Law	.08	.06	.03
128	Gary Allenson	.08	.06	.03
129	Art Howe	.08	.06	.03
130	Larry Gura	.10	.08	.04
131	Keith Moreland	.60	.45	.25
132	Tommy Boggs	.08	.06	.03
133	Jeff Cox	.08	.06	.03
134	Steve Mura	.08	.06	.03
135	Gorman Thomas	.15	.11	.06
136	Doug Capilla	.08	.06	.03
137	Hosken Powell	.08	.06	.03
138	Rich Dotson	.30	.25	.12
139	Oscar Gamble	.10	.08	.04
140	Bob Forsch	.12	.09	.05
141	Miguel Dilone	.08	.06	.03
142	Jackson Todd	.08	.06	.03
143	Dan Meyer	.08	.06	.03
144	Allen Ripley	.08	.06	.03
145	Mickey Rivers	.12	.09	.05
146	Bobby Castillo	.08	.06	.03
147	Dale Berra	.08	.06	.03
148	Randy Niemann	.08	.06	.03
149	Joe Nolan	.08	.06	.03
150	Mark Fidrych	.12	.09	.05
151	Claudell Washington	.12	.09	.05
152	John Urrea	.08	.06	.03
153	Tom Poquette	.08	.06	.03
154	Rick Langford	.08	.06	.03
155	Chris Chambliss	.12	.09	.05
156	Bob McClure	.08	.06	.03
157	John Wathan	.12	.09	.05
158	Fergie Jenkins	.30	.25	.12
159	Brian Doyle	.08	.06	.03
160	Garry Maddox	.12	.09	.05
161	Dan Graham	.08	.06	.03
162	Doug Corbett	.10	.08	.04
163	Billy Almon	.08	.06	.03
164	Lamarr Hoyt (LaMarr)	.20	.15	.08
165	Tony Scott	.08	.06	.03
166	Floyd Bannister	.12	.09	.05
167	Terry Whitfield	.08	.06	.03
168	Don Robinson	.08	.06	.03
169	John Mayberry	.10	.08	.04
170	Ross Grimsley	.10	.08	.04
171	Gene Richards	.08	.06	.03
172	Gary Woods	.08	.06	.03
173	Bump Wills	.08	.06	.03
174	Doug Rau	.08	.06	.03
175	Dave Collins	.10	.08	.04
176	Mike Krukow	.12	.09	.05
177	Rick Peters	.08	.06	.03
178	Jim Essian	.08	.06	.04
179	Rudy May	.10	.08	.04
180	Pete Rose	3.25	2.50	1.25
181	Elias Sosa	.08	.06	.03
182	Bob Grich	.15	.11	.06
183	Dick Davis	.08	.06	.03
184	Jim Dwyer	.08	.06	.03
185	Dennis Leonard	.10	.08	.04
186	Wayne Nordhagen	.08	.06	.03
187	Mike Parrott	.08	.06	.03
188	Doug DeCinces	.15	.11	.06
189	Craig Swan	.08	.06	.03
190	Cesar Cedeno	.15	.11	.06
191	Rick Sutcliffe	.60	.45	.25
192	Braves Future Stars (Terry Harper, Ed Miller, Rafael Ramirez)	.25	.20	.10
193	Pete Vuckovich	.10	.08	.04
194	Rod Scurry	.10	.08	.04
195	Rich Murray	.08	.06	.03
196	Duffy Dyer	.08	.06	.03
197	Jim Kern	.08	.06	.03
198	Jerry Dybzinski	.08	.06	.03
199	Chuck Rainey	.08	.06	.03
200	George Foster	.25	.20	.10
201	Record Breaker (Johnny Bench)	.40	.30	.15
202	Record Breaker (Steve Carlton)	.40	.30	.15
203	Record Breaker (Bill Gullickson)	.15	.11	.06
204	Record Breaker (Ron LeFlore, Rodney Scott)	.10	.08	.04
205	Record Breaker (Pete Rose)	.80	.60	.30
206	Record Breaker (Mike Schmidt)	.50	.40	.20
207	Record Breaker (Ozzie Smith)	.20	.15	.08
208	Record Breaker (Willie Wilson)	.20	.15	.08
209	Dickie Thon	.10	.08	.04
210	Jim Palmer	.80	.60	.30
211	Derrel Thomas	.08	.06	.03
212	Steve Nicosia	.08	.06	.03
213	Al Holland	.12	.09	.05
214	Angels Future Stars (Ralph Botting, Jim Dorsey, John Harris)	.08	.06	.03
215	Larry Hisle	.10	.08	.04
216	John Henry Johnson	.08	.06	.03
217	Rich Hebner	.08	.06	.03
218	Paul Splittorff	.10	.08	.04
219	Ken Landreaux	.10	.08	.04
220	Tom Seaver	1.25	.90	.50
221	Bob Davis	.08	.06	.03
222	Jorge Orta	.08	.06	.03
223	Roy Lee Jackson	.08	.06	.03
224	Pat Zachry	.08	.06	.03
225	Ruppert Jones	.08	.06	.03

	MT	NR MT	EX
226 Manny Sanguillen	.08	.06	.03
227 Fred Martinez	.08	.06	.03
228 Tom Paciorek	.10	.08	.04
229 Rollie Fingers	.60	.45	.25
230 George Hendrick	.12	.09	.05
231 Joe Beckwith	.08	.06	.03
232 Mickey Klutts	.08	.06	.03
233 Skip Lockwood	.08	.06	.03
234 Lou Whitaker	.50	.40	.20
235 Scott Sanderson	.12	.09	.05
236 Mike Ivie	.08	.06	.03
237 Charlie Moore	.08	.06	.03
238 Willie Hernandez	.12	.09	.05
239 Rick Miller	.08	.06	.03
240 Nolan Ryan	1.25	.90	.50
241 Checklist 122-242	.08	.06	.03
242 Chet Lemon	.12	.09	.05
243 Sal Butera	.08	.06	.03
244 Cardinals Future Stars (Tito Landrum, Al Olmsted, Andy Rincon)	.15	.11	.06
245 Ed Figueroa	.08	.06	.03
246 Ed Ott	.08	.06	.03
247 Glenn Hubbard	.10	.08	.04
248 Joey McLaughlin	.08	.06	.03
249 Larry Cox	.08	.06	.03
250 Ron Guidry	.50	.40	.20
251 Tom Brookens	.10	.08	.04
252 Victor Cruz	.08	.06	.03
253 Dave Bergman	.08	.06	.03
254 Ozzie Smith	.60	.45	.25
255 Mark Littell	.08	.06	.03
256 Bombo Rivera	.08	.06	.03
257 Rennie Stennett	.08	.06	.03
258 Joe Price	.12	.09	.05
259 Mets Future Stars (Juan Berenguer, Hubie Brooks, Mookie Wilson)	2.00	1.50	.80
260 Ron Cey	.15	.11	.06
261 Rickey Henderson	3.50	2.75	1.50
262 Sammy Stewart	.08	.06	.03
263 Brian Downing	.12	.09	.05
264 Jim Norris	.08	.06	.03
265 John Candelaria	.12	.09	.05
266 Tom Herr	.15	.11	.06
267 Stan Bahnsen	.08	.06	.03
268 Jerry Royster	.08	.06	.03
269 Ken Forsch	.10	.08	.04
270 Greg Luzinski	.20	.15	.08
271 Bill Castro	.08	.06	.03
272 Bruce Kimm	.08	.06	.03
273 Stan Papi	.08	.06	.03
274 Craig Chamberlain	.08	.06	.03
275 Dwight Evans	.25	.20	.10
276 Dan Spillner	.08	.06	.03
277 Alfredo Griffin	.12	.09	.05
278 Rick Sofield	.08	.06	.03
279 Bob Knepper	.12	.09	.05
280 Ken Griffey	.15	.11	.06
281 Fred Stanley	.08	.06	.03
282 Mariners Future Stars (Rick Anderson, Greg Biercevicz, Rodney Craig)	.08	.06	.03
283 Billy Sample	.08	.06	.03
284 Brian Kingman	.08	.06	.03
285 Jerry Turner	.08	.06	.03
286 Dave Frost	.08	.06	.03
287 Lenn Sakata	.08	.06	.03
288 Bob Clark	.08	.06	.03
289 Mickey Hatcher	.10	.08	.04
290 Bob Boone	.08	.06	.03
291 Aurelio Lopez	.08	.06	.03
292 Mike Squires	.08	.06	.03
293 Charlie Lea	.12	.09	.05
294 Mike Tyson	.08	.06	.03
295 Hal McRae	.15	.11	.06
296 Bill Nahorodny	.08	.06	.03
297 Bob Bailor	.08	.06	.03
298 Buddy Solomon	.08	.06	.03
299 Elliott Maddox	.08	.06	.03
300 Paul Molitor	.30	.25	.12
301 Matt Keough	.08	.06	.03
302 Dodgers Future Stars (Jack Perconte, Mike Scioscia, Fernando Valenzuela)	6.00	4.50	2.50
303 Johnny Oates	.08	.06	.03
304 John Castino	.08	.06	.03
305 Ken Clay	.08	.06	.03
306 Juan Beniquez	.08	.06	.03
307 Gene Garber	.08	.06	.03
308 Rick Manning	.08	.06	.03
309 Luis Salazar	.10	.08	.04
310 Vida Blue	.08	.06	.03
311 Freddie Patek	.08	.06	.03
312 Rick Rhoden	.15	.11	.06

	MT	NR MT	EX
313 Luis Pujols	.08	.06	.03
314 Rich Dauer	.08	.06	.03
315 Kirk Gibson	3.25	2.50	1.25
316 Craig Minetto	.08	.06	.03
317 Lonnie Smith	.10	.08	.04
318 Steve Yeager	.08	.06	.03
319 Rowland Office	.08	.06	.03
320 Tom Burgmeier	.08	.06	.03
321 Leon Durham	1.00	.70	.40
322 Neil Allen	.10	.08	.04
323 Jim Morrison	.08	.06	.03
324 Mike Willis	.08	.06	.03
325 Ray Knight	.12	.09	.05
326 Biff Pocoroba	.08	.06	.03
327 Moose Haas	.08	.06	.03
328 Twins Future Stars (Dave Engle, Greg Johnston, Gary Ward)	.12	.09	.05
329 Twins Future Stars (Joaquin Andujar)	.12	.09	.05
330 Frank White	.15	.11	.06
331 Dennis Lamp	.08	.06	.03
332 Lee Lacy	.08	.06	.03
333 Sid Monge	.08	.06	.03
334 Dane Iorg	.08	.06	.03
335 Rick Cerone	.10	.08	.04
336 Eddie Whitson	.10	.08	.04
337 Lynn Jones	.08	.06	.03
338 Checklist 243-363	.25	.20	.10
339 John Ellis	.08	.06	.03
340 Bruce Kison	.08	.06	.03
341 Dwayne Murphy	.12	.09	.05
342 Eric Rasmussen	.08	.06	.03
343 Frank Taveras	.08	.06	.03
344 Byron McLaughlin	.08	.06	.03
345 Warren Cromartie	.08	.06	.03
346 Larry Christenson	.08	.06	.03
347 Harold Baines	2.75	2.00	1.00
348 Bob Sykes	.08	.06	.03
349 Glenn Hoffman	.10	.08	.04
350 J.R. Richard	.12	.09	.05
351 Otto Velez	.08	.06	.03
352 Dick Tidrow	.08	.06	.03
353 Terry Kennedy	.12	.09	.05
354 Mario Soto	.12	.09	.05
355 Bob Horner	.50	.40	.20
356 Padres Future Stars (George Stablein, Craig Stimac, Tom Tellmann)	.08	.06	.03
357 Jim Slaton	.08	.06	.03
358 Mark Wagner	.08	.06	.03
359 Tom Hausman	.08	.06	.03
360 Willie Wilson	.30	.25	.12
361 Joe Strain	.08	.06	.03
362 Bo Diaz	.10	.08	.04
363 Geoff Zahn	.08	.06	.03
364 Mike Davis	.50	.40	.20
365 Graig Nettles	.12	.09	.05
366 Mike Ramsey	.08	.06	.03
367 Denny Martinez	.10	.08	.04
368 Leon Roberts	.08	.06	.03
369 Frank Tanana	.12	.09	.05
370 Dave Winfield	1.00	.70	.40
371 Charlie Hough	.15	.11	.06
372 Jay Johnstone	.12	.09	.05
373 Pat Underwood	.08	.06	.03
374 Tom Hutton	.08	.06	.03
375 Dave Concepcion	.20	.15	.08
376 Ron Reed	.10	.08	.04
377 Jerry Morales	.08	.06	.03
378 Dave Rader	.08	.06	.03
379 Lary Sorensen	.08	.06	.03
380 Willie Stargell	1.00	.70	.40
381 Cubs Future Stars (Carlos Lezcano, Steve Macko, Randy Martz)	.08	.06	.03
382 Paul Mirabella	.08	.06	.03
383 Eric Soderholm	.08	.06	.03
384 Mike Sadek	.08	.06	.03
385 Joe Sambito	.08	.06	.03
386 Dave Edwards	.08	.06	.03
387 Phil Niekro	.70	.50	.30
388 Andre Thornton	.15	.11	.06
389 Marty Pattin	.08	.06	.03
390 Cesar Geronimo	.08	.06	.03
391 Dave Lemanczyk	.08	.06	.03
392 Lance Parrish	.70	.50	.30
393 Broderick Perkins	.08	.06	.03
394 Woodie Fryman	.10	.08	.04
395 Scot Thompson	.08	.06	.03
396 Bill Campbell	.08	.06	.03
397 Julio Cruz	.08	.06	.03
398 Ross Baumgarten	.08	.06	.03

		MT	NR MT	EX
399	Orioles Future Stars (Mike Boddicker, Mark Corey, Floyd Rayford)	1.75	1.25	.70
400	Reggie Jackson	1.50	1.25	.60
401	A.L. Championships (Royals Sweep Yankees)	.50	.40	.20
402	N.L. Championships (Phillies Squeak Past Astros)	.40	.30	.15
403	World Series (Phillies Beat Royals In 6)	.25	.20	.10
404	World Series Summary (Phillies Win First World Series)	.25	.20	.10
405	Nino Espinosa	.08	.06	.03
406	Dickie Noles	.08	.06	.03
407	Ernie Whitt	.10	.08	.04
408	Fernando Arroyo	.08	.06	.03
409	Larry Herndon	.10	.08	.04
410	Bert Campaneris	.12	.09	.05
411	Terry Puhl	.08	.06	.03
412	Britt Burns	.12	.09	.05
413	Tony Bernazard	.10	.08	.04
414	John Pacella	.08	.06	.03
415	Ben Oglivie	.12	.09	.05
416	Gary Alexander	.08	.06	.03
417	Dan Schatzeder	.08	.06	.03
418	Bobby Brown	.08	.06	.03
419	Tom Hume	.08	.06	.03
420	Keith Hernandez	.80	.60	.30
421	Bob Stanley	.10	.08	.04
422	Dan Ford	.08	.06	.03
423	Shane Rawley	.15	.11	.06
424	Yankees Future Stars (Tim Lollar, Bruce Robinson, Dennis Werth)	.12	.09	.05
425	Al Bumbry	.10	.08	.04
426	Warren Brusstar	.08	.06	.03
427	John D'Acquisto	.08	.06	.03
428	John Stearns	.08	.06	.03
429	Mick Kelleher	.08	.06	.03
430	Jim Bibby	.08	.06	.03
431	Dave Roberts	.08	.06	.03
432	Len Barker	.10	.08	.04
433	Rance Mulliniks	.08	.06	.03
434	Roger Erickson	.08	.06	.03
435	Jim Spencer	.08	.06	.03
436	Gary Lucas	.12	.09	.05
437	Mike Heath	.08	.06	.03
438	John Montefusco	.10	.08	.04
439	Denny Walling	.08	.06	.03
440	Jerry Reuss	.15	.11	.06
441	Ken Reitz	.08	.06	.03
442	Ron Pruitt	.08	.06	.03
443	Jim Beattie	.08	.06	.03
444	Garth Iorg	.08	.06	.03
445	Ellis Valentine	.08	.06	.03
446	Checklist 364-484	.25	.20	.10
447	Junior Kennedy	.08	.06	.03
448	Tim Corcoran	.08	.06	.03
449	Paul Mitchell	.08	.06	.03
450	Dave Kingman	.10	.08	.04
451	Indians Future Stars (Chris Bando, Tom Brennan, Sandy Wihtol)	.15	.11	.06
452	Renie Martin	.08	.06	.03
453	Rob Wilfong	.08	.06	.03
454	Andy Hassler	.08	.06	.03
455	Rick Burleson	.10	.08	.04
456	Jeff Reardon	1.25	.90	.50
457	Mike Lum	.08	.06	.03
458	Randy Jones	.10	.08	.04
459	Greg Gross	.08	.06	.03
460	Rich Gossage	.40	.30	.15
461	Dave McKay	.08	.06	.03
462	Jack Brohamer	.08	.06	.03
463	Milt May	.08	.06	.03
464	Adrian Devine	.08	.06	.03
465	Bill Russell	.12	.09	.05
466	Bob Molinaro	.08	.06	.03
467	Dave Stieb	.50	.40	.20
468	Johnny Wockenfuss	.08	.06	.03
469	Jeff Leonard	.35	.25	.14
470	Manny Trillo	.10	.08	.04
471	Mike Vail	.08	.06	.03
472	Dyar Miller	.08	.06	.03
473	Jose Cardenal	.08	.06	.03
474	Mike LaCoss	.10	.08	.04
475	Buddy Bell	.15	.11	.06
476	Jerry Koosman	.15	.11	.06
477	Luis Gomez	.08	.06	.03
478	Juan Eichelberger	.08	.06	.03
479	Expos Future Stars (Bobby Pate, Tim Raines, Roberto Ramos)	8.50	6.50	3.50
480	Carlton Fisk	.40	.30	.15
481	Bob Lacey	.08	.06	.03

		MT	NR MT	EX
482	Jim Gantner	.10	.08	.04
483	Mike Griffin	.08	.06	.03
484	Max Venable	.08	.06	.03
485	Garry Templeton	.12	.09	.05
486	Marc Hill	.08	.06	.03
487	Dewey Robinson	.08	.06	.03
488	Damaso Garcia	.30	.25	.12
489	John Littlefield	.08	.06	.03
490	Eddie Murray	1.50	1.25	.60
491	Gordy Pladson	.08	.06	.03
492	Barry Foote	.08	.06	.03
493	Dan Quisenberry	.30	.25	.12
494	Bob Walk	.15	.11	.06
495	Dusty Baker	.15	.11	.06
496	Paul Dade	.08	.06	.03
497	Fred Norman	.08	.06	.03
498	Pat Putnam	.08	.06	.03
499	Frank Pastore	.08	.06	.03
500	Jim Rice	1.00	.70	.40
501	Tim Foli	.08	.06	.03
502	Giants Future Stars (Chris Bourjos, Al Hargesheimer, Mike Rowland)	.08	.06	.03
503	Steve McCatty	.08	.06	.03
504	Dale Murphy	2.50	2.00	1.00
505	Jason Thompson	.10	.08	.04
506	Phil Huffman	.08	.06	.03
507	Jamie Quirk	.08	.06	.03
508	Rob Dressler	.08	.06	.03
509	Pete Mackanin	.08	.06	.03
510	Lee Mazzilli	.12	.09	.05
511	Wayne Garland	.08	.06	.03
512	Gary Thomasson	.08	.06	.03
513	Frank LaCorte	.08	.06	.03
514	George Riley	.08	.06	.03
515	Robin Yount	1.00	.70	.40
516	Doug Bird	.08	.06	.03
517	Richie Zisk	.10	.08	.04
518	Grant Jackson	.08	.06	.03
519	John Tamargo	.08	.06	.03
520	Steve Stone	.12	.09	.05
521	Sam Mejias	.08	.06	.03
522	Mike Colbern	.08	.06	.03
523	John Fulgham	.08	.06	.03
524	Willie Aikens	.10	.08	.04
525	Mike Torrez	.10	.08	.04
526	Phillies Future Stars (Marty Bystrom, Jay Loviglio, Jim Wright)	.10	.08	.04
527	Danny Goodwin	.08	.06	.03
528	Gary Matthews	.15	.11	.06
529	Dave LaRoche	.08	.06	.03
530	Steve Garvey	1.25	.90	.50
531	John Curtis	.08	.06	.03
532	Bill Stein	.08	.06	.03
533	Jesus Figueroa	.08	.06	.03
534	Dave Smith	.40	.30	.15
535	Omar Moreno	.08	.06	.03
536	Bob Owchinko	.08	.06	.03
537	Ron Hodges	.08	.06	.03
538	Tom Griffin	.08	.06	.03
539	Rodney Scott	.08	.06	.03
540	Mike Schmidt	1.00	.70	.40
541	Steve Swisher	.08	.06	.03
542	Larry Bradford	.08	.06	.03
543	Terry Crowley	.08	.06	.03
544	Rich Gale	.08	.06	.03
545	Johnny Grubb	.08	.06	.03
546	Paul Moskau	.08	.06	.03
547	Mario Guerrero	.08	.06	.03
548	Dave Goltz	.10	.08	.04
549	Jerry Remy	.08	.06	.03
550	Tommy John	.50	.40	.20
551	Pirates Future Stars (Vance Law, Tony Pena, Pascual Perez)	1.50	1.25	.60
552	Steve Trout	.12	.09	.05
553	Tim Blackwell	.08	.06	.03
554	Bert Blyleven	.35	.25	.14
555	Cecil Cooper	.20	.15	.08
556	Jerry Mumphrey	.10	.08	.04
557	Chris Knapp	.08	.06	.03
558	Barry Bonnell	.08	.06	.03
559	Willie Montanez	.08	.06	.03
560	Joe Morgan	.60	.45	.25
561	Dennis Littlejohn	.08	.06	.03
562	Checklist 485-605	.25	.20	.10
563	Jim Kaat	.30	.25	.12
564	Ron Hassey	.08	.06	.03
565	Burt Hooton	.10	.08	.04
566	Del Unser	.08	.06	.03
567	Mark Bomback	.08	.06	.03
568	Dave Revering	.08	.06	.03
569	Al Williams	.08	.06	.03

		MT	NR MT	EX
570	Ken Singleton	.12	.09	.05
571	Todd Cruz	.08	.06	.03
572	Jack Morris	.60	.45	.25
573	Phil Garner	.10	.08	.04
574	Bill Caudill	.10	.08	.04
575	Tony Perez	.35	.25	.14
576	Reggie Cleveland	.08	.06	.03
577	Blue Jays Future Stars (Luis Leal, Brian Milner, Ken Schrom)	.25	.20	.10
578	Bill Gullickson	.50	.40	.20
579	Tim Flannery	.08	.06	.03
580	Don Baylor	.20	.15	.08
581	Roy Howell	.08	.06	.03
582	Gaylord Perry	.70	.50	.30
583	Larry Milbourne	.08	.06	.03
584	Randy Lerch	.08	.06	.03
585	Amos Otis	.12	.09	.05
586	Silvio Martinez	.08	.06	.03
587	Jeff Newman	.08	.06	.03
588	Gary Lavelle	.08	.06	.03
589	Lamar Johnson	.08	.06	.03
590	Bruce Sutter	.25	.20	.10
591	John Lowenstein	.08	.06	.03
592	Steve Comer	.08	.06	.03
593	Steve Kemp	.12	.09	.05
594	Preston Hanna	.08	.06	.03
595	Butch Hobson	.08	.06	.03
596	Jerry Augustine	.08	.06	.03
597	Rafael Landestoy	.08	.06	.03
598	George Vukovich	.08	.06	.03
599	Dennis Kinney	.08	.06	.03
600	Johnny Bench	1.25	.90	.50
601	Don Aase	.10	.08	.04
602	Bobby Murcer	.15	.11	.06
603	John Verhoeven	.08	.06	.03
604	Rob Picciolo	.08	.06	.03
605	Don Sutton	.70	.50	.30
606	Reds Future Stars (Bruce Berenyi, Geoff Combe, Paul Householder)	.08	.06	.03
607	Dave Palmer	.12	.09	.05
608	Greg Pryor	.08	.06	.03
609	Lynn McGlothen	.08	.06	.03
610	Darrell Porter	.10	.08	.04
611	Rick Matula	.08	.06	.03
612	Duane Kuiper	.08	.06	.03
613	Jim Anderson	.08	.06	.03
614	Dave Rozema	.08	.06	.03
615	Rick Dempsey	.12	.09	.05
616	Rick Wise	.10	.08	.04
617	Craig Reynolds	.08	.06	.03
618	John Milner	.08	.06	.03
619	Steve Henderson	.08	.06	.03
620	Dennis Eckersley	.12	.09	.05
621	Tom Donohue	.08	.06	.03
622	Randy Moffitt	.08	.06	.03
623	Sal Bando	.12	.09	.05
624	Bob Welch	.15	.11	.06
625	Bill Buckner	.15	.11	.06
626	Tigers Future Stars (Dave Steffen, Jerry Ujdur, Roger Weaver)	.08	.06	.03
627	Luis Tiant	.20	.15	.08
628	Vic Correll	.08	.06	.03
629	Tony Armas	.12	.09	.05
630	Steve Carlton	1.25	.90	.50
631	Ron Jackson	.08	.06	.03
632	Alan Bannister	.08	.06	.03
633	Bill Lee	.10	.08	.04
634	Doug Flynn	.08	.06	.03
635	Bobby Bonds	.15	.11	.06
636	Al Hrabosky	.10	.08	.04
637	Jerry Narron	.08	.06	.03
638	Checklist 606-726	.25	.20	.10
639	Carney Lansford	.15	.11	.06
640	Dave Parker	.60	.45	.25
641	Mark Belanger	.10	.08	.04
642	Vern Ruhle	.08	.06	.03
643	Lloyd Moseby	1.75	1.25	.70
644	Ramon Aviles	.08	.06	.03
645	Rick Reuschel	.15	.11	.06
646	Marvis Foley	.08	.06	.03
647	Dick Drago	.08	.06	.03
648	Darrell Evans	.25	.20	.10
649	Manny Sarmiento	.08	.06	.03
650	Bucky Dent	.15	.11	.06
651	Pedro Guerrero	1.25	.90	.50
652	John Montague	.08	.06	.03
653	Bill Fahey	.08	.06	.03
654	Ray Burris	.08	.06	.03
655	Dan Driessen	.12	.09	.05
656	Jon Matlack	.10	.08	.04
657	Mike Cubbage	.08	.06	.03

		MT	NR MT	EX
658	Milt Wilcox	.10	.08	.04
659	Brewers Future Stars (John Flinn, Ed Romero, Ned Yost)	.08	.06	.03
660	Gary Carter	1.25	.90	.50
661	Orioles Team (Earl Weaver)	.30	.25	.12
662	Red Sox Team (Ralph Houk)	.30	.25	.12
663	Angels Team (Jim Fregosi)	.25	.20	.10
664	White Sox Team (Tony LaRussa)	.25	.20	.10
665	Indians Team (Dave Garcia)	.25	.20	.10
666	Tigers Team (Sparky Anderson)	.30	.25	.12
667	Royals Team (Jim Frey)	.25	.20	.10
668	Brewers Team (Bob Rodgers)	.25	.20	.10
669	Twins Team (John Goryl)	.25	.20	.10
670	Yankees Team (Gene Michael)	.35	.25	.14
671	A's Team (Billy Martin)	.30	.25	.12
672	Mariners Team (Maury Wills)	.25	.20	.10
673	Rangers Team (Don Zimmer)	.25	.20	.10
674	Blue Jays Team (Bobby Mattick)	.25	.20	.10
675	Braves Team (Bobby Cox)	.25	.20	.10
676	Cubs Team (Joe Amalfitano)	.25	.20	.10
677	Reds Team (John McNamara)	.25	.20	.10
678	Astros Team (Bill Virdon)	.25	.20	.10
679	Dodgers Team (Tom Lasorda)	.35	.25	.14
680	Expos Team (Dick Williams)	.25	.20	.10
681	Mets Team (Joe Torre)	.30	.25	.12
682	Phillies Team (Dallas Green)	.25	.20	.10
683	Pirates Team (Chuck Tanner)	.25	.20	.10
684	Cardinals Team (Whitey Herzog)	.30	.25	.12
685	Padres Team (Frank Howard)	.25	.20	.10
686	Giants Team (Dave Bristol)	.25	.20	.10
687	Jeff Jones	.08	.06	.03
688	Kiko Garcia	.08	.06	.03
689	Red Sox Future Stars (Bruce Hurst, Keith MacWhorter, Reid Nichols)	1.25	.90	.50
690	Bob Watson	.10	.08	.04
691	Dick Ruthven	.08	.06	.03
692	Lenny Randle	.08	.06	.03
693	Steve Howe	.25	.20	.10
694	Bud Harrelson	.08	.06	.03
695	Kent Tekulve	.10	.08	.04
696	Alan Ashby	.08	.06	.03
697	Rick Waits	.08	.06	.03
698	Mike Jorgensen	.08	.06	.03
699	Glenn Abbott	.08	.06	.03
700	George Brett	2.25	1.75	.90
701	Joe Rudi	.12	.09	.05
702	George Medich	.08	.06	.03
703	Alvis Woods	.08	.06	.03
704	Bill Travers	.08	.06	.03
705	Ted Simmons	.25	.20	.10
706	Dave Ford	.08	.06	.03
707	Dave Cash	.08	.06	.03
708	Doyle Alexander	.15	.11	.06
709	Alan Trammell	.30	.25	.12
710	Ron LeFlore	.08	.06	.03
711	Joe Ferguson	.08	.06	.03
712	Bill Bonham	.08	.06	.03
713	Bill North	.08	.06	.03
714	Pete Redfern	.08	.06	.03
715	Bill Madlock	.25	.20	.10
716	Glenn Borgmann	.08	.06	.03
717	Jim Barr	.08	.06	.03
718	Larry Biittner	.08	.06	.03
719	Sparky Lyle	.15	.11	.06
720	Fred Lynn	.35	.25	.14
721	Toby Harrah	.10	.08	.04
722	Joe Niekro	.20	.15	.08
723	Bruce Bochte	.08	.06	.03
724	Lou Piniella	.20	.15	.08
725	Steve Rogers	.10	.08	.04
726	Rick Monday	.15	.11	.06

1981 Topps Home Team 5x7 Photos

Once again testing the popularity of large cards, Topps issued 4⅞" by 6⅞" cards in two different sets. The Home Team cards featured a large color photo, facsimile autograph and white border on the front. Backs had the player name, team, position and a checklist at the bottom. The 102 cards were sold in limited areas corresponding to the teams' geographic home. It was also possible to order the whole set by mail. Eleven teams were involved in the issue with the number of players from each team ranging from six to

MARIO SOTO
Cincinnati Reds
PITCHER

12. Although it is an attractive set featuring many stars, ready availability and many collectors' aversion to large cards keep prices relatively low today.

		MT	NR MT	EX
	Complete Set:	40.00	30.00	16.00
	Common Player:	.20	.15	.08
(1)	Dusty Baker	.30	.25	.12
(2)	Don Baylor	.50	.40	.20
(3)	Rick Burleson	.30	.25	.12
(4)	Rod Carew	.90	.70	.35
(5)	Ron Cey	.40	.30	.15
(6)	Steve Garvey	.90	.70	.35
(7)	Bobby Grich	.40	.30	.15
(8)	Butch Hobson	.20	.15	.08
(9)	Burt Hooton	.25	.20	.10
(10)	Steve Howe	.25	.20	.10
(11)	Dave Lopes	.30	.25	.12
(12)	Fred Lynn	.50	.40	.20
(13)	Rick Monday	.30	.25	.12
(14)	Jerry Reuss	.40	.30	.15
(15)	Bill Russell	.30	.25	.12
(16)	Reggie Smith	.40	.30	.15
(17)	Bob Welch	.40	.30	.15
(18)	Steve Yeager	.20	.15	.08
(19)	Buddy Bell	.40	.30	.15
(20)	Cesar Cedeno	.40	.30	.15
(21)	Jose Cruz	.40	.30	.15
(22)	Art Howe	.20	.15	.08
(23)	Jon Matlack	.25	.20	.10
(24)	Al Oliver	.50	.40	.20
(25)	Terry Puhl	.20	.15	.08
(26)	Mickey Rivers	.30	.25	.12
(27)	Nolan Ryan	.70	.50	.30
(28)	Jim Sundberg	.30	.25	.12
(29)	Don Sutton	.60	.45	.25
(30)	Bump Wills	.20	.15	.08
(31)	Tim Blackwell	.20	.15	.08
(32)	Bill Buckner	.50	.40	.20
(33)	Britt Burns	.20	.15	.08
(34)	Ivan DeJesus	.20	.15	.08
(35)	Rich Dotson	.30	.25	.12
(36)	Leon Durham	.50	.40	.20
(37)	Ed Farmer	.20	.15	.08
(38)	Lamar Johnson	.20	.15	.08
(39)	Dave Kingman	.50	.40	.20
(40)	Mike Krukow	.30	.25	.12
(41)	Ron LeFlore	.25	.20	.10
(42)	Chet Lemon	.30	.25	.12
(43)	Bob Molinaro	.20	.15	.08
(44)	Jim Morrison	.20	.15	.08
(45)	Wayne Nordhagen	.20	.15	.08
(46)	Ken Reitz	.20	.15	.08
(47)	Rick Reuschel	.40	.30	.15
(48)	Mike Tyson	.20	.15	.08
(49)	Neil Allen	.20	.15	.08
(50)	Rick Cerone	.25	.20	.10
(51)	Bucky Dent	.40	.30	.15
(52)	Doug Flynn	.20	.15	.08
(53)	Rich Gossage	.60	.45	.25
(54)	Ron Guidry	.60	.45	.25
(55)	Reggie Jackson	.90	.70	.35
(56)	Tommy John	.50	.40	.20
(57)	Ruppert Jones	.20	.15	.08
(58)	Rudy May	.20	.15	.08
(59)	Lee Mazzilli	.25	.20	.10
(60)	Graig Nettles	.50	.40	.20
(61)	Willie Randolph	.40	.30	.15
(62)	Rusty Staub	.50	.40	.20

		MT	NR MT	EX
(63)	Frank Taveras	.20	.15	.08
(64)	Alex Trevino	.20	.15	.08
(65)	Bob Watson	.25	.20	.10
(66)	Dave Winfield	.90	.70	.35
(67)	Bob Boone	.30	.25	.12
(68)	Larry Bowa	.40	.30	.15
(69)	Steve Carlton	.70	.50	.30
(70)	Greg Luzinski	.50	.40	.20
(71)	Garry Maddox	.30	.25	.12
(72)	Bake McBride	.25	.20	.10
(73)	Tug McGraw	.50	.40	.20
(74)	Pete Rose	1.75	1.25	.70
(75)	Dick Ruthven	.20	.15	.08
(76)	Mike Schmidt	.90	.70	.35
(77)	Manny Trillo	.30	.25	.12
(78)	Del Unser	.20	.15	.08
(79)	Tom Burgmeier	.20	.15	.08
(80)	Dennis Eckersley	.30	.25	.12
(81)	Dwight Evans	.50	.40	.20
(82)	Carlton Fisk	.60	.45	.25
(83)	Glenn Hoffman	.20	.15	.08
(84)	Carney Lansford	.30	.25	.12
(85)	Tony Perez	.60	.45	.25
(86)	Jim Rice	.90	.70	.35
(87)	Bob Stanley	.30	.25	.12
(88)	Dave Stapleton	.20	.15	.08
(89)	Frank Tanana	.30	.25	.12
(90)	Carl Yastrzemski	1.25	.90	.50
(91)	Johnny Bench	.90	.70	.35
(92)	Dave Collins	.25	.20	.10
(93)	Dave Concepcion	.50	.40	.20
(94)	Dan Driessen	.30	.25	.12
(95)	George Foster	.50	.40	.20
(96)	Ken Griffey	.40	.30	.15
(97)	Tom Hume	.20	.15	.08
(98)	Ray Knight	.30	.25	.12
(99)	Joe Nolan	.20	.15	.08
(100)	Ron Oester	.20	.15	.08
(101)	Tom Seaver	.70	.50	.30
(102)	Mario Soto	.30	.25	.12

1981 Topps National 5x7 Photos

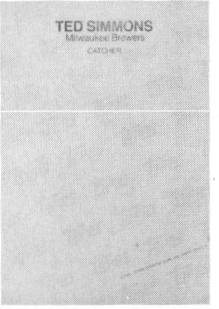

TED SIMMONS
Milwaukee Brewers
CATCHER

The other half of the Topps efforts with large cards in 1981. Measuring 4⅞'' by 6⅞,'' the National photo issue was limited to 15 cards. They were sold in areas not covered by the Home Team sets and featured ten cards which carried the same photos as found in the Home Team set, but with no checklist on the backs. Five cards were unique to the National set: George Brett, Cecil Cooper, Jim Palmer, Dave Parker and Ted Simmons. With their wide distribution and a limited demand, there are currently plenty of these cards to meet the demand thus keeping prices fairly low.

		MT	NR MT	EX
	Complete Set:	5.00	3.75	2.00
	Common Player:	.30	.25	.12
(1)	Buddy Bell	.30	.25	.12
(2)	Johnny Bench	.60	.45	.25
(3)	George Brett	.90	.70	.35
(4)	Rod Carew	.60	.45	.25
(5)	Cecil Cooper	.50	.40	.20

		MT	NR MT	EX
(6)	Steve Garvey	.70	.50	.30
(7)	Rich Gossage	.40	.30	.15
(8)	Reggie Jackson	.70	.50	.30
(9)	Jim Palmer	.70	.50	.30
(10)	Dave Parker	.60	.45	.25
(11)	Jim Rice	.50	.40	.20
(12)	Pete Rose	1.25	.90	.50
(13)	Mike Schmidt	.70	.50	.30
(14)	Tom Seaver	.60	.45	.25
(15)	Ted Simmons	.50	.40	.20

1981 Topps Traded

 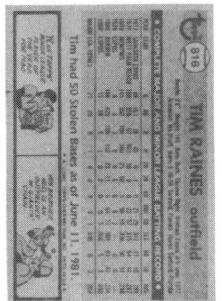

Popularly known as "'81 Updates" these 2½" by 3½," the 132 cards in this extension set are numbered from 727 to 858 technically making them a high-number series of the regular Topps set. The set was not packaged in gum packs, but rather placed in a red box and sold through baseball card dealers only. While many complained about the method, the fact remains, even at higher prices, the set has done well for its owners as it features not only mid-season trades, but also single-player rookie cards of some of the hottest prospects.

		MT	NR MT	EX
Complete Set:		20.00	15.00	8.00
Common Player:		.10	.08	.04
727	Danny Ainge	.50	.40	.20
728	Doyle Alexander	.25	.20	.10
729	Gary Alexander	.10	.08	.04
730	Billy Almon	.10	.08	.04
731	Joaquin Andujar	.15	.11	.06
732	Bob Bailor	.10	.08	.04
733	Juan Beniquez	.10	.08	.04
734	Dave Bergman	.10	.08	.04
735	Tony Bernazard	.15	.11	.06
736	Larry Biittner	.10	.08	.04
737	Doug Bird	.10	.08	.04
738	Bert Blyleven	.60	.45	.25
739	Mark Bomback	.10	.08	.04
740	Bobby Bonds	.20	.15	.08
741	Rick Bosetti	.10	.08	.04
742	Hubie Brooks	1.25	.90	.50
743	Rick Burleson	.15	.11	.06
744	Ray Burris	.10	.08	.04
745	Jeff Burroughs	.15	.11	.06
746	Enos Cabell	.15	.11	.06
747	Ken Clay	.10	.08	.04
748	Mark Clear	.15	.11	.06
749	Larry Cox	.10	.08	.04
750	Hector Cruz	.10	.08	.04
751	Victor Cruz	.10	.08	.04
752	Mike Cubbage	.10	.08	.04
753	Dick Davis	.10	.08	.04
754	Brian Doyle	.10	.08	.04
755	Dick Drago	.10	.08	.04
756	Leon Durham	.70	.50	.30
757	Jim Dwyer	.10	.08	.04
758	Dave Edwards	.10	.08	.04
759	Jim Essian	.10	.08	.04
760	Bill Fahey	.10	.08	.04
761	Rollie Fingers	.70	.50	.30
762	Carlton Fisk	.60	.45	.25
763	Barry Foote	.10	.08	.04
764	Ken Forsch	.15	.11	.06

		MT	NR MT	EX
765	Kiko Garcia	.10	.08	.04
766	Cesar Geronimo	.10	.08	.04
767	Gary Gray	.10	.08	.04
768	Mickey Hatcher	.15	.11	.06
769	Steve Henderson	.10	.08	.04
770	Marc Hill	.10	.08	.04
771	Butch Hobson	.10	.08	.04
772	Rick Honeycutt	.15	.11	.06
773	Roy Howell	.10	.08	.04
774	Mike Ivie	.10	.08	.04
775	Roy Lee Jackson	.10	.08	.04
776	Cliff Johnson	.10	.08	.04
777	Randy Jones	.15	.11	.06
778	Ruppert Jones	.10	.08	.04
779	Mick Kelleher	.10	.08	.04
780	Terry Kennedy	.20	.15	.08
781	Dave Kingman	.40	.30	.15
782	Bob Knepper	.15	.11	.06
783	Ken Kravec	.10	.08	.04
784	Bob Lacey	.10	.08	.04
785	Dennis Lamp	.10	.08	.04
786	Rafael Landestoy	.10	.08	.04
787	Ken Landreaux	.15	.11	.06
788	Carney Lansford	.20	.15	.08
789	Dave LaRoche	.10	.08	.04
790	Joe Lefebvre	.10	.08	.04
791	Ron LeFlore	.15	.11	.06
792	Randy Lerch	.10	.08	.04
793	Sixto Lezcano	.10	.08	.04
794	John Littlefield	.10	.08	.04
795	Mike Lum	.10	.08	.04
796	Greg Luzinski	.25	.20	.10
797	Fred Lynn	.50	.40	.20
798	Jerry Martin	.10	.08	.04
799	Buck Martinez	.10	.08	.04
800	Gary Matthews	.20	.15	.08
801	Mario Mendoza	.10	.08	.04
802	Larry Milbourne	.10	.08	.04
803	Rick Miller	.10	.08	.04
804	John Montefusco	.15	.11	.06
805	Jerry Morales	.10	.08	.04
806	Jose Morales	.10	.08	.04
807	Joe Morgan	1.00	.70	.40
808	Jerry Mumphrey	.15	.11	.06
809	Gene Nelson	.20	.15	.08
810	Ed Ott	.10	.08	.04
811	Bob Owchinko	.10	.08	.04
812	Gaylord Perry	1.25	.90	.50
813	Mike Phillips	.10	.08	.04
814	Darrell Porter	.15	.11	.06
815	Mike Proly	.10	.08	.04
816	Tim Raines	6.00	4.50	2.50
817	Lenny Randle	.10	.08	.04
818	Doug Rau	.10	.08	.04
819	Jeff Reardon	.50	.40	.20
820	Ken Reitz	.10	.08	.04
821	Steve Renko	.10	.08	.04
822	Rick Reuschel	.25	.20	.10
823	Dave Revering	.10	.08	.04
824	Dave Roberts	.10	.08	.04
825	Leon Roberts	.10	.08	.04
826	Joe Rudi	.20	.15	.08
827	Kevin Saucier	.10	.08	.04
828	Tony Scott	.10	.08	.04
829	Bob Shirley	.10	.08	.04
830	Ted Simmons	.40	.30	.15
831	Lary Sorensen	.10	.08	.04
832	Jim Spencer	.10	.08	.04
833	Harry Spilman	.10	.08	.04
834	Fred Stanley	.10	.08	.04
835	Rusty Staub	.30	.25	.12
836	Bill Stein	.10	.08	.04
837	Joe Strain	.10	.08	.04
838	Bruce Sutter	.50	.40	.20
839	Don Sutton	1.25	.90	.50
840	Steve Swisher	.10	.08	.04
841	Frank Tanana	.20	.15	.08
842	Gene Tenace	.15	.11	.06
843	Jason Thompson	.10	.08	.04
844	Dickie Thon	.15	.11	.06
845	Bill Travers	.10	.08	.04
846	Tom Underwood	.10	.08	.04
847	John Urrea	.10	.08	.04
848	Mike Vail	.10	.08	.04
849	Ellis Valentine	.15	.11	.06
850	Fernando Valenzuela	5.00	3.75	2.00
851	Pete Vuckovich	.15	.11	.06
852	Mark Wagner	.10	.08	.04
853	Bob Walk	.10	.08	.04
854	Claudell Washington	.15	.11	.06
855	Dave Winfield	1.75	1.25	.70

		MT	NR MT	EX
856	Geoff Zahn	.10	.08	.04
857	Richie Zisk	.15	.11	.06
858	Checklist 727-858	.10	.08	.04

1982 Topps

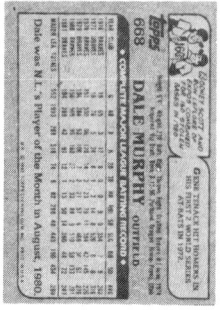

BRAVES
DALE MURPHY

At 792 cards, this was the largest issue produced up to that time, eliminating the need for double-printed cards. The 2½'' by 3½'' cards featured a front color photo with a pair of stripes down the left side. Under the player's photo were found his name, team and position. A facsimile autograph runs across the front of the picture. Specialty cards included great performances of the previous season, All-Stars, statistical leaders and "In Action" cards (indicated by "IA" in listings below). Managers joined hitting and pitching leaders on a card while rookies were known as "Future Stars" on group cards.

		MT	NR MT	EX
	Complete Set:	75.00	56.00	30.00
	Common Player:	.08	.06	.03
1	1981 Highlight (Steve Carlton)	.50	.40	.20
2	1981 Highlight (Ron Davis)	.08	.06	.03
3	1981 Highlight (Tim Raines)	.30	.25	.12
4	1981 Highlight (Pete Rose)	.70	.50	.30
5	1981 Highlight (Nolan Ryan)	.30	.25	.12
6	1981 Highlight (Fernando Valenzuela)	.30	.25	.12
7	Scott Sanderson	.10	.08	.04
8	Rich Dauer	.08	.06	.03
9	Ron Guidry	.35	.25	.14
10	Ron Guidry IA	.15	.11	.06
11	Gary Alexander	.08	.06	.03
12	Moose Haas	.08	.06	.03
13	Lamar Johnson	.08	.06	.03
14	Steve Howe	.12	.09	.05
15	Ellis Valentine	.08	.06	.03
16	Steve Comer	.08	.06	.03
17	Darrell Evans	.25	.20	.10
18	Fernando Arroyo	.08	.06	.03
19	Ernie Whitt	.10	.08	.04
20	Garry Maddox	.12	.09	.05
21	Orioles Future Stars (Bob Bonner, Cal Ripken, Jeff Schneider)	10.00	7.50	4.00
22	Jim Beattie	.08	.06	.03
23	Willie Hernandez	.10	.08	.04
24	Dave Frost	.08	.06	.03
25	Jerry Remy	.08	.06	.03
26	Jorge Orta	.08	.06	.03
27	Tom Herr	.12	.09	.05
28	John Urrea	.08	.06	.03
29	Dwayne Murphy	.10	.08	.04
30	Tom Seaver	.60	.45	.25
31	Tom Seaver IA	.30	.25	.12
32	Gene Garber	.08	.06	.03
33	Jerry Morales	.08	.06	.03
34	Joe Sambito	.08	.06	.03
35	Willie Aikens	.08	.06	.03
36	Rangers Batting & Pitching Ldrs. (George Medich, Al Oliver)	.12	.09	.05
37	Dan Graham	.08	.06	.03
38	Charlie Lea	.10	.08	.04
39	Lou Whitaker	.35	.25	.14
40	Dave Parker	.35	.25	.14

		MT	NR MT	EX
41	Dave Parker IA	.15	.11	.06
42	Rick Sofield	.08	.06	.03
43	Mike Cubbage	.08	.06	.03
44	Britt Burns	.10	.08	.04
45	Rick Cerone	.10	.08	.04
46	Jerry Augustine	.08	.06	.03
47	Jeff Leonard	.15	.11	.06
48	Bobby Castillo	.08	.06	.03
49	Alvis Woods	.08	.06	.03
50	Buddy Bell	.15	.11	.06
51	Cubs Future Stars (Jay Howell, Carlos Lezcano, Ty Waller)	.30	.25	.12
52	Larry Andersen	.12	.09	.05
53	Greg Gross	.08	.06	.03
54	Ron Hassey	.08	.06	.03
55	Rick Burleson	.10	.08	.04
56	Mark Littell	.08	.06	.03
57	Craig Reynolds	.08	.06	.03
58	John D'Acquisto	.08	.06	.03
59	Rich Gedman	.70	.50	.30
60	Tony Armas	.12	.09	.05
61	Tommy Boggs	.08	.06	.03
62	Mike Tyson	.08	.06	.03
63	Mario Soto	.12	.09	.05
64	Lynn Jones	.08	.06	.03
65	Terry Kennedy	.12	.09	.05
66	Astros Batting & Pitching Ldrs. (Art Howe, Nolan Ryan)	.25	.20	.10
67	Rich Gale	.08	.06	.03
68	Roy Howell	.08	.06	.03
69	Al Williams	.08	.06	.03
70	Tim Raines	1.75	1.25	.70
71	Roy Lee Jackson	.08	.06	.03
72	Rick Auerbach	.08	.06	.03
73	Buddy Solomon	.08	.06	.03
74	Bob Clark	.08	.06	.03
75	Tommy John	.30	.25	.12
76	Greg Pryor	.08	.06	.03
77	Miguel Dilone	.08	.06	.03
78	George Medich	.08	.06	.03
79	Bob Bailor	.08	.06	.03
80	Jim Palmer	.60	.45	.25
81	Jim Palmer IA	.30	.25	.12
82	Bob Welch	.15	.11	.06
83	Yankees Future Stars (Steve Balboni, Andy McGaffigan, Andre Robertson)	.50	.40	.20
84	Rennie Stennett	.08	.06	.03
85	Lynn McGlothen	.08	.06	.03
86	Dane Iorg	.08	.06	.03
87	Matt Keough	.08	.06	.03
88	Biff Pocoroba	.08	.06	.03
89	Steve Henderson	.08	.06	.03
90	Nolan Ryan	.80	.60	.30
91	Carney Lansford	.12	.09	.05
92	Brad Havens	.08	.06	.03
93	Larry Hisle	.10	.08	.04
94	Andy Hassler	.08	.06	.03
95	Ozzie Smith	.35	.25	.14
96	Royals Batting & Pitching Ldrs. (George Brett, Larry Gura)	.35	.25	.14
97	Paul Moskau	.08	.06	.03
98	Terry Bulling	.08	.06	.03
99	Barry Bonnell	.08	.06	.03
100	Mike Schmidt	1.25	.90	.50
101	Mike Schmidt IA	.60	.45	.25
102	Dan Briggs	.08	.06	.03
103	Bob Lacey	.08	.06	.03
104	Rance Mulliniks	.08	.06	.03
105	Kirk Gibson	.70	.50	.30
106	Enrique Romo	.08	.06	.03
107	Wayne Krenchicki	.08	.06	.03
108	Bob Sykes	.08	.06	.03
109	Dave Revering	.08	.06	.03
110	Carlton Fisk	.35	.25	.14
111	Carlton Fisk IA	.15	.11	.06
112	Billy Sample	.08	.06	.03
113	Steve McCatty	.08	.06	.03
114	Ken Landreaux	.10	.08	.04
115	Gaylord Perry	.40	.30	.15
116	Jim Wohlford	.08	.06	.03
117	Rawly Eastwick	.08	.06	.03
118	Expos Future Stars (Terry Francona, Brad Mills, Bryn Smith)	.25	.20	.10
119	Joe Pittman	.08	.06	.03
120	Gary Lucas	.08	.06	.03
121	Ed Lynch	.10	.08	.04
122	Jamie Easterly	.08	.06	.03
123	Danny Goodwin	.08	.06	.03
124	Reid Nichols	.08	.06	.03
125	Danny Ainge	.20	.15	.08

#	Name	MT	NR MT	EX
126	Braves Batting & Pitching Ldrs. (Rick Mahler, Claudell Washington)	.12	.09	.05
127	Lonnie Smith	.10	.08	.04
128	Frank Pastore	.08	.06	.03
129	Checklist 1-132	.12	.09	.05
130	Julio Cruz	.08	.06	.03
131	Stan Bahnsen	.08	.06	.03
132	Lee May	.10	.08	.04
133	Pat Underwood	.08	.06	.03
134	Dan Ford	.08	.06	.03
135	Andy Rincon	.08	.06	.03
136	Lenn Sakata	.08	.06	.03
137	George Cappuzzello	.08	.06	.03
138	Tony Pena	.30	.25	.12
139	Jeff Jones	.08	.06	.03
140	Ron LeFlore	.10	.08	.04
141	Indians Future Stars (Chris Bando, Tom Brennan, Von Hayes)	1.25	.90	.50
142	Dave LaRoche	.08	.06	.03
143	Mookie Wilson	.15	.11	.06
144	Fred Breining	.08	.06	.03
145	Bob Horner	.50	.40	.20
146	Mike Griffin	.08	.06	.03
147	Denny Walling	.08	.06	.03
148	Mickey Klutts	.08	.06	.03
149	Pat Putnam	.08	.06	.03
150	Ted Simmons	.20	.15	.08
151	Dave Edwards	.08	.06	.03
152	Ramon Aviles	.08	.06	.03
153	Roger Erickson	.08	.06	.03
154	Dennis Werth	.08	.06	.03
155	Otto Velez	.08	.06	.03
156	A's Batting & Pitching Ldrs. (Rickey Henderson, Steve McCatty)	.25	.20	.10
157	Steve Crawford	.08	.06	.03
158	Brian Downing	.12	.09	.05
159	Larry Biittner	.08	.06	.03
160	Luis Tiant	.15	.11	.06
161	Batting Leaders (Carney Lansford, Bill Madlock)	.20	.15	.08
162	Home Run Leaders (Tony Armas, Dwight Evans, Bobby Grich, Eddie Murray, Mike Schmidt)	.35	.25	.14
163	Runs Batted In Leaders (Eddie Murray, Mike Schmidt)	.40	.30	.15
164	Stolen Base Leaders (Rickey Henderson, Tim Raines)	.35	.25	.14
165	Victory Leaders (Denny Martinez, Steve McCatty, Jack Morris, Tom Seaver, Pete Vuckovich)	.20	.15	.08
166	Strikeout Leaders (Len Barker, Fernando Valenzuela)	.20	.15	.08
167	Earned Run Avg. Leaders (Steve McCatty, Nolan Ryan)	.20	.15	.08
168	Leading Relievers (Rollie Fingers, Bruce Sutter)	.20	.15	.08
169	Charlie Leibrandt	.12	.09	.05
170	Jim Bibby	.08	.06	.03
171	Giants Future Stars (Bob Brenly, Chili Davis, Bob Tufts)	1.25	.90	.50
172	Bill Gullickson	.15	.11	.06
173	Jamie Quirk	.08	.06	.03
174	Dave Ford	.08	.06	.03
175	Jerry Mumphrey	.10	.08	.04
176	Dewey Robinson	.08	.06	.03
177	John Ellis	.08	.06	.03
178	Dyar Miller	.08	.06	.03
179	Steve Garvey	.80	.60	.30
180	Steve Garvey IA	.40	.30	.15
181	Silvio Martinez	.08	.06	.03
182	Larry Herndon	.10	.08	.04
183	Mike Proly	.08	.06	.03
184	Mick Kelleher	.08	.06	.03
185	Phil Niekro	.50	.40	.20
186	Cardinals Batting & Pitching Ldrs. (Bob Forsch, Keith Hernandez)	.25	.20	.10
187	Jeff Newman	.08	.06	.03
188	Randy Martz	.08	.06	.03
189	Glenn Hoffman	.08	.06	.03
190	J.R. Richard	.12	.09	.05
191	Tim Wallach	2.00	1.50	.80
192	Broderick Perkins	.08	.06	.03
193	Darrell Jackson	.08	.06	.03
194	Mike Vail	.08	.06	.03
195	Paul Molitor	.25	.20	.10
196	Willie Upshaw	.15	.11	.06
197	Shane Rawley	.15	.11	.06
198	Chris Speier	.10	.08	.04
199	Don Aase	.10	.08	.04
200	George Brett	1.50	1.25	.60
201	George Brett IA	.70	.50	.30
202	Rick Manning	.08	.06	.03
203	Blue Jays Future Stars (Jesse Barfield, Brian Milner, Boomer Wells)	4.50	3.50	1.75
204	Gary Roenicke	.10	.08	.04
205	Neil Allen	.08	.06	.03
206	Tony Bernazard	.10	.08	.04
207	Rod Scurry	.08	.06	.03
208	Bobby Murcer	.15	.11	.06
209	Gary Lavelle	.08	.06	.03
210	Keith Hernandez	.60	.45	.25
211	Dan Petry	.12	.09	.05
212	Mario Mendoza	.08	.06	.03
213	Dave Stewart	.60	.45	.25
214	Brian Asselstine	.08	.06	.03
215	Mike Krukow	.10	.08	.04
216	White Sox Batting & Pitching Ldrs. (Dennis Lamp, Chet Lemon)	.12	.09	.05
217	Bo McLaughlin	.08	.06	.03
218	Dave Roberts	.08	.06	.03
219	John Curtis	.08	.06	.03
220	Manny Trillo	.10	.08	.04
221	Jim Slaton	.08	.06	.03
222	Butch Wynegar	.10	.08	.04
223	Lloyd Moseby	.30	.25	.12
224	Bruce Bochte	.08	.06	.03
225	Mike Torrez	.10	.08	.04
226	Checklist 133-264	.12	.09	.05
227	Ray Burris	.08	.06	.03
228	Sam Mejias	.08	.06	.03
229	Geoff Zahn	.08	.06	.03
230	Willie Wilson	.20	.15	.08
231	Phillies Future Stars (Mark Davis, Bob Dernier, Ozzie Virgil)	.50	.40	.20
232	Terry Crowley	.08	.06	.03
233	Duane Kuiper	.08	.06	.03
234	Ron Hodges	.08	.06	.03
235	Mike Easler	.12	.09	.05
236	John Martin	.08	.06	.03
237	Rusty Kuntz	.08	.06	.03
238	Kevin Saucier	.08	.06	.03
239	Jon Matlack	.10	.08	.04
240	Bucky Dent	.15	.11	.06
241	Bucky Dent IA	.10	.08	.04
242	Milt May	.08	.06	.03
243	Bob Owchinko	.08	.06	.03
244	Rufino Linares	.08	.06	.03
245	Ken Reitz	.08	.06	.03
246	Mets Batting & Pitching Ldrs. (Hubie Brooks, Mike Scott)	.20	.15	.08
247	Pedro Guerrero	.70	.50	.30
248	Frank LaCorte	.08	.06	.03
249	Tim Flannery	.08	.06	.03
250	Tug McGraw	.15	.11	.06
251	Fred Lynn	.30	.25	.12
252	Fred Lynn IA	.15	.11	.06
253	Chuck Baker	.08	.06	.03
254	Jorge Bell	12.00	9.00	4.75
255	Tony Perez	.30	.25	.12
256	Tony Perez IA	.15	.11	.06
257	Larry Harlow	.08	.06	.03
258	Bo Diaz	.10	.08	.04
259	Rodney Scott	.08	.06	.03
260	Bruce Sutter	.20	.15	.08
261	Tigers Future Stars (Howard Bailey, Marty Castillo, Dave Rucker)	.08	.06	.03
262	Doug Bair	.08	.06	.03
263	Victor Cruz	.08	.06	.03
264	Dan Quisenberry	.25	.20	.10
265	Al Bumbry	.10	.08	.04
266	Rick Leach	.15	.11	.06
267	Kurt Bevacqua	.08	.06	.03
268	Rickey Keeton	.08	.06	.03
269	Jim Essian	.08	.06	.03
270	Rusty Staub	.20	.15	.08
271	Larry Bradford	.08	.06	.03
272	Bump Wills	.08	.06	.03
273	Doug Bird	.08	.06	.03
274	Bob Ojeda	.80	.60	.30
275	Bob Watson	.10	.08	.04
276	Angels Batting & Pitching Ldrs. (Rod Carew, Ken Forsch)	.25	.20	.10
277	Terry Puhl	.08	.06	.03
278	John Littlefield	.08	.06	.03
279	Bill Russell	.10	.08	.04
280	Ben Oglivie	.10	.08	.04
281	John Verhoeven	.08	.06	.03
282	Ken Macha	.08	.06	.03
283	Brian Allard	.08	.06	.03
284	Bob Grich	.15	.11	.06
285	Sparky Lyle	.12	.09	.05
286	Bill Fahey	.08	.06	.03

		MT	NR MT	EX
287	Alan Bannister	.08	.06	.03
288	Garry Templeton	.12	.09	.05
289	Bob Stanley	.10	.08	.04
290	Ken Singleton	.12	.09	.05
291	Pirates Future Stars (Vance Law, Bob Long, Johnny Ray)	1.25	.90	.50
292	Dave Palmer	.10	.08	.04
293	Rob Picciolo	.08	.06	.03
294	Mike LaCoss	.10	.08	.04
295	Jason Thompson	.08	.06	.03
296	Bob Walk	.08	.06	.03
297	Clint Hurdle	.08	.06	.03
298	Danny Darwin	.10	.08	.04
299	Steve Trout	.10	.08	.04
300	Reggie Jackson	1.00	.70	.40
301	Reggie Jackson IA	.50	.40	.20
302	Doug Flynn	.08	.06	.03
303	Bill Caudill	.08	.06	.03
304	Johnnie LeMaster	.08	.06	.03
305	Don Sutton	.50	.40	.20
306	Don Sutton IA	.25	.20	.10
307	Randy Bass	.08	.06	.03
308	Charlie Moore	.08	.06	.03
309	Pete Redfern	.08	.06	.03
310	Mike Hargrove	.10	.08	.04
311	Dodgers Batting & Pitching Leaders (Dusty Baker, Burt Hooton)	.15	.11	.06
312	Lenny Randle	.08	.06	.03
313	John Harris	.08	.06	.03
314	Buck Martinez	.08	.06	.03
315	Burt Hooton	.10	.08	.04
316	Steve Braun	.08	.06	.03
317	Dick Ruthven	.08	.06	.03
318	Mike Heath	.08	.06	.03
319	Dave Rozema	.08	.06	.03
320	Chris Chambliss	.10	.08	.04
321	Chris Chambliss IA	.10	.08	.04
322	Garry Hancock	.08	.06	.03
323	Bill Lee	.10	.08	.04
324	Steve Dillard	.08	.06	.03
325	Jose Cruz	.15	.11	.06
326	Pete Falcone	.08	.06	.03
327	Joe Nolan	.08	.06	.03
328	Ed Farmer	.08	.06	.03
329	U.L. Washington	.08	.06	.03
330	Rick Wise	.10	.08	.04
331	Benny Ayala	.08	.06	.03
332	Don Robinson	.10	.08	.04
333	Brewers Future Stars (Frank DiPino, Marshall Edwards, Chuck Porter)	.15	.11	.06
334	Aurelio Rodriguez	.10	.08	.04
335	Jim Sundberg	.10	.08	.04
336	Mariners Batting & Pitching Ldrs. (Glenn Abbott, Tom Paciorek)	.12	.09	.05
337	Pete Rose AS	.80	.60	.30
338	Dave Lopes AS	.12	.09	.05
339	Mike Schmidt AS	.50	.40	.20
340	Dave Concepcion AS	.12	.09	.05
341	Andre Dawson AS	.25	.20	.10
342a	George Foster AS (no autograph)	2.25	1.75	.90
342b	George Foster AS (autograph on front)	.40	.30	.15
343	Dave Parker AS	.20	.15	.08
344	Gary Carter AS	.35	.25	.14
345	Fernando Valenzuela AS	.35	.25	.14
346	Tom Seaver AS	.35	.25	.14
347	Bruce Sutter AS	.12	.09	.05
348	Derrel Thomas	.08	.06	.03
349	George Frazier	.08	.06	.03
350	Thad Bosley	.08	.06	.03
351	Reds Future Stars (Scott Brown, Geoff Combe, Paul Householder)	.08	.06	.03
352	Dick Davis	.08	.06	.03
353	Jack O'Connor	.08	.06	.03
354	Roberto Ramos	.08	.06	.03
355	Dwight Evans	.25	.20	.10
356	Denny Lewallyn	.08	.06	.03
357	Butch Hobson	.08	.06	.03
358	Mike Parrott	.08	.06	.03
359	Jim Dwyer	.08	.06	.03
360	Len Barker	.10	.08	.04
361	Rafael Landestoy	.08	.06	.03
362	Jim Wright	.08	.06	.03
363	Bob Molinaro	.08	.06	.03
364	Doyle Alexander	.15	.11	.06
365	Bill Madlock	.25	.20	.10
366	Padres Batting & Pitching Ldrs. (Juan Eichelberger, Luis Salazar)	.12	.09	.05
367	Jim Kaat	.25	.20	.10
368	Alex Trevino	.08	.06	.03
369	Champ Summers	.08	.06	.03

		MT	NR MT	EX
370	Mike Norris	.08	.06	.03
371	Jerry Don Gleaton	.08	.06	.03
372	Luis Gomez	.08	.06	.03
373	Gene Nelson	.15	.11	.06
374	Tim Blackwell	.08	.06	.03
375	Dusty Baker	.12	.09	.05
376	Chris Welsh	.08	.06	.03
377	Kiko Garcia	.08	.06	.03
378	Mike Caldwell	.08	.06	.03
379	Rob Wilfong	.08	.06	.03
380	Dave Stieb	.25	.20	.10
381	Red Sox Future Stars (Bruce Hurst, Dave Schmidt, Julio Valdez)	.25	.20	.10
382	Joe Simpson	.08	.06	.03
383a	Pascual Perez (no position on front)	35.00	26.00	14.00
383b	Pascual Perez (position on front)	.12	.09	.05
384	Keith Moreland	.20	.15	.08
385	Ken Forsch	.10	.08	.04
386	Jerry White	.08	.06	.03
387	Tom Veryzer	.08	.06	.03
388	Joe Rudi	.12	.09	.05
389	George Vukovich	.08	.06	.03
390	Eddie Murray	1.25	.90	.50
391	Dave Tobik	.08	.06	.03
392	Rick Bosetti	.08	.06	.03
393	Al Hrabosky	.10	.08	.04
394	Checklist 265-396	.12	.09	.05
395	Omar Moreno	.08	.06	.03
396	Twins Batting & Pitching Ldrs. (Fernando Arroyo, John Castino)	.12	.09	.05
397	Ken Brett	.10	.08	.04
398	Mike Squires	.08	.06	.03
399	Pat Zachry	.08	.06	.03
400	Johnny Bench	.80	.60	.30
401	Johnny Bench IA	.40	.30	.15
402	Bill Stein	.08	.06	.03
403	Jim Tracy	.08	.06	.03
404	Dickie Thon	.10	.08	.04
405	Rick Reuschel	.15	.11	.06
406	Al Holland	.08	.06	.03
407	Danny Boone	.08	.06	.03
408	Ed Romero	.08	.06	.03
409	Don Cooper	.08	.06	.03
410	Ron Cey	.15	.11	.06
411	Ron Cey IA	.10	.08	.04
412	Luis Leal	.08	.06	.03
413	Dan Meyer	.08	.06	.03
414	Elias Sosa	.08	.06	.03
415	Don Baylor	.20	.15	.08
416	Marty Bystrom	.08	.06	.03
417	Pat Kelly	.08	.06	.03
418	Rangers Future Stars (John Butcher, Bobby Johnson, Dave Schmidt)	.20	.15	.08
419	Steve Stone	.12	.09	.05
420	George Hendrick	.12	.09	.05
421	Mark Clear	.10	.08	.04
422	Cliff Johnson	.08	.06	.03
423	Stan Papi	.08	.06	.03
424	Bruce Benedict	.08	.06	.03
425	John Candelaria	.12	.09	.05
426	Orioles Batting & Pitching Ldrs. (Eddie Murray, Sammy Stewart)	.35	.25	.14
427	Ron Oester	.08	.06	.03
428	Lamarr Hoyt (LaMarr)	.12	.09	.05
429	John Wathan	.12	.09	.05
430	Vida Blue	.15	.11	.06
431	Vida Blue IA	.10	.08	.04
432	Mike Scott	.25	.20	.10
433	Alan Ashby	.08	.06	.03
434	Joe Lefebvre	.08	.06	.03
435	Robin Yount	.70	.50	.30
436	Joe Strain	.08	.06	.03
437	Juan Berenguer	.10	.08	.04
438	Pete Mackanin	.08	.06	.03
439	Dave Righetti	2.00	1.50	.80
440	Jeff Burroughs	.10	.08	.04
441	Astros Future Stars (Danny Heep, Billy Smith, Bobby Sprowl)	.08	.06	.03
442	Bruce Kison	.08	.06	.03
443	Mark Wagner	.08	.06	.03
444	Terry Forster	.10	.08	.04
445	Larry Parrish	.12	.09	.05
446	Wayne Garland	.08	.06	.03
447	Darrell Porter	.10	.08	.04
448	Darrell Porter IA	.10	.08	.04
449	Luis Aguayo	.12	.09	.05
450	Jack Morris	.50	.40	.20
451	Ed Miller	.08	.06	.03
452	Lee Smith	.90	.70	.35
453	Art Howe	.08	.06	.03

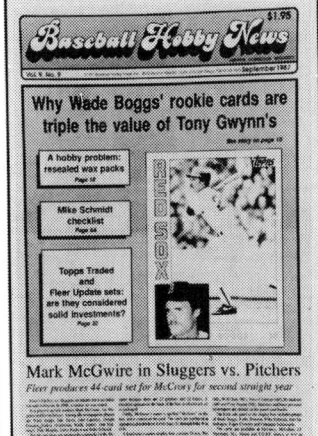

		MT	NR MT	EX
454	Rick Langford	.08	.06	.03
455	Tom Burgmeier	.08	.06	.03
456	Cubs Batting & Pitching Ldrs. (Bill Buckner, Randy Martz)	.15	.11	.06
457	Tim Stoddard	.08	.06	.03
458	Willie Montanez	.08	.06	.03
459	Bruce Berenyi	.08	.06	.03
460	Jack Clark	.30	.25	.12
461	Rich Dotson	.12	.09	.05
462	Dave Chalk	.08	.06	.03
463	Jim Kern	.08	.06	.03
464	Juan Bonilla	.12	.09	.05
465	Lee Mazzilli	.10	.08	.04
466	Randy Lerch	.08	.06	.03
467	Mickey Hatcher	.10	.08	.04
468	Floyd Bannister	.12	.09	.05
469	Ed Ott	.08	.06	.03
470	John Mayberry	.10	.08	.04
471	Royals Future Stars (Atlee Hammaker, Mike Jones, Darryl Motley)	.25	.20	.10
472	Oscar Gamble	.10	.08	.04
473	Mike Stanton	.08	.06	.03
474	Ken Oberkfell	.10	.08	.04
475	Alan Trammell	.50	.40	.20
476	Brian Kingman	.08	.06	.03
477	Steve Yeager	.08	.06	.03
478	Ray Searage	.08	.06	.03
479	Rowland Office	.08	.06	.03
480	Steve Carlton	.80	.60	.30
481	Steve Carlton IA	.40	.30	.15
482	Glenn Hubbard	.10	.08	.04
483	Gary Woods	.08	.06	.03
484	Ivan DeJesus	.08	.06	.03
485	Kent Tekulve	.10	.08	.04
486	Yankees Batting & Pitching Ldrs. (Tommy John, Jerry Mumphrey)	.20	.15	.08
487	Bob McClure	.08	.06	.03
488	Ron Jackson	.08	.06	.03
489	Rick Dempsey	.10	.08	.04
490	Dennis Eckersley	.12	.09	.05
491	Checklist 397-528	.12	.09	.05
492	Joe Price	.08	.06	.03
493	Chet Lemon	.10	.08	.04
494	Hubie Brooks	.20	.15	.08
495	Dennis Leonard	.10	.08	.04
496	Johnny Grubb	.08	.06	.03
497	Jim Anderson	.08	.06	.03
498	Dave Bergman	.08	.06	.03
499	Paul Mirabella	.08	.06	.03
500	Rod Carew	.80	.60	.30
501	Rod Carew IA	.40	.30	.15
502	Braves Future Stars (Steve Bedrosian, Brett Butler, Larry Owen)	1.00	.70	.40
503	Julio Gonzalez	.08	.06	.03
504	Rick Peters	.08	.06	.03
505	Graig Nettles	.25	.20	.10
506	Graig Nettles IA	.12	.09	.05
507	Terry Harper	.08	.06	.03
508	Jody Davis	.70	.50	.30
509	Harry Spilman	.08	.06	.03
510	Fernando Valenzuela	1.50	1.25	.60
511	Ruppert Jones	.08	.06	.03
512	Jerry Dybzinski	.08	.06	.03
513	Rick Rhoden	.15	.11	.06
514	Joe Ferguson	.08	.06	.03
515	Larry Bowa	.20	.15	.08
516	Larry Bowa IA	.12	.09	.05
517	Mark Brouhard	.08	.06	.03
518	Garth Iorg	.08	.06	.03
519	Glenn Adams	.08	.06	.03
520	Mike Flanagan	.12	.09	.05
521	Billy Almon	.08	.06	.03
522	Chuck Rainey	.08	.06	.03
523	Gary Gray	.08	.06	.03
524	Tom Hausman	.08	.06	.03
525	Ray Knight	.12	.09	.05
526	Expos Batting & Pitching Ldrs. (Warren Cromartie, Bill Gullickson)	.12	.09	.05
527	John Henry Johnson	.08	.06	.03
528	Matt Alexander	.08	.06	.03
529	Allen Ripley	.08	.06	.03
530	Dickie Noles	.08	.06	.03
531	A's Future Stars (Rich Bordi, Mark Budaska, Kelvin Moore)	.08	.06	.03
532	Toby Harrah	.10	.08	.04
533	Joaquin Andujar	.12	.09	.05
534	Dave McKay	.08	.06	.03
535	Lance Parrish	.50	.40	.20
536	Rafael Ramirez	.10	.08	.04
537	Doug Capilla	.08	.06	.03
538	Lou Piniella	.20	.15	.08

		MT	NR MT	EX
539	Vern Ruhle	.08	.06	.03
540	Andre Dawson	.50	.40	.20
541	Barry Evans	.08	.06	.03
542	Ned Yost	.08	.06	.03
543	Bill Robinson	.08	.06	.03
544	Larry Christenson	.08	.06	.03
545	Reggie Smith	.15	.11	.06
546	Reggie Smith IA	.10	.08	.04
547	Rod Carew AS	.35	.25	.14
548	Willie Randolph AS	.12	.09	.05
549	George Brett AS	.60	.45	.25
550	Bucky Dent AS	.12	.09	.05
551	Reggie Jackson AS	.50	.40	.20
552	Ken Singleton AS	.12	.09	.05
553	Dave Winfield AS	.40	.30	.15
554	Carlton Fisk AS	.20	.15	.08
555	Scott McGregor AS	.12	.09	.05
556	Jack Morris AS	.20	.15	.08
557	Rich Gossage AS	.20	.15	.08
558	John Tudor	.30	.25	.12
559	Indians Batting & Pitching Ldrs. (Bert Blyleven, Mike Hargrove)	.15	.11	.06
560	Doug Corbett	.08	.06	.03
561	Cardinals Future Stars (Glenn Brummer, Luis DeLeon, Gene Roof)	.10	.08	.04
562	Mike O'Berry	.08	.06	.03
563	Ross Baumgarten	.08	.06	.03
564	Doug DeCinces	.15	.11	.06
565	Jackson Todd	.08	.06	.03
566	Mike Jorgensen	.08	.06	.03
567	Bob Babcock	.08	.06	.03
568	Joe Pettini	.08	.06	.03
569	Willie Randolph	.15	.11	.06
570	Willie Randolph IA	.10	.08	.04
571	Glenn Abbott	.08	.06	.03
572	Juan Beniquez	.08	.06	.03
573	Rick Waits	.08	.06	.03
574	Mike Ramsey	.08	.06	.03
575	Al Cowens	.08	.06	.03
576	Giants Batting & Pitching Ldrs. (Vida Blue, Milt May)	.15	.11	.06
577	Rick Monday	.12	.09	.05
578	Shooty Babitt	.08	.06	.03
579	Rick Mahler	.30	.25	.12
580	Bobby Bonds	.15	.11	.06
581	Ron Reed	.10	.08	.04
582	Luis Pujols	.08	.06	.03
583	Tippy Martinez	.08	.06	.03
584	Hosken Powell	.08	.06	.03
585	Rollie Fingers	.30	.25	.12
586	Rollie Fingers IA	.15	.11	.06
587	Tim Lollar	.08	.06	.03
588	Dale Berra	.08	.06	.03
589	Dave Stapleton	.08	.06	.03
590	Al Oliver	.20	.15	.08
591	Al Oliver IA	.10	.08	.04
592	Craig Swan	.08	.06	.03
593	Billy Smith	.08	.06	.03
594	Renie Martin	.08	.06	.03
595	Dave Collins	.10	.08	.04
596	Damaso Garcia	.12	.09	.05
597	Wayne Nordhagen	.08	.06	.03
598	Bob Galasso	.08	.06	.03
599	White Sox Future Stars (Jay Loviglio, Reggie Patterson, Leo Sutherland)	.08	.06	.03
600	Dave Winfield	.50	.40	.20
601	Sid Monge	.08	.06	.03
602	Freddie Patek	.08	.06	.03
603	Rich Hebner	.08	.06	.03
604	Orlando Sanchez	.08	.06	.03
605	Steve Rogers	.10	.08	.04
606	Blue Jays Batting & Pitching Ldrs. (John Mayberry, Dave Stieb)	.15	.11	.06
607	Leon Durham	.25	.20	.10
608	Jerry Royster	.08	.06	.03
609	Rick Sutcliffe	.25	.20	.10
610	Rickey Henderson	1.50	1.25	.60
611	Joe Niekro	.20	.15	.08
612	Gary Ward	.10	.08	.04
613	Jim Gantner	.10	.08	.04
614	Juan Eichelberger	.08	.06	.03
615	Bob Boone	.12	.09	.05
616	Bob Boone IA	.10	.08	.04
617	Scott McGregor	.12	.09	.05
618	Tim Foli	.08	.06	.03
619	Bill Campbell	.08	.06	.03
620	Ken Griffey	.15	.11	.06
621	Ken Griffey IA	.10	.08	.04
622	Dennis Lamp	.08	.06	.03
623	Mets Future Stars (Ron Gardenhire, Terry Leach, Tim Leary)	.35	.25	.14

		MT	NR MT	EX
624	Fergie Jenkins	.25	.20	.10
625	Hal McRae	.15	.11	.06
626	Randy Jones	.10	.08	.04
627	Enos Cabell	.10	.08	.04
628	Bill Travers	.08	.06	.03
629	Johnny Wockenfuss	.08	.06	.03
630	Joe Charboneau	.10	.08	.04
631	Gene Tenace	.10	.08	.04
632	Bryan Clark	.08	.06	.03
633	Mitchell Page	.08	.06	.03
634	Checklist 529-660	.12	.09	.05
635	Ron Davis	.10	.08	.04
636	Phillies Batting & Pitching Ldrs. (Steve Carlton, Pete Rose)	.50	.40	.20
637	Rick Camp	.08	.06	.03
638	John Milner	.08	.06	.03
639	Ken Kravec	.08	.06	.03
640	Cesar Cedeno	.15	.11	.06
641	Steve Mura	.08	.06	.03
642	Mike Scioscia	.10	.08	.04
643	Pete Vuckovich	.12	.09	.05
644	John Castino	.08	.06	.03
645	Frank White	.12	.09	.05
646	Frank White IA	.10	.08	.04
647	Warren Brusstar	.08	.06	.03
648	Jose Morales	.08	.06	.03
649	Ken Clay	.08	.06	.03
650	Carl Yastrzemski	1.25	.90	.50
651	Carl Yastrzemski IA	.60	.45	.25
652	Steve Nicosia	.08	.06	.03
653	Angels Future Stars (Tom Brunansky, Luis Sanchez, Daryl Sconiers)	2.25	1.75	.90
654	Jim Morrison	.08	.06	.03
655	Joel Youngblood	.08	.06	.03
656	Eddie Whitson	.08	.06	.03
657	Tom Poquette	.08	.06	.03
658	Tito Landrum	.08	.06	.03
659	Fred Martinez	.08	.06	.03
660	Dave Concepcion	.15	.11	.06
661	Dave Concepcion IA	.10	.08	.04
662	Luis Salazar	.08	.06	.03
663	Hector Cruz	.08	.06	.03
664	Dan Spillner	.08	.06	.03
665	Jim Clancy	.15	.11	.06
666	Tigers Batting & Pitching Ldrs. (Steve Kemp, Dan Petry)	.15	.11	.06
667	Jeff Reardon	.30	.25	.12
668	Dale Murphy	2.00	1.50	.80
669	Larry Milbourne	.08	.06	.03
670	Steve Kemp	.12	.09	.05
671	Mike Davis	.15	.11	.06
672	Bob Knepper	.12	.09	.05
673	Keith Drumright	.08	.06	.03
674	Dave Goltz	.10	.08	.04
675	Cecil Cooper	.20	.15	.08
676	Sal Butera	.08	.06	.03
677	Alfredo Griffin	.12	.09	.05
678	Tom Paciorek	.08	.06	.03
679	Sammy Stewart	.08	.06	.03
680	Gary Matthews	.12	.09	.05
681	Dodgers Future Stars (Mike Marshall, Ron Roenicke, Steve Sax)	3.25	2.50	1.25
682	Jesse Jefferson	.08	.06	.03
683	Phil Garner	.10	.08	.04
684	Harold Baines	.70	.50	.30
685	Bert Blyleven	.25	.20	.10
686	Gary Allenson	.08	.06	.03
687	Greg Minton	.08	.06	.03
688	Leon Roberts	.08	.06	.03
689	Lary Sorensen	.08	.06	.03
690	Dave Kingman	.20	.15	.08
691	Dan Schatzeder	.08	.06	.03
692	Wayne Gross	.08	.06	.03
693	Cesar Geronimo	.08	.06	.03
694	Dave Wehrmeister	.08	.06	.03
695	Warren Cromartie	.08	.06	.03
696	Pirates Batting & Pitching Ldrs. (Bill Madlock, Buddy Solomon)	.15	.11	.06
697	John Montefusco	.08	.06	.03
698	Tony Scott	.08	.06	.03
699	Dick Tidrow	.08	.06	.03
700	George Foster	.25	.20	.10
701	George Foster IA	.12	.09	.05
702	Steve Renko	.08	.06	.03
703	Brewers Batting & Pitching Ldrs. (Cecil Cooper, Pete Vuckovich)	.15	.11	.06
704	Mickey Rivers	.12	.09	.05
705	Mickey Rivers IA	.10	.08	.04
706	Barry Foote	.08	.06	.03
707	Mark Bomback	.08	.06	.03
708	Gene Richards	.08	.06	.03

		MT	NR MT	EX
709	Don Money	.10	.08	.04
710	Jerry Reuss	.15	.11	.06
711	Mariners Future Stars (Dave Edler, Dave Henderson, Reggie Walton)	.25	.20	.10
712	Denny Martinez	.10	.08	.04
713	Del Unser	.08	.06	.03
714	Jerry Koosman	.15	.11	.06
715	Willie Stargell	.60	.45	.25
716	Willie Stargell IA	.30	.25	.12
717	Rick Miller	.08	.06	.03
718	Charlie Hough	.12	.09	.05
719	Jerry Narron	.08	.06	.03
720	Greg Luzinski	.20	.15	.08
721	Greg Luzinski IA	.12	.09	.05
722	Jerry Martin	.08	.06	.03
723	Junior Kennedy	.08	.06	.03
724	Dave Rosello	.08	.06	.03
725	Amos Otis	.12	.09	.05
726	Amos Otis IA	.10	.08	.04
727	Sixto Lezcano	.08	.06	.03
728	Aurelio Lopez	.08	.06	.03
729	Jim Spencer	.08	.06	.03
730	Gary Carter	.80	.60	.30
731	Padres Future Stars (Mike Armstrong, Doug Gwosdz, Fred Kuhaulua)	.08	.06	.03
732	Mike Lum	.08	.06	.03
733	Larry McWilliams	.08	.06	.03
734	Mike Ivie	.08	.06	.03
735	Rudy May	.10	.08	.04
736	Jerry Turner	.08	.06	.03
737	Reggie Cleveland	.08	.06	.03
738	Dave Engle	.08	.06	.03
739	Joey McLaughlin	.08	.06	.03
740	Dave Lopes	.12	.09	.05
741	Dave Lopes IA	.10	.08	.04
742	Dick Drago	.08	.06	.03
743	John Stearns	.08	.06	.03
744	Mike Witt	1.75	1.25	.70
745	Bake McBride	.08	.06	.03
746	Andre Thornton	.15	.11	.06
747	John Lowenstein	.08	.06	.03
748	Marc Hill	.08	.06	.03
749	Bob Shirley	.08	.06	.03
750	Jim Rice	.90	.70	.35
751	Rick Honeycutt	.10	.08	.04
752	Lee Lacy	.10	.08	.04
753	Tom Brookens	.08	.06	.03
754	Joe Morgan	.40	.30	.15
755	Joe Morgan IA	.20	.15	.08
756	Reds Batting & Pitching Ldrs. (Ken Griffey, Tom Seaver)	.30	.25	.12
757	Tom Underwood	.08	.06	.03
758	Claudell Washington	.12	.09	.05
759	Paul Splittorff	.10	.08	.04
760	Bill Buckner	.15	.11	.06
761	Dave Smith	.12	.09	.05
762	Mike Phillips	.08	.06	.03
763	Tom Hume	.08	.06	.03
764	Steve Swisher	.08	.06	.03
765	Gorman Thomas	.15	.11	.06
766	Twins Future Stars (Lenny Faedo, Kent Hrbek, Tim Laudner)	3.50	2.75	1.50
767	Roy Smalley	.10	.08	.04
768	Jerry Garvin	.08	.06	.03
769	Richie Zisk	.10	.08	.04
770	Rich Gossage	.35	.25	.14
771	Rich Gossage IA	.15	.11	.06
772	Bert Campaneris	.12	.09	.05
773	John Denny	.10	.08	.04
774	Jay Johnstone	.12	.09	.05
775	Bob Forsch	.12	.09	.05
776	Mark Belanger	.10	.08	.04
777	Tom Griffin	.08	.06	.03
778	Kevin Hickey	.08	.06	.03
779	Grant Jackson	.08	.06	.03
780	Pete Rose	2.25	1.75	.90
781	Pete Rose IA	1.00	.70	.40
782	Frank Taveras	.08	.06	.03
783	Greg Harris	.15	.11	.06
784	Milt Wilcox	.10	.08	.04
785	Dan Driessen	.12	.09	.05
786	Red Sox Batting & Pitching Ldrs. (Carney Lansford, Mike Torrez)	.12	.09	.05
787	Fred Stanley	.08	.06	.03
788	Woodie Fryman	.10	.08	.04
789	Checklist 661-792	.12	.09	.05
790	Larry Gura	.10	.08	.04
791	Bobby Brown	.08	.06	.03
792	Frank Tanana	.12	.09	.05

1982 Topps Traded

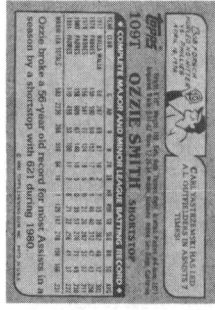

Topps released its second straight 132-card Traded set in September of 1982. Again, the 2½'' by 3½'' cards featured not only players who had been traded during the season, but also promising rookies who were given their first individual cards. The cards follow the basic design of the regular issues, but had their backs printed in red rather than the regular-issue green. As in 1981, the cards were not available in normal retail outlets and could only be purchased through regular baseball card dealers. Unlike the previous year, the cards are numbered 1-132 with the letter "T" following the number.

		MT	NR MT	EX
Complete Set:		20.00	15.00	8.00
Common Player:		.10	.08	.04
1T	Doyle Alexander	.25	.20	.10
2T	Jesse Barfield	3.25	2.50	1.25
3T	Ross Baumgarten	.10	.08	.04
4T	Steve Bedrosian	.80	.60	.30
5T	Mark Belanger	.15	.11	.06
6T	Kurt Bevacqua	.10	.08	.04
7T	Tim Blackwell	.10	.08	.04
8T	Vida Blue	.25	.20	.10
9T	Bob Boone	.20	.15	.08
10T	Larry Bowa	.25	.20	.10
11T	Dan Briggs	.10	.08	.04
12T	Bobby Brown	.10	.08	.04
13T	Tom Brunansky	1.50	1.25	.60
14T	Jeff Burroughs	.15	.11	.06
15T	Enos Cabell	.15	.11	.06
16T	Bill Campbell	.10	.08	.04
17T	Bobby Castillo	.10	.08	.04
18T	Bill Caudill	.15	.11	.06
19T	Cesar Cedeno	.25	.20	.10
20T	Dave Collins	.15	.11	.06
21T	Doug Corbett	.10	.08	.04
22T	Al Cowens	.15	.11	.06
23T	Chili Davis	1.25	.90	.50
24T	Dick Davis	.10	.08	.04
25T	Ron Davis	.15	.11	.06
26T	Doug DeCinces	.20	.15	.08
27T	Ivan DeJesus	.10	.08	.04
28T	Bob Dernier	.25	.20	.10
29T	Bo Diaz	.15	.11	.06
30T	Roger Erickson	.10	.08	.04
31T	Jim Essian	.10	.08	.04
32T	Ed Farmer	.10	.08	.04
33T	Doug Flynn	.10	.08	.04
34T	Tim Foli	.10	.08	.04
35T	Dan Ford	.10	.08	.04
36T	George Foster	.40	.30	.15
37T	Dave Frost	.10	.08	.04
38T	Rich Gale	.10	.08	.04
39T	Ron Gardenhire	.10	.08	.04
40T	Ken Griffey	.25	.20	.10
41T	Greg Harris	.10	.08	.04
42T	Von Hayes	1.50	1.25	.60
43T	Larry Herndon	.15	.11	.06
44T	Kent Hrbek	3.25	2.50	1.25
45T	Mike Ivie	.10	.08	.04
46T	Grant Jackson	.10	.08	.04
47T	Reggie Jackson	2.25	1.75	.90
48T	Ron Jackson	.10	.08	.04
49T	Fergie Jenkins	.40	.30	.15

		MT	NR MT	EX
50T	Lamar Johnson	.10	.08	.04
51T	Randy Johnson	.10	.08	.04
52T	Jay Johnstone	.15	.11	.06
53T	Mick Kelleher	.10	.08	.04
54T	Steve Kemp	.15	.11	.06
55T	Junior Kennedy	.10	.08	.04
56T	Jim Kern	.10	.08	.04
57T	Ray Knight	.20	.15	.08
58T	Wayne Krenchicki	.10	.08	.04
59T	Mike Krukow	.15	.11	.06
60T	Duane Kuiper	.10	.08	.04
61T	Mike LaCoss	.15	.11	.06
62T	Chet Lemon	.15	.11	.06
63T	Sixto Lezcano	.10	.08	.04
64T	Dave Lopes	.20	.15	.08
65T	Jerry Martin	.10	.08	.04
66T	Renie Martin	.10	.08	.04
67T	John Mayberry	.15	.11	.06
68T	Lee Mazzilli	.15	.11	.06
69T	Bake McBride	.10	.08	.04
70T	Dan Meyer	.10	.08	.04
71T	Larry Milbourne	.10	.08	.04
72T	Eddie Milner	.30	.25	.12
73T	Sid Monge	.10	.08	.04
74T	Jose Morales	.10	.08	.04
75T	Keith Moreland	.15	.11	.06
76T	John Montefusco	.15	.11	.06
77T	Jim Morrison	.10	.08	.04
78T	Rance Mulliniks	.10	.08	.04
79T	Steve Mura	.10	.08	.04
80T	Gene Nelson	.10	.08	.04
81T	Joe Nolan	.10	.08	.04
82T	Dickie Noles	.10	.08	.04
83T	Al Oliver	.30	.25	.12
84T	Jorge Orta	.10	.08	.04
85T	Tom Paciorek	.15	.11	.06
86T	Larry Parrish	.20	.15	.08
87T	Jack Perconte	.10	.08	.04
88T	Gaylord Perry	1.25	.90	.50
89T	Rob Picciolo	.10	.08	.04
90T	Joe Pittman	.10	.08	.04
91T	Hosken Powell	.10	.08	.04
92T	Mike Proly	.10	.08	.04
93T	Greg Pryor	.10	.08	.04
94T	Charlie Puleo	.15	.11	.06
95T	Shane Rawley	.20	.15	.08
96T	Johnny Ray	.80	.60	.30
97T	Dave Revering	.10	.08	.04
98T	Cal Ripken	7.50	5.75	3.00
99T	Allen Ripley	.10	.08	.04
100T	Bill Robinson	.10	.08	.04
101T	Aurelio Rodriguez	.15	.11	.06
102T	Joe Rudi	.20	.15	.08
103T	Steve Sax	1.75	1.25	.70
104T	Dan Schatzeder	.10	.08	.04
105T	Bob Shirley	.10	.08	.04
106T	Eric Show	.30	.25	.12
107T	Roy Smalley	.15	.11	.06
108T	Lonnie Smith	.15	.11	.06
109T	Ozzie Smith	.70	.50	.30
110T	Reggie Smith	.20	.15	.08
111T	Lary Sorensen	.10	.08	.04
112T	Elias Sosa	.10	.08	.04
113T	Mike Stanton	.10	.08	.04
114T	Steve Stroughter	.10	.08	.04
115T	Champ Summers	.10	.08	.04
116T	Rick Sutcliffe	.40	.30	.15
117T	Frank Tanana	.20	.15	.08
118T	Frank Taveras	.10	.08	.04
119T	Garry Templeton	.20	.15	.08
120T	Alex Trevino	.10	.08	.04
121T	Jerry Turner	.10	.08	.04
122T	Ed Vande Berg	.15	.11	.06
123T	Tom Veryzer	.10	.08	.04
124T	Ron Washington	.10	.08	.04
125T	Bob Watson	.15	.11	.06
126T	Dennis Werth	.10	.08	.04
127T	Eddie Whitson	.15	.11	.06
128T	Rob Wilfong	.10	.08	.04
129T	Bump Wills	.10	.08	.04
130T	Gary Woods	.10	.08	.04
131T	Butch Wynegar	.15	.11	.06
132T	Checklist 1-132	.10	.08	.04

Definitions for grading conditions are located in the Introduction of this price guide.

1983 Topps

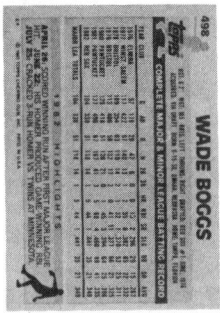

The 1983 Topps set totaled 792 cards. Missing among the regular 2½" by 3½" cards were some form of future stars cards, as Topps was saving them for the now established late season "Traded" set. The '83 cards carried a large color photo as well as a smaller color photo on the front, quite similar in design to the 1963 set. Team colors framed the card which at the bottom had the player's name, position and team. At the upper right-hand corner was a Topps logo. The backs were horizontal and included statistics, personal information and 1982 highlights. Specialty cards included record-break performances, league leaders, All-Stars, numbered checklists, "Team Leaders" and "Super Veteran" cards which were horizontal with a current and first-season picture of the honored player.

		MT	NR MT	EX
Complete Set:		80.00	60.00	32.00
Common Player:		.08	.06	.03
1	Record Breaker (Tony Armas)	.12	.09	.05
2	Record Breaker (Rickey Henderson)			
		.35	.25	.14
3	Record Breaker (Greg Minton)	.10	.08	.04
4	Record Breaker (Lance Parrish)	.20	.15	.08
5	Record Breaker (Manny Trillo)	.10	.08	.04
6	Record Breaker (John Wathan)	.10	.08	.04
7	Gene Richards	.08	.06	.03
8	Steve Balboni	.12	.09	.05
9	Joey McLaughlin	.08	.06	.03
10	Gorman Thomas	.15	.11	.06
11	Billy Gardner	.08	.06	.03
12	Paul Mirabella	.08	.06	.03
13	Larry Herndon	.10	.08	.04
14	Frank LaCorte	.08	.06	.03
15	Ron Cey	.15	.11	.06
16	George Vukovich	.08	.06	.03
17	Kent Tekulve	.10	.08	.04
18	Super Veteran (Kent Tekulve)	.10	.08	.04
19	Oscar Gamble	.10	.08	.04
20	Carlton Fisk	.25	.20	.10
21	Orioles Batting & Pitching Ldrs. (Eddie Murray, Jim Palmer)	.35	.25	.14
22	Randy Martz	.08	.06	.03
23	Mike Heath	.08	.06	.03
24	Steve Mura	.08	.06	.03
25	Hal McRae	.15	.11	.06
26	Jerry Royster	.08	.06	.03
27	Doug Corbett	.08	.06	.03
28	Bruce Bochte	.08	.06	.03
29	Randy Jones	.10	.08	.04
30	Jim Rice	.70	.50	.30
31	Bill Gullickson	.12	.09	.05
32	Dave Bergman	.08	.06	.03
33	Jack O'Connor	.08	.06	.03
34	Paul Householder	.08	.06	.03
35	Rollie Fingers	.30	.25	.12
36	Super Veteran (Rollie Fingers)	.15	.11	.06
37	Darrell Johnson	.08	.06	.03
38	Tim Flannery	.08	.06	.03
39	Terry Puhl	.08	.06	.03
40	Fernando Valenzuela	.50	.40	.20
41	Jerry Turner	.08	.06	.03
42	Dale Murray	.08	.06	.03
43	Bob Dernier	.10	.08	.04

		MT	NR MT	EX
44	Don Robinson	.10	.08	.04
45	John Mayberry	.10	.08	.04
46	Richard Dotson	.12	.09	.05
47	Dave McKay	.08	.06	.03
48	Lary Sorensen	.08	.06	.03
49	Willie McGee	2.50	2.00	1.00
50	Bob Horner	.35	.25	.14
51	Cubs Batting & Pitching Ldrs. (Leon Durham, Fergie Jenkins)	.15	.11	.06
52	Onix Concepcion	.10	.08	.04
53	Mike Witt	.50	.40	.20
54	Jim Maler	.08	.06	.03
55	Mookie Wilson	.12	.09	.05
56	Chuck Rainey	.08	.06	.03
57	Tim Blackwell	.08	.06	.03
58	Al Holland	.08	.06	.03
59	Benny Ayala	.08	.06	.03
60	Johnny Bench	.60	.45	.25
61	Super Veteran (Johnny Bench)	.30	.25	.12
62	Bob McClure	.08	.06	.03
63	Rick Monday	.12	.09	.05
64	Bill Stein	.08	.06	.03
65	Jack Morris	.35	.25	.14
66	Bob Lillis	.08	.06	.03
67	Sal Butera	.08	.06	.03
68	Eric Show	.30	.25	.12
69	Lee Lacy	.10	.08	.04
70	Steve Carlton	.60	.45	.25
71	Super Veteran (Steve Carlton)	.30	.25	.12
72	Tom Paciorek	.08	.06	.03
73	Allen Ripley	.08	.06	.03
74	Julio Gonzalez	.08	.06	.03
75	Amos Otis	.10	.08	.04
76	Rick Mahler	.12	.09	.05
77	Hosken Powell	.08	.06	.03
78	Bill Caudill	.08	.06	.03
79	Mick Kelleher	.08	.06	.03
80	George Foster	.20	.15	.08
81	Yankees Batting & Pitching Ldrs. (Jerry Mumphrey, Dave Righetti)	.15	.11	.06
82	Bruce Hurst	.15	.11	.06
83	Ryne Sandberg	6.00	4.50	2.50
84	Milt May	.08	.06	.03
85	Ken Singleton	.12	.09	.05
86	Tom Hume	.08	.06	.03
87	Joe Rudi	.12	.09	.05
88	Jim Gantner	.10	.08	.04
89	Leon Roberts	.08	.06	.03
90	Jerry Reuss	.12	.09	.05
91	Larry Milbourne	.08	.06	.03
92	Mike LaCoss	.10	.08	.04
93	John Castino	.08	.06	.03
94	Dave Edwards	.08	.06	.03
95	Alan Trammell	.50	.40	.20
96	Dick Howser	.10	.08	.04
97	Ross Baumgarten	.08	.06	.03
98	Vance Law	.10	.08	.04
99	Dickie Noles	.08	.06	.03
100	Pete Rose	1.75	1.25	.70
101	Super Veteran (Pete Rose)	.80	.60	.30
102	Dave Beard	.08	.06	.03
103	Darrell Porter	.10	.08	.04
104	Bob Walk	.08	.06	.03
105	Don Baylor	.20	.15	.08
106	Gene Nelson	.08	.06	.03
107	Mike Jorgensen	.08	.06	.03
108	Glenn Hoffman	.08	.06	.03
109	Luis Leal	.08	.06	.03
110	Ken Griffey	.15	.11	.06
111	Expos Batting & Pitching Ldrs. (Al Oliver, Steve Rogers)	.15	.11	.06
112	Bob Shirley	.08	.06	.03
113	Ron Roenicke	.08	.06	.03
114	Jim Slaton	.08	.06	.03
115	Chili Davis	.25	.20	.10
116	Dave Schmidt	.10	.08	.04
117	Alan Knicely	.08	.06	.03
118	Chris Welsh	.08	.06	.03
119	Tom Brookens	.08	.06	.03
120	Len Barker	.10	.08	.04
121	Mickey Hatcher	.10	.08	.04
122	Jimmy Smith	.08	.06	.03
123	George Frazier	.08	.06	.03
124	Marc Hill	.08	.06	.03
125	Leon Durham	.15	.11	.06
126	Joe Torre	.10	.08	.04
127	Preston Hanna	.08	.06	.03
128	Mike Ramsey	.08	.06	.03
129	Checklist 1-132	.12	.09	.05
130	Dave Stieb	.20	.15	.08
131	Ed Ott	.08	.06	.03

		MT	NR MT	EX
132	Todd Cruz	.08	.06	.03
133	Jim Barr	.08	.06	.03
134	Hubie Brooks	.15	.11	.06
135	Dwight Evans	.25	.20	.10
136	Willie Aikens	.08	.06	.03
137	Woodie Fryman	.10	.08	.04
138	Rick Dempsey	.10	.08	.04
139	Bruce Berenyi	.08	.06	.03
140	Willie Randolph	.12	.09	.05
141	Indians Batting & Pitching Ldrs. (Toby Harrah, Rick Sutcliffe)	.15	.11	.06
142	Mike Caldwell	.08	.06	.03
143	Joe Pettini	.08	.06	.03
144	Mark Wagner	.08	.06	.03
145	Don Sutton	.40	.30	.15
146	Super Veteran (Don Sutton)	.20	.15	.08
147	Rick Leach	.10	.08	.04
148	Dave Roberts	.08	.06	.03
149	Johnny Ray	.20	.15	.08
150	Bruce Sutter	.20	.15	.08
151	Super Veteran (Bruce Sutter)	.12	.09	.05
152	Jay Johnstone	.12	.09	.05
153	Jerry Koosman	.15	.11	.06
154	Johnnie LeMaster	.08	.06	.03
155	Dan Quisenberry	.25	.20	.10
156	Billy Martin	.12	.09	.05
157	Steve Bedrosian	.25	.20	.10
158	Rob Wilfong	.08	.06	.03
159	Mike Stanton	.08	.06	.03
160	Dave Kingman	.20	.15	.08
161	Super Veteran (Dave Kingman)	.10	.08	.04
162	Mark Clear	.10	.08	.04
163	Cal Ripken	2.00	1.50	.80
164	Dave Palmer	.10	.08	.04
165	Dan Driessen	.10	.08	.04
166	John Pacella	.08	.06	.03
167	Mark Brouhard	.08	.06	.03
168	Juan Eichelberger	.08	.06	.03
169	Doug Flynn	.08	.06	.03
170	Steve Howe	.10	.08	.04
171	Giants Batting & Pitching Ldrs. (Bill Laskey, Joe Morgan)	.15	.11	.06
172	Vern Ruhle	.08	.06	.03
173	Jim Morrison	.08	.06	.03
174	Jerry Ujdur	.08	.06	.03
175	Bo Diaz	.10	.08	.04
176	Dave Righetti	.35	.25	.14
177	Harold Baines	.25	.20	.10
178	Luis Tiant	.15	.11	.06
179	Super Veteran (Luis Tiant)	.10	.08	.04
180	Rickey Henderson	.80	.60	.30
181	Terry Felton	.08	.06	.03
182	Mike Fischlin	.08	.06	.03
183	Ed Vande Berg	.12	.09	.05
184	Bob Clark	.08	.06	.03
185	Tim Lollar	.08	.06	.03
186	Whitey Herzog	.12	.09	.05
187	Terry Leach	.12	.09	.05
188	Rick Miller	.08	.06	.03
189	Dan Schatzeder	.08	.06	.03
190	Cecil Cooper	.20	.15	.08
191	Joe Price	.08	.06	.03
192	Floyd Rayford	.08	.06	.03
193	Harry Spilman	.08	.06	.03
194	Cesar Geronimo	.08	.06	.03
195	Bob Stoddard	.08	.06	.03
196	Bill Fahey	.08	.06	.03
197	Jim Eisenreich	.20	.15	.08
198	Kiko Garcia	.08	.06	.03
199	Marty Bystrom	.08	.06	.03
200	Rod Carew	.70	.50	.30
201	Super Veteran (Rod Carew)	.35	.25	.14
202	Blue Jays Batting & Pitching Ldrs. (Damaso Garcia, Dave Stieb)	.15	.11	.06
203	Mike Morgan	.08	.06	.03
204	Junior Kennedy	.08	.06	.03
205	Dave Parker	.35	.25	.14
206	Ken Oberkfell	.10	.08	.04
207	Rick Camp	.08	.06	.03
208	Dan Meyer	.08	.06	.03
209	Mike Moore	.30	.25	.12
210	Jack Clark	.30	.25	.12
211	John Denny	.12	.09	.05
212	John Stearns	.08	.06	.03
213	Tom Burgmeier	.08	.06	.03
214	Jerry White	.08	.06	.03
215	Mario Soto	.12	.09	.05
216	Tony LaRussa	.10	.08	.04
217	Tim Stoddard	.08	.06	.03
218	Roy Howell	.08	.06	.03
219	Mike Armstrong	.08	.06	.03
220	Dusty Baker	.12	.09	.05
221	Joe Niekro	.15	.11	.06
222	Damaso Garcia	.12	.09	.05
223	John Montefusco	.08	.06	.03
224	Mickey Rivers	.12	.09	.05
225	Enos Cabell	.08	.06	.03
226	Enrique Romo	.08	.06	.03
227	Chris Bando	.08	.06	.03
228	Joaquin Andujar	.12	.09	.05
229	Phillies Batting & Pitching Ldrs. (Steve Carlton, Bo Diaz)	.20	.15	.08
230	Fergie Jenkins	.25	.20	.10
231	Super Veteran (Fergie Jenkins)	.12	.09	.05
232	Tom Brunansky	.30	.25	.12
233	Wayne Gross	.08	.06	.03
234	Larry Andersen	.08	.06	.03
235	Claudell Washington	.10	.08	.04
236	Steve Renko	.08	.06	.03
237	Dan Norman	.08	.06	.03
238	Bud Black	.25	.20	.10
239	Dave Stapleton	.08	.06	.03
240	Rich Gossage	.30	.25	.12
241	Super Veteran (Rich Gossage)	.15	.11	.06
242	Joe Nolan	.08	.06	.03
243	Duane Walker	.08	.06	.03
244	Dwight Bernard	.08	.06	.03
245	Steve Sax	.30	.25	.12
246	George Bamberger	.08	.06	.03
247	Dave Smith	.12	.09	.05
248	Bake McBride	.08	.06	.03
249	Checklist 133-264	.12	.09	.05
250	Bill Buckner	.15	.11	.06
251	Alan Wiggins	.20	.15	.08
252	Luis Aguayo	.08	.06	.03
253	Larry McWilliams	.08	.06	.03
254	Rick Cerone	.10	.08	.04
255	Gene Garber	.08	.06	.03
256	Super Veteran (Gene Garber)	.08	.06	.03
257	Jesse Barfield	.90	.70	.35
258	Manny Castillo	.08	.06	.03
259	Jeff Jones	.08	.06	.03
260	Steve Kemp	.12	.09	.05
261	Tigers Batting & Pitching Ldrs. (Larry Herndon, Dan Petry)	.12	.09	.05
262	Ron Jackson	.08	.06	.03
263	Renie Martin	.08	.06	.03
264	Jamie Quirk	.08	.06	.03
265	Joel Youngblood	.08	.06	.03
266	Paul Boris	.08	.06	.03
267	Terry Francona	.10	.08	.04
268	Storm Davis	.40	.30	.15
269	Ron Oester	.08	.06	.03
270	Dennis Eckersley	.12	.09	.05
271	Ed Romero	.08	.06	.03
272	Frank Tanana	.12	.09	.05
273	Mark Belanger	.10	.08	.04
274	Terry Kennedy	.12	.09	.05
275	Ray Knight	.12	.09	.05
276	Gene Mauch	.10	.08	.04
277	Rance Mulliniks	.08	.06	.03
278	Kevin Hickey	.08	.06	.03
279	Greg Gross	.08	.06	.03
280	Bert Blyleven	.25	.20	.10
281	Andre Robertson	.08	.06	.03
282	Reggie Smith	.12	.09	.05
283	Super Veteran (Reggie Smith)	.10	.08	.04
284	Jeff Lahti	.08	.06	.03
285	Lance Parrish	.40	.30	.15
286	Rick Langford	.08	.06	.03
287	Bobby Brown	.08	.06	.03
288	Joe Cowley	.20	.15	.08
289	Jerry Dybzinski	.08	.06	.03
290	Jeff Reardon	.15	.11	.06
291	Pirates Batting & Pitching Ldrs. (John Candelaria, Bill Madlock)	.15	.11	.06
292	Craig Swan	.08	.06	.03
293	Glenn Gulliver	.08	.06	.03
294	Dave Engle	.08	.06	.03
295	Jerry Remy	.08	.06	.03
296	Greg Harris	.08	.06	.03
297	Ned Yost	.08	.06	.03
298	Floyd Chiffer	.08	.06	.03
299	George Wright	.08	.06	.03
300	Mike Schmidt	1.00	.70	.40
301	Super Veteran (Mike Schmidt)	.50	.40	.20
302	Ernie Whitt	.10	.08	.04
303	Miguel Dilone	.08	.06	.03
304	Dave Rucker	.08	.06	.03
305	Larry Bowa	.15	.11	.06
306	Tom Lasorda	.12	.09	.05
307	Lou Piniella	.20	.15	.08

#	Player	MT	NR MT	EX
308	Jesus Vega	.08	.06	.03
309	Jeff Leonard	.15	.11	.06
310	Greg Luzinski	.15	.11	.06
311	Glenn Brummer	.08	.06	.03
312	Brian Kingman	.08	.06	.03
313	Gary Gray	.08	.06	.03
314	Ken Dayley	.15	.11	.06
315	Rick Burleson	.10	.08	.04
316	Paul Splittorff	.10	.08	.04
317	Gary Rajsich	.08	.06	.03
318	John Tudor	.15	.11	.06
319	Lenn Sakata	.08	.06	.03
320	Steve Rogers	.10	.08	.04
321	Brewers Batting & Pitching Ldrs. (Pete Vuckovich, Robin Yount)	.20	.15	.08
322	Dave Van Gorder	.08	.06	.03
323	Luis DeLeon	.08	.06	.03
324	Mike Marshall	.25	.20	.10
325	Von Hayes	.25	.20	.10
326	Garth Iorg	.08	.06	.03
327	Bobby Castillo	.08	.06	.03
328	Craig Reynolds	.08	.06	.03
329	Randy Niemann	.08	.06	.03
330	Buddy Bell	.15	.11	.06
331	Mike Krukow	.10	.08	.04
332	Glenn Wilson	.90	.70	.35
333	Dave LaRoche	.08	.06	.03
334	Super Veteran (Dave LaRoche)	.08	.06	.03
335	Steve Henderson	.08	.06	.03
336	Rene Lachemann	.08	.06	.03
337	Tito Landrum	.08	.06	.03
338	Bob Owchinko	.08	.06	.03
339	Terry Harper	.08	.06	.03
340	Larry Gura	.10	.08	.04
341	Doug DeCinces	.15	.11	.06
342	Atlee Hammaker	.10	.08	.04
343	Bob Bailor	.08	.06	.03
344	Roger LaFrancois	.08	.06	.03
345	Jim Clancy	.12	.09	.05
346	Joe Pittman	.08	.06	.03
347	Sammy Stewart	.08	.06	.03
348	Alan Bannister	.08	.06	.03
349	Checklist 265-396	.12	.09	.05
350	Robin Yount	.50	.40	.20
351	Reds Batting & Pitching Ldrs. (Cesar Cedeno, Mario Soto)	.12	.09	.05
352	Mike Scioscia	.10	.08	.04
353	Steve Comer	.08	.06	.03
354	Randy Johnson	.08	.06	.03
355	Jim Bibby	.08	.06	.03
356	Gary Woods	.08	.06	.03
357	Len Matuszek	.10	.08	.04
358	Jerry Garvin	.08	.06	.03
359	Dave Collins	.10	.08	.04
360	Nolan Ryan	.60	.45	.25
361	Super Veteran (Nolan Ryan)	.30	.25	.12
362	Bill Almon	.08	.06	.03
363	John Stuper	.12	.09	.05
364	Brett Butler	.20	.15	.08
365	Dave Lopes	.12	.09	.05
366	Dick Williams	.10	.08	.04
367	Bud Anderson	.08	.06	.03
368	Richie Zisk	.10	.08	.04
369	Jesse Orosco	.15	.11	.06
370	Gary Carter	.60	.45	.25
371	Mike Richardt	.08	.06	.03
372	Terry Crowley	.08	.06	.03
373	Kevin Saucier	.08	.06	.03
374	Wayne Krenchicki	.08	.06	.03
375	Pete Vuckovich	.10	.08	.04
376	Ken Landreaux	.10	.08	.04
377	Lee May	.10	.08	.04
378	Super Veteran (Lee May)	.10	.08	.04
379	Guy Sularz	.08	.06	.03
380	Ron Davis	.08	.06	.03
381	Red Sox Batting & Pitching Ldrs. (Jim Rice, Bob Stanley)	.25	.20	.10
382	Bob Knepper	.12	.09	.05
383	Ozzie Virgil	.10	.08	.04
384	Dave Dravecky	.70	.50	.30
385	Mike Easler	.12	.09	.05
386	Rod Carew AS	.35	.25	.14
387	Bob Grich AS	.12	.09	.05
388	George Brett AS	.50	.40	.20
389	Robin Yount AS	.25	.20	.10
390	Reggie Jackson AS	.40	.30	.15
391	Rickey Henderson AS	.40	.30	.15
392	Fred Lynn AS	.15	.11	.06
393	Carlton Fisk AS	.15	.11	.06
394	Pete Vuckovich AS	.10	.08	.04
395	Larry Gura AS	.10	.08	.04
396	Dan Quisenberry AS	.12	.09	.05
397	Pete Rose AS	.70	.50	.30
398	Manny Trillo AS	.10	.08	.04
399	Mike Schmidt AS	.50	.40	.20
400	Dave Concepcion AS	.12	.09	.05
401	Dale Murphy AS	.70	.50	.30
402	Andre Dawson AS	.20	.15	.08
403	Tim Raines AS	.35	.25	.14
404	Gary Carter AS	.35	.25	.14
405	Steve Rogers AS	.10	.08	.04
406	Steve Carlton AS	.35	.25	.14
407	Bruce Sutter AS	.12	.09	.05
408	Rudy May	.10	.08	.04
409	Marvis Foley	.08	.06	.03
410	Phil Niekro	.40	.30	.15
411	Super Veteran (Phil Niekro)	.20	.15	.08
412	Rangers Batting & Pitching Ldrs. (Buddy Bell, Charlie Hough)	.15	.11	.06
413	Matt Keough	.08	.06	.03
414	Julio Cruz	.08	.06	.03
415	Bob Forsch	.10	.08	.04
416	Joe Ferguson	.08	.06	.03
417	Tom Hausman	.08	.06	.03
418	Greg Pryor	.08	.06	.03
419	Steve Crawford	.08	.06	.03
420	Al Oliver	.20	.15	.08
421	Super Veteran (Al Oliver)	.12	.09	.05
422	George Cappuzzello	.08	.06	.03
423	Tom Lawless	.10	.08	.04
424	Jerry Augustine	.08	.06	.03
425	Pedro Guerrero	.35	.25	.14
426	Earl Weaver	.10	.08	.04
427	Roy Lee Jackson	.08	.06	.03
428	Champ Summers	.08	.06	.03
429	Eddie Whitson	.10	.08	.04
430	Kirk Gibson	.35	.25	.14
431	Gary Gaetti	2.75	2.00	1.00
432	Porfirio Altamirano	.08	.06	.03
433	Dale Berra	.08	.06	.03
434	Dennis Lamp	.08	.06	.03
435	Tony Armas	.12	.09	.05
436	Bill Campbell	.08	.06	.03
437	Rick Sweet	.08	.06	.03
438	Dave LaPoint	.20	.15	.08
439	Rafael Ramirez	.10	.08	.04
440	Ron Guidry	.30	.25	.12
441	Astros Batting & Pitching Ldrs. (Ray Knight, Joe Niekro)	.15	.11	.06
442	Brian Downing	.12	.09	.05
443	Don Hood	.08	.06	.03
444	Wally Backman	.25	.20	.10
445	Mike Flanagan	.12	.09	.05
446	Reid Nichols	.08	.06	.03
447	Bryn Smith	.10	.08	.04
448	Darrell Evans	.20	.15	.08
449	Eddie Milner	.20	.15	.08
450	Ted Simmons	.20	.15	.08
451	Super Veteran (Ted Simmons)	.12	.09	.05
452	Lloyd Moseby	.15	.11	.06
453	Lamar Johnson	.08	.06	.03
454	Bob Welch	.12	.09	.05
455	Sixto Lezcano	.08	.06	.03
456	Lee Elia	.08	.06	.03
457	Milt Wilcox	.10	.08	.04
458	Ron Washington	.08	.06	.03
459	Ed Farmer	.08	.06	.03
460	Roy Smalley	.10	.08	.04
461	Steve Trout	.12	.09	.05
462	Steve Nicosia	.08	.06	.03
463	Gaylord Perry	.40	.30	.15
464	Super Veteran (Gaylord Perry)	.20	.15	.08
465	Lonnie Smith	.10	.08	.04
466	Tom Underwood	.08	.06	.03
467	Rufino Linares	.08	.06	.03
468	Dave Goltz	.08	.06	.03
469	Ron Gardenhire	.08	.06	.03
470	Greg Minton	.08	.06	.03
471	Royals Batting & Pitching Ldrs. (Vida Blue, Willie Wilson)	.15	.11	.06
472	Gary Allenson	.08	.06	.03
473	John Lowenstein	.08	.06	.03
474	Ray Burris	.08	.06	.03
475	Cesar Cedeno	.12	.09	.05
476	Rob Picciolo	.08	.06	.03
477	Tom Niedenfuer	.15	.11	.06
478	Phil Garner	.10	.08	.04
479	Charlie Hough	.12	.09	.05
480	Toby Harrah	.10	.08	.04
481	Scot Thompson	.08	.06	.03
482	Tony Gwynn	15.00	11.00	6.00
483	Lynn Jones	.08	.06	.03

		MT	NR MT	EX
484	Dick Ruthven	.08	.06	.03
485	Omar Moreno	.08	.06	.03
486	Clyde King	.08	.06	.03
487	Jerry Hairston	.08	.06	.03
488	Alfredo Griffin	.10	.08	.04
489	Tom Herr	.12	.09	.05
490	Jim Palmer	.50	.40	.20
491	Super Veteran (Jim Palmer)	.20	.15	.08
492	Paul Serna	.08	.06	.03
493	Steve McCatty	.08	.06	.03
494	Bob Brenly	.10	.08	.04
495	Warren Cromartie	.08	.06	.03
496	Tom Veryzer	.08	.06	.03
497	Rick Sutcliffe	.15	.11	.06
498	Wade Boggs	30.00	22.00	12.00
499	Jeff Little	.10	.08	.04
500	Reggie Jackson	.70	.50	.30
501	Super Veteran (Reggie Jackson)	.35	.25	.14
502	Braves Batting & Pitching Ldrs. (Dale Murphy, Phil Niekro)	.50	.40	.20
503	Moose Haas	.08	.06	.03
504	Don Werner	.08	.06	.03
505	Garry Templeton	.12	.09	.05
506	Jim Gott	.15	.11	.06
507	Tony Scott	.08	.06	.03
508	Tom Filer	.10	.08	.04
509	Lou Whitaker	.35	.25	.14
510	Tug McGraw	.15	.11	.06
511	Super Veteran (Tug McGraw)	.10	.08	.04
512	Doyle Alexander	.15	.11	.06
513	Fred Stanley	.08	.06	.03
514	Rudy Law	.08	.06	.03
515	Gene Tenace	.10	.08	.04
516	Bill Virdon	.10	.08	.04
517	Gary Ward	.10	.08	.04
518	Bill Laskey	.08	.06	.03
519	Terry Bulling	.08	.06	.03
520	Fred Lynn	.25	.20	.10
521	Bruce Benedict	.08	.06	.03
522	Pat Zachry	.08	.06	.03
523	Carney Lansford	.10	.08	.04
524	Tom Brennan	.08	.06	.03
525	Frank White	.12	.09	.05
526	Checklist 397-528	.12	.09	.05
527	Larry Biittner	.08	.06	.03
528	Jamie Easterly	.08	.06	.03
529	Tim Laudner	.10	.08	.04
530	Eddie Murray	.80	.60	.30
531	Athletics Batting & Pitching Ldrs. (Rickey Henderson, Rick Langford)	.30	.25	.12
532	Dave Stewart	.15	.11	.06
533	Luis Salazar	.08	.06	.03
534	John Butcher	.08	.06	.03
535	Manny Trillo	.10	.08	.04
536	Johnny Wockenfuss	.08	.06	.03
537	Rod Scurry	.08	.06	.03
538	Danny Heep	.08	.06	.03
539	Roger Erickson	.08	.06	.03
540	Ozzie Smith	.30	.25	.12
541	Britt Burns	.08	.06	.03
542	Jody Davis	.15	.11	.06
543	Alan Fowlkes	.08	.06	.03
544	Larry Whisenton	.08	.06	.03
545	Floyd Bannister	.12	.09	.05
546	Dave Garcia	.08	.06	.03
547	Geoff Zahn	.08	.06	.03
548	Brian Giles	.08	.06	.03
549	Charlie Puleo	.15	.11	.06
550	Carl Yastrzemski	.80	.60	.30
551	Super Veteran (Carl Yastrzemski)	.40	.30	.15
552	Tim Wallach	.30	.25	.12
553	Denny Martinez	.10	.08	.04
554	Mike Vail	.08	.06	.03
555	Steve Yeager	.08	.06	.03
556	Willie Upshaw	.12	.09	.05
557	Rick Honeycutt	.10	.08	.04
558	Dickie Thon	.10	.08	.04
559	Pete Redfern	.08	.06	.03
560	Ron LeFlore	.10	.08	.04
561	Cardinals Batting & Pitching Ldrs. (Joaquin Andujar, Lonnie Smith)	.12	.09	.05
562	Dave Rozema	.08	.06	.03
563	Juan Bonilla	.08	.06	.03
564	Sid Monge	.08	.06	.03
565	Bucky Dent	.10	.08	.04
566	Manny Sarmiento	.08	.06	.03
567	Joe Simpson	.08	.06	.03
568	Willie Hernandez	.12	.09	.05
569	Jack Perconte	.08	.06	.03
570	Vida Blue	.15	.11	.06
571	Mickey Klutts	.08	.06	.03

		MT	NR MT	EX
572	Bob Watson	.10	.08	.04
573	Andy Hassler	.08	.06	.03
574	Glenn Adams	.08	.06	.03
575	Neil Allen	.08	.06	.03
576	Frank Robinson	.12	.09	.05
577	Luis Aponte	.08	.06	.03
578	David Green	.08	.06	.03
579	Rich Dauer	.08	.06	.03
580	Tom Seaver	.60	.45	.25
581	Super Veteran (Tom Seaver)	.30	.25	.12
582	Marshall Edwards	.08	.06	.03
583	Terry Forster	.10	.08	.04
584	Dave Hostetler	.08	.06	.03
585	Jose Cruz	.15	.11	.06
586	Frank Viola	1.75	1.25	.70
587	Ivan DeJesus	.08	.06	.03
588	Pat Underwood	.08	.06	.03
589	Alvis Woods	.08	.06	.03
590	Tony Pena	.12	.09	.05
591	White Sox Batting & Pitching Ldrs. (LaMarr Hoyt, Greg Luzinski)	.15	.11	.06
592	Shane Rawley	.12	.09	.05
593	Broderick Perkins	.08	.06	.03
594	Eric Rasmussen	.08	.06	.03
595	Tim Raines	.50	.40	.20
596	Randy Johnson	.08	.06	.03
597	Mike Proly	.08	.06	.03
598	Dwayne Murphy	.10	.08	.04
599	Don Aase	.10	.08	.04
600	George Brett	1.00	.70	.40
601	Ed Lynch	.08	.06	.03
602	Rich Gedman	.12	.09	.05
603	Joe Morgan	.35	.25	.14
604	Super Veteran (Joe Morgan)	.15	.11	.06
605	Gary Roenicke	.10	.08	.04
606	Bobby Cox	.08	.06	.03
607	Charlie Leibrandt	.10	.08	.04
608	Don Money	.10	.08	.04
609	Danny Darwin	.10	.08	.04
610	Steve Garvey	.70	.50	.30
611	Bert Roberge	.08	.06	.03
612	Steve Swisher	.08	.06	.03
613	Mike Ivie	.08	.06	.03
614	Ed Glynn	.08	.06	.03
615	Garry Maddox	.12	.09	.05
616	Bill Nahorodny	.08	.06	.03
617	Butch Wynegar	.10	.08	.04
618	LaMarr Hoyt	.10	.08	.04
619	Keith Moreland	.10	.08	.04
620	Mike Norris	.08	.06	.03
621	Mets Batting & Pitching Ldrs. (Craig Swan, Mookie Wilson)	.12	.09	.05
622	Dave Edler	.08	.06	.03
623	Luis Sanchez	.08	.06	.03
624	Glenn Hubbard	.10	.08	.04
625	Ken Forsch	.10	.08	.04
626	Jerry Martin	.08	.06	.03
627	Doug Bair	.08	.06	.03
628	Julio Valdez	.08	.06	.03
629	Charlie Lea	.08	.06	.03
630	Paul Molitor	.25	.20	.10
631	Tippy Martinez	.08	.06	.03
632	Alex Trevino	.08	.06	.03
633	Vicente Romo	.08	.06	.03
634	Max Venable	.08	.06	.03
635	Graig Nettles	.20	.15	.08
636	Super Veteran (Graig Nettles)	.12	.09	.05
637	Pat Corrales	.10	.08	.04
638	Dan Petry	.12	.09	.05
639	Art Howe	.08	.06	.03
640	Andre Thornton	.12	.09	.05
641	Billy Sample	.08	.06	.03
642	Checklist 529-660	.12	.09	.05
643	Bump Wills	.08	.06	.03
644	Joe Lefebvre	.08	.06	.03
645	Bill Madlock	.20	.15	.08
646	Jim Essian	.08	.06	.03
647	Bobby Mitchell	.08	.06	.03
648	Jeff Burroughs	.10	.08	.04
649	Tommy Boggs	.08	.06	.03
650	George Hendrick	.10	.08	.04
651	Angels Batting & Pitching Ldrs. (Rod Carew, Mike Witt)	.30	.25	.12
652	Butch Hobson	.08	.06	.03
653	Ellis Valentine	.08	.06	.03
654	Bob Ojeda	.20	.15	.08
655	Al Bumbry	.10	.08	.04
656	Dave Frost	.08	.06	.03
657	Mike Gates	.08	.06	.03
658	Frank Pastore	.08	.06	.03
659	Charlie Moore	.08	.06	.03

		MT	NR MT	EX
660	Mike Hargrove	.10	.08	.04
661	Bill Russell	.10	.08	.04
662	Joe Sambito	.08	.06	.03
663	Tom O'Malley	.08	.06	.03
664	Bob Molinaro	.08	.06	.03
665	Jim Sundberg	.10	.08	.04
666	Sparky Anderson	.12	.09	.05
667	Dick Davis	.08	.06	.03
668	Larry Christenson	.08	.06	.03
669	Mike Squires	.08	.06	.03
670	Jerry Mumphrey	.10	.08	.04
671	Lenny Faedo	.08	.06	.03
672	Jim Kaat	.20	.15	.08
673	Super Veteran (Jim Kaat)	.12	.09	.05
674	Kurt Bevacqua	.08	.06	.03
675	Jim Beattie	.08	.06	.03
676	Biff Pocoroba	.08	.06	.03
677	Dave Revering	.08	.06	.03
678	Juan Beniquez	.08	.06	.03
679	Mike Scott	.20	.15	.08
680	Andre Dawson	.40	.30	.15
681	Dodgers Batting & Pitching Ldrs. (Pedro Guerrero, Fernando Valenzuela)	.25	.20	.10
682	Bob Stanley	.10	.08	.04
683	Dan Ford	.08	.06	.03
684	Rafael Landestoy	.08	.06	.03
685	Lee Mazzilli	.10	.08	.04
686	Randy Lerch	.08	.06	.03
687	U.L. Washington	.08	.06	.03
688	Jim Wohlford	.08	.06	.03
689	Ron Hassey	.08	.06	.03
690	Kent Hrbek	.60	.45	.25
691	Dave Tobik	.08	.06	.03
692	Denny Walling	.08	.06	.03
693	Sparky Lyle	.12	.09	.05
694	Super Veteran (Sparky Lyle)	.10	.08	.04
695	Ruppert Jones	.08	.06	.03
696	Chuck Tanner	.10	.08	.04
697	Barry Foote	.08	.06	.03
698	Tony Bernazard	.10	.08	.04
699	Lee Smith	.20	.15	.08
700	Keith Hernandez	.50	.40	.20
701	Batting Leaders (Al Oliver, Willie Wilson)	.15	.11	.06
702	Home Run Leaders (Reggie Jackson, Dave Kingman, Gorman Thomas)	.25	.20	.10
703	Runs Batted In Leaders (Hal McRae, Dale Murphy)	.35	.25	.14
704	Stolen Base Leaders (Rickey Henderson, Tim Raines)	.35	.25	.14
705	Victory Leaders (Steve Carlton, LaMarr Hoyt)	.20	.15	.08
706	Strikeout Leaders (Floyd Bannister, Steve Carlton)	.20	.15	.08
707	Earned Run Average Leaders (Steve Rogers, Rick Sutcliffe)	.12	.09	.05
708	Leading Firemen (Dan Quisenberry, Bruce Sutter)	.15	.11	.06
709	Jimmy Sexton	.08	.06	.03
710	Willie Wilson	.20	.15	.08
711	Mariners Batting & Pitching Ldrs. (Jim Beattie, Bruce Bochte)	.12	.09	.05
712	Bruce Kison	.08	.06	.03
713	Ron Hodges	.08	.06	.03
714	Wayne Nordhagen	.08	.06	.03
715	Tony Perez	.25	.20	.10
716	Super Veteran (Tony Perez)	.12	.09	.05
717	Scott Sanderson	.10	.08	.04
718	Jim Dwyer	.08	.06	.03
719	Rich Gale	.08	.06	.03
720	Dave Concepcion	.15	.11	.06
721	John Martin	.08	.06	.03
722	Jorge Orta	.08	.06	.03
723	Randy Moffitt	.08	.06	.03
724	Johnny Grubb	.08	.06	.03
725	Dan Spillner	.08	.06	.03
726	Harvey Kuenn	.10	.08	.04
727	Chet Lemon	.10	.08	.04
728	Ron Reed	.10	.08	.04
729	Jerry Morales	.08	.06	.03
730	Jason Thompson	.08	.06	.03
731	Al Williams	.08	.06	.03
732	Dave Henderson	.12	.09	.05
733	Buck Martinez	.08	.06	.03
734	Steve Braun	.08	.06	.03
735	Tommy John	.25	.20	.10
736	Super Veteran (Tommy John)	.12	.09	.05
737	Mitchell Page	.08	.06	.03
738	Tim Foli	.08	.06	.03
739	Rick Ownbey	.08	.06	.03
740	Rusty Staub	.15	.11	.06

		MT	NR MT	EX
741	Super Veteran (Rusty Staub)	.10	.08	.04
742	Padres Batting & Pitching Ldrs. (Terry Kennedy, Tim Lollar)	.12	.09	.05
743	Mike Torrez	.10	.08	.04
744	Brad Mills	.08	.06	.03
745	Scott McGregor	.12	.09	.05
746	John Wathan	.12	.09	.05
747	Fred Breining	.08	.06	.03
748	Derrel Thomas	.08	.06	.03
749	Jon Matlack	.10	.08	.04
750	Ben Oglivie	.10	.08	.04
751	Brad Havens	.08	.06	.03
752	Luis Pujols	.08	.06	.03
753	Elias Sosa	.08	.06	.03
754	Bill Robinson	.08	.06	.03
755	John Candelaria	.12	.09	.05
756	Russ Nixon	.08	.06	.03
757	Rick Manning	.08	.06	.03
758	Aurelio Rodriguez	.10	.08	.04
759	Doug Bird	.08	.06	.03
760	Dale Murphy	1.50	1.25	.60
761	Gary Lucas	.08	.06	.03
762	Cliff Johnson	.08	.06	.03
763	Al Cowens	.08	.06	.03
764	Pete Falcone	.08	.06	.03
765	Bob Boone	.12	.09	.05
766	Barry Bonnell	.08	.06	.03
767	Duane Kuiper	.08	.06	.03
768	Chris Speier	.08	.06	.03
769	Checklist 661-792	.12	.09	.05
770	Dave Winfield	.50	.40	.20
771	Twins Batting & Pitching Ldrs. (Bobby Castillo, Kent Hrbek)	.20	.15	.08
772	Jim Kern	.08	.06	.03
773	Larry Hisle	.10	.08	.04
774	Alan Ashby	.08	.06	.03
775	Burt Hooton	.10	.08	.04
776	Larry Parrish	.12	.09	.05
777	John Curtis	.08	.06	.03
778	Rich Hebner	.08	.06	.03
779	Rick Waits	.08	.06	.03
780	Gary Matthews	.12	.09	.05
781	Rick Rhoden	.12	.09	.05
782	Bobby Murcer	.12	.09	.05
783	Super Veteran (Bobby Murcer)	.10	.08	.04
784	Jeff Newman	.08	.06	.03
785	Dennis Leonard	.10	.08	.04
786	Ralph Houk	.10	.08	.04
787	Dick Tidrow	.08	.06	.03
788	Dane Iorg	.08	.06	.03
789	Bryan Clark	.08	.06	.03
790	Bob Grich	.12	.09	.05
791	Gary Lavelle	.08	.06	.03
792	Chris Chambliss	.10	.08	.04

1983 Topps All-Star Glossy Set of 40

This set was a "consolation prize" in a scratch-off contest in regular packs of 1983 cards. The 2½" by 3½" cards have a large color photo surrounded by a yellow frame on the front. In very small type on a white border is printed the player's name. Backs carried the player's name, team, position and the card number along with a Topps identification. A major feature was that the surface of the front was glossy, which most collectors find very attractive. With many top stars, the set is a popular one, and the price has not moved too far above the issue price.

		MT	NR MT	EX
Complete Set:		12.00	9.00	4.75
Common Player:		.15	.11	.06
1	Carl Yastrzemski	1.00	.70	.40
2	Mookie Wilson	.15	.11	.06
3	Andre Thornton	.15	.11	.06
4	Keith Hernandez	.40	.30	.15
5	Robin Yount	.40	.30	.15
6	Terry Kennedy	.15	.11	.06
7	Dave Winfield	.60	.45	.25
8	Mike Schmidt	1.00	.70	.40
9	Buddy Bell	.20	.15	.08
10	Fernando Valenzuela	.50	.40	.20
11	Rich Gossage	.25	.20	.10
12	Bob Horner	.25	.20	.10
13	Toby Harrah	.15	.11	.06
14	Pete Rose	1.25	.90	.50
15	Cecil Cooper	.20	.15	.08
16	Dale Murphy	1.00	.70	.40
17	Carlton Fisk	.30	.25	.12
18	Ray Knight	.15	.11	.06
19	Jim Palmer	.40	.30	.15
20	Gary Carter	.50	.40	.20
21	Richard Zisk	.15	.11	.06
22	Dusty Baker	.15	.11	.06
23	Willie Wilson	.20	.15	.08
24	Bill Buckner	.15	.11	.06
25	Dave Stieb	.20	.15	.08
26	Bill Madlock	.20	.15	.08
27	Lance Parrish	.30	.25	.12
28	Nolan Ryan	.50	.40	.20
29	Rod Carew	.60	.45	.25
30	Al Oliver	.20	.15	.08
31	George Brett	1.00	.70	.40
32	Jack Clark	.25	.20	.10
33	Rickey Henderson	.70	.50	.30
34	Dave Concepcion	.20	.15	.08
35	Kent Hrbek	.30	.25	.12
36	Steve Carlton	.50	.40	.20
37	Eddie Murray	.70	.50	.30
38	Ruppert Jones	.15	.11	.06
39	Reggie Jackson	.70	.50	.30
40	Bruce Sutter	.20	.15	.08

1983 Topps Foldouts

Another Topps test issue, these 3-1/2'' by 5-5/16'' cards were printed in booklets like souvenir post-cards. Each of the booklets had a theme of currently playing statistical leaders in a specific category such as home runs. The cards feature a color player photo on each side. A black strip at the bottom gives the player's name, position and team along with statistics in the particular category. A facsimile autograph crosses the photograph. Booklets carried nine cards with eight having players on both sides and one doubling as the back cover, for a total of 17 cards per booklet. There were 85 cards in the set, although some players appear in more than one category. Naturally, most of the players pictured are stars. Even so, the set is a problem as it seems to be most valuable when complete and seldom, so the cards are difficult to display.

		MT	NR MT	EX
Complete Set:		6.00	4.50	2.50
Common Folder:		1.00	.70	.40

1   Pitching Leaders (Vida Blue, Bert Blyleven, Steve Carlton, Fergie Jenkins, Tommy John, Jim Kaat, Jerry Koosman, Joe Niekro, Phil Niekro, Jim Palmer, Gaylord Perry, Jerry Reuss, Nolan Ryan, Tom Seaver, Paul Splittorff, Don Sutton, Mike Torrez)

	MT	NR MT	EX
	1.75	1.25	.70

2   Home Run Leaders (Johnny Bench, Ron Cey, Darrell Evans, George Foster, Reggie Jackson, Dave Kingman, Greg Luzinski, John Mayberry, Rick Monday, Bobby Murcer, Graig Nettles, Tony Perez, Jim Rice, Mike Schmidt, Rusty Staub, Carl Yastrzemski)

	MT	NR MT	EX
	2.50	2.00	1.00

3   Batting Leaders (George Brett, Rod Carew, Cecil Cooper, Steve Garvey, Ken Griffey, Pedro Guerrero, Keith Hernandez, Dane Iorg, Fred Lynn, Bill Madlock, Bake McBride, Al Oliver, Dave Parker, Jim Rice, Pete Rose, Lonnie Smith, Willie Wilson)

	MT	NR MT	EX
	2.50	2.00	1.00

4   Relief Aces (Tom Burgmeier, Bill Campbell, Ed Farmer, Rollie Fingers, Terry Forster, Gene Garber, Rich Gossage, Jim Kern, Gary Lavelle, Tug McGraw, Greg Minton, Randy Moffitt, Dan Quisenberry, Ron Reed, Elias Sosa, Bruce Sutter, Kent Tekulve)

	MT	NR MT	EX
	1.00	.70	.40

5   Stolen Base Leaders (Don Baylor, Larry Bowa, Al Bumbry, Rod Carew, Cesar Cedeno, Dave Concepcion, Jose Cruz, Julio Cruz, Rickey Henderson, Ron LeFlore, Davey Lopes, Garry Maddox, Omar Moreno, Joe Morgan, Amos Otis, Mickey Rivers, Willie Wilson)

	MT	NR MT	EX
	1.00	.70	.40

1983 Topps Traded

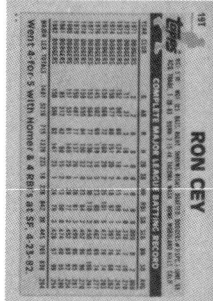

These 2½'' by 3½'' cards mark a continuation of the traded set introduced in 1981. The 132 cards retain the basic design of the year's regular issue, with their numbering being 1-132 with the ''T'' suffix. Cards in the set include traded players, new managers ad promising rookies. Sold only through dealers, the set was in heavy demand as it contained the first cards of Darryl Strawberry, Ron Kittle, Julio Franco and Mel Hall. While some of these cards were very hot in 1983, it seems likely that some of the rookies may not live up to their initial promise.

		MT	NR MT	EX
Complete Set:		38.00	28.00	15.00
Common Player:		.10	.08	.04
1T	Neil Allen	.10	.08	.04
2T	Bill Almon	.10	.08	.04
3T	Joe Altobelli	.10	.08	.04
4T	Tony Armas	.20	.15	.08
5T	Doug Bair	.10	.08	.04
6T	Steve Baker	.10	.08	.04
7T	Floyd Bannister	.20	.15	.08
8T	Don Baylor	.30	.25	.12
9T	Tony Bernazard	.15	.11	.06

		MT	NR MT	EX
10T	Larry Biittner	.10	.08	.04
11T	Dann Bilardello	.10	.08	.04
12T	Doug Bird	.10	.08	.04
13T	Steve Boros	.10	.08	.04
14T	Greg Brock	.50	.40	.20
15T	Mike Brown	.10	.08	.04
16T	Tom Burgmeier	.10	.08	.04
17T	Randy Bush	.20	.15	.08
18T	Bert Campaneris	.20	.15	.08
19T	Ron Cey	.25	.20	.10
20T	Chris Codiroli	.15	.11	.06
21T	Dave Collins	.15	.11	.06
22T	Terry Crowley	.10	.08	.04
23T	Julio Cruz	.10	.08	.04
24T	Mike Davis	.15	.11	.06
25T	Frank DiPino	.10	.08	.04
26T	Bill Doran	1.00	.70	.40
27T	Jerry Dybzinski	.10	.08	.04
28T	Jamie Easterly	.10	.08	.04
29T	Juan Eichelberger	.10	.08	.04
30T	Jim Essian	.10	.08	.04
31T	Pete Falcone	.10	.08	.04
32T	Mike Ferraro	.10	.08	.04
33T	Terry Forster	.15	.11	.06
34T	Julio Franco	1.25	.90	.50
35T	Rich Gale	.10	.08	.04
36T	Kiko Garcia	.10	.08	.04
37T	Steve Garvey	1.50	1.25	.60
38T	Johnny Grubb	.10	.08	.04
39T	Mel Hall	.70	.50	.30
40T	Von Hayes	.60	.45	.25
41T	Danny Heep	.10	.08	.04
42T	Steve Henderson	.10	.08	.04
43T	Keith Hernandez	.90	.70	.35
44T	Leo Hernandez	.10	.08	.04
45T	Willie Hernandez	.20	.15	.08
46T	Al Holland	.10	.08	.04
47T	Frank Howard	.15	.11	.06
48T	Bobby Johnson	.10	.08	.04
49T	Cliff Johnson	.10	.08	.04
50T	Odell Jones	.10	.08	.04
51T	Mike Jorgensen	.10	.08	.04
52T	Bob Kearney	.10	.08	.04
53T	Steve Kemp	.15	.11	.06
54T	Matt Keough	.10	.08	.04
55T	Ron Kittle	.60	.45	.25
56T	Mickey Klutts	.10	.08	.04
57T	Alan Knicely	.10	.08	.04
58T	Mike Krukow	.15	.11	.06
59T	Rafael Landestoy	.10	.08	.04
60T	Carney Lansford	.15	.11	.06
61T	Joe Lefebvre	.10	.08	.04
62T	Bryan Little	.10	.08	.04
63T	Aurelio Lopez	.10	.08	.04
64T	Mike Madden	.15	.11	.06
65T	Rick Manning	.10	.08	.04
66T	Billy Martin	.20	.15	.08
67T	Lee Mazzilli	.15	.11	.06
68T	Andy McGaffigan	.10	.08	.04
69T	Craig McMurtry	.15	.11	.06
70T	John McNamara	.10	.08	.04
71T	Orlando Mercado	.10	.08	.04
72T	Larry Milbourne	.10	.08	.04
73T	Randy Moffitt	.10	.08	.04
74T	Sid Monge	.10	.08	.04
75T	Jose Morales	.10	.08	.04
76T	Omar Moreno	.10	.08	.04
77T	Joe Morgan	1.00	.70	.40
78T	Mike Morgan	.10	.08	.04
79T	Dale Murray	.10	.08	.04
80T	Jeff Newman	.10	.08	.04
81T	Pete O'Brien	1.25	.90	.50
82T	Jorge Orta	.10	.08	.04
83T	Alejandro Pena	.20	.15	.08
84T	Pascual Perez	.15	.11	.06
85T	Tony Perez	.60	.45	.25
86T	Broderick Perkins	.10	.08	.04
87T	Tony Phillips	.20	.15	.08
88T	Charlie Puleo	.10	.08	.04
89T	Pat Putnam	.10	.08	.04
90T	Jamie Quirk	.10	.08	.04
91T	Doug Rader	.10	.08	.04
92T	Chuck Rainey	.10	.08	.04
93T	Bobby Ramos	.10	.08	.04
94T	Gary Redus	.40	.30	.15
95T	Steve Renko	.10	.08	.04
96T	Leon Roberts	.10	.08	.04
97T	Aurelio Rodriguez	.15	.11	.06
98T	Dick Ruthven	.10	.08	.04
99T	Daryl Sconiers	.10	.08	.04
100T	Mike Scott	.50	.40	.20

		MT	NR MT	EX
101T	Tom Seaver	1.25	.90	.50
102T	John Shelby	.25	.20	.10
103T	Bob Shirley	.10	.08	.04
104T	Joe Simpson	.10	.08	.04
105T	Doug Sisk	.15	.11	.06
106T	Mike Smithson	.15	.11	.06
107T	Elias Sosa	.10	.08	.04
108T	Darryl Strawberry	24.00	18.00	9.50
109T	Tom Tellmann	.10	.08	.04
110T	Gene Tenace	.15	.11	.06
111T	Gorman Thomas	.25	.20	.10
112T	Dick Tidrow	.10	.08	.04
113T	Dave Tobik	.10	.08	.04
114T	Wayne Tolleson	.20	.15	.08
115T	Mike Torrez	.15	.11	.06
116T	Manny Trillo	.15	.11	.06
117T	Steve Trout	.20	.15	.08
118T	Lee Tunnell	.15	.11	.06
119T	Mike Vail	.10	.08	.04
120T	Ellis Valentine	.10	.08	.04
121T	Tom Veryzer	.10	.08	.04
122T	George Vukovich	.10	.08	.04
123T	Rick Waits	.10	.08	.04
124T	Greg Walker	1.25	.90	.50
125T	Chris Welsh	.10	.08	.04
126T	Len Whitehouse	.10	.08	.04
127T	Eddie Whitson	.15	.11	.06
128T	Jim Wohlford	.10	.08	.04
129T	Matt Young	.25	.20	.10
130T	Joel Youngblood	.10	.08	.04
131T	Pat Zachry	.10	.08	.04
132T	Checklist 1-132	.10	.08	.04

1984 Topps

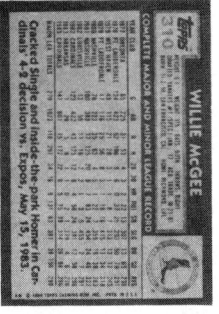

Another 792-card regular set from Topps. For the second straight year, the 2½'' by 3½'' cards featured a color action photo on the front along with a small portrait photo in the lower left. The team name ran in big letters down the left side, while the player's name and position ran under the large action photo. In the upper right-hand corner was the Topps logo. Backs have a team logo in the upper-right corner along with statistics, personal information and a few highlights. The backs have an unusual and hard to read red-and-purple coloring. Specialty cards include past season highlights, team leaders, major league statistical leaders, All-Stars, active career leaders and numbered checklists. Again, promising rookies were saved for the traded set. Late in 1984, Topps introduced a specially-boxed ''Tiffany'' edition of the '84 set, with the cards printed on white cardboard with a glossy finish. A total of 10,000 sets were produced. Prices for Tiffany edition superstars can run from six to eight times the value of the ''regular'' edition, while common cards sell in the 40¢ range.

		MT	NR MT	EX
	Complete Set:	75.00	56.00	30.00
	Common Player:	.08	.06	.03
1	1983 Highlight (Steve Carlton)	.30	.25	.12
2	1983 Highlight (Rickey Henderson)	.30	.25	.12
3	1983 Highlight (Dan Quisenberry)	.12	.09	.05

#	Name	MT	NR MT	EX
4	1983 Highlight (Steve Carlton, Gaylord Perry, Nolan Ryan)	.30	.25	.12
5	1983 Highlight (Bob Forsch, Dave Righetti, Mike Warren)	.15	.11	.06
6	1983 Highlight (Johnny Bench, Gaylord Perry, Carl Yastrzemski)	.40	.30	.15
7	Gary Lucas	.08	.06	.03
8	Don Mattingly	27.00	20.00	11.00
9	Jim Gott	.08	.06	.03
10	Robin Yount	.40	.30	.15
11	Twins Batting & Pitching Leaders (Kent Hrbek, Ken Schrom)	.20	.15	.08
12	Billy Sample	.08	.06	.03
13	Scott Holman	.08	.06	.03
14	Tom Brookens	.08	.06	.03
15	Burt Hooton	.10	.08	.04
16	Omar Moreno	.08	.06	.03
17	John Denny	.10	.08	.04
18	Dale Berra	.08	.06	.03
19	Ray Fontenot	.12	.09	.05
20	Greg Luzinski	.12	.09	.05
21	Joe Altobelli	.08	.06	.03
22	Bryan Clark	.08	.06	.03
23	Keith Moreland	.10	.08	.04
24	John Martin	.08	.06	.03
25	Glenn Hubbard	.10	.08	.04
26	Bud Black	.10	.08	.04
27	Daryl Sconiers	.08	.06	.03
28	Frank Viola	.30	.25	.12
29	Danny Heep	.08	.06	.03
30	Wade Boggs	7.00	5.25	2.75
31	Andy McGaffigan	.08	.06	.03
32	Bobby Ramos	.08	.06	.03
33	Tom Burgmeier	.08	.06	.03
35	Don Sutton	.30	.25	.12
36	Denny Walling	.08	.06	.03
37	Rangers Batting & Pitching Leaders (Buddy Bell, Rick Honeycutt)	.12	.09	.05
38	Luis DeLeon	.08	.06	.03
39	Garth Iorg	.08	.06	.03
40	Dusty Baker	.12	.09	.05
41	Tony Bernazard	.10	.08	.04
42	Johnny Grubb	.08	.06	.03
43	Ron Reed	.10	.08	.04
44	Jim Morrison	.08	.06	.03
45	Jerry Mumphrey	.10	.08	.04
46	Ray Smith	.08	.06	.03
47	Rudy Law	.08	.06	.03
48	Julio Franco	.40	.30	.15
49	John Stuper	.08	.06	.03
50	Chris Chambliss	.10	.08	.04
51	Jim Frey	.08	.06	.03
52	Paul Splittorff	.10	.08	.04
53	Juan Beniquez	.08	.06	.03
54	Jesse Orosco	.10	.08	.04
55	Dave Concepcion	.15	.11	.06
56	Gary Allenson	.08	.06	.03
57	Dan Schatzeder	.08	.06	.03
58	Max Venable	.08	.06	.03
59	Sammy Stewart	.08	.06	.03
60	Paul Molitor	.20	.15	.08
61	Chris Codiroli	.12	.09	.05
62	Dave Hostetler	.08	.06	.03
63	Ed Vande Berg	.08	.06	.03
64	Mike Scioscia	.08	.06	.03
65	Kirk Gibson	.35	.25	.14
66	Astros Batting & Pitching Leaders (Jose Cruz, Nolan Ryan)	.25	.20	.10
67	Gary Ward	.10	.08	.04
68	Luis Salazar	.08	.06	.03
69	Rod Scurry	.08	.06	.03
70	Gary Matthews	.12	.09	.05
71	Leo Hernandez	.08	.06	.03
72	Mike Squires	.08	.06	.03
73	Jody Davis	.12	.09	.05
74	Jerry Martin	.08	.06	.03
75	Bob Forsch	.10	.08	.04
76	Alfredo Griffin	.10	.08	.04
77	Brett Butler	.12	.09	.05
78	Mike Torrez	.10	.08	.04
79	Rob Wilfong	.08	.06	.03
80	Steve Rogers	.10	.08	.04
81	Billy Martin	.12	.09	.05
82	Doug Bird	.08	.06	.03
83	Richie Zisk	.10	.08	.04
84	Lenny Faedo	.08	.06	.03
85	Atlee Hammaker	.10	.08	.04
86	John Shelby	.20	.15	.08
87	Frank Pastore	.08	.06	.03
88	Rob Picciolo	.08	.06	.03
89	Mike Smithson	.12	.09	.05
90	Pedro Guerrero	.35	.25	.14
91	Dan Spillner	.08	.06	.03
92	Lloyd Moseby	.15	.11	.06
93	Bob Knepper	.10	.08	.04
94	Mario Ramirez	.08	.06	.03
95	Aurelio Lopez	.08	.06	.03
96	Royals Batting & Pitching Leaders (Larry Gura, Hal McRae)	.12	.09	.05
97	LaMarr Hoyt	.10	.08	.04
98	Steve Nicosia	.08	.06	.03
99	Craig Lefferts	.20	.15	.08
100	Reggie Jackson	.60	.45	.25
101	Porfirio Altamirano	.08	.06	.03
102	Ken Oberkfell	.10	.08	.04
103	Dwayne Murphy	.10	.08	.04
104	Ken Dayley	.08	.06	.03
105	Tony Armas	.12	.09	.05
106	Tim Stoddard	.08	.06	.03
107	Ned Yost	.08	.06	.03
108	Randy Moffitt	.08	.06	.03
109	Brad Wellman	.08	.06	.03
110	Ron Guidry	.30	.25	.12
111	Bill Virdon	.08	.06	.03
112	Tom Niedenfuer	.10	.08	.04
113	Kelly Paris	.08	.06	.03
114	Checklist 1-132	.08	.06	.03
115	Andre Thornton	.12	.09	.05
116	George Bjorkman	.08	.06	.03
117	Tom Veryzer	.08	.06	.03
118	Charlie Hough	.12	.09	.05
119	Johnny Wockenfuss	.08	.06	.03
120	Keith Hernandez	.40	.30	.15
121	Pat Sheridan	.15	.11	.06
122	Cecilio Guante	.10	.08	.04
123	Butch Wynegar	.10	.08	.04
124	Damaso Garcia	.10	.08	.04
125	Britt Burns	.08	.06	.03
126	Braves Batting & Pitching Leaders (Craig McMurtry, Dale Murphy)	.25	.20	.10
127	Mike Madden	.10	.08	.04
128	Rick Manning	.08	.06	.03
129	Bill Laskey	.08	.06	.03
130	Ozzie Smith	.15	.11	.06
131	Batting Leaders (Wade Boggs, Bill Madlock)	.40	.30	.15
132	Home Run Leaders (Jim Rice, Mike Schmidt)	.40	.30	.15
133	Runs Batted In Leaders (Cecil Cooper, Dale Murphy, Jim Rice)	.40	.30	.15
134	Stolen Base Leaders (Rickey Henderson, Tim Raines)	.30	.25	.12
135	Victory Leaders (John Denny, LaMarr Hoyt)	.10	.08	.04
136	Strikeout Leaders (Steve Carlton, Jack Morris)	.25	.20	.10
137	Earned Run Average Leaders (Atlee Hammaker, Rick Honeycutt)	.10	.08	.04
138	Leading Firemen (Al Holland, Dan Quisenberry)	.12	.09	.05
139	Bert Campaneris	.12	.09	.05
140	Storm Davis	.10	.08	.04
141	Pat Corrales	.08	.06	.03
142	Rich Gale	.08	.06	.03
143	Jose Morales	.08	.06	.03
144	Brian Harper	.08	.06	.03
145	Gary Lavelle	.08	.06	.03
146	Ed Romero	.08	.06	.03
147	Dan Petry	.10	.08	.04
148	Joe Lefebvre	.08	.06	.03
149	Jon Matlack	.10	.08	.04
150	Dale Murphy	1.00	.70	.40
151	Steve Trout	.10	.08	.04
152	Glenn Brummer	.08	.06	.03
153	Dick Tidrow	.08	.06	.03
154	Dave Henderson	.08	.06	.03
155	Frank White	.12	.09	.05
156	Athletics Batting & Pitching Leaders (Tim Conroy, Rickey Henderson)	.25	.20	.10
157	Gary Gaetti	.50	.40	.20
158	John Curtis	.08	.06	.03
159	Darryl Cias	.08	.06	.03
160	Mario Soto	.10	.08	.04
161	Junior Ortiz	.08	.06	.03
162	Bob Ojeda	.12	.09	.05
163	Lorenzo Gray	.08	.06	.03
164	Scott Sanderson	.10	.08	.04
165	Ken Singleton	.12	.09	.05
166	Jamie Nelson	.08	.06	.03
167	Marshall Edwards	.08	.06	.03
168	Juan Bonilla	.08	.06	.03
169	Larry Parrish	.12	.09	.05

#	Player	MT	NR MT	EX
170	Jerry Reuss	.12	.09	.05
171	Frank Robinson	.12	.09	.05
172	Frank DiPino	.08	.06	.03
173	Marvell Wynne	.15	.11	.06
174	Juan Berenguer	.08	.06	.03
175	Graig Nettles	.20	.15	.08
176	Lee Smith	.15	.11	.06
177	Jerry Hairston	.08	.06	.03
178	Bill Krueger	.10	.08	.04
179	Buck Martinez	.08	.06	.03
180	Manny Trillo	.10	.08	.04
181	Roy Thomas	.08	.06	.03
182	Darryl Strawberry	9.00	6.75	3.50
183	Al Williams	.08	.06	.03
184	Mike O'Berry	.08	.06	.03
185	Sixto Lezcano	.08	.06	.03
186	Cardinals Batting & Pitching Leaders (Lonnie Smith, John Stuper)	.12	.09	.05
187	Luis Aponte	.08	.06	.03
188	Bryan Little	.08	.06	.03
189	Tim Conroy	.12	.09	.05
190	Ben Oglivie	.10	.08	.04
191	Mike Boddicker	.15	.11	.06
192	Nick Esasky	.35	.25	.14
193	Darrell Brown	.08	.06	.03
194	Domingo Ramos	.08	.06	.03
195	Jack Morris	.30	.25	.12
196	Don Slaught	.12	.09	.05
197	Garry Hancock	.08	.06	.03
198	Bill Doran	.80	.60	.30
199	Willie Hernandez	.12	.09	.05
200	Andre Dawson	.35	.25	.14
201	Bruce Kison	.08	.06	.03
202	Bobby Cox	.08	.06	.03
203	Matt Keough	.08	.06	.03
204	Bobby Meacham	.20	.15	.08
205	Greg Minton	.08	.06	.03
206	Andy Van Slyke	.90	.70	.35
207	Donnie Moore	.10	.08	.04
208	Jose Oquendo	.15	.11	.06
209	Manny Sarmiento	.08	.06	.03
210	Joe Morgan	.30	.25	.12
211	Rick Sweet	.08	.06	.03
212	Broderick Perkins	.08	.06	.03
213	Bruce Hurst	.12	.09	.05
214	Paul Householder	.08	.06	.03
215	Tippy Martinez	.08	.06	.03
216	White Sox Batting & Pitching Leaders (Richard Dotson, Carlton Fisk)	.15	.11	.06
217	Alan Ashby	.08	.06	.03
218	Rick Waits	.08	.06	.03
219	Joe Simpson	.08	.06	.03
220	Fernando Valenzuela	.40	.30	.15
221	Cliff Johnson	.08	.06	.03
222	Rick Honeycutt	.10	.08	.04
223	Wayne Krenchicki	.08	.06	.03
224	Sid Monge	.08	.06	.03
225	Lee Mazzilli	.10	.08	.04
226	Juan Eichelberger	.08	.06	.03
227	Steve Braun	.08	.06	.03
228	John Rabb	.08	.06	.03
229	Paul Owens	.08	.06	.03
230	Rickey Henderson	.60	.45	.25
231	Gary Woods	.08	.06	.03
232	Tim Wallach	.15	.11	.06
233	Checklist 133-264	.08	.06	.03
234	Joe Niekro, Rafael Ramirez	.10	.08	.04
235	Matt Young	.15	.11	.06
236	Ellis Valentine	.08	.06	.03
237	John Castino	.08	.06	.03
238	Reid Nichols	.08	.06	.03
239	Jay Howell	.10	.08	.04
240	Eddie Murray	.60	.45	.25
241	Billy Almon	.08	.06	.03
242	Alex Trevino	.08	.06	.03
243	Pete Ladd	.08	.06	.03
244	Candy Maldonado	.25	.20	.10
245	Rick Sutcliffe	.15	.11	.06
246	Mets Batting & Pitching Leaders (Tom Seaver, Mookie Wilson)	.25	.20	.10
247	Onix Concepcion	.08	.06	.03
248	Bill Dawley	.15	.11	.06
249	Jay Johnstone	.10	.08	.04
250	Bill Madlock	.15	.11	.06
251	Tony Gwynn	1.75	1.25	.70
252	Larry Christenson	.08	.06	.03
253	Jim Wohlford	.08	.06	.03
254	Shane Rawley	.12	.09	.05
255	Bruce Benedict	.08	.06	.03
256	Dave Geisel	.08	.06	.03
257	Julio Cruz	.08	.06	.03

#	Player	MT	NR MT	EX
258	Luis Sanchez	.08	.06	.03
259	Sparky Anderson	.12	.09	.05
260	Scott McGregor	.12	.09	.05
261	Bobby Brown	.08	.06	.03
262	Tom Candiotti	.20	.15	.08
263	Jack Fimple	.08	.06	.03
264	Doug Frobel	.08	.06	.03
265	Donnie Hill	.15	.11	.06
266	Steve Lubratich	.08	.06	.03
267	Carmelo Martinez	.25	.20	.10
268	Jack O'Connor	.08	.06	.03
269	Aurelio Rodriguez	.10	.08	.04
270	Jeff Russell	.12	.09	.05
271	Moose Haas	.08	.06	.03
272	Rick Dempsey	.10	.08	.04
273	Charlie Puleo	.08	.06	.03
274	Rick Monday	.10	.08	.04
275	Len Matuszek	.08	.06	.03
276	Angels Batting & Pitching Leaders (Rod Carew, Geoff Zahn)	.20	.15	.08
277	Eddie Whitson	.08	.06	.03
278	Jorge Bell	1.50	1.25	.60
279	Ivan DeJesus	.08	.06	.03
280	Floyd Bannister	.12	.09	.05
281	Larry Milbourne	.08	.06	.03
282	Jim Barr	.08	.06	.03
283	Larry Biittner	.08	.06	.03
284	Howard Bailey	.08	.06	.03
285	Darrell Porter	.10	.08	.04
286	Lary Sorensen	.08	.06	.03
287	Warren Cromartie	.08	.06	.03
288	Jim Beattie	.08	.06	.03
289	Randy Johnson	.08	.06	.03
290	Dave Dravecky	.12	.09	.05
291	Chuck Tanner	.10	.08	.04
292	Tony Scott	.08	.06	.03
293	Ed Lynch	.08	.06	.03
294	U.L. Washington	.08	.06	.03
295	Mike Flanagan	.12	.09	.05
296	Jeff Newman	.08	.06	.03
297	Bruce Berenyi	.08	.06	.03
298	Jim Gantner	.10	.08	.04
299	John Butcher	.08	.06	.03
300	Pete Rose	1.50	1.25	.60
301	Frank LaCorte	.08	.06	.03
302	Barry Bonnell	.08	.06	.03
303	Marty Castillo	.08	.06	.03
304	Warren Brusstar	.08	.06	.03
305	Roy Smalley	.10	.08	.04
306	Dodgers Batting & Pitching Leaders (Pedro Guerrero, Bob Welch)	.15	.11	.06
307	Bobby Mitchell	.08	.06	.03
308	Ron Hassey	.08	.06	.03
309	Tony Phillips	.15	.11	.06
310	Willie McGee	.35	.25	.14
311	Jerry Koosman	.12	.09	.05
312	Jorge Orta	.08	.06	.03
313	Mike Jorgensen	.08	.06	.03
314	Orlando Mercado	.08	.06	.03
315	Bob Grich	.12	.09	.05
316	Mark Bradley	.08	.06	.03
317	Greg Pryor	.08	.06	.03
318	Bill Gullickson	.10	.08	.04
319	Al Bumbry	.10	.08	.04
320	Bob Stanley	.10	.08	.04
321	Harvey Kuenn	.10	.08	.04
322	Ken Schrom	.08	.06	.03
323	Alan Knicely	.08	.06	.03
324	Alejandro Pena	.15	.11	.06
325	Darrell Evans	.15	.11	.06
326	Bob Kearney	.08	.06	.03
327	Ruppert Jones	.08	.06	.03
328	Vern Ruhle	.08	.06	.03
329	Pat Tabler	.20	.15	.08
330	John Candelaria	.12	.09	.05
331	Bucky Dent	.12	.09	.05
332	Kevin Gross	.35	.25	.14
333	Larry Herndon	.10	.08	.04
334	Chuck Rainey	.08	.06	.03
335	Don Baylor	.15	.11	.06
336	Mariners Batting & Pitching Leaders (Pat Putnam, Matt Young)	.12	.09	.05
337	Kevin Hagen	.08	.06	.03
338	Mike Warren	.10	.08	.04
339	Roy Lee Jackson	.08	.06	.03
340	Hal McRae	.12	.09	.05
341	Dave Tobik	.08	.06	.03
342	Tim Foli	.08	.06	.03
343	Mark Davis	.08	.06	.03
344	Rick Miller	.08	.06	.03
345	Kent Hrbek	.40	.30	.15

		MT	NR MT	EX
346	Kurt Bevacqua	.08	.06	.03
347	Allan Ramirez	.08	.06	.03
348	Toby Harrah	.10	.08	.04
349	Bob Gibson	.08	.06	.03
350	George Foster	.20	.15	.08
351	Russ Nixon	.08	.06	.03
352	Dave Stewart	.12	.09	.05
353	Jim Anderson	.08	.06	.03
354	Jeff Burroughs	.10	.08	.04
355	Jason Thompson	.08	.06	.03
356	Glenn Abbott	.08	.06	.03
357	Ron Cey	.12	.09	.05
358	Bob Dernier	.10	.08	.04
359	Jim Acker	.15	.11	.06
360	Willie Randolph	.12	.09	.05
361	Dave Smith	.10	.08	.04
362	David Green	.08	.06	.03
363	Tim Laudner	.08	.06	.03
364	Scott Fletcher	.12	.09	.05
365	Steve Bedrosian	.12	.09	.05
366	Padres Batting & Pitching Leaders (Dave Dravecky, Terry Kennedy)	.12	.09	.05
367	Jamie Easterly	.08	.06	.03
368	Hubie Brooks	.15	.11	.06
369	Steve McCatty	.08	.06	.03
370	Tim Raines	.40	.30	.15
371	Dave Gumpert	.08	.06	.03
372	Gary Roenicke	.08	.06	.03
373	Bill Scherrer	.08	.06	.03
374	Don Money	.10	.08	.04
375	Dennis Leonard	.08	.06	.03
376	Dave Anderson	.15	.11	.06
377	Danny Darwin	.10	.08	.04
378	Bob Brenly	.08	.06	.03
379	Checklist 265-396	.08	.06	.03
380	Steve Garvey	.50	.40	.20
381	Ralph Houk	.10	.08	.04
382	Chris Nyman	.08	.06	.03
383	Terry Puhl	.08	.06	.03
384	Lee Tunnell	.12	.09	.05
385	Tony Perez	.20	.15	.08
386	George Hendrick AS	.10	.08	.04
387	Johnny Ray AS	.12	.09	.05
388	Mike Schmidt AS	.35	.25	.14
389	Ozzie Smith AS	.15	.11	.06
390	Tim Raines AS	.25	.20	.10
391	Dale Murphy AS	.40	.30	.15
392	Andre Dawson AS	.20	.15	.08
393	Gary Carter AS	.30	.25	.12
394	Steve Rogers AS	.10	.08	.04
395	Steve Carlton AS	.25	.20	.10
396	Jesse Orosco AS	.10	.08	.04
397	Eddie Murray AS	.35	.25	.14
398	Lou Whitaker AS	.20	.15	.08
399	George Brett AS	.35	.25	.14
400	Cal Ripken AS	.35	.25	.14
401	Jim Rice AS	.30	.25	.12
402	Dave Winfield AS	.30	.25	.12
403	Lloyd Moseby AS	.12	.09	.05
404	Ted Simmons AS	.15	.11	.06
405	LaMarr Hoyt AS	.10	.08	.04
406	Ron Guidry AS	.20	.15	.08
407	Dan Quisenberry AS	.12	.09	.05
408	Lou Piniella	.15	.11	.06
409	Juan Agosto	.12	.09	.05
410	Claudell Washington	.10	.08	.04
411	Houston Jimenez	.08	.06	.03
412	Doug Rader	.08	.06	.03
413	Spike Owen	.20	.15	.08
414	Mitchell Page	.08	.06	.03
415	Tommy John	.25	.20	.10
416	Dane Iorg	.08	.06	.03
417	Mike Armstrong	.08	.06	.03
418	Ron Hodges	.08	.06	.03
419	John Henry Johnson	.08	.06	.03
420	Cecil Cooper	.15	.11	.06
421	Charlie Lea	.08	.06	.03
422	Jose Cruz	.12	.09	.05
423	Mike Morgan	.08	.06	.03
424	Dann Bilardello	.08	.06	.03
425	Steve Howe	.10	.08	.04
426	Orioles Batting & Pitching Leaders (Mike Boddicker, Cal Ripken)	.25	.20	.10
427	Rick Leach	.08	.06	.03
428	Fred Breining	.08	.06	.03
429	Randy Bush	.15	.11	.06
430	Rusty Staub	.12	.09	.05
431	Chris Bando	.08	.06	.03
432	Charlie Hudson	.25	.20	.10
433	Rich Hebner	.08	.06	.03
434	Harold Baines	.25	.20	.10
435	Neil Allen	.08	.06	.03
436	Rick Peters	.08	.06	.03
437	Mike Proly	.08	.06	.03
438	Biff Pocoroba	.08	.06	.03
439	Bob Stoddard	.08	.06	.03
440	Steve Kemp	.10	.08	.04
441	Bob Lillis	.08	.06	.03
442	Byron McLaughlin	.08	.06	.03
443	Benny Ayala	.08	.06	.03
444	Steve Renko	.08	.06	.03
445	Jerry Remy	.08	.06	.03
446	Luis Pujols	.08	.06	.03
447	Tom Brunansky	.20	.15	.08
448	Ben Hayes	.08	.06	.03
449	Joe Pettini	.08	.06	.03
450	Gary Carter	.50	.40	.20
451	Bob Jones	.08	.06	.03
452	Chuck Porter	.08	.06	.03
453	Willie Upshaw	.12	.09	.05
454	Joe Beckwith	.08	.06	.03
455	Terry Kennedy	.10	.08	.04
456	Cubs Batting & Pitching Leaders (Fergie Jenkins, Keith Moreland)	.15	.11	.06
457	Dave Rozema	.08	.06	.03
458	Kiko Garcia	.08	.06	.03
459	Kevin Hickey	.08	.06	.03
460	Dave Winfield	.40	.30	.15
461	Jim Maler	.08	.06	.03
462	Lee Lacy	.10	.08	.04
463	Dave Engle	.08	.06	.03
464	Jeff Jones	.08	.06	.03
465	Mookie Wilson	.12	.09	.05
466	Gene Garber	.08	.06	.03
467	Mike Ramsey	.08	.06	.03
468	Geoff Zahn	.08	.06	.03
469	Tom O'Malley	.08	.06	.03
470	Nolan Ryan	.40	.30	.15
471	Dick Howser	.10	.08	.04
472	Mike Brown	.08	.06	.03
473	Jim Dwyer	.08	.06	.03
474	Greg Bargar	.08	.06	.03
475	Gary Redus	.30	.25	.12
476	Tom Tellmann	.08	.06	.03
477	Rafael Landestoy	.08	.06	.03
478	Alan Bannister	.08	.06	.03
479	Frank Tanana	.12	.09	.05
480	Ron Kittle	.25	.20	.10
481	Mark Thurmond	.15	.11	.06
482	Enos Cabell	.08	.06	.03
483	Fergie Jenkins	.20	.15	.08
484	Ozzie Virgil	.10	.08	.04
485	Rick Rhoden	.12	.09	.05
486	Yankees Batting & Pitching Leaders (Don Baylor, Ron Guidry)	.15	.11	.06
487	Ricky Adams	.08	.06	.03
488	Jesse Barfield	.35	.25	.14
489	Dave Von Ohlen	.08	.06	.03
490	Cal Ripken	.60	.45	.25
491	Bobby Castillo	.08	.06	.03
492	Tucker Ashford	.08	.06	.03
493	Mike Norris	.08	.06	.03
494	Chili Davis	.15	.11	.06
495	Rollie Fingers	.25	.20	.10
496	Terry Francona	.08	.06	.03
497	Bud Anderson	.08	.06	.03
498	Rich Gedman	.12	.09	.05
499	Mike Witt	.15	.11	.06
500	George Brett	.70	.50	.30
501	Steve Henderson	.08	.06	.03
502	Joe Torre	.08	.06	.03
503	Elias Sosa	.08	.06	.03
504	Mickey Rivers	.10	.08	.04
505	Pete Vuckovich	.10	.08	.04
506	Ernie Whitt	.10	.08	.04
507	Mike LaCoss	.10	.08	.04
508	Mel Hall	.15	.11	.06
509	Brad Havens	.08	.06	.03
510	Alan Trammell	.40	.30	.15
511	Marty Bystrom	.08	.06	.03
512	Oscar Gamble	.10	.08	.04
513	Dave Beard	.08	.06	.03
514	Floyd Rayford	.08	.06	.03
515	Gorman Thomas	.12	.09	.05
516	Expos Batting & Pitching Leaders (Charlie Lea, Al Oliver)	.15	.11	.06
517	John Moses	.08	.06	.03
518	Greg Walker	.70	.50	.30
519	Ron Davis	.08	.06	.03
520	Bob Boone	.12	.09	.05
521	Pete Falcone	.08	.06	.03
522	Dave Bergman	.08	.06	.03

	MT	NR MT	EX
523 Glenn Hoffman	.08	.06	.03
524 Carlos Diaz	.08	.06	.03
525 Willie Wilson	.15	.11	.06
526 Ron Oester	.08	.06	.03
527 Checklist 397-528	.08	.06	.03
528 Mark Brouhard	.08	.06	.03
529 Keith Atherton	.20	.15	.08
530 Dan Ford	.08	.06	.03
531 Steve Boros	.08	.06	.03
532 Eric Show	.10	.08	.04
533 Ken Landreaux	.10	.08	.04
534 Pete O'Brien	1.00	.70	.40
535 Bo Diaz	.10	.08	.04
536 Doug Bair	.08	.06	.03
537 Johnny Ray	.15	.11	.06
538 Kevin Bass	.15	.11	.06
539 George Frazier	.08	.06	.03
540 George Hendrick	.10	.08	.04
541 Dennis Lamp	.08	.06	.03
542 Duane Kuiper	.08	.06	.03
543 Craig McMurtry	.10	.08	.04
544 Cesar Geronimo	.08	.06	.03
545 Bill Buckner	.15	.11	.06
546 Indians Batting & Pitching Leaders (Mike Hargrove, Lary Sorensen)	.12	.09	.05
547 Mike Moore	.08	.06	.03
548 Ron Jackson	.08	.06	.03
549 Walt Terrell	.50	.40	.20
550 Jim Rice	.40	.30	.15
551 Scott Ullger	.08	.06	.03
552 Ray Burris	.08	.06	.03
553 Joe Nolan	.08	.06	.03
554 Ted Power	.15	.11	.06
555 Greg Brock	.20	.15	.08
556 Joey McLaughlin	.08	.06	.03
557 Wayne Tolleson	.10	.08	.04
558 Mike Davis	.10	.08	.04
559 Mike Scott	.20	.15	.08
560 Carlton Fisk	.20	.15	.08
561 Whitey Herzog	.10	.08	.04
562 Manny Castillo	.08	.06	.03
563 Glenn Wilson	.12	.09	.05
564 Al Holland	.08	.06	.03
565 Leon Durham	.15	.11	.06
566 Jim Bibby	.08	.06	.03
567 Mike Heath	.08	.06	.03
568 Pete Filson	.08	.06	.03
569 Bake McBride	.08	.06	.03
570 Dan Quisenberry	.20	.15	.08
571 Bruce Bochy	.08	.06	.03
572 Jerry Royster	.08	.06	.03
573 Dave Kingman	.15	.11	.06
574 Brian Downing	.12	.09	.05
575 Jim Clancy	.12	.09	.05
576 Giants Batting & Pitching Leaders (Atlee Hammaker, Jeff Leonard)	.12	.09	.05
577 Mark Clear	.10	.08	.04
578 Lenn Sakata	.08	.06	.03
579 Bob James	.20	.15	.08
580 Lonnie Smith	.10	.08	.04
581 Jose DeLeon	.25	.20	.10
582 Bob McClure	.08	.06	.03
583 Derrel Thomas	.08	.06	.03
584 Dave Schmidt	.10	.08	.04
585 Dan Driessen	.10	.08	.04
586 Joe Niekro	.15	.11	.06
587 Von Hayes	.20	.15	.08
588 Milt Wilcox	.10	.08	.04
589 Mike Easler	.10	.08	.04
590 Dave Stieb	.15	.11	.06
591 Tony LaRussa	.10	.08	.04
592 Andre Robertson	.08	.06	.03
593 Jeff Lahti	.08	.06	.03
594 Gene Richards	.08	.06	.03
595 Jeff Reardon	.15	.11	.06
596 Ryne Sandberg	1.25	.90	.50
597 Rick Camp	.08	.06	.03
598 Rusty Kuntz	.08	.06	.03
599 Doug Sisk	.12	.09	.05
600 Rod Carew	.50	.40	.20
601 John Tudor	.12	.09	.05
602 John Wathan	.10	.08	.04
603 Renie Martin	.08	.06	.03
604 John Lowenstein	.08	.06	.03
605 Mike Caldwell	.08	.06	.03
606 Blue Jays Batting & Pitching Leaders (Lloyd Moseby, Dave Stieb)	.15	.11	.06
607 Tom Hume	.08	.06	.03
608 Bobby Johnson	.08	.06	.03
609 Dan Meyer	.08	.06	.03
610 Steve Sax	.20	.15	.08
611 Chet Lemon	.10	.08	.04
612 Harry Spilman	.08	.06	.03
613 Greg Gross	.08	.06	.03
614 Len Barker	.10	.08	.04
615 Garry Templeton	.12	.09	.05
616 Don Robinson	.10	.08	.04
617 Rick Cerone	.10	.08	.04
618 Dickie Noles	.08	.06	.03
619 Jerry Dybzinski	.08	.06	.03
620 Al Oliver	.20	.15	.08
621 Frank Howard	.10	.08	.04
622 Al Cowens	.08	.06	.03
623 Ron Washington	.08	.06	.03
624 Terry Harper	.08	.06	.03
625 Larry Gura	.10	.08	.04
626 Bob Clark	.08	.06	.03
627 Dave LaPoint	.08	.06	.03
628 Ed Jurak	.08	.06	.03
629 Rick Langford	.08	.06	.03
630 Ted Simmons	.15	.11	.06
631 Denny Martinez	.10	.08	.04
632 Tom Foley	.08	.06	.03
633 Mike Krukow	.10	.08	.04
634 Mike Marshall	.15	.11	.06
635 Dave Righetti	.25	.20	.10
636 Pat Putnam	.08	.06	.03
637 Phillies Batting & Pitching Leaders (John Denny, Gary Matthews)	.12	.09	.05
638 George Vukovich	.08	.06	.03
639 Rick Lysander	.08	.06	.03
640 Lance Parrish	.35	.25	.14
641 Mike Richardt	.08	.06	.03
642 Tom Underwood	.08	.06	.03
643 Mike Brown	.08	.06	.03
644 Tim Lollar	.08	.06	.03
645 Tony Pena	.15	.11	.06
646 Checklist 529-660	.08	.06	.03
647 Ron Roenicke	.08	.06	.03
648 Len Whitehouse	.08	.06	.03
649 Tom Herr	.12	.09	.05
650 Phil Niekro	.30	.25	.12
651 John McNamara	.08	.06	.03
652 Rudy May	.10	.08	.04
653 Dave Stapleton	.08	.06	.03
654 Bob Bailor	.08	.06	.03
655 Amos Otis	.10	.08	.04
656 Bryn Smith	.10	.08	.04
657 Thad Bosley	.08	.06	.03
658 Jerry Augustine	.08	.06	.03
659 Duane Walker	.08	.06	.03
660 Ray Knight	.12	.09	.05
661 Steve Yeager	.08	.06	.03
662 Tom Brennan	.08	.06	.03
663 Johnnie LeMaster	.08	.06	.03
664 Dave Stegman	.08	.06	.03
665 Buddy Bell	.15	.11	.06
666 Tigers Batting & Pitching Leaders (Jack Morris, Lou Whitaker)	.15	.11	.06
667 Vance Law	.10	.08	.04
668 Larry McWilliams	.08	.06	.03
669 Dave Lopes	.10	.08	.04
670 Rich Gossage	.25	.20	.10
671 Jamie Quirk	.08	.06	.03
672 Ricky Nelson	.08	.06	.03
673 Mike Walters	.08	.06	.03
674 Tim Flannery	.08	.06	.03
675 Pascual Perez	.10	.08	.04
676 Brian Giles	.08	.06	.03
677 Doyle Alexander	.15	.11	.06
678 Chris Speier	.08	.06	.03
679 Art Howe	.08	.06	.03
680 Fred Lynn	.25	.20	.10
681 Tom Lasorda	.12	.09	.05
682 Dan Morogiello	.08	.06	.03
683 Marty Barrett	1.25	.90	.50
684 Bob Shirley	.08	.06	.03
685 Willie Aikens	.08	.06	.03
686 Joe Price	.08	.06	.03
687 Roy Howell	.08	.06	.03
688 George Wright	.08	.06	.03
689 Mike Fischlin	.08	.06	.03
690 Jack Clark	.25	.20	.10
691 Steve Lake	.12	.09	.05
692 Dickie Thon	.10	.08	.04
693 Alan Wiggins	.08	.06	.03
694 Mike Stanton	.08	.06	.03
695 Lou Whitaker	.30	.25	.12
696 Pirates Batting & Pitching Leaders (Bill Madlock, Rick Rhoden)	.15	.11	.06
697 Dale Murray	.08	.06	.03
698 Marc Hill	.08	.06	.03

		MT	NR MT	EX
699	Dave Rucker	.08	.06	.03
700	Mike Schmidt	.70	.50	.30
701	NL Active Career Batting Leaders (Bill Madlock, Dave Parker, Pete Rose)	.35	.25	.14
702	NL Active Career Hit Leaders (Tony Perez, Pete Rose, Rusty Staub)	.35	.25	.14
703	NL Active Career Home Run Leaders (Dave Kingman, Tony Perez, Mike Schmidt)	.30	.25	.12
704	NL Active Career RBI Leaders (Al Oliver, Tony Perez, Rusty Staub)	.15	.11	.06
705	NL Active Career Stolen Bases Leaders (Larry Bowa, Cesar Cedeno, Joe Morgan)	.12	.09	.05
706	NL Active Career Victory Leaders (Steve Carlton, Fergie Jenkins, Tom Seaver)	.30	.25	.12
707	NL Active Career Strikeout Leaders (Steve Carlton, Nolan Ryan, Tom Seaver)	.35	.25	.14
708	NL Active Career ERA Leaders (Steve Carlton, Steve Rogers, Tom Seaver)	.25	.20	.10
709	NL Active Career Save Leaders (Gene Garber, Tug McGraw, Bruce Sutter)	.12	.09	.05
710	AL Active Career Batting Leaders (George Brett, Rod Carew, Cecil Cooper)	.30	.25	.12
711	AL Active Career Hit Leaders (Bert Campaneris, Rod Carew, Reggie Jackson)	.30	.25	.12
712	AL Active Career Home Run Leaders (Reggie Jackson, Greg Luzinski, Graig Nettles)	.20	.15	.08
713	AL Active Career RBI Leaders (Reggie Jackson, Graig Nettles, Ted Simmons)	.20	.15	.08
714	AL Active Career Stolen Bases Leaders (Bert Campaneris, Dave Lopes, Omar Moreno)	.10	.08	.04
715	AL Active Career Victory Leaders (Tommy John, Jim Palmer, Don Sutton)	.25	.20	.10
716	AL Active Strikeout Leaders (Bert Blyleven, Jerry Koosman, Don Sutton)	.15	.11	.06
717	AL Active Career ERA Leaders (Rollie Fingers, Ron Guidry, Jim Palmer)	.15	.11	.06
718	AL Active Career Save Leaders (Rollie Fingers, Rich Gossage, Dan Quisenberry)	.15	.11	.06
719	Andy Hassler	.08	.06	.03
720	Dwight Evans	.20	.15	.08
721	Del Crandall	.08	.06	.03
722	Bob Welch	.12	.09	.05
723	Rich Dauer	.08	.06	.03
724	Eric Rasmussen	.08	.06	.03
725	Cesar Cedeno	.12	.09	.05
726	Brewers Batting & Pitching Leaders (Moose Haas, Ted Simmons)	.12	.09	.05
727	Joel Youngblood	.08	.06	.03
728	Tug McGraw	.15	.11	.06
729	Gene Tenace	.10	.08	.04
730	Bruce Sutter	.20	.15	.08
731	Lynn Jones	.08	.06	.03
732	Terry Crowley	.08	.06	.03
733	Dave Collins	.10	.08	.04
734	Odell Jones	.08	.06	.03
735	Rick Burleson	.10	.08	.04
736	Dick Ruthven	.08	.06	.03
737	Jim Essian	.08	.06	.03
738	Bill Schroeder	.25	.20	.10
739	Bob Watson	.10	.08	.04
740	Tom Seaver	.40	.30	.15
741	Wayne Gross	.08	.06	.03
742	Dick Williams	.10	.08	.04
743	Don Hood	.08	.06	.03
744	Jamie Allen	.08	.06	.03
745	Dennis Eckersley	.12	.09	.05
746	Mickey Hatcher	.10	.08	.04
747	Pat Zachry	.08	.06	.03
748	Jeff Leonard	.12	.09	.05
749	Doug Flynn	.08	.06	.03
750	Jim Palmer	.40	.30	.15
751	Charlie Moore	.08	.06	.03
752	Phil Garner	.10	.08	.04
753	Doug Gwosdz	.08	.06	.03
754	Kent Tekulve	.10	.08	.04
755	Garry Maddox	.12	.09	.05
756	Reds Batting & Pitching Leaders (Ron Oester, Mario Soto)	.12	.09	.05
757	Larry Bowa	.15	.11	.06
758	Bill Stein	.08	.06	.03
759	Richard Dotson	.12	.09	.05
760	Bob Horner	.30	.25	.12
761	John Montefusco	.08	.06	.03
762	Rance Mulliniks	.08	.06	.03

		MT	NR MT	EX
763	Craig Swan	.08	.06	.03
764	Mike Hargrove	.10	.08	.04
765	Ken Forsch	.10	.08	.04
766	Mike Vail	.08	.06	.03
767	Carney Lansford	.10	.08	.04
768	Champ Summers	.08	.06	.03
769	Bill Caudill	.08	.06	.03
770	Ken Griffey	.15	.11	.06
771	Billy Gardner	.08	.06	.03
772	Jim Slaton	.08	.06	.03
773	Todd Cruz	.08	.06	.03
774	Tom Gorman	.08	.06	.03
775	Dave Parker	.30	.25	.12
776	Craig Reynolds	.08	.06	.03
777	Tom Paciorek	.08	.06	.03
778	Andy Hawkins	.20	.15	.08
779	Jim Sundberg	.10	.08	.04
780	Steve Carlton	.50	.40	.20
781	Checklist 661-792	.08	.06	.03
782	Steve Balboni	.10	.08	.04
783	Luis Leal	.08	.06	.03
784	Leon Roberts	.08	.06	.03
785	Joaquin Andujar	.12	.09	.05
786	Red Sox Batting & Pitching Leaders (Wade Boggs, Bob Ojeda)	.40	.30	.15
787	Bill Campbell	.08	.06	.03
788	Milt May	.08	.06	.03
789	Bert Blyleven	.20	.15	.08
790	Doug DeCinces	.12	.09	.05
791	Terry Forster	.10	.08	.04
792	Bill Russell	.10	.08	.04

1984 Topps All-Star Glossy Set of 22

These 2½'' by 3½'' cards were a result of the success of Topps efforts the previous year with glossy cards on a mail-in basis. A 22-card set, the cards were divided evenly between the two leagues. Each starter for both leagues, the managers and the honorary team captains had an All-Star Glossy card. The cards featured a large color photo on the front with an All-Star banner across the top and the league emblem in the lower left. The player's name and position appeared below the photo. Backs have a name, team, position and card number along with the phrase ''1983 All-Star Game Commemorative Set.'' The '84 Glossy All-Stars were distributed one card per pack in Topps rak-paks that year.

		MT	NR MT	EX
	Complete Set:	6.00	4.50	2.50
	Common Player:	.20	.15	.08
1	Harvey Kuenn	.20	.15	.08
2	Rod Carew	.50	.40	.20
3	Manny Trillo	.20	.15	.08
4	George Brett	.80	.60	.30
5	Robin Yount	.40	.30	.15
6	Jim Rice	.50	.40	.20
7	Fred Lynn	.25	.20	.10
8	Dave Winfield	.50	.40	.20
9	Ted Simmons	.25	.20	.10
10	Dave Stieb	.25	.20	.10

		MT	NR MT	EX
11	Carl Yastrzemski	.80	.60	.30
12	Whitey Herzog	.20	.15	.08
13	Al Oliver	.25	.20	.10
14	Steve Sax	.30	.25	.12
15	Mike Schmidt	.60	.45	.25
16	Ozzie Smith	.30	.25	.12
17	Tim Raines	.50	.40	.20
18	Andre Dawson	.30	.25	.12
19	Dale Murphy	.90	.70	.35
20	Gary Carter	.50	.40	.20
21	Mario Soto	.20	.15	.08
22	Johnny Bench	.60	.45	.25

		MT	NR MT	EX
36	Robin Yount	.40	.30	.15
37	Tim Raines	.50	.40	.20
38	Dan Quisenberry	.20	.15	.08
39	Mike Schmidt	1.00	.70	.40
40	Carlton Fisk	.30	.25	.12

1984 Topps All-Star Glossy Set of 40

For the second straight year in 1984, Topps produced a 40-card All-Star "Collector's Edition" set as a "consolation prize" for its sweepstakes game. By collecting game cards and sending them in with a bit of cash, the collector could receive one of eight different five-card series. As the previous year, the 2½" by 3½" cards featured a nearly full-frame color photo on its glossy finish front. Backs were printed in red and blue.

		MT	NR MT	EX
	Complete Set:	14.00	10.50	5.50
	Common Player:	.15	.11	.06
1	Pete Rose	1.25	.90	.50
2	Lance Parrish	.30	.25	.12
3	Steve Rogers	.15	.11	.06
4	Eddie Murray	.70	.50	.30
5	Johnny Ray	.20	.15	.08
6	Rickey Henderson	.70	.50	.30
7	Atlee Hammaker	.15	.11	.06
8	Wade Boggs	3.00	2.25	1.25
9	Gary Carter	.50	.40	.20
10	Jack Morris	.30	.25	.12
11	Darrell Evans	.20	.15	.08
12	George Brett	1.00	.70	.40
13	Bob Horner	.25	.20	.10
14	Ron Guidry	.30	.25	.12
15	Nolan Ryan	.50	.40	.20
16	Dave Winfield	.60	.45	.25
17	Ozzie Smith	.25	.20	.10
18	Ted Simmons	.20	.15	.08
19	Bill Madlock	.20	.15	.08
20	Tony Armas	.15	.11	.06
21	Al Oliver	.20	.15	.08
22	Jim Rice	.50	.40	.20
23	George Hendrick	.15	.11	.06
24	Dave Stieb	.20	.15	.08
25	Pedro Guerrero	.30	.25	.12
26	Rod Carew	.60	.45	.25
27	Steve Carlton	.50	.40	.20
28	Dave Righetti	.30	.25	.12
29	Darryl Strawberry	1.50	1.25	.60
30	Lou Whitaker	.30	.25	.12
31	Dale Murphy	1.00	.70	.40
32	LaMarr Hoyt	.15	.11	.06
33	Jesse Orosco	.15	.11	.06
34	Cecil Cooper	.20	.15	.08
35	Andre Dawson	.35	.25	.14

1984 Topps Super

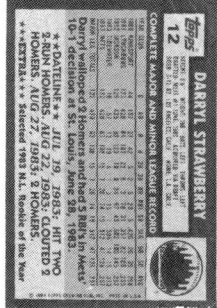

The next installment in Topps continuing production of large-format cards, these 4⅞" by 6⅞" cards were available in limited geographical areas. They were sold in cellophane packs with a complete set being 30 cards. Other than their size and the change in card number on the back, there is nothing to distinguish the Supers from the regular 1984 Topps cards of the same players. One plus is that the players are all big name stars, and are likely to remain in demand.

		MT	NR MT	EX
	Complete Set:	10.00	7.50	4.00
	Common Player:	.20	.15	.08
1	Cal Ripken	.70	.50	.30
2	Dale Murphy	.90	.70	.35
3	LaMarr Hoyt	.20	.15	.08
4	John Denny	.20	.15	.08
5	Jim Rice	.50	.40	.20
6	Mike Schmidt	.90	.70	.35
7	Wade Boggs	1.25	.90	.50
8	Bill Madlock	.25	.20	.10
9	Dan Quisenberry	.25	.20	.10
10	Al Holland	.20	.15	.08
11	Ron Kittle	.20	.15	.08
12	Darryl Strawberry	1.25	.90	.50
13	George Brett	.90	.70	.35
14	Bill Buckner	.25	.20	.10
15	Carlton Fisk	.25	.20	.10
16	Steve Carlton	.50	.40	.20
17	Ron Guidry	.35	.25	.14
18	Gary Carter	.50	.40	.20
19	Rickey Henderson	.70	.50	.30
20	Andre Dawson	.35	.25	.14
21	Reggie Jackson	.60	.45	.25
22	Steve Garvey	.50	.40	.20
23	Fred Lynn	.35	.25	.14
24	Pedro Guerrero	.25	.20	.10
25	Eddie Murray	.60	.45	.25
26	Keith Hernandez	.50	.40	.20
27	Dave Winfield	.50	.40	.20
28	Nolan Ryan	.50	.40	.20
29	Robin Yount	.40	.30	.15
30	Fernando Valenzuela	.40	.30	.15

1984 Topps Traded

The popular Topps Traded set returned for its fourth year in 1984 with another 132-card set. The 2½" by 3½" cards have an identical design to the regular Topps cards except that the back cardboard is white and the card numbers carry a "T" suffix. As before the set was sold only through hobby dealers. Also as before, players who changed teams, new man-

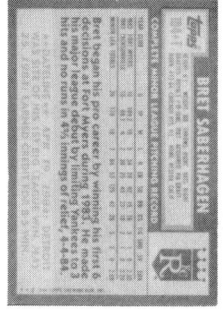

BRET SABERHAGEN P

agers and promising rookies are included in the set. The presence of several promising young rookies in especially high demand from investors and speculators has made this one of the most expensive Topps issues of recent years. A glossy-finish "Tiffany" version of the set was also issued, valued at four to five times the price of the normal Traded cards.

	MT	NR MT	EX
Complete Set:	75.00	56.00	30.00
Common Player:	.10	.08	.04
1T Willie Aikens	.10	.08	.04
2T Luis Aponte	.10	.08	.04
3T Mike Armstrong	.10	.08	.04
4T Bob Bailor	.10	.08	.04
5T Dusty Baker	.20	.15	.08
6T Steve Balboni	.15	.11	.06
7T Alan Bannister	.10	.08	.04
8T Dave Beard	.10	.08	.04
9T Joe Beckwith	.10	.08	.04
10T Bruce Berenyi	.10	.08	.04
11T Dave Bergman	.10	.08	.04
12T Tony Bernazard	.15	.11	.06
13T Yogi Berra	.20	.15	.08
14T Barry Bonnell	.10	.08	.04
15T Phil Bradley	3.00	2.25	1.25
16T Fred Breining	.10	.08	.04
17T Bill Buckner	.25	.20	.10
18T Ray Burris	.10	.08	.04
19T John Butcher	.10	.08	.04
20T Brett Butler	.20	.15	.08
21T Enos Cabell	.15	.11	.06
22T Bill Campbell	.10	.08	.04
23T Bill Caudill	.10	.08	.04
24T Bob Clark	.10	.08	.04
25T Bryan Clark	.10	.08	.04
26T Jaime Cocanower	.10	.08	.04
27T Ron Darling	6.00	4.50	2.50
28T Alvin Davis	3.00	2.25	1.25
29T Ken Dayley	.10	.08	.04
30T Jeff Dedmon	.15	.11	.06
31T Bob Dernier	.10	.08	.04
32T Carlos Diaz	.10	.08	.04
33T Mike Easler	.15	.11	.06
34T Dennis Eckersley	.15	.11	.06
35T Jim Essian	.10	.08	.04
36T Darrell Evans	.25	.20	.10
37T Mike Fitzgerald	.15	.11	.06
38T Tim Foli	.10	.08	.04
39T George Frazier	.10	.08	.04
40T Rich Gale	.10	.08	.04
41T Barbaro Garbey	.10	.08	.04
42T Dwight Gooden	35.00	26.00	14.00
43T Rich Gossage	.40	.30	.15
44T Wayne Gross	.10	.08	.04
45T Mark Gubicza	.40	.30	.15
46T Jackie Gutierrez	.10	.08	.04
47T Mel Hall	.20	.15	.08
48T Toby Harrah	.15	.11	.06
49T Ron Hassey	.10	.08	.04
50T Rich Hebner	.10	.08	.04
51T Willie Hernandez	.30	.25	.12
52T Ricky Horton	.40	.30	.15
53T Art Howe	.10	.08	.04
54T Dane Iorg	.10	.08	.04
55T Brook Jacoby	1.50	1.25	.60
56T Mike Jeffcoat	.15	.11	.06
57T Dave Johnson	.15	.11	.06
58T Lynn Jones	.10	.08	.04

	MT	NR MT	EX
59T Ruppert Jones	.10	.08	.04
60T Mike Jorgensen	.10	.08	.04
61T Bob Kearney	.10	.08	.04
62T Jimmy Key	2.50	2.00	1.00
63T Dave Kingman	.40	.30	.15
64T Jerry Koosman	.30	.25	.12
65T Wayne Krenchicki	.10	.08	.04
66T Rusty Kuntz	.10	.08	.04
67T Rene Lachemann	.10	.08	.04
68T Frank LaCorte	.10	.08	.04
69T Dennis Lamp	.10	.08	.04
70T Mark Langston	2.50	2.00	1.00
71T Rick Leach	.10	.08	.04
72T Craig Lefferts	.15	.11	.06
73T Gary Lucas	.10	.08	.04
74T Jerry Martin	.10	.08	.04
75T Carmelo Martinez	.25	.20	.10
76T Mike Mason	.20	.15	.08
77T Gary Matthews	.25	.20	.10
78T Andy McGaffigan	.10	.08	.04
79T Larry Milbourne	.10	.08	.04
80T Sid Monge	.10	.08	.04
81T Jackie Moore	.10	.08	.04
82T Joe Morgan	1.00	.70	.40
83T Graig Nettles	.50	.40	.20
84T Phil Niekro	1.00	.70	.40
85T Ken Oberkfell	.15	.11	.06
86T Mike O'Berry	.10	.08	.04
87T Al Oliver	.35	.25	.14
88T Jorge Orta	.10	.08	.04
89T Amos Otis	.15	.11	.06
90T Dave Parker	.80	.60	.30
91T Tony Perez	.60	.45	.25
92T Gerald Perry	.60	.45	.25
93T Gary Pettis	.40	.30	.15
94T Rob Picciolo	.10	.08	.04
95T Vern Rapp	.10	.08	.04
96T Floyd Rayford	.10	.08	.04
97T Randy Ready	.20	.15	.08
98T Ron Reed	.15	.11	.06
99T Gene Richards	.10	.08	.04
100T Jose Rijo	.40	.30	.15
101T Jeff Robinson	.30	.25	.12
102T Ron Romanick	.20	.15	.08
103T Pete Rose	6.00	4.50	2.50
104T Bret Saberhagen	10.00	7.50	4.00
105T Juan Samuel	2.25	1.75	.90
106T Scott Sanderson	.15	.11	.06
107T Dick Schofield	.40	.30	.15
108T Tom Seaver	2.00	1.50	.80
109T Jim Slaton	.10	.08	.04
110T Mike Smithson	.10	.08	.04
111T Lary Sorensen	.10	.08	.04
112T Tim Stoddard	.10	.08	.04
113T Champ Summers	.10	.08	.04
114T Jim Sundberg	.15	.11	.06
115T Rick Sutcliffe	.50	.40	.20
116T Craig Swan	.10	.08	.04
117T Tim Teufel	.40	.30	.15
118T Derrel Thomas	.10	.08	.04
119T Gorman Thomas	.25	.20	.10
120T Alex Trevino	.10	.08	.04
121T Manny Trillo	.15	.11	.06
122T John Tudor	.20	.15	.08
123T Tom Underwood	.10	.08	.04
124T Mike Vail	.10	.08	.04
125T Tom Waddell	.15	.11	.06
126T Gary Ward	.15	.11	.06
127T Curt Wilkerson	.10	.08	.04
128T Frank Williams	.25	.20	.10
129T Glenn Wilson	.30	.25	.12
130T Johnny Wockenfuss	.10	.08	.04
131T Ned Yost	.10	.08	.04
132T Checklist 1-132	.10	.08	.04

1985 Topps

Holding the line at 792 cards, Topps did initiate some major design changes in its 2½'' by 3½'' cards in 1985. The use of two photos on the front was discontinued in favor of one large color photo. The Topps logo appeared in the upper-lefthand corner. At the bottom ran a diagonal rectangular box with the team name. It joined a team logo, and below that point ran the player's position and name. The backs feature statistics, biographical information and a

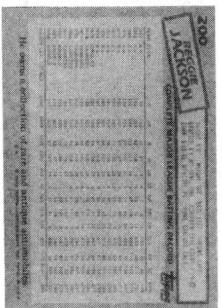

trivia question. Some interesting specialty sets were introduced in 1985 including the revival of the father-son theme from 1976, a subset of the 1984 U.S. Olympic Baseball Team members and a set featuring #1 draft choices since the inception of the baseball draft in 1965. Again in 1985, a glossy-finish "Tiffany" edition of the regular set was produced, though the number was cut back to 5,000 sets. Values range from four times regular value for common cards to five-six times for high-demand stars and rookie cards.

		MT	NR MT	EX
Complete Set:		90.00	67.00	36.00
Common Player:		.06	.05	.02
1	Record Breaker (Carlton Fisk)	.15	.11	.06
2	Record Breaker (Steve Garvey)	.20	.15	.08
3	Record Breaker (Dwight Gooden)	1.00	.70	.40
4	Record Breaker (Cliff Johnson)	.08	.06	.03
5	Record Breaker (Joe Morgan)	.15	.11	.06
6	Record Breaker (Pete Rose)	.60	.45	.25
7	Record Breaker (Nolan Ryan)	.30	.25	.12
8	Record Breaker (Juan Samuel)	.20	.15	.08
9	Record Breaker (Bruce Sutter)	.15	.11	.06
10	Record Breaker (Don Sutton)	.20	.15	.08
11	Ralph Houk	.08	.06	.03
12	Dave Lopes	.08	.06	.03
13	Tim Lollar	.06	.05	.02
14	Chris Bando	.06	.05	.02
15	Jerry Koosman	.10	.08	.04
16	Bobby Meacham	.06	.05	.02
17	Mike Scott	.15	.11	.06
18	Mickey Hatcher	.06	.05	.02
19	George Frazier	.06	.05	.02
20	Chet Lemon	.08	.06	.03
21	Lee Tunnell	.06	.05	.02
22	Duane Kuiper	.06	.05	.02
23	Bret Saberhagen	3.25	2.50	1.25
24	Jesse Barfield	.25	.20	.10
25	Steve Bedrosian	.12	.09	.05
26	Roy Smalley	.06	.05	.02
27	Bruce Berenyi	.06	.05	.02
28	Dann Bilardello	.06	.05	.02
29	Odell Jones	.06	.05	.02
30	Cal Ripken	.50	.40	.20
31	Terry Whitfield	.06	.05	.02
32	Chuck Porter	.06	.05	.02
33	Tito Landrum	.06	.05	.02
34	Ed Nunez	.15	.11	.06
35	Graig Nettles	.15	.11	.06
36	Fred Breining	.06	.05	.02
37	Reid Nichols	.06	.05	.02
38	Jackie Moore	.06	.05	.02
39	Johnny Wockenfuss	.06	.05	.02
40	Phil Niekro	.25	.20	.10
41	Mike Fischlin	.06	.05	.02
42	Luis Sanchez	.06	.05	.02
43	Andre David	.06	.05	.02
44	Dickie Thon	.08	.06	.03
45	Greg Minton	.06	.05	.02
46	Gary Woods	.06	.05	.02
47	Dave Rozema	.06	.05	.02
48	Tony Fernandez	1.00	.70	.40
49	Butch Davis	.06	.05	.02
50	John Candelaria	.10	.08	.04
51	Bob Watson	.08	.06	.03
52	Jerry Dybzinski	.06	.05	.02
53	Tom Gorman	.06	.05	.02
54	Cesar Cedeno	.10	.08	.04
55	Frank Tanana	.10	.08	.04

		MT	NR MT	EX
56	Jim Dwyer	.06	.05	.02
57	Pat Zachry	.06	.05	.02
58	Orlando Mercado	.06	.05	.02
59	Rick Waits	.06	.05	.02
60	George Hendrick	.08	.06	.03
61	Curt Kaufman	.06	.05	.02
62	Mike Ramsey	.06	.05	.02
63	Steve McCatty	.06	.05	.02
64	Mark Bailey	.12	.09	.05
65	Bill Buckner	.12	.09	.05
66	Dick Williams	.08	.06	.03
67	Rafael Santana	.20	.15	.08
68	Von Hayes	.12	.09	.05
69	Jim Winn	.15	.11	.06
70	Don Baylor	.12	.09	.05
71	Tim Laudner	.06	.05	.02
72	Rick Sutcliffe	.12	.09	.05
73	Rusty Kuntz	.06	.05	.02
74	Mike Krukow	.08	.06	.03
75	Willie Upshaw	.08	.06	.03
76	Alan Bannister	.06	.05	.02
77	Joe Beckwith	.06	.05	.02
78	Scott Fletcher	.08	.06	.03
79	Rick Mahler	.06	.05	.02
80	Keith Hernandez	.30	.25	.12
81	Lenn Sakata	.06	.05	.02
82	Joe Price	.06	.05	.02
83	Charlie Moore	.06	.05	.02
84	Spike Owen	.06	.05	.02
85	Mike Marshall	.12	.09	.05
86	Don Aase	.08	.06	.03
87	David Green	.06	.05	.02
88	Bryn Smith	.08	.06	.03
89	Jackie Gutierrez	.06	.05	.02
90	Rich Gossage	.20	.15	.08
91	Jeff Burroughs	.08	.06	.03
92	Paul Owens	.06	.05	.02
93	Don Schulze	.10	.08	.04
94	Toby Harrah	.08	.06	.03
95	Jose Cruz	.10	.08	.04
96	Johnny Ray	.12	.09	.05
97	Pete Filson	.06	.05	.02
98	Steve Lake	.06	.05	.02
99	Milt Wilcox	.08	.06	.03
100	George Brett	.50	.40	.20
101	Jim Acker	.06	.05	.02
102	Tommy Dunbar	.06	.05	.02
103	Randy Lerch	.06	.05	.02
104	Mike Fitzgerald	.08	.06	.03
105	Ron Kittle	.10	.08	.04
106	Pascual Perez	.08	.06	.03
107	Tom Foley	.06	.05	.02
108	Darnell Coles	.15	.11	.06
109	Gary Roenicke	.06	.05	.02
110	Alejandro Pena	.06	.05	.02
111	Doug DeCinces	.10	.08	.04
112	Tom Tellmann	.06	.05	.02
113	Tom Herr	.10	.08	.04
114	Bob James	.06	.05	.02
115	Rickey Henderson	.40	.30	.15
116	Dennis Boyd	.20	.15	.08
117	Greg Gross	.06	.05	.02
118	Eric Show	.06	.05	.02
119	Pat Corrales	.06	.05	.02
120	Steve Kemp	.08	.06	.03
121	Checklist 1-132	.06	.05	.02
122	Tom Brunansky	.12	.09	.05
123	Dave Smith	.08	.06	.03
124	Rich Hebner	.06	.05	.02
125	Kent Tekulve	.08	.06	.03
126	Ruppert Jones	.06	.05	.02
127	Mark Gubicza	.30	.25	.12
128	Ernie Whitt	.08	.06	.03
129	Gene Garber	.06	.05	.02
130	Al Oliver	.12	.09	.05
131	Father - Son (Buddy Bell, Gus Bell)	.12	.09	.05
132	Father - Son (Dale Berra, Yogi Berra)	.20	.15	.08
133	Father - Son (Bob Boone, Ray Boone)	.12	.09	.05
134	Father - Son (Terry Francona, Tito Francona)	.08	.06	.03
135	Father - Son (Bob Kennedy, Terry Kennedy)	.08	.06	.03
136	Father - Son (Bill Kunkel, Jeff Kunkel)	.08	.06	.03
137	Father - Son (Vance Law, Vern Law)	.10	.08	.04
138	Father - Son (Dick Schofield, Dick Schofield)	.08	.06	.03

		MT	NR MT	EX
139	Father - Son (Bob Skinner, Joel Skinner)	.08	.06	.03
140	Father - Son (Roy Smalley, Roy Smalley)	.08	.06	.03
141	Father - Son (Dave Stenhouse, Mike Stenhouse)	.08	.06	.03
142	Father - Son (Dizzy Trout, Steve Trout)	.08	.06	.03
143	Father - Son (Ossie Virgil, Ozzie Virgil)	.08	.06	.03
144	Ron Gardenhire	.06	.05	.02
145	Alvin Davis	1.50	1.25	.60
146	Gary Redus	.08	.06	.03
147	Bill Swaggerty	.06	.05	.02
148	Steve Yeager	.06	.05	.02
149	Dickie Noles	.06	.05	.02
150	Jim Rice	.35	.25	.14
151	Moose Haas	.06	.05	.02
152	Steve Braun	.06	.05	.02
153	Frank LaCorte	.06	.05	.02
154	Argenis Salazar	.08	.06	.03
155	Yogi Berra	.12	.09	.05
156	Craig Reynolds	.06	.05	.02
157	Tug McGraw	.10	.08	.04
158	Pat Tabler	.08	.06	.03
159	Carlos Diaz	.06	.05	.02
160	Lance Parrish	.25	.20	.10
161	Ken Schrom	.06	.05	.02
162	Benny Distefano	.10	.08	.04
163	Dennis Eckersley	.08	.06	.03
164	Jorge Orta	.06	.05	.02
165	Dusty Baker	.08	.06	.03
166	Keith Atherton	.08	.06	.03
167	Rufino Linares	.06	.05	.02
168	Garth Iorg	.06	.05	.02
169	Dan Spillner	.06	.05	.02
170	George Foster	.15	.11	.06
171	Bill Stein	.06	.05	.02
172	Jack Perconte	.06	.05	.02
173	Mike Young	.15	.11	.06
174	Rick Honeycutt	.08	.06	.03
175	Dave Parker	.25	.20	.10
176	Bill Schroeder	.08	.06	.03
177	Dave Von Ohlen	.06	.05	.02
178	Miguel Dilone	.06	.05	.02
179	Tommy John	.20	.15	.08
180	Dave Winfield	.35	.25	.14
181	Roger Clemens	9.00	6.75	3.50
182	Tim Flannery	.06	.05	.02
183	Larry McWilliams	.06	.05	.02
184	Carmen Castillo	.10	.08	.04
185	Al Holland	.06	.05	.02
186	Bob Lillis	.06	.05	.02
187	Mike Walters	.06	.05	.02
188	Greg Pryor	.06	.05	.02
189	Warren Brusstar	.06	.05	.02
190	Rusty Staub	.12	.09	.05
191	Steve Nicosia	.06	.05	.02
192	Howard Johnson	.70	.50	.30
193	Jimmy Key	.70	.50	.30
194	Dave Stegman	.06	.05	.02
195	Glenn Hubbard	.06	.05	.02
196	Pete O'Brien	.20	.15	.08
197	Mike Warren	.06	.05	.02
198	Eddie Milner	.06	.05	.02
199	Denny Martinez	.06	.05	.02
200	Reggie Jackson	.40	.30	.15
201	Burt Hooton	.08	.06	.03
202	Gorman Thomas	.12	.09	.05
203	Bob McClure	.06	.05	.02
204	Art Howe	.06	.05	.02
205	Steve Rogers	.08	.06	.03
206	Phil Garner	.08	.06	.03
207	Mark Clear	.08	.06	.03
208	Champ Summers	.06	.05	.02
209	Bill Campbell	.06	.05	.02
210	Gary Matthews	.10	.08	.04
211	Clay Christiansen	.06	.05	.02
212	George Vukovich	.06	.05	.02
213	Billy Gardner	.06	.05	.02
214	John Tudor	.10	.08	.04
215	Bob Brenly	.06	.05	.02
216	Jerry Don Gleaton	.06	.05	.02
217	Leon Roberts	.06	.05	.02
218	Doyle Alexander	.10	.08	.04
219	Gerald Perry	.12	.09	.05
220	Fred Lynn	.20	.15	.08
221	Ron Reed	.06	.05	.02
222	Hubie Brooks	.10	.08	.04
223	Tom Hume	.06	.05	.02
224	Al Cowens	.06	.05	.02
225	Mike Boddicker	.12	.09	.05
226	Juan Beniquez	.06	.05	.02
227	Danny Darwin	.08	.06	.03
228	Dion James	.25	.20	.10
229	Dave LaPoint	.06	.05	.02
230	Gary Carter	.40	.30	.15
231	Dwayne Murphy	.08	.06	.03
232	Dave Beard	.06	.05	.02
233	Ed Jurak	.06	.05	.02
234	Jerry Narron	.06	.05	.02
235	Garry Maddox	.08	.06	.03
236	Mark Thurmond	.06	.05	.02
237	Julio Franco	.12	.09	.05
238	Jose Rijo	.20	.15	.08
239	Tim Teufel	.10	.08	.04
240	Dave Stieb	.12	.09	.05
241	Jim Frey	.06	.05	.02
242	Greg Harris	.06	.05	.02
243	Barbaro Garbey	.06	.05	.02
244	Mike Jones	.06	.05	.02
245	Chili Davis	.10	.08	.04
246	Mike Norris	.06	.05	.02
247	Wayne Tolleson	.06	.05	.02
248	Terry Forster	.08	.06	.03
249	Harold Baines	.15	.11	.06
250	Jesse Orosco	.08	.06	.03
251	Brad Gulden	.06	.05	.02
252	Dan Ford	.06	.05	.02
253	Sid Bream	.40	.30	.15
254	Pete Vuckovich	.08	.06	.03
255	Lonnie Smith	.08	.06	.03
256	Mike Stanton	.06	.05	.02
257	Brian Little (Bryan)	.06	.05	.02
258	Mike Brown	.06	.05	.02
259	Gary Allenson	.06	.05	.02
260	Dave Righetti	.20	.15	.08
261	Checklist 133-264	.06	.05	.02
262	Greg Booker	.12	.09	.05
263	Mel Hall	.08	.06	.03
264	Joe Sambito	.06	.05	.02
265	Juan Samuel	.50	.40	.20
266	Frank Viola	.12	.09	.05
267	Henry Cotto	.12	.09	.05
268	Chuck Tanner	.08	.06	.03
269	Doug Baker	.10	.08	.04
270	Dan Quisenberry	.15	.11	.06
271	1968 #1 Draft Pick (Tim Foli)	.08	.06	.03
272	1969 #1 Draft Pick (Jeff Burroughs)	.08	.06	.03
273	1969 #1 Draft Pick (Bill Almon)	.08	.06	.03
274	1976 #1 Draft Pick (Floyd Bannister)	.10	.08	.04
275	1977 #1 Draft Pick (Harold Baines)	.15	.11	.06
276	1978 #1 Draft Pick (Bob Horner)	.15	.11	.06
277	1979 #1 Draft Pick (Al Chambers)	.08	.06	.03
278	1980 #1 Draft Pick (Darryl Strawberry)	.50	.40	.20
279	1981 #1 Draft Pick (Mike Moore)	.08	.06	.03
280	1982 #1 Draft Pick (Shawon Dunston)	.75	.60	.30
281	1983 #1 Draft Pick (Tim Belcher)	.08	.06	.03
282	1984 #1 Draft Pick (Shawn Abner)	.40	.30	.15
283	Fran Mullins	.06	.05	.02
284	Marty Bystrom	.06	.05	.02
285	Dan Driessen	.08	.06	.03
286	Rudy Law	.06	.05	.02
287	Walt Terrell	.12	.09	.05
288	Jeff Kunkel	.12	.09	.05
289	Tom Underwood	.06	.05	.02
290	Cecil Cooper	.15	.11	.06
291	Bob Welch	.10	.08	.04
292	Brad Komminsk	.10	.08	.04
293	Curt Young	.50	.40	.20
294	Tom Nieto	.12	.09	.05
295	Joe Niekro	.10	.08	.04
296	Ricky Nelson	.06	.05	.02
297	Gary Lucas	.06	.05	.02
298	Marty Barrett	.20	.15	.08
299	Andy Hawkins	.06	.05	.02
300	Rod Carew	.40	.30	.15
301	John Montefusco	.06	.05	.02
302	Tim Corcoran	.06	.05	.02
303	Mike Jeffcoat	.06	.05	.02
304	Gary Gaetti	.20	.15	.08
305	Dale Berra	.06	.05	.02
306	Rick Reuschel	.10	.08	.04
307	Sparky Anderson	.08	.06	.03
308	John Wathan	.08	.06	.03
309	Mike Witt	.12	.09	.05
310	Manny Trillo	.08	.06	.03

#	Name	MT	NR MT	EX
311	Jim Gott	.06	.05	.02
312	Marc Hill	.06	.05	.02
313	Dave Schmidt	.08	.06	.03
314	Ron Oester	.06	.05	.02
315	Doug Sisk	.06	.05	.02
316	John Lowenstein	.06	.05	.02
317	Jack Lazorko	.10	.08	.04
318	Ted Simmons	.12	.09	.05
319	Jeff Jones	.06	.05	.02
320	Dale Murphy	.60	.45	.25
321	Ricky Horton	.30	.25	.12
322	Dave Stapleton	.06	.05	.02
323	Andy McGaffigan	.06	.05	.02
324	Bruce Bochy	.06	.05	.02
325	John Denny	.06	.05	.02
326	Kevin Bass	.12	.09	.05
327	Brook Jacoby	.30	.25	.12
328	Bob Shirley	.06	.05	.02
329	Ron Washington	.06	.05	.02
330	Leon Durham	.10	.08	.04
331	Bill Laskey	.06	.05	.02
332	Brian Harper	.06	.05	.02
333	Willie Hernandez	.08	.06	.03
334	Dick Howser	.08	.06	.03
335	Bruce Benedict	.06	.05	.02
336	Rance Mulliniks	.06	.05	.02
337	Billy Sample	.06	.05	.02
338	Britt Burns	.06	.05	.02
339	Danny Heep	.06	.05	.02
340	Robin Yount	.35	.25	.14
341	Floyd Rayford	.06	.05	.02
342	Ted Power	.08	.06	.03
343	Bill Russell	.08	.06	.03
344	Dave Henderson	.06	.05	.02
345	Charlie Lea	.06	.05	.02
346	Terry Pendleton	.70	.50	.30
347	Rick Langford	.06	.05	.02
348	Bob Boone	.08	.06	.03
349	Domingo Ramos	.06	.05	.02
350	Wade Boggs	3.25	2.50	1.25
351	Juan Agosto	.06	.05	.02
352	Joe Morgan	.20	.15	.08
353	Julio Solano	.10	.08	.04
354	Andre Robertson	.06	.05	.02
355	Bert Blyleven	.15	.11	.06
356	Dave Meier	.06	.05	.02
357	Rich Bordi	.06	.05	.02
358	Tony Pena	.10	.08	.04
359	Pat Sheridan	.06	.05	.02
360	Steve Carlton	.40	.30	.15
361	Alfredo Griffin	.08	.06	.03
362	Craig McMurtry	.06	.05	.02
363	Ron Hodges	.06	.05	.02
364	Richard Dotson	.10	.08	.04
365	Danny Ozark	.06	.05	.02
366	Todd Cruz	.06	.05	.02
367	Keefe Cato	.06	.05	.02
368	Dave Bergman	.06	.05	.02
369	R.J. Reynolds	.35	.25	.14
370	Bruce Sutter	.15	.11	.06
371	Mickey Rivers	.08	.06	.03
372	Roy Howell	.06	.05	.02
373	Mike Moore	.06	.05	.02
374	Brian Downing	.10	.08	.04
375	Jeff Reardon	.15	.11	.06
376	Jeff Newman	.06	.05	.02
377	Checklist 265-396	.06	.05	.02
378	Alan Wiggins	.06	.05	.02
379	Charles Hudson	.08	.06	.03
380	Ken Griffey	.10	.08	.04
381	Roy Smith	.06	.05	.02
382	Denny Walling	.06	.05	.02
383	Rick Lysander	.06	.05	.02
384	Jody Davis	.10	.08	.04
385	Jose DeLeon	.08	.06	.03
386	Dan Gladden	.40	.30	.15
387	Buddy Biancalana	.15	.11	.06
388	Bert Roberge	.06	.05	.02
389	1984 United States Baseball Team (Rod Dedeaux)	.06	.05	.02
390	1984 United States Baseball Team (Sid Akins)	.10	.08	.04
391	1984 United States Baseball Team (Flavio Alfaro)	.06	.05	.02
392	1984 United States Baseball Team (Don August)	.12	.09	.05
393	1984 United States Baseball Team (Scott Bankhead)	.35	.25	.14
394	1984 United States Baseball Team (Bob Caffrey)	.10	.08	.04

#	Name	MT	NR MT	EX
395	1984 United States Baseball Team (Mike Dunne)	1.50	1.25	.60
396	1984 United States Baseball Team (Gary Green)	.12	.09	.05
397	1984 United States Baseball Team (John Hoover)	.10	.08	.04
398	1984 United States Baseball Team (Shane Mack)	.80	.60	.30
399	1984 United States Baseball Team (John Marzano)	1.50	1.25	.60
400	1984 United States Baseball Team (Oddibe McDowell)	1.50	1.25	.60
401	1984 United States Baseball Team (Mark McGwire)	15.00	11.00	6.00
402	1984 United States Baseball Team (Pat Pacillo)	.25	.20	.10
403	1984 United States Baseball Team (Cory Snyder)	8.00	6.00	3.25
404	1984 United States Baseball Team (Billy Swift)	.20	.15	.08
405	Tom Veryzer	.06	.05	.02
406	Len Whitehouse	.06	.05	.02
407	Bobby Ramos	.06	.05	.02
408	Sid Monge	.06	.05	.02
409	Brad Wellman	.06	.05	.02
410	Bob Horner	.25	.20	.10
411	Bobby Cox	.06	.05	.02
412	Bud Black	.06	.05	.02
413	Vance Law	.08	.06	.03
414	Gary Ward	.08	.06	.03
415	Ron Darling	1.25	.90	.50
416	Wayne Gross	.06	.05	.02
417	John Franco	.50	.40	.20
418	Ken Landreaux	.08	.06	.03
419	Mike Caldwell	.06	.05	.02
420	Andre Dawson	.30	.25	.12
421	Dave Rucker	.06	.05	.02
422	Carney Lansford	.08	.06	.03
423	Barry Bonnell	.06	.05	.02
424	Al Nipper	.25	.20	.10
425	Mike Hargrove	.08	.06	.03
426	Verne Ruhle	.06	.05	.02
427	Mario Ramirez	.06	.05	.02
428	Larry Andersen	.06	.05	.02
429	Rick Cerone	.08	.06	.03
430	Ron Davis	.06	.05	.02
431	U.L. Washington	.06	.05	.02
432	Thad Bosley	.06	.05	.02
433	Jim Morrison	.06	.05	.02
434	Gene Richards	.06	.05	.02
435	Dan Petry	.10	.08	.04
436	Willie Aikens	.06	.05	.02
437	Al Jones	.06	.05	.02
438	Joe Torre	.08	.06	.03
439	Junior Ortiz	.06	.05	.02
440	Fernando Valenzuela	.35	.25	.14
441	Duane Walker	.06	.05	.02
442	Ken Forsch	.06	.05	.02
443	George Wright	.06	.05	.02
444	Tony Phillips	.06	.05	.02
445	Tippy Martinez	.06	.05	.02
446	Jim Sundberg	.08	.06	.03
447	Jeff Lahti	.06	.05	.02
448	Derrel Thomas	.06	.05	.02
449	Phil Bradley	1.50	1.25	.60
450	Steve Garvey	.40	.30	.15
451	Bruce Hurst	.10	.08	.04
452	John Castino	.06	.05	.02
453	Tom Waddell	.10	.08	.04
454	Glenn Wilson	.10	.08	.04
455	Bob Knepper	.08	.06	.03
456	Tim Foli	.06	.05	.02
457	Cecilio Guante	.06	.05	.02
458	Randy Johnson	.06	.05	.02
459	Charlie Leibrandt	.08	.06	.03
460	Ryne Sandberg	.40	.30	.15
461	Marty Castillo	.06	.05	.02
462	Gary Lavelle	.06	.05	.02
463	Dave Collins	.08	.06	.03
464	Mike Mason	.10	.08	.04
465	Bob Grich	.10	.08	.04
466	Tony LaRussa	.08	.06	.03
467	Ed Lynch	.06	.05	.02
468	Wayne Krenchicki	.06	.05	.02
469	Sammy Stewart	.06	.05	.02
470	Steve Sax	.20	.15	.08
471	Pete Ladd	.06	.05	.02
472	Jim Essian	.06	.05	.02
473	Tim Wallach	.12	.09	.05
474	Kurt Kepshire	.06	.05	.02
475	Andre Thornton	.10	.08	.04

		MT	NR MT	EX
476	Jeff Stone	.20	.15	.08
477	Bob Ojeda	.10	.08	.04
478	Kurt Bevacqua	.06	.05	.02
479	Mike Madden	.06	.05	.02
480	Lou Whitaker	.25	.20	.10
481	Dale Murray	.06	.05	.02
482	Harry Spilman	.06	.05	.02
483	Mike Smithson	.06	.05	.02
484	Larry Bowa	.12	.09	.05
485	Matt Young	.08	.06	.03
486	Steve Balboni	.08	.06	.03
487	Frank Williams	.20	.15	.08
488	Joel Skinner	.08	.06	.03
489	Bryan Clark	.06	.05	.02
490	Jason Thompson	.06	.05	.02
491	Rick Camp	.06	.05	.02
492	Dave Johnson	.08	.06	.03
493	Orel Hershiser	1.75	1.25	.70
494	Rich Dauer	.06	.05	.02
495	Mario Soto	.08	.06	.03
496	Donnie Scott	.06	.05	.02
497	Gary Pettis	.20	.15	.08
498	Ed Romero	.06	.05	.02
499	Danny Cox	.35	.25	.14
500	Mike Schmidt	.50	.40	.20
501	Dan Schatzeder	.06	.05	.02
502	Rick Miller	.06	.05	.02
503	Tim Conroy	.06	.05	.02
504	Jerry Willard	.06	.05	.02
505	Jim Beattie	.06	.05	.02
506	Franklin Stubbs	.60	.45	.25
507	Ray Fontenot	.06	.05	.02
508	John Shelby	.08	.06	.03
509	Milt May	.06	.05	.02
510	Kent Hrbek	.25	.20	.10
511	Lee Smith	.10	.08	.04
512	Tom Brookens	.06	.05	.02
513	Lynn Jones	.06	.05	.02
514	Jeff Cornell	.06	.05	.02
515	Dave Concepcion	.12	.09	.05
516	Roy Lee Jackson	.06	.05	.02
517	Jerry Martin	.06	.05	.02
518	Chris Chambliss	.08	.06	.03
519	Doug Rader	.06	.05	.02
520	LaMarr Hoyt	.08	.06	.03
521	Rick Dempsey	.08	.06	.03
522	Paul Molitor	.15	.11	.06
523	Candy Maldonado	.10	.08	.04
524	Rob Wilfong	.06	.05	.02
525	Darrell Porter	.08	.06	.03
526	Dave Palmer	.08	.06	.03
527	Checklist 397-528	.06	.05	.02
528	Bill Krueger	.06	.05	.02
529	Rich Gedman	.10	.08	.04
530	Dave Dravecky	.08	.06	.03
531	Joe Lefebvre	.06	.05	.02
532	Frank DiPino	.06	.05	.02
533	Tony Bernazard	.08	.06	.03
534	Brian Dayett	.08	.06	.03
535	Pat Putnam	.06	.05	.02
536	Kirby Puckett	9.00	6.75	3.50
537	Don Robinson	.08	.06	.03
538	Keith Moreland	.08	.06	.03
539	Aurelio Lopez	.06	.05	.02
540	Claudell Washington	.08	.06	.03
541	Mark Davis	.06	.05	.02
542	Don Slaught	.06	.05	.02
543	Mike Squires	.06	.05	.02
544	Bruce Kison	.06	.05	.02
545	Lloyd Moseby	.10	.08	.04
546	Brent Gaff	.06	.05	.02
547	Pete Rose	.60	.45	.25
548	Larry Parrish	.10	.08	.04
549	Mike Scioscia	.06	.05	.02
550	Scott McGregor	.10	.08	.04
551	Andy Van Slyke	.15	.11	.06
552	Chris Codiroli	.06	.05	.02
553	Bob Clark	.06	.05	.02
554	Doug Flynn	.06	.05	.02
555	Bob Stanley	.08	.06	.03
556	Sixto Lezcano	.06	.05	.02
557	Len Barker	.08	.06	.03
558	Carmelo Martinez	.10	.08	.04
559	Jay Howell	.08	.06	.03
560	Bill Madlock	.12	.09	.05
561	Darryl Motley	.06	.05	.02
562	Houston Jimenez	.06	.05	.02
563	Dick Ruthven	.06	.05	.02
564	Alan Ashby	.06	.05	.02
565	Kirk Gibson	.30	.25	.12
566	Ed Vande Berg	.06	.05	.02

		MT	NR MT	EX
567	Joel Youngblood	.06	.05	.02
568	Cliff Johnson	.06	.05	.02
569	Ken Oberkfell	.08	.06	.03
570	Darryl Strawberry	1.75	1.25	.70
571	Charlie Hough	.08	.06	.03
572	Tom Paciorek	.06	.05	.02
573	Jay Tibbs	.15	.11	.06
574	Joe Altobelli	.06	.05	.02
575	Pedro Guerrero	.25	.20	.10
576	Jaime Cocanower	.06	.05	.02
577	Chris Speier	.06	.05	.02
578	Terry Francona	.06	.05	.02
579	Ron Romanick	.15	.11	.06
580	Dwight Evans	.12	.09	.05
581	Mark Wagner	.06	.05	.02
582	Ken Phelps	.20	.15	.08
583	Bobby Brown	.06	.05	.02
584	Kevin Gross	.10	.08	.04
585	Butch Wynegar	.08	.06	.03
586	Bill Scherrer	.06	.05	.02
587	Doug Frobel	.06	.05	.02
588	Bobby Castillo	.06	.05	.02
589	Bob Dernier	.06	.05	.02
590	Ray Knight	.10	.08	.04
591	Larry Herndon	.08	.06	.03
592	Jeff Robinson	.25	.20	.10
593	Rick Leach	.06	.05	.02
594	Curt Wilkerson	.08	.06	.03
595	Larry Gura	.08	.06	.03
596	Jerry Hairston	.06	.05	.02
597	Brad Lesley	.06	.05	.02
598	Jose Oquendo	.08	.06	.03
599	Storm Davis	.08	.06	.03
600	Pete Rose	1.00	.70	.40
601	Tom Lasorda	.10	.08	.04
602	Jeff Dedmon	.15	.11	.06
603	Rick Manning	.06	.05	.02
604	Daryl Sconiers	.06	.05	.02
605	Ozzie Smith	.15	.11	.06
606	Rich Gale	.06	.05	.02
607	Bill Almon	.06	.05	.02
608	Craig Lefferts	.08	.06	.03
609	Broderick Perkins	.06	.05	.02
610	Jack Morris	.25	.20	.10
611	Ozzie Virgil	.08	.06	.03
612	Mike Armstrong	.06	.05	.02
613	Terry Puhl	.06	.05	.02
614	Al Williams	.06	.05	.02
615	Marvell Wynne	.06	.05	.02
616	Scott Sanderson	.08	.06	.03
617	Willie Wilson	.12	.09	.05
618	Pete Falcone	.06	.05	.02
619	Jeff Leonard	.10	.08	.04
620	Dwight Gooden	7.50	5.75	3.00
621	Marvis Foley	.06	.05	.02
622	Luis Leal	.06	.05	.02
623	Greg Walker	.12	.09	.05
624	Benny Ayala	.06	.05	.02
625	Mark Langston	.70	.50	.30
626	German Rivera	.06	.05	.02
627	Eric Davis	17.00	12.50	6.75
628	Rene Lachemann	.06	.05	.02
629	Dick Schofield	.15	.11	.06
630	Tim Raines	.35	.25	.14
631	Bob Forsch	.08	.06	.03
632	Bruce Bochte	.06	.05	.02
633	Glenn Hoffman	.06	.05	.02
634	Bill Dawley	.06	.05	.02
635	Terry Kennedy	.08	.06	.03
636	Shane Rawley	.10	.08	.04
637	Brett Butler	.08	.06	.03
638	Mike Pagliarulo	2.25	1.75	.90
639	Ed Hodge	.06	.05	.02
640	Steve Henderson	.06	.05	.02
641	Rod Scurry	.06	.05	.02
642	Dave Owen	.06	.05	.02
643	Johnny Grubb	.06	.05	.02
644	Mark Huismann	.08	.06	.03
645	Damaso Garcia	.08	.06	.03
646	Scot Thompson	.06	.05	.02
647	Rafael Ramirez	.06	.05	.02
648	Bob Jones	.06	.05	.02
649	Sid Fernandez	1.00	.70	.40
650	Greg Luzinski	.10	.08	.04
651	Jeff Russell	.06	.05	.02
652	Joe Nolan	.06	.05	.02
653	Mark Brouhard	.06	.05	.02
654	Dave Anderson	.06	.05	.02
655	Joaquin Andujar	.08	.06	.03
656	Chuck Cottier	.06	.05	.02
657	Jim Slaton	.06	.05	.02

		MT	NR MT	EX
658	Mike Stenhouse	.06	.05	.02
659	Checklist 529-660	.06	.05	.02
660	Tony Gwynn	.60	.45	.25
661	Steve Crawford	.06	.05	.02
662	Mike Heath	.06	.05	.02
663	Luis Aguayo	.06	.05	.02
664	Steve Farr	.15	.11	.06
665	Don Mattingly	9.00	6.75	3.50
666	Mike LaCoss	.08	.06	.03
667	Dave Engle	.06	.05	.02
668	Steve Trout	.08	.06	.03
669	Lee Lacy	.08	.06	.03
670	Tom Seaver	.30	.25	.12
671	Dane Iorg	.06	.05	.02
672	Juan Berenguer	.06	.05	.02
673	Buck Martinez	.06	.05	.02
674	Atlee Hammaker	.06	.05	.02
675	Tony Perez	.15	.11	.06
676	Albert Hall	.20	.15	.08
677	Wally Backman	.08	.06	.03
678	Joey McLaughlin	.06	.05	.02
679	Bob Kearney	.06	.05	.02
680	Jerry Reuss	.08	.06	.03
681	Ben Oglivie	.08	.06	.03
682	Doug Corbett	.06	.05	.02
683	Whitey Herzog	.08	.06	.03
684	Bill Doran	.12	.09	.05
685	Bill Caudill	.06	.05	.02
686	Mike Easler	.08	.06	.03
687	Bill Gullickson	.08	.06	.03
688	Len Matuszek	.06	.05	.02
689	Luis DeLeon	.06	.05	.02
690	Alan Trammell	.35	.25	.14
691	Dennis Rasmussen	.12	.09	.05
692	Randy Bush	.06	.05	.02
693	Tim Stoddard	.06	.05	.02
694	Joe Carter	1.25	.90	.50
695	Rick Rhoden	.10	.08	.04
696	John Rabb	.06	.05	.02
697	Onix Concepcion	.06	.05	.02
698	Jorge Bell	.60	.45	.25
699	Donnie Moore	.06	.05	.02
700	Eddie Murray	.50	.40	.20
701	Eddie Murray AS	.30	.25	.12
702	Damaso Garcia AS	.08	.06	.03
703	George Brett AS	.35	.25	.14
704	Cal Ripken AS	.30	.25	.12
705	Dave Winfield AS	.20	.15	.08
706	Rickey Henderson AS	.30	.25	.12
707	Tony Armas AS	.08	.06	.03
708	Lance Parrish AS	.15	.11	.06
709	Mike Boddicker AS	.08	.06	.03
710	Frank Viola AS	.10	.08	.04
711	Dan Quisenberry AS	.10	.08	.04
712	Keith Hernandez AS	.20	.15	.08
713	Ryne Sandberg AS	.20	.15	.08
714	Mike Schmidt AS	.30	.25	.12
715	Ozzie Smith AS	.12	.09	.05
716	Dale Murphy AS	.35	.25	.14
717	Tony Gwynn AS	.30	.25	.12
718	Jeff Leonard AS	.10	.08	.04
719	Gary Carter AS	.20	.15	.08
720	Rick Sutcliffe AS	.12	.09	.05
721	Bob Knepper AS	.08	.06	.03
722	Bruce Sutter AS	.12	.09	.05
723	Dave Stewart	.10	.08	.04
724	Oscar Gamble	.08	.06	.03
725	Floyd Bannister	.10	.08	.04
726	Al Bumbry	.08	.06	.03
727	Frank Pastore	.06	.05	.02
728	Bob Bailor	.06	.05	.02
729	Don Sutton	.30	.25	.12
730	Dave Kingman	.15	.11	.06
731	Neil Allen	.06	.05	.02
732	John McNamara	.06	.05	.02
733	Tony Scott	.06	.05	.02
734	John Henry Johnson	.06	.05	.02
735	Garry Templeton	.10	.08	.04
736	Jerry Mumphrey	.08	.06	.03
737	Bo Diaz	.08	.06	.03
738	Omar Moreno	.06	.05	.02
739	Ernie Camacho	.06	.05	.02
740	Jack Clark	.20	.15	.08
741	John Butcher	.06	.05	.02
742	Ron Hassey	.06	.05	.02
743	Frank White	.10	.08	.04
744	Doug Bair	.06	.05	.02
745	Buddy Bell	.12	.09	.05
746	Jim Clancy	.10	.08	.04
747	Alex Trevino	.06	.05	.02
748	Lee Mazzilli	.08	.06	.03

		MT	NR MT	EX
749	Julio Cruz	.06	.05	.02
750	Rollie Fingers	.20	.15	.08
751	Kelvin Chapman	.06	.05	.02
752	Bob Owchinko	.06	.05	.02
753	Greg Brock	.10	.08	.04
754	Larry Milbourne	.06	.05	.02
755	Ken Singleton	.08	.06	.03
756	Rob Picciolo	.06	.05	.02
757	Willie McGee	.30	.25	.12
758	Ray Burris	.06	.05	.02
759	Jim Fanning	.06	.05	.02
760	Nolan Ryan	.40	.30	.15
761	Jerry Remy	.06	.05	.02
762	Eddie Whitson	.06	.05	.02
763	Kiko Garcia	.06	.05	.02
764	Jamie Easterly	.06	.05	.02
765	Willie Randolph	.10	.08	.04
766	Paul Mirabella	.06	.05	.02
767	Darrell Brown	.06	.05	.02
768	Ron Cey	.10	.08	.04
769	Joe Cowley	.06	.05	.02
770	Carlton Fisk	.20	.15	.08
771	Geoff Zahn	.06	.05	.02
772	Johnnie LeMaster	.06	.05	.02
773	Hal McRae	.10	.08	.04
774	Dennis Lamp	.06	.05	.02
775	Mookie Wilson	.10	.08	.04
776	Jerry Royster	.06	.05	.02
777	Ned Yost	.06	.05	.02
778	Mike Davis	.08	.06	.03
779	Nick Esasky	.08	.06	.03
780	Mike Flanagan	.10	.08	.04
781	Jim Gantner	.08	.06	.03
782	Tom Niedenfuer	.08	.06	.03
783	Mike Jorgensen	.06	.05	.02
784	Checklist 661-792	.06	.05	.02
785	Tony Armas	.10	.08	.04
786	Enos Cabell	.06	.05	.02
787	Jim Wohlford	.06	.05	.02
788	Steve Comer	.06	.05	.02
789	Luis Salazar	.06	.05	.02
790	Ron Guidry	.25	.20	.10
791	Ivan DeJesus	.06	.05	.02
792	Darrell Evans	.12	.09	.05

1985 Topps All-Star Glossy
Set of 22

The second straight year for this set of 22 cards featuring the starting players, the honorary captains and the managers in the All-Star Game. The set is virtually identical to that of the previous year in design with a color photo, All-Star banner, league emblem, and player's name and position on the front. What makes the cards special is their high gloss finish. The cards were available as inserts in Topps rak-paks. With their combination of attractive appearance and big-name stars, these 2½" by 3½" cards will probably continue to enjoy a great deal of popularity.

		MT	NR MT	EX
Complete Set:		6.00	4.50	2.50
Common Player:		.20	.15	.08
1	Paul Owens	.20	.15	.08
2	Steve Garvey	.50	.40	.20

		MT	NR MT	EX
3	Ryne Sandberg	.60	.45	.25
4	Mike Schmidt	.60	.45	.25
5	Ozzie Smith	.25	.20	.10
6	Tony Gwynn	.60	.45	.25
7	Dale Murphy	.90	.70	.35
8	Darryl Strawberry	.70	.50	.30
9	Gary Carter	.50	.40	.20
10	Charlie Lea	.20	.15	.08
11	Willie McCovey	.35	.25	.14
12	Joe Altobelli	.20	.15	.08
13	Rod Carew	.50	.40	.20
14	Lou Whitaker	.30	.25	.12
15	George Brett	.80	.60	.30
16	Cal Ripken	.60	.45	.25
17	Dave Winfield	.50	.40	.20
18	Chet Lemon	.20	.15	.08
19	Reggie Jackson	.60	.45	.25
20	Lance Parrish	.30	.25	.12
21	Dave Stieb	.25	.20	.10
22	Hank Greenberg	.20	.15	.08

		MT	NR MT	EX
26	Jack Morris	.30	.25	.12
27	Don Mattingly	3.50	2.75	1.50
28	Eddie Murray	.70	.50	.30
29	Tony Gwynn	.60	.45	.25
30	Charlie Lea	.15	.11	.06
31	Juan Samuel	.30	.25	.12
32	Phil Niekro	.35	.25	.14
33	Alejandro Pena	.15	.11	.06
34	Harold Baines	.25	.20	.10
35	Dan Quisenberry	.20	.15	.08
36	Gary Carter	.50	.40	.20
37	Mario Soto	.15	.11	.06
38	Dwight Gooden	2.50	2.00	1.00
39	Tom Brunansky	.20	.15	.08
40	Dave Stieb	.20	.15	.08

1985 Topps All-Star Glossy Set of 40

Similar to previous years' glossy sets, the 1985 All-Star "Collector's Edition" glossy set of 40 could be obtained through the mail in eight five-card subsets. To obtain the 2½'' by 3½'' cards, collectors had to accumulate sweepstakes insert cards from Topps packs, and pay 75¢ postage and handling. Under the circumstances, the complete set of 40 cards was not inexpensive. They are however, rather attractive and popular cards, and the set size enabled Topps to include some players who didn't make their 22-card set.

		MT	NR MT	EX
Complete Set:		14.00	10.50	5.50
Common Player:		.15	.11	.06
1	Dale Murphy	1.00	.70	.40
2	Jesse Orosco	.15	.11	.06
3	Bob Brenly	.15	.11	.06
4	Mike Boddicker	.20	.15	.08
5	Dave Kingman	.25	.20	.10
6	Jim Rice	.50	.40	.20
7	Frank Viola	.20	.15	.08
8	Alvin Davis	.35	.25	.14
9	Rick Sutcliffe	.20	.15	.08
10	Pete Rose	1.25	.90	.50
11	Leon Durham	.20	.15	.08
12	Joaquin Andujar	.15	.11	.06
13	Keith Hernandez	.40	.30	.15
14	Dave Winfield	.60	.45	.25
15	Reggie Jackson	.70	.50	.30
16	Alan Trammell	.35	.25	.14
17	Bert Blyleven	.20	.15	.08
18	Tony Armas	.15	.11	.06
19	Rich Gossage	.25	.20	.10
20	Jose Cruz	.20	.15	.08
21	Ryne Sandberg	.40	.30	.15
22	Bruce Sutter	.20	.15	.08
23	Mike Schmidt	1.00	.70	.40
24	Cal Ripken	.70	.50	.30
25	Dan Petry	.15	.11	.06

1985 Topps All-Time Record Holders

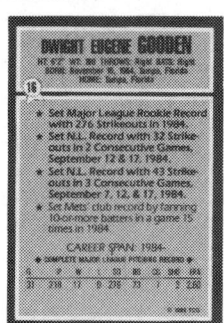

This 44-card boxed set was produced by Topps for the Woolworth's chain stores. Many hobbyists refer to this as the "Woolworth's" set, but that name does not appear anywhere on the cards. Featuring a combination of black-and-white and color photos of baseball record holders from all eras, the set was in the standard 2½'' by 3½'' format. Backs, printed in blue and orange, give career details and personal data. Because it combined old-timers with current players, the set did not achieve a great deal of collector popularity.

		MT	NR MT	EX
Complete Set:		5.00	3.75	2.00
Common Player:		.05	.04	.02
1	Hank Aaron	.20	.15	.08
2	Grover Alexander	.10	.08	.04
3	Ernie Banks	.12	.09	.05
4	Yogi Berra	.15	.11	.06
5	Lou Brock	.12	.09	.05
6	Steve Carlton	.12	.09	.05
7	Jack Chesbro	.07	.05	.03
8	Ty Cobb	.25	.20	.10
9	Sam Crawford	.07	.05	.03
10	Rollie Fingers	.07	.05	.03
11	Whitey Ford	.12	.09	.05
12	Johnny Frederick	.05	.04	.02
13	Frankie Frisch	.07	.05	.03
14	Lou Gehrig	.25	.20	.10
15	Jim Gentile	.05	.04	.02
16	Dwight Gooden	.40	.30	.15
17	Rickey Henderson	.15	.11	.06
18	Rogers Hornsby	.12	.09	.05
19	Frank Howard	.07	.05	.03
20	Cliff Johnson	.05	.04	.02
21	Walter Johnson	.15	.11	.06
22	Hub Leonard	.05	.04	.02
23	Mickey Mantle	.80	.60	.30
24	Roger Maris	.12	.09	.05
25	Christy Mathewson	.12	.09	.05
26	Willie Mays	.20	.15	.08
27	Stan Musial	.20	.15	.08
28	Dan Quisenberry	.07	.05	.03
29	Frank Robinson	.12	.09	.05

		MT	NR MT	EX
30	Pete Rose	.40	.30	.15
31	Babe Ruth	.50	.40	.20
32	Nolan Ryan	.12	.09	.05
33	George Sisler	.10	.08	.04
34	Tris Speaker	.10	.08	.04
35	Ed Walsh	.07	.05	.03
36	Lloyd Waner	.07	.05	.03
37	Earl Webb	.05	.04	.02
38	Ted Williams	.30	.25	.12
39	Maury Wills	.10	.08	.04
40	Hack Wilson	.07	.05	.03
41	Owen Wilson	.05	.04	.02
42	Willie Wilson	.07	.05	.03
43	Rudy York	.05	.04	.02
44	Cy Young	.15	.11	.06

		MT	NR MT	EX
36	Keith Hernandez	.50	.40	.20
37	Robin Yount	.40	.30	.15
38	Joaquin Andujar	.20	.15	.08
39	Lloyd Moseby	.20	.15	.08
40	Chili Davis	.20	.15	.08
41	Kent Hrbek	.35	.25	.14
42	Dave Parker	.35	.25	.14
43	Jack Morris	.35	.25	.14
44	Pedro Guerrero	.30	.25	.12
45	Mike Witt	.20	.15	.08
46	George Brett	.90	.70	.35
47	Ozzie Smith	.30	.25	.12
48	Cal Ripken	.70	.50	.30
49	Rich Gossage	.25	.20	.10
50	Jim Rice	.50	.40	.20
51	Harold Baines	.25	.20	.10
52	Fernando Valenzuela	.40	.30	.15
53	Buddy Bell	.25	.20	.10
54	Jesse Orosco	.20	.15	.08
55	Lance Parrish	.35	.25	.14
56	Jason Thompson	.20	.15	.08
57	Tom Brunansky	.25	.20	.10
58	Dave Righetti	30	.25	.12
59	Dave Kingman	.25	.20	.10
60	Dave Winfield	.50	.40	.20

1985 Topps Super

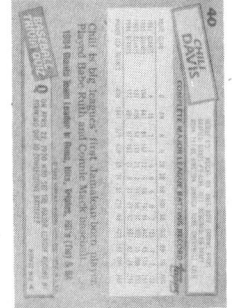

Still trying to sell collectors on the idea of jumbo-sized cards, Topps returned for a second year with its 4⅞'' by 6⅞'' "Super" set. In fact, the set size was doubled from the previous year, to 60 cards. As in '84, the Supers were identical to the regular-issue '85 cards of the same players, only the card numbers on back were changed. The cards were again sold three per pack for 50¢.

		MT	NR MT	EX
Complete Set:		14.00	10.50	5.50
Common Player:		.20	.15	.08
1	Ryne Sandberg	.50	.40	.20
2	Willie Hernandez	.20	.15	.08
3	Rick Sutcliffe	.25	.20	.10
4	Don Mattingly	2.25	1.75	.90
5	Tony Gwynn	.70	.50	.30
6	Alvin Davis	.35	.25	.14
7	Dwight Gooden	2.00	1.50	.80
8	Dan Quisenberry	.25	.20	.10
9	Bruce Sutter	.25	.20	.10
10	Tony Armas	.20	.15	.08
11	Dale Murphy	.90	.70	.35
12	Mike Schmidt	.90	.70	.35
13	Gary Carter	.50	.40	.20
14	Rickey Henderson	.70	.50	.30
15	Tim Raines	.50	.40	.20
16	Mike Boddicker	.20	.15	.08
17	Alejandro Pena	.20	.15	.08
18	Eddie Murray	.60	.45	.25
19	Gary Matthews	.20	.15	.08
20	Mark Langston	.30	.25	.12
21	Mario Soto	.20	.15	.08
22	Dave Stieb	.20	.15	.08
23	Nolan Ryan	.50	.40	.20
24	Steve Carlton	.50	.40	.20
25	Alan Trammell	.40	.30	.15
26	Steve Garvey	.50	.40	.20
27	Kirk Gibson	.35	.25	.14
28	Juan Samuel	.35	.25	.14
29	Reggie Jackson	.60	.45	.25
30	Darryl Strawberry	.90	.70	.35
31	Tom Seaver	.50	.40	.20
32	Pete Rose	1.25	.90	.50
33	Dwight Evans	.30	.25	.12
34	Jose Cruz	.20	.15	.08
35	Bert Blyleven	.25	.20	.10

1985 Topps 3-D

These 4¼'' by 6'' cards were something new. Printed on plastic, rather than paper, the player picture on the card was actually raised above the surface much like might be found on a relief map; a true 3-D baseball card. The plastic cards include the player's name, a Topps logo and card number across the top, and a team logo on the side. Backs are blank but have two peel-off adhesive strips so that the card may be attached to a flat surface. There are 30 cards in the set, the bulk of whom are stars.

		MT	NR MT	EX
Complete Set:		14.00	10.50	5.50
Common Player:		.20	.15	.08
1	Mike Schmidt	.90	.70	.35
2	Eddie Murray	.70	.50	.30
3	Dale Murphy	.90	.70	.35
4	George Brett	.90	.70	.35
5	Pete Rose	1.25	.90	.50
6	Jim Rice	.60	.45	.25
7	Ryne Sandberg	.50	.40	.20
8	Don Mattingly	2.25	1.75	.90
9	Darryl Strawberry	.90	.70	.35
10	Rickey Henderson	.80	.60	.30
11	Keith Hernandez	.50	.40	.20
12	Dave Kingman	.20	.15	.08
13	Tony Gwynn	.80	.60	.30
14	Reggie Jackson	.70	.50	.30
15	Gary Carter	.60	.45	.25
16	Cal Ripken	.80	.60	.30
17	Tim Raines	.50	.40	.20
18	Dave Winfield	.60	.45	.25
19	Dwight Gooden	2.00	1.50	.80
20	Dave Stieb	.20	.15	.08
21	Fernando Valenzuela	.50	.40	.20
22	Mark Langston	.30	.25	.12
23	Bruce Sutter	.25	.20	.10
24	Dan Quisenberry	.25	.20	.10

		MT	NR MT	EX
25	Steve Carlton	.60	.45	.25
26	Mike Boddicker	.20	.15	.08
27	Goose Gossage	.30	.25	.12
28	Jack Morris	.40	.30	.15
29	Rick Sutcliffe	.30	.25	.12
30	Tom Seaver	.60	.45	.25

1985 Topps Traded

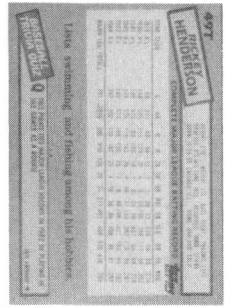

By 1985, the Topps Traded set had become a yearly feature, and Topps continued the tradition with another 132-card set. The 2½'' by 3½'' cards followed the pattern of being virtually identical in design to the regular cards issued by Topps. Sold only through established hobby dealers, the set featured traded veterans and promising rookies. A glossy-finish ''Tiffany'' edition of the set is valued at four times normal Traded card value for commons, up to five or six times normal value for superstars and hot rookies.

		MT	NR MT	EX
Complete Set:		14.00	10.50	5.50
Common Player:		.10	.08	.04

1T	Don Aase	.15	.11	.06
2T	Bill Almon	.10	.08	.04
3T	Benny Ayala	.10	.08	.04
4T	Dusty Baker	.15	.11	.06
5T	George Bamberger	.10	.08	.04
6T	Dale Berra	.10	.08	.04
7T	Rich Bordi	.10	.08	.04
8T	Daryl Boston	.20	.15	.08
9T	Hubie Brooks	.20	.15	.08
10T	Chris Brown	1.75	1.25	.70
11T	Tom Browning	.40	.30	.15
12T	Al Bumbry	.10	.08	.04
13T	Ray Burris	.10	.08	.04
14T	Jeff Burroughs	.15	.11	.06
15T	Bill Campbell	.10	.08	.04
16T	Don Carman	.40	.30	.15
17T	Gary Carter	.80	.60	.30
18T	Bobby Castillo	.10	.08	.04
19T	Bill Caudill	.10	.08	.04
20T	Rick Cerone	.10	.08	.04
21T	Bryan Clark	.10	.08	.04
22T	Jack Clark	.35	.25	.14
23T	Pat Clements	.20	.15	.08
24T	Vince Coleman	4.00	3.00	1.50
25T	Dave Collins	.15	.11	.06
26T	Danny Darwin	.15	.11	.06
27T	Jim Davenport	.10	.08	.04
28T	Jerry Davis	.10	.08	.04
29T	Brian Dayett	.10	.08	.04
30T	Ivan DeJesus	.10	.08	.04
31T	Ken Dixon	.20	.15	.08
32T	Mariano Duncan	.25	.20	.10
33T	John Felske	.10	.08	.04
34T	Mike Fitzgerald	.10	.08	.04
35T	Ray Fontenot	.10	.08	.04
36T	Greg Gagne	.50	.40	.20
37T	Oscar Gamble	.15	.11	.06
38T	Scott Garrelts	.30	.25	.12
39T	Bob Gibson	.10	.08	.04
40T	Jim Gott	.10	.08	.04
41T	David Green	.10	.08	.04
42T	Alfredo Griffin	.15	.11	.06

		MT	NR MT	EX
43T	Ozzie Guillen	.80	.60	.30
44T	Eddie Haas	.10	.08	.04
45T	Terry Harper	.10	.08	.04
46T	Toby Harrah	.15	.11	.06
47T	Greg Harris	.10	.08	.04
48T	Ron Hassey	.10	.08	.04
49T	Rickey Henderson	1.00	.70	.40
50T	Steve Henderson	.10	.08	.04
51T	George Hendrick	.15	.11	.06
52T	Joe Hesketh	.25	.20	.10
53T	Teddy Higuera	2.50	2.00	1.00
54T	Donnie Hill	.10	.08	.04
55T	Al Holland	.10	.08	.04
56T	Burt Hooton	.15	.11	.06
57T	Jay Howell	.15	.11	.06
58T	Ken Howell	.15	.11	.06
59T	LaMarr Hoyt	.15	.11	.06
60T	Tim Hulett	.20	.15	.08
61T	Bob James	.10	.08	.04
62T	Steve Jeltz	.15	.11	.06
63T	Cliff Johnson	.10	.08	.04
64T	Howard Johnson	.90	.70	.35
65T	Ruppert Jones	.10	.08	.04
66T	Steve Kemp	.15	.11	.06
67T	Bruce Kison	.10	.08	.04
68T	Alan Knicely	.10	.08	.04
69T	Mike LaCoss	.15	.11	.06
70T	Lee Lacy	.15	.11	.06
71T	Dave LaPoint	.10	.08	.04
72T	Gary Lavelle	.10	.08	.04
73T	Vance Law	.15	.11	.06
74T	Johnnie LeMaster	.10	.08	.04
75T	Sixto Lezcano	.10	.08	.04
76T	Tim Lollar	.10	.08	.04
77T	Fred Lynn	.30	.25	.12
78T	Billy Martin	.20	.15	.08
79T	Ron Mathis	.15	.11	.06
80T	Len Matuszek	.10	.08	.04
81T	Gene Mauch	.15	.11	.06
82T	Oddibe McDowell	1.00	.70	.40
83T	Roger McDowell	.90	.70	.35
84T	John McNamara	.10	.08	.04
85T	Donnie Moore	.10	.08	.04
86T	Gene Nelson	.10	.08	.04
87T	Steve Nicosia	.10	.08	.04
88T	Al Oliver	.30	.25	.12
89T	Joe Orsulak	.25	.20	.10
90T	Rob Picciolo	.10	.08	.04
91T	Chris Pittaro	.15	.11	.06
92T	Jim Presley	2.00	1.50	.80
93T	Rick Reuschel	.20	.15	.08
94T	Bert Roberge	.10	.08	.04
95T	Bob Rodgers	.10	.08	.04
96T	Jerry Royster	.10	.08	.04
97T	Dave Rozema	.10	.08	.04
98T	Dave Rucker	.10	.08	.04
99T	Vern Ruhle	.10	.08	.04
100T	Paul Runge	.15	.11	.06
101T	Mark Salas	.20	.15	.08
102T	Luis Salazar	.10	.08	.04
103T	Joe Sambito	.10	.08	.04
104T	Rick Schu	.25	.20	.10
105T	Donnie Scott	.10	.08	.04
106T	Larry Sheets	1.25	.90	.50
107T	Don Slaught	.10	.08	.04
108T	Roy Smalley	.15	.11	.06
109T	Lonnie Smith	.15	.11	.06
110T	Nate Snell	.15	.11	.06
111T	Chris Speier	.10	.08	.04
112T	Mike Stenhouse	.10	.08	.04
113T	Tim Stoddard	.10	.08	.04
114T	Jim Sundberg	.15	.11	.06
115T	Bruce Sutter	.25	.20	.10
116T	Don Sutton	.60	.45	.25
117T	Kent Tekulve	.15	.11	.06
118T	Tom Tellmann	.10	.08	.04
119T	Walt Terrell	.15	.11	.06
120T	Mickey Tettleton	.15	.11	.06
121T	Derrel Thomas	.10	.08	.04
122T	Rich Thompson	.10	.08	.04
123T	Alex Trevino	.10	.08	.04
124T	John Tudor	.20	.15	.08
125T	Jose Uribe	.25	.20	.10
126T	Bobby Valentine	.10	.08	.04
127T	Dave Von Ohlen	.10	.08	.04
128T	U.L. Washington	.10	.08	.04
129T	Earl Weaver	.15	.11	.06
130T	Eddie Whitson	.10	.08	.04
131T	Herm Winningham	.20	.15	.08
132T	Checklist 1-132	.10	.08	.04

1986 Topps

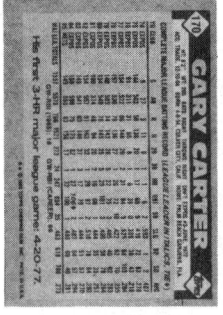

GARY CARTER

The 1986 Topps set consists of 792 cards. Fronts of the 2½'' by 3½'' cards feature color photos with the Topps logo in the upper right-hand corner while the player's position is in the lower left-hand corner. Above the picture is the team name, while below it is the player's name. The borders were a departure from previous practice, as the top ⅞'' was black, while the remainder was white. There are no card #s 51 and 171 in the set; the card that should have been #51, Bobby Wine, shares #57 with Bill Doran, while #171, Bob Rodgers, shares #141 with Chuck Cottier. Once again, a 5,000-set glossy-finish "Tiffany" edition was produced. Values are four to six times higher than the same card in the regular issue.

		MT	NR MT	EX
Complete Set:		28.00	21.00	11.00
Common Player:		.05	.04	.02
1	Pete Rose	.90	.70	.35
2	Rose Special 1963-66	.30	.25	.12
3	Rose Special 1967-70	.30	.25	.12
4	Rose Special 1971-74	.30	.25	.12
5	Rose Special 1975-78	.30	.25	.12
6	Rose Special 1979-82	.30	.25	.12
7	Rose Special 1983-85	.30	.25	.12
8	Dwayne Murphy	.07	.05	.03
9	Roy Smith	.05	.04	.02
10	Tony Gwynn	.40	.30	.15
11	Bob Ojeda	.10	.08	.04
12	Jose Uribe	.25	.20	.10
13	Bob Kearney	.05	.04	.02
14	Julio Cruz	.05	.04	.02
15	Eddie Whitson	.05	.04	.02
16	Rick Schu	.07	.05	.03
17	Mike Stenhouse	.05	.04	.02
18	Brent Gaff	.05	.04	.02
19	Rich Hebner	.05	.04	.02
20	Lou Whitaker	.20	.15	.08
21	George Bamberger	.05	.04	.02
22	Duane Walker	.05	.04	.02
23	Manny Lee	.15	.11	.06
24	Len Barker	.07	.05	.03
25	Willie Wilson	.12	.09	.05
26	Frank DiPino	.05	.04	.02
27	Ray Knight	.10	.08	.04
28	Eric Davis	4.00	3.00	1.50
29	Tony Phillips	.05	.04	.02
30	Eddie Murray	.40	.30	.15
31	Jamie Easterly	.05	.04	.02
32	Steve Yeager	.05	.04	.02
33	Jeff Lahti	.05	.04	.02
34	Ken Phelps	.12	.09	.05
35	Jeff Reardon	.15	.11	.06
36	Tigers Leaders (Lance Parrish)	.15	.11	.06
37	Mark Thurmond	.05	.04	.02
38	Glenn Hoffman	.05	.04	.02
39	Dave Rucker	.05	.04	.02
40	Ken Griffey	.10	.08	.04
41	Brad Wellman	.05	.04	.02
42	Geoff Zahn	.05	.04	.02
43	Dave Engle	.05	.04	.02
44	Lance McCullers	.20	.15	.08
45	Damaso Garcia	.07	.05	.03
46	Billy Hatcher	.25	.20	.10
47	Juan Berenguer	.05	.04	.02

		MT	NR MT	EX
48	Bill Almon	.05	.04	.02
49	Rick Manning	.05	.04	.02
50	Dan Quisenberry	.12	.09	.05
51	Not Issued			
52	Chris Welsh	.05	.04	.02
53	Len Dykstra	.70	.50	.30
54	John Franco	.10	.08	.04
55	Fred Lynn	.20	.15	.08
56	Tom Niedenfuer	.07	.05	.03
57a	Bobby Wine	.05	.04	.02
57b	Bill Doran	.10	.08	.04
58	Bill Krueger	.05	.04	.02
59	Andre Thornton	.07	.05	.03
60	Dwight Evans	.12	.09	.05
61	Karl Best	.07	.05	.03
62	Bob Boone	.07	.05	.03
63	Ron Roenicke	.05	.04	.02
64	Floyd Bannister	.10	.08	.04
65	Dan Driessen	.07	.05	.03
66	Cardinals Leaders (Bob Forsch)	.07	.05	.03
67	Carmelo Martinez	.07	.05	.03
68	Ed Lynch	.05	.04	.02
69	Luis Aguayo	.05	.04	.02
70	Dave Winfield	.30	.25	.12
71	Ken Schrom	.05	.04	.02
72	Shawon Dunston	.20	.15	.08
73	Randy O'Neal	.10	.08	.04
74	Rance Mulliniks	.05	.04	.02
75	Jose DeLeon	.07	.05	.03
76	Dion James	.12	.09	.05
77	Charlie Leibrandt	.07	.05	.03
78	Bruce Benedict	.05	.04	.02
79	Dave Schmidt	.07	.05	.03
80	Darryl Strawberry	.50	.40	.20
81	Gene Mauch	.07	.05	.03
82	Tippy Martinez	.05	.04	.02
83	Phil Garner	.07	.05	.03
84	Curt Young	.10	.08	.04
85	Tony Perez	.15	.11	.06
86	Tom Waddell	.05	.04	.02
87	Candy Maldonado	.10	.08	.04
88	Tom Nieto	.05	.04	.02
89	Randy St. Claire	.07	.05	.03
90	Garry Templeton	.10	.08	.04
91	Steve Crawford	.05	.04	.02
92	Al Cowens	.05	.04	.02
93	Scot Thompson	.05	.04	.02
94	Rick Bordi	.05	.04	.02
95	Ozzie Virgil	.07	.05	.03
96	Blue Jay Leaders (Jim Clancy)	.07	.05	.03
97	Gary Gaetti	.20	.15	.08
98	Dick Ruthven	.05	.04	.02
99	Buddy Biancalana	.05	.04	.02
100	Nolan Ryan	.30	.25	.12
101	Dave Bergman	.05	.04	.02
102	Joe Orsulak	.12	.09	.05
103	Luis Salazar	.05	.04	.02
104	Sid Fernandez	.12	.09	.05
105	Gary Ward	.07	.05	.03
106	Ray Burris	.05	.04	.02
107	Rafael Ramirez	.05	.04	.02
108	Ted Power	.07	.05	.03
109	Len Matuszek	.05	.04	.02
110	Scott McGregor	.07	.05	.03
111	Roger Craig	.07	.05	.03
112	Bill Campbell	.05	.04	.02
113	U.L. Washington	.05	.04	.02
114	Mike Brown	.05	.04	.02
115	Jay Howell	.07	.05	.03
116	Brook Jacoby	.10	.08	.04
117	Bruce Kison	.05	.04	.02
118	Jerry Royster	.05	.04	.02
119	Barry Bonnell	.05	.04	.02
120	Steve Carlton	.30	.25	.12
121	Nelson Simmons	.10	.08	.04
122	Pete Filson	.05	.04	.02
123	Greg Walker	.10	.08	.04
124	Luis Sanchez	.05	.04	.02
125	Dave Lopes	.07	.05	.03
126	Mets Leaders (Mookie Wilson)	.07	.05	.03
127	Jack Howell	.50	.40	.20
128	John Wathan	.07	.05	.03
129	Jeff Dedmon	.07	.05	.03
130	Alan Trammell	.30	.25	.12
131	Checklist 1-132	.05	.04	.02
132	Razor Shines	.05	.04	.02
133	Andy McGaffigan	.05	.04	.02
134	Carney Lansford	.07	.05	.03
135	Joe Niekro	.10	.08	.04
136	Mike Hargrove	.07	.05	.03
137	Charlie Moore	.05	.04	.02

		MT	NR MT	EX
138	Mark Davis	.05	.04	.02
139	Daryl Boston	.10	.08	.04
140	John Candelaria	.10	.08	.04
141a	Bob Rodgers	.05	.04	.02
141b	Chuck Cottier	.05	.04	.02
142	Bob Jones	.05	.04	.02
143	Dave Van Gorder	.05	.04	.02
144	Doug Sisk	.05	.04	.02
145	Pedro Guerrero	.20	.15	.08
146	Jack Perconte	.05	.04	.02
147	Larry Sheets	.30	.25	.12
148	Mike Heath	.05	.04	.02
149	Brett Butler	.07	.05	.03
150	Joaquin Andujar	.07	.05	.03
151	Dave Stapleton	.05	.04	.02
152	Mike Morgan	.05	.04	.02
153	Ricky Adams	.05	.04	.02
154	Bert Roberge	.05	.04	.02
155	Bob Grich	.10	.08	.04
156	White Sox Leaders (Richard Dotson)			
		.07	.05	.03
157	Ron Hassey	.05	.04	.02
158	Derrel Thomas	.05	.04	.02
159	Orel Hershiser	.35	.25	.14
160	Chet Lemon	.07	.05	.03
161	Lee Tunnell	.05	.04	.02
162	Greg Gagne	.20	.15	.08
163	Pete Ladd	.05	.04	.02
164	Steve Balboni	.07	.05	.03
165	Mike Davis	.07	.05	.03
166	Dickie Thon	.07	.05	.03
167	Zane Smith	.25	.20	.10
168	Jeff Burroughs	.07	.05	.03
169	George Wright	.05	.04	.02
170	Gary Carter	.30	.25	.12
171	Not Issued			
172	Jerry Reed	.10	.08	.04
173	Wayne Gross	.05	.04	.02
174	Brian Snyder	.05	.04	.02
175	Steve Sax	.15	.11	.06
176	Jay Tibbs	.05	.04	.02
177	Joel Youngblood	.05	.04	.02
178	Ivan DeJesus	.05	.04	.02
179	Stu Cliburn	.07	.05	.03
180	Don Mattingly	3.50	2.75	1.50
181	Al Nipper	.07	.05	.03
182	Bobby Brown	.05	.04	.02
183	Larry Andersen	.05	.04	.02
184	Tim Laudner	.05	.04	.02
185	Rollie Fingers	.20	.15	.08
186	Astros Leaders (Jose Cruz)	.07	.05	.03
187	Scott Fletcher	.07	.05	.03
188	Bob Dernier	.05	.04	.02
189	Mike Mason	.05	.04	.02
190	George Hendrick	.07	.05	.03
191	Wally Backman	.07	.05	.03
192	Milt Wilcox	.07	.05	.03
193	Daryl Sconiers	.05	.04	.02
194	Craig McMurtry	.05	.04	.02
195	Dave Concepcion	.12	.09	.05
196	Doyle Alexander	.10	.08	.04
197	Enos Cabell	.05	.04	.02
198	Ken Dixon	.07	.05	.03
199	Dick Howser	.07	.05	.03
200	Mike Schmidt	.40	.30	.15
201	Record Breaker (Vince Coleman)	.30	.25	.12
202	Record Breaker (Dwight Gooden)	.40	.30	.15
203	Record Breaker (Keith Hernandez)	.20	.15	.08
204	Record Breaker (Phil Niekro)	.15	.11	.06
205	Record Breaker (Tony Perez)	.10	.08	.04
206	Record Breaker (Pete Rose)	.40	.30	.15
207	Record Breaker (Fernando Valenzuela)			
		.20	.15	.08
208	Ramon Romero	.05	.04	.02
209	Randy Ready	.07	.05	.03
210	Calvin Schiraldi	.15	.11	.06
211	Ed Wojna	.10	.08	.04
212	Chris Speier	.05	.04	.02
213	Bob Shirley	.05	.04	.02
214	Randy Bush	.05	.04	.02
215	Frank White	.10	.08	.04
216	A's Leaders (Dwayne Murphy)	.07	.05	.03
217	Bill Scherrer	.05	.04	.02
218	Randy Hunt	.05	.04	.02
219	Dennis Lamp	.05	.04	.02
220	Bob Horner	.20	.15	.08
221	Dave Henderson	.05	.04	.02
222	Craig Gerber	.05	.04	.02
223	Atlee Hammaker	.05	.04	.02
224	Cesar Cedeno	.10	.08	.04
225	Ron Darling	.15	.11	.06

		MT	NR MT	EX
226	Lee Lacy	.07	.05	.03
227	Al Jones	.05	.04	.02
228	Tom Lawless	.05	.04	.02
229	Bill Gullickson	.07	.05	.03
230	Terry Kennedy	.07	.05	.03
231	Jim Frey	.05	.04	.02
232	Rick Rhoden	.10	.08	.04
233	Steve Lyons	.07	.05	.03
234	Doug Corbett	.05	.04	.02
235	Butch Wynegar	.07	.05	.03
236	Frank Eufemia	.05	.04	.02
237	Ted Simmons	.12	.09	.05
238	Larry Parrish	.10	.08	.04
239	Joel Skinner	.05	.04	.02
240	Tommy John	.20	.15	.08
241	Tony Fernandez	.20	.15	.08
242	Rich Thompson	.05	.04	.02
243	Johnny Grubb	.05	.04	.02
244	Craig Lefferts	.05	.04	.02
245	Jim Sundberg	.07	.05	.03
246	Phillies Leaders (Steve Carlton)	.15	.11	.06
247	Terry Harper	.05	.04	.02
248	Spike Owen	.05	.04	.02
249	Rob Deer	.50	.40	.20
250	Dwight Gooden	2.00	1.50	.80
251	Rich Dauer	.05	.04	.02
252	Bobby Castillo	.05	.04	.02
253	Dann Bilardello	.05	.04	.02
254	Ozzie Guillen	.40	.30	.15
255	Tony Armas	.07	.05	.03
256	Kurt Kepshire	.05	.04	.02
257	Doug DeCinces	.10	.08	.04
258	Tim Burke	.30	.25	.12
259	Dan Pasqua	.50	.40	.20
260	Tony Pena	.10	.08	.04
261	Bobby Valentine	.05	.04	.02
262	Mario Ramirez	.05	.04	.02
263	Checklist 133-264	.05	.04	.02
264	Darren Daulton	.15	.11	.06
265	Ron Davis	.05	.04	.02
266	Keith Moreland	.07	.05	.03
267	Paul Molitor	.15	.11	.06
268	Mike Scott	.15	.11	.06
269	Dane Iorg	.05	.04	.02
270	Jack Morris	.20	.15	.08
271	Dave Collins	.07	.05	.03
272	Tim Tolman	.07	.05	.03
273	Jerry Willard	.05	.04	.02
274	Ron Gardenhire	.05	.04	.02
275	Charlie Hough	.10	.08	.04
276	Yankees Leaders (Willie Randolph)	.10	.08	.04
277	Jaime Cocanower	.05	.04	.02
278	Sixto Lezcano	.05	.04	.02
279	Al Pardo	.05	.04	.02
280	Tim Raines	.30	.25	.12
281	Steve Mura	.05	.04	.02
282	Jerry Mumphrey	.07	.05	.03
283	Mike Fischlin	.05	.04	.02
284	Brian Dayett	.05	.04	.02
285	Buddy Bell	.10	.08	.04
286	Luis DeLeon	.05	.04	.02
287	John Christensen	.10	.08	.04
288	Don Aase	.07	.05	.03
289	Johnnie LeMaster	.05	.04	.02
290	Carlton Fisk	.20	.15	.08
291	Tom Lasorda	.07	.05	.03
292	Chuck Porter	.05	.04	.02
293	Chris Chambliss	.07	.05	.03
294	Danny Cox	.10	.08	.04
295	Kirk Gibson	.25	.20	.10
296	Geno Petralli	.10	.08	.04
297	Tim Lollar	.05	.04	.02
298	Craig Reynolds	.05	.04	.02
299	Bryn Smith	.07	.05	.03
300	George Brett	.50	.40	.20
301	Dennis Rasmussen	.07	.05	.03
302	Greg Gross	.05	.04	.02
303	Curt Wardle	.05	.04	.02
304	Mike Gallego	.10	.08	.04
305	Phil Bradley	.20	.15	.08
306	Padres Leaders (Terry Kennedy)	.07	.05	.03
307	Dave Sax	.05	.04	.02
308	Ray Fontenot	.05	.04	.02
309	John Shelby	.07	.05	.03
310	Greg Minton	.05	.04	.02
311	Dick Schofield	.05	.04	.02
312	Tom Filer	.05	.04	.02
313	Joe DeSa	.05	.04	.02
314	Frank Pastore	.05	.04	.02
315	Mookie Wilson	.10	.08	.04
316	Sammy Khalifa	.07	.05	.03

#	Player	MT	NR MT	EX
317	Ed Romero	.05	.04	.02
318	Terry Whitfield	.05	.04	.02
319	Rick Camp	.05	.04	.02
320	Jim Rice	.30	.25	.12
321	Earl Weaver	.07	.05	.03
322	Bob Forsch	.07	.05	.03
323	Jerry Davis	.05	.04	.02
324	Dan Schatzeder	.05	.04	.02
325	Juan Beniquez	.05	.04	.02
326	Kent Tekulve	.07	.05	.03
327	Mike Pagliarulo	.25	.20	.10
328	Pete O'Brien	.10	.08	.04
329	Kirby Puckett	1.25	.90	.50
330	Rick Sutcliffe	.12	.09	.05
331	Alan Ashby	.05	.04	.02
332	Darryl Motley	.05	.04	.02
333	Tom Henke	.15	.11	.06
334	Ken Oberkfell	.07	.05	.03
335	Don Sutton	.25	.20	.10
336	Indians Leaders (Andre Thornton)	.07	.05	.03
337	Darnell Coles	.07	.05	.03
338	Jorge Bell	.35	.25	.14
339	Bruce Berenyi	.05	.04	.02
340	Cal Ripken	.40	.30	.15
341	Frank Williams	.07	.05	.03
342	Gary Redus	.07	.05	.03
343	Carlos Diaz	.05	.04	.02
344	Jim Wohlford	.05	.04	.02
345	Donnie Moore	.05	.04	.02
346	Bryan Little	.05	.04	.02
347	Teddy Higuera	1.25	.90	.50
348	Cliff Johnson	.05	.04	.02
349	Mark Clear	.07	.05	.03
350	Jack Clark	.20	.15	.08
351	Chuck Tanner	.07	.05	.03
352	Harry Spilman	.05	.04	.02
353	Keith Atherton	.05	.04	.02
354	Tony Bernazard	.07	.05	.03
355	Lee Smith	.10	.08	.04
356	Mickey Hatcher	.05	.04	.02
357	Ed Vande Berg	.05	.04	.02
358	Rick Dempsey	.07	.05	.03
359	Mike LaCoss	.07	.05	.03
360	Lloyd Moseby	.10	.08	.04
361	Shane Rawley	.10	.08	.04
362	Tom Paciorek	.05	.04	.02
363	Terry Forster	.07	.05	.03
364	Reid Nichols	.05	.04	.02
365	Mike Flanagan	.10	.08	.04
366	Reds Leaders (Dave Concepcion)	.07	.05	.03
367	Aurelio Lopez	.05	.04	.02
368	Greg Brock	.10	.08	.04
369	Al Holland	.05	.04	.02
370	Vince Coleman	1.75	1.25	.70
371	Bill Stein	.05	.04	.02
372	Ben Oglivie	.07	.05	.03
373	Urbano Lugo	.07	.05	.03
374	Terry Francona	.05	.04	.02
375	Rich Gedman	.10	.08	.04
376	Bill Dawley	.05	.04	.02
377	Joe Carter	.20	.15	.08
378	Bruce Bochte	.05	.04	.02
379	Bobby Meacham	.05	.04	.02
380	LaMarr Hoyt	.07	.05	.03
381	Ray Miller	.05	.04	.02
382	Ivan Calderon	.50	.40	.20
383	Chris Brown	.80	.60	.30
384	Steve Trout	.07	.05	.03
385	Cecil Cooper	.12	.09	.05
386	Cecil Fielder	.20	.15	.08
387	Steve Kemp	.07	.05	.03
388	Dickie Noles	.05	.04	.02
389	Glenn Davis	1.25	.90	.50
390	Tom Seaver	.30	.25	.12
391	Julio Franco	.10	.08	.04
392	John Russell	.07	.05	.03
393	Chris Pittaro	.12	.09	.05
394	Checklist 265-396	.05	.04	.02
395	Scott Garrelts	.07	.05	.03
396	Red Sox Leaders (Dwight Evans)	.10	.08	.04
397	Steve Buechele	.20	.15	.08
398	Earnie Riles	.30	.25	.12
399	Bill Swift	.07	.05	.03
400	Rod Carew	.30	.25	.12
401	Turn Back The Clock (Fernando Valenzuela)	.15	.11	.06
402	Turn Back The Clock (Tom Seaver)	.15	.11	.06
403	Turn Back The Clock (Willie Mays)	.20	.15	.08
404	Turn Back The Clock (Frank Robinson)	.15	.11	.06
405	Turn Back The Clock (Roger Maris)	.20	.15	.08
406	Scott Sanderson	.07	.05	.03
407	Sal Butera	.05	.04	.02
408	Dave Smith	.07	.05	.03
409	Paul Runge	.07	.05	.03
410	Dave Kingman	.15	.11	.06
411	Sparky Anderson	.07	.05	.03
412	Jim Clancy	.10	.08	.04
413	Tim Flannery	.05	.04	.02
414	Tom Gorman	.05	.04	.02
415	Hal McRae	.10	.08	.04
416	Denny Martinez	.05	.04	.02
417	R.J. Reynolds	.10	.08	.04
418	Alan Knicely	.05	.04	.02
419	Frank Wills	.05	.04	.02
420	Von Hayes	.12	.09	.05
421	Dave Palmer	.07	.05	.03
422	Mike Jorgensen	.05	.04	.02
423	Dan Spillner	.05	.04	.02
424	Rick Miller	.05	.04	.02
425	Larry McWilliams	.05	.04	.02
426	Brewers Leaders (Charlie Moore)	.07	.05	.03
427	Joe Cowley	.05	.04	.02
428	Max Venable	.05	.04	.02
429	Greg Booker	.05	.04	.02
430	Kent Hrbek	.20	.15	.08
431	George Frazier	.05	.04	.02
432	Mark Bailey	.05	.04	.02
433	Chris Codiroli	.05	.04	.02
434	Curt Wilkerson	.05	.04	.02
435	Bill Caudill	.05	.04	.02
436	Doug Flynn	.05	.04	.02
437	Rick Mahler	.05	.04	.02
438	Clint Hurdle	.05	.04	.02
439	Rick Honeycutt	.07	.05	.03
440	Alvin Davis	.20	.15	.08
441	Whitey Herzog	.07	.05	.03
442	Ron Robinson	.12	.09	.05
443	Bill Buckner	.10	.08	.04
444	Alex Trevino	.05	.04	.02
445	Bert Blyleven	.15	.11	.06
446	Lenn Sakata	.05	.04	.02
447	Jerry Don Gleaton	.05	.04	.02
448	Herm Winningham	.20	.15	.08
449	Rod Scurry	.05	.04	.02
450	Graig Nettles	.15	.11	.06
451	Mark Brown	.05	.04	.02
452	Bob Clark	.05	.04	.02
453	Steve Jeltz	.07	.05	.03
454	Burt Hooton	.07	.05	.03
455	Willie Randolph	.10	.08	.04
456	Braves Leaders (Dale Murphy)	.25	.20	.10
457	Mickey Tettleton	.10	.08	.04
458	Kevin Bass	.10	.08	.04
459	Luis Leal	.05	.04	.02
460	Leon Durham	.10	.08	.04
461	Walt Terrell	.07	.05	.03
462	Domingo Ramos	.05	.04	.02
463	Jim Gott	.05	.04	.02
464	Ruppert Jones	.05	.04	.02
465	Jesse Orosco	.07	.05	.03
466	Tom Foley	.05	.04	.02
467	Bob James	.05	.04	.02
468	Mike Scioscia	.05	.04	.02
469	Storm Davis	.05	.04	.02
470	Bill Madlock	.12	.09	.05
471	Bobby Cox	.05	.04	.02
472	Joe Hesketh	.10	.08	.04
473	Mark Brouhard	.05	.04	.02
474	John Tudor	.10	.08	.04
475	Juan Samuel	.12	.09	.05
476	Ron Mathis	.10	.08	.04
477	Mike Easler	.07	.05	.03
478	Andy Hawkins	.05	.04	.02
479	Bob Melvin	.12	.09	.05
480	Oddibe McDowell	.40	.30	.15
481	Scott Bradley	.10	.08	.04
482	Rick Lysander	.05	.04	.02
483	George Vukovich	.05	.04	.02
484	Donnie Hill	.05	.04	.02
485	Gary Matthews	.10	.08	.04
486	Angels Leaders (Bob Grich)	.07	.05	.03
487	Bret Saberhagen	.50	.40	.20
488	Lou Thornton	.12	.09	.05
489	Jim Winn	.05	.04	.02
490	Jeff Leonard	.10	.08	.04
491	Pascual Perez	.07	.05	.03
492	Kelvin Chapman	.05	.04	.02
493	Gene Nelson	.05	.04	.02
494	Gary Roenicke	.05	.04	.02
495	Mark Langston	.12	.09	.05
496	Jay Johnstone	.07	.05	.03

#	Player	MT	NR MT	EX
497	John Stuper	.05	.04	.02
498	Tito Landrum	.05	.04	.02
499	Bob Gibson	.05	.04	.02
500	Rickey Henderson	.40	.30	.15
501	Dave Johnson	.07	.05	.03
502	Glen Cook	.07	.05	.03
503	Mike Fitzgerald	.05	.04	.02
504	Denny Walling	.05	.04	.02
505	Jerry Koosman	.10	.08	.04
506	Bill Russell	.07	.05	.03
507	Steve Ontiveros	.20	.15	.08
508	Alan Wiggins	.05	.04	.02
509	Ernie Camacho	.05	.04	.02
510	Wade Boggs	2.25	1.75	.90
511	Ed Nunez	.05	.04	.02
512	Thad Bosley	.05	.04	.02
513	Ron Washington	.05	.04	.02
514	Mike Jones	.05	.04	.02
515	Darrell Evans	.12	.09	.05
516	Giants Leaders (Greg Minton)	.07	.05	.03
517	Milt Thompson	.40	.30	.15
518	Buck Martinez	.05	.04	.02
519	Danny Darwin	.07	.05	.03
520	Keith Hernandez	.30	.25	.12
521	Nate Snell	.07	.05	.03
522	Bob Bailor	.05	.04	.02
523	Joe Price	.05	.04	.02
524	Darrell Miller	.10	.08	.04
525	Marvell Wynne	.05	.04	.02
526	Charlie Lea	.05	.04	.02
527	Checklist 397-528	.05	.04	.02
528	Terry Pendleton	.15	.11	.06
529	Marc Sullivan	.10	.08	.04
530	Rich Gossage	.20	.15	.08
531	Tony LaRussa	.07	.05	.03
532	Don Carman	.30	.25	.12
533	Billy Sample	.05	.04	.02
534	Jeff Calhoun	.05	.04	.02
535	Toby Harrah	.07	.05	.03
536	Jose Rijo	.07	.05	.03
537	Mark Salas	.07	.05	.03
538	Dennis Eckersley	.07	.05	.03
539	Glenn Hubbard	.05	.04	.02
540	Dan Petry	.10	.08	.04
541	Jorge Orta	.05	.04	.02
542	Don Schulze	.05	.04	.02
543	Jerry Narron	.05	.04	.02
544	Eddie Milner	.05	.04	.02
545	Jimmy Key	.15	.11	.06
546	Mariners Leaders (Dave Henderson)	.07	.05	.03
547	Roger McDowell	.40	.30	.15
548	Mike Young	.07	.05	.03
549	Bob Welch	.10	.08	.04
550	Tom Herr	.10	.08	.04
551	Dave LaPoint	.05	.04	.02
552	Marc Hill	.05	.04	.02
553	Jim Morrison	.05	.04	.02
554	Paul Householder	.05	.04	.02
555	Hubie Brooks	.10	.08	.04
556	John Denny	.05	.04	.02
557	Gerald Perry	.07	.05	.03
558	Tim Stoddard	.05	.04	.02
559	Tommy Dunbar	.05	.04	.02
560	Dave Righetti	.20	.15	.08
561	Bob Lillis	.05	.04	.02
562	Joe Beckwith	.05	.04	.02
563	Alejandro Sanchez	.05	.04	.02
564	Warren Brusstar	.05	.04	.02
565	Tom Brunansky	.12	.09	.05
566	Alfredo Griffin	.07	.05	.03
567	Jeff Barkley	.05	.04	.02
568	Donnie Scott	.05	.04	.02
569	Jim Acker	.05	.04	.02
570	Rusty Staub	.10	.08	.04
571	Mike Jeffcoat	.05	.04	.02
572	Paul Zuvella	.05	.04	.02
573	Tom Hume	.05	.04	.02
574	Ron Kittle	.10	.08	.04
575	Mike Boddicker	.10	.08	.04
576	Expos Leaders (Andre Dawson)	.12	.09	.05
577	Jerry Reuss	.07	.05	.03
578	Lee Mazzilli	.07	.05	.03
579	Jim Slaton	.05	.04	.02
580	Willie McGee	.15	.11	.06
581	Bruce Hurst	.10	.08	.04
582	Jim Gantner	.07	.05	.03
583	Al Bumbry	.05	.04	.02
584	Brian Fisher	.35	.25	.14
585	Garry Maddox	.07	.05	.03
586	Greg Harris	.05	.04	.02
587	Rafael Santana	.05	.04	.02
588	Steve Lake	.05	.04	.02
589	Sid Bream	.10	.08	.04
590	Bob Knepper	.07	.05	.03
591	Jackie Moore	.05	.04	.02
592	Frank Tanana	.10	.08	.04
593	Jesse Barfield	.25	.20	.10
594	Chris Bando	.05	.04	.02
595	Dave Parker	.20	.15	.08
596	Onix Concepcion	.05	.04	.02
597	Sammy Stewart	.05	.04	.02
598	Jim Presley	.40	.30	.15
599	Rick Aguilera	.35	.25	.14
600	Dale Murphy	.50	.40	.20
601	Gary Lucas	.05	.04	.02
602	Mariano Duncan	.20	.15	.08
603	Bill Laskey	.05	.04	.02
604	Gary Pettis	.07	.05	.03
605	Dennis Boyd	.07	.05	.03
606	Royals Leaders (Hal McRae)	.07	.05	.03
607	Ken Dayley	.05	.04	.02
608	Bruce Bochy	.05	.04	.02
609	Barbaro Garbey	.05	.04	.02
610	Ron Guidry	.20	.15	.08
611	Gary Woods	.05	.04	.02
612	Richard Dotson	.10	.08	.04
613	Roy Smalley	.05	.04	.02
614	Rick Waits	.05	.04	.02
615	Johnny Ray	.10	.08	.04
616	Glenn Brummer	.05	.04	.02
617	Lonnie Smith	.07	.05	.03
618	Jim Pankovits	.05	.04	.02
619	Danny Heep	.05	.04	.02
620	Bruce Sutter	.12	.09	.05
621	John Felske	.05	.04	.02
622	Gary Lavelle	.05	.04	.02
623	Floyd Rayford	.05	.04	.02
624	Steve McCatty	.05	.04	.02
625	Bob Brenly	.05	.04	.02
626	Roy Thomas	.05	.04	.02
627	Ron Oester	.05	.04	.02
628	Kirk McCaskill	.35	.25	.14
629	Mitch Webster	.40	.30	.15
630	Fernando Valenzuela	.30	.25	.12
631	Steve Braun	.05	.04	.02
632	Dave Von Ohlen	.05	.04	.02
633	Jackie Gutierrez	.05	.04	.02
634	Roy Lee Jackson	.05	.04	.02
635	Jason Thompson	.05	.04	.02
636	Cubs Leaders (Lee Smith)	.07	.05	.03
637	Rudy Law	.05	.04	.02
638	John Butcher	.05	.04	.02
639	Bo Diaz	.07	.05	.03
640	Jose Cruz	.10	.08	.04
641	Wayne Tolleson	.05	.04	.02
642	Ray Searage	.05	.04	.02
643	Tom Brookens	.05	.04	.02
644	Mark Gubicza	.07	.05	.03
645	Dusty Baker	.07	.05	.03
646	Mike Moore	.05	.04	.02
647	Mel Hall	.07	.05	.03
648	Steve Bedrosian	.12	.09	.05
649	Ronn Reynolds	.10	.08	.04
650	Dave Stieb	.12	.09	.05
651	Billy Martin	.12	.09	.05
652	Tom Browning	.12	.09	.05
653	Jim Dwyer	.05	.04	.02
654	Ken Howell	.07	.05	.03
655	Manny Trillo	.07	.05	.03
656	Brian Harper	.05	.04	.02
657	Juan Agosto	.05	.04	.02
658	Rob Wilfong	.05	.04	.02
659	Checklist 529-660	.05	.04	.02
660	Steve Garvey	.30	.25	.12
661	Roger Clemens	3.00	2.25	1.25
662	Bill Schroeder	.05	.04	.02
663	Neil Allen	.05	.04	.02
664	Tim Corcoran	.05	.04	.02
665	Alejandro Pena	.05	.04	.02
666	Rangers Leaders (Charlie Hough)	.07	.05	.03
667	Tim Teufel	.07	.05	.03
668	Cecilio Guante	.05	.04	.02
669	Ron Cey	.10	.08	.04
670	Willie Hernandez	.07	.05	.03
671	Lynn Jones	.05	.04	.02
672	Rob Picciolo	.05	.04	.02
673	Ernie Whitt	.07	.05	.03
674	Pat Tabler	.07	.05	.03
675	Claudell Washington	.07	.05	.03
676	Matt Young	.05	.04	.02
677	Nick Esasky	.05	.04	.02

		MT	NR MT	EX
678	Dan Gladden	.10	.08	.04
679	Britt Burns	.05	.04	.02
680	George Foster	.15	.11	.06
681	Dick Williams	.07	.05	.03
682	Junior Ortiz	.05	.04	.02
683	Andy Van Slyke	.10	.08	.04
684	Bob McClure	.05	.04	.02
685	Tim Wallach	.12	.09	.05
686	Jeff Stone	.07	.05	.03
687	Mike Trujillo	.12	.09	.05
688	Larry Herndon	.07	.05	.03
689	Dave Stewart	.10	.08	.04
690	Ryne Sandberg	.30	.25	.12
691	Mike Madden	.05	.04	.02
692	Dale Berra	.05	.04	.02
693	Tom Tellmann	.05	.04	.02
694	Garth Iorg	.05	.04	.02
695	Mike Smithson	.05	.04	.02
696	Dodgers Leaders (Bill Russell)	.07	.05	.03
697	Bud Black	.05	.04	.02
698	Brad Komminsk	.05	.04	.02
699	Pat Corrales	.05	.04	.02
700	Reggie Jackson	.35	.25	.14
701	Keith Hernandez AS	.15	.11	.06
702	Tom Herr AS	.07	.05	.03
703	Tim Wallach AS	.10	.08	.04
704	Ozzie Smith AS	.10	.08	.04
705	Dale Murphy AS	.30	.25	.12
706	Pedro Guerrero AS	.12	.09	.05
707	Willie McGee AS	.12	.09	.05
708	Gary Carter AS	.20	.15	.08
709	Dwight Gooden AS	.40	.30	.15
710	John Tudor AS	.07	.05	.03
711	Jeff Reardon AS	.10	.08	.04
712	Don Mattingly AS	.90	.70	.35
713	Damaso Garcia AS	.07	.05	.03
714	George Brett AS	.30	.25	.12
715	Cal Ripken AS	.25	.20	.10
716	Rickey Henderson AS	.25	.20	.10
717	Dave Winfield AS	.20	.15	.08
718	Jorge Bell AS	.20	.15	.08
719	Carlton Fisk AS	.12	.09	.05
720	Bret Saberhagen AS	.20	.15	.08
721	Ron Guidry AS	.12	.09	.05
722	Dan Quisenberry AS	.10	.08	.04
723	Marty Bystrom	.05	.04	.02
724	Tim Hulett	.07	.05	.03
725	Mario Soto	.07	.05	.03
726	Orioles Leaders (Rick Dempsey)	.07	.05	.03
727	David Green	.05	.04	.02
728	Mike Marshall	.10	.08	.04
729	Jim Beattie	.05	.04	.02
730	Ozzie Smith	.15	.11	.06
731	Don Robinson	.07	.05	.03
732	Floyd Youmans	.60	.45	.25
733	Ron Romanick	.05	.04	.02
734	Marty Barrett	.10	.08	.04
735	Dave Dravecky	.07	.05	.03
736	Glenn Wilson	.10	.08	.04
737	Pete Vuckovich	.07	.05	.03
738	Andre Robertson	.05	.04	.02
739	Dave Rozema	.05	.04	.02
740	Lance Parrish	.20	.15	.08
741	Pete Rose	.40	.30	.15
742	Frank Viola	.12	.09	.05
743	Pat Sheridan	.05	.04	.02
744	Lary Sorensen	.05	.04	.02
745	Willie Upshaw	.07	.05	.03
746	Denny Gonzalez	.05	.04	.02
747	Rick Cerone	.05	.04	.02
748	Steve Henderson	.05	.04	.02
749	Ed Jurak	.05	.04	.02
750	Gorman Thomas	.10	.08	.04
751	Howard Johnson	.12	.09	.05
752	Mike Krukow	.07	.05	.03
753	Dan Ford	.05	.04	.02
754	Pat Clements	.15	.11	.06
755	Harold Baines	.15	.11	.06
756	Pirates Leaders (Rick Rhoden)	.07	.05	.03
757	Darrell Porter	.07	.05	.03
758	Dave Anderson	.05	.04	.02
759	Moose Haas	.05	.04	.02
760	Andre Dawson	.20	.15	.08
761	Don Slaught	.05	.04	.02
762	Eric Show	.05	.04	.02
763	Terry Puhl	.05	.04	.02
764	Kevin Gross	.07	.05	.03
765	Don Baylor	.12	.09	.05
766	Rick Langford	.05	.04	.02
767	Jody Davis	.10	.08	.04
768	Vern Ruhle	.05	.04	.02

		MT	NR MT	EX
769	Harold Reynolds	.30	.25	.12
770	Vida Blue	.10	.08	.04
771	John McNamara	.05	.04	.02
772	Brian Downing	.07	.05	.03
773	Greg Pryor	.05	.04	.02
774	Terry Leach	.07	.05	.03
775	Al Oliver	.10	.08	.04
776	Gene Garber	.05	.04	.02
777	Wayne Krenchicki	.05	.04	.02
778	Jerry Hairston	.05	.04	.02
779	Rick Reuschel	.10	.08	.04
780	Robin Yount	.30	.25	.12
781	Joe Nolan	.05	.04	.02
782	Ken Landreaux	.07	.05	.03
783	Ricky Horton	.07	.05	.03
784	Alan Bannister	.05	.04	.02
785	Bob Stanley	.07	.05	.03
786	Twins Leaders (Mickey Hatcher)	.07	.05	.03
787	Vance Law	.07	.05	.03
788	Marty Castillo	.05	.04	.02
789	Kurt Bevacqua	.05	.04	.02
790	Phil Niekro	.25	.20	.10
791	Checklist 661-792	.05	.04	.02
792	Charles Hudson	.07	.05	.03

1986 Topps All-Star Glossy
Set of 22

As in previous years, Topps continued to make the popular glossy surfaced cards as an insert in rak-paks. The All-Star Glossy set of 22 2½'' by 3½'' cards shows little design change from previous years. Cards feature a front color photo and All-Star banner at the top. The bottom has the player's name and position. The set included the All-Star starting teams as well as the managers and honorary captains.

		MT	NR MT	EX
Complete Set:		6.00	4.50	2.50
Common Player:		.20	.15	.08
1	Sparky Anderson	.20	.15	.08
2	Eddie Murray	.50	.40	.20
3	Lou Whitaker	.30	.25	.12
4	George Brett	.80	.60	.30
5	Cal Ripken	.60	.45	.25
6	Jim Rice	.50	.40	.20
7	Rickey Henderson	.60	.45	.25
8	Dave Winfield	.50	.40	.20
9	Carlton Fisk	.30	.25	.12
10	Jack Morris	.30	.25	.12
11	A.L. All-Star Team	.20	.15	.08
12	Dick Williams	.20	.15	.08
13	Steve Garvey	.50	.40	.20
14	Tom Herr	.25	.20	.10
15	Graig Nettles	.25	.20	.10
16	Ozzie Smith	.25	.20	.10
17	Tony Gwynn	.60	.45	.25
18	Dale Murphy	.90	.70	.35
19	Darryl Strawberry	.60	.45	.25
20	Terry Kennedy	.20	.15	.08
21	LaMarr Hoyt	.20	.15	.08
22	N.L. All-Star Team	.20	.15	.08

1986 Topps All-Star Glossy Set of 60

		MT	NR MT	EX
45	Nolan Ryan	.50	.40	.20
46	Ozzie Smith	.25	.20	.10
47	Jorge Bell	.50	.40	.20
48	Gorman Thomas	.15	.11	.06
49	Tom Browning	.20	.15	.08
50	Larry Sheets	.30	.25	.12
51	Pete Rose	1.25	.90	.50
52	Brett Butler	.15	.11	.06
53	John Tudor	.20	.15	.08
54	Phil Bradley	.35	.25	.14
55	Jeff Reardon	.20	.15	.08
56	Rich Gossage	.25	.20	.10
57	Tony Gwynn	.60	.45	.25
58	Ozzie Guillen	.25	.20	.10
59	Glenn Davis	.35	.25	.14
60	Darrell Evans	.20	.15	.08

The Topps All-Star & Hot Prospects Glossy Set of 60 cards represents an expansion of a good idea. The 2½'' by 3½'' cards had a good following when they were limited to stars, but Topps realized that the addition of top young players would spice up the set even further, so in 1986 it was expanded from 40 to 60 cards. The cards themselves are basically all color glossy picture with the player's name in very small print in the lower left-hand corner. To obtain the set you needed to send $1 plus six special offer cards from wax packs to Topps for each series. At 60 cards, that meant the process had to be repeated six times as there were 10 cards in each series, making the set quite expensive from the outset.

		MT	NR MT	EX
Complete Set:		15.00	11.00	6.00
Common Player:		.15	.11	.06
1	Oddibe McDowell	.35	.25	.14
2	Reggie Jackson	.70	.50	.30
3	Fernando Valenzuela	.35	.25	.14
4	Jack Clark	.25	.20	.10
5	Rickey Henderson	.70	.50	.30
6	Steve Balboni	.15	.11	.06
7	Keith Hernandez	.40	.30	.15
8	Lance Parrish	.30	.25	.12
9	Willie McGee	.25	.20	.10
10	Chris Brown	.40	.30	.15
11	Darryl Strawberry	.70	.50	.30
12	Ron Guidry	.30	.25	.12
13	Dave Parker	.25	.20	.10
14	Cal Ripken	.70	.50	.30
15	Tim Raines	.50	.40	.20
16	Rod Carew	.60	.45	.25
17	Mike Schmidt	.90	.70	.35
18	George Brett	.90	.70	.35
19	Joe Hesketh	.15	.11	.06
20	Dan Pasqua	.25	.20	.10
21	Vince Coleman	1.00	.70	.40
22	Tom Seaver	.50	.40	.20
23	Gary Carter	.50	.40	.20
24	Orel Hershiser	.30	.25	.12
25	Pedro Guerrero	.30	.25	.12
26	Wade Boggs	1.25	.90	.50
27	Bret Saberhagen	.35	.25	.14
28	Carlton Fisk	.25	.20	.10
29	Kirk Gibson	.35	.25	.14
30	Brian Fisher	.20	.15	.08
31	Don Mattingly	3.00	2.25	1.25
32	Tom Herr	.20	.15	.08
33	Eddie Murray	.70	.50	.30
34	Ryne Sandberg	.40	.30	.15
35	Dan Quisenberry	.20	.15	.08
36	Jim Rice	.50	.40	.20
37	Dale Murphy	.90	.70	.35
38	Steve Garvey	.50	.40	.20
39	Roger McDowell	.30	.25	.12
40	Earnie Riles	.20	.15	.08
41	Dwight Gooden	1.25	.90	.50
42	Dave Winfield	.50	.40	.20
43	Dave Stieb	.20	.15	.08
44	Bob Horner	.25	.20	.10

1986 Topps Box Panels

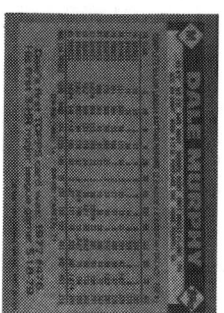

Following the lead of Donruss which introduced the concept in 1985, Topps produced special cards on the bottom panels of wax boxes. Individual cards measure 2½'' by 3½'', the same as regular cards. Design of the cards is virtually identical with regular '86 Topps, though the top border is in red, rather than black. The cards are lettered ''A'' through ''P,'' rather than numbered on the back.

		MT	NR MT	EX
Complete Panel Set:		12.00	9.00	4.75
Complete Singles Set:		4.75	3.50	2.00
Common Panel:		2.00	1.50	.80
Common Single Player:		.15	.11	.06
Panel		3.50	2.75	1.50
A	Jorge Bell	.25	.20	.10
B	Wade Boggs	.50	.40	.20
C	George Brett	.35	.25	.14
D	Vince Coleman	.35	.25	.14
Panel		2.00	1.50	.80
E	Carlton Fisk	.15	.11	.06
F	Dwight Gooden	.40	.30	.15
G	Pedro Guerrero	.15	.11	.06
H	Ron Guidry	.15	.11	.06
Panel		3.50	2.75	1.50
I	Reggie Jackson	.30	.25	.12
J	Don Mattingly	.80	.60	.30
K	Oddibe McDowell	.20	.15	.08
L	Willie McGee	.15	.11	.06
Panel		3.00	2.25	1.25
M	Dale Murphy	.35	.25	.14
N	Pete Rose	.50	.40	.20
O	Bret Saberhagen	.15	.11	.06
P	Fernando Valenzuela	.25	.20	.10

1986 Topps Gallery of Champions

While Topps had experimented in previous years with miniature metal versions of its past and current cards as a dealer-ordering incentive, 1986 saw the expansion of the idea to a full set of 12 tops stars,

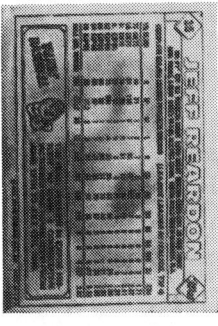

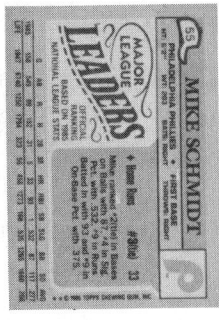

MIKE SCHMIDT

minted 1/4-size (approximately 1¼'' by 1¾'') in silver, aluminum and bronze. The metallic cards faithfully capture much of the details of the originals, but have not caught on well with collectors.

	MT	NR MT	EX
Complete Aluminum Set:	25.00	18.50	10.00
Complete Bronze Set:	150.00	112.00	60.00
Complete Silver Set:	600.00	450.00	240.00
(1a) Wade Boggs (aluminum)	2.00	1.50	.80
(1b) Wade Boggs (bronze)	20.00	15.00	8.00
(1c) Wade Boggs (silver)	100.00	75.00	40.00
(2a) Vince Coleman (aluminum)	1.25	.90	.50
(2b) Vince Coleman (bronze)	12.00	9.00	4.75
(2c) Vince Coleman (silver)	50.00	37.00	20.00
(3a) Darrell Evans (aluminum)	.70	.50	.30
(3b) Darrell Evans (bronze)	7.50	5.75	3.00
(3c) Darrell Evans (silver)	20.00	15.00	8.00
(4a) Dwight Gooden (aluminum)	2.00	1.50	.80
(4b) Dwight Gooden (bronze)	20.00	15.00	8.00
(4c) Dwight Gooden (silver)	100.00	75.00	40.00
(5a) Ozzie Guillen (aluminum)	.70	.50	.30
(5b) Ozzie Guillen (bronze)	7.50	5.75	3.00
(5c) Ozzie Guillen (silver)	20.00	15.00	8.00
(6a) Don Mattingly (aluminum)	5.00	3.75	2.00
(6b) Don Mattingly (bronze)	35.00	26.00	14.00
(6c) Don Mattingly (silver)	150.00	112.00	60.00
(7a) Willie McGee (aluminum)	1.00	.70	.40
(7b) Willie McGee (bronze)	10.00	7.50	4.00
(7c) Willie McGee (silver)	30.00	22.00	12.00
(8a) Dale Murphy (aluminum)	1.50	1.25	.60
(8b) Dale Murphy (bronze)	15.00	11.00	6.00
(8c) Dale Murphy (silver)	80.00	60.00	32.00
(9a) Dan Quisenberry (aluminum)	.70	.50	.30
(9b) Dan Quisenberry (bronze)	7.50	5.75	3.00
(9c) Dan Quisenberry (silver)	20.00	15.00	8.00
(10a) Jeff Reardon (aluminum)	.70	.50	.30
(10b) Jeff Reardon (bronze)	7.50	5.75	3.00
(10c) Jeff Reardon (silver)	20.00	15.00	8.00
(11a) Pete Rose (aluminum)	2.50	2.00	1.00
(11b) Pete Rose (bronze)	25.00	18.50	10.00
(11c) Pete Rose (silver)	110.00	82.00	44.00
(12a) Bret Saberhagen (aluminum)	1.00	.70	.40
(12b) Bret Saberhagen (bronze)	10.00	7.50	4.00
(12c) Bret Saberhagen (silver)	30.00	22.00	12.00

1986 Topps Mini
League Leaders

Topps had long experimented with bigger cards, but in 1986, they also decided to try smaller ones. These 2-1/8'' by 2-15/16'' cards featured top players in a number of categories. Sold in plastic packs as a regular Topps issue, the 66-card set was attractive as well as innovative. The cards featured color photos and a minimum of added information on the fronts where only the player's name and Topps logo appeared. Backs had limited information as well, but did feature whatever information was required to justify the player's inclusion in a set of league leaders. Whether collectors will accept the format remains to be seen, but it is attractive and is loaded with top names.

	MT	NR MT	EX
Complete Set:	6.50	5.00	2.50
Common Player:	.09	.07	.04
1 Eddie Murray	.40	.30	.15
2 Cal Ripken	.40	.30	.15
3 Wade Boggs	.80	.60	.30
4 Dennis Boyd	.09	.07	.04
5 Dwight Evans	.20	.15	.08
6 Bruce Hurst	.15	.11	.06
7 Gary Pettis	.09	.07	.04
8 Harold Baines	.20	.15	.08
9 Floyd Bannister	.15	.11	.06
10 Britt Burns	.09	.07	.04
11 Carlton Fisk	.25	.20	.10
12 Brett Butler	.15	.11	.06
13 Darrell Evans	.20	.15	.08
14 Jack Morris	.25	.20	.10
15 Lance Parrish	.25	.20	.10
16 Walt Terrell	.15	.11	.06
17 Steve Balboni	.09	.07	.04
18 George Brett	.50	.40	.20
19 Charlie Leibrandt	.15	.11	.06
20 Bret Saberhagen	.25	.20	.10
21 Lonnie Smith	.09	.07	.04
22 Willie Wilson	.15	.11	.06
23 Bert Blyleven	.20	.15	.08
24 Mike Smithson	.09	.07	.04
25 Frank Viola	.15	.11	.06
26 Ron Guidry	.25	.20	.10
27 Rickey Henderson	.40	.30	.15
28 Don Mattingly	1.25	.90	.50
29 Dave Winfield	.30	.25	.12
30 Mike Moore	.09	.07	.04
31 Gorman Thomas	.15	.11	.06
32 Toby Harrah	.09	.07	.04
33 Charlie Hough	.15	.11	.06
34 Doyle Alexander	.15	.11	.06
35 Jimmy Key	.15	.11	.06
36 Dave Stieb	.15	.11	.06
37 Dale Murphy	.50	.40	.20
38 Keith Moreland	.15	.11	.06
39 Ryne Sandberg	.30	.25	.12
40 Tom Browning	.15	.11	.06
41 Dave Parker	.20	.15	.08
42 Mario Soto	.09	.07	.04
43 Nolan Ryan	.30	.25	.12
44 Pedro Guerrero	.20	.15	.08
45 Orel Hershiser	.15	.11	.06
46 Mike Scioscia	.09	.07	.04
47 Fernando Valenzuela	.25	.20	.10
48 Bob Welch	.15	.11	.06
49 Tim Raines	.30	.25	.12
50 Gary Carter	.30	.25	.12
51 Sid Fernandez	.15	.11	.06
52 Dwight Gooden	.70	.50	.30
53 Keith Hernandez	.25	.20	.10
54 Juan Samuel	.20	.15	.08
55 Mike Schmidt	.50	.40	.20
56 Glenn Wilson	.15	.11	.06
57 Rick Reuschel	.15	.11	.06
58 Joaquin Andujar	.09	.07	.04
59 Jack Clark	.20	.15	.08
60 Vince Coleman	.60	.45	.25
61 Danny Cox	.15	.11	.06
62 Tom Herr	.15	.11	.06
63 Willie McGee	.20	.15	.08
64 John Tudor	.15	.11	.06
65 Tony Gwynn	.40	.30	.15
66 Checklist	.09	.07	.04

1986 Topps Stickers

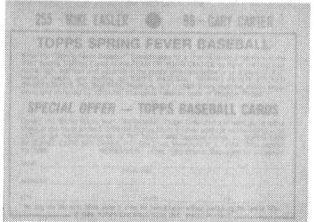

The 1986 Topps stickers are 2⅛'' by 3.'' The 200-piece set features 316 different subjects, with some stickers including two or three players. Numbers run only to 315, however. The set includes some specialty stickers such as League Championships and World Series themes. Stickers are numbered both front and back and included a chance to win a trip to spring training as well as an offer to buy a complete 1986 Topps regular set. An album for the stickers was available in stores.

		MT	NR MT	EX
Complete Set:		15.00	11.00	6.00
Common Player:		.03	.02	.01
Sticker Album:		.40	.30	.15
1	Pete Rose	.25	.20	.10
2	Pete Rose	.25	.20	.10
3	George Brett	.12	.09	.05
4	Rod Carew	.10	.08	.04
5	Vince Coleman	.12	.09	.05
6	Dwight Gooden	.15	.11	.06
7	Phil Niekro	.08	.06	.03
8	Tony Perez	.06	.05	.02
9	Nolan Ryan	.10	.08	.04
10	Tom Seaver	.10	.08	.04
11	N.L. Championship Series (Ozzie Smith)			
		.06	.05	.02
12	N.L. Championship Series (Bill Madlock)			
		.04	.03	.02
13	N.L. Championship Series (Cardinals Celebrate)	.03	.02	.01
14	A.L. Championship Series (Al Oliver)			
		.04	.03	.02
15	A.L. Championship Series (Jim Sundberg)			
		.03	.02	.01
16	A.L. Championship Series (George Brett)			
		.10	.08	.04
17	World Series (Bret Saberhagen)	.06	.05	.02
18	World Series (Dane Iorg)	.03	.02	.01
19	World Series (Tito Landrum)	.03	.02	.01
20	World Series (John Tudor)	.04	.03	.02
21	World Series (Buddy Biancalana)	.03	.02	.01
22	World Series (Darryl Motley, Darrell Porter)	.03	.02	.01
23	World Series (George Brett, Frank White)	.10	.08	.04
24	Nolan Ryan	.15	.11	.06
25	Bill Doran	.08	.06	.03
26	Jose Cruz	.04	.03	.02
27	Mike Scott	.08	.06	.03
28	Kevin Bass	.04	.03	.02
29	Glenn Davis	.10	.08	.04
30	Mark Bailey	.06	.05	.02
31	Dave Smith	.10	.08	.04
32	Phil Garner	.03	.02	.01
33	Dickie Thon	.06	.05	.02
34	Bob Horner	.12	.09	.05

		MT	NR MT	EX
35	Dale Murphy	.25	.20	.10
36	Glenn Hubbard	.04	.03	.02
37	Bruce Sutter	.08	.06	.03
38	Ken Oberkfell	.04	.03	.02
39	Claudell Washington	.04	.03	.02
40	Steve Bedrosian	.04	.03	.02
41	Terry Harper	.03	.02	.01
42	Rafael Ramirez	.06	.05	.02
43	Rick Mahler	.03	.02	.01
44	Joaquin Andujar	.06	.05	.02
45	Willie McGee	.10	.08	.04
46	Ozzie Smith	.06	.05	.02
47	Vince Coleman	.12	.09	.05
48	Danny Cox	.04	.03	.02
49	Tom Herr	.04	.03	.02
50	Jack Clark	.08	.06	.03
51	Andy Van Slyke	.04	.03	.02
52	John Tudor	.08	.06	.03
53	Terry Pendleton	.03	.02	.01
54	Keith Moreland	.06	.05	.02
55	Ryne Sandberg	.15	.11	.06
56	Lee Smith	.04	.03	.02
57	Steve Trout	.06	.05	.02
58	Jody Davis	.08	.06	.03
59	Gary Matthews	.04	.03	.02
60	Leon Durham	.04	.03	.02
61	Rick Sutcliffe	.06	.05	.02
62	Dennis Eckersley	.04	.03	.02
63	Bob Dernier	.03	.02	.01
64	Fernando Valenzuela	.15	.11	.06
65	Pedro Guerrero	.12	.09	.05
66	Jerry Reuss	.06	.05	.02
67	Greg Brock	.06	.05	.02
68	Mike Scioscia	.03	.02	.01
69	Ken Howell	.04	.03	.02
70	Bill Madlock	.04	.03	.02
71	Mike Marshall	.06	.05	.02
72	Steve Sax	.06	.05	.02
73	Orel Hershiser	.06	.05	.02
74	Andre Dawson	.12	.09	.05
75	Tim Raines	.12	.09	.05
76	Jeff Reardon	.06	.05	.02
77	Hubie Brooks	.04	.03	.02
78	Bill Gullickson	.04	.03	.02
79	Bryn Smith	.04	.03	.02
80	Terry Francona	.04	.03	.02
81	Vance Law	.03	.02	.01
82	Tim Wallach	.04	.03	.02
83	Herm Winningham	.04	.03	.02
84	Jeff Leonard	.06	.05	.02
85	Chris Brown	.20	.15	.08
86	Scott Garrelts	.03	.02	.01
87	Jose Uribe	.04	.03	.02
88	Manny Trillo	.04	.03	.02
89	Dan Driessen	.04	.03	.02
90	Dan Gladden	.06	.05	.02
91	Mark Davis	.04	.03	.02
92	Bob Brenly	.03	.02	.01
93	Mike Krukow	.04	.03	.02
94	Dwight Gooden	.35	.25	.14
95	Darryl Strawberry	.25	.20	.10
96	Gary Carter	.10	.08	.04
97	Wally Backman	.06	.05	.02
98	Ron Darling	.06	.05	.02
99	Keith Hernandez	.12	.09	.05
100	George Foster	.06	.05	.02
101	Howard Johnson	.06	.05	.02
102	Rafael Santana	.04	.03	.02
103	Roger McDowell	.06	.05	.02
104	Steve Garvey	.15	.11	.06
105	Tony Gwynn	.20	.15	.08
106	Graig Nettles	.06	.05	.02
107	Rich Gossage	.10	.08	.04
108	Andy Hawkins	.04	.03	.02
109	Carmelo Martinez	.04	.03	.02
110	Garry Templeton	.04	.03	.02
111	Terry Kennedy	.06	.05	.02
112	Tim Flannery	.08	.06	.03
113	LaMarr Hoyt	.03	.02	.01
114	Mike Schmidt	.25	.20	.10
115	Ozzie Virgil	.06	.05	.02
116	Steve Carlton	.10	.08	.04
117	Garry Maddox	.03	.02	.01
118	Glenn Wilson	.06	.05	.02
119	Kevin Gross	.03	.02	.01
120	Von Hayes	.04	.03	.02
121	Juan Samuel	.06	.05	.02
122	Rick Schu	.08	.06	.03
123	Shane Rawley	.06	.05	.02
124	Johnny Ray	.06	.05	.02
125	Tony Pena	.06	.05	.02

		MT	NR MT	EX			MT	NR MT	EX
126	Rick Reuschel	.12	.09	.05	217	Phil Bradley	.10	.08	.04
127	Sammy Khalifa	.06	.05	.02	218	Alvin Davis	.06	.05	.02
128	Marvell Wynne	.04	.03	.02	219	Jim Presley	.08	.06	.03
129	Jason Thompson	.03	.02	.01	220	Matt Young	.04	.03	.02
130	Rick Rhoden	.04	.03	.02	221	Mike Moore	.04	.03	.02
131	Bill Almon	.03	.02	.01	222	Dave Henderson	.06	.05	.02
132	Joe Orsulak	.06	.05	.02	223	Ed Nunez	.04	.03	.02
133	Jim Morrison	.06	.05	.02	224	Spike Owen	.03	.02	.01
134	Pete Rose	.40	.30	.15	225	Mark Langston	.06	.05	.02
135	Dave Parker	.12	.09	.05	226	Cal Ripken	.20	.15	.08
136	Mario Soto	.03	.02	.01	227	Eddie Murray	.20	.15	.08
137	Dave Concepcion	.10	.08	.04	228	Fred Lynn	.06	.05	.02
138	Ron Oester	.03	.02	.01	229	Lee Lacy	.03	.02	.01
139	Buddy Bell	.06	.05	.02	230	Scott McGregor	.04	.03	.02
140	Ted Power	.03	.02	.01	231	Storm Davis	.04	.03	.02
141	Tom Browning	.06	.05	.02	232	Rick Dempsey	.06	.05	.02
142	John Franco	.08	.06	.03	233	Mike Boddicker	.06	.05	.02
143	Tony Perez	.06	.05	.02	234	Mike Young	.06	.05	.02
144	Willie McGee	.08	.06	.03	235	Sammy Stewart	.06	.05	.02
145	Dale Murphy	.15	.11	.06	236	Pete O'Brien	.08	.06	.03
146	Tony Gwynn	.40	.30	.15	237	Oddibe McDowell	.15	.11	.06
147	Tom Herr	.15	.11	.06	238	Toby Harrah	.04	.03	.02
148	Steve Garvey	.30	.25	.12	239	Gary Ward	.04	.03	.02
149	Dale Murphy	.40	.30	.15	240	Larry Parrish	.04	.03	.02
150	Darryl Strawberry	.40	.30	.15	241	Charlie Hough	.04	.03	.02
151	Graig Nettles	.15	.11	.06	242	Burt Hooton	.03	.02	.01
152	Terry Kennedy	.15	.11	.06	243	Don Slaught	.04	.03	.02
153	Ozzie Smith	.20	.15	.08	244	Curt Wilkerson	.04	.03	.02
154	LaMarr Hoyt	.15	.11	.06	245	Greg Harris	.03	.02	.01
155	Rickey Henderson	.40	.30	.15	246	Jim Rice	.15	.11	.06
156	Lou Whitaker	.25	.20	.10	247	Wade Boggs	.60	.45	.25
157	George Brett	.40	.30	.15	248	Rich Gedman	.04	.03	.02
158	Eddie Murray	.40	.30	.15	249	Dennis Boyd	.04	.03	.02
159	Cal Ripken	.40	.30	.15	250	Marty Barrett	.04	.03	.02
160	Dave Winfield	.30	.25	.12	251	Dwight Evans	.06	.05	.02
161	Jim Rice	.30	.25	.12	252	Bill Buckner	.04	.03	.02
162	Carlton Fisk	.25	.20	.10	253	Bob Stanley	.03	.02	.01
163	Jack Morris	.25	.20	.10	254	Tony Armas	.04	.03	.02
164	Wade Boggs	.15	.11	.06	255	Mike Easler	.10	.08	.04
165	Darrell Evans	.06	.05	.02	256	George Brett	.25	.20	.10
166	Mike Davis	.06	.05	.02	257	Dan Quisenberry	.06	.05	.02
167	Dave Kingman	.08	.06	.03	258	Willie Wilson	.06	.05	.02
168	Alfredo Griffin	.04	.03	.02	259	Jim Sundberg	.06	.05	.02
169	Carney Lansford	.04	.03	.02	260	Bret Saberhagen	.12	.09	.05
170	Bruce Bochte	.10	.08	.04	261	Bud Black	.06	.05	.02
171	Dwayne Murphy	.08	.06	.03	262	Charlie Leibrandt	.06	.05	.02
172	Dave Collins	.04	.03	.02	263	Frank White	.04	.03	.02
173	Chris Codiroli	.10	.08	.04	264	Lonnie Smith	.06	.05	.02
174	Mike Heath	.03	.02	.01	265	Steve Balboni	.06	.05	.02
175	Jay Howell	.12	.09	.05	266	Kirk Gibson	.15	.11	.06
176	Rod Carew	.20	.15	.08	267	Alan Trammell	.15	.11	.06
177	Reggie Jackson	.20	.15	.08	268	Jack Morris	.10	.08	.04
178	Doug DeCinces	.10	.08	.04	269	Darrell Evans	.04	.03	.02
179	Bob Boone	.12	.09	.05	270	Dan Petry	.04	.03	.02
180	Ron Romanick	.15	.11	.06	271	Larry Herndon	.04	.03	.02
181	Bob Grich	.08	.06	.03	272	Lou Whitaker	.06	.05	.02
182	Donnie Moore	.06	.05	.02	273	Lance Parrish	.08	.06	.03
183	Brian Downing	.10	.08	.04	274	Chet Lemon	.03	.02	.01
184	Ruppert Jones	.10	.08	.04	275	Willie Hernandez	.10	.08	.04
185	Juan Beniquez	.04	.03	.02	276	Tom Brunansky	.08	.06	.03
186	Dave Stieb	.06	.05	.02	277	Kent Hrbek	.12	.09	.05
187	Jorge Bell	.20	.15	.08	278	Mark Salas	.03	.02	.01
188	Willie Upshaw	.08	.06	.03	279	Bert Blyleven	.06	.05	.02
189	Tom Henke	.04	.03	.02	280	Tim Teufel	.03	.02	.01
190	Damaso Garcia	.10	.08	.04	281	Ron Davis	.04	.03	.02
191	Jimmy Key	.06	.05	.02	282	Mike Smithson	.06	.05	.02
192	Jesse Barfield	.10	.08	.04	283	Gary Gaetti	.08	.06	.03
193	Dennis Lamp	.03	.02	.01	284	Frank Viola	.06	.05	.02
194	Tony Fernandez	.06	.05	.02	285	Kirby Puckett	.12	.09	.05
195	Lloyd Moseby	.04	.03	.02	286	Carlton Fisk	.12	.09	.05
196	Cecil Cooper	.08	.06	.03	287	Tom Seaver	.15	.11	.06
197	Robin Yount	.15	.11	.06	288	Harold Baines	.06	.05	.02
198	Rollie Fingers	.08	.06	.03	289	Ron Kittle	.04	.03	.02
199	Ted Simmons	.04	.03	.02	290	Bob James	.03	.02	.01
200	Ben Oglivie	.04	.03	.02	291	Rudy Law	.04	.03	.02
201	Moose Haas	.04	.03	.02	292	Britt Burns	.03	.02	.01
202	Jim Gantner	.03	.02	.01	293	Greg Walker	.06	.05	.02
203	Paul Molitor	.06	.05	.02	294	Ozzie Guillen	.06	.05	.02
204	Charlie Moore	.03	.02	.01	295	Tim Hulett	.03	.02	.01
205	Danny Darwin	.06	.05	.02	296	Don Mattingly	.70	.50	.30
206	Brett Butler	.06	.05	.02	297	Rickey Henderson	.20	.15	.08
207	Brook Jacoby	.08	.06	.03	298	Dave Winfield	.10	.08	.04
208	Andre Thornton	.12	.09	.05	299	Butch Wynegar	.03	.02	.01
209	Tom Waddell	.04	.03	.02	300	Don Baylor	.06	.05	.02
210	Tony Bernazard	.04	.03	.02	301	Eddie Whitson	.03	.02	.01
211	Julio Franco	.08	.06	.03	302	Ron Guidry	.06	.05	.02
212	Pat Tabler	.04	.03	.02	303	Dave Righetti	.08	.06	.03
213	Joe Carter	.08	.06	.03	304	Bobby Meacham	.06	.05	.02
214	George Vukovich	.03	.02	.01	305	Willie Randolph	.08	.06	.03
215	Rich Thompson	.04	.03	.02	306	Vince Coleman	.15	.11	.06
216	Gorman Thomas	.06	.05	.02	307	Oddibe McDowell	.15	.11	.06

		MT	NR MT	EX
308	Larry Sheets	.06	.05	.02
309	Ozzie Guillen	.06	.05	.02
310	Earnie Riles	.04	.03	.02
311	Chris Brown	.10	.08	.04
312	Brian Fisher, Roger McDowell	.08	.06	.03
313	Tom Browning	.04	.03	.02
314	Glenn Davis	.10	.08	.04
315	Mark Salas	.03	.02	.01

1986 Topps Super

 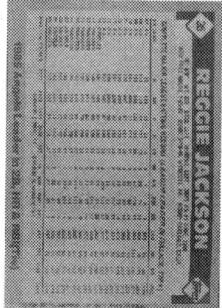

REGGIE JACKSON

A third year of oversize, 4⅞" by 6⅞," versions of Topps' regular issue cards saw the set once again hit the 60-card mark. Besides being four times the size of a normal card, the Supers differed only in the number on the back of the card.

		MT	NR MT	EX
Complete Set:		9.00	6.75	3.50
Common Player:		.20	.15	.08
1	Don Mattingly	2.25	1.75	.90
2	Willie McGee	.35	.25	.14
3	Bret Saberhagen	.35	.25	.14
4	Dwight Gooden	1.75	1.25	.70
5	Dan Quisenberry	.25	.20	.10
6	Jeff Reardon	.25	.20	.10
7	Ozzie Guillen	.25	.20	.10
8	Vince Coleman	.70	.50	.30
9	Harold Baines	.25	.20	.10
10	Jorge Bell	.60	.45	.25
11	Bert Blyleven	.25	.20	.10
12	Wade Boggs	1.25	.90	.50
13	Phil Bradley	.25	.20	.10
14	George Brett	.80	.60	.30
15	Hubie Brooks	.20	.15	.08
16	Tom Browning	.20	.15	.08
17	Bill Buckner	.20	.15	.08
18	Brett Butler	.20	.15	.08
19	Gary Carter	.50	.40	.20
20	Cecil Cooper	.25	.20	.10
21	Darrell Evans	.25	.20	.10
22	Dwight Evans	.25	.20	.10
23	Carlton Fisk	.30	.25	.12
24	Steve Garvey	.50	.40	.20
25	Kirk Gibson	.35	.25	.14
26	Rich Gossage	.25	.20	.10
27	Pedro Guerrero	.30	.25	.12
28	Ron Guidry	.30	.25	.12
29	Tony Gwynn	.70	.50	.30
30	Rickey Henderson	.70	.50	.30
31	Keith Hernandez	.50	.40	.20
32	Tom Herr	.25	.20	.10
33	Orel Hershiser	.30	.25	.12
34	Jay Howell	.20	.15	.08
35	Reggie Jackson	.60	.45	.25
36	Bob James	.20	.15	.08
37	Charlie Leibrandt	.20	.15	.08
38	Jack Morris	.35	.25	.14
39	Dale Murphy	.80	.60	.30
40	Eddie Murray	.60	.45	.25
41	Dave Parker	.35	.25	.14
42	Tim Raines	.50	.40	.20
43	Jim Rice	.50	.40	.20
44	Dave Righetti	.30	.25	.12
45	Cal Ripken	.70	.50	.30
46	Pete Rose	1.00	.70	.40
47	Nolan Ryan	.50	.40	.20
48	Ryne Sandberg	.50	.40	.20
49	Mike Schmidt	.80	.60	.30

		MT	NR MT	EX
50	Tom Seaver	.50	.40	.20
51	Bryn Smith	.20	.15	.08
52	Lee Smith	.20	.15	.08
53	Ozzie Smith	.30	.25	.12
54	Dave Stieb	.20	.15	.08
55	Darryl Strawberry	.80	.60	.30
56	Gorman Thomas	.20	.15	.08
57	John Tudor	.20	.15	.08
58	Fernando Valenzuela	.40	.30	.15
59	Willie Wilson	.25	.20	.10
60	Dave Winfield	.50	.40	.20

1986 Topps Super Star

 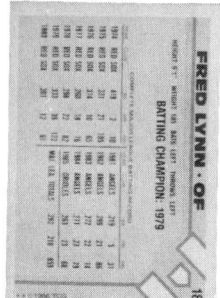

Labeled "Topps' Collector Series" in a red band at the top of the front, this set marked the second year of Topps' production of a special boxed set for the Woolworth chain of stores, though Woolworth's name does not appear anywhere on the card. The cards, which measure 2½" by 3½," feature a color photo with its lower right corner rolled up to reveal the words "Super Star" on a bright yellow border. The player's name appears in the lower left corner. The 66-card set features stars and should retain a certain measure of popularity on that basis.

		MT	NR MT	EX
Complete Set:		5.00	3.75	2.00
Common Player:		.09	.07	.04
1	Tony Armas	.09	.07	.04
2	Don Baylor	.12	.09	.05
3	Wade Boggs	.70	.50	.30
4	George Brett	.40	.30	.15
5	Bill Buckner	.09	.07	.04
6	Rod Carew	.30	.25	.12
7	Gary Carter	.30	.25	.12
8	Cecil Cooper	.12	.09	.05
9	Darrell Evans	.12	.09	.05
10	Dwight Evans	.15	.11	.06
11	George Foster	.12	.09	.05
12	Bobby Grich	.09	.07	.04
13	Tony Gwynn	.35	.25	.14
14	Keith Hernandez	.25	.20	.10
15	Reggie Jackson	.30	.25	.12
16	Dave Kingman	.12	.09	.05
17	Carney Lansford	.09	.07	.04
18	Fred Lynn	.12	.09	.05
19	Bill Madlock	.12	.09	.05
20	Don Mattingly	1.25	.90	.50
21	Willie McGee	.20	.15	.08
22	Hal McRae	.09	.07	.04
23	Dale Murphy	.40	.30	.15
24	Eddie Murray	.35	.25	.14
25	Ben Oglivie	.09	.07	.04
26	Al Oliver	.12	.09	.05
27	Dave Parker	.20	.15	.08
28	Jim Rice	.30	.25	.12
29	Pete Rose	.90	.70	.35
30	Mike Schmidt	.40	.30	.15
31	Gorman Thomas	.09	.07	.04
32	Willie Wilson	.12	.09	.05
33	Dave Winfield	.30	.25	.12

1986 Topps Tattoos

Topps returned to tattoos in 1986 marketing a set of 24 different tattoo sheets. Each sheet of tattoos measures 3-7/16" by 14" and includes both player

		MT	NR MT	EX
	Reardon, Bryn Smith, Gorman Thomas			
		.30	.25	.12
23	Carlton Fisk, Bob Grich, Pedro Guerrero, Willie McGee, Paul Molitor, Mike Scott, Dave Stieb, Lou Whitaker	.20	.15	.08
24	Bert Blyleven, Damaso Garcia, Phil Garner, Tony Gwynn, Rickey Henderson, Ben Oglivie, Nolan Ryan, Fernando Valenzuela			
		.30	.25	.12

and smaller action tattoos. As the action tattoos were uniform and not of any particular player, they add little value to the sheet. The player tattoos measure 1-3/16'' by 2-3/8.'' With 24 sheets, eight players per sheet, there are 192 players represented in the set. The sheets are numbered.

		MT	NR MT	EX
Complete Set:		5.00	3.75	2.00
Common Player:		.20	.15	.08
1	Julio Franco, Rich Gossage, Keith Hernandez, Charlie Leibrandt, Jack Perconte, Lee Smith, Dickie Thon, Dave Winfield	.25	.20	.10
2	Jesse Barfield, Shawon Dunston, Dennis Eckersley, Brian Fisher, Moose Haas, Mike Moore, Dale Murphy, Bret Saberhagen	.30	.25	.12
3	George Bell, Bob Brenly, Steve Carlton, Jose DeLeon, Bob Horner, Bob James, Dan Quisenberry, Andre Thornton	.25	.20	.10
4	Mike Davis, Leon Durham, Darrell Evans, Glenn Hubbard, Johnny Ray, Cal Ripken, Ted Simmons	.25	.20	.10
5	John Candelaria, Rick Dempsey, Steve Garvey, Ozzie Guillen, Gary Matthews, Jesse Orosco, Tony Pena	.25	.20	.10
6	Bruce Bochte, George Brett, Cecil Cooper, Sammy Khalifa, Ron Kittle, Scott McGregor, Pete Rose, Mookie Wilson	.45	.35	.20
7	John Franco, Carney Lansford, Don Mattingly, Graig Nettles, Rick Reuschel, Mike Schmidt, Larry Sheets, Don Sutton	.45	.35	.20
8	Cecilio Guante, Willie Hernandez, Mike Krukow, Fred Lynn, Phil Niekro, Ed Nunez, Ryne Sandberg, Pat Tabler	.25	.20	.10
9	Brett Butler, Chris Codiroli, Jim Gantner, Charlie Hough, Dave Parker, Rick Rhoden, Glenn Wilson, Robin Yount	.20	.15	.08
10	Tom Browning, Ron Darling, Von Hayes, Chet Lemon, Tom Seaver, Mike Smithson, Bruce Sutter, Alan Trammell	.25	.20	.10
11	Tony Armas, Jose Cruz, Jay Howell, Rick Mahler, Jack Morris, Rafael Ramirez, Dave Righetti, Mike Young	.20	.15	.08
12	Alvin Davis, Doug DeCinces, Andy Hawkins, Dennis Lamp, Keith Moreland, Jim Presley, Mario Soto, John Tudor	.20	.15	.08
13	Hubie Brooks, Jody Davis, Dwight Evans, Ron Hassey, Charles Hudson, Kirby Puckett, Jose Uribe	.20	.15	.08
14	Tony Bernazard, Phil Bradley, Bill Buckner, Brian Downing, Dan Driessen, Ron Guidry, LaMarr Hoyt, Garry Maddox	.20	.15	.08
15	Buddy Bell, Joe Carter, Tony Fernandez, Tito Landrum, Jeff Leonard, Hal McRae, Willie Randolph, Juan Samuel	.20	.15	.08
16	Dennis Boyd, Vince Coleman, Scott Garrelts, Alfredo Griffin, Donnie Moore, Tony Perez, Ozzie Smith, Frank White	.25	.20	.10
17	Rich Gedman, Kent Hrbek, Reggie Jackson, Mike Marshall, Terry Pendleton, Tim Raines, Mark Salas, Claudell Washington	.25	.20	.10
18	Chris Brown, Tom Brunansky, Glenn Davis, Ron Davis, Burt Hooton, Darryl Strawberry, Frank Viola, Tim Wallach	.30	.25	.12
19	Jack Clark, Bill Doran, Toby Harrah, Bill Madlock, Pete O'Brien, Larry Parrish, Mike Scioscia, Garry Templeton	.20	.15	.08
20	Gary Carter, Andre Dawson, Dwight Gooden, Orel Hershiser, Oddibe McDowell, Roger McDowell, Dwayne Murphy, Jim Rice	.40	.30	.15
21	Steve Balboni, Mike Easler, Charlie Lea, Lloyd Moseby, Steve Sax, Rick Sutcliffe, Gary Ward, Willie Wilson	.20	.15	.08
22	Wade Boggs, Dave Concepcion, Kirk Gibson, Tom Herr, Lance Parrish, Jeff			

1986 Topps Traded

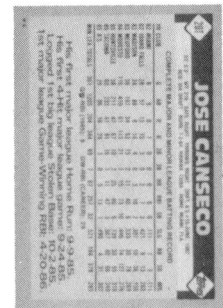

JOSE CANSECO

This 132-card set of 2½'' by 3½'' cards is one of the most popular sets of recent times. As always, the set features traded veterans, including such players as Phil Niekro and Tom Seaver. They are not, however, the reason for the excitement. The demand is there because of a better than usual crop of rookies who also appear in the sets. Among those are Jose Canseco, Wally Joyner, Pete Incaviglia, Todd Worrell and the first card of Bo Jackson. As in the previous two years, a glossy-finish ''Tiffany'' edition of 5,000 Traded sets was produced. The ''Tiffany'' cards are worth four to six times the value of the regular Traded cards.

		MT	NR MT	EX
Complete Set:		14.00	10.50	5.50
Common Player:		.08	.06	.03
1T	Andy Allanson	.20	.15	.08
2T	Neil Allen	.08	.06	.03
3T	Joaquin Andujar	.12	.09	.05
4T	Paul Assenmacher	.20	.15	.08
5T	Scott Bailes	.25	.20	.10
6T	Don Baylor	.15	.11	.06
7T	Steve Bedrosian	.15	.11	.06
8T	Juan Beniquez	.08	.06	.03
9T	Juan Berenguer	.08	.06	.03
10T	Mike Bielecki	.08	.06	.03
11T	Barry Bonds	.80	.60	.30
12T	Bobby Bonilla	.40	.30	.15
13T	Juan Bonilla	.08	.06	.03
14T	Rich Bordi	.08	.06	.03
15T	Steve Boros	.08	.06	.03
16T	Rick Burleson	.12	.09	.05
17T	Bill Campbell	.08	.06	.03
18T	Tom Candiotti	.08	.06	.03
19T	John Cangelosi	.30	.25	.12
20T	Jose Canseco	4.00	3.00	1.50
21T	Carmen Castillo	.08	.06	.03
22T	Rick Cerone	.08	.06	.03
23T	John Cerutti	.35	.25	.14
24T	Will Clark	3.00	2.25	1.25
25T	Mark Clear	.12	.09	.05
26T	Darnell Coles	.15	.11	.06
27T	Dave Collins	.12	.09	.05
28T	Tim Conroy	.08	.06	.03
29T	Joe Cowley	.08	.06	.03
30T	Joel Davis	.15	.11	.06
31T	Rob Deer	.20	.15	.08
32T	John Denny	.08	.06	.03
33T	Mike Easler	.12	.09	.05
34T	Mark Eichhorn	.35	.25	.14
35T	Steve Farr	.08	.06	.03
36T	Scott Fletcher	.12	.09	.05
37T	Terry Forster	.12	.09	.05
38T	Terry Francona	.08	.06	.03
39T	Jim Fregosi	.08	.06	.03

		MT	NR MT	EX
40T	Andres Galarraga	1.25	.90	.50
41T	Ken Griffey	.15	.11	.06
42T	Bill Gullickson	.12	.09	.05
43T	Jose Guzman	.35	.25	.14
44T	Moose Haas	.08	.06	.03
45T	Billy Hatcher	.15	.11	.06
46T	Mike Heath	.08	.06	.03
47T	Tom Hume	.08	.06	.03
48T	Pete Incaviglia	2.00	1.50	.80
49T	Dane Iorg	.08	.06	.03
50T	Bo Jackson	3.00	2.25	1.25
51T	Wally Joyner	3.75	2.75	1.50
52T	Charlie Kerfeld	.20	.15	.08
53T	Eric King	.30	.25	.12
54T	Bob Kipper	.15	.11	.06
55T	Wayne Krenchicki	.08	.06	.03
56T	John Kruk	1.25	.90	.50
57T	Mike LaCoss	.12	.09	.05
58T	Pete Ladd	.08	.06	.03
59T	Mike Laga	.08	.06	.03
60T	Hal Lanier	.08	.06	.03
61T	Dave LaPoint	.08	.06	.03
62T	Rudy Law	.08	.06	.03
63T	Rick Leach	.08	.06	.03
64T	Tim Leary	.08	.06	.03
65T	Dennis Leonard	.12	.09	.05
66T	Jim Leyland	.08	.06	.03
67T	Steve Lyons	.12	.09	.05
68T	Mickey Mahler	.08	.06	.03
69T	Candy Maldonado	.15	.11	.06
70T	Roger Mason	.12	.09	.05
71T	Bob McClure	.08	.06	.03
72T	Andy McGaffigan	.08	.06	.03
73T	Gene Michael	.08	.06	.03
74T	Kevin Mitchell	.60	.45	.25
75T	Omar Moreno	.08	.06	.03
76T	Jerry Mumphrey	.12	.09	.05
77T	Phil Niekro	.40	.30	.15
78T	Randy Niemann	.08	.06	.03
79T	Juan Nieves	.40	.30	.15
80T	Otis Nixon	.12	.09	.05
81T	Bob Ojeda	.15	.11	.06
82T	Jose Oquendo	.08	.06	.03
83T	Tom Paciorek	.08	.06	.03
84T	Dave Palmer	.12	.09	.05
85T	Frank Pastore	.08	.06	.03
86T	Lou Piniella	.12	.09	.05
87T	Dan Plesac	.40	.30	.15
88T	Darrell Porter	.12	.09	.05
89T	Rey Quinones (Quinonez)	.25	.20	.10
90T	Gary Redus	.12	.09	.05
91T	Bip Roberts	.12	.09	.05
92T	Billy Jo Robidoux	.15	.11	.06
93T	Jeff Robinson	.12	.09	.05
94T	Gary Roenicke	.08	.06	.03
95T	Ed Romero	.08	.06	.03
96T	Argenis Salazar	.08	.06	.03
97T	Joe Sambito	.08	.06	.03
98T	Billy Sample	.08	.06	.03
99T	Dave Schmidt	.12	.09	.05
100T	Ken Schrom	.08	.06	.03
101T	Tom Seaver	.60	.45	.25
102T	Ted Simmons	.20	.15	.08
103T	Sammy Stewart	.08	.06	.03
104T	Kurt Stillwell	.50	.40	.20
105T	Franklin Stubbs	.15	.11	.06
106T	Dale Sveum	.50	.40	.20
107T	Chuck Tanner	.12	.09	.05
108T	Danny Tartabull	1.00	.70	.40
109T	Tim Teufel	.08	.06	.03
110T	Bob Tewksbury	.25	.20	.10
111T	Andres Thomas	.25	.20	.10
112T	Milt Thompson	.12	.09	.05
113T	Robby Thompson	.35	.25	.14
114T	Jay Tibbs	.08	.06	.03
115T	Wayne Tolleson	.08	.06	.03
116T	Alex Trevino	.08	.06	.03
117T	Manny Trillo	.12	.09	.05
118T	Ed Vande Berg	.08	.06	.03
119T	Ozzie Virgil	.12	.09	.05
120T	Bob Walk	.08	.06	.03
121T	Gene Walter	.15	.11	.06
122T	Claudell Washington	.12	.09	.05
123T	Bill Wegman	.30	.25	.12
124T	Dick Williams	.12	.09	.05
125T	Mitch Williams	.30	.25	.12
126T	Bobby Witt	.40	.30	.15
127T	Todd Worrell	1.00	.70	.40
128T	George Wright	.08	.06	.03
129T	Ricky Wright	.08	.06	.03
130T	Steve Yeager	.08	.06	.03

		MT	NR MT	EX
131T	Paul Zuvella	.08	.06	.03
132T	Checklist	.08	.06	.03

1986 Topps 3-D

A second effort in the production of over-size (4½'' by 6'') plastic cards on which the player figure is embossed. Cards were sold one per pack for approximately 50¢. The 30 players in the set were among the game's top stars. The embossed color photo is bordered at bottom by a strip of contrasting color on which the player name appears. At top, a row of white baseballs each contain a letter of the team nickname. Backs have no printing, and contain two self-adhesive strips with which the cards can be attached to a hard surface.

		MT	NR MT	EX
	Complete Set:	11.00	8.25	4.50
	Common Player:	.20	.15	.08
1	Bert Blyleven	.30	.25	.12
2	Gary Carter	.60	.45	.25
3	Wade Boggs	1.25	.90	.50
4	Dwight Gooden	1.25	.90	.50
5	George Brett	.80	.60	.30
6	Rich Gossage	.30	.25	.12
7	Darrell Evans	.25	.20	.10
8	Pedro Guerrero	.30	.25	.12
9	Ron Guidry	.30	.25	.12
10	Keith Hernandez	.50	.40	.20
11	Rickey Henderson	.70	.50	.30
12	Orel Hershiser	.30	.25	.12
13	Reggie Jackson	.60	.45	.25
14	Willie McGee	.30	.25	.12
15	Don Mattingly	2.25	1.75	.90
16	Dale Murphy	.80	.60	.30
17	Jack Morris	.30	.25	.12
18	Dave Parker	.30	.25	.12
19	Eddie Murray	.60	.45	.25
20	Jeff Reardon	.30	.25	.12
21	Dan Quisenberry	.25	.20	.10
22	Pete Rose	1.00	.70	.40
23	Jim Rice	.50	.40	.20
24	Mike Schmidt	.80	.60	.30
25	Bret Saberhagen	.30	.25	.12
26	Darryl Strawberry	.80	.60	.30
27	Dave Stieb	.20	.15	.08
28	John Tudor	.20	.15	.08
29	Dave Winfield	.50	.40	.20
30	Fernando Valenzuela	.40	.30	.15

1987 Topps

Many collectors feel that Topps' 1987 set of 792 cards is a future classic. The 2½'' by 3½'' design is closely akin to the 1962 set in that the player photo is set against a woodgrain border. Instead of a rolling corner, as in 1962, the player photos in '87 feature a couple of clipped corners at top left and bottom right, where the team logo and player name appear. Position is not given on the front of the card for the first

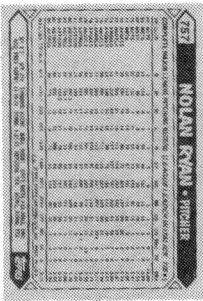

time in many years. For the first time in several years, the trophy which designates members of Topps All-Star Rookie Team have returned to the card design. As in the previous three years, Topps issued a glossy-finish "Tiffany" edition of their 792-card set. However, it was speculated that as many as 50,000 sets were produced as opposed to the 5,000 sets printed in 1985 and 1986. Because of the large print run, the values for the Tiffany cards are only 3-4 times higher than the same card in the regular issue.

		MT	NR MT	EX
Complete Set:		24.00	18.00	9.50
Common Player:		.04	.03	.02
1	Record Breaker (Roger Clemens)	.35	.25	.14
2	Record Breaker (Jim Deshaies)	.10	.08	.04
3	Record Breaker (Dwight Evans)	.08	.06	.03
4	Record Breaker (Dave Lopes)	.06	.05	.02
5	Record Breaker (Dave Righetti)	.08	.06	.03
6	Record Breaker (Ruben Sierra)	.20	.15	.08
7	Record Breaker (Todd Worrell)	.08	.06	.03
8	Terry Pendleton	.08	.06	.03
9	Jay Tibbs	.04	.03	.02
10	Cecil Cooper	.10	.08	.04
11	Indians Leaders	.06	.05	.02
12	Jeff Sellers	.20	.15	.08
13	Nick Esasky	.04	.03	.02
14	Dave Stewart	.10	.08	.04
15	Claudell Washington	.06	.05	.02
16	Pat Clements	.06	.05	.02
17	Pete O'Brien	.10	.08	.04
18	Dick Howser	.06	.05	.02
19	Matt Young	.04	.03	.02
20	Gary Carter	.25	.20	.10
21	Mark Davis	.04	.03	.02
22	Doug DeCinces	.06	.05	.02
23	Lee Smith	.10	.08	.04
24	Tony Walker	.10	.08	.04
25	Bert Blyleven	.12	.09	.05
26	Greg Brock	.08	.06	.03
27	Joe Cowley	.04	.03	.02
28	Rick Dempsey	.06	.05	.02
29	Jimmy Key	.10	.08	.04
30	Tim Raines	.25	.20	.10
31	Braves Leaders	.06	.05	.02
32	Tim Leary	.04	.03	.02
33	Andy Van Slyke	.08	.06	.03
34	Jose Rijo	.04	.03	.02
35	Sid Bream	.08	.06	.03
36	Eric King	.20	.15	.08
37	Marvell Wynne	.04	.03	.02
38	Dennis Leonard	.06	.05	.02
39	Marty Barrett	.08	.06	.03
40	Dave Righetti	.15	.11	.06
41	Bo Diaz	.04	.03	.02
42	Gary Redus	.06	.05	.02
43	Gene Michael	.04	.03	.02
44	Greg Harris	.04	.03	.02
45	Jim Presley	.12	.09	.05
46	Danny Gladden	.06	.05	.02
47	Dennis Powell	.04	.03	.02
48	Wally Backman	.06	.05	.02
49	Terry Harper	.04	.03	.02
50	Dave Smith	.06	.05	.02
51	Mel Hall	.06	.05	.02
52	Keith Atherton	.04	.03	.02
53	Ruppert Jones	.04	.03	.02
54	Bill Dawley	.04	.03	.02
55	Tim Wallach	.10	.08	.04
56	Brewers Leaders	.06	.05	.02

		MT	NR MT	EX
57	Scott Nielsen	.12	.09	.05
58	Thad Bosley	.04	.03	.02
59	Ken Dayley	.04	.03	.02
60	Tony Pena	.08	.06	.03
61	Bobby Thigpen	.20	.15	.08
62	Bobby Meacham	.04	.03	.02
63	Fred Toliver	.06	.05	.02
64	Harry Spilman	.04	.03	.02
65	Tom Browning	.06	.05	.02
66	Marc Sullivan	.04	.03	.02
67	Bill Swift	.04	.03	.02
68	Tony LaRussa	.06	.05	.02
69	Lonnie Smith	.06	.05	.02
70	Charlie Hough	.06	.05	.02
71	Mike Aldrete	.35	.25	.14
72	Walt Terrell	.06	.05	.02
73	Dave Anderson	.04	.03	.02
74	Dan Pasqua	.10	.08	.04
75	Ron Darling	.12	.09	.05
76	Rafael Ramirez	.04	.03	.02
77	Bryan Oelkers	.04	.03	.02
78	Tom Foley	.04	.03	.02
79	Juan Nieves	.12	.09	.05
80	Wally Joyner	2.25	1.75	.90
81	Padres Leaders	.06	.05	.02
82	Rob Murphy	.15	.11	.06
83	Mike Davis	.06	.05	.02
84	Steve Lake	.04	.03	.02
85	Kevin Bass	.08	.06	.03
86	Nate Snell	.04	.03	.02
87	Mark Salas	.04	.03	.02
88	Ed Wojna	.04	.03	.02
89	Ozzie Guillen	.10	.08	.04
90	Dave Stieb	.10	.08	.04
91	Harold Reynolds	.10	.08	.04
92a	Urbano Lugo (no trademark on front)			
		.30	.25	.12
92b	Urbano Lugo (trademark on front)	.06	.05	.02
93	Jim Leyland	.04	.03	.02
94	Calvin Schiraldi	.06	.05	.02
95	Oddibe McDowell	.10	.08	.04
96	Frank Williams	.04	.03	.02
97	Glenn Wilson	.08	.06	.03
98	Bill Scherrer	.04	.03	.02
99	Darryl Motley	.04	.03	.02
100	Steve Garvey	.20	.15	.08
101	Carl Willis	.10	.08	.04
102	Paul Zuvella	.04	.03	.02
103	Rick Aguilera	.08	.06	.03
104	Billy Sample	.04	.03	.02
105	Floyd Youmans	.10	.08	.04
106	Blue Jays Leaders	.06	.05	.02
107	John Butcher	.04	.03	.02
108	Jim Gantner (photo reversed)	.06	.05	.02
109	R.J. Reynolds	.06	.05	.02
110	John Tudor	.08	.06	.03
111	Alfredo Griffin	.06	.05	.02
112	Alan Ashby	.04	.03	.02
113	Neil Allen	.04	.03	.02
114	Billy Beane	.04	.03	.02
115	Donnie Moore	.04	.03	.02
116	Bill Russell	.06	.05	.02
117	Jim Beattie	.04	.03	.02
118	Bobby Valentine	.04	.03	.02
119	Ron Robinson	.04	.03	.02
120	Eddie Murray	.30	.25	.12
121	Kevin Romine	.15	.11	.06
122	Jim Clancy	.08	.06	.03
123	John Kruk	.90	.70	.35
124	Ray Fontenot	.04	.03	.02
125	Bob Brenly	.04	.03	.02
126	Mike Loynd	.15	.11	.06
127	Vance Law	.06	.05	.02
128	Checklist 1-132	.04	.03	.02
129	Rick Cerone	.04	.03	.02
130	Dwight Gooden	.80	.60	.30
131	Pirates Leaders	.06	.05	.02
132	Paul Assenmacher	.15	.11	.06
133	Jose Oquendo	.04	.03	.02
134	Rich Yett	.12	.09	.05
135	Mike Easler	.06	.05	.02
136	Ron Romanick	.04	.03	.02
137	Jerry Willard	.04	.03	.02
138	Roy Lee Jackson	.04	.03	.02
139	Devon White	1.25	.90	.50
140	Bret Saberhagen	.20	.15	.08
141	Herm Winningham	.06	.05	.02
142	Rick Sutcliffe	.10	.08	.04
143	Steve Boros	.04	.03	.02
144	Mike Scioscia	.04	.03	.02
145	Charlie Kerfeld	.10	.08	.04

		MT	NR MT	EX
146	Tracy Jones	.50	.40	.20
147	Randy Niemann	.04	.03	.02
148	Dave Collins	.06	.05	.02
149	Ray Searage	.04	.03	.02
150	Wade Boggs	1.25	.90	.50
151	Mike LaCoss	.06	.05	.02
152	Toby Harrah	.06	.05	.02
153	Duane Ward	.12	.09	.05
154	Tom O'Malley	.04	.03	.02
155	Eddie Whitson	.04	.03	.02
156	Mariners Leaders	.06	.05	.02
157	Danny Darwin	.06	.05	.02
158	Tim Teufel	.04	.03	.02
159	Ed Olwine	.10	.08	.04
160	Julio Franco	.10	.08	.04
161	Steve Ontiveros	.06	.05	.02
162	Mike LaValliere	.20	.15	.08
163	Kevin Gross	.06	.05	.02
164	Sammy Khalifa	.04	.03	.02
165	Jeff Reardon	.12	.09	.05
166	Bob Boone	.06	.05	.02
167	Jim Deshaies	.30	.25	.12
168	Lou Piniella	.06	.05	.02
169	Ron Washington	.04	.03	.02
170	Bo Jackson	1.50	1.25	.60
171	Chuck Cary	.12	.09	.05
172	Ron Oester	.04	.03	.02
173	Alex Trevino	.04	.03	.02
174	Henry Cotto	.04	.03	.02
175	Bob Stanley	.06	.05	.02
176	Steve Buechele	.06	.05	.02
177	Keith Moreland	.06	.05	.02
178	Cecil Fielder	.06	.05	.02
179	Bill Wegman	.08	.06	.03
180	Chris Brown	.12	.09	.05
181	Cardinals Leaders	.06	.05	.02
182	Lee Lacy	.06	.05	.02
183	Andy Hawkins	.04	.03	.02
184	Bobby Bonilla	.30	.25	.12
185	Roger McDowell	.10	.08	.04
186	Bruce Benedict	.04	.03	.02
187	Mark Huismann	.04	.03	.02
188	Tony Phillips	.04	.03	.02
189	Joe Hesketh	.04	.03	.02
190	Jim Sundberg	.06	.05	.02
191	Charles Hudson	.06	.05	.02
192	Cory Snyder	1.00	.70	.40
193	Roger Craig	.06	.05	.02
194	Kirk McCaskill	.10	.08	.04
195	Mike Pagliarulo	.10	.08	.04
196	Randy O'Neal	.04	.03	.02
197	Mark Bailey	.04	.03	.02
198	Lee Mazzilli	.06	.05	.02
199	Mariano Duncan	.06	.05	.02
200	Pete Rose	.60	.45	.25
201	John Cangelosi	.20	.15	.08
202	Ricky Wright	.04	.03	.02
203	Mike Kingery	.20	.15	.08
204	Sammy Stewart	.04	.03	.02
205	Graig Nettles	.10	.08	.04
206	Twins Leaders	.06	.05	.02
207	George Frazier	.04	.03	.02
208	John Shelby	.06	.05	.02
209	Rick Schu	.04	.03	.02
210	Lloyd Moseby	.08	.06	.03
211	John Morris	.06	.05	.02
212	Mike Fitzgerald	.04	.03	.02
213	Randy Myers	.20	.15	.08
214	Omar Moreno	.04	.03	.02
215	Mark Langston	.10	.08	.04
216	B.J. Surhoff	1.00	.70	.40
217	Chris Codiroli	.04	.03	.02
218	Sparky Anderson	.06	.05	.02
219	Cecilio Guante	.04	.03	.02
220	Joe Carter	.12	.09	.05
221	Vern Ruhle	.04	.03	.02
222	Denny Walling	.04	.03	.02
223	Charlie Leibrandt	.06	.05	.02
224	Wayne Tolleson	.04	.03	.02
225	Mike Smithson	.04	.03	.02
226	Max Venable	.04	.03	.02
227	Jamie Moyer	.20	.15	.08
228	Curt Wilkerson	.04	.03	.02
229	Mike Birkbeck	.12	.09	.05
230	Don Baylor	.10	.08	.04
231	Giants Leaders	.06	.05	.02
232	Reggie Williams	.15	.11	.06
233	Russ Morman	.12	.09	.05
234	Pat Sheridan	.04	.03	.02
235	Alvin Davis	.10	.08	.04
236	Tommy John	.15	.11	.06

		MT	NR MT	EX
237	Jim Morrison	.04	.03	.02
238	Bill Krueger	.04	.03	.02
239	Juan Espino	.04	.03	.02
240	Steve Balboni	.06	.05	.02
241	Danny Heep	.04	.03	.02
242	Rick Mahler	.04	.03	.02
243	Whitey Herzog	.06	.05	.02
244	Dickie Noles	.04	.03	.02
245	Willie Upshaw	.06	.05	.02
246	Jim Dwyer	.04	.03	.02
247	Jeff Reed	.06	.05	.02
248	Gene Walter	.06	.05	.02
249	Jim Pankovits	.04	.03	.02
250	Teddy Higuera	.15	.11	.06
251	Rob Wilfong	.04	.03	.02
252	Denny Martinez	.04	.03	.02
253	Eddie Milner	.04	.03	.02
254	Bob Tewksbury	.15	.11	.06
255	Juan Samuel	.10	.08	.04
256	Royals Leaders	.06	.05	.02
257	Bob Forsch	.06	.05	.02
258	Steve Yeager	.04	.03	.02
259	Mike Greenwell	1.50	1.25	.60
260	Vida Blue	.08	.06	.03
261	Ruben Sierra	1.25	.90	.50
262	Jim Winn	.04	.03	.02
263	Stan Javier	.06	.05	.02
264	Checklist 133-264	.04	.03	.02
265	Darrell Evans	.10	.08	.04
266	Jeff Hamilton	.15	.11	.06
267	Howard Johnson	.10	.08	.04
268	Pat Corrales	.04	.03	.02
269	Cliff Speck	.04	.03	.02
270	Jody Davis	.08	.06	.03
271	Mike Brown	.04	.03	.02
272	Andres Galarraga	.15	.11	.06
273	Gene Nelson	.04	.03	.02
274	Jeff Hearron	.10	.08	.04
275	LaMarr Hoyt	.06	.05	.02
276	Jackie Gutierrez	.04	.03	.02
277	Juan Agosto	.04	.03	.02
278	Gary Pettis	.06	.05	.02
279	Dan Plesac	.35	.25	.14
280	Jeffrey Leonard	.08	.06	.03
281	Reds Leaders	.08	.06	.03
282	Jeff Calhoun	.04	.03	.02
283	Doug Drabek	.25	.20	.10
284	John Moses	.04	.03	.02
285	Dennis Boyd	.06	.05	.02
286	Mike Woodard	.06	.05	.02
287	Dave Von Ohlen	.04	.03	.02
288	Tito Landrum	.04	.03	.02
289	Bob Kipper	.06	.05	.02
290	Leon Durham	.08	.06	.03
291	Mitch Williams	.20	.15	.08
292	Franklin Stubbs	.10	.08	.04
293	Bob Rodgers	.04	.03	.02
294	Steve Jeltz	.04	.03	.02
295	Len Dykstra	.12	.09	.05
296	Andres Thomas	.20	.15	.08
297	Don Schulze	.04	.03	.02
298	Larry Herndon	.06	.05	.02
299	Joel Davis	.06	.05	.02
300	Reggie Jackson	.30	.25	.12
301	Luis Aquino	.10	.08	.04
302	Bill Schroeder	.04	.03	.02
303	Juan Berenguer	.04	.03	.02
304	Phil Garner	.06	.05	.02
305	John Franco	.06	.05	.02
306	Red Sox Leaders	.06	.05	.02
307	Lee Guetterman	.25	.20	.10
308	Don Slaught	.04	.03	.02
309	Mike Young	.06	.05	.02
310	Frank Viola	.10	.08	.04
311	Turn Back The Clock (Rickey Henderson)	.10	.08	.04
312	Turn Back The Clock (Reggie Jackson)	.10	.08	.04
313	Turn Back The Clock (Roberto Clemente)	.15	.11	.06
314	Turn Back The Clock (Carl Yastrzemski)	.10	.08	.04
315	Turn Back The Clock (Maury Wills)	.06	.05	.02
316	Brian Fisher	.08	.06	.03
317	Clint Hurdle	.04	.03	.02
318	Jim Fregosi	.06	.05	.02
319	Greg Swindell	.40	.30	.15
320	Barry Bonds	.50	.40	.20
321	Mike Laga	.04	.03	.02
322	Chris Bando	.04	.03	.02
323	Al Newman	.12	.09	.05

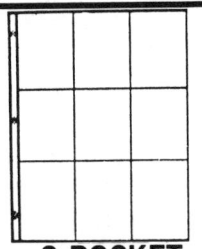
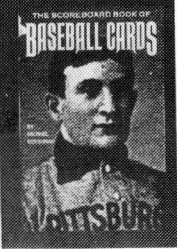

		MT	NR MT	EX
324	Dave Palmer	.06	.05	.02
325	Garry Templeton	.08	.06	.03
326	Mark Gubicza	.06	.05	.02
327	Dale Sveum	.30	.25	.12
328	Bob Welch	.08	.06	.03
329	Ron Roenicke	.04	.03	.02
330	Mike Scott	.12	.09	.05
331	Mets Leaders	.08	.06	.03
332	Joe Price	.04	.03	.02
333	Ken Phelps	.06	.05	.02
334	Ed Correa	.25	.20	.10
335	Candy Maldonado	.08	.06	.03
336	Allan Anderson	.10	.08	.04
337	Darrell Miller	.06	.05	.02
338	Tim Conroy	.04	.03	.02
339	Donnie Hill	.04	.03	.02
340	Roger Clemens	.90	.70	.35
341	Mike Brown	.04	.03	.02
342	Bob James	.04	.03	.02
343	Hal Lanier	.04	.03	.02
344a	Joe Niekro (copyright outside yellow on back)	.30	.25	.12
344b	Joe Niekro (copyright inside yellow on back)	.08	.06	.03
345	Andre Dawson	.20	.15	.08
346	Shawon Dunston	.08	.06	.03
347	Mickey Brantley	.08	.06	.03
348	Carmelo Martinez	.06	.05	.02
349	Storm Davis	.04	.03	.02
350	Keith Hernandez	.20	.15	.08
351	Gene Garber	.04	.03	.02
352	Mike Felder	.08	.06	.03
353	Ernie Camacho	.04	.03	.02
354	Jamie Quirk	.04	.03	.02
355	Don Carman	.08	.06	.03
356	White Sox Leaders	.06	.05	.02
357	Steve Fireovid	.10	.08	.04
358	Sal Butera	.04	.03	.02
359	Doug Corbett	.04	.03	.02
360	Pedro Guerrero	.15	.11	.06
361	Mark Thurmond	.04	.03	.02
362	Luis Quinones	.12	.09	.05
363	Jose Guzman	.12	.09	.05
364	Randy Bush	.04	.03	.02
365	Rick Rhoden	.08	.06	.03
366	Mark McGwire	3.50	2.75	1.50
367	Jeff Lahti	.04	.03	.02
368	John McNamara	.04	.03	.02
369	Brian Dayett	.04	.03	.02
370	Fred Lynn	.15	.11	.06
371	Mark Eichhorn	.25	.20	.10
372	Jerry Mumphrey	.06	.05	.02
373	Jeff Dedmon	.04	.03	.02
374	Glenn Hoffman	.04	.03	.02
375	Ron Guidry	.15	.11	.06
376	Scott Bradley	.04	.03	.02
377	John Henry Johnson	.04	.03	.02
378	Rafael Santana	.04	.03	.02
379	John Russell	.04	.03	.02
380	Rich Gossage	.15	.11	.06
381	Expos Leaders	.06	.05	.02
382	Rudy Law	.04	.03	.02
383	Ron Davis	.04	.03	.02
384	Johnny Grubb	.04	.03	.02
385	Orel Hershiser	.12	.09	.05
386	Dickie Thon	.06	.05	.02
387	T.R. Bryden	.12	.09	.05
388	Geno Petralli	.04	.03	.02
389	Jeff Robinson	.06	.05	.02
390	Gary Matthews	.08	.06	.03
391	Jay Howell	.06	.05	.02
392	Checklist 265-396	.04	.03	.02
393	Pete Rose	.40	.30	.15
394	Mike Bielecki	.04	.03	.02
395	Damaso Garcia	.06	.05	.02
396	Tim Lollar	.04	.03	.02
397	Greg Walker	.08	.06	.03
398	Brad Havens	.04	.03	.02
399	Curt Ford	.10	.08	.04
400	George Brett	.35	.25	.14
401	Billy Jo Robidoux	.08	.06	.03
402	Mike Trujillo	.04	.03	.02
403	Jerry Royster	.04	.03	.02
404	Doug Sisk	.04	.03	.02
405	Brook Jacoby	.10	.08	.04
406	Yankees Leaders	.06	.05	.02
407	Jim Acker	.04	.03	.02
408	John Mizerock	.04	.03	.02
409	Milt Thompson	.08	.06	.03
410	Fernando Valenzuela	.25	.20	.10
411	Darnell Coles	.06	.05	.02

		MT	NR MT	EX
412	Eric Davis	2.00	1.50	.80
413	Moose Haas	.04	.03	.02
414	Joe Orsulak	.06	.05	.02
415	Bobby Witt	.30	.25	.12
416	Tom Nieto	.04	.03	.02
417	Pat Perry	.08	.06	.03
418	Dick Williams	.06	.05	.02
419	Mark Portugal	.12	.09	.05
420	Will Clark	1.50	1.25	.60
421	Jose DeLeon	.06	.05	.02
422	Jack Howell	.10	.08	.04
423	Jaime Cocanower	.04	.03	.02
424	Chris Speier	.04	.03	.02
425	Tom Seaver	.25	.20	.10
426	Floyd Rayford	.04	.03	.02
427	Ed Nunez	.04	.03	.02
428	Bruce Bochy	.04	.03	.02
429	Tim Pyznarski	.12	.09	.05
430	Mike Schmidt	.35	.25	.14
431	Dodgers Leaders	.06	.05	.02
432	Jim Slaton	.04	.03	.02
433	Ed Hearn	.12	.09	.05
434	Mike Fischlin	.04	.03	.02
435	Bruce Sutter	.12	.09	.05
436	Andy Allanson	.15	.11	.06
437	Ted Power	.06	.05	.02
438	Kelly Downs	.30	.25	.12
439	Karl Best	.04	.03	.02
440	Willie McGee	.10	.08	.04
441	Dave Leiper	.12	.09	.05
442	Mitch Webster	.08	.06	.03
443	John Felske	.04	.03	.02
444	Jeff Russell	.04	.03	.02
445	Dave Lopes	.06	.05	.02
446	Chuck Finley	.12	.09	.05
447	Bill Almon	.04	.03	.02
448	Chris Bosio	.20	.15	.08
449	Pat Dodson	.15	.11	.06
450	Kirby Puckett	.30	.25	.12
451	Joe Sambito	.04	.03	.02
452	Dave Henderson	.04	.03	.02
453	Scott Terry	.12	.09	.05
454	Luis Salazar	.04	.03	.02
455	Mike Boddicker	.08	.06	.03
456	A's Leaders	.06	.05	.02
457	Len Matuszek	.04	.03	.02
458	Kelly Gruber	.08	.06	.03
459	Dennis Eckersley	.06	.05	.02
460	Darryl Strawberry	.35	.25	.14
461	Craig McMurtry	.04	.03	.02
462	Scott Fletcher	.06	.05	.02
463	Tom Candiotti	.04	.03	.02
464	Butch Wynegar	.04	.03	.02
465	Todd Worrell	.40	.30	.15
466	Kal Daniels	1.25	.90	.50
467	Randy St. Claire	.04	.03	.02
468	George Bamberger	.04	.03	.02
469	Mike Diaz	.25	.20	.10
470	Dave Dravecky	.06	.05	.02
471	Ronn Reynolds	.04	.03	.02
472	Bill Doran	.08	.06	.03
473	Steve Farr	.04	.03	.02
474	Jerry Narron	.04	.03	.02
475	Scott Garrelts	.04	.03	.02
476	Danny Tartabull	.90	.70	.35
477	Ken Howell	.04	.03	.02
478	Tim Laudner	.04	.03	.02
479	Bob Sebra	.15	.11	.06
480	Jim Rice	.25	.20	.10
481	Phillies Leaders	.06	.05	.02
482	Daryl Boston	.04	.03	.02
483	Dwight Lowry	.12	.09	.05
484	Jim Traber	.15	.11	.06
485	Tony Fernandez	.10	.08	.04
486	Otis Nixon	.04	.03	.02
487	Dave Gumpert	.04	.03	.02
488	Ray Knight	.08	.06	.03
489	Bill Gullickson	.06	.05	.02
490	Dale Murphy	.40	.30	.15
491	Ron Karkovice	.15	.11	.06
492	Mike Heath	.04	.03	.02
493	Tom Lasorda	.06	.05	.02
494	Barry Jones	.15	.11	.06
495	Gorman Thomas	.08	.06	.03
496	Bruce Bochte	.04	.03	.02
497	Dale Mohorcic	.20	.15	.08
498	Bob Kearney	.04	.03	.02
499	Bruce Ruffin	.25	.20	.10
500	Don Mattingly	2.25	1.75	.90
501	Craig Lefferts	.04	.03	.02
502	Dick Schofield	.04	.03	.02

		MT	NR MT	EX
503	Larry Andersen	.04	.03	.02
504	Mickey Hatcher	.04	.03	.02
505	Bryn Smith	.06	.05	.02
506	Orioles Leaders	.06	.05	.02
507	Dave Stapleton	.04	.03	.02
508	Scott Bankhead	.20	.15	.08
509	Enos Cabell	.04	.03	.02
510	Tom Henke	.06	.05	.02
511	Steve Lyons	.04	.03	.02
512	Dave Magadan	.70	.50	.30
513	Carmen Castillo	.04	.03	.02
514	Orlando Mercado	.04	.03	.02
515	Willie Hernandez	.06	.05	.02
516	Ted Simmons	.10	.08	.04
517	Mario Soto	.06	.05	.02
518	Gene Mauch	.06	.05	.02
519	Curt Young	.06	.05	.02
520	Jack Clark	.15	.11	.06
521	Rick Reuschel	.08	.06	.03
522	Checklist 397-528	.04	.03	.02
523	Earnie Riles	.06	.05	.02
524	Bob Shirley	.04	.03	.02
525	Phil Bradley	.12	.09	.05
526	Roger Mason	.04	.03	.02
527	Jim Wohlford	.04	.03	.02
528	Ken Dixon	.04	.03	.02
529	Alvaro Espinoza	.10	.08	.04
530	Tony Gwynn	.35	.25	.14
531	Astros Leaders	.06	.05	.02
532	Jeff Stone	.04	.03	.02
533	Argenis Salazar	.04	.03	.02
534	Scott Sanderson	.06	.05	.02
535	Tony Armas	.06	.05	.02
536	Terry Mulholland	.10	.08	.04
537	Rance Mulliniks	.04	.03	.02
538	Tom Niedenfuer	.06	.05	.02
539	Reid Nichols	.04	.03	.02
540	Terry Kennedy	.06	.05	.02
541	Rafael Belliard	.10	.08	.04
542	Ricky Horton	.06	.05	.02
543	Dave Johnson	.06	.05	.02
544	Zane Smith	.08	.06	.03
545	Buddy Bell	.08	.06	.03
546	Mike Morgan	.04	.03	.02
547	Rob Deer	.10	.08	.04
548	Bill Mooneyham	.10	.08	.04
549	Bob Melvin	.04	.03	.02
550	Pete Incaviglia	1.25	.90	.50
551	Frank Wills	.04	.03	.02
552	Larry Sheets	.10	.08	.04
553	Mike Maddux	.15	.11	.06
554	Buddy Biancalana	.04	.03	.02
555	Dennis Rasmussen	.06	.05	.02
556	Angels Leaders	.06	.05	.02
557	John Cerutti	.25	.20	.10
558	Greg Gagne	.08	.06	.03
559	Lance McCullers	.06	.05	.02
560	Glenn Davis	.25	.20	.10
561	Rey Quinones (Quinonez)	.15	.11	.06
562	Bryan Clutterbuck	.10	.08	.04
563	John Stefero	.04	.03	.02
564	Larry McWilliams	.04	.03	.02
565	Dusty Baker	.06	.05	.02
566	Tim Hulett	.04	.03	.02
567	Greg Mathews	.30	.25	.12
568	Earl Weaver	.06	.05	.02
569	Wade Rowdon	.10	.08	.04
570	Sid Fernandez	.10	.08	.04
571	Ozzie Virgil	.06	.05	.02
572	Pete Ladd	.04	.03	.02
573	Hal McRae	.08	.06	.03
574	Manny Lee	.04	.03	.02
575	Pat Tabler	.06	.05	.02
576	Frank Pastore	.04	.03	.02
577	Dann Bilardello	.04	.03	.02
578	Billy Hatcher	.06	.05	.02
579	Rick Burleson	.06	.05	.02
580	Mike Krukow	.06	.05	.02
581	Cubs Leaders	.06	.05	.02
582	Bruce Berenyi	.04	.03	.02
583	Junior Ortiz	.04	.03	.02
584	Ron Kittle	.08	.06	.03
585	Scott Bailes	.15	.11	.06
586	Ben Oglivie	.06	.05	.02
587	Eric Plunk	.06	.05	.02
588	Wallace Johnson	.04	.03	.02
589	Steve Crawford	.04	.03	.02
590	Vince Coleman	.25	.20	.10
591	Spike Owen	.04	.03	.02
592	Chris Welsh	.04	.03	.02
593	Chuck Tanner	.06	.05	.02

		MT	NR MT	EX
594	Rick Anderson	.10	.08	.04
595	Keith Hernandez AS	.12	.09	.05
596	Steve Sax AS	.08	.06	.03
597	Mike Schmidt AS	.20	.15	.08
598	Ozzie Smith AS	.08	.06	.03
599	Tony Gwynn AS	.20	.15	.08
600	Dave Parker AS	.10	.08	.04
601	Darryl Strawberry AS	.20	.15	.08
602	Gary Carter AS	.15	.11	.06
603a	Dwight Gooden AS (no trademark on front)	.80	.60	.30
603b	Dwight Gooden AS (trademark on front)	.30	.25	.12
604	Fernando Valenzuela AS	.12	.09	.05
605	Todd Worrell AS	.12	.09	.05
606a	Don Mattingly AS (no trademark on front)	1.50	1.25	.60
606b	Don Mattingly AS (trademark on front)	.70	.50	.30
607	Tony Bernazard AS	.06	.05	.02
608	Wade Boggs AS	.40	.30	.15
609	Cal Ripken AS	.15	.11	.06
610	Jim Rice AS	.15	.11	.06
611	Kirby Puckett AS	.15	.11	.06
612	George Bell AS	.15	.11	.06
613	Lance Parrish AS	.10	.08	.04
614	Roger Clemens AS	.30	.25	.12
615	Teddy Higuera AS	.10	.08	.04
616	Dave Righetti AS	.10	.08	.04
617	Al Nipper	.04	.03	.02
618	Tom Kelly	.08	.06	.03
619	Jerry Reed	.04	.03	.02
620	Jose Canseco	2.25	1.75	.90
621	Danny Cox	.08	.06	.03
622	Glenn Braggs	.40	.30	.15
623	Kurt Stillwell	.35	.25	.14
624	Tim Burke	.06	.05	.02
625	Mookie Wilson	.08	.06	.03
626	Joel Skinner	.04	.03	.02
627	Ken Oberkfell	.06	.05	.02
628	Bob Walk	.04	.03	.02
629	Larry Parrish	.08	.06	.03
630	John Candelaria	.08	.06	.03
631	Tigers Leaders	.06	.05	.02
632	Rob Woodward	.06	.05	.02
633	Jose Uribe	.06	.05	.02
634	Rafael Palmeiro	.40	.30	.15
635	Ken Schrom	.04	.03	.02
636	Darren Daulton	.04	.03	.02
637	Bip Roberts	.10	.08	.04
638	Rich Bordi	.04	.03	.02
639	Gerald Perry	.06	.05	.02
640	Mark Clear	.06	.05	.02
641	Domingo Ramos	.04	.03	.02
642	Al Pulido	.04	.03	.02
643	Ron Shepherd	.04	.03	.02
644	John Denny	.04	.03	.02
645	Dwight Evans	.12	.09	.05
646	Mike Mason	.04	.03	.02
647	Tom Lawless	.04	.03	.02
648	Barry Larkin	.60	.45	.25
649	Mickey Tettleton	.04	.03	.02
650	Hubie Brooks	.08	.06	.03
651	Benny Distefano	.04	.03	.02
652	Terry Forster	.06	.05	.02
653	Kevin Mitchell	.40	.30	.15
654	Checklist 529-660	.04	.03	.02
655	Jesse Barfield	.15	.11	.06
656	Rangers Leaders	.06	.05	.02
657	Tom Waddell	.04	.03	.02
658	Robby Thompson	.30	.25	.12
659	Aurelio Lopez	.04	.03	.02
660	Bob Horner	.12	.09	.05
661	Lou Whitaker	.15	.11	.06
662	Frank DiPino	.04	.03	.02
663	Cliff Johnson	.04	.03	.02
664	Mike Marshall	.08	.06	.03
665	Rod Scurry	.04	.03	.02
666	Von Hayes	.08	.06	.03
667	Ron Hassey	.04	.03	.02
668	Juan Bonilla	.04	.03	.02
669	Bud Black	.04	.03	.02
670	Jose Cruz	.08	.06	.03
671a	Ray Soff (no "D" before copyright line)	.20	.15	.08
671b	Ray Soff ("D" before copyright line)	.10	.08	.04
672	Chili Davis	.08	.06	.03
673	Don Sutton	.15	.11	.06
674	Bill Campbell	.04	.03	.02
675	Ed Romero	.04	.03	.02
676	Charlie Moore	.04	.03	.02

		MT	NR MT	EX
677	Bob Grich	.08	.06	.03
678	Carney Lansford	.06	.05	.02
679	Kent Hrbek	.12	.09	.05
680	Ryne Sandberg	.20	.15	.08
681	George Bell	.30	.25	.12
682	Jerry Reuss	.06	.05	.02
683	Gary Roenicke	.04	.03	.02
684	Kent Tekulve	.06	.05	.02
685	Jerry Hairston	.04	.03	.02
686	Doyle Alexander	.08	.06	.03
687	Alan Trammell	.25	.20	.10
688	Juan Beniquez	.04	.03	.02
689	Darrell Porter	.06	.05	.02
690	Dane Iorg	.04	.03	.02
691	Dave Parker	.15	.11	.06
692	Frank White	.08	.06	.03
693	Terry Puhl	.04	.03	.02
694	Phil Niekro	.20	.15	.08
695	Chico Walker	.12	.09	.05
696	Gary Lucas	.04	.03	.02
697	Ed Lynch	.04	.03	.02
698	Ernie Whitt	.06	.05	.02
699	Ken Landreaux	.06	.05	.02
700	Dave Bergman	.04	.03	.02
701	Willie Randolph	.08	.06	.03
702	Greg Gross	.04	.03	.02
703	Dave Schmidt	.06	.05	.02
704	Jesse Orosco	.06	.05	.02
705	Bruce Hurst	.08	.06	.03
706	Rick Manning	.04	.03	.02
707	Bob McClure	.04	.03	.02
708	Scott McGregor	.06	.05	.02
709	Dave Kingman	.10	.08	.04
710	Gary Gaetti	.12	.09	.05
711	Ken Griffey	.08	.06	.03
712	Don Robinson	.06	.05	.02
713	Tom Brookens	.04	.03	.02
714	Dan Quisenberry	.10	.08	.04
715	Bob Dernier	.04	.03	.02
716	Rick Leach	.04	.03	.02
717	Ed Vande Berg	.04	.03	.02
718	Steve Carlton	.25	.20	.10
719	Tom Hume	.04	.03	.02
720	Richard Dotson	.08	.06	.03
721	Tom Herr	.08	.06	.03
722	Bob Knepper	.06	.05	.02
723	Brett Butler	.06	.05	.02
724	Greg Minton	.04	.03	.02
725	George Hendrick	.06	.05	.02
726	Frank Tanana	.06	.05	.02
727	Mike Moore	.04	.03	.02
728	Tippy Martinez	.04	.03	.02
729	Tom Paciorek	.04	.03	.02
730	Eric Show	.04	.03	.02
731	Dave Concepcion	.10	.08	.04
732	Manny Trillo	.06	.05	.02
733	Bill Caudill	.04	.03	.02
734	Bill Madlock	.10	.08	.04
735	Rickey Henderson	.30	.25	.12
736	Steve Bedrosian	.10	.08	.04
737	Floyd Bannister	.08	.06	.03
738	Jorge Orta	.04	.03	.02
739	Chet Lemon	.06	.05	.02
740	Rich Gedman	.08	.06	.03
741	Paul Molitor	.12	.09	.05
742	Andy McGaffigan	.04	.03	.02
743	Dwayne Murphy	.06	.05	.02
744	Roy Smalley	.04	.03	.02
745	Glenn Hubbard	.04	.03	.02
746	Bob Ojeda	.08	.06	.03
747	Johnny Ray	.08	.06	.03
748	Mike Flanagan	.08	.06	.03
749	Ozzie Smith	.12	.09	.05
750	Steve Trout	.06	.05	.02
751	Garth Iorg	.04	.03	.02
752	Dan Petry	.06	.05	.02
753	Rick Honeycutt	.06	.05	.02
754	Dave LaPoint	.04	.03	.02
755	Luis Aguayo	.04	.03	.02
756	Carlton Fisk	.15	.11	.06
757	Nolan Ryan	.25	.20	.10
758	Tony Bernazard	.06	.05	.02
759	Joel Youngblood	.04	.03	.02
760	Mike Witt	.10	.08	.04
761	Greg Pryor	.04	.03	.02
762	Gary Ward	.06	.05	.02
763	Tim Flannery	.04	.03	.02
764	Bill Buckner	.08	.06	.03
765	Kirk Gibson	.20	.15	.08
766	Don Aase	.06	.05	.02

		MT	NR MT	EX
767	Ron Cey	.08	.06	.03
768	Dennis Lamp	.04	.03	.02
769	Steve Sax	.12	.09	.05
770	Dave Winfield	.25	.20	.10
771	Shane Rawley	.06	.05	.02
772	Harold Baines	.12	.09	.05
773	Robin Yount	.20	.15	.08
774	Wayne Krenchicki	.04	.03	.02
775	Joaquin Andujar	.06	.05	.02
776	Tom Brunansky	.10	.08	.04
777	Chris Chambliss	.06	.05	.02
778	Jack Morris	.20	.15	.08
779	Craig Reynolds	.04	.03	.02
780	Andre Thornton	.06	.05	.02
781	Atlee Hammaker	.04	.03	.02
782	Brian Downing	.06	.05	.02
783	Willie Wilson	.10	.08	.04
784	Cal Ripken	.30	.25	.15
785	Terry Francona	.04	.03	.02
786	Jimy Williams	.04	.03	.02
787	Alejandro Pena	.04	.03	.02
788	Tim Stoddard	.04	.03	.02
789	Dan Schatzeder	.04	.03	.02
790	Julio Cruz	.04	.03	.02
791	Lance Parrish	.15	.11	.06
792	Checklist 661-792	.04	.03	.02

1987 Topps All-Star Glossy
Set of 22

For the fourth consecutive year, Topps produced an All-Star Game commemorative set of 22 cards. The glossy cards, which measure 2½'' by 3½'', were included in rack packs. Using the same basic card design as in previous efforts with a few minor changes, the 1987 edition featured American and National League logos on the card fronts. Card #'s 1-12 feature representatives from the American League, while #'s 13-22 are National Leaguers.

		MT	NR MT	EX
Complete Set:		5.00	3.75	2.00
Common Player:		.15	.11	.06
1	Whitey Herzog	.15	.11	.06
2	Keith Hernandez	.40	.30	.15
3	Ryne Sandberg	.40	.30	.15
4	Mike Schmidt	.60	.45	.25
5	Ozzie Smith	.25	.20	.10
6	Tony Gwynn	.50	.40	.20
7	Dale Murphy	.70	.50	.30
8	Darryl Strawberry	.60	.45	.25
9	Gary Carter	.40	.30	.15
10	Dwight Gooden	.60	.45	.25
11	Fernando Valenzuela	.30	.25	.12
12	Dick Howser	.15	.11	.06
13	Wally Joyner	1.25	.90	.50
14	Lou Whitaker	.25	.20	.10
15	Wade Boggs	.80	.60	.30
16	Cal Ripken	.50	.40	.20
17	Dave Winfield	.40	.30	.15
18	Rickey Henderson	.50	.40	.20
19	Kirby Puckett	.35	.25	.14
20	Lance Parrish	.30	.25	.12
21	Roger Clemens	.60	.45	.25
22	Teddy Higuera	.30	.25	.12

1987 Topps All-Star Glossy Set of 60

Using the same design as the previous year, the 1987 Topps All-Star Glossy set included 48 All-Star performers plus 12 potential superstars branded as "Hot Prospects." The card fronts are uncluttered, save the player's name found in very small print at the bottom. The set was available via a mail-in offer. Six sub-sets made up the 60-card set, with each subset available for $1.00 plus six special offer cards that were found in wax packs.

		MT	NR MT	EX
Complete Set:		14.00	10.50	5.50
Common Player:		.15	.11	.06
1	Don Mattingly	3.50	2.75	1.50
2	Tony Gwynn	.60	.45	.25
3	Gary Gaetti	.25	.20	.10
4	Glenn Davis	.30	.25	.12
5	Roger Clemens	.70	.50	.30
6	Dale Murphy	.90	.70	.35
7	Lou Whitaker	.30	.25	.12
8	Roger McDowell	.15	.11	.06
9	Cory Snyder	.70	.50	.30
10	Todd Worrell	.25	.20	.10
11	Gary Carter	.50	.40	.20
12	Eddie Murray	.70	.50	.30
13	Bob Knepper	.15	.11	.06
14	Harold Baines	.20	.15	.08
15	Jeff Reardon	.20	.15	.08
16	Joe Carter	.25	.20	.10
17	Dave Parker	.25	.20	.10
18	Wade Boggs	1.25	.90	.50
19	Danny Tartabull	.35	.25	.14
20	Jim Deshaies	.20	.15	.08
21	Rickey Henderson	.70	.50	.30
22	Rob Deer	.20	.15	.08
23	Ozzie Smith	.25	.20	.10
24	Dave Righetti	.25	.20	.10
25	Kent Hrbek	.30	.25	.12
26	Keith Hernandez	.40	.30	.15
27	Don Baylor	.15	.11	.06
28	Mike Schmidt	.90	.70	.35
29	Pete Incaviglia	.70	.50	.30
30	Barry Bonds	.40	.30	.15
31	George Brett	.90	.70	.35
32	Darryl Strawberry	.70	.50	.30
33	Mike Witt	.25	.20	.10
34	Kevin Bass	.15	.11	.06
35	Jesse Barfield	.25	.20	.10
36	Bob Ojeda	.15	.11	.06
37	Cal Ripken	.70	.50	.30
38	Vince Coleman	.25	.20	.10
39	Wally Joyner	1.75	1.25	.70
40	Robby Thompson	.25	.20	.10
41	Pete Rose	1.25	.90	.50
42	Jim Rice	.50	.40	.20
43	Tony Bernazard	.15	.11	.06
44	Eric Davis	1.25	.90	.50
45	George Bell	.50	.40	.20
46	Hubie Brooks	.15	.11	.06
47	Jack Morris	.30	.25	.12
48	Tim Raines	.50	.40	.20
49	Mark Eichhorn	.20	.15	.08
50	Kevin Mitchell	.30	.25	.12

		MT	NR MT	EX
51	Dwight Gooden	.80	.60	.30
52	Doug DeCinces	.15	.11	.06
53	Fernando Valenzuela	.35	.25	.14
54	Reggie Jackson	.70	.50	.30
55	Johnny Ray	.15	.11	.06
56	Mike Pagliarulo	.20	.15	.08
57	Kirby Puckett	.40	.30	.15
58	Lance Parrish	.30	.25	.12
59	Jose Canseco	1.25	.90	.50
60	Greg Mathews	.25	.20	.10

1987 Topps Baseball Highlights

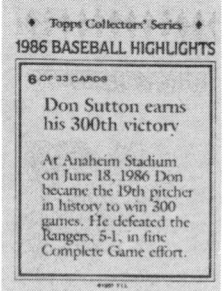

The "Baseball Highlights" boxed set of 33 cards was prepared by Topps for distribution at stores in the Woolworth's chain. Each card measures 2½" by 3½" in size and features a memorable baseball event that occurred during the 1986 season. The glossy set sold for $1.99 in Woolworth's stores.

		MT	NR MT	EX
Complete Set:		5.00	3.75	2.00
Common Player:		.09	.07	.04
1	Steve Carlton	.30	.25	.12
2	Cecil Cooper	.12	.09	.05
3	Rickey Henderson	.35	.25	.14
4	Reggie Jackson	.30	.25	.12
5	Jim Rice	.30	.25	.12
6	Don Sutton	.20	.15	.08
7	Roger Clemens	.50	.40	.20
8	Mike Schmidt	.35	.25	.14
9	Jesse Barfield	.15	.11	.06
10	Wade Boggs	.70	.50	.30
11	Tim Raines	.30	.25	.12
12	Jose Canseco	.70	.50	.30
13	Todd Worrell	.15	.11	.06
14	Dave Righetti	.15	.11	.06
15	Don Mattingly	1.00	.70	.40
16	Tony Gwynn	.35	.25	.14
17	Marty Barrett	.09	.07	.04
18	Mike Scott	.12	.09	.05
19	World Series Game #1 (Bruce Hurst)	.09	.07	.04
20	World Series Game #1 (Calvin Schiraldi)	.09	.07	.04
21	World Series Game #2 (Dwight Evans)	.12	.09	.05
22	World Series Game #2 (Dave Henderson)	.09	.07	.04
23	World Series Game #3 (Len Dykstra)	.12	.09	.05
24	World Series Game #3 (Bob Ojeda)	.09	.07	.04
25	World Series Game #4 (Gary Carter)	.30	.25	.12
26	World Series Game #4 (Ron Darling)	.15	.11	.06
27	Jim Rice	.30	.25	.12
28	Bruce Hurst	.09	.07	.04
29	World Series Game #6 (Darryl Strawberry)	.35	.25	.14
30	World Series Game #6 (Ray Knight)	.09	.07	.04

		MT	NR MT	EX
31	World Series Game #6 (Keith Hernandez)			
		.25	.20	.10
32	World Series Games #7 (Mets Celebrate)			
		.12	.09	.05
33	Ray Knight	.09	.07	.04

1987 Topps Box Panels

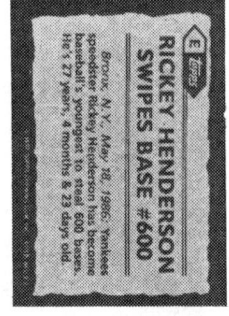

Offering baseball cards on retail boxes for a second straight year, Topps reduced the size of the cards to 2⅛'' by 3''. Four different wax pack boxes were available, each featuring two cards that were placed on the sides of the boxes. The card fronts are identical in design to the regular issue cards. The backs are printed in blue and yellow and carry a commentary imitating a newspaper format. The cards are numbered A through H.

		MT	NR MT	EX
Complete Panel Set:		5.00	3.75	2.00
Complete Singles Set:		2.00	1.50	.80
Common Panel:		.75	.60	.30
Common Single Player:		.15	.11	.06
Panel		1.25	.90	.50
A	Don Baylor	.15	.11	.06
B	Steve Carlton	.30	.25	.12
Panel		.75	.60	.30
C	Ron Cey	.15	.11	.06
D	Cecil Cooper	.15	.11	.06
Panel		1.75	1.25	.70
E	Rickey Henderson	.40	.30	.15
F	Jim Rice	.30	.25	.12
Panel		1.25	.90	.50
G	Don Sutton	.20	.15	.08
H	Dave Winfield	.30	.25	.12

1987 Topps Coins

For the first time since 1971, Topps issued a set of baseball "coins." Similar in design to the 1964 edition of Topps coins, the metal discs measure 1½'' in diameter. The aluminum coins were sold on a limited basis in retail outlets. Three coins and three sticks of gum were found in a pack. The coin fronts feature a full-color photo along with the player's name, team and position in a white band at the bottom of the coin.

Gold-colored rims are found for American League players; National League players have silver-colored rims. Backs are silver in color and carry the coin number, player's name and personal and statistical information.

		MT	NR MT	EX
Complete Set:		10.00	7.50	4.00
Common Player:		.15	.11	.06
1	Harold Baines	.15	.11	.06
2	Jesse Barfield	.15	.11	.06
3	George Bell	.25	.20	.10
4	Wade Boggs	.60	.45	.25
5	George Brett	.30	.25	.12
6	Jose Canseco	.50	.40	.20
7	Joe Carter	.15	.11	.06
8	Roger Clemens	.40	.30	.15
9	Alvin Davis	.15	.11	.06
10	Rob Deer	.15	.11	.06
11	Kirk Gibson	.20	.15	.08
12	Rickey Henderson	.25	.20	.10
13	Kent Hrbek	.20	.15	.08
14	Pete Incaviglia	.30	.25	.12
15	Reggie Jackson	.25	.20	.10
16	Wally Joyner	.60	.45	.25
17	Don Mattingly	1.00	.70	.40
18	Jack Morris	.20	.15	.08
19	Eddie Murray	.25	.20	.10
20	Kirby Puckett	.25	.20	.10
21	Jim Rice	.25	.20	.10
22	Dave Righetti	.20	.15	.08
23	Cal Ripken	.25	.20	.10
24	Cory Snyder	.25	.20	.10
25	Danny Tartabull	.20	.15	.08
26	Dave Winfield	.25	.20	.10
27	Hubie Brooks	.15	.11	.06
28	Gary Carter	.25	.20	.10
29	Vince Coleman	.20	.15	.08
30	Eric Davis	.70	.50	.30
31	Glenn Davis	.15	.11	.06
32	Steve Garvey	.25	.20	.10
33	Dwight Gooden	.40	.30	.15
34	Tony Gwynn	.25	.20	.10
35	Von Hayes	.15	.11	.06
36	Keith Hernandez	.20	.15	.08
37	Dale Murphy	.30	.25	.12
38	Dave Parker	.20	.15	.08
39	Tony Pena	.15	.11	.06
40	Nolan Ryan	.25	.20	.10
41	Ryne Sandberg	.20	.15	.08
42	Steve Sax	.20	.15	.08
43	Mike Schmidt	.30	.25	.12
44	Mike Scott	.15	.11	.06
45	Ozzie Smith	.15	.11	.06
46	Darryl Strawberry	.30	.25	.12
47	Fernando Valenzuela	.20	.15	.08
48	Todd Worrell	.15	.11	.06

1987 Topps Gallery of Champions

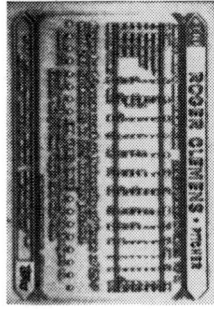

Designed as a tribute to the 1986 season's winners of baseball's most prestigious awards, the Gallery of Champions are metal "cards" that are one-quarter size replicas of the regular issue Topps cards. The bronze and silver sets were issued in leather-like velvet-lined display cases; the aluminum sets came cello wrapped. Hobby dealers who purchased one bronze set or a 16-set case of aluminum "cards" received one free Jose Canseco pewter metal mini-card. The purchase of a silver set included five Canseco pewters.

		MT	NR MT	EX
	Complete Aluminum Set:	25.00	18.50	10.00
	Complete Bronze Set:	150.00	112.00	60.00
	Complete Silver Set:	600.00	450.00	240.00
(1a)	Jesse Barfield (aluminum)	1.00	.70	.40
(1b)	Jesse Barfield (bronze)	10.00	7.50	4.00
(1c)	Jesse Barfield (silver)	30.00	22.00	12.00
(2a)	Wade Boggs (aluminum)	2.00	1.50	.80
(2b)	Wade Boggs (bronze)	20.00	15.00	8.00
(2c)	Wade Boggs (silver)	100.00	75.00	40.00
(3a)	Jose Canseco (aluminum)	2.00	1.50	.80
(3b)	Jose Canseco (bronze)	20.00	15.00	8.00
(3c)	Jose Canseco (silver)	100.00	75.00	40.00
(4a)	Joe Carter (aluminum)	.70	.50	.30
(4b)	Joe Carter (bronze)	7.50	5.75	3.00
(4c)	Joe Carter (silver)	20.00	15.00	8.00
(5a)	Roger Clemens (aluminum)	1.50	1.25	.60
(5b)	Roger Clemens (bronze)	15.00	11.00	6.00
(5c)	Roger Clemens (silver)	80.00	60.00	32.00
(6a)	Tony Gwynn (aluminum)	1.25	.90	.50
(6b)	Tony Gwynn (bronze)	12.00	9.00	4.75
(6c)	Tony Gwynn (silver)	50.00	37.00	20.00
(7a)	Don Mattingly (aluminum)	5.00	3.75	2.00
(7b)	Don Mattingly (bronze)	35.00	26.00	14.00
(7c)	Don Mattingly (silver)	150.00	112.00	60.00
(8a)	Tim Raines (aluminum)	1.00	.70	.40
(8b)	Tim Raines (bronze)	10.00	7.50	4.00
(8c)	Tim Raines (silver)	30.00	22.00	12.00
(9a)	Dave Righetti (aluminum)	1.00	.70	.40
(9b)	Dave Righetti (bronze)	10.00	7.50	4.00
(9c)	Dave Righetti (silver)	30.00	22.00	12.00
(10a)	Mike Schmidt (aluminum)	1.50	1.25	.60
(10b)	Mike Schmidt (bronze)	15.00	11.00	6.00
(10c)	Mike Schmidt (silver)	80.00	60.00	32.00
(11a)	Mike Scott (aluminum)	.70	.50	.30
(11b)	Mike Scott (bronze)	7.50	5.75	3.00
(11c)	Mike Scott (silver)	20.00	15.00	8.00
(12a)	Todd Worrell (aluminum)	.70	.50	.30
(12b)	Todd Worrell (bronze)	10.00	7.50	4.00
(12c)	Todd Worrell (silver)	20.00	15.00	8.00

1987 Topps Glossy Rookies

The 1987 Topps Glossy Rookies set of 22 cards was introduced with Topps' new 100-card "Jumbo Packs." Intended for sale in supermarkets, the jumbo packs contained one glossy card. Measuring the standard 2½" by 3½" size, the special insert cards featured the top rookies from the previous season.

		MT	NR MT	EX
	Complete Set:	10.00	7.50	4.00
	Common Player:	.20	.15	.08
1	Andy Allanson	.30	.25	.12
2	John Cangelosi	.40	.30	.15
3	Jose Canseco	2.00	1.50	.80

		MT	NR MT	EX
4	Will Clark	1.50	1.25	.60
5	Mark Eichhorn	.50	.40	.20
6	Pete Incaviglia	1.00	.70	.40
7	Wally Joyner	2.00	1.50	.80
8	Eric King	.40	.30	.15
9	Dave Magadan	1.00	.70	.40
10	John Morris	.20	.15	.08
11	Juan Nieves	.40	.30	.15
12	Rafael Palmeiro	.80	.60	.30
13	Billy Jo Robidoux	.20	.15	.08
14	Bruce Ruffin	.50	.40	.20
15	Ruben Sierra	1.25	.90	.50
16	Cory Snyder	.80	.60	.30
17	Kurt Stillwell	.60	.45	.25
18	Dale Sveum	.50	.40	.20
19	Danny Tartabull	.80	.60	.30
20	Andres Thomas	.50	.40	.20
21	Robby Thompson	.50	.40	.20
22	Todd Worrell	.60	.45	.25

1987 Topps Mini League Leaders

Returning for 1987, the Topps "Major League Leaders" set was increased in size from 66 to 76 cards. The 2⅛" by 3" cards feature wood grain borders that encompass a white-bordered full-color photo. The card backs are printed in yellow, orange and brown and list the player's official ranking based on his 1986 American or National statistics. The players featured are those who finished the top five in their leagues' various batting and pitching statistics. The cards were sold in plastic packs, seven cards plus a game card per pack.

		MT	NR MT	EX
	Complete Set:	6.00	4.50	2.50
	Common Player:	.09	.07	.04
1	Bob Horner	.20	.15	.08
2	Dale Murphy	.50	.40	.20
3	Lee Smith	.15	.11	.06
4	Eric Davis	.80	.60	.30
5	John Franco	.15	.11	.06
6	Dave Parker	.20	.15	.08
7	Kevin Bass	.15	.11	.06
8	Glenn Davis	.20	.15	.08
9	Bill Doran	.15	.11	.06
10	Bob Knepper	.09	.07	.04
11	Mike Scott	.20	.15	.08
12	Dave Smith	.09	.07	.04
13	Mariano Duncan	.09	.07	.04
14	Orel Hershiser	.15	.11	.06
15	Steve Sax	.20	.15	.08
16	Fernando Valenzuela	.25	.20	.10
17	Tim Raines	.30	.25	.12
18	Jeff Reardon	.15	.11	.06
19	Floyd Youmans	.15	.11	.06
20	Gary Carter	.30	.25	.12
21	Ron Darling	.20	.15	.08
22	Sid Fernandez	.15	.11	.06
23	Dwight Gooden	.60	.45	.25
24	Keith Hernandez	.25	.20	.10
25	Bob Ojeda	.15	.11	.06

		MT	NR MT	EX
26	Darryl Strawberry	.50	.40	.20
27	Steve Bedrosian	.15	.11	.06
28	Von Hayes	.15	.11	.06
29	Juan Samuel	.20	.15	.08
30	Mike Schmidt	.50	.40	.20
31	Rick Rhoden	.15	.11	.06
32	Vince Coleman	.20	.15	.08
33	Danny Cox	.15	.11	.06
34	Todd Worrell	.20	.15	.08
35	Tony Gwynn	.40	.30	.15
36	Mike Krukow	.09	.07	.04
37	Candy Maldonado	.15	.11	.06
38	Don Aase	.09	.07	.04
39	Eddie Murray	.40	.30	.15
40	Cal Ripken	.40	.30	.15
41	Wade Boggs	.80	.60	.30
42	Roger Clemens	.60	.45	.25
43	Bruce Hurst	.15	.11	.06
44	Jim Rice	.30	.25	.12
45	Wally Joyner	.80	.60	.30
46	Donnie Moore	.09	.07	.04
47	Gary Pettis	.09	.07	.04
48	Mike Witt	.15	.11	.06
49	John Cangelosi	.15	.11	.06
50	Tom Candiotti	.09	.07	.04
51	Joe Carter	.20	.15	.08
52	Pat Tabler	.15	.11	.06
53	Kirk Gibson	.25	.20	.10
54	Willie Hernandez	.09	.07	.04
55	Jack Morris	.25	.20	.10
56	Alan Trammell	.30	.25	.12
57	George Brett	.50	.40	.20
58	Willie Wilson	.15	.11	.06
59	Rob Deer	.15	.11	.06
60	Teddy Higuera	.15	.11	.06
61	Bert Blyleven	.20	.15	.08
62	Gary Gaetti	.20	.15	.08
63	Kirby Puckett	.30	.25	.12
64	Rickey Henderson	.40	.30	.15
65	Don Mattingly	1.25	.90	.50
66	Dennis Rasmussen	.09	.07	.04
67	Dave Righetti	.20	.15	.08
68	Jose Canseco	.80	.60	.30
69	Dave Kingman	.15	.11	.06
70	Phil Bradley	.15	.11	.06
71	Mark Langston	.15	.11	.06
72	Pete O'Brien	.15	.11	.06
73	Jesse Barfield	.20	.15	.08
74	George Bell	.30	.25	.12
75	Tony Fernandez	.15	.11	.06
76	Tom Henke	.15	.11	.06
77	Checklist	.09	.07	.04

1987 Topps Stickers

 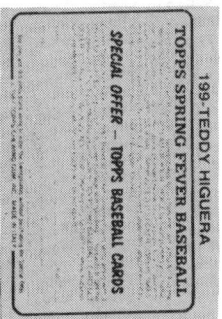

For the seventh consecutive year, Topps issued stickers to be housed in a specially designed yearbook. The stickers, which measure 2⅛" by 3", offer a full-color front with a peel-off back printed in blue ink on white stock. The sticker fronts feature either one full-size player picture or two half-size individual stickers. The sticker yearbook measures 9" by 10¾" and contains 36 glossy, magazine-style pages, all printed in full color. Mike Schmidt, 1986 National League MVP, is featured on the cover. The yearbook sold in retail outlets for 35¢, while stickers were sold five in a pack for 25¢.

		MT	NR MT	EX
Complete Set:		15.00	11.00	6.00
Common Player:		.03	.02	.01
Sticker Album:		.40	.30	.15
1	Jim Deshaies	.04	.03	.02
2	Roger Clemens	.15	.11	.06
3	Roger Clemens	.15	.11	.06
4	Dwight Evans	.06	.05	.02
5	Dwight Gooden	.15	.11	.06
6	Dwight Gooden	.15	.11	.06
7	Dave Lopes	.04	.03	.02
8	Dave Righetti	.06	.05	.02
9	Dave Righetti	.10	.08	.04
10	Ruben Sierra	.25	.20	.10
11	Todd Worrell	.06	.05	.02
12	Todd Worrell	.08	.06	.03
13	N.L. Championship Series (Lenny Dykstra)	.06	.05	.02
14	N.L. Championship Series (Gary Carter)	.08	.06	.03
15	N.L. Championship Series (Mike Scott)	.06	.05	.02
16	A.L. Championship Series (Gary Pettis)	.03	.02	.01
17	A.L. Championship Series (Jim Rice)	.08	.06	.03
18	A.L. Championship Series (Bruce Hurst)	.04	.03	.02
19	1986 World Series (Bruce Hurst)	.04	.03	.02
20	1986 World Series (Wade Boggs)	.15	.11	.06
21	1986 World Series (Lenny Dykstra)	.06	.05	.02
22	1986 World Series (Gary Carter)	.08	.06	.03
23	1986 World Series (Dave Henderson)	.03	.02	.01
24	1986 World Series (Howard Johnson)	.06	.05	.02
25	1986 World Series (Mets Celebrate)	.08	.06	.03
26	Glenn Davis	.15	.11	.06
27	Nolan Ryan	.10	.08	.04
28	Charlie Kerfeld	.04	.03	.02
29	Jose Cruz	.04	.03	.02
30	Phil Garner	.06	.05	.02
31	Bill Doran	.06	.05	.02
32	Bob Knepper	.03	.02	.01
33	Denny Walling	.10	.08	.04
34	Kevin Bass	.04	.03	.02
35	Mike Scott	.10	.08	.04
36	Dale Murphy	.25	.20	.10
37	Paul Assenmacher	.06	.05	.02
38	Ken Oberkfell	.06	.05	.02
39	Andres Thomas	.08	.06	.03
40	Gene Garber	.03	.02	.01
41	Bob Horner	.12	.09	.05
42	Rafael Ramirez	.04	.03	.02
43	Rick Mahler	.03	.02	.01
44	Omar Moreno	.04	.03	.02
45	Dave Palmer	.03	.02	.01
46	Ozzie Smith	.10	.08	.04
47	Bob Forsch	.03	.02	.01
48	Willie McGee	.06	.05	.02
49	Tom Herr	.06	.05	.02
50	Vince Coleman	.08	.06	.03
51	Andy Van Slyke	.06	.05	.02
52	Jack Clark	.08	.06	.03
53	John Tudor	.04	.03	.02
54	Terry Pendleton	.03	.02	.01
55	Todd Worrell	.10	.08	.04
56	Lee Smith	.06	.05	.02
57	Leon Durham	.04	.03	.02
58	Jerry Mumphrey	.04	.03	.02
59	Shawon Dunston	.06	.05	.02
60	Scott Sanderson	.06	.05	.02
61	Ryne Sandberg	.15	.11	.06
62	Gary Matthews	.04	.03	.02
63	Dennis Eckersley	.03	.02	.01
64	Jody Davis	.06	.05	.02
65	Keith Moreland	.04	.03	.02
66	Mike Marshall	.04	.03	.02
67	Bill Madlock	.06	.05	.02
68	Greg Brock	.04	.03	.02
69	Pedro Guerrero	.08	.06	.03
70	Steve Sax	.12	.09	.05
71	Rick Honeycutt	.03	.02	.01
72	Franklin Stubbs	.04	.03	.02
73	Mike Scioscia	.20	.15	.08
74	Mariano Duncan	.03	.02	.01
75	Fernando Valenzuela	.15	.11	.06
76	Hubie Brooks	.06	.05	.02
77	Andre Dawson	.10	.08	.04

		MT	NR MT	EX				MT	NR MT	EX
78	Tim Burke	.04	.03	.02		169	Bruce Bochte	.03	.02	.01
79	Floyd Youmans	.04	.03	.02		170	Dwayne Murphy	.06	.05	.02
80	Tim Wallach	.04	.03	.02		171	Carney Lansford	.30	.25	.12
81	Jeff Reardon	.06	.05	.02		172	Joaquin Andujar	.04	.03	.02
82	Mitch Webster	.15	.11	.06		173	Dave Kingman	.08	.06	.03
83	Bryn Smith	.03	.02	.01		174	Wally Joyner	.40	.30	.15
84	Andres Galarraga	.12	.09	.05		175	Gary Pettis	.15	.11	.06
85	Tim Raines	.15	.11	.06		176	Dick Schofield	.15	.11	.06
86	Chris Brown	.08	.06	.03		177	Donnie Moore	.06	.05	.02
87	Bob Brenly	.03	.02	.01		178	Brian Downing	.15	.11	.06
88	Will Clark	.25	.20	.10		179	Mike Witt	.08	.06	.03
89	Scott Garrelts	.04	.03	.02		180	Bob Boone	.15	.11	.06
90	Jeffrey Leonard	.06	.05	.02		181	Kirk McCaskill	.04	.03	.02
91	Robby Thompson	.06	.05	.02		182	Doug DeCinces	.06	.05	.02
92	Mike Krukow	.03	.02	.01		183	Don Sutton	.10	.08	.04
93	Danny Gladden	.03	.02	.01		184	Jessie Barfield	.10	.08	.04
94	Candy Maldonado	.04	.03	.02		185	Tom Henke	.25	.20	.10
95	Chili Davis	.03	.02	.01		186	Willie Upshaw	.06	.05	.02
96	Dwight Gooden	.30	.25	.12		187	Mark Eichhorn	.08	.06	.03
97	Sid Fernandez	.04	.03	.02		188	Damaso Garcia	.10	.08	.04
98	Len Dykstra	.06	.05	.02		189	Jim Clancy	.04	.03	.02
99	Bob Ojeda	.04	.03	.02		190	Lloyd Moseby	.04	.03	.02
100	Wally Backman	.04	.03	.02		191	Tony Fernandez	.06	.05	.02
101	Gary Carter	.15	.11	.06		192	Jimmy Key	.06	.05	.02
102	Keith Hernandez	.10	.08	.04		193	George Bell	.20	.15	.08
103	Darryl Strawberry	.15	.11	.06		194	Rob Deer	.06	.05	.02
104	Roger McDowell	.08	.06	.03		195	Mark Clear	.03	.02	.01
105	Ron Darling	.08	.06	.03		196	Robin Yount	.10	.08	.04
106	Tony Gwynn	.20	.15	.08		197	Jim Gantner	.04	.03	.02
107	Dave Dravecky	.04	.03	.02		198	Cecil Cooper	.06	.05	.02
108	Terry Kennedy	.08	.06	.03		199	Teddy Higuera	.08	.06	.03
109	Rich Gossage	.10	.08	.04		200	Paul Molitor	.08	.06	.03
110	Garry Templeton	.04	.03	.02		201	Dan Plesac	.08	.06	.03
111	Lance McCullers	.04	.03	.02		202	Billy Jo Robidoux	.03	.02	.01
112	Eric Show	.03	.02	.01		203	Earnie Riles	.04	.03	.02
113	John Kruk	.20	.15	.08		204	Ken Schrom	.03	.02	.01
114	Tim Flannery	.06	.05	.02		205	Pat Tabler	.04	.03	.02
115	Steve Garvey	.15	.11	.06		206	Mel Hall	.03	.02	.01
116	Mike Schmidt	.25	.20	.10		207	Tony Bernazard	.03	.02	.01
117	Glenn Wilson	.06	.05	.02		208	Joe Carter	.10	.08	.04
118	Kent Tekulve	.06	.05	.02		209	Ernie Camacho	.06	.05	.02
119	Gary Redus	.08	.06	.03		210	Julio Franco	.06	.05	.02
120	Shane Rawley	.04	.03	.02		211	Tom Candiotti	.08	.06	.03
121	Von Hayes	.06	.05	.02		212	Brook Jacoby	.06	.05	.02
122	Don Carman	.04	.03	.02		213	Cory Snyder	.30	.25	.12
123	Bruce Ruffin	.06	.05	.02		214	Jim Presley	.08	.06	.03
124	Steve Bedrosian	.06	.05	.02		215	Mike Moore	.08	.06	.03
125	Juan Samuel	.06	.05	.02		216	Harold Reynolds	.04	.03	.02
126	Sid Bream	.08	.06	.03		217	Scott Bradley	.03	.02	.01
127	Cecilio Guante	.03	.02	.01		218	Matt Young	.04	.03	.02
128	Rick Reuschel	.04	.03	.02		219	Mark Langston	.04	.03	.02
129	Tony Pena	.04	.03	.02		220	Alvin Davis	.06	.05	.02
130	Rick Rhoden	.06	.05	.02		221	Phil Bradley	.06	.05	.02
131	Barry Bonds	.10	.08	.04		222	Ken Phelps	.04	.03	.02
132	Joe Orsulak	.03	.02	.01		223	Danny Tartabull	.20	.15	.08
133	Jim Morrison	.12	.09	.05		224	Eddie Murray	.20	.15	.08
134	R.J. Reynolds	.04	.03	.02		225	Rick Dempsey	.03	.02	.01
135	Johnny Ray	.06	.05	.02		226	Fred Lynn	.06	.05	.02
136	Eric Davis	.40	.30	.15		227	Mike Boddicker	.04	.03	.02
137	Tom Browning	.10	.08	.04		228	Don Aase	.04	.03	.02
138	John Franco	.06	.05	.02		229	Larry Sheets	.06	.05	.02
139	Pete Rose	.20	.15	.08		230	Storm Davis	.04	.03	.02
140	Bill Gullickson	.04	.03	.02		231	Lee Lacy	.08	.06	.03
141	Ron Oester	.03	.02	.01		232	Jim Traber	.03	.02	.01
142	Bo Diaz	.25	.20	.10		233	Cal Ripken	.20	.15	.08
143	Buddy Bell	.06	.05	.02		234	Larry Parrish	.06	.05	.02
144	Eddie Milner	.10	.08	.04		235	Gary Ward	.04	.03	.02
145	Dave Parker	.10	.08	.04		236	Pete Incaviglia	.20	.15	.08
146	Kirby Puckett	.35	.25	.14		237	Scott Fletcher	.03	.02	.01
147	Rickey Henderson	.40	.30	.15		238	Greg Harris	.10	.08	.04
148	Wade Boggs	.60	.45	.25		239	Pete O'Brien	.06	.05	.02
149	Lance Parrish	.25	.20	.10		240	Charlie Hough	.04	.03	.02
150	Wally Joyner	.70	.50	.30		241	Don Slaught	.04	.03	.02
151	Cal Ripken	.40	.30	.15		242	Steve Buechele	.04	.03	.02
152	Dave Winfield	.30	.25	.12		243	Oddibe McDowell	.06	.05	.02
153	Lou Whitaker	.25	.20	.10		244	Roger Clemens	.15	.11	.06
154	Roger Clemens	.50	.40	.20		245	Bob Stanley	.03	.02	.01
155	Tony Gwynn	.40	.30	.15		246	Tom Seaver	.12	.09	.05
156	Ryne Sandberg	.25	.20	.10		247	Rich Gedman	.03	.02	.01
157	Keith Hernandez	.25	.20	.10		248	Jim Rice	.15	.11	.06
158	Gary Carter	.30	.25	.12		249	Dennis Boyd	.25	.20	.10
159	Darryl Strawberry	.40	.30	.15		250	Bill Buckner	.04	.03	.02
160	Mike Schmidt	.40	.30	.15		251	Dwight Evans	.06	.05	.02
161	Dale Murphy	.40	.30	.15		252	Don Baylor	.06	.05	.02
162	Ozzie Smith	.20	.15	.08		253	Wade Boggs	.35	.25	.14
163	Dwight Gooden	.50	.40	.20		254	George Brett	.25	.20	.10
164	Jose Canseco	.40	.30	.15		255	Steve Farr	.03	.02	.01
165	Curt Young	.06	.05	.02		256	Jim Sundberg	.03	.02	.01
166	Alfredo Griffin	.20	.15	.08		257	Dan Quisenberry	.04	.03	.02
167	Dave Stewart	.06	.05	.02		258	Charlie Leibrandt	.04	.03	.02
168	Mike Davis	.08	.06	.03		259	Argenis Salazar	.06	.05	.02

			MT	NR MT	EX
260	Frank White		.04	.03	.02
261	Willie Wilson		.04	.03	.02
262	Lonnie Smith		.10	.08	.04
263	Steve Balboni		.04	.03	.02
264	Darrell Evans		.06	.05	.02
265	Johnny Grubb		.15	.11	.06
266	Jack Morris		.08	.06	.03
267	Lou Whitaker		.08	.06	.03
268	Chet Lemon		.04	.03	.02
269	Lance Parrish		.08	.06	.03
270	Alan Trammell		.10	.08	.04
271	Darnell Coles		.04	.03	.02
272	Willie Hernandez		.04	.03	.02
273	Kirk Gibson		.15	.11	.06
274	Kirby Puckett		.20	.15	.08
275	Mike Smithson		.03	.02	.01
276	Mickey Hatcher		.20	.15	.08
277	Frank Viola		.06	.05	.02
278	Bert Blyleven		.06	.05	.02
279	Gary Gaetti		.10	.08	.04
280	Tom Brunansky		.06	.05	.02
281	Kent Hrbek		.08	.06	.03
282	Roy Smalley		.04	.03	.02
283	Greg Gagne		.04	.03	.02
284	Harold Baines		.10	.08	.04
285	Ron Hassey		.06	.05	.02
286	Floyd Bannister		.06	.05	.02
287	Ozzie Guillen		.06	.05	.02
288	Carlton Fisk		.08	.06	.03
289	Tim Hulett		.03	.02	.01
290	Joe Cowley		.04	.03	.02
291	Greg Walker		.04	.03	.02
292	Neil Allen		.10	.08	.04
293	John Cangelosi		.06	.05	.02
294	Don Mattingly		.70	.50	.30
295	Mike Easler		.03	.02	.01
296	Rickey Henderson		.12	.09	.05
297	Dan Pasqua		.04	.03	.02
298	Dave Winfield		.10	.08	.04
299	Dave Righetti		.12	.09	.05
300	Mike Pagliarulo		.06	.05	.02
301	Ron Guidry		.20	.15	.08
302	Willie Randolph		.04	.03	.02
303	Dennis Rasmussen		.03	.02	.01
304	Jose Canseco		.25	.20	.10
305	Andres Thomas		.06	.05	.02
306	Danny Tartabull		.10	.08	.04
307	Robby Thompson		.06	.05	.02
308	Pete Incaviglia, Cory Snyder		.20	.15	.08
309	Dale Sveum		.06	.05	.02
310	Todd Worrell		.08	.06	.03
311	Andy Allanson		.03	.02	.01
312	Bruce Ruffin		.06	.05	.02
313	Wally Joyner		.30	.25	.12

1987 Topps Traded

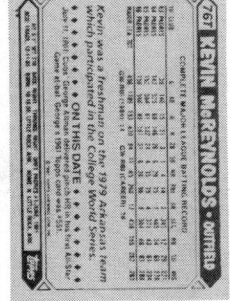

The Topps Traded set consists of 132 cards as have all Traded sets issued by Topps since 1981. The cards measure the standard 2½'' by 3½'' and are identical in design to the regular edition set. The purpose of the set is to update player trades and feature rookies not included in the regular issue. As they had done the previous three years, Topps produced a glossy-coated ''Tiffany'' edition of the Traded set. The Tiffany edition cards are valued at two to three times greater than the regular Traded cards.

		MT	NR MT	EX
Complete Set:		9.50	7.25	3.75
Common Player:		.06	.05	.02
1T	Bill Almon	.06	.05	.02
2T	Scott Bankhead	.08	.06	.03
3T	Eric Bell	.20	.15	.08
4T	Juan Beniquez	.06	.05	.02
5T	Juan Berenguer	.06	.05	.02
6T	Greg Booker	.06	.05	.02
7T	Thad Bosley	.06	.05	.02
8T	Larry Bowa	.10	.08	.04
9T	Greg Brock	.10	.08	.04
10T	Bob Brower	.20	.15	.08
11T	Jerry Browne	.20	.15	.08
12T	Ralph Bryant	.15	.11	.06
13T	DeWayne Buice	.20	.15	.08
14T	Ellis Burks	1.50	1.25	.60
15T	Ivan Calderon	.12	.09	.05
16T	Jeff Calhoun	.06	.05	.02
17T	Casey Candaele	.15	.11	.06
18T	John Cangelosi	.08	.06	.03
19T	Steve Carlton	.30	.25	.12
20T	Juan Castillo	.10	.08	.04
21T	Rick Cerone	.06	.05	.02
22T	Ron Cey	.10	.08	.04
23T	John Christensen	.06	.05	.02
24T	Dave Cone	.12	.09	.05
25T	Chuck Crim	.15	.11	.06
26T	Storm Davis	.06	.05	.02
27T	Andre Dawson	.40	.30	.15
28T	Rick Dempsey	.08	.06	.03
29T	Doug Drabek	.10	.08	.04
30T	Mike Dunne	.50	.40	.20
31T	Dennis Eckersley	.10	.08	.04
32T	Lee Elia	.06	.05	.02
33T	Brian Fisher	.10	.08	.04
34T	Terry Francona	.06	.05	.02
35T	Willie Fraser	.20	.15	.08
36T	Billy Gardner	.06	.05	.02
37T	Ken Gerhart	.30	.25	.12
38T	Danny Gladden	.08	.06	.03
39T	Jim Gott	.06	.05	.02
40T	Cecilio Guante	.06	.05	.02
41T	Albert Hall	.06	.05	.02
42T	Terry Harper	.06	.05	.02
43T	Mickey Hatcher	.06	.05	.02
44T	Brad Havens	.06	.05	.02
45T	Neal Heaton	.08	.06	.03
46T	Mike Henneman	.35	.25	.14
47T	Donnie Hill	.06	.05	.02
48T	Guy Hoffman	.06	.05	.02
49T	Brian Holton	.15	.11	.06
50T	Charles Hudson	.08	.06	.03
51T	Danny Jackson	.20	.15	.08
52T	Reggie Jackson	.40	.30	.15
53T	Chris James	.60	.45	.25
54T	Dion James	.12	.09	.05
55T	Stan Jefferson	.30	.25	.12
56T	Joe Johnson	.10	.08	.04
57T	Terry Kennedy	.08	.06	.03
58T	Mike Kingery	.10	.08	.04
59T	Ray Knight	.10	.08	.04
60T	Gene Larkin	.20	.15	.08
61T	Mike LaValliere	.08	.06	.03
62T	Jack Lazorko	.06	.05	.02
63T	Terry Leach	.12	.09	.05
64T	Tim Leary	.06	.05	.02
65T	Jim Lindeman	.30	.25	.12
66T	Steve Lombardozzi	.15	.11	.06
67T	Bill Long	.20	.15	.08
68T	Barry Lyons	.20	.15	.08
69T	Shane Mack	.35	.25	.14
70T	Greg Maddux	.15	.11	.06
71T	Bill Madlock	.15	.11	.06
72T	Joe Magrane	.80	.60	.30
73T	Dave Martinez	.25	.20	.10
74T	Fred McGriff	.40	.30	.15
75T	Mark McLemore	.12	.09	.05
76T	Kevin McReynolds	.50	.40	.20
77T	Dave Meads	.20	.15	.08
78T	Eddie Milner	.06	.05	.02
79T	Greg Minton	.06	.05	.02
80T	John Mitchell	.20	.15	.08
81T	Kevin Mitchell	.15	.11	.06
82T	Charlie Moore	.06	.05	.02
83T	Jeff Musselman	.25	.20	.10
84T	Gene Nelson	.06	.05	.02
85T	Graig Nettles	.15	.11	.06
86T	Al Newman	.08	.06	.03
87T	Reid Nichols	.06	.05	.02
88T	Tom Niedenfuer	.08	.06	.03

		MT	NR MT	EX
89T	Joe Niekro	.12	.09	.05
90T	Tom Nieto	.06	.05	.02
91T	Matt Nokes	2.00	1.50	.80
92T	Dickie Noles	.06	.05	.02
93T	Pat Pacillo	.20	.15	.08
94T	Lance Parrish	.20	.15	.08
95T	Tony Pena	.12	.09	.05
96T	Luis Polonia	.35	.25	.14
97T	Randy Ready	.06	.05	.02
98T	Jeff Reardon	.15	.11	.06
99T	Gary Redus	.08	.06	.03
100T	Jeff Reed	.06	.05	.02
101T	Rick Rhoden	.12	.09	.05
102T	Cal Ripken, Sr.	.08	.06	.03
103T	Wally Ritchie	.20	.15	.08
104T	Jeff Robinson	.25	.20	.10
105T	Gary Roenicke	.06	.05	.02
106T	Jerry Royster	.06	.05	.02
107T	Mark Salas	.06	.05	.02
108T	Luis Salazar	.06	.05	.02
109T	Benny Santiago	1.25	.90	.50
110T	Dave Schmidt	.08	.06	.03
111T	Kevin Seitzer	2.50	2.00	1.00
112T	John Shelby	.08	.06	.03
113T	Steve Shields	.08	.06	.03
114T	John Smiley	.30	.25	.12
115T	Chris Speier	.06	.05	.02
116T	Mike Stanley	.30	.25	.12
117T	Terry Steinbach	.40	.30	.15
118T	Les Straker	.30	.25	.12
119T	Jim Sundberg	.08	.06	.03
120T	Danny Tartabull	.35	.25	.14
121T	Tom Trebelhorn	.08	.06	.03
122T	Dave Valle	.12	.09	.05
123T	Ed Vande Berg	.06	.05	.02
124T	Andy Van Slyke	.10	.08	.04
125T	Gary Ward	.08	.06	.03
126T	Alan Wiggins	.06	.05	.02
127T	Bill Wilkinson	.20	.15	.08
128T	Frank Williams	.08	.06	.03
129T	Matt Williams	.35	.25	.14
130T	Jim Winn	.06	.05	.02
131T	Matt Young	.06	.05	.02
132T	Checklist 1T-132T	.06	.05	.02

1988 Topps

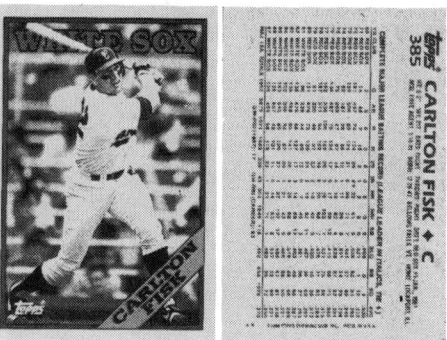

The 1988 Topps set features a clean, attractive design that should prove to be very popular with collectors for many years to come. The full color player photo is surrounded by a thin yellow frame which is encompassed by a white border. The player's name appears in the lower right corner in a colored band which appears to wrap around the player photo. The player's team nickname is located in large letters at the top of the card. The Topps logo is placed in the lower left corner of the card. The card backs feature black print on orange and grey stock and includes the usual player personal and career statistics. Many of the cards contain a new feature entitled "This Way To The Clubhouse", which explains how the player joined his current team, be it by trade, free agency, etc. The 792-card set includes a number of special subsets including "Future Stars", "Turn Back The Clock", All-Star teams, All-Star rookie selections, and Record Breakers. All cards measure 2½" by 3½".

		MT	NR MT	EX
Complete Set:		18.00	13.50	7.25
Common Player:		.03	.02	.01
1	'87 Record Breakers (Vince Coleman)	.08	.06	.03
2	'87 Record Breakers (Don Mattingly)	.60	.45	.25
3	'87 Record Breakers (Mark McGwire)	.50	.40	.20
4	'87 Record Breakers (Eddie Murray)	.10	.08	.04
5	'87 Record Breakers (Joe Niekro, Phil Niekro)	.10	.08	.04
6	'87 Record Breakers (Nolan Ryan)	.10	.08	.04
7	'87 Record Breakers (Benito Santiago)	.20	.15	.08
8	Kevin Elster	.30	.25	.12
9	Andy Hawkins	.03	.02	.01
10	Ryne Sandberg	.15	.11	.06
11	Mike Young	.06	.05	.02
12	Bill Schroeder	.03	.02	.01
13	Andres Thomas	.08	.06	.03
14	Sparky Anderson	.06	.05	.02
15	Chili Davis	.08	.06	.03
16	Kirk McCaskill	.06	.05	.02
17	Ron Oester	.03	.02	.01
18	Al Leiter (photo not Leiter)	.30	.25	.12
19	Mark Davidson	.12	.09	.05
20	Kevin Gross	.06	.05	.02
21	Red Sox Leaders	.10	.08	.04
22	Greg Swindell	.10	.08	.04
23	Ken Landreaux	.03	.02	.01
24	Jim Deshaies	.08	.06	.03
25	Andres Galarraga	.08	.06	.03
26	Mitch Williams	.06	.05	.02
27	R.J. Reynolds	.06	.05	.02
28	Jose Nunez	.20	.15	.08
29	Argenis Salazar	.03	.02	.01
30	Sid Fernandez	.08	.06	.03
31	Bruce Bochy	.03	.02	.01
32	Mike Morgan	.03	.02	.01
33	Rob Deer	.08	.06	.03
34	Ricky Horton	.06	.05	.02
35	Harold Baines	.10	.08	.04
36	Jamie Moyer	.06	.05	.02
37	Ed Romero	.03	.02	.01
38	Jeff Calhoun	.03	.02	.01
39	Gerald Perry	.06	.05	.02
40	Orel Hershiser	.08	.06	.03
41	Bob Melvin	.03	.02	.01
42	Bill Landrum	.12	.09	.05
43	Dick Schofield	.03	.02	.01
44	Lou Piniella	.06	.05	.02
45	Kent Hrbek	.12	.09	.05
46	Darnell Coles	.06	.05	.02
47	Joaquin Andujar	.06	.05	.02
48	Alan Ashby	.03	.02	.01
49	Dave Clark	.10	.08	.04
50	Hubie Brooks	.08	.06	.03
51	Orioles Leaders	.06	.05	.02
52	Don Robinson	.03	.02	.01
53	Curt Wilkerson	.03	.02	.01
54	Jim Clancy	.06	.05	.02
55	Phil Bradley	.10	.08	.04
56	Ed Hearn	.03	.02	.01
57	Tim Crews	.25	.20	.10
58	Dave Magadan	.15	.11	.06
59	Danny Cox	.08	.06	.03
60	Rickey Henderson	.25	.20	.10
61	Mark Knudson	.12	.09	.05
62	Jeff Hamilton	.08	.06	.03
63	Jimmy Jones	.08	.06	.03
64	Ken Caminiti	.30	.25	.12
65	Leon Durham	.06	.05	.02
66	Shane Rawley	.06	.05	.02
67	Ken Oberkfell	.03	.02	.01
68	Dave Dravecky	.06	.05	.02
69	Mike Hart	.15	.11	.06
70	Roger Clemens	.50	.40	.20
71	Gary Pettis	.03	.02	.01
72	Dennis Eckersley	.06	.05	.02
73	Randy Bush	.03	.02	.01
74	Tom Lasorda	.06	.05	.02
75	Joe Carter	.10	.08	.04
76	Denny Martinez	.03	.02	.01
77	Tom O'Malley	.03	.02	.01
78	Dan Petry	.06	.05	.02

		MT	NR MT	EX			MT	NR MT	EX
79	Ernie Whitt	.06	.05	.02	170	Rich Gossage	.12	.09	.05
80	Mark Langston	.08	.06	.03	171	Cubs Leaders	.03	.02	.01
81	Reds Leaders	.06	.05	.02	172	Lloyd McClendon	.15	.11	.06
82	Darrel Akerfelds	.20	.15	.08	173	Eric Plunk	.03	.02	.01
83	Jose Oquendo	.03	.02	.01	174	Phil Garner	.03	.02	.01
84	Cecilio Guante	.03	.02	.01	175	Kevin Bass	.06	.05	.02
85	Howard Johnson	.08	.06	.03	176	Jeff Reed	.03	.02	.01
86	Ron Karkovice	.06	.05	.02	177	Frank Tanana	.06	.05	.02
87	Mike Mason	.03	.02	.01	178	Dwayne Henry	.08	.06	.03
88	Earnie Riles	.03	.02	.01	179	Charlie Puleo	.03	.02	.01
89	Gary Thurman	.30	.25	.12	180	Terry Kennedy	.06	.05	.02
90	Dale Murphy	.30	.25	.12	181	Dave Cone	.06	.05	.02
91	Joey Cora	.15	.11	.06	182	Ken Phelps	.06	.05	.02
92	Len Matuszek	.03	.02	.01	183	Tom Lawless	.03	.02	.01
93	Bob Sebra	.06	.05	.02	184	Ivan Calderon	.08	.06	.03
94	Chuck Jackson	.20	.15	.08	185	Rick Rhoden	.06	.05	.02
95	Lance Parrish	.12	.09	.05	186	Rafael Palmeiro	.10	.08	.04
96	Todd Benzinger	.60	.45	.25	187	Steve Kiefer	.08	.06	.03
97	Scott Garrelts	.03	.02	.01	188	John Russell	.03	.02	.01
98	Rene Gonzales	.15	.11	.06	189	Wes Gardner	.15	.11	.06
99	Chuck Finley	.06	.05	.02	190	Candy Maldonado	.06	.05	.02
100	Jack Clark	.12	.09	.05	191	John Cerutti	.08	.06	.03
101	Allan Anderson	.03	.02	.01	192	Devon White	.25	.20	.10
102	Barry Larkin	.10	.08	.04	193	Brian Fisher	.06	.05	.02
103	Curt Young	.06	.05	.02	194	Tom Kelly	.06	.05	.02
104	Dick Williams	.06	.05	.02	195	Dan Quisenberry	.08	.06	.03
105	Jesse Orosco	.06	.05	.02	196	Dave Engle	.03	.02	.01
106	Jim Walewander	.15	.11	.06	197	Lance McCullers	.06	.05	.02
107	Scott Bailes	.06	.05	.02	198	Franklin Stubbs	.06	.05	.02
108	Steve Lyons	.03	.02	.01	199	Dave Meads	.15	.11	.06
109	Joel Skinner	.03	.02	.01	200	Wade Boggs	.80	.60	.30
110	Teddy Higuera	.08	.06	.03	201	Rangers Leaders	.06	.05	.02
111	Expos Leaders	.06	.05	.02	202	Glenn Hoffman	.03	.02	.01
112	Les Lancaster	.20	.15	.08	203	Fred Toliver	.03	.02	.01
113	Kelly Gruber	.03	.02	.01	204	Paul O'Neill	.10	.08	.04
114	Jeff Russell	.03	.02	.01	205	Nelson Liriano	.20	.15	.08
115	Johnny Ray	.06	.05	.02	206	Domingo Ramos	.03	.02	.01
116	Jerry Don Gleaton	.03	.02	.01	207	John Mitchell	.20	.15	.08
117	James Steels	.12	.09	.05	208	Steve Lake	.03	.02	.01
118	Bob Welch	.06	.05	.02	209	Richard Dotson	.06	.05	.02
119	Robbie Wine	.20	.15	.08	210	Willie Randolph	.06	.05	.02
120	Kirby Puckett	.25	.20	.10	211	Frank DiPino	.03	.02	.01
121	Checklist 1-132	.03	.02	.01	212	Greg Brock	.06	.05	.02
122	Tony Bernazard	.03	.02	.01	213	Albert Hall	.03	.02	.01
123	Tom Candiotti	.03	.02	.01	214	Dave Schmidt	.03	.02	.01
124	Ray Knight	.06	.05	.02	215	Von Hayes	.08	.06	.03
125	Bruce Hurst	.06	.05	.02	216	Jerry Reuss	.06	.05	.02
126	Steve Jeltz	.03	.02	.01	217	Harry Spilman	.03	.02	.01
127	Jim Gott	.03	.02	.01	218	Dan Schatzeder	.03	.02	.01
128	Johnny Grubb	.03	.02	.01	219	Mike Stanley	.08	.06	.03
129	Greg Minton	.03	.02	.01	220	Tom Henke	.06	.05	.02
130	Buddy Bell	.08	.06	.03	221	Rafael Belliard	.03	.02	.01
131	Don Schulze	.03	.02	.01	222	Steve Farr	.03	.02	.01
132	Donnie Hill	.03	.02	.01	223	Stan Jefferson	.10	.08	.04
133	Greg Mathews	.08	.06	.03	224	Tom Trebelhorn	.03	.02	.01
134	Chuck Tanner	.06	.05	.02	225	Mike Scioscia	.03	.02	.01
135	Dennis Rasmussen	.06	.05	.02	226	Dave Lopes	.06	.05	.02
136	Brian Dayett	.03	.02	.01	227	Ed Correa	.08	.06	.03
137	Chris Bosio	.06	.05	.02	228	Wallace Johnson	.03	.02	.01
138	Mitch Webster	.06	.05	.02	229	Jeff Musselman	.06	.05	.02
139	Jerry Browne	.06	.05	.02	230	Pat Tabler	.06	.05	.02
140	Jesse Barfield	.10	.08	.04	231	Pirates Leaders	.06	.05	.02
141	Royals Leaders	.06	.05	.02	232	Bob James	.03	.02	.01
142	Andy Van Slyke	.06	.05	.02	233	Rafael Santana	.03	.02	.01
143	Mickey Tettleton	.03	.02	.01	234	Ken Dayley	.03	.02	.01
144	Don Gordon	.12	.09	.05	235	Gary Ward	.06	.05	.02
145	Bill Madlock	.10	.08	.04	236	Ted Power	.06	.05	.02
146	Donell Nixon	.20	.15	.08	237	Mike Heath	.03	.02	.01
147	Bill Buckner	.08	.06	.03	238	Luis Polonia	.20	.15	.08
148	Carmelo Martinez	.03	.02	.01	239	Roy Smalley	.03	.02	.01
149	Ken Howell	.03	.02	.01	240	Lee Smith	.08	.06	.03
150	Eric Davis	.80	.60	.30	241	Damaso Garcia	.06	.05	.02
151	Bob Knepper	.06	.05	.02	242	Tom Niedenfuer	.03	.02	.01
152	Jody Reed	.25	.20	.10	243	Mark Ryal	.06	.05	.02
153	John Habyan	.03	.02	.01	244	Jeff Robinson	.03	.02	.01
154	Jeff Stone	.03	.02	.01	245	Rich Gedman	.06	.05	.02
155	Bruce Sutter	.08	.06	.03	246	Mike Campbell	.25	.20	.10
156	Gary Matthews	.06	.05	.02	247	Thad Bosley	.03	.02	.01
157	Atlee Hammaker	.03	.02	.01	248	Storm Davis	.03	.02	.01
158	Tim Hulett	.03	.02	.01	249	Mike Marshall	.08	.06	.03
159	Brad Arnsberg	.20	.15	.08	250	Nolan Ryan	.20	.15	.08
160	Willie McGee	.10	.08	.04	251	Tom Foley	.03	.02	.01
161	Bryn Smith	.06	.05	.02	252	Bob Brower	.06	.05	.02
162	Mark McLemore	.03	.02	.01	253	Checklist 133-264	.03	.02	.01
163	Dale Mohorcic	.06	.05	.02	254	Lee Elia	.03	.02	.01
164	Dave Johnson	.06	.05	.02	255	Mookie Wilson	.06	.05	.02
165	Robin Yount	.15	.11	.06	256	Ken Schrom	.03	.02	.01
166	Rick Rodriguez	.15	.11	.06	257	Jerry Royster	.03	.02	.01
167	Rance Mulliniks	.03	.02	.01	258	Ed Nunez	.03	.02	.01
168	Barry Jones	.03	.02	.01	259	Ron Kittle	.06	.05	.02
169	Ross Jones	.15	.11	.06	260	Vince Coleman	.15	.11	.06

	MT	NR MT	EX			MT	NR MT	EX
261	Giants Leaders	.06	.05	.02	352	Billy Ripken	.30	.25	.12
262	Drew Hall	.10	.08	.04	353	Ed Olwine	.03	.02	.01
263	Glenn Braggs	.10	.08	.04	354	Marc Sullivan	.03	.02	.01
264	Les Straker	.15	.11	.06	355	Roger McDowell	.06	.05	.02
265	Bo Diaz	.03	.02	.01	356	Luis Aguayo	.03	.02	.01
266	Paul Assenmacher	.06	.05	.02	357	Floyd Bannister	.06	.05	.02
267	Billy Bean	.15	.11	.06	358	Rey Quinones	.06	.05	.02
268	Bruce Ruffin	.08	.06	.03	359	Tim Stoddard	.03	.02	.01
269	Ellis Burks	1.50	1.25	.60	360	Tony Gwynn	.25	.20	.10
270	Mike Witt	.08	.06	.03	361	Greg Maddux	.08	.06	.03
271	Ken Gerhart	.08	.06	.03	362	Juan Castillo	.06	.05	.02
272	Steve Ontiveros	.03	.02	.01	363	Willie Fraser	.08	.06	.03
273	Garth Iorg	.03	.02	.01	364	Nick Esasky	.03	.02	.01
274	Junior Ortiz	.03	.02	.01	365	Floyd Youmans	.08	.06	.03
275	Kevin Seitzer	1.25	.90	.50	366	Chet Lemon	.06	.05	.02
276	Luis Salazar	.03	.02	.01	367	Tim Leary	.03	.02	.01
277	Alejandro Pena	.03	.02	.01	368	Gerald Young	.30	.25	.12
278	Jose Cruz	.06	.05	.02	369	Greg Harris	.03	.02	.01
279	Randy St. Claire	.03	.02	.01	370	Jose Canseco	.60	.45	.25
280	Pete Incaviglia	.25	.20	.10	371	Joe Hesketh	.03	.02	.01
281	Jerry Hairston	.03	.02	.01	372	Matt Williams	.30	.25	.12
282	Pat Perry	.03	.02	.01	373	Checklist 265-396	.03	.02	.01
283	Phil Lombardi	.08	.06	.03	374	Doc Edwards	.03	.02	.01
284	Larry Bowa	.06	.05	.02	375	Tom Brunansky	.08	.06	.03
285	Jim Presley	.08	.06	.03	376	Bill Wilkinson	.15	.11	.06
286	Chuck Crim	.12	.09	.05	377	Sam Horn	.90	.70	.35
287	Manny Trillo	.06	.05	.02	378	Todd Frohwirth	.20	.15	.08
288	Pat Pacillo	.20	.15	.08	379	Rafael Ramirez	.03	.02	.01
289	Dave Bergman	.03	.02	.01	380	Joe Magrane	.35	.25	.14
290	Tony Fernandez	.10	.08	.04	381	Angels Leaders	.06	.05	.02
291	Astros Leaders	.06	.05	.02	382	Keith Miller	.25	.20	.10
292	Carney Lansford	.06	.05	.02	383	Eric Bell	.08	.06	.03
293	Doug Jones	.15	.11	.06	384	Neil Allen	.03	.02	.01
294	Al Pedrique	.15	.11	.06	385	Carlton Fisk	.12	.09	.05
295	Bert Blyleven	.10	.08	.04	386	Don Mattingly AS	.60	.45	.25
296	Floyd Rayford	.03	.02	.01	387	Willie Randolph AS	.06	.05	.02
297	Zane Smith	.06	.05	.02	388	Wade Boggs AS	.35	.25	.14
298	Milt Thompson	.06	.05	.02	389	Alan Trammell AS	.08	.06	.03
299	Steve Crawford	.03	.02	.01	390	George Bell AS	.12	.09	.05
300	Don Mattingly	1.25	.90	.50	391	Kirby Puckett AS	.12	.09	.05
301	Bud Black	.03	.02	.01	392	Dave Winfield AS	.12	.09	.05
302	Jose Uribe	.03	.02	.01	393	Matt Nokes AS	.50	.40	.20
303	Eric Show	.03	.02	.01	394	Roger Clemens AS	.15	.11	.06
304	George Hendrick	.06	.05	.02	395	Jimmy Key AS	.06	.05	.02
305	Steve Sax	.12	.09	.05	396	Tom Henke AS	.06	.05	.02
306	Billy Hatcher	.06	.05	.02	397	Jack Clark AS	.06	.05	.02
307	Mike Trujillo	.06	.05	.02	398	Juan Samuel AS	.06	.05	.02
308	Lee Mazzilli	.06	.05	.02	399	Tim Wallach AS	.06	.05	.02
309	Bill Long	.20	.15	.08	400	Ozzie Smith AS	.08	.06	.03
310	Tom Herr	.06	.05	.02	401	Andre Dawson AS	.10	.08	.04
311	Scott Sanderson	.03	.02	.01	402	Tony Gwynn AS	.15	.11	.06
312	Joey Meyer	.10	.08	.04	403	Tim Raines AS	.12	.09	.05
313	Bob McClure	.03	.02	.01	404	Benny Santiago AS	.25	.20	.10
314	Jimy Williams	.03	.02	.01	405	Dwight Gooden AS	.15	.11	.06
315	Dave Parker	.12	.09	.05	406	Shane Rawley AS	.06	.05	.02
316	Jose Rijo	.03	.02	.01	407	Steve Bedrosian AS	.10	.08	.04
317	Tom Nieto	.03	.02	.01	408	Dion James	.06	.05	.02
318	Mel Hall	.06	.05	.02	409	Joel McKeon	.06	.05	.02
319	Mike Loynd	.06	.05	.02	410	Tony Pena	.06	.05	.02
320	Alan Trammell	.15	.11	.06	411	Wayne Tolleson	.03	.02	.01
321	White Sox Leaders	.06	.05	.02	412	Randy Myers	.06	.05	.02
322	Vicente Palacios	.25	.20	.10	413	John Christensen	.03	.02	.01
323	Rick Leach	.03	.02	.01	414	John McNamara	.03	.02	.01
324	Danny Jackson	.06	.05	.02	415	Don Carman	.08	.06	.03
325	Glenn Hubbard	.03	.02	.01	416	Keith Moreland	.06	.05	.02
326	Al Nipper	.03	.02	.01	417	Mark Ciardi	.12	.09	.05
327	Larry Sheets	.08	.06	.03	418	Joel Youngblood	.03	.02	.01
328	Greg Cadaret	.15	.11	.06	419	Scott McGregor	.06	.05	.02
329	Chris Speier	.03	.02	.01	420	Wally Joyner	.70	.50	.30
330	Eddie Whitson	.03	.02	.01	421	Ed Vande Berg	.03	.02	.01
331	Brian Downing	.06	.05	.02	422	Dave Concepcion	.06	.05	.02
332	Jerry Reed	.03	.02	.01	423	John Smiley	.20	.15	.08
333	Wally Backman	.06	.05	.02	424	Dwayne Murphy	.03	.02	.01
334	Dave LaPoint	.03	.02	.01	425	Jeff Reardon	.10	.08	.04
335	Claudell Washington	.06	.05	.02	426	Randy Ready	.03	.02	.01
336	Ed Lynch	.03	.02	.01	427	Paul Kilgus	.15	.11	.06
337	Jim Gantner	.03	.02	.01	428	John Shelby	.03	.02	.01
338	Brian Holton	.08	.06	.03	429	Tigers Leaders	.06	.05	.02
339	Kurt Stillwell	.10	.08	.04	430	Glenn Davis	.12	.09	.05
340	Jack Morris	.15	.11	.06	431	Casey Candaele	.06	.05	.02
341	Carmen Castillo	.03	.02	.01	432	Mike Moore	.03	.02	.01
342	Larry Andersen	.03	.02	.01	433	Bill Pecota	.15	.11	.06
343	Greg Gagne	.06	.05	.02	434	Rick Aguilera	.06	.05	.02
344	Tony LaRussa	.03	.02	.01	435	Mike Pagliarulo	.08	.06	.03
345	Scott Fletcher	.06	.05	.02	436	Mike Bielecki	.03	.02	.01
346	Vance Law	.03	.02	.01	437	Fred Manrique	.20	.15	.08
347	Joe Johnson	.06	.05	.02	438	Rob Ducey	.15	.11	.06
348	Jim Eisenreich	.08	.06	.03	439	Dave Martinez	.15	.11	.06
349	Bob Walk	.03	.02	.01	440	Steve Bedrosian	.08	.06	.03
350	Will Clark	.60	.45	.25	441	Rick Manning	.03	.02	.01
351	Cardinals Leaders	.06	.05	.02	442	Tom Bolton	.15	.11	.06

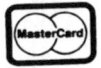

#	Name	MT	NR MT	EX
443	Ken Griffey	.06	.05	.02
444	Cal Ripken, Sr.	.03	.02	.01
445	Mike Krukow	.06	.05	.02
446	Doug DeCinces	.06	.05	.02
447	Jeff Montgomery	.20	.15	.08
448	Mike Davis	.06	.05	.02
449	Jeff Robinson	.20	.15	.08
450	Barry Bonds	.10	.08	.04
451	Keith Atherton	.03	.02	.01
452	Willie Wilson	.08	.06	.03
453	Dennis Powell	.03	.02	.01
454	Marvell Wynne	.03	.02	.01
455	Shawn Hillegas	.20	.15	.08
456	Dave Anderson	.03	.02	.01
457	Terry Leach	.06	.05	.02
458	Ron Hassey	.03	.02	.01
459	Yankees Leaders	.06	.05	.02
460	Ozzie Smith	.10	.08	.04
461	Danny Darwin	.03	.02	.01
462	Don Slaught	.03	.02	.01
463	Fred McGriff	.10	.08	.04
464	Jay Tibbs	.03	.02	.01
465	Paul Molitor	.10	.08	.04
466	Jerry Mumphrey	.06	.05	.02
467	Don Aase	.03	.02	.01
468	Darren Daulton	.03	.02	.01
469	Jeff Dedmon	.03	.02	.01
470	Dwight Evans	.10	.08	.04
471	Donnie Moore	.03	.02	.01
472	Robby Thompson	.08	.06	.03
473	Joe Niekro	.06	.05	.02
474	Tom Brookens	.03	.02	.01
475	Pete Rose	.20	.15	.08
476	Dave Stewart	.06	.05	.02
477	Jamie Quirk	.03	.02	.01
478	Sid Bream	.06	.05	.02
479	Brett Butler	.06	.05	.02
480	Dwight Gooden	.40	.30	.15
481	Mariano Duncan	.03	.02	.01
482	Mark Davis	.03	.02	.01
483	Rod Booker	.15	.11	.06
484	Pat Clements	.03	.02	.01
485	Harold Reynolds	.06	.05	.02
486	Pat Keedy	.15	.11	.06
487	Jim Pankovits	.03	.02	.01
488	Andy McGaffigan	.03	.02	.01
489	Dodgers Leaders	.06	.05	.02
490	Larry Parrish	.06	.05	.02
491	B.J. Surhoff	.20	.15	.08
492	Doyle Alexander	.08	.06	.03
493	Mike Greenwell	.60	.45	.25
494	Wally Ritchie	.15	.11	.06
495	Eddie Murray	.25	.20	.10
496	Guy Hoffman	.03	.02	.01
497	Kevin Mitchell	.08	.06	.03
498	Bob Boone	.06	.05	.02
499	Eric King	.08	.06	.03
500	Andre Dawson	.15	.11	.06
501	Tim Birtsas	.06	.05	.02
502	Danny Gladden	.06	.05	.02
503	Junior Noboa	.15	.11	.06
504	Bob Rodgers	.03	.02	.01
505	Willie Upshaw	.06	.05	.02
506	John Cangelosi	.06	.05	.02
507	Mark Gubicza	.06	.05	.02
508	Tim Teufel	.03	.02	.01
509	Bill Dawley	.03	.02	.01
510	Dave Winfield	.20	.15	.08
511	Joel Davis	.03	.02	.01
512	Alex Trevino	.03	.02	.01
513	Tim Flannery	.03	.02	.01
514	Pat Sheridan	.03	.02	.01
515	Juan Nieves	.08	.06	.03
516	Jim Sundberg	.03	.02	.01
517	Ron Robinson	.03	.02	.01
518	Greg Gross	.03	.02	.01
519	Mariners Leaders	.06	.05	.02
520	Dave Smith	.06	.05	.02
521	Jim Dwyer	.03	.02	.01
522	Bob Patterson	.15	.11	.06
523	Gary Roenicke	.03	.02	.01
524	Gary Lucas	.03	.02	.01
525	Marty Barrett	.06	.05	.02
526	Juan Berenguer	.03	.02	.01
527	Steve Henderson	.03	.02	.01
528	Checklist 397-528	.03	.02	.01
529	Tim Burke	.06	.05	.02
530	Gary Carter	.20	.15	.08
531	Rich Yett	.03	.02	.01
532	Mike Kingery	.06	.05	.02
533	John Farrell	.25	.20	.10
534	John Wathan	.03	.02	.01
535	Ron Guidry	.12	.09	.05
536	John Morris	.03	.02	.01
537	Steve Buechele	.03	.02	.01
538	Bill Wegman	.03	.02	.01
539	Mike LaValliere	.06	.05	.02
540	Bret Saberhagen	.15	.11	.06
541	Juan Beniquez	.03	.02	.01
542	Paul Noce	.15	.11	.06
543	Kent Tekulve	.06	.05	.02
544	Jim Traber	.06	.05	.02
545	Don Baylor	.08	.06	.03
546	John Candelaria	.06	.05	.02
547	Felix Fermin	.12	.09	.05
548	Shane Mack	.25	.20	.10
549	Braves Leaders	.06	.05	.02
550	Pedro Guerrero	.12	.09	.05
551	Terry Steinbach	.10	.08	.04
552	Mark Thurmond	.03	.02	.01
553	Tracy Jones	.10	.08	.04
554	Mike Smithson	.03	.02	.01
555	Brook Jacoby	.08	.06	.03
556	Stan Clarke	.15	.11	.06
557	Craig Reynolds	.03	.02	.01
558	Bob Ojeda	.06	.05	.02
559	Ken Williams	.20	.15	.08
560	Tim Wallach	.08	.06	.03
561	Rick Cerone	.03	.02	.01
562	Jim Lindeman	.10	.08	.04
563	Jose Guzman	.06	.05	.02
564	Frank Lucchesi	.03	.02	.01
565	Lloyd Moseby	.08	.06	.03
566	Charlie O'Brien	.12	.09	.05
567	Mike Diaz	.08	.06	.03
568	Chris Brown	.08	.06	.03
569	Charlie Leibrandt	.06	.05	.02
570	Jeffrey Leonard	.06	.05	.02
571	Mark Williamson	.15	.11	.06
572	Chris James	.10	.08	.04
573	Bob Stanley	.03	.02	.01
574	Graig Nettles	.08	.06	.03
575	Don Sutton	.12	.09	.05
576	Tommy Hinzo	.15	.11	.06
577	Tom Browning	.06	.05	.02
578	Gary Gaetti	.10	.08	.04
579	Mets Leaders	.06	.05	.02
580	Mark McGwire	1.00	.70	.40
581	Tito Landrum	.03	.02	.01
582	Mike Henneman	.20	.15	.08
583	Dave Valle	.06	.05	.02
584	Steve Trout	.06	.05	.02
585	Ozzie Guillen	.08	.06	.03
586	Bob Forsch	.03	.02	.01
587	Terry Puhl	.03	.02	.01
588	Jeff Parrett	.15	.11	.06
589	Geno Petralli	.03	.02	.01
590	George Bell	.20	.15	.08
591	Doug Drabek	.06	.05	.02
592	Dale Sveum	.08	.06	.03
593	Bob Tewksbury	.06	.05	.02
594	Bobby Valentine	.03	.02	.01
595	Frank White	.06	.05	.02
596	John Kruk	.20	.15	.08
597	Gene Garber	.03	.02	.01
598	Lee Lacy	.03	.02	.01
599	Calvin Schiraldi	.03	.02	.01
600	Mike Schmidt	.30	.25	.12
601	Jack Lazorko	.03	.02	.01
602	Mike Aldrete	.10	.08	.04
603	Rob Murphy	.06	.05	.02
604	Chris Bando	.03	.02	.01
605	Kirk Gibson	.15	.11	.06
606	Moose Haas	.03	.02	.01
607	Mickey Hatcher	.03	.02	.01
608	Charlie Kerfeld	.03	.02	.01
609	Twins Leaders	.06	.05	.02
610	Keith Hernandez	.15	.11	.06
611	Tommy John	.12	.09	.05
612	Curt Ford	.03	.02	.01
613	Bobby Thigpen	.06	.05	.02
614	Herm Winningham	.03	.02	.01
615	Jody Davis	.06	.05	.02
616	Jay Aldrich	.12	.09	.05
617	Oddibe McDowell	.08	.06	.03
618	Cecil Fielder	.06	.05	.02
619	Mike Dunne	.30	.25	.12
620	Cory Snyder	.15	.11	.06
621	Gene Nelson	.03	.02	.01
622	Kal Daniels	.15	.11	.06
623	Mike Flanagan	.06	.05	.02
624	Jim Leyland	.03	.02	.01

		MT	NR MT	EX
625	Frank Viola	.08	.06	.03
626	Glenn Wilson	.06	.05	.02
627	Joe Boever	.12	.09	.05
628	Dave Henderson	.03	.02	.01
629	Kelly Downs	.08	.06	.03
630	Darrell Evans	.08	.06	.03
631	Jack Howell	.06	.05	.02
632	Steve Shields	.12	.09	.05
633	Barry Lyons	.15	.11	.06
634	Jose DeLeon	.03	.02	.01
635	Terry Pendleton	.06	.05	.02
636	Charles Hudson	.03	.02	.01
637	Jay Bell	.15	.11	.06
638	Steve Balboni	.03	.02	.01
639	Brewers Leaders	.06	.05	.02
640	Garry Templeton	.06	.05	.02
641	Rick Honeycutt	.03	.02	.01
642	Bob Dernier	.03	.02	.01
643	Rocky Childress	.15	.11	.06
644	Terry McGriff	.06	.05	.02
645	Matt Nokes	1.25	.90	.50
646	Checklist 529-660	.03	.02	.01
647	Pascual Perez	.06	.05	.02
648	Al Newman	.03	.02	.01
649	DeWayne Buice	.15	.11	.06
650	Cal Ripken	.25	.20	.10
651	Mike Jackson	.15	.11	.06
652	Bruce Benedict	.03	.02	.01
653	Jeff Sellers	.06	.05	.02
654	Roger Craig	.06	.05	.02
655	Len Dykstra	.08	.06	.03
656	Lee Guetterman	.06	.05	.02
657	Gary Redus	.06	.05	.02
658	Tim Conroy	.03	.02	.01
659	Bobby Meacham	.03	.02	.01
660	Rick Reuschel	.08	.06	.03
661	Turn Back The Clock (Nolan Ryan)	.08	.06	.03
662	Turn Back The Clock (Jim Rice)	.08	.06	.03
663	Turn Back The Clock (Ron Blomberg)	.03	.02	.01
664	Turn Back The Clock (Bob Gibson)	.08	.06	.03
665	Turn Back The Clock (Stan Musial)	.12	.09	.05
666	Mario Soto	.06	.05	.02
667	Luis Quinones	.03	.02	.01
668	Walt Terrell	.06	.05	.02
669	Phillies Leaders	.06	.05	.02
670	Dan Plesac	.10	.08	.04
671	Tim Laudner	.03	.02	.01
672	John Davis	.20	.15	.08
673	Tony Phillips	.03	.02	.01
674	Mike Fitzgerald	.03	.02	.01
675	Jim Rice	.20	.15	.08
676	Ken Dixon	.03	.02	.01
677	Eddie Milner	.03	.02	.01
678	Jim Acker	.03	.02	.01
679	Darrell Miller	.03	.02	.01
680	Charlie Hough	.06	.05	.02
681	Bobby Bonilla	.08	.06	.03
682	Jimmy Key	.08	.06	.03
683	Julio Franco	.08	.06	.03
684	Hal Lanier	.03	.02	.01
685	Ron Darling	.10	.08	.04
686	Terry Francona	.03	.02	.01
687	Mickey Brantley	.03	.02	.01
688	Jim Winn	.03	.02	.01
689	Tom Pagnozzi	.15	.11	.06
690	Jay Howell	.06	.05	.02
691	Dan Pasqua	.08	.06	.03
692	Mike Birkbeck	.03	.02	.01
693	Benny Santiago	.50	.40	.20
694	Eric Nolte	.15	.11	.06
695	Shawon Dunston	.08	.06	.03
696	Duane Ward	.03	.02	.01
697	Steve Lombardozzi	.06	.05	.02
698	Brad Havens	.03	.02	.01
699	Padres Leaders	.06	.05	.02
700	George Brett	.30	.25	.12
701	Sammy Stewart	.03	.02	.01
702	Mike Gallego	.03	.02	.01
703	Bob Brenly	.03	.02	.01
704	Dennis Boyd	.06	.05	.02
705	Juan Samuel	.10	.08	.04
706	Rick Mahler	.03	.02	.01
707	Fred Lynn	.10	.08	.04
708	Gus Polidor	.06	.05	.02
709	George Frazier	.03	.02	.01
710	Darryl Strawberry	.30	.25	.12
711	Bill Gullickson	.06	.05	.02
712	John Moses	.03	.02	.01
713	Willie Hernandez	.06	.05	.02
714	Jim Fregosi	.03	.02	.01

		MT	NR MT	EX
715	Todd Worrell	.10	.08	.04
716	Lenn Sakata	.03	.02	.01
717	Jay Baller	.08	.06	.03
718	Mike Felder	.03	.02	.01
719	Denny Walling	.03	.02	.01
720	Tim Raines	.20	.15	.08
721	Pete O'Brien	.06	.05	.02
722	Manny Lee	.03	.02	.01
723	Bob Kipper	.03	.02	.01
724	Danny Tartabull	.15	.11	.06
725	Mike Boddicker	.06	.05	.02
726	Alfredo Griffin	.06	.05	.02
727	Greg Booker	.03	.02	.01
728	Andy Allanson	.06	.05	.02
729	Blue Jays Leaders	.06	.05	.02
730	John Franco	.06	.05	.02
731	Rick Schu	.03	.02	.01
732	Dave Palmer	.03	.02	.01
733	Spike Owen	.03	.02	.01
734	Craig Lefferts	.03	.02	.01
735	Kevin McReynolds	.08	.06	.03
736	Matt Young	.03	.02	.01
737	Butch Wynegar	.03	.02	.01
738	Scott Bankhead	.03	.02	.01
739	Daryl Boston	.03	.02	.01
740	Rick Sutcliffe	.10	.08	.04
741	Mike Easler	.06	.05	.02
742	Mark Clear	.03	.02	.01
743	Larry Herndon	.03	.02	.01
744	Whitey Herzog	.06	.05	.02
745	Bill Doran	.06	.05	.02
746	Gene Larkin	.12	.09	.05
747	Bobby Witt	.08	.06	.03
748	Reid Nichols	.03	.02	.01
749	Mark Eichhorn	.08	.06	.03
750	Bo Jackson	.30	.25	.12
751	Jim Morrison	.03	.02	.01
752	Mark Grant	.03	.02	.01
753	Danny Heep	.03	.02	.01
754	Mike LaCoss	.03	.02	.01
755	Ozzie Virgil	.06	.05	.02
756	Mike Maddux	.08	.06	.03
757	John Marzano	.50	.40	.20
758	Eddie Williams	.25	.20	.10
759	A's Leaders	.06	.05	.02
760	Mike Scott	.10	.08	.04
761	Tony Armas	.06	.05	.02
762	Scott Bradley	.03	.02	.01
763	Doug Sisk	.03	.02	.01
764	Greg Walker	.06	.05	.02
765	Neal Heaton	.06	.05	.02
766	Henry Cotto	.03	.02	.01
767	Jose Lind	.30	.25	.12
768	Dickie Noles	.03	.02	.01
769	Cecil Cooper	.08	.06	.03
770	Lou Whitaker	.12	.09	.05
771	Ruben Sierra	.35	.25	.14
772	Sal Butera	.03	.02	.01
773	Frank Williams	.03	.02	.01
774	Gene Mauch	.03	.02	.01
775	Dave Stieb	.08	.06	.03
776	Checklist 661-792	.03	.02	.01
777	Lonnie Smith	.03	.02	.01
778a	Keith Comstock (white team letters)	.25	.20	.10
778b	Keith Comstock (blue team letters)	.15	.11	.06
779	Tom Glavine	.30	.25	.12
780	Fernando Valenzuela	.15	.11	.06
781	Keith Hughes	.15	.11	.06
782	Jeff Ballard	.15	.11	.06
783	Ron Roenicke	.03	.02	.01
784	Joe Sambito	.03	.02	.01
785	Alvin Davis	.10	.08	.04
786	Joe Price	.03	.02	.01
787	Bill Almon	.03	.02	.01
788	Ray Searage	.03	.02	.01
789	Indians Leaders	.06	.05	.02
790	Dave Righetti	.12	.09	.05
791	Ted Simmons	.08	.06	.03
792	John Tudor	.06	.05	.02

Definitions for grading conditions are located in the Introduction of this price guide.

1987 Toys "R" Us

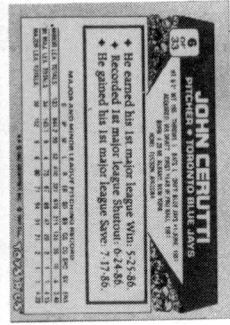

Marked as a collectors' edition set and titled "Baseball Rookies", the 1987 Toys "R" Us issue was produced by Topps for the toy store chain. The set is comprised of 33 glossy-coated cards, each measuring 2½" by 3½". The card fronts are very colorful, employing nine different colors including deep black borders. The backs, printed in blue and orange, contain career highlights and composite minor and major league statistics. The set was distributed in a specially designed box and sold for $1.99 in retail outlets.

		MT	NR MT	EX
1	Andy Allanson	.12	.09	.05
2	Paul Assenmacher	.12	.09	.05
3	Scott Bailes	.15	.11	.06
4	Barry Bonds	.30	.25	.12
5	Jose Canseco	1.00	.70	.40
6	John Cerutti	.15	.11	.06
7	Will Clark	.60	.45	.25
8	Kal Daniels	.20	.15	.08
9	Jim Deshaies	.15	.11	.06
10	Mark Eichhorn	.15	.11	.06
11	Ed Hearn	.09	.07	.04
12	Pete Incaviglia	.40	.30	.15
13	Bo Jackson	.60	.45	.25
14	Wally Joyner	1.00	.70	.40
15	Charlie Kerfeld	.09	.07	.04
16	Eric King	.15	.11	.06
17	John Kruk	.40	.30	.15
18	Barry Larkin	.30	.25	.12
19	Mike LaValliere	.15	.11	.06
20	Greg Mathews	.15	.11	.06
21	Kevin Mitchell	.20	.15	.08
22	Dan Plesac	.20	.15	.08
23	Bruce Ruffin	.15	.11	.06
24	Ruben Sierra	.50	.40	.20
25	Cory Snyder	.40	.30	.15
26	Kurt Stillwell	.20	.15	.08
27	Dale Sveum	.15	.11	.06
28	Danny Tartabull	.30	.25	.12
29	Andres Thomas	.15	.11	.06
30	Robby Thompson	.15	.11	.06
31	Jim Traber	.09	.07	.04
32	Mitch Williams	.15	.11	.06
33	Todd Worrell	.30	.25	.12

1969 Transogram

Produced by the Transogram toy company, the 2½" by 3½" cards were printed on the bottom of toy baseball player statue boxes. The cards featured a color photo of the player surrounded by a rounded white border. Below the photo was the player's name in red and his team and other personal details all printed in black. The overall background was yellow. The cards had to be cut off the box, but collectors prefer to find the box intact and better still, with the statue inside. Although the 60-card set featured a lot of stars, and is fairly scarce, it does not have a lot of popularity today.

		NR MT	EX	VG
	Complete Set:	375.00	187.00	112.00
	Common Player:	.80	.40	.25
(1)	Hank Aaron	20.00	10.00	6.00
(2)	Richie Allen	4.00	2.00	1.25
(3)	Felipe Alou	3.00	1.50	.90
(4)	Matty Alou	3.00	1.50	.90
(5)	Luis Aparicio	10.00	5.00	3.00
(6)	Joe Azcue	2.00	1.00	.60
(7)	Ernie Banks	8.00	4.00	2.50
(8)	Lou Brock	15.00	7.50	4.50
(9)	John Callison	3.00	1.50	.90
(10)	Jose Cardenal	2.00	1.00	.60
(11)	Danny Cater	2.00	1.00	.60
(12)	Roberto Clemente	15.00	7.50	4.50
(13)	Willie Davis	1.00	.50	.30
(14)	Mike Epstein	2.00	1.00	.60
(15)	Jim Fregosi	1.00	.50	.30
(16)	Bob Gibson	6.00	3.00	1.75
(17)	Tom Haller	2.00	1.00	.60
(18)	Ken Harrelson	3.00	1.50	.90
(19)	Willie Horton	3.00	1.50	.90
(20)	Frank Howard	1.50	.70	.45
(21)	Tommy John	8.00	4.00	2.50
(22)	Al Kaline	8.00	4.00	2.50
(23)	Harmon Killebrew	8.00	4.00	2.50
(24)	Bobby Knoop	2.00	1.00	.60
(25)	Jerry Koosman	.80	.40	.25
(26)	Jim Lefebvre	2.00	1.00	.60
(27)	Mickey Mantle	80.00	40.00	24.00
(28)	Juan Marichal	6.00	3.00	1.75
(29)	Lee May	3.00	1.50	.90
(30)	Willie Mays	20.00	10.00	6.00
(31)	Bill Mazeroski	4.00	2.00	1.25
(32)	Tim McCarver	4.00	2.00	1.25
(33)	Willie McCovey	8.00	4.00	2.50
(34)	Denny McLain	1.50	.70	.45
(35)	Dave McNally	3.00	1.50	.90
(36)	Rick Monday	3.00	1.50	.90
(37)	Blue Moon Odom	.80	.40	.25
(38)	Tony Oliva	1.50	.70	.45
(39)	Camilo Pascual	3.00	1.50	.90
(40)	Tony Perez	6.00	3.00	1.75
(41)	Rico Petrocelli	1.00	.50	.30
(42)	Rick Reichardt	.80	.40	.25
(43)	Brooks Robinson	20.00	10.00	6.00
(44)	Frank Robinson	8.00	4.00	2.50
(45)	Cookie Rojas	2.00	1.00	.60
(46)	Pete Rose	35.00	17.50	10.50
(47)	Ron Santo	1.50	.70	.45
(48)	Tom Seaver	8.00	4.00	2.50
(49)	Rusty Staub	4.00	2.00	1.25
(50)	Mel Stottlemyre	1.00	.50	.30
(51)	Ron Swoboda	.80	.40	.25
(52)	Luis Tiant	3.00	1.50	.90
(53)	Joe Torre	4.00	2.00	1.25
(54)	Cesar Tovar	2.00	1.00	.60
(55)	Pete Ward	2.00	1.00	.60
(56)	Roy White	3.00	1.50	.90
(57)	Billy Williams	10.00	5.00	3.00
(58)	Don Wilson	2.00	1.00	.60
(59)	Jim Wynn	.80	.40	.25
(60)	Carl Yastrzemski	25.00	12.50	7.50

NOTE: A card number in parentheses ( ) indicates the set is unnumbered.

1970 Transogram

ROBERTO CLEMENTE
OUTFIELD
PITTSBURGH PIRATES

Like the 1969 cards, the 1970 Transogram cards were available on boxes of Transogram baseball statues. The cards were slightly larger at 2-9/16'' by 3-1/2''. The 30-card set has the same pictures as the 1969 set except for Joe Torre. All players in the '70 set were included in the '69 Transogram issue except for Reggie Jackson, Sam McDowell and Boog Powell. Three cards and three statues were part of each Transogram box in 1970. When available, most collectors prefer to find the cards as uncut panels of three, or better yet, as complete boxes.

		NR MT	EX	VG
Complete Set:		200.00	100.00	60.00
Common Player:		.75	.40	.25
(1)	Hank Aaron	20.00	10.00	6.00
(2)	Ernie Banks	8.00	4.00	2.50
(3)	Roberto Clemente	15.00	7.50	4.50
(4)	Willie Davis	1.00	.50	.30
(5)	Jim Fregosi	1.00	.50	.30
(6)	Bob Gibson	6.00	3.00	1.75
(7)	Frank Howard	1.50	.70	.45
(8)	Reggie Jackson	35.00	17.50	10.50
(9)	Cleon Jones	.80	.40	.25
(10)	Al Kaline	8.00	4.00	2.50
(11)	Harmon Killebrew	8.00	4.00	2.50
(12)	Jerry Koosman	.80	.40	.25
(13)	Willie McCovey	8.00	4.00	2.50
(14)	Sam McDowell	3.00	1.50	.90
(15)	Denny McLain	1.50	.70	.45
(16)	Juan Marichal	6.00	3.00	1.75
(17)	Willie Mays	20.00	10.00	6.00
(18)	Blue Moon Odom	.80	.40	.25
(19)	Tony Oliva	1.50	.70	.45
(20)	Rico Petrocelli	1.00	.50	.30
(21)	Boog Powell	4.00	2.00	1.25
(22)	Rick Reichardt	.80	.40	.25
(23)	Frank Robinson	8.00	4.00	2.50
(24)	Pete Rose	35.00	17.50	10.50
(25)	Ron Santo	1.50	.70	.45
(26)	Tom Seaver	8.00	4.00	2.50
(27)	Mel Stottlemyre	1.00	.50	.30
(28)	Joe Torre	4.00	2.00	1.25
(29)	Jim Wynn	.80	.40	.25
(30)	Carl Yastrzemski	25.00	12.50	7.50

1970 Transogram Mets

The Transogram Mets set is a second set that the company produced in 1970. The cards are 2-9/16'' by 3-1/2'' and feature members of the World Championship Mets team. There are 15 cards in the set which retains the basic color picture with player's names in red and team, position and biographical details in black format. As with the other Transogram sets, the cards are most valuable when they are still part of their original box with the statues. Values decrease for them if the cards are removed from the box. While the Mets set does not have the attraction

JERRY KOOSMAN
PITCHER
NEW YORK METS

of many Hall of Famers as was the case with the regular set, it does make a very nice item for the Mets team collector.

		NR MT	EX	VG
Complete Set:		60.00	30.00	18.00
Common Player:		.75	.40	.25
(1)	Tommie Agee	3.00	1.50	.90
(2)	Ken Boswell	2.00	1.00	.60
(3)	Donn Clendenon	3.00	1.50	.90
(4)	Gary Gentry	2.00	1.00	.60
(5)	Jerry Grote	3.00	1.50	.90
(6)	Bud Harrelson	3.00	1.50	.90
(7)	Cleon Jones	.80	.40	.25
(8)	Jerry Koosman	.80	.40	.25
(9)	Ed Kranepool	3.00	1.50	.90
(10)	Tug McGraw	6.00	3.00	1.75
(11)	Nolan Ryan	30.00	15.00	9.00
(12)	Art Shamsky	2.00	1.00	.60
(13)	Tom Seaver	8.00	4.00	2.50
(14)	Ron Swoboda	.80	.40	.25
(15)	Al Weis	2.00	1.00	.60

1983 True Value White Sox

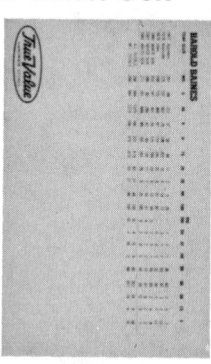

HAROLD BAINES
Right Field 3

Issued by the Chicago White Sox and True Value hardware stores these 2⅝'' by 4⅛'' cards are a rather expensive and scarce regional set. The 23-card set was originally scheduled as part of a promotion in which cards were given out at special Tuesday night games. The idea was sound, but rainouts forced the cancellation of some games so those scheduled cards were never given out. They were, however, smuggled out to hobby channels making it possible, although not easy, to assemble complete sets. The cards feature a large color photo with a wide white border. A red and blue White Sox logo is in the lower left corner, while the player's name, position and team number are in the lower right. Backs feature a True Value ad along with statistics. The three cards which were never given out through the normal channels are considered more scarce than the others. They are Marc Hill, Harold Baines and Salome Barojas.

		MT	NR MT	EX
Complete Set:		30.00	22.00	12.00
Common Player:		.40	.30	.15
1	Scott Fletcher	.60	.45	.25
2	Harold Baines	5.00	3.75	2.00
5	Vance Law	.40	.30	.15
7	Marc Hill	3.25	2.50	1.25
10	Tony LaRussa	.50	.40	.20
11	Rudy Law	.40	.30	.15
14	Tony Bernazard	.50	.40	.20
17	Jerry Hairston	.40	.30	.15
19	Greg Luzinski	1.00	.70	.40
24	Floyd Bannister	.70	.50	.30
25	Mike Squires	.40	.30	.15
30	Salome Barojas	3.25	2.50	1.25
31	LaMarr Hoyt	.70	.50	.30
34	Richard Dotson	.70	.50	.30
36	Jerry Koosman	.70	.50	.30
40	Britt Burns	.70	.50	.30
41	Dick Tidrow	.40	.30	.15
42	Ron Kittle	1.75	1.25	.70
44	Tom Paciorek	.50	.40	.20
45	Kevin Hickey	.40	.30	.15
53	Dennis Lamp	.40	.30	.15
67	Jim Kern	.40	.30	.15
72	Carlton Fisk	2.25	1.75	.90

		MT	NR MT	EX
32	Tim Hulett	.70	.50	.30
34	Richard Dotson	.60	.45	.25
40	Britt Burns	.60	.45	.25
41	Tom Seaver	3.00	2.25	1.25
42	Ron Kittle	1.25	.90	.50
44	Tom Paciorek	.50	.40	.20
50	Juan Agosto	.40	.30	.15
59	Tom Brennan	.40	.30	.15
72	Carlton Fisk	2.00	1.50	.80
---	Minnie Minoso	2.00	1.50	.80
---	Luis Aparicio	2.00	1.50	.80
---	Nancy Faust (organist)	.40	.30	.15
---	The Coaching Staff (Ed Brinkman, Dave Duncan, Art Kusnyer, Tony LaRussa, Jim Leyland, Dave Nelson, Joe Nossek)	.40	.30	.15

1986 True Value

A 30-card set of 2½'' by 3½'' cards was available in three-card packets at True Value hardware stores with a purchase of $5 or more purchase. Cards feature a photo enclosed by stars and a ball and bat at the bottom. The player's name and team are in the lower left while his position and a Major League Baseball logo are in the lower right. The True Value logo is in the upper left. Above the picture runs the phrase ''Collector Series.'' Backs feature some personal information and brief 1985 statistics. Along with the player cards, the folders contained a sweepstakes card offering trips to post-season games and other prizes.

1984 True Value White Sox

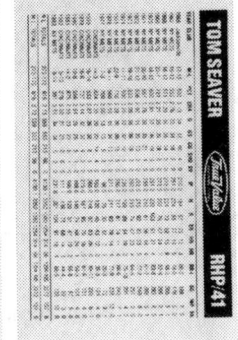

TOM SEAVER
Pitcher 41

True Value hardware stores and the Chicago White Sox gave their Tuesday night baseball card promotion at Comiskey Park another try in 1984. The cards measure 2⅝'' by 4⅛'' with 30 cards comprising the set. In addition to the players, there was a card for manager Tony LaRussa, one for the coaching staff, and for former Sox greats Luis Aparicio and Minnie Minoso. Cards designs were very similar to the 1983 cards. As the cards were given out two at a time, it was very difficult to acquire a complete set. Additionally, as numbers available vary based on attendance, some cards are scarcer than others.

		MT	NR MT	EX
Complete Set:		25.00	18.50	10.00
Common Player:		.40	.30	.15
1	Scott Fletcher	.60	.45	.25
3	Harold Baines	2.25	1.75	.90
5	Vance Law	.40	.30	.15
7	Marc Hill	.40	.30	.15
8	Dave Stegman	.40	.30	.15
10	Tony LaRussa	.50	.40	.20
11	Rudy Law	.40	.30	.15
16	Julio Cruz	.60	.45	.25
17	Jerry Hairston	.40	.30	.15
19	Greg Luzinski	1.00	.70	.40
20	Jerry Dybzinski	.40	.30	.15
24	Floyd Bannister	.70	.50	.30
25	Mike Squires	.40	.30	.15
27	Ron Reed	.50	.40	.20
29	Greg Walker	2.00	1.50	.80
30	Salome Barojas	.40	.30	.15
31	LaMarr Hoyt	.60	.45	.25

		MT	NR MT	EX
Complete Panel Set:		9.00	6.75	3.50
Complete Singles Set:		3.00	2.25	1.25
Common Panel:		.40	.30	.15
Common Single Player:		.05	.04	.02
Panel		1.00	.70	.40
1	Pedro Guerrero	.08	.06	.03
2	Steve Garvey	.15	.11	.06
3	Eddie Murray	.20	.15	.08
Panel		2.00	1.50	.80
4	Pete Rose	.30	.25	.12
5	Don Mattingly	.50	.40	.20
6	Fernando Valenzuela	.10	.08	.04
Panel		.60	.45	.25
7	Jim Rice	.15	.11	.06
8	Kirk Gibson	.08	.06	.03
9	Ozzie Smith	.05	.04	.02
Panel		1.00	.70	.40
10	Dale Murphy	.20	.15	.08
11	Robin Yount	.10	.08	.04
12	Tom Seaver	.15	.11	.06
Panel		.80	.60	.30
13	Reggie Jackson	.15	.11	.06
14	Ryne Sandberg	.10	.08	.04
15	Bruce Sutter	.05	.04	.02
Panel		1.00	.70	.40
16	Gary Carter	.15	.11	.06
17	George Brett	.20	.15	.08
18	Rick Sutcliffe	.05	.04	.02
Panel		.40	.30	.15
19	Dave Stieb	.05	.04	.02
20	Buddy Bell	.05	.04	.02
21	Alvin Davis	.08	.06	.03

Panel		MT	NR MT	EX
22	Cal Ripken, Jr.	.60	.45	.25
23	Bill Madlock	.20	.15	.08
24	Kent Hrbek	.08	.06	.03
Panel		.10	.08	.04
25	Lou Whitaker	.50	.40	.20
26	Nolan Ryan	.08	.06	.03
27	Dwayne Murphy	.15	.11	.06
Panel		.05	.04	.02
28	Mike Schmidt	1.25	.90	.50
29	Andre Dawson	.20	.15	.08
30	Wade Boggs	.10	.08	.04
		.35	.25	.14

		NR MT	EX	VG
31	Vernon (Lefty) Gomez	300.00	150.00	90.00
32	George (Babe) Ruth	2000.00	1000.00	600.00

1931 W517

1932 U.S. Caramel

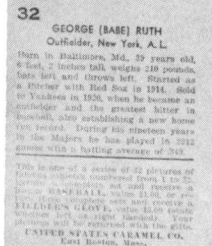

Produced by the U.S. Caramel Company, Boston, this set was not limited to baseball. Rather, it was a set of 31 "Famous Athletes" of which some 26 were baseball players. The 2½" by 3" cards had a black-and-white picture on the front with a red background and white border. The player's name appeared in white above the picture. The back featured the player's name, position, team and league as well as a redemption ad and card number. The cards were among the last of the caramel card sets and are very scarce today. This is probably due to a rather limited production, although the cards could also be redeemed for a baseball and a baseball glove. Card #16 is unknown and was probably never issued.

		NR MT	EX	VG
Complete Set:		10000.00	5000.00	3000.
Common Player:		200.00	100.00	60.00
1	Edward T. (Eddie) Collins	375.00	187.00	112.00
2	Paul (Big Poison) Waner	250.00	125.00	75.00
4	William (Bill) Terry	300.00	150.00	90.00
5	Earl B. Combs (Earle)	250.00	125.00	75.00
6	William (Bill) Dickey	400.00	200.00	120.00
7	Joseph (Joe) Cronin	300.00	150.00	90.00
8	Charles (Chick) Hafey	250.00	125.00	75.00
10	Walter (Rabbit) Maranville	250.00	125.00	75.00
11	Rogers (Rajah) Hornsby	450.00	225.00	135.00
12	Gordon (Mickey) Cochrane	300.00	150.00	90.00
13	Lloyd (Little Poison) Waner	250.00	125.00	75.00
14	Tyrus (Ty) Cobb	1000.00	500.00	300.00
17	Al. Simmons	250.00	125.00	75.00
18	Anthony (Tony) Lazzeri	250.00	125.00	75.00
19	Walter (Wally) Berger	200.00	100.00	60.00
20	Charles (Large Charlie) Ruffing	250.00	125.00	75.00
21	Charles (Chuck) Klein	250.00	125.00	75.00
23	James (Jimmy) Foxx	450.00	225.00	135.00
24	Frank J. (Lefty) O'Doul	200.00	100.00	60.00
26	Henry (Lou) Gehrig	1200.00	600.00	360.00
27	Robert (Lefty) Grove	375.00	187.00	112.00
28	Edward Brant (Brandt)	200.00	100.00	60.00
29	George Earnshaw	200.00	100.00	60.00
30	Frank (Frankie) Frisch	300.00	150.00	90.00

The 54-card W517 set is a scarce issue of 3" by 4" cards which are generally found in a sepia color. There are, however, other known colors of W517s, and they tend to bring higher prices from specialists. The cards feature a player picture as well as his name and team. The card number appears in a small circle on the front, while backs are blank. The set is heavy in stars of the period including two Babe Ruths (#4 and #20). Not actively collected by many, the set is a relatively inexpensive way to obtain cards of many contemporary Hall of Famers.

		NR MT	EX	VG
Complete Set:		3000.00	1500.00	900.00
Common Player:		25.00	12.50	7.50
1	Earl Combs (Earle)	60.00	30.00	18.00
2	Pie Traynor	50.00	25.00	15.00
3	Eddie Rausch (Roush)	50.00	25.00	15.00
4	Babe Ruth	400.00	200.00	120.00
5a	Chalmer Cissell (Chicago)	25.00	12.50	7.50
5b	Chalmer Cissell (Cleveland)	25.00	12.50	7.50
6	Bill Sherdel	25.00	12.50	7.50
7	Bill Shore	25.00	12.50	7.50
8	Geo. Earnshaw	25.00	12.50	7.50
9	Bucky Harris	40.00	20.00	12.00
10	Charlie Klein	50.00	25.00	15.00
11a	Geo. Kelly (Reds)	50.00	25.00	15.00
11b	Geo. Kelly (Brooklyn)	50.00	25.00	15.00
12	Travis Jackson	50.00	25.00	15.00
13	Willie Kamm	25.00	12.50	7.50
14	Harry Heilman (Heilmann)	50.00	25.00	15.00
15	Grover Alexander	60.00	30.00	18.00
16	Frank Frisch	50.00	25.00	15.00
17	Jack Quinn	25.00	12.50	7.50
18	Cy Williams	30.00	15.00	9.00
19	Kiki Cuyler	50.00	25.00	15.00
20	Babe Ruth	400.00	200.00	120.00
21	Jimmie Foxx	80.00	40.00	24.00
22	Jimmy Dykes	25.00	12.50	7.50
23	Bill Terry	60.00	30.00	18.00
24	Freddy Lindstrom	50.00	25.00	15.00
25	Hughey Critz	25.00	12.50	7.50
26	Pete Donahue	25.00	12.50	7.50
27	Tony Lazzeri	40.00	20.00	12.00
28	Heine Manush (Heinie)	50.00	25.00	15.00
29a	Chick Hafey (Cardinals)	50.00	25.00	15.00
29b	Chick Hafey (Cincinnati)	50.00	25.00	15.00
30	Melvin Ott	70.00	35.00	21.00
31	Bing Miller	25.00	12.50	7.50

		NR MT	EX	VG
32	Geo. Haas	25.00	12.50	7.50
33a	Lefty O'Doul (Phillies)	30.00	15.00	9.00
33b	Lefty O'Doul (Brooklyn)	30.00	15.00	9.00
34	Paul Waner	50.00	25.00	15.00
35	Lou Gehrig	275.00	137.00	82.00
36	Dazzy Vance	50.00	25.00	15.00
37	Mickey Cochrane	50.00	25.00	15.00
38	Rogers Hornsby	80.00	40.00	24.00
39	Lefty Grove	60.00	30.00	18.00
40	Al Simmons	50.00	25.00	15.00
41	Rube Walberg	25.00	12.50	7.50
42	Hack Wilson	50.00	25.00	15.00
43	Art Shires	25.00	12.50	7.50
44	Sammy Hale	25.00	12.50	7.50
45	Ted Lyons	50.00	25.00	15.00
46	Joe Sewell	50.00	25.00	15.00
47	Goose Goslin	50.00	25.00	15.00
48	Lou Fonseca (Lew)	30.00	15.00	9.00
49	Bob Muesel (Meusel)	30.00	15.00	9.00
50	Lu Blue	25.00	12.50	7.50
52	Eddy Collins (Eddie)	60.00	30.00	18.00
53	Joe Judge	25.00	12.50	7.50
54	Mickey Cochrane	60.00	30.00	18.00

1938 W711-1 Reds

WALLY BERGER
Outfielder

Ever since he came into the league in 1930 Berger has been one of the circuit's most dangerous hitters. Led the league in home runs in 1935 and has hit more homers than any player in the league except Mel Ott and Chuck Klein. Was acquired by the Reds in a trade with the Giants in June.

This 32-card set is a challenging one of particular interest to Cincinnati team collectors. The 2'' by x3'' cards were sold at the ballpark. Fronts feature a picture of the player while backs have the player's name, position and a generally flattering description of the player's talents. Cards are not numbered.

		NR MT	EX	VG
Complete Set:		200.00	100.00	60.00
Common Player:		7.00	3.50	2.00
(1)	Wally Berger ("... in a trade with the Giants in June.")	9.00	4.50	2.75
(2)	Joe Cascarella	8.00	4.00	2.50
(3)	Allen "Dusty" Cooke	8.00	4.00	2.50
(4)	Harry Craft	7.00	3.50	2.00
(5)	Ray "Peaches" Davis	7.00	3.50	2.00
(6)	Paul Derringer ("Won 22 games ... this season.")	10.00	5.00	3.00
(7)	Linus Frey ("... only 25 now.")	8.00	4.00	2.50
(8)	Lee Gamble ("... Syracuse last year.")	8.00	4.00	2.50
(9)	Ival Goodman (no mention of 30 homers)	8.00	4.00	2.50
(10)	Harry "Hank" Gowdy	7.00	3.50	2.00
(11)	Lee Grissom (no mention of 1938)	8.00	4.00	2.50
(12)	Willard Hershberger	9.00	4.50	2.75
(13)	Ernie Lombardi (no mention of 1938 MVP)	18.00	9.00	5.50
(14)	Frank McCormick	9.00	4.50	2.75
(15)	Bill McKechnie ("Last year he led ...")	15.00	7.50	4.50
(16)	Lloyd "Whitey" Moore ("... last year with Syracuse.")	8.00	4.00	2.50
(17)	Billy Myers ("... in his fourth year.")	8.00	4.00	2.50
(18)	Lee Riggs ("... in his fourth season ...")	8.00	4.00	2.50
(19)	Eddie Roush	18.00	9.00	5.50

		NR MT	EX	VG
(20)	Gene Schott	8.00	4.00	2.50
(21)	Johnny Vander Meer (pitching pose)	12.00	6.00	3.50
(22)	Wm. "Bucky" Walter ("... won 14 games ...")	9.00	4.50	2.75
(23)	Jim Weaver	7.00	3.50	2.00

1939 W711-1 Reds

WALLY BERGER
Outfielder

Ever since he came into the league in 1930, Berger has been one of the circuit's most dangerous hitters. Led the league in home runs in 1935 and has hit more homers than any player in the league except Mel Ott and Chuck Klein. Was acquired by the Reds in a trade with the Giants in June, 1938.

An updating by one season of the team-issued 1938 W711-1 issue, most of the players and poses on the 2'' by 3'' cards remained the same. A close study of the career summary on the card's back is necessary to determine which year of issue is at hand.

		NR MT	EX	VG
Complete Set:		325.00	162.00	97.00
Common Player:		7.00	3.50	2.00
(1)	Wally Berger ("... in a trade with the Giants in June, 1938.")	9.00	4.50	2.75
(2)	Nino Bongiovanni	25.00	12.50	7.50
(3)	Stanley 'Frenchy' Bordagaray	25.00	12.50	7.50
(4)	Harry Craft	7.00	3.50	2.00
(5)	Ray "Peaches" Davis	7.00	3.50	2.00
(6)	Paul Derringer ("Won 22 games ... last year.")	10.00	5.00	3.00
(7)	Linus Frey ("... only 26 now.")	8.00	4.00	2.50
(8)	Lee Gamble ("... Syracuse in 1937.")	8.00	4.00	2.50
(9)	Ival Goodman (mentions hitting 30 homers)	8.00	4.00	2.50
(10)	Harry "Hank" Gowdy	7.00	3.50	2.00
(11)	Lee Grissom (mentions 1938)	8.00	4.00	2.50
(12)	Willard Hershberger	9.00	4.50	2.75
(13)	Eddie Joost	8.00	4.00	2.50
(14)	Wes Livengood	75.00	37.00	22.00
(15)	Ernie Lombardi (mentions MVP of 1938)	18.00	9.00	5.50
(16)	Frank McCormick	9.00	4.50	2.75
(17)	Bill McKechnie ("In 1937 he led ...")	15.00	7.50	4.50
(18)	Lloyd "Whitey" Moore ("... in 1937 with Syracuse.")	8.00	4.00	2.50
(19)	Billy Myers ("... in his fifth year ...")	8.00	4.00	2.50
(20)	Lee Riggs ("... in his fifth season...")	8.00	4.00	2.50
(21)	Les Scarsella	10.00	5.00	3.00
(22)	Eugene "Junior" Thompson	8.00	4.00	2.50
(23)	Johnny Vander Meer (portrait)	12.00	6.00	3.50
(24)	Wm. "Bucky" Walters ("Won 15 games ...")	9.00	4.50	2.75
(25)	Jim Weaver	7.00	3.50	2.00
(26)	Bill Werber	8.00	4.00	2.50
(27)	Jimmy Wilson	8.00	4.00	2.50

1940 W711-2 Harry Hartman Reds

Another early set of the Cincinnati Reds, this 32-card set of 2⅛'' by 2⅝'' cards contains a number of

interesting items. The black-and-white cards carry no numbers and feature a picture of the player on the front and name, position and biographical information on the back. As the Reds were World Champions in 1940 after defeating Detroit 4-3, the set features special cards for the World Series title making it one of the first to feature events as well as individuals. The set takes its name from Reds' announcer Harry Hartman, who has a card in the issue and supposedly was instrumental in its issue.

		NR MT	EX	VG
Complete Set:		250.00	125.00	75.00
Common Player:		7.00	3.50	2.00
(1)	Morris Arnovich	7.00	3.50	2.00
(2)	William (Bill) Baker	7.00	3.50	2.00
(3)	Joseph Beggs	7.00	3.50	2.00
(4)	Harry Craft	7.00	3.50	2.00
(5)	Paul Derringer	9.00	4.50	2.75
(6)	Linus Frey	7.00	3.50	2.00
(7)	Ival Goodman	7.00	3.50	2.00
(8)	Harry (Hank) Gowdy	7.00	3.50	2.00
(9)	Witt Guise	7.00	3.50	2.00
(10)	Harry (Socko) Hartman	7.00	3.50	2.00
(11)	Willard Hershberger	8.00	4.00	2.50
(12)	John Hutchings	7.00	3.50	2.00
(13)	Edwin Joost	7.00	3.50	2.00
(14)	Ernie Lombardi	18.00	9.00	5.50
(15)	Frank McCormick	9.00	4.50	2.75
(16)	Myron McCormick	7.00	3.50	2.00
(17)	William Boyd McKechnie	15.00	7.50	4.50
(18)	Lloyd (Whitey) Moore	7.00	3.50	2.00
(19)	William (Bill) Myers	7.00	3.50	2.00
(20)	Lewis Riggs	7.00	3.50	2.00
(21)	Elmer Riddle	7.00	3.50	2.00
(22)	James A. Ripple	7.00	3.50	2.00
(23)	Milburn Shoffner	7.00	3.50	2.00
(24)	Eugene Thompson	7.00	3.50	2.00
(25)	James Turner	7.00	3.50	2.00
(26)	John Vander Meer	12.00	6.00	3.50
(27)	Wm. (Bucky) Walters	9.00	4.50	2.75
(28)	William (Bill) Werber	7.00	3.50	2.00
(29)	James Wilson	8.00	4.00	2.50
(30)	The Cincinnati Reds	7.00	3.50	2.00
(31)	The Cincinnati Reds World Champions	7.00	3.50	2.00
(32)	Tell The World About The Cincinnati Reds	7.00	3.50	2.00
(33)	Tell The World About The Cincinnati Reds World Champions	7.00	3.50	2.00
(34)	Results 1940 World's Series	8.00	4.00	2.50
(35)	Debt of Gratitude to Wm. Koehl Co.	7.00	3.50	2.00

1941 W753 Browns

Measuring 2⅛'' by 2⅝'' this unnumbered set of cards features the St. Louis Browns in black-and-white portrait photos. There were 29 cards in the set which featured a photo on the front and the player's name, position and personal and statistical information. There were also cards for coaches and one of the club's two managers that season (Luke Sewell). As the Browns weren't much of a team in 1941 (or in most seasons for that matter) there are no major stars in the set.

		NR MT	EX	VG
Complete Set:		250.00	125.00	75.00
Common Player:		9.00	4.50	2.75
(1)	Johnny Allen	9.00	4.50	2.75
(2)	Elden Auker (Eldon)	9.00	4.50	2.75
(3)	Donald L Barnes	9.00	4.50	2.75
(4)	Johnny Berardino	12.00	6.00	3.50
(5)	George Caster	9.00	4.50	2.75
(6)	Harlond Benton (Darky) Clift	9.00	4.50	2.75
(7)	Roy J. Cullenbine	9.00	4.50	2.75
(8)	William O. DeWitt	9.00	4.50	2.75
(9)	Roberto Estalella	9.00	4.50	2.75
(10)	Richard Benjamin (Rick) Ferrell	20.00	10.00	6.00
(11)	Dennis W. Galehouse	9.00	4.50	2.75
(12)	Joseph L. Grace	9.00	4.50	2.75
(13)	Frank Grube	9.00	4.50	2.75
(14)	Robert A. Harris	9.00	4.50	2.75
(15)	Donald Henry Heffner	9.00	4.50	2.75
(16)	Fred Hofmann	9.00	4.50	2.75
(17)	Walter Franklin Judnich	9.00	4.50	2.75
(18)	John Henry (Jack) Kramer	9.00	4.50	2.75
(19)	Chester (Chet) Laabs	9.00	4.50	2.75
(20)	John Lucadello	9.00	4.50	2.75
(21)	George Hartley McQuinn	9.00	4.50	2.75
(22)	Robert Cleveland Muncrief, Jr.	9.00	4.50	2.75
(23)	John Niggeling	9.00	4.50	2.75
(24)	Fred Raymond (Fritz) Ostermueller	9.00	4.50	2.75
(25)	James Luther (Luke) Sewell	10.00	5.00	3.00
(26)	Alan Cochran Strange (Cochrane)	9.00	4.50	2.75
(27)	Robert Virgil (Bob) Swift	9.00	4.50	2.75
(28)	James W. (Zack) Taylor	9.00	4.50	2.75
(29)	William Felix (Bill) Trotter	9.00	4.50	2.75
(30)	Presentation Card/Order Form	15.00	7.50	4.50

1941 W754 Cardinals

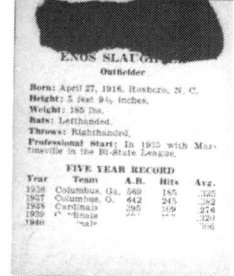

A companion set to W753, this time featuring the other team in St. Louis. Cards measure 2⅛'' by 2⅝'' and are unnumbered. Like the Browns set, there are 29 cards featuring black-and-white photos on the front and the individual's name, position and personal and statistical information on the back. One interesting addition to the set is a card of Branch Rickey which coupled with cards of Enos Slaughter and Johnny Mize gives the set a bit more appeal than the Browns set.

	NR MT	EX	VG
Complete Set:	300.00	150.00	90.00
Common Player:	9.00	4.50	2.75

		NR MT	EX	VG
(1)	Sam Breadon	9.00	4.50	2.75
(2)	James Brown	9.00	4.50	2.75
(3)	Morton Cooper	9.00	4.50	2.75
(4)	William Walker Cooper	9.00	4.50	2.75
(5)	Estel Crabtree	9.00	4.50	2.75
(6)	Frank Crespi	9.00	4.50	2.75
(7)	William Crouch	9.00	4.50	2.75
(8)	Miguel Mike Gonzalez	9.00	4.50	2.75
(9)	Harry Gumbert	9.00	4.50	2.75
(10)	John Hopp	9.00	4.50	2.75
(11)	Ira Hutchinson	9.00	4.50	2.75
(12)	Howard Krist	9.00	4.50	2.75
(13)	Edward E. Lake	9.00	4.50	2.75
(14)	Hubert Max Lanier	10.00	5.00	3.00
(15)	Gus Mancuso	9.00	4.50	2.75
(16)	Martin Marion	15.00	7.50	4.50
(17)	Steve Mesner	9.00	4.50	2.75
(18)	John Mize	25.00	12.50	7.50
(19)	Capt. Terry Moore	12.00	6.00	3.50
(20)	Sam Nahem	9.00	4.50	2.75
(21)	Don Padgett	9.00	4.50	2.75
(22)	Branch Rickey	25.00	12.50	7.50
(23)	Clyde Shoun	9.00	4.50	2.75
(24)	Enos Slaughter	25.00	12.50	7.50
(25)	William H. (Billy) Southworth	9.00	4.50	2.75
(26)	Herman Coaker Triplett	9.00	4.50	2.75
(27)	Clyde Buzzy Wares	9.00	4.50	2.75
(28)	Lou Warneke	9.00	4.50	2.75
(29)	Ernest White	9.00	4.50	2.75
(30)	Presentation Card/Order Form	15.00	7.50	4.50

1985 Wendy's Tigers

 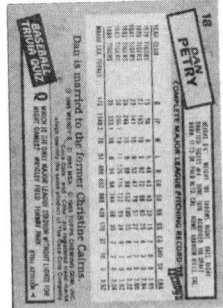

This 22-card set of cards measuring 2½'' by 3½,'' which carried both Wendy's Hamburgers and Coca-Cola logos was produced by Topps. The cards feature a color photo with the player's team, name and position underneath the picture and the Wendy's logo in the lower left and Coke logo in the upper right. Backs are identical to 1985 Topps cards except they have different card numbers and are done in a red and black color scheme. Cards were distributed three to a pack along with a "Header" checklist in a cellophane package at selected Wendy's outlets in Michigan only.

		MT	NR MT	EX
Complete Set:		8.00	6.00	3.25
Common Player:		.15	.11	.06
1	Sparky Anderson	.30	.25	.12
2	Doug Bair	.15	.11	.06
3	Juan Berenguer	.15	.11	.06
4	Dave Bergman	.15	.11	.06
5	Tom Brookens	.15	.11	.06
6	Marty Castillo	.15	.11	.06
7	Darrell Evans	.50	.40	.20
8	Barbaro Garbey	.15	.11	.06
9	Kirk Gibson	.80	.60	.30
10	Johnny Grubb	.15	.11	.06
11	Willie Hernandez	.25	.20	.10
12	Larry Herndon	.20	.15	.08
13	Rusty Kuntz	.15	.11	.06
14	Chet Lemon	.20	.15	.08
15	Aurelio Lopez	.15	.11	.06
16	Jack Morris	.70	.50	.30

		MT	NR MT	EX
17	Lance Parrish	.70	.50	.30
18	Dan Petry	.30	.25	.12
19	Bill Scherrer	.15	.11	.06
20	Alan Trammell	.80	.60	.30
21	Lou Whitaker	.70	.50	.30
22	Milt Wilcox	.15	.11	.06

1951 Wheaties

Printed as the backs of boxes on individual serving boxes of Wheaties, the six-card 1951 set includes three baseball players and one each football player, basketball player and golfer. Well-trimmed cards measure 2½'' by 3¼.'' The cards feature blue line drawings of the athletes, with a facsimile autograph and descriptive title below. There is a wide white border.

		NR MT	EX	VG
Complete Set:		225.00	112.00	67.00
Common Player:		20.00	10.00	6.00
(1)	Bob Feller (baseball)	75.00	37.00	22.00
(2)	John Lujack (football)	25.00	12.50	7.50
(3)	George K. Mikan (basketball)	25.00	12.50	7.50
(4)	Stan Musial (baseball)	100.00	50.00	30.00
(5)	Sam Snead (golfer)	20.00	10.00	6.00
(6)	Ted Williams (baseball)	125.00	62.00	37.00

1952 Wheaties

These 2'' by 2¾'' cards appeared on the back of the popular cereal boxes. Actually, sports figures had been appearing on the backs of the boxes for many years, but in 1952, of the 30 athletes depicted, 10 were baseball players. That means there were 20 baseball cards, as each player appeared in both a portrait and an action drawing. The cards have a blue line drawing on an orange background with a white border. The player's name, team, and position appear at the bottom. The cards have rounded corners and are not widely collected because they have an outdated look, are mixed with other athletes and are often poorly cut from the boxes.

		NR MT	EX	VG
Complete Set:		450.00	225.00	135.00
Common Player:		10.00	5.00	3.00
(1)	Larry "Yogi" Berra (portrait)	30.00	15.00	9.00
(2)	Larry "Yogi" Berra (action pose)	30.00	15.00	9.00
(3)	Roy Campanella (portrait)	30.00	15.00	9.00
(4)	Roy Campanella (action pose)	30.00	15.00	9.00
(5)	Bob Feller (portrait)	25.00	12.50	7.50
(6)	Bob Feller (action pose)	25.00	12.50	7.50
(7)	George Kell (portrait)	12.00	6.00	3.50
(8)	George Kell (action pose)	12.00	6.00	3.50
(9)	Ralph Kiner (portrait)	15.00	7.50	4.50
(10)	Ralph Kiner (action pose)	15.00	7.50	4.50
(11)	Bob Lemon (portrait)	15.00	7.50	4.50
(12)	Bob Lemon (action pose)	15.00	7.50	4.50
(13)	Stan Musial (portrait)	50.00	25.00	15.00
(14)	Stan Musial (action pose)	50.00	25.00	15.00
(15)	Phil Rizzuto (portrait)	18.00	9.00	5.50
(16)	Phil Rizzuto (action pose)	18.00	9.00	5.50
(17)	Elwin "Preacher" Roe (portrait)	10.00	5.00	3.00
(18)	Elwin "Preacher" Roe (action pose)			
		10.00	5.00	3.00
(19)	Ted Williams (portrait)	60.00	30.00	18.00
(20)	Ted Williams (action pose)	60.00	30.00	18.00

1982 Wheaties Indians

TOBY HARRAH
Infield

GET THE

EATIES FOR WHEATIES

—that undeniable, irresistible urge for the crispy, crunchy whole wheat taste of

WHEATIES

The Breakfast of Champions.

These 2-13/16'' by 4-1/8'' cards were given out 10 at a time during three special promotional games; later the complete set was placed on sale at the Indian's gift shop. The 30-card set represented the first time in 30 years that Wheaties had produced a baseball card set. The cards featured color photos surrounded by a wide white border with the player's name and position below the picture. The Indians logo is in the lower left corner while the Wheaties logo is in the lower right. Card backs have a Wheaties ad.

		MT	NR MT	EX
Complete Set:		7.50	5.75	3.00
Common Player:		.15	.11	.06
(1)	Chris Bando	.15	.11	.06
(2)	Alan Bannister	.15	.11	.06
(3)	Len Barker	.25	.20	.10
(4)	Bert Blyleven	.60	.45	.25
(5)	Tom Brennan	.15	.11	.06
(6)	Joe Charboneau	.25	.20	.10
(7)	Rodney Craig	.15	.11	.06
(8)	John Denny	.25	.20	.10
(9)	Miguel Dilone	.15	.11	.06
(10)	Jerry Dybzinski	.15	.11	.06
(11)	Mike Fischlin	.15	.11	.06
(12)	Dave Garcia	.15	.11	.06
(13)	Johnny Goryl	.15	.11	.06
(14)	Mike Hargrove	.25	.20	.10
(15)	Toby Harrah	.25	.20	.10
(16)	Ron Hassey	.15	.11	.06
(17)	Von Hayes	.90	.70	.35
(18)	Dennis Lewallyn	.15	.11	.06
(19)	Rick Manning	.15	.11	.06
(20)	Bake McBride	.15	.11	.06
(21)	Tommy McCraw	.15	.11	.06
(22)	Jack Perconte	.15	.11	.06
(23)	Mel Queen	.15	.11	.06
(24)	Dennis Sommers	.15	.11	.06

		MT	NR MT	EX
(25)	Lary Sorensen	.15	.11	.06
(26)	Dan Spillner	.15	.11	.06
(27)	Rick Sutcliffe	.60	.45	.25
(28)	Andre Thornton	.50	.40	.20
(29)	Rick Waits	.15	.11	.06
(30)	Eddie Whitson	.20	.15	.08

1983 Wheaties Indians

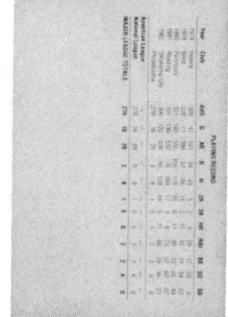

JULIO FRANCO
Infield

WHEATIES

A 32-card set marking the second year of Wheaties involvement with the Indians. Distribution of the 2-13/16'' by 4-1/8'' cards changed slightly in that the entire set was given away on the day of the special promotional game. As happened in 1982, the set was then placed on sale at the team's gift shop. The set includes 27 players, four coaches and the manager. The format of the cards remained basically the same on the front although the backs of player cards were changed to include complete major and minor league statistics.

		MT	NR MT	EX
Complete Set:		7.50	5.75	3.00
Common Player:		.15	.11	.06
(1)	Bud Anderson	.15	.11	.06
(2)	Jay Baller	.20	.15	.08
(3)	Chris Bando	.15	.11	.06
(4)	Alan Bannister	.15	.11	.06
(5)	Len Barker	.25	.20	.10
(6)	Bert Blyleven	.60	.45	.25
(7)	Wil Culmer	.15	.11	.06
(8)	Miguel Dilone	.15	.11	.06
(9)	Juan Eichelberger	.15	.11	.06
(10)	Jim Essian	.15	.11	.06
(11)	Mike Ferraro	.15	.11	.06
(12)	Mike Fischlin	.15	.11	.06
(13)	Julio Franco	.90	.70	.35
(14)	Ed Glynn	.15	.11	.06
(15)	Johnny Goryl	.15	.11	.06
(16)	Mike Hargrove	.25	.20	.10
(17)	Toby Harrah	.25	.20	.10
(18)	Ron Hassey	.15	.11	.06
(19)	Neal Heaton	.35	.25	.14
(20)	Rick Manning	.15	.11	.06
(21)	Bake McBride	.15	.11	.06
(22)	Don McMahon	.15	.11	.06
(23)	Ed Napoleon	.15	.11	.06
(24)	Broderick Perkins	.15	.11	.06
(25)	Dennis Sommers	.15	.11	.06
(26)	Lary Sorensen	.15	.11	.06
(27)	Dan Spillner	.15	.11	.06
(28)	Rick Sutcliffe	.60	.45	.25
(29)	Andre Thornton	.50	.40	.20
(30)	Manny Trillo	.25	.20	.10
(31)	George Vukovich	.15	.11	.06
(32)	Rick Waits	.15	.11	.06

1984 Wheaties Indians

The 2-13/16'' by 4-1/8'' cards again were given out at Municipal Stadium as part of a promotion

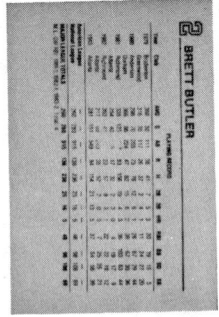

BRETT
BUTLER
Outfield

The 2⅝" by 3¾" cards are among the most popular and difficult to find baseball card sets issued with hot dogs during the 1950s. The cards featured color-added photos on the front where the player's name, team and position appear at the top. The front also has a facsimile autograph and a color picture of a package of Wilson's hot dogs. The card backs feature personal information, a short career summary and 1953 and career statistics. The 20-card set includes players from a number of teams and was distributed nationally in the hot dog packages. The problem with such distribution is that the cards are very tough to find without grease stains from the hot dogs.

involving Wheaties and the Indians on July 22. The set is down from 32 cards in 1983 to 29. There were 26 players as well as cards for the manager, coaches and team mascot Tom-E-Hawk. Designs of the cards were identical to prior years. The 1984 set is numbered by uniform number. A total of 15,000 sets were printed and any left over from the promotion were placed on sale in the team's gift shop.

		MT	NR MT	EX
	Complete Set	7.50	5.75	3.00
	Common Player	.15	.11	.06
2	Brett Butler	.40	.30	.15
4	Tony Bernazard	.20	.15	.08
8	Carmelo Castillo	.15	.11	.06
10	Pat Tabler	.50	.40	.20
13	Ernie Camacho	.15	.11	.06
14	Julio Franco	.70	.50	.30
15	Broderick Perkins	.15	.11	.06
16	Jerry Willard	.15	.11	.06
18	Pat Corrales	.15	.11	.06
21	Mike Hargrove	.25	.20	.10
22	Mike Fischlin	.15	.11	.06
23	Chris Bando	.15	.11	.06
24	George Vukovich	.15	.11	.06
26	Brook Jacoby	.80	.60	.30
27	Steve Farr	.25	.20	.10
28	Bert Blyleven	.60	.45	.25
29	Andre Thornton	.50	.40	.20
30	Joe Carter	.90	.70	.35
31	Steve Comer	.15	.11	.06
33	Roy Smith	.15	.11	.06
34	Mel Hall	.40	.30	.15
36	Jamie Easterly	.15	.11	.06
37	Don Schulze	.20	.15	.08
38	Luis Aponte	.15	.11	.06
44	Neal Heaton	.25	.20	.10
46	Mike Jeffcoat	.15	.11	.06
54	Tom Waddell	.20	.15	.08
---	Coaching Staff (Bobby Bonds, John Goryl, Don McMahon, Ed Napoleon, Dennis Sommers)	.15	.11	.06
---	Tom-E-Hawk (mascot)	.15	.11	.06

		NR MT	EX	VG
	Complete Set:	3200.00	1600.00	960.00
	Common Player:	75.00	37.00	22.00
(1)	Roy Campanella	375.00	187.00	112.00
(2)	Del Ennis	75.00	37.00	22.00
(3)	Carl Erskine	90.00	45.00	27.00
(4)	Ferris Fain	75.00	37.00	22.00
(5)	Bob Feller	300.00	150.00	90.00
(6)	Nelson Fox	125.00	62.00	37.00
(7)	Johnny Groth	75.00	37.00	22.00
(8)	Stan Hack	75.00	37.00	22.00
(9)	Gil Hodges	225.00	112.00	67.00
(10)	Ray Jablonski	75.00	37.00	22.00
(11)	Harvey Kuenn	100.00	50.00	30.00
(12)	Roy McMillan	75.00	37.00	22.00
(13)	Andy Pafko	75.00	37.00	22.00
(14)	Paul Richards	75.00	37.00	22.00
(15)	Hank Sauer	75.00	37.00	22.00
(16)	Red Schoendienst	90.00	45.00	27.00
(17)	Enos Slaughter	150.00	75.00	45.00
(18)	Vern Stephens	75.00	37.00	22.00
(19)	Sammy White	75.00	37.00	22.00
(20)	Ted Williams	1100.00	550.00	330.00

1954 Wilson Franks

GIL HODGES
first base BROOKLYN DODGERS

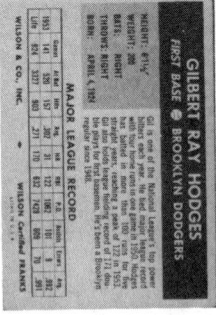

TED WILLIAMS
outfield BOSTON RED SOX

CARL ERSKINE
pitcher BROOKLYN DODGERS

ROY CAMPANELLA
catcher BROOKLYN DODGERS

VERN STEPHENS
third base BALTIMORE ORIOLES

1954 Wilson Franks Cards

Index

Advertisers Index

1988 sneak peek: Donruss

Lester Lancaster P

Don Mattingly 1B

Al Leiter P

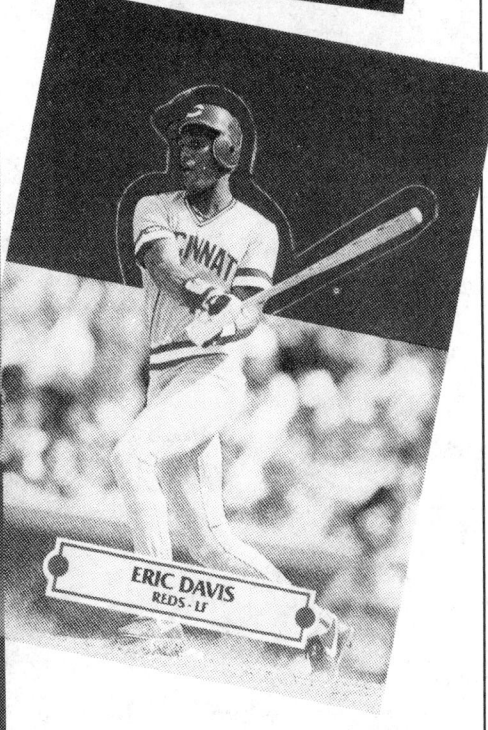

ERIC DAVIS
REDS · LF

1988 sneak peek: Fleer

1988 sneak peek: Score

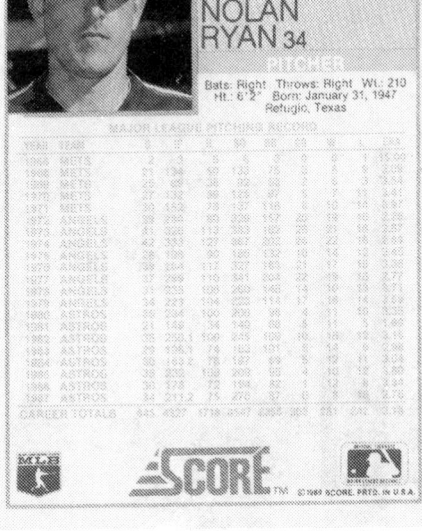

1988 sneak peek: Topps

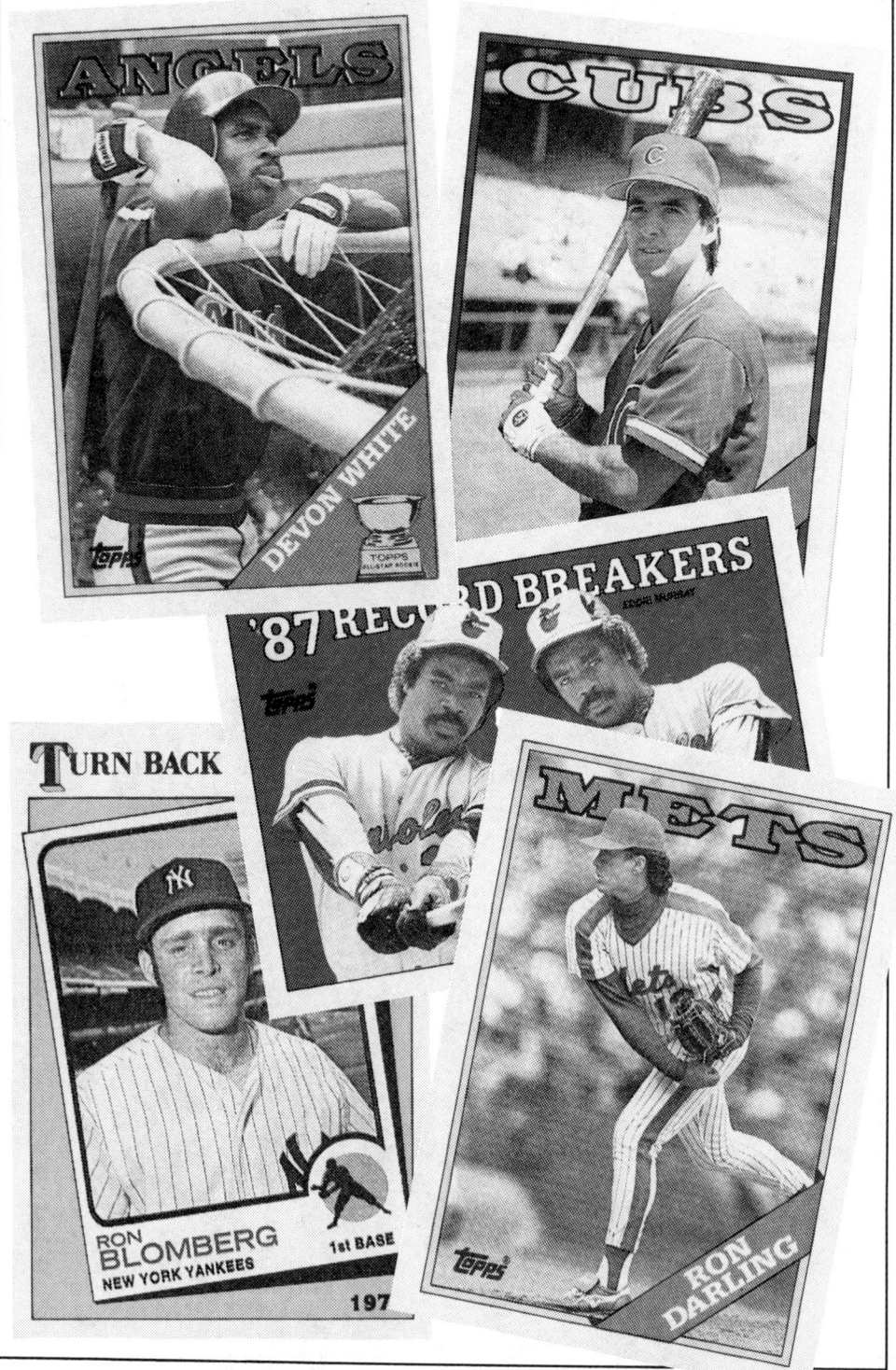

NOTES:

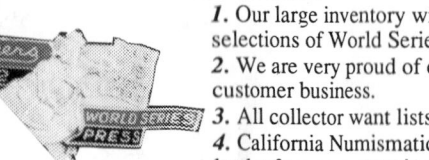
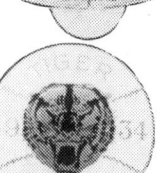

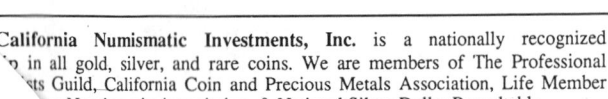